THE
CHAMBERS
THESAURUS

Edited by

Martin H Manser

CHAMBERS

CHAMBERS

7 Hopetoun Crescent
Edinburgh EH7 4AY

Copyright © Chambers Harrap Publishers Ltd 1996
Reprinted 1997, 1998, 1999 (twice)

A CIP catalogue record for this book is available from the British Library.

ISBN 0-550-18308-6

The editor wishes to thank the following for their contributions to this project:
Rosalind Desmond, Lynda Drury, Karen Dunnell, Rosalind Fergusson, Jenny
Roberts, Gloria Wren for their help in editing and keyboarding the text; the
editors of the *Chambers 20th Century Thesaurus*, on which this work is based;
many individuals who have sent in suggestions for additional entries to the
publishers; and staff at the publishers for their invaluable assistance and support:
Megan Thomson, Robert Allen, Elaine Higgleton, Ilona Morison and Martin
Mellor.

Typeset by Chambers Harrap Publishers Ltd, Edinburgh
Printed in France by Partenaires

Introduction

A thesaurus is a dictionary that provides alternatives to a particular word or phrase. It is the essential companion for anyone who wants to create something satisfying out of words — a quick, convenient source of synonyms and related terms that will help users express themselves in as precise, succinct and yet varied a manner as possible.

It was in 1852 that Peter Mark Roget published his *Thesaurus*. Its full original title was *The Thesaurus of English Words and Phrases Classified and Arranged so as to Facilitate the Expression of Ideas and Assist in Literary Composition*. His purpose was to provide readers not only with synonyms for a word, but, more generally, with a wide choice of expressions relevant to a particular concept. His method was to classify these within a framework of ideas on 17th-century philosophical and scientific principles. This meant that a very full alphabetical index was needed to open up the classified lists to the user. It was probably the complications of this system that ensured the continued popularity of the more 'user-friendly' type of word-finding book already in production in Roget's time — the simple alphabetical list of words, each followed by its own group of synonyms. More recently there has emerged the type of thesaurus that, while preserving the alphabetical arrangement, acknowledges the value of Roget's approach by supplying related words within each entry on a rather broader, more comprehensive basis than that of mere synonymity.

Chambers English Thesaurus belongs to this last type — it lists the commonest, most synonym-rich words in the language, arranged alphabetically, each with a plentiful supply of alternative and connected expressions. Selected antonyms have also been added wherever appropriate. It has all the recognized usefulness of any thesaurus — but its special advantage is that it draws on the resources of *The Chambers Dictionary*, known to dictionary connoisseurs and word-game enthusiasts alike as a mine of useful, interesting and diverting items of vocabulary.

This thesaurus is a completely rewritten version of earlier editions of the *Chambers Thesaurus*. Many obsolete and rarer words have been deleted and thousands of new words have been added. Entries have been fully restructured to give a more focused treatment of synonyms, and also many new features have been included to help make the thesaurus even more useful.

Special features include:
- listing of synonyms by range of context ('register') to show the appropriate styles at which words are used, eg *formal*, *colloq*. (informal) or *slang*, or *technical* to show a word that is restricted to a particular subject field
- example phrases or sentences based on citations from the British National Corpus
- senses within an entry distinguished by numbered sections and either by a key synonym in SMALL CAPITALS or by an example in ***bold italics***, eg **sad 1** UNHAPPY, sorrowful ... **2 *sad news*** upsetting, distressing ...
- inclusion of related adjectives, eg the related adjective of *meaning* is 'semantic'
- hundreds of special panels showing word families ('hyponyms') giving lists of related words that present examples of, for example, **flowers** and **sports**, or informative encyclopedic information, eg **rivers**, **mountains** and **volcanoes**.
- concise notes on words easily confused, eg *censor* or *censure*, *fatal* or *fateful*.

A thesaurus jogs the memory — it offers help to the person struggling to encapsulate a meaning in a forgotten *mot juste* that might remain tantalizingly on the tip of the tongue. It is indispensable to the student, writer or reporter. A thesaurus is fun to use, and with the fun comes the opportunity to enhance a personal command of words and increase general knowledge. Words that may not be well known to the reader will trigger off investigations in a dictionary, leading to an exploration of the remoter corners of the language. Finally, a thesaurus is a tool that the word-gamester — player, solver or compiler — cannot do without.

It is recommended that the *Chambers English Thesaurus* should be used in conjunction with a dictionary, since the words listed are only rarely completely interchangeable alternatives. *Chambers 21st Century Dictionary* will be a useful standard companion; the obscurer terms will be found in the fuller *Chambers Dictionary*.

It is hoped that readers will enjoy using this thesaurus not only to discover the exact word or phrase for an appropriate context but also to appreciate more fully the rich diversity of the English language.

Martin H Manser
Aylesbury 1997

Abbreviations

adj	adjective	*prep*	preposition
adv	adverb	*pron*	pronoun
Austral.	Australian English	®	trademark
colloq.	colloquial	*Scot.*	Scottish English
conj	conjunction	*US*	American English
interj	interjection	*v*	verb
n	noun		

How to use the Thesaurus

headwords appear in bold type at the beginning of each entry	**box**[1] *n, v* ▶ *n boxes of books* container, receptacle, case, carton, packet, present, bijou, casket, pyxis, pyx, chest, coffret
many examples are given of word families (hyponyms)	*Types of box include*: bin, caddy, canister, cartridge, casket, coffer, coffin, crate, locker, pack, package, punnet, sarcophagus, tea chest, tin, trunk; ballot-box, black box, box-file, cardboard box, cigarette box, collection-box, cool-box, dispatch box, hatbox, jewellery box, knife box, matchbox, pencilbox, pillbox, pillar box, postbox, safe, sewing box, shoebox, snuffbox, strongbox, suggestion box, toolbox, trinket box, vesta, writing-slope.
phrases are highlighted separately	▶ *v* package, pack, wrap, case, encase ▷ **box in** enclose, surround, block in, cordon off, hem in, shut in, fence in, corner, trap, confine, restrain, coop up, restrict, imprison, cage, contain; *formal* circumscribe
numbered sections show separate meanings of the word	**box**[2] *v* **1** *learn to box* fight, spar, engage in fisticuffs **2** *box someone's ears* punch, hit, strike, slap, batter, thump, buffet, cuff
register labels show different contexts in which synonyms can be used	*colloq.* clout, wallop, whack, slug; *slang* sock
	boxer *n* fighter, prizefighter, sparring partner *formal* pugilist
informative encyclopedic lists included	*Weight divisions in professional boxing*: heavyweight, cruiserweight/junior-heavyweight, light-heavyweight, super-middleweight, middleweight, light-middleweight/junior-middleweight, welterweight, light-welterweight/junior-welterweight, lightweight, junior-lightweight/superfeatherweight, featherweight, super-bantamweight/junior-featherweight, bantamweight, super-flyweight/junior-bantamweight, flyweight, light-flyweight/junior-flyweight, mini-flyweight/straw-weight/minimum weight.
synonyms or alternative words are listed after the headword	**boxing** *n* prizefighting, fisticuffs, sparring *formal* pugilism *Related adjective*: pugilistic
synonyms are arranged according to shades of meaning	**boycott** *v* refuse, reject, embargo, black, ban, prohibit, disallow, bar, exclude, blacklist, proscribe, outlaw, ostracize, ignore, avoid, spurn *formal* eschew *colloq.* cold-shoulder, send to Coventry ⴲ encourage, support, advocate, defend, champion, patronize
parts of speech are listed after the headword and treated in order within the entry	**brace**[1] *n, v* ▶ *n fit braces to strengthen a wall* support, stay, strap, prop, clamp, fastener, vice, beam, strut, reinforcement, truss, buttress, shoring *formal* stanchion ▶ *v* strengthen, reinforce, bolster, buttress, prop (up), shore (up), support, hold up, steady, secure, tighten, fasten, tie, strap, bind, bandage *formal* fortify
words that have different histories but are spelt in the same way are highlighted by raised numbers and also by examples or key synonyms	**brace**[2] *n* *a brace of pheasant* pair, couple, twosome, duo
	bracing *adj* fresh, crisp, refreshing, reviving, strengthening, fortifying, tonic, rousing, stimulating, exhilarating, invigorating, enlivening, energizing, brisk, energetic,

vigorous

≠ weakening, draining, debilitating; *formal* enervating

> *the sign* **≠** *indicates antonyms - words that mean the opposite of another word*

brag *v*

bluster, boast, show off, swagger, vaunt
formal hyperbolize
colloq. blow your own trumpet, US blow your own horn, crow, talk big, lay it on thick/with a trowel
≠ be modest; *formal* deprecate; *colloq.* run down

> *American English vocabulary included*

brain *n*

1 *have a good brain*
mind, head, intellect, intelligence, wit, reason, sense, common sense, shrewdness, understanding
technical encephalon
formal acumen, sagacity, sensorium
colloq. grey matter, brains, nous, savvy
Related adjective: cerebral

> *technical synonyms listed separately*

> *related adjectives noted*

Parts of the brain include: brainstem, cerebellum, cerebral cortex (grey matter), cerebrum, corpus callosum, forebrain, frontal lobe, hindbrain, hypothalamus, medulla oblongata, mesencephalon, midbrain, occipital lobe, optic thalamus, parietal lobe, pineal body, pituitary gland, pons, spinal cord, temporal lobe, thalamus.

> *examples in numbered sections help you find the meaning that you want*

2 *the real brain in the family*
mastermind, intellectual, scholar, expert, pundit, highbrow, genius, prodigy
colloq. egghead, boffin, brainbox, cleverclogs
≠ 2 simpleton, idiot

brand *n, v*

▶ *n* **1** *different brands of soap*
MAKE, brand-name, tradename, trademark, logo, symbol, sign, emblem, label, stamp, hallmark
2 KIND, quality, class, kind, type, sort, line, variety, species
3 *identify cattle by their brand*
MARK , tag, identification, identifying mark
▶ *v* **1** *branded as a troublemaker*
mark, stamp, label, typecast, stigmatize, stain, taint, disgrace, discredit, denounce, censure
formal besmirch
2 *brand cattle*
mark, stamp, burn (in), scar

> *key synonyms in small capitals in numbered sections help you find the meaning that you want*

brash *adj*

1 BRAZEN, forward, impertinent, impudent, insolent, rude, cocky, self-confident, assertive, assured, bold, audacious
formal temerarious
colloq. pushy
2 RECKLESS, rash, impetuous, impulsive, hasty, foolhardy, incautious, indiscreet
formal incautious, precipitate
≠ 1 reserved, unassuming, modest, unobtrusive **2** cautious, wary, prudent

> *antonyms are given at the end of many entries, with numbered sections corresponding to those for the synonyms*

bravery *n*

courage, pluck, fearlessness, boldness, daring, stalwartness, hardiness, fortitude, resolution, tenacity, stout-heartedness, valour, gallantry, heroism, indomitability, mettle, spirit, dauntlessness, audacity
formal intrepidity, valiance
colloq. guts, grit, spunk
≠ cowardice, fearfulness, faint-heartedness, timidity

⚠ **bravery** or **bravado** ?
Bravery is courage: *soldiers decorated for bravery.*
Bravado is a boastful act of bravery intended to impress or intimidate or a boastful pretence of bravery aimed at concealing cowardice: *She felt her defiant bravado disintegrate like shattered glass.*

> *the sign* ⚠ *indicates a note on words easily confused*

A

abandon *v, n*
▶ *v* **1** *abandon a baby*
DESERT, leave (behind), maroon, strand, walk out on
formal forsake
colloq. run out on, jilt, ditch, chuck, dump, leave in the
lurch, give the elbow to, break (it) off with, leave high
and dry
2 *abandon the boat*
vacate, evacuate, leave, depart from, withdraw from, go
away from, bail out, escape, get out, break free from,
break away, break loose
colloq. quit
3 *abandon an activity/your responsibilities*
give up, stop (doing), let go, leave, abort, resign (from),
surrender, waive, sacrifice
formal renounce, part with, desist, cease, discontinue,
forego, forswear, relinquish, abdicate, yield, cede
colloq. drop, scrap, leave it at that, quit, jack in, pack
in, kick the habit
4 *abandon yourself to despair*
give way to, give yourself up to, yield to, be overcome by
E3 **1** support, maintain, stay (with), remain (with)
3 start, begin, continue
▶ *n* carelessness, recklessness, unrestraint, wildness,
impetuosity, thoughtlessness
E3 restraint, caution, inhibition(s), moderation, care,
carefulness

abandoned *adj*
1 *abandoned buildings*
DESERTED, unoccupied, unused, empty, vacant,
derelict, neglected, forlorn, desolate
formal forsaken
2 *abandoned young people*
DISSOLUTE, wild, crazy, uninhibited, mad, wanton,
wicked, debauched, immoral, corrupt
formal reprobate, profligate
E3 **1** (well-)kept, occupied **2** restrained, (self-)
controlled

abandonment *n*
1 DESERTION, leaving (behind), neglect, marooning,
stranding
formal forsaking, decampment, dereliction
colloq. running out on, jilting, ditching
2 *abandonment of an activity*
giving-up, stopping, resignation (from), surrender,
waiving, sacrifice
formal renunciation, relinquishment, cessation,
discontinuation, discontinuance, abdication, cession
colloq. dropping, scrapping

abase *v*
humble, humiliate
formal debase, demean, mortify, belittle, malign,
disparage
E3 elevate, honour, raise

abashed *adj*
ashamed, shamefaced, embarrassed, mortified,
humiliated, humbled, affronted, confused, taken

aback, bewildered, nonplussed, confounded,
dumbfounded
formal perturbed, discomposed, disconcerted,
discomfited, discountenanced
colloq. floored
E3 composed, at ease; *formal* audacious

abate *v*
1 *the storm abated*
DECREASE, subside, reduce, lessen, sink, dwindle, die
down, ease, moderate, taper off, fall off, wane
formal diminish, decline, attenuate
colloq. let up
2 *abate anger/pain*
MODERATE, ease, relieve, lessen, decrease, alleviate,
soothe, mitigate, pacify, quell, subside, weaken, wane,
slacken, slow, fade
formal remit
colloq. let up
E3 **1** increase, strengthen

abatement *n*
1 *the abatement of the storm; noise abatement*
reduction, lessening, subsidence, dying-down,
dwindling, easing, lowering
formal decline, diminution, attenuation
2 *abatement of anger*
moderation, easing, relief, lessening, decrease,
alleviation, mitigation, weakening, wane, slackening
formal remission, assuagement, palliation

abbey *n*
monastery, priory, friary, seminary, convent, nunnery,
cloister, minster, cathedral

abbreviate *v*
shorten, cut (down), trim, clip, abridge, summarize,
précis, abstract, digest, condense, compress, reduce,
lessen, shrink, contract
formal truncate, curtail, constrict
E3 extend, lengthen, expand, amplify

abbreviation *n*
shortening, short form, shortened form, contraction,
acronym, initialism, clipping, curtailment,
abridgement, summary, synopsis, résumé, précis,
abstract, digest, compression, reduction
formal truncated form, summarization, truncation
E3 long form, extension, expansion, amplification

abdicate *v*
1 *the king abdicated*
resign, resign from the throne, stand down, give up,
give up the throne
formal retire, relinquish/renounce the throne
colloq. quit
2 *abdicate responsibility*
abandon, give up, reject, refuse to accept any longer,
surrender, disown
formal renounce, relinquish, cede, yield, forego,
abjure, abnegate, repudiate

colloq. shirk, quit, turn your back on, wash your hands of

abdication   *n*
1 *the abdication of the king*
resignation, retirement, standing-down, giving up of the throne
formal renunciation/relinquishment of the throne
2 *abdication of responsibilities*
abandonment, rejection, refusal, surrender, giving-up, disowning
formal renunciation, relinquishment, abjuration, abnegation, repudiation

abdomen   *n*
belly, stomach, midriff
colloq. guts, tummy, tum, paunch, pot belly, corporation
Related adjectives: coeliac, abdominal

abdominal   *adj*
coeliac, ventral, intestinal, visceral, ventricular, gastric, colic

abduct   *v*
kidnap, seize, take (away) by force, carry off, make off with, snatch, shanghai, take as hostage, hold to ransom, spirit away, lay hold of, seduce, rape
formal appropriate
colloq. run away/off with

aberrant   *adj*
deviant, deviating, divergent, different, irregular, anomalous, odd, peculiar, eccentric, rogue, defective, corrupt
formal incongruous, atypical
colloq. freakish, quirky
E3 regular, normal, typical

aberration   *n*
1 *an aberration in behaviour*
deviation, straying, wandering, divergence, instability, irregularity, abnormality, nonconformity, oversight, anomaly, oddity, peculiarity, eccentricity, lapse, delusion
2 *scientific aberrations*
deviation, divergence, irregularity, abnormality, variation, anomaly, oddity, peculiarity, mistake
E3 1 conformity, regularity, normality

abet   *v*
help, aid, assist, support, encourage, endorse, promote, sanction, spur, condone
formal succour
colloq. egg on
E3 prevent, hinder, discourage

abeyance   *n*
▷ **in abeyance**   no longer in use, cancelled temporarily, not in operation, disused, suspended, in (a state of) suspension, pending
formal dormant
colloq. hanging fire, on ice, shelved
E3 in use, in operation, continued

abhor   *v*
hate, detest, loathe, recoil from, spurn, despise, have an aversion to, can't abide/bear, shudder at, shrink from
formal abominate, execrate
colloq. hate someone's guts, can't stand
E3 love, adore

abhorrence   *n*
hate, hatred, aversion, loathing, horror, revulsion, disgust, distaste, contempt

formal abomination, repugnance, execration, detestation, animosity, enmity, malice, odium
E3 love, adoration

abhorrent   *adj*
repugnant, detestable, loathsome, abominable, obnoxious, hated, hateful, horrible, horrid, offensive, repellent, repulsive, revolting, nauseating, disgusting, distasteful
formal execrable, heinous, odious
E3 delightful, attractive

abide   *v*
1 *I can't abide that smell*
BEAR, put up with, tolerate, accept, take, brook, endure
colloq. stand, stomach
2 *truths that abide*
REMAIN, last, endure, continue, persist
▷ **abide by**   obey, observe, follow, go along with, carry out, stand by, hold to, keep to, agree to, accept, respect, uphold, fulfil; *formal* comply with, adhere to, conform to, submit to, discharge; *colloq.* go by the book, stick to the rules, toe the line
E3 ignore, reject; *colloq.* flout

abiding   *adj*
lasting, enduring, constant, continual, continuous, long-lasting, long-term, long-running, lifelong, persistent, unchanging, unchangeable, eternal, everlasting, immortal, unending, chronic, permanent, stable, firm, durable
formal immutable
E3 short-lived, short-term; *formal* ephemeral, transient

ability   *n*
1 *the ability to teach*
CAPABILITY, capacity, faculty, facility, power(s), resources
formal potentiality, potential, propensity
2 *someone of great ability*
SKILL, competence, proficiency, qualification, talent, gift, calibre, endowment, expertise, forte, strength, dexterity, aptitude, deftness, adeptness, adroitness, prowess, motivation
formal competency
colloq. knack, flair, touch, know-how, genius, the hang, the knack, what it takes, *savoir-faire,* savvy
E3 1 inability **2** incompetence, weakness

⚠ **ability** or **capability** ?
Ability is the more general term, referring to the possession of particular skills, knowledge, powers, etc or the simple fact of something being possible: *his ability to write a catchy tune; our ability to work together. Capability* may refer to the possession of an aptitude, especially one that derives from a person's character: *my mother's organizational capabilities.*

---

abject   *adj*
1 *abject poverty*
miserable, wretched, forlorn, hopeless, shameful, humiliating, pitiable, pathetic, outcast, degraded
formal execrable
2 *an abject coward*
contemptible, worthless, base, low, mean, dishonourable, deplorable, despicable, vile, sordid, debased, degenerate, submissive, servile, grovelling
formal ignoble, ignominious
E3 2 proud, exalted

abjure *v*
renounce, abandon, disown, deny, reject
formal relinquish, retract, forswear, abdicate,
abnegate, disavow, disclaim, renege on
E3 agree, assent, support

ablaze *adj*
1 BURNING, blazing, flaming, in flames, on fire,
ignited, lighted, alight, incandescent
formal aflame, afire
2 *a house ablaze with lights*
illuminated, luminous, glowing, aglow, radiant,
flashing, gleaming, sparkling, brilliant, lit up
formal incandescent
3 *eyes ablaze with passion*
impassioned, passionate, fervent, ardent, fiery,
enthusiastic, excited, exhilarated, stimulated, aroused,
angry, furious, fuming, raging, incensed, frenzied

able *adj*
capable, competent, fit, fitted, dexterous, adroit, deft,
adept, proficient, qualified, practised, experienced,
skilled, accomplished, clever, intelligent, expert,
masterly, skilful, ingenious talented, gifted, strong,
powerful, effective, efficient
colloq. all there, on the ball, up to it, wised up, cut out
for
E3 unable, incapable, incompetent, ineffective

able-bodied *adj*
fit, healthy, sound, in good health, strong, robust,
hardy, tough, vigorous, powerful, hale, hearty, hale and
hearty, fine, lusty, sturdy, rugged, strapping, stout,
burly, stalwart, staunch
E3 disabled, handicapped, infirm, delicate

abnegation *n*
abstinence, self-denial, surrender, self-sacrifice,
giving-up, temperance
formal renunciation, relinquishment, forbearance,
abjuration, repudiation, eschewal

abnormal *adj*
odd, strange, peculiar, curious, queer, weird,
eccentric, idiosyncratic, paranormal, unnatural,
uncanny, extraordinary, exceptional, unusual,
uncommon, unexpected, irregular, erratic, wayward,
deviant, divergent, different
formal singular, anomalous, aberrant, atypical, outré,
preternatural
colloq. oddball
E3 normal, regular, typical

abnormality *n*
oddity, peculiarity, eccentricity, strangeness,
bizarreness, unnaturalness, unusualness, irregularity,
exception, anomaly, deformity, flaw, malformation,
dysfunction, deviation, divergence, difference
formal singularity, aberration, atypicality
E3 normality, regularity

abode *n*
home, dwelling, dwelling-place, lodgings, habitation,
habitat
formal residence, domicile
colloq. pad

abolish *v*
cancel, end, stop, do away with, quash, repeal, revoke,
annul, invalidate, rescind, suppress, destroy, eliminate,
put an end to, exterminate, annihilate, obliterate,
eradicate, overthrow, blot out, wipe out, get rid of,
stamp out, subvert, overturn
formal terminate, discontinue, nullify, vitiate,

abrogate, expunge
colloq. axe
E3 create, introduce, establish, institute, retain,
authorize, continue

abolition *n*
cancellation, ending, doing away with, repeal,
suppression, destruction, elimination, annihilation,
extinction, overthrow, blotting-out, quashing,
withdrawal
formal termination, annulment, invalidation,
nullification, voiding, rescindment, revocation,
abrogation, rescission, obliteration, extermination,
eradication, extirpation, dissolution, subversion
colloq. axe
E3 creation, introduction, retention, authorization,
continuation

abominable *adj*
loathsome, detestable, hateful, horrid, horrible,
abhorrent, offensive, repulsive, repellent, disgusting,
revolting, obnoxious, nauseating, foul, base, vile,
atrocious, appalling, terrible, contemptible,
despicable, wretched, cursed, damnable
formal execrable, odious, repugnant, heinous,
reprehensible
E3 delightful, pleasant, desirable

abominate *v*
abhor, hate, loathe, detest, despise, have an aversion to,
condemn
formal execrate
E3 love, adore

abomination *n*
1 *murder is an abomination*
OUTRAGE, offence, disgrace, horror, atrocity, evil,
curse, plague, torment
formal anathema
2 HATE, hatred, loathing, revulsion, disgust, distaste,
aversion, hostility
formal abhorrence, execration, detestation,
repugnance, odium
E3 **2** adoration, delight

aboriginal *adj*
native, indigenous, original, earliest, first, primal,
primeval, primitive, ancient, local
formal autochthonous

abort *v*
1 *abort a pregnancy*
TERMINATE, miscarry, have a miscarriage
2 *abort a plan*
end, bring/come to an end, stop, suspend, halt, call off,
cut short, check, frustrate, thwart, fail
formal nullify
colloq. axe, pull the plug on
E3 **2** continue, start, begin

abortion *n*
termination, miscarriage

abortive *adj*
failed, unsuccessful, fruitless, unproductive, barren,
sterile, vain, idle, futile, useless, ineffective
formal unavailing, ineffectual
E3 successful, fruitful

abound *v*
be plentiful, flourish, swell, increase, swarm, teem,
crowd, be full, brim over, overflow
formal proliferate, thrive, superabound, exuberate,
luxuriate

about *prep, adv*
▶ *prep* **1** *write about a subject*
REGARDING, on, on the subject of, concerning, relating to, connected with, concerned with, as regards, referring to, with regard to, with respect to, with reference to, in the matter of, re, dealing with
formal apropos of
2 *somewhere about the house*
close to, near, nearby, beside, adjacent to
3 *walk about the town*
round, around, surrounding, throughout, all over
formal encircling, encompassing
▶ *adv* **1** *about twenty*
around, approximately, roughly, in the region of, more or less, almost, nearly, approaching, nearing
formal circa
2 *run about*
to and fro, here and there, from place to place
old use hither and thither
▷ **about to** going to, on the point of, on the verge of, all but, ready to, soon to, intending to, preparing to

about-turn *n*
about-face, volte-face, (complete) reversal, turnabout
formal enantiodromia
colloq. U-turn

above *prep, adv, adj*
▶ *prep* **1** *above the clouds*
over, higher than, on top of
formal atop
2 *above the rank of sergeant*
superior to, senior to, higher than, over
3 *temperatures above the average*
in excess of, exceeding, beyond
formal surpassing
4 *above suspicion*
beyond, not liable to, not open to, superior to
⊟ **1** below, under **2** below
▶ *adv* **1** *noise from above*
overhead, high up, higher
formal aloft, on high
2 *as mentioned above*
earlier, before, previously
⊟ **1** below, underneath **2** below
▶ *adj* above-mentioned, previous, earlier, preceding
formal above-stated, foregoing, prior, aforementioned, aforesaid

above-board *adj*
honest, legitimate, straight, true, open, frank, candid, straightforward, forthright, truthful, trustworthy, honourable, reputable, upright
formal guileless, veracious
colloq. on the level, fair and square, square
⊟ dishonest, underhand, shady

abrade *v*
rub, graze, scratch, scrape, scour, grate, grind, chafe, erode, wear away/down

abrasion *n*
graze, scratch, cut, scratching, scraping, scrape, scouring, grating, grinding, abrading, chafing, chafe, friction, rubbing, erosion, wearing away, wearing-down
formal excoriation

abrasive *adj*
1 *abrasive material*
rough, scratching, scraping, grating, rough, harsh, chafing, corrosive
formal erosive, frictional, attritional, erodent

2 *an abrasive person*
harsh, brusque, caustic, sharp, biting, hurtful, nasty, unpleasant, irritating, annoying
⊟ **1** smooth **2** pleasant, kind

abreast *adj*
1 *walk abreast*
side by side, level, beside/alongside each other, next to each other
2 *keep abreast of the news*
acquainted, informed, knowledgeable, *au courant*, up to date, in touch, *au fait*, familiar, well up
formal conversant
colloq. in the picture, on the ball, with your finger on the pulse
⊟ **2** unaware, out of touch, unfamiliar

abridge *v*
shorten, cut (down), prune, curtail, abbreviate, contract, reduce, decrease, lessen, summarize, précis, abstract, digest, condense, compress, concentrate
formal synopsize
colloq. clip, lop
⊟ expand, amplify; *colloq.* pad out

abridgement *n*
1 *the abridgement of the story*
SHORTENING, cutting, reduction, decrease, diminishing, concentration, contraction, restriction
formal diminution, truncation
2 *an abridgement of a report*
SUMMARY, synopsis, résumé, short version, shortened ⟍ version, outline, précis, abstract, digest, epitome
formal conspectus, abrégé
⊟ **1** expansion; *colloq.* padding (out)

abroad *adv*
1 *go abroad on business*
OVERSEAS, in/to a foreign country, in/to foreign parts, out of the country, far and wide, widely
2 *news spread abroad*
AT LARGE, widely, publicly, around, about, circulating, extensively, current
⊟ **1** at home

abrogate *v*
abolish, cancel, end, stop, repeal, revoke, do away with, annul, invalidate, reverse
formal countermand, rescind, retract, dissolve, repudiate, disenact
colloq. axe, scrap
⊟ establish, institute, introduce

abrupt *adj*
1 *come to an abrupt end*
sudden, unexpected, unforeseen, unannounced, unceremonious, surprising, dramatic, quick, rapid, swift, hasty, hurried, instant, instantaneous
formal precipitate
colloq. snap
2 *an abrupt manner*
BRUSQUE, curt, terse, brisk, gruff, rough, rude, offhand, impolite, blunt, direct, uncivil
colloq. short, snappy, snappish
3 *an abrupt slope*
sheer, steep, sharp
formal precipitous, declivitous
⊟ **1** gradual, slow, leisurely **2** friendly, expansive, ceremonious, polite

abscond *v*
run away, run off, make off, decamp, flee, fly, escape, disappear, vanish, bolt
formal take French leave

colloq. quit, scram, skedaddle, vamoose, clear out, make a quick getaway, beat it, run for it, do a runner, do a bunk, do a moonlight flit

absence *n*
1 *absence from school*
non-attendance, non-appearance, truancy, absenteeism, non-existence
2 LACK, need, deficiency, scarcity, unavailability, default, omission, vacancy
formal want, dearth, privation, paucity, vacuity
E3 **1** presence, attendance, appearance **2** presence

absent *adj*
1 *absent from the meeting*
MISSING, not present, not here, not there, not around, away, out, off, unavailable, gone, lacking, truant
formal in absentia
colloq. when someone's back is turned
2 INATTENTIVE, daydreaming, dreamy, faraway, elsewhere, absent-minded, blank, preoccupied, unaware, oblivious, unheeding
formal vacant, distracted
E3 **1** present, here, there **2** attentive, alert, aware

absent-minded *adj*
forgetful, scatterbrained, having a bad memory, absent, withdrawn, faraway, distracted, preoccupied, absorbed, engrossed, musing, dreaming, dreamy, wool-gathering, inattentive, unaware, oblivious, unconscious, heedless, unheeding, unthinking, impractical, abstracted, pensive
formal distrait(e)
colloq. with a memory like a sieve, not all there, somewhere else, dead to the world, miles away, in a world of your own, scatty
E3 attentive

absolute *adj*
1 *in absolute confidence*
utter, total, complete, entire, full, thorough, exhaustive, supreme, definitive, conclusive, final, definite, unquestionable, unambiguous, undivided, unlimited, categorical, decided, decisive, positive, sure, certain, genuine, pure, perfect, sheer, unmixed, unadulterated, unqualified, unconditional, unmitigated, unrestrained, unequivocal, unrestricted, downright, rank, out-and-out, outright
formal consummate, indubitable, peremptory
2 *absolute power/ruler*
supreme, totalitarian, autocratic, tyrannical, despotic, dictatorial, sovereign, authoritarian, almighty, unlimited, unrestricted, plenary
formal omnipotent, autarchical

absolutely *adv*
utterly, totally, completely, entirely, fully, wholly, thoroughly, exhaustively, perfectly, supremely, unconditionally, finally, categorically, definitely, positively, in every way/respect, wholeheartedly, conclusively, unequivocally, unambiguously, unquestionably, decidedly, decisively, surely, certainly, infallibly, genuinely, truly, purely, exactly, precisely
colloq. dead

absolution *n*
forgiveness, pardon, deliverance, freedom, liberation, release, mercy, redemption, acquittal, amnesty, emancipation
formal exoneration, remission, vindication, discharge, exculpation, purgation, shrift

absolve *v*
excuse, clear, forgive, pardon, deliver, free, set free,

liberate, release, loose, have mercy on, show mercy towards, emancipate
formal exonerate, vindicate, justify, acquit, discharge, exculpate, remit
colloq. let off

absorb *v*
1 *absorb liquid/heat*
take in, draw in, soak up, drink in, suck up, assimilate, engulf
formal ingest, imbibe, consume
colloq. devour
2 *absorb facts*
take in, digest, assimilate, understand, receive, hold, retain
3 *absorb your attention*
ENGROSS, involve, fascinate, enthral, captivate, engage, hold, preoccupy, occupy, fill (up), monopolize
colloq. not be able to put down
4 *absorbed into a bigger company*
incorporate, integrate, assimilate
colloq. swallow up
E3 **1** give out; *formal* exude

absorbed *adj*
engrossed, involved, fascinated, interested, enthralled, captivated, preoccupied, occupied, taken up with, riveted

absorbent *adj*
receptive, porous, permeable, pervious, soaking, blotting, retentive
formal absorptive, assimilative, sorbefacient, resorbent
E3 water-repellent, water-proof

absorbing *adj*
interesting, amusing, entertaining, enjoyable, diverting, engrossing, preoccupying, intriguing, fascinating, captivating, enthralling, spellbinding, gripping, riveting, compelling, compulsive
colloq. unputdownable
E3 boring, off-putting

absorption *n*
1 *the absorption of liquid/heat*
taking-in, drawing-in, soaking-up, assimilation
technical osmosis
formal ingestion, consumption
colloq. devouring
2 *absorption of your attention*
ENGROSSING, involvement, captivating, riveting, engagement, holding, preoccupation, occupation, attentiveness, concentration, intentness, monopoly

abstain *v*
1 *abstain from food*
refuse, reject, resist, shun, avoid, keep from, give up, do/go without, stop, stop short of, hold back, keep from
formal refrain, decline, renounce, forbear, forego, desist, deny yourself, eschew
colloq. think twice before doing something
2 *abstain in an election*
not vote, refuse to vote
E3 **1** indulge

abstemious *adj*
temperate, moderate, self-denying, self-disciplined, disciplined, sober, sparing, frugal, austere, ascetic, restrained
formal abstinent, self-abnegating
E3 intemperate, gluttonous, luxurious

abstention *n*
not voting, refusal to vote, declining to vote

abstinence *n*
1 *abstinence from sensual desires*
abstaining, self-denial, non-indulgence, avoidance, refusal, giving-up, going-without, restraint, self-restraint, self-control, self-discipline
formal abstemiousness, continence, forbearance, refraining, declension, renunciation, desistance, eschewal
2 *abstinence from alcohol*
TEETOTALISM, temperance, moderation, frugality, asceticism
formal sobriety, nephalism
E3 **1** indulgence, self-indulgence

abstract *adj, n, v*
▶ *adj* **1** *abstract nouns*
non-concrete, conceptual, notional
2 *abstract reasoning*
theoretical, conceptual, notional, intellectual, hypothetical, unpractical, unrealistic, general, generalized, indefinite, metaphysical, philosophical, academic, complex, deep, profound, subtle
formal abstruse, arcane, recondite
3 *abstract paintings*
non-realistic, non-representational, contrived
E3 **1, 2** concrete **2** real, actual, practical **3** representational, realistic, figurative
▶ *n* synopsis, outline, summary, recapitulation, résumé, précis, digest, abridgement, compression
formal epitome, conspectus
▶ *v* **1** *abstract a report*
summarize, outline, précis, digest, condense, compress, abridge, abbreviate, shorten, cut (down)
2 *abstract coal from the ground*
EXTRACT, remove, take away/out, withdraw, isolate, detach, separate
formal dissociate
E3 **1** expand, lengthen **2** insert, put in

abstracted *adj*
preoccupied, absent-minded, distracted, forgetful, scatterbrained, absent, withdrawn, absorbed, engrossed, pensive, musing, dreaming, dreamy, bemused, wool-gathering, inattentive, unaware, oblivious, unconscious, heedless, unheeding, unthinking, impractical
colloq. scatty
E3 attentive, alert; *colloq.* on the ball

abstraction *n*
1 IDEA, notion, concept, thought, conception, theory, hypothesis, theorem, formula, generalization, generality
2 INATTENTION, dream, dreaminess, absent-mindedness, preoccupation, remoteness, withdrawal
formal distraction, pensiveness, absorption, bemusedness
3 EXTRACTION, withdrawal, isolation, separation

abstruse *adj*
obscure, difficult to understand, deep, profound, complex, mysterious, cryptic, unfathomable, incomprehensible, perplexing, puzzling
formal arcane, esoteric, inscrutable, enigmatic, recondite
E3 simple, obvious

absurd *adj*
ridiculous, ludicrous, preposterous, fantastic, illogical, paradoxical, unreasonable, irrational, nonsensical, meaningless, senseless, foolish, silly, stupid, idiotic, crazy, farcical, inane, comical, funny, humorous, harebrained, laughable, derisory
formal incongruous, implausible, untenable, risible, asinine
colloq. daft
E3 reasonable, logical, rational, sensible

absurdity *n*
ridiculousness, ludicrousness, illogicality, unreasonableness, meaninglessness, senselessness, foolishness, folly, silliness, fatuousness, idiocy, stupidity, craziness, inanity, paradox, humour, farce, charade, travesty, joke, nonsense, rubbish
formal incongruity, irrationality, implausibility
colloq. daftness, twaddle, gibberish, drivel, claptrap, balderdash
E3 reasonableness, logicality, rationality, (good) sense

abundance *n*
plenty, fullness, great supply, wealth, generosity, richness, riches, lavishness, overflow, land of milk and honey, glut, extravagance, excess, bonanza, fortune
formal amplitude, bounty, plethora, copiousness, profusion, exuberance, luxuriance, munificence, plenitude, prodigality, opulence, affluence
colloq. bags, heaps, masses, piles, loads, stacks, lashings, oodles, lots, *US* scads
E3 shortage, scarcity; *formal* dearth, paucity

abundant *adj*
plentiful, in plenty, full, filled, ample, copious, profuse, bountiful, exuberant, more than enough, well-supplied, ample, generous, rich, affluent, lavish, teeming, overflowing, galore
formal bounteous, luxuriant, opulent
E3 scarce, sparse, scant, insufficient

abuse *n, v*
▶ *n* **1** *the abuse of drugs*
misuse, exploitation, imposition, oppression, wrong, ill-treatment, maltreatment
formal misapplication
2 *child abuse*
mistreatment, maltreatment, ill-treatment, cruelty, hurt, injury, molestation, damage, harm, beating, torture
3 *shout abuse*
insult(s), swearing, swear-word, cursing, curse, offence, defamation, libel, slander, reproach, censure, scolding
formal affront, upbraiding, invective, castigation, malediction, vilification, vituperation, calumniation, calumny, contumely, denigration, derision, disparagement, tirade, diatribe, vitriol
E3 **2** care, attention **3** compliment(s), praise
▶ *v* **1** *abuse authority*
misuse, exploit, take advantage of
formal misapply
2 *abuse children*
ILL-TREAT, maltreat, hurt, injure, damage, harm, beat, hit, batter, oppress, exploit, wrong, torture, molest, rape, harass sexually
3 *abuse immigrants*
INSULT, swear at, curse, hurl abuse at, call names, be rude to, defame, libel, slander, pick on, bully, smear, scold, rail, victimize
formal malign, revile, upbraid, calumniate, castigate, denigrate, disparage, oppugn
colloq. slate, treat like dirt
E3 **2** cherish, care for, look after **3** compliment, praise

⚠ **abuse** or **misuse** ?
Abuse refers to the use of something for the wrong purposes: *substance abuse,* eg glue-sniffing. *Misuse* refers to the use of substances or objects in an incorrect way: *Bacteria may acquire resistance to a particular antibiotic by its overuse or misuse.*

abusive *adj*
insulting, offensive, rude, scathing, hurtful, harmful, injurious, cruel, brutal, destructive, scathing, defamatory, libellous, slanderous, derogatory, disparaging, pejorative, maligning, reviling, reproachful, scolding, blasphemous
formal vilifying, censorious, upbraiding, railing, vituperative, castigating, calumniating, contumelious, denigrating, opprobrious
🔁 complimentary, polite

abut *v*
border, be next to, verge on, join, touch, impinge
formal adjoin, conjoin

abysmal *adj*
dismal, shocking, disgraceful, dreadful, appalling, awful, complete, utter

abyss *n*
fall into an abyss; the abyss of war
gulf, chasm, crevasse, fissure, gorge, canyon, crater, pit, bottomless pit, depth(s), void
formal barathrum

academic *adj, n*
▶ *adj* **1** *academic qualifications*
educational, instructional, scholastic
formal pedagogical
2 *she's very academic*
SCHOLARLY, intellectual, educated, well-educated, learned, well-read, studious, bookish, literary, highbrow, serious, donnish
formal erudite
colloq. brainy, smart
3 *an academic, not practical, approach*
THEORETICAL, hypothetical, speculative, abstract, impractical, irrelevant, ivory-tower
formal conjectural, notional
🔁 **3** practical, relevant
▶ *n* teacher, professor, don, master, fellow, lecturer, tutor, educator, instructor, trainer, student, scholar, man/woman of letters, pedant, bookworm

accede *v*
1 *accede to a request*
ACCEPT, bow to, agree to, admit, give in, back down
formal consent to, assent to, comply with, acquiesce, concur
2 *accede to the throne*
come to, inherit
formal assume, attain, succeed (to)

accelerate *v*
1 *the car/driver accelerated*
quicken, speed, speed up, drive faster, go faster, pick up/gather speed, gain momentum
colloq. open up, put your foot down, step on it/the gas/ the juice, put on a spurt
2 *accelerate a process*
speed up, hurry, step up, stimulate, facilitate, advance, further, promote, spur on, forward
technical festinate
formal hasten, expedite, precipitate
🔁 **1, 2** decelerate, slow down, delay

acceleration *n*
1 *the acceleration of a car*
speeding-up, rate of increase, momentum
2 *acceleration of a process*
speeding-up, stepping-up, stimulation, promotion, forwarding
formal advancement, furtherance, hastening, expedition
🔁 **1, 2** deceleration, slowing-down, delay

accent *n*
1 *speak with a strong Irish accent*
PRONUNCIATION, articulation, brogue, tone, pitch, intonation, inflection, accentuation, stress, emphasis, intensity, force, rhythm, beat, pulse
formal enunciation, diction, modulation, cadence, pulsation
colloq. twang
2 *the accent is on ease of use*
EMPHASIS, prominence, importance, priority, underlining, highlighting

accentuate *v*
accent, stress, emphasize, put the emphasis on, underline, underscore, highlight, give prominence to, heighten, intensify, strengthen, deepen
colloq. point up, drive the point home, make great play of, show up
🔁 weaken; *colloq.* play down

accept *v*
1 *accept a job/an offer*
take, take up, receive, obtain, acquire, gain, secure, get, say yes to, not say no to
formal reply in the affirmative
colloq. jump at
2 *accept advice*
take, welcome
formal embrace
colloq. take on board, take someone's point
3 *accept a decision*
acknowledge, recognize, admit, allow, approve, agree to, take on, adopt, bow to, go along with, give in, back down
formal abide by, accede to, consent to, acquiesce in, concur with, comply with
4 *accept responsibility/blame*
take on, undertake, bear, be responsible for, admit, acknowledge
5 *accept an explanation*
believe (in), trust, be certain of
colloq. buy, swallow, fall for
6 *accept into the family*
WELCOME, receive, receive warmly, integrate
7 *accept ill-treatment*
TOLERATE, stand, bear, abide, face up to, take, endure, put up with, yield to, resign yourself to, be resigned to, come to terms with, let go of
colloq. stomach, swallow, make the best of
🔁 **1** refuse, turn down **2, 3, 4, 5, 6** reject

acceptable *adj*
1 *homework that is just acceptable*
SATISFACTORY, tolerable, moderate, passable, adequate, reasonable, all right, unexceptionable
colloq. OK, so-so
2 *acceptable not to smoke*
admissible, allowable, permissible, tolerable, agreeable, appropriate, desirable
colloq. the done thing
3 *a most acceptable present*

welcome, delightful, pleasant, desirable, gratifying
F3 1 unacceptable, unsatisfactory 2 unacceptable

acceptance *n*
1 *acceptance of a job/an offer*
taking (up), accepting, receipt, obtaining, getting,
acquiring, gaining, securing
2 *acceptance of advice*
taking, welcoming
formal embracing
colloq. taking on board, taking someone's point
3 *acceptance of the decision*
acknowledgement, admission, recognition, approval,
agreement, taking on, adoption, going along with,
giving-in, backing-down
formal consent, assent, affirmation, accession,
acquiescence, concurrence, endorsement, ratification
colloq. stamp of approval, OK
4 *acceptance of responsibility/blame*
taking on, undertaking, assumption, admission,
acknowledgement
5 *the idea gained acceptance*
credence, belief, trust, faith
6 *acceptance into the family*
welcome, receiving, recognition, integration
7 *acceptance of your situation*
tolerance, bearing, facing up to, endurance,
resignation, putting up with
colloq. making the best of
F3 1 refusal 2, 3, 4, 5, 6 rejection

accepted *adj*
recognized, established, authorized, approved,
ratified, sanctioned, agreed, acknowledged, admitted,
confirmed, acceptable, correct, appropriate,
conventional, orthodox, traditional, customary, time-
honoured, received, universal, regular, standard,
normal, usual, common
F3 unconventional, unorthodox, controversial

access *n*
1 *gain access to the building*
means of approach/entry, entry, entering, entrance,
gateway, door, way in, key, approach, passage, road,
path, drive, driveway, course
2 *deny access to the prisoner*
admission, admittance, right of entry, permission to
enter/see, accessibility
formal entrée, ingress
F3 1 exit, outlet; *formal* egress

accessible *adj*
1 *accessible from the motorway*
reachable, attainable, achievable
colloq. get-at-able
2 *financial help that is accessible to everyone*
obtainable, available, on hand, ready, handy,
convenient, near, nearby
formal procurable
3 *an accessible book/painting*
UNDERSTANDABLE, intelligible, easy to understand
formal user-friendly
F3 1 inaccessible, remote; *colloq.* out of the way, off
the beaten track 3 incomprehensible, unintelligible

accession *n*
1 *accession to the throne*
inheritance
formal assumption, attaining, succession
2 *accessions to the library*
addition, acquisition, increase, possession, purchase,
gift

accessory *n, adj*
▶ *n* 1 *computer accessories*
extra, supplement, addition, attachment, extension,
component, fitting
formal appendage, adjunct
2 *accessories to match an outfit*
decoration, adornment, ornament, frill, trimming,
supplement, complement, gloves, hat, belt, shoes,
handbag, jewellery
formal embellishment
3 *an accessory to a crime*
ACCOMPLICE, partner, associate, colleague,
confederate, assistant, helper, help, aid
technical accessory before the fact, accessory after the
fact, particeps criminis
formal abettor, conniver
▶ *adj* additional, extra, supplementary, subsidiary,
contributory, incidental, secondary, ancillary,
auxiliary, subordinate
formal supplemental

accident *n*
1 *an accident with boiling water*
mishap, casualty, calamity, disaster, tragedy
formal misfortune, mischance, misadventure
colloq. blow
2 *a car accident*
collision, crash, fatality
formal contretemps
colloq. pile-up, smash-up, wreck; *slang* shunt, prang
3 *happen by accident*
CHANCE, hazard, luck, good luck, fortune, good
fortune, fate, coincidence
formal fortuity, serendipity, contingency,
happenstance
colloq. fluke

accidental *adj*
unintentional, unintended, inadvertent, unplanned,
uncalculated, unpremeditated, unwitting,
unexpected, unanticipated, unforeseen, unlooked-for,
chance, uncertain, haphazard, random, casual,
incidental
formal fortuitous, adventitious, serendipitous,
aleatory
colloq. fluky
F3 intentional, deliberate, calculated, premeditated

accidentally *adv*
unintentionally, inadvertently, unexpectedly, by
chance, by accident, by mistake, unwittingly,
haphazardly, randomly, incidentally
formal fortuitously, bechance, adventitiously,
serendipitously
F3 intentionally, deliberately

acclaim *v, n*
▶ *v* praise, commend, extol, exalt, honour, hail,
salute, welcome, applaud, clap, cheer, celebrate,
fanfare, toast
formal laud, eulogize
colloq. rave about, give rave reviews to, give a good
press to
F3 condemn, criticize; *colloq.* give a bad press to
▶ *n* praise, commendation, homage, tribute,
exaltation, honour, welcome, approval, bouquets,
applause, ovation, clapping, cheers, cheering,
shouting, celebration
formal acclamation, approbation, eulogy, extolment,
laudation, plaudits
F3 criticism, disapproval, condemnation;
formal vituperation; *colloq.* brickbats, bad press

acclamation *n*
praise, commendation, homage, tribute, exaltation, honour, welcome, approval, congratulations, applause, ovation, clapping, cheering, bravos, shouting, celebration, enthusiasm
formal approbation, eulogy, felicitations, paean, panegyric
F∃ criticism, disapproval, condemnation

acclimatize *v*
adjust, adapt, accustom, get used to, find your way around, accommodate, familiarize, attune, conform
formal habituate, acculturate, inure, naturalize
colloq. find/get your bearings, find your feet

accolade *n*
award, honour, tribute, praise

accommodate *v*
1 *accommodate someone in a hotel*
PUT UP, take in, house, shelter, provide shelter for, cater for, lodge, board, billet
formal domicile
colloq. put a roof over someone's head
2 *the hall accommodates 400*
take, hold, have room/space for
3 *accommodate customers*
help, be helpful to, oblige, assist, aid, serve, provide, supply, comply, conform
colloq. give/lend a (helping) hand to
4 *accommodate yourself to new developments*
adapt, accustom, acclimatize, adjust, modify, fit, harmonize, reconcile, settle, compose

accommodating *adj*
obliging, indulgent, helpful, co-operative, agreeable, willing, kind, considerate, unselfish, sympathetic, friendly, hospitable
formal complaisant, pliable
F∃ disobliging, selfish

accommodation *n*
1 *find accommodation*
housing, shelter, board, quarter(s), lodging
colloq. a roof over someone's head
2 *reach an accommodation*
agreement, compromise, negotiation(s), reconciliation, settlement, harmony, conformity

> *Types of accommodation include*: flat, apartment, bedsit, bedsitter, *colloq.* digs, lodgings, hostel, halls of residence, rooms, residence, dwelling, shelter, *colloq.* pad, *colloq.* squat, bed and breakfast, board, guest house, hotel, youth hostel, villa, timeshare, motel, inn, pension, boarding-house, barracks, billet, married quarters. *See also* **house**; **room**.

accompaniment *n*
1 *a musical accompaniment*
support, background, backing, backup
technical obbligato, vamp
2 *wine as an accompaniment to food*
complement, accessory, supplement, addition
formal concomitant, adjunct, coexistence

accompany *v*
1 *accompany someone on holiday*
escort, attend, go (along) with, associate with, come (along) with, partner, chaperone, usher, conduct, follow
formal consort, convoy, squire
colloq. hang around with
2 *a book accompanied by a study guide*

complement, supplement, belong to, go with
formal coexist, coincide
3 *accompany someone on the guitar*
play with, provide backing/support for

accomplice *n*
assistant, helper, abettor, mate, henchman, conspirator, collaborator, ally, confederate, partner, associate, colleague, aide, participator, accessory, right-hand man
colloq. sidekick

accomplish *v*
achieve, attain, do, perform, carry out, manage, execute, fulfil, discharge, finish, complete, conclude, realize, bring about, bring off, engineer, produce, obtain
formal consummate, effect, effectuate
colloq. hack it, pull it off, deliver the goods, bring home the bacon

accomplished *adj*
skilled, professional, practised, proficient, gifted, talented, skilful, experienced, adroit, adept, expert, masterly, polished, cultivated
formal consummate
F∃ unskilled, inexpert, incapable

accomplishment *n*
1 *the accomplishment of a task*
achievement, attainment, doing, performance, carrying-out, execution, fulfilment, finishing, completion, management, conclusion, perfection, realization, fruition, production
formal discharge, consummation, effecting, futurition
2 *her great accomplishments*
SKILL, talent, ability, capability, proficiency, gift, forte, art
formal aptitude, faculty
3 *no mean accomplishment*
feat, achievement, deed, triumph, exploit
colloq. stroke

accord *v, n*
▶ *v* **1** *not accord with the truth*
correspond, agree, harmonize, be in agreement/harmony, match, conform, suit
formal concur
2 *accord someone recognition*
grant, give, tender, allow, endow, confer
formal bestow, vouchsafe
F∃ 1 disagree **2** deny
▶ *n* agreement, assent, unanimity, unity, correspondence, conformity, harmony, sympathy
formal congruence, congruity, concurrence, accordance, concert
F∃ conflict, discord, disharmony
▷ **of your own accord** voluntarily, of your own free will, freely, willingly, without being asked/forced
▷ **with one accord** unanimously, of one mind, in complete agreement

accordance *n*
▷ **in accordance with** in agreement with, consistent with, in keeping with, obedient to, in conformity with, in line with, in proportion to, in relation to, after, in the light of, in the manner of
formal commensurate with, in concert with, in consonance with

according *adj*
▷ **according to 1** *according to this book* as claimed by, as said/claimed/stated by, on the report of **2** *play according to the rules* in accordance with, in keeping

with, obedient to, in conformity with, in line with, consistent with, after, in the light of, in the manner of, after the manner of, as per **3** *be paid according to experience* in proportion to, in relation to, depending on, as per; *formal* commensurate with

accordingly *adv*
1 *he was dishonest and was distrusted accordingly*
correspondingly, so, as a result, for that reason, consequently, in consequence, therefore
formal thus, hence, ergo
2 *act accordingly*
appropriately, properly, suitably, consistently

accost *v*
approach, confront, waylay, stop, halt, detain, importune, solicit, attack, molest
colloq. buttonhole

account *n, v*
▶ *n* **1** *an account of what happened*
story, tale, commentary, narrative, chronicle, history, memoir, record, statement, report, communiqué write-up, version, narration, portrayal, sketch, description, presentation, explanation, detail(s)
2 *pay an account*
BILL, statement, invoice, tab, charges
3 *the accounts of a business*
ledger, books, register, inventory
4 *a matter of no account*
importance, significance, consequence
formal distinction, esteem, import, regard
▷ **on account of** because of, owing to, the reason is
▷ **on no account** under no circumstances, certainly not
▶ *v* consider, assess, believe, count, hold, reckon, look upon, view as, value
formal adjudge, appraise, deem, esteem
▷ **account for 1** *account for the missing money*
EXPLAIN, give reasons for, come up with an explanation, illuminate, clear up, rationalize, justify, answer for, say why; *formal* elucidate, vindicate **2** *exports account for half our income*
make up, be responsible for, represent, supply, provide, give; *formal* constitute **3** *account for an enemy*
defeat, destroy, kill

accountability *n*
responsibility, answerability, liability, amenability, reporting, obligation

accountable *adj*
responsible, answerable, liable, amenable, obliged, bound, charged with, chargeable
formal obligated

accoutrements *n*
paraphernalia, gear, equipment, decorations, fittings, fixtures, furnishings, appointments, kit, outfit, trimmings, adornments
formal appurtenances, caparison
colloq. bits and pieces, odds and ends

accredited *adj*
recognized, official, authorized, qualified, endorsed, appointed, approved, certified, licensed, commissioned
formal certificated, deputed

accrue *v*
accumulate, increase, mount (up), be added, build up, collect, amass
formal augment

accumulate *v*
gather, build up, assemble, collect, amass, accrue, grow, increase, multiply, pile up, hoard, stockpile, store, gain, acquire
formal aggregate, augment, cumulate
colloq. stash, snowball
F∃ *formal* disseminate, diffuse

accumulation *n*
gathering, build-up, building-up, collection, growth, increase, multiplication, hoard, mass, pile, stockpile, store, stack, stock, reserve, conglomeration, gain, accrual, assembly, acquisition
formal aggregate, augmentation, cumulation
F∃ *formal* dissemination

accuracy *n*
correctness, precision, exactness, authenticity, truth, truthfulness, closeness, faithfulness, carefulness, meticulousness
formal veracity, fidelity, exactitude, scrupulosity, verity, veridicality
F∃ inaccuracy

accurate *adj*
1 *an accurate report/translation*
faithful, true, correct, exact, strict, literal, word-for-word, word-perfect, close, sound, truthful, valid, authentic, unerring, faultless, perfect, fair
formal veracious, letter-perfect, veridical
2 *accurate calculations*
correct, precise, right, valid, rigorous, meticulous
colloq. spot on, bang on
3 *an accurate gun/throw*
well-aimed, well-directed, precise
F∃ 1, 2, 3 inaccurate **2** imprecise, inexact

accursed *adj*
damned, wretched, hateful, despicable, abominable, condemned, doomed, bewitched
formal execrable, anathematized, bedevilled
F∃ blessed

accusation *n*
charge, allegation, denunciation, impeachment, recrimination, complaint, incrimination, blame, indictment
formal imputation, arraignment, inculpation, citation, crimination, gravamen, delation

accuse *v*
1 *accused of murder*
make accusations, bring/press charges, prosecute, put on trial, allege, make allegations, denounce, impeach, confront, attribute, indict, incriminate, implicate, inform against
formal impugn, impute, arraign, cite, criminate
colloq. frame, book
2 *accuse someone of cheating*
blame, hold responsible
formal censure, recriminate
colloq. point the finger at, throw the book at

accustom *v*
familiarize, adjust, adapt, accommodate, get used to, get familiar with, get acquainted with, conform
formal habituate, inure, attune

accustomed *adj*
1 *accustomed to the dark*
used, in the habit of, given, acclimatized, acquainted
formal habituated, inured, wont
colloq. at home
2 *sitting in her accustomed chair*

normal, usual, ordinary, familiar, everyday,
conventional, routine, regular, customary, traditional,
established, fixed, prevailing, general
formal habitual, wonted, consuetudinary
F3 1 unaccustomed, unused

ace *n, adj*
▶ *n* champion, expert, genius, master, maestro,
winner, virtuoso
colloq. dab hand, hotshot, whizz
▶ *adj* brilliant, excellent, first-class, superb,
outstanding, great, perfect

acerbic *adj*
sharp, harsh, biting, stinging, abrasive, caustic,
acrimonious
formal astringent, vitriolic, mordant, rancorous,
trenchant
F3 mild, friendly, kind

ache *v, n*
▶ *v* **1** *my legs ache*
HURT, be sore, pain, be painful, suffer, be in agony,
agonize, throb, pound, twinge, smart, sting
colloq. kill
2 *aching to tell her*
LONG, yearn, pine, hanker, desire, crave, hunger,
thirst, itch
▶ *n* **1** *an ache in my neck*
PAIN, hurt, soreness, suffering, anguish, agony, throb,
throbbing, pounding, pang, twinge, smarting, stinging
2 *an ache for the past*
longing, yearning, craving, itch, hankering

achieve *v*
accomplish, do, attain, reach, get, obtain, acquire,
gain, earn, win, succeed, manage, do, perform, carry
out, execute, fulfil, finish, complete, bring about,
realize, produce
formal procure, consummate, effect, effectuate
F3 miss, fail

achievement *n*
1 *the achievement of our aims*
accomplishment, attainment, performance,
execution, fulfilment, completion, success,
realization, fruition
formal procurement, consummation, acquirement,
fruition
2 *great achievements*
accomplishment, act, action, activity, deed,
performance, exploit, feat, effort

achiever *n*
doer, performer, succeeder
colloq. high flyer, go-getter, success story

acid *n, adj*
▶ *n*

Types of acid include: acetic, acrylic, amino, aqua for-
tis, aqua regia, ascorbic, benzoic, boric, carbolic,
chloric, citric, DNA (deoxyribonucleic acid), fatty,
folic, formic, hydrochloric, hydrocyanic, lactic, malic,
nitric, nitrohydrochloric, nitrous, palmitic, pectic,
phenol, phosphoric, prussic, RNA (ribonucleic
acid), salicylic, spirits of salt, stearic, sulphuric, tan-
nic, tartaric, uric. *See also* **amino acid**.

▶ *adj* **1** *an acid taste*
acidic, sour, bitter, tart, vinegary, sharp, pungent,
acerbic, caustic, corrosive
formal acetic, acetous, acidulous
2 *an acid remark*
bitter, unkind, critical, sarcastic, stinging, biting,

cutting, incisive, harsh, morose, hurtful
formal acerbic, astringent, mordant, trenchant,
vitriolic
F3 1 alkaline **2** kind, complimentary

acknowledge *v*
1 *acknowledge a fact/an error*
ADMIT, recognize, accept, agree to, declare, grant,
allow, confess, own up to, concede
formal acquiesce, accede, affirm, avouch
2 *acknowledge him with a nod*
greet, address, notice, recognize
formal salute, hail
3 *acknowledge a letter*
answer, write back, reply to, respond to, react to,
confirm
4 *acknowledge someone's help*
thank, say thank you, express/show your appreciation,
be grateful, express your thanks/gratitude, recognize
F3 1 deny, disagree with **2** ignore

acknowledged *adj*
recognized, accepted, approved, accredited, declared,
professed, confirmed
formal attested, avowed

acknowledgement *n*
1 *an acknowledgement of defeat*
recognition, admission, confession, declaration,
profession, acceptance
2 *a gesture of acknowledgement*
greeting, notice, recognition, nod, smile, wave
formal salutation
3 *an acknowledgement of a letter*
answer, reply, response, reaction
formal affirmation
4 *an acknowledgement of assistance*
expression of gratitude/appreciation/thanks,
gratefulness, tribute, credit

acme *n*
high point, height, peak, pinnacle, climax,
culmination, crown, optimum, summit
formal apex, zenith, apogee
F3 low point; *formal* nadir

acolyte *n*
follower, assistant, helper, attendant, adherent

acoustic *adj*
·hearing, sound
formal auditory, aural, audile

acquaint *v*
familiarize, let know, accustom, tell, notify, advise,
inform, make aware of, brief, enlighten, divulge,
disclose, reveal, announce
formal make conversant, apprise

acquaintance *n*
1 *friends and acquaintances*
associate, companion, colleague, friend, contact
formal confrère
2 *my acquaintance with them*
FAMILIARITY, association, relationship, intimacy,
association, social contact, fellowship, companionship
3 *some acquaintance with art*
familiarity, awareness, knowledge, understanding,
experience
formal cognizance

acquainted *adj*
1 *acquainted with him*
FRIENDLY, on friendly terms, on good terms
2 *acquainted with that book*

FAMILIAR, well-versed, knowledgeable, aware, abreast, *au fait*
formal conversant, cognizant, apprised
colloq. in the know
E 2 unfamiliar, unaware, ignorant

acquiesce *v*
consent, submit, agree, accept, allow, approve, defer
formal concur, accede
colloq. give in
E disagree, object, resist

acquiescence *n*
consent, agreement, acceptance, approval, submission, yielding, deference
formal concurrence, compliance, assent
E disagreement, resistance

acquiescent *adj*
consenting, agreeable, agreeing, accepting, approving, amenable, obedient, submissive, yielding, deferential, servile
formal acceding, concurrent, compliant, complaisant

acquire *v*
buy, purchase, obtain, get, come by, receive, collect, gather, amass, accumulate, net, gain, secure, earn, win, achieve, attain, realize
formal procure, appropriate
colloq. pick up, snap up, splash out on; *slang* bag, cop, collar
E relinquish, forfeit, sell

acquisition *n*
1 *his latest acquisition*
PURCHASE, buy, gain, possession, accession, takeover, property
2 *the acquisition of a skill*
securing, gaining, obtaining, achievement, attainment
formal procurement, appropriation

acquisitive *adj*
greedy, covetous, grasping
formal avaricious, avid, predatory, rapacious, voracious

acquisitiveness *n*
greed, covetousness, graspingness
formal avarice, avidity, predatoriness, rapacity, voracity

acquit *v*
1 *acquitted of the crime*
clear, reprieve, excuse, free, liberate, deliver, relieve, release, dismiss, discharge, settle, satisfy, repay
formal absolve, exonerate, exculpate, vindicate
colloq. let off, let off the hook
2 *acquit yourself well*
perform, behave, act, do, conduct
formal comport, bear
colloq. make a good/bad job
E 1 convict, condemn

acquittal *n*
clearance, reprieve, excusing, freeing, liberation, deliverance, relief, release, dismissal, discharge
formal absolution, exoneration, exculpation, vindication, compurgation
E conviction, condemnation

acrid *adj*
1 *an acrid smell*
pungent, sharp, stinging, acid, sour, tart, harsh, burning, caustic, acerbic
2 *an acrid comment*

caustic, biting, cutting, incisive, sarcastic, sardonic, bitter, acrimonious, harsh, nasty, malicious, venomous
formal acerbic, astringent, mordant, trenchant, virulent, vitriolic

acrimonious *adj*
bitter, biting, cutting, caustic, sharp, virulent, severe, spiteful, censorious, abusive, ill-tempered, waspish, venomous
formal acerbic, astringent, rancorous, trenchant, vitriolic, splenetic, irascible, petulant
colloq. crabbed
E peaceable, kindly; *formal* irenic

acrimony *n*
bitterness, resentment, spite, ill-will, gall, ill temper, sarcasm, harshness, venom
formal causticity, rancour, petulance, irascibility, mordancy, trenchancy, vitriol, spleen, astringency, acerbity, asperity, acridity, virulence

acrobat *n*
gymnast, tumbler, balancer, somersaulter, contortionist, trapeze artist, rope-walker, rope-dancer, stuntman, stuntwoman
formal funambulist, aerialist, equilibrist

act *v, n*
▶ *v* **1** *act in a certain way; act fast*
behave, be, move, do, take action, take steps, take measures, be active, be busy, go about, react
formal conduct yourself, acquit yourself, exert yourself, comport yourself
2 *the drug will act soon*
TAKE EFFECT, have an effect, work, operate, function
formal be efficacious
3 *the gear acts as a brake*
work, function, serve, operate, do, do the job of
4 *act upset*
pretend, fake, put on
formal feign, affect, assume, simulate, dissemble, dissimulate
colloq. sham
5 *act in a play*
perform, go on the stage, play, portray, represent, mime, characterize, enact, mimic, imitate, impersonate
▷ **act on** **1** *act on orders* CARRY OUT, fulfil, comply with, conform to, obey, follow, heed, take **2** AFFECT influence, alter, modify, change, transform
▷ **act up** not work, misbehave, behave badly, cause trouble, give bother; *colloq.* play up, mess about, muck around
▶ *n* **1** *acts of bravery*
DEED, action, undertaking, enterprise, operation, manoeuvre, move, step, doing, execution, accomplishment, achievement, exploit, feat, stroke
2 *put on an act*
pretence, make-believe, counterfeit, fake
formal feigning, dissimulation, dissemblance, affectation
colloq. sham, show, front
3 *an act of parliament*
law, statute, ordinance, edict, decree, resolution, measure, ruling, bill
4 *a juggler's act*
turn, item, routine, sketch, performance
colloq. skit, gig

acting *adj, n*
▶ *adj* temporary, provisional, interim, stopgap, supply, stand-by, stand-in, standing in for, in place of,

covering, deputy, substitute, reserve, relief, pro tem, surrogate

▶ *n* theatre, drama, performing, performing arts, stagecraft, artistry, performance, play-acting, melodrama, dramatics, theatricals, histrionics, footlights, portrayal, characterization, impersonation, imitating

action *n*
1 *his prompt action*
act, move, deed, exploit, step, measure, course of action, feat, accomplishment, achievement, performance, effort, endeavour, enterprise, undertaking, proceeding, process, activity
2 *put an idea into action*
OPERATION, practice, effect, force, functioning, doing, performance, exercise, exertion, work, mechanism, movement, motion
3 *the action of a chemical on metal*
EFFECT, operation, influence
4 *people of action*
vitality, liveliness, spirit, energy, vigour, power, force, activity
colloq. get-up-and-go
5 *killed in action*
warfare, battle, conflict, combat, fight, fray, engagement, encounter, skirmish, clash
formal affray
6 *a legal action*
litigation, lawsuit, suit, case, prosecution

activate *v*
start, start working, set off, fire, switch/turn/put on, set in motion, mobilize, propel, move, stir, rouse, arouse, get going, set going, trigger (off), trip, stimulate, initiate, motivate, prompt, energize, excite, galvanize
formal actuate, animate, impel, bestir
colloq. push/press the button, throw the switch
⊟ deactivate, stop, arrest

active *adj*
1 *an active person*
BUSY, occupied, industrious, diligent, hard-working, forceful, spirited, vital, vibrant, forward, hyperactive, manic, frenetic
formal indefatigable, astir
colloq. on the go
2 *active for his age*
agile, nimble, spry, sprightly, light-footed, quick, alert, animated, lively, energetic, vigorous
3 *active members*
devoted, engaged, involved, committed, contributing, militant, activist, enterprising, enthusiastic
4 *the system is active*
in operation, functioning, working, running, in force
⊟ 1 passive 3 inactive

activity *n*
1 *the office is full of activity*
business, liveliness, life, activeness, action, motion, movement, commotion, bustle, industry, labour, exertion, exercise
colloq. hurly-burly, a hive of activity/industry, comings and goings, toing and froing
2 *holiday activities*
pursuit, hobby, pastime, interest, diversion, distraction, something to do, occupation, job, work, act, deed, project, scheme, task, venture, enterprise, endeavour, undertaking
formal avocation
⊟ 1 inactivity, passivity

actor, actress *n*
play actor, film actor, film star, movie star, comedian, tragedian, player, performer, stage performer, artist, dramatic artist, leading lady, leading man, understudy, extra, walk-on, impersonator, mime, mime artist, mummer
formal Thespian, Roscius
colloq. ham

actual *adj*
real, existent, substantial, tangible, material, physical, concrete, positive, definite, absolute, certain, unquestionable, indisputable, confirmed, verified, factual, truthful, true, genuine, legitimate, bona fide, authentic, realistic
formal de facto
colloq. real live
⊟ theoretical, apparent, imaginary

actuality *n*
reality, fact, substance, truth
formal factuality, historicity, corporeality, materiality, substantiality

actually *adv*
1 *Did you actually see him fall?*
in fact, as a matter of fact, as it happens, in truth, in reality, really, truly, indeed, absolutely
formal de facto
2 *she took her degree eventually and actually got a first class*
even, though it may seem strange, surprisingly, as it happens

actuate *v*
move, stir, stimulate, activate, motivate, instigate, prompt, rouse, arouse, kindle, start, start working, set off, set going, trigger (off), switch/turn on, set in motion

acumen *n*
astuteness, shrewdness, sharpness, keenness, quickness, penetration, insight, intuition, discrimination, discernment, judgement, perception, sense, wit, wisdom, intelligence, cleverness, ingenuity
formal judiciousness, percipience, perspicacity, perspicuity, sagacity, sapience
colloq. smartness, gumption

acute *adj*
1 *an acute shortage*
SEVERE, intense, extreme, violent, critical, dangerous, serious, grave, urgent, crucial, vital, decisive, sharp, cutting, poignant, distressing
2 *an acute mind*
SHARP, keen, incisive, penetrating, astute, shrewd, canny, judicious, discerning, clever, observant, perceptive, insightful, sensitive
formal percipient, perspicacious, sapient
colloq. smart
3 *an acute illness*
severe, serious, intense, dangerous, critical, grave
⊟ 1 mild, slight 3 mild, chronic, persistent

acutely *adv*
very, intensely, extremely, strongly, seriously, gravely, sharply, keenly

adage *n*
maxim, saying, axiom, proverb, byword, precept, saw
formal aphorism, apophthegm, paroemia

adamant *adj*
hard, resolute, determined, set, firm, insistent, rigid, stiff, inflexible, unbending, unrelenting, unyielding,

stubborn, uncompromising, tough, fixed, immovable, unshakable
formal intransigent, obdurate
E3 hesitant, flexible, yielding

adapt *v*
1 *adapt to a new environment*
ADJUST, acclimatize yourself, familiarize yourself, orientate yourself, accommodate yourself, get used/accustomed *formal* habituate yourself
2 *adapt a building*
ALTER, change, qualify, modify, adjust, convert, remodel, customize, fit, tailor, fashion, shape, harmonize, match, suit, conform, comply, prepare

adaptable *adj*
flexible, compliant, amenable, easy-going, versatile, plastic, malleable, alterable, changeable, variable, modifiable, adjustable, convertible, conformable
E3 inflexible; *formal* refractory

adaptation *n*
1 *adaptation to a different situation*
ADJUSTMENT, acclimatization, familiarization, accommodation, getting used/accustomed
formal habituation
2 *adaptation of a novel for TV*
ALTERATION, change, modification, shift, transformation, revision, variation, adjustment, conversion, remodelling, customization, fitting, refitting, fashioning, refashioning, reworking, shaping, reshaping, harmonization, matching, conformity, preparation

add *v*
1 *add an introduction to the book*
put on, put in, include, increase, complete, improve, attach, supplement, combine, build on
formal adjoin, affix, append, annex, augment
colloq. throw in
2 *add numbers*
count (up), total, work out/calculate the total
colloq. tot up
3 *'Thanks,' I added*
tack on, continue, go on to say, carry on
E3 1 take away, reduce, decrease **2** subtract, take (away), deduct, remove
▷ **add up 1** *add up numbers* add, sum up, add together, total, tally, count (up), reckon, calculate, compute; *colloq.* tot up **2** *the total adds up to 100* amount, come to, include, spell; *formal* constitute **3** *it doesn't add up* be consistent, hang together, fit, be plausible, be reasonable, stand to reason, make sense, mean, signify, indicate, ring true
E3 1 subtract

added *adj*
additional, supplementary, extra, more, another, fresh, further, new, spare
formal adjunct

addendum *n*
appendix, addition, postscript, supplement
formal codicil, adjunct, appendage, augmentation, attachment, endorsement, allonge

addict *n*
1 *a drug addict*
drug taker, drug user
colloq. junkie, user, dope-fiend; *slang* freak, head, coke-head, tripper, mainliner
2 *a chess addict*
enthusiast, fan, devotee, follower, adherent
colloq. buff, fiend, freak

addicted *adj*
1 *addicted to drugs*
dependent, drug-dependent
colloq. hooked, strung out
2 *addicted to TV*
obsessed, absorbed, devoted, dedicated, fond, inclined
colloq. hooked

addiction *n*
1 *alcohol addiction*
dependence, craving, habit
slang monkey
2 *addiction to chocolate*
craving, habit, obsession, compulsive behaviour, mania

addition *n*
1 *the index is a welcome addition*
supplement, attachment, extra, increment, additive, rider, afterthought, postscript, annexe, addendum, appendix, accessory
formal adjunct, appendage, appurtenance
2 *the addition of a separate phone line*
adding, extension, enlargement, increasing, increase, gain
formal annexation, accession, accretion
3 *addition of numbers*
summing-up, totalling, counting, reckoning, inclusion, computation
colloq. totting-up
E3 2 removal, taking-away **3** subtraction, deduction
▷ **in addition** additionally, too, also, as well, besides, moreover, further, furthermore, over and above, too, not to mention
colloq. into the bargain

additional *adj*
added, extra, supplementary, spare, more, further, increased, other, new, fresh, another
formal adscititious, adventitious, supervenient, excrescent

additionally *adv*
in addition, too, also, as well, besides, moreover, further, furthermore, over and above
colloq. into the bargain, for good measure

additive *n*
supplement, addition, extra, preservative

addled *adj*
confused, befuddled, bewildered, flustered, muddled, mixed-up, perplexed
E3 clear

address *n, v*
▶ *n* **1** *write down an address and phone number*
home, house, flat, apartment, lodging, directions, inscription, whereabouts, location, situation, place, poste restante, dwelling
formal (place of) residence, abode
2 SPEECH, talk, lecture, sermon, oration, discourse, monologue, soliloquy, dissertation
formal diatribe, philippic, apostrophe, disquisition
3 *forms of address*
greeting, welcome
formal salutation, invocation
▶ *v* **1** *address an audience*
lecture, speak to, talk to, give a talk/speech to, make/deliver a speech
formal sermonize, harangue, orate
2 *address a remark to someone*
communicate, direct, convey, send, intend for

formal remit
3 *How should I address a duke?*
call, speak/write to, designate
▷ **address (yourself) to** deal with, give your attention to, apply yourself to, devote yourself to, attend to, undertake, concentrate on, focus on, engage in, take care of

adduce *v*
cite, mention, allude to, refer to, put forward, point out, present
formal proffer, evidence

adept *adj, n*
▶ *adj* skilled, accomplished, expert, masterly, experienced, versed, practised, polished, proficient, competent, capable, good, clever, able, adroit, deft, nimble
colloq. ace, sharp, hot stuff, no flies on someone
✪ bungling, incompetent, inept
▶ *n* master, expert, genius, maestro
colloq. dab hand, hot stuff, nobody's fool, wizard
✪ bungler, incompetent

adequacy *n*
sufficiency, suitability, fitness, ability, competence, capability, serviceability, acceptability, satisfactoriness, reasonableness, passability, tolerability, tolerableness, fairness, indifference, mediocrity
formal commensurateness, requisiteness
✪ inadequacy, insufficiency

adequate *adj*
1 *adequate amounts of food*
enough, sufficient
formal commensurate, requisite
2 *adequate work*
acceptable, satisfactory, passable, reasonable, tolerable, unexceptional, indifferent, undistinguished, average, suitable, fit, able, competent, capable, serviceable
colloq. all right, OK, will do, could be better/worse, patchy, fair to middling, run of the mill, nothing (much) to write home about, not set the Thames on fire
✪ **1** insufficient **2** inadequate

adhere *v*
1 STICK, stick together, glue, paste, cement, grip, fix, fasten, attach, join, link, combine, coalesce, cohere, hold, cling
formal cleave to, accrete
2 *adhere to the agreement*
OBSERVE, follow, abide by, comply with, fulfil, obey, keep, heed, respect, stand by
colloq. stick
3 *adhere to an opinion*
support, hold, defend, stand by, go along with, stick up for
formal espouse

adherent *n*
supporter, upholder, advocate, partisan, follower, disciple, satellite, henchman, devotee, admirer, fan, enthusiast
formal votary, aficionado, sectary
colloq. hanger-on, buff, freak, nut

adhesion *n*
adherence, adhesiveness, holding together, sticking together, bond, attachment, grip, cohesion

adhesive *adj, n*
▶ *adj* sticky, stick-on, tacky, self-adhesive, gummed,

adhering, sticking, clinging, holding, attaching, cohesive
formal adherent, glutinous, mucilaginous
colloq. gummy, gluey
▶ *n* glue, gum, fixative, paste, cement, tape, sticky tape, Sellotape®, Elastoplast®, Band-aid®, Superglue®, Blue-tak®
formal mucilage

adieu *n*
goodbye, farewell, leave-taking, *au revoir*
formal valediction, valedictory
colloq. cheerio, cheers

adjacent *adj*
adjoining, touching, bordering, alongside, beside, next-door, neighbouring, next, closest, nearest, close, near
formal abutting, contiguous, juxtaposed, conterminant, conterminate, conterminous, proximate, vicinal
✪ remote, distant

adjoin *v*
touch, meet, border, verge, neighbour, interconnect, link, connect, join, combine, unite, couple, attach, add, annex
formal abut, append, juxtapose

adjoining *adj*
adjacent, touching, bordering, near, neighbouring, next, next door, verging, interconnecting, linking, connecting, joining, combining, uniting
formal contiguous, impinging, abutting, proximate, juxtaposed, conjoining, vicinal

adjourn *v*
1 *adjourn a meeting*
stop temporarily, interrupt, suspend, break off, delay, stay, defer, postpone, put off, pause
formal discontinue, prorogue
2 *adjourn to the lounge*
withdraw
formal retire, repair
✪ **1** assemble, convene

adjournment *n*
interruption, suspension, break, pause, interval, delay, stay, postponement, putting-off, *US* recess, intermission
formal discontinuation, deferment, deferral, dissolution, prorogation

adjudicate *v*
judge, arbitrate, umpire, referee, settle, determine, decide, pronounce
formal adjudge

adjust *v*
1 *adjust to new circumstances*
become/grow accustomed, adapt, acclimatize yourself, become acclimatized, orientate yourself, accommodate yourself, reconcile yourself, harmonize, conform
formal habituate yourself
colloq. get used to
2 MODIFY, change, adapt, alter, convert, dispose, shape, remodel, fit, accommodate, suit, measure, amend, revise, make adjustments, rectify, regulate, balance, repair, reshape, refashion, temper, tune, fix, set, arrange, align, compose, settle, shape, square
formal coapt
colloq. fine-tune, tweak
✪ **2** upset; *formal* disarrange

adjustable *adj*
adaptable, modifiable, convertible, flexible, movable
🔁 fixed, immovable

adjustment *n*
1 *minor adjustments to the engine*
MODIFICATION, change, adaptation, alteration,
conversion, remodelling, shaping, fitting,
accommodation, amendment, revision, rectification,
regulation, tuning, fixing, setting, arranging,
rearranging, arrangement, rearrangement, ordering,
settlement
2 *adjustment to a new job*
orientation, adaptation, acclimatization,
accommodation, naturalization, reconciliation,
harmonization, conforming, getting used to
formal habituation

ad-lib *v, adj, adv*
▶ *v* improvise, make up, invent
formal extemporize
colloq. speak off the cuff/off the top of your head
▶ *adj* impromptu, improvised, unprepared, without
preparation, unpremeditated, unrehearsed,
spontaneous, made-up
formal extempore, extemporaneous, extemporized
colloq. off-the-cuff, off the top of your head
🔁 prepared
▶ *adv* impromptu, spontaneously, impulsively
formal extempore, extemporaneously
colloq. off the cuff, off the top of your head

administer *v*
1 *administer a country/law/project*
organize, direct, conduct, manage, run, control,
regulate, superintend, supervise, oversee, govern, rule,
lead, head, preside over, officiate
2 *administer a drug*
GIVE, provide, supply, distribute, give out, measure
out, mete out, execute, impose, apply
formal dispense, disburse, adhibit
colloq. dole out

administration *n*
1 *reduce the cost of administration*
administering, management, running, paperwork,
organization, direction, control, superintendence,
supervision, overseeing, governing, ruling, leadership,
execution
colloq. red tape
2 *a country's administration*
government, governing body, regime, ministry,
leadership, directorship, management, executive, term
of office

administrative *adj*
management, managerial, governmental, legislative,
authoritative, executive, organizational, regulatory,
supervisory
formal directorial, gubernatorial

> *Administrative areas include*:
> area, borough, city, constituency, county, district,
> division, enclave, parish, precinct, province, region,
> sector, shire, state, territory, town, village, ward.

administrator *n*
manager, organizer, director, controller,
superintendent, supervisor, overseer, governor, ruler,
leader, president, chairman, chief executive, executive,
managing director, head, chief
formal custodian, guardian, trustee
colloq. boss

admirable *adj*
praiseworthy, commendable, creditable, deserving,
worthy, praiseworthy, respected, fine, excellent,
superior, wonderful, exquisite, choice, rare, masterly,
valuable
formal estimable, laudable, meritorious
🔁 contemptible, despicable, deplorable

admiration *n*
respect, (high) regard, reverence, worship, idolism,
adoration, affection, adulation, approval, praise,
appreciation, kudos, pleasure, delight, wonder,
astonishment, amazement, surprise
formal (high) esteem, approbation, veneration, fureur
colloq. yen
🔁 contempt, disrespect, scorn

admire *v*
1 *admire his honesty*
respect, think highly of, have a high opinion of, look up
to, like very much, revere, worship, idolize, revere,
adore, approve, praise, applaud
formal hold in high regard/esteem, esteem (highly),
venerate, laud, prize, iconize
colloq. think the world of, hero-worship, put on a
pedestal, take your hat off to; *slang* think the sun
shines out of someone's arse
2 *admire a car*
appreciate, value, like, approve of
🔁 **1** despise, censure

admirer *n*
1 *a great admirer of classical music*
follower, disciple, adherent, supporter, fan, enthusiast,
devotee, worshipper, idolizer, idolater
formal aficionado
colloq. buff, fiend, freak
2 *a woman's admirers*
suitor, boyfriend, girlfriend, sweetheart, lover
formal beau, wooer, gallant
🔁 **1** critic, opponent

admissible *adj*
acceptable, allowable, permissible, allowed,
permitted, lawful, legitimate, justifiable, tolerable,
tolerated, passable
formal licit
🔁 inadmissible, illegitimate

admission *n*
1 *refuse admission*
permission, entrance, access, right of access
formal ingress
2 *admission is £5*
admission fee, entrance, entrance fee, entry charge
3 *an admission of guilt*
CONFESSION, granting, acknowledgement,
recognition, acceptance, allowance, concession,
affirmation, declaration, profession, disclosure,
divulgence, revelation, exposé
formal avowal, *mea culpa*, peccavi
🔁 **1** exclusion, prohibition **3** denial, contradiction

> ⚠ **admission** or **admittance** ?
> Each word means 'the act of entering' or 'permission
> to enter', but *admittance* is used in more formal styles:
> *Admission by ticket only; gain admittance to the palace
> of the President.*

admit *v*
1 *admit I was wrong*
CONFESS, own up, grant, acknowledge, recognize,

accept, allow, concede, agree, declare, profess,
disclose, unburden yourself, divulge, reveal
formal affirm
colloq. blurt out, eat your words, come clean
2 *be admitted to the palace*
LET IN, allow to enter, give access, give admission,
accept, receive, take in, introduce, initiate
formal intromit
F3 1 deny, hide **2** shut out, exclude, let out

admittance *n*
admitting, admission, letting in, (right of) access,
entrance, (right of) entry, acceptance, reception,
introduction, initiation
formal ingress
F3 exclusion

admixture *n*
mixture, compound, combination, blend,
amalgamation, mix, fusion, amalgam, alloy
formal commixture, intermixture, tincture

admonish *v*
scold, rebuke, reprimand, discipline, correct, reprove,
warn, upbraid, chide, censure, exhort, counsel
formal berate
colloq. tell off

admonition *n*
rebuke, reprimand, reproof, scolding, correction,
warning, censure, exhortation, counsel
formal berating, reprehension
colloq. telling-off

adolescence *n*
teens, teenage years, puberty, youth, minority,
boyhood, girlhood, development, immaturity,
youthfulness, boyishness, girlishness
formal pubescence, juvenescence, juvenility
Related adjective: neanic

adolescent *adj, n*
▶ *adj* **1** *an adolescent son*
teenage, young, youthful, juvenile, boyish, girlish,
growing, developing
formal pubescent, juvenescent
2 *adolescent behaviour*
immature, puerile, childish
▶ *n* teenager, youth, young person, young adult,
juvenile, minor

adopt *v*
1 *adopt children*
take in, take as your own, foster
2 *adopt a policy*
TAKE UP, take on, accept, assume, follow, choose,
select, nominate, support, maintain, back, endorse,
ratify, approve
formal appropriate, embrace, espouse
F3 1 disown **2** reject

adoption *n*
1 *the adoption of children*
taking as your own, taking-in, (long-term) fostering
2 *the adoption of a suggestion*
taking-on, acceptance, taking-up, choice, selection,
support, backing, endorsement, ratification, approval
formal appropriation, approbation, embracement,
embracing, espousal

adorable *adj*
lovable, dear, darling, precious, appealing, sweet,
winsome, charming, enchanting, captivating, winning,
delightful, pleasing, attractive, wonderful, fetching,

bewitching
F3 hateful, abominable

adoration *n*
1 *adoration for someone*
love, admiration, devotion, cherishing, doting on,
(high)regard
formal esteem
2 *adoration of God*
worship, praise, reverence, veneration, homage,
idolizaton, exaltation, magnification, glorification
F3 2 abhorrence, detestation

adore *v*
1 *adore your parents*
love, cherish, be devoted to, dote on, hold dear, be fond
of, admire, honour, revere, worship
formal esteem (highly), venerate
colloq. think the world of
2 *adore apricots*
love, like very much, enjoy greatly, be fond of, enjoy,
relish, be partial to
colloq. have a weakness for, not be able to resist
F3 1, 2 hate; *formal* abhor

adorn *v*
decorate, deck, ornament, crown, trim, garnish, gild,
enhance, embellish, enrich, grace, trim
formal festoon, bedeck, emblazon, furbish, gild,
adonize, apparel, array, beautify, bedight, bedizen,
begem, bejewel, bestick, impearl, miniate
colloq. doll up, tart up

adornment *n*
1 *bodily adornment*
beautification, decorating, ornamentation,
ornateness, enrichment, embellishment
formal bedizenment, garniture
2 *gold adornments*
accessory, ornament, decoration, jewellery, frill,
trappings, trimmings, garnish, flounce, frippery
formal falbala, fallal, fallalery, fandangle, figgery,
furbelow, garnishry, gilding

adrift *adj*
1 *the boat had been cut adrift*
at sea, drifting, off course, anchorless
2 *feel adrift and lonely*
aimless, rootless, directionless, goalless, insecure,
unsettled
F3 1 anchored **2** stable

adroit *adj*
skilful, adept, able, clever, expert, masterful,
proficient, deft, dexterous
F3 clumsy, inept, maladroit

adroitness *n*
skill, skilfulness, adeptness, ability, cleverness,
expertise, mastery, facility, finesse, proficiency,
competence, deftness, dexterity
F3 clumsiness, ineptitude

adulation *n*
flattery, idolization, personality cult, hero worship,
praise, sycophancy, bootlicking, fawning
formal blandishment

adulatory *adj*
flattering, praising, bootlicking, fawning, servile,
sycophantic
formal blandishing, fulsome, obsequious, unctuous
F3 unflattering

adult *adj*
1 *adult responsibilities*
grown-up, of age, full-grown, fully-grown, developed, mature, ripe, ripened
2 *adult magazines*
sexually explicit, pornographic, obscene
⊟ 1 immature
Related adjective: ephebic

adulterate *v*
contaminate, pollute, taint, corrupt, defile, debase, degrade, dilute, water down, weaken, devalue, deteriorate, make impure
formal attenuate, bastardize, vitiate
⊟ purify, refine

adultery *n*
unfaithfulness, infidelity, affair, extramarital relations/ relationship, extramarital sex, entanglement, flirtation, unchastity
colloq. cheating, a bit on the side; *slang* playing around, playing the field
⊟ faithfulness, fidelity

advance *v, n*
▶ *v* 1 PROCEED, go forward, move on, move forward, come forward, surge forward, go ahead, progress, make progress, make headway, forge ahead
colloq. make great strides, come on in leaps and bounds
2 *advance the date of the wedding*
bring forward, make earlier
3 ACCELERATE, speed (up), send forward
formal hasten, expedite
4 FURTHER, promote, upgrade, foster, support, assist, help, benefit, facilitate, increase, grow
5 *advance an idea*
PRESENT, submit, put forward, suggest, allege, cite, bring forward, offer, provide, supply, furnish
formal proffer, adduce
6 *advance a sum of money*
lend, loan, pay, pay beforehand, pay in advance, give
⊟ 1 retreat 2 put back 3 *formal* retard
4 impede, hinder
▶ *n* 1 *recent advances in medicine*
PROGRESS, forward movement, onward movement, moving forward, going forward, marching forward, headway, step, breakthrough, development, progression, growth, increase, improvement
formal advancement, furtherance, betterment, amelioration
2 *an advance of £500*
deposit, down payment, prepayment, credit, loan, retainer
⊟ 1 retreat, recession
▷ **in advance** beforehand, previously, early, earlier, sooner, ahead, in front, in the lead, in the forefront; *colloq.* up front
⊟ later, behind

advanced *adj*
1 *an advanced design*
up-to-date, leading, foremost, ahead, forward, precocious, progressive, forward-looking, hi-tech, state-of-the art, avant-garde, ultra-modern, ahead of the times, sophisticated, complex, higher, at the cutting/leading edge
2 *an advanced course of studies*
high-level, complex
⊟ 1 backward, retarded 2 elementary

advancement *n*
1 *advancement in a career*

PROMOTION, furtherance, betterment
formal preferment
2 *the advancement of science*
improvement, development, growth, rise, gain, advance, progress, headway
⊟ 1 demotion 2 retardation

advances *n*
overtures, addresses, approach(es), attentions, moves, proposition

advantage *n*
1 *the advantages of electric light*
asset, blessing, benefit, good, good point, plus, plus point, virtue, pro, boon, fruit, welfare, interest, service, help, aid, assistance, use, convenience, usefulness, utility, profit, gain
formal avail
colloq. beauty, pay-off
2 *an advantage over other candidates*
edge, lead, upper hand, superiority, precedence, dominance, pre-eminence, sway, leverage
colloq. head start, everything going for you, the odds in your favour
⊟ 1 disadvantage, drawback, hindrance

advantageous *adj*
beneficial, favourable, convenient, helpful, of assistance, of service, useful, worthwhile, valuable, profitable, gainful, remunerative, rewarding
formal opportune, propitious, furthersome
⊟ disadvantageous, adverse, damaging

advent *n*
coming, appearance, approach, arrival, entrance, introduction, occurrence, onset, dawn, birth, beginning
formal accession, inception

adventure *n*
1 *exciting adventures*
exploit, venture, undertaking, enterprise, risk, hazard, chance, speculation, experience, incident, occurrence
2 *a life of adventure*
excitement, enterprise, risk, danger, peril, romance

adventurer *n*
opportunist, hero, heroine, traveller, venturer, voyager, wanderer

adventurous *adj*
1 *an adventurous person*
daring, intrepid, bold, headstrong, audacious, impetuous, reckless, rash, risky, venturesome, enterprising
colloq. spunky, gutsy
2 *an adventurous life*
exciting, enterprising, risky, dangerous, perilous, hazardous, romantic
⊟ 1, 2 unadventurous 1 cautious, chary, prudent

adversary *n*
enemy, opponent, antagonist, assailant, attacker, competitor, contestant, foe, opposer, rival
⊟ ally, supporter, friend

adverse *adj*
unfavourable, disadvantageous, hostile, antagonistic, opposing, opposite, counter, contrary, conflicting, counter-productive, negative, unfortunate, unlucky, detrimental, harmful, injurious, hurtful, unfriendly, uncongenial
formal inauspicious, inopportune, unpropitious, inexpedient, untoward
⊟ advantageous, favourable

⚠ **adverse** or **averse** ?
Adverse means 'unfavourable, hostile, harmful':
adverse criticism. Averse means 'having a dislike,
disinclined': *She's not averse to walking all over people
to get what she wants.*

---

adversity *n*
misfortune, ill fortune, bad luck, ill luck, reverse,
hardship, hard times, misery, wretchedness, affliction,
suffering, distress, sorrow, woe, trouble, trial, calamity,
disaster, catastrophe
formal tribulation
colloq. hell, living hell; *slang* the pits
F3 prosperity

advertise *v*
1 *advertise a product*
publicize, promote, market, merchandise, sell, praise,
tout
colloq. push, plug, hype
2 *advertise the time of a performance*
announce, declare, proclaim, broadcast, publish,
display, make known, make public, inform, notify
formal promulgate

advertisement *n*
commercial, publicity, promotion, marketing, jingle,
display, blurb, announcement, notice, poster, bill,
placard, leaflet, handbill, circular, handout,
propaganda, trailer
colloq. advert, ad, plug, hype

advice *n*
1 *give someone advice*
warning, caution, dos and don'ts, injunction,
instruction, counsel, counselling, help, guidance,
direction, suggestion, recommendation, opinion,
view, tip, wisdom, word, constructive criticism,
encouragement
2 *a remittance advice*
notification, notice, memorandum, communication,
information

advisability *n*
desirability, suitability, appropriateness, aptness,
wisdom, judiciousness, prudence, soundness
formal expediency
F3 inadvisability, folly

advisable *adj*
suggested, recommended, sensible, wise, wisest,
prudent, judicious, sound, profitable, beneficial, best,
desirable, suitable, appropriate, apt, fitting, fit, proper,
correct
formal politic
F3 inadvisable, foolish

advise *v*
1 COUNSEL, guide, give guidance, warn, forewarn,
caution, instruct, teach, tutor, suggest, give/offer/
make suggestions, recommend, give/offer/make
recommendations, commend, urge
formal enjoin, forewarn
2 NOTIFY, inform, tell, acquaint, make known,
report, give notice
formal apprise

adviser *n*
counsellor, consultant, authority, guide, teacher, tutor,
instructor, coach, helper, aide, right-hand man/
woman, therapist, mentor, guru, confidant(e), counsel,
lawyer

advisory *adj*
advising, consultative, consulting, counselling,
helping, recommending
formal consultatory

advocacy *n*
support, backing, adoption, campaigning, promotion,
championing, defence, encouragement, patronage,
proposal, recommendation, justification, upholding,
propagation
formal espousal, advancement, promulgation

advocate *v, n*
▶ *v* defend, champion, campaign for, press for, argue
for, plead for, justify, urge, encourage, advise,
recommend, propose, promote, endorse, back (up),
support, uphold, patronize, adopt, subscribe to,
favour, believe in, sympathize with, lobby
formal espouse, countenance
colloq. be behind, be pro, throw your weight behind
F3 *formal* impugn, disparage, deprecate
▶ *n* **1** *an advocate of an idea*
defender, supporter, upholder, champion,
campaigner, pleader, vindicator, proponent,
exponent, promoter, speaker, spokesperson
2 *the advocate in a court of law*
lawyer, barrister, counsel, attorney
F3 **1** opponent, critic

aegis *n*
support, backing, auspices, guardianship, patronage,
sponsorship, wing, advocacy, championship, favour

aeroplane *n*
See panel at **aircraft**.

affability *n*
friendliness, amiability, approachability, openness,
geniality, good humour, good nature, mildness,
benevolence, kindliness, graciousness, obligingness,
courtesy, amicability, congeniality, cordiality, warmth,
sociability, pleasantness
formal benignity, conversableness
F3 unfriendliness, reserve, reticence, coolness

affable *adj*
friendly, amiable, approachable, open, expansive,
genial, good-humoured, good-natured, mild,
benevolent, kindly, gracious, obliging, courteous,
amicable, congenial, cordial, warm, sociable, pleasant,
agreeable
F3 unfriendly, reserved, reticent, cool

affair *n*
1 BUSINESS, transaction, operation, proceeding,
undertaking, activity, project, responsibility, interest,
concern, matter, question, issue, subject, topic,
circumstance, happening, occurrence, incident,
episode, event
2 *have an affair*
relationship, liaison, intrigue, love affair, romance,
amour; *colloq.* fling

affect *v*
1 *changes that affect the schedule*
have an effect/influence on, concern, regard, involve,
relate to, apply to, do to, bear upon, impinge upon, act
on, change, transform, alter, modify, influence, sway,
prevail over, impact
2 *deeply affected by the poverty*
move, touch, impress, interest, stir, upset, disturb,
trouble, overcome; *formal* perturb
3 *a disease affects the body*
attack, strike, take hold of

4 *affect an attitude*
adopt, put on, simulate, imitate, fake, counterfeit, sham, pretend, profess
formal feign, assume

⚠ **affect** or **effect** ?
Affect is always a verb. Its most common meaning is 'to have an influence on; change the circumstances, etc of': *The accident affected his eyesight. Effect* is used as a noun or a verb: as a noun it means 'result or consequence': *recover from the effects of his illness.* As a verb it is used in formal styles to mean 'to cause or bring about': *effect a reconciliation with his parents.*

---

affectation *n*
airs, pretentiousness, mannerism, pose, act, show, appearance, façade, pretence, sham, false display, simulation, imitation, artificiality, insincerity, theatricism, airs and graces
E3 artlessness, ingenuousness

affected *adj*
put-on, simulated, artificial, fake, counterfeit, sham, contrived, studied, precious, mannered, contrived, pretentious, pompous, stiff, unnatural, insincere, twee
formal assumed, feigned, literose, minikin
colloq. la-di-da, phoney
E3 genuine, natural

affecting *adj*
moving, touching, impressive, piteous, pitiable, pitiful, poignant, pathetic, sad, stirring, troubling

affection *n*
fondness, attachment, devotion, love, tenderness, care, caring, warmth, feeling, kindness, friendliness, goodwill, favour, liking, partiality, inclination, passion, desire
formal amity, penchant, predilection, predisposition, proclivity, propensity
E3 dislike, antipathy

affectionate *adj*
fond, attached, devoted, doting, loving, tender, caring, warm, warm-hearted, kind, friendly, amiable, cordial
E3 cold, undemonstrative

affiliate *v*
join, associate, ally, amalgamate, unite, annex, combine, connect, incorporate, join, merge, syndicate, band together
formal confederate, conjoin

affiliation *n*
connection, relationship, link, tie, bond, alliance, union, amalgamation, association, coalition, combination, confederation, federation, incorporation, membership, joining, league, merger

affinity *n*
1 RAPPORT, attraction, compatibility, fondness, liking, good terms, bond, partiality
formal predisposition, propensity
colloq. chemistry
2 RESEMBLANCE, similarity, likeness, correspondence, analogy, comparability
formal similitude
E3 **1** hatred **2** dissimilarity

affirm *v*
confirm, corroborate, endorse, ratify, certify, witness, testify, swear, maintain, state, assert, declare, pronounce
formal asseverate, attest, aver, avouch, avow
E3 refute, deny

affirmation *n*
assertion, statement, declaration, attestation, certification, confirmation, corroboration, endorsement, ratification, oath, pronouncement, testimony, witness
formal affirmance, asseveration, averment, deposition, avouchment, avowal

affirmative *adj*
agreeing, concurring, approving, assenting, consenting, positive, confirming, corroborative, emphatic
E3 negative, dissenting

affix *v*
stick, glue, paste, pin on, tack, attach, add, annex, append, bind, connect, fasten, join, tag
formal adjoin, subjoin
E3 detach

afflict *v*
strike, visit, trouble, burden, oppress, distress, grieve, pain, hurt, wound, harm, try, harass, plague, torment, torture; *old use* smite; *formal* beset
E3 comfort; *formal* solace

⚠ **afflict** or **inflict** ?
Afflict means 'to cause pain or distress to': *Pre-fight nerves afflict almost everyone. Inflict* means 'to impose something unpleasant or unwanted': *They inflicted heavy casualties on the enemy.*

---

affliction *n*
distress, grief, sorrow, misery, depression, suffering, pain, torment, disease, illness, sickness, plague, curse, cross, ordeal, trial, trouble, hardship, adversity, misfortune, calamity, disaster, woe, wretchedness
formal tribulation
E3 comfort, blessing; *formal* consolation, solace

affluence *n*
wealthiness, wealth, riches, fortune, substance, property, prosperity, abundance, profusion, plenty
colloq. tidy sum; *slang* megabucks
formal opulence
E3 poverty

affluent *adj*
wealthy, rich, moneyed, well-off, prosperous, well-to-do, comfortable
formal opulent
colloq. well-heeled, flush, in the money, rolling in it; *slang* loaded
E3 poor, impoverished

afford *v*
1 *afford school fees*
have enough for, pay for, be able to pay, spare, allow, manage, sustain, bear
2 *privileges afforded by the membership*
provide, supply, furnish, give, grant, offer, impart, produce, yield, generate

affray *n*
brawl, brush, contest, disturbance, fight, quarrel, riot, row feud, fracas, fray, melee, scuffle, set-to, skirmish, squabble, tussle, wrangle
colloq. fisticuffs, scrap, free-for-all

affront *v, n*
▶ *v* offend, insult, abuse, snub, slight, provoke,

displease, irritate, annoy, anger, vex, incense, outrage, pique

E3 compliment, appease

▶ *n* offence, insult, slur, rudeness, discourtesy, disrespect, indignity, snub, slight, wrong, injury, abuse, provocation, vexation, outrage
formal aspersion
colloq. slap in the face, kick in the teeth

E3 compliment

afoot   *adj*
about, around, circulating, current, going about, in the air, in the wind, brewing
formal abroad
colloq. in the pipeline

afraid   *adj*
1 *afraid of spiders*
FRIGHTENED, scared, alarmed, terrified, petrified, panic-stricken, fearful, timorous, daunted, intimidated, faint-hearted, cowardly, craven, reluctant, apprehensive, anxious, nervous, timid, distrustful, suspicious
formal tremulous, aghast
2 *I'm afraid she's badly hurt*
sorry, concerned, regretful

E3 1 unafraid, brave, bold, confident

afresh   *adv*
anew, again, once again, once more, newly, over again

after   *prep*
1 *life after death*
following, subsequent to
2 *named after his mother*
in honour of, given the same name as
3 *after the way I've been treated*
because of, owing to, in consequence of, as a result of

E3 1 before

aftermath   *n*
after-effects, effects, results, outcome, consequences, end, repercussions, upshot, wake

afterwards   *adv*
next, later (on), subsequently, after that, then

again   *adv*
once more, once again, yet again, one more time, another time, over again, afresh, anew, encore
▷ **again and again** repeatedly, continually, constantly, over and over again, time and time again, time and again

against   *prep*
1 *against the wall*
adjacent to, close up to, touching, in contact with, on
formal abutting
2 *against corporal punishment*
opposing, versus, opposed to, in opposition to, antagonistic to, hostile to, resisting, in defiance of, opposite to, facing, fronting, in the face of, confronting, in contrast to
colloq. anti

E3 2 in favour of, for; *colloq.* pro

age   *n, v*
▶ *n* **1** *the Ice Age*
era, epoch, day, days, generation, date, time, period, duration, span, years, aeon
2 *the experience of age*
old age, maturity, elderliness, seniority, dotage, senility, decline, advancing/declining years
formal senescence, decrepitude

E3 2 youth; *colloq.* salad days

▶ *v* grow old/up, come of age, mature, ripen, mellow, season, decline, deteriorate, degenerate, wither

E3 obsolesce

aged   *adj*
old, elderly, advanced (in years), ageing, geriatric, grey, hoary, patriarchal, superannuated
formal senescent
colloq. getting on, past it, over the hill, have seen better days, no spring chicken, not as young as you were, with one foot in the grave, ancient

E3 young, youthful

agency   *n*
1 *a recruitment agency*
bureau, office, department, organization, business, firm, company, work
2 MEANS, medium, instrumentality, power, force, influence, effect, intervention, action, activity, operation, mechanism, workings

agenda   *n*
list, plan, programme, schedule, calendar, diary, timetable, to-do list, scheme of work, menu

agent   *n*
1 *a travel agent*
representative, broker, middleman, go-between, intermediary, negotiator, substitute, deputy, delegate, envoy, emissary, minister, proxy, trustee, assignee, mover, doer, performer, operator, operative, functionary, worker, factor
colloq. rep
2 *a secret agent*
spy, double agent, *US* operative
colloq. mole
3 *water-purifying agents*
instrument, vehicle, channel, means, agency, cause, force

agglomeration   *n*
accumulation, build-up, collection, gathering, increase, store, aggregate
formal augmentation, aggregation

aggrandize   *v*
make richer, make more powerful, advance, dignify, elevate, enhance, enlarge, ennoble, enrich, exaggerate, exalt, glamorize, glorify, inflate, amplify, magnify, promote, upgrade, widen

E3 belittle, debase

aggravate   *v*
1 *aggravate the problem*
worsen, make worse, compound, inflame, increase, intensify, heighten, magnify, exaggerate
formal exacerbate
colloq. add fuel to the fire/flames, add insult to injury, rub salt in the wound
2 ANNOY, irritate, vex, irk, exasperate, incense, provoke, tease, pester, harass
colloq. get on someone's nerves, get up someone's nose, rub up the wrong way, needle

E3 1 improve, alleviate **2** soothe, appease, mollify

aggravation   *n*
annoyance, exasperation, irritation, provocation, teasing, vexation, irksomeness
colloq. hassle, thorn in the flesh

aggregate   *n*
total, sum, sum total, grand total, amount, total/whole amount, whole, totality, entirety, generality, combination, collection, accumulation

aggression *n*
1 ANTAGONISM, provocation, offence, injury, attack, offensive, assault, onslaught, raid, incursion, strike, encroachment, infringement, invasion, intrusion
2 AGGRESSIVENESS, militancy, belligerence, combativeness, hostility
formal pugnacity, bellicosity
F3 1 peace, resistance 2 passivity, gentleness

aggressive *adj*
1 *an aggressive person*
argumentative, quarrelsome, contentious, belligerent, hostile, offensive, provocative, intrusive, invasive, ruthless, brutal, savage, ferocious, destructive
formal pugnacious
colloq. cut-throat
2 *an aggressive sales rep*
bold, assertive, go-ahead, forceful, vigorous, zealous
colloq. pushy; *slang* in-your-face
F3 1 peaceable, friendly, submissive, 2 unassertive, timid

aggressor *n*
invader, attacker, assailant, assaulter, intruder, offender, provoker
F3 victim

aggrieved *adj*
bitter, resentful, pained, distressed, saddened, unhappy, upset, annoyed, wronged, offended, hurt, injured, insulted, maltreated, ill-used
F3 pleased, happy

aghast *adj*
shocked, appalled, horrified, horror-struck, thunderstruck, stunned, stupefied, amazed, astonished, astounded, startled, confounded, dismayed

agile *adj*
1 *an agile person*
active, lively, nimble, spry, sprightly, mobile, athletic, flexible, limber, lithe, fleet, quick, swift, brisk
2 *an agile mind*
astute, sharp, acute, alert, quick-witted, clever
F3 1 clumsy, stiff 2 slow

agility *n*
1 *agility of movement*
activeness, liveliness, nimbleness, mobility, flexibility, quickness, swiftness, briskness
2 *agility of thought*
astuteness, sharpness, alertness, quick-wittedness
F3 1 clumsiness, stiffness 2 slowness

agitate *v*
1 *the news agitated them*
worry, trouble, upset, alarm, disturb, unsettle, disquiet, discompose, fluster, ruffle, flurry, unnerve, confuse, distract, disconcert
formal perturb
2 *agitate for reform*
campaign, argue, fight, rouse, arouse, stir up, excite, stimulate, incite, inflame, ferment, work up
3 *agitate the mixture*
shake, rattle, rock, stir, beat, churn, toss, whisk
F3 1 calm, tranquillize

agitated *adj*
worried, troubled, upset, disturbed, anxious, unsettled, flustered, ruffled, distraught, unnerved, disconcerted, nervous
colloq. in a lather
F3 calm, composed

agitator *n*
troublemaker, activist, subversive, rabble-rouser, revolutionary, *agent provocateur*, inciter, instigator, firebrand, fomenter
colloq. stirrer

agnostic *n*
unbeliever, sceptic, doubter
colloq. doubting Thomas

ago *adv*
from that time, gone, past, since, previously, earlier

agog *adj*
eager, excited, curious, enthralled, enthusiastic, impatient, in suspense, keen, avid
colloq. on the edge of your seat, on tenterhooks
F3 incurious

agonize *v*
worry, labour, strain, strive, struggle, trouble, wrestle

agonizing *adj*
distressing, excruciating, harrowing, painful, tormenting, torturous, worrying, racking

agony *n*
anguish, torment, torture, pain, spasm, throes, suffering, affliction, tribulation, distress, hurt, woe, misery, wretchedness

agree *v*
1 *agree with someone*
CONCUR, get on, settle, be of one mind, be of the same opinion, share the view, be at one, come to/reach an agreement, compromise, make concessions
formal accord
colloq. see eye to eye, go along with, go with, meet halfway
2 *agree to your request*
CONSENT, allow, permit, accept, grant, admit, concede, yield, comply, say yes to
formal assent, accede, acquiesce in
colloq. give the go-ahead, give the thumbs-up, rubber-stamp
3 *the reports do not agree*
match, suit, fit, tally, correspond, conform
F3 1 disagree 2 refuse 3 disagree, differ, conflict

agreeable *adj*
1 *agreeable weather*
pleasant, enjoyable, delightful, fine, nice, acceptable
2 *an agreeable person*
pleasant, congenial, likable, nice, attractive, delightful, charming, friendly, good-natured, amicable, sympathetic
3 *agreeable to a suggestion*
willing, amenable, compliant
F3 1 disagreeable, nasty 2 unpleasant
3 unwilling, reluctant to accept

agreement *n*
1 *a trade agreement*
settlement, covenant, treaty, pact, contract, deed, deal, bargain, arrangement, understanding
formal concordat, compact, indenture
2 *be in agreement*
unanimity, union, harmony, sympathy, consensus, affinity
formal assent, complaisance
3 *the agreement of the reports*
matching, fitting, tally, correspondence, consistency, conformity, compatibility, similarity
formal concurrence, accord, concord, consonance
F3 2 disagreement 3 inconsistency

agricultural *adj*
agronomic, agrarian, farming, farmed, cultivated, rural, pastoral
formal bucolic, geoponic, georgic, praedial

agriculture *n*
farming, husbandry, cultivation, tillage
technical agribusiness, agronomics, agronomy, agroscience, geoponics
Related adjective: geoponic

Types of agricultural implement and machinery include: axe, chainsaw, clover broadcaster, fertilizer distributor, field sprinkler, fork, hayfork, pitchfork, hoe, potato planter, rake, hayrake, reaping hook, saw, scythe, shovel, sickle, spade, wheelbarrow, whetstone; all-terrain vehicle (ATV), baler, bale wrapper, cultivator, drill, corn drill, seed drill, fertilizer spreader, fork-lift truck, front end loader, harrow, combination seed-harrow, disc harrow, harvester, combine harvester, hedgecutter, irrigator, milking machine, mower, flail mower, muckspreader, potato planter, plough, reversible plough, wheel plough, power lift, rotary hoe, Rotovator®, scarifier, slurry tanker, sprayer, tedder, tractor, trailer.

aground *adj & adv*
ashore, beached, foundered, grounded, high and dry, marooned, stranded, stuck, wrecked, on the rocks
E3 afloat

ahead *adv*
1 *glance ahead*
forward, onward, leading, at the head, in front
2 *ahead on points*
in the lead, winning, at an advantage, advanced, superior, to the fore, in the forefront
3 *plan ahead*
in advance, before, earlier on

aid *v, n*
▶ *v* **1** *aid an invalid*
help, assist, rally round, relieve, support, subsidize, sustain, second, serve, favour, co-operate with
formal succour, oblige, accommodate
2 *aid a process*
promote, boost, encourage, facilitate, speed up, ease
formal expedite, hasten
E3 1 *colloq.* not lift a finger **2** hinder, impede, obstruct
▶ *n* **1** *aid for refugees*
relief, benefit, assistance, subsidy, donation, gift, contribution, funding, grant, sponsorship, patronage, favour, encouragement, service
formal subvention
2 *turn to someone for aid*
help, assistance, prop, support, backup, boost
formal succour
colloq. (helping) hand, a shot in the arm, a leg up
E3 2 hindrance, impediment, obstruction

aide *n*
adviser, assistant, right-hand person, right-hand man, supporter, adjutant, advocate, aide-de-camp, attaché, confidant, disciple, follower

ail *v*
afflict, trouble, upset, bother, distress, fail, irritate, pain, sicken, weaken, worry
E3 comfort, flourish

ailing *adj*
unwell, ill, sick, poorly, suffering, languishing, sickly, diseased, invalid, infirm, unsound, unfit, frail, weak, feeble, failing
formal indisposed, debilitated
colloq. out of sorts, under the weather, off-colour
E3 healthy, fit, thriving, flourishing

ailment *n*
illness, sickness, complaint, malady, disease, infection, disorder, affliction, infirmity, disability, weakness
formal indisposition

aim *v, n*
▶ *v* **1** POINT, direct, take aim, shoot at, level, train, sight, target
colloq. zero in on
2 *aim to achieve*
plan, aspire, want, wish, seek, resolve, purpose, intend, propose, mean, design, strive, try, attempt, endeavour, set your sights on
formal resolve
▶ *n* purpose, motive, end, intention, object, objective, target, mark, goal, direction, course, plan, design, scheme, aspiration, mission, mission statement, ambition, hope, dream, desire, wish

aimless *adj*
pointless, purposeless, goalless, futile, unmotivated, irresolute, directionless, rambling, drifting, wandering, undirected, unguided, unsettled, stray, chance, random, haphazard, erratic, unpredictable, wayward
E3 purposeful, positive, determined

air *n, v*
▶ *n* **1** *birds flying in the air*
atmosphere, oxygen, sky, heavens
formal ether
Related adjective: aerial
2 *the air we breathe*
breath, fresh air, puff, waft, draught, breeze, wind, blast
formal zephyr
Related adjective: pneumatic
3 APPEARANCE, look, aspect, aura, bearing, manner, character, effect, impression, feeling, carriage
formal ambience, demeanour
▶ *v* **1** *air a room*
ventilate, aerate, freshen
2 *air an opinion*
utter, voice, express, give vent to, make known, communicate, tell, declare, state, reveal, disclose, divulge, expose, make public, broadcast, publish, circulate, disseminate, publicize
colloq. speak your mind, have your say

aircraft *n*

Types of aircraft include: aeroplane, plane, jet, jumbo, Concorde, airbus, helicopter, monoplane, two-seater, air-ambulance, freighter, sea-plane, glider, hang-glider, microlight, hot-air balloon; fighter, spitfire, bomber, *colloq.* kite, jump-jet, dive-bomber, *colloq.* chopper, spy plane, delta-wing, swing-wing, troop-carrier, airship, turbojet, VTOL (vertical take-off and landing), warplane, zeppelin.

airing *n*
1 *give clothes an airing*
ventilation, aeration, freshening
2 *the airing of opinions*
expression, making known, communication, declaration, statement, revelation, disclosure,

divulgence, exposure, uttering, voicing, broadcast, publication, circulation
formal dissemination

airless *adj*
unventilated, badly/poorly ventilated, stuffy, musty, stale, suffocating, stifling, sultry, muggy, close, heavy, oppressive
E∃ airy, fresh

airs *n*
arrogance, artificiality, haughtiness, posing, pretensions, pretentiousness, superciliousness
formal affectation, affectedness, hauteur, pomposity
colloq. swank

airtight *adj*
closed, sealed, impenetrable, impermeable, tight-fitting

airy *adj*
1 *an airy room*
roomy, spacious, open, well-ventilated, draughty, breezy, blowy, windy, gusty
2 CASUAL, cheerful, happy, light-hearted, high-spirited, lively, jaunty, nonchalant, offhand
E∃ **1** airless, stuffy, close, heavy, oppressive

aisle *n*
gangway, corridor, passage, passageway, alleyway, walkway, path, lane

alarm *n, v*
▶ *n* **1** FRIGHT, scare, fear, terror, panic, horror, shock, consternation, dismay, distress, anxiety, nervousness, apprehension, trepidation, uneasiness
formal perturbation
2 *a burglar alarm*
danger signal, alert, warning, distress signal, siren, bell, alarm-bell
formal tocsin
E∃ **1** calmness, composure
▶ *v* frighten, scare, startle, terrify, panic, make afraid, unnerve, daunt, dismay, distress, agitate
formal perturb, affright
colloq. put the wind up, rattle
E∃ reassure, calm, soothe

alarming *adj*
frightening, scary, startling, terrifying, unnerving, daunting, ominous, worrying, threatening, dismaying, disturbing, distressing, shocking, dreadful
formal perturbing
E∃ reassuring

alarmist *n*
scaremonger, pessimist, doomwatcher
E∃ optimist

alcohol *n*
drink, liquor, spirits, strong drink, intoxicant
colloq. hard stuff, the bottle, Dutch courage, fire-water; *slang* booze

alcoholic *adj, n*
▶ *adj* intoxicating, inebriating, brewed, fermented, distilled, strong, hard, ardent, having a drink problem
▶ *n* drunk, drunkard, inebriate, drinker, hard drinker, heavy drinker, dipsomaniac
colloq. tippler; *slang* boozer, wino, lush, alkie, dipso, soak, piss artist, toper, tosspot

alcove *n*
niche, nook, recess, bay, corner, cubbyhole, compartment, cubicle, booth, carrel

alert *adj, v*
▶ *adj* attentive, awake, wide-awake, watchful, vigilant, on the lookout, sharp-eyed, observant, perceptive, sharp-witted, active, lively, spirited, quick, brisk, agile, nimble, ready, prepared, careful, heedful, circumspect, wary
formal on the qui vive
colloq. with your eyes open/peeled, on the ball, on your toes
E∃ slow, listless, unprepared
▶ *v* warn, forewarn, notify, inform, tip off, signal, alarm

algae *n*

Types of algae and lichen include: anabaena, badderlocks, bladderwrack, bull kelp, carrageen, Ceylon moss, chlorella, conferva, desmid, diatom, dinaflagellate, dulse, euglena, fucoid, fucus, gulfweed, Irish moss, kelp, laminaria, laver, lecanora, nostoc, nullipore, oak moss, oarweed, peacock's tail, redware, reindeer moss, rock tripe, rockweed, sargassum, sea lace, sea lettuce, sea tangle, seaware, sea wrack, Spanish moss, spirogyra, stonewort, wrack.

alias *n, adv*
▶ *n* pseudonym, false name, assumed name, *nom de guerre*, *nom de plume*, pen name, stage name, nickname
formal sobriquet, allonym, anonym
▶ *adv* also known as, also called, otherwise, otherwise known as, under the name of, formerly
colloq. aka

alibi *n*
defence, justification, story, explanation, excuse, cover-up, pretext, reason

alien *adj, n*
▶ *adj* **1** *an alien culture*
foreign, exotic, extraterrestrial, extraneous, remote
2 *alien surroundings*
strange, unfamiliar, outlandish, incongruous
3 *alien to her nature*
opposed, contrary, conflicting, antagonistic, incompatible
formal repugnant, inimical
▶ *n* foreigner, immigrant, newcomer, stranger, outsider
E∃ native, resident

alienate *v*
antagonize, estrange, set against, turn away, turn off, make hostile, separate, divorce
formal disaffect
E∃ unite

alienation *n*
antagonization, estrangement, turning away, indifference, remoteness, rupture, separation, isolation, severance, divorce, disunion, diversion
formal disaffection
E∃ endearment

alight[1] *adj*
1 *set the rubbish alight*
lighted, lit, ignited, on fire, burning, blazing, ablaze, flaming, fiery
2 *eyes alight with excitement*
lit up, illuminated, bright, radiant, shining, brilliant, lively, alive

alight² *v*
passengers alighting from buses
descend, get down, get off, land, touch down, come down, come to rest, settle, light, perch
formal dismount, disembark, debark
E3 ascend, board, get on, get onto, rise

align *v*
1 *align yourself with a political party*
ally, side, sympathize, associate, affiliate, join, co-operate, agree, join forces, combine, unite
2 *align two pieces of wood*
arrange, straighten, range, line up, make parallel, even (up), adjust, regulate, regularize, order, co-ordinate

alignment *n*
1 *alignment with a political party*
affiliation, association, alliance, co-operation, agreement, sympathy, siding
2 *alignment of the pieces*
arrangement, straightening, line, lining up, order, ranging

alike *adj, adv*
▶ *adj* similar, resembling, comparable, akin, corresponding, equivalent, equal, the same, much the same, identical, indistinguishable, duplicate, parallel, even, uniform
formal analogous, cognate
E3 dissimilar, unlike, different
▶ *adv* similarly, in the same way, analogously, correspondingly, equally, in common

alive *adj*
1 *Are your parents alive still?*
LIVING, having life, live, animate, breathing, existent, in existence
formal extant
colloq. (still) going strong, in the land of the living
2 *I like her because she is so alive*
LIVELY, animated, spirited, awake, alert, active, brisk, energetic, full of life, vigorous, zestful, vivacious, vibrant, vital
3 *alive with tourists*
full of, teeming with, abounding in, overflowing with
colloq. crawling with, swarming with
4 *alive to the danger*
aware of, heedful of, alert to, sensitive to
formal cognizant of
E3 **1** dead, extinct **2** lifeless, apathetic **4** unaware of, blind to, deaf to

all *adj, n, adv*
▶ *adj* **1** *all people are equal*
each, every, each and every, every single, every one of, the whole of, every bit of, in its entirety, from start to finish
2 *run with all speed*
complete, entire, full, total, utter, outright, perfect, greatest
E3 **1** no, none
▶ *n* everything, everyone, everybody, sum, total, aggregate, total amount, whole amount, whole, entirety, utmost, comprehensiveness, universality
colloq. the lot
E3 nothing, none
▶ *adv* completely, entirely, wholly, fully, totally, utterly, altogether, wholesale

allay *v*
alleviate, relieve, soothe, ease, smooth, calm, tranquillize, compose, quiet, quell, pacify, mollify, soften, blunt, lessen, reduce, diminish, check,
moderate
E3 exacerbate, intensify

allegation *n*
accusation, charge, claim, profession, assertion, affirmation, declaration, statement, testimony, plea
formal avowal, deposition, asseveration

allege *v*
assert, affirm, declare, state, maintain, insist, hold, put forward, contend, claim, profess, plead
formal attest

alleged *adj*
supposed, reputed, inferred, so-called, professed, declared, stated, claimed, described, designated, doubtful, dubious, suspect
formal ostensible, putative

allegiance *n*
loyalty, fidelity, faithfulness, constancy, duty, obligation, obedience, devotion, support, adherence, solidarity, friendship
formal fealty
E3 disloyalty, enmity

allegorical *adj*
figurative, representative, symbolic, metaphorical, symbolizing, typical
formal parabolic, emblematic, significative

allegory *n*
analogy, comparison, metaphor, symbol, parable, story, fable, myth, legend, tale, symbolism
formal emblem, apologue

allergic *adj*
1 *allergic to shellfish*
sensitive, hypersensitive, susceptible, affected
2 *allergic to Mondays*
averse, disinclined, opposed, hostile, antagonistic
formal dyspathetic

allergy *n*
1 *an allergy to dogs*
sensitivity, hypersensitivity, susceptibility
2 *an allergy to work*
opposition, hostility, antagonism, aversion
formal antipathy, disinclination, dyspathy

alleviate *v*
relieve, soothe, ease, mitigate, soften, cushion, dull, deaden, allay, abate, lessen, assuage, reduce, diminish, check, moderate, mollify, temper, subdue
formal palliate
E3 aggravate

alleviation *n*
relief, soothing, easing, mitigation, dulling, deadening, abatement, lessening, assuagement, reduction, moderation, mollification
formal palliation, diminution
E3 aggravation

alley *n*
alleyway, back street, lane, street, road, mall, passage, passageway, pathway, close, gate, walk

alliance *n*
partnership, confederation, federation, association, affiliation, coalition, league, bloc, cartel, conglomerate, consortium, syndicate, guild, union, marriage, agreement, compact, bond, pact, treaty, combination, connection
E3 separation, divorce, estrangement, enmity, hostility

allied *adj*
associated, connected, linked, bound, combined, in league, joined, joint, kindred, related, affiliated, amalgamated, coupled, unified, united, married, wed
colloq. hand in glove, in cahoots
🔁 estranged

allocate *v*
assign, designate, budget, allow, earmark, set aside, allot, apportion, share out, distribute, dispense, divide, parcel out, mete (out), ration
formal admeasure

allocation *n*
1 *the allocation of funds*
apportionment, distribution, giving-out, allotment
2 *an allocation of tickets*
share, measure, lot, portion, stint, ration, quota, budget, allowance, grant
colloq. cut, slice of the cake

allot *v*
divide, ration, apportion, share out, distribute, dispense, mete, allocate, assign, designate, budget, allow, grant, earmark, set aside
formal admeasure
colloq. dole out

allotment *n*
1 *dig an allotment*
land, plot of land
2 *an allotment of funds*
division, partition, allocation, apportionment, measure, percentage, lot, portion, share, stint, ration, quota, allowance, grant
formal apportionment

all-out *adj*
complete, full, total, undivided, comprehensive, exhaustive, thorough, intensive, thoroughgoing, wholesale, vigorous, powerful, full-scale, maximum, utmost, unlimited, unrestrained, unremitting, unstinted, resolute, determined
colloq. no-holds-barred
🔁 perfunctory, half-hearted

allow *v*
1 PERMIT, let, enable, authorize, sanction, warrant, approve, say yes to, agree to, give leave, tolerate, put up with, endure, suffer
formal give your consent (to), consent (to)
colloq. OK, okay, give the go-ahead, give the green light
2 ADMIT, confess, own, acknowledge, concede, grant, agree
3 *allow two hours for the journey*
allot, allocate, assign, apportion, afford, give, provide, spare
🔁 1 forbid, prevent 2 deny
▷ **allow for** take into account, make provision for, make allowances for, provide for, foresee, plan for, arrange for, bear in mind, keep in mind, consider, include
🔁 discount

allowable *adj*
permissible, acceptable, admissible, justifiable, all right, appropriate, approved, legal, legitimate, lawful
formal licit, sanctionable
colloq. legit
🔁 unacceptable

allowance *n*
1 PAYMENT, remittance, pocket money, grant,

income, maintenance, subsistence allowance, expenses, expense allowance, contribution, benefit, stipend, pension, annuity
2 REBATE, reduction, deduction, discount, concession, subsidy, weighting
3 ALLOCATION, lot, amount, portion, share, ration, quota
▷ **make allowances** 1 TAKE INTO ACCOUNT, take into consideration, bear/keep in mind, consider
2 *make allowances for her inexperience* EXCUSE, pardon, forgive

alloy *n*
blend, compound, composite, amalgam, combination, mixture, fusion, coalescence
formal admixture, composite

all right *adj, adv*
▶ *adj* 1 SATISFACTORY, passable, unobjectionable, acceptable, reasonable, good enough, allowable, adequate, fair, average
colloq. OK
2 *Are you all right?*
well, healthy, unhurt, uninjured, unharmed, unimpaired, whole, sound, safe, secure
colloq. right as rain
🔁 1 unacceptable, inadequate
▶ *adv* satisfactorily, well enough, passably, unobjectionably, acceptably, suitably, appropriately, adequately, reasonably
colloq. OK
🔁 unsatisfactorily, unacceptably

allude *v*
mention, refer, remark, speak of, hint, imply, infer, insinuate, intimate, suggest, touch on/upon
formal adumbrate

⚠ **allude** or **elude** ?
If you *allude* to something, you refer to it; if something *eludes* you, you cannot remember it or understand it.

allure *v, n*
▶ *v* lure, entice, seduce, lead on, tempt, coax, cajole, persuade, win over, disarm, charm, enchant, attract, interest, fascinate, captivate, entrance, beguile
colloq. give the come-on, work on
🔁 repel
▶ *n* lure, enticement, seduction, temptation, appeal, attraction, magnetism, fascination, glamour, captivation, charm, enchantment

alluring *adj*
attractive, fascinating, intriguing, interesting, captivating, winning, enchanting, engaging, enticing, arousing, beguiling, bewitching, fetching, seductive, sensuous, sexy, desirable, tempting
colloq. come-hither
🔁 repellent, unattractive

allusion *n*
mention, reference, citation, quotation, remark, observation, suggestion, hint, intimation, implication, insinuation

⚠ **allusion** or **illusion** ?
An *allusion* to something is an indirect reference to it; an *illusion* is a false belief or appearance.

ally *n, v*
▶ *n* supporter, associate, consort, confederate, partner, colleague, co-worker, collaborator, helper,

accomplice, accessory, friend
colloq. sidekick
E3 enemy, antagonist
▶ *v* associate, collaborate, join forces, band together, team up, go into partnership, fraternize, confederate, affiliate, league, side, join, connect, link, marry, unite, unify, amalgamate, combine
E3 estrange, separate

almanac *n*
yearbook, annual, calendar, register

almighty *adj*
1 *almighty God*
all-powerful, supreme, absolute, great, invincible
formal omnipotent, plenipotent
2 ENORMOUS, severe, intense, overwhelming, overpowering, terrible, awful, desperate
E3 **1** impotent, weak

almost *adv*
nearly, practically, virtually, just about, as good as, all but, well-nigh, more or less, to all intents and purposes, close to/on, not far from, approaching, nearing, not quite, about, approximately
formal quasi-
colloq. pretty much/well

alone *adj*
only, sole, single, unique, solitary, separate, detached, unconnected, isolated, cloistered, apart, by yourself, by itself, on your own, lonely, lonesome, deserted, abandoned, forsaken, forlorn, desolate, unaccompanied, unescorted, unattended, solo, single-handed, unaided
formal sequestered
colloq. on your tod
E3 together, accompanied, escorted

aloof *adj*
distant, remote, offish, standoffish, haughty, supercilious, unapproachable, inaccessible, detached, forbidding, cool, chilly, cold, unsympathetic, unresponsive, indifferent, uninterested, reserved, unforthcoming, unfriendly, unsociable, antisocial, formal
E3 sociable, friendly, concerned

aloud *adv*
out loud, audibly, intelligibly, clearly, plainly, distinctly, loudly, resoundingly, sonorously, noisily, vociferously
E3 silently

alphabet *n*

Alphabets and writing systems include: Arabic, Byzantine, Chalcidian alphabet, cuneiform, Cyrillic, devanagari, estrangelo, finger-alphabet, futhark, Georgian, Glagol, Glossic, Greek, Gurmukhi, Hebrew, hieroglyphs, hiragana, ideograph, Initial Teaching Alphabet, (i.t.a.), International Phonetic Alphabet (IPA), kana, kanji, katakana, Kufic, linear A, linear B, logograph, nagari, naskhi, ogam, pictograph, romaji, Roman, runic, syllabary.

already *adv*
1 *I've read the book already*
before now, beforehand, just now, previously
formal heretofore, hitherto
2 *he can already count*
even now, even then, so soon (as this), so early by now, by that time, by then, by this time

also *adv*
too, as well, and, plus, along with, including, as well as, additionally, in addition, besides, further, furthermore, moreover

alter *v*
change, vary, diversify, modify, qualify, shift, transpose, make different, adjust, adapt, convert, turn, transform, reform, reshape, remodel, recast, revise, amend, emend
formal metamorphose, transmute
E3 fix

alteration *n*
change, variation, variance, difference, diversification, shift, transposition, modification, adjustment, adaptation, conversion, transformation, transfiguration, reformation, reshaping, remodelling, revision, amendment
formal metamorphosis, transmutation, vicissitude
E3 fixity

altercation *n*
argument, dispute, clash, disagreement, discord, dissension, fracas, quarrel, row, squabble, wrangle
formal logomachy

alternate *v, adj*
▶ *v* interchange, reciprocate, rotate, take turns, take it in turns, follow one another, replace each other, substitute, change, alter, vary, oscillate, fluctuate, intersperse
colloq. chop and change
▶ *adj* **1** *alternate weekends*
alternating, every other, every second
2 *alternate bouts of depression and happiness*
(repeated) one after the other, in turns, consecutive, interchanging, reciprocal, rotating

⚠ **alternate** or **alternative** ?
Alternate refers to something happening or coming every second day, week, etc or in turns: *He visits them on alternate Tuesdays; alternate bursts of hot and cold water. Alternative* refers to the choice of two possibilities: *If that doesn't work, we'll have to think of an alternative plan.*

alternative *n, adj*
▶ *n* option, choice, selection, preference, other, recourse, substitute, back-up
▶ *adj* **1** *an alternative possibility*
substitute, second, another, other, different
2 *alternative medicine*
unorthodox, unconventional, fringe, nontraditional
E3 **2** conventional, traditional, orthodox, standard, regular

although *conj*
though, even though, despite/in spite of the fact that, while, even if, even supposing, granted that
formal albeit, whilst, howbeit, notwithstanding

altitude *n*
height, elevation, loftiness, tallness, stature, depth

altogether *adv*
1 *altogether more efficient*
totally, completely, entirely, wholly, fully, utterly, absolutely, quite, perfectly, thoroughly
2 *the meal came to £40 altogether*
in total, in all, all told, *in toto,* all in all

altruistic *adj*
selfless, unselfish, self-sacrificing, disinterested,

public-spirited, philanthropic, charitable, humanitarian, benevolent, generous, considerate, humane
₣₃ selfish

always *adv*
1 *always be home by 6 o'clock*
every time, all the time, consistently, invariably, without exception, habitually, unfailingly, regularly, perpetually, in perpetuum, evermore
2 *always criticizing others*
again and again, continually, constantly, repeatedly, forever, endlessly, unceasingly, eternally
₣₃ 1 never

amalgam *n*
mixture, blend, fusion, alloy, compound, coalescence, synthesis, combination, union
formal admixture, aggregate, commixture

amalgamate *v*
merge, blend, mingle, intermix, incorporate, alloy, integrate, compound, fuse, coalesce, synthesize, combine, unite, unify, ally
formal commingle, homogenize
₣₃ separate

amalgamation *n*
merger, blend, incorporation, integration, joining, compound, fusion, coalescence, synthesis, combination, unity, union, unification, alliance
formal admixture, commingling, homogenization
₣₃ separation

amass *v*
accumulate, accrue, assemble, collect, gather, heap (up), hoard, pile (up), store (up), gain, acquire
formal agglomerate, agglutinate, aggregate, foregather, garner

amateur *n*
non-professional, layman, lay person, dilettante, dabbler, enthusiast, fancier
colloq. ham, buff
₣₃ professional

amateurish *adj*
non-professional, lay, unpaid, unqualified, untrained, unskilful, inexpert, unprofessional, clumsy, crude, inept
₣₃ professional, expert, skilled

amaze *v*
surprise, startle, astonish, astound, stun, stupefy, daze, stagger, dumbfound, shock, dismay, disconcert, confound, bewilder
colloq. floor, flabbergast, bowl over, gobsmack, wow, blow your mind, knock for six, knock you down with a feather, strike dumb

amazement *n*
surprise, astonishment, shock, dismay, confusion, perplexity, bewilderment, admiration, wonder, marvel
formal stupefaction, wonderment

ambassador *n*
1 *a country's ambassador*
envoy, diplomat, consul
formal emissary, legate, plenipotentiary
2 *an ambassador of peace*
representative, agent, deputy, delegate, minister

ambience *n*
atmosphere, air, aura, climate, milieu, mood, spirit, surroundings, environment, character, feel, feeling,

flavour, impression, tenor, tone
colloq. vibes, vibrations

ambiguity *n*
double meaning, *double entendre*, ambivalence, polysemy, equivocality, equivocation, confusion, obscurity, unclearness, vagueness, woolliness, imprecision, indeterminateness, dubiousness, doubt, doubtfulness, uncertainty, enigma, puzzle, paradox
formal dubiety
₣₃ clarity

ambiguous *adj*
double-meaning, equivocal, multivocal, double-edged, two-edged, back-handed, cryptic, enigmatic, paradoxical, puzzling, confusing, obscure, unclear, vague, indefinite, imprecise, woolly, confused, dubious, doubtful, uncertain, inconclusive, indeterminate
₣₃ clear, definite

ambit *n*
scope, extent, range, compass, confines

ambition *n*
1 ASPIRATION, aim, goal, target, objective, intent, purpose, design, object, ideal, dream, hope, wish, desire, yearning, longing, hankering, craving, hunger
2 *a woman of ambition*
enterprise, drive, push, thrust, striving, eagerness, commitment, initiative, zeal
colloq. get-up-and-go, what it takes
₣₃ 2 apathy, diffidence

ambitious *adj*
1 ASPIRING, hopeful, desirous, intent, purposeful, bold, assertive, enterprising, driving, energetic, enthusiastic, eager, keen, striving, industrious, zealous
colloq. power-hungry, go-ahead, pushy, full of go, not backward in coming forward
2 FORMIDABLE, hard, difficult, arduous, strenuous, demanding, challenging, bold, exacting, impressive, grandiose, elaborate
₣₃ 1 lazy, unassuming 2 modest, uninspiring

ambivalence *n*
contradiction, conflict, clash, opposition, inconsistency, confusion, fluctuation, wavering, hesitation, irresoluteness, uncertainty, doubt, inconclusiveness
formal vacillation
₣₃ certainty

ambivalent *adj*
contradictory, conflicting, clashing, warring, opposed, inconsistent, mixed, confused, fluctuating, wavering, hesitant, irresolute, undecided, unresolved, unsettled, uncertain, unsure, doubtful, debatable, inconclusive
formal vacillating
₣₃ unequivocal

amble *v*
walk, saunter, stroll, dawdle, wander, drift, meander, ramble
formal perambulate, promenade
colloq. mosey along, toddle
₣₃ stride, march

ambush *n, v*
▶ *n* waylaying, surprise attack, trap, snare
formal ambuscade
▶ *v* lie in wait, waylay, lay a trap for, surprise, trap, attack, ensnare, bushwhack
formal ambuscade
colloq. turn on, pounce on, jump

ameliorate *v*
alleviate, improve, better, amend, benefit, ease, elevate, enhance, mend, mitigate, promote, relieve
🔳 exacerbate, worsen

amenable *adj*
accommodating, flexible, willing, open, agreeable, persuadable, compliant, submissive, responsive, susceptible, liable, responsible
formal tractable, acquiescent, complaisant
🔳 unwilling, intractable

amend *v*
revise, correct, rectify, fix, repair, mend, remedy, redress, reform, change, alter, adjust, modify, qualify, enhance, improve, better
formal emend, emendate, ameliorate
🔳 impair, worsen

⚠ **amend** or **emend** ?
If you *amend* a document, you alter or improve it; if you *emend* a text you correct errors in it.

amendment *n*
revision, correction, remedy, reform, change, alteration, adjustment, modification, improvement, qualification, enhancement, clarification, addition, attachment, adjunct
formal corrigendum, rectification, emendation, addendum
🔳 impairment, deterioration

amends *n*
atonement, expiation, requital, satisfaction, recompense, compensation, indemnification, indemnity, reparation, redress, restoration, restitution

amenity *n*
facility, advantage, convenience, service, utility, resource

amiable *adj*
affable, friendly, approachable, genial, warm, cheerful, good-tempered, good-natured, kind, easy to get along/on with, obliging, charming, engaging, likable, pleasant, agreeable, congenial, companionable, sociable
🔳 unfriendly, curt, hostile

⚠ **amiable** or **amicable** ?
Amiable is used to describe a person who is friendly, good-tempered and pleasant; *amicable* is used to describe relationships or agreements that are conducted in a friendly way without anger.

amicable *adj*
friendly, cordial, good-natured, civil, harmonious civilised, peaceful
🔳 hostile

amid *prep*
amidst, midst, in the midst of, in the thick of, among, amongst, in the middle of, surrounded by

amino acid *n*
Amino acids include: alanine, arginine, asparagine, aspartic acid, cysteine, glutamic acid, glutamine, glycine, histidine, isoleucine, leucine, lysine, methionine, phenylalanine, proline, serine, threonine, trytophan, tyrosine, valine.

amiss *adj*
wrong, awry, defective, false, faulty, improper, out of order, inaccurate, inappropriate, incorrect, unsuitable, untoward, imperfect, out of kilter
colloq. wonky
🔳 right, well

amity *n*
peace, peacefulness, understanding, accord, concord, cordiality, fellowship, fraternity, brotherliness, friendliness, friendship, goodwill, harmony, kindness, sympathy
formal comity
🔳 discord, hostility

ammunition *n*
missiles, bullets, shells, rockets, projectiles, cartridges, slugs, grenades, bombs, shot, mine, gunpowder

amnesty *n*
pardon, forgiveness, absolution, mercy, lenience, indulgence, reprieve, remission, dispensation, immunity

amok *adv*
berserk, crazy, in a frenzy, frenzied, insanely, like a lunatic, madly, wildly, uncontrollably, violently

among *prep*
amongst, between, in the middle of, surrounded by, amid, amidst, midst, in the midst of, in the thick of, with, together with

amorous *adj*
passionate, loving, affectionate, tender, fond, erotic, impassioned, in love, lovesick, lustful
formal amatory
colloq. randy
🔳 cold, indifferent

amorphous *adj*
formless, nebulous, shapeless, featureless, indeterminate, indistinct, irregular, undefined, unformed, unshapen, unstructured, vague
formal inchoate
🔳 definite, distinctive, shapely

amount *n*
quantity, number, sum, total, sum total, whole, entirety, aggregate, lot, quota, supply, volume, mass, bulk, measure, magnitude, extent, expanse
▷ **amount to 1** *amount to a total* add up to, total, aggregate, come to, make, equal, run to; *colloq.* tot up, tot up to **2** *giving presents to potential customers amounts to bribery* mean, be tantamount to, be equivalent to, correspond to, come down to, boil down to

amphibian *n*
Amphibians include: frog, bullfrog, tree frog, toad, horned toad, midwife toad, natterjack, newt, eft, salamander, conger eel, axolotl.

ample *adj*
1 *ample opportunity/space*
(more than) enough, sufficient, considerable, substantial, plentiful, plenty, abundant, unrestricted, profuse, spacious, great, copious
formal commodious
2 *of ample proportions*
large, big, extensive, expansive, broad, wide, full, generous substantial,
formal voluminous
🔳 **1** insufficient, inadequate, meagre

amplify *v*
1 *amplify sound*
MAKE LOUDER, increase, heighten, enhance, boost, intensify, strengthen, deepen, raise
2 *amplify a statement*
enlarge on, expand, fill out, bulk out, add to, supplement, augment, increase, extend, lengthen, widen, broaden, develop, elaborate on, go into details, flesh out
formal expatiate on
E3 1 reduce, decrease, soften

amplitude *n*
expanse, vastness, volume, bulk, capacity, extent, fullness, greatness, largeness, magnitude, mass, profusion, spaciousness, width
formal copiousnessplenitude capaciousness

amputate *v*
cut off, remove, sever, dissever, separate, dock, lop, curtail, truncate

amulet *n*
charm, talisman, fetish, juju, lucky charm
formal braxas, pentacle, periapt, phylactery

amuse *v*
1 *the joke amused them*
make laugh, cheer (up), gladden, charm, delight, please, enthral
colloq. tickle, crease, crack, tickle your funny bone
2 *amuse yourselves while I'm away*
OCCUPY, entertain, divert, regale, engross, absorb, interest, recreate, relax
formal disport
E3 1 displease 2 bore

amusement *n*
1 *a look of amusement at the joke*
fun, enjoyment, pleasure, delight, merriment, mirth, hilarity, laughter,
2 *to the amusement of the onlookers*
entertainment, diversion, distraction
3 PASTIME, game, sport, recreation, hobby, interest

amusing *adj*
funny, humorous, hilarious, comical, laughable, ludicrous, droll, witty, facetious, jocular, jolly, waggish, enjoyable, pleasant, charming, delightful, entertaining, interesting
E3 dull, boring

anaemic *adj*
bloodless, ashen, chalky, livid, pasty, pallid, sallow, whey-faced, pale, wan, colourless, insipid, weak, feeble, ineffectual, enervated, frail, infirm, sickly
E3 ruddy, sanguine, full-blooded

anaesthetic *n*
painkiller, sedative, analgesic, anodyne, narcotic, opiate, palliative, soporific, epidural, stupefacient, stupefactive, premedication, local anaesthetic, general anaesthetic

anaesthetize *v*
desensitize, numb, deaden, dull, drug, dope, stupefy

analogous *adj*
comparable, similar, like, resembling, matching, kindred, parallel, corresponding, equivalent, relative, correlative, agreeing
E3 disparate

analogy *n*
comparison, simile, metaphor, likeness, resemblance, similarity, parallel, correspondence, equivalence,

relation, correlation, agreement
formal similitude, semblance

analyse *v*
break down, separate, divide, take apart, dissect, reduce, resolve, sift, investigate, inquire, study, examine, scrutinize, review, interpret, test, judge, evaluate, estimate, consider
formal anatomize, assay

analysis *n*
breakdown, separation, division, dissection, reduction, resolution, sifting, investigation, inquiry, study, examination, inspection, scrutiny, review, check, check-up, exposition, explication, explanation, interpretation, test, judgement, opinion, evaluation, estimation, reasoning
formal anatomization, assay

analytical *adj*
analytic, detailed, in-depth, searching, critical, questioning, inquiring, inquisitive, investigative, dissecting, diagnostic, systematic, methodical, logical, rational, interpretative, explanatory, expository, studious

anarchic *adj*
lawless, ungoverned, anarchistic, libertarian, nihilist, revolutionary, rebellious, mutinous, riotous, chaotic, disordered, confused, disorganized
E3 submissive, orderly

anarchist *n*
revolutionary, rebel, insurgent, libertarian, nihilist, terrorist

anarchy *n*
lawlessness, unrule, misrule, anarchism, revolution, rebellion, insurrection, mutiny, riot, pandemonium, chaos, disorder, confusion
E3 rule, control, order

anathema *n*
aversion, abhorrence, abomination, object of loathing, *bête noire*, bugbear, bane, curse, proscription, taboo

anatomy *n*
dissection, vivisection, zootomy, analysis, make-up, composition, constitution, construction, frame, framework, build, structure

Anatomical terms include: aural, biceps, bone, cardiac, cartilage, cerebral, dental, diaphragm, dorsal, duodenal, elbow, epidermis, epiglottis, Fallopian tubes, foreskin, funny bone, gastric, genitalia, gingival, gristle, groin, gullet, hamstring, helix, hepatic, hock, intercostal, jugular, lachrymal, ligament, lumbar, mammary, membral, muscle, nasal, neural, ocular, oesophagus, optical, pectoral, pedal, pulmonary, renal, spine, tendon, triceps, umbilicus, uterus, uvula, voice-box, vulva, windpipe, womb. *See also* **bone; brain; ear; eye; gland; heart; mouth; muscle; tooth; vein.**

ancestor *n*
forebear, forefather, progenitor, predecessor, forerunner, precursor, antecedent
formal primogenitor
E3 descendant

ancestral *adj*
familial, parental, genealogical, hereditary, genetic
formal lineal

ancestry *n*
ancestors, forebears, forefathers, progenitors,

parentage, family, family tree, lineage, line, descent, blood, race, stock, roots, pedigree, genealogy, extraction, derivation, origin, heritage, heredity

anchor *v*
moor, berth, tie up, make fast, fasten, attach, affix, fix

Types of anchor include: car, double fluked, drogue, grapnel, kedge, killick, mushroom, navy, sea, stocked, stockless, yachtsman.

ancient *adj*
1 *ancient history*
early, antediluvian, prehistoric, fossilized, primeval, primordial, immemorial old, aged, time-worn, age-old, antique
formal pristine
colloq. as old as the hills
2 OLD-FASHIONED, out-of-date, antiquated, archaic, outmoded, *passé*, obsolete, bygone, early, original
formal superannuated, atavistic
F∃ 1 recent, contemporary **2** modern, up-to-date

ancillary *adj*
auxiliary, supporting, helping, accessory, contributory, extra, secondary, subordinate, additional, subsidiary, supplementary
formal adjuvant, adminicular

and *conj*
also, too, together (with), besides, as well (as), in addition (to), plus, including, furthermore, moreover, by the way, then
colloq. what's more

anecdote *n*
story, tale, yarn, sketch, reminiscence

anew *adv*
afresh, again, once again, once more

angel *n*
1 *angel of God*
divine messenger, heavenly messenger, heavenly being, principality, power
2 DARLING, treasure, saint, paragon, gem, ideal
F∃ 1 devil, fiend

The nine orders of angels are: seraph, cherub, throne, domination/dominion, virtue, power, principality, archangel, angel.

angelic *adj*
cherubic, seraphic, celestial, heavenly, divine, holy, pious, saintly, pure, innocent, unworldly, virtuous, lovely, beautiful, adorable
formal beatific, ethereal, empyrean
F∃ devilish, fiendish

anger *n, v*
▶ *n* annoyance, irritation, antagonism, displeasure, irritability, temper, pique, vexation, ire, rage, fury, wrath, exasperation, chagrin, outrage, indignation, gall, bitterness, rancour, resentment, fit of anger, paroxysm
formal choler, dudgeon
US colloq. conniption
F∃ forgiveness, forbearance
▶ *v* annoy, irritate, irk, vex, rile, make angry, needle, nettle, bother, ruffle, provoke, antagonize, offend, affront, gall, madden, enrage, incense, infuriate, exasperate, outrage
colloq. aggravate, wind up, miff, make your blood boil;

slang nark, piss off
F∃ please, appease, calm

angle *n, v*
▶ *n* **1** CORNER, intersection, projection, nook, bend, flexure, hook, crook, elbow, knee, crotch, edge, point, gradient, inclination
2 ASPECT, outlook, facet, side, approach, direction, position, standpoint, viewpoint, point of view, slant, perspective
▶ *v* face, point, turn, direct, slant
▷ **angle for** seek, aim, try to get, go for, shoot for, make a bid for

angry *adj*
annoyed, cross, in a temper, irritated, displeased, irate, enraged, incensed, livid, seething, infuriated, furious, raging, passionate, heated, hot, exasperated, outraged, indignant, bitter, resentful
old use choleric, rancorous, splenetic, foribund, wrathful
colloq. aggravated, uptight, mad, hopping mad, seeing red, in a lather, disgruntled, up in arms, hot under the collar, on the warpath, in a paddy; *slang* pissed off
F∃ content, happy, calm

Colloquial ways of expressing becoming angry and losing your temper include: blow up, blow a fuse, blow a gasket, blow your cool, blow your stack, blow your top, boil over, burst a blood vessel, do your nut, explode, flip your lid, fly into a rage, fly off the handle, go mad, go off the deep end, go up the wall, hit the ceiling, hit the roof, lose your cool, lose your patience, lose your rag, raise Cain, raise hell, see red, throw a tantrum, throw a wobbly, foam at the mouth, get all steamed up, *US* go ape, go ballistic, lose your marbles.

anguish *n*
agony, anxiety, desolation, distress, suffering, torment, torture, grief, heartache, heartbreak, misery, pain, pang, rack, sorrow, tribulation, woe, wretchedness
formal dole, dolour
F∃ happiness, solace

anguished *adj*
afflicted, tormented, stressed, distressed, harrowed, miserable, stricken, suffering, tortured, wretched
formal dolorous

angular *adj*
bony, thin, gaunt, gawky, lank, lanky, lean, rawboned, scrawny, skinny, spare

animal *n, adj*
▶ *n* **1** *wild animals*
creature, mammal, beast
2 *that man is an animal*
beast, brute, barbarian, savage, monster
colloq. swine, pig
▶ *adj* **1** *animal fats*
formal animalic, zoic
2 *animal instincts*
bestial, brutish, inhuman, savage, wild, instinctive, bodily, physical, carnal, fleshly, sensual
Related adjective: zoic

Animals include: cat, dog, hamster, gerbil, mouse, rat, rabbit, hare, fox, badger, beaver, mole, otter, weasel, ferret, ermine, mink, hedgehog, squirrel, horse, pig, cow, bull, goat, sheep; monkey, lemur, gibbon, ape, chimpanzee, orang-utan, baboon, gorilla; seal, sealion, dolphin, walrus, whale; lion, tiger, cheetah, puma, panther, cougar, jaguar, ocelot, leopard; aardvark, armadillo, wolf, wolverine, hyena, mongoose, skunk, racoon, wombat, platypus, koala, polecat; deer, antelope, gazelle, eland, impala, reindeer, elk, caribou, moose; wallaby, kangaroo, bison, buffalo, gnu, camel, zebra, llama, panda, giant panda, grizzly bear, polar bear, giraffe, hippopotamus, rhinoceros, elephant. *See also* **amphibian; bird; butterfly; cat; cattle; dog; fish; horse; insect; invertebrate; mammal; marsupial; mollusc; monkey; moth; reptile; rodent**. *See also* animal sounds *at* sound [1]. *See also* **collective nouns**.

animate *adj, v*
▶ *adj* alive, living, live, breathing, conscious
◱ inanimate
▶ *v* activate, enliven, arouse, instigate, invigorate, galvanize, goad, spur, impel, stimulate, incite, energize, excite, fire, kindle, move, quicken, reactivate, revive, rouse, spark, stir, urge, vitalize, encourage, inspire
formal embolden, vivify, inspirit
colloq. buck up
◱ dull, inhibit

animated *adj*
lively, spirited, buoyant, vibrant, ebullient, vivacious, alive, vital, quick, brisk, vigorous, energetic, active, passionate, impassioned, vehement, ardent, fervent, glowing, radiant, excited, enthusiastic, eager
colloq. full of beans, bright and breezy
◱ lethargic, sluggish, inert

animation *n*
liveliness, spirit, action, activity, ebullience, passion, elation, energy, enthusiasm, excitement, exhilaration, fervour, high spirits, life, radiance, sparkle, sprightliness, verve, vibrancy, vigour, vitality, zeal, zest
colloq. pep, zing
◱ dullness, inertia

animosity *n*
ill feeling, ill-will, acrimony, bitterness, rancour, resentment, spite, malice, malignity, malevolence, hate, hatred, loathing, abhorrence, antagonism, hostility, enmity, feud
formal odium, animus
◱ goodwill

annals *n*
archives, chronicles, records, registers, history, journals, memoirs, reports

annex *v*
1 ADD, append, affix, attach, fasten, adjoin, join, connect, unite, incorporate
2 SEIZE,
appropriate, acquire, usurp, occupy, conquer, take over
formal arrogate

⚠ **annex** or **annexe** ?
Annex, stressed on the second syllable, is a verb meaning to add or acquire: *The USSR annexed Latvia in World War II.* The noun, stressed on the first syllable, may be spelt *annex* or *annexe,* but the form with *-e* is more common.

annexation *n*
seizure, appropriation, acquisition, usurping, occupation, conquest, takeover
formal arrogation

annexe *n*
wing, extension, attachment, addition, supplement, expansion

annihilate *v*
eliminate, eradicate, obliterate, erase, wipe out, murder, assassinate, exterminate, extinguish, raze, destroy, abolish, conquer, defeat, rout
formal extirpate
colloq. liquidate, rub out, thrash, trounce, bring to their knees

annihilation *n*
elimination, eradication, obliteration, erasure, murder, assassination, extermination, extinction, destruction, abolition, defeat
formal extirpation
colloq. liquidation

anniversary *n*

Names of wedding anniversary include: 1st cotton, 2nd paper, 3rd leather, 4th flowers/fruit, 5th wood, 6th iron/sugar, 7th copper/wool, 8th bronze/pottery, 9th pottery/willow, 10th tin, 11th steel, 12th silk/linen, 13th lace, 14th ivory, 15th crystal, 20th china, 25th silver, 30th pearl, 35th coral, 40th ruby, 45th sapphire, 50th gold, 55th emerald, 60th diamond, 70th platinum.

annotate *v*
note, gloss, comment, explain, interpret, elucidate
formal marginalize, explicate

annotation *n*
note, footnote, gloss, comment, commentary, exegesis, explanation, elucidation
formal explication

announce *v*
declare, proclaim, report, state, make/issue a statement, reveal, disclose, divulge, make known, make public, notify, intimate, give out, publish, broadcast, advertise, publicize, blazon (abroad)
formal promulgate, propound, preconize
◱ suppress

announcement *n*
1 *make an announcement*
statement, declaration, proclamation, report, communiqu , dispatch, bulletin, message, information, notification, intimation, revelation, disclosure, divulgence, publication, broadcast, advertisement, publicity
2 *the announcement of the news*
declaration, proclamation, reporting, revelation, disclosure, divulgence, making known/public, notification, intimation, giving-out, publication, publicizing

announcer *n*
broadcaster, newscaster, newsreader, commentator, compre, host, master of ceremonies, MC, presenter, anchorman, anchorwoman, town crier, herald, messenger

annoy *v*
irritate, rile, displease, anger, vex, irk, madden, exasperate, tease, provoke, ruffle, gall, trouble, nag, disturb, bother, pester, plague, harass, molest
colloq. aggravate, bug, hassle, rub up the wrong way, wind up, get someone's blood up, make your blood boil, get on your nerves, get up your nose, get under your skin, get someone's goat, get on your wick, drive crazy/nuts, drive bananas, drive up the wall, drive

round the bend/twist, get your back up, brass off, cheese off, make someone's hackles rise, give someone the hump, get your dander up, *US* tick/hack off
F3 please, gratify, comfort

annoyance *n*
1 NUISANCE, pest, disturbance, bother, trouble, bore, tease, provocation, irritant
colloq. bind, drag, headache, pain, pain in the neck;
slang pain in the backside/arse, *US* pain in the ass/butt
2 *express your annoyance*
irritation, displeasure, anger, vexation, exasperation, harassment
colloq. aggravation
F3 2 pleasure

annoyed *adj*
irritated, cross, upset, displeased, angry, vexed, piqued, exasperated, provoked, indignant, harassed
colloq. peeved, miffed, narked, bugged, hassled, driven crazy, driven nuts, cheesed off, got the hump, in a huff
F3 pleased

annoying *adj*
irritating, vexatious, irksome, troublesome, bothersome, tiresome, trying, maddening, exasperating, galling, offensive, teasing, provoking, disturbing, intrusive, unwelcome, harassing, *US* pesky
colloq. aggravating
F3 pleasing, welcome

annual *n, adj*
▶ *n* yearbook, almanac, calendar, register
▶ *adj* yearly

annul *v*
nullify, invalidate, void, rescind, abrogate, suspend, cancel, abolish, quash, repeal, revoke, countermand, negate, declare null and void, retract, recall, reverse
F3 enact, restore

annulment *n*
invalidation, voiding, rescindment, abrogation, suspension, cancellation, abolition, quashing, repeal, countermand, negation, nullification, recall, reverse
formal revocation, rescission
F3 enactment, restoration

anodyne *adj*
bland, inoffensive, neutral, deadening

anoint *v*
1 OIL, grease, lubricate, apply oil/lubrication, rub, smear, daub
old use anele
formal embrocate
2 BLESS, consecrate, sanctify, dedicate, ordain

anomalous *adj*
abnormal, atypical, exceptional, irregular, inconsistent, incongruous, deviant, freakish, eccentric, peculiar, odd, unusual, singular, rare
colloq. freak
F3 normal, regular, ordinary

anomaly *n*
abnormality, exception, irregularity, inconsistency, incongruity, aberration, deviation, divergence, departure, freak, misfit, eccentricity, peculiarity, oddity, rarity

anonymous *adj*
unnamed, nameless, unsigned, unacknowledged, unspecified, unidentified, unknown, incognito, faceless, impersonal, nondescript, unexceptional

formal unattested, innominate
F3 named, signed, identifiable, distinctive

another *adj*
1 ADDITIONAL, further, extra, more, added, spare, second
2 DIFFERENT, other, some other, alternative, not the same, variant

answer *n, v*
▶ *n* 1 REPLY, acknowledgement, response, reaction, rejoinder, retort, riposte, retaliation, rebuttal
formal replication
colloq. comeback
2 SOLUTION, explanation, result, key, resolution unravelling
colloq. quick fix
▶ *v* 1 REPLY, acknowledge, respond, write back, react, refute, retaliate
colloq. get/come back to
2 *answer a need*
fulfil, fill, meet, satisfy, match up to
3 *answer (to) a description*
fit, correspond to, correlate, conform, agree, suit, serve, pass
▷ **answer back** talk back, be cheeky to, retort, riposte, retaliate, retort, contradict, disagree, argue, dispute, rebut; *US colloq.* sass
▷ **answer for** 1 *answer for her loyalty* vouch for, be responsible for, be liable for, speak for 2 *answer for the crimes* pay for, be punished for

answerable *adj*
liable, responsible, accountable, chargeable, blameworthy, to blame

antagonism *n*
hostility, opposition, enmity rivalry, antipathy, ill feeling, ill-will, animosity, friction, discord, dissension, contention, conflict
F3 rapport, sympathy, agreement

antagonist *n*
opponent, adversary, enemy, foe, rival, competitor, contestant, contender
F3 ally, supporter

antagonistic *adj*
conflicting, opposed, adverse, at variance, incompatible, hostile, belligerent, contentious, unfriendly, ill-disposed, averse,
F3 sympathetic, friendly

antagonize *v*
alienate, estrange, disaffect, repel, embitter, offend, insult, provoke, annoy, irritate, anger, incense
formal disaffect
F3 disarm

antecedent *n*
1 *antecedents of the aeroplane*
precursor, forerunner, precedent
2 *with Welsh antecedents*
ancestors, forebears, forefathers, extraction, genealogy

anthem *n*
hymn, song, chorale, psalm, song of praise, canticle, chant
formal paean

anthology *n*
selection, collection, compilation, compendium, digest, treasury, miscellany, omnibus edition
formal spicilege

anticipate *v*
1 FORESTALL, pre-empt, intercept, prevent
formal obviate, preclude
colloq. beat to it
2 EXPECT, foresee, predict, forecast, think likely,
look for, await, look forward to, hope for, bank on,
count on/upon, reckon on, prepare for, *US* figure on

anticipation *n*
1 *in anticipation of the shortage*
expectation, preparation, prediction
2 *eager anticipation*
excitement, expectancy, hope
colloq. bated breath

anticlimax *n*
comedown, let-down, disappointment, fiasco
formal bathos
colloq. non-event, damp squib, not all that it was
cracked up to be

antics *n*
foolery, tomfoolery, silliness, buffoonery, clowning,
horseplay, frolics, capers, skylarking, playfulness,
mischief, tricks, monkey-tricks, pranks, stunts, doings

antidote *n*
1 *an antidote to a sting*
cure, counter-agent, antitoxin, neutralizer,
countermeasure
technical antivenin, mithridate, theriac
2 *an antidote to depression*
remedy, cure, corrective

antipathy *n*
aversion, dislike, hate, hatred, loathing, abhorrence,
distaste, disgust, repulsion, antagonism, animosity, ill-
will, bad blood, enmity, hostility, opposition,
incompatibility
formal animus, odium
F3 sympathy, affection, rapport

antiquated *adj*
obsolete, old-fashioned, outdated, outmoded, out-of-
date, dated, bygone, anachronistic, ancient,
antediluvian, archaic, démodé, fossilized, outworn,
passé
colloq. on the way out, old hat
F3 forward-looking, modern

antique *adj, n*
▶ *adj* antiquarian, ancient, old, veteran, vintage,
quaint, antiquated, old-fashioned, outdated, archaic,
obsolete
▶ *n* antiquity, relic, bygone, period piece, heirloom,
curio, museum piece, curiosity, rarity, object of virtu

antiquity *n*
1 ancient times, time immemorial, distant past, olden
days
2 *of great antiquity*
age, old age, oldness, agedness
F3 1 modernity, novelty

antiseptic *adj, n*
▶ *adj* disinfectant, medicated, aseptic, germ-free,
clean, pure, unpolluted, uncontaminated, sterile,
sterilized, sanitized, sanitary, hygienic
▶ *n* disinfectant, germicide, bactericide, purifier,
cleanser

antisocial *adj*
1 *an antisocial person*
unfriendly, unsociable, uncommunicative, reserved,
retiring, withdrawn, alienated, unapproachable
2 *antisocial behaviour*
asocial, unacceptable, disruptive, disorderly,
rebellious, lawless, belligerent, antagonistic, hostile,
anarchic
F3 1 sociable, gregarious 2 acceptable

antithesis *n*
1 OPPOSITE, converse, reverse, opposite extreme
2 OPPOSITION, contrast, contradiction, reversal

anxiety *n*
worry, concern, care, distress, nervousness,
apprehension, disquiet, dread, anguish, foreboding,
misgiving, uneasiness, restlessness, fretfulness,
impatience, suspense, tension, stress, strain
formal disquietude, worriment
F3 calm, composure, serenity

anxious *adj*
1 APPREHENSIVE, worried, concerned, nervous,
afraid, fearful, uneasy, restless, fretful, impatient, in
suspense, on tenterhooks, tense, taut, distressed,
dismayed, disturbed, troubled, tormented,
overwrought, tortured
formal solicitous
colloq. in a stew, having butterflies in your stomach/
tummy, tearing your hair out
2 EAGER, keen, longing, eager, enthusiastic,
yearning, expectant
F3 1 calm, composed

apace *adv*
speedily, swiftly, double-quick, fast, hastily, quickly,
rapidly, at full speed, at top speed, without delay

apart *adv*
1 *stand apart from the others*
aside, to one side, away, afar, distant, aloof, excluded,
isolated, cut off, separated, separate, distinct,
piecemeal
2 *live apart*
SEPARATELY, independently, separated, divorced, not
together, not living together, individually, singly, alone,
on your own, by yourself, privately
3 *tear apart*
to pieces, to bits, into parts, in pieces, in bits, piecemeal
F3 2 connected 3 together
▷ **apart from** except (for), not counting, excepted,
aside from, excluding, with the exception of, but for

apathetic *adj*
uninterested, uninvolved, indifferent, blasé, cool,
unemotional, emotionless, impassive, unmoved,
unconcerned, cold, unfeeling, numb, unresponsive,
passive, listless, lethargic, unambitious, lukewarm,
half-hearted
F3 enthusiastic, involved, concerned, feeling,
responsive

apathy *n*
uninterestedness, indifference, coolness, impassivity,
unconcern, lack of interest, lack of concern, lack of
enthusiasm, coldness, insensibility, passivity,
listlessness, lethargy, sluggishness, torpor, inertia
formal languor, acedia, accidie
F3 enthusiasm, interest, concern

ape *v, n*
▶ *v* copy, imitate, echo, mirror, parrot, mimic, take
off, caricature, parody, mock, counterfeit, affect
▶ *n* monkey, chimpanzee, gibbon, gorilla, baboon,
orang-utan
Related adjective: simian

aperture *n*
gap, hole, opening, passage, perforation, breach, chink, cleft, crack, eye, fissure, rent, slit, slot, space, vent, mouth
technical orifice, foramen,
formal interstice

apex *n*
top, high point, peak, pinnacle, point, summit, tip, climax, consummation, crest, crown, crowning point, culmination, height
technical acme, fastigium, apogee, vertex, zenith
F3 nadir

aphorism *n*
maxim, adage, axiom, dictum, maxim, precept, proverb, saw, saying, witticism
formal apothegm, epigram, gnome

aphrodisiac *n, adj*
▶ *n* love potion, stimulant
▶ *adj* stimulant, erogenous, erotic
formal amative, amatory, erotogenous, venerous

aplomb *n*
composure, calmness, equanimity, poise, balance, coolness, confidence, assurance, self-assurance, audacity
F3 discomposure

aplomb *n*
poise, assurance, calmness, composure, confidence, coolness, equanimity, sang-froid, savoir faire, self-assurance, self-confidence, self-possession
F3 discomposure

apocryphal *adj*
unauthenticated, unverified, unsubstantiated, unsupported, questionable, spurious, equivocal, doubtful, dubious, fabricated, concocted, fictitious, imaginary, legendary, mythical
F3 authentic, true

apologetic *adj*
sorry, repentant, penitent, contrite, remorseful, conscience-stricken, regretful, rueful
F3 unrepentant, impenitent, defiant

apologize *v*
say you are sorry, say sorry, regret, be apologetic, ask forgiveness, ask pardon, beg someone's pardon, acknowledge, confess, explain, justify, plead
colloq. swallow your pride, eat your words, eat humble pie

apology *n*
saying sorry, acknowledgement, confession, excuse, regrets, explanation, justification, vindication, defence, plea
formal palliation
F3 defiance

apostasy *n*
defection, desertion, disloyalty, faithfulness, falseness, renunciation, treachery, unfaithfulness, heresy
formal perfidy, recreance, recreancy, renegation, recidivism
F3 loyalty, orthodoxy

apostate *n*
renegade, defector, deserter, traitor, turncoat, heretic
formal recidivist, recreant, tergiversator
F3 follower

apostle *n*
1 *Jesus Christ's apostles*
disciple, messenger, preacher, evangelist, missionary, reformer, proselytizer
2 *apostles of a united Europe*
advocate, champion, supporter, crusader, pioneer, proponent,

appal *v*
horrify, shock, outrage, disgust, dismay, disconcert, daunt, intimidate, unnerve, alarm, scare, frighten, terrify
F3 reassure, encourage

appalling *adj*
horrifying, horrific, harrowing, shocking, outrageous, atrocious, disgusting, awful, dreadful, frightful, terrible, dire, grim, hideous, ghastly, horrible, horrid, loathsome, daunting, intimidating, unnerving, alarming, frightening, terrifying, nightmarish
F3 reassuring, encouraging

apparatus *n*
1 *gym apparatus*
appliance, gadget, device, contraption, equipment, gear, tackle, outfit, tools, implements, utensils, materials, machine, machinery
2 *the apparatus of government*
system, structure, network, set-up, mechanism, framework, means

apparel *n*
clothing, clothes, clothing, garments, dress, costume, garb, outfit, wardrobe

apparent *adj*
1 *his distrust was all too apparent*
visible, evident, noticeable, perceptible, plain, clear, distinct, marked, unmistakable, conspicuous, be standing out, obvious, manifest, patent, open, declared
2 *their apparent calmness*
seeming, superficial, outward, visible, ostensible
F3 1 hidden, obscure

apparently *adv*
seemingly, ostensibly, outwardly, on the face of it, to all appearances, superficially, on the surface, reputedly, plainly, clearly, obviously, manifestly, patently

apparition *n*
ghost, spectre, phantom, spirit, vision, manifestation, materialization, presence
formal chimera, visitant
colloq. spook

appeal *n, v*
▶ *n* 1 REQUEST, application, claim, approach, petition, suit, solicitation, plea, entreaty, supplication, prayer, invocation
formal imploration, adjuration, orison
2 ATTRACTION, allure, interest, fascination, enchantment, charm, attractiveness, winsomeness, beauty, charisma, magnetism
3 *an appeal in a lawcourt*
retrial, reconsideration, review, re-evaluation, re-examination
▶ *v* 1 *appeal for help*
ask (for), request, call, apply, claim, address, petition, solicit, plead, beg, beseech, implore, entreat, pray, invoke, call upon
formal supplicate, sue
2 ATTRACT, draw, allure, lure, tempt, entice, invite, interest, engage, fascinate, charm, please

appear *v*
1 ARRIVE, enter, turn up, attend, be present, materialize, develop, show (up), come into sight, come

into view, come along, loom, rise, surface, arise, occur, crop up, come to light, come out, emerge, issue, be published
2 SEEM, look, give the impression of being, come across as, show signs of, take the guise of, turn out
colloq. pop up
3 *appear in a show*
act, perform, play, take part, be a guest in, be on stage
4 *his book appeared in the shops*
be published, come out, become available
E3 1 disappear, vanish

appearance *n*
1 APPEARING, arrival, advent, coming, coming into view, rise, emergence, début, introduction, attendance, presence
2 LOOK, expression, face, aspect, air, bearing, manner, looks, figure, (outward) form, complexion, image
formal mien, visage, demeanour
3 *keep up an appearance*
pretence, semblance, show, front, guise, illusion, impression, outward impression, façade, image
E3 1 disappearance

appease *v*
placate, pacify, reconcile, satisfy, mitigate, make peace with, conciliate, propitiate
E3 aggravate

appellation *n*
epithet, name, title, designation, description
formal sobriquet

append *v*
add, affix, attach, fasten, join, tack on
formal adjoin, annex, conjoin, subjoin

appendage *n*
addendum, appendix, addition, supplement, adjunct, tailpiece

appendix *n*
addition, appendage, adjunct, addendum, supplement, epilogue, codicil, postscript, rider

appetite *n*
1 *a good appetite*
hunger, stomach, relish, zest, taste
2 *appetite for sensation*
hunger, taste, thirst, inclination, liking, desire, longing, propensity, yearning, craving, lust, eagerness, passion, zeal

appetizing *adj*
mouthwatering, tempting, inviting, appealing, palatable, tasty, delicious, succulent, piquant, savoury
colloq. scrumptious
E3 disgusting, distasteful

applaud *v*
1 *the audience applauded*
clap, cheer, put your hands together for, give an ovation/a standing ovation to, give a round of applause, show your appreciation to
colloq. give a big hand to
2 *applaud the government's efforts*
acclaim, compliment, congratulate, approve, commend, praise
formal laud, eulogize, extol

applause *n*
ovation, standing ovation, clapping, cheering, cheers, bravos, acclaim, acclamation, accolade, congratulation, approval, commendation, praise

formal encomium
colloq. a big hand
E3 criticism, censure

appliance *n*
machine, device, contrivance, contraption, gadget, tool, implement, instrument, apparatus, mechanism

applicable *adj*
relevant, apt, appropriate, fitting, suited, useful, suitable, fit, proper, valid, legitimate
formal pertinent, apposite
E3 inapplicable, inappropriate

applicant *n*
candidate, interviewee, claimant, contestant, competitor, aspirant, suitor, petitioner, inquirer
technical postulant

application *n*
1 REQUEST, appeal, petition, suit, claim, inquiry, demand
2 RELEVANCE, function, purpose, use, value, bearing, significance, praxis, aptness, germaneness
formal pertinence
3 DILIGENCE, hard work, industry, effort, commitment, dedication, perseverance, keenness, attentiveness
formal assiduity, sedulousness

apply *v*
1 REQUEST, ask for, requisition, put in for, put in an application for, fill in a form for, order, write away/off for, appeal, petition, solicit, sue, claim, inquire
2 *apply yourself to a task*
address, buckle down, settle down, commit, devote, dedicate, give, direct, concentrate, study, persevere, be industrious, work hard, make an effort, commit/devote yourself
3 USE, exercise, utilize, employ, bring into play, put into practice/operation, draw on, engage, harness, ply, wield, administer, execute, implement, assign, direct, bring to bear, exert, practise, resort to
4 REFER, relate, be relevant, be significant, fit, suit
formal pertain, appertain
5 *apply ointment*
put on, spread on, lay on, cover with, paint, anoint, smear, rub, treat with
old use appose
formal adhibit

appoint *v*
1 NAME, nominate, be shortlisted, elect, install, choose, select, pick, engage, employ, take on, hire, recruit, commission, co-opt, delegate, assign, allot, designate, command, direct, charge, detail
2 DECIDE, determine, arrange, settle, fix, set, establish, ordain, decree, destine, designate, allot
E3 1 reject, dismiss, discharge

appointed *adj*
determined, decided, chosen, assigned, arranged, settled, fixed, set, established, ordained, decreed, destined, preordained, designated, allotted

appointment *n*
1 ARRANGEMENT, engagement, date, meeting, arrangement to meet, interview, consultation, rendezvous
old use tryst, assignation
2 JOB, position, situation, post, office, place
3 NAMING, nomination, election, choosing, choice, selection, commissioning, delegation

apportion *v*
assign, allocate, allot, distribute, divide, dispense, deal (out), hand out, grant, measure out, mete(out), ration (out), share (out)
formal admeasure
colloq. dole out

apportionment *n*
allocation, allotment, distribution, division, dispensation, assignment, dealing, grant, ration(ing), share
colloq. handout

apposite *adj*
relevant, applicable, appropriate, apt, germane, suitable, suited, to the point, to the purpose
formal pertinent, apropos, befitting
E3 inapposite

appraisal *n*
evaluation, assessment, survey, inspection, review, examination, estimate, estimation, judgement, reckoning, opinion, appreciation, valuation, rating
formal assay
colloq. once-over

appraise *v*
evaluate, assess, survey, inspect, review, examine, estimate, sum up, judge, value, rate
formal assay
colloq. size up, once-over

⚠ **appraise** or **apprise** ?
If you *appraise* someone or something, you form an opinion about their quality, value, etc. If you are *apprised* of something, you are told about it.
---

appreciable *adj*
noticeable, significant, considerable, substantial, definite perceptible, discernible, recognizable
E3 insignificant, imperceptible, negligible

appreciate *v*
1 ENJOY, relish, savour, prize, treasure, value, cherish, admire, respect, regard, esteem, like, welcome, take kindly to, think highly of
2 UNDERSTAND, comprehend, perceive, realize, recognize, grasp, be aware of, be conscious of, be sensitive to, acknowledge, sympathize with, know, see
3 *I appreciate your help*
be grateful for, express your gratitude/appreciation, thank, be appreciative, be indebted to
4 *appreciate in value*
grow, increase, rise, mount, go up, inflate, gain, strengthen, improve, enhance
E3 1 despise, hate 2 overlook, ignore 4 depreciate, go down

appreciation *n*
1 ENJOYMENT, relish, admiration, liking, respect, regard, esteem, valuing,
2 *send a present to show your appreciation*
gratitude, gratefulness, thankfulness, indebtedness, obligation
3 UNDERSTANDING, comprehension, perception, awareness, realization, recognition, grasp, acknowledgement, sympathy, sensitivity, responsiveness, valuation, assessment, estimation, judgement, knowledge
formal cognizance
4 REVIEW, critique, evaluation, analysis, assessment, commentary, notice, praise
5 GROWTH, increase, rise, inflation, gain,

improvement, escalation, enhancement
E3 1 ingratitude 5 depreciation

appreciative *adj*
1 GRATEFUL, thankful, obliged, indebted, pleased
formal beholden
2 ADMIRING, encouraging, enthusiastic, respectful, sensitive, responsive, perceptive, knowledgeable, conscious, mindful
E3 1 ungrateful

apprehend *v*
1 CATCH, arrest, capture, detain, seize
colloq. bust, nick, collar, grab, nab, run in
2 UNDERSTAND, comprehend, grasp, believe, conceive, perceive, realize, recognize, see
colloq. twig

apprehension *n*
1 ANXIETY, dread, foreboding, misgiving, qualm, uneasiness, worry, concern, disquiet, concern, nervousness, alarm, fear, trepidation, doubt, suspicion, mistrust
formal perturbation
colloq. butterflies (in your stomach), the willies
2 ARREST, capture, detention, seizure, taking
3 UNDERSTANDING, comprehension, grasp, belief, conception, perception, discernment, realization, recognition

apprehensive *adj*
nervous, anxious, worried, concerned, uneasy, doubtful, suspicious, mistrustful, distrustful, bothered, alarmed, afraid, fearful
colloq. on tenterhooks
E3 assured, confident

apprentice *n*
trainee, probationer, student, pupil, learner, novice, beginner, starter, recruit, newcomer, tyro
US colloq. rookie
E3 expert

apprise *v*
inform, notify, acquaint, advise, brief, communicate, enlighten, intimate, tell, warn
colloq. tip off

⚠ **apprise** or **appraise** ? *See panel at* **appraise**.
---

approach *v, n*
▶ *v* 1 GET CLOSER TO, come nearer/closer, advance towards, move towards, draw near, near, gain on, catch up, reach, meet, arrive
2 SPEAK TO, address, make conversation with, greet, accost
3 TACKLE, deal with, begin, commence, set about, embark on, undertake, introduce, mention, treat
4 APPLY TO, appeal to, sound out, contact, get in touch with, get onto, invite, make advances, make overtures, broach
5 *a speed approaching 200 km/h*
REACH, come close to, come near to, compare with, approximate
▶ *n* 1 *the approach of winter*
advance, coming, coming near/close, advent, arrival
2 ACCESS, road, avenue, drive, driveway, way, passage, entrance, doorway, threshold
3 APPLICATION, appeal, overture(s), advances, invitation, proposition, proposal, request, plea
4 METHOD, manner, style, technique, procedure, means, *modus operandi*, strategy, system, tactics, course of action

approachable *adj*
1 FRIENDLY, easy to get on/along with, sociable, congenial, warm, affable, agreeable, open, informal
2 ACCESSIBLE attainable, reachable
colloq. get-at-able
F⁊ 1 aloof, unapproachable
2 inaccessible, remote

appropriate *adj, v*
▶ *adj* suitable, applicable, relevant, to the point, well-chosen, apt, fitting, fit, befitting, germane, seemly, becoming, proper, right, correct, accepted, well-timed, timely, seasonable, opportune
formal pertinent, appurtenant, apropos, meet, felicitous
colloq. spot-on
F⁊ inappropriate, irrelevant, unsuitable
▶ *v* 1 SEIZE, take, take possession of, commandeer, requisition, confiscate, impound, assume, usurp
formal expropriate, arrogate
2 STEAL, pocket, filch, pilfer, embezzle, misappropriate, thieve, make off with
formal purloin, peculate
colloq. nick, pinch, swipe

approval *n*
1 ADMIRATION, esteem, regard, respect, good opinion, liking, appreciation, acceptance, favour, recommendation, praise, commendation, acclaim, acclamation, honour, applause
formal approbation
2 AGREEMENT, acceptance, assent, consent, permission, leave, sanction, authorization, licence, mandate, endorsement, blessing, certification, ratification, validation, confirmation, support
formal approbation, concurrence, imprimatur
colloq. go-ahead, green light, OK, rubber stamp, nod, wink, thumbs-up
F⁊ 1 disapproval, condemnation

approve *v*
1 ADMIRE, esteem, regard, like, think well/highly of, hold in high regard, be pleased with, appreciate, favour, recommend, praise, commend, acclaim, applaud
2 *approve a proposal*
agree to, assent to, consent to, accede to, allow, permit, pass, sanction, authorize, mandate, bless, countenance, ratify, validate, endorse, support, uphold, second, back, accept, adopt, carry, confirm
formal concur
colloq. give the go-ahead to, give the green light to, OK, rubber-stamp, give the nod to, give the thumbs-up to, buy
F⁊ 1 disapprove, condemn 2 reject

approved *adj*
accepted, authorized, orthodox, official, recommended, sanctioned, correct, favoured, permissible, permitted, preferred, proper, recognized
F⁊ unauthorized, unorthodox

approximate *adj, v*
▶ *adj* estimated, guessed, rough, inexact, loose, close, near, like, similar, relative
colloq. ballpark
F⁊ exact
▶ *v* approach, come close to, border on, verge on, be tantamount to, resemble, be similar to

approximately *adv*
roughly, around, about, some, something like, odd, circa, more or less, loosely, round about, or

thereabouts, approaching, close to, nearly, just about, not far off, in the region/neighbourhood/vicinity of, somewhere in the region of, in round numbers, rounded up/down
colloq. give or take
F⁊ exactly

approximation *n*
1 ESTIMATE, rough calculation, rough idea, guess, conjecture
colloq. guesstimate, ballpark figure
2 *an approximation to a dress*
semblance, likeness, resemblance, correspondence

apropos *adj, prep*
▶ *adj* suitable, applicable, relevant, to the point, well-chosen, apt, fitting, befitting, seemly, becoming, proper, right, correct, accepted, timely, seasonable, opportune
formal pertinent, felicitous
F⁊ inappropriate
▶ *prep* with reference to, with regard to, with respect to, in relation to, in respect of, on the subject of, in connection with, re, regarding, respecting

apt *adj*
1 RELEVANT, applicable, apposite, appropriate, fitting, acceptable, suitable, fit, germane, seemly, proper, correct, accurate, timely, seasonable
colloq. spot-on
2 *apt to do something*
INCLINED, liable, prone, given, disposed, tending, likely, given, ready, subject
F⁊ 1 inapt, unsuitable

aptitude *n*
ability, natural ability, capability, capacity, faculty, gift, talent, flair, facility, skill, proficiency, cleverness, intelligence, quickness, bent, inclination, leaning, disposition, tendency
F⁊ inaptitude

aquatic *adj*
water, sea, river, marine, maritime, nautical, watery, fluid, liquid
formal fluvial

arable *adj*
cultivable, ploughable, tillable, fertile, productive, fruitful
formal fecund

Types of arable crop include: *US* alfalfa, barley, bean, mung bean, soya bean, corn, popcorn, sweetcorn, fodder beet, mangel wurzel, sugar beet, cassava, kale, lucerne, linseed, millet, oats, oilseed rape, pea, potato, sweet potato, yam, rice, rye, sorghum, swede, turnip, wheat.

arbiter *n*
1 ADJUDICATOR, judge, referee, umpire
2 *an arbiter of style*
authority, expert, pundit, master, controller

arbitrary *adj*
1 RANDOM, chance, capricious, whimsical, inconsistent, discretionary, subjective, personal, instinctive, unreasoned, illogical, irrational, unreasonable
2 DESPOTIC, tyrannical, dictatorial, autocratic, absolute, imperious, magisterial, domineering, overbearing, high-handed, dogmatic
F⁊ 1 reasoned, rational, circumspect

arbitrate *v*
judge, adjudicate, pass judgement, sit in judgement, referee, umpire, mediate, settle, decide, determine

arbitration *n*
judgement, adjudication, intervention, mediation, negotiation, settlement, decision, determination
formal arbitrament

arbitrator *n*
judge, adjudicator, arbiter, referee, umpire, moderator, mediator, negotiator, intermediary, go-between

arc *n*
curve, curved line, bend, arch, bow, curvature, semicircle

arcade *n*
gallery, cloister, colonnade, covered way, mall, piazza, portico, precinct, shopping mall, shopping precinct
technical loggia, peristyle, stoa

arcane *adj*
secret, mysterious, concealed, obscure, hidden, abstruse, mystical, cryptic, enigmatic, esoteric, recondite, occult, profound

arch *n, v, adj*
▶ *n* **1** *the arches of a bridge*
archway, bridge, span, dome, vault, concave
2 ARC, bend, curve, curvature, bow, semicircle
▶ *v* bend, curve, bow, arc, vault, camber
▶ *adj* mischievous, playful, mysterious, cunning, sly arch

Types of arch include: basket handle, convex, corbel, equilateral, four-centre, Gothic, horseshoe, keel, lancet, Norman, ogee, parabolic, round, segmental, shouldered, skew, stilted, tented, trefoil, Tudor.

archaeology *n*

Archaeological terms include: agger, amphitheatre, amphora, artefact, barrow, beaker, blade, bogman, bowl, bracteate, burin, cairn, cartouche, cave art/rock art, cist, cromlech, cup, dolmen, earthwork, eolith, flake, flask, flint, handaxe, henge, hieroglyph, hill fort, hoard, hypocaust, incised decoration, jar, jug, kitchen-midden, kurgan, ley lines, loom weight, lynchet, megalith, microlith, mosaic, mound, mummy, neolith, obelisk, palmette, palstave, papyrus, potassium-argon dating, radiocarbon dating, rock shelter, sondage, spindle, stele, stone circle, tell, tumulus, urn, vallum, whorl.

archaic *adj*
antiquated, old-fashioned, outmoded, *passé*, outdated, out-of-date, obsolete, old, ancient, antique, quaint, bygone, primitive, medieval, antediluvian
colloq. old hat, out of the ark
E3 modern, recent

archetypal *adj*
model, standard, typical, representative, characteristic, original, classic, ideal, stock
formal exemplary

archetype *n*
pattern, model, standard, form, type, prototype, original, precursor, classic, paradigm, ideal, epitome, stereotype
formal exemplar

architect *n*
1 *the architect of the building*
designer, planner, master builder, draughtsman

2 *the architect of modern economics*
creator, author, inventor, engineer, maker, constructor, prime mover, originator, founder, instigator, shaper
colloq. mastermind

architecture *n*
1 *study architecture*
designing, planning, building, construction
technical architectonics
2 *Victorian architecture*
style, design, composition, structure, arrangement, make-up, framework

Architectural and building terms include: alcove, annexe, architrave, baluster, barge-board, baroque, bas relief, capstone, classical, coping stone, Corinthian, corner-stone, cornice, coving, dado, dogtooth, dome, Doric, drawbridge, dry-stone, duplex, Early English, eaves, Edwardian, elevation, Elizabethan, façade, fascia, festoon, fillet, finial, flamboyant, Flemish bond, fletton, fluting, frieze, frontispiece, gargoyle, gatehouse, Georgian, Gothic, groin, groundplan, half-timbered, Ionic, jamb, lintel, mullion, Norman, pagoda, pantile, parapet, pinnacle, plinth, Queen-Anne, rafters, Regency, reveal, ridge, rococo, Romanesque, roof, rotunda, roughcast, sacristy, scroll, soffit, stucco, terrazzo, Tudor, Tuscan, wainscot, weathering. *See also* **arch; roof; tower; wall; window**.

archives *n*
records, annals, chronicles, memorials, papers, documents, deeds, ledgers, registers, memorabilia, roll

arctic *adj*
1 *the Arctic Ocean*
polar, far north
formal boreal, hyperborean
2 *arctic weather*
freezing, freezing cold, bitterly cold, frozen, glacial, subzero
E3 1 Antarctic

ardent *adj*
fervent, fiery, warm, passionate, impassioned, fierce, avid, vehement, intense, strong, spirited, enthusiastic, eager, keen, dedicated, devoted, zealous, hot, fervid
E3 apathetic, unenthusiastic

ardour *n*
fervour, passion, fire, heat, warmth, avidity, vehemence, intensity, spirit, enthusiasm, eagerness, animation, zest, keenness, dedication, devotion, zeal, lust
formal empressement
E3 apathy, coolness, indifference

arduous *adj*
hard, difficult, tough, rigorous, severe, harsh, formidable, strenuous, tiring, taxing, fatiguing, wearying, daunting, exhausting, backbreaking, punishing, gruelling, uphill, laborious, onerous, burdensome, heavy
colloq. be a slog, be murder
E3 easy

area *n*
1 *the Muslim areas of the city*
locality, neighbourhood, quarter, environment, environs, patch, terrain, district, region, parish, zone, sector, department, precinct, province, enclave, catchment area, reserve area
2 *an area of land*
expanse, width, breadth, stretch, part, portion, section, tract

3 *an area of activity/knowledge*
FIELD, sphere, domain, world, realm, territory, department, province, branch, range, scope, compass, size, extent

arena *n*
1 STADIUM, field, ground, bowl, ring, area, amphitheatre, coliseum, hippodrome
2 *the political arena*
sphere, scene, domain, world, realm, department, province, battlefield, battleground, area of conflict

arguable *adj*
debatable, open to question, questionable, disputable, contentious, uncertain, undecided, moot
formal controvertible
F∃ incontrovertible, indisputable, certain

argue *v*
1 QUARREL, squabble, bicker, row, have a row, wrangle, haggle, remonstrate, take/join issue, fight, feud, fall out, disagree, dispute
formal altercate
colloq. be at each other's throats, be at loggerheads, have it out (with), have words, cross swords, have a bone to pick
2 REASON, assert, contend, hold, declare, maintain, claim, plead
formal expostulate
3 *argue the point*
question, debate, discuss
4 *argued them out of leaving*
persuade, talk out of, convince
5 BE EVIDENCE FOR, exhibit, display, show, manifest, demonstrate, indicate, denote, prove, suggest, imply

argument *n*
1 QUARREL, squabble, row, wrangle, controversy, debate, discussion, dispute, disagreement, clash, difference of opinion, heated exchange, conflict, fight, feud, rumpus, ruckus, *US* spat
formal altercation
colloq. tiff, barney, argy-bargy, running battle, shouting-match, slanging-match, set-to, dust-up, ding-dong, bust-up
2 REASONING, reason, logic, rationale, assertion, declaration, contention, claim, demonstration, evidence, argumentation, debate, defence, case
formal expostulation
Related adjective: elenctic
3 *the argument of the book*
synopsis, summary, theme, outline, plot, thesis

argumentative *adj*
quarrelsome, contentious, polemical, opinionated, belligerent, perverse, contrary, cantankerous
formal captious, disputatious, litigious, dissentious
colloq. stroppy
F∃ complaisant

arid *adj*
1 *an arid landscape*
dry, parched, waterless, moistureless, desiccated, torrid, dehydrated, baked, shrivelled up, barren, infertile, unproductive, desert, waste
formal torrefied
2 DULL, uninteresting, boring, monotonous, tedious, dry, sterile, dreary, drab, colourless, lifeless, spiritless, uninspired, vapid, jejune
F∃ 1 fertile **2** lively, exciting

aright *adv*
rightly, accurately, exactly, properly, correctly, truly, fitly, suitably, aptly

arise *v*
1 OCCUR, emerge, issue, appear, come to light, come up, present itself, happen, begin, start, commence, come into being/existence
colloq. crop up
2 *points that arose from the report*
result, be a result of, be caused by, ensue, follow, derive, stem, come, spring, proceed, flow
3 RISE, get up, stand up, get to your feet, rise up, go up, ascend, climb, mount, lift, soar, tower

aristocracy *n*
upper class, privileged class, gentry, nobility, noblemen, noblewomen, peerage, ruling class, gentility, high society, elite
formal patriciate, patricians, optimates, *haute monde*
colloq. top drawer, upper crust
F∃ common people, lower classes, working class, proletariat; *colloq.* plebs, hoi polloi, riff-raff, proles

aristocrat *n*
noble, nobleman, noblewoman, peer, peeress, lord, lady, patrician,
formal grandee, eupatrid, optimate
colloq. toff, nob
F∃ commoner

aristocratic *adj*
upper-class, highborn, well-born, noble, patrician, blue-blooded, titled, lordly, courtly, elite, dignified, elegant, refined, thoroughbred
colloq. upper-crust
F∃ plebeian, vulgar

arm¹ *n*
1 *with folded arms*
limb, upper limb, appendage
technical brachium
Related adjective: brachial
2 *the air arm of the fighting forces*
wing, section, division, detachment, department, branch, offshoot, extension, projection
3 *an arm of the sea*
inlet, estuary, bay, channel, firth, passage, cove, creek

arm² *v*
arm someone with weapons/information
provide, supply, issue, equip, rig, outfit, prime, prepare, forearm, rearm, gird, steel, brace, reinforce, strengthen, protect
formal array, furnish, fortify, accoutre

armada *n*
fleet, flotilla, navy, naval force, squadron

armaments *n*
weapons, arms, artillery, guns, cannon, munitions, ammunition, ordnance, weaponry

armed services

Units in the armed services include: task-force, militia, garrison; *air force*: wing, squadron, flight; *army*: patrol, troop, corps, platoon, squad, battery, company, brigade, battalion, regiment; *marines*: Royal Marines, commandos; *navy*: fleet, flotilla, squadron, convoy. *See also* **rank¹**.

armistice *n*
ceasefire, truce, peace, peace treaty, agreement to end/cease/suspend hostilities

armour *n*
protective covering, panoply, mail, chain mail, iron-cladding

armoured *adj*
armour-plated, steel-plated, iron-clad, reinforced, protected, bullet-proof, bomb-proof

armoury *n*
arsenal, ordnance depot, ammunition dump, magazine, (arms) depot, repository, stock, stockpile, garderobe

arms *n*
1 WEAPONS, weaponry, firearms, guns, artillery, instruments of war, armaments, ordnance, munitions, ammunition
2 COAT-OF-ARMS, armorial bearings, insignia, heraldic device, escutcheon, shield, crest, heraldry, blazonry

army *n*
1 *a captain in the army*
armed force, military, militia, land forces, soldiers, troops, infantry
Related adjective: military
2 *an army of workers*
legions, cohorts, multitude, throng, host, horde, pack, mob, crowd, swarm

aroma *n*
smell, odour, scent, perfume, fragrance, bouquet, savour
formal fumet(te), redolence

aromatic *adj*
perfumed, fragrant, sweet-smelling, fresh, scented, balmy, savoury, spicy, pungent
formal redolent, odoriferous
E3 acrid, foul-smelling

around *prep, adv*
▶ *prep* 1 SURROUNDING, round, encircling, encompassing, enclosing, on all sides of, on every side of, about, framed by
formal circumambient, circumjacent
2 *around a dozen*
approximately, roughly, about, circa, more or less, close to, nearly
▶ *adv* 1 EVERYWHERE, all over, in all directions, on all sides, throughout, about, here and there, to and fro
2 CLOSE, close by, near, nearby, at hand

arouse *v*
1 *arouse suspicion*
cause, instigate, induce, summon up, call forth, spark, kindle, inflame, whet, sharpen, quicken, animate, excite, prompt, provoke, stimulate, trigger, incur
2 *arouse someone to anger*
provoke, incite, agitate, stir up, excite, evoke, rouse, startle, galvanize, goad, spur, whip up, get going
3 *arouse from sleep*
wake up, waken, awaken
4 *arouse sexually*
stimulate, excite, get going
colloq. turn on
E3 2 calm, lull, quieten

arraign *v*
accuse, call to account, charge, impeach, indict, prosecute, impugn, incriminate

arrange *v*
1 *arrange a meeting*
decide, settle on, agree, plan, organize, set up, make (an appointment)
colloq. fix (up), pencil in
2 ORGANIZE, co-ordinate, prepare, fix, plan, project, design, devise, contrive, determine, settle
3 ORDER, tidy, range, array, marshal, dispose, distribute, position, set out, lay out, align, line up, group, class, classify, categorize, sort (out), sift, grade, list, file, systematize, catalogue, codify, methodize, regulate, adjust
4 *arrange music*
adapt, set, score, orchestrate, instrument, harmonize
E3 3 untidy, disorganize, muddle

arrangement *n*
1 *make arrangements*
plan(s), preparation(s), detail(s), planning, preparing, groundwork
2 AGREEMENT, settlement, contract, terms, compromise, *modus vivendi*
3 ORDER, array, display, disposition, layout, line-up, positioning, grouping, classification, structure, system, method, set-up, organization, preparation, planning, plan, scheme, design, format, schedule
4 ADAPTATION, version, interpretation, setting, score, orchestration, instrumentation, harmonization

arrant *adj*
absolute, complete, utter, downright, extreme, out-and-out, outright, rank, thorough, thoroughgoing, brazen, flagrant, gross, blatant, unmitigated, incorrigible, infamous, notorious, barefaced, vile
formal egregious

array *n, v*
▶ *n* arrangement, display, show, exhibition, exposition, assortment, collection, muster, order, formation, line-up, parade, disposition, marshalling
formal assemblage
▶ *v* 1 ARRANGE, order, range, dispose, position, group, line up, align, draw up, marshal, assemble, muster, parade, display, show, exhibit
2 CLOTHE, dress, robe, deck, adorn, decorate
formal attire, accoutre, apparel, bedizen, habilitate

arrears *n*
debt(s), liabilities, outstanding payment/amount, sum of money owed, amount owed, liabilities, balance, deficit
▷ **in arrears** owing, outstanding, behind(hand), in debt, overdue, late

arrest *v, n*
▶ *v* 1 *arrest a criminal*
capture, catch, seize, apprehend, detain, take into custody,
colloq. bust, nick, collar, grab, nab, book, run in, pick up, do, nail
2 STOP, stem, check, restrain, inhibit, halt, interrupt, stall, delay, slow (down), retard, block, obstruct, impede, hinder
colloq. nip in the bud
3 *arrest your attention*
capture, attract, catch, grip, engage, absorb, engross, rivet, fascinate, intrigue
▶ *n* capture, apprehension, detention, taking into custody, seizure
▷ **under arrest** in custody, helping police with their inquiries, in captivity

arresting *adj*
striking, amazing, surprising, stunning, extraordinary, impressive, remarkable, engaging, notable, noteworthy, conspicuous, noticeable,

outstanding
F3 inconspicuous, unremarkable

arrival   *n*
1 *the arrival of the president/fresh supplies*
appearance, entrance, entry, coming, approach,
occurrence, emergence
formal advent
2 *welcome new arrivals*
newcomer, incomer, visitor, guest, entrant,
débutant(e), fresher, *US* freshman
formal visitant
F3 **1** departure

arrive   *v*
1 *arrive at the airport*
come, reach, get to, get there, get here, be present, reach
your destination, appear, put in an appearance, land,
touch down, dock, pull in, come in, check in, clock in,
materialize, enter, come on the scene, occur, happen
colloq. show (up), turn up, make it, drop in, blow in,
roll up, surface
2 APPEAR, become available, come on the market, be
produced
3 *arrive at a decision*
reach, come to
4 *he thinks he's really arrived*
succeed
colloq. make it, get to the top
F3 **1** depart, leave

arrogance   *n*
pride, conceit, boasting, haughtiness, vanity,
superciliousness, disdain, scorn, contempt,
superiority, egotism, condescension, lordiness,
pomposity, high-handedness, imperiousness, self-
importance, snobbishness, presumption, insolence
formal hauteur, hubris, contumely
colloq. nerve
F3 humility, unassumingness, bashfulness

arrogant   *adj*
proud, conceited, boastful, full of yourself, haughty,
supercilious, disdainful, scornful, contemptuous,
superior, egotistic, condescending, patronizing,
imperious, lordly, overbearing, high-handed,
imperious, self-important, snobbish, presumptuous,
assuming, insolent
formal hubristic
colloq. big-headed, stuck-up, high and mighty, uppity,
toffee-nosed, hoity-toity
F3 humble, unassuming, bashful

arrogate   *v*
appropriate, seize, usurp, assume, presume,
commandeer, misappropriate, possess yourself of

arrow   *n*
1 *shoot with an arrow*
shaft, bolt, dart, flight
2 *follow the arrows*
marker, indicator, pointer
Related adjective: sagittal

arsenal   *n*
armouryl, ordnance depot, ammunition dump,
magazine, (arms) depot, repository, stock, stockpile,
garderobe

arson   *n*
fire-raising, incendiarism, pyromania

arsonist   *n*
fire-raiser, fire-bug, incendiary, pyromaniac

art   *n*
1 FINE ART, painting, sculpture, drawing, artwork,
design, visual arts, craft, artistry, draughtsmanship,
craftsmanship
2 *the art of public speaking*
SKILL, knack, technique, craft, method, aptitude,
facility, talent, flair, gift, dexterity, finesse, ingenuity,
mastery, expertise, virtuosity, adroitness, profession,
trade
3 ARTFULNESS, cunning, craftiness, slyness, guile,
deceit, trickery, astuteness, shrewdness, wiliness

Schools of art include: abstract, action painting,
Aestheticism, Art Deco, Art Nouveau, Barbizon,
Baroque, Bohemian, Byzantine, classical revival,
classicism, Conceptual Art, Constructivism,
Cubism, Dadaism, Etruscan art, Expressionism,
Fauvism, Florentine, folk art, Futurism, Gothic,
Hellenistic, Impressionism, junk art, Mannerism,
medieval art, Minimal Art, Modernism, the Nabis,
Naturalism, Neoclassicism, Neoexpressionism,
Neoimpressionism, Neo-Plasticism, Op Art, plastic
art, Pop Art, Postimpressionism, Post-Modernism,
Purism, quattrocento, Realism, renaissance,
Rococo, Romanesque, Romanticism,
Suprematism, Surrealism, Symbolism, Venetian,
Vorticism. *See also* **painting; picture; sculpture**.

Arts and crafts include: painting, oil painting,
watercolour, fresco, portraiture; architecture,
drawing, sketching, caricature, illustration;
graphics, film, video; sculpture, modelling,
woodcarving, woodcraft, marquetry, metalwork,
enamelling, cloisonne, engraving, etching, pottery,
ceramics, mosaic, jewellery, stained glass,
photography, lithography, calligraphy, collage,
origami, spinning, weaving, batik, silk-screen
printing, needlework, tapestry, embroidery,
patchwork, crochet, knitting. *See also* **embroidery**.

artefact   *n*
thing, something, object, item, tool, piece of jewellery

artery   *n*
See panel at **vein**.

artful   *adj*
cunning, crafty, sly, foxy, wily, tricky, scheming,
designing, deceitful, devious, subtle, sharp, shrewd,
smart, clever, masterly, ingenious, resourceful, skilful,
dexterous
formal vulpine
F3 artless, nave, ingenuous

article   *n*
1 *articles in a magazine*
feature, report, story, account, piece, item, review,
commentary, write-up, composition, essay, paper,
monograph, offprint
2 ITEM, thing, something, object, commodity, unit,
artefact, part, constituent, piece, portion,
colloq. thingummy, thingummyjig, thingummybob
3 *article 25 of the contract*
paragraph, section, clause, point

articulate   *adj, v*
▶ *adj* distinct, well-spoken, eloquent, clear, lucid,
intelligible, comprehensible, understandable,
coherent, fluent, vocal, expressive, meaningful
F3 inarticulate, incoherent
▶ *v* say, utter, speak, talk, express, voice, vocalize,
verbalize, state, pronounce, enunciate, breathe

articulated adj
coupled, linked, hinged, interlocked, joined, attached, connected, fastened, fitted together, joint

articulation n
saying, utterance, speaking, talking, expression, voicing, vocalization, verbalization, pronunciation, enunciation, diction, delivery

artifice n
1 TRICK, device, dodge, ruse, scheme, stratagem, strategy, subterfuge, tactic, wile, contrivance,
2 DECEIT, trickery, artfulness, deception, fraud, guile, craft, craftiness, cunning, slyness, subtlety, chicanery, cleverness

artificial adj
1 artificial flowers
SYNTHETIC, imitation, mock, plastic, man-made, manufactured, simulated, non-natural, processed
2 an artificial smile
false, fake, bogus, counterfeit, spurious, specious, sham, insincere, assumed, affected, mannered, studied, forced, contrived, made-up, feigned, pretended, simulated
colloq. phoney, pseudo, pseud
E3 1 natural, real 2 genuine

artisan n
craftsman, craftswoman, artificer, journeyman, expert, skilled worker, mechanic, technician, operative
Related adjective: banausic

artist n

Types of artist include: architect, graphic designer, designer, draughtsman, draughtswoman, illustrator, cartoonist, photographer, printer, engraver, goldsmith, silversmith, blacksmith, carpenter, potter, weaver, sculptor, painter; craftsman, craftswoman, master.

⚠ **artist** or **artiste** ?
An artist is someone who paints pictures or is skilled in one of the fine arts. An artiste, or artist, is a performer in a theatre or circus or on television; artiste is now regarded as old-fashioned or affected.

artiste n
performer, entertainer, variety artist, vaudevillian, comic, comedian, comedienne, player, trouper, actor, actress, dancer, singer

artistic adj
1 an artistic person
CREATIVE, sensitive, refined, cultured, gifted, cultivated, skilled, talented, imaginative
2 an artistic design
aesthetic, ornamental, decorative, beautiful, attractive, exquisite, elegant, stylish, tasteful, graceful, harmonious
E3 2 inelegant

artistry n
craftsmanship, workmanship, skill, craft, talent, flair, ability, brilliance, genius, finesse, style, mastery, expertise, proficiency, accomplishment, deftness, touch, sensitivity, creativity
E3 ineptitude

artless adj
simple, natural, unpretentious, genuine, guileless, honest, ingenuous, sincere, straightforward, open, plain, pure, childlike, innocent, nave, direct, frank, candid, true, trusting, unsophisticated, unwary, unworldly
E3 artful, cunning

as conj & prep
1 WHILE, when, whilst, at the same time (that/as), simultaneously
2 SUCH AS, for example, for instance, like,
3 IN THE SAME MANNER THAT, in the same way that, like
4 BECAUSE, since, seeing that, considering that, inasmuch as, being, the reason is …, through, on account of, as a result of, owing to
▷ **as for** with reference to, as regards, with regard to, on the subject of, in connection with, in relation to, with relation to, with respect to
▷ **as it were** so to speak, in a manner of speaking, in a way, in some way, so to say, as it might be

ascend v
rise, take off, lift off, go up, move up, gain height, slope upwards, climb, scale, mount, tower, float up, fly up, soar, arise
E3 descend, go down

ascendancy n
dominance, domination, authority, command, control, power, dominion, superiority, lordship, mastery, supremacy, edge, predominance, pre-eminence, influence, prevalence, sway
formal hegemony
colloq. upper hand
E3 decline, subordination

ascent n
1 ASCENDING, ascension, climb, climbing, scaling, escalation, rise, rising, mounting
2 SLOPE, gradient, incline, ramp, hill, elevation
formal acclivity
3 their rapid ascent to power
rise, advance, progress
formal advancement
E3 1 descent

ascertain v
find out, learn, discover, get to know, determine, fix, establish, settle, locate, detect, identify, verify, confirm, make certain
colloq. suss out, pin down

ascetic adj, n
▶ adj self-denying, self-disciplined, austere, abstemious, abstinent, self-controlled, stern, strict, severe, rigorous, harsh, plain, puritanical, Spartan
▶ n hermit, recluse, solitary, anchorite, abstainer, celibate, monk, nun, puritan, fakir, dervish, yogi

ascribe v
attribute, credit, give credit to, put down, assign, charge
formal accredit, impute

ashamed adj
1 ashamed of your behaviour
sorry, apologetic, remorseful, contrite, guilty, conscience-stricken, sheepish, embarrassed, blushing, red-faced, mortified, humiliated, discomfited, abashed, humbled, crestfallen, distressed, discomposed, confused
colloq. not able to look someone in the face, having your tail between your legs
2 ashamed to admit his mistakes
reluctant, hesitant, unwilling, self-conscious, bashful,

modest
F3 1 shameless, proud, defiant 2 proud

ashen *adj*
pallid, pale, pasty, wan, white, anaemic, blanched,
bleached, colourless, ghastly, grey, leaden, livid, pallid
F3 ruddy

aside *adv, n*
▶ *adv* 1 *move aside*
to one side, on one side, alongside, apart, away, out of
the way, separately, in isolation, alone, privately,
secretly
2 *his money aside*
apart, notwithstanding
▶ *n* digression, parenthesis, departure, soliloquy,
monologue, stage whisper, whisper

asinine *adj*
silly, stupid, foolish, senseless, nonsensical, idiotic,
moronic, imbecilic, absurd, half-witted, fatuous, inane
colloq. daft, potty, gormless
F3 intelligent, sensible

ask *v*
1 *ask a question*
inquire, query, question, put a question to, pose, put
forward, want to know the answer to, interrogate,
propose, suggest, cross-examine, cross-question, poll,
canvass, interview, press
formal posit, postulate, propound
colloq. grill, give a grilling to, pump, quiz, put on the
spot
2 *ask for advice*
REQUEST, appeal, petition, sue, plead, beg, entreat,
implore, clamour, beseech, pray, supplicate, crave,
demand, order, bid, require, seek, approach, solicit,
invite, summon, requisition
3 *ask them to dinner*
invite, have round/over, entertain,

askance *adv*
suspiciously, disapprovingly, contemptuously,
scornfully, disdainfully, distrustfully, doubtfully,
dubiously, mistrustfully, sceptically, indirectly,
sideways, obliquely

askew *adv & adj*
crooked, lopsided, sideways, oblique, at an oblique
angle, off-centre, out of line, asymmetric, crookedly
colloq. skew, skew-whiff
F3 straight, level

asleep *adj*
sleeping, napping, snoozing, fast asleep, sound asleep,
resting, inactive, inert, unconscious, numb, dozing
formal dormant, reposing
colloq. flaked out, comatose, dead to the world, out like
a light, having forty winks

aspect *n*
1 *many aspects of life*
angle, direction, side, facet, feature, point, factor,
dimension, position, standpoint, point of view, view,
outlook, light
2 *take on a more promising aspect*
appearance, look, air, manner, bearing, face,
expression, countenance
3 *a house with a northern aspect*
direction, position, standpoint, point of view, view,
outlook

asperity *n*
sharpness, acerbity, harshness, roughness, severity,
acrimony, astringency, bitterness, churlishness,

crabbedness, crossness, irascibility, irritability,
peevishness, sourness
formal causticity
F3 mildness

aspersion *n*
▷ **cast aspersions on** make critical comments
about, criticize, censure, defame, disparage, reproach,
slander; *formal* denigrate, deprecate, vilify;
colloq. throw/sling mud at, slur, smear
F3 commend, compliment

asphyxiate *v*
suffocate, choke, smother, stifle, strangle, strangulate,
throttle

aspiration *n*
aim, intent, purpose, endeavour, object, objective,
goal, ambition, hope, dream, ideal, wish, desire,
yearning, longing, craving, hankering

aspire *v*
aim, intend, purpose, seek, pursue, hope, dream, wish,
have as an ambition/aim/goal, desire, yearn, long,
crave, hanker

aspiring *adj*
would-be, aspirant, striving, endeavouring, ambitious,
enterprising, budding, keen, eager, hopeful,
optimistic, wishful, longing

ass *n*
1 *ride an ass*
donkey, mule, burro, hinny, jackass, pony
colloq. moke
2 *call someone an ass*
fool, idiot, imbecile
colloq. blockhead, nincompoop, ninny, nitwit,
numskull, twerp, twit, dimwit; *slang* wally, dipstick,
nerd
Related adjective: asinine

assail *v*
1 *assailed by the newspapers/foreign army*
attack, criticize, lay into, set about, set upon, malign,
maltreat, strike, invade, bombard
colloq. tear into
2 *assailed by doubts*
beset, plague, worry, trouble, torment, bedevil, perplex

assailant *n*
attacker, invader, opponent, adversary, enemy, mugger,
aggressor, assailer, assaulter, abuser, reviler

assassin *n*
murderer, killer, slayer, cut-throat, executioner,
gunman
colloq. hatchet man, liquidator, contract man, hit-man

assassinate *v*
murder, kill, slay, dispatch, take someone's life
colloq. eliminate, liquidate, hit, bump off, do in

assault *n, v*
▶ *n* 1 ATTACK, offensive, onslaught, blitz, strike,
raid, invasion, incursion, storm, storming, charge, act
of aggression
2 *charged with assault*
battery, violent act, grievous bodily harm, rape, abuse,
molestation
colloq. GBH, mugging
▶ *v* attack, charge, invade, strike, hit, set upon, fall on,
rape, molest, interfere with, abuse, bombard
colloq. go for, lay into, beat up, do over, mug

assemblage *n*
accumulation, collection, gathering, group, mass, multitude, rally, crowd, flock, throng

assemble *v*
1 GATHER, congregate, muster, summons, rally, convene, meet, join up, flock, group, collect, accumulate, amass, bring/come together, get together, round up, marshal, mobilize, mass
2 CONSTRUCT, build, put together, piece together, fit together, compose, make, connect, join, fabricate, manufacture, set up, collate
🖃 1 scatter, disperse 2 dismantle

assembly *n*
1 GATHERING, rally, meeting, convention, conference, congress, council, group, body, body of people, company, congregation, flock, crowd, multitude, throng, collection, assemblage
technical agora, synod, gemot, gorsedd, indaba, kgotla
formal convocation, panegyry
2 CONSTRUCTION, building, fabrication, manufacture, putting together, construction

assent *v, n*
▶ *v* agree, approve, accept, allow, consent, grant, permit, sanction, submit, subscribe, yield
formal accede, acquiesce, comply, concede, concur
🖃 disagree
▶ *n* agreement, approval, acceptance, capitulation, concession, consent, permission, sanction, submission
formal accord, acquiescence, compliance, concurrence, approbation

assert *v*
1 *assert a fact*
DECLARE, state, pronounce, profess, affirm, confirm, attest, argue, swear, testify to
2 *assert your rights*
maintain, insist on, establish, stress, protest, defend, vindicate, uphold, claim, stand up for, contend
🖃 1 deny, refute
▷ **assert yourself** behave confidently, make your presence felt, make people sit up and take notice, make people sit up and listen

assertion *n*
affirmation, attestation, word, allegation, claim, contention, insistence, vindication, declaration, profession, statement, pronouncement
formal avowal, predication
🖃 denial

assertive *adj*
bold, confident, self-confident, self-assured, sure of yourself, positive, forward, insistent, emphatic, forceful, firm, decided, strong-willed, dogmatic, opinionated, presumptuous, assuming, overbearing, domineering, dominant, aggressive
colloq. pushy, not backward in coming forward
🖃 timid, diffident

assess *v*
1 *assess a situation*
evaluate, gauge, estimate, appraise, review, judge, consider, weigh, size up
colloq. check out
2 *assess the value of something*
compute, calculate, determine, estimate, fix, value, rate, tax, levy, impose, demand

assessment *n*
1 *the assessment of a situation*
evaluation, estimation, appraisal, review, testing, judgement, consideration, opinion,
colloq. recce
2 *a tax assessment*
levy, computation, valuation, rate, toll, tariff, imposition, demand

asset *n*
1 *an asset to the school*
strength, strong point, resource, virtue, benefit, advantage, blessing, boon, help, aid, liability
colloq. plus, plus point
2 *the assets of a company*
estate, property, possessions, goods, holdings, securities, money, wealth, capital, funds, reserves, savings, valuables, resources, means

assiduous *adj*
industrious, diligent, hard-working, conscientious, constant, dedicated, devoted, attentive, persevering, persistent, steady, studious, unflagging, indefatigable, untiring
formal sedulous
🖃 negligent

assign *v*
1 ALLOCATE, apportion, grant, give, dispense, distribute, allot, consign, delegate, name, nominate, designate, appoint, choose, select, detail, commission, install, determine, set, fix, specify, stipulate
2 ATTRIBUTE, ascribe, put down
formal accredit, impute
colloq. chalk up to

assignation *n*
secret meeting, appointment, arrangement, date, engagement, rendezvous
old use tryst

assignment *n*
1 *written assignments*
task, project, job, position, post, duty, responsibility, obligation, commission, errand, charge
2 *his assignment to the job*
appointment, delegation, designation, nomination, selection, allocation, consignment, grant, distribution

assimilate *v*
1 *assimilate new ideas*
ABSORB, take in, pick up, incorporate, learn
2 INTEGRATE, absorb
blend, mix, mingle, unite, accustom, adapt, adjust, acclimatise, accommodate
🖃 1, 2 reject

assist *v*
1 *assist with someone's work/expenses*
HELP, aid, give/lend a hand, abet, rally round, co-operate, collaborate, back (up), second, support, reinforce, sustain, relieve
formal succour
colloq. do your bit, give a leg up to
2 *assist in the operation of a task*
facilitate, make easier, expedite, benefit, encourage, serve, enable, further, advance
🖃 1 hinder 2 thwart

assistance *n*
help, aid, co-operation, collaboration, backing, support, reinforcement, relief, benefit, service, boost, furtherance
colloq. a helping hand, a leg up

formal succour

EJ hindrance, resistance

assistant *n*
1 DEPUTY, subordinate, right-hand man, auxiliary, ancillary, backer, second, second-in-command, supporter, driving force
2 *a personal assistant*
helper, aide, accomplice, accessory, abettor, collaborator, colleague, partner, ally, confederate, associate
3 *a shop assistant*
salesperson, salesman, saleswoman, checkout person, *US* sales clerk

associate *v, n*
▶ *v* 1 CONNECT, link, think of together, couple, correlate, pair, identify
colloq. think of in the same breath, go hand in hand
2 *associate with bad company*
socialize, mingle, mix, keep company, fraternize, be involved
formal consort
colloq. hang around/out, hobnob, rub shoulders
3 AFFILIATE, confederate, ally, league, join, amalgamate, combine, unite, link, connect, relate, couple, attach, band together, syndicate, yoke
▶ *n* partner, ally, confederate, affiliate, collaborator, co-worker, mate, colleague, peer, compeer, fellow, comrade, companion, friend, assistant, helper, follower
colloq. sidekick

association *n*
1 ORGANIZATION, corporation, company, partnership, league, alliance, coalition, confederation, confederacy, federation, affiliation, consortium, cartel, syndicate, union, society, club, fraternity, fellowship, guild, clique, group, band
formal sodality
2 BOND, tie, connection, link, correlation, relation, relationship, involvement, intimacy, friendship, companionship, familiarity

assorted *adj*
miscellaneous, mixed, varied, different, differing, diverse, sundry, motley, various, several, manifold
formal variegated, heterogeneous, multifarious

assortment *n*
miscellany, medley, potpourri, jumble, mix, mixture, variety, diversity, collection, selection, choice, arrangement, group(ing), lot, bunch
technical salmagundi, olla-podrida
old use farrago

assuage *v*
1 *assuage grief/pain*
relieve ease, lessen, reduce, soften, allay, alleviate, calm, lighten, lower, lull, mitigate, moderate, soothe, mollify, pacify, palliate
2 *assuage your thirst*
alleviate, quench, satisfy, appease
formal slake
EJ 1 exacerbate, worsen

assume *v*
1 PRESUME, surmise, accept, take for granted, take as read, expect, understand, deduce, infer, guess, suppose, presuppose, think, believe, imagine, fancy
formal postulate
colloq. take it ..., take someone's word for it
2 AFFECT, take on, feign, counterfeit, simulate, put on, pretend

3 *assume great importance*
take on, adopt, come to have
4 *assume command*
undertake, adopt, enter upon, take upon yourself, embrace, seize, arrogate, commandeer, appropriate, usurp, pre-empt, take over

assumed *adj*
false, bogus, counterfeit, fake, sham, affected, feigned, simulated, pretended, made-up, fictitious, hypothetical
formal supposititious, putative, pseudonymous
colloq. phoney
EJ true, real, actual

assumption *n*
1 *make an assumption*
presumption, surmise, inference, supposition, presupposition, guess, conjecture, theory, hypothesis, premise, postulate, idea, notion, belief, expectation, fancy
formal postulation
2 *her assumption of power*
undertaking, adoption, taking upon yourself, embarkation, embrace, seizure, commandeering, takeover
formal arrogation, appropriation, usurpation, pre-emption

assurance *n*
1 GUARANTEE, pledge, promise, security, vow, declaration, affirmation, assertion, word, undertaking, oath
2 CONFIDENCE, self-confidence, self-assurance, assuredness, aplomb, boldness, self-reliance, belief in yourself, audacity, courage, nerve, conviction, sureness, certainty
EJ 2 shyness, doubt, uncertainty

assure *v*
1 *assured me he would be safe*
convince, persuade, encourage, hearten, reassure, soothe, comfort,
2 *success is assured*
guarantee, warrant, pledge, promise, seal, secure, ensure, confirm, affirm, vow, swear, certify, attest

assured *adj*
1 SURE, certain, indisputable, irrefutable, confirmed, promised, positive, definite, settled, fixed, ensured, guaranteed, secure
colloq. cut and dried
2 SELF-ASSURED, confident, self-confident, self-possessed, sure of yourself, bold, audacious, assertive
EJ 1 uncertain 2 shy, bashful

astonish *v*
surprise, startle, amaze, astound, stun, stupefy, daze, stagger, dumbfound, take aback, take your breath away, shock, confound, bewilder
colloq. floor, flabbergast, wow

astonished *adj*
surprised, startled, amazed, astounded, stunned, dazed, staggered, dumbfounded, taken aback, shocked, confounded, bewildered
colloq. knocked for six, bowled over, flabbergasted

astonishing *adj*
surprising, startling, amazing, astounding, stunning, breathtaking, impressive, striking, startling, staggering, shocking, bewildering
colloq. mind-boggling

astonishment *n*
surprise, amazement, shock, disbelief, dismay,
consternation, confusion, bewilderment, wonder
formal stupefaction

astound *v*
surprise, startle, amaze, astonish, stun, take your
breath away, stupefy, overwhelm, shock, bewilder
colloq. knock for six, bowl over

astounding *adj*
surprising, startling, amazing, astonishing, stunning,
breathtaking, stupefying, overwhelming, staggering,
shocking, bewildering

astray *adv*
adrift, off course, lost, missing, miss, wrong, awry, off
the mark
colloq. off the rails

astringent *adj*
1 *an astringent liquid*
acerbic, acid, caustic
technical styptic
2 *astringent criticism*
caustic, biting, trenchant, scathing, hard, harsh,
severe, stern
formal mordant
E 1, 2 bland

astronaut *n*
spaceman, spacewoman, space traveller, cosmonaut

astute *adj*
shrewd, prudent, sagacious, wise, canny, knowing,
intelligent, sharp, penetrating, keen, perceptive,
discerning, subtle, clever, crafty, cunning, sly, wily
formal perspicacious, sagacious
E stupid, slow

asylum *n*
1 *seek political asylum*
haven, sanctuary, refuge, shelter, retreat, place of safety
colloq. port in a storm
2 *an asylum for the mentally ill*
mental hospital, psychiatric hospital, institution
colloq. funny farm, loony bin, madhouse, nuthouse

asymmetrical *adj*
unsymmetrical, unbalanced, uneven, lopsided,
crooked, awry, unequal, disproportionate, irregular,
distorted, malformed
E symmetrical

asymmetry *n*
imbalance, unevenness, crookedness, lopsidedness,
inequality, disproportionateness, irregularity,
distortion, malformation
E symmetry

atheism *n*
unbelief, non-belief, disbelief, scepticism, irreligion,
ungodliness, godlessness, impiety, infidelity,
paganism, heathenism, freethinking, rationalism
technical nihilism

atheist *n*
unbeliever, non-believer, humanist, rationalist,
disbeliever, sceptic, infidel, heretic, pagan, heathen,
freethinker
technical nihilist
formal nullifidian

athlete *n*
sportsman, sportswoman, runner, gymnast,
competitor, contestant, contender, player

athletic *adj*
1 *an athletic person*
fit, energetic, vigorous, active, sporty, muscular,
sinewy, brawny, strapping, robust, sturdy, strong,
powerful, well-knit, well-proportioned, wiry
2 *athletic events*
sports, gymnastic, games
E 1 puny

athletics *n*
sports, games, matches, races, track events, field
events, exercises, gymnastics
technical aerobics, callisthenics

atmosphere *n*
1 AIR, sky, aerospace, heavens, ether
2 AMBIENCE, environment, surroundings, setting,
milieu, background, air, aura, feel, feeling, mood,
climate, spirit, tone, tenor, character, quality, flavour
Related adjective: epedaphic

The different layers of the atmosphere are: tropo-
sphere, stratosphere, mesosphere, thermosphere,
ionosphere, exosphere.

atom *n*
molecule, particle, bit, morsel, crumb, fragment, grain,
spot, speck, mite, shred, scrap, hint, trace, scintilla,
jot, iota, whit

Subatomic particles include: photon, electron,
positron, neutrino, anti-neutrino, muon, pion,
kaon, proton, anti-proton, neutron, anti-neutron,
lambda particle, sigma particle, omega particle, psi
particle.

atone *v*
make amends, pay for, remedy, indemnify, reconcile,
repent, compensate, recompense, make up for, make
right, make good, offset, redeem, redress, appease,
propitiate, expiate

atonement *n*
amends, reparation, repayment, reimbursement,
requital, restitution, restoration, satisfaction,
compensation, indemnity, payment, penance,
recompense, redress, appeasement, propitiation,
expiation
colloq. eye for an eye

atrocious *adj*
atrocious behaviour/weather
shocking, appalling, abominable, dreadful, terrible,
horrible, horrendous, hideous, ghastly, grievous,
savage, vicious, monstrous, fiendish, wicked, brutal,
cruel, ruthless, merciless
formal heinous, nefarious, flagitious
E admirable, fine

atrocity *n*
outrage, abomination, enormity, horror, monstrosity,
savagery, barbarity, brutality, cruelty, viciousness, evil,
villainy, wickedness, violation, vileness, hideousness,
atrociousness
formal heinousness, flagitiousness

atrophy *n, v*
▶ *n* withering, shrivelling, wasting (away),
emaciation, decay, decline, degeneration,
deterioration, diminution
technical marasmus, tabefaction
▶ *v* wither, shrivel, waste (away), emaciate, decay,
decline, degenerate, deteriorate, diminish, dwindle,

fade, shrink
technical tabefy

attach *v*

1 *attach a label*
affix, stick, adhere, fasten, fix, secure, tie, bind, pin, nail, weld, join, unite, connect, link, couple, add, annex, make secure
2 *attach yourself to a group*
join, affiliate with, associate with, combine with, ally, unite
colloq. latch onto
3 ASCRIBE, attribute, assign, put, place, associate, relate to, belong
formal impute
4 *a centre attached to the university*
link, affiliate, associate, connect, assign, second
F3 1 detach, unfasten

attached *adj*

1 *very attached to her family*
affectionate fond, loving, tender, liking, friendly, devoted
2 *Is she attached?*
married, engaged, spoken for, in a relationship, involved with someone
colloq. going steady
F3 1 unloving **2** single, unattached, on your own

attachment *n*

1 ACCESSORY, fitting, fixture, extension, extra, supplement, supplementary part, addition, adjunct, codicil
formal appendage, appurtenance, accoutrement
2 FONDNESS, affection, tenderness, love, liking, partiality, loyalty, devotion, friendship, affinity, attraction, bond, tie, link

attack *v, n*

▶ *v* **1** *attack a country/person*
raid, strike, storm, rush, charge, assail, assault, besiege, set about, set upon, fall on, lay into, go for, pounce on, ambush
colloq. beat up, do over, mug, make a dead set at, jump, leave for dead; *slang* knock into the middle of next week, have your guts for garters, take to the cleaners
2 CRITICIZE, find fault with, censure, blame, denounce, revile, malign, abuse, reprove, rebuke, *formal* berate, impugn, revile, fulminate against, vilify, calumniate, decry
colloq. slate, slam, knock, pan, tear/pull to pieces, tear to shreds, pick holes in, have a go at, run down, bitch about, slag off
3 *the disease attacks the nerves*
destroy, affect, infect
4 *attack a task*
tackle, deal with, begin, start, get started on, commence, set about, embark on, undertake
F3 1 defend, protect
▶ *n* **1** OFFENSIVE, blitz, bombardment, invasion, incursion, foray, raid, strike, charge, storming, rush, onslaught, assault, sortie, push, sally, act of aggression, battery
formal irruption
2 *an attack on his reputation*
criticism, censure, abuse
formal invective, impugnment, revilement, vilification
colloq. slating, slamming, knocking, flak
3 SEIZURE, fit, convulsion, bout, paroxysm, spasm, stroke
formal access

attacker *n*

assailant, aggressor, invader, raider, critic, detractor, reviler, abuser, persecutor
colloq. mugger
F3 defender, supporter

attain *v*

accomplish, achieve, fulfil, complete, effect, realize, earn, reach, touch, arrive at, hit, grasp, find, get, acquire, obtain, procure, secure, gain, win, net

attainable *adj*

achievable, feasible, viable, manageable, obtainable, possible, potential, practicable, probable, reachable, realistic, within reach, at hand, accessible, imaginable, conceivable
colloq. doable
F3 unattainable

attainment *n*

1 *artistic attainments*
ACCOMPLISHMENT, achievement, feat, success, ability, capability, competence, proficiency, skill, art, talent, gift, aptitude, facility,
2 *the attainment of his ambitions*
fulfilment, completion, consummation, realization, accomplishment, mastery
formal procurement, acquirement

attempt *v, n*

▶ *v* try, have a try, endeavour, aspire, set out, seek, strive, undertake, tackle, venture, aim, experiment, see if you can do, try your hand
colloq. have a go/shot/crack/stab, give it a go/try/whirl, try your hand at, do your level best
▶ *n* try, endeavour, go, push, effort, struggle, bid, undertaking, venture, trial, experiment
colloq. shot, stab, bash, crack

attend *v*

1 *attend a meeting*
be present, be here, be there, go/come along, appear, put in/make an appearance, go to, frequent, visit
colloq. turn up, show (up)
2 PAY ATTENTION, concentrate, listen, hear, heed, mind, mark, watch, note, notice, take note/notice, follow, observe
3 ESCORT, chaperone, accompany, usher, follow, guard
4 *attend the sick*
look after, take care of, care for, nurse, tend, minister to, help, serve, wait upon
▷ **attend to** deal with, see to, take care of, look after, manage, handle, process, direct, control, oversee, supervise, follow up (on), heed

attendance *n*

presence, appearance, audience, house, crowd, gate
colloq. turnout, showing (up)

attendant *n, adj*

▶ *n* assistant, aide, helper, auxiliary, steward, waiter, servant, page, retainer, guide, marshal, usher, escort, companion, follower, guard, custodian
▶ *adj* accompanying, attached, associated, related, incidental, resultant, consequent, subsequent
formal concomitant

attention *n*

▶ **1** *let your attention wander*
alertness, vigilance, concentration, heed, notice, observation, regard, mind, mindfulness, awareness, recognition, thought, focus of your thoughts, contemplation, consideration, preoccupation

formal advertence, advertency
2 *attract great public attention*
notice, observation, regard, awareness, recognition, thought, contemplation, consideration, heed concern
colloq. limelight, high profile
3 *receive medical attention*
care, treatment, therapy, help, service
4 *flattered by his attentions*
respect, courtesy, politeness, compliments, gallantry
F3 1 inattention, disregard, daydreaming
2 inattention, disregard **3** carelessness
▷ **pay attention to** concentrate on, focus your mind/thoughts on, focus on, devote your attention to, take notice, listen/watch carefully

attentive *adj*
1 ALERT, awake, vigilant, aware, watchful, watching, observant, noticing, concentrating, heedful, mindful, careful, conscientious, on the qui vive, listening
formal advertent
colloq. all ears
2 CONSIDERATE, thoughtful, kind, obliging, accommodating, civil polite, courteous, devoted, gracious, conscientious, chivalrous, gallant
F3 1 inattentive, heedless **2** inconsiderate

attest *v*
prove, confirm, corroborate, demonstrate, show, display, manifest, endorse, certify, affirm, assert, certify, declare, demonstrate, vouch for, bear witness to, verify
formal adjure, aver, asseverate, evince, evidence

attic *n*
loft, garret, mansard

attire *n*
dress, clothes, clothing, wear, garments, outfit, garb, costume finery
formal habit, accoutrements, apparel, habilements
colloq. gear, togs, rig-out

attired *adj*
clothed, dressed, arrayed, adorned, turned out
formal habilitated
colloq. decked out, rigged out

attitude *n*
1 OPINION, feeling, disposition, mood, aspect, manner, position, point of view, view, outlook, perspective, approach, way of thinking, mentality, mindset, world-view, *Weltanschauung*
2 POSTURE, bearing, pose, posture, stance, stand
formal deportment, carriage

attract *v*
pull, draw, lure, allure, entice, seduce, tempt, invite, induce, incline, appeal to, bring in, pull in, magnetize, interest, engage, fascinate, enchant, charm, bewitch, captivate, excite
F3 repel, disgust

attraction *n*
1 *the attraction of an exotic lifestyle*
pull, draw, magnetism, lure, allure, bait, enticement, inducement, seduction, temptation, invitation, appeal, affinity, interest, fascination, enchantment, charm, captivation
2 *tourist attractions*
sight, feature, building, activity, entertainment
F3 1 repulsion

attractive *adj*
1 *an attractive person*
pretty, fair, fetching, good-looking, handsome,

beautiful, gorgeous, striking, stunning, glamorous, elegant, lovely, pleasant, charismatic, picturesque, pleasing, cute, engaging, prepossessing, winsome, desirable, sexy, *Scot.* bonny
old use comely, dashing
2 *an attractive suggestion*
agreeable, appealing, winsome, winning, enticing, seductive, tempting, inviting, interesting, engaging, fascinating, charming, captivating, irresistible, magnetic

attribute *v, n*
▶ *v* ascribe, credit, assign, put down, blame, charge, refer, apply
formal accredit, impute
▶ *n* property, quality, virtue, point, aspect, facet, feature, trait, characteristic, idiosyncrasy, peculiarity, quirk, note, mark, side, streak, sign, indicator, symbol

attrition *n*
1 FRICTION, abrasion, rubbing, scraping, chafing, erosion
formal detrition
2 *a war of attrition*
wearing away, wearing down, grinding, harassment,
formal attenuation

attuned *adj*
acclimatized, assimilated, accustomed, familiarized, adapted, adjusted, regulated, co-ordinated, harmonized, set, tuned

atypical *adj*
uncharacteristic, unusual, exceptional, untypical, aberrant, abnormal, anomalous, deviant, divergent, eccentric, extraordinary, freakish
F3 typical

auburn *adj*
reddish-brown, chestnut, tawny, russet, copper, rust, henna, Titian

audacious *adj*
adventurous, daring, enterprising, courageous, rash, reckless, risky, assuming, assured, unabashed, bold, brave, fearless, intrepid, dauntless, valiant, plucky, disrespectful, impertinent, forward, presumptuous, impudent, insolent, cheeky, pert, brazen, rude, shameless
formal venturesome
F3 cautious, reserved, timid

audacity *n*
adventurousness, daring, enterprise, courage, rashness, recklessness, risk, boldness, bravery, fearlessness, intrepidity, dauntlessness, valour, pluck, disrespectfulness, impertinence, forwardness, presumption, impudence, insolence, cheek, pertness, brazenness, effrontery, defiance, rudeness, shamelessness
F3 caution, reserve, timidity

audible *adj*
clear, distinct, recognizable, perceptible, discernible, detectable, appreciable, hearable, heard
F3 inaudible, silent, unclear

audience *n*
1 *members of the audience*
spectators, onlookers, house, auditorium, listeners, viewers, crowd, turnout, gathering, assembly, congregation, fans, devotees, regulars, following, public, ratings
2 MEETING, interview, hearing, consultation, reception, conference

audit *n, v*
▶ *n* examination, inspection, check, verification, investigation, scrutiny, analysis, review, statement, balancing
▶ *v* examine, inspect, check, verify, investigate, scrutinize, analyse, review, go over, go through, work through, balance

augment *v*
add to, amplify, boost, enlarge, build up, put on, expand, extend, grow, increase, make greater, magnify, multiply, raise, inflate, enhance, heighten, intensify, reinforce, strengthen, swell
◼ decrease

augur *v*
herald, prophesy, foretell, predict, promise, be a sign of, signify
formal forebode, betoken, harbinger, bode, presage, portend

augury *n*
omen, herald, prophecy, prediction, foreboding, prognostication, forerunner, forewarning, harbinger, token, warning, portent, promise, sign
formal haruspication, prodrome

august *adj*
dignified, exalted, solemn, noble, impressive, imposing, glorious, grand, lofty, magnificent, majestic, stately, awe-inspiring

aura *n*
air, ambience, atmosphere, mood, quality, emanation, feel, feeling, hint, suggestion, vibrations
formal nimbus
colloq. vibes

auspices *n*
▷ **under the auspices of** under the aegis of, under the authority of, with the patronage/sponsorship of, with the backing/support/approval of, under the supervision/control/influence/guidance of, in the charge/care of

auspicious *adj*
favourable, encouraging, cheerful, bright, rosy, promising, hopeful, optimistic, fortunate, lucky, opportune, timely, happy, prosperous
formal propitious, felicitous
◼ unfavourable, inauspicious, ominous

austere *adj*
1 STARK, bleak, plain, simple, basic, unadorned, unornamented, grim, forbidding, sombre
2 SEVERE, stern, strict, cold, formal, distant, rigid, rigorous, stringent, exacting, hard, harsh, spartan, grave, serious, solemn, sober, abstemious, unfeeling, unbending, inflexible, self-denying, restrained, economical, frugal, ascetic, self-disciplined, puritanical, chaste
formal self-abnegating
◼ 1 ornate, elaborate 2 genial

austerity *n*
plainness, simplicity, severity, coldness, formality, hardness, harshness, solemnity, abstemiousness, abstinence, economy, asceticism, self-denial, self-discipline, inflexibility, puritanism
◼ elaborateness, extravagance, materialism

authentic *adj*
1 *an authentic signature*
genuine, real, actual, certain, bona fide, lawful, legal, legitimate, valid

colloq. the real thing, the genuine article, the real McCoy
2 *an authentic description*
accurate, factual, true, true-to-life, correct, faithful, reliable, dependable, trustworthy, honest, credible
colloq. kosher
◼ 1 false, fake, counterfeit, spurious 2 inaccurate, unfaithful

authenticate *v*
verify, validate, certify, endorse, confirm, ratify, corroborate, guarantee, warrant, vouch for, attest, authorize, prove, substantiate
formal accredit

authenticity *n*
genuineness, certainty, authoritativeness, validity, truth, veracity, truthfulness, honesty, accuracy, correctness, faithfulness, fidelity, reliability, dependability, credibility, trustworthiness, legality, legitimacy
◼ spuriousness, invalidity

author *n*
1 WRITER, novelist, biographer, dramatist, playwright, poet, essayist, composer, contributor, screenwriter, librettist, lyricist, songwriter, reporter, journalist, pen, penman, penwoman
Related adjective: auctorial
2 CREATOR, founder, originator, initiator, parent, prime mover, mover, inventor, designer, architect, planner, maker, producer

authoritarian *adj*
strict, disciplinarian, severe, harsh, rigid, tough, inflexible, unyielding, dogmatic, doctrinaire, absolute, autocratic, dictatorial, totalitarian, despotic, tyrannical, oppressive, domineering, imperious
◼ liberal

⚠ **authoritarian** or **authoritative**?
You describe a person or government as *authoritarian* if they try to control people instead of letting them have the freedom to make their own decisions. An *authoritative* account of something is one that is reliable; an *authoritative* person is one who inspires attention and obedience from others.

---

authoritative *adj*
1 *an authoritative person*
self-confident, confident, self-assured, self-possessed, sure of yourself, bold, audacious, assertive, imposing, masterful
2 *an authoritative study*
scholarly, learned, official, authorized, legitimate, valid, approved, sanctioned, accepted, definitive, decisive, authentic, factual, true, truthful, accurate, faithful, convincing, sound, reliable, dependable, trustworthy
◼ 2 unofficial, unreliable

authority *n*
1 GOVERNMENT, administration, establishment, management, officialdom, state, council, bureaucracy
colloq. they, the powers that be
2 SOVEREIGNTY, supremacy, rule, sway, control, dominion, influence, command, power, force, jurisdiction
colloq. clout, muscle
3 AUTHORIZATION, permission, sanction, permit, warrant, licence, credentials, right, power, prerogative, carte blanche

4 *an authority on antiques*
expert, pundit, connoisseur, specialist, professional, master, scholar, sage
colloq. buff

authorization *n*
authority, permission, consent, sanction, approval, mandate, validation, ratification, confirmation, licence, entitlement, empowering, commission, warranty, permit, leave, credentials
formal accreditation
colloq. OK, okay, go-ahead, green light

authorize *v*
legalize, make legal, validate, ratify, confirm, license, entitle, empower, give authority to, enable, commission, warrant, permit, give permission, allow, let, consent to, sanction, approve
formal accredit
colloq. OK, okay, give the go-ahead, give the green light

autobiography *n*
memoirs, life story, story of your life, diary, journal

autocracy *n*
absolutism, totalitarianism, dictatorship, despotism, tyranny, authoritarianism, fascism
🖾 democracy

autocrat *n*
absolutist, totalitarian, dictator, despot, tyrant, authoritarian, fascist
old use panjandrum
colloq. (little) Hitler

autocratic *adj*
absolute, all-powerful, totalitarian, despotic, tyrannical, authoritarian, dictatorial, domineering, overbearing, imperious
🖾 democratic, liberal

autograph *n, v*
▶ *n* signature, name, initials, countersignature, inscription, endorsement, mark
▶ *v* sign, write your name, initial, countersign, endorse, put your mark

automatic *adj*
1 AUTOMATED, self-activating, mechanical, mechanized, programmed, self-regulating, computerized, push-button, robotic, self-propelling, unmanned
2 SPONTANEOUS, reflex, involuntary, mechanical, unwilled, unconscious, unthinking, natural, instinctive, routine, necessary, certain, inevitable, unavoidable, inescapable, uncontrollable
colloq. knee-jerk

autonomy *n*
self-government, self-rule, home rule, sovereignty, independence, self-determination, self-sufficiency, autarky, freedom, free will
🖾 subjection, compulsion

auxiliary *n, adj*
▶ *n* ancillary, subordinate, helper, partner, supporter, right-hand man, backer, second, second-in-command
old use foederatus
▶ *adj* ancillary, assistant, subsidiary, accessory, secondary, supporting, supportive, helping, assisting, aiding, extra, supplementary, spare, reserve, back-up, emergency, substitute

available *adj*
free, vacant, unoccupied, untaken, to hand, within

reach, at hand, accessible, handy, convenient, on hand, at your disposal, disposable, ready, obtainable, usable, forthcoming
formal procurable
colloq. on tap, up your sleeve, up for grabs, yours for the asking/taking
🖾 unavailable, taken

avalanche *n*
landslide, landslip, cascade, torrent, deluge, flood, inundation, wave, barrage

avant-garde *adj*
innovative, innovatory, pioneering, experimental, unconventional, original, progressive, advanced, forward-looking, futuristic, enterprising, inventive, modern, contemporary
colloq. go-ahead ; *slang* far-out, way-out
🖾 conservative

avarice *n*
covetousness, acquisitiveness, greed, greediness, meanness, miserliness, selfishness, materialism
🖾 generosity, liberality

avaricious *adj*
covetous, grasping, acquisitive, greedy, mercenary, mean, miserly
formal rapacious, pleonectic
🖾 generous, liberal

avenge *v*
take revenge for, take vengeance for, punish, requite, repay, pay back, retaliate
colloq. get even with, get back at, get your own back

average *n, adj*
▶ *n* mean, mid-point, median, norm, mode, standard, centre, rule, par, medium, mode, run
🖾 extreme, exception
▶ *adj* **1** *the average age*
mean, medial, median, middle, intermediate, medium
2 *the average reader*
ordinary, everyday, common, usual, normal, regular, standard, typical, routine, unexceptional
3 *an average performance*
mediocre, moderate, satisfactory, fair, middling, fair to middling, indifferent, passable, tolerable, undistinguished, unexceptional, nothing special
colloq. run-of-the-mill, so-so, not up to much, nothing much to write home about, not much cop, no great shakes
🖾 **1** extreme **3** exceptional, remarkable

averse *adj*
reluctant, unwilling, loath, disinclined, ill-disposed, hostile, opposed, antagonistic, unfavourable
formal antipathetic
🖾 willing, keen, sympathetic

⚠ **averse** or **adverse** ? *See panel at* **adverse**.

aversion *n*
dislike, hate, hatred, loathing, abomination, horror, phobia, reluctance, unwillingness, distaste, disgust, revulsion, repulsion, hostility, opposition, antagonism
formal detestation, abhorrence, repugnance, disinclination
🖾 liking, sympathy, desire

avert *v*
turn away, deflect, turn aside, parry, head off, fend off, ward off, stave off, forestall, frustrate, prevent, avoid,

evade, stop
formal obviate, preclude

aviation *n*
aeronautics, flying, flight, aircraft industry
aviation

Aviation terms include: aeronautics, aeroplane,
aerospace, aileron, aircraft, airfield, air hostess,
airline, air-miss, *US* airplane, airport, airship,
airspace, air steward, airstrip, air-traffic control,
airway, altitude, automatic pilot, biplane, black
box, captain, *colloq.* chocks away, cockpit, console,
control tower, crash-dive, crash-landing, dive, drag,
fixed-wing, flap, flight, flight crew, flight deck,
flight recorder, fly-by, fly-by-wire, fly-past,
fuselage, *slang* George, glider, ground-control,
ground-speed, hangar, helicopter, hop, hot-air
balloon, jet, jet engine, jet propulsion, jetstream,
joystick, jumbo jet, landing, landing-gear, landing-
strip, lift-off, loop-the-loop, Mach number, maiden
flight, mid-air collision, monoplane, night-flying,
nose dive, overshoot, parachute, pilot, plane,
pressurised cabin, *slang* prang, propeller, rotor
blade, rudder, runway, solo flight, sonic boom,
sound barrier, spoiler, supersonic, swing-wing,
take-off, taxi, test flight, test pilot, thrust,
touchdown, undercarriage, undershoot, vapour
trail, vertical take-off and landing (VTOL),
windsock, wingspan. *See also* **aircraft**.

avid *adj*
eager, earnest, keen, enthusiastic, fanatical, devoted,
dedicated, zealous, ardent, fervent, intense, great,
passionate, insatiable, ravenous, hungry, thirsty,
greedy, grasping, covetous
colloq. crazy, mad
Ƒ3 indifferent

avoid *v*
evade, stay/keep away from, elude, sidestep, escape,
run away from, get out of, bypass, get round, balk,
prevent, avert, shun, abstain from, hold back from, shy
away from, steer clear of, make a detour, keep your
distance from
formal eschew, circumvent, refrain from, forbear
colloq. hedge, duck, dodge, shirk, wriggle/worm your
way out of, give a miss, give a wide berth to

avoidable *adj*
escapable, preventable
formal avertible, eludible
Ƒ3 inevitable, inescapable

avowed *adj*
sworn, declared, professed, self-proclaimed, self-
confessed, confessed, admitted, acknowledged, open,
overt

await *v*
wait for, expect, hope for, look forward to, look for, be
in store for, lie in wait

awake *adj, v*
▶ *adj* wakeful, wide awake, stirring, aroused, alert,
vigilant, watchful, observant, attentive, conscious,
aware, sensitive, alive
colloq. tossing and turning, not sleeping a wink
Ƒ3 asleep, sleeping
▶ *v* awaken, waken, wake, wake up, rouse, stir, arouse

awakening *n*
awaking, wakening, waking, rousing, arousal,
stimulation, animating, enlivening, activation, revival,
birth
formal vivification

award *n, v*
▶ *n* **1** *an award for bravery*
prize, trophy, decoration, medal, certificate,
presentation, commendation, citation
slang gong
2 *an award for compensation*
endowment, gift, grant, allotment, allowance,
dispensation, bestowal, conferral, adjudication,
judgement, decision, order
▶ *v* give, present, distribute, dispense, bestow, confer,
accord, endow, gift, grant, allot, allocate, assign, allow,
determine
formal apportion, adjudge

aware *adj*
1 *aware of the problem*
conscious, alive to, sensitive, appreciative, mindful,
heedful, attentive, observant, sharp, alert, vigilant
formal sentient, sensible
2 *politically aware*
familiar, conversant, acquainted, informed,
enlightened, au courant, knowing, knowledgeable,
shrewd
formal cognizant, apprised
colloq. clued up, in the know, on the ball
Ƒ3 **1** unaware, oblivious, insensitive

awe *n*
wonder, reverence, respect, honour, admiration,
amazement, astonishment, fear, terror, dread,
apprehension
formal veneration, stupefaction
Ƒ3 contempt

awe-inspiring *adj*
wonderful, sublime, magnificent, stupendous,
overwhelming, breathtaking, striking, spectacular,
stupefying, stunning, astonishing, amazing,
impressive, dazzling, imposing, majestic, solemn,
exalted, sublime, moving, awesome, formidable,
daunting, intimidating, fearsome
formal numinous
Ƒ3 contemptible, tame

awful *adj*
awful weather/injuries
terrible, dreadful, fearful, frightful, ghastly,
unpleasant, nasty, horrible, horrid, hideous, ugly,
gruesome, dire, abysmal, unpleasant, atrocious,
horrific, horrifying, shocking, appalling, alarming,
disgusting, distressing, spine-chilling
formal heinous
Ƒ3 wonderful, excellent

awkward *adj*
1 CLUMSY, gauche, inept, inexpert, unskilful,
bungling, ham-fisted, unco-ordinated, ungainly,
graceless, ungraceful, ungainly, inelegant,
cumbersome, unwieldy, lubberly
formal maladroit
colloq. all thumbs
2 *feeling awkward in their presence*
uncomfortable, ill at ease, embarrassed, shy
3 *put me in an awkward position*
difficult, tricky, embarrassing, uncomfortable,
delicate, troublesome, perplexing, problematic,
annoying, inconvenient, fiddly
4 OBSTINATE, stubborn, unco-operative, irritable,
touchy, prickly, oversensitive, rude, unpleasant
Ƒ3 **1** graceful, elegant, convenient,
handy **2** comfortable, relaxed, at
ease **3** straightforward, easy **4** amenable, pleasant

awry *adv & adj*
1 *clothing left awry*
askew, asymmetrical, cock-eyed, crooked, misaligned, oblique, off-centre, skew-whiff, twisted, uneven, *colloq.* wonky
2 *plans gone awry*
wrong, amiss
⊟ 1 straight, symmetrical

axe *n, v*
▶ *n* hatchet, chopper, cleaver, tomahawk, battle-axe
▷ **get the axe** be cancelled; *colloq.* get the boot, get the chop
▶ *v* **1** CUT DOWN, fell, hew, chop, cleave, split
2 CANCEL, terminate, discontinue, remove, withdraw, eliminate, get rid of, throw out, dismiss, discharge
colloq. cut, sack, fire

axiom *n*
principle, fundamental, truth, truism, precept, dictum, byword, maxim, adage, aphorism

axiomatic *adj*
manifest, assumed, certain, given, granted, self-evident, understood, unquestioned, presupposed, fundamental, accepted, proverbial
formal indubitable, aphoristic, apophthegmatic, gnomic

axis *n*
centre-line, vertical, horizontal, pivot, hinge

axle *n*
shaft, spindle, rod, pin, pivot

B

babble *v, n*
▶ *v* **1** CHATTER, gabble, jabber, gibber, cackle, prate, mutter, mumble, murmur
colloq. rabbit on, waffle
2 *the stream babbled*
burble, gurgle
▶ *n* chatter, gabble, clamour, hubbub, babel, gibberish, burble, murmur

babe *n*
baby, child, infant, babe in arms

babel *n*
babble, hubbub, clamour, bedlam, hullabaloo, chaos, commotion, confusion, din, disorder, pandemonium, tumult, turmoil, uproar

baby *n, adj*
▶ *n* babe, infant, newborn baby, suckling, child, tiny, toddler, tiny tot, *Scot.* bairn
technical neonate
slang sprog
▶ *adj* miniature, small-scale, midget, small, little, tiny, minute, diminutive, dwarf, *Scot.* wee
colloq. mini

babyish *adj*
childish, juvenile, puerile, infantile, silly, foolish, baby, young, immature, naïve
colloq. soft, sissy
E3 mature, precocious

back *n, v, adj, adv*
▶ *n* **1** *lie on your back*
backbone, spine
technical dorsum, tergum
Related adjective: dorsal
2 *the back of an envelope*
rear, stern, end, rear end, tail, tail end, hind part, hindquarters, posterior, backside, reverse, reverse side, other side
E3 front, face
▷ **behind your back** secretly, without your knowledge, deceitfully, slyly, furtively, covertly, sneakily, surreptitiously
▶ *v* **1** GO BACKWARDS, reverse, recede, backtrack, retreat, retire, withdraw, back away, recoil
formal regress
2 SUPPORT, sustain, assist, help, aid, abet, side with, champion, advocate, encourage, promote, boost, favour, confirm, bolster, sanction, countenance, endorse, second, countersign, sponsor, finance, subsidize, underwrite
colloq. throw your weight behind, get/be behind
E3 **1** advance, approach **2** discourage, weaken
▷ **back away** retreat, withdraw, draw back, fall back, move back, give ground, recoil, step back, recede
▷ **back down** abandon, yield, submit, surrender concede, give in, submit, retreat, withdraw, back-pedal, backtrack, climb down
▷ **back out** abandon, give up, withdraw, resign,

recant, go back on, cancel; *colloq.* pull out, get cold feet, chicken out
▷ **back up** support, confirm, corroborate, bear out, validate, substantiate, endorse, second, champion, reinforce, bolster, assist, aid
▶ *adj* **1** *the back door*
rear, end, tail, posterior, hind, hindmost, reverse, other
2 *back copies*
past, previous, earlier, former, outdated, elapsed, bygone, out of date, obsolete
E3 **1** front
▶ *adv* backwards, to the rear, behind
E3 forwards

backbiting *n*
criticism, slander, libel, defamation, abuse, disparagement, gossip, malice, scandalmongering, spite, spitefulness
formal aspersion, calumny, denigration, revilement, detraction, vilification, vituperation
colloq. bitchiness, cattiness, slagging off, mud-slinging
E3 praise

backbone *n*
1 SPINE, spinal column, vertebrae, vertebral column
Related adjective: vertebrate
2 *the backbone of an organization*
mainstay, support, core, foundation, basis, nucleus
3 COURAGE, mettle, pluck, nerve, grit, determination, resolve, (strength of) character, firmness, tenacity, steadfastness, willpower, toughness, stamina, strength, power
colloq. bottle
E3 **3** spinelessness, weakness

backbreaking *adj*
arduous, exhausting, gruelling, strenuous, hard, heavy, crushing, killing, laborious, punishing
E3 easy

backer *n*
advocate, benefactor, promoter, second, seconder, sponsor, subscriber, supporter, underwriter, champion, patron, well-wisher, patron

backfire *v*
1 *the engine backfired*
explode, discharge, blow up, detonate
2 *the plans backfired*
recoil, rebound, ricochet, boomerang, miscarry, fail, defeat itself, be self-defeating, be counterproductive
colloq. flop, come home to roost, score an own goal, blow up in your face

background *n*
1 SETTING, backdrop, backcloth, scene, surroundings, environment, milieu, context, framework, circumstances, influences, factors
2 HISTORY, record, credentials, experience, qualifications, grounding, preparation, education,

upbringing, family, (family) circumstances, breeding, social standing, status, origins, culture, tradition

backhanded *adj*
ambiguous, double-edged, two-edged, indirect, oblique, dubious, equivocal, ironic, sarcastic, sardonic
F∃ sincere, wholehearted

backing *n*
support, accompaniment, aid, assistance, help, helpers, championing, advocacy, encouragement, moral support, commendation, favour, approval, sanction, promotion, endorsement, seconding, patronage, sponsorship, finance, funds, grant, subsidy

backlash *n*
reaction, response, repercussion, reprisal, retaliation, recoil, kickback, backfire, boomerang

backlog *n*
accumulation, stock, supply, resources, reserve, reserves, heap, excess, hoard
colloq. mountain

back-pedal *v*
take back, retract, change your mind, have second thoughts, abandon, yield, submit, surrender, concede, give in, submit, retreat, withdraw, backtrack, climb down
formal tergiversate
colloq. do a U-turn

backslide *v*
lapse, relapse, default, defect, turn away, turn your back, fall from grace, renege, desert, revert, go back, sin, slip, stray, go astray
formal apostatize, regress, tergiversate
colloq. leave the straight and narrow
F∃ persevere

backslider *n*
apostate, defaulter, defector, deserter, renegade, reneger, turncoat
formal recidivist, recreant, tergiversator

backsliding *n*
lapse, relapse, apostasy, defection, desertion, defaulting
formal regression, tergiversation

backup *n*
support, help, assistance, aid, encouragement, confirmation, endorsement, reinforcement, additional equipment/resources

backward *adj*
1 *a backward step*
rearward, reverse, to the back, retrograde, retrogressive, regressive
2 *a backward country/society*
undeveloped, underdeveloped, unsophisticated
3 SHY, bashful, retiring, reluctant, unwilling, hesitant, hesitating, shrinking, timid, wavering
4 *a backward child*
slow, immature, retarded, having learning difficulties, subnormal
F∃ 1 forward 2 advanced, developed 3 precocious

backwards *adv*
rearwards, to the back, retrogressively, regressively

backwash *n*
1 *the backwash of a ship*
wash, flow, swell, waves, wake, path

2 REPERCUSSIONS, aftermath, after effect(s), result(s), consequence(s), reverberations

backwoods *n*
back of beyond, bush, outback
colloq. middle of nowhere, sticks

bacteria *n*
germs, viruses, microbes, micro-organisms, parasites, bacilli
colloq. bugs

bad *adj*
1 UNPLEASANT, disagreeable, nasty, dreadful, appalling, atrocious, undesirable, unfortunate, distressing, adverse, detrimental, harmful, damaging, hurtful, dangerous, injurious, unhealthy, unwholesome, destructive, ruinous
formal deleterious
2 EVIL, wicked, sinful, criminal, corrupt, dishonest, shameful, immoral, vile, offensive, degenerate, outrageous, deplorable
formal reprehensible, reprobate
3 *bad workmanship; bad at speaking French*
poor, inferior, inadequate, weak, mediocre, substandard, imperfect, faulty, defective, deficient, unsatisfactory, unacceptable, second-rate, third-rate, useless, hopeless, incompetent, mismanaged, ineffective
formal ineffectual
colloq. awful, terrible, botched, lousy, pathetic, ropy, a load of rubbish, a load of garbage; *slang* poxy, crummy, naff, crappy, a load of crap/shit
4 *feel bad today*
unwell, sick, ill, poorly, indisposed, diseased, painful, in pain, aching, unhappy, despondent, gloomy
colloq. under the weather
5 ROTTEN, mouldy, decayed, spoilt, putrid, rancid, sour, off, tainted, contaminated, high
formal putrefactive, putrescent
6 *a bad child*
naughty, mischievous, badly-behaved, ill-behaved, disobedient, unruly, wayward
formal refractory
colloq. stroppy, bolshie
7 *have a bad cold*
serious, grave, severe, intense, critical, acute, harsh
8 *a bad time to call*
inconvenient, unfortunate, unfavourable, unsuitable, inappropriate
formal inauspicious
F∃ 1 good, pleasant, mild 2 virtuous 3 skilled, skilful 4 well, happy 5 fresh 6 well-behaved, obedient 7 good, convenient, favourable;
formal auspicious
▷ **not bad** quite good, all right, tolerable, passable, fair, average, adequate, reasonable, satisfactory;
colloq. OK, so-so

badge *n*
1 *a school badge*
identification, emblem, device, insignia, crest, shield, escutcheon, sign, mark, token, stamp, brand, trademark, logo, ensign
2 *a badge of power*
sign, mark, token, symbol, indicator, indication

badger *v*
pester, plague, torment, harass, bait, bully, chivvy, goad, harry, hound, nag
formal importune
colloq. hassle

badinage *n*
banter, repartee, word-play, jocularity, teasing,
waggery, chaff, drollery, give and take, humour,
mockery, raillery
formal persiflage
colloq. ribbing

badly *adv*
1 *a badly directed play*
poorly, inadequately, imperfectly, defectively,
unsatisfactorily, unacceptably, uselessly,
incompetently, wrongly, incorrectly, improperly,
defectively, faultily, imperfectly, inadequately,
unsatisfactorily, poorly, incompetently, negligently,
carelessly
formal ineffectually
colloq. awfully, terribly, pathetically
2 *badly hurt*
SERIOUSLY, acutely, bitterly, painfully, desperately,
severely, critically, gravely, crucially
3 WICKEDLY, criminally, immorally, shamefully,
dishonestly, sinfully, evilly, offensively, unfairly
4 UNFAVOURABLY, adversely, unfortunately,
unsuccessfully, unhappily
5 *want something badly*
very much, greatly, exceedingly, enormously,
tremendously, desperately, intensely extremely, deeply
⊟ **2** slightly, mildly **3** well **4** favourably,
fortunately

bad-tempered *adj*
irritable, cross, snappy, quick-tempered, grumpy,
fractious, in a (bad) mood, narky, impatient, choleric
formal querulous, cantankerous, petulant
colloq. stroppy, in a huff, in a sulk, having got out of bed
on the wrong side, having a short fuse, cross as a bear
with a sore head, crotchety, crabbed, crabby, grouchy,
shirty, ratty
⊟ good-tempered, genial, equable

baffle *v*
puzzle, perplex, mystify, bemuse, bewilder, confuse,
mystify, confound, dumbfound, daze, upset,
disconcert, foil, thwart, frustrate, hinder, block, bar,
check, defeat
colloq. bamboozle, flummox, stump, throw
⊟ enlighten, help

baffling *adj*
puzzling, perplexing, mysterious, bewildering,
confusing, stupefying, perplexing, disconcerting,
surprising, amazing, astounding, bemusing,
extraordinary, unfathomable
⊟ enlightening, explanatory

bag *v, n*
▶ *v* **1** CATCH, capture, trap, land, kill, shoot
2 OBTAIN, acquire, get, gain, come by, corner, take,
grab, appropriate, commandeer, reserve
▶ *n* container, receptacle

Types of bag include: attaché-case, backpack,
bumbag, carrier bag, carry all, case, clutch bag,
duffel bag, flight bag, grip, handbag, haversack,
hold-all, kitbag, knapsack, pack, rucksack, sack,
saddlebag, satchel, shoulder-bag, suitcase, valise,
vanity bag.

baggage *n*
luggage, suitcases, bags, belongings, things,
equipment, gear, paraphernalia, effects
formal impedimenta, accoutrements

baggy *adj*
loose, loose-fitting, slack, roomy, ill-fitting, billowing,
bulging, ballooning, floppy, shapeless, sagging,
droopy, oversize, extra large
⊟ tight, firm

bail *n*
security, surety, pledge, bond, guarantee, warranty,
collateral
▷ **bail out** **1** HELP, aid, assist, relieve, rescue,
finance **2** (*also* **bale out**) withdraw, retreat, quit,
back out, escape, get out, get clear

bait *n, v*
▶ *n* lure, incentive, inducement, bribe, temptation,
snare, enticement, allurement, incitement, attraction
⊟ disincentive
▶ *v* tease, provoke, goad, irritate, annoy, hound, irk,
harass, persecute, torment, badger, plague, harry
colloq. needle, hassle, give a hard time to

balance *v, n*
▶ *v* **1** STEADY, poise, stabilize, level, square,
equalize, equate, match
2 *balance the cost against the benefits*
equalize, equate, match, counterbalance, counteract,
counterweigh, neutralize, offset, set, adjust, juggle,
compensate for
3 COMPARE, consider, weigh, estimate, evaluate,
appraise, review
⊟ **1** unbalance, overbalance
▶ *n* **1** EQUILIBRIUM, steadiness, stability, evenness,
symmetry, equality, parity, equity, equivalence,
correspondence, uniformity
technical stasis
formal equipoise
2 COMPOSURE, calmness, self-possession, poise,
assurance, level-headedness, cool-headedness,
equanimity
formal aplomb, sangfroid
3 REMAINDER, rest, residue, surplus, excess,
difference
⊟ **1** imbalance, instability

balanced *adj*
1 *a balanced report*
objective, fair, impartial, unbiased, unprejudiced,
equitable
2 *a balanced diet*
well-rounded, healthy, complete
3 *a balanced person*
calm, self-possessed, assured, level-headed, cool-
headed, equitable, even-handed, sensible
⊟ **1** prejudiced, biased
▷ **on balance** in conclusion, all in all, taking
everything into consideration

balcony *n*
terrace, veranda, portico, loggia, gallery, upper circle,
gods

bald *adj*
1 BALD-HEADED, hairless, smooth, uncovered
technical glabrous, glabrate
formal depilated
colloq. bald as a coot
2 BARE, naked, unadorned, plain, simple, severe,
stark, barren, exposed, treeless, unsheltered, bleak
3 *a bald statement*
forthright, direct, straight, blunt, outright, downright,
straightforward, outspoken, simple, plain, unadorned
⊟ **1** hairy, hirsute
3 adorned

balderdash *n*
rubbish, nonsense, drivel, gibberish, trash, tripe,
twaddle
colloq. bunk, bunkum, claptrap, piffle, bilge,
poppycock, hot air, cobblers, rot, tommyrot;
slang balls, bollocks, shit, bullshit

balding *adj*
receding, losing your hair, thin on top, bald

baldness *n*
bald-headedness, bareness, hair loss, hairlessness,
starkness
technical calvities, calvousness, glabrousness, psilosis
formal alopecia
F3 hirsuteness

bale *n, v*
▶ *n* bundle, truss, pack, package, parcel
▶ *v* ▷ **bale out** *see* **bail out** 2.

baleful *adj*
deadly, harmful, threatening, destructive, evil, hurtful,
injurious, malevolent, malignant, menacing,
mournful, noxious, ominous, pernicious, ruinous,
sinister, venomous
F3 favourable

balk, baulk *v*
1 FLINCH, recoil, shrink, jib, boggle, hesitate, refuse,
resist, dodge, evade, shirk
formal eschew
2 THWART, frustrate, foil, forestall, disconcert,
baffle, hinder, obstruct, check, stall, bar, prevent,
impede, defeat, counteract

ball¹ *n*
a golf ball
sphere, globe, orb, globule, drop, conglomeration,
projectile, pellet, pill, shot, bullet
colloq. slug
▷ **play ball** co-operate, collaborate, go along, play
along, show, respond, reciprocate, willing

ball² *n*
an invitation to a ball
dance, dinner-dance, party, soirée, masquerade,
carnival, assembly

ballad *n*
poem, song, folk-song, shanty, carol, ditty

ballet *n*
ballet-dancing, dancing, leg-business

Terms used in ballet include: à pointe, arabesque,
attitude, ballerina, prima ballerina, ballon, barre,
battement, batterie, battu, bourrée, capriole, chassé,
choreography, ciseaux, company, corps de ballet,
coryphée, divertissement, écarté, élévation,
entrechat, fish dive, five positions, fouetté, fouetté en
tournant, glissade, jeté, grande jeté, leotard, pas de
deux, pas de seul, pirouette, plié, pointes, sur les
pointes, ports de bras, principal male dancer,
régisseur, répétiteur, ballet shoe, point shoe, splits,
stulchak, tutu.

balloon *v*
bag, belly, billow, blow up, bulge, dilate, enlarge,
expand, inflate, puff out, swell, rocket, soar
formal distend

ballot *n*
poll, polling, vote, voting, election, referendum,
plebiscite

ballyhoo *n*
fuss, hubbub, to-do, hullabaloo, clamour, commotion,
excitement, disturbance, noise, racket, tumult, hue and
cry, agitation, build-up, promotion, propaganda,
publicity, advertising, hype

balm *n*
soothing balm for the skin/a troubled spirit
cream, lotion, salve, sedative, unguent, balsam,
bromide, calmative, curative, embrocation, emollient,
lenitive, ointment, palliative, restorative, anodyne,
comfort, consolation
F3 irritant, vexation

balmy *adj*
warm, summery, gentle, mild, pleasant, soft,
temperate, clement, soothing
F3 inclement

bamboozle *v*
puzzle, perplex, mystify, bemuse, bewilder, confuse,
mystify, confound, dumbfound, daze, upset,
disconcert, trick, cheat, dupe, deceive, hoodwink, fool,
swindle
colloq. con, gull

ban *v, n*
▶ *v* forbid, prohibit, disallow, bar, exclude, ostracize,
outlaw, banish, suppress, veto, restrict, censor,
disqualify
formal proscribe
F3 allow, permit, authorize
▶ *n* prohibition, embargo, injunction, sanctions, veto,
boycott, stoppage, restriction, suppression,
censorship, outlawry, bar, banishment, condemnation,
denunciation, curse, taboo
formal interdiction, proscription
F3 permission, dispensation

banal *adj*
trite, commonplace, ordinary, everyday, mundane,
humdrum, boring, dull, unimaginative, nondescript,
bland, hackneyed, clichéed, stock, stereotyped, stale,
overused, threadbare, tired, unoriginal, inane,
wearing thin, empty, vapid
colloq. corny
F3 original, fresh, imaginative

banality *n*
triteness, ordinariness, dullness, unimaginativeness,
staleness, tiredness, unoriginality, inaneness,
emptiness, vapidity, fatuity, cliché, commonplace,
bromide, platitude, prosaicism, triviality, truism
F3 originality

band¹ *n*
a metal band
strip, belt, ribbon, tape, bandage, binding, tie, ligature,
bond, strap, cord, chain, connection, link, shackle,
manacle, fetter

band² *n, v*
▶ *n* 1 *bands of looters*
TROOP, gang, crew, group, troop, herd, flock, party,
body, gathering, crowd, throng, horde, contingent,
association, company, society, club, clique
2 *the band played on*
group, music/musical group, pop group, orchestra,
ensemble
▶ *v* group, gather, join, unite, join forces, close ranks,
stand together, pull together, ally, collaborate,
consolidate, amalgamate, merge, affiliate, federate
colloq. stick together
F3 disband, disperse

bandage *n, v*
▶ *n* dressing, plaster, gauze, compress, ligature, tourniquet, swathe, swaddle
▶ *v* bind (up), dress, cover, swathe, swaddle

bandit *n*
robber, thief, brigand, marauder, plunderer, outlaw, highwayman, pirate, buccaneer, hijacker, cowboy, gunman, desperado, gangster, crook, criminal, racketeer

bandy¹ *v*
bandy words about
exchange, swap, trade, barter, interchange, reciprocate, pass, toss, throw

bandy² *adj*
bandy-legged
bow-legged, curved, bowed, bent, misshapen, crooked

bane *n*
ruin, adversity, destruction, scourge, affliction, torment, trial, trouble, vexation, woe, annoyance, *bête noire*, blight, burden, calamity, curse, disaster, distress, downfall, evil, irritation, misery, misfortune, nuisance, ordeal, plague, pest, pestilence
E blessing

bang *n, v, adv*
▶ *n* **1** *a loud bang*
explosion, detonation, pop, boom, clap, peal, clang, clash, thud, thump, slam, noise, report, shot
formal report
2 *a nasty bang on the head*
BLOW, hit, knock, bump, crash, collision, crack, smack, punch, thump, stroke, bash
colloq. wallop, whack, sock
▶ *v* **1** STRIKE, hit, bump into, crash into, bash, knock, bump, rap, drum, hammer, pound, thump, stamp
2 EXPLODE, burst, detonate, boom, echo, resound, crash, slam, clatter, clang, peal, thunder
▶ *adv* straight, directly, headlong, right, exactly, precisely, absolutely, slap, smack, hard, noisily, suddenly, abruptly

banish *v*
1 *banish someone from their country*
EXPEL, eject, evict, deport, transport, drive away, cast out, throw out, exile, outlaw, ban, bar, debar, exclude, shut out, ostracize, excommunicate, expatriate, repatriate, extradite
formal rusticate
2 *banish thoughts from your mind*
dismiss, oust, dislodge, remove, get rid of, drive away, send away, shut out, discard, dispel, dislodge, eliminate, eradicate
E **1** recall, welcome

banishment *n*
expulsion, eviction, deportation, expatriation, transportation, exile, exclusion, ostracism, excommunication, extradition
formal outlawry
E return, recall, welcome

banisters *n*
railing, rail, handrail, balustrade

bank¹ *n, v*
▶ *n* **1** *a bank account*
financial institution, high-street bank, clearing bank, merchant bank, savings bank, building society, finance company/house
2 *a blood bank*

accumulation, fund, pool, reservoir, depository, repository, treasury, savings, reserve, store, stock, stockpile, hoard, cache
▶ *v* deposit, save (up), keep, store, accumulate, stockpile, lay by, put aside
colloq. save for a rainy day
E spend
▷ **bank on** depend on, rely on, count on, bet on, trust, believe in; *colloq.* pin your hopes on

bank² *n, v*
▶ *n* **1** *the banks of a river*
side, embankment, slope, tilt, edge, shore, margin
Related adjective: riparian
2 *a bank of ground*
mound, earthwork, ridge, hillock, knoll, rampart, levee, parados, slope, rise, incline, heap, pile, mass
▶ *v* **1** SLOPE, incline, pitch, slant, tilt, tip
2 HEAP, pile, stack, mass, amass, accumulate, mound, drift

bank³ *n*
a bank of switches
row, series, array, panel, bench, group, tier, rank, line, succession, sequence, train

banknote *n*
bill, note, paper money, treasury note, *US* greenback
slang flimsy

bankrupt *adj, v, n*
▶ *adj* **1** *the company went bankrupt*
insolvent, in liquidation, ruined, failed, folded, beggared, destitute, impoverished, spent
formal penurious, impecunious
colloq. bust, broke, hard up, gone to the wall, gone under, in the red, on the rocks, on your uppers
2 *bankrupt philosophies of life*
deficient, lacking, wanting, deprived, exhausted, depleted
E **1** solvent, wealthy, flourishing, prospering, rich; *colloq.* in the black
▶ *v* ruin, cripple
▶ *n* insolvent, debtor, pauper, beggar

bankruptcy *n*
insolvency, (financial) ruin, liquidation, disaster, exhaustion, failure, indebtedness, lack
formal penury, beggary, ruination
E solvency, wealth

banner *n*
flag, standard, colours, ensign, pennant, streamer, placard, sign, banderol, burgee, fanion, pennon, labarum, gonfalon, vexillum

banquet *n*
feast, dinner, dinner party, meal, party, treat, spread

banter *n, v*
▶ *n* joking, jesting, pleasantry, badinage, repartee, word play, chaff, chaffing, derision, mockery, ridicule, raillery, persiflage
colloq. kidding, ribbing
▶ *v* joke, jest, chaff, deride, mock, ridicule, make fun of
colloq. kid, rib, rag, pull someone's leg

baptism *n*
1 *the child's baptism*
christening, immersion, sprinkling, affusion, aspersion, purification, naming, dedication
2 *a baptism of fire*
beginning, initiation, introduction, début, launch, launching, inauguration

baptize *v*
christen, immerse, sprinkle, purify, cleanse, name, call, term, style, title, introduce, initiate, enrol, recruit

bar *n, v, prep*
▶ *n* **1** PUBLIC HOUSE, inn, tavern, saloon, taproom, lounge, lounge bar, grill, brasserie, counter, table
colloq. pub, hostelry, watering-hole; *slang* boozer
2 ROD, stick, shaft, pole, stake, stanchion, batten, crosspiece, rail, railing, paling, barricade
3 SLAB, cake, block, lump, chunk, wedge, ingot, nugget
4 OBSTACLE, impediment, hindrance, obstruction, barrier, stop, check, deterrent, drawback
5 *called to the Bar*
barristers, lawyers, counsel, court, tribunal
▶ *v* **1** EXCLUDE, debar, ban, forbid, prohibit, prevent, hinder, obstruct, block, blockade, restrain, check, stop, disqualify, suspend
formal preclude
2 *bar the door*
barricade, lock, bolt, latch, fasten, secure, padlock
▶ *prep* except, with the exception of, excepting, apart from, save, but for, excluding, omitting

barb *n*
1 *the barb on a fish hook*
arrow, point, spike, needle, thorn, prickle, bristle, fluke
2 *critical barbs at leaders*
gibe, insult, affront, sneer, rebuff, sarcasm, scorn
colloq. dig

barbarian *n, adj*
▶ *n* savage, brute, wild person, ruffian, hooligan, vandal, lout, oaf, boor, philistine, ignoramus, illiterate
▶ *adj* savage, brute, wild, rough, brutish, coarse, crude, uncivilized, uncouth, uncultivated, uncultured, unsophisticated, vulgar, loutish, hooligan
formal tramontane

barbaric *adj*
barbarous, primitive, wild, savage, fierce, ferocious, vicious, cruel, inhuman, brutal, brutish, bestial, murderous, ruthless, uncivilized, uncouth, vulgar, coarse, crude, rude
E3 humane, civilized, gracious

barbarism *n*
wildness, savagery, fierceness, ferocity, viciousness, cruelty, inhumanness, brutality, brutishness, bestiality, murderousness, ruthlessness, uncivilizedness, corruption, enormity, uncouthness, vulgarity, coarseness, crudeness, rudeness

barbarity *n*
barbarousness, wildness, savagery, ferocity, viciousness, cruelty, inhumanity, brutality, ruthlessness, brutishness, atrocity, outrage, enormity
E3 civilization, humanity, civility

barbarous *adj*
1 *barbarous behaviour*
wild, savage, fierce, ferocious, vicious, cruel, inhuman, barbarian, barbaric, brutal, brutish, bestial, murderous, ruthless, heartless
2 *barbarous by modern standards*
primitive, ignorant, uncivilized, unrefined, unsophisticated, uncultured, unlettered, vulgar, rough, rude, crude
E3 **2** civilized, cultured, educated

barbed *adj*
1 PRICKLY, spiny, thorny, spiked, pronged, hooked, jagged, toothed, pointed

2 *a barbed remark*
cutting, caustic, acid, hurtful, unkind, nasty, snide, hostile, critical

bare *adj*
1 NAKED, nude, in the nude, unclothed, undressed, with nothing on, stripped, denuded, uncovered, exposed
colloq. in your birthday suit, in the raw
2 *bare shelves/rooms*
empty, vacant, unfurnished
3 *a bare tree/landscape*
barren, denuded, exposed, bleak, desolate, unsheltered, treeless, unforested, unwooded, woodless
formal defoliated
4 *the bare facts/minimum*
PLAIN, simple, unadorned, barren, bald, stark, basic, essential, straightforward, cold, hard, sheer, absolute, mere
E3 **1** clothed **2** full, decorated **3** wooded, sheltered, forested **4** detailed

barefaced *adj*
brazen, shameless, blatant, bold, brash, flagrant, glaring, arrant, impudent, insolent, unabashed, undisguised, unconcealed, audacious, naked, obvious, manifest, open, palpable, patent, transparent, bald

barefooted *adj*
barefoot, shoeless, unshod
formal discalced
E3 shod

barely *adv*
hardly, scarcely, no sooner, only just, just, almost
colloq. be a near/close thing, by the skin of your teeth, by a whisker

bargain *n, v*
▶ *n* **1** DEAL, transaction, contract, treaty, pact, pledge, promise, covenant, agreement, understanding, arrangement, negotiation
formal concordat
2 DISCOUNT, reduction, special offer, good buy, value for money
colloq. snip, giveaway, steal
▷ **into the bargain** as well, besides, additionally
▶ *v* negotiate, haggle, beat down, deal, trade, traffic, barter, buy, sell, transact, settle, clinch
▷ **bargain for** expect, anticipate, plan for, be prepared for, include, reckon on, take into account, look for, foresee, imagine, contemplate, consider, figure on

bargaining *n*
negotiation, haggling, dealing(s), trade, trafficking, barter(ing), buying, selling, transaction, horsetrading, wheeling and dealing, wheeler-dealing

barge *n, v*
▶ *n* canal-boat, flatboat, narrow-boat, houseboat, lighter
▶ *v* push (in), push your way, force your way, shove, rush, bump, hit, collide, press, jostle, elbow, smash, plough
▷ **barge in** interrupt, butt in, burst in, break in, cut in, gatecrash, intrude, interfere

bark¹ *v, n*
▶ *v* **1** *the dog barked*
yap, woof, yelp, snap, snarl, growl, bay, howl
2 *bark orders at someone*

yell, shout, cry, bawl, thunder, snap, snarl
▶ *n* yap, woof, yelp, snap, snarl, growl, bay, howl

bark² *n*
the bark of a tree
covering, casing, crust, husk, rind, peel, skin, hide, shell
technical cortex, integument

barmy *adj*
crazy, foolish, idiotic, insane, mad, odd, silly, stupid
colloq. daft, batty, dippy, dotty, loony, loopy, nuts, crackers, nutty, off your head/rocker/nutter, need your head examining, round the bend/twist, off your trolley, out to lunch
🔁 rational, sane, sensible, of sound mind

baroque *adj*
elaborate, ornate, rococo, florid, flamboyant, embellished, exuberant, vigorous, bold, convoluted, decorated, overdecorated, overwrought, extravagant, showy, fanciful, fantastic, whimsical, grotesque
🔁 plain, simple, unadorned, austere

barrack *v*
heckle, jeer, shout down, interrupt

barracks *n*
garrison, camp, encampment, fort, guardhouse, quarters, billet, lodging, accommodation, casern

barrage *n*
a barrage of fire/criticism
bombardment, shelling, gunfire, cannonade, battery, volley, salvo, burst, broadside, assault, attack, onset, onslaught, deluge, torrent, flood, stream, storm, hail, rain, shower, mass, abundance, profusion

barrel *n*
cask, keg, tun, butt, water-butt, tierce, rundlet

barren *adj*
1 *barren land/activity*
ARID, dry, desert, desolate, waste, uncultivable, empty, flat, dull, vapid, uninteresting, uninspiring, uninformative, uninstructive, unrewarding, unproductive, profitless, unfruitful, fruitless, pointless, useless, valueless, purposeless
2 INFERTILE, sterile, childless, unprolific, unbearing
formal infecund
🔁 1 fertile, productive, fruitful, useful 2 fertile

barricade *n, v*
▶ *n* blockade, obstruction, obstacle, barrier, bar, fence, stockade, bulwark, rampart, palisade, protection, defence
▶ *v* block, obstruct, bar, close (up), shut (off), fortify, strengthen, defend, protect

barrier *n*
1 WALL, fence, railing, barricade, bar, gate, blockade, stockade, obstacle, roadblock, boom, rampart, fortification, ditch, frontier, boundary, bar, check
2 *a barrier to success*
obstacle, hurdle, stumbling-block, impediment, obstruction, hindrance, handicap, limitation, restriction, drawback, check, restraint, difficulty

barring *prep*
except (for), except (in the event of), if, unless

bartender *n*
barman, barmaid, barkeeper, publican

barter *v, n*
▶ *v* trade, exchange, bargain, swap, traffic, deal,

haggle, negotiate, sell
▶ *n* trade, trading, exchange, bargaining, swapping, trafficking, dealing, haggling, negotiation

base¹ *n, v*
▶ *n* 1 *the base of the statue*
BOTTOM, foot, pedestal, plinth, stand, stay, rest, support, prop, foundation, foundation stone, keystone, underneath, substructure, understructure, bed, groundwork
technical fundus
2 BASIS, foundation, fundamental, essential, component, principal, key, heart, core, essence, root, origin, source
3 HEADQUARTERS, centre, post, station, camp, settlement, depot, home, starting-point
▶ *v* 1 *research based on fact*
found, establish, ground, build, construct, derive, have as a basis, depend, rest, hinge
2 *based in Edinburgh*
locate, station, position, situate, site, install

base² *adj*
base behaviour
abject, contemptible, despicable, wicked, corrupt, immoral, evil, vile, reprobate, vulgar, shameful, sordid, depraved, unprincipled, disgraceful, disreputable, wretched, worthless, ignominious, infamous, scandalous, low, lowly, low-minded, mean, miserable, pitiful, poor, valueless

baseless *adj*
groundless, unfounded, unsupported, unsubstantiated, unauthenticated, unconfirmed, unjustified, uncalled-for, gratuitous
🔁 justifiable, substantiated

basement *n*
cellar, crypt, vault

bash *v, n*
▶ *v* hit, strike, knock, punch, belt, smash, smack, slug, break, crash
colloq. wallop, whack, sock
▶ *n* 1 *have a bash at something*
attempt, go, try
colloq. crack, whirl, shot, stab
2 *throw a bash*
party, rave-up
colloq. thrash

bashful *adj*
shy, coy, retiring, backward, reticent, reserved, unforthcoming, hesitant, shrinking, nervous, timid, timorous, diffident, modest, self-effacing, inhibited, self-conscious, embarrassed, blushing, abashed, shamefaced, sheepish
🔁 bold, confident, aggressive, assertive

bashfulness *n*
shyness, coyness, reticence, reserve, hesitancy, nervousness, timidity, diffidence, modesty, self-effacement, inhibition, self-consciousness, embarrassment, blushes, shamefacedness, sheepishness
🔁 boldness, confidence, assertiveness

basic *adj*
1 FUNDAMENTAL, elementary, primary, radical, root, underlying, key, central, inherent, intrinsic, essential, indispensable, vital, necessary, important, first, preparatory
2 *basic rate of pay*
standard, minimum, lowest level, starting

3 *basic accommodation*
primitive, elementary, plain, simple, staple, unadorned, spartan, stark, austere, crude, unsophisticated
E3 **1** inessential, minor, peripheral **2** with commission, premium

basically *adv*
fundamentally, essentially, in essence, at bottom, at heart, inherently, radically, intrinsically, principally, primarily, substantially, mainly, in the main, when it comes down to it

basics *n*
fundamentals, essentials, rudiments, (first) principles, introduction, facts, necessaries, practicalities, realities, bedrock, rock bottom, core
colloq. brass tacks, nitty-gritty, nuts and bolts

basin *n*
1 *a pudding basin*
bowl, dish, sink
2 *the basin of a river*
bed, crater, cavity, hollow, depression, channel, dip

basis *n*
1 *research that forms the basis of the book*
foundation, support, base, bottom, footing, ground(s), groundwork, cornerstone, bedrock, key, keynote, reason(s), rationale, fundamental(s), fundamental point, starting-point, premise, principle, first principles, main ingredient, alpha and omega, essential(s), essence, heart, core, thrust
formal quintessence, hypostasis
2 *on a particular basis*
arrangement, procedure, method, system, principle, condition(s), terms, way, approach

bask *v*
1 *bask in the sun*
sunbathe, lie, lounge, relax, laze, loll
2 *bask in someone's approval*
revel, delight in, enjoy, take pleasure in, relish, savour, lap up, wallow
formal luxuriate

basket *n*
hamper, creel, pannier, punnet, bassinet, coop, skep, trug

bass *adj*
deep, deep-pitched, deep-toned, low, low-pitched, low-toned, grave, rich, resonant, sonorous

bastard *n*
illegitimate, illegitimate child, love child, natural child

bastardize *v*
adulterate, pervert, defile, contaminate, corrupt, debase, degrade, demean, depreciate, devalue, cheapen, distort

bastion *n*
stronghold, citadel, fortress, defence, bulwark, mainstay, support, prop, pillar, rock, protection, defence
formal redoubt

batch *n*
lot, consignment, parcel, pack, bunch, set, assortment, collection, assemblage, cluster, accumulation, mass, group, conglomeration, contingent, amount, quantity, aggregate, crowd

bath *n, v*
▶ *n* **1** *be in the bath*

bathtub, tub, sauna, steam bath, Jacuzzi®, whirlpool, bath, slipper bath, Turkish bath, steam room, spa, hamman, thermae
formal balneary
Related adjective: balneal
2 *have/take a bath*
wash, scrub, soak, shower, douche, tub, dip,
▶ *v* bathe, have/take a bath, wash, clean, soak, shower

bathe *v, n*
▶ *v* **1** *bathe in the sea*
swim, bath, take a dip
2 *bathe a wound*
wet, moisten, immerse, wash, cleanse, rinse, soak, steep, flood, cover, suffuse
▶ *n* swim, dip, paddle, wash, rinse, soak

bathos *n*
anticlimax, comedown, let-down

baton *n*
stick, rod, staff, truncheon

battalion *n*
1 *an infantry battalion*
army, force, garrison, brigade, regiment, squadron, company, platoon, division, detachment, section, contingent, legion, troops, unit
2 *a battalion of people*
horde, multitude, throng, host, mass, herd

batten *n, v*
▶ *n* strip, bar, board
▶ *v* barricade, board up, clamp down, fasten, fix, nail down, secure, tighten

batter *v*
1 *waves battering the pier*
beat, pound, pummel, buffet, smash, dash, pelt, lash, damage, wear down, wear out, erode, mangle
2 *battering his wife*
abuse, maltreat, ill-treat, hit, strike, knock about, club, bash, beat, assault, hurt, injure, bruise, disfigure
colloq. wallop, thrash, whack
▷ **batter down** break down, smash, demolish, destroy, ruin, wreck

battered *adj*
1 *a battered child*
beaten, abused, ill-treated, injured, bruised
2 *a battered old shed*
weather-beaten, dilapidated, tumbledown, ramshackle, shabby, crumbling, damaged, crushed

battery *n*
1 *a battery of tests/cameras*
sequence, series, set, cycle, succession
2 *assault and battery*
attack, beating, grievous bodily harm, force, striking, thrashing, violence
colloq. mugging
3 *the military battery*
artillery, cannon, cannonry, emplacements, guns

battle *n, v*
▶ *n* *a battle against the enemy/cancer*
war, warfare, hostilities, action, conflict, armed conflict, strife, combat, fight, engagement, final battle, Armageddon, encounter, attack, fray, skirmish, brawl, clash, struggle, free-for-all, contest, tournament, campaign, drive, race, competition, crusade, row, disagreement, confrontation, dispute, debate, controversy
formal altercation

▶ *v*   *battle against the enemy/authorities*
fight, combat, war, feud, contend, struggle, strive, combat, campaign, crusade, agitate, clamour, contest, argue, quarrel, disagree, dispute

battle-axe *n*
dragon, disciplinarian, harridan, martinet, Tartar, termagant, virago

battle-cry *n*
war cry, war song, rallying cry/call, slogan, motto, watchword, catchword

battlefield *n*
battleground, field of battle, front, front line, war/combat zone, theatre of operations, arena

batty *adj*
crazy, foolish, idiotic, insane, mad, demented, odd, eccentric, peculiar, silly, stupid
colloq. daft, barmy, bats, bonkers, dippy, dotty, loony, loopy, nuts, crackers, nutty, off your head/rocker/nutter, need your head examining, round the bend/twist, out to lunch
E3 rational, sane, sensible

bauble *n*
knick-knack, trinket, toy, plaything, trifle, ornament, bagatelle, bibelot, flamfew, gewgaw, gimcrack, kickshaw, tinsel

baulk *see* **balk.**

bawd *n*
brothel-keeper, madam, panderess, pimp, procuress

bawdy *adj*
lewd, blue, pornographic, coarse, dirty, rude, vulgar, erotic, obscene, gross, improper, indecent, indecorous, indelicate, lecherous, lascivious, licentious, lustful, ribald, risqué, smutty, suggestive
formal libidinous, prurient, salacious
E3 chaste, clean

bawl *v*
1 *the baby bawled*
cry, weep sob, blubber, wail, snivel, squall
2 *bawl loudly at someone*
yell, shout, cry (out), bellow, howl, roar, call (out), scream, screech
formal vociferate
colloq. holler
▷ **bawl out** scold, rebuke, reprimand, yell at

bay¹ *n*
moor the ship in a bay
gulf, bight, arm, sound, firth, inlet, indentation, cove, lagoon, estuary, loch

bay² *n*
a bay in the lounge
recess, alcove, niche, nook, opening, compartment, cubicle, booth, stall, carrel

bay³ *v*
baying for blood
howl, clamour, roar, bellow, bell, bawl, cry, bark, yelp
colloq. holler

bayonet *n, v*
▶ *n*   knife, blade, pike, spear, dagger, poniard
▶ *v*   stab, impale, knife, pierce, spear, stick

bazaar *n*
market, marketplace, mart, exchange, sale, fair, fête, bring-and-buy, souk

be *v*
1 EXIST, breathe, live, be alive, inhabit, be situated, be located, stand, lie, reside, dwell
2 STAY, remain, abide, last, endure, persist, continue, survive, stand, prevail, obtain
3 HAPPEN, occur, arise, come about, take place, come to pass, develop, transpire
formal befall
4 REPRESENT, constitute, make (up), form, amount to, add up to, account for

beach *n*
sand, sands, shingle, shore, strand, seashore, seaside, water's edge, coast, coastline, seaboard
formal littoral
Related adjective: littoral

beachcomber *n*
forager, loafer, loiterer, scavenger, scrounger, wayfarer

beacon *n*
signal, fire, watch fire, bonfire, light, beam, lighthouse, watchtower, flare, rocket, sign, warning light, danger signal
old use fanal
formal pharos

bead *n*
1 *a string of beads*
ball, pearl, jewel, pellet globule, spheroid
2 *beads of sweat*
drop, droplet, drip, blob, dot, bubble
colloq. glob

beak *n*
bill, mandibles, nib, neb, rostrum, nose, proboscis, snout

beaker *n*
glass, tumbler, jar, cup, mug, tankard

beam *n, v*
▶ *n* **1** *a beam of light*
ray, shaft, gleam, stream, flash, flare, glint, glimmer, glow, bar
2 PLANK, board, timber, rafter, joist, girder, spar, boom, bar, support, stanchion, transom, lintel, cantilever, stringer, summer, lath, scantling
▶ *v* **1** *beam a TV signal*
TRANSMIT, emit, broadcast, send, aim, direct, relay
2 *sunlight beaming through the window*
shine, emit, radiate, glare, gleam, glitter, glow, glimmer, flash, sparkle
formal effulge
3 SMILE, grin

bean *n*
Related adjectives: fabaceous, leguminous

Varieties of bean and pulse include: adzuki bean, alfalfa, beansprout, black-eyed pea, broad bean, butter bean, carob bean, chick pea, chilli bean, dal, dwarf runner bean, fava bean, French bean, garbanzo pea, green bean, haricot bean, kidney bean, legume, lentil, *US* lima bean, locust bean, mange tout, marrowfat pea, mung bean, *US* navy bean, okra, pea, *US* pinto bean, red kidney bean, runner bean, *US* scarlet runner, snap bean, soya bean, split pea, string bean, sugar bean, tonka bean, *US* wax bean.

bear *v*
1 CARRY, convey, transport, move, take, bring, fetch
colloq. hump, tote
2 SUPPORT, hold (up), shoulder, uphold, sustain

3 *bear children*
give birth to, breed, propagate, beget, engender, produce, generate, develop, yield, bring forth, give up
4 TOLERATE, stand, put up with, endure, abide, suffer, like, permit, allow, admit, endorse, accept, take, live with
colloq. stomach
5 *bear signs of a struggle*
carry, show, display, have
6 *bear the cost*
pay, accept, support, shoulder
7 *bear someone malice*
hold, have, maintain, entertain, harbour, cherish
8 *bear left at the junction*
veer, turn, move, go, drive, diverge, deviate, bend, curve
▷ **bear in mind** keep in, mind, remember, be mindful of, consider, note, take into account, make a mental note
▷ **bear out** confirm, endorse, support, back up, uphold, prove, demonstrate, corroborate, substantiate, validate, warrant, ratify, vindicate, justify, verify
▷ **bear up** persevere, cope, soldier on, carry on, suffer, endure, survive, withstand; *colloq.* grin and bear it, keep your pecker up
▷ **bear with** tolerate, put up with, endure, suffer, forbear, be patient with, make allowances for

bearable *adj*
tolerable, endurable, sufferable, supportable, sustainable, passable, acceptable, admissible, manageable
F3 unbearable, intolerable

beard *n, v*
▶ *n* facial hair, stubble, bristle, beaver, goatee, imperial, vandyke, moustache, whiskers, five o'clock shadow, mutton chops, sideburns, sideboards, tuft
▶ *v* brave, challenge, confront, dare, defy, face, oppose, stand up against

bearded *adj*
unshaven, bristly, stubbly, whiskered, bewhiskered, tufted, hairy, hirsute, shaggy, bushy
technical pogoniate
F3 beardless, clean-shaven, smooth

bearer *n*
1 *the bearer of bad news*
conveyor, courier, messenger, runner
2 *the bearers of a coffin*
carrier, conveyor, porter, transporter
3 *the bearer of a document*
holder, possessor, beneficiary, consignee, payee

bearing *n*
1 *have no bearing on the matter*
influence, relevance, significance, connection, relation, concern, reference
formal pertinence
2 MANNER, manner, air, aspect, attitude, behaviour, poise, carriage, gait, posture, stature
formal demeanour, comportment, deportment, mien
3 *find your bearings*
orientation, position, situation, location, whereabouts, course, track, way, direction, aim

beast *n*
1 *birds and beasts*
animal, creature, brute
2 *You selfish beast!*
brute, monster, savage, barbarian, pig, swine, devil,

ogre, fiend
Related adjectives: bestial, theriomorphous

beastly *adj*
horrible, horrid, terrible, unpleasant, disagreeable, awful, nasty, rotten, foul, repulsive, rotten, brutal, cruel

beat *v, n, adj*
▶ *v* **1** HIT, flog, lash, whip, flay, cane, birch, strap, thrash, lay into, punch, strike, swipe, knock, bang, wham, club, bash, slap, smack, pound, hammer, batter, thump, drub, welt, thwack, buffet, pelt, bruise, box, cudgel, lambast, pummel
old use contuse, knubble, knout, vapulate
colloq. tan, wallop, whack, belt, clout, biff, fill in
2 *hear his heart beating*
PULSATE, pulse, throb, thump, pound, race, palpitate, flutter, vibrate, quiver, tremble, shake, quake
3 *waves beating against the rocks*
pound, strike, dash, batter
4 *beat a drum*
hit, strike, bang
5 *a bird's wings beating*
flap, flutter, shake, swing, quiver, vibrate
6 *beat the eggs*
stir, mix, whisk, blend, combine
7 *beat metal*
hammer, forge, knock, fashion, form, shape, stamp
formal malleate
8 DEFEAT, trounce, best, worst, conquer, overcome, overwhelm, overpower, subdue, rout, annihilate, outplay, outwit, outsmart, be more than a match for, have the edge on, drub
formal vanquish, subjugate
colloq. hammer, slaughter, clobber, lick, thrash, wipe the floor with
9 *beat the record*
surpass, excel, exceed, outdo, outstrip, outrun, transcend,
▷ **beat up** attack, assault, knock about, knock around, batter
colloq. do over, mug, rough up, knock someone's block off, beat the living daylights out of, knock into the middle of next week, batter
▶ *n* **1** *the beat of a drum*
hit, stroke, strike, striking, bang, blow, knocking, pounding
2 PULSATION, pulse, stroke, throb, pounding, thump, palpitation, vibration, flutter
3 RHYTHM, time, tempo, metre, measure, rhyme, stress, accent
formal cadence
4 *a police officer's beat*
round, rounds, territory, circuit, course, journey, way, path, route, walk
▶ *adj* exhausted, fatigued, tired, wearied, worn out, zonked
colloq. jiggered; *slang* zonked (out)

beaten *adj*
1 *beaten metal*
HAMMERED, stamped, forged, wrought, worked, formed, shaped, fashioned
2 *beaten paths*
trampled, trodden, well-trodden, well-worn, well-used
3 WHISKED, whipped, mixed, blended, frothy, foamy

beatific *adj*
blissful, blessed, divine, exalted, sublime, glorious, heavenly, joyful, ecstatic, rapturous, angelic, seraphic

beatify *v*
sanctify, bless, exalt, glorify
formal macarize

beating *n*
1 CORPORAL PUNISHMENT, hitting, whipping,
flogging, caning, the cane/birch/strap, thrashing,
lashing, drubbing, punching, clubbing, slapping,
smacking, battering, thumping, bruising,
chastisement,
colloq. tanning, whacking, walloping
2 DEFEAT, conquest, rout, ruin, downfall, overthrow,
trouncing, overwhelming, overpowering,
annihilation, outwitting, outsmarting
formal vanquishing
colloq. hammering, slaughter, clobbering, thrashing

beau *n*
admirer, suitor, sweetheart, boyfriend, lover, escort,
fiancé
colloq. guy

beautician *n*
beauty specialist, cosmetician, hairdresser, friseur
formal visagiste

beautiful *adj*
attractive, fair, pretty, lovely, good-looking, handsome,
gorgeous, radiant, ravishing, voluptuous, striking,
stunning, pleasing, appealing, alluring, charming,
pleasing, delightful, fine, graceful, exquisite, seemly,
becoming, magnificent
Scot. bonny
formal comely, pulchritudinous
colloq. smashing, out of this world
🔁 ugly, plain, hideous

beautify *v*
embellish, smarten (up), enhance, improve, grace, gild,
garnish, decorate, ornament, deck, bedeck, adorn,
array, glamorize, spruce up
colloq. titivate, tart up, doll up
🔁 disfigure, spoil

beauty *n*
1 *the beauty of a woman/poem*
attractiveness, prettiness, loveliness, (good) looks,
handsomeness, gorgeousness, radiance, appeal, allure,
charm, delight, grace, gracefulness, exquisiteness,
seemliness, excellence, harmony, symmetry
formal pulchritude
Related adjective: pulchritudinous
2 *think her a real beauty*
belle, charmer, siren, Venus, *femme fatale*
colloq. good-looker, smasher, corker, cracker,
knockout, stunner, peach
3 *the beauties of the plan*
attraction, advantage, benefit, good thing, plus point,
good point, virtue, merit, glory, boon, blessing, bonus,
dividend
🔁 **1** ugliness, repulsiveness **2** frump
3 disadvantage

beaver *v*
▷ **beaver away** work hard, work at, put a lot of effort
in, persist, persevere
colloq. slog, plug away, slave away

becalmed *adj*
at a standstill, at a halt, idle, motionless, still, stranded,
marooned, stuck

because *conj*
as, for, since, owing to, due to, on account of, as a result
of, the reason is ..., through, thanks to, in view of the

fact that
formal by reason of, by virtue of, forasmuch
colloq. seeing as

beckon *v*
1 *beckon to someone*
summon, motion, gesture, signal, nod, wave,
gesticulate
2 *fame beckons*
call, invite, attract, pull, draw, lure, allure, entice,
tempt, induce, persuade, coax

become *v*
1 *become old-fashioned*
turn, grow (into), get, change into, be changed into,
develop into, mature into, pass into, come to be, turn
out to be, wax
2 SUIT, befit, flatter, look good on, enhance, grace,
embellish, ornament, set off, harmonize

becoming *adj*
1 *a hat in a more becoming style*
attractive, charming, flattering, graceful, elegant,
tasteful, fetching, pretty, comely
2 *becoming behaviour*
APPROPRIATE, suitable, fit, fitting, befitting,
consistent, congruous compatible
🔁 **1, 2** unbecoming

bed *n, v*
▶ *n* **1** *get out of bed*
divan, couch, bunk
slang sack, hay, kip
2 LAYER, stratum, substratum, matrix, base, basis,
bottom, floor, foundation, groundwork, watercourse,
channel
3 *bed of flowers*
garden, border, patch, area, space, strip, row, plot
▷ **go to bed with** sleep with, have sex with, have
sexual intercourse with, make love to

Kinds of bed include: berth, box bed, bunk bed,
camp-bed, cot, cradle, crib, day bed, divan bed,
double bed, foldaway bed, folding bed, four-poster,
hammock, mattress, pallet, palliasse, Put-u-up®,
put-you-up, single bed, sofa bed, trucklebed,
trundlebed, twin bed, water-bed, Z-bed.

▶ *v* base, embed, establish, fix, found, ground,
implant, inlay, insert, bury, plant, settle
▷ **bed down** sleep, go to bed, settle down, turn in;
slang doss down, hit the hay/sack, kip down

bedclothes *n*
bedding, bed-linen, covers

Kinds of bedclothes include: mattress cover, pillow,
pillow sham, bolster, pillowcase, pillowslip, sheet,
fitted sheet, valanced sheet, valance, blanket,
cellular blanket, electric blanket, quilt, patchwork
quilt, duvet, quilt cover, duvet cover, eiderdown,
bedspread, candlewick bedspread, throwover,
counterpane, coverlet, *US* comforter, bed canopy,
sleeping-bag, bedroll.

bedeck *v*
beautify, decorate, deck, adorn, embellish, festoon,
garnish, ornament, array, trick out, trim

bedevil *v*
afflict, torment, confound, frustrate, harass, irk,
pester, plague, tease, annoy, besiege, torture, trouble,
distress, vex, fret, worry, irritate

bedlam *n*
chaos, pandemonium, madhouse, commotion,
confusion, furore, clamour, hubbub, hullabaloo, noise,
tumult, turmoil, uproar, babel, anarchy
F3 calm

bedraggled *adj*
untidy, unkempt, dishevelled, disordered, scruffy,
slovenly, messy, dirty, muddy, muddied, soiled, wet,
soaked, soaking (wet), sodden, dripping, drenched
F3 neat, tidy, clean

bedridden *adj*
confined to bed, incapacitated
colloq. laid up, flat on your back

bedrock *n*
the bedrock of a building/your life
foundation, support, basis, base, bottom, footing,
reason(s), rationale, fundamentals, basics, essentials,
fundamental point, starting-point, premise, first
principles, essence, heart

beef *v*
complain, criticize, grumble, moan, grouse, object,
dispute, disagree
colloq. gripe
F3 approve
▷ **beef up** strengthen, consolidate, give new energy
to, toughen, invigorate, build up, establish, reinforce,
substantiate, flesh out
F3 weaken

beefy *adj*
brawny, muscular, bulky, burly, fat, fleshy, heavy, hefty,
hulking, stalwart, stocky, robust, sturdy
formal corpulent
F3 slight

beer *n*
ale, bitter, stout, real ale, light ale, draught, bottled
beer, lager, Pils, Pilsener, mild

beetle *v*
dash, hurry, nip, run, rush, scamper, scoot, scurry,
tear, zip

beetling *adj*
overhanging, protruding, poking out, projecting,
jutting, leaning over, sticking out
formal pendent

befall *v*
happen, take place, occur, arrive, chance, result, ensue,
fall, follow, materialize
formal betide, supervene

befitting *adj*
appropriate, suitable, becoming, apt, correct, decent,
fit, fitting, proper, right, seemly
old use meet
F3 unbecoming

before *prep, adv*
▶ *prep* **1** *before breakfast*
earlier than, previous to, prior to, not later than, sooner
than, in preparation for, in anticipation of, on the eve of
2 *perform before the king*
in front of, in the presence of, in the sight of
3 *all of his life before him*
in front of, ahead of
▶ *adv* **1** *have been here before*
earlier, formerly, previously, already
2 *go on before*
ahead, in front, in advance

beforehand *adv*
in advance, preliminarily, already, before, previously,
earlier, sooner

befriend *v*
help, aid, assist, succour, back, support, protect,
defend, look after, stand by, uphold, sustain, comfort,
encourage, welcome, favour, benefit, take under your
wing, keep an eye on, make friends with, make a friend
of, get to know, fall in with, stick up for
formal succour
F3 neglect, oppose

befuddle *v*
confuse, muddle, baffle, bewilder, daze, disorient,
puzzle, stupefy

beg *v*
1 *beg someone to do something*
ask for, beseech, request, require, desire, crave, plead,
appeal, turn to, entreat, implore, pray, supplicate,
petition, solicit, importune
2 *beg for money*
ask for money, cadge
colloq. bum, scrounge, sponge, *US* mooch (off)

beget *v*
1 CAUSE, bring about, create, breed, give rise to,
occasion, result in, engender
formal effect
2 *beget a child*
breed, father, generate, procreate, produce, propagate,
sire, spawn

beggar *n, v*
▶ *n* mendicant, supplicant, pauper, down-and-out,
tramp, vagrant, panhandler
colloq. cadger, scrounger, sponger, freeloader, bum;
US moocher; *slang* bludger, *US* schnorrer
▶ *v* defy, baffle, challenge, exceed, surpass, transcend
Related adjective: mendicant

beggarly *adj*
stingy, abject, meagre, mean, miserly, contemptible,
despicable, inadequate, low, needy, niggardly, paltry,
pathetic, pitiful, wretched
F3 affluent, generous

begin *v*
start, commence, set about, embark on, set in motion,
get going, launch into, do first, activate, actuate, set off,
originate, initiate, introduce, found, institute, open,
instigate, arise, spring, emerge, appear, crop up
colloq. kick off, get cracking, set the ball rolling, take
the plunge
F3 end, stop, finish, cease, conclude

beginner *n*
novice, tiro, starter, learner, trainee, apprentice,
student, probationer, initiate, freshman, fresher,
recruit, raw recruit, cub, tenderfoot, fledgling,
neophyte
old use abecedarian
colloq. greenhorn, rookie
F3 veteran, old hand, expert

beginning *n*
start, commencement, onset, outset, first part,
opening part, opening, preface, prelude, introduction,
initiation, establishment, inauguration, institution,
launch, inception, starting-point, birth, dawn, origin,
source, fountainhead, root, seed, conception, genesis,
emergence, rise, fresh start, new beginnings, pastures
new
formal inchoation, incipience

colloq. the word go, day one, square one, first base, kick-off, intro, new leaf
E3 end, finish, conclusion

begrudge *v*
resent, grudge, mind, object to, envy, covet, be jealous of, stint
E3 allow

beguile *v*
1 CHARM, enchant, bewitch, captivate, delight, attract, amuse, entertain, divert, distract, occupy, engross
2 DECEIVE, fool, hoodwink, dupe, trick, cheat, delude, mislead, seduce, cozen

beguiling *adj*
alluring, appealing, attractive, bewitching, captivating, charming, delightful, diverting, enchanting, entertaining, interesting, intriguing, enticing, seductive
E3 offensive, repulsive

behalf *n*
▷ **on behalf of** for, representing, acting for, for the benefit/good of, for the sake of, in the name/authority of, for the good of, in the interests of, to the advantage/profit of

behave *v*
1 *behave aggressively*
act, conduct yourself, be, acquit yourself, respond, react, perform
formal comport yourself
2 *tell the children to behave themselves*
be good, be well behaved, act properly/politely, be on your best behaviour, mind your manners, stay out of trouble
colloq. act your age, keep your nose clean, not mess about/muck about, stop fooling around, mind your p's and q's, not put a foot wrong
3 *electrons behave like this*
function, operate, work, act, perform, react
E3 2 misbehave, get into trouble; *colloq.* act up, be up to no good

behaviour *n*
1 *the child's behaviour*
conduct, manner, manners, ways, habits, dealings, way of acting, response, reaction, attitudes
formal demeanour, comportment, deportment
2 *the behaviour of chemical elements*
operation, performance, functioning, action, reaction

behead *v*
decapitate, execute, guillotine

behest *n*
▷ **at the behest of** with the authority of, at the bidding of, at the order/command of, at the request of, on the instruction(s) of, on the wishes of

behind *prep, adv, n*
▶ *prep* 1 *a shed behind the garage*
at the back of, at the rear of, on the other side of, *US* in back of
2 *walk behind the others*
after, following, at the back of, at the rear of, close on
3 *behind schedule*
late, later than, running late, overdue, slow, slower than usual
4 *we are behind you in your decision*
supporting, backing, endorsing, for, on the side of
5 *the reasons behind the change in policy*
responsible for, explaining, accounting for, instigating,

causing, initiating, giving rise to, at the bottom of
E3 1 in front of 2 ahead of
▶ *adv* 1 *with a garden behind*
at the back/rear, in the rear
2 *with the stragglers following behind*
after, following, at the back, next, subsequently
3 *be behind with work/payments*
behindhand, late, overdue, in arrears, in debt
▶ *n* bottom, buttocks, backside
colloq. bum, posterior, arse, *US* ass, *US* butt

behindhand *adv*
delayed, late, remiss, slow, tardy, backward
formal dilatory

behold *v, interj*
▶ *v* consider, contemplate, descry, discern, espy, look at, see, watch, note, observe, mark, perceive, regard, scan, gaze at, survey, view, witness
▶ *interj* look, mark, observe, see, watch, *voici*, *voila*, *ecce*, lo

beholden *adj*
indebted, obligated, obliged, under obligation, bound, grateful, owing, thankful

behove *v*
befit, be seemly, be proper, be to your advantage, benefit, profit, be advantageous, be necessary, be essential

beige *adj*
buff, fawn, mushroom, camel, sandy, khaki, coffee, oatmeal, tan, ecru, greige, neutral

being *n*
1 EXISTENCE, actuality, reality, life, animation, essence, substance, nature, soul, spirit
technical haecceity, esse
2 CREATURE, animal, beast, human being, human, man, woman, mortal, person, individual, thing, entity

belabour *v*
hit, attack, beat, flog, thrash, whip, belt, flay

belated *adj*
late, tardy, overdue, delayed, behindhand, unpunctual
E3 punctual, timely

belch *v, n*
▶ *v* 1 *the baby belched*
burp, hiccup, bring up wind
formal eructate
2 *chimneys belching out smoke*
emit, give out, give off, discharge, vent, eject, disgorge, spew
▶ *n* burp, hiccup
formal eructatation

beleaguered *adj*
1 *a beleaguered person*
harassed, pestered, badgered, bothered, worried, vexed, plagued, persecuted, beset
2 *a beleaguered city*
BESIEGED, under siege, surrounded, blockaded

belie *v*
1 *the statistics belie the theory*
disprove, contradict, deny, refute, negate, run counter to
formal gainsay, confute
2 *her looks belie her age*
conceal, disguise, misrepresent, falsify, mislead, deceive

belief *n*
1 OPINION, persuasion, feeling, intuition, impression, notion, theory, view, viewpoint, point of view, conviction, judgement
2 CONFIDENCE, reliance, trust, faith, credit, assurance, certainty, sureness, presumption, expectation
3 IDEOLOGY, faith, creed, doctrine, teaching, dogma, theory, ism, tenet, principle
E3 2 disbelief, doubt

believable *adj*
credible, imaginable, conceivable, acceptable, plausible, possible, likely, probable, authoritative, reliable, trustworthy, (well) within the bounds of possibility, not beyond the realms of possibility, with a ring of truth
E3 unbelievable, incredible, inconceivable, implausible, unconvincing

believe *v*
1 *I believe she's a professor*
think, be of the opinion that, accept, suppose, gather, reckon, assume, consider, hold, maintain, understand, speculate, conjecture, guess, imagine, judge
formal deem, postulate, opine
2 *believe him/that he is telling the truth*
accept, trust, be convinced by, be persuaded by, be certain of, take someone's word for it
colloq. take on board, swallow, fall for, buy, wear, fall for/swallow hook line and sinker
E3 2 disbelieve, doubt, question
▷ **believe in 1** *believe in God* be sure of the existence/reality of, be convinced of **2** *believe in hard work* approve of, favour, be in favour of, recommend, encourage, swear by, trust, be persuaded by, value highly, depend on, rely on, have confidence in, trust, accept the importance of; *formal* set great store by; *colloq.* rate

believer *n*
convert, proselyte, disciple, follower, adherent, devotee, zealot, supporter, upholder
E3 unbeliever, sceptic

belittle *v*
demean, minimize, play down, trivialize, dismiss, underrate, understate, undervalue, underestimate, lessen, diminish, detract from, decry, disparage, run down, deride, scorn, ridicule
formal deprecate
E3 exaggerate, praise

bellicose *adj*
aggressive, militant, argumentative, quarrelsome, contentious, combative, violent, bullying, antagonistic, warring, warlike
formal pugnacious
E3 peaceable

belligerence *n*
aggression, militancy, argumentativeness, provocation, quarrelsomeness, unfriendliness, contentiousness, combativeness, violence, bullying, antagonism, war, war-mongering, sabre-rattling
formal pugnacity
E3 complaisance

belligerent *adj*
aggressive, militant, argumentative, provocative, quarrelsome, contentious, combative, violent, bullying, antagonistic, warring, warlike, war-mongering, sabre-rattling

formal pugnacious, disputatious, truculent
E3 peaceable

bellow *v*
roar, yell, shout, bawl, cry, scream, shriek, howl, clamour, raise your voice
colloq. holler

belly *n*
stomach, abdomen, gut, guts, insides, intestines, paunch, pot-belly, beer belly
technical venter
colloq. tummy, corporation; *slang* bread basket
Related adjective: alvine

belong *v*
1 *this book belongs to me*
be owned by, be the possession of, be the property of, be under the ownership of, be yours
2 *belong to a rugby club*
be a member of, be affiliated to, be connected with, be associated with, be in, be an adherent of
3 *this lid belongs to that pan*
fit, go with, be part of, attach to, link up with, tie up with, be connected with, relate to
4 *Where do these toys belong?*
have as its place/home, go, fit in, be sorted, be categorized, be classified, be included

belonging *n*
rapport, closeness, acceptance, affinity, association, attachment, compatibility, fellow-feeling, fellowship, kinship, link(s), loyalty, relationship
E3 antipathy

belongings *n*
possessions, property, chattels, goods, (personal) effects, paraphernalia
formal appurtenances, accoutrements
colloq. gear, stuff, things

beloved *adj, n*
▶ *adj* loved, much loved, adored, cherished, treasured, prized, precious, pet, favourite, dearest, dear, darling, admired, revered, worshipped
▶ *n* sweetheart, darling, dear, dearest, love, fiancé, fiancée, betrothed, boyfriend, girlfriend, special friend, partner, spouse, husband, wife, favourite, lover, pet, precious, sweet
formal inamorata, inamorato

below *adv, prep*
▶ *adv* **1** *the flat below mine*
beneath, under, underneath, down, lower, lower down
2 *see below for details*
later, at a later place, further on
E3 1, 2 above
▶ *prep* **1** UNDER, underneath, beneath, lower than
2 INFERIOR TO, lower (in rank) than, lesser than, subordinate to, subject to
E3 1, 2 above

belt *n, v*
▶ *n* **1** SASH, girdle, waistband, girth, strap
formal cummerbund, baldric, ceinture, cestus, cincture, cingulum
2 STRIP, area, region, district, zone, swathe, stretch, tract, extent, layer
3 THUMP, hit, punch, strike, swipe, knock, bang, bashing, slap, smack, pelt, bruise, box
colloq. tan, wallop, whack, clout
▶ *v* **1** HIT, strap, flog, lash, whip, flay, cane, birch, punch, strike, swipe, knock, bang, bash, slap, smack, thump, thwack, pelt, bruise, box

colloq. tan, wallop, whack, clout, biff
2 *belt along the road*
dash, tear, fly, rush, career, zip, charge, speed
▷ **belt up** shut up, be quiet; *colloq.* pipe down, cut it
out; *slang* put a sock in it, keep your trap shut, shut
your mouth/face

bemoan *v*
lament, mourn, bewail, deplore, grieve for, regret, rue,
sigh for, sorrow over, weep for
F3 gloat

bemuse *v*
confuse, bewilder, puzzle, perplex, daze, muddle,
befuddle, stupefy
F3 enlighten, illuminate

bemused *adj*
bewildered, confused, puzzled, perplexed,
disconcerted, dazed, overwhelmed, muddled,
befuddled, stupefied, astounded, astonished
F3 clear-headed, clear, lucid

bench *n*
1 SEAT, form, settle, pew, ledge
2 *work at a bench*
counter, table, stall, board, workbench, worktable
3 COURT, courtroom, tribunal, judiciary, judicature,
judge, magistrate

benchmark *n*
criterion, example, level, model, norm, pattern,
reference, reference-point, point of reference,
guideline(s), standard, scale, touchstone, yardstick

bend *v, n*
▶ *v* **1** *bend down to pick up a pin*
stoop, crouch, lean, incline, bow, kneel
2 *bend the wire*
curve, make curved, turn, deflect, twist, contort, flex,
shape, mould, arch, bow, loop, contort, buckle, warp
3 *the road bends*
curve, turn, deflect, veer, diverge, twist, wind,
meander, zigzag, swerve, deviate
formal incurve
4 *bend to their will*
mould, shape, persuade, influence, affect, sway,
compel
F3 **2** straighten
▶ *n* curvature, curve, arc, bow, loop, hook, crook,
elbow, angle, corner, hairpin bend, dog-leg, turn,
twist, kink, zigzag, divergence, deflection
technical flexure
formal incurvation

beneath *adv, prep*
▶ *adv* below, under, underneath, lower, lower down
F3 above
▶ *prep* **1** UNDER, underneath, below, lower than
2 UNWORTHY OF, unbefitting, unbecoming
F3 **1** above

benediction *n*
blessing, prayer, thanksgiving, consecration, favour,
grace, invocation
formal benison
F3 anathema, curse; *formal* execration

benefactor *n*
patron, sponsor, backer, supporter, promoter, donor,
contributor, subscriber, provider, subsidizer,
philanthropist, helper, friend, well-wisher, giver
colloq. angel
F3 opponent, persecutor

beneficent *adj*
altruistic, liberal, benevolent, benign, bountiful,
charitable, compassionate, generous, helpful, kind,
unselfish
formal munificent
F3 mean

beneficial *adj*
advantageous, favourable, useful, helpful, promising,
profitable, serviceable, rewarding, valuable,
improving, edifying, wholesome, salutary
formal propitious
F3 harmful, detrimental, useless

beneficiary *n*
payee, receiver, recipient, inheritor, legatee, heir,
heiress, successor

benefit *n, v*
▶ *n* **1** *the benefits of exercise*
advantage, good, good point, gain, profit, asset,
blessing, boon, interest, favour, bonus, dividend,
fringe benefit, perk
colloq. pay-off
2 *of benefit to children*
good help, aid, assistance, service, use, avail, welfare
3 *child benefit; unemployment benefit*
income, allowance, pension, sick pay, payment, social
security, credit, support, Job Seekers Allowance (JSA),
unemployment benefit, income support
colloq. dole; *US* welfare
F3 **1** disadvantage **2** harm, damage
▶ *v* help, aid, assist, serve, be of service to, avail, be of
advantage to, do good to, profit, improve, enhance,
better, further, advance, promote
F3 hinder, harm, undermine

benevolence *n*
philanthropy, humanitarianism, charitableness,
generosity, liberality, magnanimity, altruism,
humaneness, goodwill, kindness, kind-heartedness,
friendliness, compassion, pity, mercy, grace, tolerance,
care, considerateness
formal munificence
F3 meanness

benevolent *adj*
philanthropic, humanitarian, charitable, generous,
liberal, magnanimous, altruistic, benign, humane,
kind, kind-hearted, soft-hearted, friendly, kindly, well-
disposed, compassionate, merciful, gracious, tolerant,
caring, considerate
formal munificent
F3 mean, selfish, malevolent

benighted *adj*
ignorant, unenlightened, inexperienced, unknowing,
uneducated, unschooled, uncultured, backward,
illiterate, unlettered, unfortunate

benign *adj*
1 BENEVOLENT, charitable, good, gracious, gentle,
kind, obliging, friendly, amiable, affable, genial,
cordial, generous, liberal, sympathetic
2 *benign conditions/climate*
FAVOURABLE, opportune, providential, beneficial,
agreeable, temperate, mild, warm, refreshing, healthy,
restorative, wholesome
formal auspicious, propitious, salubrious
3 *a benign tumour*
curable, harmless, non-malignant, treatable
F3 **1** hostile **2** harmful, unpleasant **3** malignant,
dangerous

bent *adj, n*
▶ *adj* **1** ANGLED, curved, bowed, arched, crooked, folded, doubled, twisted, hunched, stooped, warped, contorted
2 DISHONEST, illegal, criminal, corrupt, fraudulent, untrustworthy
colloq. crooked
F3 1 straight, upright **2** honest, trustworthy
▷ **bent on** determined to, resolved to, set on, fixed on, insistent on, intent on, inclined to, disposed to
▶ *n* tendency, inclination, disposition, leaning, preference, ability, capacity, faculty, aptitude, facility, gift, talent, fondness, knack, flair, forte
formal predisposition, predilecton, penchant, proclivity, propensity
colloq. cup of tea

bequeath *v*
1 *bequeathed in her will*
leave, bestow, will, make over, give, endow, grant, consign, transfer, assign, entrust, commit
2 *social problems bequeathed by past generations*
hand down, pass on, impart, transmit

bequest *n*
legacy, inheritance, heritage, trust, endowment, gift, donation, estate, settlement
formal devisal, bestowal, bequeathal

berate *v*
scold, chide, reprimand, rebuke, tell off, reproach, reprove, censure, chastise, chide, criticize, rail at, revile, upbraid
formal castigate, fulminate, vituperate
colloq. blast, slate, read the riot act to, jump down the throat of, dress down, tear a strip off, give a rocket to, give hell, *US* chew out
F3 praise

bereaved *adj*
deprived, lost, dispossessed, divested, robbed, orphaned, widowed

bereavement *n*
loss, death, passing, passing-away, deprivation, dispossession, sadness, sorrow, grief

bereft *adj*
▷ **bereft of** deprived of, robbed of, stripped of, destitute of, devoid of, lacking, wanting, parted from, cut off from, minus

berserk *adj*
mad, crazy, demented, insane, deranged, frantic, frenzied, crazed, wild, raging, furious, violent, rabid, manic, maniacal, raving, hysterical, uncontrollable
colloq. out of your mind, off your head
F3 sane, calm

berth *n, v*
▶ *n* **1** BED, bunk, hammock, billet
2 MOORING, anchorage, quay, wharf, dock, harbour, port
▶ *v* anchor, dock, drop/cast anchor, land, moor, tie up
F3 weigh anchor, up anchor

beseech *v*
beg, call on, entreat, implore, ask, petition, plead, pray, solicit, appeal to, supplicate, crave, desire
formal adjure, importune, obsecrate, sue, exhort

beset *v*
assail, attack, harass, entangle, worry, pester, plague,

torment, bedevil, hem in, surround
colloq. hassle

besetting *adj*
compulsive, habitual, persistent, dominant, inveterate, irresistible, uncontrollable, obsessive, prevalent, constant, recurring, troublesome, harassing

beside *prep*
next to, by, alongside, abreast of, adjacent, abutting, bordering, neighbouring, next door to, close to, near, overlooking
▷ **beside the point** irrelevant, immaterial, extraneous, inapplicable, incidental, inconsequential, pointless, unimportant, unrelated
▷ **beside yourself** berserk, insane, mad, crazy, crazed, delirious, demented, deranged, frantic, frenetic, frenzied, distraught, unbalanced, unhinged

besides *adv, prep*
▶ *adv* also, as well, too, in addition, additionally, further, furthermore, moreover
colloq. what's more
▶ *prep* apart from, other than, aside from, in addition to, over and above, as well as, excluding

besiege *v*
1 LAY SIEGE TO, blockade, surround, encircle, encompass, confine, beleaguer
2 *besieged by reporters*
surround, encircle, encompass, confine, shut in, hem in
3 TROUBLE, worry, bother, importune, assail, beset, beleaguer, harass, pester, badger, nag, hound, plague

besmirch *v*
defame, defile, dishonour, slander, smear, soil, dirty, blacken, damage, stain, sully, tarnish
F3 enhance

besotted *adj*
infatuated, doting, obsessed, smitten, hypnotized, spellbound, stupefied, bewitched, intoxicated
F3 indifferent, disenchanted

bespeak *v*
demonstrate, indicate, reveal, show, signify, denote, display, exhibit, evidence, evince, attest, proclaim, suggest, imply

best *adj, adv, n, v*
▶ *adj* optimum, optimal, first, foremost, leading, top, ultimate, prime, record-breaking, unequalled, unsurpassed, unrivalled, unbeatable, matchless, peerless, incomparable, supreme, pre-eminent, of highest quality, greatest, highest, largest, finest, worthiest, excellent, outstanding, superlative, first-rate, first-class, ideal, perfect
formal nonpareil
colloq. ace, star, number one, (the) tops, second to none, the pick of the bunch, one in a million, a cut above the rest
F3 worst
▶ *adv* greatly, extremely, exceptionally, excellently, outstandingly, superlatively, unsurpassedly, matchlessly, incomparably, supremely, most, to the greatest/highest degree
F3 worst, least
▶ *n* **1** *students who are the best in their year*
finest, cream, prime, elite, top, first, pick, choice, favourite, star, highlight
colloq. the pick of the bunch
2 *do your best*
hardest, utmost, greatest effort

colloq. damnedest

▪ **1** worst

▶ *v* defeat, trounce, worst, conquer, overcome, overwhelm, overpower, subdue, rout, annihilate, outplay, outwit, outsmart, be more than a match for, have the edge on

formal vanquish

colloq. hammer, slaughter, clobber, lick, thrash

bestial *adj*
cruel, savage, brutal, animal, barbaric, barbarous, beastly, inhuman, brutish, carnal, depraved, degraded, gross, sensual, sordid, vile
formal feral
▪ civilized, humane

bestir *v*
arouse, exert, awaken, stimulate, energize, galvanize, incite, motivate, activate, actuate, animate
▪ calm, lull, quell

bestow *v*
award, present, grant, confer, endow, bequeath, commit, entrust, impart, transmit, allot, apportion, accord, give, donate, lavish
▪ withhold, deprive

bestride *v*
dominate, command, overshadow, bestraddle, sit astride, stand astride, straddle

bet *v, n*
▶ *v* **1** *bet money on a horse*
wager, gamble, punt, speculate, risk, hazard, chance, venture, lay, stake, bid, pledge, back, put, place
colloq. play for money, have a flutter
2 *I bet she did it on purpose*
be certain, be sure, be convinced, expect, not be surprised
▶ *n* **1** *place a bet*
wager, gamble, speculation, risk, venture, stake, ante, bid, pledge, lottery, sweepstake, accumulator
colloq. flutter
2 *my bet is that he'll stay*
opinion, feeling, intuition, impression, notion, theory, view, viewpoint, point of view, conviction, judgement
3 *your best bet*
choice, option, course of action, alternative

bête noire *n*
bugbear, bane, abomination, anathema, aversion, curse, pet hate, pet aversion
▪ favourite

betide *v*
befall, chance, develop, ensue, happen, occur, overtake
formal supervene

betoken *v*
signal, indicate, signify, suggest, augur, bespeak, bode, forebode, portend, presage, declare, denote, evidence, represent, manifest, mark, prognosticate, promise

betray *v*
1 *betray a friend*
inform on, double-cross, desert, abandon, forsake, turn traitor, be disloyal to, be unfaithful to, break faith with, deceive, delude, mislead, dupe
colloq. tell on, sell (out), sell down the river, stab in the back, squeal on, blow the whistle on, shop, walk out on; *slang* grass
2 DISCLOSE, give away, tell, divulge, expose, reveal, show, manifest, let slip, bring to light, unmask
▪ **1** defend, protect, be loyal to **2** conceal, hide

betrayal *n*
treachery, treason, sell-out, disloyalty, unfaithfulness, double-dealing, double-crossing, duplicity, deception, trickery, duping, falseness, breaking faith
formal perfidy
▪ loyalty, faithfulness, protection

betrayer *n*
traitor, Judas, informer, double-crosser, deceiver, conspirator, renegade, apostate
colloq. whistle-blower; *slang* grass, supergrass
▪ protector, supporter

betrothal *n*
engagement, proposal of marriage, promise, vow(s), plighting of your troth, troth
formal espousal, fiançailles

betrothed *adj*
engaged, engaged to be married, contracted, promised
formal affianced, espoused

better *adj, v*
▶ *adj* **1** SUPERIOR, bigger, larger, longer, greater, worthier, of higher quality, finer, surpassing, preferable, more acceptable, more fitting, more advantageous, more valuable
colloq. a cut above
2 IMPROVING, progressing, on the mend, recovering, fitter, healthier, stronger, (fully) recovered, restored, cured, healed, well
colloq. on the mend
▪ **1** inferior **2** worse
▶ *v* **1** IMPROVE, enhance, raise, make better, further, promote, forward, reform, mend, correct, rectify, enrich
formal ameliorate
2 SURPASS, top, beat, outdo, exceed, improve on, outstrip, overtake, cap, go one better than
▪ **1** worsen, deteriorate

betterment *n*
improvement, furtherance, advancement, edification, enhancement, enrichment
formal amelioration, melioration
▪ deterioration, impairment

between *prep*
in the middle (of), among, halfway, mid, amid, amidst, amongst

bevel *n, v*
▶ *n* oblique, slant, slope, tilt, angle, bias, diagonal, mitre, basil, bezel, cant, chamfer
▶ *v* slant, slope, tilt, angle, mitre, bias, cant, chamfer

beverage *n*
drink, draught, liquor, liquid, refreshment
formal potation, potable

bevy *n*
gathering, group, band, company, assembly, collection, troupe, flock, gaggle, pack, bunch, crowd, throng

bewail *v*
grieve over, sorrow over, lament, bemoan, cry over, moan, mourn, regret, repent, rue, sigh over, deplore, keen
▪ gloat, glory, vaunt

beware *v*
watch out, look out, mind (out), be careful, be cautious, be wary, take heed, steer clear of, avoid, shun, guard against, be on your guard, be on the lookout for

bewilder *v*
confuse, muddle, mix up, disconcert, confound, baffle, puzzle, perplex, mystify, daze, stupefy, bemuse, disorient
colloq. bamboozle, stump

bewildered *adj*
confused, muddled, uncertain, disoriented, nonplussed, baffled, puzzled, perplexed, mystified, taken aback, bemused, surprised, speechless, stunned
colloq. bamboozled, (all) at sea
F3 unperturbed, collected

bewilderment *n*
perplexity, confusion, uncertainty, daze, disconcertion, disorientation, mystification, puzzlement, stupefaction, surprise, awe
F3 composure, confidence

bewitch *v*
charm, enchant, allure, beguile, spellbind, possess, enthral, captivate, enrapture, delight, obsess, fascinate, intrigue, tantalize, seduce, entrance, mesmerize, hypnotize, transfix
F3 disenchant, repel

beyond *prep*
1 *the fields beyond the house*
on the far side of, on the other side of, further than, away from, remote from, apart from
2 *beyond the age of 16*
after, past, later than, above, over, greater than, upwards of
3 *beyond me/my understanding*
out of reach of, out of range of, further than the limitations of

bias *n, v*
▶ *n* **1** *racial bias*
PREJUDICE, partiality, favouritism, one-sidedness, unfairness, bigotry, intolerance, stereotyping, distortion, bent, leaning, inclination, tendency
formal propensity, proclivity, predilection
2 *cut on the bias*
diagonal, angle, slant, oblique, cross
F3 1 impartiality, fairness
▶ *v* prejudice, influence, sway, predispose, distort, jaundice, twist, angle, load, slant, warp, weight
old use earwig
colloq. load the dice

biased *adj*
prejudiced, one-sided, unfair, bigoted, blinkered, jaundiced, influenced, swayed, partial, predisposed, tendentious, subjective, partisan, slanted, angled, distorted, warped, twisted, loaded, weighted
F3 impartial, fair, objective

Bible *n*
1 *study the Christian Bible*
Scriptures, holy Scriptures, Holy Bible, holy writ, Old Testament, New Testament, Apocrypha, writings, canon, revelation, Pentateuch, law, prophets, Gospels, epistles, letters
colloq. good book

The books of the Bible are: the Old Testament: Genesis, Exodus, Leviticus, Numbers, Deuteronomy, Joshua, Judges, Ruth, 1 Samuel, 2 Samuel, 1 Kings, 2 Kings, 1 Chronicles, 2 Chronicles, Ezra, Nehemiah, Esther, Job, Psalms, Proverbs, Ecclesiastes, Song of Solomon (Song of Songs), Isaiah, Jeremiah, Lamentations, Ezekiel, Daniel, Hosea, Joel, Amos, Obadiah, Jonah, Micah,

Nahum, Habakkuk, Zephaniah, Haggai, Zechariah, Malachi; *the New Testament:* Matthew, Mark, Luke, John, Acts of the Apostles, Romans, 1 Corinthians, 2 Corinthians, Galatians, Ephesians, Philippians, Colossians, 1 Thessalonians, 2 Thessalonians, 1 Timothy, 2 Timothy, Titus, Philemon, Hebrews, James, 1 Peter, 2 Peter, 1 John, 2 John, 3 John, Jude, Revelation; *the Apocrypha:* 1 Esdras, 2 Esdras, Tobit, Judith, Additions to Esther, Wisdom of Solomon, Ecclesiasticus, Baruch, Letter of Jeremiah, Prayer of Azariah, Song of the Three Young Men, History of Susanna, Bel and the Dragon, Prayer of Manasseh, 1 Maccabees, 2 Maccabees.

2 *the gardener's bible; the cyclist's bible*
manual, handbook, authority, reference book, encyclopedia, dictionary, lexicon, guidebook, directory, companion, textbook, primer

bibliography *n*
book list, list of books, record, catalogue

bicker *v*
squabble, row, quarrel, wrangle, argue, spar, fight, clash, disagree, dispute, fall out
formal altercate
colloq. scrap
F3 agree, make up

bicycle *n*
cycle, two-wheeler, racer, mountain bike, all-terrain bike, tandem, unicycle
colloq. bike, push-bike

bid *v, n*
▶ *v* **1** *bid for a painting*
offer, proffer, tender, submit, put forward, advance, propose
2 ASK, request, desire, instruct, direct, command, order, require, charge, call (for), demand, tell, summon, invite, solicit
formal enjoin
3 *bid them farewell*
wish, greet, say, call, tell, wave
▶ *n* **1** OFFER, tender, sum, amount, price, advance, submission, proposal
2 ATTEMPT, effort, try, endeavour, venture
colloq. go

bidding *n*
request, desire, instruction, direction, command, order, charge, call, demand, summons, requirement, invitation, injunction
formal behest

big *adj*
1 *a big house*
large, great, sizable, considerable, substantial, huge, enormous, immense, vast, massive, colossal, gigantic, giant, mammoth, extensive, spacious, cavernous, extra large
formal voluminous
colloq. whopping, jumbo, bumper, ginormous, humungous; *slang* mega
2 *a big person*
large, burly, tall, huge, enormous, bulky, hulking, massive, beefy, brawny, muscular, fat, stout, obese
formal corpulent
colloq. hefty
3 *love your big brother*
older, elder, grown-up, adult
4 *a big decision*
important, significant, momentous, major, serious, weighty, salient, critical, radical, fundamental

5 *a big name in the fashion world*
important, significant, well-known, famous, leading, main, principal, eminent, distinguished, prominent, influential, outstanding, noteworthy, valued
6 *that's big of you*
generous, magnanimous, gracious, kind-hearted, benevolent, unselfish
E3 1, 2 small, little **3** younger **4** insignificant **5** insignificant, unknown **6** mean, miserly, selfish

bigot *n*
sectarian, dogmatist, fanatic, zealot, chauvinist, racist, sexist, male chauvinist pig (MCP)
E3 liberal, humanitarian

bigoted *adj*
prejudiced, biased, intolerant, fanatical, illiberal, narrow-minded, narrow, blinkered, closed, dogmatic, opinionated, obstinate, jaundiced, influenced, swayed, partial, warped, twisted
E3 tolerant, liberal, broad-minded, enlightened

bigotry *n*
prejudice, discrimination, bias, injustice, unfairness, intolerance, partiality, narrow-mindedness, dogmatism, fanaticism, chauvinism, jingoism, sectarianism, racism, racialism, sexism
E3 tolerance

bigwig *n*
celebrity, dignitary, personage, somebody, VIP, notable, mogul, panjandrum
colloq. big gun, big noise, big shot, big cheese, heavyweight, nob
E3 nobody, nonentity

bile *n*
anger, bitterness, bad temper, short temper, ill-humour, irascibility, irritability, testiness, peevishness, rancour, choler, gall, spleen

bilge *n*
rubbish, nonsense, drivel, gibberish, trash, tripe, twaddle
colloq. claptrap, piffle, codswallop, poppycock, hot air, cobblers, rot, tommyrot

bilious *adj*
1 IRRITABLE, bad-tempered, short-tempered, ill-tempered, ill-humoured, choleric, cross, grumpy, crotchety, testy, grouchy, edgy, crabby, peevish
2 SICK, queasy, nauseated, sickly
colloq. out of sorts
3 *bilious colours*
sickly, disgusting, nauseating, garish

bilk *v*
cheat, deceive, defraud, trick, swindle
colloq. con, do, do out of, diddle, bamboozle;
slang fleece, sting

bill¹ *n, v*
▶ *n* **1** INVOICE, statement, account, charges, reckoning, tally, score, *US* check
US colloq. tab
2 CIRCULAR, leaflet, handout, bulletin, handbill, broadsheet, advertisement, notice, announcement, poster, flyer, placard, playbill, programme
colloq. advert, ad
3 *parliamentary bill*
proposal, measure, (piece of) legislation, statute, act
▶ *v* **1** *bill you at the end of the month*
invoice, charge, debit, list costs, send a statement, send an account/invoice

2 *be billed to appear in a show*
advertise, announce, give notice, post

bill² *n*
a bird's bill
beak, mandible, neb, nib, rostrum

billet *n, v*
▶ *n* **1** ACCOMMODATION, quarters, living quarters, barracks, lodging, housing, berth
2 EMPLOYMENT, post, job, post, position, situation, office, occupation
▶ *v* accommodate, lodge, quarter, station

billow *v, n*
▶ *v* swell, expand, bulge, puff out, fill out, balloon, rise, heave, surge, roll, undulate
▶ *n* cloud, mass, surge, rush, wave, flood, breaker

billowy *adj*
billowing, swelling, surging, heaving, rippling, rolling, tossing, swirling, undulating, waving

bin *n*
container, receptacle, box, basket, chest

bind *v, n*
▶ *v* **1** FASTEN, tie, attach, fasten, secure, clamp, stick, lash, truss, rope, strap, fetter, tether, shackle, chain, bandage, cover, dress, wrap, tape
2 OBLIGE, force, compel, constrain, impel, require, necessitate, restrict, confine, restrain, hamper, yoke
3 *bound together by a common grief*
UNITE, join, tie, unify, bond, stand together, pull together, close ranks
▶ *n* bore, difficulty, inconvenience, irritation, dilemma, embarrassment, hole, impasse, nuisance, predicament, quandary
colloq. drag, spot, tight spot

binding *adj, n*
▶ *adj* obligatory, compulsory, mandatory, necessary, requisite, permanent, conclusive, irrevocable, unalterable, indissoluble, unbreakable, strict, stringent, rigorous, tight, valid
▶ *n* cover, covering, wrapping, border, edging, trimming, tape, bandage

binge *n*
spree, bout, fling, orgy, jag, guzzle
colloq. do, beano, bender, blind
E3 fast

biography *n*
life story, life, history, autobiography, memoirs, journals, diaries, letters, recollections, profile, curriculum vitae, cv, account, record, biopic
formal prosopography

biology *n*

Biological terms include: bacteriology, biochemistry, biology, bionics, botany, cybernetics, cytology, Darwinism, neo-Darwinism, ecology, embryology, endocrinology, evolution, Haeckel's law, genetics, Mendelism, Lamarckism, marine biology, natural history, palaeontology, pathology, physiology, systematics, taxonomy, zoology; amino acid, anatomy, animal behaviour, animal kingdom, bacillus, bacteria, biologist, botanist, cell, chromosome, class, coccus, conservation, corpuscle, cultivar, cytoplasm, deoxyribonucleic acid (DNA), diffusion, ecosystem, ectoplasm, embryo, endoplasmic reticulum (ER), enzyme, evolution, excretion, extinction, flora and fauna, food chain, fossil, gene, genetic engineering, genetic fingerprinting, population genetics, germ, Golgi apparatus, hereditary factor, homeostasis, living world, meiosis, membrane, metabolism, micro-organism, microbe, mitosis, molecule, mutation, natural selection, nuclear membrane, nucleus, nutrition, order, organism, osmosis, parasitism, photosynthesis, pollution, protein, protoplasm, reproduction, respiration, reticulum, ribonucleic acid (RNA), ribosome, secretion, survival of the fittest, symbiosis, virus.

bird *n*
Related adjectives: avian, avine, volucrine, ornithoid

Birds include: sparrow, thrush, starling, blackbird, bluetit, chaffinch, greenfinch, bullfinch, dunnock, robin, wagtail, swallow, tit, wren, martin, swift, crow, magpie, dove, pigeon, skylark, nightingale, linnet, warbler, jay, jackdaw, rook, raven, cuckoo, woodpecker, yellowhammer; duck, mallard, eider, teal, swan, goose, heron, stork, flamingo, pelican, kingfisher, moorhen, coot, lapwing, peewit, plover, curlew, snipe, avocet, seagull, guillemot, tern, petrel, crane, bittern, petrel, albatross, gannet, cormorant, auk, puffin, dipper; eagle, owl, hawk, sparrowhawk, falcon, kestrel, osprey, buzzard, vulture, condor; emu, ostrich, kiwi, peacock, penguin; chicken, grouse, partridge, pheasant, quail, turkey; canary, budgerigar, *colloq.* budgie, cockatiel, cockatoo, lovebird, parakeet, parrot, macaw, toucan, myna bird, mockingbird, kookaburra, bird of paradise.

birth *n*
1 CHILDBIRTH, labour, confinement, delivery, arrival, nativity
formal parturition
colloq. patter of tiny feet
Related adjective: natal
2 *of noble birth*
ancestry, family, parentage, origin(s), descent, line, lineage, genealogy, derivation, pedigree, blood, stock, race, strain, house, extraction, background, breeding
3 BEGINNING, rise, emergence, arrival, appearance, origin(s), start, starting-point, commencement, source, dawn, derivation, fountainhead, root, seed, genesis
formal advent
E3 1 death **3** end, finish, conclusion

birthday *n*
anniversary, day of birth
Related adjectives: natalitial, genethliac

birthmark *n*
blemish, discoloration, mole, patch, naevus
Related adjective: naevoid

birthplace *n*
place of origin, place of birth, native town, native country, fatherland, mother country, home, home town, root(s), provenance, source, fount, cradle

birthright *n*
privilege, prerogative, due, inheritance, legacy

biscuit *n*
cake, cookie, cracker, rusk, wafer, hardtack

bisect *v*
halve, cut in half, divide, divide into two, separate, split, intersect, cross, fork
formal bifurcate

bisexual *adj*
androgynous, hermaphrodite
technical gynandromorphic, gynandromorphous,

monoclinous, epicene
colloq. AC/DC, ambidextrous, bi, swinging both ways
E3 heterosexual, homosexual

bishop *n*
prelate, archbishop, primate, diocesan, metropolitan, patriarch, suffragan
Related adjective: episcopal

bit *n*
fragment, part, segment, portion, piece, small piece, slice, crumb, grain, morsel, mouthful, drop, dash, chunk, lump, scrap, particle, atom, mite, whit, jot, iota, tittle, shred, grain, flake, chip, sliver, speck, touch, hint, trace, scintilla, soupçon, vestige
▷ **a bit 1** *a bit boring* slightly, rather, a little, not much, not very **2** *wait a bit* a while, a moment, a short time, minute, few minutes, moment, few moments; *colloq.* jiffy, tick
▷ **bit by bit** gradually, little by little, in stages, step by step, slowly, piecemeal
E3 all at once, wholesale

bitch *n, v*
▶ *n* **1** *a bitch and her puppies*
female dog
2 *that woman's a bitch*
vixen, shrew, harpy, virago
slang cow; *colloq.* cat
▶ *v* complain, moan, grumble, criticize, find fault with, talk about behind their back
colloq. gripe, whinge, whine, slag off, bad-mouth

bitchy *adj*
catty, snide, nasty, mean, spiteful, malicious, vindictive, cutting, backbiting, venomous, shrewish, vixenish, cruel, vicious
formal rancorous
E3 kind, loving

bite *v, n*
▶ *v* **1** CHEW, eat, munch, gnaw, nibble, peck, champ, crunch, crush
formal masticate
2 *the dog bit her hand*
nip, snap, pierce, wound, tear, rend, sink/get your teeth into
3 SMART, sting, tingle
4 *the rise in costs was beginning to bite*
GRIP, take effect, work, grip, hold, seize, pinch
▶ *n* **1** NIP, snap, wound, sting, smarting, pinch, prick, puncture, lesion
Related adjective: morsal
2 *have a bite to eat*
snack, light meal, refreshment, mouthful, morsel, taste, piece, bit
3 PUNGENCY, piquancy, spiciness
colloq. kick, punch

biting *adj*
1 COLD, freezing, sharp, bitter, harsh, severe, penetrating, piercing, nipping, stinging
2 CUTTING, incisive, bitter, piercing, penetrating, raw, stinging, sharp, tart, caustic, scathing, cynical, hurtful
formal trenchant, mordant
E3 1 mild **2** bland

bitter *adj*
1 ACID, tart, sharp, sour, vinegary, unsweetened, pungent, tangy
formal acrid, astringent, acerbic
2 RESENTFUL, embittered, begrudging, indignant, aggrieved, angry, sour, morose, jaundiced, cynical,

sullen, hostile, spiteful, vindictive, venomous, scathing, caustic
formal acrimonious, acerbic, rancorous, malevolent, vitriolic, vituperative, virulent
colloq. with a chip on your shoulder
3 INTENSE, severe, harsh, fierce, cruel, savage, merciless, painful, sad, unhappy, disappointing, tragic, distressing, harrowing, heartbreaking, heart-rending
4 *bitter winds*
stinging, biting, sharp, freezing, freezing cold, arctic, raw, harsh, piercing, penetrating
E3 1 sweet **2** contented **3** mild, happy **4** warm

bitterness *n*
1 ACIDITY, tartness, sharpness, sourness, vinegar, pungency, tanginess
2 RESENTMENT, embitterment, grudge, indignation, anger, sourness, moroseness, jaundice, cynicism, sullenness, hostility, spite, vindictiveness, venom
formal acrimony, acerbity, rancour, malevolence, virulence
3 INTENSITY, severity, harshness, ferocity, cruelty, pain, painfulness, sadness, unhappiness, disappointment, tragedy, distress, heartbreaking, heart-rending
4 *the bitterness of the winter*
sharpness, coldness, rawness, harshness, penetration, bite

bizarre *adj*
strange, odd, queer, curious, weird, peculiar, eccentric, outlandish, ludicrous, ridiculous, fantastic, comical, extravagant, grotesque, freakish, abnormal, deviant, unusual, uncommon, unconventional, extraordinary
colloq. offbeat, oddball, wacky; *slang* way-out
E3 normal, ordinary, standard

blab *v*
blurt out, tell, reveal, disclose, divulge, let slip, gossip, tattle
colloq. squeal, leak
E3 hide, hush up

black *adj, v, n*
▶ *adj* **1** JET-BLACK, coal-black, pitch-black, jet, ebony, raven, sable, inky, sooty, dusky, swarthy
formal nigrescent
colloq. black as coal
2 *black athletes*
dark-skinned, coloured, Negro, Negroid, swarthy
technical melanistic
3 DARK, unlit, unilluminated., moonless, starless, overcast, dingy, dusky, dim, gloomy, overcast, sombre, funereal, pitch-black
formal crepuscular, tenebrous, fuliginous, subfusc, Cimmerian, Stygian
4 FILTHY, dirty, soiled, stained, grimy, sooty, grubby, muddy, unclean
5 *the future looks black*
bleak, gloomy, sad, depressing, distressing, melancholy, dismal, hopeless, sombre, mournful, funereal, awful
6 *in a black mood*
miserable, depressed, resentful, bitter, sullen, angry, threatening, menacing
formal lugubrious
E3 1 white **2** white **3** bright **4** clean **5** bright
▶ *v* **1** *black someone's eye*
bruise, blacken, punch, hit, injure
2 *they blacked the imported goods*

boycott, embargo, blacklist, ban, bar, taboo
▷ **black out 1** FAINT, pass out, lose consciousness, collapse; *colloq.* flake out **2** DARKEN, eclipse, cover up **3** CENSOR, conceal, suppress, withhold, censor, gag
▶ *n* ▷ **in the black** in credit, without debt, solvent; *colloq.* with your head above water

blackball *v*
vote against, ban, bar, blacklist, ostracize, shut out, drum out, throw out, exclude, expel, oust, reject, repudiate, snub, veto
colloq. give the cold shoulder to

blacken *v*
1 DARKEN, dirty, make dirty, soil, smudge, cloud
2 DEFAME, malign, slander, libel, revile, detract, smear, besmirch, sully, stain, tarnish, taint, defile, discredit, dishonour
formal impugn, calumniate, vilify, decry
colloq. run down
E3 2 praise, enhance

blackguard *n*
scoundrel, rascal, rogue, villain, devil, knave, miscreant, reprobate, wretch
colloq. bleeder, blighter, bounder, rotter, stinker, swine, scumbag

blacklist *v*
debar, disallow, exclude, ban, outlaw, bar, boycott, expel, ostracize, reject, shut out, repudiate, snub, taboo, veto
formal preclude, proscribe
E3 accept, allow

blackmail *n, v*
▶ *n* extortion, intimidation, exaction, bribery, ransom
formal chantage
colloq. hush money
▶ *v* extort, exact, hold to ransom, threaten, force, compel, coerce, demand
colloq. bleed, milk, squeeze, lean on

blackmailer *n*
bloodsucker, extortioner, extortionist, vampire

blackout *n*
1 POWER FAILURE, power cut, electricity failure
2 FAINT, coma, unconsciousness, loss of consciousness, swoon, oblivion
technical syncope
colloq. flaking-out
3 *a news blackout*
suppression, embargo, censorship, withholding, concealment, secrecy
colloq. cover-up

blade *n*
edge, cutting edge, knife, dagger, sword, scalpel, razor, vane

blame *v, n*
▶ *v* hold responsible, say something is someone's fault, accuse, charge, tax, reprimand, chide, reprove, upbraid, reprehend, admonish, rebuke, reproach, censure, attribute liability, criticize, find fault with, find guilty, disapprove, condemn, scapegoat
formal berate
colloq. tear into, point the finger at
E3 exonerate, vindicate
▶ *n* censure, criticism, reprimand, reproof, reproach, recrimination, condemnation, accusation, charge, incrimination, guilt, fault, responsibility,

accountability, liability, onus
formal culpability, berating
slang stick, rap

blameless *adj*
innocent, guiltless, clear, faultless, without fault,
perfect, unblemished, stainless, virtuous, sinless,
upright, above reproach, irreproachable, unblamable,
unimpeachable
E3 guilty, blameworthy

blameworthy *adj*
at fault, guilty, discreditable, disreputable, shameful,
unworthy, indefensible, inexcusable, reprehensible,
reproachable
formal culpable, flagitious
E3 blameless

blanch *v*
1 *blanch at the sight*
grow/become/turn pale, go/become/turn white,
whiten, grow/become pallid
2 *blanch vegetables*
boil, scald
E3 1 colour, blush, redden

bland *adv*
1 *a bland person/statement*
boring, monotonous, humdrum, tedious, dull,
uninspiring, uninteresting, unexciting, nondescript,
characterless, ordinary, mundane, inoffensive, flat,
weak
2 TASTELESS, insipid, flavourless, weak, mild
E3 1 exciting, lively, stimulating **2** tasty, piquant,
rich

blandishments *n*
flattery, compliments, enticements, fawning,
inducements, ingratiation, blarney, cajolery, coaxing,
persuasiveness, sycophancy, wheedling
formal inveiglement
colloq. soft soap, sweet talk

blank *adj, n*
▶ *adj* **1** *a blank page*
empty, unfilled, void, clear, bare, unmarked,
unwritten, plain, clean, white
2 EXPRESSIONLESS, deadpan, poker-faced,
impassive, emotionless, without feeling, lifeless,
apathetic, uninterested, indifferent, glazed, empty,
vacant, vacuous, inscrutable, uncomprehending
▶ *n* space, gap, break, void, emptiness, empty space,
vacancy, vacuity, nothingness, vacuum

blanket *n, v, adj*
▶ *n* **1** *blankets on a bed*
cover, covering, bedcover, coverlet, bedspread
2 *a blanket of snow*
covering, coating, coat, layer, film, carpet, cloak,
mantle, cover, sheet, film, envelope, overlay, wrapper,
wrapping
▶ *v* cover, coat, overlay, eclipse, hide, conceal, mask,
cloak, surround, muffle, deaden, obscure, suppress,
cloud
▶ *adj* across-the-board, all-embracing, all-inclusive,
comprehensive, inclusive, overall, global, total,
sweeping, wide-ranging

blare *v*
trumpet, clamour, roar, blast (out), boom (out),
resound, sound loudly, thunder, ring, peal, clang, hoot,
toot, honk

blarney *n*
blandishments, cajolery, coaxing, flattery,

persuasiveness, wheedling
colloq. soft soap, spiel, sweet talk

blasé *adj*
nonchalant, offhand, unimpressed, unmoved,
unexcited, jaded, weary, bored, uninterested,
uninspired, apathetic, indifferent, cool, lukewarm,
unconcerned
formal phlegmatic
E3 excited, enthusiastic, responsive

blaspheme *v*
swear, curse, profane, utter profanities, utter oaths,
desecrate, damn, revile, abuse
formal execrate, imprecate, anathematize
colloq. cuss

blasphemous *adj*
profane, impious, sacrilegious, godless, ungodly,
irreligious, irreverent
formal imprecatory

blasphemy *n*
profanity, profaneness, curse, expletive, cursing,
swearing, oaths, impiety, impiousness, ungodliness,
irreverence, unholiness, sacrilege, desecration,
violation, outrage
formal execration, imprecation

blast *n, v*
▶ *n* **1** EXPLOSION, detonation, bang, crash, clap,
crack, volley, burst, outburst, discharge
2 *a blast of cold air*
draught, gust, rush, gale, squall, storm, tempest
3 SOUND, blow, blare, blaring, roar, roaring, boom,
booming, thunder, clamour, bellow, peal, hoot, toot,
honk, wail, scream, shriek, clang
▶ *v* **1** EXPLODE, blow up, blow to pieces, burst,
shatter, destroy, demolish, ruin, assail, attack
2 SOUND, blare (out), boom(out), roar, thunder, peal,
bellow, hoot, toot, honk, wail, scream, shriek, clang
3 CRITICIZE, reprimand, rebuke, tell off, reprove,
upbraid
formal berate
▷ **blast off** take off, lift off, be launched

blatant *adj*
flagrant, brazen, barefaced, arrant, open, overt,
undisguised, ostentatious, glaring, conspicuous,
manifest, patent, obtrusive, prominent, pronounced,
obvious, sheer, outright, unmitigated, out and out

⚠ **blatant** or **flagrant** ?
Blatant means 'glaringly or shamelessly obvious': *a
blatant lie/liar. Flagrant* implies a greater degree of
condemnation and means 'scandalous, very obvious
and wicked': *a flagrant misuse of his powers.*

---

blaze *n, v*
▶ *n* **1** FIRE, flames, inferno, bonfire, flare-up,
explosion, blast
formal conflagration
2 *a blaze of colour*
radiance, brilliance, beam, glare, flash, gleam, glitter,
glow, light, burst, outburst
▶ *v* **1** *the fire was blazing*
burn, flame, flare (up), ignite, catch fire, burst into
flames
2 *blazing with light*
shine, beam, glare, flash, flare, gleam, glitter, glow,
light, burst, be radiant, be brilliant
3 *eyes blazing with anger*
blow up, explode, erupt, burst, burn, fire, flash, rage,

boil, seethe
colloq. see red

blazon *v*
proclaim, publicize, announce, make known, broadcast, celebrate, flourish, trumpet, flaunt, vaunt
E∃ deprecate, hush up

bleach *v*
whiten, make white, blanch, decolour, decolorize, fade, pale, make pale, lighten
technical etiolate, peroxide

bleak *adj*
1 GLOOMY, sombre, leaden, grim, dreary, dismal, dark, drab, depressing, miserable, wretched, desperate, grim, joyless, cheerless, comfortless, hopeless, discouraging, disheartening, unpromising
2 *a bleak landscape*
unsheltered, windy, windswept, exposed, open, barren, bare, empty, desolate, chilly, cold
3 COLD, chilly, raw, weather-beaten, dreary, dull
E∃ **1** bright, cheerful **3** bright, fine, pleasant

bleary *adj*
bleary-eyed, blurred, blurry, cloudy, dim, tired, watery, rheumy

bleat *v*
1 *sheep bleating*
baa, bray, cry, call, *US* blat
2 *bleating about price increases*
complain, grumble, moan
colloq. whine, whinge

bleed *v*
1 HAEMORRHAGE, lose blood, shed blood, gush, spurt, flow, run, exude, weep, ooze, seep, trickle
technical exsanguinate, phlebotomize, extravasate
2 DRAIN, suck dry, exhaust, squeeze, milk, sap, reduce
formal deplete
3 *bleed money*
extort, extract
colloq. milk, squeeze

blemish *n, v*
▶ *n* **1** *a blemish on her skin*
deformity, disfigurement, mark, speck, smudge, blotch, blot, stain, discoloration

Kinds of blemish include: acne, birthmark, blackhead, blister, boil, bump, bunion, callus, carbuncle, chilblain, corn, freckle, mole, naevus, pimple, pockmark, pustule, scab, scar, spot, strawberry mark, verruca, wart, whitehead, *slang* zit.

2 *a blemish on his character*
flaw, imperfection, defect, fault, stain, taint, disgrace, dishonour
▶ *v* tarnish, flaw, deface, disfigure, spoil, mar, damage, impair, spot, mark, blot, stain, sully, taint, compromise

blench *v*
falter, hesitate, recoil, flinch, shrink, shudder, cower, shy, start, wince, quail, quake, quiver

blend *v, n*
▶ *v* **1** MERGE, combine, mix, mingle, amalgamate, coalesce, compound, synthesize, fuse, unite, homogenize, alloy, interweave, intertwine, stir, beat, whisk
formal intermix, admix, commix, commingle
2 HARMONIZE, complement, fit, match, go (well)

with, go together, suit, set off
E∃ **1** separate, divide
▶ *n* compound, composite, alloy, amalgam, amalgamation, merging, synthesis, fusion, combination, union, uniting, mix, mixture, cross between two things, concoction
formal admixture, commixture

bless *v*
1 ANOINT, sanctify, consecrate, hallow, dedicate, ordain
2 PRAISE, extol, magnify, glorify, exalt, thank
formal laud
3 *the priest blessed the congregation*
ask God's favour for, as God's protection for
E∃ **1** curse **2** condemn

blessed *adj*
1 HOLY, sacred, hallowed, sanctified, revered, adored, divine
2 HAPPY, contented, glad, joyful, joyous, lucky, fortunate, prosperous
3 *blessed with a good memory*
favoured, endowed, graced, provided
E∃ **1** cursed **2** unhappy, sad

blessing *n*
1 CONSECRATION, dedication, benediction, grace, thanksgiving, commendation
technical darshan, kiddush
formal invocation, benison
2 BENEFIT, advantage, favour, godsend, windfall, gift, gain, profit, help, service, bounty, good thing, good fortune
3 *give a proposal your blessing*
approval, backing, support, agreement, authority, sanction, consent, permission, leave
formal approbation, concurrence
E∃ **2** curse, blight **3** condemnation

blight *n, v*
▶ *n* **1** *affected by planning blight*
curse, misfortune, woe, trouble, calamity, bane, evil, scourge, affliction, decay, pollution, contamination, corruption
2 *potato blight*
disease, fungus, mildew, rot, infestation, cancer, canker,
E∃ **1** blessing, boon
▶ *v* spoil, mar, injure, undermine, ruin, wreck, crush, dash, shatter, destroy, damage, kill, annihilate, blast, wither, shrivel, frustrate, disappoint
E∃ bless

blind *adj, v, n*
▶ *adj* **1** SIGHTLESS, unsighted, unseeing, visionless, eyeless

Ways of describing sight impairment include: amaurotic, astigmatic, having cataracts, colour-blind, far-sighted, glaucomatous, half-blind, hemeralopic, hypermetropic, long-sighted, myopic, near-sighted, night-blind, nyctalopic, partially-sighted, presbyopic, purblind, sand-blind, short-sighted, snow-blind, stone-blind, trachomatous, visually handicapped, visually impaired, *colloq.* blind as a bat.

2 *blind to their needs*
UNAWARE, ignorant, oblivious, unconscious, unobservant, imperceptive, slow, inattentive, neglectful, indifferent, insensitive, thoughtless, inconsiderate
3 *love is blind*

UNREASONING, uncritical, unthinking, irrational, injudicious, indiscriminate, heedless, mindless, impulsive, hasty, rash, impetuous, reckless, wild, mad, careless
4 CLOSED, obstructed, hidden, concealed, out of sight, obscured
Ⓔ **1** sighted **2** aware, sensitive **3** careful, cautious
▶ v **1** *blinded in the accident*
make blind, cause to lose your vision, deprive of sight, deprive of vision, put the eyes out of, gouge the eyes out of
2 *blinded by the car's headlights*
dazzle, block your vision, obscure your vision
3 *tolerance blinds you to faults*
cause to lose reason/sense, deceive, mislead, trick, trap
▶ n **1** *a window blind*
screen, cover, curtain, (window) shade, shutter, roller blind, Austrian blind, Venetian blind
2 *operate as a blind for illegal activities*
cloak, mask, camouflage, masquerade, front, façade, distraction, smokescreen, cover
colloq. cover-up

blindly *adv*
1 *feel your way blindly*
without vision, without sight, sightlessly, unseeingly
2 UNCRITICALLY, unthinkingly, irrationally, indiscriminately, mindlessly, senselessly, thoughtlessly, impulsively, rashly, impetuously, recklessly, wildly, madly, carelessly, incautiously
Ⓔ **2** critically, cautiously

blink *v*
1 *his eyes blinked*
wink
formal nictate, nictitate
2 *the light blinked*
flash, flicker, twinkle, shine, gleam, glimmer, glitter, sparkle, scintillate

bliss *n*
blissfulness, ecstasy, euphoria, rapture, joy, elation, happiness, gladness, blessedness, paradise, heaven, seventh heaven, utopia, nirvana
Ⓔ misery, hell, damnation

blissful *adj*
ecstatic, euphoric, elated, enraptured, idyllic, rapturous, delighted, enchanted, joyful, joyous, happy
Ⓔ miserable, wretched

blister *n*
sore, swelling, cyst, boil, abscess, ulcer, pustule, pimple, canker, carbuncle
technical bleb, bulla, furuncle, papilla, papula, pompholyx, vesicle, vesicula, wen
Related adjective: vesicant

blistering *adj*
1 *blistering heat*
hot, scorching, withering, intense, extreme
2 *blistering criticism*
cruel, vicious, savage, fierce, caustic, scathing, sarcastic

blithe *adj*
casual, unthinking, thoughtless, careless, heedless, uncaring, unconcerned, carefree, untroubled, cheerful, cheery, light-hearted
Ⓔ morose, thoughtful, serious

blitz *n*
1 *the blitz during the war*
bombardment, attack, offensive, raid, strike,

campaign, onslaught, blitzkrieg
2 *have a blitz on the garden*
effort, all-out effort, attack, exertion, attempt, endeavour, campaign

blizzard *n*
snowstorm, squall, storm, tempest

bloated *adj*
swollen, puffy, blown up, inflated, dilated, expanded, enlarged, full, stuffed
formal distended
Ⓔ thin, shrunken, shrivelled

blob *n*
drop, droplet, globule, bead, pearl, bubble, dab, spot, splash, gob, lump, mass, ball, pellet, pill
colloq. glob

bloc *n*
alliance, group, league, coalition, federation, union, ring, syndicate, entente, axis, cabal, cartel, clique, faction

block *n, v*
▶ n **1** *a block of offices*
building, development, structure
2 *a block of stone*
piece, lump, mass, slab, chunk, hunk, square, cube, wedge, cake, brick, bar
3 *a block of seats/tickets*
batch, cluster, quantity, series, section
4 OBSTACLE, barrier, bar, jam, blockage, stoppage, resistance, obstruction, impediment, hindrance, drawback, deterrent, stumbling-block, let, delay
▶ v *block a pipe/progress*
choke, clog, stop up, dam up, close, seal, bar, obstruct, be in the way, impede, hinder, stonewall, stop, check, arrest, halt, thwart, frustrate, scotch, deter
colloq. bung up

blockade *n, v*
▶ n barrier, barricade, siege, obstruction, restriction, obstacle, block, stoppage, closure, encirclement
technical investment
▶ v keep from, prevent, hinder, stop, check, obstruct, prevent entering/reaching, prevent using, besiege, encircle, surround

blockage *n*
obstruction, blocking, stoppage, occlusion, block, clot, jam, log-jam, congestion, hindrance, impediment
formal occlusion

blockhead *n*
fool, idiot, imbecile, dunce
colloq. nincompoop, ninny, nitwit, numskull, twerp, twit, dimwit; *slang* wally, jerk, dipstick, nerd, dork, geek
Ⓔ brain, genius

bloke *n*
man, boy, fellow, male, individual, character
colloq. chap, guy

blond, blonde *adj*
fair, flaxen, golden, fair-haired, golden-haired, light-coloured, tow-coloured, bleached

blood *n*
1 *lose blood*
lifeblood, vital fluid, gore
Related adjectives: haemal, haemic, haematic, sanguineous
2 *of aristocratic blood*

extraction, birth, descent, lineage, family, kindred, relations, ancestry, descendants, kinship, relationship

bloodcurdling *adj*
horrifying, chilling, spine-chilling, hair-raising, terrifying, frightening, scary, dreadful, fearful, appalling, horrible, horrid, horrendous

bloodless *adj*
1 *a bloodless coup*
peaceful, non-violent, strife-free, unwarlike
2 *her bloodless face*
ASHEN, anaemic, colourless, pale, pallid, pasty, sallow, sickly, wan, chalky, cold, drained, feeble, insipid, languid, lifeless, listless, unfeeling, unemotional, passionless, spiritless, torpid
Ⅎ 1 bloody, violent 2 bloody, ruddy, vigorous

bloodshed *n*
killing, murder, slaughter, slaying, massacre, blood-bath, butchery, carnage, pogrom, gore, bloodletting, decimation

bloodsucker *n*
blackmailer, extortioner, extortionist
colloq. leech, parasite, sponger

bloodthirsty *adj*
murderous, homicidal, warlike, savage, barbaric, barbarous, brutal, ferocious, vicious, cruel, inhuman, ruthless
formal sanguinary

bloody *adj*
bleeding, bloodstained, gory, murderous, bloodthirsty, savage, brutal, ferocious, fierce, cruel
formal sanguinary, sanguine, sanguineous, sanguinolent

bloom *n, v*
▶ *n* 1 BLOSSOM, flower, bud
technical efflorescence, florescence
2 PRIME, heyday, perfection, blush, flush, glow, rosiness, beauty, radiance, lustre, health, vigour, strength, freshness
▶ *v* 1 *the flowers were blooming*
bud, sprout, blossom, flower, open
2 *the children are blooming*
flourish, develop, mature, grow, blossom, prosper, thrive, glow
Ⅎ 1 fade, wither

blooming *adj*
blossoming, healthy, flowering, rosy, ruddy, bonny
technical florescent
Ⅎ ailing

blossom *n, v*
▶ *n* bloom, flower, bud
technical efflorescence, florescence
▶ *v* 1 *the trees were blossoming*
bloom, flower
formal burgeon
2 *blossom into a beautiful young woman*
develop, mature, bloom, flourish, thrive, prosper, succeed
formal burgeon
Ⅎ 2 fade, wither

blot *n, v*
▶ *n* 1 *an ink blot*
spot, stain, smudge, blotch, smear, mark, splodge, speck, blemish
2 *a blot on his reputation*
blemish, flaw, fault, defect, imperfection, taint, stain,

disgrace, tarnishing, black mark
▶ *v* 1 *blot a surface*
spot, mark, stain, smudge, blur, dry (up), soak(up), absorb
2 *blotted his character*
sully, taint, tarnish, spoil, mar, disfigure, disgrace
▷ **blot out** obliterate, cancel, delete, erase, darken, obscure, hide, conceal, screen, shadow, eclipse;
formal efface, expunge

blotch *n*
patch, splodge, splotch, splash, smudge, blot, spot, mark, stain, blemish

blotchy *adj*
spotty, spotted, patchy, uneven, smeary, blemished, reddened, inflamed

blow[1] *v, n*
▶ *v* 1 *the wind was blowing*
gust, blast, flurry
2 *blow leaves along the road*
waft, fan, flutter, float, flow, stream, rush, whirl, whisk, sweep, fling, buffet, drive, blast
3 BREATHE, breathe out, pant, puff (out)
formal exhale
4 *blow a horn*
play, sound, pipe, trumpet, toot, blare, blast
5 *blow a lot of money*
fritter away, misspend, spend freely
formal dissipate
colloq. spend like water, pour down the drain
6 *blow a chance/opportunity*
waste, spoil, ruin, wreck, make a mess of, miss out on
colloq. miss the boat; *slang* screw up
▶ *n* puff, draught, flurry, gust, blast, wind, gale, squall, tempest
▷ **blow out** put out, smother, snuff out;
formal extinguish
▷ **blow over** die down, subside, end, finish, cease, pass, vanish, disappear, be forgotten, fizzle out, peter out; *formal* dissipate
▷ **blow up** 1 EXPLODE, go off, go up, detonate, burst, blast, bomb 2 INFLATE, pump up, swell, fill (out), puff up, balloon, bloat, dilate, expand, enlarge, magnify, exaggerate, overstate; *formal* distend
3 LOSE YOUR TEMPER, become angry, get into a rage, take leave of your senses; *colloq.* blow your top, hit the roof, fly off the handle, go mad, go ballistic, flip (your lid); *US slang* go ape

blow[2] *n*
1 *a blow on the head*
hit, concussion, box, cuff, clip, swipe, bash, slap, smack, buffet, bang, clap, knock, rap, stroke, thump, punch, hook
colloq. clout, whack, wallop, belt; *slang* biff, sock
2 MISFORTUNE, affliction, reverse, setback, comedown, disappointment, upset, jolt, shock, bombshell, calamity, catastrophe, disaster
colloq. shocker, bolt from the blue, rude awakening

blow-out *n*
1 PUNCTURE, flat tyre, burst tyre
colloq. flat
2 PARTY, celebration, feast
colloq. binge, bash, knees-up, rave, rave-up, beanfeast

blowy *adj*
breezy, windy, fresh, blustery, gusty, squally, stormy

blowzy *adj*
sloppy, slovenly, unkempt, untidy, bedraggled,

dishevelled, ungroomed, tousled, messy, slipshod
F3 neat, smart

blubber *v*
cry, weep, blub, sob, snivel, sniffle, whimper

bludgeon *v, n*
▶ *v* **1** BEAT, strike, club, batter, hit, beat, cudgel
colloq. clobber, cosh
2 FORCE, coerce, compel, intimidate, bulldoze,
badger, hector, harass, browbeat, bully, dragoon,
pressurize, terrorize
▶ *n* club, baton, cosh, cudgel, truncheon

blue *adj*
1 AZURE, sky-blue, royal blue, sapphire, cobalt,
ultramarine, navy blue, navy, indigo, aquamarine,
turquoise, cyan, cerulean
2 DEPRESSED, low, dejected, downcast, dispirited,
downhearted, despondent, gloomy, glum, dismal, sad,
unhappy, miserable, melancholy, morose
colloq. fed up, down in the dumps
3 *a blue joke*
obscene, offensive, indecent, improper, coarse, vulgar,
lewd, dirty, pornographic, erotic, bawdy, smutty, risqué
colloq. adult, raunchy, steamy, near the bone, near the
knuckle
F3 2 cheerful, happy **3** decent, clean

blueprint *n*
design, outline, draft, sketch, pilot, guide, plan,
scheme, strategy, project, programme, archetype,
prototype, representation, model, pattern

blues *n*
depression, despondency, gloom, gloominess,
moodiness, glumness, melancholy, miseries, dejection,
doldrums
colloq. dumps
F3 euphoria

bluff[1] *v, n*
▶ *v* *was only bluffing*
lie, pretend, feign, sham, fake, deceive, delude,
mislead, hoodwink, blind, fool
colloq. bamboozle
▶ *n* lie, idle boast, bravado, humbug, pretence, show,
sham, fake, fraud, trick, subterfuge, deceit, deception,
feint
formal braggadocio

bluff[2] *adj, n*
▶ *adj* *a bluff man*
blunt, candid, direct, downright, open, outspoken,
plain-spoken, straightforward, frank, genial, good-
natured, hearty, affable
F3 diplomatic, refined
▶ *n* cliff, crag, escarpment, peak, precipice,
promontory, foreland, bank, brow, headland, height,
ridge, scarp, escarp

blunder *n, v*
▶ *n* mistake, error, inaccuracy, misjudgement, slip,
indiscretion, gaffe, *faux pas*, oversight, fault
formal solecism
colloq. howler, bloomer, clanger, boob, booboo, slip-
up; *slang* cock-up
▶ *v* make a mistake, stumble, flounder, bumble, err,
miscalculate, misjudge, get wrong, go wrong, bungle,
mismanage
colloq. botch, slip up, fluff, goof; *slang* cock up, screw
up

blunt *adj, v*
▶ *adj* **1** UNSHARPENED, not sharp, dull, worn,

pointless, edgeless, rounded, stubbed
2 FRANK, candid, direct, forthright, unceremonious,
explicit, plain-spoken, honest, straightforward,
downright, outspoken, tactless, insensitive, rude,
impolite, uncivil, brusque, curt, stark, abrupt
colloq. calling a spade a spade, speaking your mind,
not beating about the bush, not mincing your words
F3 1 sharp, pointed **2** subtle, tactful
▶ *v* dull, take the edge off, dampen, soften, deaden,
numb, anaesthetize, alleviate, allay, abate, weaken
formal hebetate
F3 sharpen, intensify

blur *v, n*
▶ *v* **1** *the windscreen blurred*
smear, smudge, spot, blotch, stain
2 *blurred memories/views*
obscure, make vague/indistinct, mask, conceal, mist,
fog, befog, cloud, becloud, veil, dim, dull, darken,
soften
▶ *n* **1** *a blur on the picture*
smear, smudge, spot, blotch, stain
2 *my memories are a blur*
haze, mist, fog, cloudiness, fuzziness, indistinctness,
obscurity, muddle, confusion, dimness

blurb *n*
advertisement, commendation, copy, puff
colloq. hype, spiel

blurred *adj*
out of focus, fuzzy, unclear, indistinct, vague,
ill-defined, lacking definition, faint, hazy, misty, foggy,
cloudy, clouded, bleary, dim, obscure, confused
F3 clear, distinct

blurt *v*
▷ **blurt out** exclaim, cry (out), call out, come out
with, gush, spout, utter, tell, reveal, disclose, divulge,
let out, leak, let slip; *formal* ejaculate; *colloq.* blab, let
the cat out of the bag, give the game away, spill the
beans
F3 bottle up, hush up

blush *v, n*
▶ *v* flush, redden, go red, turn red, colour, glow,
blanch
▶ *n* flush, reddening, rosiness, ruddiness, colour,
glow

blushing *adj*
flushed, red, rosy, glowing, confused, embarrassed,
ashamed, modest
formal erubescence
F3 pale, white, composed

bluster *v, n*
▶ *v* boast, brag, crow, swagger, strut, vaunt, show off,
rant, roar, storm, bully, harangue, hector
colloq. talk big
▶ *n* boasting, crowing, bravado, bluff, swagger,
domineering
formal braggadocio

blustery *adj*
windy, gusty, squally, stormy, tempestuous, violent,
wild, boisterous
F3 calm

board *n, v*
▶ *n* **1** *a wooden board*
sheet, panel, slab, plank, beam, timber, slat
2 COMMITTEE, council, panel, jury, commission,
directorate, directors, trustees, governors, advisers,
advisory group, working party, management, head

office
3 MEALS, food, sustenance, provisions, rations
formal victuals
slang grub, nosh
▶ *v* get on, get in/into, embark, mount, enter, catch
formal embus, emplane, entrain
▷ **board up** close (up), cover (up), shut (up), seal

boast *v, n*
▶ *v* **1** *boasts about his qualifications*
brag, crow, claim, exaggerate, overstate, bluster,
trumpet, vaunt, strut, swagger, prate, show off, sing
your own praises
formal gasconade, rodomontade
colloq. swank, talk big, loudmouth, blow your own
trumpet, *US* blow your own horn
2 *boasts a new sauna*
exhibit, possess, enjoy, pride yourself on
◨ **1** *formal* belittle, deprecate
▶ *n* brag, crowing, blustering, self-praise,
overstatement, claim, vaunt, pride, joy, gem, treasure
formal fanfaronade, gasconade, gasconism,
rodomontade, jactation
colloq. hot air, swank

boastful *adj*
proud, conceited, vain, puffed up, bragging, crowing,
cocky, swaggering, arrogant, self-flattering, egotistical
formal vainglorious
colloq. big-headed, swollen-headed, swanky
◨ modest, self-effacing, humble

boat *n*

Types of boat or ship include: canoe, dinghy, lifeboat,
rowing-boat, kayak, coracle, skiff, punt, sampan,
dhow, gondola, pedalo, catamaran, trimaran, yacht;
cabin-cruiser, motor-boat, motor-launch,
speedboat, trawler, barge, scow, narrow boat,
houseboat, dredger, junk, smack, lugger;
hovercraft, hydrofoil; clipper, cutter, ketch, packet,
brig, schooner, square-rigger, galleon; ferry,
paddle-steamer, tug, freighter, liner, container-ship,
tanker; warship, battleship, destroyer, submarine,
U-boat, frigate, aircraft-carrier, cruiser,
dreadnought, corvette, minesweeper, man-of-war.

boatman *n*
ferryman, oarsman, oarswoman, rower, sailor,
yachtsman, yachtswoman, waterman, bargee,
gondolier, voyageur

bob *v*
1 *a raft bobbing up and down*
bounce, float, move up and down shake, quiver, wobble
formal oscillate
2 *bobbed back into the house*
leap, spring, jump, jerk, jolt, twitch, nod, bow, curtsy,
hop, skip
▷ **bob up** appear, emerge, arrive, materialize, rise,
surface, pop up, spring up, crop up, arise;
colloq. show up

bode *v*
predict, foretell, prophesy, indicate, signify, intimate,
herald, threaten, warn
formal augur, forebode, foreshadow, foreshow,
forewarn, presage, betoken, portend, purport

bodily *adj, adv*
▶ *adj* physical, carnal, fleshly, real, actual, tangible,
substantial, concrete, material
formal corporeal
◨ spiritual

▶ *adv* altogether, en masse, collectively, as a whole, as
one, completely, fully, wholly, entirely, totally, in toto
◨ piecemeal

body *n*
1 *his whole body was aching*
physique, build, form, frame, figure, anatomy,
skeleton, trunk, torso
Related adjective: corporal
2 CORPSE, cadaver, carcase, dead body
slang stiff
3 *sit in the body of the church*
main part, central part, largest part
4 ORGANIZATION, association, society,
corporation, company, confederation, council,
authority, bloc, cartel, syndicate, congress, collection,
group, band, crowd, throng, multitude, mob, mass,
phalanx
5 CONSISTENCY, density, solidity, firmness, bulk,
mass, substance, essence, fullness, richness

bodyguard *n*
guard, protector, defender, guardian
slang minder

boffin *n*
scientist, engineer, designer, planner, inventor,
mastermind, genius, brain, intellect, intellectual,
thinker
colloq. egghead, wizard, backroom-boy

bog *n, v*
▶ *n* marsh, swamp, fen, mire, quagmire, quag,
slough, morass, quicksands, marshland, swampland,
wetlands
▶ *v* ▷ **bog down** encumber, hinder, overwhelm,
deluge, sink, stick, slow down, slow up, delay, halt, hold
up, set back, stall; *formal* impede, retard, mire

boggle *v*
astound, startle, amaze, surprise, overwhelm, stagger,
alarm, confuse
colloq. bowl over, flabbergast

boggy *adj*
marshy, miry, swampy, muddy, oozy, morassy, quaggy,
soft, spongy, waterlogged, fenny
formal paludal
◨ arid

bogus *adj*
false, fake, counterfeit, forged, fraudulent, spurious,
sham, make-believe, artificial, imitation, dummy
colloq. phoney, pseudo, pseud
◨ genuine, true, real, valid

bohemian *adj, n*
▶ *adj* artistic, unconventional, unorthodox,
nonconformist, alternative, original, avant-garde,
eccentric, offbeat, bizarre, exotic
colloq. arty, oddball, off-the-wall; *slang* way-out
◨ bourgeois, conventional, orthodox
▶ *n* beatnik, hippie, drop-out, nonconformist
◨ conformist

boil[1] *v*
1 *boil water*
SIMMER, stew, cook, heat, seethe, bring/come to the
boil, brew, gurgle, bubble, fizz, effervesce, froth, foam,
steam
2 *boil with anger*
erupt, explode, rage, rave, storm, fume
formal fulminate
colloq. blow your top, fly into a rage, go off the deep
end, hit the roof

▷ **boil down** amount, reduce, concentrate, distil, condense, digest, abstract, summarize, abridge

boil² *n*
a boil on the skin
pustule, abscess, gumboil, ulcer, tumour, pimple, carbuncle, blister, inflammation

boiling *adj*
1 *boiling water*
turbulent, gurgling, bubbling, steaming, scalding
2 HOT, baking, roasting, scorching, sweltering, blistering, torrid, *US* broiling
3 ANGRY, indignant, incensed, infuriated, enraged, furious, fuming, flaming

boisterous *adj*
exuberant, rollicking, romping, bouncy, active, hyperactive, lively, spirited, turbulent, energetic, tumultuous, loud, noisy, clamorous, rowdy, rough, disorderly, riotous, wild, unrestrained, unruly, obstreperous
colloq. rumbustious
E quiet, calm, restrained, docile

bold *adj*
1 BRAVE, dauntless, daring, audacious, fearless, undaunted, courageous, valiant, intrepid, heroic, gallant, intrepid, adventurous, venturesome, enterprising, plucky, spirited, confident, outgoing
formal valorous
colloq. bold as a lion
2 BRAZEN, brash, forward, shameless, unabashed, impudent, insolent, barefaced
colloq. cheeky, saucy, brassy, pert, bold as brass
3 EYE-CATCHING, striking, conspicuous, prominent, strong, pronounced, distinct, definite, bright, vivid, colourful, loud, flashy, showy, flamboyant
E **1** cowardly, nervous, cautious, timid, shy **2** timid, modest, shy, diffident **3** faint, restrained

bolshie *adj*
awkward, obstinate, unhelpful, difficult, stubborn, unco-operative, irritable, touchy, prickly, oversensitive, rude, unpleasant, problem
colloq. stroppy, bloody-minded
E amenable, pleasant, co-operative, helpful

bolster *v, n*
▶ *v* boost, aid, assist, help, maintain, prop, reinforce, strengthen, supplement, support, brace, buoy up, buttress, firm up, shore up, stay, stiffen, revitalize, invigorate
formal augment
E undermine
▶ *n* pillow, support, cushion

bolt *n, v*
▶ *n* **1** *a bolt on a door*
bar, rod, shaft, fastener, latch, catch, lock
2 *nuts and bolts*
screw, pin, peg, rivet
▶ *v* **1** FASTEN, secure, bar, latch, lock, rivet, pin, screw
2 *bolt for the door*
escape, flee, fly, run (away), run off, sprint, rush, dash, hurtle
formal abscond
3 *bolt your food down*
gulp, wolf (down), gobble, gorge, guzzle, devour, cram, stuff

bomb *n, v*
▶ *n* atom bomb, nuclear bomb, hydrogen bomb, petrol bomb, neutron bomb, shell, bombshell, explosive, charge, grenade, mine, incendiary, fire-bomb, torpedo, depth charge, plastic bomb, time bomb, rocket, shell, missile, projectile, Molotov cocktail, stink bomb, car bomb, fire-bomb, letter bomb
▶ *v* bombard, shell, torpedo, attack, blow up, destroy

bombard *v*
1 *bombard the airport*
attack, assail, pelt, pound, strafe, blast, bomb, shell, torpedo, stone, blitz, raid, besiege
2 *bombard with criticism*
attack, hound, bother, harass, pester

bombardment *n*
1 *aerial bombardment*
attack, assault, air raid, bombing, shelling, blitz, barrage, cannonade, fusillade, salvo, fire, flak
2 *bombardment of questions*
attack, onslaught, besieging, hounding, bothering, harassing, pestering

bombastic *adj*
pompous, pretentious, grandiose, verbose, wordy, turgid, ostentatious, affected, high-flown, inflated, bloated, windy
formal grandiloquent, magniloquent, portentous, euphuistic, fustian
E reserved, restrained

bona fide *adj*
genuine, real, valid, true, actual, authentic, lawful, legal, legitimate, kosher, honest
colloq. the real McCoy
E bogus

bonanza *n*
windfall, sudden wealth, godsend, stroke of luck, blessing, boon

bond *n, v*
▶ *n* **1** *bonds of friendship*
CONNECTION, relation, relationship, link, tie(s), binding, union, affiliation, attachment, rapport, affinity, chemistry
formal vinculum
2 CONTRACT, covenant, agreement, pledge, promise, pact, transaction, deal, treaty, word, obligation
3 FETTER, shackle, manacle, chain, cord, band, binding
▶ *v* connect, fasten, bind, unite, fuse, join, stick, attach, glue, gum, paste, weld, seal

bondage *n*
imprisonment, captivity, confinement, restraint, slavery, enslavement, serfdom, servitude, subservience, subjection, subjugation, yoke
formal incarceration, thraldom, vassalage
E freedom, independence

bone *n*
Related adjectives: osseous, osteal

Human bones include: clavicle, coccyx, collar-bone, femur, fibula, hip-bone, humerus, ilium, ischium, mandible, maxilla, metacarpal, metatarsal, patella, pelvic girdle, pelvis, pubis, radius, rib, scapula, shoulder-blade, skull, sternum, stirrup-bone, temporal, thigh-bone, tibia, ulna, vertebra.

bonny *adj*
attractive, lovely, beautiful, pretty, fine, fair, blooming, bouncing, cheerful, cheery, joyful, merry
F3 ugly

bonus *n*
1 *pay a bonus*
commission, dividend, premium, prize, reward, honorarium, tip, gratuity, gift, fringe benefits, handout
formal lagniappe
2 *the good weather is a bonus*
advantage, benefit, gain, extra
formal perquisite
colloq. plus, perk
F3 **2** disadvantage, disincentive

bony *adj*
thin, lean, angular, lanky, gawky, gangling, skinny, scrawny, scraggy, emaciated, skeletal, rawboned, gaunt, drawn
F3 fat, plump

book *n, v*
▶ *n* volume, tome, publication, work, booklet, tract

Types of book include: hardback, paperback, bestseller; fiction, novel, story, thriller, detective, romantic novel, penny dreadful; children's book, primer, picture-book, annual; reference book, encyclopedia, dictionary, lexicon, thesaurus, concordance, anthology, compendium, omnibus, atlas, guidebook, gazetteer, directory, anthology, pocket companion, handbook, manual, cookbook, yearbook, almanac, catalogue; notebook, exercise book, textbook, scrapbook, album, sketchbook, diary, jotter, pad, ledger; libretto, manuscript, hymn-book, hymnal, prayer-book, psalter, missal, lectionary. *See also* **literature**.

▶ *v* **1** *book a ticket*
arrange (in advance), reserve, make a reservation for, engage, charter, procure, order, organize, schedule, programme
colloq. bag
2 *booked for assault*
charge, accuse (of), blame
F3 **1** cancel
▷ **book in** register, enrol, check in, record your arrival

bookbinding *n*

Terms used in bookbinding include: adhesive binding, all edges gilt (aeg), backboard, backbone, back cornering, back lining, *US* binder's board, binder's brass, *US* binder's die, binding, blind blocking, blocking, boards, bolts, book block, buckram, case, casebound, casing-in, cloth-lined board, comb-binding, drawn-on, dust cover, embossing, endpaper, flyleaf, fore edge, front board, full bound, gather, half bound, hardback, head, headband, headcap, hinge, jacket, laminating, library binding, limp, lining, Linson®, loose-leaf, mechanical binding, millboard, morocco, notch binding, open-flat, paperback, pasteboard, perfect binding, quarter bound, raised band, ring binding, rounding and backing, saddle-stitch, sewing, shoulder, side-stitch, signature, smashing, soft-cover, spine, spiral binding, square back, stab-stitch, *US* stamping, strawboard, tail, tailband, thermoplastic binding, thread sewing, unsewn binding, varnishing, whole bound, wire binding, wire stitching, wiro binding, yapp.

bookish *adj*
studious, well-read, academic, scholarly, cultured, erudite, highbrow, intellectual, learned, literary, scholastic, lettered, donnish, bluestocking, pedantic
F3 lowbrow, unlettered

books *n*
accounts, ledgers, records, financial statement, balance sheet

boom *v, n*
▶ *v* **1** BANG, crash, roar, blare, thunder, roll, bellow, rumble, resound, reverberate, blast, explode
2 FLOURISH, thrive, prosper, succeed, develop, grow, do well, increase, gain, progress, expand, swell, surge, leap, escalate, intensify, strengthen, go from strength to strength, mushroom, explode
F3 **2** fail, collapse, slump
▶ *n* **1** BANG, clap, crash, roar, thunder, rumble, reverberation, blast, blare, bellow, roll, explosion, burst, loud noise
2 INCREASE, growth, expansion, gain, upsurge, jump, surge, leap, spurt, boost, upturn, upswing, improvement, advance, progress, success, development, escalation, explosion
F3 **2** failure, collapse, slump, recession, depression

boomerang *v*
rebound, bounce back, spring back, recoil, ricochet, backfire

boon *n*
blessing, advantage, benefit, bonus, help, godsend, windfall, favour, kindness, gift, present, grant, gratuity
colloq. plus
F3 disadvantage, blight

boor *n*
oaf, lout, barbarian, philistine, vulgarian, rustic, yahoo
colloq. peasant, country bumpkin, clod, clodhopper, yokel

boorish *adj*
uncouth, oafish, loutish, ill-mannered, ill-bred, rude, coarse, rough, crude, vulgar, unrefined, uncivilized, gruff, impolite, rustic, uneducated, ignorant
F3 polite, refined, cultured, genteel

boost *v, n*
▶ *v* **1** *boost confidence*
bolster, lift, encourage, inspire, uplift, foster, support
2 *boost sales*
increase, raise, put up, improve, enhance, develop, enlarge, expand, supplement, amplify, advance, help, aid, assist, maximize, promote, encourage, further, heighten
formal augment
3 *boost a product*
advertise, promote, publicize, praise
colloq. plug, hype
F3 **1** undermine **2** lower, deteriorate, hinder
▶ *n* **1** *a boost to morale*
lift, uplift, fillip, encouragement, inspiration, stimulus, support
colloq. shot in the arm, ego-trip
2 *a boost to sales*
increase, rise, improvement, enhancement, development, enlargement, expansion, increment, addition, supplement, amplification, advance, help, aid, assistance, furtherance
formal augmentation
3 *a boost for a product*
advertisement, promotion, publicity, praise
colloq. plug, hype
F3 **1** setback, blow **2** setback, deterioration

boot¹ *n, v*
▶ *n* gumboot, wellington, galosh, overshoe, walking-boot, climbing-boot, riding-boot, football boot, Doc Martens®, wader, bootee
▶ *v* kick, shove
▷ **boot out** dismiss, eject, expel, lay off, suspend, shed, give notice, make redundant; *colloq.* kick out, fire, sack, give someone their cards, give the heave

boot² *v*
▷ **to boot** as well, in addition
colloq. into the bargain

booth *n*
cubicle, compartment, carrel, stall, stand, kiosk, hut, box

bootless *adj*
fruitless, futile, vain, ineffective, useless, pointless, profitless, sterile, unavailing, unsuccessful, worthless unproductive, barren
⊟ profitable, useful

booty *n*
loot, plunder, pillage, spoil(s), haul, gains, takings, pickings, prize, profits, takings, winnings
slang swag

border *n, v*
▶ *n* **1** BOUNDARY, frontier, line, state line, marchlands, marches
2 *herbaceous borders*
bed, edge, rim, brim, verge, margin, fringe, periphery, surround, perimeter, circumference, bound, bounds, confine, confines, limit, demarcation, borderline, brink
technical limb
3 HEM, frill, valance, skirt, trimming, frieze
▶ *v* **1** *Sweden borders Norway*
lie/be next to, be adjacent to, join, touch, connect
formal adjoin, abut, impinge
2 *streets bordered with trees*
edge, bound, skirt, flank, fringe, rim, surround, trim, hem
formal circumscribe
▷ **border on** verge on, be almost, be nearly, resemble, approximate to, approach

borderline *adj*
marginal, problematic, indefinite, doubtful, uncertain, indecisive, indeterminate, ambivalent
colloq. iffy
⊟ certain, definite, clear-cut

bore¹ *v, n*
▶ *v* *the speech bored them*
tire, make tired, weary, wear out, fatigue, exhaust, pall on, be tedious to, jade, trouble, bother, worry, irritate, annoy, vex, irk
colloq. turn off, send to sleep, bore the pants off
⊟ interest, excite
▶ *n* nuisance, bother
colloq. bind, drag, turn-off, headache, pain, pain in the neck
⊟ pleasure, delight

bore² *v*
bore a hole
drill, mine, pierce, perforate, penetrate, puncture, sink, dig (out), burrow, hollow (out), tap, tunnel, undermine, sap

bored *adj*
uninterested, unexcited, tired, wearied, exhausted
formal ennuied, ennuyé

colloq. bored to tears, bored stiff, bored out of your mind, cheesed off, fed up, turned off, sick and tired, in a rut, brassed off, browned off
⊟ interested, excited

boredom *n*
tedium, tediousness, monotony, humdrum, dullness, sameness, flatness, apathy, listlessness, weariness, world-weariness, frustration
formal ennui, malaise, acedia
⊟ interest, excitement

boring *adj*
tedious, dull, monotonous, routine, repetitious, uninteresting, unexciting, uneventful, dreary, humdrum, tiring, tiresome, unvaried, commonplace, trite, unimaginative, uninspired, dry, stale, flat, insipid, prosaic, long-winded
old use stultifying, jejune
colloq. samey, dull as ditchwater, soul-destroying, with the novelty worn off
⊟ interesting, exciting, stimulating, original

borrow *v*
1 *borrow a friend's car*
have the use of, take/have on loan, use temporarily, scrounge, cadge, take out a loan, rent, hire, charter, lease
colloq. sponge
2 *borrow words/ideas*
adopt, take (over), draw, derive, obtain, use, acquire
formal appropriate
⊟ **1** lend

borrowing *n*
1 *borrowing of money*
use, temporary use, loan, rental, hire, charter, leasing
2 *English borrowings in German*
loan, loan-translation, loan-word, adoption, takeover, derivation, use, acquisition
technical calque
⊟ **1** lending

bosom *n, adj*
▶ *n* **1** BUST, breasts, chest, breast
slang boob, bristol, knocker, tit
2 *in the bosom of the family*
HEART, core, centre, midst, protection, shelter, sanctuary
▶ *adj* close, intimate, dear, devoted, loving, faithful, confidential

boss *n, v*
▶ *n* employer, master, owner, captain, head, chief, leader, supremo, administrator, executive, director, manager, superior, foreman, superintendent, overseer, governor, supervisor
colloq. gaffer
▶ *v* order around, order about, domineer, tyrannize, bully, bulldoze, browbeat, give orders to, dominate
colloq. push around, throw your weight about, lay down the law

bossy *adj*
authoritarian, autocratic, tyrannical, despotic, dictatorial, domineering, overbearing, oppressive, lordly, high-handed, dominating, imperious, insistent, assertive, demanding, exacting
⊟ unassertive

botch *v, n*
▶ *v* bungle, mess (up), make a mess of, blunder, mar, mismanage, ruin, spoil, patch
colloq. foul up, fluff, muff, make a hash of, make a bad

job of, goof; *slang* louse up, screw up, cock up, balls up; *taboo slang* fuck up
E3 accomplish, succeed
▶ *n* blunder, bungle, failure, muddle, mess, miscarriage
colloq. farce, shambles, hash; *slang* cock-up, balls-up
E3 success

both *adj*
the two, each, the pair, the one and the other

bother *v, n*
▶ *v* **1** *not bother to reply*
concern yourself, trouble, make the/an effort, think necessary
2 *the heat bothered us*
concern, annoy, worry, upset, trouble dismay, alarm, distress, vex
colloq. bug
3 *don't bother her*
disturb, inconvenience, put out, trouble, pester, plague, harass, nag, annoy, irritate, molest
formal incommode
colloq. hassle
▶ *n* **1** *not worth the bother*
trouble, inconvenience, effort, problem, difficulty, fuss, exertion, pains, bustle, flurry
colloq. hassle
2 *office paperwork is a real bother*
nuisance, annoyance, irritation, problem, difficulty, vexation, worry, strain
colloq. aggravation, pest, pain in the neck

bothersome *adj*
troublesome, annoying, irksome, irritating, infuriating, vexatious, vexing, inconvenient, distressing, exasperating, laborious, boring, tedious, tiresome, wearisome
colloq. aggravating

bottle *n, v*
▶ *n* container

Types of bottle include: ampulla, calabash, carafe, carboy, decanter, demijohn, flacon, flagon, flask, gourd, jack, phial, pitcher, vial; apothecary bottle, beer bottle, cruet, feeding bottle, hip flask, hot-water bottle, milk bottle, scent bottle, snuff bottle, Thermos® flask, vinegar bottle, wine bottle. *See also* **wine-bottle sizes**.

▶ *v* ▷ **bottle up** hide, conceal, restrain, curb, keep back, hold back, keep in check, suppress, inhibit, restrict, shut in, enclose, contain, disguise
E3 unbosom, unburden

bottleneck *n*
hold-up, traffic jam, snarl-up, congestion, clogging, blockage, obstruction, block, obstacle, restriction, constriction, narrowing

bottom *n, adj*
▶ *n* **1** UNDERSIDE, underneath, sole, base, foot, plinth, pedestal, support, foundation, substructure, underpinning, ground, nadir
2 *at the bottom of the sea*
floor, bed, depths
3 *at the bottom of the garden*
end, far end, furthest end, farthest end
4 *children at the bottom of the class*
lowest level, least important position
5 *sitting on his bottom*
rear, behind, buttocks, seat, rump
colloq. posterior backside, bum; *US* butt, tail, ass;

slang arse
E3 **1** top **2** surface **4** top
▶ *adj* lowest, lower, underside, undermost

bottomless *adj*
a bottomless pit/supply of funds
deep, profound, fathomless, unfathomed, unplumbed, immeasurable, measureless, infinite, boundless, limitless, unlimited, inexhaustible
E3 shallow, limited

bough *n*
branch, limb

boulder *n*
rock, stone

boulevard *n*
avenue, mall, parade, promenade, drive, prospect, thoroughfare

bounce *v, n*
▶ *v* **1** *bounce a ball*
rebound, spring back, bob, ricochet, recoil, throw
2 *children bouncing about*
spring, jump, leap, bound
▷ **bounce back** recover, get better, get back to normal, improve
▶ *n* **1** SPRING, bound, springiness, elasticity, give, resilience, rebound, recoil
2 EBULLIENCE, exuberance, vitality, vivacity, energy, vigour, animation, dynamism, spiritedness, liveliness
colloq. go, get-up-and-go, zip

bouncing *adj*
healthy, lively, robust, strong, vigorous, thriving, blooming, bonny

bound¹ *adj*
1 *bound to go wrong*
sure, certain, definite, fated, destined, doomed
2 LIABLE, committed, duty-bound, pledged, obliged, required, forced, compelled, constrained, beholden
3 FASTENED, secured, fixed, tied (up), chained, roped, fettered, tethered, held, attached, clamped, lashed, trussed, strapped, shackled, restricted, bandaged
▷ **bound up with** tied up with, connected with, linked with, related to, associated with, dependent on; *colloq.* (going) hand in hand with

bound² *adj*
be bound for Norway
heading, headed, off (to), on your way to, travelling, going, coming, proceeding

bound³ *v, n*
▶ *v* *she bounded down the stairs*
jump, leap, vault, hurdle, spring, bounce, bob, hop, skip, dance, frisk, gambol, frolic, caper, prance
▶ *n* jump, leap, vault, spring, bounce, bob, hop, skip, gambol, frolic, caper, dance, prance

bound⁴ *n, v*
▶ *n* **1** BORDER, line, limit, borderline, demarcation, confine(s), margin, verge, brink, edge, perimeter, circumference, extremity, termination
2 LIMITATION, limit, restriction, check, curb, restraint
▷ **out of bounds** forbidden, off-limits, disallowed, banned, barred, prohibited, taboo
▶ *v* **1** BORDER, outline, limit, enclose, edge, skirt, flank, fringe, surround
2 RESTRICT, regulate, control, moderate, restrain,

contain
formal circumscribe

boundary *n*
border, frontier, barrier, line, borderline, demarcation, bounds, confines, limits, margin, fringe, verge, brink, edge, perimeter, extremity, termination, point of no return, Rubicon
Related adjectives: perimetric, peripheral

bounded *adj*
enclosed, surrounded, bordered, edged, encircled, encompassed, limited, restrained, restricted, confined, walled in, hemmed in, controlled, defined, demarcated
formal circumscribed, delimited

bounder *n*
cad, cheat, blackguard, rogue, miscreant, cur, dastard, knave
colloq. blighter, rotter, pig, swine, rat, dirty dog

boundless *adj*
unbounded, limitless, unlimited, illimitable, unconfined, countless, incalculable, numberless, innumerable, untold, incalculable, vast, immense, measureless, immeasurable, infinite, endless, unending, never-ending, interminable, everlasting, inexhaustible, unflagging, indefatigable
E3 limited, restricted

bounds *n*
restrictions, confines, limits, borders, marches, demarcations, margins, fringes, boundaries, periphery, circumference, perimeter, edges, extremities, parameters, scope
▷ **out of bounds** off limits, prohibited, forbidden, not allowed

bountiful *adj*
abundant, plentiful, exuberant, profuse, ample, prolific, overflowing, ungrudging, unstinting, boundless, copious, generous, lavish, liberal, open-handed, princely
formal magnanimous, munificent, bounteous, plenteous, luxuriant
E3 meagre, mean, sparse

bounty *n*
1 REWARD, recompense, premium, bonus, gratuity, tip, gift, present, donation, grant, allowance
2 GENEROSITY, liberality, largesse, almsgiving, charity, philanthropy, kindness
formal munificence, beneficence

bouquet *n*
1 *a bouquet of flowers*
bunch, posy, nosegay, spray, corsage, buttonhole, boutonnière, wreath, garland
2 AROMA, smell, odour, scent, perfume, fragrance
formal redolence, odoriferousness

bourgeois *adj*
middle-class, materialistic, money-orientated, conservative, traditional, conformist, conventional, hide-bound, unadventurous, ordinary, dull, humdrum, banal, commonplace, trite, pedestrian, uninspired, unoriginal, uncreative, unimaginative, uncultured
E3 bohemian, unconventional, original

bout *n*
1 PERIOD, spell, time, stint, turn, term, stretch, run, course, session, spree
colloq. go

2 *a bout of illness*
attack, fit, touch
3 FIGHT, battle, engagement, encounter, struggle, set-to, match, contest, competition, round, heat

bovine *adj*
1 *bovine animals*
cattlelike, cowlike
2 *his bovine response*
stupid, slow, dull, slow-witted, dim-witted
colloq. dense, dumb, thick, doltish
E3 2 quick

bow[1] *v, n*
▶ *v* 1 *bow your head*
incline, bend, nod, bob, curtsy, kowtow, salaam, stoop, curve, arch, crook, crouch
formal genuflect, make obeisance
2 YIELD, give in, give way to, consent, surrender, capitulate, submit, succumb, concede, accept, comply, defer
formal accede, acquiesce
3 SUBDUE, overpower, conquer, crush, humble, humiliate
formal subjugate, vanquish
▷ **bow out** withdraw, pull out, desert, abandon, defect, back out, retire, resign, leave, stand down, step down, give up; *colloq.* chicken out, quit
▶ *n* inclination, bending, nod, bob, curtsy, arc, kowtow, salaam, salutation, acknowledgement
formal genuflexion, obeisance, prostration

bow[2] *n*
the bow of a ship
front, beak, head, prow, stem, rostrum
E3 stern

bowdlerize *v*
censor, cut, edit, excise, expunge, expurgate, purge, clean up, purify, modify, blue-pencil

bowels *n*
1 INTESTINES, entrails, guts, colon
technical viscera
colloq. insides, innards
2 *in the bowels of the earth*
DEPTHS, interior, inside, middle, centre, core, heart, belly, cavity

bower *n*
arbour, shelter, alcove, grotto, bay, recess, retreat, sanctuary

bowl[1] *n*
a washing-up bowl
receptacle, container, vessel, dish, basin, sink

bowl[2] *v*
bowl a ball
throw, hurl, fling, pitch, roll, spin, whirl, rotate, revolve
▷ **bowl over** 1 *bowled over by the news* overwhelm, affect deeply, impress greatly, surprise, amaze, astound, astonish, stagger, stun, dumbfound; *colloq.* flabbergast, floor 2 *bowl over a person* knock down, fell, topple, unbalance, push into

box[1] *n, v*
▶ *n* *boxes of books*
container, receptacle, case, carton, packet, present, bijou, casket, pyxis, pyx, chest, coffret

Types of box include: bin, caddy, canister, cartridge, casket, coffer, coffin, crate, locker, pack, package, punnet, sarcophagus, tea chest, tin, trunk; ballot-box, black box, box-file, cardboard box, cigarette

box 86 **brainless**

box, collection-box, cool-box, dispatch box, hatbox, jewellery box, knife box, matchbox, pencilbox, pillbox, pillar box, postbox, safe, sewing box, shoebox, snuffbox, strongbox, suggestion box, toolbox, trinket box, vesta, writing-slope.

▶ *v* package, pack, wrap, case, encase
▷ **box in** enclose, surround, block in, cordon off, hem in, shut in, fence in, corner, trap, confine, restrain, coop up, restrict, imprison, cage, contain;
formal circumscribe

box² *v*
1 *learn to box*
fight, spar, engage in fisticuffs
2 *box someone's ears*
punch, hit, strike, slap, batter, thump, buffet, cuff
colloq. clout, wallop, whack, slug; *slang* sock

boxer *n*
fighter, prizefighter, sparring partner
formal pugilist

Weight divisions in professional boxing:
heavyweight, cruiserweight/junior-heavyweight, light-heavyweight, super-middleweight, middleweight, light-middleweight/junior-middleweight, welterweight, light-welterweight/junior-welterweight, lightweight, junior-lightweight/superfeatherweight, featherweight, super-bantamweight/junior-featherweight, bantamweight, super-flyweight/junior-bantamweight, flyweight, light-flyweight/junior-flyweight, mini-flyweight/straw-weight/minimum weight.

boxing *n*
prizefighting, fisticuffs, sparring
formal pugilism
Related adjective: pugilistic

boy *n*
son, lad, youngster, stripling, youth, junior, schoolboy, fellow, child, adolescent, teenager, young man
colloq. kid, nipper, whippersnapper, guttersnipe

boycott *v*
refuse, reject, embargo, black, ban, prohibit, disallow, bar, exclude, blacklist, proscribe, outlaw, ostracize, ignore, avoid, spurn
formal eschew
colloq. cold-shoulder, send to Coventry
⊟ encourage, support, advocate, defend, champion, patronize

boyfriend *n*
young man, man, admirer, sweetheart, lover, suitor, fiancé, beau, partner, cohabitee, live-in lover, common-law spouse
colloq. fellow, bloke, date, toyboy, steady, significant other

boyish *adj*
youthful, childlike, adolescent, childish, immature, innocent, juvenile, puerile, tomboy, unfeminine, unmaidenly, young
colloq. green

brace¹ *n, v*
▶ *n fit braces to strengthen a wall*
support, stay, strap, prop, clamp, fastener, vice, beam, strut, reinforcement, truss, buttress, shoring
formal stanchion
▶ *v* strengthen, reinforce, bolster, buttress, prop (up), shore (up), support, hold up, steady, secure, tighten,

fasten, tie, strap, bind, bandage
formal fortify

brace² *n*
a brace of pheasant
pair, couple, twosome, duo

bracelet *n*
bangle, band, circlet
Related adjective: armillary

bracing *adj*
fresh, crisp, refreshing, reviving, strengthening, fortifying, tonic, rousing, stimulating, exhilarating, invigorating, enlivening, energizing, brisk, energetic, vigorous
⊟ weakening, draining, debilitating;
formal enervating

brackish *adj*
bitter, briny, saline, salt, saltish, salty
⊟ fresh, clean, clear

brag *v*
bluster, boast, show off, swagger, vaunt
formal hyperbolize
colloq. blow your own trumpet, *US* blow your own horn, crow, talk big, lay it on thick/with a trowel
⊟ be modest; *formal* deprecate; *colloq.* run down

braggart *n*
boaster, bluffer, blusterer, show-off, boaster, braggadocio, fanfaron, gascon, rodomontader, swaggerer, swashbuckler
colloq. big mouth, windbag, loud-mouth

bragging *n*
showing-off, bluster, boastfulness, boasting, bravado, exaggeration
formal vauntery
colloq. hot air
⊟ modesty, unobtrusiveness

braid *v*
plait, interweave, interlace, intertwine, weave, lace, twine, entwine, ravel, twist, wind
⊟ undo, unravel

brain *n*
1 *have a good brain*
mind, head, intellect, intelligence, wit, reason, sense, common sense, shrewdness, understanding
technical encephalon
formal acumen, sagacity, sensorium
colloq. grey matter, brains, nous, savvy
Related adjective: cerebral

Parts of the brain include: brainstem, cerebellum, cerebral cortex (grey matter), cerebrum, corpus callosum, forebrain, frontal lobe, hindbrain, hypothalamus, medulla oblongata, mesencephalon, midbrain, occipital lobe, optic thalamus, parietal lobe, pineal body, pituitary gland, pons, spinal cord, temporal lobe, thalamus.

2 *the real brain in the family*
mastermind, intellectual, scholar, expert, pundit, highbrow, genius, prodigy
colloq. egghead, boffin, brainbox, cleverclogs
⊟ 2 simpleton, idiot

brainless *adj*
silly, stupid, crazy, daft, foolish, incompetent, half-witted, idiotic, inept, mindless, thoughtless, senseless
⊟ sensible, shrewd, wise

brainteaser *n*
riddle, puzzle, problem, conundrum, mind-bender,
poser

brainwashing *n*
indoctrination, conditioning, pressurizing,
re-education, grilling, indoctrination, intellectual
suicide, mind-bending, persuasion
formal menticide

brainy *adj*
intellectual, intelligent, clever, gifted, smart, bright,
brilliant, wise
formal sapient
F3 dull, stupid

brake *n, v*
▶ *n* check, curb, rein, restraint, control, restriction,
constraint, drag
formal retardment
▶ *v* slow, decelerate, reduce speed, retard, drag,
slacken, moderate, check, halt, stop, pull up
formal retard
F3 accelerate

branch *n*
1 *the branches of a tree*
BOUGH, limb sprig, shoot, stem, offshoot, arm, wing,
prong
technical ramus
Related adjectives: ramal, rameal, rameous, ramous
2 *a different branch of the company*
DEPARTMENT, office, local/regional office, part,
section, division, subsidiary, subsection, subdivision,
wing, discipline
▷ **branch off** divide, fork, diverge, separate;
formal bifurcate, furcate
▷ **branch out** diversify, subdivide, vary, develop,
expand, enlarge, extend, add to, broaden out, increase,
multiply, proliferate; *formal* ramify

brand *n, v*
▶ *n* **1** *different brands of soap*
MAKE, brand-name, tradename, trademark, logo,
symbol, sign, emblem, label, stamp, hallmark
2 KIND, quality, class, kind, type, sort, line, variety,
species
3 *identify cattle by their brand*
MARK , tag, identification, identifying mark
▶ *v* **1** *branded as a troublemaker*
mark, stamp, label, typecast, stigmatize, stain, taint,
disgrace, discredit, denounce, censure
formal besmirch
2 *brand cattle*
mark, stamp, burn (in), scar

brandish *v*
wave, flourish, shake, raise, swing, wield, flash, flaunt,
exhibit, display, parade

brash *adj*
1 BRAZEN, forward, impertinent, impudent,
insolent, rude, cocky, self-confident, assertive,
assured, bold, audacious
formal temerarious
colloq. pushy
2 RECKLESS, rash, impetuous, impulsive, hasty,
foolhardy, incautious, indiscreet
formal incautious, precipitate
F3 **1** reserved, unassuming, modest,
unobtrusive **2** cautious, wary, prudent

brass *n*
brazenness, impertinence, impudence, insolence, gall,

rudeness, presumption, audacity
formal effrontery, temerity
colloq. cheek, nerve, chutzpah, brass neck, brass nerve
F3 timidity; *formal* circumspection

brassy *adj*
1 *brassy music*
NOISY, loud, blaring, dissonant, grating, hard, harsh,
jangling, jarring, piercing, raucous, strident
2 *a brassy blonde*
shameless, forward, brash, insolent, bold, loud, brazen
colloq. pushy, loud-mouthed, saucy

brat *n*
kid, youngster, rascal
colloq. nipper, guttersnipe, jackanapes, puppy,
whippersnapper

bravado *n*
swagger, boasting, bragging, bluster, talk, boast,
showing-off, parade, show, pretence
formal vaunting, bombast, braggadocio, fanfaronade,
rodomontade
F3 modesty, restraint

brave *adj, v*
▶ *adj* courageous, plucky, unafraid, fearless,
undaunted, unflinching, bold, daring, intrepid,
stalwart, hardy, stoical, resolute, stout-hearted, lion-
hearted, valiant, gallant, heroic, indomitable
formal dauntless, audacious, valorous, doughty
colloq. gutsy, spunky, gritty
F3 cowardly, afraid, timid, craven, faint-hearted;
colloq. yellow, spineless, wimpish, chicken
▶ *v* face, confront, defy, challenge, dare, stand up to,
face up to, suffer, endure, bear, withstand
colloq. put up with, face the music, keep a stiff upper
lip, put a bold/brave face on it, not turn a hair, keep
your chin up
F3 yield, capitulate, give in; *colloq.* get cold feet,
chicken out

bravery *n*
courage, pluck, fearlessness, boldness, daring,
stalwartness, hardiness, fortitude, resolution, tenacity,
stout-heartedness, valour, gallantry, heroism,
indomitability, mettle, spirit, dauntlessness, audacity
formal intrepidity, valiance
colloq. guts, grit, spunk
F3 cowardice, fearfulness, faint-heartedness, timidity

⚠ **bravery** or **bravado** ?
Bravery is courage: *soldiers decorated for bravery.*
Bravado is a boastful act of bravery intended to
impress or intimidate or a boastful pretence of
bravery aimed at concealing cowardice: *She felt her
defiant bravado disintegrate like shattered glass.*

brawl *n, v*
▶ *n* fight, scrap, scuffle, melee, free-for-all, fray,
affray, broil, skirmish, fracas, rumpus, disorder, row,
argument, quarrel, squabble, dispute, clash, fisticuffs,
Donnybrook
formal altercation
colloq. punch-up, bust-up, dust-up, *US* ruckus
▶ *v* fight, scuffle, wrestle, tussle, argue, quarrel,
squabble, wrangle, dispute
formal altercate
colloq. scrap, row

brawn *n*
strength, might, muscle, muscles, bulk, bulkiness,

muscularity, power, robustness, sinews
colloq. beef, beefiness

brawny *adj*
muscular, sinewy, athletic, well-built, burly, hefty, solid, bulky, hulking, massive, strapping, strong, powerful, vigorous, sturdy, robust, hardy, stalwart
colloq. beefy, husky
F3 slight, frail, skinny, weak, weedy

bray *v*
neigh, whinny, heehaw, blare, hoot, roar, screech, trumpet, bell, bellow

brazen *adj*
blatant, flagrant, brash, brassy, bold, forward, saucy, pert, barefaced, impudent, insolent, defiant, shameless, unashamed, unabashed, immodest
formal audacious
colloq. pushy, brassy
F3 shy, shamefaced, modest, cautious
▷ **brazen it out** be unashamed, defy, be defiant, be impenitent; *colloq.* put a brave/bold face on it

breach *n, v*
▶ *n* **1** *a breach of the rules*
breaking, violation, contravention, infringement, trespass, disobedience, offence, transgression, lapse, disruption
formal infraction
2 *a breach in international relations*
quarrel, disagreement, dissension, difference, variance, schism, rift rupture, split, division, separation, parting, severance, alienation, dissociation
formal disaffection, estrangement
3 *a breach in the defences*
break, crack, rift, rupture, fissure, cleft, crevice, opening, aperture, gap, space, hole, gulf, chasm
▶ *v* **1** *breach an agreement*
violate, break, contravene, infringe
2 *breach the sea wall*
rupture, break (open), open up, burst through, split

bread *n*
1 *bread and jam*
crusts, roll, loaf, bap, plait, cob, sandwich, nan, chapati, paratha, pitta, matzo, croissant, baguette, brioche, bagel, French stick, pumpernickel
Related adjective: panary
2 *our daily bread*
food, provisions, diet, fare, nourishment, necessities
formal nutriment, sustenance, subsistence, victuals
3 *earn your daily bread*
cash, money, funds

breadth *n*
1 *the breadth of the garden*
WIDTH, broadness, wideness, latitude, thickness, size, magnitude, measure
2 *a great breadth of interests*
RANGE, scale, reach, scope, compass, span, sweep, extent, expanse, spread, comprehensiveness, extensiveness, vastness
formal amplitude

break *v, n*
▶ *v* **1** *break a plate*
fracture, crack, snap, split, sever, separate, divide, rend, smash, disintegrate, splinter, shiver, shatter, ruin, destroy, demolish
2 *break the law*
violate, contravene, infringe, breach, disobey, flout, dishonour
3 *the television has broken*

stop working, fail
formal malfunction
colloq. go on the blink, pack up, conk out, go kaput, crash, cut out
4 *break for lunch*
PAUSE, halt, stop, interrupt, suspend, rest
formal discontinue
5 *break a silence*
INTERRUPT, suspend, interfere with, bring to an end
formal discontinue
colloq. cut off
6 *the news broke his spirit*
overcome, subdue, tame, weaken, enfeeble, impair, undermine, demoralize
7 *the injury broke her skin*
pierce, perforate, puncture, open (up)
8 *break the news*
tell, inform, impart, divulge, disclose, reveal, announce
9 *break a record*
EXCEED, beat, better, excel, surpass, outdo, outstrip
10 *the weather broke*
change (for the better/worse), vary, improve, worsen
11 *break a code*
CRACK, decipher, solve, work/figure out
F3 **1** mend, put together **2** keep, obey, observe, abide by **3** mend **4** start again **6** encourage, strengthen
▶ *n* **1** *a break in the defences/diplomatic relations*
fracture, crack, split, rift, rupture, schism, separation, tear, gash, fissure, cleft, crevice, opening, gap, hole, breach
formal estrangement
2 *have a break for coffee*
interval, intermission, interlude, interruption, stop, pause, halt, lull, respite, rest
colloq. let-up, breather, time-out
3 *go away for a short break*
time off, holiday, *US* vacation
4 *a lucky break*
opportunity, chance, advantage, fortune, (stroke of) luck, opening
▷ **break away** separate, split (off), part company, detach, secede, leave, depart, quit, run away, escape, flee, fly; *colloq.* make a run for it
▷ **break down 1** *the van broke down* fail, stop, stop working, give way, collapse; *colloq.* pack up, conk out, seize up **2** *negotiations broke down* fail, collapse, founder; *colloq.* fall through **3** *break down in tears* lose control, be overcome, collapse; *colloq.* go to pieces, crack up **4** *break down the figures* analyse, dissect, separate, itemize, detail
▷ **break in 1** *break in with unhelpful remarks* INTERRUPT, butt in, cut in, interject, intervene, intrude, encroach, impinge; *formal* interpose
2 *break in and steal the money* BURGLE, rob, raid, enter illegally **3** *break in a horse/pair of walking boots* train, condition, wear, accustom, get used to
▷ **break off 1** *break off a piece of ice* DETACH, separate, part, divide, disconnect, sever; *formal* dissever; *colloq.* snap off **2** *break off as the phone rang; break off a relationship* pause, interrupt, suspend, halt, stop, cease, end, finish, bring to an end; *formal* discontinue, terminate
▷ **break out 1** *war broke out in 1939* START, begin (suddenly), arise, emerge, happen, occur, erupt; *formal* commence; *colloq.* flare up, burst out **2** *break out of prison* ESCAPE, bolt, flee; *formal* abscond
3 *'Just a minute,' she broke out* exclaim, shout; *colloq.* burst out **4** *break out into a rash* erupt, come

out in

▷ **break through** emerge, gain ground, leap forward, make headway, pass, penetrate, progress, succeed, overcome

▷ **break up** 1 *break up a monopoly* dismantle, take apart, demolish, destroy, disintegrate, splinter, sever, divide, split (up), part, separate 2 *the couple broke up* separate, divorce, finish; *colloq.* split up 3 *the meeting broke up* disband, disperse, dissolve, adjourn, suspend, stop, finish; *formal* discontinue, terminate

▷ **break with** finish with, part with, reject, separate from; *formal* renounce, repudiate; *colloq.* drop, jilt, ditch

breakable *adj*
brittle, fragile, delicate, flimsy, insubstantial, frail
formal friable, frangible
colloq. jerry-built
E3 unbreakable, durable, sturdy, long-lasting, shatterproof

breakaway *adj*
rebel, dissenting, renegade, heretical
formal apostate, schismatic, seceding, secessionist

breakdown *n*
1 *the breakdown of the talks/car*
failure, collapse, disintegration, interruption, stoppage
formal malfunction
2 *a nervous breakdown*
collapse
colloq. going to pieces, cracking-up
3 ANALYSIS, dissection, itemization, classification, categorization

breaker *n*
wave, roller, billow, white horses

break-in *n*
burglary, house-breaking, robbery, raid, invasion, intrusion, trespass, larceny

breakthrough *n*
discovery, find, finding, invention, innovation, advance, progress, headway, step, gain, leap, step/leap forward, quantum leap (forward), development, improvement, milestone

break-up *n*
divorce, separation, parting, split, rift, finish, dispersal, disintegration, crumbling
formal dissolution, termination
colloq. splitting-up

breakwater *n*
groyne, mole, jetty, pier, quay, spur, wharf, dock

breast *n*
1 *beat your breasts in sorrow*
bosom, bust, chest, front, heart, thorax
2 *a woman's breasts*
bust, nipple, teat, cleavage
technical mamma
slang boob, bristol, knocker, tit
Related adjective: mammary

breath *n*
1 *take deep breaths to relax*
air, breathing, respiration, sigh, gasp, pant, gulp
formal flatus, inhalation, exhalation
Related adjectives: respiratory, aspiratory
2 *a breath of fresh air*
breeze, puff, waft, gust
formal pneuma

3 *a breath of autumn in the air*
aroma, smell, odour, whiff
4 *a breath of scandal*
HINT, suggestion, suspicion, undertone, whisper, murmur

breathe *v*
1 *breathe deeply*
sigh, gasp, pant, puff, snore
formal inhale, exhale, respire, expire
2 *not breathe a word to anyone*
express, voice, murmur, whisper, tell, articulate, utter, impart
3 *breathe new life into a project*
instil, imbue, infuse, inject, inspire
formal transfuse

breather *n*
break, rest, constitutional, pause, halt, recess, relaxation, rest, walk
formal respite
colloq. breathing-space

breathless *adj*
1 *breathless from climbing*
short-winded, out of breath, panting, puffing, puffed (out), exhausted, winded, gasping, wheezing, choking
2 *breathless anticipation*
expectant, impatient, in suspense, eager, agog, excited, feverish, anxious

breathtaking *adj*
awe-inspiring, impressive, magnificent, spectacular, overwhelming, amazing, astonishing, stunning, exciting, thrilling, stirring, moving

breed *v, n*
▶ *v* 1 *breed dogs*
REPRODUCE, procreate, multiply, hatch, bear, give birth to, rear, raise, bring up, bring forth
formal propagate, pullulate
2 *breed suspicion*
PRODUCE, create, originate, arouse, cause, occasion, give rise to, generate, make, foster, nurture, nourish, cultivate, develop
formal engender
▶ *n* 1 *breeds of cattle*
SPECIES, strain, variety, family, stamp, stock, race, line, lineage, pedigree, hybrid
formal progeny
2 *the new breed of leader*
kind, type, class

breeding *n*
1 *the breeding of cattle*
REPRODUCTION, nurture, development, rearing, raising, upbringing, ancestry, lineage, stock, genetic engineering
formal procreation
2 *have breeding*
(good) manners, politeness, gentility, refinement, culture, polish, education, training
formal civility, urbanity
E3 2 vulgarity, bad manners

breeding-ground *n*
nest, nursery, school, training ground
colloq. hotbed

breeze *n, v*
▶ *n* wind, gust, flurry, waft, puff, breath, draught, air
▶ *v* glide, sail, hurry, sweep, trip, wander
colloq. flit, sally

breezy _adj_
1 _a breezy day_
WINDY, blowing, fresh, airy, gusty, blustery, squally
2 _a breezy manner_
LIVELY, confident, animated, jaunty, buoyant, blithe, debonair, carefree, cheerful, casual, informal, light, bright, exhilarating, vivacious
colloq. easy-going
🔄 **1** still, calm, windless **2** staid, serious, quiet, sad

brevity _n_
1 _the brevity of the speech_
briefness, shortness, conciseness, succinctness, pithiness, economy, crispness, incisiveness, abruptness, curtness
formal terseness, concision, laconism
2 _the brevity of life_
briefness, shortness
formal impermanence, ephemerality, transience, transitoriness
🔄 **1** long-windedness, wordiness; _formal_ verbosity, prolixity **2** permanence; _formal_ longevity

brew _v, n_
▶ _v_ **1** _brew tea_
stew, boil, prepare, soak, steep, cook
formal infuse, seethe, ferment, prepare
2 _brew beer_
ferment
3 _trouble/a storm is brewing_
build up, gather, develop, plot, scheme, plan, project, devise, contrive, concoct, hatch, excite, foment
▶ _n_ **1** _boil up a hot brew_
drink, liquor, potion
formal beverage, infusion
2 _a powerful brew of sex and violence_
mixture, blend, preparation, fermentation, distillation
formal concoction

bribe _n, v_
▶ _n_ incentive, inducement, allurement, enticement, kickback, douceur
colloq. back-hander, refresher, sweetener, hush money, pay-off, slush fund, protection money, _US_ payola, boodle
▶ _v_ corrupt, reward, suborn, square
colloq. buy/pay off, grease, grease someone's palm, fix, take care of

bribery _n_
corruption, inducement, protection
colloq. palm-greasing, graft

bric-à-brac _n_
knick-knacks, ornaments, curios, antiques, trinkets, baubles, trumpery

brick _n_
1 _bricks and mortar_
breeze block, adobe, firebrick, block, briquette, header, klinker, stretcher, rock, stone
2 _be a real brick for helping_
mate, pal, real friend, chum, _US_ buddy

bridal _adj_
wedding, nuptial, marriage, matrimonial, marital, conjugal
formal connubial

bride _n_
honeymooner, newly-wed, wife, spouse, marriage partner, war bride, GI bride

bridegroom _n_
honeymooner, newly-wed, husband, spouse, marriage partner, groom

bridge _n, v_
▶ _n_ **1** _a bridge over the river_
arch, span, causeway, link

Types of bridge include: suspension bridge, arch bridge, cantilever bridge, flying bridge, flyover, overpass, footbridge, railway bridge, viaduct, aqueduct, humpback bridge, toll bridge, pontoon bridge, Bailey bridge, rope bridge, drawbridge, swing bridge.

2 _act as a bridge between the different factions_
link, connection, bond, tie
▶ _v_ span, cross, go over, reach across, fill, link, connect, couple, join, unite, bind
formal traverse

bridle _v, n_
▶ _v_ **1** _bridle your temper_
check, curb, restrain, control, govern, master, subdue, moderate, repress, contain
2 _bridle at someone's anger_
bristle, become indignant, be offended by
▶ _n_ check, halter, control, curb, restraint

brief _adj, n, v_
▶ _adj_ **1** _a brief report/visit_
short, terse, succinct, concise, pithy, crisp, compressed, condensed, abridged, thumbnail
formal aphoristic
2 _a brief manner_
ABRUPT, sharp, short, brusque, blunt, curt, surly
formal laconic
3 _this brief life_
short-lived, momentary, ephemeral, transient, fleeting, passing, transitory, temporary, limited, cursory, hasty, quick, swift
formal fugacious
🔄 **1** lengthy, long-winded, extensive; _formal_ verbose, protracted
▶ _n_ **1** _with a brief to reduce crime_
RESPONSIBILITY, orders, instructions, directions, remit, mandate, directive, advice, briefing, data, information
2 _a brief of the day's events_
outline, summary, précis, abstract, abridgement, digest
3 _a legal brief_
dossier, case, defence, argument, evidence, data
▶ _v_ instruct, direct, explain, guide, advise, prepare, prime, inform
colloq. fill in, gen up, give someone the run-down/low-down, put someone in the picture

briefing _n_
meeting, conference, preparation, priming, information, advice, guidance, directions, instructions, orders
formal intimation
colloq. filling-in, gen, run-down, low-down

briefly _adv_
1 _speak briefly_
concisely, succinctly, cursorily, precisely, quickly, summarily, tersely, to the point
2 _briefly, the answer is no_
in brief, in a word, in a few words
colloq. in a nutshell
🔄 **1** at length, fully

brigade *n*
group, band, body, company, unit, corps, crew, force, party, squad, team, troop, contingent

brigand *n*
bandit, robber, desperado, gangster, outlaw, marauder, plunderer, ruffian, highwayman, freebooter

bright *adj*
1 *bright lights/colours*
BRILLIANT, luminous, illuminated, radiant, shining, beaming, flashing, gleaming, glistening, glittering, sparkling, twinkling, shimmering, glowing, glorious, splendid, dazzling, blinding, glaring, blazing, intense, vivid
formal resplendent, effulgent, refulgent, lustrous, incandescent
2 *look bright*
HAPPY, cheerful, glad, joyful, merry, jolly, lively
formal vivacious
3 *the future looks bright*
PROMISING, favourable, rosy, optimistic, hopeful, encouraging
formal propitious, auspicious
4 *bright students*
CLEVER, smart, intelligent, quick-witted, quick, sharp, acute, keen, astute, perceptive
colloq. brainy, bright as a button
5 *a bright day*
FINE, sunny, cloudless, unclouded, pleasant
F₃ 1 dull, drab, colourless, pale, dim, soft **2** sad, gloomy, depressed; *colloq.* down **3** depressing; gloomy; *formal* inauspicious **4** stupid; *colloq.* thick **5** dark, overcast, cloudy

brighten *v*
1 *brighten up a room*
light up, illuminate, lighten, make bright
2 *brighten up the silver*
polish, burnish, rub (up), shine, gleam, glow
3 *brighten at the prospect*
CHEER UP, gladden, hearten, encourage, liven up
formal enliven
colloq. buck up, perk up, pep up
F₃ 1 darken, shadow **2** dull, tarnish

brilliance *n*
1 *brilliance at the piano*
talent, virtuosity, genius, greatness, distinction, excellence, aptitude, cleverness, distinction
2 *the brilliance of the sun*
RADIANCE, brightness, sparkle, dazzle, intensity, vividness, gloss, lustre, sheen, glamour, glory, magnificence, splendour
formal resplendence, effulgence, refulgence, fulgency, coruscation

brilliant *adj*
1 *a brilliant flautist*
gifted, talented, accomplished, expert, skilful, masterly, exceptional, outstanding, superb, illustrious, famous, celebrated
2 *a brilliant light/show*
sparkling, glittering, scintillating, dazzling, glaring, blazing, intense, vivid, bright, shining, glossy, showy, glorious, magnificent, splendid
formal resplendent, effulgent, refulgent, fulgent
3 *a brilliant mind*
clever, bright, intelligent, quick, astute
formal erudite
colloq. brainy
4 *a brilliant performance*
clever, skilful, masterly, remarkable, resourceful,

enterprising
5 *What a brilliant game!*
great, fantastic, superb, wonderful
F₃ 1 undistinguished, untalented **2** dull **3** stupid **4** ordinary; *colloq.* run-of-the-mill **5** awful, bad

brim *n, v*
▶ *n* rim, perimeter, circumference, lip, edge, margin, border, brink, verge, top, limit
▶ *v* be full with, be (packed) full with, be filled with, overflow with, be overflowing with

bring *v*
1 *bring a drink; bring you home later*
take, carry, transport, fetch, deliver, escort, accompany, usher, guide, conduct, lead, convey
formal bear
2 *bring misery*
cause, produce, result in, create, prompt, provoke, force
formal engender
▷ **bring about** cause, occasion, create, produce, generate, accomplish, achieve, fulfil, realize, manage; *formal* effect
▷ **bring down 1** *bring down the government*
OVERTHROW, unseat, oust, defeat, destroy; *formal* vanquish; *colloq.* topple, knock down, shoot down **2** *bring down blood pressure/unemployment*
REDUCE, lower, cause to fall/drop
▷ **bring forward** advance, put forward, make earlier
F₃ postpone, put back
▷ **bring in 1** *bring in new laws* INTRODUCE, initiate, originate, pioneer, set up, usher in; *formal* inaugurate **2** *bring in £4,000* earn, net, gross, produce, fetch, return, yield; *formal* accrue, realize
▷ **bring off** succeed in, achieve, fulfil, perform, accomplish, win; *formal* execute, discharge; *colloq.* pull off
▷ **bring on 1** *bring on a headache* cause, lead to, give rise to, generate, inspire, prompt, provoke; *formal* occasion, induce, precipitate **2** *bring on the plant's growth* ADVANCE, accelerate, foster, nurture, improve; *formal* expedite
▷ **bring out 1** *bring out a point in a story*
EMPHASIZE, stress, highlight, enhance, draw out, make someone aware of **2** *bring out a book* publish, print, issue, launch, introduce, produce
▷ **bring round 1** *bring round someone who is unconscious* REVIVE, resuscitate, bring to, rouse, awaken **2** *bring someone round to your way of thinking* PERSUADE, convince, win over, convert, coax, cajole
▷ **bring up 1** *bring up children* care for, raise, foster, nurture, educate, teach, train, form; *formal* rear **2** *bring up a matter for discussion*
RAISE, introduce, broach, mention, submit, propose **3** *bring up food* vomit, regurgitate; *colloq.* throw up, puke

brink *n*
on the brink of the cliff edge/war
verge, threshold, edge, margin, fringe, border, boundary, limit, extremity, lip, rim, brim, bank

brisk *adj*
1 *go for a brisk walk*
energetic, vigorous, quick, snappy, lively, spirited, active, busy, bustling, agile, nimble, alert
2 *a brisk manner*
lively, quick, businesslike

colloq. no-nonsense
3 *brisk business*
busy, rapid, good
4 *brisk weather*
invigorating, exhilarating, stimulating, bracing, refreshing, cold, fresh, crisp
E3 **1** unenergetic, slow **2** slow, lethargic **3** slow, sluggish

bristle *n, v*
▶ *n* **1** *shave off bristles*
hair, whisker, stubble
2 *bristles on an animal's back*
spine, prickle, barb, quill, thorn, awn
▶ *v* **1** *bristling with anger*
seethe (with), draw oneself up, bridle at, be incensed at
technical horripilate
2 *bristling with police*
teem with, swarm with
formal abound in
colloq. be thick with, hum with

bristly *adj*
hairy, whiskered, bearded, unshaven, stubbly, rough, spiny, prickly, spiky, thorny
technical hispid, barbellate
formal hirsute
E3 clean-shaven, smooth

brittle *adj*
1 BREAKABLE, easily broken, fragile, delicate, frail, hard, crisp, crumbly, crumbling, shattery
formal friable, frangible
2 *a brittle situation*
unstable, fragile, delicate
3 *a brittle manner*
tense, curt, irritable, nervous
colloq. nervy
4 *a brittle laugh*
short hard, sharp, harsh, grating
E3 **1** durable, resilient, sturdy **2** stable, secure, constant

broach *v*
introduce, raise, mention, propose, suggest, hint at

broad *adj*
1 *broad avenues/valleys*
WIDE, large, vast, roomy, spacious, ample, extensive, widespread
formal capacious, latitudinous
2 *a broad education*
WIDE-RANGING, far-reaching, encyclopedic, extensive, all-embracing, inclusive, comprehensive, general, sweeping, universal, unlimited
formal catholic, eclectic, compendious
3 *the broad meaning of the term*
general, vague, not detailed
4 *broad support*
WIDESPREAD, extensive, general
5 *a broad hint*
obvious, clear, plain, undisguised, unconcealed
E3 **1** narrow **2** limited, restricted **3** narrow, detailed, specific, precise **4** limited **5** veiled, disguised

⚠ **broad** or **wide** ?
Broad refers to the extent across something and often has the connotation of spaciousness or ampleness, whereas *wide* refers to the distance separating, or the gap between, sides or edges: *a person's broad back; broad shoulders; wide sleeves; a wide doorway.*

broadcast *v, n*
▶ *v* **1** *broadcast TV programmes*
TRANSMIT, air, show, beam, relay, televise, cable
2 *broadcast the decision widely*
make known, report, announce, publicize, advertise, publish, circulate, spread, scatter
formal promulgate, disseminate
▶ *n* transmission, programme, show, access television, community broadcasting, simulcast, simultaneous transmission, television première, teletext, satellite programme

broaden *v*
the road broadens out; broaden the scope of the inquiry
widen, spread, enlarge, expand, extend, stretch, increase, develop, report, branch out, diversify
formal augment
E3 narrow, reduce, restrict

broad-minded *adj*
liberal, tolerant, permissive, forbearing, enlightened, free-thinking, progressive, indulgent, impartial, open-minded, receptive, unbiased, unprejudiced, dispassionate
E3 narrow-minded, intolerant, biased, prejudiced

broadside *n*
1 *fire a broadside at a ship*
attack, assault, volley, battering, cannonade, blast, bombardment, counterblast
2 *verbal broadsides*
criticism, denunciation
formal philippic, diatribe, fulmination, harangue, invective
colloq. brickbat, stick

brochure *n*
leaflet, booklet, pamphlet, prospectus, broadsheet, handbill, circular, handout, folder, flyer

broil *v*
grill, cook, fry, barbecue, roast

broiling *adj*
sweltering, boiling, baking, roasting, scorching, blistering

broke *adj*
penniless, bankrupt, ruined, poor, impoverished, poverty-stricken, destitute
formal insolvent, impecunious, penurious, indigent
colloq. bust, skint, stony-broke, strapped (for cash), cleaned out, on your uppers, on your beam ends, not having two pennies to rub together
E3 rich, affluent, solvent

broken *adj*
1 *a broken pipe*
fractured, burst, ruptured, severed, separated, shattered, smashed, destroyed, demolished
colloq. broken to smithereens
2 *broken machinery*
faulty, damaged, defective, out of order/action, not working, gone wrong
formal malfunctioning, inoperative
colloq. bust, kaput, duff, on the blink, wonky
3 *broken sleep*
disjointed, disconnected, fragmentary, interrupted, intermittent, spasmodic, erratic
formal discontinuous
4 *speak broken German*
hesitating, stammering, halting, imperfect, disjointed
5 *a broken man*
beaten, defeated, crushed, demoralized, weak, feeble,

exhausted, tamed, subdued, oppressed
formal vanquished
colloq. down, knackered
E3 **1** mended, intact, whole **2** mended, in order/
action, working **3** continuous, uninterrupted
4 fluent

broken-down *adj*
1 *a broken-down machine*
faulty, damaged, defective, out of order
formal inoperative
colloq. on the blink, bust, kaput, duff
2 *a broken-down old house*
DILAPIDATED, in disrepair, decrepit, ruined,
decayed, collapsed

broken-hearted *adj*
heartbroken, inconsolable, devastated, grief-stricken,
desolate, despairing, miserable, wretched, mournful,
sorrowful, sad, unhappy, dejected, despondent,
crestfallen, disappointed
formal dolorous, forlorn, wretched, disconsolate,
prostrated
colloq. down, down in the dumps

broker *n*
agent, middleman, dealer, factor, handler,
intermediary, negotiator, stockbroker, jobber,
stockjobber
technical arbitrageur

bromide *n*
platitude, banality, cliché, commonplace, stereotype,
truism
formal anodyne

bronze *adj*
copper, copper-coloured, auburn, chestnut,
reddish-brown, rust, tan, Titian

brooch *n*
badge, pin, clip, clasp, breastpin, tiepin

brood *v, n*
▶ *v* **1** *brood over lost opportunities*
ponder, meditate, muse, mull over, go over, dwell on,
worry about, sulk, agonize
formal, rehearse, ruminate
colloq. fret, mope
2 *hens brood*
incubate, sit, hatch
▶ *n* **1** *a brood of birds*
clutch, chicks, hatch, litter, young, offspring, issue,
progeny
2 *a brood of children*
children, family

brook¹ *n*
a brook running by the cottage
stream, rivulet, beck, burn, watercourse, channel,
inlet, gill, runnel

brook² *v*
will brook no interference
tolerate, allow, accept, allow, permit, bear, endure,
stand, put up with, support, withstand
formal countenance
colloq. stomach

brothel *n*
bordello, bawdy-house, house of ill fame, house of ill
repute, red light, whorehouse, bagnio
slang knocking-shop, *US* cathouse

brother *n*
1 *brothers and sisters*

sibling, blood-brother, relation, relative
Related adjective: fraternal
2 *brothers in the struggle against injustice*
comrade, friend, mate, partner, colleague, associate,
fellow, companion
colloq. chum, mate, pal
3 *brothers in a monastery*
monk, friar

brotherhood *n*
1 *feelings of brotherhood*
fellowship, comradeship, friendship, friendliness
camaraderie
2 *a brotherhood of monks*
fraternity, association, society, league, confederation,
confederacy, alliance, union, guild, fellowship,
community, clique

brotherly *adj*
fraternal, loyal, affectionate, amicable, caring,
sympathetic, friendly, kind, loving, benevolent,
philanthropic
E3 callous, unbrotherly

brow *n*
1 *sweat on your brow*
forehead, temples
2 *the brow of the hill*
summit, ridge, top, tip, peak, verge, brink, cliff

browbeat *v*
bully, coerce, force, intimidate, threaten, tyrannize,
hound, dragoon, domineer, overbear, oppress
colloq. bulldoze
E3 coax, flatter; *colloq.* sweet-talk

brown *adj, v*
▶ *adj* **1** *brown in colour*
mahogany, chocolate, coffee, hazel, bay, chestnut,
auburn, umber, sepia, ginger, beige, fawn, tan, tawny,
russet, rust, rusty, brunette, dark, dusky
2 *brown from lying in the sun*
sunburnt, tanned, bronze, bronzed, browned
▶ *v* cook, seal, fry, grill, toast

browned off *adj*
bored, fed up, discontented, discouraged,
disheartened, weary
colloq. bored stiff, brassed off, cheesed off,
disgruntled; *slang* pissed off
E3 fascinated, interested, intrigued

browse *v*
1 *browse through a book*
survey, scan, leaf through, flick through, dip into, skim
formal peruse
2 *sheep browsing in the fields*
GRAZE, pasture, feed, eat, nibble

bruise *v, n*
▶ *v* **1** *bruise your leg*
discolour, blacken, mark, blemish, injure, wound
2 *bruise someone's feelings*
hurt, injure, insult, offend, grieve, upset, crush
3 *bruise fruit*
damage, mark, spoil, blemish, crush
▶ *n* discoloration, mark, blemish, injury
technical ecchymosis
formal contusion
colloq. black eye, shiner

brunt *n*
burden, thrust, (main) force, impact, impetus,
pressure, (full) weight, shock, strain

brush¹ *n, v*

▶ *n* *sweep the room with a brush*
broom, sweeper, besom, whisk
▶ *v* **1** *brush the room*
clean, clean, sweep, flick, burnish, polish, shine
2 *brush against the table*
touch, contact, graze, kiss, stroke, rub, scrape
▷ **brush aside** dismiss, ignore, flout, disregard, override; *formal* belittle; *colloq.* pooh-pooh
▷ **brush off** disregard, ignore, slight, snub, rebuff, dismiss, spurn, reject, repulse, disown; *formal* repudiate; *colloq.* cold-shoulder
▷ **brush up 1** *brush up your Spanish* revise, relearn, improve, polish up, study, read up; *colloq.* swot, bone up on, cram **2** *go and brush up* refresh (yourself), freshen up, clean (yourself up), tidy (up)

brush² *n*

a ball lost in the brush
bush, scrub, thicket, bushes, shrubs, brushwood, undergrowth, ground cover

brush³ *n*

a brush with the police
confrontation, encounter, disagreement, argument, clash, conflict, fight, skirmish, tussle, fracas
colloq. dust-up, set-to, scrap

brush-off *n*

discouragement, dismissal, rebuff, refusal, rejection, repudiation, repulse, slight, snub
formal repudiation
colloq. cold shoulder; *US slang* kiss-off
E3 encouragement

brusque *adj*

abrupt, sharp, short, terse, curt, gruff, surly, discourteous, impolite, uncivil, blunt, tactless, uncivil, undiplomatic
E3 courteous, polite, tactful

brutal *adj*

1 *a brutal murder/attacker*
savage, bloodthirsty, vicious, ferocious, cruel, inhumane, animal, inhuman, beastly, brutish, remorseless, pitiless, merciless, ruthless, callous
formal bestial
2 *brutal frankness*
harsh, insensitive, unfeeling, heartless, severe
E3 1 kindly, humane, civilized **2** kind, gentle, sensitive

brutality *n*

savagery, bloodthirstiness, viciousness, ferocity, cruelty, inhumanity, violence, atrocity, ruthlessness, callousness, roughness, coarseness, barbarism, barbarity, brutishness
formal callosity
E3 gentleness, kindness

brute *n, adj*

▶ *n* animal, beast, swine, creature, monster, ogre, devil, fiend, savage, sadist, bully, lout, yahoo
▶ *adj* physical, senseless, unthinking, bodily, carnal, coarse, depraved, fleshly, gross, instinctive, mindless, sensual

brutish *adj*

brutal, uncivilized, barbarian, barbaric, barbarous, coarse, crass, crude, cruel, gross, loutish, savage, stupid, uncouth, vulgar
formal bestial, feral, ferine
E3 refined, civilized, polite

bubble *n, v*

▶ *n* **1** *soap bubbles*
ball (of air), drop, droplet, bead, blister, fizz, foam, froth, head, lather, suds, effervescence, globule, spume
formal vesicle
2 *the bubble of all their dreams burst*
delusion, fantasy, fraud, illusion, trifle, vanity
▶ *v* **1** SPARKLE, froth, foam, seethe, boil, burble, gurgle, effervesce
colloq. fizz
2 *bubble with enthusiasm*
be filled, be excited, sparkle, be elated
colloq. bounce

bubbly *adj*

1 SPARKLING, carbonated, frothy, foaming, sudsy, effervescent
colloq. fizzy
2 LIVELY, happy, merry, elated, excited, exuberant, vivacious
formal animated, ebullient
colloq. bouncy
E3 1 flat, still **2** lethargic

buccaneer *n*

pirate, corsair, filibuster, freebooter, privateer, sea-robber, sea-rover, sea-wolf

buck *v*

▷ **buck up 1** *buck someone up* cheer (up), encourage, improve, rally, stimulate, take heart, hearten, enliven; *formal* inspirit; *colloq.* perk up
2 *Buck up or we'll be late!* hurry (up); *formal* hasten; *colloq.* get a move on, get your skates on, step on it
E3 1 discourage **2** slow down

bucket *n*

pail, can, bail, scuttle, pitcher, vessel

buckle *n, v*

▶ *n* **1** *a buckle on a belt*
clasp, clip, catch, fastener, hasp
2 *a buckle in metal*
bulge, warp, distortion, twist, kink
formal contortion
▶ *v* **1** *buckle your belt*
FASTEN, clasp, catch, hook, hitch, connect, close, secure
2 *the metal buckled*
bend, warp, twist, distort, bulge, fold, wrinkle, crumple, collapse
colloq. cave in

bucolic *adj*

pastoral, rural, agrarian, agricultural, country
formal rustic
colloq. countrified
E3 industrial, urban

bud *n, v*

▶ *n* shoot, sprout, sprig, germ, embryo
formal knosp, plumule
▶ *v* shoot, sprout, develop, grow
formal burgeon, pullulate
E3 wither, waste away

budding *adj*

potential, promising, embryonic, developing, growing, flowering, fledgling
formal incipient, nascent, burgeoning
E3 experienced, mature

budge *v*

1 *the door won't budge*

move, stir, shift, remove, dislodge, push, roll, slide
2 *not budge from your position*
change, bend, yield, give (way), give in, change your
mind, not compromise, sway, influence, persuade,
convince

budget *n, v*
▶ *n* finances, funds, resources, economics, means,
allowance, allotment, quota, allocation, (financial)
estimate, what you can afford
▶ *v* plan, estimate, allow, allot, allocate, set aside,
ration, afford
formal apportion

buff¹ *adj, v*
▶ *adj* *buff-coloured envelopes*
yellowish-brown, yellowish, straw, sandy, fawn, khaki,
tan
▶ *v* polish, burnish, shine, smooth, rub, brush

buff² *n*
a computer buff
expert, connoisseur, enthusiast, fan, admirer, devotee,
addict, aficionado, *US* maven
colloq. freak, fiend

buffer *n*
shock-absorber, bumper, fender, pad, cushion, pillow,
intermediary, screen, shield, bulwark

buffet¹ *n*
1 *a railway buffet*
snackbar, counter, café, cafeteria
2 *a buffet supper*
self-service, cold meal, smorgasbord
colloq. help yourself

buffet² *v, n*
▶ *v* *was buffeted by the storm*
batter, hit, strike, knock, bang, bump, push, pound,
pummel, beat, shove, thump, box, cuff, slap
colloq. clout
▶ *n* blow, knock, bang, bump, jar, jolt, push, thump,
box, cuff, clout, slap, smack, shove, thump, box, cuff,
slap, smack
colloq. clout

buffoon *n*
clown, comedian, comic, fool, harlequin, jester, joker,
wag, droll

buffoonery *n*
clowning, jesting, pantomime, tomfoolery,
waggishness, drollery, nonsense, silliness

bug *n, v*
▶ *n* **1** INSECT, flea
colloq. creepy-crawly
2 *a stomach bug*
virus, bacterium, germ, microbe, micro-organism,
infection, disease
3 *a bug in a computer program*
fault, defect, flaw, blemish, imperfection, failing, error
colloq. gremlin
4 *bitten by the decorating bug*
craze, fad, obsession
5 *put a bug in a room*
hidden microphone, listening device
colloq. wire-tap, phone-tap
▶ *v* **1** *their attitude bugs me*
ANNOY, irritate, vex, irk, bother, disturb, harass
colloq. needle, wind up
2 *bug an office*
tap, listen in (on/to)

formal eavesdrop (on)
colloq. wire-tap, phone-tap

bugbear *n*
anathema, bane, *bête noire*, pet hate, dread, fiend,
horror, nightmare

build *v, n*
▶ *v* **1** *build a new hotel*
construct, put up, erect, raise, fabricate, make, form,
constitute, assemble, put together, knock together,
shape, fashion
2 *build a fairer society*
develop, enlarge, extend, increase, escalate, intensify
formal augment
FA 1 destroy, demolish; *colloq.* knock down
2 lessen
▶ *n* physique, figure, body, form, shape, size, frame,
structure
▷ **build up 1** *build up a navy* ASSEMBLE, put
together, piece together, extend, enlarge **2** *build up
your strength* reinforce, extend, expand, develop,
amplify, increase, escalate, intensify, heighten, boost,
improve, enhance; *formal* fortify **3** *build a person up
as important* publicize, advertise, promote;
colloq. plug, hype

building *n*
construction, development, fabrication, structure,
erection, architecture
formal edifice, dwelling
Related adjective: tectonic

Types of building include: house, bungalow, cottage,
block of flats, apartment, *US* condominium, cabin,
farmhouse, villa, mansion, chateau, castle, palace;
church, chapel, cathedral, abbey, monastery, temple,
pagoda, mosque, synagogue; shop, store, garage,
factory, warehouse, silo, office block, tower block,
skyscraper, theatre, cinema, gymnasium, sports
hall, restaurant, café, hotel, *colloq.* pub, public
house, inn, school, college, museum, library,
hospital, prison, power station, observatory;
barracks, fort, fortress, monument, mausoleum;
shed, barn, outhouse, stable, mill, lighthouse, pier,
pavilion, boat-house, beach-hut, summerhouse,
gazebo, dovecote, windmill. *See also* **house;
restaurant; shop**.

Types of building material include: aluminium,
ashlar, asphalt, bitumen, breeze block, brick,
building block, cast iron, cement, chipboard, clay,
concrete, reinforced concrete, fixings, flagstone,
girder, glass, glass fibre, gravel, granite, grout,
gypsum, hardboard, hard core, insulation, foam
insulation, loose fill insulation, lagging, lintel, *US*
lumber, marble, mortar, paving stone, pavior,
plaster, plasterboard, plastic, plywood, sand,
sandstone, shingle, slate, stainless steel, steel, steel
beam, stone, tarmac, thatch, tile, floor tile, roof tile,
timber, wattle and daub, wood.

build-up *n*
1 *a build-up of fat*
enlargement, expansion, development, increase, gain,
growth, accumulation, escalation
formal accretion
2 *build-up of nuclear weapons*
ACCUMULATION, mass, load, heap, stack, drift,
store, stockpile
3 *build-up to the competition*
publicity, promotion
colloq. plug, hype
FA 1 reduction, decrease, contraction

built-in *adj*
1 *built-in wardrobes*
FITTED, integral, in-built, included
2 *built-in safeguards*
inherent, included, incorporated, implicit, in-built, inseparable, integral, intrinsic, essential, fundamental, necessary

bulb *n*

Plants grown from bulbs and corms include: acidanthera, allium, amarylis, anemone, bluebell (endymion), chincherinchee, chionodoxa, crocosmia, crocus, autumn crocus (colchicum), cyclamen, daffodil, crown imperial (fritillaria), galtonia, garlic, gladioli, grape hyacinth (muscari), hyacinth, iris, ixia, jonquil, lily, montbretia, narcissus, nerine, ranunculus, scilla, snowdrop (galanthus), sparaxis, tulip, winter aconite.

bulbous *adj*
rounded, swollen, swelling, bulging, convex, bloated
technical pulvinate(d)
formal distended

bulge *n, v*
▶ *n* **1** *a bulge on the wall*
swelling, bump, lump, hump
formal projection, protuberance, distension
2 *a bulge in the production figures*
rise, increase, surge, upsurge, intensification
▶ *v* swell, hump, expand, enlarge, bulb, project, protrude,
formal dilate, distend
colloq. puff out, sag

bulk *n*
1 *the vast bulk of the ship*
size, magnitude, dimensions, extent, bigness, largeness, immensity, volume, mass, weight, substance, body
formal amplitude
2 *the bulk of the recruits*
MAJORITY, most, nearly all, preponderance
colloq. lion's share

bulky *adj*
substantial, big, large, huge, enormous, immense, mammoth, massive, colossal, hulking, hefty, heavy, weighty, unmanageable, unwieldy, awkward, cumbersome
formal voluminous
▣ insubstantial, small, handy

bulldoze *v*
1 *bulldoze buildings*
clear, flatten, level, raze
colloq. knock down
2 *bulldoze someone into buying; bulldoze plans through a committee*
FORCE, push (through), intimidate, browbeat
formal coerce
colloq. bully, steamroller

bullet *n*
shot, pellet, ball, missile, propellant, cartridge, cartouche
formal projectile
colloq. slug

bulletin *n*
1 *televison news bulletins*
REPORT, newsflash, dispatch, communiqué, statement, announcement, notification,

communication, message
2 *an office bulletin*
news sheet, newspaper, newsletter, leaflet

bullish *adj*
optimistic, confident, hopeful, positive, cheeful, buoyant
formal sanguine
colloq. upbeat

bully *n, v*
▶ *n* persecutor, tormentor, browbeater, intimidator, bully-boy, ruffian, thug, bouncer
colloq. heavy, tough
▶ *v* persecute, torment, terrorize, bulldoze, coerce, browbeat, bullyrag, intimidate, cow, tyrannize, pick on, victimize, domineer, overbear, oppress
colloq. push around
▣ coax, persuade, encourage

bulwark *n*
bastion, buttress, defence, guard, safeguard, security, support, mainstay, outwork, buffer, embankment, fortification, partition, rampart
technical redoubt

bumbling *adj*
bungling, awkward, inept, blundering, botching, clumsy, inefficient, incompetent, lumbering, muddled, stumbling
formal maladroit
▣ competent, efficient

bump *v, n*
▶ *v* **1** *bump into the wall/against the table*
hit, strike, knock, bang, crash, collide (with)
colloq. slam, prang
2 *bump along a track*
jolt, jerk, jar, jostle, rattle, shake, bounce
▶ *n* **1** *hear a bump*
blow, hit, knock, bang, thump, thud, smash, crash, collision, impact, jolt, jar, shock
2 *a bump on your head*
lump, swelling, bulge, injury, hump
technical papilla, knur, nodule
formal protrusion, protuberance, tumescence
3 *a bump on a road*
lump, bulge, hump, protuberance, sleeping policeman
▷ **bump into** come across, meet (unexpectedly), meet by chance, encounter; *formal* chance upon, happen upon, light upon; *colloq.* run into
▷ **bump off** kill, murder, assassinate, remove; *colloq.* eliminate, liquidate, do in, rub out, blow away, top

bumper *adj*
plentiful, abundant, large, great, enormous, massive, excellent, exceptional
▣ small, tiny

bumpkin *n*
country bumpkin, country yokel, boor, clodhopper, rustic, oaf, peasant, provincial
colloq. hillbilly, hick, hayseed

bumptious *adj*
self-important, pompous, officious, overbearing, pushy, assertive, over-confident, presumptuous, forward, full of yourself, impudent, arrogant, cocky, conceited, swaggering, boastful, full of yourself, egotistic
colloq. cocky, pushy
▣ humble, modest, unassertive

bumpy *adj*
1 ***a bumpy road***
rough, lumpy, pot-holed, knobbly, knobby, uneven, irregular
2 ***a bumpy ride***
rough, uneven jerky, jolting, bouncy, choppy
E3 **1** smooth, level **2** smooth, even, uncomfortable

bunch *n, v*
▶ *n* **1** ***a bunch of grapes***
bundle, sheaf, tuft, clump, cluster
2 ***a bunch of keys/papers***
batch, lot, wad, heap, pile, stack, mass, number, quantity, collection, assortment
formal agglomeration, fascicle, fascicule
3 ***a bunch of flowers***
BOUQUET, posy, spray, nosegay, corsage
4 ***a bunch of people***
gang, band, troop, crew, team, party, gathering, flock, swarm, crowd, mob, multitude
▶ *v* group, bundle, cluster, collect, gather, flock, herd, crowd, mass, pack, huddle
formal assemble, congregate
E3 disperse, scatter, spread out

bundle *n, v*
▶ *n* **1** ***a bundle of sticks***
bunch, sheaf, roll, bale, truss, faggot
formal fascicle, fascicule
2 ***carry bundles of clothes***
pack, batch, parcel, package, packet, carton, box, bag
formal consignment
3 ***a bundle of books/paper***
group, set, collection, assortment, quantity, mass, accumulation, pile, stack, heap
▶ *v* **1** ***bundle papers together***
pack, wrap, bale, truss, cluster, gather, parcel, bind, tie, fasten
2 ***bundle someone into a van***
rush, hurry, push roughly, shove

bungle *v*
mismanage, make a mess of, ruin, spoil, mar, fudge, blunder
colloq. foul up, mess up, louse up, bodge, botch, fluff, boob, muff; *slang* cock up, screw up

bungler *n*
incompetent, blunderer
colloq. botcher, butterfingers, duffer

bungling *adj*
awkward, clumsy, incompetent, inept, unskilful
formal maladroit
colloq. blundering, botching, cack-handed, ham-fisted, ham-handed

bunkum *n*
nonsense, rubbish
colloq. balderdash, baloney, bilge, bosh, bunk, garbage, cobblers, hooey, horsefeathers, piffle, poppycock, rot, stuff and nonsense, tommyrot, trash, tripe, twaddle, *US* hogwash, horsefeathers; *slang* balls

buoy *n*
float, marker, signal, beacon, mooring
▷ **buoy up** support, sustain, raise, lift, boost, encourage, cheer (up), hearten
E3 depress, discourage

buoyant *adj*
1 ***a buoyant mood***
light-hearted, carefree, bright, cheerful, optimistic, happy, joyful, lively, blithe, bullish, debonair, animated, vivacious
colloq. bouncy, peppy
2 ***a buoyant raft***
floatable, floating, afloat, light, weightless
E3 **1** depressed, despairing **2** heavy

burble *v*
babble, gurgle, lap murmur, purl

burden *n, v*
▶ *n* **1** ***put down a heavy burden***
cargo, load, weight, dead-weight,
2 ***the burdens of office***
OBLIGATION, responsibility, duty, onus, millstone, pressure, strain, stress, worry, anxiety, weight, care, trouble, trial, affliction, sorrow
formal encumbrance
▶ *v* ***burdened with a heavy load/worldly cares***
weigh down, handicap, bother, worry, tax, strain, overload, lie heavy/hard on, oppress, overwhelm, crush
formal encumber
E3 unburden, relieve

burdensome *adj*
onerous, crushing, difficult, weighty, exacting, heavy, irksome, oppressive, taxing, troublesome, trying, wearisome
E3 easy, light

bureau *n*
1 ***the Federal Bureau of Investigation***
office, service, agency, branch, department, division, counter
2 ***sit at a bureau***
desk, writing-desk

bureaucracy *n*
1 ***a bureaucracy of thousands of civil servants***
administration, government, ministry, civil service, the authorities, the system
2 ***try to reduce bureaucracy***
administration, rules and regulations, officialdom, officiousness, beadledom
colloq. red tape

bureaucrat *n*
officer, official, office-holder, administrator, civil servant, functionary, (government) minister, committee member, mandarin, apparatchik

bureaucratic *adj*
official, administrative, governmental, ministerial, complicated, procedural, inflexible

burglar *n*
housebreaker, robber, thief, pilferer, trespasser, cat-burglar

burglary *n*
housebreaking, break-in, robbery, theft, stealing, trespass, pilferage, larceny
colloq. heist

burial *n*
burying, funeral
formal interment, entombment, obsequies, exequies, inhumation

burial place *n*
graveyard, cemetery, churchyard, God's acre, vault, crypt, catacomb, mausoleum, necropolis, tumulus

burlesque *n, adj*
▶ *n* caricature, mock, mockery, parody, ridicule, satire, travesty

colloq. take-off, send-up, spoof, mickey-taking
▶ *adj* comic, derisive, farcical, mocking, parodying, satirical
formal caricatural, hudibrastic
F3 serious

burly *adj*
well-built, thickset, hulking, hefty, heavy, stocky, big, sturdy, brawny, beefy, muscular, athletic, strapping, strong, powerful
F3 small, puny, thin, slim

burn *v*
1 *the fire's burning*
be on/catch fire, be in flames, burst into flames, blaze, be/catch ablaze, go up in smoke, flame, flare (up), flash, glow, flicker, smoulder, smoke
2 *burn rubbish*
ignite, light, set fire to, put a match to, kindle, incinerate, cremate, consume, corrode, burn down, destroy, go up in flames, gut
formal conflagrate, deflagrate
3 *burn your hand on the oven; burn a hole in a cardigan*
SCALD, scorch, parch, shrivel, singe, char, toast, brand, sear
formal cauterize
4 *make your throat burn*
smart, sting, bite, hurt, tingle
5 *burn with anger*
FUME, simmer, seethe
6 *burn to be with someone*
long, desire, yearn, itch, be eager

burning *adj*
1 *a burning skyscraper*
ablaze, aflame, afire, fiery, flaming, blazing, flashing, gleaming, glowing, smouldering, alight, lit, illuminated
2 *a burning forehead; a burning hot day*
hot, scalding, scorching
3 *a burning sensation*
searing, piercing, acute, smarting, stinging, prickling, tingling, biting, caustic, pungent
formal acrid
4 *burning desire*
PASSIONATE, ardent, fervent, eager, earnest, intense, vehement, impassioned, frantic, frenzied, consuming
formal fervid
5 *a burning issue*
URGENT, pressing, important, significant, crucial, essential, vital
F3 2 cold 4 apathetic 5 unimportant

burnish *v*
polish (up), brighten, buff, glaze, shine

burp *v*
belch, bring up wind
formal eructate

burrow *n, v*
▶ *n* warren, hole, earth, set, den, lair, retreat, shelter, tunnel
▶ *v* **1** *burrow into the sand*
TUNNEL, dig, delve, excavate, mine, undermine
2 *burrow for the keys*
RUMMAGE, delve, search

burst *v, n*
▶ *v* **1** *the tyre burst*
puncture, rupture, tear, split, crack, break (open), fragment, shatter, shiver, disintegrate
2 *the dam burst*
gush, spout, rush, erupt

3 *burst into a room*
rush, run, hurry, race, dart, break in on
colloq. barge, push your way
4 *the bomb burst*
explode, blow up
▶ *n* **1** *have a burst on the motorway*
puncture
colloq. blow-out
2 *a burst of gunfire; a sudden burst of activity*
discharge, volley, gush, spurt, surge, rush, spate, torrent, outpouring, outburst, outbreak, fit
formal fusillade
▷ **burst out 1** *burst out crying* begin, start;
formal commence **2** *"That's what I've been trying to tell you," she burst out* EXCLAIM, cry (out), call out, utter; *colloq.* blurt out

bury *v*
1 *bury the dead*
lay to rest, shroud
formal inter, entomb, sepulchre, inhume, inearth
colloq. put six feet under
2 *bury your face in your hands; bury a memory*
sink, submerge, plant, implant, embed, conceal, hide, cover, engulf, immerse, enclose
formal enshroud
3 *buried yourself in work*
immerse, engross, occupy, engage, absorb
F3 **1** formal disinter, exhume **2** uncover, discover, expose

bush *n*
1 *a rose bush*
shrub, hedge, plant, thicket
2 *go camping in the bush*
scrub, brush, scrubland, backwoods, brush, wilds
▷ **not beat about the bush** speak plainly/openly;
colloq. call a spade a spade

bushy *adj*
shaggy, thick, bristling, bristly, fluffy, fuzzy, luxuriant, spreading, stiff, unruly, rough, wiry
formal dasyphyllous, dumose, dumous
F3 thin, neat, tidy, trim, well-kept

busily *adv*
actively, diligently, assiduously, earnestly, energetically, hard, industriously, purposefully, briskly, speedily, strenuously

business *n*
1 *do business*
trade, commerce, industry, manufacturing dealings, transactions, bargaining, trading, buying, selling, merchandising
2 *set up a new business*
COMPANY, firm, industry, corporation, establishment, organization, concern, operation, franchise, enterprise, private enterprise, flagship, industry, venture, management buyout, consortium, syndicate, holding company, parent/subsidiary company, conglomerate, multinational
3 *a line of business*
job, occupation, work, employment, trade, profession, line, calling, career, vocation, duty, task, responsibility, métier
4 *none of your business*
affair, matter, issue, subject, topic, question, problem, point
5 *the business of the meeting*
topic, subject, issue, question, matter

businesslike *adj*
professional, efficient, thorough, systematic, methodical, organized, orderly, well-ordered, painstaking, practical, pragmatic, matter-of-fact, precise, correct, formal, impersonal
E3 inefficient, wasteful, disorganized; *colloq.* sloppy

businessman, businesswoman *n*
executive, entrepreneur, industrialist, trader, merchant, tycoon, magnate, capitalist, financier, employer

busker *n*
street-entertainer, street-musician

bust *n*
1 *a bust of the President*
SCULPTURE, head, torso, statue
2 *a woman's bust*
bosom, breasts, chest, breast
slang boobs, bristols, knockers, tits

bustle *v, n*
▶ *v* hurry, dash, rush, scamper, scurry, rush to and fro, scramble, fuss
formal hasten, bestir
colloq. tear, belt, to and fro
▶ *n* activity, stir, commotion, tumult, agitation, excitement, fuss, scramble, flurry, hurry, hurly-burly, hustle and bustle, rush hour, the rush
formal haste, pother, ado
colloq. a hive of activity, comings and goings

bustling *adj*
lively, active, energetic, busy, hectic, buzzing, rushing, crowded, eventful, full, humming, restless, stirring, swarming, teeming
formal astir, thronged
E3 quiet, sleepy, restful

busy *adj, v*
▶ *adj* **1** *be busy at the moment*
occupied, engaged, otherwise engaged, employed, unavailable, working, having a previous engagement/prior appointment
colloq. tied up, hard at it, busy as a bee
2 *a very busy day*
active, lively, energetic, strenuous, tiring, full, crowded, swarming, vibrant, teeming, bustling, hectic, frantic, eventful
3 *busy preparing for the meeting*
occupied, involved, engrossed, working
4 *a busy person*
active, having a lot to do, energetic, lively, diligent, industrious, assiduous, restless, tireless
formal sedulous
colloq. on the go, having a lot on, having your hands full, fully stretched, rushed off your feet, under pressure, snowed under, up to your eyes in something
E3 1 free, available **2** quiet, leisured, empty **3** unoccupied **4** lazy, idle; *colloq.* at a loose end
▶ *v* occupy, involve, engage, employ, engross, absorb, immerse, interest, concern

busybody *n*
meddler, interferer, intruder, pry, gossip, eavesdropper, snoop, snooper, troublemaker, scandalmonger
formal pantopragmatic, quidnunc
colloq. nosy parker

butcher *n, v*
▶ *n* **1** *buy meat from the butcher's*
meat counter, meat retailer, supermarket

2 *known as the Butcher*
SLAUGHTERER, destroyer, killer, (mass) murderer, slayer
▶ *v* slaughter, massacre, assassinate, destroy, exterminate, kill, liquidate, mutilate, slay, destroy

butchery *n*
slaughter, massacre, (mass) murder, carnage, killing, mass destruction, blood-letting, bloodshed

butt[1] *n*
1 *the butt of a gun/tool*
end, butt end, base, foot, shaft, stock, handle, haft
2 *the butt of a cigarette*
stub, tip, tail end
colloq. fag-end, dog-end
3 *sit on your butt*
bottom, buttocks
colloq. bum, posterior; *slang* arse

butt[2] *n*
the butt of jokes
target, mark, object, subject, victim, laughing-stock, dupe, scapegoat

butt[3] *v*
butt someone with its horns
hit, bump, knock, buffet, push, ram, thrust, shove, punch, jab, prod, poke
▷ **butt in** interrupt, cut in, intrude, meddle, interfere; *formal* interpose, interject; *colloq.* stick your nose in, put your oar in

butter *v*
▷ **butter up** flatter, praise, blarney, cajole, coax, pander to, wheedle, kowtow
colloq. suck up to, soft-soap

butterfly *n*
Related adjectives: papilionaceous, rhopaloceral, rhopalocerous

Types of butterfly include: red admiral, white admiral, apollo, cabbage white, chalkhill blue, common blue, brimstone, meadow brown, Camberwell beauty, clouded yellow, comma, large copper, small copper, fritillary, Duke of Burgundy fritillary, heath fritillary, gatekeeper, grayling, hairstreak, purple hairstreak, white letter hairstreak, hermit, monarch, orange-tip, painted lady, peacock, purple emperor, ringlet, grizzled skipper, swallowtail, tortoiseshell.

buttocks *n*
bottom, rump, hindquarters, rear, seat, breech, haunches, derrière
technical gluteus, nates
colloq. bum, behind, posterior; *US* butt; *slang* arse, *US* ass
Related adjective: gluteal

button *n*
1 *buttons on a shirt*
fastener, fastening, catch, clasp
2 *press the button*
knob, disc, switch

buttonhole *v*
accost, waylay, catch, take aside, detain
formal importune
colloq. grab, nab, corner

buttress *n, v*
▶ *n* support, prop, shore, stay, brace, pier, strut, mainstay, reinforcement

formal abutment, stanchion
▶ *v* support, prop up, shore up, hold up, back up, brace, underpin, strengthen, reinforce, bolster up, sustain
E3 undermine, weaken

buxom *adj*
plump, ample, bosomy, busty, chesty, well-endowed, well-rounded
formal voluptuous, comely
colloq. busty
E3 petite, slim, small

buy *v, n*
▶ *v* **1** *buy a car*
pay for, acquire, obtain, get, go shopping, do the shopping, shop around, shop for, stock up on, invest in, speculate
formal purchase, procure
colloq. snap up, pick up, splash out on
2 *buy the tax man*
bribe, buy off, suborn
colloq. fix, grease someone's palm
E3 **1** sell
▶ *n* purchase, acquisition, bargain, deal

buyer *n*
purchaser, shopper, consumer, customer, client, patron
formal patron, vendee, emptor
E3 seller; *formal* vendor

buzz *v, n*
▶ *v* **1** *bees buzzing round*
hum, whirr, drone, murmur
formal bombilate, bombinate, susurrate
2 *buzz with excitement*
hum, throb, pulse, bustle, race
▶ *n* **1** *the buzz of bees*
hum, whirr, buzzing, drone, murmur, purr
technical tinnitus
formal bombilation, bombination, susurration, susurrus
2 *give someone a buzz*
ring, (phone) call
3 *the latest buzz*
rumour, gossip, scandal, latest, hearsay
4 *winning gives me a buzz*
THRILL, excitement, stimulation
colloq. kick(s), high

by *prep, adv*
▶ *prep* **1** *a low table by the chair*
near, next to, close to, beside, alongside
2 *enter by the window*
along, over, through, via
3 *earn money by working hard*
by means of, through the agency of, through
formal under the aegis of
4 *get home by noon*
before, no later than, at
5 *by any standard*
according to, in relation to
▶ *adv* near, close (by), handy, at hand, past, beyond, away, aside

bygone *adj*
past, ancient, departed, forgotten, former, previous, lost, olden, one-time, antiquated
formal erstwhile, forepast
E3 modern, recent, future, forthcoming

bypass *v, n*
▶ *v* avoid, find a way round, sidestep, ignore, neglect, omit
formal circumvent
colloq. dodge, skirt
▶ *n* ring road, detour, diversion

by-product *n*
1 *cattle feed is a by-product of whisky*
derivative, spin-off
2 *by-products of modern life*
consequence, result, side effect, repercussion, after-effect
colloq. fallout

bystander *n*
spectator, onlooker, looker-on, watcher, observer, witness, eyewitness, passer-by
colloq. rubberneck
E3 participant

byword *n*
1 *a byword for efficiency*
SLOGAN, catchword, dictum, maxim, motto
2 PROVERB, saw, saying, precept, adage, aphorism
formal apophthegm

C

cab *n*
1 *hire a cab*
taxi, taxicab, minicab, hackney carriage,
2 *the cab in a lorry*
compartment, driver's compartment, cabin, quarters

cabal *n*
clique, faction, party, plotters, coalition, league, set,
coterie, conclave junta, junto

cabaret *n*
entertainment, show, dancing, singing, comedy

cabin *n*
1 *a log cabin*
HUT, shack, shanty, lodge, chalet, cottage, shed,
shelter, *Scot.* bothy, refuge
2 BERTH, quarters, sleeping quarters, compartment,
room, stateroom

cabinet *n*
1 *a medicine cabinet*
cupboard, closet, dresser, case, store, chest, locker
2 *Cabinet ministers*
government, ministers, leadership, senate,
administration, executive

cable *n, v*
▶ *n* **1** *tie with cable*
line, rope, cord, chain, guy, stay, hawser
2 *electric cable*
wire, flex, lead
3 *send a message by cable*
telegram, telegraph, Telemessage®, wire, fax, facsimile
▶ *v* send a telegram/telemessage/wire, send by
telegraph, telegraph, wire, radio, fax

cache *n*
store, accumulation, collection, fund, hoard, reserve,
stock, stockpile, storehouse, supply, garner, treasure-
store, hidden treasure
formal repository
colloq. stash

cachet *n*
estimation, prestige, reputation, approval, favour,
distinction, eminence
formal esteem
colloq. street cred

cackle *v & n*
laugh loudly, laugh unpleasantly, chortle, chuckle,
crow, giggle, snigger, titter

cacophonous *adj*
raucous, strident, grating, harsh, discordant,
dissonant, inharmonious, jarring
formal horrisonant
E3 harmonious, pleasant

cacophony *n*
raucousness, stridency, harshness, discord,
dissonance, disharmony, jarring, caterwauling

formal horrisonance
E3 harmony

cad *n*
blackguard, scoundrel, rascal, rogue, villain, devil,
knave, deceiver, miscreant, reprobate, wretch
colloq. bleeder, blighter, bounder, rotter, stinker, rat,
swine, scumbag

cadaver *n*
dead body, body, corpse, remains, carcase
slang stiff

cadaverous *adj*
corpse-like, death-like, pale, ashen, wan, ghostly,
gaunt, haggard, thin, emaciated, skeletal,
colloq. like death warmed up

cadence *n*
intonation, lilt, modulation, inflection, accent,
rhythm, beat, stress, tempo, measure, metre, pattern,
swing, pulse, throb, rate

cadge *v*
scrounge, beg
colloq. sponge, bum

café *n*
coffee shop, tea shop, tea room, coffee bar, cybercafé,
cafeteria, snackbar, bistro, wine bar, brasserie,
restaurant, buffet

cafeteria *n*
self-service café, self-service restaurant, self-service
canteen, café, canteen, restaurant, buffet

cage *n*
aviary, coop, hutch, enclosure, pen, pound, lock-up,
corral

caged *adj*
encaged, cooped up, shut up, confined, restrained,
fenced in, imprisoned, impounded, locked up
formal incarcerated
E3 released, let out, free

cagey *adj*
careful, chary, cautious, discreet, guarded,
non-committal, secretive, shrewd, wary, wily
formal circumspect
colloq. playing your cards close to your chest
E3 frank, indiscreet, open

cajole *v*
coax, persuade, get round, wheedle, flatter, tempt, lure,
seduce, entice, beguile, mislead, dupe
formal inveigle
colloq. sweet-talk, butter up, soft-soap
E3 bully, force, compel

cajolery *n*
coaxing, persuasion, wheedling, flattery, blarney,
enticement, inducement(s), beguilement, misleading,
duping
formal blandishments, inveigling

colloq. sweet talk, soft soap
E3 bullying, force, compulsion

cake *n, v*
▶ *n* **1** *tea and cakes*
gateau, fancy, pastry, madeleine, bun, pie, tart, flan
2 LUMP, mass, bar, slab, block, cube, chunk, loaf
▶ *v* coat, cover, encrust, plaster, dry, harden, solidify,
consolidate, coagulate, congeal, thicken

calamitous *adj*
disastrous, catastrophic, ruinous, devastating, deadly,
fatal, cataclysmic, dire, ghastly, dreadful, wretched,
tragic, woeful, grievous
E3 good, fortunate, happy

calamity *n*
disaster, catastrophe, mishap, misadventure,
mischance, misfortune, adversity, scourge, reverse,
trial, tribulation, affliction, distress, tragedy, ruin,
downfall, trouble
E3 blessing, godsend

calculate *v*
1 WORK OUT, compute, count, enumerate, reckon
(up), figure, determine, make, derive, measure, weigh,
rate, value, estimate, gauge
2 *a plan calculated to make him jealous*
judge, consider, plan, intend, aim, design

calculated *adj*
considered, deliberate, intended, intentional, planned,
purposeful, wilful, premeditated
formal purposed
E3 unintended, unplanned

calculating *adj*
crafty, cunning, sly, devious, scheming, designing,
contriving, manipulative, sharp, shrewd,
Machiavellian
E3 artless, naïve

calculation *n*
sum, computation, working-out, answer, result,
reckoning, figuring, estimate, estimation, forecast,
judgement, planning, deliberation

calibre *n*
1 DIAMETER, bore, gauge, size, measure
2 *candidates of the right calibre*
talent, gifts, strength, worth, merit, quality, character,
ability, capacity, faculty, excellence, competence,
endowments, stature, distinction

call *v, n*
▶ *v* **1** NAME, christen, baptize, title, entitle, dub,
style, term, label, brand, describe as, designate,
rename
formal denominate
2 SHOUT, yell, exclaim, cry (out), scream, shriek,
bellow, roar, bawl
3 TELEPHONE, phone (up), ring (up), contact,
give someone a ring
colloq. buzz, give someone a buzz, give someone a
tinkle
4 *call a doctor*
ask to come in/round, ask for, send for, contact, order
formal summon
5 *call to collect the money*
call in/round, drop in, pay a visit, stop by, come by
colloq. pop in
6 *call a meeting*
invite, bid, assemble
formal convene, summon
▷ **call for** **1** FETCH, collect, pick up, go for

2 DEMAND, require, need, make necessary, justify,
involve, occasion, suggest, press for, push for;
formal entail, necessitate, warrant
▷ **call off** cancel, drop, abandon, discontinue, break
off, withdraw; *formal* rescind, revoke; *colloq.* scrub,
shelve
▷ **call on** **1** *call on a friend* pay someone a (short)
visit, visit, look in on, go and see **2** *call on the
government to resign* appeal, appeal to, ask, bid, ask,
demand, urge, request, plead, press for;
formal request, summon, supplicate, entreat
▶ *n* **1** CRY, exclamation, shout, yell, scream, shriek
2 VISIT, ring, summons, invitation
3 *a telephone call*
ring
colloq. buzz, tinkle, bell
4 *calls for his resignation*
APPEAL, request, plea, order, command, claim,
announcement, signal
5 *there's no call for it*
demand, need, occasion, cause, excuse, justification,
reason, grounds, right, run
▷ **on call** ready, on standby, standing by, on duty

call girl *n*
prostitute, whore, harlot, loose woman, woman of the
streets, street-walker, lady of the night
colloq. hooker, hustler

calling *n*
mission, vocation, career, profession, occupation, job,
trade, business, line, line of business/work, work,
employment, field, province, pursuit, métier

callous *adj*
heartless, hard-hearted, cold, cold-hearted,
cold-blooded, harsh, tough, indifferent, uncaring,
unsympathetic, unfeeling, insensitive, hardened, stony,
stony-hearted, thick-skinned
formal obdurate, indurate, insensate
E3 kind, caring, sympathetic, sensitive

callow *adj*
inexperienced, immature, naïve, innocent, guileless,
juvenile, puerile, raw, fledgling, uninitiated,
unsophisticated, unfledged, untried
formal jejune
colloq. green
E3 experienced

calm *adj, v, n*
▶ *adj* **1** COMPOSED, self-possessed, self-controlled,
collected, quiet, serene, cool, cool-headed,
dispassionate, unemotional, impassive, unmoved,
placid, sedate, poised, imperturbable, unexcitable,
relaxed, unexcited, unruffled, unflustered,
unperturbed, undisturbed, untroubled,
unapprehensive, steady
colloq. laid back, unflappable
2 *calm waters/weather*
smooth, still, waveless, windless, unclouded, mild,
tranquil, serene, peaceful, quiet, undisturbed, restful
E3 **1** excitable, worried, anxious, upset **2** rough,
wild, windy, stormy
▶ *v* compose, soothe, relax, sedate, tranquillize, hush,
lull, quieten, still, settle (down), allay, pacify
formal mollify, placate, appease, assuage
colloq. cool down, simmer down, keep your head,
lighten up
E3 excite, worry, upset
▶ *n* calmness, stillness, tranquillity, restfulness,
composure, contentment, serenity, peacefulness,
peace, quiet, hush, impassiveness, impassivity,

presence of mind
formal quietude, repose, placidity, equanimity,
sang-froid, ataraxia
colloq. unflabbability, cool
⊟ storminess, restlessness, trouble, excitement

calumny *n*
slander, abuse, aspersion, backbiting, defamation,
insult, libel, lying, misrepresentation
formal denigration, obloquy, revilement, derogation,
detraction, disparagement, vilification, vituperation
colloq. slagging-off, smear

camaraderie *n*
brotherhood, brotherliness, companionship,
comradeship, *esprit de corps*, fellowship,
fraternization, good fellowship, sociability, closeness,
affinity, intimacy, togetherness

camera *n*

Types of camera include: automatic, bellows,
binocular, box Brownie®, camcorder, camera
obscura, cine, cinematographic, compact,
daguerreotype, disc, disposable, film, Instamatic®,
large-format, miniature, subminiature, panoramic,
plate, dry-plate, half-plate, quarter-plate, wet-plate,
point-and-press, Polaroid®, press, reflex, folding
reflex, single-lens reflex (SLR), twin-lens reflex
(TLR), security, sliding box, sound, still, stereo,
Super 8®, TV, video. *See also* **photographic**.

camouflage *n, v*
▶ *n* disguise, guise, masquerade, mask, cloak, screen,
blind, front, cover, cover-up, protective colouring,
concealment, deception, façade
▶ *v* disguise, mask, cloak, veil, screen, cover,
cover up, conceal, hide, obscure
⊟ uncover, reveal

camp¹ *n, v*
▶ *n* **1** *a Scout camp*
campsite, camping-site, camping-ground,
encampment, tents, bivouac
2 *the union camp*
side, faction, group, party, section, set, crowd, caucus,
clique
▶ *v* pitch tents, set up camp, sleep outdoors
colloq. rough it

camp² *adj*
camp behaviour
affected, artificial, campy, exaggerated, mannered,
ostentatious, posturing, theatrical, effeminate, queer,
homosexual
colloq. over the top, poncy

campaign *n, v*
▶ *n* *the election campaign; a bombing campaign*
crusade, movement, promotion, drive, push, course of
action, strategy, offensive, attack, battle, expedition,
operation, war
▶ *v* crusade, promote, push, drive, advocate, work,
fight, strive, struggle, battle, attack

camp-follower *n*
hanger-on, henchman, lackey, toady

can *n*
tin, container, receptacle, canister, jar, jerrycan,
pail

canal *n*
1 *the Grand Union canal*

waterway, watercourse, channel, zanja
2 *the alimentary canal*
tube, channel, passage

cancel *v*
1 *cancel a concert*
call off, abort, abandon, drop, postpone
colloq. scrap, scrub, shelve, axe
2 *cancel a reservation/debt*
abolish, annul, quash, stop, break off, repeal, delete,
erase, obliterate, eliminate, dissolve, override
formal discontinue, countermand, rescind, revoke,
annul, nullify, invalidate, retract, abrogate, vitiate
▷ **cancel out** offset, compensate, make up for,
redeem, counterbalance, balance, neutralize,
counteract, nullify

cancellation *n*
calling-off, abandoning, abandonment, abolition,
dropping, stopping, deletion, elimination,
neutralization, quashing, repeal
formal annulment, revocation, invalidation, nullifying
colloq. shelving, scrubbing

cancer *n*
1 TUMOUR, growth, malignancy, malignant growth
technical carcinoma
2 EVIL, blight, canker, pestilence, sickness, disease,
plague, scourge, corruption, rot

candelabrum *n*
candlestick, menorah

candid *adj*
frank, open, truthful, honest, sincere, forthright,
straightforward, ingenuous, guileless, simple, plain,
plain-spoken, clear, unequivocal, blunt, outspoken
⊟ guarded, evasive, devious

candidate *n*
1 *candidates for a job*
applicant, aspirant, contender, contestant, competitor,
seeker, runner, possibility, nominee
2 *candidates for an exam*
entrant

candle *n*
taper, tallow-candle, cerge, wax-light

candour *n*
frankness, openness, truthfulness, honesty, plain-
dealing, sincerity, forthrightness, straightforwardness,
directness, brusqueness, ingenuousness, guilelessness,
naïvety, artlessness, simplicity, plainness,
unequivocalness, bluntness, outspokenness
⊟ guardedness, evasiveness, deviousness

candy *n*
sweets, confectionery, chocolates, toffees

cane *n*
stick, staff, crook, rod, walking-stick, alpenstock
formal ferule

canker *n*
1 EVIL, blight, cancer, pestilence, sickness, disease,
plague, scourge, bane, corrosion, corruption, rot
2 *canker in an animal's ear*
sore, ulcer, boil, infection, lesion

cannabis *n*
marijuana, hemp, hashish, bhang
colloq. dope, ganja, grass, hash, pot, spliff, puff, tea,
kef; *slang* blow, weed, skunk, punk, leaf, *US* locoweed

cannibal   *n*
people-eater, man-eater
technical anthropophagite

cannibalism   *n*
man-eating, people-eating
technical anthropophagy, endophagy, exophagy

cannon   *n*
gun, mortar, field gun, howitzer, artillery, battery,
ordnance
colloq. big gun

> ⚠ **cannon** or **canon** ?
> A *cannon* is a large gun. A *canon* is a Christian priest
> who helps to run the work of a cathedral and also a
> general rule or belief: *the canons of literary taste.*

cannonade   *n*
barrage, bombardment, shelling, volley, broadside,
pounding, salvo

canny   *adj*
shrewd, acute, sharp, astute, careful, cautious,
prudent, clever, knowing, skilful, sly, subtle, wise,
worldly-wise, artful, pawky
formal circumspect, perspicacious, judicious,
sagacious
colloq. no flies on someone
🖃 foolish, imprudent

canon   *n*
1 *a cathedral canon*
prebendary, clergyman, vicar, priest, minister,
reverend
2 *the canons of literary taste*
principle, rule, regulation, statute, criterion, standard,
precept, dictate, yardstick

canonical   *adj*
authorized, recognized, accepted, sanctioned,
approved, authoritative, orthodox, regular

Names of canonical hours include: matins, lauds,
terce, sext, none, vespers, compline.

canopy   *n*
awning, cover, covering, shade, shelter, sunshade,
umbrella, tester, tilt, baldachin

cant   *n*
1 *insincere cant*
insincerity, hypocrisy, pretentiousness,
sanctimoniousness
2 *underworld cant*
argot, jargon, lingo, slang, vernacular

cantankerous   *adj*
irritable, irascible, grumpy, grouchy, crusty, testy,
bad-tempered, quick-tempered, ill-humoured, cross,
peevish, difficult, perverse, contrary, quarrelsome
colloq. crabbed, crabby, crotchety
🖃 good-natured, pleasant; *colloq.* easy-going

canter   *n & v*
amble, trot, jog, jogtrot, lope, gallop, run

canvass   *v*
1 ELECTIONEER, agitate, campaign, solicit votes,
ask for votes, seek votes, poll, drum up support
2 EXAMINE, inspect, find out, scrutinize, study, scan,
investigate, explore, survey, examine, inquire into,
analyse, sift, evaluate, poll, discuss, debate

canyon   *n*
gorge, ravine, gully, valley, chasm, abyss

cap   *n, v*
▶ *n* **1** HAT, bonnet, skullcap, beret, tam-o'-shanter,
tammy, flat cap, school cap, peaked cap, baseball cap,
balmoral, kalpak, forage-cap, glengarry, muffin-cap,
kepi
2 LID, top, cover, stopper, plug, bung
▶ *v* **1** *cap someone's story*
exceed, excel, surpass, transcend, better, beat, outdo,
outstrip, outshine, eclipse
2 *mountains capped with snow*
crown, top, cover, coat
3 *rate-cap a council*
limit, restrict, curb, restrain, control

capability   *n*
ability, capacity, faculty, power, potential, means,
facility, competence, qualification, skill, skilfulness,
accomplishment, proficiency, talent, aptitude,
efficiency
🖃 inability, incompetence

> ⚠ **capability** or **ability** ? *See panel at* **ability**.

capable   *adj*
1 *a capable person*
able, competent, efficient, qualified, experienced,
accomplished, skilful, adept, proficient, gifted,
talented, masterly, clever, intelligent, smart,
businesslike
2 *capable of winning*
fitted, suited, apt to, liable to, disposed to, inclined to,
tending to, having the inclination/tendency to,
allowing, needing
🖃 **1** incompetent, useless **2** incapable

capacious   *adj*
ample, big, vast, wide, broad, huge, large, roomy,
sizable, spacious, comfortable, comprehensive,
expansive, extensive, generous, liberal, substantial
formal commodious, voluminous
🖃 cramped, small

capacity   *n*
1 CAPABILITY, ability, faculty, power, potential,
competence, proficiency, efficiency, skill, gift, talent,
genius, cleverness, intelligence, aptitude, resources,
readiness
2 VOLUME, space, room, size, dimensions,
proportions, magnitude, extent, largeness, compass,
range, scope
3 *in her capacity as president*
role, function, position, office, post, appointment, job

cape¹   *n*
wear a cape
cloak, shawl, wrap, mantle, robe, poncho, pelisse,
pelerine, coat

cape²   *n*
the Cape of Good Hope
headland, head, promontory, point, ness, neck,
tongue, peninsula

caper   *v, n*
▶ *v* cavort, frisk, frolic, gambol, bounce, bound,
dance, hop, jump, leap, romp, skip, spring
▶ *n* antic, escapade, high jinks, jest, lark, mischief,
prank, stunt, jape, affair, business
US colloq. dido

capital   *n, adj*
▶ *n* **1** *need capital to expand the business*
funds, finance, principal, money, cash, savings,
investment(s), wealth, means, wherewithal, resources,
assets, liquid assets, property, stock, reserves
2 *the capital of France*
most important city, administrative centre, seat of
government
3 *write in capitals*
block letter, block capital, capital letter, upper-case
letter
formal majuscule, uncial
▶ *adj* **1** PRINCIPAL, important, leading, primary,
prime, main, major, cardinal, central, chief, first,
foremost
2 *a capital offence*
serious, punishable by death
E3 **1** minor, unimportant **2** minor

capitalism   *n*
private enterprise, free enterprise, private ownership,
laissez-faire

capitalist   *n*
banker, financier, investor, moneyman, tycoon,
magnate, mogul, person of means, plutocrat
colloq. moneybags, money-spinner; *slang* fat cat

capitalize   *v*
▷ **capitalize on**   take advantage of, profit from,
make the most of, exploit; *colloq.* cash in on

capitulate   *v*
surrender, yield, give in, give up, relent, back down,
submit, succumb
colloq. throw in the towel/sponge

capitulation   *n*
surrender, yielding, giving-in, giving-up, relenting,
backing-down, submission, succumbing

caprice   *n*
whim, fad, fancy, impulse, whimsy, fantasy, notion,
quirk, vagary, vapour, fickleness, fitfulness,
inconstancy

capricious   *adj*
changeable, inconstant, mercurial, erratic, fickle,
uncertain, unpredictable, variable, wayward, fitful,
fanciful, whimsical, freakish, impulsive, odd, queer,
quirky
E3 sensible, steady

capsize   *v*
overturn, turn over, turn turtle, invert, keel over,
tip over, roll over, upset

capsule   *n*
1 *a capsule of medicine*
pill, tablet, lozenge, receptacle, container
2 *a seed capsule*
shell, sheath, pod
3 *a space capsule*
craft, module, probe

captain   *n*
officer, commander, master, skipper, pilot, head,
chief, leader
colloq. boss

caption   *n*
heading, note, title, legend, wording, inscription

captivate   *v*
charm, enchant, bewitch, beguile, fascinate, delight,
enthral, hypnotize, mesmerize, lure, allure, seduce,

win, attract, enamour, infatuate, enrapture, dazzle
E3 repel, disgust, appal

captivating   *adj*
attractive, charming, fascinating, beautiful,
enchanting, bewitching, beguiling, delightful,
enthralling, alluring, seductive, winsome, dazzling
E3 ugly, unattractive

captive   *n, adj*
▶ *n* prisoner, hostage, slave, detainee, internee,
convict, jailbird
▶ *adj* imprisoned, caged, confined, restricted,
secure, locked up/away, shut up, interned, detained,
held in custody, restrained, enchained, enslaved,
ensnared, in bondage
formal incarcerated
E3 free, liberated

captivity   *n*
custody, detention, imprisonment, internment,
confinement, restraint, constraint, bondage, duress,
slavery
formal incarceration, servitude
E3 freedom, liberation

capture   *v, n*
▶ *v* **1** *capture a prisoner*
catch, trap, entrap, hunt down, snare, ensnare, take,
take possession of, seize, arrest, apprehend, imprison,
recapture, pick up, secure, win
colloq. nab, collar, nick
2 *capture a mood*
encapsulate, represent, record, embrace
▶ *n* catching, trapping, taking, taking captive, taking
prisoner, seizure, arrest, imprisonment
colloq. nabbing, collaring, nicking

car   *n*
automobile, motor car, motor vehicle, motor, vehicle

Types of car include: saloon, hatchback, fastback,
estate, sports car, cabriolet, convertible, limousine,
colloq. limo, *colloq.* wheels, *colloq.* banger, Mini®,
bubble-car, coupé, station wagon, shooting brake,
veteran car, vintage car, jalopy, *colloq.* Beetle, four-
wheel drive, jeep, buggy, Land Rover®, Range
Rover®, panda car, patrol car, taxi, cab. *See also*
motor vehicle.

carafe   *n*
bottle, decanter, flagon, flask, jug, pitcher

carbuncle   *n*
boil, inflammation, pimple, sore, anthrax

carcase   *n*
1 *the carcase of an animal*
body, dead body, corpse, cadaver, remains
2 *the carcase of a building*
shell, structure, framework, hulk, skeleton

card   *n*
▷ **on the cards**   likely, probable, possible, being a
strong possibility, looking like, looking as if
colloq. the chances are

cardinal   *adj*
chief, main, principal, fundamental, greatest, highest,
important, key, leading, paramount, pre-eminent,
primary, prime, central, essential, first, foremost,
capital

care   *n, v*
▶ *n* **1** *handle with care*

CAREFULNESS, caution, forethought, watchfulness, pains, meticulousness, accuracy
formal prudence, vigilance, circumspection
2 *children need care*
looking-after, regard, concern, attention, tending, minding, watching-over, heed, regard, consideration, interest, protection
3 *in their care*
keeping, safekeeping, custody, guardianship, protection, ward, charge, responsibility, control, supervision, tutelage
4 *forget all your cares*
WORRY, anxiety, stress, strain, pressure, responsibility, burden, concern, trouble, distress, affliction, fear, disquiet
formal tribulation, vexation
colloq. hang-up
E3 1 carelessness **2** carelessness, thoughtlessness, inattention, neglect
▶ *v* worry, mind, bother, be concerned, be interested
colloq. give a damn
E3 neglect, ignore, be indifferent; *slang* not give a hoot/hang/hoot/damn/toss, not give a monkey's, not give a tinker's cuss/brass farthing
▷ **care for 1** LOOK AFTER, take care of, nurse, tend, mind, watch over, protect, provide for, minister to, attend, tend, maintain **2** *care for someone* BE FOND OF, feel affection for, love, be in love with, be keen on, be close to, enjoy, delight in, cherish **3** *Would you care for a cup of tea?* like, want, desire

career *n, v*
▶ *n* vocation, calling, life-work, occupation, pursuit, profession, trade, job, employment, métier, livelihood
▶ *v* rush, dash, tear, hurtle, race, run, gallop, speed, shoot, bolt

carefree *adj*
unworried, untroubled, unconcerned, blithe, breezy, happy-go-lucky, cheery, light-hearted, cheerful, happy
formal insouciant, nonchalant
colloq. easy-going, laid back
E3 worried, anxious, troubled, distressed, despondent

careful *adj*
1 CAUTIOUS, aware, wary, chary, vigilant, watchful, alert, attentive, mindful, heedful, discreet, tactful, guarded
formal prudent, circumspect, judicious,
2 METICULOUS, painstaking, conscientious, diligent, assiduous, scrupulous, fastidious, rigorous, thorough, detailed, showing great attention to detail, methodical, systematic, particular, accurate, precise, thoughtful
formal punctilious
E3 1 careless, inattentive, thoughtless, reckless
2 careless

careless *adj*
1 UNTHINKING, thoughtless, inattentive, inconsiderate, uncaring, unconcerned, heedless, unmindful, forgetful, remiss, negligent, absent-minded, irresponsible, reckless, indiscreet, tactless, unguarded
2 *careless work*
inaccurate, messy, untidy, disorganized, disorderly, neglectful, slack, lax, slipshod, slapdash, hasty, perfunctory, cursory, superficial, offhand, casual
colloq. sloppy
3 *careless charm*
casual, carefree, unworried, untroubled, simple,

artless, breezy, light-hearted, cheerful, happy-go-lucky
formal insouciant, nonchalant
colloq. easy-going, laid back
E3 1 thoughtful, careful **2** careful, accurate, meticulous

caress *v, n*
▶ *v* stroke, pet, fondle, cuddle, hug, embrace, kiss, touch, rub, nuzzle
colloq. canoodle, grope
▶ *n* stroke, touch, pat, fondle, cuddle, hug, embrace, kiss, petting
colloq. slap and tickle

caretaker *n*
janitor, porter, watchman, keeper, custodian, curator, warden, superintendent, concierge, steward, ostiary, doorkeeper

careworn *adj*
tired, weary, worn, worn-out, exhausted, fatigued, gaunt, haggard
E3 lively, sprightly

cargo *n*
freight, load, pay-load, haul, lading, tonnage, shipment, consignment, contents, goods, merchandise, baggage

caricature *n, v*
▶ *n* cartoon, parody, lampoon, burlesque, satire, mimicry, imitation, representation, distortion, travesty
colloq. send-up, take-off
▶ *v* parody, mock, ridicule, satirize, mimic, distort, exaggerate
colloq. send up, take off

carnage *n*
bloodshed, bloodbath, butchery, slaughter, killing, murder, mass murder, massacre, genocide, ethnic cleansing, holocaust

carnal *adj*
sensual, sexual, erotic, fleshly, physical, human, natural, animal, bodily, impure, lascivious, lecherous, lewd, licentious, lustful
formal corporeal, libidinous
E3 chaste, pure, spiritual

carnival *n*
festival, fiesta, gala, jamboree, fête, fair, holiday, jubilee, celebration, merrymaking, revelry

carnivorous *adj*
meat-eating
technical creophagous, zoophagous

carol *n*
Christmas song, noel, song, hymn, strain, wassail, chorus

carouse *v*
make merry, revel, drink, drink freely, party, celebrate, quaff, roister, wassail
formal imbibe
slang booze

carousing *n*
celebrating, drinking, merrymaking, partying

carp *v*
complain, criticize, censure, reproach, find faults, nag, quibble
formal ultracrepidate
colloq. knock, nit-pick
E3 praise, compliment

carpenter *n*
woodworker, joiner, cabinet-maker

carpet *n*
1 *fit a new carpet*
floor-covering, covering, mat, rug, matting,
Axminster, Aubusson, Wilton, Kidderminster, kali,
kilim
2 *a carpet of leaves*
layer, blanket, covering, bed

carriage *n*
1 COACH, wagon, cab, trap, hackney, hansom, gig,
landau, car, vehicle
2 POSTURE, bearing, air, manner, attitude, stance,
presence, guise, behaviour, conduct
formal deportment, demeanour, mien
3 CARRYING, conveyance, transport,
transportation, delivery, freight, postage

carrier *n*
bearer, conveyor, delivery-person, roundsperson,
messenger, porter, runner, transmitter, transporter,
vehicle, vector

carry *v*
1 BRING, convey, transport, haul, move, transfer,
relay, release, take, drive, fetch, shift, conduct, pipe,
deliver, hand over
colloq. lug, cart, hump, tote
2 BEAR, shoulder, support, underpin, maintain, hold
(up), uphold, sustain, suffer, stand, take someone's
weight
3 *carry a disease*
transmit, pass on, be infected with
4 *the proposal was carried*
pass, vote for, vote in favour, accept, adopt, authorize,
ratify, sanction
5 *drug-smuggling carries a risk*
bear, involve, have (as a consequence), lead to, mean
formal entail
6 *the newspaper carried the story*
cover, contain, display, show, present, communicate,
print, release, broadcast
formal disseminate
7 *carry several brands*
stock, sell, retail, have, have for sale
▷ **carry on** **1** CONTINUE, proceed, last, endure,
maintain, go on, keep on, keep up, persist, persevere,
progress, return to, resume, restart **2** *carry on a
business* operate, run, manage, conduct,
administer **3** *children carrying on* misbehaving,
behave foolishly; *colloq.* mess around, play up
4 *carrying on with a colleague at work* have an affair,
be involved
1 stop, finish **3** behave (well)
▷ **carry out** do, perform, undertake, discharge,
conduct, execute, implement, fulfil, accomplish,
achieve, realize, bring off, put into effect/operation/
practice; *formal* effect; *colloq.* deliver (the goods)

cart *n, v*
▶ *n* barrow, handcart, wheelbarrow, wagon, truck,
dray
▶ *v* move, convey, transport, haul, bear, carry,
transfer, shift
colloq. lug, hump, tote

carton *n*
box, packet, pack, case, container, package, parcel

cartoon *n*
1 *newspaper cartoons*
sketch, drawing, picture, bubble, balloon, caricature,

parody, lampoon, burlesque
colloq. send-up, take-off
2 *watch cartoons on TV*
comic strip, animation, animated film

cartridge *n*
cassette, canister, cylinder, tube, container, case,
capsule, shell, magazine, round, charge

carve *v*
1 *carve meat*
cut (up), slice, chop, hack
2 *carve stone*
sculpt, sculpture, shape, form, fashion, mould, hew,
whittle, chisel, cut, chip
3 *carve a design*
etch, engrave, incise, notch, indent
▷ **carve up** divide, share (out), separate, partition,
parcel out, distribute, split (up)

carving *n*
bust, incision, sculpture, statue, statuette
technical dendroglyph, lithoglyph, petroglyph
Related adjective: glyptic

cascade *n, v*
▶ *n* rush, gush, outpouring, flood, deluge, torrent,
avalanche, cataract, waterfall, falls, fountain, chute,
shower, trickle
▶ *v* rush, gush, surge, flood, overflow, spill, tumble,
fall, descend, shower, pour, plunge, pitch

case¹ *n*
1 OCCURRENCE, circumstances, context, state,
condition, position, situation, occasion, event,
specimen, example, instance, illustration, point
formal contingency
2 LAWSUIT, suit, trial, proceedings, action, process,
cause, argument, dispute
3 *a doctor's case*
patient, invalid, victim, client

case² *n*
1 CONTAINER, receptacle, holder, trunk, crate, box,
carton, casket, chest, cabinet, showcase, casing,
cartridge, shell, capsule, sheath, cover, jacket, wrapper
2 SUITCASE, briefcase, vanity-case, bag, holdall,
portmanteau, valise, overnight-bag, flight bag, hand-
luggage, travel bag, attaché case, portfolio, trunk

cash *n, v*
▶ *n* **1** *pay by cash*
money, hard money, ready money, banknotes, notes,
coins, change, legal tender, currency, hard currency,
bullion
2 *have no cash for a holiday*
funds, resources, capital, wherewithal
slang bread, dough, dosh, readies, ready, lolly
▶ *v* exchange, realize, liquidate, turn into cash,
encash

cashier¹ *n*
a bank cashier
clerk, bank clerk, teller, treasurer, bursar, purser,
banker, accountant, financial controller

cashier² *v*
be cashiered from the army
discharge, dismiss, drum out, expel, break, discard,
throw out, get rid of
colloq. sack, give someone the boot, unfrock

cask *n*
barrel, tun, keg, hogshead, firkin, vat, tub, butt
old use Kilderkin

casket *n*
1 *keep jewels in a casket*
box, case, chest, coffer, jewel-box, kist, pyxis
2 COFFIN, box, sarcophagus
slang pine overcoat, wooden overcoat

cast *v, n*
▶ *v* **1** THROW, hurl, lob, pitch, fling, toss, sling,
heave, shy, launch, impel, drive,
2 *cast light*
direct, project, shed, emit, give out, give off, radiate,
diffuse, spread, scatter
3 *cast your eyes/a glance*
look (at), glimpse, glance, see, view, catch sight
4 *cast doubt/suspicion*
place, put, throw, put in jeopardy
colloq. put a question mark over
5 *cast your vote*
vote, register, record, mark with a cross
6 MOULD, shape, form, model, fashion, found
▷ **cast down** depress, discourage, dishearten,
deject, sadden, crush, desolate
F3 cheer up, encourage
▶ *n* **1** COMPANY, troupe, actors, players, performers,
entertainers, characters, dramatis personae
2 CASTING, mould, shape, form, model, covering

caste *n*
class, social class, social standing, order, group,
position, rank, station, status, grade, lineage,
background, degree, estate, stratum, race

castigate *v*
criticize, reprimand, chasten, chastise, rebuke, scold,
discipline, punish, correct, censure, chide, reprove,
upbraid, berate
colloq. dress down, haul over the coals, rap on the
knuckles, tear a strip off

castle *n*
stronghold, fort, fortress, citadel, keep, tower, château,
palace, mansion, stately home, country house

Parts of a castle include: approach, bailey, barbican,
bartizan, bastion, battlements, brattice, buttress,
chapel, corbel, courtyard, crenel, crenellation,
curtain wall, ditch, donjon, drawbridge, dungeon,
embrasure, enclosure wall, fosse, gatehouse, inner
wall, keep, merlon, moat, motte, mound, outer
bailey, parapet, portcullis, postern, rampart, scarp,
stockade, tower, lookout tower, turret, ward,
watchtower.

castrate *v*
emasculate, geld, neuter, unman, unsex
formal evirate

casual *adj*
1 UNCONCERNED, nonchalant, blasé, lackadaisical,
lukewarm, negligent, apathetic, indifferent, informal,
offhand, relaxed
formal insouciant
colloq. couldn't-care-less, easy-going, laid back,
happy-go-lucky, free-and-easy
2 *casual clothes*
informal, comfortable, relaxed, leisure
3 *casual work*
temporary, irregular, intermittent, occasional, part-
time, short-term, provisional
4 *a casual meeting*
chance, fortuitous, accidental, unintentional,
unpremeditated, unexpected, unforeseen, irregular,

random, occasional, incidental, superficial, cursory
formal serendipitous
F3 **1** worried, concerned
2 formal
3 permanent, regular, full-time
4 deliberate, planned

casualty *n*
injury, loss, death, fatality, victim, sufferer, injured,
injured person, wounded, dead person, missing

casuistry *n*
chicanery, sophism, sophistry, speciousness,
equivocation

cat *n*
tabby, kitten, mouser, tomcat
colloq. puss, pussy, pussy cat, mog, moggy
old use grimalkin
Related adjective: feline

Breeds of cat include: Abyssinian, American
shorthair, Balinese, Birman, Bombay, British
longhair, British shorthair, Burmese, Carthusian,
chinchilla, Cornish rex, Cymric, Devon rex,
domestic tabby, Egyptian Mau, Exotic shorthair,
Foreign Blue, Foreign spotted shorthair, Foreign
White, Havana, Himalayan, Japanese Bobtail,
Korat, Maine Coon, Manx, Norwegian Forest,
Persian, rag-doll, rex, Russian Blue, Scottish Fold,
Siamese, silver tabby, Singapura, Somali, Tiffany,
Tonkinese, Tortoiseshell, Turkish Angora, Turkish
Van.

cataclysm *n*
disaster, calamity, catastrophe, debacle, devastation,
upheaval, blow, collapse, convulsion

catacomb *n*
underground passages, underground rooms,
underground tunnels, burial-vault, vault, tomb, crypt
formal ossuary

catalogue *n, v*
▶ *n* list, inventory, roll, register, roster, schedule,
checklist, record, table, classification, index, directory,
gazetteer, brochure, guide, prospectus, manifest,
calendar, bulletin
▶ *v* list, compile/make a list, register, record, index,
classify, alphabetize, file

catapult *v*
propel, hurl, fling, throw, pitch, toss, sling, hurtle,
launch, shoot, fire

cataract *n*
waterfall, falls, rapids, force, cascade, downpour,
torrent, deluge

catastrophe *n*
disaster, calamity, debacle, fiasco, failure, ruin,
devastation, tragedy, blow, reverse, mischance,
misfortune, adversity, trouble, upheaval
formal cataclysm, affliction

catastrophic *adj*
disastrous, tragic, fatal, calamitous, devastating,
terrible, dreadful, awful
formal cataclysmic

catcall *n*
jeer, boo, gibe, hiss, whistle, barracking,
colloq. raspberry

catch *v, n*
▶ *v* **1** *catch a ball*
hold, grab, take, seize, grasp, snatch, grip, clutch
2 *catch an animal/a prisoner*
capture, trap, entrap, hunt down, snare, ensnare, hook,
net, seize, lay hold of, arrest, apprehend, corner, round
up, recapture
colloq. nab, collar, nick
3 *catch what someone says*
HEAR, make out, perceive, recognize, understand,
follow, take in, fathom, grasp, comprehend
colloq. get the hang of, twig
4 *catch someone doing something wrong*
SURPRISE, catch red-handed/in the act, expose,
unmask, startle, find (out), discover, detect, discern
5 *catch a cold*
get, develop, go down with, pick up, become infected
with, become ill with
formal contract, succumb to
6 *catch someone's attention*
attract, draw, grasp, hold
◨ **1** drop, release, free **3** miss
▷ **catch on 1** *the new style is catching on quickly*
become popular, become fashionable; *colloq.* become
all the rage **2** *catch on to what she said* understand,
follow, take in, fathom, grasp, comprehend
▷ **catch up** draw level, gain on, overtake
▶ *n* **1** FASTENER, clip, hook, clasp, hasp, latch, lock,
bolt, *Northern Eng* sneck
2 DISADVANTAGE, drawback, snag, hitch, obstacle,
problem, difficulty
colloq. fly in the ointment

catch phrase *n*
saying, slogan, motto, jingle, watchword, byword,
catchword, formula, password

catching *adj*
infectious, contagious, communicable, transmittable,
transmissible

catchy *adj*
memorable, unforgettable, haunting, popular,
melodic, tuneful, attractive, captivating, appealing
◨ dull, boring, instantly forgettable

catechize *v*
instruct, interrogate, question, cross-examine,
examine, test, drill
colloq. grill, give the third degree

categorical *adj*
absolute, total, utter, unqualified, unreserved,
unconditional, downright, positive, definite, emphatic,
unequivocal, clear, conclusive, explicit, express, direct
◨ tentative, qualified, vague

categorize *v*
class, classify, group, sort, grade, rank, order, arrange,
list, tabulate, stereotype, pigeonhole

category *n*
class, classification, group, grouping, kind, sort, type,
variety, genre, section, division, department, chapter,
head, heading, title, rubric, grade, rank, order, list,
listing

cater *v*
1 *cater for people's needs/interests*
provide, supply, furnish, serve
formal provision, victual
2 *cater to someone's desires*
indulge, pander

caterwaul *v*
wail, scream, cry, screech, shriek, bawl, howl, miaow,
squall, yowl

catharsis *n*
cleansing, purging, purification, purifying, release
technical abreaction, abstersion, epuration, lustration

cathartic *adj*
cleansing, purging, purifying, release
technical abreactive, abstersive, lustral

cathedral *n*
minster, dome, duomo

catholic *adj*
broad, broad-based, diverse, wide, wide-ranging,
widespread, varied, universal, global, general,
comprehensive, inclusive, all-inclusive, all-embracing,
all-encompassing, liberal, tolerant, open-minded,
broad-minded
formal eclectic
◨ narrow, limited, narrow-minded, bigoted

cattle *n*
cows, bulls, oxen, livestock, stock, beasts
Related adjective: bovine

Breeds of cattle include: Aberdeen Angus,
Africander, Alderney, Ankole, Ayrshire, Blonde
d'Aquitaine, Brahman, Brown Swiss, cattabu,
cattalo, Charolais, Chillingham, Devon, dexter,
Durham, Friesian, Galloway, Guernsey, Hereford,
Highland, Holstein, Jersey, Latvian, Limousin,
Longhorn, Luing, Red Poll, Romagnola, Santa
Gertrudis, Shetland, Shorthorn, Simmenthaler,
Teeswater, Ukrainian, Welsh Black.

catty *adj*
bitchy, malicious, spiteful, venomous, vicious, mean,
ill-natured, malevolent, back-biting
formal rancorous
◨ kind, pleasant

caucus *n*
assembly, meeting, session, convention, gathering,
conclave, get-together, parley, set, clique

causative *adj*
causing, root
technical factitive, factive

cause *n, v*
▶ *n* **1** SOURCE, origin, beginning, root, basis, factor,
spring, mainspring, originator, creator, producer,
maker, author, mover, prime mover, agent, agency
2 REASON, motive, grounds, justification,
explanation, basis, motivation, stimulus, incentive,
inducement, impulse
3 *a worthy cause*
object, purpose, end, aim, ideal, principle, belief,
conviction, movement, undertaking, enterprise
◨ **1** effect, result, consequence
▶ *v* begin, give rise to, be the cause of, be at the root of,
lead to, result in, occasion, bring about, make, make
happen, produce, generate, originate, create, breed,
precipitate, trigger (off), motivate, stimulate, provoke,
incite, induce, prompt, force, compel
formal effect, render
◨ stop, prevent

caustic *adj*
1 *caustic chemicals*
corrosive, acid, destructive, burning, stinging

2 *a caustic remark*
biting, cutting, stinging, keen, pungent, bitter, sarcastic, scathing, virulent, severe, snide
formal acrimonious, astringent, mordant, trenchant
E3 1 soothing **2** mild, kind

cauterize *v*
burn, sterilize, disinfect, scorch, sear, singe, carbonize

caution *n, v*
▶ *n* **1** CARE, carefulness, watchfulness, alertness, mindfulness, heed, heedfulness, discretion, forethought, deliberation, wariness
formal prudence, vigilance, circumspection
2 WARNING, injunction, advice, counsel
formal admonition, caveat
colloq. tip-off
E3 1 carelessness, recklessness
▶ *v* warn, advise, counsel, urge, alert, deter
formal admonish
colloq. tip off

cautious *adj*
careful, watchful, alert, heedful, shrewd, discreet, tactful, chary, wary, guarded, tentative, unadventurous
formal prudent, circumspect, judicious, vigilant
colloq. cagey softly-softly, gingerly
E3 reckless, rash, foolhardy

cavalcade *n*
procession, parade, march-past, troop, array, retinue, cortège, train

cavalier *n, adj*
▶ *n* **1** HORSEMAN, equestrian, horse soldier, cavalryman, knight, chevalier, Bashi-Bazouk, chasseur, Ironside, spahi
2 GENTLEMAN, gallant, escort, partner
▶ *adj* supercilious, patronizing, condescending, lordly, haughty, lofty, arrogant, swaggering, insolent, scornful, disdainful, curt, offhand, casual, free-and-easy

cavalry *n*
horsemen, equestrians, horse soldiers, cavalrymen, troopers, dragoons, hussars, lancers

cave *n, v*
▶ *n* cavern, grotto, hole, pothole, tunnel, dugout, underground chamber, hollow, cavity
▶ *v* ▷ **cave in** collapse, subside, give way, yield, fall (in), slip
Related adjective: speleological

caveat *n*
caution, warning, alarm
formal admonition

cavern *n*
cave, cavity, den, grotto, hollow, pothole, vault, tunnel, dugout, underground chamber

cavernous *adj*
hollow, concave, gaping, yawning, echoing, resonant, deep, unfathomable, bottomless, huge, immense, vast, spacious, dark, gloomy, sunken, depressed

cavil *v*
complain, carp, criticize, censure, reproach, find faults, nag, quibble
colloq. nit-pick
E3 praise, compliment

cavity *n*
hole, gap, dent, hollow, crater, pit, well, sinus
technical orifice, ventricle, aperture, lacuna

cavort *v*
caper, frolic, gambol, prance, skip, dance, frisk, sport, romp

cease *v*
stop, refrain, halt, call a halt, come/bring to a halt, break off, leave (off), finish, end, come/bring to an end, conclude, terminate, suspend, let up, abate, fail, die
formal discontinue, desist
colloq. fizzle out, peter out, pack in, quit
E3 begin, start, commence

ceaseless *adj*
endless, unending, never-ending, eternal, everlasting, continuous, non-stop, incessant, unceasing, interminable, constant, perpetual, continual, persistent, untiring, uninterrupted, unremitting
E3 occasional, irregular

cede *v*
surrender, give up, resign, abandon, yield, relinquish, convey, transfer, hand over, turn over, grant, deliver, allow, concede
formal abdicate, renounce

ceiling *n*
1 *a decorated ceiling*
vault, plafond, roof, overhead, overhead covering, rafters, beams, awning, canopy
2 LIMIT, upper limit, maximum, most, cut-off point

celebrate *v*
1 *celebrate a birthday*
commemorate, remember, observe, keep, mark, honour, do something in someone's honour, have/throw a party, rejoice, enjoy yourself, have fun, go out, toast, drink to, extol, revel
colloq. rave, binge, have a ball, live it up, whoop it up, go out on the town, go on the razzle, paint the town red, kill the fatted calf, put the flags out
2 *the priest celebrated Communion*
bless, perform, solemnize

celebrated *adj*
famous, well-known, famed, renowned, illustrious, glorious, eminent, distinguished, great, notable, noted, prominent, outstanding, legendary, popular, acclaimed, exalted, revered
colloq. with your name in lights
E3 unknown, obscure, forgotten

celebration *n*
observance, merrymaking, jollification, revelry, festivity
colloq. rave, rave-up, binge, spree

Celebrations include: anniversary, banquet, baptism, bar mitzvah, birthday, centenary, christening, coming-of-age, commemoration, feast, festival, fête, gala, graduation, harvest festival, homecoming, Independence Day, jubilee, marriage, May Day, name-day, party, reception, remembrance, retirement, reunion, saint's day, thanksgiving, tribute, wedding. *See also* **anniversary; party**.

celebrity *n*
star, personality, name, dignitary, famous person, superstar, legend, legend in their own lifetime, living legend, household name
formal personage, notable, luminary, worthy,
colloq. VIP, big name, bigwig, big shot
E3 nobody, unknown, nonentity

celerity *n*
rapidity, fastness, quickness, speed, swiftness, velocity, dispatch, expedition, fleetness, haste, promptness
🖃 slowness

celestial *adj*
heavenly, divine, godlike, spiritual, angelic, seraphic, elysian, empyrean, ethereal, paradisaic, eternal, immortal, sublime, supernatural, transcendental, astral, starry
🖃 earthly, mundane

celibacy *n*
singleness, bachelorhood, spinsterhood, virginity, chastity, purity, self-denial, self-restraint, abstinence, continence
formal abnegation

celibate *adj*
chaste, pure, abstinent, virgin, single, bachelor, spinster

cell *n*
1 *a prison cell*
prison, jail, dungeon, lock-up, room, cubicle, chamber, compartment, enclosure
2 *living cells*
unit, organism
technical protoplasm, cytoplasm, protoplast, gamete, zygote, spore, nucleus, matrix
Related adjective: cytoid
3 *a political cell*
faction, nucleus, group, party, unit, section, set, crowd, caucus, clique

cellar *n*
basement, crypt, vault, storeroom, wine cellar

cement *n, v*
▶ *n* plaster, mortar, concrete, screed, pointing, grouting, matrix, bonding, adhesive, glue, paste
▶ *v* stick, bond, weld, solder, join, cohere, unite, combine, bind, affix, attach, glue, gum

cemetery *n*
burial ground, burial place, burial site, graveyard, churchyard, graves, tombs
formal necropolis, charnel house, God's acre

censor *v, n*
▶ *v* cut, make cuts, ban, edit, delete, blue-pencil, bowdlerize, expurgate
▶ *n* inspector, examiner, editor, bowdlerizer, expurgater

⚠ **censor** or **censure**?
To *censor* books, films, etc is to examine them, deleting parts of them or forbidding publication: *His letters home were censored.* To *censure* someone is to criticize them severely: *The President was severely censured for abusing his powers.*

censorious *adj*
condemnatory, disapproving, disparaging, fault-finding, carping, cavilling, critical, hypercritical, severe
formal captious
🖃 complimentary, approving

censure *v, n*
▶ *v* condemn, denounce, blame, criticize, disapprove of, reprehend, reprove, reproach, rebuke, reprimand, scold
formal castigate, admonish, remonstrate, upbraid

colloq. tell off, haul over the coals, come down heavy on, pull to pieces
🖃 praise, compliment, approve
▶ *n* condemnation, blame, disapproval, criticism, denunciation, reprehension, reproof, reproach, rebuke, reprimand, scolding
formal admonition, admonishment, castigation, upbraiding, remonstrance, obloquy, vituperation
colloq. telling-off
🖃 praise, compliments, approval

central *adj*
1 MIDDLE, mid, inner, interior, medial, median
2 PRINCIPAL, main, major, most important, chief, key, primary, fundamental, foremost, dominant, vital, crucial, significant, focal, pivotal, basic, essential, core, prime
🖃 **1** peripheral **2** minor, secondary

centralize *v*
concentrate, converge, bring/gather together, incorporate, rationalize, focus, streamline, amalgamate, compact, condense, unify
🖃 decentralize

centre *n, v*
▶ *n* middle, midpoint, heart, core, nucleus, kernel, pivot, hub, focus, focal point, crux, linchpin, arena
colloq. bull's-eye
🖃 edge, periphery, outskirts
▶ *v* focus, concentrate, converge, gravitate, revolve, pivot, hinge

ceramics *n*
pottery, earthenware, ware, bisque, faience, ironstone, porcelain, raku
See panel at **pottery**.

cereal *n*
1 *cereal crops*
barley, grain, corn, wheat, maize, millet, oats, rye, sorghum
2 *breakfast cereal*
cornflakes, muesli, porridge, oatmeal
Related adjective: farinaceous

ceremonial *adj, n*
▶ *adj* formal, official, stately, solemn, dignified, ritual, ritualistic
🖃 informal, casual
▶ *n* ceremony, formality, protocol, custom, solemnity, ritual, rite

⚠ **ceremonial** or **ceremonious**?
Ceremonial means 'relating to or appropriate for a ceremony': *ceremonial dress; a ceremonial occasion.* *Ceremonious* means 'very formal or polite': *He ushered her through with a ceremonious bow.*

ceremonious *adj*
stately, dignified, grand, solemn, ritual, civil, official, polite, courteous, deferential, courtly, formal, stiff, starchy, exact, precise, scrupulous
formal punctilious
colloq. starchy
🖃 unceremonious, informal, relaxed

ceremony *n*
1 *wedding ceremony*
service, rite, sacrament, ordinance, liturgy, commemoration, observance, festival, celebration, formality, function, custom, tradition, parade, anniversary, inauguration, dedication, induction,

initiation, graduation, investiture, bar mitzvah, unveiling
2 ETIQUETTE, formality, protocol, form, niceties, ceremonial, ritual, pomp, pageantry, show
formal decorum, propriety

certain *adj*
1 *I'm certain he's telling the truth*
SURE, positive, assured, confident, convinced, persuaded
2 *it's certain that she left yesterday*
indisputable, unquestionable, undeniable, undoubted, evident, obvious, clear, plain, conclusive, absolute, convincing, true
formal indubitable, incontrovertible, irrefutable
colloq. no two ways about it, no ifs and buts, sure as eggs is eggs
3 *success is certain*
INEVITABLE, unavoidable, inescapable, bound, bound to happen, meant to happen, destined, fated, doomed
formal inexorable, ineluctable
colloq. cut and dried, open-and-shut, home and dry, in the bag
4 *below a certain income*
SPECIFIC, special, particular, individual, precise, express, fixed, established, settled, decided, definite, determined
5 *to a certain extent*
some, partial
E3 1 uncertain, unsure, hesitant, doubtful
3 unlikely

certainly *adv*
surely, of course, naturally, obviously, clearly, plainly, definitely, for sure, undoubtedly, without a doubt, no doubt, undeniably, unquestionably, absolutely, by all means, doubtlessly, assuredly, positively

certainty *n*
1 *identify someone with certainty*
sureness, positiveness, assurance, confidence, conviction, faith, trust, assurance, assuredness
2 *it's a certainty that she'll get the job*
inevitability, foregone conclusion, truth, validity, fact, reality
colloq. sure thing, safe bet, dead cert
E3 1 uncertainty, doubt, hesitation

certificate *n*
document, award, diploma, qualification, credentials, testimonial, guarantee, endorsement, warrant, licence, authorization, pass, voucher

certify *v*
declare, assure, guarantee, endorse, confirm, pronounce, vouch, testify, witness, bear witness to, substantiate, verify, authenticate, validate, warrant, ratify, authorize, recognize, license
formal attest, aver, corroborate, accredit

certitude *n*
(full) assurance, assuredness, certainty, confidence, conviction sureness, positiveness
formal plerophoria, plerophory
E3 doubt

cessation *n*
halt, halting, ceasing, discontinuation, discontinuing, end, ending, remission, respite, rest, standstill, stay, stoppage, stopping, conclusion, suspension, termination, pause, recess, break, let-up, interruption, intermission, interval

formal abeyance, desistance, discontinuance, hiatus
E3 beginning, start, commencement

chafe *v*
1 *chafe someone's skin*
rub, grate, irritate, rasp, scrape, inflame, scratch, wear
formal abrade, excoriate
2 *chafing at the rules*
anger, annoy, enrage, exasperate, incense, provoke, inflame, vex
colloq. peeve, get on someone's nerves, get on someone's wick

chaff *n*
husks, shells, pods, cases
Related adjective: paleaceous

chagrin *n, v*
▶ *n* annoyance, exasperation, indignation, disappointment, displeasure, irritation, vexation, disquiet, dissatisfaction, embarrassment, mortification, humiliation, shame, fretfulness
formal discomfiture, discomposure
E3 delight, pleasure
▶ *v* annoy, exasperate, disappoint, displease, irritate, vex, irk, disquiet, dissatisfy, embarrass, humiliate, mortify
colloq. peeve

chain *n, v*
▶ *n* **1** FETTER, manacle, restraint, bond, shackle, trammel, link, coupling, union
2 *a hotel chain*
group, company, firm
3 *a chain of islands*
string, line, row, train, set
formal concatenation
4 *a chain of events*
series, sequence, succession, progression
▶ *v* tether, fasten, secure, bind, tie, hitch, restrain, confine, fetter, shackle, manacle, handcuff, enslave
E3 free, release, liberate
Related adjective: catenary

chair *n, v*
▶ *n* **1** *sit on a chair*
armchair, recliner, swivel-chair, seat, stool, bench, form
2 *Sally is the new chair*
chairperson, chairman, chairwoman, president, convenor, organizer, director, master of ceremonies, MC, toastmaster, speaker
▶ *v* lead, act as chairperson/chairman/ chairwoman, convene, direct, supervise, preside over

chalk *v*
▷ **chalk up** achieve, attain, gain, log, score, tally, register, record, accumulate, ascribe, attribute, charge, credit, put down

chalky *adj*
ashen, pale, pallid, white, wan, colourless, powdery
formal calcareous, cretaceous

challenge *v, n*
▶ *v* **1** DARE, defy, confront, brave, summon, invite, accost, provoke
colloq. throw down the gauntlet
2 *challenged his authority*
QUESTION, dispute, query, protest, disagree with, object to, take exception to, call into question
formal demur
3 *challenged my ability*
test, tax, try, stretch

▶ n 1 *the new job is a real challenge*
test, trial, hurdle, obstacle, problem, risk, hazard, opportunity
2 *take up the challenge to fight*
dare, defiance, confrontation, provocation, call, summons, bidding
3 *a challenge to their powers*
dispute, protest, opposition, defiance, disagreement, objection, calling into question, questioning, interrogation, stand, confrontation, ultimatum

challenging *adj*
exciting, exacting, demanding, testing, taxing, stretching
E3 undemanding

chamber *n*
1 HALL, assembly room, auditorium, meeting-place
2 ROOM, apartment, compartment, bedroom, boudoir
3 *the chambers of the heart*
cavity, ventricle, compartment
4 *the upper chamber of parliament*
assembly, legislature, parliament, council, house

champion *n, v*
▶ n 1 *the school chess champion*
winner, victor, conqueror, title-holder, hero, ace
colloq. champ
2 *a champion of animal rights*
guardian, protector, defender, vindicator, patron, backer, supporter, upholder, advocate
colloq. angel
▶ v defend, stand up for, back, support, protect, maintain, uphold, advocate, promote
formal espouse

chance *n, v, adj*
▶ n 1 *meet someone by chance*
ACCIDENT, coincidence, luck, fortune, providence, fate, destiny, risk, gamble, speculation
formal fortuity, serendipity
colloq. fluke
2 *there's a chance that I'll be late*
possibility, prospect, probability, likelihood, odds
3 *a second chance*
opportunity, opening, occasion, time
colloq. break, golden opportunity, chance of a lifetime, your best shot
E3 1 certainty
▶ v 1 RISK, hazard, take a chance, gamble, wager, stake, try, speculate, venture
colloq. chance your luck, push your luck, play a hunch, bet your boots/life, bet your bottom dollar
2 HAPPEN, occur, come about, take place, arise, crop up, develop, result, follow
▷ **chance on/upon** meet, meet unexpectedly, find by chance, discover, come across, stumble on;
colloq. run into, bump into
▶ adj fortuitous, casual, accidental, inadvertent, unintentional, unintended, unforeseen, unexpected, unanticipated, unlooked-for, random, arbitrary, haphazard, incidental
formal serendipitous
colloq. flukey
E3 deliberate, intentional, foreseen, certain

chancy *adj*
risky, speculative, tricky, uncertain, fraught, hazardous, dangerous, problematical
colloq. dicey, dodgy
E3 safe, secure

change *v, n*
▶ v 1 *water changes into ice; prices keep changing*
make/become different, alter, vary, convert, turn, go, become, move, develop, modify, reorganize, reform, restructure, remodel, revise, renew, amend, adapt, customize, adjust, transform, evolve, transfer, move, shift, fluctuate, vacillate, be in a state of flux
technical mutate, transmutate, metamorphose, transfigure
2 *change one thing for another*
substitute, replace, alternate, interchange, rotate, transpose, exchange, swap, trade, switch, barter
colloq. chop and change
3 *change buses*
transfer, connect, make a connection
▶ n 1 *a change in the weather*
difference, alteration, variation, conversion, modification, reorganization, shake-up, transition, trend, movement, diversion, novelty, innovation, variety, revolution, upheaval, development, reform, restructuring, remodelling, reconstruction, revision, renewal, amendment, adaptation, customization, adjustment, transformation, evolution, transfer, move, shift, fluctuation, vacillation, state of flux, reversal, about-turn, about-face, volte-face, turnabout, ebb and flow
technical mutation, transmutation, metamorphosis, transfiguration
formal vicissitude
colloq. U-turn
2 *a change of government*
exchange, transposition, interchange, substitution, substitute, replacement, alternation, rotation, swap, trade, switch, barter
3 *Have you got any change?*
coins, cash, silver, coppers

changeable *adj*
variable, varying, fluctuating, fluid, kaleidoscopic, shifting, mobile, unsettled, unstable, uncertain, unpredictable, unreliable, erratic, irregular, inconstant, fickle, capricious, volatile, unstable, unsteady, wavering, vacillating, mercurial, labile, chameleonic, chamelion-like, Protean
formal mutable, vicissitudinous
E3 constant, settled, reliable

channel *n, v*
▶ n 1 *a channel for rainwater; irrigation channels*
passage, duct, conduit, main, groove, furrow, trough, gutter, gully, canal, flume, watercourse, waterway, strait, neck, sound
2 *channels of communication*
route, course, path, avenue, way, means, medium, approach, passage, agent, agency
▶ v direct, guide, conduct, convey, send, transmit, force, concentrate, focus

chant *n, v*
▶ n 1 *the football supporters' chants*
shout, cry, slogan, warcry
2 *a religious chant*
plainsong, psalm, song, melody, chorus, refrain, ditty, incantation, recitation, mantra
▶ v sing, chorus, recite
formal intone

chaos *n*
disorder, confusion, disorganization, anarchy, lawlessness, tumult, upheaval, disruption, pandemonium, uproar, riot, bedlam, madhouse, mess
formal tohu bohu

colloq. pig's breakfast, dog's dinner, shambles; *US slang* snafu
🔁 order

chaotic *adj*
disordered, confused, disorganized, topsy-turvy, deranged, anarchic, lawless, orderless, riotous, tumultuous, unruly, uncontrolled, disrupted
colloq. shambolic, at sixes and sevens, all over the place/shop, higgledy-piggledy; *US slang* snafu
🔁 ordered, organized

chap *n*
fellow, man, boy, person, individual, character, sort, type
colloq. bloke, guy

chaperone, chaperon *n, v*
▶ *n* companion, escort, duenna
▶ *v* escort, accompany, attend, guard, protect, safeguard, shepherd, take care of, look after, mind watch over

chapped *adj*
sore, chafed, cracked, raw, cracked

chapter *n*
1 *read chapter 3*
section, division, part, clause, portion, topic
2 *a new chapter in my life*
EPISODE, period, phase, stage, time

char *v*
burn, cauterize, scorch, sear, singe, carbonize, brown

character *n*
1 *the cruel side of his character; the character of the countryside*
nature, essential quality, essence, ethos, personality, disposition, temperament, temper, constitution, make-up, individuality, identity, peculiarity, feature, attributes, characteristics, quality, property, type, stamp, calibre, reputation, psyche, status, position, trait, image
formal persona
colloq. what makes someone tick
2 *he has character; this house has character*
strength, strength of purpose, determination, courage, honesty, integrity, uprightness, moral fibre, charm, appeal, attractiveness, attractive features, distinctive features, arresting qualities, specialness, style, interest
3 ECCENTRIC, eccentric person, original, oddity
colloq. oddball, case
4 *the characters in a play*
individual, person, human being, role, part, sort, type,
5 LETTER, figure, symbol, sign, mark, type, device, logo, emblem, cipher, rune, hieroglyph, ideograph

characteristic *n, adj*
▶ *n* feature, trait, attribute, property, quality, essential quality, mark, hallmark, factor, peculiarity, idiosyncrasy, mannerism, symptom
▶ *adj* distinctive, distinguishing, individual, idiosyncratic, peculiar, specific, special, typical, representative, symbolic, symptomatic
🔁 uncharacteristic, untypical

characterize *v*
1 *materialism that characterizes life*
typify, mark, stamp, brand, identify, distinguish, indicate, specify, designate
2 DESCRIBE, represent, portray, present

charade *n*
farce, mockery, parody, pretence, fake, travesty, sham, pantomime

charge *v, n*
▶ *v* 1 *charge a high price*
ask, ask for, ask someone to pay, demand, demand in payment, set/fix a price, levy, exact, debit, bill, put down to
2 ACCUSE, indict, impeach, incriminate, blame
formal arraign
3 ATTACK, assail, assault, storm, rush (forward), tear
▶ *n* 1 PRICE, cost, fee, rate, amount, expense, expenditure, outlay, payment, rent, rental, dues, toll, levy, tax
2 ACCUSATION, indictment, allegation, impeachment, blame, incrimination
formal arraignment, imputation
3 ATTACK, assault, onslaught, sortie, incursion, storming, rush, onrush
4 *in your charge*
custody, keeping, care, safekeeping, guardianship, ward, protection, trust, responsibility, duty, burden, obligation
▷ **in charge of** responsible for, managing, leading, controlling, directing, supervising, overseeing, heading up, looking after, taking care of

charitable *adj*
philanthropic, humanitarian, benevolent, benign, kind, compassionate, sympathetic, understanding, considerate, generous, open-handed, liberal, tolerant, broad-minded, kindly, lenient, forgiving, indulgent, gracious
formal magnanimous, beneficent, bounteous, eleemosynary
🔁 uncharitable, inconsiderate, unforgiving

charity *n*
1 fund, trust, foundation, caritas, voluntary organization
2 *live on charity*
gift, donation, handout, aid, relief, contribution, funding, assistance, alms
3 GENEROSITY, goodwill, bountifulness, almsgiving, philanthropy, unselfishness, altruism, benevolence, benignness, kindness, goodness, humanity, compassion, considerateness, thoughtfulness, tender-heartedness, love, affection, tolerance, clemency, indulgence
formal beneficence
🔁 3 selfishness, malice

Charities in the UK which have the largest income: National Trust, Royal National Lifeboat Institution (RNLI), Oxfam, Imperial Cancer Research Fund (ICRF), Cancer Research Campaign, Salvation Army, Save the Children Fund, Barnardo's, Help the Aged, Guide Dogs for the Blind Association, Royal Society for the Prevention of Cruelty to Animals (RSPCA), British Heart Foundation, National Society for the Prevention of Cruelty to Children (NSPCC), British Red Cross Society, Royal National Institute for the Blind (RNIB), Marie Curie Memorial Foundation, Capability Scotland, Christian Aid, World Wide Fund for Nature (WWFN), ActionAid, Jewish Philanthropic Association, Cancer Relief Macmillan fund, Royal Society for the Protection of Birds (RSPB), Tear Fund, People's Dispensary for Sick Animals (PDSA).

charlatan *n*
impostor, cheat, fake, fraud, confidence, trickster, pretender, bogus caller/official, quack, sham, swindler, mountebank
colloq. phoney, con man

charm *n, v*
▶ *n* **1** ATTRACTION, allure, allurement, magnetism, appeal, delightfulness, attractiveness, desirability, fascination, enchantment, captivation
colloq. what it takes
2 *lucky charm*
trinket, ornament, talisman, mascot, amulet, fetish, idol, grisgris, juju, obi, periapt, porte-bonheur
3 *the magician's charm*
spell, sorcery, magic, abracadabra
▶ *v* please, delight, enrapture, captivate, fascinate, beguile, enchant, bewitch, mesmerize, attract, draw, allure, intrigue, cajole, win, enamour, seduce
🖃 repel, disgust

charming *adj*
pleasing, delightful, pleasant, lovely, captivating, enchanting, attractive, fetching, appealing, tasteful, sweet, cute, winsome, alluring, engaging, tempting, seductive, winning, irresistible
formal delectable
🖃 ugly, unattractive, repulsive

chart *n, v*
▶ *n* **1** *a chart showing the patient's temperature*
diagram, table, graph, map, plan, blueprint, bar chart, flow chart, pie chart, flow sheet
technical nomogram, nomograph
2 *number one in the charts*
hit parade, top twenty, list, league
▶ *v* **1** *chart an area*
map, map out, sketch, draw, draft, outline, delineate, mark, plot, place
2 MONITOR, document, record, keep a record of, put on record, note, register, observe, follow

charter *n, v*
▶ *n* right, privilege, prerogative, authority, authorization, permit, licence, franchise, concession, contract, covenant, indenture, deed, bond, warrant, sanction, document
formal accreditation
▶ *v* hire, rent, lease, commission, engage, employ, authorize, sanction, license

chary *adj*
careful, cautious, wary, guarded, heedful, uneasy, unwilling, reluctant, slow, suspicious, leery
formal prudent, circumspect
🖃 heedless, unwary

chase *v, n*
▶ *v* pursue, follow, hunt, run after, give chase, track, trail, tail, shadow, hound, drive, expel, send away, rush, hurry
colloq. be hot on someone's heels
▶ *n* pursuit, trail, running after, hunt, hunting, coursing, rush

chasm *n*
1 *a chasm in the rocks*
crack, rift, split, cleft, fissure, crevasse, canyon, gorge, ravine, gap, opening, gulf, abyss, void, hollow, cavity, crater, breach
2 *a chasm between two people*
rift, split, gulf, gap, opening, gulf, breach, divorce, separation, estrangement, alienation, disagreement, quarrel

chassis *n*
framework, bodywork, frame, fuselage, skeleton, structure, substructure, undercarriage

chaste *adj*
1 *a chaste person*
pure, virginal, unsullied, undefiled, immaculate, abstinent, continent, celibate, unmarried, single, virtuous, moral, innocent
2 *a chaste style*
modest, decent, plain, simple, restrained, austere, unadorned, unembellished
🖃 **1** promiscuous, immoral, corrupt
2 unrestrained, decorated

chasten *v*
humble, humiliate, tame, subdue, repress, curb, restrain, moderate, soften, discipline, punish, correct, reprove
formal chastise, castigate

chastise *v*
punish, discipline, reprimand, correct, reprove, admonish, scold, censure, beat, flog, whip, lash, scourge, smack, spank, strap, cane
formal castigate, upbraid, berate
colloq. haul over the coals, dress down, take to task, wallop
🖃 praise, encourage

chastity *n*
purity, virginity, maidenhood, modesty, abstinence, temperateness, continence, celibacy, unmarried state, singleness, virtue, innocence, immaculateness
🖃 promiscuity, immorality

chat *v, n*
▶ *v* talk, gossip, chatter, tittle-tattle
formal converse
colloq. natter, jabber, babble, rabbit (on), gas, waffle, prattle, chinwag, jaw, chew the rag/fat
▶ *n* talk, conversation, gossip, tête-à-tête, heart-to-heart, cosy chat, small talk, tittle-tattle
colloq. natter, confab, chinwag

chatter *v, n*
▶ *v* babble, chat, gossip, tattle, tittle-tattle
colloq. pass the time of day, natter, jabber, witter, babble, rabbit (on), gab, gas, waffle, prattle, chinwag, jaw, talk the hind legs off a donkey
▶ *n* talk, conversation, gossip, tête-à-tête, chit-chat, natter, jabber, witter, prattle, babble, tittle-tattle, jaw
colloq. natter, confab, chinwag

chatterbox *n*
chatterer, babbler, gossipper, gossip, conversationalist, jabberer, tittle-tattler, tattler
colloq. natterer, windbag, gasbag, gabber, big mouth, blabbermouth, loudmouth

chatty *adj*
1 *a chatty person*
talkative, gossipy, conversational, garrulous, gushing, effusive, verbose, long-winded, glib
formal loquacious
colloq. gabby, mouthy
2 *a chatty letter*
newsy, friendly, informal, colloquial, conversational, familiar
🖃 quiet, taciturn

chauvinism *n*
jingoism, nationalism, bias, prejudice, partisanship, flag-waving, sexism, male chauvinism

chauvinist *adj*
jingoist, nationalist, biased, prejudiced, flag-waving, sexist, male chauvinist

cheap *adj*
1 INEXPENSIVE, reasonable, dirt-cheap, low-price, low-cost, affordable, bargain, reduced, cut-price, knock-down, marked-down, discounted, slashed, rock-bottom, giveaway, budget, economy, sale, economical, no-frills, cheap-rate, reduced rate, concessional rate, on special offer, value for money, a good buy
colloq. a snip, a steal, going for a song, dirt-cheap, ten a penny, on a shoestring
2 SHODDY, cheap and nasty, tatty, tawdry, inferior, second-rate, worthless, vulgar, tasteless, common, poor, cheapjack, paltry, two-bit
colloq. cheapo, tacky
3 *cheap comments*
mean, contemptible, despicable, low, vulgar, sordid
E3 1 expensive, costly, dear **2** superior, good quality **3** noble, admirable

cheapen *v*
devalue, degrade, lower, demean, depreciate, belittle, disparage, discredit, downgrade
formal denigrate, derogate

cheat *v, n*
▶ *v* **1** *cheat someone*
defraud, swindle, diddle, short-change, double-cross, mislead, deceive, dupe, fool, trick, hoodwink, gull, beguile, cozen, fiddle, fake, bluff, welsh
colloq. do, do one over on, rip off, con, sting, fleece, take for a ride, take to the cleaners, pull the wool over someone's eyes, two-time, bilk, fix, rig, bamboozle
2 *cheated out of their inheritance*
prevent, deprive, deny, thwart, frustrate, check
colloq. do, have
▶ *n* **1** cheater, dodger, crook, fraud, swindler, extortioner, double-crosser, impostor, charlatan, deceiver, trickster, confidence trickster, rogue, cozener
colloq. con man, shark

check *v, n*
▶ *v* **1** EXAMINE, inspect, scrutinize, look at (closely), go through, scan, investigate, probe, inquire into, test, monitor, police, study, research, analyse, compare, cross-check, screen, take stock, make sure, confirm, verify
formal corroborate, substantiate, validate
colloq. give the once-over
2 *check an impulse*
curb, bridle, restrain, control, limit, contain, rein in, repress, inhibit, damp, thwart, hinder, impede, obstruct, bar, delay, slow (down), stop, staunch, stem, arrest, halt, bring to a standstill
formal retard
▷ **check in** register, book in, enrol, record your arrival
▷ **check out 1** *check out of a hotel* leave, pay the bill, settle up **2** *check out the procedure* examine, investigate, test, study, look into; *colloq.* recce
▷ **check up** investigate, inspect, evaluate, assess, analyse, probe, inquire into, ascertain, make sure, confirm, verify
▶ *n* **1** EXAMINATION, inspection, scrutiny, check-up, investigation, inquiry, audit, test, research, monitoring, analysis, probe, confirmation, verification
colloq. once-over
2 BILL, invoice, statement, account, charges, reckoning, tally, *US* tab

check-up *n*
examination, inspection, scrutiny, investigation, inquiry, audit, test, research, monitoring, analysis, evaluation, appraisal, probe, confirmation, verification

cheek *n*
impertinence, impudence, insolence, disrespect, brazenness, audacity, gall
formal effrontery, temerity
colloq. nerve, sauce, gall, lip, mouth, brass neck, chutzpah

cheeky *adj*
impertinent, impudent, insolent, disrespectful, forward, brazen, pert, audacious, overfamiliar
colloq. fresh, saucy, lippy, *US* sassy
E3 respectful, polite

cheer *v, n*
▶ *v* **1** ACCLAIM, hail, clap, applaud, salute, welcome, celebrate, fanfare, shout, support
colloq. root for
2 COMFORT, console, brighten, gladden, warm, uplift, raise/lift the spirits of, elate, exhilarate, encourage, hearten, enliven, buoy up
formal solace, inspirit
colloq. buck up, perk up
▷ **cheer up** comfort, console, encourage, brighten, hearten, liven (up), take heart, rally; *colloq.* buck up, perk up
E3 1 boo, jeer **2** dishearten, discourage
▶ *n* **1** *the cheers of the crowd*
acclamation, hurrah, bravo, applause, clapping, ovation
formal plaudits
2 CHEERFULNESS, gladness, happiness, hopefulness, joyfulness, high spirits, light-heartedness, merriment, merrymaking, revelry
E3 criticism

cheerful *adj*
1 *a cheerful person*
happy, glad, contented, joyful, joyous, blithe, carefree, light-hearted, cheery, good-humoured, sunny, optimistic, enthusiastic, hearty, genial, jovial, jolly, gay, merry, lively, animated, exuberant, bright, smiling, laughing, spirited, in good spirits, chirpy, breezy, jaunty, buoyant, sparkling
2 *painted in a cheerful yellow*
attractive, pleasing, pleasant, agreeable, delightful, warm, sunny, bright, comforting, encouraging, heartening, inspiring, stirring
E3 1 sad, dejected, depressed **2** depressing, disheartening

cheerio *interj*
goodbye, farewell, adieu, *au revoir*
colloq. cheers, so long, bye, bye-bye, see you, see you later, ta-ta

cheerless *adj*
gloomy, dismal, dreary, dull, depressing, dejected, despondent, austere, barren, desolate, forlorn, grim, bleak, cold, sad, unhappy, sombre, sorrowful, comfortless, joyless, lonely, melancholy, miserable, mournful, dank, dark, dingy, disconsolate, drab, sullen, sunless, winterly, uninviting
formal dolorous
E3 bright, cheerful

cheers *interj*
1 *say cheers as a toast*
bottoms up, here's to you, your good health, here's

looking to you, here's mud in your eye, here's to..., to absent friends, down the hatch, happy landings, all the best, *prosit, skol, slàinte*

2 THANK YOU, thank you very much, bless you, much obliged
colloq. many thanks, thanks a lot, ta
3 GOODBYE, farewell, adieu, *au revoir*
colloq. so long, bye, bye-bye, see you, see you later, ta-ta

cheery *adj*
happy, glad, contented, joyful, carefree, light-hearted, cheerful, optimistic, enthusiastic, hearty, genial, jovial, jolly, gay, merry, lively, animated, exuberant, bright, smiling, laughing, spirited, in good spirits, chirpy, breezy, jaunty, buoyant, sparkling
E3 downcast, sad

cheese *n*
Related adjective: caseous

Varieties of cheese include: Amsterdam, Bel Paese, Bleu d'Auvergne, Blue Cheshire, Blue Vinny, Boursin, Brie, Caboc, Caerphilly, Camembert, Carré, Cheddar, Cheshire, Churnton, cottage cheese, cream cheese, Crowdie, curd cheese, Danish blue, Derby, Dolcelatte, Dorset Blue, Double Gloucester, Dunlop, Edam, Emmental, Emmentaler, ewe-cheese, Feta, fromage frais, Gloucester, Gorgonzola, Gouda, Gruyère, Huntsman, Jarlsberg, Killarney, Lancashire, Leicester, Limburg(er), Lymeswold, mascarpone, mouse-trap, mozzarella, Neufchâtel, Orkney, Parmesan, Petit Suisse, Pont-l'Éveque, Port Salut, processed cheese, quark, Red Leicester, Red Windsor, ricotta, Roquefort, sage Derby, Saint-Paulin, Stilton, stracchino, vegetarian cheese, Vacherin, Wensleydale.

chemical elements

The chemical elements (with their symbols) are: actinium (Ac), aluminium (Al), americium (Am), antimony (Sb), argon (Ar), arsenic (As), astatine (At), barium (Ba), berkelium (Bk), beryllium (Be), bismuth (Bi), boron (B), bromine (Br), cadmium (Cd), caesium (Cs), calcium (Ca), californium (Cf), carbon (C), cerium (Ce), chlorine (Cl), chromium (Cr), cobalt (Co), copper (Cu), curium (Cm), dysprosium (Dy), einsteinium (Es), erbium (Er), europium (Eu), fermium (Fm), fluorine (F), francium (Fr), gadolinium (Gd), gallium (Ga), germanium (Ge), gold (Au), hafnium (Hf), hahnium (Ha), helium (He), holmium (Ho), hydrogen (H), indium (In), iodine (I), iridium (Ir), iron (Fe), krypton (Kr), lanthanum (La), lawrencium (Lr), lead (Pb), lithium (Li), lutetium (Lu), magnesium (Mg), manganese (Mn), mendelevium (Md), mercury (Hg), molybdenum (Mo), neodymium (Nd), neon (Ne), neptunium (Np), nickel (Ni), niobium (Nb), nitrogen (N), nobelium (No), osmium (Os), oxygen (O), palladium (Pd), phosphorus (P), platinum (Pt), plutonium (Pu), polonium (Po), potassium (K), praseodymium (Pr), promethium (Pm), protactinium (Pa), radium (Ra), radon (Rn), rhenium (Re), rhodium (Rh), rubidium (Rb), ruthenium (Ru), rutherfordium (Rf), samarium (Sm), scandium (Sc), selenium (Se), silicon (Si), silver (Ag), sodium (Na), strontium (Sr), sulphur (S), tantalum (Ta), technetium (Tc), tellurium (Te), terbium (Tb), thallium (Tl), thorium (Th), thulium (Tm), tin (Sn), titanium (Ti), tungsten (W), uranium (U), vanadium (V), xenon (Xe), ytterbium (Yb), yttrium (Y), zinc (Zn), zirconium (Zr).

chemistry *n*

Terms used in chemistry include: analytical chemistry, biochemistry, inorganic chemistry, organic chemistry, physical chemistry; acid, alkali, analysis, atom, atomic number, atomic structure, subatomic particles, base, bond, buffer, catalysis, catalyst, chain reaction, chemical bond, chemical compound, chemical element, chemical equation, chemical reaction, chemist, chlorination, combustion, compound, corrosion, covalent bond, crystal, cycle, decomposition, diffusion, dissociation, distillation, electrochemical cell, electrode, electron, electrolysis, emulsion, fermentation, fixation, formula, free radical, gas, halogen, hydrolysis, immiscible, indicator, inert gas, ion, ionic bond, isomer, isotope, lipid, liquid, litmus paper, litmus test, mass, matter, metallic bond, mixture, mole, molecule, neutron, noble gas, nucleus, oxidation, periodic table, pH, polymer, proton, radioactivity, reaction, reduction, respiration, salt, solids, solution, solvent, substance, suspension, symbol, synthesis, valency, zwitterion.
See also **acid; chemical elements; gas; minerals**.

chequered *adj*
varied, mixed, diverse, with good and bad parts, with ups and downs, with sad and happy downs, with its fair share of rough and tumble

cherish *v*
1 *cherish someone*
care for, look after, love, take (good) care of, hold dear, treasure, adore, support, foster, nurture, nourish, nurse, sustain
2 *cherish a tradition/privilege*
foster, nurture, sustain, hold dear, value, prize, treasure
3 *cherish hopes/memories*
harbour, shelter, entertain, hold dear, value, prize, treasure

cherub *n*
angel, seraph

cherubic *adj*
adorable, appealing, cute, sweet, innocent, lovable, lovely, heavenly, angelic, seraphic

chest *n*
1 *a man with a hairy chest*
breast
technical sternum, thorax
Related adjective: pectoral, thoracic
2 *a treasure chest*
trunk, crate, box, case, casket, coffer, strongbox

chew *v*
bite, gnaw, munch, champ, chomp, crunch, grind
formal masticate
▷ **chew over** consider, meditate on, mull over, ponder, weigh up, muse on, deliberate upon; *formal* ruminate on; *colloq.* put on your thinking cap

chic *adj*
elegant, fashionable, sophisticated, modish, smart, stylish, dapper, à la mode

colloq. snazzy, trendy
⊟ outmoded, unfashionable

chicanery *n*
trickery, deception, fraud, deceitfulness, dishonesty, deviousness, cheating, double-dealing, guile, hoodwinking, duplicity, artifice, intrigue, sharp practice, underhandedness, sophistry, subterfuge, wiles
colloq. dodge, jiggery-pokery,

chide *v*
scold, tell off, blame, criticize, censure, lecture, rebuke, reprehend, reprimand, reproach, reprove
formal admonish, berate, upbraid, objurgate
⊟ praise

chief *adj, n*
▶ *adj* leading, foremost, uppermost, highest, supreme, grand, arch, head, premier, principal, main, key, central, prime, prevailing, predominant, dominant, pre-eminent, outstanding, vital, most important, essential, primary, major, controlling, directing, supervising
⊟ minor, unimportant
▶ *n* ruler, chieftain, lord, overlord, master, supremo, head, principal, leader, commander, captain, governor, boss, director, manager, premier, prime minister, president, suzerain, chair, chairperson, chairman, chairwoman, chief executive, managing director, superintendent, superior, ringleader
colloq. boss, gaffer, top dog, big cheese, big noise, big gun

chiefly *adv*
mainly, mostly, for the most part, in the main, predominantly, principally, primarily, essentially, especially, generally, on the whole, usually

child *n*
youngster, young person, little one, young one, baby, infant, toddler, minor, juvenile, boy, little boy, girl, little girl, son, daughter, adolescent, teenager, youth, young adult, descendant
formal offspring, issue, progeny
colloq. tot, tiny tot, kid, nipper, brat, sprog

childbirth *n*
labour, delivery, confinement, child-bearing, lying-in, pregnancy, maternity
technical parturition
formal travail, accouchement, puerperal

childhood *n*
babyhood, infancy, boyhood, girlhood, schooldays, youth, adolescence, minority, immaturity

childish *adj*
babyish, boyish, girlish, infantile, puerile, juvenile, immature, irresponsible, silly, foolish, frivolous
⊟ mature, sensible

⚠ **childish** or **childlike** ?
You describe someone as *childish* if you think they are behaving in a silly immature way: *Stop being so childish! Childlike* is a neutral term: *childlike innocence.*

---

childlike *adj*
innocent, naïve, ingenuous, artless, guileless, credulous, trusting, trustful, simple, natural

chill *n, v, adj*
▶ *n* **1** *a wintry chill in the air*
coolness, cold, coldness, rawness, bite, nip, crispness, iciness
2 *catch a chill*
cold, fever, flu, influenza, virus
3 *a chill ran down my spine*
shiver, fear, anxiety, apprehension, dread
⊟ 1 warmth
▶ *v* **1** COOL, cool down, refrigerate, make/become cold(er), freeze, ice
2 FRIGHTEN, terrify, dismay, scare, dishearten, discourage, depress, dampen
⊟ 1 warm, heat
▷ **chill out** calm down, relax, have a rest;
colloq. take it easy
▶ *adj* cold, cool, raw, sharp, biting, icy, freezing, wintry, chilly, frigid, depressing, bleak
colloq. nippy, parky
⊟ warm, hot

chilly *adj*
1 *chilly weather*
cold, fresh, brisk, crisp, cool, raw, sharp, biting, icy, freezing, frigid, wintry
colloq. nippy, parky
2 *a chilly response*
cool, frigid, unsympathetic, unwelcoming, aloof, stony, distant, unresponsive, unfriendly, unenthusiastic, hostile
⊟ 1 warm **2** friendly

chime *v*
sound, strike, toll, ring, peal, clang, ding, dong, jingle, tinkle, reverberate, boom, resound
formal tintinnabulate
▷ **chime in 1** *chime in when someone is talking* interrupt; *colloq.* chip in, butt in, cut in **2** *his analysis chimed in with mine* fit in, harmonize, correspond, blend, agree, be consistent, be similar

chimera *n*
illusion, fantasy, delusion, dream, fancy, idle fancy, figment of the imagination, hallucination, will-o'-the-wisp, spectre

chimney *n*
shaft, vent, flue, funnel, cleft, crevice, lum, femerall

china *n*
1 *a vase made of china*
porcelain, ceramic, pottery, earthenware, terracotta
2 *serve the best china*
crockery, plates, dishes, cups and saucers, tableware, dinner service

Chinese calendar

The animals representing the years in which people are born: rat, buffalo, tiger, rabbit (or hare), dragon, snake, horse, goat (or sheep), monkey, rooster, dog, pig.

chink *n*
crack, rift, cleft, fissure, crevice, cut, split, slit, slot, cavity, opening, aperture, gap, space

chip *n, v*
▶ *n* **1** *fish and chips*
fried potato, (French) fry
2 NOTCH, nick, crack, scratch, dent, flaw
3 FRAGMENT, scrap, wafer, splinter, sliver, flake, shred, shard, shaving, paring
4 *gambling chips*
counter, disc, token

▶ *v* chisel, whittle, nick, crack, fragment, break (off), crumble, notch, gash, snick, damage
▷ **chip in** 1 CONTRIBUTE, make a donation, donate, club together, have a collection, pay, subscribe; *colloq.* have a whip-round 2 *chime in when someone is talking* interrupt; *formal* interpose; *colloq.* chime in, butt in, cut in

chirp *v & n*
chirrup, tweet, cheep, peep, trill, twitter, warble, sing, pipe, whistle

chirpy *adj*
cheerful, cheery, bright, happy, merry, gay, jaunty, blithe
colloq. perky
E꜡ downcast, sad

chit-chat *n*
chat, chatter, talk, conversation, gossip, idle gossip, tête-à-tête, heart-to-heart, cosy chat, small talk, tittle-tattle
colloq. natter, confab, chinwag

chivalrous *adj*
gentlemanly, polite, courteous, well-mannered, gallant, heroic, valiant, brave, courageous, bold, gracious, noble, honourable
E꜡ ungallant, cowardly

chivalry *n*
gentlemanliness, politeness, courtesy, graciousness, good manners, courtliness, gallantry, bravery, courage, boldness, honour, truthfulness, integrity

chivvy *v*
badger, harass, annoy, hound, goad, nag, urge, pester, plague, pressure, hurry (up), prod, torment
formal importune
colloq. hassle

choice *n, adj*
▶ *n* 1 *a choice of several dishes; make a choice between two things*
selection, variety, range, choosing, opting, picking, preference, decision, election, discrimination, 2 *have no choice but to go*
option, alternative, answer, solution
▶ *adj* select, best, superior, prime, plum, excellent, first-class, first-rate, fine, exquisite, exclusive, hand-picked, special, prize, valuable, precious
E꜡ inferior, poor

choke *v*
1 STRANGLE, throttle, asphyxiate, suffocate, stifle, smother, suppress, overpower, overwhelm
2 OBSTRUCT, constrict, congest, clog, block, dam (up), bar, close, stop, plug
formal occlude
3 COUGH, gag, retch
▷ **choke back** suppress, restrain, contain, control, check, curb, repress, inhibit, fight back

choleric *adj*
fiery, hot-tempered, angry, bad-tempered, ill-tempered, quick-tempered, testy, touchy, irascible, irritable, petulant
colloq. crabbed, crabby, crotchety
E꜡ calm, placid

choose *v*
1 *choose a new dress*
pick (out), select, single out, take, go for, opt for, vote for, decide on, settle on, fix on, designate, adopt, take up, appoint, elect, predestine

formal espouse
colloq. plump for
2 *choose to do something*
decide, prefer, wish, desire, make up your mind, want, favour, see fit

choosy *adj*
selective, discriminating, fussy, particular, finicky, fastidious, exacting, faddy
colloq. picky, pernickety
undemanding

chop *v*
cut, hack, fell, hew, lop, saw, sever, truncate, slice, carve, cleave, divide, dissect, split, slash, axe
▷ **chop up** cut (up), cut into pieces, slice (up), divide, cube, dice, shred, mince, grind, grate

choppy *adj*
rough, turbulent, tempestuous, stormy, squally, blustery, ruffled, wavy, uneven, broken
E꜡ calm, still, peaceful

chore *n*
task, job, errand, routine, duty, burden, piece of work

chortle *v*
cackle, chuckle, guffaw, laugh, crow, snigger, snort

chorus *n*
1 REFRAIN, response, burden, strain, call, shout
2 CHOIR, choristers, singers, vocalists, ensemble, choral group

christen *v*
1 *christen a baby*
baptize, name, give a name to, sprinkle, immerse,
2 *christened it 'the emerald forest'*
name, call, dub, title, style, term, designate
3 *christen the wine glasses*
inaugurate, use for the first time, begin using

Christmas *n*
Xmas, Noel, Yule, Yuletide

chronic *adj*
1 *a chronic illness*
PERSISTENT, deep-seated, recurring, incessant, constant, continual, long-lasting, long-standing, long-term, ingrained, deep-rooted
2 *a chronic worrier*
inveterate, confirmed, habitual, hardened
3 *the film was chronic*
awful, terrible, dreadful, appalling, atrocious
E꜡ 1 temporary 3 excellent

chronicle *n, v*
▶ *n* account, record, register, annals, archives, diary, calendar, history, journal, narrative, story, saga, epic
▶ *v* recount, narrate, relate, report, tell, write down, set down, record, put on record, register, enter, list

chronicler *n*
historian, archivist, annalist, diarist, narrator, recorder, reporter, scribe, historiographer, chronographer, chronologer

chronological *adj*
consecutive, sequential, in sequence, progressive, ordered, in order, serial, historical

chubby *adj*
plump, fat, podgy, fleshy, flabby, stout, portly, round, full, tubby, paunchy
formal rotund
E꜡ slim, skinny

chuck *v*
1 THROW, cast, toss, fling, heave, hurl, jettison, pitch, shy, sling
2 *chuck a habit/your boyfriend*
give up, abandon, reject, discard, get rid of, jilt
formal forsake
colloq. quit, dump, pack in, give the brush-off, give the elbow

chuckle *v*
laugh, laugh quietly, giggle, titter, snigger, chortle, snort, cackle, crow

chum *n*
friend, companion, comrade
colloq. mate, pal, crony, buddy
E3 enemy

chummy *adj*
friendly, affectionate, close, intimate, sociable
colloq. matey, pally, thick

chunk *n*
lump, hunk, mass, wedge, block, slab, piece, dollop, portion
colloq. wodge

church *n*
1 *go to church*
place of worship, chapel, house of God, Lord's house, house of prayer, cathedral, minster, abbey, tabernacle, meeting-house, bethel, kirk, chantry, shrine
2 *the Methodist Church*
denomination, tradition, grouping, sect, cult
3 CONGREGATION, assembly, fellowship, community, people of God, body of Christ, bride of Christ
Related adjective: ecclesiastical

Parts of a church or cathedral include: aisle, almonry, altar, ambulatory, apse, arcade, arch, belfry, bell screen, bell tower, chancel, chapel, choir, clerestory, cloister, confessional, credence, crossing, crypt, fenestella, font, frontal, gallery, keystone, lectern, narthex, nave, parvis, pew, pinnacle, piscina, porch, portal, predella, presbytery, pulpit, reredos, ringing chamber, rood, rood screen, sacristy, sanctuary, sedile, shrine, slype, spire, squint, stall, steeple, stoup, tomb, tower, transept, triforium, vault, vestry.

Names of church services include: baptism, christening, Christingle, communion, Holy Communion, confirmation, dedication, Eucharist, evening service, evensong, funeral, Lord's Supper, marriage, Mass, High Mass, Midnight Mass, nuptial Mass, Requiem Mass, Holy Matrimony, memorial service, morning prayers, morning service. *See also* **canonical.** *See also* **places of worship** *at* **worship.**

churlish *adj*
bad-tempered, ill-tempered, harsh, impolite, morose, rough, brusque, rude, sullen, surly, uncivil, unmannerly, ill-mannered, ill-bred, discourteous, unneighbourly, unsociable, loutish, boorish, oafish
colloq. crabbed
E3 polite, urbane

churn *v*
1 *my stomach is churning*
heave, turn, vomit, be sick, retch
colloq. throw up, puke

2 *churn up mud*
move about violently, agitate, beat, swirl, toss, writhe, convulse, boil, foam, froth, seethe
▷ **churn out** turn out, produce in great quantities, pump out, throw together, knock up

chute *n*
channel, incline, slide, slope, ramp, runway, shaft, funnel, gutter, trough

cigarette *n*
cigar, menthol, filter-tip, king-size, high-tar, low-tar, roll-up, roll-your-own, smoke, whiff
colloq. cig, ciggy, fag, fag end, dog end, gasper, joint, spliff; *slang* cancer-stick, coffin-nail

cinch *n*
colloq. child's play, doddle, piece of cake, snip, stroll, walkover, pushover, like falling off a log

cinders *n*
embers, ashes, clinker, charcoal, coke, slag

cinema *n*
1 FILMS, pictures, movies
colloq. or *old use* flicks
colloq. big screen, silver screen
2 PICTURE-HOUSE, film theatre, movie theatre, movies, entertainment centre, multiplex, picture-palace
colloq. fleapit

cipher *n*
1 CODE, secret system, coded message, cryptogram, cryptograph
2 NONENTITY, nobody, yes-man

circle *n, v*

Types of circle include: annulus, ball, band, belt, circuit, circumference, coil, compass, cordon, coronet, crown, curl, cycle, disc, discus, eddy, ellipse, epicycle, girdle, globe, gyration, halo, hoop, lap, loop, orb, orbit, oval, perimeter, plate, revolution, ring, rotation, round, saucer, sphere, spiral, turn, tyre, vortex, wheel, whirlpool, whirlwind, wreath.

▶ *n* *circle of friends*
group, band, company, crowd, set, clique, coterie, gang, club, society, assembly, fellowship, fraternity
Related adjective: circular
▶ *v* **1** RING, loop, encircle, surround, belt, gird, encompass, enclose, envelop, hem in, hedge in
formal circumscribe, circumnavigate
2 ROTATE, revolve, move round, pivot, gyrate, circulate, whirl, turn, swivel, pivot, coil, wind

circuit *n*
1 *a racing circuit; run a circuit*
race track, track, running-track, lap, orbit, revolution, course, route, round, beat
formal perambulation
2 *the circuit of the gardens*
circumference, boundary, bounds, limit, range, compass, ambit
3 *a judge's circuit*
tour, district, area, region

circuitous *adj*
roundabout, indirect, oblique, devious, tortuous, winding, meandering, rambling
formal periphrastic, labyrinthine
E3 direct, straight

circular *adj, n*
▶ *adj* round, annular, ring-shaped, hoop-shaped,

disc-shaped, spherical
▶ *n* handbill, leaflet, pamphlet, notice, announcement, advertisement, letter, flyer

circulate *v*
1 *circulate information*
spread (around), diffuse, broadcast, transmit, publicize, publish, issue, give out, propagate, pass round, distribute, go/get around
formal disseminate, promulgate
2 GO ROUND, rotate, revolve, gyrate, whirl, swirl, flow

circulation *n*
1 BLOOD-FLOW, flow, motion, movement, rotation, circling
2 SPREAD, transmission, publication, readership, distribution, publicity, propagation
formal dissemination

circumference *n*
circuit, perimeter, rim, edge, girth, outline, boundary, border, bounds, limits, confines, extremity, margin, verge, fringe, periphery, circuit

circumlocution *n*
diffuseness, discursiveness, tautology, indirectness, euphemism, redundancy, roundaboutness, wordiness
formal convolution, periphrasis, pleonasm, verbosity, prolixity

circumlocutory *adj*
diffuse, discursive, tautological, indirect, euphemistic, redundant, roundabout, wordy
formal convoluted, periphrastic, pleonastic, verbose, prolix

circumscribe *v*
bound, limit, restrain, restrict, confine, curtail, trim, define, delimit, delineate, demarcate, surround, encircle, enclose, encompass, hem in, pen in

circumspect *adj*
careful, cautious, attentive, deliberate, discreet, guarded, observant, wary, canny, watchful, discriminating, wise
formal prudent, sagacious, judicious, vigilant, politic
F3 unguarded, unwary, reckless

circumspection *n*
care, caution, deliberation, discretion, guardedness, canniness, chariness, wariness
formal prudence, vigilance
F3 recklessness

circumstance *n*
1 *died in mysterious circumstances*
condition, fact, factor, situation, position, state, state of affairs, background, environment, arrangement, detail, particular, item, thing, element, event, occurrence, happening, respect, lie of the land, how the land lies
2 *in impoverished circumstances*
situation, means, resources, status, financial position, case, lifestyle, plight
3 *a victim of circumstance*
fate, fortune, lot

circumstantial *adj*
conjectural, presumed, deduced, contingent, hearsay, incidental, indirect, provisional, inferential
formal evidential, presumptive

circumvent *v*
avoid, get round, get out of, get past, evade, bypass, sidestep, steer clear of, thwart, outwit

cistern *n*
tank, reservoir, sink, basin, vat

citadel *n*
fortress, stronghold, bastion, castle, keep, tower, fortification, acropolis

citation *n*
1 AWARD, commendation, honour
2 QUOTATION, quote, cutting, excerpt, illustration, mention, passage, reference, source

cite *v*
quote, mention, refer to, name, specify, allude to, exemplify, give an example, enumerate, advance, bring up
formal adduce, evidence

citizen *n*
city-dweller, townsman, townswoman, inhabitant, denizen, resident, householder, voter, taxpayer, freeman, burgher, subject, urbanite, local
formal denizen, oppidan

city *n*
metropolis, town, urban district, conurbation, megalopolis, metropolitan area, inner city, city centre, downtown, concrete jungle, urban sprawl, precinct, ghetto, suburbia, megalopolis, municipality
colloq. big smoke
Related adjectives: civic, urban

civic *adj*
city, metropolitan, urban, suburban, municipal, borough, local, public, communal, community

civil *adj*
1 *civil affairs*
domestic, home, national, internal, interior, state, municipal, civic, public, communal, local, community, secular, civilian
2 POLITE, courteous, well-mannered, mannerly, well-bred, cultivated, courtly, refined, civilized, polished, urbane, affable, respectful, complaisant, obliging, accommodating
F3 1 international, military, religious **2** uncivil, discourteous, rude

civility *n*
politeness, courteousness, courtesy, breeding, refinement, (good) manners, respect, urbanity, tact, graciousness, affability, pleasantness, amenity
formal comity
F3 discourtesy, rudeness, uncouthness

civilization *n*
1 *ancient civilizations*
society, human society, culture, community, people
2 *modern western civilization*
progress, advancement, development, education, enlightenment, cultivation, refinement, sophistication, urbanity
F3 2 barbarity, primitiveness

civilize *v*
educate, enlighten, educate, instruct, cultivate, refine, polish, sophisticate, socialize, improve, perfect, tame, humanize

civilized *adj*
1 *a civilized society*
advanced, developed, educated, enlightened, cultured, refined, sophisticated, cultivated, urbane, polite, sociable
2 *a polite, civilized manner*
reasonable, sensible, polite, cultivated

E3 1 uncivilized, barbarous, primitive **2** harsh, coarse, unreasonable, unsophisticated

clad *adj*
clothed, wearing, covered, dressed
formal attired

claim *v, n*
▶ *v* **1** MAINTAIN, allege, profess, state, affirm, assert, maintain, contend, hold, insist, pretend, profess
formal avow, aver, postulate, purport, assume
2 *claim a refund*
ask, request, put in for, require, need, demand, exact, take, collect, lay claim to, have a right to, be entitled to, deserve
formal requisition
3 *claimed the lives of three people*
take, cause, kill
▶ *n* **1** ALLEGATION, pretension, affirmation, assertion, contention, declaration, profession, insistence
formal avowal, averment
2 APPLICATION, petition, request, requirement, demand, call, right, privilege, entitlement

claimant *n*
applicant, candidate, petitioner, suppliant, supplicant, litigant, pretendant, pretender

clairvoyance *n*
psychic powers, ESP, extrasensory perception, telepathy fortune-telling

clairvoyant *adj, n*
▶ *adj* psychic, prophetic, visionary, telepathic, extra-sensory
▶ *n* psychic, fortune-teller, prophet, prophetess, visionary, seer, soothsayer, augur, oracle, diviner, telepath

clamber *v*
scramble, claw, climb, scrabble, shin, scale, mount, ascend, *US* shinny

clammy *adj*
damp, moist, sweaty, sweating, sticky, slimy, dank, muggy, heavy, close

clamorous *adj*
noisy, blaring, vociferous, deafening, lusty, riotous, tumultuous, uproarious, vehement, insistent
E3 quiet, silent

clamour *v, n*
▶ *v* demand, ask for noisily, call for, press for, claim, insist, urge
▶ *n* noise, uproar, commotion, shouting, din, racket, blare, agitation, hubbub, outcry, complaints
formal vociferation
E3 quietness, silence

clamp *n, v*
▶ *n* vice, grip, press, brace, clasp, bracket, fastener, immobilizer
▶ *v* fasten, secure, fix, clinch, clench, squeeze, press, grip, hold, brace, immobilize
▷ **clamp down on** control, limit, crack down on, come down hard on, restrict, confine, restrain, suppress, stop, put a stop to

clan *n*
1 *the Macleod clan*
tribe, family, house, race, line, sept
2 GROUP, circle, society, brotherhood, fraternity, confraternity, sect, faction, band, set, clique, coterie

clandestine *adj*
secret, surreptitious, undercover, underhand, concealed, hidden, covert, fraudulent, sly, sneaky, stealthy, underground, closet, furtive, private
colloq. backroom, behind-door, cloak-and-dagger, under-the-counter
E3 open

clang *v & n*
clash, jangle, clank, clink, clunk, clatter, peal, bong, chime, resound, reverberate, ring, toll

clanger *n*
mistake, error, blunder, inaccuracy, misjudgement, slip, indiscretion, gaffe, *faux pas*, oversight, fault
formal solecism
colloq. howler, bloomer, boob, booboo, slip-up;
slang cock-up

clank *v & n*
clang, clash, jangle, clink, clunk, clatter, resound, reverberate, ring, toll

clannish *adj*
cliquey, cliquish, unfriendly, select, exclusive, insular, narrow, parochial, sectarian
E3 friendly, open

clap *v*
1 APPLAUD, acclaim, cheer, put your hands together for
2 SLAP, smack, strike, pat, bang
colloq. wallop, whack

claptrap *n*
rubbish, nonsense, drivel, gibberish, trash, tripe, twaddle, blarney
colloq. bunk, bunkum, claptrap, piffle, bilge, poppycock, hot air, cobblers, codswallop, rot, tommyrot;

clarification *n*
explanation, simplification, interpretation, exposition, definition, gloss, illumination
formal elucidation
E3 *formal* obfuscation

clarify *v*
1 EXPLAIN, make clear, throw light on, simplify, resolve, spell out, clear up, make plain, define, illuminate, gloss
formal elucidate
2 REFINE, purify, filter, clear
E3 1 obscure, confuse **2** cloud

clarity *n*
1 *clarity of thought*
lucidity, simplicity, intelligibility, comprehensibility, plainness, explicitness, unambiguousness, obviousness
2 *clarity of the water/her diction*
clearness, transparency, precision, sharpness, definition
E3 1 vagueness **2** obscurity, imprecision

clash *v, n*
▶ *v* **1** CRASH, bang, strike, clank, clang, jangle, clatter, rattle, jar
2 CONFLICT, disagree, quarrel, wrangle, grapple, fight, contend, feud, war
3 *two events clash*
happen at the same time, coincide
formal co-occur
4 *the styles clash*
not match, not go with, not go together, look

unpleasant, be incompatible, be discordant, jar
F3 4 match, be compatible, harmonize, go well
together
▶ *n* **1** CRASH, striking, bang, clank, clank, jangle,
clatter, noise
2 *a clash with the police*
confrontation, showdown, conflict, disagreement,
fight, brush, collision, warring, fighting, feud, quarrel,
wrangle

clasp *n, v*
▶ *n* **1** FASTENER, buckle, clip, pin, hasp, hook,
fastening, catch
2 HOLD, grip, grasp, embrace, hug, cuddle
▶ *v* **1** HOLD, grip, grasp, clutch, embrace, enfold,
hug, squeeze, press, cling to
2 FASTEN, connect, attach, grapple, hook, clip, pin

class *n, v*
▶ *n* **1** *a French class*
lesson, period, lecture, seminar, tutorial, workshop,
teach-in, course, year, form, grade, study group, set
2 *a social class*
social order, social status, status, (social) standing,
standing in society, social division, rank, level, (social)
background, caste

Social classes/groups include: aristocracy, nobility,
gentry, landed gentry, gentlefolk, elite, *colloq.* nob,
high society, *colloq.* top drawer, upper class, ruling
class, jet set, middle class, lower class, working class,
bourgeoisie, proletariat, hoi-polloi, commoner,
serf, plebeian, *colloq.* pleb. *See also* **nobility**.

3 CATEGORY, classification, group, set, section,
division, department, sphere, grouping, order, league,
rank, status, caste, quality, grade, type, genre, sort, kind,
species, genus, style
technical phylum
formal denomination
4 *he has class*
taste, style, stylishness, elegance, sophistication,
distinction
▶ *v* categorize, classify, group, sort, rank, arrange,
order, grade, rate, pigeonhole, designate, brand

classic *adj, n*
▶ *adj* **1** *a classic film*
first-class, first-rate, outstanding, brilliant, ideal, best,
finest, definitive, masterly, excellent
formal consummate
2 TYPICAL, prime, representative, characteristic,
standard, regular, usual, true
formal paradigmatic, quintessential
3 *classic style*
traditional, time-honoured, established, archetypal,
model, exemplary, ageless, timeless, immortal,
undying, lasting, enduring, abiding
F3 1 second-rate **2** unrepresentative
▶ *n* standard, model, prototype, exemplar,
masterwork, masterpiece, established work, great,
pièce de résistance

classical *adj*
1 *classical style/form*
traditional, elegant, refined, excellent, plain, pure,
restrained, well-proportioned, symmetrical,
harmonious
2 *classical music*
serious, traditional, concert, symphonic
3 *classical Greece*
ancient Greek, Grecian, Hellenic, ancient Roman,

Latin, Attic
F3 1 modern

classification *n*
categorization, sorting, classing, grading, grouping,
arrangement, systematization, codification,
tabulation, cataloguing
technical taxonomy

classify *v*
categorize, class, group, pigeonhole, sort, grade, rank,
arrange, order, type, distribute, systematize, codify,
tabulate, file, catalogue
formal dispose

classy *adj*
stylish, elegant, sophisticated, up-market, expensive,
exclusive, exquisite, fine, grand, high-class, select,
superior, gorgeous
colloq. posh, ritzy, swanky
F3 dowdy, plain, unstylish

clatter *n & v*
bang, strike, clank, clunk, clang, jangle, crash, rattle,
jar

clause *n*
article, item, part, section, subsection, paragraph,
heading, chapter, passage, phrase, condition, proviso,
provision, rider, specification, point, loophole

claw *n, v*
▶ *n* talon, nail, pincer, nipper, gripper
technical chela, unguis
▶ *v* scratch, scrabble, scrape, graze, tear, rip, lacerate,
maul, mangle

clean *adj, adv*
▶ *adj* **1** WASHED, laundered, sterile, aseptic,
antiseptic, hygienic, sanitary, sterilized, sterile,
cleansed, laundered, decontaminated, purified, pure,
unadulterated, fresh, unpolluted, uncontaminated,
immaculate, spotless, unspotted, unstained, unsoiled,
unsullied, perfect, speckless, spick and span, faultless,
flawless, unblemished
colloq. clean as a new pin
2 *a clean life*
innocent, guiltless, virtuous, pure, good, upright,
moral, honest, honourable, righteous, reputable,
upstanding, respectable, decent, chaste
colloq. squeaky-clean
3 *a clean sheet of paper*
blank, new, fresh, unmarked, unused
4 *a clean game*
fair, just, according to the rules, even-handed, proper
colloq. above board
5 *clean lines*
simple, well-defined, clean-cut, smooth, regular,
straight, neat, tidy
F3 1 dirty, polluted **2** dishonourable, indecent
4 dirty, rough **5** ragged
▶ *adv* completely, straight, directly, entirely, fully,
totally, quite

Ways to clean include: bath, bathe, bleach, brush,
buff, cleanse, clear, comb, decontaminate,
deodorize, disinfect, distil, dry-clean, dust, filter,
floss, flush, freshen, freshen up, fumigate, groom,
Hoover®, launder, mop, muck out, pasteurize, pick,
polish, purge, purify, refine, rinse, rub, sandblast,
sanitize, scour, scrape, scrub, shampoo, shine,
shower, soak, soap, sponge, spring-clean, spruce,
spruce up, steep, sterilize, swab, sweep, swill, tidy,
vacuum, valet, wash, wipe.

cleaner *n*
char, charlady, charwoman, daily

cleanse *v*
1 *cleanse a wound*
disinfect, sterilize, clean, bathe, wash, rinse
formal deterge
2 *cleansed from sin/cleanse your soul*
absolve, purify, purge, make free from, clear
formal lustrate
E3 1 dirty 2 defile

cleanser *n*
soap, soap powder, detergent, cleaner, solvent, scourer,
scouring powder, purifier, disinfectant

clear *adj, v*
▶ *adj* 1 PLAIN, distinct, comprehensible,
intelligible, coherent, lucid, explicit, precise,
unambiguous, well-defined, apparent, evident, patent,
obvious, manifest, conspicuous, unmistakable,
unquestionable, explicit, sure, unequivocal,
incontrovertible, beyond question, crystal-clear,
beyond doubt, certain, positive, definite, convinced
2 *clear thinking*
sharp, keen, perceptive, penetrating, quick, sensible,
reasonable, logical
3 *clear water*
transparent, limpid, crystalline, glassy, translucent,
see-through, clean, unclouded, colourless
formal pellucid, diaphonous
4 *a clear day*
cloudless, unclouded, fine, fair, bright, sunny, light,
luminous, undimmed
5 UNOBSTRUCTED, unblocked, open, free, empty,
unhindered, unimpeded
6 *a clear conscience*
guiltless, innocent, blameless, in the clear
formal having no qualms, having/feeling no
compunction
7 AUDIBLE, perceptible, pronounced, distinct,
recognizable
colloq. clear as a bell
E3 1 unclear, vague, ambiguous, confusing, unsure
2 muddled 3 opaque, cloudy 4 dull, cloudy, rainy,
misty 5 blocked 6 guilty 7 inaudible, indistinct,
faint
▶ *v* 1 *clear the dishes/room*
remove, take away, empty, unload, vacate, evacuate,
move, shift, get rid of, rid, free, clean, fine, filter, tidy,
wipe, erase, cleanse, refine, filter
2 UNBLOCK, unclog, unstop, decongest, free, rid,
extricate, disentangle, loosen
3 *clear a fence*
jump (over), vault, leap over, go over
4 ACQUIT, exonerate, absolve, pardon, vindicate,
excuse, justify, free, liberate, release, let go
formal exculpate
5 *cleared for publication*
permit, give permission, allow, authorize, approve,
pass, sanction
colloq. give the green light, give the go-ahead
6 *clear £100*
earn, take home, net, make a profit, make, gain,
bring (in)
E3 1 dirty 2 block 4 condemn 5 prohibit
▷ **clear out** 1 *been told to clear out* get out, leave, go
away, depart, withdraw; *colloq.* beat it, clear off, push
off, shove off, hop it; *slang* get lost, piss off 2 *clear out
a cupboard* tidy(up), empty, sort (out), throw out
▷ **clear up** 1 EXPLAIN, clarify, elucidate, unravel,
solve, resolve, answer, straighten (out), sort out, iron

out; *colloq.* crack 2 TIDY, order, sort, rearrange, put
in order, straighten (up), remove 3 *the weather
cleared up* clear, become fine, become sunny, stop
raining, brighten(up), improve

clearance *n*
1 *clearance of old buildings*
demolition, removal, taking-away, emptying,
unloading, vacating, evacuation, clearing, moving,
shifting, freeing, cleansing
2 AUTHORIZATION, sanction, endorsement,
permission, consent, leave
colloq. OK, go-ahead, green light, say-so
3 SPACE, gap, room, headroom, margin, allowance

clear-cut *adj*
definite, explicit, well-defined, clear, precise, specific,
straightforward, unambiguous, unequivocal, distinct,
trenchant, plain
colloq. cut and dried
E3 ambiguous, vague

clearing *n*
space, gap, opening, glade, dell

clearly *adv*
obviously, without doubt, undoubtedly, undeniably,
evidently, incontestably, incontrovertibly, indisputably,
unmistakably, manifestly, plainly, patently, distinctly,
openly, markedly

cleave[1] *v*
cleave the tree in two
split, divide, separate, sever, cut, slice, chop, crack,
disunite, halve, hew, open, part, pierce, rend
formal dissever, sunder
E3 join, unite

cleave[2] *v*
cleave to your marriage partner
adhere, cling, cohere, hold, stick, remain, attach, unite

cleft *n*
fissure, opening, gap, fracture, breach, break, chasm,
chink, crack, cranny, crevice, rent, split

clemency *n*
mercy, mercifulness, pity, compassion, forbearance,
forgiveness, generosity, humanity, indulgence,
kindness, sympathy, leniency, mildness, moderation,
soft-heartedness, tenderness
formal magnanimity
E3 harshness, ruthlessness

clench *v*
grip, hold, clasp, close (tightly), seal, fasten, shut,
clutch, double, grasp, grit

clergy *n*
clergymen, churchmen, clerics, the church, the cloth,
ministry, priesthood, holy orders
Related adjective: clerical

clergyman *n*
churchman, cleric, ecclesiastic, divine, man of God,
man of the cloth, minister, priest, reverend, father,
vicar, pastor, padre, parson, rector, canon, dean,
deacon, deaconess, chaplain, curate, presbyter, rabbi,
imam, muezzin, mullah

clerical *adj*
1 ADMINISTRATIVE, office, secretarial, white-
collar, official, filing, typing, keyboarding
colloq. pen-pushing
2 ECCLESIASTICAL, pastoral, ministerial, priestly,
episcopal, canonical, sacerdotal

Types of clerical vestment include: alb, amice, biretta, cassock, chasuble, chimere, clerical collar, *colloq.* dog-collar, cope, cotta, cowl, dalmatic, ephod, frock, Geneva bands, Geneva gown, habit, hood, maniple, mantle, mitre, mozzetta, pallium, rochet, scapular, scarf, skullcap, soutane, stole, surplice, tallith, tippet, tunicle, wimple, yarmulka.

clerk *n*
account-keeper, record-keeper, assistant, official, administrative officer, administrator, notary, receptionist, secretary, typist, stenographer, shop-assistant, writer, copyist, protocolist
colloq. pen- pusher

clever *adj*
1 *a clever student*
intelligent, bright, brilliant, smart, witty, gifted, talented, expert, knowledgeable, adroit, apt, able, capable, quick, quick-witted, sharp, sharp-witted, keen, shrewd, knowing, perceptive, discerning, cunning
formal sapient, sagacious
colloq. brainy
2 *a clever plan*
inventive, resourceful, sensible, rational, ingenious, shrewd
E3 **1** foolish, stupid, senseless, ignorant **2** foolish

cliché *n*
platitude, hackneyed phrase/expression, commonplace, banality, truism, bromide, (old) chestnut, stereotype

click *v, n*
▶ *v* **1** *the machine clicked*
clack, clink, snap, snick, snip, tick, beat
2 *it suddenly clicked*
(begin to) understand, make sense, fall into place
colloq. twig, cotton on
▶ *n* beat, clack, clink, snap, snick, snip, tick

client *n*
customer, patron, regular, buyer, purchaser, shopper, consumer, user, patient, applicant

clientèle *n*
business, clients, customers, following, market, patronage, patrons, regulars, trade, buyers, purchasers, shoppers, consumers, users

cliff *n*
precipice, overhang, bluff, face, rock-face, scar, scarp, escarpment, crag, tor, promontory

climactic *adj*
decisive, critical, crucial, exciting, paramount
E3 trivial

climate *n*
1 *a cold climate*
weather, weather conditions, temperature
2 *a hostile political climate*
atmosphere, feeling, mood, temper, disposition, setting, milieu, environment, ambience, tendency, trend

climax *n*
culmination, height, high point, highlight, acme, zenith, peak, pinnacle, summit, apex, top, head
formal apogee
E3 low point; *formal* nadir

climb *v*
1 *climb the stairs*
go up, ascend, scale, shin up, clamber, mount, surmount
2 *climb into the car*
move, stir, shift, clamber, scramble
3 *unemployment is climbing*
increase, go up, rise, soar, shoot up, top
▷ **climb down** retract, back down, admit that you are wrong, concede, retreat; *colloq.* eat your words,

clinch *v*
settle, secure, seal, close, conclude, decide, determine, confirm, verify
colloq. land

cling *v*
1 *cling to a branch*
clasp, clutch, grasp, grip, hold on to, stick, adhere, cleave, fasten, embrace, hug
2 *cling to old ideas*
adhere, stick to, support, hold to, defend, stand by, be faithful to, stay true to

clinic *n*
medical centre, health centre, hospital, infirmary, doctor's, outpatients' department

clinical *adj*
1 *clinical trials of the drug*
medical, hospital, patient
2 *a clinical design*
simple, plain, austere, stark, basic, unadorned
3 *a clinical attitude*
impersonal, analytic, business-like, cold, emotionless, unemotional, unfeeling, detached, disinterested, dispassionate, uninvolved, impassive, objective, scientific
E3 **2** decorated, ornamented **3** warm, biased, subjective

clip *n, v*
▶ *n* **1** *a paper clip*
fastener, staple, pin
2 *a clip from a newspaper*
cutting, snippet, quotation, citation, passage, section, excerpt, extract
3 *a clip round the ear*
punch, slap, cuff, box
colloq. clout, thump, wallop, whack
▶ *v* **1** *clipped the pen to her pocket*
pin, staple, fasten, attach, fix, hold
2 *clip a bush*
trim, snip, cut, cut short, prune, pare, shear, crop, dock, poll, pollard, truncate, curtail, shorten, abbreviate

clipping *n*
cutting, snippet, quotation, citation, passage, section, excerpt, extract, clip

clique *n*
circle, set, coterie, group, circle, bunch, band, pack, gang, crowd, in-crowd, society, fraternity, faction, clan

cloak *n, v*
▶ *n* **1** *wear a cloak*
cape, mantle, robe, wrap, shawl, cope, coat, cover
2 *a cloak of secrecy*
coat, cover, shield, mask, front, screen, blind, veil, mantle, shroud, pretext
▶ *v* cover, veil, mask, screen, hide, conceal, obscure, shroud, disguise, shield, camouflage

clock *n, v*
▶ *n*

▶ *v* ▷ **clock up** reach, record, register, archive, attain, chalk up, notch up

clog *v*
block, choke, stop up, bung up, dam (up), congest, jam, obstruct, impede, hinder, hamper, encumber, burden
formal occlude
☒ unblock, free

cloister *n*
walkway, pavement, corridor, aisle, arcade, portico, ambulatory

cloistered *adj*
sheltered, secluded, confined, restricted, enclosed, shielded, withdrawn, insulated, protected, isolated
formal reclusive, sequestered, cloistral, hermitic
☒ open

close¹ *v, n*
▶ *v* **1** SHUT, shut up, fasten, secure, lock (up), bar, bolt, padlock
2 *close a road/bottle*
obstruct, block, shut, clog, plug, cork, stop up, fill, seal
formal occlude
3 END, bring to an end, draw to an end, finish, complete, conclude, terminate, adjourn, wind up, round off, stop
formal cease, discontinue
4 *the shop closes at 6 o'clock*
shut, close for the night
5 *the factory closed in March*
close down, close permanently, cease operating, cease operations, shut down, go bankrupt, fail
colloq. fold, go bust, go to the wall
6 *close a gap*
join, unite, fuse, seal, narrow, lessen
7 *close a deal*
settle, secure, seal, clinch, conclude, decide, determine, establish, confirm, verify
☒ **1** open, separate **3** start, begin **4** open, open for business **6** widen
▷ **close in** come nearer, draw near, approach, surround, encircle
▶ *n* end, finish, completion, conclusion, culmination, ending, finale, dénouement, termination, adjournment, winding-up, stop, pause
formal cessation
☒ start, beginning

close² *n*
live in a close
courtyard, enclosure, quadrangle, square, place, court, row, terrace, lane, mews, cul-de-sac

close³ *adj*
1 NEAR, close by, nearby, at hand, not far, neighbouring, adjacent, adjoining, in the vicinity, in close proximity, impending, imminent
colloq. on your doorstep, in your own backyard, a stone's throw
2 INTIMATE, dear, familiar, attached, inseparable,

devoted, loving, close-knit, tight, best, good, bosom
3 *a close resemblance*
strong, near, similar, like, comparable, corresponding
4 *a close game*
evenly matched, well-matched, hard-fought
colloq. neck and neck
5 OPPRESSIVE, heavy, stuffy, fuggy, muggy, humid, sultry, sweltering, airless, stifling, suffocating, stuffy, unventilated, sticky
6 MISERLY, mean, stingy, niggardly, penny-pinching
formal parsimonious
colloq. tight
7 SECRETIVE, uncommunicative, unforthcoming, quiet, taciturn, reticent, private, secret, confidential
8 *a close translation*
exact, precise, accurate, strict, literal, faithful, true
9 *pay close attention*
fixed, concentrated, thorough, rigorous, painstaking, detailed, methodical, careful, intense, keen, searching
10 DENSE, compact, condensed, solid, packed, crowded, cramped
☒ **1** far, distant **2** cool, unfriendly, distant **5** fresh, airy, well-ventilated **6** generous **7** open **8** rough, loose

closet *n, adj*
▶ *n* cupboard, wardrobe, storage room
▶ *adj* secret, private, unrevealed, hidden, covert, furtive, underground, surreptitious, undercover
☒ open, having come out

closure *n*
1 *the closure of the factory*
closing-down, permanent closing, shutdown, failure, bankruptcy
formal cessation of operations
colloq. folding
2 *the closure of the road*
obstruction, block, blocking, shutting, stopping-up

clot *n, v*
▶ *n* lump, mass, glob, clump, thrombus, thrombosis, clotting, obstruction, coagulation
▶ *v* coalesce, curdle, coagulate, congeal, thicken, solidify, set, gel

cloth *n*
1 FABRIC, material, stuff, textile, upholstery
2 RAG, face-cloth, flannel, dish-cloth, floorcloth, duster, towel

clothe *v*
dress, put on, robe, deck, outfit, fit out, rig, vest, drape, cover
formal attire, apparel, accoutre, habit, invest, bedizen, caparison
☒ undress, strip, disrobe

clothes *n*
clothing, garments, wear, garb, outfit, dress, costume, wardrobe, vestments
formal attire, apparel, raiment, habiliments, vesture
colloq. gear, clobber, togs, get-up, hand-me-downs, cast-offs
Related adjectives: sartorial, habilatory

sweat-shirt, tee-shirt, T-shirt, waistcoat, blouse, smock, tabard, tunic; uniform; trousers, jeans, Levis®, 501s®, denims, slacks, cords, flannels, drainpipes, bell-bottoms, dungarees, leggings, pedal-pushers, breeches, plus-fours, jodhpurs, Bermuda shorts, hot pants, shorts; lingerie, bra, brassière, body stocking, camisole, liberty bodice, corset, girdle, garter, suspender belt, suspenders, shift, slip, petticoat, teddy, basque, briefs, pants, panties, French knickers, camiknickers, hosiery, pantihose, tights, stockings; underpants, boxer-shorts, Y-fronts, vest, string vest, singlet; swimsuit, bathing-costume, bikini, swimming costume, swimming trunks, leotard, salopette; nightdress, *colloq.* nightie, pyjamas, bed-jacket, bedsocks, dressing-gown, housecoat, negligee; scarf, glove, mitten, muffler, earmuffs, leg-warmers, sock, tie, bow-tie, necktie, cravat, stole, shawl, belt, braces, cummerbund, veil, yashmak. *See also* **clerical; footwear; hat.**

cloud *n, v*
▶ *n*

Types of cloud include: cirrus, cirrostratus, cirrocumulus, altocumulus, altostratus, cumulus, stratocumulus, nimbostratus, fractostratus, fractocumulus, cumulonimbus, stratus.

▶ *v* mist, fog, blur, dull, dim, darken, shade, shadow, overshadow, eclipse, cover, veil, shroud, mantle, obscure, muddle, confuse
formal obfuscate
F3 clear
Related adjective: nubiform

cloudy *adj*
1 *a cloudy sky*
overcast, dull, dark, murky, gloomy, sombre, grey, leaden, heavy, lowering, dim, sunless, hazy, misty, foggy
2 *a cloudy liquid*
opaque, milky, muddy
3 *cloudy issues*
indistinct, obscure, nebulous, hazy, misty, foggy, blurred, blurry, confused, muddled
F3 1 bright, sunny, cloudless 2 clear 3 clear, distinct, plain

clout *v, n*
▶ *v* punch, strike, smack, hit, slap, cuff, box
colloq. thump, wallop, whack; *slang* sock, slug
▶ *n* 1 *gave him a clout*
punch, strike, smack, hit, slap, cuff, box
colloq. thump, wallop, whack; *slang* sock, slug
2 *political clout*
influence, weight, authority, power, standing, prestige
colloq. pull, muscle

cloven *adj*
divided, split, bisected, cleft
F3 solid

clown *n, v*
▶ *n* 1 *clowns at a circus*
buffoon, comic, comedian, joker, jester, fool, harlequin, pierrot, zany
2 *some clown has parked in front of the gates*
fool, idiot, blockhead, imbecile
colloq. nincompoop, ninny, nitwit, numskull, twerp, twit, dimwit; *slang* wally, jerk, dipstick, nerd, dork, geek

▶ *v* fool around, act foolishly, act/play the fool, jest, joke
colloq. mess around, muck about

cloying *adj*
disgusting, nauseating, sickening, sickly, excessive, choking, oversweet, fulsome
F3 pleasing, pleasant

club *n, v*
▶ *n* 1 ASSOCIATION, society, organization, group, league, guild, order, union, auxiliary, fraternity, federation, company, brotherhood, set, circle, clique, social club
2 STICK, staff, bat, bludgeon, truncheon, cudgel, mace, *US* blackjack
colloq. cosh
▶ *v* hit, strike, beat (up), bash, clout, bludgeon, batter, pummel
colloq. clobber, clout, cosh
▷ **club together** give money, share the cost, contribute, chip in; *colloq.* have a whip-round

clue *n*
hint, tip, suggestion, idea, notion, lead, tip-off, pointer, sign, indication, evidence, trace, suspicion, inkling, intimation

clump *n, v*
▶ *n* cluster, bundle, bunch, tuft, thicket, mass, accumulation, collection, lot, group
formal agglomeration, agglutination
▶ *v* 1 *clump around*
tramp, clomp, stamp, stomp, stumble, plod, trudge, lumber, thump, thud
2 *clump together*
group, accumulate, amass, cluster, bunch, bundle

clumsy *adj*
1 *a clumsy person*
awkward, unco-ordinated, bungling, ham-fisted, accident-prone, unhandy, heavy-handed, unskilful, inept, bungling, blundering, lumbering, gauche, ungainly, ungraceful, wooden
formal maladroit
colloq. gawky, all thumbs
2 *clumsy objects*
awkward, unwieldy, ungainly, heavy, bulky, cumbersome, ill-made, shapeless
3 *a clumsy attempt to comfort her*
insensitive, rude, tactless, awkward, uncouth, rough, crude,
F3 1 co-ordinated, skilful, careful, graceful, natural 2 elegant 3 sensitive, tactful

cluster *n, v*
▶ *n* bunch, clump, batch, group, knot, band, mass, crowd, gathering, huddle, collection, assembly, assortment
technical inflorescence, raceme, panicle, truss
formal assemblage, agglomeration
▶ *v* bunch, group (together), gather, collect, assemble, congregate, come together, flock

clustered *adj*
bunched, gathered, grouped, assembled, massed
formal glomerate

clutch *v, n*
▶ *v* hold, get/take hold of, clasp, grip, hang on to, grasp, cling to, clench, seize, snatch, grab, catch, grapple, embrace
▶ *n* 1 *in someone's clutches*
control, grasp, grip, power, sway, dominion,

possession, hands, keeping, custody, embrace, mercy, claws, jaws
2 *a clutch of eggs*
set, setting, group, hatching, incubation

clutter *n, v*
▶ *n* litter, mess, jumble, untidiness, disorder, disarray, muddle, chaos, confusion
▶ *v* litter, encumber, fill (untidily), mess (up), make a mess, make untidy, cover, strew, scatter

coach *n, v*
▶ *n* **1** *travel by coach*
express coach, bus, *US* Greyhound
old use charabanc, motor-bus, motor-coach
2 *a train of twelve coaches*
carriage, car, wagon
3 *a football coach*
trainer, instructor, tutor, teacher, educator, mentor
4 *a coach and horses*
carriage, wagon, cab, trap, hackney, hansom, gig, landau, brougham
▶ *v* train, drill, instruct, teach, tutor, prime, cram, prepare

coagulate *v*
congeal, thicken, solidify, gel, melt, clot, curdle

coalesce *v*
amalgamate, join (together), blend, mix, unite, combine, consolidate, cohere, fuse, incorporate, integrate, merge, affiliate
formal commingle, commix

coalition *n*
alliance, merger, amalgamation, combination, integration, fusion, joining, league, bloc, compact, federation, confederation, confederacy, association, affiliation, union
formal conjunction, compact

coarse *adj*
1 ROUGH, unpolished, unfinished, uneven, lumpy, unpurified, unrefined, unprocessed, rugged, hairy, bristly, scaly, prickly
2 *coarse humour*
bawdy, ribald, earthy, obscene, smutty, vulgar, crude, offensive, foul-mouthed, boorish, loutish, rude, impolite, ill-mannered, rough, gross, rank, indelicate, improper, indecent, immodest
colloq. blue, raunchy
🔄 **1** smooth, fine **2** refined, sophisticated, polite, clean

coarsen *v*
roughen, thicken, blunt, deaden, desensitize, dull, harden
formal indurate
🔄 sensitize

coarseness *n*
bawdiness, ribaldry, obscenity, smut, smuttiness, vulgarity, crassitude, crudity, earthiness, indelicacy, offensiveness, indecency, immodesty
🔄 delicacy, politeness, sophistication

coast *n, v*
▶ *n* coastline, seaboard, shore, seashore, beach, seaside, strand, foreshore
formal littoral
Related adjectives: littoral, orarian
▶ *v* freewheel, glide, slide, sail, cruise, taxi, drift

coat *n, v*
▶ *n*

Types of coat include: overcoat, greatcoat, redingote, car-coat, duffel coat, fur coat, Afghan, blanket, frock-coat, tail-coat, jacket, bomber jacket, dinner-jacket, donkey-jacket, hacking-jacket, reefer, pea-jacket, shooting-jacket, safari jacket, Eton jacket, matinee jacket, tuxedo, blazer, raincoat, trench-coat, mackintosh, *colloq.* mac, Burberry, parka, anorak, cagoul, windcheater, jerkin, blouson, cape, cloak, poncho.

1 FUR, hair, fleece, wool, pelt, hide, skin
2 LAYER, coating, covering, cover, overlay, film, blanket, sheet, mantle, glaze, varnish, finish, veneer, laminate, lamination, cladding
technical integument, pellicle
▶ *v* cover, paint, spread, layer, smear, daub, apply, put on/over, plaster, pave, cake, encrust

coating *n*
covering, layer, dusting, wash, coat, blanket, sheet, membrane, film, skin, finish, overlay, veneer, glaze, varnish, enamel, lamination, crust
formal patina

coax *v*
persuade, cajole, wheedle, get round, talk into, win over/round, flatter, beguile, allure, induce, entice, tempt, prevail upon
formal inveigle
colloq. sweet-talk, soft-soap

cobble *v*
▷ **cobble together** make/produce roughly, make/produce quickly, improvise, knock up, put together

cock *n, v*
▶ *n* rooster, capon, cockerel, chicken, chanticleer
▶ *v* lift, raise, point, slant, incline, tip

cock-eyed *adj*
1 CROOKED, lopsided, askew, asymmetrical, awry, skew-whiff
2 SENSELESS, absurd, crazy, ludicrous, nonsensical, preposterous
colloq. daft, barmy
🔄 **2** sensible, sober

cocky *adj*
arrogant, self-important, conceited, vain, swollen-headed, egotistical, swaggering, brash, cocksure, self-assured, self-confident, overconfident, bumptious
formal hubristic
🔄 humble, modest, shy

cocoon *v*
protect, overprotect, isolate, preserve, defend, envelop, cushion, insulate, wrap, cover, cloister

coddle *v*
pamper, pet, spoil, protect, overprotect, mollycoddle, cosset, humour, indulge, baby

code *n*
1 ETHICS, rules, regulations, laws, principles, morals, morality, system, custom, convention, etiquette, manners, practice, conduct
2 *written in code*
cipher, secret language, secret writing, secret message, cryptograph, cryptogram, Morse code
3 *a book's code number*
numbers, letters, signs, symbols, bar code, postcode, postal code, zip code, dialling code, local code, national code, international code, machine code

coerce *v*
force, use force, drive, compel, constrain, pressurize, pressure, bully, intimidate, browbeat, bludgeon, dragoon, pressgang
colloq. bulldoze, strongarm, twist someone's arm, lean on

coercion *n*
force, duress, compulsion, constraint, pressure, bullying, intimidation, threats, direct action, browbeating, duress, strongarm tactics

coffer *n*
casket, case, box, chest, trunk, safe, strongbox, treasury, moneybox, repository

cogent *adj*
convincing, compelling, conclusive, potent, powerful, strong, forceful, forcible, influential, weighty, irresistible, persuasive, unanswerable, effective, urgent
E3 weak, ineffective, unsound

cogitate *v*
think deeply, consider, contemplate, deliberate, meditate, muse, ponder, reflect, mull over
formal ruminate, cerebrate

cognate *adj*
related, affiliated, associated, connected, kindred, akin, alike, allied, analogous, corresponding, similar
technical agnate, consanguine, congeneric
E3 unrelated, unconnected

cognition *n*
perception, awareness, consciousness, knowledge, apprehension, learning, discernment, insight, comprehension, understanding, thinking, intelligence, enlightenment, reason, reasoning, rationality

cognizance *n*
▷ **take cognizance of** acknowledge, regard, recognize, take notice of, become aware of, accept

cognizant *adj*
aware, conscious, conversant, familiar, informed, knowledgeable, acquainted, versed, witting
E3 unaware

cohabit *v*
live together, live together as man and wife, live with, sleep together
colloq. live in sin; *slang* shack up

cohere *v*
1 STICK, adhere, cling, fuse, unite, bind, combine, coalesce, consolidate
2 *the argument does not cohere*
agree, square, correspond, harmonize, hold, hang together, make sense, add up
E3 separate

coherence *n*
agreement, harmony, consistency, correspondence, connection, sense, union, unity
formal congruity, consonance, concordance
E3 incoherence

coherent *adj*
articulate, intelligible, comprehensible, easy to understand, meaningful, lucid, clear, consistent, logical, reasoned, rational, sensible, orderly, systematic, organized, well-structured, well-planned
E3 incoherent, unintelligible, meaningless

cohesion *n*
union, unity, whole, agreement, harmony, consistency, correspondence, connection, sense

cohort *n*
1 *Roman cohorts*
troop, division, legion, regiment, squadron, band, brigade, squad, body, column, company, contingent
2 COMPANION, partner, accomplice, assistant, supporter, associate, follower, myrmidon
colloq. mate, buddy, sidekick

coil *v, n*
▶ *v* wind, spiral, curl, loop, twist, writhe, snake, wreathe, twine, entwine
formal convolute
▶ *n* roll, curl, loop, ring, spiral, corkscrew, helix, twist, whorl
formal convolution, volution

coin *n, v*
▶ *n* piece, bit, money, cash, change, small change, loose change, silver, copper
formal specie
Related adjectives: numismatic, nummulary, nummary

Types of coin include: angel, bezant, *colloq.* bob, copper, crown, dandiprat, denarius, dime, doubloon, ducat, farthing, florin, groat, guilder, guinea, half-crown, half guinea, halfpenny, half sovereign, ha'penny, krugerrand, louis d'or, moidore, napoleon, nickel, noble, obol, penny, pound, *colloq.* quid, rap, real, sesterce, shilling, sixpence, solidus, sou, sovereign, spade guinea, stater, *colloq.* tanner, thaler, threepenny bit.

▶ *v* 1 *coin a new word*
invent, make up, think up, conceive, dream up, devise, formulate, originate, create, fabricate, produce, neologize
2 *coin money*
produce, mint, forge

coincide *v*
1 *the two events coincided*
happen at the same time, happen together, clash, take place simultaneously, synchronize
formal concur
2 *our opinions coincide*
be the same, agree, correspond, square, tally, accord, harmonize, be consistent with, match
formal concur

coincidence *n*
1 CHANCE, accident, luck, eventuality
formal fortuity, serendipity
colloq. fluke
2 COEXISTENCE, correspondence, happening at the same time, happening together, clash, clashing, taking place simultaneously, synchronization
formal concurrence, conjunction, correlation

coincidental *adj*
accidental, chance, casual, unintentional, unplanned, lucky
formal fortuitous, serendipitous
colloq. flukey
E3 deliberate, planned, arranged

coitus *n*
sexual intercourse, sex, union, copulation, coupling, love-making, marriage-bed, sleeping with someone, going to bed with someone, mating
formal coition

cold   *adj, n*

▶ *adj* **1** UNHEATED, cool, chilled, ice-cold, chilly, chill, shivery, raw, biting, bitter, fresh, wintry, frigid, frosty, icy, rimy, glacial, arctic, Siberian, polar, freezing, frozen, numbed, keen
old use frore
formal gelid, brumal, brumous
colloq. nippy, parky
2 UNFEELING, unmoved, unsympathetic, unemotional, frigid, unfriendly, distant, remote, aloof, standoffish, reserved, clinical, undemonstrative, unresponsive, passionless, unexcitable, indifferent, lukewarm, stony, callous, insensitive, heartless, uncaring, antagonistic, hostile
formal phlegmatic
E3 1 hot, warm **2** friendly, responsive, warm
▶ *n* coldness, chill, chilliness, coolness, frigidity, iciness, rawness, winter, frost, snow, ice
E3 warmth, heat

cold-blooded   *adj*

cruel, inhuman, brutal, savage, barbaric, barbarous, merciless, ruthless, pitiless, callous, unfeeling, heartless
E3 compassionate, merciful

cold-hearted   *adj*

unfeeling, unkind, uncaring, insensitive, unsympathetic, uncompassionate, callous, stony-hearted, cold, heartless, indifferent, detached, flinty, inhuman
E3 warm-hearted

collaborate   *v*

1 WORK TOGETHER, co-operate, join, join forces, work jointly, work as partners, combine forces, team up, associate with, unite, participate
2 *collaborate with the enemy*
conspire, collude, fraternize, betray, turn traitor

collaboration   *n*

1 *in collaboration with local industry*
association, alliance, partnership, teamwork, co-operation, participation, union, combined/joint/collective effort
2 *collaboration with the enemy*
conspiring, collusion, fraternizing

collaborator   *n*

1 *collaborators in the research*
co-worker, associate, partner, team-mate, colleague, assistant
2 *traitors and collaborators*
conspirator, accomplice, traitor, turncoat, betrayer, colluder, fraternizer, quisling, renegade

collapse   *v, n*

▶ *v* **1** *the bridge collapsed*
fall down, fall in, fall to pieces, come apart, fall apart, sink, founder, disintegrate, crumble, subside, give way, cave in
2 *the business collapsed*
fail, founder, break down, fall through, finish, disintegrate, come to an end, come to nothing, slump
colloq. fold, flop
3 *collapse with exhaustion*
faint, pass out, lose consciousness, black out, keel over, swoon, crumple
▶ *n* **1** *the collapse of the roof*
falling-down, falling-in, falling to pieces, coming apart, sinking, foundering, disintegration, subsidence, giving way, cave-in
2 *the collapse of the talks*

failure, foundering, breakdown, falling-through, disintegration, downfall, ruin, debacle
colloq. flop
3 *his collapse in the street*
fainting, passing-out, loss of consciousness, blackout, keeling-over, swoon

collar   *n, v*

▶ *n* neckband, ring, dog-collar, gorget, ruff, bertha, rebato, ruche
▶ *v* stop, grab, capture, catch, seize, arrest, apprehend
colloq. nab, nick

collate   *v*

gather, collect, sort, arrange, order, put in order, organize, compare, compose

collateral   *n*

security, guarantee, pledge, surety, assurance, deposit, funds

colleague   *n*

workmate, co-worker, team-mate, partner, collaborator, ally, associate, confederate, confrère, comrade, fellow worker, companion, aide, helper, assistant, auxiliary

collect   *v*

1 *collect firewood*
gather, accumulate, amass, heap, hoard, pile up, stockpile,
formal aggregate
2 *a crowd collected*
gather, form, come together, amass, mass, converge, congregate, assemble, convene, muster, rally
3 *collect them from the station*
fetch, pick up, meet, get, call for, come for, go and get, go and take, go and bring
4 *collect for a charity*
raise money, ask for money, ask people to give, solicit, acquire
5 *collect stamps*
acquire, save, amass, have as a hobby, be interested in
6 *collect your thoughts*
compose, gather (together), assemble, prepare
E3 2 disperse, scatter **3** drop off

collected   *adj*

composed, controlled, self-controlled, self-possessed, placid, serene, calm, unruffled, unshaken, unperturbed, imperturbable, poised, cool
E3 anxious, worried, agitated

collection   *n*

1 *an art collection; the collection of information*
group, cluster, accumulation, gathering, assembly, conglomeration, mass, heap, pile, hoard, stockpile, store, assortment, job-lot
formal assemblage
2 *a collection of poems*
set, anthology, compilation, collected works
3 *a collection for charity*
donation(s), gift(s), contribution(s), subscription, offering, offertory
colloq. whip-round

collective   *adj, n*

▶ *adj* united, combined, concerted, co-operative, collaborative, joint, common, shared, corporate, democratic, composite, aggregate, unanimous, cumulative
E3 individual
▶ *n* commune, co-operative, community, kibbutz, kolkhoz, moshav

collective nouns

Collective nouns (by animal) include: shrewdness of *apes*, cete of *badgers*, sloth of *bears*, swarm of *bees*, obstinacy of *buffalos*, clowder of *cats*, drove of *cattle*, brood of *chickens*, bask of *crocodiles*, murder of *crows*, herd of *deer*, pack of *dogs*, school of *dolphins*, dole of *doves*, team of *ducks*, parade of *elephants*, busyness of *ferrets*, charm of *finches*, shoal of *fish*, skulk of *foxes*, army of *frogs*, gaggle/skein of *geese*, tribe of *goats*, husk of *hares*, cast of *hawks*, brood of *hens*, bloat of *hippopotami*, string of *horses*, pack of *hounds*, troop of *kangaroos*, kindle of *kittens*, exaltation of *larks*, leap of *leopards*, pride of *lions*, swarm of *locusts*, tittering of *magpies*, troop of *monkeys*, watch of *nightingales*, family of *otters*, parliament of *owls*, pandemonium of *parrots*, covey of *partridges*, muster of *peacocks*, muster of *penguins*, nye of *pheasants*, litter of *pigs*, school of *porpoises*, bury of *rabbits*, colony of *rats*, unkindness of *ravens*, crash of *rhinoceros*, building of *rooks*, pod of *seals*, flock of *sheep*, murmuration of *starlings*, ambush of *tigers*, rafter of *turkeys*, turn of *turtles*, descent of *woodpeckers*, gam of *whales*, rout of *wolves*, zeal of *zebras*.

collector *n*

Names of collectors and enthusiasts include: zoophile (*animals*), antiquary (*antiques*), tegestollogist (*beer mats*), campanologist (*bell-ringing*), ornithologist (*birds*), bibliophile (*books*), audiophile (*broadcast sound*), lepidopterist (*butterflies*), cartophilist (*cigarette cards*), numismatist (*coins/medals*), conservationist (*countryside*), environmentalist (*the environment*), xenophile (*foreigners*), gourmet (*good food*), gastronome (*good living*), discophile (*gramophone records*), chirographist (*handwriting*), hippophile (*horses*), entomologist (*insects*), phillumenist (*matches/matchboxes*), monarchist (*the monarchy*), deltiologist (*postcards*), arachnologist (*spiders/arachnids*), philatelist (*stamps*), arctophile (*teddy bears*), etymologist (*words*).

college *n*

educational institution, educational establishment, university, *formerly* polytechnic, *formerly* poly, institute, college of further education, technical college, adult education centre, academy, school, seminary
Related adjective: collegiate

collide *v*

1 *the cars collided*
crash (into), meet head on, smash (into), bump (into), run into, go into, plough into, hit
colloq. prang
2 *their opinions collided*
CLASH, conflict, be in conflict, disagree, quarrel, wrangle, grapple, fight, contend, feud, war

collision *n*

1 *in collision with a lorry*
CRASH, impact, bump, smash, accident, pile-up, wreck, disaster
colloq. prang
2 *a collision of interests*
CLASH, conflict, confrontation, opposition, showdown, disagreement, fight, brush, collision, warring, fighting, feud, quarrel, wrangle

colloquial *adj*

conversational, informal, familiar, everyday, vernacular, casual, idiomatic, chatty, popular
formal demotic
E∃ formal

collude *v*

conspire, plot, connive, collaborate, scheme, intrigue
formal machinate

collusion *n*

complicity, deceit, conspiracy, plot, connivance, collaboration, league, scheme, scheming, intrigue, artifice
formal machination
colloq. cahoots

colonist *n*

colonial, settler, immigrant, emigrant, pioneer

colonize *v*

settle, occupy, people, pioneer, found, populate

colonnade *n*

arcade, cloisters, portico, covered walk, stoa
formal columniation, peristyle

colony *n*

1 *Britain's former colonies*
settlement, outpost, dependency, dominion, protectorate, possession, satellite, satellite state, territory, province
2 *a colony of birds*
group, association, community, settlement

colossal *adj*

huge, enormous, immense, vast, massive, great, gigantic, mammoth, monstrous, monumental, herculean, gargantuan
formal Brobdingnagian
colloq. whopping
E∃ tiny, minute

colour *n, v*

▶ *n* **1** HUE, shade, tinge, tone, tincture, tint, dye, paint, wash, pigment, pigmentation, colorant, coloration, complexion
2 *the colour of her cheeks*
rosiness, ruddiness, pinkness, glow
3 VIVIDNESS, liveliness, life, richness, brilliance, animation
4 *a nation's colours*
flag, standard, banner, emblem, ensign, insignia, badge

The range of colours includes: red, crimson, scarlet, vermillion, cherry, cerise, magenta, maroon, burgundy, ruby, orange, tangerine, apricot, coral, salmon, peach, amber, brown, chestnut, mahogany, bronze, auburn, rust, umber, copper, cinnamon, chocolate, tan, sepia, taupe, beige, fawn, yellow, lemon, canary, ochre, saffron, topaz, gold, chartreuse, green, eau de nil, emerald, jade, bottle, avocado, sage, khaki, turquoise, aquamarine, cobalt, blue, sapphire, gentian, indigo, anil, navy, violet, purple, mauve, plum, lavender, lilac, pink, rose, magnolia, cream, ecru, milky, white, grey, silver, charcoal, ebony, jet, black.

▶ *v* **1** PAINT, crayon, dye, tint, stain, tinge, wash, highlight
2 BLUSH, flush, redden, go/turn red
3 *colour your judgement*
affect, bias, prejudice, influence, sway, distort, slant,

pervert, exaggerate, overstate, misrepresent, falsify, taint
Related adjective: chromatic

colourful   *adj*
1 MULTICOLOURED, kaleidoscopic, variegated, many-coloured, parti-coloured, vivid, bright, brilliant, rich, deep, intense, vibrant, gaudy, garish
2 *a colourful description*
vivid, graphic, picturesque, animated, lively, stimulating, exciting, interesting, rich, vibrant
F3 **1** colourless, drab

colourless   *adj*
1 TRANSPARENT, neutral, uncoloured, monochrome, in black and white, bleached, washed out, faded, pale, ashen, sickly, anaemic, wan
2 INSIPID, lacklustre, dull, dreary, drab, plain, characterless, unmemorable, boring, uninteresting, tame
F3 **1** colourful **2** bright, exciting

column   *n*
1 PILLAR, post, shaft, upright, support, pier, obelisk
technical asta, caryatid, telamon, Atlas, pilaster
2 *a column of people*
line, row, rank, file, procession, queue, string, parade, list
3 *a column in a newspaper*
article, item, piece, feature, story
Related adjectives: columnal, columnar

columnist   *n*
journalist, reporter, reviewer, writer, correspondent, critic, editor

coma   *n*
unconsciousness, hypnosis, insensibility, lethargy, oblivion, stupor, torpor, trance, drowsiness
technical catalepsy, sopor
formal somnolence

comatose   *adj*
unconscious, out, out cold, in a coma, insensible, lethargic, drowsy, sleepy, sluggish, stupefied, stunned, dazed, torpid
technical cataleptic, soporose
formal somnolent
F3 conscious

comb   *v*
1 *comb your hair*
groom, neaten, tidy, arrange, dress, untangle
2 SEARCH, hunt, scour, sweep, sift, screen, rake, rummage, ransack, go through
colloq. go over with a fine-tooth comb, turn upside down

combat   *n, v*
▶ *n* war, warfare, hostilities, action, battle, fight, fighting, skirmish, struggle, conflict, clash, encounter, engagement, contest, bout, duel
▶ *v* fight, battle, do battle, war, wage war, take up arms, strive, struggle, contend, contest, oppose, resist, withstand, defy

combatant   *n*
fighter, warrior, soldier, serviceman, servicewoman, enemy, opponent, adversary, antagonist, belligerent, contender

combative   *adj*
aggressive, antagonistic, belligerent, argumentative, contentious, militant, quarrelsome, warlike

formal bellicose, pugnacious, truculent
F3 pacific, peaceful

combination   *n*
1 *in combination with other subjects*
association, co-operation, conjunction, co-ordination, union, amalgamation, coalition, unification, alliance, federation, confederation, confederacy, combine, consortium, syndicate, merger, integration, synergy
2 BLEND, mix, mixture, composite, cross, amalgam, amalgamation, fusion, coalescence, collection, connection, group, synthesis, compound, solution

combine   *v*
merge, amalgamate, bring together, put together, club together, unify, blend, stir, mix, mingle, integrate, incorporate, synthesize, compound, alloy, fuse, bond, bind, weld, join, join forces, connect, link, marry, unite, pool, ally, associate, team up, co-operate
formal admix, homogenize
F3 divide, separate, detach

combustible   *adj*
1 *combustible gas*
explosive, flammable, incendiary, ignitable, inflammable
2 *a combustible temper*
excitable, sensitive, explosive, stormy, tense, volatile, charged
F3 incombustible, non-flammable, flameproof

combustion   *n*
burning, igniting, ignition, firing

come   *v*
1 *they came to me*
advance, move towards, travel towards, move forward, approach, near, draw near
2 *come to the river/party*
reach, attain, arrive, enter, get here, appear, put in an appearance, attend, materialize
colloq. turn up, show up, surface, burst in, barge in
3 *come to power*
reach, attain, achieve, gain, secure, pass into
4 *the time for action has come*
arrive, occur, take place, happen, come about, present itself, come to pass, transpire
5 *she comes from Belgium*
originate, be, be a native of, be ... by birth, have as your home, hail, have as its source/origin
6 *his arrogance comes from his insecurity*
result from, be caused by, follow, issue, develop, arise, stem, evolve
7 *it may come to war*
pass into, become, turn, evolve into, develop into, enter, go as far as
8 *the idea came to me*
think of, remember, strike, occur to, come to the mind of, dawn on
F3 **1** go **2** depart, leave **3** fall from **8** forget
▷ **come about** happen, occur, come to pass, take place, result, arise, transpire; *formal* befall
▷ **come across** find (by chance), discover, meet by chance, stumble across, encounter, notice;
formal chance upon, happen upon; *colloq.* run into, bump into
▷ **come along** progress, make progress, develop, get better, improve, show an improvement, make headway, advance, rally, mend, recover, recuperate
▷ **come apart** collapse, disintegrate, fall to bits/pieces, break (up), separate, split, tear, crumble
▷ **come between** separate, part, divide, split up,

disunite, alienate, cause a rift between
formal estrange
▷ **come by** acquire, get, get hold of, obtain, secure, come into someone's possession, fall into someone's hands; *formal* procure
▷ **come clean** acknowledge, admit, confess, own up, reveal, tell all; *colloq.* make a clean breast of something, spill the beans
▷ **come down** decrease, fall, drop, reduce, descend, decline, deteriorate, worsen, degenerate
▷ **come down on** blame, criticize, rebuke, reprimand, find fault with, chide, reprove, upbraid, reprehend, admonish; *formal* berate; *colloq.* slate, tear into
▷ **come down to** mean, be tantamount to, be equivalent to, correspond to, amount to, boil down to
▷ **come down with** catch, fall ill with, get, develop, go down with, pick up, become infected with, become ill with; *formal* contract, succumb to
▷ **come forward** offer (yourself), offer your services, volunteer, step forward
▷ **come in** enter, appear, arrive, finish, receive; *colloq.* show up
🔁 go out
▷ **come in for** receive, get, suffer, endure, bear, undergo, experience, be subjected to
▷ **come into** inherit, be left, have bequeathed to you, acquire, receive
▷ **come off** succeed, be successful, be effective, go well, work (out), happen, occur, take place, end up
▷ **come on** begin, appear, advance, proceed, progress, make progress, develop, improve, show an improvement, get better, thrive, succeed rally, mend, recover, recuperate
▷ **come out 1** *the magazine comes out monthly* be published, appear, be produced, become available, become known **2** *everything came out all right in the end* result, end (up), finish, conclude, terminate **3** *gay people coming out* come out of the closet, declare yourself to be, declare openly, admit, be outed by someone
▷ **come out with** say, state, affirm, declare, exclaim, disclose, divulge, exclaim, blurt out
▷ **come round 1** *come around from the anaesthetic* recover, recover/regain consciousness, wake, awake **2** YIELD, change your mind, agree, be converted to, be persuaded, be won over, relent, concede, allow, grant, accede
🔁 **1** pass out
▷ **come through** endure, withstand, survive, prevail, triumph, succeed, accomplish, achieve
▷ **come to 1** *come to after the operation* recover, recover/regain consciousness, wake, awake **2** *come to a total* add up to, total, aggregate, amount to, make, equal, run to
▷ **come up** rise, arise, happen, occur, present itself, crop up, turn up
▷ **come up to** reach, meet, match up to, measure up to, live up to, make the grade, compare with, approach, bear comparison with
▷ **come up with** suggest, put forward, propose, offer, present, think of, dream up, conceive, advance, produce, submit

comeback *n*
return, reappearance, resurgence, revival, recovery, rally

comedian *n*
comic, clown, humorist, funny man, funny woman,

entertainer, wit, joker
colloq. wag, gagster

comedown *n*
anticlimax, let-down, disappointment, deflation, blow, reverse, reversal, decline, descent, demotion, humiliation, degradation

comedy *n*
1 *comedy on TV*
farce, entertainment, pantomime, burlesque, vaudeville, slapstick, satire, situation comedy, sitcom
2 *the comedy of the situation*
humour, hilarity, funniness, drollery, clowning, wit, joking, jesting, facetiousness
🔁 **1** tragedy

comely *adj*
attractive, beautiful, pretty, lovely, good-looking, blooming, bonny, buxom, fair, graceful, pleasing, winsome
formal pulchritudinous

come-on *n*
encouragement, inducement, enticement, lure, allurement, temptation

come-uppance *n*
deserts, just deserts, what you deserve, dues, merit, punishment, rebuke, chastening, recompense, requital, retribution

comfort *n, v*
▶ *n* **1** EASE, relaxation, luxury, plenty, snugness, cosiness, wellbeing, satisfaction, contentment, enjoyment, freedom from pain, freedom from worry/ unhappiness, freedom from difficulties
formal repose, opulence
2 CONSOLATION, compensation, cheer, reassurance, encouragement, condolence, alleviation, relief, help, aid, support
formal solace, succour
🔁 **1** discomfort **2** distress
▶ *v* ease, soothe, relieve, alleviate, assuage, console, cheer, gladden, reassure, hearten, encourage, help, support, sympathize, empathize, invigorate, strengthen, enliven, refresh
formal bring solace to, succour

comfortable *adj*
1 SNUG, cosy, relaxing, restful, easy, convenient, pleasant, agreeable, enjoyable, delightful
colloq. comfy
2 *comfortable clothes*
well-fitting, loose-fitting, roomy
3 AFFLUENT, well-off, well-to-do, without financial problems, pleasant, prosperous, luxurious
formal opulent
4 *not feel comfortable talking about it*
relaxed, at ease, unembarrassed, confident, happy, contented, safe
🔁 **1** uncomfortable, unpleasant **2** uncomfortable, tight **3** poor **4** uneasy, nervous, offended, embarrassed, threatened

comforting *adj*
soothing, reassuring, encouraging, heartening, heart-warming, helpful, cheering, consolatory, consoling, encouraging
formal inspiriting
🔁 worrying

comic *adj, n*
▶ *adj* funny, hilarious, side-splitting, comical, droll, humorous, witty, amusing, entertaining, diverting,

joking, facetious, jocular, light, farcical, ridiculous, ludicrous, absurd, laughable, zany
colloq. priceless, rich
🗲 tragic, serious
▶ *n* comedian, clown, humorist, funny man, funny woman, entertainer, wit, joker, buffoon
colloq. wag, gagster

comical *adj*
funny, hilarious, droll, humorous, witty, amusing, entertaining, diverting, laughable, farcical, absurd, ridiculous, ludicrous
🗲 sad, unamusing

coming *adj, n*
▶ *adj* 1 *in the coming months*
next, forthcoming, upcoming, impending, imminent, due, approaching, advancing, near, nearing, future
2 *the coming man*
aspiring, promising, rising, up-and-coming
▶ *n* advent, approach, arrival, nearing, birth, dawn, accession

command *v, n*
▶ *v* 1 ORDER, bid, give orders to, charge, enjoin, direct, instruct, require, demand, compel
formal adjure
2 LEAD, head, rule, reign, govern, control, have charge/command/control of, direct, dominate, manage, superintend, supervise, preside over
3 *command respect*
be given, gain, receive, get, obtain, secure
▶ *n* 1 COMMANDMENT, decree, edict, precept, mandate, order, bidding, charge, injunction, dictate, directive, direction, instruction, requirement
formal behest
2 *be in command*
power, authority, leadership, control, charge, domination, dominion, mastery, rule, sway, government, ascendancy, management, supervision, superintendence

commandeer *v*
seize, take possession of, confiscate, impound, hijack, usurp
formal appropriate, requisition, expropriate, arrogate, sequester, sequestrate

commander *n*
leader, head, chief, director, commander-in-chief, general, admiral, captain, commanding officer, officer
colloq. boss

commanding *adj*
1 *in a commanding lead*
powerful, strong, superior, advantageous, dominant, dominating, controlling, directing
2 *a commanding personality*
authoritative, forceful, powerful, assertive, confident, autocratic
formal peremptory
3 *the castle's commanding position*
dominating, imposing, impressive, lofty

commemorate *v*
celebrate, solemnize, remember, mark, honour, pay tribute to, salute, immortalize, observe, keep, recognize
formal memorialize

commemoration *n*
celebration, observance, remembrance, memory, tribute, honour, honouring, ceremony, salute, recognition, dedication

commemorative *adj*
memorial, celebratory, remembering, marking, honouring, saluting, dedicatory, in memory of, in memoriam, in remembrance of, in honour of, as a tribute to, in recognition of

commence *v*
begin, make a beginning, start, make a start, embark on, originate, initiate, inaugurate, open, launch, go ahead
🗲 finish, end
formal cease

commend *v*
1 PRAISE, compliment, acclaim, extol, applaud, speak highly of
formal laud, eulogize
2 *commend this book*
recommend, suggest, approve, propose, advocate, put in a good word for
3 COMMIT, entrust, trust, confide, consign, hand over, give, deliver, yield
🗲 1 criticize, censure

commendable *adj*
admirable, excellent, noble, praiseworthy, worthy, creditable, exemplary, deserving, estimable
formal laudable, meritorious
🗲 blameworthy, poor

commendation *n*
praise, acclaim, acclamation, accolade, applause, high/good opinion, good word, approval, credit, recognition, encouragement, recommendation, special mention
formal approbation, encomium, panegyric
🗲 blame, criticism

commensurate *adj*
proportionate, equivalent, corresponding, comparable, in proportion to, according to, corresponding to, consistent with, appropriate to, compatible with, acceptable, adequate, sufficient, due, fitting

comment *v, n*
▶ *v* remark, give an opinion, observe, note, mention, say, point out, explain, interpret
formal interpose, interject, elucidate, opine
▶ *n* opinion, statement, remark, observation, view, note, annotation, footnote, marginal note, explanation, illustration, exposition, commentary, criticism
formal elucidation

commentary *n*
1 *a commentary on a football match*
narration, voice-over, analysis, description, report, account, review
2 *a Bible commentary*
explanation, interpretation, analysis, notes, annotation, treatise, critique
formal elucidation, exegesis, exposition

commentator *n*
1 *a sports commentator*
broadcaster, reporter, correspondent, sportscaster, newscaster, narrator, commenter
2 *a commentator on the text*
annotator, interpreter, critic
formal expositor, exegete

commerce *n*
trade, business, industry, private enterprise, buying

and selling, dealings, relations, dealing, traffic, trafficking, exchange, marketing, merchandising

commercial *adj, n*
▶ *adj* **1** *buildings for commercial use*
trade, trading, business, industrial
2 *a commercial success*
profitable, profit-making, sellable, saleable, popular, monetary, financial, entrepreneurial, profit-orientated, materialistic, mercenary, venal
▶ *n* advertisement, publicity, promotion, marketing, jingle, display, blurb, announcement, notice, poster, bill, placard, leaflet, handbill, circular, handout, propaganda
colloq. advert, ad, plug, hype

commiserate *v*
express/offer sympathy, send/offer condolences, sympathize, comfort, understand, console, show consideration

commiseration *n*
pity, sympathy, compassion, consolation, comfort, consideration, understanding, condolence
formal solace

commission *n, v*
▶ *n* **1** ASSIGNMENT, mission, errand, task, job, duty, function, appointment, employment, mandate, work, piece of work, warrant, authority, charge, trust, responsibility
2 COMMITTEE, board, delegation, council, advisory group/body, deputation, representative
3 *commission on a sale*
percentage, share, royalty, allowance, fee, brokerage, compensation
colloq. cut, rake-off
▶ *v* nominate, select, appoint, arrange, contract, engage, employ, assign, authorize, empower, delegate, depute, send, order, place/put in an order for, request, ask for, mandate

commit *v*
1 *commit a crime*
do, carry out, get up to, indulge in, perform, execute, enact
formal effect, perpetrate
2 ENTRUST, trust, confide, commend, consign, deliver, hand over, give, assign, deposit
3 *commit yourself to do something*
promise, pledge, bind, engage, decide, dedicate, bind, covenant, cross the Rubicon
formal obligate

commitment *n*
1 *show commitment*
DEDICATION, involvement, adherence, devotion, allegiance, loyalty, hard work, effort
2 *too many commitments*
DUTY, responsibility, undertaking, obligation, engagement, liability, tie
3 *make a commitment*
UNDERTAKING, guarantee, assurance, promise, word, covenant, pledge, vow
🔁 **1** vacillation, wavering

committed *adj*
active, dedicated, devoted, loyal, involved, enthusiastic, zealous, fervent, red-hot, hardworking, diligent, industrious, studious
colloq. card-carrying
formal engagé
🔁 apathetic, uncommitted

committee *n*

Types of committee include: advisory group/body, assembly, board, caucus, commission, congress, council, delegation, deputation, discussion group, group, jury, legation, mission, panel, quango, quorum, steering committee, steering group, sub-committee, synod, task-force, team, *colloq.* think tank, working party, workshop.

commodious *adj*
roomy, spacious, large, ample, comfortable, expansive, extensive
formal capacious
🔁 cramped

commodity *n*
product, thing, article, item, goods, merchandise, output, produce, stock, wares

common *adj*
1 *a common name*
frequent, familiar, customary, habitual, usual, daily, everyday, routine, regular
colloq. two a penny
2 *have a common belief*
mutual, shared, joint, collective
3 *common land*
communal, community, public
4 *common knowledge*
widespread, prevalent, general, universal, conventional, accepted, popular, commonplace
5 *the common cold*
ordinary, standard, average, plain, simple, workaday, run-of-the-mill, undistinguished, unexceptional
6 VULGAR, coarse, unrefined, crude, inferior, low, ill-bred, uncouth, loutish, plebeian
colloq. common as muck
🔁 **1** uncommon, unusual, rare, noteworthy
5 different, special **6** tasteful, refined

commonly *adv*
generally, normally, usually, typically, routinely, as a rule, for the most part
🔁 rarely

commonplace *adj*
ordinary, unexceptional, everyday, common, routine, humdrum, pedestrian, banal, trite, widespread, frequent, hackneyed, stock, stale, obvious, worn out, boring, uninteresting, threadbare, mundane
🔁 memorable, exceptional

common sense *n*
good sense, sense, sensibleness, level-headedness, sanity, soundness, reason, pragmatism, hard-headedness, realism, experience, discernment, wisdom, shrewdness, astuteness, judgement, native intelligence, practicality
formal prudence, judiciousness
colloq. gumption, nous, savvy
🔁 folly, stupidity

common-sense *adj*
commonsensical, matter-of-fact, sensible, level-headed, sane, sound, reasonable, practical, down-to-earth, pragmatic, hard-headed, realistic, experienced, wise, discerning, shrewd, astute
formal prudent, judicious
🔁 foolish, unreasonable, unrealistic

commonwealth   *n*

Members of the Commonwealth are: Antigua and Barbuda, Australia, the Bahamas, Bangladesh, Barbados, Belize, Botswana, Brunei, Canada, Cyprus, Dominica, the Gambia, Ghana, Grenada, Guyana, India, Jamaica, Kenya, Kiribati, Lesotho, Malawi, Malaysia, the Maldives, Malta, Mauritius, Namibia, Nauru, New Zealand, Nigeria, Pakistan, Papua New Guinea, St Christopher and Nevis, St Lucia, St Vincent and the Grenadines, Seychelles, Sierra Leone, Singapore, Solomon Islands, South Africa, Sri Lanka, Swaziland, Tanzania, Tonga, Trinidad and Tobago, Tuvalu, Uganda, United Kingdom, Vanuatu, Western Samoa, Zambia, Zimbabwe.

commotion   *n*

agitation, hurly-burly, turmoil, tumult, excitement, ferment, fuss, bustle, ado, uproar, furore, racket, hubbub, rumpus, row, clamour, fracas, upheaval, disturbance, confusion, disorder, disquiet, riot, stir *colloq.* ballyhoo, hullabaloo, to-do, brouhaha, bust-up

communal   *adj*

public, community, shared, joint, collective, general, common
E3 private, personal

commune   *n, v*

▶ *n* collective, co-operative, kibbutz, community, fellowship, colony, settlement
▶ *v* converse, discourse, communicate, make contact, feel/get close to, feel/get in touch, relate spiritually

communicable   *adj*

infectious, contagious, transmittable, transmissible, transferable, conveyable, catching, spreadable
formal infective

communicate   *v*

1 ANNOUNCE, impart, inform, acquaint, intimate, notify, publish, broadcast, relay, spread, diffuse, pass on, transmit, convey, declare, proclaim, make known, report, reveal, disclose, divulge, unfold, express
formal disseminate
2 TALK, speak, converse, commune, correspond, write, phone, telephone, contact, get/be in touch, keep the lines open

communication   *n*

information, intelligence, intimation, disclosure, contact, connection, transmission
formal dissemination

Forms of communication include: media, mass media, broadcasting, radio, wireless, television, TV, cable TV, satellite, subscription TV, pay TV, pay-per-view, video, video-on-demand, teletext; telecommunications, data communication, information technology (IT); the Internet, the net, World Wide Web; newspaper, press, news, newsflash, magazine, journal, advertising, publicity, poster, leaflet, pamphlet, brochure, catalogue; post, dispatch, correspondence, letter, postcard, aerogram, e-mail, telegram, Telemessage®, cable, *colloq.* wire, chain letter, junk mail, mailshot; conversation, word, message, dialogue, speech, gossip, *colloq.* grapevine; notice, bulletin, announcement, communiqué, circular, memo, note, report, statement, press release; telephone, intercom, answering machine, walkie-talkie, bleeper, tannoy, telex, teleprinter, facsimile, fax, computer, word processor, typewriter, dictaphone, megaphone, loud-hailer; radar, Morse code, semaphore, Braille, sign language. *See also* **telephone**.

communicative   *adj*

talkative, voluble, expansive, informative, chatty, sociable, friendly, forthcoming, outgoing, extrovert, unreserved, free, open, frank, candid
E3 quiet, reserved, reticent, secretive

communion   *n*

1 *communion with nature*
sharing thoughts, sharing feelings, communing, closeness, sympathy, empathy, togetherness, unity, harmony, fellowship, participation, rapport, affinity
formal accord, concord, intercourse
2 *Holy Communion*
Lord's Supper, Eucharist, Mass, Sacrament

communiqué   *n*

announcement, bulletin, (official) communication, dispatch, message, report, statement, newsflash

communism   *n*

collectivism, sovietism, revisionism, socialism, totalitarianism, Bolshevism, Leninism, Marxism, Stalinism, Trotskyism, Maoism, Titoism

community   *n*

1 *the local community*
district, locality, neighbourhood, population, people, populace, public, residents
2 *the Bangladeshi community*
population, people, populace, public, residents, nation, state, section, group, colony, fellowship, brotherhood, fraternity
3 *a religious community*
commune, kibbutz, society, association, fellowship, brotherhood, sisterhood, fraternity
Related adjectives: communal, civil

commute   *v*

1 *commute by train*
travel to work, travel to and from, journey, shuttle
2 *commute the death sentence*
REDUCE, decrease, shorten, curtail, lighten, soften, mitigate, remit, adjust, modify

commuter   *n*

traveller, passenger
colloq. strap-hanger, suburbanite

compact¹   *adj, v*

▶ *adj* *a compact book*
small, neat, short, brief, terse, succinct, concise, pithy, condensed, pocket, little, compressed, pressed together, close, dense, impenetrable, solid, firm
E3 large, rambling, diffuse
▶ *v* compress, press down, press together, condense, consolidate, pack down, cram, flatten, ram, squeeze, tamp

compact²   *n*

the compact between the nations
agreement, alliance, pact, treaty, arrangement, transaction, deal, settlement, bargain, understanding, bond, indenture, concordat, contract, covenant, entente

companion   *n*

fellow, comrade, friend, intimate, confidant(e), ally, confederate, colleague, associate, partner, consort,

escort, chaperon, attendant, aide, assistant, accomplice, follower
colloq. mate, pal, buddy, crony, sidekick

companionable   *adj*
friendly, affable, sympathetic, familiar, genial, amiable, congenial, convivial, sociable, extrovert, outgoing, approachable, gregarious, informal, neighbourly
F3 unfriendly

companionship   *n*
fellowship, comradeship, camaraderie, *esprit de corps*, support, friendship, company, togetherness, conviviality, association, social intercourse, intimacy, sympathy, rapport
Related adjective: contubernal

company   *n*
1 *a manufacturing company*
firm, business, business organization, concern, association, corporation, establishment, house, partnership, syndicate, cartel, trust, consortium, conglomerate, multinational, holding company, subsidiary, public limited company (PLC or plc), private limited company, limited company, limited liability company
2 TROUPE, group, band, ensemble, set, circle, crowd, throng, body, troop, crew, party, assembly, gathering, community, society, team
3 GUESTS, visitors, callers
4 *be glad of company*
friendship, companionship, support, togetherness, fellowship, comradeship, conviviality, attendance, contact, presence

comparable   *adj*
similar, like, alike, related, akin, corresponding, analogous, equivalent, tantamount, proportional, proportionate, commensurate, parallel, equal
formal cognate
F3 dissimilar, unlike, unequal

> ⚠ **comparable** or **comparative** ?
> *Comparable* means 'of the same kind, to the same degree, etc': *cheaper than any comparable hotel.*
> *Comparative* means 'judged by comparing with something else': *After they had stopped playing so noisily there was a period of comparative silence.*

comparative   *adj*
relative, by/in comparison

compare   *v*
1 *compare the new edition with the old one*
contrast, juxtapose, balance, weigh, measure, note the differences between, correlate
2 *compare her to an angel*
liken, equate, link, correlate, regard as the same, show the similarities between, draw analogies with, draw a parallel between
formal analogize
3 *not compare with his predecessor*
resemble, match, equal, parallel, bear comparison, be comparable to, be as good as, match
colloq. hold a candle to

comparison   *n*
juxtaposition, analogy, parallel, correlation, relationship, likeness, resemblance, similarity, comparability, contrast, differences, differentiation, distinction

compartment   *n*
section, division, subdivision, part, category, pigeonhole, cubbyhole, niche, alcove, bay, area, stall, booth, cubicle, locker, partition, carrel, cell, chamber, berth, carriage

compass   *n*
limit(s), range, scope, stretch, space, extent, sphere, area, reach, field, realm(s), boundary, bounds, circle, circuit, circumference, enclosure, round, scale, zone

compassion   *n*
kindness, gentleness, tenderness, tender-heartedness, fellow-feeling, humanity, mercy, pity, leniency, sympathy, commiseration, condolence, sorrow, benevolence, consideration, concern, care, understanding
F3 cruelty, indifference

compassionate   *adj*
kind-hearted, kindly, tender-hearted, tender, gentle, caring, warm-hearted, benevolent, humanitarian, humane, merciful, clement, lenient, pitying, sympathetic, understanding, supportive
F3 cruel, indifferent

compatible   *adj*
harmonious, in harmony, consistent, matching, suitable, suited, reconcilable, adaptable, conformable, sympathetic, having rapport, like-minded, well-matched, well-suited, similar
formal congruous, congruent, accordant, consonant
F3 incompatible, antagonistic, contradictory

compatriot   *n*
fellow citizen, fellow national, countryman, fellow countryman, countrywoman, fellow countrywoman

compel   *v*
force, make, constrain, oblige, necessitate, drive, urge, impel, insist on, coerce, pressure, pressurize, hustle, browbeat, bully, intimidate, press-gang, dragoon
colloq. bulldoze, strongarm, twist someone's arm, lean on, put the screws on

compelling   *adj*
1 *a compelling story*
fascinating, gripping, riveting, enthralling, spellbinding, absorbing, mesmeric, irresistible, compulsive
colloq. unputdownable
2 *compelling reasons*
forceful, imperative, urgent, pressing, overriding, powerful, cogent, persuasive, convincing, weighty, conclusive, incontrovertible, irrefutable
F3 **1** boring **2** weak, unconvincing

compendium   *n*
companion, handbook, manual, digest, summary, synopsis, vade-mecum

compensate   *v*
1 *compensate you for any loss*
repay, refund, reimburse, indemnify, recompense, reward, remunerate
2 *compensate for doing wrong*
make amends, make reparation, make good, make up for, restore, requite atone, redeem, redress, satisfy
3 COUNTERACT, balance, counterbalance, cancel, neutralize, nullify, offset
formal countervail, counterpoise

compensation   *n*
1 *pay compensation*
recompense, reward, payment, remuneration, requital,

repayment, refund, reimbursement, indemnification, indemnity, damages, reparation, return
2 *make compensation for wrongdoing*
amends, redress, satisfaction, restoration, restitution, atonement, consolation, comfort

compère *n*
host, link person, presenter, master of ceremonies, MC, emcee, announcer, anchorman, anchorwoman

compete *v*
1 *compete against/with other firms*
vie, contest, contend, fight, battle, struggle, strive, oppose, challenge, pit yourself, rival, jostle
2 *compete in a contest*
contend, participate, enter, run, race, take part, go in for

competence *n*
ability, proficiency, capability, aptitude, capacity, skill, technique, experience, expertise, facility, fitness
F3 incompetence

competent *adj*
1 *competent to deal with them*
capable, able, adept, efficient, trained, qualified, well-qualified, skilled, skilful, accomplished, experienced, proficient, expert, masterly, equal
2 *competent work*
satisfactory, acceptable, reasonable, passable, respectable, adequate, sufficient, fit, suitable, appropriate
F3 1 incompetent, incapable, unable, inefficient
2 excellent, outstanding

competition *n*
1 CONTEST, championship, tournament, cup, event, race, match, game, quiz, bout, meet
2 RIVALRY, opposition, challenge, contest, contention, conflict, struggle, strife, vying, competitiveness, combativeness
3 COMPETITORS, rivals, opponents, opposition, challengers, field

competitive *adj*
combative, contentious, antagonistic, aggressive, ambitious, keen,
colloq. pushy, cut-throat, dog-eat-dog

competitiveness *n*
combativeness, contentiousness, antagonism, assertiveness, challenge, aggression, aggressiveness, rivalry, ambitious, ambitiousness, keenness
formal pugnacity
colloq. pushiness, rat race, survival of the fittest
F3 backwardness, sluggishness

competitor *n*
contestant, contender, entrant, candidate, participant, challenger, player, opponent, adversary, antagonist, rival, emulator, competition, opposition

compilation *n*
composition, collection, accumulation, collation, anthology, selection, organization, arrangement, thesaurus, treasury, album, compendium, miscellany, omnibus, potpourri, corpus, opus, work
formal assemblage, amassment, collectanea, florilegium, chrestomathy

compile *v*
compose, put together, collect, gather, garner, cull, accumulate, amass, assemble, collate, marshal, organize, arrange

complacency *n*
smugness, self-satisfaction, gloating, triumph, pleasure, pride, self-righteousness, serenity, self-assurance, gratification, contentment, satisfaction
F3 diffidence, discontent

complacent *adj*
smug, self-satisfied, gloating, triumphant, proud, self-righteous, serenity, unconcerned, serene, self-assured, pleased, gratified, contented, satisfied
F3 diffident, concerned, discontented

⚠ **complacent** or **complaisant** ?
Complacent means 'smugly pleased with yourself or your own abilities': *One of the dangers of success is that you can become complacent. Complaisant* means 'being cheerfully willing to do what others want': *Franca's complaisant kindness was too much for him.*

---

complain *v*
1 *complain to the manager; always complaining*
criticize, find fault, file/lodge a complaint, take something up with someone, kick up a fuss, object, protest, air your grievances, grumble, carp, fuss, lament, bemoan, bewail, moan, nag, whine, groan, growl
formal remonstrate, expostulate, repine
colloq. beef, belly-ache, grouse, gripe, bleat, whinge, have a bone to pick
2 *complain of an illness*
suffer from, endure, be in pain, feel pain, hurt, ache

complainer *n*
grumbler, moaner, niggler
colloq. belly-acher, grouser, fuss-pot, nit-picker, whiner, whinger

complaint *n*
1 PROTEST, objection, grumble, moan, grievance, dissatisfaction, annoyance, fault-finding, criticism, carping, censure, accusation, charge, representation
colloq. beefing, belly-aching, grouse, gripe, bleating, whingeing
2 *a chest complaint*
ailment, illness, sickness, disease, disorder, trouble, upset, condition
formal indisposition, affliction, malady, malaise

complaisant *adj*
agreeable, amenable, amiable, accommodating, obliging, solicitous, biddable, compliant, deferential, conciliatory, docile, obedient, conformable
formal tractable
F3 obstinate, perverse

⚠ **complaisant** or **complacent** ?
See panel at **complacent**.

---

complement *n, v*
▶ *n* **1** *wine as a complement to the dinner*
companion, counterpart, addition, accessory, completion
formal consummation
2 *the ship's complement*
allowance, quota, total, totality, aggregate, sum, capacity, entirety
▶ *v* go well with, go well together, combine well with, match, set off, contrast, round off, complete, crown

---

⚠ **complement, compliment** or **supplement** ?
One thing is a *complement* to another when it makes a pleasant contrast or makes the combination of the

two things pleasantly balanced: *Yoghurt can be used as a complement to spicy dishes.* You pay someone a *compliment* when you praise them. A *supplement* is something added to something else that is already complete or to make up for a deficiency: *a magazine supplement; take vitamin supplements.*

complementary *adj*
finishing, completing, perfecting, reciprocal, interdependent, correlative, interrelated, corresponding, matching, twin, fellow, companion,
F3 contradictory, incompatible

⚠ **complementary, complimentary** or **supplementary** ?
Two things are *complementary* if they complement each other: *use complementary colours in all the furnishings.* You say something *complimentary* to someone as an expression of admiration or praise to them; a *complimentary* ticket is one given free of charge. You use *supplementary* to describe something that is added: *ask a supplementary question.*

---

complete *adj, v*
▶ *adj* **1** ENTIRE, integral, whole, entire, full, unbroken, undivided, total, intact, plenary, unabbreviated, unabridged, unshortened, unedited, unexpurgated, detailed, comprehensive, exhaustive
2 FINISHED, ended, completed, concluded, over, done, accomplished, finalized, settled, achieved
formal terminated
3 UTTER, total, absolute, outright, downright, out-and-out, thorough, unqualified, unmitigated, unconditional, perfect
F3 **1** abridged **2** incomplete **3** partial
▶ *v* **1** *complete the work*
finish, end, close, conclude, finalize, settle, perform, discharge, execute, fulfil, realize, accomplish, achieve, make up, crown, cap, round off, wind up, perfect
formal terminate, consummate
colloq. polish off, clinch
2 *complete a form*
fill in, fill out, answer

completely *adv*
totally, utterly, wholly, fully, in full, absolutely, perfectly, quite, thoroughly, through and through, altogether, entirely, solidly
colloq. in every respect, lock stock and barrel, from first to last, root and branch, every inch, heart and soul, hook line and sinker

completion *n*
finish, end, close, conclusion, finalization, settlement, discharge, execution, fulfilment, realization, accomplishment, achievement, attainment, fruition, culmination, perfection
formal termination, consummation

complex *adj, n*
▶ *adj* complicated, intricate, elaborate, involved, difficult, circuitous, tortuous, devious, mixed, varied, diverse, multiple, composite, compound, ramified
formal convoluted, Byzantine
F3 simple, easy
▶ *n* **1** NETWORK, structure, system, scheme, composite, organization, establishment, institute, development
formal aggregation
2 FIXATION, obsession, preoccupation, phobia,

disorder, neurosis
colloq. hang-up, thing

complexion *n*
1 SKIN, colour, colouring, tone, pigmentation
2 LOOK, appearance, aspect, attitude, guise, light, character, nature, cast, type, stamp, kind

complexity *n*
complication, intricacy, elaboration, involvement, circuitousness, tortuousness, deviousness, multifariousness, multiplicity, variety, diverseness, compositeness, entanglement, ramification, repercussion
formal convolution
F3 simplicity

compliance *n*
obedience, submissiveness, submission, agreement, assent, conformability, deference, passivity, yielding
formal acquiescence, complaisance, concurrence
F3 defiance, disobedience

compliant *adj*
obedient, submissive, subservient, pliable, accommodating, agreeable, biddable, conformable, deferential, passive, docile, yielding, indulgent
formal acquiescent, complaisant, tractable
F3 disobedient, intractable

complicate *v*
compound, elaborate, make difficult, involve, make involved, muddle, mix up, confuse, jumble, tangle, entangle
F3 simplify

complicated *adj*
complex, intricate, elaborate, involved, tortuous, difficult, puzzling, perplexing, problematic, cryptic
formal convoluted
colloq. fiddly
F3 simple, easy

complication *n*
difficulty, problem, drawback, snag, obstacle, problem, ramification, repercussion, complexity, intricacy, elaboration, convolution, tangle, web, confusion, mixture

complicity *n*
collusion, collaboration, connivance, involvement, agreement, approval, knowledge
formal concurrence, abetment
F3 ignorance, innocence

compliment *n, v*
▶ *n* **1** *pay someone a compliment*
flattery, flattering remarks, admiration, favour, approval, congratulations, tribute, honour, accolade, bouquet, commendation, praise
formal eulogy, homage, felicitation, encomium, laudation
2 *sends his compliments*
greetings, regards, best wishes, congratulations, remembrances, respects
formal salutation, devoirs
F3 **1** insult, criticism
▶ *v* flatter, admire, commend, speak highly/well of, praise, extol, congratulate, applaud, salute
formal felicitate, laud, eulogize
F3 insult, condemn

⚠ **compliment, complement** or **supplement** ?
See panel at **complement**.

---

complimentary *adj*
1 FLATTERING, admiring, favourable, approving, appreciative, congratulatory, commendatory
formal eulogistic, panegyrical
2 *complimentary ticket*
free, gratis, honorary, courtesy
colloq. on the house
E3 **1** insulting, unflattering, critical

⚠ **complimentary** or **complementary** ?
See panel at **complementary**.
---

comply *v*
agree, consent, assent, yield, submit, defer, respect, observe, obey, abide by, all in, conform, follow, perform, discharge, fulfil, satisfy, meet, oblige, accommodate
formal acquiesce, accord, accede
E3 defy, disobey

component *n, adj*
▶ *n* part, constituent, constituent part, integral part, ingredient, element, factor, item, unit, piece, section, module, bit, spare part
▶ *adj* constituent, integral, essential, basic, intrinsic, inherent

comport *v*
acquit, conduct, carry, bear, act, behave, perform
formal demean, deport

compose *v*
1 *the board is composed of four directors*
MAKE UP, constitute, form, comprise
2 CREATE, write, arrange, produce, make (up), think of/up, devise, form, fashion, build, construct, frame, invent, concoct, put together, assemble
3 CALM, calm down, soothe, quiet, collect, still, settle, steady, tranquillize, quell, assuage, pacify, control

composed *adj*
calm, calmed down, tranquil, quite, quietened down, serene, relaxed, unworried, unruffled, level-headed, cool, collected, cool and collected, self-possessed, controlled, self-controlled, confident, imperturbable, placid, sedate, at ease
colloq. unflappable, cool as a cucumber
E3 agitated, worried, troubled

composer *n*
musician, arranger, songwriter, songsmith, tunesmith, author, writer, creator, maker, originator, producer, poet, bard

composite *adj, n*
▶ *adj* compound, conglomerate, complex, blended, combined, fused, mixed, patchwork, synthesized
formal heterogeneous, agglutinate
E3 homogeneous, uniform
▶ *n* compound, conglomerate, blend, combination, alloy, amalgam, fusion, mixture, synthesis, pastiche, patchwork
formal agglutination

composition *n*
1 CONSTITUTION, make-up, combination, mixture, form, structure, configuration, layout, arrangement, organization, character, harmony, consonance, balance, symmetry
formal conformation
2 *a musical composition*
creation, work, work of art, opus, piece, arrangement,

adaptation, accompaniment, symphony, opera, study, exercise, poem, picture, painting, drawing, story, novel
3 MAKING, production, formation, creation, invention, arranging, devising, putting together, concoction, design, formulation, writing, compilation, proportion

compost *n*
fertilizer, humus, mulch, manure, peat, dressing

composure *n*
calm, tranquillity, serenity, ease, coolness, self-possession, self-control, level-headedness, confidence, assurance, self-assurance, aplomb, poise, dignity, imperturbability, placidity, equanimity, dispassion, impassivity
formal aplomb
E3 agitation, nervousness, discomposure

compound¹ *n, adj, v*
▶ *n* *a chemical compound*
blend, mixture, medley, hybrid, composite, amalgam, alloy, synthesis, fusion, composition, amalgamation, combination, conglomerate
technical admixture
▶ *adj* composite, blended, combined, fused, mixed, synthesized, multiple, complex, complicated, intricate, conglomerate
▶ *v* **1** COMBINE, put together, amalgamate, unite, fuse, coalesce, synthesize, alloy, blend, mix, mingle, intermingle
2 WORSEN, exacerbate, aggravate, make matters worse, complicate, intensify, heighten, magnify, add to, increase
formal augment
colloq. add insult to injury

compound² *n*
a prison compound
enclosure, yard, pen, fold, pound, paddock, stockade, corral, court

comprehend *v*
1 UNDERSTAND, conceive, see, grasp, make sense of, fathom, penetrate, realize, appreciate, know, apprehend, perceive, discern, take in, assimilate
colloq. tumble to, twig
2 INCLUDE, comprise, take in, encompass, involve, contain, embrace, cover
E3 **1** misunderstand

comprehensible *adj*
understandable, easy to understand, intelligible, graspable, discernible, conceivable, coherent, explicit, clear, lucid, plain, simple, accessible, straightforward
E3 incomprehensible, obscure

comprehension *n*
understanding, conception, grasp, realization, appreciation, knowledge, apprehension, perception, discernment, judgement, sense, insight, intelligence
colloq. ken
E3 incomprehension, unawareness

comprehensive *adj*
thorough, exhaustive, full, complete, encyclopedic, compendious, broad, wide, widespread, extensive, sweeping, general, blanket, inclusive, overall, all-inclusive, all-embracing, across-the-board
E3 partial, incomplete, selective

compress *v*
1 *compress petrol and air*
press, squeeze, crush, squash, flatten, jam, wedge, cram, tamp, stuff, compact, condense, constrict,

consolidate, impact, pressurize, concentrate
2 *compress an article*
abridge, condense, contract, telescope, shorten, abbreviate, reduce, summarize, synopsize
old use astrict
formal coarctate
F3 2 expand, diffuse

comprise *v*
1 *the flat comprises three rooms*
consist of, be composed of, include, contain, take in, incorporate, embody, involve, encompass, cover
formal comprehend, embrace
2 *the countries that comprise Great Britain*
make up, constitute, compose, form

compromise *v, n*
▶ *v* **1** NEGOTIATE, bargain, arbitrate, settle, agree, concede, make concessions, meet halfway, come to/reach an understanding, give and take, adapt, adjust
2 *compromise your principles*
weaken, undermine, expose, endanger, imperil, jeopardize, risk, prejudice
3 DISHONOUR, discredit, shame, bring shame to, bring into disrepute, damage, embarrass, involve, implicate
▶ *n* settlement, agreement, concession, negotiation, mediation, understanding, bargain, deal, co-operation, accommodation, adjustment, trade-off, give-and-take, balance
F3 disagreement, intransigence

compulsion *n*
1 *use compulsion to obtain something*
force, coercion, duress, constraint, obligation, pressure, demand, insistence
2 *feel a compulsion to do something*
urge, drive, impulse, desire, longing, need, necessity, temptation, obsession, preoccupation

compulsive *adj*
1 IRRESISTIBLE, overwhelming, overpowering, uncontrollable, obsessive, compelling, driving, besetting, urgent
2 *a compulsive gambler*
obsessive, habitual, addicted, dependent, hardened, incorrigible, irredeemable, incurable, hopeless
colloq. pathological, hooked
3 *compulsive viewing*
compelling, fascinating, gripping, riveting, enthralling, spellbinding, absorbing, mesmeric, irresistible

compulsory *adj*
obligatory, mandatory, imperative, forced, set, stipulated, binding, contractual, essential, necessary, required, requisite, *de rigueur*
F3 optional, voluntary, discretionary

compunction *n*
remorse, regret, repentance, penitence, shame, contrition, sorrow, qualm, misgiving, guilt, reluctance, hesitation, unease, uneasiness
F3 callousness, defiance

compute *v*
calculate, count (up), sum, tally, add up, total, enumerate, reckon, estimate, assess, evaluate, figure, measure, rate

computer *n*

Computer terms include: mainframe, microcomputer, minicomputer, PC (personal computer), Applemac®; hardware, CPU (central processing unit), Pentium® processor, disk drive, joystick, keyboard, lap-top, light pen, microprocessor, modem, monitor, mouse, mouse mat, notebook computer, printer, bubblejet printer, daisywheel printer, dot-matrix printer, ink-jet printer, laser printer, screen, VDU (visual display unit); software, program, Windows®, WordPerfect®, Wordstar®, disk, magnetic disk, floppy disk, hard disk, optical disk, magnetic tape; programming language, BASIC, COBOL, FORTRAN; memory, backing storage, external memory, immediate access memory, internal memory, RAM (Random Access Memory), ROM (Read Only Memory), multimedia, CD-ROM (Compact Disc Read Only Memory); access, ASCII, backup, bit, boot, buffer, byte, kilobyte, megabyte, character, chip, silicon chip, printed circuit board, motherboard, computer game, computer graphics, computer literate, computer simulation, computer terminal, cursor, icon, graphical user interface (GUI), data, databank, database, default, desktop publishing (DTP), digitizer, directory, DOS (disk operating system), electronic mail, e-mail, the Internet, the net, World Wide Web, JANET®, format, function, grammar checker, graphics, hacking, hypertext, interface, macro, menu, MSDOS (Microsoft® disk operating system), network, peripheral, pixel, scrolling, spellchecker, spreadsheet, template, toggle, toolbar, user-friendly, user interface, video game, virtual reality (VR), virus, window, word-processing, work station, WYSIWYG (what you see is what you get).

comrade *n*
fellow, companion, friend, intimate, confidant(e), ally, confederate, colleague, associate, partner, consort, escort, chaperon, attendant, aide, assistant, accomplice, follower
colloq. mate, pal, buddy, crony, sidekick

con *v, n*
▶ *v* trick, cheat, hoax, dupe, deceive, mislead, hoodwink, double-cross, swindle, defraud, rook
formal inveigle
colloq. rip off, fleece, do, bamboozle
▶ *n* confidence trick, trick, bluff, deception, swindle, cheating, fraud, racket
colloq. fiddle, scam

concatenation *n*
sequence, series, course, progress, progression, succession, string, chain, connection, interlinking, interlocking, linking, nexus, thread, trail, procession, train

concave *adj*
hollow, hollowed, curved in, bending inwards, cupped, scooped, excavated, sunken, indented, depressed
formal incurvate, incurved
F3 convex

conceal *v*
1 *conceal a body*
hide, obscure, disguise, camouflage, mask, screen, veil, cloak, shroud, cover, bury, submerge, keep hidden, keep out of sight, tuck away
formal secrete
colloq. stash
2 *conceal a secret*
hide, keep dark, keep secret, keep quiet, suppress
formal dissemble

colloq. cover up, hush up, sweep under the carpet, put the lid on, whitewash
F3 1 uncover 2 reveal, disclose

concealed *adj*
hidden, covered, screened, unseen, covert, disguised, inconspicuous, latent, tucked away
F3 clear, plain

concealment *n*
1 *concealment of guns*
hideaway, hideout, hiding, disguise, camouflage, mask, protection, screen, veil, shroud, cloak, cover, secrecy, shelter
formal secretion
2 *concealment of information*
hiding, suppression, keeping dark, secrecy
colloq. cover-up, whitewash, smokescreen
F3 1 uncovering 2 openness, revelation

concede *v*
1 ADMIT, confess, acknowledge, recognize, own (up), grant, allow, accept
formal accede
2 YIELD, give up, surrender, relinquish, forfeit, sacrifice, hand over
formal cede
F3 1 deny

conceit *n*
conceitedness, pride, arrogance, vanity, haughtiness, immodesty, boastfulness, swagger, egotism, self-love, narcissism, self-importance, self-admiration, superciliousness, cockiness, self-satisfaction, complacency
formal vainglory
F3 modesty, diffidence

conceited *adj*
vain, proud, arrogant, haughty, boastful, swollen-headed, immodest, egotistical, narcissistic, self-important, full of yourself, puffed up, supercilious, self-satisfied, complacent, smug
formal vainglorious
colloq. cocky, big-headed, stuck-up, toffee-nosed, too big for your boots
F3 modest, self-effacing, diffident, humble

conceivable *adj*
imaginable, credible, believable, thinkable, tenable, possible, likely, probable
F3 inconceivable, unimaginable

conceive *v*
1 IMAGINE, envisage, visualize, see, picture, grasp, understand, perceive, apprehend, comprehend, realize, appreciate, believe, think, fancy, suppose
2 INVENT, design, devise, formulate, think of/up, come up with, create, originate, form, contrive, produce, develop
3 *conceive a baby*
become pregnant, become fertilized, be fertile, become impregnated, become inseminated, reproduce, give birth to

concentrate *v, n*
▶ *v* **1** FOCUS, converge, centre, centralize, rivet, consolidate, cluster, crowd, congregate, gather, collect, accumulate, amass
2 APPLY YOURSELF, think, give your (undivided) attention, pay/devote attention, attend, put/keep your mind, consider, mind
3 CONDENSE, evaporate, boil down, reduce, compress, distil, thicken, intensify

F3 1 disperse 3 dilute
▶ *n* essence, extract, distillation, juice
technical apozem, decoction, decocture
formal quintessence, elixir

concentrated *adj*
1 *concentrated liquid*
condensed, evaporated, reduced, thickened, compressed, dense, rich, strong, undiluted
2 INTENSE, intensive, all-out, concerted, vigorous, hard, deep
F3 1 diluted 2 half-hearted

concentration *n*
1 ATTENTION, deep/close thought, heed, absorption, application, mind, devotion, single-mindedness, engrossment, intensity
2 CONVERGENCE, centralization, focusing, cluster, crowd, grouping, collection, congregation, accumulation, consolidation, conglomeration
formal agglomeration
3 COMPRESSION, evaporation, boiling-down, distillation, reduction, consolidation, denseness, thickness
F3 1 distraction 2 dispersal 3 dilution

concept *n*
idea, notion, plan, theory, hypothesis, thought, abstraction, conception, conceptualization, visualization, image, view, picture, impression

conception *n*
1 CONCEPT, idea, notion, thought, plan, theory, hypothesis, image, view, picture, impression
2 KNOWLEDGE, understanding, appreciation, perception, visualization, image, picture, impression, idea, inkling, clue
3 INVENTION, design, birth, beginning, origin, origination, outset, initiation, inauguration, formation, launching
4 *from conception to birth*
impregnation, insemination, fertilization, pregnancy, reproduction, sexual intercourse
formal fecundation

concern *v, n*
▶ *v* **1** WORRY, distress, trouble, disturb, bother, upset, alarm, make worried, make anxious, prey on your mind
formal perturb
2 *concern yourself with their problems*
give your attention to, involve, interest, busy, devote, affect, touch
3 BE ABOUT, relate to, refer to, regard, deal with, be connected with, have to do with, involve, apply to, bear on
formal appertain to, pertain to
▶ *n* **1** *a cause for concern*
anxiety, worry, unease, disquiet, care, sorrow, distress, apprehension, disturbance, strain, pressure, anguish
formal perturbation
2 REGARD, consideration, attention, attentiveness, care, heed, thought
3 *it's not my concern*
duty, responsibility, charge, job, task, field, business, affair, matter, problem, interest, involvement
4 COMPANY, firm, business, corporation, association, establishment, enterprise, organization, partnership, syndicate
F3 1 joy 2 indifference

concerned *adj*
1 ANXIOUS, worried, uneasy, apprehensive, upset,

unhappy, distressed, troubled, disturbed, bothered
formal perturbed
2 *concerned teachers*
attentive, caring, considerate, kind, thoughtful,
helpful, charitable, unselfish, altruistic, gracious,
sensitive
3 CONNECTED, related, involved, implicated,
interested, involved, affected
F3 1 unconcerned, indifferent, apathetic
2 inconsiderate, thoughtless, selfish

concerning *prep*
about, regarding, with regard to, as regards, respecting,
with respect to, with reference to, referring to, relating
to, relevant to, in the matter of, on the subject of, re
formal apropos

concert *n*
1 *a musical concert*
performance, entertainment, presentation,
production, show, recital, appearance, engagement,
rendering, rendition, gig, jam session, prom, soirée
2 *work in concert with others*
agreement, harmony, unanimity, union, unison
formal accord, concord, concordance, consonance
F3 2 disunity

concerted *adj*
combined, united, joint, collective, shared, co-
operative, collaborative, co-ordinated, interactive,
organized, concentrated, prearranged, planned
F3 separate, unco-ordinated, disorganized

concession *n*
1 YIELDING, giving-up, surrender, relinquishment,
forfeit, sacrifice, handover, admission,
acknowledgement, recognition, grant, allowance,
compromise, adjustment, acceptance
formal ceding
colloq. sop
2 *tax concessions*
reduction, decrease, cut, (special) right, (special)
privilege, favour, grant, allowance, exception
colloq. bending of the rules

conciliate *v*
reconcile, pacify, placate, appease, restore harmony to,
satisfy, soften, soothe, disarm, disembitter, mollify,
propitiate
F3 antagonize

conciliation *n*
reconciliation, peacemaking, pacification, placation,
appeasement, mollification, propitiation
F3 alienation, antagonization

conciliator *n*
reconciler, mediator, negotiator, peacemaker,
intermediary, intercessor, dove
F3 troublemaker

conciliatory *adj*
reconciliatory, peacemaking, peaceable, appeasing,
disarming, mollifying, pacific, assuaging
formal irenic, pacificatory, placatory, propitiative,
propitiatory
F3 antagonistic

concise *adj*
short, brief, terse, succinct, pithy, crisp, compendious,
compact, compressed, condensed, abridged,
abbreviated, summary, to the point
formal synoptic, epigrammatic
F3 diffuse, wordy

conclave *n*
assembly, (secret) meeting, council, conference,
session cabinet, cabal
formal confabulation
colloq. powwow, parley

conclude *v*
1 END, bring/come/draw to an end, close, finish,
complete, culminate
formal consummate, cease, terminate, discontinue
colloq. wind up, polish off
2 INFER, deduce, come to the conclusion, assume,
surmise, reason, gather, suppose, reckon, judge, decide
formal conjecture, surmise
3 SETTLE, resolve, close, decide, establish, determine,
negotiate, accomplish, agree, arrange, work out
formal effect
colloq. wrap up, pull off, clinch
F3 1 begin, start, commence

conclusion *n*
1 INFERENCE, deduction, assumption, opinion,
conviction, judgement, verdict, decision, resolution,
settlement, result, consequence, outcome, upshot,
issue, answer, solution
2 END, close, finish, completion, culmination, finale
formal consummation, cessation, termination,
discontinuance
3 SETTLING, resolution, decision, establishment,
determination, negotiation, accomplishment,
agreement, arrangement, working-out
formal effecting
colloq. pulling-off, clinching

conclusive *adj*
final, ultimate, definitive, decisive, clear, convincing,
definite, undeniable, irrefutable, indisputable,
incontrovertible, unarguable, unanswerable
F3 inconclusive, questionable

concoct *v*
1 *concoct a meal*
put together, mix, prepare, make, develop, blend,
cook (up), brew
colloq. rustle up
2 *concoct a story*
fabricate, invent, devise, contrive, formulate, plan,
plot, hatch
formal decoct
colloq. cook up

concoction *n*
brew, potion, preparation, mixture, blend,
combination, compound, creation

concomitant *adj, n*
▶ *adj* complementary, accompanying, associative,
attendant, co-existent, coincidental, incidental,
simultaneous, synchronous, concurrent, contributing
formal contemporaneous, conterminous, syndromic
F3 accidental, unrelated
▶ *n* accompaniment, by-product, incidental,
secondary, symptom, side effect
formal epiphenomenon

concord *n*
harmony, accord, agreement, friendship, entente,
consensus, unanimity, unison, amicability, peace,
compact, treaty, rapport
formal amity, consonance
F3 discord

concourse *n*
1 *the station concourse*

hall, entrance, foyer, lobby, lounge, piazza, plaza
2 *a concourse of people*
gathering, multitude, crowd, swarm, throng, assembly, collection, meeting, crush, press

concrete *adj*
1 *concrete objects*
real, actual, solid, physical, material, substantial, tangible, touchable, perceptible, visible
2 *concrete evidence*
firm, definite, positive, specific, explicit, genuine, factual, solid
F3 **2** abstract, vague

concubine *n*
mistress, kept woman, paramour, lover, courtesan, leman, lorette, apple-squire

concupiscence *n*
appetite, desire, libido, lasciviousness, lechery, lewdness, lust, lustfulness
formal libidinousness, lubricity
colloq. randiness, horniness

concupiscent *adj*
lascivious, lecherous, lewd, lustful
formal libidinous, lubricious
colloq. randy, horny

concur *v*
agree, approve, comply, consent, co-operate, harmonize, be in harmony
formal accede, assent, accord, acquiesce
F3 disagree

concurrence *n*
1 *concurrence on the decision*
agreement, association, convergence, common ground, acceptance, approval
formal assent, acquiescence
2 *the concurrence of the two events*
coincidence, coexistence, synchrony
formal contemporaneity, juxtaposition, simultaneity
F3 **1** difference, disagreement

concurrent *adj*
simultaneous, synchronous, contemporaneous, coinciding, coincident, concomitant, coexisting, coexistent

condemn *v*
1 *condemn his actions*
disapprove, criticize, reproach, blame, revile, deplore, denounce
formal reprehend, reprove, deprecate, berate, upbraid, castigate, disparage, censure
colloq. slam, slate
2 *condemn a prisoner*
sentence, give/pass a sentence, punish, convict, judge, damn
3 *condemned to a life of poverty*
doom, compel, coerce, force, consign, ordain
4 *condemn a building*
declare unsafe, declare unfit, demolish, destroy, bar, ban
F3 **1** praise, approve **2** acquit, pardon

condemnation *n*
disapproval, criticism, reproof, reproach, blame, denunciation, damnation, conviction, sentence, judgement
formal castigation, censure, deprecation, disparagement
colloq. thumbs-down
F3 praise, approval

condemnatory *adj*
critical, disapproving, discouraging, incriminating, unfavourable, accusatory, accusing, damnatory
formal censorious, denunciatory, deprecatory, proscriptive, reprobative, reprobatory
F3 approving, complimentary, indulgent;
formal laudatory

condensation *n*
1 *condensation of liquid*
distillation, liquefaction, precipitation, concentration, evaporation, reduction, boiling-down, consolidation
technical deliquescence
2 ABRIDGEMENT, précis, synopsis, digest, contraction, compression, curtailment

condense *v*
1 *condense a book*
shorten, cut (down), curtail, abbreviate, abridge, précis, summarize, encapsulate, contract, compress, compact
2 DISTIL, precipitate, concentrate, evaporate, reduce, thicken, solidify, coagulate, compress, boil down, intensify
technical deliquesce
F3 **1** expand **2** dilute

condensed *adj*
1 *a condensed book*
shortened, cut (down), curtailed, abridged abbreviated, summarized, abstracted, reduced, contracted, compact, concise
2 *condensed liquid*
concentrated, evaporated, reduced, thickened, compressed, clotted, coagulated, dense, rich, strong, undiluted
F3 **1** expanded **2** diluted

condescend *v*
1 *condescend to do something*
deign, see fit, stoop, bend, lower yourself, demean yourself, humble yourself, descend
2 *condescend to people*
patronize, talk down to, treat condescendingly, be snobbish to

condescending *adj*
patronizing, disdainful, supercilious, snooty, snobbish, haughty, lofty, superior, lordly, imperious
colloq. stuck-up, toffee-nosed
F3 gracious, humble

condescension *n*
disdain, haughtiness, superciliousness, superiority, loftiness, snobbishness, lordliness, airs
F3 humility

condition *n, v*
▶ *n* **1** STATE, circumstances, factor(s), case, position, situation, predicament, plight, quandary
2 *the conditions in which people work*
surroundings, environment, milieu, setting, atmosphere, climate, background, context, circumstances, factors, way of life, situation, state, set-up
3 REQUIREMENT, obligation, prerequisite, terms, stipulation, demand, necessity, essential, precondition, provision, proviso, qualification, limit, limitation, restriction, rule
4 *out of condition*
fitness, health, state, state of health, shape, form, order, working order, fettle, kilter
colloq. nick
5 *a heart condition*

disorder, defect, weakness, infirmity, problem, complaint, disease, illness, ailment
formal malady
▶ *v* **1** *a shampoo that conditions*
tone, make healthy, restore, revive, treat, improve groom
2 *conditioned by experience*
influence, mould, educate, train, groom, equip, prepare, prime, accustom, familiarize, season, temper, adapt, adjust, tune, indoctrinate, brainwash

conditional *adj*
provisional, qualified, limited, restricted, tied, relative, subject, based, dependent, contingent
F3 unconditional, absolute

condolence *n*
sympathy, commiseration, compassion, pity, consolation, support
F3 congratulation

condom *n*
sheath, protective, female condom, Femidom®
slang French letter, johnnie, rubber, *US* scumbag

condone *v*
forgive, pardon, excuse, overlook, ignore, disregard, tolerate, brook, let pass, allow
colloq. turn a blind eye to
F3 condemn, censure

conducive *adj*
leading, tending, contributing, contributory, productive, promoting, advantageous, beneficial, favourable, helpful, useful, instrumental, encouraging
F3 detrimental, adverse, unfavourable

conduct *v, n*
▶ *v* **1** CARRY OUT, perform, do, administer, manage, run, organize, direct, orchestrate, chair, control, be in charge of, handle, regulate
2 ACCOMPANY, show, take, bring, escort, usher, lead, guide, direct, pilot, steer
3 *conduct heat*
convey, carry, bear, transmit
4 *conduct yourself*
behave, acquit, act
formal comport
▶ *n* **1** *good conduct*
behaviour, actions, ways, manners, bearing, practice, attitude
formal comportment, demeanour, deportment
2 ADMINISTRATION, management, direction, running, organization, operation, control, supervision, leadership, guidance

conduit *n*
channel, pipe, tunnel, passage, passageway, duct, tube, drain, gutter, culvert, ditch, flume, chute, watercourse, waterway, canal, main

confectionery *n*
sweets, chocolates, candy, toffees, rock, truffle, fudge, *Scot.* tablet, Turkish delight, bonbon

confederacy *n*
union, federation, alliance, coalition, confederation, league, partnership
formal compact

confederate *n, adj*
▶ *n* accomplice, ally, assistant, associate, colleague, friend, partner, supporter, collaborator, abettor, accessory, conspirator

▶ *adj* federate, federal, allied, associated, combined, united

confederation *n*
union, federation, alliance, association, coalition, amalgamation, confederacy, league, partnership
formal compact

confer *v*
1 DISCUSS, debate, deliberate, consult, talk, converse, exchange views
2 BESTOW, award, present, give (out), grant, accord, impart, lend

conference *n*
meeting, convention, congress, summit, symposium, forum, discussion, debate, consultation, dialogue, colloquium, seminar
formal convocation

confess *v*
admit, confide, own (up), accept blame, accept responsibility, grant, concede, acknowledge, recognize, affirm, assert, profess, declare, disclose, make known, divulge, expose, unbosom, unburden
colloq. come clean, make a clean breast of, get off your chest, come out with it, spill the beans, tell all
F3 deny, conceal

confession *n*
admission, acknowledgement, owning-up, affirmation, assertion, profession, declaration, disclosure, making known, divulgence, exposure, revelation, unbosoming, unburdening
F3 denial, concealment

confidant, confidante *n*
friend, close friend, bosom friend, intimate, companion
colloq. crony, pal, mate

confide *v*
confess, admit, tell a secret, reveal, disclose, divulge, whisper, breathe, tell, impart, intimate, unburden, unbosom, pour out your heart to
colloq. get off your chest
F3 hide, suppress, conceal

confidence *n*
1 *have confidence in someone*
TRUST, faith, reliance, dependence, credence, belief, conviction, certainty
2 SELF-ASSURANCE, assurance, composure, calmness, self-possession, self-confidence, self-reliance, self-assurance, belief in yourself, poise, boldness, courage
formal aplomb
3 SECRET, confidential matter, private matter, intimacy
F3 **1** distrust **2** diffidence
▷ **in confidence** privately, in privacy, in private, confidentially, in secret, personally, between ourselves, *entre nous,* behind closed doors, within these four walls; *colloq.* between you and me, between you me and the gatepost/bedpost
F3 openly

confident *adj*
1 *confident that it will happen*
sure, certain, positive, convinced, definite, unhesitating
2 *a confident person*
assured, sure of yourself, composed, self-possessed, calm, cool, self-confident, self-reliant, self-assured, unselfconscious, bold, courageous, fearless, positive,

optimistic, dauntless, unabashed
colloq. upbeat
≡ 1 doubtful **2** diffident, insecure

confidential *adj*
secret, top secret, classified, restricted, off-the-record,
private, personal, intimate, sensitive
old use privy
colloq. hush-hush

confidentially *adv*
privately, in privacy, in private, in confidence, in secret,
personally, between ourselves, *entre nous*, behind
closed doors, on the quiet, within these four walls
formal in camera
colloq. between you and me, between you me and the
gatepost/bedpost
≡ openly

configuration *n*
arrangement, composition, figure, form, outline,
shape, contour, cast
formal conformation, disposition

confine *v, n*
▶ *v* **1** *confine a disease; confine yourself to something*
restrict, limit, keep within limits, bound, bind,
constrain, control, fix, regulate
formal circumscribe
2 *confine in prison*
imprison, cage, enclose, shut (up), hold prisoner, hold
captive, hold in custody, intern, impound, keep in, lock
up/away, coop up, bind, shackle, trammel, restrain,
repress, inhibit
formal incarcerate, immure
≡ 1 derestrict **2** free
▶ *n* limit, limitation, restriction, scope, parameter,
bound, boundary, frontier, border, circumference,
perimeter, edge

confined *adj*
restricted, limited, narrow, constrained, controlled,
enclosed, housebound
formal circumscribed
≡ free, unrestricted

confinement *n*
1 IMPRISONMENT, internment, custody, detention,
captivity, house arrest
formal incarceration
2 CHILDBIRTH, birth, labour, delivery
technical parturition
≡ 1 freedom, liberty

confirm *v*
1 PROVE, corroborate, substantiate, verify, check,
validate, authenticate, give credence to, evidence,
demonstrate, endorse, back, support
2 ESTABLISH, fix, settle, ratify, sanction, approve,
authorize, warrant, endorse
colloq. clinch
3 *confirm that he will go*
affirm, assert, assure, pledge, promise, guarantee
formal asseverate, aver
4 *confirmed me in my decision*
strengthen, reinforce, harden, support, uphold
formal fortify
≡ 1 refute, deny

confirmation *n*
affirmation, validation, authentication,
corroboration, substantiation, verification, proof,
evidence, testimony, ratification, sanction, approval,
assent, acceptance, agreement, endorsement, backing,

support
formal accreditation
≡ denial

confirmed *adj*
inveterate, entrenched, dyed-in-the-wool, rooted,
fixed, set, established, long-established, long-
standing, habitual, chronic, through and through,
seasoned, hardened, incorrigible, incurable
formal inured

confiscate *v*
seize, remove, take away, take possession of, impound,
commandeer
formal appropriate, expropriate, arrogate, sequester
≡ return, restore

confiscation *n*
seizure, removal, takeover, impounding,
commandeering
formal appropriation, distrainment, distraint, escheat,
expropriation, sequestration, forfeiture
≡ restoration

conflagration *n*
blaze, fire, inferno, holocaust
formal deflagration

conflict *n, v*
▶ *n* **1** DISAGREEMENT, quarrel, dissension,
dispute, opposition, antagonism, hostility, friction,
strife, unrest, confrontation, feud, discord, contention,
ill-will, difference of opinion, variance, clash, row
formal antipathy
colloq. bust-up
2 BATTLE, war, warfare, combat, fight, contest,
engagement, skirmish, fracas, brawl, quarrel, feud,
encounter, row, clash
colloq. set-to, bust-up, scrap
≡ 1 agreement, harmony, concord
▶ *v* differ, clash, collide, disagree, be at variance, be at
loggerheads, be at odds, be inconsistent with,
contradict, oppose, be in opposition, contest, fight,
combat, battle, war, strive, struggle, contend
≡ agree, harmonize

confluence *n*
convergence, junction, meeting, meeting-point,
concurrence, union, watersmeet
formal conflux

conform *v*
1 *conform to a law*
obey, follow, comply, fall in with, observe, adapt,
adjust, accommodate
2 *conform in your behaviour*
follow, be conventional, be uniform, do the same thing
colloq. follow the crowd, go with the flow/stream, toe
the line, jump on the bandwagon
3 *conform to a pattern*
agree, accord, harmonize, match, correspond, tally,
square
≡ 1 disobey **2** rebel **3** differ, conflict

conformist *n*
conventionalist, traditionalist
colloq. yes-man, stick-in-the-mud, rubber-stamp
≡ bohemian, nonconformist

conformity *n*
1 *in conformity with the law*
compliance, observance, obedience, allegiance
adaptation, adjustment, accommodation, affinity,
agreement, harmony, correspondence, likeness,
similarity, resemblance

formal consonance, congruity
2 *conformity in behaviour*
conventionality, orthodoxy, traditionalism, uniformity
E3 1 disobedience **2** nonconformity, rebellion

confound *v*
1 CONFUSE, bewilder, baffle, perplex, mystify, puzzle, nonplus, surprise, startle, amaze, astonish, astound, dumbfound, stun, stupefy
formal discomfit
colloq. bamboozle, flabbergast, flummox
2 *confound their plans*
thwart, frustrate, upset, beat, defeat, overwhelm, overthrow, destroy, demolish, ruin

confront *v*
1 *confront a problem*
face, face up to, brave, tackle, address, deal with, cope with, contend with, reckon with, come to terms with
colloq. come to grips with, meet head on, face the music
2 *confront the enemy*
face, face up to, meet, encounter, stand up to, challenge, oppose, brave, defy, resist, withstand, attack, assault, accost
3 *confront him with the facts*
challenge, present, show

confrontation *n*
encounter, clash, conflict, collision, showdown, disagreement, fight, battle, quarrel, engagement, contest
colloq. set-to

confuse *v*
1 BEWILDER, baffle, perplex, mystify, confound, puzzle, bemuse, disorient, disconcert, fluster, discompose, upset, embarrass, mortify
colloq. throw, floor, tie in knots
2 MUDDLE, mix up, mistake, jumble, disarrange, disorder, tangle, entangle, involve, mingle
3 *to confuse matters further*
complicate, make more difficult, compound, elaborate, make difficult, involve, make involved,
E3 1 enlighten, clarify **3** simplify

confused *adj*
1 BEWILDERED, baffled, perplexed, mystified, confounded, puzzled, bemused, nonplussed, disconcerted, flustered, disorientated, dazed, unbalanced
colloq. flummoxed, floored, not knowing whether you are coming or going, up a gumtree, in a flat spin, in a flap, all at sea, like a headless chicken
2 MUDDLED, jumbled, disarranged, disordered, untidy, disorderly, chaotic, disorganized, mixed-up, out of order
colloq. higgledy-piggledy, at sixes and sevens, have your wires crossed; *slang* have your knickers in a twist
E3 2 orderly

confusing *adj*
puzzling, baffling, bewildering, muddling, perplexing, unclear, difficult, ambiguous, complicated, involved, contradictory, inconclusive, inconsistent, misleading, cryptic, tortuous
E3 clear, definite

confusion *n*
1 DISORDER, disarray, untidiness, mess, clutter, jumble, muddle, mix-up, disorganization, disarrangement, chaos, turmoil, commotion, upheaval
colloq. shambles
2 MISUNDERSTANDING, puzzlement, perplexity,

mystification, bewilderment, bafflement, muddle
E3 1 order **2** clarity

congeal *v*
clot, curdle, coalesce, coagulate, thicken, stiffen, harden, concentrate, fuse, solidify, set, cake, gel, freeze
E3 dissolve, melt, liquefy

congenial *adj*
agreeable, pleasant, pleasing, relaxing, delightful, favourable, friendly, companionable, genial, sympathetic, homely, compatible, complaisant, cosy, like-minded, suitable, well-suited
E3 disagreeable, unpleasant

congenital *adj*
1 *a congenital disease*
hereditary, inborn, inbred, inherited, innate, inherent, constitutional, natural
technical connate
2 *a congenital liar*
inveterate, entrenched, habitual, chronic, seasoned, hardened, incorrigible, incurable, complete, thorough, utter
formal inured

congested *adj*
1 *congested roads*
blocked, clogged, jammed, packed, stuffed, crammed, full, crowded, overcrowded, overflowing, teeming
2 *a congested nose*
blocked, clogged, choked
E3 1, 2 clear

congestion *n*
1 *congestion on the roads*
clogging, blockage, overcrowding, jam, traffic jam, snarl-up, gridlock, bottleneck
2 *nasal congestion*
clogging, blockage, blocking, choking

conglomerate *n*
corporation, multinational, merger, cartel, trust, consortium, company, firm, business, business organization, concern, association, partnership, corporation, establishment

conglomeration *n*
mass, agglomeration, aggregation, accumulation, collection, assemblage, composite, medley, hotchpotch

congratulate *v*
praise, compliment, say well done to, wish well, wish happiness to, send/offer good wishes to, send/off best wishes to
formal felicitate
colloq. take your hat off to, pat on the back
E3 commiserate

congratulations *n*
compliments, good wishes, best wishes, greetings
formal felicitations
colloq. pat on the back, bouquet(s)
E3 commiserations, condolences

congregate *v*
gather, assemble, collect, muster, rally, rendezvous, meet, convene, converge, flock, crowd, throng, form, mass, accumulate, cluster, clump
E3 disperse

congregation *n*
assembly, crowd, group, throng, mass, multitude, host, meeting, flock, parishioners, parish, laity, fellowship

congress n
assembly, conference, convention, council, legislature, meeting, gathering, forum, parliament, synod, diet
formal conclave, convocation

congruence n
correspondence, consistency, agreement, conformity, coincidence, harmony, compatibility, similarity, resemblance, identity, match, parallelism
formal concinnity, concurrence
E3 incongruity

conical adj
cone-shaped, pyramidal, pyramid-shaped, funnel-shaped, tapering, tapered, pointed
formal infundibular, infundibulate, turbinate

conjectural adj
hypothetical, assumed, surmised, tentative, theoretical, speculative, supposed, academic, suppositional
formal posited, postulated
E3 factual, real

conjecture v, n
▶ *v* speculate, theorize, hypothesize, guess, estimate, reckon, fancy, suppose, presuppose, surmise, assume, presume, infer, imagine, suspect
▶ *n* speculation, theory, hypothesis, fancy, notion, guesswork, guess, estimate, supposition, presupposition, surmise, suspicion, assumption, presumption, conclusion, inference, extrapolation, projection
colloq. guesstimate

conjugal adv
matrimonial, marital, nuptial, married, wedded, bridal
formal connubial, epithalamic, spousal, hymeneal

conjunction n
coincidence, co-occurrence, coexistence, combination, amalgamation, association, union, unification
formal concurrence, juxtaposition
▷ **in conjunction with** together with, with, along with, alongside, combined with, in partnership with, in collaboration with, in association with, in company with

conjure v
1 *conjuring at the children's party*
do tricks, perform tricks, do magic, perform magic
2 *conjure handkerchiefs from a hat*
summon, invoke, call up, evoke, make appear, rouse, raise, bewitch, charm, fascinate, compel
▷ **conjure up** evoke, create, produce, excite, awaken, recollect, recall, call/bring to mind

conjurer n
magician, illusionist, miracle-worker, sorcerer, wizard
formal prestidigitator, prestigiator, thaumaturge

conk v
▷ **conk out** break down, collapse, fail
colloq. pack up, go on the blink, go haywire

connect v
connect two objects; connected with the murder
join, link, unite, couple, bridge, combine, fasten, secure, affix, tie, clamp, fuse, attach, relate (to), correlate, associate, bracket, identify, ally
formal concatenate
E3 disconnect, cut off, detach

connected adj
joined, linked, united, coupled, tied, combined, fastened, secured, related, akin, associated, affiliated, allied
E3 disconnected, unconnected

connection n
1 *a connection between pipes; a connection between smoking and cancer*
junction, coupling, joint, fastening, attachment, clasp, bond, tie, link, association, alliance, relation, relationship, interrelation, contact, communication, parallel, correlation, analogy, correspondence, relevance, reference
2 *use your connections to get a job*
friend, acquaintance, relation, relative, contact, sponsor, person of influence, person of importance
E3 1 disconnection

connivance n
collusion, complicity, condoning, consent, abetment, abetting

connive v
1 *connive with someone to commit an offence*
collude, conspire, intrigue, plot, scheme
formal complot, cabal, coact
2 *connive at wrongdoing*
overlook, ignore, disregard, condone, tolerate, brook, let go, let pass, pass over, gloss over, allow, wink at
colloq. turn a blind eye to

conniving adj
scheming, colluding, conspiring, plotting, nasty, immoral, unscrupulous, corrupt

connoisseur n
authority, specialist, expert, judge, arbiter, pundit, specialist, devotee, aficionado, cognoscente, gourmet, gastronome, epicure, virtuoso, aesthete
colloq. buff

connotation n
implication, suggestion, intimation, hint, nuance, allusion, undertone, overtone, insinuation, colouring, association

connote v
imply, suggest, intimate, hint at, allude to, insinuate, signify, indicate, associate
formal import, purport, betoken

conquer v
1 *conquer an enemy/your fears*
DEFEAT, beat, overthrow, overpower, rout, crush, subdue, quell, overrun, best, get the better of, worst, get the better of, overcome, surmount, win, succeed, triumph over, prevail over, rise above, master, suppress, humble
formal vanquish, subjugate
colloq. trounce
2 SEIZE, take, annex, occupy, possess, take possession of, acquire, obtain, win
formal appropriate
E3 1 surrender, yield, give in

conqueror n
victor, winner, champion, hero, master, lord
formal vanquisher, subjugator, conquistador
colloq. champ

conquest n
1 *the conquest of the country*
victory, triumph, win, success, defeat, beating, overthrow, overpowering, coup, rout, crushing,

mastery, subjection, invasion, overrunning, possession, occupation, capture, seizing, annexation, acquisition
formal appropriation, subjugation, vanquishment
colloq. trouncing
2 *his latest conquest*
captive, lover, catch, acquisition

conscience *n*
principles, standards, morals, ethics, sense of right, sense of right and wrong, moral sense, moral code, still small voice, voice within, scruples, qualms

conscience-stricken *adj*
ashamed, sorry, contrite, guilt-ridden, guilty, penitent, regretful, remorseful, repentant, disturbed, troubled
formal compunctious
E3 unashamed, unrepentant

conscientious *adj*
diligent, hard-working, scrupulous, painstaking, methodical, thorough, meticulous, punctilious, dedicated, assiduous, particular, careful, attentive, responsible, upright, honest, faithful, dutiful
E3 careless, irresponsible, unreliable

conscious *adj*
1 AWAKE, alive, responsive, sensible, rational, reasoning, alert
formal sentient
2 AWARE, self-conscious, heedful, mindful, alert
formal cognizant, percipient, sensible
3 *a conscious effort to be polite*
deliberate, intentional, on purpose, calculated, premeditated, studied, knowing, wilful, voluntary
formal volitional
E3 **1** unconscious **2** unaware **3** involuntary, unintentional

consciousness *n*
1 *enter his consciousness*
awareness, mind, knowledge, intuition, perception, apprehension, realization, recognition
formal cognizance, sentience, sensibility
2 *lose consciousness*
being awake, wakefulness, awareness, alertness
E3 **2** unconsciousness

conscript *v, n*
▶ *v* recruit, enlist, draft, call up, take on, round up, muster
E3 volunteer
▶ *n* recruit, enlistee, draftee
E3 volunteer

consecrate *v*
sanctify, bless, anoint, hallow, make holy, dedicate, devote, vow, ordain, venerate, revere, exalt

consecutive *adj*
successive, sequential, serial, continuous, unbroken, uninterrupted, following, succeeding, running, one after the other, in turn, straight
formal seriate
colloq. on the trot, back to back
E3 discontinuous

consensus *n*
agreement, consent, harmony, majority view, unanimity, unity
formal concord, concurrence, consentience
E3 disagreement

consent *v, n*
▶ *v* agree, accept, approve, permit, allow, authorize,

grant, admit, concede, yield, go along with, comply
formal concur, assent, accede, acquiesce
colloq. give the go-ahead, give the green light, give the thumbs-up
E3 refuse, decline, oppose
▶ *n* agreement, acceptance, approval, authorization, permission, clearance, sanction, concession, compliance
formal concurrence, assent, acquiescence
colloq. go-ahead, green light
E3 disagreement, refusal, opposition
Related adjective: consensual

consequence *n*
1 RESULT, outcome, issue, end, upshot, effect, side effect, eventuality, implication, repercussion, reverberation
2 *of no consequence*
importance, significance, concern, value, weight, substance, note, eminence, prominence, distinction
formal import, moment
E3 **1** cause **2** unimportance, insignificance

consequent *adj*
resultant, resulting, ensuing, subsequent, following, successive, sequential

consequently *adv*
as a result, therefore, with the result that, so that, accordingly, consequentially, necessarily, subsequently, then
formal inferentially, ergo, hence, thus

conservation *n*
keeping, safe-keeping, custody, saving, care, economy, husbandry, maintenance, upkeep, preservation, protection, safeguarding, ecology, environmentalism
E3 destruction

conservatism *n*
conservativeness, conventionalism, orthodoxy, traditionalism
E3 radicalism

conservative *adj, n*
▶ *adj* **1** *conservative politicians*
Tory, right-wing, hidebound, die-hard, reactionary, establishmentarian
2 *conservative opinions/estimates*
unprogressive, conventional, traditional, traditionalist, orthodox, inflexible, set in your ways, moderate, middle-of-the-road, careful, cautious, guarded, sober
E3 **1** left-wing, radical **2** innovative
▶ *n* Tory, right-winger, die-hard, stick-in-the-mud, reactionary, traditionalist, moderate
E3 left-winger, radical

conservatory *n*
1 *grow plants in the conservatory*
greenhouse, glasshouse, hothouse
2 *study music at the conservatory*
conservatoire, school, college, academy, institute, music school, drama college

conserve *v*
keep, keep back, keep in reserve, save, store up, hoard, maintain, preserve, protect, take care of, guard, safeguard
E3 use, waste, squander

consider *v*
1 PONDER, deliberate, reflect, contemplate, meditate, muse, mull over, examine, study, weigh (up), respect, remember, note, make a mental note of, give thought

to, bear/keep in mind, take into account/consideration
formal cogitate, ruminate
colloq. chew over, toy with
2 *consider it an honour*
regard as, think, believe, judge, rate, count, hold, feel
formal deem

considerable *adj*
great, large, big, sizable, substantial, ample, plentiful, abundant, lavish, generous, marked, noticeable, perceptible, appreciable, reasonable, tolerable, respectable, important, significant, noteworthy, distinguished, influential
colloq. tidy
FͿ small, slight, insignificant, unremarkable

considerably *adv*
significantly, substantially, greatly, markedly, much, noticeably, remarkably, appreciably, abundantly
FͿ slightly

considerate *adj*
kind, thoughtful, caring, attentive, obliging, helpful, charitable, unselfish, concerned, selfless, altruistic, gracious, sympathetic, compassionate, generous, sensitive, tactful, discreet, solicitous
FͿ inconsiderate, thoughtless, selfish

consideration *n*
1 THOUGHT, deliberation, reflection, contemplation, meditation, examination, analysis, scrutiny, review, inspection, attention, notice, heed, regard, reckoning, account
formal cogitation, rumination
2 KINDNESS, thoughtfulness, care, attention, regard, respect, helpfulness, unselfishness, concern, selflessness, altruism, graciousness, sympathy, compassion, generosity, sensitivity, tact, discretion
3 *the cost is a major consideration*
fact, circumstance, factor, issue, point
FͿ **1** disregard **2** thoughtlessness

considering *prep*
1 *considering her age*
taking into account/consideration, bearing in mind, making allowances for, in view of, in the light of
2 *he's very well, considering*
all things considered, all in all

consign *v*
entrust, assign, commend, commit, devote, hand over, give over, transfer, transmit, deliver, convey, ship, banish, relegate

consignment *n*
cargo, shipment, load, batch, delivery, goods

consist *v*
1 *a jury consists of twelve people*
comprise, be composed of, be made up of, contain, include, incorporate, embody, be formed of, embrace, involve, amount to
2 *the poem's beauty consists in its simplicity*
inhere, lie, reside, be contained, have as its main feature

consistency *n*
1 *the consistency of the porridge*
thickness, density, firmness, cohesion, smoothness
technical viscosity
2 STEADINESS, regularity, evenness, uniformity, sameness, identity, constancy, steadfastness, stability, persistence, dependability, reliability, unchangeableness, lack of change
3 AGREEMENT, accordance, correspondence,

compatibility, harmony
formal congruity, consonance
FͿ **3** inconsistency

consistent *adj*
1 STEADY, stable, regular, uniform, unchanging, undeviating, constant, same, persistent, unfailing, dependable
2 *not consistent with his colleague's version*
agreeing, compatible, corresponding, coinciding, matching, harmonious, conforming, logical
formal accordant, consonant, congruous
FͿ **1** irregular, erratic **2** inconsistent

consolation *n*
comfort, cheer, encouragement, help, support, reassurance, aid, sympathy, commiseration, relief, ease, soothing, alleviation
formal solace, succour, assuagement
FͿ discouragement

console[1] *v*
console the bereaved
comfort, cheer, hearten, encourage, help, support, reassure, sympathize with, commiserate with, relieve, soothe, calm
formal solace, succour
FͿ upset, agitate

console[2] *n*
an instrument console
panel, control panel, board, dashboard, keyboard, instruments, controls, switches, knobs, dials, buttons, levers

consolidate *v*
1 *consolidate power/support*
reinforce, strengthen, make strong(er), secure, make (more) secure, stabilize, make (more) stable, cement
formal fortify
2 *consolidate businesses*
unite, join, combine, amalgamate, merge, unify, fuse

consolidation *n*
1 *consolidation of power*
reinforcement, strengthening, securing, stabilization, cementing
formal fortification
2 *consolidation of businesses*
uniting, joining, combination, amalgamation, merger, unification, affiliation, alliance, association, confederation, federation, fusion

consonance *n*
compatibility, agreement, consistency, conformity, correspondence, harmony, suitability
formal accordance, congruity, concord
FͿ dissonance

consonant *adj*
compatible, consistent, correspondent, conforming, harmonious, in harmony, agreeing, suitable, in accordance, according
formal accordant, congruous
FͿ dissonant

consort *n, v*
▶ *n* partner, companion, associate, escort, spouse, husband, wife
▶ *v* associate, spend time, keep company, fraternize, mingle, mix

consortium *n*
partnership, confederation, federation, association, affiliation, coalition, league, corporation, company,

bloc, cartel, conglomerate, alliance, organization, syndicate, guild, union, marriage, agreement, compact, bond, pact, treaty, combination

conspicuous *adj*
apparent, visible, noticeable, easily seen/noticed, marked, clear, obvious, evident, recognizable, observable, discernible, perceptible, patent, manifest, prominent, striking, blatant, flagrant, glaring, ostentatious, showy, flashy, garish
colloq. standing out a mile
⊟ inconspicuous, concealed, hidden

conspiracy *n*
plot, scheme, intrigue, stratagem, league, cabal, collusion, collaboration, connivance, treason
formal machination
colloq. fix, frame-up

conspirator *n*
conspirer, plotter, schemer, intriguer, colluder, collaborator, traitor

conspire *v*
1 *conspire to oust the president*
plot, hatch a plot, scheme, intrigue, manoeuvre, connive, collude, collaborate
formal machinate
2 *events conspiring for their harm*
combine, join, join forces, work/act together, connect, link, unite, ally, associate, co-operate

constancy *n*
1 STABILITY, steadiness, permanence, unchangeability, firmness, regularity, uniformity
2 LOYALTY, faithfulness, fidelity, devotion, steadfastness, dependability, trustworthiness, firmness, steadiness, persistence, resolution, perseverance, tenacity
⊟ 1 change, irregularity 2 fickleness

constant *adj*
1 *a constant barrage of questions*
CONTINUAL, unbroken, never-ending, non-stop, endless, interminable, incessant, eternal, everlasting, perpetual, persistent, chronic, continuous, unremitting, uninterrupted, unbroken, without respite, relentless, unflagging, unwavering
formal ceaseless
2 *his temperature is constant*
stable, steady, unchanging, unvarying, changeless, invariable, unalterable, permanent, firm, even, regular, uniform
formal immutable
3 *a constant friend*
loyal, faithful, staunch, steadfast, dependable, trustworthy, true, devoted, firm, steady, persistent, resolute, persevering
1 fitful, occasional 2 variable, irregular 3 disloyal, fickle

constantly *adv*
always, continually, all the time, for ever, permanently, continuously, endlessly, non-stop, everlastingly, incessantly, interminably, invariably, perpetually, relentlessly, ad nauseam
formal ceaselessly
⊟ occasionally

constellation *n*

The constellations (with common English names) are: Andromeda, Antlia (Air Pump), Apus (Bird of Paradise), Aquarius (Water Bearer), Aquila (Eagle), Ara (Altar), Aries (Ram), Auriga (Charioteer), Boötes (Herdsman), Caelum (Chisel), Camelopardalis (Giraffe), Cancer (Crab), Canes Venatici (Hunting Dogs), Canis Major (Great Dog), Canis Minor (Little Dog), Capricornus (Sea Goat), Carina (Keel), Cassiopeia, Centaurus (Centaur), Cepheus, Cetus (Whale), Chamaeleon (Chameleon), Circinus (Compasses), Columba (Dove), Coma Berenices (Berenice's Hair), Corona Australis (Southern Crown), Corona Borealis (Northern Crown), Corvus (Crow), Crater (Cup), Crux (Southern Cross), Cygnus (Swan), Delphinus (Dolphin), Dorado (Swordfish), Draco (Dragon), Equuleus (Little Horse), Eridanus (River Eridanus), Fornax (Furnace), Gemini (Twins), Grus (Crane), Hercules, Horologium (Clock), Hydra (Sea Serpent), Hydrus (Water Snake), Indus (Indian), Lacerta (Lizard), Leo (Lion), Leo Minor (Little Lion), Lepus (Hare), Libra (Scales), Lupus (Wolf), Lynx, Lyra (Harp), Mensa (Table), Microscopium (Microscope), Monoceros (Unicorn), Musca (Fly), Norma (Level), Octans (Octant), Ophiuchus (Serpent Bearer), Orion, Pavo (Peacock), Pegasus (Winged Horse), Perseus, Phoenix, Pictor (Easel), Pisces (Fishes), Piscis Austrinus (Southern Fish), Puppis (Ship's Stern), Pyxis (Mariner's Compass), Reticulum (Net), Sagitta (Arrow), Sagittarius (Archer), Scorpius (Scorpion), Sculptor, Scutum (Shield), Serpens (Serpent), Sextans (Sextant), Taurus (Bull), Telescopium (Telescope), Triangulum (Triangle), Triangulum Australe (Southern Triangle), Tucana (Toucan), Ursa Major (Great Bear), Ursa Minor (Little Bear), Vela (Sails), Virgo (Virgin), Volans (Flying Fish), Vulpecula (Fox). *See also* **star**.

consternation *n*
alarm, dismay, anxiety, fear distress, dread, horror, fright, shock, terror, panic, awe, bewilderment
formal disquietude, perturbation, trepidation
⊟ composure

constituent *n, adj*
▶ *n* 1 *voting by constituents*
elector, voter
2 *the constituents of the mixture*
ingredient, element, factor, principle, component, component part, part, content, bit, section, unit
⊟ 2 whole
▶ *adj* component, integral, essential, basic, intrinsic, inherent

constitute *v*
1 *six counties constitute the province*
comprise, make up, form, compose
2 *his remarks constitute a challenge to the leadership*
be, represent, mean, form, make, be equivalent to, amount to, add up to, be tantamount to, be regarded as
3 *constitute a committee*
form, create, establish, set up, found, institute, appoint, authorize, commission, charter, empower

constitution *n*
1 *a country's constitution*
laws, rules, statutes, basic principles, code, charter, codified law, bill of rights
2 *the constitution of the committee*
COMPOSITION, make-up, structure, organization, formation
formal configuration

3 HEALTH, condition, physique, physical condition, make-up, disposition, temperament, character, nature

constitutional *adj, n*
▶ *adj* statutory, by law, according to the law, legal, legitimate, lawful, legislative, governmental, authorized, vested, codified, ratified
▶ *n* walk, stroll, saunter, amble, promenade, turn, airing

constrain *v*
1 *feel constrained to tell the whole truth*
FORCE, compel, coerce, oblige, necessitate, drive, impel, pressurize, pressure, urge
2 *constrained by responsibilities*
LIMIT, confine, constrict, restrain, check, curb, bind, restrict, hinder, hold back

constrained *adj*
uneasy, embarrassed, inhibited, reticent, reserved, guarded, stiff, forced, unnatural
E3 relaxed, free

constraint *n*
1 FORCE, duress, compulsion, coercion, pressure, necessity, obligation, demand, insistence
2 RESTRICTION, limitation, hindrance, restraint, check, curb, damper, impediment

constrict *v*
1 *constrict an air passage*
squeeze, compress, pinch, cramp, narrow, make narrow, tighten, contract, shrink, choke, strangle, strangulate
2 *constricted by lower budgets*
limit, restrict, confine, constrain, check, curb, bind, hinder, impede, hold back, obstruct, hamper, inhibit
E3 1 expand

constriction *n*
1 *feel a constriction in the chest*
squeezing, narrowing, pressure, tightness, tightening, compression, cramp, blockage
technical stricture, stenosis
formal constringency
2 *constrictions in the budget*
restriction, constraint, limitation, reduction, check, curb, hindrance, impediment
E3 1 expansion

construct *v*
1 *construct a building*
build, erect, raise, elevate, make, manufacture, fabricate, assemble, establish, put up, set up
2 *construct a theory*
compose, form, put together, shape, fashion, fabricate, model, devise, design, engineer, create, found, establish, formulate
E3 1 demolish, destroy

construction *n*
1 *houses under construction*
building, erection, fabrication, assembly, elevation, making, manufacture, establishment
2 *the cathedral is a magnificent construction*
structure, building, edifice, assembly, fabric, form, shape, framework, figure, model
3 *the construction put on his remarks*
INTERPRETATION, meaning, inference, deduction, reading
E3 1 demolition, destruction

constructive *adj*
practical, productive, positive, helpful, useful,

valuable, beneficial, advantageous
E3 destructive, negative, unhelpful

construe *v*
interpret, explain, understand, see as, regard as, read, render, take to mean, deduce, infer, analyse
formal expound

consult *v*
1 *consult an expert*
ask/seek advice, ask/seek information, ask someone's opinion, question, interrogate, turn to
colloq. pick someone's brains
2 *consult with business partners*
confer, discuss, debate, deliberate
3 *consult a map*
look up, refer to, turn to

consultant *n*
adviser, expert, authority, specialist

consultation *n*
discussion, deliberation, talk, dialogue, conference, meeting, hearing, interview, examination, appointment, forum, session

consultative *adj*
advisory, advising, consulting, counselling, helping, recommending
formal consultatory

consume *v*
1 EAT, eat up, drink (up), swallow, devour, gobble, take
formal ingest
colloq. tuck in, guzzle, scoff, polish off, touch
2 USE UP, absorb, spend, get through, go through, drain, exhaust, use, squander, waste, fritter away
formal deplete, dissipate, expend, utilize
3 DESTROY, demolish, annihilate, devastate, gut, ravage, lay waste
4 *consumed with jealousy*
devour, dominate, absorb, engross, preoccupy, grip, obsess, monopolize, overwhelm, torment
colloq. eat up

consumer *n*
user, end-user, customer, buyer, purchaser, shopper, patron, client

consuming *adj*
dominating, compelling, absorbing, preoccupying, devouring, engrossing, gripping, obsessive, immoderate, monopolizing, overwhelming, tormenting

consummate *adj, v*
▶ *adj* absolute, complete, total, utter, perfect, supreme superior, ultimate, superb, transcendent, unqualified, skilled, accomplished, gifted, practised, proficient, distinguished, matchless, polished
E3 imperfect
▶ *v* perfect, accomplish, fulfil, realize, complete, perform, achieve, crown, cap, end, finish, conclude
formal terminate, execute, effectuate

consummation *n*
perfection, accomplishment, fulfilment, realization, completion, performance, achievement, culmination, crowning, capping, end, finish, conclusion
formal termination, execution, actualization, effectuation

consumption *n*
1 EATING, drinking, swallowing, devouring
formal ingestion
colloq. tucking-in, guzzling, scoffing

2 USING-UP, absorption, spending, getting-through, going-through, draining, exhaustion, squandering, waste
formal depletion, expending, expenditure, utilization

contact *n, v*
▶ *n* **1** *in contact with an object*
touching, touch, impact, meeting, junction, union, proximity
formal juxtaposition, contiguity
2 *in contact with old friends*
touch, communication, connection, association
3 *use your contacts to get a job*
friend, acquaintance, relation, relative, connection, sponsor, person of influence, person of importance, network of contacts
▶ *v* approach, get onto, apply to, reach, get hold of, get in touch with, get through to, communicate with, notify, write to, speak to, telephone, phone, ring, call, fax

contagious *adj*
1 *a contagious disease*
infectious, catching, communicable, transmissible, transmittable, spreading, epidemic, pandemic
2 *contagious laughter*
infectious, compelling, irresistible, catching, spreading

contain *v*
1 INCLUDE, take in, comprise, incorporate, embody, involve, embrace, enclose, have inside, hold, carry, take, accommodate, seat
2 *contain your feelings*
repress, suppress, stifle, restrain, control, keep under control, keep back, hold in, check, keep in check, curb, limit, stop, prevent from spreading
⊟ **1** exclude

container *n*
receptacle, vessel, holder
formal repository

Types of container include: bag, barrel, basin, basket, bath, beaker, bin, bottle, bowl, box, bucket, can, canister, carton, case, cask, casket, cauldron, chest, churn, cistern, crate, crock, cup, cylinder, dish, drum, dustbin, glass, hamper, jar, jug, keg, kettle, locker, mug, pack, packet, pail, pan, pannier, pitcher, pot, punnet, purse, sack, suitcase, tank, tea caddy, tea chest, teapot, tin, trough, trunk, tub, tube, tumbler, tureen, urn, vase, vat, waste bin, waste-paper basket, water-butt, well. *See also* **box**[1].

contaminate *v*
infect, pollute, decay, adulterate, taint, soil, sully, defile, corrupt, harm, foul, spoil, make impure, deprave, debase, stain, tarnish
formal vitiate
⊟ purify

contamination *n*
infection, pollution, decay, adulteration, taint, soiling, sullying, defilement, desecration, corruption, harm, foulness, rottenness, spoiling, filth, impurity, debasement, stain, tarnish
formal vitiation
⊟ purification

contemplate *v*
1 *contemplate leaving; contemplate the meaning of life*
CONSIDER, think about, deliberate, reflect on, ponder, meditate, muse, mull over, dwell, examine,

study, weigh (up), turn over in your mind, have in mind/view, expect, foresee, envisage, plan, design, propose, intend
formal cogitate, ruminate
2 *contemplate the view*
look at, regard, view, observe, scrutinize, survey, examine, inspect

contemplation *n*
1 *religious contemplation*
CONSIDERATION, thought, deliberation, reflection, pondering, meditation, musing, mulling-over, dwell, examination, study, weighing (up)
formal cogitation, rumination, cerebration
2 *contemplation of the view*
gazing, regard, view, observation, scrutiny, survey, examination, inspection

contemplative *adj*
thoughtful, reflective, meditative, introspective, musing, pensive, rapt, intent, deep in thought
formal cerebral, ruminative
⊟ impulsive, thoughtless

contemporary *adj*
1 MODERN, current, present, present-day, present-time, today's, topical, recent, latest, up-to-date, fashionable, up-to-the-minute, ultra-modern, avant-garde, futuristic
colloq. trendy, new-fangled, with it
2 CONTEMPORANEOUS, coexistent, synchronous, simultaneous
formal concurrent, coetaneous, coeval
⊟ **1** out-of-date, old-fashioned

contempt *n*
scorn, disdain, condescension, derision, ridicule, mockery, disrespect, dishonour, disregard, neglect, dislike, loathing, hatred
formal detestation, contumely
⊟ respect, admiration, regard

contemptible *adj*
despicable, shameful, low, mean, vile, base, detestable, lamentable, loathsome, abject, wretched, degenerate, unworthy, pitiful, paltry, worthless
formal ignominious
⊟ admirable, honourable

contemptuous *adj*
scornful, disdainful, sneering, supercilious, condescending, disdainful, arrogant, haughty, high and mighty, cynical, derisive, derisory, insulting, mocking, jeering, disrespectful, insolent, withering
formal contumelious
⊟ respectful, polite, humble

contend *v*
1 *contend with a problem*
deal, cope, grapple face, face up to, brave, tackle, address, reckon, come to terms
colloq. come to grips, meet head on
2 MAINTAIN, state, hold, argue, allege, assert, declare, affirm, profess, claim
formal aver, asseverate
3 COMPETE, vie, contest, dispute, clash, wrestle, grapple, struggle, strive, tussle, oppose, challenge, fight, battle, combat, war

content[1] *n*
1 *the contents of the package*
constituents, parts, elements, ingredients, components, component parts, load, items, what is contained, things inside

2 *the contents of the book*
CHAPTER, division, section, subject, subject matter, topic, theme
3 SUBSTANCE, matter, material, essence, gist, meaning, significance, text, theme, subject matter, ideas, contents, load, burden
4 CAPACITY, volume, size, measure

content^2 *adj, n, v*
▶ *adj* *content with the arrangements*
satisfied, fulfilled, contented, comfortable, unworried, untroubled, pleased, happy, glad, cheerful, willing, at ease
F∃ dissatisfied, troubled
▶ *n* comfort, contentment, satisfaction, fulfilment, delight, pleasure, happiness, gladness, cheerfulness, peace, peacefulness, ease, serenity, gratification
formal equanimity
F∃ discontent
▶ *v* satisfy, humour, indulge, gratify, please, be happy, be pleased, be glad, delight, appease, pacify, placate
F∃ displease

contented *adj*
happy, glad, pleased, cheerful, comfortable, relaxed, content, satisfied, fulfilled, unworried, untroubled
F∃ discontented, troubled, unhappy, annoyed

contention *n*
1 *it is my contention that …*
belief, contention, opinion, persuasion, feeling, intuition, impression, notion, theory, view, viewpoint, point of view, thesis, conviction, claim, judgement, stand, position, assertion, argument
2 *a matter of contention*
disagreement, argument, controversy, dispute, debate, discord, dissension, enmity, feuding, hostility, strife, struggle, rivalry, wrangling

contentious *adj*
1 *a contentious issue*
controversial, polemical, disputed, doubtful, questionable, debatable, disputable
2 *a contentious person*
argumentative, antagonistic, quarrelsome, hostile, perverse, querulous, bickering, captious
formal pugnacious
F∃ **1** uncontroversial **2** co-operative, peaceable

contentment *n*
contentedness, happiness, gladness, cheerfulness, pleasure, gratification, comfort, ease, complacency, peace, peacefulness, serenity, equanimity, content, satisfaction, gratification, fulfilment
F∃ unhappiness, discontent, dissatisfaction

contest *n, v*
▶ *n* competition, game, match, race, championship, tournament, event, encounter, fight, battle, combat, conflict, struggle, skirmish, combat, dispute, vying, debate, controversy
colloq. set-to
▶ *v* **1** DISPUTE, debate, question, call into question, doubt, challenge, oppose, argue against, deny, refute
technical litigate
2 COMPETE, be in competition with, vie, contend, strive, struggle, fight, battle, try to beat, tussle
F∃ **1** accept

contestant *n*
competitor, contender, player, participant, entrant, candidate, aspirant, rival, opponent, adversary

context *n*
background, setting, surroundings, framework, frame of reference, state of affairs, situation, general situation, position, circumstances, factors, conditions

contiguous *adj*
adjacent, adjoining, touching, beside, bordering, near, close, neighbouring, next, tangential
technical vicinal
formal abutting, conjoining, conterminous, juxtaposed, juxtapositional

continent *n*
mainland, terra firma

> *The continents of the world are*: Africa, Antarctica, Asia, Australia, Europe, North America, South America.

contingency *n*
eventuality, possibility, accident, randomness, arbitrariness, chance, chance event, emergency, event, happening, incident, uncertainty
formal fortuity, juncture

contingent *n, adj*
▶ *n* body, company, deputation, delegation, mission, representatives, detachment, section, division, group, set, batch, quota, party, complement
▶ *adj* dependent, conditional, subject, based, relative

continual *adj*
constant, perpetual, incessant, interminable, eternal, everlasting, regular, frequent, recurrent, repeated, repetitive, persistent
F∃ occasional, intermittent, temporary

> ⚠ **continual** or **continuous** ?
> *Continual* means 'very frequent, happening again and again': *I've had continual interruptions all morning. Continuous* means 'without a pause or break': *continuous rain.*

continually *adv*
constantly, perpetually, incessantly, interminably, forever, eternally, everlastingly, always, endlessly, non-stop, regularly, frequently, recurrently, repeatedly, persistently, habitually, all the time
formal ceaselessly
F∃ occasionally, intermittently

continuance *n*
continuation, duration, endurance, period, term, permanence, persistence
formal protraction

continuation *n*
1 *continuation after a pause*
resumption, recommencement, starting again, renewal, maintenance, development, furtherance, addition, supplement, sequel
2 *the continuation of the road*
prolongation, lengthening, extension
formal protraction
F∃ **1** *formal* cessation, termination

continue *v*
1 *continue doing something*
go on, carry on, not stop, keep on (with), proceed, persist in, persevere in, progress, press on
colloq. stick at, soldier on
2 *the course continues next term*
resume, recommence, renew, proceed (again), start

again, begin again, take up again, carry on, go on
colloq. pick up the threads, pick up where you have left off
3 *if the storm continues*
last, endure, remain, abide, survive, hold out, stay, rest, pursue, sustain, maintain, lengthen, prolong, extend, persist, keep on, project
4 *'I'm not sure,' she continued*
start talking again, resume, go on
5 *continue on your way*
keep going, keep travelling, keep walking, keep moving, keep on, carry on
E3 **1, 2, 3, 4** stop

continuity *n*
flow, progression, succession, sequence, linkage, interrelationship, connection, cohesion, continuousness, uninterruptedness, unchangeableness
E3 discontinuity

continuous *adj*
unbroken, uninterrupted, consecutive, non-stop, not stopping, without a break, endless, ceaseless, unending, never-ending, solid, unceasing, interminable, constant, unremitting, prolonged, extended, continued, lasting
colloq. with no let-up
E3 discontinuous, broken, sporadic

⚠ **continuous** or **continual** ?
See panel at **continual.**

contort *v*
twist, distort, warp, wrench, disfigure, deform, misshape, bend out of shape, gnarl, knot, writhe, squirm, wriggle
formal convolute

contortionist *n*
acrobat, gymnast, tumbler, balancer, somersaulter, trapeze artist, rope-walker, rope-dancer, stuntman, stuntwoman
formal funambulist, aerialist, equilibrist

contour *n*
outline, silhouette, shape, form, figure, curve, lines, relief, profile, character, aspect

contraband *n*
banned/black-market goods, smuggling, forbidden/ illegal traffic, bootlegging, prohibited/unlawful goods
formal proscribed goods
colloq. hot goods

contraceptive *n*

Contraceptives and other forms of birth control include: barrier contraceptive, barrier method, cervical cap, coil, coitus interruptus, condom, contraceptive ring, contraceptive sponge, diaphragm, Dutch cap, female condom, Femidom®, *slang* French letter, injectable contraceptive, intrauterine device (IUD), *slang* johnnie, loop, minipill, morning-after pill, oral contraceptive, pill, *US* prophylactic, protective, rhythm method, *slang* rubber, sheath, spermicide, vaginal ring, withdrawal method.

contract *v, n*
▶ *v* **1** SHRINK, lessen, diminish, reduce, decrease, shorten, become shorter, become smaller, curtail, abbreviate, abridge, condense, compress, constrict,

narrow, tighten, tense, draw in, shrivel, wrinkle
2 *contract pneumonia*
catch, get, go/come down with, develop, pick up, become infected with, become ill with
formal succumb to
3 PLEDGE, promise, undertake, engage, agree, stipulate, arrange, agree terms, settle, negotiate, bargain
E3 **1** expand, enlarge, lengthen
▶ *n* agreement, bond, commitment, engagement, covenant, treaty, convention, pact, transaction, deal, bargain, settlement, arrangement, understanding
formal compact, concordat

contraction *n*
1 *'Don't' is a contraction of 'do not'*
abbreviation, shortening, shortened form, abridgement
2 *the contraction of muscles*
constriction, compression, narrowing, tightening, tensing, drawing-in, shrivelling, shrinkage, lessening, reduction, curtailment
technical astringency
E3 **2** expansion, growth

contradict *v*
1 *contradict someone*
deny, challenge, oppose, dispute, rebut, counter, go against
formal disaffirm, confute, refute, impugn, gainsay
2 *one statement contradicts another*
disagree, clash, conflict, contrast, go against, be at variance, be at odds, be in conflict, be inconsistent with
formal negate
colloq. fly in the face of
E3 **1, 2** agree **2** confirm; *formal* corroborate

contradiction *n*
1 *the contradiction between theory and practice*
clash, variance, odds, conflict, inconsistency, disagreement, paradox
formal incongruity, negation, antithesis
2 *contradiction of an earlier report*
denial, challenge, opposition, dispute, rebuttal, counter-argument
formal disaffirmance, disaffirmation, confutation, refutation
E3 **1, 2** agreement

contradictory *adj*
contrary, opposite, opposing, paradoxical, conflicting, clashing, inconsistent, incompatible, antagonistic, irreconcilable, opposed
formal discrepant, dissentient, repugnant, incongruous, antithetical
E3 consistent

contraption *n*
contrivance, device, gadget, apparatus, rig, machine, mechanism, invention
colloq. thingumajig

contrary *adj, n*
▶ *adj* **1** OPPOSITE, counter, reverse, conflicting, clashing, inconsistent, incompatible, irreconcilable, antagonistic, opposed, opposing, adverse, hostile
2 PERVERSE, awkward, disobliging, difficult, wayward, obstinate, headstrong, intractable, cantankerous
formal refractory
colloq. stroppy
E3 **1** like **2** obliging
▶ *n* opposite, converse, reverse

formal antithesis
▷ **on the contrary** quite/just the reverse, quite/just the opposite

contrast *n, v*
▶ *n* difference, dissimilarity, divergence, distinction, differentiation, comparison, foil, opposite, opposition, relief
formal disparity, dissimilitude, antithesis
F3 similarity, resemblance
▶ *v* **1** *contrast two people*
compare, differentiate, distinguish, discriminate
2 *her expression contrasted sharply with her dress*
disagree, contradict, clash, conflict, differ, oppose, go against, be at variance, be at odds, be in conflict, be inconsistent with
▷ **in contrast to** as distinguished from, opposed to, in opposition to, rather than, as against

contravene *v*
infringe, violate, break, breach, disobey, defy, flout
formal transgress
F3 uphold, observe, obey

contretemps *n*
clash, brush, tiff, difficulty, accident, misadventure, misfortune, mishap, hitch, predicament

contribute *v*
1 *contribute money to charity*
give, donate, give a donation, subscribe, grant, present, endow, provide, supply, furnish
formal bestow
colloq. chip in
2 *poor design contributed to the disaster*
cause, play a part in, give rise to, lead to, result in, occasion, bring about, make, make happen, produce, generate, originate, create, promote, help, add to, be instrumental in
formal conduce
3 *contribute an article for a magazine*
write, compose, create, compile, prepare, edit, supply, provide

contribution *n*
1 *a contribution of £1000*
donation, subscription, gift, gratuity, handout, grant, present, endowment, offering, input, addition
formal bestowal
2 *a contribution to a magazine*
article, story, feature, item, piece, column, report, review

contributor *n*
1 DONOR, subscriber, giver, patron, benefactor, sponsor, backer, supporter
2 WRITER, author, journalist, reporter, compiler, correspondent, reviewer, critic, columnist, freelance

contrite *adj*
sorry, regretful, remorseful, repentant, penitent, penitential, guilt-ridden, conscience-stricken, chastened, humble, ashamed

contrition *n*
remorse, sorrow, regret, shame, humiliation, penitence, repentance, sackcloth and ashes, self-reproach
formal compunction

contrivance *n*
1 INVENTION, device, contraption, gadget, implement, appliance, machine, mechanism, tool, apparatus, equipment, gear

2 STRATAGEM, ploy, trick, dodge, ruse, expedient, plan, design, project, scheme, plot, intrigue
formal machination, artifice

contrive *v*
1 *somehow contrived to blame me*
manage, succeed, arrange, bring about, create, design, devise, find a way
2 *contrive a meeting between them*
engineer, manoeuvre, orchestrate, stage-manage, plan, plot, scheme, fabricate, create, devise, invent, concoct, construct
colloq. set up, wangle

contrived *adj*
unnatural, artificial, false, forced, strained, laboured, mannered, elaborate, overdone
colloq. set-up
F3 natural, genuine, spontaneous

control *n, v*
▶ *n* **1** POWER, charge, authority, command, mastery, dominance, sway, supremacy, government, rule, reign, direction, management, oversight, supervision, superintendence, discipline, guidance, influence
formal jurisdiction
2 RESTRAINT, self-restraint, self-control, self-discipline, constraint, check, curb, repression
3 *price controls*
restriction, constraint, limitation, regulation, limit, reduction, brake, check, curb, hindrance, impediment
4 INSTRUMENT, dial, switch, button, knob, lever
▶ *v* **1** LEAD, be in charge of, have authority over, govern, rule, command, direct, manage, head, oversee, preside over, dominate, supervise, superintend
colloq. be the boss, be in the driving seat, be in the saddle, pull the strings, rule the roost, run the show, call the tune/shots, wear the trousers
2 *control a machine/the temperature*
run, operate, work, make go, regulate, adjust, monitor, verify
3 *control wages*
restrict, limit, regulate, constrain, reduce, check, curb
colloq. keep a tight rein on, put the brakes on
4 *control your temper*
restrain, check, curb, subdue, repress, hold back, keep, contain

controversial *adj*
contentious, polemical, disputed, doubtful, questionable, debatable, disputable, at issue

controversy *n*
debate, discussion, war of words, difference of opinion, dispute, disagreement, argument, quarrel, squabble, wrangle, strife, contention, discord, friction, dissension
formal polemic, altercation
F3 accord, agreement
Related adjective: eristic

contusion *n*
bruise, bump, discoloration, mark, blemish, injury, knock, lump, swelling
technical ecchymosis

conundrum *n*
puzzle, problem, enigma, poser, riddle, word game, anagram, brainteaser

convalescence *n*
recuperation, getting better, improvement, recovery, rehabilitation, restoration

convene *v*
1 *convene a meeting*
call (together), rally, summon
2 *the court convened*
assemble, meet, gather, collect, congregate, muster
formal convoke

convenience *n*
1 ACCESSIBILITY, availability, handiness, usefulness, use, ease of use, utility, serviceability, service, benefit, advantage, advantageousness, help, suitability, fitness, appropriateness, opportuneness
formal expediency, propitiousness, propinquity
2 *all modern conveniences*
facility, amenity, appliance, device, labour-saving device, gadget, service, resource
F3 1 inconvenience

convenient *adj*
nearby, at hand, near/close at hand, within reach, within walking/driving distance, accessible, available, handy, useful, beneficial, helpful, labour-saving, adapted, fitted, suited, suitable, fit, fitting, appropriate, opportune, timely, well-timed
formal expedient
colloq. just/only round the corner, at your fingertips
F3 inconvenient, awkward

convention *n*
1 CUSTOM, tradition, practice, usage, protocol, etiquette, formality, matter of form, code
formal propriety, punctilio
2 ASSEMBLY, congress, conference, meeting, gathering, council, delegates, representatives, synod
formal convocation, conclave
3 *the Geneva convention*
agreement, bond, commitment, engagement, covenant, treaty, pact, transaction, deal, bargain, settlement, arrangement, understanding
formal compact, concordat

conventional *adj*
traditional, orthodox, formal, correct, proper, prevalent, prevailing, accepted, received, expected, unoriginal, conformist, conservative, ritual, routine, usual, customary, regular, standard, normal, ordinary, mainstream, straight, stereotyped, trite, hidebound, pedestrian, commonplace, common
colloq. common or garden, run-of-the-mill
F3 unconventional, unusual, exotic, alternative

converge *v*
1 *crowds converged on the car*
approach, move towards, gather, close in, form, mass, focus, concentrate
2 *the roads converge at the bridge*
meet, join, combine, merge, coincide, unite, come together
F3 1 disperse **2** diverge

convergence *n*
concentration, approach, merging, combination, blending, meeting, coincidence, junction, intersection, union
formal confluence
F3 divergence, separation

conversant *adj*
▷ **conversant with** familiar with, acquainted with, experienced in, informed about, knowledgeable about, practised in, proficient in, skilled in, versed in, *au fait* with
formal apprised of
F3 ignorant of

conversation *n*
talk, chat, gossip, discussion, discourse, dialogue, exchange, communication, tête-à-tête, heart-to-heart, cosy chat, small talk
formal colloquy
colloq. chinwag, natter, confab

conversational *adj*
informal, chatty, colloquial, communicative, relaxed, casual

converse[1] *v*
converse with people
talk, discuss, confer, communicate, chat, gossip, chatter
formal commune, discourse

converse[2] *n, adj*
▶ *n the converse is true*
opposite, reverse, contrary, obverse
formal antithesis
colloq. other way round, other side of the coin
▶ *adj* opposite, opposing, reverse, counter, contrary, reversed, transposed, obverse
formal antithetical

conversion *n*
1 *a loft conversion*
alteration, change, transformation, turning, adaptation, modification, remodelling, reshaping, reconstruction, reorganization, customization, adjustment,
technical metamorphosis, transfiguration, mutation, transmutation
2 *conversion of pounds into francs*
change, exchange, substitution, switch
3 *conversion to Judaism*
persuasion, conviction, reformation, regeneration, rebirth, proselytization, preaching

convert *v, n*
▶ *v* **1** *convert the building*
ALTER, change, turn, transform, make, adapt, customize, adjust, modify, go over to, transfer, switch, reform, restructure, remodel, reshape, refashion, restyle, revise, reorganize, rebuild, reconstruct
technical metamorphose, transfigure, mutate, transmute
2 *convert inches into centimetres*
change, exchange, substitute, turn into, switch from
3 WIN OVER, convince, persuade, cause to change beliefs/religion, reform, proselytize
▶ *n* disciple, believer, new person, changed person, proselyte, neophyte, adherent

convertible *adj*
adaptable, adjustable, exchangeable, modifiable, interchangeable
formal permutable

convex *adj*
rounded, curved out, bending outwards, bulging, swelling, protuberant, gibbous
F3 concave, hollow

convey *v*
1 *convey feelings*
COMMUNICATE, express, tell, relate, reveal, disclose, announce, make known, transmit, hand on, pass on
formal impart
2 TRANSPORT, carry, bear, bring, fetch, move, transport, drive, shift, send, forward, deliver, transfer, conduct, guide, channel, pipe

conveyance n
1 VEHICLE, car, bus, coach, bicycle, motorcycle, lorry, truck, van, wagon, carriage
2 *the conveyance of bicycles*
transport, transportation, movement, transfer, transference
3 *the conveyance of property*
transfer, transference, granting, transmission, consignment, delivery, bequeathal, ceding

convict v, n
▶ v condemn, find guilty, sentence, judge, imprison
▶ n criminal, law-breaker, felon, culprit, villain, offender, wrongdoer, prisoner, inmate, burglar, thief, robber
colloq. crook, jailbird; *slang* lag

conviction n
1 BELIEF, view, opinion, faith, creed, tenet, principle
2 *speak with conviction*
assurance, confidence, fervour, earnestness, certainty, firmness, persuasion
formal certitude
3 *previous convictions*
condemnation, pronouncement of guilt, sentence, judgement, imprisonment

convince v
assure, persuade, prove to, sway, talk into, win over, bring round, influence, prompt
formal prevail upon

convincing adj
persuasive, powerful, telling, impressive, credible, plausible, likely, probable, conclusive, compelling, forceful, incontrovertible
formal cogent
⊟ unconvincing, improbable

convivial adj
friendly, sociable, genial, cheerful, cordial, festive, hearty, jolly, jovial, lively, merry, fun-loving
⊟ taciturn

conviviality n
geniality, cheer, cordiality, sociability, gaiety, jollity, joviality, bonhomie, liveliness, mirth, festivity, merrymaking

convocation n
congress, convention, council, assembly, congregation, meeting, diet, synod
formal conclave, forgathering, assemblage

convoluted adj
convoluted carvings/ideas
twisting, winding, meandering, tortuous, involved, complicated, complex
⊟ straight, straightforward

convolution n
1 *convolutions in the design*
coil, twist, whorl, turn, spiral, helix, loop, coiling, winding, sinuousness, sinuosity
technical gyrus
formal curlicue
2 *convolutions in relationships*
complexity, intricacy, complication, entanglement, involvement, tortuousness

convoy n
fleet, line, escort, guard, protection, attendance, train, group, company

convulse v
suffer a fit/seizure, shake uncontrollably/violently, jerk, seize, unsettle, disturb

convulsion n
1 FIT, seizure, attack, paroxysm, spasm, cramp, contraction, tic, tremor
2 *major political convulsions*
ERUPTION, outburst, furore, disturbance, unrest, disorder, commotion, tumult, turmoil, agitation, turbulence, upheaval

convulsive adj
jerky, spasmodic, fitful, sporadic, uncontrolled, violent

cook v
prepare, heat, warm, put on, put together, improvise, undercook, underdo, overcook, overdo, burn
colloq. rustle up

Ways of cooking include: bake, barbecue, boil, braise, broil, brown, casserole, coddle, curry, deep-fry, fricassee, fry, grill, microwave, oven-roast, parboil, poach, pot-roast, roast, sauté, scramble, simmer, spit-roast, steam, stew, stir-fry, toast.

▷ **cook up** concoct, prepare, brew, invent, make up, fabricate, contrive, devise, plan, plot, scheme

cool adj, v, n
▶ adj 1 CHILLY, fresh, breezy, nippy, cold, bracing, crisp, draughty
2 *a cool drink*
cold, chilled, iced, ice-cold, refreshing
3 CALM, unruffled, unexcited, composed, self-possessed, level-headed, collected, unemotional, dispassionate, quiet, relaxed, impassive, unmoved, placid, sedate, poised, imperturbable, unexcitable, unflustered, unperturbed, undisturbed, untroubled, unapprehensive
colloq. laid back, unflappable, cool as a cucumber
4 *a cool reception*
unfriendly, unwelcoming, cold, frigid, frosty, lukewarm, half-hearted, unenthusiastic, apathetic, uninterested, unresponsive, uncommunicative, undemonstrative, reserved, distant, aloof, standoffish
5 *look cool in that outfit*
sophisticated, fashionable, elegant, smart, stylish
colloq. trendy, streetwise
6 *a really cool party*
great, wonderful, excellent, fantastic, marvellous
⊟ 1 warm, hot 2 hot 3 excited, angry
4 friendly, welcoming
▶ v 1 CHILL, refrigerate, ice, freeze, make cold, make colder, get/turn cold, get/turn colder, fan, air-condition
2 MODERATE, lessen, temper, dampen, diminish, reduce, quiet, calm, allay
formal abate, assuage
⊟ 1 warm, heat 2 excite
▶ n 1 *keep/lose your cool*
composure, coolness, calmness, collectedness, poise, self-possession, self-discipline, self-control, control, temper
2 *the cool of the early morning*
chill, freshness, breeze, nippiness, cold, crispness, draught
technical defervescence, defervescency

cooling n, adj
▶ n chilling, refrigeration, air-conditioning, ventilation
technical defervescence, defervescency

☰ heating, warming
▶ *adj* freezing, refrigerant, refrigerative, refrigeratory
☰ warming

coop *n, v*
▶ *n* cage, box, enclosure, pen, hutch, pound
▶ *v* ▷ **coop up** imprison, cage, enclose, shut (up), impound, keep in, lock up/away, pen, imprison
formal incarcerate, immure

co-operate *v*
collaborate, work together, pull together, band together, team up, help, assist, aid, contribute, participate, combine, unite, join forces, share, pool, conspire
colloq. play ball

co-operation *n*
helpfulness, help, helping hand, assistance, aid, contribution, participation, collaboration, teamwork, working together, unity, co-ordination, joint action, concerted action, give-and-take
☰ opposition, rivalry, competition

co-operative *adj*
1 COLLECTIVE, joint, shared, combined, united, concerted, co-ordinated, collaborative, working together
2 HELPFUL, helping, assisting, supportive, responsive, obliging, accommodating, willing
formal coactive, compliant
☰ 2 unco-operative, rebellious

co-ordinate *v*
organize, arrange, systematize, order, work together, co-operate, collaborate, tabulate, integrate, mesh, synchronize, harmonize, match, correlate, regulate
colloq. mix 'n' match

cope *v*
manage, carry on, survive, get by, get through, make do, succeed, take in your stride
▷ **cope with** deal with, encounter, contend with, struggle with, grapple with, wrestle with, handle, manage, treat, weather, endure
☰ *colloq.* not hack it

copious *adj*
abundant, plentiful, inexhaustible, overflowing, profuse, rich, lavish, bountiful, liberal, full, ample, generous, extensive, great, huge
formal plenteous, bounteous, luxuriant
colloq. bags of
☰ scarce, meagre

cop-out *n*
dodge, evasion, fraud, pretence, pretext, alibi
colloq. shirking, passing the buck

copse *n*
coppice, wood, thicket, grove, bush, brush

copulate *v*
mate, make love, have sex, have sexual intercourse, enjoy, gender, horse, line
colloq. go to bed with; *slang* get your leg over, go all the way, have, lay, make it with, have it off with, bed; *taboo slang* bonk, screw, hump, bang, shag, stuff, fuck

copy *n, v*
▶ *n* 1 *copies of the letter*
duplicate, facsimile, fax, carbon copy, photocopy, Photostat®, Xerox®, reproduction, print, tracing, transcript, transcription, replica, model, pattern, archetype, representation, image, likeness, counterfeit, forgery, fake, imitation, borrowing, plagiarism, crib

2 *buy a copy of the magazine*
issue, sample, example, specimen
☰ 1 original
▶ *v* duplicate, photocopy, Photostat®, Xerox®, reproduce, print, trace, transcribe, fax, scan, forge, counterfeit, pirate, simulate, imitate, impersonate, mimic, ape, parrot, repeat, echo, mirror, follow, emulate, borrow, plagiarize, crib
formal replicate

coquettish *adj*
flirtatious, amorous, dallying, flighty, flirty, inviting, teasing
colloq. come-hither, vampish

cord *n*
string, twine, rope, line, cable, flex, connection, link, bond, tie
Related adjective: funicular

cordial *adj*
friendly, amicable, affable, affectionate, agreeable, cheerful, genial, sociable, pleasant, heartfelt, warm, warm-hearted, welcoming, wholehearted, earnest, hearty, stimulating, invigorating
☰ hostile, aloof, cool

cordiality *n*
friendliness, affability, affection, agreeableness, cheerfulness, geniality, sociability, heartiness, warmth, welcome, wholeheartedness, earnest, sincerity
☰ coolness, hostility

cordon *n, v*
▶ *n* line, ring, barrier, chain, fence
▶ *v* ▷ **cordon off** close off, fence off, isolate, separate, encircle, enclose, surround

core *n*
kernel, nucleus, heart, centre, middle, nub, crux, essence, substance, gist
formal quintessence
colloq. nitty-gritty
☰ surface, exterior

corn *n*
arable crop, cereal crop, cereal, wheat, barley, oats, rye, maize, grain
Related adjective: frumentarious

corner *n, v*
▶ *n* 1 *round the corner*
angle, joint, crook, bend, curve, turning, fork, junction, intersection
2 NOOK, cranny, niche, recess, crevice, cavity, hole, hideout, hideaway, retreat
3 *in a tight corner*
predicament, plight, situation, hardship, straits
colloq. tight spot, nowhere to turn, hole, pickle
▶ *v* 1 *corner an animal*
force into a place, trap, hunt down, catch, cut off, block off, run to earth, confine
2 *corner the market*
monopolize, control, dominate, have sole rights in
colloq. hog

corny *adj*
banal, commonplace, hackneyed, stale, overused, stereotyped, trite, clichéd, sentimental, dull, feeble, maudlin, mawkish, old-fashioned, platitudinous
☰ new, original

corollary *n*
consequence, conclusion, result, upshot, deduction,

induction, inference
formal illation

coronation *n*
enthronement, crowning, accession to the throne

coronet *n*
crown, diadem, tiara, circlet, wreath, garland

corporal *adj*
anatomical, bodily, fleshly, carnal, material, physical,
tangible, corporeal
formal somatic
EJ spiritual

corporate *adj*
combined, collective, concerted, joint, communal,
merged, pooled, shared, united, allied, amalgamated,
collaborative

corporation *n*
1 *a business corporation*
firm, company, business, concern, association,
organization, establishment, house, partnership,
syndicate, cartel, trust, consortium, conglomerate,
multinational, industry, holding company
2 *the Corporation of London*
council, authority, authorities, governing body

corporeal *adj*
actual, material, physical, substantial, tangible, bodily,
fleshly, human, mortal
EJ spiritual

corps *n*
band, body, detachment, unit, squad, team, division,
brigade, company, contingent, crew, regiment,
squadron

corpse *n*
body, dead body, carcase, cadaver, skeleton, remains,
mummy, zombie
slang stiff

corpulent *adj*
fat, fattish, large, obese, overweight, plump, stout,
beefy, bulky, burly, fleshy, portly, pot-bellied, podgy,
roly-poly, tubby, well-padded
formal rotund, adipose
EJ thin

corpus *n*
collection, compilation, body, entirety, whole
formal aggregation

corral *n*
enclosure, fold, pound, stall, coop, sty, kraal

correct *adj, v*
▶ *adj* 1 *the correct answer*
right, accurate, precise, exact, strict, true, truthful,
actual, real, faithful, word-perfect, faultless, flawless,
unerring
colloq. spot on, bang on
2 PROPER, acceptable, accepted, standard, regular,
just, appropriate, suitable, fitting, conventional
old use seemly
colloq. OK
EJ 1 incorrect, wrong, inaccurate
▶ *v* 1 *correct an error*
rectify, put right, right, set right, put straight, remedy,
cure, debug, redress, adjust, regulate, revise, improve,
amend
formal emend, ameliorate, disabuse
colloq. put the record straight
2 PUNISH, discipline, reprimand, reprove, scold,

rebuke, reform
formal admonish

correction *n*
1 *corrections to the text*
rectification, remedying, adjustment, alteration,
modification, amendment, improvement
formal emendation, amelioration
2 PUNISHMENT, discipline, reprimand,
chastisement, reproof, scolding, rebuke, reformation
formal admonition

corrective *adj*
1 *corrective measures*
remedial, curative, medicinal, palliative, restorative,
therapeutic
formal emendatory
2 DISCIPLINARY, disciplinary penal, punitive,
reformatory, rehabilitative

correlate *v*
associate, compare, connect, show a connection/
relationship, co-ordinate, correspond, agree, equate,
interact, link, parallel, relate, link, tie in

correlation *n*
association, connection, relationship,
correspondence, equivalence, interaction,
interchange, interdependence, interrelationship,
link, reciprocity

correspond *v*
1 MATCH, match up, fit (together), answer, conform,
tally, square, agree, be in agreement, be consistent,
coincide, harmonize, dovetail, complement, be
similar, be equivalent
formal concur, correlate, accord, be analogous
2 COMMUNICATE, write, pen, exchange letters,
keep in touch

correspondence *n*
1 COMMUNICATION, writing, letters, post, mail
2 CONFORMITY, agreement, coincidence, relation,
analogy, comparison, comparability, similarity,
resemblance, equivalence, conformity, harmony,
match
formal concurrence, correlation, congruity,
consonance
EJ 2 divergence, incongruity

correspondent *n*
journalist, reporter, contributor, writer

corresponding *adj*
matching, complementary, reciprocal, interrelated,
comparable, equivalent, similar, like, matching,
parallel, identical
formal analogous

corridor *n*
aisle, passageway, passage, hallway, hall, lobby

corroborate *v*
confirm, prove, bear out, verify, support, back up,
endorse, ratify, certify, substantiate, validate,
authenticate, document, underpin, uphold, sustain
formal evidence
EJ contradict

corroborative *adj*
confirming, confirmatory, supporting, supportive,
verifying, endorsing, substantiating, validating
formal confirmative, evidential, evidentiary,
verificatory

corrode   *v*

erode, wear away, eat away, consume, destroy, waste, rust, oxidize, tarnish, impair, deteriorate, rot, crumble, disintegrate
formal abrade

corrosive   *adj*

corroding, acid, caustic, cutting, abrasive, wearing, consuming, destructive, wasting
technical erosive

corrugated   *adj*

ridged, fluted, grooved, channelled, furrowed, wrinkled, folded, crinkled, rumpled, creased
technical striate

corrupt   *adj, v*

▶ *adj* rotten, unscrupulous, unprincipled, unethical, immoral, evil, wicked, fraudulent, dishonest, untrustworthy, bribable, venal, depraved, degenerate, dissolute, tainted, contaminated
colloq. shady, bent, crooked
E3 ethical, virtuous, upright, honest, fair, trustworthy
▶ *v* contaminate, pollute, adulterate, taint, infect, mar, blight, defile, debase, debauch, pervert, deprave, warp, be a bad influence, lure, bribe, suborn
formal vitiate
colloq. lead astray, buy (off), grease someone's palm
E3 purify

corruption   *n*

unscrupulousness, immorality, impurity, depravity, degeneration, degradation, perversion, debauchery, distortion, dishonesty, fraud, bribery, subornation, extortion, sharp practice, vice, wickedness, iniquity, evil, criminality, villainy, contamination, pollution, rottenness, *US* graft
colloq. wheeling and dealing, crookedness, shadiness
E3 honesty, virtue, fairness, trustworthiness

corset   *n*

girdle, panty girdle, belt, bodice, corselet, foundation garment, stays

cortège   *n*

procession, retinue, suite, train, column, entourage, cavalcade, parade

cosmetic   *adj*

1 *a cosmetic substance*
make-up, beauty, beautifying
2 *cosmetic changes*
superficial, surface, external, shallow, peripheral, minor, slight, trivial
E3 2 basic, essential

cosmetics   *n*

Types of cosmetics include: blusher, cleanser, eyebrow pencil, eyelash dye, eyeliner, eye shadow, face cream, face mask, face pack, face powder, false eyelashes, foundation, greasepaint, kohl pencil, lip gloss, lip liner, lipstick, loose powder, maquillage, mascara, moisturizer, nail polish, nail varnish, pancake make-up, pressed powder, rouge, toner, *colloq.* war paint.

cosmic   *adj*

1 *cosmic forces*
worldwide, universal, in/from space, infinite, limitless, measureless
2 *changes of cosmic proportion*

immense, vast, huge, grandiose, infinite, limitless, immeasurable, measureless

cosmonaut   *n*

astronaut, spaceman, spacewoman, space traveller

cosmopolitan   *adj*

1 *a very cosmopolitan city*
international, universal, multiracial, multicultural
2 *a very cosmopolitan outlook*
worldly, worldly-wise, well-travelled, broad-minded, sophisticated, cultured, urbane
E3 2 insular, parochial

cosmos   *n*

universe, creation, galaxy, system, worlds

cosset   *v*

coddle, mollycoddle, baby, pamper, indulge, spoil, pet, fondle, cuddle, cherish

cost   *n, v*

▶ *n* 1 EXPENSE, outlay, payment, expenditure, charge, price, selling price, asking price, rate, fee, quotation, amount, figure, value, valuation, worth
formal disbursement
colloq. damage
2 *cover costs*
budget, expenses, expenditure, spending, outgoings, outlay, overheads
3 *the cost to her health*
harm, injury, hurt, loss, suffering, deprivation, detriment, sacrifice, penalty, price
▶ *v* 1 *it costs £500*
pay, charge, be priced at, ask for, sell for, retail at, buy for, be valued at, be worth, fetch, go for, come to, amount to
colloq. set back, knock back
2 *cost a job*
price, estimate, cost out, quote, value, calculate, work out
3 *cost him his life*
cause the loss/sacrifice of, cause harm/injury, deprive, harm, injure, hurt, be a high price to pay

costly   *adj*

1 EXPENSIVE, dear, exorbitant, excessive, lavish, rich, splendid, valuable, precious, high-cost, high-priced, priceless
colloq. pricey, steep
2 HARMFUL, damaging, destructive, detrimental, disastrous, ruinous, catastrophic, loss-making
formal deleterious
E3 1 cheap, inexpensive

costume   *n*

outfit, uniform, livery, ensemble, robes, vestments, dress, style of dress, fashion, clothes, clothing, garments, habit, fancy dress
formal apparel, attire
colloq. get-up

cosy   *adj*

snug, comfortable, warm, sheltered, secure, safe, homely, congenial, intimate
colloq. comfy
E3 uncomfortable, cold

coterie   *n*

set, circle, clique, group, club, association, community, faction, camp, caucus, cabal, gang

cottage   *n*

lodge, chalet, bungalow, hut, cabin, shack

couch   *n, v*
▶ *n*   sofa, settee, chesterfield, chaise-longue, ottoman, divan, bed, day bed, sofa bed
▶ *v*   express, frame, phrase, word, set, bear, support, utter, cradle

cough   *v, n*
▶ *v*   clear your throat, bark, hack, hawk, hem
▷ **cough up**   pay up, pay, pay out, give; *colloq.* fork out, shell out, stump up
▶ *n*   bark, hack, hawking, hem, clearing your throat
technical tussis
colloq. frog in your throat

council   *n*
1 *the town council*
local authority, cabinet, ministry, parliament, government, governing body, senate, administration
2 *the Arts Council*
advisory body, advisory group, committee, panel, jury, commission, directorate, directors, trustees, governors, advisers, board, working party, management
3 *a ministerial council*
congress, assembly, convention, conference, gathering, rally, meeting, convocation, group, body, body of people, company, congregation, flock, crowd, multitude, throng
formal convocation
Related adjective: conciliar

⚠ **council** or **counsel** ?
A *council* is 'a body of people who organize, control, advise or take decisions': *a county council. Counsel* is a rather formal word for 'advice': *give wise counsel.*

---

counsel   *n, v*
▶ *n* **1** ADVICE, suggestion, recommendation, guidance, direction, information, consultation, deliberation, consideration, forethought, opinion, viewpoint, suggestion
formal exhortation, admonition
2 *counsel for the defence*
lawyer, advocate, solicitor, attorney, barrister
▶ *v*   advise, warn, caution, suggest, recommend, advocate, urge, exhort, guide, give guidance, direct, instruct, give your opinion
formal exhort, admonish

count   *v, n*
▶ *v* **1** NUMBER, enumerate, list, include, reckon, calculate, compute, tell, check, add (up), total, score, tally
colloq. tot up
2 MATTER, be important, signify, qualify, carry weight, make a difference, make an impression, mean something
colloq. cut some ice, make waves
3 *count yourself lucky*
consider, regard, judge, think, reckon, look upon, hold
formal esteem, deem
4 *if you count children*
include, take account of, take into account, allow for
▷ **count on**   depend on, rely on, bank on, lean on, reckon on, expect, believe, trust
▷ **count out**   exclude, eliminate, ignore, leave out, omit, pass over, disregard, include out
🇪🇿 include, consider
▶ *n*   numbering, enumeration, poll, reckoning, calculation, computation, sum, total, tally, whole, full

amount
colloq. totting-up

countenance   *n, v*
▶ *n*   face, expression, appearance, features, look
formal mien, physiognomy, visage
▶ *v*   tolerate, agree, allow, approve, brook, stand for, put up with, back, condone, endorse, endure, sanction

counter¹   *n*
1 *serve at the counter*
worktop, surface, work surface, table, stand
2 *a counter in a game*
disc, token, chip, piece, coin, marker

counter²   *v, adv, adj*
▶ *v*   *counter someone's argument*
parry, resist, oppose, combat, dispute, offset, answer, respond, retaliate, retort, hit back at, return, meet
▶ *adv*   against, in opposition, contrary to, conversely
▶ *adj*   contrary, opposite, opposing, conflicting, contradictory, contrasting, opposed, against, adverse

counteract   *v*
neutralize, counterbalance, offset, act against, oppose, resist, hinder, check, thwart, frustrate, foil, defeat, undo, annul, invalidate
formal negate, countervail
🇪🇿 support, assist

counterbalance   *v*
balance, compensate for, make up for, equalize, neutralize, offset, undo
formal counterpoise, countervail

counterfeit   *adj, n, v*
▶ *adj*   fake, faked, false, forged, copied, pirate, fraudulent, bogus, sham, spurious, imitation, artificial, simulated, pretended
formal feigned
colloq. phoney, pseud, pseudo
🇪🇿 genuine, authentic, real
▶ *n*   fake, forgery, copy, reproduction, imitation, fraud, sham
▶ *v*   fake, forge, fabricate, copy, imitate, reproduce, pirate, impersonate, falsify, pretend, simulate, sham
formal feign

countermand   *v*
cancel, reverse, annul, override, overturn, quash, repeal
formal abrogate, rescind, revoke

counterpart   *n*
equivalent, opposite number, equal, complement, supplement, parallel, match, fellow, mate, twin, duplicate, copy, obverse

countless   *adj*
innumerable, myriad, numberless, unnumbered, untold, incalculable, infinite, endless, without end, immeasurable, measureless, inexhaustible, limitless, boundless
colloq. umpteen
🇪🇿 finite, limited

countrified   *adj*
rural, rustic, pastoral, provincial, idyllic, agricultural, agrarian, outback
formal bucolic
colloq. hick
🇪🇿 urban; *formal* oppidan

country   *n, adj*
▶ *n* **1** STATE, nation, kingdom, realm, republic, power, community, principality, inhabitants, people,

population, populace, residents, citizens, voters, electors
2 COUNTRYSIDE, green belt, farmland, moorland, rural area, outback, bush
colloq. provinces, backwater, backwoods, wilds, sticks, back of beyond, middle of nowhere
Related adjective: rural
3 TERRAIN, land, territory, region, area, district, neighbourhood, locality
F∃ **2** town, city
▶ *adj* rural, rustic, pastoral, landed, provincial, idyllic, agricultural, agrarian
formal bucolic
F∃ urban

countryman, countrywoman *n*
1 *fellow countrywomen*
compatriot, fellow citizen, fellow national
2 *local countrymen's skills*
farmer, yokel, boor, clodhopper, rustic, peasant, provincial, backwoodsman, bushwhacker, *Scot.* hind
colloq. bumpkin, hillbilly, hick, hayseed

countryside *n*
landscape, scenery, country, green belt, farmland, moorland, rural area, outdoors

county *n*
shire, province, region, area, state, territory, district
Related adjective: comital

coup *n*
1 *a military coup*
coup d'état, overthrow, revolution, (military) takeover, uprising, palace revolution, putsch, rebellion, revolt
2 *a big coup for the company*
feat, masterstroke, stroke, accomplishment, deed, exploit, stunt, action, manoeuvre, tour de force

coup de grâce *n*
death blow
formal quietus
colloq. clincher, kiss of death, come-uppance, kibosh, kill

coup d'état *n*
coup, overthrow, revolution, (military) takeover, uprising, palace revolution, putsch, rebellion, revolt

couple *n, v*
▶ *n* pair, husband and wife, newlyweds, partners, lovers, brace, twosome, duo,
▶ *v* pair, match, marry, wed, unite, join, link, connect, combine, ally, associate, attach, fasten, hitch, clasp, bind, buckle, yoke
formal conjoin

coupon *n*
voucher, token, slip, check, stub, ticket, certificate, form

courage *n*
bravery, pluck, fearlessness, dauntlessness, heroism, gallantry, valour, boldness, audacity, intrepidity, daring, determination, resolution, spirit, mettle, backbone
formal fortitude
colloq. nerve, guts, bottle, spunk, grit
F∃ cowardice, fear

courageous *adj*
brave, plucky, fearless, dauntless, indomitable, heroic, gallant, valiant, lion-hearted, stout-hearted, hardy, bold, audacious, lion-hearted, daring, intrepid, adventurous, determined, resolute

formal valorous
colloq. gutsy, spunky
F∃ cowardly, afraid

courier *n*
1 *the courier delivered the parcels*
messenger, carrier, dispatch rider, runner, bearer, emissary, envoy, representative, herald, legate, nuncio, estafette, pursuivant
2 *a guided tour by the courier*
guide, travel guide, tour guide, escort, company representative

course *n, v*
▶ *n* **1** CURRICULUM, syllabus, programme, schedule, classes, lessons, lectures, studies
2 FLOW, movement, advance, march, rise, progress, development, unfolding, furtherance, order, sequence, series, succession, progression
3 DURATION, time, period, lapse, term, spell, span, passing, passage
4 ROUTE, direction, way, passage, path, track, tack, road, lane, run, channel, trail, line, circuit, orbit, ambit, trajectory, flight path
5 *course of action*
plan, schedule, programme, policy, procedure, system, process, manner, method, way, approach, tack
formal mode
6 *the last hole on the course*
golf course, racecourse, racetrack, track, ground, circuit
7 *chicken for main course*
dish, part, stage, remove, starters, hors d'oeuvres, appetizer, entrée, main course, dessert, sweet, pudding, entremets
colloq. afters
8 *a course of medical treatment*
sequence, series, programme, schedule, regimen
▷ **in due course** in time, in due time, sooner or later, in the course of time, finally, eventually, to be sure
▷ **of course** naturally, certainly, surely, by all means, definitely, without a doubt, no doubt, undoubtedly, doubtlessly, needless to say; *formal* indubitably
▶ *v* **1** *tears coursing down her cheeks*
flow, run, move, pour, gush, stream, surge, dash
2 *coursing hares*
chase, hunt, pursue, run after, follow, track, race

court *n, v*
▶ *n* **1** LAWCOURT, bench, bar, judiciary, tribunal, trial, session, assizes

Types of court include: Admiralty Division, assizes, Central Criminal Court, Chancery Division, children's court, circuit court, civil court, coroner's court, county court, court-martial, court of appeals, court of claims, Court of Common Pleas, Court of Exchequer, court of justice, Court of Protection, Court of Session, criminal court, crown court, district court, divorce court, European Court of Justice, family court, federal court, High Court, High Court of Justiciary, House of Lords, Industrial tribunals, International Court of Justice, juvenile court, Lord Chancellor's Court, magistrates' court, municipal court, Old Bailey, police court, Privy Council, sheriff court, small claims court, Supreme Court.

2 *tennis courts*
playing area, game area, enclosure, track, ground, arena, ring, alley, green
3 COURTYARD, yard, quadrangle, square, patio,

cloister, forecourt, enclosure, plaza, esplanade
colloq. quad
4 *at the king's court*
palace, castle, royal residence
5 ENTOURAGE, attendants, household, retinue, suite,
train, cortège
▶ *v* **1** *court a young lady*
woo, pursue, chase, go out, go with
colloq. date, go steady
2 *court support/publicity*
cultivate, try to win, solicit, flatter, pander to, attract,
prompt, provoke, incite, seek, invite

courteous *adj*
polite, civil, respectful, well-mannered, well-bred,
deferential, ladylike, gentlemanly, mannerly, gracious,
obliging, considerate, kind, diplomatic, tactful,
attentive, gallant, chivalrous, courtly, urbane,
debonair, refined, polished
F3 discourteous, impolite, rude

courtesy *n*
politeness, civility, respect, (good) manners, (good)
breeding, deference, graciousness, consideration,
kindness, favour, generosity, tact, attention, gallantry,
chivalry, refinement, urbanity
F3 discourtesy, rudeness

courtier *n*
noble, nobleman, lord, lady, lady-in-waiting, steward,
page, attendant, cup-bearer, train-bearer, subject,
liegeman, follower, flatterer, sycophant, toady

courtly *adj*
gracious, dignified, polite, refined, obliging, polished,
elegant, stately, aristocratic, high-bred, lordly,
ceremonious, gallant, chivalrous, civil, formal,
decorous, flattering
F3 inelegant, provincial, rough

courtship *n*
wooing, pursuit, courting, chasing, going-out, dating,
going steady, romance, affair

courtyard *n*
yard, quadrangle, area, enclosure, court, square,
cloister, forecourt, plaza, patio, esplanade, atrium
colloq. quad

cove *n*
bay, bight, inlet, estuary, firth, fiord, creek

covenant *n, v*
▶ *n* arrangement, promise contract, bond,
commitment, deed, engagement, pact, pledge, treaty,
trust, convention, stipulation, undertaking
formal indenture, compact, concordat
▶ *v* agree, contract, promise, stipulate, undertake,
engage, pledge

cover *v, n*
▶ *v* **1** HIDE, put/place over, conceal, bury, obscure,
shroud, veil, wreathe, screen, mask, disguise,
camouflage
2 *covered with mud*
be over, coat, spread, daub, plaster, cake, encase, wrap,
envelop, blanket, swaddle, clothe, dress, overlay
formal attire, accoutre
3 SHELTER, put/place over, protect, shield, guard,
safeguard, defend
4 *cover a topic*
deal with, treat, consider, examine, investigate, give
details of, review, survey, report, describe, encompass,
embrace, incorporate, embody, involve, include,
contain, comprise, take in

5 *cover 25 miles*
travel (over), cross, go, go across, journey, go, do
formal traverse
6 *cover for a colleague*
stand in for, deputize, relieve, replace, take over from,
be a replacement/substitute for
7 *the estate covers some 500 acres*
extend over, stretch, continue, stretch, measure
8 *£50 to cover expenses*
pay for, be enough for, recompense, make up for
9 *the insurance will cover it*
protect, insure, provide for
formal indemnify
F3 **1** uncover **2** strip **3** expose **4** exclude
▷ **cover up** conceal, hide, suppress, keep secret,
keep dark, repress, gloss over; *formal* dissemble;
colloq. whitewash, hush up
F3 disclose, reveal
▶ *n* **1** SHELTER, refuge, protection, shield, guard,
defence, concealment, hiding-place, sanctuary, refuge,
disguise, camouflage
2 COVERING, coating, top, lid, cup, jacket, wrapper,
binding, case, envelope, package, coat, layer, film,
skin, carpet, mantle, clothing, dress, bedclothes,
blankets, duvet, bedspread, canopy
3 *as a cover for illegal activity*
cover-up, concealment, screen, smokescreen, veil,
screen, mask, front, façade, pretence, conspiracy,
complicity
colloq. whitewash
4 *insurance cover*
protection, insurance, compensation, assurance
formal indemnity, indemnification

coverage *n*
reporting, report(s), description, account,
investigation, analysis, item, story, reportage

covering *n, adj*
▶ *n* layer, coat, coating, blanket, carpet, film, veneer,
skin, crust, case, shell, casing, housing, wrapping,
clothing, protection, shelter, mask, overlay, cover, top,
shelter, roof, roofing
▶ *adj* accompanying, explanatory, descriptive,
introductory

covert *adj*
hidden, secret, private, clandestine, concealed,
disguised, veiled, sneaky, stealthy, sidelong,
surreptitious, unsuspected, ulterior, underhand
formal dissembled, subreptitious
colloq. under the table
F3 open

cover-up *n*
concealment, screen, smokescreen, front, façade,
pretence, conspiracy, complicity
colloq. whitewash

covet *v*
desire, crave, long for, yearn for, hanker for, want,
hunger/thirst for, lust after, envy, begrudge
colloq. fancy

covetous *adj*
yearning, craving, wanting, longing, hankering,
hungering, thirsting, acquisitive, grasping, greedy,
insatiable, jealous, envious
formal desirous, avaricious, rapacious
F3 generous, temperate

covey *n*
cluster, flight, flock, group, bevy, nid, skein

cow *v*
intimidate, domineer, browbeat, bully, terrorize,
frighten, scare, overawe, subdue, unnerve, daunt,
dishearten, dismay
colloq. rattle
F3 encourage

coward *n*
craven, faint-heart, poltroon, renegade, deserter
old use recreant
colloq. chicken, scaredy-cat, yellow-belly, sissy,
cry-baby, wimp, *Austral.* sook
F3 hero

cowardice *n*
cowardliness, faint-heartedness, timorousness,
spinelessness
formal pusillanimity
F3 courage, bravery, valour

cowardly *adj*
faint-hearted, craven, fearful, timorous, scared,
unheroic, chicken-hearted, chicken-livered, spineless,
weak, weak-kneed, soft, jittery
formal pusillanimous
colloq. chicken, gutless, wimpish, yellow-bellied,
yellow, lily-livered
F3 brave, courageous, bold

cowboy *n*
1 *cowboys to look after cattle*
drover, cattleman, cowhand, herdsman, cattleherder,
herder, stockman, rancher, ranchero
US bronco-buster, buckaroo, cowpoke, cowpuncher,
gaucho, vaquero, waddy, wrangler
2 *a cowboy plumbing firm*
bungler, incompetent, rascal, rogue, scoundrel
F3 2 professional

cower *v*
crouch, grovel, skulk, shrink, flinch, draw back, recoil,
wince, cringe, quail, tremble, quake, shake, shiver

coy *adj*
modest, demure, prudish, prim, diffident, shy, bashful,
timid, shrinking, backward, retiring, self-effacing,
withdrawn, reserved, reticence, evasive, arch,
flirtatious, coquettish, skittish, kittenish
F3 bold, forward

crabbed, crabby *adj*
bad-tempered, cross, ill-tempered, irritable, morose,
snappish, cantankerous, petulant, perverse, acrid,
acrimonious, awkward, difficult, harsh, tough, sour,
captious, churlish, fretful, snappy, surly, tart, testy
formal iracund, iracundulous, irascible, misanthropic,
splenetic
colloq. crotchety, grouchy, prickly
F3 calm, placid

crack *v, n, adj*
▶ *v* 1 SPLIT, burst, fracture, break, snap, shatter,
splinter, split, fragment, chip
2 EXPLODE, go bang, bang, detonate, boom, burst,
pop, crackle, snap, crash, bash, hit, clap, slap, bump
colloq. whack, wallop, clout
3 *crack under pressure*
lose control, collapse, break down, go to pieces
4 *crack a code*
decipher, work out, solve, unravel, figure out, find the
answer to
▷ **crack down on** clamp down on, end, stop, put a
stop to, crush, suppress, check, control, limit, restrict,
confine, repress, act against

▷ **crack up** lose control, go to pieces, have a nervous
breakdown, break down, collapse, go mad, go ballisitic
▶ *n* 1 BREAK, fracture, flaw, chip, split, rift, breach,
rupture, gap, crevice, fissure, cleft, cavity, chink, line,
cranny
2 EXPLOSION, bang, boom, detonation, burst, pop,
snap, crash, clap, blow, smack, slap, hit, bump
formal report
colloq. whack, clout
3 *have a crack at something*
attempt, go, try
colloq. bash, shot, stab, whirl
4 JOKE, quip, witticism, one-liner, wisecrack, gibe,
repartee
colloq. gag, dig
▶ *adj* first-class, first-rate, excellent, outstanding,
brilliant, superior, choice, hand-picked, expert
colloq. top-notch

crackdown *n*
clampdown, crushing, end, check, stop, repression,
suppression

cracked *adj*
1 *a cracked glass*
broken, chipped, damaged, defective, flawed,
imperfect, faulty, fissured, split, torn
2 *they're cracked*
crazy, insane, deranged, crazed, foolish, idiotic
colloq. daft, barmy, batty, crackbrained, crackpot,
loony, nuts, nutty, off your rocker, round the bend
F3 1 flawless, perfect 2 sane

crackers *adj*
cracked, crazy, mad, foolish, idiotic
colloq. daft, batty, crackbrained, crackpot, loony,
nuts, nutty, round the bend
F3 sane

crackle *v, n*
▶ *v* snap, crack, sizzle, rustle
formal crepitate, decrepitate
▶ *n* snap, crack, sizzle, rustle
formal crepitation, crepitus, decrepitation

crackpot *n*
idiot, fool
colloq. freak, loony, weirdo, oddball, nutter;
slang dork

cradle *n, v*
▶ *n* 1 COT, carry-cot, travel-cot, crib, bassinet, bed
2 SOURCE, origin, spring, wellspring, fount,
fountain-head, birthplace, starting-point, beginning
▶ *v* hold, support, rock, lull, nestle, nurse, shelter,
nurture, tend

craft *n*
1 SKILL, expertise, mastery, talent, knack, flair,
ability, skilfulness, expertness, aptitude, dexterity,
cleverness, artistry, art, handicraft, handiwork,
workmanship, technique
2 TRADE, business, calling, vocation, job,
occupation, work, employment, line, pursuit
3 VESSEL, boat, ship, aircraft, spacecraft, spaceship,
landing craft

craftsman, craftswoman *n*
artist, artisan, technician, expert, master, maker,
skilled worker, wright, smith

craftsmanship *n*
artistry, workmanship, skill, technique, dexterity,
expertise, mastery

crafty *adj*
sly, cunning, artful, wily, foxy, devious, subtle,
scheming, calculating, conniving, designing, deceitful,
fraudulent, sharp, shrewd, astute, canny
formal duplicitous
colloq. crooked
E3 artless, naïve, guileless

crag *n*
bluff, cliff, escarpment, scarp, ridge, peak, pinnacle,
rock, tor

craggy *adj*
1 *a craggy cliff*
precipitous, rocky, rough, rugged, cragged, stony,
jagged, uneven
2 *a craggy face*
rough, rugged, jagged, uneven
E3 **2** smooth

cram *v*
1 *cram sweets into your mouth*
stuff, jam, ram, force, press, squeeze, crush, compress,
pack, crowd, overcrowd, fill (up), overfill, glut, gorge
formal compact
2 *cram for an exam*
revise, study hard
colloq. swot, mug up, bone up on, grind

cramp *n, v*
▶ *n* pain, ache, twinge, pang, contraction,
convulsion, spasm, muscular contraction, crick, stitch,
pins and needles, stiffness
▶ *v* hinder, hamper, obstruct, impede, inhibit,
handicap, thwart, frustrate, check, restrict, limit,
bridle, hamstring, arrest, constrain, restrain, confine,
stymie, shackle, tie

cramped *adj*
narrow, tight, small, uncomfortable, restricted,
confined, crowded, packed, squashed, squeezed,
closed in, hemmed in, overcrowded, full, overfull,
jam-packed, congested
colloq. poky, no room to swing a cat
E3 spacious

crane *n*
derrick, hoist, tackle, winch, block and tackle, davit

crank *n*
eccentric, character, madman, idiot
colloq. freak, weirdo, oddball, nutter, crackpot;
slang loony

cranky *adj*
1 ECCENTRIC, odd, peculiar, unconventional,
strange, bizarre, freakish, idiosyncratic
colloq. wacky, dotty
2 BAD-TEMPERED, cross, ill-tempered, irritable,
cantankerous, awkward, difficult, harsh, snappy, surly,
tart, testy
colloq. crabby, crotchety, prickly
E3 **1** normal, sensible **2** calm, placid

cranny *n*
chink, cleft, crack, crevice, fissure, rent, gap, hole,
nook, opening, cleavage
formal interstice

crash *n, v, adj*
▶ *n* **1** *a car crash*
accident, collision, bump, pile-up, wreck
colloq. smash, smash-up, prang
2 BANG, clash, clatter, clang, clank, thud, thump,
boom, explosion, thunder, smash, racket, din

3 *stock-market crash*
collapse, failure, ruin, downfall, fall, bankruptcy,
depression
▶ *v* **1** COLLIDE, hit, knock, bump, bang, run into, go
into, drive into, smash into, plough into
2 BREAK, fracture, smash, batter, dash, shatter,
splinter, shiver, fragment, disintegrate
3 FALL, topple, pitch, plunge, collapse, fail, fold (up),
founder, go under, go into liquidation
colloq. go bust, go to the wall
4 *the computer crashed*
cut out, break down, stop working, fail
formal malfunction
colloq. pack up, go on the blink
▶ *adj* intensive, rapid, accelerated, concentrated,
telescoped, emergency, immediate, round-the-clock,
urgent

crass *adj*
stupid, indelicate, insensitive, tactless, unrefined,
unsophisticated, blundering, rude, crude, coarse,
dense, oafish, unsubtle, witless
formal obtuse
E3 refined, sensitive

crate *n*
container, box, case, tea chest, packing-box, packing-
case

crater *n*
hollow, depression, hole, dip, pit, cavity, chasm, abyss

crave *v*
hunger for, thirst for, long for, yearn for, pine for, sigh
for, hanker after, pant for, lust after, desire, covet, want,
dream of, wish, need, require
colloq. be dying for, fancy
E3 dislike

craven *adj*
cowardly, faint-hearted, fearful, timorous, scared,
afraid, unheroic, chicken-hearted, chicken-livered,
lily-livered, mean-spirited, spineless, weak, weak-
kneed, soft
old use recreant, poltroon
formal pusillanimous
colloq. chicken, gutless, yellow
E3 brave, courageous, bold

craving *n*
appetite, hunger, thirst, longing, yearning, pining,
sighing, hankering, panting, lust, desire, wish, need,
urge
E3 dislike, distaste

crawl *v*
1 CREEP, go on all fours, move on your hands and
knees, inch, edge, slither, wriggle, squirm, writhe,
drag, move/advance slowly
2 GROVEL, cringe, toady, fawn, flatter, bow and
scrape, curry favour
colloq. be all over, suck up, creep
3 *the city centre crawling with police*
teem, swarm, seethe, bristle, be full of

craze *n*
fad, novelty, fashion, vogue, mode, trend, obsession,
preoccupation, mania, frenzy, passion, infatuation,
whim, enthusiasm
colloq. rage, the latest, thing

crazed *adj*
mad, insane, lunatic, unbalanced, deranged,
demented, crazy, wild, berserk, unhinged, out of your
mind

colloq. loony, nuts, off your rocker, round the bend, round the twist

crazy *adj*
1 MAD, insane, lunatic, unbalanced, disturbed, deranged, demented, crazed, wild, berserk, unhinged, out of your mind
colloq. loony, loopy, bonkers, nuts, nutty, nutty as a fruitcake, doolally, off your rocker, out to lunch, needing your head examining, round the bend, round the twist, not all there, having lost your marbles, having several cards short of a full deck, with one sandwich short of a picnic
2 *What a crazy idea!*
silly, foolish, idiotic, stupid, senseless, unwise, imprudent, nonsensical, absurd, odd, peculiar, ludicrous, ridiculous, preposterous, outrageous, impracticable, unrealistic, foolhardy, irresponsible, wild
colloq. daft, barmy, batty, potty, half-baked, hare-brained, crackbrained, crackpot
3 *crazy about golf*
enthusiastic, fanatical, zealous, devoted, fond, keen, avid, ardent, passionate, infatuated, enamoured, smitten, mad, wild
colloq. daft, nuts
F3 1 sane **2** sensible **3** indifferent
▷ **go crazy** go mad, blow up; *colloq.* go ballistic, flip (your lid), lose your marbles; *US slang* go ape

creak *v*
squeak, groan, grate, scrape, rasp, scratch, grind, squeal, screech

creaky *adj*
squeaky, squeaking, groaning, grating, scraping, rasping, scratching, grinding, squealing, screeching, rusty, unoiled

cream *n, adj*
▶ *n* **1** PASTE, emulsion, oil, lotion, ointment, salve, cosmetic
technical emollient, liniment, unguent
2 BEST, pick, elite, flower, choice/select part, prime, pick of the bunch, *crème de la crème*
▶ *adj* yellowish-white, whitish-yellow, off-white, pale, pasty

creamy *adj*
1 CREAM-COLOURED, creamy, off-white, yellowish-white, whitish-yellow, pale, pasty
2 MILKY, buttery, oily, smooth, velvety, rich, thick

crease *v, n*
▶ *v* fold, pleat, wrinkle, pucker, crumple, rumple, crinkle, crimp, tuck, corrugate, groove, furrow, ridge
▷ **crease up** make laugh, amuse; *colloq.* make someone fall about, make someone split their sides, have rolling in the aisles
▶ *n* fold, line, pleat, tuck, wrinkle, pucker, ruck, crinkle, corrugation, furrow, ridge, groove

create *v*
invent, coin, formulate, compose, design, devise, concoct, hatch, originate, initiate, found, establish, set up, institute, cause, cause to happen, bring about, occasion, give rise to, produce, bring into being, bring into existence, generate, engender, make, form, shape, mould, develop, build, construct, erect, frame, fabricate, appoint, install, invest, inaugurate, ordain, lead to, result in
F3 destroy

creation *n*
1 MAKING, formation, constitution, invention, concoction, origination, foundation, establishment, institution, production, generation, origin, conception, initiation, birth, development, construction, fabrication
formal procreation, genesis
2 *God's creation*
world, universe, cosmos, nature, life, everything
3 INVENTION, innovation, brainchild, concept, product, achievement, work, work of art, handiwork, masterpiece, composition, design, *pièce de résistance*, *chef d'oeuvre*
F3 1 destruction

creative *adj*
artistic, inventive, original, imaginative, inspired, visionary, full of ideas, talented, gifted, clever, ingenious, resourceful, fertile, productive, intuitive
F3 unimaginative

creativity *n*
artistry, inventiveness, originality, imagination, imaginativeness, inspiration, vision, talent, gift, cleverness, ingenuity, resourcefulness, fertility, productiveness
F3 unimaginativeness

creator *n*
maker, inventor, designer, architect, author, originator, producer, initiator, builder, composer, founder, father, mother, prime mover, first cause, God

creature *n*
animal, beast, bird, fish, insect, organism, being, living thing, mortal, individual, person, human being, human, man, woman, body, soul, mortal

credence *n*
belief, confidence, trust, faith, dependence, reliance, support, credibility, credit
F3 distrust

credentials *n*
diploma, certificate, reference, testimonial, recommendation, authorization, warrant, licence, permit, passport, identity card, proof of identity, papers, documents, deed, title
formal accreditation

credibility *n*
integrity, reliability, trustworthiness, plausibility, probability, likelihood, reasonableness
F3 implausibility

credible *adj*
believable, imaginable, convincing, conceivable, thinkable, tenable, plausible, likely, probable, possible, reasonable, persuasive, convincing, sincere, honest, trustworthy, reliable, dependable
colloq. with a ring of truth
F3 incredible, unbelievable, implausible, unreliable

> ⚠ **credible, creditable** or **credulous** ?
> *Credible* means 'believable, even if untrue': *a credible theory. Creditable* means 'worthy of praise or respect': *a very creditable performance. Credulous* means 'too easily convinced; easily fooled': *Only the most credulous of voters would believe all the party's election promises.*

credit *n, v*
▶ *n* **1** *get the credit for his success*
acknowledgement, recognition, thanks, approval,

commendation, praise, acclaim, tribute
formal laudation
2 *your loyalty does you credit*
glory, fame, prestige, distinction, honour, reputation, asset, boast, pride, esteem, estimation
colloq. feather in your cap, pride and joy
3 *give someone credit for their ability*
belief, trust, faith, credence, confidence
4 *be in credit*
money in your bank account
colloq. in the black
E3 1 blame, discredit, shame **4** overdraft, insolvency; *colloq.* in the red
▷ **on credit** on account, by instalments, by deferred payment, on hire purchase; *colloq.* on tick, on the slate, on the tab, on the never-never
▶ *v* **1** *credited with the invention*
attribute, ascribe, put down, assign, charge
formal accredit, impute
2 *the reports are difficult to credit*
believe, accept, subscribe to, trust, have faith, rely on
colloq. swallow, fall for, buy
E3 2 disbelieve

creditable *adj*
honourable, reputable, respectable, estimable, admirable, commendable, praiseworthy, good, excellent, exemplary, worthy, deserving
formal laudable, meritorious
E3 shameful, blameworthy

creditor *n*
person/business you owe money to, lender
formal debtee
colloq. loan shark
E3 debtor

credulity *n*
naïvety, gullibility, credulousness, dupability, silliness, simplicity, stupidity, uncriticalness
E3 scepticism

credulous *adj*
naïve, gullible, wide-eyed, trusting, overtrusting, dupable, unsuspecting, uncritical
E3 sceptical, suspicious

⚠ **credulous**, **credible** or **creditable** ?
See panel at **credible**.

creed *n*
belief, faith, persuasion, credo, catechism, doctrine, teaching, principles, tenets, articles, canon, dogma

creek *n*
inlet, estuary, cove, bay, bight, firth, fiord

creep *v, n*
▶ *v* crawl, inch, edge, tiptoe, steal, sneak, slink, move unnoticed, slither, worm, wriggle, squirm, grovel, writhe
▶ *n* **1** *You little creep!*
sneak, fawner, sycophant, toady
colloq. yes-man, bootlicker
2 *gave me the creeps*
fear, horror, revulsion, terror, alarm, unease, disquiet

creeper *n*
climber, climbing plant, trailer, trailing plant, plant, rambler, runner, trailing, vine, liana

creepy *adj*
eerie, sinister, threatening, frightening, terrifying, hair-raising, bloodcurdling, spine-chilling,
nightmarish, macabre, gruesome, horrible, horrifying, horrific, unpleasant, menacing, ominous, disturbing, weird
colloq. scary, spooky

crescent-shaped *adj*
bow-shaped, sickle-shaped
formal falcate, falcated, falciform, lunate, lunated, lunular

crest *n*
1 *the crest of the hill*
ridge, crown, top, peak, summit, pinnacle, head
formal apex
2 TUFT, tassel, plume, comb, cockscomb, mane, aigrette, caruncle, panache
3 INSIGNIA, regalia, device, symbol, emblem, badge, coat of arms

crestfallen *adj*
disappointed, downhearted, dejected, sad, depressed, despondent, discouraged, disheartened, dispirited, downcast
formal disconsolate
colloq. cheesed off, in the doldrums, down in the dumps
E3 elated

crevasse *n*
abyss, chasm, cleft, crack, fissure, gap, bergschrund

crevice *n*
crack, fissure, split, rift, cleft, slit, chink, cranny, gap, hole, opening, break
formal interstice

crew *n*
team, party, squad, troop, corps, company, complement, force, corps, gang, band, pack, group, unit, bunch, crowd, mob, set, lot

crib *n, v*
▶ *n* carry-cot, cot, crib, travel-cot, crib, bassinet, bed
▶ *v* copy, cheat, steal, pirate, plagiarize
formal purloin
colloq. lift, pinch

crick *n*
pain, spasm, stiffness, convulsion, cramp, twinge

crier *n*
announcer, proclaimer, messenger, bearer of tidings, herald, town crier

crime *n*
law-breaking, lawlessness, delinquency, illegal act, unlawful act, offence, felony, misdemeanour, misdeed, wrongdoing, misconduct, transgression, violation, sin, iniquity, vice, villainy, wickedness, atrocity, outrage
formal malfeasance

Crimes include: theft, robbery, burglary, larceny, pilfering, mugging, poaching; assault, rape, grievous bodily harm, *colloq.* GBH, battery, manslaughter, homicide, murder, assassination; fraud, bribery, corruption, embezzlement, extortion, blackmail; arson, treason, terrorism, hijack, piracy, computer hacking, kidnapping, sabotage, vandalism, hooliganism, drug-smuggling, forgery, counterfeiting, perjury, joy-riding, drink-driving, drunk and disorderly.

criminal *n, adj*
▶ *n* law-breaker, felon, delinquent, offender, wrongdoer, miscreant, culprit, villain, convict,

prisoner, gang, ring, (criminal) syndicate, underworld
formal malefactor

Types of criminal include: armed robber, arsonist, assassin, bandit, batterer, bigamist, blackmailer, bootlegger, brigand, buccaneer, burglar, car-thief, cat burglar, counterfeiter, cracksman, crook, dope pusher, drink-driver, drug-smuggler, embezzler, extortionist, fire-raiser, forger, gangster, gunman, highwayman, hijacker, *slang* hood, hoodlum, housebreaker, *colloq.* jailbird, joyrider, kerb-crawler, kidnapper, killer, *slang* lag, larcenist, *US* mobster, mugger, murderer, perjurer, pickpocket, pirate, poacher, racketeer, ram-raider, rapist, receiver, robber, rustler, saboteur, safecracker, sexual abuser, shoplifter, smuggler, strangler, swindler, terrorist, thief, thug, trespasser, vandal, war criminal.

▶ *adj* **1** *a criminal offence*
illegal, unlawful, illicit, lawless, law-breaking, wrong, indictable, dishonest, villainous, corrupt, wicked, evil, iniquitous
formal culpable, felonious, nefarious
colloq. crooked, bent
2 *a criminal waste*
scandalous, deplorable, disgraceful, outrageous, infamous, disgusting, shameful, reprehensible
colloq. obscene
E3 **1** legal, lawful, honest, upright

crimp *v*
flute, pleat, fold, gather, furrow, ridge, corrugate, groove, wrinkle, pucker, crease, crumple, rumple, crinkle, tuck

cringe *v*
1 *the sight made me cringe*
shrink, recoil, shy, start, flinch, draw back, wince, blench, quail, tremble, quiver, cower, crouch, bend, bow, stoop
2 GROVEL, toady, fawn, flatter, bow and scrape, curry favour
colloq. crawl, creep, be all over, suck up

crinkle *n, v*
▶ *n* fold, line, pleat, crease, tuck, ruffle, rumple, twist, wave, wrinkle, pucker, ruck, crinkle, corrugation, furrow, ridge, groove
▶ *v* fold, pleat, crease, wrinkle, pucker, curl, twist, crumple, rumple, crinkle, crimp, tuck, corrugate, groove, furrow, ridge

crinkly *adj*
fluted, pleated, folded, gathered, furrowed, ridged, corrugated, grooved, wrinkled, wrinkly, puckered, curly, frizzy, kinky, creased, crimped, crumpled, rumpled, crinkled, tucked
E3 smooth, straight

cripple *v*
crippled by the accident/the tax increase
lame, paralyse, disable, handicap, injure, maim, mutilate, damage, impair, spoil, ruin, destroy, sabotage, weaken, hamstring, hamper, impede, spoil
formal incapacitate, debilitate, vitiate

crippled *adj*
lame, paralysed, disabled, handicapped, deformed
formal incapacitated

crisis *n*
emergency, extremity, catastrophe, disaster, calamity, critical situation, dilemma, quandary, predicament,

difficulty, trouble, problem
formal exigency
colloq. crunch, mess, scrape, pickle, jam, fix, hole, hot water

crisp *adj*
1 *a crisp biscuit*
crispy, crunchy, brittle, crumbly, breakable, firm, hard
formal friable
2 BRACING, invigorating, refreshing, fresh, brisk, chilly, cool
3 BRIEF, pithy, terse, brief, short, succinct, clear, incisive
colloq. snappy
E3 **1** soggy, limp, flabby **2** muggy **3** wordy, vague

criterion *n*
standard, norm, touchstone, benchmark, yardstick, measure, gauge, rule, scale, law, principle, model, canon, test
formal exemplar

critic *n*
1 *a music critic*
reviewer, commentator, analyst, pundit, authority, expert, judge
2 *a critic of the government*
judge, censor, censurer, carper, fault-finder, attacker
colloq. backbiter, carper, nit-picker, knocker

critical *adj*
1 *at the critical moment*
crucial, vital, essential, important, all-important, momentous, major, deciding, decisive, historic, fateful, pivotal, urgent, serious, compelling, pressing
formal exigent, climacteric
2 *in a critical condition*
dangerous, serious, grave, precarious
formal perilous
3 UNCOMPLIMENTARY, derogatory, disparaging, judgemental, disapproving, censorious, scathing, carping, fault-finding, captious, niggling, quibbling, hypercritical, venomous, vitriolic
formal vituperative
colloq. cavilling, nit-picking
4 ANALYTICAL, diagnostic, penetrating, probing, discerning, evaluative, explanatory, perceptive
formal expository
E3 **1** unimportant **3** complimentary, appreciative

criticism *n*
1 CONDEMNATION, disapproval, disparagement, fault-finding, censure, reproof, blame
formal animadversion
colloq. brickbat, flak, slating, slamming, nit-picking, niggle, knocking, stick
2 REVIEW, critique, assessment, evaluation, appraisal, judgement, analysis, commentary, write-up, appreciation, explanation, interpretation
formal exposition, explication
colloq. bad press
E3 **1** praise, commendation

criticize *v*
1 CONDEMN, disparage, carp, disapprove of, find fault with, denounce, attack, censure, blame
formal animadvert, excoriate, decry, denigrate, vituperate
colloq. nag, slate, slam, knock, snipe, run down, come down on, give someone some stick, go to town on, haul over the coals, pick holes in, pan, pull to pieces, tear to shreds, tear a strip off, nit-pick, do a hatchet job on, slag off, badmouth, rubbish, put the boot in

2 REVIEW, assess, evaluate, appraise, judge, analyse, explain, interpret
▨ **1** praise, commend

critique *n*
review, essay, assessment, evaluation, appraisal, judgement, analysis, commentary, write-up, appreciation, explanation, interpretation
formal exposition, explication

croak *v*
rasp, squawk, caw, wheeze, speak harshly, rasp, gasp, grunt

crock *n*
jar, pot, vessel

crockery *n*
dishes, tableware, china, porcelain, earthenware, stoneware, pottery

Items of crockery include: cup, saucer, coffee cup, mug, beaker, plate, side plate, dinner plate, bowl, cereal bowl, soup bowl, salad-bowl, sugar bowl, jug, milk-jug, basin, pot, teapot, coffee pot, percolator, cafétière, cakestand, meat dish, butter-dish, tureen, gravy boat, cruet, teaset, dinner service.

croft *n*
farm, plot, smallholding, farmland

crony *n*
friend, companion, associate, colleague, accomplice, ally, comrade, follower, sidekick
colloq. mate, pal, chum, buddy

crook *n, v*
▶ *n* criminal, thief, robber, law-breaker, swindler, cheat, rogue, fraud, villain
colloq. shark, con man
▶ *v* bend, twist, tilt, slant, angle, hook, curve, flex, bow, distort, warp, deform

crooked *adj*
1 ASKEW, awry, lopsided, asymmetric, irregular, uneven, off-centre, tilted, slanting, bent, angled, hooked, curved, bowed, warped, distorted, misshapen, deformed, contorted, twisted, buckled, tortuous, sinuous, winding, zigzag
formal anfractuous
colloq. skew-whiff
2 CRIMINAL, illegal, unlawful, illicit, criminal, dishonest, deceitful, corrupt, fraudulent, shifty, underhand, treacherous, unscrupulous, unprincipled, unethical
formal nefarious
colloq. bent, shady
▨ **1** straight **2** honest

croon *v*
sing, hum, warble, lilt, vocalize

crop *n, v*
▶ *n* **1** *grow crops*
growth, yield, produce, fruits, harvest, vintage, gathering, reaping, gleaning
See also **arable crop**.
2 *this year's crop of graduates*
batch, group, lot, set, collection
▶ *v* cut, snip, clip, shear, trim, pare, prune, mow, lop, shorten, reduce, curtail
▷ **crop up** arise, emerge, appear, arrive, occur, happen, come up, turn up, present itself, come to pass, take place

cross *n, v, adj*
▶ *n* **1** BURDEN, load, misfortune, trouble, adversity, worry, disaster, catastrophe, trial, grief, misery, pain, suffering, woe
formal affliction, tribulation
2 CROSSBREED, hybrid, mongrel, blend, mix, mixture, amalgam, combination
Related adjective: crucial

Types of cross include: ankh, Avelian, botoné, Calvary, capital, cardinal, Celtic, Constantinian, Cornish, crosslet, crucifix, encolpion, fleury, fylfot, Geneva, Greek, Jerusalem, Latin, Lorraine, Maltese, moline, papal, patriarchal, potent, quadrate, rood, Russian, saltire, St Andrew's, St Anthony's, St George's, St Peter's, swastika, tau, Y-cross.

▶ *v* **1** *cross the river*
go across, travel across, pass over, ford, bridge, span
formal traverse
2 INTERSECT, meet, join, converge, criss-cross, lace, interweave, intertwine
3 CROSSBREED, interbreed, mongrelize, hybridize, cross-fertilize, cross-pollinate, blend, mix
4 THWART, frustrate, foil, hinder, hamper, impede, obstruct, block, check, resist, oppose
▶ *adj* **1** IRRITABLE, annoyed, angry, vexed, bad-tempered, ill-tempered, grumpy, put out, irascible, short, snappy, snappish, surly, sullen, fractious, cantankerous, awkward, difficult, harsh, fretful, disagreeable, impatient
formal splenetic
colloq. peeved, shirty, crotchety, grouchy, crabby, prickly
2 TRANSVERSE, crosswise, oblique, diagonal, intersecting, opposite, reciprocal
▨ **1** placid, pleasant

cross-examine *v*
interrogate, question, cross-question, quiz, examine
colloq. grill, pump, give someone the third degree,

crossing *n*
1 *meet at the crossing*
junction, intersection, crossroads
2 *a pedestrian crossing*
pedestrian crossing, zebra crossing, pelican crossing, Toucan crossing, *US* crosswalk
3 *a sea crossing*
journey, trip, passage, voyage

crosswise *adv*
diagonally, crossways, crisscross, across, over, sideways, transversely, aslant, obliquely, athwart, awry
formal catercorner, catercornered

crotchety *adj*
grumpy, awkward, bad-tempered, cross, irritable, difficult, disagreeable, obstreperous, peevish, prickly, surly, testy, petulant, fractious, irascible, cantankerous, contrary, crusty
formal iracund, iracundulous
colloq. crabby, crabbed, grouchy
▨ calm, placid, pleasant

crouch *v*
squat, kneel, stoop, bend, bow, hunch, duck, cower, cringe

crow *v*
bluster, boast, brag, show off, gloat, rejoice, triumph, exult, flourish, vaunt
colloq. blow your own trumpet, *US* blow your own horn

crowd *n, v*
▶ *n* **1** THRONG, multitude, army, host, mob, masses, populace, people, public, riff-raff, rabble, horde, swarm, flock, herd, drove, pack, press, crush, squash, assembly, collection, company
2 *all the college crowd*
group, bunch, lot, set, circle, clique, fraternity
3 SPECTATORS, viewers, listeners, gate, attendance, audience, house, turnout
▶ *v* **1** *crowd around the pop star*
cluster, gather, congregate, muster, converge, huddle, mass, mob, throng, swarm, flock, surge, stream
2 *crowd into a van*
push, shove, elbow, jostle, thrust, press, squeeze, bundle, pile, pack, cram, jam, stuff, compress, congest, overflow

crowded *adj*
full, filled, packed, jammed, congested, crammed, cramped, crushed, overfull, overcrowded, overpopulated, busy, teeming, swarming, overflowing
colloq. full to bursting, jam-packed, packed like sardines, chock-a-block, thick on the ground
E3 empty, deserted

crown *n, v*
▶ *n* **1** CORONET, diadem, tiara, circlet, wreath, garland
Related adjective: coronal
2 PRIZE, trophy, reward, honour, distinction, glory, kudos, garland, laurels
3 SOVEREIGN, monarch, king, queen, emperor, empress, ruler, sovereignty, monarchy, royalty, empire
4 TOP, tip, crest, summit, pinnacle, peak, climax, height, culmination
formal acme, apex
▶ *v* **1** *crown the king*
enthrone, invest, induct, install, anoint, adorn, festoon, honour, dignify, reward
2 TOP, cap, complete, perfect, fulfil, finalize, round off, perfect, be the culmination of
formal consummate

crowning *adj, n*
▶ *adj* culminating, final, perfect, supreme, top, ultimate, unmatched, unsurpassed, paramount, sovereign
formal climactic, consummate
▶ *n* coronation, enthronement, installation, investiture
formal incoronation

crucial *adj*
urgent, pressing, vital, essential, key, pivotal, central, important, momentous, major, deciding, decisive, critical, trying, testing, compelling, pressing searching, historic, pivotal
E3 unimportant, trivial

crucify *v*
1 *Christ was crucified*
kill on the cross, execute, put to death on a cross
2 *crucified by the critics*
criticize, mock, ridicule, persecute, torment, punish, torture, rack
colloq. slam, slate, tear to pieces

crude *adj*
1 RAW, unprocessed, unrefined, rough, coarse, unfinished, unpolished
2 *a crude cabin*
rough, natural, primitive, makeshift, unfinished, undeveloped, simple, basic, rudimentary

formal rude
3 *a crude remark*
vulgar, coarse, rude, indecent, obscene, uncouth, risqué, offensive, gross, dirty, lewd, earthy, bawdy, smutty
colloq. raunchy, blue, hot, juicy
E3 **1** refined, finished **2** polite, decent, tasteful

cruel *adj*
fierce, ferocious, vicious, savage, barbarous, barbaric, bloodthirsty, murderous, cold-blooded, sadistic, brutal, inhuman, inhumane, unkind, nasty, mean, evil, fiendish, spiteful, malicious, callous, heartless, unfeeling, merciless, pitiless, flinty, hard-hearted, stony-hearted, implacable, ruthless, remorseless, unrelenting, inexorable, grim, hellish, atrocious, bitter, severe, cutting, painful, excruciating
formal malevolent, vengeful, indurate
E3 kind, compassionate, merciful

cruelty *n*
ferocity, viciousness, savagery, barbarity, bloodthirstiness, murderousness, violence, sadism, abuse, bullying, brutality, bestiality, inhumanity, spite, malice, venom, callousness, heartlessness, hard-heartedness, mercilessness, ruthlessness, tyranny, unkindness, meanness, harshness, severity
E3 kindness, compassion, mercy

cruise *n, v*
▶ *n* holiday, voyage, sail, journey, trip
▶ *v* **1** *cruising round the Mediterranean*
sail, travel, journey
2 *cruising along comfortably*
sail, coast, drift, freewheel, glide, slide, taxi

crumb *n*
piece, scrap, morsel, bit, titbit, particle, grain, atom, flake, speck, iota, jot, mite, shred, sliver, snippet, soupçon

crumble *v*
1 *the plaster is crumbling*
fragment, break up, come away, decompose, disintegrate, decay, degenerate, deteriorate, collapse, crush, pound, grind, powder, pulverize
2 *the organization began to crumble*
collapse, fail, fall to pieces, fall apart, disintegrate, decay, degenerate, deteriorate, break down, rot

crumbly *adj*
brittle, powdery, short
formal friable, pulverulent

crummy *adj*
inferior, miserable, poor, rotten, shoddy, trashy, cheap, useless, weak, worthless, contemptible, second-rate, third-rate
colloq. grotty, pathetic, rubbishy, half-baked;
slang crappy
E3 excellent

crumple *v*
crush, wrinkle, pucker, crinkle, rumple, crease, fold, collapse, fall

crunch *v, n*
▶ *v* **1** *crunch a biscuit*
munch, chomp, champ, chew, bite, grind, crush
formal masticate
2 *snow crunching*
grind, crush, scrunch, smash
▶ *n* crisis, crux, critical situation, emergency, test, moment of truth
colloq. pinch

crusade *n, v*
▶ *n* **1** *the Crusades*
holy war, jihad
2 *the crusade against nuclear power*
campaign, drive, struggle, push, movement, cause,
undertaking, expedition, strategy, offensive
▶ *v* campaign, promote, push, drive, advocate, work,
fight, strive, struggle, battle, attack

crusader *n*
advocate, campaigner, champion, promoter,
enthusiast, reformer, zealot, fighter, missionary

crush *v, n*
▶ *v* **1** SQUASH, compress, squeeze, mash, press,
pulp, break (up), smash, mill, pound, pulverize,
shatter, screw up, grind, crunch, crumble, crumple,
crinkle, wrinkle
formal comminute, triturate
2 *the rebels were crushed*
conquer, demolish, devastate, overpower, overwhelm,
overcome, quash, quell, suppress, subdue, put down
formal vanquish
3 *crushed by the criticism*
upset, devastate, humiliate, shame, abash
colloq. put down
▶ *n* **1** *injured in the crush*
crowd, pack, press, squash, jam
2 *a crush on the French teacher*
infatuation, passion, obsession, love, liking
colloq. pash

crust *n*
surface, exterior, outside, covering, topping, coat,
coating, layer, film, casing, mantle, skin, rind, shell,
husk, scab, caking
technical incrustation, concretion

crusty *adj*
1 *crusty bread*
crispy, crunchy, brittle, crumbly, breakable, firm, hard,
well-done, baked, well-baked
formal friable
2 *a crusty old man*
grumpy, awkward, bad-tempered, short-tempered,
brusque, gruff, cross, irritable, difficult, disagreeable,
obstreperous, peevish, prickly, surly, testy, touchy,
petulant, fractious, irascible, cantankerous, contrary
formal splenetic
colloq. crabby, crabbed, grouchy
🖃 **1** soft, soggy **2** calm, placid, pleasant

crux *n*
nub, heart, core, essence, centre, kernel, nucleus
colloq. the bottom line

cry *v, n*
▶ *v* **1** WEEP, sob, be in/shed tears, blubber, wail,
howl, bawl, whimper, whine, snivel
colloq. burst into tears, cry your eyes out
2 SHOUT, call (out), exclaim, roar, bellow, yell,
scream, howl, bawl, shriek, screech
▷ **cry off** cancel, withdraw, excuse yourself, back
out, decide against, change your mind
▷ **cry out for** need, call for, demand, want, require;
formal necessitate
▶ *n* **1** WEEP, weeping, sob, sobbing, tears, blubber,
wail, howl, bawl, whimper, whine, snivel
2 SHOUT, call, plea, exclamation, roar, bellow, yell,
scream, howl, bawl, shriek, screech

crypt *n*
tomb, vault, burial chamber, catacomb, mausoleum,

undercroft
Related adjective: cryptal

cryptic *adj*
enigmatic, ambiguous, equivocal, puzzling,
perplexing, mysterious, strange, bizarre, secret,
hidden, veiled, obscure, dark, occult
formal abstruse, esoteric
🖃 straightforward, clear, obvious

crystallize *v*
1 *the substance crystallized*
solidify, harden, materialize form
2 *the idea crystallized*
make/become clear, make/become definite, clarify,
appear, emerge, form

cub *n*
1 *fox cubs*
offspring, pup, puppy, whelp, baby
2 *a cub reporter*
beginner, novice, tiro, starter, learner, trainee,
apprentice, student, probationer, initiate, freshman,
fresher, recruit, raw recruit, tenderfoot, fledgling,
neophyte, youngster, youth
colloq. greenhorn, rookie

cubbyhole *n*
compartment, niche, pigeonhole, slot, recess, den,
hideaway, hole, tiny room

cube *n*
dice, die, solid, block, cuboid, hexahedron

cuddle *v*
hug, embrace, clasp, hold, enfold, nurse, nestle,
snuggle, pet, fondle, caress
colloq. snog, canoodle, neck, smooch

cuddly *adj*
cuddlesome, lovable, huggable, plump, soft, warm,
cosy

cudgel *n, v*
▶ *n* club, stick, mace, bludgeon, bat, truncheon,
shillelagh, alpeen, bastinado
colloq. cosh
▶ *v* hit, strike, beat, club, bash, clout, thwack, pound,
bludgeon, batter
colloq. clobber, cosh

cue *n*
signal, sign, nod, hint, suggestion, intimation,
indication, reminder, prompt, incentive, stimulus

cuff *v*
hit, thump, box, clip, knock, buffet, slap, smack, strike,
clout, beat
colloq. biff, clobber, belt, whack
▷ **off the cuff** impromptu, extempore, without
preparation, ad lib, spontaneously, improvised,
unprepared, unrehearsed, unscripted; *colloq.* off the
top of your head, on the spur of the moment

cuisine *n*
cooking, cookery, *haute cuisine, cordon bleu, nouvelle
cuisine*

cul-de-sac *n*
no through road, dead end, blind alley

cull *v*
1 *cull information*
collect, gather, choose, pick (out), select, sift, glean,
pluck, amass
2 *cull wild animals*
kill, destroy, slaughter, thin (out)

culminate v
climax, come to a climax, end (up), terminate, close, conclude, finish, peak
formal consummate
colloq. wind up
E3 start, begin

culmination n
climax, height, high point, peak, pinnacle, summit, top, crown, perfection, finale, conclusion, completion
formal consummation, apex, acme, zenith
E3 start, beginning

culpable adj
to blame, wrong, in the wrong, at fault, responsible, guilty, liable, offending, answerable, blamable, blameworthy, censurable, reprehensible, sinful
formal peccant
E3 blameless, innocent

culprit n
guilty party, offender, wrongdoer, miscreant, law-breaker, criminal, felon, delinquent, convict, villain

cult n
1 SECT, denomination, religion, faith, belief, affiliation, school, movement, party, faction
2 CRAZE, fad, fashion, vogue, obsession, trend
colloq. in-thing

cultivate v
1 FARM, till, work, plough, dig, prepare, grow, sow, plant, tend, raise, bring on, fertilize, produce, harvest
2 FOSTER, nurture, cherish, help, aid, assist, support, back, encourage, promote, further, forward, advance, enhance, work on, pursue, court, woo, develop, train, prepare, polish, refine, improve, enrich, enlighten
E3 2 neglect

cultivated adj
refined, cultured, civilized, sophisticated, polished, genteel, urbane, advanced, enlightened, educated, well-read, well-informed, scholarly, highbrow, discerning, discriminating

cultural adj
1 *cultural events*
artistic, aesthetic, liberal, civilizing, humanizing, enlightening, educational, educative, edifying, improving, broadening, developmental, enriching, elevating
2 *cultural heritage*
communal, national, ethnic, folk, tribal, traditional, time-honoured
technical anthropological
formal societal

culture n
1 *popular culture*
the arts, humanities, painting, philosophy, music, literature, history, learning
2 CIVILIZATION, society, lifestyle, way of life, customs, traditions, heritage, habits, behaviour
formal mores
3 *cell culture*
growth, production, crop, tendering, nurturing

cultured adj
cultivated, civilized, advanced, enlightened, educated, well-educated, well-read, well-informed, learned, scholarly, highbrow, intellectual, erudite, artistic, well-bred, refined, polite, polished, sophisticated, genteel, tasteful, urbane
colloq. arty
E3 uncultured, uneducated, ignorant

culvert n
channel, conduit, drain, duct, gutter, sewer, watercourse

cumbersome adj
1 *a cumbersome machine*
awkward, inconvenient, bulky, unwieldy, unmanageable, burdensome, onerous, heavy, weighty
formal incommodious, cumbrous
2 *a cumbersome process*
complicated, complex, involved, difficult, inefficient, badly organized, wasteful, slow
E3 1 convenient, manageable 2 simple, efficient

cumulative adj
increasing, growing, mounting, multiplying, enlarging, growing, collective
colloq. snowballing

cunning adj, n
▶ adj 1 *a cunning person*
crafty, sly, artful, wily, tricky, devious, subtle, deceitful, guileful, manipulative, sharp, shrewd, astute, canny, knowing, deep
colloq. shifty, cunning as a fox
2 *a cunning plan*
clever, imaginative, ingenious, skilful, inventive, resourceful, deft, dexterous, fiendish
E3 1 naïve, ingenuous, gullible
▶ n craftiness, slyness, artfulness, trickery, deviousness, subtlety, deceit, deceitfulness, guile, wiles, sharpness, shrewdness, astuteness, ingenuity, cleverness, imaginativeness, skill, inventiveness, resourcefulness, deftness, finesse, adroitness, fiendishness

cup n
1 *drink from a cup*
mug, tankard, beaker, goblet, chalice
2 *win a cup*
trophy, award, medal, prize, reward
3 *claret cup*
punch, wine

cupboard n
cabinet, locker, closet, wardrobe, pantry, sideboard, tallboy, dresser, Welsh dresser, chest, chest of drawers

cupidity n
acquisitiveness, greed, greediness, avarice, graspingness, covetousness, eagerness, hunger, hankering, itching, longing, yearning
formal avidity, rapaciousness, rapacity, voracity

curative adj
healing, healthful, health-giving, therapeutic, tonic, medicinal, remedial, restorative, corrective, salutary
technical febrifugal
formal alleviative, vulnerary

curator n
keeper, attendant, conservator, custodian, caretaker, steward, warden, warder, guardian

curb v, n
▶ v restrain, constrain, restrict, contain, control, keep under control, check, keep in check, moderate, reduce, bridle, muzzle, hold back, suppress, subdue, repress, inhibit, hinder, impede, hamper
formal retard
E3 encourage, foster
▶ n limitation, restriction, check, control, constraint, restraint, brake, rein, bridle, deterrent, damper, holding-back, suppression, repression, hindrance,

hamper, impediment
formal retardant

curdle *v*
coagulate, congeal, clot, solidify, thicken, turn, sour,
turn sour, ferment

cure *v, n*
▶ *v* **1** HEAL, remedy, correct, restore, treat, repair,
fix, rectify, mend, relieve, ease, alleviate, remedy, help,
make better, make well
2 PRESERVE, dry, smoke, salt, pickle, kipper
▶ *n* remedy, antidote, panacea, cure-all, solution,
medicine, corrective, restorative, healing, treatment,
therapy, alleviation, recovery
technical specific
formal elixir

curio *n*
antique, bygone, curiosity, knick-knack, trinket,
bibelot, *objet d'art*, object of virtu, *objet de vertu*

curiosity *n*
1 INQUISITIVENESS, interest, questioning,
querying, search, inquiry, prying, snooping,
interference
colloq. nosiness
2 CURIO, *objet d'art*, antique, bygone, novelty, trinket,
knick-knack
3 ODDITY, rarity, freak, phenomenon, spectacle,
wonder, marvel, exotica

curious *adj*
1 INQUISITIVE, questioning, querying, searching,
inquiring, interested, intrigued, fascinated, keen to
know, wanting to learn, prying, meddling, snooping,
meddlesome, interfering
colloq. nosy
2 *a curious sight*
odd, queer, funny, strange, peculiar, bizarre,
mysterious, puzzling, extraordinary, out of the
ordinary, unusual, remarkable, rare, unique, novel,
exotic, unconventional, weird, freakish, unorthodox,
quaint
▣ **1** uninterested, indifferent **2** ordinary, usual,
normal

curl *v, n*
▶ *v* crimp, frizz, wave, crinkle, ripple, kink, bend,
curve, meander, loop, turn, twist, wind, wreathe, twirl,
twine, coil, spiral, snake, corkscrew, scroll
▣ uncurl
▶ *n* wave, kink, swirl, twist, ring, ringlet, coil,
curlicue, helix, spiral, whorl

curly *adj*
curled, crimped, permed, frizzy, fuzzy, wavy, kinky,
curling, looping, turning, twisting, winding,
wreathing, twirling, coiling, spiralled, spiralling,
corkscrew
▣ straight

currency *n*
1 MONEY, legal tender, coinage, coins, notes, cash,
bills

Currencies of the world include: baht (*Thailand*),
bolivar (*Venezuela*), cent (*US, Canada, Australia,
New Zealand, South Africa*, etc), centavo
(*Portugal, Brazil, Mexico*, etc), centime (*France,
Belgium, Algeria*, etc), dinar (*Bosnia-Hercegovina,
Yugoslavia, Iraq, Jordan*, etc), dirham (*Morocco*),
dollar (*US, Canada, Australia, New Zealand*, etc),
dong (*Vietnam*), drachma (*Greece*), dram

(*Armenia*), ecu (*European Union*), escudo
(*Portugal*), euro (*European Union*), fils (*Iraq,
Jordan*, etc), franc (*France, Belgium, Switzerland*,
etc), guilder (*Netherlands*), karbovanets
(*Ukraine*), kopek (*Russia, Belarus, Tajikistan*),
koruna (*Czech Republic, Slovakia*), krona
(*Sweden*), króna (*Iceland*), krone (*Denmark,
Norway*), kroon (*Estonia*), kunar (*Croatia*), kyat
(*Myanmar*), lari (*Georgia*), lats (*Latvia*), lek
(*Albania*), leu (*Romania, Moldova*), lev (*Bulgaria*),
lira (*Italy*), litas (*Lithuania*), manat (*Azerbaijan,
Turkmenistan*), mark (*Germany*), pence (*UK*),
peseta (*Spain*), peso (*Mexico, Chile*, etc), pfennig
(*Germany*), piastre (*Egypt, Syria*, etc), pound (*UK,
Egypt*, etc), punt (*Ireland*), rand (*South Africa*),
real (*Brazil*), rial (*Iran*), riyal (*Saudi Arabia*),
rouble (*Russia, Belarus, Tajikistan*), rupee (*India,
Pakistan*, etc), schilling (*Austria*), shekel (*Israel*),
shilling (*Kenya, Uganda*, etc), som (*Kyrgyzstan*),
sterling (*UK*), sucre (*Ecuador*), sum (*Uzbekistan*),
tenge (*Kazakhstan*), tolar (*Slovenia*), won
(*N Korea, S Korea*), yen (*Japan*), yuan (*China*),
zaïre (*Zaire*), zloty (*Poland*).

2 ACCEPTANCE, publicity, popularity, vogue,
circulation, prevalence, exposure
formal dissemination

current *adj, n*
▶ *adj* **1** *current events*
present, ongoing, existing, contemporary, present-day,
present-time, modern, fashionable, in fashion, up-to-
date, up-to-the-minute, in vogue, popular
formal extant
colloq. trendy, in
2 *still current in the 1800s*
(generally) accepted, widespread, prevalent, common,
popular, general, prevailing, reigning, in circulation
colloq. going around
▣ **1** obsolete, old-fashioned
▶ *n* draught, stream, mainstream, jet, flow, swirl,
movement, drift, ebb, tide, course, progress, trend,
direction, tendency, undercurrent, tenor, mood,
feeling

curriculum *n*
syllabus, core curriculum, national curriculum,
subjects, course of studies, discipline, course, course of
study, module, educational programme, timetable

curse *v, n*
▶ *v* **1** SWEAR, use bad language, blaspheme, damn,
condemn, denounce, blast
formal accurse, imprecate, anathematize, fulminate
colloq. cuss, put a jinx on
2 BLIGHT, plague, scourge, afflict, harm, ruin,
trouble, beset, torment
▣ **2** bless
▶ *n* **1** SWEAR-WORD, oath, expletive, blasphemy,
obscenity, profanity, bad language
formal anathema, imprecation, execration
colloq. four-letter word
2 JINX, spell, anathema, bane, evil, plague, scourge,
affliction, trouble, torment, ordeal, calamity,
misfortune, disaster
formal malediction, execration, tribulation
▣ **2** blessing, advantage

cursed *adj*
damned, detestable, abominable, confounded,
infernal, hateful, loathsome, odious, vile, fiendish,
annoying, unpleasant, pernicious, infamous

formal execrable
colloq. blasted, blooming, flipping, dashed, dratting

cursory *adj*
brief, slight, summary, superficial, desultory, quick, rapid, fleeting, hasty, hurried, offhand, dismissive, passing, perfunctory, careless, casual, slapdash
E∃ painstaking, thorough

curt *adj*
abrupt, blunt, rude, sharp, brusque, gruff, laconic, offhand, short, short-spoken, tart, terse, snappish, unceremonious, uncivil, ungracious, brief, pithy, concise, succinct, summary
E∃ voluble

curtail *v*
reduce, limit, restrict, shorten, truncate, cut, cut down, cut short, cut back (on), trim, shrink, abridge, abbreviate, lessen, decrease, pare, pare down/back, prune, slim, guillotine
E∃ lengthen, extend, increase

curtailment *n*
reduction, limitation, restriction, shortening, truncation, cut, cutback, trimming, shrinkage, abridgement, abbreviation, contraction, lessening, decrease, paring, docking, pruning, slimming, guillotine
formal retrenchment
E∃ extension, lengthening, increase

curtain *n*
blind, screen, cover, shutter, net curtain, hanging, window hanging, backdrop, portière, drapery, tapestry, *US* drape

curtsy *v*
bob, bow, kowtow, salaam
formal genuflect

curvaceous *adj*
shapely, well-proportioned, well-rounded, well-stacked, buxom, comely, curvy, bosomy, voluptuous
E∃ skinny

curve *v, n*
▶ *v* bend, arch, arc, bow, bulge, swell, hook, crook, turn, wind, twist, round, swerve, loop, spiral, coil
formal incurve
▶ *n* bend, turn, bow, loop, arc, arch, circle, crescent, trajectory, helix, spiral, winding, meandering, camber, kink, curvature, flexure

curved *adj*
bent, arched, bowed, rounded, humped, bulging, swelling, convex, concave, bending, cupped, scooped, crooked, twisted, warped, sweeping, sinuous, tortuous, serpentine
technical arcuate, curviform
E∃ straight

cushion *n, v*
▶ *n* pillow, bolster, headrest, squab, beanbag, hassock, pad, padding, mat, buffer, shock absorber
technical pulvinus
Related adjectives: pulvillar, pulvinar
▶ *v* soften, deaden, dampen, absorb, muffle, stifle, suppress, lessen, reduce, diminish, mitigate, protect, bolster, buttress, prop up, support

cushy *adj*
comfortable, easy, undemanding
colloq. jammy, soft, plum
E∃ demanding, tough

custodian *n*
caretaker, conservator, curator, guard, guardian, warden, warder, keeper, overseer, superintendent, watchdog, watchman, protector, castellan

custody *n*
1 KEEPING, possession, charge, care, safekeeping, protection, preservation, custodianship, trusteeship, guardianship, wardship, guidance, supervision, responsibility
2 DETENTION, confinement, imprisonment, captivity, arrest
formal incarceration

custom *n*
1 *national customs*
tradition, usage, use, habit, routine, procedure, practice, policy, way, manner, style, form, fashion, way of behaving, convention, etiquette, ethos, formality, procedure, observance, ritual, rite, usage, institution
2 *take my custom elsewhere*
business, trade
formal patronage

customarily *adv*
traditionally, conventionally, habitually, routinely, regularly, as a rule, usually, normally, ordinarily, commonly, generally, popularly, fashionably
E∃ unusually, occasionally, rarely

customary *adj*
traditional, conventional, accepted, established, set, habitual, routine, regular, usual, normal, ordinary, everyday, familiar, common, general, popular, fashionable, prevailing
E∃ unusual, rare

customer *n*
client, patron, regular, consumer, shopper, buyer, purchaser, clientele, prospect
colloq. punter

customize *v*
adapt, convert, modify, tailor, alter, adjust, suit, fit, transform
colloq. fine-tune

cut *v, n*
▶ *v* **1** *cut the paper/your finger; cut a hole*
slit, pierce, slice, sever, chop, hack, hew, carve, split, dock, lop, prune, excise
2 *cut meat*
dissect, divide, carve, slice, chop (up), dice, mince, shred, grate
formal cleave
3 *cut hair/grass*
shorten, trim, clip, crop, snip, shear, mow, shave, pare, prune, dock
4 *cut glass*
engrave, incise, chisel, score
5 *cut someone's throat*
stab, wound, nick, slash, lacerate
6 *cut costs*
reduce, decrease, lower, diminish, curtail, curb, prune
colloq. slash, axe
7 *cut a story/broadcast*
shorten, make shorter, curtail, abbreviate, abridge, condense, précis, summarize, edit, delete, omit
formal excise, expurgate
8 *cut someone dead*
IGNORE, spurn, avoid, pretend not to see/notice, snub, slight, rebuff, insult, scorn
colloq. cut dead, cold-shoulder, look right through, send to Coventry, not give someone the time of day

▷ **cut across** transcend, surmount, go beyond, rise above, leave behind

▷ **cut back** check, crop, curb, curtail, decrease, economize, lessen, lop, lower, prune, reduce, trim, scale down; *formal* retrench; *colloq.* slash, downsize

▷ **cut down** 1 *cut down a tree* fell, chop down, hew, saw, lop, level, raze 2 REDUCE, decrease, lower, lessen, diminish, curtail, curb, prune

▷ **cut in** interrupt, break in, butt in, intervene, intrude; *formal* interpose, interject; *colloq.* barge in

▷ **cut off** 1 *cut off his head* remove, sever, detach, amputate, chop off, take off, break off, tear off 2 *feel cut off from friends* separate, isolate, keep apart, detach, seclude, sever, insulate, shelter 3 *cut off a supply* STOP, end, bring to an end, halt, suspend, disconnect, break off, block, obstruct, intercept; *formal* discontinue 4 *get cut off on the phone* disconnect, break off, unhook, separate, detach, intercept, interrupt

▷ **cut out** 1 *cut out a coupon* extract, remove, separate, take out, tear out; *formal* excise 2 omit, cut, exclude, leave out, drop, delete, edit; *formal* excise 3 stop, refrain; *formal* cease, desist, discontinue; *colloq.* quit, leave off, lay off, knock off, pack in 4 *the engine cut out* stop working, fail, break down, go wrong; *formal* malfunction; *colloq.* pack up; *slang* conk out

▷ **cut up** carve, slice(up), chop (up), dice, mince, dissect, dismember, divide, slash

▶ *n* 1 INCISION, wound, nick, gash, slit, slash, rip, laceration, notch, score

2 *go for a cut at the barber's* trim, clip, crop, shave

3 *spending cuts* reduction, decrease, lowering, cutback, saving, economy, lessening
formal retrenchment

4 *a cut of meat* section, slice, piece, bit, part

5 *a power cut* failure, fault, breakdown, breaking-down, cutting-out
formal malfunctioning

6 *a cut of the profits* SHARE, allocation, proportion, portion, quota, ration
colloq. slice, slice of the cake, whack

7 *the cut of a garment* shape, style, fashion, form, profile

▷ **cut out for** suitable, suited, right, appropriate, qualified, made, good

▷ **cut and dried** clear, definite, certain, settled, fixed, organized, prearranged, automatic; *formal* predetermined; *colloq.* sewn up

cutback *n*
cut, saving, economy, reduction, decrease, curtailment, lowering, lessening
formal retrenchment
colloq. slashing

cutlery *n*

Items of cutlery include: knife, butter-knife, carving-knife, fish knife, steak knife, cheese knife, breadknife, vegetable knife, fork, fish fork, carving fork, spoon, dessert-spoon, tablespoon, teaspoon, soup-spoon, caddy spoon, salt spoon, apostle spoon, ladle, salad servers, fish slice, cake server, sugar tongs, chopsticks, canteen of cutlery.

cut-price *adj*
reduced, sale, discount, bargain, cheap, low-priced, cut-rate

cutter *n*

Types of cutter include: axe, billhook, blade, chisel, chopper, clippers, guillotine, hedgetrimmer, knife, flick knife, penknife, pocket knife, Stanley knife®, Swiss army knife, lopper, machete, mower, lawnmower, plane, razor, saw, chainsaw, fretsaw, hacksaw, jigsaw, scalpel, scissors, scythe, secateurs, shears, pinking shears, sickle, Strimmer®, sword. *See also* **cutlery; saw[1]; weapon.**

cut-throat *adj*
ruthless, pitiless, relentless, fierce, highly/fiercely competitive, keen, keenly contested, cruel, brutal
colloq. dog-eat-dog

cutting *adj, n*
▶ *adj* *a cutting wind/comment*
bitter, raw, chill, sharp, keen, pointed, incisive, penetrating, piercing, wounding, hurtful, stinging, biting, caustic, acid, scathing, sarcastic, snide, malicious
formal mordant, trenchant
colloq. bitchy
▶ *n* clipping, extract, excerpt, piece

cycle *n*
circle, round, rotation, oscillation, rhythm, biorhythm, body clock, revolution, rota, series, sequence, order, pattern, succession, phase, period, era, age, epoch, aeon

cyclone *n*
hurricane, monsoon, tempest, tropical storm, storm, tornado, typhoon, whirlwind

cylinder *n*
column, barrel, drum, reel, bobbin, spool, spindle

cynic *n*
sceptic, doubter, pessimist, killjoy, scoffer
formal misanthrope
colloq. knocker, spoilsport

cynical *adj*
sceptical, doubtful, doubting, distrustful, disillusioned, disenchanted, pessimistic, negative, critical, scornful, derisive, suspicious, contemptuous, sneering, surly, scoffing, mocking, sarcastic, sardonic, ironic

cynicism *n*
scepticism, doubt, disbelief, distrust, disillusionment, disenchantment, pessimism, scorn, suspicion, contempt, sneering, scoffing, mocking, sarcasm, irony
formal misanthropy

cyst *n*
growth, sac, vesicle, blister, wen, bladder, bleb
technical atheroma, utricle

D

dab *v, n*
▶ *v* pat, daub, swab, wipe, touch, press, tap
▶ *n* **1** BIT, drop, dash, speck, spot, trace, tinge, smear, smudge, fleck
colloq. dollop
2 TOUCH, pat, stroke, tap, press
▷ **dab hand** expert, pastmaster, wizard, ace, adept

dabble *v*
1 TRIFLE, play, tinker, toy, dally, potter
2 PADDLE, moisten, wet, dampen, sprinkle, dip, splash, splatter

dabbler *n*
amateur, lay person, dilettante, trifler, dallier, tinkerer
🔁 professional, expert

daft *adj*
1 FOOLISH, crazy, silly, stupid, absurd, ridiculous, ludicrous, preposterous, outrageous, nonsensical, senseless, unwise, imprudent, odd, peculiar, impracticable, unrealistic, foolhardy, irrational, irresponsible, wild, idiotic, fatuous, inane
colloq. dotty, dumb, barmy, batty, potty, half-baked, hare-brained, crackbrained, crackpot, wacky
2 INSANE, mad, lunatic, simple, crazy, unbalanced, disturbed, deranged, demented, crazed, wild, berserk, touched, unhinged, out of your mind
colloq. mental, loony, loopy, bonkers, nuts, nutty, nutty as a fruitcake, off your rocker, needing your head examining, round the bend, round the twist
3 INFATUATED, passionate, enamoured, smitten, mad, wild, enthusiastic, fanatical, zealous, devoted, fond, keen, avid, ardent
colloq. daft, nuts, potty, sweet
🔁 **1** sensible **2** sane **3** indifferent

dagger *n*
bayonet, poniard, stiletto, knife, blade, skean, dirk, skene-dhu, kris, kukri, jambiya, misericord, yatagan

daily *adj, adv*
▶ *adj* **1** REGULAR, routine, everyday, customary, common, commonplace, ordinary, habitual
2 EVERYDAY
formal diurnal, quotidian, circadian
▶ *adv* every day, day after day, day by day

dainty *adj, n*
▶ *adj* **1** DELICATE, elegant, pretty, exquisite, petite, little, small, refined, fine, graceful, neat, trim, charming
2 *a dainty morsel*
tasty, delectable, delightful, enjoyable, appetizing, palatable mouth-watering, luscious, succulent, juicy, savoury
3 FASTIDIOUS, fussy, particular, discriminating, finicky, scrupulous
colloq. choosy
🔁 **1** gross, clumsy **2** unpalatable
▶ *n* delicacy, fancy, titbit, sweetmeat, bonbon, bonne-bouche

dais *n*
platform, stage, rostrum, podium, stand

dale *n*
valley, vale, glen, dell, coomb, dingle, gill, glen, strath

dally *v*
1 DAWDLE, linger, loiter, delay
formal procrastinate, tarry
2 *dally with an idea*
toy, play, flirt, trifle, frivol
🔁 **1** hasten, hurry

dam *n, v*
▶ *n* barrier, barrage, embankment, wall, blockage, barricade, obstruction, hindrance
▶ *v* block, confine, restrict, check, barricade, staunch, stem, obstruct

damage *v, n*
▶ *v* harm, injure, hurt, spoil, ruin, destroy, impair, mar, abuse, wreck, deface, vandalize, sabotage, desecrate, mutilate, weaken, tamper with, play/wreak havoc with, incapacitate
formal vitiate
🔁 mend, repair, fix
▶ *n* **1** *extensive damage after the fire*
harm, injury, hurt, destruction, ruin, devastation, havoc, loss, abuse, suffering, mischief, mutilation, impairment, detriment, defacement, vandalism
2 *pay damages*
compensation, fine, indemnity, reimbursement, reparation, restitution, satisfaction
🔁 **1** repair

damaging *adj*
harmful, hurtful, injurious, unfavourable, bad, detrimental, disadvantageous, pernicious, prejudicial, ruinous
formal deleterious
🔁 favourable, helpful

dame *n*
1 *Dame Edith Evans*
lady, noblewoman, baroness, dowager, peeress, aristocrat
2 *US slang* WOMAN, female, broad

damn *v, n*
▶ *v* **1** CURSE, swear, blast, doom, blaspheme, use bad language
formal accurse, imprecate, execrate, maledict, anathematize, fulminate
2 CONDEMN, revile, denounce, criticize, censure, denunciate
formal berate, castigate, inveigh, excoriate, decry, denigrate
colloq. slam, slate, pan, knock, run down, come down on, pick holes in, pan, pull to pieces, tear to shreds
🔁 **1** bless **2** praise, commend
▶ *n* iota, jot

slang dash, hoot, toss, monkey's, brass farthing, two hoots, tinker's cuss

damnable *adj*
abominable, atrocious, horrible, despicable, detestable, iniquitous, cursed, infernal, offensive, wicked
formal execrable
E3 admirable, praiseworthy

damnation *n*
condemnation, doom, denunciation, hell, perdition, excommunication, anathema
formal proscription

damned *adj*
1 *the damned in hell*
condemned, doomed, lost, cursed, accursed, reprobate, anathematized
2 *a damned disgrace*
cursed, detestable, despicable, abominable, confounded, infernal, hateful, loathsome, odious, vile, fiendish, annoying, unpleasant, pernicious
formal execrable
colloq. blasted, blooming, flipping, darned, dashed, dratting; *taboo slang* fucking
E3 1 blessed

damning *adj*
incriminating, condemning, implicating
formal accusatorial, condemnatory, damnatory, implicative, inculpatory

damp *adj, n, v*
▶ *adj* moist, wet, clammy, dank, humid, dewy, muggy, rainy, drizzly, misty, soggy, vaporous, rheumy
E3 dry, arid
▶ *n* dampness, moisture, clamminess, dankness, humidity, wet, wetness, dew, rain, drizzle, fog, mist, vapour
E3 dryness
▶ *v* ▷ **damp down** calm, dull, deaden, restrain, check, reduce, lessen, moderate, decrease, diminish

dampen *v*
1 MOISTEN, wet, spray, damp
2 DISCOURAGE, dishearten, damp down, deter, dash, dull, deaden, restrain, check, depress, dismay, reduce, lessen, moderate, decrease, diminish, put a damper on, muffle, inhibit, stifle, smother
E3 1 dry **2** encourage

damper *n*
▷ **put a damper on** discourage, dishearten, damp down, deter, dash, dull, deaden, restrain, check, depress, dismay, reduce, lessen, moderate, decrease, diminish, muffle, inhibit, stifle, smother
E3 encourage

dampness *n*
damp, moisture, clamminess, dankness, humidity, wet, wetness, dew, rain, drizzle, fog, mist, vapour

damsel *n*
maiden, girl, lass, young woman, young lady

dance *v, n*
▶ *v* **1** *learn to dance*
move to music, rock, spin, sway, twirl, pirouette, whirl, trip the light fantastic
colloq. hoof it, hop, jig, shake a leg
2 *dance for joy*
skip, leap, jump, bounce, frisk, caper, frolic, gambol, juke, kantikoy, prance, skip, spin, stomp, sway, swing, tread a measure, whirl

3 *lights dancing on the water*
leap, sway, flicker, twinkle, flash, shimmer, sparkle, waver, play, move lightly
▶ *n* ball, social
colloq. hop, knees-up, shindig
Related adjective: orchestic

Dances include: waltz, quickstep, foxtrot, tango, polka, one-step, military two-step, valeta, Lancers, rumba, samba, mambo, bossanova, beguine, fandango, flamenco, mazurka, bolero, paso doble, can-can; rock 'n' roll, jive, twist, stomp, bop, jitterbug, mashed potato; black bottom, Charleston, cha-cha, turkey-trot; Circassian circle, Paul Jones, jig, reel, quadrille, Highland fling, morris-dance, clog dance, hoe-down, hokey-cokey, Lambeth Walk, conga, belly-dance; galliard, gavotte, minuet.

Types of dancing include: ballet, tap, ballroom, old-time, disco, folk, country, Irish, Highland, Latin-American, flamenco, clog-dancing, morris dancing, limbo-dancing, break-dancing, robotics. *See also* **ballet**.

Dance functions include: disco, dance, social, tea dance, ceilidh, barn dance, ball, fancy dress ball, charity ball, hunt ball, *colloq.* hop, *colloq.* knees-up, *colloq.* shindig, *colloq.* rave, *US* prom.

dancer *n*
ballerina, ballet dancer, danseur, danseuse, coryphee, tap-dancer, belly-dancer

dandy *n, adj*
▶ *n* fop, coxcomb, beau, man about town, Adonis, beau, blade, dapperling, dude, exquisite, peacock, popinjay, swell, toff
▶ *adj* fine, capital, excellent, first-rate, great, splendid

danger *n*
1 *in danger of falling*
insecurity, jeopardy, precariousness, liability, vulnerability
formal endangerment, imperilment
2 *the dangers of smoking*
risk, threat, peril, hazard, menace, pitfall
E3 1 safety, security **2** safety

dangerous *adj*
unsafe, insecure, risky, high-risk, fraught with danger, threatening, breakneck, hazardous, chancy, perilous, precarious, reckless, treacherous, vulnerable, defenceless, menacing, ominous, exposed, susceptible, alarming, critical, severe, serious, grave, daring, nasty
formal minacious
colloq. dicey, hairy
E3 safe, secure, harmless

dangle *v*
1 HANG, droop, swing, sway, flap, trail
2 TEMPT, entice, flaunt, flourish, lure, hold out, tantalize

dank *adj*
damp, moist, wet, clammy, sticky, dewy, slimy, soggy
E3 dry

dapper *adj*
trim, well-dressed, well-turned-out, well-groomed, chic, dainty, neat, smart, spruce, stylish, nimble, active, brisk, spry
colloq. natty
E3 dishevelled, dowdy, scruffy, shabby, sloppy

dappled adj
speckled, mottled, spotted, stippled, dotted, flecked, freckled, variegated, bespeckled, piebald, pied, chequered

dare v, n
▶ v **1** RISK, venture, brave, be brave/bold enough, have the courage, hazard, adventure, endanger, stake, gamble
2 CHALLENGE, goad, provoke, taunt
colloq. throw down the gauntlet
3 DEFY, face, brave, confront, resist, flout, stand up to
▶ n challenge, venture, risk, provocation, taunt, goad, ultimatum, gauntlet

daredevil n, adj
▶ n adventurer, desperado, madcap, stuntman
F3 coward
▶ adj adventurous, daring, bold, fearless, dauntless, intrepid, brave, plucky, audacious, dauntless, reckless, rash, impetuous, impulsive, valiant

daring adj, n
▶ adj bold, adventurous, intrepid, courageous, fearless, brave, plucky, audacious, valiant, dauntless, undaunted, reckless, wild, rash, impulsive, foolhardy
F3 cautious, timid, afraid
▶ n boldness, fearlessness, courage, bravery, adventurousness, audacity, intrepidity, valour, defiance, pluck, spirit, gall, prowess, wildness, rashness, foolhardiness
colloq. guts, nerve, grit
F3 caution, timidity, cowardice

dark adj, n
▶ adj **1** *a dark room/day*
unlit, badly/poorly/dimly lit, overcast, black, dim, unilluminated, shady, shadowy, overcast, sunless, cloudy, misty, murky, misty, foggy, dusky, gloomy, dingy
formal tenebrous
2 *dark hair/skin*
black, brown, dark-haired, brunette, dark-skinned
3 *a dark manner*
gloomy, grim, sad, cheerless, joyless, drab, dismal, bleak, forbidding, sombre, sinister, dejected, mournful, morose, ominous, menacing
4 *the dark days of war*
unpleasant, awful, worrying, sad, gloomy, distressing, hopeless, frightening, bleak, dismal, black
5 *dark secrets*
hidden, mysterious, obscure, secret, unintelligible, puzzling, enigmatic, intricate, cryptic
formal abstruse, arcane, recondite, esoteric
F3 **1** light, bright, clear **2** fair, light **3** bright, cheerful **4** happy, joyful **5** comprehensible
▶ n **1** DARKNESS, dimness, night, night-time, nightfall, evening, blackness, gloom, dusk, twilight, half-light, shadows, shade, shadiness, murkiness, sunlessness, cloudiness, mist, fog
formal tenebrity, tenebrosity
2 IGNORANCE, secrecy, privacy, concealment, obscurity, mystery
F3 **1** light, brightness, daylight, lightness
2 enlightenment, openness

darken v
1 DIM, become/grow darker, obscure, blacken, cloud (over), fog, shadow, overshadow, shade, fade, eclipse
old use obnubilate
2 DEPRESS, sadden, deject, make gloomy, grow/become angry, look angry, frown
F3 **1** lighten **2** brighten

darling n, adj
▶ n **1** *come here, darling*
beloved, dear, dearest, favourite, sweetheart, love, pet, honey, angel, treasure
2 *the darling of the fashion world*
FAVOURITE, pet, apple of your eye
colloq. blue-eyed boy, teacher's pet
▶ adj dear, dearest, beloved, adored, cherished, precious, treasured

darn v
mend, repair, stitch, sew (up)

dart v, n
▶ v **1** DASH, bound, sprint, flit, flash, fly, rush, run, race, spring, leap, tear, bolt, scurry
colloq. scoot
2 THROW, cast, hurl, fling, shoot, toss, sling, launch, project, propel, send
▶ n bolt, arrow, barb, feather, flight, shaft

dash v, n
▶ v **1** RUSH, fly, hurry, tear, dart, dive, race, sprint, run, speed, bolt, bound, hurtle
colloq. nip, pop
2 *waves dashing against rocks*
smash, strike, lash, pound, beat, break, throw, crash, slam, hurl, fling
3 *dash your hopes*
crush, smash, shatter, disappoint, discourage, dishearten, let down, depress, sadden, dampen, confound, blight, ruin, destroy, spoil, frustrate, thwart, destroy, devastate, ruin
▷ **dash off** scribble, jot down, scrawl
▶ n **1** DROP, pinch, grain, touch, flavour, soupçon, trace, suggestion, hint, tinge, bit, little
colloq. smidgen
2 SPRINT, dart, bolt, rush, spurt, race, run

dashing adj
1 LIVELY, vigorous, spirited, energetic, animated, gallant, daring, bold, plucky, exuberant
2 SMART, stylish, fashionable, elegant, debonair, showy, flamboyant, attractive
F3 **1** lethargic **2** dowdy

dastardly adj
wicked, low, mean, base, contemptible, underhand, vile, cowardly, craven, despicable, faint-hearted, lily-livered
formal pusillanimous
F3 heroic, noble

data n
information, documents, facts, input, statistics, figures, details, material, research, particulars

date n, v
▶ n **1** TIME, age, period, era, stage, epoch, day, week, month, year, decade, century, millennium
2 APPOINTMENT, engagement, meeting, rendezvous
formal assignation
3 FRIEND, boyfriend, girlfriend, partner, escort
colloq. steady
▷ **out of date** old-fashioned, unfashionable, outdated, obsolete, dated, outmoded, antiquated, archaic, *passé*
F3 fashionable, modern
▷ **to date** so far, until now, until the present time, up to now, up to the present
▷ **up to date** fashionable, modern, current, contemporary, up to the minute; *colloq.* trendy
F3 old-fashioned, dated
▶ v **1** *date back to the 18th century*

originate, go back, come/exist from, belong to
2 *buy styles that won't date*
become old-fashioned/obsolete, go out, go out of use
formal obsolesce
3 *date someone*
go out with, take out, be together, go steady, court

dated *adj*
old-fashioned, obsolete, outdated, outmoded, out-of-date, *passé*, superseded, unfashionable, obsolescent, antiquated, archaic
colloq. old hat
E3 fashionable, up-to-the-minute

daub *v, n*
▶ *v* smear, plaster, coat, paint, cover, smirch, smudge, spatter, splatter, stain, sully
▶ *n* smear, splash, splodge, splotch, spot, stain, blot, blotch

daughter *n*
girl, child, lass, lassie, offspring, descendant, inhabitant, disciple

daunt *v*
intimidate, unnerve, alarm, dismay, frighten, scare, disconcert, cow, overawe, take aback, discourage, dishearten, demoralize, disillusion, put off, dispirit, deter
E3 encourage, hearten

dauntless *adj*
fearless, undaunted, resolute, brave, courageous, bold, intrepid, daring, plucky, valiant
E3 discouraged, disheartened

dawdle *v*
delay, loiter, lag, go slowly, go at a snail's pace, hang about, linger, dally, take your time, take too long, trail, potter
formal tarry
colloq. dilly-dally
E3 hurry

dawn *n, v*
▶ *n* **1** SUNRISE, daybreak, break of day, morning, daylight, first light, crack of dawn
Related adjectives: auroral, aurorean
2 BEGINNING, start, emergence, onset, origin, birth, arrival, rise
formal commencement, advent, inception, genesis
E3 **1** dusk **2** end
▶ *v* **1** BREAK, brighten, lighten, become/grow light, gleam, glimmer
2 BEGIN, appear, emerge, open, develop, originate, be born, come into being, rise
formal commence
▷ **dawn on** realize, strike, occur to, sink in, come into your mind; *colloq.* hit, click

day *n*
1 DAYTIME, daylight
2 AGE, period, time, date, era, generation, epoch
E3 **1** night
▷ **day after day** regularly, continually, endlessly, persistently, monotonously, perpetually, relentlessly
▷ **day by day** gradually, progressively, slowly but surely, steadily
▷ **have had its day** be no longer fashionable/popular, be no longer useful/successful, be out of date; *colloq.* be past it
Related adjective: diurnal

daybreak *n*
sunrise, dawn, break of day, morning, daylight, first

light, crack of dawn, cock-crow(ing), sun-up
E3 sunset, sundown

daydream *n, v*
▶ *n* fantasy, imagining, reverie, castles in the air, pipe dream, vision, musing, wish, dream, inattention, figment
▶ *v* fantasize, imagine, muse, fancy, dream, be lost in space, not pay attention, let your thoughts wander, stare into space
colloq. switch off

daylight *n*
1 *during daylight hours*
light, natural light, day, daytime, sunlight
2 SUNRISE, dawn, daybreak, break of day, morning, first light, crack of dawn
E3 **1** night, dark

daze *v, n*
▶ *v* **1** STUN, stupefy, shock, numb, paralyse
2 DAZZLE, bewilder, blind, confuse, baffle, dumbfound, amaze, surprise, shock, stun, startle, perplex, astonish, astound, stagger, take aback
colloq. flabbergast
▶ *n* bewilderment, confusion, stupor, numbness, trance, shock, distraction

dazed *adj*
1 STUNNED, stupefied, shocked, numbed, paralysed, unconscious
colloq. out
2 DAZZLED, bewildered, confused, baffled, dumbfounded, speechless, amazed, surprised, shocked, stunned, startled, perplexed, astonished, astounded, staggered, taken aback
colloq. flabbergasted

dazzle *v, n*
▶ *v* **1** DAZE, blind, confuse, blur
2 SPARKLE, fascinate, impress, strike, overwhelm, awe, overawe, overpower, scintillate, bedazzle, amaze, astonish, bewitch, hypnotize, dumbfound, stupefy
colloq. bowl over, knock out, wow
▶ *n* sparkle, brilliance, brightness, magnificence, splendour, scintillation, glitter, gleam, glare
colloq. razzmatazz

dazzling *adj*
brilliant, splendid, impressive, stunning, awe-inspiring, breathtaking, spectacular, glaring, glittering, shining, sparkling, glorious, radiant, ravishing, scintillating, sensational, grand, superb

dead *adj, adv*
▶ *adj* **1** LIFELESS, inanimate, defunct, departed, perished, extinct, late, gone, no more
formal deceased
colloq. dead as a doornail
2 *dead leaves*
inanimate, lifeless, inert
formal insentient, insensate, exanimate
3 *a dead language*
obsolete, extinct, discontinued, no longer spoken
4 *that issue is dead*
dated, out of date, *passé*, no longer of interest
colloq. old hat, dead as a dodo
5 *this town is dead*
boring, dull, humdrum, tedious, uninteresting, unexciting, with nothing happening, quiet
6 *my fingers have gone dead*
numb, unfeeling, not feeling anything, gone to sleep, paralysed
7 UNRESPONSIVE, apathetic, dull, indifferent,

insensitive, numb, cold, emotionless, frigid, lukewarm, unsympathetic, torpid
8 *dead centre*
EXACT, absolute, perfect, unqualified, utter, outright, complete, entire, total, downright, thorough
9 EXHAUSTED, tired, tired out, worn out
colloq. knackered, dead beat, ready to drop
F3 **1** alive **3** living **7** lively **9** refreshed
▶ *adv* absolutely, completely, entirely, exactly, precisely, perfectly, very, quite, totally, thoroughly, utterly

deaden *v*
reduce, blunt, muffle, dull, lessen, quieten, suppress, weaken, numb, diminish, stifle, mitigate, alleviate, soothe, moderate, take the edge off, anaesthetize, desensitize, smother, check, abate, allay, assuage, subdue, dampen, hush, mute, paralyse
F3 heighten

deadlock *n*
standstill, stalemate, checkmate, impasse, dead end, halt, stoppage

deadly *adj, adv*
▶ *adj* **1** *deadly poison*
lethal, fatal, dangerous, venomous, toxic, destructive, pernicious, noxious, malignant, murderous, mortal
2 *deadly enemies*
implacable, mortal, murderous, hated, grim, fierce, savage
3 *in deadly earnest*
great, serious, marked, intense, extreme
4 *a deadly lecture*
dull, boring, uninteresting, unexciting, tedious, monotonous
5 *deadly aim*
unerring, unfailing, precise, accurate, sure, effective, true
F3 **1** harmless **4** exciting
▶ *adv* utterly, thoroughly, dreadfully, absolutely, completely, entirely, perfectly, quite, totally, utterly

deadpan *adj*
blank, empty, expressionless, unexpressive, impassive, inexpressive, inscrutable, poker-faced, straight-faced, dispassionate

deaf *adj*
1 HARD OF HEARING, stone-deaf, with impaired hearing
colloq. deaf as a post
2 UNCONCERNED, indifferent, impervious, unmoved, oblivious, heedless, unmindful
F3 **2** aware, conscious

deafening *adj*
piercing, very loud, very noisy, ear-splitting, booming, resounding, thunderous, ringing, reverberating, roaring, overwhelming
F3 quiet

deal *v, n*
▶ *v* **1** DISTRIBUTE, give out, share, dole out, divide, allot, dispense, assign, mete out
formal apportion, bestow
2 TRADE, do business, buy and sell, negotiate, traffic, export, bargain, handle, treat, operate, market, stock
3 *deal a blow*
deliver, administer, direct, mete, inflict
▷ **deal with** **1** *deal with a situation* attend to, concern, see to, manage, handle, tackle, cope with, get to grips with, take care of, look after, sort out, process **2** *her novel deals with the future* treat,

consider, be about, concern, cover
▶ *n* **1** QUANTITY, lot, load, amount, extent, degree, portion, share
2 AGREEMENT, contract, understanding, pact, transaction, bargain, buy, arrangement
3 ROUND, hand, distribution

dealer *n*
trader, salesman, saleswoman, salesperson, merchant, retailer, wholesaler, marketer, merchandiser, vendor, trafficker
colloq. pusher, tout

dealings *n*
business, commerce, trade, operations, traffic, trafficking, transactions, negotiations, relations
formal intercourse
colloq. truck

dear *adj, n*
▶ *adj* **1** LOVED, beloved, treasured, valued, cherished, adored, favoured, precious, favourite, intimate, respected, close, darling, familiar, endearing
formal esteemed
2 EXPENSIVE, high-priced, costly, high-cost, overpriced, exorbitant, not cheap
colloq. pricey, steep
F3 **1** disliked, hated **2** cheap
▶ *n* beloved, loved one, precious, darling, pet, sweetheart, honey, angel, treasure

dearly *adv*
1 *he loves her dearly*
fondly, affectionately, with affection, lovingly, devotedly, adoringly, tenderly, intimately, with favour/ respect
2 *I wish it dearly*
greatly, extremely, very much, deeply, profoundly
3 *pay dearly for something*
at a great cost, at a high price, with great loss

dearth *n*
scarcity, shortage, deficiency, insufficiency, inadequacy, deficiency, lack, absence, scantiness, sparsity, need, poverty, famine
formal paucity, want
F3 excess, abundance

death *n*
1 *people in danger of death*
loss, departure, loss of life, fatality, passing, passing away, perishing, end, finish, the grave
formal expiration, decease, demise, quietus
colloq. last farewell, curtains
2 *the death of the welfare state*
ruin, destruction, end, finish, undoing, annihilation, downfall, extermination, dissolution, extinction
formal demise, obliteration, eradication, extirpation, termination, cessation
F3 **1** life, birth
▷ **put to death** execute, kill, hang, electrocute, shoot, guillotine, behead, exterminate, martyr
Related adjective: mortal

deathless *adj*
immortal, imperishable, eternal, everlasting, undying, never-ending, timeless, incorruptible, memorable, unforgettable

deathly *adj*
1 ASHEN, grim, haggard, pale, pallid, ghastly, wan, colourless, cadaverous
2 FATAL, deadly, mortal, intense, extreme, utmost

debacle *n*
fiasco, catastrophe, failure, collapse, defeat,
devastation, disaster, downfall, havoc, cataclysm,
overthrow, reversal, rout, turmoil, disintegration, ruin,
ruination, stampede, farce

debar *v*
ban, bar, forbid, prohibit, eject, exclude, shut out, keep
out, expel, stop, hamper, hinder, obstruct, prevent,
segregate, restrain, deny, blackball
formal preclude, proscribe
Ⅎ admit, allow

debase *v*
degrade, demean, devalue, disgrace, dishonour,
discredit, shame, humble, humiliate, cheapen, lower,
reduce, abase, defile, contaminate, pollute, corrupt,
adulterate, alloy, dilute, taint
formal vitiate
Ⅎ elevate, purify

debased *adj*
degraded, devalued, disgraced, dishonoured,
discredited, shamed, humbled, humiliated,
cheapened, abased, defiled, contaminated, impure,
polluted, perverted, corrupt, debauched, fallen, low,
degenerate, adulterated, tainted, base, sordid, vile
Ⅎ elevated, pure

debasement *n*
degradation, devaluation, disgrace, dishonour, shame,
humiliation, cheapening, depravation, abasement,
defilement, contamination, pollution, perversion,
corruption, degeneration, adulteration
Ⅎ elevation, purification

debatable *adj*
questionable, arguable, uncertain, unsure, disputable,
contestable, controversial, open to question, doubtful,
contentious, undecided, unsettled, problematical,
dubious, moot
Ⅎ unquestionable, certain, incontrovertible

debate *n, v*
▶ *n* discussion, argument, controversy, deliberation,
consideration, forum, contention, dispute, reflection,
polemic
formal disputation, altercation
▶ *v* 1 DISPUTE, argue, reason, discuss, talk about/
over, contend, contest, wrangle
formal altercate
colloq. kick around
2 CONSIDER, think over, deliberate, ponder, reflect,
meditate on, mull over, weigh
formal cogitate

debauch *v*
corrupt, lead astray, deprave, over-indulge, pervert,
pollute, subvert, ravish, ruin, seduce, violate
formal vitiate
Ⅎ cleanse, purge, purify

debauched *adj*
depraved, abandoned, immoral, corrupt, corrupted,
debased, perverted, degenerate, degraded,
intemperate, overindulgent, dissipated, dissolute,
excessive, decadent, promiscuous, wanton, lewd,
carousing, riotous
formal licentious
Ⅎ decent, pure, virtuous

debauchery *n*
depravity, immorality, corruption, degeneracy,
degradation, intemperance, overindulgence,
rakishness, dissoluteness, excess, decadence,

wantonness, lewdness, carousal, orgy, revel, lust, riot
formal dissipation, licentiousness, libertinism,
Ⅎ restraint, temperance

debilitate *v*
weaken, undermine, sap, incapacitate, wear out,
exhaust, impair, cripple
formal enervate, enfeeble, devitalize
Ⅎ strengthen, invigorate, energize

debilitating *adj*
weakening, undermining, incapacitating, wearing out,
fatiguing, tiring, exhausting, impairing, crippling
formal enervating, enervative, enfeebling
Ⅎ invigorating, strengthening

debility *n*
weakness, infirmity, tiredness, fatigue, exhaustion,
faintness, feebleness, frailty, incapacity, infirmity, lack
of energy/vitality
Ⅎ strength, vigour
technical asthenia, atonicity, atony
formal decrepitude, enervation, enfeeblement,
languor, malaise

debonair *adj*
suave, refined, urbane, well-bred, smooth, dashing,
elegant, affable, breezy, buoyant, charming, courteous,
cheerful, jaunty, light-hearted

debris *n*
remains, ruins, rubbish, waste, wreck, wreckage, litter,
fragments, rubble, trash, pieces, bits, sweepings, drift
formal detritus

debt *n*
1 *£500 in debt*
arrears, overdraft, money owing/due, due, liability,
debit, duty, bill, hock, claim, score
colloq. the red, Queer Street
2 *in someone's debt for their kindness*
indebtedness, obligation, commitment, liability
Ⅎ 1 credit, asset

debtor *n*
borrower, bankrupt, insolvent, defaulter, mortgagor
Ⅎ creditor

debunk *v*
expose, deflate, puncture, show up, ridicule, mock,
explode, disprove, lampoon
colloq. cut down to size

début *n*
first appearance, first performance, first night, first
recording, first time, introduction, launching,
beginning, entrance, presentation, inauguration,
première, coming-out, initiation

decadence *n*
corruption, debasement, debauchery, depravity,
dissolution, immorality, degeneracy, degenerateness,
degeneration, deterioration, self-indulgence,
debasement, decay, decline, fall, perversion
formal dissipation, licentiousness, retrogression
Ⅎ flourishing, rise

decadent *adj*
1 CORRUPT, debased, debauched, depraved,
dissolute, dissipated, immoral, degenerate, degraded,
self-indulgent
formal licentious
2 DECAYING, declining, degenerating, deteriorating,
debased
Ⅎ 1 moral

decamp v
make off, run away, take off, abscond, bolt, desert, escape, flee, flit, fly
colloq. scarper, skedaddle, vamoose, do a runner, do a bunk, do a moonlight flit, hightail it, absquatulate

decapitate v
behead, execute, guillotine, unhead

decay v, n
▶ v **1** ROT, go bad, decompose, spoil, fester, perish, rust, corrode
formal putrefy
2 DECLINE, deteriorate, disintegrate, corrode, crumble, waste away, degenerate, atrophy, wear away, weaken, dwindle, fail, shrivel, wither, sink
F3 2 flourish, grow
▶ n **1** ROT, going bad, decomposition, rotting, perishing
formal putrefaction, putrescence, putridity
2 DECLINE, deterioration, disintegration, degeneration, collapse, crumbling, decadence, weakening, wasting, failing, atrophy, withering, fading

decayed adj
rotten, bad, off, stale, sour, rank, addled, carious, decomposed, spoiled, mouldy, mildewed, perished, corroded, carrion, wasted, withered
formal putrefied, putrid

decease n
death, dying, demise, departure, passing, passing away, dissolution
formal expiration, demise

deceased adj, n
▶ adj dead, departed, former, late, lost, defunct, expired, gone, finished, extinct
▶ n dead, departed

deceit n
deception, pretence, cheating, misrepresentation, fraud, trickery, fraudulence, double-dealing, underhandedness, chicanery, fake, guile, sham, subterfuge, swindle, treachery, hypocrisy, artifice, ruse, cunning, slyness, craftiness, wiliness, stratagem, wile, imposition, feint, abuse
formal duplicity
F3 honesty, openness, frankness

deceitful adj
dishonest, untruthful, lying, deceptive, deceiving, false, insincere, untrustworthy, double-dealing, fraudulent, treacherous, duplicitous, guileful, underhand, sneaky, counterfeit, crafty, sly, cunning, hypocritical, designing, illusory, knavish
formal mendacious, duplicitous, dissembling, perfidious
colloq. two-faced, tricky
F3 honest, open

deceive v
mislead, delude, cheat (on), betray, fool, trick, hoax, bluff, dupe, swindle, outsmart, outwit, impose upon, lead on, misguide, outwit, hoodwink, beguile, set a trap for, entrap, ensnare, camouflage, abuse, seduce, gull
formal dissemble
colloq. con, kid, bamboozle, have on, take for a ride, string along, double-cross, two-time, pull someone's leg, pull a fast one on, pull the wool over someone's eyes, put up a smokescreen, lead up the garden path, put one over on

deceiver n
deluder, cheat, betrayer, fake, fraud, hypocrite, trickster, hoaxer, swindler, impostor, charlatan, abuser, seducer, mountebank
formal dissembler, inveigler
colloq. con man, diddler, crook, double-dealer

decelerate v
slow down, brake, put the brakes on, reduce speed

decency n
respectability, uprightness, integrity, civility, correctness, fitness, good taste, etiquette, courtesy, modesty, helpfulness
old use seemliness
formal propriety, decorum
F3 impropriety, discourtesy

decent adj
1 *decent behaviour*
RESPECTABLE, upright, worthy, proper, fitting, tasteful, chaste, virtuous, ethical, suitable, modest, appropriate, presentable, pure, fit, becoming, befitting, nice
old use seemly
formal decorous
2 *a decent person*
KIND, obliging, courteous, helpful, accommodating, generous, thoughtful, polite, gracious
3 ADEQUATE, acceptable, satisfactory, reasonable, sufficient, tolerable, competent
colloq. OK
F3 1 indecent **2** disobliging

decentralize n
devolve, regionalize, localize, delegate, deconcentrate, spread downwards/outwards
F3 centralize

deception n
deceit, pretence, deceptiveness, insincerity, treachery, hypocrisy, cheating, misrepresentation, trickery, fraudulence, double-dealing, underhandedness, chicanery, trick, cheat, imposture, lie, hoax, fraud, bluff, ruse, snare, guile, sham, subterfuge, artifice, swindle, stratagem, illusion, wile, craftiness, cunning
formal dissembling, duplicity
colloq. con, put-up job, leg-pull, flim-flam
F3 openness, honesty

deceptive adj
misleading, dishonest, false, fraudulent, cheating, cunning, sly, crooked, crafty, underhand, misleading, unreliable, illusive, fake, illusory, spurious, specious, mock, bogus, sham, ambiguous, specious
F3 genuine, artless, open
formal fallacious, dissembling, duplicitous

decide v
1 *decide to do something*
MAKE UP YOUR MIND, come to/arrive at a decision, reach/make a decision, come to/reach a conclusion, determine, resolve
2 *decide an issue/a case*
settle, resolve, determine, conclude, fix, establish, adjudicate, arbitrate, judge, rule, give a judgement/ruling
3 *decide on a new car*
choose, pick, select, opt for, settle
colloq. go for, plump for

decided adj
1 DEFINITE, clear, certain, marked, obvious, undeniable, indisputable, unequivocal, absolute,

clear-cut, pronounced, undisputed, unmistakable, unquestionable, positive, unambiguous, categorical, express, absolute, distinct, emphatic
2 RESOLUTE, decisive, determined, purposeful, firm, unhesitating, unswerving, unwavering, deliberate, forthright
🔁 **1** inconclusive **2** irresolute

decidedly *adv*
very, absolutely, certainly, downright, positively, quite, unquestionably, unequivocally, unmistakably, clearly, definitely, distinctly, obviously, decisively

decider *n*
clincher, *coup de grâce*, determiner, floorer

deciding *adj*
decisive, determining, conclusive, critical, crucial, significant, final, chief, influential, prime, principal, supreme
colloq. crunch
🔁 insignificant

decipher *v*
decode, unscramble, unravel, interpret, translate, make out, work out, understand, transliterate
formal construe
colloq. crack, figure out
🔁 encode

decision *n*
1 CONCLUSION, result, outcome, verdict, finding, settlement, resolution, judgement, arbitration, adjudication, ruling, decree, pronouncement, opinion
2 DETERMINATION, decisiveness, firmness, resolve, forcefulness, purpose, strong-mindedness

decisive *adj*
1 CONCLUSIVE, deciding, definite, definitive, determining, absolute, final, critical, crucial, influential, significant, momentous, prime, principal, fateful
2 *a decisive person*
DETERMINED, resolute, decided, positive, firm, forceful, forthright, purposeful, strong, strong-minded, unwavering, unswerving
🔁 **1** inconclusive, insignificant **2** indecisive

deck *v*
decorate, ornament, adorn, beautify, embellish, trim, garnish, garland, festoon, grace, enrich, prettify, trick out
formal array, bedeck
colloq. tart up, rig, tog

declaim *v*
speak boldly/dramatically, proclaim, hold forth, lecture, harangue, rant, sermonize
formal orate, perorate
colloq. spiel, spout

declamation *n*
speech, address, lecture, oration, sermon, harangue, tirade, rant, speechifying

declamatory *adj*
bold, dramatic, rhetorical, bombastic, discursive, grandiloquent, grandiose, high-flown, inflated, oratorical, overblown, pompous, stagy, theatrical, stilted
formal magniloquent, orotund, fustian

declaration *n*
1 ANNOUNCEMENT, notification, pronouncement, statement, proclamation, edict, decree, manifesto, broadcast

formal promulgation
2 AFFIRMATION, acknowledgement, assertion, statement, confession, testimony, confirmation, disclosure, profession, revelation
formal attestation, avowal, affidavit, averment

declare *v*
1 ANNOUNCE, proclaim, make known, pronounce, decree, publish, broadcast
formal promulgate
2 AFFIRM, assert, claim, profess, maintain, state, certify, pronounce, confess, confirm, disclose, make known, reveal, show, swear, testify, witness, validate
formal aver, avow, attest

decline *v, n*
▶ *v* **1** DIMINISH, become/get less, go/come down, decrease, dwindle, lessen, fade, fall, sink, subside, slide, drop, wane, weaken, wither, fade, ebb, flag, plummet, plunge
formal abate
2 REFUSE, turn down, say no to, reject, deny, repudiate, forego, avoid, balk
colloq. give the thumbs-down to
3 DECAY, deteriorate, worsen, degenerate, sink, rot, slip, fall off, lapse
formal regress
4 DESCEND, sink, slope, dip, slant
🔁 **1** grow, increase **2** accept **3** improve **4** rise
▶ *n* **1** DETERIORATION, dwindling, lessening, decrease, reduction, decay, degeneration, weakening, worsening, failing, failure, downturn, dwindling, waning, fall, falling-off, recession, slump
formal diminution, abatement
2 DESCENT, dip, declination, hill, slope, incline, divergence, deviation
formal declivity
🔁 **1** improvement **2** rise

decode *v*
decipher, interpret, unscramble, unravel, translate, make out, work out, understand, transliterate, uncipher
formal construe
colloq. crack, figure out
🔁 encode

decomposable *adj*
biodegradable, degradable, destructible, decompoundable

decompose *v*
disintegrate, rot, decay, break down, break up, crumble, spoil, dissolve, separate, fester
formal putrefy

decomposition *n*
rot, going bad, decay, rotting, perishing, corruption, disintegration, dissolution
formal putrefaction, putrescence, putridity
🔁 combination, unification

décor *n*
decoration, ornamentation, furnishings, colour scheme, ornamentation, scenery

decorate *v*
1 ORNAMENT, adorn, beautify, embellish, trim, garnish, deck, garland, festoon, grace, enrich, prettify, trick out
formal array, bedizen, bedaub
colloq. tart up
2 RENOVATE, paint, paper, wallpaper, colour, smarten, refurbish

colloq. do up
3 HONOUR, crown, cite, give a medal/honour to, give an award to, garland, bemedal

decoration *n*
1 ORNAMENT, adornment, ornamentation, trimming, embellishment, beautification, enhancement, décor, furnishings, mural, colour scheme, garnish, flourish, enrichment, elaboration, bunting, frill, scroll, trinket, bauble, knick-knack
2 AWARD, medal, order, badge, garland, crown, colours, ribbon, cross, laurel, wreath, star, emblem, insignia, honour, title

decorative *adj*
ornamental, fancy, adorning, beautifying, embellishing, non-functional, pretty, ornate, elaborate, enhancing, rococo
Ea plain

decorous *adj*
polite, refined, correct, courtly, decent, dignified, proper, well-behaved, appropriate, suitable, becoming, befitting, comely, *comme il faut*, fit, mannerly, modest, sedate, staid
old use seemly
Ea indecorous

decorum *n*
good manners, good form, etiquette, respectability, conformity, protocol, behaviour, decency, dignity, restraint, politeness, modesty, grace, breeding
old use seemliness
formal propriety, deportment
Ea bad manners; *formal* impropriety

decoy *n, v*
▶ *n* lure, trap, snare, pitfall, enticement, inducement, ensnarement, allurement, pretence, attraction, temptation, bait, diversion, dummy
▶ *v* bait, lure, entrap, entice, ensnare, allure, tempt, deceive, attract, seduce, lead, draw
formal inveigle

decrease *v, n*
▶ *v* lessen, make/become less, go/come down, lower, diminish, dwindle, decline, fall (off), reduce, subside, slide, plummet, plunge, cut back/down, contract, drop, ease, shrink, taper (off), wane, slim (down), let up, slacken, peter out, curtail, scale down, trim
formal abate
Ea increase
▶ *n* lessening, reduction, decline, lowering, drop, fall, falling-off, dwindling, loss, cutback, contraction, downturn, ebb, shrinkage, subsidence, step-down
formal diminution, abatement
Ea increase

decree *n, v*
▶ *n* order, command, law, ordinance, regulation, ruling, judgement, directive, rule, statute, act, enactment, edict, fiat, proclamation, mandate, manifesto, precept
formal interlocution, indiction, firman, rescript, psephism, irade, hatti-sherif
Related adjective: decretal
▶ *v* order, command, rule, lay down, dictate, direct, decide, determine, ordain, prescribe, proclaim, pronounce, enact
formal enjoin

decrepit *adj*
1 *a decrepit building*
dilapidated, run-down, ramshackle, rickety, broken-down, battered, worn-out, old, in bad condition/ shape, tumbledown, crumbling, falling apart/to bits
colloq. clapped-out
2 *a decrepit person*
weak, aged, feeble, frail, worn-out, infirm, elderly, doddering, tottering
formal senescent

decrepitude *n*
ruin, dilapidation, decay, degeneration, deterioration, disability, debility, weakness, feebleness, infirmity, incapacity, dotage, old age, senility
formal senescence
Ea good repair, youth

decry *v*
criticize, condemn, disparage, carp, disapprove of, find fault with, denounce, attack, belittle, blame, depreciate, devalue, underrate, undervalue
formal censure, declaim against, animadvert, excoriate, derogate, inveigh against, denigrate, traduce
colloq. slate, knock, snipe, run down, come down on, pan, pull to pieces, tear to shreds, tear a strip off, nit-pick, do a hatchet job on
Ea praise, value

dedicate *v*
1 DEVOTE, commit, assign, give, give over to, pledge, present, offer, sacrifice, surrender
2 *dedicate a book*
inscribe, address, name
3 CONSECRATE, bless, sanctify, set apart, hallow, make holy

dedicated *adj*
1 *a dedicated teacher*
devoted, committed, enthusiastic, single-minded, wholehearted, single-hearted, zealous, given over to, purposeful, hard working, industrious, diligent
2 CUSTOMIZED, custom-built, bespoke
Ea **1** uncommitted, apathetic

dedication *n*
1 COMMITMENT, devotion, single-mindedness, wholeheartedness, allegiance, attachment, adherence, faithfulness, loyalty, enthusiasm, zeal, self-sacrifice
2 INSCRIPTION, address
3 CONSECRATION, hallowing, blessing, sanctification, presentation
Ea **1** apathy

deduce *v*
derive, infer, gather, conclude, come to the conclusion, reason, surmise, understand, draw, glean

deduct *v*
subtract, take away/off, remove, reduce by, decrease by, withdraw
colloq. knock off
Ea add

deduction *n*
1 INFERENCE, reasoning, finding, conclusion, corollary, surmising, assumption, presumption, result
2 SUBTRACTION, reduction, decrease, taking away/ off, withdrawal, removal, discount, allowance
formal diminution, abatement
Ea **2** addition, increase

deed *n*
1 ACTION, act, activity, achievement, performance, accomplishment, undertaking, exploit, feat, fact, truth, reality
2 DOCUMENT, contract, agreement, record, title,

transaction
formal indenture

deem *v*
judge, believe, suppose, think, conceive, consider, estimate, hold, imagine, account, reckon, regard
formal adjudge, esteem

deep *adj, adv, n*
▶ *adj* **1** *a deep river/pit*
PROFOUND, bottomless, unplumbed, fathomless, unfathomed, immeasurable, yawning, cavernous, immersed
2 *a deep sleep/crisis/feeling*
INTENSE, serious, earnest, extreme, profound, very great, severe, heart-felt, passionate, fervent, ardent, strong, vigorous, grave
3 *a deep person*
PERCEPTIVE, discerning, profound, wise, learned, astute, clever, serious, intellectual, quiet, reserved
formal sagacious, perspicacious
colloq. deep as a well
4 LOW, low-pitched, bass, resonant, sonorous, resounding, booming, rich, strong, powerful
5 *a deep colour*
STRONG, intense, rich, vivid, brilliant, warm, glowing, dark
6 OBSCURE, mysterious, difficult
formal abstruse, esoteric, recondite
🔄 **1** shallow, open **2** light **3** superficial, shallow, frivolous **4** high, high-pitched **5** light, pale **6** clear, plain, open
▶ *adv* far, a long way, a great distance
▶ *n* sea, high seas, ocean, main
colloq. briny

deepen *v*
1 INTENSIFY, grow, increase, strengthen, reinforce, heighten, extend, magnify, build up, deteriorate, worsen, get worse
2 EXCAVATE, hollow, dig out, scoop out

deeply *adv*
intensely, seriously, earnestly, extremely, completely, thoroughly, profoundly, very much, severely, passionately, fervently, ardently, movingly, strongly, vigorously, acutely, distressingly, feelingly, gravely, mournfully, sadly, to the quick
colloq. from the bottom of your heart
🔄 slightly

deep-seated *adj*
ingrained, entrenched, deep-rooted, fixed, confirmed, deep, settled
🔄 eradicable, temporary

deer *n*
buck, doe, hart, reindeer, roe, stag
Related adjective: cervine

deface *v*
damage, spoil, disfigure, blemish, impair, mutilate, mar, sully, tarnish, vandalize, deform, obliterate, injure, destroy
🔄 repair

de facto *adv & adj*
actually, in effect, really; actual, existing, real
🔄 de jure

defamation *n*
slander, libel, disparagement, slur, smear, smear campaign, innuendo, scandal, backbiting
formal vilification, aspersion, calumny, traducement, denigration, derogation, obloquy, opprobrium,

malediction
🔄 commendation, praise

defamatory *adj*
slanderous, libellous, disparaging, pejorative, insulting, injurious, derogatory
formal vilifying, denigrating, contumelious, calumnious, maledictory
🔄 complimentary, appreciative

defame *v*
slander, libel, discredit, disgrace, dishonour, besmirch, disparage, libel, malign, blacken, smear, speak evil of, stigmatize
old use infame
formal cast aspersions, denigrate, asperse, calumniate, traduce, vilify, vituperate
colloq. run down, drag through the mud, sling/throw mud at
🔄 compliment, praise

default *v, n*
▶ *v* fail, evade, defraud, neglect, dodge, swindle, backslide
▶ *n* failure, absence, neglect, negligence, non-payment, omission, deficiency, lapse, fault, lack, defect
formal want, dereliction

defaulter *n*
non-payer, offender, absentee, non-appearer

defeat *v, n*
▶ *v* **1** CONQUER, beat, overcome, overpower, get the better of, eclipse, excel, surpass, subdue, overthrow, worst, repel, overwhelm, rout, ruin, crush, quell, bring someone to their knees, reject, throw out
formal subjugate, vanquish
colloq. thrash, lick, hammer, thump, trounce, annihilate, smash, devastate, slaughter, make mincemeat (out) of, run rings round
2 FRUSTRATE, confound, balk, get the better of, disappoint, foil, thwart, baffle, puzzle, perplex, checkmate, block, obstruct
▶ *n* **1** CONQUEST, beating, overthrow, overcoming, rout, repulsion, ruin, crushing, rejection, debacle
formal subjugation, vanquishment
colloq. trouncing, thrashing
2 FRUSTRATION, failure, setback, reverse, breakdown, downfall, disappointment, thwarting, checkmate

defeatist *n, adj*
▶ *n* pessimist, quitter, yielder, doomwatcher, prophet of doom
🔄 optimist
▶ *adj* pessimistic, resigned, fatalistic, despondent, helpless, hopeless, despairing, gloomy
🔄 optimistic

defecate *v*
empty/move your bowels, evacuate, excrete, pass a motion, relieve yourself, void excrement, ease yourself
formal egest
colloq. poo, do number two; *slang* shit, crap

defect *n, v*
▶ *n* imperfection, fault, flaw, deficiency, failing, mistake, error, inadequacy, blemish, taint, deformity, error, shortcoming, shortfall, weakness, frailty, lack, spot, weak spot, snag, absence, omission
formal want
colloq. bug
▶ *v* desert, abandon, break faith, change sides, rebel,

revolt, turn traitor
formal renege, apostatize, tergiversate

defection *n*
desertion, abandonment, disloyalty, backsliding, rebellion, revolt, mutiny, betrayal, treason
formal renegation, apostasy, defalcation, dereliction, perfidy, tergiversation

defective *adj*
faulty, imperfect, out of order, flawed, deficient, broken, in disrepair, abnormal
formal malfunctioning
colloq. bust, duff, on the blink
E3 in order, working; *formal* operative

⚠ **defective** or **deficient** ?
Defective means 'having a fault or flaw': *The crash was caused by defective wiring in the signalling system.* *Deficient* means 'inadequate, lacking in what is needed': *a diet deficient in essential vitamins and minerals.*

---

defector *n*
deserter, traitor, turncoat, betrayer, rebel, Judas, quisling, mutineer, recreant, backslider
formal renegade, apostate, tergiversator
colloq. rat

defence *n*
1 PROTECTION, resistance, security, fortification, cover, safeguard, shelter, guard, shield, screen, deterrence, deterrent, barricade, bastion, keep, fortress, outpost, stronghold, garrison, immunity, bulwark, rampart, buttress
2 *a country's defences*
military resources, armed forces, army, navy, air force, troops, soldiers, military, weapons, armaments
3 JUSTIFICATION, explanation, excuse, argument, plea, vindication, pleading, testimony, alibi, case
formal apologia, explication, extenuation, exoneration
E3 1 attack, assault **3** accusation, attack

defenceless *adj*
unprotected, undefended, unarmed, unguarded, vulnerable, exposed, open to attack, weak, helpless, powerless, impotent
E3 protected, guarded

defend *v*
1 PROTECT, guard, safeguard, watch over, shelter, secure, preserve, shield, screen, cover, resist, withstand, oppose, keep from harm, contest, deter, barricade, garrison, buttress
formal fortify
2 SUPPORT, stand up for, stand by, back, uphold, endorse, vindicate, champion, bolster, argue for, speak up for, make a case for, explain, justify, plead
formal exonerate
colloq. stick up for
E3 1 attack **2** accuse, attack

defendant *n*
accused, offender, prisoner
technical litigant, appellant, respondent

defender *n*
1 PROTECTOR, guard, bodyguard, keeper
2 SUPPORTER, guardian, advocate, vindicator, backer, endorser, upholder, preserver, champion, patron, sponsor, counsel, apologist
E3 1 attacker **2** accuser

defensible *adj*
justifiable, tenable, arguable, permissible, plausible, valid, maintainable, safe, secure, unassailable, impregnable, pardonable, vindicable
E3 indefensible, insecure

defensive *adj*
1 PROTECTIVE, defending, safeguarding, protecting, wary, opposing, cautious, watchful
2 SELF-JUSTIFYING, apologetic, self-defensive

defer¹ *v*
defer a meeting
delay, postpone, put off, adjourn, hold over, put back, shelve, suspend, waive
formal procrastinate, prorogue, protract
colloq. put on ice, put on the back burner, take a raincheck on
E3 bring forward

defer² *v*
defer to an expert opinion
yield, give way, comply, submit, surrender, give in, capitulate, respect, bow
formal accede, acquiesce

deference *n*
1 RESPECT, regard, honour, reverence, courtesy, civility, politeness, attentiveness, consideration, thoughtfulness
formal esteem
2 SUBMISSION, submissiveness, obedience, yielding
formal compliance, acquiescence
E3 1 contempt **2** resistance

deferential *adj*
respectful, reverent, reverential, courteous, civil, dutiful, polite, attentive, considerate, thoughtful, ingratiating
formal morigerous, regardful, complaisant, obeisant, obsequious
E3 arrogant, immodest

deferment *n*
delay, postponement, putting-off, adjournment, holding-over, shelving, suspension, stay, moratorium, waiving
formal procrastination, prorogation

defiance *n*
opposition, confrontation, resistance, challenge, disobedience, rebelliousness, contempt, insubordination, disregard, insolence
formal recalcitrance, truculence, contumacy
E3 compliance, acquiescence, submissiveness

defiant *adj*
challenging, resistant, antagonistic, aggressive, rebellious, insubordinate, disobedient, intransigent, bold, insolent, contemptuous, scornful, obstinate, unco-operative, militant, provocative
formal recalcitrant, refractory, truculent, contumacious
E3 compliant, acquiescent, submissive

deficiency *n*
1 SHORTAGE, lack, inadequacy, scarcity, insufficiency, dearth, want, scantiness, absence, deficit
2 IMPERFECTION, shortcoming, weakness, fault, defect, flaw, failing, frailty
E3 1 excess, surfeit **2** perfection

deficient *adj*
inadequate, insufficient, scarce, short, lacking, meagre, scanty, skimpy, incomplete, unsatisfactory,

inferior, weak
formal wanting, exiguous
F3 excessive

⚠ **deficient** or **defective** ? *See panel at* **defective**.

---

deficit *n*
shortage, shortfall, deficiency, loss, arrears, lack, default
F3 excess

defile *v, n*
▶ *v* pollute, violate, contaminate, degrade, dishonour, desecrate, defame, debase, soil, dirty, infect, stain, spoil, sully, tarnish, taint, make impure/unclean, profane, treat sacrilegiously, corrupt, blacken, disgrace
formal denigrate, vitiate, inquinate
F3 clean, cleanse, purify
▶ *n* pass, gorge, valley, gully, passage, ravine

definable *adj*
ascertainable, definite, identifiable, describable, determinable, perceptible, definite, fixed, specific, exact, precise
formal explicable
F3 indefinable

define *v*
1 *define the boundaries*
bound, limit, delimit, establish, demarcate, mark out, fix
formal circumscribe, delineate
2 *define the meaning*
explain, characterize, describe, interpret, determine, designate, specify, spell out, detail, clarify
formal expound, elucidate

definite *adj*
1 CLEAR, clear-cut, exact, precise, specific, explicit, particular, firm, obvious, marked, noticeable
2 CERTAIN, settled, sure, positive, fixed, decided, determined, assured, guaranteed
F3 1 vague 2 indefinite, provisional

⚠ **definite** or **definitive** ?
Definite means 'clear' or 'certain': *I'll give you a definite answer later. Definitive* means 'final, settling things once and for all': *a definitive study of Ben Jonson.*

---

definitely *adv*
positively, surely, unquestionably, without question, absolutely, certainly, categorically, undeniably, clearly, undoubtedly, doubtless, without doubt, no denying, unmistakably, plainly, obviously, indeed, easily
formal indubitably

definition *n*
1 EXPLANATION, meaning, significance, sense, description, interpretation, clarification, determination
formal exposition, elucidation
2 DISTINCTNESS, clarity, precision, clearness, focus, sharpness, visibility, contrast

definitive *adj*
decisive, conclusive, final, authoritative, standard, correct, ultimate, reliable, exhaustive, perfect, exact, absolute, complete, categorical
F3 interim

deflate *v*
1 FLATTEN, puncture, collapse, let down, exhaust, squash, empty, contract, void, shrink, squeeze

2 *deflate his opinion of himself*
humiliate, debunk, dash, disappoint, dispirit, humble, mortify, chasten, disconcert
colloq. put down
3 DEPRECIATE, devalue, reduce, lessen, lower, diminish, decrease, depress
F3 1 inflate 2 boost 3 inflate, increase

deflect *v*
deviate, diverge, turn (aside), swerve, veer, change course, sidetrack, drift, twist, avert, wind, glance off, bend, ricochet

deflection *n*
deviation, divergence, turning, turning aside, swerve, veer, changing course, sidetracking, drift, twisting, glancing-off, bend, ricochet
formal aberration, refraction

deflower *v*
violate, assault, defile, rape, seduce, spoil, desecrate, force, harm, mar, molest, ruin
formal ravish, despoil

deform *v*
distort, contort, disfigure, deface, malform, misshape, warp, mar, pervert, ruin, spoil, damage, maim, mutilate, twist, buckle

deformation *n*
bend, curve, distortion, contortion, disfiguration, defacement, malformation, misshapenness, mutilation, twist, twisting, warp, buckle
technical diastrophism

deformed *adj*
distorted, misshapen, malformed, contorted, disfigured, crippled, crooked, gnarled, bent, twisted, warped, buckled, defaced, mangled, maimed, marred, ruined, mutilated, perverted, corrupted

deformity *n*
distortion, misshapenness, malformation, disfigurement, defacement, abnormality, irregularity, imperfection, misproportion, defect, ugliness, crookedness, vileness, grossness, monstrosity, corruption, perversion

defraud *v*
cheat, swindle, dupe, rob, trick, rook, deceive, delude, mislead, fool, hoodwink, outwit, embezzle, beguile
formal cozen
colloq. fiddle, fleece, sting, rip off, do, diddle, con

defray *v*
reimburse, refund, repay, recompense, discharge, meet, pay, settle
F3 incur

deft *adj*
adept, handy, dexterous, nimble, skilful, adroit, agile, expert, nifty, proficient, able, neat, clever
F3 clumsy, awkward

defunct *adj*
1 DEAD, deceased, departed, gone, expired, extinct
2 OBSOLETE, invalid, expired, *passé*, outmoded, bygone
formal inoperative
F3 1 alive, live 2 functioning; *formal* operative

defy *v*
1 *defy the authorities*
challenge, confront, resist, dare, brave, face, repel, spurn, beard, flout, slight, withstand, stand up to, disobey, rebel against, disrespect, disregard, ignore,

scorn, despise, defeat, beard, provoke, frustrate, thwart
2 *her writings defy categorization*
elude, avoid, frustrate, baffle, foil
⊟ 1 obey **2** permit, allow

degeneracy *n*
dissoluteness, debauchery, depravation, degradation,
debasement, decadence, corruption, fallenness,
immorality, vileness, wickedness, sinfulness,
degeneration, perversion, deterioration
formal effeteness
⊟ morality, uprightness

degenerate *adj, v*
▶ *adj* dissolute, debauched, depraved, degraded,
debased, base, low, abandoned, decadent, corrupt,
fallen, immoral, mean, ignoble, vile, wicked, sinful,
degenerated, perverted, deteriorated
formal effete, profligate
⊟ moral, upright
▶ *v* decline, deteriorate, sink, decay, rot, fail, slip,
worsen, fall off, lapse, decrease
formal regress
colloq. go downhill, go to pot, go down the tube
⊟ improve

degeneration *n*
decline, deterioration, debasement, decay, failure, slip,
worsening, falling-off, sinking, drop, slide, lapse,
atrophy, decrease
formal regression
⊟ improvement

degradation *n*
1 ABASEMENT, humiliation, mortification,
dishonour, disgrace, shame, ignominy, decadence,
degeneracy, dissoluteness, debauchery, depravation,
debasement, corruption, fallenness, immorality,
vileness, wickedness, sinfulness, degeneration,
perversion
2 DETERIORATION, degeneration, decline,
downgrading, demotion
⊟ 1 enhancement **2** virtue

degrade *v*
1 DISHONOUR, disgrace, debase, abase, shame,
humiliate, humble, discredit, mortify, demean, belittle,
lower, devalue, weaken, impair, deteriorate, cheapen,
adulterate, pervert, sully, defile, corrupt
2 DEMOTE, depose, downgrade, deprive, cashier,
reduce/lower in rank, relegate, unseat
colloq. drum out, take down a peg or two
⊟ 1 exalt **2** promote

degrading *adj*
humiliating, dishonourable, disgraceful, debasing,
base, shameful, contemptible, discrediting, mortifying,
demeaning, belittling, cheapening, ignoble,
undignified, unworthy
⊟ enhancing

degree *n*
1 *to a great degree*
EXTENT, measure, range, stage, step, level, amount,
intensity, strength, standard
2 GRADE, class, rank, rung, order, position,
standing, status, stage, level, limit, unit, point, mark

dehydrate *v*
dry, dry up, dry out, evaporate, lose water, drain, parch
formal desiccate, exsiccate, effloresce,

deification *n*
exaltation, elevation, worship, glorification,
idolization, extolling, immortalization, ennoblement,
idealization
formal veneration, apotheosis, divinification,
divinization

deify *v*
exalt, elevate, worship, glorify, idolize, extol,
immortalize, ennoble, idealize
formal aggrandize, venerate

deign *v*
condescend, stoop, lower yourself, consent, demean
yourself

deity *n*
god, goddess, divinity, divine being, supreme being,
godhead, idol, demigod, spirit, power, eternal,
immortal

dejected *adj*
downcast, despondent, depressed, downhearted,
discouraged, disheartened, down, low, melancholy,
sad, miserable, cast down, gloomy, glum, crestfallen,
crushed, demoralized, dismal, wretched, doleful,
morose, spiritless, dispirited
formal disconsolate
colloq. blue, down in the dumps
⊟ cheerful, high-spirited, happy

dejection *n*
despondency, depression, downheartedness,
discouragement, low spirits, despair, melancholy,
sadness, sorrow, unhappiness, misery, gloom,
gloominess, wretchedness, dolefulness, moroseness,
dispiritedness
formal disconsolateness, disconsolation
colloq. blues, dumps
⊟ happiness, high spirits

de jure *adv & adj*
legally, rightfully, legal, rightful
⊟ de facto

delay *v, n*
▶ *v* **1** OBSTRUCT, hinder, impede, hamper, hold up,
check, hold back, set back, stop, halt, detain,
stonewall, filibuster, keep, restrain
2 POSTPONE, put off, defer, suspend, shelve, hold
over, adjourn, stall
formal procrastinate
colloq. put on ice, put on the back burner
3 DAWDLE, hang on, linger, lag (behind), loiter,
dither, hold back
formal tarry
colloq. dilly-dally
⊟ 1 accelerate **2** bring forward **3** hurry, keep up
▶ *n* **1** OBSTRUCTION, hindrance, impediment,
hold-up, check, setback, stay, stoppage, halt,
interruption, lull, interval, wait
2 POSTPONEMENT, deferment, putting-off,
adjournment, holding-over, shelving, suspension, stay,
respite, moratorium, waiving, reprieve
formal procrastination, cunctation, mora
3 DAWDLING, lingering, loitering, stalling
formal tarrying
colloq. dilly-dallying
⊟ 1 hastening, continuation **3** hurry

delectable *adj*
1 DELICIOUS, appetizing, palatable, tasty, dainty,
luscious, mouth-watering, succulent, flavoursome,
savoury
colloq. scrumptious, yummy
2 ATTRACTIVE, pleasant, delightful, adorable,
charming, enchanting, engaging, exciting, pleasing,

agreeable
🔁 **1** unpalatable **2** unpleasant

delectation *n*
enjoyment, delight, happiness, pleasure, comfort, contentment, gratification, refreshment, relish, satisfaction, amusement, diversion, entertainment
🔁 distaste

delegate *n, v*
▶ *n* representative, agent, envoy, messenger, deputy, ambassador, spokesperson, spokesman, spokeswoman, legate, emissary, proxy, commissioner
▶ *v* authorize, appoint, depute, charge, commission, commit, give, pass on/over, assign, empower, entrust, devolve, consign, leave, designate, ordain, nominate, name, hand over

delegation *n*
1 DEPUTATION, representatives, commission, legation, mission, contingent, embassy
2 *delegation of responsibility*
committal, transference, consignment, passing on/over, devolution, empowerment

delete *v*
erase, remove, cross out, cancel, rub out, strike (out), take out, obliterate, edit (out), cut (out), blot out, blue-pencil
formal excise, efface, expunge
🔁 add, insert

deleterious *adj*
destructive, detrimental, harmful, hurtful, injurious, bad, damaging, ruinous, pernicious, prejudicial
formal noxious
🔁 enhancing, helpful

deliberate *adj, v*
▶ *adj* **1** INTENTIONAL, planned, calculated, prearranged, premeditated, preplanned, preconceived, willed, conscious, designed, considered, advised
2 CAREFUL, unhurried, thoughtful, methodical, cautious, studied, prudent, slow, ponderous, steady, leisurely, measured, heedful, resolute, unhesitating, unwavering
formal circumspect
🔁 **1** unintentional, accidental **2** hasty
▶ *v* consider, ponder, reflect, think (over), meditate, mull over, muse, debate, discuss, evaluate, weigh (up), consult
formal cogitate, ruminate, excogitate

deliberately *adv*
1 INTENTIONALLY, on purpose, consciously, pointedly, calculatingly, by design, in cold blood, knowingly, wittingly, wilfully, with malice aforethought
2 CAREFULLY, unhurriedly, thoughtfully, methodically, cautiously, prudently, slowly, ponderously, steadily
formal circumspectly
🔁 **1** unintentionally, by accident, accidentally, by mistake **2** hastily

deliberation *n*
1 CONSIDERATION, reflection, thought, calculation, forethought, meditation, pondering, musing, mullling, brooding, study, evaluation, weighing-up
formal cogitation, rumination, excogitate
2 *secret deliberations*
debate, discussion, consultation, conferring
3 CARE, carefulness, caution, thoughtfulness,

unhurriedness, slowness, steadiness, prudence
formal circumspection

delicacy *n*
1 DAINTINESS, fineness, elegance, exquisiteness, lightness, fragility, precision
2 SENSITIVITY, tact, diplomacy, discretion, care, consideration, subtlety, finesse, discrimination, niceness
3 TITBIT, dainty, taste, treat, luxury, sweetmeat, savoury, relish, speciality
🔁 **1** coarseness, roughness **2** tactlessness

delicate *adj*
1 FINE, dainty, exquisite, elegant, slight, graceful
2 FRAIL, sickly, weak, ailing, infirm, unwell, in poor health, faint
formal debilitated
3 *delicate china*
fragile, breakable, easily damaged/broken, frail, flimsy, brittle, insubstantial
4 *a delicate situation*
sensitive, tricky, difficult, problematic, critical, awkward, touchy, controversial
5 *needs delicate handling*
tactful, sensitive, diplomatic, careful, considerate, discreet
colloq. softly-softly, kid-glove
6 SUBTLE, muted, pastel, pale, muted, subdued, soft, faint, mild, bland
7 *a delicate instrument*
precision, sensitive, precise, exact, accurate
🔁 **1** coarse **2** healthy, strong **3** strong **4** easy
6 strong, bold

delicious *adj*
1 TASTY, palatable, appetizing, mouth-watering, juicy, succulent, toothsome, savoury, good, choice, tempting
formal delectable, nectareous, ambrosial
colloq. morish, scrumptious, yummy
2 ENJOYABLE, pleasant, agreeable, delightful, charming, enchanting, captivating, pleasurable, pleasing, gratifying, entertaining, fascinating
🔁 **1** unpalatable **2** unpleasant

delight *n, v*
▶ *n* happiness, joy, pleasure, contentment, enjoyment, gladness, glee, rapture, transport, bliss, euphoria, ecstasy, elation, gratification, jubilation, amusement, entertainment
🔁 disgust, displeasure
▶ *v* **1** *the prospect of being parents delighted them*
please, charm, gratify, cheer, gladden, excite, enchant, captivate, enrapture, tickle, thrill, ravish, amuse, entertain
colloq. bowl over, tickle pink
2 *delight in something*
enjoy, relish, like, love, appreciate, revel in, take pleasure in, take pride in, glory in, boast of, wallow in, savour
🔁 **1** disappoint, displease, dismay **2** dislike, hate

delighted *adj*
happy, pleased, glad, enchanted, captivated, enraptured, entranced, elated, euphoric, ecstatic, thrilled, excited, joyful, overjoyed, gleeful, jubilant, gratified, charmed
formal joyous
colloq. over the moon, tickled pink, happy as Larry/a sandboy, pleased as Punch
🔁 disappointed, dismayed

delightful *adj*
charming, enchanting, captivating, enjoyable, pleasant, thrilling, exciting, agreeable, pleasurable, engaging, attractive, pleasing, gratifying, appealing, fascinating, amusing, diverting, entertaining
formal delectable
colloq. out of this world, great, magic, ace, divine, the tops
🖃 nasty, unpleasant

delimit *v*
bound, demarcate, determine, establish, fix, mark, define

delineate *v*
describe, define, depict, portray, set forth, outline, draw, sketch, trace, design, chart, render, represent, define, mark, bound, determine, establish, fix

delinquency *n*
crime, offence, misdeed, wrongdoing, misbehaviour, misconduct, law-breaking, misdemeanour, criminality
formal transgression

delinquent *n, adj*
▶ *n* offender, criminal, wrongdoer, law-breaker, hooligan, young offender, culprit, ruffian, vandal
formal miscreant
▶ *adj* criminal, offending, law-breaking, lawless, guilty, negligent
formal remiss, culpable
🖃 blameless, careful

delirious *adj*
1 *delirious because of fever*
demented, raving, incoherent, beside yourself, irrational, deranged, frenzied, light-headed, wild, mad, frantic, insane, crazy, unhinged, babbling, out of your mind
2 *delirious with excitement*
ecstatic, euphoric, overjoyed, elated, jubilant, beside yourself, carried away
colloq. over the moon
🖃 1 sane

delirium *n*
1 *feverish delirium*
derangement, raving, incoherence, irrationality, fever, frenzy, passion, wildness, madness, insanity, lunacy, craziness, hallucination, hysteria
colloq. jimjams
2 *the delirium of first love*
ecstasy, euphoria, joy, elation, excitement, jubilation, wildness, passion
🖃 1 sanity

deliver *v*
1 *deliver a parcel*
convey, bring, take, send, give, carry, supply, distribute, give out
formal dispatch
2 SURRENDER, hand over, relinquish, yield, transfer, grant, entrust, commit
formal cede
3 *deliver a speech*
UTTER, make, speak, proclaim, declare, announce, pronounce, express, voice, give voice to
formal enunciate
4 ADMINISTER, deal, give, inflict, launch, direct, aim, strike
5 *deliver the promised benefits*
FULFIL, provide, supply, do, carry out, implement

6 SET FREE, liberate, save, rescue, release
formal emancipate, ransom, redeem

deliverance *n*
rescue, liberation, salvation, freedom, release, escape, extrication
formal emancipation, ransom, redemption

delivery *n*
1 CONVEYANCE, supply, distribution, transport, transportation, carriage, consignment, transmission, transfer, shipment
formal dispatch
2 ARTICULATION, speech, utterance, intonation, elocution
formal enunciation
3 CHILDBIRTH, labour, confinement
formal parturition, travail

dell *n*
valley, vale, hollow, dean, dingle

delude *v*
deceive, mislead, beguile, dupe, fool, take in, lead on, trick, hoodwink, hoax, cheat, misguide, misinform
colloq. bamboozle, have on, take for a ride, double-cross, two-time, pull someone's leg, pull a fast one on, pull the wool over someone's eyes

deluge *n, v*
▶ *n a deluge of rain/letters*
flood, inundation, downpour, overflowing, torrent, avalanche, spate, rush, wave
▶ *v deluged by rain/queries* flood, inundate, drench, drown, overwhelm, soak, swamp, engulf, submerge

delusion *n*
illusion, hallucination, fancy, misconception, misapprehension, false belief/impression, deception, misbelief, fallacy, misinformation, tricking

> ⚠ **delusion** or **illusion** ?
> A *delusion* is a false belief arising in your own mind, whereas an *illusion* is a false impression coming into your mind from the world outside it.

de luxe, deluxe *adj*
luxury, luxurious, select, choice, quality, expensive, costly, special, exclusive, grand, lavish, fine, elegant, palatial, rich, splendid, sumptuous, superior
formal opulent
colloq. plush

delve *v*
burrow, rummage, search, dig into, hunt in/through, poke, ransack, root, probe, examine, explore, investigate, go/look into, research

demagogue *n*
agitator, orator, firebrand, haranguer, rabble-rouser, tub-thumper

demand *v, n*
▶ *v* 1 ASK, request, tell, call for, insist on, urge, press for, hold out for, order, dictate, stipulate, solicit, claim, petition, exact, inquire, question, interrogate
2 REQUIRE, need, take, call for, involve, cry out for
formal necessitate
▶ *n* 1 REQUEST, question, claim, petition, plea, order, inquiry, desire, pressure, insistence, clamour, interrogation
2 NEED, necessity, call, requirement, want
formal exigency

▷ **in demand** popular, fashionable, asked for, requested, sought after; *colloq.* big, trendy

demanding *adj*
hard, difficult, challenging, exacting, taxing, tough, exhausting, wearing, back-breaking, insistent, nagging, harassing, pressing, testing, urgent, trying
formal exigent
colloq. a tall order
Ea easy, undemanding, easy-going

demarcate *v*
determine, establish, fix, mark (out), delimit, define, bound

demarcation *n*
boundary, bound, differentiation, distinction, division, separation, enclosure, limit, line, margin, determination, establishment, fixing, marking off/out, delimitation, definition

demean *v*
lower, humble, degrade, belittle, deprecate, humiliate, debase, abase, descend, demote, stoop, condescend
Ea exalt, enhance

demeanour *n*
manner, conduct, behaviour, air
formal bearing, deportment, mien, comportment

demented *adj*
made, insane, lunatic, unbalanced, disturbed, deranged, crazed, wild, berserk, unhinged, out of your mind
colloq. loony, loopy, bonkers, nuts, nutty, nutty as a fruitcake, off your rocker, needing your head examining, round the bend, round the twist
Ea sane

demise *n*
1 DEATH, decease, end, passing, departure
formal termination, expiration, cessation
2 DOWNFALL, fall, collapse, failure, ruin

democracy *n*
self-government, commonwealth, autonomy, republic

democratic *adj*
self-governing, representative, egalitarian, autonomous, popular, populist, republican

demolish *v*
1 DESTROY, dismantle, knock down, pull down, flatten, bulldoze, raze, tear down, break up, pulverize, level
2 *demolish the opponents*
beat, overcome, overpower, get the better of, conquer, excel, surpass, subdue, overthrow, repel, overwhelm, rout, ruin, crush, quell, bring someone to their knees
formal subjugate, vanquish
colloq. thrash, lick, hammer, annihilate, devastate, slaughter
3 *demolish an argument*
destroy, ruin, wreck, overturn, undo
Ea 1 build up, erect, construct

demolition *n*
1 DESTRUCTION, dismantling, knocking-down, pulling-down, flattening, razing, tearing-down, breaking-up, levelling, razing
2 *demolition of the opposing team*
beating, overpowering, surpassing, overthrow, overwhelming, rout
colloq. thrashing, licking, hammering, annihilation, slaughter

demon *n*
1 DEVIL, fiend, evil spirit, fallen angel, imp, ghoul, daemon, cacodemon, afrit, rakshas, incubus, succubus
2 VILLAIN, devil, rogue, monster, fiend, beast, savage, brute
3 *a demon chess player*
addict, fanatic, fiend, buff, wizard,
colloq. ace, freak, dab hand

demonic *adj*
fiendish, devilish, diabolical, hellish, infernal, satanic, possessed, mad, maniacal, manic, crazed, frantic, frenetic, frenzied, furious

demonstrable *adj*
verifiable, provable, arguable, attestable, self-evident, obvious, evident, certain, clear, positive
formal evincible
Ea unverifiable

demonstrate *v*
1 PROVE, determine, show, establish, verify
formal validate, substantiate
2 SHOW, display, exhibit, express, indicate, register, betray
formal manifest, testify to, bear witness to, evince, betoken, bespeak
3 EXPLAIN, illustrate, describe, show, teach, make clear
formal expound
4 PROTEST, march, parade, rally, picket, sit in

demonstration *n*
1 DISPLAY, expression, indication, exhibition, proof, confirmation, evidence, testimony, verification
formal manifestation, evincement, affirmation, substantiation, validation
2 EXPLANATION, illustration, description, presentation, test, trial
formal exposition, elucidation
3 PROTEST, march, rally, mass rally, picket, sit-in, parade, picket, civil disobedience
colloq. demo

demonstrative *adj*
affectionate, expressive, extrovert, unreserved, effusive, gushing, expansive, emotional, open, loving, warm
Ea reserved, introvert, cold, restrained

demoralize *v*
1 DISCOURAGE, dishearten, dispirit, undermine, depress, deject, cast down, crush, disconcert, make despondent, daunt, lower, undermine, weaken
2 CORRUPT, deprave, debase, pervert, contaminate, defile
Ea 1 encourage, inspire confidence 2 improve

demote *v*
downgrade, reduce in rank, degrade, relegate, humble, cashier
Ea promote, upgrade

demotic *adj*
popular, vernacular, colloquial, vulgar
formal enchorial, enchoric

demur *v, n*
▶ *v* disagree, dissent, object, take exception, refuse, protest, dispute, balk, cavil, scruple, doubt, express doubts, hesitate, be unwilling, refuse
▶ *n* disagreement, dissent, hesitation, objection, protest, misgiving, qualm, reservation, doubt, scruple
formal compunction, demurral

demure *adj*
modest, reserved, unassuming, reticent, coy, shy,
timid, quiet, serious, retiring, prissy, grave, prudish,
sober, strait-laced, prim, staid
F3 wanton, forward

den *n*
1 *a wolf's den*
lair, hideout, hole, hollow
2 *a den of forgers*
haunt, meeting-place, patch, pitch
colloq. dive, joint
3 *study in his den*
retreat, study, hideaway, shelter, sanctuary

denial *n*
1 CONTRADICTION, opposition, disagreement,
dissent, repudiation, disclaimer, dismissal,
renunciation
formal negation, disavowal, disaffirmation, abjuration

2 REFUSAL, rebuff, rejection, dismissal, prohibition,
veto
3 *denial of your parents*
disowning, renunciation, repudiation, disavowal

denigrate *v*
run down, slander, belittle, abuse, assail, criticize,
deprecate
formal disparage, revile, defame, malign, vilify, decry,
besmirch, impugn, calumniate, vilipend, cast
aspersions on
colloq. fling/sling throw mud, pick holes in
F3 praise, acclaim

denizen *n*
citizen, dweller, inhabitant, occupant, resident,
habitant, habitué

denomination *n*
1 RELIGION, persuasion, Church, sect, religious
body/group, belief, faith, creed, communion, cult,
school, order, constituency
2 *the denomination of a banknote*
value, face value, worth, unit, grade, class, kind, sort,
designation

denote *v*
indicate, be a sign of, stand for, signify, represent,
symbolize, mean, refer to, express, designate, typify,
mark, show, imply, suggest
formal betoken

dénouement *n*
climax, culmination, conclusion, outcome, upshot,
finale, resolution, clarification, unravelling, finish, last
act, solution, close
colloq. pay-off

denounce *v*
condemn, censure, accuse, attack, criticize, inform
against, betray, indict
formal deplore, revile, decry, castigate, impugn, vilify,
arraign, declaim, fulminate, inculpate
F3 acclaim, praise

dense *adj*
1 *a dense crowd/forest*
solid, packed, crammed, jammed together, close-
packed, tightly packed, crowded, thick, compact,
compressed, condensed, close, close-knit, heavy
2 *dense smoke*
thick, opaque, impenetrable, concentrated
3 STUPID, crass, dull, slow, slow-witted
formal obtuse

colloq. thick, dim, dim-witted
F3 **1** thin, sparse **3** quick-witted, clever

density *n*
body, mass, bulk, closeness, compactness, consistency,
denseness, solidity, solidness, thickness, tightness,
impenetrability
F3 sparseness

dent *n, v*
► *n* hollow, depression, dip, concavity, indentation,
crater, dimple, dint, pit
► *v* depress, gouge, push in, indent

denude *v*
strip, divest, expose, uncover, bare, deforest, defoliate
F3 cover, clothe

denunciation *n*
condemnation, denouncement, censure, accusation,
incrimination, attack, criticism
formal invective, decrial, castigation, obloquy,
fulmination
F3 acclaim, praise

deny *v*
1 *deny the allegations*
contradict, oppose, disagree with, disprove, repudiate,
rebut
formal refute, disaffirm, negate, nullify, abjure, gainsay

2 *deny him access to his children*
REFUSE, turn down, forbid, prohibit, reject, withhold,
dismiss, rebuff, veto
formal decline
3 *deny your parents*
disown, disclaim, renounce, repudiate, turn your back
on
formal disavow, recant
F3 **1** admit **2** allow

deodorant *n*
anti-perspirant, deodorizer, air-freshener,
disinfectant, fumigant, fumigator

deodorize *v*
freshen, purify, refresh, sweeten, disinfect, fumigate,
aerate, ventilate

depart *v*
1 GO, leave, withdraw, exit, make off, decamp, take
your leave, absent yourself, set off, set out, start out,
pull out, get going, remove, retreat, migrate, escape,
disappear, retire, vanish
colloq. push along/off, make tracks, quit, scat, scoot,
scram, take off, take to your heels, make yourself
scarce, shove off, bunk off, clear off, split, scarper,
skedaddle, vamoose, skive, do a runner, do a bunk, do a
moonlight flit, hit the road/trail, make a bolt/break for
it, up sticks, hightail it, sling your hook
2 DEVIATE, digress, differ, diverge, fork, branch off,
swerve, turn aside, veer, vary
F3 **1** arrive, return **2** keep to

departed *adj*
dead, gone, late, passed away
formal deceased, expired

department *n*
1 DIVISION, branch, subdivision, section, sector,
wing, office, bureau, agency, organization, station,
unit, branch, region, district
2 SPHERE, realm, province, domain, field, area,
concern, responsibility, interest, function, speciality,
line

departure n

1 EXIT, going, going away/off, leaving, leave-taking, removal, withdrawal, retirement, retreat, escape, exodus, setting-off, setting-out
2 DEVIATION, digression, divergence, variation, innovation, branching (out), forking, difference, change, shift, veering
F **1** arrival, return

depend v

1 *the cost depends on the quantity*
HINGE ON, be dependent on, rest on, revolve around, be subject to, hang on, be decided by, be determined by, be based on, ride on
formal turn on, be contingent on
2 *depend on her for support*
RELY ON, count on, calculate on, reckon on, build upon, trust in, have confidence in, lean on, need, not manage without, expect
colloq. bank on

dependable adj

reliable, trustworthy, steady, trusty, responsible, faithful, unfailing, sure, honest, conscientious, steadfast, certain, stable
colloq. tried and tested, a safe pair of hands
F unreliable, fickle

dependant n

child, minor, relative, charge, protégé, ward, client, hanger-on, henchman, minion, subordinate, parasite

dependence n

1 RELIANCE, confidence, faith, trust, need, expectation
2 ADDICTION, attachment, subservience, abuse, helplessness, subordination
F **1** independence

dependency n

1 COLONY, province, protectorate
2 RELIANCE, helplessness, weakness, immaturity, support, subordination
3 ADDICTION, attachment, habit, subservience, abuse

dependent adj

1 RELIANT, helpless, weak, immature, subject, sustained, leaning, supported, subordinate, vulnerable
2 *the profit is dependent on the quantity bought*
conditional, decided, determined, controlled, dictated, based, influenced, relative, subject, subordinate
formal contingent
F **1, 2** independent

depict v

1 *depicted in a painting*
portray, illustrate, sketch, outline, draw, picture, paint, trace, show, represent, describe
2 *novels depicting Victorian life*
portray, describe, recount, characterize, detail, illustrate, outline, trace, show, represent, render, reproduce, record
formal delineate

depiction n

portrayal, description, characterization, detailing, drawing, illustration, image, likeness, picture, caricature, sketch, outline, representation, rendering
formal delineation

deplete v

empty, drain, exhaust, impoverish, bankrupt, weaken, evacuate, use up, consume, spend, expend, run down, reduce, lessen, decrease, diminish, eat into, erode, whittle away
formal attenuate
F increase; *formal* augment

depletion n

exhaustion, impoverishment, weakening, evacuation, consumption, expenditure, reduction, lessening, decrease, deficiency, dwindling, lowering, shrinkage
formal attenuation, diminution
F increase, supply; *formal* augmentation

deplorable adj

disgraceful, reprehensible, scandalous, outrageous, shameful, dishonourable, disreputable, blameworthy, abominable, despicable, lamentable, pitiable, grievous, regrettable, unfortunate, wretched, distressing, sad, miserable, heartbreaking, melancholy, disastrous, dire, appalling
F excellent, commendable

deplore v

1 DISAPPROVE OF, condemn, criticize, reproach, blame, revile, denounce
formal reprehend, reprove, deprecate, berate, upbraid, castigate, disparage, censure
colloq. slam, slate
2 GRIEVE FOR, lament, mourn, regret, bemoan, bewail, pine, rue, weep, cry, shed tears
F **1** extol

deploy v

arrange, position, station, spread out, scatter, use, utilize, distribute
formal dispose

depopulate v

empty, dispeople, unpeople

deport¹ v

deported from a country
expel, banish, exile, extradite, repatriate, transport, oust, ostracize

deport² v

deport yourself well
conduct, bear, behave, carry, hold, manage, act
formal acquit, comport

deportation n

expulsion, banishment, exile, extradition, repatriation, transportation, ousting, ostracism

deportment n

manner, air, appearance, aspect, bearing, behaviour, carriage, conduct, pose, posture, stance, etiquette
formal comportment, demeanour, mien

depose v

oust, overthrow, dismiss, remove, unseat, topple, disestablish, displace, demote, dethrone, discharge, downgrade
colloq. sack, fire

deposit v, n

▶ *v* **1** LAY, drop, plant, place, put (down), set (down), settle, park, sit, locate
technical precipitate
colloq. dump, bung
2 SAVE, store, hoard, bank, amass, consign, entrust, lodge, file, stow, put away, put by
▶ *n* **1** SECURITY, stake, down payment, pledge, retainer, instalment, part payment, money
old use gage
formal earnest
2 SEDIMENT, accumulation, dregs, lees, silt, warp

technical alluvium, precipitate, precipitation
sublimate
formal deposition

deposition *n*
1 *the deposition of the ruler*
ousting, dismissal, removal, unseating, toppling,
displacement, dethronement
2 *the witness's deposition*
affidavit, declaration, statement, testimony, evidence,
information

depository *n*
storehouse, store, warehouse, bonded warehouse,
depot, repository, arsenal

depot *n*
1 *military depot*
storehouse, store, warehouse, depository, repository,
cache, arsenal
2 *bus depot*
station, garage, terminal, terminus

deprave *v*
corrupt, debauch, debase, degrade, pervert, subvert,
infect, demoralize, lead astray, seduce, pollute, defile,
contaminate
E₃ improve, reform

depraved *adj*
corrupt, debauched, degenerate, perverted, debased,
reprobate, dissolute, immoral, obscene, base,
shameless, wicked, sinful, vile, evil, iniquitous,
criminal
E₃ moral, upright
formal licentious

depravity *n*
corruption, debauchery, degeneracy, perversion,
debasement, reprobacy, dissoluteness, immorality,
baseness, wickedness, sinfulness, vileness, evil,
iniquity, vice
formal turpitude
E₃ uprightness

deprecate *v*
condemn, disapprove of, criticize, object to, protest at,
reject, reproach, blame, revile, denounce
formal deplore, reprehend, reprove, deprecate, berate,
upbraid, castigate, disparage, censure
colloq. slam, slate, knock
E₃ approve, commend

> ⚠ **deprecate** or **depreciate** ?
> *Deprecate* is a formal word meaning 'to disapprove
> of': *The government deprecated the soldiers' actions.*
> *Depreciate* most commonly means 'to fall or cause to
> fall in value': *Property shares have depreciated rapidly.*
> A rarer meaning of *depreciate* is 'to speak of as having
> little value or importance': *to depreciate your
> achievements.*

deprecatory *adj*
disapproving, reproachful, dismissive, protesting,
apologetic, regretful
formal censorious, condemnatory
E₃ encouraging; *formal* commendatory

depreciate *v*
1 DEVALUE, deflate, downgrade, decrease/fall/go
down in value, reduce, lower, drop, fall, lessen, decline,
slump
2 BELITTLE, undervalue, underestimate, underrate,
slight, run down, make light of

formal disparage, denigrate, revile, defame, malign
E₃ 1 appreciate 2 overrate

depreciation *n*
1 DEVALUATION, deflation, depression, slump, fall,
reduction in price/value, mark-down, cheapening
2 BELITTLEMENT, underestimation
formal disparagement, denigration

depredation *n*
desolation, destruction, devastation, laying waste,
ravaging, marauding, pillage, looting, plunder,
raiding, ransacking, harrying, robbery, theft
formal despoiling, denudation

depress *v*
1 DEJECT, sadden, make sadden, dishearten,
discourage, cast down, bring down, weigh down,
oppress, upset, daunt, burden, overburden
colloq. get down, break someone's heart
2 WEAKEN, undermine, sap, tire, drain, exhaust,
weary, impair, reduce, lessen, press, lower, level
formal enervate, debilitate
3 DEVALUE, bring down, reduce, lower, cut,
depreciate, cheapen
colloq. slash
E₃ 1 cheer 2 vitalize; *formal* fortify 3 increase,
raise

depressant *n*
sedative, tranquillizer, downer, relaxant, calmant,
calmative
E₃ stimulant

depressed *adj*
1 DEJECTED, low-spirited, melancholy, dispirited,
sad, unhappy, low, low in spirits, down, downcast,
disheartened, miserable, moody, cast down,
discouraged, gloomy, glum, downhearted, distressed,
despondent, morose, crestfallen, pessimistic
colloq. fed up, blue, down in the dumps
2 POOR, disadvantaged, deprived, needy, run-down,
destitute, poverty-stricken
3 SUNKEN, recessed, concave, hollow, indented,
dented, pushed in
E₃ 1 cheerful 2 thriving, affluent 3 convex,
protuberant

depressing *adj*
dejecting, dismal, bleak, gloomy, saddening, cheerless,
dreary, disheartening, unhappy, sad, melancholy,
sombre, grey, black, daunting, discouraging,
dispiriting, heartbreaking, distressing, hopeless, grave
E₃ cheerful, happy, encouraging

depression *n*
1 DEJECTION, despair, despondency, melancholy,
low spirits, unhappiness, sadness, gloom, gloominess,
doldrums, glumness, downheartedness, pessimism,
hopelessness, desolation, discouragement
technical melancholia
colloq. blues, dumps
2 RECESSION, slump, stagnation, crash, hard times,
decline, inactivity, slowdown, standstill
3 INDENTATION, hollow, hole, dip, concavity, dent,
dimple, valley, pit, sink, dint, bowl, cavity, basin,
impression, dish, excavation
E₃ 1 cheerfulness, happiness, euphoria
2 prosperity, boom 3 convexity;
formal protuberance

deprivation *n*
1 *deprivation of sleep*
denial, withdrawal, withholding, removal, lack,

dispossession
2 *deprivation in inner cities*
hardship, poverty, want, need, disadvantage
formal destitution, privation, penury

deprive *v*
take away, dispossess, strip, divest, rob, confiscate,
bereave, deny, withhold, refuse
formal denude, expropriate
E⃞ endow, provide

deprived *adj*
poor, needy, in need, underprivileged, disadvantaged,
impoverished, destitute, lacking, bereft
E⃞ prosperous

depth *n*
1 DEEPNESS, profoundness, extent, measure, drop
formal profundity
2 *depth of feeling*
INTENSITY, strength, thoroughness, seriousness,
severity, gravity, earnestness, passion, vigour, fervour
3 *a person of great depth*
WISDOM, insight, discernment, perception,
penetration, awareness, intuition, astuteness,
cleverness, shrewdness, acumen
formal profundity
4 *the depths of their knowledge*
extent, extensiveness, scope, amount
formal profundity
5 *depth of colour*
intensity, strength, richness, vividness, brilliance,
warmth, glow, darkness
6 *the depths of the sea*
remotest area, bed, floor, bottom, abyss, deep, gulf,
middle, midst
E⃞ **1** shallowness **6** surface
▷ **in depth** comprehensively, thoroughly,
exhaustively, extensively, in detail
E⃞ superficially, broadly

deputation *n*
commission, delegation, embassy, mission,
representatives, legation, committee

depute *v*
appoint, authorize, charge, commission, second,
designate, nominate, empower, entrust, mandate,
delegate, consign, hand over
formal accredit

deputize *n*
represent, stand in for, take over, substitute, replace,
act for, understudy, take the place of, double, relieve,
cover
colloq. sub for

deputy *n, adj*
▶ *n* representative, agent, delegate, proxy, substitute,
stand-in, second-in-command, ambassador, envoy,
commissioner, lieutenant, legate, surrogate,
subordinate, assistant, locum, spokesperson, vice-
president, vice-chairperson, vice-regent
▶ *adj* assistant, representative, substitute, stand-in,
surrogate, subordinate, vice-, suffragan, coadjutor,
depute

deranged *adj*
disordered, demented, crazy, mad, lunatic, insane, of
unsound mind, *non compos mentis*, unbalanced,
unhinged, unsettled, disturbed, irrational, confused,
frantic, delirious, distraught, berserk, out of your mind
colloq. loony, loopy, bonkers, nuts, nutty, nutty as a
fruitcake, off your rocker, needing your head

examining, round the bend, round the twist, out to
lunch
E⃞ sane, calm

derangement *n*
aberration, agitation, confusion, delirium, dementia,
disorder, distraction, disturbance, frenzy,
hallucination, mania, insanity, lunacy, madness
E⃞ order, sanity

derelict *adj, n*
▶ *adj* abandoned, neglected, deserted, forsaken,
desolate, discarded, dilapidated, falling to pieces,
ramshackle, tumbledown, run-down, ruined, in
disrepair
▶ *n* tramp, vagrant, dosser, beggar, wretch, down-
and-out, drifter, hobo, outcast, no-good, good-for-
nothing, no-hoper, ne'er-do-well

dereliction *n*
1 DILAPIDATION, abandonment, neglect, desertion,
forsaking, desolation, ruin(s), disrepair
2 *dereliction of duty*
abdication, abandonment, desertion, evasion, failure,
faithlessness, forsaking, betrayal, neglect, negligence,
relinquishment, remissness, renunciation
formal apostasy, renegation
E⃞ **2** devotion, faithfulness, fulfilment

deride *v*
ridicule, mock, scoff, scorn, jeer, sneer, make fun of,
satirize, gibe, insult, belittle, disdain, taunt, tease, rag
formal disparage
colloq. knock, pooh-pooh
E⃞ respect, praise

de rigueur *adj*
conventional, fitting, necessary, correct, decent, done,
proper, required, right
formal decorous
colloq. the done thing

derision *n*
ridicule, mockery, scorn, contempt, scoffing, hissing,
satire, sneering, taunting, disrespect, insult, teasing,
ragging, disdain
formal disparagement
E⃞ respect, praise

derisive *adj*
mocking, scornful, contemptuous, scoffing,
disrespectful, insulting, irreverent, jeering, disdainful,
taunting
E⃞ respectful, flattering

⚠ **derisive** or **derisory** ?
Derisive means 'mocking; showing derision': *derisive
laughter. Derisory* means 'ridiculous; deserving
mockery or derision': *The management offered a
derisory pay increase.*

---

derisory *adj*
laughable, ludicrous, absurd, ridiculous, contemptible,
insulting, outrageous, preposterous, tiny, paltry
formal risible

derivation *n*
source, origin, root, beginning, etymology, extraction,
foundation, genealogy, ancestry, basis, descent,
deduction, inference

derivative *adj, n*
▶ *adj* unoriginal, acquired, copied, borrowed,
derived, imitative, obtained, second-hand, secondary,

plagiarized, hackneyed, trite
colloq. cribbed, rehashed
🔄 original, inventive, innovative
▶ *n* derivation, offshoot, by-product, development, branch, outgrowth, spin-off, product, descendant

derive *v*
1 *derive pleasure from something*
GAIN, obtain, get, draw, extract, receive, acquire, borrow
formal procure
2 ORIGINATE, arise, spring, flow, have as the source, have its origin/roots in, descend, stem, issue, follow, develop, evolve
formal emanate, proceed

derogatory *adj*
insulting, pejorative, belittling, offensive, critical, disapproving, unfavourable, slighting, uncomplimentary, injurious
formal disparaging, depreciative, defamatory, vilifying, denigratory
🔄 flattering, favourable, complimentary

descend *v*
1 GO DOWN, move down, drop, fall, plummet, plunge, tumble, swoop, sink, arrive, alight, dismount, dip, slope, incline, subside
2 CONDESCEND, deign, sink, stoop, lower yourself
3 DEGENERATE, deteriorate, decline
colloq. go downhill, go to the dogs
4 ORIGINATE, issue, spring, stem
formal proceed, emanate
5 *family descended on us*
invade, arrive suddenly, swoop, take over
🔄 1 ascend, rise

descendants *n*
offspring, children, issue, progeny, successors, lineage, line, scions, posterity
formal seed
🔄 ancestors

descent *n*
1 FALL, going-down, drop, plunge, sinking, subsiding, dip, decline, incline, slope, slant, gradient
formal declivity
2 COMEDOWN, debasement, degradation, deterioration, decline, degeneracy, decadence
3 ANCESTRY, parentage, heredity, family tree, genealogy, lineage, line, stock, extraction, origin
🔄 1 ascent, rise

describe *v*
1 *describe a situation*
portray, depict, illustrate, characterize, specify, draw, define, detail, give details of, explain, express, tell, talk, write, narrate, outline, relate, recount, present, represent, report
formal delineate, elucidate
2 *describe someone as clever*
call, portray, consider, think, style, label, designate, brand, hail
3 *skaters describing circles on the ice*
mark out, draw, sketch, trace, outline
formal delineate

description *n*
1 PORTRAYAL, representation, characterization, account, depiction, sketch, portrait, presentation, report, statement, outline, explanation, narration, commentary, chronicle, profile
formal delineation, exposition, elucidation
2 SORT, type, kind, variety, specification, order, class, designation, category, breed, brand, make

descriptive *adj*
illustrative, explanatory, expressive, detailed, graphic, colourful, pictorial, striking, vivid, detailed
formal elucidatory

descry *v*
discern, catch sight of, mark, notice, observe, perceive, recognize, discover, distinguish, glimpse, see, spot, detect
old use espy

desecrate *v*
defile, violate, pervert, pollute, profane, contaminate, debase, dishallow, dishonour, insult, abuse, blaspheme, vandalize, violate

desecration *n*
defilement, violation, blasphemy, debasement, dishonouring, pollution, profanation, sacrilege, impiety, insult

desert¹ *n, adj*
▶ *n the Sahara desert*
wasteland, wilderness, wilds, barrenness, void
▶ *adj* bare, barren, waste, wild, uninhabited, empty, uncultivated, dry, dried up, arid, parched, moistureless, infertile, unproductive, desolate, sterile, lonely, solitary
Related adjective: eremic

Deserts of the world, with locations, include: Sahara, N Africa; Arabian, SW Asia; Gobi, Mongolia and NE China; Patagonian, Argentina; Great Basin, SW USA; Chihuahuan, Mexico; Great Sandy, NW Australia; Nubian, Sudan; Great Victoria, SW Australia; Thar, India/Pakistan; Sonoran, SW USA; Kara Kum, Turkmenistan; Kyzyl-Kum, Kazakhstan; Takla Makan, N China; Kalahari, SW Africa.

desert² *v*
1 *desert his family*
abandon, leave, maroon, strand, give up, walk out on
formal renounce, forsake, relinquish, cast off, abscond
colloq. jilt, quit, run out on, leave in the lurch, leave high and dry, rat on
2 *the soldier deserted*
decamp, defect, run away, fly, flee, go AWOL
formal abscond
3 *desert a political party*
abandon, give up, turn your back on, deny, betray, change sides
formal forsake, relinquish, renounce, recant, apostasize, tergiversate
🔄 1 stand by, support 3 support

desert³ *n*
1 DUE, right, reward, deserts, what you deserve, return, retribution, payment, recompense, remuneration
colloq. come-uppance
2 WORTH, merit, virtue

deserted *adj*
abandoned, empty, derelict, desolate, God-forsaken, neglected, underpopulated, stranded, isolated, bereft, left, vacant, betrayed, lonely, solitary, uninhabited, unoccupied
formal forsaken
🔄 populous

deserter *n*
runaway, absconder, escapee, truant, renegade,

defector, traitor, turncoat, fugitive, betrayer, backslider, delinquent
formal apostate
colloq. rat

desertion *n*
1 *desertion of his family*
abandonment, leaving, give up
formal forsaking, relinquishment, absconding, casting-off, renunciation
colloq. jilting, quitting
2 *desertions from the armed forces*
defection, decamping, running-away, flight, going AWOL, truancy
formal absconding, dereliction
3 *desertion of a political party*
abandonment, giving-up, denial, betrayal
formal renunciation, forsaking, relinquishment, apostasy, renegation, tergiversation
F3 3 support

deserve *v*
earn, be worthy of, merit, be entitled to, warrant, justify, have a right to, win, rate, incur

deserved *adj*
due, earned, merited, justifiable, justified, warranted, right, rightful, well-earned, suitable, proper, fitting, fair, just, appropriate, apt, legitimate
formal meet, apposite, condign
F3 gratuitous, undeserved

deserving *adj*
worthy, estimable, exemplary, praiseworthy, admirable, commendable, upright, righteous, virtuous
formal laudable, meritorious
F3 undeserving, unworthy

desiccated *adj*
dehydrated, drained, dried, dry, arid, dead, lifeless, parched, powdered, sterile
formal exsiccated

desiccation *n*
dehydration, dryness, aridity, parching, sterility
formal exsiccation, xeransis

design *v, n*
▶ *v* **1** DRAW, plan, sketch, draw up, draft, outline, plot
formal delineate
2 INVENT, originate, conceive, create, think up, develop, construct, fashion, form, model, fabricate, hatch, make
3 INTEND, plot, plan, devise, purpose, contrive, aim, scheme, shape, project, propose, tailor, mean, gear
▶ *n* **1** BLUEPRINT, draft, pattern, plan, prototype, sketch, drawing, outline, map, diagram, scheme, model, guide
formal delineation
2 MOTIF, style, pattern, logo, shape, form, figure, device, emblem, monogram, cipher, format, structure, organization, arrangement, composition, make-up, construction
3 AIM, intention, goal, purpose, plan, end, object, objective, scheme, plot, project, meaning, target, point, wish, desire, hope, dream, enterprise, undertaking
▷ **by design** intentionally, deliberately, on purpose, consciously, pointedly, calculatingly, knowingly, wittingly, wilfully

designate *v*
1 *designated as a listed building*

call, name, title, entitle, term, dub, style, describe, christen
2 *designated to be chairman*
choose, appoint, nominate, select, elect, assign, specify, define, stipulate, earmark, set aside, show, denote, indicate

designation *n*
1 NAME, title, term, label, epithet, nickname, description, style, sobriquet
formal appellation
colloq. tag
2 INDICATION, specification, description, definition, denoting, marking, classification, category, stipulation
3 NOMINATION, appointment, selection, election

designer *n*
deviser, originator, maker, stylist, inventor, creator, contriver, producer, fashioner, planner, architect, author

designing *adj*
artful, crafty, scheming, conspiring, calculating, devious, intriguing, plotting, tricky, wily, sly, deceitful, cunning, guileful, underhand, sharp, shrewd
F3 artless, naïve

desirability *n*
1 *the desirability of qualifications*
ADVANTAGE, profit, advisability, benefit, preference, usefulness, merit, worth, excellence, popularity
2 *the desirability of the woman*
ATTRACTIVENESS, attraction, allure, seductiveness
colloq. sexiness
F3 1 disadvantage, inadvisability, undesirability

desirable *adj*
1 *a desirable qualification*
ADVANTAGEOUS, sought-after, profitable, worthwhile, advisable, appropriate, expedient, beneficial, preferable, sensible, eligible, good, pleasing, pleasant, agreeable, popular, in demand
2 *a desirable woman*
ATTRACTIVE, alluring, seductive, fetching, tempting, tantalizing
colloq. sexy; *slang* beddable
F3 1 undesirable **2** unattractive

desire *v, n*
▶ *v* **1** WANT, wish for, covet, long for, like, need, crave, hunger for, yearn for, set your heart on, fancy, hanker after
colloq. be dying for, set your heart on, have your eyes on, have designs on, give the world for
2 *desire a man*
lust after, burn for, take to
colloq. fancy, be crazy about, have a crush on, take a shine to
▶ *n* **1** WANT, longing, wish, need, fancy, yearning, craving, hankering, lust, appetite, preference, aspiration
formal predilection, predisposition, proclivity
colloq. itch, yen
2 LUST, passion, sexual attraction, sexuality, sex drive, ardour, libido, sensuality, lasciviousness
formal concupiscence
Related adjective: epithymetic

desired *adj*
required, proper, accurate, appropriate, correct, exact, expected, fitting, necessary, particular, right
F3 undesired, unintentional

desirous *adj*
ready, willing, ambitious, aspiring, avid, burning,
craving, itching, eager, enthusiastic, hopeful, hoping,
keen, longing, anxious, wishing, yearning
F∃ reluctant, unenthusiastic

desist *v*
stop, leave off, refrain, end, break off, give up, halt,
abstain, suspend, pause, peter out
formal cease, discontinue, remit, forbear
F∃ continue, resume

desk *n*
bureau, lectern, reading-desk, davenport, écritoire,
secretaire, writing-table, ambo

desolate *adj, v*
▶ *adj* 1 DESERTED, uninhabited, unoccupied,
abandoned, unfrequented, barren, bare, arid, bleak,
gloomy, dismal, dreary, lonely, solitary, isolated,
God-forsaken, forsaken, waste, depressing
2 FORLORN, bereft, depressed, dejected, forsaken,
despondent, distressed, melancholy, miserable,
melancholy, gloomy, unhappy, sad, disheartened,
dismal, downcast, broken-hearted, heartbroken,
wretched
F∃ 1 populous 2 cheerful
▶ *v* devastate, upset, disconcert, overwhelm, take
aback, confound, nonplus, get down
formal discomfit
colloq. shatter, floor

desolation *n*
1 DESTRUCTION, ruin, devastation, ravages, laying
waste
2 BARRENNESS, bleakness, emptiness, forlornness,
loneliness, isolation, solitude, remoteness, wildness
3 DEJECTION, despair, despondency, gloom, misery,
sadness, melancholy, sorrow, unhappiness, broken-
heartedness, anguish, depression, grief, distress,
wretchedness

despair *v, n*
▶ *v* lose heart, lose hope, give up, give in, be
despondent, be discouraged, collapse, surrender
colloq. hit rock bottom, throw in the towel
F∃ hope
▶ *n* despondency, gloom, hopelessness, desperation,
dejection, anguish, distress, inconsolableness,
melancholy, misery, depression, pessimism,
wretchedness
F∃ cheerfulness, resilience

despairing *adj*
despondent, distraught, inconsolable, desolate,
desperate, heartbroken, suicidal, grief-stricken,
hopeless, depressed, discouraged, disheartened,
dejected, miserable, anguished, wretched, sorrowful,
pessimistic, dismayed, downcast
formal disconsolate
F∃ cheerful, hopeful

desperado *n*
bandit, criminal, brigand, terrorist, gangster,
gunman, outlaw, ruffian, thug, cut-throat, law-breaker
colloq. hoodlum, mugger

desperate *adj*
1 HOPELESS, inconsolable, wretched, despondent,
abandoned, distraught, desolate, heartbroken,
suicidal, grief-stricken, depressed, discouraged,
disheartened, dejected, miserable, anguished,
sorrowful, pessimistic, dismayed, downcast
formal disconsolate

2 RECKLESS, rash, impetuous, bold, audacious,
daring, dangerous, do-or-die, foolhardy, risky,
hazardous, hasty, wild, violent, frantic, frenzied,
incautious, determined
formal precipitate
3 CRITICAL, dire, acute, crucial, serious, grave,
severe, extreme, urgent, compelling, pressing, great,
dangerous
4 *desperate to leave school*
wanting very much, needing very much, crying out for,
in great need
colloq. dying
F∃ 1 hopeful 2 cautious

desperately *adv*
dangerously, critically, gravely, acutely, hopelessly,
seriously, severely, badly, dangerously, urgently, greatly,
extremely, dreadfully, fearfully, frightfully

desperation *n*
despair, despondency, anguish, hopelessness, gloom,
misery, agony, distress, pain, wretchedness, sorrow,
trouble, worry, anxiety, depression

despicable *adj*
contemptible, vile, worthless, detestable, disgusting,
mean, degrading, wretched, disgraceful, disreputable,
shameful, abominable, loathsome, reprobate
old use caitiff
formal reprehensible
F∃ admirable, noble

despise *v*
scorn, look down on, disdain, condemn, spurn,
undervalue, slight, dislike, hate, detest, loathe, shun,
mock, sneer
formal abhor, revile, deplore, deride
F∃ admire

despite *prep*
in spite of, regardless of, in the face of, undeterred by,
against, defying
formal notwithstanding

despoil *v*
destroy, devastate, loot, maraud, pillage, plunder,
ransack, ravage, deprive, dispossess, divest, rifle, rob,
strip, vandalize, wreck
formal denude, depredate, spoliate
F∃ adorn, enrich

despondency *n*
broken-heartedness, dejection, depression, despair,
desperation, discouragement, dispiritedness,
downheartedness, gloom, glumness, hopelessness,
inconsolability, melancholia, melancholy, distress,
misery, sadness, sorrow, grief, wretchedness
formal disconsolateness
colloq. blues, heartache
F∃ cheerfulness, hopefulness

despondent *adj*
depressed, dejected, disheartened, downcast, down,
low, gloomy, glum, discouraged, distressed, miserable,
melancholy, sad, sorrowful, doleful, despairing,
heartbroken, inconsolable, mournful, wretched
colloq. down in the dumps, blue
F∃ cheerful, heartened, hopeful

despot *n*
autocrat, tyrant, dictator, oppressor, absolute ruler,
absolutist, boss

despotic *adj*
autocratic, tyrannical, imperious, oppressive,

dictatorial, authoritarian, domineering, high-handed, absolute, overbearing, arbitrary, arrogant
F3 democratic, egalitarian, liberal, tolerant

despotism *n*
autocracy, totalitarianism, tyranny, dictatorship, absolutism, oppression, repression
F3 democracy, egalitarianism, liberalism, tolerance

dessert *n*
sweet, sweet dish, sweet course, pudding
colloq. afters, pud

destination *n*
1 GOAL, aim, objective, object, purpose, target, end, intention, aspiration, design, ambition
2 JOURNEY'S END, terminus, station, stop, final port of call, end of the line

destined *adj*
1 FATED, doomed, inevitable, certain, meant, unavoidable, inescapable, intended, designed, appointed, set apart
formal predetermined, ordained, foreordained
2 BOUND, directed, routed, en route, headed, heading, scheduled, assigned, booked

destiny *n*
fate, future, doom, fortune, luck, karma, kismet
formal lot, portion, predestination, predestiny

destitute *adj*
1 POOR, hard up, badly off, penniless, poverty-stricken, impoverished, distressed, bankrupt
formal impecunious, indigent, penurious
colloq. broke, stony-broke, down and out, on the breadline, cleaned out, strapped for cash, with your back to the wall, on your beam-ends; *slang* skint
2 LACKING, needy, wanting, innocent of, deprived, deficient, depleted
formal devoid of, bereft
F3 1 prosperous, rich

destitution *n*
poverty, pennilessness, impoverishment, distress, bankruptcy, beggary, starvation, straits
formal impecuniousness, indigence, penury, pauperdom
colloq. down and out, on the breadline
F3 prosperity, wealth

destroy *v*
1 DEMOLISH, ruin, shatter, wreck, devastate, smash, break, crush, subdue, overthrow, sabotage, undo, stamp out, dismantle, knock down, pull down, tear down, flatten, obliterate, thwart, undermine, waste, lay waste, gut, level, spoil, ravage, raze, ransack, torpedo, unshape
formal extirpate
2 KILL, annihilate, eliminate, extinguish, eradicate, dispatch, slaughter, put down, put to sleep, put out of its misery
formal slay, nullify, vitiate
colloq. decimate
F3 1 build up 2 create

destroyer *n*
wrecker, annihilator, demolisher, desolater, despoiler, ransacker, ravager, vandal, locust, kiss of death
F3 creator

destruction *n*
1 RUIN, devastation, shattering, smashing, crushing, wreckage, demolition, knocking-down, pulling-down, tearing-down, vandalism, defeat, downfall, overthrow,

ruination, desolation, obliteration, undoing, wastage, razing, levelling, dismantling, havoc, ravagement
formal depredation
2 ANNIHILATION, killing, extermination, eradication, elimination, extinction, slaughter, murder, massacre, end, liquidation
formal nullification
F3 2 creation

destructive *adj*
1 *destructive storms*
devastating, damaging, catastrophic, disastrous, deadly, harmful, fatal, disruptive, lethal, ruinous, injurious, detrimental, hurtful, malignant, pernicious, mischievous
formal noxious, nullifying, deleterious, baneful, slaughterous
2 *destructive criticism*
adverse, hostile, negative, discouraging, unfavourable, unfriendly, disparaging, contrary, derogatory, undermining, subversive, vicious
formal denigrating
F3 1 creative 2 constructive, favourable

desultory *adj*
random, erratic, aimless, disorderly, chaotic, haphazard, irregular, half-hearted, spasmodic, inconsistent, undirected, unco-ordinated, unsystematic, unmethodical, fitful, disconnected, rambling, loose
formal capricious
F3 systematic, methodical

detach *v*
1 *detach the reply slip*
separate, take/tear off, disconnect, unfasten, disjoin, cut off, disengage, remove, undo, uncouple, unhitch, sever, dissociate, isolate, loosen, free, unfix, unhitch, segregate, divide, disentangle
2 *detach yourself from something*
separate, sever, split, cut off, dissociate, isolate, loosen, free, segregate
formal estrange
F3 1 attach 2 involve

detached *adj*
1 SEPARATE, disconnected, dissociated, severed, free, loose, divided, discrete
2 ALOOF, remote, dispassionate, impersonal, neutral, impartial, independent, indifferent, unconcerned, disinterested, cold, clinical, unemotional, objective
F3 1 connected 2 involved

detachment *n*
1 ALOOFNESS, remoteness, coolness, reserve, unconcern, indifference, impassivity, disinterestedness, neutrality, dispassionateness, lack of emotion, impartiality, objectivity, lack of bias, fairness
2 SEPARATION, disconnection, unfastening, uncoupling, disengagement, removal, withdrawal, undoing, severance, isolation, loosening, disentangling
formal disunion
3 SQUAD, unit, force, corps, brigade, patrol, task force
F3 1 concern, bias, prejudice

detail *n, v*
▶ *n* particular, item, factor, element, aspect, component, feature, point, fact, circumstance, respect, specific, specification, ingredient, attribute, count, respect, technicality, complication, intricacy, small

print, complexity, ins and outs, minutiae, triviality, nicety, thoroughness, elaboration, meticulousness, refinement
colloq. ins and outs, nitty-gritty, nuts and bolts
▷ **in detail** point by point, carefully, thoroughly, comprehensively, exhaustively, fully, item by item, at length, in depth
▶ *v* **1** LIST, set out, enumerate, itemize, specify, catalogue, spell out, tabulate, describe, portray, depict, point out, recount, relate
formal delineate, rehearse
2 ASSIGN, appoint, choose, allocate, charge, delegate, commission

detailed *adj*
comprehensive, exhaustive, full, itemized, thorough, minute, in-depth, exact, precise, specific, particular, itemized, intricate, elaborate, complex, complicated, meticulous, descriptive
formal convoluted
colloq. blow-by-blow
⊟ cursory, general

detain *v*
1 DELAY, hold (up), make late, hold back, keep (back), hinder, impede, check, slow, stay, stop
formal retard, inhibit
2 CONFINE, arrest, intern, hold, restrain, keep, keep/hold in custody, lock up, put in prison, imprison
formal incarcerate
⊟ **2** release

detect *v*
1 NOTICE, ascertain, note, observe, perceive, make out, recognize, discern, distinguish, identify, sight, catch, spot, spy
2 UNCOVER, catch, discover, disclose, expose, find, turn up, track down, uncover, unearth, unmask, reveal, bring to light

detection *n*
1 NOTICING, ascertaining, note, observation, perception, recognition, discernment, distinguishing, identification, sighting, *US* operative
2 UNCOVERING, discovery, disclosure, exposé, exposure, tracking-down, smelling-out, sniffing-out, uncovering, unearthing, unmasking, revelation

detective *n*
police officer, (private) investigator, plain-clothes officer
colloq. private eye, sleuth, sleuth-hound, gumshoe, shamus, dick, tail

detention *n*
1 DETAINMENT, custody, confinement, imprisonment, captivity, restraint, constraint, internment, quarantine, punishment
formal incarceration,
2 DELAY, hindrance, holding-back, slowing-up
⊟ **1** release

deter *v*
discourage, put off, talk out of, inhibit, frighten, intimidate, scare off, daunt, check, caution, warn, restrain, hinder, frighten, prevent, prohibit, stop
formal dissuade, disincline
colloq. turn off
⊟ encourage

detergent *n*
cleaner, cleanser, soap, washing powder, washing-up liquid
technical abstergent

deteriorate *v*
1 WORSEN, get worse, decline, degenerate, depreciate, drop, fail, fall off, lapse, slide, relapse, slip, wane, ebb
formal retrograde, retrogress
colloq. go downhill, go to pot, go down the tube, go/ run to seed
2 DECAY, disintegrate, decompose, go bad, break up, fall apart, fall to pieces, weaken, fade
⊟ **1** improve, get better

deterioration *n*
worsening, decline, degeneration, drop, failure, falling-off, downturn, lapse, slide, relapse, slipping, waning, ebb, atrophy, corrosion, debasement, degradation, disintegration
formal retrogression, exacerbation, pejoration
⊟ improvement

determinate *adj*
fixed, absolute, certain, clear-cut, distinct, explicit, express, conclusive, decided, decisive, defined, settled, specific, specified, definite, definitive, established, positive, precise, quantified
⊟ indeterminate

determination *n*
1 RESOLUTENESS, tenacity, firmness, willpower, perseverance, persistence, purpose, resolve, backbone, steadfastness, single-mindedness, will, insistence, conviction, dedication, push, drive, stamina, moral fibre, strength of character, firmness of purpose
formal fortitude
colloq. guts, grit, stay the course, hang on like grim death, hold your ground, dig your heels in
2 DECISION, judgement, settlement, conclusion, decree, verdict, opinion
formal resolution
⊟ **1** irresolution

Colloquial expressions showing determination include: mean business, stick to your guns, go to great lengths, go all out, go to extremes, go the whole hog, go for it, move heaven and earth, stop at nothing, do your utmost, give your all, leave no stone unturned, pull out all the stops, put your heart and soul into, strain every nerve, be hell-bent, get stuck into.

determine *v*
1 AFFECT, influence, govern, control, condition, dictate, direct, guide, prompt, impel, regulate, ordain
2 DISCOVER, establish, find out, learn, ascertain, identify, check, detect, verify
3 DECIDE, settle, make up your mind, choose, conclude, agree on, establish, fix on, elect, finish
formal resolve, purpose
colloq. clinch

determined *adj*
resolute, firm, purposeful, strong-willed, single-minded, persevering, persistent, strong, strong-minded, steadfast, tenacious, dogged, insistent, intent, set, resolved, fixed, bent, dedicated, convinced, decided, unflinching, unwavering, uncompromising, stubborn
colloq. hell-bent, dead set, out
⊟ irresolute, wavering

deterrent *n*
hindrance, impediment, obstacle, repellent, check, bar, barrier, block, discouragement, disincentive, obstruction, curb, restraint, difficulty
⊟ incentive, encouragement

detest *v*
hate, loathe, dislike, recoil from, deplore, despise
formal abhor, abominate, execrate
colloq. can't stand
F3 adore, love

detestable *adj*
hateful, loathsome, repellent, obnoxious, despicable, odious, contemptible, revolting, repulsive, repugnant, offensive, vile, disgusting, distasteful, heinous, shocking, sordid
formal abhorrent, abominable, execrable, accursed, reprehensible
F3 adorable, admirable

detestation *n*
hate, hatred, loathing, dislike, anathema, animosity, hostility, antipathy, aversion, repugnance, revulsion
formal abhorrence, abomination, execration, odium
F3 adoration, approval, love

dethrone *v*
depose, oust, topple, unseat, unthrone, uncrown
F3 crown, enthrone

detonate *v*
blow up, discharge, blast, explode, ignite, kindle, set off, let off, spark off
formal fulminate

detonation *n*
bang, blast, explosion, blow-up, boom, burst, discharge, igniting, ignition
formal fulmination, report

detour *n*
deviation, diversion, indirect route, circuitous route, roundabout route, scenic route, digression, byroad, byway, bypath, bypass

detract *v*
diminish, subtract from, take away from, spoil, mar, reduce, lessen, lower, devaluate, depreciate, belittle
formal disparage
F3 add to, enhance, praise

detractor *n*
backbiter, belittler, defamer, slanderer, muck-raker, reviler, scandalmonger, enemy
formal denigrator, disparager, traducer, vilifier
F3 flatterer, supporter, defender

detriment *n*
damage, harm, hurt, disadvantage, loss, ill, injury, impairment, disservice, wrong, evil, mischief, prejudice
F3 advantage, benefit

detrimental *adj*
damaging, harmful, hurtful, adverse, disadvantageous, prejudicial, mischievous, pernicious, destructive
formal injurious, inimical
F3 advantageous, favourable, beneficial

detritus *n*
remains, rubbish, debris, rubble, fragments, garbage, junk, litter, scum, waste, wreckage

devalue *v*
deflate, devaluate, lower, reduce, decrease
formal devalorize

devastate *v*
1 DESTROY, desolate, lay waste, demolish, spoil, despoil, wreck, ruin, ravage, waste, ransack, plunder, level, flatten, raze, pillage, sack
2 DISCONCERT, overwhelm, overcome, shock, take

aback, confound, nonplus, discompose, traumatize
formal perturb, discomfit
colloq. shatter, floor

devastating *adj*
1 *devastating storms*
destructive, disastrous, damaging, harmful, catastrophic
2 *a devastating argument*
effective, incisive, overwhelming, shocking, stunning
colloq. shattering

devastation *n*
destruction, desolation, waste, havoc, ruin(s), damage, wreckage, ravages, demolition, annihilation, pillage, plunder, spoliation

develop *v*
1 ADVANCE, grow, evolve, expand, enlarge, progress, foster, nurture, flourish, mature, prosper, improve, branch out, spread
2 ELABORATE, amplify, argument, enhance, unfold, work out, expand on
formal dilate on
3 ACQUIRE, begin, start, generate, create, invent, produce, originate, establish, set about/off, found, institute
formal contract, commence
4 RESULT, come about, grow, ensue, arise, follow, happen
5 *develop an illness*
catch, get, go down with, pick up, become infected with, become ill with
formal contract, succumb to

development *n*
1 GROWTH, evolution, advance, blossoming, elaboration, furtherance, progress, progression, unfolding, expansion, enlargement, extension, spread, increase, improvement, maturity, flourishing, prosperity, promotion, refinement, issue
2 OCCURRENCE, happening, event, incident, circumstance, change, outcome, situation, result, phenomenon
3 *property development*
complex, centre, block, estate, land, area

deviant *adj, n*
▶ *adj* divergent, aberrant, anomalous, abnormal, irregular, variant, bizarre, eccentric, anomalous, quirky, freakish, perverse, perverted, twisted, wayward, bent,
formal disparity
colloq. kinky, oddball, with a screw loose, with bats in the belfry
F3 normal
▶ *n* freak, oddity, misfit, dropout, odd sort, pervert
colloq. oddball, kook, crank, weirdo; *slang* geek, goof
F3 straight

deviate *v*
diverge, veer, turn (aside), digress, swerve, deflect, change, vary, differ, depart, stray, yaw, wander, err, go astray, drift, part
colloq. go off the rails

deviation *n*
divergence, aberration, departure, abnormality, irregularity, difference, variance, variation, digression, eccentricity, anomaly, deflection, turning-aside, alteration, discrepancy, detour, fluctuation, inconsistency, change, drift, quirk, shift, freak
formal disparity
F3 conformity, regularity

device *n*
1 TOOL, implement, appliance, gadget, contrivance, contraption, apparatus, utensil, instrument, machine, mechanism
colloq. gizmo
2 SCHEME, ruse, strategy, stratagem, plan, plot, ploy, gambit, manoeuvre, wile, trick, artifice, stunt, manoeuvre
formal machination
colloq. dodge
3 EMBLEM, symbol, motif, logo, colophon, design, insignia, crest, badge, shield, seal, token, coat of arms

devil *n*
1 DEMON, Satan, fiend, evil spirit, arch-fiend, Lucifer, imp, Evil One, Prince of Darkness, Adversary, Beelzebub, Mephistopheles
colloq. Old Nick, Old Harry
Related adjective: diabolic
2 BRUTE, rogue, monster, ogre, savage, beast, demon, terror, imp, rascal, wretch

devilish *adj*
diabolical, diabolic, fiendish, satanic, demonic, hellish, damnable, evil, infernal, wicked, vile, atrocious, dreadful, outrageous, shocking, disastrous, excruciating, accursed
formal execrable, nefarious

devil-may-care *adj*
careless, reckless, casual, cavalier, easy-going, flippant, frivolous, happy-go-lucky, heedless, nonchalant, unconcerned, unworried, swaggering, swashbuckling
formal insouciant

devious *adj*
1 UNDERHAND, deceitful, dishonest, double-dealing, unscrupulous, scheming, insidious, insincere, designing, calculating, crafty, cunning, evasive, wily, sly, artful, surreptitious, treacherous, misleading
formal disingenuous
colloq. tricky, slippery, crooked
2 INDIRECT, circuitous, rambling, roundabout, wandering, winding, deviating, tortuous, erratic
F3 1 straightforward 2 direct

devise *v*
invent, contrive, plan, plot, design, conceive, come up with, work out, think up, dream up, put together, arrange, formulate, imagine, scheme, construct, originate, create, concoct, forge, fabricate, hatch, frame, project, shape, form, compose, create
colloq. cook up

devoid *adj*
lacking, wanting, without, free, bereft, destitute, deprived, bare, barren, empty, vacant, void
formal deficient
F3 endowed

devolution *n*
decentralization, delegation of power, distribution, transference of power, dispersal
F3 centralization

devolve *v*
hand down, delegate, transfer, consign, convey, deliver, depute, entrust, commission, fall to, rest with

devote *v*
dedicate, consecrate, commit, give yourself, set apart, set aside, reserve, consign, apply, allocate, allot, sacrifice, enshrine, assign, appropriate, surrender, offer, give, put in, pledge

devoted *adj*
dedicated, ardent, committed, loyal, faithful, devout, loving, staunch, steadfast, true, constant, fond, unswerving, tireless, concerned, attentive, caring
F3 indifferent, disloyal

devotee *n*
enthusiast, fan, fanatic, addict, aficionado, follower, supporter, zealot, adherent, admirer, disciple, hound
colloq. buff, freak, merchant, fiend

devotion *n*
1 DEDICATION, commitment, consecration, ardour, loyalty, allegiance, adherence, trueness, staunchness, constancy, solidarity, zeal, support, love, passion, fervour, fondness, attachment, admiration, warmness, closeness, adoration, affection, faithfulness, reverence, steadfastness, regard, earnestness
formal fidelity
2 DEVOUTNESS, piety, godliness, faith, holiness, spirituality, sanctity
3 PRAYER, worship, observance
F3 1 inconstancy 2 irreverence

devotional *adj*
devout, holy, pietistic, religious, reverential, sacred, solemn, spiritual, dutiful, pious

devour *v*
1 EAT, eat up, consume, finish off, guzzle, gulp, gorge, gobble, bolt, swallow, cram, gormandize, feast on, relish, revel in
colloq. wolf down, stuff, polish off, tuck into, scoff, put away, knock back
2 DESTROY, devastate, lay waste, consume, absorb, engulf, envelop, ravage, dispatch
3 *devour a book*
be engrossed in, take in, drink in, appreciate, enjoy, relish, feast on

devout *adj*
1 PIOUS, godly, religious, reverent, prayerful, saintly, holy, orthodox, church-going, committed, practising
2 SINCERE, earnest, devoted, fervent, genuine, staunch, steadfast, ardent, passionate, serious, wholehearted, constant, faithful, intense, vehement, heartfelt, zealous, unswerving, deep, profound
F3 1 irreligious 2 insincere

devoutly *adv*
1 *devoutly religious*
piously, religiously, reverently, prayerfully
2 SINCERELY, deeply, earnestly, fervently, staunchly, steadfastly, ardently, passionately, wholeheartedly, faithfully, zealously

dewy *adj*
blooming, innocent, starry-eyed, youthful
formal roral, roric, rorid, roscid

dexterity *n*
deftness, adeptness, address, adroitness, agility, handiness, nimbleness, proficiency, mastery, readiness, skilfulness, ability, skill, expertise, aptitude, art, artistry, expertness, facility, knack, finesse, legerdemain, sleight, ingenuity, effortlessness
F3 clumsiness, awkwardness, ineptitude

dexterous *adj*
deft, adept, adroit, agile, able, nimble, proficient, skilful, clever, expert, accomplished, nippy, handy, facile, nimble-fingered, neat-handed
colloq. nifty
F3 clumsy, inept, awkward

diabolical *adj*
devilish, fiendish, demonic, hellish, damnable, evil,
infernal, satanic, wicked, vile, sinful, dreadful,
outrageous, shocking, appalling, disastrous,
monstrous, excruciating, atrocious, nasty
formal execrable

diadem *n*
circlet, coronet, crown, tiara, headband, mitre, round

diagnose *v*
identify, determine, recognize, pinpoint, distinguish,
analyse, explain, isolate, detect, interpret, investigate

diagnosis *n*
identification, verdict, explanation, conclusion,
answer, interpretation, judgement, analysis, opinion,
investigation, recognition, detection, examination,
scrutiny

diagnostic *adj*
analytical, indicative, interpretative, interpretive,
recognizable, symptomatic, demonstrative,
distinguishing

diagonal *adj*
oblique, slanting, cross, crossing, crosswise, sloping,
crooked, angled, cornerways

diagonally *adv*
obliquely, crossways, crosswise, at an angle,
cornerwise, on the cross, on the slant, slantwise, aslant,
on the bias

diagram *n*
plan, sketch, chart, bar chart, pie chart, flow chart,
drawing, figure, representation, schema, illustration,
outline, draft, graph, picture, exploded view, cutaway,
layout, table
formal delineation

diagrammatic *adj*
diagrammatical, schematic, graphic, illustrative,
representational, tabular
◪ imaginative, impressionistic

dial *n, v*
▶ *n* circle, disc, face, clock, control
▶ *v* phone, telephone, ring, call (up)
colloq. give a buzz/a bell

dialect *n*
idiom, language, regionalism, localism, patois,
provincialism, vernacular, variety, argot, jargon,
accent, speech, diction
colloq. lingo

dialectic *adj, n*
▶ *adj* dialectical, logical, rational, argumentative,
analytical, rationalistic, logistic, polemical, inductive,
deductive
formal disputatious
▶ *n* dialectics, logic, reasoning, rationale, analysis,
debate, argumentation, contention, discussion,
polemics, deduction
formal disputation, induction, ratiocination

dialogue *n*
1 CONVERSATION, communication, talk, chat,
tête-à-tête, gossip, exchange, discussion, discourse,
conference
formal interchange, converse, debate, colloquy,
interlocution
2 LINES, script

diametrically *adv*
directly, completely, absolutely, utterly
formal antithetical

diaphanous *adj*
cobwebby, delicate, filmy, fine, gauzy, gossamer,
gossamery, chiffony, light, see-through, sheer, thin,
translucent, transparent, veily
formal pellucid
◪ heavy, opaque, thick

diarrhoea *n*
looseness of the bowels, gippy tummy, holiday tummy,
Montezuma's revenge, dysentery
colloq. the runs, the trots, Spanish tummy, Delhi belly
◪ constipation

diary *n*
journal, day-book, logbook, chronicle, year-book,
appointment book, engagement book, Filofax®

diatribe *n*
tirade, abuse, harangue, attack, onslaught,
denunciation, criticism, insult, reviling, upbraiding,
reproof, reprimand, rebuke
formal invective, vituperation, philippic
colloq. knocking, slating, slamming, running-down
◪ praise, eulogy

dicey *adj*
risky, chancy, unpredictable, uncertain, tricky,
problematic, dangerous, difficult, dubious
colloq. iffy, hairy, dodgy
◪ certain

dicky *adj*
unsound, unsteady, weak, ailing, frail, infirm, shaky
◪ healthy, robust

dictate *v, n*
▶ *v* **1** SAY, read, read aloud, read out, speak, utter,
announce, pronounce, transmit
2 COMMAND, lay down, set down, impose, demand,
insist, order, direct, decree, instruct, rule
formal prescribe, promulgate
▶ *n* command, decree, precept, principle, rule,
direction, charge, injunction, edict, order, ruling,
statute, requirement, law, bidding, mandate,
ultimatum, word
formal ordinance, behest, promulgation

dictator *n*
despot, absolute ruler, autocrat, tyrant, oppressor
formal autarchist
colloq. supremo, Big Brother

dictatorial *adj*
tyrannical, despotic, totalitarian, all powerful,
authoritarian, autocratic, oppressive, imperious,
domineering, absolute, unlimited, unrestricted,
repressive, overbearing, arbitrary, dogmatic
formal omnipotent, peremptory, autarchic
colloq. bossy
◪ democratic, egalitarian, liberal

dictatorship *n*
tyranny, despotism, totalitarianism, authoritarianism,
autocracy, absolute rule, fascism, police state, reign of
terror, Hitlerism
◪ democracy, egalitarianism

diction *n*
speech, articulation, language, elocution, intonation,
pronunciation, inflection, fluency, delivery,
expression, phrasing
formal enunciation

dictionary n
lexicon, glossary, thesaurus, vocabulary, wordbook, encyclopedia, concordance

dictum n
1 RULING, pronouncement, decree, dictate, edict, precept, command, order
formal fiat
2 SAYING, maxim, axiom, utterance, proverb, aphorism

didactic adj
instructive, educational, informative, prescriptive, pedantic, moralizing, moral
formal educative, pedagogic

die v
1 *he died in terrible pain*
pass away, pass on, depart, depart this life, breathe your last, draw your last breath, lose your life, perish
formal expire
colloq. peg out, bite the dust, pop off, give up the ghost, have had it, meet your maker, push up daisies, go the way of all flesh, shuffle off this mortal coil; *slang* snuff it, cash in your chips, kick the bucket
2 DWINDLE, fade, pass, ebb, sink, wane, wilt, wither, decline, decay, decrease, finish, lapse, end, come to an end, disappear, vanish, subside, dissolve, melt away
colloq. peter out
3 *the machine died*
stop, break down, fail, lose power
slang conk out
4 LONG FOR, pine for, yearn, desire, be desperate
colloq. be crazy, be mad, be nuts, be wild, be raring
▷ **die away** fade, become weak, become faint, disappear
▷ **die down** decrease, subside, decline, quieten, stop
▷ **die out** become rarer/less common, disappear, vanish; *colloq.* peter out
F■ 1 live

die-hard n
reactionary, hardliner, ultra-conservative, rightist, fanatic, zealot
formal intransigent
colloq. blimp, old fogey, stick-in-the-mud

diet n, v
▶ n 1 FOOD, nutrition, rations, foodstuffs, fare, subsistence
old use provisions
formal sustenance, victuals, comestibles, viands
2 FAST, abstinence, regimen
▶ v lose weight, slim, fast, reduce, abstain
colloq. weight-watch

differ v
1 VARY, diverge, deviate, depart from, be a departure from, contradict, contrast, be unlike, be dissimilar
2 DISAGREE, argue, conflict, oppose, dispute, be at odds with, be at variance, clash, quarrel, fall out, debate, contend, not see eye to eye, take issue
formal dissent, altercate
F■ 1 conform 2 agree

difference n
1 DISSIMILARITY, unlikeness, discrepancy, divergence, diversity, variation, variance, variety, distinctness, distinction, deviation, differentiation, contrast, singularity, exception
formal dissimilitude, antithesis, incongruity, disparity
2 DISAGREEMENT, clash, dispute, conflict, argument, misunderstanding, quarrel, row, set-to, contention

formal controversy, disputation, altercation
3 REMAINDER, rest, balance, residue
F■ 1 conformity 2 agreement

different adj
1 DISSIMILAR, unlike, contrasting, divergent, inconsistent, deviating, at odds, at variance, clashing, opposed
colloq. a far cry, poles/worlds apart, different as chalk and cheese
2 VARIED, various, varying, separate, diverse, miscellaneous, assorted, many, numerous, several, sundry, other, another
formal disparate, discrete
colloq. mixed bag
3 UNUSUAL, unconventional, unique, distinct, distinctive, extraordinary, individual, original, special, strange, remarkable, odd, peculiar, rare, bizarre, anomalous, out of the ordinary
F■ 1 similar, identical 2 same 3 conventional, ordinary

differentiate v
distinguish, tell apart, discriminate, contrast, separate, mark off, individualize, particularize

differentiation n
distinction, distinguishing, discrimination, contrast, separation, demarcation, individualization, particularization, modification
F■ assimilation, association, confusion, connection

difficult adj
1 HARD, laborious, demanding, arduous, strenuous, tough, gruelling, tiring, wearisome, exhausting, back-breaking, uphill, formidable, exacting, burdensome, onerous
2 COMPLEX, complicated, intricate, hard, involved, obscure, dark, knotty, thorny, problematical, puzzling, perplexing, abstract, baffling, tricky
formal abstruse, intractable, recondite, arcane, esoteric
3 UNMANAGEABLE, awkward, perverse, troublesome, trying, demanding, unco-operative, tiresome, stubborn, obstinate
formal intractable, recalcitrant, refractory
F■ 1 easy 2 straightforward, simple, intelligible
3 manageable, helpful

difficulty n
1 HARDSHIP, trouble, labour, strain, arduousness, strenuousness, painfulness, trial, struggle, awkwardness
formal tribulation, exigency
2 PROBLEM, predicament, complication, snag, dilemma, quandary, perplexity, embarrassment, plight, distress, hang-up, obstacle, hindrance, hurdle, impediment, objection, opposition, block, barrier, obstruction, pitfall, stumbling-block, cleft stick
colloq. fix, mess, jam, spot, hiccup, hole, dire straits, pickle, tall order, hot/deep water, fly in the ointment, catch-22, how-d'you-do, devil, tight spot, pretty pass; *slang* bitch, bugger, pain in the arse, shit creek
F■ 1 ease
▷ **in difficulties** having problems, in trouble; *colloq.* up against it, stumped, at the end of your tether, out of your depth, not knowing which way to turn, in the soup, in a fix/mess/jam/hole, in dire straits, in a scrape, in hot/deep water, in a tight spot; *slang* up shit creek (without a paddle)

diffidence n
unassertiveness, modesty, shyness, self-consciousness,

self-effacement, timidity, insecurity, reserve, bashfulness, humility, inhibition, meekness, self-distrust, self-doubt, hesitancy, reluctance, backwardness
E3 confidence

diffident *adj*
unassertive, modest, shy, timid, self-conscious, self-effacing, insecure, nervous, bashful, abashed, meek, reserved, withdrawn, tentative, shrinking, inhibited, hesitant, reluctant, unsure, shamefaced, sheepish
E3 assertive, confident

diffuse *v, adj*
▶ *v* spread, scatter, disperse, distribute, propagate, dispense, disseminate, permeate, circulate
formal dissipate, promulgate
E3 concentrate
▶ *adj* **1** *diffuse outbreaks of rain*
scattered, unconcentrated, diffused, dispersed, disconnected
2 *a diffuse prose style*
verbose, imprecise, wordy, rambling, long-winded, profuse, vague, discursive
formal prolix, loquacious, periphrastic, circumlocutory
colloq. waffling
E3 **1** concentrated **2** succinct

dig *v, n*
▶ *v* **1** EXCAVATE, penetrate, burrow, make a hole, mine, quarry, scoop, hollow, channel, tunnel, till, turn over, work, cultivate, harrow, plough, gouge, delve, pierce
2 POKE, prod, jab, punch
3 INVESTIGATE, probe, go into, research, search, delve
▷ **dig up** discover, unearth, uncover, root out, bring to light, disinter, expose, extricate, find, retrieve, track down; *formal* exhume
E3 bury, obscure
▶ *n* **1** *a dig in the ribs*
poke, prod, jab, punch
2 GIBE, jeer, sneer, taunt, crack, insinuation, insult, wisecrack, compliment

digest *v, n*
▶ *v* **1** ABSORB, assimilate, incorporate, process, dissolve, break down
formal macerate, macera
2 TAKE IN, absorb, understand, assimilate, grasp, study, consider, contemplate, meditate, mull over, ponder
3 SHORTEN, summarize, condense, compress, reduce, abridge
formal comprehend
▶ *n* summary, abridgement, abstract, précis, synopsis, résumé, reduction, abbreviation, compression, compendium

digestion *n*
absorption, assimilation, breaking-down, transformation
formal ingestion, eupepsia

dignified *adj*
stately, solemn, imposing, grand, majestic, noble, august, lordly, courtly, ceremonious, lofty, exalted, formal, distinguished, grave, impressive, reserved, honourable
formal decorous
E3 undignified, lowly

dignify *v*
honour, distinguish, grace, exalt, enhance, adorn, glorify, advance, elevate, ennoble, promote, raise
formal aggrandize, apotheosize
E3 degrade, demean

dignitary *n*
worthy, notable, high-up, personage, somebody
formal luminary
colloq. VIP, bigwig, big name, big gun, big shot, top brass

dignity *n*
stateliness, solemnity, nobleness, courtliness, self-possession, grandeur, loftiness, majesty, honour, eminence, importance, excellence, honourability, nobility, self-respect, self-esteem, self-importance, standing, poise, respectability, greatness, elevation, status, pride
formal propriety, decorum

digress *v*
diverge, deviate, stray, wander, go off at a tangent, go off the subject, drift, depart, ramble, turn aside, be sidetracked

digression *n*
divergence, deviation, straying, wandering, aside, departure, diversion, footnote, parenthesis
formal apostrophe, divagation, *obiter dictum*, excursus

dilapidated *adj*
ramshackle, shabby, broken-down, neglected, tumbledown, uncared-for, rickety, shaky, decrepit, crumbling, run-down, worn-out, ruined, in ruins, decayed, decaying, falling apart

dilapidation *n*
decay, ruin, disrepair, collapse, demolition, destruction, deterioration, disintegration, waste

dilate *v*
enlarge, expand, spread (out), broaden, widen, increase, extend, stretch, swell, bloat, inflate
formal distend
E3 contract, constrict, shorten

dilatory *adj*
delaying, slow, sluggish, lingering, dawdling, lazy, lackadaisical, slack, snail-like, time-wasting, postponing, stalling
formal procrastinating, tardy, tarrying
E3 prompt

dilemma *n*
quandary, conflict, predicament, problem, vicious circle, difficulty, puzzle, embarrassment, mess, perplexity, plight
colloq. catch-22, spot, no-win situation, tight corner

dilettante *n*
dabbler, amateur, trifler, potterer
formal aesthete, sciolist
E3 professional

diligence *n*
assiduity, assiduousness, industry, conscientiousness, attention, care, thoroughness, dedication, attentiveness, application, constancy, earnestness, intentness, laboriousness, perseverance
formal pertinacity, sedulousness
E3 laziness

diligent *adj*
assiduous, industrious, hard-working, conscientious, painstaking, busy, attentive, tireless, careful, thorough,

dedicated, meticulous, persevering, persistent, studious, earnest, constant
formal sedulous
E3 negligent, lazy

dilly-dally *v*
dally, dawdle, delay, falter, hesitate, hover, linger, loiter, dither, potter, vacillate, waver, take your time
formal procrastinate, tarry
colloq. shilly-shally

dilute *v*
adulterate, water down, thin (out), make thinner, weaken, make weaker, diffuse, diminish, decrease, lessen, reduce, temper, moderate, tone down
formal attenuate, mitigate
E3 concentrate

dim *adj, v*
▶ *adj* **1** DARK, dull, dusky, cloudy, overcast, grey, shadowy, gloomy, leaden, sombre, dingy, unlit, lacklustre, feeble
formal crepuscular, tenebrous
2 INDISTINCT, blurred, hazy, ill-defined, obscure, misty, unclear, foggy, fuzzy, vague, faint, weak, feeble, pale, confused, imperfect
formal obfuscated
3 STUPID, dense, obtuse, slow-witted, doltish
colloq. thick, dumb, gormless, dim-witted
4 *dim prospects*
unpromising, unfavourable, gloomy, discouraging, adverse
formal inauspicious
E3 **1** bright **2** distinct **3** bright, intelligent **4** hopeful, promising
▶ *v* darken, dull, obscure, cloud, blur, become blurred, fade, become faint, pale, tarnish, shade
E3 brighten, illuminate

dimension *n*
1 *the dimensions of the room*
extent, measurement, measure, size, length, width, breadth, height, depth, area, proportions, scope, magnitude, largeness, volume, capacity, mass
2 *the dimensions of a problem*
extent, size, scale, range, bulk, importance, magnitude, greatness
3 *add a new dimension to the matter*
aspect, facet, side, factor, element, feature

diminish *v*
1 DECREASE, lessen, become/grow less, reduce, lower, contract, decline, dwindle, shrink, recede, taper off, wane, weaken, become/grow weaker, fade, sink, subside, deflate, ebb, slacken, die away, die out, cut
formal abate, retrench
colloq. peter out
2 BELITTLE, devalue, defame
formal disparage, deprecate, denigrate, derogate, vilify
E3 **1** increase, grow **2** exaggerate

diminution *n*
reduction, lessening, contraction, decline, ebb, decrease, cut, cutback, curtailment, deduction, decay, subsidence, weakening, shortening, shrinkage
formal abatement, retrenchment
E3 enlargement, increase, growth

diminutive *adj*
small-scale, tiny, little, undersized, small, miniature, minute, microscopic, infinitesimal, elfin, petite, midget, compact, Lilliputian, pocket(-sized), pygmy, dwarfish

Scot. wee
formal homuncular
colloq. mini, teeny, teeny-weeny, dinky, pint-size(d)
E3 big, large, oversized

dimple *n*
concavity, depression, dint, hollow
technical fovea, umbilicus

dimwit *n*
idiot, fool, blockhead, nitwit, dunce, dullard, dunderhead, ignoramus
colloq. bonehead, numskull, twit

din *n*
noise, loud noise, row, racket, clash, clatter, clamour, clangour, pandemonium, uproar, tumult, commotion, crash, hubbub, brouhaha, outcry, shout, shouting, yelling, babble
colloq. hullabaloo
E3 quiet, calm

dine *v*
eat, have dinner, feast, sup, lunch, banquet, feed

dingy *adj*
dark, drab, grimy, murky, faded, dull, dim, shabby, soiled, discoloured, dirty, grimy, dreary, gloomy, dismal, cheerless, seedy, sombre, obscure, run-down, colourless, murky, dusky, worn
E3 bright, clean

dinky *adj*
dainty, fine, small, petite, neat, trim, miniature
colloq. natty, mini

dinner *n*
meal, main meal, evening meal, supper, tea, banquet, feast, spread
formal repast, refection
colloq. blow-out
Related adjective: prandial

dinosaur *n*

Dinosaurs include: Ornithischia, Saurischia; Allosaurus, Ankylosaurus, Apatosaurus, Barosaurus, Brachiosaurus, Brontosaurus, Camptosaurus, Coelophysis, Compsognathus, Corythosaurus, Deinonychus, Diplodocus, Heterodontosaurus, Iguanodon, Ophiacodon, Ornithomimus, Pachycephalosaurus, Parasaurolophus, Plateosaurus, Stegosaurus, Styracosaurus, Triceratops, Tyrannosaurus.

dint *n*
dent, indentation, impression, hollow, depression, blow, concavity, stroke
▷ **by dint of** by means of, by the agency of, through the medium of, with the assistance of; *formal* by virtue of

dip *v, n*
▶ *v* **1** PLUNGE, immerse, submerge, duck, dunk, lower, bathe, soak, douse, souse, sink
2 DESCEND, go down, decline, drop, fall, decrease, subside, slump, sink, lower
3 *the track dips*
slope, descend, go down, decline, drop, fall, sink
▷ **dip into 1** *dip into a book* look at, leaf through, look through, run through, flick through, thumb through, skim, browse **2** *dip into your savings* spend, draw on, use
▶ *n* **1** HOLLOW, basin, decline, hole, drop, concavity, incline, descent, indentation, dent, depression, fall,

slope, decrease, slump, lowering
2 BATHE, immersion, plunge, soaking, ducking,
swim, drenching, dive
formal infusion
3 *an avocado dip*
sauce, cream, dressing

diplomacy *n*
1 TACT, tactfulness, finesse, sensitivity, delicacy,
discretion, savoir-faire, cleverness, subtlety, skill, craft
formal judiciousness, prudence
2 STATECRAFT, statesmanship, international
relations, politics, negotiation, manoeuvring

diplomat *n*
go-between, mediator, negotiator, ambassador, envoy,
emissary, legate, attaché, consul, plenipotentiary,
chargé d'affaires, conciliator, peacemaker, arbitrator,
moderator, politician, statesman

diplomatic *adj*
1 *diplomatic relations*
consular, ambassadorial
2 TACTFUL, politic, discreet, subtle, sensitive, clever,
skilful
formal judicious, prudent
F3 tactless

dire *adj*
1 DISASTROUS, dreadful, terrible, frightful, awful,
appalling, calamitous, catastrophic, horrible,
atrocious, shocking, alarming, distressing
2 DESPERATE, urgent, grave, drastic, crucial,
extreme, vital, pressing, ominous

direct *adj, v*
▶ *adj* **1** STRAIGHT, undeviating, unswerving,
through, uninterrupted, non-stop, unbroken
2 STRAIGHTFORWARD, outspoken, blunt, bluff,
frank, straight, forthright, plainspoken, unequivocal,
sincere, candid, honest, explicit, unambiguous
colloq. up-front
3 IMMEDIATE, first-hand, face-to-face, personal
F3 **1** indirect, circuitous **2** equivocal **3** indirect
▶ *v* **1** CONTROL, be in control of, manage, run,
administer, be in charge of, organize, lead, govern,
regulate, superintend, preside over, oversee, supervise,
handle, mastermind
colloq. call the shots, be the boss of
2 INSTRUCT, command, order, give orders, issue
instructions, charge
formal adjure
3 GUIDE, lead, conduct, point, show, steer, show/
point the way, escort, usher
4 AIM, point, focus, turn, intend, mean, level

direction *n*
1 CONTROL, administration, management,
government, running, handling, supervision,
guidance, leadership, superintendency, overseeing,
regulation
2 ROUTE, way, line, road, course, path, track, bearing,
orientation
3 *change the direction of your career*
course, trend, tendency, inclination, drift, tenor,
current aim, orientation
4 *give someone directions*
instructions, guidelines, orders, brief, briefing,
guidance, recommendations, indication, plan, rules,
regulations

directive *n*
command, instruction, order, regulation, ruling,
imperative, dictate, decree, charge, bidding, mandate,

injunction, ordinance, edict, notice
formal fiat

directly *adv*
1 IMMEDIATELY, instantly, at once, promptly, right
away, speedily, forthwith, instantaneously, quickly,
soon, presently, straightaway, without delay, as soon as
possible, straight, right, exactly
colloq. pronto
2 FRANKLY, bluntly, candidly, honestly,
straightforwardly, unequivocally, sincerely, clearly,
plainly, explicitly, unambiguously

director *n*
manager, managing director, board of directors, head,
boss, chief, controller, executive, chief executive,
principal, governor, leader, president, superintendent,
organizer, supervisor, overseer, administrator,
producer, chairman, chairwoman, chairperson, chair,
conductor, régisseur
colloq. top dog

dirge *n*
elegy, lament, funeral song, requiem, dead-march,
coronach, threnody, monody

dirt *n*
1 EARTH, soil, clay, dust, mud, loam
2 FILTH, grime, soot, pollution, muck, mire,
excrement, stain, smudge, sludge, slime, tarnish
colloq. gunge, yuck, grot; *slang* crud, gunk, grunge,
crap
3 INDECENCY, impurity, obscenity, pornography,
lewdness, sordidness, salaciousness
colloq. smut, sleaze

dirty *adj, v*
▶ *adj* **1** FILTHY, grimy, grubby, mucky, soiled,
greasy, unclean, unwashed, unhygienic, foul, messy,
muddy, dusty, sooty, polluted, slimy, squalid, dull, miry,
scruffy, shabby, sullied, stained, defiled, tarnished,
clouded, cloudy, dark, dull
colloq. grotty, yucky, flea-bitten, cruddy
2 INDECENT, improper, obscene, coarse, filthy,
smutty, sordid, salacious, suggestive, risqué, vulgar,
pornographic, contaminated, corrupt, lewd, bawdy,
ribald
colloq. blue, raunchy, sleazy
F3 **1** clean **2** decent **3** honest
▶ *v* pollute, soil, stain, foul, mess up, defile,
contaminate, adulterate, smear, smirch, spoil, smudge,
splash, sully, tarnish, muddy, blacken
formal besmirch, begrime
F3 clean, cleanse

disability *n*
handicap, disablement, disorder, inability, incapability,
incapacity, infirmity, defect, unfitness,
disqualification, illness, ailment, complaint, weakness
formal impairment, affliction, malady

disable *v*
1 *disable a person*
cripple, lame, damage, handicap, hamstring, make
unfit, disqualify, weaken, immobilize, invalidate,
paralyse, prostrate
formal incapacitate, impair, debilitate, enfeeble
2 *disable a machine*
immobolize, paralyse, stop, deactivate, put out of
action
formal render inoperative

disabled *adj*
handicapped, infirm, unfit, crippled, lame,

immobilized, maimed, weak, weakened, out of action, paralysed, bed-ridden, wrecked
formal incapacitated, impaired, indisposed, debilitated, enfeebled
colloq. physically challenged
F3 able, able-bodied

disadvantage *n*
1 DRAWBACK, snag, hindrance, liability, handicap, impediment, limitation, inconvenience, flaw, defect, nuisance, weakness, weak point, trouble, penalty
colloq. downside, minus, hang-up, spanner in the works, fly in the ointment, weak link in the chain, chink in your armour, Achilles heel
2 HARM, damage, detriment, hurt, injury, loss, prejudice, hardship, lack, disservice
formal privation
F3 1 advantage, benefit, asset

disadvantaged *adj*
deprived, underprivileged, poor, poverty stricken, handicapped, impoverished, struggling, in need, in distress, in want
F3 privileged

disadvantageous *adj*
unfavourable, harmful, detrimental, inopportune, prejudicial, adverse, unfortunate, unlucky, damaging, hurtful, injurious, inconvenient, ill-timed, inexpedient
formal hapless, deleterious
F3 advantageous, favourable; *formal* auspicious

disaffected *adj*
disloyal, hostile, alienated, antagonistic, rebellious, mutinous, dissatisfied, disgruntled, discontented, unfriendly, seditious
formal estranged
F3 loyal, friendly, satisfied

disaffection *n*
disloyalty, hostility, alienation, discontentment, resentment, ill-will, dissatisfaction, animosity, coolness, unfriendliness, antagonism, disharmony, discord, disagreement, aversion, dislike
formal estrangement
F3 loyalty, contentment

disagree *v*
1 *disagree with someone; the two sides disagree*
conflict, contradict, diverge, differ, clash, agree to differ, not see eye to eye with, be at odds with, be at loggerheads with, quarrel, argue, bicker, wrangle, fight, squabble, contend, dispute, contest, take issue, beg to differ
formal dissent
colloq. fall out
2 *disagree with an idea*
disapprove of, think wrong, oppose, object, contradict, take issue with, argue against, be against
formal dissent
3 *food disagreeing with you*
upset, make unwell, cause illness
F3 1 agree 2 approve, accept 3 agree

disagreeable *adj*
1 *a disagreeable old man*
bad-tempered, ill-humoured, impolite, difficult, unfriendly, ill-natured, awkward, unhelpful, peevish, rude, surly, churlish, irritable, nasty, disobliging, contrary, cross, brusque
colloq. grouchy
2 *a disagreeable taste*
disgusting, unpleasant, offensive, repulsive, repellent, obnoxious, unsavoury, horrible, dreadful, abominable,

objectionable, nasty
formal repugnant
F3 1 amiable, pleasant 2 agreeable, pleasant

disagreement *n*
1 DISPUTE, argument, difference of opinion, friction, conflict, quarrel, row, clash, dissent, contention, strife, dissension, misunderstanding, squabble, wrangle
formal altercation, discord, disputation
colloq. falling-out, tiff
2 DIFFERENCE, variance, unlikeness, discrepancy, deviation, conformity, dissimilarity, incompatibility, inconsistency, divergence, diversity
formal disparity, incongruity, dissimilitude
F3 1 agreement, harmony 2 similarity, conformity

disallow *v*
ban, cancel, forbid, prohibit, refuse, reject, debar, dismiss, embargo, disown, rebuff, repudiate, veto, say no to, exclude
formal abjure, disaffirm, disavow, disclaim, proscribe, interdict
F3 allow, permit

disappear *v*
1 VANISH, wane, recede, fade, evaporate, melt away, dissolve, ebb, go out of sight, pass from sight, get lost, go missing, dematerialize
formal evanesce
colloq. make tracks
2 GO, depart, withdraw, retire, exit, flee, fly, escape, hide
colloq. scarper, vamoose
3 END, perish, pass, die out, die away, become extinct
formal expire, cease
F3 1 appear 3 emerge, start, begin

disappearance *n*
1 VANISHING, fading, passing from sight, evaporation, melting away, departure, withdrawal, exit, loss, going, passing, desertion, flight
2 END, passing, dying-out, expiry, extinction
formal expiry, evanescence
F3 1 appearance, manifestation 2 start, beginning

disappoint *v*
let down, fail, dissatisfy, disillusion, dismay, discourage, depress, dispirit, disenchant, sadden, thwart, vex, baffle, frustrate, foil, dishearten, disgruntle, disconcert, hamper, hinder, deceive, defeat, delude, dash someone's hopes
F3 satisfy, please, delight

disappointed *adj*
let-down, frustrated, thwarted, disenchanted, deflated, disillusioned, dissatisfied, upset, vexed, discouraged, disgruntled, disheartened, distressed, downhearted, saddened, cast down, despondent, depressed, disenchanted
colloq. miffed
F3 pleased, satisfied

disappointing *adj*
unsatisfactory, inferior, inadequate, insufficient, unworthy, pathetic, sad, sorry, unhappy, discouraging, disconcerting, depressing, disagreeable, anticlimactic
colloq. not all it's cracked up to be, underwhelming
F3 encouraging, pleasant, satisfactory

disappointment *n*
1 FRUSTRATION, dissatisfaction, failure, disenchantment, disillusionment, displeasure, discouragement, discontent, distress, regret, chagrin, sadness, despondency, dispiritedness

colloq. cold comfort, bitter pill (to swallow)
2 FAILURE, let-down, anticlimax, setback, comedown, non-event, blow, misfortune, fiasco, disaster, calamity
colloq. washout, wipeout, damp squib, swiz, swizzle
▣ **1** pleasure, satisfaction, delight **2** success

disapprobation *n*
blame, censure, condemnation, criticism, denunciation, disapproval, disfavour, dissatisfaction, dislike, displeasure, objection, exception, reproach, reproof
formal remonstration, disparagement
▣ approval; *formal* approbation

disapproval *n*
censure, condemnation, criticism, blame, displeasure, reproach, exception, objection, dissatisfaction, denunciation, dislike, rejection, veto, rebuke, reproof
formal remonstration, disparagement
colloq. disapprobation, the thumbs-down
▣ approval; *formal* approbation

disapprove *v*
censure, condemn, blame, take exception to, be against, object to, find unacceptable, deplore, denounce, disparage, dislike, reject, veto, spurn, look down on, think little of, hold in contempt, frown on, take a dim view of, take exception to, think badly of, have a low opinion of, not hold with
formal deprecate, discountenance, disallow, animadvert
colloq. look down your nose at, give the thumbs-down
▣ approve, agree, have a high opinion of

disapproving *adj*
censorious, condemnatory, critical, reproachful, derogatory, pejorative
formal deprecatory, disparaging, disapprobative, disapprobatory, improbative, improbatory

disarm *v*
1 DISABLE, unarm, demilitarize, demobilize, deactivate, disband, immobilize, lay down arms/weapons, make powerless, put out of action
formal render inoperative
2 APPEASE, conciliate, win over, mollify, placate, persuade, charm
▣ **1** arm

disarmament *n*
demilitarization, demobilization, deactivation, laying-down of arms/weapons, arms control/limitation/reduction

disarming *adj*
charming, winning, persuasive, conciliatory, irresistible, likeable, mollifying

disarrange *v*
untidy, disorganize, disorder, confuse, disturb, jumble, mess, dislocate, shuffle, unsettle, derange
▣ arrange, tidy

disarray *n*
disorder, confusion, chaos, mess, muddle, disorganization, clutter, untidiness, dishevelment, unruliness, unsettledness, jumble, clutter, indiscipline, tangle, upset
colloq. shambles
▣ order

disaster *n*
calamity, catastrophe, misfortune, reverse, reversal, adversity, tragedy, blow, accident, act of God,
cataclysm, debacle, mishap, misadventure, setback, failure, fiasco, ruin, stroke, trouble, mischance, ruination
colloq. flop, wash out
▣ success, triumph

disastrous *adj*
calamitous, catastrophic, cataclysmic, devastating, ravaging, ruinous, tragic, unlucky, unfortunate, adverse, dreadful, dire, terrible, appalling, shocking, destructive, harmful, injurious, ill-fated, ill-starred, fatal, miserable
▣ successful; *formal* auspicious

disavowal *n*
repudiation, denial, contradiction, renunciation, rejection, dissent
formal disaffirmation, abjuration

disband *v*
disperse, break up, scatter, dismiss, demobilize, part company, separate, dissolve, go separate ways
colloq. demob
▣ assemble, gather, muster

disbelief *n*
unbelief, incredulity, doubt, scepticism, questioning, suspicion, distrust, mistrust, discredit, rejection
formal dubiety
▣ belief, conviction

Colloquial expressions of disbelief include: a good one!; a likely story!; come, come!; come off it!; do me a favour!; don't give me that!; don't make me laugh!; don't tell me!; do you mean to say?; excuses, excuses!; fancy that!; get along (with you)!; get away (with you)!; go on!; go on with you!; good heavens!; good Lord!; goodness gracious me!; goodness me!; heavens above!; I ask you!; I bet!; I don't think; I'll eat my hat!; I've heard that one before!; if you believe that, you'd believe anything!; just fancy!; make me laugh!; my (giddy) aunt!; my foot!; my goodness!; my hat!; no kidding!; oh, yeah!; promises, promises!; pull the other one, it's got bells on!; says who?; says you!; sez who?; sez you!; stone me!; stone the crows!; strike a light!; strike me dead!; strike me pink!; stuff and nonsense!; tell it to the marines!; tell me another!; that's a tall story!; that's news to me!; that's rich!; the devil you do!; the hell you say!; what a load of cobblers!; you can't be serious!; you don't say!; you'll be lucky!; you must be joking!; you must be kidding!; you're kidding!; you're pulling my leg!; you what!

disbelieve *v*
discount, discredit, repudiate, reject, distrust, mistrust, suspect, question, doubt, be unconvinced
colloq. take something with a pinch of salt
▣ believe, trust, give credence to, accept

disbeliever *n*
doubter, agnostic, atheist, unbeliever, questioner, sceptic, scoffer, doubting Thomas
formal nullifidian
▣ believer

disburse *v*
pay out, spend, lay out
formal expend
colloq. fork out, shell out, cough up

disbursement *n*
payment, outlay, spending, expenditure
formal disbursal, disposal

disc *n*
1 CIRCLE, face, plate, ring, saucer, counter, discus

2 RECORD, album, LP, CD, vinyl, gramophone record
3 DISK, diskette, hard disk, floppy disk, compact disk, CD-ROM, microfloppy

discard v
reject, abandon, dispose of, get rid of, throw away, throw out, jettison, dispense with, cast aside, toss out, drop, scrap, shed, remove, relinquish, repudiate
formal forsake
colloq. ditch, dump, chuck away/out
Ea retain, adopt

discern v
perceive, make out, observe, detect, recognize, see, ascertain, notice, determine, discover, distinguish, differentiate, judge, discriminate
formal descry

discernible adj
perceptible, noticeable, detectable, appreciable, distinct, distinguishable, observable, recognizable, visible, apparent, clear, obvious, plain, conspicuous, patent, discoverable
formal manifest
Ea imperceptible

discerning adj
discriminating, perceptive, astute, clear-sighted, sensitive, shrewd, wise, ingenious, intelligent, clever, quick, sharp, subtle, penetrating, acute, piercing, critical, eagle-eyed, sound
formal sagacious, perspicacious, percipient, prudent, sapient
Ea dull, obtuse

discernment n
judgement, discrimination, perception, perceptiveness, acuteness, clear-sightedness, shrewdness, wisdom, sharpness, ingenuity, insight, intelligence, cleverness, understanding, awareness, acumen, keenness, (good) taste, penetration
formal ascertainment, percipience, perspicacity, sagacity

discharge v, n
▶ v 1 LIBERATE, free, set free, let go, pardon, release, clear, absolve, acquit, relieve, dismiss
formal exonerate, exculpate
2 *discharge from employment*
remove, dismiss, expel, get rid of, discard, oust, eject
colloq. sack, fire, turf out, boot out, give the boot to, give the elbow, axe
3 FULFIL, carry out, perform, do, fulfil
formal dispense
4 FIRE, shoot, let off, detonate, explode, set off
5 *discharge fumes*
emit, let off/out, give off, release, exude, ooze, leak, disgorge, gush
formal excrete, disembogue
6 *discharge a debt*
settle, pay, clear, honour, satisfy, meet
Ea 1 detain 2 appoint, hire 3 neglect
▶ n 1 LIBERATION, release, acquittal, clearance, absolution
formal exoneration, exculpation
2 *discharge from employment*
dismissal, removal, expulsion, ousting, cashiering
colloq. sacking, the sack, firing, the boot, the elbow
3 EMISSION, secretion, ejection, flow, exuding, release, pus
formal excretion, suppuration
4 FULFILMENT, accomplishment, performance,

doing, execution, achievement
5 *discharge of a debt*
settling, payment, clearance, honouring
Ea 1 confinement, detention 2 hiring, appointment 3 absorption 4 neglect

disciple n
follower, convert, proselyte, adherent, believer, devotee, supporter, upholder, learner, pupil, student, votary

disciplinarian n
authoritarian, (hard) taskmaster, autocrat, stickler, despot, tyrant, martinet

discipline n, v
▶ n 1 TRAINING, exercise, drill, practice, routine, regimen
2 PUNISHMENT, correction
formal chastisement, castigation
3 STRICTNESS, control, self-control, restraint, self-restraint, regulation, orderliness
4 SUBJECT, area of study, field of study, course of study, branch, speciality
Ea 3 indiscipline
▶ v 1 TRAIN, instruct, drill, educate, exercise, break in, ground
formal inculcate, inure
2 CHECK, control, correct, restrain, govern, regulate, limit, restrict
3 PUNISH, chasten, rebuke, reprove, penalize, correct, reprimand, make an example of, teach someone a lesson
formal chastise, castigate

disclaim v
deny, disown, repudiate, abandon, renounce, reject, decline, refuse
formal abjure, disavow
colloq. wash your hands of
Ea accept, confess

disclaimer n
denial, repudiation, renunciation, rejection, contradiction
formal abjuration, abnegation, disavowal, disaffirmation, disownment, retraction

disclose v
make known, reveal, tell, confess, let slip, blurt out, relate, publish, broadcast, communicate, make public, expose, reveal, show, exhibit, uncover, lay bare, unveil, bring to light, discover
formal divulge, impart
colloq. leak, blab, squeal, let the cat out of the bag, spill the beans
Ea conceal

disclosure n
revelation, exposure, exposé, uncovering, publication, discovery, admission, confession, acknowledgement, announcement, publication, broadcast, declaration, bringing to light, laying bare
formal divulgence
colloq. leak

discoloration n
blemish, stain, spot, streak, mark, patch, blot, blotch, splotch
technical dyschroa, ecchymosis

discolour v
disfigure, fade, stain, soil, mark, mar, rust, streak, tarnish, tinge, weather

discomfit *v*
embarrass, disconcert, discompose, unsettle, demoralize, abash, confound, baffle, confuse, perplex, fluster, ruffle, frustrate, thwart, outwit
formal perturb, rattle
colloq. faze

discomfiture *n*
unease, embarrassment, confusion, abashment, discomposure, demoralization, frustration, disappointment, humiliation, chagrin

discomfort *n*
1 ACHE, pain, soreness, hurt, twinge, pang
formal malaise
2 UNEASE, embarrassment, trouble, distress, disquiet, hardship, vexation, irritation, annoyance, worry, apprehension, restlessness
3 INCONVENIENCE, difficulty, trouble, disadvantage, drawback, worry, nuisance, bother, irritation, annoyance
F3 2 comfort, ease

discomposure *n*
unease, upset, agitation, restlessness, fluster, disturbance, anxiety, irritation, annoyance
formal disquietude, inquietude, perturbation
F3 *formal* composure

disconcert *v*
unsettle, disturb, confuse, upset, unnerve, put off/out, shake, alarm, startle, take aback, throw off balance, surprise, fluster, ruffle, bewilder, nonplus, embarrass, baffle, perplex, dismay
formal perturb
colloq. faze, rattle, put someone's nose out of joint;
US slang discombobulate

disconcerting *adj*
disturbing, confusing, upsetting, unnerving, daunting, alarming, bewildering, distracting, embarrassing, awkward, baffling, perplexing, dismaying, bothersome
formal perturbing
colloq. off-putting

disconnect *v*
cut off, disengage, uncouple, sever, separate, detach, unplug, undo, unhook, unhitch, part, divide, split
F3 attach, connect, join, unite

disconnected *adj*
confused, incoherent, garbled, rambling, unco-ordinated, unintelligible, loose, wandering, rambling, irrational, disjointed, illogical, jumbled, mixed-up, abrupt, staccato
F3 coherent, connected

disconsolate *adj*
desolate, dejected, dispirited, sad, melancholy, depressed, unhappy, wretched, miserable, despondent, gloomy, downcast, forlorn, inconsolable, low, low-spirited, down, crushed, heavy-hearted, hopeless, heartbroken, wretched, grief-stricken
colloq. down in the dumps
F3 cheerful, joyful

discontent *n*
uneasiness, dissatisfaction, disquiet, disaffection, restlessness, fretfulness, unrest, impatience, vexation, regret, displeasure, misery, unhappiness, wretchedness
F3 content, satisfaction, happiness

discontented *adj*
dissatisfied, disgruntled, unhappy, restless, inpatient, disaffected, miserable, wretched, exasperated,

displeased, complaining
colloq. fed up, browned off, cheesed off;
slang pissed off
F3 contented, satisfied, happy

discontinue *v*
stop, come to a stop, end, come to an end, finish, break off, refrain, do away with, halt, drop, suspend, abolish, abandon, cancel, interrupt
formal cease, terminate
colloq. quit, scrap
F3 begin, continue, produce

discontinuity *n*
disjointedness, disconnectedness, incoherence, interruption, breach, disconnection, disruption, disunion, rupture
F3 continuity, coherence

discontinuous *adj*
intermittent, broken, disconnected, fitful, interrupted, irregular, spasmodic, periodic, punctuated
F3 continuous

discord *n*
1 CONFLICT, disagreement, dissension, clashing, disunity, incompatibility, difference, difference of opinion, dispute, contention, friction, division, opposition, strife, split, wrangling, argument, row, dissent
formal discordance
2 DISCORD OF SOUNDS, disharmony, jangle, jangling, jarring, harshness
formal dissonance, cacophony
F3 1 concord, agreement 2 harmony

discordant *adj*
1 DISAGREEING, conflicting, at odds, at variance, opposing, clashing, hostile, contradictory, differing, dissenting, incompatible, inconsistent
formal incongruous
2 DISSONANT, grating, jangling, jarring, harsh, strident, sharp, flat
technical atonal
formal cacophonous
F3 1 agreeing 2 harmonious

discount *n, v*
▶ *n* reduction, rebate, allowance, cut price, cut, concession, deduction, mark-down
▶ *v* 1 DISREGARD, ignore, overlook, disbelieve, pass over, gloss over
2 REDUCE, deduct, mark down, take off
colloq. knock off, slash
F3 1 pay attention to 2 increase

discourage *v*
1 DISHEARTEN, dampen, dispirit, depress, demoralize, dismay, unnerve, put off, daunt, deject, disappoint, cast down, put a damper on
2 DETER, dissuade, hinder, put off, restrain, prevent, hold back, talk out of, advise against
F3 1 encourage, hearten 2 encourage, persuade

discouraged *adj*
disheartened, let-down, deflated, dispirited, depressed, demoralized, dejected, dismayed, downcast, glum, pessimistic, daunted, dashed, crestfallen
F3 encouraged, heartened

discouragement *n*
1 DOWNHEARTEDNESS, despondency, pessimism, dismay, depression, dejection, despair, disappointment, hopelessness, gloom

2 DETERRENT, damper, setback, impediment, obstacle, curb, barrier, disincentive, opposition, hindrance, restraint, rebuff
F3 1 encouragement **2** incentive

discouraging adj
disheartening, dispiriting, depressing, disappointing, demoralizing, off-putting, unfavourable, dampening, daunting
formal dehortatory, dissuasive, dissuasory, inauspicious, unpropitious
F3 encouraging, heartening

discourse n, v
▶ *n* **1** CONVERSATION, dialogue, chat, communication, talk, discussion
formal converse, colloquy, confabulation
2 SPEECH, address, lecture, sermon, essay, treatise, dissertation, homily
formal oration, disquisition
▶ *v* converse, talk, speak, discuss, debate, confer, lecture, preach

discourteous adj
rude, bad-mannered, ill-mannered, impolite, boorish, uncouth, disrespectful, unpleasant, offensive, ill-bred, uncivil, unmannerly, ungracious, unceremonious, impertinent, impudent, insolent, offhand, curt, brusque, abrupt, short, gruff
F3 courteous, polite

discourtesy n
rudeness, bad manners, impoliteness, disrespectfulness, ill-breeding, unmannerliness, ungraciousness, incivility, impertinence, insolence, curtness, brusqueness, rebuff, slight, snub, insult, affront
formal indecorousness, indecorum
F3 courtesy, politeness

discover v
1 FIND OUT ABOUT, determine, realize, notice, recognize, perceive, see, spot, discern, establish, learn, detect, come to know, fathom (out)
formal ascertain
colloq. twig, suss out, get wise to, rumble, get onto, get wind of
2 FIND, come across, uncover, unearth, dig up, disclose, reveal, stumble across/on, turn up, come to light, ferret out, light on, locate
3 ORIGINATE, invent, pioneer, devise, create, work out, compose
F3 1 conceal, cover (up) **2** miss

discoverer n
explorer, finder, founder, pioneer, initiator, inventor, originator, author, deviser, creator

discovery n
1 FINDING, determination, realization, recognition, discernment, learning, disclosure, detection, revelation, location
2 BREAKTHROUGH, find, finding(s), origination, introduction, innovation, research, invention, devising, exploration, pioneering

discredit v, n
▶ *v* **1** *discredit someone*
dishonour, degrade, defame, damage, disgrace, bring into disrepute, give someone a bad name, belittle, slander, slur, smear, tarnish, reproach, reflect (badly) on, put in a bad light
formal disparage, vilify, cast aspersions on
2 *discredit a theory*

DISBELIEVE, distrust, doubt, question, mistrust, challenge, invalidate, deny, discard, reject, explode, debunk, shake your faith in
formal refute
F3 1 honour **2** believe
▶ *n* dishonour, disrepute, censure, disgrace, blame, shame, reproach, slur, stigma, smear, scandal, infamy, humiliation
formal aspersion, opprobrium, ignominy

discreditable adj
improper, dishonourable, disreputable, disgraceful, scandalous, blameworthy, shameful, infamous, degrading
formal reprehensible
F3 creditable

discreet adj
tactful, careful, diplomatic, cautious, delicate, reserved, guarded, wary, sensible, wise, considerate
formal politic, prudent, judicious, circumspect
F3 tactless, indiscreet

⚠ **discreet** or **discrete** ?
Discreet means 'prudent, cautious, not saying or doing anything that might cause trouble': *My secretary won't ask awkward questions; she's very discreet. Discrete* means 'separate, not attached to others': *a suspension of discrete particles in a liquid.*

---

discrepancy n
inconsistency, difference, variance, variation, dissimilarity, deviation, divergence, disagreement, conflict, contradiction, inequality
formal disparity, discordance, incongruity

discrete adj
separate, distinct, detached, disconnected, unattached, individual, discontinuous, disjoined
formal disjunct

discretion n
1 TACT, diplomacy, caution, wisdom, discernment, judgement, good sense, care, carefulness, reserve, consideration, wariness, guardedness
formal judiciousness, prudence, circumspection, volition, predilection
2 CHOICE, freedom, preference, will, wish, desire, inclination
F3 1 indiscretion

discretionary adj
optional, voluntary, elective, open
F3 fixed, mandatory, compulsory, automatic

discriminate v
1 DISTINGUISH, differentiate, discern, tell apart, tell/recognize the differences, draw/make a distinction, segregate, separate
2 BE PREJUDICED, be biased, victimize, treat differently, be intolerant
F3 1 confuse, confound **2** favour

discriminating adj
discerning, fastidious, selective, critical, perceptive, particular, tasteful, keen, astute, shrewd, sensitive, cultivated

discrimination n
1 BIAS, prejudice, intolerance, unfairness, bigotry, favouritism, narrow-mindedness, inequity, segregation, racism, sexism, male chauvinism, ageism, homophobia
2 DISCERNMENT, judgement, acumen, perception,

acuteness, insight, shrewdness, astuteness,
penetration, subtlety, keenness, sensitivity, refinement,
taste
formal perspicacity

discriminatory *adj*
biased, prejudiced, favouring, inequitable, prejudicial,
unfair, unjust, discriminative, partial, partisan,
preferential, loaded, weighted, one-sided
F3 fair, impartial, unbiased

discursive *adj*
rambling, digressing, wandering, wordy, long-winded,
meandering, wide-ranging, circuitous, diffuse, verbose
formal prolix
F3 terse

discuss *v*
debate, talk about/over, confer, argue, consider, go
into, weigh up, deliberate, converse, consult, exchange
views on, examine, study, review, analyse
old use parley
formal discourse, confabulate
colloq. kick around, put your heads together

discussion *n*
debate, conference, argument, conversation, talk,
talks, dialogue, exchange, consultation, forum,
negotiations, deliberation, consideration, analysis,
review, examination, study, scrutiny, seminar,
symposium
old use parley
formal discourse, colloquium
colloq. powwow

disdain *n, v*
▶ *n* scorn, contempt, arrogance, haughtiness,
derision, sneering, dislike, snobbishness
formal disparagement, deprecation, contumely
F3 admiration, respect
▶ *v* scorn, look down on, despise, slight, disregard,
snub, ignore, reject, spurn, rebuff, turn down, belittle,
sneer at, undervalue
formal contemn, deride, disavow
colloq. pooh-pooh, cold shoulder
F3 admire, respect

disdainful *adj*
scornful, contemptuous, derisive, haughty, aloof,
arrogant, supercilious, sneering, slighting, pompous,
superior, proud, insolent
formal disparaging
F3 respectful

disease *n*
illness, sickness, ill-health, infirmity, complaint,
disorder, ailment, indisposition, condition, disability,
infection, contagion, epidemic
formal malady, affliction
colloq. bug, virus
F3 health

Diseases and disorders include: Addison's disease,
AIDS, alopecia, Alzheimer's disease, anaemia,
angina, anorexia nervosa, anthrax, arthritis,
asbestosis, asthma, athlete's foot, autism, Bell's Palsy,
beriberi, Black Death, botulism, Bright's disease,
bronchitis, brucellosis, bubonic plague, bulimia,
cancer, cerebral palsy, chickenpox, cholera, cirrhosis,
coeliac disease, common cold, consumption, croup,
cystic fibrosis, diabetes, diphtheria, dropsy,
dysentery, eclampsia, emphysema, encephalitis,
endometriosis, enteritis, farmer's lung, *colloq.* flu,
foot-and-mouth disease, gangrene, German measles,
gingivitis, glandular fever, glaucoma, gonorrhoea,

haemophilia, herpes, hepatitis, Hodgkin's disease,
Huntington's chorea, hydrophobia, impetigo,
influenza, Lassa fever, Legionnaires' disease, leprosy,
leukaemia, lockjaw, malaria, mastoiditis, measles,
meningitis, motor neuron disease, multiple sclerosis
(MS), mumps, muscular dystrophy, myalgic
encephalomyelitis (ME), nephritis, osteomyelitis,
osteoporosis, Paget's disease, Parkinson's disease,
peritonitis, pneumonia, poliomyelitis, psittacosis,
psoriasis, pyorrhoea, rabies, rheumatic fever,
rheumatoid arthritis, rickets, ringworm, rubella,
scabies, scarlet fever, schistosomiasis, schizophrenia,
scurvy, septicaemia, shingles, silicosis, smallpox,
syphilis, tapeworm, tetanus, thrombosis, thrush,
tinnitus, tuberculosis (TB), typhoid, typhus, vertigo,
whooping cough, yellow fever.

diseased *adj*
sick, ill, unhealthy, unwell, infirm, ailing, unsound,
contaminated, infected, blighted
F3 healthy, well

disembark *v*
land, arrive, dismount, leave, get off, step off
formal alight, debark, detrain, deplane
F3 embark

disembodied *adj*
bodiless, ghostly, phantom, spiritual, immaterial,
intangible
formal incorporeal, discarnate, spectral

disembowel *v*
disbowel, draw, embowel, gut, gralloch, paunch
formal eviscerate, exenterate

disenchanted *adj*
disillusioned, disappointed, let down, discouraged,
jaundiced, cynical, soured, blasé, indifferent
colloq. fed up

disenchantment *n*
disillusionment, disillusion, disappointment,
cynicism, revulsion

disengage *v*
disconnect, disunite, detach, loosen, free, extricate,
undo, unfasten, untie, uncouple, unhitch, unhook,
release, liberate, separate, loosen, disentangle,
withdraw
F3 connect, engage, unite

disengaged *adj*
detached, liberated, loose, released, free(d),
disentangled, separate(d), unattached, unconnected,
unhitched
F3 connected, joined, united

disentangle *v*
1 LOOSE, release, free, extricate, disconnect,
untangle, unwind, unfasten, disengage, detach,
unravel, unsnarl, untwist, undo, unknot, separate,
unfold, straighten
2 RESOLVE, clarify, simplify, distinguish, separate,
distance
F3 1 entangle

disfavour *n*
1 *fall into disfavour*
unpopularity, discredit, disrepute
formal ignominy, opprobrium
2 *look with disfavour at someone*
dislike, disapproval, displeasure, distaste,
dissatisfaction, disregard, low opinion
formal disapprobation, disesteem
F3 1, 2 favour

disfigure *v*
deface, blemish, mutilate, maim, scar, mar, deform, scar, distort, damage, injure, ruin, spoil, flaw, make ugly
🔁 adorn, embellish

disfigurement *n*
blemish, defacement, defect, deformity, mutilation, scar, spot, blotch, stain, disgrace, impairment, injury, distortion, uglification
🔁 adornment

disgorge *v*
discharge, empty, eject, expel, vomit, spew, spout, belch, regurgitate, relinquish, renounce, surrender
formal effuse
colloq. throw up

disgrace *n, v*
▶ *n* shame, disrepute, disrespect, dishonour, disfavour, humiliation, loss of face, defamation, degradation, infamy, discredit, scandal, reproach, blot, slur, smear, stain, stigma, black mark
formal ignominy, debasement, disapprobation, opprobrium, obloquy
colloq. skeleton in the cupboard
🔁 honour, esteem
▶ *v* shame, bring shame on, put to shame, dishonour, abase, defame, humiliate, cause to lose face, put someone's nose out of joint, blot someone's copybook, disfavour, degrade, debase, belittle, discredit, reproach, blame, slur, sully, taint, stain, stigmatize
formal disparage, denigrate
colloq. drag through the mud
🔁 honour, respect

disgraced *adj*
discredited, shamed, dishonoured, humiliated, degraded, branded, stigmatized
colloq. in the doghouse
🔁 honoured, respected

disgraceful *adj*
shameful, dishonourable, disreputable, scandalous, outrageous, despicable, contemptible, blameworthy, shocking, unworthy, dreadful, terrible, awful, appalling
formal ignominious, culpable, reprehensible
🔁 honourable, respectable

disgruntled *adj*
discontented, dissatisfied, displeased, annoyed, exasperated, grumpy, irritated, peeved, peevish, resentful, sulky, sullen, testy, vexed, put out, petulant
formal malcontent
colloq. fed up, hacked off, cheesed off, browned off, brassed off
🔁 pleased, satisfied

disguise *n, v*
▶ *n* concealment, camouflage, cloak, cover, costume, mask, front, façade, masquerade, deception, misrepresentation, false picture, pretence, travesty, screen, veil, shroud
▶ *v* **1** CONCEAL, cover, cover up, be under cover, camouflage, mask, hide, dress up, impersonate, cloak, screen, veil, shroud, suppress, repress
colloq. put on a brave face
2 FALSIFY, deceive, pretend, misrepresent, gloss over, fake, fudge
formal dissemble, feign
colloq. cook the books, whitewash, put up a smokescreen
🔁 **1** reveal, expose

disguised *adj*
camouflaged, cloaked, veiled, hidden, made up, masked, incognito, undercover, unrecognizable, fake, false
formal covert, feigned

disgust *v, n*
▶ *v* offend, displease, nauseate, revolt, sicken, repel, outrage, put off, make your gorge rise
colloq. turn off, turn your stomach
🔁 delight, please
▶ *n* revulsion, repulsion, distaste, aversion, nausea, loathing, hatred, disapproval, displeasure
formal repugnance, abhorrence, detestation

disgusted *adj*
repelled, repulsed, revolted, sickened, offended, appalled, outraged, put off
colloq. up in arms
🔁 attracted, delighted

disgusting *adj*
repellent, repulsive, revolting, offensive, sickening, nauseating, nauseous, off-putting, odious, foul, unappetizing, unpalatable, distasteful, unpleasant, bad, vile, obscene, abominable, detestable, disgraceful, appalling, objectionable, nasty, shocking, outrageous
formal repugnant, rebarbative
colloq. yucky, gross
🔁 delightful, pleasant, acceptable

dish *n, v*
▶ *n* plate, bowl, platter, food, fare, recipe, speciality, delicacy, course
▶ *v* ▷ **dish out** distribute, give out, share out, hand out, hand round, pass round, dole out, allocate, mete out, inflict
▷ **dish up** serve, present, ladle, spoon, scoop, dispense, offer, present

disharmony *n*
conflict, clash, discord, friction, incompatibility
formal disaccord, discordance, dissonance
🔁 harmony

dishearten *v*
discourage, dispirit, dampen, cast down, depress, make depressed, dismay, dash, disappoint, deject, weigh down, daunt, crush, deter, put a damper on
🔁 encourage, hearten

disheartened *adj*
discouraged, dispirited, downcast, depressed, disappointed, dismayed, downhearted, dejected, daunted, crestfallen, crushed
🔁 encouraged, heartened

dishevelled *adj*
tousled, unkempt, uncombed, untidy, bedraggled, messy, in a mess, ruffled, rumpled, slovenly, disordered
formal disarranged
🔁 neat, tidy

dishonest *adj*
untruthful, fraudulent, deceitful, false, lying, deceptive, double-dealing, cheating, treacherous, untrustworthy, unscrupulous, unprincipled, swindling, corrupt, disreputable, dishonourable, crafty, cunning, sly, devious, irregular
formal perfidious, mendacious, duplicitous
colloq. crooked, shady, bent, shifty, fishy, iffy
🔁 honest, trustworthy, scrupulous

dishonesty *n*
deceit, falsehood, falsity, fraudulence, fraud,

criminality, insincerity, untruthfulness, treachery, cheating, double-dealing, corruption, unscrupulousness, trickery, chicanery, sharp practice, irregularity
formal duplicity, improbity, perfidy
colloq. crookedness, shadiness, dirty trick
E3 honesty, truthfulness

dishonour *v, n*
▶ *v* **1** *dishonour the family's name*
disgrace, shame, humiliate, debase, defile, degrade, defame, discredit, stain, sully, abuse, insult, offend, affront, demean, debauch
2 *dishonour an agreement/a cheque*
refuse, reject, turn down
E3 **1** honour **2** honour, accept
▶ *n* disgrace, abasement, humiliation, shame, degradation, disrepute, infamy, indignity, reproach, slight, slur, scandal, stigma, insult, offence, outrage, abuse, discourtesy
formal discredit, ignominy, disfavour, aspersion, debasement, opprobrium
E3 honour

dishonourable *adj*
disreputable, unprincipled, unscrupulous, untrustworthy, unethical, unworthy, corrupt, discreditable, treacherous, scandalous, shameful, shameless, disgraceful, contemptible, despicable, infamous, ignoble
formal ignominious, perfidious
colloq. shady
E3 honourable

disillusion *v*
disenchant, disappoint
formal disabuse

disillusioned *adj*
disenchanted, undeceived, disappointed, let-down
formal disabused

disincentive *n*
deterrent, barrier, constraint, damper, determent, discouragement, dissuasion, hindrance, impediment, obstacle, repellent, restriction, turn-off
E3 encouragement, incentive

disinclination *n*
reluctance, unwillingness, hesitation, dislike, loathness, objection, opposition, resistance, alienation, averseness, aversion,
formal antipathy, repugnance
E3 inclination, enthusiasm

disinclined *adj*
reluctant, unwilling, resistant, indisposed, unenthusiastic, loath, opposed, hesitant
formal averse
E3 inclined, willing, enthusiastic

disinfect *v*
sterilize, fumigate, sanitize, decontaminate, cleanse, purify, purge, clean
E3 contaminate, infect

disinfectant *n*
antiseptic, sterilizer, sanitizer, fumigant, decontaminant, bactericide, germicide

disingenuous *adj*
insincere, deceitful, dishonest, devious, designing, guileful, wily, sly, crafty, artful, cunning, two-faced, shifty, insidious, uncandid

E3 artless, frank, ingenuous, naïve
formal duplicitous, feigned

disinherit *v*
cut off, renounce, reject, abandon, dispossess, impoverish, repudiate, cut someone out of your will
colloq. cut off without a penny, turn your back on

disintegrate *v*
break up, decompose, fall apart, break apart, crumble, rot, decay, moulder, separate, shatter, smash, splinter, fall to pieces

disinterest *n*
disinterestedness, impartiality, neutrality, detachment, unbiasedness, dispassionateness, fairness

disinterested *adj*
unbiased, neutral, impartial, objective, unprejudiced, dispassionate, detached, uninvolved, open-minded, fair, equitable, just, even-handed, unselfish
E3 biased, prejudiced, concerned

⚠ **disinterested** or **uninterested** ?
Disinterested means 'not biased, not influenced by private feelings or selfish motives': *I think we need the opinions of a few disinterested observers. Uninterested* means 'not interested, not showing any interest': *uninterested in politics.*

disjointed *adj*
1 INCOHERENT, aimless, directionless, confused, disordered, loose, unconnected, bitty, wandering, rambling, spasmodic
2 DISCONNECTED, dislocated, divided, separated, disunited, displaced, broken, fitful, split, disarticulated
E3 **1** coherent

dislike *n, v*
▶ *n* aversion, hatred, hostility, distaste, disapproval, displeasure, resentment, animosity, antagonism, enmity, detestation, disgust, loathing
formal repugnance, disinclination, disapprobation, disesteem, antipathy, animus
E3 liking; *formal* predilection
▶ *v* hate, detest, object to, loathe, abominate, disapprove, regard with distaste, shun, despise, scorn
formal abhor, execrate, disfavour, disrelish
colloq. not stand the sight of, not be someone's cup of tea, be sick to the back teeth of, be no love lost between
E3 like, favour

dislocate *v*
1 *dislocate a bone*
disjoint, put out of joint/place, displace, misplace, twist, strain, sprain, pull, disengage, put out, disorder, shift, disconnect, disunite
technical luxate
colloq. do in
2 *dislocate plans*
DISRUPT, disturb, disorganize, confuse, throw into confusion

dislocation *n*
disruption, disturbance, disarray, disorder, disorganization
E3 order

dislodge *v*
displace, eject, remove, oust, extricate, force out, shift, move, uproot

disloyal *adj*
treacherous, faithless, false, traitorous, deceitful,

double-dealing, two-faced, unfaithful, untrue, unpatriotic
formal apostate, perfidious
■ loyal, faithful, trustworthy, constant

disloyalty *n*
treachery, unfaithfulness, falseness, falsity, breach of trust, betrayal, treason, double-dealing, deceit, infidelity, adultery
formal apostasy, inconstancy, perfidiousness, perfidy, sedition
■ loyalty, faithfulness

dismal *adj*
dreary, gloomy, depressing, bleak, cheerless, dull, dark, dingy, drab, low-spirited, melancholy, desolate, sad, cheerless, sombre, forlorn, despondent, miserable, sorrowful, hopeless, discouraging
formal lugubrious
colloq. long-faced
■ cheerful, bright

dismantle *v*
demolish, take apart, disassemble, strip (down), pull apart, separate, take to pieces
■ assemble, put together

dismay *n, v*
▶ *n* alarm, distress, agitation, dread, fear, fright, horror, terror, discouragement, disappointment
formal consternation, apprehension, trepidation
■ boldness, encouragement
▶ *v* alarm, daunt, frighten, unnerve, unsettle, upset, scare, put off, dispirit, cast down, distress, disconcert, disturb, shock, take aback, dishearten, discourage, disillusion, depress, horrify, worry, bother, concern, disappoint
formal perturb
■ encourage, hearten

dismember *v*
disjoint, amputate, dissect, dislocate, mutilate, sever, divide, separate, break up
■ assemble, join, unify

dismiss *v*
1 *the class was dismissed*
discharge, free, let go, release, send away, remove, dissolve, drop, discord, banish
2 *dismiss employees*
make redundant, give notice, suspend, give someone their papers, lay off, discharge, relegate, expel, remove, cashier
colloq. send packing, boot out, sack, fire, give someone their cards, give someone the sack/push/boot/elbow, show someone the door
3 *dismiss it from your mind*
discount, disregard, banish, reject, repudiate, set aside, put away, put out of your mind, shelve, spurn, pour cold water on
■ **1** retain, gather **2** appoint, hire **3** accept, think about

dismissal *n*
notice, redundancy, laying-off, discharge, removal, expulsion, marching-orders
colloq. papers, sacking, firing, sack, push, boot, elbow
■ appointment, hiring

dismissive *adj*
contemptuous, disdainful, scornful, sneering, off-hand
formal dismissory
■ concerned, interested

dismount *v*
descend, get down
formal alight, disembark, light, unmount
■ mount

disobedience *n*
unruliness, waywardness, defiance, rebellion, wilfulness, contrariness, indiscipline, mutiny, revolt
formal contumacity, contumacy, infraction, insubordination, recalcitrance
■ obedience

disobedient *adj*
unruly, wayward, defiant, rebellious, wilful, contrary, disorderly, obstreperous, naughty, mischievous
formal contumacious, froward, insubordinate, intractable, refractory, recalcitrant, recusant
■ obedient

disobey *v*
infringe, go against someone's wishes, overstep, step out of line, flout, disregard, defy, ignore, resist, rebel
formal contravene, violate, transgress
■ obey, comply with

disobliging *adj*
unhelpful, unwilling, unco-operative, unaccommodating, awkward, disagreeable, discourteous, rude, uncivil, bloody-minded
■ obliging, helpful

disorder *n*
1 CONFUSION, chaos, muddle, disarray, mess, untidiness, clutter, disorganization, disorderliness, jumble
colloq. shambles,
2 DISTURBANCE, unrest, tumult, riot, breach of the peace, confusion, disruption, commotion, uproar, fracas, brawl, fight, rumpus, rout, clamour, quarrel, brouhaha, melee
3 ILLNESS, complaint, disease, sickness, disability, ailment, condition
formal affliction, malady
■ **1** neatness, order **2** law and order, peace

disordered *adj*
1 UNTIDY, messy, confused, muddled, disorganized, jumbled, cluttered, upside-down
2 DISTURBED, deranged, confused, troubled, upset, maladjusted, unbalanced
■ **1** organized, tidy

disorderly *adj*
1 DISORGANIZED, confused, chaotic, irregular, messy, untidy, jumbled, cluttered, in disarray
colloq. at sixes and sevens
2 UNRULY, undisciplined, unmanageable, uncontrollable, obstreperous, rowdy, rough, boisterous, tumultuous, turbulent, rebellious, wild, lawless, disobedient
formal refractory
■ **1** neat, tidy **2** well-behaved

disorganization *n*
disarray, chaos, confusion, disorder, disruption, untidiness, muddle
colloq. shambles
■ order, tidiness

disorganize *v*
disorder, disrupt, disturb, disarrange, muddle, upset, confuse, discompose, jumble, play havoc with, unsettle, break up, mess up, mix up, destroy
■ organize

disorganized *adj*
1 CONFUSED, disordered, haphazard, jumbled, muddled, chaotic, unsorted, unsystematized, topsy-turvy
colloq. shambolic
2 UNMETHODICAL, unorganized, unstructured, unsystematic, careless, muddled
colloq. untogether
F3 1 organized, tidy 2 organized, methodical

disorientate *v*
confuse, disorient, mislead, perplex, puzzle, upset, muddle
colloq. faze

disorientated *adj*
disoriented, confused, bewildered, mixed up, muddled, perplexed, puzzled, unsettled, unbalanced, lost, adrift, astray, at sea, upset

disown *v*
repudiate, renounce, disclaim, deny, cast off, disallow, reject, turn your back on, abandon
formal forsake, disavow, abnegate
F3 accept, acknowledge

disparage *v*
belittle, criticize, defame, slander, decry, degrade, detract from, disdain, discredit, dishonour, malign, ridicule, scorn, run down, minimize, dismiss, underestimate, underrate, undervalue
formal denigrate, deprecate, deride, vilify, traduce, vilipend, derogate, calumniate, cast aspersions on
F3 praise

disparagement *n*
belittlement, condemnation, criticism, slander, contempt, denunciation, discredit, disdain, ridicule, scorn, debasement, degradation, detraction, underestimation
formal derision, deprecation, aspersion, derogation, decrial, decrying, contumely, vilification
F3 praise

disparaging *adj*
derisive, derogatory, mocking, scornful, critical, insulting, dismissive
formal deprecatory, derisive
colloq. snide
F3 flattering, praising

disparate *adj*
contrasting, different, dissimilar, unequal, unlike, contrary, diverse, distinct
formal discrepant
F3 equal, similar

disparity *n*
difference, contrast, discrepancy, gap, gulf, dissimilarity, distinction, imbalance, inequality, unevenness, unlikeness, disproportion, bias, unfairness
formal dissimilitude, incongruity, inequity
F3 equality, similarity, parity

dispassionate *adj*
detached, objective, impartial, neutral, disinterested, unbiased, unprejudiced, equitable, impersonal, fair, cool, calm, calm and collected, composed, unemotional, unexcited, self-possessed, self-controlled
F3 biased, emotional, involved

dispatch, despatch *v, n*
▶ *v* 1 SEND, mail, post, express, transmit, forward,

consign, expedite, convey, remit, accelerate
2 DISPOSE OF, finish, perform, discharge, conclude, settle, perform
3 KILL, murder, execute, put to death, assassinate, slaughter
colloq. bump off, knock off, do in
F3 1 receive
▶ *n* 1 COMMUNICATION, message, report, bulletin, communiqué, news, letter, article, account, item, piece
2 PROMPTNESS, speed, expedition, celerity, haste, rapidity, swiftness
formal alacrity, promptitude
F3 2 slowness

dispel *v*
banish, drive away, chase away, get rid of, rid, dismiss, disperse, allay, eliminate, expel, rout, scatter, melt away
formal dissipate, disseminate

dispensable *adj*
unnecessary, disposable, expendable, inessential, non-essential, replaceable, superfluous, needless, gratuitous, useless
F3 indispensable, essential

dispensation *n*
1 PERMISSION, exemption, exception, release, remission, relief, reprieve, immunity, licence
2 ISSUE, distribution, allocation, allotment, apportionment, handing out, sharing out
formal endowment, bestowal
3 AUTHORITY, order, system, organization, arrangement, plan, scheme, direction, administration, discharge, application
formal economy

dispense *v*
1 DISTRIBUTE, give out, deal out, hand out, dole out, share out, apportion, allot, allocate, assign, share, divide out, mete out, bestow
formal confer
2 ADMINISTER, carry out, apply, implement, enforce, discharge, execute, operate
formal effectuate
▷ **dispense with** dispose of, get rid of, abolish, do away with, do without, not need, discard, omit, disregard, give up, cancel, forego, ignore, waive, renounce, relinquish; *formal* rescind, revoke

disperse *v*
scatter, dispel, spread, distribute, diffuse, dissolve, break up, melt away, thin out, dismiss, disband, separate, go their separate ways
formal dissipate, disseminate
F3 gather

dispersion *n*
spreading, scattering, distribution, circulation, dispersal, diffusion, broadcast
technical diaspora
formal dissemination, dissipation

dispirit *v*
dishearten, discourage, deject, depress, dash, dampen, damp, sadden, put a damper on, deter
F3 encourage, hearten

dispirited *adj*
disheartened, discouraged, dejected, depressed, despondent, sad, downcast, cast down, crestfallen, gloomy, glum, morose, low
colloq. fed up, cheesed off, down, down in the dumps, brassed off, browned off,
F3 encouraged

displace *v*
1 DISLODGE, move, shift, misplace, disturb, dislocate, relocate
2 DEPOSE, oust, remove, force out, dislodge, replace, dismiss, discharge, supplant, eject, expel, evict, succeed, supersede
colloq. turf out, boot out

displacement *n*
disarrangement, dislodging, dislocation, shifting, moving, disturbance, misplacement
technical ectopia, ectopy, heterotaxis, heterotopia
E3 order, arrangement

display *v, n*
▶ *v* 1 EXHIBIT, present, demonstrate, show, put on show, unveil, advertise, promote, publicize
2 BETRAY, disclose, reveal, show, expose
formal evince, manifest
3 SHOW OFF, flourish, parade, flaunt, boast, blazon
E3 1 conceal 2 disguise
▶ *n* show, exhibition, exhibit, demonstration, presentation, parade, spectacle, pageant, array, revelation, evidence, disclosure
formal manifestation, evincement

displease *v*
offend, annoy, irritate, anger, upset, dissatisfy, infuriate, offend, provoke, exasperate, incense, irk, vex, disturb
formal perturb, discompose
colloq. put out, aggravate, bug
E3 please, satisfy

displeased *n*
annoyed, angry, exasperated, furious, infuriated, irritated, offended, upset, disgruntled, peeved, piqued
colloq. aggravated, put out
E3 pleased

displeasure *n*
offence, annoyance, disapproval, irritation, resentment, discontentment, disfavour, dissatisfaction, distaste, disgust, anger, exasperation, indignation, chagrin, ire, pique, wrath
formal disapprobation, perturbation
E3 pleasure

disport *v*
divert, amuse, entertain, cheer, delight, play, revel, romp, frisk, frolic, cavort, gambol, sport

disposable *adj*
disposable plastic cups
throwaway, expendable, non-returnable, biodegradable

disposal *n*
1 ARRANGEMENT, grouping, order
2 CONTROL, direction, command
3 REMOVAL, riddance, throwing-away, clearance, discarding, jettisoning, scrapping
▷ **at someone's disposal** available, obtainable, at/to hand, ready; *colloq.* on tap

dispose *v*
1 *dispose of a problem*
DEAL WITH, decide, settle, determine, finish, attend to, see to, handle, tackle, look after, take care of, sort out
2 *dispose of old books*
GET RID OF, discard, throw away/out, shed, scrap, destroy, jettison, clear out
colloq. dump, get shot of, chuck out
3 *dispose troops*

arrange, align, group, place, position, put, situate, order, organize, line up
4 *dispose of a person*
kill, murder, destroy, do away with, put to death
colloq. do in, bump off
E3 2 keep

disposed *adj*
liable, inclined, prone, likely, apt, minded, subject, ready, prepared, willing, eager
formal predisposed
E3 *formal* disinclined

disposition *n*
1 *a friendly disposition; a disposition to obey*
character, nature, temperament, inclination, make-up, bent, leaning, constitution, habit, mood, temper, spirit, humour, tendency, proneness
formal predisposition, propensity, predilection, proclivity
colloq. what makes someone tick
2 *the disposition of troops*
arrangement, alignment, placing, positioning, order, line-up, pattern, grouping, sequence, system
3 *the disposition of property*
distribution, giving-over, allocation, disposal, transfer, conveyance

dispossess *v*
deprive, take away, divest, strip, rob, eject, evict, expel, oust, dislodge
E3 give, provide

disproportion *n*
inequality, unevenness, imbalance, lopsidedness, discrepancy, inadequacy, insufficiency
formal asymmetry, disparity, incommensurateness
E3 balance, equality

disproportionate *adj*
unequal, uneven, unbalanced, excessive, unreasonable, out of proportion
formal incommensurate
E3 balanced ; *formal* commensurate

disprove *v*
rebut, discredit, invalidate, contradict, prove false, deny, expose, give the lie to
formal refute, negate, controvert, confute
colloq. debunk
E3 confirm, prove

disputable *adj*
arguable, debatable, questionable, controversial, doubtful, dubious, uncertain, moot
formal litigious
E3 indisputable, unquestionable

disputation *n*
debate, argument, argumentation, controversy, dispute, deliberation, polemics
technical quodlibet
formal dissension

disputatious *adj*
argumentative, contentious, polemical, quarrelsome, cantankerous, captious
formal litigious, pugnacious

dispute *v, n*
▶ *v* argue, debate, question, call into question, contend, challenge, contest, discuss, doubt, contest, contradict, deny, quarrel, clash, wrangle, bicker, squabble
E3 agree

▶ *n* argument, debate, disagreement, controversy, conflict, contention, quarrel, row, wrangle, feud, strife, squabble
formal altercation
F3 agreement, settlement

disqualified *adj*
eliminated, ineligible, struck off
formal debarred, precluded, disentitled
F3 accepted, eligible, qualified

disqualify *v*
1 *disqualified from the competition*
rule out, declare ineligible, eliminate, prohibit, suspend, strike off
formal preclude, disentitle, debar
2 INCAPACITATE, disable, invalidate, immobilize, handicap
formal impair, debilitate
F3 **1** qualify, accept

disquiet *n, v*
▶ *n* anxiety, worry, concern, uneasiness, nervousness, uneasiness, restlessness, alarm, distress, agitation, fretfulness, fear, foreboding, anguish, dread, disturbance, upset, trouble
formal disquietude, inquietude, perturbation
F3 calm, reassurance
▶ *v* worry, make anxious, unsettle, make uneasy, unnerve, distress, agitate, annoy, bother, trouble, upset, concern, disturb, fret, shake, ruffle, harass, pester, plague, vex
formal discompose, incommode, perturb
colloq. hassle
F3 calm, reassure

disquisition *n*
explanation, dissertation, paper, essay, thesis, treatise, monograph, sermon
formal discourse, exposition

disregard *v, n*
▶ *v* **1** IGNORE, overlook, discount, neglect, take no notice of, pass over, gloss over, disobey, flout, make light of, set aside, brush aside
colloq. turn a blind eye to, laugh off
2 SLIGHT, snub, shun, insult, despise, disdain
formal disparage, denigrate
colloq. cold shoulder
F3 **1** heed, pay attention to, listen to **2** respect
▶ *n* neglect, negligence, carelessness, inattention, oversight, indifference, disrespect, contempt, disdain
formal denigration
colloq. brush-off
F3 attention, heed, notice

disrepair *n*
dilapidation, deterioration, decay, collapse, ruin, rack and ruin, shabbiness
F3 good repair

disreputable *adj*
1 DISGRACEFUL, discreditable, dubious, suspicious, dishonourable, unprincipled, unrespectable, notorious, infamous, scandalous, outrageous, shameful, unworthy, base, contemptible, corrupt, low, mean, shocking
formal ignominious, opprobrious
colloq. shady, shifty, dodgy
2 SCRUFFY, shabby, seedy, unkempt, slovenly, untidy, dishevelled
F3 **1** honourable, respectable **2** smart

disrepute *n*
disgrace, dishonour, shame, disfavour, discredit, disreputation, infamy
formal disesteem, ignominy, obloquy
F3 honour; *formal* esteem

disrespect *n*
impoliteness, disregard, discourtesy, incivility, irreverence, rudeness, dishonour, contempt, scorn, insolence, impertinence, impudence, cheek
formal misesteem
F3 respect, politeness, civility, consideration

disrespectful *adj*
rude, discourteous, inconsiderate, impertinent, impolite, impudent, insolent, uncivil, unmannerly, cheeky, insulting, irreverent, contemptuous
US colloq. sassy
F3 polite, respectful, civil, considerate

disrobe *v*
undress, unclothe, take off, bare, uncover, strip, remove, shed, denude
formal divest, disapparel
F3 cover, dress

disrupt *v*
disturb, disorganize, confuse, cause confusion in, interfere with, interrupt, butt in, break up, unsettle, intrude, upset, throw into disorder/disarray, disarrange, hamper, impede, sabotage
colloq. throw a spanner in the works, put a spoke in someone's wheel

disruption *n*
disorder, confusion, disorganization, turmoil, disarray, disorderliness, disturbance, interference, interruption, stoppage, upheaval, upset

disruptive *adj*
troublesome, unruly, undisciplined, obstreperous, disorderly, boisterous, noisy, turbulent, distracting, disturbing, unsettling, upsetting
F3 well-behaved, manageable

dissatisfaction *n*
discontent, displeasure, dislike, discomfort, disappointment, disapproval, frustration, restlessness, anger, annoyance, irritation, exasperation, unhappiness, regret, resentment, vexation, chagrin
formal disapprobation
F3 satisfaction

dissatisfied *adj*
discontented, displeased, disgruntled, disappointed, disillusioned, disenchanted, frustrated, angry, annoyed, irritated, exasperated, unfulfilled, unhappy, unsatisfied
colloq. fed up, cheesed off, brassed off, browned off ;
slang pissed off
F3 fulfilled, satisfied

dissatisfy *v*
displease, disappoint, discontent, disgruntle, anger, annoy, irritate, exasperate, frustrate, put out, vex

dissect *v*
1 DISMEMBER, cut up, vivisect
formal anatomize
2 ANALYSE, break down, investigate, scrutinize, examine, inspect, study, probe, explore, pore over

dissection *n*
1 dismemberment, cutting up, vivisection
technical autopsy, necropsy
2 analysis, breakdown, investigation, scrutiny,

examination, inspection, study, probe, exploration
Related adjective: prosectorial

dissemble *v*
feign, pretend, hide, conceal, disguise, simulate, camouflage, cloak, mask, counterfeit, fake, falsify, sham, play possum
formal affect, dissimulate
colloq. cover up
F3 admit

dissembler *n*
pretender, deceiver, hypocrite, impostor, trickster, charlatan, fake, feigner, fraud, whited sepulchre
formal dissimulator
colloq. con man

disseminate *v*
circulate, distribute, spread, broadcast, scatter, sow, diffuse, disperse, publish, publicize, propagate, proclaim
formal promulgate

dissemination *n*
circulation, distribution, spread, broadcasting, publishing, publication, diffusion, dispersion, propagation
formal promulgation

dissension *n*
disagreement, discord, dissent, dispute, contention, argument, conflict, strife, friction, quarrel, variance, difference of opinion
F3 agreement

dissent *v, n*
▶ *v* disagree, differ, protest, object, dispute, refuse, quibble
F3 assent
▶ *n* disagreement, difference, dissension, discord, friction, dispute, difference of opinion, controversy, resistance, opposition, objection, protest
F3 agreement, conformity

dissenter *n*
dissident, objector, protestant, protester, demonstrator, nonconformist, disputant, rebel, recusant, heretic, revolutionary, sectary, schismatic

dissentient *adj*
disagreeing, dissenting, dissident, opposing, protesting, conflicting, differing, rebellious, heretical, revolutionary, recusant
F3 arguing

dissertation *n*
thesis, treatise, critique, essay, monograph, paper
technical prolegomena, propaedeutic
formal discourse, disquisition, exposition

disservice *n*
disfavour, injury, wrong, bad turn, harm, hurt, unkindness, injustice, sharp practice
colloq. dirty trick, con trick, kick in the teeth
F3 favour

dissidence *n*
disagreement, discordance, dispute, dissent, feud, recusancy, rupture, schism, variance
F3 agreement, peace

dissident *adj, n*
▶ *adj* disagreeing, differing, discordant, nonconformist, opposing, protesting, conflicting, rebellious, heretical, revolutionary
formal dissenting, heterodox

F3 acquiescent, orthodox
▶ *n* dissenter, protester, objector, nonconformist, rebel, agitator, revolutionary, heretic, schismatic, recusant
F3 assenter

dissimilar *adj*
unlike, different, divergent, deviating, unrelated, contrasting, incompatible, mismatched, distinct, diverse, varying, various
formal disparate, heterogeneous
F3 similar, like, alike

dissimilarity *n*
unlikeness, difference, discrepancy, divergence, distinction, unrelatedness, contrast, incomparability, diversity, variety, incompatibility
formal disparity, dissimilitude, heterogeneity
F3 compatibility, similarity

dissimulate *v*
feign, pretend, hide, lie, fake, conceal, mask, cloak, disguise, camouflage
formal dissemble, affect
colloq. cover up

dissipate *v*
1 *he dissipated his inheritance*
spend, waste, exhaust, squander, use up, expend, consume, lavish, drain, deplete, fritter away, burn up, run/get through
2 *the clouds dissipated*
disperse, drive away, scatter, break up, vanish, disappear, dispel, diffuse, evaporate, dissolve, melt away
F3 **1** accumulate **2** appear, gather

dissipated *adj*
dissolute, debauched, abandoned, self-indulgent, rakish, wasted, corrupt, wild, depraved, degenerate
formal intemperate, profligate, licentious
F3 conserved, virtuous, upright

dissipation *n*
1 *the dissipation of all fears*
dispersal, diffusion, evaporation, disappearance, squandering, expenditure, consumption, depletion
2 DEBAUCHERY, extravagance, licence, immorality, abandonment, self-indulgence, excess, prodigality, corruption, depravity
formal intemperance, licentiousness
F3 **1** conservation **2** virtue

dissociate *v*
1 *dissociate one thing from another*
separate, detach, break off/up, disunite, disassociate, disengage, disconnect, cut off, sever, disband, set apart, divorce, disrupt, isolate, segregate
2 *dissociate yourself from something*
distance, disconnect, cut off, withdraw, separate
formal secede
colloq. quit
F3 associate, join

dissociation *n*
separation, detachment, break, division, divorce, disconnection, disengagement, dissevering, distancing, segregation, isolation, setting apart, cutting-off, severance, severing, split
formal disunion
F3 association, union

dissolute *adj*
dissipated, debauched, degenerate, depraved, wanton, self-indulgent, abandoned, corrupt, immoral, lewd,

rakish, unrestrained, wild
formal intemperate, profligate, licentious
◨ restrained, virtuous

dissolution *n*
1 *the dissolution of an organization/a marriage*
ending, break-up, conclusion, suspension, divorce,
annulment
formal termination, discontinuation
2 *the dissolution of the monarchy*
break-up, destruction, overthrow
3 *dissolution of family life*
break-up, disintegration, collapse, decomposition,
separation, division, disposal, evaporation,
disappearance

dissolve *v*
1 *sugar dissolves in water*
liquefy, melt, go into solution
technical deliquesce, solvate
2 *the marriage/partnership dissolved*
end, bring to an end, finish, break up, disintegrate,
wind up, dismiss, disband, separate, disperse
formal terminate, discontinue
3 *my fears gradually dissolved*
disappear, vanish, evaporate, disperse, dwindle,
melt away, crumble
formal dissipate, evanesce
4 *dissolve into tears*
collapse, be overcome with, lose control, break, burst,
begin, start

dissonance *n*
discord, clash, disagreement, dissension, difference,
incompatibility, inconsistency, variance, disharmony,
discordance, discrepancy, harshness, jangle, stridency,
grating, jarring, cacophony
formal disparity, incongruity
◨ harmony, agreement

dissonant *adj*
discordant, clashing, jarring, disagreeing, jangling,
grating, differing, harsh, incompatible, irregular,
inconsistent, irreconcilable, raucous, strident,
cacophonous, unmusical, tuneless, unmelodious
formal anomalous, incongruous
◨ compatible, harmonious

dissuade *v*
deter, discourage, put off, stop, discourage,
persuade not to, talk out of, disincline
◨ persuade

dissuasion *n*
discouragement, deterrence, deterring, caution
formal expostulation, remonstrance, remonstration
◨ persuasion

distance *n, v*
▶ *n* 1 SPACE, interval, gap, separation, extent,
stretch, range, reach, span, length, width, breadth,
depth, height
2 REMOTENESS, farness, inaccessibility
3 ALOOFNESS, reserve, coolness, coldness,
remoteness, formality, unfriendliness, stiffness
◨ 1 closeness 2 accessibility 3 approachability,
closeness, warmth
▶ *v* separate, cut off, dissociate, remove, withdraw,
break
formal secede

distant *adj*
1 FAR, faraway, far-flung, far-off, out-of-the-way,
remote, outlying, isolated, abroad, dispersed

colloq. back of beyond
2 *a distant relative*
not close, slight, remote
3 ALOOF, cool, reserved, formal, cold, unfriendly,
restrained, detached, stiff, unapproachable,
uncommunicative, unresponsive, antisocial,
withdrawn
colloq. stand-offish
◨ 1 close, nearby 2 close 3 approachable, warm

distaste *n*
dislike, aversion, disgust, revulsion, horror, loathing,
disfavour, displeasure
formal repugnance, abhorrence, antipathy
◨ liking

distasteful *adj*
disagreeable, offensive, displeasing, unpleasant,
disgusting, revolting, objectionable, repellent,
repulsive, obnoxious, undesirable, uninviting,
unsavoury, detestable, loathsome, abhorrent
formal repugnant
◨ pleasing

distend *v*
bloat, swell, dilate, enlarge, expand, fill out, inflate,
bulge, balloon, puff, stretch, widen
technical intumesce
◨ deflate

distended *adj*
bloated, swollen, dilated, enlarged, expanded,
inflated, puffed-out, puffy, stretched, astrut
technical emphysematous, tumescent, varicose
◨ deflated

distension *n*
swelling, bloating, enlargement, expansion, extension,
spread, dilation
technical emphysema, intumescence, tumescence

distil *v*
vaporize, evaporate, condense, extract, press out, draw
out, derive, express, drip, trickle, leak, flow, purify,
refine
technical rectify, sublimate,

distillation *n*
extract, extraction, evaporation, condensation,
essence, spirit

distinct *adj*
1 CLEAR, plain, evident, obvious, clear-cut, apparent,
marked, defined, well-defined, sharp, definite,
noticeable, recognizable, unambiguous, unmistakable
formal manifest
2 SEPARATE, different, detached, individual,
dissimilar, unconnected, unassociated
formal discrete, disparate
◨ 1 indistinct, vague

⚠ **distinct** or **distinctive** ?
Distinct means 'definite', 'clearly or easily seen, heard,
smelt, etc': *a distinct smell of alcohol; a distinct
Scottishness in her pronunciation. Distinctive* means
'characteristic', 'distinguishing one person or thing
from others': *She has a very distinctive walk; the
distinctive call of a barn owl.*

distinction *n*
1 DIFFERENTIATION, discrimination,
discernment, separation, difference, dissimilarity,
division, contrast
formal contradistinction, dissimilitude

2 EXCELLENCE, renown, fame, celebrity, prominence, eminence, importance, significance, reputation, greatness, honour, prestige, repute, superiority, worth, merit, credit, quality
formal consequence
3 CHARACTERISTIC, peculiarity, individuality, feature, quality, mark
E3 2 unimportance, obscurity

distinctive *adj*
characteristic, distinguishing, individual, peculiar, different, typical, unique, particular, special, original, noteworthy, extraordinary, idiosyncratic
formal singular
E3 ordinary, common

distinctly *adv*
clearly, plainly, obviously, evidently, definitely, markedly, noticeably, unmistakably, unambiguously
formal manifestly

distinguish *v*
1 DIFFERENTIATE, tell apart, set apart, discriminate, determine, tell the difference between, single out, mark off, characterize, particularize, typify, mark, stamp, categorize, characterize, classify
2 DISCERN, perceive, identify, ascertain, make out, recognize, see, detect, notice, pick out, discriminate
formal descry
3 *distinguish yourself academically*
excel, do well, acquit yourself well, bring fame to, bring honour to, bring acclaim to, glorify, dignify

distinguishable *adj*
recognizable, discernible, clear, plain, plainly seen, evident, noticeable, conspicuous, obvious, perceptible, appreciable, observable
formal manifest
E3 indistinguishable

distinguished *adj*
famous, eminent, celebrated, well-known, acclaimed, illustrious, prominent, notable, noted, renowned, famed, honoured, acclaimed, outstanding, striking, marked, extraordinary, noble, aristocratic, refined, conspicuous
formal esteemed
E3 insignificant, obscure, unimpressive

distinguishing *adj*
differentiating, different, distinctive, individual, individualistic, marked, peculiar, typical, characteristic, unique, discriminative, discriminatory
formal singular, diacritical

distort *v*
1 DEFORM, contort, bend, misshape, disfigure, twist, warp, buckle
2 FALSIFY, misrepresent, pervert, slant, twist, bias, colour, garble, tamper with
colloq. cook the books

distorted *adj*
1 DEFORMED, bent, misshapen, out of shape, disfigured, twisted, warped, awry, skew, skewed, wry
2 FALSE, biased, perverted, misrepresented
E3 1 straight **2** accurate

distortion *n*
1 DEFORMITY, twist, bend, buckle, contortion, crookedness, skew, slant, warp
2 MISREPRESENTATION, falsification, perversion, bias, twisting, colouring, garbling

distract *v*
1 DIVERT, sidetrack, deflect, draw away, turn aside/away, put off
2 AMUSE, occupy, divert, entertain, engross
3 CONFUSE, disconcert, bewilder, confound, disturb, perplex, puzzle, fluster, discompose

distracted *adj*
1 DISTRAUGHT, agitated, anxious, overwrought, upset, distressed, grief-stricken, beside yourself, worked up, frantic, hysterical, raving, mad, wild, crazy
2 *their attention was distracted*
abstracted, wandering, absent-minded, preoccupied, inattentive, dreaming
colloq. miles away, not with it
E3 1 calm, untroubled **2** attentive

distracting *adj*
disturbing, disconcerting, confusing, bewildering, annoying, irritating
formal perturbing
colloq. off-putting

distraction *n*
1 DISTURBANCE, interrupted, diversion, interference, confusion
formal derangement
2 DIVERSION, amusement, entertainment, game, sport, hobby, pastime, recreation, divertissement
▷ **drive someone to distraction** upset, annoy, anger, madden, exasperate; *colloq.* drive crazy, get someone's blood up, make your blood boil

distraught *adj*
agitated, anxious, overwrought, upset, distressed, distracted, beside yourself, worked up, frantic, hysterical, raving, mad, wild, crazy
colloq. in a state, het up
E3 calm, untroubled

distress *n, v*
▶ *n* **1** ANGUISH, grief, misery, sorrow, heartache, suffering, discomfort, torment, wretchedness, sadness, worry, anxiety, unease, desolation, pain, agony, torture
formal woe, tribulation, affliction, perturbation
2 ADVERSITY, hardship, poverty, need, destitution, calamity, misfortune, trouble, difficulties, trial
formal privation, indigence, penury
E3 1 content **2** comfort, ease
▶ *v* upset, cause suffering to, grieve, disturb, trouble, sadden, make miserable, worry, make anxious, pain, vex, torment, harass, harrow, hurt, agonize, break someone's heart
formal afflict, perturb
colloq. cut up
E3 comfort

distribute *v*
1 DISPENSE, allocate, give out, hand out, pass round, dole out, dish out, share, deal (out), divide, measure out, mete out, allot, issue
formal apportion
2 DELIVER, supply, hand out, spread, issue, circulate, pass round
3 SCATTER, diffuse, disperse
formal disseminate
E3 2 collect

distribution *n*
1 DELIVERY, supply, transport, transportation, dealing, handling, conveyance
2 ALLOCATION, giving-out, handing-out, division, sharing
formal apportionment

3 CIRCULATION, spreading, scattering, dispersal, *formal* dissemination
4 ARRANGEMENT, grouping, classification, organization, placement, position
🖅 **1** collection

district *n*
region, area, quarter, neighbourhood, locality, sector, precinct, zone, block, parish, place, locale, community, vicinity, ward, constituency, domain, territory

distrust *v, n*
▶ *v* mistrust, doubt, have doubts about, disbelieve, suspect, be suspicious of, question, be sceptical about, discredit
🖅 trust
▶ *n* mistrust, doubt, doubtfulness, disbelief, suspicion, misgiving, wariness, scepticism, question, questioning, qualm, chariness, discredit
🖅 trust, confidence, faith

distrustful *adj*
mistrustful, distrusting, doubtful, doubting, dubious, disbelieving, suspicious, wary, sceptical, untrustful, untrusting, chary, uneasy, cynical
🖅 trustful, unsuspecting

disturb *v*
1 DISRUPT, interrupt, put off, distract, bother, butt in on, break someone's train of thought, pester
2 AGITATE, trouble, unsettle, upset, distress, worry, make anxious, fluster, annoy, bother, concern, disconcert, dismay, discompose, stir
formal discomfit, perturb
3 DISARRANGE, disorder, confuse, upset, disorganize, muddle, unsettle, throw into confusion
🖅 **2** reassure **3** order

disturbance *n*
1 DISRUPTION, agitation, interference, interruption, distraction, intrusion, upheaval, upset, confusion, disorder, muddle, annoyance, bother, trouble, hindrance
2 DISORDER, uproar, commotion, tumult, turmoil, fracas, fray, brawl, riot, row, rumpus, hullabaloo, racket
3 *emotional disturbance*
illness, sickness, disorder, complaint, neurosis
🖅 **1** peace **2** order

disturbed *adj*
1 *disturbed by the news*
anxious, apprehensive, bothered, concerned, troubled, worried, upset, confused, discomposed, uneasy, flustered
2 *emotionally disturbed*
maladjusted, neurotic, unbalanced, psychotic, mentally ill, paranoid, upset
colloq. screwed-up, hung-up
🖅 **1** calm

disturbing *adj*
alarming, distressing, troubling, unsettling, upsetting, worrying, disconcerting, bewildering, confusing, dismaying, disquieting, discouraging, agitating, frightening, startling, threatening
formal disturbant, disturbative, perturbing
🖅 reassuring, comforting

disunited *adj*
divided, split, separated, disrupted, alienated
formal estranged
🖅 unify

disunity *n*
disagreement, conflict, discord, division, dissension, dissent, rupture, schism, split, strife, party spirit, alienation, breach
formal estrangement, discordance
🖅 unity

disuse *n*
neglect, abandonment, decay
formal desuetude, discontinuance
🖅 use

disused *adj*
unused, neglected, abandoned, decayed
formal discontinued
🖅 used

ditch *n, v*
▶ *n* trench, dyke, channel, canal, gully, gutter, furrow, moat, drain, level, watercourse
▶ *v* abandon, get rid of, throw away/out, discard, dispose of, drop, jettison, scrap
colloq. dump, chuck

dither *v, n*
▶ *v* hesitate, waver, vacillate, hang back, delay, take your time
colloq. be in two minds, shilly-shally, dilly-dally
▶ *n* panic, indecision, bother, flutter, fluster
colloq. flap, pother, stew, tizzy
🖅 decision

divan *n*
couch, settee, sofa, chaise-longue, day bed, lounge, lounger, ottoman, chesterfield

dive *v, n*
▶ *v* **1** *dive into water*
plunge, jump, plummet, dip, submerge, leap, nose-dive, fall, drop, swoop, descend, go down/under, pitch
2 *dive for cover*
move quickly, leap, dash, rush, hurry, fly, tear, bolt
▶ *n* **1** PLUNGE, lunge, header, jump, leap, plummet, nose-dive, swoop, dash, spring, fall, drop
2 *make a dive for the door*
leap, dash, rush, dart
3 BAR, club, pub, saloon, nightclub
colloq. dump, joint, hole

diverge *v*
1 DIVIDE, branch (off), fork, part, separate, spread (out), split, subdivide, radiate
formal bifurcate
2 DIFFER, vary, disagree, dissent, conflict, clash, contradict, be at variance
3 DEVIATE, digress, stray, wander, depart, drift
formal divagate
🖅 **1** converge **2** agree

divergence *n*
difference, disagreement, variation, clash, conflict, deviation, separation, parting, deflection, departure, digression, branching-out
formal disparity
🖅 agreement

divergent *adj*
different, differing, disagreeing, conflicting, dissimilar, variant, varying, separate, diverging, diverse, deviating, tangential
🖅 similar

divers *adj*
varying, varied, various, different, many, numerous,

several, some, miscellaneous, sundry
formal manifold, multifarious

diverse *adj*
various, varied, varying, sundry, all means of,
different, differing, assorted, mixed, unlike, dissimilar,
contrasting, miscellaneous, separate, several, distinct
formal discrete, heterogeneous
🖃 similar, identical

diversify *v*
vary, change, expand, extend, branch out, bring variety
to, spread out, modify, alter, mix, assort
formal variegate

diversion *n*
1 DEVIATION, detour, alternative route, redirection,
rerouteing, switching
2 AMUSEMENT, entertainment, distraction, hobby,
pastime, recreation, relaxation, play, game, sport, fun,
divertissement
3 ALTERATION, change, redirection, deviation

diversionary *adj*
distracting, deflecting, divertive

diversity *n*
variety, dissimilarity, difference, diversification,
variance, assortment, miscellany, range, mixture,
medley
formal variegation, dissimilitude, pluralism,
heterogeneity
🖃 similarity, likeness

divert *v*
1 DEFLECT, redirect, reroute, switch, sidetrack,
avert, distract, deflect, draw/turn away
2 AMUSE, entertain, occupy, distract, delight, occupy,
interest, absorb, engross, intrigue

diverting *adj*
enjoyable, entertaining, amusing, fun, pleasant,
pleasurable, funny, humorous, witty
🖃 irritating

divest *v*
divest of power/clothes
deprive, strip, remove, dispossess, undress, unclothe,
disrobe
old use doff
formal denude, despoil
🖃 clothe

divide *v*
1 SPLIT, separate, sever, part, cut (up), break up/
down, detach, bisect, disconnect, detach, segregate,
diverge, branch, fork
2 DISTRIBUTE, share, allocate, deal out, allot,
dispense, hand out, dole out, measure out
formal apportion
3 DISUNITE, separate, alienate, split (up), break up,
come between, set someone against another
formal estrange
4 CLASSIFY, group, sort, grade, arrange, order, rank,
categorize, segregate
🖃 1 join 2 collect 3 unite
▷ **divide up** share (out), allocate, allot, dole out,
measure out, parcel out; *formal* apportion

dividend *n*
1 *shareholders' dividends*
share, bonus, portion, surplus, gain
colloq. cut, divvy, whack
2 BENEFIT, bonus, extra, gain, plus

divination *n*
clairvoyance, divining, foretelling, prophecy,
prediction, fortune-telling, dukkeripen, second sight,
soothsaying, augury, -mancy, presage
Scot. taghairm
formal hariolation, prognostication, rhabdomancy
Related adjective: mantic

divine *adj, n, v*
▶ *adj* 1 GODLIKE, godly, superhuman,
supernatural, mystical, celestial, heavenly, angelic,
seraphic, saintly, spiritual
2 HOLY, sacred, sanctified, consecrated, spiritual,
transcendent, exalted, glorious, religious, supreme
3 DELIGHTFUL, beautiful, charming, lovely,
wonderful, excellent, glorious, heavenly
🖃 1 human 2 mundane
▶ *n* churchman, churchwoman, clergyman,
clergywoman, minister, priest, pastor, parson,
reverend, cleric, ecclesiastic, prelate
▶ *v* guess, deduce, suppose, infer, surmise, suspect,
understand, foretell, apprehend, perceive
formal conjecture, intuit, prognosticate

diviner *n*
astrologer, augur, oracle, prophet, seer, soothsayer,
haruspex, sibyl, water-finder, dowser
old use divinator

divinity *n*
1 *worship a divinity; claims to divinity*
god, goddess, deity, divineness, godliness, holiness,
sanctity, godhead, spirit
2 THEOLOGY, religious studies, religious education,
religious knowledge, religion

division *n*
1 SEPARATION, dividing, detaching, parting, cutting
(up), disunion, severance
2 BREACH, rupture, split, schism, rift, disunion,
disagreement, feud, discord, conflict, alienation,
difference of opinion
formal estrangement
3 DISTRIBUTION, sharing (out), allotment,
allocation
formal apportionment
4 SECTION, group, sector, segment, part,
department, category, class, compartment, branch,
arm
5 BOUNDARY, divide, dividing-line, frontier, border,
partition, demarcation line
🖃 1 union 2 unity 3 collection 4 whole

divisive *adj*
alienating, damaging, injurious, disruptive,
troublesome, troublemaking, inharmonious
formal discordant, estranging
🖃 harmonious, unifying

divorce *n, v*
▶ *n* dissolution, annulment, break-up, split-up, split,
rupture, separation, breach, division, partition,
disunion, severance
▶ *v* separate, part, annul, break up, split up, sever,
dissolve, divide, detach, dissociate, disconnect,
disunite, isolate
colloq. bust up
🖃 marry, unite

divulge *v*
reveal, disclose, make known, tell, communicate,
broadcast, publish, proclaim, confess, declare, let slip,
betray, expose, uncover
formal impart, promulgate

colloq. leak, break the news, let the cat out of the bag, spill the beans, blow the gaff, put your cards on the table

dizzy *adj*
1 GIDDY, faint, light-headed, wobbly, shaky, reeling, off-balance, weak at the knees, with your head swimming
formal vertiginous
colloq. woozy
2 CONFUSED, bewildered, dazed, muddled
3 *a dizzy blonde*
silly, irresponsible, foolish, feather-brained, scatterbrained
US colloq. ditsy

do *v, n*
▶ *v* 1 PERFORM, carry out, execute, accomplish, achieve, fulfil, implement, complete, discharge, undertake, work, put on, present, end, finish, put into practice
formal conclude, effectuate
2 BEHAVE, act, conduct yourself
formal comport yourself
3 *do the tea*
prepare, get ready, fix, organize, arrange, deal with, look after, take care of, manage, be in charge of, be responsible for, produce, make, create, cause, proceed
4 *Will this do?*
be enough, be adequate, be sufficient, be satisfactory, fit the bill, satisfy, serve
formal suffice
5 *What do you do?*
have a job, work as, be employed as, earn a living as
6 *do something about a problem*
try to solve, deal with, work out, find the answer to, sort out, figure out, tackle
formal resolve
colloq. crack, get to the bottom of
7 *do French at school*
study, learn, master, read, work at/on, take, major in
8 *do deliveries for you*
provide, supply, furnish, offer
9 *do 150 kph*
travel at, go at, reach, achieve
10 *do well/badly; How are you doing?*
get on, get along, come on, come along, fare, progress, develop, manage, make a good/bad job of
11 CHEAT, defraud, swindle, trick, deceive, dupe, hoodwink
colloq. con, rip off, have, fleece, take for a ride
▷ **do away with** 1 GET RID OF, discard, dispose of, abolish, remove, eliminate; *formal* discontinue, nullify, annul 2 KILL, murder, slaughter, slay, exterminate, assassinate; *colloq.* do in, knock off, bump off
▷ **do down** critcize, condemn, blame, censure, find fault with
▷ **do in** kill, murder, slaughter, slay, exterminate, assassinate; *colloq.* knock off, bump off
▷ **do out of** prevent from having, deprive of, cheat out of, trick out of, swindle out of; *colloq.* con out of, diddle out of, fleece
▷ **do up** 1 FASTEN, tie, lace, button, zip up, pack 2 RENOVATE, redecorate, decorate, restore, modernize, repair, recondition
▷ **do without** go without, manage without, give up, dispense with, deny yourself, refrain; *formal* forego, abstain from, relinquish
▶ *n* function, affair, event, gathering, party, celebration, soirée, occasion

colloq. bash, knees-up, rave-up
▷ **dos and don'ts** rules, regulations, code, instructions, standards, customs, etiquette

docile *adj*
tractable, co-operative, manageable, submissive, obedient, amenable, controllable, controlled, obliging, yielding
formal compliant
🗲 truculent, unco-operative

docility *n*
amenability, tractability, manageability, submissiveness, obedience, biddableness, meekness, pliability, pliancy
formal complaisance, compliance, ductility
🗲 truculence, unco-operativeness

dock[1] *n, v*
▶ *n* *the ship is in dock*
harbour, wharf, quay, boat-yard, pier, waterfront, jetty, marina
▶ *v* anchor, moor, drop anchor, land, berth, put in, tie up

dock[2] *v*
1 *dock an animal's tail*
crop, clip, cut, shorten, curtail, truncate
2 *dock someone's pay*
deduct, reduce, lessen, withhold, decrease, subtract, remove, diminish

docket *n, v*
▶ *n* certificate, ticket, label, receipt, tab, tag, bill, chit, chitty, counterfoil, tally, documentation, paperwork
▶ *v* label, mark, tab, tag, ticket, register, catalogue, file, index

doctor *n, v*
▶ *n* physician, medical officer, consultant, clinician
colloq. medic

Types of medical doctor include: general practitioner, GP, family doctor, family practitioner, locum, hospital doctor, houseman, intern, resident, registrar, consultant, medical officer (MO), *colloq.* doc, *colloq.* bones, *colloq.* quack, dentist, veterinary surgeon, *colloq.* vet. *See also* **medical specialists; surgeon**.

▶ *v* 1 ALTER, tamper with, interfere with, falsify, misrepresent, pervert, adulterate, change, disguise, dilute
2 CONTAMINATE, drug, weaken, lace, add drugs/poison to, adulterate
colloq. spike
3 STERILIZE, castrate, spay, neuter

doctrinaire *adj*
dogmatic, inflexible, rigid, insistent, opinionated, pedantic, biased, fanatical
🗲 flexible

doctrine *n*
dogma, creed, belief, tenet, principle, teaching, precept, conviction, opinion, canon, credo

document *n, v*
▶ *n* paper, certificate, deed, record, proof, evidence, report, form, charter
technical affidavit
formal instrument
▶ *v* 1 RECORD, put on record, keep on record, report, chronicle, list, detail, register, cite, chart
2 SUPPORT, back up, prove, verify, give weight to
formal corroborate, substantiate, validate

documentary *adj*
recorded, chronicled, detailed, charted, written

doddering *adj*
decrepit, weak, aged, feeble, frail, infirm, elderly, tottering

doddery *adj*
unsteady, shaky, weak, faltering, doddering, tottery, feeble, infirm, aged
F3 hale, youthful

dodge *v, n*
▶ *v* avoid, elude, evade, swerve, jump away, bypass, get out of, get round, side-step, shirk, shun, shift, steer clear of, fend off, veer
colloq. duck
▶ *n* trick, ruse, ploy, wile, scheme, stratagem, manoeuvre, device, contrivance, subterfuge, deception, sharp practice
formal machination

dodger *n*
evader, avoider, shirker, trickster, slacker, layabout, dreamer
colloq. lead-swinger, skiver, slyboots, lazybones

dodgy *adj*
chancy, dangerous, delicate, dubious, disreputable, difficult, problematical, risky, ticklish, tricky, uncertain, suspect, unreliable, unsafe
colloq. dicey, dicky, shifty
F3 easy, safe

doer *n*
achiever, activist, organizer, worker, accomplisher, executor, bustler, dynamo
colloq. go-getter, live wire, power-house
F3 thinker, contemplatist

doff *v*
take off, discard, remove, shed, throw off, lift, raise, tip, touch
F3 don

dog *n, v*
▶ *n* **1** *cats and dogs*
hound, cur, mongrel, canine, puppy, pup, bitch
colloq. mutt, pooch
2 VILLAIN, scoundrel, rascal, rogue, wretch
Related adjective: canine

Breeds of dog include: Afghan hound, alsatian, basset-hound, beagle, Border collie, borzoi, bulldog, bull-mastiff, bull-terrier, cairn terrier, chihuahua, chow, cocker spaniel, collie, corgi, dachshund, Dalmatian, Doberman pinscher, foxhound, fox-terrier, German Shepherd, golden retriever, Great Dane, greyhound, husky, Irish wolfhound, Jack Russell, King Charles spaniel, Labrador, lhasa apso, lurcher, Maltese, Old English sheepdog, Pekingese, pit bull terrier, pointer, poodle, pug, Rottweiler, saluki, sausage-dog, schnauzer, Scottie, Scottish-terrier, Sealyham, setter, sheltie, shih tzu, springer spaniel, St Bernard, terrier, West Highland terrier, Westie, whippet, wolf-hound, Yorkshire terrier.

▶ *v* pursue, follow, trail, track, tail, hound, shadow, plague, harry, haunt, trouble, worry

dogged *adj*
determined, resolute, persistent, persevering, intent, tenacious, firm, steadfast, staunch, single-minded, tireless, indefatigable, steady, unshakable, stubborn, obstinate, relentless, unyielding, unflagging, unfaltering

formal indomitable, obdurate, pertinacious
F3 irresolute, apathetic

doggedness *n*
determination, resolution, persistence, perseverance, tenaciousness, tenacity, firmness, steadfastness, steadiness, single-mindedness, stubbornness, obstinacy, relentlessness, endurance
formal indomitability, pertinacity

dogma *n*
doctrine, creed, belief, precept, principle, code (of belief), article (of faith), credo, tenet, conviction, teaching, opinion, maxim

dogmatic *adj*
opinionated, assertive, authoritative, canonical, positive, doctrinaire, domineering, dictatorial, doctrinal, categorical, emphatic, overbearing, arbitrary, insistent, arrogant, imperious, intolerant, authoritarian, ex cathedra, unquestionable, unchallengeable, pontifical

dogmatism *n*
opinionatedness, assertiveness, imperiousness, dictatorialness, bigotry, presumption, arbitrariness, positiveness
formal peremptoriness

dogsbody *n*
gofer, drudge, slave, lackey, doormat, galley-slave, menial, factotum, maid-of-all-work, man-of-all-work
colloq. skivvy

doings *n*
activities, actions, acts, exploits, feats, achievements, enterprises, deeds, events, goings-on, happenings, dealings, affairs, concerns, adventures, handiwork, proceedings, transactions

doldrums *n*
depression, dejection, downheartedness, gloom, listlessness, low-spiritedness, apathy, boredom, tedium, dullness, inertia, stagnation, sluggishness, torpor
formal ennui, lassitude, malaise, acedia
colloq. blues, dumps

dole *n, v*
▶ *n* benefit, Job Seekers Allowance (JSA), unemployment benefit, social security, allowance, payment, income, credit, support
▶ *v* ▷ **dole out** distribute, allocate, give out, hand out, dish out, apportion, allot, mete out, share (out), divide (up), deal (out), issue, ration, dispense, administer, assign; *formal* apportion

doleful *adj*
cheerless, depressing, distressing, dismal, dreary, forlorn, gloomy, melancholy, miserable, wretched, sad, sorrowful, mournful, sombre, rueful, painful, pathetic, pitiful, woeful
formal dolorous, lugubrious, woebegone, disconsolate
colloq. blue, down in the dumps
F3 cheerful

doll *n*
figure, puppet, marionette, plaything, toy, figurine, moppet, dolly, Barbie®, Sindy®
▷ **doll up** dress up, preen, primp, deck out, trick out, titivate; *colloq.* tart up

dollop *n*
lump, blob, clump, bunch, ball, glob, gob, gobbet

dolorous *adj*
anguished, distressing, melancholy, miserable, wretched, sad, sorrowful, doleful, grievous, harrowing, heart-rending, painful, mournful, rueful, sombre, woeful
formal lugubrious, woebegone
E3 happy

dolour *n*
anguish, distress, grief, misery, sadness, sorrow, heartache, heartbreak, mourning, suffering, lamentation

dolt *n*
fool, idiot, imbecile, simpleton
colloq. ass, blockhead, nincompoop, ninny, nitwit, numskull, twerp, dope, chump, clot, nutcase, twit, dimwit; *slang* wally, dipstick, nerd

domain *n*
1 DOMINION, kingdom, realm, territory, region, empire, estate, lands, province
2 FIELD, area, speciality, concern, section, department, region, province, realm, sphere, world, discipline, jurisdiction

dome *n*
cupola, vault, rotunda, mound, hemisphere

domestic *adj, n*
▶ *adj* 1 HOME, family, household, home-loving, stay-at-home, homely, domesticated, house-trained, tame, pet, private, personal
formal domiciliary
2 INTERNAL, indigenous, native, home
E3 2 foreign, international, export
▶ *n* servant, maid, charwoman, char, daily help, domestic help, daily, au pair

domestic appliance

Types of domestic appliance include: washing machine, washer, washer/drier, tumble-drier, clothes airer, iron, steam iron, steam press, trouser press; dishwasher, vacuum cleaner, upright cleaner, cylinder cleaner, wet-and-dry cleaner, Hoover®, floor polisher, carpet sweeper, carpet shampooer; oven, Aga®, barbecue, cooker, Dutch oven, electric cooker, fan oven, gas stove, kitchen range, microwave oven, stove, hob, hotplate, grill, electric grill, griddle, rotisserie, spit, waffle iron, deep fryer, slow cooker, sandwich maker, toaster; food processor, mixer, blender, liquidizer, ice-cream maker, juicer, juice extractor, food slicer, electric knife, knife sharpener, kettle, tea/coffee maker, percolator, coffee mill, electric tin opener, timer, water filter; refrigerator, *colloq.* fridge, icebox, fridge/freezer, freezer, deep-freeze; hostess-trolley, humidifier, ionizer, fire extinguisher. *See also* **kitchen utensils**.

domesticate *v*
tame, house-train, break, break in, train, accustom, familiarize, acclimatize, naturalize, assimilate
formal habituate

domesticated *adj*
tame, tamed, pet, house-trained, broken (in), domestic, home-loving, homely, house-proud, housewifely, naturalized
E3 feral, wild

domesticity *n*
homemaking, housecraft, homecraft, housekeeping, home economics, domestic science, domestication

domicile *n, v*
▶ *n* home, house, residence, lodging(s), residency, mansion, quarters, settlement
formal abode, dwelling, habitation
▶ *v* make your home, settle, establish, take up residence, put down roots

dominance *n*
supremacy, authority, power, command, pre-eminence, control, rule, domination, sway, leadership, mastery, government
formal ascendancy, hegemony, paramountcy

dominant *adj*
1 AUTHORITATIVE, controlling, governing, ruling, powerful, all-powerful, strong, assertive, influential
2 PRINCIPAL, main, outstanding, chief, major, key, important, most important, predominant, primary, paramount, prime, prominent, outstanding, leading, pre-eminent, supreme, prevailing, prevalent, commanding
E3 1 submissive 2 subordinate

dominate *v*
1 CONTROL, domineer, govern, preside, rule, direct, command, monopolize, predominate, master, lead, overrule, prevail, overbear, intimidate, tyrannize
formal have ascendancy over
colloq. have the upper/whip hand over, have under your thumb, have over a barrel, throw your weight around
2 OVERSHADOW, eclipse, dwarf, overlook, tower over

domination *n*
command, control, authority, influence, power, leadership, rule, sway, mastery, supremacy, superiority, despotism, dictatorship, oppression, subjection, subordination, suppression, repression, tyranny, pre-eminence, predominance
formal ascendancy

domineering *adj*
overbearing, authoritarian, imperious, autocratic, dictatorial, despotic, masterful, high-handed, iron-handed, forceful, coercive, oppressive, tyrannical, arrogant, haughty, aggressive
formal peremptory
colloq. bossy, pushy
E3 meek, servile

dominion *n*
1 POWER, authority, domination, command, control, rule, direction, sway, jurisdiction, government, lordship, mastery, supremacy, sovereignty
formal ascendancy
2 DOMAIN, country, territory, province, colony, realm, kingdom, empire

don *v, n*
▶ *v* put on, get into, dress in, slip into, clothe yourself in
E3 doff
▶ *n* lecturer, teacher, tutor, academic, scholar, professor

Don Juan *n*
ladies' man, lady-killer, womanizer, lover, Casanova, philander(er), romeo, gigolo

donate *v*
give, give away, contribute, present, make a gift, make a donation, pledge, bequeath, subscribe
formal bestow, confer

colloq. cough up, fork out, chip in, club together, shell out
▣ receive

donation *n*
gift, present, offering, grant, gratuity, largess(e), contribution, presentation, subscription, alms, charity, bequest
formal benefaction

done *adj, interj*
▶ *adj* **1** FINISHED, over, accomplished, complete, completed, ended, settled, realized, fulfilled, executed
formal concluded, terminated, consummated
2 CONVENTIONAL, acceptable, proper, right, correct, suitable, appropriate, fitting
old use seemly
formal decorous
3 COOKED, well-done, ready, prepared, finished, baked, boiled, browned, friend, roasted, stewed
▷ **done for** ruined, destroyed, finished, lost, wrecked, undone, doomed, beaten, broken, dashed, defeated, foiled; *formal* vanquished; *colloq.* for the high jump
▷ **done in** exhausted, tired out, weary, fatigued; *colloq.* all in, bushed, dead, dead beat, dog-tired, fagged out, knackered, pooped, zonked, on your last legs, bushed, flaked out, shattered, worn to a frazzle
▷ **have done with** finished with, over with, thrash with, no longer involved/associated with; *colloq.* over and done with
▶ *interj* settled, agreed, accepted, arranged, decided, right, absolutely
colloq. OK

donkey *n*
ass, mule, burro, hinny, jackass, jenny
colloq. moke
Related adjective: asinine

donnish *adj*
academic, serious, intellectual, bookish, erudite, learned, pedantic, scholarly, scholastic, formalistic, pedagogic

donor *n*
giver, donator, benefactor, backer, supporter, contributor, philanthropist, provider
colloq. fairy godmother, angel
▣ beneficiary

doom *n, v*
▶ *n* **1** FATE, fortune, destiny, portion, lot
2 DESTRUCTION, catastrophe, downfall, disaster, ruin, ruination, death, death-knell, rack and ruin
3 CONDEMNATION, judgement, sentence, verdict, pronouncement
▶ *v* condemn, damn, consign, judge, sentence, decree, pronounce, destine, fate, destine
formal predestine

doomed *adj*
condemned, damned, fated, ill-fated, star-crossed, ill-omened, cursed, destined, ruined, hopeless, unlucky, luckless, ill-starred, bedevilled

door *n*
1 *the door of the house*
opening, entrance, entry, exit, doorway, portal, hatch
2 OPPORTUNITY, open door, entrance, opening, way in, access, route, way, gateway, road

doorkeeper *n*
commissionaire, doorman, gatekeeper, usher, janitor, porter, concierge, ostiary

dope *n, v*
▶ *n* **1** NARCOTIC, drugs, marijuana, cannabis, opiate, hallucinogen, barbiturate, amphetamine, crack, acid, LSD
colloq. grass, weed, hash, pot, speed, coke;
slang Ecstasy, E
2 FOOL, dolt, idiot, dunce, simpleton
colloq. half-wit, dimwit, clot, blockhead, nincompoop, ninny, nitwit, twerp, twit
3 INFORMATION, facts, inside information, details, specifics, particulars
colloq. low-down, info, gen
▶ *v* drug, sedate, anaesthetize, stupefy, medicate, narcotize, inject, knock out, doctor
colloq. spike

dopey *adj*
1 SLEEPY, dozy, groggy, drowsy, nodding, lethargic
formal somnolent, torpid
2 STUPID, foolish, silly, daft, dozy, simple
▣ **1** awake, alert **2** clever, bright

dormant *adj*
1 INACTIVE, asleep, sleeping, inert, resting, slumbering, sluggish, hibernating, latent, fallow
technical comatose
formal torpid, quiescent
2 LATENT, unrealized, potential, undeveloped, undisclosed
▣ **1** active, awake **2** realized, developed

dose *n, v*
▶ *n* measure, dosage, amount, portion, quantity, draught, potion, prescription, shot
▶ *v* medicate, administer, prescribe, dispense, treat

dot *n, v*
▶ *n* point, spot, speck, mark, fleck, dab, circle, pin-point, atom, particle, decimal point, full stop, iota, jot
▷ **on the dot** punctually, promptly, precisely, exactly on time, sharp
▶ *v* spot, speckle, mark, scatter, pepper, sprinkle, stud, dab, stipple, punctuate

dotage *n*
old age, senility, second childhood, infirmity, weakness, feebleness, imbecility
formal decrepitude

dote *v*
▷ **dote on** adore, idolize, worship, treasure, admire, love, hold dear, indulge, pamper, spoil

doting *adj*
adoring, devoted, fond, loving, affectionate, tender, soft, indulgent

dotty *adj*
crazy, eccentric, feeble-minded, peculiar, touched, weird
colloq. daft, barmy, batty, loony, potty
▣ sensible

double *adj, v, n*
▶ *adj* **1** *double doors; a double yellow line*
dual, twofold, twice, duplicate, twin, paired, doubled, two-ply, coupled
formal bifarious, binal, binate
2 AMBIGUOUS, double-meaning, double-edged, two-edged, ambivalent, equivocal, paradoxical
▣ single, half
▶ *v* **1** *double your income*
duplicate, enlarge, increase, twofold, repeat, multiply by two, fold, magnify
2 *double as someone/something*

have a second job/purpose, have a dual/second role
3 *double for someone*
substitute, stand in, understudy, be an understudy
▷ **double back**   return, reverse, backtrack, circle, dodge, evade, loop, go back the way you came, retrace your steps
▶ *n*   twin, duplicate, copy, clone, replica, doppelgänger, lookalike, match, image, facsimile, counterpart, impersonator
colloq. spitting image, ringer
▷ **at the double**   immediately, at once, without delay, right away, straight away, quickly, at full speed

double-cross   *v*
cheat, swindle, defraud, trick, hoodwink, betray, mislead
colloq. con, two-time, pull a fast one on, take for a ride

double-dealing   *n*
cheating, swindling, betrayal, treachery, defrauding, tricking, hoodwinking, misleading, two-facedness, two-timing
formal dissembling, duplicity, perfidy, mendacity
colloq. two-timing, crookedness

double entendre   *n*
double meaning, innuendo, suggestiveness, ambiguity, play on words, wordplay, pun

doubly   *adv*
twice, twofold, again, especially, extra
formal bis

doubt   *n, v*
▶ *n* **1** DISTRUST, suspicion, mistrust, scepticism, reservation, misgiving, qualm, mixed feeling, incredulity, apprehension, hesitation, uneasiness
2 UNCERTAINTY, difficulty, confusion, ambiguity, problem, indecision, hesitation, perplexity, dilemma, quandary
E3 **1** trust, confidence, faith **2** certainty, belief
▷ **in doubt**   uncertain, undecided, unresolved, unreliable, ambiguous, in question, open to question, questionable, open to debate, debatable; *colloq.* up in the air
▷ **no doubt**   doubtless, without doubt, undoubtedly, definitely, unquestionably, certainly, surely, of course, no denying, probably, most likely, presumably
▶ *v* **1** DISTRUST, mistrust, query, question, suspect, be suspicious, have misgivings/qualms about, fear
formal disbelieve
colloq. take with a pinch of salt
2 BE UNCERTAIN, be dubious, hesitate, vacillate, waver, be undecided
formal demur
E3 **1** believe, trust, have confidence in **2** be certain, decide

doubter   *n*
questioner, sceptic, disbeliever, unbeliever, agnostic, doubting Thomas, cynic, scoffer
E3 believer

doubtful   *adj*
1 *it is doubtful that he will win*
unlikely, improbable, uncertain, in doubt, open to question, debatable
colloq. touch and go
2 *doubtful about his future*
uncertain, unsure, undecided, suspicious, distrustful, uneasy, apprehensive, having reservations/misgivings, irresolute, wavering, hesitant, vacillating, tentative, sceptical
colloq. in two minds

3 *writing of doubtful origin*
dubious, questionable, suspect, unclear, inconclusive, ambiguous, vague, obscure, debatable
colloq. fishy, shady, iffy
E3 **1** certain **2** certain, decided, confident
3 definite, settled, trustworthy

doubtless   *adv*
certainly, without doubt, undoubtedly, unquestionably, indisputably, no doubt, clearly, surely, of course, truly, precisely, probably, presumably, most likely, seemingly, supposedly

dour   *adj*
1 GLOOMY, dismal, forbidding, grim, morose, unfriendly, unsmiling, dreary, austere, sour, sullen, churlish, gruff
2 HARD, harsh, inflexible, unyielding, rigid, severe, stern, rigorous, strict, obstinate
E3 **1** cheerful, bright **2** easy-going

douse, dowse   *v*
1 SOAK, pour water over, saturate, flood, deluge, steep, submerge, immerse, immerge, wet, dip, souse, duck, drench, dunk, plunge, splash
2 EXTINGUISH, put out, blow out, smother, quench, snuff

dovetail   *v*
fit together, correspond, match, coincide, conform, agree, tally, harmonize, join, interlock, link
formal accord

dowdy   *adj*
unfashionable, ill-dressed, frumpish, drab, shabby, frowsy, dingy, old-fashioned, slovenly
colloq. tatty, tacky
E3 fashionable, smart

down¹   *prep, adv, adj, v*
▶ *prep & adv*
down the road
to a lower level/position, to the ground, to the floor, to the bottom
E3 up
▷ **down with**   get rid of, away with
▶ *adj* **1** SAD, depressed, unhappy, melancholy, miserable, downhearted, dejected, downcast, dispirited, wretched, low
colloq. blue, down in the dumps
2 *the computer is down*
out of order, out of action, not working, crashed
formal inoperative
colloq. bust; *slang* conked out
E3 **1** happy **2** operational
▶ *v* **1** KNOCK DOWN, fell, floor, bring down, prostrate, throw, topple
2 SWALLOW, consume, drink, gulp
colloq. swig, put away, knock back, toss of, swill

down²   *n*
quilts made of down
soft feathers, fine hair, wool, pile, shag, nap, fluff, floss, fuzz, floccus, flue, bloom
technical pappus
Related adjectives: pappose, pappous

down-and-out   *adj, n*
▶ *adj*   derelict, destitute, impoverished, on your uppers, penniless, ruined
▶ *n*   tramp, vagrant, vagabond
US hobo
colloq. loser; *slang* dosser

down-at-heel *adj*
shabby, poor, ill-dressed, frayed, tattered, ragged, drab, frowsy, dowdy, dingy, run-down, slovenly
colloq. tatty, tacky, seedy

downbeat *adj*
1 RELAXED, calm, low, downcast, informal, casual, nonchalant, unhurried, unworried
formal insouciant
colloq. laid back
2 GLOOMY, pessimistic, fearing the worst, negative, depressed, low, downcast, despondent, cheerless, cynical
E3 1 upbeat 2 happy

downcast *adj*
dejected, depressed, despondent, sad, unhappy, wretched, miserable, down, low, disheartened, downhearted, dispirited, discouraged, disappointed, crestfallen, daunted, dismayed, glum, gloomy
formal disconsolate
colloq. blue, fed up
E3 cheerful, happy, elated

downfall *n*
fall, ruin, failure, collapse, destruction, disgrace, debasement, degradation, debacle, undoing, overthrow
E3 rise

downgrade *v*
1 DEGRADE, demote, lower, humble, reduce/lower in rank, relegate, depose, deflate
formal disparage, denigrate
colloq. take down a peg or two, take the wind out of someone's sails
2 BELITTLE, decry, minimize, defame, make light of
colloq. run down, do down, sell short
E3 1 upgrade, improve 2 praise

downhearted *adj*
depressed, dejected, despondent, sad, downcast, disappointed, discouraged, disheartened, dispirited, low-spirited, daunted, unhappy, gloomy, glum, dismayed, disappointed
formal disconsolate
E3 cheerful, enthusiastic

downpour *n*
cloudburst, deluge, rainstorm, flood, inundation, torrent

downright *adv, adj*
▶ *adv* absolutely, plainly, utterly, clearly, completely, totally, thoroughly, categorically
▶ *adj* outright, complete, total, out-and-out, absolute, plain, utter, clear, sheer, thorough, wholesale, categorical, unqualified, unequivocal

down-to-earth *adj*
commonsense, commonsensical, hard-headed, matter-of-fact, mundane, no-nonsense, plain-spoken, practical, realistic, sane, sensible, unsentimental, idealistic
E3 fantastic, impractical

down-trodden *adj*
oppressed, subservient, exploited, trampled on, weighed-down, burdened, overwhelmed, abused, tyrannized, bullied, victimized, helpless, powerless
formal subjugated

downward *adj*
descending, declining, going/moving down, downhill, sliding, slipping
E3 upward

dowry *n*
marriage settlement, marriage portion, inheritance, legacy, portion, provision, share, wedding-dower, dot, dower, endowment, faculty, gift, talent

doze *v, n*
▶ *v* sleep, nap, catnap, take a nap, drift off, go off, nod off, drop off
colloq. snooze, kip; *slang* zizz
▶ *n* nap, catnap, siesta,
colloq. snooze, forty winks, kip, shut-eye; *slang* zizz

drab *adj*
dull, dingy, dreary, dismal, gloomy, flat, grey, colourless, lacklustre, cheerless, lifeless, sombre, shabby, featureless, tedious, boring
E3 bright, cheerful

draft *n, v*
▶ *n* 1 OUTLINE, sketch, rough sketch, plan, abstract, rough, preliminary version, drawing, blueprint
formal delineation, protocol
2 *a bank draft*
bill of exchange, cheque, money order, letter of credit, postal order
▶ *v* draw (up), outline, sketch, plan, design, formulate, compose
formal delineate

drag *v, n*
▶ *v* 1 DRAW, pull, haul, lug, tug, trail, tow, yank
2 GO SLOWLY, creep, crawl, lag, become boring/tedious, wear on, go on and on, go on for ever
▷ **drag out** spin out, prolong, draw out, extend, hang on, lengthen, persist; *formal* protract
▷ **drag up** rake up, remind, bring up, raise, mention, introduce, revive
▶ *n* bore, annoyance, nuisance, bother, pest, trouble
colloq. pain, pain in the neck, bind, headache

dragoon *v*
coerce, compel, constrain, drive, force, harass, impel, intimidate, browbeat, bully
colloq. strongarm

drain *v, n*
▶ *v* 1 EMPTY, remove, evacuate, draw off, pump off, extract, withdraw, strain, dry, milk, bleed, tap
formal void
2 *waste draining into the stream*
trickle, flow out, seep out, leak, ooze
formal discharge, exude, effuse
3 EXHAUST, consume, sap, use up, drink up, swallow, strain, tax
formal deplete
E3 1 fill
▶ *n* 1 CHANNEL, conduit, culvert, duct, outlet, trench, ditch, outlet, pipe, gutter, sewer
2 *a drain on resources*
exhaustion, consumption, sap, strain, tax
formal depletion

drama *n*
1 PLAY, acting, theatre, show, piece, spectacle, stagecraft, scene, comedy, melodrama, tragedy, dramatics, dramaturgy
2 EXCITEMENT, thrill, sensation, crisis, dilemma, tension, turmoil, histrionics

dramatic *adj*
1 *a dramatic change*
striking, sudden, marked, significant, abrupt,

noticeable, distinct
2 EXCITING, striking, stirring, thrilling, tense, spectacular, vivid, graphic, sensational, expressive, effective, impressive, unexpected
3 HISTRIONIC, theatrical, exaggerated, melodramatic, flamboyant, artificial
4 *dramatic art*
theatrical, stage, Thespian

dramatist *n*
playwright, scriptwriter, play-writer, screen writer, comedian, dramaturge, dramaturgist, tragedian

dramatize *v*
1 STAGE, put on, adapt, present as a play/film, arrange for
2 EXAGGERATE, play-act, act, overdo, overstate
colloq. ham (up), lay it on thick, blow up out of all proportion, make a big thing of

drape *v*
hang, cover, wrap, envelop, overlay, shroud, cloak, veil, arrange, decorate, adorn, fold, drop, droop, suspend

drapery *n*
cloth, covering(s), curtain(s), hanging(s), blind(s), arras, backdrop, tapestry, valance

drastic *adj*
extreme, radical, strong, forceful, severe, harsh, rigorous, far-reaching, desperate, dire, Draconian
F3 moderate, cautious

draught *n*
1 PUFF, current, flow, movement
formal influx
2 DRINK, quantity, cup, potion
3 PULLING, dragging, drawing, traction

draw *v, n*
▶ *v* **1** *draw a picture*
sketch, portray, trace, pencil, paint, represent, map out, depict, design, chart, scribble, doodle
formal delineate
2 *the procession drew nearer*
MOVE, go, proceed, progress, travel, come, approach, advance
3 PULL, drag, haul, tow, tug, lug, trail
4 *draw a knife; draw water from a well*
take out, pull out, bring out, produce, extract, remove, withdraw
5 *draw a breath*
breath in
formal inhale, respire, inspire
6 *draw money from a bank*
take, get, receive, obtain
formal procure
7 *draw attention to something*
ATTRACT, allure, lure, entice, bring in, influence, persuade, elicit, prompt
8 *draw a conclusion*
conclude, deduce, infer, gather, come to, reason
9 *draw lots*
pick, choose, select, decide on, go for
colloq. plump for
10 TIE, be equal, be even
colloq. be all square
F3 3 push **7** repel
▷ **draw back** recoil, wince, flinch, shrink, start back, withdraw, retract, retreat
▷ **draw on** make use of, use, put to use, exploit, apply, employ, quarry, rely on, have recourse to;
formal utilize
▷ **draw out 1** *the train drew out of the station* pull

out, move out, set out, depart, leave,
start **2** EXTEND, prolong, lengthen, spin out, elongate, stretch; *formal* protract **3** *draw someone out* encourage to talk, induce to talk/speak, put at ease, make feel less nervous, make
F3 2 shorten
▷ **draw up 1** DRAFT, compose, formulate, prepare, frame, write out, put in writing **2** PULL UP, stop, halt, run in
▶ *n* **1** ATTRACTION, enticement, lure, allure, appeal, bait, interest, magnetism
2 TIE, stalemate, dead heat

drawback *n*
disadvantage, snag, hitch, obstacle, hurdle, barrier, impediment, hindrance, difficulty, problem, flaw, fault, catch, stumbling-block, nuisance, trouble, defect, weak spot, handicap, deficiency, liability, limitation, imperfection, damper, discouragement
colloq. fly in the ointment
F3 advantage, benefit

drawing *n*
sketch, picture, outline, representation, portrayal, illustration, cartoon, graphic, portrait, composition, depiction, diagram, study
formal delineation

drawl *v*
speak slowly, draw out your vowels, drone, haw-haw, protract, twang

drawn *adj*
tired, fatigued, worn, haggard, gaunt, pinched, strained, stressed, taut, tense, fraught, harassed, sapped, washed out
colloq. hassled

dread *v, n, adj*
▶ *v* fear, shrink from, quail, cringe at, flinch, shy, shudder, tremble, be afraid of, be scared of, be terrified by, be frightened (to death) by, be anxious/worried about
colloq. get cold feet about
F3 look forward to
▶ *n* fear, apprehension, misgiving, dismay, alarm, horror, terror, fright, fit of terror, blind panic, cold sweat, hair standing on end, disquiet, worry, qualm
formal trepidation, perturbation
colloq. (blue) funk
F3 confidence, security
▶ *adj* dreaded, feared, frightening, frightful, terrifying, terrible, dreadful, awful, awe-inspiring, alarming, ghastly, grisly, gruesome, horrible, dire

dreadful *adj*
awful, terrible, frightful, horrible, appalling, dire, shocking, outrageous, frightening, terrifying, alarming, ghastly, horrendous, horrific, grim, tragic, grievous, hideous, unpleasant, nasty
formal heinous
F3 wonderful, comforting

dream *n, v, adj*
▶ *n* **1** VISION, illusion, reverie, trance, fantasy, daydream, nightmare, hallucination, delusion, imagination, phantasmagoria
Related adjectives: oneiric, somnial
2 ASPIRATION, ambition, wish, hope, desire, yearning, ideal, goal, design, aim, plan, speculation, expectation, castles in the air
3 DAYDREAM, fantasy, reverie, pipe dream, inattention

4 *their new house is a dream*
ideal, beauty, perfection, joy, marvel
▶ *v* **1** *dream during sleep*
imagine, envisage, fantasize, fancy, hallucinate
2 DAYDREAM, fantasize, imagine, muse, fancy, be
lost in space, not pay attention, let your thoughts
wander, stare into space
colloq. switch off
3 *dream of becoming a doctor*
want very much, long, desire, yearn, crave
▷ **dream up** invent, devise, conceive, think up,
conjure up, imagine, concoct, hatch, create, fabricate,
spin, contrive
▷ **not dream of** not think, not imagine, not
consider, not conceive
▶ *adj* perfect, ideal, model, supreme, superb,
excellent, wonderful

dreamer *n*
idealist, visionary, fantasist, romancer, daydreamer,
star-gazer, theorizer, romantic, Utopian
E∃ realist, pragmatist

dreamlike *adj*
surreal, illusory, unreal, trance-like, hallucinatory,
insubstantial, unsubstantial, visionary, chimerical,
phantom, phantasmagoric, phantasmagorical
formal ethereal

dreamy *adj*
1 FANTASTIC, unreal, imaginary, shadowy, unclear,
indistinct, vague, misty, hazy, faint, ethereal, dim
2 IMPRACTICAL, fanciful, daydreaming,
fantasizing, romantic, idealistic, visionary, faraway,
absent, musing, pensive, thoughtful, absent-minded,
preoccupied, abstracted
colloq. with your head in the clouds
3 *dreamy music*
relaxing, soothing, lulling, calming, gentle, soft,
romantic
E∃ 1 real, clear **2** practical, down-to-earth

dreary *adj*
gloomy, depressing, drab, dismal, bleak, sombre,
cheerless, sad, mournful, overcast, dark, boring,
tedious, uninteresting, uneventful, dull, humdrum,
routine, monotonous, unvaried, wearisome,
commonplace, colourless, lifeless, featureless,
run-of-the-mill
E∃ cheerful, interesting

dredge *v*
▷ **dredge up** dig up, discover, uncover, unearth,
raise, drag up, draw up, fish up, rake up, scoop up

dregs *n*
1 SEDIMENT, deposit, residue, lees, grounds,
scourings, scum, dross, trash, waste
technical precipitate, sublimate
formal residuum, detritus
2 OUTCASTS, rabble, riff-raff, scum, down-and-outs,
tramps, vagrants
slang dossers

drench *v*
soak, soak to the skin, saturate, steep, wet, douse,
souse, immerse, inundate, duck, flood, swamp, imbue,
drown, permeate

dress *n, v*
▶ *n* **1** FROCK, gown, robe
2 CLOTHES, clothing, garment(s), outfit, costume,
ensemble, garb
formal attire, apparel, habiliment

colloq. get-up, gear, togs
Related adjective: sartorial
▶ *v* **1** CLOTHE, put on, get into, slip into, garb, rig,
robe, wear, don, decorate, deck, garnish, trim, adorn,
turn out, fit (out), drape
formal attire, array, accoutre
colloq. throw on
2 *dress your hair*
ARRANGE, adjust, dispose, prepare, groom,
straighten, tidy, comb, do, primp, preen
3 BANDAGE, bind up, put a plaster on, clean, cover,
tend, treat, swathe
4 *dress meat*
clean, prepare, get ready
E∃ 1 strip, undress
▷ **dress down** rebuke, reprimand, reprove, scold,
chide; *formal* berate, castigate, upbraid;
colloq. carpet, haul over the coals, tear off a strip, tell
off, give someone an earful
▷ **dress up** beautify, improve, adorn, decorate,
ornament, embellish, deck, gild, disguise;
colloq. doll up, tart up, tog up

dressing *n*
1 *a salad dressing*
sauce, condiment, relish, salad dressing, French
dressing, Thousand Island dressing
2 BANDAGE, plaster, Elastoplast®, gauze, lint,
compress, poultice, tourniquet, pad, spica, ligature

dressmaker *n*
tailor, tailoress, couturier, modiste, needlewoman,
seamstress, sewing woman, midinette

dressy *adj*
elegant, formal, smart, stylish, elaborate, ornate
colloq. classy, natty, ritzy, swish
E∃ dowdy, scruffy

dribble *v, n*
▶ *v* **1** TRICKLE, drip, leak, run, seep, drop, ooze
formal exude
2 DROOL, slaver, slobber, drivel
▶ *n* drip, trickle, droplet, leak, seepage, sprinkling

dried *adj*
arid, dehydrated, desiccated, drained, parched, wilted,
withered, wizened, shrivelled, mummified
formal exsiccated

drift *v, n*
▶ *v* **1** WANDER, waft, stray, float, freewheel, coast,
go with the stream, be carried along, roam, rove
2 GATHER, accumulate, pile up, bank, drive, amass
▶ *n* **1** ACCUMULATION, mound, pile, bank, mass,
heap, accumulation
2 TREND, tendency, course, direction, flow,
movement, current, variation, digression, rush, sweep
3 MEANING, intention, implication, gist, vein, tenor,
thrust, course, direction, trend, tendency, significance,
essence, core, substance, aim, point, design, scope
formal import, purport

drifter *n*
wanderer, traveller, nomad, vagrant, itinerant, rover,
tramp, vagabond, rolling stone, swagman,
beachcomber
US hobo

drill *n, v*
▶ *n* **1** BORER, awl, bit, gimlet
2 INSTRUCTION, training, practice, coaching,
grounding, exercise, repetition, tuition, preparation,
discipline, indoctrination, procedure, routine

formal inculcation
▶ *v* **1** TEACH, train, instruct, coach, practise, school, rehearse, exercise, discipline, ground, put someone through their paces
formal inculcate
2 BORE, pierce, make a hole in, penetrate, puncture, perforate, prick, punch

drink *v, n*
▶ *v* **1** IMBIBE, swallow, have, sip, drain, down, gulp, sup, quaff, absorb, guzzle, swill
formal partake of
colloq. swig, knock back
2 GET DRUNK, have one too many, have (a drop) too much, indulge, carouse, revel, be a hard drinker, be a heavy drinker, have a drink problem
colloq. tipple, tank up, have one over the eight, drink like a fish, hit the bottle, knock back a few, polish off;
slang booze, get pissed, lush
3 *drink someone's health*
drink to, toast, propose a toast to, salute, wish someone success
▶ *n* **1** BEVERAGE, liquid, brew, infusion, soft drink, cold drink, hot drink, thirst-quencher, refreshment, draught, sip, swallow, gulp
colloq. swig

> *Types of non-alcoholic drink include*: Assam, Indian, Earl Grey, China tea, lapsang souchong, green tea, herbal tea, fruit tea, camomile tea, peppermint tea, rosehip tea, lemon tea, tisane, julep, mint-julep; coffee, café au lait, café filtre, café noir, cappuccino, expresso, Irish coffee, Turkish coffee; cocoa, hot chocolate, Horlicks®, Ovaltine®, milk, milk shake, float; fizzy drink, *colloq.* pop, cherryade, Coca Cola®, *colloq.* coke, cream soda, ginger beer, lemonade, limeade, Pepsi®, root beer, sarsaparilla, cordial, squash, barley water, Ribena®, fruit juice, mixer, bitter lemon, Canada Dry®, ginger ale, soda water, tonic water, mineral water, Perrier®, seltzer, Vichy water, Lucozade®, Wincarnis®, beef tea.

2 ALCOHOL, strong drink, spirits, liquor, tot
colloq. tipple, the bottle, stiffener, hard stuff;
slang booze

> *Alcoholic drinks include*: ale, beer, cider, lager, shandy, stout, Guinness®; alcopop; aquavit, Armagnac, bourbon, brandy, Calvados, Cognac, gin, gin-and-tonic, G&T, pink gin, sloe gin, rum, grog, rye, vodka, whisky, Scotch and soda, hot toddy; wine, red wine, vin rouge, vin rosé, white wine, vin blanc, champagne, *colloq.* bubbly, hock, mead, perry, *colloq.* vino, *colloq.* plonk, absinthe, advocaat, Benedictine, Chartreuse, black velvet, bloody Mary, Buck's fizz, Campari, cherry brandy, cocktail, Cointreau®, crème de menthe, daiquiri, eggnog, ginger wine, kirsch, Marsala, Martini®, ouzo, Pernod®, pina colada, port, punch, retsina, sake, sangria, schnapps, sherry, snowball, tequila, Tom Collins, vermouth. *See also* **wine**.

drinkable *adj*
clean, safe, fit to drink, potable

drinker *n*
hard/serious drinker, heavy drinker, drunk, drunkard, inebriate, dipsomaniac, imbiber
colloq. tippler; *slang* boozer, wino, lush, alkie, dipso, soak, piss artist, toper, tosspot
E3 abstainer, teetotaller

drip *v, n*
▶ *v* drop, dribble, trickle, leak, ooze, plop, drizzle, splash, sprinkle, weep, filter, percolate

▶ *n* **1** DROP, trickle, dribble, leak, splash, plop, bead, tear
2 WEAKLING, bore
colloq. wimp, softy, wet, ninny

drive *v, n*
▶ *v* **1** STEER, ride, travel (by car), go/come (by car), motor, be behind/at the wheel, be at the controls
2 TRANSPORT, take, convey, carry, move, send, run, chauffeur, give someone a lift, take someone somewhere
3 PROPEL, impel, direct, control, manage, operate, run, handle, hurl, press, thrust
4 FORCE, compel, impel, coerce, constrain, press, move, push, urge, spur, prod, herd, round up, dragoon, goad, guide, oblige, leave someone with no choice/option
5 MOTIVATE, force, compel, pressure, pressurize, impel, lead, prompt, actuate, incite, provoke, persuade, move, spur
6 STRIKE, hammer, knock, thump, dash, dig, sink, ram, thrust, plunge
7 OVERBURDEN, overwork, tax, overtax, work too hard, overdo it, burden
colloq. kill yourself
▷ **drive at** imply, allude to, intimate, mean, suggest, hint, have in mind, intend, refer to, signify, insinuate, indicate, aim at; *colloq.* get at
▶ *n* **1** EXCURSION, outing, journey, ride, run, trip, jaunt
colloq. spin, turn
2 AVENUE, driveway, road, roadway
3 ENERGY, enterprise, ambition, initiative, vigour, verve, motivation, determination, will, resolve, spirit, effort, action
formal tenacity
colloq. get-up-and-go, pizazz, zip; *slang* vim
4 CAMPAIGN, crusade, appeal, effort, action, fight, struggle, battle
colloq. push
5 POWER, thrust, surge, pressure, propulsion, transmission, propeller shaft
6 URGE, instinct, impulse, pressure, need, desire

drivel *n*
nonsense, rubbish, gibberish, gobbledygook, garbage
old use balderdash
colloq. bunkum, mumbo-jumbo, waffle, rot, poppycock, tripe, hogwash, claptrap, twaddle;
slang crap

driver *n*
motorist, motorcyclist, rider, chauffeur, cabbie, trucker

driving *adj*
compelling, forceful, vigorous, dynamic, energetic, forthright, heavy, violent, sweeping

drizzle *n, v*
▶ *n* mist, mizzle, (light) rain, spray, shower, mizzle
▶ *v* spit, spray, sprinkle, rain, spot, shower, mizzle

droll *adj*
bizarre, odd, queer, eccentric, peculiar, comical, amusing, humorous, ridiculous, laughable, ludicrous, funny, clownish, zany, farcical, waggish, whimsical, witty, comic, diverting, entertaining, jocular
formal risible

drone *v, n*
▶ *v* **1** HUM, buzz, purr, thrum, vibrate, whirr, drawl, chant, bombilate, bombinate
2 *the lecturer droned on and on*

go on and on, speak interminably, talk monotonously, intone
▶ *n* **1** HUM, buzz, purr, thrum, vibration, whirr, whirring, murmuring, chant
2 LAZY PERSON, idler, loafer, slacker, dreamer, layabout, parasite, leech, hanger-on
colloq. lazybones, sponger, scrounger

drool *v*
1 DRIBBLE, slobber, slaver, salivate, drivel, salivate, slaver, slobber, water at the mouth
2 *drool over the new baby*
dote, enthuse, gloat, gush, slobber over

droop *v*
1 HANG DOWN, dangle, sag, bend, wilt, stoop, bow, fall down, sink, drop, slump
2 LANGUISH, decline, flag, falter, slump, lose heart, wilt, wither, drop, faint, fall down, fade, slouch
E3 1 straighten **2** flourish, rise

drop *v, n*
▶ *v* **1** FALL, sink, decline, plunge, plummet, tumble, dive, descend, droop
2 LOWER, let fall, let go
3 DRIP, trickle, leak, dribble, plop
4 LOWER, decrease, lessen, weaken, diminish, decline, dwindle, slacken off, plummet, plunge, sink
5 ABANDON, give up, desert, reject, jilt, disown, walk out on
formal forsake, relinquish, repudiate, renounce
colloq. chuck, ditch, run out on, throw over
6 END, stop, finish, leave out, miss out, omit, exclude
formal cease, dispense with, discontinue, terminate, forego, relinquish, repudiate, renounce
colloq. quit
7 DISMISS, discharge, make redundant
colloq. sack, fire, turf out, boot out
E3 1 rise
▷ **drop back** fall behind, lag (behind), fall back; *formal* retreat
▷ **drop in** call (round), call by, come over, come round, visit, come by; *colloq.* pop in
▷ **drop off 1** FALL ASLEEP, drift off, go off, catnap; *colloq.* nod off, doze, snooze, have forty winks **2** DECLINE, fall off, plummet, decrease, dwindle, lessen diminish, slacken off, plummet, plunge, sink **3** DELIVER, set down, deposit, unload, hand in
E3 1 wake up **2** increase
▷ **drop out** withdraw, leave, give up, abandon; *formal* renounce, forsake; *colloq.* back out, cry off, quit
▷ **drop out of** back out of, withdraw from, leave, opt out, pull out, abandon; *formal* renounce, renege; *colloq.* cry off from, quit
▶ *n* **1** DROPLET, bead, tear, drip, bubble, blob, globule, trickle
formal goutte, globulet, spheroid, gutta
2 LITTLE, mouthful, sprinkle, bit, pinch, sip, nip, tot, trace, dab, splash
US tad
formal modicum
colloq. dash, spot, smidgen
3 DESCENT, fall, precipice, cliff, slope, chasm, abyss, plunge
formal dcclivity
4 DECLINE, falling-off, fall-off, lowering, downturn, decrease, reduction, cutback, slump, plunge, depreciation, devaluation, deterioration

dropout *n*
non-conformist, rebel, Bohemian, dissenter, hippie, loner, deviant
formal dissentient, malcontent, renegade

droppings *n*
excrement, dung, manure, ordure, spraint
technical excreta, stools
formal egesta, faeces

dross *n*
rubbish, remains, refuse, trash, waste, scum, debris, dregs, impurity, lees, slag
technical scoria

drought *n*
dryness, aridity, parchedness, dehydration, shortage, want
formal desiccation

drove *n*
herd, horde, gathering, crowd, multitude, swarm, throng, flock, pack, host, company, mob, press, crush

drown *v*
1 SUBMERGE, immerse, inundate, go under, flood, sink, deluge, engulf, drench
2 OVERWHELM, overpower, overcome, swamp, wipe out, extinguish

drowsiness *n*
sleepiness, tiredness, weariness, lethargy, sluggishness
formal oscitancy, somnolence, torpor
colloq. dopiness, doziness, grogginess,

drowsy *adj*
sleepy, tired, weary, lethargic, nodding, dreamy, dozy, yawning, half-asleep, hardly able to keep your eyes open
formal somnolent, torpid
colloq. dopey
E3 alert, awake

drubbing *n*
defeat, beating, flogging, pounding, pummelling, trouncing, walloping, whipping, hammering
colloq. clobbering, licking, thrashing

drudge *n, v*
▶ *n* toiler, menial, hack, labourer, toiler, servant, slave, factotum, worker, galley-slave, lackey
colloq. dogsbody, skivvy
▶ *v* plod, toil, work, slave, labour
colloq. plug away, grind, beaver, slog away, keep your nose to the grindstone, work your fingers to the bone
E3 idle, laze

drudgery *n*
labour, menial work, hack-work, slavery, sweat, sweated labour, toil, skivvying, chore
colloq. donkeywork, slog, grind

drug *n, v*
▶ *n* medication, medicine, remedy, potion, cure

Types of drug include: anaesthetic, analgesic, antibiotic, antidepressant, antihistamine, barbiturate, narcotic, opiate, hallucinogenic, sedative, steroid, stimulant, tranquillizer; chloroform, aspirin, codeine, paracetamol, morphine, penicillin, diazepam, Valium®, cortisone, insulin, digitalis, laudanum, quinine, progesterone, oestrogen, cannabis, marijuana, smack, LSD, acid, ecstasy, *slang* E, heroin, opium, cocaine, crack, *colloq.* dope, amphetamine, downer, *slang* speed.
See also **medicine**.

▶ *v* medicate, sedate, tranquillize, anaesthetize, make unconscious, dose, stupefy, deaden, numb
colloq. dope, knock out

drug addict *n*
colloq. junkie, user, dope-fiend; *slang* freak, head, coke-head, tripper, mainliner

drugged *adj*
stupefied
technical comatose
colloq. knocked out, high, spaced out, turned on, doped, zonked, on a trip; *slang* stoned

drum *v*
beat, pulsate, tap, throb, thrum, tattoo, reverberate, rap, knock
▷ **drum into** din into, drive home, hammer, harp on, instil, reiterate, inculcate
▷ **drum out** expel, discharge, dismiss; *colloq.* throw out
▷ **drum up** obtain, round up, collect, gather, summon, solicit, canvass, petition, attract, get

drunk *adj, n*
▶ *adj* under the influence, drunken
formal inebriated, intoxicated, crapulent
colloq. merry, tight, tipsy, tiddly, well-oiled, blotto, drunk as a lord/newt, blind drunk, roaring drunk, the worse for drink, soused, squiffy, happy, legless, plastered, sozzled, pickled, bibulous, woozy, one over the eight, under the table, bevvied, have had a few; *slang* stoned, tanked up, loaded, lit up, canned, paralytic, sloshed, smashed, pissed, stewed, bombed, wasted, wrecked
ᴇᴈ sober, temperate, abstinent, teetotal
▶ *n* drunkard, alcoholic, inebriated, drinker, hard drinker, heavy drinker, dipsomaniac
colloq. tippler; *slang* boozer, wino, lush, alkie, dipso, soak, piss artist, toper, sot, tosspot

drunkard *n*
drunk, alcoholic, inebriated, drinker, hard drinker, heavy drinker, dipsomaniac
colloq. tippler; *slang* boozer, wino, lush, alkie, dipso, soak, piss artist, toper, sot, tosspot

drunken *adj*
1 DRUNK
formal inebriate, intoxicated, crapulent
colloq. merry, tight, tipsy, tiddly, happy; *slang* boozy, stoned, loaded, lit up, sloshed, pissed, bombed
2 *a drunken party*
debauched, dissipated, riotous, intemperate, baccanalian
formal crapulent
ᴇᴈ **1** sober

drunkenness *n*
intemperance, alcoholism, hard/serious drinking, debauchery, dipsomania
formal inebriation, inebriety, insobriety, intoxication, crapulence
colloq. bibulousness, tipsiness
ᴇᴈ sobriety

dry *adj, v*
▶ *adj* **1** ARID, parched, scorched, thirsty, dehydrated, barren, unwatered, rainless, moistureless, torrid, shrivelled, withered, wilted
technical xeric
formal desiccated
colloq. dry as a bone
2 BORING, dull, dreary, tedious, monotonous, uninteresting, wearisome, flat

colloq. dry as dust
3 *dry humour*
witty, ironic, subtle, cynical, droll, deadpan, sarcastic, cutting, low-key, laconic
ᴇᴈ **1** wet, damp **2** interesting, imaginative
▶ *v* dehydrate, parch, scorch, drain, shrivel, wither, wilt
formal desiccate
ᴇᴈ soak, wet
▷ **dry up 1** FAIL, stop being productive, come to an end, disappear, stop, fade, die out **2** STOP TALKING, forget your lines, shut up, someone's mind goes blank

dryness *n*
aridity, aridness, drought, barrenness, dehydration, thirst, thirstiness
ᴇᴈ wetness

dual *adj*
double, twofold, duplicate, duplex, binary, combined, paired, coupled, twin, two-piece, matched

dub *v*
name, call, entitle, confer, designate, label, nickname, style, tag, term, christen
formal bestow

dubiety *n*
doubt, doubtfulness, indecision, uncertainty, misgiving, scepticism, suspicion, mistrust, qualm, hesitation
formal incertitude
ᴇᴈ certainty

dubious *adj*
1 DOUBTFUL, uncertain, undecided, unsure, wavering, vacillating, unsettled, suspicious, sceptical, hesitant, irresolute
2 QUESTIONABLE, debatable, unreliable, untrustworthy, ambiguous, suspect, suspicious, obscure
colloq. fishy, shady, iffy, shifty
ᴇᴈ **1** certain **2** trustworthy

duck *v*
1 CROUCH, stoop, bob, bend, bow down, drop, squat
2 AVOID, evade, shirk, shun, sidestep, steer clear of, elude
colloq. dodge, wriggle out of, worm your way out of
3 DIP, immerse, plunge, dunk, dive, submerge, douse, souse, wet, lower

duct *n*
pipe, tube, channel, conduit, passage, vessel, canal, funnel

ductile *adj*
amenable, biddable, flexible, plastic, malleable, manageable, pliable, pliant, tractable, manipulable, yielding
formal compliant
ᴇᴈ intractable; *formal* refractory

dud *n, adj*
▶ *n* failure, flop
colloq. washout
▶ *adj* broken, failed, valueless, worthless
formal inoperative, nugatory
colloq. bust, duff, kaput
ᴇᴈ working

due *adj, adv, n*
▶ *adj* **1** OWED, owing, payable, unpaid, outstanding, in arrears

2 RIGHTFUL, right, fitting, appropriate, proper, merited, deserved, justified, suitable, correct
3 ADEQUATE, enough, sufficient, ample, plenty of
formal requisite
4 EXPECTED, scheduled, anticipated, long-awaited, required
F3 1 paid **3** inadequate
▷ **due to** owing to, as a result of, caused by, because of
▶ *adv* exactly, direct(ly), precisely, straight
colloq. dead
▶ *n* **1** *give him his due*
rights, (just) deserts, merits, prerogative, privilege, birthright
colloq. come-uppance,
2 *pay dues*
charge(s), contribution, fee, membership fee, levy, subscription

duel *n*
affair of honour, combat, contest, fight, clash, struggle, battle, competition, rivalry, engagement, encounter

duffer *n*
bungler, blunderer, fool, idiot, ignoramus, oaf
colloq. bonehead, clod, clot, dolt, dimwit

dulcet *adj*
sweet, sweet-sounding, gentle, pleasant, melodious, harmonious, mellow, soothing, soft, agreeable
formal mellifluous

dull *adj, v*
▶ *adj* **1** BORING, uninteresting, unexciting, flat, dreary, monotonous, stereotyped, tedious, tiresome, wearisome, stultifying, uneventful, humdrum, unimaginative, pedestrian, dismal, lifeless, plain, bland, insipid, heavy, ponderous
colloq. dull as ditchwater
2 DARK, sombre, gloomy, drab, dreary, murky, indistinct, grey, dark, cloudy, lacklustre, matt, opaque, dim, overcast
3 UNINTELLIGENT, dense, dim, stupid, slow
colloq. dimwitted, thick, dumb, bird-brained, slow on the uptake
4 *dull weather*
overcast, grey, cloudy, dim, dark, leaden, dreary, sombre, gloomy
5 *feel dull*
sluggish, slow, inactive, inert, idle, heavy, lethargic
formal torpid
6 *a dull pain*
weak, faint, mild, troublesome, uncomfortable, distressing
7 *a dull sound/thud*
muted, indistinct, weak, feeble, muffled
8 BLUNT, unsharpened, edgeless
F3 1 interesting, exciting, lively **2** bright
3 intelligent, clever **4** fine, sunny **5** lively, energetic **6** sharp, intense, acute **7** sharp **8** sharp
▶ *v* **1** BLUNT, alleviate, moderate, lessen, reduce, decrease, diminish, relieve, soften, allay, assuage, tone down
formal mitigate
2 DEADEN, numb, paralyse, stupefy, drug, tranquillize
3 DISCOURAGE, dampen, subdue, sadden, dishearten, depress, deject
4 DIM, obscure, darken, fade, wash out

dullard *n*
idiot, imbecile, ignoramus, moron, oaf, simpleton, dunce

colloq. blockhead, bonehead, chump, clod, clot, dimwit, dolt, dope, dunderhead, nitwit, numskull,
F3 brain

dullness *n*
dreariness, emptiness, flatness, dryness, plainness, monotony, slowness, tedium, sluggishness
formal torpor, vacuity, vapidity
F3 excitement, interest, sharpness, brightness, clarity

duly *adv*
accordingly, appropriately, correctly, fitly, fittingly, properly, rightfully, suitably, sure enough, deservedly
formal befittingly, decorously

dumb *adj*
1 *deaf and dumb*
silent, mute, soundless, speechless, tongue-tied, inarticulate, without speech, at a loss for words, lost for words
colloq. mum; *slang* shtoom
2 STUPID, unintelligent, foolish, dense
colloq. dim-witted, thick, brainless, gormless

dumbfounded *adj*
astonished, amazed, astounded, overwhelmed, speechless, taken aback, startled, stunned, overcome, confounded, lost for words, staggered, confused, baffled, bewildered, dumb, nonplussed, paralysed
colloq. thrown, flabbergasted, bowled over, floored, gobsmacked, knocked for six

dummy *n, adj*
▶ *n* **1** COPY, duplicate, imitation, counterfeit, substitute, representation, reproduction, sample
2 MODEL, lay-figure, mannequin, figure, form
3 TEAT, pacifier
4 IDIOT, imbecile, fool, oaf
colloq. blockhead, chump, clot, dimwit, numskull, nitwit
▶ *adj* **1** ARTIFICIAL, fake, imitation, false, bogus, mock, sham
colloq. phoney
2 *a dummy run*
SIMULATED, practice, trial

dump *v, n*
▶ *v* **1** DEPOSIT, put down, place, drop, offload, throw down, let fall, fling down, unload, empty out, tip out, discharge, pour out, park
colloq. plonk, bung
2 GET RID OF, discard, scrap, throw away, throw out, dispose of, ditch, tip, jettison
colloq. chuck away
3 *he dumped his girlfriend*
leave, abandon, walk out on
formal forsake
colloq. ditch, chuck
▶ *n* **1** RUBBISH TIP, junkyard, rubbish heap, tip, scrapyard
2 HOVEL, slum, shack, shanty, mess
colloq. hole, joint, tip, pigsty
▷ **down in the dumps** sad, depressed, unhappy, melancholy, miserable, downhearted, dejected, downcast, dispirited, low; *colloq.* blue

dumpy *adj*
short, plump, stout, chubby, chunky, podgy, pudgy, squab, squat, stubby, tubby
F3 tall

dun *adj*
greyish-brown, dull, dingy, mud-coloured, mouse-coloured

dunce *n*
fool, idiot, imbecile
colloq. blockhead, bonehead, nincompoop, ninny, nitwit, numskull, twerp, twit, dimwit; *slang* wally, dipstick, nerd
🔁 brain, intellectual

dung *n*
excrement, animal waste, droppings, manure, ordure, spraint
formal faeces

dungeon *n*
cell, prison, jail, gaol, cage, lock-up, keep, oubliette, vault

dupe *v, n*
▶ *v* deceive, delude, fool, trick, outwit, cheat, hoax, swindle, take in, hoodwink, defraud
colloq. con, rip off, bamboozle
▶ *n* victim, fool, gull, pawn, puppet, instrument, simpleton
colloq. sucker, mug, push-over, fall guy, stooge

duplicate *v, adj, n*
▶ *v* copy, reproduce, repeat, do again, photocopy, Xerox®, fax, facsimile, double, clone, echo
formal replicate
▶ *adj* identical, matching, twin, twofold, corresponding, paired, matched
▶ *n* copy, replica, reproduction, model, photocopy, Xerox®, carbon (copy), match, mate, facsimile, fax, double, twin, clone, imitation, forgery
colloq. lookalike, (dead) ringer, spitting image

duplication *n*
repetition, copy(ing), photocopy(ing), reproduction, doubling, clone, cloning
formal dittography, gemination, replication

duplicity *n*
deceit, deception, dishonesty, falsehood, fraud, guile, hypocrisy, double-dealing, treachery, betrayal, artifice, chicanery
formal dissimulation, mendacity, perfidy

durability *n*
permanence, imperishability, persistence, stability, strength, endurance, constancy, lastingness
🔁 fragility, impermanence, weakness
formal durableness, longevity

durable *adj*
lasting, enduring, long-lasting, abiding, hard-wearing, heavy-duty, reinforced, strong, solid, sturdy, tough, robust, unchanging, unfading, substantial, sound, reliable, dependable, stable, resistant, persistent, persisting, constant, permanent, firm, fixed, fast
🔁 changeable, perishable, weak, fragile

duration *n*
time, time span, time scale, extent, continuation, continuance, perpetuation, prolongation, fullness, length, length of time, period, span, spell, stretch
🔁 shortening

duress *n*
constraint, coercion, compulsion, pressure, restraint, threat, force, enforcement, exaction
colloq. arm-twisting

during *conj*
at/in the time of, for the time of, in, throughout, in the course of, all the while

dusk *n*
twilight, sunset, nightfall, evening, sundown, gloaming, darkness, dark, gloom, shadows, shade
🔁 dawn, brightness

dusky *adj*
1 SHADOWY, dark, dim, gloomy, murky, cloudy, foggy, misty, hazy, twilit
formal crepuscular, tenebrous, fuliginous, subfusc
2 DARK-SKINNED, dark-coloured, dark-complexioned, swarthy, tawny, black, brown
🔁 1 bright 2 white

dust *n, v*
▶ *n* powder, particles, dirt, earth, soil, ground, clay, grit, grime, soot, smut
▶ *v* 1 CLEAN, wipe, brush, mop, burnish, polish, spray
2 SPRINKLE, powder, scatter, cover, spread

dust-up *n*
conflict, disagreement, quarrel, argument, disturbance, encounter, fight, fracas, brawl, brush, commotion, scuffle, skirmish, tussle
colloq. argy-bargy, punch-up, scrap, set-to

dusty *adj*
1 DIRTY, grubby, grimy, filthy, dust-covered, sooty
2 POWDERY, granular, crumbly, chalky, sandy
formal friable
🔁 1 clean 2 solid, hard

dutiful *adj*
obedient, respectful, conscientious, devoted, filial, reverential, deferential, submissive, thoughtful, considerate
formal compliant

duty *n*
1 OBLIGATION, responsibility, burden, onus, assignment, calling, charge, part, role, task, job, chore, business, function, work, office, service, commission, mission, requirement
2 OBEDIENCE, respect, loyalty, allegiance, faithfulness
formal fidelity
3 TAX, toll, tariff, levy, customs, excise, dues
▷ **off duty** not working, on holiday, off, off work, free, resting, inactive
▷ **on duty** at work, working, on call, engaged, busy, occupied, active; *colloq.* tied up

dwarf *n, adj, v*
▶ *n* 1 PERSON OF RESTRICTED GROWTH, midget, pygmy, Tom Thumb, Lilliputian
2 GNOME, goblin
▶ *adj* miniature, small, tiny, pocket, diminutive, petite, Lilliputian, baby, pygmy, stunted, undersized
colloq. mini
🔁 large
▶ *v* 1 STUNT, retard, check, arrest
formal atrophy
2 OVERSHADOW, tower over, dominate
colloq. stand head and shoulders above

dwell *v*
live, inhabit, stay, settle, populate, people, lodge, rest
formal reside, abide, be domiciled
colloq. hang out
▷ **dwell on** brood on, think about, meditate on, turn over in your mind, reflect on, mull over, harp on, linger over, elaborate, emphasize; *formal* expatiate, ruminate on
🔁 pass over

dweller   *n*
inhabitant, occupant, occupier, resident
formal denizen

dwelling   *n*
home, house, establishment, residence, quarters,
dwelling-house, lodge, lodging, cottage, hut, shanty,
tent
formal abode, domicile, habitation

dwindle   *v*
diminish, decrease, decline, become/grow less, lessen,
subside, ebb, fade, weaken, taper off, tail off, shrink,
fall, wane, waste away, die out, wither, shrivel, vanish,
disappear
colloq. peter out
E∃ increase, grow

dye   *n, v*
▶ *n* colour, colouring, agent, stain, wash, pigment,
tint, shade, hue, tinge
▶ *v* colour, tint, stain, shade, pigment, tinge, imbue
Related adjective: tinctorial

dyed-in-the-wool   *adj*
entrenched, inveterate, deep-rooted, die-hard,
established, long-standing, settled, fixed, hard-core,
hardened, inflexible, unchangeable, uncompromising,
unshakable, through and through, thorough,
confirmed, complete, card-carrying
E∃ superficial

dying   *adj*
passing, final, going, mortal, close/near to death, not
long for this world, at death's door, on your deathbed,
perishing, failing, fading, vanishing, ebbing
formal moribund
colloq. with one foot in the grave, on your last legs
E∃ reviving

dynamic   *adj*
forceful, powerful, active, strong, energetic, full of
energy, vigorous, high-powered, driving, effective,
self-starting, spirited, vital, lively, active, potent
colloq. go-ahead, magnetic, go-getting
E∃ inactive, apathetic

dynamism   *n*
energy, forcefulness, drive, initiative, liveliness, vigour,
enterprise
colloq. get-up-and-go, go, pep, pizzazz, push, vim,
zap, zip
E∃ apathy, inactivity, slowness

dynasty   *n*
house, line, succession, dominion, regime,
government, authority, rule, jurisdiction, empire,
sovereignty

dyspeptic   *adj*
bad-tempered, crabbed, crabby, crotchety, gloomy,
grouchy, indigested, peevish, short-tempered,
snappish, testy, touchy

E

each *adj, pron, adv*
▶ *adj* every, every single, every individual
▶ *pron* each one, each in their own way, each and every one
▶ *adv* apiece, individually, per capita, per head, per person, respectively, separately, singly

eager *adj*
1 ENTHUSIASTIC, keen, fervent, intent, earnest, wholehearted, zealous, impatient, avid, ardent, diligent
2 LONGING, yearning, anxious, keen, intent, wishing, greedy, thirsty, hungry
🗲 **1** unenthusiastic, indifferent, reluctant

eagerly *adv*
keenly, enthusiastically, fervently, intently, earnestly, wholeheartedly, impatiently, ardently, avidly, zealously, greedily
🗲 apathetically, listlessly

eagerness *n*
keenness, enthusiasm, fervency, fervour, intentness, earnestness, wholeheartedness, impatience, ardour, avidity, impetuosity, zeal, longing, yearning, greediness, hunger, thirst
formal fervidity
🗲 apathy, disinterest

ear *n*
1 ATTENTION, heed, notice, regard, attentiveness
2 *an ear for language*
perception, sensitivity, discrimination, appreciation, hearing, skill, ability, taste
▷ **play it by ear** ad-lib, extemporize, improvise; *colloq.* take things as they come, think on your feet
Related adjectives: aural, auricular, otic

> *Parts of the ear include*: anvil (incus), auditory canal, auditory nerve, auricle, cochlea, concha, eardrum, eustachian tube, hammer (malleus), helix, labyrinth, lobe, oval window, pinna, round window, semicircular canal, stirrup (stapes), tragus, tympanum, vestibular nerve, vestibule.

early *adj, adv*
▶ *adj* **1** *early symptoms/stages*
forward, advanced, premature, untimely, undeveloped, precocious, first, initial, opening
2 *early theatre*
primitive, ancient
technical autochthonous
formal primeval, primordial
▶ *adv* **1** *early in the day*
in the (early) morning, at dawn, at daybreak
2 AHEAD OF TIME, ahead of schedule, in good time, beforehand, before the usual/arranged/expected time, with time to spare, in advance, too soon, prematurely
🗲 **1** late

earmark *v*
set aside, put aside, designate, allocate, keep back, reserve, label, mark out, tag

earn *v*
1 *earn a good salary*
receive, be/get paid, obtain, make, get, draw, clear, gain, realize, gross, net, collect, pocket, take home, reap
colloq. bring in, pull in
2 *earn your reputation*
deserve, merit, be owed, be someone's by right, warrant, win, rate, obtain, secure, attain, achieve
🗲 **1** spend, lose

earnest¹ *adj*
1 SERIOUS, sincere, solemn, grave, heartfelt, intense, dedicated, committed, thoughtful, zealous
formal assiduous
2 RESOLUTE, devoted, ardent, conscientious, intent, keen, fervent, firm, fixed, eager, enthusiastic, steady
🗲 **1** frivolous, flippant **2** apathetic
▷ **in earnest 1** SERIOUSLY, resolutely, ardently, conscientiously, intently, steadily, wholeheartedly, passionately **2** SINCERE, genuine, serious, not joking
🗲 **2** in jest, as a joke

earnest² *n*
the earnest of heavenly gifts
deposit, down payment, guarantee, pledge, token, security, assurance, determination, promise, resolution, seriousness, sincerity, truth

earnestly *adv*
seriously, sincerely, intently, resolutely, firmly, keenly, eagerly, fervently, warmly, zealously
🗲 flippantly, listlessly

earnestness *n*
seriousness, sincerity, gravity, purposefulness, resolution, intentness, determination, ardour, devotion, eagerness, enthusiasm, fervency, fervour, zeal, keenness, passion, vehemence, warmth
🗲 apathy, flippancy

earnings *n*
pay, income, salary, wages, profits, take home pay, net pay, gross pay, gain, proceeds, reward, receipts, return, revenue, fee, remuneration, honorarium, stipend
formal emolument
🗲 expenditure, outgoings

earth *n*
1 WORLD, planet, globe, sphere, orb
Related adjectives: terrestrial, telluric
2 LAND, ground, soil, turf, clay, loam, sod, humus, dirt

earthenware *n*
pottery, ceramics, crockery, stoneware, pots

earthly *adj*
1 *our earthly life*
material, physical, human, worldly, mortal, mundane, fleshly, secular, sensual, materialistic, profane, temporal
formal terrestrial, tellurian, telluric
2 *no earthly explanation*
possible, likely, imaginable, conceivable, slightest, feasible
F≡ **1** spiritual, heavenly

earthquake *n*
earth-tremor, tremor, quake, seism, shake, upheaval, aftershock
Related adjectives: seismic, seismal, terremotive

earthy *adj*
crude, coarse, rude, vulgar, bawdy, rough, ribald, robust, down-to-earth, natural, unsophisticated, uninhibited
formal indecorous
colloq. raunchy, blue
F≡ refined, modest, inhibited

ease *n, v*
▶ *n* **1** FACILITY, effortlessness, skilfulness, deftness, adroitness, dexterity, naturalness, cleverness
2 COMFORT, contentment, enjoyment, peace, affluence, prosperity, wealth, leisure, relaxation, rest, quiet, happiness, lap of luxury
formal repose, opulence
colloq. bed of roses, easy street, life of Riley
F≡ **1** difficulty **2** discomfort
▷ **at ease** relaxed, natural, composed, calm, secure, at home, comfortable
▶ *v* **1** *ease the pain*
alleviate, moderate, grow/become less, lessen, reduce, diminish, lighten, relieve, relent, allay, assuage, relax, comfort, calm, soothe, facilitate, smooth, quieten, salve
formal mitigate, abate, ameliorate, palliate
2 *ease it into position*
inch, steer, edge, slide, manoeuvre, guide
F≡ **1** aggravate, intensify, worsen
▷ **ease off** decrease, become less, die away, die down, diminish, moderate, relent, slacken, subside, wane; *formal* abate
F≡ increase

easily *adv*
1 EFFORTLESSLY, comfortably, readily, simply, fluently, straightforwardly
2 *easily the best*
BY FAR, undoubtedly, indisputably, definitely, certainly, doubtlessly, clearly, far and away, undeniably, simply, surely, probably, well
F≡ **1** laboriously

easy *adj*
1 SIMPLE, effortless, uncomplicated, undemanding, straightforward, foolproof, manageable, painless, natural
colloq. cushy, a cinch, a doddle, a piece of cake, a pushover, easy as ABC, child's play, like falling off a log
2 RELAXED, carefree, easy-going, comfortable, informal, calm, natural, leisurely, casual, unforced
colloq. laid-back
F≡ **1** difficult, hard, demanding, exacting **2** tense, uneasy

easy-going *adj*
relaxed, tolerant, lenient, amenable, undemanding, carefree, nonchalant, calm, even-tempered, serene,

placid
formal insouciant, imperturbable
colloq. laid-back, happy-go-lucky
F≡ strict, intolerant, critical

eat *v*
1 CONSUME, feed, swallow, devour, chew, munch, have a snack, breakfast, lunch, dine, gulp down, bolt down, gobble
formal ingest, partake of
colloq. scoff, put away, wolf down, tuck into, polish off, graze
2 CORRODE, erode, wear away, decay, rot, crumble, dissolve, undermine

eatable *adj*
edible, palatable, good, wholesome, digestible
formal comestible
F≡ inedible, unpalatable

⚠ **eatable** or **edible** ?
If something is *edible,* it is by nature safe or good to eat, whereas if it is *eatable,* it is in a condition that makes it possible to eat it (whether or not it is safe to do so). Poisonous mushrooms are *eatable* but they are not *edible,* while a bag of flour is perfectly *edible* but would scarcely be *eatable.*
---

eavesdrop *v*
listen in, spy, overhear, monitor
colloq. snoop, tap, bug

eavesdropper *n*
listener, monitor, spy
colloq. snoop, snooper

ebb *v, n*
▶ *v* **1** *the tide ebbed*
fall, fall back, flow back, go out, recede
formal retrocede
2 *his confidence ebbed away*
decline, decrease, diminish, drop, dwindle, flag, weaken, deteriorate, decay, degenerate, fade away, shrink, sink, slacken, subside, recede, lessen, wane
formal abate
colloq. peter out
F≡ **1** rise **2** increase, rise
▶ *n* **1** *at ebb tide*
low tide, low water, ebb tide, fall, going out, flowing-back, retreat
2 *her health is at a low ebb*
decline, decrease, drop, decay, lagging, lessening, deterioration, degeneration, slackening, weakening, subsidence, wane, waning, dwindling
F≡ **1** rise, flow **2** increase

ebony *adj*
black, dark, jet, jet-black, jetty, sable, sooty

ebullience *n*
exhilaration, effusiveness, enthusiasm, excitement, exuberance, brightness, buoyancy, elation, vivacity, high spirits, breeziness, zest
colloq. chirpiness
F≡ apathy, dullness, lifelessness

ebullient *adj*
exhilarated, effusive, enthusiastic, excited, exuberant, bright, buoyant, elated, gushing, vivacious, effervescent, breezy, irrepressible, zestful
colloq. chirpy
F≡ apathetic, dull, lifeless

eccentric *adj, n*
▶ *adj* odd, peculiar, abnormal, unconventional, strange, quirky, weird, queer, outlandish, idiosyncratic, bizarre, freakish, erratic, singular
formal aberrant
colloq. way-out, wacky, dotty, off-beat, nutty, loony, loopy, *US* kooky
🔁 conventional, orthodox, normal
▶ *n* nonconformist, oddity
colloq. oddball, crank, freak, character, case, nut, nutter, weirdo, crackpot, *US* kook, odd fish, square peg in a round hole, fish out of water; *slang* geek

eccentricity *n*
unconventionality, strangeness, peculiarity, nonconformity, abnormality, oddity, bizarreness, weirdness, idiosyncrasy, singularity, quirk, freakishness, anomaly
formal aberration, capriciousness
🔁 conventionality, ordinariness

ecclesiastic *n*
churchman, churchwoman, cleric, clergyman, clergywoman, man/woman of God, man/woman of the cloth, minister, priest, reverend, father, vicar, pastor, padre, parson, rector, canon, dean, deacon, deaconess, chaplain, curate, presbyter

ecclesiastical *adj*
church, churchly, religious, clerical, priestly, holy, divine, spiritual, pastoral
formal sacerdotal
🔁 secular, temporal

echelon *n*
level, rank, grade, rung, tier, degree, position, place, status

echo *n, v*
▶ *n* 1 REVERBERATION, ringing, resounding, reiteration, repetition, reflection
2 IMITATION, copy, reproduction, reflection, mirror image, image, parallel, repeat, clone, duplicate
3 REMINDER, memory, remembrance, allusion, hint, trace
formal evocation
Related adjective: phonocamptic
▶ *v* 1 REVERBERATE, resound, repeat, reflect, reiterate, ring
2 IMITATE, copy, reproduce, mirror, reflect, resemble, mimic, repeat, parallel, parrot

éclat *n*
effect, glory, brilliance, lustre, ostentation, show, distinction, display, success, splendour, acclaim, renown, acclamation, applause, approval, fame, celebrity
formal plaudits
🔁 disapproval, dullness

eclectic *adj*
diverse, wide-ranging, many-sided, catholic, broad, comprehensive, diversified, general, all-embracing, liberal, varied, selective
formal heterogeneous, multifarious
🔁 narrow, one-sided, exclusive

eclipse *v, n*
▶ *v* 1 BLOT OUT, obscure, cloud, cover, conceal, veil, shroud, darken, dim, cast a shadow over
2 OUTDO, overshadow, outshine, surpass, exceed, transcend, excel, dwarf, put into the shade, leave someone standing
colloq. run rings around

▶ *n* 1 OVERSHADOWING, blotting-out, darkening, concealing, covering, veiling, shading, dimming
formal obscuration
2 DECLINE, failure, fall, loss, ebb, weakening

economic *adj*
1 COMMERCIAL, business, industrial, trade
2 FINANCIAL, budgetary, fiscal, monetary
3 PROFITABLE, profit-making, money-making, productive, cost-effective, viable, remunerative

⚠ **economic** or **economical** ?
Economic means 'relating to economics or the economy of a country': *economic history; the country's economic future*. It also means 'giving an adequate profit or fair return', as in *We must charge an economic rent/price*. *Economical* means 'thrifty', 'not wasteful, expensive, or extravagant': *This car is very economical on petrol; the economical use of limited supplies*.

economical *adj*
1 THRIFTY, careful, saving, sparing, frugal, scrimping, skimping
formal prudent, parsimonious
2 CHEAP, inexpensive, low-priced, low-cost, low-budget, reasonable, cost-effective, budget, modest, efficient
🔁 1 wasteful 2 expensive, uneconomical

economize *v*
save, cut back, budget, cut expenditure, use less, buy cheaply, keep down costs, live on the cheap, cut costs, be economical, scrimp and save
formal retrench
colloq. tighten your belt, cut corners, cut your coat according to your cloth
🔁 waste, squander

economy *n*
1 *the country's economy*
system of wealth, financial state, financial resources, financial system, financial organization, business resources
2 THRIFT, saving, restraint, carefulness, care, frugality, parsimony, providence, husbandry, scrimping, skimping
formal prudence
🔁 2 extravagance

ecstasy *n*
delight, rapture, bliss, elation, joy, jubilation, euphoria, frenzy, exultation, fervour, transports of delight, pleasure
🔁 misery, torment

ecstatic *adj*
elated, blissful, joyful, jubilant, rapturous, enraptured, overjoyed, euphoric, delirious, frenzied, fervent
formal rhapsodic
colloq. jumping for joy, on cloud nine, in seventh heaven, over the moon, tickled pink, high as a kite
🔁 downcast

eddy *n, v*
▶ *n* whirlpool, swirl, swirling, vortex, twist, maelstrom
▶ *v* swirl, whirl

edge *n, v*
▶ *n* 1 BORDER, rim, boundary, frontier, limit, brim, threshold, brink, fringe, margin, outline, outer limit, side, verge, line, extremity, perimeter, periphery, lip

2 ADVANTAGE, superiority, force, dominance
formal ascendancy
colloq. upper hand, whip hand
3 SHARPNESS, acuteness, keenness, incisiveness, severity, zest, bite, sting
formal pungency, acerbity, causticity, trenchancy
▷ **on edge** nervous, tense, anxious, apprehensive, ill at ease, keyed-up, touchy, edgy, irritable;
colloq. uptight, nervy
E3 calm, at ease
▶ *v* creep, crawl, inch, ease, steal, sidle, elbow, worm, pick your way

edgy *adj*
on edge, nervous, tense, anxious, ill at ease, keyed-up, touchy, irritable
colloq. uptight, nervy
E3 calm, at ease

edible *adj*
eatable, fit to eat, palatable, digestible, wholesome, good, harmless
formal comestible
E3 inedible

⚠ **edible** or **eatable** ? *See panel at* **eatable**.

edict *n*
command, order, proclamation, law, decree, regulation, pronouncement, rule, ruling, act, mandate, statute, fiat, injunction, manifesto, pronunciamento, ukase

edification *n*
instruction, improvement, enlightenment, guidance, education, teaching, coaching, upbuilding, elevation, uplifting

edifice *n*
building, construction, structure, erection

edify *v*
instruct, build up, improve, enlighten, inform, guide, educate, tutor, nurture, teach, school, coach, elevate, uplift

edit *v*
1 *edit a text*
correct, revise, rewrite, rephrase, reorder, rearrange, adapt, modify, check, compile, rephrase, select, polish, annotate, blue pencil
formal emend, redact
2 *edit a newspaper*
be in charge of, direct, head (up), be responsible for

edition *n*
copy, volume, impression, printing, publication, issue, version, number

educable *adj*
instructible, teachable, trainable
E3 ineducable

educate *v*
teach, train, instruct, tutor, coach, school, inform, cultivate, edify, enlighten, drill, improve, prepare, prime, discipline, indoctrinate, develop
formal inculcate

educated *adj*
learned, taught, schooled, literate, trained, knowledgeable, enlightened, informed, instructed, lettered, well-read, cultured, civilized, cultivated, wise, tutored, refined, well-bred
formal erudite, sagacious

colloq. brainy, all there, clever-clever
E3 uneducated, uncultured

education *n*
teaching, training, schooling, tuition, tutoring, coaching, guidance, instruction, informing, drilling, cultivation, culture, letters, scholarship, improvement, enlightenment, edification, knowledge, nurture, preparation, fostering, upbringing, development, indoctrination
formal inculcation

educational *adj*
academic, learning, teaching, cultural, edifying, enlightening, educative, improving, informative, instructive
formal didactic, scholastic, pedagogic, pedagogical
E3 uninformative

Educational establishments include: kindergarten, nursery school, infant school, primary school, middle school, combined school, comprehensive school, secondary school, secondary modern, upper school, high school, grammar school, grant-maintained school, preparatory school, public school, private school, boarding-school, college, sixth-form college, college of further education, polytechnic, poly, city technical college, CTC, technical college, university, adult-education centre, academy, seminary, finishing school, business school, secretarial college, Sunday school, convent school, summer-school.

Educational terms include: adult education, assisted places scheme, A-level, (international) baccalaureate, board of governors, break time, bursar, campus, catchment area, certificate, classroom, coeducation, common entrance, course, course of studies, curriculum, degree, diploma, discipline, double-first, educational programme, eleven-plus, enrolment, examination, exercise book, final exam, finals, further education, GCSE (General Certificate of Secondary Education), governor, graduation, half-term, head boy, head girl, head teacher, higher education, homework, intake, invigilator, lecture, literacy, matriculation, matron, mixed-ability teaching, modular course, module, national curriculum, newly qualified teacher, NVQ (national vocational qualification), numeracy, O-level, opting out, parent governor, PTA (parent teacher association), playground, playtime, prefect, primary education, proctor, professor, pupil, quadrangle, qualification, refresher course, register, report, scholarship, school term, secondary education, special education, statemented, streaming, student, student grant, student loan, study, subject, syllabus, teacher, teacher training, test paper, textbook, thesis, timetable, truancy, university entrance, work experience, YTS (Youth Training Scheme).

educative *adj*
instructive, improving, informative, edifying, educational, enlightening
formal catechetic, catechismal, catechistic(al), didactic
E3 uninformative

educator *n*
instructor, teacher, tutor, schoolteacher, schoolmaster, schoolmistress, educationalist, lecturer, professor, academic, trainer, coach
formal pedagogue

eerie adj
weird, strange, unnatural, unearthly, mysterious, uncanny, ghostly, frightening, scaring, scary, bloodcurdling
colloq. spooky, creepy, spine-chilling

efface v
remove, destroy, delete, rub out, wipe out, cancel, eliminate, eradicate, obliterate, erase, blank out, blot out, cross out
formal excise, expunge, extirpate

effect n, v
▶ *n* 1 OUTCOME, result, conclusion, consequence, upshot, fruit, impact, aftermath, issue
2 POWER, force, impact, impression, strength, influence
formal efficacy
3 MEANING, significance, sense, drift, tenor
formal import, purport
4 *personal effects*
belongings, possessions, property, goods, movables, paraphernalia, baggage, luggage, things, trappings
formal chattels, accoutrements
colloq. gear, things, stuff
▷ **in effect** in fact, actually, in actual fact, really, in reality, in truth, to all intents and purposes, in practice, for all practical purposes, essentially, effectively, virtually
▷ **take effect** be effective, become operative, come into force, come into operation, be implemented, become valid, begin, work, produce results, function
▶ *v* cause, execute, bring about, carry out, create, achieve, accomplish, perform, produce, make, initiate, give rise to, fulfil, complete
formal generate, effectuate

⚠ effect or affect ? *See panel at* **affect**.

effective adj
1 EFFICIENT, productive, adequate, capable, useful, successful
formal efficacious
2 OPERATIVE, in force, functioning, valid, current, active
3 STRIKING, impressive, forceful, powerful, exciting, attractive, persuasive, convincing, potent, telling
formal cogent
4 ACTUAL, practical, virtual, essential
F3 1 ineffective, powerless 4 theoretical

⚠ **effective** or **effectual** ?
Effective has a number of meanings: 'producing, or likely to produce, the intended result': *Aspirin is effective against many types of pain*; 'impressive', 'powerful': *He's a very effective speaker*; 'in operation, in force': *The new regulations become effective at midnight*; 'in reality, even if not in theory': *Although not the king, he was the effective ruler of the country for twenty years. Effectual* puts more emphasis on the actual achievement of the desired result than *effective* does. If the police take *effective* measures to combat the rising crime rate, these measures have the desired effect, or are expected to, whereas if the police take *effectual measures,* there is no doubt that these measures are succeeding in reducing the crime rate.

effectiveness n
success, strength, force, influence, use, power, ability, capability, efficiency, validity, vigour, weight
formal cogency, efficacy, potency

colloq. clout
F3 ineffectiveness, uselessness

effectual adj
1 *an effectual plan*
successful, effective, useful, capable, influential, serviceable, operative, sound, powerful, productive, forcible
2 *effectual contracts*
binding, authoritative, lawful, legal, valid
F3 1 ineffective, useless

effeminate adj
unmanly, womanly, womanish, feminine, delicate
colloq. sissy, wimpish
F3 manly

effervesce v
1 *mineral water effervescing*
sparkle, bubble, fizz, boil, foam, froth, ferment
2 *effervescing with conversation*
be lively, be vivacious, be animated, be exhilarated
formal ebullient

effervescence n
1 SPARKLE, bubbles, bubbling, fizz, foam, foaming, froth, frothing, ferment, fermentation
2 LIVELINESS, vivacity, vitality, animation, buoyancy, enthusiasm, high spirits, excitedness, excitement, exhilaration, exuberance
formal ebullience
colloq. vim, zing, zip

effervescent adj
1 BUBBLY, bubbling, sparkling, fizzy, fizzing, frothy, carbonated, foaming, fermenting
2 LIVELY, vivacious, animated, buoyant, exhilarated, enthusiastic, exuberant, sparkling, excited, vital
formal ebullient
F3 1 flat 2 dull

effete adj
weak, feeble, enfeebled, exhausted, drained, fruitless, unfruitful, unproductive, played out, spent, sterile, tired out, worn out, spoiled, used up, unprolific, wasted, decayed, barren, corrupt, debased, decrepit, degenerate, decadent
formal debilitated, enervated, ineffectual, infecund
F3 vigorous

efficacious adj
effective, productive, capable, useful, successful, competent, powerful, potent, strong, adequate, sufficient, active, effectual, operative
F3 ineffective, useless

efficacy n
effectiveness, effect, usefulness, use, success, power, energy, force, influence, potency, strength, capability, ability, competence, virtue
F3 ineffectiveness, uselessness

efficiency n
effectiveness, competence, proficiency, skill, expertise, skilfulness, capability, ability, productivity, organization
F3 inefficiency, incompetence

efficient adj
effective, competent, proficient, skilful, capable, able, productive, organized, well-organized, well-ordered, streamlined, rationalized, businesslike, workmanlike, powerful, well-run, well-conducted, expert
F3 inefficient, incompetent

effigy *n*
figure, statue, carving, representation, likeness, picture, portrait, image, icon, idol, dummy, guy

effluent *n*
waste, discharge, sewage, emission, outflow, pollutant, pollution
formal effluence, effluvium, efflux, emanation, exhalation

effort *n*
1 EXERTION, strain, application, struggle, sweat, trouble, energy, hard work, power, force, stress, toil, striving, pains, labour, muscle power
formal travail
colloq. elbow grease, sweat of your brow, beef, muscles
2 ATTEMPT, try, endeavour
colloq. go, shot, stab, crack, bash, whirl
3 ACHIEVEMENT, accomplishment, feat, attainment, exploit, production, creation, deed, product, result, work, opus

effortless *adj*
easy, simple, undemanding, facile, painless, uncomplicated, unexacting, straightforward, smooth
🗲 difficult, complicated, exacting, demanding

effrontery *n*
audacity, impertinence, insolence, impudence, temerity, boldness, brazenness, cheekiness, gall, nerve, presumption, disrespect, arrogance, brashness
colloq. cheek, nerve, face, brass, lip, chutzpah
🗲 respect, timidity

effulgent *adj*
brilliant, radiant, shining, glowing, splendid, glorious
formal resplendent, refulgent, incandescent

effusion *n*
outpouring, outburst, outflow, gush, discharge, emission, stream, shedding
formal effluence, efflux, voidance

effusive *adj*
fulsome, gushing, unrestrained, unreserved, expansive, demonstrative, profuse, overflowing, enthusiastic, exuberant, extravagant, lavish, talkative, voluble, lyrical
formal ebullient, rhapsodic
colloq. gabby, gassy, over the top, OTT, all mouth, big-mouthed
🗲 reserved, restrained

egg *v*
▷ **egg on** encourage, incite, push, urge, drive, excite, stimulate, spur, prompt, coax, talk into, goad, prod, prick; *formal* exhort
🗲 discourage

egghead *n*
boffin, brain, intellect, intellectual, academic, thinker, scholar, bookworm, genius, Einstein
colloq. know-all, know-it-all

ego *n*
self, (sense of) identity, self-esteem, self-importance, self-confidence, self-image, self-worth

egoism *n*
self-interest, self-centredness, self-importance, self-absorption, self-love, self-regard, self-seeking, selfishness, narcissism, egocentricity, egomania, egotism, amour-propre
🗲 altruism

egoist *n*
self-seeker, narcissist, egotist, egomaniac

egoistic *adj*
self-absorbed, self-important, self-involved, self-centred, self-pleasing, self-seeking, narcissistic, egocentric, egoistical, egotistic, egotistical, egomaniacal
🗲 altruistic

egotism *n*
egoism, egomania, self-centredness, no thought for others, self-importance, egocentricity, selfishness, superiority, conceitedness, self-regard, self-love, self-conceit, narcissism, self-admiration, pride, boastfulness, vanity, snobbery
formal braggadocio
colloq. bigheadedness, swank, blowing your own trumpet; *US* blowing your own horn
🗲 humility

egotist *n*
boaster, bluffer, show-off, self-admirer, braggart, egoist, egomaniac, swaggerer, braggadocio
colloq. bighead, big mouth, smart alec, clever clogs, clever dick

egotistic *adj*
egoistic, egocentric, self-centred, selfish, self-important, self-admiring, narcissistic, conceited, superior, vain, proud, boasting, bragging
colloq. swollen-headed, bigheaded
🗲 humble

egregious *adj*
grievous, outrageous, scandalous, shocking, gross, rank, infamous, notorious, insufferable, intolerable, monstrous, flagrant, glaring, arrant, heinous
🗲 slight

egress *n*
exit, way out, outlet, vent, issue, exodus, emergence, leaving, departure, escape

ejaculate *v*
1 DISCHARGE, eject, spurt, emit, release, expel
colloq. come
2 EXCLAIM, call (out), blurt (out), cry (out), shout (out), yell, utter, scream

ejaculation *n*
1 *ejaculation of semen*
discharge, ejection, emission, spurt, release, expulsion, orgasm, climax
colloq. coming
2 EXCLAMATION, call, cry, scream, shout, yell, utterance

eject *v*
1 EMIT, expel, discharge, release, spout, spew, disgorge, evacuate, vomit
formal exude, excrete
2 OUST, evict, get rid of, throw out, drive out, turn out, expel, remove, banish, deport, dismiss, discharge, exile, kick out
colloq. fire, sack, boot out, turf out, chuck out, give someone their cards, show someone the door
3 BAIL OUT, propel, thrust out, throw out, get out

ejection *n*
eviction, expulsion, removal, banishment, dismissal, discharge, exile, deportation, ousting
colloq. firing, sacking, the boot, the sack

eke *v*
▷ **eke out** 1 *eke out supplies* make something

stretch, stretch, spin out, fill out, husband, economize on, be economical with, add to, increase, supplement; *colloq.* go easy with **2** *eke out a living* scrimp and save, scrape, scratch, get by, survive; *colloq.* live from hand to mouth, feel the pinch

elaborate *adj, v*
▶ *adj* **1** *elaborate plans*
detailed, complicated, complex, careful, thorough, exact, extensive, painstaking, precise, perfected, minute, laboured, studied
2 *elaborate designs*
intricate, complex, complicated, involved, ornamental, ornate, fancy, decorated, extravagant, ostentatious, showy, fussy, rococo
⊟ 2 simple, plain
▶ *v* amplify, develop, enlarge on, expand on, flesh out, polish, improve, refine, enhance, devise, explain
formal expatiate
⊟ précis, simplify

élan *n*
panache, liveliness, flair, flourish, style, spirit, verve, vigour, vivacity, animation, confidence, zest, dash, esprit
colloq. brio, oomph, pizzazz
⊟ apathy, lifelessness

elapse *v*
pass, lapse, go by, go on, slip away, slip by

elastic *adj*
1 PLIABLE, flexible, stretchable, stretchy, supple, resilient, yielding, springy, rubbery, pliant, plastic, bouncy, buoyant
2 ADAPTABLE, accommodating, flexible, tolerant, adjustable, fluid
formal compliant
colloq. easy
⊟ 1 rigid **2** inflexible

elasticity *n*
1 PLIABILITY, flexibility, resilience, stretch, stretchiness, springiness, suppleness, plasticity, bounce, buoyancy
colloq. give
2 ADAPTABILITY, flexibility, tolerance, adjustability
⊟ 1 rigidity **2** inflexibility

elated *adj*
exhilarated, excited, delighted, euphoric, ecstatic, rapturous, exultant, jubilant, overjoyed, joyful, blissful
formal joyous, rhapsodic
colloq. over the moon, on cloud nine
⊟ despondent, downcast

elation *n*
exhilaration, delight, transports of delight, euphoria, ecstasy, rapture, bliss, exultation, glee, high spirits, joy, joyfulness, jubilation
formal joyousness
⊟ depression, despondency

elbow *v*
jostle, nudge, push, bump, knock, crowd, shoulder
colloq. shove, barge

elbow-room *n*
space, room, breathing-space, play, scope, leeway, freedom, latitude, Lebensraum

elder *adj*
older, senior, first-born, ancient
⊟ younger

elderly *adj, n*
▶ *adj* aging, aged, old, grey-haired, hoary, senile
formal senescent
colloq. not as young as you were, not getting any younger, over the hill, long in the tooth, past it, not long for this world
⊟ young, youthful
▶ *n* old people, older generation, older adults, senior citizens, retired people, pensioners, old-age pensioners, OAPs
colloq. oldies, wrinklies, has-beens; *slang* fossils

eldest *adj*
first, first-born, oldest
⊟ youngest

elect *v, adj*
▶ *v* choose, pick, opt for, select, vote for, cast a vote, go to the polls, decide on, prefer, adopt, designate, appoint, determine
colloq. plump for
▶ *adj* *the elect; the president-elect*
choice, elite, chosen, designated, designate, picked, prospective, selected, to be, preferred, hand-picked

election *n*
choice, selection, vote, voting, ballot, poll, hustings, referendum, appointment, determination, decision, preference, choosing, picking

elector *n*
voter, selector, constituent, electorate

electric *adj*
1 *an electric light*
electric-powered, mains-operated, battery-operated, rechargeable, cordless, powered, live
2 *the atmosphere was electric*
electrifying, exciting, stimulating, thrilling, startling, charged, dynamic, stirring, tense, rousing
⊟ 2 unexciting, flat

electrical components

Types of electrical components and devices include: adaptor, ammeter, armature, battery, bayonet fitting, cable, ceiling rose, circuit breaker, conduit, continuity tester, copper conductor, dimmer switch, dry-cell battery, earthed plug, electrical screwdriver, electricity meter, extension lead, fluorescent tube, fuse, fusebox, fuse carrier, high voltage tester, insulating tape, lampholder, light bulb, multimeter, neon lamp, socket, test lamp, three-core cable, three-pin plug, transducer, transformer, two-pin plug, universal test meter, voltage doubler, wire strippers.

electricity and electronic terms

Electricity and electronic terms include: alternating current (AC), alternator, amp, ampere, amplifier, analogue signal, anode, band-pass filter, battery, bioelectricity, capacitance, capacitor, cathode, cathode-ray tube, cell, commutator, condenser, conductivity, coulomb, digital signal, diode, direct current (DC), Dolby (system), dynamo, eddy current, electrode, electrolyte, electromagnet, electron tube, farad, Faraday cage, Foucault current, frequency modulation, galvanic, galvanometer, generator, grid system, henry, impedance, induced current, inductance, integrated circuit, isoelectric, isoelectronic, logic gate, loudspeaker, microchip, mutual induction, ohm, optoelectronics, oscillator, oscilloscope, piezoelectricity, polarity, power station, reactance, resistance, resistor, rheostat, semiconductor, siemens, silicon chip, solenoid, solid state circuit, static electricity, step-down transformer, superconductivity, switch, thermionics, thermistor, thyristor, transformer, transistor, triode, truth table, turboalternator, tweeter, valve, volt, voltaic, voltage amplifier, watt, Wheatstone bridge, woofer.

electrify *v*
thrill, excite, shock, charge, invigorate, animate, stimulate, stir, rouse, fire, jolt, galvanize, amaze, astonish, astound, stagger
F3 bore

elegance *n*
style, chic, fashionableness, sophistication, smartness, refinement, polish, beauty, dignity, distinction, grace, gracefulness, discernment, taste, gentility, politeness, tastefulness, poise, exquisiteness, grandeur, luxury, sumptuousness
formal propriety
F3 inelegance

elegant *adj*
stylish, chic, fashionable, modish, smart, refined, polished, cultivated, genteel, charming, sophisticated, smooth, tasteful, lovely, fine, exquisite, beautiful, cultured, graceful, handsome, delicate, neat, artistic
F3 inelegant, unrefined, unfashionable

elegiac *adj*
lamenting, funereal, mournful, doleful, melancholic, sad, plaintive, valedictory, keening
formal threnetic, threnetical, threnodial, threnodic
F3 happy

elegy *n*
dirge, lament, requiem, funeral poem, funeral song, plaint
formal threnody, threnode
Related adjectives: epicedial, epicedian

element *n*
1 *the elements of our discussion*
factor, component, constituent, ingredient, member, part, piece, fragment, feature, strand
2 *the elements of a subject*
BASICS, foundations, fundamentals, principles, rudiments, essentials
3 *an element of truth*
small amount, grain, trace, touch, hint, suspicion, soupçon
4 *the criminal element in society*
individual(s), group, faction, set, party, clique
5 *exposed to the elements*
weather, wind and rain, storms, climate, atmospheric conditions, atmospheric forces
F3 1 whole

elemental *adj*
basic, fundamental, natural, rudimentary, primitive, radical, immense, powerful, forceful, uncontrolled

elementary *adj*
basic, fundamental, rudimentary, principal, primary, clear, easy, introductory, straightforward, uncomplicated, simple
F3 advanced, complicated

elephantine *adj*
large, vast, immense, huge, enormous, massive, bulky, hulking, heavy, weighty, awkward, clumsy, lumbering

elevate *v*
1 LIFT, raise, hoist, uplift, heighten, intensify, magnify, exalt

colloq. hike up
2 PROMOTE, advance, exalt, aggrandize, refine, ennoble, upgrade
colloq. move up the ladder, put on a pedestal, kick upstairs
3 UPLIFT, rouse, boost, buoy up, brighten, cheer, gladden, give a lift to
F3 1 lower 2 downgrade 3 depress

elevated *adj*
1 IMPORTANT, great, lofty, exalted, grand, noble, dignified
2 *elevated thoughts*
advanced, lofty, exalted, grand, noble, dignified, moral
formal sublime
3 *elevated ground*
raised, lifted (up), rising, high, hoisted, uplifted

elevation *n*
1 RISE, promotion, advancement, preferment, upgrading, aggrandizement
colloq. step up the ladder, leg-up, go-getting
2 EXALTATION, loftiness, grandeur, eminence, nobility, dignity
formal sublimity
3 HEIGHT, altitude, tallness, hill, rise, mound, mount
F3 1 demotion 3 dip

elf *n*
fairy, sprite, imp, goblin, hobgoblin, gnome, brownie, leprechaun, troll, banshee, puck
Related adjectives: elfish, elfin, elfvan, elvish

elfin *adj*
small, petite, delicate, charming, elfish, elflike, frolicsome, sprightly, playful, impish, mischievous, puckish

elicit *v*
evoke, draw out, bring out, derive, extract, obtain, exact, extort, cause, wrest
formal call forth, educe
colloq. worm out

eligible *adj*
qualified, fit, fitting, appropriate, suitable, acceptable, worthy, proper, desirable
F3 ineligible

eliminate *v*
1 GET RID OF, remove, cut out, take out, exclude, delete, dispense with, put an end/a stop to, rub out, omit, reject, disregard, dispose of, drop, do away with, eradicate, expel, extinguish, stamp out
2 DEFEAT, conquer, beat, overwhelm
colloq. knock out, thrash, lick, hammer, annihilate
3 KILL, murder, do away with, exterminate
colloq. wipe out, liquidate, rub out, bump off, do in
F3 1 include, accept

elite *n, adj*
▶ *n* best, pick, cream, elect, aristocracy, upper classes, nobility, gentry, crème de la crème, establishment, high society
colloq. pick of the bunch, jet set
▶ *adj* choice, best, exclusive, selected, first-class, aristocratic, noble, upper-class

elixir *n*
cure-all, panacea, remedy, solution, mixture, concentrate, essence, extract, pith, potion, principle, quintessence, syrup, tincture, nostrum

elliptical *adj*
1 OVAL, egg-shaped, oviform, ovoid(al)
2 OBLIQUE, cryptic, obscure, ambiguous, incomprehensible, unfathomable, concise, concentrated, condensed, laconic, terse
formal abstruse, recondite
🖃 2 clear, direct

elocution *n*
delivery, articulation, diction, pronunciation, voice production, rhetoric, speech, utterance, phrasing
formal enunciation, oratory

elongate *v*
lengthen, extend, draw out, prolong, make longer, stretch
formal protract

elongated *adj*
lengthened, extended, prolonged, protracted, stretched, long

elope *v*
run off, run away, decamp, bolt, make off, abscond, flee, escape, slip away, steal away, leave, disappear
colloq. do a bunk

eloquence *n*
expressiveness, fluency, flow of words, expression, persuasiveness, articulateness, diction, facility, forcefulness, oratory, rhetoric
formal facundity
colloq. gift of the gab, blarney, gassiness
🖃 inarticulateness

eloquent *adj*
articulate, fluent, well-expressed, well-spoken, glib, expressive, vocal, voluble, persuasive, moving, forceful, graceful, plausible, stirring, effective, vivid
🖃 inarticulate, tongue-tied

elsewhere *adv*
somewhere else, in/to another place, not here, absent, removed, abroad
🖃 here, present

elucidate *v*
explain, clarify, make clear, clear up, interpret, spell out, simplify, state simply, illustrate, illuminate, unfold, throw/shed light on, fill in, exemplify, give an example
formal explicate, expound
🖃 confuse

elucidation *n*
explanation, clarification, comment, commentary, illumination, illustration, interpretation, footnote, gloss, annotation, marginalia
formal explication, exposition

elude *v*
1 AVOID, escape, evade, shirk, shake off, flee, get away from, give someone the slip, throw someone off the scent
formal circumvent
colloq. dodge, duck, slip through someone's fingers
2 PUZZLE, frustrate, baffle, confound, thwart, stump, foil

elusive *adj*
1 INDEFINABLE, difficult to describe, intangible, unanalysable, subtle, puzzling, baffling, deceptive, misleading, transient, transitory
2 EVASIVE, difficult to find, hard to catch, slippery, tricky
colloq. shifty, dodgy

emaciated *adj*
thin, gaunt, lean, haggard, drawn, wasted, anorexic, scrawny, skinny, skeletal, pinched, meagre
formal attenuated, cadaverous
colloq. thin as a rake, all skin and bone
🖃 plump, well-fed

emaciation *n*
thinness, gauntness, leanness, haggardness, scrawniness
formal atrophy
🖃 plumpness

emanate *v*
1 RADIATE, send out, emit, give out, give off, discharge
formal exhale
2 ORIGINATE, proceed, arise, derive, issue, spring, stem, flow, come, emerge

emanation *n*
discharge, emission, flow, effluent, effluence, radiation
formal effluvium, efflux, effluxion, effusion

emancipate *v*
free, liberate, release, set free, enfranchise, deliver, discharge, loose, set loose, unchain, untie, unshackle, unfetter, unyoke
formal manumit
🖃 enslave

emancipation *n*
liberation, freedom, setting free, release, deliverance, liberty, discharge, enfranchisement, unbinding, unfettering, unchaining
formal manumission
🖃 enslavement

emasculate *v*
1 CASTRATE, geld, neuter, spay
2 WEAKEN, impoverish, cripple, debilitate, soften
formal enervate
🖃 2 boost, vitalize

embalm *v*
preserve, mummify, store, lay out, enshrine, cherish, consecrate, conserve, treasure

embankment *n*
causeway, dam, rampart, levee, earthwork

embargo *n, v*
▶ *n* restriction, ban, prohibition, restraint, bar, barrier, impediment, check, hindrance, obstruction, blockage, stoppage, seizure
formal proscription, interdiction
▶ *v* restrict, ban, bar, prohibit, restrain, block, check, impede, obstruct, seize, stop
formal interdict, proscribe
🖃 allow

embark *v*
board (ship), go aboard, take ship
🖃 disembark
▷ **embark on** begin, start, commence, set about, launch into, undertake, venture into, enter (on), initiate, engage
🖃 complete, finish

embarrass *v*
make awkward/ashamed, disconcert, mortify, show up, discompose, fluster, humiliate, shame, distress, upset, confuse
formal discomfit, discountenance

embarrassed *adj*
awkward, uncomfortable, self-conscious, upset, confused, distressed, disconcerted, ashamed, shamed, guilty, shown up, humiliated, mortified, abashed
formal discomfited
colloq. sheepish
◨ unembarrassed

embarrassing *adj*
awkward, uncomfortable, disconcerting, distressing, upsetting, sensitive, mortifying, humiliating, shameful, shaming, tricky, compromising, painful
formal discomfiting, indelicate, discountenancing
colloq. touchy

embarrassment *n*
1 DISCOMPOSURE, self-consciousness, mortification, humiliation, shame, guilt, awkwardness, confusion, distress, bashfulness
formal chagrin, discomfiture
2 DIFFICULTY, constraint, predicament, distress, dilemma, mess, plight
colloq. fix, scrape, pickle
3 *an embarrassment of riches*
abundance, surplus, excess, superabundance
formal profusion

embassy *n*
consulate, legation, ministry, delegation, deputation, mission

embed *v*
implant, plant, fix, insert, root, set, sink, hammer, drive

embellish *v*
adorn, ornament, decorate, deck, dress up, beautify, gild, garnish, trim, festoon, elaborate, embroider, enrich, exaggerate, enhance, varnish, grace
formal bedeck, bespangle
◨ simplify; *formal* denude

embellishment *n*
adornment, ornament, ornamentation, decoration, elaboration, garnish, trimming, gilding, enrichment, enhancement, embroidery, exaggeration

embers *n*
ashes, cinders, charcoal, residue

embezzle *v*
steal, swindle, pilfer, rob,
formal appropriate, misappropriate, purloin, defalcate, peculate
colloq. filch, pinch, nab, nick, rip off, have your fingers/hand in the till

embezzlement *n*
pilfering, fraud, stealing, theft
formal appropriation, misappropriation, defalcation
colloq. filching, nabbing, nicking

embezzler *n*
cheat, fraud, thief, robber
formal defalcator, peculator
colloq. crook, diddler, con man

embittered *adj*
bitter, resentful, disaffected, sour, disillusioned, disenchanted, angry, exasperated, piqued, rankled

emblazon *v*
1 DECORATE, adorn, ornament, blazon, embellish, depict, colour, illuminate, paint
2 PROCLAIM, publicize, publish, extol, praise,

glorify, trumpet
formal laud

emblem *n*
symbol, sign, token, representation, logo, insignia, device, crest, mark, badge, figure, image

emblematic *adj*
representative, representing, symbolic, symbolical, figurative, emblematical

embodiment *n*
incarnation, personification, exemplification, expression, epitome, example, type, model, incorporation, realization, representation, concentration
formal manifestation

embody *v*
1 PERSONIFY, exemplify, represent, stand for, typify, symbolize, incorporate, express
formal manifest
2 INCLUDE, contain, integrate, incorporate, assimilate, collect, combine, bring together, take in

embolden *v*
encourage, inspire, make brave/bold, give courage to, invigorate, reassure, rouse, stimulate, stir, strengthen, vitalize, animate, fire, cheer, hearten, inflame, nerve
◨ dishearten

embrace *v, n*
▶ *v* 1 HUG, clasp, cuddle, hold, grasp, put/throw your arms around, take into your arms, squeeze
colloq. neck, canoodle, smooch
2 INCLUDE, encompass, incorporate, contain, cover, involve, take in, span
formal comprise
3 ACCEPT, take up, welcome, receive eagerly, receive wholeheartedly
formal espouse
colloq. take on board
▶ *n* hug, cuddle, hold, clasp, squeeze
colloq. clinch, necking, slap and tickle, smooch

embrocation *n*
cream, lotion, ointment, salve
formal epithem

embroider *v*
1 DECORATE, sew, stitch
2 EMBELLISH, enrich, exaggerate, colour, enhance, elaborate, dress up, garnish

embroidery *n*
fancywork, needlework, sewing, tapestry, tatting, needlepoint

Types of embroidery stitch include: backstitch, blanket, bullion, chain, chevron, cross, feather, fishbone, French knot, half-cross, herringbone, lazy-daisy, longstitch, long-and-short, moss, Oriental couching, Romanian couching, running, satin, stem, straight, Swiss darning, tent.

embroil *v*
involve, implicate, entangle, enmesh, mix up, catch up in, draw into, incriminate

embryo *n*
1 UNBORN CHILD, foetus
2 *the embryo of the plan*
nucleus, germ, beginning, root, rudiments, basics

embryonic *adj*
undeveloped, rudimentary, immature, beginning,

unformed, early, germinal, elementary, primary
formal incipient, inchoate
🔁 developed

emend *v*
correct, rectify, edit, revise, rewrite, polish, refine,
improve, alter, amend
formal redact

⚠ **emend** or **amend** ? *See panel at* **amend**.

emendation *n*
correction, editing, revision, rewriting, refinement,
improvement, alteration, amendment
formal corrigendum, rectification, redaction

emerge *v*
1 *emerge from the office*
come out, come forth, come into view, emanate, issue,
proceed, arise, rise, surface, appear, develop, turn up,
materialize
2 *the facts emerged*
become known, come out, come to light, appear,
transpire, turn out
colloq. crop up
🔁 **1** disappear

emergence *n*
appearance, rise, coming, dawn, development, arrival,
springing-up, unfolding, disclosure, issue
formal advent
🔁 disappearance

emergency *n, adj*
▶ *n* crisis, danger, accident, catastrophe, disaster,
calamity, difficulty, predicament, plight, pinch, strait,
dilemma, quandary
formal exigency
colloq. scrape, mess, pickle, fix, hot water
▶ *adj* alternative, back-up, reserve, spare, substitute,
extra, fall-back

emergent *adj*
budding, coming (out), developing, emerging,
embryonic, rising, independent
🔁 declining, disappearing

emetic *adj, n*
▶ *adj* emetical, vomitive, vomitory
▶ *n* vomit, vomitary, vomitive

emigrate *n*
migrate, move abroad, relocate, move, depart, leave
your home/native country, resettle

emigration *n*
moving abroad, migration, removal, departure,
exodus, journey, relocation, expatriation

eminence *n*
distinction, fame, pre-eminence, prominence,
renown, reputation, illustriousness, greatness,
importance, esteem, celebrity, notability, note,
prestige, dignity, rank

eminent *adj*
distinguished, famous, prominent, illustrious,
outstanding, notable, pre-eminent, prestigious,
celebrated, renowned, noteworthy, conspicuous,
esteemed, important, well-known, elevated,
respected, great, high-ranking, grand, superior
🔁 unknown, obscure, unimportant

eminently *adv*
highly, well, very, greatly, exceedingly, exceptionally,

extremely, outstandingly, prominently, remarkably,
notably, signally, strikingly, conspicuously,
surpassingly, par excellence

emissary *n*
ambassador, agent, envoy, messenger, delegate, herald,
courier, representative, scout, deputy, intermediary,
go-between, spy

emission *n*
discharge, issue, ejection, emanation, giving-out,
giving-off, diffusion, transmission, exhalation,
radiation, release, production, exudation, vent

emit *v*
discharge, issue, eject, emanate, exude, pour out, give
out, throw out, give off, send out, send forth, diffuse,
radiate, release, shed, vent, ooze, leak, produce, let out,
express
formal excrete
🔁 absorb

emollient *adj, n*
▶ *adj* **1** SOOTHING, assuaging, mollifying,
softening
formal assuasive, balsamic, demulcent, lenitive,
mitigative
2 CONCILIATORY, placatory, appeasing, calming
formal propitiatory
▶ *n* cream, lotion, moisturizer, oil, ointment, balm,
poultice, salve
formal lenitive, liniment, unguent

emolument *n*
pay, salary, wages, payment, remuneration, return,
reward, allowance, benefit, earnings, fee, gain,
profit(s), hire, honorarium, stipend, compensation,
recompense

emotion *n*
feeling, passion, sensation, sense, sentiment, ardour,
fervour, warmth, reaction, vehemence, excitement, joy,
happiness, ecstasy, sadness, sorrow, grief, fear, despair,
dread, hate, anger

emotional *adj*
1 FEELING, passionate, sensitive, responsive, loving,
ardent, tender, warm, roused, demonstrative,
excitable, enthusiastic, fervent, impassioned, moved,
sentimental, zealous, hot-blooded, heated,
tempestuous, overcharged, temperamental, fiery
2 EMOTIVE, moving, poignant, thrilling, touching,
stirring, heart-warming, soul-stirring, exciting,
sentimental, pathetic
colloq. tear-jerking, soppy, schmaltzy
🔁 **1** unemotional, cold, detached, calm

emotionless *adj*
cold, cold-blooded, cool, distant, undemonstrative,
unemotional, unfeeling, impassive, detached, clinical,
indifferent, remote, blank, toneless, frigid, glacial
formal imperturbable, phlegmatic
🔁 emotional

emotive *adj*
controversial, delicate, inflammatory, sensitive,
awkward, touchy

empathize *v*
share, identify with, feel for, comfort, support,
understand, be sensitive towards
colloq. put yourself in someone's shoes

emperor *n*
ruler, sovereign, imperator, kaiser, mikado, shogun,

tsar
Related adjective: imperial

emphasis *n*
1 IMPORTANCE, stress, weight, significance, priority, underscoring, accent, accentuation, force, power, prominence, pre-eminence, attention, intensity, strength, urgency, positiveness, insistence, mark, moment
2 *the emphasis is on the second syllable*
stress, accent, weight, force

emphasize *v*
1 *emphasize the differences*
stress, accentuate, underline, highlight, call attention to, accent, feature, dwell on, weight, point up, spotlight, play up, insist on, press home, intensify, heighten, strengthen, punctuate, bring to the fore
colloq. drive the point home
2 *emphasize a syllable*
put stress on, accent, stress, accentuate
F3 1 play down, understate

emphatic *adj*
forceful, positive, insistent, certain, definite, decided, unequivocal, absolute, categorical, earnest, marked, pronounced, significant, unmistakable, distinctive, strong, striking, vigorous, distinct, energetic, forcible, important, impressive, momentous, powerful, punctuated, telling, vivid, direct
F3 tentative, hesitant, understated

empire *n*
1 DOMAIN, dominion, kingdom, realm, province, commonwealth, territory
2 SUPREMACY, sovereignty, rule, authority, dominion, command, government, jurisdiction, control, power, sway
Related adjective: imperial

empirical *adj*
practical, pragmatic, experimental, observed
formal experiential
F3 theoretical, conjectural, speculative

employ *v*
1 ENGAGE, hire, appoint, take on, recruit, sign up, enlist, commission, put on the payroll, retain, fill, occupy, take up, apprentice
2 USE, utilize, make use of, put to use, apply, draw on, exploit, bring to bear, bring into play, ply, exercise, exert

employed *adj*
working, in work, in employment, with a job, earning, hired, occupied, engaged, active, preoccupied, busy
F3 unemployed, jobless

employee *n*
worker, working man, working woman, working person, blue-collar worker, white-collar worker, office worker, member of staff, job-holder, hand, wage-earner, assistant, labourer, operative, artisan, craftsman, tradesman

employer *n*
proprietor, owner, manager, head, management, director, executive, company, firm, business, establishment, organization
colloq. boss, skipper, gaffer

employment *n*
1 JOB, work, occupation, situation, business, calling, profession, vocation, trade, service, métier, pursuit, craft

colloq. line
2 ENLISTMENT, employ, engagement, hire, hiring, taking-on, recruitment, apprenticeship, signing-up
F3 1 unemployment

emporium *n*
shop, store, establishment, bazaar, market, market-place, mart, fair

empower *v*
1 AUTHORIZE, warrant, enable, license, certify, sanction, permit, entitle, commission, delegate, qualify
formal accredit
2 EQUIP, enable, give power/means to

emptiness *n*
1 VACUUM, vacantness, void, voidness, hollowness, hunger, bareness, barrenness, desolation
formal hiatus
2 FUTILITY, meaninglessness, uselessness, worthlessness, aimlessness, purposelessness, senselessness, ineffectiveness, insubstantiality, unreality
F3 1 fullness

empty *adj, v*
▶ *adj* 1 VACANT, with nothing in it, containing nothing, void, unoccupied, free, available, uninhabited, unfilled, deserted, barren, bare, hollow, desolate, blank, clear
2 *an empty gesture*
FUTILE, aimless, meaningless, senseless, trivial, vain, idle, worthless, useless, fruitless, unreal, insubstantial, ineffective, insincere
formal ineffectual
3 *an empty period of life*
aimless, meaningless, senseless, purposeless, futile, vain, hollow, worthless, useless
4 VACUOUS, inane, expressionless, blank, vacant, deadpan
F3 1 full 2 meaningful 3 interesting, eventful
▶ *v* drain, exhaust, discharge, issue, clear, turn out, evacuate, vacate, leave, go out, pour out, flow out, use up, unload, void, gut
F3 fill

empty-headed *adj*
inane, silly, stupid, foolish, frivolous
colloq. scatter-brained, scatty, feather-brained, daft, dopey, batty, dotty
F3 intelligent

emulate *v*
match, copy, mimic, follow, imitate, model yourself on, echo, compete with, contend with, rival, vie with
colloq. take a leaf out of someone's book

emulation *n*
copying, mimicry, following, imitation, echoing, matching, challenge, competition, contention, contest, rivalry, strife

enable *v*
1 AUTHORIZE, equip, qualify, entitle, empower, sanction, warrant, allow, permit, prepare, equip, fit, license, commission, endue
formal accredit, validate
2 FACILITATE, make possible, make easier, allow, permit, help, further, clear/pave the way for
F3 prevent, inhibit, forbid

enact *v*
1 DECREE, ordain, order, authorize, command, legislate, rule, sanction, ratify, pass, make law, establish

2 ACT OUT, perform, play, portray, represent, depict, appear as
F3 **1** repeal, rescind

enactment *n*
1 PASSING, authorization, approval, sanction, ratification, legislation, rule, bill, act, statute, law, order, decree, edict, command, commandment, ordinance, regulation
2 PERFORMANCE, play, playing, performing, acting, portrayal, representation, staging
F3 **1** repeal

enamoured *adj*
charmed, infatuated, in love with, enchanted, captivated, entranced, bewitched, enthralled, smitten, keen, wild, mad, taken, fascinated, fond

encampment *n*
camp, camping-ground, campsite, base, bivouac, quarters, tents

encapsulate *v*
sum up, summarize, typify, exemplify, epitomize, capture, include, contain, take in, represent, condense, digest, abridge, compress, précis

enchant *v*
1 CAPTIVATE, charm, fascinate, enrapture, enamour, attract, allure, appeal, delight, thrill
2 ENTRANCE, enthral, bewitch, beguile, spellbind, hypnotize, mesmerize
F3 **1** repel

enchanter *n*
conjurer, magician, magus, mesmerist, necromancer, reim-kennar, sorcerer, spellbinder, warlock, witch, wizard

enchanting *adj*
charming, delightful, attractive, fascinating, appealing, lovely, pleasant, wonderful, alluring, bewitching, captivating, endearing, entrancing, irresistible, mesmerizing, ravishing, winsome
F3 boring, repellent

enchantment *n*
1 DELIGHT, fascination, charm, appeal, attractiveness, allure, allurement, glamour, bliss, rapture, ecstasy
2 SPELL, magic, witchcraft, wizardry, hypnotism, sorcery, incantation, charm, mesmerism
formal conjuration, necromancy
F3 **1** disenchantment

enchantress *n*
1 SORCERESS, magician, spellbinder, witch, conjurer, Circe, lamia
formal necromancer
2 SEDUCTRESS, charmer, siren, vamp, femme fatale

encircle *v*
surround, encompass, compass, ring, circle, orbit, girdle, enclose, enfold, envelop, crowd, close in, hem in
formal circumscribe, gird

enclose *v*
1 SURROUND, encircle, encompass, ring, circle, fence, hedge, hem in, bound, encase, embrace, envelop, confine, frame, cage, cocoon, hold, shut in, close in, wrap, pen, cover, corral
formal circumscribe
2 INCLUDE, insert, contain, put in, send with
formal comprehend

enclosure *n*
1 *herded into the enclosure*
pen, pound, compound, paddock, fold, stockade, sty, run, arena, area, corral, kraal, court, yard, ring, fencing, close, cloister
2 INSERTION, inclusion, addition

encompass *v*
1 ENCIRCLE, circle, ring, surround, envelop, close in, shut in, hem in, confine, enclose, hold
formal gird, circumscribe
2 INCLUDE, cover, embrace, contain, take in, admit, incorporate, involve, embody, span
formal comprise, comprehend

encore *n*
repeat, repetition, additional/extra performance

encounter *v, n*
▶ *v* **1** *encounter difficulties*
confront, face, be faced with, experience, be/come up against, deal with, cope with
2 MEET, come across, run across, stumble across
formal happen on, chance upon
colloq. run into, bump into
3 FIGHT, clash with, combat, engage, grapple with, struggle, strive, contend, tussle, do battle with, come into conflict with
colloq. cross swords with
▶ *n* **1** MEETING, contact, rendezvous, brush, confrontation
2 CLASH, fight, combat, conflict, struggle, contest, battle, dispute, engagement, action, skirmish, run-in, collision
colloq. set-to

encourage *v*
1 HEARTEN, stimulate, motivate, spur, reassure, rally, give moral support to, be supportive to, animate, stir, inspire, incite, buoy up, cheer, urge, rouse, comfort, embolden, console
formal exhort
2 *encourage someone to do something*
persuade, influence, sway, win over, convince, prompt, talk into
formal exhort
colloq. egg on
3 PROMOTE, advance, aid, boost, forward, further, foster, back, support, help, assist, advocate, favour, strengthen
F3 **1** discourage, depress **2** discourage, dissuade **3** discourage

encouragement *n*
1 REASSURANCE, inspiration, motivation, cheer, incitement, urging, persuasion, stimulation, consolation
formal exhortation, succour
colloq. pep talk
2 PROMOTION, help, aid, assistance, boost, incentive, support, backing, stimulus, furtherance
colloq. shot in the arm
F3 **1** discouragement, disapproval

encouraging *adj*
heartening, promising, hopeful, reassuring, stimulating, inspiring, uplifting, cheering, comforting, bright, rosy, cheerful, satisfactory
formal auspicious
F3 discouraging

encroach *v*
intrude, invade, impinge, trespass, infringe, usurp,

overstep, overrun, infiltrate, make inroads
colloq. muscle in on, tread on someone's toes

encroachment *n*
intrusion, invasion, trespassing, infringement,
overstepping, infiltration
formal incursion

encumber *v*
1 BURDEN, overload, weigh down, saddle, strain,
stress, oppress, handicap, hamper, hinder, impede,
restrain, slow down, obstruct, constrain,
inconvenience, prevent, check, cramp
formal retard
2 BLOCK, congest, jam, pack, stuff, cram

encumbrance *n*
burden, load, weight, cross, millstone, albatross,
difficulty, restraint, constraint, handicap, impediment,
obstruction, obstacle, inconvenience, strain, stress,
hindrance, liability, obligation, responsibility
formal cumbrance

encyclopedic *adj*
complete, exhaustive, comprehensive, thorough, wide-
ranging, vast, all-inclusive, broad, all-embracing, all-
encompassing, universal, compendious
F3 incomplete, narrow

end *n, v*
▶ *n* 1 FINISH, conclusion, close, ending,
completion, culmination, epilogue, finale,
dénouement
formal termination, cessation
2 EXTREMITY, boundary, border, edge, limit,
margin, tip
3 REMAINDER, tip, butt, left-over, remnant, stub,
scrap, vestige, fragment, leftovers
4 AIM, object, objective, purpose, intention, goal,
target, point, reason, motive, design
formal intent
5 RESULT, outcome, consequence, issue, upshot
6 DEATH, destruction, extermination, downfall,
doom, ruin, extinction, dissolution
formal demise
7 PART, aspect, side, area, field, section, department,
branch
F3 1 beginning, start 6 birth
▷ **the end** intolerable, unbearable, unendurable, too
much, enough, beyond endurance, insufferable, the
worst; *colloq.* the limit, the last straw, the final blow
▶ *v* 1 FINISH, come/bring to an end, close, stop, be
over, expire, complete, round off, culminate, break off,
die out, fade away, run out
formal cease, conclude, terminate, discontinue
colloq. wind up
2 DESTROY, annihilate, exterminate, extinguish,
ruin, abolish, dissolve
F3 1 begin, start; *formal* commence

endanger *v*
hazard, risk, put at risk, jeopardize, put in jeopardy,
expose, threaten, put in danger, compromise
formal imperil
F3 protect

endearing *adj*
lovable, charming, appealing, attractive, winsome,
engaging, delightful, sweet, adorable, captivating,
enchanting

endearment *n*
love, affection, fondness, attachment, diminutive,

pet-name, sweet nothing
formal hypocorism

endeavour *v, n*
▶ *v* attempt, try, strive, struggle, aim, aspire,
undertake, venture, try your hand at, labour, take
pains, do your best
formal seek
▶ *n* attempt, effort, try, undertaking, enterprise, aim,
venture, striving
colloq. go, shot, stab, bash, crack

ending *n*
end, close, finish, completion, conclusion,
culmination, climax, resolution, dénouement, finale,
epilogue
formal termination, consummation, cessation
F3 beginning, start

endless *adj*
1 INFINITE, without end, unending, boundless,
limitless, unlimited, measureless
2 EVERLASTING, perpetual, constant, continual,
continuous, undying, eternal, interminable, boring,
monotonous
formal ceaseless
3 UNBROKEN, continuous, constant, uninterrupted,
entire, whole
F3 1 finite, limited 2 temporary

endorse *v*
1 APPROVE, sanction, authorize, support, back, be/
get behind, favour, ratify, confirm, vouch for, advocate,
uphold, warrant, recommend, subscribe to, sustain,
adopt
formal affirm
colloq. throw your weight behind
2 SIGN, countersign

endorsement *n*
1 APPROVAL, sanction, authorization, support,
backing, ratification, confirmation, advocacy,
warrant, recommendation, commendation, seal of
approval, testimonial
formal affirmation
colloq. OK
2 SIGNATURE, countersignature

endow *v*
1 LEAVE, will, give, donate, grant, boast, present,
award, finance, fund, support, make over, furnish,
provide, supply
formal bestow, bequeath, confer
2 HAVE, possess, give, provide, present, enjoy, boast,
be endued with, be blessed with

endowment *n*
1 LEGACY, award, grant, fund, finance, gift, present,
provision, settlement, donation, dowry, income,
revenue
formal bequest, bestowal, benefaction
2 TALENT, attribute, faculty, gift, aptitude, capability,
ability, quality, flair, power, capacity, genius,
qualification, attribute

endurable *adj*
bearable, tolerable, supportable, manageable,
withstandable, sustainable, sufferable
F3 intolerable, unbearable

endurance *n*
patience, staying power, stamina, resignation,
stoicism, sufferance, tenacity, perseverance,
resolution, stability, durability, backbone, persistence,
strength, toleration

formal fortitude
colloq. guts, spunk, bottle, stickability

endure *v*
1 *endure hardship*
bear, stand, put up with, tolerate, abide, weather, brave, cope with, face, go through, encounter, meet, experience, submit to, suffer, sustain, swallow, undergo, withstand, take, stick, allow, permit, support
colloq. stomach
2 *a peace that will endure for ever*
last, remain, live, survive, stay, persist, continue, hold, prevail
formal abide

enduring *adj*
lasting, long-lasting, durable, permanent, perpetual, abiding, remaining, continuing, long-standing, stable, steady, firm, steadfast, persistent, persisting, chronic, prevailing, surviving, unfaltering, unwavering, eternal, immortal, imperishable
Ⓕ changeable, fleeting

enemy *n*
adversary, opponent, rival, antagonist, the opposition, competitor, the competition, opposer, other side
formal foe
Ⓕ friend, ally

energetic *adj*
lively, vigorous, active, animated, dynamic, spirited, tireless, boisterous, zestful, brisk, strong, forceful, potent, powerful, strenuous, high-powered, indefatigable
colloq. bursting with energy, full of beans, go-getting, zippy, punchy
Ⓕ lethargic, sluggish, inactive, idle

energize *v*
stimulate, arouse, stir, motivate, enliven, invigorate, liven, quicken, animate, vitalize, vivify, activate, electrify, galvanize
colloq. pep up
Ⓕ daunt

energy *n*
liveliness, vigour, activity, animation, drive, dynamism, enthusiasm, life, spirit, verve, vivacity, vitality, sparkle, effervescence, zest, zeal, ardour, fire, efficiency, force, forcefulness, effectiveness, strength, power, potency, intensity, exertion, stamina
formal might
colloq. get-up-and-go, zip, push, brio, pizzazz
Ⓕ lethargy, inertia, weakness

enervated *adj*
tired, weak, exhausted, feeble, fatigued, worn out, weakened, incapacitated, paralysed, undermined, unmanned, unnerved, sapped, devitalized, limp, spent
formal debilitated, effete, enfeebled
colloq. done in, run-down, washed-out
Ⓕ active, energetic

enfeeble *v*
weaken, exhaust, fatigue, reduce, diminish, wear out, sap, geld, undermine, unhinge, unnerve, deplete, devitalize
formal debilitate, enervate
Ⓕ strengthen

enfold *v*
1 ENCLOSE, envelop, shroud, swathe, encircle, encompass, fold, enwrap, wrap (up)
2 EMBRACE, clasp, hug, hold

enforce *v*
1 IMPOSE, administer, implement, carry out, apply, execute, discharge, fulfil
2 COMPEL, insist on, oblige, urge, constrain, require, necessitate, force, pressure, pressurize, coerce, prosecute, reinforce

enforced *adj*
compulsory, binding, necessary, required, unavoidable, imposed, involuntary, forced, obliged, compelled, constrained, dictated, ordained, prescribed

enforcement *n*
imposition, administration, implementation, application, execution, discharge, fulfilment, insistence, coercion, obligation, compulsion, constraint, pressure, prosecution, requirement
formal coaction

enfranchise *v*
give the right to vote to, give the vote to, free, liberate, release
formal emancipate, manumit, give suffrage to
Ⓕ disenfranchise

enfranchisement *n*
giving the right to vote, voting rights, freedom, freeing, liberating, liberation, release
formal emancipation, manumission, suffrage
Ⓕ disenfranchisement

engage *v*
1 PARTICIPATE, take part, embark on, take up, practise, do, enter into, undertake, join in, involve, become involved in/with
2 ATTRACT, allure, draw, win, gain, captivate, charm, catch
3 OCCUPY, engross, absorb, employ, fill, hold, preoccupy, busy, tie up, grip
4 EMPLOY, hire, appoint, take on, sign up/on, enlist, enrol, commission, recruit, contract, put on the payroll
5 INTERLOCK, mesh, enmesh, interconnect, join, fit together, interact, attach
6 FIGHT, battle with, attack, take on, encounter, assail, clash with, combat, join in battle with, wage war with
Ⓕ **2** repel **4** dismiss, discharge **5** disengage

engaged *adj*
1 *engaged in his work*
occupied, busy, engrossed, immersed, absorbed, preoccupied, involved, active, employed
colloq. tied up
2 *engaged to be married*
promised, pledged, committed
formal betrothed, affianced, plighted, espoused
colloq. spoken for
3 *the phone is engaged*
busy, unavailable, in use, taken
colloq. tied up

engagement *n*
1 APPOINTMENT, meeting, interview, date, arrangement, commitment, assignation, fixture, rendezvous
2 PROMISE, pledge, commitment, obligation, agreement, contract, bond, assurance, vow
formal betrothal, troth
3 FIGHT, battle, combat, conflict, attack, clash, war, assault, strife, struggle, offensive, action, encounter, confrontation, contest

engaging *adj*
charming, attractive, appealing, captivating, pleasing, delightful, winsome, winning, lovable, adorable, sweet, likable, pleasant, fetching, fascinating, enchanting, agreeable
🔁 repulsive, repellent

engender *v*
cause, produce, occasion, bring about, give rise to, instigate, lead to, incite, induce, create, inspire, generate, arouse, excite, encourage, nurture, kindle, breed, propagate, provoke
old use beget
formal effect

engine *n*
motor, machine, machinery, mechanism, appliance, contraption, apparatus, device, instrument, tool, implement, locomotive, generator, dynamo

Types of engine include: diesel, donkey, fuel-injection, internal-combustion, jet, petrol, steam, turbine, turbojet, turboprop, V-engine.

Parts of an automotive engine and its ancillaries include: air filter, alternator, camshaft, camshaft cover, carburettor, choke, connecting rod, *colloq.* con-rod, cooling fan, crankshaft, crankshaft pulley, cylinder block, cylinder head, drive belt, exhaust manifold, exhaust valve, fan belt, flywheel, fuel and ignition ECU (electronic control unit), fuel injector, gasket, ignition coil, ignition distributor, inlet manifold, inlet valve, oil filter, oil pump, oil seal, petrol pump, piston, piston ring, power-steering pump, push-rod, radiator, rocker arm, rocker cover, rotor arm, spark plug, starter motor, sump, tappet, thermostat, timing belt, timing pulley, turbocharger.

engineer *n, v*
▶ *n* **1** MECHANIC, technician, operator, driver, engine driver
2 DESIGNER, originator, planner, builder, inventor, deviser, mastermind, architect, civil engineer, electrical engineer, mechanical engineer, chemical engineer, sound engineer
▶ *v* plan, contrive, devise, manoeuvre, cause, manipulate, control, direct, bring about, mastermind, originate, arrange, orchestrate, plot, scheme, stage-manage, manage, create, rig
formal effect

engrave *v*
1 INSCRIBE, cut, carve, chisel, etch, mark, print, imprint, impress, incise, chase
2 *engraved on her mind*
imprint, impress, fix, stamp, lodge, set, embed, engrain, brand

engraving *n*
print, impression, imprint, inscription, carving, etching, cutting, cut, woodcut, plate, block, cutting, chiselling, mark
technical dry-point, intaglio

engross *v*
absorb, occupy, engage, interest, grip, hold, preoccupy, rivet, fascinate, captivate, enthral, arrest, involve, intrigue
🔁 bore

engrossed *adj*
absorbed, occupied, taken up, preoccupied, gripped, engaged, caught up, enthralled, fascinated, captivated, immersed, intent, intrigued, rapt, riveted, mesmerized, wrapped, lost, fixated
🔁 bored, disinterested

engrossing *adj*
absorbing, fascinating, enthralling, captivating, intriguing, gripping, interesting, compelling, riveting, suspenseful
colloq. unputdownable
🔁 boring

engulf *v*
overwhelm, swamp, flood, deluge, drown, inundate, plunge, immerse, submerge, overrun, overtake, swallow up, devour, consume, bury, absorb, engross, envelop

enhance *v*
heighten, intensify, increase, improve, upgrade, elevate, add to, enrich, magnify, swell, exalt, raise, lift, boost, strengthen, emphasize, stress, reinforce, embellish
formal augment
🔁 reduce, minimize

enhancement *n*
heightening, increase, improvement, elevation, enrichment, magnification, intensification, boost, emphasis, stress, reinforcement
formal augmentation

enigma *n*
mystery, riddle, puzzle, paradox, conundrum, problem, dilemma, quandary, brain-teaser
colloq. poser

enigmatic *adj*
mysterious, mystifying, puzzling, cryptic, obscure, strange, baffling, perplexing, paradoxical, incomprehensible, inexplicable, unfathomable
formal arcane, esoteric, recondite
🔁 simple, straightforward

enjoin *v*
1 ORDER, command, demand, urge, direct, instruct, decree, ordain, advise, require, charge
2 PROHIBIT, forbid, ban, bar
formal disallow, interdict, proscribe

enjoy *v*
1 *enjoy dancing*
take pleasure in, delight in, appreciate, like, relish, revel in, love, be fond of, rejoice in, savour
colloq. fancy
2 *enjoy a benefit*
have, possess, be blessed with, be endowed with, be favoured with
🔁 **1** dislike, hate
▷ **enjoy yourself** have a good time, have fun, make merry; *colloq.* have a whale of a time, live it up, let your hair down, paint the town red

enjoyable *adj*
pleasant, agreeable, delightful, pleasing, entertaining, amusing, fun, pleasurable, delicious, fine, lovely, good, nice, satisfying
formal gratifying, delectable
🔁 disagreeable

enjoyment *n*
1 PLEASURE, delight, amusement, entertainment, relish, joy, fun, gladness, happiness, diversion, recreation, indulgence, zest, satisfaction
formal gratification, delectation
2 POSSESSION, use, advantage, benefit, privilege,

favour, blessing
F3 1 displeasure

enlarge v
1 *enlarge the garden; glands enlarging*
make/become larger, make/become bigger, increase,
expand, extend, magnify, add to, supplement, inflate,
swell, stretch, multiply, develop, amplify, widen,
broaden, lengthen, heighten
technical distend, dilate, intumesce
formal augment, elongate
2 *enlarge a photograph*
make bigger, blow up
3 *enlarge on something*
expand on, go into details, elaborate on
formal expatiate on, dilate on
F3 1 diminish, shrink

enlargement n
1 *enlargement of the building/a gland*
increase, expansion, extension, magnification,
inflation swelling, stretching, multiplication,
development, amplification
technical distension, dilation, intumescence, oedema
formal augmentation
2 *a photographic enlargement*
blow up, magnification
F3 2 contraction, decrease, reduction

enlighten v
instruct, edify, cultivate, educate, inform, illuminate,
teach, tutor, counsel, apprise, advise, make aware
F3 confuse

enlightened adj
informed, aware, knowledgeable, educated, civilized,
cultivated, refined, cultured, sophisticated,
conversant, wise, learned, intellectual, reasonable,
liberal, broad-minded, open-minded, literate
formal erudite
F3 ignorant, confused

enlightenment n
awareness, knowledge, teaching, understanding,
education, instruction, wisdom, information, insight,
comprehension, civilization, cultivation, refinement,
learning, literacy, edification, sophistication, broad-
mindedness, open-mindedness
formal erudition, sapience
F3 confusion, ignorance

enlist v
enlist in the army; enlist someone's help
engage, enrol, register, sign up, recruit, conscript, hire,
take on, employ, volunteer, join (up), gather, muster,
secure, obtain, enter
formal procure

enliven v
excite, exhilarate, brighten, cheer (up), gladden,
hearten, invigorate, rouse, wake up, liven (up),
stimulate, revitalize, inspire, animate, buoy up, fire,
kindle, quicken, spark
formal vivify
colloq. pep up, perk up, give a lift to
F3 subdue

en masse adv
all at once, all together, as a group, as a whole, as one,
ensemble, in a body, together, en bloc, wholesale

enmity n
animosity, hostility, antagonism, discord, strife, feud,
antipathy, bitterness, hate, hatred, aversion, ill-will,
bad blood, rancour, malice, venom

formal acrimony, malevolence
F3 friendship, reconciliation

ennoble v
dignify, uplift, elevate, raise, exalt, enhance, glorify,
honour, magnify
formal aggrandize, nobilitate

ennui n
boredom, tiredness, dissatisfaction, tedium, lassitude,
listlessness, languor
formal accidie, acedia
colloq. the doldrums

enormity n
atrocity, outrage, iniquity, horror, evil, crime,
abomination, violation, monstrosity, outrageousness,
wickedness, vileness, depravity, evilness,
atrociousness, viciousness

⚠ **enormity** or **enormousness**?
Of these two nouns, only *enormousness* should be
used when referring to size: *the enormousness of his
ambitions.* *Enormity* means 'great wickedness,
seriousness (of a crime, etc)': *the enormity of his
assault on the little girl.*

---

enormous adj
huge, immense, vast, gigantic, massive, colossal, large-
scale, gross, gargantuan, astronomic, monstrous,
mammoth, considerable, tremendous, stupendous,
prodigious
colloq. jumbo, great big, whopping
F3 small, tiny

enormously adv
extremely, to a vast/huge/immense extent, hugely,
exceptionally, extraordinarily, exceedingly, massively,
tremendously, immensely

enormousness n
hugeness, immenseness, vastness, massiveness,
largeness, greatness, magnitude, expanse,
extensiveness

enough adj, n, adv
▶ *adj* sufficient, adequate, ample, plenty, abundant
F3 insufficient, inadequate
▶ *n* sufficiency, adequacy, plenty, abundance, ample
supply
formal amplitude
▶ *adv* sufficiently, adequately, reasonably, tolerably,
passably, moderately, fairly, satisfactorily, amply

en passant adv
in passing, by the way, while on the subject,
incidentally, cursorily

enquire, enquirer, enquiring, enquiry *see*
inquire, inquirer, inquiring, inquiry.

enrage v
incense, infuriate, anger, make angry, annoy, madden,
provoke, incite, inflame, agitate, exasperate, irritate,
rile, irk, vex
colloq. needle, bug, wind up, drive someone up the
wall, drive someone round the bend, make someone's
blood boil, make someone's hackles rise, put/get
someone's back up, push too far
F3 calm, placate

enraged adj
incensed, infuriated, angry, angered, furious, livid,
raging, storming, inflamed, annoyed, irritated, irate,
exasperated, fuming

colloq. aggravated, mad, wild
◨ calm

enrapture *v*
enchant, fascinate, charm, thrill, delight, captivate, bewitch, beguile, enthral, entrance, spellbind, transport, ravish

enrich *v*
1 ENDOW, enhance, improve, refine, develop, cultivate, add to, supplement
formal augment, aggrandize, ameliorate
2 ADORN, ornament, beautify, embellish, decorate, garnish, grace, gild
◨ 1 impoverish

enrol *v*
1 REGISTER, enlist, sign on, sign up, join up, recruit, go in for, enter, put your name down, engage, admit
2 RECORD, list, note, enter, put down
formal inscribe

enrolment *n*
registration, recruitment, enlistment, enlisting, signing on/up, joining up, admission, acceptance

en route *adv*
in transit, on the move, on the way, on the road

ensconce *v*
install, settle, establish, entrench, nestle, put, place, lodge, protect, shelter, shield, screen, locate

ensemble *n*
1 WHOLE, total, entirety, sum, set, group, collection, accumulation
formal aggregate
colloq. whole caboodle, whole (bang) shoot
2 OUTFIT, costume, suit, co-ordinates
colloq. get-up, rig-out
3 GROUP, band, company, troupe, circle, chorus, cast

enshrine *v*
preserve, protect, guard, shield, treasure, cherish, immortalize, consecrate, dedicate, exalt, hallow, revere, sanctify, idolize, embalm
formal apotheosize

enshroud *v*
cloak, cloud, shroud, veil, pall, wrap, conceal, hide, cover, enclose, enfold, envelop, enwrap, obscure

ensign *n*
banner, standard, flag, colours, pennant, jack, badge, crest, shield, coat of arms

enslave *v*
subject, dominate, bind, enchain, yoke, trap
formal subjugate
◨ free, emancipate

enslavement *n*
slavery, subjection, servitude, bondage, captivity, oppression, repression, serfdom, vassalage
formal dulosis, enthralment, subjugation, thraldom
◨ emancipation

ensnare *v*
trap, catch, capture, net, snare, embroil, enmesh, entangle, entrap

ensue *v*
follow, issue, proceed, succeed, result, arise, happen, occur, transpire, turn out, flow, derive, stem, come next
formal befall
◨ precede

ensure *v*
1 MAKE CERTAIN, make sure, guarantee, warrant, secure, certify
formal effect
2 PROTECT, make safe, guard, safeguard, secure

entail *v*
involve, necessitate, occasion, need, require, call for, demand, cause, produce, bring about, give rise to, lead to, result in

entangle *v*
1 *entangled in the net*
tangle, twist, knot, ravel, intertwine, enmesh, ensnare, snare, mix up
2 EMBROIL, involve, implicate, complicate, confuse, jumble, muddle
◨ 1, 2 disentangle

entanglement *n*
1 TANGLE, knot, mesh, tie, trap, jumble, ensnarement, entrapment, snare
2 INVOLVEMENT, complication, embarrassment, confusion, muddle, snarl-up, difficulty, mess, mix-up, predicament, liaison, affair
◨ 1, 2 disentanglement

entente *n*
agreement, arrangement, friendship, deal, pact, treaty, understanding, entente cordiale
formal compact

enter *v*
1 COME IN TO, go in (to), get in (to), arrive, cross the threshold, burst in, sneak in, break in, worm your way in, insert, introduce, board, infiltrate, penetrate, occupy
colloq. pop in
2 JOIN, become a member of, enlist, set about, sign up, put your name down for, take up, participate, take part, go in for, undertake, embark upon, enrol, start, begin, engage in
formal commence
3 RECORD, log, note, list, register, put down, take down, set down, inscribe, lodge, put on record, submit, input
◨ 1 depart 3 delete

enterprise *n*
1 UNDERTAKING, venture, project, plan, effort, operation, campaign, programme, endeavour, task, scheme
2 INITIATIVE, resourcefulness, drive, adventurousness, courage, boldness, ambition, energy, enthusiasm, strong feeling, spirit, vitality
colloq. get-up-and-go, push, oomph
3 BUSINESS, company, firm, establishment, operation, concern, industry
◨ 2 apathy

enterprising *adj*
venturesome, adventurous, bold, daring, imaginative, resourceful, entrepreneurial, self-reliant, enthusiastic, energetic, keen, eager, zealous, ambitious, aspiring, spirited, vigorous, active
colloq. go-ahead, pushy
◨ unenterprising, lethargic

entertain *v*
1 AMUSE, divert, please, delight, cheer, interest, occupy, engage, engross, charm, captivate
2 RECEIVE, have guests, ask over/round, have round, invite over/round, accommodate, play host to, provide hospitality, put up, treat, host, regale

3 HARBOUR, contemplate, consider, think about, imagine, conceive, foster, nurture, cherish
formal countenance
F3 1 bore **3** reject

entertainer *n*

Entertainers include: acrobat, actor, actress, artiste, busker, chat-show host, clown, comedian, comic, conjuror, dancer, disc jockey, *colloq.* DJ, escapologist, game-show host, hypnotist, ice-skater, impressionist, jester, juggler, magician, mime artist, mimic, mind-reader, minstrel, musician, performer, player, presenter, singer, song-and-dance act, stand-up comic, striptease-artist, *colloq.* stripper, trapeze-artist, tight-rope walker, ventriloquist. See also **musician; singer**.

entertaining *adj*
amusing, diverting, fun, recreational, enjoyable, delightful, interesting, pleasant, pleasing, pleasurable, humorous, funny, comical, witty
F3 boring

entertainment *n*
1 AMUSEMENT, diversion, recreation, enjoyment, play, hobby, pastime, fun, sport, leisure, activity, distraction, pleasure
2 SHOW, spectacle, performance, play, presentation, extravaganza

Forms of entertainment include: cinema, cartoon show, video, radio, television, theatre, pantomime; dance, disco, discothèque, concert, recital, musical, opera, variety show, music hall, revue, karaoke, cabaret, night-club, casino; magic-show, puppet show, Punch-and-Judy show, circus, gymkhana, waxworks, laser-light show, zoo, rodeo, carnival, pageant, fête, festival, firework party, barbecue, show business, *colloq.* show biz. See also **performance; theatrical**.

enthral *v*
captivate, entrance, enchant, fascinate, charm, beguile, bewitch, thrill, enrapture, delight, intrigue, spellbind, hypnotize, mesmerize, engross, grip, rivet, absorb
F3 1 bore

enthralling *adj*
captivating, entrancing, enchanting, fascinating, intriguing, beguiling, charming, thrilling, riveting, gripping, compulsive, compelling, spellbinding, hypnotizing, mesmerizing, mesmeric
F3 boring

enthuse *v*
praise, rave, wax lyrical, gush, drool, excite, inspire, motivate, fire, bubble over, effervesce

enthusiasm *n*
1 ZEAL, ardour, fervour, passion, keenness, eagerness, vehemence, warmth, zest, frenzy, fire, excitement, earnestness, relish, spirit, wholeheartedness, commitment, devotion
2 INTEREST, hobby, pastime, passion, craze, mania, rage
colloq. thing
F3 1 apathy

enthusiast *n*
devotee, zealot, admirer, fan, supporter, follower, fanatic, aficionado, lover
colloq. buff, freak, fiend

enthusiastic *adj*
keen, ardent, eager, fervent, vehement, passionate, warm, wholehearted, zealous, vigorous, spirited, earnest, devoted, avid, committed, excited, fanatical, exuberant
formal ebullient
colloq. crazy, mad, wild, daft, nuts, potty
F3 unenthusiastic, apathetic

entice *v*
tempt, lure, attract, seduce, lead on, draw, coax, persuade, induce, beguile, cajole
formal inveigle
colloq. sweet-talk

enticement *n*
inducement, lure, attraction, seduction, bait, persuasion, coaxing, temptation, decoy, allurement, beguilement, cajolery
formal blandishments, inveiglement
colloq. come-on, sweet-talk

entire *adj*
complete, whole, total, full, absolute, intact, sound, perfect
F3 incomplete, partial

entirely *adv*
completely, wholly, totally, fully, utterly, unreservedly, absolutely, in toto, thoroughly, altogether, perfectly, only, solely, exclusively, in every respect, in every way, every inch
F3 partially

entirety *n*
totality, fullness, completeness, wholeness, whole

entitle *v*
1 AUTHORIZE, give someone the right, qualify, empower, enable, make eligible, allow, permit, license, warrant, sanction
formal accredit
2 NAME, call, term, title, give the title, know as, style, christen, dub, label, designate

entity *n*
being, existence, thing, body, creature, individual, organism, substance, object

entombment *n*
burial, interment
formal inhumation, sepulture

entourage *n*
retinue, attendants, company, companions, followers, following, escort, staff, suite, court, train, retainers, associates, cortège, coterie

entrails *n*
intestines, offal, viscera, bowels, internal organs, vital organs, giblets, umbles
colloq. guts, innards, insides

entrance[1] *n*
1 OPENING, way in, entry, access, door, doorway, gate, gateway, approach, threshold, drive, driveway, passageway, lobby, porch, hall, vestibule, foyer, anteroom
2 ARRIVAL, appearance, debut, initiation, introduction, start
3 ACCESS, admission, admittance, entry, right of entry, entrée
formal ingress
F3 1 exit **2** departure

entrance[2] *v*
entranced by her beauty
charm, enchant, enrapture, captivate, enthral, bewitch, beguile, spellbind, fascinate, charm, delight, ravish, transport, hypnotize, mesmerize
E3 repel

entrant *n*
1 NOVICE, beginner, starter, newcomer, new arrival, initiate, convert, probationer, apprentice, fresher, freshman, learner, student, pupil, trainee
2 COMPETITOR, candidate, contestant, contender, entry, applicant, participant, player, rival, opponent

entrap *v*
1 CATCH, trap, capture, snare, ensnare, entangle, enmesh, embroil, ambush, net
2 TRICK, deceive, delude, entice, seduce, implicate, beguile, allure, lure
formal inveigle

entreat *v*
beg, implore, plead with, crave, pray, ask, petition, solicit, request, appeal to
formal beseech, supplicate, invoke, importune

entreaty *n*
appeal, plea, prayer, petition, suit, cry, solicitation, request
formal supplication, invocation

entrench *v*
establish, fix, embed, dig in, ensconce, install, lodge, root, ingrain, settle, seat, plant, anchor, set, stop a gap, take up position
E3 dislodge

entrenched *adj*
deep-rooted, deep-seated, rooted, well-established, firm, fixed, implanted, ingrained, inbred, set, inflexible, diehard, unshakable, dyed-in-the-wool, indelible, ineradicable
formal intransigent
colloq. stick-in-the-mud

entrepreneur *n*
business executive, businessman, businesswoman, financier, industrialist, middleman, promoter, agent, dealer, broker, contractor, magnate, tycoon, speculator, money-maker, manager, impresario

entrepreneurial *adj*
business, commercial, industrial, trade, contractual, managerial, financial, monetary, economic, budgetary, professional

entrust *v*
trust, commit, make someone responsible for, put in charge, confide, consign, authorize, charge, assign, turn over, hand over, commend, depute, invest, delegate, deliver

entry *n*
1 ENTRANCE, appearance, admittance, admission, access, entrée, introduction
2 RECORD, item, minute, note, memorandum, description, statement, account, listing
3 ENTRANT, competitor, contestant, candidate, applicant, participant, player, rival, opponent
4 OPENING, entrance, door, doorway, access, threshold, way in, passage, gate, gateway, approach, lobby, porch, hall, vestibule, foyer, anteroom
E3 4 exit

entwine *v*
wind, twist, intertwine, interlace, interlink,

interweave, intwine, braid, knit, plait, twine, weave, wreathe, knot, ravel, entangle, embroil
E3 unravel

enumerate *v*
list, name, itemize, cite, detail, specify, count, number, relate, recount, spell out, tell, mention, calculate, quote, recite, reckon

enunciate *v*
1 ARTICULATE, pronounce, vocalize, voice, express, say, speak, utter, sound
2 STATE, declare, express, utter, proclaim, announce, put forward
formal affirm, propound, promulgate

envelop *v*
wrap, enfold, enwrap, encase, cover, swathe, shroud, engulf, enclose, encircle, encompass, surround, cloak, veil, blanket, conceal, obscure, hide

envelope *n*
wrapper, wrapping, cover, case, casing, sheath, covering, shell, skin, holder, jacket, coating

enviable *adj*
desirable, privileged, favoured, blessed, fortunate, lucky, desirable, advantageous, sought-after, excellent, fine
E3 unenviable

envious *adj*
covetous, jealous, resentful, green (with envy), dissatisfied, grudging, begrudging, jaundiced
colloq. green-eyed

environment *n*
surroundings, conditions, climate, circumstances, milieu, atmosphere, habitat, situation, element, medium, background, ambience, scene, setting, locale, context, mood, influences, territory, domain
colloq. the lie of the land, which way the wind is blowing

environmentalist *n*
conservationist, ecologist, preservationist, Friends of the Earth
colloq. ecofreak, econut, green

environs *n*
neighbourhood, surroundings, surrounding area, vicinity, outskirts, suburbs, district, locality, precincts, purlieus
formal circumjacencies, vicinage

envisage *v*
visualize, imagine, picture, see coming, envision, conceive of, preconceive, predict, anticipate, foresee, image, see, think of, contemplate

envoy *n*
agent, representative, ambassador, diplomat, messenger, legate, consul, attaché, emissary, minister, delegate, deputy, courier, mediator, intermediary, go-between

envy *n, v*
▶ *n* covetousness, jealousy, resentfulness, resentment, dissatisfaction, grudge, ill-will, malice, spite
▶ *v* covet, resent, begrudge, grudge, crave

ephemeral *adj*
transient, short-lived, fleeting, brief, momentary, passing, short, temporary, transitory, impermanent, flitting
formal evanescent, fugacious, fungous
E3 enduring, lasting, perpetual

epic *adj, n*
▶ *adj* heroic, grand, majestic, elevated, exalted, lofty, imposing, impressive, vast, ambitious, long, large, large-scale, great, colossal, huge
formal grandiloquent, sublime
◳ ordinary
▶ *n* long story/poem, narrative, history, legend, saga, myth

epicure *n*
gourmet, connoisseur, *bon vivant, bon viveur,* gastronome, epicurean, gourmand, glutton, hedonist, sensualist, Sybarite, voluptuary

epicurean *adj*
gourmet, gastronomic, gourmandizing, sensual, voluptuous, luxurious, self-indulgent, gluttonous, luscious, lush, unrestrained, hedonistic, Sybaritic, libertine

epidemic *adj, n*
▶ *adj* widespread, prevalent, extensive, rife, rampant, sweeping, wide-ranging, pervasive, prevailing, endemic
formal pandemic
▶ *n* plague, outbreak, scourge, spread, rash, spate, upsurge, growth, increase, rise, wave

epigram *n*
witticism, quip, *bon mot,* saying, proverb, maxim, aphorism, gnome
technical apophthegm

epigrammatic *adj*
concise, succinct, brief, short, terse, laconic, pithy, aphoristic, incisive, piquant, pointed, sharp, pungent, witty, ironic

epilogue *n*
afterword, postscript, PS, appendix, coda, conclusion, swan song
◳ foreword, prologue, preface

episode *n*
1 INCIDENT, event, occurrence, happening, occasion, circumstance, experience, adventure, affair, matter, business
2 INSTALMENT, part, chapter, passage, section, scene
Related adjective: episodic

episodic *adj*
periodic, intermittent, irregular, occasional, spasmodic, sporadic, disconnected, disjointed, digressive, anecdotal
formal picaresque

epistle *n*
letter, communication, message, missive, correspondence, bulletin, note, line, encyclical

epitaph *n*
commemoration, inscription, rest in peace, RIP, obituary, funeral oration
technical lapidary expression

epithet *n*
description, descriptive adjective, descriptive phrase/expression, designation, name, nickname, tag, title, sobriquet
formal appellation, denomination

epitome *n*
1 PERSONIFICATION, embodiment, representation, model, example, archetype, type, prototype, essence
formal quintessence, exemplar
2 SUMMARY, abstract, abridgement, digest, synopsis, outline, précis, résumé

epitomize *v*
1 PERSONIFY, embody, represent, exemplify, encapsulate, illustrate, typify, symbolize, sum up
formal incarnate
2 ABRIDGE, shorten, summarize, abbreviate, abstract, précis, reduce, compress, condense, contract, curtail, cut
◳ 2 elaborate, expand

epoch *n*
age, era, period, time, date

equable *adj*
1 *an equable person*
even-tempered, placid, calm, cool and collected, serene, unexcitable, tranquil, composed, level-headed, easy-going
formal imperturbable
colloq. unflappable, unfazed, laid-back
2 *an equable climate*
uniform, even, consistent, constant, regular, moderate, temperate, unchanging, unvarying, steady, stable, smooth
◳ 1 excitable 2 variable, extreme

⚠ **equable** or **equitable** ?
Equable means 'even-tempered': *That child would infuriate the most equable parent*; 'not extreme and without great variation': *an equable climate.* *Equitable* means 'fair, just': *a more equitable distribution of profits.*

equal *adj, n, v*
▶ *adj* 1 IDENTICAL, the same, alike, like, equivalent, corresponding, commensurate, comparable
2 EVEN, uniform, regular, constant, level, unchanging, symmetrical, unvarying, balanced, well balanced, matched, evenly matched, on an equal footing
colloq. fifty-fifty, neck and neck
3 IMPARTIAL, fair, just, unbiased, neutral, non-partisan
4 *equal to a task*
COMPETENT, able, adequate, sufficient, fit, strong, capable, suitable, suited
◳ 1 different 2 unequal 3 biased 4 unsuitable
▶ *n* peer, counterpart, equivalent, coequal, match, parallel, twin, fellow, mate, compeer
▶ *v* 1 *equal a number*
match, correspond to, be the same as, add up to, amount to, balance, parallel, square with, tally with, coincide with, equalize, equate with, make, total
2 *equal someone's score*
match, rival, emulate, be level with, be on a par with, measure up to, come up to

equality *n*
1 UNIFORMITY, evenness, equivalence, correspondence, comparability, parallelism, balance, parity, par, symmetry, proportion, identity, sameness, likeness, similarity
2 IMPARTIALITY, fairness, justice, neutrality, partisanship, equal rights, equal opportunities, egalitarianism
◳ 2 inequality

equalize *v*
level, even up, make even, even out, match, equal,

equate, draw level, keep pace, balance, redress the balance, square, standardize, regularize, compensate, smooth

equanimity *n*
composure, calm, tranquillity, serenity, ease, coolness, self-possession, self-control, level-headedness, confidence, assurance, self-assurance, pose, dignity, placidity, impassivity
formal imperturbability, aplomb, sangfroid
colloq. unflappability
E3 alarm, anxiety, discomposure

equate *v*
1 *equate wealth with happiness*
compare with, liken to, match with, identify with, connect with, link with, pair with, juxtapose with, regard as the same, bracket together
2 *costs equate to a quarter of the income*
correspond to, correspond with, balance, parallel, equalize, be equal, offset, square with, agree with, tally with

equation *n*
equality, correspondence, equivalence, balancing, agreement, parallel, pairing, comparison, match, matching, likeness, identity, similarity
formal juxtaposition

equestrian *n, adj*
▶ *n* horseman, horsewoman, rider, courier, cavalryman, knight, cavalier, hussar, trooper, cowboy, cowgirl, rancher, herder, jockey
▶ *adj* mounted, riding, horse-riding
formal equine

equilibrium *n*
1 BALANCE, poise, symmetry, evenness, stability, steadiness
technical stasis
formal equipoise, counterpoise
2 EQUANIMITY, self-possession, composure, calmness, coolness, serenity, tranquillity, self-control, level-headedness, confidence, assurance, self-assurance, poise, dignity
formal imperturbability, aplomb, sangfroid
colloq. unflappability
E3 1 imbalance, instability **2** anxiety

equip *v*
provide, fit out, supply, furnish, prepare, arm, issue, fit up, kit out, stock, endow, rig, dress, deck out
formal array, accoutre

equipment *n*
apparatus, gear, supplies, tackle, kit, tools, material, furnishings, luggage, baggage, outfit, paraphernalia, stuff, things, accessories, furniture
formal accoutrements
colloq. rig-out

equipoise *n*
equilibrium, balance, evenness, stability, steadiness, symmetry, poise, ballast, counterbalance, counter-weight
formal counterpoise, equibalance, equiponderance
E3 imbalance

equitable *adj*
even-handed, fair, proper, reasonable, right, rightful, due, fair-and-square, square, honest, ethical, impartial, just, unbiased, unprejudiced, legitimate, disinterested, dispassionate, objective
E3 inequitable, unfair

⚠ **equitable** or **equable** ? *See panel at* **equable**.

equity *n*
even-handedness, equitableness, fairness, fair play, fair-mindedness, reasonableness, righteousness, uprightness, honesty, integrity, justice, justness, objectivity, impartiality, disinterestedness
formal rectitude
E3 inequity

equivalence *n*
identity, correspondence, agreement, likeness, equality, interchangeability, comparability, similarity, substitutability, correlation, parallel, conformity, sameness
formal parity
E3 unlikeness, dissimilarity

equivalent *adj, n*
▶ *adj* equal, same, similar, identical, substitutable, corresponding, alike, like, comparable, interchangeable, even, twin
technical homologous
formal tantamount, commensurate
E3 unlike, different
▶ *n* counterpart, opposite number, equal, parallel, match, fellow, double, twin, peer, alternative, correspondent
technical homologue
formal correlative

equivocal *adj*
ambiguous, uncertain, ambivalent, obscure, vague, indefinite, evasive, oblique, misleading, dubious, questionable, suspicious, confusing, indefinite
E3 unequivocal, clear, definite

equivocate *v*
prevaricate, evade, dodge, fence, hedge, mislead, change your mind
formal tergiversate, vacillate
colloq. shilly-shally, pussyfoot, waffle, chop and change, change your tune, beat about the bush, hedge your bets, run with the hare and hunt with the hounds

equivocation *n*
prevarication, evasion, dodging the issue, hedging, double talk, quibbling, shifting, shuffling
formal tergiversation
colloq. waffle, weasel words, pussyfooting
E3 directness

era *n*
age, epoch, period, date, day, days, time, times, generation, aeon, season, cycle, stage, century

eradicate *v*
eliminate, annihilate, get rid of, remove, root out, uproot, suppress, destroy, exterminate, extinguish, weed out, stamp out, wipe out, crack down on, abolish, erase, obliterate
formal efface, expunge, extirpate

eradication *n*
elimination, annihilation, removal, riddance, obliteration, abolition, suppression, destruction, extermination, extinction
formal effacement, extirpation, deracination, expunction

erasable *adj*
removable, washable, eradicable
formal effaceable
E3 permanent, ineradicable

erase *v*
obliterate, rub out, delete, blot out, wipe out, cancel, get rid of, remove, eradicate, put out of your mind
formal expunge, efface, excise

erasure *n*
obliteration, deletion, elimination, eradication, removal, cancellation, cleansing
formal erasement, effacement, expunction

erect *v, adj*
▶ *v* **1** BUILD, construct, put up, put together, establish, set up, elevate, assemble, raise, rear, lift, mount, pitch, create
2 *erect an organization*
found, form, institute, initiate, put up, create, organize, establish
▶ *adj* **1** UPRIGHT, straight, vertical, upstanding, standing, raised
2 RIGID, hard, firm, stiff

erection *n*
1 BUILDING, construction, edifice, structure, assembly, establishment, manufacture, fabrication, creation, elevation, raising
colloq. pile
2 RIGIDITY, stiffness
technical tumescence

ergo *adv*
therefore, consequently, accordingly, for this reason, in consequence, so, then, this being the case
formal hence, thus

erode *v*
wear away, eat away, eat into, wear down, corrode, consume, grind down, destroy, disintegrate, deteriorate, fragment, deplete, spoil, undermine
formal abrade, excoriate

erosion *n*
wear, wearing away, corrosion, disintegration, deterioration, destruction, undermining
formal abrasion, attrition, denudation, excoriation

erotic *adj*
aphrodisiac, seductive, sensual, titillating, pornographic, lascivious, stimulating, suggestive, erogenous, sexually arousing, amorous, venereal, carnal, lustful, voluptuous
formal amatory
colloq. sexy, adult, blue, raunchy, steamy, dirty

err *v*
1 MAKE A MISTAKE, be wrong, be incorrect, miscalculate, mistake, misjudge, make a slip, blunder, misunderstand, misconstrue
colloq. slip up, boob, make a booboo, bark up the wrong tree, get hold of the wrong end of the stick, put your foot in it; *slang* louse up, balls up, cock up
2 DO WRONG, sin, misbehave, go astray, offend, deviate, fall from grace
formal transgress

errand *n*
task, job, duty, chore, commission, charge, mission, undertaking, assignment, message

errant *adj*
1 WAYWARD, wrong, erring, stray, straying, deviant, offending, criminal, lawless, disobedient, sinful, sinning, loose
formal aberrant, peccant
2 ROAMING, rambling, roving, itinerant, journeying, wandering, nomadic
formal peripatetic

erratic *adj*
changeable, variable, fitful, fluctuating, inconsistent, intermittent, sporadic, irregular, unsteady, unstable, shifting, varying, inconstant, unpredictable, volatile, unsettled, unreliable, abnormal, eccentric, wandering, meandering
formal aberrant, capricious, desultory
F3 steady, consistent, stable

erring *adj*
wayward, wrong, errant, stray, straying, deviant, offending, criminal, lawless, disobedient, guilty, sinful, sinning, loose
formal peccant

erroneous *adj*
incorrect, wrong, mistaken, false, untrue, spurious, specious, inaccurate, inexact, invalid, illogical, unfounded, faulty, flawed, misguided, misplaced
formal fallacious
F3 correct, right

error *n*
mistake, inaccuracy, slip, blunder, gaffe, *faux pas*, lapse, slip of the tongue, mix-up, miscalculation, misunderstanding, misinterpretation, misjudgement, misconception, misapprehension, misprint, literal, spelling mistake, oversight, omission, fallacy, flaw, fault, wrong
formal solecism, aberration
colloq. slip-up, howler, boob

ersatz *adj*
fake, substitute, imitation, artificial, synthetic, man-made, simulated, counterfeit, sham, bogus
colloq. phoney

erstwhile *adj*
one-time, former, sometime, ex, late, old, once, past, previous, bygone

erudite *adj*
learned, scholarly, well-educated, knowledgeable, lettered, educated, well-read, literate, academic, cultured, intellectual, wise, highbrow, profound
colloq. brainy
F3 illiterate, ignorant

erudition *n*
learning, scholarship, education, knowledge, facts, knowledgeableness, learnedness, scholarliness, wisdom, culture, letters
formal profundity, reconditeness

erupt *v*
break out, explode, belch, pour forth, discharge, burst, gush, spew, spout, eject, vent, expel, emit, flare up, vomit, break
formal eruct, eructate

eruption *n*
1 OUTBURST, discharge, ejection, emission, venting, explosion, flare-up
2 RASH, outbreak, inflammation

escalate *v*
increase, intensify, grow, accelerate, rise, step up, heighten, raise, spiral, magnify, mushroom, enlarge, expand, extend, develop, mount, ascend, climb, soar, amplify
colloq. rocket, go through the roof, hit the roof
F3 decrease, diminish

escalator *n*
lift, elevator, moving staircase, moving walkway, travolator

escapable *adj*
avoidable, evadable, avertible, eludible
⊟ inevitable

escapade *n*
adventure, exploit, fling, prank, frolic, caper, romp, spree, antic, stunt, trick
colloq. lark, skylarking

escape *v, n*
▶ *v* **1** GET AWAY, break free, run away, make your escape, make your getaway, bolt, abscond, flee, fly, decamp, break loose, break out, flit, slip away, shake off, slip
colloq. scoot, scram, scat, scarper, do a runner/bunk, do a moonlight flit, make a bolt/break for it, take to your heels, run for your life, slip through someone's fingers
2 AVOID, evade, elude, skip, shun, steer clear of, sidestep
formal circumvent
colloq. dodge, duck
3 LEAK, seep, flow, drain, spurt, gush, issue, discharge, ooze, trickle, pour out/forth, pass
4 *his name escapes me*
forget, not place, not be remembered/recalled, not know
colloq. be on the tip of your tongue, not be able to put your finger on
▶ *n* **1** GETAWAY, flight, bolt, flit, breakout, absconding, decampment, jailbreak
colloq. bunk
2 AVOIDANCE, evasion
formal circumvention
colloq. dodging, ducking
3 LEAK, seepage, leakage, outflow, gush, drain, discharge, issue, emission, spurt, outpour, emanation
formal efflux
4 ESCAPISM, diversion, distraction, dreaming, fantasy, fantasizing, wishful thinking, recreation, relaxation, pastime, safety-valve

escapee *n*
absconder, jailbreaker, defector, deserter, fugitive, runaway, truant, refugee

escapism *n*
diversion, distraction, dreaming, fantasy, fantasizing, wishful thinking, recreation, relaxation, pastime, safety-valve
⊟ realism

escapist *n*
dreamer, daydreamer, fantasizer, wishful thinker, non-realist
colloq. ostrich
⊟ realist

eschew *v*
avoid, give up, refrain from, abandon, keep clear of, repudiate, shun, spurn, disdain
formal abjure, abstain from, forgo, forswear, renounce
⊟ embrace

escort *n, v*
▶ *n* **1** COMPANION, chaperon(e), partner, attendant, aide, squire, guide, bodyguard, protector, defender, beau
colloq. date
2 ENTOURAGE, company, retinue, suite, train, guard,

convoy, cortège, attendants
▶ *v* accompany, partner, chaperon(e), bring, come (along) with, take, take out, attend on, guide, lead, usher, conduct, guard, protect, defend, shepherd, walk

esoteric *adj*
obscure, cryptic, inscrutable, mysterious, mystic, mystical, occult, hidden, secret, confidential, private, inside
formal recondite, abstruse, arcane
⊟ well-known, familiar

especial *adj*
particular, special, marked, specific, striking, pre-eminent, notable, noteworthy, exceptional, outstanding, express, unique, exclusive, extraordinary, peculiar, singular, signal, uncommon, unusual, remarkable

especially *adv*
1 PARTICULARLY, specially, markedly, notably, exceptionally, outstandingly, expressly, supremely, uniquely, exclusively, unusually, extraordinarily, uncommonly, remarkably, strikingly, very
2 CHIEFLY, mainly, principally, primarily, pre-eminently, above all, most of all

espionage *n*
counter-intelligence, infiltration, intelligence, investigation, probing, reconnaissance, spying, surveillance, intercepting, industrial espionage, undercover operations/work, fifth column
colloq. snooping, bugging, wiretapping

espousal *n*
adoption, embracing, support, advocacy, backing, promotion, choice, defence, championing, championship, maintenance

espouse *v*
take up, adopt, embrace, support, advocate, back, choose, stand up for, defend, champion, patronize, maintain, opt for

espy *v*
notice, see, catch sight of, glimpse, observe, detect, discern, perceive, make out, sight, spot, spy, discover, distinguish, behold

essay *n, v*
▶ *n* composition, dissertation, paper, article, assignment, thesis, piece, commentary, critique, treatise, review, leader, tract
formal discourse, disquisition
▶ *v* try, attempt, endeavour, test, go for, take on, strain, strive, struggle, tackle, undertake
colloq. have a bash, have a crack, have a go, have a stab

essence *n*
1 NATURE, character, essential character, being, substance, reality, actuality, soul, spirit, core, centre, heart, meaning, point, quality, significance, life, entity, crux, kernel, marrow, pith, characteristics, attributes, principle
formal quintessence
2 CONCENTRATE, extract, concentration, distillation, spirits
formal distillate
▷ **in essence** basically, fundamentally, essentially, substantially, to all intents and purposes
▷ **of the essence** crucial, indispensable, necessary, vital, requisite, required, needed, important

essential *adj, n*
▶ *adj* **1** FUNDAMENTAL, basic, intrinsic, inherent,

innate, underlying, principal, main, key, central, characteristic, definitive, typical, constituent
2 CRUCIAL, indispensable, necessary, vital, requisite, required, needed, important
◨ **1** incidental **2** dispensable, inessential
▶ *n* necessity, prerequisite, requisite, requirement, basic, fundamental, necessary, principle, gist, main point(s), key point(s)
formal sine qua non
colloq. must

establish *v*
1 SET UP, found, start, form, institute, bring into being, open, create, begin, organize, inaugurate, introduce, install, plant, settle, secure, lodge, base
2 PROVE, demonstrate, show, authenticate, ratify, verify, certify, confirm, attest
formal substantiate, validate, corroborate, affirm
◨ **1** uproot **2** refute

established *adj*
respected, experienced, traditional, conventional, secure, settled, entrenched, ensconced, fixed, steadfast, proved, proven, tried and tested
◨ impermanent, unreliable

establishment *n*
1 FORMATION, setting up, founding, forming, creation, foundation, installation, institution, organization, inauguration
formal inception
2 BUSINESS, company, firm, institute, organization, concern, institution, corporation, enterprise, shop, store
3 RULING CLASS, the system, the authorities, the powers that be

estate *n*
1 POSSESSIONS, effects, assets, belongings, holdings, property, goods, lands, landholding, real estate, manor
2 AREA, development, centre, land, region, tract
3 STATUS, standing, situation, position, class, place, condition, state, rank

estate agent *n*
property agent
US realtor, real-estate agent

esteem *n, v*
▶ *n* respect, regard, good opinion, appreciation, estimation, judgement, admiration, honour, consideration, reverence, credit, reckoning, count, account, love
formal veneration, approbation
▶ *v* respect, admire, honour, regard highly, revere, reverence, value, cherish, reckon, rate, regard, think, view, consider, treasure, count, judge, hold, believe, account
formal adjudge, deem, venerate

esteemed *adj*
admired, respected, well-respected, well-thought-of, worthy, highly-regarded, honoured, revered, treasured, valued, honourable, admirable, reputable, respectable, distinguished, excellent, prized
formal venerated

estimable *adj*
esteemed, respected, worthy, creditable, admirable, commendable, distinguished, reputable, respectable, honourable, excellent, good, notable, noteworthy, praiseworthy, valuable, valued
formal laudable, meritorious
◨ despicable, insignificant

estimate *v, n*
▶ *v* assess, reckon, evaluate, calculate roughly, work out approximately, gauge, guess, value
formal conjecture
▶ *n* **1** ROUGH CALCULATION, approximate cost/price/value/quantity, quotation, reckoning, valuation, judgement, (rough) guess, approximation, assessment, estimation, evaluation, computation
colloq. guesstimate, ballpark figure
2 JUDGEMENT, consideration, opinion, belief, view, thinking, conclusion, evaluation, assessment, reckoning

estimation *n*
1 JUDGEMENT, opinion, belief, consideration, estimate, view, (way of) thinking, feeling, evaluation, assessment, reckoning, conception, calculation, computation, conclusion
2 RESPECT, regard, appreciation, esteem, credit
3 ROUGH CALCULATION, approximate cost/price/value/quantity, valuation, (rough) guess, assessment, estimate, evaluation

estrange *v*
alienate, disaffect, antagonize, disunite, divide, divorce, split up, break up, separate, sever, drive apart, part, set at variance, set against, withhold, withdraw
colloq. drive a wedge between, put a barrier between
◨ attract, bind, unite

estranged *adj*
divided, separate, separated, divorced, alienated, disaffected, antagonized
◨ reconciled, united

estrangement *n*
alienation, disaffection, antagonization, disunity, division, dissociation, parting, separation, severance, split, breach, break-up, hostility, unfriendliness, antipathy, withdrawal, withholding

estuary *n*
inlet, mouth, firth, fjord, creek, cove, bay, arm, sea-loch

et cetera *adv*
and so on, and so forth, and the like, and the rest, &c, and suchlike, et al
colloq. and what have you, and/or whatever

etch *v*
cut, carve, engrave, burn, furrow, dig, groove, impress, imprint, incise, ingrain, inscribe, bite, corrode, stamp

etching *n*
carving, cut, engraving, inscription, impression, imprint, print, sketch

eternal *adj*
1 *eternal bliss*
unending, endless, ceaseless, everlasting, never-ending, infinite, limitless, immortal, deathless, undying, imperishable, indestructible
2 *eternal truths*
unchanging, timeless, enduring, lasting, perennial, abiding
3 *eternal quarrelling*
constant, continuous, perpetual, persistent, incessant, interminable, endless, never-ending, non-stop, relentless, remorseless
formal unremitting
◨ **1** ephemeral, temporary **2** changeable

eternally *adv*
1 EVERLASTINGLY, endlessly, ceaselessly,

indestructibly, for ever
2 INTERMINABLY, constantly, lastingly, always, for ever, perpetually, incessantly
🖙 briefly, temporarily

eternity n
1 EVERLASTINGNESS, endlessness, everlasting, imperishability, infinity, timelessness, perpetuity, immutability, after-life, hereafter, immortality, deathlessness, everlasting life, heaven, paradise, next world, world to come, world without end
2 AGE, ages, long time, ages and ages
colloq. donkey's years

ethereal adj
1 DELICATE, immaterial, dainty, exquisite, fine, light, gossamer, subtle, tenuous, insubstantial, intangible, airy-fairy, impalpable
formal diaphanous
2 HEAVENLY, spiritual, celestial, refined, rarefied, unearthly, unworldly, elemental
formal empyreal, empyrean
🖙 **2** earthly, solid

ethical adj
moral, principled, just, right, proper, virtuous, honourable, fair, upright, decent, above reproach, righteous, honest, good, correct, high-minded, commendable, fitting, noble
old use seemly
formal decorous
🖙 unethical

ethics n
moral values, values, morality, morals, principles, moral principles, standards, moral standards, code, moral code, moral philosophy, rules, beliefs, conscience, equity, principles of behaviour, principles of right and wrong
formal propriety

ethnic adj
racial, native, indigenous, traditional, tribal, folk, cultural, national, aboriginal
formal autochthonous

ethos n
attitude, beliefs, standards, manners, ethics, morality, code, principles, spirit, tenor, flavour, rationale, character, disposition

etiquette n
code, code of behaviour, formalities, standards, correctness, conventions, customs, code of practice, code of conduct, rules, manners, good manners, form, good form, politeness, courtesy, ceremony, decency, unwritten law
formal protocol, civility, decorum, propriety

etymology n
word history, word origins, word-lore, linguistics, origin, derivation, source, philology, semantics, lexicology

eulogize v
praise, acclaim, sing/sound the praises of, wax lyrical, applaud, approve, celebrate, exalt, extol, glorify, honour, magnify, commend, compliment, congratulate
formal laud, panegyrize
colloq. rave about, hype, plug
🖙 condemn

eulogy n
praise, tribute, acclaim, acclamation, accolade, commendation, exaltation, glorification, compliment, applause, plaudit
formal encomium, laud, laudation, laudatory, paean, panegyric
🖙 condemnation

euphemism n
evasion, polite term, indirect expression, substitution, softening, genteelism, politeness, understatement
🖙 dysphemism

euphemistic adj
polite, neutral, vague, indirect, evasive, soft-toned, genteel, understated

euphonious adj
harmonious, melodious, melodic, musical, silvery, soft, sweet, dulcet, mellow, sweet-sounding, sweet-toned, tuneful, clear
formal canorous, consonant, dulcifluous, dulciloquent, euphonic, mellifluous, symphonious
🖙 cacophonous

euphoria n
elation, ecstasy, bliss, rapture, high spirits, buoyancy, well-being, exhilaration, exultation, joy, intoxication, jubilation, transport, glee, exaltation, enthusiasm, cheerfulness
colloq. high
🖙 depression, despondency

euphoric adj
elated, ecstatic, blissful, rapturous, exhilarated, enraptured, enthusiastic, buoyant, intoxicated, exultant, exulted, joyful, gleeful, happy, cheerful, jubilant
formal joyous
colloq. high
🖙 depressed, despondent

euthanasia n
mercy killing, release, happy/merciful release, quietus

evacuate v
1 LEAVE, go away from, depart, withdraw, remove, move out of, retreat, retire from, abandon, desert, vacate, decamp, relinquish
formal forsake
colloq. quit, clear (out), pull out of
2 EMPTY, make empty, eject, void, clear, expel, discharge, eliminate, purge
formal defecate, excrete

evacuation n
1 DEPARTURE, leaving, withdrawal, retreat, exodus, flight, removal, desertion, abandonment, clearance, relinquishment, retirement, vacating
formal forsaking
colloq. quitting
2 EMPTYING, expulsion, ejection, discharge, elimination, purging, urination
formal defecation

evade v
1 *evade your duties*
elude, avoid, escape, shirk, steer clear of, shun, sidestep, get round, balk, fend off
formal circumvent
colloq. dodge, duck, skive, chicken out, cop out
2 *evade a question*
prevaricate, equivocate, fence, fudge, avoid, parry, quibble
colloq. hedge, dodge, duck, beat about the bush
🖙 **1** confront, face

evaluate *v*
value, assess, estimate, reckon, calculate, gauge, measure, judge, determine, rate, size up, weigh, compute, rank
formal appraise

evaluation *n*
valuation, assessment, estimation, estimate, judgement, reckoning, calculation, opinion, determination, computation
formal appraisal

evanescent *adj*
ephemeral, fading, fleeting, brief, short-lived, transient, transitory, impermanent, momentary, temporary, unstable, disappearing, vanishing, passing, evaporating, insubstantial, perishable
E∃ permanent

evangelical *adj*
1 *evangelical Christianity*
biblical, Bible-believing, scriptural, orthodox, fundamentalist, missionary, crusading
colloq. Bible-bashing, Bible-thumping, Bible-punching
2 ENTHUSIASTIC, zealous, campaigning, crusading, evangelistic, missionary, propagandizing, propagandist, proselytizing

evangelist *n*
preacher, missionary, missioner, revivalist, crusader, campaigner

evangelize *v*
preach, campaign, spread the word, crusade, convert, proselytize, baptize, gospelize, missionarize, missionize, propagandize

evaporate *v*
1 DISAPPEAR, dematerialize, vanish, melt (away), dissolve, disperse, dispel, fade
formal dissipate, evanesce
2 VAPORIZE, dry, dehydrate, exhale
formal desiccate

evaporation *n*
vaporization, drying, dehydration, condensation, distillation, dematerialization, dissolution, fading, melting, vanishing
formal desiccation

evasion *n*
1 AVOIDANCE, equivocation, prevarication, escape, shirking, trickery, subterfuge, fencing, steering clear of, shunning
formal circumvention, tergiversation
colloq. hedging, ducking
2 *evasions rather than straight answers*
excuse, quibble, deception, deceit, trickery, fudging, prevarication, equivocation
colloq. ducking, hedging, dodge, dodging
E∃ **1** frankness, directness

evasive *adj*
equivocating, indirect, vague, prevaricating, devious, unforthcoming, misleading, deceitful, deceptive, fudging, quibbling, oblique, secretive, tricky, cunning
colloq. shifty, slippery, cagey, waffling
E∃ direct, frank

eve *n*
day before, time before, period before, verge, brink, edge, threshold

even *adj, adv, v*
▶ *adj* **1** LEVEL, flat, smooth, horizontal, flush, parallel, uniform, true, plane
2 STEADY, unvarying, unchanging, stable, constant, regular, uniform, consistent, unwavering
3 EQUAL, balanced, matching, same, similar, like, alike, evenly matched, on an equal footing, symmetrical, level, side by side
colloq. fifty-fifty, neck and neck
4 EVEN-TEMPERED, calm, placid, serene, tranquil, composed, cool, equable, unruffled, unexcitable
formal unperturbable
colloq. unflappable
5 EVEN-HANDED, balanced, equitable, fair, impartial, just, neutral, non-partisan
E∃ **1** uneven **3** unequal
▶ *adv* **1** *even worse*
all the more, still, yet, more, to a greater extent/degree
2 *even a child could do that*
surprisingly, unexpectedly, unusually, oddly, as well, also, too, still more, likewise
3 *sad, even depressed*
more exactly, more precisely, indeed
4 *not even write his own name*
hardly, scarcely, at all, so much as
▷ **even so** however, but, all the same, despite that, in spite of that, however that may be, nevertheless, nonetheless, still, yet; *formal* notwithstanding that
▶ *v* smooth, flatten, level, plane, match, regularize, balance, equalize, make equal, make uniform, align, square, stabilize, steady, straighten
colloq. strike a balance

even-handed *adj*
fair, just, impartial, balanced, disinterested, dispassionate, equitable, neutral, unbiased, unprejudiced, reasonable, non-discriminatory, square, fair and square, without fear or favour
E∃ inequitable, discriminatory

evening *n*
nightfall, dusk, close of day, eve, eventide, twilight, sunset, sundown

event *n*
1 HAPPENING, occurrence, incident, occasion, affair, circumstance, episode, experience, matter, case, adventure, business, fact, possibility, milestone
formal eventuality
2 GAME, match, fixture, competition, contest, round, race, tournament, engagement, meeting, item
3 CONSEQUENCE, result, outcome, conclusion, end, aftermath, upshot, effect, issue
formal termination

even-tempered *adj*
calm, level-headed, equable, placid, stable, tranquil, serene, composed, cool, cool and collected, steady, peaceful, peaceable
formal imperturbable
colloq. unflappable, unfazed, laid-back
E∃ excitable, erratic

eventful *adj*
busy, exciting, lively, active, full, interesting, remarkable, important, significant, memorable, momentous, historic, crucial, critical, notable, noteworthy, unforgettable
colloq. action-packed
E∃ dull, ordinary

eventual *adj*
final, ultimate, last, resulting, closing, concluding, ensuing, future, later, subsequent, prospective, projected, planned, impending

eventuality *n*
possibility, probability, likelihood, chance,
contingency, event, happening, circumstance, case,
outcome, crisis, emergency, mishap
formal happenstance

eventually *adv*
finally, ultimately, at last, in the end, at length,
subsequently, after all, sooner or later, in the long run,
in the fullness of time
colloq. at the end of the day, when all is said and done,
in the final analysis

ever *adv*
1 ALWAYS, evermore, for ever, perpetually,
permanently, constantly, at all times, continually,
incessantly, endlessly, eternally, until the end of time,
till doomsday, till your dying day
colloq. till the cows come home, till hell freezes over
2 AT ANY TIME, in any case, in any circumstances,
at all, on any account, on any occasion
E3 1 never
▷ **ever so**   very, very much, really, extremely

everlasting *adj*
1 ETERNAL, undying, never-ending, endless,
immortal, infinite, imperishable, constant,
permanent, perpetual, indestructible, timeless
2 *everlasting noise*
constant, continuous, perpetual, persistent, incessant,
interminable, endless, never-ending, non-stop,
relentless, remorseless
formal unremitting
E3 temporary, transient

evermore *adv*
always, for ever, eternally, ever, ever after, for ever and a
day, for ever and ever, unceasingly, to the end of time,
till doomsday
formal henceforth, hereafter, in perpetuum

every *adj*
1 EACH, every single, every individual
2 *make every effort*
all possible, as much as possible
3 *have every confidence*
all, complete, total, full, entire

everybody *n*
everyone, one and all, each one, each person, every
person, all and sundry, the whole world

everyday *adj*
ordinary, common, commonplace, day-to-day,
familiar, run-of-the-mill, regular, standard, basic,
plain, routine, usual, workaday, normal, average,
customary, stock, accustomed, conventional, daily,
habitual, monotonous, unimaginative, frequent,
simple, informal
colloq. common-or-garden
E3 unusual, exceptional, special

everyone *n*
everybody, one and all, each one, each person, every
person, all and sundry, the whole world
colloq. all the world and his wife, every Tom, Dick and
Harry, every man Jack, Uncle Tom Cobleigh and all

everything *n*
all, all things, each thing, the lot, the whole lot, the
entirety, the sum, the total, lock, stock and barrel
formal the aggregate
colloq. the whole caboodle, the whole kit and
caboodle, the whole shooting-match, the whole

shebang, the whole bag of tricks, the works, everything
but the kitchen sink

everywhere *adv*
all around, in/to all places, in/to each place, the world
over, all over, throughout, far and near, near and far, far
and wide, high and low, ubiquitous
colloq. left, right and centre, here there and
everywhere; *US* every place

evict *v*
expel, eject, dispossess, put out, turn out, throw out,
force out, force to leave, remove, cast out, oust,
dislodge
formal expropriate
colloq. turf out, kick out, chuck out, show someone the
door, throw out on the streets, turn out of house and
home

eviction *n*
expulsion, ejection, dispossession, removal, clearance,
dislodgement
formal defenestration, expropriation
colloq. the bum's rush, the boot, the push, the elbow

evidence *n, v*
▶ *n* **1** PROOF, verification, confirmation, grounds,
support, documentation, data
formal affirmation, substantiation, corroboration
2 TESTIMONY, declaration
technical affidavit
formal attestation
3 INDICATION, suggestion, sign, trace, mark, hint,
demonstration, token, symptom
formal manifestation
▷ **in evidence**   clear, obvious, apparent, plain,
patent, visible, conspicuous, noticeable, clear-cut,
unmistakable
▶ *v* show, indicate, reveal, demonstrate, display,
exhibit, prove, witness, signify, confirm, establish,
betray
formal affirm, attest, denote, evince, manifest

evident *adj*
clear, obvious, apparent, plain, patent, visible,
conspicuous, noticeable, clear-cut, unmistakable,
perceptible, distinct, discernible, tangible, undoubted,
incontestable, indisputable, incontrovertible
formal manifest

evidently *adv*
1 CLEARLY, apparently, plainly, patently, obviously,
undoubtedly, doubtless(ly), indisputably
formal manifestly
2 SEEMINGLY, apparently, outwardly, as it would
seem/appear, so it seems/appears, to all appearances
formal ostensibly

evil *adj, n*
▶ *adj* **1** WICKED, wrong, sinful, bad, immoral,
vicious, vile, cruel, base, corrupt, malicious,
malignant, devilish, demonic, diabolic, depraved,
mischievous, sinister, black
formal malevolent, iniquitous, reprehensible,
nefarious, heinous
2 HARMFUL, pernicious, destructive, injurious,
deadly, detrimental, hurtful, bad, poisonous
formal deleterious
3 DISASTROUS, ruinous, calamitous, catastrophic,
adverse, dire, unfortunate, unlucky
formal inauspicious, unpropitious
4 OFFENSIVE, noxious, foul, stinking
formal noisome
E3 1 good **3** fortunate

▶ *n* **1** WICKEDNESS, wrongdoing, wrong, immorality, misconduct, badness, sin, sinfulness, vice, viciousness, vileness, depravity, baseness, corruption, devilishness, mischief
formal iniquity, malignity, heinousness
2 ADVERSITY, calamity, disaster, misfortune, suffering, sorrow, ruin, catastrophe, blow, curse, distress, hurt, harm, ill, pain, injury, misery, woe
formal affliction

evildoer *n*
wrongdoer, bad person, criminal, delinquent, offender, miscreant, reprobate, sinner, scoundrel, rogue, villain

evince *v*
show, reveal, indicate, display, exhibit, express, signify, demonstrate, confess, declare, betray, establish
formal attest, bespeak, betoken, evidence, manifest
⊟ conceal, suppress

eviscerate *v*
disembowel, gut, draw, gralloch
formal exenterate

evocation *n*
summoning-up, calling, elicitation, invocation, inducing, arousal, stirring, stimulation, suggestion, activation, excitation, kindling, recall, echo

evocative *adj*
suggestive, expressive, indicative, reminiscent, vivid, graphic, memorable
formal redolent

evoke *v*
summon (up), call, elicit, invoke, induce, arouse, stir, raise, kindle, stimulate, bring about, cause, call forth, call up, conjure up, awaken, provoke, excite, recall, bring back memories of, make someone think of
⊟ suppress

evolution *n*
development, growth, progression, progress, expansion, increase, ripening, derivation, descent, unrolling, unfolding, unravelling, working-out, opening-out

evolve *v*
develop, grow, increase, mature, progress, unravel, unroll, unfold, work out, open out, expand, enlarge, emerge, descend, derive, result, elaborate

exacerbate *v*
aggravate, worsen, make worse, make things/matters worse, compound the problem, heighten, increase, provoke, sharpen, intensify, exaggerate, inflame, exasperate, deepen, embitter, enrage, infuriate, irritate, vex
colloq. add fuel to the fire/flames, fan the flames, add insult to injury, rub salt in the wound
⊟ soothe

exact *adj, v*
▶ *adj* **1** PRECISE, accurate, correct, faithful, literal, flawless, faultless, right, true, definite, explicit, detailed, specific, strict, unerring, close, just, factual, identical, express, word-perfect
formal veracious
colloq. blow-by-blow, on the nail, spot on, bang on, on the button
2 CAREFUL, scrupulous, particular, rigorous, precise, methodical, meticulous, orderly, exacting, painstaking, thorough
formal punctilious

⊟ **1** inexact, imprecise **2** careless
▶ *v* extort, extract, claim, insist on, wrest, wring, compel, demand, command, call for, force, impose, require, squeeze
colloq. milk, bleed

exacting *adj*
demanding, challenging, difficult, hard, laborious, arduous, onerous, stringent, tiring, rigorous, taxing, tough, harsh, firm, painstaking, severe, strict, stern, unsparing, unyielding
⊟ easy

exactitude *n*
accuracy, precision, exactness, correctness, faultlessness, carefulness, care, meticulousness, orderliness, rigorousness, rigour, scrupulousness, thoroughness, conscientiousness, painstakingness, perfectionism, strictness, detail
⊟ inaccuracy, carelessness, imprecision

exactly *adv, interj*
▶ *adv* **1** PRECISELY, accurately, literally, faithfully, correctly, specifically, rigorously, scrupulously, verbatim, carefully, faultlessly, without error, unerringly, strictly, religiously, to the letter, particularly, methodically, explicitly, expressly
formal veraciously
colloq. dead
2 ABSOLUTELY, definitely, precisely, indeed, certainly, truly, quite, just, unequivocally
colloq. bang on, spot on, on the dot, on the button, on the nail, to a T, smash, plumb
⊟ **1** inaccurately, roughly, vaguely
▶ *interj* precisely, quite, of course, just so, indeed, absolutely, agreed, certainly, right, true

exactness *n*
accuracy, precision, exactitude, correctness, faultlessness, carefulness, care, meticulousness, orderliness, rigorousness, rigour, scrupulousness, thoroughness, strictness
⊟ inaccuracy, carelessness, imprecision

exaggerate *v*
overstate, overdo, magnify, overemphasize, emphasize, stress, make too much of, dramatize, overdramatize, embellish, embroider, colour, stretch the truth, enlarge, amplify, enhance, oversell, overplay
formal aggrandize
colloq. lay/pile it on, lay/pile in on thick, lay/pile it on with a trowel, make a mountain out of a molehill, blow something up out of all proportion, shoot a line, make a drama out of a crisis
⊟ understate, play down

exaggerated *adj*
overstated, overdone, overestimated, overcharged, excessive, extravagant, pretentious, embellished, amplified, bombastic, inflated, overblown, caricatured, burlesqued, exalted
technical euphuistic
formal hyperbolic
colloq. tall
⊟ understated, played down

exaggeration *n*
overstatement, overemphasis, emphasis, magnification, overestimation, excess, extravagance, embellishment, enlargement, pretentiousness, amplification, burlesque, caricature, parody
formal hyperbole
⊟ meiosis, understatement

exalt *v*
1 PRAISE, extol, glorify, magnify, acclaim, applaud, bless, honour, adore, revere, worship, reverence, eulogize
formal laud, venerate
2 DELIGHT, elate, overjoy, transport, promote, raise, prefer, elevate, upgrade, enliven, excite, exhilarate
formal aggrandize

exaltation *n*
1 ELATION, ecstasy, rapture, bliss, joy, jubilation, excitement, exhilaration, high spirits
2 PRAISE, glorification, acclaim, honour, glory, reverence, worship, adoration, eulogy
formal veneration

exalted *adj*
1 LOFTY, high, elevated, grand, regal, lordly, eminent, stately, noble, idealistic, virtuous, moral
2 ELATED, ecstatic, blissful, joyful, happy, jubilant, rapturous, in high spirits
colloq. in seventh heaven

exam *n*
test, examination, exercises, questions, multiple-choice questions, practical, quiz, paper, viva, oral, final

examination *n*
1 INSPECTION, inquiry, scrutiny, study, survey, search, analysis, assessment, exploration, investigation, probe, observation, research, review, scan, perusal, check, check-up, audit, critique, post-mortem
formal appraisal
colloq. once-over
2 TEST, exam, quiz, questioning, cross-examination, cross-questioning, trial, inquisition, interrogation, viva, oral

examine *v*
1 INSPECT, investigate, scrutinize, study, look at, look into, observe, survey, analyse, explore, inquire, consider, probe, research, review, scan, check (out), check over, ponder, pore over, sift, vet, weigh up, assess, audit, peruse
technical assay
formal appraise
slang case
2 TEST, quiz, question, cross-examine, cross-question, interrogate
formal catechize
colloq. grill, pump, give the third degree to, give someone a roasting, go to town on, put the screws on

examinee *n*
entrant, candidate, competitor, contestant, applicant, interviewee

examiner *n*
adjudicator, assessor, tester, inspector, interviewer, judge, marker, questioner, reviewer, reader, analyst, censor, critic, auditor, arbiter, scrutineer, scrutinizer
technical assayer
formal examinant, interlocutor, scrutator

example *n*
1 SAMPLE, specimen, prototype
formal exemplar, archetype
2 INSTANCE, case, case in point, illustration, exemplification, representation/typical case, epitome
3 MODEL, role model, guide, pattern, ideal, standard, criterion, type
formal precedent, paradigm

4 LESSON, warning, caution, punishment
formal admonition
▷ **for example** eg, for instance, as an example/instance, say, to illustrate, by way of illustration, to give as an illustration

exasperate *v*
infuriate, annoy, anger, incense, irritate, madden, provoke, enrage, irk, rile, rankle, rouse, goad, vex, gall
colloq. get on someone's nerves, get to, needle, bug, wind up, drive up the wall, make someone's blood boil, put someone's back up
F₃ appease, pacify

exasperated *adj*
infuriated, annoyed, angry, indignant, angered, incensed, irritated, maddened, provoked, riled, vexed, piqued, irked, galled, goaded
colloq. aggravated, at the end of your tether, bugged, fed up, needled, nettled, peeved
F₃ calm, satisfied

exasperating *adj*
infuriating, annoying, bothersome, maddening, provoking, troublesome, disagreeable, irksome, irritating, vexing, galling, pernicious, vexatious
colloq. aggravating

excavate *v*
dig (out), dig up, hollow, burrow, tunnel, delve, unearth, mine, quarry, disinter, cut, gouge, scoop, reveal, uncover
formal exhume

excavation *n*
hole, hollow, pit, quarry, mine, colliery, dugout, dig, diggings, burrow, cavity, crater, trench, trough, shaft, ditch, cutting

exceed *v*
surpass, go beyond, be greater/larger than, be more than, outnumber, outdo, outstrip, beat, better, be superior to, pass, overtake, top, outshine, eclipse, outreach, outrun, outweigh, transcend, cap, overdo, overstep, go over

exceedingly *adv*
very, very much, extremely, greatly, highly, unusually, exceptionally, especially, enormously, excessively, hugely, immensely, vastly, inordinately, unprecedentedly, superlatively, surpassingly, amazingly, astonishingly, extraordinarily

excel *v*
1 BE EXCELLENT, succeed, shine, stand out, be outstanding, be skilful, be pre-eminent, predominate
2 SURPASS, outdo, beat, be superior to, outclass, outperform, outrank, outrival, eclipse, better, be better than

excellence *n*
superiority, pre-eminence, distinction, merit, supremacy, quality, worth, value, fineness, skill, eminence, goodness, greatness, virtue, perfection, purity, transcendence

excellent *adj*
wonderful, brilliant, marvellous, fantastic, superior, first-class, first-rate, high-quality, very good, prime, superlative, unequalled, unparalleled, matchless, exceptional, outstanding, surpassing, remarkable, distinguished, great, eminent, flawless, faultless, perfect, good, exemplary, select, superb, admirable, commendable, splendid, pre-eminent, praiseworthy, noteworthy, notable, noted, fine, worthy, inspired

formal sterling
colloq. top-notch, smashing, terrific, neat, ace, brill, out of this world, second to none; *slang* mega, cool, wicked, stonking, radical, crucial, way-out, shit-hot, groovy
E3 inferior, second-rate

except *prep, v*
▶ *prep* excepting, but, but for, apart from, other than, with the exception of, aside from, save, omitting, not counting, leaving out, excluding, except for, besides, bar, barring, minus, less
▶ *v* leave out, omit, bar, exclude, reject, rule out, pass over

exception *n*
oddity, deviation, departure, abnormality, irregularity, peculiarity, inconsistency, rarity, special case, freak, quirk
formal anomaly
▷ **with the exception of** excepting, but, apart from, other than, save, omitting, not counting, leaving out, excluding, except for, besides, bar, barring, minus, less

exceptionable *adj*
objectionable, unpleasant, disagreeable, offensive, unacceptable, disgusting, deplorable, abhorrent
formal repugnant
E3 acceptable, agreeable

exceptional *adj*
1 OUTSTANDING, remarkable, marvellous, excellent, extraordinary, brilliant, phenomenal, notable, noteworthy, superior, unequalled
formal prodigious
2 ABNORMAL, unusual, strange, odd, irregular, extraordinary, out of the ordinary, peculiar, special, rare, atypical, uncommon
formal anomalous, aberrant, singular
E3 **1** mediocre **2** normal

exceptionally *adv*
1 EXTREMELY, extraordinarily, notably, outstandingly, especially, amazingly, remarkably, wonderfully
2 UNUSUALLY, uncommonly, irregularly, abnormally, rarely

excerpt *n*
extract, passage, portion, section, selection, quote, quotation, part, piece, cutting, clip, clipping, citation, scrap, fragment
technical pericope

excess *n, adj*
▶ *n* **1** SURFEIT, too much, more than enough, overabundance, oversupply, glut, superabundance, surplus, backlog, overflow, overkill, remainder, residue, leftovers
formal plethora, superfluity
colloq. bellyful
2 OVERINDULGENCE, dissoluteness, immoderateness, immoderation, extravagance, unrestraint, debauchery
formal dissipation, intemperance, prodigality
E3 **1** deficiency **2** restraint
▶ *adj* extra, surplus, too much, spare, redundant, remaining, residual, left-over, additional, superfluous
formal supernumerary
E3 inadequate

excessive *adj*
immoderate, inordinate, extreme, too much, undue,

uncalled-for, disproportionate, overdone, unnecessary, unneeded, needless, unwarranted, superfluous, superabundant, unreasonable, lavish, exorbitant, extravagant
colloq. steep, over the top, OTT
E3 insufficient

excessively *adv*
immoderately, inordinately, extremely, too much, to a fault, unduly, unreasonably, overly, overmuch, disproportionately, unnecessarily, needlessly, superfluously, exorbitantly, exaggeratedly, extravagantly, intemperately
E3 insufficiently, inadequately

exchange *v, n*
▶ *v* barter, change, trade, swap, switch, replace, interchange, convert, commute, transpose, substitute, stand in for, reciprocate, bargain, bandy
▶ *n* **1** INTERCHANGE, swap, switch, replacement, substitution
formal reciprocity
colloq. give and take
2 TRADE, commerce, dealing, market, traffic, barter, bargain, trade-off
3 CONVERSATION, discussion, chat, argument
Related adjective: catallactic

excise¹ *n*
excise duty
duty, tax, VAT, customs, levy, surcharge, tariff, toll
formal impost

excise² *v*
excise sensitive material
cut, cut out, remove, extract, destroy, eradicate, erase, delete, exterminate
formal expunge, expurgate, extirpate, rescind

excision *n*
removal, deletion, eradication, destruction, expunction
formal expurgation, extermination, extirpation

excitable *adj*
temperamental, volatile, passionate, emotional, highly-strung, fiery, hot-headed, hasty, nervous, hot-tempered, irascible, quick-tempered, sensitive, susceptible
formal choleric, mercurial
colloq. edgy
E3 calm, stable

excite *v*
1 *excite a feeling*
stir up, thrill, impress, touch, move, agitate, disturb, upset, arouse, rouse, animate, awaken, evoke, engender, inspire, kindle, fire, inflame, ignite
colloq. turn on
2 *excite an action*
provoke, motivate, stimulate, bring about, instigate, incite, induce, galvanize, generate, sway
3 *excite sexually*
arouse, stimulate, awaken, titillate
colloq. turn on
E3 **1** calm

excited *adj*
aroused, roused, stimulated, stirred, exhilarated, thrilled, elated, in high spirits, enthusiastic, eager, moved, beside yourself, animated, worked up, wrought-up, overwrought, agitated, restless, frantic, frenzied, wild
colloq. high, on the edge of your seat, on tenterhooks,

thrilled to bits, turned on, uptight, hyper, fired up
E3 calm, apathetic

excitement n

1 *the excitement of winning*
thrill, passion, adventure, emotion, pleasure,
animation, elation, enthusiasm, restlessness, ferment,
fever, eagerness, stimulation, agitation, discomposure,
exhilaration
formal perturbation
colloq. kick(s)
2 UNREST, ado, action, activity, commotion, stir, fuss,
tumult, flurry, furore
E3 **1** apathy **2** calm

exciting adj

stimulating, stirring, intoxicating, exhilarating,
thrilling, dramatic, rousing, moving, enthralling,
electrifying, striking, breathtaking, sensational,
provocative, inspiring, interesting
colloq. nail-biting, cliff-hanging, action-packed, sexy
E3 dull, unexciting

exclaim v

cry (out), declare, come out with, blurt (out), call, yell,
shout, roar, shriek, bellow, proclaim, utter
formal vociferate, ejaculate

exclamation n

cry, call, yell, shout, expletive, interjection, outcry,
utterance, roar, shriek, bellow
formal ejaculation

exclude v

1 BAN, bar, prohibit, refuse, disallow, veto, forbid,
blacklist
formal interdict
2 OMIT, leave out, miss out, delete, keep out, refuse,
reject, ignore, shut out, rule out, ostracize, eliminate
formal preclude
colloq. drop, skip
3 EXPEL, eject, evict, throw out, remove,
excommunicate
colloq. boot out, turf out, kick out
E3 **1** admit **2** include, consider

exclusion n

1 OMISSION, rejection, elimination, ruling out,
refusal, repudiation
formal preclusion
2 BAN, bar, prohibition, embargo, veto, boycott
formal interdict, proscription
3 EJECTION, expulsion, eviction, removal
boycott, exception
E3 **1** inclusion **2** allowance **3** admittance

exclusive adj

1 SOLE, single, individual, unique, only, undivided,
unshared, complete, whole, total, peculiar
2 RESTRICTED, limited, closed, private, narrow,
restrictive, choice, select, discriminative, cliquey, chic,
elegant, fashionable, up-market, upper crust, snobbish
colloq. classy, posh, snazzy, ritzy, plush, swish
▷ **exclusive of** except, except for, with the exception
of, excepting, excluding, not including, not counting,
omitting, leaving out, ruling out, barring, debarring
E3 inclusive of

excommunicate v

ban, banish, eject, denounce, exclude, expel, remove,
bar, blacklist, debar, outlaw, repudiate, disfellowship,
unchurch
formal anathematize, proscribe, execrate

excoriate v

condemn, carp, disapprove of, find fault with,
denounce, attack, censure, blame
formal animadvert, disparage, decry, denigrate,
vituperate
colloq. nag, slate, slam, knock, snipe, run down, come
down on, give someone some stick, nit-pick

excrement n

waste matter, excretion, dung, ordure, droppings, turd
technical egesta, frass, scats, guano
formal faeces, stool
slang crap, shit, poop
Related adjective: excrementitious

excrescence n

1 GROWTH, swelling, bump, lump, knob, appendage,
outgrowth, projection, prominence, tumour, wart,
boil, cancer
formal intumescence, protuberance
2 MONSTROSITY, blot, disfigurement, eyesore

excrete v

void, pass, eject, discharge, expel, evacuate, exude,
secrete
formal defecate, urinate
slang crap, shit

excretion n

discharge, excrement, droppings, dung, evacuation,
ordure, perspiration
formal defecation, excreta, urination, faeces, stool
slang crap, shit

excruciating adj

agonizing, painful, severe, tormenting, unbearable,
insufferable, acute, intolerable, intense, sharp,
piercing, extreme, atrocious, racking, harrowing,
savage, burning, bitter

exculpate v

clear, discharge, excuse, free, justify, let off, pardon,
release, vindicate, forgive, deliver, absolve, acquit
formal exonerate
E3 blame, condemn

excursion n

1 OUTING, trip, day trip, jaunt, expedition, journey,
tour, airing, breather, ride, drive, walk, ramble
colloq. junket
2 DIGRESSION, departure, straying, wandering,
detour, diversion

excusable adj

understandable, minor, slight, allowable, permissible,
defensible, explainable, forgivable, pardonable,
justifiable
E3 blameworthy

excuse v, n

▶ *v* **1** FORGIVE, pardon, overlook, absolve, acquit,
tolerate, make allowances for, ignore, indulge
formal exonerate, exculpate
2 RELEASE, free, discharge, liberate, let off, relieve,
spare, exempt
3 CONDONE, explain, justify, vindicate, defend,
apologize for
formal mitigate
E3 **1** criticize **2** punish
▶ *n* justification, explanation, grounds, defence, plea,
alibi, reason, vindication, apology, pretext, pretence,
evasion, shift, substitute
formal exoneration, mitigation, mitigating
circumstances
colloq. cop-out, front, cover-up

execrable *adj*

deplorable, abhorrent, abominable, disgusting, foul, appalling, atrocious, despicable, detestable, offensive, shocking, repulsive, revolting, horrible, loathsome, vile, nauseous, obnoxious, odious, damnable, accursed, hateful
formal heinous
F3 admirable, esteemable

execrate *v*

deplore, hate, abhor, loathe, abominate, condemn, denounce, denunciate, despise, detest, revile, curse, damn, imprecate
formal excoriate, fulminate, inveigh against, vilify, anathematize
colloq. blast
F3 commend, praise

execute *v*

1 PUT TO DEATH, kill, hang, electrocute, shoot, guillotine, behead, crucify
formal decapitate
colloq. liquidate
2 CARRY OUT, perform, do, accomplish, achieve, fulfil, complete, bring off, discharge, put into effect, put into practice, enact, deliver, enforce, finish, implement, administer, engineer, realize, dispatch, validate, serve, render, stage
formal effect, consummate, expedite

execution *n*

1 DEATH PENALTY, death sentence, capital punishment, putting to death, killing

Means of execution include: beheading, burning, crucifixion, decapitation, electrocution, firing squad, garrotting, gassing, guillotining, hanging, lethal injection, lynching, shooting, stoning, *colloq.* stringing up.

2 ACCOMPLISHMENT, operation, performance, completion, achievement, administration, effect, enactment, implementation, realization, fulfilment, discharge, dispatch, enforcement
formal consummation, effecting
3 STYLE, technique, rendition, rendering, delivery, performance, staging, manner, mode, presentation

executioner *n*

hangman, firing squad, headsman, axeman, killer, murderer, exterminator, assassin, slayer
colloq. hit man, liquidator

executive *n, adj*

▶ *n* **1** ADMINISTRATOR, manager, organizer, leader, controller, director, governor, official
2 ADMINISTRATION, management, government, leadership, hierarchy
colloq. top brass, big guns, big shots
▶ *adj* administrative, managerial, controlling, supervisory, regulating, decision-making, governing, law-making, organizing, directing, directorial, organizational, leading, guiding

exegesis *n*

explanation, interpretation, clarification, opening-up
formal exposition, expounding, explication

exemplar *n*

example, standard, model, pattern, type, ideal, prototype, paragon, copy, criterion, yardstick, epitome, illustration, instance, specimen
formal archetype, embodiment, exemplification, paradigm

exemplary *adj*

1 MODEL, ideal, perfect, admirable, excellent, faultless, flawless, correct, good, commendable, praiseworthy, worthy, honourable
formal laudable, estimable, meritorious
2 CAUTIONARY, warning
formal admonitory
F3 **1** imperfect, unworthy

exemplify *v*

illustrate, be an example of, demonstrate, show, instance, cite, represent, typify, characterize, embody, personify, epitomize, exhibit, depict, display
formal manifest

exempt *v, adj*

▶ *v* excuse, release, relieve, let off, free, grant immunity to, absolve, discharge, dismiss, liberate, spare, exclude, waive, make an exception
formal exonerate
▶ *adj* excused, not liable, not subject, immune, released, spared, absolved, discharged, excluded, free, liberated, dismissed, clear
F3 liable

exemption *n*

exception, exclusion, immunity, privilege, indulgence, release, freedom, indemnity, discharge
formal absolution, dispensation, exoneration
F3 liability

exercise *v, n*

▶ *v* **1** USE, utilize, employ, make use of, apply, exert, practise, implement, bring to bear, bring into play, wield, try, discharge, exploit
2 TRAIN, do exercises, drill, practise, keep fit, exert yourself
colloq. work out
3 WORRY, disturb, trouble, upset, burden, distress, vex, annoy, agitate, afflict, preoccupy
formal perturb
▶ *n* **1** TRAINING, drill, movement, practice, effort, exertion, activity, keep-fit, aerobics, sports, gymnastics, PE, physical education, PT, physical training, warm-up, jogging, running, isometrics, eurhythmics, callisthenics, labour
colloq. physical jerks, workout
2 USE, utilization, employment, application, implementation, practice, operation, discharge, assignment, fulfilment, accomplishment, exertion
3 TASK, lesson, work, discipline, problem, piece of work

exert *v*

use, utilize, employ, apply, exercise, bring to bear, bring into play, wield, spend, expend
▷ **exert yourself** strive, struggle, try hard, strain, make every effort, take pains, do your best/utmost, toil, labour, work, endeavour, apply yourself, give your all; *colloq.* sweat, go all out, pull out all the stops

exertion *n*

1 EFFORT, industry, labour, toil, work, exercise, struggle, diligence, assiduousness, perseverance, pains, endeavour, attempt, strain, stress, trial
formal travail
2 USE, utilization, employment, application, exercise, operation, action
F3 **1** idleness, rest

exhale *v*

breathe (out), give off, blow, discharge, emit, expel, issue, respire, steam, evaporate

formal emanate, expire
F3 inhale

exhaust *v, n*
▶ *v* **1** TIRE (OUT), weary, fatigue, tax, sap, drain, strain, weaken, overwork, overtax, wear out
formal enervate
colloq. do in, fag out, knock out, whack, take it out of, nearly/almost kill
2 CONSUME, empty, drain, sap, spend, expend, waste, squander, impoverish, use up, finish, dry, bankrupt
formal deplete, dissipate
F3 **1** refresh **2** renew
▶ *n* emission, exhalation, discharge, fumes, smoke, steam, vapour
formal emanation

exhausted *adj*
1 TIRED OUT, dead tired, worn out, fatigued, weak, washed-out, drained, jaded
formal enfeebled, enervated
colloq. dead-beat, all in, done (in), whacked, fagged out, knackered, bushed, burnt out, dog-tired, ready to drop, zonked
2 EMPTY, finished, consumed, spent, used up, drained, dry, worn out, void
formal depleted
F3 **1** vigorous **2** fresh

exhausting *adj*
tiring, strenuous, taxing, wearing, gruelling, arduous, hard, laborious, backbreaking, draining, severe, testing, punishing, formidable
formal debilitating, enervating
F3 refreshing, invigorating

exhaustion *n*
fatigue, tiredness, weariness, weakness, feebleness, lethargy, jet-lag
formal debility, enervation
F3 freshness, liveliness

exhaustive *adj*
comprehensive, all-embracing, all-inclusive, far-reaching, complete, total, extensive, encyclopedic, full-scale, thorough, full, in-depth, intensive, detailed, definitive, all-out, sweeping
F3 incomplete, restricted

exhibit *v, n*
▶ *v* display, put on display, show, present, demonstrate, expose, unveil, parade, reveal, express, make clear, make plain, reveal, disclose, indicate, air, flaunt, offer, set out, set forth
formal manifest, array
F3 conceal, hide
▶ *n* display, exhibition, show, showing, demonstration, illustration, model, presentation

exhibition *n*
display, show, demonstration, exhibit, presentation, spectacle, showing, fair, performance, airing, representation, showcase, indication, expression, revelation, disclosure
formal manifestation, exposition
colloq. expo

exhibitionist *n*
show-off, extrovert, poseur, poser, self-advertiser

exhilarate *v*
thrill, excite, make excited, elate, make happy, cheer up, delight, gladden, animate, enliven, invigorate, vitalize, revitalize, raise/lift the spirits of, stimulate, brighten, lift

colloq. perk up
F3 bore, discourage

exhilarating *adj*
thrilling, exciting, delightful, cheerful, gladdening, cheering, enlivening, stimulating, revitalizing, invigorating, heady, breathtaking
colloq. mind-blowing
F3 boring, discouraging

exhilaration *n*
excitement, thrill, happiness, cheerfulness, gladness, delight, elation, joy, joyfulness, exaltation, glee, high spirits, liveliness, vivacity, zeal, enthusiasm, animation, ardour, invigoration, revitalization, stimulation, gusto, dash, gaiety, mirth, hilarity
formal élan
F3 boredom, discouragement

exhort *v*
urge, persuade, encourage, implore, goad, incite, inflame, inspire, instigate, spur, warn, bid, call upon, press, advise, counsel, caution, prompt
formal admonish, beseech, enjoin, entreat

exhortation *n*
urging, persuasion, encouragement, goading, incitement, advice, caution, warning, counsel, bidding, lecture, sermon
formal admonition, beseeching, enjoinder, entreaty, paraenesis, protreptic

exhume *v*
disinter, dig up, disentomb, excavate, unbury, unearth, resurrect
formal disinhume
F3 bury

exigency *n*
1 DEMAND, requirement, need, necessity
2 EMERGENCY, urgency, crisis, criticalness, difficulty, distress, imperativeness, pressure, plight, quandary, predicament, stress

exigent *adj*
urgent, demanding, insistent, necessary, pressing, stringent, exacting, critical, crucial

exiguous *adj*
meagre, insufficient, scant, scanty, negligible, sparse, slight, slim, bare

exile *n, v*
▶ *n* **1** BANISHMENT, deportation, expatriation, expulsion, uprooting, ostracism, separating, separation, transportation
2 EXPATRIATE, refugee, émigré, ex-pat, deportee, displaced person, outcast, outlaw, pariah
▶ *v* banish, expel, deport, extradite, expatriate, repatriate, drive out, cast out, uproot, separate, ostracize, oust, excommunicate, eject, outlaw, ban, bar

exist *v*
1 BE, live, have life, abide, continue, endure, have being, have existence, breathe, have breath
2 SUBSIST, survive, live, eke out a living, eke out an existence
3 BE PRESENT, occur, happen, be available, remain, last, continue, prevail

existence *n*
1 BEING, life, living, reality, actuality, fact, continuance, continuation, endurance, survival, breath, subsistence
2 WAY OF LIFE, way of living, life, lifestyle
formal mode of living

3 ENTITY, creature, being, thing
4 CREATION, the world
E∃ 1 death, non-existence

existent *adj*
existing, actual, real, current, present, living, alive,
enduring, remaining, surviving, standing, abiding,
prevailing
formal obtaining, extant
colloq. around
E∃ non-existent

exit *n, v*
▶ *n* **1** DEPARTURE, going, leaving, retreat,
withdrawal, leave-taking, retirement, farewell, exodus,
flight
2 DOOR, way out, doorway, gate, vent, outlet
formal egress
E∃ 1 entrance, arrival **2** entrance
▶ *v* depart, leave, go, retire, withdraw, take your leave,
retreat, issue
E∃ arrive, enter

exodus *n*
departure, evacuation, mass departure, mass
evacuation, flight, fleeing, escape, leaving, migration,
retirement, long march, retreat, withdrawal, exit,
hegira

exonerate *v*
1 ABSOLVE, acquit, clear, excuse, vindicate, justify,
pardon, declare innocent, discharge
formal exculpate
2 EXEMPT, excuse, spare, let off, free, liberate,
discharge, release, relieve
E∃ 1 incriminate

exoneration *n*
1 ACQUITTAL, clearing, excusing, vindication,
justification, pardon, discharge, amnesty, absolution,
dismissal
formal exculpation
2 EXEMPTION, excusing, discharge, liberation,
freeing, release, relief, immunity, indemnity
E∃ 1 incrimination

exorbitant *adj*
excessive, unreasonable, unwarranted, undue,
inordinate, immoderate, extravagant, extortionate,
enormous, preposterous, monstrous
colloq. daylight robbery, a rip-off
E∃ reasonable, moderate, fair

exorcism *n*
casting out, deliverance, freeing, expulsion,
purification
old use exsufflation
formal adjuration

exorcize *v*
cast out, drive out, free, expel, purify
old use exsufflate
formal adjure

exotic *adj*
1 FOREIGN, alien, imported, introduced, tropical,
external, non-native
2 UNUSUAL, striking, different, remarkable,
unfamiliar, extraordinary, bizarre, curious, strange,
impressive, fascinating, colourful, glamorous,
peculiar, outlandish, extravagant, outrageous,
sensational
E∃ 1 native **2** ordinary, common

expand *v*
increase, grow, become/make larger/bigger, extend,
enlarge, develop, amplify, spread, stretch, swell, widen,
lengthen, thicken, intensify, escalate, magnify, multiply,
inflate, amplify, broaden, blow up, open out, fill out,
fatten, puff out, unfold, unfurl, pad, branch out,
diversify
formal distend, dilate, intumesce
E∃ contract
▷ **expand on** enlarge on, elaborate on, embroider,
go into details; *formal* expatiate on, dilate on

expanse *n*
extent, space, area, breadth, range, stretch, region,
sweep, field, plain, tract, vastness, extensiveness

expansion *n*
growth, increase, extension, development,
amplification, spread, expanse, swelling, enlargement,
lengthening, thickening, broadening, magnification,
multiplication, inflation, unfolding, unfurling,
diversification
formal augmentation, diffusion, dilation, distension,
dilatation
E∃ contraction

expansive *adj*
1 EXTENSIVE, broad, comprehensive, wide,
wide-ranging, widespread, all-embracing, thorough
2 FRIENDLY, genial, outgoing, open, affable,
sociable, talkative, warm, communicative, effusive,
uninhibited
formal loquacious
3 EXPANDING, growing, increasing, enlarging,
developing, diversifying, magnifying, multiplying
E∃ 1 restricted, narrow **2** reserved, cold
3 contracting

expatiate *v*
expand, enlarge, amplify, elaborate, embellish,
develop, expound, dwell on
formal dilate

expatriate *n, v, adj*
▶ *n* emigrant, émigré, exile, refugee, displaced
person, ex-pat, outcast
▶ *v* banish, exile, deport, extradite, drive out, uproot,
expel, oust, repatriate, ostracize
formal proscribe
▶ *adj* banished, exiled, deported, expelled, uprooted,
emigrant, émigré

expect *v*
1 *expect you're right*
suppose, assume, believe, think, presume, imagine,
reckon, trust
formal surmise, conjecture
colloq. guess
2 *expect the money soon*
anticipate, await, look forward to, hope for, look for,
watch for, bank on, bargain for, envisage, predict,
forecast, contemplate, project, foresee
3 *expect you to comply*
require, want, wish, insist on, demand, call for,
look for, hope for, rely on, count on

expectancy *n*
anticipation, eagerness, expectation, hope, suspense,
waiting, curiosity
formal conjecture

expectant *adj*
1 AWAITING, anticipating, looking forward, hopeful,
in suspense, ready, apprehensive, anxious, watchful,

eager, on tenterhooks, with bated breath, curious
2 PREGNANT, going to have a baby
technical gravid
formal with child, enceinte
colloq. expecting, in the family way, in the club;
slang preggers, with a bun in the oven

expectantly *adv*
in anticipation, eagerly, expectingly, hopefully, in
suspense, apprehensively, optimistically

expectation *n*
hope, belief, anticipation, assumption, presumption,
surmise, supposition, calculation, forecast, projection,
prediction, eagerness, requirement, demand,
insistence, promise, want, wish, reliance, trust,
prospect, confidence, assurance, suspense, optimism,
possibility, probability, outlook
formal conjecture

expecting *adj*
pregnant, going to have a baby, expectant
technical gravid
formal with child, enceinte
colloq. in the family way, in the club

expedience *n*
convenience, suitability, appropriateness, fitness,
aptness, advantageousness, effectiveness, desirability,
helpfulness, properness, profitableness, usefulness,
practicality, pragmatism, advisability, benefit,
advantage, profitability, expediency, utility,
utilitarianism
formal judiciousness, propriety, prudence

expedient *adj, n*
▶ *adj* convenient, suitable, appropriate, fitting,
opportune, politic, in your own interest, profitable,
useful, beneficial, advantageous, advisable, sensible,
practical, pragmatic, tactical
formal prudent
▣ inexpedient
▶ *n* stratagem, scheme, means, method, tactic, ploy,
manoeuvre, plan, trick, shift, contrivance, device,
stopgap
colloq. dodge

expedite *v*
speed up, accelerate, step up, quicken, hasten, hurry,
further, facilitate, assist, promote, press, dispatch,
discharge, hurry through
formal precipitate
▣ delay

expedition *n*
1 JOURNEY, excursion, trip, voyage, tour, outing,
exploration, trek, safari, hike, sail, ramble, raid, quest,
pilgrimage, adventure, undertaking, enterprise,
project, campaign, mission, crusade
2 TEAM, group, party, crew, company
3 PROMPTNESS, speed, swiftness, haste
formal alacrity, celerity

expeditious *adj*
quick, efficient, rapid, speedy, swift, fast, hasty,
immediate, instant, diligent, prompt, active, alert,
brisk, ready
colloq. meteoric
▣ slow

expel *v*
1 DRIVE OUT, eject, evict, banish, throw out, cast out,
ban, bar, oust, dismiss, reject, exile, outlaw, expatriate
formal proscribe
colloq. boot out, chuck out, kick out

2 DISCHARGE, eject, belch, evacuate, void, cast out,
spew out
▣ **1** welcome

expend *v*
1 SPEND, pay, buy, afford, overspend, waste, fritter,
squander
formal purchase, disburse, procure
colloq. fork out, lay out, shell out, blow, splash out
2 CONSUME, use (up), get through, go through,
exhaust, empty, drain, sap, employ, utilize
formal dissipate, deplete
▣ **1** save **2** conserve

expendable *adj*
dispensable, disposable, replaceable, unimportant,
unnecessary, inessential, non-essential
▣ indispensable, necessary

expenditure *n*
1 *huge amounts of public expenditure*
spending, expense, expenses, costs, outlay, outgoings,
payment, output, waste, squandering
formal disbursement
2 *the expenditure of effort*
use, application, consumption, draining, sapping,
employment, utilization
formal dissipation
▣ income

expense *n*
1 *underestimate the expense of moving house*
spending, expenditure, outlay, payment, paying-out,
loss, cost, price, charge, fee, rate
formal disbursement
2 *expenses will be reimbursed*
costs, outgoings, incidentals, outlay, overheads,
incidental expenses, out-of-pocket expenses,
miscellaneous expenses, spending
3 *at the expense of his life*
cost, sacrifice, loss, harm, disadvantage, detriment
Related adjective: sumptuary

expensive *adj*
dear, high-priced, costly, costing a lot, exorbitant,
extortionate, overpriced, extravagant, lavish
colloq. steep, pricey, sky-high, costing an arm and a
leg, costing the earth, costing a bomb, daylight robbery
▣ cheap, inexpensive

experience *n, v*
▶ *n* **1** KNOWLEDGE, familiarity, contact, skill,
involvement, exposure, participation, practice,
training, understanding, learning, observation
colloq. know-how
2 INCIDENT, event, episode, happening, encounter,
occurrence, circumstance, adventure, affair, case,
ordeal
▣ **1** inexperience
▶ *v* undergo, go through, live through, suffer, feel,
endure, encounter, face, meet, know, try, perceive,
sustain, become familiar with, participate in

experienced *adj*
1 PRACTISED, knowledgeable, familiar, capable,
competent, proficient, adept, well-versed, expert,
accomplished, qualified, skilful, skilled, tried,
trained, professional, *au fait*, *au courant*
2 MATURE, seasoned, wise, veteran, sophisticated,
worldly wise
colloq. around, streetwise
▣ **1** inexperienced, unskilled **2** inexperienced,
unsophisticated

experiment *n, v*
▶ *n* trial, test, testing, investigation, experimentation, research, inquiry, demonstration, examination, observation, analysis, trial run, venture, try-out, trial and error, attempt, procedure, proof, pilot study, piloting, dummy run, dry run
▶ *v* try (out), test, investigate, examine, research, sample, verify, observe, explore, carry out tests, conduct an experiment

experimental *adj*
trial, test, exploratory, tentative, provisional, investigative, observational, speculative, pilot, preliminary, trial-and-error, at the trial/exploratory stage
formal empirical, peirastic

expert *n, adj*
▶ *n* specialist, connoisseur, authority, pundit, master, past master, old master, professional, maestro, virtuoso
colloq. pro, dab hand, old hand, ace, buff, egghead, wise guy, *US* mavin, *US* maven
▶ *adj* proficient, adept, skilled, skilful, knowledgeable, experienced, able, practised, professional, accomplished, masterly, excellent, brilliant, specialist, qualified, virtuoso, dexterous
colloq. top-notch, up on, well up on, crack, ace
FE amateurish, novice

expertise *n*
expertness, proficiency, ability, skill, skilfulness, deftness, knowledge, professionalism, mastery, command, dexterity, facility, cleverness, virtuosity, savoir-faire
colloq. know-how, knack
FE inexperience, inexpertness

expiate *v*
atone for, make amends for, purge, do penance for, make up for, pay for, redress

expiation *n*
atonement, redemption, ransom, reparation, redress, penance, amends, recompense, shrift

expire *v*
1 END, come to an end, cease, finish, stop, close, run out, be no longer valid, lapse
formal terminate, conclude, discontinue
2 DIE, depart, perish, pass away, pass on, depart this life, breathe your last, lose your life
formal decease
colloq. peg out, bite the dust, pop off, give up the ghost, have had it, meet your maker; *slang* snuff it, cash in your chips, kick the bucket
FE 1 begin, be valid 2 live, be born

expiry *n*
end, finish, close, expiration, lapse
formal cessation, conclusion, termination, discontinuation
FE beginning, continuation

explain *v*
1 INTERPRET, clarify, describe, define, make clear, throw/shed light on, simplify, resolve, solve, spell out, translate, elaborate, unfold, unravel, untangle, decipher, decode, illustrate, demonstrate, disclose, teach, set out
formal elucidate, expound, delineate, explicate
2 JUSTIFY, excuse, account for, rationalize, vindicate, defend, give a reason for, explain away, lie behind
FE 1 obscure, confound

explanation *n*
1 INTERPRETATION, clarification, definition, illustration, demonstration, account, description, note, comment, commentary, gloss, footnote, annotation, unfolding, deciphering, decoding
formal elucidation, exegesis, expounding, delineation, explication
2 JUSTIFICATION, excuse, reason, account, motive, meaning, answer, warrant, rationalization, vindication, defence, alibi
formal apologia

explanatory *adj*
descriptive, demonstrative, illustrative, justifying
formal interpretative, interpretive, explicative, expository, exegetical, elucidatory

expletive *n*
swear-word, oath, curse, blasphemy, obscenity, profanity, bad language
formal anathema, imprecation, execration
colloq. four-letter word

explicable *adj*
explainable, accountable, definable, determinable, intelligible, justifiable, resolvable, understandable, solvable
formal interpretable, exponible

explicate *v*
explain, interpret, clarify, describe, define, make clear, illustrate, demonstrate, spell out, set forth, unfold, unravel, untangle, work out
formal elucidate, expound
FE confuse, obscure

explicit *adj*
1 CLEAR, distinct, clearly expressed, exact, categorical, absolute, direct, certain, positive, precise, specific, unequivocal, unambiguous, express, definite, declared, detailed, stated, straightforward
2 OPEN, direct, frank, candid, outspoken, straightforward, forthright, unreserved, unrestrained, uninhibited, plain, plain-spoken
FE 1 implicit, unspoken, vague 2 reserved, restrained

explode *v*
1 BLOW UP, burst, go off, go up, set off, detonate, discharge, blast
formal erupt
colloq. go bang
2 *explode with rage*
blow up, erupt, flare up, burst out
colloq. blow a fuse, blow your cool, blow your top, boil over, burst a blood vessel, do your nut, fly into a rage, fly off the handle, go off the deep end, go up the wall, hit the ceiling, hit the roof, lose your cool, lose your rag, see red
3 DISCREDIT, disprove, give the lie to, debunk, invalidate, rebut, repudiate
formal refute
4 GROW RAPIDLY, increase suddenly, escalate, accelerate, boom, leap, surge, mushroom, rocket
FE 3 prove, confirm

exploit *n, v*
▶ *n* deed, feat, adventure, achievement, accomplishment, attainment, activity, action, act, stunt
▶ *v* 1 USE, apply, employ, draw on, put to good use, utilize, capitalize on, use to good advantage, profit by, turn to account, take advantage of, make capital out of, tap

colloq. cash in on, milk
2 MISUSE, abuse, take advantage of, take liberties, profiteer, oppress, ill-treat, impose on, manipulate
colloq. rip off, fleece, milk, bleed, take for a ride, put something across someone, pull a fast one on, walk all over, play off against

exploration *n*
1 INVESTIGATION, examination, inquiry, research, scrutiny, study, inspection, observation, analysis, probe
2 EXPEDITION, survey, reconnaissance, search, trip, tour, voyage, travel, safari

exploratory *adj*
investigative, fact-finding, experimental, pilot, probing, searching, analytic, tentative, trial

explore *v*
1 INVESTIGATE, examine, look into, study, inspect, research, scrutinize, probe, analyse, consider, survey, inquire into, review
2 TRAVEL, tour, search, reconnoitre, prospect, scout, survey
formal traverse
colloq. see the world, do

explorer *n*
traveller, discoverer, navigator, tourer, prospector, scout, surveyor, reconnoitrer

explosion *n*
1 DETONATION, blast, burst, outburst, discharge, eruption, bang, boom, outbreak, clap, crack, thunder, rumble, roll, fit
formal report
2 *population explosion*
boom, surge, leap, sudden increase, dramatic growth
3 *explosion of anger*
outburst, eruption, fit, flare-up, rage, tantrum, paroxysm

explosive *n, adj*
▶ *n* dynamite, gelignite, gunpowder, jelly, nitroglycerine, TNT, cordite, Semtex®
▶ *adj* 1 *an explosive device*
charged, hazardous, dangerous, unstable, volatile
formal perilous
2 *an explosive situation*
tense, sensitive, fraught, charged, critical, nerve-racking, unstable, volatile
3 FIERY, angry, unstable, volatile, overwrought, worked-up, violent, stormy, unrestrained, wild, raging, sensitive, touchy
4 *explosive growth*
sudden, dramatic, rapid, unexpected, mushrooming, rocketing, burgeoning, abrupt
colloq. meteoric
F∃ 1, 2 stable, calm 3 composed

exponent *n*
1 ADVOCATE, promoter, supporter, upholder, defender, backer, adherent, spokesman, spokeswoman, spokesperson, champion
formal proponent
2 PRACTITIONER, adept, expert, master, specialist, player, performer

export *v, n*
▶ *v* trade, deal with, sell abroad/overseas, traffic in, transport
▶ *n* exported product/commodity/goods, transfer, trade, foreign trade, international trade

expose *v*
1 REVEAL, show, exhibit, display, disclose, uncover, bring to light, bring out into the open, make known, present, detect, divulge, betray, unveil, unmask, unearth, lay bare, denounce
formal manifest
colloq. blow the whistle, take the lid off
2 ENDANGER, jeopardize, imperil, risk, hazard, put at risk, put in jeopardy, make vulnerable
3 *expose the public to art*
familiarize with, bring into contact with, acquaint with, introduce to, lay open to, subject to
F∃ 1 conceal, cover up 2 protect

exposé *n*
disclosure, divulgence, exposure, revelation, uncovering, account, article

exposed *adj*
bare, open, in the open, revealed, laid bare, unprotected, without protection, open to the elements, vulnerable, exhibited, on display, on show, on view, shown, susceptible
F∃ covered, sheltered

exposition *n*
1 EXPLANATION, description, analysis, unfolding, clarification, illumination, commentary, interpretation, account, illustration, critique, presentation, paper, study, thesis, monograph
formal discourse, elucidation, exegesis, explication
2 EXHIBITION, show, fair, display, demonstration
colloq. expo

expository *adj*
explanatory, descriptive, illustrative, interpretative
technical exegetic, hermeneutic
formal declaratory, elucidative, explicatory, interpretive

expostulate *v*
protest, argue, plead, reason, dissuade
formal remonstrate

exposure *n*
1 REVELATION, uncovering, disclosure, exposé, showing, unmasking, unveiling, display, airing, exhibition, presentation, publicity, discovery, detection, divulgence, denunciation
formal manifestation
2 FAMILIARITY, experience, knowledge, contact, acquaintance, awareness
3 JEOPARDY, danger, hazard, risk, vulnerability, susceptibility
4 PUBLICITY, public attention, advertising, promotion
colloq. plug, hype

expound *v*
explain, analyse, dissect, unfold, unravel, untangle, clarify, illuminate, describe, illustrate, interpret, comment on, set forth, set out, spell out, preach, sermonize
formal elucidate, explicate

express *v, adj*
▶ *v* 1 ARTICULATE, verbalize, put into words, utter, voice, give voice to, say, speak, state, communicate, put/get over, pronounce, word, tell, announce, report, assert, declare, put across, formulate, point out, intimate, testify, convey, vent, ventilate, air
formal enunciate
2 SHOW, demonstrate, exhibit, disclose, divulge, reveal, indicate, denote, depict, embody, couch

formal manifest
3 SYMBOLIZE, stand for, represent, signify, designate
▶ *adj* **1** SPECIFIC, explicit, exact, definite, clear, categorical, precise, distinct, well-defined, clear-cut, certain, plain, particular, stated, unambiguous, unequivocal, special, sole
formal manifest
2 FAST, speedy, rapid, quick, swift, high-speed, brisk, non-stop
formal expeditious
🔁 **1** vague

expression *n*
1 LOOK, air, aspect, appearance, scowl, grimace, gesture
formal countenance, mien
2 REPRESENTATION, demonstration, indication, exhibition, communication, illustration, embodiment, show, sign, symbol, style
formal manifestation
3 UTTERANCE, verbalization, voicing, communication, articulation, statement, assertion, proclamation, announcement, declaration, pronouncement, speech, wording, intimation
4 PHRASE, word, wording, term, turn of phrase, saying, set phrase, phrasing, idiom, language
5 TONE, intonation, delivery, style, idiom, diction, enunciation, modulation, phrasing
formal locution
6 FEELING, emotion, passion, depth, force, power, vigour, vividness, intensity, imagination, artistry, creativity

expressionless *adj*
dull, blank, deadpan, impassive, emotionless, straight-faced, inscrutable, empty, vacuous, glassy
colloq. poker-faced
🔁 expressive

expressive *adj*
1 ELOQUENT, articulate, meaningful, forceful, telling, revealing, informative, communicative, demonstrative, emphatic, moving, evocative, poignant, lively, striking, animated, suggestive, significant, thoughtful, vivid, sympathetic
2 INDICATIVE, showing, demonstrating, revealing, suggesting

expressly *adv*
specifically, explicitly, exactly, definitely, clearly, categorically, absolutely, precisely, distinctly, plainly, particularly, unambiguously, unequivocally, specially, solely, especially, decidedly, intentionally, on purpose, purposely, pointedly
formal manifestly

expropriate *v*
take, take away, seize, commandeer, confiscate, impound, usurp, assume, dispossess, annex, unhouse
technical disseise
formal appropriate, arrogate, requisition, sequester

expulsion *n*
1 EJECTION, eviction, exile, banishment, removal, discharge, exclusion, dismissal, throwing out, rejection
colloq. sacking, the sack, the boot
2 DISCHARGE, ejection, belching, evacuation, voiding, excretion

expunge *v*
erase, remove, wipe out, cancel, obliterate, eradicate, destroy, exterminate, extinguish, raze, get rid of, abolish, annihilate, annul, blot out, delete, cross out,

rub out
formal efface, extirpate

expurgate *v*
censor, cut, emend, clean up, blue-pencil, bowdlerize, purge, purify, sanitize

exquisite *adj*
1 BEAUTIFUL, attractive, dainty, delicate, fine, charming, elegant, delightful, lovely, pretty, pleasing, fragile
2 PERFECT, flawless, fine, excellent, choice, precious, rare, outstanding
3 REFINED, discriminating, meticulous, sensitive, discerning, cultivated, cultured, impeccable
4 INTENSE, keen, sharp, acute, piercing, poignant
🔁 **1** ugly **2** flawed **3** unrefined

extant *adj*
surviving, remaining, existent, existing, in existence, alive, living, subsistent, subsisting
🔁 extinct, non-existent, dead

extempore *adv, adj*
▶ *adv* impromptu, ad lib, on the spur of the moment, spontaneously
colloq. off the cuff, off the top of your head
▶ *adj* impromptu, improvised, ad-lib, unscripted, spontaneous, unplanned, unrehearsed, unprepared, extemporaneous
colloq. off-the-cuff
🔁 planned

extemporize *v*
ad-lib, improvise, play it by ear, think on your feet, make up

extend *v*
1 SPREAD, stretch, reach, continue, carry on, run, last, come (up/down) to, go as far as, go down/up to
2 ENLARGE, increase, expand, develop, amplify, intensify, step up, lengthen, widen, broaden, draw out, stretch, prolong, spin out, drag out, unwind
formal elongate, protract, augment
3 OFFER, give, grant, hold out, reach out, impart, present
formal bestow, confer, proffer
🔁 **2** contract, shorten **3** withhold

extended *adj*
lengthy, long, lengthened, increased, enlarged, expanded, developed, amplified

extension *n*
1 ENLARGEMENT, increase, stretching, broadening, widening, lengthening, expansion, development, enhancement, continuation, prolongation
formal elongation, protraction
2 ADDITION, supplement, appendix, annexe, wing, add-on, adjunct
formal addendum
3 DELAY, postponement, more/additional time

extensive *adj*
1 BROAD, comprehensive, far-reaching, large-scale, thorough, wide, wide-ranging, widespread, universal, complete, extended, all-inclusive, unlimited, boundless, general, pervasive, prevalent
2 LARGE, huge, roomy, spacious, vast, long, lengthy, wide, substantial, fair-sized, sizeable
formal capacious, commodious, voluminous
🔁 **1** restricted, narrow **2** small

extent *n*
1 DIMENSION(s), amount, magnitude, expanse, size,

area, bulk, degree, level, breadth, quantity, spread, coverage, stretch, volume, width, measure, length, duration, term, time
2 LIMIT, bounds, lengths, range, reach, scope, compass, stretch, sphere, play, sweep

extenuate *v*
diminish, excuse, lessen, minimize, modify, qualify, soften
formal mitigate

extenuating *adj*
moderating, qualifying, justifying, palliative, diminishing, excusing, lessening, minimizing, modifying, softening
formal exculpatory, extenuative, extenuatory, mitigating

exterior *n, adj*
▶ *n* outside, surface, outer surface, covering, coating, face, façade, shell, skin, finish, externals, external surface, appearance
F3 inside, interior
▶ *adj* outer, outside, outermost, surface, external, superficial, surrounding, outward, peripheral, extrinsic
F3 inside, interior

exterminate *v*
annihilate, kill, eradicate, destroy, eliminate, massacre, slaughter, abolish, wipe out
formal extirpate

extermination *n*
annihilation, killing, eradication, elimination, destruction, massacre, genocide
formal extirpation

external *adj*
1 OUTER, surface, outside, exterior, superficial, outward, outermost, apparent, visible, extraneous, peripheral, extrinsic
2 *external students*
extramural, independent, visiting, non-resident, outside
F3 **1** internal **2** resident

extinct *adj*
1 DEFUNCT, dead, died out, non-existent, gone, obsolete, ended, exterminated, terminated, vanished, lost, wiped out, abolished
2 EXTINGUISHED, quenched, inactive, out, burnt out
3 OBSOLETE, invalid, expired, *passé*, outmoded, bygone, antiquated
formal terminated
F3 **1** living, existing, existent **2** active, erupting

extinction *n*
annihilation, extermination, death, dying-out, vanishing, eradication, obliteration, destruction, abolition, excision
formal termination

extinguish *v*
1 PUT OUT, blow out, snuff out, stifle, smother, choke, douse, quench, dampen down, stub out
2 ANNIHILATE, exterminate, eliminate, destroy, kill, eradicate, erase, abolish, remove, end, suppress
formal expunge, extirpate

extirpate *v*
destroy, annihilate, eliminate, wipe out, eradicate, cut out, remove, root out, uproot, abolish, exterminate,

extinguish, erase
formal deracinate, expunge

extol *v*
praise, acclaim, exalt, magnify, glorify, sing the praises of, applaud, celebrate, commend
formal laud, eulogize, rhapsodize
F3 blame; *formal* denigrate

extort *v*
extract, wring, exact, coerce, force, get out of, wrest, blackmail, squeeze, bully
colloq. milk, bleed

extortion *n*
force, coercion, blackmail, oppression, demand, exaction, racketeering
colloq. milking

extortionate *adj*
exorbitant, excessive, outrageous, grasping, exacting, immoderate, unreasonable, inordinate, preposterous, oppressive, severe, hard, harsh
formal rapacious

extra *adj, n, adv*
▶ *adj* **1** ADDITIONAL, added, auxiliary, supplementary, new, another, more, further, ancillary, fresh, other, subsidiary
2 EXCESS, excessive, spare, superfluous, surplus, unused, unneeded, unnecessary, left-over, reserve, redundant
formal supernumerary
F3 **1** integral **2** essential
▶ *n* **1** ADDITION, supplement, extension, accessory, appendage, bonus, complement, additive, adjunct, attachment
formal addendum
2 *employ extras in the film*
bit player, supernumerary, spear-carrier, walk-on part, minor role
▶ *adv* **1** ESPECIALLY, exceptionally, extraordinarily, particularly, unusually, remarkably, uncommonly, extremely
2 IN ADDITION, also, as well, together with, along with, besides, too, additionally, and so on, not to mention, not forgetting, let alone, above and beyond
colloq. into the bargain

extract *v, n*
▶ *v* **1** REMOVE, take out, draw out, cut out, get out, pull out, exact, uproot, prize, pluck, wrench, withdraw
formal deracinate
2 DERIVE, draw, distil, obtain, get, gather, glean, wrest, wring, elicit, worm
3 CHOOSE, select, cull, abstract, copy, cite, quote, reproduce
F3 **1** insert
▶ *n* **1** DISTILLATION, essence, concentrate, spirits, decoction, juice
formal distillate
2 EXCERPT, passage, selection, clip, clipping, cutting, quotation, abstract, citation

extraction *n*
1 REMOVAL, taking out, uprooting, drawing, pulling, withdrawal, separation, obtaining, derivation
2 ORIGIN, descent, ancestry, birth, blood, lineage, derivation, family, stock, parentage, pedigree, race
F3 **1** insertion

extradite *v*
send back, send home, deport, repatriate, banish, expel, exile

extradition n
sending back, deportation, banishment, expulsion, exile

extraneous adj
superfluous, supplementary, redundant, irrelevant, immaterial, inapplicable, inappropriate, inessential, inapt, incidental, tangential, needless, unnecessary, unneeded, non-essential, unessential, unrelated, unconnected, extra, additional, peripheral, exterior, external, extrinsic, alien, strange, foreign
formal inapposite
🖃 integral, essential

extraordinary adj
remarkable, unusual, exceptional, notable, noteworthy, outstanding, unique, special, unexpected, strange, peculiar, odd, bizarre, curious, unconventional, rare, uncommon, surprising, amazing, astounding, wonderful, unprecedented, marvellous, fantastic, significant, particular
formal singular
colloq. out of this world
🖃 commonplace, ordinary

extravagance n
1 OVERSPENDING, squandering, waste, wastefulness, thriftlessness, recklessness
formal profligacy, prodigality, improvidence, imprudence
2 EXCESS, exaggeration, immoderation, recklessness, profusion, outrageousness, folly, wildness, pretentiousness, lavishness
🖃 1 thrift 2 moderation, restraint

extravagant adj
1 WASTEFUL, spendthrift, squandering, thriftless, reckless
formal prodigal, profligate, improvident, imprudent
2 IMMODERATE, exaggerated, excessive, flamboyant, preposterous, outrageous, ostentatious, pretentious, lavish, ornate, fanciful, fantastic, wild, unrestrained
colloq. flashy, over the top, OTT
3 OVERPRICED, exorbitant, expensive, excessive, extortionate, costly, dear
colloq. steep
🖃 1 thrifty 2 moderate, restrained 3 reasonable

extravaganza n
spectacular, pageant, display, show, spectacle

extreme adj, n
▶ *adj* 1 INTENSE, great, immoderate, inordinate, utmost, uttermost, out-and-out, maximum, acute, downright, extraordinary, exceptional, greatest, highest, supreme, ultimate, unreasonable, remarkable
2 FARTHEST, far-off, faraway, distant, endmost, outermost, outlying, remotest, most remote, uttermost, final, last, terminal, ultimate, endmost
3 RADICAL, zealous, extremist, fanatical, hardline, immoderate, excessive, unreasonable
4 DRASTIC, dire, uncompromising, unrelenting, unyielding, stern, strict, rigid, severe, harsh, stringent, Draconian
🖃 1 mild 3 moderate
▶ *n* extremity, limit, maximum, ultimate, utmost, excess, top, mark, line, pinnacle, peak, height, end, climax, depth, edge, pole
formal termination, acme, apex, zenith
▷ **in the extreme** exceedingly, excessively, very, exceptionally, extraordinarily, intensely, remarkably,

utterly, greatly, highly, immoderately, uncommonly, inordinately

extremely adv
exceedingly, excessively, very, really, exceptionally, extraordinarily, intensely, thoroughly, remarkably, utterly, greatly, highly, unusually, unreasonably, immoderately, uncommonly, inordinately, acutely, severely, decidedly
old use jolly
colloq. awfully, terribly, dreadfully, frightfully, terrifically

extremism n
fanaticism, radicalism, zeal, excessiveness, unreasonableness, terrorism
formal zealotry
🖃 moderation

extremist n
fanatic, hardliner, fundamentalist, militant, radical, zealot, diehard, ultra, terrorist
🖃 moderate

extremity n
1 EXTREME, limit, boundary, brink, verge, periphery, bound, border, frontier, height, tip, top, edge, excess, end, termination, peak, pinnacle, margin, terminal, terminus, ultimate, pole, maximum, minimum, depth
formal apex, acme, zenith, apogee
3 *extremities of the body*
limb, arm, hand, finger, foot, leg, toe
3 CRISIS, danger, emergency, plight, hardship, adversity, misfortune, trouble
formal indigence, exigency

extricate v
disentangle, extract, clear, disengage, detach, let loose, free, deliver, liberate, release, rescue, relieve, remove, get out, withdraw
🖃 involve

extrinsic adj
external, extraneous, exterior, outside, alien, exotic, foreign, imported
🖃 intrinsic

extrovert n
mixer, socializer, mingler, outgoing person, sociable person, conversationalist, joiner, life and soul of the party

extroverted adj
outgoing, friendly, sociable, amicable, amiable, exuberant, hearty, demonstrative
🖃 introverted

extrude v
force out, squeeze out, press out, mould

exuberance n
1 LIVELINESS, vitality, high spirits, zest, effervescence, enthusiasm, eagerness, excitement, animation, elation, buoyancy, exhilaration, effusiveness, cheerfulness, fulsomeness, life, vigour, energy
formal ebullience, vivacity
colloq. pizzazz
2 ABUNDANCE, copiousness, lushness, richness, superabundance, lavishness, luxuriance, rankness, exaggeration, excessiveness
formal plenitude, prodigality, profusion
🖃 1 apathy, lifelessness 2 scantiness

exuberant adj
1 LIVELY, vivacious, spirited, zestful, high-spirited,

effervescent, enthusiastic, sparkling, excited, animated, elated, buoyant, exhilarated, effusive, cheerful, full of life, vigorous, energetic, unrestrained, fulsome, irrepressible, exaggerated
formal ebullient
2 PLENTIFUL, lavish, overflowing, luxurious, lush, rich, profuse, abundant, thriving, rank
formal plenteous
F3 1 apathetic 2 scarce

exude *v*
1 *exude confidence*
radiate, ooze, display, show, emanate, emit, exhibit
formal manifest
2 DISCHARGE, issue, flow out, bleed, excrete, leak, secrete, seep, perspire, sweat, trickle, weep, well

exult *v*
rejoice, revel, delight, be joyful, be delighted, glory, celebrate, relish, crow, gloat, triumph
colloq. be over the moon

exultant *adj*
delighted, rejoicing, revelling, elated, exulting, gleeful, joyful, overjoyed, jubilant, transporting, enraptured, triumphant
formal joyous
colloq. cock-a-hoop, over the moon
F3 depressed

exultation *n*
rejoicing, joy, delight, elation, glee, revelling, glory, glorying, joyfulness, jubilation, merriness, transport, triumph, celebration, crowing, gloating
formal joyousness, paean, eulogy
F3 depression

eye *n, v*
▶ *n* 1 APPRECIATION, discrimination, discernment, perception, awareness, recognition, judgement, sensitivity, taste
2 VISION, sight, eyesight, power of seeing, faculty of sight, observation
3 VIEWPOINT, opinion, view, point of view, judgement, mind, estimation, belief
4 WATCH, observation, lookout, view, notice, watchfulness, vigilance, surveillance

▷ **keep an eye on** watch closely, mind, attend to, take responsibility for, look after, take care of, monitor, keep tabs on
▷ **see eye to eye** agree, be of one mind, be at one, reach an agreement; *colloq.* go along with, go with, speak the same language, be on the same wavelength
▷ **set eyes on** see, notice, observe, come across, come upon, lay eyes on, clap eyes on, meet, encounter; *formal* behold
▷ **up to your eyes** busy, occupied, involved, engrossed, overwhelmed, inundated; *colloq.* snowed under, fully stretched, overstretched, having your hands full, tied up
F3 free, idle
Related adjectives: ocular, ophthalmic, optical

Parts of the eye include: anterior chamber, aqueous humour, blind spot, choroid, ciliary body, cone, conjunctiva, cornea, eyelash, fovea, iris, lacrimal duct, lens, lower eyelid, ocular muscle, optic nerve, papilla, pupil, posterior chamber, retina, rod, sclera, suspension ligament, upper eyelid, vitreous humour.

▶ *v* look at, watch, regard, observe, stare at, gaze at, glance at, view, scrutinize, scan, examine, peruse, study, survey, inspect, contemplate, look up and down, assess

eye-catching *adj*
striking, arresting, attractive, spectacular, captivating, beautiful, stunning, gorgeous, imposing, impressive, showy, conspicuous, noticeable, prominent
F3 plain, unattractive

eyesight *n*
vision, sight, perception, observation, power of seeing, faculty of sight, view
Related adjectives: optical, ocular, visual

eyesore *n*
ugliness, blemish, scar, monstrosity, blot, blot on the landscape, disfigurement, defacement, horror, blight, disgrace, atrocity, mess, carbuncle

eyewitness *n*
witness, observer, spectator, looker-on, onlooker, bystander, viewer, passer-by, watcher

F

fable *n*
Aesop's fables; fact or fable?
allegory, parable, story, tale, moral tale, yarn, myth,
legend, epic, saga, fiction, fabrication, invention, lie,
untruth, falsehood, yarn
colloq. tall story, old wives' tale
formal apologue

fabled *adj*
legendary, renowned, famous, famed, remarkable
E∃ unknown

fabric *n*
1 CLOTH, material, textile, stuff, web, texture
2 STRUCTURE, framework, construction, make-up,
constitution, organization, infrastructure, foundations

> *Fabrics include*: alpaca, angora, astrakhan,
> barathea, bouclé, cashmere, chenille, duffel, felt,
> flannel, fleece, Harris tweed®, mohair, paisley,
> serge, sheepskin, Shetland wool, tweed, vicuña,
> wool, worsted; brocade, buckram, calico, cambric,
> candlewick, canvas, chambray, cheesecloth, chino,
> chintz, cord, corduroy, cotton, crepe, denim, drill,
> jean, flannelette, gaberdine, gingham, jersey, lawn,
> linen, lisle, madras, moleskin, muslin, needlecord,
> piqué, poplin, sateen, seersucker, terry towelling,
> ticking, Viyella®, webbing, winceyette; brocade,
> grosgrain, damask, Brussels lace, chiffon, georgette,
> gossamer, voile, organza, organdie, tulle, net, crepe
> de Chine, silk, taffeta, shantung, velvet, velour;
> polycotton, polyester, rayon, nylon, Crimplene®,
> Terylene®, Lurex®, lamé; hessian, horsehair,
> chamois, kid, leather, leather-cloth, sharkskin,
> suede.

fabricate *v*
1 FAKE, falsify, forge, counterfeit, invent, make up,
trump up, concoct, hatch
colloq. cook up
2 MANUFACTURE, make, construct, assemble, build,
erect, put together, produce, form, shape, fashion,
create, frame, devise
E∃ 2 demolish, destroy

fabrication *n*
1 FAKE, falsehood, forgery, invention, concoction,
fable, fiction, figment, story, myth, untruth
colloq. cock-and-bull story, fairy story
2 MANUFACTURE, assembly, building, construction,
erection, production
formal assemblage
E∃ 1 truth

fabulous *adj*
1 WONDERFUL, marvellous, fantastic, remarkable,
great, superb, breathtaking, spectacular, phenomenal,
amazing, astounding, astonishing, unbelievable,
incredible, inconceivable, unimaginable
colloq. out of this world, top-notch, great, super, cool,
magic, radical; *slang* way-out

2 *a fabulous beast*
mythical, legendary, fabled, fantastic, fictitious,
fictional, invented, made-up, imaginary, unreal
E∃ 2 real

façade *n*
1 FRONT, exterior, frontage, face
2 SHOW, semblance, appearance, cover, cloak, veil,
guise, mask, disguise, pretence, veneer

face *n, v*
▶ *n* **1** *she has a lovely face*
features, façade
formal countenance, visage, physiognomy
colloq. mug, kisser, phiz, pan, clock, dial; *slang* puss
2 EXPRESSION, look, appearance, air, aspect
formal mien, demeanour
3 *pull a face*
grimace, frown, scowl, pout
4 EXTERIOR, outside, surface, cover, front, frontage,
façade, aspect, side
5 *changing the face of the city*
appearance, nature, look(s), aspect, form
6 *save/lose face*
reputation, prestige, name, standing, respect, honour,
admiration
▷ **face to face** opposite, facing, eye to eye,
confronting, in confrontation; *colloq.* eyeball to
eyeball
▷ **fly in the face of** contradict, oppose, disagree,
clash, conflict, contrast, go against, be at variance,
be at odds, be in conflict, be inconsistent with
▷ **on the face of it** apparently, seemingly, ostensibly,
outwardly, to all appearances, superficially,
on the surface, reputedly, plainly, clearly, obviously,
manifestly, patently
▷ **pull a face** frown, grimace, lour, pout, scowl, sulk,
glower, knit your brows
Related adjective: facial
▶ *v* **1** BE OPPOSITE, give on to, front, overlook,
look onto
2 CONFRONT, face up to, deal with, come up against,
cope with, tackle, brave, defy, oppose, brave, resist,
withstand, have to reckon with, encounter, meet,
experience
3 COVER, line, coat, dress, clad, overlay, smooth,
polish, veneer
▷ **face up to** accept, come to terms with, resign
yourself to, acknowledge, recognize, cope with,
deal with, confront, meet head-on, stand up to

facelift *n*
1 COSMETIC SURGERY, plastic surgery
technical rhytidectomy
2 REDECORATION, renovation, restoration

facet *n*
surface, plane, slant, side, face, aspect, element, angle,
point, feature, characteristic, factor

facetious *adj*
flippant, frivolous, playful, jocular, jocose, jesting,
joking, tongue-in-cheek, light-hearted, funny,
amusing, humorous, comic, comical, droll, witty
E3 serious

facile *adj*
shallow, superficial, easy, simple, simplistic,
uncomplicated, ready, quick, hasty, glib, fluent,
smooth, slick, plausible
E3 complicated, profound

facilitate *v*
ease, help, assist, encourage, further, smooth, smooth
the way, promote, advance, forward, accelerate,
speed up
formal expedite

facility *n*
1 *a facility for learning languages*
effortlessness, ease, readiness, quickness, fluency,
eloquence, articulateness, smoothness, proficiency,
skill, skilfulness, talent, gift, knack, ability, dexterity
2 *sports facilities*
amenity, service, utility, convenience, resource,
prerequisite, appliance, equipment, means,
opportunity, advantage, aid
colloq. mod con

facing *n*
coating, covering, lining, cladding, dressing,
reinforcement, façade, overlay, surface, trimming,
veneer, false front
technical revetment

facsimile *n*
copy, imitation, reproduction, repro, replica, carbon
copy, carbon, duplicate, image, fax, photocopy,
Photostat®, Xerox®, mimeograph, transcript, print

fact *n*
1 *facts and figures*
information, datum, detail, particular, specific, point,
item, feature, factor, circumstance, component,
element, event, incident, occurrence, happening, act,
deed, fait accompli
colloq. gen, info, low-down, score, ins and outs
2 REALITY, actuality, factuality, certainty, truth
E3 2 fiction
▷ **in fact** actually, in actual fact, in point of fact, as a
matter of fact, in practice, in reality, really, indeed,
truly, in truth

faction *n*
1 SPLINTER GROUP, ginger group, minority,
division, section, contingent, party, band, side, group,
camp, set, sector, ring, caucus, clique, coterie, cabal,
junta, lobby, pressure group
2 DISAGREEMENT, conflict, argument, friction,
quarrels, discord, disharmony, division, trouble,
contention, infighting, strife

factious *adj*
conflicting, clashing, divisive, partisan, sectarian,
quarrelsome, discordant, quarrelling, at odds, at
loggerheads, warring, troublemaking, turbulent,
tumultuous, dissident, rival, contentious, mutinous,
seditious, insurrectionary, rebellious
formal disputatious, refractory
E3 calm, co-operative

factor *n*
cause, influence, circumstance, contingency,
consideration, element, ingredient, component,
constituent, part, point, aspect, facet, fact, item, detail,

characteristic, feature
formal determinant

factory *n*
works, plant, mill, shop floor, assembly line, workshop,
foundry, manufactory

factotum *n*
do-all, handyman, jack-of-all-trades, maid-of-all-
work, Man (or Girl) Friday, odd-jobman

factual *adj*
true, historical, actual, real, genuine, authentic, true-
to-life, correct, accurate, truthful, precise, exact,
literal, faithful, close, strict, detailed, realistic,
unbiased, unprejudiced, objective
E3 false, fictitious, imaginary, fictional

faculties *n*
wits, senses, intelligence, reason, powers, capabilities

faculty *n*
1 ABILITY, capability, capacity, power, facility,
proficiency, knack, flair, gift, talent, skill, aptitude,
bent
2 *Faculty of Medicine*
department, organization, division, section

fad *n*
craze, mania, (passing) fashion, mode, vogue, trend,
enthusiasm, whim, fancy
formal affectation
colloq. rage

faddy *adj*
fussy, particular, fastidious, finicky, hard-to-please,
exact
colloq. pernickety, choosy, picky, nit-picking

fade *v*
1 DISCOLOUR, lose colour, bleach, blanch, blench,
pale, become paler, lose colour, tone down, whiten,
dim, dull, wash out
technical etiolate
colloq. go as white as a sheet
2 DECLINE, fall, diminish, dwindle, ebb (away),
wane, fail, waste away, disappear, vanish, recede, melt
(away), dissolve, pale, flag, weaken, become weaker,
droop, wilt, wither, shrivel, perish, die (away)
formal evanesce
colloq. peter out, fizzle out
E3 brighten

faeces *n*
waste matter, body waste, excrement, droppings, dung,
ordure, turd
technical excreta, stools
slang shit, crap
Related adjectives: stercoraceous, stercoral

fag *n*
1 CIGARETTE, filter-tip, king-size, high-tar, low-tar,
roll-up, roll-your-own, smoke, whiff
colloq. cig, ciggy, fag end, dog end, gasper, joint;
slang cancer-stick, coffin-nail
2 NUISANCE, inconvenience, irritation, bind, bore,
bother, chore, pest
colloq. drag

fagged *adj*
exhausted, fatigued, weary, worn out, jaded, wasted
colloq. all in, beat, knackered, on your last legs;
slang zonked
E3 refreshed

fail *v*

1 GO WRONG, be unsuccessful, break down, collapse, miscarry, abort, fall through, founder, come to grief, come to nothing, get nowhere
colloq. flop, fold, flunk, not come off, not make it, not come up to scratch, fall flat, blow it, blow your chances, bite the dust, come a cropper, come unstuck, come undone, not come up with the goods, fizzle out, score an own goal, *US* bomb
2 *fail to pay the bill*
omit, neglect, forget, not do something
3 LET DOWN, disappoint, leave, desert, neglect, abandon
formal forsake
4 *the engine failed*
break down, go wrong, stop, not work, cut out, not start
formal malfunction
colloq. pack up, crash, go kaput; *slang* conk out
5 *the business failed*
collapse, founder, go bankrupt, go bust, go under, become insolvent, sink
colloq. fold, flop, crash, go bust, go broke, go to the wall, go into the red, *US* go belly-up
6 *his health failed*
weaken, fade, wane, ebb, sink, collapse, flag, decline, dwindle, diminish, decay, deteriorate, droop
E3 **1** succeed **4** work **5** prosper
without fail without exception, unfailingly, constantly, regularly, dependably, conscientiously, reliably, faithfully, predictably, punctually, religiously; *colloq.* like clockwork
E3 unpredictably, unreliably

failing *n, prep*

▶ *n* weakness, foible, fault, defect, imperfection, flaw, blemish, drawback, deficiency, shortcoming, failure, lapse, error, weak spot
E3 strength, advantage
▶ *prep* in the absence of, lacking, without, in default of, wanting

failure *n*

1 *our efforts ended in failure*
lack of success, defeat, collapse, breakdown, downfall, miscarriage, abortion, frustration, coming to nothing
colloq. flop, washout, let-down, mess
2 *the plan was a failure*
disappointment, misfortune, disaster, calamity, miss, fiasco
colloq. flop, washout, shambles, slip-up, no go, wipeout
3 *his failure to return home*
omission, neglect, negligence, disregard, oversight, forgetfulness, default
formal dereliction
4 *feel that you are a failure*
loser, born loser, misfit, reject, victim
colloq. dropout, non-starter, washout, write-off, no-hoper, also-ran, flop, has-been, dead loss, waste of space
5 *the failure of the machine*
breakdown, cutting-out, shutdown, stopping, stalling
formal malfunctioning
colloq. crash, packing-up; *slang* conking-out
6 *the failure of the business*
collapse, bankruptcy, ruin, insolvency, foundering
colloq. crash, folding, flop, going under, going to the wall
7 *the failure of his health*
weakening, fading, decline, sinking, flagging, waning, ebbing, collapse, breakdown, deterioration

E3 **1, 2** success **3** observance **4** success **6** prosperity

faint *adj, v, n*

▶ *adj* **1** SLIGHT, weak, feeble, soft, low, hushed, muffled, subdued, muted, faded, bleached, mild, light, pale, dull, dim, hazy, indistinct, unclear, obscure, blurred, vague
2 *I feel faint*
dizzy, giddy, unsteady, light-headed, weak, feeble, exhausted
colloq. woozy
3 *a faint smile*
slight, feeble, weak, unenthusiastic, half-hearted
E3 **1** strong, clear
▶ *v* black out, lose consciousness, pass out, collapse, drop
old use swoon
colloq. flake out, keel over
▶ *n* blackout, loss of consciousness, collapse, unconsciousness
technical syncope
old use swoon

faint-hearted *adj*

timid, timorous, weak, lily-livered, spiritless, diffident, half-hearted, irresolute
colloq. yellow
E3 courageous, confident

faintly *adv*

slightly, vaguely, a little, a bit, weakly, feebly, softly

fair¹ *adj*

1 JUST, equitable, square, even-handed, dispassionate, impartial, objective, disinterested, unbiased, unprejudiced, detached, right, proper, above board, lawful, legitimate, honest, trustworthy, upright, honourable
colloq. on the level, straight up, legit, kosher, going/done/played by the book
2 *a fair number; a fair chance of success*
reasonable, moderate, respectable, satisfactory, modest, decent, sporting
3 FAIR-HAIRED, fair-headed, blond(e), yellow, light, light-haired
4 *fair skin*
pale, cream, light
5 ADEQUATE, sufficient, middling, not bad, all right, satisfactory, acceptable, tolerable, reasonable, passable, mediocre
colloq. OK, so-so
6 *fair weather*
fine, dry, sunny, bright, clear, cloudless, unclouded
E3 **1** unfair **3** dark **5** excellent, poor **6** inclement, cloudy

fair² *n*

a trade fair
exhibition, show, exposition, trade fair, market, craft fair, bazaar, exchange, fête, festival, carnival, gala
colloq. expo
Related adjective: nundinal

fairly *adv*

1 QUITE, rather, somewhat, reasonably, tolerably, moderately, adequately, pretty
2 POSITIVELY, absolutely, impartially, really, fully, veritably
3 JUSTLY, equitably, honestly, objectively, unbiasedly, properly, legally, lawfully
E3 **3** unfairly

fairness n

justice, equitableness, equity, even-handedness, unbiasedness, impartiality, legitimacy, rightfulness, rightness, uprightness, disinterestedness, decency, legitimateness
E3 unfairness

fairy n

elf, fay, pixie, imp, brownie, leprechaun, sprite, Robin Goodfellow, Puck, hob, hobgoblin, nymph, rusalka, peri, fée

fairy tale n

1 FAIRY STORY, folk-tale, myth, romance, fiction, fantasy
2 LIE, untruth, invention, fabrication
colloq. cock-and-bull story, tall story

faith n

1 BELIEF, trust, reliance, dependence, conviction, confidence, assurance
formal credit, credence
2 RELIGION, denomination, persuasion, church, belief, creed, teaching, doctrine, dogma, sect
3 FAITHFULNESS, fidelity, loyalty, obedience, commitment, devotion, dedication, honour, sincerity, honesty, truthfulness
old use allegiance, fealty
E3 1 mistrust **3** unfaithfulness, treachery

faithful adj, n

▶ *adj* **1** LOYAL, devoted, committed, dedicated, staunch, steadfast, constant, trusty, trustworthy, reliable, dependable, unwavering, unflagging, unswerving, obedient, true
2 *a faithful description*
accurate, precise, exact, strict, close, strict, true, truthful
E3 1 disloyal, treacherous **2** inaccurate, vague
▶ *n* adherents, followers, supporters, believers, congregation, communicants, brethren

faithfulness n

1 LOYALTY, fidelity, devotion, dedication, commitment, allegiance, steadfastness, constancy, trustworthiness, reliability, dependability, staunchness
old use fealty
2 ACCURACY, closeness, exactness, strictness, scrupulousness
E3 1 disloyalty, treachery **2** inaccuracy

faithless adj

1 DISLOYAL, unfaithful, inconstant, fickle, false, false-hearted, unreliable, untrue, untrustworthy, untruthful, traitorous, treacherous, adulterous
formal perfidious
2 UNBELIEVING, doubting, disbelieving
formal nullifidian
E3 believing, faithful

faithlessness n

unfaithfulness, disloyalty, deceit, infidelity, fickleness, inconstancy, treachery, betrayal, adultery, apostasy
formal perfidy
E3 belief, faithfulness

fake adj, v, n

▶ *adj* forged, counterfeit, false, spurious, pseudo, bogus, fraudulent, assumed, sham, artificial, simulated, mock, imitation, reproduction
formal affected
colloq. phoney, pseud, pretend
E3 genuine
▶ *v* forge, fabricate, counterfeit, copy, pirate, imitate,

simulate, feign, sham, pretend, put on, assume
formal affect
▶ *n* forgery, copy, reproduction, replica, imitation, mountebank, simulation, sham, counterfeit, hoax, fraud, impostor, charlatan
colloq. phoney, quack

fall v, n

▶ *v* **1** TUMBLE, stumble, trip, fall down, slip, topple, keel over, collapse, slump, crash, slide, pitch (forward)
2 DESCEND, go down, come down, drop, slope, incline, slant, slide, sink, dive, plunge, plummet, nose-dive, pitch
3 DECREASE, lessen, decline, go down, diminish, dwindle, fall off, subside, recede, slump, plummet, plunge, dive, nose-dive
4 *fall asleep*
pass (into), become, grow (into), turn, come to be
5 *fall in battle*
be killed, die, perish, lose your life
formal be slain
6 *the town fell in the battle*
lose control, be defeated, be conquered, be taken, surrender, yield, capitulate, give in, pass into enemy hands
formal be vanquished
7 *my birthday falls on a Tuesday this year*
happen, occur, take place, come about
E3 2 rise **3** increase
▷ **fall apart** break, break into pieces, fall to bits/ pieces, come/go to pieces, go to bits, break up, come away, shatter, disintegrate, collapse, dissolve, crack up, crumble, decompose, decay, rot
▷ **fall back** retreat, withdraw, recoil, draw back, pull back, disengage, depart
▷ **fall back on** resort to, make use of, have recourse to, use, employ, turn to, look to, call on, call into play
▷ **fall behind** lag (behind), trail, drop back, not keep up
E3 keep up, make progress, keep pace
▷ **fall for 1** FALL IN LOVE WITH, be attached to, become infatuated with, desire, take to; *colloq.* fancy, be crazy about, have a crush on, fall head over heels in love with **2** ACCEPT, be taken in by, be fooled by, be deceived by; *colloq.* swallow, buy
▷ **fall in** cave in, come down, collapse, crash, give way, subside, sink
▷ **fall in with** agree with, go along with, accept, comply with, co-operate with, support
formal assent to
▷ **fall off** decrease, lessen, drop (off), slump, decline, deteriorate, worsen, slow, slacken
▷ **fall on** attack, descend on, set upon, lay into, pounce on, snatch, assail, assault
▷ **fall out** quarrel, argue, squabble, bicker, fight, clash, disagree, differ
E3 agree
▷ **fall through** come to nothing, go wrong, fail, miscarry, abort, founder, collapse, come to grief
E3 come off, succeed
▷ **fall to** apply yourself, begin, get stuck in, set about, set to, start
formal commence
▶ *n* **1** TUMBLE, stumble, trip, topple, keeling-over, collapse, slip, slide, crash
2 DROP, fall-off, decrease, decline, cut, reduction, lessening, dwindling, slump, crash, plunge, plummeting, nose-dive
3 DEFEAT, capture, conquest, overthrow, loss of control, downfall, collapse, ruin, failure, destruction, surrender, capitulation, yielding, giving-in,

resignation
formal demise

fallacious *adj*
false, wrong, untrue, incorrect, mistaken, deceptive,
erroneous, inaccurate, inexact, illogical, misleading,
spurious, delusive, delusory, illusory, fictitious
formal casuistical, sophistic, sophistical
E3 correct, true

fallacy *n*
misconception, misapprehension, miscalculation,
delusion, mistake, mistaken belief, error, flaw,
inconsistency, falsehood, false idea, illusion, myth
formal casuistry, sophism, sophistry
E3 truth

fallen *adj*
1 *fallen in battle*
killed, died, dead, lost, perished, slaughtered
formal slain
2 *fallen women*
immoral, loose, promiscuous, degenerate, shamed,
disgraced
E3 2 chaste

fallible *adj*
imperfect, errant, erring, frail, weak, flawed, human,
mortal, ignorant, uncertain
E3 infallible

fallow *adj*
uncultivated, unploughed, unplanted, unsown,
undeveloped, unused, idle, inactive, unproductive,
dormant, resting, barren

false *adj*
1 WRONG, incorrect, mistaken, untrue, erroneous,
inaccurate, inexact, misleading, faulty, invalid, illusory
formal fallacious
2 ARTIFICIAL, synthetic, imitation, simulated,
mock, fake, counterfeit, fraudulent, forged, fabricated,
invented, feigned, pretended, sham, bogus, assumed,
fictitious
colloq. phoney, pretend, trumped-up
3 *false friends*
disloyal, unfaithful, faithless, lying, unreliable,
deceitful, dishonest, insincere, untrustworthy,
hypocritical, two-faced, double-dealing, treacherous,
traitorous
formal duplicitous, perfidious
E3 1 true, right **2** real, genuine **3** faithful, reliable,
genuine

falsehood *n*
untruth, lie, fib, story, fairy story, fiction, fabrication,
invention, untruthfulness, deceit, deception,
dishonesty, insincerity, hypocrisy, two-facedness,
double dealing, treachery
technical perjury
formal duplicity, perfidy
colloq. tall story; *slang* bullshit
E3 truth, truthfulness

falsification *n*
alteration, tampering, distortion, perversion,
misrepresentation, change, adulteration, deceit,
forgery
formal dissimulation

falsify *v*
alter, tamper with, doctor, distort, adulterate, twist,
pervert, misrepresent, misstate, forge, counterfeit,
fake, rig, fiddle, manipulate, massage
colloq. cook

falter *v*
1 TOTTER, stumble, be unsteady, be shaky
2 *falter while talking*
stammer, stutter, stumble
colloq. fluff your lines
3 HESITATE, waver, vacillate, delay, flinch, quail,
shake, tremble, flag, fail
colloq. shilly-shally, dilly-dally, be in two minds, sit on
the fence, drag your feet, take your time

faltering *adj*
uncertain, hesitant, unsteady, weak, tentative,
irresolute, stammering, stumbling, timid, broken,
failing, flagging
E3 firm, strong

fame *n*
renown, celebrity, stardom, prominence, distinction,
eminence, notability, note, illustriousness, glory,
honour, greatness, importance, reputation, name
formal esteem

famed *adj*
renowned, well-known, widely-known, famous,
recognized, noted, celebrated, acclaimed
formal esteemed
E3 unknown

familiar *adj*
1 EVERYDAY, usual, routine, repeated, conventional,
household, common, commonplace, ordinary,
accustomed, customary, frequent, habitual, run-of-
the-mill, well-known, known, recognizable,
unmistakable
2 INTIMATE, close, near, dear, confidential, friendly,
informal, free, free-and-easy, easy, relaxed, casual,
comfortable, sociable, open, natural, unceremonious,
unreserved
colloq. pally, chummy
3 *familiar with the procedure*
aware, acquainted, abreast, knowledgeable, versed,
conversant, well up, *au fait*, *au courant*
4 FORWARD, over-familiar, over-friendly,
presumptuous, impertinent, bold, disrespectful
colloq. pushy, smarmy
E3 1 unfamiliar, strange **2** formal, reserved
3 unfamiliar, ignorant

familiarity *n*
1 INTIMACY, liberty, closeness, nearness,
friendliness, ease, sociability, openness, naturalness,
informality, casualness, unceremoniousness
colloq. palliness, chumminess
2 AWARENESS, acquaintance, experience, skill,
knowledge, understanding, comprehension, grasp,
mastery
3 FORWARDNESS, over-familiarity, over-
friendliness, presumption, liberty, liberties,
impertinence, boldness, disrespect, impudence,
intrusiveness
colloq. pushiness

familiarize *v*
accustom, acclimatize, make familiar, make aware,
make acquainted, teach, school, train, coach, instruct,
indoctrinate, prime, brief
formal habituate

family *n*
1 RELATIVES, relations, household, nuclear family,
extended family, one-parent family, single-parent
family, next of kin, kin, kindred, kinsmen, people,
parents, your own flesh and blood, you and yours,
ancestors, forebears, children, offspring, issue,

progeny, descendants, scions, stirps
colloq. folk, little ones, kids, patter of tiny feet
2 CLAN, tribe, race, dynasty, house, pedigree, ancestry, parentage, descent, line, lineage, extraction, blood, stock, strain, birth
3 CLASS, group, species, genus, type, class, kind, classification
technical stirps
▷ **family tree** ancestry, pedigree, genealogy, line, lineage, extraction, background

Members of a family include: ancestor, forebear, forefather, descendant, offspring, heir; husband, wife, spouse, parent, father, dad, *colloq.* daddy, *colloq.* old man, mother, *colloq.* mum, *colloq.* mummy, *US colloq.* mom, grandparent, grandfather, grandmother, granny, *colloq.* nanny, grandchild, son, daughter, brother, half-brother, sister, half-sister, sibling, uncle, aunt, nephew, niece, cousin, godfather, godmother, godchild, stepfather, stepdad, stepmother, stepmum, foster-parent, foster-child.

famine *n*
starvation, hunger, malnutrition, lack, deprivation, scarcity, shortage of food, dearth, lack, death
formal destitution, want
E3 plenty

famished *adj*
starved, starving, famishing, ravenous, hungry, undernourished, voracious
E3 sated

famous *adj*
well-known, famed, renowned, celebrated, acclaimed, world-famous, noted, great, distinguished, illustrious, eminent, honoured, respected, acclaimed, glorious, legendary, remarkable, notable, popular, prominent, signal, venerable, having (made) a name for yourself, someone's name be on everyone's lips, notorious, infamous
formal esteemed
E3 unheard-of, unknown, obscure

fan[1] *n*
football fans
enthusiast, admirer, supporter, backer, follower, adherent, devotee, addict, lover, aficionado
colloq. buff, fiend, freak, nut

fan[2] *v, n*
▶ *v* **1** COOL, ventilate, air, air-condition, air-cool, blow, freshen, refresh
2 INCREASE, provoke, intensify, stimulate, incite, instigate, rouse, arouse, excite, agitate, ignite, kindle, stir up, work up, whip up
▷ **fan out** spread out, move out, open out, unfold, unfurl
▶ *n* extractor fan, ventilator, air-conditioner, blower, cooler, air cooler, propeller, vane

fanatic *n*
zealot, devotee, enthusiast, addict, maniac, visionary, radical, bigot, extremist, militant, activist, fundamentalist
colloq. fiend, freak

fanatical *adj*
overenthusiastic, extreme, passionate, zealous, fervent, burning, mad, wild, frenzied, rabid, obsessive, fundamentalist, activist, militant, immoderate, extremist, radical, single-minded, bigoted,

narrow-minded, dogmatic
E3 moderate, unenthusiastic

fanaticism *n*
extremism, monomania, single-mindedness, fundamentalism, activism, militancy, obsessiveness, madness, wildness, frenzy, infatuation, bigotry, narrow-mindedness, zeal, fervour, dogmatism, enthusiasm, dedication
E3 moderation

fanciful *adj*
1 IMAGINARY, mythical, flighty, fabulous, fantastic, legendary, visionary, romantic, unrealistic, unreal, make-believe, illusory, fairy-tale, airy-fairy, vaporous, whimsical, wild
2 ELABORATE, ornate, decorated, extravagant, wild, creative, imaginative, fantastic, curious
E3 **1** real, ordinary, realistic **2** simple, plain

fancy *v, n, adj*
▶ *v* **1** LIKE, want, feel like, wish, prefer, favour, desire, take a liking to, take to, go for, have in mind, not mind, not say no to, long for, yearn for
2 BE ATTRACTED TO, find attractive, desire, take to, go for, have a soft spot for, think the world of, be interested in, lust after
colloq. have a crush on, have eyes for, be mad about, want; *slang* have the hots for
3 THINK, conceive, imagine, dream of, picture, believe, suppose, reckon, guess
formal conjecture, surmise
E3 **1** dislike
▶ *n* **1** DESIRE, whim, caprice, raving, urge, want, wish, liking, fondness, longing, yearning, inclination, preference
formal penchant, predilection
colloq. itch, yen
2 NOTION, thought, idea, opinion, impression, imagination, creativity, dream, fantasy, vision, illusion, delusion
E3 **1** dislike, aversion **2** fact, reality
▶ *adj* elaborate, ornate, decorated, adorned, ornamented, embellished, rococo, baroque, elegant, extravagant, ostentatious, showy, lavish, fantastic, fanciful, far-fetched
E3 plain, ordinary, simple

fanfare *n*
flourish, trumpet call, trump, fanfarade
old use tucket

fang *n*
tooth, prong, tusk, tang, venom-tooth

fantasize *v*
imagine, daydream, dream, hallucinate, invent, romance
colloq. build castles in the air, live in a dream

fantastic *adj*
1 WONDERFUL, marvellous, sensational, superb, excellent, first-rate, tremendous, terrific, great, brilliant, incredible, unbelievable, amazing, overwhelming, enormous, extreme
colloq. top notch, super, cool, magic, ace, radical, brill, out of this world, *US* neat
2 STRANGE, weird, odd, eccentric, bizarre, exotic, outlandish, extravagant, wild, absurd, fanciful, fabulous, imaginary, illusory, unreal, imaginative, visionary, romantic
E3 **1** ordinary **2** real

fantasy *n*
dream, daydream, reverie, pipe-dream, nightmare, vision, hallucination, illusion, mirage, apparition, figment of the imagination, invention, fancy, flight of fancy, myth, speculation, delusion, misconception, creativity, imagination, originality, unreality, moonshine
colloq. cloud-cuckoo-land, pie in the sky
⊟ reality

far *adv, adj*
▶ *adv* a long way, a good way, great distance, some distance, nowhere near, much, very much, greatly, considerably, extremely, markedly, decidedly, incomparably, immeasurably
colloq. miles
⊟ near, close
▷ **far and wide** extensively, far and near, widely, everywhere, in/from all places, all about, broadly, worldwide
▷ **far out** extreme, strange, exotic, radical, bizarre, weird, outlandish; *colloq.* way out
⊟ orthodox, conventional
▷ **go far** be successful, achieve success, get on; *colloq.* get on in the world, make your mark, make a name for yourself, go places
▷ **so far** up to now, up to this point, up to the present moment, till now, to date; *formal* thus far, hitherto
▶ *adj* distant, far-off, faraway, far-flung, outlying, remote, inaccessible, secluded, out-of-the-way, God-forsaken, removed, far-removed, further, opposite, other
US colloq. in the boondocks/boonies
⊟ nearby, close, accessible

faraway *adj*
1 DISTANT, remote, outlying, far-flung, far-off, far
2 DREAMY, absent-minded, absent, abstracted, preoccupied, lost
⊟ alert, nearby

farce *n*
1 COMEDY, slapstick, buffoonery, satire, parody, burlesque
2 TRAVESTY, sham, parody, joke, mockery, ridiculousness, absurdity, nonsense
colloq. shambles

farcical *adj*
ridiculous, absurd, ludicrous, preposterous, nonsensical, stupid, laughable, comic, silly, derisory, diverting
⊟ sensible

fare *n, v*
▶ *n* **1** *pay your fare*
charge, cost, price, fee, ticket, passage
2 FOOD, eatables, nourishment, nutriment, rations, meals, diet, menu, board, table
old use provisions
formal sustenance, victuals, viands
colloq. nosh, eats
▶ *v* be, do, get along, get on, go, go on, happen, make out, manage, proceed, progress, prosper, succeed, turn out

far-fetched *adj*
implausible, unrealistic, improbable, unlikely, dubious, incredible, unbelievable, unconvincing, fantastic, fanciful, preposterous, crazy
⊟ plausible

farm *n, v*
▶ *n* ranch, farmstead, grange, croft, homestead, station, co-operative, land, farmland, holding, acreage, acres

Types of farm include: arable farm, cattle ranch, dairy farm, fish farm, mixed farm, organic farm, pig farm, sheep station, croft, smallholding, estate, plantation.

▶ *v* cultivate, till, plough, work the land, plant, operate
▷ **farm out** subcontract, pass/give to others, delegate, contract out

farmer *n*
agriculturist, crofter, smallholder, husbandman, rancher, crofter, grazier, yeoman
technical agronomist

farming *n*
agriculture, cultivation, husbandry, tilling, crofting
technical agribusiness, agronomy, agroscience geoponics

farrago *n*
hotchpotch, jumble, medley, miscellany, mixture, mélange, pot-pourri, hash, mishmash, gallimaufry, salmagundi
colloq. dog's breakfast

far-reaching *adj*
broad, extensive, widespread, sweeping, important, wide-ranging, wide, comprehensive, thorough, global, significant, momentous
⊟ limited, restricted, insignificant

far-sighted *adj*
wise, forward-looking, far-seeing, shrewd, discerning, cautious, acute, canny, provident
formal circumspect, judicious, politic, prescient, prudent
⊟ imprudent, unwise

farther *adj, adv*
▶ *adj* further, more distant, remoter, more extreme
▶ *adv* to a greater distance, to a more distant/remote/onward/advanced point

farthest *adj*
furthest, most distant, remotest, most extreme

fascinate *v*
absorb, engross, intrigue, delight, charm, allure, lure, draw, attract entice, captivate, enchant, beguile, spellbind, enthral, enrapture, rivet, transfix, hypnotize, mesmerize
⊟ bore, repel

fascinated *adj*
absorbed, engrossed, curious, intrigued, delighted, charmed, enticed, spellbound, enthralled, entranced, captivated, bewitched, beguiled, hypnotized, mesmerized, infatuated, smitten
colloq. hooked
⊟ bored, uninterested

fascinating *adj*
intriguing, gripping, exciting, interesting, engaging, engrossing, irresistible, compelling, alluring, bewitching, captivating, enchanting, riveting, enticing, seductive, tempting, charming, absorbing, stimulating, delightful, mesmerizing
⊟ boring, uninteresting

fascination *n*
interest, attraction, delight, appeal, lure, allure, compulsion, magnetism, pull, draw, charm,

captivation, enchantment, spell, sorcery, magic
E3 boredom, repulsion

fascism *n*
autocracy, dictatorship, absolutism, authoritarianism,
totalitarianism, Hitlerism

fascist *adj, n*
▶ *adj* autocratic, absolutist, authoritarian,
totalitarian, Hitlerist, Hitlerite
▶ *n* autocrat, absolutist, authoritarian, totalitarian,
Blackshirt, Hitlerite, Hitlerist

fashion *n, v*
▶ *n* **1** MANNER, way, method, mode, approach, style,
system, shape, form, make, design, pattern, line, cut,
look, appearance, type, sort, kind
2 VOGUE, trend, mode, style, fad, craze, custom,
tendency, practice, convention
colloq. rage, latest
3 COUTURE, clothes, clothes industry, haute couture,
fashion business, high fashion, designer label
colloq. rag trade
▷ **after a fashion** not very well, to some extent, in a
manner of speaking
▶ *v* create, form, shape, mould, model, design, fit,
tailor, alter, adjust, adapt, suit

fashionable *adj*
chic, smart, elegant, stylish, designer, modish, à la
mode, in vogue, in, popular, prevailing, current, latest,
up-to-the-minute, up-to-date, contemporary, modern
colloq. trendy, all the rage, natty, glitzy, ritzy, snazzy,
swanky, funky, hip, with it, swinging, in thing, cool,
dressed to the nines
E3 unfashionable

fast¹ *adj, adv*
▶ *adj* **1** QUICK, swift, rapid, brisk, accelerated,
speedy, express, high-speed, hasty, hurried,
flying
colloq. nippy
2 FASTENED, shut, closed, secure, fixed, immovable,
immobile, firm, tight
E3 **1** slow, unhurried **2** loose
▶ *adv* **1** QUICKLY, swiftly, rapidly, speedily, hastily,
hurriedly, in a hurry, apace, presto
colloq. like a flash, like a shot, as fast as your legs will
carry you, before you can say Jack Robinson, at a rate
of knots, hell for leather, like greased lightning
2 FIRMLY, securely, tightly, immovably, fixedly,
resolutely, doggedly, stubbornly
colloq. like mad/crazy, like the wind, like lightning,
like a bat out of hell, like the clappers, lickety-spit
3 *fast asleep*
sound, deeply, fully
E3 **1** slowly, gradually

fast² *v, n*
▶ *v* *fast for religious reasons*
go hungry, diet, slim, deny yourself, starve, refrain
formal abstain
▶ *n* fasting, diet, starvation, abstinence
E3 gluttony, self-indulgence

fasten *v*
1 FIX, affix, attach, clamp, grip, anchor, rivet, nail,
pin, clip, tack, seal, close, latch, shut, lock, bolt, secure,
tie, tether, hitch, bind, chain, link, interlock, connect,
join, unite, do up, button, zip up, lace, buckle
2 *fasten your attention*
focus, direct, concentrate, fix, rivet, point aim
E3 **1** unfasten, untie, undo

fastener *n*

Types of fastener include: bond, button, catch, clasp,
clip, collar stud, cotter, cufflink, eyelet, frog, hasp,
hinge, holder, hook, hook-and-eye, knot, lace, latch,
link, lock, loop, nail, paperclip, press stud, rivet,
screw, shoelace, split pin, staple, stitch, stud, tie,
toggle, treasury tag, Velcro®, zip, *US* zipper.

fastidious *adj*
fussy, particular, finicky, hard-to-please, faddy,
discriminating, hypercritical, meticulous, precise,
punctilious, overnice, squeamish, difficult, dainty
colloq. choosy, pernickety, picky
E3 undemanding

fat *adj, n*
▶ *adj* **1** PLUMP, overweight, obese, tubby, dumpy,
stout, portly, round, paunchy, well-endowed, pot-
bellied, large, heavy, solid, chubby, podgy, fleshy,
buxom, sonsy
formal rotund, corpulent, steatopygous
colloq. beefy, flabby, gross, fat as a pig
2 FATTY, oily, pinguid, greasy
formal oleaginous, adipose, sebaceous
3 *a fat book*
thick, wide, broad, big, heavy, solid, substantial
4 *fat profits*
large, handsome, considerable, generous, sizeable
E3 **1** thin, slim **2** low-fat **3** narrow, slim, thin
4 slim, meagre, miserable, poor
▶ *n* **1** FATNESS, obesity, plumpness, stoutness,
solidness, bulk, chubbiness, overweight, paunch,
pot (belly), blubber
formal corpulence
colloq. flab
2 *fats such as cream*
butter, margarine, cream, cheese, lard, suet, animal
fat, vegetable fat, polyunsaturated fat, tallow, blubber

fatal *adj*
deadly, lethal, mortal, killing, incurable, malignant,
terminal, final, destructive, calamitous, catastrophic,
disastrous
E3 harmless

⚠ **fatal** or **fateful** ?
Fatal means 'causing death or disaster': *a fatal
accident; She made the fatal mistake of telling him what
she really thought. Fateful* means 'of great importance,
having important consequences, etc', as in: *At last the
fateful day arrived, the day she was to be married.*

fatalism *n*
resignation, stoicism, acceptance, passivity, endurance
formal predestination, preordination, foreordination

fatality *n*
death, mortality, loss, casualty, dead, deadliness,
lethality, disaster, catastrophe

fate *n*
destiny, providence, God's will, kismet, karma,
chance, future, luck, fortune, horoscope, stars, lot,
doom, end, issue, outcome, ruin, disaster, destruction,
catastrophe, defeat, death

fated *adj*
doomed, destined, predestined, preordained,
foreordained, unavoidable, inevitable, inescapable,
certain, sure

formal ineluctable
F3 avoidable

fateful *adj*
crucial, critical, decisive, important, momentous,
significant, pivotal
F3 unimportant

⚠ **fateful** or **fatal** ? *See panel at* **fatal**.

father *n, v*
▶ *n* **1** PARENT, patriarch, ancestor
formal begetter, procreator, progenitor, sire,
paterfamilias, pater
colloq. dad, daddy, pop, pa, papa, old man
Related adjective: paternal
2 ANCESTOR, patriarch, elder, forefather, forebear,
predecessor, progenitor
3 FOUNDER, creator, originator, inventor, initiator,
maker, architect, author, patron, leader, prime mover
4 PRIEST, padre, pastor, parson, clergyman, abbé,
curé
▶ *v* produce, engender, give life to
old use beget, sire
formal procreate

fatherland *n*
native land, home, homeland, land of your birth,
mother-country, motherland, old country

fatherly *adj*
paternal, kind, kindly, affectionate, protective,
supportive, benevolent, benign, tender, forbearing,
indulgent, patriarchal
formal avuncular
F3 cold, harsh, unkind

fathom *v*
1 MEASURE, gauge, plumb, sound, probe, estimate
2 UNDERSTAND, comprehend, grasp, see, perceive,
work out, search out, interpret, penetrate, get to the
bottom of

fatigue *n, v*
▶ *n* tiredness, weariness, exhaustion, lethargy,
listlessness, lassitude, weakness
formal debility, enervation
F3 energy
▶ *v* tire, wear out, weary, exhaust, drain, sap, tax,
weaken, overwork
formal debilitate, enervate
colloq. take it out of
F3 invigorate, refresh

fatigued *adj*
exhausted, jaded, jiggered, overtired, tired, tired out,
wasted, weary
colloq. all in, beat, bushed, dead-beat, fagged (out),
knackered, whacked, zonked, done in
F3 refreshed

fatness *n*
plumpness, overweight, obesity, bulk, bulkiness,
heaviness, largeness, tubbiness, stoutness, portliness,
podginess, grossness
formal corpulence, rotundity
colloq. flab

fatten *v*
feed, feed up, nourish, nurture, build up, overfeed,
cram, stuff, bloat, swell, fill out, spread, expand,
widen, broaden, thicken, pinguefy

fatty *adj*
fat, greasy, oily, creamy, buttery, fleshy, waxy, pinguid
formal oleaginous, oleic, adipose, sebaceous, lipoid,
unctuous

fatuous *adj*
idiotic, foolish, silly, stupid, ludicrous, ridiculous,
absurd, daft, inane, mindless, vacuous, moronic,
puerile, brainless, lunatic, dense, asinine,
weak-minded, witless
F3 sensible

fault *n, v*
▶ *n* **1** DEFECT, flaw, blemish, imperfection,
deficiency, shortcoming, weak point, weakness,
failing, foible, negligence, omission, oversight
colloq. bug, glitch, hitch
2 ERROR, mistake, blunder, slip, lapse, indiscretion,
peccadillo, foible, misdeed, offence, wrong,
wrongdoing, sin
formal misdemeanour
colloq. slip-up, boob, booboo
3 *it's your fault*
responsibility, accountability, liability, answerability,
blameworthiness
formal culpability
▷ **at fault** (in the) wrong, blameworthy, to blame,
responsible, accountable, guilty; *formal* culpable
▷ **to a fault** excessively, extremely, too much,
inordinately, unduly, unnecessarily,
disproportionately, in the extreme, to extremes,
immoderately, out of all proportion; *colloq.* over the
top
▶ *v* find fault with, criticize, censure, blame, call to
account
formal impugn
colloq. pick holes in, knock, slate, slam, pull to pieces
F3 praise, approve

fault-finding *n, adj*
▶ *n* criticism, grumbling, complaining, carping,
quibbling, cavilling, nagging, niggling, hypercriticism
formal ultracrepidation
colloq. finger-pointing, hair-splitting, nit-picking
F3 praise
▶ *adj* critical, grumbling, nagging, captious, carping,
cavilling, censorious, hypercritical
old use pettifogging
formal querulous, ultracrepidarian
colloq. nit-picking
F3 complimentary

faultless *adj*
perfect, flawless, unblemished, spotless, immaculate,
impeccable, unsullied, pure, blameless, exemplary,
model, correct, accurate
F3 faulty, imperfect, flawed

faulty *adj*
1 NOT WORKING, defective, imperfect, damaged,
out of order, out of action, broken
formal malfunctioning, inoperative
colloq. on the blink, bust, kaput, duff
2 FLAWED, idefective, inaccurate, incorrect, wrong,
erroneous, illogical, invalid, weak
formal fallacious, casuistic
F3 **1** working **2** sound

faux pas *n*
blunder, gaffe, indiscretion, mistake
formal impropriety, solecism
colloq. boob, booboo, clanger, goof, slip-up, howler

favour *n, v*
▶ *n* **1** APPROVAL, support, backing, sympathy, kindness, friendliness, goodwill, patronage, assistance, aid, favouritism, preference, partiality
formal esteem, approbation
2 *he did me a favour*
kindness, service, good turn, good deed, courtesy, benefit
F3 **1** disapproval
▷ **in favour of** for, all for, pro, supporting, on the side of, backing, behind
F3 against
▶ *v* **1** PREFER, choose, select, opt for, like, pick, approve, support, back, recommend, endorse, advocate, champion, sanction, take kindly to
colloq. go for, plump for
2 HELP, assist, aid, benefit, promote, encourage, pamper, spoil, indulge
formal succour
F3 **1** dislike **2** mistreat

favourable *adj*
1 *a favourable reaction*
positive, sympathetic, agreeable, well-disposed, approving, complimentary, enthusiastic, friendly, amicable, kind, understanding, encouraging, reassuring, heartening
2 *a favourable impression*
positive, good, agreeable, pleasing, effective, promising
3 *favourable conditions*
good, advantageous, beneficial, promising, fair, encouraging, convenient, suitable, appropriate, opportune
formal auspicious, propitious
F3 **1** negative **2** negative **3** unhelpful

favourably *adv*
well, positively, sympathetically, agreeably, approvingly, enthusiastically, helpfully, advantageously, fortunately, conveniently, opportunely, profitably
formal auspiciously, propitiously
F3 unfavourably

favoured *adj*
preferred, chosen, selected, recommended, favourite, privileged, advantaged, blessed, elite
formal predilected

favourite *adj, n*
▶ *adj* preferred, favoured, pet, best-loved, most-liked, dearest, beloved, treasured, chosen, special
formal esteemed
F3 hated
▶ *n* preference, choice, first choice, number one, pick, pet, beloved, darling, idol
colloq. blue-eyed boy, teacher's pet, the apple of your eye
F3 *bête noire*, pet hate

favouritism *n*
nepotism, preferential treatment, preference, partiality, prejudice, inequality, inequity, one-sidedness, partisanship, bias, unfairness, injustice
F3 impartiality, equality

fawn¹ *adj*
a fawn coat
beige, buff, yellowish-brown, sand-coloured, sandy, khaki

fawn² *v*
fawning over someone famous

flatter, grovel, bow and scrape, court, curry favour, dance attendance, kowtow, pay court, ingratiate yourself, toady
colloq. bootlick, crawl, creep, cringe, smarm, lick someone's boots, suck up to, butter up, soft-soap

fawning *adj*
obsequious, servile, sycophantic, deferential, flattering, grovelling, ingratiating, bowing and scraping, abject, toadying, toadyish
formal unctuous
colloq. bootlicking, crawling, cringing,
F3 cold, proud

fear *n, v*
▶ *n* **1** TERROR, dread, alarm, fright, panic, fearfulness, agitation, apprehension, foreboding, dismay, distress, trembling, shaking, quivering, phobia, aversion, terror, horror, nightmare, *bête noire*
formal trepidation, consternation
2 ANXIETY, worry, concern, unease, uneasiness, qualms, misgivings, disquiet, suspicion, doubt
formal solicitude
3 AWE, reverence, respect, wonder, honour, fear, fear of God, terror, dread
formal veneration
4 *no fear of being misunderstood*
chance, risk, likelihood, possibility, probability, prospect, expectation, scope
F3 **1** courage, bravery, confidence **3** contempt
▶ *v* BE AFRAID OF, be scared of, dread, shudder at, shrink from tremble, lose your nerve, take fright at, have a horror of, have a phobia about, panic
colloq. have your heart in your mouth, your heart melts, your stomach turns, get the wind up, be in a cold sweat, freak out, lose your bottle
2 WORRY, be anxious about, be uneasy about, be concerned about, have misgivings/qualms about, tremble for
3 *fear God*
stand in awe of, revere, hold in reverence, reverence, wonder at
formal venerate
4 *I fear I can't help you*
be afraid, suspect, expect, foresee, anticipate

fearful *adj*
1 FRIGHTENED, afraid, scared, alarmed, in dread, nervous, anxious, tense, uneasy, apprehensive, agitated, trembling, shaking, quivering, petrified, hesitant, nervy, panicky, faint-hearted, timid
colloq. spineless, yellow
2 TERRIBLE, dreadful, awful, frightful, atrocious, shocking, dire, harrowing, distressing, appalling, horrific, monstrous, gruesome, hideous, ghastly, horrible, grim
formal fearsome
F3 **1** brave, courageous, fearless **2** wonderful, delightful

fearfully *adv*
1 APPREHENSIVELY, anxiously, nervously, hesitantly, timidly, in fear and trembling
2 *fearfully insecure*
extremely, highly, intensely, unusually, exceedingly
colloq. awfully, terribly, frightfully, dreadfully

fearless *adj*
bold, brave, confident, courageous, daring, intrepid, valiant, heroic, gallant, plucky, dauntless, unafraid, unapprehensive, unabashed, undaunted, unflinching, lion-hearted, unblenching, unblinking
formal doughty, indomitable, valorous

colloq. game, gutsy, spunky, gritty, spunky
🖃 afraid, timid

fearsome *adj*
formidable, awe-inspiring, awesome, awful, daunting,
frightening, frightful, hair-raising, horrendous,
horrible, horrific, horrifying, menacing, terrible,
unnerving, alarming, appalling, dismaying
🖃 delightful

feasibility *n*
practicability, achievability, workability,
reasonableness, possibility, viability, expedience

feasible *adj*
practicable, practical, workable, doable, achievable,
attainable, realizable, accomplishable, viable,
expedient, reasonable, possible, likely, realistic
🖃 impossible

feast *n, v*
▶ *n* **1** BANQUET, dinner, spread, junket
formal repast
colloq. blow-out, binge, beano, slap-up meal
2 *a feast for the eyes*
wealth, abundance, cornucopia
formal profusion
3 FESTIVAL, holiday, gala, fête, celebration, saint's
day, feast day, religious festival, holy day, revels,
festivities
Related adjective: festal
▶ *v* gorge, eat your fill, wine and dine, indulge in,
treat, entertain, regale
formal partake of

feat *n*
exploit, deed, act, action, accomplishment,
achievement, attainment, performance

feather *n*
plume, quill, down, tuft, crest
technical penna, plumule, plumula, aigrette, egret,
pinion
Related adjectives: pennaceous, plumose, plumous

feathery *adj*
1 *feathery birds*
feathered, featherlike, fleecy, fluffy, wispy, downy
technical pennaceous, penniform, plumate, plumed,
plumose, plumous, plumy
2 *feathery clouds*
soft, light, delicate, fluffy, wispy

feature *n, v*
▶ *n* **1** ASPECT, facet, point, factor, attribute, quality,
property, side, trait, characteristic, peculiarity, mark,
hallmark, speciality, highlight, attraction, focal point
2 *a person's facial features*
face, looks
formal countenance, lineaments, physiognomy, visage
colloq. mug, phiz, kisser, pan, clock, dial
3 *a magazine feature*
column, article, report, story, piece, item, comment
▶ *v* **1** EMPHASIZE, highlight, spotlight, play up,
accentuate, promote, show, present
2 APPEAR, figure, participate, act, perform, star

febrile *adj*
feverish, delirious, fevered, flushed, fiery, hot,
inflamed, burning
formal pyretic

feckless *adj*
incompetent, weak, feeble, useless, worthless, aimless,
futile, hopeless, irresponsible

formal ineffectual
🖃 efficient, sensible

fecund *adj*
fertile, productive, fruitful, prolific, teeming
formal feracious, fructiferous, fructuous
🖃 infertile

fecundity *n*
fertility, productiveness, fruitfulness
formal feracity, fructiferousness
🖃 infertility

fed up *adj*
depressed, bored, discontented, annoyed, dismal,
dissatisfied, gloomy, glum, tired, weary, have had
enough
colloq. blue, brassed off, browned off, cheesed off,
down, sick and tired, hacked off, have had it up to here,
at the end of your tether; *slang* pissed off
🖃 contented

federal *adj*
confederated, amalgamated, allied, integrated,
united, unified, in league, combined, associated

federate *v*
confederate, amalgamate, integrate, join together,
league, syndicate, unify, unite, combine, associate
🖃 disunite, separate

federation *n*
confederation, confederacy, alliance, league,
amalgamation, association, coalition, combination,
syndicate, union, copartnership, federacy

fee *n*
charge, terms, bill, account, pay, remuneration,
payment, cost, price, retainer, subscription, reward,
recompense, hire, rent, retainer, honorarium, toll
formal emolument

feeble *adj*
1 WEAK, faint, exhausted, frail, slight, delicate, puny,
sickly, infirm, ailing, failing, powerless, helpless,
decrepit
formal effete, debilitated, enervated
2 *a feeble excuse*
inadequate, lame, poor, weak, futile, thin, flimsy,
unconvincing, tame, ineffective, unsuccessful
formal ineffectual
3 *a feeble person*
ineffective, weak, incompetent, indecisive
formal ineffectual
colloq. wimpish, wet
🖃 **1** strong, powerful

feeble-minded *adj*
slow-witted, half-witted, stupid, moronic, simple,
weak-minded, retarded, deficient, idiotic, imbecilic
colloq. dim-witted, dumb, slow on the uptake, soft in
the head, two bricks short of a load
🖃 bright, intelligent

feed *v, n*
▶ *v* **1** *feed the baby*
give food to, nurture, nourish, cater for, provide for,
suckle, eat, dine (on), consume, take in
formal partake of
2 *animals feeding*
graze, pasture, browse, crop
formal ruminate
3 *feed your sense of self-worth*
strengthen, gratify, fuel, foster, nurture, encourage
4 *feed data into a computer*

put, insert, give, introduce, provide, supply, slide, slip
▶ *n* food, fodder, forage, pasture, silage, provender

feel *v, n*
▶ *v* **1** EXPERIENCE, be, go through, live through, undergo, suffer, bear, endure, be overcome by, give way to, harbour, nurse, know, enjoy
2 TOUCH, finger, handle, manipulate, hold, contact, stroke, massage, rub, caress, fondle, paw, maul, poke, fumble, grope, clutch, grasp
3 *feel soft*
seem, appear, look
4 THINK, believe, consider, reckon, judge, hold
formal deem
5 SENSE, perceive, notice, observe, know, understand, realize, be aware of, feel in your bones
▷ **feel for** pity, sympathize (with), empathize with, commiserate (with), be sorry for, be moved by, grieve for, weep for, pity
▷ **feel like** want, desire, wish, fancy
▶ *n* **1** *the feel of the material*
texture, surface, finish, touch, consistency
2 *have a feel for computer-programming*
touch, knack, ability, skill, aptitude, gift, talent, faculty, flair, bent
3 *the feel of a place*
atmosphere, impression, feeling, quality, mood, air, aura, ambience
colloq. vibes

feeler *n*
1 ANTENNA, horn, tentacle, sense-organ
technical palp, palpus
2 *put out feelers*
advance, approach, overture(s), probe, trial balloon, ballon d'essai

feeling *n*
1 EMOTION, passion, intensity, warmth, compassion, love, sympathy, understanding, pity, concern, affection, fondness, ardour, sentiment, sentimentality, susceptibility, sensibility, sensitivity, appreciation, fervour, intensity
formal sentience
2 SENSE, perception, sensation, instinct, intuition, hunch, theory, suspicion, inkling, impression, idea, thought, notion, opinion, view, point of view, way of thinking
3 *hurt someone's feelings*
emotions, passions, self-esteem, sensitivities, susceptibilities, ego
formal affections
4 AIR, aura, atmosphere, mood, quality, feel, impression
colloq. vibes

feign *v*
simulate, assume, fabricate, fake, forge, imitate, pretend, put on, put it on, sham, make a show of, invent, counterfeit, act
formal affect, dissemble, dissimulate

feint *n*
play, pretence, ruse, artifice, distraction, expedient, gambit, manoeuvre, stratagem, subterfuge, blind, bluff, deception, mock-assault, wile
colloq. dodge

felicitous *adj*
1 APPOSITE, appropriate, apt, fitting, suitable, well-chosen, opportune, timely, well-timed, well-turned, fortunate
formal apropos

2 DELIGHTFUL, happy, inspired, fortunate
formal propitious
◲ inappropriate

felicity *n*
1 BLISS, joy, delight, ecstasy, happiness
formal delectation
2 APPROPRIATENESS, applicability, aptness, eloquence, suitability, suitableness
formal propriety
◲ **1** sadness **2** inappropriateness

feline *adj*
catlike, graceful, sleek, slinky, smooth, stealthy, seductive, sensual, sinuous, leonine

fell *v*
cut down, hew, knock down, strike down, floor, level, flatten, raze, raze to the ground, demolish, overthrow

fellow *n, adj*
▶ *n* **1** MAN, male, boy, individual, person, character
colloq. chap, bloke, guy, lad
2 PEER, compeer, equal, partner, associate, colleague, co-worker, confrère, contemporary, compatriot, companion, comrade, friend, counterpart, match, mate, twin, double
colloq. crony, pal, chum, buddy
▶ *adj* co-, associate, associated, related, like, similar

fellow feeling *n*
commiseration, compassion, sympathy, understanding, empathy

fellowship *n*
1 COMPANIONSHIP, camaraderie, comradeship, communion, familiarity, friendship, amiability, affability, intimacy
colloq. chumminess, matiness, palliness
2 ASSOCIATION, league, guild, society, club, union, affiliation, fraternity, brotherhood, sisterhood, order

female *adj*
feminine, she-, girlish, womanly, ladylike
◲ male

Female terms include: girl, lass, maiden, woman, lady, daughter, sister, girlfriend, fiancée, bride, wife, mother, aunt, niece, grandmother, matriarch, godmother, widow, dowager, dame, madam, mistress, virgin, spinster, old-maid, crone, *slang* bird, *slang* chick, lesbian, *slang* bitch, prostitute, whore, harlot; cow, heifer, bitch, duck, doe, ewe, hen, mare, filly, nanny-goat, sow, tigress, vixen.

feminine *adj*
1 FEMALE, womanly, ladylike, pretty, graceful, gentle, tender, delicate
2 EFFEMINATE, unmanly, womanish, girlish, weak
colloq. sissy
◲ **1** masculine **2** manly

femininity *n*
feminineness, womanhood, womanishness, womanliness, girlishness, effeminacy, prettiness, gracefulness, gentleness, tenderness, delicacy
colloq. sissiness
◲ masculinity

feminism *n*
women's movement, women's lib(eration), female emancipation, women's rights

femme fatale *n*
charmer, seductress, enchantress, temptress, siren, vamp

fen *n*
bog, marsh, morass, moss, quag, quagmire, slough, swamp

fence *n, v*
▶ *n* barrier, railing, rail, paling, wall, hedge, windbreak, guard, defence, barricade, stockade, enclosure, rampart, palisade
▶ *v* **1** SURROUND, encircle, bound, hedge, wall, enclose, shut in, pen, coop, confine, restrict, separate, protect, secure, guard, defend
formal fortify, circumscribe
2 PARRY, evade, hedge, equivocate, quibble, stonewall, prevaricate
formal vacillate, tergiversate
colloq. dodge, pussyfoot, shilly-shally, beat about the bush
▷ **sit on the fence** be irresolute, be uncommitted, be undecided, be unsure, be uncertain, vacillate, dither; *colloq.* shilly-shally

fencing *n*

Fencing terms include: appel, attack, balestra, barrage, coquille, disengage, en garde, épée, feint, flèche, foible, foil, forte, hit, lunge, on guard, parry, counter-parry, pink, piste, plastron, remise, reprise, riposte, counter-riposte, sabre, tac-au-tac, thrust, touch, touché, volt.

fend *v*
1 *fend for yourself*
look after, take care of, support, maintain, sustain, provide
2 *fend off an attack*
ward off, beat off, parry, deflect, divert, avert, resist, repel, repulse, hold at bay, keep off, stave off, shut out, turn aside

feral *adj*
wild, ferocious, fierce, savage, vicious, brutal, brutish, bestial, undomesticated, unbroken, untamed
E3 tame, domesticated

ferment *v, n*
▶ *v* **1** BUBBLE, effervesce, froth, foam, boil, seethe, smoulder, fester, work, brew, rise
2 ROUSE, arouse, stir up, excite, work up, agitate, foment, incite, provoke, inflame, cause, heat
▶ *n* unrest, agitation, turbulence, stir, excitement, turmoil, disruption, commotion, confusion, fuss, tumult, hubbub, stew, uproar, furore, brouhaha, frenzy, fever
E3 calm

ferocious *adj*
1 VICIOUS, savage, fierce, wild, untamed, barbarous, barbaric, brutal, inhuman, cruel, sadistic, murderous, bloodthirsty, violent, merciless, pitiless, bitter, ruthless
formal feral
2 INTENSE, wild, vigorous, strong, extreme, severe, deep
E3 **1** tame **2** gentle, mild

ferocity *n*
savagery, fierceness, violence, bloodthirstiness, ruthlessness, cruelty, inhumanity, brutality, viciousness, sadism, barbarity, wildness, intensity,
severity, extremity
E3 gentleness, mildness

ferret *v*
search, rummage, hunt, go through, scour, forage, rifle
▷ **ferret out** discover, search out, find, hunt down, track down, trace, elicit, extract, unearth, dig up, nose out, root out, worm out, run to earth; *colloq.* suss out

ferry *n, v*
▶ *n* ferry-boat, car ferry, ship, boat, vessel, packet, packet boat, shuttle
▶ *v* transport, ship, convey, carry, take, shuttle, taxi, drive, run, move, shift, ply

fertile *adj*
1 *fertile soil*
fruitful, productive, rich, abundant
formal fecund, luxuriant
2 *a fertile imagination*
creative, resourceful, inventive, prolific, productive, imaginative, inspired, visionary
3 *fertile animals*
generative, prolific, able to have children, potent, reproductive, virile
formal fecund
E3 **1** unfruitful, unproductive **2** barren **3** sterile, infertile, barren

fertility *n*
1 FRUITFULNESS, productiveness, abundance, richness
formal luxuriance, fecundity
2 *fertility tests*
generativeness, prolificness, potency, reproductiveness, virility
E3 **1** aridity **2** barrenness, sterility

fertilization *n*
impregnation, implantation, insemination, pollination, propagation
formal fecundation, procreation

fertilize *v*
1 IMPREGNATE, inseminate, pollinate, make pregnant, make fruitful
formal procreate, fecundate, fructify
2 *fertilize land*
enrich, feed, dress, compost, manure, dung, mulch, top-dress

fertilizer *n*
dressing, compost, manure, dung, top-dressing, plant food, mulch, bone meal, humus

fervent *adj*
ardent, earnest, eager, sincere, enthusiastic, wholehearted, excited, energetic, vigorous, fiery, spirited, intense, vehement, passionate, full-blooded, zealous, devout, impassioned, heartfelt, emotional, warm
E3 cool, indifferent, apathetic

fervour *n*
ardour, eagerness, earnestness, sincerity, enthusiasm, excitement, animation, energy, vigour, spirit, verve, intensity, wholeheartedness, fire, vehemence, passion, emotion, zeal, warmth
E3 apathy, indifference

fester *v*
1 *the wound was festering*
infect, ulcerate, gather, suppurate, discharge
technical maturate

2 *the food was festering*
rot, decay, go bad, decompose, perish
formal putrefy
3 *hatred was festering*
rankle, irk, chafe, anger, annoy, gall, rankle, smoulder

festival *n*
celebration, commemoration, anniversary, jubilee,
holiday, feast, gala, gala day, fair, fête, carnival, fiesta,
party, merrymaking, entertainment, festivities

festive *adj*
celebratory, holiday, gala, carnival, festal, happy,
joyful, merry, hearty, cheerful, cheery, light-hearted,
jolly, jovial, cordial, jubilant, convivial
formal joyous
E3 gloomy, sombre, sober

festivity *n*
celebration, jubilation, feasting, banqueting, fun,
enjoyment, pleasure, entertainment, festival, party, fun
and games, carousal, junketing, sport, amusement,
cheerfulness, cheeriness, merriment, merrymaking,
revelry, revel, jollity, joviality, conviviality

festoon *v, n*
▶ *v* adorn, deck, garland, wreathe, drape, hang,
swathe, decorate, ornament, garnish
formal bedeck, array
▶ *n* garland, wreath, swathe, chaplet, swag

fetch *v*
1 *fetch a bucket*
get, go and get, collect, bring, carry, transport, deliver,
escort, convey, conduct
2 SELL FOR, go for, bring in, yield, realize, make, earn

fetching *adj*
attractive, pretty, sweet, cute, charming, enchanting,
fascinating, captivating, alluring, winsome
E3 repellent

fête *n, v*
▶ *n* fair, bazaar, sale of work, garden party, gala,
carnival, festival
▶ *v* entertain, treat, regale, welcome, honour, lionize

fetid *adj*
stinking, disgusting, foul, filthy, sickly, nauseating,
smelly, odorous, offensive, rancid, rank, reeking
formal malodorous, noisome, noxious, mephitic
E3 fragrant

fetish *n*
1 FIXATION, obsession, mania, *idée fixe*
colloq. thing
2 CHARM, amulet, talisman, idol, image, cult object,
ju-ju, totem

fetter *v*
hamper, restrain, hinder, obstruct, restrict, impede,
constrain, bind, chain, confine, encumber, curb,
shackle, tie (up), hamstring, manacle, truss, entrammel
E3 free

fetters *n*
1 CONSTRAINTS, obstructions, restraints,
restrictions, hindrances, checks, curbs, inhibitions,
captivity, bondage
2 CHAINS, bonds, bracelets, handcuffs, irons,
shackles, manacles

feud *n, v*
▶ *n* vendetta, quarrel, row, argument, disagreement,
dispute, bickering, conflict, strife, discord, animosity,
ill will, bitterness, enmity, hostility, antagonism,

rivalry, bad blood
E3 agreement, peace
▶ *v* quarrel, argue, row, squabble, bicker, clash,
contend, dispute, duel, fight, brawl, war, wrangle,
be at odds
formal altercate
E3 agree

fever *n*
1 FEVERISHNESS, (high) temperature, delirium,
ague
technical pyrexia
old use calenture
Related adjective: febrile
2 EXCITEMENT, agitation, turmoil, unrest,
restlessness, heat, passion, ecstasy, frenzy, ferment

feverish *adj*
1 DELIRIOUS, with a temperature, hot, burning,
flushed, red
2 EXCITED, impatient, agitated, restless, nervous,
overwrought, worked up, passionate, frenzied, frantic,
hectic, rushed, hasty, hurried, flustered, troubled,
bothered
colloq. hot and bothered, in a kerfuffle, in a tizzy, in a
tizz, in a dither
E3 1 cool **2** calm

few *adj, pron*
▶ *adj* scarce, rare, uncommon, sporadic, infrequent,
sparse, thin, scant, scanty, meagre, negligible,
inconsiderable, inadequate, insufficient, in short
supply
colloq. thin on the ground
E3 many
▶ *pron* not many, hardly any, scarcely any, one or two,
a couple, a small number of, scattering, sprinkling,
handful, some, a minority
E3 many

fiancé, fiancée *n*
betrothed, intended, husband-to-be, bridegroom-to-
be, future/prospective husband, wife-to-be, bride-to-
be, future/prospective wife

fiasco *n*
failure, catastrophe, calamity, collapse, debacle,
disaster, ruin, rout, mess
colloq. cropper, damp squib, flop, washout
E3 success

fiat *n*
order, command, directive, edict, decree, injunction,
mandate, sanction, warrant, authorization, ordinance,
permission, dictate, precept, dictum, proclamation,
diktat
colloq. OK

fib *n, v*
▶ *n* lie, untruth, white lie, falsehood, story, tale, yarn,
concoction, fantasy, fiction, invention,
misrepresentation, evasion, prevarication
colloq. whopper
▶ *v* evade, fabricate, falsify, fantasize, invent, lie,
prevaricate, sidestep
formal dissemble

fibre *n*
1 FILAMENT, strand, thread, tendril, fibril, nerve,
sinew, pile, texture, material, cloth, substance, stuff
2 *moral fibre*
character, nature, make-up, disposition, temperament,
calibre, backbone, strength, stamina, toughness,

courage, resolution, determination, resoluteness, willpower, strength of character, firmness (of purpose)

fickle *adj*
inconstant, disloyal, unfaithful, faithless, treacherous, unreliable, unpredictable, variable, changeable, irresolute, vacillating, volatile, unstable, unsteady, inconstant, flighty
formal capricious, mercurial, labile
E3 constant, steady, stable

fickleness *n*
inconstancy, disloyalty, unfaithfulness, faithlessness, treachery, unreliability, unpredictability, changeability, changeableness, volatility, unsteadiness, instability, fitfulness, flightiness
formal capriciousness
E3 constancy

fiction *n*
1 *read fiction*
novels, fantasy, romance, story, tale, yarn, fable, parable, legend, myth, story-telling
2 PRETENCE, lie, falsehood, untruth, fabrication, invention, concoction
colloq. fib, tall story, cock-and-bull story
E3 **1** non-fiction **2** fact, truth

fictional *adj*
literary, invented, made-up, imaginary, make-believe, legendary, mythical, mythological, fabulous, non-existent, unreal
E3 factual, real

fictitious *adj*
false, untrue, invented, made-up, fabricated, fake, apocryphal, imaginary, non-existent, bogus, counterfeit, sham, spurious, assumed, supposed, concocted, improvised
E3 true, genuine

fiddle *v, n*
▶ *v* **1** *fiddling with her necklace*
play, tinker, toy, trifle, tamper, mess around, fool around, meddle, interfere, fidget, fuss
2 CHEAT, falsify, swindle, juggle, manoeuvre, racketeer
colloq. cook the books, diddle, graft
▶ *n* swindle, fraud, racket, sharp practice
colloq. con, rip-off, graft, fix

fiddling *adj*
trifling, petty, trivial, insignificant, negligible, paltry
E3 important, significant

fidelity *n*
1 FAITHFULNESS, loyalty, allegiance, devotion, devotedness, constancy, reliability, dependability, trustworthiness
2 ACCURACY, exactness, precision, closeness, adherence, strictness, faithfulness, authenticity
E3 **1** disloyalty, unfaithfulness, infidelity, inconstancy, treachery **2** inaccuracy

fidget *v*
squirm, wriggle, writhe, toss and turn, shuffle, twitch, jerk, jump, jiggle, twiddle, fret, fuss, bustle, fiddle, mess about, play around, tinker, toy, trifle, tamper

fidgety *adj*
restless, impatient, uneasy, nervous, agitated, excited, jumpy, twitchy, on edge
formal restive
colloq. jittery, uptight, afraid of your shadow, like a cat

on hot bricks
E3 still

field *n, v*
▶ *n* **1** GRASSLAND, meadow, pasture, paddock, playing-field, ground, pitch, green, lawn
old use lea, mead, sward, glebe
Related adjectives: agrestic, campestral
2 RANGE, scope, bounds, limits, confines, territory, area, province, domain, sphere, environment, department, discipline, speciality, line, forte, regime, scene
3 PARTICIPANTS, entrants, contestants, competitors, contenders, runners, candidates, applicants, opponents, opposition, competition, possibles
▶ *v* **1** CATCH, retrieve, stop, pick up, return
2 ANSWER, cope with, deal with, handle, parry, deflect

fiend *n*
1 EVIL SPIRIT, demon, devil, monster, savage, beast, brute, ogre
2 *a health fiend*
enthusiast, fanatic, fan, addict, devotee, aficionado
colloq. freak, nut, buff

fiendish *adj*
1 *a fiendish person/plot*
devilish, diabolical, infernal, wicked, malevolent, cunning, cruel, inhuman, savage, brutal, aggressive, vicious, ferocious, ruthless, bloodthirsty, barbaric, monstrous, unspeakable
2 *a fiendish problem/plan*
difficult, intricate, involved, complex, complicated, obscure, horrendous, challenging, cunning, clever, imaginative, ingenious, resourceful

fierce *adj*
1 FEROCIOUS, vicious, savage, cruel, brutal, wild, merciless, ruthless, aggressive, dangerous, bloodthirsty, murderous, frightening, menacing, threatening, stern, grim, terrible, relentless
2 INTENSE, strong, powerful, passionate, wild, raging, violent, furious, tempestuous, severe, grave, keen, cut-throat, hot, uncontrolled, relentless
E3 **1** gentle, kind **2** calm

fiercely *adv*
ferociously, viciously, savagely, cruelly, brutally, wildly, mercilessly, murderously, ruthlessly, aggressively, dangerously, menacingly, threateningly, sternly, terribly, intensely, implacably, fanatically, bitterly, strongly, powerfully, passionately, relentlessly, violently, furiously, tempestuously, severely, keenly
colloq. tooth and nail
E3 gently, kindly

fiery *adj*
1 BURNING, afire, flaming, aflame, blazing, ablaze, red-hot, glowing, aglow, flushed, hot, torrid, sultry
2 PASSIONATE, inflamed, ardent, fervent, impatient, excitable, impetuous, impulsive, hot-headed, fierce, violent, heated
3 SPICY, spiced, seasoned, hot, pungent, piquant, sharp
E3 **1** cold **2** impassive

fight *v, n*
▶ *v* **1** WRESTLE, box, fence, joust, brawl, punch, hit, set about, take on, scuffle, tussle, skirmish, combat, battle, do battle, war, wage war, make war, be at war, clash, cross swords, engage, attack, grapple, struggle, contend, come to blows
colloq. scrap, lay into, weigh into

2 QUARREL, argue, have a row, dispute, squabble, bicker, wrangle, feud, be at odds
formal altercate
colloq. fall out, be at each other's throats
3 OPPOSE, contest, campaign against, champion, work for, resist, withstand, defy, hold out against, stand up to, dispute, object to, take issue with, strive
▷ **fight back 1** RETALIATE, defend yourself, resist, put up a fight, counter-attack, hold out against, retort, reply **2** *fight back tears* hold back, force back, restrain, curb, control, repress, contain, suppress, check; *colloq.* bottle up
▷ **fight off** hold off, keep/hold at bay, ward off, stave off, resist, repel, rebuff, beat off, rout, put to flight
▶ *n* **1** BOUT, contest, duel, combat, action, battle, war, warfare, bloodshed, hostilities, attack, brawl, scuffle, tussle, struggle, brush, skirmish, exchange, clash, engagement, encounter, confrontation, conflict, fray, row, disturbance, free-for-all, fracas, rout, ruckus, ruction, riot, melee, ruffle, shindy, Donnybrook
colloq. aggro, bovver, scrap, set-to, punch-up, pasting, bashing
2 QUARREL, row, disagreement, difference of opinion, argument, dispute
colloq. dust-up
formal dissension, discord, altercation
3 *the fight for freedom*
campaign, crusade, movement, drive, struggle, battle
4 *lose all his fight*
determination, willpower, tenacity, firmness, resoluteness, drive, spirit, aggression, will to live

fighter *n*
combatant, contestant, contender, rival, opponent, adversary, antagonist, attacker, disputant, boxer, wrestler, prizefighter, sparring partner, soldier, trouper, mercenary, warrior, man-at-arms, swordsman, gladiator
formal pugilist

figment *n*
▷ **a figment of your imagination** invention, fabrication, falsehood, fancy, fiction, illusion, delusion, improvisation, fable, deception, concoction

figurative *adj*
metaphorical, symbolic, emblematic, representative, allegorical, parabolic, descriptive, pictorial, naturalistic
Ⓔ literal

figure *n, v*
▶ *n* **1** NUMBER, numeral, digit, integer, sum, amount, total
2 *good at figures*
arithmetics, mental arithmetic, calculations, mathematics, maths, statistics
3 SHAPE, form, outline, silhouette
4 BODY, frame, build, physique, torso
5 *public figure*
dignitary, celebrity, leader, personality, character, person, personage, notable, worthy
6 DIAGRAM, illustration, picture, drawing, sketch, image, representation, symbol, sign, emblem, design, pattern
▷ **figure of speech** figure, image, imagery, rhetorical device, turn of phrase
See panel at **rhetorical**.
▶ *v* **1** RECKON, guess, estimate, judge, think, believe, consider, conclude
2 FEATURE, appear, crop up, be mentioned in, be included in

▷ **figure out** work out, calculate, make, compute, reckon, count, estimate, puzzle out, resolve, fathom, reason, understand, see, make out, decipher; *colloq.* twig, tumble to, latch onto, get the picture

figurehead *n*
1 *the president is merely a figurehead*
front man, name, mouthpiece, dummy, puppet, image, man of straw, nominal head, titular head, token
2 *a figurehead on a ship's prow*
figure, bust, carving

filament *n*
fibre, strand, thread, hair, whisker, wire, tendril, string, cord, cable, pile

filch *v*
steal, take, pilfer, thieve, rob, embezzle, palm, crib
formal misappropriate, peculate, purloin
colloq. lift, nick, pinch, rip off, knock off, snaffle, snitch, swipe

file¹ *n, v*
▶ *n* **1** FOLDER, dossier, papers, portfolio, binder, case, box, record, document, data, information, particulars, details
2 LINE, queue, column, row, procession, cortège, train, string, stream, trail
▶ *v* **1** *file papers*
record, register, note, enter, process, store, classify, categorize, pigeonhole, organize, catalogue, put in place
2 *file a complaint/file for divorce*
make, put in, submit, apply ask
3 *file out of the building*
walk in line, trail, process, stream, march, parade, troop

file² *v*
file a rough surface
rub (down), sand, abrade, scour, scrape, grate, rasp, hone, whet, shave, plane, smooth, polish, shape

filial *adj*
dutiful, loyal, respectful, devoted, affectionate, loving, fond, daughterly
Ⓔ disloyal, unfilial

filibuster *n, v*
▶ *n* delay, impediment, obstruction, postponement, hindrance
formal procrastination, speechifying, peroration
▶ *v* delay, obstruct, impede, put off, prevent, hinder
formal procrastinate, speechify, perorate
Ⓔ expedite

filigree *n*
fretwork, lacework, lattice, latticework, interlace, lace, scrollwork, tracery, wirework

fill *v, n*
▶ *v* **1** *fill a bucket with water*
MAKE FULL, stock, supply, furnish, satisfy, provide, pack, crowd, occupy, cram, stuff, congest, block, clog, plug, bung, cork, stop (up), close, seal
formal replenish
2 PERVADE, imbue, permeate, soak, impregnate, saturate, charge, spread throughout, riddle
formal suffuse
3 *fill a post*
take up, hold, occupy, fulfil, complete, perform
Ⓔ **1** empty, drain
▷ **fill in 1** *fill in a form* complete, fill out, answer
2 STAND IN, deputize, understudy, substitute, replace, represent, act for **3** INFORM, brief, advise,

acquaint, bring up to date
▷ **fill out 1** *fill out a form* complete, fill in, answer
2 *the child filled out* become/grow fatter, put on/gain weight, become plumper/chubbier
▶ *n* enough, abundance, ample, plenty, sufficiency, sufficient, all you want, more than enough, all you can take

filling *n, adj*
▶ *n* contents, inside, stuffing, padding, wadding, filler, substance
▶ *adj* satisfying, nutritious, rich, square, solid, stodgy, substantial, heavy, large, big, generous, ample
 insubstantial

fillip *n*
boost, incentive, stimulus, inducement, encouragement, motivation, goad, impetus, spur, prod, push
colloq. shove
 damper

film *n, v*
▶ *n* **1** MOTION PICTURE, picture, video, cassette, videocassette, cartridge, reel, spool, feature film, short, documentary, screenplay, footage
colloq. movie, flick
Related adjective: cinematic

Kinds of film include: action, adult, adventure, animated, avant-garde, biopic, B-movie, black comedy, blockbuster, *colloq.* blue, buddy, burlesque, Carry-on, cartoon, chapter-play, Charlie Chaplin, cinéma-vérité, classic, cliff-hanger, comedy, comedy thriller, comic-book hero, cowboy and Indian, crime, cult, detective, disaster, Disney, documentary, Ealing comedy, epic, erotic, escapist, ethnographic, expressionist, family, fantasy, farce, film à clef, film noir, flashback, gangster, gay-lesbian, historical romance, Hitchcock, Hollywood, horror, James Bond, kitchen sink, love story, low-budget, medieval, melodrama, multiple-story, murder, murder mystery, musical remake, newsreel, new wave, nouvelle vague, passion, period epic, police, police thriller, political, pornographic, psychological thriller, realist, re-make, rites of passage, robbery, romantic, romantic tragedy, satirical, science-fiction, screenplay, serial, sexual fantasy, short, silent, social comedy, social problem, space-age, space exploration, Spielberg, spy, surrealist, *colloq.* tear-jerker, thriller, thrillomedy, tragedy, tragicomedy, travelogue, underground, Victorian adaptation, *colloq.* vogue, war, war hero, western, whodunnit.

2 LAYER, covering, cover, dusting, coat, coating, glaze, skin, membrane, tissue, sheet, veil, blanket, screen, cloud, mist, haze, veil
▶ *v* photograph, shoot, record on film, televise, video, videotape
▷ **film over** cloud over, mist over, glaze, become blurred, blur, dull

filmy *adj*
cobwebby, delicate, fragile, fine, gauzy, gossamer, gossamery, light, chiffony, see-through, sheer, shimmering, thin, translucent, transparent, insubstantial, flimsy, floaty
formal diaphanous
 opaque

filter *v, n*
▶ *v* strain, sieve, sift, riddle, screen, refine, purify,

clarify, percolate, ooze, seep, leak, trickle, dribble, drain, leach
formal filtrate
▶ *n* strainer, sieve, sifter, colander, mesh, netting, gauze, riddle, membrane

filth *n*
1 DIRT, grime, muck, dung, manure, excrement, sewage, refuse, rubbish, garbage, trash, slime, sludge, effluent, pollution, contamination, corruption, defilement, impurity, uncleanness, foulness, sordidness, squalor
formal faeces, putrefaction, putrescence
colloq. gunge, yuck, grot; *slang* crud, gunk, grunge, crap
2 OBSCENITY, pornography, indecency, vulgarity, coarseness, dirty books
colloq. smut, sleaze, porn, hard porn, blue films, sexploitation, raunchiness
 1 cleanness, cleanliness, purity

filthy *adj*
1 DIRTY, soiled, unwashed, grimy, grubby, black, mucky, muddy, slimy, sooty, unclean, contaminated, polluted, decaying, rotten, impure, foul, gross, sordid, squalid, vile, low, mean, base, nasty, contemptible, despicable
formal faecal, putrid, putrefying
colloq. yucky; *slang* crappy
2 OBSCENE, dirty, foul, pornographic, smutty, bawdy, suggestive, indecent, explicit, offensive, foul-mouthed, vulgar, coarse, lewd, corrupt, depraved
colloq. blue, adult
3 DESPICABLE, contemptible, worthless, wretched, nasty, vile, low
 1 clean, pure **2** decent

final *adj*
1 LAST, latest, closing, concluding, finishing, end, ultimate, terminal, dying, last-minute, eventual
formal terminating
2 CONCLUSIVE, definitive, decisive, definite, settled, incontrovertible, indisputable, irrevocable, irrefutable
formal determinate
 1 first, initial

finale *n*
climax, dénouement, culmination, crowning glory, end, ending, conclusion, close, final act, curtain, epilogue

finality *n*
conclusiveness, conviction, decidedness, decisiveness, definiteness, certitude, firmness, resolution, inevitability, inevitableness, unavoidability, incontrovertibility, irreversibility, irrevocability
formal ultimacy

finalize *v*
conclude, finish, complete, round off, work out, resolve, settle, agree, decide, close
colloq. clinch, sew up, wrap up, put the icing on the cake, put the finishing touches to

finally *adv*
lastly, in conclusion, to conclude, ultimately, eventually, at last, at length, in the end, conclusively, once and for all, for ever, for good, permanently, irreversibly, irrevocably, decisively, definitely
colloq. when all is said and done

finance *n, v*
▶ *n* **1** *corporate finance*
economics, money management, accounting,

banking, investment, stock market, business, commerce, trade, money, funding, sponsorship, subsidy
2 *the company's finances*
accounts, affairs, budget, bank account, income, revenue, liquidity, resources, funding, assets, means, capital, wealth, money, cash, funds, wherewithal, savings
▶ *v* pay for, fund, sponsor, back, support, underwrite, guarantee, subsidize, capitalize, float, set up

financial *adj*
monetary, money, economic, fiscal, budgetary, commercial, entrepreneurial
formal pecuniary

financier *n*
financialist, banker, stockbroker, money-maker, investor, speculator

find *v, n*
▶ *v* **1** DISCOVER, locate, track down, trace, retrieve, recover, regain, get back, unearth, uncover, dig out, turn up, expose, reveal, bring to light, come across, come by, stumble across/on, meet, encounter, detect, recognize, notice, observe, perceive, realize, learn
formal happen upon, chance upon
2 ATTAIN, achieve, win, reach, gain, earn, acquire, obtain, get
formal procure
3 *find it difficult*
consider, think, judge, rate, gauge, declare
formal deem
F3 1 lose
▷ **find out 1** LEARN, ascertain, establish, identify, pinpoint, discover, detect, note, observe, perceive, see, gather, realize; *colloq.* get wind of, suss out
2 UNMASK, expose, show up, uncover, reveal, disclose, get at, detect, bring to light, lay bare, catch; *colloq.* suss out, tumble to; *slang* rumble
▶ *n* acquisition, asset, catch, coup, discovery, boon, godsend, bargain, good buy

finding *n*
1 FIND, discovery, breakthrough, innovation
2 DECISION, conclusion, judgement, verdict, order, pronouncement, decree, recommendation, award

fine¹ *adj*
1 EXCELLENT, outstanding, exceptional, first-class, great, superior, exquisite, splendid, magnificent, admirable, brilliant, beautiful, handsome, attractive, lovely, nice, good, select, choice
2 HEALTHY, in good health, well, fit, strong, flourishing, vigorous
3 SATISFACTORY, acceptable, all right, agreeable, good; *colloq.* OK
4 *fine weather*
bright, sunny, clear, cloudless, dry, fair, clement, temperate
5 THIN, slender, slim, slight, sheer, gauzy, powdery, flimsy, light, fragile, delicate, dainty, narrow
6 POWDERY, ground, crushed, fine-grained, gossamer
7 EXPENSIVE, elegant, smart, fashionable, stylish
8 *a fine distinction*
EXACT, precise, accurate, nice, critical
colloq. hair-splitting
F3 1 mediocre **4** cloudy, dull, inclement, stormy
5 thick, coarse

fine² *n, v*
▶ *n* *a speeding fine*

penalty, punishment, forfeit, forfeiture, damages
formal amercement, mulct
▶ *v* penalize, punish
formal amerce, mulct
colloq. sting

finery *n*
decorations, frippery, best clothes, Sunday best, jewellery, ornaments, showiness, splendour, gaudery, trappings
formal bedizenment
colloq. glad rags, best bib and tucker

finesse *n, v*
▶ *n* skill, flair, expertise, deftness, adeptness, adroitness, cleverness, delicacy, diplomacy, tact, discretion, subtlety, *savoir-faire*, elegance, gracefulness, polish, neatness, refinement, sophistication, quickness
colloq. know-how
▶ *v* bluff, evade, manipulate, manoeuvre, trick

finger *v*
touch, handle, manipulate, feel, stroke, caress, fondle, paw, fiddle with, toy with, play about with, meddle with
▷ **put your finger on** pinpoint, indicate, isolate, pin down, hit upon, identify, discover, find out, remember, place, locate, recall; *colloq.* hit the nail on the head

finicky *adj*
1 PARTICULAR, finickety, fussy, fastidious, meticulous, scrupulous, critical, hypercritical, selective, discriminating, faddy
colloq. pernickety, choosy, nit-picking, picky
2 FIDDLY, intricate, tricky, difficult, delicate
F3 1 easy-going **2** easy

finish *v, n*
▶ *v* **1** END, bring/come to an end, stop, be over, complete, accomplish, attain, achieve, fulfil, carry out, discharge, deal with, do, close, settle, round off, culminate, perfect
formal conclude, terminate, cease, discontinue
colloq. wind up, polish off, pack in, wrap up, sew up, be done with, get shot of, be through, call it a day
2 USE UP, use, consume, devour, eat, drink, exhaust, drain, empty, run out of
formal deplete, expend
3 DESTROY, ruin, exterminate, get rid of, annihilate, defeat, overcome, overwhelm, overpower, conquer, rout, overthrow, crush, bring down, get the better of
colloq. wipe out
F3 1 begin, start; *formal* commence
▶ *n* **1** END, completion, conclusion, close, ending, finale, culmination, accomplishment, achievement, perfection, fulfilment, discharge, ruin, destruction
formal termination, cessation
colloq. winding-up, wind-up, curtains
2 SURFACE, appearance, texture, grain, polish, shine, gloss, glaze, coating, veneer, lacquer, lustre, smoothness
F3 1 beginning, start; *formal* commencement

finished *adj*
1 COMPLETED, complete, concluded, dealt with, over, at an end
colloq. over and done with, through, wrapped up, sewn up
2 USELESS, defeated, ruined, doomed, drained, exhausted, empty, spent, undone, unwanted, unpopular
colloq. done for, played out, zonked

3 *a finished performance*
accomplished, proficient, professional, expert, polished, impeccable, faultless, flawless, perfect, masterly, consummate, refined, sophisticated, urbane, virtuoso
E3 1 unfinished, incomplete **2** useful, productive **3** incompetent; *colloq.* hopeless

finite *adj*
limited, restricted, bounded, demarcated, terminable, definable, fixed, measurable, calculable, countable, numbered
E3 infinite

fire *n, v*
▶ *n* **1** FLAMES, blaze, bonfire, inferno, burning, combustion, holocaust
formal conflagration
Related adjective: igneous
2 GUNFIRE, attack, bombing, shelling, sniping, bombardment, barrage, cannonade, fusillade, salvo, fire, flak
3 HEATER, radiator, convector, fan
4 PASSION, feeling, ardour, excitement, eagerness, enthusiasm, spirit, energy, liveliness, life, vigour, animation, vivacity, verve, fervour, intensity, heat, radiance, inventiveness, creativity, sparkle
▶ *v* **1** IGNITE, light, put a match to, kindle, set fire to, set on fire, set alight, set ablaze
2 *fire a missile*
shoot, launch, set off, let off, detonate, discharge, explode, trigger, hurl
3 DISMISS, discharge, eject, get rid of
colloq. sack, axe, boot out, show someone the door, give someone their cards, give someone the sack/push/boot/elbow
4 EXCITE, whet, enliven, galvanize, electrify, stir (up), arouse, rouse, motivate, stimulate, inspire, animate, inflame, incite, spark off, trigger off
▷ **on fire 1** IN FLAMES, burning, alight, ignited, flaming, aflame, blazing, ablaze, fiery
2 ENTHUSIASTIC, passionate, excited, eager, ardent, energetic, creative, inventive, sparkling, inspired

firearm *n*
gun, weapon, automatic, handgun, pistol, revolver, rifle, shotgun, musket

fireplace *n*

Types of fireplace include: backboiler, boiler, bonfire, brazier, campfire, electric fire, firebox, forge, furnace, gas fire, grate, hearth, incinerator, kiln, open fire, oven, stove, paraffin stove, wood burning stove.

fireworks *n*
1 PYROTECHNICS, explosions, illuminations, feux d'artifice
2 UPROAR, trouble, outburst, frenzy, fit, rage, rows, storm, temper, sparks, hysterics

Types of firework include: banger, Catherine wheel, cracker, Chinese cracker, firecracker, fountain, golden rain, indoor firework, jumping-jack, pinwheel, rocket, roman candle, sky-rocket, sparkler, squib.

firm¹ *adj*
1 *firm ground*
dense, compressed, compact, close-grained, concentrated, set, solid, solidified, substantive, hard,

hardened, unyielding, stiff, rigid, inflexible, inelastic
2 FIXED, embedded, established, fast, tight, secure, fastened, anchored, riveted, immovable, tight, motionless, unshakable, stationary, steady, stable, set, sturdy, strong
3 *a firm decision*
definite, settled, fixed, decided, established, unchangeable, unalterable
4 ADAMANT, unshakable, resolute, resolved, decided, determined, dogged, unwavering, unfaltering, unswerving, unflinching, strict, hard, inflexible, stubborn, obstinate, constant, steadfast, staunch, tenacious
formal obdurate
5 *firm friends*
close, dependable, true, sure, committed, unchanging, constant, long-standing, long-lasting, steady, stable, steadfast, staunch
E3 1 soft, flabby **2** unsteady **3** changeable **4** hesitant

firm² *n*
a firm of accountants
company, corporation, business, enterprise, concern, house, establishment, institution, organization, association, partnership, syndicate, conglomerate

firmly *adv*
securely, tightly, steadily, stably, sturdily, strongly, robustly, unshakably, unwaveringly, strictly, immovably, unalterably, unchangeably, unflinchingly, resolutely, inflexibly, decisively, definitely, determinedly, doggedly, enduringly, staunchly, steadfastly
E3 hesitantly, uncertainly, unsoundly

firmness *n*
1 STIFFNESS, hardness, rigidity, solidity, density, compactness, inflexibility, inelasticity, tautness, tension, fixity, immovability, tightness
2 STRENGTH, strength of will, determination, resolution, resolve, dependability, reliability, staunchness, steadfastness, steadiness, willpower, constancy, conviction, changelessness, stability, strictness, resistance, sureness, doggedness
formal indomitability, obduracy
E3 1 softness **2** uncertainty

first *adj, adv, n*
▶ *adj* **1** INITIAL, opening, introductory, preliminary, beginning, inaugural, elementary, primary, basic, fundamental
2 ORIGINAL, earliest, earlier, prior, primitive, oldest, eldest, senior
formal primeval, primordial
3 CHIEF, main, key, cardinal, principal, head, leading, foremost, ruling, sovereign, highest, greatest, uppermost, paramount, best, prime, supreme, predominant, pre-eminent
E3 1 last, final
▶ *adv* initially, to begin with, at first, first of all, in the first place, to start with, first and foremost, at the outset, beforehand, before anything else, originally, in preference, rather, sooner
▶ *n* beginning, start, opening, introduction, outset, origin(s), original, prototype, unveiling, première
formal commencement, inception
colloq. the word go, square one

first-born *adj*
elder, eldest, older, oldest, senior
old use eigne, primogenit

formal ané(e), primogenital, primogenitary,
primogenitive

firsthand   *adj & adv*
direct(ly), immediate(ly), personal(ly), in service,
on the job
colloq. straight from the horse's mouth, hands-on
🔁 indirect(ly)

first name   *n*
forename, Christian name, given name, baptismal
name

first-rate   *adj*
first-class, second-to-none, matchless, peerless, top,
top-flight, leading, supreme, superior, prime,
excellent, outstanding, superlative, premier,
exceptional, splendid, superb, fine, admirable
colloq. super, top-notch, A1, ace, crack, out of this
world; *slang* way-out, cool, radical, mega
🔁 inferior

fiscal   *adj*
financial, monetary, money, economic, budgetary,
treasury, capital
formal pecuniary

fish   *n, v*
▶ *n*

> *Types of fish include*: bloater, brisling, cod, coley,
> Dover sole, haddock, hake, halibut, herring, jellied
> eel, kipper, mackerel, pilchard, plaice, rainbow
> trout, salmon, sardine, sole, sprat, trout, tuna,
> turbot, whitebait; bass, Bombay duck, bream, brill,
> carp, catfish, chub, conger eel, cuttlefish, dab, dace,
> dogfish, dory, eel, goldfish, guppy, marlin, minnow,
> monkfish, mullet, octopus, perch, pike, piranha,
> roach, shark, skate, snapper, squid, stickleback,
> stingray, sturgeon, swordfish, tench, whiting; clam,
> cockle, crab, crayfish, *US* crawfish, kingprawn,
> lobster, mussel, oyster, prawn, scallop, shrimp,
> whelk. *See also* **shark**.

Related adjectives: piscine, ichthyic, ichthyoid
▶ *v* **1** GO FISHING, angle, trawl
2 *fished in her bag for a pen*
delve, hunt, search, grope
▷ **fish out** produce, take out, extract, find, retrieve,
haul out, pull out, come up with, dredge up

fisherman   *n*
angler, fisher, rodfisher, rodman, rodsman, rodster
formal piscator, piscatorian

fishing   *n*
angling, trawling
Related adjectives: piscatorial, piscatory, halieutic

fishy   *adj*
1 *a fishy taste*
fish-like
formal piscatorial, piscatory, piscine
2 ODD, suspicious, questionable, shady, suspect,
doubtful, dubious, implausible, improbable, funny,
irregular, queer
🔁 honest, legitimate

fission   *n*
splitting, breaking, division, rupture, parting, rending,
schism, severance, scission, cleavage

fissure   *n*
crack, opening, cleft, fracture, breach, break, cranny,
crevasse, crevice, rent, rift, rupture, chasm, hole, gap,
gash, slit, split, chink, fault

technical grike, foramen, sulcus
formal cleavage, interstice, scissure

fist   *n*
palm, hand
colloq. paw; *slang* mitt

fit¹   *adj, v*
▶ *adj* **1** HEALTHY, well, in good health, able-
bodied, in good form, in good shape, in shape, in good
condition, in trim, sound, sturdy, strong, hardy, robust,
vigorous, flourishing, hale and hearty
2 SUITABLE, appropriate, apt, fitting, correct, right,
proper, due, convenient, ready, prepared, able, capable,
competent, qualified, equipped, trained, eligible,
worthy
old use seemly
formal decorous, pertinent
🔁 **1** unfit **2** unsuitable, unworthy
▶ *v* **1** *Do the shoes fit you?*
get into, be the right size for, be the right shape for,
be a good fit
colloq. fit like a glove
2 MATCH, correspond, conform, follow, agree, tally,
suit, be suitable, harmonize, go, be right, be consistent,
belong, dovetail, interlock, connect, join, put together,
meet, accommodate
formal concur, be consonant
3 *fit a washing-machine*
install, insert, put in, arrange, position, place, put in
position/place, attach, arrange, fix
4 ALTER, modify, change, adjust, adapt, regulate,
tailor, shape, fashion, accommodate
5 EQUIP, qualify, train, make suitable, prepare, make
ready, prime, condition, arm, coach, groom, tailor
▷ **fit in** match, correspond, conform, agree, square,
belong, slot, squeeze; *formal* accord, concur
▷ **fit out** equip, rig out, kit out, outfit, provide,
supply, furnish, prepare, arm; *formal* accoutre

fit²   *n*
1 SEIZURE, convulsion, spasm, paroxysm, attack
technical ictus
2 OUTBREAK, bout, spell, burst, surge, outburst,
eruption, explosion, tantrum
▷ **in fits and starts** sporadically, fitfully,
intermittently, occasionally, irregularly, unevenly,
brokenly, erratically, off and on
🔁 regularly, steadily

fitful   *adj*
sporadic, intermittent, occasional, spasmodic, erratic,
irregular, disconnected, haphazard, uneven, broken,
disturbed
🔁 steady, regular

fitness   *n*
1 SUITABILITY, qualifications, readiness,
preparedness, eligibility, appropriateness, aptness,
competence, adequacy, applicability, condition
formal pertinence
2 HEALTH, healthiness, strength, vigour, condition,
shape, trim, good health, robustness, haleness
🔁 **1** unsuitability **2** unfitness

fitted   *adj*
1 *fitted wardrobe*
built-in, permanent, fixed
2 EQUIPPED, rigged out, provided, furnished,
appointed, prepared, armed, tailored
3 SUITED, right, suitable, fit, qualified, cut out

fitting   *adj, n*
▶ *adj* apt, appropriate, suitable, fit, correct, right,

proper, desirable, deserved
old use seemly, meet
formal decorous
⊟ unsuitable, improper
▶ *n* **1** *light fittings*
attachment, accessory, connection, part, component,
piece, unit, fitment, fixture, unit
2 *the price includes fittings*
equipment, furnishings, furniture, fixtures,
installations, fitments, accessories, extras
formal accoutrements, appointments

fix *v, n*
▶ *v* **1** FASTEN, secure, tie, bind, attach, join,
connect, link, couple, anchor, clamp, pin, nail, screw,
rivet, stick, glue, cement, set, harden, solidify, stiffen,
stabilize, plant, root, implant, embed, establish,
install, station, locate, situate, position
2 *fix a date*
arrange, set, specify, define, agree on, decide,
determine, name, settle, resolve, finalize, arrive at, sort
3 MEND, repair, patch up, correct, rectify, adjust,
restore, remedy, see to, put right
4 *fix your eyes/attention*
direct, aim, focus, concentrate, turn, level
5 *fix your hair*
arrange, tidy, groom, adjust, dress, prepare, put in
order, order, do, straighten, comb
6 *fix a race*
rig, falsify, fake, manoeuvre, tamper with, manipulate
7 *fix some food for you*
prepare, make, get ready, put together, cook
⊟ **1** move, shift **3** damage **5** untidy
▷ **fix up** arrange, organize, settle, agree on, plan,
lay on, provide, supply, furnish, equip, settle, sort out,
produce, bring about
▶ *n* **1** DILEMMA, quandary, predicament, plight,
difficulty, corner, mess, muddle
colloq. hole, (tight) spot, bind, pickle, scrape, jam,
the soup
2 INJECTION, dose, shot, hit
colloq. score, slug, bang

fixation *n*
preoccupation, obsession, mania, fetish, infatuation,
compulsion, complex, *idée fixe*, phobia
colloq. thing, hang-up

fixed *adj*
decided, settled, established, constant, definite,
arranged, planned, set, firm, rigid, inflexible,
entrenched, immobile, steady, secure, fast, rooted,
permanent
colloq. cast/set in stone
⊟ variable, varying, flexible, mobile

fixity *n*
permanence, persistence, constancy, stability,
steadiness, fixedness
formal immutability

fixture *n*
1 *fixtures and fittings*
equipment, furnishings, furniture, installations
2 *a sports fixture*
event, match, game, competition, contest, race, round,
meeting

fizz *v*
effervesce, sparkle, bubble, froth, foam, fizzle, hiss

fizzle *v*
▷ **fizzle out** collapse, come to nothing, die away, die
down, fall through, fail, come to grief, stop, subside,

disappear, evaporate, taper off
formal dissipate
colloq. fold, peter out, flop

fizzy *adj*
effervescent, sparkling, aerated, carbonated, gassy,
bubbly, bubbling, frothy, foaming

flabbergasted *adj*
amazed, confounded, astonished, astounded,
staggered, dumbfounded, speechless, stunned, dazed,
nonplussed, overcome, overwhelmed
colloq. bowled over

flabby *adj*
fleshy, soft, yielding, flaccid, limp, floppy, drooping,
hanging, sagging, slack, loose, lax, weak, feeble, fat,
overweight, plump
⊟ firm, strong, lean, toned

flaccid *adj*
limp, drooping, flabby, floppy, lax, loose, sagging,
slack, soft, toneless, weak, nerveless, relaxed, clammy
⊟ firm, hard

flag[1] *n, v*
▶ *n* *fly the Japanese flag*
Related adjective: vexillary

Types of flag include: banderol, banner, bunting,
burgee, colours, cornet, ensign, gonfalon, jack,
oriflamme, pennant, pilot flag, signal flag,
standard, streamer, swallow tail, vexillum.

Names of flag include: Blue Ensign, Blue Peter,
Crescent, Hammer and Sickle, Jolly Roger, Old
Glory, Olympic Flag, Red Ensign, Rising Sun, Skull
and Crossbones, Star Spangled Banner, Stars and
Stripes, Tricolour, Union Jack, White Ensign, Yellow
Jack.

▶ *v* **1** SIGNAL, wave, salute, motion, hail, wave down,
signal to stop
2 MARK, indicate, label, tag, note

flag[2] *v*
spirits were beginning to flag
lessen, diminish, decline, fall (off), subside, wane, ebb,
sink, slump, dwindle, peter out, taper off, fade, fail,
weaken, slow, falter, tire, grow tired, weary, wilt, droop,
hang down, sag, flop, faint, die
formal abate
⊟ revive

flagellation *n*
beating, whipping, flogging, lashing, scourging,
thrashing, flaying, whaling
old use verberation
formal castigation, chastisement, vapulation

flagging *adj*
lessening, diminishing, declining, subsiding, sinking,
dwindling, ebbing, waning, decreasing, fading, failing,
weakening, slowing, faltering, sagging, tiring,
drooping, faltering, wilting
formal abating
⊟ returning, reviving

flagon *n*
bottle, decanter, carafe, jug, pitcher, flask, ewer, vessel

flagrant *adj*
scandalous, outrageous, glaring, disgraceful, dreadful,
shameless, blatant, ostentatious, open, atrocious,
enormous, heinous, infamous, notorious, bold,

brazen, audacious, barefaced, conspicuous, unashamed, undisguised, overt, rank, gross, arrant
formal egregious
F3 covert, secret

⚠ **flagrant** or **blatant** ? *See panel at* **blatant**.

flail *v*
wave uncontrolledly, swing wildly, thresh, thrash, batter, beat, whip, strike

flair *n*
skill, ability, natural ability, aptitude, faculty, gift, talent, bent, facility, knack, mastery, genius, feel, taste, discernment, acumen, style, elegance, stylishness, panache
F3 inability, ineptitude

flak *n*
criticism, blame, censure, complaints, disapproval, fault-finding, hostility, opposition, abuse, condemnation
formal animadversions, aspersions, disapprobation, disparagement, invective
colloq. bad press, brickbats, stick

flake *n, v*
▶ *n* scale, peeling, paring, shaving, scurf, sliver, wafer, chip, splinter, bit, particle, fragment
technical desquamation, exfoliation, furfur
▶ *v* scale, peel, chip, splinter, blister
technical desquamate, exfoliate
▷ **flake out** collapse, pass out, faint, keel over, drop, fall asleep, relax completely

flaky *adj*
dry, scaly, scurfy, laminar, layered
technical desquamative, desquamatory, exfoliative, furfuraceous, scabrous

flamboyance *n*
showiness, ostentation, colour, brilliance, glamour, extravagance, style, dash, élan, panache, theatricality
colloq. pizzazz
F3 diffidence, restraint

flamboyant *adj*
showy, ostentatious, flashy, gaudy, bright, colourful, brilliant, exciting, dazzling, striking, dashing, extravagant, rich, glamorous, elaborate, ornate, florid, theatrical
F3 modest, restrained

flame *v, n*
▶ *v* burn, catch fire, flare, blaze, burst into flames, glare, flash, beam, shine, glow, sparkle, gleam, radiate
▶ *n* **1** FIRE, blaze, light, brightness, gleam, glow, heat, warmth
formal conflagration
2 PASSION, ardour, fervour, warmth, fervency, excitement, enthusiasm, eagerness, keenness, zeal, intensity, radiance, fire
3 *an old flame*
lover, partner, boyfriend, girlfriend, sweetheart

flaming *adj*
1 *a flaming torch*
burning, alight, aflame, blazing, on fire, in flames, fiery, brilliant, scintillating, red-hot, glowing, raging, smouldering
2 *a flaming red*
intense, vivid, bright, brilliant, blazing
3 *a flaming temper*

furious, angry, enraged, raging, infuriated, incensed, mad, violent

flammable *adj*
inflammable, ignitable, combustible
F3 non-flammable, incombustible, flameproof, fire-resistant, flame-resistant

flank *n, v*
▶ *n the animal's/enemy's flank*
side, edge, quarter, wing, loin, haunch, hip, thigh
▶ *v* edge, fringe, skirt, line, border, bound, confine, wall, screen

flannel *n*
nonsense, rubbish, flattery, blarney
colloq. waffle, rot, sweet talk, soft soap

flap *v, n*
▶ *v* flutter, vibrate, wave, agitate, shake, wag, waggle, swing, sway, swish, thrash, thresh, beat, move up and down, move from side to side
▶ *n* **1** FOLD, fly, lapel, overhang, overlap, covering, tab, lug, tag, tail, skirt, apron, aileron, lappet
2 FLUTTER, fluttering, wave, shake, wag, waggle, swing, sway, swish
3 PANIC, fuss, commotion, fluster, agitation, flutter, dither
colloq. state, tizzy, stew

flare *v, n*
▶ *v* **1** FLAME, burn, blaze, glare, glow, gleam, glitter, sparkle, flash, flicker, burst, explode, erupt
2 BROADEN, widen, flare out, spread out, splay
▷ **flare up** erupt, break out, blaze, burst out, lose your temper, lose control; *colloq.* explode, blow up, boil over, lose your cool
▶ *n* **1** FLAME, blaze, glare, flash, flicker, burst, glimmer, gleam, dazzle
2 SIGNAL, distress signal, warning signal, beacon, light, rocket, beam
3 BROADENING, widening, spread, splay

flash *v, n, adj*
▶ *v* **1** BEAM, shine, light up, flare, blaze, glare, gleam, glimmer, glisten, glint, flicker, twinkle, sparkle, glitter, shimmer, scintillate, dance
formal coruscate, fulgurate
2 *the train flashed past*
streak, fly, shoot, speed, dart, race, dash, tear, zoom, rush, bolt, career, bound
3 *flashed her engagement ring*
flourish, brandish, flaunt, show off, display
▶ *n* **1** *flash of lightning*
beam, ray, shaft, spark, blaze, flare, burst, streak, glare, glimmer, glitter, gleam, glint, flicker, twinkle, sparkle, shimmer
2 *a flash of inspiration*
burst, outburst, outbreak, sudden appearance, show, display, exhibition
▷ **in a flash** in an instant, in a moment, in a split second, in a twinkling, in the twinkling of an eye, in no time (at all), in less than no time, in a trice; *colloq.* pronto, in a jiffy, in two shakes of a lamb's tail, before you can say Jack Robinson
▶ *adj* showy, ostentatious, smart, fashionable, expensive, glamorous, gaudy, kitsch, pretentious

flashy *adj*
showy, ostentatious, flamboyant, glamorous, bold, loud, garish, gaudy, jazzy, flash, pretentious, tawdry, cheap, vulgar, tasteless, kitsch, showing poor taste
colloq. tacky, glitzy
F3 plain, tasteful

flask *n*
bottle, carafe, flagon, decanter, matrass, flacket, lekythos

flat *n, adj, adv*
▶ *n* apartment, penthouse, maisonette, tenement, flatlet, rooms, suite, bed-sit(ter)
colloq. pad
▶ *adj* **1** LEVEL, plane, even, smooth, uniform, unbroken, levelled, horizontal, outstretched, prostrate, prone, recumbent, reclining, low, spread-eagled
technical homaloidal
formal supine
colloq. flat as a pancake
2 SHALLOW, not deep, not thick, not tall
3 *a flat tyre*
punctured, burst, deflated, collapsed, ruptured
colloq. blown-out
4 DULL, boring, monotonous, tedious, uninteresting, unexciting, stale, lifeless, dead, spiritless, lacklustre, vapid, insipid, bland, weak, watery, empty, pointless
5 *a flat refusal*
absolute, utter, total, unequivocal, categorical, positive, unconditional, unqualified, outright, out and out, downright, point-blank, direct, straight, explicit, plain, final, definite, complete
6 *feel flat*
depressed, low, discouraged, dejected, downcast, miserable, inactive, sluggish, slack, slow
colloq. down
7 *charge a flat price*
set, fixed, standard, definite, stock, firm, rigid, planned, arranged
▣ 1 bumpy, vertical, upright **2** deep, thick, tall **4** exciting, full **5** equivocal **6** happy, cheerful, lively **7** variable, negotiable
▶ *adv* directly, outright, categorically, absolutely, straight, point-blank, completely, totally, utterly, entirely, exactly, plainly, precisely
▷ **flat out** at top speed, at full speed, all out, for all you are worth

flatly *adv*
categorically, point-blank, positively, absolutely, completely, uncompromisingly, unconditionally, unhesitatingly
formal peremptorily

flatness *n*
1 EVENNESS, levelness, smoothness, horizontality, uniformity
2 DULLNESS, monotony, tedium, boredom, staleness, emptiness, tastelessness, insipidity, vapidity
formal languor

flatten *v*
1 SMOOTH, iron, press, roll, crush, squash, compress, plane, level, make flat, make even, even out
2 KNOCK DOWN, knock to the ground, prostrate, floor, fell, demolish, raze, tear down, overwhelm, subdue

flatter *v*
1 PRAISE, compliment, adulate, fawn, sing the praises of, wheedle, toady, kowtow, humour, play up to, court, curry favour with
formal sycophantize, eulogize, inveigle
colloq. sweet-talk, butter up, creep, suck up to, make up to, soft-soap, play up to
2 *that dress flatters you*
show off, make someone look attractive, look good on, become, suit, enhance, embellish, grace, show to advantage, befit
▣ 1 criticize

flatterer *n*
adulator, fawner, groveller, lackey, toady, bootlicker, lickspittle
formal encomiast, sycophant, eulogizer
colloq. back-scratcher, creeper, crawler
▣ critic, opponent

flattering *adj*
complimentary, kind, favourable, enhancing, gratifying, becoming, adulatory, ingratiating, fawning, fulsome, effusive, servile, smooth-spoken, smooth-tongued, honeyed, honey-tongued, sugared, sugary
old use gnathonic
formal laudatory, obsequious, sycophantic, unctuous
▣ candid, uncompromising, unflattering

flattery *n*
adulation, praise, blarney, fulsomeness, compliments, cajolery, fawning, toadyism, ingratiation, servility
formal eulogy, sycophancy, blandishments, laudation
colloq. sweet talk, soft soap, flannel
▣ criticism

flatulence *n*
wind, windiness, gas, gassiness
formal eructation, flatus, borborygmus, ventosity
colloq. farting

flatulent *v*
windy, gassy
formal ventose

flaunt *v*
show off, display, parade, flourish, brandish, exhibit, boast, air, sport, vaunt, wield, dangle, flash
old use disport

⚠ **flaunt** or **flout** ?
To *flaunt* something is 'to show it off or display it ostentatiously': *She was flaunting her new fur coat in front of her colleagues. Flout* means 'to treat with contempt, to refuse to obey or comply with': *He constantly flouts authority/the law.*

flavour *n, v*
▶ *n* **1** TASTE, tang, smack, savour, relish, piquancy, zest, aroma, odour
colloq. zing
2 QUALITY, property, character, style, aspect, feeling, feel, atmosphere, tone, spirit, essence, nature, soul
3 HINT, suggestion, touch, tinge, tone
▶ *v* season, spice, ginger up, infuse, imbue, lace

flavouring *n*
seasoning, flavour, zest, tang, relish, piquancy, essence, extract, additive
colloq. zing

flaw *n*
defect, imperfection, fault, weakness, weak spot, foible, shortcoming, failing, fallacy, lapse, slip, error, mistake, blemish, spot, mark, speck, crack, crevice, fissure, cleft, rent, split, tear, rift, chip, break, fracture

flawed *adj*
imperfect, defective, faulty, blemished, marked, damaged, spoilt, marred, cracked, chipped, broken, unsound, fallacious, erroneous
▣ flawless, perfect

flawless *adj*
perfect, faultless, unblemished, spotless, immaculate,

impeccable, stainless, sound, intact, whole, unbroken, undamaged, unimpaired
🔄 flawed, imperfect, blemished

flay *v*
skin, skin alive, upbraid, revile, scourge, flog
formal excoriate, castigate, execrate, lambast
colloq. pull to pieces, tear a strip off

fleck *v, n*
▶ *v* dot, spot, mark, speckle, dapple, mottle, stipple, freckle, streak, sprinkle, dust, spatter
▶ *n* dot, point, spot, mark, speck, speckle, freckle, streak

fledgling *n*
beginner, newcomer, novice, apprentice, learner, recruit, trainee, tiro, neophyte, novitiate, tenderfoot
colloq. greenhorn, rookie

flee *v*
run away, bolt, fly, take flight, take off, make off, cut and run, escape, get away, rush, decamp, abscond, leave, depart, withdraw, retreat, vanish, disappear, make yourself scarce
colloq. clear off, take to your heels, scarper, scoot, scram, vamoose
🔄 stay

fleece *n, v*
▶ *n* down, coat, wool
▶ *v* swindle, rob, steal, cheat, defraud, overcharge, plunder, mulct, bilk
colloq. bleed, con, diddle, rip off, squeeze, sting, fiddle, gull, have someone on, string along, take for a ride, take to the cleaners, pull a fast one

fleecy *adj*
downy, woolly, soft, velvety, shaggy, nappy, fluffy, hairy
formal floccose, flocculate, lanuginose, pilose, eriophorous
🔄 bald, smooth

fleet *n, adj*
▶ *n* flotilla, armada, navy, task force, naval force, squadron
▶ *adj* swift, fast, quick, rapid, nimble, flying, speedy, light-footed, winged, mercurial, meteoric
formal expeditious
🔄 slow

fleeting *adj*
short, brief, flying, short-lived, short, quick, sudden, rushed, momentary, ephemeral, transient, transitory, passing, temporary
formal evanescent, fugacious
colloq. here today and gone tomorrow
🔄 lasting, permanent

flesh *n, v*
▶ *n* **1** *an animal's flesh*
body, tissue, fat, muscle, brawn, skin, meat, pulp
2 SUBSTANCE, matter, physicality, pith, stuff, solidity, significance, weight
3 *pleasures of the flesh*
human nature, physical nature, sinful nature, carnal nature, carnality, physicality, corporeality, sensuality
▷ **flesh and blood** family, relative, relations, kin;
colloq. folks
▷ **in the flesh** in person, in real life, in actual life, before your own eyes
Related adjectives: carnal, carneous, carnose
▶ *v* ▷ **flesh out** add/give details, elaborate, make complete, make more substantial

fleshly *adj*
wordly, earthy, physical, earthly, corporal, corporeal, bodily, human, animal, sensual, sexual, bestial, carnal, lustful, erotic, material, brutish
🔄 spiritual

fleshy *adj*
fat, ample, beefy, chubby, chunky, brawny, hefty, meaty, obese, plump, podgy, portly, tubby, stout, paunchy, overweight, well-padded
formal corpulent, rotund
colloq. flabby
🔄 thin, slim

flex *n, v*
▶ *n* cable, wire, lead, cord
▶ *v* bend, bow, curve, angle, crook, ply, double up, stretch, tighten, contract
🔄 straighten, extend

flexibility *n*
1 BENDABILITY, pliability, pliancy, elasticity, resilience, spring, springiness, suppleness, give, flexion
formal tensility
2 ADAPTABILITY, agreeability, adjustability, amenability
formal complaisance
🔄 **1, 2** inflexibility

flexible *adj*
1 BENDABLE, pliable, pliant, plastic, malleable, mouldable, elastic, stretchy, springy, yielding, supple, lithe, limber, double-jointed, agile, mobile
colloq. bendy
2 ADAPTABLE, adjustable, changeable, amenable, accommodating, variable, open, open-ended, yielding, manageable
🔄 **1** inflexible, rigid **2** fixed, inflexible, rigid

flick *v, n*
▶ *v* hit, strike, rap, tap, touch, dab, flip, swish, snap, click, jerk, whip, lash
▷ **flick through** flip through, browse through, thumb through, leaf through, glance at, glance over, skip, skim, scan
▶ *n* rap, tap, touch, dab, flip, jerk, click, snap, swish

flicker *v, n*
▶ *v* flash, blink, wink, twinkle, sparkle, glimmer, glitter, flare, glint, shimmer, gutter, flutter, vibrate, bat, quiver, waver
▶ *n* flash, gleam, glint, twinkle, glimmer, glitter, sparkle, spark, trace, drop, iota, atom, indication

flight[1] *n*
a seagull in flight
1 FLYING, aviation, aeronautics, air transport, air travel
2 JOURNEY, trip, voyage, shuttle, globe-trotting
3 *a flight of steps*
staircase, set, stairway, stairs, steps

flight[2] *n*
his flight from the police
fleeing, escape, running away/off, getaway, breakaway, rush, absconding, exit, departure, exodus, retreat, withdrawal
▷ **take flight** run away, bolt, fly, take off, make off, cut and run, escape, get away, rush, decamp, abscond, leave, depart, withdraw, retreat, vanish, disappear

flighty *adj*
inconstant, scatterbrained, impetuous, impulsive, changeable, irresponsible, silly, skittish, thoughtless,

fickle, frivolous, light-headed, rattle-brained, rattle-headed, unstable, unsteady, volatile, unbalanced, wild, mercurial
formal capricious
colloq. bird-brained, hare-brained
F3 steady, responsible, sensible

flimsy *adj*
1 *flimsy clothing/structures*
thin, fine, light, slight, insubstantial, ethereal, lightweight, fragile, delicate, filmy, sheer, shaky, rickety, ramshackle, jerry-built, makeshift
2 *flimsy excuse*
weak, feeble, meagre, inadequate, shallow, superficial, trivial, poor, thin, trifling, unconvincing, implausible
F3 1 sturdy, strong **2** convincing, plausible

flinch *v*
wince, start, cringe, cower, crouch, quail, tremble, shake, quake, shudder, shiver, shrink, blench, recoil, draw back, pull back, balk, shy away, shirk, withdraw, retreat, flee
colloq. duck, dodge

fling *v, n*
▶ *v* throw, hurl, pitch, lob, toss, cast, sling, catapult, launch, propel, send, send flying, let fly, heave, jerk
colloq. chuck
▶ *n* **1** THROW, hurl, pitch, lob, toss, cast, shot, heave
2 SPREE, venture, indulgence, gamble, binge, whirl, go, trial, try, turn, attempt
colloq. crack

flip *v, n*
▶ *v* flick, spin, twirl, twist, turn, toss, throw, cast, pitch, jerk, flap, click, snap
▷ **flip through** flick through, browse through, thumb through, leaf through, glance at, glance over, skip, skim, scan
▶ *n* flick, spin, twirl, twist, turn, toss, jerk, flap, click, snap

flippancy *n*
facetiousness, light-heartedness, frivolity, superficiality, shallowness, thoughtlessness, disrespect, disrespectfulness, glibness, pertness, impertinence, irreverence, levity
formal persiflage
colloq. cheek, cheekiness, sauciness
F3 earnestness, seriousness

flippant *adj*
facetious, light-hearted, frivolous, superficial, shallow, thoughtless, offhand, flip, glib, pert, impudent, impertinent, rude, disrespectful, irreverent, irresponsible
formal insouciant
colloq. saucy, cheeky
F3 serious, respectful

flirt *v, n*
▶ *v* chat up, make eyes at, ogle, eye up, make a pass at, make up to, lead on, philander, dally
▷ **flirt with** consider, entertain, toy with, play with, trifle with, dabble in, try
▶ *n* tease, vamp, trifler, heart-breaker, philanderer, wanton, hussy, coquet(te), gillet
old use gillflirt
slang chippy

flirtation *n*
affair, chatting up, dalliance, dallying, philandering, coquetry, intrigue, teasing, toying, trifling, sport
formal amour

flirtatious *adj*
provocative, coquettish, flirty, loose, promiscuous, teasing, sportive, amorous, wanton
colloq. come-hither, come-on

flit *v*
dart, speed, dash, rush, flash, fly, wing, flutter, flitter, whisk, skim, slip, pass, bob, dance

float *v*
1 GLIDE, stay afloat, sail, swim, bob, be buoyant, slide, drift, waft, hover, wander, hang, suspend
2 LAUNCH, initiate, set up, establish, promote, get going, get off the ground, be in at the beginning of, get the show on the road
3 *float an idea with you*
suggest, recommend, put forward, submit, present, propose
F3 1 sink

floating *adj*
1 AFLOAT, buoyant, unsinkable, sailing, swimming, bobbing, drifting, wafting, hovering
2 VARIABLE, fluctuating, movable, migratory, transitory, wandering, unsettled, unattached, free, uncommitted
F3 1 sinking, submerged **2** fixed, settled

flock *v, n*
▶ *v* herd, swarm, troop, converge, mass, bunch, cluster, huddle, mill, crowd, throng, group, assemble, come together, gather, collect, congregate
▶ *n* herd, pack, crowd, throng, drove, fold, host, multitude, mass, bunch, cluster, group, gathering, collection, assembly, congregation

flog *v*
1 BEAT, whip, lash, scourge, birch, cane, strap, flay, drub, thrash, belt, chastise, punish, horsewhip
formal flagellate
colloq. whack, wallop
2 SELL, deal in, handle, trade, peddle, hawk, offer for sale, put up for sale

flogging *n*
beating, whipping, lashing, scourging, birching, caning, flaying, strapping, belting, thrashing, hiding, horsewhipping
formal flagellation
colloq. whacking, walloping

flood *v, n*
▶ *v* **1** DELUGE, inundate, soak, drench, saturate, fill, overflow, surge, swell, brim over, immerse, submerge, engulf, swamp, overwhelm, drown, smother
2 FLOW, pour, stream, rush, surge, gush, saturate
▶ *n* **1** DELUGE, inundation, downpour, torrent, flash flood, flow, tide, stream, rush, spate, outpouring, overflow
2 EXCESS, torrent, abundance, glut
formal profusion, superfluity, plethora
F3 1 drought, trickle **2** trickle, dearth, lack

floor *n, v*
▶ *n* **1** FLOORING, ground, base, basis
2 *on the third floor*
storey, level, stage, landing, deck, tier
▶ *v* **1** BAFFLE, defeat, overwhelm, beat, frustrate, confound, perplex, nonplus, dumbfound, puzzle, bewilder, disconcert, throw
formal discomfit
colloq. stump
2 KNOCK DOWN, strike down, fell, level, prostrate

flop *v, n*
▶ *v* **1** COLLAPSE, slump, tumble, droop, hang, dangle, sag, drop, fall, topple
2 FAIL, be unsuccessful, collapse, misfire, fall flat, founder, sink
colloq. fold, pack up, crash, go bust, go broke, go to the wall, go into the red, *US* bomb
▶ *n* failure, fiasco, debacle, disaster
colloq. wash-out, non-starter, shambles, slip-up, no-hoper, also-ran, has-been

floppy *adj*
droopy, hanging, dangling, sagging, limp, loose, baggy, soft, flabby
🔁 firm

flora *n*
botany, plant life, plants, vegetable kingdom, vegetation, herbage, plantage

florid *adj*
1 FLOWERY, ornate, elaborate, fussy, overelaborate, extravagant, embellished, verbose, pompous, bombastic, baroque, rococo, flamboyant
technical melismatic
formal grandiloquent
2 *a florid complexion*
ruddy, red, red-faced, reddish, blushing, flushed, purple
formal rubicund
🔁 **1** plain, simple **2** pale

flotsam *n*
jetsam, wreckage, floating wreckage, debris, rubbish, junk, oddments, odds and ends
formal detritus

flounce¹ *v*
bounce, spring, stamp, storm, toss, jerk, twist, throw, fling, bob

flounce² *n*
frill, fringe, ruffle, trimming, valance, falbala
old use furbelow

flounder *v*
wallow, thresh about, flail about, struggle, grope, fumble, blunder, stagger, stumble, falter, dither, be confused, be in difficulties, go under, be out of your depth, not know which way to turn

flourish *v, n*
▶ *v* **1** THRIVE, grow, wax, increase, flower, blossom, bloom, bear fruit, be strong, develop, progress, get on, do well, prosper, succeed, boom
formal burgeon
2 BRANDISH, wave, shake, twirl, swing, swish, wag, display, wield, flaunt, show off, parade, exhibit, vaunt
🔁 **1** decline, languish, fail
▶ *n* **1** DISPLAY, parade, show, gesture, wave, sweep, fanfare, ornament, decoration, panache, élan
colloq. pizzazz
2 *a flourish on the lettering*
swirl, curlicue, serif, twist

flourishing *adj*
thriving, blooming, blossoming, prosperous, successful, booming

flout *v*
defy, disobey, break, disregard, spurn, treat with contempt, show contempt for, disdain, reject, scorn, jeer at, scoff at, sneer at, mock, laugh at, ridicule
formal violate
🔁 obey, respect, regard

flow *v, n*
▶ *v* **1** CIRCULATE, move, run, proceed, ooze, seep, trickle, ripple, bubble, well, spout, spew, spurt, squirt, gush, jet, leak, drip, spill, pour, cascade, rush, stream, teem, flood, overflow, surge, sweep, drift, slip, slide, babble, gurgle, glide, roll, swirl, whirl
2 ORIGINATE, derive, arise, spring, emerge, issue, result, stem, proceed
formal emanate
▶ *n* course, flux, tide, current, drift, outpouring, stream, deluge, cascade, spurt, gush, outpouring, flood, spate, abundance, plenty
formal effusion, plethora

flower *n, v*
▶ *n* **1** BLOOM, blossom, bud, floret, floweret
technical efflorescence, florescence, inflorescence
2 BEST, cream, pick, finest, choice, select, elite, crème de la crème
Related adjective: floral

Parts of a flower include: anther, calyx, capitulum, carpel, corolla, corymb, dichasium, filament, gynoecium, monochasium, nectary, ovary, ovule, panicle, pedicel, petal, pistil, raceme, receptacle, sepal, spadix, spike, stalk, stamen, stigma, style, thalamus, torus, umbel.

Flowers include: African violet, alyssum, anemone, aster, aubrietia, azalea, begonia, bluebell, busy lizzie (impatiens), calendula, candytuft, carnation, chrysanthemum, cornflower, cowslip, crocus, cyclamen, daffodil, dahlia, daisy, delphinium, forget-me-not, foxglove (digitalis), freesia, fuchsia, gardenia, geranium, gladioli, hollyhock, hyacinth, iris (flag), lily, lily-of-the-valley, lobelia, lupin, marigold, narcissus, nasturtium, nemesia, nicotiana, night-scented stock, orchid, pansy, petunia, pink (dianthus), phlox, poinsettia, polyanthus, poppy, primrose, primula, rose, salvia, snapdragon (antirrhinum), snowdrop, stock, sunflower, sweet pea, sweet william, tulip, verbena, viola, violet, wallflower, zinnia. *See also* **bulb; plant; shrub; wild flower**.

▶ *v* bud, bloom, blossom, open, sprout, come out, develop, grow, mature, prosper, thrive, flourish, succeed
formal burgeon

flowery *adj*
florid, ornate, elaborate, fancy, baroque, rhetorical, high-flown, verbose, pompous, bombastic
technical euphuistic
formal grandiloquent
🔁 plain, simple

flowing *adj*
1 *flowing rivers/traffic*
moving, oozing, seeping, bubbling, welling, gushing, pouring, rushing, cascading, streaming, surging, sweeping, overflowing
2 FLUENT, effortless, easy, smooth, continuous, uninterrupted, unbroken
3 *flowing hair*
hanging, hanging loose, hanging freely, falling, rolling

fluctuate *v*
vary, change, alter, shift, rise and fall, seesaw, go up and down, ebb and flow, alternate, swing, sway, undulate, vacillate, waver, hesitate
formal oscillate

colloq. chop and change
E3 be steady

fluctuation *n*
variation, change, shift, swing, alternation, variability,
instability, unsteadiness, wavering, irresolution,
inconstancy, ambivalence, fickleness
formal oscillation, capriciousness, vacillation

flue *n*
shaft, pipe, duct, vent, channel, passage, chimney

fluency *n*
ease, eloquence, smoothness, articulateness,
assurance, command, control, facility, readiness,
glibness, slickness
formal facundity, volubility
E3 incoherence

fluent *adj*
flowing, smooth, easy, effortless, fluid, natural,
graceful, elegant, articulate, eloquent, silver-tongued,
slick, glib, ready
formal voluble, mellifluous
E3 broken, inarticulate, tongue-tied

fluff *n, v*
► *n* down, nap, pile, fuzz, floss, lint, dust
► *v* botch, do badly, make a bad job of, mismanage,
bungle, mess up, make a mess of, muck up, muddle,
fumble, muff, spoil
colloq. blot your copybook, boob, put your foot in it,
foul up, mess up, blow; *slang* balls up, cock up, screw
up
E3 bring off

fluffy *adj*
furry, fuzzy, downy, feathery, fleecy, woolly, hairy,
shaggy, velvety, silky, soft

fluid *n, adj*
► *n* liquid, solution, liquor, juice, gas, vapour
► *adj* 1 LIQUID, liquefied, aqueous, watery, flowing,
running, runny, melted, molten
2 *a fluid situation*
variable, changeable, unstable, inconstant, shifting,
mobile, adjustable, adaptable, flexible, open,
unsettled, fluctuating, unsteady, unstable
formal protean
3 *fluid movements*
flowing, smooth, effortless, easy, graceful, elegant,
natural
E3 1 solid 2 inflexible, fixed

fluke *n*
stroke, stroke of luck, lucky break, accident, quirk,
blessing, windfall, break, chance, coincidence
formal fortuity, serendipity
colloq. freak

fluky *adj*
accidental, lucky, chance, fortunate, coincidental,
uncertain, incalculable
formal fortuitous, serendipitous
colloq. freakish

flummox *v*
confuse, confound, baffle, bewilder, mystify, perplex,
puzzle, nonplus, fox, stump, defeat, stymie
colloq. bamboozle

flummoxed *adj*
baffled, confounded, bewildered, confused,
perplexed, puzzled, mystified, nonplussed, stumped,
foxed, stymied, at a loss, at sea

flunkey *n*
lackey, assistant, menial, minion, slave, manservant,
valet, underling, drudge, footman, hanger-on, cringer,
toady, bootlicker, yes-man

flurry *n, v*
► *n* **1** BURST, outbreak, spell, shower, bout, spurt,
gust, blast, squall
2 BUSTLE, hurry, hubbub, fluster, fuss, commotion,
tumult, whirl, disturbance, agitation, excitement, stir
formal perturbation
colloq. to-do, flap
► *v* fluster, hurry, hustle, agitate, bewilder, bother,
bustle, flutter, fuss, unsettle, upset, confuse, ruffle,
disconcert, disturb
formal discountenance, perturb
colloq. hassle, rattle

flush[1] *v, n, adj*
► *v* **1** BLUSH, go/turn red, redden, crimson, colour,
burn, glow, flame
formal suffuse
2 CLEANSE, wash, rinse, hose, swab, clear, empty,
eject, evacuate, expel
► *n* bloom, freshness, vigour, glow, blush, colour,
redness, rosiness, ruddiness
old use rud
► *adj* **1** ABUNDANT, lavish, generous, full,
overflowing, rich, wealthy, moneyed, prosperous,
well-off, well-heeled, well-to-do
2 LEVEL, even, smooth, flat, plane, square, true

flush[2] *v*
flush the enemy out of the forest
force out, drive out, run to earth, discover, uncover,
expel, eject, start, rouse, disturb

flushed *adj*
1 RED, rosy, ruddy, blushing, burning, crimson,
scarlet, aflame, ablaze, glowing, aglow, hot,
embarrassed
formal rubicund
2 ELATED, thrilled, enthused, excited, exhilarated,
exultant, animated, aroused, inspired, intoxicated,
sanguine
E3 1 pale

fluster *v, n*
► *v* bother, upset, embarrass, disturb, agitate, ruffle,
discompose, confuse, confound, unsettle, unnerve,
make nervous, disconcert, put off, distract
formal perturb
colloq. rattle, faze
E3 calm
► *n* flurry, bustle, commotion, disturbance,
confusion, agitation, upset, turmoil, agitation, panic,
embarrassment
formal perturbation
colloq. state, flap, dither, tizzy, tizz
E3 calm

fluted *adj*
grooved, furrowed, channelled, corrugated, ribbed,
ridged

flutter *v, n*
► *v* flap, wave, beat, bat, flicker, vibrate, palpitate,
agitate, shake, tremble, quiver, shiver, ruffle, flitter,
ripple, twitch, pulsate, toss, waver, fluctuate, dance,
hover
► *n* **1** FLAPPING, wave, beat, flicker, vibration,
palpitation, tremble, tremor, quiver, shiver, shudder,
twitch, ripple, ruffle
2 BET, gamble, wager, speculation, risk

flux *n*
fluctuation, instability, unrest, change, alteration, modification, fluidity, flow, movement, motion, transition, development, mutation
🔁 stability, rest

fly¹ *v*
1 TAKE OFF, rise, ascend, mount, soar, glide, float, hover, flit, flutter, wing
2 *fly an aeroplane*
control, operate, pilot, guide, manoeuvre, steer
3 *fly a flag*
show, wave, display, exhibit, present, reveal
4 RACE, sprint, dash, tear, rush, go/pass quickly, slip by, hurry, speed, zoom, shoot, bolt, dart, career, jet
formal hasten
▷ **fly at** attack, go for, fall upon, hit, strike, lay into, charge, lash out at, let someone have it, let fly; *colloq.* bite someone's head off, jump down someone's throat

fly² *adj*
he's a fly fellow
alert, artful, sharp, shrewd, astute, canny, careful, cunning
formal prudent, sagacious
colloq. nobody's fool, on the ball, smart

fly-by-night *adj*
cowboy, discreditable, disreputable, questionable, shady, unreliable, untrustworthy, undependable, irresponsible, dubious, ephemeral, short-lived
colloq. here today gone tomorrow
🔁 reliable

flying *adj*
1 *flying insects*
gliding, floating, hovering, flapping, fluttering, airborne, winged, winging, wind-borne, soaring, mobile
2 *a flying visit*
BRIEF, hurried, fleeting, rapid, fast, hasty, rushed, speedy

foam *n, v*
▶ *n* froth, lather, suds, head, bubbles, fizz, spume, effervescence
▶ *v* froth, lather, bubble, effervesce, fizz, boil, seethe, spume

foamy *adj*
frothy, lathery, bubbly, foaming, spumy, sudsy
formal spumescent

fob *v*
▷ **fob off** foist, pass off, get rid of, dump, unload, inflict, impose, deceive, put off; *colloq.* palm off

focus *n, v*
▶ *n* focal point, target, centre, heart, core, nucleus, kernel, crux, hub, axis, linchpin, pivot, hinge
▷ **in focus** clear, share, distinct, well-defined
▷ **out of focus** blurred, ill-defined, indistinct, hazy, fuzzy, blurry, muzzy
▶ *v* concentrate, aim, direct, turn, fix, spotlight, pinpoint, home in, zoom in, converge, meet, join, centre, bring into focus
colloq. zero in

fodder *n*
feed, food, foodstuff, forage, nourishment, rations, silage, provender, lucerne, browsing, proviant, pabulum

foe *n*
enemy, adversary, antagonist, opponent, combatant, rival, ill-wisher
🔁 friend

foetus *n*
unborn child, embryo
Related adjective: foetal

fog *n, v*
▶ *n* **1** MIST, haze, mistiness, haziness, cloud, gloom, murkiness, smog, pea-souper
2 PERPLEXITY, puzzlement, confusion, bewilderment, bafflement, disorientation, daze, trance, stupor, vagueness, obscurity, blur, haze
▶ *v* mist, steam up, cloud, dull, dim, darken, obscure, blur, confuse, muddle, bewilder, baffle, perplex
formal obfuscate

foggy *adj*
misty, hazy, smoggy, cloudy, clouded, overcast, murky, dark, grey, shadowy, gloomy, dim, indistinct, vague, obscure, unclear
🔁 clear

foible *n*
quirk, weakness, weak point, idiosyncrasy, imperfection, eccentricity, oddity, failing, fault, defect, oddness, peculiarity, shortcoming, strangeness, habit

foil¹ *v*
foil someone's plans
defeat, outwit, frustrate, thwart, prevent, baffle, counter, nullify, stop, check, baulk, obstruct, block, elude, hinder, hamper
formal circumvent
colloq. scuttle, scupper
🔁 abet

foil² *n*
a foil to her dark hair
contrast, complement, balance, setting, background, relief
formal antithesis

foist *v*
force, impose, introduce, thrust, unload, pass off, get rid of, fob off, wish on
colloq. palm off

fold¹ *v, n*
▶ *v* **1** BEND, ply, double, overlap, tuck, pleat, crease, gather, turn under, turn down, crumple, crimp, crinkle
2 ENFOLD, embrace, hug, clasp, squeeze, envelop, wrap (up), enclose, entwine, intertwine
3 *the business folded*
fail, shut down, close, collapse, crash, go out of business
colloq. flop, pack up, go to the wall, go bust
▶ *n* bend, turn, layer, ply, overlap, tuck, pleat, gather, crease, knife-edge, line, wrinkle, crinkle, pucker, furrow, corrugation

fold² *n*
1 ENCLOSURE, pen, pound, compound, paddock, stockade, court, yard, ring, kraal
2 CONGREGATION, church, assembly, flock, gathering, parishioners, fellowship

folder *n*
file, binder, folio, portfolio, envelope, holder, wallet, pocket

foliage *n*
leaves, greenery, leafage, vegetation, foliation

technical frondescence, foliature, vernation
formal verdure

folk *n, adj*

▶ *n* **1** PEOPLE, society, nation, public, population, race, tribe, clan, ethnic group
2 RELATIONS, family, parents, relatives, kin, kindred
▶ *adj* ethnic, national, traditional, popular, native, indigenous, tribal, ancestral

folklore *n*

fables, folktales, legends, myths, mythology, lore, stories, tales, customs, beliefs, tradition, superstitions

follow *v*

1 *night follows day*
come after, succeed, come next, replace, supersede, supplant, take the place of, step into the shoes of
2 CHASE, pursue, go after, run after, hunt, track, trail, shadow, tail, stalk, dog, give chase, hound, catch, be at someone's heels
3 ACCOMPANY, go (along) with, escort, attend, trail, go behind, walk behind, tread behind, tag along
4 RESULT, ensue, develop, emanate, arise, issue, spring, flow, proceed
5 OBEY, adhere to, heed, mind, observe, note, accept, yield to, conform to, carry out, practise
formal comply with
6 GRASP, understand, comprehend, fathom, take in, appreciate
colloq. twig, latch onto
7 KEEP UP WITH, support, be interested in, be devoted to, be a fan of, be a supporter of, keep up to date with
E3 1 precede **3** abandon, desert **5** disobey
▷ **follow through** continue, pursue, see through, finish, complete, conclude, fulfil, implement, bring to completion
▷ **follow up** investigate, check out, look into, research, continue, pursue, reinforce, consolidate

follower *n*

backer, supporter, admirer, enthusiast, fan, devotee, disciple, apostle, pupil, imitator, emulator, adherent, hanger-on, believer, convert, attendant, retainer, helper, companion, escort
colloq. sidekick, freak, buff

following *adj, n*

▶ *adj* subsequent, next, succeeding, successive, resulting, ensuing, consequent, later
E3 previous
▶ *n* followers, suite, retinue, entourage, circle, fans, admirers, adherents, supporters, support, body of support, backing, backers, patrons, patronage, clientèle, audience, public, coterie

folly *n*

1 FOOLISHNESS, stupidity, senselessness, rashness, recklessness, irresponsibility, indiscretion, craziness, inanity, madness, lunacy, insanity, idiocy, imbecility, silliness, ludicrousness, ridiculousness, absurdity, nonsense, illogicality
formal imprudence, fatuousness
2 MONUMENT, tower, whim, belvedere, gazebo
E3 1 wisdom, prudence, sanity

foment *v*

incite, instigate, excite, stir up, agitate, arouse, rouse, encourage, kindle, promote, prompt, provoke, raise, activate, stimulate, spur, quicken, goad, whip up, work up, foster, brew
E3 quell

fond *adj*

1 *fond of someone/something*
liking, partial to, attached to, keen on, having a soft spot for, addicted to
formal enamoured of
colloq. hooked on
2 AFFECTIONATE, warm, tender, caring, loving, adoring, devoted, doting, indulgent, amorous
3 *fond expectations*
foolish, naïve, deluded, credulous, absurd, impractical, over-optimistic, vain

fondle *v*

caress, stroke, pat, pet, hug, cuddle
colloq. touch up

fondness *n*

affection, devotion, kindness, tenderness, love, liking, fancy, attachment, enthusiasm, inclination, leaning, partiality, preference, weakness, soft spot, taste, susceptibility
formal penchant, predilection
E3 aversion, hate

food *n*

1 FOODSTUFFS, comestibles, provisions, meals, stores, rations, refreshments, sustenance, nourishment, nutrition, nutriment, subsistence, feed, fodder, diet, fare, dish, speciality, delicacy, cooking, cuisine, menu, board, table
formal viands, victuals
colloq. eatables, eats, tuck; *slang* grub, nosh, chow, scoff
2 *food for thought*
mental stimulation, something to be seriously considered, something to think about

Kinds of food include: soup, broth, minestrone, bouillabaisse, borsch, cockaleekie, consommé, gazpacho, goulash, vichyssoise; chips, French fries, ratatouille, sauerkraut, bubble-and-squeak, nut cutlet, cauliflower cheese, chilladas, hummus, macaroni cheese; pasta, cannelloni, fettuccine, ravioli, spaghetti bolognese, tortellini, lasagne; fish and chips, fishcake, fish-finger, fisherman's pie, kedgeree, gefilte fish, kipper, pickled herring, scampi, calamari, prawn cocktail, caviar; meat, casserole, cassoulet, hotpot, shepherd's pie, cottage pie, chilli con carne, biriani, chop suey, moussaka, paella, samosa, pizza, ragout, risotto, tandoori, vindaloo, Wiener schnitzel, smorgasbord, stroganoff, Scotch woodcock, welsh rarebit, faggot, haggis, sausage, frankfurter, hot dog, fritter, hamburger, McDonald's®, Big Mac®, Wimpy®, bacon, egg, omelette, quiche, tofu, Quorn®, Yorkshire pudding, toad-in-the-hole; ice cream, charlotte russe, egg custard, fruit salad, fruit cocktail, gateau, millefeuilles, pavlova, profiterole, Sachertorte, soufflé, summer pudding, Bakewell tart, trifle, yogurt, sundae, syllabub, queen of puddings, Christmas pudding, tapioca, rice pudding, roly-poly pudding, spotted dick, zabaglione; doughnut, Chelsea bun, Eccles cake, éclair, flapjack, fruitcake, Danish pastry, Genoa cake, Battenburg cake, Madeira cake, lardy cake, hot-cross-bun, ginger nut, gingerbread, ginger snap, macaroon, digestive, digestive biscuit, oatcake, Garibaldi biscuit; bread, French bread, French toast, pumpernickel, cottage loaf, croissant; baguette, brioche, bagel, gravy, fondue, salad cream, mayonnaise, French dressing; sauces: tartare, Worcestershire, bechamel, white, barbecue, tomato ketchup, hollandaise, Tabasco®, apple, mint, cranberry, horseradish, pesto. *See also* **cheese; fish; fruit; meat; nut; pasta; pastry; sugar; sweet; vegetable**.

fool   *n, v*
▶ *n* blockhead, fat-head, dunce, dimwit, simpleton, halfwit, idiot, cretin, imbecile, ignoramus, moron, dupe, stooge, butt, laughing-stock, clown, comic, buffoon, jester
colloq. nincompoop, ass, chump, ninny, clot, dope, twit, nitwit, nit, sucker, mug, twerp, birdbrain; *slang* wally, jerk, dumbo, pillock, prat, dork, geek, plonker, prick, git
▷ **play the fool** fool around, fool about, mess about, mess around, clown around, monkey around; *colloq.* act the fool
▶ *v* **1** DECEIVE, take in, delude, mislead, beguile, make a fool of, dupe, gull, hoodwink, put one over on, trick, hoax, cheat, swindle, bluff, tease, joke, jest, play tricks, pretend, feign, sham
colloq. con, diddle, string along, have on, kid, bamboozle, make believe
2 *fooling about*
lark about, play about, monkey about, monkey around
colloq. horse around, mess about, mess around

foolery   *n*
silliness, folly, fooling, nonsense, tomfoolery, antics, buffoonery, drollery, waggery, zanyism, capers, carry-on, clowning, farce, childishness, horseplay, larks, high jinks, mischief, practical jokes, pranks, monkey tricks, shenanigans

foolhardy   *adj*
rash, reckless, ill-advised, irresponsible, incautious, impulsive, bold, daring, daredevil
formal imprudent, temerarious
E3 cautious; *formal* prudent

foolish   *adj*
stupid, senseless, silly, absurd, ridiculous, ludicrous, nonsensical, unwise, ill-advised, ill-considered, short-sighted, half-baked, crazy, mad, insane, idiotic, moronic, hare-brained, half-witted, simple-minded, simple, ignorant, unintelligent, inept, inane, pointless, unreasonable
formal fatuous, risible, injudicious
colloq. daft, crack-brained, gormless, dumb, dotty, potty, batty, barmy, nutty, not in your right mind, out of your mind, with a screw missing, needing to have your head examined
E3 wise; *formal* prudent, judicious

foolishly   *adv*
stupidly, senselessly, absurdly, ridiculously, unwisely, ill-advisedly, idiotically, incautiously, indiscreetly, mistakenly, ineptly, short-sightedly
formal fatuously, imprudently, injudiciously
E3 wisely

foolishness   *n*
stupidity, silliness, senselessness, absurdity, irresponsibility, weakness, craziness, madness, lunacy, nonsense, rubbish, folly, foolery, inanity, ineptitude, indiscretion
formal imprudence, incaution, unreason, unwisdom
colloq. bunkum, claptrap, baloney, daftness, hogwash, rot, piffle, poppycock, bunk, bunkum, claptrap, bilge, cobblers; *slang* crap, balls, bullshit
E3 wisdom; *formal* prudence

foolproof   *adj*
idiot-proof, infallible, unfailing, safe, fail-safe, sure, certain, dependable, trustworthy, guaranteed
colloq. sure-fire
E3 unreliable

foot   *n*
1 *an animal's feet*
paw, hoof, pad, trotter, leg, toe, sole, heel
technical pes
Related adjectives: pedal, pedate
2 *at the foot of the hill*
bottom, end, far end, limit, extremity, border, foundation
E3 2 head, top, summit

footing   *n*
1 BASIS, base, foundation, ground, relations, relationship, terms, conditions, state, standing, status, grade, rank, position
2 FOOTHOLD, balance, support, position, grip

footling   *adj*
paltry, trifling, minor, trivial, insignificant, petty, irrelevant
colloq. piffling

footnotes   *n*
annotation, note, marginal note, gloss, commentary, marginalia
formal scholia

footprint   *n*
footmark, track, trail, trace, step, tread
formal vestige

footstep   *n*
footmark, track, step, tread, footfall, plod, tramp, trudge

footwear   *n*

Types of footwear include: shoe, court-shoe, brogue, casual, *colloq.* lace-up, *colloq.* slip-on, slingback, sandal, espadrille, stiletto heel, platform heel, moccasin, Doc Martens®, slipper, mule, pantofle, *colloq.* flip-flop, boot, walking-boot, climbing-boot, riding-boot, overshoe, football boot, wader, bootee, wellington boot, *colloq.* welly, galosh, gumboot, football boot, rugby boot, tennis shoe, plimsoll, pump, sneaker, trainer, ballet shoe, clog, sabot, snow-shoe, *slang* beetle-crushers, *slang* brothel-creepers.

fop   *n*
dandy, coxcomb, beau, popinjay, dude, exquisite, peacock, swell, toff
old use muscadin

foppish   *adj*
dapper, dressy, spruce, overdressed, preening, vain, dandyish, dandified, affected, dainty, finical
colloq. la-di-da, natty
E3 unkempt

forage   *n, v*
▶ *n* fodder, pasturage, feed, food, foodstuffs, provender
▶ *v* rummage, search, seek, cast about, scour, scratch, hunt, scavenge, ransack, plunder, assault, ravage, loot, raid, invade

foray   *n*
raid, offensive, attack, assault, ravage, sortie, sally, swoop, invasion, inroad, incursion, reconnaissance

forbear *v*
refrain, avoid, decline, hesitate, hold, hold back, keep from, stop, withhold, stay, restrain yourself, omit, pause
formal abstain, desist, cease, eschew

forbearance *n*
self-control, patience, moderation, endurance, leniency, mildness, restraint, temperance, tolerance, toleration, avoidance, clemency, long-suffering, resignation, refraining, sufferance
formal abstinence
⊟ intolerance

forbearing *adj*
long-suffering, patient, moderate, lenient, self-controlled, restrained, tolerant, merciful, mild, easy, forgiving, indulgent, clement
⊟ intolerant, merciless

forbid *v*
prohibit, disallow, not allow, not let, ban, veto, refuse, deny, outlaw, debar, blacklist, exclude, rule out, prevent, block, hinder, inhibit
formal proscribe, interdict, preclude
⊟ allow, permit, let, approve

forbidden *adj*
prohibited, banned, excluded, taboo, vetoed, debarred, illicit, outlawed, out of bounds
formal proscribed

forbidding *adj*
stern, formidable, awesome, severe, harsh, grim, unfriendly, daunting, off-putting, uninviting, menacing, threatening, ominous, sinister, foreboding, frightening
⊟ approachable, friendly, congenial

force *v, n*
▶ *v* **1** COMPEL, make, oblige, urge, coerce, constrain, press, pressure, pressurize, put pressure on, pressgang, bulldoze, bully, railroad, drive, propel, impel, push, thrust, impose, inflict
formal necessitate
colloq. lean on, put the screws on, twist someone's arm, breathe down someone's neck
2 PRISE, force open, crack, blast, wrench, wrest, extort, exact, wring, extract
▶ *n* **1** COMPULSION, impulse, necessity, influence, coercion, constraint, pressure, duress, enforcement, violence, aggression
colloq. arm-twisting, strongarm tactics, the screws, the third degree
2 POWER, might, strength, intensity, effort, energy, vigour, exertion, stamina, muscle, momentum, impetus, drive, dynamo, dynamism, vitality, passion, vehement, determination, stress, emphasis, influence, power, significance, persuasiveness, effectiveness
3 MEANING, sense, substance, significance, gist, essence, thrust
4 ARMY, troop, body, corps, regiment, squad, platoon, squadron, battalion, division, unit, detachment, patrol
⊟ **2** weakness
▷ **in force 1** IN OPERATION, functioning, valid, binding, working, effective, current, on the statute book; *formal* operative **2** IN STRENGTH, in crowds, in large/great numbers, in flocks, in droves

forced *adj*
1 UNNATURAL, stiff, wooden, stilted, laboured, strained, false, artificial, contrived, feigned, insincere, overdone

formal affected
2 COMPULSORY, obligatory, involuntary, enforced, compelled
formal mandatory
⊟ **1** spontaneous, natural, sincere

forceful *adj*
strong, mighty, powerful, potent, effective, compelling, convincing, impressive, persuasive, telling, valid, weighty, urgent, emphatic, vehement, forcible, dynamic, assertive, energetic, vigorous
formal cogent
⊟ weak, feeble

forcible *adj*
1 VIOLENT, aggressive, coercive, forced, by/using force
2 POWERFUL, strong, compelling, compulsory, effective, impressive, telling, weighty, cogent, energetic, forceful, vehement, mighty, potent
⊟ **1, 2** feeble, weak

forcibly *adv*
violently, by force, using force, against your will, compulsorily, obligatorily, under compulsion, under duress, vigorously, vehemently, emphatically, willy-nilly

ford *n*
causeway, crossing, drift

forebear *n*
ancestor, forefather, father, predecessor, forerunner, antecedent
formal progenitor, primogenitor
⊟ descendant

foreboding *n*
misgiving, anxiety, worry, apprehension, apprehensiveness, suspicion, dread, fear, omen, sign, token, premonition, warning, prediction, intuition, feeling, sixth sense
formal presentiment, prognostication

forecast *v, n*
▶ *v* predict, prophesy, foretell, foresee, forewarn, anticipate, expect, tip off, estimate, calculate
formal conjecture, prognosticate, portend, divine, augur
▶ *n* prediction, prophecy, expectation, forewarning, outlook, projection, guess, tip, speculation
formal prognosis, conjecture, prognostication, augury
colloq. guesstimate

forefather *n*
ancestor, forebear, father, predecessor, forerunner, antecedent
formal progenitor, primogenitor
⊟ descendant

forefront *n*
front, front line, firing line, van, vanguard, spearhead, lead, fore, leading/foremost position, avant-garde
⊟ rear

forego *v*
give up, yield, surrender, sacrifice, forfeit, waive, abandon, resign, pass up, do without, go without, refrain from
formal relinquish, renounce, abstain from, eschew, abjure

foregoing *adj*
preceding, above, previous, earlier, former, prior

formal antecedent, precedent, aforementioned
▣ following

foregone *adj*
foreseen, fixed, inevitable, anticipated, predictable,
cut-and-dried, open-and-shut
formal predetermined, preordained
▣ unpredictable

foreground *n*
fore, forefront, front, prominence, leading/foremost
position, centre, limelight
▣ background

forehead *n*
brow, temples, front
technical metope
Related adjectives: metopic, frontal

foreign *adj*
alien, immigrant, imported, international, external,
outside, overseas, exotic, ethnic, migrant, faraway,
distant, remote, strange, unfamiliar, outlandish,
peculiar, odd, unknown, uncharacteristic,
unconnected, extraneous, borrowed
formal incongruous, inapposite
▣ native, indigenous

foreigner *n*
alien, immigrant, incomer, stranger, outsider,
newcomer, visitor
▣ native

foreknowledge *n*
foresight, premonition, forewarning, clairvoyance,
second sight
technical precognition, prescience
formal prevision, prognostication

foreman *n*
supervisor, superintendent, manager, leader, overseer,
steward, ganger, overman, charge hand
colloq. boss, gaffer, *US* honcho

foremost *adj*
first, leading, most important, front, chief, main,
principal, primary, first, top, cardinal, paramount,
central, highest, advanced, uppermost, supreme,
prime, premier, pre-eminent

foreordained *adj*
fated, destined, appointed, preordained, prearranged,
foredoomed
formal predestined, predetermined

forerunner *n*
precursor, predecessor, ancestor, antecedent,
forefather, harbinger, herald, envoy, sign, token
▣ successor, follower

foresee *v*
envisage, anticipate, expect, forecast, predict,
prophesy, foretell, foreknow, forebode
formal prognosticate, divine

foreshadow *v*
predict, prophesy, signal, indicate, signify, mean,
suggest, promise
formal bode, prefigure, presage, augur, portend

foresight *n*
anticipation, planning, forward planning,
forethought, far-sightedness, vision, caution,
discernment, discrimination, care, readiness,
preparedness, provision, precaution
formal prudence, circumspection, perspicacity,

judiciousness
▣ improvidence

forest *n*
wood, woodland, woods, trees, greenwood, monte,
plantation, urman

forestall *v*
pre-empt, anticipate, stop, avert, head off, ward off,
stave off, parry, balk, frustrate, thwart, obstruct,
hinder, prevent, impede, intercept, get ahead of
formal preclude, obviate

forestry *n*
forestation, woodcraft, woodmanship, forest
management
technical afforestation, arboriculture, dendrology,
silviculture

foretaste *n*
forewarning, foretoken, preview, trailer, sample,
appetizer, specimen, example, whiff, indication,
warning, premonition

foretell *v*
prophesy, forecast, predict, foresee, signify,
foreshadow, indicate, forewarn
formal prognosticate, augur, presage, divine

forethought *n*
preparation, planning, forward planning, provision,
precaution, anticipation, foresight, far-sightedness,
caution, discernment
formal circumspection, prudence, perspicacity,
judiciousness
▣ improvidence, carelessness

forever *adv*
1 ETERNALLY, always, ever, evermore, for all time,
permanently, till the end of time
colloq. till kingdom come, till the cows come home,
for good, until hell freezes over
2 CONTINUALLY, constantly, always, persistently,
incessantly, perpetually, endlessly
formal interminably
colloq. all the time

forewarn *v*
alert, advise, caution, tip off, give advance warning to
formal apprise, admonish, dissuade, previse

foreword *n*
preface, introduction, preliminary matter, prelims,
frontmatter, prologue
formal prolegomenon
▣ appendix, postscript, epilogue

forfeit *v, n*
▶ *v* lose, give up, hand over, surrender, sacrifice,
forego, abandon
formal relinquish, renounce
▶ *n* penalty, loss, surrender, confiscation, fine,
damages, relinquishment
technical sequestration, amercement

forfeiture *n*
giving up, surrender, confiscation, loss,
relinquishment, sacrifice, foregoing
technical escheat, attainder, sequestration
formal déchéance

forge¹ *v*
1 MAKE, mould, cast, shape, form, fashion, found,
beat out, hammer out, beat into shape, work, create,
construct, invent, frame, devise, put together

2 *forge a document*
fake, counterfeit, falsify, copy, imitate, simulate, feign

forge²
▷ **forge ahead** *building is forging ahead* progress, make progress, move steadily, advance, go/move forward, make headway, push forward

forger *n*
counterfeiter, contriver, faker, falsifier, framer, coiner, fabricator

forgery *n*
fake, counterfeit, copy, replica, reproduction, imitation, sham, fraud, faking, falsification, counterfeiting
colloq. dud, phoney
🗲 original

forget *v*
omit, fail, fail to remember, have no recollection of, neglect, let slip, overlook, disregard, ignore, lose sight of, dismiss, think no more of, unlearn, not place, slip your mind, put out of your mind, put behind you, put aside
colloq. go in one ear and out the other, have a memory like a sieve
🗲 remember, recall, recollect
▷ **forget yourself** misbehave, behave badly, be guilty of misconduct

forgetful *adj*
absent-minded, scatterbrained, preoccupied, distracted, abstracted, dreamy, inattentive, oblivious, negligent, neglectful, remiss, lax, careless, heedless, unheeding
formal pensive
colloq. with a memory like a sieve, not all there
🗲 attentive, mindful, heedful

forgetfulness *n*
absent-mindedness, inattention, obliviousness, oblivion, dreaminess, heedlessness, carelessness, wool-gathering, abstraction, amnesia, lapse, laxness
formal obliviscence
🗲 attentiveness, heedfulness

forgivable *adj*
excusable, pardonable, minor, petty, slight, trifling, innocent, venial
🗲 unforgivable

forgive *v*
pardon, absolve, excuse, acquit, remit, let off, let it go, clear, spare, overlook, condone, forgive and forget, let bygones be bygones
formal exonerate, exculpate
colloq. shake hands, shake on it, think no more of, bury the hatchet
🗲 punish, censure

forgiveness *n*
pardon, absolution, acquittal, remission, amnesty, mercy, clemency, leniency
formal exoneration
🗲 punishment, censure, blame

forgiving *adj*
merciful, clement, lenient, tolerant, forbearing, indulgent, kind, humane, compassionate, soft-hearted, mild
formal magnanimous
🗲 merciless, censorious, harsh

forgo *see* **forego**.

forgotten *adj*
unremembered, unrecalled, blotted out, disregarded, ignored, neglected, obliterated, overlooked, omitted, out of mind, past recollection, past recall, gone, left behind, buried, bygone, past, lost, irrecoverable, irretrievable, unretrieved
🗲 remembered

fork *v, n*
▶ *v* split, divide, part, separate, diverge, branch (off), go separate ways
formal bifurcate, divaricate
▷ **fork out** pay (up), give; *colloq.* cough up, shell out, stump up
▶ *n* branching, divergence, separation, split, division, junction, intersection
formal bifurcation, divarication, furcation

forked *adj*
branched, branching, divided, split, separated, Y-shaped, pronged
formal tined, bifurcate, divaricated, forficate, furcate, furcal, furcular

forlorn *adj*
deserted, abandoned, forsaken, forgotten, neglected, bereft, friendless, lonely, lost, homeless, uncared-for, destitute, desolate, desperate, despairing, hopeless, cheerless, unhappy, miserable, sad, wretched, helpless, pathetic, pitiable
formal disconsolate
🗲 cheerful

form *n, v*
▶ *n* **1** APPEARANCE, shape, mould, cast, cut, guise, outline, silhouette, figure, build, construction, frame, framework, structure, format, formation, model, pattern, design, arrangement, planning, order, organization, system
formal configuration, disposition, manifestation
2 *a form of punishment*
type, kind, sort, order, species, genus, variety, genre, style, manner, nature, character, description
3 CLASS, year, grade, stream
4 *on top form*
health, fitness, shape, trim, fettle, condition, spirits
5 ETIQUETTE, protocol, custom, convention, ritual, behaviour, polite behaviour, manners
colloq. the done thing
6 QUESTIONNAIRE, document, application (form), paper, sheet
▶ *v* **1** SHAPE, mould, model, fashion, forge, make, manufacture, produce, create, found, establish, build, construct, assemble, put together, set up, devise, arrange, organize, order, line up, develop, acquire
2 COMPRISE, constitute, make (up), compose, serve as, be a part of
3 APPEAR, take shape, materialize, crystallize, come into existence, show up, grow, develop, become visible

formal *adj*
1 OFFICIAL, ceremonial, ritual, stately, solemn, conventional, customary, traditional, established, orthodox, correct, prescribed, approved, proper, fixed, set, standard, regular, ordered, organized, methodical
2 PRIM, starchy, stiff, strait-laced, strict, rigid, inflexible, unbending, precise, exact, punctilious, ceremonious, stilted, remote, reserved, aloof
3 *a formal garden*
symmetrical, ordered, controlled, regular, conventional
🗲 **2** informal, casual

formality *n*
custom, convention, ceremony, ceremoniousness,
ritual, procedure, rule, custom, form, matter of form,
bureaucracy, red tape, protocol, etiquette, form,
correctness, politeness
formal decorum, propriety, punctilio
F3 informality

format *n*
appearance, form, order, presentation, design, layout,
pattern, plan, shape, structure, style, arrangement,
make-up, look, type, construction, dimensions
formal configuration

formation *n*
1 STRUCTURE, construction, composition,
constitution, format, order, organization,
arrangement, layout, make-up, grouping, pattern,
design, figure
formal configuration, disposition, phalanx
2 CREATION, generation, production, construction,
building, making, shaping, manufacture, appearance,
development, starting, founding, institution,
establishment, inauguration

formative *adj*
determining, controlling, influential, dominant,
shaping, growing, guiding, moulding, developmental,
impressionable, teachable, malleable, mouldable,
pliant, susceptible, sensitive
formal determinative
F3 destructive

former *adj*
past, ex-, one-time, sometime, late, departed, old,
old-time, ancient, bygone, historical, earlier, prior,
previous, preceding, long ago, long-gone, first,
first-mentioned, antecedent, foregoing, above
formal erstwhile, quondam, of yore
F3 current, present, future, following

formerly *adv*
once, in the past, previously, historically, earlier,
at an earlier time, before, at one time, once
formal heretofore, hitherto, erst, erstwhile
F3 currently, now, later

formidable *adj*
daunting, redoubtable, challenging, redoubtable,
intimidating, threatening, menacing, frightening,
terrifying, horrifying, alarming, terrific, frightful,
horrific, fearful, great, huge, colossal, mammoth,
tremendous, impressive, powerful, awesome, dreadful,
overwhelming, staggering
formal prodigious
colloq. scary, mind-blowing, spooky

formless *adj*
amorphous, shapeless, confused, chaotic,
disorganized, indefinite, indeterminate, incoherent,
nebulous, vague, unshaped, unformed
formal inchoate, indigest
F3 definite, orderly

formula *n*
recipe, prescription, proposal, blueprint, code, fixed/
set expression, wording, rubric, rule, principle, form,
precept, procedure, technique, convention, method,
way

formulate *v*
devise, create, compose, prepare, conceive, think up,
invent, originate, found, form, give form to, work out,
plan, design, map out, draw up, frame, define, express,
articulate, state, set down, put down, specify, detail,
itemize, develop, evolve

fornication *n*
sexual intercourse, sex, sexual relations, making love,
love-making, going to bed/sleeping with someone
formal coitus, copulation

forsake *v*
desert, abandon, throw over, discard, jettison, cast off,
reject, repudiate, set aside, disown, leave, give up,
surrender
formal relinquish, renounce, forego
colloq. jilt, quit, ditch, leave in the lurch, have done
with, turn your back on

forsaken *adj*
abandoned, deserted, neglected, God-forsaken,
remote, isolated, desolate, forlorn, lonely, marooned,
solitary, derelict, dreary, destitute, cast off, discarded,
disowned, rejected, shunned, outcast, ignored,
friendless
colloq. jilted, left in the lurch

forswear *v*
abandon, give up, repudiate, drop, disown, disclaim,
reject, deny, do without, renege, lie, perjure yourself
formal forsake, forego, renounce, recant, disavow,
abjure, retract
colloq. cut out, pack in, jack in
F3 revert to

fort *n*
fortress, castle, tower, watchtower, citadel, keep,
stronghold, fortification, turret, battlements, parapet,
garrison, station, camp, donjon, redoubt

forte *n*
strong point, strength, skill, speciality, gift, talent,
aptitude, bent, métier
F3 weak point, inadequacy

forth *adv*
out, away, off, outside, onwards, forwards, into
existence, into view

forthcoming *adj*
1 *their forthcoming wedding*
impending, imminent, approaching, coming, future,
prospective, projected, expected
2 AVAILABLE, accessible, obtainable, ready, at your
disposal
colloq. on tap, up for grabs, yours for the asking/taking
3 COMMUNICATIVE, talkative, chatty,
conversational, sociable, informative, expansive, open,
frank, direct
formal loquacious, voluble
F3 3 reticent, reserved

forthright *adj*
direct, straightforward, blunt, frank, candid, plain,
plain-spoken, open, honest, bold, outspoken
F3 devious, secretive

forthwith *adv*
immediately, at once, directly, instantly, straightaway,
right away, without delay, quickly
colloq. pronto

fortification *n*
defence, strengthening, reinforcement, protection,
castle, citadel, fort, fortress, keep, stronghold,
earthwork, rampart, bulwark, bastion, battlements,
parapet, barricade, palisade, buttressing,
embattlement, entrenchment, munition, outwork,
redoubt, stockade

fortify *v*
1 STRENGTHEN, reinforce, brace, shore up, buttress, garrison, defend, guard, protect, secure, cover, embattle
2 INVIGORATE, sustain, support, boost, revive, energize, brace, encourage, hearten, cheer, reassure, strengthen, buoy up
E3 1 weaken

fortitude *n*
courage, bravery, valour, pluck, nerve, resolution, determination, tenacity, perseverance, patience, firmness, strength of mind, backbone, mettle, willpower, hardihood, endurance, stoicism
formal forbearance
colloq. grit, spine
E3 cowardice, fear

fortress *n*
stronghold, castle, citadel, fortification, fastness, tower, keep, garrison, battlements

fortuitous *adj*
accidental, chance, random, arbitrary, casual, haphazard, incidental, unforeseen, unexpected, unplanned, unintentional, lucky, fortunate, providential
colloq. fluky
E3 intentional, planned, anticipated

fortunate *adj*
lucky, providential, happy, prosperous, flourishing, successful, well-off, timely, well-timed, opportune, convenient, advantageous, favourable, encouraging, promising, profitable, blessed, favoured
formal felicitous, propitious, auspicious, providential
E3 unlucky, unfortunate, unhappy

fortunately *adv*
luckily, happily, conveniently, encouragingly
formal providentially
E3 unfortunately

fortune *n*
1 WEALTH, riches, treasure, income, means, substance, assets, estate, property, possessions, affluence, prosperity, success
formal opulence
colloq. mint, pile, packet, bundle, bomb; *slang* megabucks, big bucks
2 LUCK, chance, coincidence, accident, providence, fate, destiny, doom, lot, portion, cup, life, history, future
formal serendipity
3 *the fortunes of the company*
experience, circumstances, position, condition, situation, state of affairs

fortune-teller *n*
prophet, prophetess, visionary, soothsayer, seer, augur, diviner, oracle, sibyl, psychic, telepath

forum *n*
meeting, meeting-place, arena, rostrum, stage, assembly, conference, discussion, debate, symposium

forward *adj, adv, v*
▶ *adj* 1 FIRST, head, front, fore, foremost, leading, advance, onward, advancing, progressing, progressive, prospective, future, forward-looking, enterprising
formal frontal
colloq. go-ahead
2 CONFIDENT, over-confident, assertive, over-assertive, bold, audacious, brazen, brash, barefaced, impudent, impertinent, familiar, overfamiliar,

presumptuous, presuming, aggressive, thrusting
colloq. cheeky, fresh, cocky, pushy
3 EARLY, advance, precocious, premature, advanced, well-advanced, well-developed
E3 1 backward, retrograde 2 shy, modest 3 late, retarded
▶ *adv* forwards, ahead, on, onward, onwards, out, forth, into view, into the open
▶ *v* advance, promote, further, foster, encourage, support, back, favour, help, assist, aid, facilitate, accelerate, speed (up), step up, hurry, hasten, dispatch, send (on), pass on, post, mail, transport, deliver, ship
formal expedite
E3 impede, obstruct, hinder, slow

forward-looking *adj*
far-sighted, enterprising, progressive, reforming, modern, innovative, dynamic, enlightened, avant-garde, liberal
colloq. go-getting, goey, go-ahead
E3 conservative, retrograde

forwardness *n*
confidence, over-confidence, boldness, audacity, brashness, brazenness, pertness, presumption, presumptuousness, impertinence, impudence, aggressiveness
colloq. cheek, cheekiness, pushiness
E3 reserve, retiring

forwards *adv*
forward, ahead, on, onwards, out, forth

fossil *n*
remains, remnant, petrified remains/impression, ammonite, relic, reliquiae
technical graptolite, coprolite, trilobite

fossilized *adj*
1 HARDENED, petrified, ossified, stony
2 OUT OF DATE, archaic, obsolete, old-fashioned, *passé*, outmoded, prehistoric, antediluvian, anachronistic, antiquated, extinct, dead
E3 2 up-to-date

foster *v*
raise, rear, bring up, nurse, care for, take care of, look after, nourish, feed, sustain, help, assist, aid, back, support, uphold, promote, advance, encourage, stimulate, further, boost, cultivate, nurture, hold, cherish, entertain, harbour
E3 neglect, discourage

foul *adj, v*
▶ *adj* 1 DISGUSTING, offensive, repulsive, revolting, dirty, soiled, filthy, unclean, tainted, infected, impure, defiled, polluted, contaminated, rank, fetid, stinking, smelly, foul-smelling, putrid, decayed, rotting, rotten, sickening, nauseating, abominable, loathsome, odious, squalid
formal fetid, putrescent, putrefactive
2 *foul language*
obscene, lewd, smutty, dirty, filthy, indecent, coarse, off-colour, ribald, lewd, indelicate, vulgar, gross, low, blasphemous, profane, offensive, abusive
colloq. blue
3 NASTY, disagreeable, wicked, vicious, vile, base, mean, low, loathsome, despicable, offensive, revolting, repulsive, disgusting, abhorrent, detestable, horrible, disgraceful, shameful, contemptible
formal iniquitous, heinous, execrable, nefarious
4 *foul weather*
bad, nasty, unpleasant, disagreeable, rainy, wet, stormy, squally, blustery, rough, dirty, wild

⊟ 1 clean 2 clean 4 fine
▷ **foul play** criminal violence, crime, unfair/
dishonest behaviour, breach of the rules, deception,
dirty work, double-dealing; *colloq.* funny business,
sharp practice
⊟ fair play, justice
▶ *v* 1 DIRTY, soil, stain, sully, muddy, blacken, defile,
taint, pollute, contaminate
2 ENTANGLE, catch, snarl, twist, ensnare, tangle
3 BLOCK, obstruct, clog, choke, jam, foul up
⊟ 1 clean 2 disentangle 3 clear

foul-mouthed *adj*
coarse, obscene, offensive, profane, abusive,
blasphemous
formal foul-spoken

found *v*
1 START, originate, create, bring into being, organize,
initiate, institute, inaugurate, set up, constitute,
develop, establish, endow
2 BASE, ground, bottom, root, rest, set, ground, settle,
fix, plant, locate, position, raise, build, erect, construct

foundation *n*
1 BASE, foot, bottom, ground, bedrock, substance,
basis, footing, underpinning, understructure,
substructure, substratum
2 BASIS, support, base, groundwork, bedrock, key,
keynote, reason(s), rationale, fundamental(s),
fundamental point, starting-point, premise, principle,
first principles, main ingredient, alpha and omega,
essential(s), essence, heart, core, thrust
formal quintessence, hypostasis
3 SETTING-UP, establishment, founding, institution,
inauguration, initiation, creation, constitution,
endowment, organization, groundwork

founder[1] *n*
the founder of the university
originator, initiator, father, mother, benefactor,
creator, author, architect, designer, inventor, prime
mover, maker, builder, constructor, organizer,
institutor, establisher, developer, discoverer

founder[2] *v*
the ship/plan foundered
sink, go down, go to the bottom, submerge, capsize,
subside, collapse, break down, fall, come to grief, fail,
misfire, miscarry, abort, fall through, come to nothing,
go wrong
⊟ succeed

foundling *n*
stray, orphan, waif, outcast, urchin, enfant trouvé

fountain *n*
1 SPRAY, jet, spout, spring, spurt, fount, well,
wellspring, source, reservoir, waterworks
2 SOURCE, origin, fount, rise, well, cause, birth,
beginning, mainspring, fountainhead, wellhead
formal commencement, inception

four-square *adv*
firmly, squarely, resolutely, solidly, frankly, honestly

fowl *n*
bird, duck, chicken, cock, hen, bantam, goose, turkey,
pheasant, wildfowl, poultry
Related adjective: gallinaceous

foxy *adj*
crafty, canny, devious, cunning, artful, astute, sharp,
shrewd, sly, tricky, wily, fly, knowing, guileful
⊟ naïve, open

foyer *n*
entrance hall, hall, reception, lobby, vestibule,
antechamber, anteroom

fracas *n*
brawl, disturbance, fight, free-for-all, quarrel, riot,
trouble, uproar, row, rumpus, scuffle, barney, affray,
ruckus, ruction, rout, ruffle, shindy, melee
formal Donnybrook
colloq. aggro

fraction *n*
proportion, amount, ratio, subdivision, part, bit

fractious *adj*
awkward, quarrelsome, cross, irritable, touchy, bad-
tempered, petulant, testy, unruly, captious, fretful,
peevish
formal choleric, querulous, recalcitrant, refractory
colloq. crabby, crotchety, grouchy, grumpy
⊟ complaisant, placid

fracture *n, v*
▶ *n* break, breakage, crack, fissure, cleft, rupture,
split, splitting, rift, rent, schism, breach, gap, opening,
aperture, slit
▶ *v* break, crack, rupture, split, splinter, chip
⊟ join

fragile *adj*
1 BRITTLE, breakable, frail, delicate, flimsy, dainty,
fine, slight, insubstantial, unstable
formal frangible
2 *feel fragile after an illness*
weak, feeble, infirm
⊟ 1 robust, tough, durable, sturdy 2 strong

fragility *n*
brittleness, breakableness, delicacy, frailty, weakness,
feebleness, infirmity
formal frangibility
⊟ durability, robustness, strength

fragment *n, v*
▶ *n* piece, bit, part, portion, fraction, particle, crumb,
morsel, scrap, remainder, remains, remnant, shred,
snip, snippet, chip, splinter, shiver, sliver, chink, shard
▶ *v* break, shatter, splinter, shiver, crumble,
disintegrate, come to pieces, come apart, break up,
divide, split (up), disunite, smash to pieces/smithereens
⊟ hold together, join

fragmentary *adj*
bitty, piecemeal, scrappy, broken, disjointed,
disconnected, separate, scattered, sketchy, partial,
incomplete, uneven, discontinuous, incoherent
⊟ whole, complete

fragrance *n*
perfume, scent, smell, sweet smell, odour, aroma,
bouquet, balm, attar, otto
formal redolence

fragrant *adj*
perfumed, scented, sweet-smelling, sweet, balmy,
aromatic, odorous
formal redolent, odoriferous
⊟ unscented

frail *adj*
delicate, brittle, breakable, easily broken, fragile,
flimsy, insubstantial, slight, puny, weak, feeble, infirm,
unwell, unsound, vulnerable, susceptible
formal frangible
⊟ robust, tough, strong

frailty *n*
weakness, weak point, foible, failing, deficiency,
shortcoming, fault, defect, flaw, blemish,
imperfection, infirmity, fallibility, susceptibility,
vulnerability, brittleness, fragility, delicacy
E3 strength, robustness, toughness

frame *n, v*
▶ *n* **1** STRUCTURE, fabric, framework, skeleton,
carcase, shell, casing, chassis, substructure,
foundation, construction, support, bodywork, body,
build, form, physique, figure, size, shape
2 MOUNT, mounting, setting, surround, border, edge
▷ **frame of mind** state (of mind), mood, condition,
humour, temper, disposition, spirit, outlook, attitude
▶ *v* **1** COMPOSE, formulate, conceive, establish,
create, devise, contrive, concoct, plan, map out, plot,
sketch, draw up, draft, shape, form, model, fashion,
mould, forge, assemble, put together, build, set up,
erect, construct, fabricate, make, manufacture
colloq. cook up
2 SURROUND, enclose, box in, case, encase, mount
3 *I've been framed*
trap, incriminate, plant
colloq. set up, fit up, pin on, cook up a charge

frame-up *n*
fabrication, trap
colloq. fit-up, fix, put-up job, trumped-up charge

framework *n*
structure, fabric, bare bones, skeleton, shell, frame,
casing, outline, plan, foundation, groundwork,
substructure, trestle, trestlework, lattice, rack, scheme,
constraints, parameters

franchise *n*
concession, licence, charter, warrant, authorization,
permission, privilege, right, prerogative, liberty,
freedom, immunity, exemption
formal consent, suffrage, enfranchisement

frank *adj, v*
▶ *adj* honest, truthful, sincere, genuine, candid,
blunt, open, free, plain, plain-spoken, direct,
forthright, straight, straightforward, downright,
outspoken, explicit, bluff
colloq. straight from the shoulder, up-front
E3 insincere, evasive
▶ *v* stamp, mark, postmark, cancel

frankly *adv*
to be frank, to be honest, to be blunt, in truth, honestly,
candidly, bluntly, truthfully, openly, freely, plainly,
directly, straight, explicitly
E3 insincerely, evasively

frankness *n*
bluntness, candour, forthrightness, plain speaking,
openness, directness, sincerity, outspokenness,
truthfulness
formal ingenuousness
E3 reserve

frantic *adj*
agitated, overwrought, fraught, desperate, beside
yourself, furious, raging, mad, wild, raving, frenzied,
berserk, frenetic, distressed, distracted, distraught,
out of control, panic-stricken, hectic
colloq. at your wits' end
E3 calm, composed

fraternity *n*
comradeship, brotherhood, kinship, camaraderie,
companionship, set, society, association, circle, club,
company, guild, order, league, union, fellowship, clan

fraternize *v*
mix, mingle, socialize, associate, keep company,
go around, affiliate, unite, sympathize
formal consort
colloq. hang about, hobnob, pal up with, gang up with,
rub shoulders
E3 shun, ignore

fraud *n*
1 DECEIT, deception, guile, fraudulence, cheating,
swindling, double-dealing, sharp practice,
embezzlement, fake, counterfeit, forgery, sham, hoax,
trick, trickery, racket
formal duplicity, chicanery
colloq. con, rip-off, riddle, scam, fix, diddle, swiz
2 CHARLATAN, impostor, pretender, sham, fake,
bluffer, hoaxer, cheat, swindler, embezzler, double-
dealer, trickster, quack, mountebank
colloq. phoney, con man

fraudulent *adj*
dishonest, criminal, deceitful, deceptive, false, bogus,
sham, counterfeit, swindling, cheating, double-
dealing, unscrupulous, exploitative, shameless
formal duplicitous
colloq. crooked, shady, phoney
E3 honest, genuine

fraught *adj*
1 FULL, filled, charged, abounding, accompanied,
attended, bristling
formal laden, replete
2 ANXIOUS, tense, agitated, worried, under stress,
distressed, distraught, overwrought
colloq. uptight, stressed out
E3 calm, untroublesome

fray *v, n*
▶ *v* **1** *the rope is fraying*
become ragged, become threadbare, wear, unravel,
wear thin
2 *tempers were fraying*
irritate, vex, strain, stress, tax, overtax, make tense,
make nervous, push too far, put on edge
▶ *n* brawl, scuffle, free-for-all, set-to, clash, conflict,
fight, combat, battle, quarrel, row, rumpus,
disturbance, riot, excitement, challenge
colloq. dust-up

frayed *adj*
ragged, tattered, worn, threadbare, unravelled, thin,
worn thin

freak *n, adj*
▶ *n* **1** MONSTER, mutant, mutation, freak of nature,
monstrosity, deformity, irregularity
formal malformation
2 ANOMALY, abnormality, aberration, oddity,
curiosity, quirk, whim, vagary, twist, turn
formal caprice
colloq. oddball, weirdo
3 ENTHUSIAST, fanatic, addict, devotee, fan,
aficionado
colloq. buff, fiend, nut
▶ *adj* abnormal, atypical, unusual, exceptional, odd,
queer, bizarre, erratic, unpredictable, unexpected,
surprise, chance
formal aberrant, capricious, fortuitous
colloq. fluky
E3 normal, common

freakish adj
unusual, odd, abnormal, strange, unconventional, unpredictable, weird, outlandish, freaky, whimsical, fanciful, fantastic, grotesque, monstrous, malformed, arbitrary, fitful, changeable, erratic
formal aberrant, capricious
F3 ordinary, normal

free adj, v, adv
▶ *adj* **1** *free tickets*
gratis, without charge, free of charge, for nothing, at no cost, at no extra cost, complimentary
colloq. on the house; *slang* buckshee
2 *free to move*
AT LIBERTY, at large, loose, on the loose, unattached, unrestrained, unconfined, out
colloq. free as a bird
3 *a free country*
LIBERATED, emancipated, sovereign, independent, democratic, self-governing, self-ruling, autonomous
4 *free of dirt*
lacking, without, unaffected by, immune to, exempt from, safe from, clear of
formal devoid of
5 *free time; a free seat*
spare, available, idle, unemployed, unoccupied, with time on your hands, untaken, vacant, empty
6 CLEAR, unobstructed, unimpeded, open, unblocked, unhampered
7 GENEROUS, liberal, open-handed, lavish, charitable, giving, hospitable, unstinting
formal munificent
8 *with his free hand*
unattached, unfastened, loose, unsecured
9 *a free translation*
loose, rough, general, broad, vague, inexact, imprecise
10 *his free manner; free movement*
easy, relaxed, easy-going, smooth, natural, uninhibited, casual, spontaneous, fluid
colloq. doing your own thing, doing as you please
F3 **2** imprisoned, bound, tied, fettered, confined, restricted **4** liable to, affected by **5** busy, occupied, at work, reserved, engaged; *colloq.* tied up
6 blocked, obstructed **7** mean, stingy
8 attached **9** literal, rigorous, exact, precise
10 inhibited, formal, tense
▷ **free and easy** casual, informal, easy-going, relaxed, happy-go-lucky, carefree, spontaneous, tolerant; *colloq.* laid-back
F3 inhibited, formal
▷ **free hand** authority, freedom, latitude, liberty, carte blanche, permission, power, scope, discretion
▶ *v free a prisoner; free someone trapped; free someone from debt*
release, let go, let out, loose, turn loose, set loose, set free, untie, unbind, unchain, unleash, liberate, emancipate, rescue, deliver, save, ransom, disentangle, disengage, extricate, clear, make available, rid, relieve, unburden, exempt, excuse, except, absolve, acquit
F3 imprison, confine
▶ *adv* **1** FOR NOTHING, for free, without charge, gratis, freely, for love
2 GENEROUSLY, liberally, lavishly, extravagantly, abundantly, copiously
F3 **2** meanly

free will n
freedom, liberty, independence, self-determination, self-sufficiency, spontaneity
technical autarky
formal volition, autonomy

freedom n
1 LIBERTY, emancipation, deliverance, release, exemption, immunity, impunity
2 INDEPENDENCE, autonomy, self-government, sovereignty, democracy, emancipation, home rule
3 RANGE, scope, play, leeway, margin, latitude, licence, privilege, right, power, prerogative, free rein, free hand, opportunity, informality, flexibility
F3 **1** captivity, confinement **3** restriction

freely adv
1 READILY, willingly, voluntarily, of your own volition, of your own free will, spontaneously, easily
2 *give freely*
generously, liberally, lavishly, extravagantly, amply, abundantly
3 *speak freely*
frankly, candidly, bluntly, unreservedly, openly, plainly
F3 **2** grudgingly **3** evasively, cautiously

freethinker n
rationalist, sceptic, agnostic, doubter, deist, unbeliever, infidel

freeze v, n
▶ *v* **1** ICE OVER, ice up, congeal, solidify, set, harden, stiffen
technical glaciate
2 DEEP-FREEZE, ice, refrigerate, chill, cool
3 GET COLD, shiver, quiver, catch a chill, turn blue with cold, your teeth be chattering
4 STOP, suspend, fix, immobilize, halt, stand still, stop dead in your tracks, hold
5 FIX, hold, suspend, peg
▶ *n* **1** FROST, freeze-up
2 STOPPAGE, halt, standstill, shutdown, suspension, interruption, postponement, stay, embargo, moratorium

freezing adj
icy, frosty, glacial, arctic, polar, Siberian, wintry, raw, bitter, bitterly cold, biting, cutting, piercing, penetrating, numbing, stinging, numb, cold, chilly
F3 hot, warm

freight n
cargo, load, lading, payload, contents, goods, merchandise, consignment, shipment, transportation, conveyance, carriage, haulage, freightage, portage

frenetic adj
frantic, wild, frenzied, hectic, overwrought, demented, distraught, excited, unbalanced, mad, insane, berserk, hysterical, maniacal, obsessive, hyperactive
F3 calm, placid

frenzied adj
frantic, frenetic, hectic, feverish, desperate, furious, overwrought, distraught, distracted, crazed, wild, uncontrolled, mad, berserk, amok, raving, demented, hysterical, panic-stricken, out of control, uncontrolled, beside yourself, obsessive, at your wits' end
F3 calm, composed

frenzy n
1 TURMOIL, agitation, wildness, distraction, madness, lunacy, insanity, mania, hysteria, delirium, fever
old use derangement
2 BURST, fit, bout, spasm, paroxysm, convulsion, seizure, outburst, transport, passion, rage, fury
F3 **1** calm, composure

frequency n
frequentness, incidence, prevalence, recurrence, repetition, commonness, oftenness, constancy
formal periodicity
🔁 infrequency

frequent *adj, v*
▶ *adj* common, commonplace, happening often, normal, everyday, familiar, usual, customary, habitual, prevailing, prevalent, predominant, numerous, countless, incessant, constant, continual, persistent, repeated, recurring, regular
🔁 infrequent
▶ *v* visit, go to frequently, go to regularly, patronize, attend, haunt, associate with
colloq. hang out at, hang about with, hang out with

frequenter n
regular, regular visitor, customer, client, patron, haunter, habitué

frequently *adv*
often, commonly, many times, much, many a time, over and over, repeatedly, persistently, continually, habitually, customarily, oftentimes
colloq. nine times out of ten, more times than you've had hot dinners
🔁 infrequently, seldom

fresh *adj*
1 ADDITIONAL, supplementary, extra, more, further, other
2 NEW, novel, innovative, original, different, brand-new, unconventional, revolutionary, modern, up-to-date, recent, latest, exciting, unusual
colloq. new-fangled
3 REFRESHING, bracing, invigorating, brisk, crisp, keen, cool, chilly, fair, bright, clean, clear, pure, unfaded, unpolluted
4 *fresh fruit*
RAW, natural, unprocessed, crude, unpreserved, uncured, undried
5 REFRESHED, revived, restored, renewed, rested, invigorated, stimulated, energetic, vigorous, lively, vibrant, alert, vital, bouncing
colloq. raring to go, ready for more, yourself again, a new person, fresh as a daisy
6 *a fresh complexion*
HEALTHY, glowing, bright, clear, blooming, fair, pink, rosy
7 PERT, disrespectful, impudent, insolent, bold, brazen, forward, familiar, overfamiliar, presumptuous
colloq. saucy, cheeky, cocky
🔁 2 old, hackneyed 3 stale 4 preserved, tinned, processed 5 tired

freshen *v*
1 AIR, ventilate, purify, clean, clear, deodorize
2 REFRESH, restore, revitalize, revive, reinvigorate, liven (up), enliven, stimulate, rouse
colloq. tart up
🔁 2 tire
▷ **freshen up** tidy yourself up, wash yourself, get washed, spruce yourself up, get spruced up

freshman n
first-year, fresher, underclassman

freshness n
brightness, cleanness, clearness, newness, originality, novelty, bloom, shine, glow, sparkle, vigour, wholesomeness
🔁 staleness, tiredness

fret *v*
1 WORRY, be anxious, be upset, agonize, anguish, be distressed, brood, pine, mope, brood, make a fuss
2 VEX, irritate, nettle, bother, trouble, anger, annoy, exasperate, infuriate, rile, torment

fretful *adj*
worried, anxious, unhappy, upset, distressed, disturbed, uneasy, fearful, tense, restless, troubled
colloq. edgy, uptight
🔁 calm

friable *adj*
brittle, crumbly, crisp, powdery
formal pulverizable
🔁 solid

friar n
monk, religioner, mendicant, religious, prior, abbot, brother

friction n
1 DISAGREEMENT, dispute, disharmony, clashing, conflict, strife, quarrelling, arguing, antagonism, hostility, opposition, rivalry, animosity, bad/ill feeling, bad blood, resentment
formal dissension, discord, disputation
2 RUBBING, chafing, irritation, scraping, grating, rasping, erosion, gnawing, wearing away, resistance, traction
formal abrasion, abrading, attrition, excoriation

friend n
1 COMPANION, good friend, close friend, best friend, intimate, confidant(e), bosom friend, soul mate, comrade, ally, partner, associate, familiar, playmate, pen-friend, acquaintance, well-wisher
colloq. mate, pal, chum, buddy, crony
2 SUPPORTER, backer, patron, well-wisher, sponsor, benefactor, subscriber
🔁 1 enemy 2 opponent

friendless *adj*
alone, companionless, unpopular, unloved, unbefriended, solitary, shunned, ostracized, lonely, isolated, forlorn, abandoned, lonesome, lonely-heart, deserted, forsaken, unattached, unbeloved, by yourself, with no one to turn to
colloq. cold shouldered

friendliness n
affability, amiability, companionability, congeniality, conviviality, approachability, kindness, kindliness, warmth, neighbourliness, sociability, geniality, *Gemütlichkeit*
colloq. matiness
🔁 coldness, unsociableness

friendly *adj*
1 AMIABLE, affable, genial, convivial, cordial, kind, kindly, warm, neighbourly, helpful, sympathetic, fond, affectionate, familiar, intimate, inseparable, close, companionable, sociable, outgoing, approachable, receptive, hospitable, comradely, amicable, peaceable, well-disposed, favourable, agreeable, good-natured, sympathetic
colloq. maty, pally, chummy, thick, tight
2 *a friendly atmosphere*
convivial, congenial, cordial, welcoming, warm, close, amicable, familiar
🔁 1 hostile, unsociable, unfriendly 2 cold

friendship n
companionship, closeness, intimacy, familiarity, amiability, affinity, rapport, attachment, affection,

fondness, warmth, love, harmony, concord, understanding, goodwill, friendliness, kindliness, friendly relationship, alliance, fellowship, comradeship
formal amity
Ⅎ enmity, animosity

fright *n*
shock, scare, alarm, dismay, dread, apprehension, fear, fearfulness, terror, horror, panic, disquiet
formal trepidation, consternation, perturbation
colloq. blind panic, cold sweat, hair standing on end, blood running cold, knocking knees, shivers, jitters, creeps, willies, heebie-jeebies, funk, blue funk, bombshell, bolt from the blue

frighten *v*
alarm, daunt, unnerve, unman, dismay, intimidate, terrorize, scare, startle, scare stiff, give someone a fright, terrify, petrify, horrify, appal, shock, panic
colloq. rattle, scare out of your wits, make your blood run cold, scare the living daylights out of, make your hair stand on end, make someone jump out of their skin, put the frighteners on, put the wind up;
slang scare the shit out of
Ⅎ reassure, calm

frightened *adj*
afraid, dismayed, scared, terrified, unnerved, terrorized, terror-stricken, alarmed, cowed, frozen, petrified, scared stiff, startled, trembly, quivery, panicky, panic-stricken
colloq. scared out of your wits, scared to death, having kittens, in a blue funk, shaking like a leaf, with your heart in your mouth
Ⅎ calm, courageous

frightening *adj*
alarming, daunting, formidable, grim, fearsome, forbidding, terrifying, hair-raising, creepy, bloodcurdling, spine-chilling, petrifying, traumatic
colloq. scary, hairy, spooky

frightful *adj*
unpleasant, disagreeable, awful, nasty, dreadful, fearful, terrible, alarming, appalling, shocking, harrowing, unspeakable, dire, grim, ghastly, hideous, horrible, horrid, grisly, macabre, gruesome, revolting, repulsive, abhorrent, odious, loathsome, unbearable
Ⅎ pleasant, agreeable

frigid *adj*
1 FROZEN, bitter, freezing, icy, frosty, glacial, arctic, cold, chill, chilly, wintry, polar, Siberian
2 UNFEELING, unresponsive, passionless, unloving, cool, chilly, icy, distant, formal, aloof, passive, lifeless
Ⅎ 1 hot 2 responsible, enthusiastic, approachable

frigidity *n*
unresponsiveness, unapproachability, frostiness, iciness, impassivity, lifelessness, passivity, stiffness, cold-heartedness, coldness, aloofness, chill, chilliness
Ⅎ responsiveness, warmth

frill *n*
1 *a blouse with frills*
flounce, gathering, ruff, ruffle, trimming, tuck, valance, fold, fringe, furbelow, ruche, ruching, purfle, orphrey
2 *the basic model without the frills*
TRIMMINGS, addition, extra, ornamentation, decoration, embellishment, fanciness, accessory, ostentation, superfluity, finery, frilliness, fandangle, frippery

frilly *adj*
ruffled, crimped, gathered, frilled, trimmed, lacy, fancy, ornate
Ⅎ plain

fringe *n, adj, v*
▶ *n* 1 MARGIN, periphery, outskirts, edge, perimeter, limit, rim, border, verge, borderline
2 BORDER, edging, trimming, tassel, frill, valance
▶ *adj* unconventional, unorthodox, unofficial, alternative, avant-garde, experimental
Ⅎ conventional, mainstream
▶ *v* border, edge, trim, skirt, surround, enclose

fringed *adj*
bordered, edged, fringy, trimmed, tasselled, tasselly
technical fimbriated

frippery *n*
finery, adornments, decorations, ornaments, ostentation, pretentiousness, showiness, gaudiness, fanciness, flashiness, frilliness, fussiness, tawdriness, triviality, baubles, fandangles, trinkets, knickknacks, gewgaws, trifles, trivia, frills, froth, nonsense, glad rags, foppery
formal meretriciousness
Ⅎ plainness, simplicity

frisk *v*
1 JUMP, leap, skip, hop, bounce, prance, caper, dance, gambol, frolic, romp, cavort, play, sport, trip
2 BODY-SEARCH, search, inspect, check, *US* shake down

frisky *adj*
lively, active, spirited, high-spirited, in high spirits, exuberant, dashing, frolicsome, playful, romping, rollicking, bouncy
colloq. high, alive and kicking, full of beans, hyper
Ⅎ quiet, subdued

fritter *v*
waste, squander, go through, get through, idle, misuse, misspend, overspend,
formal dissipate
colloq. spend like water; *slang* blow

frivolity *n*
fun, gaiety, flippancy, facetiousness, jest, light-heartedness, levity, triviality, superficiality, inanity, silliness, folly, foolishness, pettiness, nonsense, senselessness
Ⅎ seriousness

frivolous *adj*
trifling, trivial, unimportant, petty, shallow, superficial, inane, light, merry, zany, flippant, jocular, light-hearted, juvenile, puerile, flighty, facetious, foolish, silly, idle, vain, pointless, senseless, futile
Ⅎ serious, sensible

frizzy *adj*
curled, curly, crimped, crisp, frizzed, wiry, corrugated
Ⅎ straight

frolic *v, n*
▶ *v* gambol, caper, romp, play, lark around, rollick, make merry, frisk, prance, cavort, dance, leap, skip, hop, bounce, sport
▶ *n* fun, fun and games, amusement, sport, game, gaiety, jollity, merriment, mirth, revel, romp, prank, lark, caper, spree, high jinks, antics, escapade
colloq. razzle, razzle-dazzle

frolicsome *adj*
playful, frisky, lively, merry, gay, sprightly, sportive,

rollicking, coltish, skittish
E3 quiet, serious, solemn

front *n, adj, v*
▶ *n* **1** *the front of the building*
face, aspect, frontage, façade, outside, exterior, facing, cover, obverse, top, head, lead, vanguard, forefront, front line, firing line, foreground, forepart, bow
2 PRETENCE, show, air, appearance, look, expression, manner, exterior, façade, cover, mask, disguise, pretext, cover-up, blind
formal countenance
E3 1 back, rear
▶ *adj* leading, foremost, head, first, fore
E3 back, rear, last
▷ **in front** leading, ahead, first, in advance, to the fore, before, preceding
E3 behind
▶ *v* face, confront, look over, look out on, meet, oppose, overlook

frontier *n*
border, boundary, borderline, limit, edge, perimeter, confines, marches, bounds, verge

frost *n*
freeze, freeze-up, Jack Frost, hoar-frost, rime, coldness

frosty *adj*
1 ICY, frozen, freezing, frigid, wintry, cold, bitterly cold, chilly, rimy, glacial, frigid, arctic, Siberian, polar
colloq. nippy, parky
2 UNFRIENDLY, unwelcoming, cool, cold, icy, aloof, standoffish, stiff, discouraging, hostile
E3 1 warm, hot **2** warm, friendly responsive, welcoming, enthusiastic

froth *n, v*
▶ *n* bubbles, effervescence, fizz, foam, lather, suds, head, scum, spume
▶ *v* foam, lather, ferment, fizz, effervesce, bubble, spume
Related adjectives: spumous, spumy

frothy *adj*
1 BUBBLING, bubbly, foaming, foamy, yeasty, sudsy
formal spumescent, spumous, spumy
colloq. fizzy
2 INSUBSTANTIAL, empty, trivial, frivolous, trifling, slight, vain
E3 1 flat **2** substantial, significant

frown *v, n*
▶ *v* scowl, glower, lour, glare, grimace, pout
colloq. give someone a dirty look, look daggers at
▷ **frown on** disapprove of, object to, dislike, discourage, take a dim view of, not take kindly to, think badly of, have a low opinion of, raise your eyebrows
E3 approve of, go along with
▶ *n* scowl, glower, glare, grimace, raised eyebrow
colloq. dirty look

frowsy *adj*
untidy, dishevelled, unwashed, unkempt, ungroomed, dirty, messy, frumpish, frumpy, slatternly, sloppy, slovenly, sluttish
E3 well-groomed

frozen *adj*
iced, chilled, icy, frosty, icebound, ice-covered, arctic, ice-cold, bitterly cold, raw, polar, Siberian, frigid, freezing, numb, hard, frosted, solidified, stiff, frozen-stiff, rigid, fixed
E3 warm

frugal *adj*
thrifty, penny-wise, niggardly, penny-pinching, miserly, stingy, careful, provident, saving, economical, sparing, meagre, paltry, scanty, inadequate
formal parsimonious, prudent
colloq. scrimping and saving
E3 wasteful, generous

fruit *n*
1 CROP, harvest, produce, fruitage

Varieties of fruit include: apple, Bramley, Cox's Orange Pippin, Golden Delicious, Granny Smith, crab apple; pear, William, Conference; orange, Jaffa, mandarin, mineola, clementine, satsuma, tangerine, Seville; apricot, peach, plum, nectarine, cherry, sloe, damson, greengage, grape, gooseberry, *colloq.* goosegog, rhubarb, tomato; banana, pineapple, olive, lemon, lime, ugli fruit, star fruit, lychee, passion fruit, date, fig, grapefruit, kiwi fruit, mango, avocado; melon, honeydew, cantaloupe, watermelon; strawberry, raspberry, blackberry, bilberry, loganberry, elderberry, blueberry, boysenberry, cranberry; redcurrant, blackcurrant.

2 BENEFIT, consequence, advantage, effect, outcome, reward, return, result, yield, product, profit

fruitful *adj*
1 FERTILE, rich, teeming, plentiful, abundant, prolific, productive, fruit-bearing
formal fecund, feracious
2 REWARDING, profitable, advantageous, beneficial, effective, worthwhile, well-spent, useful, successful, productive
formal effectual, efficacious
E3 1 barren **2** fruitless

fruitfulness *n*
productiveness, profitability, fertility, usefulness
formal fecundity, feracity
E3 fruitlessness

fruition *n*
realization, fulfilment, attainment, achievement, completion, maturity, ripeness, perfection, success, enjoyment
formal consummation

fruitless *adj*
unsuccessful, abortive, useless, futile, pointless, vain, idle, hopeless, worthless, unproductive, barren, sterile
formal ineffectual
E3 fruitful, successful, profitable, productive

fruity *adj*
1 *a fruity voice*
rich, mellow, resonant, full
2 INDECENT, bawdy, indelicate, juicy, suggestive, saucy, risqué, titillating, vulgar, salacious, spicy, sexy, smutty, racy
colloq. blue
E3 2 decent

frumpy *adj*
dowdy, dreary, drab, badly-dressed, dingy, ill-dressed, dated, out of date
E3 chic, well-groomed

frustrate *v*
1 DISAPPOINT, discourage, dishearten, dissatisfy, embitter, depress, anger, annoy, irritate
formal circumvent
colloq. stymie
2 THWART, foil, balk, baffle, block, check, stop,

defeat, hinder, obstruct, hamper, impede, forestall, counter, nullify, neutralize, inhibit
colloq. spike, nobble
E3 1 encourage 2 further, promote

frustrated *adj*
disappointed, discontented, discouraged, dissatisfied, disheartened, embittered, resentful, angry, annoyed, thwarted, blighted, repressed
E3 fulfilled, satisfied

frustration *n*
1 DISAPPOINTMENT, discouragement, dissatisfaction, resentment, annoyance, anger, vexation, irritation
2 THWARTING, foiling, balking, blocking, defeat, curbing, failure, non-fulfilment, obstruction, contravention
formal circumvention
E3 1 fulfilment 2 furthering, promoting

fuddled *adj*
hazy, confused, muddled, stupefied, muzzy, bemused, drunk, groggy, woozy, inebriated, intoxicated, sozzled, tipsy
E3 clear, sober

fuddy-duddy *n, adj*
▶ *n* conservative, museum piece, fossil
colloq. old fogey, stick-in-the-mud, square, back number, stuffed shirt
▶ *adj* old-fashioned, old-fogeyish, stick-in-the-mud, stuffy, carping, censorious, prim
E3 up-to-date

fudge *v*
avoid, dodge, equivocate, evade, hedge, stall, shuffle, misrepresent, fake, falsify
colloq. cook, fiddle, fix

fuel *n, v*
▶ *n* 1 COMBUSTIBLE, propellant, motive power
2 PROVOCATION, incitement, encouragement, ammunition, goading, incentive, stimulus, material

Fuels include: gas, calor gas®, propane, butane, methane, acetylene, electricity, coal, coke, anthracite, charcoal, oil, petrol, gasoline, diesel, derv, paraffin, kerosine, methylated spirit, wood, logs, peat, fossil fuel, nuclear power.

▶ *v* incite, inflame, fire, encourage, fan, feed, nourish, sustain, stoke up
E3 discourage, damp down

fug *n*
stuffiness, staleness, reek, stink, frowstiness, fustiness
formal fetidness
E3 airiness

fuggy *adj*
stuffy, airless, close, stale, suffocating, unventilated, foul, fetid, frowsty, fusty
formal noisome, noxious
E3 airy

fugitive *n, adj*
▶ *n* escapee, runaway, deserter, refugee
▶ *adj* 1 RUNAWAY, refugee, deserter
2 FLEETING, transient, transitory, passing, short, short-lived, momentary, brief, flying, temporary, ephemeral, elusive
formal evanescent, fugacious
E3 2 permanent

fulfil *v*
complete, finish, perfect, realize, achieve, accomplish, perform, execute, discharge, implement, carry out, comply with, observe, keep, obey, conform to, satisfy, fill, meet, answer
formal conclude, consummate, effect
E3 fail, break

fulfilled *adj*
satisfied, gratified, pleased, happy, content
E3 dissatisfied, discontented, unhappy

fulfilment *n*
completion, perfection, realization, achievement, accomplishment, success, performance, execution, discharge, implementation, observance, satisfaction
formal consummation
E3 failure

full *adj, adv, n*
▶ *adj* 1 FILLED, loaded, laden, packed, crowded, crammed, stuffed, overflowing, bulging, well-stocked, flush, jammed, filled to capacity, full to the brim
colloq. chock-a-block, packed out, bursting at the seams, packed like sardines
2 ENTIRE, whole, intact, total, complete, unabridged, unexpurgated
3 THOROUGH, comprehensive, exhaustive, all-inclusive, broad, vast, extensive, detailed, ample, filled, generous, abundant, plentiful, copious, profuse, sufficient
4 *feel full*
satisfied, gorged, sated, stuffed
formal satiated, replete
colloq. bursting
5 *a full sound*
rich, resonant, loud, deep, clear, strong, distinct, fruity
6 *at full speed*
maximum, top, highest, greatest, utmost
7 *lead a full life*
busy, active, lively, eventful, tiring, hectic, frantic
8 *a full figure*
plump, chubby, stout, fat, overweight, large, round, shapely, buxom, obese
formal corpulent, rotund
9 *a full skirt*
wide, baggy, loose-fitting
formal voluminous
E3 1 empty 2 partial, incomplete 3 superficial
4 hungry 6 minimum 7 unoccupied, empty
▶ *adv* directly, squarely, straight, right, exactly
colloq. bang, smack
▶ *n* ▷ **in full** fully, completely, wholly, in detail, with all the details, in its entirety, in total, uncut, with nothing missed out
▷ **to the full** to the greatest possible extent, to the utmost, fully, completely, entirely, thoroughly, utterly

full-blooded *adj*
committed, dedicated, devoted, enthusiastic, wholehearted, thorough, vigorous, hearty
E3 half-hearted

full-grown *adj*
adult, grown-up, fully-grown, of age, mature, ripe, developed, fully-developed, fully-fledged, full-blown, full-scale
E3 young, undeveloped

fullness *n*
1 THOROUGHNESS, comprehensiveness, vastness, extensiveness, abundance, plenty, profusion, ampleness, completeness, totality, richness, resonance,

strength, loudness, wholeness, variety
2 SATISFACTION, glut, fill, satedness
formal satiation, satiety, repletion
3 BREADTH, wideth, largeness, shapeliness, plumpness, curvaceousness
4 SWELLING, enlargement, inflammation, growth
technical tumescence
formal dilation
E3 1 incompleteness **2** emptiness
▷ **in the fullness of time** eventually, in due course, finally, ultimately, in the end; *colloq.* when all is said and done, in the final analysis

full-scale *adj*
exhaustive, extensive, complete, sweeping, thorough, thoroughgoing, wide-ranging, comprehensive, all-out, in-depth, all-encompassing, intensive, major
E3 partial

fully *adv*
completely, totally, utterly, wholly, entirely, in all respects, thoroughly, altogether, quite, positively, without reserve, unreservedly, perfectly, satisfactorily, sufficiently
E3 partly

fully-fledged *adj*
professional, qualified, trained, senior, graduate, mature, proficient, experienced, fully-developed, full-blown
E3 inexperienced

fulminate *v*
criticize, condemn, curse, denounce, protest, rage, rail, fume, thunder
formal animadvert, inveigh, vituperate, declaim, decry
E3 praise

fulmination *n*
condemnation, criticism, denunciation, thundering, tirade, detonation
formal diatribe, invective, obloquy, philippic, decrial
E3 praise

fulsome *adj*
extravagant, excessive, immoderate, overdone, gross, inordinate, insincere, adulatory, effusive, fawning, ingratiating, sycophantic, unctuous, sickening, nauseating, cloying, nauseous, offensive, saccharine
colloq. smarmy, slimy, buttery, over the top
E3 sincere

fumble *v*
grope, feel, scrabble, blunder, bungle, botch, mishandle, mismanage, flounder, spoil

fume *v*
1 SMOKE, smoulder, boil, steam
2 RAGE, be furious, storm, rant, rave, seethe, boil, be livid
colloq. rant and rave, blow your cool, burst a blood vessel, hit the roof

fumes *n*
exhaust, smoke, gas, vapour, haze, fog, smog, pollution, stink, smell, stench, reek
formal exhalation

fumigate *v*
deodorize, disinfect, sterilize, purify, cleanse, sanitize

fuming *adj*
angry, enraged, furious, livid, incensed, raging, seething, boiling

colloq. steamed up
E3 calm

fun *n, adj*
▶ *n* enjoyment, pleasure, amusement, entertainment, relaxation, diversion, distraction, recreation, play, sport, game, foolery, tomfoolery, buffoonery, horseplay, skylarking, romp, merrymaking, celebration, laughter, laughs, mirth, cheerfulness, gladness, jollity, jocularity, hilarity, joy, joking, jesting
▷ **for fun** for a laugh, for enjoyment, for no particular reason; *colloq.* for kicks, for the hell of it
▷ **in fun** as a joke, jokingly, for a laugh, to tease, in jest, mischievously, teasingly, tongue in cheek
▷ **make fun of** ridicule, mock, jeer at, scoff at, sneer at, tease, taunt, humiliate, poke fun at; *formal* deride; *colloq.* rib, send up, pull someone's leg, take the mickey; *slang* take the piss
▶ *adj* entertaining, amusing, diverting, recreational, delightful, pleasurable, enjoyable, lively, witty

function *n, v*
▶ *n* **1** ROLE, part, office, duty, charge, responsibility, concern, capacity, job, post, chore, task, occupation, situation, employment, business, activity, purpose, mission, use
2 RECEPTION, party, gathering, affair, dinner, luncheon
colloq. do
▶ *v* work, be in working order, operate, run, go, serve, act, perform, behave, play the part of, have the job of
E3 break down; *formal* malfunction; *slang* conk out

functional *adj*
working, operational, operative, running, working, practical, useful, utilitarian, utility, plain, hard-wearing, serviceable
E3 useless, decorative

functionary *n*
bureaucrat, employee, officer, official, office-bearer, office-holder, dignitary

fund *n, v*
▶ *n* **1** *contribute to the restoration fund*
pool, kitty, reserve, treasury, grant, endowment, foundation, investment
2 *raise funds for the repairs*
money, finance, backing, capital, resources, savings, wealth, cash, means, assets
3 *a fund of funny stories*
reserve, repository, storehouse, store, stock, collection, accumulation, hoard, cache, stack, mine, well, source, supply, reservoir
▶ *v* finance, provide finance for, capitalize, endow, subsidize, pay for, underwrite, sponsor, back, support, promote, float

fundamental *adj*
basic, primary, first, elementary, underlying, integral, central, principal, cardinal, prime, main, chief, key, essential, indispensable, vital, necessary, crucial, important, initial, original, profound
formal rudimentary, basal, elemental

fundamentally *adv*
basically, essentially, in essence, at bottom, at heart, deep down, inherently, intrinsically, primarily

fundamentals *n*
basics, essentials, first principles, laws, rules, rudiments, facts, necessaries, practicalities
colloq. brass tacks, nitty-gritty, nuts and bolts

funeral n

burial, cremation, wake
formal interment, entombment, inhumation, exequies, obsequies

funereal adj

solemn, serious, grave, mournful, sad, sombre, depressing, dismal, dreary, gloomy, lamenting, woeful, sepulchral, dark, deathlike
formal exequial, funeral, funebrial, lugubrious
F3 happy, lively

fungus n

Related adjective: fungous

Types of fungus include: black spot, blight, botritis, brown rot, candida, downy mildew, ergot, grey mould, mushroom, orange-peel fungus, penicillium, potato blight, powdery mildew, rust, saprophyte, scab, smut, sooty mould, toadstool, yeast, brewer's yeast. *See also* **mushrooms and toadstools**.

funk v

balk at, flinch from, recoil from, blench, duck out of, shirk from
colloq. chicken out of, cop out, dodge

funnel v

channel, direct, convey, move, transfer, pass, go, pour, siphon, filter

funny adj

1 HUMOROUS, amusing, entertaining, diverting, comic, comical, hilarious, witty, facetious, droll, farcical, laughable, ridiculous, absurd, silly, hysterical, side-splitting, riotous, uproarious, riotous, rich
formal risible
colloq. killing, corny, rum, a scream, a hoot
2 ODD, strange, peculiar, curious, queer, weird, bizarre, unusual, remarkable, puzzling, perplexing, mysterious, suspicious, dubious
colloq. shady, oddball, way-out, off-beat, wacky
F3 1 serious, solemn, sad 2 normal, ordinary, usual

fur n

coat, hair, hide, down, fleece, pelt, fell, skin, wool, pelage

furious adj

1 ANGRY, livid, indignant, irate, enraged, infuriated, incensed, inflamed, raging, fuming, boiling, seething, frenzied, purple with rage
colloq. mad, hopping mad, sizzling, up in arms, in a stew, in a paddy, in a lather, in a huff, gone off the deep end, hot under the collar, foaming at the mouth
2 VIOLENT, wild, fierce, intense, vigorous, frantic, boisterous, stormy, tempestuous, vehement
F3 1 calm, pleased 2 restrained

furnish v

equip, fit out, decorate, rig, appoint, stock, provide, supply, afford, grant, give, offer, present, endue, appoint
formal bestow
F3 divest

furniture n

equipment, appliances, furnishings, fittings, appointments, fitments, household goods, movables, possessions, effects, things

Types of furniture include: table, dining-table, gateleg table, refectory table, lowboy, side-table, coffee-table, card table; chair, easy chair, armchair, rocking-chair, recliner, dining-chair, carver, kitchen chair, stool, swivel-chair, high-chair, suite, settee, sofa, couch, studio couch, chesterfield, pouffe, footstool, bean-bag; bed, four-poster, chaise-longue, daybed, bed-settee, divan, camp-bed, bunk, water-bed, cot, cradle; desk, bureau, secretaire, bookcase, cupboard, cabinet, china cabinet, Welsh dresser, sideboard, buffet, dumb-waiter, fireplace, overmantel, fender, firescreen, hallstand, umbrella-stand, mirror, magazine rack; wardrobe, armoire, dressing-table, vanity unit, washstand, chest-of-drawers, tallboy, chiffonier, commode, ottoman, chest, coffer, blanket box.

Styles of furniture include: Adam, Anglo-Colonial, Anglo-Indian, Art Deco, Art Nouveau, Baroque, Biedermeier, boulle, buhl, Charles II, Chippendale, Colonial, Continental Empire, Cromwellian, Dutch Colonial, Dutch Neoclassical, Edwardian, Empire, French Provincial, French Second Empire, Gainsborough, Georgian, Gothic, Hepplewhite, Louis Philippe, Louis-Quatorze, Louis-Quinze, provincial, Queen Anne, Regency, Restoration, rococo, Sheraton, Shibayama, Transitional, Vernis Martin, Victorian, William and Mary, William IV, Windsor.

furore n

uproar, disturbance, outcry, commotion, fuss, frenzy, fury, hullabaloo, outburst, rage, stir, to-do, tumult, storm, excitement
colloq. flap
F3 calm

furrow n, v

▶ n 1 GROOVE, channel, trench, hollow, trough, rut, track
technical sulcus
2 WRINKLE, line, crease, crinkle, crow's foot
▶ v crease, wrinkle, draw together, knit, seam, flute, channel, corrugate, gouge, plough, groove
Related adjective: sulcal

further adj, v, adv

▶ adj 1 MORE, additional, supplementary, extra, fresh, new, other
2 FARTHER, more distant, remoter, more extreme
F3 2 nearer
▶ v advance, forward, promote, champion, encourage, foster, help, aid, assist, ease, facilitate, speed (up), hasten, accelerate
formal expedite
colloq. push
F3 stop, frustrate
▶ adv moreover, furthermore, besides, in addition, additionally, also, as well, too
colloq. what's more

furtherance n

advancement, promotion, advancing, backing, boosting, encouragement, help, facilitation, carrying-out, championship, promoting, advocacy, pursuit
formal preferment

furthermore adv

moreover, in addition, further, besides, also, too, as well, additionally
colloq. what's more

furthest *adj*
farthest, furthermost, remotest, outermost, outmost, extreme, ultimate, utmost, uttermost
E3 nearest

furtive *adj*
surreptitious, sly, stealthy, secretive, underhand, hidden, cloaked, veiled, covert, secret, sneaky
formal clandestine
E3 open

fury *n*
anger, rage, wrath, ire, frenzy, madness, passion, vehemence, fierceness, ferocity, violence, wildness, intensity, severity, force, turbulence, power
E3 calm, peacefulness

fuse *v*
combine, integrate, unite, join, amalgamate, blend, coalesce, meld, melt, solder, weld, smelt, merge, synthesize, intermix
formal agglutinate, commingle, intermingle

fusillade *n*
barrage, volley, discharge, burst, fire, hail, outburst, salvo, broadside

fusion *n*
melting, smelting, welding, union, synthesis, blending, coalescence, amalgamation, integration, merger, federation

fuss *n, v*
▶ *n* bother, trouble, palaver, furore, squabble, row, commotion, stir, fluster, confusion, upset, worry, agitation, excitement, bustle, flurry, hurry
colloq. hassle, to-do, hoo-ha, flap, carry-on, kerfuffle, ballyhoo, tizzy, a song and dance, storm in a teacup
E3 calm
▶ *v* complain, grumble, fret, worry, panic, take pains, bother, bustle, fidget
colloq. flap, stir, make a song and dance, be in a tizzy

fussiness *n*
choosiness, finicality, finicalness, pernicketiness, perfectionism, meticulousness, niceness, niggling, particularity, busyness
E3 unfastidiousness

fusspot *n*
worrier, perfectionist, hyper-critic, stickler, fidget
colloq. nit-picker, old woman

fussy *adj*
1 PARTICULAR, fastidious, scrupulous, finicky, finical, difficult, hard to please, discriminating, faddy, demanding, quibbling, pettifogging, pedantic, selective
colloq. pernickety, choosy, picky, nit-picking
2 FANCY, elaborate, ornate, overdecorated, cluttered, busy, baroque, rococo
E3 1 casual, uncritical 2 plain, simple

fusty *adj*
1 OLD-FASHIONED, antiquated, archaic, outdated, out-of-date, *passé*
colloq. old-fogeyish
2 STALE, damp, dank, airless, stuffy, unventilated, fuggy, ill-smelling, musty, mouldy, mouldering, frowsty, rank
formal malodorous
E3 1 up-to-date 2 airy

futile *adj*
pointless, useless, worthless, vain, in vain, idle, wasted, fruitless, profitless, unavailing, to no avail, unsuccessful, abortive, unprofitable, unproductive, ineffective, barren, empty, hollow, forlorn
formal ineffectual
E3 fruitful, profitable

futility *n*
pointlessness, uselessness, fruitlessness, worthlessness, ineffectiveness, waste, unproductiveness, vanity, emptiness, hollowness, barrenness, aimlessness
E3 use, purpose, success

future *n, adj*
▶ *n* hereafter, tomorrow, time to come, coming times, outlook, prospects, expectations
E3 past
▶ *adj* prospective, next, designate, to be, to come, forthcoming, in the offing, imminent, impending, coming, approaching, expected, planned, unborn, later, subsequent, eventual, fated, destined
E3 past

fuzz *n*
down, floss, fluff, fug, hair, lint, nap, pile, fibre, flock

fuzzy *adj*
1 FRIZZY, fluffy, furry, woolly, fleecy, downy, linty, velvety, napped
2 BLURRED, unfocused, ill-defined, indefinite, unclear, indistinct, vague, faint, hazy, foggy, shadowy, woolly, muffled, distorted, fuddled, confused
colloq. muzzy
E3 2 clear, distinct, focused

G

gab *v, n*
▶ *v* chatter, talk, drivel, gossip, jaw, prattle, tattle, babble, blabber, jabber, blather, blether, buzz
colloq. yak
▶ *n* chat, chatter, chitchat, conversation, prattle, prattling, gossip, blab, blarney, blethering, small talk, tittle-tattle, tongue-wagging
formal loquacity
colloq. yackety-yak, yak

gabble *v, n*
▶ *v* babble, chatter, jabber, prattle, spout, splutter, cackle, sputter, gaggle, gibber, rattle, blab, blabber, blether
▶ *n* babble, chatter, blabber, cackling, prattle, twaddle, blethering, waffle, nonsense, drivel, gibberish

gad *v*
▷ **gad about** gallivant, run around, travel, roam, wander, range, rove, flit about, ramble, stray, traipse, dot about

gadabout *n*
gallivanter, rambler, rover, runabout, wanderer, pleasure-seeker
Scot. stravaiger

gadget *n*
tool, implement, appliance, device, instrument, apparatus, mechanism, contrivance, invention, contraption, thing, novelty, gimmick
colloq. thingummy, gismo, widget, whatsit, whatnot

gaffe *n*
blunder, mistake, slip, indiscretion, *faux pas*, gaucherie
formal solecism
colloq. bloomer, boob, boo-boo, brick, clanger, goof, howler

gaffer *n*
foreman, manager, overseer, superintendent, supervisor, overman, ganger
colloq. boss

gag¹ *v*
1 SILENCE, muffle, muzzle, quiet, stifle, smother, block, plug, clog, put a gag on, throttle, suppress, restrain, curb, check, still
2 RETCH, choke, heave, nearly vomit

gag² *n*
a comedian telling gags
joke, jest, quip, wisecrack, one-liner, pun, witticism
colloq. crack, funny

gaiety *n*
happiness, glee, cheerfulness, joy, pleasure, delight, *joie de vivre*, jollity, merriment, mirth, gladness, blitheness, hilarity, fun, merrymaking, revelry, festivity, celebration, frolics, joviality, good humour, high spirits, light-heartedness, liveliness, exuberance, buoyancy, brightness, brilliance, sparkle, glitter, colour, colourfulness, show, showiness
formal vivacity
E₃ sadness, drabness

gaily *adv*
happily, joyfully, merrily, cheerfully, blithely, light-heartedly, brightly, brilliantly, colourfully, flamboyantly
E₃ sadly, dully

gain *v, n*
▶ *v* **1** EARN, make, produce, realize, gross, net, clear, profit, yield, bring in, reap, harvest, gather, win, achieve, capture, secure, get, obtain, acquire
formal procure
2 REACH, arrive at, come to, get to, attain, achieve, realize
3 *gain speed*
increase, pick up, gather, collect, add, advance, progress, improve
E₃ 1 lose **3** lose
▷ **gain on** close with, close in on, narrow the gap, approach, get nearer/closer to, catch up, level with, overtake, outdistance
E₃ leave behind
▷ **gain time** delay, stall, temporize;
formal procrastinate; *colloq.* drag your feet, dilly-dally
▶ *n* earnings, proceeds, income, revenue, winnings, pickings, proceeds, takings, profit, return, reward, yield, interest, dividend, growth, addition, increase, increment, rise, advance, progress, headway, improvement, advantage, benefit, attainment, achievement, acquisition
formal emolument, advancement, augmentation, accretion
E₃ loss

gainful *adj*
profitable, beneficial, advantageous, fruitful, lucrative, remunerative, moneymaking, paying, productive, rewarding, financially rewarding, useful, worthwhile
formal fructuous
E₃ useless

gainsay *v*
deny, contradict, disagree with, dispute, oppose, challenge
formal contravene, controvert, disaffirm
E₃ agree

gait *n*
walk, pace, step, stride, tread, bearing, carriage, manner

gala *n*
festivity, celebration, party, festival, carnival, jubilee, jamboree, fête, fair, pageant, procession

galaxy *n*
1 STARS, star system, solar system, the Milky Way, constellation, cluster, nebula

2 ARRAY, host, collection, gathering, group assembly, mass

gale *n*
1 WIND, squall, storm, hurricane, tornado, typhoon, cyclone
2 BURST, outburst, outbreak, fit, eruption, explosion, blast

gall¹ *n*
had the gall to ask for more money
1 IMPERTINENCE, impudence, brazenness, insolence, presumption, presumptuousness
formal effrontery
colloq. nerve, neck, cheek, chutzpah, sauciness, brass, brass neck
2 BITTERNESS, rancour, sourness, spite, animosity, hostility, enmity, antipathy, malice, venom, virulence
formal acrimony, animus, malevolence
F∃ **1** modesty, reserve **2** friendliness

gall² *v*
it galls me to have to ask his permission
annoy, irritate, irk, exasperate, vex, bother, get to, nettle, peeve, pester, provoke, plague, rile, rankle, ruffle, harass, nag
colloq. aggravate
F∃ please

gallant *adj*
chivalrous, gentlemanly, courteous, polite, gracious, attentive, thoughtful, considerate, courtly, noble, honourable, dashing, manly, heroic, valiant, brave, courageous, fearless, dauntless, intrepid, audacious, bold, daring, plucky
F∃ ungentlemanly, cowardly

gallantry *n*
chivalry, gentlemanliness, courtesy, courteousness, politeness, graciousness, attentiveness, thoughtfulness, consideration, courtliness, nobility, honour, manliness, heroism, valour, bravery, courage, courageousness, spirit, fearlessness, dauntlessness, boldness, intrepidity, audacity, pluck, daring
formal valiance
F∃ cowardice, ungentlemanliness

gallery *n*
art gallery, exhibition area, museum, arcade, passage, walk, balcony, circle, spectators
colloq. gods

galling *adj*
annoying, irritating, irksome, exasperating, humiliating, infuriating, vexing, provoking, nettling, plaguing, rankling, vexatious, bitter, embittering, bothersome, harassing
colloq. aggravating
F∃ pleasing

gallivant *v*
gad about, run around, travel, roam, wander, ramble, range, rove, stray, traipse, flit about, dot about
Scot. stravaig

gallop *v*
bolt, canter, run, sprint, race, career, fly, dash, tear, speed, zoom, scurry, shoot, dart, rush, hurry
formal hasten
F∃ amble

gallows *n*
scaffold, gibbet, the rope
Related adjective: patibulary

galore *adv*
in abundance, lots of, plenty, in numbers, to spare, everywhere
formal in profusion
colloq. heaps of, tons of, stacks of, millions of
F∃ scarce

galvanize *v*
electrify, shock, jolt, prod, spur, urge, provoke, stimulate, stir, startle, move, arouse, rouse, awaken, excite, fire, inspire, enliven, animate, invigorate, vitalize, energize

gambit *n*
device, manoeuvre, move, ploy, tactic(s), ruse, play, stratagem, trick, wile, artifice
formal machination

gamble *v, n*
▶ *v* bet, wager, try your luck, put money on, back, punt, play, play for money, play the horses, game, stake, chance, chance it, take a chance, risk, take a risk, hazard, venture, speculate, back
colloq. have a flutter
▶ *n* bet, wager, punt, lottery, chance, risk, hazard, venture, speculation, pot luck
colloq. flutter, leap in the dark, toss-up

gambler *n*
better, punter, risk-taker, tipster, bookmaker, turf accountant, desperado, daredevil

gambol *v*
caper, frolic, frisk, cavort, dance, skip, leap, romp, jump, bound, spring, hop, bounce, prance

game¹ *n*
1 RECREATION, play, sport, pastime, diversion, distraction, entertainment, amusement, merriment, fun, frolic, romp, joke, jest, prank, trick

Types of indoor game include: board game, backgammon, US checkers, chess, Cluedo®, draughts, halma, ludo, mah-jong, Monopoly®, nine men's morris, Scrabble®, snakes and ladders, Trivial Pursuit®; card game, baccarat, beggar-my-neighbour, bezique, blackjack, brag, bridge, canasta, chemin de fer, *colloq.* crib, cribbage, faro, gin rummy, rummy, happy families, *colloq.* nap, napoleon, newmarket, old maid, patience, Pelmanism, picquet, poker, draw poker, stud poker, pontoon, vingt-et-un, snap, solitaire, twenty- one, whist, partner whist, solo whist; bagatelle, pinball, billiards, snooker, pool, bowling, ten-pin bowling, bowls, darts, dice, craps, dominoes, roulette, shove ha'penny, table tennis, ping pong.

Types of children's games include: battleships, blind man's buff, charades, Chinese whispers, consequences, fivestones, forfeits, hangman, hide-and-seek, I-spy, jacks, jackstraws, musical chairs, noughts and crosses, pass the parcel, piggy-in-the-middle, pin the tail on the donkey, postman's knock, sardines, Simon says, spillikins, spin the bottle, tiddlywinks.

2 COMPETITION, contest, match, round, tournament, event, meeting, meet, bout, round
3 GAME BIRDS, animals, wild animals, meat, flesh, wild fowl, prey, quarry, bag, spoils

Types of game (killed for sport) include: antelope, badger, bear, blackcock, boar, wild boar, caribou, deer, fallow deer, red deer, roe deer, duck, elk, fox, grouse, hazel grouse, wood grouse, hare, lion, moose, mountain lion, partridge, pheasant, quail, rabbit, snipe, squirrel, stag, tiger, waterfowl.

4 ACTIVITY, business, enterprise, profession, occupation, line, trade
5 SCHEME, trick, intention, ploy, plot, strategy, device, stratagem, tactic(s), ruse

game² *adj*
1 *game for anything*
willing, inclined, interested, ready, prepared, eager, enthusiastic
formal desirous
2 BOLD, daring, intrepid, brave, courageous, fearless, resolute, spirited, unflinching, gallant, plucky, valiant, lion-hearted
Ⅎ 1 unwilling **2** cowardly, afraid, fearful

gamekeeper *n*
keeper, warden
old use venerer

gamut *n*
scale, series, range, sweep, scope, compass, spectrum, sequence, field, area, variety

gang *n*
group, band, ring, pack, herd, mob, crowd, gathering, horde, circle, clique, coterie, set, lot, club, team, crew, squad, shift, party, troupe, company

gangling *adj*
lanky, gawky, gangly, skinny, spindly, bony, angular, raw-boned, loose-jointed, awkward, tall, ungainly, rangy, gauche

gangster *n*
mobster, desperado, hoodlum, ruffian, rough, tough, thug, terrorist, racketeer, bandit, brigand, robber, criminal
colloq. crook; *slang* heavy

gaol *see* jail.

gaoler *see* jailer.

gap *n*
1 SPACE, blank, void, hole, cavity, aperture, opening, crack, chink, crevice, cleft, cranny, breach, rift, fracture, rent, divide, gulf, divergence, difference
formal orifice, lacuna, vacuity, discontinuity, disparity
2 INTERRUPTION, break, recess, pause, lull, interlude, intermission, interval, hiatus

gape *v*
1 STARE, gaze, wonder, goggle
colloq. gawp, gawk
US slang rubberneck
2 OPEN, yawn, part, split, crack

gaping *adj*
open, yawning, broad, wide, vast, cavernous
Ⅎ tiny

garage *n*
lock-up, car port, petrol station, service station

garb *n, v*
▶ *n* **1** CLOTHES, clothing, garment, costume, dress, outfit, wear, robes, uniform, vestments, habiliment
formal apparel, array, attire, raiment
colloq. gear, get-up, rig-out, togs
2 APPEARANCE, guise, aspect, look, form, fashion, style
▶ *v* clothe, cover, dress, robe
formal apparel, array, attire, habilitate
colloq. rig out

garbage *n*
1 WASTE, rubbish, refuse, remains, leftovers, scourings, scraps, slops, swill, filth, muck, debris, dross, junk, litter, bits and pieces, odds and ends, sweepings
formal detritus
Scot. trash
2 NONSENSE, rubbish, gibberish, trash, tripe, twaddle
colloq. bunk, bunkum, claptrap, piffle, bilge, poppycock, hot air, cobblers, rot, tommyrot; *slang* balls, bollocks, shit, bullshit

garble *v*
confuse, muddle, jumble, scramble, mix up, twist, distort, corrupt, pervert, warp, slant, doctor, misrepresent, misinterpret, falsify, tamper with, mutilate
Ⅎ decipher

garden *n*
yard, backyard, plot, park

Types of garden include: allotment, alpine garden, arboretum, arbour, beer garden, border, botanical garden, bottle garden, cottage garden, fruit garden, garden of rest, hanging garden, herbaceous border, herb garden, hop garden, indoor garden, Japanese garden, kitchen garden, knot garden, lawn, market garden, orchard, ornamental garden, raised bed, rockery, rock garden, rose arbour, rose bed, rose garden, shrubbery, sink garden, sunken garden, tea garden, terrarium, vegetable plot, wall garden, water garden, window box, winter garden.

gargantuan *adj*
colossal, huge, enormous, giant, gigantic, massive, immense, vast, tremendous, towering, mammoth, large, big, monumental, titanic, monstrous, elephantine
formal leviathan, prodigious, Brobdingnagian
Ⅎ small, tiny, minute

garish *adj*
gaudy, lurid, loud, glaring, flashy, showy, flaunting, tawdry, vulgar, tasteless, cheap, glittering, tinselly, raffish
formal meretricious
colloq. glitzy, flash
Ⅎ quiet, tasteful

garland *n, v*
▶ *n* wreath, festoon, decoration, flowers, laurels, honours, crown, coronet, coronal, headband, lei, bays, chaplet, stemma
▶ *v* wreathe, festoon, decorate, deck, adorn, crown

garments *n*
clothes, clothing, wear, outfit, dress, costume, uniform
formal attire, apparel
colloq. gear, togs, get-up, garb

garner *v*
gather, collect, accumulate, amass, assemble, heap, pile up, stack up, hoard, lay up, put by, reserve, save, stockpile, cull, store, stow away, deposit, treasure, husband
Ⅎ dissipate

garnish *v, n*
▶ *v* decorate, adorn, ornament, trim, deck (out), festoon, embellish, enhance, grace, set off, beautify
Ⅎ divest
▶ *n* decoration, ornament, ornamentation,

adornment, trimming, embellishment, enhancement, relish

garret *n*
attic, loft, mansard

garrison *n, v*
▶ *n* **1** ARMED FORCE, detachment, troops, unit, command
2 FORT, fortress, fortification, stronghold, station, post, base, barracks, camp, encampment, casern, zareba
Related adjective: presidiary
▶ *v* **1** PROTECT, defend, guard
2 OCCUPY, position, place, mount, station, assign, furnish, man, post

garrulous *adj*
talkative, chatty, windy, long-winded, verbose, wordy, gabby, gassy, glib, yabbering, gossiping, gushing, chattering, babbling, effusive, prattling, prating, mouthy
formal loquacious, prolix, voluble
F3 taciturn, terse

gas *n*
Related adjective: pneumatic

Types of gas include: acetylene, ammonia, black damp, butane, carbon dioxide, carbon monoxide, chloroform, choke damp, CS gas, cyanogen, ether, ethylene, fire damp, helium, hydrogen sulphide, krypton, laughing gas, marsh gas, methane, mustard gas, natural gas, neon, nerve gas, niton, nitrous oxide, ozone, propane, radon, tear gas, town gas, xenon.

gash *v, n*
▶ *v* cut, wound, slash, slit, incise, lacerate, tear, rend, split, score, gouge, nick
▶ *n* cut, wound, slash, slit, incision, laceration, tear, rent, split, score, gouge, nick

gasp *v, n*
▶ *v* pant, puff, blow, breathe, catch your breath, wheeze, heave, choke, gulp
▶ *n* pant, puff, blow, breath, choke, gulp, exclamation

gastric *adj*
stomach, intestinal, abdominal, coeliac, stomachic, enteric

gate *n*
barrier, door, doorway, gateway, opening, entrance, exit, access, passage
formal portal

gather *v*
1 CONGREGATE, convene, muster, rally, round up, assemble, summon, marshal, collect, come/bring together, meet, group, crowd, cluster, attract, draw, pull in, amass, mass, accumulate, converge, hoard, stockpile, heap, pile up, hoard up, build, rake in, garner
colloq. stash away
2 INFER, deduce, conclude, surmise, assume, understand, learn, hear, believe
3 *gather flowers*
pick, pluck, cull, select, reap, harvest, crop, glean, collect, garner
4 *gather speed*
gain, increase, grow, pick up, build up, add, advance, progress, improve, develop
5 FOLD, pleat, tuck, pucker, ruffle, shirr
F3 **1** scatter, dissipate

gathering *n*
assembly, convention, meeting, round-up, rally, get-together, jamboree, party, group, band, company, congregation, mass, crowd, flock, throng, mob, horde, turnout
formal convocation, conclave, assemblage

gauche *adj*
awkward, clumsy, shy, ungainly, inelegant, ungraceful, unpolished, gawky, graceless, uncultured, unsophisticated, ignorant, ill-bred, ill-mannered, insensitive, inept, farouche, tactless
formal maladroit
F3 graceful, elegant, urbane

gaudy *adj*
bright, too bright, brilliant, colourful, multicoloured, glaring, garish, loud, shrieking, harsh, stark, flashy, showy, kitsch, flaunting, ostentatious, tinselly, tawdry, vulgar, tasteless, raffish
formal meretricious
colloq. glitzy, flash, snazzy
F3 drab, plain, simple

gauge *v, n*
▶ *v* estimate, guess, judge, assess, evaluate, value, rate, reckon, figure, calculate, compute, count, measure, weigh, determine, check
formal apprise, ascertain
colloq. guesstimate
▶ *n* **1** STANDARD, basic, guide, norm, criterion, benchmark, yardstick, touchstone, rule, guideline, indicator, measure, meter, test, sample, example, model, pattern
formal exemplar
2 SIZE, magnitude, measure, capacity, bore, calibre, thickness, width, span, extent, area, scope, height, depth, degree
See panel at **measuring instruments**.

gaunt *adj*
1 HAGGARD, hollow-eyed, angular, bony, thin, lean, lank, skinny, skin and bones, scraggy, scrawny, spindly, skeletal, emaciated, wasted
formal cadaverous
2 BLEAK, stark, bare, barren, desolate, forlorn, dismal, dreary, forbidding, grim, harsh
F3 **1** plump

gauzy *adj*
filmy, flimsy, delicate, sheer, thin, transparent, light, see-through, gossamer, insubstantial, unsubstantial
formal diaphanous
F3 heavy, thick

gawk *v*
gape, goggle, stare, gaze, look, ogle

gawky *adj*
awkward, clumsy, gauche, inept, loutish, oafish, ungainly, gangling, lanky, unco-ordinated, graceless, lumbering
formal maladroit
F3 graceful

gay *adj, n*
▶ *adj* **1** HOMOSEXUAL, lesbian, bisexual
colloq. camp, butch; *slang* queer, bent, dykey
2 HAPPY, joyful, jolly, merry, cheerful, bright, blithe, sunny, carefree, debonair, fun-loving, pleasure-seeking, vivacious, lively, animated, exuberant, sprightly, playful, light-hearted, in good/high spirits
3 *gay colours*
vivid, rich, bright, brilliant, sparkling, festive,

colourful, gaudy, garish, flashy, showy, flamboyant
⊟ 1 heterosexual; *slang* straight   **2** sad, gloomy
▶ *n* homosexual, lesbian
slang queer, poof, dyke, faggot, fag, fairy, bent, pansy,
queen, homo, nancy, pansy, woofter
⊟ heterosexual; *colloq.* straight

gaze   *v, n*
▶ *v* stare, stare fixedly/intently, contemplate, regard,
watch, view, look, gape, wonder, goggle, eye
colloq. gawk
▶ *n* stare, look, fixed look, gape

gazebo   *n*
belvedere, summerhouse, shelter, pavilion, hut

gazette   *n*
newspaper, journal, magazine, news-sheet, periodical,
paper, organ, dispatch, notice

gear   *n, v*
▶ *n* **1** EQUIPMENT, kit, outfit, tackle, apparatus,
tools, implements, instruments, appliances,
accessories, supplies, utensils, contrivances
formal accoutrements
colloq. stuff, things
2 GEARWHEEL, cogwheel, tooth-wheel, toothed
wheel, ratchet, cog, gearing, mechanism, machinery,
works
formal engrenage
3 BELONGINGS, possessions, personal possessions,
things, baggage, luggage, paraphernalia, kit
formal effects
colloq. stuff
4 CLOTHES, clothing, garments, dress
formal attire, apparel
colloq. garb, togs, get-up
▶ *v* adapt, fit, design, tailor, devise, prepare, organize

gel, jell   *v*
set, congeal, coagulate, crystallize, harden, thicken,
solidify, materialize, come together, finalize, form,
take shape

gelatinous   *adj*
jelly-like, jellied, congealed, rubbery, glutinous,
gummy, gluey, sticky, viscous, viscid
formal mucilaginous
colloq. gooey

geld   *v*
emasculate, castrate, neuter, unman, unsex

gem   *n*
1 GEMSTONE, precious stone, stone, jewel
2 TREASURE, prize, masterpiece, *pièce de résistance*,
crème de la crème
colloq. pride and joy

> *Gems and gemstones include*: diamond, white
> sapphire, zircon, cubic zirconia, marcasite,
> rhinestone, pearl, moonstone, onyx, opal, mother-of-
> pearl, amber, citrine, fire opal, topaz, agate, tiger's
> eye, jasper, morganite, ruby, garnet, rose quartz,
> beryl, cornelian, coral, amethyst, sapphire,
> turquoise, lapis lazuli, emerald, aquamarine,
> bloodstone, jade, peridot, tourmaline, jet.

gen   *n, v*
▶ *n* information, facts, details, data, knowledge,
background
colloq. info, low-down, dope
▶ *v* ▷ **gen up on**   find out about, be well-informed
about, research, read up on, study; *colloq.* swot up on,
bone up on, brush up on

genealogy   *n*
family tree, family history, pedigree, lineage, ancestry,
descent, derivation, extraction, family, dynasty, line,
birth, parentage, breeding

general   *adj*
1 *a general statement*
broad, sweeping, blanket, all-inclusive,
comprehensive, universal, global, total, across-the-
board, widespread, wide-ranging, prevailing,
prevalent, extensive, overall, accepted, popular,
panoramic
2 VAGUE, broad, ill-defined, indefinite, imprecise,
inexact, approximate, loose, rough, unspecific
3 USUAL, regular, normal, typical, ordinary,
standard, everyday, customary, conventional,
common, habitual, public
4 *a general store*
mixed, varied, assorted, diverse, miscellaneous
formal heterogeneous, variegated
⊟ 1 particular, limited   **2** specific, detailed, precise
3 rare

generality   *n*
1 GENERALIZATION, sweeping statement, general
statement, impreciseness, indefiniteness, inexactness,
looseness, approximateness, vagueness
2 COMMONNESS, extensiveness, popularity,
prevalence, universality, comprehensiveness, breadth,
catholicity, ecumenicity, miscellaneity
⊟ 1 detail, exactness, particular   **2** uncommonness

generally   *adv*
usually, normally, in general, ordinarily, commonly,
habitually, customarily, as a rule, by and large, for the
most part, on the whole, mostly, in most cases,
predominantly, mainly, chiefly, broadly, largely,
at large, universally

generate   *v*
produce, engender, whip up, arouse, cause, bring
about, bring into being, give rise to, create, originate,
initiate, occasion, make, form, breed, propagate
⊟ prevent

generation   *n*
1 AGE GROUP, age, days, era, epoch, period, time
2 PRODUCTION, creation, origination, formation,
engendering, reproduction, propagation, breeding
formal genesis, procreation

generic   *adj*
1 GENERAL, common, comprehensive, inclusive,
universal, sweeping, wide, all-inclusive,
all-encompassing, blanket, collective
2 *generic drugs*
unbranded, non-trademarked, non-registered,
non-proprietary
⊟ 1 particular   **2** branded, trademarked,
registered, proprietary

generosity   *n*
liberality, open-handedness, bounty, charity,
magnanimity, philanthropy, kindness, big-
heartedness, benevolence, goodness, lavishness,
unselfishness, selflessness
formal munificence
⊟ meanness, selfishness

generous   *adj*
1 LIBERAL, free, bountiful, open-handed, free-
handed, unstinting, unsparing, lavish
2 MAGNANIMOUS, charitable, philanthropic,
public-spirited, unselfish, selfless, altruistic, kind, big-

hearted, benevolent, good, high-minded, noble, lofty
formal beneficent, munificent
colloq. big
3 AMPLE, lavish, full, plentiful, abundant, rich,
copious, overflowing
E3 1 mean, miserly **2** selfish **3** meagre

genesis *n*
origin, beginning, birth, outset, root, source, start,
foundation, founding, generation, initiation,
engendering, formation, propagation, creation, dawn
formal commencement, inception
E3 end, finish

genial *adj*
affable, amiable, friendly, amicable, convivial, cordial,
kindly, kind, sociable, warm-hearted, warm, hearty,
jovial, jolly, cheerful, happy, good-natured, good-
humoured, agreeable, pleasant
colloq. easy-going
E3 cold, unfriendly

geniality *n*
affability, amiability, friendliness, conviviality,
congenialness, cordiality, kindliness, kindness, warm-
heartedness, warmth, joviality, jollity, cheerfulness,
happiness, gladness, cheeriness, good nature,
agreeableness, pleasantness
E3 coldness, unfriendliness

genie *n*
spirit, fairy, demon, jinni, jinnee, jann

genitals *n*
sexual organs, reproductive organs, private parts,
vulva, clitoris, labia majora/minora, vagina, womb,
uterus, penis, scrotum, testicles
technical pudenda, pudendum
formal genitalia
colloq. privates, willy; *slang* fanny, pussy, cunt, cock,
prick, dick, balls

genius *n*
1 VIRTUOSO, maestro, prodigy, master, past master,
expert, adept, intellectual, mastermind, brain,
intellect, sage
colloq. egghead, brains, boffin
2 INTELLIGENCE, brightness, brilliance,
cleverness, fine mind, intellect, wisdom, ability,
aptitude, gift, talent, flair, knack, bent, inclination,
capacity, faculty
formal propensity
colloq. brains, nous, grey matter, little grey cells

genocide *n*
extermination, massacre, slaughter, ethnocide, ethnic
cleansing

genre *n*
type, form, style, class, fashion, brand, group, kind,
sort, variety, category, character, school, strain
technical genus

genteel *adj*
respectable, refined, cultivated, polished, elegant,
polite, stylish, fashionable, cultured, aristocratic,
formal, civil, gentlemanly, graceful, mannerly, well-
mannered, well-bred, courteous, courtly, ladylike,
urbane
E3 crude, rough, unpolished, vulgar

gentility *n*
1 NOBILITY, aristocracy, high birth, gentle birth,
good family, upper class, nobles, rank, breeding, elite,
gentry, blue blood

2 COURTESY, respectability, formality, elegance,
politeness, etiquette, civility, courtliness, manners,
mannerliness, refinement, culture, urbanity
formal decorum, propriety
E3 crudeness, discourteousness, roughness

gentle *adj*
1 KIND, kindly, amiable, tender, tender-hearted, soft-
hearted, compassionate, sympathetic, lenient,
humane, merciful, charitable, benign, mild, placid,
calm, tranquil, serene, soft
2 *a gentle slope*
gradual, slow, easy, smooth, moderate, slight, light,
imperceptible
3 SOOTHING, peaceful, serene, quiet, soft, smooth
4 *gentle winds*
mild, light, moderate, calm, pleasant, balmy
E3 1 unkind, rough, harsh, wild **2** steep, severe
4 strong, violent

gentlemanly *adj*
courteous, polite, refined, polished, urbane, well-bred,
well-mannered, cultivated, civilized, civil, honourable,
mannerly, gentlemanlike, noble, gallant, genteel,
reputable, suave, obliging
E3 impolite, rough

gentry *n*
nobility, nobles, upper class, aristocracy, elite, gentility

genuine *adj*
1 REAL, actual, natural, pure, original, authentic,
factual, veritable, true, sound, bona fide, legitimate,
legal, lawful, unadulterated, pukka
colloq. real McCoy
2 HONEST, sincere, frank, candid, earnest, with
integrity, truthful, open, natural
E3 1 artificial, false, fake, counterfeit **2** insincere,
deceitful

genus *n*
species, race, breed, genre, order, sort, set, type,
division, subdivision, kind, group, category, class
technical taxon

geological timescale

*A scale into which the Earth's geological history can be
subdivided*: *Cenozoic*: Quaternary (2 million years
ago to present: Holocene, Pleistocene), Tertiary (65
million years ago to 2 million years ago: Pliocene,
Miocene, Oligocene, Eocene, Palaeocene); *Mesozoic*:
Cretaceous (140 million years ago to 65 million years
ago), Jurassic (210 million yeas ago to 140 million
years ago), Triassic (250 million years ago to 210
million years ago); *Palaeozoic*: Permian (290 million
years ago to 250 million years ago), Carboniferous
(360 million years ago to 290 million years ago:
Pennsylvanian, Mississippian), Devonian (410
million yeas ago to 360 million years ago), Silurian
(440 million years ago to 410 million years ago),
Ordovician (505 million years ago to 440 million
years ago), Cambrian (580 million years ago to 505
million years ago); *Precambrian* (before 580 million
years ago).

germ *n*
1 MICRO-ORGANISM, microbe, bacterium, bacillus,
virus
colloq. bug
2 BEGINNING, start, origin, source, fountain, cause,
spark, rudiment, nucleus, root, seed, embryo, bud,
sprout
formal commencement, inception

germane *adj*
relevant, appropriate, suitable, apt, applicable, fitting, material, proper, related, connected, akin, allied
formal pertinent, apposite, apropos
F3 irrelevant

germinal *adj*
generative, developing, embryonic, seminal, preliminary, rudimentary, undeveloped

germinate *v*
bud, sprout, shoot, develop, originate, grow, swell, spring up, take root
formal burgeon

gestation *n*
development, incubation, pregnancy, conception, evolution, ripening, planning, drafting
formal maturation

gesticulate *v*
wave, signal, gesture, motion, indicate, sign, make a sign

gesticulation *n*
wave, signal, gesture, motion, movement, indication, sign
formal chironomy

gesture *n, v*
▶ *n* movement, motion, indication, sign, signal, wave, gesticulation, act, action
▶ *v* indicate, sign, motion, beckon, point, signal, wave, gesticulate

get *v*
1 OBTAIN, acquire, come by, receive, be given, earn, gain, buy, bring in, clear, make, win, secure, achieve, realize
formal procure, purchase
2 *it's getting dark*
become, turn, go, grow, come to be
3 *get him to help*
persuade, coax, induce, talk into, urge, influence, sway, win over, convince
formal prevail upon
4 MOVE, go, come, reach, arrive
5 FETCH, collect, pick up, bring, take, catch, capture, seize, grab
6 *get a disease*
catch, pick up, develop, come down with, become infected with, be afflicted by
formal contract
7 *get to see the exhibition*
succeed, manage, have the opportunity, organize, arrange
8 *get breakfast*
prepare, get ready, cook, put together
US fix
colloq. rustle up
9 *get a joke*
understand, see, follow, grasp, fathom
formal comprehend
colloq. twig, get the hang of, get the point, get it
10 *get a thief/an animal*
catch, capture, trap, hunt down, snare, lay hold of, arrest, hit, kill
colloq. nab, collar, nick
11 *his snoring really gets me*
annoy, irritate, infuriate, exasperate, vex, provoke, bother
colloq. bug, get on someone's nerves, rub someone up the wrong way, drive crazy
F3 1 lose **4** leave

▷ **get about** move about, move around, go/travel (widely)
▷ **get across** communicate, transmit, convey, impart, put across, put over, get over, bring home to
▷ **get ahead** advance, progress, get on, thrive, flourish, prosper, do well, succeed, make good, make it; *colloq.* go places, get there, get somewhere, go great guns, make the big time, make your mark, go up in the world
F3 fall behind, fail
▷ **get along 1** COPE, manage, get by, survive, fare, progress, develop **2** AGREE, be on friendly terms, harmonize, get on, be on the same wavelength; *colloq.* hit it off
▷ **get at 1** REACH, attain, find, discover, obtain **2** BRIBE, suborn, corrupt, influence **3** MEAN, intend, imply, insinuate, hint, suggest **4** CRITICIZE, find fault with, pick on, attack, make fun of; *colloq.* knock, slate, slam, pick holes in
▷ **get away** escape, get out, break out, break away, break free, run away, flee, depart, leave
▷ **get back 1** RETURN, go/come back, go/come home **2** RECOVER, regain, recoup, repossess, retrieve **3** PAY BACK, retaliate, get even with, take vengeance on, avenge yourself on
▷ **get by** cope, get along, manage, survive, exist, fare; *formal* subsist; *colloq.* make ends meet, scrape through, hang on, keep your head above water, keep the wolf from the door, weather the storm, see it through
▷ **get down 1** DEPRESS, sadden, dishearten, dispirit **2** DESCEND, dismount, disembark, alight, get off
F3 1 encourage **2** board
▷ **get even** pay back, reciprocate, repay, requite, revenge yourself; *colloq.* get your own back, settle a score
▷ **get in** enter, penetrate, infiltrate, arrive, come, land, embark
▷ **get off 1** *get off a train* alight, leave, get out (of), dismount, climb off, descend; *formal* disembark **2** REMOVE, detach, separate, shed, get down
F3 1 get on **2** put on
▷ **get on 1** BOARD, climb on, get in, get into, embark, mount, ascend **2** COPE, manage, fare, get along, make out, prosper, succeed, be on friendly terms with; *colloq.* hit it off with **3** CONTINUE, proceed, press on, advance, progress
F3 1 get off
▷ **get out 1** ESCAPE, flee, break out, extricate yourself, free yourself, leave, depart, withdraw, vacate, evacuate, clear out; *colloq.* quit, clear off **2** *she got out a pen* take out, produce **3** *the news got out* become public, become known, come out, leak out, be leaked, spread, circulate
▷ **get out of** avoid, escape, evade, shirk; *colloq.* dodge, skive
▷ **get over 1** RECOVER FROM, shake off, recuperate from, pull through, get well/better, respond to treatment, be restored, survive **2** SURMOUNT, overcome, master, get round, defeat, deal with, complete **3** COMMUNICATE, get across, convey, put over, impart, explain
▷ **get ready** prepare, arrange, fix up, ready, rehearse, set out
▷ **get rid of** do away with, dispense with, dispose of, throw away, rid yourself of, shake off, remove, unload, dump, eject, eliminate, expel, jettison; *colloq.* get shot of
F3 accumulate, acquire
▷ **get round 1** BYPASS, bypass, evade, avoid;

formal circumvent **2** PERSUADE, win over, talk round, coax, induce, sway; *formal* prevail upon
▷ **get there** advance, arrive, prosper, succeed, make good; *colloq.* go places, make it
▷ **get together** meet, assemble, collect, gather, congregate, rally, join, unite, collaborate, organize
▷ **get up** stand (up), arise, rise, ascend, climb, mount, scale

getaway *n*
escape, breakout, flight, start, absconding, decampment, break

get-together *n*
party, reception, meeting, reunion, function, gathering, rally, assembly, social, soirée
colloq. do

get-up *n*
set, outfit, clothes, clothing, garments
colloq. rig-out, gear, togs

ghastly *adj*
1 AWFUL, dreadful, frightful, frightening, terrifying, terrible, grim, gruesome, hideous, horrible, horrid, horrendous, loathsome, nasty, repellent, shocking, appalling
2 *look/feel ghastly*
ill, sick, unwell, poorly, rotten, dreadful, awful, terrible
colloq. lousy, ropy, off colour, under the weather
3 *a ghastly mistake*
serious, bad, grave, critical, dangerous, awful, terrible, dreadful, frightful, shocking, appalling, unrepeatable
F3 1 delightful, attractive **2** well, healthy

ghost *n*
1 SPECTRE, phantom, apparition, visitant, spirit, wraith, soul, shade, shadow, presence
colloq. spook
2 TRACE, suggestion, hint, shadow, impression, semblance

ghostly *adj*
eerie, creepy, weird, supernatural, unearthly, ghostlike, spectral, wraith-like, phantom, illusory, shadowy
colloq. spooky

ghoulish *adj*
grisly, gruesome, macabre, morbid, unhealthy, unwholesome, revolting, sick

giant *n, adj*
▶ *n* monster, titan, colossus, Goliath, Hercules, behemoth, ogre, Cyclops
▶ *adj* gigantic, colossal, titanic, mammoth, king-size, huge, enormous, massive, immense, vast, monumental, prodigious, gargantuan, cyclopean, Brobdingnagian, large
colloq. jumbo, great big, whopping

gibber *v*
babble, blab, blabber, blather, gabble, jabber, prattle, chatter, cackle, cant

gibberish *n*
nonsense, rubbish, drivel, jargon, twaddle, balderdash, prattle, yammer
colloq. gobbledygook, mumbo-jumbo, poppycock, tommyrot, cobblers, bunkum
F3 sense

gibe, jibe *n, v*
▶ *n* jeer, sneer, mockery, ridicule, teasing, taunt, derision, scoff, poke, quip
colloq. dig, crack
▶ *v* jeer, sneer, mock, ridicule, taunt, tease, scoff,

make fun of
formal deride

giddiness *n*
1 DIZZINESS, faintness, light-headedness, wooziness, wobbliness, nausea, vertigo
2 EXCITEMENT, dizziness, frenzy, exhilaration, thrill, animation

giddy *adj*
1 DIZZY, faint, light-headed, unsteady, reeling
formal vertiginous
colloq. woozy
2 EXCITED, wild, dizzy, exhilarated, stirred, stimulated, thrilled, elated, frenzied
colloq. high

gift *n, v*
▶ *n* **1** PRESENT, offering, donation, contribution, bounty, largesse, gratuity, tip, bonus, inheritance, legacy, bequest, endowment
colloq. freebie
2 TALENT, genius, flair, skill, aptitude, aptness, bent, knack, facility, endowment, proficiency, power, faculty, attribute, ability, capability, capacity, turn
▶ *v* present, offer, contribute, donate
formal bestow, confer

gifted *adj*
talented, endowed, adept, skilful, expert, masterly, skilled, accomplished, able, capable, proficient, clever, intelligent, bright, brilliant, sharp
colloq. smart

gigantic *adj*
huge, enormous, immense, vast, giant, massive, colossal, king-size, monumental, titanic, mammoth, gargantuan, Brobdingnagian
colloq. jumbo, great big, whopping
F3 tiny, Lilliputian

giggle *v & n*
titter, snigger, chuckle, chortle, laugh, snicker

gild *v*
enhance, ornament, deck, enrich, adorn, grace, beautify, embellish, embroider, festoon, garnish, brighten, dress up, paint, coat, trim
formal array, bedeck

gilded *adj*
gilt, gold, golden, gold-plated, gold-layered

gimcrack *adj*
cheap, shoddy, tawdry, trashy, rubbishy, trumpery
colloq. tacky
F3 solid, well-made

gimmick *n*
attraction, publicity, novelty, ploy, stratagem, ruse, scheme, trick, stunt, dodge, device, contrivance, gadget

gingerly *adv*
tentatively, hesitantly, warily, watchfully, cautiously, with caution, carefully, charity, attentively, delicately
formal judiciously, prudently
F3 boldly, carelessly

Gipsy *see* **Gypsy.**

gird *v*
1 PREPARE, ready, get ready, brace, steel
formal fortify
2 FASTEN, belt, bind, girdle, hem in, pen, surround, encircle, enclose, ring, encompass, enfold

girdle *n, v*
▶ *n* belt, sash, band, waistband, corset
formal cummerbund, ceinture, cestus, cincture, cingulum
▶ *v* surround, encircle, circle, enclose, encompass, go round, gird, bind, bound, hem, ring

girl *n*
lass, young woman, young lady, schoolgirl, girlfriend, sweetheart, maiden, madam, daughter, child, teenager, adolescent, au pair
colloq. kid, nipper

girlfriend *n*
young lady, girl, lass, partner, date, sweetheart, lover, fiancée, mistress, old flame, cohabitee, live-in lover, common-law spouse
colloq. date, steady, significant other; *slang* bird, chick

girlish *adj*
youthful, childlike, adolescent, childish, immature, innocent, unmasculine

girth *n*
circumference, perimeter, measure, size, bulk, strap, band

gist *n*
pith, essence, marrow, substance, matter, meaning, significance, sense, idea, drift, direction, point, crux, nucleus, nub, core, keynote
formal import, quintessence

give *v*
1 PRESENT, award, let someone have, slip, offer, lend, donate, contribute, provide, supply, distribute, administer, furnish, grant, endow, gift, make over, hand over, turn over, deliver, entrust, bequeath, leave, will, commit, devote
formal confer, bestow, accord, proffer
2 *give news*
communicate, transmit, transfer, convey, tell, utter, announce, declare, pronounce, publish, set forth
formal impart
3 CONCEDE, allow, admit, yield, give way, give up, surrender
formal cede
4 *give trouble*
cause, occasion, make, create, produce, do, perform
5 *give an impression*
show, indicate, display, present, exhibit, reveal, set forth
formal manifest
6 *give attention to something*
concentrate, direct, aim, focus, turn
7 *give someone a fright*
cause to experience/undergo, make, do, perform, occasion, create, give rise to
8 *give something a value*
allow, offer, estimate, grant
9 SINK, yield, bend, buckle, give way, break (down), collapse, fall, fall apart
10 *give a party*
organize, arrange, put on, be responsible for, take charge of, lay on
colloq. throw
11 *be given to understand something*
lead, made, cause, move, dispose, incline, prompt, induce
E3 1 take, withhold **5** withstand
▷ **give away** betray, inform on, expose, uncover, divulge, let slip, disclose, reveal, leak, let out, let slip, concede

E3 keep
▷ **give in** surrender, capitulate, submit, yield, give way, concede, admit/concede defeat, give up, succumb; *colloq.* quit, throw in the towel/sponge, chuck it in, pack it in, jack in, call it a day, show the white flag
E3 hold out
▷ **give off** emit, discharge, release, give out, send out, throw out, pour out, exhale, vent, exude, produce
▷ **give on to** lead to, open on to, overlook
▷ **give out 1** DISTRIBUTE, disperse, hand out, pass around, share out, dole out, mete out, allot, deal; *colloq.* dish out **2** ANNOUNCE, declare, broadcast, publish, make known, circulate, disseminate, communicate, transmit, impart, notify, advertise **3** STOP WORKING, break down; *colloq.* pack up; *slang* conk out **4** RUN OUT, come to an end, be (all) mixed up, be exhausted; *formal* depleted
▷ **give up 1** STOP, resign, abandon, renounce, waive, leave off, sacrifice; *formal* cease, relinquish, discontinue, forswear; *colloq.* quit, cut out
2 SURRENDER, capitulate, give in, concede, concede defeat; *colloq.* quit, throw in the towel, turn in
E3 1 start **2** hold out

give-and-take *n*
adaptability, compromise, negotiation, flexibility, goodwill, willingness, compliance

given *adj, prep*
▶ *adj* **1** *a given number*
specified, particular, definite, specific, individual, distinct
2 INCLINED, disposed, likely, liable, prone
▶ *prep* considering, taking into account/consideration, bearing in mind, making allowances for, in view of, in the light of, assuming

giver *n*
benefactor, patron, sponsor, backer, supporter, promoter, donor, contributor, subscriber, provider, subsidizer, philanthropist, helper, friend, well-wisher
colloq. angel, fairy godmother
E3 opponent, persecutor

glacial *adj*
1 FREEZING, frozen, biting, bitter, chill, chilly, cold, frosty, raw, wintry, stiff, frigid, icy, piercing, polar, arctic, Siberian
formal brumous, gelid
2 UNFRIENDLY, antagonistic, cold, icy, hostile
formal inimical
E3 warm

glad *adj*
1 PLEASED, delighted, gratified, contented, satisfied, happy, joyful, overjoyed, thrilled, elated, merry, cheerful, cheery, gleeful, welcome, bright
colloq. over the moon, chuffed, tickled pink
2 WILLING, eager, keen, ready, prepared, inclined, happy, pleased
formal disposed
E3 1 sad, unhappy **2** unwilling, reluctant

gladden *v*
brighten, cheer, encourage, delight, please, hearten, gratify, rejoice, elate, enliven, exhilarate, raise the spirits of
colloq. buck up
E3 sadden

gladly *adv*
happily, cheerfully, freely, willingly, readily, with good

grace, with pleasure
old use fain
ⴳ sadly, unwillingly, reluctantly

gladness *n*
happiness, joy, cheerfulness, delight, pleasure,
brightness, high spirits, jollity, glee, hilarity, mirth,
gaiety
formal felicity, joyousness
ⴳ sadness

glamorous *adj*
smart, elegant, well-dressed, attractive, beautiful,
lovely, gorgeous, enchanting, captivating, alluring,
charming, appealing, fascinating, exciting, thrilling,
dazzling, glittering, glossy, colourful
colloq. glitzy, flashy, ritzy
ⴳ plain, drab, boring

glamour *n*
attraction, attractiveness, allure, appeal, fascination,
excitement, thrill, captivation, enchantment, charm,
magic, beauty, elegance, glitter, prestige

glance *v, n*
▶ *v* peep, peek, glimpse, catch a glimpse of, view,
look, look quickly/briefly at, scan, skim, leaf, flip, flick,
thumb, dip, browse
▷ **glance off** bounce off, rebound, ricochet,
spring back
▶ *n* peep, peek, glimpse, look, quick/brief look
colloq. butcher's, dekko, gander

gland *n*
Related adjectives: adenoid, glandular

Types of gland include: adrenal, apocrine, cortex,
eccrine, endocrine, exocrine, holocrine, lachrymal,
lymph, lymph node, mammary, medulla, merocrine,
ovary, pancreas, parathyroid, parotid, pineal,
pituitary, prostate, sebaceous, testicle, thymus,
thyroid.

glare *v, n*
▶ *v* **1** GLOWER, look frown, scowl, stare, frown
colloq. daggers, give someone a dirty look
2 DAZZLE, blaze, flame, flare, shine, beam, reflect
▶ *n* **1** *his fiery glare*
frown, scowl, stare, look
colloq. dirty look, black look
2 BRIGHTNESS, brilliance, glow, blaze, flame, flare,
dazzle, spotlight

glaring *adj*
blatant, flagrant, open, conspicuous, patent, obvious,
over, outrageous, gross, lurid
formal manifest
ⴳ hidden, concealed, minor

glass *n*
1 BEAKER, tumbler, goblet
2 CRYSTAL, glassware, vitrics
3 SPECTACLES, lens, contact lenses, lorgnette,
eyeglasses, opera-glasses, pince-nez, monocle
colloq. specs
Related adjectives: vitreous, hyaline
See also **spectacles**.

glassy *adj*
1 GLASSLIKE, smooth, polished, slippery, icy, shiny,
glossy, transparent, clear, crystal clear, mirrorlike
2 *a glassy stare*
expressionless, blank, empty, vacant, dazed,

unmoving, fixed, deadpan, glazed, vacuous, cold,
lifeless, dull

glaze *v, n*
▶ *v* coat, cover, enamel, gloss, varnish, lacquer,
polish, burnish
▶ *n* coat, coating, finish, enamel, varnish, lacquer,
polish, shine, lustre, gloss

gleam *n, v*
▶ *n* glint, flash, beam, ray, shaft, flare, flicker,
glimmer, shimmer, sparkle, glitter, gloss, glow, lustre,
brightness
▶ *v* glint, flash, glance, flare, shine, radiate, beam,
glisten, glimmer, glitter, sparkle, scintillate, shimmer,
glow

glean *v*
gather, collect, find out, learn, pick (up), select,
accumulate, amass, harvest, garner, reap, cull

glee *n*
delight, cheerfulness, pleasure, fun, joy, joyfulness,
merriment, mirth, gladness, liveliness, exhilaration,
exuberance, exultation, elation, hilarity, jocularity,
jollity, joviality, gaiety, gratification, triumph, verve
formal joyousness

gleeful *adj*
delighted, cheerful, pleased, happy, beside yourself,
joyful, overjoyed, elated, exuberant, exultant, merry,
mirthful, jubilant, jovial, gratified, triumphant
formal joyous
colloq. over the moon, cock-a-hoop
ⴳ sad

glib *adj*
fluent, easy, facile, quick, ready, talkative, plausible,
insincere, smooth, slick, suave, smooth-tongued,
smooth-talking, silver-tongued
formal loquacious, voluble
colloq. with the gift of the gab, gabby, gassy
ⴳ tongue-tied, implausible

glide *v*
slide, move smoothly/effortlessly, slip, skate, skim, fly,
float, drift, sail, coast, roll, run, flow, pass

glimmer *v, n*
▶ *v* glow, shimmer, glisten, glitter, sparkle, twinkle,
wink, blink, flash, flicker, gleam, shine
▶ *n* **1** GLOW, shimmer, shine, sparkle, twinkle,
flicker, glint, gleam, ray, flash
2 TRACE, hint, suggestion, inkling, grain, flicker, ray

glimpse *n, v*
▶ *n* peep, peek, squint, glance, look, quick/brief
look, sight, sighting, view
▶ *v* spy, espy, spot, catch sight of, sight, view

glint *v, n*
▶ *v* flash, gleam, shine, reflect, glitter, sparkle,
glisten, twinkle, glimmer, shimmer, scintillate
▶ *n* flash, gleam, shine, reflection, glitter, sparkle,
glistening, twinkle, glimmer, shimmer

glisten *v*
shine, gleam, glint, glitter, flash, sparkle, twinkle,
flicker, glimmer, shimmer
formal coruscate

glitter *v, n*
▶ *v* sparkle, spangle, scintillate, twinkle, shimmer,
glimmer, flicker, glisten, glint, gleam, flash, shine,
dazzle
formal coruscate

► *n* **1** SPARKLE, scintillation, twinkle, shimmer, glimmer, flicker, glint, gleam, flash, shine, lustre, sheen, brightness, radiance, brilliance, splendour
formal coruscation
2 SHOWINESS, glamour, tinsel, flashiness
colloq. glitz, razzle-dazzle, razzmatazz

gloat *v*
triumph, glory, exult, rejoice, revel in, delight in, relish, crow, boast, vaunt
colloq. rub it in

global *adj*
1 WORLDWIDE, universal, international
2 GENERAL, all-encompassing, total, thorough, exhaustive, comprehensive, all-inclusive, encyclopedic, wide-ranging
F3 1 parochial **2** limited

globe *n*
world, earth, planet, sphere, ball, orb, round

globular *adj*
ball-shaped, round, globate, spherical
formal orbicular, spheroid

globule *n*
bead, ball, bubble, drop, droplet, globulet, pearl, pellet, particle
technical vesicle, vesicula

gloom *n*
1 DARK, darkness, blackness, shade, shadow, dusk, twilight, dimness, obscurity, cloud, cloudiness, dullness, murkiness
2 DEPRESSION, low spirits, despondency, dejection, sadness, unhappiness, glumness, melancholy, grief, sorrow, woe, misery, hopelessness, pessimism, desolation, despair
colloq. the blues
F3 1 brightness **2** cheerfulness, happiness

gloomy *adj*
1 DARK, sombre, shadowy, dim, obscure, overcast, dull, dreary, dismal, dingy, unlit
formal tenebrous, crepuscular
2 DEPRESSED, down, low, despondent, dejected, downcast, dispirited, down-hearted, sad, miserable, glum, morose, dreary, drear, pessimistic, cheerless, melancholy, sorrowful, dismal, depressing, desolate, in low spirits
formal disconsolate
colloq. down in the dumps
F3 1 bright **2** happy, cheerful

glorify *v*
1 *glorify God*
praise, worship, exalt, adore, honour, thank, bless, magnify, revere, extol, sanctify
formal laud, venerate
2 *glorify violence/war*
celebrate, praise, magnify, hail, lionize, idolize, elevate, enshrine, immortalize, romanticize, panegyrize
formal eulogize
F3 1 denounce; *formal* vilify

glorious *adj*
1 ILLUSTRIOUS, eminent, distinguished, famous, renowned, honoured, noted, great, noble, celebrated, famed, splendid, magnificent, grand, majestic, supreme, excellent, victorious, triumphant
2 MARVELLOUS, splendid, beautiful, gorgeous, superb, perfect, splendid, excellent, wonderful, delightful, dazzling, heavenly

colloq. super, terrific, great
3 *glorious weather*
FINE, bright, radiant, shining, brilliant
F3 1 unknown

glory *n, v*
► *n* **1** FAME, renown, celebrity, illustriousness, greatness, eminence, distinction, honour, recognition, acclaim, prestige, accolade, kudos, triumph
2 PRAISE, homage, tribute, worship, veneration, adoration, exaltation, blessing, thanksgiving, gratitude
3 BRIGHTNESS, radiance, brilliance, beauty, splendour, resplendence, magnificence, pomp, grandeur, majesty, dignity, impressiveness
► *v* revel, delight, exult, pride yourself, rejoice, triumph, relish, boast, crow, gloat

gloss¹ *n, v*
► *n* **1** SHEEN, polish, varnish, lustre, shine, brightness, gleam, shimmer, sparkle, brilliance
2 SHOW, appearance, semblance, surface, front, façade, veneer, camouflage, mask, disguise, veil, window-dressing
► *v* ▷ **gloss over** conceal, hide, veil, draw a veil over, mask, disguise, camouflage, cover up, whitewash, explain away, evade, avoid, ignore, smooth over, deal with quickly

gloss² *n, v*
► *n* *glosses to the text*
annotation, note, footnote, explanation, interpretation, translation, definition, comment, commentary
formal elucidation, explication, scholion
► *v* annotate, add glosses to, define, explain, interpret, construe, translate, comment
formal elucidate

glossy *adj*
shiny, sheeny, lustrous, sleek, silky, smooth, glassy, polished, burnished, glazed, gleaming, enamelled, bright, shining, shimmering, sparkling, brilliant
F3 matt

glove *n*
mitten, mitt, gauntlet, gage, mousquetaire glove, oven glove

glow *n, v*
► *n* **1** LIGHT, gleam, glimmer, radiance, brightness, vividness, richness, brilliance, splendour
technical phosphorescence
formal luminosity, incandescence
2 ARDOUR, fervour, intensity, warmth, passion, enthusiasm, excitement, happiness, satisfaction
3 FLUSH, blush, rosiness, redness, reddening, pinkness, burning
► *v* **1** SHINE, radiate, gleam, glimmer, burn, smoulder
2 *their faces glowed*
flush, blush, colour, redden, grow/look pink

glower *v, n*
► *v* glare, frown, scowl, stare, frown
colloq. look daggers, give someone a dirty look
► *n* glare, frown, scowl, stare, look
colloq. black look, dirty look

glowing *adj*
1 BRIGHT, luminous, vivid, vibrant, rich, warm, flushed, red, ruddy, flaming, smouldering
technical phosphorescent
formal incandescent

2 *a glowing review*
complimentary, enthusiastic, favourable, ecstatic, rhapsodic
formal laudatory, eulogistic, panegyrical
colloq. rave
F3 1 dull, colourless **2** restrained

glue *n, v*
▶ *n* adhesive, gum, paste, size, cement, fixative, mortar
▶ *v* stick, affix, gum, paste, seal, bond, cement, fix
formal agglutinate

gluey *adj*
adhesive, gummy, sticky, viscid, viscous
formal glutinous

glum *adj*
gloomy, unhappy, forlorn, sad, miserable, depressed, despondent, moody, dejected, morose, pessimistic, doleful, crestfallen, sour, sulky, sullen, surly, grumpy, gruff, ill-humoured, churlish, crabbed
colloq. down, low, down in the dumps
F3 ecstatic, happy

glut *n, v*
▶ *n* surplus, excess, superfluity, surfeit, overabundance, superabundance, saturation, overflow
F3 scarcity, lack
▶ *v* saturate, oversupply, overload, inundate, flood, deluge, overfeed, sate, satiate, stuff, gorge, fill, cram, choke, clog

glutinous *adj*
adhesive, sticky, cohesive, gluey, gummy, mucous, viscous
formal mucilaginous, viscid

glutton *n*
gourmand, gormandizer, gobbler
colloq. guzzler, greedy guts, gorger, pig
F3 ascetic

gluttonous *adj*
greedy, gluttonish, voracious, ravenous, insatiable, gormandizing
formal edacious, esurient, omnivorous, rapacious
colloq. gutsy, hoggish, piggish
F3 abstemious, ascetic

gluttony *n*
gourmandise, gourmandism, greed, greediness, voracity, insatiability
formal edacity, esurience
colloq. piggishness
F3 abstinence, asceticism

gnarled *adj*
gnarly, knotted, knotty, bumpy, lumpy, twisted, contorted, distorted, rough, wrinkled, rugged, weather-beaten, leathery

gnash *v*
grind, grate, grit, scrape

gnaw *v*
1 BITE, nibble, munch, chew, crunch, eat, devour, consume, erode, wear, haunt
formal masticate
2 WORRY, nag, niggle, fret, trouble, plague, prey, torment, harass, harry

go *v, n*
▶ *v* **1** MOVE, pass, advance, progress, proceed, make for, head, drive, travel, journey, walk, start, begin, go away, depart, leave, take your leave, set off, set out,

retreat, withdraw, disappear, vanish, melt away
formal repair
colloq. quit, scat, scoot, scram, make tracks
2 OPERATE, function, work, run, act, perform, be in working order
3 EXTEND, spread, stretch, reach, lead, span, continue, unfold
4 *time goes quickly*
pass, elapse, lapse, proceed, roll on, go by, slip away, tick away
5 *go mad*
become, turn, get, grow, come to be, be changed into
6 *the machine goes 'beep'*
emit, sound, make a sound, give off, send out, release
7 *the books go here*
belong, have as its usual place, fit in, be found, be located, be situated
8 *the interview went well*
turn out, work out, progress, proceed, manage, fare, occur, result, end up
formal eventuate
colloq. pan out
9 *Where does all the money go?*
be used up, be spent, be finished, be exhausted, be consumed
10 *100 jobs will go*
get rid of, be discarded, be thrown away, be dismissed, be made redundant
colloq. be axed, be sacked, be fired, be given their cards, be down the door
11 *most of the income goes on rent*
be spent on, be given to, be allotted to, be assigned to, be awarded to
12 *the hat goes well with the dress*
match, harmonize, co-ordinate, blend, go together, complement, suit, fit, correspond, go with each other
formal accord
F3 1 stop **2** break down, fail **12** clash
▷ **go about** approach, begin, set about, address, tackle, attend to, undertake, do, engage in, perform
▷ **go ahead** begin, proceed, carry on, continue, advance, progress, make progress, move
▷ **go along with** accept, agree with, obey, follow, support, abide by; *formal* comply with, concur with
▷ **go around** circulate, be spread around, be passed round, be talked about, go about
▷ **go at** set about, tackle, attack, blame, criticize, argue
▷ **go away** depart, leave, abscond, withdraw, retreat, disappear, vanish; *colloq.* get knotted, sling your hook

Colloquial expressions telling someone to go away include: away!, away with you!, be off!, beat it!, buzz off!, clear off!, clear out!, do me a favour!, get out of here!, get out!, get the hell out of here!, go and jump in the lake!, go fly a kite!, never darken my door again!, off with you!, off you go!, on your way!, out of my sight!, push off!, run along!, scarper!, scat!, scram!, shove off!, skeddadle!, take a running jump!, vamoose!

Slang expressions telling someone to go away include: bugger off!, fuck off!, get lost!, naff off!, piss off!, sod off!

▷ **go back** return, revert, backslide, retreat
▷ **go back on** renege on, default on, deny, break your promise
▷ **go by** **1** PASS, elapse, lapse, flow **2** *go by the rules* observe, follow, obey, heed; *formal* comply with

▷ **go down** 1 DESCEND, descend, sink, be submerged, set, fall (down), drop, decrease, be reduced, decline, deteriorate, degenerate, fail, founder, go under, collapse; *colloq.* fold 2 LOSE, be beaten, be defeated, suffer defeat, fail; *colloq.* come a cropper 3 *the joke went down badly* be received, have as a response, be reacted to, be met with, sustain

▷ **go for** 1 CHOOSE, select, prefer, favour, aim for, like, admire, enjoy 2 ATTACK, assail, assault, rush at, set about, lunge at

▷ **go in for** enter, take part in, participate in, engage in, go into, take up, embrace, adopt, undertake, practise, pursue, follow; *formal* espouse

▷ **go into** discuss, consider, review, examine, study, research, look into, scrutinize, investigate, inquire into, check out, probe, delve into, analyse, dissect

▷ **go off** 1 DEPART, leave, set out, abscond, vanish, disappear; *colloq.* quit 2 EXPLODE, blow up, blast, burst, detonate, be fired, be discharged; *colloq.* go bang 3 *the milk has gone off* deteriorate, turn, sour, go bad, rot, go stale

▷ **go on** 1 CONTINUE, carry on, proceed, persist, stay, endure, last, remain 2 CHATTER, ramble on; *colloq.* rabbit, witter, natter, gab, gas, talk the hind legs off a donkey 3 HAPPEN, occur, take place

▷ **go out** 1 EXIT, depart, leave, withdraw 2 *go out with a boy* go with, court, see each other; *colloq.* date, go steady

▷ **go over** examine, peruse, study, revise, scan, read, look over, inspect, discuss, think about, check, review, repeat, rehearse, list

▷ **go through** 1 SUFFER, undergo, experience, bear, tolerate, endure, withstand, stand, be subjected to 2 INVESTIGATE, check, examine, look through, search, hunt, explore 3 USE UP, consume, exhaust, spend, squander, get through

▷ **go together** match, harmonize, fit, suit, blend, co-ordinate, complement; *formal* accord

▷ **go under** 2 CLOSE DOWN, collapse, default, die, fail, go out of business, founder, go bankrupt; *colloq.* fold, flop, go to the wall, go bust 2 SINK, go down, founder, submerge, succumb, drown

▷ **go with** 1 MATCH, harmonize, co-ordinate, blend, complement, suit, fit, correspond 2 ACCOMPANY, escort, take, usher
▣ 1 clash

▷ **go without** abstain, deny yourself, forego, do without, manage without, lack, want

▶ *n* 1 *have a go* attempt, try, bid, turn, endeavour, effort *colloq.* shot, bash, stab, whirl 2 ENERGY, vitality, life, force, spirit, dynamism, vigour, animation *colloq.* get-up-and-go, push, pizzazz

goad *v*
prod, prick, spur, impel, push, drive, jolt, provoke, incite, induce, instigate, arouse, stimulate, inspire, motivate, pressurize, prompt, urge, nag, hound, harass, taunt, annoy, irritate, vex

go-ahead *n, adj*
▶ *n* permission, authorization, clearance, sanction, approval, assent, consent, warranty, agreement, confirmation
colloq. green light, OK, thumbs-up
▣ ban, veto, embargo
▶ *adj* enterprising, pioneering, progressive, ambitious, forward, forward-looking, opportunist, up-and-coming, dynamic, vigorous, energetic, aggressive

colloq. go-getting, pushy
▣ unenterprising, sluggish

goal *n*
target, mark, objective, aim, intention, object, purpose, end, design, ambition, ideal, aspiration

gobble *v*
bolt, guzzle, gorge, cram, stuff, devour, consume, swallow, gulp
colloq. put away, wolf, scoff

gobbledygook *n*
jargon, journalese, computerese, psychobabble, buzz words, nonsense, rubbish, drivel, twaddle, balderdash, prattle

go-between *n*
intermediary, mediator, liaison, contact, middleman, broker, dealer, agent, factor, messenger, medium

goblin *n*
imp, brownie, fiend, hobgoblin, gnome, elf, sprite, spirit, gremlin, nixie, red-cap, bogey, kelpie, kobold, demon

God *n*
Deity, Supreme Being, Divine Being, Godhead, prime mover, Creator, Maker, Providence, Lord, King, Almighty, Holy One, Jehovah, Yahweh, Father, Allah, Brahma, Zeus, Holy One, Judge, Saviour, Eternal, Everlasting
Related adjective: divine

god, goddess *n*
deity, divine being, divinity, spirit, power, icon, idol, graven image
Related adjective: divine

God-forsaken *adj*
remote, isolated, lonely, bleak, desolate, abandoned, deserted, forlorn, dismal, dreary, gloomy, miserable, wretched, depressing

godless *adj*
ungodly, atheistic, heathen, pagan, irreligious, agnostic, faithless, unholy, unrighteous, impious, sacrilegious, profane, irreverent, bad, evil, sinful, wicked
formal nullifidian
▣ godly, pious

godlike *adj*
divine, celestial, heavenly, exalted, saintly, holy, sacred, perfect, sublime, transcendent, superhuman
formal deiform, theomorphic

godly *adj*
religious, holy, pious, devout, God-fearing, believing, righteous, good, moral, virtuous, righteous, saintly, pure, innocent
▣ godless, impious

godsend *n*
blessing, boon, stroke of luck, bonanza, windfall, benediction, miracle
▣ blow, setback

goggle *v*
stare, gaze, wonder
colloq. gawp, gawk

going-over *n*
1 EXAMINATION, inspection, investigation, study, survey, analysis, check, check-up, review, scrutiny 2 BEATING, attack, criticism, reprimand, scolding, rebuke, pasting, chiding, thrashing, whipping, row

formal castigation, chastisement
colloq. dressing-down, trouncing

goings-on *n*
events, activities, occurrences, happenings, affair,
scenes, business, misbehaviour, mischief
colloq. funny business

gold *n*
bullion, nugget, bar, ingot, precious metal
Related adjectives: auric, aural

golden *adj*
1 GOLD, gilded, gilt, gold-coloured, yellow, blond(e),
fair, flaxen, bright, shining, gleaming, brilliant,
dazzling, lustrous
formal resplendent
2 PROSPEROUS, successful, glorious, excellent,
treasured, precious, happy, joyful, delightful, rosy,
favourable, promising, flourishing, bright, rewarding
formal auspicious, propitious

golf club *n*

Types of golf club include: driver, brassie, spoon,
wood, iron, driving iron, midiron, midmashie,
mashie iron, mashie, spade mashie, mashie niblick,
pitching niblick, niblick, putter, pitching wedge, sand
wedge.

gone *adj*
departed, absent, away, astray, defunct, disappeared,
vanished, lost, missing, finished, done, over, elapsed,
past, used, spent, dead, extinct
colloq. over and done with

goo *n*
matter, ooze, slime, stickiness, slush, sludge, mud,
scum, mire, muck, grease, grime
colloq. gunge, yuck, grot; *slang* crud, gunk, grunge

good *adj, n, interj*
▶ *adj* 1 *have a good day; do good work*
enjoyable, cheerful, pleasing, pleasurable, satisfying,
commendable, excellent, first-class, first-rate,
superior, fine, wonderful, marvellous, fantastic,
terrific, superb, exceptional, acceptable, satisfactory,
pleasant, agreeable, nice, adequate, passable,
reasonable, tolerable, desirable
colloq. great, super
2 *good at her job*
competent, proficient, skilled, expert, accomplished,
professional, skilful, clever, talented, gifted, fit,
brilliant, able, capable, dependable, reliable, efficient,
adept, dexterous
3 KIND, considerate, gracious, friendly, sympathetic,
benevolent, charitable, altruistic, philanthropic,
kind-hearted, well-disposed
4 VIRTUOUS, exemplary, moral, upright, honest,
trustworthy, worthy, honourable, noble, admirable,
righteous, ethical
colloq. salt of the earth
5 ADVANTAGEOUS, beneficial, favourable, helpful,
useful, worthwhile, profitable, convenient,
appropriate, suitable, fitting, lucky, fortunate
formal auspicious, propitious
6 WELL-BEHAVED, obedient, well-mannered,
polite, respectful, under control
formal compliant
colloq. good as gold
7 *in good health*
fine, healthy, strong, vigorous, sound, hale and hearty
colloq. in the pink, the picture of health, fit as a fiddle

8 *a good reason*
sound, sensible, valid, right, genuine
9 *be good friends*
close, dear, intimate, best, loving, bosom
10 THOROUGH, complete, whole, substantial,
considerable, sizeable, large
🔁 1 bad, poor 2 incompetent 3 unkind,
inconsiderate 4 wicked, immoral 5 inconvenient,
useless 6 naughty, disobedient 7 poor 8 bad
▷ **make good** 1 PUT RIGHT, make amends for,
make recompense for, compensate for, make
restitution for 2 SUCCEED, get ahead, go far,
progress, be successful, get on in the world 3 *make
good a threat/promise* fulfil, carry out, do, live up to,
put into action; *formal* effect
▶ *n* 1 VIRTUE, morality, goodness, integrity, honesty,
honour, uprightness, righteousness, right, ethics,
morals
formal rectitude
2 USE, purpose, avail, advantage, profit, gain, worth,
merit, usefulness, service
3 *for your own good*
benefit, welfare, wellbeing, interest, sake, behalf,
convenience
▷ **for good** for ever, always, ever, evermore, for all
time, permanently, till the end of time, eternally;
colloq. till kingdom come, till the cows come home
▶ *interj* fine, perfect, all right, very well, right,
agreed, indeed, just so
colloq. OK

goodbye *interj, n*
▶ *interj* farewell, adieu, *au revoir, auf Wiedersehen,
ciao*
colloq. cheerio, bye, bye-bye, cheers, see you (later), see
you around, be seeing you, all the best, mind how you
go, take care, have a nice day, ta-ta, so long
▶ *n* farewell, adieu, *au revoir*, leave-taking, parting,
swan song
formal valediction

good-for-nothing *adj, n*
▶ *adj* lazy, useless, worthless, idle, irresponsible,
reprobate, no-good
formal profligate, indolent, feckless
🔁 conscientious, successful
▶ *n* layabout, ne'er-do-well, reprobate, idler, waster,
wastrel
formal profligate
colloq. black sheep, lazy-bones, loafer; *slang* bum
🔁 achiever, success, winner

good-humoured *adj*
cheerful, happy, jovial, genial, affable, amiable,
friendly, congenial, pleasant, good-tempered,
approachable
🔁 ill-humoured

good-looking *adj*
attractive, handsome, beautiful, fair, pretty, lovely,
personable, presentable
old use comely
🔁 ugly, plain

goodly *adj*
substantial, sizeable, considerable, ample, large, good,
significant, sufficient
colloq. tidy
🔁 inadequate

good-natured *adj*
kind, kindly, kind-hearted, sympathetic, benevolent,
generous, helpful, neighbourly, gentle, good-tempered,

warm-hearted, approachable, friendly, tolerant, patient
Ǝ ill-natured

goodness *n*
virtue, uprightness, integrity, righteousness, honesty, kindness, compassion, graciousness, mercy, goodwill, excellence, benefit, benevolence, unselfishness, generosity, altruism, friendliness, helpfulness, wholesomeness
formal rectitude, probity, beneficence
Ǝ badness, wickedness, selfishness

goods *n*
1 PROPERTY, chattels, effects, possessions, belongings, paraphernalia, things
colloq. gear, stuff
formal accoutrements, appurtenances
2 MERCHANDISE, wares, commodities, products, things, lines, stock, freight

goodwill *n*
benevolence, kindness, compassion, generosity, favour, friendliness, friendship, zeal
formal amity
Ǝ ill-will

goody-goody *adj*
self-righteous, sanctimonious, pious, priggish
formal unctuous, ultra-virtuous

gooey *adj*
1 STICKY, soft, gluey, glutinous, viscous, tacky, thick, syrupy
formal mucilaginous, viscid
colloq. gungy
2 SENTIMENTAL, slushy, sloppy, syrupy, nauseating, maudlin, mawkish

gore *v, n*
▶ *v* pierce, penetrate, stab, spear, stick, impale, wound
▶ *n* blood, bloodiness, bloodshed, slaughter, butchery, carnage
technical cruor, grume

gorge *n, v*
▶ *n* canyon, ravine, gully, defile, chasm, abyss, crevice, cleft, fissure, rift, gap, pass
▶ *v* feed, guzzle, gobble, devour, bolt, gulp, swallow, cram, stuff, fill, sate, surfeit, glut, overeat
colloq. wolf
Ǝ fast

gorgeous *adj*
1 MAGNIFICENT, splendid, grand, glorious, superb, fine, impressive, rich, sumptuous, luxurious, brilliant, dazzling, resplendent, marvellous, wonderful, delightful, pleasing, lovely, enjoyable, good, showy, glamorous
formal opulent
2 ATTRACTIVE, beautiful, pretty, fine, sweet, glamorous, handsome, good-looking, lovely
formal pulchritudinous
colloq. sexy, stunning, ravishing
Ǝ dull, plain

gory *adj*
bloody, bloodstained, blood-soaked, grisly, brutal, savage, violent, murderous
formal sanguinary

gospel *n*
1 LIFE OF CHRIST, teaching of Christ, message of Christ, good news, New Testament

2 TEACHING, doctrine, creed, credo, certainty, truth, fact
technical kerygma
formal evangel, verity

gossamer *adj*
thin, light, delicate, flimsy, fine, cobwebby, insubstantial, sheer, shimmering, silky, airy, transparent, see-through, translucent, gauzy
formal diaphanous
Ǝ heavy, opaque, thick

gossip *n, v*
▶ *n* 1 IDLE TALK, prattle, chitchat, tittle-tattle, rumour, hearsay, report, whisper, scandal
colloq. mud-slinging, smear campaign
2 GOSSIP-MONGER, scandalmonger, whisperer, prattler, babbler, chatterbox, busybody, talebearer, tell-tale, tattler, blether
colloq. nosey parker
▶ *v* talk, chat, natter, chatter, blether, blather, gabble, prattle, babble, tattle, spread gossip, tell tales, whisper, rumour, spread/circulate a rumour
colloq. jabber, rabbit (on), gas, waffle, chinwag, jaw, chew the rag/fat

gouge *v*
chisel, cut, hack, incise, score, groove, scratch, claw, gash, slash, dig, scoop, hollow, extract

gourmand *n*
glutton, gormandizer
formal omnivore
colloq. gorger, guzzler, hog, pig
Ǝ ascetic

> ⚠ **gormand** or **gourmet** ?
> A *gourmand* is a glutton; a person who enjoys eating large quantities of food. A *gourmet* is a person who has an expert knowledge of, and a passion for, good food and wine.

gourmet *n*
gastronome, epicure, epicurean, connoisseur, bon vivant
colloq. foodie

govern *v*
1 RULE, reign, be in power, hold office, direct, manage, administer, be responsible for, superintend, supervise, oversee, preside, lead, head, be in charge of, command, order, control, influence, guide, conduct, steer, pilot
2 *govern your temper*
dominate, master, control, regulate, curb, check, keep in check, hold/keep back, restrain, contain, quell, constrain, bridle, rein in, subdue, tame, discipline

governess *n*
teacher, guide, instructress, tutoress, tutress, mentor, companion, duenna
old use gouvernante

governing *adj*
ruling, controlling, regulatory, commanding, reigning, guiding, leading, supreme, uppermost, dominant, overriding, predominant, prevailing, transcendent
formal dominative

government *n*
1 *blame the government*
administration, executive, ministry, Establishment, authorities, state, régime, congress, parliament, council, cabinet, leadership

colloq. powers that be
2 RULE, sovereignty, sway, direction, management, superintendence, supervision, surveillance, command, charge, authority, power, guidance, conduct, domination, dominion, control, regulation, restraint

Government systems include: absolutism, autocracy, commonwealth, communism, democracy, despotism, dictatorship, empire, federation, hierocracy, junta, kingdom, monarchy, plutocracy, puppet government, republic, theocracy, triumvirate. *See also* **parliaments and political assemblies.**

governor *n*
ruler, commissioner, administrator, executive, director, manager, leader, head, chief, president, viceroy, commander, superintendent, supervisor, commander, master, regulator, guide, warden, overseer, controller
colloq. boss
Related adjective: gubernatorial

gown *n*
robe, dress, frock, dressing-gown, garment, habit, costume
colloq. garb

grab *v, n*
▶ *v* seize, snatch, take, pluck, snap up, catch/take/lay hold of, grasp, clutch, grip, catch, capture, commandeer, usurp, annex
formal appropriate
colloq. nab, bag, collar, nail, swipe
▶ *n* grasp, grip, clutch, snatch, catch, capture
▷ **up for grabs** available, obtainable, at hand; *colloq.* for the asking, to be had

grace *n, v*
▶ *n* **1** GRACEFULNESS, poise, beauty, attractiveness, loveliness, shapeliness, smoothness, elegance, ease, fluency, finesse, tastefulness, good taste, refinement, polish, breeding, cultivation, manners, etiquette, decorum, decency, consideration, courtesy, charm
old use comeliness
formal propriety
2 KINDNESS, kindliness, compassion, consideration, goodness, virtue, generosity, charity, benevolence, goodwill, favour, forgiveness, indulgence, mercy, mercifulness, leniency, pardon, reprieve, quarter
formal beneficence, clemency
3 *say grace*
blessing, benediction, thanksgiving, prayer
◫ **2** cruelty, harshness
▶ *v* favour, honour, dignify, distinguish, embellish, enhance, enrich, set off, trim, garnish, decorate, ornament, adorn
◫ spoil, detract from

graceful *adj*
easy, flowing, fluid, easy, smooth, supple, agile, deft, nimble, natural, slender, fine, tasteful, elegant, beautiful, attractive, appealing, charming, tasteful, cultured, refined, polished, cultivated, suave
◫ graceless, awkward, clumsy, ungainly

graceless *adj*
clumsy, awkward, unattractive, forced, gauche, gawky, ungainly, ungraceful, inelegant, rough, rude, vulgar, coarse, crude, uncouth, unsophisticated, impolite, improper, unmannerly, ill-mannered, barbarous,

shameless
formal indecorous
◫ graceful, refined

gracious *adj*
1 POLITE, courteous, well-mannered, refined, considerate, sweet, obliging, accommodating, kind, compassionate, kind-hearted, kindly, friendly, pleasant, benevolent, generous, magnanimous, charitable, hospitable, forgiving, indulgent, lenient, mild, clement, merciful
formal beneficent
2 ELEGANT, luxurious, comfortable, tasteful, sumptuous
◫ **1** ungracious

gradation *n*
change, progression, degree, grading, sorting, ordering, progress, succession, arrangement, sequence, series, stage, step, level, mark, shading, rank
formal array

grade *n, v*
▶ *n* rank, status, standing, station, place, position, level, stage, degree, step, rating, rung, notch, mark, brand, quality, standard, condition, size, order, group, type, class, category, classification
formal echelon
▷ **make the grade** succeed, pass, come/win through, reach the expected standard
▶ *v* sort, arrange, categorize, order, group, class, rate, size, rank, range, classify, evaluate, assess, value, mark, brand, label, pigeonhole, type

gradient *n*
slope, incline, hill, bank, rise, grade
formal acclivity, declivity

gradual *adj*
slow, leisurely, unhurried, easy, gentle, moderate, regular, even, measured, steady, continuous, progressive, step-by-step
◫ sudden, steep, precipitate

gradually *adv*
little by little, bit by bit, imperceptibly, inch by inch, step by step, successively, continuously, progressively, by degrees, piecemeal, slowly, gently, cautiously, gingerly, moderately, regularly, evenly, steadily

graduate *v, n*
▶ *v* **1** *graduate from medical school*
pass, qualify, complete studies
2 CALIBRATE, mark off, measure out, proportion, grade, arrange, range, order, rank, sort, group, classify, categorize
3 PROGRESS, move up, move forward, advance, be promoted, make headway, go/forge ahead
▶ *n* qualified/skilled person, expert, specialist, consultant, professional, bachelor, doctor, master, fellow, member, graduand, alumna, alumnus, valedictorian
colloq. whizz kid

graft[1] *v, n*
▶ *v* *grafted onto a tree*
engraft, implant, insert, transplant, join, splice
formal affix
▶ *n* implant, implantation, transplant, growth, splice, bud, sprout, shoot, scion

graft[2] *n*
1 EFFORT, hard word, toil, labour
colloq. sweat of your brow, slog
2 BRIBERY, corruption, dishonesty, extortion

colloq. con tricks, shady business, dirty tricks/ dealings, wheeling and dealing, sharp practices, rip-off, sting; *slang* scam

grain *n*
1 BIT, piece, fragment, scrap, morsel, crumb, granule, particle, molecule, atom, jot, iota, mite, speck, modicum, trace, hint, suggestion, soupçon, scintilla
2 SEED, kernel, corn, cereals, wheat, rye, barley, oats, maize
3 TEXTURE, fabric, fibre, weave, pattern, marking, surface, nap

grand *adj*
1 MAJESTIC, regal, stately, palatial, splendid, magnificent, glorious, superb, sublime, exalting, fine, excellent, outstanding, first-rate, impressive, imposing, striking, monumental, large, luxurious, lavish, sumptuous, noble, lordly, lofty, pompous, pretentious, grandiose, showy, ostentatious, ambitious
formal opulent
2 SUPREME, pre-eminent, leading, head, chief, main, principal, arch, highest, senior, great, illustrious
3 *have a grand day out*
excellent, wonderful, splendid, marvellous, fantastic, superb, enjoyable, delightful, outstanding, first-rate
colloq. great, super, terrific, smashing; *slang* mega, cool, wicked
4 *a grand total*
complete, final, comprehensive, inclusive, all-inclusive, in full
◨ 1 humble, plain, simple common, poor

grandeur *n*
majesty, stateliness, pomp, state, dignity, splendour, magnificence, impressiveness, luxuriousness, lavishness, nobility, greatness, illustriousness, importance, fame, renown, eminence, prominence
formal opulence
◨ humbleness, lowliness, simplicity

grandfather *n*
grandpa, grand(d)ad, grand(d)addy

grandiloquent *adj*
exaggerated, pretentious, high-flown, high-sounding, inflated, pompous, bombastic, flowery, rhetorical, fustian, euphuistic, swollen, turgid
formal grandiloquous, magniloquent, orotund
◨ plain, restrained, simple

grandiose *adj*
pompous, pretentious, high-flown, high-sounding, lofty, ambitious, extravagant, ostentatious, showy, flamboyant, grand, majestic, splendid, striking, stately, magnificent, impressive, imposing, monumental
colloq. over-the-top
◨ unpretentious

grandmother *n*
grandma, granny, gran, nan

grant *v, n*
▶ *v* 1 GIVE, donate, present, award, impart, transmit, dispense, assign, allot, allocate, provide, supply, contribute
formal confer, bestow, apportion, furnish
2 ADMIT, acknowledge, concede, allow, permit, accept, agree to
formal consent to, accede to, vouchsafe
◨ 1 withhold 2 deny
▶ *n* allowance, subsidy, concession, award, bursary,

scholarship, gift, donation, endowment, bequest, annuity, pension, honorarium, contribution

granule *n*
piece, particle, grain, scrap, crumb, bead, speck, fragment, iota, jot, atom, molecule, pellet, seed

granular *adj*
grainy, granulated, gritty, sandy, lumpy, rough, crumbly, friable

graph *n*
diagram, chart, table, grid, plot, curve, bar graph, bar chart, pie chart, scatter diagram
technical nomogram, nomograph

graphic *adj*
1 VIVID, descriptive, expressive, striking, telling, lively, realistic, explicit, effective, clear, lucid, specific, detailed, well-defined, blow-by-blow
formal cogent
2 VISUAL, pictorial, diagrammatic, drawn, illustrative, representational
formal delineative
◨ vague, impressionistic

grapple *v*
1 GRASP, seize, snatch, grab, grip, clutch, clasp, hold, lay hold of, wrestle, tussle, struggle, contend, battle, fight, combat, clash, engage, close
2 *grapple with a problem*
face, confront, encounter, tackle, address, deal with, cope with, get to grips with
◨ release, avoid, evade

grasp *v, n*
▶ *v* 1 HOLD, clasp, clutch, grip, grapple, seize, snatch, grab, catch, lay hold of, clench
2 *grasp a concept*
understand, comprehend, follow, see, perceive, master, realize, take in, catch on, latch onto
formal apprehend
colloq. get
▶ *n* 1 GRIP, clasp, hold, embrace, clutches, possession, control, power, command, rule, dominion, mastery
2 UNDERSTANDING, comprehension, apprehension, mastery, familiarity, knowledge, awareness, perception

grasping *adj*
greedy, acquisitive, covetous, mercenary, mean, selfish, miserly, close-fisted, tight-fisted, stingy, niggardly
formal avaricious, rapacious, parsimonious
◨ generous

grass *n*
turf, lawn, green, grassland, common, field, meadow, pasture, downs, prairie, pampas, savanna, steppe, veld, veldt
old use lea, mead, sward
Related adjective: graminaceous

> *Types of grass include*: bamboo, barley, beard grass, bent, buckwheat, cane, cocksfoot, corn, couch grass, English ryegrass, esparto, fescue, Italian ryegrass, kangaroo grass, Kentucky bluegrass, knot grass, maize, marijuana, marram grass, meadow foxtail, meadow grass, millet, oats, paddy, pampas grass, papyrus, rattan, reed, rice, rye, ryegrass, sorghum, squirrel-tail grass, sugar cane, switch grass, twitch grass, wheat, wild oat.

grate *v*
1 GRIND, shred, mince, pulverize, rub, rasp, scrape,

scratch
formal triturate
2 JAR, set your teeth on edge, annoy, irritate, vex, irk, exasperate, gall, rankle
colloq. aggravate, peeve, get on your nerves, get under your skin, get someone's goat

grateful *adj*
thankful, appreciative, indebted, obliged, obligated
formal beholden
E3 ungrateful

gratification *n*
pleasure, satisfaction, contentment, delight, elation, enjoyment, joy, thrill, relish, indulgence, glee
colloq. kicks
E3 frustration, disappointment

gratify *v*
1 PLEASE, cheer, charm, gladden, delight, thrill, make happy
2 SATISFY, fulfil, indulge, pander to, humour, favour, pamper, spoil, cosset, placate
E3 1 frustrate **2** thwart

grating¹ *adj*
a grating noise
harsh, rasping, scraping, grinding, scratching, squeaky, screeching, strident, discordant, raucous, jarring, annoying, irritating, galling, unpleasant, disagreeable, offensive, exasperating, irksome
E3 harmonious, pleasing

grating² *n*
a grating over a window
grate, grille, grid, lattice, trellis, frame
technical graticule

gratis *adv*
free, without charge, free of charge, for nothing, at no cost, complimentary
colloq. on the house; *slang* buckshee

gratitude *n*
gratefulness, thankfulness, thanks, appreciation, acknowledgement, recognition, indebtedness, obligation
E3 ingratitude, ungratefulness

gratuitous *adj*
1 VIOLENCE, wanton, unnecessary, needless, superfluous, unwarranted, unjustified, groundless, unfounded, undeserved, unprovoked, uncalled-for, unasked-for, unmerited, unsolicited, without reason
2 VOLUNTARY, free, free of charge, gratis, for nothing, complimentary, unrewarded, unpaid
E3 justified, provoked

gratuity *n*
tip, bonus, gift, present, donation, reward, recompense, bounty, boon, largesse, baksheesh, pourboire
formal perquisite
colloq. perk

grave¹ *n*
1 *buried in a grave*
burial place, tomb, vault, crypt, last resting-place, sepulchre, mausoleum, pit, burial mound, burial site, barrow, tumulus, cairn
2 DEATH, loss of life, loss, departure, fatality, passing, passing away
formal expiration, decease, demise
colloq. last farewell, curtains

grave² *adj*
1 SOLEMN, dignified, sober, sedate, serious, earnest, sombre, severe, thoughtful, pensive, grim, gloomy, long-faced, quiet, reserved, subdued, restrained, staid
2 *a grave mistake*
important, significant, weighty, momentous, serious, critical, vital, crucial, urgent, pressing, acute, severe, menacing, threatening, dangerous, hazardous
formal exigent, perilous
E3 1 cheerful, smiling **2** trivial, light, slight

gravel *n*
shingle, grit, pebbles, stones, chesil, hogging
old use grail

gravelly *adj*
1 GRAINY, granular, pebbly, shingly, gritty
old use glareous
formal sabulose, sabulous
2 *a gravelly voice*
harsh, rough, thick, hoarse, guttural, throaty, grating, gruff
E3 2 clear, fine

gravestone *n*
tombstone, headstone, stone, memorial

graveyard *n*
cemetery, burial ground, burial place, burial site, churchyard
formal necropolis, charnel house, God's acre

gravitate *v*
fall, descend, drop, head for, move, precipitate, sink, incline, lean, tend, drift, be attached to, be drawn to, settle

gravity *n*
1 IMPORTANCE, significance, seriousness, weightiness, momentousness, consequence, urgency, acuteness, severity, danger, hazard
formal exigency, peril
2 SOLEMNITY, dignity, seriousness, earnestness, severity, thoughtfulness, sombreness, grimness, gloominess, reserve, restraint
formal sobriety
3 GRAVITATION, attraction, pull, weight, heaviness
E3 1 triviality **2** levity

graze¹ *v*
the cattle are grazing
crop, feed, fodder, pasture, browse
formal ruminate

graze² *v, n*
▶ *v* **1** SCRATCH, scrape, skin, bruise, rub, chafe
formal abrade
2 BRUSH, skim, touch, kiss, shave, glance off
▶ *n* scratch, scrape, abrasion

grease *n*
oil, lubrication, fat, lard, dripping, tallow

greasy *adj*
oily, fatty, lardy, buttery, smeary, slimy, slippery, smooth, waxy
formal oleaginous, oleic, adipose, sebaceous, unctuous

great *adj*
1 LARGE, big, huge, enormous, massive, colossal, gigantic, mammoth, immense, vast, extensive, boundless, spacious, impressive
colloq. great big, whopping, jumbo, ginormous;
slang mega

2 *with great care*
considerable, pronounced, substantial, sizeable, extreme, excessive, inordinate
3 FAMOUS, renowned, celebrated, famed, illustrious, eminent, distinguished, prominent, noteworthy, notable, noted, remarkable, outstanding
formal august
4 FINE, grand, glorious, impressive, imposing, magnificent, splendid
5 IMPORTANT, significant, serious, major, crucial, critical, principal, primary, main, chief, leading, essential, momentous, vital, paramount, salient
6 EXCELLENT, excellent, first-rate, superb, wonderful, marvellous, admirable, splendid, tremendous, fantastic, fabulous
colloq. super, terrific, smashing, ace, top-notch;
slang cool, mega, wicked
7 EXPERT, proficient, adept, skilled, skilful, knowledgeable, experienced, able, practised, professional, accomplished, masterly, excellent, brilliant, specialist, qualified, virtuoso, dexterous
colloq. top-notch, up on, well up on, crack, ace
E3 1 small, limited **2** slight **3** unknown
5 unimportant, insignificant **7** amateurish, novice

greatly *adv*
much, considerably, enormously, highly, extremely, immensely, vastly, noticeably, significantly, remarkably, impressively, notably, substantially, markedly, mightily, tremendously, hugely, powerfully, exceedingly, abundantly

greatness *n*
fame, renown, illustriousness, eminence, heroism, distinction, note, significance, importance, weight, momentousness, seriousness, power, magnitude, intensity, excellence, glory, genius, grandeur
E3 insignificance, pettiness, smallness

greed *n*
1 HUNGER, ravenousness, gluttony, gourmandism, insatiability
formal voracity, edacity, esurience
colloq. piggishness, hoggishness, bingeing, stuffing yourself
2 ACQUISITIVENESS, covetousness, desire, craving, longing, eagerness, impatience, selfishness
formal avarice, rapacity, cupidity
E3 1 abstemiousness, self-restraint

greedy *adj*
1 HUNGRY, starving, ravenous, gluttonous, gormandizing, insatiable
formal voracious, edacious, esurient, omnivorous
colloq. hoggish, piggish, bingeing
2 ACQUISITIVE, covetous, desirous, craving, grabbing, eager, impatient, grasping, selfish
formal avaricious, rapacious, cupidinous
colloq. on the make, grabby
E3 1 abstemious

green *adj, n*
▶ *adj* **1** GRASSY, leafy, unripe, lush, unseasoned, tender, raw, fresh, budding, blooming, flourishing, healthy, vigorous
old use virent
formal verdant, glaucous, viridescent, virescent, verdurous
2 ECOLOGICAL, environmental, conservationist, eco-friendly, environmentally aware, environmentally friendly
3 IMMATURE, naïve, simple, unsophisticated, ignorant, unqualified, inexperienced, untrained,

inexpert, unversed, raw, new, recent, young
colloq. wet behind the ears
4 *green with envy*
envious, covetous, jealous, grudging, resentful
E3 3 mature, experienced, qualified, expert
▶ *n* common, lawn, grass, turf, field, grassland, meadow, pasture
old use sward, lea

greenery *n*
foliage, vegetation, greenness
formal verdure, verdancy, viridity, viridescence, virescence

greenhorn *n*
novice, apprentice, beginner, learner, initiate, recruit, neophyte, tenderfoot, tiro, newcomer, fledgling
colloq. rookie
E3 veteran; *colloq.* old hand

greenhouse *n*
glasshouse, hothouse, conservatory, pavilion, vinery, orangery

greet *v*
salute, acknowledge, hail, address, say hello to, shake hands with, kiss, wave to, nod to, accost, meet, receive, welcome
E3 ignore

greeting *n*
salutation, acknowledgement, wave, hallo, nod, handshake, the time of day, seasonal greeting, address, reception, welcome

greetings *n*
regards, kind/warm regards, respects, compliments, best wishes, good wishes, congratulations, respects, love, salutations

gregarious *adj*
sociable, outgoing, extrovert, friendly, affable, social, companionable, convivial, cordial, warm, hospitable
E3 unsociable

grey *adj*
1 *a grey colour*
neutral, colourless, pale, pallid, ashen, wan, leaden
2 *a grey morning*
dull, cloudy, overcast, dim, dark, dismal, dreary, bleak, cheerless, foggy, misty, murky
3 GLOOMY, dismal, cheerless, depressing, dreary, bleak, dull, uninteresting, colourless
4 *a grey area*
unclear, uncertain, doubtful, ambiguous, debatable, open to question

grid *n*
grating, frame, grille, grill, gridiron, lattice, trellis
technical graticule

grief *n*
sorrow, sadness, unhappiness, depression, dejection, desolation, despondency, despair, distress, misery, woe, heartbreak, mourning, bereavement, heartache, anguish, agony, pain, suffering, trouble, regret, remorse
formal affliction, lamentation, tribulation
E3 happiness, delight

grief-stricken *adj*
sorrowful, sad, unhappy, sorrowing, grieving, mourning, depressed, dejected, desolate, despondent, distressed, despairing, broken, broken-hearted, heartbroken, inconsolable, overcome, overwhelmed, devastated, crushed, anguished, troubled, wretched

formal disconsolate, woebegone, afflicted
◳ overjoyed, delighted

grievance *n*
complaint, resentment, objection, protest, charge,
wrong, injustice, unfairness, offence, injury, damage,
trouble, hardship, trial
formal affliction, tribulation
colloq. moan, grumble, grouse, gripe, bone to pick

grieve *v*
1 SORROW, lament, mourn, wail, cry, weep, sob,
mope, brood, pine away, ache, suffer
2 SADDEN, upset, dismay, distress, afflict, pain, hurt,
wound, crush, horrify, offend, shock, break someone's
heart
◳ **1** rejoice **2** please, gladden

grievous *adj*
1 SEVERE, grave, tragic, appalling, distressing,
dreadful, atrocious, burdensome, calamitous,
devastating, damaging, shameful, harmful,
outrageous, overwhelming, shocking, deplorable,
intolerable, unbearable, monstrous, flagrant, glaring
formal sorrowful
2 WOUNDING, injurious, hurtful, painful, damaging,
sore
formal afflicting

grim *adj*
1 STERN, severe, harsh, dour, forbidding, formidable,
fierce, menacing, threatening, surly, sullen, morose,
gloomy, depressing, unattractive
2 UNPLEASANT, horrible, horrid, horrendous, dire,
ghastly, gruesome, grisly, sinister, dreadful, awful,
frightening, fearsome, terrible, shocking, appalling,
harrowing, unspeakable
3 RESOLUTE, determined, dogged, tenacious,
persistent, stubborn, inexorable, unyielding,
unshakable
formal obdurate
◳ **1** attractive **2** pleasant

grimace *n, v*
▶ *n* frown, scowl, pout, smirk, sneer, face
▶ *v* pull a face, make a face, frown, scowl, pout,
smirk, mouth, sneer

grime *n*
dirt, muck, filth, soot, dust, mud
colloq. gunge, yuck, grot; *slang* crud, grunge

grimy *adj*
dirty, mucky, grubby, soiled, stained, filthy, sooty,
smutty, dusty, muddy, smudgy
formal besmirched
◳ clean

grind *v, n*
▶ *v* **1** CRUSH, pound, pulverize, crumble, powder,
mill, granulate, grate, scrape, gnash
formal kibble, levigate, comminute, triturate
2 SHARPEN, whet, smooth, polish, sand, file, rub,
abrade
3 GRATE, scrape, rub, rasp, grind
▷ **grind down** wear down, oppress, crush, trouble,
persecute, plague, torment, harass, harry, hound,
tyrannize; *formal* afflict
▶ *n* drudgery, chore, toil, labour, round, routine,
exertion, task, slavery, sweat

grip *n, v*
▶ *n* **1** HOLD, grasp, clasp, clutch, embrace, clench,
hug
2 CONTROL, power, command, influence, mastery,

domination, clutches
3 BAG, case, hold-all, kitbag, shoulder-bag, valise,
suitcase, overnight bag, travelling bag
▷ **come/get to grips with** deal with, tackle, cope
with, take care of, look after, encounter, confront,
face up to, take on, grasp
▶ *v* **1** HOLD, grasp, clasp, get/catch/grab hold of,
clutch, clench, latch onto, cling, seize, grab, catch
2 FASCINATE, thrill, enthral, spellbind, mesmerize,
hypnotize, entrance, rivet, engross, absorb, involve,
engage, compel

gripe *v, n*
▶ *v* complain, grumble, protest, moan, nag, groan
colloq. beef, bellyache, carp, grouch, grouse, whine,
whinge, bitch, have a bone to pick
▶ *n* complaint, groan, grumble, moan, objection,
protest, grievance
colloq. beef, grouch, grouse, griping, bitch

gripping *adj*
fascinating, thrilling, enthralling, compelling,
compulsive, exciting, suspenseful, spellbinding,
entrancing, riveting, engrossing, absorbing
colloq. unputdownable

grisly *adj*
gruesome, gory, grim, macabre, horrid, horrible,
horrifying, ghastly, awful, frightful, terrible, dreadful,
repulsive, revolting, disgusting, hideous, macabre,
loathsome, abhorrent, abominable, appalling,
shocking
◳ delightful

grit *n, v*
▶ *n* **1** GRAVEL, pebbles, shingle, sand, dust
Related adjectives: sabulous, sabulose
2 DETERMINATION, courage, bravery, strength,
resolve, resolution, hardness, toughness, mettle,
endurance, perseverance, doggedness, steadfastness,
tenacity
colloq. backbone, guts
▶ *v* clench, gnash, grate, rasp, scrape, grind

gritty *adj*
1 GRAINY, dusty, gravelly, sandy, shingly, pebbly,
powdery, granular, rough, abrasive
formal sabulous, sabulose
2 DETERMINED, courageous, brave, resolute, hardy,
tough, mettlesome, dogged, tenacious, steadfast,
spirited, plucky
colloq. spunky
◳ **1** fine, smooth **2** cowardly; *colloq.* spineless

grizzle *v*
cry, whimper, whine, whinge, sniffle, snivel, snuffle,
fret, moan, complain, grumble

grizzled *adj*
grey, grey-haired, grey-headed, greying, hoary, hoar,
pepper-and-salt
technical griseous
formal canescent

groan *n, v*
▶ *n* **1** MOAN, sigh, cry, whine, whimper, wail, lament
2 COMPLAINT, grumble, objection, protest, outcry,
grievance, moan
colloq. beef, grouch, grouse, griping
▶ *v* **1** MOAN, sigh, cry, whine, whimper, wail, lament
2 COMPLAIN, grumble, object, protest
colloq. whine, whinge, beef, bellyache, grouse

grocer *n*
dealer, storekeeper, supplier, supermarket,

greengrocer
formal purveyor, victualler

groggy *adj*
weak, dopey, unsteady, wobbly, shaky, staggering,
stunned, dazed, confused, befuddled, bewildered,
stupefied, punch-drunk, dizzy, faint, reeling
colloq. muzzy, woozy
E3 healthy, strong, lucid

groom *v, n*
▶ *v* **1** SMARTEN, neaten, tidy (up), spruce up,
prepare, put in order, arrange, adjust, fix, do, smooth
2 CLEAN, brush, curry, preen, dress
3 *groomed for her new post*
prepare, make ready, train, school, teach, educate,
instruct, tutor, drill, coach, prime
▶ *n* **1** BRIDEGROOM, honeymooner, newly-wed,
husband, spouse, marriage partner
2 STABLEBOY, stableman, stable lad/lass, stable hand

groove *n*
furrow, rut, track, slot, channel, canal, chamfer, gutter,
trough, ditch, trench, hollow, gouge, indentation, cut,
score, ridge
technical rabbet, rebate, sulcus
Related adjective: sulcal

grooved *adj*
channelled, fluted, furrowed, rutted, scored,
chamfered
technical rabbeted, scrobiculate
formal sulcal, sulcate, exarate
E3 ridged

grope *v*
1 FUMBLE, feel, scrabble, flounder, pick
2 SEARCH, hunt, scrabble, fish, probe, cast about

gross *adj, v*
▶ *adj* **1** *gross misconduct*
serious, grievous, blatant, flagrant, glaring, obvious,
plain, sheer, utter, outright, shameful, shocking,
outrageous
formal manifest, egregious
2 OBSCENE, lewd, improper, dirty, filthy, risqué,
pornographic, indecent, offensive, rude, coarse, crude,
vulgar, ribald, bawdy, smutty, earthy, improper,
tasteless
colloq. blue
3 FAT, obese, overweight, big, large, huge, colossal,
immense, massive, hulking, bulky, heavy
formal corpulent
4 TASTELESS, vulgar, unpleasant, uncultured,
unsophisticated, unrefined, insensitive, coarse,
boorish
5 *gross earnings*
inclusive, all-inclusive, total, entire, complete,
comprehensive, whole, before deductions, before tax
formal aggregate
E3 **2** polite **3** slight **4** tasteful **5** net
▶ *v* earn, make, take, bring in, accumulate, total
formal aggregate
colloq. rake in

grotesque *adj*
bizarre, odd, weird, strange, peculiar, unnatural,
freakish, monstrous, hideous, ugly, unsightly,
misshapen, deformed, malformed, distorted, twisted,
fantastic, fanciful, whimsical, extravagant, ridiculous,
ludicrous, absurd, outlandish, surreal, macabre
E3 normal, graceful

grotto *n*
cave, cavern, chamber, catacomb, underground
chamber, subterranean (chamber)

grouch *n*
1 COMPLAINER, grumbler, moaner, fault-finder,
murmurer, mutterer, grouser
formal malcontent
colloq. belly-acher, crosspatch, whiner, whinger,
2 COMPLAINT, grievance, grumble, objection, moan
colloq. gripe, grouse, whinge

grouchy *adj*
bad-tempered, irritable, cross, dissatisfied,
discontented, grumpy, sulky, surly, complaining,
grumbling, testy, ill-tempered, irascible, captious,
churlish, peevish, petulant
formal cantankerous, querulous, truculent
colloq. crotchety
E3 contented

ground *n, v*
▶ *n* **1** EARTH, soil, clay, loam, dirt, dust, dry land,
terra firma, land, terrain, bottom, foundation, surface
2 *a football ground*
field, pitch, stadium, arena, park
3 *the palace grounds*
estate, property, territory, domain, gardens, park,
campus, surroundings, fields, acres, land, terrain,
holding, plot
4 *no grounds for such harsh treatment*
base, foundation, justification, excuse, vindication,
reason, motive, inducement, cause, occasion, call,
score, account, argument, principle, basis
5 *coffee grounds*
dregs, sediment, deposit, residue, lees, scourings
technical precipitate
▶ *v* **1** BASE, found, establish, set, fix, settle
2 PREPARE, introduce, initiate, familiarize with,
acquaint with, inform, instruct, teach, educate, train,
drill, coach, tutor

groundless *adj*
baseless, unfounded, unsubstantiated, unsupported,
empty, imaginary, false, illusory, unjustified,
unwarranted, unprovoked, uncalled-for, without
reason
E3 well-founded, reasonable, justified

groundwork *n*
basis, base, essentials, foundation, fundamentals,
preparation, preliminaries, research, homework,
cornerstone, footing, spadework, underpinnings

group *n, v*
▶ *n* band, gang, pack, team, crew, troop, squad,
detachment, unit, party, faction, set, circle, clique,
coterie, contingent, club, society, association, guild,
league, organization, company, gathering,
congregation, body, assembly, crowd, flock, collection,
bunch, clump, cluster, knot, batch, lot, combination,
element, bracket, formation, grouping, class, category,
classification, genus, species, family, school
formal conglomeration
▶ *v* **1** GATHER, collect, assemble, congregate, mass,
cluster, clump, bunch, huddle
2 *group them according to size*
sort, range, arrange, marshal, line up, organize, order,
rank, grade, class, classify, categorize, band, bracket,
link, associate

grouse *v, n*
▶ *v* complain, grumble, moan, find fault
colloq. beef, bellyache, carp, grouch, gripe, whine,

whinge, bitch
🔁 acquiesce
► *n* complaint, groan, grumble, moan, objection, protest, grievance
colloq. bellyache, gripe, grouch, whine, whinge

grove *n*
wood, woodland, thicket, spinney, coppice, copse, plantation, covert, arbour, avenue
Related adjective: nemoral

grovel *v*
1 INGRATIATE YOURSELF, crawl, creep, toady, flatter, fawn, cringe, cower, kowtow, defer, demean yourself
colloq. butter someone up, suck up, bow and scrape, lick someone's boots, kiss up to
2 CRAWL, creep, kneel, crouch, stoop, lie low, prostrate yourself, lie down, bow down, cower, fall on your knees

grow *v*
1 BECOME LARGER, become taller/bigger, increase in size/height, extend, develop, expand, enlarge, lengthen, elongate, widen, broaden, thicken, deepen, swell, fill out
2 GERMINATE, shoot, sprout, spring, bud, flower, mature, develop
formal burgeon
3 INCREASE, rise, expand, enlarge, swell, spread, extend, stretch, develop, multiply, escalate, mushroom, wax
formal proliferate
4 *grow cold*
become, get, go, turn, come to be, change, develop
5 PROGRESS, thrive, flourish, prosper, succeed, improve, advance, make headway
6 ORIGINATE, arise, issue, stem, spring
7 CULTIVATE, farm, produce, propagate, breed, raise, sow, plant, harvest
🔁 1 shrink 3 decrease 5 fail

growl *v*
snarl, snap, yap, bark, howl, yelp, rumble, roar

grown-up *adj, n*
► *adj* adult, mature, of age, full-grown, fully-grown, fully-developed, fully-fledged
🔁 young, immature
► *n* adult, man, woman
🔁 child

growth *n*
1 INCREASE, rise, extension, enlargement, expansion, spread, multiplication, magnification, amplification, deepening, development, evolution, progress, advance, improvement, success, headway, prosperity
formal proliferation, augmentation, aggrandizement
2 GERMINATION, shooting, sprouting, springing, budding, flowering, development
formal maturation, burgeoning
3 TUMOUR, tumour, lump, swelling, protuberance, outgrowth
technical intumescence, excrescence
🔁 1 decrease, decline, failure

grub *v, n*
► *v* dig, burrow, delve, excavate, probe, root, rummage, forage, ferret, hunt, search, scour, unearth, uncover, explore
► *n* 1 LARVA, maggot, worm, pupa, caterpillar, chrysalis
2 FOOD, provision, meals, refreshment(s),

sustenance, nutrition
colloq. eats, tuck; *slang* nosh

grubby *adj*
dirty, soiled, unwashed, mucky, grimy, filthy, squalid, seedy, messy, scruffy, shabby
🔁 clean

grudge *n, v*
► *n* resentment, bitterness, envy, jealousy, pique, spite, malice, enmity, antagonism, hate, hatred, venom, dislike, animosity, antipathy, aversion, ill-will, hard feelings, grievance
formal malevolence, rancour, animus
🔁 favour
► *v* begrudge, resent, envy, covet, be jealous of, dislike, take exception to, object to, mind

grudging *adj*
reluctant, unwilling, hesitant, half-hearted, unenthusiastic, resentful, envious, jealous

gruelling *adj*
hard, difficult, taxing, demanding, tiring, exhausting, laborious, arduous, strenuous, trying, backbreaking, draining, crushing, grinding, harsh, severe, tough, punishing
🔁 easy

gruesome *adj*
horrible, disgusting, repellent, repugnant, repulsive, revolting, sickening, hideous, grisly, macabre, grim, ghastly, awful, terrible, horrific, horrid, frightful, dreadful, appalling, shocking, monstrous, abhorrent, abominable, loathsome
🔁 pleasant

gruff *adj*
1 CURT, brusque, abrupt, blunt, rude, surly, sour, sullen, grumpy, bad-tempered, churlish, testy, tetchy, rude, impolite, unfriendly, discourteous
colloq. crotchety, crabbed
2 *a gruff voice*
rough, harsh, rasping, guttural, throaty, husky, hoarse, croaking, thick
🔁 1 friendly, courteous, polite

grumble *v, n*
► *v* 1 COMPLAIN, moan, object, protest, bleat, find fault
colloq. bellyache, beef, grouch, gripe, whine, whinge, carp
2 RUMBLE, murmur, gurgle, growl
► *n* 1 COMPLAINT, moan, grievance, objection, protest
colloq. beef, gripe, grouch, grouse, whinge, bleat, bitch
2 RUMBLE, murmur, muttering, gurgle, growl, roar

grumpy *adj*
bad-tempered, ill-tempered, churlish, cross, irritable, surly, sullen, sulky, tetchy, snappy, petulant, discontented
formal cantankerous
colloq. crotchety, crabbed, grouchy, ratty, in a huff, in a sulk, having got out of bed on the wrong side
🔁 contented

guarantee *n, v*
► *n* warranty, insurance, assurance, promise, word of honour, pledge, oath, bond, covenant, contract, security, collateral, surety, endorsement, testimonial
formal earnest
► *v* assure, give an assurance, promise, pledge, swear, vouch for, answer for, warrant, certify, underwrite, provide security/collateral/surety for, endorse,

support, back, sponsor, secure, protect, insure, ensure, make sure, make certain

guarantor *n*
underwriter, guarantee, sponsor, supporter, backer, surety, warrantor, referee, voucher, bondsman, bailsman, covenantor
colloq. angel

guard *v, n*
▶ *v* protect, safeguard, save, preserve, shield, secure, screen, shelter, cover, defend, patrol, police, escort, supervise, oversee, watch, keep watch, be alert, look out, take care, mind, beware
▶ *n* **1** PROTECTOR, defender, custodian, warder, escort, bodyguard, keeper, conductor, watch, scout, watchman, lookout, sentry, sentinel, picket, patrol, security, guardian
slang minder
2 PROTECTION, safeguard, defence, wall, barrier, fence, screen, shield, bumper, fender, buffer, pad, cushion
▷ **off your guard** careless, unprepared, unaware(s), unready, unwary, inattentive, napping, unsuspecting, surprised, with your defences down; *colloq.* red-handed, with your pants down
▷ **on your guard** alert, watchful, vigilant, cautious, careful, ready, prepared, attentive, on the lookout, wary, wide awake, on the alert; *formal* circumspect

guarded *adj*
cautious, wary, chary, careful, watchful, discreet, non-committal, reluctant, reticent, reserved, restrained, secretive
formal circumspect
colloq. cagey
F∃ communicative, frank

guardian *n*
trustee, curator, custodian, steward, caretaker, keeper, warden, protector, preserver, defender, champion, guard, warder, escort, attendant

guardianship *n*
trust, care, guidance, trusteeship, curatorship, custodianship, custody, tutelage, stewardship, patronage, attendance, guard, hands, keeping, wardenship, wardship, preservation, protection, safekeeping, defence
formal aegis

guerrilla *n*
freedomfighter, terrorist, irregular, resistance fighter, partisan, sniper, guerrillero, franc-tireur, haiduck, bushwhacker, maquisard

guess *v, n*
▶ *v* speculate, make a guess, predict, estimate, judge, reckon, hypothesize, work out, put something at, suppose, assume, think, believe, judge, consider, imagine, fancy, feel, suspect
formal conjecture, surmise, postulate
colloq. guesstimate
▶ *n* prediction, estimate, speculation, assumption, belief, judgement, reckoning, fancy, idea, notion, theory, hypothesis, guesswork, opinion, feeling, suspicion, intuition, hunch
formal conjecture, supposition, surmise
colloq. guesstimate, ballpark figure, shot in the dark

guesswork *n*
speculation, estimation, reckoning, prediction, assumption, intuition, theory, hypothesis

formal conjecture, supposition, surmise
colloq. guesstimate

guest *n*
visitor, caller, boarder, lodger, resident, patron, regular
formal visitant

guesthouse *n*
boarding-house, hostel, hostelry, inn, hotel, pension, rooming-house
formal xenodochium

guidance *n*
leadership, direction, management, rule, charge, control, teaching, instruction, advice, counsel, counselling, help, assistance, information, instructions, directions, guidelines, indication(s), pointer(s), hint(s), tip(s), recommendation(s), suggestion(s)

guide *v, n*
▶ *v* **1** LEAD, conduct, direct, navigate, point, steer, pilot, manoeuvre, usher, escort, show, show the way, accompany, attend; *colloq.* hold someone's hand
2 CONTROL, govern, manage, direct, be in charge of, rule, preside over, oversee, supervise, superintend, command
3 ADVISE, counsel, give directions/recommendations to, influence, educate, teach, instruct, train
▶ *n* **1** MANUAL, handbook, guidebook, catalogue, directory, key, ABC
2 LEADER, courier, navigator, pilot, helmsman, steersman, conductor, director, ranger, usher, escort, chaperon, attendant, companion
3 ADVISER, counsellor, mentor, guru, teacher, instructor, tutor
4 GUIDELINE, example, model, pattern, norm, gauge, standard, criterion, measure, benchmark, yardstick, tombstone, indication, pointer, signpost, sign, signal, key, marker, mark, beacon
formal exemplar, archetype

guideline *n*
instruction, recommendation, suggestion, direction, advice, information, indication rule, regulation, standard, criterion, measure, benchmark, yardstick, touchstone, framework, parameter, constraint, procedure, principle, terms

guild *n*
organization, association, alliance, federation, society, club, union, fellowship, league, order, company, chapel, brotherhood, lodge, fraternity, sorority, corporation, incorporation

guile *n*
deceit, deception, cunning, treachery, double-dealing, fraud, trickery, trickiness, wiliness, cleverness, slyness, craft, craftiness, deviousness, artfulness, artifice, ruse, gamesmanship, knavery
formal duplicity
F∃ artlessness, guilelessness

guileless *adj*
artless, direct, straight, straightforward, genuine, honest, frank, sincere, trusting, truthful, innocent, naïve, candid, natural, open, simple, transparent, unreserved, unsophisticated, unworldly
formal ingenuous
F∃ artful, cunning

guilt *n*
1 *he confessed his guilt*
responsibility, blame, blameworthiness, disgrace, dishonour, wrong, wrongdoing, criminality, misconduct, unlawfulness
formal culpability
2 *a feeling of guilt*
guilty conscience, conscience, disgrace, dishonour, shame, self-condemnation, self-reproach, self-accusation, regret, remorse, contrition, repentance, penitence
formal compunction
◳ **1** innocence, righteousness **2** shamelessness

guiltless *adj*
blameless, innocent, clear, clean, pure, irreproachable, above reproach, sinless, spotless, faultless, stainless, immaculate, impeccable, unblamable, unimpeachable, undefiled, unspotted, unsullied, untainted, untarnished
formal inculpable
◳ guilty, tainted

guilty *adj*
1 *guilty of a crime*
responsible, blamable, blameworthy, to blame, at fault, offending, wrong, illegal, unlawful, illicit, sinful, wicked, delinquent, criminal, convicted, evil
formal culpable
2 CONSCIENCE-STRICKEN, ashamed, guilt-ridden, bad, with a bad conscience, shamefaced, sheepish, sorry, regretful, remorseful, contrite, penitent, repentant
formal compunctious
◳ **1** innocent, guiltless, blameless **2** shameless

guise *n*
appearance, form, shape, features, likeness, manner, disguise, mask, pretence, show, façade, front, behaviour, custom, air, aspect, face, semblance
formal demeanour

gulf *n*
1 BAY, bight, cove, inlet, basin
2 GAP, opening, separation, division, rift, split, breach, cleft, fissure, crevice, chasm, gorge, hole, ravine, abyss, void, hollow, canyon

gullet *n*
throat, craw, crop, maw
technical oesophagus
old use weasand
Related adjective: oesophageal

gullibility *n*
credulity, innocence, simplicity, naïvety, trustfulness, foolishness
◳ astuteness

gullible *adj*
credulous, suggestible, impressionable, trusting, trustful, ingenuous, unsuspecting, easily deceived, foolish, naïve, green, inexperienced, unsophisticated, innocent
colloq. wet behind the ears
◳ astute

gully *n*
channel, ravine, gorge, valley, canyon, watercourse, gutter, ditch

gulp *v, n*
▶ *v* swallow, swig, swill, quaff, bolt, gobble, guzzle, devour, stuff
colloq. knock back, wolf, tuck into

◳ sip, nibble
▶ *n* swallow, swig, draught, mouthful

gum *n, v*
▶ *n* adhesive, glue, paste, cement, fixative, resin
Related adjective: mucilaginous
▶ *v* stick, glue, paste, fix, cement, seal, clog
formal affix
▷ **gum up** obstruct, hinder, impede, choke, clog

gummy *adj*
sticky, adhesive, gluey, gooey, tacky, viscous
formal viscid

gumption *n*
common sense, initiative, resourcefulness, cleverness, astuteness, nous, enterprise, shrewdness, wit, discernment, acumen, ability, acuteness
formal sagacity
colloq. savvy
◳ foolishness

gun *n*
firearm, handgun, pistol, revolver, automatic repeater, Colt®, Winchester®, rifle, shotgun, machine-gun, airgun, carbine, bazooka, howitzer, flintlock, blunderbuss, musket, cannon, mortar, machine-gun, fusil
colloq. shooter, shooting iron

gunman *n*
assassin, terrorist, thug, killer, murderer, bandit, gangster, sniper, mobster, shootist, bravo, desperado, gunslinger
colloq. hatchet man, hit man

gurgle *v, n*
▶ *v* **1** BABBLE, bubble, burble, murmur, ripple, lap, splash, plash, crow
2 BURBLE, crow, babble
▶ *n* **1** BABBLE, bubbling, murmur, ripple
2 BURBLE, crow, babble

guru *n*
expert, authority, instructor, master, teacher, tutor, leader, mentor, luminary, guiding light, pundit, maharishi, Svengali, swami, sage

gush *v, n*
▶ *v* **1** FLOW, run, pour, stream, surge, cascade, flood, rush, burst, spurt, spout, jet, well, issue
2 ENTHUSE, effervesce, bubble over, effuse, chatter, babble, fuss, jabber, blather, drivel
colloq. go on
▶ *n* flow, outflow, stream, surge, torrent, cascade, flood, tide, rush, burst, outburst, spurt, spout, outpouring, spate, jet

gushing *adj*
effusive, over-enthusiastic, excessive, cloying, emotional, saccharine, sentimental, sickly, fulsome, gushy, mawkish
◳ restrained, sincere

gust *n, v*
▶ *n* blast, burst, rush, flurry, blow, puff, breeze, wind, gale, storm, squall, surge, outburst, outbreak, fit, eruption
▶ *v* blast, blow, puff, squall, bluster, breeze, rush, surge, burst out, erupt

gusto *n*
zest, relish, appreciation, enjoyment, pleasure, delight, enthusiasm, exhilaration, exuberance, energy, fervour, élan, verve, zeal
◳ distaste, apathy

gusty *adj*
stormy, blowy, squally, windy, blustering, blustery, breezy, tempestuous
F3 calm

gut *n, v, adj*
▶ *n* **1** INTESTINES, bowels, viscera, entrails, vital organs, insides, belly, stomach
colloq. innards
Related adjectives: enteral, enteric, splanchnic
2 *have the guts to own up*
courage, bravery, pluck, boldness, audacity, tenacity, nerve, mettle
formal fortitude
colloq. grit, backbone, bottle, spunk
▶ *v* **1** *gut fish*
disembowel, draw, clean (out)
formal eviscerate, exenterate
2 STRIP, clear, empty, rifle, ransack, plunder, loot, sack, rob, destroy, devastate, ravage, clear out
▶ *adj* instinctive, intuitive, emotional, unthinking, basic, deep-seated, heartfelt, innate, involuntary, natural, spontaneous, strong

gutless *adj*
weak, cowardly, feeble, irresolute, timid, faint-hearted, craven, abject
colloq. chicken, chicken-hearted, chicken-livered, lily-livered, spineless
F3 courageous

gutsy *adj*
bold, brave, courageous, determined, resolute, plucky, indomitable, mettlesome, passionate, spirited, staunch, gallant, game
F3 quiet, timid

gutter *n*
drain, sluice, sewer, ditch, trench, trough, channel, duct, conduit, culvert, passage, pipe, tube

guttersnipe *n*
urchin, waif, ragamuffin, gamin, mudlark, tatterdemalion

guttural *adj*
rasping, throaty, croaking, hoarse, harsh, gruff, rough, grating, gravelly, husky, deep, low, thick
F3 dulcet

guy *n*
fellow, man, boy, youth, lad, person, individual, character
colloq. bloke, chap

guzzle *v*
bolt, devour, gobble, gormandize, stuff, cram, gulp, swallow, swill, quaff, swig
colloq. wolf, scoff, polish off, put away, tuck into, knock back

Gypsy, Gipsy *n*
Romany, traveller, rom, rye, wanderer, roamer, rover, rambler, hawker, huckster, nomad, tzigany, Zigeuner, Zincalo, Zingaro, Bohemian, tinker, diddicoy

gyrate *v*
turn, revolve, rotate, twirl, pirouette, spin, whirl, wheel, swirl, swivel, circle, spiral

gyration *n*
turn, revolution, rotation, twirl, pirouette, spin, spinning, whirl, whirling, swirl, swivel, wheeling, circle, spiral
formal convolution

H

habit *n*
1 CUSTOM, usage, practice, routine, rule, procedure, matter of course, second nature, way(s), manner, mannerism, mode, policy, wont, inclination, tendency, leaning, bent, mannerism, quirk
formal propensity, proclivity
2 ADDICTION, dependence, fixation, obsession, weakness
3 GARMENT, costume, dress, clothing, outfit, uniform, robe, vestment
colloq. get-up, gear, togs

habitable *adj*
fit to live in, suitable to live in, good enough to live in, inhabitable

habitat *n*
home, domain, element, environment, surroundings, dwelling, locality, territory, terrain
formal abode

habitation *n*
1 OCCUPANCY, occupation, quarters, residence, tenancy, housing, lodging, inhabitance, inhabitancy, inhabitation
2 HOME, house, cottage, accommodation, flat, apartment, hut, quarters, living quarters, lodging, mansion
formal abode, domicile, dwelling, dwelling-place, residence, residency
colloq. digs, pad, joint, roof over your head

habitual *adj*
1 CUSTOMARY, traditional, accustomed, routine, usual, ordinary, common, natural, normal, set, standard, regular, recurrent, fixed, established, familiar
formal wonted
2 *habitual drinker*
confirmed, inveterate, chronic, hardened, addicted, dependent, constant, persistent, obsessive
F3 1 occasional, infrequent

habituate *v*
acclimatize, accustom, make used to, adapt, familiarize, make familiar with, break in, condition, train, school, discipline, tame, harden, inure, season

habitué *n*
regular, regular customer, frequenter, patron, denizen

hack¹ *v*
hacked them to death
cut, chop, hew, fell, saw, clear, notch, gash, slash, lacerate, mutilate, mangle

hack² *n*
write as a hack
scribbler, writer, journalist, drudge, slave

hackle *n*
▷ **make someone's hackles rise** anger, annoy, irritate, irk, vex, rile, make angry, needle, nettle,

bother, ruffle, provoke, antagonize, offend, affront, gall, madden, enrage, incense, infuriate, exasperate, outrage; *colloq.* aggravate, miff, make your blood boil, bug, hassle, rub up the wrong way, get someone's blood up, get on your nerves

hackneyed *adj*
stale, overworked, overused, tired, worn-out, time-worn, threadbare, wearing thin, unoriginal, cliché-ridden, clichéed, stereotyped, stock, banal, trite, commonplace, common, pedestrian, uninspired, unimaginative
formal platitudinous
colloq. corny, run-of-the-mill, yawn-making
F3 original, new, fresh

hag *n*
crone, witch, shrew, gorgon, termagant, vixen, virago, harridan, fury, harpy
colloq. battle-axe

haggard *adj*
drawn, gaunt, careworn, thin, wasted, drained, shrunken, pinched, hollow-cheeked, pale, pallid, wan, ghastly
F3 hale

haggle *v*
bargain, negotiate, barter, beat down, chaffer, higgle, wrangle, squabble, bicker, quarrel, dispute
US dicker

hail¹ *v*
1 GREET, address, acknowledge, salute, say hello to, nod to, wave to
2 SIGNAL TO, flag down, wave to, call out to
3 ACCLAIM, applaud, honour, welcome, praise, cheer, exalt
formal laud
4 *hail from Malawi*
come, originate, have your home/roots in, be born in

hail² *n, v*
▶ *n a hail of arrows*
barrage, bombardment, volley, torrent, shower, rain, storm
▶ *v* pelt, bombard, shower, rain, batter, attack, assail

hair *n*
locks, tresses, shock, mop, mane, fleece, wool, coat, fur, pelt, hide
▷ **let your hair down** relax, let yourself go, throw off your inhibitions; *colloq.* hang loose, loosen up; *slang* let it all hang out, chill out
▷ **not turn a hair** calm, remain composed; *colloq.* see it coming, not bat an eyelid, keep your cool, stay cool
▷ **split hairs** find fault, quibble, cavil, argue over unimportant details; *colloq.* nit-pick
Related adjectives: pilose, pileous, crinal, capillaceous, trichoid

hair's-breadth *n*
fraction, hair, inch, jot
colloq. whisker
⊟ mile

hairdo *n*
hairstyle, coiffure, cut, haircut, style, set

hairdresser *n*
hairstylist, stylist, barber, coiffeur, coiffeuse

hairless *adj*
bald, bald-headed, shorn, tonsured, shaven, clean-shaven, beardless
⊟ hairy, hirsute

hair-raising *adj*
frightening, scary, terrifying, horrifying, shocking, bloodcurdling, spine-chilling, petrifying, eerie, alarming, startling, thrilling, exciting
colloq. creepy

hairstyle *n*
style, coiffure, cut, haircut, set
colloq. hairdo

Hairstyles include: Afro, backcombed, bangs, beehive, bob, bouffant, braid, bun, chignon, corn rows, cowlick, crewcut, crimped, crop, curled, dreadlocks, duck's arse, DA, Eton crop, French pleat, fringe, frizette, marcel wave, mohican, pageboy, perm, pigtail, plait, pompadour, ponytail, pouffe, quiff, ringlets, shingle, short back and sides, sideboards, sideburns, skinhead, tonsure, topknot, undercut; hair-piece, toupee, wig.

hairy *adj*
hirsute, bearded, shaggy, bushy, fuzzy, furry, woolly, fleecy, unshaven
formal pilose, crinose, crinigerous, crinite
⊟ bald, clean-shaven

halcyon *adj*
peaceful, happy, flourishing, prosperous, carefree, calm, balmy, mild, gentle, golden, pacific, placid, quiet, serene, still, tranquil, undisturbed
⊟ stormy

hale *adj*
healthy, fit, well, youthful, strong, sound, vigorous, robust, flourishing, athletic, hearty, able-bodied, blooming
colloq. in the pink, in fine fettle
⊟ ill

half *n, adj, adv*
▶ *n* fifty per cent, equal part/share, bisection, hemisphere, semicircle, section, segment, portion, share, fraction
▶ *adj* semi-, halved, divided, divided in two, bisected, hemispherical, fractional, part, partial, incomplete, moderate, limited, slight
⊟ whole
▶ *adv* partly, partially, incompletely, inadequately, insufficiently, moderately, slightly, barely
⊟ completely
▷ **by half** very, considerably, excessively, too
▷ **by halves** incompletely, imperfectly, inadequately, insufficiently
⊟ thoroughly
▷ **not half 1** *not half as clever* not at all, not nearly
2 *not half get into trouble* very, very much, really, indeed

half-baked *adj*
impractical, stupid, ill-conceived, unplanned, undeveloped, ill-judged, short-sighted, silly, crazy, foolish, senseless
colloq. harebrained, crackpot
⊟ sensible, thought out

half-caste *n*
Creole, griff(e), mestee, mestiza, mestizo, metif, Métis, Métisse, miscegen, miscegene, miscegine, mongrel, mulatta, mulatto, mulattress, quadroon, quarteroon, quarter-blood, quintroon, sambo

half-hearted *adj*
lukewarm, cool, weak, feeble, passive, apathetic, lacklustre, listless, uninterested, unenthusiastic, indifferent, unconcerned, neutral
⊟ whole-hearted, enthusiastic

halfway *adv, adj*
▶ *adv* midway, in/to the middle, centrally
▶ *adj* middle, central, equidistant, mid, midway, intermediate, mean, median
▷ **meet someone halfway** compromise, negotiate, make concessions, come to/reach an understanding, give and take, steer a middle course, find a happy medium, make a deal; *colloq.* go fifty-fifty with, split the difference

halfwit *n*
fool, blockhead, fat-head, dunce, dimwit, simpleton, idiot, cretin, imbecile, ignoramus, moron, dupe, stooge, butt, laughing-stock, clown, comic, buffoon, jester
colloq. nincompoop, ass, chump, ninny, clot, dope, twit, nitwit, nit, sucker, mug, twerp, birdbrain;
slang wally, dumbo, pillock, prat, dork, geek, plonker, prick
⊟ brain

half-witted *adj*
simple-minded, feeble-minded, silly, foolish, idiotic, stupid, crazy, dull, moronic, simple
colloq. dim-witted, crack-brained, crackpot, dumb, dotty, potty, batty, barmy, nutty, two bricks short of a load
⊟ clever

hall *n*
1 HALLWAY, corridor, passage, passageway, entrance-hall, foyer, vestibule, lobby
2 CONCERT-HALL, auditorium, chamber, assembly room, conference hall

hallmark *n*
1 *a hallmark on gold*
official mark/stamp, mark/stamp of authenticity
2 *the hallmark of her music*
typical quality, distinctive feature, stamp, mark, trademark, brand-name, sign, indication, indicator, symbol, emblem, device, badge

hallowed *adj*
honoured, revered, sacred, sacrosanct, blessed, sanctified, consecrated, holy, dedicated, established, inviolable, age-old

hallucinate *v*
dream, imagine, imagine things, see things, see visions, daydream, fantasize
slang freak out, trip

hallucination *n*
illusion, mirage, vision, apparition, dream, daydream, fantasy, figment, figment of the imagination, delusion,

delirium, phantasmagoria
slang freak-out, trip

halo *n*
circle of light, crown, ring, corona, glory, nimbus, radiance, aura, aureole, aureola, gloria, gloriole, halation

halt *v, n*
▶ *v* stop, come/bring to a stop, draw up, pull up, pause, wait, rest, break off, finish, bring/draw to a close, end, put an end to, check, stem, curb, obstruct, block, arrest, crush, hold back, impede
formal discontinue, cease, desist, terminate
colloq. quit, call it a day
E3 start, continue
▶ *n* stop, stoppage, arrest, interruption, break, interval, pause, rest, respite, breathing-space, standstill, end, close, deadlock, stalemate
formal termination, cessation, discontinuance, discontinuation, desistance
E3 start, continuation

halting *adj*
hesitant, stuttering, stammering, faltering, stumbling, fumbling for words, uncertain, broken, imperfect, laboured, awkward, unsteady
E3 fluent, certain

halve *v*
bisect, cut in half, split in two, divide, divide equally, split, sever, share, cut down, reduce, lessen
formal dichotomize

halved *adj*
divided, split, cut, shared, bisected
formal dimidiate

hammer *v, n*
▶ *v* **1** HIT, strike, beat, drum, bang, bash, hit, slap, pound, batter, knock, drive, shape, form, make, mould, fashion
2 CRITICIZE, condemn, attack, blame, censure
formal decry, denigrate
colloq. slate, slam, knock, run down, tear a strip off
3 *hammer the opposition*
BEAT, trounce, defeat, overcome, overwhelm, rout, annihilate, outplay
colloq. clobber, slaughter, lick, thrash
4 *hammer an idea into someone*
FORCE, drum, din, drive home, instil, reiterate
5 *hammer away at his essay*
PERSEVERE, pound, persist, keep on, labour, plug, grind, drudge, slog
▷ **hammer out** settle, sort out, negotiate, thrash out, achieve eventually, produce, bring about, work out, carry through, accomplish, complete, finish, resolve
▶ *n* mallet, gavel, beetle

hamper *v, n*
▶ *v* hinder, impede, obstruct, slow down, hold up, stop, inhibit, frustrate, thwart, baulk, prevent, handicap, hamstring, shackle, cramp, restrict, curb, restrain, block, check, bridle, encumber, fetter, foil
E3 aid, facilitate
formal retard
colloq. stymie
▶ *n* basket, box, container, creel, pannier

hamstring *v*
hinder, impede, hold up, stop, frustrate, baulk, thwart, cramp, restrict, restrain, block, check, encumber, foil,

cripple, disable, handicap, incapacitate, paralyse
colloq. stymie

hand *n, v*
▶ *n* **1** FIST, palm
technical manus
colloq. paw; *slang* mitt, fin
Related adjective: manual
2 *give me a hand*
HELP, helping hand, aid, assistance, support, participation, part, influence
formal succour
3 *in someone's hands*
RESPONSIBILITY, care, custody, possession, charge, authority, command, control, power, management, supervision, clutches
4 *give someone a hand*
APPLAUSE, clapping, handclap, cheering, acclaim, ovation
5 INDICATOR, pointer, needle, arrow, marker
6 HANDWRITING, writing, script, penmanship, calligraphy
colloq. fist
7 WORKER, employee, operative, workman, labourer, farm-hand, hireling
▷ **at hand** near, close, to hand, handy, accessible, available, at someone's disposal, ready, imminent, about to happen
▷ **by hand** manually, using your hands
▷ **from hand to mouth** precariously, dangerously, insecurely, uncertainly, in poverty, from day to day; *colloq.* on the breadline
▷ **hand in glove** very closely, in close collaboration/co-operation, in close association
▷ **hand in hand** **1** HOLDING HANDS, with hands joined/clasped/held **2** CLOSELY RELATED, closely together, in close association
▷ **in hand** **1** BEING DEALT WITH, under way, considered, attended to, under control **2** SPARE, in reserve, put by, ready, available
▷ **to hand** near, close, at hand, near, close, handy, accessible, available, at someone's disposal, ready, imminent, about to happen
▷ **try your hand** attempt, try, seek, strive, see if you can do; *colloq.* have a go, have a shot/crack/stab
▷ **win hands down** win easily/effortlessly, win without effort
▶ *v* give, pass, offer, submit, present, yield, deliver, hand over, transmit, conduct, convey
▷ **hand down** bequeath, will, pass on, pass down, transfer, give, grant, leave
▷ **hand out** distribute, deal out, pass out, give out, share out, mete out; *formal* dispense, disseminate; *colloq.* dish out
▷ **hand over** yield, relinquish, surrender, turn over, deliver, consign, release, give, donate, present, pass, transfer
E3 keep, retain

handbill *n*
circular, leaflet, pamphlet, flyer, notice, announcement, advertisement, letter

handbook *n*
manual, instruction book, book of directions, ABC, guide, guidebook, companion, prospectus

handcuff *v*
fetter, shackle, manacle, fasten, secure, tie

handcuffs *n*
manacles, fetters, cuffs, shackles, wristlets,
colloq. darbies

handful *n*
1 SMALL NUMBER, few, little, small amount, sprinkling, scattering, smattering
2 NUISANCE, bother, pest
colloq. pain in the neck, thorn in the flesh, pain
E3 1 a lot, many

handicap *n, v*
▶ *n* obstacle, obstruction, check, block, barrier, impediment, stumbling-block, hindrance, encumbrance, constraint, drawback, disadvantage, restriction, limitation, penalty, disability, impairment, abnormality, defect, shortcoming
E3 assistance, advantage
▶ *v* impede, hinder, disadvantage, put at a disadvantage, hold back, hamper, impair, obstruct, block, check, bridle, curb, burden, encumber, restrict, limit, disable
formal retard
E3 help, assist

handicraft *n*
craft, art, craftwork, craftsmanship, skill, handwork, handiwork, workmanship

handiwork *n*
work, doing, responsibility, achievement, action, product, result, design, invention, creation, production, skill, workmanship, craftsmanship, artisanship, handicraft, craft, art, craftwork

handle *n, v*
▶ *n* grip, handgrip, knob, stock, shaft, hilt, haft
Related adjective: manubrial
▶ *v* **1** TOUCH, finger, feel, fondle, pick up, hold, grasp, grip
colloq. paw
2 *handle a situation*
tackle, treat, deal with, manage, cope with, control, supervise, be in charge of, take care of
3 *handle a car*
operate, control, drive, steer, work
4 TRADE IN, do business in, deal in, market, stock, traffic, operate

handling *n*
management, conduct, approach, operation, running, treatment, direction, administration, discussion, transaction, manipulation

handout *n*
1 CHARITY, alms, gifts, dole, largesse, share, issue, free sample
colloq. freebie
2 LEAFLET, circular, bulletin, statement, press release, brochure, pamphlet, literature

hand-picked *adj*
choice, select, selected, chosen, elect, elite, picked, screened, recherché

handsome *adj*
1 GOOD-LOOKING, attractive, fair, personable, elegant, fine, dignified, stately
colloq. gorgeous, dishy, hunky
2 GENEROUS, liberal, large, considerable, ample, lavish, plentiful, abundant, bountiful, sizeable, magnanimous, unsparing, unstinting
E3 1 ugly, unattractive **2** mean

handsomely *adv*
generously, lavishly, plentifully, richly, amply, abundantly, bountifully, liberally, magnanimously, unsparingly, unstintingly

formal munificently
E3 stingily

handwriting *n*
writing, script, hand, penmanship, calligraphy, autograph
colloq. fist, scrawl, scribble

handy *adj*
1 CONVENIENT, practical, useful, helpful, functional, practicable
2 AVAILABLE, to hand, ready, at hand, near, nearly, accessible, within reach
colloq. at your fingertips
3 SKILFUL, proficient, expert, skilled, clever, practical, dexterous, adroit, adept, nimble
E3 2 inconvenient **3** clumsy

handyman *n*
DIYer, odd-jobman, odd-jobber, Jack-of-all-trades, factotum

hang *v*
1 SUSPEND, be suspended, hang down, put up, dangle, swing, drape, drop, flop, droop, sag, trail, lean, bend
2 FASTEN, attach, fix, stick, glue, past, cement
formal affix, append
3 *hang in the air*
float, drift, hover, flit, flutter, linger, remain, cling
4 *the prisoners were hanged*
execute, lynch, put to death, send to the gallows/scaffold/gibbet, kill
colloq. string up
▷ **get the hang** understand, grasp, comprehend, fathom, get the knack of; *colloq.* twig
▷ **hang about** hang around, linger, loiter, dawdle, waste time, associate with, keep company with, frequent, haunt
▷ **hang back** hold back, be reluctant, hesitate, shy away, shrink back, recoil, stay behind; *formal* demur
▷ **hang fire** hold back, hang back, delay, hold on, stall, stick, stop, wait; *formal* procrastinate, vacillate
E3 press on
▷ **hang on 1** WAIT, hold on, remain, hold out, endure, continue, carry on, persevere, persist
2 GRIP, grasp, cling, clutch, hold fast
3 DEPEND ON, hinge on, turn on, rest on, be conditional on, be determined by; *formal* be contingent on
E3 1 give up
▷ **hang over** impend, loom, menace, threaten, approach

hangdog *adj*
abject, browbeaten, defeated, guilty, shamefaced, cowed, cringing, downcast, miserable, wretched, sneaking, furtive
E3 bold

hanger-on *n*
follower, minion, henchman, lackey, toady, sycophant, parasite, lackey, freeloader, dependant
colloq. sponger

hanging *adj, n*
▶ *adj* suspended, dangling, swinging, draping, drooping, flopping, floppy, flapping, loose, unattached, unsupported
formal pendent, pendulous, pensile
▶ *n* drape, drapery, drop, frontal, drop-scene, dossal, dossel

hang-out *n*
haunt, den, meeting-place, home, patch, local
colloq. dive, joint, watering-hole

hangover *n*
after-effects, katzenjammer, morning after, the morning after the night before
formal crapulence

hang-up *n*
inhibition, difficulty, problem, obsession, preoccupation, fixation, phobia, *idée fixe*, block, mental block
colloq. thing

hank *n*
skein, coil, loop, length, roll, piece, twist
Scot. fank

hanker *v*
▷ **hanker after/for** crave, hunger for, thirst for, want, wish for, desire, covet, yearn for, long for, pine for, itch for, set your heart on; *colloq.* be dying for

hankering *n*
craving, hunger, thirst, wish, desire, yearning, longing, pining, itch, urge

hanky-panky *n*
mischief, trickery, tricks, deception, dishonesty, jiggery-pokery, nonsense, cheating, chicanery, subterfuge, devilry
formal machinations
colloq. funny business, monkey business, shenanigans
⇄ openness

haphazard *adj*
random, chance, casual, arbitrary, hit-or-miss, indiscriminate, irregular, aimless, orderless, unsystematic, disorganized, disorderly, careless, slapdash, slipshod, unmethodical, unplanned
⇄ methodical, orderly

hapless *adj*
unlucky, unhappy, unfortunate, wretched, miserable, ill-fated, ill-starred, cursed, luckless, jinxed, star-crossed
⇄ lucky

happen *v*
1 OCCUR, take place, fall, arise, crop up, develop, present itself, turn up, go on, come about, come true, result, ensue, follow, turn out, appear, come into being
formal transpire, supervene, eventuate
colloq. materialize
2 ***happen to do something***
have the good/bad luck to, have the good/bad fortune to
3 ***happen on something***
find, discover, hit on, light on, stumble on, come across, chance on

happening *n*
occurrence, phenomenon, event, incident, episode, occasion, adventure, experience, accident, chance, proceedings, circumstance, case, affair, thing, action, scene, business
formal eventuality

happily *adv*
1 GLADLY, joyfully, merrily, cheerfully, gleefully, heartily, delightedly, contentedly, agreeably, enthusiastically, willingly
formal joyously
2 FORTUNATELY, luckily, providentially, by chance, fittingly
formal auspiciously, opportunely, propitiously
⇄ **1, 2** unhappily

happiness *n*
joy, joyfulness, gladness, cheerfulness, cheeriness, contentment, pleasure, delight, enjoyment, gaiety, glee, merriment, merriness, light-heartedness, exuberance, high spirits, good spirits, elation, bliss, ecstasy, euphoria
formal blitheness, felicity
⇄ unhappiness, sadness

happy *adj*
1 JOYFUL, jolly, merry, cheerful, glad, pleased, delighted, thrilled, elated, ecstatic, rapturous, overjoyed, exuberant, gleeful, euphoric, satisfied, gratified, in good/high spirits, in a good mood, content, contented, gay, carefree, light-hearted, jovial, radiant, smiling, untroubled, unconcerned, unworried
formal joyous, blithe
colloq. cock-a-hoop, on top of the world, happy as Larry/a sandboy, over the moon, on cloud nine, in seventh heaven, walking/floating on air, tickled pink
2 ***a happy coincidence***
lucky, fortunate, favourable, advantageous, convenient, helpful, beneficial, appropriate, apt, fitting, proper, opportune
formal felicitous, auspicious, propitious, apposite
⇄ **1** unhappy, sad, discontented **2** unfortunate, inappropriate

happy-go-lucky *adj*
easy-going, carefree, casual, nonchalant, cheerful, devil-may-care, light-hearted, unconcerned, untroubled, unworried, reckless, irresponsible, heedless, improvident
formal blithe, insouciant
⇄ anxious, wary

harangue *n, v*
▶ *n* diatribe, tirade, lecture, speech, address
formal peroration, exhortation
▶ *v* lecture, preach, hold forth, spout, address
formal declaim

harass *v*
pester, badger, harry, plague, torment, hound, dragoon, persecute, exasperate, vex, annoy, nag, provoke, antagonize, irritate, fret, bother, disturb, trouble, worry, stress, tire, wear out, exhaust, fatigue
colloq. hassle, have it in for, put the wind up, put the frighteners on, drive round the bend/twist

harassed *adj*
distraught, pressurized, pressured, stressed, under pressure, under stress, strained, distressed, troubled, worried, careworn, hounded, pestered, plagued, tormented, harried, vexed
colloq. hassled, stressed out, uptight
⇄ carefree

harassment *n*
annoyance, nuisance, pestering, trouble, molest, molestation, persecution, pressuring, torment, bother, distress, aggravation, badgering, bedevilment, irritation, vexation
colloq. hassle
⇄ assistance

harbinger *n*
herald, forerunner, precursor, messenger, omen, portent, warning, sign, indication, *avant-courier*
formal foretoken

harbour *n, v*

▶ *n* port, dock, quay, wharf, marina, mooring, anchorage, haven, shelter, refuge

▶ *v* **1** HIDE, conceal, protect, shield, shelter, house, taken in

2 *harbour a feeling*
hold, retain, cling to, entertain, maintain, foster, nurse, nurture, cherish, believe, imagine

hard *adj, adv*

▶ *adj* **1** SOLID, firm, unyielding, tough, strong, dense, condensed, compressed, compact, compacted, impenetrable, resistant, stiff, rigid, inflexible, unpliable
colloq. hard as stone/iron/rock

2 *a hard question/problem*
COMPLICATED, difficult, complex, involved, intricate, knotty, baffling, puzzling, perplexing, bewildering

3 *building a wall is hard work*
STRENUOUS, difficult, arduous, onerous, laborious, tough, tiring, toilsome, exhausting, backbreaking, tiring, heavy, exacting, rigorous

4 HARSH, severe, strict, callous, unfeeling, unsympathetic, cruel, cold-hearted, hard-hearted, stern, tyrannical, oppressive, pitiless, merciless, ruthless, implacable, unsparing, unyielding, unrelenting, distressing, painful, unpleasant
formal obdurate
colloq. hard as flint, standing no nonsense, ruling with a rod of iron

5 *hard times*
tough, unpleasant, difficult, harsh, grim, severe, painful, distressing, uncomfortable, disagreeable, austere

6 *a hard worker*
hard-working, industrious, diligent, assiduous, conscientious, zealous, enthusiastic, keen, busy, energetic
formal sedulous

7 *a hard push*
forceful, powerful, strong, intense, heavy, sharp, violent

8 *a hard winter*
cold, severe, harsh, raw, bitter, freezing

9 *hard evidence*
true, indisputable, undeniable, unquestionable, definite, actual, certain, real, verified

10 *hard drugs*
addictive, harmful, habit-forming, narcotic, heavy, strong, potent

🔃 **1** soft, yielding **2** easy, simple **4** kind, pleasant, compassionate, gentle **5** easy, comfortable **6** lazy, idle **8** mild **9** uncertain

▶ *adv* **1** FORCEFULLY, powerfully, energetically, intensely, strongly, heavily, sharply, violently, vigorously
formal with all your might

2 *work hard*
diligently, industriously, assiduously, conscientiously, energetically, intensely, busily, enthusiastically, eagerly, keenly

3 *look/think hard*
carefully, attentively, closely, intently, sharply, keenly

4 *a hard-won victory*
with difficulty, arduously, strenuously, laboriously, after a struggle, vigorously

5 *snowing hard*
intensely, severely, strongly, heavily, steadily

🔃 **3** carelessly **4** effortlessly **5** lightly

▷ **hard and fast** binding, fixed, definite, immutable,
incontrovertible, inflexible, invariable, rigid, set, strict, stringent, unalterable, unchangeable, unchanging, uncompromising

🔃 flexible

▷ **hard up** penniless, impoverished, in the red, bankrupt, short, lacking; *formal* impecunious; *colloq.* broke, bust, stony broke, skint, cleaned out, strapped (for cash), on your uppers, on your beam ends, not having two pennies to rub together

🔃 rich

hard-bitten *adj*
callous, case-hardened, cynical, down-to-earth, hard-boiled, hard-headed, hard-nosed, toughened, inured, matter-of-fact, practical, realistic, ruthless, shrewd, tough, unsentimental

🔃 callow

hard-boiled *adj*
tough, cynical, hard-headed, down-to-earth, unsentimental

hard-core *adj*
steadfast, dedicated, blatant, obstinate, rigid, staunch, explicit, extreme, intransigent, dyed-in-the-wool, diehard

🔃 moderate

harden *v*
solidify, set, freeze, congeal, bake, cake, stiffen, petrify, strengthen, reinforce, buttress, brace, steel, gird, nerve, toughen, temper, deaden, season, accustom, train, inure
technical anneal, vulcanize
formal fortify, habituate, indurate

🔃 soften, weaken

hardened *adj*
incorrigible, inveterate, irredeemable, seasoned, set, shameless, toughened, inured, reprobate, habitual, accustomed, habituated, chronic, unfeeling, callous
formal obdurate

🔃 soft, callow

hard-headed *adj*
shrewd, astute, businesslike, sharp, level-headed, clear-thinking, cool-headed, sensible, realistic, rational, pragmatic, practical, hard-bitten, hard-boiled, tough, unsentimental, down-to-earth
colloq. hard-nosed

🔃 unrealistic, sentimental, idealistic, impractical

hard-hearted *adj*
callous, unfeeling, uncaring, unconcerned, unkind, cold, hard, stony, stony-hearted, heartless, hard, unsympathetic, cruel, inhuman, pitiless, merciless

🔃 kind, merciful, compassionate, concerned

hard-hitting *adj*
condemnatory, critical, unsparing, boldly, directly, frankly, straight, vigorous, forceful, tough, uncompromising
colloq. no-holds-barred, pulling no punches

🔃 mild

hardiness *n*
robustness, toughness, resilience, resolution, boldness, courage, valour, ruggedness, sturdiness, intrepidity
formal fortitude

🔃 timidity

hardline *adj*
strict, tough, extreme, immoderate, inflexible, militant, uncompromising, unyielding, undeviating

formal intransigent
⟷ moderate, flexible

hardly *adv*
barely, scarcely, just, only just, not quite, not at all, almost not, by no means

hardness *n*
toughness, severity, harshness, sternness, firmness, rigidity, difficulty, laboriousness, insensitivity, pitilessness, inhumanity, coldness
⟷ ease, mildness, softness

hard-pressed *adj*
hard-pushed, hard put, harassed, harried, pushed, under pressure, overburdened, overtaxed
colloq. up against it, in a corner, with your back to the wall
⟷ untroubled

hardship *n*
misfortune, adversity, trouble, difficulty, affliction, pain, distress, suffering, burdens, trial, want, need, austerity, poverty, destitution, deprivation, misery
formal tribulation, privation
⟷ ease, comfort, prosperity

hard-wearing *adj*
durable, lasting, well-made, made/built to last, strong, tough, sturdy, stout, rugged, resilient
⟷ delicate

hard-working *adj*
industrious, diligent, assiduous, conscientious, enthusiastic, keen, zealous, busy, energetic
formal sedulous
colloq. with your nose to the grindstone
⟷ idle, lazy

hardy *adj*
1 STRONG, tough, sturdy, durable, heavy-duty, robust, vigorous, fit, sound, healthy
2 BRAVE, courageous, plucky, fearless, undaunted, bold, daring, intrepid, stalwart, stoical, stout, stout-hearted, heroic, indomitable
⟷ weak, unhealthy

hare-brained *adj*
foolish, stupid, silly, wild, daft, ill-conceived, careless, rash, reckless, inane, giddy
colloq. half-baked, crackpot, scatty, scatterbrained
⟷ sensible

hark *v*
listen, hear, give ear, mark, note, notice, pay attention, pay heed
old use hearken
▷ **hark back** remember, recall, recollect, go back, turn back, revert; *formal* regress

harlequin *n & adj*
fool, jester, clown, comic, buffoon, zany, jester, joker

harlot *n*
prostitute, callgirl, whore
old use hussy, strumpet
colloq. fallen woman, loose woman, pro, streetwalker, tramp, hooker; *slang* scrubber, tart

harm *n, v*
▶ *n* damage, loss, injury, hurt, pain, detriment, ill, misfortune, adversity, suffering, ruin, destruction, loss, wrong, abuse, impairment, disservice
⟷ benefit, service
▶ *v* damage, impair, work against, blemish, spoil, mar, ruin, hurt, destroy, injure, wound, ill-treat,

maltreat, abuse, molest, misuse, be detrimental to
⟷ benefit, improve

harmful *adj*
damaging, detrimental, bad, pernicious, unhealthy, unwholesome, injurious, wounding, dangerous, hazardous, poisonous, toxic, destructive
formal noxious, deleterious
⟷ harmless

harmless *adj*
safe, innocuous, non-toxic, inoffensive, gentle, mild, blameless, innocent, -friendly
⟷ harmful, dangerous, destructive

harmonious *adj*
1 MELODIOUS, tuneful, musical, sweet-sounding, harmonizing, rhythmic, symphonious, euphonious, pleasant, mellow
formal mellifluous
2 MATCHING, co-ordinated, balanced, compatible
formal congruous, concordant
3 *a harmonious relationship*
agreeable, cordial, amiable, amicable, friendly, sympathetic, like-minded, peaceful, peaceable, compatible
⟷ 1 discordant

harmonize *v*
match, co-ordinate, balance, mix, blend, fit in, suit, tone, blend, correspond, go together, get on with, agree, reconcile, coincide, accommodate, adapt, arrange, compose
formal be congruous, be congruent, accord
⟷ clash, conflict

harmony *n*
1 TUNEFULNESS, tune, melody, melodiousness, euphony
formal mellifluousness
2 *live in harmony*
AGREEMENT, unison, unanimity, oneness, unity, compatibility, like-mindedness, peace, goodwill, rapport, sympathy, understanding, amicability, friendliness, co-operation
formal accord, concord, amity, assent, concurrence
3 CO-ORDINATION, balance, blending, symmetry, correspondence, conformity
formal concord, consonance
⟷ 1 discord 2 conflict

harness *n, v*
▶ *n* tackle, gear, equipment, reins, straps, tack
formal accoutrements
▶ *v* control, channel, use, utilize, exploit, make use of, employ, mobilize, apply
▷ **in harness** 1 CO-OPERATING, in co-operation, collaborating, together 2 *back in harness* at work, working, busy, active, employed

harp *v*
▷ **harp on** keep talking about, dwell on, labour, press, reiterate, renew, repeat, nag
colloq. go on and on about

harpoon *n*
arrow, barb, dart, spear, trident, grains

harridan *n*
virago, vixen, witch, dragon, harpy, nag, scold, shrew, tartar, fury, gorgon, termagant, Xanthippe, hell-cat
colloq. battle-axe

harried *adj*
worried, anxious, agitated, troubled, bothered,

distressed, harassed, hard-pressed, pressured, pressurized, plagued, tormented, ravaged, beset
colloq. hassled
F3 untroubled

harrowing *adj*
distressing, upsetting, heart-rending, disturbing, alarming, daunting, tormenting, frightening, terrifying, nerve-racking, traumatic, agonizing, excruciating
formal perturbing
F3 encouraging, heartening

harry *v*
badger, pester, nag, chivvy, harass, oppress, plague, torment, persecute, annoy, vex, worry, trouble, bother, disturb, molest
colloq. hassle

harsh *adj*
1 SEVERE, austere, barren, stark, bitter, bleak, grim, comfortless, desolate, wild, inhospitable, Spartan
2 CRUEL, strict, abrasive, severe, stern, grim, savage, brutal, unsympathetic, unfeeling, hard, inhuman, pitiless, ruthless, merciless, Draconian
formal acerbic
3 *a harsh sound*
RASPING, rough, coarse, croaking, guttural, hoarse, gruff, grinding, grating, jarring, jangling, discordant, strident, ear-piercing, raucous, sharp, shrill, unpleasant, dissonant, metallic
4 BRIGHT, dazzling, glaring, showy, flashy, gaudy, lurid, garish, bold
F3 1 mild, comfortable, lenient 2 compassionate, feeling 3 harmonious, soft, gentle 4 gentle

harshness *n*
bitterness, coarseness, roughness, severity, ill-temper, rigour, starkness, sternness, strictness, hardness, sourness, abrasiveness, brutality
formal acerbity, acrimony, asperity
F3 mildness, softness, gentleness

harum-scarum *adj*
reckless, hasty, rash, impetuous, irresponsible, ill-considered, wild, careless, haphazard, erratic
formal imprudent, precipitate
colloq. hare-brained, scatterbrained, scatty
F3 sensible

harvest *n, v*
▶ *n* 1 HARVEST-TIME, ingathering, reaping, harvesting, collection, store, supply, stock, accumulation, horde
2 CROP, yield, return, produce, product, fruits, result, consequence, effect, returns
▶ *v* reap, mow, pick, glean, pluck, garner, gather (in), collect, accumulate, amass, horde, gain, obtain, acquire, secure

hash *n*
1 MESS, botch, muddle, bungle, mix-up, jumble, confusion, mismanagement, hotchpotch, mishmash
2 GOULASH, stew, hotpot, lobscouse, lob's course

hashish *n*
hash, hemp, marijuana, bhang, cannabis
colloq. dope, ganja, grass, pot

hassle *n, v*
▶ *n* bother, inconvenience, nuisance, difficulty, trouble, problem, struggle, argument, disagreement, quarrel, squabble, trial, upset, fight, dispute, bickering, wrangle
formal altercation

colloq. aggro
F3 agreement, peace
▶ *v* bother, pester, trouble, annoy, badger, harass, hound, harry, chivvy
colloq. bug
F3 assist, calm

haste *n*
hurry, rush, hustle, bustle, speed, velocity, rapidity, swiftness, quickness, briskness, fastness, urgency, rashness, recklessness, carelessness, foolhardiness, impulsiveness, impetuosity
formal alacrity, celerity, expeditiousness
F3 slowness

hasten *v*
hurry (up), be quick, go fast/quickly, rush, run, sprint, dash, tear, race, fly, bolt, accelerate, speed (up), quicken, dispatch, urge, assist, help, aid, boost, press, advance, forward, step up, push forward
old use make haste
formal expedite, precipitate
colloq. get a move on, step on it/the gas, hotfoot it, put your foot down
F3 dawdle, delay

hastily *adv*
1 RASHLY, recklessly, hurriedly, impetuously, heedlessly, impulsively
formal precipitately
2 FAST, quickly, rapidly, speedily, promptly, straightaway, apace
colloq. double-quick, chop-chop
F3 1 carefully, deliberately 2 slowly

hasty *adj*
1 *a hasty decision*
hurried, rushed, rash, reckless, heedless, thoughtless, careless, impetuous, impulsive, impatient, headlong, hot-headed
formal precipitate
2 FAST, quick, rapid, swift, speedy, rushed, hurried, brisk, prompt, short, brief, cursory, fleeting, transitory, perfunctory
formal expeditious
F3 1 careful, deliberate 2 slow

hat *n*

Hats include: trilby, bowler, fedora, top-hat, Homburg, *US* derby, pork-pie hat, flat-cap, beret, bonnet, tam-o'-shanter, tammy, deerstalker, hunting-cap, stovepipe hat, stetson, ten-gallon hat, boater, sunhat, panama, straw hat, picture-hat, pill-box, cloche, *US* beanie, poke-bonnet, mob-cap, turban, fez, sombrero, sou'wester, glengarry, bearskin, busby, peaked cap, sailor-hat, baseball cap, balaclava, hood, snood, toque, helmet, mortar-board, skullcap, yarmulka, mitre, biretta.

hatch *v*
1 INCUBATE, brood, sit on, breed
2 CONCOCT, formulate, originate, think up, dream up, invent, conceive, devise, contrive, plot, scheme, design, plan, project

hatchet *n*
axe, chopper, cleaver, tomahawk, battle-axe, mattock, pickaxe, machete

hate *v, n*
▶ *v* 1 DISLIKE, despise, detest, loathe, not stand, recoil from, have an aversion to, feel revulsion at

formal abhor, abominate, execrate
colloq. hate someone's guts
2 *I hate to disturb you*
regret, apologize, be sorry, be reluctant, be unwilling, be loath
🔲 **1** like, love
▶ *n* hatred, aversion, dislike, loathing, animosity, ill-will, grudge, bitterness, resentment, antagonism, hostility, enmity
formal abhorrence, abomination, rancour
🔲 liking, love

hateful *adj*
horrid, horrible, loathsome, detestable, abominable, offensive, disgusting, obnoxious, odious, revolting, repulsive, nasty, unpleasant, disagreeable, despicable, vile, contemptible, foul, evil, heinous
formal abhorrent, execrable, repellent, repugnant
🔲 pleasing

hatred *n*
hate, aversion, dislike, loathing, disgust, revulsion, animosity, ill-will, grudge, bitterness, resentment, antagonism, hostility, enmity
formal detestation, repugnance, abhorrence, abomination, execration, rancour, antipathy, animus
🔲 liking, love

haughtiness *n*
arrogance, pride, conceit, contempt, contemptuousness, disdain, aloofness, loftiness, snobbishness, superciliousness, airs, hauteur, insolence, pomposity
colloq. snootiness
🔲 friendliness, humility

haughty *adj*
arrogant, proud, conceited, vain, swollen-headed, lofty, imperious, high and mighty, supercilious, cavalier, contemptuous, disdainful, scornful, superior, self-important, egotistical, overbearing, condescending, patronizing, snobbish
colloq. snooty, stuck-up, high and mighty, on your high horse
🔲 humble, modest

haul *v, n*
▶ *v* pull, heave, tug, draw, tow, drag, trail, move, transport, convey, ship, convoy, carry, cart, lug, push
colloq. hump
▶ *n* loot, booty, plunder, spoils, takings, gain, yield, find
slang swag

haunches *n*
thighs, hips, buttocks, nates, huckles, hucks, hunkers

haunt *v, n*
▶ *v* **1** *a ghost haunts the house*
walk, visit, appear often in, materialize, spook, possess, curse
colloq. show up
2 FREQUENT, patronize, visit (regularly)
colloq. hang about/around in
3 *memories haunted her*
plague, torment, trouble, disturb, worry, burden, recur, prey on, beset, harry, oppress, obsess, possess
▶ *n* resort, stamping-ground, den, local, meeting-place, rendezvous, favourite spot
colloq. hangout

haunted *adj*
1 POSSESSED, cursed, eerie, ghostly, jinxed, hag-ridden

colloq. spooky
2 TROUBLED, worried, plagued, tormented, obsessed, preoccupied

haunting *adj*
memorable, unforgettable, persistent, recurrent, evocative, nostalgic, atmospheric, poignant
🔲 unmemorable

have *v*
1 OWN, possess, get, obtain, gain, be given, acquire, secure, take, receive, accept, keep, hold, use
formal procure
2 FEEL, experience, enjoy, suffer, undergo, submit to, be subjected to, endure, tolerate, put up with, go through, find, meet, encounter
3 CONTAIN, include, take in, embody, incorporate, consist of
formal comprise, embrace, comprehend
4 *have a party*
hold, arrange, organize, take part in, participate in
5 *have to go now*
must, be forced, be compelled, be obliged, be required, ought, should
6 *have someone do something*
cause, make, arrange, get, oblige, require, persuade, talk into, ask, tell, request, order, command, bid, force, compel, coerce
formal enjoin, prevail upon
7 *have pity on someone*
show, demonstrate, display, exhibit, express, feel
formal manifest
8 *have food/drink*
eat, swallow, consume, take, drink, devour, down, gulp, guzzle
formal partake of
colloq. put away, tuck into, knock back
9 *have a baby*
give birth to, bear, bring into the world, be delivered of
old use beget
10 *I won't have such behaviour*
tolerate, put up with, take, accept, allow, permit, stand, abide, brook
11 *you've been had*
deceive, dupe, fool, trick, cheat, swindle, take in
colloq. con, diddle
🔲 **1** lack
▷ **have done with** finish with, give up, stop, be through with; *formal* cease, desist; *colloq.* throw over, wash your hands of
▷ **have had it** be in trouble, have no hope, be defeated, be exhausted, be lost, have no chance of success; *colloq.* bite the dust, come to a sticky end
▷ **have on** **1** WEAR, be dressed in, be clothed in **2** *What have you got on this week?* have an engagement, have an appointment, have arranged, have planned **3** TEASE, trick, play a joke on; *colloq.* kid, rag, pull someone's leg

haven *n*
harbour, port, dock, bay, anchorage, shelter, refuge, sanctuary, asylum, retreat, oasis

haversack *n*
backpack, rucksack, knapsack, kitbag

havoc *n*
chaos, confusion, disorder, disruption, mayhem, damage, destruction, ruin, ruination, wreck, wreckage, rack and ruin, devastation, waste, ravaging, desolation
formal despoliation
colloq. shambles

hawk¹ *n*

hawks and other birds of prey
buzzard, kite, harrier, sparrowhawk, falcon, haggard, goshawk, tercel
Related adjective: accipitrine

hawk² *v*

hawking goods at people's houses
sell, offer for sale, peddle, market, offer, cry, tout, vend, bark

hawker *n*

pedlar, vendor, door-to-door salesman, crier, huckster, colporteur, barrow-boy, chapman, costermonger, coster

haywire *adj*

wrong, out of control, crazy, mad, wild, chaotic, confused, disordered, disorganized, tangled, topsy-turvy

hazard *n, v*

▶ *n* risk, danger, jeopardy, menace, threat, deathtrap, pitfall, accident, chance, luck
formal peril
F3 safety
▶ *v* **1** RISK, endanger, jeopardize, expose to danger, put at risk, put in jeopardy
2 CHANCE, gamble, stake, venture, suggest, put forward, submit, offer, speculate

hazardous *adj*

risky, dangerous, unsafe, precarious, menacing, threatening, insecure, chancy, uncertain, unpredictable, difficult, tricky
formal perilous
colloq. hairy
F3 safe, secure

haze *n*

1 MIST, fog, smog, cloud, steam, vapour, film, mistiness, fogginess, cloudiness, smokiness, dimness, obscurity
2 BLUR, confusion, muddle, bewilderment, uncertainty, indistinctness, vagueness

hazy *adj*

misty, foggy, smoky, clouded, cloudy, overcast, milky, fuzzy, blurred, muzzy, ill-defined, veiled, obscure, dim, faint, unclear, indistinct, vague, indefinite, uncertain
F3 clear, bright, definite

head *n, adj, v*

▶ *n* **1** SKULL, cranium
technical caput
colloq. noddle, nut, conk, bonce
Related adjectives: capital, cephalic
2 MIND, brain, mentality, mental abilities, intellect, intelligence, wit(s), sense, understanding, wisdom, thought, reasoning, common sense
colloq. brains, loaf, noddle, little grey cells, grey matter, upper storey
3 TOP, peak, summit, crown, crest, tip, apex, vertex, height, climax
4 FRONT, fore, forefront, vanguard, van, lead
5 LEADER, chief, captain, commander, director, manager, managing director, superintendent, supervisor, principal, head teacher, headmaster, headmistress, ruler, controller, administrator, president, governor, chair, chairman, chairwoman, chairperson
colloq. boss
6 COMMAND, control(s), leadership, directorship,

management, supervision, charge
7 *come to a head*
CRISIS, critical point, climax, emergency, catastrophe, calamity, dilemma
colloq. crunch
8 *the head of a river*
source, origin, fount, spring, rise, wellspring, wellhead
9 *no head on the beer*
froth, foam, bubbles, fizz, suds, lather
F3 **1** foot, tail **3** base, foot **4** back **5** subordinate
▷ **go to your head** **1** MAKE DRUNK, intoxicate, inebriate, make dizzy, befuddle; *colloq.* make woozy
2 *success has gone to his head* make arrogant, make conceited, make proud, make someone full of themselves; *colloq.* puff up
▷ **head over heels** completely, utterly, uncontrollably, wholeheartedly, recklessly, thoroughly, intensely, wildly
▷ **keep your head** keep calm, stay calm and collected, keep control of yourself, keep/maintain your composure; *colloq.* keep your cool
▷ **lose your head** panic, lose control of yourself, lose your composure; *colloq.* lose your cool, flap, go round like a headless chicken
▶ *adj* leading, front, foremost, first, chief, main, prime, principal, top, topmost, highest, supreme, premier, dominant, pre-eminent
▶ *v* **1** *head the queue*
be at the front of, be first in, go first, lead
2 LEAD, rule, govern, command, direct, be in charge of, be in control of, manage, run, superintend, oversee, supervise, administer, control, guide, steer
▷ **head for** make for, go/move/travel towards, direct towards, go in the direction of, aim for, point to, turn for, steer for
▷ **head off** forestall, intercept, intervene, deflect, divert, turn aside, cut off, fend off, ward off, avert, prevent, stop; *formal* interpose
▷ **head up** lead, direct, manage, be in charge of, take charge of, be responsible for

headache *n*

1 *suffer from headaches*
migraine, neuralgia
technical cephalalgia, hemicrania
2 BOTHER, nuisance, trouble, inconvenience, problem, worry, pest, vexation, bane
colloq. hassle

heading *n*

title, name, headline, rubric, caption, section, division, classification, subject, category, class, head

headland *n*

promontory, cape, head, point, ness, foreland

headlong *adj, adv*

▶ *adj* hasty, impetuous, impulsive, rash, reckless, careless, impetuous, impulsive, dangerous, breakneck, head-first
formal precipitate
▶ *adv* head first, hurriedly, hastily, prematurely, rashly, recklessly, carelessly, heedlessly, impetuously, impulsively, thoughtlessly, without thinking, wildly
formal precipitately

headman *n*

chief, leader, captain, ruler, muqaddam, sachem

head-on *adj*

a head-on crash/confrontation
direct, full-frontal, straight-on, straight
colloq. eyeball-to-eyeball

headquarters *n*
HQ, base (camp), head office, main office, centre of operations, nerve centre

headstrong *adj*
stubborn, obstinate, intractable, wayward, pigheaded, wilful, self-willed, not listening to reason, perverse, contrary, unruly, ungovernable
formal obdurate, refractory, recalcitrant, intransient
E3 tractable, docile

headway *n*
advance, progress, ground, way, improvement, development

heady *adj*
intoxicating, strong, stimulating, overpowering, exhilarating, invigorating, thrilling, exciting, ecstatic, euphoric, rousing

heal *v*
cure, make better, make well, remedy, mend, restore, improve, treat, soothe, comfort, salve, settle, reconcile, make good, patch up, put/set right
formal assuage, palliate

health *n*
fitness, constitution, form, shape, trim, fettle, condition, tone, state, healthiness, good condition, wellbeing, welfare, good shape, soundness, robustness, strength, vigour
E3 illness, infirmity

healthy *adj*
1 WELL, fit, good, fine, in condition, in good shape, in fine fettle, sound, sturdy, robust, strong, vigorous, hale and hearty, blooming, flourishing, thriving, able-bodied
colloq. hardy, fit as a fiddle, right as rain, in the pink, a picture of health
2 *healthy food*
wholesome, nutritious, nourishing, bracing, good, beneficial, invigorating, healthful
3 *healthy fresh air*
bracing, invigorating, refreshing, stimulating
formal salubrious
4 *a healthy economy*
successful, strong, sound, robust, vigorous
5 *a healthy respect for authority*
wise, sensible, sound
formal prudent, judicious
E3 **1** ill, sick, infirm **2** *colloq.* junk **3** ailing

heap *n, v*
▶ *n* **1** MOUND, pile, stack, mountain, lot, mass, bundle, accumulation, collection, hoard, stockpile, supply, store
formal assemblage, agglomeration
2 A LOT, great deal, plenty, abundance, quantities, lots, mass, lashings
colloq. load(s), stack(s), tons, oodles, pot(s), millions, scores
▶ *v* **1** PILE, stack, mound, bank, build, amass, accumulate, collect, gather, assemble, hoard, stockpile, store (up), load, burden
2 *heap criticism/praise on someone*
shower, lavish
formal confer, bestow

hear *v*
1 LISTEN, catch, pick up, make out, perceive, be in touch with, overhear, eavesdrop, heed, pay attention, take in
colloq. latch onto

2 LEARN, find out, discover, pick up, understand, gather, be informed, be told
formal ascertain
3 JUDGE, pass judgement, try, examine, investigate, consider, inquire, adjudicate

hearing *n*
1 EARSHOT, sound, range, hearing distance, reach, ear, perception
2 TRIAL, inquiry, investigation, examination, review, judgement, inquest, inquisition, adjudication, audition, interview, audience

hearsay *n*
rumour, word of mouth, talk, common talk, common knowledge, gossip, tittle-tattle, report
colloq. buzz

heart *n*
1 SOUL, mind, character, disposition, nature, temperament
2 FEELING, emotion, sentiment, love, affection, passion, tenderness, kindness, compassion, concern, sympathy, pity, responsiveness, warmth
3 *lose heart*
courage, bravery, boldness, heroism, fearlessness, intrepidity, pluck, stout-heartedness, spirit, resolution, determination, enthusiasm, eagerness, keenness
formal fortitude
colloq. guts
4 CENTRE, middle, core, substance, kernel, nucleus, nub, crux, essence, essential part, pith, marrow
formal quintessence
E3 **3** cowardice **4** periphery
Related adjective: cardiac

Parts of the heart include: aortic valve, ascending aorta, bicuspid valve, carotid artery, descending thoracic aorta, inferior vena cava, left atrium, left pulmonary artery, left pulmonary veins, left ventricle, mitral valve, myocardium, papillary muscle, pulmonary valve, right atrium, right pulmonary artery, right pulmonary veins, right ventricle, superior vena cava, tricuspid valve, ventricular septum.

▷ **at heart** basically, really, fundamentally, essentially, in essence, at bottom
▷ **by heart** by rote, parrot-fashion, pat, off pat, word for word, verbatim
▷ **change of heart** change of mind, rethink, second thoughts
▷ **from the bottom of your heart** deeply, sincerely, earnestly, profoundly, devoutly
▷ **heart and soul** eagerly, enthusiastically, completely, unreservedly, wholeheartedly, devotedly, gladly, heartily, absolutely, entirely
▷ **set your heart on** wish for, long for, desire, yearn, crave
▷ **take heart** be encouraged, brighten up, cheer up, rally, revive; *colloq.* buck up, perk up
▷ **take to heart** be affected by, be moved by, be upset by, be disturbed by

heartache *n*
sorrow, anxiety, worry, grief, despair, anguish, agony, heartbreak, pain, suffering, despondency, dejection, bitterness, distress, remorse, torment, torture
formal affliction

heartbreak *n*
distress, sadness, suffering, sorrow, dejection, despair, pain, grief, misery, agony, anguish, desolation
E3 elation, joy, relief

heartbreaking *adj*
distressing, sad, tragic, harsh, harrowing, heart-rending, pitiful, agonizing, painful, excruciating, grievous, bitter, cruel, disappointing, poignant
🖃 heartwarming, heartening

heartbroken *adj*
broken-hearted, desolate, sad, miserable, sorrowful, in low spirits, dejected, despondent, downcast, suffering, crestfallen, disappointed, disheartened, dispirited, grieved, desolate, crushed, anguished
🖃 delighted, elated

hearten *v*
comfort, console, reassure, cheer (up), encourage, boost, inspire, invigorate, stimulate, energize, revitalize, animate, rouse, raise the spirits of
colloq. buck up, pep up
🖃 dishearten, depress, dismay

heartfelt *adj*
deep, profound, sincere, honest, genuine, unfeigned, devout, earnest, ardent, fervent, wholehearted, warm, compassionate
🖃 insincere, false

heartily *adv*
1 ENTHUSIASTICALLY, eagerly, earnestly, deeply, profoundly, warmly, gladly, cordially, feelingly, sincerely, resolutely, unfeignedly, zealously, vigorously, genuinely
2 ABSOLUTELY, completely, very, totally, thoroughly

heartless *adj*
unfeeling, uncaring, cold, hard, hard-hearted, cold-hearted, cold-blooded, callous, unkind, cruel, inhuman, harsh, brutal, ruthless, pitiless, merciless, unsympathetic, unmoved, inconsiderate
🖃 kind, considerate, sympathetic, merciful

heart-rending *adj*
harrowing, heartbreaking, agonizing, pitiful, piteous, pathetic, tragic, sad, harrowing, distressing, moving, affecting, poignant

heartsick *adj*
sad, heavy-hearted, despondent, dejected, disappointed, depressed, downcast, melancholy, glum

heart-throb *n*
pin-up, star, idol
colloq. dreamboat

heart-to-heart *n*
cosy chat, private conversation, tête-à-tête, friendly talk, honest talk, personal conversation

heartwarming *adj*
cheering, heartening, encouraging, uplifting, gladdening, touching, moving, affecting, pleasing, gratifying, rewarding, satisfying
🖃 heartbreaking

hearty *adj*
1 ENTHUSIASTIC, eager, wholehearted, unreserved, heartfelt, sincere, genuine, unfeigned, warm, affable, friendly, cordial, jovial, cheerful, ebullient, effusive, exuberant
2 *a hearty breakfast*
large, sizeable, substantial, filling, solid, nourishing, nutritious, ample, abundant, generous
3 STRONG, energetic, vigorous, boisterous, robust, healthy, sound, hardy, stalwart
🖃 1 inhibited, reserved, cold, half-hearted 3 weak, feeble

heat *n, v*
▶ *n* 1 HOTNESS, warmth, sultriness, torridness, swelter, closeness, heaviness, high temperature, fever, feverishness
technical calefaction
Related adjectives: calorific, thermal
2 ARDOUR, fervour, fervency, fieriness, passion, warmth, intensity, vehemence, fury, anger, excitement, impetuosity, earnestness, eagerness, enthusiasm, zeal
🖃 1 cold(ness) 2 coolness
▶ *v* 1 WARM, boil, toast, cook, microwave, bake, roast, reheat, warm up
technical calefy
2 INFLAME, excite, animate, stir, rouse, arouse, stimulate, enrage, annoy, flush, glow
🖃 1 cool (down), chill

heated *adj*
angry, furious, raging, passionate, impassioned, fiery, stormy, tempestuous, bitter, fierce, intense, vehement, violent, frenzied, enraged, inflamed, excited, animated, stirred, fired, roused, stimulated
colloq. worked-up
🖃 calm

heathen *n, adj*
▶ *n* pagan, unbeliever, infidel, philistine, nations, idolater, idolatress, barbarian, savage
formal nullifidian
🖃 believer
▶ *adj* pagan, unbelieving, infidel, philistine, uncivilized, unenlightened, idolatrous, godless, irreligious, savage, barbaric
formal nullifidian
🖃 godly, believing

heave *v*
1 PULL, haul, drag, tug, raise, lift, hitch, hoist, lever, rise, surge
2 THROW, fling, hurl, cast, toss, send, pitch, let fly
colloq. chuck, sling
3 RETCH, vomit, be sick, spew, gag
colloq. throw up
4 *heave a sigh*
give, utter, express, let out, breathe

heaven *n*
1 PARADISE, home of God, bliss, next world, hereafter, life to come, afterlife, utopia, Elysium, elysian fields, happy hunting-ground, Zion, nirvana, Valhalla, Swarga
formal abode of God
colloq. up there
2 SKY, firmament, skies, the blue, ether
3 ECSTASY, rapture, bliss, happiness, complete happiness, joy, delight, transports of delight
colloq. seventh heaven
🖃 1 hell

heavenly *adj*
1 CELESTIAL, unearthly, supernatural, extraterrestrial, cosmic, other-worldly, spiritual, divine, godlike, angelic, seraphic, cherubic, immortal, holy, sublime, blessed, beatific
formal empyreal, empyrean
2 BLISSFUL, wonderful, glorious, marvellous, rapturous, beautiful, lovely, exquisite, perfect, enchanting, delightful, enjoyable
colloq. out of this world, divine
🖃 1 infernal, mundane 2 hellish

heavily *adv*
1 PONDEROUSLY, slowly, clumsily, awkwardly,

laboriously, painfully, hard, sluggishly, weightily, woodenly
2 COMPACTLY, closely, densely, solidly, thick, thickly
3 COMPLETELY, utterly, decisively, thoroughly, roundly, soundly
4 EXCESSIVELY, to excess, too much, abundantly, copiously
F3 1 lightly **2** loosely

heaviness *n*
1 WEIGHT, weightiness, ponderousness, heftiness, bulk, density, solidity, thickness
2 *a heaviness in the air*
dejection, depression, despondency, melancholy, sadness, seriousness, oppression, oppressiveness, burdensomeness, onerousness, drowsiness, sleepiness, sluggishness, deadness, gloom, gloominess
formal languor, lassitude, somnolence
F3 2 lightness, liveliness

heavy *adj*
1 WEIGHTY, hefty, ponderous, burdensome, cumbersome, awkward, massive, substantial, large, bulky, hulking, solid, dense, thick
colloq. weighing a ton, heavy as lead
2 *heavy work*
hard, difficult, tough, arduous, laborious, strenuous, troublesome, demanding, taxing, exacting, harsh, severe
3 SERIOUS, intense, serious, grave, sombre, deep, profound, dull, tedious, dry, uninteresting
4 *heavy fighting; a heavy shower*
severe, intense, extreme, excessive, considerable, strong, great, immoderate, inordinate
5 *a heavy blow on the head*
forceful, hard, powerful, strong, intense, sharp, violent
6 *heavy responsibilities*
burdensome, onerous, unbearable, intolerable, crushing, difficult, weighty, exacting, irksome, oppressive, taxing, troublesome, trying, wearisome
7 *with a heavy heart*
sad, miserable, despondent, depressed, discouraged, downcast, gloomy, crushed
8 *a heavy meal*
filling, substantial, solid, big, large, stodgy, indigestible, starchy
9 *tables heavy with food*
laden, loaded, full, burdened, weighed down, encumbered, groaning
10 *the weather is heavy*
sultry, humid, oppressive, muggy, close, steamy, sticky
11 *a heavy sky*
dark, cloudy, overcast, dull, grey, gloomy, leaden
F3 1 light **2** easy **3** light **4** light **5** gentle
6 light **8** light **10** cool, fresh **11** bright

heavy-handed *adj*
clumsy, awkward, blundering, bungling, unsubtle, tactless, insensitive, thoughtless, inept, oppressive, forceful, severe, harsh, stern, overbearing, domineering, autocratic, despotic
formal maladroit
colloq. ham-fisted, cack-handed, all fingers and thumbs, like a bull in a china shop
F3 skilful

heavy-hearted *adj*
sorrowful, sad, depressed, discouraged, disappointed, disheartened, downcast, downhearted, despondent, gloomy, miserable, morose, mournful, melancholy, glum, forlorn, crushed, heartsick
F3 light-hearted

heckle *v*
barrack, shout down, interrupt, disrupt, jeer, taunt, pester, gibe, catcall, bait

hectic *adj*
busy, frantic, frenetic, chaotic, fast, feverish, excited, bustling, heated, furious, frenzied, tumultuous, turbulent, wild
F3 leisurely

hector *v*
bully, intimidate, badger, chivvy, harass, menace, threaten, nag, provoke, worry, browbeat, bluster, bullyrag, huff
colloq. bulldoze

hedge *n, v*
▶ *n* **1** FENCE, hedgerow, screen, windbreak, barrier, protection, dyke, boundary
2 SAFEGUARD, protection, shield, cover, guard
▶ *v* **1** SURROUND, enclose, encircle, edge, hem in, confine, restrict, limit, guard, shield, protect, safeguard, cover, insure
formal fortify
2 STALL, equivocate, dodge, sidestep, evade, quibble, prevaricate
formal temporize
colloq. duck, dodge

hedonism *n*
gratification, luxuriousness, self-indulgence, sensualism, sensuality, voluptuousness, pleasure-seeking, Epicureanism, epicurism, *dolce vita*, sybaritism
F3 asceticism

hedonist *n*
pleasure-seeker, sensualist, voluptuary, epicure, epicurean, *bon vivant, bon viveur*, sybarite
F3 ascetic

hedonistic *adj*
luxurious, pleasure-seeking, self-indulgent, voluptuous, epicurean, sybaritic
F3 ascetic, austere

heed *v, n*
▶ *v* listen, pay attention, mind, mark, attend to, take note/notice, take into account, take into consideration, bear in mind, consider, note, regard, observe, follow, obey
F3 ignore, disregard
▶ *n* attention, regard, note, notice, consideration, mind, thought, watchfulness, care, caution, heedfulness, respect, ear
formal animadversion
F3 inattention, indifference, unconcern

heedful *adj*
attentive, watchful, mindful, observant, careful, cautious, vigilant, chary, wary
formal circumspect, prudent, regardful
F3 heedless, unthinking

heedless *adj*
oblivious, unthinking, careless, negligent, rash, reckless, foolhardy, inattentive, unobservant, unwary, thoughtless, regardless, unconcerned, unmindful
formal precipitate
F3 heedful, mindful, attentive, watchful, vigilant

hefty *adj*
1 LARGE, big, huge, strapping, burly, hulking, beefy, muscular, brawny, strong, powerful, vigorous, robust, massive, stout

2 *a hefty blow*
FORCEFUL, hard, heavy, weighty, powerful, vigorous, solid, substantial, massive, immense, colossal, bulky, awkward, unwieldy
3 *a hefty sum of money*
SUBSTANTIAL, considerable, generous, ample, sizeable
🔲 **1** small, slight **2** weak **3** small

height *n*
1 HIGHNESS, altitude, elevation, tallness, loftiness, stature
2 TOP, summit, peak, pinnacle, mountain top, hill top, apex, crest, crown, culmination, climax, perfection, extremity, maximum, limit, ultimate, uttermost, ceiling
technical vertex, zenith, apogee
🔲 **1** depth

heighten *v*
raise, elevate, lift, increase, add to, build up, magnify, intensify, strengthen, sharpen, improve, boost, amplify, enhance, exalt
formal augment
🔲 lower, decrease, diminish

heinous *adj*
evil, monstrous, atrocious, abominable, detestable, loathsome, contemptible, despicable, iniquitous, outrageous, shocking, flagrant, vicious, wicked, awful, hideous, villainous, revolting, hateful, odious, infamous, unspeakable, grave
formal abhorrent, execrable, facinorous, nefarious

heir, heiress *n*
beneficiary, co-heir, inheritor, inheritress, inheritrix, successor, scion
technical parcener, legatee

helix *n*
spiral, twist, coil, curl, whorl, loop, wreathe, screw, corkscrew
technical curlicue, volute

hell *n*
1 *heaven and hell*
underworld, inferno, infernal regions, lower regions, nether world, abyss, fire, bottomless pit, Hades, Acheron, Gehenna, Tophet, Abaddon, Tartarus, Malebolge
formal perdition, abode of the devil
colloq. down there, blazes
2 TORTURE, suffering, anguish, agony, torment, ordeal, nightmare, misery, wretchedness
formal tribulation
🔲 **1** heaven
▷ **give someone hell** trouble, annoy, torment, pester, vex, harass, punish, scold, beat, flog
▷ **hell for leather** very fast, hurriedly, quickly, rapidly, swiftly, recklessly, rashly, wildly, post-haste; *formal* precipitately
▷ **raise hell** object noisily, protest loudly, be very angry, be furious; *colloq.* hit the roof

hell-bent *adj*
determined, bent, intent, fixed, resolved, set, settled, tenacious, dogged, inflexible, unhesitating, unwavering
formal intransigent, obdurate

hellish *adj, adv*
▶ *adj* infernal, devilish, satanic, diabolical, demonic, fiendish, accursed, damnable, monstrous, savage, barbaric, wicked, cruel, abominable, atrocious,

dreadful, nasty, disagreeable, unpleasant
formal nefarious, execrable
🔲 heavenly
▶ *adv* dreadfully, awfully, extremely, unpleasantly

helm *n*
tiller, rudder, wheel
▷ **at the helm** in control, in command, in charge, leading, directing, in the driving seat, holding the reins, in the saddle

help *v, n*
▶ *v* **1** AID, assist, be of assistance, lend a hand, do something for, do someone a good turn, serve, be of use, guide, collaborate, co-operate, back, stand by, rally round, support, back, encourage, oblige, contribute to, promote, nurse, give a boost to
colloq. do your bit
2 IMPROVE, relieve, soothe, assuage, cure, heal, remedy, ease, facilitate, further
formal ameliorate, alleviate, mitigate
3 *can't help laughing*
be able to stop, control, prevent yourself
formal be able to refrain/abstain
🔲 **1** hinder **2** worsen
▶ *n* **1** AID, assistance, helping hand, collaboration, co-operation, encouragement, boost, backup, support, backing, advice, guidance, service, charity, relief, use, utility, avail, benefit, advantage
formal succour
colloq. shot in the arm, tower of strength
2 REMEDY, relief, cure, healing, improvement, restorative, moderator, balm, salve
formal alleviation, amelioration, mitigation
colloq. oil on troubled waters
🔲 **1** hindrance

helper *n*
assistant, deputy, auxiliary, subsidiary, attendant, aide, adjutant, right-hand man/woman, PA, mate, helpmate, partner, associate, colleague, collaborator, accomplice, worker, co-worker, subordinate, ally, supporter, second, second-in-command, employee, man/girl Friday, maid, servant

helpful *adj*
1 USEFUL, of use, practical, of service, constructive, worthwhile, valuable, beneficial, profitable, advantageous
2 *a helpful person*
CO-OPERATIVE, obliging, accommodating, neighbourly, friendly, caring, considerate, kind, benevolent, charitable, sympathetic, supportive
🔲 **1** useless, futile **2** unfriendly, cruel

helping *n*
serving, portion, share, ration, amount, plateful, bowlful, spoonful, piece
colloq. dollop

helpless *adj*
weak, feeble, powerless, dependent, vulnerable, exposed, unprotected, defenceless, abandoned, friendless, destitute, forlorn, desolate, incapable, incompetent, infirm, disabled, impotent, paralysed
formal debilitated
colloq. helpless as a newborn babe
🔲 strong, independent, competent

helpmate *n*
partner, support, assistant, associate, companion, consort, helper, helpmeet, better half, other half, spouse, husband, wife

helter-skelter *adv, adj*
▶ *adv* carelessly, confusedly, recklessly, wildly, hastily, hurriedly, pell-mell, rashly, impulsively, headlong
▶ *adj* confused, disordered, disorganized, jumbled, muddled, random, unsystematic, hit-or-miss, haphazard, topsy-turvy, higgledy-piggledy

hem *n, v*
▶ *n* edge, edging, border, margin, fringe, trim, trimming, frill, valance, flounce
technical fimbria
▶ *v* fringe, edge, trim, bind, border, skirt, fold
technical fimbriate
▷ **hem in** surround, enclose, box in, close in, shut in, confine, restrict, limit, hedge in, pen in, trap, constrain

hence *adv*
therefore, thus, for this reason, accordingly, consequently
formal ergo

henceforth *adv*
from now on, from this time on, in the future, henceforward, hereafter, hereinafter, hence

henchman *n*
aide, associate, subordinate, supporter, attendant, follower, right-hand man/woman, minion, bodyguard, lackey, underling
colloq. heavy, hit man, hatchet man, crony, minder, sidekick

henpecked *adj*
dominated, subjugated, browbeaten, bullied, intimidated, criticized, harassed, pestered, badgered, tormented, meek, timid
colloq. under someone's thumb, tied to someone's apron strings, like a puppet on a string
🔄 dominant

herald *n, v*
▶ *n* messenger, courier, announcer, crier, forerunner, precursor, usher, omen, token, signal, sign, indication
formal harbinger, portent, augury
▶ *v* **1** ANNOUNCE, proclaim, broadcast, advertise, publicize, make known, make public, trumpet
formal promulgate
2 PRECEDE, usher in, show, indicate, promise, foreshadow
formal harbinger, augur, portend, a presage
colloq. pave the way

heraldry *n*

Heraldic terms include: shield, crest, coat of arms, arms, badge, hatchment, emblazonry, emblem, ensign, insignia, regaliamantling, helmet, supporters, field, charge, compartment, motto, dexter, centre, sinister, annulet, fleur-de-lis, martlet, mullet, rampant, passant, sejant, caboched, statant, displayed, couchant, dormant, urinant, volant, chevron, pile, pall, saltire, quarter, orle, bordure, gyronny, lozenge, impale, escutcheon, antelope, camelopard, cockatrice, eagle, griffin, lion, phoenix, unicorn, wivern, addorsed, bezant, blazon, canton, cinquefoil, quatrefoil, roundel, semé, tierced, undee, urdé.

herbs and spices

Herbs and spices include: angelica, anise, basil, bay, bergamot, borage, camomile, catmint, chervil, chives, comfrey, cumin, dill, fennel, garlic, hyssop, lavender, lemon balm, lovage, marjoram, mint, oregano, parsley, rosemary, sage, savory, sorrel, tarragon, thyme; allspice, caper, caraway seeds, cardamon, cayenne pepper, chilli, cinnamon, cloves, coriander, curry, ginger, mace, mustard, nutmeg, paprika, pepper, saffron, sesame, turmeric, vanilla.

herculean *adj*
arduous, laborious, onerous, toilsome, demanding, strong, tough, exacting, difficult, enormous, powerful, exhausting, strenuous, tremendous, colossal, large, gigantic, massive, great, huge, mammoth, formidable, daunting, gruelling, heavy, hard

herd *n, v*
▶ *n* drove, flock, swarm, pack, collection, press, crush, mass, horde, throng, multitude, crowd, mob, host, the masses, rabble
colloq. riff-raff, plebs, proles
▶ *v* **1** FLOCK, congregate, gather, collect, get together, assemble, rally, huddle, muster
2 LEAD, guide, shepherd, round up, urge, drive, goad, force

herdsman *n*
shepherd, cowherd, cowman, drover, stockman, grazier, wrangler
US vaquero

here *adv*
1 *come here*
in/to/at this place, present, around, in
2 *I must finish here*
at this point, at this time, now, at this stage
🔄 **1** there, away, absent, missing **2** then

here and there *adv*
in different places, hither and thither, to and fro, sporadically
colloq. from pillar to post

hereafter *adv, n*
▶ *adv* from now on, from this time forward/onwards, hence, henceforth, henceforward, in the future, later, eventually
▶ *n* afterlife, heaven, paradise, life after death, life to come, next world, elysian fields, happy hunting-ground

hereditary *adj*
1 *a hereditary title*
inherited, bequeathed, handed down, family, ancestral, left, willed, transferred
2 *hereditary diseases*
inborn, inbred, innate, inherent, inherited, natural, congenital, genetic, transmissible

heresy *n*
heterodoxy, unorthodoxy, nonconformity, free-thinking, apostasy, dissidence, dissent, unbelief, atheism, agnosticism, scepticism, schism, error, sectarianism, separatism, revisionism, blasphemy
old use recusance
🔄 orthodoxy

heretic *n*
free-thinker, nonconformist, apostate, dissident, dissenter, unbeliever, atheist, agnostic, sceptic, revisionist, separatist, schismatic, sectarian, renegade
old use recusant
🔄 conformist

heretical *adj*
heterodox, unorthodox, free-thinking, dissident,

dissenting, revisionist, separatist, sectarian, renegade, unbelieving, atheistic, agnostic, sceptical, revisionist, rationalistic, schismatic, impious, irreverent, iconoclastic, blasphemous
old use recusant
F3 orthodox, conventional, conformist

heritage *n*
1 INHERITANCE, legacy, bequest, endowment, lot, portion, share, estate, birthright, due
2 HISTORY, past, tradition, culture, cultural, traditions, background, ancestry, descent, lineage, family, extraction, dynasty

hermetic *adj*
airtight, sealed, watertight, shut, hermetical

hermit *n*
recluse, solitary, loner, monk, ascetic, anchorite, anchoress, ancress, eremite, stylite, pillarist, pillar-saint

hermitage *n*
retreat, refuge, haven, sanctuary, cloister, shelter, asylum, hideaway, hideout, hiding-place

hero *n*
1 *the hero of a play*
protagonist, leading male role/part, leading actor, male lead, lead
2 *heroes in battle*
conqueror, victor, champion, man/person of courage, cavalier, lion, celebrity
colloq. goody
3 IDOL, star, superstar, pin-up, ideal, paragon, celebrity, god
colloq. heart-throb
F3 1 villain

heroic *adj*
brave, courageous, fearless, dauntless, undaunted, lion-hearted, stout-hearted, valiant, bold, daring, intrepid, adventurous, gallant, chivalrous, noble, determined, selfless
formal valorous, doughty
F3 cowardly, timid

heroine *n*
1 *the heroine of a play*
protagonist, leading female role/part, leading actress/lady, female lead, lead, diva, prima donna, prima ballerina
2 *heroines in battle*
conqueror, victor, champion, woman/person of courage, cavalier, lion, celebrity
colloq. goody
3 IDOL, star, superstar, pin-up, ideal, paragon, celebrity, goddess
F3 1 villain

heroism *n*
bravery, courage, valour, fearlessness, dauntlessness, boldness, daring, intrepidity, gallantry, chivalry, prowess, selflessness, determination, stout-heartedness, lion-heartedness
formal fortitude, doughtiness
F3 cowardice, timidity; *formal* pusillanimity

hero-worship *n*
admiration, idolization, adoration, worship, exaltation, glorification, adulation, idealization, deification
formal veneration
colloq. putting on a pedestal

hesitancy *n*
reluctance, misgiving, qualm, scruples, unwillingness, doubt, doubtfulness, reservation, uncertainty, indecision, wavering
formal disinclination, demur, irresolution
F3 willingness, certainty

hesitant *adj*
hesitating, reluctant, unwilling, half-hearted, uncertain, unsure, doubtful, sceptical, dubious, indecisive, irresolute, vacillating, delaying, stalling, wavering, tentative, wary, shy, timid, halting, stammering, stuttering
formal disinclined, demurring
F3 decisive, resolute, confident, fluent

hesitate *v*
1 PAUSE, delay, wait, think twice, hold back, hang back, falter, stumble, halt, stammer, stutter
2 BE RELUCTANT, be unwilling, shrink from, scruple, boggle, vacillate, waver, stall, be uncertain, dither
formal demur, be disinclined
colloq. shilly-shally, dilly-dally
F3 2 decide

hesitation *n*
pause, delay, holding-back, hanging-back, waiting, reluctance, unwillingness, hesitance, scruple(s), qualm(s), misgivings, doubt, doubtfulness, scepticism, second thoughts, vacillation, wavering, uncertainty, unsureness, indecision, stalling, faltering, stumbling, stammering, stuttering
formal irresolution, disinclination, demure, cunctation
colloq. dilly-dallying, shilly-shallying
F3 eagerness, assurance

heterodox *adj*
unorthodox, unsound, dissident, dissenting, free-thinking, heretical, schismatic, iconoclastic, revisionist
F3 orthodox

heterogeneous *adj*
diverse, varied, miscellaneous, assorted, different, mixed, motley, diversified, divergent, catholic, opposed, unlike, unrelated, dissimilar, contrary, contrasted, discrepant
technical polymorphic
formal multiform, disparate, incongruous
F3 homogeneous

heterosexual *adj & n*
colloq. straight; *slang* hetero, breeder
F3 homosexual, gay

hew *v*
1 CHOP cut, fell, saw, axe, lop, hack, sever, prune, trim, split
2 FORM, carve, sculpt, sculpture, chip, whittle, chisel, hammer, fashion, model, shape, make

heyday *n*
peak, pinnacle, prime, flush, bloom, flowering, culmination, golden age, boom time

hiatus *n*
break, gap, breach, opening, rift, space, void, chasm, blank, discontinuity, pause, rest, lull, interruption, interval, lapse, suspension
formal aperture, discontinuance, lacuna

hidden *adj*
1 *a hidden door*

CONCEALED, covered, shrouded, veiled, masked, disguised, camouflaged, unseen, secret, out of sight
2 OBSCURE, dark, occult, secret, covert, close, cryptic, indistinct, mysterious, abstruse, mystical, latent, ulterior
formal arcane, recondite
colloq. under wraps
⊟ 1 showing, apparent, revealed, visible, on view **2** obvious, clear, distinct

hide¹ *v*
1 CONCEAL, cover, cloak, shroud, veil, draw a veil over, put out of sight, screen, mask, disguise, camouflage, obscure, shadow, eclipse, darken, cloud, obstruct, bury, store, stow, secrete, withhold, keep dark, suppress
formal dissemble
colloq. stash away, bottle up, keep under your hat, sweep under the carpet, keep under wraps
2 TAKE COVER, shelter, conceal yourself, lie low, go to ground, go into hiding, keep out of sight, cover your tracks, lurk
colloq. hole up, disappear into thin air, keep a low profile, lie doggo, lay a false scent
⊟ 1 reveal, show, display

hide² *n*
the hide of an animal
skin, pelt, fell, fur, coat, fleece, leather

hideaway *n*
retreat, hiding-place, hideout, refuge, sanctuary, shelter, cloister, hermitage, haven, nest, den, lair, hole

hidebound *adj*
set, rigid, fixed, entrenched, narrow, narrow-minded, intolerant, strait-laced, conventional, ultra-conservative, bigoted, uncompromising, reactionary
formal intractable
⊟ liberal, progressive

hideous *adj*
ugly, repulsive, repellent, grotesque, monstrous, unsightly, horrid, ghastly, awful, dreadful, frightful, terrible, grim, gruesome, macabre, abominable, terrifying, shocking, outrageous, appalling, horrifying, disgusting, revolting, horrible, horrendous
⊟ beautiful, attractive

hideout *n*
retreat, hiding-place, hideaway, refuge, sanctuary, shelter, cloister, hermitage, haven, nest, den, lair, hole

hiding¹ *n*
go into hiding
concealment, cover, veiling, screening, disguise, shroud, veil, mask, camouflage

hiding² *n*
give someone a good hiding
beating, flogging, whipping, caning, spanking, thrashing, drubbing, battering
colloq. walloping, tanning, whacking, belting, licking

hidingplace *n*
hideaway, hideout, lair, den, hole, hide, nest, cache, cover, shelter, refuge, haven, sanctuary, retreat, cloister

hierarchy *n*
pecking order, ranking, grading, scale, series, ladder, echelons, strata, system, structure

higgledy-piggledy *adv, adj*
▶ *adv* any old how, anyhow, indiscriminately, untidily, confusedly, haphazardly, pell-mell, topsy-turvy
▶ *adj* confused, disorderly, disorganized, untidy, jumbled, muddled, haphazard, indiscriminate, topsy-turvy

high *adj, n*
▶ *adj* **1** TALL, lofty, elevated, soaring, towering
2 GREAT, strong, powerful, forceful, vigorous, violent, intense, extreme
3 IMPORTANT, influential, powerful, eminent, distinguished, notable, prominent, chief, top, principal, leading, senior, high-ranking, elevated, exalted
4 *a higher form of life*
advanced, complex, elaborate, progressive, ultra-modern, hi-tech
5 *a high standard*
good, excellent, fine, outstanding, great, perfect, exemplary, commendable, noteworthy, first-class, first-rate, superior, superlative, surpassing, unequalled, unparalleled, select, choice, quality, de luxe, gilt-edged, tiptop, top-class, blue-chip
colloq. classy
6 *have a high opinion of someone*
favourable, good, positive, well-disposed, approving, complimentary, admiring, agreeable, appreciative
7 *high moral principles*
noble, moral, ethical, lofty, virtuous, upright, admirable, honourable, worthy
8 *a high price*
expensive, dear, costly, exorbitant, excessive, inflated, extortionate
colloq. steep
9 HIGH-PITCHED, soprano, treble, falsetto, sharp, shrill, tinny, piping, piercing, penetrating, acute
10 *high on drugs*
intoxicated, inebriated, hallucinating
colloq. turned on, having your mind blown, doped, on a trip, stoned, freaked out, spaced out, wasted, zonked; *US* wired; *slang* bombed, loaded, blitzed, blasted, out of it
11 *meat going high*
bad, off, rotting, smelling, decayed, putrid, rancid
⊟ 1 low, short **2** low, slight **3** unimportant, lowly **4** low **5** low, poor, inferior **6** low, poor, bad **7** low **8** cheap **9** deep, low
▷ **high and dry** abandoned, marooned, stranded, helpless, bereft, destitute; *colloq.* ditched, dumped
▷ **high and mighty** arrogant, conceited, haughty, overbearing, self-important, snobbish, superior, proud, egotistic, condescending, patronizing, disdainful, cavalier, imperious, overweening; *colloq.* stuck-up, swanky
▶ *n* **1** *feeling on a high*
intoxication, inebriation, hallucination
colloq. trip, turn-on, freak-out
2 RECORD, height, summit, peak, top
formal zenith
⊟ 1, 2 low

high spirits *n*
boisterousness, exhilaration, exuberance, ebullience, animation, energy, spirit, boldness, liveliness, sparkle, good cheer, vivacity, capers, hilarity, buoyancy, *joie de vivre*
colloq. bounce

high-born *adj*
noble, aristocratic, blue-blooded, thoroughbred, well-born, patrician
⊟ low-born

highbrow *n, adj*
▶ *n* intellectual, scholar, genius, mastermind,

academic
colloq. egghead, brains, brainbox, know-it-all, clever clogs, boffin
▶ *adj* intellectual, sophisticated, cultured, cultivated, academic, scholarly, bookish, deep, profound, serious, classical
colloq. brainy
Ⴆ lowbrow

high-class *adj*
upper-class, top-class, top-flight, high-quality, quality, de luxe, luxurious, élite, elegant, superior, excellent, first-rate, choice, select, exclusive
colloq. posh, classy, super
Ⴆ ordinary, mediocre

highfalutin, highfaluting *adj*
pretentious, pompous, supercilious, bombastic, grandiose, high-flown, high-sounding, lofty
formal affected, magniloquent
colloq. la-di-da, swanky

high-flown *adj*
florid, extravagant, exaggerated, elaborate, flamboyant, ornate, ostentatious, pretentious, high-sounding, grandiose, pompous, bombastic, turgid, artificial, stilted, affected, lofty, highfalutin, supercilious
formal grandiloquent
colloq. la-di-da

high-handed *adj*
overbearing, domineering, arrogant, haughty, imperious, dictatorial, autocratic, despotic, tyrannical, oppressive, arbitrary
formal peremptory
colloq. bossy

highland *n*
mountain, hill, upland, elevation, rise, mound, mount, height, ridge, plateau

highlight *n, v*
▶ *n* high point, high spot, most interesting/exciting part, most significant feature, focus, peak, climax, best, cream
▶ *v* underline, emphasize, put emphasis on, stress, accentuate, accent, play up, point up, spotlight, illuminate, show up, set off, focus on, feature, call attention to

highly *adv*
1 VERY, very much, greatly, considerably, decidedly, extremely, certainly, immensely, vastly, hugely, tremendously, exceptionally, extraordinarily
2 *think highly of someone*
favourably, approvingly, enthusiastically, warmly, well, appreciatively

highly-strung *adj*
sensitive, neurotic, nervous, easily upset, nervy, jumpy, edgy, on edge, temperamental, excitable, restless, overwrought, tense, stressed
colloq. wound up, uptight
Ⴆ calm

high-minded *adj*
lofty, noble, pure, moral, ethical, principled, idealistic, elevated, virtuous, upright, righteous, honourable, fair, good, worthy
Ⴆ immoral, unscrupulous

high-pitched *adj*
soprano, treble, falsetto, sharp, shrill, tinny, piping,

piercing, penetrating, acute
Ⴆ deep, low

high-powered *adj*
powerful, forceful, driving, aggressive, insistent, dynamic, ambitious, enterprising, assertive, energetic, vigorous
colloq. go-ahead, pushy

high-priced *adj*
expensive, dear, costly, exorbitant, excessive, extortionate, high, pricey, unreasonable
colloq. steep, stiff
Ⴆ cheap

high-sounding *adj*
grandiose, flamboyant, ostentatious, overblown, pompous, florid, artificial, bombastic, extravagant, high-flown, ponderous, pretentious, stilted, strained
formal affected, grandiloquent, magniloquent, orotund

high-spirited *adj*
boisterous, bouncy, exuberant, effervescent, frolicsome, ebullient, sparkling, animated, vigorous, vibrant, vivacious, lively, active, dynamic, energetic, spirited, dashing, bold, daring
Ⴆ quiet, sedate, placid
colloq. full of beans

highwayman *n*
bandit, robber, land-pirate, rank-rider, knight of the road, footpad

hijack *v*
commandeer, skyjack, seize, take over
formal expropriate

hike *v, n*
▶ *v* 1 RAMBLE, walk, trek, wander, march, tramp, trudge, plod
2 RAISE, increasse, put up, lift, pull up
colloq. jack up, push up
3 *hike up your clothing*
pull, tug, jerk, hoist, jack, hitch, raise, lift
colloq. yank
▶ *n* ramble, walk, trek, wander, tramp, trudge, march

hilarious *adj*
funny, amusing, comical, humorous, side-splitting, farcical, laughable, riotous, uproarious, noisy, boisterous, rollicking, merry, entertaining, jolly, jovial
formal risible
colloq. hysterical, killing, a scream
Ⴆ serious, grave

hilarity *n*
mirth, laughter, fun, amusement, comedy, comedy, levity, frivolity, merriment, jollity, conviviality, high spirits, boisterousness, exuberance, exhilaration
Ⴆ seriousness, gravity

hill *n*
1 HILLOCK, knoll, mound, hummock, prominence, eminence, elevation, rise, rising ground, hilltop, foothill, down, fell, tor, mountain, mount, height
US mesa
2 *a steep hill*
slope, incline, gradient, ramp, rise, ascent, drop, descent, declivity
formal acclivity

hillock *n*
mound, hummock, knoll, dune, barrow, knap, knob, monticle, monticulus, tump
Scot. knowe

hilt *n*
handle, grip, handgrip, shaft, haft, heft, helve
▷ **to the hilt** completely, fully, as fully as possible,
wholly, entirely, utterly, to the full, to the end, to the
maximum extent, in every respect; *colloq.* all the way,
from first to last, from beginning to end

hind *adj*
rear, back, hinder, tail, after, posterior, caudal
F3 fore

hinder *v*
hamper, obstruct, block, impede, encumber,
handicap, hamstring, hold up, delay, slow down, hold
back, check, curb, halt, stop, forestall, arrest, prevent,
foil, frustrate, thwart, balk, oppose, inhibit, interfere
with, interrupt
formal retard
colloq. stymie, put a spoke in someone's wheel
F3 help, aid, assist

hindmost *adj*
last, farthest behind, furthest back, rearmost, tail,
endmost, furthest, final, remotest, trailing, ultimate,
concluding, terminal
F3 foremost

hindrance *n*
obstruction, impediment, handicap, encumbrance,
obstacle, stumbling-block, block, barrier, bar, check,
curb, restraint, restriction, thwarting, interference,
interruption, stoppage, hold-up, delay, limitation,
difficulty, drag, snag, hitch, drawback, disadvantage,
inconvenience, deterrent, foil
F3 help, aid, assistance

hinge *v*
centre, turn, revolve, pivot, hang, depend, rest
formal be contingent

hint *n, v*
▶ *n* **1** TIP, advice, suggestion, help, clue, inkling,
suspicion, tip-off, cue, reminder, indication, sign,
pointer, mention, allusion, intimation, whisper,
insinuation, implication, innuendo
colloq. wrinkle
2 *a hint of garlic*
touch, trace, tinge, taste, dash, soupçon, sprinkling,
speck, whiff, suspicion, suggestion, nuance
▶ *v* suggest, prompt, indicate, signal, imply,
insinuate, intimate, allude, mention
colloq. tip off, tip someone the wink

hinterland *n*
interior, hinderland, back-country, backveld,
back-blocks

hip *n*
haunch, loin, pelvis, hindquarters, posterior, buttocks,
rump, croup, huck, huckle

hippie *n*
beatnik, flower child, rebel, loner, bohemian, deviant
colloq. dropout

hire *v, n*
▶ *v* **1** RENT, let, lease, charter, commission, book,
reserve
2 EMPLOY, take on, sign up, sign on, engage, appoint,
enlist, retain
F3 **2** dismiss; *colloq.* fire
▶ *n* rental, rent, lease, fee, charge, pay, cost, price,
salary, wage

hire-purchase *n*
instalment plan, easy terms
colloq. never-never

hirsute *adj*
hairy, bearded, unshaven, bristly, bewhiskered, shaggy
technical hispid
formal crinal, crinate, crinigerous, crinose, crinite
F3 bald, hairless

hiss *v, n*
▶ *v* **1** WHISTLE, shrill, whizz, sizzle
formal sibilate
2 JEER, mock, scoff at, scorn, ridicule, taunt, boo,
hoot, shout down, catcall
formal deride
colloq. blow raspberries
▶ *n* **1** WHISTLE, hissing, buzz
formal sibilance, sibilation
2 JEER, mockery, scoffing, scorn, taunting,
contempt, hoot, boo, catcall
formal derision
colloq. raspberry

historian *n*
chronicler, archivist, annalist, diarist, narrator,
recorder, historiographer, chronologer

historic *adj*
famous, famed, renowned, celebrated, momentous,
important, significant, epoch-making, notable,
memorable, remarkable, outstanding, extraordinary
formal consequential
colloq. red-letter
F3 unimportant, insignificant, unknown

⚠ **historic** or **historical** ?
Historic means 'famous or important in history': *a
historic battle. Historical* means 'of or about history':
books on military and historical topics; or 'having
actually happened or lived, in contrast to existing
only in legend or fiction': *Is Macbeth a historical
person?*

---

historical *adj*
1 *of historical interest*
past, old, former, prior, ancient, bygone
formal of yore
2 REAL, actual, authentic, factual, documented,
recorded, chronicled, confirmed, verified, verifiable
formal attested
F3 **2** legendary, fictional

history *n*
1 PAST, bygone/olden days, former times, days of old,
the (good) old days, antiquity, yesterday
formal yesteryear, days of yore
2 CHRONICLE, record(s), annals, archives,
chronology, account, study, report(s), narrative, story,
tale, saga, biography, life, autobiography, memoirs
3 BACKGROUND, experience, record, credentials,
qualifications, education, family, circumstances

histrionic *adj*
dramatic, exaggerated, theatrical, melodramatic,
insincere, sensational, unnatural, forced, artificial,
bogus, ham
formal affected

histrionics *n*
overacting, theatricality, dramatics, performance,
artificiality, insincerity, unnaturalness,
sensationalism, staginess, tantrums, scene

formal affectation
colloq. ranting and raving

hit   *v, n*
▶ *v* **1** STRIKE, knock, tap, smack, slap, thrash, bash, bat, thump, punch, beat, pound, batter, buffet, cuff, box, thrash
colloq. whack, belt, wallop, clout, biff, sock, clobber, zap
2 BUMP, collide with, bang, crash into, smash into, run into, meet head-on, plough into, damage, harm
3 AFFECT, have an effect on, upset, disturb, trouble, overwhelm, move, touch
formal perturb
colloq. knock for six
4 *the thought hit me*
come to mind, come to, strike, be remembered, be thought of, occur to, dawn on
▷ **hit back** retaliate, reciprocate, counter-attack, strike back, criticize in return
▷ **hit it off** get along with, get on (well) with, be/become friendly with, become friends, warm to, grow to like, relate well to each other, get on good terms with;
colloq. become thick as thieves
▷ **hit on** realize, arrive at, guess, think of, chance on, stumble on, light on, uncover, discover, invent
▷ **hit out** lash out, assail, attack, rail, strike out, denounce, condemn, criticize; *formal* denounce, inveigh, vilify
▶ *n* **1** STROKE, shot, blow, knock, tap, slap, smack, buffet, thrashing, beating, punch, cuff, box, bash, bump, collision, impact, crash, smash
colloq. clout, whack, belt, wallop, clobbering, biff, sock
2 SUCCESS, triumph
colloq. winner
F3 **2** failure

hitch   *v, n*
▶ *v* **1** FASTEN, attach, tie, harness, tether, bind, yoke, couple, connect, join, unite
2 PULL, heave, tug, jerk, hoist
colloq. yank, hike (up)
F3 **1** unhitch, unfasten
▶ *n* snag, delay, hold-up, trouble, problem, difficulty, mishap, setback, hiccup, drawback, catch, impediment, hindrance, obstacle, block, check, barrier, obstruction

hitherto   *adv*
until now, up to now, till now, so far, previously, beforehand, thus far
formal heretofore

hit-or-miss   *adj*
disorganized, haphazard, indiscriminate, undirected, unplanned, careless, offhand, casual, aimless, random, trial-and-error, perfunctory, lackadaisical, apathetic, cursory, uneven
F3 directed, planned, organized

hoard   *n, v*
▶ *n* collection, accumulation, mass, heap, pile, fund, reservoir, supply, reserve, store, stockpile, cache, treasure-trove
formal aggregation, conglomeration
colloq. stash
▶ *v* collect, gather, amass, accumulate, heap (up), stack up, buy up, save, set aside, put by, put away, lay in, lay up, store, stock up, stockpile, pile up, keep, treasure
colloq. stash away
F3 use, spend, squander

⚠ **hoard** or **horde** ?
A *hoard* is a store or hidden stock of something: *He had a hoard of chocolate bars under the bed*. A *horde* is a crowd or large number of people, etc: *Hordes of tourists come here every year.*

hoarder   *n*
collector, saver, gatherer, miser, niggard, magpie, squirrel

hoary   *adj*
1 WHITE-HAIRED, white, grey, grey-haired, silvery, grizzled, venerable, old, aged, ancient, antique, antiquated
formal canescent, senescent
2 *that hoary old joke*
old, familiar, ancient, archaic
colloq. old-hat

hoarse   *adj*
husky, croaky, croaking, throaty, guttural, gravelly, gruff, growling, rough, harsh, rasping, raspy, grating, raucous, discordant
F3 clear, smooth

hoax   *n, v*
▶ *n* trick, prank, practical joke, put-on, joke, jest, ruse, fake, fraud, deception, bluff, humbug, cheat, swindle
colloq. leg-pull, con, put-up job, frame-up, fast one, scam, spoof
▶ *v* trick, deceive, play a practical joke on, take in, fool, dupe, gull, delude, swindle, cheat, hoodwink, bluff
colloq. con, bamboozle, have on, pull someone's leg, take for a ride, lead up the garden path, pull the wool over someone's eyes, pull a fast one on, double-cross, two-time

hoaxer   *n*
joker, practical joker, prankster, trickster, hoodwinker, mystifier, humbug
colloq. bamboozler, spoofer

hobble   *v*
limp, walk with a limp, stumble, falter, stagger, totter, reel, dodder, shuffle, walk awkwardly, walk lamely

hobby   *n*
pastime, interest, diversion, recreation, relaxation, pursuit, leisure, activity/pursuit, sideline, game, sport, entertainment, amusement, divertissement

hobgoblin   *n*
goblin, imp, elf, dwarf, gnome, spectre, spirit, evil spirit, sprite, apparition, bugbear, bogey, bugaboo

hobnob   *v*
associate, fraternize, keep company, mingle, mix, go around, socialize
formal consort
colloq. hang about, pal around

hocus-pocus   *n*
trickery, swindle, deception, delusion, chicanery, gibberish, humbug, imposture, nonsense, mumbo-jumbo, rigmarole, sleight of hand, legerdemain, trompe-l'oeil, artifice, cant, jargon, gobbledygook, abracadabra, cheat, hoax, deceit, conjuring
formal prestidigitation

hog   *n, v*
▶ *n* pig, boar, wild boar, porker, grunter, swine

▶ *v* monopolize, control, dominate, corner, take over, keep to yourself

hogwash *n*
rubbish, nonsense, drivel, gibberish, trash, tripe, twaddle
colloq. bunk, bunkum, claptrap, piffle, bilge, poppycock, hot air, cobblers, eyewash, hooey, tosh, balderdash, rot, tommyrot; *slang* balls, bollocks, shit, bullshit

hoi polloi *n*
the common people, the ordinary people, the masses, the proletariat, the third estate
formal the populace
colloq. riff-raff, the plebs, the peasants, the rabble, the herd, the great unwashed, the proles
Ⅎ aristocracy, élite, nobility

hoist *v, n*
▶ *v* lift, elevate, raise, erect, jack up, winch up, heave, rear, uplift
▶ *n* jack, winch, crane, tackle, pulley, capstan, lift, elevator

hoity-toity *adj*
arrogant, proud, overweening, conceited, haughty, scornful, snobbish, supercilious, lofty, disdainful, pompous
colloq. stuck-up, high and mighty, toffee-nosed, snooty, uppity

hold *v, n*
▶ *v* **1** GRIP, have in your hand(s), grasp, clutch, clasp, seize, cling to, embrace, enfold, hug, have, own, possess, keep, retain
2 *hold a meeting*
run, organize, conduct, carry on, continue, call, summon, convene, assemble, preside over
3 *hold someone's attention*
keep, engage, occupy, maintain, catch, arrest, absorb, engross, fascinate, enthral, captivate, rivet, fill, monopolize
4 CONSIDER, regard, judge, reckon, suppose, view, treat, think, believe, maintain, assume, presume
formal esteem, deem
5 BEAR, support, hold up, keep up, sustain, carry, take, buttress, prop up, brace
6 IMPRISON, detain, confine, impound, imprison, hold in custody, lock up, stop, arrest, check, curb, restrain
formal incarcerate
7 CLING, stick, adhere, stay, remain
8 *the memories that they held dear*
cherish, treasure, value, prize, hold dear
9 *the bus holds 53 passengers*
contain, accommodate, take, have a capacity of
formal compromise
10 *hold office as prime minister*
occupy, fill, take up, continue, fulfil, have, hold down
11 *the fine weather will hold*
continue, carry on, last, remain, stay, keep up
12 *the invitation/theory still holds*
stay, apply, remain, remain valid/true, be in force/ operation, hold up
Ⅎ **1** drop **5** collapse, fall, break **6** release, free, liberate
▷ **hold back 1** CONTROL, keep back, curb, check, bar, restrain, impede, stop, delay, prevent, obstruct, suppress, stifle, retain, withhold, repress, contain, inhibit; *formal* retard **2** HESITATE, delay, shrink, refuse; *formal* desist, refrain, forbear
Ⅎ **1** release, disclose

▷ **hold down 1** *hold down a job* keep, have, occupy, continue in **2** *hold someone down* keep down, oppress, dominate, tyrannize, suppress
▷ **hold forth** speak, talk, lecture, discourse, preach, harangue; *formal* orate, declaim; *colloq.* spout
▷ **hold off 1** FEND OFF, fight off, ward off, stave off, keep off, keep at bay, repel, rebuff **2** DELAY, postpone, put off, defer, avoid, wait
▷ **hold on 1** GRASP, grip, clutch, clasp, seize, cling to **2** CONTINUE, endure, remain, persevere, carry on, keep going, survive; *colloq.* hang on
▷ **hold out 1** OFFER, give, present, extend; *formal* proffer **2** LAST, last out, continue, carry on, persist, endure, persevere, stand fast, stand firm, resist, withstand; *colloq.* hang on
Ⅎ **2** give in, yield
▷ **hold over** defer, postpone, put off, delay, adjourn, suspend, shelve
▷ **hold up 1** SUPPORT, bear, carry, hold, sustain, brace, shore up, prop up, lift, raise **2** DELAY, detain, slow, hinder, impede, obstruct, set/put back; *formal* retard **3** ROB, steal from, burgle, knock over, break into; *US* burglarize; *colloq.* mug, stick up, knock off, nobble
▷ **hold water** bear scrutiny/examination, convince, be convincing, make sense, ring true, work, stand up, pass the test; *colloq.* wash
▷ **hold with** agree with, go along with, approve of, support, subscribe to, accept; *formal* countenance
▷ **hold your own** resist, withstand, survive, stand fast, stand firm, stand your ground; *colloq.* keep your head above water
Ⅎ be defeated, lose ground
▶ *n* **1** GRIP, grasp, clasp, embrace, hug
2 INFLUENCE, power, sway, mastery, dominance, dominion, authority, control, grip, leverage
colloq. clout
▷ **get hold of 1** OBTAIN, get, acquire, get your hands on **2** CONTACT, reach, speak to, communicate with, get through to
▷ **put on hold** delay, postpone, put off, hold off, defer; *colloq.* put on the back burner

holder *n*
1 *holders of tickets*
bearer, owner, possessor, proprietor, keeper, purchaser, custodian, occupant, incumbent
2 CONTAINER, receptacle, case, housing, casing, cover, sheath, rest, stand

holdings *n*
investments, shares, stocks, securities, bonds, assets, resources, land, real estate, possessions, property, estate, tenure

hold-up *n*
1 DELAY, wait, hitch, setback, snag, difficulty, problem, trouble, obstruction, stoppage, (traffic) jam, bottleneck
2 ROBBERY, burglary, theft, break-in, raid
colloq. mugging; *slang* heist, stick-up, stick-up job

hole *n, v*
▶ *n* **1** *dig a hole*
dent, dimple, depression, excavation, crater, mine, shaft, pothole, scoop, hollow, cavity, pit, chasm, cave, cavern, chamber, pocket, recess
2 *a hole in the roof*
aperture, opening, space, break, gap, pore, puncture, perforation, eyelet, tear, split, crack, fissure, breach, rift, vent, notch, slit, gash, rent, outlet, shaft, slot
formal orifice

3 *an animal's hole*
burrow, nest, lair, den, covert, set
4 *a hole in a theory*
flaw, fault, mistake, error, defect, loophole,
inconsistency, discrepancy, weakness
5 HOVEL, slum, shack
colloq. dump, tip, pigsty
6 *in a hole*
predicament, difficulty, quandary, snag, plight
colloq. fix, mess, jam, spot, pickle, hot/deep water,
pretty pass
▷ **pick holes in** criticize, find fault with; *colloq.* run
down, pull to pieces, nit-pick
▶ *v* puncture, perforate, pierce, breach, break, crack,
stab, spike, slit, gash, rent
▷ **hole up** hide, conceal yourself, take cover, lie low,
go to ground, go into hiding

hole-and-corner *adj*
secretive, secret, underhand, clandestine, covert,
furtive, stealthy, surreptitious
colloq. back-door, backstairs, hush-hush, sneaky,
under-the-counter
E3 open, public

holiday *n*
1 *go on holiday*
vacation, trip, recess, leave, leave of absence, time off,
day off, break, rest, half-term, furlough
2 *a national holiday*
public holiday, bank holiday, legal holiday, feast day,
festival, celebration, anniversary, saint's day, holy day
Related adjectives: ferial, festal

holier-than-thou *adj*
self-righteous, sanctimonious, self-satisfied,
complacent, self-approving, smug, priggish, pietistic,
pious, religiose
formal unctuous
colloq. goody-goody,
E3 humble, modest, meek

holiness *n*
sacredness, sanctity, spirituality, divinity, piety,
devoutness, godliness, consecration, dedication,
saintliness, blessedness, religiousness, goodness,
virtuousness, righteousness, purity, perfection,
sinlessness
E3 impiety

holler *n & v*
yell, shout, bawl, bellow, roar, call, cheer, shriek,
clamour, cry, howl, yelp, yowl, whoop

hollow *adj, n, v*
▶ *adj* **1** CONCAVE, indented, depressed, caved-in,
sunken, deep-set, deep, cavernous, empty, vacant,
void, unfilled
formal incurvate
2 FALSE, artificial, deceptive, insincere, hypocritical,
pretended, deceitful, sham, meaningless, empty, vain,
futile, fruitless, useless, pointless, profitless, worthless,
valueless, unavailing, of no avail, Pyrrhic
3 *a hollow sound*
dull, flat, low, muffled, deep, rumbling, echoing,
reverberant
E3 1 solid **2** real
▷ **beat someone hollow** defeat soundly/
convincingly, rout, overwhelm, crash; *colloq.* thrash,
lick, hammer, trounce, annihilate, devastate,
slaughter
▶ *n* **1** HOLE, pit, well, cavity, crater, excavation,
cavern, cave, depression, basin, bowl, cup, dimple,

dent, dip, niche, recess, nook, cranny, indentation,
groove, channel, trough
formal concavity
2 VALLEY, gorge, ravine, dell, glen, dale, cirque
▶ *v* dig, excavate, burrow, tunnel, scoop, gouge,
channel, groove, furrow, pit, dent, indent

holocaust *n*
conflagration, flames, inferno, destruction,
devastation, annihilation, extermination, extinction,
massacre, carnage, mass murder, genocide, ethnic
cleansing, sacrifice, slaughter, pogrom, hecatomb
formal immolation

holy *adj*
1 *holy ground*
sacred, hallowed, consecrated, sanctified, sacrosanct,
dedicated, blessed, venerated, revered, religious,
spiritual, divine
2 PIOUS, religious, devout, godly, God-fearing,
pietistic, saintly, virtuous, good, righteous, moral,
faithful, pure, perfect, sinless
E3 1 unsanctified **2** impious, irreligious

homage *n*
recognition, acknowledgement, tribute, honour,
praise, adulation, admiration, regard, respect,
deference, reverence, adoration, awe, worship,
devotion
formal esteem, veneration

home *n, adj, v*
▶ *n* **1** *invite someone to your home*
HOUSE, flat, apartment, bungalow, cottage, address
formal residence, abode, domicile, dwelling,
dwelling-place, habitation
colloq. pad, digs, semi-, roof over your head,
somewhere to live
2 BIRTHPLACE, roots, home town, native town,
homeland, native country, country of origin,
mother country, motherland, fatherland
3 INSTITUTION, residential home, nursing home,
retirement home, old people's home, sheltered
housing, children's home, Dr Barnardo's home, refuge,
hostel, centre, retreat, asylum, safe place
4 *the home of jazz*
PLACE OF ORIGIN, birthplace, source, fount, cradle,
habitat, natural environment, element
▷ **at home 1** COMFORTABLE, relaxed, at
ease **2** FAMILIAR, knowledgeable, experienced,
skilled, conversant, competent; *colloq.* well up
▷ **bring home** make someone understand, make
someone aware, impress, emphasize, instil, inculcate
▷ **nothing to write home about** not interesting,
not exciting, dull, drab, boring, ordinary, mediocre,
inferior, predictable; *colloq.* not enough to set the
Thames on fire, no great shakes, nothing
earthshattering
Related adjective: domestic
▶ *adj* domestic, household, family, internal, local,
national, native, inland, interior
E3 foreign, international, overseas
▶ *v* ▷ **home in on** pinpoint, aim, direct, focus,
concentrate, zero in on, zoom in on

homeland *n*
native land, country of origin, native country,
fatherland, motherland, mother country

homeless *adj, n*
▶ *adj* itinerant, travelling, nomadic, wandering,
vagrant, rootless, unsettled, displaced, dispossessed,
evicted, exiled, outcast, abandoned, forsaken,

destitute
formal of no fixed abode
colloq. down-and-out; *slang* dossing
▶ *n* travellers, vagabonds, vagrants, tramps, squatters
formal derelicts
colloq. down-and-outs; *slang* dossers

homely *adj*
1 *a homely room*
HOMELIKE, homey, comfortable, cosy, snug, relaxed,
informal, friendly, welcoming, cheerful, hospitable,
intimate, familiar
2 SIMPLE, plain, everyday, ordinary, domestic,
natural, modest, unassuming, unpretentious,
unsophisticated, folksy, homespun
3 *a homely person*
PLAIN, unattractive, unlovely, ugly, unprepossessing
colloq. not much to look at
◳ 1 grand, formal 3 attractive, lovely, good-
looking

homespun *adj*
plain, simple, uncomplicated, unpolished, unrefined,
unsophisticated, rough, rude, crude, rustic, homely,
home-made, inelegant, amateurish, coarse, artless,
folksy
◳ sophisticated

homicidal *adj*
deadly, lethal, murderous, violent, bloodthirsty,
mortal, death-dealing, maniacal
formal sanguinary

homicide *n*
murder, manslaughter, assassination, killing,
bloodshed, slaughter, slaying

homily *n*
sermon, lecture, talk, speech, address, harangue,
preaching
formal discourse, postil, oration
colloq. spiel

homogeneity *n*
uniformity, consistency, identicalness, similarity,
sameness, resemblance, likeness, oneness,
correspondence, agreement, analogousness,
comparability
formal consonancy, similitude
◳ difference, disagreement

homogeneous *adj*
uniform, consistent, unvarying, unvaried, identical,
similar, alike, (all) the same, of the same kind, all of a
piece, akin, kindred, analogous, corresponding,
comparable, harmonious, compatible
formal cognate, correlative
◳ heterogeneous, different

homogenize *v*
blend, merge, combine, amalgamate, coalesce, fuse,
unite

homologous *adj*
related, matching, similar, parallel, comparable,
analogous, equivalent, like, correspondent,
corresponding
◳ different, dissimilar

homosexual *n, adj*
▶ *n* gay, lesbian, invert, bisexual
slang queer, poof, dyke, faggot, fag, fairy, bent, pansy,
queen, homo, nancy, pansy, woofter
◳ heterosexual; *colloq.* straight
See also **lesbian, gay**.

▶ *adj* gay, lesbian
colloq. camp, butch; *slang* queer, bent, dykey

hone *v*
sharpen, whet, point, edge, grind, file, polish, develop

honest *adj*
1 LAW-ABIDING, virtuous, upright, upstanding,
ethical, moral, principled, high-minded, right-
minded, scrupulous, honourable, dependable,
reputable, respectable, reliable, trustworthy,
incorruptible, true, genuine, real
2 TRUTHFUL, sincere, frank, candid, blunt,
outspoken, direct, straight, outright, forthright,
straightforward, plain, simple, open, plain-speaking
colloq. up front
3 FAIR, just, impartial, objective, equitable, above-
board, legitimate, legal, lawful
colloq. on the level, fair and square, honest as the day is
long, straight as a die
◳ 1 dishonourable 2 dishonest 3 unjust

honestly *adv*
1 REALLY, truly, truthfully, sincerely, frankly, to be
honest, directly, outright, plainly, openly
colloq. straight up, not to put too fine a point on it
2 LEGITIMATELY, legally, lawfully, morally, ethically,
fairly, justly, objectively, honourably, in good faith
colloq. on the level
◳ 2 dishonestly, dishonourably

honesty *n*
1 VIRTUE, uprightness, honour, integrity, morality,
morals, ethics, principles, righteousness,
incorruptibility, scrupulousness, trustworthiness,
genuineness, veracity
formal probity, rectitude
2 TRUTHFULNESS, sincerity, frankness, candour,
bluntness, outspokenness, forthrightness,
straightforwardness, plain-speaking, explicitness,
openness
3 FAIRNESS, legitimacy, legality, equity, justness,
objectivity, impartiality, balance, even-handedness
◳ 2 dishonesty 3 bias, prejudice, partiality

honorarium *n*
fee, pay, salary, remuneration, recompense, reward
formal emolument

honorary *adj*
unpaid, unofficial, titular, nominal, in name only,
honorific, ex officio, formal
◳ paid

honour *n, v*
▶ *n* 1 REPUTATION, good name, repute, renown,
fame, glory, distinction, regard, respect, credit, dignity,
self-respect, pride, integrity, uprightness, honesty,
morals, ethics, principles, virtue, goodness, morality,
decency, righteousness, trustworthiness, truthfulness
formal esteem, rectitude, probity
2 AWARD, accolade, decoration, prize, reward,
trophy, crown, title, distinction, laurel, commendation,
acknowledgement, compliment, recognition, tribute,
favour, privilege
3 PRAISE, acclaim, acclamation, applause, homage,
admiration, reverence, worship, adoration
◳ 1 dishonour, disgrace
▶ *v* 1 PRAISE, acclaim, applaud, commend, have a
high regard for, compliment, exalt, glorify, pay homage
to, pay tribute to, acknowledge, recognize, decorate,
crown, celebrate, commemorate, remember, admire,
respect, revere, worship, prize, value
formal esteem, venerate

2 *honour a promise*
KEEP, observe, respect, fulfil, carry out, discharge, execute, perform, be true to
3 *honour a cheque/bill*
PAY, accept, clear
F3 **1** dishonour, disgrace

honourable *adj*
great, eminent, distinguished, renowned, famous, notable, noted, illustrious, respected, worthy, prestigious, trusty, reputable, respectable, admirable, virtuous, upright, upstanding, straight, honest, trustworthy, truthful, true, sincere, dependable, reliable, noble, high-minded, principled, high-principled, moral, ethical, fair, just, right, righteous, good, decent
F3 dishonourable, unworthy, dishonest

hood *n*
cowl, scarf, capuche, capeline, domino

hoodlum *n*
1 HOOLIGAN, ruffian, rowdy, vandal, mobster, thug, tough, lout, brute
colloq. mugger; *slang* bovver boy, yob
2 CRIMINAL, law-breaker, felon, offender, gangster, armed robber, gunman
US colloq. mobster, hood

hoodwink *v*
deceive, dupe, fool, take in, delude, mislead, outwit, hoax, trick, cheat, rook, gull, defraud, swindle, get the better of
colloq. bamboozle, have on, con, take for a ride, pull a fast one on, pull the wool over someone's eyes

hoof *n*
foot, trotter, cloven hoof, cloot
technical ungula

hoofed *adj*
cloven-footed, cloven-hoofed
technical ungulate, unguligrade

hook *n, v*
▶ *n* **1** *a hook on a door/dress*
CATCH, peg, barb, fastener, clasp, hasp, clip
2 SICKLE, scythe
3 BEND, curve, crook, angle, loop, elbow, bow, arc
4 BLOW, hit, stroke, box, thump, punch, cuff, clip, knock, rap
colloq. clout, wallop
▷ **off the hook** cleared, acquitted, in the clear;
formal exonerated, vindicated; *colloq.* scot free
▶ *v* **1** BEND, crook, curve, curl
2 CATCH, capture, bag, grab, trap, entrap, snare, ensnare, enmesh, entangle
3 FASTEN, clasp, hitch, fix, secure

hooked *adj*
1 CURVED, bent, curled, beaked, barbed, beaky, aquiline, sickle-shaped
formal falcate, hamate, hamose, hamous, hamular, hamulate, uncate, unciform, uncinate
2 ADDICTED, dependent, devoted, obsessed, enamoured

hooligan *n*
ruffian, rowdy, hoodlum, mobster, thug, tough, rough, lout, vandal, delinquent
colloq. mugger; *slang* bovver boy, yob

hoop *n*
ring, circle, round, loop, wheel, band, girdle, circlet

hoot *v, n*
▶ *v* **1** *an owl hooting*
call, cry, whoop, screech, tu-whit tu-whoo
formal ululate
2 *the car hooted*
toot, beep, whistle
3 *the audience hooted*
shout, shriek, whoop, howl, sneer, ridicule, taunt, mock, jeer, boo, hiss, howl down
▶ *n* **1** *the hoot of an owl*
call, cry, whoop, screech, tu-whit tu-whoo
2 *the hoot of a car*
toot, beep, whistle
3 *the hoots of the audience*
shout, shriek, whoop, howl, sneer, ridicule, taunt, mock, jeer, boo, hiss

hop *v, n*
▶ *v* **1** JUMP, leap, spring, bound, vault, skip, dance, prance, frisk, limp, hobble
2 *hop over to Paris*
pop, nip, fly quickly
▶ *n* **1** JUMP, leap, spring, bound, vault, bounce, step, skip, dance
2 *a quick hop by plane*
(quick) flight, trip, journey, excursion, jaunt
3 DANCE, disco, social, party
colloq. knees-up, rave, shindig

hope *n, v*
▶ *n* hopefulness, optimism, ambition, aspiration, wish, desire, longing, yearning, craving, dream, expectation, anticipation, prospect, promise, belief, confidence, assurance, conviction, assumption, faith
F3 pessimism, despair
▶ *v* aspire, wish, desire, long, yearn, crave, dream, expect, be hopeful, await, look forward to, anticipate, be ambitious, contemplate, foresee, believe, trust, have confidence, rely, reckon on, assume
colloq. keep your fingers crossed, pin your hopes on, hope against hope
F3 despair

hopeful *adj*
1 OPTIMISTIC, confident, assured, expectant, sanguine, cheerful, buoyant, aspiring, aspirant, positive
colloq. bullish
2 *a hopeful sign*
promising, encouraging, heartening, gladdening, reassuring, optimistic, pleasant, favourable, positive, rosy, bright, cheerful
formal propitious, auspicious
F3 **1** pessimistic, despairing **2** discouraging

hopefully *adv*
1 *hopefully the weather will improve*
I hope, if all goes well, with luck, all being well, probably, conceivably, it is to be hoped that
2 EXPECTANTLY, with hope, with anticipation, confidently, eagerly, optimistically, expectedly
formal sanguinely
colloq. bullishly

hopeless *adj*
1 PESSIMISTIC, defeatist, negative, despairing, desperate, gloomy, demoralized, downhearted, dejected, downcast, despondent, forlorn, wretched
2 UNATTAINABLE, unachievable, impracticable, impossible, vain, grave, foolish, futile, useless, pointless, worthless, poor, helpless, lost, irreversible, irremediable, beyond remedy, irreparable, beyond repair, incurable

3 *hopeless at speaking French*
useless, incompetent, bad, weak
colloq. lousy, pathetic, awful
E3 **1** hopeful, optimistic **2** curable **3** skilled, expert

horde *n*
band, gang, pack, troop, crew, herd, drove, flock, swarm, crowd, mob, throng, mass, multitude, host, army

⚠ **horde** or **hoard** ? *See panel at* **hoard**.

horizon *n*
1 SKYLINE, vista, prospect, range, range of vision
2 *widen your horizons*
scope, perspective, compass, outlook, perception

horizontal *adj*
level, flat, plane, smooth, levelled, on its side
formal supine

horny *adj*
1 *a horny shell*
hard, corny, callous
technical ceratoid
formal corneous
2 LUSTFUL, ardent, sexy, lascivious, lecherous, ruttish
formal concupiscent, libidinous
colloq. randy
E3 **2** cold, frigid

horrendous *adj*
horrific, shocking, appalling, horrifying, terrifying, frightening, terrible, dreadful, frightful

horrible *adj*
1 *horrible scenes of murder*
horrific, shocking, appalling, horrifying, terrifying, frightening, harrowing, bloodcurdling, hair-raising, terrible, dreadful, frightful, repulsive, revolting, abominable, grim, hideous, gruesome, ghastly, awful
colloq. scary
2 *that fish smells horrible*
unpleasant, disagreeable, nasty, unkind, obnoxious, horrid, disgusting, revolting, loathsome, repulsive, detestable, abominable, offensive, ghastly, awful, terrible, dreadful, frightful
E3 **1** attractive **2** pleasant, agreeable, lovely

horrid *adj*
1 HORRIFIC, shocking, appalling, horrifying, terrifying, frightening, harrowing, bloodcurdling, hair-raising, terrible, dreadful, frightful, repulsive, revolting, abominable, grim, hideous, gruesome, ghastly, awful
2 UNKIND, mean, nasty, awful, cruel, dreadful, obnoxious, hateful
colloq. beastly
E3 **1, 2** lovely, pleasant

horrific *adj*
horrifying, shocking, appalling, awful, terrible, frightful, dreadful, ghastly, gruesome, terrifying, frightening, harrowing, bloodcurdling
colloq. scary

horrify *v*
shock, appal, offend, outrage, scandalize, disgust, repel, revolt, sicken, nauseate, dismay, alarm, startle, scare, panic, frighten, terrify, terrorize, intimidate
colloq. make your blood run cold, make your hair stand on end, put the wind up, put the frighteners on,

scare out of your wits, scare the living daylights out of, scare to death
E3 please, delight

horror *n*
1 *recoil in horror*
shock, outrage, disgust, distaste, revulsion, repugnance, abhorrence, loathing, abomination, hate, dismay, alarm, fright, fear, terror, panic, dread, apprehension
formal consternation, trepidation, detestation
2 GHASTLINESS, awfulness, frightfulness, hideousness, unpleasantness
E3 **1** approval, delight

horror-struck *adj*
appalled, shocked, frightened, horrified, terrified, horror-stricken, aghast, stunned, petrified
E3 delighted, pleased

horse *n*
steed, mount, stallion, nag, mustang, mare, colt, filly, bay, sorrel, roan, hack, bronc(h)o, charger, cob, dobbin, hackney, centaur
Related adjectives: equine, caballine, hippic

Breeds of horse include: Akhal-Teké, Alter-Réal, American Quarter Horse, American Saddle Horse, American Trotter, Andalusian, Anglo-Arab, Anglo-Norman, Appaloosa, Arab, Ardennias, Auxois, Barb, Bavarian Warmblood, Boulonnais, Brabançon, Breton, British Warmblood, Brumby, Budyonny, Calabrese, Charollais Halfbred, Cleveland Bay, Clydesdale, Comtois, Criollo, Danubian, Døle Gudbrandsdal, Døle Trotter, Don, Dutch Draught, East Bulgarian, East Friesian, Einsiedler, Finnish, Frederiksborg, Freiberger, French Saddle Horse, French Trotter, Friesian, Furioso, Gelderland, German Trotter, Groningen, Hanoverian, Hispano, Holstein, Iomud, Irish Draught, Irish Hunter, Italian Heavy Draught, Jutland, Kabardin, Karabair, Karabakh, Kladruber, Knabstrup, Kustanair, Latvian Harness Horse, Limousin Halfbred, Lipizzaner, Lithuanian Heavy Draught, Lokai, Lusitano, Mangalarga, Maremmana, Masuren, Mecklenburg, Metis Trotter, Morgan, Muraköz, Murgese, Mustang, New Kirgiz, Nonius, North Swedish, Oldenburg, Orlov Trotter, Palomino, Paso Fino, Percheron, Peruvian Stepping Horse, Pinto, Pinzgauer Noriker, Plateau Persian, Poitevin, Rhineland Heavy Draught, Russian Heavy Draught, Salerno, Sardinian, Shagya Arab, Shire, Suffolk Punch, Swedish Halfbred, Tchenaran, Tennessee Walking Horse, Tersky, Thoroughbred, Toric, Trait du Nord, Trakehner, Vladimir Heavy Draught, Waler, Welsh Cob, Württemberg.

Breeds of pony include: Connemara, Dales, Dartmoor, Exmoor, Falabella, Fell, Hackney, Highland, New Forest, Przewalski's Horse, Shetland, Welsh Mountain Pony, Welsh Pony.

horseman, horsewoman *n*
equestrian, rider, jockey, cavalryman, horse soldier, hussar, dragoon, knight

horseplay *n*
clowning, buffoonery, foolery, fooling, fooling around, tomfoolery, skylarking, pranks, capers, antics, high jinks, practical jokes, fun and games,

rough-and-tumble
colloq. monkey business

hortatory *adj*
encouraging, edifying, heartening, inspiriting,
instructive, practical, stimulating, homiletic
formal didactic, exhortative, exhortatory, hortative,
preceptive
colloq. pep

horticulture *n*
gardening, cultivation
formal arboriculture, floriculture

hosanna *n*
praise, worship, alleluia, save us
formal laudation

hose *n*
pipe, tube, tubing, channel, conduit, duct

hosiery *n*
socks, stockings, tights, leggings, leg-coverings, hose

hospitable *adj*
friendly, sociable, welcoming, neighbourly, receptive,
cordial, amicable, congenial, convivial, genial, warm,
helpful, kind, kind-hearted, gracious, generous,
open-handed, liberal, bountiful
E3 inhospitable, unfriendly, hostile

hospital *n*
medical centre, health centre, clinic, infirmary,
institute, sanatorium, hospice
Related adjective: nosocomial

hospitality *n*
friendliness, sociability, welcome, neighbourliness,
accommodation, entertainment, congeniality,
conviviality, warmth, cheer, generosity, kindness,
liberality, helpfulness, open-handedness
E3 unfriendliness, hostility
Related adjective: xenial

host¹ *n, v*
▶ *n* **1** COMPÈRE, master of ceremonies, MC,
presenter, announcer, anchorman, anchorwoman,
linkman, media personality
colloq. emcee
2 PUBLICAN, innkeeper, landlord, landlady,
proprietor, proprietress
▶ *v* present, introduce, give, compère

host² *n*
a host of letters
multitude, myriad, array, army, horde, crowd, throng,
mass, swarm, pack, troop, herd, mob, crush, band

hostage *n*
prisoner, captive, pawn, surety, security, pledge

hostel *n*
youth hostel, bed and breakfast, boarding-house,
guesthouse, hotel, inn, motel, pension
formal residence
slang dosshouse

hostile *adj*
1 BELLIGERENT, warlike, ill-disposed,
unsympathetic, unfriendly, inhospitable, inimical,
antagonistic, opposed
formal bellicose, malevolent
2 ADVERSE, unfavourable, contrary, opposite
formal inauspicious
E3 1 receptive, friendly, welcoming **2** favourable

hostilities *n*
war, warfare, battle, fighting, conflict, strife, action,
bloodshed

hostility *n*
opposition, aggression, belligerence, militancy,
enmity, antagonism, animosity, unfriendliness, cruelty,
ill-will, malice, resentment, hate, hatred, dislike,
aversion
formal estrangement, abhorrence, bellicosity,
malevolence
E3 friendliness, friendship

hot *adj*
1 WARM, heated, fiery, burning, scalding, scorching,
blistering, red hot, roasting, baking, boiling, piping,
steaming, sizzling, sweltering, parching, searing,
sultry, torrid, tropical
2 SPICY, peppery, piquant, sharp, pungent, strong,
fiery
3 FEVERISH, delirious, burning, flushed, red,
with a temperature
4 *his hot temper*
fiery, furious, angry, indignant, raging, boiling,
seething, fuming, livid, violent, heated, inflamed,
incensed, enraged
5 *hot competition*
fierce, intense, strong, furious, keen, cut-throat
6 *not very hot on the idea*
keen, enthusiastic, eager, warm, earnest, zealous,
diligent, devoted
7 *hot news*
recent, new, fresh, latest, up-to-date, exciting
8 *hot goods*
illegally obtained/imported, contraband, stolen,
pilfered, ill-gotten
E3 1 cold, cool, chilly **2** mild, bland **4** calm
7 old, stale
▷ **hot air** nonsense, empty talk, emptiness, mere
words, blather, blether, bluster, bombast, vapour,
foam, froth; *formal* verbiage; *colloq.* balderdash,
bosh, bunk, bunkum, claptrap, gas, cobblers, piffle,
bilge; *slang* bullshit
E3 wisdom

hotbed *n*
breeding-ground, den, hive, nest, seedbed, cradle,
nursery, school, forcing-house

hot-blooded *adj*
temperamental, excitable, spirited, wild, rash,
impulsive, impetuous, high-spirited, heated, fervent,
fiery, bold, eager, ardent, passionate, lustful, sensual,
lusty
formal perfervid, precipitate
E3 cool, dispassionate

hotchpotch *n*
mishmash, medley, miscellany, collection, mix,
mixture, melange, jumble, confusion, mess
US hodgepodge

hotel *n*
boarding-house, guesthouse, pension, motel, inn,
public house, tavern, hostel, hostelry
colloq. pub

hotfoot *adv*
speedily, at top speed, quickly, rapidly, swiftly,
without delay, hurriedly, in haste, hastily, posthaste,
helter-skelter, pell-mell
E3 slowly; *formal* dilatorily

hothead *n*

tearaway, terror, madcap, madman, daredevil, desperado, hotspur

hotheaded *adj*

headstrong, impetuous, impulsive, hasty, rash, foolhardy, reckless, wild, fiery, excitable, volatile, explosive, volcanic, hot-tempered, quick-tempered, short-tempered, irascible

F3 cool, calm

hothouse *n*

greenhouse, glasshouse, conservatory, orangery, vinery

hot-tempered *adj*

fiery, choleric, explosive, quick-tempered, short-tempered, violent, volcanic, testy, hasty, irascible, irritable, petulant

F3 calm, cool; *formal* imperturbable

hound *v*

chase, pursue, follow, hunt (down), track, stalk, trail, drive, force, goad, prod, urge, chivvy, nag, pester, disturb, bully, badger, harry, harass, provoke, persecute

house *n, v*

▶ *n* **1** BUILDING, home

formal dwelling, residence, domicile, habitation

2 HOUSEHOLD, family, family circle, home, ménage

3 *a publishing/design house*

firm, company, establishment, business, enterprise, corporation, organization

4 ASSEMBLY, body, chamber, legislature, parliament, congress

5 *a full house at the theatre*

audience, auditorium, gathering, assembly, turnout, spectators, onlookers, listeners, viewers

6 DYNASTY, family, clan, tribe, line, lineage, ancestry, blood, strain, race, kindred

▷ **on the house** free, free of charge, without charge/ cost, for nothing, at no (extra) cost

Related adjectives: domestic, domal

Types of house include: semi-detached, *colloq.* semi, detached, terraced, town-house, council house, cottage, thatched cottage, *colloq.* prefab, pied-à-terre, bungalow, chalet bungalow; flat, bedsit, apartment, studio, maisonette, penthouse, granny flat, *US* duplex, *US* condominium, manor, hall, lodge, grange, villa, mansion, rectory, vicarage, parsonage, manse, croft, farmhouse, homestead, ranchhouse, chalet, log cabin, shack, shanty, hut, igloo, hacienda.

▶ *v* **1** LODGE, quarter, billet, board, accommodate, put up, take in, have room/space for, shelter, harbour

2 HOLD, contain, protect, cover, guard, shelter, sheathe, place, keep, store

household *n, adj*

▶ *n* family, family circle, house, home, ménage, establishment, set-up

▶ *adj* domestic, home, family, ordinary, plain, everyday, common, familiar, well-known, established

householder *n*

resident, tenant, occupier, occupant, owner, landlady, freeholder, leaseholder, proprietor, landlord, home-owner, head of the household

housekeeping *n*

home economics, domestic science, household management, running a home, domestic work/ matters, homemaking, housewifery

houseman *n*

1 DOCTOR, house-physician, house-surgeon, intern(e), resident

2 MANSERVANT, servant, butler, valet, retainer, gentleman's gentleman

house-trained *adj*

domesticated, tame, tamed, well-mannered, house-broken

F3 unsocial

housing *n*

1 ACCOMMODATION, houses, homes, shelter

formal dwellings, habitation

2 CASING, case, container, holder, covering, guard, cover, sheath, jacket, protection

hovel *n*

shack, shanty, cabin, hut, shed

colloq. dump, hole

hover *v*

1 HANG, poise, float, drift, fly, flutter, flap

2 *he hovered by the door*

pause, linger, hang about, hesitate, waver, fluctuate, alternate, seesaw

formal vacillate, oscillate

however *adv*

nevertheless, nonetheless, still, yet, even so, regardless, though, anyhow, just the same

formal notwithstanding

howl *n & v*

wail, cry, shriek, scream, bawl, shout, yell, roar, bellow, bay, yelp, yowl, hoot, moan, groan

howler *n*

error, mistake, blunder, gaffe, malapropism

formal solecism

colloq. bloomer, clanger, boob

hub *n*

centre, middle, focus, focal point, axis, pivot, linchpin, nerve centre, core, heart

hubbub *n*

noise, racket, din, clamour, commotion, disturbance, riot, uproar, hullabaloo, rumpus, confusion, disorder, tumult, hurly-burly, chaos, pandemonium

F3 peace, quiet

huckster *n*

hawker, dealer, salesperson, barker, tinker, vendor, haggler, packman, pedlar, pitcher

huddle *v, n*

▶ *v* cluster, gravitate, converge, meet, gather, congregate, crowd, flock, cram, pack, herd, throng, press, squeeze, cuddle, snuggle, nestle, curl up, crouch, hunch

F3 disperse

▶ *n* **1** CLUSTER, clump, knot, mass, crowd, heap, muddle, jumble

2 MEETING, conclave, conference, discussion, consultation

colloq. powwow

hue *n*

colour, shade, tint, dye, tinge, nuance, tone, complexion, aspect, light

hue and cry *n*

furore, fuss, hullabaloo, outcry, rumpus, uproar, brouhaha, clamour, ado, chase

colloq. ruction, to-do

huff *n*
pique, sulks, mood, bad mood, anger, rage, passion

huffy *adj*
cross, angry, resentful, snappy, disgruntled, grumpy, irritable, offended, sulky, surly, testy, touchy, moping, morose, moody, crusty, short, peevish, petulant, waspish
formal querulous
colloq. crabbed, crotchety, miffed, shirty
🖃 cheery, happy

hug *v, n*
▶ *v* embrace, cuddle, squeeze, enfold, hold, hold close, press, clasp, clutch, grip, cling to, stay close to, follow closely, enclose
▶ *n* embrace, cuddle, squeeze, clasp, hold, clinch

huge *adj*
immense, vast, enormous, massive, colossal, titanic, giant, gigantic, mammoth, monumental, tremendous, stupendous, great, big, large, extensive, monstrous, Herculean, gargantuan, titanic, bulky, heavy, unwieldy
formal prodigious
colloq. jumbo
🖃 tiny, minute

hulk *n*
1 WRECK, shipwreck, remains, derelict, frame, hull, shell
2 LOUT, lump, lubber, oaf
colloq. clod

hulking *adj*
massive, heavy, weighty, unwieldy, cumbersome, bulky, awkward, clumsy, lumbering, ungainly
🖃 small, delicate

hull¹ *n*
the hull of a ship
body, frame, framework, skeleton, structure, casing, covering

hull² *n, v*
▶ *n*   *the hull of a fruit*
husk, pod, capsule, legume, skin, rind, peel, shell
US shuck
technical epicarp
▶ *v* husk, pare, peel, shell, strip, skin, trim
US shuck

hullabaloo *n*
fuss, palaver, outcry, furore, hue and cry, noise, din, racket, brouhaha, uproar, pandemonium, rumpus, disturbance, commotion, hubbub, turmoil, tumult
colloq. to-do, ruction
🖃 calm, peace

hum *v, n*
▶ *v* 1 BUZZ, whirr, purr, drone, thrum, croon, sing
2 MURMUR, mumble
3 *humming with activity*
throb, pulse, vibrate, buzz
▶ *n* buzz, buzzing, whirr, whirring, purring, thrum, drone, murmur, mumble, throb, throbbing, pulsation, vibration

human *adj, n*
▶ *adj* 1 MORTAL, physical, fleshly, fallible, flesh and blood, weak, susceptible, vulnerable, reasonable, rational
formal anthropoid
2 KIND, considerate, understanding, humane, compassionate, sympathetic
🖃 2 inhuman

▶ *n* human being, mortal, man, woman, child, person, individual, body, soul
technical homo sapiens

humane *adj*
kind, compassionate, sympathetic, understanding, kind-hearted, good-natured, considerate, gentle, tender, loving, mild, lenient, merciful, forgiving, forbearing, kindly, generous, benevolent, charitable, humanitarian, good, benign
🖃 inhumane, cruel

humanitarian *adj, n*
▶ *adj* benevolent, charitable, philanthropic, public-spirited, welfare, compassionate, humane, kind, sympathetic, understanding, considerate, generous, altruistic, unselfish
🖃 selfish, self-seeking
▶ *n* philanthropist, benefactor, good Samaritan, do-gooder, altruist
🖃 egoist, self-seeker

humanitarianism *n*
benevolence, charitableness, charity, goodwill, philanthropy, humanism, compassionateness, generosity, loving-kindness
formal beneficence
🖃 egoism, self-seeking

humanity *n*
1 HUMAN RACE, humankind, mankind, womankind, mortals, mortality, people, man
technical homo sapiens
2 HUMANENESS, kindness, compassion, fellow-feeling, brotherly love, understanding, tenderness, sympathy, gentleness, tenderness, thoughtfulness, benevolence, tolerance, generosity, goodwill, kind-heartedness, goodness, pity, mercy
🖃 2 inhumanity, cruelty

humanize *v*
improve, better, polish, refine, domesticate, tame, civilize, cultivate, educate, enlighten, edify

humble *adj, v*
▶ *adj* 1 MEEK, submissive, unassertive, modest, unassuming, self-effacing, polite, respectful, deferential, servile, subservient, sycophantic, obsequious, prideless
2 LOWLY, low, mean, insignificant, unimportant, common, commonplace, ordinary, poor, inferior, low-ranking, plain, simple, modest, unassuming, unpretentious, unostentatious, undistinguished, unrefined
🖃 1 proud, assertive 2 important, pretentious
▶ *v* bring down, lower, bring low, abase, demean, sink, discredit, belittle, disgrace, shame, put to shame, humiliate, mortify, chasten, crush, deflate, subdue
formal disparage
colloq. put someone in their place, bring/take someone down a peg or two
🖃 exalt

humbly *adv*
modestly, unassumingly, meekly, respectfully, simply, submissively, unpretentiously, deferentially, diffidently, docilely, obsequiously, subserviently, servilely
colloq. sheepishly, cap in hand
🖃 confidently, defiantly

humbug *n*
1 DECEPTION, pretence, sham, fraud, swindle, trick, hoax, deceit, trickery, cheating
colloq. con

2 NONSENSE, rubbish, bluff, cant, hypocrisy
colloq. bunkum, claptrap, eyewash, balderdash, poppycock, cobblers, rot; *slang* baloney, balls, shit
3 CHARLATAN, fraud, cheat, bluffer, actor, swindler, impostor, fake, sham, trickster, rogue
colloq. con man, swank, poser

humdrum *adj*
boring, tedious, monotonous, routine, dull, repetitious, tiresome, dreary, uninteresting, uneventful, unvaried, ordinary, mundane, everyday, commonplace, run-of-the-mill, banal
Ε3 varied, lively, unusual, exceptional

humid *adj*
damp, moist, dank, wet, clammy, sticky, close, heavy, oppressive, muggy, sultry, steamy
Ε3 dry

humidity *n*
humidness, damp, dampness, moisture, moistness, dankness, wetness, stickiness, closeness, heaviness, clamminess, mugginess, sultriness, steaminess, sogginess, vaporousness, dew, mist
formal vaporosity
Ε3 dryness

humiliate *v*
mortify, embarrass, confound, crush, break, deflate, chasten, shame, put to shame, bring shame on, disgrace, abash, discredit, degrade, demean, humble, bring low, abase
formal discomfit
colloq. put down, put someone in their place, make someone lose face, bring/take someone down a peg or two, cut someone down to size, take the wind out of someone's sails
Ε3 dignify, exalt

humiliating *adj*
humbling, mortifying, shaming, crushing, chastening, deflating, degrading, embarrassing, disgraceful, ignominious, inglorious, disgracing, snubbing
formal discomfiting, humiliant, humiliative, humiliatory
Ε3 gratifying, triumphant

humiliation *n*
mortification, embarrassment, shame, disgrace, chastening, crushing, confounding, dishonour, discredit, indignity, ignominy, abasement, humbling, degradation, deflation, snub, rebuff, affront
formal discomfiture
colloq. put-down, loss of face, humble pie
Ε3 gratification, triumph

humility *n*
modesty, unassertiveness, unassumingness, self-effacement, diffidence, meekness, submissiveness, deference, self-abasement, servility, humbleness, lowliness, unpretentiousness
Ε3 pride, arrogance, assertiveness

hummock *n*
hillock, hump, knoll, mound, barrow, elevation, prominence

humorist *n*
wit, satirist, caricaturist, cartoonist, comedian, comic, joker, wag, jester, clown

humorous *adj*
funny, amusing, comic, entertaining, witty, satirical, facetious, playful, waggish, droll, whimsical, comical, farcical, ludicrous, absurd, ridiculous, laughable,
hilarious, side-splitting
formal jocular, risible
colloq. zany
Ε3 serious, humourless

humour *n, v*
► *n* **1** WIT, wittiness, gags, drollery, jokes, jesting, badinage, repartee, facetiousness, absurdity, ridiculousness, hilarity, satire, comedy, farce, fun, amusement
formal jocularity
colloq. wisecracks
2 *in a bad humour*
mood, temper, frame/state of mind, spirits, disposition, temperament
► *v* go along with, comply with, accommodate, satisfy, gratify, indulge, pamper, spoil, cosset, favour, permit, please, mollify, flatter, pander to, tolerate
formal acquiesce in

humourless *adj*
boring, tedious, dull, dry, solemn, serious, grave, sombre, glum, morose, unsmiling, unlaughing, grim, long-faced
Ε3 humorous, witty

hump *n, v*
► *n* **1** HUNCH, lump, knob, bump, projection, protuberance, outgrowth, bulge, swelling, mound, mass, prominence, protrusion
formal excrescence, intumescence
2 *get/give the hump*
unhappiness, annoyance, irritation, vexation, exasperation, sadness, depression, gloom
formal aggravation
► *v* **1** ARCH, curve, crook
2 CARRY, lug, lift, heave, hoist, shoulder

hump-backed *adj*
crookbacked, hunchbacked, hunched, crooked, stooped, humped, deformed, misshapen, gibbous
technical kyphotic
Ε3 straight, upright

humped *adj*
arched, bent, curved, crooked, hunched, gibbous
Ε3 flat, straight

hunch *n, v*
► *n* premonition, intuition, suspicion, feeling, impression, idea, inkling, guess, sixth sense
formal presentiment
► *v* hump, bend, curve, arch, stoop, crouch, squat, huddle, draw in, curl up

hunger *n, v*
► *n* **1** HUNGRINESS, emptiness, starvation, malnutrition, famine, famishment, appetite, ravenousness, greed, greediness
formal voracity, esurience, esuriency
2 *hunger for power*
desire, craving, longing, yearning, pining, hankering, want, need, yen, itch, thirst, appetite
► *v* starve, want, wish, desire, need, crave, have a craving for, hanker, long, have a longing for, yearn, pine, ache, itch, thirst

hungry *adj*
1 STARVING, underfed, undernourished, malnourished, empty, hollow, famished, ravenous, greedy, insatiable
formal voracious
colloq. peckish, could eat a horse

2 *hungry for knowledge*
desirous, craving, longing, aching, yearning, pining, hankering, itching, thirsty, eager, avid, needing, covetous
F₃ 1 satisfied, full

hunk *n*
chunk, lump, piece, block, slab, wedge, mass, dollop, clod, gobbet

hunt *v, n*
▶ *v* **1** CHASE, pursue, follow, shadow, hound, dog, stalk, track, trail
2 SEEK, look for, search, try to find, scour, rummage, fish, ferret, forage, investigate
▶ *n* chase, pursuit, search, stalking, tracking, scouring, rummaging, quest, investigation

hunter *n*
huntsman, chaser, chasseur, woodman, woodsman, jäger, montero, venator, venerer

hurdle *n*
jump, fence, wall, hedge, railing, bar, barrier, barricade, obstacle, obstruction, stumbling-block, hindrance, impediment, handicap, problem, snag, difficulty, complication

hurl *v*
throw, toss, fling, sling, pitch, cast, heave, catapult, project, propel, fire, launch, send, let fly
colloq. chuck

hurly-burly *n*
bustle, hustle, commotion, confusion, trouble, disorder, disruption, unrest, pandemonium, uproar, chaos, furore, upheaval, tumult, turbulence, turmoil, frenzy, distraction, agitation, hubbub, brouhaha, bedlam
colloq. hassle

hurricane *n*
gale, tornado, typhoon, cyclone, whirlwind, squall, storm, tempest

hurried *adj*
rushed, hectic, hasty, speedy, fast, quick, breakneck, swift, rapid, passing, fleeting, transient, transitory, brief, short, cursory, superficial, offhand, perfunctory, shallow, careless, slapdash
formal precipitate
colloq. rush job
F₃ leisurely, unhurried

hurry *v, n*
▶ *v* rush, dash, run, fly, hasten, make haste, press on, quicken, speed (up), accelerate, hustle, push
formal expedite
colloq. get a move on, run like hell, show your heels, get cracking, cut and run, put your foot down, step on it, go all out, pull your finger out, shake a leg
F₃ slow down, delay
▶ *n* rush, haste, quickness, swiftness, fastness, rapidity, speed, urgency, hustle, bustle, flurry, commotion, hubbub, confusion
old use dispatch
formal expedition, celerity
F₃ leisureliness, calm

hurt *v, n, adj*
▶ *v* **1** *my leg hurts*
ACHE, be painful, be sore, pain, throb, sting, smart, burn, tingle
2 INJURE, wound, maltreat, ill-treat, bruise, cut, scratch, lacerate, damage, burn, torture, maim, impair,

disable
formal debilitate
3 DAMAGE, impair, harm, mar, spoil, blemish, blight
4 UPSET, sadden, cause sadness, grieve, distress, wound, offend, annoy
formal afflict
▶ *n* pain, soreness, aching, throbbing, burning, tingling, smarting, discomfort, suffering, injury, wound, cut, bruise, scratch, damage, harm, distress, sadness, upset, sorrow, grief, misery
formal affliction
▶ *adj* **1** INJURED, wounded, bruised, grazed, cut, scarred, lacerated, maimed, painful, sore, aching, throbbing, burning, tingling, smarting
2 UPSET, sad, saddened, sorrowful, grief-stricken, miserable, in anguish, distressed, aggrieved, annoyed, offended, affronted

hurtful *adj*
1 UPSETTING, wounding, vicious, cruel, mean, unkind, nasty, malicious, spiteful, catty, derogatory, offensive, distressing, scathing, cutting
formal injurious, malefactory
2 HARMFUL, damaging, pernicious, destructive, ruinous
formal injurious, deleterious
F₃ 1 helpful, kind, innocuous **2** advantageous

hurtle *v*
dash, tear, race, fly, shoot, speed, rush, career, charge, plunge, dive, crash, rattle

husband *n, v*
▶ *n* spouse, partner, mate, groom, married man
colloq. hubby, better half, other half
▶ *v* conserve, economize, eke out, use sparingly, use carefully, preserve, reserve, put aside, put by, budget, save, save up, store, ration, hoard
F₃ squander, waste

husbandry *n*
1 FARMING, agriculture, cultivation, tillage, land management, farm management, conservation
technical agribusiness, agronomics, agronomy
2 MANAGEMENT, saving, thrift, thriftiness, frugality, economy, good housekeeping
F₃ 2 wastefulness, squandering

hush *v, n, interj*
▶ *v* quieten, silence, shush, still, settle, compose, calm, soothe, mollify, subdue
colloq. pipe down, shut up, cut the cackle, dry up
F₃ disturb, rouse
▷ **hush up** keep dark, keep secret, suppress, conceal, cover up, stifle, smother, gag
F₃ publicize
▶ *n* quietness, quiet, silence, peace, peacefulness, stillness, calm, calmness, tranquillity, serenity
formal repose
F₃ noise, clamour
▶ *interj* quiet, hold your tongue, shut up, not another word

hush-hush *adj*
secret, confidential, classified, restricted, top-secret
colloq. under wraps
F₃ open, public

husk *n*
covering, case, shell, pod, capsule, legume, hull, rind, peel, skin, bran, chaff
US shuck
technical epicarp

husky *adj*

1 HOARSE, croaky, croaking, low, deep, throaty, guttural, gruff, gravelly, rasping, rough, thick, coarse, harsh
2 BRAWNY, muscular, burly, hefty, strong, strapping, well-built
colloq. beefy

hussy *n*

loose woman, minx, temptress
colloq. floosie, vamp; *slang* slut, tart, scrubber, tramp, slag

hustle *v, n*

▶ *v* rush, hurry, dash, fly, bustle, hasten, force, pressurize, push, shove, thrust, bundle, elbow, nudge, jostle, crowd
▶ *n* bustle, activity, stir, commotion, tumult, agitation, fuss, hurry, rush, hurly-burly

hut *n*

cabin, shack, shanty, booth, shed, lean-to, shelter, den

hybrid *n, adj*

▶ *n* cross, crossbreed, half-breed, half-blood, mongrel, composite, combination, mixture, amalgam, compound
formal conglomeration
▶ *adj* crossbred, mongrel, composite, combined, mixed, heterogeneous, compound
E3 pure-bred

hybridize *v*

crossbreed, cross, interbreed, bastardize, reproduce together

hygiene *n*

sanitariness, sanitation, sterility, disinfection, cleanliness, purity, wholesomeness
E3 insanitariness

hygienic *adj*

sanitary, sterile, sterilized, aseptic, germ-free, disinfected, clean, pure, healthy, wholesome
formal salubrious
E3 unhygienic, insanitary, contaminated, polluted

hymn *n*

song of praise, song, chorus, spiritual, psalm, anthem, carol, chant, cantata, canticle, motet, doxology, introit, choral(e), offertory, paean, paraphrase

hype *n, v*

▶ *n* publicity, advertisement, advertising, promotion, puffing, ballyhoo, build-up, racket, fuss
colloq. plugging, razzmatazz
▶ *v* promote, publicize, advertise, build up
colloq. plug

hyperbole *n*

overstatement, exaggeration, excess, magnification, extravagance, overkill
E3 understatement; *technical* meiosis

hypercritical *adj*

fault-finding, over-particular, pedantic, finicky, fussy, quibbling, hair-splitting, niggling, captious, carping, strict, cavilling, censorious
formal ultracrepidarian
colloq. nit-picking, pernickety, choosy, picky
E3 tolerant, uncritical

hypnotic *adj*

mesmerizing, soporific, sleep-inducing, sedative, numbing, spellbinding, fascinating, compelling,
irresistible, magnetic
formal somniferous, stupefactive

hypnotism *n*

hypnosis, mesmerism, suggestion, auto-suggestion

hypnotize *v*

mesmerize, put into a state of unconsciousness, put to sleep, spellbind, bewitch, enchant, entrance, fascinate, captivate, beguile, magnetize

hypochondria *n*

neurosis, hypochondrianism, hypochondriasis
formal valetudinarianism

hypochondriac *n, adj*

▶ *n* hypochondriast
formal valetudinarian
▶ *adj* hypochondriacal, neurotic
formal valetudinarian

hypocrisy *n*

insincerity, double-talk, double-dealing, two-facedness, dishonesty, falsity, deceit, deceitfulness, deception, pretence, pretended goodness, lip service, cant, pharisaism
formal dissembling, duplicity
colloq. phoneyness
E3 sincerity

hypocrite *n*

deceiver, fraud, impostor, pretender, mountebank, Pharisee, canter, charlatan, whited sepulchre, Holy Willie
formal dissembler
colloq. phoney, pseud, pseudo

hypocritical *adj*

insincere, two-faced, self-righteous, sanctimonious, double-dealing, false, specious, hollow, deceptive, fraudulent, spurious, deceitful, dishonest, lying, pharisaical, Pecksniffian
formal dissembling, perfidious, duplicitous
colloq. phoney
E3 sincere, genuine, truthful

hypothesis *n*

theory, thesis, theorem, axiom, proposition, supposition, presumption, assumption, speculation
formal premise, postulate, conjecture

hypothetical *adj*

theoretical, imaginary, imagined, supposed, assumed, presumed, proposed, speculative
formal conjectural
E3 real, actual

hysteria *n*

agitation, frenzy, panic, hysterics, neurosis, mania, delirium, madness
colloq. (screaming) habdabs
E3 calm, composure, control

hysterical *adj*

1 FRANTIC, frenzied, berserk, out of control, uncontrollable, mad, raving, crazed, beside yourself, delirious, demented, overwrought, neurotic, in a panic
2 HILARIOUS, extremely funny, uproarious, side-splitting
colloq. priceless, rich
E3 **1** calm, composed, self-possessed

hysterics *n*

agitation, frenzy, panic, hysteria, neurosis, mania, delirium, madness
colloq. (screaming) habdabs

I

ice *n, v*
▶ *n* **1** FROZEN WATER, frost, rime, icicle, glacier
2 ICINESS, frostiness, coldness, chill, coolness,
unresponsiveness, distance
▷ **put on ice** shelve, delay, postpone, put off, defer;
formal hold/leave in abeyance; *colloq.* put on the back
burner
▶ *v* freeze (over), refrigerate, chill, cool, frost, glaze,
harden

ice-cold *adj*
frozen, iced, chilled, icy, frosty, icebound, arctic,
bitterly cold, raw, polar, glacial, Siberian, frigid,
freezing, numb, hard, frosted, solidified, stiff,
frozen-stiff, chilled to the bone, rigid, fixed
technical algid
formal gelid
E3 warm, hot

icon *n*
idol, portrait, image, likeness, figure, representation,
symbol, portrait, portrayal

iconoclast *n*
critic, denouncer, dissenter, denunciator, dissident,
radical, sceptic, rebel, opponent, questioner, heretic,
unbeliever, image-breaker
E3 devotee, believer

iconoclastic *adj*
critical, dissident, irreverent, innovative, questioning,
radical, rebellious, sceptical, subversive, heretical,
impious
formal denunciatory, dissentient
E3 uncritical, unquestioning, trustful

icy *adj*
1 ICE-COLD, glacial, freezing, frozen, frosty, raw,
bitter, biting, cold, chill, chilly, frigid, arctic, polar,
Siberian
formal gelid
2 *icy roads*
frosty, slippery, glassy, frozen, icebound, frostbound,
rimy, slippy
3 HOSTILE, cold, stony, cool, frigid, frosty,
indifferent, unfriendly, aloof, stiff, reserved,
restrained, distant, formal
E3 1 hot **3** friendly, warm, welcoming, responsive

idea *n*
1 THOUGHT, concept, notion, theory, hypothesis,
guess, belief, opinion, feeling, view, viewpoint,
judgement, conception, conceptualization, vision,
image, impression, perception, interpretation,
understanding, inkling, suspicion, fancy, clue
formal conjecture, abstraction
2 *a good idea*
brainwave, suggestion, proposal, proposition,
recommendation, plan, scheme, design
3 AIM, intention, purpose, reason, point, end, goal,
target, object, objective

ideal *n, adj*
▶ *n* **1** PERFECTION, epitome, paragon, example,
model, pattern, prototype, type, image, criterion,
standard, yardstick, benchmark
formal acme, exemplar, archetype, nonpareil
2 PRINCIPLE, morals, ethics, moral standards/
values, ethical standards/values
▶ *adj* **1** PERFECT, dream, utopian, best, optimum,
optimal, supreme, highest, complete, absolute, model
formal archetypal, quintessential, consummate
2 UNREAL, imaginary, conceptual, philosophical,
theoretical, hypothetical, abstract, unattainable,
impractical, visionary, romantic, fanciful, idealistic,
utopian

idealism *n*
impracticality, perfectionism, romanticism,
utopianism
E3 pragmatism, realism

idealist *n*
perfectionist, visionary, dreamer, optimist, romantic,
romanticist
E3 realist, pragmatist

idealistic *adj*
perfectionist, utopian, visionary, romantic, quixotic,
starry-eyed, optimistic, unrealistic, impractical,
impracticable
E3 realistic, pragmatic, practical

idealization *n*
romanticization, romanticizing, glamorization,
glorification, worship, exaltation, idolization,
ennoblement
formal apotheosis

idealize *v*
utopianize, romanticize, glamorize, glorify, exalt,
worship, idolize
E3 caricature

ideally *adv*
perfectly, in a perfect world, in an ideal world, at best,
in theory, theoretically, hypothetically

idée fixe *n*
fixation, obsession, complex, hang-up, leitmotiv,
fixed idea
formal monomania

identical *adj*
same, self-same, one and the same, indistinguishable,
interchangeable, twin, duplicate, like, alike, similar,
corresponding, matching, equal, equivalent
colloq. as like as two peas in a pod
E3 different

identifiable *adj*
recognizable, discernible, noticeable, known,
perceptible, detectable, distinguishable, unmistakable
formal ascertainable
E3 unidentifiable, indefinable, unfamiliar, unknown

identification *n*
1 RECOGNITION, detection, spotting, pointing-out, diagnosis, naming, labelling, classification
2 EMPATHY, association, involvement, connection, rapport, relationship, sympathy, fellow feeling
3 IDENTITY CARD, documents, ID, papers, credentials, badge

identify *v*
1 RECOGNIZE, know, pick out, single out, point out, distinguish, perceive, make out, discern, discover, find out, establish, notice, detect, diagnose, name, label, tag, specify, pinpoint, spot, place, catalogue, classify
formal ascertain
2 ASSOCIATE, connect, relate, involve, place, think of together, couple
3 *identify with other sufferers*
empathize with, relate to, associate with, respond to, sympathize with, feel for

identity *n*
1 INDIVIDUALITY, particularity, distinctiveness, uniqueness, self, selfhood, personhood, name, ego, personality, character, existence
formal singularity
2 SAMENESS, likeness, selfsameness, closeness, similarity, resemblance, indistinguishability, interchangeability, correspondence, equality, equivalence

ideologist *n*
thinker, theorist, visionary, philosopher, teacher, doctrinaire, ideologue

ideology *n*
philosophy, world-view, ideas, principles, teaching, theory, tenets, doctrine(s), convictions, belief(s), opinion(s), faith, dogma, thesis
formal creed, credo

idiocy *n*
folly, stupidity, silliness, senselessness, lunacy, craziness, absurdity, foolhardiness, insanity, inanity
formal fatuousness
colloq. daftness
F3 wisdom, sanity

idiom *n*
phrase, expression, colloquialism, language, turn of phrase, phraseology, style, usage, jargon, speech, talk, vernacular
formal locution

idiomatic *adj*
colloquial, everyday, vernacular, native, grammatical, correct, dialectal, dialectical, idiolectal
F3 unidiomatic

idiosyncrasy *n*
peculiarity, individuality, speciality, oddity, eccentricity, freak, quirk, habit, mannerism, trait, feature, characteristic, quality
formal singularity

idiosyncratic *adj*
personal, individual, characteristic, distinctive, peculiar, odd, eccentric, quirky
formal singular
F3 general, common

idiot *n*
fool, imbecile, fat-head, dunce, dimwit, simpleton, halfwit, cretin, clown, ignoramus
colloq. thickhead, numskull, nincompoop, ass, chump, ninny, clot, dope, twit, nitwit, nit, sucker, mug,

twerp, birdbrain; *slang* jerk, nerd, wally, dumbo, pillock, prat, dork, geek, plonker, prick

idiotic *adj*
foolish, stupid, senseless, silly, absurd, ridiculous, ludicrous, nonsensical, unwise, ill-advised, ill-considered, short-sighted, half-baked, crazy, mad, insane, idiotic, moronic, hare-brained, half-witted, simple-minded, simple, ignorant, unintelligent, inept, inane, pointless, unreasonable
formal fatuous, risible, injudicious
colloq. thick-headed, daft, crack-brained, dumb, dotty, potty, batty, barmy, nutty
F3 sensible, sane

idle *adj, v*
▶ *adj* 1 INACTIVE, not working, inoperative, unused, dormant, dead, mothballed, unoccupied, unemployed, jobless, redundant
colloq. on the dole
2 LAZY, work-shy, lethargic, sluggish, lackadaisical, do-nothing, loafish
formal indolent, slothful
3 *idle threats*
empty, futile, vain, pointless, useless, worthless, pointless, fruitless, unsuccessful, ineffective, unproductive
formal ineffectual
4 *idle gossip*
casual, trivial, petty, foolish, shallow, unimportant, insignificant
F3 1 active, hardworking 2 busy 4 important, deep
▶ *v* 1 DO NOTHING, laze, lounge, while, take it easy, sit back, relax, kill time, while away, potter, loiter, dawdle, dally, fritter, waste, loaf, slack, shirk
colloq. skive, horse around; *slang* sod about, bum around, fart about, arse around
2 *the engine is idling*
tick over, be operational, be ready to work/run, move
F3 1 work, be busy

idleness *n*
laziness, lazing, sluggishness, torpor, inaction, inactivity, inertia, vegetating, shiftlessness, leisure, loafing, pottering, ease, unemployment
formal indolence, sloth, slothfulness
colloq. skiving
F3 activity, employment, occupation

idler *n*
loafer, dawdler, slacker, lounger, malingerer, shirker, good-for-nothing, laggard, sluggard, waster, wastrel, layabout, do-nothing, drone, clock-watcher
formal sloth
colloq. dodger, lazybones, skiver

idol *n*
1 HERO, heroine, favourite, darling, star, superstar, pet, beloved
colloq. blue-eyed boy, pin-up
2 *worship idols*
effigy, icon, image, graven image, likeness, god, deity, fetish, mammet

idolater *n*
admirer, worshipper, adorer, devotee, idol-worshipper, idolatress, idolist, iconolater, votary

idolatrous *adj*
adoring, worshipping, glorifying, lionizing, adulatory, idolizing, idol-worshipping, reverential, uncritical, pagan, heretical

idolatry *n*
worshipping, admiration, reverence, adoration, adulation, deification, exaltation, glorification, hero-worship, idolizing, idolism, iconolatry, icon worship, paganism, heathenism, fetishism
🗲 vilification

idolize *v*
hero-worship, lionize, exalt, glorify, worship, deify, revere, admire, adore, adulate, reverence, love, dote on
formal venerate
colloq. put on a pedestal
🗲 despise

idyllic *adj*
perfect, idealized, heavenly, blissful, delightful, wonderful, charming, picturesque, pastoral, rustic, unspoiled, peaceful, romantic, happy
🗲 unpleasant, spoiled, noisy

if *conj*
in the event of, in case of, on condition that, as/so long as, provided, providing, assuming (that), supposing (that)

iffy *adj*
uncertain, doubtful, dubious, undecided, unsettled
colloq. dodgy

ignite *v*
set fire to, set alight, light, catch fire, flare up, burn, burst into flames, conflagrate, fire, inflame, kindle, touch off, put a match to, spark off
🗲 quench

ignoble *adj*
low, mean, petty, base, vulgar, wretched, contemptible, despicable, shameful, vile, infamous, disgraceful, dishonourable
formal heinous
🗲 noble, worthy, honourable

ignominious *adj*
humiliating, mortifying, degrading, undignified, shameful, dishonourable, discreditable, sorry, disreputable, disgraceful, despicable, infamous, abject, base, despicable, contemptible, scandalous, embarrassing
🗲 triumphant, honourable, glorious

ignominy *n*
humiliation, mortification, degradation, shame, dishonour, discredit, disgrace, disrepute, reproach, scandal, contempt, indignity, infamy, stigma
formal obloquy, odium, opprobrium
🗲 credit, honour, dignity

ignoramus *n*
dunce, dimwit, halfwit, imbecile, simpleton, fool, illiterate, know-nothing, blockhead, dullard
colloq. numskull, bonehead, ass, duffer, dolt
🗲 scholar, intellectual, highbrow

ignorance *n*
unintelligence, illiteracy, unawareness, unconsciousness, oblivion, unfamiliarity, inexperience, innocence, naïvety, stupidity
colloq. greenness, thickness
🗲 knowledge, wisdom, education, intelligence

ignorant *adj*
uneducated, illiterate, innumerate, backward, unread, untaught, untrained, inexperienced, unschooled, unlearned, stupid, uninitiated, unenlightened, uninformed, ill-informed, unwitting, unaware, unfamiliar, unacquainted, unconscious, oblivious,
blind, innocent, naïve
formal nescient
colloq. clueless, dense, thick, thick as two short planks, dumb, in the dark, not all there, a brick short of a load
🗲 educated, knowledgeable, learned, clever, wise;
formal conversant

ignore *v*
disregard, take no notice of, not take any notice of, overlook, take for granted, pay no attention to, be oblivious to, pass over, neglect, omit, brush aside, shrug off, reject, snub, spurn, slight, cut (dead)
colloq. close/shut your eyes to, turn a blind eye to, look the other way, turn a deaf ear to, not listen to, cold-shoulder, turn your back on, keep in the dark, bury your head in the sand, run away from
🗲 notice, observe, pay attention to

ilk *n*
kind, sort, type, make, style, variety, brand, breed, class, stamp, character, description

ill *adj, n, adv*
▶ *adj* **1** SICK, poorly, unwell, laid up, ailing, off-colour, seedy, queasy, diseased, unhealthy, infirm, frail, weak, feeble, bedridden
formal afflicted, indisposed, valetudinarian
colloq. in a bad way, dicky, out of sorts, under the weather, run down, rough, groggy, like death warmed up
2 *an ill omen*
bad, evil, damaging, harmful, unpleasant, injurious, destructive, ruinous, detrimental, adverse, unfavourable, unpromising, sinister, ominous, threatening, unlucky, unfortunate, difficult, harsh, severe
formal inauspicious, unpropitious, infelicitous, deleterious
3 *ill feelings*
unkind, unfriendly, antagonistic, hostile, resentful, belligerent
🗲 **1** well, healthy **2** good, favourable, fortunate
3 kind, friendly
▷ **ill at ease** uncomfortable, awkward, fidgety, hesitant, embarrassed, self-conscious, strange, unsure, nervous, on edge, restless, tense, unrelaxed, unsettled, uneasy, worried, anxious, disquieted, disturbed;
colloq. edgy, like a cat on hot bricks, on tenterhooks
🗲 at ease
▶ *n* trouble, problem, trial(s), pain, misfortune, suffering, disaster, unpleasantness, harm, evil, hurt, cruelty, destruction, injury, sorrow
formal tribulation, affliction
🗲 good, benefit
▶ *adv* **1** BADLY, unfavourably, unkindly, disapprovingly, adversely, unfortunately, unsuccessfully, unluckily, wrongfully
formal inauspiciously
2 SCARCELY, hardly, barely, by no means, insufficiently, inadequately, poorly, scantily, amiss
🗲 **1** well

ill-advised *adj*
unwise, foolish, ill-considered, thoughtless, careless, hasty, rash, reckless, short-sighted, misguided, inappropriate
formal imprudent, injudicious
🗲 wise, sensible, well-advised, cautious;
formal politic, circumspect

ill-assorted *adj*
incompatible, inharmonious, discordant, unsuited, mismatched, uncongenial, misallied

formal incongruous
⊟ harmonious, well-matched

ill-bred *adj*
bad-mannered, ill-mannered, discourteous, impolite, rude, loutish, boorish, coarse, crude, vulgar, crass, uncouth, indelicate, uncivil, uncivilized
formal unseemly
⊟ well-bred, polite, gentlemanly, ladylike

ill-considered *adj*
ill-advised, ill-judged, careless, foolish, hasty, heedless, rash, unwise, overhasty
formal improvident, imprudent, injudicious, precipitate
⊟ sensible, wise

ill-defined *adj*
indistinct, unclear, vague, nebulous, imprecise, indefinite, blurred, fuzzy, hazy, woolly, blurry, dim, shadowy
⊟ clear

ill-disposed *adj*
unfriendly, unsympathetic, hostile, antagonistic, opposed, unco-operative, unwelcoming, against
formal averse, inimical
colloq. anti
⊟ well-disposed

illegal *adj*
unlawful, illicit, criminal, wrong, forbidden, prohibited, illegitimate, fraudulent, banned, outlawed, barred, unauthorized, under-the-counter, black-market, unconstitutional, wrongful
formal felonious, proscribed, interdicted
⊟ legal, lawful, permitted, allowed

illegality *n*
wrong, wrongfulness, wrongness, crime, criminality, illegitimacy, illicitness, lawlessness, unconstitutionality, unlawfulness
technical felony
⊟ legality

illegible *adj*
unreadable, indecipherable, hard to read, scrawled, obscure, faint, indistinct, unintelligible, hieroglyphic
⊟ legible, clear

illegitimate *adj*
1 *an illegitimate child*
natural, love, bastard, fatherless, misbegotten, adulterine, unfathered
formal born out of wedlock
colloq. born on the wrong side of the blanket
2 ILLEGAL, unlawful, illicit, lawless, unauthorized, unwarranted, unlicensed, improper
3 ILLOGICAL, incorrect, inadmissible, spurious, invalid, unsound
⊟ **1** legitimate **2** legal **3** well-reasoned

ill-fated *adj*
doomed, ill-starred, ill-omened, blighted, unfortunate, unlucky, luckless, unhappy
formal hapless
⊟ lucky

ill-favoured *adj*
hideous, plain, repulsive, ugly, unattractive, unlovely, unprepossessing, unsightly
US homely
⊟ beautiful, attractive

ill-feeling *n*
ill-will, bad blood, bitterness, grudge, hard feelings,

resentment, sourness, spite, malice, hostility, enmity, animosity, antagonism, dissatisfaction, frustration, offence, anger, indignation, wrath, disgruntlement, dudgeon
formal animus, odium, rancour
⊟ friendship, goodwill

ill-founded *adj*
baseless, groundless, without foundation, unjustified, unsupported, unconfirmed
⊟ substantiated, verified

ill-humoured *adj*
bad-tempered, cross, impatient, irascible, quick-tempered, irritable, sharp, snappy, snappish, disagreeable, grumpy, sulky, sullen, huffy, moody, morose, peevish, tart, testy, waspish
formal acrimonious, cantankerous, petulant
colloq. crabbed, crabby, crotchety, grouchy
⊟ amiable

illiberal *adj*
mean, narrow-minded, intolerant, petty, prejudiced, reactionary, small-minded, bigoted, hidebound, ungenerous, uncharitable, stingy, miserly, niggardly, close-fisted, tight
formal parsimonious
colloq. tightfisted
⊟ broad-minded, liberal

illicit *adj*
illegal, unlawful, criminal, wrong, illegitimate, improper, forbidden, prohibited, banned, barred, unauthorized, unlicensed, black-market, contraband, ill-gotten, under-the-counter, furtive, clandestine, secretive, surreptitious, stealthy
⊟ legal, permissible

illiterate *adj*
ignorant, uneducated, unschooled, unlearned, untaught, unlettered, untutored, uncultured
technical analphabetic
formal benighted
⊟ literate

ill-judged *adj*
ill-advised, ill-considered, short-sighted, unwise, foolish, foolhardy, misguided, hasty, overhasty, rash, reckless, incautious, indiscreet, wrong-headed
formal impolitic, imprudent, injudicious
colloq. daft
⊟ sensible

ill-mannered *adj*
rude, impolite, badly-behaved, insolent, discourteous, ill-bred, ill-behaved, unmannerly, uncivil, loutish, uncouth, boorish, churlish, coarse, crude, insensitive
⊟ polite, well-mannered

ill-natured *adj*
spiteful, vindictive, nasty, perverse, mean, surly, sulky, sullen, unfriendly, unkind, unpleasant, vicious, bad-tempered, cross, disagreeable, malicious, malignant, churlish
formal malevolent, petulant
colloq. crabbed
⊟ good-natured

illness *n*
disease, disorder, complaint, condition, ailment, sickness, ill/poor health, indisposition, infirmity, disability, attack, bout, touch
formal malady, affliction
See panel at **disease**.

illogical adj

irrational, unreasonable, unscientific, untenable, invalid, unsound, faulty, specious, spurious, inconsistent, fallible, senseless, meaningless, absurd, incorrect, wrong
formal fallacious, sophistical, casuistic
🔁 logical, rational, reasonable

illogicality n

irrationality, unreasonableness, unreason, unsoundness, absurdity, senselessness, speciousness, fallacy, inconsistency, invalidity
formal fallaciousness
🔁 logicality

ill-starred adj

doomed, ill-fated, unfortunate, unhappy, unlucky, star-crossed, blighted
formal inauspicious, hapless
🔁 fortunate

ill-tempered adj

bad-tempered, cross, ill-natured, ill-humoured, impatient, irritable, irascible, spiteful, vicious, curt, grumpy, testy, tetchy, touchy, choleric, sharp
🔁 good-tempered

ill-timed adj

inopportune, inconvenient, inappropriate, unseasonable, untimely, wrong-timed, unwelcome, unfortunate, awkward, tactless, inept, crass
🔁 well-timed

ill-treat v

mistreat, abuse, maltreat, injure, harm, damage, neglect, mishandle, misuse, wrong, oppress

ill-treatment n

abuse, mistreatment, maltreatment, damage, harm, injury, ill-use, manhandling, mishandling, misuse, neglect
🔁 care

illuminate v

1 LIGHT, light up, shine on, throw light on, floodlight, brighten
formal illumine
2 CLARIFY, clear up, elucidate, illustrate, explain, edify, instruct, enlighten
3 DECORATE, ornament, adorn, embellish, illustrate
🔁 1 darken 2 mystify

illuminating adj

informative, instructive, helpful, edifying, enlightening, revealing
formal explanatory, revelatory
🔁 unhelpful

illumination n

1 LIGHT, lights, lighting, beam, ray, irradiation, brightness, radiance
2 ENLIGHTENMENT, awareness, insight, understanding, instruction, perception, learning, education, revelation
3 DECORATION, ornamentation, adornment, embellishment, illustration
🔁 1 darkness

illusion n

apparition, mirage, spectre, phantom, will-o'-the-wisp, hallucination, figment of the imagination, fantasy, fancy, delusion, misapprehension, misconception, misjudgement, error, false impression, deception

formal chimera, fallacy
🔁 reality, truth

⚠ **illusion** or **allusion**? *See panel at* **allusion**.

⚠ **illusion** or **delusion**? *See panel at* **delusion**.

illusory adj

illusive, illusionary, deceptive, misleading, apparent, seeming, deluding, delusive, unreal, delusory, fancied, imagined, specious, unsubstantial, sham, false, untrue, mistaken, erroneous
formal chimerical, fallacious
🔁 real, actual

illustrate v

1 DEMONSTRATE, exemplify, instance, explain, interpret, clarify, draw, sketch, depict, picture, show, exhibit
formal elucidate
2 ILLUMINATE, decorate, ornament, adorn, embellish
formal miniate

illustrated adj

decorated, embellished, illuminated, pictorial
formal miniated

illustration n

1 PICTURE, plate, half-tone, photograph, drawing, sketch, figure, diagram, chart, artwork, design, representation, decoration, ornamentation, adornment, embellishment
2 EXAMPLE, specimen, instance, case, sample, analogy, demonstration, exemplification, explanation, interpretation, clarification
formal exemplar, elucidation

illustrative adj

explanatory, descriptive, representative, typical, exemplifying, sample, specimen, diagrammatic, graphic, pictorial, interpretative
formal explicatory, expository, delineative, illustrational, illustratory

illustrious adj

great, noble, eminent, distinguished, celebrated, acclaimed, honoured, famous, famed, renowned, well-known, noted, prominent, outstanding, pre-eminent, remarkable, notable, brilliant, excellent, splendid, magnificent, glorious, exalted
formal esteemed
🔁 ignoble, inglorious

ill-will n

hostility, antagonism, bad blood, enmity, unfriendliness, malevolence, malice, spite, animosity, ill-feeling, resentment, hard feelings, bad blood, grudge, dislike, aversion, hatred, antipathy, anger, indignation, wrath
formal animus, rancour, odium
🔁 goodwill, friendship

image n

1 IDEA, notion, concept, conception, thought, fancy, impression, perception, vision
2 REPRESENTATION, likeness, resemblance, picture, portrait, icon, graven image, effigy, figure, figurine, statue, statuette, bust, idol, replica, doll
3 REPRODUCTION, reflection, photograph, picture, copy, facsimile
4 *the image of his father*
likeness, representation, double, twin, duplicate, copy,

clone, replica, doppelgänger, lookalike, match
colloq. spitting image, (dead) ringer
5 *images in a poem*
figure of speech, figurative expression, turn of phrase, rhetorical device, imagery, simile, metaphor

imaginable *adj*
conceivable, thinkable, believable, credible, supposable, feasible, plausible, likely, possible, probable
E∃ unimaginable, inconceivable

imaginary *adj*
imagined, fanciful, fancied, illusory, hallucinatory, visionary, pretend, make-believe, dreamy, shadowy, ghostly, spectral, insubstantial, unreal, non-existent, fictional, fantastic, fabulous, legendary, mythological, mythical, made-up, invented, fictitious, assumed, supposed, hypothetical, notional
formal chimerical
E∃ real

imagination *n*
1 CREATIVITY, imaginativeness, inventiveness, fancifulness, originality, inspiration, insight, ingenuity, resourcefulness, enterprise, wit, vision
2 *see them in my imagination*
mind's eye, fancy, illusion, vision, dream, conceptualization
formal chimera
E∃ 1 unimaginativeness **2** reality

imaginative *adj*
creative, inventive, innovative, full of ideas, original, inspired, visionary, ingenious, clever, resourceful, enterprising, fanciful, whimsical, fantastic, vivid
E∃ unimaginative

imagine *v*
1 PICTURE, form a picture of, visualize, see, see in your mind's eye, envisage, conceive, fancy, fantasize, daydream, dream, pretend, make believe, conjure up, dream up, think up, invent, devise, create, scheme, plan, project
2 *I imagine so*
think, believe, judge, suppose, guess, reckon, assume, presume, gather, fancy
formal conjecture, deem, surmise
colloq. take it

imbalance *n*
unevenness, inequality, disproportion, unfairness, partiality, bias
formal disparity, inequity
E∃ balance, parity

imbecile *n, adj*
▶ *n* idiot, halfwit, simpleton, moron, cretin, fool, blockhead, bungler, dunce, dimwit
colloq. ass, clot, twit, nitwit
▶ *adj* stupid, silly, foolish, idiotic, inane, ludicrous, absurd, crazy, moronic, witless, asinine
formal fatuous
colloq. doltish, thick, daft, dotty, dopey, barmy
E∃ intelligent, sensible

imbecility *n*
foolishness, idiocy, inanity, stupidity, incompetence, cretinism, asininity, childishness
technical amentia
formal fatuity
E∃ intelligence, sense

imbibe *v*
1 DRINK, consume, swallow, gulp, sip

formal ingest
colloq. knock back, quaff, swig
2 ABSORB, take in, assimilate, drink in, receive, soak up, acquire, gain, gather
colloq. lap up

imbroglio *n*
entanglement, tangle, involvement, confusion, difficulty, dilemma, muddle, mess, quandary, embroilment
colloq. scrape

imbue *v*
permeate, impregnate, pervade, suffuse, fill, saturate, inject, ingrain, inspire, charge, steep, inculcate, instil, tinge, tint

imitate *v*
1 COPY, take as a model, follow, follow suit, do likewise, ape, mimic, impersonate, do an impression of, caricature, parody, mock, parrot, repeat, echo, mirror
formal emulate
colloq. take off, send up, spoof, take a leaf out of someone's book
2 REPRODUCE, duplicate, simulate, copy, fake, counterfeit, forge
formal replicate

imitation *n, adj*
▶ *n* **1** MIMICRY, impersonation, aping, apery, impression, caricature, parody, mocking, mockery, travesty
colloq. take-off, send-up, spoof
2 COPY, duplicate, reproduction, replica, simulation, counterfeit, fake, forgery, sham, likeness, resemblance, reflection, dummy
formal emulation
▶ *adj* artificial, synthetic, man-made, ersatz, fake, mock, reproduction, simulated, sham, dummy
colloq. phoney, pseudo
E∃ genuine

imitative *adj*
copying, mimicking, parrot-like, unoriginal, derivative, plagiarized, second-hand, simulated, mock
formal emulating, mimetic
colloq. me-too
E∃ original

imitator *n*
mimic, impersonator, impressionist, parrot, ape, echo, parodist, plagiarist, copier, copyist, follower, epigone
formal emulator
colloq. copycat

immaculate *adj*
perfect, unblemished, flawless, faultless, impeccable, spotless, unsoiled, clean, spick and span, pure, unsullied, undefiled, incorrupt, untainted, stainless, blameless, guiltless, sinless, innocent
colloq. squeaky clean
E∃ blemished, stained, contaminated

immaterial *adj*
irrelevant, insignificant, unimportant, minor, trivial, petty, trifling, inconsequential, of no account
E∃ relevant, important

immature *adj*
young, under-age, adolescent, juvenile, childish, puerile, infantile, babyish, raw, crude, callow, inexperienced, naïve, unripe, undeveloped, unmellowed, incomplete, unready, unprepared
formal ingenuous

colloq. wet behind the ears, innocent as a newborn babe, green

E∃ mature, fully-developed, grown-up

immaturity *n*
youth, adolescence, juvenility, childishness, puerility, babyishness, rawness, crudeness, crudity, callowness, inexperience, immatureness, unpreparedness, imperfection, unripeness, greenness

E∃ maturity, mellowness

immeasurable *adj*
vast, immense, infinite, limitless, unlimited, illimitable, boundless, fathomless, unfathomable, unbounded, endless, never ending, interminable, bottomless, inexhaustible, incalculable, inestimable

E∃ limited

immediacy *n*
urgency, importance, criticalness, instancy, spontaneity, instantaneity, promptness, swiftness, simultaneity, directness, imminence

E∃ remoteness, distance

immediate *adj*
1 INSTANT, instantaneous, direct, sudden, without delay, prompt, swift, speedy
2 URGENT, pressing, important, vital, crucial, critical, current, present, existing, pressing
colloq. top-priority, high-priority
3 NEAREST, closest, next, adjacent, next-door, near, close, recent
formal adjoining, abutting
4 *the immediate cause of death*
direct, primary, basic, fundamental, chief, main, principal

E∃ 1 delayed 3 distant 4 indirect

immediately *adv*
now, straight away, right away, right now, at once, instantly, instantaneously, directly, speedily, quickly, forthwith, without delay, no sooner ... than, as soon as, promptly, unhesitatingly, without hesitation, without question, this minute/instant
colloq. pronto, yesterday, before you know it, before you can say Jack Robinson, in two shakes of a lamb's tail, like a shot

E∃ eventually, never

immemorial *adj*
age-old, timeless, ancient, archaic, long-standing, fixed, time-honoured, hoary, traditional, ancestral
formal of yore

E∃ recent

immense *adj*
vast, great, extremely large, huge, enormous, massive, giant, gigantic, colossal, extensive, cosmic, tremendous, monumental, mammoth, herculean, elephantine, titanic, Brobdingnagian
colloq. whopping, bumper, jumbo, ginormous, humungous, mega

E∃ tiny, minute

immensely *adv*
enormously, greatly, extremely, extraordinarily, massively

immensity *n*
magnitude, bulk, expanse, vastness, greatness, hugeness, enormousness, massiveness, giganticness, extensiveness

E∃ minuteness

immerse *v*
1 PLUNGE, submerge, submerse, sink, duck, dip, dunk, douse, souse, saturate, drench, soak, bathe, baptize
2 ENGROSS, preoccupy, occupy, absorb, bury, wrap up in, engage, involve, engulf

immersed *adj*
absorbed, engrossed, involved, occupied, preoccupied, consumed, buried, busy, deep, taken up, wrapped up, rapt, sunk

immersion *n*
1 SUBMERSION, plunging, sinking, ducking, dip, dipping, dunking, dousing, saturation, drenching, soaking, baptism, bathe
2 PREOCCUPATION, absorption, engrossing, engagement, involvement, concentration

immigrant *n*
incomer, settler, migrant, newcomer, new arrival, alien

E∃ native

immigrate *v*
come in, move in, migrate, settle, resettle, remove

E∃ emigrate

imminence *n*
approach, nearness, closeness, immediacy, instancy, menace, threat
formal propinquity

E∃ remoteness

imminent *adj*
impending, forthcoming, in the offing, approaching, fast approaching, coming, on the way, near, close, looming, menacing, threatening, brewing, in the air, at hand, about to happen, almost upon you, on the horizon
colloq. round the corner

E∃ remote, far-off

immobile *adj*
motionless, stationary, unmoving, immobilized, at rest, still, stock-still, static, immovable, rooted, fixed, frozen, rigid, stiff, riveted

E∃ mobile, moving

immobility *n*
motionlessness, immovability, steadiness, stillness, firmness, fixedness, fixity, stability, inertness, disability

E∃ mobility

immobilize *v*
stop, halt, inactivate, freeze, transfix, paralyse, cripple, disable, put out of action/operation

E∃ mobilize

immoderate *adj*
excessive, unreasonable, unjustified, unwarranted, undue, exaggerated, fulsome, enormous, exorbitant, lavish, extravagant, extreme, wanton, inordinate, uncalled-for, uncontrolled, unrestrained, outrageous, unlimited, unrestricted, unbridled, uncurbed, intemperate, self-indulgent
formal unconscionable, profligate, hubristic, distemperate, egregious
colloq. over the top, OTT, steep

E∃ moderate

immoderately *adv*
excessively, exorbitantly, extravagantly, extremely, inordinately, exaggeratedly, unduly, unjustifiably, unrestrainedly, without measure, unreasonably,

wantonly
🔁 moderately

immoderation *n*
excess, excessiveness, exorbitance, extravagance, lavishness, immoderateness, intemperance, overindulgence, unreason, unrestraint
formal prodigality, dissipation
🔁 moderation

immodest *adj*
indecent, revealing, shameless, forward, bold, boastful, impudent, brazen, improper, immoral, obscene, lewd, coarse, risqué
formal indecorous
colloq. cheeky, fresh, cocky, saucy
🔁 modest

immodesty *n*
audacity, boldness, forwardness, gall, impudence, shamelessness, temerity, bawdiness, coarseness, impurity, lewdness, obscenity, indelicacy
formal indecorousness, indecorum
colloq. brass
🔁 modesty

immoral *adj*
unethical, wrong, wrongdoing, bad, sinful, evil, wicked, unscrupulous, unprincipled, dishonest, vile, corrupt, depraved, base, degenerate, debauched, reprobate, dissolute, loose, lewd, indecent, pornographic, obscene, licentious, impure
formal iniquitous, nefarious
colloq. blue, raunchy, juicy
🔁 moral, right, good

immorality *n*
wrong, wrongdoing, badness, sin, sinfulness, evil, wickedness, dishonesty, vileness, corruption, vice, depravity, dissoluteness, debauchery, impurity, lewdness, indecency, pornography, obscenity, licentiousness
formal iniquity, profligacy, turpitude
🔁 morality

immortal *adj, n*
▶ *adj* **1** UNDYING, deathless, imperishable, indestructible, unfading, eternal, everlasting, perpetual, endless, ceaseless, lasting, enduring, abiding, constant, perennial, timeless, ageless
formal sempiternal
2 *recall those immortal words*
memorable, unforgettable, well-known, celebrated, famous, honoured, distinguished
🔁 **1** mortal
▶ *n* deity, god, goddess, divinity, great, hero, genius, Olympian

immortality *n*
1 ETERNAL LIFE, everlasting life, eternity, endlessness, deathlessness, incorruptibility, imperishability, indestructibility, timelessness, perpetuity
2 FAME, glorification, gloriousness, glory, greatness, renown, celebrity, honour, distinction
🔁 **1** mortality

immortalize *v*
celebrate, commemorate, memorialize, perpetuate, glorify, enshrine, eternalize
formal laud

immovable *adj*
1 FIXED, rooted, immobile, stuck, fast, secure, stable, moored, riveted, anchored, jammed, constant, firm, set
2 STEADFAST, determined, resolute, adamant, unshakable, stubborn, obstinate, uncompromising, unyielding, set, firm, constant, inflexible, dogged, unwavering, unswerving
formal intransigent
🔁 **1** movable **2** flexible

immune *adj*
invulnerable, unsusceptible, resistant, proof, protected, safe, exempt, free, clear, secure, spared, excused, released, relieved, absolved
🔁 susceptible, liable, subject, affected

immunity *n*
resistance, protection, immunization, vaccination, inoculation, safety, exemption, indemnity, exception, impunity, freedom, liberty, release, licence, franchise, privilege, right, permission
formal exoneration
🔁 susceptibility

immunization *n*
vaccination, inoculation, injection, protection, jab

immunize *v*
vaccinate, inoculate, inject, protect, safeguard, shield

immure *v*
enclose, confine, wall in, shut up, cage, imprison, incarcerate, jail, cloister, enwall
🔁 free

immutability *n*
changelessness, immutableness, invariability, unalterableness, unchangeableness, permanence, constancy, durability, fixedness, stability
🔁 mutability

immutable *adj*
changeless, inflexible, invariable, unalterable, unchangeable, perpetual, permanent, abiding, constant, enduring, fixed, lasting, stable, steadfast, sacrosanct
🔁 mutable, changeable

imp *n*
1 SPRITE, demon, devil, goblin, hobgoblin, gnome, puck
2 MISCHIEVOUS CHILD, rascal, rogue, scamp, brat, minx, troublemaker, mischief-maker, trickster, prankster, flibbertigibbet, gamin, urchin

impact *n, v*
▶ *n* **1** *the impact of the reforms*
effect, consequences, results, repercussions, impression, power, influence, significance, meaning
2 COLLISION, crash, smash, bang, bump, blow, knock, whack, contact, clash, jolt, force, shock, brunt
▶ *v* **1** COLLIDE, crash, hit, clash, crush, fix, strike, press together
2 AFFECT, have an effect on, influence, apply to, impinge

impair *v*
damage, harm, injure, hinder, mar, spoil, cripple, disable, worsen, deteriorate, undermine, weaken, reduce, decrease, lessen, diminish, blunt
formal debilitate, enervate, vitiate, enfeeble
🔁 improve, enhance

impaired *adj*
defective, faulty, flawed, poor, weak, disabled, imperfect, damaged, spoilt, unsound
formal vitiated
🔁 enhanced

impairment *n*
disability, disablement, injury, weakness, damage, deterioration, reduction, harm, hurt, fault, flaw, ruin
formal dysfunction, vitiation
E3 enhancement

impale *v*
pierce, puncture, perforate, run through, spear, lance, spike, skewer, spit, stick, stab, prick, transfix, disembowel

impalpable *adj*
imperceptible, inapprehensible, insubstantial, unsubstantial, elusive, indistinct, intangible, shadowy, tenuous, thin, fine, delicate, airy
formal incorporeal
E3 palpable

impart *v*
1 CONVEY, tell, relate, communicate, make known, transmit, disclose, divulge, reveal, report, pass on
2 GIVE, grant, offer, contribute, lend, assign
formal confer, bestow, accord
E3 1, 2 withhold

impartial *adj*
objective, dispassionate, detached, disinterested, neutral, non-partisan, unbiased, unprejudiced, open-minded, fair, fair-minded, just, equitable, even-handed, equal
colloq. having an axe to grind
E3 biased, prejudiced

impartiality *n*
neutrality, non-partisanship, objectivity, unbiasedness, fairness, justice, even-handedness, open-mindedness, detachment, disinterest, disinterestedness, dispassion, equality, equity
E3 bias, prejudice, favouritism, discrimination

impassable *adj*
blocked, closed, obstructed, unnavigable, unpassable, pathless, trackless, impenetrable, insurmountable, insuperable, unassailable, invincible
E3 passable

impasse *n*
deadlock, stalemate, checkmate, dead end, cul-de-sac, blind alley, halt, standstill

impassioned *adj*
fervent, ardent, passionate, intense, inspired, stirring, spirited, rousing, emotional, enthusiastic, eager, excited, fervid, vigorous, forceful, violent, furious, fiery, vehement, animated, glowing, inflamed, heated, blazing
E3 apathetic, mild

impassive *adj*
expressionless, emotionless, calm, composed, unruffled, unconcerned, apathetic, cool, unfeeling, unemotional, unmoved, unruffled, unexcitable, stoical, indifferent, dispassionate
formal imperturbable, phlegmatic
colloq. unflappable, laid back
E3 responsive, moved

impatience *n*
eagerness, keenness, excitability, restlessness, agitation, anxiety, nervousness, edginess, uneasiness, irritability, intolerance, shortness, brusqueness, abruptness, curtness, tenseness, haste, rashness, impetuosity
E3 patience

impatient *adj*
eager, keen, excitable, restless, fidgety, fretful, agitated, anxious, nervous, edgy, irritable, jittery, snappy, testy, hot-tempered, quick-tempered, angry, intolerant, brusque, abrupt, short, curt, tense, impetuous, hasty, headlong
formal restive, querulous, precipitate
colloq. champing at the bit, straining/panting at the leash
E3 patient

impeach *v*
accuse, charge, denounce, criticize, revile, attack, censure, blame
technical indict, arraign
formal impugn, disparage

impeachment *n*
accusation, charge
technical arraignment, indictment
formal disparagement

impeccable *adj*
perfect, faultless, precise, exact, correct, exemplary, flawless, unblemished, stainless, immaculate, pure, upright, irreproachable, blameless, innocent
E3 faulty, flawed, corrupt

impecunious *adj*
poor, poverty-stricken, insolvent, destitute, impoverished, penniless, needy
formal indigent, penurious
colloq. broke, stony-broke, skint, cleaned out
E3 rich

impede *v*
hinder, hamper, obstruct, block, handicap, clog, slow (down), hold up, hold back, delay, check, curb, restrain, thwart, disrupt, stop, bar
formal retard
E3 aid, promote, further

impediment *n*
1 HINDRANCE, obstacle, obstruction, barrier, bar, block, setback, stumbling-block, snag, difficulty, handicap, burden, encumbrance, check, curb, restraint, restriction
2 *a speech impediment*
DEFECT, handicap, stutter, stammer
E3 1 aid

impedimenta *n*
baggage, luggage, equipment, gear, belongings
formal effects, accoutrements
colloq. things, stuff, bits and pieces

impel *v*
urge, force, oblige, compel, constrain, drive, propel, get going, push, press, pressure, pressurize, spur, prod, goad, prompt, incite, stimulate, excite, instigate, motivate, inspire, move
E3 deter, dissuade

impending *adj*
imminent, forthcoming, in the offing, approaching, coming, close, near, at hand, on the way, looming, menacing, threatening, brewing, in the air, about to happen, on the horizon
E3 remote, far-off

impenetrable *adj*
1 *impenetrable jungle*
impassable, solid, thick, dense, overgrown
2 UNINTELLIGIBLE, incomprehensible, unfathomable, indiscernible, puzzling, baffling,

mysterious, cryptic, enigmatic, obscure, dark, inscrutable
formal abstruse, recondite
E≡ **2** accessible, understandable

impenitence *n*
impenitency, stubbornness, defiance, hard-heartedness, incorrigibility
formal obduracy
E≡ penitence

impenitent *adj*
unrepentant, unremorseful, uncontrite, unashamed, defiant, hardened, incorrigible, remorseless, unabashed, unreformed, unregenerate
formal obdurate
E≡ penitent, contrite

imperative *adj*
vital, essential, crucial, pressing, urgent, compulsory, critical, necessary, obligatory, indispensable
E≡ optional, unimportant

imperceptible *adj*
inappreciable, indiscernible, unapparent, indistinguishable, undetectable, inaudible, unapparent, faint, slight, muffled, negligible, impalpable, infinitesimal, microscopic, minute, tiny, minuscule, small, fine, subtle, gradual, unclear, obscure, vague, indistinct, indefinite
E≡ perceptible, noticeable, clear

imperceptibly *adv*
inappreciably, indiscernibly, unnoticeably, unobtrusively, unseen, slowly, subtly, gradually, bit by bit, little by little
formal insensibly
E≡ perceptibly

imperfect *adj*
faulty, flawed, defective, damaged, broken, blemished, impaired, chipped, deficient, inadequate, insufficient, incomplete
E≡ perfect, whole

imperfection *n*
fault, flaw, defect, blemish, deformity, crack, dent, break, tear, cut, scratch, blot, blotch, stain, taint, spot, deficiency, impairment, shortcoming, foible, weakness, failing, inadequacy, insufficiency
E≡ perfection

imperial *adj*
sovereign, supreme, absolute, royal, regal, monarchical, kingly, queenly, majestic, grand, magnificent, glorious, splendid, great, noble, lofty, stately

---

⚠ **imperial** or **imperious** ?
Imperial means 'of an empire or emperor': *the imperial crown. Imperious* means 'proud and overbearing', 'behaving as if expecting to be, or in the habit of being, obeyed': *She disliked his imperious manner.*

---

imperialism *n*
empire-building, colonialism, expansionism, acquisitiveness, adventurism

imperil *v*
endanger, put in danger, jeopardize, put in jeopardy, risk, expose to risk, hazard, take a chance, expose, compromise, threaten

imperious *adj*
overbearing, domineering, autocratic, despotic, tyrannical, dictatorial, high-handed, lordly, masterful, commanding, assertive, arrogant, haughty
formal peremptory, overweening
E≡ humble

imperishable *adj*
enduring, permanent, incorruptible, indestructible, inextinguishable, undying, unfading, unforgettable, abiding, perpetual, perennial, eternal, everlasting, immortal, deathless
E≡ perishable

impermanent *adj*
transient, temporary, passing, short-lived, momentary, transitory, inconstant, brief, elusive, fleeting, flying, unfixed, unsettled, unstable, mortal, perishable, fugitive
formal ephemeral, evanescent, fugacious
colloq. fly-by-night
E≡ permanent

impermeable *adj*
impervious, impenetrable, impassable, sealed, hermetic, non-porous, damp-proof, waterproof, proof, water-resistant, resistant, water-repellent
E≡ permeable, porous

impersonal *adj*
1 COLD, cool, frigid, formal, official, aloof, remote, distant, clinical, stiff, stuffy, businesslike, detached, unemotional, unfeeling
2 OBJECTIVE, neutral, dispassionate, detached, unbiased, unprejudiced
E≡ **1** friendly, informal **2** biased

impersonate *v*
imitate, mimic, parody, caricature, mock, ape, masquerade as, pose as, pass off as, act, portray
colloq. take off

impersonation *n*
imitation, impression, mimicry, parody, caricature, aping, apery, burlesque
colloq. take-off

impertinence *n*
rudeness, impoliteness, disrespect, discourtesy, insolence, impudence, effrontery, audacity, boldness, brazenness, forwardness, presumption, shamelessness
colloq. cheek, brass, brass neck, nerve, sauce, lip, gall, face, mouth
E≡ politeness, respect, civility

impertinent *adj*
rude, impolite, ill-mannered, unmannerly, discourteous, disrespectful, insolent, impudent, pert, bold, audacious, brash, brazen, forward, presumptuous, shameless
colloq. cheeky, saucy, fresh; *US* sassy; *slang* smart-arsed
E≡ polite, respectful

imperturbability *n*
calmness, composure, coolness, complacency, self-possession, tranquillity
formal equanimity
E≡ jitteriness, touchiness

imperturbable *adj*
unexcitable, calm, tranquil, composed, collected, even-tempered, self-possessed, cool, impassive, unmoved, unruffled, untroubled, complacent

colloq. unflappable, calm and collected
E3 excitable, ruffled

impervious *adj*
1 IMPERMEABLE, waterproof, damp-proof, proof,
non-porous, watertight, hermetic, closed, sealed,
resistant, impenetrable
2 *impervious to criticism*
immune, invulnerable, untouched, unaffected,
unmoved, closed, resistant
E3 1 porous, pervious 2 responsive, vulnerable

impetuosity *n*
impetuousness, impulsiveness, rashness, haste,
hastiness, spontaneity, foolhardiness, recklessness,
thoughtlessness, impatience, dash, élan, vehemence
formal precipitateness
E3 caution, wariness; *formal* circumspection

impetuous *adj*
impulsive, spontaneous, unplanned, unthinking,
unpremeditated, spur-of-the-moment, hasty,
impatient, headlong, uncontrolled, brash, foolhardy,
rash, reckless, thoughtless, unthinking, ill-conceived,
unreasoned
formal precipitate
E3 cautious, wary; *formal* circumspect

impetuously *adv*
rashly, impulsively, unthinkingly, recklessly,
spontaneously, passionately, vehemently
formal precipitately
E3 cautiously

impetus *n*
stimulus, incentive, motivation, influence,
encouragement, inspiration, actuation, impulse,
momentum, force, energy, power, drive, urging, boost,
push, goad, spur

impiety *n*
irreverence, irreligion, profaneness, profanity,
sinfulness, ungodliness, unholiness, unrighteousness,
wickedness, godlessness, blasphemy, sacrilege,
sacrilegiousness
formal iniquity, hubris
E3 piety, reverence

Impinge *v*
encroach, infringe, affect, influence, hit, touch (on),
intrude, trespass, invade

impious *adj*
irreverent, irreligious, profane, sinful, ungodly,
godless, unholy, unrighteous, wicked, blasphemous,
sacrilegious
formal iniquitous, hubristic
E3 pious, reverent

impish *adj*
mischievous, naughty, roguish, rascally, sportive,
devilish, elfin, gamin, tricksome, frolicsome, tricksy,
pranksome, waggish

implacability *n*
implacableness, inexorability, relentlessness,
remorselessness, mercilessness, pitilessness,
ruthlessness, unforgivingness, vengefulness,
irreconcilability, inflexibility
formal intransigence, intractability, rancorousness
E3 placability

implacable *adj*
inexorable, relentless, unrelenting, remorseless,
merciless, pitiless, unappeasable, irreconcilable,
vengeful, cruel, heartless, unforgiving, ruthless,

inflexible, adamant, uncompromising, unyielding
formal intransigent, intractable, rancorous
E3 compassionate, forgiving

implant *v*
1 *implant ideas in someone's mind*
sow, plant, fix, root, instil, inculcate, introduce
2 *implant a new heart/new skin tissue*
insert, place, put, engraft, graft, transplant
3 EMBED, fix, sow, plant, place, root

implausible *adj*
improbable, unlikely, hard to believe, unbelievable,
inconceivable, incredible, far-fetched, dubious,
doubtful, questionable, suspect, unconvincing, weak,
flimsy, thin, transparent
E3 plausible, likely, reasonable

implement *n, v*
▶ *n* tool, instrument, utensil, gadget, device,
apparatus, appliance, contrivance
▶ *v* enforce, bring about, carry out, perform, do,
fulfil, complete, accomplish, realize, put into effect,
put into action/operation
formal discharge, execute, effect

implementation *n*
carrying out, performance, performing, fulfilling,
fulfilment, accomplishment, completion, operation,
action, enforcement, realization
formal discharge, effecting, execution

implicate *v*
involve, embroil, entangle, incriminate, compromise,
include, concern, connect, associate, be a part of,
be (a) party to
formal inculpate
E3 absolve; *formal* exonerate

implicated *adj*
involved, embroiled, entangled, incriminated,
compromised, included, concerned, connected,
associated, responsible, party to, suspected
formal inculpated
E3 exonerated

implication *n*
1 INFERENCE, deduction, insinuation, suggestion,
meaning, significance, overtone, undertone,
ramification, repercusssion, effect, consequence,
conclusion
2 INVOLVEMENT, entanglement, embroilment,
incrimination, connection, association
formal inculpation

implicit *adj*
1 IMPLIED, inferred, deducible, insinuated,
suggested, hinted, indirect, unsaid, unspoken,
unexpressed, unstated, tacit, understood, inherent,
hidden, latent
2 *implicit belief*
unquestioning, unhesitating, utter, total, full, entire,
complete, absolute, perfect, sheer, positive,
unqualified, unreserved, unconditional, steadfast,
wholehearted
E3 1 explicit 2 half-hearted

implicitly *adv*
absolutely, totally, utterly, completely, unconditionally,
unhesitatingly, unquestioningly, unreservedly,
steadfastly, wholeheartedly, firmly
E3 explicitly

implied *adj*
implicit, tacit, indirect, insinuated, suggested, hinted,

assumed, understood, unspoken, unexpressed, unstated, undeclared, inherent
F3 stated

implore *v*
beg, entreat, ask, appeal, request, press, crave, plead, pray
formal importune, solicit, supplicate, beseech

imply *v*
suggest, insinuate, hint, intimate, infer, say indirectly, give someone to understand/believe, mean, signify, point to, indicate, signal, involve, require, entail, state
formal denote

> ⚠ **imply** or **infer** ?
> *Imply* means 'to suggest or hint at (something) without actually stating it': *Are you implying that I'm a liar?* *Infer* means 'to form an opinion by reasoning from what you know': *I inferred from your silence that you were angry.*

impolite *adj*
rude, discourteous, bad-mannered, unmannerly, ill-mannered, ill-bred, uncivil, unrefined, ungentlemanly, unladylike, indecorous, ungracious, inconsiderate, disrespectful, impertinent, insolent, rough, loutish, boorish, coarse, crude, vulgar, abrupt
colloq. cheeky
F3 polite, courteous

impoliteness *n*
rudeness, discourtesy, bad manners, unmannerliness, disrespect, insolence, impertinence, incivility, inconsiderateness, boorishness, churlishness, crassness, indelicacy, roughness, coarseness, abruptness, gaucherie
F3 politeness, courtesy

impolitic *adj*
unwise, ill-advised, inexpedient, ill-judged, misguided, ill-considered, short-sighted, undiplomatic, indiscreet, rash, foolish
formal injudicious, imprudent, maladroit
colloq. daft
F3 wise; *formal* politic, prudent

import *n, v*
▶ *n* **1** *exports and imports*
imported product/commodity/goods, foreign product/commodity/goods, foreign trade
2 IMPORTANCE, consequence, significance, weight, substance
3 CONTENT, sense, substance, nub, meaning, implication, intention, thrust, message, drift, essence, gist
formal purport
▶ *v* betoken, bring in, imply, indicate, introduce, mean, purport, signify

importance *n*
1 MOMENTOUSNESS, significance, urgency, criticalness, graveness, substance, matter, concern, interest, usefulness, value, worth, weight
formal consequence
2 *people of importance in society*
influence, power, mark, prominence, eminence, distinction, noteworthiness, prestige, status, standing
formal esteem
F3 **1, 2** unimportance, insignificance

important *adj*
1 MOMENTOUS, noteworthy, significant, meaningful,

relevant, material, salient, urgent, critical, paramount, crucial, vital, essential, key, central, primary, principal, major, main, chief, priority, substantial, valuable, valued, weighty, serious, grave, far-reaching, pivotal, historic, fateful
formal seminal
2 *the most important person in the school*
LEADING, foremost, high-level, high-ranking, influential, chief, main, powerful, pre-eminent, prestigious, prominent, outstanding, eminent, notable, distinguished, valued, noted
formal esteemed
F3 **1** unimportant, insignificant, trivial
2 powerless

importunate *adj*
insistent, persistent, troublesome, impatient, tenacious, dogged, pressing, urgent
formal pertinacious

importune *v*
pester, badger, harass, hound, cajole, plague, appeal, request, press, urge, plead with, solicit, beset
formal supplicate

importunity *n*
insistence, persistence, pressing, pestering, harassing, hounding, urgency, urging, solicitation, harassment, cajolery, entreaties

impose *v*
1 ENFORCE, exact, levy, apply, charge, set, fix, put (on), place (on), lay (on), introduce, institute, establish, decree, inflict, burden, encumber, saddle, force, thrust, foist
2 FOIST, force yourself, thrust yourself, intrude, butt in, break in, encroach, trespass, obtrude, presume, exploit, put upon, abuse, mislead, take liberties, take advantage of

imposing *adj*
impressive, striking, grand, stately, majestic, splendid, dignified, lofty, august
F3 unimposing, modest

imposition *n*
1 ENFORCEMENT, introduction, infliction, exaction, levying, application, setting, fixing, establishment, decree, institution
2 CHARGE, tax, tariff, toll, burden, constraint, load, encumbrance, duty, task, punishment
3 INTRUSION, encroachment, trespassing

impossibility *n*
hopelessness, impracticability, unattainableness, unobtainableness, unacceptability, untenability, unviability, inability, inconceivability, preposterousness, absurdity, ludicrousness, ridiculousness
F3 possibility

impossible *adj*
hopeless, impracticable, unworkable, unattainable, unachievable, unobtainable, insoluble, unreasonable, unacceptable, beyond you, inconceivable, unimaginable, unthinkable, out of the question, preposterous, incredible, unbelievable, absurd, ludicrous, ridiculous, outlandish, intolerable, unbearable
colloq. out, not by any stretch of the imagination, and pigs might fly
F3 possible

impostor *n*
fraud, fake, quack, charlatan, sham, mountebank,

impersonator, pretender, deceiver, deluder, hoodwinker, swindler, cheat, trickster, defrauder, rogue
colloq. phoney, con man

imposture *n*
deception, fraud, impersonation, quackery, swindle, trick, counterfeit, cheat, hoax, artifice
colloq. con, con trick

impotence *n*
powerlessness, helplessness, uselessness, inability, inadequacy, incapacity, incompetence, ineffectiveness, weakness, feebleness, frailty, disability, infirmity, paralysis
formal enervation, inefficacy, impuissance
E3 strength

impotent *adj*
powerless, helpless, useless, worthless, futile, unable, incapable, ineffective, incompetent, inadequate, weak, feeble, frail, worn out, exhausted, infirm, disabled, incapacitated, paralysed, crippled
formal debilitated, enervated, impuissant
E3 potent, strong

impound *v*
1 CONFISCATE, seize, remove, take away, take possession of, commandeer
formal appropriate, expropriate
2 CONFINE, shut up, cage, keep in, lock up, coop up, hem in
formal incarcerate, immure

impoverish *v*
bankrupt, break, ruin, beggar, weaken, reduce, deplete, exhaust, drain, diminish, denude
formal pauperize
E3 enrich

impoverished *adj*
1 POOR, needy, poverty-stricken, destitute, down-and-out, bankrupt, penniless, ruined
formal impecunious, penurious, indigent
colloq. bust, skint, stony-broke, cleaned out, on your uppers, on your beam ends, not having two pennies to rub together
2 WEAKENED, drained, exhausted, desolate, empty, waste, dead, barren, bare
E3 **1** rich

impracticability *n*
unworkability, infeasibility, unsuitableness, unviability, uselessness, impossibility, futility, hopelessness
E3 practicability

impracticable *adj*
unworkable, unfeasible, unattainable, unachievable, impossible, out of the question, unviable, useless, unserviceable, inoperable
E3 practicable, feasible

⚠ **impracticable** or **impractical** ?
Impracticable means 'that cannot be carried out or put into practice': *The whole project has become completely impracticable.* When referring to suggestions, plans, etc, *impractical* means 'possible to carry out but not sensible or convenient': *In a modern economy barter is totally impractical*; 'not able to do or make things in a sensible and efficient way': *He was impractical and dreamy, with a head full of foolish notions.*

---

impractical *adj*
unrealistic, idealistic, romantic, starry-eyed, visionary, theoretical abstract, academic, ivory-tower, impracticable, unworkable, impossible, awkward, inconvenient, unserviceable
E3 practical, realistic, sensible

impracticality *n*
idealism, romanticism, unworkability, unworkableness, impossibility, hopelessness, infeasibility
E3 practicality

imprecation *n*
curse, blasphemy, denunciation, abuse, anathema
formal execration, malediction, profanity, vituperation, vilification

imprecise *adj*
inexact, inaccurate, approximate, estimated, rough, loose, indefinite, vague, woolly, blurred, hazy, ill-defined, sloppy, inexplicit, ambiguous, equivocal
E3 precise, exact

impregnable *adj*
impenetrable, unconquerable, invincible, unbeatable, unassailable, indestructible, inviolable, fortified, strong, solid, secure, safe, invulnerable, unquestionable, irrefutable
E3 vulnerable

impregnate *v*
1 SOAK, steep, saturate, drench, fill, permeate, pervade, suffuse, imbue, infuse, penetrate
2 INSEMINATE, fertilize, make pregnant
formal fecundate

impregnation *n*
fertilization, fertilizing, insemination, saturation, imbuing
formal fructification, fructifying, fecundation

impresario *n*
manager, organizer, director, producer, promoter, exhibitor

impress *v*
1 *I'm not impressed*
strike, move, touch, sway, affect, influence, stir, inspire, rouse, excite
colloq. grab
2 STAMP, imprint, print, engrave, mark, indent, instil, inculcate, fix deeply, emphasize, stress, highlight, underline, bring home

impressed *adj*
moved, excited, affected, struck, influenced, marked, taken, touched, stamped, stirred, overawed
colloq. grabbed, turned on, knocked out
E3 unimpressed

impression *n*
1 FEELING, awareness, consciousness, sense, sensation, illusion, idea, notion, opinion, belief, thought, conviction, suspicion, fancy, hunch, memory, recollection
colloq. funny feeling, gut feeling, vibes
2 *make a good impression*
effect, impact, influence, power, control, sway
3 STAMP, mark, print, dent, indentation, imprint, pressure, outline
4 IMPERSONATION, imitation, parody, mimicry, caricature, burlesque
colloq. take-off, send-up

impressionability *n*
naïvety, gullibility, susceptibility, vulnerability, sensitivity, receptiveness, receptivity, suggestibility, greenness
formal ingenuousness

impressionable *adj*
naïve, gullible, persuadable, susceptible, vulnerable, sensitive, pliable, mouldable, responsive, open, receptive
formal ingenuous

impressive *adj*
striking, imposing, grand, breathtaking, spectacular, powerful, effective, dazzling, awe-inspiring, awesome, stirring, inspiring, exciting, rousing, moving, affecting, touching
■ unimpressive, uninspiring

imprint *n, v*
▶ *n* print, mark, stamp, impression, indentation, sign, logo, emblem, badge, colophon
▶ *v* stamp, print, mark, brand, impress, fix, establish, engrave, emboss, etch

imprison *v*
put in prison, send to prison, jail, intern, detain, lock up, cage, pen, confine, shut in
formal incarcerate, immure
colloq. send down, put away, bang up
■ release, free

imprisoned *adj*
jailed, locked up, behind bars, confined, caged, captive
formal incarcerated, immured
colloq. inside, put away, sent down, doing time, doing bird; *slang* doing porridge
■ free

imprisonment *n*
internment, detention, custody, captivity, confinement
formal incarceration
■ freedom, liberty

improbability *n*
uncertainty, doubt, doubtfulness, dubiousness, unlikelihood, unlikeliness, far-fetchedness, preposterousness, ridiculousness, implausibility
formal dubiety
■ probability

improbable *adj*
uncertain, questionable, doubtful, unlikely, dubious, implausible, unconvincing, far-fetched, preposterous, ridiculous, unbelievable, incredible
■ probable, likely, convincing

impromptu *adj, adv*
▶ *adj* improvised, extempore, ad-lib, off the cuff, unscripted, unrehearsed, unprepared, spontaneous
■ rehearsed
▶ *adv* without preparation, extempore, ad lib, spontaneously
colloq. on the spur of the moment, off the top of your head, off the cuff

improper *adj*
1 INDECENT, rude, vulgar, shocking, risqué, indelicate
formal unseemly, indecorous, unbecoming
2 WRONG, incorrect, irregular, false, erroneous, unlawful
3 UNSUITABLE, inappropriate, unfitting, inopportune, inadequate, out of place
formal incongruous

■ 1 decent 2 correct, lawful 3 suitable, appropriate

impropriety *n*
mistake, lapse, slip, blunder, *faux pas*, gaffe, bad taste, vulgarity, gaucherie, immodesty, indecency, unsuitability
formal incongruity, indecorousness, indecorum, solecism, unseemliness
■ *formal* propriety

improve *v*
better, make better, ameliorate, enhance, enrich, perfect, polish, touch up, mend, rectify, put right, set right, correct, amend, revise, reform, help, upgrade, modernize, streamline, revamp, increase, rise, pick up, develop, look up, advance, grow, progress, make headway, get better, recover, convalesce, recuperate, rally, rehabilitate, gain strength
colloq. be on the up and up, get your act together, turn over a new leaf, mend your ways, perk up, look up, give a facelift to, do up, fix up
■ worsen, deteriorate, decline

improvement *n*
betterment, enhancement, rectification, rectifying, correction, amendment, revision, reform, reformation, rehabilitation, upgrading, modernizing, increase, rise, upswing, gain, development, advance, growth, progress, headway, furtherance, recovery, rally, upswing
formal amelioration
■ deterioration, decline, worsening

improvident *adj*
thriftless, unthrifty, spendthrift, extravagant, shiftless, uneconomical, wasteful, careless, reckless, heedless, inattentive, thoughtless, negligent, unprepared, underprepared, Micawberish
formal imprudent, prodigal, profligate
■ thrifty, economical

improvisation *n*
ad-lib, ad-libbing, extemporizing, impromptu, invention, spontaneity, makeshift, expedient, vamp
formal autoschediasm

improvise *v*
1 CONTRIVE, devise, concoct, invent, put together quickly, make do
colloq. throw together, cobble together, knock up, rig up, run up
2 EXTEMPORIZE, ad-lib, compose/perform without preparation, vamp
colloq. say whatever comes into your head/mind, speak off the cuff, speak off the top of your head, play by ear, have a brainwave

improvised *adj*
extempore, ad-lib, spontaneous, extemporaneous, extemporized, makeshift, off-the-cuff, unrehearsed, unprepared, unscripted
■ rehearsed

imprudent *adj*
unwise, ill-advised, ill-considered, ill-judged, foolish, foolhardy, short-sighted, rash, reckless, hasty, irresponsible, unthinking, careless, heedless, thoughtless, indiscreet
formal impolitic, injudicious, improvident
■ wise, cautious, wary; *formal* prudent

impudence *n*
impertinence, boldness, brazenness, pertness, insolence, rudeness, presumption

formal effrontery
colloq. cheek, nerve, sauciness, lip, face, mouth, brass neck
≢ politeness

impudent *adj*
impertinent, bold, forward, shameless, immodest, cocky, brazen, insolent, rude, impolite, disrespectful, presumptuous, audacious, pert
colloq. cheeky, saucy, fresh; *slang* smart-arsed
≢ polite

impugn *v*
challenge, attack, assail, question, call in question, criticize, oppose, resist, dispute
formal berate, censure, revile, vilify, vituperate, traduce, vilipend
≢ praise, compliment

impulse *n*
1 URGE, wish, desire, inclination, whim, notion, caprice, instinct, feeling, passion, drive
2 IMPETUS, momentum, force, pressure, drive, thrust, propulsion, impulsion, surge, push, incitement, incentive, inducement, stimulation, stimulus, motive, motivation

impulsive *adj*
impetuous, rash, reckless, foolhardy, thoughtless, unthinking, impatient, madcap, headstrong, hasty, quick, sudden, ill-judged, ill-considered, spontaneous, automatic, instinctive, emotional, passionate, intuitive
formal precipitate
≢ cautious, premeditated

impulsiveness *n*
impetuosity, impetuousness, rashness, recklessness, foolhardiness, thoughtlessness, impatience, haste, hastiness, quickness, suddenness, spontaneity, instinct, emotion, passion, intuitiveness
formal precipitateness, precipitation
≢ caution

impunity *n*
exemption, freedom, immunity, liberty, licence, dispensation, permission, security, amnesty, excusal
≢ liability

impure *adj*
1 UNREFINED, adulterated, alloyed, mixed, blended, combined, diluted, contaminated, polluted, tainted, infected, corrupt, defiled, debased, sullied, unclean, dirty, foul, filthy
2 OBSCENE, indecent, dirty, crude, coarse, vulgar, offensive, immoral, shameless, improper, promiscuous, depraved, unchaste, sexy, immodest, lustful, lewd, lecherous, licentious, risqué, suggestive, pornographic, erotic, smutty, bawdy, ribald
≢ 1 pure 2 chaste, decent

impurity *n*
1 *impurities in the petrol*
adulteration, mixture, blend, dilution, contamination, pollution, taint, infection, corruption, debasement, dirtiness, contaminant, pollutant, dirt, filth, grime, foulness, dross, foreign body, mark, spot
2 OBSCENITY, indecency, crudity, coarseness, vulgarity, offensiveness, immorality, shamelessness, impropriety, promiscuity, unchastity, looseness, immodesty, lustfulness, lewdness, licentiousness, pornography, eroticism, smut
≢ 2 purity

impute *v*
ascribe, assign, attribute, put down to, charge, credit, refer
formal accredit

in *adj*
fashionable, in vogue, popular, current, smart, stylish, modish
colloq. all the rage, trendy, cool

inability *n*
incapability, incapacity, powerlessness, impotence, inadequacy, incompetence, ineffectiveness, weakness, ineptitude, handicap, disability, uselessness
≢ ability

inaccessible *adj*
isolated, remote, out of the way, God-forsaken, unfrequented, unapproachable, unreachable, out of reach, beyond reach, unattainable, impenetrable, unavailable
colloq. unget-at-able
≢ accessible

inaccuracy *n*
mistake, error, miscalculation, slip, blunder, gaffe, fault, defect, imprecision, inexactness, unreliability, erroneousness, mistakenness
formal corrigendum, erratum, fallaciousness
colloq. boo-boo, slip-up, howler
≢ accuracy, precision

inaccurate *adj*
incorrect, wrong, erroneous, mistaken, false, faulty, flawed, imperfect, defective, imprecise, inexact, out, loose, unreliable, unfaithful, untrue, unsound
formal fallacious
≢ accurate, correct, true, right, sound

inaccurately *adv*
incorrectly, wrongly, erroneously, falsely, imperfectly, defectively, imprecisely, inexactly, unreliably, unfaithfully, loosely, wildly, carelessly, clumsily
≢ accurately, correctly

inaction *n*
inactivity, immobility, motionlessness, inertia, rest, idleness, passivity, slowness, lifelessness, sluggishness, lethargy, stagnation
formal torpor
≢ action

inactivate *v*
disable, immobilize, paralyse, stop, cripple, mothball, stabilize
colloq. knock the bottom out of, scupper
≢ activate

inactive *adj*
immobile, motionless, stationary, inert, idle, unused, unemployed, dormant, passive, sedentary, lazy, slow, lifeless, lethargic, sluggish, vegetating, stagnant, sleepy
formal inoperative, indolent, torpid, quiescent
≢ active, working, busy, working, functioning, in use

inactivity *n*
immobility, inaction, inertia, inertness, idleness, unemployment, dormancy, passivity, laziness, sluggishness, lifelessness, lethargy, sloth, vegetation, stagnation, hibernation, languor, dullness, heaviness
technical stasis
formal indolence, lassitude, quiescence, dilatoriness, torpor, abeyance
≢ activeness

inadequacy *n*
1 INSUFFICIENCY, lack, shortage, deficit, dearth, deficiency, scarcity, scantiness, meagreness
formal want, paucity
2 DEFECTIVENESS, ineffectiveness, inability, incapability, incompetence, ineffectiveness
formal inefficacy
3 *the inadequacies of the system*
fault, defect, imperfection, weakness, foible, failing, shortcoming, flaw
F3 1 adequacy 3 strong point

inadequate *adj*
1 INSUFFICIENT, short, wanting, deficient, too little/few, scanty, scant, scarce, skimpy, sparse, meagre, niggardly
2 INCOMPETENT, bad, incapable, inexpert, unproficient, careless, not good enough, unequal, unqualified, ineffective, faulty, defective, imperfect, unsatisfactory, unfit, substandard, disappointing
formal ineffectual, inefficacious
colloq. not up to scratch
F3 1 adequate, enough 2 satisfactory

inadequately *adv*
insufficiently, poorly, meagrely, scantily, sketchily, skimpily, sparsely, thinly, imperfectly, badly, carelessly
F3 adequately

inadmissible *adj*
unacceptable, irrelevant, immaterial, inappropriate, disallowed, prohibited, improper
formal precluded, inapposite
F3 admissible

inadvertent *adj*
accidental, chance, unintentional, unintended, unplanned, unpremeditated, uncalculated, careless, negligent, thoughtless, unwitting, unconscious, involuntary
F3 deliberate, conscious, careful

inadvertently *adv*
accidentally, by accident, by mistake, by chance, unintentionally, unthinkingly, unwittingly, unconsciously, involuntarily, carelessly, heedlessly, negligently, mistakenly, remissly, thoughtlessly
F3 deliberately

inadvisable *adj*
unwise, foolish, silly, ill-advised, ill-judged, ill-considered, inexpedient, misguided, indiscreet
formal imprudent, injudicious
F3 advisable, wise

inalienable *adj*
inherent, inviolable, unassailable, non-negotiable, non-transferable, untransferable, unremovable, permanent, sacrosanct, absolute
F3 impermanent

inane *adj*
senseless, foolish, stupid, unintelligent, silly, idiotic, absurd, ridiculous, ludicrous, frivolous, trifling, puerile, mindless, nonsensical, vapid, empty, vacuous, vain, worthless, futile
formal fatuous
F3 sensible

inanimate *adj*
lifeless, dead, defunct, extinct, unconscious, inactive, lazy, inert, dormant, immobile, stagnant, spiritless, dull, apathetic, lethargic, wooden
technical insentient, insensate
formal torpid
F3 animate, living, alive

inanity *n*
senselessness, folly, foolishness, stupidity, silliness, absurdity, ridiculousness, ludicrousness, frivolity, puerility, imbecility, vapidity, vacuity, asininity, emptiness
formal fatuity
colloq. daftness, waffle
F3 sense

inapplicable *adj*
irrelevant, immaterial, inapt, inappropriate, unsuitable, unsuited, unrelated, unconnected
formal inapposite, inconsequent
F3 applicable; *formal* germane, pertinent

inapposite *adj*
unsuitable, inappropriate, irrelevant, immaterial, unsuitable, out of place

inappropriate *adj*
unsuitable, inapt, ill-suited, ill-fitted, irrelevant, out of place, untimely, ill-timed, inopportune, tactless, improper, unbecoming, unfitting, tasteless
formal inapposite, incongruous, unseemly, indecorous
F3 appropriate, suitable

inapt *adj*
inappropriate, unsuitable, unsuited, ill-suited, ill-fitted, irrelevant, out of place, ill-timed, inopportune, unfortunate
formal inapposite, infelicitous
F3 apt

inarticulacy *n*
inarticulateness, incoherence, unintelligibility, incomprehensibility, mumbling, indistinctness, hesitancy, stumbling, stammering, stuttering, speechlessness, tongue-tiedness
F3 articulacy

inarticulate *adj*
incoherent, unintelligible, incomprehensible, unclear, indistinct, mumbled, blurred, muffled, hesitant, hesitating, stumbling, stammering, stuttering, trembling, shaking, quavery, faltering, disjointed, halting, tongue-tied, speechless, voiceless, dumb, mute, soundless
F3 articulate

inattention *n*
carelessness, negligence, disregard, heedlessness, thoughtlessness, unmindfulness, inattentiveness, absent-mindedness, forgetfulness, daydreaming, dreaminess, preoccupation, distraction

inattentive *adj*
distracted, dreamy, daydreaming, preoccupied, absent-minded, wool-gathering, unmindful, heedless, regardless, disregarding, careless, thoughtless, negligent, forgetful, remiss
formal distrait
colloq. miles away, in a world of your own, somewhere else
F3 attentive

inaudible *adj*
silent, noiseless, imperceptible, faint, indistinct, muffled, stifled, muted, soft, dull, low, mumbled, muttered, murmured, whispered
F3 audible, loud

inaugural *adj*
opening, introductory, first, initial, launching,

original, maiden
formal exordial

inaugurate *v*
1 *inaugurate a scheme*
institute, originate, begin, start, set up, open, launch, introduce, usher in, initiate, set in motion, put into operation, get going
formal commence
colloq. set/start the ball rolling
2 *inaugurate the president*
induct, invest, install, ordain, instate, enthrone
3 *inaugurate a new building*
dedicate, consecrate, open officially, commission

inauguration *n*
1 INSTITUTION, setting up, starting, opening, launch, launching, initiation
formal commencement
2 INDUCTION, ordination, investiture, consecration, enthronement, installation, installing

inauspicious *adj*
unfavourable, bad, unlucky, unfortunate, unpromising, untimely, ill-fated, ill-starred, discouraging, threatening, ominous, black
formal infelicitous, unpropitious
E3 promising; *formal* auspicious

inborn *adj*
innate, inherent, natural, native, congenital, inbred, hereditary, inherited, in the family, ingrained, instinctive, intuitive
formal connate
E3 learned

inbred *adj*
innate, inherent, natural, native, ingrained, constitutional
formal connate, ingenerate
E3 learned

incalculable *adj*
countless, innumerable, numberless, without number, untold, inestimable, immeasurable, measureless, limitless, boundless, unlimited, endless, infinite, immense, vast, enormous
E3 limited, restricted

incandescent *adj*
glowing, aglow, shining, dazzling, gleaming, brilliant, bright, white-hot

incantation *n*
chant, charm, spell, abracadabra, formula, magic formula, invocation, mantra, mantram, rune, hex
formal conjuration

incapable *adj*
unable, powerless, impotent, helpless, useless, weak, feeble, unfit, unsuited, unqualified, unfitted, incompetent, inept, inadequate, ineffective
formal ineffectual
colloq. not up to scratch, not hacking it, out of your league
E3 capable, experienced

incapacitate *v*
disable, cripple, paralyse, immobilize, disqualify, put out of action, lay up
formal debilitate
colloq. scupper

incapacitated *adj*
disabled, crippled, paralysed, immobilized, disqualified, out of action, unfit, unwell, hamstrung,

prostrate, drunk
formal indisposed
colloq. laid up, scuppered, tipsy
E3 operative

incapacity *n*
incapability, inability, disability, unfitness, disqualification, powerlessness, impotence, ineffectiveness, ineptitude, weakness, feebleness, inadequacy, incompetence, incompetency, uselessness
formal ineffectuality
E3 capability

incarcerate *v*
imprison, put in prison, jail, gaol, put in jail, lock up, intern, confine, impound, commit, detain, put away, restrain, restrict, cage, encage, coop up, wall in
formal immure
colloq. send down
E3 free, release

incarceration *n*
imprisonment, internment, jail, custody, detention, confinement, bondage, captivity, restraint, restriction
E3 freedom, liberation

incarnate *adj*
human, in human form, embodied, made flesh, in the flesh, fleshly, personified, typified
formal corporeal

incarnation *n*
human form, appearance in the flesh, personification, embodiment, manifestation, impersonation

incautious *adj*
careless, ill-judged, ill-advised, ill-considered, unthinking, thoughtless, inconsiderate, inattentive, unwary, unwatchful, unobservant, foolish, foolhardy, rash, reckless, hasty, impulsive
formal imprudent, injudicious, uncircumspect, precipitate
E3 cautious, careful, vigilant

incendiary *adj, n*
▶ *adj* **1** *an incendiary bomb*
fire-raising, flammable, combustible, pyromaniac
2 INCITING, inflammatory, provocative, stirring, seditious, subversive, dissentious, rabble-rousing
formal proceleusmatic
E3 **2** calming
▶ *n* **1** AGITATOR, insurgent, revolutionary, demagogue, rabble-rouser, firebrand
2 FIRE-RAISER, pyromaniac, arsonist, firebug, pétroleur, pétroleuse
3 FIRE-BOMB, bomb, explosive, charge, grenade, mine, petrol bomb

incense[1] *n*
smell the incense
perfume, scent, aroma, balm, bouquet, fragrance, joss-stick

incense[2] *v*
incense his teacher
anger, enrage, infuriate, madden, exasperate, inflame, agitate, irritate, irk, vex, nettle, rile, provoke, excite
colloq. aggravate, hassle, get someone's blood up, make someone's blood boil, get under someone's skin, drive up the wall, get someone's dander up
E3 calm

incensed *adj*
enraged, angry, fuming, furious, exasperated, mad, maddened, steamed up, indignant, infuriated, irate,

ireful, wrathful
formal furibund
colloq. in a paddy, on the warpath, up in arms
F3 calm

incentive *n*
bait, lure, enticement, reward, encouragement,
inducement, incitement, reason, motive, impetus,
spur, stimulus, goad, lure, bait, stimulant, motivation
colloq. carrot, sweetener
F3 disincentive, discouragement, deterrent

inception *n*
inauguration, initiation, opening, installation,
beginning, start, birth, origin, dawn, outset, rise
formal commencement
colloq. kick-off
F3 end

incessant *adj*
ceaseless, unceasing, endless, never-ending, unending,
continual, persistent, constant, perpetual, eternal,
everlasting, continuous, unbroken, uninterrupted,
recurrent, unremitting, non-stop
formal interminable
F3 intermittent, sporadic, periodic, temporary

incidence *n*
frequency, commonness, prevalence, extent, range,
amount, degree, rate, occurrence

incident *n*
1 EVENT, occurrence, happening, episode,
adventure, experience, proceeding, affair, matter,
occasion, instance, circumstance
2 CONFRONTATION, clash, conflict, fight, skirmish,
commotion, disturbance, scene, row, fracas, brush,
upset, mishap

incidental *adj*
accidental, chance, by chance, random, minor, non-
essential, petty, trivial, small, secondary, subordinate,
background, subsidiary, ancillary, peripheral,
supplementary, accompanying, attendant, related,
contributory
formal fortuitous, concomitant
F3 important, essential

incidentally *adv*
1 BY THE WAY, in passing, secondarily,
parenthetically, *en passant*, apropos
colloq. by the by
2 ACCIDENTALLY, by accident, coincidentally,
unexpectedly, by chance, casually, digressively
formal fortuitously

incinerate *v*
burn, cremate, reduce to ashes, carbonize

incipient *adj*
beginning, originating, starting, inaugural,
developing, rudimentary, embryonic, newborn,
impending
formal commencing, inceptive, inchoate, nascent
F3 developed

incise *v*
cut, cut into, carve, chisel, engrave, sculpt, sculpture,
etch, gash, slit, slash, nick, notch

incision *n*
cut, opening, slit, gash, notch, slash, nick

incisive *adj*
cutting, keen, sharp, acute, piercing, penetrating,
biting, stinging, pungent, caustic, acid, astute,

perceptive, shrewd, sarcastic
formal trenchant, mordant, perspicacious

incisiveness *n*
keenness, sharpness, acuteness, penetration,
astuteness, acidity, pungency, sarcasm, tartness
formal perspicacity, astucity, trenchancy

incite *v*
prompt, instigate, rouse, arouse, inflame, foment, stir
up, whip up, work up, agitate, excite, animate, provoke,
stimulate, spur, goad, prod, induce, impel, drive, urge,
encourage
colloq. egg on
F3 restrain

incitement *n*
prompting, instigation, rousing, agitation,
provocation, spur, goad, prod, impetus, stimulus,
stimulation, animation, urging, drive, motivation,
encouragement, inducement, incentive
F3 discouragement

inciting *adj*
incendiary, rabble-rousing, inflammatory,
provocative, stirring, seditious, subversive
formal proceleusmatic
F3 calming

incivility *n*
impoliteness, discourtesy, discourteousness, rudeness,
disrespect, unmannerliness, bad manners, ill-
breeding, inurbanity, boorishness, coarseness,
roughness, vulgarity
F3 civility

inclemency *n*
harshness, bitterness, rawness, severity, storminess,
tempestuousness, roughness, foulness
F3 clemency

inclement *adj*
intemperate, harsh, bitter, harsh, raw, severe, stormy,
tempestuous, rough, foul, nasty, blustery, squally
F3 fine, clement

inclination *n*
1 LIKING, fondness, affection, attraction, affinity,
taste, preference, partiality, bias, tendency, trend,
disposition, leaning
formal propensity, proclivity, predisposition,
predilection, penchant
2 *an inclination of 45 degrees*
angle, slope, gradient, incline, ascent, steepness, bank,
ramp, lift, pitch, slant, tilt, bend, bow, nod
formal acclivity, declivity
F3 1 disinclination, dislike

incline *v, n*
▶ *v* 1 DISPOSE, influence, persuade, affect, sway,
bend, bias, prejudice, tend
2 LEAN, slope, slant, bank, tilt, tip, bend, curve, list,
bow, nod, stoop, list, veer, deviate, swing
▶ *n* slope, gradient, ramp, hill, rise, ascent, dip,
descent
formal acclivity, declivity

inclined *adj*
liable, likely, tending, given, apt, disposed, of a mind,
willing
formal predisposed, wont

include *v*
comprise, incorporate, embody, contain, enclose,
hold, encompass, cover, take in, span, admit, insert,
introduce, add, enter, put in, allow for, take into

account, involve, let in on
formal comprehend, embrace, subsume
colloq. rope in, throw in
🔳 exclude, omit, eliminate

including *prep*
counting, inclusive of, with, together with, included
🔳 excluding

inclusion *n*
incorporation, involvement, embodiment,
encompassing, addition, insertion
formal comprehension
🔳 exclusion

inclusive *adj*
comprehensive, full, all-in, all-inclusive,
all-embracing, across-the-board, general,
catch-all, overall, sweeping
colloq. blanket
🔳 exclusive, narrow

incognito *adj*
in disguise, disguised, masked, veiled, camouflaged,
unmarked, unidentified, unrecognizable,
unidentifiable, keeping your identity secret, unknown,
under an assumed/a false name, nameless
🔳 undisguised

incognizant *adj*
unaware, unconscious, unacquainted, uninformed,
unenlightened, ignorant, unknowing, unobservant,
inattentive
🔳 aware; *formal* apprised

incoherence *n*
unintelligibility, incomprehensibility, inarticulateness,
stammer, stutter, mumble, mutter, brokenness,
garbledness, muddle, mix-up, jumble, confusion,
wildness, disconnectedness, disjointedness,
illogicality, inconsistency
🔳 coherence

incoherent *adj*
unintelligible, incomprehensible, inarticulate,
wandering, rambling, stammering, stuttering,
mumbled, muttered, unconnected, disconnected,
broken, garbled, scrambled, confused, muddled,
mixed-up, jumbled, disjointed, disordered, illogical,
inconsistent, unclear
🔳 coherent, intelligible

incombustible *adj*
fireproof, flameproof, fire-resistant, flame-resistant,
flame-retardant, non-flammable, non-inflammable,
unburnable
🔳 combustible

income *n*
revenue, returns, proceeds, gains, profits, interest,
takings, receipts, earnings, pay, salary, wages, means,
remuneration
🔳 expenditure, expenses

incoming *adj*
arriving, entering, approaching, coming, homeward,
returning, ensuing, succeeding, next, new
🔳 outgoing

incommensurate *adj*
disproportionate, insufficient, inadequate, unequal,
excessive, extravagant, extreme
formal inequitable, inordinate
🔳 appropriate

incommunicable *adj*
indescribable, inexpressible, unspeakable, unutterable,
unimpartable
formal ineffable
🔳 expressible, communicable

incomparable *adj*
matchless, unmatched, beyond compare, unequalled,
without equal, unparalleled, without parallel,
unrivalled, unsurpassed, peerless, inimitable,
nonpareil, paramount, supreme, superlative, superb,
brilliant
🔳 ordinary, run-of-the-mill, poor

incomparably *adv*
by far, far and away, beyond compare, immeasurably,
infinitely, easily, supremely, superbly, superlatively,
eminently, brilliantly
🔳 poorly, slightly

incompatibility *n*
irreconcilability, contradiction, clash, conflict,
variance, inconsistency, difference, disagreement,
discrepancy, antagonism, mismatch, uncongeniality
formal disparateness, disparity, incongruity
🔳 compatibility

incompatible *adj*
irreconcilable, contradictory, conflicting, at odds,
at variance, inconsistent, clashing, antagonistic,
disagreeing, discordant, ill-matched, mismatched,
unsuited, uncongenial, wrong
formal incongruous, disparate
colloq. like a fish out of water, like a square peg in a
round hole
🔳 compatible, complementary, going well together

incompetence *n*
incapability, inability, unfitness, unsuitability,
stupidity, uselessness, ineptitude, ineptness,
ineffectiveness, inefficiency, inadequacy, insufficiency,
bungling
formal ineffectuality, ineffectualness
🔳 competence

incompetent *adj*
incapable, unable, unfit, unqualified, unsuitable,
inefficient, inexpert, amateurish, unskilful, bungling,
awkward, clumsy, fumbling, stupid, useless, botched,
ineffective, inadequate, insufficient, deficient
slang not able to organize a piss-up in a brewery
🔳 competent, able

incomplete *adj*
deficient, lacking, short, unfinished, unaccomplished,
undeveloped, abridged, shortened, partial, part,
fragmentary, broken, scrappy, piecemeal, imperfect,
defective
formal wanting
🔳 complete, accomplished, exhaustive, total

incomprehensible *adj*
unintelligible, unreadable, impenetrable,
unfathomable, complex, complicated, involved, above
your head, puzzling, perplexing, baffling, deep,
profound, enigmatic, mysterious, inscrutable, obscure,
opaque
formal abstruse, recondite
🔳 comprehensible, intelligible

inconceivable *adj*
unthinkable, unimaginable, staggering, unheard-of,
impossible, unbelievable, incredible, implausible,
ridiculous, ludicrous, absurd, outrageous, shocking

colloq. mind-boggling
▣ conceivable, imaginable, not on

inconclusive *adj*
unsettled, undecided, indefinite, open, open to
question, uncertain, indecisive, ambiguous, vague,
unconvincing, unsatisfying
formal indeterminate
colloq. up in the air, left hanging
▣ conclusive; *colloq.* open-and-shut

incongruity *n*
inappropriateness, unsuitability, inconsistency,
incompatibility, conflict, clash, irreconcilability,
contradiction, discrepancy, inharmoniousness,
inaptness
formal disparity, dissociability, dissociableness
▣ consistency, harmoniousness

incongruous *adj*
inappropriate, unsuitable, out of place, out of keeping,
inconsistent, conflicting, clashing, jarring,
incompatible, irreconcilable, contradictory, contrary,
at odds, odd, absurd, strange
▣ consistent, compatible

inconsequential *adj*
minor, trivial, trifling, petty, unimportant,
insignificant, negligible, immaterial, inappreciable
▣ important, significant

inconsiderable *adj*
small, slight, negligible, trivial, petty, trifling, minor,
unimportant, insignificant, negligible
▣ considerable, large

inconsiderate *adj*
unkind, uncaring, unconcerned, uncharitable, selfish,
self-centred, egotistic, intolerant, insensitive, tactless,
rude, thoughtless, unthinking, careless, heedless,
undiscerning
▣ considerate, thoughtful, gracious, kind

inconsiderateness *n*
unkindness, unconcern, selfishness, self-centredness,
intolerance, insensitivity, tactlessness, rudeness,
thoughtlessness, carelessness
▣ considerateness, thoughtfulness, kindness

inconsistency *n*
1 CONFLICT, variance, odds, contradiction,
irreconcilability, incompatibility, discrepancy,
disagreement, divergence, paradox
formal contrariety, disparity, incongruity
2 CHANGEABLENESS, unpredictability, instability,
unsteadiness, unreliability, fickleness, inconstancy
▣ 1, 2 consistency 2 constancy

inconsistent *adj*
1 CONFLICTING, at variance, at odds, out of place/
keeping, in opposition, incompatible, contradictory,
contrary, differing, discordant, irreconcilable
formal incongruous
2 CHANGEABLE, variable, irregular, erratic,
unpredictable, varying, unstable, unsteady,
inconstant, fickle, capricious, mercurial
▣ 1, 2 consistent 2 constant

inconsolable *adj*
heartbroken, brokenhearted, devastated, desolate,
despairing, wretched, miserable, grief-stricken
formal disconsolate

inconspicuous *adj*
unobtrusive, plain, ordinary, indistinct, unremarkable,
undistinguished, discreet, low-key, hidden, concealed,

camouflaged, modest, unassuming, quiet, retiring,
insignificant, in the background
▣ conspicuous, noticeable, obtrusive

inconstant *adj*
changeable, variable, varying, changeful, erratic,
mutable, unsteady, fluctuating, inconsistent, unsettled,
unstable, volatile, wavering, uncertain, undependable,
unreliable, unfaithful, irresolute, capricious,
mercurial, wayward, fickle
formal vacillating
▣ constant

incontestable *adj*
incontrovertible, indisputable, undeniable,
unquestionable, certain, obvious, clear, evident,
self-evident, sure
formal indubitable, irrefutable
▣ uncertain

incontinent *adj*
uncontrollable, uncontrolled, ungovernable,
ungoverned, unrestrained, unbridled, unchecked,
loose, promiscuous, unchaste, dissipated, dissolute,
debauched, lewd, licentious, lascivious, lecherous,
lustful, wanton
▣ continent

incontrovertible *adj*
indisputable, unquestionable, beyond question,
beyond doubt, undeniable, beyond doubt, certain,
clear, self-evident
formal irrefutable, indubitable
▣ questionable, uncertain

inconvenience *n, v*
▶ *n* awkwardness, difficulty, problem, unsuitability,
inappropriateness, annoyance, worry, vexation,
nuisance, hindrance, drawback, bother, trouble, fuss,
upset, nuisance, disturbance, disruption,
disadvantage, burden
colloq. drag, pain, bore, bind, headache, turn-off
▣ convenience
▶ *v* bother, disturb, disrupt, put out, trouble, upset,
irk, annoy, worry, fuss, burden, impose upon
formal discommode
▣ convenience

inconvenient *adj*
awkward, ill-timed, untimely, inopportune,
unseasonable, unsuitable, inappropriate, inexpedient,
difficult, embarrassing, annoying, troublesome,
bothersome, unwieldy, unmanageable, cumbersome
▣ convenient, suitable, handy

incorporate *v*
include, embody, contain, take in, absorb, assimilate,
integrate, combine, amalgamate, unite, unify, merge,
blend, mix, fuse, coalesce, consolidate
formal subsume, embrace
▣ separate

incorporation *n*
inclusion, absorption, embodiment, assimilation,
integration, combination, amalgamation, unification,
unifying, blend, fusion, coalescence, association,
company, merger, society, federation
formal subsuming
▣ separation, splitting off

incorporeal *adj*
bodiless, unfleshy, spiritual, unreal, illusory,
intangible, ethereal, spectral, phantasmal,
phantasmic, ghostly
▣ real, fleshy

incorrect *adj*
wrong, not right, mistaken, erroneous, inaccurate,
imprecise, inexact, false, untrue, faulty,
ungrammatical, improper, illegitimate, inappropriate,
unsuitable
formal fallacious
colloq. (way) off beam
⧏ correct, accurate

incorrectness *n*
wrongness, mistakenness, erroneousness, error,
inaccuracy, imprecision, inexactitude, falseness,
faultiness, impreciseness, inexactness, speciousness,
unsoundness, unsuitability
formal fallacy
⧏ correctness, accuracy

incorrigible *adj*
irredeemable, incurable, inveterate, hardened,
hopeless, beyond, hope, beyond redemption,
dyed-in-the-wool
⧏ redeemable

incorruptibility *n*
honesty, honour, integrity, uprightness, virtue,
morality, trustworthiness, justness, nobility
formal probity
⧏ corruptibility

incorruptible *adj*
honest, straight, upright, virtuous, moral, ethical,
honourable, high-principled, trustworthy, unbribable,
just
⧏ corruptible, dishonest

increase *v, n*
▶ *v* **1** *the number of tourists has increased*
become greater, go up, be on the increase, climb, rise,
mount, soar, improve, advance, progress, grow,
develop, build up, intensify, strengthen, heighten,
extend, expand, spread, swell, multiply, proliferate,
escalate, mushroom, snowball, rocket, skyrocket,
spiral
colloq. go through the roof
2 *increase the public's awareness*
raise, boost, add to, improve, enhance, advance,
further, step up, intensify, strengthen, heighten,
develop, build up, accumulate, enlarge, magnify,
broaden, widen, deepen, extend, prolong, expand,
spread, breed, propagate, scale up
formal augment
colloq. hike up, bump up, bring to a head,
bring to the boil
⧏ **1** decline, fall **1, 2** decrease, reduce
▶ *n* rise, growth, surge, upsurge, upturn, gain, boost,
addition, increment, advance, step-up, build-up,
intensification, heightening, development,
enlargement, extension, expansion, spread,
proliferation, escalation, mushrooming, snowballing,
rocketing
formal augmentation
colloq. hike
⧏ decrease, reduction, decline

increasingly *adv*
more and more, all the more, more so, to an increasing
degree/extent, progressively, cumulatively

incredible *adj*
1 *give some incredible excuse*
unbelievable, improbable, implausible, far-fetched,
preposterous, absurd, impossible, inconceivable,
beyond/past belief, unthinkable, unimaginable
2 *walk an incredible distance*

extraordinary, amazing, surprising, astonishing,
astounding, fantastic, remarkable, exceptional,
marvellous, wonderful, great
⧏ **1** credible, believable

⚠ **incredible** or **incredulous** ?
Incredible means 'unbelievable'; *incredulous* means
'not believing, showing disbelief'. If you are told an
incredible story, you may be *incredulous*.

incredulity *n*
unbelief, disbelief, scepticism, cynicism, suspicion,
doubt, distrust, mistrust
⧏ credulity

incredulous *adj*
unbelieving, disbelieving, unconvinced, sceptical,
cynical, suspicious, doubting, distrusting, distrustful,
suspicious, dubious, doubtful, uncertain
⧏ credulous

increment *n*
increase, gain, addition, step-up, advancement,
extension, supplement, growth, enlargement,
expansion
formal accretion, accrual, accrument, addendum,
augmentation
⧏ decrease

incriminate *v*
implicate, involve, accuse, charge, impeach, blame,
put the blame on
technical indict, arraign
formal inculpate
colloq. point the finger at
⧏ exonerate

inculcate *v*
instil, drum into, hammer into, din into, drill into,
implant, fix, imprint, engrain, impress, infuse, teach,
indoctrinate

inculpate *v*
blame, put the blame on, censure, accuse, charge,
impeach, incriminate, involve, implicate, recriminate
technical indict, arraign
⧏ exonerate

incumbent *adj, n*
▶ *adj* binding, necessary, obligatory, compulsory,
prescribed, up to
formal mandatory
▶ *n* office-holder, office-bearer, official, officer,
functionary, member

incur *v*
sustain, suffer, provoke, arouse, bring upon yourself,
lay yourself open to, expose yourself to, experience,
arouse, meet with, run up, gain, earn

incurable *adj*
1 *an incurable disease*
TERMINAL, fatal, untreatable, unhealable,
inoperable, hopeless
2 INCORRIGIBLE, inveterate, hardened, hopeless,
beyond hope, beyond redemption, dyed-in-the-wool
⧏ **1** curable

incursion *n*
raid, attack, assault, invasion, onslaught, foray, sortie,
sally, infiltration, inroads, penetration
formal irruption

indebted *adj*
obliged, grateful, thankful, appreciative
formal beholden

indecency *n*
immodesty, impurity, obscenity, pornography,
lewdness, licentiousness, vulgarity, coarseness, crudity,
foulness, grossness, offensiveness
formal indecorum
⊟ decency, modesty

indecent *adj*
1 IMPURE, immodest, improper, impure, indelicate,
suggestive, offensive, obscene, pornographic, lewd,
immoral, corrupt, perverted, depraved, degenerate,
licentious, vulgar, coarse, crude, dirty, filthy, smutty,
foul, gross, bawdy, ribald, risqué, outrageous, shocking
2 *indecent haste*
improper, unbecoming, unsuitable, inappropriate
formal unseemly, indecorous
⊟ 1 decent, modest

indecipherable *adj*
indistinguishable, unreadable, illegible, unintelligible,
indistinct, unclear, tiny, crabbed, cramped
⊟ readable

indecision *n*
indecisiveness, irresolution, wavering, fluctuation,
hesitation, hesitancy, ambivalence, uncertainty,
tentativeness, doubt
formal vacillation
colloq. shilly-shallying
⊟ decisiveness, resolution

indecisive *adj*
1 UNDECIDED, irresolute, undetermined,
fluctuating, wavering, ambivalent, hesitating, hesitant,
faltering, tentative, uncertain, unsure, indefinite,
doubtful
formal vacillating
colloq. in two minds, weak-willed, pussyfooting,
shilly-shallying, wishy-washy, blowing hot and cold,
chopping and changing, sitting on the fence
2 INCONCLUSIVE, indefinite, unclear, open,
undecided, unsettled
formal indeterminate
colloq. up in the air, hanging in the balance
⊟ 1, 2 decisive 2 *colloq.* open-and-shut

indecorous *adj*
undignified, improper, immodest, indecent, rough,
impolite, rude, vulgar, in bad taste, tasteless, uncouth,
unsuitable, inappropriate, coarse, crude, uncivil,
unmannerly, ungentlemanly, unladylike,
ill-mannered, ill-bred, boorish, churlish
formal unseemly, untoward
⊟ decorous

indecorum *n*
immodesty, indecency, roughness, rudeness,
impoliteness, uncivility, tastelessness, bad taste,
coarseness, crudity, vulgarity
formal impropriety, unseemliness

indeed *adv*
really, actually, in fact, in truth, certainly, absolutely,
positively, truly, undeniably, without doubt,
undoubtedly, doubtlessly, for sure, to be sure
formal nay

indefatigable *adj*
untiring, tireless, untireable, unflagging, unfailing,
unwearied, unwearying, unweariable, unresting,
relentless, unremitting, dogged, inexhaustible,

diligent, patient, persevering, indomitable, undying
⊟ flagging, slothful

indefensible *adj*
1 UNJUSTIFIABLE, inexcusable, unforgivable,
unpardonable, insupportable, untenable, wrong,
faulty, flawed, specious
2 *an indefensible place*
vulnerable, exposed, defenceless, unshielded,
unarmed, disarmed, unprotected, unguarded,
ill-equipped
formal unfortified
⊟ 1, 2 defensible 1 excusable 2 protected,
guarded

indefinable *adj*
indescribable, inexpressible, indistinct, unrealized,
nameless, obscure, unclear, vague, subtle, dim, hazy,
impalpable
⊟ definable

indefinite *adj*
unknown, uncertain, unsettled, unresolved,
inconclusive, undecided, undetermined, unfixed,
undefined, unspecified, unlimited, ill-defined, vague,
indistinct, unclear, blurred, confused, hazy, fuzzy,
obscure, ambivalent, equivocal, ambiguous, doubtful,
imprecise, inexact, loose, general, nondescript
formal indeterminate
colloq. the jury is still out on
⊟ definite, limited, clear

indefinitely *adv*
for ever, eternally, endlessly, without limit, continually,
ad infinitum

indelible *adj*
lasting, enduring, permanent, fast, unfading,
ineffaceable, ineradicable, ingrained, imperishable,
indestructible
⊟ erasable

indelicacy *n*
immodesty, indecency, obscenity, rudeness, vulgarity,
offensiveness, suggestiveness, tastelessness, bad taste,
coarseness, crudity, grossness, smuttiness
formal impropriety
⊟ delicacy

indelicate *adj*
rude, embarrassing, suggestive, immodest, improper,
indecent, offensive, tasteless, in bad taste,
unbecoming, vulgar, coarse, crude, gross, low,
obscene, risqué
formal indecorous, unseemly, untoward
colloq. blue, off-colour
⊟ delicate

indemnify *v*
protect, secure, underwrite, guarantee, insure,
endorse, exempt, free, reimburse, compensate, repair,
repay, requite, satisfy, pay, remunerate

indemnity *n*
compensation, reimbursement, remuneration,
repayment, restitution, requital, redress, reparation,
insurance, assurance, guarantee, security, protection,
safeguard, immunity, exemption, amnesty

indent *v*
1 CUT, mark, nick, notch, dent, dint, pink, serrate,
scallop
2 ORDER, ask for, request, demand
formal requisition

indentation *n*
notch, nick, cut, serration, dent, groove, furrow, depression, dip, hollow, pit, dimple

indenture *n*
contract, agreement, certificate, deed, bond, covenant, commitment, deal, settlement

independence *n*
autonomy, self-government, self-determination, self-rule, home rule, sovereignty, freedom, liberty, individualism, separation, self-sufficiency, self-reliance
technical autarky
E3 dependence

independent *adj*
1 AUTONOMOUS, self-governing, self-determining, self-ruling, self-legislating, sovereign, absolute, non-aligned, neutral, impartial, unbiased
technical autarkic
formal autarchic
2 FREE, free-thinking, liberated, unconstrained, unrestrained, freelance, individualistic, individualist, unconventional, self-sufficient, self-supporting, self-reliant, unaided
colloq. standing on your own two feet, doing your own thing, with a mind of your own, going your own way, doing something off your own bat, paddling your own canoe
3 SEPARATE, self-contained, individual, unconnected, unattacked, unrelated, free-standing, distinct
E3 1 dependent

independently *adv*
alone, by yourself, on your own, individually, separately, solo, unaided, autonomously
colloq. under your own steam, on your tod
E3 together

indescribable *adj*
inexpressible, indefinable, unutterable, unspeakable, incredible, extraordinary, exceptional, amazing
formal ineffable
E3 describable

indestructible *adj*
unbreakable, durable, tough, strong, lasting, enduring, abiding, permanent, eternal, everlasting, immortal, endless, undecaying, inextinguishable, imperishable
formal infrangible
E3 breakable, mortal

indeterminate *adj*
indefinite, unspecified, unstated, undefined, unknown, unfixed, imprecise, inexact, unclear, vague, hazy, ill-defined, open-ended, undecided, undetermined, unpredictable, uncertain, ambiguous, equivocal, ambivalent
E3 known, specified, fixed

index *n*
1 *an index of names*
table, key, list, catalogue, directory, guide
2 INDICATOR, pointer, needle, hand, sign, token, mark, indication, hint, clue, symptom

indicate *v*
1 *shrugging shoulders indicates a lack of care*
show, reveal, display, mark, signify, mean, express, tell, make known, display, suggest, imply, represent, be symptomatic of
formal manifest, evince, denote

2 *indicate the way to someone*
point out, show, point to, designate, specify
3 *the gauge indicates temperature*
show, register, record, read

indicated *adj*
needed, required, suggested, desirable, necessary, called-for, advisable, recommended

indication *n*
sign, mark, evidence, symptom, signal, record, register, warning, omen, intimation, suggestion, hint, clue, note, explanation
formal manifestation, augury, portent

indicative *adj*
symptomatic, suggestive, demonstrative, characteristic, typical, significant, symbolic
formal denotative, exhibitive, indicatory, indicant

indicator *n*
pointer, needle, marker, hand, index, sign, symbol, token, signal, display, dial, gauge, meter, index, guide, mark, signpost
US turn signal

indict *v*
charge, accuse, impeach, summon, summons, prosecute, put on trial, incriminate
technical arraign
formal inculpate
E3 absolve; *formal* exonerate

indictment *n*
charge, accusation, impeachment, allegation, recrimination, summons, prosecution, incrimination
technical arraignment
formal inculpation
E3 exoneration

indifference *n*
apathy, unconcern, lack of concern, lack of interest, lack of feeling, coldness, coolness, inattention, disregard, heedlessness, negligence, impassivity, nonchalance, neutrality, disinterestedness
E3 interest, concern

indifferent *adj*
1 UNINTERESTED, unenthusiastic, unexcited, apathetic, unconcerned, unmoved, unresponsive, unfeeling, unemotional, uncaring, unsympathetic, blasé, callous, cold, cool, distant, aloof, detached, dispassionate, uninvolved, impassive, neutral, nonchalant, disinterested, careless, heedless
colloq. easy, all the same to you
2 MEDIOCRE, average, middling, passable, moderate, fair, adequate, undistinguished, ordinary, medium, bad, not good
colloq. OK, so-so, could be better/worse, run of the mill
E3 1 interested, caring 2 excellent

indigence *n*
poverty, distress, destitution, deprivation, necessity, need, want
formal penury, privation
E3 affluence

indigenous *adj*
native, aboriginal, original, local, home-grown
formal autochthonous
E3 foreign

indigent *adj*
poverty-stricken, impoverished, poor, destitute, needy, penniless, in dire straits, in want, in need
formal penurious, impecunious, necessitous

colloq. down and out, bust, skint, broke, stony-broke, cleaned out, on your uppers, on your beam ends, not having two pennies to rub together
₣ₐ affluent

indigestion   *n*
dyspepsia, dyspepsy, heartburn, cardialgia, acidity, pyrosis, water-brash

indignant   *adj*
annoyed, angry, irate, heated, fuming, livid, furious, incensed, infuriated, enraged, exasperated, outraged, riled, disgruntled, wrathful
colloq. mad, up in arms, peeved, miffed, narked, got the hump, in a huff
₣ₐ pleased, delighted

indignation   *n*
annoyance, anger, ire, wrath, rage, fury, exasperation, outrage, pique, scorn, contempt
₣ₐ pleasure, delight

indignity   *n*
humiliation, abuse, insult, slight, snub, affront, contempt, mistreatment, offence, disgrace, outrage, reproach, dishonour, disrespect, incivility, injury
formal contumely, obloquy, opprobrium
colloq. slap in the face, kick in the teeth, cold shoulder, putdown
₣ₐ honour

indirect   *adj*
1 ROUNDABOUT, circuitous, divergent, devious, oblique, wandering, rambling, curving, winding, meandering, zigzag, tortuous, discursive
formal periphrastic, circumlocutory
2 *an indirect effect*
secondary, incidental, unintended, subordinate, subsidiary, ancillary
₣ₐ 1 direct 2 primary

indirectly   *adv*
roundaboutly, obliquely, second-hand, deviously, in a roundabout way, hintingly
formal periphrastically, circumlocutorily
₣ₐ directly

indiscernible   *adj*
imperceptible, minuscule, minute, microscopic, tiny, undiscernible, undetectable, unapparent, indistinct, unclear, indistinct, obscure, indistinguishable, invisible, hidden, impalpable
₣ₐ clear, apparent

indiscreet   *adj*
tactless, undiplomatic, insensitive, unwise, ill-advised, ill-judged, ill-considered, foolish, foolhardy, rash, reckless, hasty, careless, heedless, unthinking, unwary, immodest, indelicate, shameless
formal impolitic, injudicious, imprudent
₣ₐ discreet, cautious

indiscretion   *n*
mistake, error, slip, *faux pas*, gaffe, blunder, lapse, tactlessness, rashness, recklessness, foolishness, folly, carelessness, immodesty, indelicacy, shamelessness
formal imprudence
colloq. boob, slip-up
₣ₐ caution, diplomacy, etiquette

indiscriminate   *adj*
general, sweeping, wholesale, random, haphazard, hit or miss, hit and miss, aimless, careless, confused, chaotic, unsystematic, unmethodical, unselective, undifferentiating, undiscriminating, mixed, varied,

diverse, motley, miscellaneous
₣ₐ selective, specific, precise

indiscriminately   *adv*
generally, wholesale, haphazardly, randomly, unselectively, aimlessly, carelessly, unsystematically, unmethodically, without fear or favour, in the mass
₣ₐ deliberately, selectively

indispensable   *adj*
vital, essential, absolutely, essential, basic, fundamental, important, key, crucial, imperative, required, requisite, needed, necessary, needful
₣ₐ dispensable, unnecessary

indisposed   *adj*
1 ILL, sick, unwell, poorly, ailing, confined to bed, laid up
formal incapacitated
colloq. groggy, under the weather, out of sorts, like death warmed up
2 RELUCTANT, unwilling, not willing, not of a mind (to), disinclined, averse, loath
₣ₐ 1 well 2 inclined

indisposition   *n*
1 ILLNESS, ailment, disease, complaint, disorder, sickness, ill health, bad health
formal malady
2 RELUCTANCE, unwillingness, hesitancy, disinclination, aversion, dislike, distaste
₣ₐ 1 health 2 inclination

indisputable   *adj*
incontrovertible, unquestionable, undeniable, incontestable, absolute, undisputed, definite, positive, certain, sure, beyond question
formal indubitable, irrefutable
₣ₐ doubtful, uncertain

indissoluble   *adj*
indestructible, permanent, inseparable, imperishable, incorruptible, enduring, lasting, eternal, fixed, inviolable, abiding, binding, solid, unbreakable
formal sempiternal
₣ₐ impermanent, short-lived

indistinct   *adj*
unclear, ill-defined, out of focus, blurred, fuzzy, misty, hazy, shadowy, obscure, dim, pale, faded, faint, low, muted, muffled, muttered, confused, unintelligible, indistinguishable, indecipherable, vague, woolly, ambiguous, indefinite, undefined
₣ₐ distinct, clear, in focus

indistinguishable   *adj*
identical, interchangeable, same, twin, alike, hard to make out the difference, cloned, tantamount
colloq. like as two peas in a pod
₣ₐ distinguishable, unalike, different, dissimilar

individual   *n, adj*
▶ *n* person, being, human being, creature, party, body, soul, mortal, type, sort, character, fellow
▶ *adj* distinctive, characteristic, typical, idiosyncratic, peculiar, unique, exclusive, original, special, personal, own, lone, solitary, isolated, proper, respective, several, separate, distinct, specific, personalized, particular, single, sole, private
formal singular
₣ₐ collective, shared, general

individualism   *n*
independence, originality, self-direction, self-interest, self-reliance, freethinking, freethought, eccentricity,

egocentricity, egoism, anarchism, libertarianism
⋳ conventionality

individualist *n*
independent, freethinker, free spirit, egoist,
egocentric, nonconformist, original, bohemian,
eccentric, maverick, loner, lone wolf, libertarian,
anarchist
⋳ conventionalist

individualistic *adj*
independent, individual, non-conformist,
unorthodox, eccentric, bohemian, original,
self-reliant, unconventional, egocentric, egoistic,
idiosyncratic, special, typical, unique, particular,
libertarian, anarchistic
⋳ conventional

individuality *n*
character, personality, distinctiveness, peculiarity,
uniqueness, originality, separateness, distinction
formal singularity
⋳ sameness

individually *adv*
separately, singly, one by one, independently,
particularly
formal severally
⋳ together

indivisible *adj*
inseparable, undividable, indissoluble, impartible
formal indiscerptible
⋳ divisible

indoctrinate *v*
brainwash, propagandize, teach, instruct, school,
ground, train, drill, impress, inculcate, instil

indoctrination *n*
brainwashing, instruction, schooling, training,
teaching, grounding, inculcation, drilling, instilling
formal catechesis, catechetics

indolence *n*
idleness, laziness, inactivity, inertia, inertness,
lethargy, heaviness, listlessness, do-nothingism,
apathy, slacking, sloth, sluggishness
formal languidness, languor, torpidity, torpidness,
torpitude, torpor
colloq. shirking
⋳ activeness, enthusiasm, industriousness

indolent *adj*
idle, lazy, inactive, inert, lethargic, listless, do-nothing,
shiftless, apathetic, slack, slow, sluggish, slothful,
sluggard, lackadaisical, lumpish
formal fainéant, languid, torpid
⋳ active, enthusiastic, industrious

indomitable *adj*
invincible, unconquerable, unbeatable, undefeatable,
impregnable, unassailable, brave, courageous, fearless,
valiant, bold, intrepid, stalwart, lion-hearted, resolute,
staunch, firm, intransigent, determined, steadfast,
undaunted, unflinching, unyielding
⋳ compliant, timid, submissive

indubitable *adj*
indisputable, beyond dispute, unanswerable,
undeniable, beyond doubt, undoubted, undoubtable,
unquestionable, unarguable, incontestable,
incontrovertible, sure, absolute, certain, obvious,
evident
formal irrefutable, irrebuttable, irrefragable
⋳ arguable

induce *v*
1 CAUSE, bring about, occasion, give rise to, lead to,
set in motion, incite, instigate, originate, prompt,
provoke, produce, generate
formal effect
2 COAX, prevail upon, encourage, press, persuade,
talk into, move, influence, draw, tempt, inspire,
motivate, urge, actuate, impel
⋳ 2 discourage, deter

inducement *n*
lure, bait, attraction, enticement, encouragement,
incentive, impetus, incitement, influence, reward,
spur, goad, stimulus, motive, reason
colloq. carrot, sweetener
⋳ disincentive

induct *v*
inaugurate, initiate, install, invest, ordain, introduce,
consecrate, enthrone, swear in

induction *n*
1 INAUGURATION, initiation, installation,
institution, investiture, ordination, introduction,
enthronement, consecration
2 INFERENCE, conclusion, deduction,
generalization

indulge *v*
1 GRATIFY, satisfy, humour, pander to, go along with,
give in to, yield to, give way to, cater to, favour, pet,
cosset, mollycoddle, pamper, spoil, treat, regale
2 *indulge in something*
give way to, give free rein to, give yourself up to, revel in,
wallow in, luxuriate in

indulgence *n*
1 EXTRAVAGANCE, luxury, treat, excess,
gratification, satisfaction, fulfilment, immoderation,
intemperance, dissipation, dissoluteness
2 FAVOUR, tolerance, generosity, lenience, pardon,
remission
⋳ 1 restraint

indulgent *adj*
tolerant, lenient, permissive, generous, forgiving,
merciful, compassionate, sympathetic, humane,
liberal, kind, fond, tender, understanding, patient,
pampering, humouring, spoiling, cosseting,
mollycoddling
formal forbearing
colloq. easy-going
⋳ strict, harsh

industrial *adj*
manufacturing, commercial, business, trade

industrialist *n*
manufacturer, producer, magnate, tycoon, baron,
captain of industry, capitalist, financier

industrious *adj*
busy, productive, hard-working, hard, diligent,
assiduous, conscientious, laborious, steady, dedicated,
studious, zealous, active, energetic, tireless,
indefatigable, persistent, persevering, determined,
dogged, vigorous
formal sedulous
colloq. busy as a bee, on the go, slogging your guts out
⋳ lazy, idle

industriously *adv*
diligently, conscientiously, assiduously, steadily, hard,
perseveringly, doggedly, sedulously

colloq. with your nose to the grindstone
E3 lazily

industry *n*
1 *the steel industry*
business, trade, commerce, manufacturing, production, service, enterprise, line, field
2 INDUSTRIOUSNESS, diligence, conscientiousness, assiduousness, assiduity, application, intentness, concentration, effort, labour, laboriousness, toil, persistence, hard work, zeal, energy, vigour, activity, perseverance, steadiness, determination, productiveness, tirelessness
formal sedulity, sedulousness
colloq. stickability

inebriated *adj*
under the influence, drunk, drunken
formal intoxicated, crapulant
colloq. merry, tight, tipsy, tiddly, well-oiled, blotto, drunk as a lord/newt, blind drunk, roaring drunk, the worse for drink, soused, squiffy, happy, legless, plastered, sozzled, pickled, bibulous, woozy, one over the eight, under the table, bevvied, have had a few;
slang stoned, tanked up, loaded, lit up, canned, paralytic, sloshed, smashed, pissed, stewed, bombed, wasted, wrecked
E3 sober, temperate, abstinent, teetotal

inedible *adj*
uneatable, unpalatable, stale, indigestible, not fit to eat, unconsumable, rotten, off, bad, rancid, harmful, noxious, poisonous, deadly
E3 edible, wholesome

ineducable *adj*
unteachable, incorrigible, indocile
E3 educable

ineffable *adj*
indescribable, inexpressible, unspeakable, unutterable, beyond words, incommunicable, unimpartible
E3 describable

ineffective *adj*
1 *an ineffective attempt*
useless, worthless, vain, idle, futile, unavailing, to no avail, abortive, profitless, fruitless, unproductive, unsuccessful
formal ineffectual
2 POWERLESS, impotent, inadequate, weak, feeble, inept, idle, lame, incompetent
E3 **1, 2** effective

ineffectual *adj*
1 *ineffectual methods*
useless, vain, futile, worthless, fruitless, unproductive, unavailing, abortive
formal inefficacious
2 *an ineffectual person*
weak, feeble, powerless, inadequate, incompetent, impotent, inept, lame
E3 **1, 2** effectual

inefficacy *n*
ineffectiveness, unproductiveness, uselessness, futility, inadequacy
formal ineffectuality, ineffectualness
E3 efficacy

inefficiency *n*
waste, wastefulness, disorganization, carelessness, negligence, slackness, laxity, ineptitude, sloppiness, incompetence, muddle
E3 efficiency

inefficient *adj*
uneconomic, wasteful, money-wasting, time-wasting, incompetent, ineffective, inexpert, unworkmanlike, slipshod, sloppy, slack, lax, inept, careless, disorganized, unorganized, negligent
E3 efficient

inelegant *adj*
graceless, ungraceful, clumsy, awkward, gauche, ungainly, laboured, ugly, unrefined, ill-bred, crude, vulgar, unpolished, rough, unsophisticated, uncultured, uncultivated, unfinished, uncouth
E3 elegant

ineligible *adj*
disqualified, ruled out, unacceptable, undesirable, unworthy, unsuitable, unfit, unfitted, unqualified, unequipped
technical incompetent
E3 eligible

inept *adj*
awkward, clumsy, bungling, heavy-handed, incompetent, incapable, inadequate, unskilful, inexpert, unsuccessful, foolish, stupid, useless, appalling
formal maladroit
colloq. pathetic, cack-handed, lousy, ham-fisted
E3 competent, skilful

ineptitude *n*
ineptness, awkwardness, clumsiness, bungling, unhandiness, gaucheness, gaucherie, incompetence, incapability, unskilfulness, inexpertness, stupidity, unfitness, uselessness, crassness
formal fatuity, incapacity
E3 aptitude, skill

inequality *n*
unequalness, imbalance, difference, discrepancy, contrast, variation, diversity, dissimilarity, nonconformity, unevenness, roughness, irregularity, disproportion, bias, prejudice, discrimination
formal disparity
E3 equality, balance

inequitable *adj*
unfair, unjust, unequal, wrongful, one-sided, biased, prejudiced, discriminatory, bigoted, intolerant, partisan, partial, preferential
E3 equitable

inequity *n*
unfairness, unjustness, injustice, maltreatment, mistreatment, abuse, inequality, wrongfulness, one-sidedness, prejudice, bias, discrimination, partiality
E3 equity

inert *adj*
1 IMMOBILE, motionless, unmoving, still, stock-still, inactive, static, stationary, inanimate, lifeless, dead, passive, cold, unresponsive
formal comatose
2 SLUGGISH, lethargic, lazy, inactive, slack, listless, dull, apathetic, idle, dormant, stagnant, torpid, sleepy
formal indolent
E3 **1** moving **2** lively, animated

inertia *n*
immobility, motionlessness, stillness, stagnation, inactivity, inaction, passivity, unresponsiveness, apathy, idleness, laziness, sloth, slothfulness, lethargy, listlessness

formal indolence, languor, torpor
⊟ activity, liveliness

inescapable *adj*
inevitable, unavoidable, destined, fated, certain, sure,
assured, irrevocable, unalterable, inexorable
formal ineluctable
⊟ escapable, preventable

inessential *adj, n*
▶ *adj* unnecessary, irrelevant, superfluous, surplus,
redundant, non-essential, needless, unasked-for,
uncalled-for, unimportant, secondary, spare,
accidental, unessential, dispensable, expendable,
extraneous, optional, extrinsic
⊟ essential, necessary
▶ *n* non-essential, extra, extravagance, luxury,
superfluity, accessory, trimming, appendage
⊟ essential

inestimable *adj*
incalculable, measureless, infinite, immeasurable,
invaluable, precious, priceless, unlimited,
uncountable, unfathomable, incomputable, immense,
vast, untold
formal prodigious
colloq. mind-boggling, worth a fortune
⊟ insignificant

inevitable *adj*
unavoidable, inescapable, necessary, definite, certain,
sure, decreed, ordained, destined, fated, automatic,
assured, fixed, settled, unalterable, irrevocable,
inexorable, unpreventable
formal predestined, ineluctable
⊟ avoidable, uncertain, alterable

inevitably *adv*
unavoidably, inescapably, irrevocably, inexorably,
necessarily, definitely, certainly, surely, automatically,
assuredly
⊟ avoidably

inexact *adj*
imprecise, approximate, inaccurate, incorrect,
erroneous, indefinite, indistinct, fuzzy, loose, woolly,
lax, muddled
formal indeterminate, fallacious
⊟ exact, accurate

inexactitude *n*
inexactness, impreciseness, imprecision, inaccuracy,
incorrectness, indefiniteness, approximation,
miscalculation, woolliness, looseness, mistake,
blunder, error
⊟ exactitude, accuracy

inexcusable *adj*
indefensible, unforgivable, unpardonable,
unjustifiable, intolerable, unacceptable, outrageous,
shameful, blameworthy
formal reprehensible
⊟ excusable, justifiable

inexhaustible *adj*
1 *an inexhaustible supply*
UNLIMITED, limitless, boundless, unbounded,
unrestricted, measureless, infinite, endless,
never-ending, abundant
formal illimitable
2 INDEFATIGABLE, tireless, untiring, unflagging,
unfailing, unwearied, unwearying, weariless
⊟ 1 limited

inexorable *adj*
relentless, unrelenting, remorseless, unalterable,
inevitable, unpreventable, unavertable, irresistible,
irrevocable, inescapable, immovable, unyielding,
unceasing, incessant, unstoppable, unfaltering,
ordained, destined, fated, definite, certain, sure
formal ineluctable
⊟ avoidable, preventable

inexorably *adv*
relentlessly, remorselessly, inescapably, irresistibly,
inevitably, irrevocably, definitely, certainly, surely,
resistlessly, implacably, pitilessly, mercilessly
formal ineluctably

inexpedient *adj*
unwise, unsuitable, inappropriate, disadvantageous,
misguided, detrimental, unadvisable, unfavourable,
indiscreet, foolish, senseless, wrong, ill-advised,
inadvisable, ill-chosen, ill-judged, inconvenient,
impractical, undesirable, undiplomatic
formal impolitic, imprudent, injudicious
⊟ expedient

inexpensive *adj*
cheap, low-priced, low-price, reasonable, modest,
bargain, budget, low-cost, cut-rate, economical,
reduced, discounted
⊟ expensive, dear

inexperience *n*
inexpertness, ignorance, unfamiliarity, strangeness,
newness, freshness, rawness, immaturity, naïveness,
innocence
⊟ experience

inexperienced *adj*
inexpert, untrained, unqualified, untutored, new to
the job, unskilled, amateur, probationary, apprentice,
unacquainted, uninformed, ignorant, unfamiliar,
unaccustomed, unseasoned, new, fresh, raw, callow,
young, immature, naïve, unsophisticated, innocent
colloq. green, wet behind the ears, out of your depth,
wide-eyed
⊟ experienced, mature

inexpert *adj*
unskilled, unskilful, untaught, untrained,
unpractised, unworkmanlike, unprofessional,
untutored, unqualified, amateur, amateurish,
awkward, clumsy, unhandy, incompetent, inept,
bungling, blundering
formal maladroit
colloq. cack-handed, ham, ham-fisted
⊟ expert

inexplicable *adj*
incomprehensible, unexplainable, unintelligible,
unaccountable, strange, mystifying, puzzling,
perplexing, baffling, bewildering, mysterious,
insoluble, enigmatic, weird, unfathomable, incredible,
unbelievable, miraculous
formal abstruse
⊟ explicable

inexplicably *adv*
incomprehensibly, unexplainably, incredibly,
unaccountably, strangely, mysteriously, mystifyingly,
bafflingly, puzzlingly, miraculously
⊟ explicably

inexpressible *adj*
indescribable, undescribable, unspeakable,
unutterable, incommunicable, indefinable, nameless,

unsayable, untellable
formal ineffable

inexpressive *adj*
unexpressive, expressionless, deadpan, poker-faced,
inscrutable, blank, vacant, empty, lifeless, dead, cold,
emotionless, impassive
F3 expressive

inextinguishable *adj*
unquenchable, indestructible, imperishable,
irrepressible, unconquerable, unquellable,
unsuppressible, deathless, enduring, lasting, eternal,
everlasting, undying, immortal
F3 impermanent, perishable

inextricable *adj*
inseparable, indissoluble, indivisible,
indistinguishable, intricate, irretrievable, irreversible

inextricably *adv*
inseparably, indissolubly, indivisibly, indistinguishably,
intricately, irresolubly, irretrievably, irreversibly

infallibility *n*
accuracy, unerringness, faultlessness, inerrancy,
perfection, dependability, reliability, safety, supremacy,
sureness, trustworthiness, impeccability,
irreproachability
formal irrefutability, omniscience
F3 fallibility

infallible *adj*
accurate, unerring, unfailing, foolproof, fail-safe,
certain, sure, reliable, dependable, trustworthy, sound,
perfect, flawless, faultless, impeccable
colloq. sure-fire
F3 fallible

infamous *adj*
notorious, ill-famed, disreputable, disgraceful,
discreditable, dishonourable, shameful, shocking,
outrageous, abominable, detestable, scandalous, evil,
bad, base, vile, wicked, hateful
old use dastardly
formal iniquitous, ignominious, egregious, nefarious
F3 illustrious, glorious

infamy *n*
notoriety, disrepute, disgrace, discredit, shame,
dishonour, discredit, wickedness, evil, baseness,
vileness, depravity, villainy
formal ignominy, turpitude
F3 glory

infancy *n*
1 BABYHOOD, childhood, youth
2 BEGINNING, start, outset, birth, dawn, cradle,
genesis, emergence, rise, origin(s), early stages
formal commencement, inception
F3 1 adulthood

infant *n, adj*
▶ *n* baby, toddler, child, little one
Scot. bairn
formal babe, babe in arms
colloq. tot
F3 adult
▶ *adj* newborn, baby, young, youthful, juvenile,
immature, beginning, growing, developing, dawning,
emergent, rudimentary, early, initial, new
formal nascent
F3 adult, mature

infantile *adj*
babyish, childish, puerile, juvenile, young, youthful,

adolescent, immature
F3 adult, mature

infatuated *adj*
besotted, obsessed, enamoured, in love, spellbound,
bewitched, mesmerized, captivated, fascinated,
enraptured, ravished, carried away
formal entêté(e)
colloq. crazy, mad, daft, nuts, sweet, wild, sold, far
gone, having a thing, smitten, head over heels in love
F3 indifferent, disenchanted

infatuation *n*
besottedness, obsession, craze, fixation, mania,
passion, love, fondness, fascination
colloq. crush, thing, pash, shine
F3 indifference, disenchantment

infect *v*
contaminate, pollute, defile, taint, blight, mar, spoil,
ulcerate, poison, corrupt, pervert, spread to, pass on,
influence, affect, excite, stimulate, animate, move,
touch, inspire

infection *n*
illness, disease, complaint, condition, virus,
bacteria, germ, epidemic, contagion, pestilence,
contamination, pollution, defilement, taint, tainting,
spoiling, fouling, blight, poison, corruption, influence
technical sepsis
colloq. bug

infectious *adj*
1 *an infectious disease*
contagious, communicable, transmissible,
transmittable, infective, catching, spreading, epidemic,
virulent, deadly, toxic, contaminating, polluting,
defiling, corrupting
technical septic
formal noxious
2 *infectious laughter*
contagious, compelling, irresistible, catching,
spreading

infelicitous *adj*
1 INAPPROPRIATE, unfitting, unsuitable,
unfortunate, inopportune, untimely, disadvantageous
formal incongruous
2 UNHAPPY, unfortunate, sad, miserable, sorrowful,
unlucky, despairing, wretched
F3 1 appropriate, apt **2** happy

infer *v*
deduce, derive, extrapolate, conclude, come to a
conclusion, reason, assume, presume, surmise, gather,
understand, allude
formal conjecture
colloq. figure out

⚠ **infer** or **imply** ? *See panel at* **imply**.

inference *n*
deduction, conclusion, consequence, assumption,
presumption, construction, interpretation, reasoning,
reading
formal extrapolation, corollary, conjecture, surmise

inferior *adj, n*
▶ *adj* **1** LOWER, lesser, minor, secondary, junior,
subordinate, ancillary, subsidiary, second-class, low,
lowly, humble, menial, subservient
colloq. not in the same league
2 *inferior work*
substandard, second-rate, low-quality, mediocre, bad,

poor, awful, unsatisfactory, imperfect, defective, incompetent, slipshod, shoddy, cheap
colloq. crummy, ropy
slang naff
🔁 **1** superior **2** excellent
▶ *n* subordinate, junior, underling, minion, vassal, menial
🔁 superior

inferiority *n*
1 SUBORDINATION, subservience, humbleness, lowliness, subservience, meanness, insignificance
2 MEDIOCRITY, imperfection, inadequacy, faultiness, defectiveness, low/poor/bad quality, unsatisfactoriness, slovenliness, shoddiness, incompetence
🔁 **1** superiority **2** excellence, perfection

infernal *adj*
1 HELLISH, satanic, devilish, diabolical, demonic, fiendish, accursed, damned, Hadean
2 WICKED, evil, vile, atrocious
formal execrable, malevolent
3 *What an infernal mess!*
damned, wretched, cursed, confounded, fiendish
colloq. blasted, flipping, blooming, darned, dashed
🔁 **1** heavenly

infertile *adj*
barren, sterile, childless, unproductive, non-productive, unfruitful, arid, parched, dried-up
formal effete, unfructuous, infecund
🔁 fertile, fruitful, productive, prolific

infertility *n*
barrenness, sterility, unfruitfulness, unproductiveness, aridity, aridness
formal effeteness, infecundity
🔁 fertility

infest *v*
swarm, teem, crawl, bristle, throng, flood, overrun, overspread, spread through, plague, take over, beset, invade, infiltrate, penetrate, permeate, pervade, ravage

infested *adj*
swarming, teeming, crawling, bristling, beset, alive, pervaded, plagued, ravaged, ridden, overrun, overspread, infiltrated, permeated, vermined

infidel *n*
pagan, heathen, disbeliever, unbeliever, heretic, sceptic, atheist, freethinker, irreligionist
formal nullifidian
🔁 believer

infidelity *n*
1 ADULTERY, unfaithfulness, cheating, falseness, affair, relationship, liaison, intrigue, romance, armour
2 DISLOYALTY, faithlessness, treachery, betrayal
formal duplicity, perfidy
colloq. fooling around, playing around
🔁 **1** fidelity **2** faithfulness

infiltrate *v*
penetrate, enter, creep into, insinuate, intrude, invade, slip, pervade, permeate, filter, percolate, seep, soak

infiltration *n*
penetration, entr(y)ism, insinuation, intrusion, pervasion, invasion, permeation, percolation
formal interpenetration

infiltrator *n*
penetrator, insinuator, intruder, spy, subversive, subverter, seditionary, entr(y)ist

infinite *adj*
limitless, unlimited, boundless, unbounded, endless, never-ending, interminable, inexhaustible, bottomless, fathomless, innumerable, numberless, without number, uncountable, countless, untold, incalculable, inestimable, immeasurable, unfathomable, vast, extensive, immense, enormous, huge, absolute, total
formal indeterminable
🔁 finite, limited

⚠ **infinite** or **infinitesimal** ?
Infinite means 'without limits', or, loosely, 'extremely large or great': *If we follow that course of action, the dangers are infinite; infinitesimal* means 'infinitely small' or, loosely, 'extremely small': *Personally, I consider the dangers infinitesimal.*

---

infinitesimal *adj*
tiny, minute, microscopic, minuscule, inconsiderable, insignificant, trifling, negligible, inappreciable, imperceptible
Scot. wee
colloq. teeny
🔁 great, large, enormous

infinity *n*
eternity, perpetuity, limitlessness, boundlessness, endlessness, inexhaustibility, countlessness, immeasurableness, extensiveness, vastness, immensity, enormousness
🔁 finiteness, limitation

infirm *adj*
weak, feeble, frail, ailing, ill, unwell, poorly, sickly, decrepit, failing, faltering, unsteady, shaky, wobbly, doddery, old, lame, disabled
formal debilitated
🔁 healthy, strong

infirmity *n*
weakness, feebleness, frailty, ailment, illness, ill health, disease, complaint, sickness, sickliness, disorder, failing, decrepitude, vulnerability, instability, dodderiness
formal debility, malady
🔁 health, strength

inflame *v*
anger, enrage, infuriate, incense, exasperate, madden, rile, provoke, stimulate, work up, stir, excite, rouse, arouse, agitate, stir (up), whip up, foment, impassion, kindle, ignite, fire, heat, fan, fuel, increase, intensify, worsen, make worse, aggravate
formal exacerbate
🔁 cool, quench

inflamed *adj*
sore, swollen, septic, infected, festered, poisoned, red, hot, heated, fevered, angry, feverish, flushed, reddened, glowing

inflammable *adj*
flammable, combustible, burnable, ignitable, ignitible
🔁 non-flammable, incombustible, flameproof, fire-resistant, flame-resistant

inflammation *n*
soreness, painfulness, tenderness, swelling, abscess, festering, infection, redness, heat, hotness, rash, sore, irritation, erruption
technical empyema, erythema, sepsis, septicity

inflammatory *adj*
1 PROVOCATIVE, incendiary, explosive, fiery, rabble-rousing, rabid, riotous, seditious, insurgent, intemperate, inciting, incitative, inflaming, instigative, anarchic, demagogic
2 SORE, painful, tender, swollen, allergic, festering, septic, infected
1 calming, pacific

inflate *v*
1 *inflate a life-jacket*
blow up, pump up, bloat, expand, dilate, enlarge, aerate, swell, puff out
formal distend
2 *inflated prices*
increase, raise, boost, step up, escalate, amplify, extend, intensify
formal augment
colloq. hike up, push up
3 *inflate the importance of something*
exaggerate, overstate, overrate, overestimate, boost, magnify
formal aggrandize
1 deflate **2** decrease, lower **3** understate, play down

inflated *adj*
1 BLOWN UP, swollen, puffed out, dilated, bloated, ballooned
formal distended, tumefied, tumid
2 INCREASED, raised, escalated, extended, intensified
3 EXAGGERATED, overblown, ostentatious, pompous, bombastic
formal grandiloquent, magniloquent, euphuistic
deflated

inflation *n*
expansion, increase, rise, escalation, hyperinflation
deflation

inflection *n*
change of tone/intonation, pitch, modulation, stress, emphasis, rhythm

inflexibility *n*
rigidity, hardness, stiffness, fixity, immovability, immutability, immutableness, inelasticity, obstinacy, stubbornness, stringency, unsuppleness
formal intractability, intransigence, obduracy
flexibility

inflexible *adj*
an inflexible mass; inflexible rules/people
rigid, stiff, hard, solid, set, fixed, unelastic, unsupple, fast, immovable, immutable, unchangeable, unvarying, uniform, standard, standardized, firm, rigorous, taut, strict, stringent, unbending, unbendable, unyielding, adamant, resolute, relentless, pitiless, merciless, implacable, intolerant, uncompromising, unaccommodating, stubborn, obstinate, steely, entrenched, dyed-in-the-wool
formal intransigent, obdurate, intractable
flexible, yielding, adaptable

inflict *v*
impose, enforce, perpetrate, wreak, administer, apply, deliver, deal (out), mete out, lay, burden, exact, levy

⚠ **inflict** or **afflict** ? *See panel at* **afflict**.

infliction *n*
imposition, enforcement, perpetration, wreaking,

administration, application, delivery, affliction, exaction, burden, punishment, trouble, worry, penalty
formal retribution, castigation, chastisement

influence *n, v*
▶ *n* power, sway, rule, authority, domination, dominance, supremacy, mastery, rule, hold, control, direction, guidance, bias, prejudice, pull, pressure, effect, impact, weight, importance, prestige, standing, mark, toll
colloq. clout, pull, whip hand, drag
▶ *v* dominate, control, manipulate, direct, guide, determine, manoeuvre, change, alter, modify, transform, affect, have an effect on, impress, move, mould, shape, stir, arouse, rouse, sway, persuade, impact on, induce, incite, instigate, prompt, impel, motivate, dispose, incline, colour, condition, bias, prejudice
colloq. have clout, carry weight, pull strings, pull wires, have under your thumb, hold over a barrel, twist someone's arm, wheel and deal

influential *adj*
dominant, controlling, leading, authoritative, charismatic, persuasive, meaningful, convincing, compelling, inspiring, moving, powerful, potent, effective, telling, strong, far-reaching, prestigious, weighty, momentous, important, significant, instrumental, guiding
ineffective, unimportant

influx *n*
inflow, inrush, invasion, arrival, intrusion, stream, flow, inflow, rush, flood, inundation
formal ingress, incursion

inform *v*
1 TELL, advise, notify, communicate, announce, relate, impart, leak, tip off, acquaint, brief, instruct, enlighten, illuminate
colloq. fill in, put in the picture, clue up, put wise, wise up, keep posted
formal apprise
2 *inform on your friends*
betray, incriminate, denounce, blab
colloq. tell on, shop, squeal, rat, blow the whistle on, sell down the river, split, snitch; *slang* grass
3 CHARACTERIZE, typify, mark, stamp, brand, identify, distinguish, permeate

informal *adj*
unofficial, unceremonious, casual, everyday, relaxed, easy, easygoing, free, natural, simple, unpretentious, familiar, colloquial, vernacular
formal, solemn, serious, official

informality *n*
unceremoniousness, casualness, congeniality, ease, freedom, familiarity, naturalness, relaxation, simplicity, unpretentiousness, approachability, homeliness, cosiness
formality, ceremony

informally *adj*
unofficially, unceremoniously, casually, easily, familiarly, simply, colloquially, freely, confidentially, privately, on the quiet
formally

information *n*
facts, details, particulars, data, input, intelligence, news, report, bulletin, communiqué, propaganda, message, word, advice, counsel, notice, briefing, instruction, knowledge, enlightenment, file, record,

dossier, database, databank, clues, evidence
formal tidings
colloq. gen, info, low-down, dope; *slang* bumf

informative *adj*
educational, instructive, edifying, enlightening,
illuminating, revealing, forthcoming, communicative,
chatty, gossipy, newsy, helpful, useful, constructive
E3 uninformative

informed *adj*
1 *we'll keep you informed*
familiar, conversant, acquainted, enlightened, briefed,
primed, posted, up to date, abreast, *au fait*
colloq. in the know
2 *an informed opinion*
well-informed, authoritative, expert, versed, well-
versed, well-read, well-briefed, erudite, learned,
knowledgeable, well-researched
E3 1 ignorant, unaware

informer *n*
informant, betrayer, traitor, Judas, tell-tale, sneak, spy
colloq. mole, rat, finger, squealer, whistle-blower,
snitch; *slang* grass, supergrass, stool pigeon, nark

infraction *n*
breaking, breach, violation, infringement,
contravention, encroachment
formal transgression
E3 observance, compliance

infrequent *adj*
exceptional, intermittent, occasional, rare, scanty,
sparse, spasmodic, sporadic, uncommon, unusual
colloq. few and far between, like gold dust
E3 frequent

infringe *v*
1 BREAK, violate, contravene, overstep, disobey,
defy, flout, ignore
formal transgress
2 INTRUDE, encroach, impinge, trespass, invade

infringement *n*
1 *infringement of the rules*
breach, breaking, disobedience, violation, defiance,
contravention, evasion, non-compliance, non-
observance
formal infraction, transgression
2 INTRUSION, encroachment, trespass, invasion

infuriate *v*
anger, vex, enrage, incense, exasperate, madden,
inflame, provoke, rouse, annoy, irritate, rile,
antagonize
colloq. bug, get, make your blood boil, rub up the
wrong way, get on someone's nerves, get under your
skin
E3 calm, pacify

infuriated *adj*
angry, exasperated, enraged, agitated, provoked,
roused, vexed, furious, incensed, irate, irritated,
violent, wild, heated, beside yourself
colloq. flaming, maddened, peeved, miffed, narked
E3 calm, gratified, pleased

infuriating *adj*
annoying, exasperating, irritating, unbearable,
intolerable, frustrating, galling, provoking, thwarting
formal vexatious
colloq. pesky, maddening, aggravating; *US* pesky
E3 agreeable, pleasing

infuse *v*
fill, breathe into, imbue, impart to, introduce, implant,
inculcate, inspire, instil, inject, steep, soak, saturate,
brew, draw

infusion *n*
implantation, inculcation, infusing, instillation,
steeping, soaking, brew

ingenious *adj*
clever, shrewd, astute, adept, adroit, cunning, crafty,
wily, sly, sharp, smart, skilful, masterly, bright,
brilliant, imaginative, creative, inventive, resourceful,
talented, gifted, original, innovative
E3 unimaginative

⚠ **ingenious** or **ingenuous** ?
Ingenious means 'clever, skilful' or 'cleverly made or
thought out': *an ingenious plan. Ingenuous* means
'frank, trusting, not cunning or deceitful': *It was
rather ingenuous of you to believe a compulsive liar
like him.*

---

ingenuity *n*
ingeniousness, cleverness, shrewdness, astuteness,
sharpness, skill, skilfulness, creativeness, adroitness,
cunning, slyness, innovativeness, invention,
inventiveness, deftness, originality, resourcefulness,
genius, gift, faculty, flair, knack
E3 clumsiness, dullness

ingenuous *adj*
artless, guileless, innocent, honest, sincere, genuine,
frank, candid, open, direct, forthright, plain, simple,
unsophisticated, naïve, trusting, trustful
formal undissembling
E3 cunning, deceitful, artful, sly

ingenuousness *n*
artlessness, guilelessness, innocence, genuineness,
honesty, openness, naïvety, trustfulness, candour,
frankness, forthrightness, directness,
unsophisticatedness, unreserve
E3 deceit, cunning, slyness, artfulness, subterfuge

inglorious *adj*
shameful, disgraceful, discreditable, dishonourable,
disreputable, humiliating, blameworthy, ignoble,
infamous, mortifying, unsuccessful, unhonoured,
unheroic, unknown, obscure, unsung
formal ignominious
E3 glorious

ingrain *v*
fix, root, entrench, engrain, embed, build in, impress,
imprint, imbue, implant, infix, instil, dye

ingrained *adj*
fixed, implanted, rooted, deep-rooted, deep-seated,
entrenched, embedded, immovable, ineradicable,
permanent, inbuilt, built-in, inborn, inbred, inherent

ingratiate *v*
curry favour, flatter, creep, crawl, grovel, fawn,
get in with, toady, play up to
colloq. suck up to, lick someone's boots, bow and
scrape, get on the right side of, get into someone's
good books

ingratiating *adj*
flattering, obsequious, servile, crawling, fawning,
toadying, unctuous, smooth-tongued, suave,
time-serving

formal sycophantic
colloq. bootlicking

ingratitude *n*
ungratefulness, thanklessness, unappreciativeness, unthankfulness, ungraciousness
◨ gratitude, thankfulness, appreciation

ingredient *n*
constituent, element, factor, unit, component, item, feature, part

ingress *n*
access, means of approach/entry, entrance, entry, admission, admittance, right of entry, permission to enter

inhabit *v*
live in, occupy, possess, colonize, settle, make your home in, people, populate, stay in
formal dwell in, reside in

inhabitant *n*
resident, citizen, native, settler, occupier, occupant, inmate, tenant, lodger
formal dweller, habitant

inhabited *adj*
lived-in, occupied, peopled, populated, settled, possessed, colonized, held, developed, tenanted, overrun
◨ uninhabited

inhalation *n*
breathing, breath, inhaling, inspiration, suction
technical respiration, spiration

inhale *v*
breathe in, draw in, draw, suck in, inspire, whiff
technical respire
formal inbreathe

inharmonious *adj*
1 UNMELODIOUS, unharmonious, tuneless, grating, harsh, strident, clashing, jangling, jarring, discordant, raucous, cacophonous, untuneful, unmusical, atonal
2 INCOMPATIBLE, conflicting, contradictory, clashing, irreconcilable, unfriendly, unsympathetic, quarrelsome, perverse
formal dissonant, antipathetic, inconsonant
colloq. stroppy
◨ 1, 2 harmonious

inherent *adj*
inborn, inbred, innate, inherited, hereditary, in the blood, native, natural, inbuilt, built-in, intrinsic, ingrained, essential, fundamental, basic

inherit *v*
succeed to, assume, take over, come into, be left, receive, be bequeathed
formal accede to

inheritance *n*
legacy, bequest, heritage, endowment, birthright, heredity, descent, succession
formal accession

inheritor *n*
heir, heiress, inheritress, inheritrix, successor, beneficiary, recipient, reversionary
technical devisee, legatee, legatary
formal heritor, heritress, heritrix

inhibit *v*
discourage, repress, hold back, suppress, curb, rein in, check, bridle, restrain, constrain, hinder, impede,
obstruct, restrict, interfere with, frustrate, thwart, hamper, balk, prevent, stop, stanch, stem, slow down
◨ encourage, assist

inhibited *adj*
repressed, self-conscious, shy, embarrassed, reticent, withdrawn, introverted, self-restrained, reserved, guarded, subdued, restrained, constrained, frustrated
colloq. uptight
◨ uninhibited, open, relaxed

inhibition *n*
1 *lose all our inhibitions*
repression, self-consciousness, shyness, reticence, reserve
colloq. hang-up
2 RESTRAINT, curb, check, hindrance, impediment, obstruction, restriction, interference, hampering, frustration, thwarting, bar
◨ 1 openness 2 freedom

inhospitable *adj*
1 *an inhospitable place*
uninhabitable, forbidding, bare, barren, bleak, desolate, empty, lonely, uncongenial, unfavourable, hostile
formal inimical
2 *an inhospitable person*
unwelcoming, unfriendly, unreceptive, unsociable, antisocial, ungenerous, unkind, unneighbourly, uncivil, cold, cool, aloof, xenophobic
◨ favourable, hospitable

inhuman *adj*
1 BARBARIC, barbarous, animal, bestial, vicious, savage, sadistic, cold-blooded, brutal, cruel, merciless, ruthless, diabolical, fiendish
2 NON-HUMAN, strange, odd, animal
◨ 1, 2 human

⚠ **inhuman or inhumane ?**
When referring to cruel conditions, treatment, behaviour, etc, *inhuman* is stronger than *inhumane*. *Inhumane* means 'unkind, cruel, showing lack of compassion', whereas *inhuman* means 'showing such cruelty and lack of compassion to a degree almost unbelievable in a human being'.

inhumane *adj*
unkind, insensitive, inconsiderate, callous, unfeeling, uncaring, unsympathetic, heartless, cold-hearted, hard-hearted, pitiless, cruel, harsh
◨ humane, kind, compassionate

inhumanity *n*
atrocity, barbarism, barbarity, savageness, brutality, brutishness, cruelty, cold-bloodedness, viciousness, pitilessness, ruthlessness, sadism, callousness, unkindness, cold-heartedness, hard-heartedness, heartlessness
◨ humanity

inimical *adj*
hostile, adverse, antagonistic, destructive, opposed, harmful, injurious, hurtful, pernicious, intolerant, unfavourable, unfriendly, unwelcoming, inhospitable, ill-disposed, disaffected, antipathetic, contrary
formal noxious, repugnant
◨ favourable, friendly, sympathetic

inimitable *adj*
unique, incomparable, matchless, unmatched, unparalleled, unrivalled, unsurpassable, unsurpassed,

unequalled, peerless, consummate, sublime, superlative, supreme, distinctive, exceptional, nonpareil, unexampled

iniquitous *adj*
evil, wicked, unrighteous, immoral, unjust, sinful, accursed, atrocious, base, vicious, awful, dreadful, criminal, abominable, infamous, reprobate
old use facinorous
formal nefarious, reprehensible, heinous, flagitious
F∃ virtuous

iniquity *n*
wickedness, injustice, offence, misdeed, wrong, wrongdoing, evil, evil-doing, sin, sinfulness, enormity, baseness, vice, viciousness, infamy, abomination, crime, lawlessness, unrighteousness, ungodliness
formal heinousness, transgression
F∃ virtue

initial *adj, v*
▶ *adj* first, beginning, opening, starting, introductory, inaugural, original, primary, prime, early, basic, elementary, foundational, formative
formal commencing, inceptive, inchoate, incipient
F∃ final, last
▶ *v* write your initials on, sign, endorse, countersign

initially *adv*
at first, at the beginning, at the start, to begin with, to start with, originally, first, firstly, first of all
F∃ finally, in the end

initiate *v, n*
▶ *v* **1** BEGIN, start, originate, pioneer, institute, set up, introduce, launch, open, inaugurate, instigate, activate, trigger, prompt, stimulate, cause
formal commence
colloq. kick off, set the ball rolling, set the wheels in motion, get off the ground, get under way, set in motion, get things moving
2 TEACH, instruct, train, drill, crash, tutor, inculcate, instil
3 *initiated into the organization*
accept, admit, let in, introduce, receive, welcome, enrol, sign up, induct, install, invest, ordain
▶ *n* member, recruit, entrant, learner, newcomer, novice, beginner, convert, catechumen, novitiate, neophyte, probationer, proselyte, tenderfoot, tiro, authority, expert, connoisseur, sage
colloq. greenhorn, rookie

initiation *n*
1 BEGINNING, start, origination, setting-up, launching, opening, inauguration
formal inception
2 ADMISSION, reception, entrance, entry, debut, introduction, admittance, enrolment, enlistment, induction, investiture, installation, ordination, inauguration, baptism, rite of passage

initiative *n*
1 ENTERPRISE, resourcefulness, inventiveness, originality, innovativeness, creativity, energy, drive, dynamism, ambition
colloq. get-up-and-go, go, push
2 SUGGESTION, recommendation, action, lead, first move, opening move, first step

inject *v*
1 *inject drugs*
inoculate, immunize, vaccinate, syringe
colloq. jab; *slang* shoot (up), mainline
2 INTRODUCE, insert, add, bring (in), infuse, instil

injection *n*
1 INOCULATION, immunization, vaccination, dose
colloq. jab, shot; *slang* fix
2 INTRODUCTION, insertion, addition, infusion, instilling

injudicious *adj*
ill-advised, ill-judged, inexpedient, ill-timed, unwise, inadvisable, incautious, inconsiderate, foolish, stupid, hasty, rash, misguided, unthinking, indiscreet, wrong-headed
formal impolitic, imprudent
F∃ wise, cautious; *formal* judicious, prudent

injunction *n*
command, order, directive, ruling, mandate, direction, instruction, precept, dictum, dictate
formal admonition

injure *v*
1 HURT, harm, damage, impair, spoil, mar, ruin, disfigure, deface, blemish, blight, weaken, undermine, mutilate, mangle, deform, wound, cut, break, fracture, maim, disable, cripple, lame
2 OFFEND, ill-treat, maltreat, abuse, wrong, upset, put out

injured *adj*
1 HURT, harmed, damaged, wounded, lame, disabled, crippled, weakened
2 OFFENDED, ill-treated, maltreated, misused, pained, put out, wronged, upset, unhappy, aggrieved, maligned, abused, defamed, insulted, grieved, displeased, disgruntled, cut to the quick

injurious *adj*
damaging, detrimental, harmful, hurtful, disadvantageous, destructive, prejudicial, unconducive, pernicious, adverse, corrupting, baneful, ruinous, unhealthy, unjust, bad, wrongful, insulting, libellous, slanderous
formal calumnious, deleterious, iniquitous, noxious
F∃ beneficial, favourable

injury *n*
1 WOUND, cut, bruise, sore, lesion, fracture, gash, abrasion, laceration, trauma, hurt, mischief, ill, harm, damage, impairment, ruin, disfigurement, mutilation
technical contusion
formal affliction
2 WRONG, ill-treatment, abuse, insult, grievance, offence, injustice

injustice *n*
unfairness, unjustness, wrong, injury, abuse, ill-treatment, offence, inequality, discrimination, oppression, bias, prejudice, one-sidedness, partisanship, partiality, favouritism
formal disparity, iniquity, inequity
F∃ justice, fairness

inkling *n*
suspicion, idea, notion, glimmering, clue, hint, intimation, insinuation, innuendo, suggestion, allusion, indication, sign, pointer
colloq. faintest, foggiest, whisper

inky *adj*
black, jet-black, coal-black, pitch-black, jet, sooty, dark-blue

inlaid *adj*
set, inset, enamelled, mosaic, tiled, lined, studded, enchased, damascened
formal tessellated, empaestic

inland *adj*
interior, inner, internal, central, domestic, up-country

inlay *n*
setting, inset, enamel, mosaic, tiling, lining, studding, damascene
formal tessellation, emblema

inlet *n*
bay, cove, bight, creek, fiord, firth, opening, entrance, passage, sound

inmate *n*
patient, prisoner, convict, detainee, case, client

inn *n*
public house, tavern, hostelry, hotel, bar
colloq. pub, local

innards *n*
1 *the innards of an animal*
insides, guts, internal organs, interior, intestines, entrails, entera, organs, umbles, viscera, vitals
2 *the innards of a machine*
works, mechanism, inner workings

innate *adj*
inborn, inbred, congenital, inherited, hereditary, inherent, intrinsic, native, indigenous, natural, instinctive, intuitive
formal connate
E3 acquired, learnt

inner *adj*
internal, interior, inside, inward, innermost, central, middle, concealed, obscure, hidden, secret, private, personal, intimate, restricted, mental, psychological, spiritual, emotional
formal esoteric
E3 outer, outward, revealed

innermost *adj*
deepest, deep, central, inmost, intimate, personal, dearest, private, secret, confidential, closest, essential, hidden, buried, basic
formal esoteric

innkeeper *n*
landlord, landlady, hotel-keeper, hotelier, publican, host, hostess, mine host, bar-keeper, restaurateur, innholder, padrone

innocence *n*
1 GUILTLESSNESS, blamelessness, irreproachability, unimpeachability, honesty, integrity, virtue, righteousness, sinlessness, faultlessness, impeccability, immaculateness, stainlessness, spotlessness, purity, chastity, virginity, incorruptibility
formal inculpability
2 ARTLESSNESS, guilelessness, ingenuousness, naïveness, naïvety, inexperience, ignorance, naturalness, simplicity, openness, frankness, unsophistication, unworldliness, childlikeness, credulity, gullibility, trustfulness
3 HARMLESSNESS, innocuousness, inoffensiveness, safety, playfulness
E3 **1** guilt **2** experience **3** harmfulness

innocent *adj, n*
▶ *adj* **1** *innocent of the crime*
guiltless, blameless, clear, irreproachable, above suspicion, unblameworthy, unimpeachable, honest, upright, virtuous, righteous, sinless, faultless, impeccable, stainless, spotless, immaculate, unsullied, unblemished, untainted, uncontaminated, pure, chaste, virginal, uncorrupted, incorrupt

formal inculpable
2 ARTLESS, guileless, ingenuous, naïve, inexperienced, fresh, natural, simple, open, frank, unsophisticated, unworldly, childlike, angelic, credulous, gullible, trusting, trustful
colloq. green, wet behind the ears, innocent as a newborn babe
3 HARMLESS, inoffensive, innocuous, safe, playful, unsuspicious
E3 **1** guilty, to blame **2** experienced, sophisticated **3** harmful, offensive
▶ *n* beginner, infant, novice, child, tenderfoot, babe, babe in arms, neophyte, ingénue, greenhorn
E3 connoisseur, expert

innocently *adv*
naïvely, artlessly, blamelessly, harmlessly, innocuously, inoffensively, unoffendingly, trustfully, trustingly, simply, ingenuously, credulously, unsuspiciously
colloq. like a lamb to the slaughter

innocuous *adj*
harmless, safe, inoffensive, unobjectionable, innocent, playful, mild, bland, unobtrusive
E3 harmful

innovation *n*
new product, new method, newness, novelty, neologism, introduction, modernization, progress, reform, change, alteration, variation, departure

innovative *adj*
new, fresh, original, creative, imaginative, inventive, resourceful, enterprising, go-ahead, progressive, reforming, bold, daring, adventurous
E3 conservative, unimaginative

innuendo *n*
insinuation, slur, whisper, hint, intimation, suggestion, implication, allusion, overtone
formal aspersion

innumerable *adj*
countless, uncountable, numerous, numberless, unnumbered, untold, incalculable, infinite, many
colloq. umpteen

inoculate *v*
immunize, vaccinate, inject, protect, safeguard
colloq. give a jab/shot to

inoculation *n*
vaccination, immunization, protection, injection
colloq. shot, jab

inoffensive *adj*
harmless, innocuous, safe, innocent, unobjectionable, peaceable, mild, bland, unobtrusive, unassertive, quiet, retiring
E3 offensive, harmful, provocative

inoperable *adj*
incurable, untreatable, unhealable, unremovable, irremovable, terminal, fatal, deadly, hopeless
formal intractable
E3 operable

inoperative *adj*
not working, not operative, out of order, out of action, out of service, out of commission, defective, broken, broken-down, non-functioning, unserviceable, unused, unworkable, useless, invalid, idle, ineffective, inadequate, inefficient, futile, worthless
formal ineffectual, inefficacious, nugatory
colloq. kaput
E3 working, operative

inopportune *adj*
untimely, inconvenient, unsuitable, inappropriate, tactless, ill-timed, ill-chosen, mistimed, wrong-timed, unfortunate, unseasonable, clumsy
formal inauspicious, infelicitous, unpropitious, infelicitous
🖪 opportune

inordinate *adj*
excessive, immoderate, extreme, exorbitant, unwarranted, unrestricted, unrestrained, undue, unreasonable, outrageous, preposterous, disproportionate, great
🖪 moderate, reasonable

input *v, n*
▶ *v* feed in, insert, key in, code, capture, process, store
▶ *n* information, data, facts, figures, statistics, material, details, particulars, resources
🖪 output

inquest *n*
inquiry, investigation, examination, hearing, post-mortem, inspection

inquietude *n*
uneasiness, restlessness, worry, anxiety, nervousness, agitation, unease, apprehension, discomposure, disquiet, jumpiness
formal disquietude, perturbation, solicitude
🖪 composure

inquire, enquire *v*
ask, question, quiz, query, investigate, look into, research, study, probe, examine, inspect, scrutinize, scan, search, explore, interrogate
colloq. snoop

inquirer, enquirer *n*
questioner, student, seeker, researcher, searcher, explorer, interrogator, investigator

inquiring, enquiring *adj*
inquisitive, interested, questioning, searching, curious, analytical, eager, investigative, investigatory, interrogatory, outward-looking, probing, prying, wondering, doubtful, sceptical
formal zetetic
colloq. nosy
🖪 incurious, unquestioning

inquiry, enquiry *n*
question, query, investigation, inquest, hearing, inquisition, interrogation, examination, inspection, scrutiny, study, survey, poll, search, probe, exploration, sounding, survey, reconnaissance

inquisition *n*
interrogation, cross-examination, cross-questioning, examination, investigation, questioning, quizzing, inquiry, inquest
colloq. grilling, third degree, witch hunt

inquisitive *adj*
curious, inquiring, questioning, probing, searching, scrutinizing, prying, peeping, peering, snooping, spying, nosy, interfering, meddlesome, intrusive
colloq. snoopy

inroad *n*
advance, progress, encroachment, foray, impingement, incursion, intrusion, trespassing, invasion, irruption, onslaught, attack, assault, offensive, charge, raid, sally, sortie, trespass

insane *adj*
1 MAD, crazy, mentally ill, lunatic, demented, deranged, unhinged, disturbed, out of your mind, *non compos mentis*
colloq. mental, crazy, loony, loopy, bonkers, nuts, nutty, nutty as a fruitcake, soft in the head, off your rocker, not all there, off your trolley, crackers, barmy, needing your head examining, round the bend, round the twist
2 FOOLISH, stupid, senseless, mad, crazy, impractical, idiotic, nonsensical, absurd, ridiculous
colloq. daft, potty, barmy
🖪 1 sane 2 sensible

insanitary *adj*
unhygienic, unsanitary, unclean, impure, unhealthy, unsanitized, dirty, dirtied, contaminated, polluted, infected, disease-ridden, filthy, foul, infested
formal unhealthful, noisome, noxious, insalubrious, feculent
🖪 sanitary, clean

insanity *n*
1 *suffer from insanity*
madness, craziness, lunacy, mental illness, neurosis, mania, dementia, delirium, frenzy, derangement
technical psychosis
2 FOLLY, madness, craziness, lunacy, foolishness, stupidity, senselessness, absurdity, ridiculousness, irresponsibility
colloq. daftness
🖪 1 sanity 2 sensibleness

insatiable *adj*
voracious, unquenchable, unsatisfiable, unappeasable, ravenous, hungry, greedy, gluttonous, craving, avid, immoderate, inordinate
formal rapacious

inscribe *v*
1 ENGRAVE, etch, carve, cut, incise, imprint, impress, stamp, brand, mark, print
2 WRITE, sign, enrol, enlist, register, record, address, autograph, dedicate

inscription *n*
engraving, etching, epitaph, caption, legend, lettering, words, writing, signature, autograph, message, dedication

inscrutable *adj*
incomprehensible, unfathomable, impenetrable, deep, unintelligible, inexplicable, unexplainable, unreadable, baffling, puzzling, mysterious, enigmatic, cryptic, hidden
formal arcane
🖪 comprehensible, expressive

insect *n*

Insects include: fly, gnat, midge, mosquito, tsetse-fly, locust, dragonfly, cranefly, *colloq.* daddy longlegs, horsefly, mayfly, butterfly, moth, bee, bumblebee, wasp, hornet, aphid, blackfly, greenfly, whitefly, froghopper, ladybird, water boatman, lacewing; beetle, cockroach, *US* roach, earwig, stick insect, grasshopper, cricket, cicada, flea, louse, nit, leatherjacket, termite, glowworm, woodworm, weevil, woodlouse.

Arachnids include: spider, black widow, tarantula, scorpion, mite, tick.

Parts of an insect: abdomen, antenna, cercus, compound eye, forewing, head, hindwing, legs, mandible, mouthpart, ocellus, ovipositor, segment, spiracle, thorax.

insecure *adj*
1 ANXIOUS, worried, nervous, uncertain, unsure, lacking confidence, afraid, apprehensive, fearful, hesitant, doubtful
2 UNSAFE, dangerous, hazardous, perilous, precarious, unsteady, unstable, shaky, loose, weak, frail, flimsy, unprotected, unguarded, defenceless, exposed, vulnerable, open to attack
E3 1 confident, self-assured 2 secure, safe, protected

insecurity *n*
1 ANXIETY, worry, nervousness, uncertainty, unsureness, apprehension, fear, uneasiness, lack of confidence
2 UNSAFETY, unsafeness, danger, hazard, peril, precariousness, unsteadiness, shakiness, instability, weakness, frailness, flimsiness, defencelessness, vulnerability
E3 1 confidence 2 safety, security

insensible *adj*
1 UNCONSCIOUS, anaesthetized, numb, senseless, unresponsive
formal insentient, comatose
colloq. out, zonked, knocked out, out for the count, dead to the world
2 UNAWARE, unconscious, oblivious, unmindful, ignorant, blind, deaf
3 CALLOUS, insensitive, unfeeling, emotionless, detached, untouched, unmoved, unaffected, cold, hard, aloof, distant
4 IMPERCEPTIBLE, indiscernible, indistinguishable, undetectable, unapparent, faint, slight
E3 1 conscious 2 aware, knowing 3 sensitive

insensitive *adj*
hardened, tough, resistant, impenetrable, impervious, immune, unsusceptible, thick-skinned, unfeeling, impassive, oblivious, indifferent, unaffected, unresponsive, unmoved, untouched, unsympathetic, uncaring, unconcerned, callous, heartless, thoughtless, tactless, crass
technical hypalgesic
E3 sensitive, responsive, affected

insensitivity *n*
hardness, toughness, resistance, impenetrability, imperviousness, immunity, unresponsiveness, hard-headedness, unconcern, bluntness, callousness, indifference, tactlessness, crassness, obtuseness
technical hypalgesia, hypalgia
E3 sensitivity, responsiveness

inseparable *adj*
indivisible, indissoluble, undividable, inextricable, close, intimate, bosom, constant, devoted
E3 separable

insert *v, n*
▶ *v* put, place, press, put in, enclose, stick in, push in, thrust in, slide in, slip in, introduce, enter, implant, embed, engraft, infix, inlay, set, inset, let in, interleave, interject
formal interpose, interpolate, intercalate
▶ *n* insertion, enclosure, inset, notice, advertisement, circular, supplement, addition, inlay

insertion *n*
addition, entry, inclusion, insert, inset, introduction, implant, supplement, intrusion
formal intercalation, interpolation, intromission

inside *n, adv, adj*
▶ *n* interior, content, contents, middle, centre, heart, core
colloq. guts, belly
E3 outside
▶ *adv* within, indoors, internally, inwardly, secretly, privately
E3 outside
▶ *adj* 1 INTERIOR, internal, inner, implicit, inherent, intrinsic, innermost, inward
2 SECRET, classified, confidential, internal, private, restricted, reserved

insider *n*
member, participant, staff member, co-worker
colloq. one of us, one of the in-crowd

insides *n*
internal organs, entrails, guts, intestines, bowels, organs, viscera, belly, stomach, abdomen
colloq. innards

insidious *adj*
subtle, sly, crafty, cunning, wily, artful, deceptive, deceitful, dishonest, devious, stealthy, surreptitious, furtive, sneaking, sneaky, tricky, treacherous, insincere, Machiavellian
formal duplicitous, perfidious
E3 direct, straightforward

insight *n*
awareness, knowledge, comprehension, understanding, realization, grasp, apprehension, perception, intuition, sensitivity, discernment, judgement, acumen, penetration, sharpness, shrewdness, observation, vision, wisdom, intelligence
formal perspicacity

insightful *adj*
perceptive, astute, sharp, shrewd, observant, penetrating, understanding, acute, discerning, intelligent, knowledgeable, wise
formal perspicacious, prudent, sagacious, percipient
E3 superficial

insignia *n*
emblem, badge, regalia, crest, sign(s), ensign, medallion, ribbon, decoration, mark, hallmark(s), symbol, trademark, brand

insignificance *n*
unimportance, irrelevance, meaninglessness, immateriality, inconsequence, inconsequentiality, negligibility, smallness, pettiness, paltriness, tininess, insubstantiality, triviality, meanness, worthlessness
formal nugatoriness
E3 significance

insignificant *adj*
unimportant, irrelevant, meaningless, immaterial, inconsequential, minor, trivial, trifling, petty, paltry, meagre, scanty, slight, small, tiny, insubstantial, inconsiderable, negligible, non-essential, peripheral, not worth mentioning
formal nugatory
colloq. piddling, cutting no ice, no great shakes, small-time
E3 significant, important

insincere *adj*
hypocritical, two-faced, double-dealing, lying, untruthful, dishonest, deceitful, underhand, devious, unfaithful, faithless, disloyal, untrue, treacherous, false, feigned, pretended, hollow
formal mendacious, disingenuous, dissembling, duplicitous, perfidious
colloq. phoney
ᴱᴬ sincere, genuine

insincerity *n*
hypocrisy, untruthfulness, dishonesty, deceitfulness, deviousness, pretence, hollowness, falseness, falsity, faithlessness, artificiality, cant, evasiveness
formal disingenuousness, dissembling, dissimulation, duplicity, mendacity, perfidy
colloq. phoniness, humbug, lip service
ᴱᴬ sincerity

insinuate *v*
imply, suggest, allude, hint, mention, intimate, indicate
colloq. get at, whisper
▷ **insinuate yourself** curry favour, get in with, ingratiate, sidle, work, worm, wriggle

insinuation *n*
suggestion, implication, allusion, hint, intimation, introduction, slant, slur, innuendo
formal aspersion

insipid *adj*
tasteless, flavourless, unsavoury, unappetizing, watery, weak, thin, bland, anaemic, colourless, drab, dull, monotonous, boring, tedious, wearisome, uninteresting, tame, flat, lifeless, inanimate, spiritless, vapid, characterless, trite, banal, unimaginative, dry
old use jejune
colloq. wishy-washy
ᴱᴬ tasty, spicy, piquant, appetizing

insist *v*
demand, require, urge, entreat, stress, emphasize, repeat, reiterate, dwell on, harp on, assert, declare, state firmly, ask for firmly, maintain, claim, contend, hold, vow, swear, persist, stand firm, stand your ground, refuse to accept an alternative
formal aver
colloq. put your foot down, not take no for an answer

insistence *n*
demand, requirement, entreaty, urging, stress, emphasis, repetition, reiteration, maintenance, assertion, declaration, claim, contention, persistence, determination, resolution, firmness
formal exhortation

insistent *adj*
demanding, importunate, emphatic, resolute, determined, emphatic, adamant, forceful, pressing, urgent, dogged, tenacious, persistent, persevering, constant, repeated, relentless, unrelenting, unremitting, unyielding, inexorable, incessant
formal importunate, exigent

insobriety *n*
drunkenness, hard drinking, intemperance, inebriation, inebriety, intoxication
formal crapulence
colloq. tipsiness
ᴱᴬ sobriety

insolence *n*
rudeness, abuse, insults, impudence, impertinence, arrogance, audacity, boldness, forwardness, pertness, presumption, presumptuousness, disrespect, contemptuousness, defiance, insubordination, offensiveness, incivility
formal hubris, effrontery, contumely
colloq. cheek, cheekiness, sauce, sauciness, gall, nerve, lip, mouth, chutzpah
ᴱᴬ politeness, respect

insolent *adj*
rude, abusive, insulting, disrespectful, ill-mannered, impertinent, impudent, bold, audacious, brazen, brash, forward, presumptuous, arrogant, defiant, contemptuous, insubordinate
colloq. cheeky, saucy, fresh
ᴱᴬ polite, respectful

insoluble *adj*
unsolvable, unexplainable, inexplicable, incomprehensible, unfathomable, impenetrable, inscrutable, enigmatic, indecipherable, complex, intricate, involved, obscure, mysterious, mystifying, puzzling, perplexing, baffling
ᴱᴬ explicable

insolvency *n*
bankruptcy, default, failure, liquidation, ruin, indebtedness, destitution, impoverishment, pennilessness
formal impecuniosity
ᴱᴬ solvency

insolvent *adj*
bankrupt, failed, in debt, liquidated, ruined, penniless, impoverished, destitute
formal impecunious
colloq. bust, broke, skint, strapped (for cash), on your beam ends, gone to the wall, gone under, in the red, on the rocks, in queer street
ᴱᴬ solvent

insomnia *n*
sleeplessness, restlessness, wakefulness
formal insomnolence
ᴱᴬ sleep

insouciance *n*
nonchalance, unconcern, carefreeness, heedlessness, indifference, light-heartedness, flippancy, airiness, breeziness, jauntiness, ease
ᴱᴬ anxiety, care

insouciant *adj*
nonchalant, unconcerned, untroubled, unworried, indifferent, heedless, carefree, casual, easy-going, free and easy, flippant, happy-go-lucky, airy, breezy, buoyant, jaunty, light-hearted
ᴱᴬ anxious, careworn

inspect *v*
check, vet, look over, go over, pore over, examine, search, investigate, appraise, assess, audit, scrutinize, study, scan, survey, view, superintend, supervise, oversee, visit, reconnoitre, see over, tour

inspection *n*
check, check-up, examination, scrutiny, scan, study, survey, review, search, investigation, vetting, analysis, appraisal, assessment, audit, supervision, visit, tour
colloq. once-over, look-over, recce, dekko

inspector *n*
supervisor, superintendent, overseer, surveyor, controller, appraiser, assessor, auditor, scrutineer, scanner, checker, tester, examiner, investigator, reviewer, critic, visitor

inspiration *n*

1 CREATIVITY, originality, imagination, genius, inventiveness, muse, influence, encouragement, stimulation, incitement, stirring, arousing, motivation, spur, goad, stimulus, fillip
2 IDEA, bright idea, stroke of genius, brainwave, insight, illumination, revelation, enlightenment, awakening

inspire *v*

encourage, hearten, influence, impress, animate, breathe, enliven, quicken, energize, galvanize, fire, kindle, inflame, stir, arouse, rouse, trigger, instigate, produce, bring about, spark off, touch off, prompt, spur, goad, motivate, provoke, stimulate, excite, exhilarate, thrill, enthral, enthuse, imbue, infuse

inspired *adj*

brilliant, impressive, superlative, wonderful, outstanding, exciting, dazzling, memorable, thrilling, enthralling, marvellous, exceptional, splendid, remarkable
Ｅ dull, uninspired

inspiring *adj*

encouraging, heartening, uplifting, invigorating, stirring, rousing, interesting, enthusiastic, invigorating, stimulating, exciting, exhilarating, thrilling, enthralling, moving, affecting, memorable, impressive
Ｅ uninspiring, dull

inspirit *v*

encourage, inspire, move, stimulate, nerve, hearten, invigorate, quicken, refresh, reinvigorate, enliven, exhilarate, fire, galvanize, incite, animate, rouse, cheer, gladden, embolden

instability *n*

unsteadiness, shakiness, vacillation, wavering, oscillation, irresolution, uncertainty, impermanence, transience, unpredictability, changeableness, variability, fluctuation, volatility, capriciousness, flightiness, fitfulness, fickleness, inconstancy, unreliability, insecurity, precariousness, unsafeness, unsoundness, flimsiness, frailty
Ｅ stability

install *v*

1 *install a new phone system*
fix, fit, lay, put (in), insert, place, position, locate, lodge, site, situate, station, plant, settle, establish, set up, introduce
2 *install her as president*
institute, inaugurate, invest, induct, ordain, consecrate, instate

installation *n*

1 FITTING, insertion, positioning, location, placing, siting
2 EQUIPMENT, machinery, plant, system
3 *her installation as president*
inauguration, investiture, instatement, induction, consecration, ordination
4 *a military installation*
base, station, post, centre, site, settlement, establishment, headquarters

instalment *n*

1 *pay in instalments*
payment, part payment, repayment, portion, hire purchase
2 EPISODE, chapter, part, section, division, portion, segment

instance *n, v*

▶ *n* **1** *several instances of bullying*
case, example, illustration, exemplification, case in point, citation, occurrence, occasion, sample
2 *at his instance*
request, urging, incitement, demand, initiative, insistence, entreaty, instigation, pressure, prompting, solicitation
formal behest, exhortation, importunity
▶ *v* mention, quote, refer to, specify, give, name, cite, point to, exemplify
formal adduce

instant *n, adj*

▶ *n* flash, twinkling, trice, moment, split second, second, minute, time, occasion, juncture
colloq. tick, jiffy, twinkling of an eye, two shakes of a lamb's tail
▶ *adj* **1** INSTANTANEOUS, immediate, on-the-spot, direct, prompt, urgent, unhesitating, quick, fast, rapid, swift
2 *instant food*
quickly prepared, easily prepared, ready mixed, convenience
Ｅ **1** slow

instantaneous *adj*

immediate, instant, direct, prompt, rapid, unhesitating, sudden, on-the-spot
Ｅ eventual

instantaneously *adv*

at once, directly, forthwith, immediately, right away, instantly, on the spot, promptly, speedily, quickly, rapidly, straight away, there and then, unhesitatingly, without hesitation, without delay
colloq. pronto, before you can say Jack Robinson, in two shakes of a lamb's tail
Ｅ eventually

instantly *adv*

immediately, instantaneously, at once, right away, straight away, there and then, forthwith, now, on the spot, without delay, directly
colloq. pronto
Ｅ eventually

instead *adv*

alternatively, preferably, rather, else, by/in contrast, as an alternative, substitute, replacement
▷ **instead of** as opposed to, in contrast to, in place of, in lieu of, on behalf of, in preference to, in favour of, as an alternative to, rather than

instigate *v*

initiate, set on, start, begin, cause, bring about, induce, press, generate, inspire, move, influence, persuade, encourage, urge, spur, prod, goad, prompt, provoke, stimulate, kindle, incite, stir up, whip up, foment, rouse, excite
colloq. egg on

instigation *n*

initiation, incitement, initiative, encouragement, prompting, urging, inducement, insistence, incentive, bidding
formal behest

instigator *n*

leader, motivator, prime mover, provoker, ringleader, spur, goad, incendiary, inciter, mischief-maker, troublemaker, *agent provocateur*, agitator, fomenter, firebrand

instil *v*
infuse, imbue, insinuate, introduce, inject, implant, inculcate, impress, teach, drill
colloq. din into

instinct *n*
1 NATURAL RESPONSE, inbred response, intuition, sixth sense, impulse, urge, drive, feeling, hunch, tendency
formal predisposition
colloq. gut feeling/reaction
2 FLAIR, knack, gift, talent, bent, feel, faculty, ability, aptitude

instinctive *adj*
natural, native, inborn, innate, inherent, intuitive, impulsive, involuntary, unintentional, automatic, mechanical, reflex, spontaneous, immediate, unlearned, untaught, unthinking, unpremeditated, visceral
colloq. gut
◘ conscious, voluntary, deliberate

instinctively *adv*
intuitively, naturally, spontaneously, unthinkingly, without thinking, automatically, involuntarily, mechanically
◘ consciously, deliberately, voluntarily

institute *v, n*
▶ *v* **1** START, originate, initiate, introduce, enact, begin, create, establish, develop, set up, organize, found, inaugurate, open, launch
formal commence
2 APPOINT, install, invest, induct, ordain, initiate
◘ **1** cancel, abolish; *formal* discontinue
▶ *n* **1** *an institute for advanced research*
school, college, academy, conservatory, seminary, foundation, institution, organization
2 LAW, principle, rule, custom, regulation, decree

institution *n*
1 ORGANIZATION, association, society, guild, league, club, concern, corporation, foundation, establishment, institute, hospital, home, centre
2 CUSTOM, tradition, usage, practice, ritual, convention, rule, law, system
3 INITIATION, starting, introduction, enactment, creation, establishment, setting-up, formation, creation, founding, foundation, installation
formal commencement, inception

institutional *adj*
established, organized, establishment, accepted, customary, conventional, formal, methodical, orderly, systematic, orthodox, regimented, set, routine, uniform, ritualistic, bureaucratic, clinical, impersonal, cold, unwelcoming, dreary, dull, drab, forbidding, monotonous, cheerless
◘ individualistic, unconventional

instruct *v*
1 TEACH, educate, tutor, coach, train, drill, ground, school, discipline, prime, prepare
2 ORDER, command, direct, demand, require, charge, mandate, tell, inform, notify, make known, advise, counsel, guide, enlighten
formal enjoin, bid

instruction *n*
1 *give someone instructions*
order, direction, recommendation, advice, guidance, information, charge, command, requirement, injunction, mandate, directive, ruling, briefing

2 EDUCATION, schooling, lesson(s), classes, tuition, tutoring, tutelage, teaching, training, coaching, drilling, grounding, preparation, priming, guidance, enlightenment
3 *read the instructions carefully*
directions, orders, recommendations, rules, brief, information, advice, key, legend, guidance, guidelines, book of words, handbook, manual

instructive *adj*
informative, educational, educative, doctrinal, uplifting, edifying, enlightening, illuminating, helpful, useful
◘ unenlightening

instructor *n*
teacher, lecturer, educator, master, mistress, tutor, coach, trainer, demonstrator, exponent, adviser, mentor, guide, pedagogue, counsellor, guru

instrument *n*
1 TOOL, implement, utensil, appliance, gadget, contraption, device, contrivance, apparatus, mechanism
colloq. gismo
2 GAUGE, meter, measure, indicator, rule, guideline, yardstick
3 AGENT, agency, vehicle, organ, medium, factor, channel, way, means
See also panels at **measuring instruments; musical instruments**.

instrumental *adj*
active, involved, contributory, conducive, influential, important, significant, useful, helpful, auxiliary, subsidiary
◘ obstructive, unhelpful

insubordinate *adj*
disobedient, rebellious, defiant, ungovernable, unruly, disorderly, undisciplined, rude, riotous, seditious, insurgent, mutinous, turbulent, impertinent, impudent,
formal contumacious, recalcitrant, refractory
◘ docile, obedient, compliant

insubordination *n*
disobedience, defiance, rebellion, insurrection, mutinousness, mutiny, revolt, riotousness, sedition, rudeness, ungovernability, indiscipline, impertinence, impudence
formal recalcitrance
◘ docility, obedience, compliance

insubstantial *adj*
1 FLIMSY, frail, feeble, weak, tenuous, poor, slight, thin
2 UNREAL, false, illusory, fanciful, imaginary, idle, vaporous, immaterial, incorporeal, moonshine
formal chimerical, ephemeral
◘ **1** solid, strong **2** real

insufferable *adj*
intolerable, unbearable, unendurable, detestable, loathsome, revolting, dreadful, shocking, outrageous, impossible, too much to bear, more than you can bear
◘ pleasant, tolerable

insufficiency *n*
inadequacy, shortage, deficiency, lack, scarcity, dearth, need, poverty, short supply
formal want
◘ sufficiency, excess

insufficient *adj*
inadequate, not enough, short, deficient, lacking, wanting, meagre, sparse, scanty, scant, scarce, in short supply
🔄 sufficient, enough, excessive

insular *adj*
parochial, provincial, cut off, detached, isolated, remote, withdrawn, separate, solitary, insulated, inward-looking, blinkered, closed, narrow-minded, narrow, limited, restricted, petty, bigoted, biased, prejudiced, xenophobic
colloq. parish-pump
🔄 open-minded

insularity *n*
isolation, detachment, narrow-mindedness, solitariness, pettiness, parochiality, parochialness, bigotry, bias, prejudice, xenophobia
🔄 open-mindedness, openness

insulate *v*
insulate water pipes; people insulated from outside influences
cushion, pad, lag, cocoon, protect, wrap, cover, shield, shelter, isolate, separate, cut off, exclude, detach, segregate, encase, envelop
formal sequester

insulation *n*
cushioning, padding, lagging, cladding, cocooning, protection, wrapping, cover, covering, stuffing, shield, shelter, isolation, separation, exclusion, detachment, segregation

insult *v, n*
▶ *v* abuse, call names, taunt, ridicule, bait, rebuff, libel, slander, malign, slight, slur, snub, injure, hurt, wound, offend, outrage, mortify
formal affront, disparage, revile, impugn, calumniate, traduce
colloq. kick in the teeth, slap in the face, give the cold shoulder
🔄 compliment, praise
▶ *n* abuse, rudeness, insolence, gibe, taunt, defamation, libel, slander, slight, slur, barb, snub, indignity, offence, outrage
formal affront, aspersions, disparagement, revilement
colloq. put-down, backhanded compliment, cold shoulder
🔄 compliment, praise

insulting *adj*
offensive, abusive, rude, hurtful, injurious, contemptuous, degrading, slighting, outrageous, insolent, scurrilous, libellous, slanderous
formal affronting, disparaging, reviling
🔄 complimentary, respectful

insuperable *adj*
insurmountable, formidable, overwhelming, invincible, unconquerable, unassailable, impassable
🔄 surmountable

insupportable *adj*
intolerable, unbearable, unendurable, insufferable, dreadful, loathsome, hateful, detestable, unacceptable, untenable, unjustifiable, indefensible
🔄 bearable

insuppressible *adj*
irrepressible, lively, unstoppable, uncontrollable, ungovernable, unruly, unsubduable, obstreperous, incorrigible, energetic

colloq. go-getting
🔄 suppressible

insurance *n*
cover, protection, assurance, safeguard, security, surety, provision, assurance, indemnity, guarantee, indemnification, warranty, policy, premium

insure *v*
cover, protect, assure, underwrite, indemnify, guarantee, warrant

insurer *n*
assurer, underwriter, protector, indemnifier, guarantor, warrantor

insurgent *n, adj*
▶ *n* rebel, revolter, revolutionary, rioter, insurrectionist, seditionist, mutineer, partisan, revolutionist, resister
▶ *adj* rebellious, revolting, revolutionary, mutinous, riotous, seditious, disobedient, insubordinate, insurrectionary, partisan

insurmountable *adj*
insuperable, unconquerable, invincible, unassailable, overwhelming, hopeless, impossible
🔄 surmountable

insurrection *n*
rising, uprising, insurgence, riot, rebellion, mutiny, revolt, revolution, sedition, coup, *coup d'état*, putsch

intact *adj*
unbroken, (all) in one piece, whole, complete, integral, entire, perfect, faultless, flawless, sound, undamaged, unharmed, unhurt, uninjured, unscathed
🔄 broken, incomplete, damaged

intangible *adj*
insubstantial, imponderable, elusive, fleeting, airy, unclear, shadowy, vague, subtle, obscure, indefinite, undefinable, indescribable, abstract, unreal, invisible, immeasurable
🔄 tangible, real

integral *adj*
1 *an integral part*
intrinsic, constituent, component, inherent, elemental, basic, fundamental, necessary, essential, indispensable
formal requisite
2 COMPLETE, entire, full, whole, total, undivided, intact
🔄 1 extra, additional, unnecessary

integrate *v*
assimilate, merge, join, unite, combine, amalgamate, consolidate, incorporate, coalesce, fuse, knit, mesh, mix, intermix, mingle, blend, homogenize, harmonize, desegregate
🔄 divide, separate, segregate

integrated *adj*
mixed, desegregated, assimilated, merged, joined, unified, unseparated, united, combined, amalgamated, consolidated, incorporated, coalesced, fused, meshed, mingled, blended, harmonized, harmonious, cohesive, connected, interrelated
colloq. part and parcel
🔄 unintegrated, segregated

integration *n*
assimilation, merger, unity, unification, combination, amalgamation, consolidation, incorporation, fusion,

blend, harmony, mix, desegregation
ⓔ separation, segregation

integrity n
1 HONESTY, uprightness, incorruptibility, purity, morality, principle, sincerity, honour, decency, virtue, goodness, fairness, righteousness, truthfulness
formal probity, rectitude
2 COMPLETENESS, wholeness, unity, entirety, totality, coherence, cohesion, unification
ⓔ 1 dishonesty 2 incompleteness

intellect n
1 *a person of considerable intellect*
mind, brain(s), brainpower, brilliance, intelligence, genius, reason, thought, understanding, comprehension, sense, wisdom, judgement
2 THINKER, academic, highbrow, mastermind, genius, intellectual
colloq. egghead
ⓔ 1 stupidity

intellectual adj, n
▶ *adj* academic, scholarly, intelligent, studious, learned, thoughtful, mental, logical, highbrow, bookish, cultural, well-educated, well-read
formal cerebral, erudite
ⓔ low-brow
▶ *n* thinker, academic, highbrow, mastermind, genius, intellect
colloq. egghead
ⓔ low-brow

intelligence n
1 INTELLECT, reason, wit(s), brainpower, cleverness, brightness, brilliance, aptitude, quickness, alertness, sharpness, acumen, discernment, perception, thought, understanding, comprehension
colloq. brain(s), grey matter, little grey cells, nous
2 INFORMATION, facts, data, knowledge, findings, notification, news, report, notice, account, rumour, warning, advice
colloq. low-down, tip-off, gen, dope
3 SURVEILLANCE, spying, espionage, observation
ⓔ 1 stupidity, foolishness

intelligent adj
clever, bright, smart, brilliant, quick, alert, quick-witted, sharp, acute, discerning, perceptive, knowing, knowledgeable, well-informed, thinking, educated, rational, sensible
formal perspicacious, sagacious
colloq. brainy, quick on the uptake, no flies on someone, knowing a thing or two, knowing how many beans make five, using your loaf, all there
ⓔ unintelligent, stupid, foolish

intelligentsia n
academics, intellectuals, cognoscenti, literati, highbrows, illuminati
colloq. brains, eggheads

intelligibility n
comprehensibility, comprehensibleness, clearness, clarity, plainness, lucidity, lucidness, explicitness, distinctness, legibility, precision, simplicity
ⓔ unintelligibility

intelligible adj
comprehensible, understandable, clear, plain, lucid, distinct, open, explicit, legible, decipherable, fathomable, penetrable
ⓔ unintelligible

intemperance n
excess, immoderation, self-indulgence, overindulgence, unrestraint, extravagance, drunkenness, intoxication, insobriety, licence
formal crapulence, inebriation
ⓔ temperance

intemperate adj
extreme, immoderate, inordinate, unrestrained, unbridled, uncontrolled, uncontrollable, irrestrainable, ungovernable, severe, violent, wild, tempestuous, passionate, excessive, unreasonable, extravagant, self-indulgent, drunken, intoxicated, dissolute, incontinent, prodigal, licentious, profligate
formal inebriated
colloq. over the top
ⓔ temperate

intend v
aim, have a mind, have in mind, contemplate, mean, be going, be looking, propose, choose, plan, project, scheme, devise, plot, design, expect, purpose, determine, be determined, destine, mark out, earmark, set apart
formal resolve

intended adj, n
▶ *adj* designated, destined, deliberate, intentional, planned, proposed, designate, future, prospective, betrothed
ⓔ accidental
▶ *n* fiancé, fiancée, husband-to-be, wife-to-be, betrothed

intense adj
1 EXTREME, great, deep, profound, strong, powerful, vigorous, potent, forceful, fierce, harsh, severe, acute, sharp, keen, enthusiastic, zealous, eager, earnest, ardent, fervent, excited, passionate, impassioned, vehement, consuming, burning, energetic, violent, intensive, concentrated, heightened
formal fervid
2 *an intense person*
serious, thoughtful, impassioned, emotional, tense, nervous, heavy
ⓔ 1 moderate, mild, weak 2 easy-going

⚠ **intense** or **intensive** ?
Intense means 'very great': *the intense heat from the furnace; intense bitterness. Intensive* means 'concentrated, thorough, taking great care': *an intense search; the intensive care ward of a hospital.*

intensely adv
extremely, deeply, very, strongly, greatly, profoundly, fiercely, ardently, fervently, passionately
colloq. with a vengeance
ⓔ mildly

intensification n
increase, stepping-up, strengthening, reinforcement, magnification, escalation, heightening, building-up, build-up, boost, aggravation, acceleration, worsening, deepening, concentration, emphasis, enhancement
formal augmentation, exacerbescence
ⓔ lessening

intensify v
increase, step up, build up, escalate, heighten, maximize, fire, boost, fuel, fan, aggravate, worsen, add to, broaden, widen, strengthen, reinforce, magnify, sharpen, whet, quicken, deepen, concentrate, emphasize, enhance

formal augment, exacerbate
colloq. hot up, bump up, hike up, add fuel to the flames, bring to a head
🔄 reduce, weaken

intensity *n*
greatness, extremity, intenseness, depth, profundity, strength, power, vigour, potency, force, fierceness, severity, acuteness, keenness, eagerness, earnestness, ardour, enthusiasm, zeal, fanaticism, fervency, fervour, fire, emotion, passion, concentration, energy, vehemence, strain, tension

intensive *adj*
concentrated, thorough, exhaustive, comprehensive, detailed, in-depth, thoroughgoing, all-out, intense
🔄 superficial

⚠ **intensive** or **intense** ? *See panel at* **intense**.

intent *adj, n*
▶ *adj* 1 *intent on doing something*
determined, resolved, set, bent, eager, keen, committed, firm
2 *an intent look*
attentive, alert, concentrating, fixed, close, hard, keen, absorbed, occupied, wrapped up, focused, engrossed, preoccupied, steady, rapt, enrapt, searching, watchful
🔄 **2** absent-minded, distracted
▶ *n* intention, purpose, meaning, objective, plan, aim, goal, target, point, idea, view, design, object, end
▷ **to all intents and purposes** almost, nearly, practically, virtually, more or less, just about, as good as, pretty much, pretty well

intention *n*
aim, purpose, object, end, point, target, goal, objective, idea, plan, design, view, intent, meaning, ambition, wish, aspiration

intentional *adj*
designed, wilful, conscious, planned, purposeful, deliberate, prearranged, premeditated, preconceived, considered, calculated, studied, intended, weighed-up, meant, on purpose
🔄 unintentional, accidental

intentionally *adv*
deliberately, on purpose, wilfully, by design, designedly, meaningly, with malice aforethought
🔄 accidentally

intently *adv*
attentively, watchfully, carefully, closely, steadily, searchingly, staringly, fixedly, hard, keenly
🔄 absent-mindedly

inter *v*
bury, lay to rest, entomb, inearth, sepulchre, inhume
formal inurn
🔄 exhume

interbreed *v*
cross, crossbreed, cross-fertilize, mongrelize, hybridize, reproduce together
formal miscegenate

interbreeding *n*
cross-breeding, crossing, hybridization
formal miscegenation

intercede *v*
mediate, arbitrate, intervene, plead, speak, petition, negotiate
formal entreat, beseech, interpose

intercept *v*
head off, ambush, interrupt, deflect, cut off, stop, arrest, catch, commandeer, take, seize, check, block, impede, obstruct, delay, frustrate, thwart

intercession *n*
mediation, arbitration, negotiation, intervention, plea, pleading, advocacy, agency, solicitation, prayer, good offices
formal beseeching, entreaty, supplication, interposition

interchange *n, v*
▶ *n* **1** EXCHANGE, trading, barter, swap, alternation, reciprocation, interplay, crossfire
colloq. give-and-take
2 INTERSECTION, junction, crossroad(s), crossing
▶ *v* exchange, swap, switch, alternate, reciprocate, replace, substitute, trade, barter, transpose, reverse

interchangeable *adj*
reciprocal, exchangeable, transposable, equivalent, corresponding, comparable, similar, identical, the same, synonymous, standard
🔄 different

intercourse *n*
1 *sexual intercourse*
sex, sexual relations, intimacy, intimate relations, love-making, copulation, carnal knowledge, sleeping with someone, going to bed with someone, the sex act
colloq. sleeping with someone, going to bed with someone, it, nookie; *taboo slang* fuck, screw, bonk, bang, shag
formal coition, coitus
2 ASSOCIATION, communication, communion, contact, connection, dealings, conversation, converse, correspondence, commerce, trade, intercommunication, congress, traffic

interdict *v, n*
▶ *v* ban, bar, debar, forbid, prohibit, prevent, embargo, rule out, veto, outlaw
formal disallow, preclude, proscribe
🔄 allow
▶ *n* ban, injunction, prohibition, bar, embargo, taboo, veto
formal disallowance, interdiction, proscription, preclusion
🔄 permission

interest *n, v*
▶ *n* **1** *have an interest in dance*
curiosity, inquisitiveness, concern, care, attention, attentiveness, notice, regard, heed, charm, allure, appeal, attraction, fascination, involvement, engagement
2 IMPORTANCE, significance, consequence, moment, consideration, magnitude, relevance, prominence, weight, value, note, urgency, priority, seriousness, gravity
3 *leisure interests*
activity, pursuit, pastime, hobby, diversion, recreation, amusement
4 ADVANTAGE, good, benefit, profit, gain
5 *business interests*
share, stake, concern, business, claim, involvement, participation, portion, investment, stock, equity
6 *earn interest*
dividend, return, profit, gain, receipts, revenue, proceeds, credits, bonus, premium, percentage
🔄 **1** boredom **2** meaninglessness **4** loss
▷ **in the interests of** for the sake of, on behalf of,

to the advantage of, for the benefit of
▶ *v* concern, involve, touch, move, attract, appeal to, divert, amuse, occupy, engage, rivet, absorb, engross, fascinate, intrigue, captivate, grip
Ea bore

interested *adj*
1 ATTENTIVE, curious, absorbed, engrossed, fascinated, intent, captivated, gripped, enthralled, riveted, intrigued, enthusiastic, keen, attracted
colloq. having the ... bug
2 CONCERNED, involved, affected, implicated
Ea **1** uninterested, indifferent, apathetic
2 disinterested, unaffected

interesting *adj*
attractive, appealing, entertaining, engaging, absorbing, engrossing, exciting, fascinating, captivating, intriguing, compelling, compulsive, gripping, riveting, stimulating, thought-provoking, amusing, curious, unusual
colloq. unputdownable
Ea uninteresting, boring, monotonous, tedious

interfere *v*
1 INTRUDE, pry, interrupt, intervene, meddle, tamper
colloq. poke/stick your nose in, stick/put your oar in, put in your two pennyworth, muscle in on, butt in; *US* put in your two cents' worth
2 HINDER, hamper, obstruct, block, check, impede, handicap, cramp, inhibit, trammel, balk, thwart, conflict, clash
colloq. get in the way of
3 MOLEST, abuse, assault, sexually assault, attack, rape
Ea **1** *colloq.* mind your own business **2** assist

interference *n*
1 INTRUSION, prying, interruption, intervention, meddling, meddlesomeness
2 OBSTRUCTION, hindrance, hampering, blocking, checking, impediment, handicap, inhibiting, trammel(s), thwarting, opposition, conflict, clashing
Ea **2** assistance

interim *adj, n*
▶ *adj* temporary, provisional, stopgap, makeshift, improvised, stand-in, acting, caretaker
colloq. pro tem
▶ *n* meantime, meanwhile, interval, interregnum

interior *adj, n*
▶ *adj* **1** INTERNAL, inside, inner, innermost, central, inward, intrinsic
2 *interior thoughts*
inner, mental, personal, private, intimate, spiritual, emotional, psychological, secret, hidden, involuntary, spontaneous, impulsive, intuitive, instinctive, innate
3 HOME, domestic, central, local, inland, up-country, remote
Ea **1** exterior, external **3** external, coastal
▶ *n* inside, inside part, centre, middle, core, heart, nucleus, depths
Ea exterior, outside

interject *v*
cry, shout, call, utter, introduce, interrupt, exclaim
formal ejaculate, interpose, interpolate

interjection *n*
exclamation, cry, shout, call, utterance, interruption
formal ejaculation, interpolation

interlace *v*
entwine, braid, twine, knit, plait, cross, enlace, interweave, interlock, intertwine, intermix, intersperse, interwreathe
formal reticulate

interlink *v*
link, link together, interconnect, lock together, interlock, mesh, knit, intergrow, intertwine, interweave, clasp together
Ea separate, divide

interlock *v*
lock together, interconnect, link, link together, mesh, clasp together, intertwine
formal interdigitate

interloper *n*
intruder, uninvited guest, trespasser, encroacher, invader
colloq. gate-crasher

interlude *n*
interval, intermission, break, breathing-space, pause, rest, recess, stop, stoppage, respite, wait, delay, halt, spell
formal hiatus
colloq. breather, let-up

intermediary *n*
mediator, go-between, negotiator, arbitrator, middleman, broker, agent

intermediate *adj*
midway, halfway, in-between, middle, mid, median, medial, mean, intermediary, intervening, transitional
Ea extreme

interment *n*
burial, burying, funeral
formal inhumation, exequies, obsequies, obsequy, sepulture
Ea exhumation

interminable *adj*
endless, never-ending, perpetual, limitless, boundless, unlimited, without end, everlasting, eternal, long, long-winded, long-drawn-out, dragging, wearisome, tedious, boring, dull, monotonous
formal ceaseless, prolix, loquacious
Ea limited, brief

intermingle *v*
mix, mix together, merge, blend, amalgamate, combine, fuse, interlace, interweave, mix up
formal commingle, commix, intermix
Ea separate

intermission *n*
interval, interlude, break, recess, rest, respite, breathing-space, pause, lull, remission, suspension, interruption, halt, stop, stoppage
formal cessation
colloq. breather, let-up

intermittent *adj*
occasional, periodic, sporadic, spasmodic, fitful, erratic, irregular, cyclic, broken, off and on
formal discontinuous
Ea continuous, constant

intern *v*
confine, detain, hold, hold in custody, jail, imprison
Ea free, release

internal *adj*
1 INSIDE, inner, interior, inward

2 HOME, domestic, in-house, local
3 *internal processes of the mind*
subjective, intimate, private, personal, spiritual, mental, emotional, psychological
F3 1 external

international *adj*
global, worldwide, intercontinental, cosmopolitan, universal, general
F3 national, local, parochial

internecine *adj*
fierce, violent, bloody, deadly, mortal, fatal, destructive, ruinous, murderous, exterminating, family, civil, internal

interplay *n*
exchange, interchange, interaction, reciprocation, alternation, transposition
colloq. give-and-take

interpolate *v*
insert, add, put in, introduce
formal interpose, interject, intercalate

interpolation *n*
insert, insertion, addition, introduction, aside
formal intercalation, interjection

interpose *v*
insert, introduce, interject, add, put in, thrust in, interrupt, intrude, interfere, come between, put/place between, intervene, step in, mediate, arbitrate, intercede
formal interpolate
colloq. barge in, butt in, muscle in, poke your nose in, put your oar in

interpret *v*
explain, clarify, make clear, throw/shed light on, define, paraphrase, translate, render, decode, decipher, solve, make sense of, understand, read, take
formal expound, elucidate, construe, explicate
colloq. read between the lines

interpretation *n*
explanation, clarification, analysis, translation, rendering, version, paraphrase, performance, reading, understanding, sense, meaning, opinion, decoding, deciphering
technical anagogy
formal expounding, exposition, elucidation, exegesis, explication, construe

interpretative *adj*
explanatory, clarificatory, interpretive
technical hermeneutic
formal exegetic, explicatory, expository

interpreter *n*
translator, linguist, commentator, annotator
technical hermeneutist
formal elucidator, exegete, exponent, expositor

interrogate *v*
question, quiz, examine, cross-examine, cross-question, debrief
colloq. grill, give a going-over, give the third degree, pump, give a roasting

interrogation *n*
questioning, quizzing, cross-questioning, examination, cross-examination, inquisition, inquiry, inquest
colloq. grilling, going-over, third degree, pumping

interrogative *adj*
questioning, quizzical, curious, inquisitive, probing, inquiring, interrogatory
formal inquisitional, inquisitorial, catechetical, erotetic

interrupt *v*
1 *interrupt a conversation*
cut in, intrude, break in, disturb, punctuate, cut in, cut short, cut off, heckle, barrack
colloq. barge in, butt in, chip in, put your oar in
2 *interrupt an event*
disturb, disrupt, hold up, stop, halt, end, suspend, delay, postpone, cancel, cut off, disconnect, break, punctuate
3 *interrupt a view*
obstruct, block, cut off, disturb, interfere with

interruption *n*
1 *work without interruption*
intrusion, interference, disturbance, cutting-in, disruption, suspension, breaking-off, delay, disconnection
formal discontinuance, cessation
colloq. barging-in, butting-in
2 *no interruptions are allowed*
question, remark, interjection, obstruction, impediment, obstacle, hitch
formal interpolation
3 PAUSE, break, halt, stop, interval, intermission, recess
colloq. breather, let-up

intersect *v*
cross, criss-cross, cut across, bisect, divide, meet, converge, overlap

intersection *n*
junction, interchange, crossroads, crossing, meeting

intersperse *v*
scatter, distribute, spread, dispense, pepper, sprinkle, dot, intermix, diversify
formal interpose, interlard

intertwine *v*
entwine, interweave, interlace, interlink, link together, connect, interwind, twirl, twist, twine, coil, cross, weave, blend, mix

interval *n*
1 BREAK, interlude, intermission, rest, pause, space, lull, gap, delay, wait, interim, period, time, recess, meantime, meanwhile
colloq. breathing-space, breather
2 SPACE, gap, opening, space, distance, period, spell, time, season

intervene *v*
1 STEP IN, mediate, arbitrate, intercede, negotiate, involve yourself in, interfere, interrupt, intrude
2 OCCUR, happen, pass, arise, come to pass
formal elapse, befall

intervening *adj*
between
formal interposing, intervenient, interjacent, mediate

intervention *n*
involvement, stepping-in, mediation, arbitration, negotiation, agency, intercession, interference, interruption, intrusion

interview *n, v*
▶ *n* discussion, audience, consultation, talk, dialogue, meeting, conference, press conference,

evaluation, appraisal, assessment, oral examination, viva
▶ *v* question, interrogate, examine, talk to, sound out, cross-examine, cross-question, evaluate, assess, vet

interviewer *n*
examiner, questioner, investigator, reporter, correspondent, evaluator, appraiser, assessor, interrogator, inquisitor
formal interlocutor, interrogant

interweave *v*
intertwine, entwine, interlace, interlink, interwind, interlock, twist, twine, coil, knit, cross, criss-cross, weave, intertangle, intertwist, interwork, interwreathe, braid, splice, blend, link together, interconnect, intermingle, connect, mix
formal reticulate

intestinal *adj*
internal, abdominal, gastric, duodenal, visceral
technical coeliac, ileac, enteric
formal stomachic

intestines *n*
bowels, guts, entrails, insides, colon, offal, viscera, vitals
colloq. innards

intimacy *n*
1 CLOSENESS, close relationship, friendship, familiarity, confidence, confidentiality, privacy, warmth, affection, love, understanding
2 SEXUAL INTERCOURSE, sexual relations, intimate relations, love-making, copulation, carnal knowledge, sleeping with someone, going to bed with someone
formal coition, coitus
🔄 distance

intimate[1] *adj, n*
▶ *adj* 1 *an intimate friend; an intimate atmosphere*
close, near, dear, bosom, cherished, friendly, informal, familiar, cosy, warm, affectionate
colloq. thick, matey, pally, chummy, tight
2 *an intimate conversation*
confidential, secret, private, personal, internal, innermost
3 *intimate knowledge of art*
deep, profound, in-depth, penetrating, detailed, exhaustive, thorough
🔄 1 unfriendly, cold, distant   3 superficial
▶ *n* friend, close friend, best friend, bosom friend, confidant(e), associate
colloq. mate, pal, chum, buddy, crony
🔄 stranger

intimate[2] *v*
initmated that he'd be willing to help
hint, insinuate, imply, suggest, indicate, signal, communicate, impart, tell, state, declare, announce, make known, let it be known

intimately *adv*
1 CLOSELY, affectionately, personally, tenderly, warmly, familiarly
2 CONFIDENTIALLY, confidingly, privately
3 DEEPLY, fully, in detail, exhaustively, thoroughly, inside out
🔄 1 coldly, distantly   3 superficially

intimation *n*
hint, inkling, insinuation, implication, suggestion, indication, announcement, communication, signal, declaration, notice, statement, reference, warning, reminder, allusion

intimidate *v*
daunt, cow, overawe, domineer, appal, dismay, alarm, scare, frighten, terrify, subdue, threaten, extort, blackmail, menace, tyrannize, terrorize, bully, browbeat, bulldoze, coerce, compel, pressure, pressurize, warn off
colloq. get at, lean on, twist someone's arm, put the screws on, put the frighteners on, turn the heat on

intimidation *n*
frightening, terrifying, menaces, threats, threatening, threatening behaviour, terrorization, terrorizing, domineering, tyrannization, bullying, browbeating, coercion, compulsion, pressure, fear, terror
colloq. arm-twisting, screws, frighteners, big stick
🔄 persuasion

intolerable *adj*
unbearable, unendurable, insupportable, unacceptable, insufferable, loathsome, detestable, impossible, more than you can bear
colloq. too bad, awful, dreadful, the limit, the end, the last straw, the straw that broke the camel's back
🔄 tolerable

intolerance *n*
impatience, prejudice, discrimination, narrowness, narrow-mindedness, small-mindedness, insularity, bigotry, opinionativeness, dogmatism, fanaticism, extremism, illiberality, uncharitableness, chauvinism, jingoism, racialism, racism, sexism, ageism, xenophobia, anti-Semitism
🔄 tolerance

intolerant *adj*
impatient, prejudiced, biased, discriminating, partisan, one-sided, bigoted, narrow, narrow-minded, small-minded, provincial, parochial, insular, opinionated, dogmatic, fanatical, extremist, illiberal, uncharitable, chauvinistic, jingoistic, racist, racialist, sexist, ageist, xenophobic, anti-Semitic
🔄 tolerant

intonation *n*
modulation, tone, accentuation, emphasis, stress, inflection, pitch, timbre, lilt, cadence

intone *v*
chant, croon, intonate, monotone, enunciate, pronounce, recite, sing, say, speak, voice, utter
formal declaim

intoxicate *n*
1 MAKE DRUNK, befuddle, fuddle, stupefy
formal inebriate
2 EXCITE, elate, exhilarate, stimulate, thrill, animate, enthuse, inspire, inflame

intoxicated *adj*
1 DRUNK, drunken, under the influence
formal inebriated, crapulent
colloq. merry, tight, tipsy, tiddly, well-oiled, blotto, drunk as a lord/newt, blind drunk, roaring drunk, the worse for drink, soused, squiffy, happy, legless, plastered, sozzled, pickled, bibulous, woozy, one over the eight, under the table, bevvied, have had a few;
slang stoned, tanked up, loaded, lit up, canned, paralytic, sloshed, smashed, pissed, stewed, bombed
2 EXCITED, elated, exhilarated, thrilled, moved, stirred, stimulated, enthusiastic, worked up, in high spirits
colloq. carried away
🔄 1 sober

intoxicating *adj*
1 *intoxicating liquor*
alcoholic, strong, stimulant
formal inebriant
colloq. going to your head
2 EXCITING, stimulating, heady, exhilarating, thrilling, stirring, dramatic, rousing, moving, enthralling, inspiring
⊟ 1 sobering

intoxication *n*
1 DRUNKENNESS, intemperance, alcoholism, hard/serious drinking, debauchery, dipsomania
technical methysis
formal inebriation, inebriety, insobriety, intoxication, crapulence
colloq. bibulousness, tipsiness
2 EXCITEMENT, elation, exhilaration, thrill, pleasure, animation, enthusiasm, stimulation, euphoria, rapture
⊟ 1 sobriety

intractability *n*
unmanageableness, uncontrollableness, ungovernability, unco-operativeness, unamenability, waywardness, stubbornness, obstinacy, perverseness, perversity, awkwardness, pig-headedness, indiscipline, incorrigibility, cantankerousness, contrariness
formal obduracy
⊟ amenability

intractable *adj*
unmanageable, uncontrollable, unyielding, unbending, unco-operative, undisciplined, ungovernable, unamenable, wild, unruly, obstinate, perverse, self-willed, wilful, wayward, pig-headed, stubborn, disobedient, awkward, difficult, fractious, headstrong, cantankerous, contrary
formal intransigent, obdurate, refractory
⊟ amenable

intransigent *adj*
stubborn, obstinate, uncompromising, unamenable, unbending, unpersuadable, unyielding, unbudgeable, unrelenting, relentless, inexorable, immovable, irreconcilable, implacable, hardline, determined, rigid, tenacious, tough
formal intractable, obdurate
colloq. uppity
⊟ amenable, flexible

intrepid *adj*
bold, daring, brave, courageous, plucky, valiant, audacious, lion-hearted, fearless, dauntless, undaunted, undismayed, unflinching, stout-hearted, spirited, stalwart, gallant, heroic
formal doughty, valorous
colloq. gutsy, spunky, gritty
⊟ cowardly, timid, afraid

intrepidness *n*
boldness, bravery, daring, intrepidity, audacity, valour, courage, heroism, dauntlessness, fearlessness, gallantry, lion-heartedness, stout-heartedness, undauntedness, pluck, prowess, spirit, nerve
formal doughtiness, fortitude
colloq. guts
⊟ cowardice, timidity

intricacy *n*
complexity, complexness, complexedness, complication, intricateness, elaborateness, entanglement, sophistication, involvement, knottiness, obscurity, enigma, involution
formal convolution(s)
⊟ simplicity, straightforwardness

intricate *adj*
complex, complicated, elaborate, sophisticated, involved, tortuous, tangled, entangled, ravelled, knotty, twisty, perplexing, baffling, puzzling, difficult, enigmatic, fancy, ornate, rococo
formal convoluted
⊟ simple, plain, straightforward

intrigue *n, v*
► *n* **1** PLOT, scheme, conspiracy, conniving, manoeuvre, stratagem, artifice, ruse, wile, trickery, cabal, double-dealing
formal collusion, machination
colloq. sharp practice, dodge
2 ROMANCE, liaison, affair, love affair, amour, intimacy
► *v* **1** FASCINATE, arouse your curiosity, rivet, tantalize, attract, pull, draw, charm, captivate, absorb, interest, puzzle
2 PLOT, scheme, conspire, connive, manoeuvre
formal machinate
⊟ 1 bore

intriguer *n*
plotter, schemer, conspirator, collaborator, conniver, Machiavellian, intrigant(e)
formal machinator
colloq. wangler, wheeler-dealer, wire-puller

intriguing *adj*
fascinating, appealing, charming, absorbing, riveting, compelling, captivating, diverting, exciting, interesting, beguiling, attractive, tantalizing, titillating, puzzling
⊟ boring, uninteresting, dull

intrinsic *adj*
basic, central, essential, fundamental, natural, underlying, built-in, in-built, inborn, inbred, interior, inherent, inward, native, indigenous, congenital, constitutional, elemental, genuine
⊟ extrinsic

introduce *v*
1 INSTITUTE, begin, start, establish, found, originate, organize, develop, inaugurate, launch, usher in, open, bring in, initiate, put/set in motion
formal commence
2 PUT FORWARD, advance, submit, offer, propose, suggest
3 PRESENT, announce, acquaint, familiarize
4 PREFACE, precede, begin, start, lead in, lead into
formal commence
⊟ 1 end, conclude **2** remove, take away
4 conclude, end, finish

introduction *n*
1 INSTITUTION, beginning, start, establishment, origination, organization, development, inauguration, launch, presentation, debut, initiation
formal commencement
2 FOREWORD, preface, preamble, prologue, preliminaries, front matter, overture, prelude, lead-in, opening
formal prolegomenon, exordium, proem
colloq. intro
3 PRESENTATION, announcement, familiarization, acquainting
4 BASICS, fundamentals, essentials, rudiments, first principles
⊟ 1 removal, withdrawal **2** appendix, conclusion

introductory *adj*
preliminary, preparatory, opening, inaugural, first, beginning, starting, initial, early, elementary, basic, fundamental, essential, rudimentary
formal prefatory, initiatory, precursory, exordial, isagogic

introspection *n*
self-examination, contemplation, pensiveness, thoughtfulness, brooding, self-analysis, self-centredness, self-observation, soul-searching, heart-searching, introversion
colloq. navel-gazing, navel-contemplation

introspective *adj*
inward-looking, contemplative, meditative, pensive, thoughtful, brooding, musing, introverted, subjective, self-centred, self-absorbed, self-examining, self-analysing, self-observing, reserved, withdrawn
⊟ outward-looking

introverted *adj*
introspective, inward-looking, self-centred, self-absorbed, self-examining, introspective, withdrawn, shy, reserved, quiet
⊟ extroverted

intrude *v*
interrupt, meddle, interfere, violate, invade, infringe, encroach, trespass
formal interject, obtrude, interlope
colloq. gatecrash, barge in, chip in, butt in
⊟ withdraw, stand back

intruder *n*
trespasser, prowler, burglar, raider, housebreaker, robber, pilferer, thief, unwelcome guest, invader, infiltrator
formal interloper
colloq. gatecrasher

intrusion *n*
interruption, interference, meddling, violation, infringement, encroachment, trespass, invasion
formal incursion, obtrusion
colloq. gatecrashing
⊟ withdrawal

intrusive *adj*
disturbing, interfering, irritating, annoying, troublesome, invasive, obtrusive, interrupting, trespassing, meddlesome, uncalled-for, unwanted, unwelcome, uninvited, forward, impertinent, officious, presumptuous
formal importunate
colloq. nosy, pushy, snooping, go-getting
⊟ unintrusive, welcome

intuition *n*
instinct, sixth sense, perception, discernment, insight, hunch, feeling, extrasensory perception
formal presentiment
colloq. gut feeling, feeling in your bones
⊟ reasoning

intuitive *adj*
instinctive, intuitional, spontaneous, involuntary, automatic, innate, inborn, unlearned, untaught
⊟ reasoned

inundate *v*
flood, deluge, swamp, engulf, submerge, soak, immerse, drown, saturate, bury, overwhelm, overburden, overrun, overflow

inundation *n*
flood, deluge, swamp, overflow, torrent, spate, tidal wave, excess, surplus, glut
⊟ trickle

inure *v*
accustom, familiarize, acclimatize, harden, temper, strengthen, desensitize, toughen, train
formal habituate

invade *v*
1 *invade a country*
enter (by force), penetrate, infiltrate, burst in, descend on, attack, assault, raid, seize, storm, maraud, plunder, pillage, occupy, take over, march into, overrun, swarm over, infest, pervade
2 *invade someone's privacy*
intrude, encroach, infringe, violate, trespass, interrupt
formal obtrude
⊟ withdraw, evacuate

invader *n*
aggressor, attacker, assailant, raider, plunderer, marauder, pillager, intruder, trespasser, infringer

invalid[1] *n, adj*
▶ *n* *visit an invalid in hospital*
patient, sufferer, convalescent
formal valetudinarian
▶ *adj* sick, ill, unwell, poorly, ailing, sickly, weak, feeble, frail, infirm, disabled, bedridden
formal debilitated, valetudinarian
⊟ healthy

invalid[2] *adj*
1 FALSE, unsound, ill-founded, unfounded, baseless, groundless, unjustified, unsubstantiated, untenable, unacceptable, unwarranted, illogical, irrational, unscientific, wrong, incorrect, weak, mistaken, erroneous
formal fallacious
2 ILLEGAL, null, void, null and void, worthless, abolished, cancelled, quashed, overturned
formal inoperative, revoked, rescinded, nullified
⊟ 1 valid, sound 2 legal, binding

invalidate *v*
annul, cancel, quash, void, veto, discredit, negate, undo, overrule, overthrow, undermine, weaken
formal abrogate, nullify, rescind, vitiate, revoke, terminate
⊟ validate

invalidity *n*
incorrectness, falsity, irrationality, unsoundness, sophism, speciousness, illogicality, inconsistency, voidness
formal fallaciousness, fallacy

invaluable *adj*
priceless, inestimable, incalculable, indispensable, precious, valuable, costly, useful
⊟ worthless, cheap

invariable *adj*
fixed, set, unvarying, unchanging, unchangeable, unalterable, changeless, permanent, constant, steady, consistent, stable, unwavering, uniform, rigid, inflexible, habitual, regular
formal immutable, invariant
⊟ variable, changeable

invariably *adv*
always, without exception, without fail, unfailingly, consistently, regularly, repeatedly, constantly,

habitually, inevitably
F3 never

invasion *n*
1 *an invasion of a country*
attack, offensive, onslaught, raid, foray, breach,
occupation, storming, penetration, infiltration
formal incursion
2 *invasion of privacy*
interference, interruption, intrusion, encroachment,
infringement, violation
F3 1 withdrawal, evacuation

invective *n*
abuse, denunciation, reproach, scolding, reprimand,
rebuke, tirade, diatribe, recrimination, sarcasm,
tongue-lashing
formal censure, revilement, fulmination, berating,
castigation, obloquy, philippic, vilification,
vituperation, contumely
F3 praise

inveigh *v*
criticize, blame, condemn, upbraid, denounce, scold,
rail, recriminate, reproach, sound off, tongue-lash
formal censure, fulminate, castigate, berate, lambast,
expostulate, vituperate
F3 praise

inveigle *v*
cajole, persuade, beguile, coax, allure, lure, seduce,
entrap, ensnare, entice, wile, decoy, manipulate,
manoeuvre, lead on, wheedle
colloq. bamboozle, con, sweet-talk

invent *v*
1 CONCEIVE, think up, design, discover, create,
originate, innovate, be the brainchild of, pioneer,
formulate, frame, devise, contrive, improvise, coin,
come up with, hit upon, dream up, fabricate
2 *invent an excuse*
make up, concoct, cook up, trump up, imagine,
dream up

invention *n*
1 *her latest invention*
design, creation, brainchild, innovation, discovery,
development, construction, device, machine, system,
contrivance, gadget
2 *the invention of the steam engine*
design, creation, discovery, development, innovation,
contriving
3 LIE, falsehood, falsification, untruth, deceit,
fabrication, concoction, fake, forgery, fiction, fantasy,
myth, figment
colloq. tall story, fib
4 INVENTIVENESS, imagination, creativity,
innovation, originality, ingenuity, resourcefulness,
skill, artistry, talent, gift, inspiration, genius
F3 3 truth

inventive *adj*
imaginative, creative, innovative, original, ingenious,
resourceful, fertile, skilful, inspired, artistic, talented,
gifted, clever

inventor *n*
designer, discoverer, creator, originator, innovator,
deviser, author, architect, developer, maker, producer,
framer, scientist, engineer, father, mother

inventory *n*
list, listing, checklist, record, register, catalogue, tally,
file, account, description, schedule, roll, roster,
equipment, supply, stock

inverse *adj, n*
▶ *adj* inverted, upside down, transposed, reversed,
opposite, other, contrary, counter, reverse, converse,
obverse
F3 converse
▶ *n* opposite, contrary, reverse, converse, obverse
colloq. the other side of the coin

inversion *n*
opposite, reversal, reverse, converse, transposal,
transposition, contrary
technical hysteron-proteron
formal antithesis, contrariety, contraposition

invert *v*
upturn, turn upside down, turn back to front, turn
inside out, turn around, overturn, capsize, turn turtle,
upset, transpose, reverse
F3 right

invertebrate *n*

Invertebrates include: *sponges:* calcareous, glass,
horny; *jellyfish, corals and sea anemones:* Portuguese
man-of-war, box jellyfish, sea wasp, dead-men's
fingers, sea pansy, sea gooseberry, Venus's girdle;
echinoderms: sea lily, feather star, starfish, crown-of-
thorns, brittle star, sea urchin, sand dollar, sea
cucumber; *worms:* annelid worm, arrow worm,
blood fluke, bristle worm, earthworm, eelworm,
flatworm, fluke, hookworm, leech, liver fluke,
lugworm, peanut worm, pinworm, ragworm,
ribbonworm, roundworm, sea mouse, tapeworm,
threadworm; *crustaceans:* acorn barnacle, barnacle,
brine shrimp, crayfish, daphnia, fairy shrimp, fiddler
crab, fish louse, goose barnacle, hermit crab, krill,
lobster, mantis shrimp, mussel shrimp, pill bug,
prawn, sand hopper, seed shrimp, spider crab, spiny
lobster, tadpole shrimp, water flea, whale louse,
woodlouse; centipede, millipede, velvet worm. *See
also* **butterfly**; **insect**; **mollusc**; **moth**.

invest *v*
1 SPEND, lay out, put in, sink, subsidize, fund
2 *invest time/energy in something*
spend, put in, devote, dedicate, give, contribute
3 PROVIDE, supply, give, endow, grant, entrust, vest,
empower, authorize, sanction
formal confer, bestow
4 *invest a person in authority*
induct, install, inaugurate, ordain

investigate *v*
inquire into, look into, consider, examine, study,
inspect, scrutinize, analyse, research, go into,
delve into, probe, explore, search, sift
colloq. check out, suss out, give the once-over, see how
the land lies, see which way the wind is blowing

investigation *n*
inquiry, inquest, hearing, consideration, examination,
study, research, survey, review, inspection, scrutiny,
analysis, probe, exploration, search, sifting,
fact-finding mission/visit

investigative *adj*
fact-finding, investigating, inspecting, research,
researching, analytical, exploratory
formal heuristic, zetetic

investigator *n*
examiner, researcher, inquirer, reviewer, inspector,
searcher, scrutineer, scrutinizer, analyst, analyser,
explorer, prober, questioner, detective,

private detective
colloq. sleuth, private eye

investiture *n*
installation, induction, inauguration, investing,
investment, ordination, coronation, enthronement,
admission, instatement

investment *n*
asset, speculation, venture, stake, risk, contribution,
outlay, expenditure, capital, cash, savings, wealth,
resources, money, funds, finance, principal, property,
stock, reserve, transaction

inveterate *adj*
chronic, habitual, hardened, diehard, dyed-in-the-
wool, entrenched, confirmed, established, hard-core,
obstinate, incorrigible, incurable, irreformable,
inured, addicted, long-standing
F3 impermanent

invidious *adj*
awkward, difficult, undesirable, unpleasant,
objectionable, hateful, obnoxious, offensive, slighting,
odious, discriminating, discriminatory
formal repugnant
F3 desirable, pleasant

invigorate *v*
vitalize, energize, animate, enliven, liven up, quicken,
strengthen, brace, motivate, stimulate, inspire,
exhilarate, excite, rouse, refresh, freshen, revitalize,
rejuvenate
formal fortify
colloq. perk up, pep up, buck up, soup up, give a new
lease of life to
F3 tire, weary, dishearten

invigorating *adj*
energizing, stimulating, refreshing, animating,
exhilarating, fresh, bracing, uplifting, rejuvenating,
vivifying, restorative, tonic, healthful, generous
formal inspiriting, salubrious
F3 tiring, disheartening, wearying

invincible *adj*
unbeatable, unconquerable, insuperable,
unsurmountable, undefeatable, unassailable,
impregnable, impenetrable, invulnerable,
indestructible, unyielding, unshakable
formal indomitable
F3 beatable, surmountable

inviolability *n*
inalienability, inviolableness, inviolacy, invulnerability,
sacrosanctness, sanctity, sacredness, holiness
F3 violability

inviolable *adj*
inalienable, unalterable, untouchable, sacred,
sacrosanct, holy, hallowed
formal intemerate
F3 violable, alienable

inviolate *adj*
entire, intact, complete, whole, undisturbed,
unbroken, unhurt, undamaged, unharmed, uninjured,
untouched, unpolluted, unprofaned, undefiled,
unstained, unsullied, unspoiled, stainless, pure,
sacred, virgin
formal intemerate
F3 sullied

invisible *adj*
unseen, out of sight, hidden, concealed, disguised,
unnoticed, unobserved, inconspicuous, indiscernible,

imperceptible, imperceivable, undetectable,
indistinguishable, infinitesimal, microscopic,
imaginary, non-existent
F3 visible

invitation *n*
request, call, summons, bidding, petition, appeal,
temptation, enticement, allurement, lure, bait, draw,
attraction, encouragement, inducement, provocation,
incitement, challenge, welcome, overture
formal solicitation
colloq. come-on

invite *v*
1 ASK, have round/over, entertain, call, summon, bid,
petition, appeal, welcome, encourage, bring on,
provoke, ask for, seek, look for
formal request, solicit, request the pleasure of
someone's company
2 ATTRACT, lead, draw, attract, tempt, entice, allure

inviting *adj*
welcoming, appealing, attractive, tempting, seductive,
enticing, alluring, pleasing, pleasant, agreeable,
delightful, captivating, fascinating, enchanting,
entrancing, intriguing, beguiling, bewitching,
tantalizing, engaging, winning, irresistible
F3 uninviting, unappealing

invocation *n*
appeal, petition, prayer
formal request, supplication, solicitation, beseeching,
entreaty, conjuration, imploration, epiclesis

invoice *n*
account bill, statement of account, charges, reckoning

invoke *v*
1 *invoke God for help*
call upon, appeal to, petition, implore, beg, pray
formal request, supplicate, beseech, entreat, solicit,
imprecate, conjure
2 *invoke a law*
turn to, resort to, have recourse to, make use of

involuntary *adj*
1 SPONTANEOUS, unconscious, automatic,
mechanical, reflex, instinctive, conditioned, impulsive,
unthinking, blind, uncontrolled, unintentional, forced
2 FORCED, compelled, coerced, reluctant, unwilling,
against your wishes
F3 **1** deliberate, intentional

involve *v*
1 REQUIRE, mean, assume, presuppose, imply, entail,
include, incorporate, encompass, cover, take in, affect,
concern
formal necessitate, denote, embrace, comprehend
2 IMPLICATE, incriminate, draw in, let yourself
in for, mix up, embroil, associate, connect, cause to
take part
formal inculpate
3 ENGAGE, interest, occupy, absorb, engross, engage,
preoccupy, hold, grip, rivet
F3 **1** exclude

involved *adj*
1 CONCERNED, associated, taking part, implicated,
incriminated, mixed up, caught up, participating
formal inculpated
colloq. in on
2 *an involved explanation*
complicated, complex, intricate, difficult, elaborate,
tangled, jumbled, knotty, tortuous, confusing,
confused

formal convoluted
F3 1 uninvolved 2 simple

involvement *n*
concern, interest, responsibility, association,
connection, participation, contribution, share, part,
implication, entanglement, attachment

invulnerability *n*
safety, security, strength, unassailability,
impenetrability, invincibility, impregnability,
inviolability, insusceptibility
F3 vulnerability

invulnerable *adj*
safe, secure, unassailable, impenetrable, invincible,
indestructible
F3 vulnerable

inward *adj*
incoming, entering, inside, interior, internal, inner,
innermost, inmost, hidden, personal, private,
intimate, secret, confidential
F3 outward, external

inwardly *adv*
inside, to yourself, within, at heart, in your heart of
hearts, deep down, deep inside you, privately, secretly
F3 externally, outwardly

iota *n*
scrap, bit, mite, jot, whit, speck, trace, hint, grain,
morsel, fraction, particle, atom
colloq. tad

irascibility *n*
snappishness, bad temper, cantankerousness,
irritability, irritation, petulance, impatience, ill-
temper, crossness, shortness, testiness, touchiness,
fieriness
colloq. crabbiness, edginess
F3 placidness

irascible *adj*
quick-tempered, short-tempered, bad-tempered, ill-
natured, ill-tempered, hot-tempered, cantankerous,
petulant, irritable, testy, touchy, choleric, cross, hasty
formal querulous, iracund, iracundulous
colloq. crabbed, crabby, narky, prickly
F3 placid

irate *adj*
annoyed, irritated, indignant, up in arms, angry,
enraged, furious, infuriated, incensed, worked up,
fuming, raging, ranting, livid, exasperated, vexed
colloq. mad
F3 calm, composed

ire *n*
anger, wrath, exasperation, annoyance, fury, rage,
indignation, passion, displeasure, choler
F3 calmness

iridescent *adj*
shimmering, sparkling, multicoloured, rainbow,
rainbow-coloured, rainbow-like, prismatic, dazzling,
glittering, shot, pearly, polychromatic
formal opalescent, variegated

irk *v*
annoy, anger, exasperate, incense, infuriate, irritate,
provoke, put out, ruffle, get, get to, vex, weary, nettle,
distress, gall, disgust, rile
colloq. aggravate, bug, miff, peeve, hassle, rub up the
wrong way, make someone's blood boil
F3 please

irksome *adj*
annoying, irritating, infuriating, exasperating, vexing,
vexatious, wearisome, bothersome, burdensome,
disagreeable, tiresome, troublesome, trying, tedious,
boring
colloq. aggravating
F3 pleasing

iron *adj, v*
▶ *adj* rigid, inflexible, adamant, determined, hard,
steely, tough, strong, firm
F3 pliable, weak
Related adjectives: ferrous, ferreous
▶ *v* press, smooth, flatten
▷ **iron out** resolve, settle, sort out, straighten out,
clear up, put right, reconcile, harmonize, deal with,
get rid of, eradicate, eliminate

ironic *adj*
ironical, sarcastic, sardonic, scornful, contemptuous,
derisive, sneering, scoffing, ridiculing, ridiculous,
mocking, satirical, wry, paradoxical
colloq. rich

irons *n*
chains, bonds, fetters, shackles, trammels, manacles

irony *n*
sarcasm, mockery, ridicule, scorn, satire, paradox,
contrariness
formal incongruity

irradiate *v*
brighten, enlighten, light up, lighten, illume,
illuminate, illumine, expose, radiate, shine on

irrational *adj*
unreasonable, unsound, illogical, inconsistent,
invalid, groundless, implausible, arbitrary, ridiculous,
absurd, crazy, wild, foolish, silly, senseless,
nonsensical, unwise
F3 rational, reasonable

irrationality *n*
unreasonableness, unreason, unsoundness,
illogicality, groundlessness, absurdity, ridiculousness,
senselessness, preposterousness, madness, lunacy,
insanity
F3 rationality

irreconcilable *adj*
incompatible, opposed, contrary, opposite, at odds,
conflicting, clashing, contradictory, inconsistent,
uncompromising, hardline, inflexible, implacable,
inexorable
formal incongruous, intransigent
F3 reconcilable

irrecoverable *adj*
irretrievable, lost, unrecoverable, unsavable,
irredeemable, irreclaimable, irremediable, irreparable,
unsalvageable
F3 recoverable

irrefutable *adj*
undeniable, incontrovertible, indisputable,
incontestable, unquestionable, beyond doubt/
question, indubitable, unanswerable, certain, sure,
definite, positive, decisive

irregular *adj*
1 ROUGH, bumpy, lumpy, uneven, pitted, crooked,
ragged, jagged, crooked, asymmetric, lopsided
2 VARIABLE, fluctuating, wavering, unsteady,
uneven, shaky, erratic, fitful, intermittent, sporadic,
spasmodic, occasional, random, haphazard,

disorganized, fragmentary, disorderly, unmethodical, unsystematic, inconsistent
3 ABNORMAL, unconventional, unorthodox, unofficial, improper, unusual, exceptional, anomalous, out of order, aberrant, extraordinary, freak, odd, strange, peculiar
4 DISHONEST, lawless, deceitful, fraudulent, false, cheating, unprincipled, immoderate, indecent, improper
▣ **1** smooth, level, uniform **2** regular **3** conventional **4** honest

irregularity   n
1 ROUGHNESS, bumpiness, unevenness, raggedness, jaggedness, crookedness, asymmetry, lopsidedness, lumpiness
2 VARIABILITY, fluctuation, wavering, fitfulness, intermittence, spasm, occasionalness, randomness, haphazardness, disorderliness, unpunctuality, inconsistency, unsteadiness, uncertainty, inconstancy, disorganization, patchiness
3 ABNORMALITY, unconventionality, unorthodoxy, anomaly, deviation, breach, aberration, oddity, peculiarity, eccentricity, freak
formal singularity
4 DISHONESTY, lawlessness, deceit, fraudulence, fraud, cheating, malpractice
▣ **1** smoothness, levelness **2** regularity **3** conventionality

irregularly   adv
occasionally, now and again, off and on, unevenly, spasmodically, haphazardly, intermittently, jerkily, unmethodically, anyhow, disconnectedly, eccentrically, erratically, fitfully
colloq. by/in fits and starts
▣ regularly

irrelevance   n
inappropriateness, inaptness, unimportance, unrelatedness, inconsequence, irrelevancy
formal inappositeness
colloq. red herring
▣ relevance, bearing

irrelevant   adj
immaterial, beside/off the point, inapplicable, inappropriate, inapt, unimportant, out of place, having no bearing, unrelated, unconnected, inconsequent, peripheral, tangential
formal inapposite
colloq. neither here nor there, not coming into it, making no difference, not matter
▣ relevant

irreligious   adj
atheistic, unbelieving, ungodly, unreligious, godless, undevout, unholy, unrighteous, agnostic, sceptical, heathenish, pagan, heathen, heretical, sacrilegious, iconoclastic, impious, irreverent, blasphemous, free-thinking, profane, rationalistic, sinful, wicked
formal nullifidian
▣ pious, religious

irremediable   adj
irreparable, irretrievable, irrecoverable, irreversible, remediless, irredeemable, incurable, inoperable, incorrigible, terminal, unmedicinable, deadly, fatal, final, hopeless, mortal
▣ remediable

Irremovable   adj
durable, immovable, indestructible, ineradicable, ingrained, inoperable, fast, fixed, set, stuck,

permanent, persistent, rooted, obstinate
formal obdurate
▣ removable

irreparable   adj
irreversible, irreclaimable, irrecoverable, irremediable, irretrievable, incurable, unrepairable
▣ recoverable, remediable

irreplaceable   adj
indispensable, essential, vital, unique, priceless, precious, peerless, matchless, unmatched, special
▣ replaceable

irrepressible   adj
ebullient, bubbly, uninhibited, buoyant, effervescent, animated, vivacious, resilient, boisterous, uncontrollable, unrestrainable, ungovernable, unstoppable, insuppressible, uncontainable

irreproachable   adj
irreprehensible, blameless, unblamable, innocent, beyond reproach, unimpeachable, faultless, guiltless, flawless, impeccable, perfect, unblemished, immaculate, stainless, spotless, sinless, pure
▣ blameworthy; *formal* culpable

irresistible   adj
1 *irresistible desire*
overwhelming, overpowering, forceful, unavoidable, inevitable, inescapable, inexorable, unpreventable, uncontrollable, irrepressible, potent, compelling, imperative, pressing, urgent
2 *irresistible beauty*
tempting, enticing, alluring, captivating, tantalizing, seductive, ravishing, enchanting, charming, fascinating
▣ **1** resistible, avoidable **2** unattractive, repulsive

irresolute   adj
indecisive, hesitating, hesitant, unsure, uncertain, doubtful, dubious, ambivalent, wavering, fluctuating, shifting, dithering, variable, weak, faint-hearted, fickle, undecided, unsettled, undetermined, unstable, unsteady, half-hearted, tentative
formal vacillating
colloq. shilly-shallying, pussyfooting, in two minds, (sitting) on the fence
▣ resolute, decisive

irrespective   adj
▷ **irrespective of** regardless of, disregarding, no matter, without considering, ignoring, not affecting, however, whatever, whichever, whoever, never mind
formal notwithstanding

irresponsible   adj
unreliable, untrustworthy, careless, negligent, thoughtless, unwise, heedless, ill-considered, rash, reckless, wild, carefree, flighty, erratic, scatterbrained, light-hearted, immature
formal injudicious
▣ responsible, dependable, cautious

irretrievable   adj
irreparable, irrecoverable, irreversible, irredeemable, irremediable, unrecoverable, unrecallable, lost, hopeless, unsalvageable, damned
formal irrevocable
▣ recoverable, reversible

irreverence   n
1 IMPIETY, godlessness, ungodliness, irreligion, heresy, profanity, sacrilege, blasphemy
2 DISRESPECT, disrespectfulness, discourtesy,

rudeness, impoliteness, insolence, impudence, impertinence, mockery, flippancy, levity, cheekiness
colloq. sauce, cheek
E3 1, 2 reverence

irreverent *adj*
1 IMPIOUS, godless, ungodly, irreligious, heretical, profane, sacrilegious, blasphemous
2 DISRESPECTFUL, discourteous, rude, impolite, impudent, impertinent, insolent, mocking, flippant
colloq. cheeky, saucy
E3 1 reverent **2** respectful, deferential

irreversible *adj*
irrevocable, unalterable, final, permanent, lasting, irreparable, irremediable, irretrievable, incurable, unrectifiable, hopeless
E3 reversible, remediable, curable

irrevocable *adj*
unalterable, unchangeable, changeless, invariable, final, fixed, settled, irreversible, irretrievable
formal immutable, predetermined
E3 alterable, flexible, reversible

irrigate *v*
water, flood, inundate, wet, soak, moisten, dampen, spray, sprinkle

irritability *n*
crossness, bad temper, ill-temper, impatience, grumpiness, prickliness, touchiness, fretfulness, edge, edginess, hypersensitivity, testiness, tetchiness, irascibility, peevishness, petulance, fractiousness
E3 cheerfulness, complacence, good humour, bonhomie

irritable *adj*
cross, bad-tempered, ill-tempered, quick-tempered, grumpy, crusty, cantankerous, testy, short-tempered, snappish, snappy, short, impatient, touchy, edgy, thin-skinned, hypersensitive, prickly, peevish, fretful, fractious, irascible
colloq. crotchety, crabby, ratty, stroppy, shirty
E3 good-tempered, cheerful

irritant *n*
annoyance, nuisance, trouble, bother, menace, provocation, vexation, goad
colloq. pain, thorn in the flesh
E3 pleasure, sweetness

irritate *v*
1 ANNOY, bother, harass, rouse, provoke, rile, irk, vex, goad, nettle, anger, enrage, infuriate, incense, exasperate, put out, grate, jar
colloq. aggravate, bug, get, get on your nerves, get your blood up, rub up the wrong way, get your back up, get under your skin, drive crazy/nuts, drive round the bend/up the wall, peeve
2 INFLAME, chafe, rub, fret, hurt, tickle, itch
E3 1 please, gratify

irritated *adj*
annoyed, bothered, angry, cross, exasperated, irked, irritable, nettled, vexed, ruffled, roused, riled, edgy, impatient, uptight, harassed, flustered, discomposed, displeased, piqued
formal exacerbated
colloq. peeved, put out, ratty, narked, miffed, in a huff
E3 composed, gratified, pleased

irritating *adj*
1 ANNOYING, infuriating, maddening, troublesome, bothersome, irksome, tiresome, grating, worrisome,

vexatious, vexing, disturbing, upsetting, nagging, displeasing, galling, provoking, thorny, trying
colloq. aggravating, pesky
2 ABRASIVE, rubbing, chafing, sore, ticklish, itchy
E3 1 pleasant, pleasing

irritation *n*
1 *express your irritation*
displeasure, dissatisfaction, annoyance, aggravation, provocation, anger, vexation, pique, indignation, fury, exasperation, irritability, crossness, testiness, snappiness, impatience
2 NUISANCE, annoyance, disturbance, bother, trouble, pest
colloq. pain, pain in the neck, thorn in the flesh, drag, bind
E3 pleasure, satisfaction, delight

island *n*
isle, islet, atoll, archipelago, eyot, holm, cay, key, skerry
Related adjective: insular

The world's largest islands include: Australia, Greenland, New Guinea, Borneo, Madagascar, Sumatra, Baffin (Canada), Honshu (Japan), Great Britain, Victoria (Canada).

isolate *v*
set apart, seclude, keep apart, segregate, quarantine, insulate, abstract, cut off, strand, maroon, detach, remove, disconnect, separate, divorce, alienate, shut out/away, ostracize, exclude
formal sequester
colloq. cold-shoulder, send to Coventry
E3 assimilate, incorporate, integrate

isolated *adj*
1 REMOTE, out-of-the-way, outlying, God-forsaken, deserted, unfrequented, secluded, detached, cut off, lonely, solitary, alone, separated, segregated, apart, single
colloq. off the beaten track
2 *an isolated occurrence*
unique, special, exceptional, atypical, untypical, solitary, single, unusual, uncommon, freak, abnormal, anomalous, unrelated
E3 1 populous **2** typical, common

isolation *n*
quarantine, solitude, solitariness, loneliness, aloneness, remoteness, seclusion, retirement, withdrawal, exile, segregation, insulation, separation, separateness, detachment, disconnection, dissociation, alienation, abstraction
formal sequestration
E3 contact

issue *n, v*
▶ *n* **1** MATTER, affair, concern, problem, point, subject, topic, question, debate, argument, dispute, controversy
2 PUBLICATION, release, distribution, supply, supplying, delivery, circulation, broadcast, announcement
formal promulgation, dissemination
3 *last week's issue*
copy, number, instalment, edition, impression, version, printing
4 RESULT, consequence, upshot, outcome, conclusion, effect, finale
colloq. pay-off
5 OFFSPRING, descendants, children, family, progeny, heirs, successors, seed, young

formal scions

6 OUTFLOW, discharge, rush, jet, spurt, gush
formal effusion, effluence
▷ **at issue** being discussed, under discussion, in question, being debated
▷ **take issue** disagree, argue, challenge, quarrel, fight, dispute, contest, protest, be at odds with, object, take exception, call into question
▶ *v* **1** PUBLISH, put out, release, distribute, supply, deliver, give out, deal out, circulate, broadcast, announce, proclaim
formal promulgate, disseminate
2 ORIGINATE, stem, result, spring, rise, emerge, burst forth, gush, flow, proceed, emanate, arise
3 COME OUT, emit, produce, discharge, emanate, emerge, burst forth, gush, flow, exude, ooze, seep

itch *v, n*
▶ *v* **1** TICKLE, irritate, tingle, prickle, crawl
2 *be itching to do something*
die, long, burn, pine, crave, hanker, yearn, ache
▶ *n* **1** ITCHINESS, tickle, irritation, prickling, tingling
Related adjective: pruritis
2 EAGERNESS, keenness, desire, ache, hunger, thirst, longing, yearning, hankering, craving, burning

itching *adj*
dying, longing, burning, hankering, aching, eager, greedy, impatient, inquisitive, avid, raring

item *n*
1 OBJECT, article, thing, piece, component, ingredient, element, factor, point, detail, particular, aspect, feature, consideration, matter, circumstance
2 *an item in the local paper*
article, piece, feature, report, story, account, notice, entry, paragraph, bulletin

itemize *v*
list, record, specify, detail, document, instance, particularize, count, mention, overname, number, enumerate, tabulate, make an inventory

itinerant *adj*
travelling, peripatetic, roving, roaming, wandering, journeying, wayfaring, drifting, rambling, nomadic, migratory, vagrant, rootless, unsettled, vagabond
▣ stationary, settled

itinerary *n*
route, course, journey, tour, circuit, plan, arrangements, programme, schedule, timetable

J

jab *v, n*
▶ *v* poke, prod, dig, nudge, stab, push, elbow, lunge, punch, box, tap, thrust
▶ *n* poke, prod, dig, nudge, stab, push, punch, box, tap, shot, injection

jabber *v*
chatter, gab, gabble, prattle, rabbit, ramble, tattle, babble, blather, blether, jaw, prate, rattle, mumble, witter, yap

jack *v*
▷ **jack up** 1 LIFT, raise, hoist, elevate 2 *jack up prices* increase, inflate, put up, push up, hike (up)

jacket *n*
CASING, cover, covering, wrapping, wrap, wrapper, case, sheath, shell, skin, envelope, folder
See panel at **coat**.

jackpot *n*
prize, first prize, winnings, kitty, pool, pot, reward, award, bonanza, stakes
colloq. big time

jaded *adj*
fatigued, exhausted, dulled, played-out, tired, tired out, weary, wearied, worn out, spent, bored, unenthusiastic
colloq. fagged, done in, bushed, fed up, cheesed off
E3 fresh, refreshed

jag *n*
barb, point, projection, protrusion, snag, notch, spur, tooth
technical denticle, dentil

jagged *adj*
uneven, irregular, notched, indented, rough, serrated, saw-edged, toothed, ragged, pointed, ridged, craggy, snagged, snaggy, barbed, spiked, nicked, broken
technical denticulate
E3 even, smooth

jail, gaol *n, v*
▶ *n* prison, jailhouse, custody, lock-up, penitentiary, detention centre, guardhouse
colloq. inside, nick; *slang* clink, cooler, slammer, quod, jug, can, choky
▶ *v* imprison, lock up, put away, send down, send to prison, confine, detain, intern, impound, immure
formal incarcerate

jailer, gaoler *n*
prison officer, warden, warder, guard, keeper, captor
slang screw

jam¹ *n*
bread and jam
conserve, preserve, jelly, spread, marmalade, confiture

jam² *v, n*
▶ *v* 1 CRAM, pack, wedge, squash, squeeze, press, crush, crowd, congest, ram, stuff, insert, confine, force,
thrust, push, press, ram
2 BLOCK, clog, obstruct, close (off), stall, stick
▶ *n* 1 CRUSH, crowd, press, crush, congestion, pack, herd, swarm, mob, throng, horde, multitude
2 *a traffic jam*
bottleneck, congestion, gridlock, hold-up, obstruction
3 PREDICAMENT, trouble, quandary, plight, straits
colloq. fix, hole, (tight) spot, bind, pickle, scrape, the soup

jamboree *n*
celebration, party, rally, festivity, festival, carnival, jubilee, junket, fête, frolic, revelry, spree, carouse, merriment, field day, gathering, get-together, convention
colloq. shindig

jangle *v, n*
▶ *v* 1 CLANK, clash, jar, clang, clatter, clink, jingle, chime, rattle, vibrate
2 *jangle someone's nerves*
upset, irritate, disturb, bother, trouble, make anxious
▶ *n* clang, clash, rattle, clatter, jar, jarring, cacophony, clink, din, discord, racket, reverberation, clangour, stridor
formal dissonance
E3 euphony

janitor *n*
caretaker, doorkeeper, doorman, custodian, concierge, porter
technical ostiary

jar¹ *n*
a jam jar
pot, container, vessel, receptacle, crock, pitcher, urn, vase, flask, flagon, carafe, jug, mug

jar² *v*
1 JOLT, agitate, rattle, shake, jerk, vibrate
2 GRATE, upset, disturb, trouble, jangle, irritate, annoy, offend, irk
colloq. nettle
3 CLASH, be in conflict, be at odds, be at variance, quarrel, disagree, bicker

jargon *n*
1 SPECIALIST LANGUAGE, journalese, computerese, computerspeak, legalese, psychobabble, buzz words, parlance, slang, cant, argot, vernacular, idiom, usage
2 NONSENSE, gibberish
colloq. gobbledegook, mumbo-jumbo

jarring *adj*
discordant, jangling, harsh, grating, irritating, cacophonous, rasping, strident, upsetting, disturbing, troubling, jolting

jaundiced *adj*
1 BITTER, cynical, pessimistic, sceptical, distrustful, disbelieving, biased, prejudiced, bigoted, envious, jealous, hostile, jaded, suspicious, resentful,

unenthusiastic, misanthropic
2 DISTORTED, biased, prejudiced, bigoted,
preconceived

jaunt *n*
trip, outing, excursion, holiday, tour, ride, drive, spin,
ramble, stroll

jaunty *adj*
sprightly, lively, perky, breezy, energetic, bouncy,
buoyant, high-spirited, self-confident, carefree, airy,
cheeky, debonair, dapper, smart, trim, showy, flashy,
spruce, stylish
F3 depressed, dowdy

jaw *n, v*
▶ *n* **1** *the lower jaw*
mandible, mouth, muzzle
technical maxilla
colloq. chops, trap
Related adjectives: maxillary, gnathic, gnathal
2 TALK, gossip, chat, conversation, discussion
colloq. chinwag, natter, confab
3 *the jaws of death*
clutches, grasp, control, power, claws, threshold
▶ *v* chat, chatter, gossip, talk, gabble
colloq. natter, rabbit (on), jabber, babble

jazz *n, v*
▶ *n*

Kinds of jazz include: acid jazz, Afro-Cuban, avant-
garde, bebop, blues, boogie-woogie, bop, cool,
Dixieland, free-form, fusion, hot jazz, jive,
mainstream, modern, New Orleans, post-bop,
ragtime, soul jazz, spiel, swing, third stream, West
Coast.

▶ *v* ▷ **jazz up**   liven up, enliven, smarten up,
brighten up

jazzy *adj*
lively, smart, spirited, stylish, bold, wild, fancy, gaudy,
vivacious, zestful
colloq. flashy, snazzy, swinging
F3 conservative, square

jealous *adj*
1 ENVIOUS, covetous, desirous, grudging,
begrudging, resentful
colloq. green, green-eyed
2 SUSPICIOUS, wary, doubting, distrustful, anxious,
possessive, insecure
3 PROTECTIVE, watchful, mindful, careful, vigilant,
wary
F3 1 contented, satisfied

jealousy *n*
1 ENVY, covetousness, grudge, grudgingness,
resentment, bitterness, spite, ill-will
colloq. green-eyed monster
2 SUSPICION, distrust, mistrust, doubt,
possessiveness, insecurity
3 PROTECTIVENESS, watchfulness, mindfulness,
carefulness, vigilance, wariness

jeer *v, n*
▶ *v* mock, scoff, taunt, gibe, ridicule, sneer, make fun
of, scorn, chaff, barrack, tease, twit, heckle, shout
down, hiss, boo, banter
formal deride
colloq. knock, *US* razz
▶ *n* mockery, ridicule, banter, taunt, gibe, sneer,
scoff, teasing, abuse, catcall, hiss, boo, hoot
formal derision
colloq. dig

jejune *adj*
1 UNSOPHISTICATED, simple, naïve, immature,
childish, juvenile, puerile, silly, callow
2 DULL, uninteresting, unoriginal, arid, trite, banal,
senseless, barren, empty, colourless, vapid, insipid,
prosaic, wishy-washy, dry, spiritless
F3 1 mature 2 meaningful

jell *see* gel.

jeopardize *v*
endanger, expose to danger, risk, put at risk, put in
jeopardy, hazard, venture, gamble, chance, take a
chance, threaten, menace, expose, stake
formal imperil
F3 protect, safeguard

jeopardy *n*
danger, risk, hazard, endangerment, venture,
vulnerability, precariousness, menace, threat,
insecurity, exposure, liability
formal peril
F3 safety, security

jerk *v, n*
▶ *v* jolt, tug, twitch, jog, yank, wrench, pull, jiggle,
lurch, pluck, thrust, shrug, throw, bounce
▶ *n* **1** JOLT, tug, twitch, jar, jog, yank, wrench, pull,
pluck, lurch, throw, thrust, shrug
2 IDIOT, fool
colloq. clot, dope, twerp, twit; *slang* nerd, wally,
pillock, prat, geek

jerky *adj*
fitful, twitchy, spasmodic, jumpy, jolting, lurching,
convulsive, disconnected, bumpy, bouncy, shaky,
shaking, rough, unco-ordinated, uncontrolled,
incoherent
F3 smooth

jerry-built *adj*
insubstantial, ramshackle, thrown together, quickly
built, built on the cheap, rickety, unstable, cheap,
shoddy, defective, faulty, flimsy, unsubstantial,
slipshod, cheapjack
F3 firm, stable, substantial

jersey *n*
sweater, jumper, pullover, sweatshirt, top, woolly

jest *n, v*
▶ *n* joke, quip, witticism, banter, fooling, prank,
practical joke, trick, hoax
colloq. wisecrack, crack, gag, kidding, leg-pull
▷ **in jest** in fun, as a joke, jokingly, to tease,
mischievously
▶ *v* joke, tell jokes, quip, fool, tease, mock, jeer
colloq. kid

jester *n*
clown, fool, comic, buffoon, comedian, humorist,
joker, wag, zany, wit, prankster, quipster, juggler,
joculator, patch, pantaloon, harlequin, merryman,
mummer, motley, merry-andrew, droll

jet¹ *n, v*
▶ *n* *a jet of water*
gush, spurt, spout, spray, spring, sprinkler, sprayer,
fountain, flow, stream, rush, squirt
▶ *v* **1** GUSH, spurt, spray, spring, flow, stream, rush,
squirt
2 FLY, zoom, rush, shoot, career

jet² *adj*
jet black
black, pitch-black, ebony, sable, raven, sooty, inky

jetsam *see* flotsam.

jettison *v*
discard, scrap, throw away, get rid of, abandon,
offload, unload, eject, expel, heave
colloq. ditch, dump, chuck
E3 load, take on

jetty *n*
breakwater, pier, dock, harbour, groyne, mole, quay,
wharf

jewel *n*
1 GEM, precious stone, gemstone, ornament
colloq. rock, sparkler
2 TREASURE, gem, find, prize, masterpiece,
showpiece, rarity, paragon, pearl, jewellery, pride and
joy, crème de la crème, *pièce de résistance*

jewellery *n*
jewels, gems, ornaments, trinkets, regalia, treasure,
bijoux, bijouterie, finery, gemmery, gauds

Types of jewellery include: bangle, bracelet, charm
bracelet, anklet, cufflink, tiepin, hatpin, brooch,
cameo, earring, stud, nose-ring, ring, signet-ring,
solitaire ring, necklace, rivière, necklet, choker,
pendant, locket, chain, beads, amulet, torque, tiara,
coronet, diadem.

Jewish calendar

The Jewish calendar and its Gregorian equivalents:
Tıshri (September-October), Hesshvan (October-
November), Kislev (November-December), Tevet
(December-January), Shevat (January-February),
Adar (February-March), Adar Sheni (leap years
only), Nisan (March-April), Iyar (April-May), Sivan
(May-June), Tammuz (June-July), Av (July-August),
Elul (August-September).

Jezebel *n*
seductress, temptress, *femme fatale*, hussy, scarlet
woman, Delilah, wanton, whore, harlot, jade,
man-eater, witch
colloq. vamp, loose woman; *slang* scrubber, tart

jib *v*
balk, shrink, recoil, back off, stall, refuse, retreat, stop
short

jibe *see* gibe.

jiffy *n*
instant, moment, second, sec, split second, flash,
twinkling, twinkling of an eye, minute, tick, two ticks,
trice, no time
colloq. two shakes of a lamb's tail
E3 age

jig *v*
jerk, prance, caper, hop, jump, leap, twitch, skip,
bounce, bob, wiggle, shake, wobble

jigger *v*
wreck, destroy, break, ruin, spoil, undermine
formal vitiate
colloq. botch up, kibosh, louse up, make a pig's ear of,
scupper; *slang* balls up, bugger up

jiggery-pokery *n*
deceit, trickery, dishonesty, fraud, deception, mischief,
subterfuge, chicanery, funny business, hanky-panky
colloq. monkey business

jiggle *v*
jerk, jump, bounce, twitch, fidget, shift, shake, agitate,
jig, jog, joggle, waggle, wiggle, wobble

jilt *v*
abandon, reject, desert, discard, brush off, leave, drop,
spurn, betray, cast aside
old use throw over
colloq. ditch, chuck, pack in

jingle *v, n*
▶ *v* clink, tinkle, ring, ding, chime, chink, jangle,
clatter, rattle
formal tintinnabulate
▶ *n* 1 CLINK, tinkle, ringing, chime, ding, clang,
rattle, jangle, clangour
formal tintinnabulation
2 RHYME, verse, song, carol, tune, ditty, doggerel,
melody, poem, chant, chorus, refrain

jingoism *n*
chauvinism, flag-waving, patriotism, nationalism,
imperialism, warmongering, insularity

jinx *n, v*
▶ *n* spell, curse, bad luck, evil eye, hex, voodoo,
hoodoo, black magic, charm, plague
formal malediction, affliction
colloq. gremlin
▶ *v* curse, bewitch, bedevil, cast a spell on, doom,
plague

jitters *n*
nerves, nervousness, tenseness, anxiety, fidgets,
agitation, trembling, uneasiness
colloq. heebie-jeebies, habdabs, the creeps, the shakes,
the shivers, the willies, jimjams

jittery *adj*
nervous, anxious, agitated, uneasy, flustered,
quivering, shaky, shivery, trembling, jumpy, fidgety,
quaking, panicky
formal perturbed
colloq. edgy, nervy
E3 calm, composed, confident

job *n*
1 *she has a good job*
work, employment, occupation, position, post,
pursuit, situation, profession, line of work/business,
career, calling, vocation, trade, métier, capacity,
business, (means of) livelihood
2 *it's a difficult job*
task, piece of work, chore, duty, responsibility, charge,
commission, assignment, mission, activity, affair,
concern, assignment, business, proceeding, project,
enterprise, office, capacity, pursuit, role, undertaking,
venture, province, part, place, share, errand, function,
contribution, stint, consignment, charge
▷ **have a job doing something** find something
difficult, find it a problem, have a hard time doing
something, find something (to be) troublesome

jobless *adj*
unemployed, out of work, without work, workless,
laid off, on the dole, inactive, idle, redundant
E3 employed

jockey *n, v*
▶ *n* equestrian, horseman, horsewoman, rider
▶ *v* manipulate, manoeuvre, engineer, negotiate,
wheedle, cajole, coax, induce, ease, edge, manage
formal inveigle

jocose adj

humorous, playful, funny, jesting, mischievous, pleasant, teasing, comical, droll, facetious, witty, sportive, waggish, jovial, joyous, merry, mirthful
formal lepid
E3 morose

jocular adj

joking, jesting, funny, joking, humorous, jovial, amusing, hilarious, comical, comic, entertaining, facetious, droll, whimsical, teasing, playful, witty, waggish, roguish
formal jocose
E3 serious

jocularity n

jesting, funniness, humour, joviality, amusement, entertainment, laughter, hilarity, merriment, gaiety, jolliness, comicality, drollery, wit, whimsicality, waggishness, pleasantry, facetiousness, playfulness, sportiveness, sport, roguishness, fooling, teasing
formal jocosity, jocoseness, desipience

jog v, n

▶ v 1 JOLT, jar, bump, jostle, jerk, joggle, nudge, poke, shake, prod, bounce, push, rock, elbow
2 PROMPT, remind, stir, arouse, activate, stimulate
3 RUN, trot, canter
▶ n 1 JOLT, bump, jerk, nudge, shove, push, poke, prod, shake
2 RUN, trot, canter

joie de vivre n

cheerfulness, enjoyment, buoyancy, joyfulness, joy, enthusiasm, merriment, mirth, pleasure, relish, zest, gaiety, gusto
formal blitheness, ebullience
colloq. bounce, get-up-and-go
E3 depression

join v

1 UNITE, connect, combine, attach, link, amalgamate, ally, unify, fasten, merge, converge, marry, couple, yoke, tie, splice, knit, weld, fuse, bind, cement, glue, add, adhere, annex
formal conjoin
2 BORDER (ON), verge on, touch, meet, coincide, march with
formal abut, adjoin, conjoin
3 ASSOCIATE, affiliate, become a member of, accompany, co-operate, collaborate, ally, enlist, enrol, enter, sign up, team up with
E3 1 divide, separate 3 leave
▷ **join in** take part in, participate, partake, co-operate, pitch in, lend a hand, help, contribute, chip in; *colloq.* muck in
▷ **join up** enlist, sign up, enrol, enter

joint n, adj, v

▶ n 1 JUNCTION, connection, union, coupling, juncture, join, intersection, hinge, knot, articulation, seam
formal nexus
2 CLUB, dive, bar, nightclub, pub, haunt, place
3 CIGARETTE
colloq. reefer, spliff, stick, roach
▶ adj combined, common, communal, joined, shared, united, collective, amalgamated, mutual, co-operative, co-ordinated, consolidated, concerted
▶ v 1 JOIN, connect, couple, unite, fasten, fit, articulate
2 CUT UP, carve, divide, sever, dismember, dissect

joke n, v

▶ n 1 JEST, quip, witticism, funny story, pun, hoot, whimsy, yarn, banter, repartee
colloq. crack, gag, wisecrack, one-liner
2 TRICK, jape, lark, prank, practical joke, hoax, spoof, fun, play, sport
▶ v jest, tell jokes, quip, clown, fool (around), pun, tease, banter, mock, laugh, frolic, gambol
colloq. kid, wisecrack, pull someone's leg, have someone on, kid, take for a ride, pull a fast one on

joker n

comedian, comic, wit, humorist, jester, trickster, quipster, prankster, hoaxer, practical joker, wag, clown, buffoon, kidder, droll, character, sport
colloq. wisecracker, card

jolly adj, adv

▶ adj 1 *a jolly person*
jovial, merry, glad, cheerful, cheery, playful, hearty, happy, exuberant, lively, gay, joyful, gleeful, mirthful
2 ENJOYABLE, happy, delightful, pleasurable, convivial, festive
E3 1 sad, unhappy
▶ adv extremely, very, exceptionally, intensely, greatly, highly, certainly

jolt v, n

▶ v 1 JAR, jerk, jog, bump, jounce, jostle, push, knock, bounce, lurch, shake, shove, push, bang, nudge
2 UPSET, startle, shock, shake (up), surprise, stun, amaze, astound, astonish, discompose, disconcert, disturb
formal perturb
▶ n 1 JAR, jerk, jog, bump, blow, bang, knock, push, shove, hit, impact, lurch, shake, start
2 SHOCK, surprise, reversal, setback, start, upset, blow, fright of your life
colloq. bombshell, thunderbolt, bolt from the blue, turn-up for the book

jostle v

1 PUSH, shove, jog, bump, elbow, hustle, jolt, crowd, shoulder, joggle, shake, squeeze, throng, bang, collide
2 COMPETE, vie, contend, fight, battle, struggle

jot n, v

▶ n iota, glimmer, trace, fraction, scrap, atom, gleam, grain, hint, speck, trifle, whit, bit, particle, mite, morsel, scintilla, tittle, ace, detail
colloq. smidgen
▶ v ▷ **jot down** write down, take down, note (down), put down, list, record, scribble, register, enter

journal n

1 MAGAZINE, periodical, newspaper, paper, publication, review, weekly, monthly
2 DIARY, gazette, daybook, log, record, account, register, chronicle

journalism n

reporting, writing, news, news coverage, reportage, feature-writing, press, Fleet Street, fourth estate, copy-writing, correspondence, media, broadcasting, radio, television

journalist n

reporter, news-writer, correspondent, editor, columnist, feature-writer, commentator, broadcaster, contributor, reviewer, editor, subeditor, newshound, paparazzo, freelance, stringer
colloq. hack, sub, journo, scribe

journey n, v

▶ n voyage, trip, travel(s), expedition, passage, trek,

tour, ramble, roving, outing, excursion, jaunt, wanderings, cruise, ride, crossing, flight, drive, safari, progress, globetrotting
formal odyssey, peregrination
▶ *v* travel, voyage, go, cruise, sail, trek, hike, tour, roam, rove, proceed, wander, tramp, ramble, range, fly, gallivant
formal peregrinate

journeyer *n*
tourist, traveller, tripper, voyager, wanderer, wayfarer, rambler, pilgrim, trekker
formal peregrinator

joust *v, n*
▶ *v* fight, spar, vie, compete, contest, quarrel, wrangle, skirmish
▶ *n* fight, encounter, contest, tournament, trial, engagement, skirmish, tilt, tourney

jovial *adj*
jolly, happy, cheerful, glad, cheery, merry, affable, animated, cordial, genial, lively, buoyant, mirthful, gleeful, gay, in good spirits, sociable
F3 gloomy, sad, depressed

joviality *n*
jollity, happiness, cheerfulness, cheeriness, gladness, merriment, mirth, glee, ebullience, fun, gaiety, affability, buoyancy, hilarity
F3 moroseness, sadness

joy *n*
1 HAPPINESS, gladness, delight, pleasure, bliss, ecstasy, elation, joyfulness, enjoyment, exultation, rejoicing, gratification, rapture, glee
formal felicitiy
colloq. seventh heaven, cloud nine
2 *the joys of childhood*
treasure, delight, pleasure, thrill, treat, prize, gem
3 *get no joy from the inquiry desk*
satisfaction, achievement, success, successful/positive result, victory, accomplishment
F3 1 despair, grief

joyful *adj*
happy, pleased, delighted, glad, elated, ecstatic, overjoyed, euphoric, thrilled, gratified, triumphant, gleeful, merry, cheerful, jubilant
colloq. tickled pink, over the moon, on top of the world, on cloud nine, in seventh heaven
F3 sorrowful, mournful

joyless *adj*
miserable, discouraging, depressing, sad, unhappy, sombre, downcast, dreary, forlorn, gloomy, glum, grim, despondent, dejected, cheerless, bleak, dismal, dispirited, doleful, dour
F3 joyful

joyous *adj*
happy, joyful, cheerful, glad, gleeful, merry, jubilant, rapturous, ecstatic, festal, festive, gladsome
F3 sad

jubilant *adj*
joyful, rejoicing, overjoyed, delighted, elated, triumphant, exuberant, exultant, excited, ecstatic, euphoric, thrilled, rhapsodic
colloq. tickled pink, over the moon, on top of the world, on cloud nine, in seventh heaven

jubilation *n*
euphoria, ecstasy, elation, triumph, excitement, exultation, jollification, joy, celebration, festivity,

jamboree, jubilee
F3 depression, lamentation

jubilee *n*
celebration, commemoration, anniversary, festival, festivity, holiday, gala, fête, carnival, feast day

Judas *n*
traitor, betrayer, deceiver, renegade, quisling, turncoat
formal tergiversator

judge *n, v*
▶ *n* 1 JUSTICE, Law Lord, magistrate, sheriff, recorder, coroner, judiciary, procurator fiscal, district attorney, seneschal, arbiter, adjudicator, arbitrator, mediator, ombudsman, moderator, referee, umpire, assessor
slang beak, his/her nibs
Related adjectives: judicial, judiciary
2 CONNOISSEUR, authority, expert, evaluator, assessor, critic, reviewer
▶ *v* 1 ADJUDICATE, arbitrate, try, sit in judgement, deliver/pronounce a verdict, referee, umpire, decree, mediate, examine, sentence, pass sentence, give a sentence, review, rule, find
formal adjudge
2 ASCERTAIN, determine, decide, assess, appraise, evaluate, estimate, value, weigh (up), gauge, review, examine, distinguish, discern, reckon, believe, think, form an opinion, consider, conclude, rate
3 CONDEMN, criticize, doom, convict, damn

judgement *n*
1 VERDICT, sentence, ruling, adjudication, decree, conclusion, decision, arbitration, finding, result, mediation, order, opinion
2 DISCERNMENT, discrimination, understanding, wisdom, common sense, good sense, sense, intelligence, taste, shrewdness, perception, penetration, acumen, enlightenment
formal prudence, judiciousness, sagacity, perspicacity
3 OPINION, assessment, evaluation, appraisal, estimate, view, belief, diagnosis, conviction
4 CONVICTION, damnation, punishment, doom, fate, misfortune
formal retribution
Related adjective: judiciary

judicial *adj*
legal, judiciary, magistral, forensic, official, discriminating, critical, impartial

⚠ **judicial** or **judicious** ?
Judicial is a formal word meaning 'relating to judges and lawcourts'. *Judicious* means 'showing wisdom and good sense': *a judicious choice of words.*

judicious *adj*
wise, careful, cautious, astute, discerning, informed, discriminating, shrewd, thoughtful, reasonable, sensible, clever, intelligent, smart, sound, well-judged, well-advised, considered, common-sense
formal prudent, sagacious, circumspect
F3 injudicious

jug *n*
pitcher, carafe, crock, ewer, flagon, urn, jar, decanter, vessel, Toby jug, container, receptacle

juggle *v*
alter, change, manipulate, falsify, tamper with, fake, rearrange, balance, equalize, adjust, massage, rig,

disguise
colloq. doctor, cook

juice *n*
liquid, fluid, extract, essence, sap, secretion, nectar, liquor, serum

juicy *adj*
1 SUCCULENT, moist, wet, lush, watery, flowing
2 INTERESTING, colourful, vivid, thrilling, exciting, sensational, racy, risqué, suggestive, scandalous, lurid, spicy
F3 1 dry

jumble *v, n*
▶ *v* disarrange, confuse, disorganize, mix (up), muddle, shuffle, tangle
F3 order
▶ *n* disorder, disarray, confusion, mess, chaos, mix-up, mixture, muddle, clutter, mixture, hotch-potch, miscellany, medley, potpourri
colloq. mishmash, shambles

jumbled *adj*
muddled, confused, chaotic, disorganized, disordered, disarrayed, mixed-up, tangled, unsorted, untidy, shuffled, tumbled, miscellaneous
F3 orderly, tidy

jumbo *adj*
gigantic, colossal, giant, extra-large, mammoth, huge, enormous, immense, vast
colloq. whopping

jump *v, n*
▶ *v* 1 LEAP, spring, bound, vault, clear, go over/across, hurdle, bounce, skip, hop, caper, cavort, frisk, romp, sport, prance, frolic, gambol
2 START, flinch, jerk, recoil, shake, quiver, twitch, jump out of your skin, wince, quail
3 OMIT, leave out, miss, skip, pass over, cut out, bypass, disregard, overlook, ignore, avoid, digress
4 RISE, increase, go up, gain, appreciate, ascend, escalate, mount, advance, surge, spiral
5 POUNCE ON, attack, assault, spring on, swoop on, set upon
colloq. mug, beat up, do over
▷ **jump at** accept, agree to, fall for, leap at, grab, seize, pounce on, snatch, swallow
▷ **jump on** criticize, blame, reprimand, rebuke, reprove, scold, chide, fly at, tick off, reproach, upbraid; *formal* berate, castigate, censure, revile
▶ *n* 1 LEAP, spring, bound, vault, hop, skip, bounce, prance, frisk, frolic, pounce
2 START, flinch, jerk, jolt, jar, lurch, shock, spasm, quiver, shiver, shake, quiver, twitch
3 BREAK, gap, space, interruption, lapse, omission, interval, breach, switch
formal hiatus, lacuna
4 RISE, increase, escalation, boost, advance, increment, upsurge, elevation, upturn, mounting
colloq. hike
5 HURDLE, fence, gate, hedge, barricade, barrier, obstacle, rail
Related adjective: saltatorial

jumper *n*
sweater, jersey, pullover, sweatshirt, woolly

jumpy *adj*
1 NERVOUS, anxious, agitated, apprehensive, uneasy, jittery, tense, panicky, fidgety, shaky, on edge
formal restive
colloq. edgy, twitchy

2 FITFUL, twitchy, spasmodic, jerky, jolting, lurching, convulsive, disconnected, bumpy, bouncy, shaky, shaking, rough, unco-ordinated, uncontrolled, incoherent
F3 1 calm, composed

junction *n*
1 *a road junction*
intersection, crossing, crossroads, interchange, meeting-point, confluence
2 JOINT, join, joining, connection, bond, seam, juncture, union, intersection, link, linking, coupling, welding

⚠ **junction** or **juncture**?
A *junction* is a point or place where things meet: *a road junction; a junction box for wires.* A *juncture* is a point in time: *at this/that juncture.*

juncture *n*
point, period, stage, time, occasion, minute, moment, crisis, emergency, crux, predicament

jungle *n*
1 *tigers in the dense jungle*
tropical forest, rainforest, equatorial rainforest, bush, growth
2 *a jungle of building regulations*
mass, heap, tangle, confusion, disorder, disarray, chaos, snarl, clutter, hotch-potch, mishmash, miscellany, medley, maze, labyrinth, web

junior *adj, n*
▶ *adj* younger, minor, lesser, lower, subordinate, secondary, subsidiary, inferior
F3 senior
▶ *n* minor, subordinate, inferior, subsidiary, minion, servant

junk *n, v*
▶ *n* rubbish, refuse, trash, debris, garbage, waste, scrap, litter, clutter, oddments, bric-à-brac, rummage, leftovers, leavings, dregs, wreckage
▶ *v* throw out, get rid of, ditch, jettison, discard, dispose of
colloq. dump, chuck

junta *n*
faction, clique, gang, group, ring, set, party, cartel, coterie, council, league, conclave, confederacy, cabal, camarilla

jurisdiction *n*
1 *under the council's jurisdiction*
power, authority, control, influence, dominion, province, sovereignty, administration, leadership, mastery, command, domination, rule, right, sway
formal prerogative
2 AREA, field, orbit, bounds, scope, range, reach, sphere, zone

jury *n*
jurors, panel, jurymen, jurywomen

just *adj, adv*
▶ *adj* 1 *a just ruler*
fair, equitable, impartial, unbiased, unprejudiced, fair-minded, even-handed, neutral, objective, disinterested, righteous, upright, virtuous, moral, ethical, truthful, sincere, honourable, good, honest, irreproachable, upstanding, principled
2 *a just punishment*
deserved, merited, earned, fitting, well-deserved, appropriate, suitable, apt, due, justified, valid, sound,

well-grounded, well-founded, proper, reasonable, rightful, lawful, legitimate, legal
E3 1 unjust 2 undeserved
▶ *adv* 1 *he's just left*
a short time ago, a moment ago, recently, lately
2 *that's just like him*
exactly, precisely, perfectly, completely, absolutely, quite
colloq. bang on, spot on, to a T
3 *she's just a child*
only, merely, simply, purely, nothing but, barely, hardly, scarcely
▷ **just about** practically, almost, virtually, nearly, as good as, all but, well-nigh, more or less, to all intents and purposes

justice *n*
1 FAIRNESS, equity, fair play, impartiality, objectivity, neutrality, equitableness, fair-mindedness, even-handedness, justness, legitimacy, honesty, honour, uprightness, integrity, right, rightfulness, rightness, righteousness, morals, ethics, justifiableness, lawfulness, validity, soundness, reasonableness
formal rectitude, propriety
2 LEGALITY, law, penalty, punishment, recompense, amends, redress, reparation, satisfaction, compensation
3 JUDGE, Justice of the Peace, JP, magistrate, sheriff
E3 1 injustice, unfairness, bias

justifiable *adj*
defensible, excusable, warranted, reasonable, within reason, sustainable, supportable, justified, lawful, legal, legitimate, acceptable, explainable, forgivable, pardonable, understandable, plausible, valid, well-founded, sound, sensible, right, proper, fit, tenable
formal explicable
E3 unjustifiable

justification *n*
defence, plea, mitigation, apology, explanation, excuse,

vindication, verification, confirmation, warrant, rationalization, reason, grounds, basis

justify *v*
vindicate, warrant, defend, acquit, absolve, clear, excuse, forgive, explain, pardon, validate, uphold, show to be right/reasonable, sustain, support, stand up for, maintain, establish, prove, rationalize, verify, confirm, bear out, deserve
formal exculpate, exonerate, substantiate

justly *adv*
properly, justifiably, duly, equitably, even-handedly, rightfully, rightly, with reason, fairly, honestly, impartially, lawfully, legitimately, conscientiously, objectively, equally
E3 unjustly

jut (out) *v*
project, protrude, stick out, overhang, extend, beetle, extrude
E3 recede

juvenile *n, adj*
▶ *n* child, youth, minor, young person, youngster, adolescent, teenager, boy, girl, infant
colloq. kid
▶ *adj* young, youthful, minor, junior, immature, inexperienced, childish, puerile, infantile, adolescent, babyish, unsophisticated, callow
colloq. green, wet behind the ears
E3 mature

juxtapose *v*
put/place together, place side by side, put next to each other

juxtaposition *n*
proximity, nearness, closeness, contact, vicinity, immediacy
formal contiguity

K

kaleidoscopic *adj*
1 MANY-COLOURED, multicoloured, many-splendoured, variegated, motley
technical poikilitic
formal polychromatic, polychrome
2 EVER-CHANGING, changeable, fluctuating, manifold, fluid
formal multifarious
🔄 1 dull, monochrome, monotonous

kaput *adj*
broken, finished, ruined, wrecked, smashed, undone, defunct, destroyed, extinct
colloq. conked out

karate *n*

Karate belts include: *junior grades (Kyu)*: red belt (beginner), white belt (8th Kyu), yellow belt (7th Kyu), orange belt (6th Kyu), green belt (5th Kyu), brown belt (4th-1st Kyu), black belt (1st Dan); *senior grades (Dans)*: black belts (1st-8th Dan).

keel *v*
▷ **keel over** 1 OVERTURN, capsize, turn upside down, turn turtle, founder, collapse, upset 2 FAINT, pass out, lose consciousness, black out, fall, drop, stagger, topple over
old use swoon

keen *adj, v*
▶ *adj* 1 EAGER, avid, fervent, enthusiastic, earnest, devoted, diligent, industrious, conscientious, assiduous, intent, impatient
2 ASTUTE, sharp, shrewd, clever, perceptive, wise, discerning, discriminating, quick, quick-witted, sharp-witted, penetrating, deep, sensitive
formal perspicacious
3 SHARP, piercing, penetrating, incisive, acute, pointed, intense, pungent, acid, biting
formal trenchant, mordant
4 *keen competition*
fierce, intense, strong, wild, ruthless, cut-throat
colloq. dog-eat-dog
5 *keen on something/someone*
fond of, devoted to, liking, attached to, loving, caring
colloq. having a soft spot for
🔄 1 apathetic 2 superficial 3 dull
▶ *v* wail, grieve, mourn, lament, sob, howl, cry, sorrow

keenness *n*
1 ENTHUSIASM, eagerness, diligence, earnestness, industriousness, industry, sedulity
2 ASTUTENESS, sharpness, shrewdness, cleverness, discernment, penetration, sensitivity, wisdom, incisiveness
formal sagacity, sapience, trenchancy
🔄 1 apathy 2 bluntness, dullness

keep *v, n*
▶ *v* 1 RETAIN, hold, preserve, hold on to, hang on to,

not part with, save, store (up), stock, deal in, carry, possess, keep possession of, amass, hoard, accumulate, collect, stack, conserve, deposit, heap, pile (up), place, maintain, furnish, sustain
2 CARRY ON, keep at/on, continue, persevere, persist, remain, stay, maintain
3 LOOK AFTER, tend, care for, keep in good order, have charge of, have custody of, maintain, provide for, subsidize, support, sustain, be responsible for, foster, superintend, mind, protect, shelter, guard, defend, watch (over), shield, safeguard, feed, nurture, manage
4 DETAIN, delay, check, hinder, hold (up), hold back, impede, obstruct, prevent, block, curb, interfere with, restrain, limit, inhibit, deter, hamper, keep back, control, constrain, arrest, withhold, confine
formal retard
5 OBSERVE, comply with, respect, obey, fulfil, adhere to, abide by, carry out, recognize, keep up, keep faith with, commemorate, celebrate, hold, maintain, perform, perpetuate, mark, honour, solemnize
formal effectuate
▷ **keep at** persevere, stick at, be steadfast, continue, carry on, complete, endure, finish, last, maintain, remain, stay, persist, plug away at, toil, grind, drudge, labour, beaver away at; *colloq.* slog at
🔄 abandon, neglect
▷ **keep back** 1 RESTRAIN, check, constrain, curb, impede, limit, prohibit, stop, control, delay;
formal retard 2 HOLD BACK, restrict, suppress, withhold, conceal, censor, hide, hush up, stifle, reserve, keep secret, retain
▷ **keep from** prevent, resist, stop, halt;
formal forbear, desist
▷ **keep in** 1 REPRESS, keep back, inhibit, bottle up, conceal, stifle, suppress, hide, control, restrain, quell, stop up 2 CONFINE, detain, shut in, coop up
🔄 1 declare 2 release
▷ **keep off** avoid, stay away from, stay off, keep away, avoid going near, not go near, keep at a distance from, steer clear of, keep at arm's length; *colloq.* give a wide berth to
▷ **keep on** continue, carry on, endure, persevere, persist, keep at it, last, remain, stay, stay the course, hold on, retain, maintain; *colloq.* soldier on, stick at it
▷ **keep on at** go on at, nag, pester, plague, pursue, badger, chivvy, harass, harry; *formal* importune
▷ **keep secret** hide, conceal, keep back, keep dark, suppress; *formal* dissemble; *colloq.* keep under your hat, keep under wraps, your lips be sealed
▷ **keep to** observe, comply with, respect, obey, fulfil, adhere to, stick to
▷ **keep track of** follow, grasp, keep up with, monitor, oversee, plot, record, trace, track, understand, watch
▷ **keep up** maintain, continue, persevere, go along with, support, sustain, preserve, keep pace, equal, contend, compete, vie, rival, match, emulate
🔄 fall behind
▶ *n* 1 SUBSISTENCE, board, board and lodgings, livelihood, living, maintenance, support, upkeep,

means, food, nourishment, sustenance, nurture
2 FORT, fortress, tower, castle, citadel, stronghold,
dungeon, donjon
▷ **for keeps** for ever, always, for all time;
colloq. for good

keeper *n*
guard, custodian, curator, caretaker, attendant,
guardian, overseer, steward, warder, jailer, gaoler,
warden, supervisor, bodyguard, escort, inspector,
defender, governor, superintendent, administrator,
surveyor
formal conservator
colloq. minder

keeping *n*
1 CUSTODY, guardianship, supervision, care, charge,
safe-keeping, retention, protection, maintenance,
surveillance, trust, tutelage, ward, cure, patronage
formal auspices, aegis
2 *in keeping with the architecture*
agreement, harmony, conformity, correspondence,
consistency, balance, proportion
formal accord, congruity

keepsake *n*
memento, souvenir, remembrance, relic, reminder,
token, pledge, emblem

keg *n*
barrel, butt, cask, drum, tun, vat, firkin, hogshead

ken *n*
knowledge, understanding, perception, awareness,
appreciation, comprehension, realization, field, grasp,
notice, range, reach, scope, acquaintance, compass
formal cognizance

kernel *n*
core, crux, grain, seed, stone, nut, nucleus, centre,
heart, nub, essence, germ, marrow, substance, gist
formal quintessence
colloq. nitty-gritty, nuts and bolts, innards

key *n, adj*
▶ *n* **1** CLUE, cue, indicator, pointer, explanation,
guide, gloss, sign, answer, solution, interpretation,
means, secret
formal explication
2 GUIDE, glossary, translation, legend, code, table,
index
3 *in a low key*
pitch, tone, style, mood
▶ *adj* important, essential, vital, crucial, necessary,
principal, decisive, central, chief, main, major,
leading, basic, fundamental

keynote *n*
core, centre, heart, substance, theme, gist, pith,
marrow, essence, emphasis, accent, stress

keystone *n*
cornerstone, core, crux, base, basis, foundation,
ground, linchpin, principle, root, mainspring, source,
spring, motive

kick *v, n*
▶ *v* **1** BOOT, hit, strike, knee, jolt
2 GIVE UP, quit, stop, leave off, abandon, desist from,
break
▷ **kick against** resist, rebel, oppose, spurn, defy,
withstand, protest, hold out against
▷ **kick around** discuss, talk about, play with, toy
with
▷ **kick off** begin, start, open, get under way, open the

proceedings, introduce, inaugurate, initiate;
formal commence; *colloq.* set/start the ball rolling
▷ **kick out** eject, evict, expel, oust, remove,
discharge, dismiss, get rid of, throw out, reject;
colloq. chuck out, sack, boot out, show someone the
door, give the sack/push/boot/elbow to
▶ *n* **1** BLOW, recoil, jolt, striking
2 STIMULATION, thrill, excitement, fun, pleasure
colloq. buzz, lift, lark, high
3 *a drink with a kick*
power, strength, potency, effect, stimulus
colloq. punch, pep, bite, zing, zip

kick-off *n*
beginning, start, outset, opening, introduction
formal commencement, inception
colloq. word go

kid[1] *n*
she has three kids
child, young one, little one, toddler, youngster, young
person, youth, juvenile, infant, girl, boy, adolescent,
teenager, lad
colloq. nipper, tot

kid[2] *v*
I was only kidding; don't kid yourself
tease, joke, hoax, fool, pretend, trick, delude, dupe,
jest, hoodwink, deceive, humbug, gull
colloq. have on, pull someone's leg, con, bamboozle

kidnap *v*
abduct, capture, seize, hold to ransom, snatch, hijack,
take/hold as hostage, steal

kill *v, n*
▶ *v* **1** SLAUGHTER, murder, take someone's life, slay,
put to death, exterminate, assassinate, stab to death,
do to death, finish off, massacre, execute, destroy,
put down, put to sleep, do away with, butcher,
annihilate, hang, execute, guillotine, behead, shoot,
electrocute, send to the electric chair
formal smite, decapitate
colloq. do in, bump off, eliminate, dispatch, liquidate,
knock off, rub out, wipe out, decimate, polish off,
take out, waste, blow away, zap
2 *kill a project*
end, destroy, put an end to, ruin, abolish, devastate,
eradicate
3 *my feet are killing me*
hurt, ache, cause pain, be painful, be sore, suffer, throb,
pound, twinge, sting, smart
4 *don't kill yourself with all this work*
strain, exhaust, tire out, weary, fatigue, sap, drain
5 *kill time*
pass, spend, occupy, fill, use (up), while away
6 *kill pain/noise*
STIFLE, deaden, dull, smother, quash, quell, suppress,
muffle
▶ *n* death, shoot-out, death-blow, end, finish, climax,
conclusion, *coup de grâce*, dénouement, dispatch,
mop-up

killer *n*
murderer, assassin, executioner, destroyer, slayer,
slaughterer, exterminator, cut-throat, gunman,
homicide
colloq. butcher, hatchet man, hit-man, liquidator

killing *n, adj*
▶ *n* **1** SLAUGHTER, murder, massacre, butchery,
genocide, homicide, assassination, execution, slaying,
manslaughter, extermination, carnage, bloodshed,
elimination, destruction, fatality

formal patricide, matricide, infanticide, fratricide, sororicide, uxoricide
colloq. liquidation
2 GAIN, fortune, windfall, booty, profit, lucky break, coup, success, stroke of luck, hit, big hit
colloq. clean-up, bonanza
▶ *adj* 1 FUNNY, hilarious, comical, amusing, uproarious, ludicrous, absurd, rib-tickling
colloq. side-splitting, a scream
2 EXHAUSTING, hard, taxing, arduous, tiring, fatiguing, wearing, draining
formal debilitating, enervating

killjoy *n*
spoilsport, moaner, complainer, dampener, damper, misery, cynic, pessimist, sceptic, grouch, whiner, prophet of doom, Weary Willie
colloq. wet blanket
E3 enthusiast, optimist, sport

kin *n*
relatives, relations, family, people, flesh and blood, cousins, blood, lineage, extraction, clan, stock, tribe
old use kindred
formal consanguinity

kind *n, adj*
▶ *n* sort, type, class, category, set, variety, character, genus, genre, style, brand, family, breed, race, nature, persuasion, description, species, strain, stamp, temperament, character, manner
▶ *adj* benevolent, kind-hearted, kindly, good-hearted, good-natured, helpful, obliging, humane, generous, magnanimous, big-hearted, compassionate, merciful, forbearing, pitying, charitable, benign, philanthropic, altruistic, humanitarian, amiable, friendly, amicable, congenial, soft-hearted, thoughtful, warm, warm-hearted, genial, considerate, courteous, sympathetic, patient, cordial, tender-hearted, loving, affectionate, understanding, lenient, mild, gentle, humane, indulgent, tolerant, unselfish, selfless, neighbourly, tactful, giving, nice, good, gracious
formal bounteous
E3 cruel, inconsiderate, unhelpful
▷ **in kind** in like manner, in return, in exchange, similarly, tit for tat

kind-hearted *adj*
kind, warm, warm-hearted, sympathetic, tender-hearted, kindly, generous, considerate, compassionate, amicable, good-hearted, good-natured, obliging, gracious, benign, big-hearted, helpful, philanthropic, altruistic, humanitarian, humane
E3 ill-natured

kindle *v*
1 IGNITE, light, set alight, set on fire, set fire to
2 INFLAME, fire, stir, thrill, stimulate, rouse, arouse, awaken, excite, fan, incite, inspire, awaken, induce, provoke

kindliness *n*
kindness, benevolence, compassion, friendliness, sympathy, warmth, generosity, charity, amiability
formal beneficence, benignity, loving-kindness
E3 cruelty, meanness, unkindness

kindly *adj*
benevolent, kind, kind-hearted, compassionate, charitable, good, good-natured, helpful, considerate, thoughtful, warm, generous, magnanimous, big-hearted, cordial, favourable, giving, indulgent, pleasant, nice, agreeable, sympathetic, understanding, tender, gentle, mild, humane, patient, friendly,

amicable, cordial, polite
E3 cruel, uncharitable

kindness *n*
1 BENEVOLENCE, kindliness, charity, magnanimity, compassion, fellow feeling, generosity, hospitality, humanity, humaneness, courtesy, friendliness, pleasantness, good will, philanthropy, altruism, humanitarianism, niceness, goodness, grace, patience, indulgence, tolerance, leniency, understanding, sympathy, considerateness, consideration, warmth, warm-heartedness, love, affection, helpfulness, thoughtfulness, gentleness, mildness
formal loving-kindness
2 FAVOUR, good turn, assistance, help, aid, service
E3 1 cruelty, inhumanity 2 disservice

kindred *n, adj*
▶ *n* relatives, relations, flesh and blood, family, people, folk, connections, clan, relationship, kinsfolk, lineage
old use kin
formal consanguinity
▶ *adj* similar, common, related, matching, like, corresponding, affiliated, connected, allied, akin
formal cognate

king *n*
1 MONARCH, ruler, sovereign, majesty, emperor, chief, chieftain, prince, lord, supremo
Related adjective: regal
2 *the king of football*
supremo, kingpin, star, chief, leader, master
colloq. leading light, top dog, big cheese/shot/noise, the greatest

kingdom *n*
monarchy, sovereignty, reign, realm, empire, dominion, commonwealth, nation, principality, state, country, domain, dynasty, province, sphere, territory, land, grouping, division

kingly *adj*
sovereign, majestic, royal, regal, imperial, imperious, lordly, noble, stately, supreme, splendid, glorious, grand, imposing, grandiose, dignified
formal august, monarchical, sublime

kink *n, v*
▶ *n* 1 CURL, twist, twirl, bend, dent, indentation, knot, loop, crimp, coil, tangle, entanglement, crinkle, wrinkle
2 QUIRK, eccentricity, idiosyncrasy, whim, foible, deviation, perversion, fetish
formal caprice
▶ *v* bend, curl, twist, curve, coil, tangle, crimp, wrinkle

kinky *adj*
1 STRANGE, odd, unconventional, freakish, eccentric, outlandish, queer, quirky, idiosyncratic, peculiar, perverted, deviant, unnatural, warped, weird, bizarre, whimsical, degenerate, depraved, licentious
formal capricious
2 CURLED, coiled, twisted, crumpled, tangled, curly, wavy, wrinkled, crimped, frizzy

kinsfolk *n*
relatives, relations, family, clan, cousins, connections
old use kin, kindred

kinship *n*
1 KIN, family, blood, relation, relationship, ties, lineage, ancestry

formal consanguinity
2 AFFINITY, similarity, association, alliance, connection, correspondence, equivalence, relationship, tie, community, likeness, kindred, conformity

kiosk *n*
booth, stall, stand, news-stand, bookstall, cabin, box, counter

kismet *n*
destiny, fate, doom, fortune, lot, portion, providence, karma
formal predestiny

kiss *v, n*
▶ *v* **1** CARESS
formal osculate
colloq. peck, give someone a peck, smooch, neck, canoodle, bill and coo; *slang* snog
2 TOUCH, touch gently/lightly, graze, glance off, brush, lick, scrape, fan
▶ *n formal* osculation
colloq. peck, smack, smacker; *slang* snog

kit *n, v*
▶ *n* **1** EQUIPMENT, gear, apparatus, supplies, tackle, provisions, outfit, implements, set, tools, trappings, rig, instruments, paraphernalia, utensils, effects, luggage, baggage
formal accoutrements, appurtenances
colloq. things, stuff
2 *football kit*
tackle, clothing, outfit, rig, colours
colloq. rig-out, gear, strip, togs, get-up, clobber
▶ *v* ▷ **kit out** equip, fit out, outfit, supply, provide, fix up, furnish, prepare, arm, deck out, dress, rig out

kitchen utensils

Kitchen utensils include: baster, blender, bottle opener, breadbin, breadboard, butter curler, butter dish, can-opener, cheese board, cheese slicer, chopping-board, colander, corer, corkscrew, cruet set, dough hook, egg separator, egg slicer, egg-timer, fish slice, flour dredger, food processor, fork, garlic press, grater, herb mill, ice-cream scoop, icing syringe, jelly mould, kitchen scales, knife block, lemon squeezer, liquidizer, mandolin, measuring jug, meat thermometer, mincer, mixing bowl, nutcracker, nutmeg grater, pasta maker, pastry board, pastry brush, pastry cutter, peeler, pepper mill, pie funnel, potato masher, pudding basin, punch bowl, rolling-pin, salad spinner, scissors, sharpening steel, shears, sieve, sifter, skewer, spatula, spice rack, stoner, storage jar, tea caddy, tea infuser, tea strainer, toast rack, tongs, tureen, vegetable brush, whisk, wine cooler, wine rack, yoghurt maker, zester; *types of knife*: boning knife, bread knife, butter-knife, carving knife, cheese knife, cleaver, cocktail knife, cook's knife, fish knife, grapefruit knife, Kitchen Devils®, palette knife, paring knife, steak knife, table knife, vegetable knife; *types of spoon*: dessert spoon, draining spoon, ladle, measuring spoon, serving spoon, skimmer, straining spoon, tablespoon, teaspoon, wooden spoon.

Types of cooking utensil include: baking sheet, bun tin, cake tin, flan tin, loaf tin, muffin tin, pie plate, quiche dish; bain-marie, brochette, casserole, cocotte, deep-fat fryer, egg coddler, egg poacher, fish kettle, fondue set, frying-pan, grill pan, milk pan, preserving pan, pressure cooker, ramekin, roasting pan, saucepan, skillet, slow cooker, soufflé dish, steamer, stockpot, terrine, vegetable steamer, wok.

kittenish *adj*
playful, sportive, frolicsome, frisky, cute, coquettish, flirtatious
☒ staid

knack *n*
flair, faculty, facility, bent, skill, competence, proficiency, talent, genius, gift, trick, ability, capability, adroitness, expertise, skilfulness, aptitude, forte, capacity, handiness, dexterity, quickness, turn
formal propensity
colloq. hang

knapsack *n*
bag, pack, haversack, rucksack, backpack, duffel bag, flight bag, hold-all, kitbag, shoulder-bag

knave *n*
rogue, scoundrel, villain, swindler, rascal, cheat, reprobate, scamp, scallywag, swine
old use blighter, bounder, dastard, rotter

knavery *n*
knavishness, mischief, roguery, trickery, villainy, devilry, corruption, deceit, deception, dishonesty, double-dealing, fraud, chicanery, imposture
formal duplicity
colloq. hanky-panky, monkey business

knavish *adj*
roguish, mischievous, rascally, fiendish, wicked, contemptible, corrupt, fraudulent, deceitful, deceptive, dishonest, dishonourable, unprincipled, unscrupulous, reprobate, scoundrelly, villainous, devilish
old use dastardly
☒ honest, honourable, scrupulous

knead *v*
manipulate, press, massage, work, ply, squeeze, shape, rub, form, mould, knuckle
formal malax, malaxate

kneel *v*
fall to your knees, bow (down), get down on your knees, stoop, bend, curtsy, revere, defer to, kowtow
formal genuflect, make obeisance

knell *n*
toll, ringing, ring, chime, peal, sound, end
old use knoll

knickers *n*
pants, panties, briefs, underwear, lingerie, bikini briefs, camiknickers, knickerbockers, Directoire knickers, bloomers
colloq. drawers, smalls

knick-knack *n*
trinket, trifle, bauble, gewgaw, gimcrack, bagatelle, ornament, bric-à-brac, plaything

knife *n, v*
▶ *n* blade, cutter, scalpel, carver, dagger, dirk, skene-dhu, penknife, pocket knife, switchblade, jackknife, machete, flick knife, craft knife, Stanley knife®, Kitchen Devils®
▶ *v* cut, rip, slash, stab, pierce, wound, lacerate, bayonet

knight *n*
cavalier, horseman, equestrian, cavalryman, man-at-arms, soldier, warrior, chevalier, gallant, freelance,

champion, knight-errant, banneret, kemper, kempery-man

knightly *adj*
chivalrous, bold, courageous, valiant, dauntless, gallant, heroic, noble, honourable, intrepid, soldierly, courtly, gracious
formal valorous
◧ cowardly, ignoble, ungallant

knit *v*
1 JOIN, unite, secure, bind, ally, connect, tie, fasten, link, draw together, mend, interlace, intertwine
2 KNOT, loop, crotchet, purl, weave
3 WRINKLE, furrow, crease, gather

knob *n*
1 HANDLE, door-handle, switch
2 LUMP, ball, boss, protrusion, bump, projection, protuberance, nub
technical umbo, capitulum
3 KNOT, knurl, gnarl, swell, knub, swelling, tumour, tuber
technical tubercle

knock *v, n*
▶ *v* **1** *knock on the door*
TAP, hit, strike, rap, thump, pound, slap, smack
2 *knock someone down*
hit, strike, smack, slap, punch, box, cuff, clip, swipe, bang, batter
colloq. clout, wallop, whack, belt
3 *knocked her head against the wall*
bang, bump, hit, strike, collide, bash, pound, thump, stamp, dash, crash, jolt
4 CRITICIZE, condemn, find fault with, attack
formal disparage, deprecate, censure
colloq. slate, slam, pan, run down, pick holes in, pull/tear to pieces
◧ **4** boost, praise
▷ **knock about 1** WANDER, travel, roam, rove, saunter, traipse, ramble, gad, gallivant, range
2 ASSOCIATE, go around; *formal* consort; *colloq.* hang around **3** BEAT UP, batter, abuse, mistreat, hurt, hit, strike, punch, bash, damage, maltreat, injure, wound, manhandle, bruise, buffet
▷ **knock down 1** DEMOLISH, destroy, fell, pull down, floor, level, wreck, raze, pound, batter, clout, smash, wallop **2** RUN OVER, hit, knock over, run down **3** *knocked down prices* reduce, lower, decrease
▷ **knock off 1** FINISH, finish/stop work, stop, clock off, clock out; *formal* cease, terminate; *colloq.* pack (it) in **2** STEAL, rob, pilfer, filch; *colloq.* pinch, nick, lift, rip off, snaffle, snitch, swipe **3** DEDUCT, take away **4** KILL, murder, slay, assassinate, get rid of, do away with; *colloq.* bump off, do in; *slang* waste
▷ **knock out 1** *knock someone out* make unconscious, floor, strike down, fell, level, prostrate; *colloq.* KO **2** *knocked out of a competition* defeat, eliminate, beat, overcome, get the better of, overwhelm, rout, crush; *colloq.* thrash, hammer, run rings round **3** STUN, astound, impress, amaze, surprise, startle, astonish, shock, overwhelm, take your breath away; *colloq.* bowl over, knock for six
◧ **1** bring round
▷ **knock up** build quickly, jerry-build, make quickly, put together hurriedly, improvise
◧ demolish
▶ *n* **1** *a knock at the door*
tap, rap, hit, pounding, banging, hammering

2 BLOW, bump, bang, box, rap, thump, cuff, clip, pounding, hammering, slap, smack
colloq. clip, whack, belt, clout, wallop
3 MISFORTUNE, blow, setback, failure, rejection, reversal, rebuff, defeat, bad experience/luck

knockout *n*
success, triumph, sensation, attraction, coup, hit, winner
colloq. smash, smash-hit, stunner
◧ flop, loser

knoll *n*
hill, hillock, mound, barrow, elevation, hummock, koppie
Scot. knowe

knot *v, n*
▶ *v* tie, secure, bind, loop, tether, leash, lash, entangle, tangle, knit, entwine, ravel, weave
▶ *n* **1** TIE, bond, joint, fastening, loop, splice, twist, ligature

Types of knot include: bend, Blackwall hitch, blood knot, bow, bowline, running bowline, carrick bend, clove hitch, common whipping, double-overhang, Englishman's tie (or knot), figure of eight, fisherman's bend, fisherman's knot, flat knot, granny knot, half hitch, highwayman's hitch, hitch, Hunter's bend, loop knot, overhand knot or thumb knot, reef knot or square knot, rolling hitch, round turn and two half hitches, seizing, sheepshank, sheet bend or common bend or swab hitch, slipknot, spade-end knot, surgeon's knot, tie, timber hitch, Turk's head, turle knot, wall knot, weaver's knot, Windsor knot.

2 BUNCH, cluster, clump, group, circle, ring, band, gathering, crowd
3 *a knot on a tree*
knob, lump, gnarl, knurl, swelling, knub

knotty *adj*
1 COMPLICATED, complex, intricate, difficult, hard, perplexing, thorny, tricky, troublesome, puzzling, baffling, mystifying, problematical, Byzantine
formal anfractuous
2 GNARLED, knobby, knotted, rugged, rough, bumpy, nodose, nodous, nodular

know *v*
1 *know French*
understand, comprehend, apprehend, perceive, sense, notice, be aware, be conscious of, fathom, be well-versed in, be conversant with, experience, realize, see, undergo, go through
formal be cognizant of
colloq. be clued up, have at your fingertips, know like the back of your hand, know what's what, have something taped
2 *I know George*
be acquainted with, be familiar with, be friends with, associate with, be on good terms with, recognize, know by sight, identify
3 *know a good wine*
distinguish, discriminate, discern, differentiate, identify, make out, tell (apart)

know-all *n*
know-it-all, wiseacre
colloq. clever clogs, clever dick, wise guy, smart alec, smartypants; *slang* smart ass/arse

know-how *n*
expertise, knowledge, experience, proficiency, competence, gumption, *savoir-faire*, ability, capability,

skill, ingenuity, dexterity, aptitude, adroitness, adeptness, talent, faculty, bent, flair, knack
colloq. savvy

knowing *adj*
meaningful, expressive, perceptive, shrewd, significant, discerning, conscious, cunning, astute, aware

knowingly *adj*
intentionally, willingly, on purpose, purposely, consciously, studiedly, wilfully, wittingly, deliberately, designedly, by design, calculatedly

knowledge *n*
1 LEARNING, scholarship, education, schooling, scholarship, letters, instruction, wisdom, tuition, enlightenment, information, data, facts
formal erudition
colloq. know-how
2 ACQUAINTANCE, familiarity, awareness, intimacy, consciousness
formal cognizance
3 UNDERSTANDING, comprehension, apprehension, recognition, judgement, discernment, wisdom, intelligence, ability, grasp, skill, expertise, proficiency, conversance
formal cognition
colloq. know-how
E3 1 ignorance 2 unawareness

knowledgeable *adj*
1 EDUCATED, scholarly, learned, informed, well-informed, well-read, lettered, intelligent, enlightened
formal erudite
colloq. a mine of information
2 AWARE, acquainted, conscious, familiar, *au fait*, conversant, experienced, expert, well-versed
colloq. in the know
E3 1 ignorant

known *adj*
acknowledged, recognized, well-known, noted, obvious, patent, plain, admitted, revealed, familiar, avowed, commonplace, published, proclaimed, confessed, celebrated, famous

knuckle *v*
▷ **knuckle down** buckle down, start to work hard, begin to study
▷ **knuckle under** submit, yield, give way, give in, succumb, surrender, capitulate, defer, buckle under; *formal* accede, acquiesce

kowtow *v*
defer, cringe, fawn, grovel, pander, curry favour, pay court, flatter, kneel
colloq. suck up, toady, bow and scrape

kudos *n*
fame, glory, applause, praise, honour, laurels, prestige, renown, repute, reputation, distinction, acclaim, plaudits
formal esteem, regard, laudation

L

label *n, v*
▶ *n* 1 TAG, ticket, docket, tab, mark, marker, sticker, trademark
2 DESCRIPTION, categorization, identification, characterization, classification, designation, tag, badge, brand, name, title, nickname, epithet
3 TRADEMARK, brand, brand name, proprietary name
▶ *v* 1 TAG, mark, stamp, attach a label to, mark, stamp, ticket
2 DESCRIBE, brand, classify, categorize, classify, characterize, identify, class, designate, define, term, call, dub, name

laboratory apparatus

Laboratory apparatus includes: autoclave, beaker, bell jar, boiling tube, Büchner funnel, Bunsen burner, burette, centrifuge, clamp, condenser, conical flask, crucible, cylinder, desiccator, distillation apparatus, dropper, evaporating dish, filter flask, filter paper, flask, fume cupboard, funnel, glove box, Kipp's apparatus, Liebig condenser, measuring cylinder, microscope, mortar, pestle, Petri dish, pipette, retort, separating funnel, slide, spatula, stand, still, stirrer, stop clock, test tube, test tube rack, thermometer, top-pan balance, tripod, trough, U-tube, volumetric flask, Woulfe bottle.

laborious *adj*
1 HARD, arduous, difficult, strenuous, tough, backbreaking, wearisome, wearying, tiresome, tiring, fatiguing, uphill, onerous, tedious, heavy, toilsome
2 HARD-WORKING, industrious, painstaking, indefatigable, diligent, careful, assiduous
🔁 1 easy, effortless 2 lazy

labour *n, v*
▶ *n* 1 WORK, task, job, employment, chore, toil, effort, hard work, exertion, drudgery, industriousness, diligence
colloq. grind, slog, sweat
2 WORKERS, employees, workforce, labourers, workmen, hands
3 CHILDBIRTH, birth, delivery, labour pains, pangs, throes, contractions
technical parturition
🔁 1 ease, leisure 2 management
▶ *v* 1 WORK, toil, work hard, drudge, slave, strive, exert yourself, endeavour, struggle, plod
formal travail
colloq. grind, sweat, kill yourself
2 OVERDO, overemphasize, dwell on, elaborate, overstress, put too much emphasis on, strain
3 *labour hard to get results*
struggle, strive, endeavour, work hard
colloq. do your best, give your all, go all out
4 *labour under a mistaken belief*
suffer, be misled, be deceived, be blinded

5 TOSS, pitch, roll, pitch, turn
🔁 1 laze, idle, lounge

laboured *adj*
awkward, unnatural, forced, difficult, complicated, heavy, overdone, overwrought, stiff, stilted, strained, ponderous, studied, contrived
formal affected
🔁 easy, natural

labourer *n*
manual worker, blue-collar worker, unskilled worker, navvy, hand, worker, workman, drudge, menial, hireling

labyrinth *n*
maze, winding, warren, complexity, intricacy, complication, network, puzzle, riddle, enigma, tangle, entanglement, jungle, confusion

labyrinthine *adj*
complex, intricate, complicated, perplexing, puzzling, involved, knotty, tangled, tortuous, winding, mazelike, confused, mazy, Byzantine
formal convoluted
🔁 simple, straightforward

lace *n, v*
▶ *n* 1 NETTING, mesh-work, open work, tatting, crochet, filigree
2 STRING, cord, twine, thong, tie, shoelace, bootlace, lacing
▶ *v* 1 TIE, do up, fasten, secure, thread, close, bind, attach, string, twine, intertwine, interweave
2 ADD TO, mix in, flavour, blend, strengthen
formal fortify
colloq. spike

lacerate *v*
tear, rip, rend, cut (open), gash, slash, wound, claw, mangle, maim, injure, mutilate, torture, torment, harrow, hurt, distress
formal afflict

laceration *n*
tear, cut, gash, rip, rent, slash, wound, injury, mutilation, maim

lachrymose *adj*
tearful, crying, weeping, weepy, mournful, sad, melancholy, sobbing, teary, woeful
formal dolorous, lugubrious
🔁 happy, laughing

lack *n, v*
▶ *n* need, scarcity, shortage, insufficiency, dearth, deficiency, absence, scantiness, vacancy, void, deprivation, destitution, emptiness
formal want, paucity, privation
🔁 abundance, profusion
▶ *v* need, have need of, not have, not have enough of, miss, be deficient in, require

formal want
colloq. be clean/fresh out of

lackadaisical *adj*
apathetic, lazy, lethargic, inert, limp, spiritless, listless, indifferent, idle, dreamy, dull, lukewarm, half-hearted, abstracted
formal enervated, indolent, languorous, languid
🔁 active, dynamic, energetic, vigorous

lackey *n*
1 FAWNER, sycophant, toady, flatterer, hanger-on, parasite, minion, pawn, instrument, tool
colloq. yes-man, doormat
2 ATTENDANT, steward, servant, manservant, footman, menial, valet

lacking *adj*
needing, without, short of, missing, minus, inadequate, deficient, defective, flawed
formal wanting

lacklustre *adj*
drab, dull, flat, boring, tedious, dry, leaden, lifeless, spiritless, uninteresting, unimaginative, uninspired, commonplace, dim, insipid, vapid
colloq. run-of-the-mill
🔁 brilliant, inspired, lively, bright

laconic *adj*
terse, succinct, pithy, concise, incisive, crisp, taciturn, short, curt, brief, economical, blunt, abrupt, to the point
🔁 verbose, wordy

lacuna *n*
gap, omission, space, void, break, blank, cavity
formal hiatus

lad *n*
1 BOY, youth, youngster, juvenile, schoolboy, son
colloq. kid
2 CHAP, fellow
colloq. guy, bloke

ladder *n*
Related adjective: scalar

Types of ladder include: accommodation ladder, companion ladder, étrier, extension ladder, folding ladder, fruit-picking ladder, gangway ladder, hook ladder, kitchen steps, loft ladder, multipurpose ladder, platform ladder, quarter ladder, ratline, rolling ladder, roof ladder, rope ladder, scale, side ladder, stepladder, stepstool, stern ladder, stile, straight ladder, tower scaffold.

laden *adj*
loaded, charged, weighed down, burdened, oppressed, packed, stuffed, weighted, full, chock-full, fraught, encumbered, hampered, taxed, jammed
🔁 empty

la-di-da *adj*
pretentious, posh, conceited, snobbish, snooty, mannered, over-refined, foppish
formal affected
colloq. highfalutin, put-on, stuck-up, toffee-nosed

ladle *v*
shovel, spoon, lade, dish, scoop, bail, dip
▷ **ladle out** hand out, distribute, disburse, dish out, dole out

lady *n*
woman, young woman, female, matron, noblewoman, dame, damsel, gentlewoman

ladylike *adj*
refined, well-bred, well-mannered, polite, courteous, proper, respectable, polished, modest, cultured, elegant, courtly, queenly, genteel, matronly
formal decorous

lag *v*
dawdle, loiter, hang back, linger, fall behind, straggle, trail, bring up the rear, saunter, delay, shuffle, idle, dally
formal tarry
colloq. shilly-shally, lounge, drag your feet, kick your heels
🔁 hurry, lead, keep up

laggard *n*
dawdler, loiterer, lingerer, straggler, sluggard, idler, saunterer, snail, loafer
colloq. slowcoach, lounger
🔁 dynamo, live wire; *colloq.* go-getter

lagoon *n*
pool, pond, shallows, lake, marsh, bog, fen, swamp
US bayou

laid up *adj*
housebound, bedridden, ill, sick, incapacitated, disabled, hors de combat, immobilized, injured, out of action, on the sick list

laid-back *adj*
relaxed, at ease, casual, leisurely, easy-going, unhurried, untroubled, unworried, calm, cool, passionless, free and easy
formal imperturbable
colloq. unflappable
🔁 tense; *colloq.* uptight

lair *n*

Lairs and homes of creatures include: sett (*badger*); den (*bear*); lodge (*beaver*); hive (*bee*); nest (*bird*); byre (*cow*); eyrie (*eagle*); coop (*fowl*); earth (*fox*); form (*hare*); den (*lion*); fortress (*mole*); hole, nest (*mouse*); holt (*otter*); sty (*pig*); dovecote (*pigeon*); burrow, warren (*rabbit*); pen, fold (*sheep*); shell (*snail*); drey (*squirrel*); nest, vespiary (*wasp*).

laissez-faire *adj*
permissive, non-interfering, non-interventionist, free-enterprise, free-market, free-trade
colloq. live and let live

lake *n*
pond, pool, lagoon, reservoir, dam, basin, mere, tarn, *Scot.* loch, *US* bayou
Related adjective: lacustrine

lam *v*
beat, batter, hit, knock, pound, thump, strike, thrash, leather, pelt, pummel
colloq. clout, wallop, clout, whack

lambaste *v*
1 CRITICIZE, reprimand, rebuke, scold, upbraid
formal berate, castigate, censure, reprove
colloq. roast
2 BEAT, whip, flog, thrash, strike, drub, thump, batter, flay, leather
colloq. clout, wallop, whack, tan

lame   *adj*

1 DISABLED, handicapped, crippled, hurt, injured, maimed, limping, hobbling, halting
formal incapacitated
colloq. gammy, poorly
2 WEAK, feeble, flimsy, inadequate, unsatisfactory, defective, poor, thin, unconvincing
E3 1 able-bodied   2 convincing

lament   *v, n*

▶ *v* mourn, bewail, grieve, sorrow, cry, weep, sob, wail, keen, complain, groan, moan, deplore, regret
formal bemoan, ululate
E3 rejoice, celebrate
▶ *n* lamentation, dirge, elegy, keen, requiem, complaint, moan, groan, wail, grieving, crying, weeping, sobbing, tears, howl
formal threnody

lamentable   *adj*

1 DEPLORABLE, regrettable, mournful, distressing, sorrowful, tragic, unfortunate, terrible, wretched, grievous, woeful
2 MEAGRE, low, inadequate, insufficient, mean, unsatisfactory, pitiful, miserable, niggardly, poor, disappointing
colloq. measly, lousy, grotty

lamentation   *n*

dirge, elegy, lament, wailing, mourning, weeping, moan, sobbing, sorrow, grief, grieving, keen, keening, jeremiad
formal ululation, deploration, threnody, plaint
E3 celebration, rejoicing

laminate   *v*

cover, layer, plate, stratify, veneer, coat, face, flake, separate, split
technical foliate
formal exfoliate

lamp   *n*

light, lantern, bulb, light bulb
See panel at **light**.

lampoon   *n, v*

▶ *n* satire, skit, caricature, parody, spoof, burlesque, travesty, pasquinade
colloq. send-up, take-off
▶ *v* satirize, caricature, parody, spoof, make fun of, ridicule, mock, burlesque, pasquinade
colloq. send up, take off

lampooner   *n*

satirist, caricaturist, parodist, pasquinader, pasquilant, pasquiler

lance   *v, n*

▶ *v* pierce, slit, cut (open), puncture, prick, incise
▶ *n* spear, javelin, pike, harpoon, bayonet, lancet

land   *n, v*

▶ *n* 1 EARTH, ground, soil, loam, terrain, dry land, terra firma
Related adjective: terrestrial
2 PROPERTY, grounds, estate, real estate, country, countryside, fields, rural area, open space, farmland, agricultural land, tract, acres, acreage, manor
Related adjectives: agrarian, praedial
3 COUNTRY, nation, region, area, district, territory, province, domain, realm, state, fatherland, motherland, native country
▶ *v* 1 ALIGHT, disembark, dismount, dock, berth, unload, touch down, come/bring in to land, bring/take down, go ashore, come to rest

2 ARRIVE, deposit, reach, get, find yourself, drop, settle, turn up
colloq. wind up, end up
3 OBTAIN, secure, gain, get, acquire, net, capture, achieve, win
formal procure
4 *land you with another bill*
saddle, weigh down, burden, oppress, trouble, tax, encumber
5 *land a blow on the ear*
hit, deal, give, catch, deliver, administer, direct, inflict
colloq. fetch

landlady, landlord   *n*

publican, innkeeper, hotelier, hotel-keeper, owner, proprietor, host, mine host, restaurateur, freeholder, tenant

landmark   *n*

feature, monument, signpost, turning-point, crisis, watershed, milestone, milepost, boundary, beacon, cairn

landscape   *n*

scene, scenery, view, panorama, outlook, vista, prospect, perspective, countryside, aspect

landslide   *n, adj*

▶ *n* landslip, earthfall, rockfall, avalanche
▶ *adj* overwhelming, decisive, emphatic, runaway

lane   *n*

way, track, passage(way), alley(way), footpath, footway, path(way), towpath, byroad, byway, driveway, avenue, channel

language   *n*

1 SPEECH, vocabulary, terminology, communication, speaking, uttering, verbalizing, vocalizing
formal parlance
2 TALK, conversation, utterance
formal discourse, converse
3 WORDING, style, phraseology, phrasing, expression, utterance, rhetoric, diction
Related adjective: linguistic

Language terms include: brogue, dialect, idiom, patois, regionalism, localism, dialect, tongue, pidgin, creole, vernacular, argot, cant, jargon, doublespeak, gobbledygook, buzz word, colloquialism, journalese, *colloq.* lingo, patter, slang, cockney rhyming slang; etymology, lexicography, lingua franca, linguistics, phonetics, semantics, syntax, usage, grammar, orthography, sociolinguistics.

languages

Languages of the world include: Aborigine, Afghan, Afrikaans, Arabic, Balinese, Bantu, Basque, Bengali, Burmese, Belorussian, Catalan, Celtic, Chinese, Cornish, Croat, Czech, Danish, Dutch, English, Eskimo, Esperanto, Estonian, Ethiopian, Farsi, Finnish, Flemish, French, Gaelic, German, Greek, Haitian, Hawaiian, Hebrew, Hindi, Hindustani, Hottentot, Hungarian, Icelandic, Indonesian, Irish, Iranian, Iraqi, Italian, Japanese, Kurdish, Lapp, Latin, Latvian, Lithuanian, Magyar, Malay, Maltese, Mandarin, Manx, Maori, Mexican, Norwegian, Persian, Polish, Portuguese, Punjabi, Romany, Romanian, Russian, Sanskrit, Scottish, Serbian, Siamese, Sinhalese, Slavonic, Slovak, Slovenian, Somali, Spanish, Swahili, Swedish, Swiss, Tamil, Thai, Tibetan, Turkish, Ukrainian, Urdu, Vietnamese, Volapük, Welsh, Yiddish, Zulu.

languid *adj*
listless, sluggish, lethargic, slow, inactive, lazy, feeble, heavy, uninterested, unenthusiastic, spiritless, indifferent, inert, lackadaisical, drooping, dull, weak, faint, weary, pining, limp, sickly
formal debilitated, enervated, languorous, torpid
F3 alert, lively, vivacious

languish *v*
1 WILT, droop, fade, fail, flag, wither, waste away, rot, deteriorate, weaken, sink, faint, decline, mope, waste, grieve, sorrow, sigh, brood, sicken
2 PINE, yearn, want, long, desire, hanker, hunger, sigh
F3 1 flourish

languor *n*
lethargy, listlessness, laziness, faintness, fatigue, weariness, silence, inertia, drowsiness, dreaminess, sleepiness, feebleness, weakness, frailty, calm, lull, relaxation, oppressiveness, heaviness, ennui, sloth, stillness
formal debility, enervation, indolence, lassitude, torpor, indolence
F3 alacrity, gusto

lank *adj*
1 *lank hair*
limp, straggling, scraggy, drooping, lifeless, lustreless
2 *lank young people*
tall, thin, long, emaciated, skinny, gaunt, lanky, lean, slender, slim, scrawny, rawboned
F3 burly

lanky *adj*
gaunt, gangling, scrawny, tall, thin, lean, slender, slim, scraggy, weedy
F3 short, squat

lap[1] *n, v*
▶ *n* 1 CIRCUIT, round, orbit, ambit, tour, loop, course, circle, compass, distance
2 *a lap on a journey*
stage, section, leg
▶ *v* wrap, fold, wind, envelop, enfold, swathe, encase, surround, cover, swaddle, overlap

lap[2] *v*
animals lapping milk
drink, sip, sup, lick
▷ **lap up** accept eagerly, take in enthusiastically, listen in, absorb

lapse *n, v*
▶ *n* 1 ERROR, slip, mistake, negligence, omission, oversight, fault, failing, indiscretion, backsliding, relapse
formal aberration, dereliction
2 FALL, descent, decline, drop, downturn, deterioration, worsening, degeneration, backslide, slipping
3 BREAK, gap, interval, lull, interruption, intermission, pause
formal hiatus
▶ *v* 1 DECLINE, fall, sink, drop, deteriorate, slide, slip, sink, drift, fail, worsen, degenerate, backslide
colloq. go downhill, go to pot, go to the dogs, go to rack and ruin, go down the tube
2 EXPIRE, run out, end, stop, become void/invalid
formal terminate, cease
3 PASS, elapse, go by, go on, slip away, slip by
F3 2 continue

lapsed *adj*
ended, expired, run out, finished, out of date, outdated, invalid, obsolete, unrenewed
formal discontinued
F3 renewed, continued

larceny *n*
stealing, theft, burglary, robbery, pilfering, piracy
formal misappropriation, purloining, expropriation
slang heist

larder *n*
pantry, storeroom, storage room, scullery

large *adj*
1 BIG, huge, immense, massive, vast, sizable, great, giant, gigantic, bulky, heavy, ample, enormous, colossal, king-sized, broad, considerable, monumental, prodigious, stupendous, mammoth, substantial, high, tall
formal commodious, voluminous
colloq. jumbo, whopping, bumper, ginormous, dirty great, humungous
2 FULL, extensive, generous, liberal, ample, roomy, plentiful, spacious, grand, far-reaching, sweeping, broad, comprehensive, exhaustive, grandiose
F3 1 small, tiny
▷ **at large** 1 GENERALLY, in general, by and large, on the whole, chiefly, mainly 2 FREE, at liberty, on the loose, on the run, independent, unconfined
▷ **by and large** on the whole, generally, mostly, generally speaking, as a rule, for the most part, all things considered

largely *adv*
mainly, in the main, principally, chiefly, generally, primarily, predominantly, mostly, for the most part, considerably, by and large, to a large extent, widely, extensively, greatly

large-scale *adj*
extensive, far-reaching, broad, nationwide, country-wide, wide, wide-ranging, expansive, wholesale, global, vast, sweeping, epic
F3 minor

largesse *n*
generosity, kindness, liberality, philanthropy, benefaction, open-handedness, bounty, donation, gift, present, aid, grant, handout, endowment, bequest, charity, allowance, alms
formal munificence
F3 meanness

lark *n, v*
▶ *n* 1 ESCAPADE, antic, fling, prank, romp, revel, mischief, fooling, horseplay, frolic, caper, cavorting, play, game
colloq. skylark
2 *this writing lark*
activity, task, job, chore
▶ *v* play, play tricks, have fun, fool around/about, mess about, cavort, frolic, caper, romp, sport, rollick, gambol
colloq. skylark

lascivious *adj*
lecherous, lewd, licentious, lustful, ribald, sensual, obscene, pornographic, crude, vulgar, coarse, bawdy, wanton, dirty, indecent, offensive, suggestive, salacious, scurrilous, unchaste
formal libidinous, prurient
colloq. blue, horny, randy, smutty

lash *n, v*
▶ *n* blow, whip, stroke, swipe, hit
▶ *v* **1** WHIP, flog, beat, hit, thrash, strike, scourge, flail, batter
colloq. wallop, whack
2 ATTACK, criticize, lay into, scold, reprove, rebuke
formal censure, fulminate, berate
colloq. bawl out, tear a strip off, tear to shreds
3 TIE, bind, fasten, secure, make fast, join, affix, rope, tether, strap
4 *waves lashing the shore*
strike, smash, dash, break, beat, pound, buffet
5 *an animal lashing its tail*
flick, swish, whip, switch, wag
▷ **lash out 1** *lash out at someone* hit out at, attack strongly, speak out against, criticize fiercely, have a go at **2** *lash out on new clothes* spend a lot of money, spend extravagantly; *colloq.* splash out on, spend a fortune on, spend money like water

lass *n*
girl, young woman, schoolgirl, lassie, miss
old use damsel, maiden
slang bird, chick

lassitude *n*
sluggishness, tiredness, weariness, lethargy, listlessness, drowsiness, apathy, dullness, exhaustion, fatigue, heaviness
formal enervation, languor, torpor
⊟ energy, vigour

last¹ *adj, adv, n*
▶ *adj* **1** *last Sunday*
most recent, latest, previous
2 FINAL, ultimate, closing, latest, rearmost, hindmost, terminal, furthest, concluding, finishing, ending, remotest, utmost, extreme
3 *the last person to expect help from*
least likely, least suitable, most unlikely, most unsuitable
⊟ **1** next **2** first, initial **3** first, most likely
▷ **last word 1** final decision, final say, final statement, conclusive/definite comment, ultimatum **2** latest, best, pick, cream, ultimate, vogue, rage, perfection, crème de la crème, *dernier cri*, *ne plus ultra; formal* quintessence
▶ *adv* finally, ultimately, behind, after, at the end, at the back/rear
⊟ first, firstly
▶ *n* finish, close, end, ending, conclusion, completion
▷ **at last** eventually, finally, in the end, in conclusion, ultimately, in due course, at length

last² *v*
it lasts six hours
continue, go on, take, endure, remain, persist, carry on, keep (on), survive, hold out, hold on, exist, wear, stay, hold on, stand up
formal abide, subsist
⊟ cease, stop, fade

last-ditch *adj*
final, desperate, frenzied, wild, last-chance, straining, struggling, frantic, heroic
colloq. all-out, eleventh-hour, last-gasp

lasting *adj*
enduring, unchanging, unceasing, unending, abiding, surviving, continuing, persisting, permanent, durable, perpetual, external, everlasting, undying, never-ending, lifelong, long-lived, long-standing, long-term

formal interminable, ceaseless
⊟ brief, fleeting, short-lived

lastly *adv*
finally, ultimately, in conclusion, in the end, to sum up
⊟ firstly

latch *n, v*
▶ *n* fastening, catch, bar, bolt, lock, hook, hasp
▶ *v* fasten, bar, bolt, lock, hook, catch, make secure
▷ **latch on to 1** ATTACH YOURSELF TO, not want to leave, follow **2** UNDERSTAND, comprehend, grasp, learn, realize; *formal* apprehend; *colloq.* twig

late *adj, adv*
▶ *adj* **1** OVERDUE, behind, behindhand, behind schedule, behind time, slow, unpunctual, delayed, last-minute
formal tardy
2 FORMER, previous, departed, dead, deceased, past, preceding, old, defunct
3 RECENT, up-to-date, current, fresh, new, up-to-the-minute, latest
⊟ **1** early, punctual
▶ *adv* unpunctually, behindhand, behind schedule, behind time, in arrears, slowly, belatedly, formerly, recently
formal dilatorily, tardily
⊟ early, punctually
▷ **of late** recently, lately, not long ago, newly, latterly

lately *adv*
recently, of late, not long ago, newly, latterly

lateness *n*
belatedness, delay, unpunctuality
formal dilatoriness, retardation, tardiness
⊟ earliness

latent *adj*
potential, possible, dormant, inactive, undeveloped, unrealized, lurking, unexpressed, unseen, unrevealed, secret, concealed, hidden, invisible, underlying, veiled, passive
formal quiescent
⊟ active, conspicuous, apparent

later *adv, adj*
▶ *adv* next, afterwards, subsequently, after, successively, in the (near) future, at a future time/date, at a later time, later on, in due course, in a while, some other time
⊟ earlier
▶ *adj* next, subsequent, following, succeeding

lateral *adj*
sideways, side, oblique, indirect, slanting, sideward, edgeways, marginal, flanking

latest *adj*
modern, newest, most recent, ultimate, up-to-date, current, now, fashionable
colloq. in, with it, up-to-the-minute
⊟ earliest

lather *n, v*
▶ *n* **1** FOAM, suds, soapsuds, froth, bubbles, soap, shampoo
2 AGITATION, fluster, anxiety, fuss, dither, flutter, fever
colloq. state, flap, tizzy, sweat, stew
▶ *v* foam, froth, rub, soap, shampoo, whip up

latitude *n*
freedom, liberty, unrestrictedness, laxity, indulgence, carte blanche, licence, leeway, scope, range, room,

space, play, clearance, breadth, width, spread, sweep, reach, span, field, extent

latter *adj*
last-mentioned, last, later, closing, final, end, concluding, ensuing, succeeding, successive, second
🔁 former

latter-day *adj*
modern, contemporary, current, present-day

latterly *adv*
lately, recently, most recently, of late
formal hitherto
🔁 formerly

lattice *n*
lattice-work, openwork, fretwork, mesh, web, grate, grating, network, espalier, grid, grille, tracery, trellis
formal reticulation

laud *v*
praise, admire, approve, magnify, acclaim, applaud, celebrate, glorify, extol, honour, hail
🔁 blame, condemn, curse, damn

laudable *adj*
praiseworthy, commendable, estimable, of note, excellent, exemplary, worthy, admirable, creditable, sterling
formal meritorious
🔁 damnable, execrable

laudation *n*
praise, acclaim, acclamation, reverence, adulation, blessing, accolade, celebrity, commendation, devotion, extolment, glorification, glory, kudos, homage, tribute
formal encomium, encomion, eulogy, panegyric, paean, veneration
🔁 condemnation, criticism

laudatory *adj*
complimentary, commendatory, adulatory, acclamatory, approving, celebratory, glorifying
formal approbatory, encomiastic(al), eulogistic, panegyrical
🔁 damning

laugh *v, n*
▶ *v* chuckle, burst out laughing, dissolve into laughter, roar/shriek with laughter, cackle, giggle, guffaw, snigger, titter, chortle, hoot, roar, peal
colloq. split your sides, fall about, crease up, break up, be rolling in the aisles, be in stitches, laugh like a drain
▷ **laugh at** mock, ridicule, make jokes about, jeer, make/poke fun of, scoff at, scorn, taunt, make a fool of;
formal deride
▷ **laugh off** dismiss, disregard, ignore, brush aside, belittle, shrug off; make little of, minimize;
colloq. pooh-pooh
▶ *n* **1** *have a good laugh*
giggle, chuckle, snigger, titter, guffaw, chortle, lark, roar, peel
colloq. scream, hoot
2 JOKE, jest, prank, hoax, trick, sport, fun, play

laughable *adj*
1 FUNNY, amusing, comical, comic, humorous, hilarious, uproarious, droll, farcical, diverting, entertaining
colloq. side-splitting
2 RIDICULOUS, absurd, ludicrous, preposterous, nonsensical, derisory, derisive
🔁 **1** serious

laughing-stock *n*
figure of fun, butt, dupe, victim, target, fair game, stooge, Aunt Sally

laughter *n*
laughing, giggling, chuckling, chortling, guffawing, sniggering, tittering, hilarity, amusement, merriment, mirth, happiness, cheerfulness, glee, convulsions
Related adjective: gelastic

launch *v*
1 PROPEL, dispatch, discharge, fire, send off, project, float, set afloat, set in motion, throw, fire
2 BEGIN, start, embark on, set up, establish, found, open, initiate, inaugurate, institute, introduce, organize, instigate
formal commence
colloq. set in motion, set the ball rolling

laundry *n*
1 WASHING, (dirty) clothes, wash
2 LAUNDERETTE, dry cleaner's
US Laundromat®

lavatory *n*
toilet, WC, bathroom, cloakroom, washroom, Ladies' room, water closet, public convenience, urinal, latrine, privy, powder room
US rest room, comfort station
colloq. loo, the ladies, the gents, bog; *slang* kazi; *US slang* john

lavish *adj, v*
▶ *adj* **1** ABUNDANT, copious, lush, luxuriant, plentiful, profuse, unlimited, prolific, splendid, grand, gorgeous, rich
2 GENEROUS, liberal, open-handed, free, bountiful, extravagant, wasteful, thriftless, prodigal, wasteful, profligate, immoderate, excessive, wild, intemperate, unsparing, unstinting
🔁 **1** scant **2** frugal, thrifty, mean
▶ *v* spend, expend, heap, pour, shower, deluge, squander, waste, dissipate
formal bestow

law *n*
1 RULE, act, legislation, decree, edict, order, directive, statute, regulation, command, commandment, pronouncement, ordinance, charter, code, constitution, enactment
2 PRINCIPLE, axiom, maxim, criterion, standard, precept, rule, formula, tenet, code, direction, instruction, canon, guideline
3 JURISPRUDENCE, legislation, lawsuit, litigation
Related adjective: legal

law-abiding *adj*
obedient, upright, orderly, lawful, complying, honest, honourable, decent, virtuous, good, righteous, upstanding, dutiful
🔁 lawless

law-breaker *n*
offender, wrongdoer, criminal, felon, miscreant, culprit, delinquent, convict, outlaw, sinner, transgressor, trespasser
formal infractor
colloq. crook

lawful *adj*
legal, legitimate, permissible, legalized, constitutional, authorized, recognized, allowable, sanctioned, warranted, valid, just, proper, rightful
formal licit
🔁 illegal, unlawful, illicit

lawless adj
disorderly, rebellious, anarchic(al), unruly, ungoverned, riotous, mutinous, insurgent, insurrectionary, rebellious, revolutionary, seditious, unrestrained, chaotic, illegal, wrongdoing, law-breaking, criminal, wild, reckless
F3 law-abiding

lawlessness n
anarchy, disorder, chaos, insurgency, insurrection, rebellion, revolution, sedition, mob-rule, piracy, racketeering
formal ochlocracy
colloq. mobocracy, rent-a-mob
F3 order

lawsuit n
litigation, suit, action, legal action, proceedings, legal proceedings, case, prosecution, dispute, process, trial, argument, contest, cause
technical indictment

lawyer n
solicitor, barrister, advocate, attorney, counsel, QC, legal adviser, legal representative
colloq. brief

lax adj
1 CASUAL, careless, heedless, easy-going, slack, lenient, indulgent, permissive, tolerant, negligent, neglectful, remiss, slipshod, sloppy, inattentive
2 IMPRECISE, inexact, indefinite, loose, inaccurate, vague, general, broad
F3 1 strict, careful 2 exact, rigorous, specific

laxative n
loosener, purgative, evacuant, purge, salts, senna, ipecacuanha
technical aperient, cathartic, eccoprotic

laxity n
1 CARELESSNESS, neglect, heedlessness, indulgence, negligence, slovenliness, slackness, sloppiness, tolerance, permissiveness, softness, leniency, freedom, indifference, nonchalance, latitude, latitudinarianism, laissez-faire
2 IMPRECISION, inexactness, indefiniteness, looseness
F3 1 severity, strictness 2 exactness

lay¹ v
1 PUT, place, deposit, set down, settle, lodge, plant, set, establish, leave
formal posit
2 ARRANGE, position, set out, locate, work out, devise, make, prepare, plan, design, present, submit, offer, put forward
formal dispose
3 ATTRIBUTE, ascribe, assign, charge, impute, allot
4 *lay a burden on someone*
impose, put, burden, inflict, apply, thrust, encumber, saddle, oppress, weigh down
5 *lay a bet*
place, bet, wager, gamble, risk, chance, hazard
6 *lay eggs*
produce, bear, deposit, give birth to, breed, engender
technical oviposit
old use beget
7 *lay a woman*
have sex with, make love with
colloq. go to bed with; *slang* make it with, have, have it off with; *taboo slang* bonk, screw, shag, fuck, bang
▷ **lay aside** 1 PUT ASIDE, save, keep, store
2 REJECT, set aside, put out of your mind, abandon, discard, dismiss, shelve, postpone, put off, cast aside
▷ **lay bare** disclose, divulge, explain, expose, reveal, show, uncover, unveil, exhibit
▷ **lay down** 1 SURRENDER, yield, give up, give, discard, drop; *formal* relinquish 2 STIPULATE, assert, postulate, affirm, state, establish, formulate, prescribe, ordain
▷ **lay down the law** dictate, crack down, emphasize, dogmatize; *formal* pontificate; *colloq.* read the riot act, rule the roost
▷ **lay hands on** 1 ATTACK, assault, beat up, lay into, seize, set on, grab, clasp, clutch, get, lay hold of, grip 2 FIND, get hold of, locate, bring to light, acquire, discover, grasp, unearth 3 BLESS, consecrate, ordain, confirm
▷ **lay in** store (up), stock up, amass, accumulate, hoard, stockpile, gather, collect, build up, glean
▷ **lay into** attack, assail, pitch into, set about, tear into, let fly at, hit out at, have a go at, lash out at
▷ **lay it on** exaggerate, overdo it, flatter, overpraise; *colloq.* butter up, soft-soap, sweet-talk
▷ **lay off** 1 DISMISS, discharge, make redundant, pay off, let go; *colloq.* sack 2 GIVE UP, drop, stop, leave off, leave alone, let up, refrain; *formal* cease, desist, discontinue; *colloq.* quit
▷ **lay on** provide, supply, cater, furnish, give, set up, organize
▷ **lay out** 1 DISPLAY, set out, put out, spread out, exhibit, arrange, plan, design 2 KNOCK OUT, fell, floor, flatten, demolish 3 SPEND, pay, give, contribute, invest; *formal* disburse; *colloq.* shell out, fork out
▷ **lay up** store up, hoard, accumulate, amass, keep, save, put away
▷ **lay waste** desolate, ravage, destroy, devastate, raze, ruin, sack, spoil, pillage, rape, vandalize; *formal* depredate, despoil

---

⚠ **lay** or **lie** ?
Lay means 'to place in a flat, prone or horizontal position'. It is a transitive verb, ie it requires an object: *If you lay the pen down there, it will roll off the table.* Lie means 'to be or move into a flat, prone or horizontal position'. It is an intransitive verb, ie, it does not have an object. The past tense is *lay*: *She went into the bedroom and lay on the bed.*

---

lay² adj
1 LAIC, secular
2 AMATEUR, non-professional, non-specialist
F3 1 clergy, ordained 2 expert, professional

lay³ n
heavenly lays
song, poem, ballad, lyric, madrigal, ode

layabout n
good-for-nothing, ne'er-do-well, waster, idler, laggard, lounger
colloq. loafer, shirker, skiver, lazy-bones, lounge-lizard

layer n
1 COVER, coating, coat, covering, film, blanket, mantle, sheet, lamina
2 STRATUM, seam, vein, band, deposit, thickness, tier, bed, plate, row, ply

layman, laywoman or layperson n
1 LAYPERSON, parishioner
2 AMATEUR, outsider, non-professional
F3 1 clergyman 2 expert, professional

lay-off *n*
redundancy, discharge, dismissal, unemployment
colloq. sack, sacking, papers, firing, push, boot, elbow

layout *n*
arrangement, design, outline, plan, format, sketch,
draft, map, geography

laze *v*
idle, lounge, sit around, lie around, loll, relax
colloq. loaf, bum around, not pull your weight
F₃ work

laziness *n*
idleness, sloth, slothfulness, inactivity, slowness,
sluggishness, lethargy, slackness
formal dilatoriness, fainéance, indolence, tardiness,
langour
F₃ industriousness

lazy *adj*
idle, slothful, slack, work-shy, inactive, inert, slow,
slow-moving, good-for-nothing, lethargic, sluggish
formal indolent, torpid, languid, languorous, tardy,
fainéant
colloq. bone idle
F₃ industrious, hard-working

lazy-bones *n*
idler, slouch, laggard, sluggard, good-for-nothing,
layabout, ne'er-do-well
colloq. loafer, lounger, shirker, skiver

leach *v*
drain, extract, filter, strain, seep, filtrate, percolate
technical osmose
formal lixiviate

lead¹ *v, n, adj*
▶ *v* **1** GUIDE, conduct, escort, steer, pilot, usher
2 RULE, govern, head, be at the head of, be in charge
of, preside over, direct, supervise, command, manage,
regulate
colloq. call the shots
3 CAUSE, result in, produce, bring about, bring on,
contribute to, call forth, tend towards, provoke
4 INFLUENCE, persuade, incline, sway, prompt,
induce, move, dispose
5 SURPASS, outdo, excel, outstrip, outrun,
outdistance, exceed, eclipse, transcend, be in lead,
be in front, come first
6 PASS, spend, live, have, undergo, experience
F₃ 1 follow
▷ **lead off** begin, commence, open, get going,
start (off), inaugurate, initiate; *colloq.* kick off, start
the ball rolling
▷ **lead on** entice, lure, seduce, tempt, draw on,
beguile, persuade, string along, deceive, trick, mislead,
dupe
▷ **lead up to** prepare (the way) for, approach,
introduce, make overtures, pave/open the way
▷ **lead the way** go in front, go first, show, show the
way, guide
▶ *n* **1** PRIORITY, precedence, first place, advance
position, start, van, vanguard, forefront, advantage,
supremacy, pre-eminence, edge, interval, gap, margin
2 LEADERSHIP, guidance, direction, example,
model, pattern
3 CLUE, hint, indication, indicator, guide, pointer,
tip, suggestion
colloq. tip-off
4 TITLE ROLE, starring part, principal, principal
part, leading role

▶ *adj* leading, first, principal, chief, main, foremost,
head, premier, primary, prime, star, top

lead² *n*
pipes made of lead
1 BULLETS, shot, ammunition, pellets, balls, slugs
2 WEIGHT, heavy weight, plumb, sinker

leaden *adj*
1 GREY, overcast, cloudy, gloomy, dingy, dismal,
dreary, ashen, greyish, oppressive, sombre
2 DULL, heavy, burdensome, onerous, laboured,
lifeless, lacklustre, listless, spiritless, sluggish,
humdrum, inert, stilted
formal languid
3 CUMBERSOME, wooden, stiff, heavy, laboured,
plodding, lead

leader *n*
1 HEAD, chief, figurehead, director, ruler, principal,
manager, governor, superintendent, overseer,
supervisor, commander, captain, superior, chieftain,
ringleader, guide, conductor, skipper, mover and
shaker
colloq. boss
2 GUIDE, courier, escort, usher
3 PIONEER, innovator, developer, expert, authority,
leading light, guiding light, discoverer, inventor,
founder, architect, trailblazer, pathfinder,
groundbreaker, front-runner
F₃ 1 follower

leadership *n*
direction, control, command, management, authority,
rule, guidance, supervision, superintendency,
domination, pre-eminence, premiership, captaincy,
administration, sway, directorship, governorship,
headship

leading *adj*
main, principal, chief, primary, first, front, supreme,
outstanding, foremost, dominant, ruling, directing,
guiding, superior, greatest, highest, governing,
paramount, top-rank, pre-eminent, number one
F₃ subordinate

leaf *n, v*
▶ *n the leaves of a tree*
1 BLADE, bract, frond, pad, calyx, needle, sepal,
leaflet
technical cotyledon, foliole
Related adjectives: foliaceous, foliar, foliose

Leaf parts include: auxiliary bud, blade,
chloroplasts, epidermis, leaf axil, leaf cells, margin,
midrib, petiole, sheath, stipule, stomata, tip, vein.

Leaf shapes include: abruptly pinnate, acerose,
ciliate, cordate, crenate, dentate, digitate, doubly
dentate, elliptic, entire, falcate, hastate, lanceolate,
linear, lobed, lyrate, obovate, orbicular, ovate,
palmate, peltate, pinnate, pinnatifid, reniform,
runcinate, sagittate, spathulate, subulate, ternate,
trifoliate.

2 PAGE, sheet, folio
▶ *v* thumb (through), browse, flip, glance, skim

leaflet *n*
pamphlet, booklet, brochure, circular, handout, bill,
handbill, flyer, tract

leafy *adj*
green, leafed, leaved, wooded, woody, shady, shaded,

bosky, frondescent, frondose
technical dasyphyllous, foliose
formal verdant

league *n, v*
▶ *n* **1** ASSOCIATION, confederation, alliance,
union, federation, confederacy, coalition, affiliation,
group, combination, band, syndicate, conglomerate,
corporation, guild, consortium, cartel, combine,
partnership, co-operative, fellowship, compact
2 CATEGORY, class, level, group
▷ **in league** allied, in co-operation, co-operating,
linked, in partnership, in alliance, in collusion, in
tandem, collaborating, conspiring; *colloq.* hand in
glove, in cahoots
⊟ at odds
▶ *v* amalgamate, associate, band together,
co-operate, collaborate, combine, confederate,
conspire, join forces, unite, link, ally, consort

leak *n, v*
▶ *n* **1** CRACK, hole, opening, puncture, crevice,
chink, fissure, break, cut
2 LEAKAGE, leaking, seeping, seepage, drip, oozing,
discharge, escape, percolation
3 DISCLOSURE, divulgence, revelation, exposure,
exposé, uncovering, bringing to light
▶ *v* **1** SEEP, drip, ooze, escape, spill, trickle,
percolate, exude, discharge
2 DISCLOSE, reveal, let slip, make known, make
public, tell, relate, give away, pass on
formal divulge, impart
colloq. blab, squeal, let on, let the cat out of the bag,
spill the beans

leaky *adj*
leaking, holey, perforated, punctured, split, cracked,
porous, permeable

lean¹ *v*
1 SLANT, slope, incline, bend, tilt, list, bank, be at an
angle
2 RECLINE, prop, rest
formal repose
3 INCLINE, favour, prefer, tend, have an inclination/
preference for
formal have a propensity for
▷ **lean on 1** RELY ON, depend on, trust in, have
confidence in, not manage without; *colloq.* bank on
2 FORCE, force, persuade, pressurize, put pressure on

lean² *adj*
1 THIN, skinny, bony, gaunt, lank, angular, slim,
slender, scraggy, scrawny, emaciated
colloq. all skin and bones
2 SCANTY, inadequate, insufficient, bare, barren,
unproductive, unfruitful, sparse, scanty, poor, arid
⊟ 1 fat, flabby

leaning *n*
tendency, inclination, preference, partiality, liking,
fondness, attraction, bent, bias, disposition, aptitude
formal propensity, proclivity, penchant, predilection

leap *v, n*
▶ *v* **1** JUMP (OVER), bound, spring, vault, clear,
skip, hop, dance, bounce, caper, gambol, romp, frisk,
frolic, cavort
2 SOAR, surge, mount, increase, rocket, skyrocket,
escalate, rise
⊟ 2 drop, fall
▷ **leap at** jump at, accept eagerly, agree to, fall for,
grab, seize, pounce on, snatch, swallow
▶ *n* **1** JUMP, bound, spring, vault, hop, skip, caper

technical entrechat
2 INCREASE, upsurge, upswing, surge, rise, soaring,
escalation
▷ **by/in leaps and bounds** rapidly, swiftly, quickly;
colloq. in no time (at all)

learn *v*
1 GRASP, comprehend, understand, master, acquire,
train, study, pick up, take in, digest, gather, assimilate,
absorb, discern, familiarize yourself in, gain
knowledge of, acquire skill in
colloq. get the hang of
2 MEMORIZE, learn by heart, commit to memory,
have off pat, remember
3 DISCOVER, find out, ascertain, understand, hear,
detect, determine, hear, see, gather, realize, become
aware of, become informed about
colloq. get wind of

learned *adj*
scholarly, erudite, well-informed, well-read, well-
educated, knowledgeable, cultured, academic,
lettered, literary, studious, literate, widely read,
intellectual, versed, pedantic
⊟ uneducated, illiterate

learner *n*
novice, beginner, student, trainee, pupil, scholar,
apprentice, tiro, neophyte
colloq. rookie, greenhorn

learning *n*
scholarship, erudition, education, schooling,
knowledge, information, letters, study, wisdom,
tuition, culture, edification, intellect, research,
pedantry

lease *v, n*
▶ *v* let, loan, rent, hire, sublet, charter
▶ *n* agreement, contract, chapter

leash *n*
lead, tether, rein, hold, cord, check, control, curb,
restraint, discipline
old use lyam

least *adj*
smallest, lowest, minimum, fewest, slightest, poorest
⊟ most

leathery *adj*
hard, hardened, durable, rough, rugged, tough,
wrinkled, wizened, leathern
technical coriaceous, corious

leave¹ *v*
1 DEPART, go, go away, set out, take your leave, pull
out, decamp, exit, move, retire, withdraw, retreat,
emigrate, disappear
colloq. push off, push along, quit, scoot, take off, make
tracks, do a bunk, up sticks, hook it
2 ABANDON, desert, forsake, give up, drop, pull out,
surrender
formal relinquish, renounce, desist, cease
colloq. run out on, ditch, jilt, chuck, damp, turn your
back on, leave high and dry
3 ASSIGN, commit, entrust, allot, consign, make
over, hand over, deliver, transmit
4 *leave property in your will*
will, hand down, leave behind, endow, give over
technical devise
formal bequeath
⊟ 1 arrive **3** receive
▷ **leave off** stop, refrain, lay off, break off, end, halt;
formal cease, discontinue, desist, abstain, terminate;

colloq. quit, give over, knock off
▷ **leave out** omit, exclude, overlook, ignore, except, disregard, pass over, count out, cut (out), eliminate, neglect, reject, cast aside, bar
⊟ include

leave² *n*
1 PERMISSION, authorization, consent, allowance, sanction, warrant, concession, indulgence, liberty, freedom
formal dispensation
colloq. say-so, OK, green light
2 HOLIDAY, time off, day off, break, leave of absence, vacation, sabbatical, furlough, sick leave, compassionate leave
⊟ **1** refusal, rejection

leaven *v*
1 RAISE, cause to rise, puff up, ferment, expand, swell, work
2 INSPIRE, stimulate, lighten, quicken, pervade, permeate, imbue, suffuse

leavings *n*
remains, remainder, residue, remnants, leftovers, dregs, detritus, dross, fragments, bits, pieces, oddments, sweepings, scraps, refuse, rubbish, debris, waste, spoil

lecher *n*
womanizer, adulterer, seducer, sensualist, debauchee, libertine, profligate, libidinist, rake, roué, fornicator, wanton, Casanova, Don Juan
colloq. dirty old man, flasher, goat, wolf

lecherous *adj*
lewd, womanizing, carnal, promiscuous, lustful, lascivious, degenerate, debauched, dissolute, dissipated, unchaste, wanton, salacious, libidinous
formal concupiscent, licentious, prurient
colloq. randy, raunchy, horny

lechery *n*
lewdness, womanizing, carnality, libertinism, debauchery, rakishness, lust, lustfulness, libidinousness, licentiousness, salaciousness, sensuality, wantonness, lasciviousness
formal concupiscence, prurience
colloq. randiness, raunchiness

lecture *n, v*
▶ *n* **1** ADDRESS, lesson, speech, talk, instruction, sermon
formal discourse, disquisition, homily
2 REPRIMAND, rebuke, reproof, scolding, harangue, censure, upbraiding, chiding, reproach
formal berating
colloq. telling-off, talking-to, dressing-down, rocket
▶ *v* **1** TALK, give a talk, teach, hold forth, speak, make a speech, expound, address, instruct, give lessons in
2 REPRIMAND, reprove, rebuke, scold, admonish, harangue, chide, censure
formal berate
colloq. tell off, haul over the coals, tear/pull to pieces, pick holes in

lecturer *n*
teacher, tutor, talker, speech-maker, speechifier, orator, expounder, speaker, reader, instructor, academic, pedagogue, sermonizer, preacher, haranguer
formal declaimer

ledge *n*
shelf, sill, mantel, mantelpiece, mantelshelf, ridge, projection, overhang, step

lee *n*
shelter, refuge, protection, cover, sanctuary

leech *n*
hanger-on, parasite, sycophant, toady, bloodsucker, freeloader, extortioner, usurer
colloq. sponger, scrounger

leer *v, n*
▶ *v* eye, ogle, look lecherously at, stare, wink, squint, gloat, goggle, grin, smirk, sneer
▶ *n* ogle, lecherous look, stare, wink, squint, grin, smirk, sneer

leery *adj*
wary, careful, cautious, guarded, uncertain, unsure, chary, suspicious, on your guard, distrustful, doubting, dubious, sceptical

lees *n*
deposit, dregs, grounds, residue, sediment, refuse, settlings, draff
formal precipitate

leeway *n*
space, room, latitude, elbow-room, play, scope, slack, margin, flexibility

left *adj*
1 LEFT-HAND, port
formal sinistral
2 LEFT-WING, socialist, radical, progressive, revolutionary, liberal, communist
colloq. red
⊟ **1** right **2** right-wing

left-handed *adj*
ambiguous, dubious, equivocal, awkward, clumsy, gauche, insincere, hypocritical, unlucky, ambidextrous
formal sinistral

left-over *n & adj*
remaining, settled, excess, surplus, unused, uneaten

leftovers *n*
leavings, remainder, remains, remnants, residue, surplus, scraps, sweepings, refuse, dregs, excess

leg *n, v*
▶ *n* **1** LIMB, member, shank
technical crus
colloq. pin, stump, peg
Related adjective: crural
2 SUPPORT, prop, upright, brace, underpinning
3 STAGE, part, bit, section, portion, stretch, segment, lap
▷ **not have a leg to stand on** be unjustified, be unproved, lack support, lack an excuse
▷ **on its last legs** weak, failing, fading fast, ailing, nearing collapse, about to fail/collapse, near to death; *colloq.* at death's door
▷ **pull someone's leg** tease, trick, joke, play a joke on, make fun of, fool, deceive; *colloq.* kid, rib, have on, wind up, lead up the garden path, pull a fast one on
▶ *v* ▷ **leg it** run, hurry, walk, go by foot; *colloq.* hoof it

legacy *n*
bequest, endowment, gift, heritage, heritance, inheritance, birthright, estate, heirloom
formal bequeathal, patrimony

legal *adj*
1 LAWFUL, legitimate, within the law, permissible, permitted, sanctioned, allowed, authorized, licensed, allowable, legalized, constitutional, valid, warranted, above-board, right, sound, proper, rightful, acceptable, admissible
formal licit
2 JUDICIAL, forensic
3 JUDICIARY, statutory, constitutional
⊟ 1 illegal

legal terms

Legal terms include: *criminal law*: acquittal, age of consent, alibi, arrest, bail, caution, charge, confession, contempt of court, dock, fine, guilty, indictment, innocent, malice aforethought, pardon, parole, plead guilty, plead not guilty, prisoner, probation, remand, reprieve, sentence; *marriage and divorce*: adultery, alimony, annulment, bigamy, decree absolute, decree nisi, divorce, maintenance, settlement; *people*: accessory, accomplice, accused, advocate, Attorney General, barrister, *colloq.* brief, clerk of the court, client, commissioner for oaths, convict, coroner, criminal, defendant, Director of Public Prosecutions, DPP, executor, felon, judge, jury, justice of the peace, JP, juvenile, Law Lord, lawyer, Lord Advocate, Lord Chancellor, Lord Chief Justice, liquidator, magistrate, notary public, offender, plaintiff, procurator fiscal, receiver, Queen's Counsel, QC, sheriff, solicitor, witness, young offender; *property or ownership*: asset, conveyance, copyright, deed, easement, endowment, estate, exchange of contracts, fee simple, foreclosure, freehold, inheritance, intestacy, lease, leasehold, legacy, local search, mortgage, patent, tenancy, title, trademark, will; *miscellaneous*: act of God, Act of Parliament, adjournment, affidavit, agreement, allegation, amnesty, appeal, arbitration, bar, bench, Bill of Rights, brief, by-law, charter, civil law, claim, codicil, common law, constitution, contract, covenant, courtcase, court martial, cross-examine, custody, damages, defence, demand, equity, eviction, evidence, extradition, grant, hearing, hung jury, indemnity, injunction, inquest, inquiry, judgment, judiciary, lawsuit, legal aid, liability, mandate, misadventure, miscarriage of justice, oath, party, penalty, power of attorney, precedent, probate, proceedings, proof, proxy, public inquiry, repeal, sanction, settlement, statute, subpoena, sue, summons, testimony, trial, tribunal, verdict, waiver, ward of court, warrant, will, writ. *See also* **court**; **crime**.

legality *n*
lawfulness, legitimacy, validity, rightness, rightfulness, soundness, admissibleness, permissibility, constitutionality
⊟ illegality

legalize *v*
legitimize, license, permit, sanction, allow, decriminalize, authorize, warrant, validate, approve, ratify, accept, admit

legate *n*
representative, ambassador, delegate, deputy, emissary, envoy, agent, commissioner, messenger, nuncio

legatee *n*
beneficiary, recipient, inheritor, heir, co-heir(ess), devisee, inheritrix

legation *n*
mission, commission, consulate, embassy, ministry, deputation, delegation, representation

legend *n*
1 MYTH, story, traditional story, tale, folk-tale, fable, fiction, romance, narrative, saga
2 INSCRIPTION, caption, motto, key, cipher, explanation

legendary *adj*
1 MYTHICAL, fabulous, fabled, story-book, fictitious, fictional, fanciful, traditional
2 FAMOUS, celebrated, renowned, well-known, illustrious, glorious, acclaimed, honoured, remembered, popular, immortal

legerdemain *n*
trickery, sleight of hand, deception, cunning, craftiness, chicanery, artifice, artfulness, subterfuge, contrivance, manipulation, manoeuvring, feint
formal prestidigitation, thaumaturgics, sophistry
colloq. hocus-pocus

legible *adj*
readable, easy to read, intelligible, decipherable, clear, distinct, neat, plain
⊟ illegible

legion *n, adj*
▶ *n* **1** *Roman legions*
army, battalion, brigade, company, division, regiment, unit, cohort, troop, force
2 *legions of foreign tourists*
host, number, multitude, myriad, swarm, throng, drove, mass, horde
▶ *adj* countless, numerous, myriad, numberless, innumerable, illimitable, multitudinous

legislate *v*
enact, ordain, decree, order, authorize, codify, establish, formulate
formal constitutionalize, prescribe

legislation *n*
1 LAW, statute, regulation, bill, act, charter, enactment, ordinance, code, authorization, ruling, rules, measure
2 LAW-MAKING, enactment, codification, formulation
formal prescription

legislative *adj*
law-making, law-giving, judicial, parliamentary, congressional, senatorial
technical jurisdictive

legislator *n*
law-maker, law-giver, member of parliament, parliamentarian, congressman, congresswoman, senator

legislature *n*
assembly, chamber, house, parliament, congress, senate

legitimate *adj*
1 LEGAL, lawful, authorized, warranted, sanctioned, statutory, rightful, proper, correct, real, genuine, acknowledged
formal licit
2 REASONABLE, sensible, rational, logical, admissible, plausible, acceptable, justifiable, justified, warranted, well-founded, sound, fair, valid, true, credible
⊟ 1 illegal **2** invalid

legitimize *v*
sanction, authorize, permit, allow, warrant, license, validate, charter, entitle, legalize, decriminalize
formal legitimate

leisure *n*
relaxation, rest, spare time, free time, time off, ease, freedom, liberty, recreation, retirement, holiday, vacation, break, time out
E3 work
▷ **at your leisure** when you want to, at your convenience, unhurriedly, in your own time, in your spare time, when you get round to it

leisurely *adj*
unhurried, slow, relaxed, comfortable, easy, easy-going, unhasty, tranquil, restful, gentle, carefree, lazy, slow, loose
colloq. laid-back
E3 rushed, hectic

lend *v*
1 LOAN, advance, allow to have, allow to use, let someone use
2 *lend your support to something*
GIVE, grant, provide, supply, contribute, donate, add
formal bestow, furnish, confer, impart
E3 1 borrow
▷ **lend an ear** listen, pay attention, take notice, heed, give ear; *formal* hearken
▷ **lend a hand** help, help out, assist, aid, give a helping hand; *colloq.* do your bit, pitch in
▷ **lend itself to** be suitable for, be appropriate for, be easily/readily used for

length *n*
1 EXTENT, distance, measure, reach, span
2 DURATION, period, term, stretch, space, span
3 PIECE, portion, section, segment
▷ **at length** 1 THOROUGHLY, in great detail, comprehensively, exhaustively 2 EVENTUALLY, finally, in due course, at last
▷ **go to any lengths** be very determined, try very hard, do anything, go to extremes

lengthen *v*
stretch, extend, draw out, grow longer, prolong, protract, spin out, eke (out), pad out, increase, expand, continue
formal elongate
E3 reduce, shorten

lengthwise *adv*
lengthways, endways, endwise, endlong, horizontally, vertically

lengthy *adj*
long, prolonged, extended, lengthened, overlong, long-drawn-out, long-winded, rambling, diffuse, wordy, verbose, drawn-out, interminable, tedious
formal protracted, prolix
E3 brief, concise

leniency *n*
lenience, tolerance, forbearance, permissiveness, indulgence, mercy, forgiveness, soft-heartedness, softness, kindness, mildness, tenderness, gentleness, compassion, humaneness, generosity, magnanimity, moderation
formal clemency
E3 severity

lenient *adj*
tolerant, forbearing, sparing, indulgent, liberal, merciful, forgiving, soft-hearted, kind, mild, tender, gentle, compassionate, humane, generous, magnanimous, moderate
E3 strict, severe

lenitive *adj*
alleviating, calming, easing, palliative, relieving, soothing, assuaging, mollifying
formal mitigating
E3 irritant

lens *n*
See panel at **spectacles**.

leper *n*
outcast, social outcast, undesirable, untouchable, pariah, lazar

lesbian *n, adj*
▶ *n* gay, homosexual, sapphist, tribade
colloq. butch, les, lez, lezzy, queer; *slang* dyke
▶ *adj* gay, homosexual, Sapphic, tribadic
colloq. butch; *slang* dykey

lesion *n*
injury, wound, abrasion, sore, scratch, scrape, bruise, cut, gash, laceration, impairment, hurt, trauma
technical contusion

less *n, adv*
▶ *n* fewer, smaller amount, not as/so much, not as/so many
E3 more
▶ *adv* to a lesser degree/extent, to a smaller extent, not as/so much
E3 more

lessen *v*
decrease, go/come down, reduce, diminish, decline, plummet, curtail, lower, ease (off), contract, die down, let up, dwindle, lighten, slow down, weaken, shrink, abridge, de-escalate, erode, minimize, narrow, moderate, subside, ebb, wane, slack, slacken, flag, fail, dull, deaden, relieve, impair
formal abate
colloq. nosedive, peter out
E3 grow, increase

lessening *n*
decrease, reduction, decline, curtailment, easing, contraction, dwindling, weakening, shrinkage, de-escalation, erosion, minimization, moderation, ebbing, waning, slackening, flagging, failure, deadening, let-up
formal abatement, diminution
colloq. petering out
E3 increase

lesser *adj*
lower, secondary, inferior, smaller, subordinate, slighter, minor
E3 greater

lesson *n*
1 CLASS, period, instruction, lecture, seminar, sermon, tutorial, teaching, coaching, course
2 ASSIGNMENT, exercise, homework, schoolwork, practice, task, drill
3 EXAMPLE, model, warning, deterrent, moral

let¹ *v*
1 PERMIT, allow, give permission, authorize, agree to, sanction, grant, enable, tolerate
formal give leave, consent to, assent to
colloq. OK, give the OK, give the go-ahead, give the green light to, give the nod, say the magic word

2 *let something happen*
allow, cause, enable, make
3 LEASE, hire, rent, let out
F3 1 prohibit, forbid
▷ **let alone** not to mention, not forgetting, never mind, apart from, also, as well as
▷ **let down** fail, disappoint, disillusion, dissatisfy, disenchant, fall short, abandon, betray, desert; *colloq.* leave in the lurch
F3 satisfy
▷ **let go** release, set free, stop holding, free, liberate, unhand; *formal* manumit
F3 catch, imprison
▷ **let in** admit, allow to enter, accept, receive, take in, include, incorporate, greet, welcome
F3 prohibit, bar, forbid
▷ **let off 1** EXCUSE, absolve, pardon, exempt, discharge, reprieve, forgive, acquit, spare, ignore, liberate, release; *formal* exonerate **2** DISCHARGE, detonate, fire, explode, emit, give off, release
F3 1 punish
▷ **let on** disclose, reveal, let slip, make known, make public, tell, relate, give away, pass on; *formal* divulge, impart; *colloq.* blab, squeal, let the cat out of the bag, spill the beans
▷ **let out 1** FREE, release, let go, discharge; *colloq.* leak **2** REVEAL, disclose, make known, utter, betray, let slip; *colloq.* blab, squeal, let the cat out of the bag, spill the beans
F3 1 keep in
▷ **let up** subside, ease (off), lessen, moderate, slacken, diminish, decrease, moderate, stop, end, halt, die down; *formal* abate, cease
F3 continue

let² *n*
without let or hindrance
check, constraint, impediment, hindrance, obstacle, obstruction, prohibition, restriction, restraint, interference
F3 assistance

let-down *n*
disappointment, anticlimax, disillusionment, setback, betrayal, desertion
colloq. washout

lethal *adj*
fatal, deadly, deathly, mortal, dangerous, poisonous, toxic, murderous, ruinous, disastrous, destructive, devastating
formal noxious
F3 harmless, safe

lethargic *adj*
listless, sluggish, dull, lifeless, inert, slow, lazy, inactive, idle, slothful, apathetic, drowsy, heavy, sleepy, weary
formal debilitated, enervated, hebetant, languid, somnolent, torpid
F3 lively

lethargy *n*
listlessness, sluggishness, dullness, lifelessness, inertia, slowness, laziness, idleness, sloth, apathy, inactivity, inaction, indifference, sleepiness, drowsiness, weariness, stupor
formal lassitude, torpor, langour, somnolence
F3 liveliness

letter *n*
1 NOTE, message, line, correspondence, dispatch, communication, chit, acknowledgement, reply, circular

formal missive, epistle
2 CHARACTER, symbol, sign
technical grapheme
3 *a woman of letters*
literature, books, culture, education, learning, humanities, writing, scholarship, academia, belles-lettres
formal erudition
▷ **to the letter** exactly, strictly, strictly speaking, word for word, literally, religiously, punctiliously, in every detail, by the book

lettered *adj*
learned, scholarly, educated, informed, knowledgeable, academic, well-educated, well-read, widely read, cultivated, cultured, literary, literate, studied, versed, accomplished
formal erudite
colloq. highbrow
F3 ignorant

let-up *n*
break, interval, lessening, pause, recess, remission, slackening, respite, lull
formal abatement, cessation
colloq. breather
F3 continuation

level *adj, n, v*
▶ *adj* **1** FLAT, smooth, even, flush, plane, uniform, horizontal, aligned, plane
2 EQUAL, balanced, aligned, even, on a par, neck and neck, matching, uniform, level pegging
3 STEADY, stable, constant, unchanging, regular, uniform
4 CALM, unemotional, steady, composed, self-possessed
colloq. unflappable
F3 1 uneven **2** unequal **3** unsteady **4** emotional
▶ *n* **1** HEIGHT, elevation, altitude, highness
2 POSITION, point, rank, status, class, degree, grade, mark, standard, standing, station, plane, layer, stratum, storey, stage, zone
formal echelon
3 MEASURE, degree, extent, quantity, size, magnitude, amount, volume
▷ **on the level** honest, open, candid, fair, straight; *colloq.* fair and square, straight-up, upfront, above board
▶ *v* **1** DEMOLISH, destroy, devastate, flatten, knock down, raze, raze to the ground, pull down, bulldoze, tear down, lay waste
2 EVEN OUT, flush, plane, smooth, equalize, even up, stabilize, make level, make flat
3 DIRECT, point, aim, train, focus, concentrate, zero in on
4 *level with someone*
admit, open up, confess, divulge, tell, tell all, speak plainly, be frank, keep nothing back
formal avow
colloq. come clean, put your cards on the table, be upfront, give it to someone straight, tell it like it is, bring out in the open

level-headed *adj*
calm, balanced, even-tempered, sensible, steady, reasonable, rational, composed, cool, cool-headed, sane, self-possessed, dependable
formal circumspect, prudent, imperturbable
colloq. unflappable

lever *n, v*
▶ *n* **1** HANDLE, bar, pull, switch, joystick

2 CROWBAR, bar, jemmy, handspike
▶ *v* force, prise, pry, raise, lift, hoist, dislodge, jemmy, shift, move, heave

leverage *n*
force, strength, power, advantage, authority, influence, rank, weight
formal ascendancy, purchase
colloq. clout, pull

leviathan *n*
giant, mammoth, hulk, colossus, monster, sea monster, behemoth, whale, Titan

levitate *v*
float, glide, waft, drift, fly, hover, suspend, hang

levity *n*
light-heartedness, light-mindedness, frivolity, carefreeness, facetiousness, flippancy, irreverence, hilarity, triviality, silliness, fun
🖃 seriousness

levy *v, n*
▶ *v* tax, impose, exact, demand, charge, raise, gather, collect
▶ *n* tax, toll, subscription, contribution, duty, customs, excise, duties, due, fee, tariff, collection, assessment, tithe
technical impost

lewd *adj*
obscene, smutty, indecent, suggestive, bawdy, pornographic, salacious, licentious, lascivious, impure, vulgar, unchaste, lustful, lecherous, carnal, promiscuous, degenerate, debauched, dissolute
formal concupiscent
colloq. blue, raunchy, randy
🖃 decent, chaste

lewdness *n*
obscenity, smut, smuttiness, indecency, bawdiness, pornography, salaciousness, licentiousness, lasciviousness, impurity, unchastity, lustfulness, lechery, vulgarity, wantonness, carnality, crudity, debauchery, depravity
formal concupiscence
colloq. randiness
🖃 chasteness, politeness

lexicon *n*
dictionary, glossary, vocabulary, wordbook, word-list, phrase book, encyclopedia

liability *n*
1 ACCOUNTABILITY, duty, obligation, responsibility, answerability, blameworthiness
formal culpability
2 DEBIT, arrears, obligation, dues, indebtedness
3 DRAWBACK, disadvantage, inconvenience, hindrance, impediment, burden, onus, nuisance, encumbrance
colloq. drag, millstone around your neck
🖃 **1** unaccountability **2** asset **3** advantage

liable *adj*
1 INCLINED, likely, apt, disposed, prone, tending, susceptible, vulnerable, exposed, subject, open
formal predisposed
2 RESPONSIBLE, answerable, accountable, amenable, changeable, to blame, at fault
🖃 **1** unlikely **2** unaccountable

liaise *v*
contact, communicate, intercommunicate,

co-operate, work together, collaborate, exchange information, relate to, network, interface

liaison *n*
1 CONTACT, connection, communication, interchange, go-between, link, co-operation, collaboration, working together, exchange of information
2 LOVE AFFAIR, affair, relationship, romance, intrigue, amour, flirtation, entanglement

liar *n*
falsifier, perjurer, deceiver, prevaricator, false witness
colloq. fibber

libation *n*
drink offering, sacrifice
formal oblation

libel *n, v*
▶ *n* defamation, false report, untrue statement, slur, smear, slander, denigration
formal disparagement, vilification, aspersion, calumny
colloq. muck-raking, mudslinging
▶ *v* defame, slander, malign, abuse, denigrate
formal cast aspersions on, vilify, revile, disparage, calumniate, traduce
colloq. slur, smear, drag someone's name through the mud, throw mud at; *US* badmouth

---

⚠ **libel** or **slander** ?
In English law, *libel* is an untrue defamatory statement made in a permanent form such as print, writing or pictures or broadcast on radio or television, whereas *slander* is one made by means of the spoken word (not broadcast) or gesture. In Scots law, both are *slander*.

---

libellous *adj*
defamatory, abusive, slanderous, derogatory, maligning, injurious, scurrilous, false, untrue, denigratory
formal vilifying, disparaging, calumniatory, traducing

liberal *adj*
1 BROAD-MINDED, open-minded, enlightened, tolerant, lenient, unprejudiced, unbiased, impartial, broad-based, wide-ranging, catholic, libertarian
2 PROGRESSIVE, reformist, forward-looking, advanced, radical, moderate
3 GENEROUS, ample, bountiful, lavish, plentiful, abundant, copious, profuse, handsome, open-handed, magnanimous, big-hearted, unsparing, munificent, philanthropic, altruistic
🖃 **1** narrow-minded **2** conservative **3** mean, miserly

liberalism *n*
progressivism, radicalism, free-thinking, humanitarianism, libertarianism, latitudinarianism
🖃 conservatism, narrow-mindedness

liberality *n*
1 GENEROSITY, benevolence, free-handedness, large-heartedness, kindness, magnanimity, open-handedness, largesse, charity, bounty, philanthropy, altruism
formal beneficence, munificence
2 BROAD-MINDEDNESS, liberalism, impartiality, open-mindedness, permissiveness, breadth, tolerance, toleration, progressivism, catholicity, libertarianism
🖃 **1** meanness **2** illiberality

liberate *v*
free, emancipate, release, let loose, set loose, let go, let out, set free, deliver, unchain, unfetter, uncage, unshackle, discharge, rescue, ransom
formal redeem, manumit
E3 imprison, enslave, restrict

liberation *n*
freedom, freeing, liberating, liberty, emancipation, release, deliverance, loosing, unchaining, uncaging, unfettering, unshackling, unpenning, ransoming, enfranchisement
formal manumission, redemption
E3 enslavement, imprisonment, restriction

liberator *n*
rescuer, deliverer, freer, saviour, ransomer, redeemer, emancipator
formal manumitter
E3 enslaver, jailer

libertine *n, adj*
▶ *n* debauchee, reprobate, seducer, sensualist, womanizer, rake, profligate, lecher, voluptary, loose-liver, roué, Don Juan, Casanova
▶ *adj* debauched, degenerate, debauched, womanizing, lecherous, reprobate, dissolute, promiscuous, lustful, salacious
formal licentious

liberty *n*
1 FREEDOM, emancipation, deliverance, release, liberation, independence, autonomy, self-government, self-rule, self-determination, sovereignty
formal manumission
2 LICENCE, permission, sanction, right, privilege, prerogative, entitlement, authorization, dispensation, franchise
3 FAMILIARITY, disrespect, overfamiliarity, presumption, impertinence, impudence, insolence
formal impropriety
E3 1 imprisonment 3 respect, politeness
▷ **at liberty** free, allowed, permitted, entitled, unconstrained, unrestricted, unhindered, without restraint, not confined

libidinous *adj*
lustful, debauched, impure, promiscuous, loose, lascivious, lecherous, carnal, lewd, salacious, unchaste, sensual, wanton, wicked
formal concupiscent, cupidinous, prurient, ruttish
colloq. randy, horny
E3 modest, temperate

libido *n*
sexual desire, sex drive, sexual appetite, sexual urge, erotic desire, passion, ardour, lust, eroticism
colloq. randiness, the hots

libretto *n*
words, text, lines, lyrics, script, book

licence *n*
1 PERMIT, warrant, certificate, charter, document, pass, authority, grant, imprimatur
2 PERMISSION, warranty, authorization, authority, sanction, certification, right, entitlement, prerogative, privilege, dispensation, carte blanche, freedom, liberty, approval, exemption, independence
formal leave, consent, accreditation
3 ABANDON, dissipation, excess, immoderation, indulgence, self-indulgence, intemperance, lawlessness, unruliness, anarchy, disorder, debauchery, decadence, dissoluteness, licentiousness, immorality,

impropriety, irresponsibility
E3 2 prohibition, restriction 3 decorum, moderation, restraint, control

license *v*
permit, give permission, allow, authorize, certify, warrant, entitle, empower, sanction, commission, franchise
formal accredit, consent
E3 ban, prohibit

licentious *adj*
debauched, dissolute, dissipated, depraved, decadent, profligate, lascivious, immoral, abandoned, lewd, lecherous, promiscuous, libertine, impure, lax, lustful, disorderly, wanton, unchaste
E3 modest, chaste

licentiousness *n*
debauchery, dissoluteness, immorality, abandon, lewdness, lechery, promiscuity, libertinism, impurity, lust, lustfulness, salaciousness, salacity, wantonness, dissipation
formal cupidinousness, prurience
E3 modesty, temperance

lick *v, n*
▶ *v* 1 *lick the chocolate*
tongue, wet, moisten, lap, taste, wash, clean
2 FLICKER, dart, play over, touch, flick, ripple
3 DEFEAT, beat, conquer
formal vanquish
colloq. thrash, hammer, trounce
▷ **lick your lips** enjoy, savour, drool over, relish, anticipate
▶ *n* bit, dab, little, speck, spot, touch, taste, stroke, sample, brush, smidgeon, hint

licking *n*
thrashing, whipping, flogging, hiding, smacking, spanking, tanning, beating, defeat, drubbing

lid *n*
top, cover, covering, cap, stopper

lie¹ *n, v*
▶ *n* *tell lies*
falsehood, untruth, perjury, falsification, fabrication, invention, fiction, half-truth, deceit, falsity, white lie, prevarication
colloq. fib, whopper, porky, tall story, made-up story, cock-and-bull story; *slang* bullshit, crap
E3 truth
▷ **give the lie to** disprove, rebut, contradict, invalidate, prove false
▶ *v* perjure, misrepresent, tell a lie, fabricate, falsify, invent, make up a story, equivocate, prevaricate
formal forswear yourself, dissemble, dissimulate
colloq. fib, lie through your teeth

lie² *v*
1 BE, exist, be located, be found, belong, extend, remain, stay, keep, stretch, reach, stand, continue
formal dwell
2 *lie down for a rest*
rest, recline, stretch out, sprawl out, lounge, couch, laze
formal repose
▷ **lie in wait for** ambush, waylay, lay a trap for, trap, attack, surprise; *formal* ambuscade
▷ **lie low** go into hiding, hide, hide away, hide out, conceal yourself, go to earth, take cover, lurk, skulk; *colloq.* hole up, lie doggo, keep a low profile

⚠ **lie or lay ?** *See panel at* **lie¹**.

lieutenant *n*
assistant, second-in-command, deputy, subordinate, right-hand man/woman

life *n*
1 BEING, existence, animation, breath, viability, aliveness, entity, soul
2 LIVING THINGS, human life, animal life, plant, fauna, flora, fauna and flora
3 *the loss of many lives*
person, individual, human being, man, woman, child
4 DURATION, lifetime, existence, life expectancy, course, span, lifespan, career
5 *the machine has a limited life*
duration, continuance, span, lifespan, time, course, period of usefulness, time of being active, lifetime
6 *see life*
(wide) experience, varied activities, travelling, meeting people
7 LIFE STORY, biography, autobiography, diary, diaries, memoirs, journal
8 LIVELINESS, vigour, vitality, vivacity, animation, high spirits, exuberance, enthusiasm, excitement, verve, zest, energy, élan, spirit, sparkle, effervescence, activity, cheerfulness
colloq. oomph, pizzazz
E3 1 death
▷ **come to life** become active, become interesting, become lively, become exciting, come alive, wake up
▷ **give your life** sacrifice yourself for, give up/sacrifice your life, offer up/surrender your life, die for, dedicate yourself to, devote yourself to
Related adjectives: vital, zoetic

life-and-death *adj*
important, all-important, crucial, vital, serious, critical

lifeblood *n*
essential part/factor, life-force, spirit, soul, core, centre, heart, inspiration

lifeless *adj*
1 DEAD, deceased, defunct, cold, unconscious, gone, inanimate, insensible, stiff
2 LETHARGIC, listless, sluggish, lacklustre, dull, apathetic, passive, insipid, uninspired, uninspiring, colourless, slow, flat, wooden, stiff
3 BARREN, bare, empty, desolate, stark, uninhabited, arid, sterile, unproductive, empty
E3 1 alive, exciting 2 lively

lifelike *adj*
realistic, true-to-life, real, true, vivid, natural, authentic, faithful, exact, graphic
E3 unrealistic, unnatural

lifelong *adj*
lifetime, for all your life, long-lasting, long-standing, persistent, lasting, enduring, abiding, permanent, constant
E3 impermanent, temporary

lifestyle *n*
way of life, life, way of living, manner of living, living conditions, position, situation

lifetime *n*
duration, existence, life, lifespan, span, period, time, course, day(s), career

lift *v, n*
▶ *v* 1 *she lifted the chair*
raise, pick up, elevate, hoist, uplift, upraise, hold up, hold high

2 *he lifted their spirits*
uplift, exalt, buoy up, boost, raise, elevate
3 *the ban has been lifted*
cancel, end, stop, relax, remove, withdraw, annul
formal revoke, rescind, terminate
4 *lift people out of the war zone*
fly, transport, move, transfer, airlift, convey, shift
5 *the fog lifted*
clear, disperse, vanish, disappear, scatter, dissolve, thin out
6 DIG UP, dig out of the ground, pull up, pick, root out, unearth
7 *lift someone else's material*
copy, plagiarize, steal, borrow
colloq. crib
E3 1 drop 2 lower 3 start 5 come down
6 plant, sow
▶ *n* 1 ELEVATOR, elevator, escalator, hoist, paternoster
2 *give you a life home*
drive, hitch, ride, run, transport
3 BOOST, fillip, encouragement, pick-me-up, uplift, spur, reassurance
colloq. shot in the arm
E3 3 discouragement

ligature *n*
band, binding, bond, link, tie, connection, cord, rope, string, thong, strap, bandage, tourniquet, ligament

light[1] *n, v, adj*
▶ *n* 1 ILLUMINATION, brightness, brilliance, radiance, glow, ray, beam, shaft, shine, glare, gleam, glint, lustre, flash, blaze
formal luminescence, effulgence, lambency
2 LAMP, lantern, lighter, match, torch, candle, taper, bulb, beacon
technical luminosity, incandescence
US flashlight
3 DAY, daybreak, daylight, daytime, dawn, sunrise, first light, crack of dawn, cockcrow
4 ENLIGHTENMENT, illumination, explanation, understanding, comprehension, insight, knowledge
formal elucidation
5 *presented in a different light*
aspect, way, approach, manner, style, angle, side, dimension, point of view
E3 1 darkness 3 night
Related adjective: photic

Sources of light include: *natural light*: aurora borealis, daylight, lightning, moonlight, starlight, sunlight; infrared, ultraviolet; *electric light*: Belisha beacon, break light, chandelier, courtesy light, fairy light, flashgun, floodlight, fluorescent light, fog lamp, footlight, halogen light, headlamp, headlight, indicator light, laser, light bulb, light buoy, lighthouse, navigation light, neon light, night light, pedestrian light, range light, runway light, searchlight, sidelight, spotlight, standard lamp, streetlight, strip light, strobe light, sun-lamp, tail-light, torch, traffic light; *fire light*: bonfire, candle, candlelight, fire, firework, flare, flame, spark, taper, gaslight, hurricane lamp, lighter, match, oil lamp, pilot light.

▶ *v* 1 IGNITE, fire, set alight, set fire to, set burning, kindle
2 ILLUMINATE, light up, lighten, floodlight, brighten, animate, cheer (up), make cheerful, switch on, turn on, put on
formal irradiate
E3 1 extinguish 2 darken

▶ *adj* **1** ILLUMINATED, bright, brilliant, luminous, glowing, shining, well-lit, sunny
2 PALE, pastel, fair, blond, blonde, bleached, faded, whitish, faint
F3 1 dark **2** black
▷ **bring to light** make known, notice, reveal, expose, discover, uncover
▷ **come to light** become obvious, be made known, be noticed, be discovered, be uncovered, be exposed
▷ **in the light of** considering, taking into consideration, taking into account, because of, in view of, bearing/keeping in mind, being mindful of, remembering
▷ **shed/throw/cast light on** clarify, make clear, explain, make plain, illuminate; *formal* elucidate

light² *adj*
1 WEIGHTLESS, insubstantial, lightweight, delicate, fine, airy, buoyant, flimsy, thin, feathery, floaty, slight
2 *light rain; light winds*
slight, mild, gentle, weak, faint
3 *light machinery*
small, portable, easily moved, easy to carry around
4 *light work*
easy, effortless, moderate, undemanding, unexacting, untaxing
5 *a light punishment*
mild, lenient, slight
6 *light movements*
graceful, quick, gentle, nimble, agile
7 TRIVIAL, inconsiderable, trifling, superficial, unimportant, inconsequential, worthless, petty
8 CHEERFUL, cheery, carefree, light-hearted, lively, happy, merry, gay
formal blithe
9 ENTERTAINING, diverting, amusing, funny, humorous, frivolous, light-hearted, witty, pleasing
10 *light food*
easy to digest, digestible, modest, delicately flavoured
11 *light soil*
easily dug, porous, loose, crumbly
F3 1 heavy, weighty, thick **2, 3, 4** heavy **5** severe, harsh **7** important, serious **8** solemn **9** serious
10 heavy, rich **11** solid, dense

light³ *v*
▷ **light on/upon** *eyes lighting upon an object* find, come across, discover, notice, hit on, spot, stumble on *formal* chance on, encounter, happen upon

lighten¹ *v*
the sky lightened
illuminate, illumine, make lighter, brighten, make brighter, light up, shine, glow
F3 darken

lighten² *v*
1 EASE, lessen, make lighter, unload, lift, relieve, reduce, calm
formal mitigate, alleviate, allay, assuage
2 BRIGHTEN, cheer (up), encourage, hearten, uplift, lift, gladden, restore, revive, elate, buoy up, inspire
formal inspirit
colloq. park up
F3 1 burden **2** depress

light-fingered *adj*
dishonest, pilfering, stealing, thieving, thievish, shoplifting, crafty, furtive, shifty, sly
colloq. crooked, filching
F3 honest

light-footed *adj*
agile, active, nimble, sprightly, spry, swift, lithe, graceful
F3 clumsy, slow

light-headed *adj*
1 FAINT, giddy, dizzy, unsteady, airy, delirious
formal vertiginous
colloq. woozy
2 FLIGHTY, foolish, frivolous, silly, superficial, shallow, empty-headed, flippant, vacuous, trifling
colloq. scatter-brained, feather-brained
F3 2 level-headed, solemn

light-hearted *adj*
cheerful, joyful, jolly, happy, happy-go-lucky, bright, in good spirits, in high spirits, carefree, untroubled, merry, sunny, glad, elated, gay, jovial, playful, frolicsome, amusing, entertaining
formal blithe
colloq. chirpy, bouncy, high
F3 sad, unhappy, serious

lighthouse *n*
beacon, tower, danger/warning signal, fanal, pharos

lightly *adv*
1 SLIGHTLY, gently, faintly, delicately, softly, thinly, sparingly, sparsely, slightingly
2 EASILY, effortlessly, readily, airily, breezily, gaily, facilely, gingerly
3 FRIVOLOUSLY, flippantly, carelessly, heedlessly, thoughtlessly
4 LENIENTLY, mildly, easily
F3 1 heavily **3** soberly

lightness *n*
1 *lightness of the clothes*
weightlessness, slightness, airiness, buoyancy, crumbliness, porosity, porousness, sandiness, delicacy, delicateness, flimsiness, thinness,
2 *lightness of movement*
grace, gracefulness, agility, gentleness, litheness, nimbleness, mildness
3 *lightness of spirit*
cheerfulness, cheeriness, light-heartedness, liveliness, gaiety, animation
formal blitheness
4 FICKLENESS, triviality, frivolity, levity
F3 1 heaviness, solidness **2** clumsiness
3 heaviness **4** sadness, severity, sobriety

lightning *n*
1 *thunder and lightning*
forked lightning, sheet lightning, ball lightning, summer lightning, lightning strike, thunderbolt, thunderclap, clap of thunder, thunderdart, thunderstorm, electric storm
2 *he works like lightning*
speedily, quickly, rapidly, hastily, immediately
colloq. wildfire, a rocket
Related adjective: fulgural

lightweight *adj*
1 LIGHT, insubstantial, delicate, flimsy, thin, feathery, weightless
2 UNIMPORTANT, insignificant, inconsequential, trivial, worthless, negligible, trifling, petty, slight, paltry
formal nugatory
F3 1 heavy **2** important, major, heavyweight

like¹ *adj, n, prep*
▶ *adj* *like minds*

similar, resembling, alike, same, much the same, having an affinity, identical, equivalent, akin, comparable, corresponding, related, relating, parallel, allied, approximating, of a kind
formal analogous
F3 unlike, dissimilar
▶ *n* equal, match, counterpart, equivalent, opposite number, fellow, mate, twin, parallel, peer
▶ *prep* in the same way/manner as, along/on the lines of, similar to

like² *v*
1 ENJOY, delight in, find enjoyable/interesting, find pleasant, take pleasure in, take to, appeal to, care for, admire, appreciate, be fond of, find attractive, be keen on, love, adore, hold dear, cherish, prize, relish, revel in, approve, welcome, take (kindly) to, be someone's liking
formal esteem
colloq. have a soft spot for, dig
2 PREFER, choose, select, decide on, feel inclined, desire, want, wish, would rather, would sooner, would more willingly/readily
colloq. go for, fancy, go a bundle on, take a shine to
F3 **1** dislike **2** reject

likeable *adj*
lovable, pleasing, appealing, nice, agreeable, charming, engaging, winsome, winning, pleasant, genial, amiable, congenial, attractive, sympathetic
F3 unpleasant, disagreeable

likelihood *n*
likeliness, probability, possibility, chance, prospect, liability
F3 improbability, unlikeliness

likely *adj, adv*
▶ *adj* **1** PROBABLE, possible, anticipated, expected, to be expected, liable, prone, tending, inclined, predictable, inclined, foreseeable
colloq. odds-on, on the cards, in the wind
2 CREDIBLE, believable, plausible, feasible, reasonable, acceptable
3 PROMISING, appropriate, acceptable, proper, fitting, fit, right, promising, hopeful, pleasing
F3 **1** unlikely **3** unsuitable
▶ *adv* probably, presumably, in all probability, no doubt, doubtlessly
colloq. (as) like as not

like-minded *adj*
agreeing, in agreement, of one mind, of the same mind, unanimous, in harmony, in rapport, compatible, harmonious
formal in accord
F3 disagreeing

liken *v*
compare, equate, match, parallel, link, relate, juxtapose, associate, set beside
formal correlate, analogize

likeness *n*
1 SIMILARITY, resemblance, comparison, affinity, correspondence, parallelism
formal similitude, analogy
2 REPRESENTATION, image, copy, reproduction, replica, facsimile, statue, bust, sculpture, effigy, drawing, painting, picture, sketch, portrait, study, photograph, icon, counterpart
3 SEMBLANCE, guise, appearance, form, shape
F3 **1** dissimilarity, unlikeness

likewise *adv*
1 SIMILARLY, in the same way, by the same token, in like manner
2 ALSO, moreover, furthermore, in addition, further, besides, too

liking *n*
fondness, love, affection, preference, partiality, affinity, taste, attraction, appreciation, proneness, inclination, tendency, bias, leaning, bent, desire, weakness, fancy
formal predilection, penchant, propensity, proclivity
colloq. soft spot, thing
F3 dislike, aversion, hatred

lilt *n*
rise and fall, rhythm, sway, swing, song, measure, beat, cadence, air

lily-white *adj*
faultless, pure, spotless, virtuous, virgin, blameless, chaste, incorrupt, innocent, irreproachable, uncorrupt, uncorrupted, unsullied, untainted, untarnished, milk-white
F3 corrupt

limb *n*
1 *stretch your limbs*
arm, leg, member, appendage, extremity
2 BRANCH, projection, offshoot, wing, fork, extension, section, part, spur, bough
▷ **out on a limb** exposed, isolated, in a weak position, vulnerable, in a risky/precarious situation
Related adjective: membral

limber *v, adj*
▶ *v* ▷ **limber up** loosen up, warm up, work out, exercise, prepare
▶ *adj* flexible, supple, pliant, plastic, elastic, agile, graceful, lithe, loose-jointed, loose-limbed, pliable, lissom
F3 stiff

limbo *n*
▷ **in limbo** in a state of uncertainty, awaiting action, left hanging, left in the air
formal in abeyance
colloq. up in the air, on the back burner

limelight *n*
fame, celebrity, spotlight, stardom, recognition, renown, attention, notice, eminence, notability, prominence, publicity, public eye

limit *n, v*
▶ *n* **1** EXTREMITY, ultimate, utmost, extreme, maximum, terminus, greatest extent, greatest amount, lid, ceiling, maximum, cut-off point, saturation point, deadline
2 BOUNDARY, confines, parameters, bound(s), brim, border, frontier, edge, brink, threshold, verge, end, perimeter, rim, compass, demarcation, termination
3 CHECK, curb, restraint, restriction, constraint, limitation
▷ **the limit** enough, intolerable, too much, the end, the worst; *colloq.* the final blow, the last straw
▶ *v* restrict, check, curb, restrain, constrain, hold in check, confine, demarcate, delimit, control, bound, hem in, ration, reduce, specify, hinder, impede
formal circumscribe

limitation *n*
1 CHECK, restriction, curb, control, constraint, restraint, delimitation, demarcation, block, hindrance, impediment
2 INADEQUACY, shortcoming, incapability, inability,

weakness, weak point, defect, disadvantage, drawback, snag, condition, qualification, reservation

F3 1 extension 2 advantage, strong point

limited *adj*

restricted, constrained, controlled, confined, checked, defined, finite, qualified, fixed, minimal, small, basic, narrow, inadequate, insufficient, scanty, incomplete, imperfect

formal circumscribed

F3 limitless, boundless

limitless *adj*

unlimited, unbounded, boundless, illimited, undefined, immeasurable, measureless, incalculable, infinite, countless, endless, never-ending, unending, interminable, inexhaustible, untold, vast, unspecified

F3 limited

limp[1] *v, n*

▶ *v* *limp down the road*

hobble, falter, stumble, hop, shuffle, shamble, stagger, totter, walk with a limp, walk unevenly

▶ *n* hobble, lameness, hitch, shuffle, uneven walk

technical claudication

limp[2] *adj*

1 FLABBY, drooping, flaccid, floppy, loose, slack, relaxed, lax, soft, flexible, pliable, limber

2 TIRED, weary, exhausted, fatigued, spent, weak, frail, feeble, worn out, lethargic

formal debilitated, enervated

F3 1 stiff, firm 2 vigorous, energetic

limpid *adj*

1 CLEAR, crystal-clear, transparent, translucent, pure, glassy, bright, still, unruffled, untroubled

formal pellucid

2 INTELLIGIBLE, comprehensible, clear, flowing, coherent, lucid

F3 1 muddy, ripply; *formal* turbid 2 unintelligible

line[1] *n, v*

▶ *n* 1 STROKE, band, bar, stripe, mark, strip, rule, dash, slash, strand, streak, seam, belt, underline, score, underscore, scratch

2 ROW, rank, queue, file, column, sequence, series, procession, parade, chain, string, trail, tier, bank

3 LIMIT, boundary, border, borderline, edge, perimeter, periphery, frontier, demarcation, margin

4 STRING, rope, cord, cable, thread, strand, filament, wire, twine

5 PROFILE, contour, outline, silhouette, figure, shape, appearance, pattern, style, formation

formal configuration, delineation

6 CREASE, wrinkle, furrow, groove, crow's feet, corrugation

7 COURSE, path, direction, track, route, channel, way, trajectory, axis

8 APPROACH, avenue, course (of action), belief, ideology, attitude, policy, system, position, practice, procedure, method, way, scheme, *modus operandi*

9 OCCUPATION, business, trade, profession, vocation, work, job, line of business/work, career, activity, interest, employment, department, calling, field, province, forte, area, activity, pursuit, specialization, specialty, specialism, speciality

10 *chat-up line*

spiel, patter, talk, sales talk, pitch

11 *drop you a line*

note, letter, card, postcard, message, word, report, memo, memorandum, information

12 WORDS, part, text, script, book, libretto

13 *a shipping line*

company, business, firm, transport business

14 *enemy lines*

defences, position, front, front line, firing-line, battleground, battlefield, battle zone

15 *a line of products*

brand, make, type, kind, sort, variety, type

16 ANCESTRY, family, descent, extraction, parentage, heritage, lineage, strain, pedigree, stock, race, breed

▷ **draw the line** refuse, say not to, exclude, limit, reject, rule out, stop short of, stand firm; *colloq.* put your foot down

▷ **in line** 1 IN A ROW, in a queue, in a column, in series 2 *bring the two systems in line with each other* in agreement, in step, in harmony; *formal* in accord 3 *in line for promotion* due, likely, being considered, in the running; *colloq.* on the cards

▷ **lay/put on the line** risk, put in jeopardy, jeopardize, endanger, imperil

▷ **toe the line** conform, keep/follow the rules, be conventional

▶ *v* 1 BORDER, skirt, verge, edge, bound, fringe, rim

2 CREASE, score, furrow, mark, draw, hatch, inscribe, rule

▷ **line up** 1 ALIGN, range, straighten, marshal, order, group, regiment, queue up, stand in line, wait in line, form ranks, fall in, assemble; *formal* array

2 ORGANIZE, arrange, prepare, produce, secure, obtain; *formal* procure; *colloq.* lay on

line[2] *v*

line a box with paper

encase, panel, cover, fill, inlay, pad, back, face, stuff, reinforce

lineage *n*

ancestry, descent, extraction, genealogy, family, line, pedigree, race, stock, birth, breed, house, heredity, ancestors, forebears, descendants, offspring, succession

lineaments *n*

features, face, lines, outline(s), appearance, aspect, profile, traits

formal countenance, visage, physiognomy, configuration

lined *adj*

1 RULED, feint

2 WRINKLED, furrowed, creased, wizened, worn

F3 1 unlined, blank 2 smooth

linen *n*

bed linen, sheets, pillowcases, tablecloths, table linen, napkins, tea towels, white goods

formal napery

line-up *n*

array, arrangement, queue, row, line, selection, cast, team, bill, list

linger *v*

1 LOITER, delay, dally, wait, remain, stay, hang on, hang around, lag, dawdle, idle, stop, take your time

formal tarry, procrastinate

colloq. dilly-dally

2 CONTINUE, endure, hold out, last, persist, survive, remain

F3 1 leave, rush

lingerie *n*

underclothes, underwear, underclothing, undergarments, panties, knickers, camiknickers, camisole, slip, half-slip, teddy, body stocking,

panty girdle, brassiere, bra, suspender belt, unmentionables, inexpressibles
colloq. frillies, undies, smalls

lingering *adj*
persistent, remaining, slow, dragging, long-drawn-out, prolonged
formal protracted
◳ quick

lingo *n*
language, tongue, patois, speech, talk, jargon, idiom, vernacular, terminology, vocabulary, parlance, dialect, argot, cant, patter

liniment *n*
cream, lotion, salve, ointment, embrocation, emollient, balm, balsam, wash
formal unguent

lining *n*
inlay, interfacing, facing, padding, backing, encasement, stiffening, panelling, reinforcement

link *n, v*
▶ *n* **1** CONNECTION, bond, tie, association, joint, relationship, tie-up, union, knot, liaison, attachment, communication, partnership
2 RING, loop, bond, tie, knot, joint
3 PART, piece, element, member, constituent, component, division
▶ *v* connect, join, attach, couple, tie, fasten, unite, bind, amalgamate, merge, associate, ally, bracket, identify, relate, yoke, attach, hook up, join forces, team up
◳ separate, unfasten
▷ **link up** connect, join (up), ally, amalgamate, meet up, join forces, merge, team up, unify, hook up, dock
◳ separate

link-up *n*
connection, alliance, amalgamation, association, relationship, partnership, merger, tie-in, union
◳ separation

lion-hearted *adj*
bold, brave, courageous, heroic, daring, gallant, intrepid, stout-hearted, valiant, fearless, dauntless, resolute, stalwart, dreadless
formal valorous
◳ cowardly

lionize *v*
glorify, hero-worship, treat as a hero, honour, idolize, magnify, fête, exalt, celebrate, praise, sing the praises of, acclaim, adulate
formal aggrandize, eulogize
colloq. put on a pedestal
◳ vilify

lip *n*
1 EDGE, brim, border, brink, rim, margin, verge
2 IMPERTINENCE, impudence, insolence, rudeness, effrontery, backchat
colloq. cheek, sauce
◳ politeness

liquefaction *n*
dissolution, dissolving, fusion, liquefying, melting, thawing
formal deliquescence
◳ solidification

liquefy *v*
dissolve, fuse, liquidize, melt, smelt, run, thaw, flux, fluidize

formal liquesce, deliquesce
◳ solidify

liquid *n, adj*
▶ *n* liquor, fluid, juice, drink, sap, solution, lotion
▶ *adj* **1** FLUID, flowing, liquefied, watery, wet, running, runny, sloppy, thin, melted, molten, thawed, clear
formal aqueous, hydrous
2 SMOOTH, flowing, steady, even, regular, unbroken, uninterrupted, mellow, melodious
◳ **1** solid, gas

liquidate *v*
1 PAY (OFF), close down, dissolve, break up, clear, discharge, wind up, sell (off), disband, cash in, convert to cash
2 ANNIHILATE, terminate, do away with, put an end to, dissolve, kill, murder, massacre, assassinate, destroy, dispatch, abolish, eliminate, exterminate, remove, finish off
colloq. rub out, wipe out

liquidize *v*
process, blend, crush, purée, mix, synthesize

liquor *n*
1 ALCOHOL, intoxicant, strong drink, spirits, drink
colloq. hard stuff, hoo(t)ch, plonk, vino, juice, Dutch courage, grog, sauce, firewater; *slang* booze, gnat's piss
2 LIQUID, juice, gravy, essence, extract, stock, broth, infusion

lissom *adj*
graceful, supple, pliable, flexible, pliant, light, nimble, agile, limber, lithe, lithesome, loose-jointed, loose-limbed, willowy
◳ stiff, awkward

list¹ *n, v*
▶ *n a shopping list*
catalogue, roll, inventory, register, enumeration, schedule, programme, agenda, index, (list of) contents, listing, record, file, directory, table, tabulation, tally, series, syllabus, calendar, recipe, roster, rota, checklist, invoice
▶ *v* enumerate, register, itemize, classify, catalogue, alphabetize, index, tabulate, record, programme, file, schedule, enrol, enter, note, bill, book, set down, write down, compile

list² *v*
the ship is listing
lean (over), incline, tilt, slope, slant, heel (over), tip, cant

listen *v*
attend, pay attention, hear, heed, hang on (someone's) words, prick up your ears, take notice, mind, lend an ear, give ear
old use hark, hearken
▷ **listen in** eavesdrop, overhear, tap, wiretap, monitor, pin back your ears, prick up your ears; *colloq.* bug

listless *adj*
sluggish, lethargic, spiritless, languishing, lackadaisical, limp, lifeless, dull, passive, inert, inactive, impassive, indifferent, uninterested, vacant, apathetic, depressed, bored, heavy
formal languid, torpid, enervated, indolent
◳ energetic, enthusiastic

listlessness *n*
lethargy, sluggishness, spiritlessness, lifelessness, sloth, inattention, indifference, ennui, apathy
formal enervation, indolence, languidness, languor, torpidity, torpor, supineness
🖅 liveliness

litany *n*
1 PRAYER, petition, supplication, devotion
formal invocation
2 CATALOGUE, account, enumeration, list, repetition, recital, recitation

literacy *n*
ability to read, ability to write, proficiency, education, culture, cultivation, intelligence, knowledge, learning, scholarship, learnedness, articulacy, articulateness
formal erudition
🖅 illiteracy

literal *adj*
1 VERBATIM, word-for-word, strict, close, actual, precise, faithful, exact, accurate, factual, true, genuine, undistorted, unexaggerated, unembellished, unvarnished
2 PROSAIC, unimaginative, uninspired, colourless, matter-of-fact, down-to-earth, humdrum, boring, dull, tedious
🖅 **1** imprecise, loose, deviating **2** imaginative

literally *adv*
1 *many people in Africa are literally starving*
actually, really, truly, certainly
2 *translate literally*
exactly, faithfully, to the letter, strictly, precisely, closely, plainly, word for word, verbatim
🖅 **2** imprecisely, loosely

literary *adj*
1 EDUCATED, well-read, bookish, learned, scholarly, lettered, literate, widely-read, cultured, cultivated, refined
formal erudite
2 *literary phrases*
formal, poetic, old-fashioned
🖅 **1** ignorant, illiterate **2** everyday, colloquial, informal

literate *adj*
able to read, able to write, proficient, educated, well-educated, cultured, intelligent, learned, intellectual, knowledgeable

literature *n*
1 WRITINGS, printed works, published works, letters, paper(s)
2 INFORMATION, facts, data, leaflet(s), pamphlet(s), circular(s), brochure(s), hand-out(s), printed matter, advertising material
colloq. bumf

Types of literature include: allegory, anti-novel, autobiography, *formal* belles-lettres, biography, classic novel, criticism, drama, epic, epistle, essay, fiction, Gothic novel, lampoon, libretto, magnum opus, non-fiction, novel, novella, parody, pastiche, *colloq.* penny dreadful, picaresque novel, poetry, polemic, postil, prose, roman novel, saga, satire, thesis, tragedy, treatise, triad, trilogy, verse. *See also* **poem; story**.

lithe *adj*
agile, supple, flexible, pliable, pliant, lissom, limber, lithesome, double-jointed, loose-jointed, loose-limbed
🖅 stiff

litigant *n*
contender, contestant, disputant, claimant, complainant, litigator, plaintiff, party

litigation *n*
lawsuit, action, dispute, suit, case, legal case, prosecution, process, contention

litigious *adj*
argumentative, quarrelsome, contentious, disputatious, disputable, belligerent
🖅 easy-going

litter *n, v*
▶ *n* **1** RUBBISH, debris, refuse, odds and ends, waste, mess, disorder, clutter, confusion, disarray, untidiness, muck, jumble, fragments, shreds
US trash, garbage
formal detritus
colloq. junk, shambles, grot
2 OFFSPRING, young, brood, family
formal progeny, issue
▶ *v* strew, scatter, mess up, make a mess of, disorder, clutter, make untidy
🖅 tidy

little *adj, adv, n*
▶ *adj* **1** SMALL, short, tiny, minute, diminutive, miniature, infinitesimal, mini, microscopic, petite, baby, midget, dwarf, Lilliputian, slender, slight, younger
colloq. wee, teeny, pint-size(d)
2 SHORT-LIVED, brief, short, fleeting, passing, momentary, transient, transitory
formal ephemeral
3 INSUFFICIENT, sparse, scant, meagre, paltry, skimpy
formal exiguous
4 INSIGNIFICANT, unimportant, inconsiderable, negligible, trivial, petty, minor, paltry, nominal, trifling
formal nugatory
colloq. peanuts
5 *a nice little house*
pleasant, attractive, nice, sweet, cute
🖅 **1** big **2** long, lengthy **3** ample
4 considerable, serious
▶ *adv* barely, hardly, scarcely, slightly, rarely, seldom, infrequently, not much, next to nothing, a drop in the ocean
🖅 frequently
▷ **little by little** gradually, bit by bit, progressively, slowly, step by step, by degrees, imperceptibly, piecemeal
🖅 all at one go, quickly
▶ *n* bit, dash, pinch, small amount, spot, trace, drop, dab, speck, touch, taste, soupçon, smattering, particle, hint, fragment, modicum, trifle, trickle
🖅 lot

liturgical *adj*
ceremonial, ritual, solemn, sacramental, formal, eucharistic
formal sacerdotal, hieratic
🖅 secular

liturgy *n*
service, office, form, formula, rite, usage, worship, ceremony, ritual, observance, sacrament, ordinance, celebration

live¹ *v*
1 BE, be alive, have life, exist, breathe, draw breath
2 LAST, endure, continue, remain, persist, stay, survive, support yourself, earn your living
formal abide
3 *live in Leeds*
have your home, be settled, inhabit, lodge, stay, squat
formal reside, abide, dwell
colloq. hang out
4 PASS, spend, lead, behave
formal comport, conduct
5 *live while you're young*
enjoy life, enjoy life to the full, see life, make the most of your life
◨ **1** die **2** cease
▷ **live it up** revel, celebrate, go on a spree;
colloq. have a ball, make merry, make whoopee, paint the town red
▷ **live on** live on fruit and vegetables, feed, live off, depend for nourishment, rely on, exist; *formal* subsist

live² *adj*
1 ALIVE, living, having life, existent, breathing, animate
2 LIVELY, vital, active, energetic, dynamic, alert, vigorous
3 BURNING, glowing, blazing, flaming, hot, ignited, alight
4 *a live TV programme*
not prerecorded, not recorded, with an audience
5 *live cables*
connected, charged, electrically charged, active
6 *a live bomb*
unexploded, explosive, unstable, volatile
7 *a live issue*
RELEVANT, current, topical, controversial, active, important, vital, lively, urgent, pressing
formal pertinent
◨ **1** dead **2** apathetic **4** prerecorded
5 disconnected **6** defused **7** irrelevant
▷ **live wire** self-starter; *colloq.* life and soul of the party; ball of fire, dynamo, go-getter, eager beaver, whizz kid
◨ wet blanket

liveable *adj*
1 INHABITABLE, habitable
2 BEARABLE, tolerable, supportable, comfortable, endurable, acceptable, adequate, satisfactory, worthwhile
◨ **1** uninhabitable **2** unbearable
▷ **liveable with** companionable, sociable, *gemütlich,* compatible, congenial, harmonious, passable, tolerable, bearable
◨ impossible, unbearable

livelihood *n*
occupation, employment, job, work, profession, trade, living, means, means of support, income, source of income, maintenance, work, support, subsistence, sustenance, upkeep

liveliness *n*
animation, energy, quickness, spirit, vitality, vivacity, dynamism, activity, boisterousness, briskness, smartness, sprightliness
colloq. brio, oomph
◨ apathy, inactivity

livelong *adj*
complete, entire, full, whole, enduring, long, protracted
◨ partial

lively *adj*
1 ANIMATED, alert, active, energetic, alive, spirited, high-spirited, enthusiastic, dynamic, vivacious, vigorous, sprightly, spry, agile, nimble, quick, keen
2 CHEERFUL, blithe, merry, frisky, perky, playful, jaunty, breezy, frolicsome, buoyant
colloq. chirpy, bouncy
3 *a lively discussion*
animated, enthusiastic, heated, interesting, exciting, stimulating
4 BUSY, bustling, quick, brisk, rapid, crowded, eventful, exciting, buzzing, teeming, swarming, hectic
5 VIVID, bright, strong, colourful, graphic, striking, exciting, imaginative, stimulating, stirring, invigorating, racy, refreshing, sparkling
◨ **1** moribund, apathetic **3** dull **4** inactive, dull

liven *v*
enliven, vitalize, put life into, rouse, invigorate, animate, energize, brighten, stir (up), spice (up)
colloq. buck up, pep up, perk up, hot up
◨ dishearten

liverish *adj*
irritable, snappy, testy, tetchy, crusty, grumpy, disagreeable, ill-humoured, quick-tempered, irascible, peevish, splenetic
colloq. crabbed, crabby, crotchety
◨ calm, easy-going

livery *n*
uniform, costume, regalia, dress, clothes, clothing, garments, vestments, suit, garb, habit
formal apparel, attire, habiliments
colloq. get-up, gear, clobber, togs

livid *adj*
1 ANGRY, furious, infuriated, irate, outraged, enraged, raging, seething, fuming, indignant, incensed, exasperated
colloq. mad
2 LEADEN, black-and-blue, bruised, discoloured, greyish, purple, purplish
3 PALE, deathly pale, pallid, ashen, blanched, white, bloodless, wan, waxy, ghastly, pasty
◨ **1** calm

living *adj, n*
▶ *adj* **1** ALIVE, breathing, existing, live, animate
2 CURRENT, surviving, continuing, active, operative, strong, vigorous, active, lively, vital, animated
formal extant
colloq. going strong
3 *a living likeness*
close, exact, identical, precise, true, genuine
◨ **1** dead **2** dead, sluggish **3** inexact
▶ *n* **1** BEING, life, animation, existence
2 LIVELIHOOD, maintenance, support, means of support, income, source of income, subsistence, sustenance, work, job, occupation, profession, trade, way of life, lifestyle
technical benefice

living-room *n*
lounge, sitting-room, drawing-room

load *n, v*
▶ *n* **1** CARGO, consignment, shipment, goods, lading, freight, contents, burden, charge
2 BURDEN, onus, responsibility, duty, obligation, encumbrance, weight, pressure, charge, trouble, worry, strain, oppression, millstone, albatross
formal tribulation

3 *loads of money*
a lot, lots, heaps, dozens, scores, hundreds, thousands, a million, millions, hordes, tons
▶ *v* **1** PACK, pile, heap, freight, fill (up), stack, lade, charge
2 BURDEN, weigh down, encumber, overburden, oppress, overwhelm, worry, trouble, weight, strain, tax, saddle with

loaded *adj*
1 BURDENED, charged, laden, full, filled, weighted, packed, piled, heaped, stacked
colloq. snowed under
2 WEIGHTED, biased, to your disadvantage
3 RICH, wealthy, well-off, affluent
colloq. well-heeled, flush, in the money, rolling in it
4 DRUNK, under the influence, drunken
formal inebriated, intoxicated, crapulant
colloq. merry, tight, tipsy, tiddly, well-oiled, blotto, drunk as a lord/newt, blind drunk, roaring drunk, the worse for drink, soused, squiffy, happy, legless, plastered, sozzled, pickled, bibulous, woozy, one over the eight, under the table, bevvied, have had a few; *slang* stoned, tanked up, lit up, canned, paralytic, sloshed, smashed, pissed, stewed, bombed

loaf¹ *n*
1 *a loaf of bread*
block, slab, brick, mass, lump, cube, cake
2 *use your loaf*
common sense, sense, head, noddle
colloq. brains, gumption, nous,

loaf² *v*
loafing about/around
stand about, idle, laze, loiter
colloq. take it easy, hang around, lounge around, mooch
F∃ toil

loafer *n*
idler, shirker, sluggard, wastrel, lounger, ne'er-do-well
colloq. layabout, skiver, lazybones

loan *n, v*
▶ *n* advance, credit, mortgage, allowance, lending
▶ *v* lend, advance, credit, allow

loath *adj*
reluctant, unwilling, resisting, disinclined, opposed, grudging, hesitant, indisposed, against
formal averse
F∃ willing

loathe *v*
hate, detest, despise, dislike, not stand, recoil from, have an aversion to, feel revulsion at
formal abominate, abhor, execrate
F∃ adore, love

loathing *n*
hatred, hate, detestation, repugnance, revulsion, repulsion, dislike, disgust, aversion, odium, ill-will, horror
formal abhorrence, abomination, antipathy, execration
F∃ affection, love

loathsome *adj*
detestable, odious, repulsive, hateful, repugnant, repellent, offensive, horrible, disgusting, odious, nauseating, vile, revolting, nasty, obnoxious, despicable, contemptible, disagreeable
formal abhorrent, abominable, execrable

lob *v*
throw, toss, hurl, pitch, fling, heave, launch, lift, shy, loft
colloq. chuck

lobby *v, n*
▶ *v* campaign for, press for, demand, persuade, call for, urge, influence, solicit, pressure, promote
colloq. push for
▶ *n* **1** VESTIBULE, foyer, porch, anteroom, hall, hallway, waiting-room, entrance hall, entrance, corridor, passage, passageway
2 PRESSURE GROUP, campaign, ginger group, lobbyists

local *adj, n*
▶ *adj* regional, provincial, community, district, neighbourhood, municipal, city, urban, town, village, parish, parochial, vernacular, small-town, limited, narrow, restricted, parish(-pump)
F∃ national
▶ *n* **1** INHABITANT, citizen, resident, native
2 PUB, bar, inn, public house, tavern
colloq. hostelry, watering-hole; *slang* boozer

locale *n*
place, position, scene, setting, site, spot, venue, area, locality, location, neighbourhood, environment, zone
formal locus

locality *n*
neighbourhood, vicinity, district, area, locale, environment, region, position, place, site, spot, scene, setting, surrounding area

localize *v*
1 IDENTIFY, specify, zero in on, narrow down, pinpoint, ascribe, assign
2 RESTRAIN, limit, restrict, confine, contain, concentrate, delimit, delimitate
formal circumscribe

locate *v*
1 FIND, discover, uncover, unearth, come across, track down, detect, pinpoint, identify
colloq. run to earth, lay your hands on, hit upon
2 SITUATE, settle, fix, establish, place, position, put, set, site, station, seat, build

location *n*
position, situation, place, whereabouts, venue, site, locale, bearings, spot, point, setting, scene
formal locus

lock¹ *n, v*
▶ *n* *fit locks to windows*
fastening, bolt, clasp, catch, padlock, mortise lock, combination lock, spring lock, Chubb® lock, Yale® lock

Parts of a lock include: barrel, bolt, cylinder, cylinder hole, dead bolt, escutcheon, face plate, hasp, key, key card, keyhole, keyway, knob, latch, latch bolt, latch follower, latch lever, mortise bolt, pin, push button, rose, sash, sash bolt, spindle, spindle hole, spring, strike plate, staple.

▶ *v* **1** FASTEN, secure, bolt, latch, bar, seal, shut, padlock
2 JOIN, unite, engage, link, mesh, entangle, entwine, clench, interlock, jam
3 CLASP, hug, embrace, grasp, encircle, enclose, clutch, grapple
F∃ unlock
▷ **lock out** shut out, refuse admittance/entrance to,

keep out, exclude, bar, debar
▷ **lock up** imprison, jail, confine, shut in, shut up, put behind bars, put under lock and key, secure, cage, pen, detain, wall in, close up; *formal* incarcerate
🔁 free

lock² *n*
locks of hair
strand, tress, tuft, plait, ringlet, curl

locker *n*
cupboard, container, cabinet, compartment

lock-up *n*
1 JAIL, gaol, prison, penitentiary, cell
slang can, clink, cooler, jug, quod
2 GARAGE, lock-up, storeroom, depository, warehouse

locomotion *n*
movement, motion, moving, progress, progression, travel, travelling, headway, action, walking
formal ambulation, perambulation

locution *n*
1 STYLE, diction, articulation, accent, intonation, inflection
2 WORDING, term, phrase, phrasing, cliché, turn of phrase, expression, idiom, collocation

lodge *n, v*
▶ *n* **1** HUT, cabin, cottage, chalet, gatehouse, house, hunting-lodge
2 BRANCH, chapter, section, group, club, society, association, meeting-place
3 HAUNT, retreat, shelter, nest, lair, den
▶ *v* **1** ACCOMMODATE, quarter, board, billet, shelter, harbour
colloq. put up
2 LIVE, stay, have your home, be settled, room
formal reside, dwell, sojourn
3 FIX, imbed, implant, get stuck, get caught
4 DEPOSIT, place, put, submit, register, bank
5 *lodge a complaint*
register, make, submit, record, file

lodger *n*
boarder, paying guest, resident, tenant, roomer, inmate, guest

lodgings *n*
accommodation, quarters, billet, board, boarding-house, rooms, place
formal dwelling, abode, residence
colloq. digs, pad, a roof over your head

lofty *adj*
1 *lofty ideals*
noble, grand, exalted, distinguished, illustrious, majestic, sublime, stately, imposing, dignified, imperial, renowned
formal esteemed
2 HIGH, tall, sky-high, elevated, raised, towering, soaring
3 ARROGANT, proud, haughty, condescending, disdainful, patronizing, supercilious, superior, lordly, snooty
colloq. high and mighty, toffee-nosed
🔁 **2** low **3** humble, lowly, modest

log *n, v*
▶ *n* **1** TIMBER, trunk, block, chunk, piece
2 RECORD, diary, journal, logbook, daybook, account, tally, register, chart

▶ *v* record, register, write up, note, set down, book, chart, tally, file

loggerheads *n*
▷ **at loggerheads** disagreeing, in conflict, at odds, in opposition, quarrelling
colloq. at daggers drawn, at each other's throats, like cat and dog

logic *n*
reasoning, reason, sense, judgement, deduction, rationale, coherence, argument, argumentation
technical dialectics
formal ratiocination

logical *adj*
reasonable, rational, reasoned, well-reasoned, well-founded, well-thought-out, coherent, consistent, relevant, valid, sound, well-founded, clear, sensible, wise, intelligent, thinking, deducible, methodical, well-organized
formal cogent, judicious
🔁 illogical, irrational

logistics *n*
organization, co-ordination, management, masterminding, orchestration, strategy, tactics, planning, plans, direction, engineering

logo *n*
symbol, sign, trademark, representation, insignia, emblem, device, mark, badge, figure, image

loiter *v*
dawdle, hang about/around, idle, waste time, take your time, linger, dally, delay, mooch, lag, saunter
formal tarry
colloq. dilly-dally, loaf, lounge

loll *v*
1 RELAX, slouch, slump, sprawl
formal recline
colloq. loaf, lounge
2 HANG, flop, droop, drop, dangle, flap, sag

lone *adj*
1 BY YOURSELF, single, sole, alone, one, only, isolated, solitary, separate, unmarried, divorced
2 *a lone parent*
by yourself, on your own, single, unmarried, unattached, divorced, separated, without a partner
3 ISOLATED, uninhabited, remote, out-of-the-way, unfrequented, secluded, abandoned, deserted, forsaken, desolate, barren
🔁 **1** accompanied

loneliness *n*
aloneness, isolation, lonesomeness, solitariness, solitude, seclusion, desolation

lonely *adj*
1 ALONE, friendless, lone, lonesome, solitary, abandoned, forsaken, companionless, reclusive, unaccompanied, destitute, rejected, outcast, sad, unhappy, miserable, wretched
2 ISOLATED, uninhabited, remote, out-of-the-way, unfrequented, secluded, abandoned, deserted, forsaken, desolate, barren, God-forsaken
colloq. off the beaten track
🔁 **1** popular **2** crowded, populous

loner *n*
individualist, recluse, solitary, hermit
formal solitudinarian
colloq. lone wolf

lonesome *adj*
1 ALONE, lonely, friendless, lone, lonesome, solitary, abandoned, forsaken, companionless, reclusive, unaccompanied, destitute, rejected, outcast, sad, unhappy, miserable, wretched
2 ISOLATED, lonely, uninhabited, remote, out-of-the-way, unfrequented, secluded, abandoned, deserted, forsaken, desolate, barren

long *adj, v*
▶ *adj* lengthy, extensive, extended, expanded, elongated, prolonged, stretched (out), spread out, sustained, expansive, far-reaching, long-drawn-out, overlong, spun out, marathon, interminable, slow
formal protracted, verbose, tardy
ﾛ short, brief, fleeting, abbreviated
▷ **before long** soon, shortly, in a short time, in a moment, in a minute or two, in the near future
▶ *v* yearn, crave, want, wish, desire, hope, dream, hanker, pine, thirst, hunger, lust, covet, itch
colloq. yen for

long-drawn-out *adj*
lengthy, long-winded, spun out, overlong, prolonged, interminable, tedious, marathon, overextended, long-drawn
formal protracted, prolix
colloq. dragging on
ﾛ brief, curtailed

longing *n, adj*
▶ *n* craving, desire, yearning, hunger, hungering, hankering, pining, thirst, wish, wanting, dream, hope, urge, coveting, itch, aspiration, ambition
colloq. yen
▶ *adj* wishful, eager, craving, pining, yearning, wistful, languishing, hungry, anxious, avid, ardent
formal desirous

long-lasting *adj*
permanent, imperishable, enduring, unchanging, unfading, continuing, abiding, chronic, lingering, long-standing, prolonged
formal protracted
ﾛ short-lived, ephemeral, transient

long-lived *adj*
enduring, lasting, durable, long-lasting, long-standing
technical macrobian, macrobiotic
formal longevous
ﾛ brief, short-lived; *formal* ephemeral

long-standing *adj*
established, long-established, well-established, long-lived, long-lasting, enduring, abiding, time-honoured, traditional

long-suffering *adj*
uncomplaining, forbearing, forgiving, tolerant, indulgent, easy-going, patient, stoical, resigned
ﾛ complaining

long-winded *adj*
lengthy, overlong, prolonged, long-drawn-out, diffuse, verbose, wordy, garrulous, long-drawn-out, discursive, repetitious, rambling, tedious
formal prolix, protracted, voluble
ﾛ brief, terse

long-windedness *n*
lengthiness, verbosity, wordiness, diffuseness, discursiveness, repetitiousness, tediousness, garrulity
formal volubility, prolixity, longueur, macrology
ﾛ brevity, curtness

look *v, n*
▶ *v* 1 WATCH, see, take a look, observe, view, survey, regard, gaze, eye, study, stare, examine, inspect, focus, check, take in, consider, scrutinize, glance, contemplate, scan, peep, gape
colloq. gawp, run your eyes over, give the once-over, give a going-over, get a load of, get an eyeful of, take a squint at, take a dekko at, take a gander at, take a butcher's at, take a shufti at; *US* eyeball
2 SEEM, appear, give the appearance of, show, exhibit, display
3 *the house looks onto the fields*
face, front, front on, give on (to), overlook, be opposite, look onto
▷ **look after** take care of, mind, care for, attend to, take charge of, maintain, tend, keep an eye on, watch over, nurse, protect, supervise, guard, babysit, sit, childmind
ﾛ neglect, disregard, ignore
▷ **look back** remember, recall, think back, reminisce, reflect on the past
▷ **look down on** despise, scorn, sneer at, hold in contempt, disdain, spurn, think of as inferior/unimportant, patronize, talk down to, act/speak condescendingly; *formal* disparage; *colloq.* look down your nose at, turn your nose up at
ﾛ esteem, approve
▷ **look for** try to find, search for, seek, quest, hunt for, hunt out, forage for
▷ **look forward to** anticipate, await, expect, hope for, long for, envisage, envision, count on, wait for, look for
▷ **look into** investigate, probe, research, study, go into, search into, examine, inquire about, ask about, explore, inspect, scrutinize, look over, plumb, fathom, dig, delve; *colloq.* check out
▷ **look like** resemble, take after, be similar (in appearance) to, have the appearance of, remind you of
▷ **look on/upon** consider, regard, think, judge, count, hold; *formal* deem
▷ **look out** pay attention, watch out, beware, be careful, be alert, be on your guard, guard yourself, keep your eyes open/peeled/skinned, be on the qui vive, keep an eye out; *colloq.* look/mind where you're going
▷ **look over** inspect, examine, check, cast an/your eye over, look through, go through, scan, read through, view, monitor; *colloq.* check out, give a once-over
▷ **look to** expect, hope for, reckon on, rely on, turn to, count on, anticipate, think about, await
▷ **look up** 1 SEARCH FOR, research, seek, consult, hunt for, find, track down 2 VISIT, call on, drop in on, look in on, pay a visit to, stop by, drop by
3 IMPROVE, get better, pick up, progress, make progress, develop, advance, make headway, come on/along; *formal* ameliorate; *colloq.* perk up
▷ **look up to** admire, respect, regard highly, revere, honour, have a high opinion of, think highly of; *formal* esteem
▶ *n* 1 VIEW, survey, inspection, examination, study, contemplation, observation, sight, review, glance, glimpse, stare, gaze, gape, peek, peep
colloq. once-over, squint, eyeful, dekko, gander, butcher's, shufti
2 APPEARANCE, aspect, manner, air, effect, impression, semblance, expression, face, guise, features, façade, complexion
formal countenance, mien, bearing

look-alike *n*
double, replica, twin, image, living image, exact likeness, clone, *doppelgänger*

colloq. spitting image, spit, (dead) ringer

lookout *n*
1 GUARD, sentry, watch, watch-tower, watchman, sentinel, tower, post, observation post
2 CONCERN, responsibility, worry, affair, business, problem
colloq. pigeon
▷ **keep a lookout** remain alert, watch, keep guard, be vigilant, be on the qui vive

loom *v*
the ship loomed out of the mist; her exams are looming
appear, emerge, take shape, become visible, menace, threaten, impend, be imminent, hang over, dominate, tower, overhang, rise, soar, mount, overshadow, overtop

loop *n, v*
▶ *n* hoop, ring, circle, noose, coil, eyelet, loophole, spiral, curve, curl, oval, kink, twist, whorl, twirl, turn, bend
formal convolution
▶ *v* coil, encircle, surround, roll, bend, circle, curve round, turn, curl, twist, spiral, wind, connect, join, tie, knot, fasten, fold, braid

loophole *n*
let-out, escape, omission, escape, clause, evasion, excuse, pretext, plea, pretence, mistake

loose *adj, v*
▶ *adj* 1 FREE, unfastened, untied, at large, unconfined, released, undone, untethered, uncoupled, unlocked, let go, escaped, off, movable, unattached, insecure, wobbly, unsteady
2 SLACK, lax, baggy, hanging, loose-fitting, sagging, flowing, shapeless, unbound, untied
3 IMPRECISE, vague, inexact, ill-defined, indefinite, inaccurate, indistinct, general, broad, rambling
4 *loose morals*
promiscuous, dissolute, lax, unchaste, fast, debauched, disreputable, immoral, corrupt, wanton, degenerate, abandoned
F3 1 firm, fixed, secure 2 tight 3 precise, specific, literal 4 chaste
▷ **at a loose end** with nothing to do, bored, out of action, idle, off duty; *colloq.* fed up, twiddling your thumbs, with time to kill
▶ *v* 1 RELEASE, set free, free, let go, liberate, loosen, unbind, unclasp, unfasten, untie, disconnect, disengage, detach, unleash, unhook, uncouple, undo, unlock, unmoor, unpen
2 RELAX, slacken, ease, moderate, lessen, loosen, weaken, diminish, reduce
F3 1 bind, fasten, fix, secure 2 tighten

loosen *v*
1 EASE, relax, loose, slacken, moderate, weaken, diminish, undo, unbind, untie, unfasten
2 FREE, set free, release, let go, set loose, let out, deliver
F3 1 tighten
▷ **loosen up** 1 RELAX, unwind, let up, go easy, lessen, ease up; *colloq.* hang loose, cool it, chill out
2 LIMBER UP, warm up, work out, exercise, prepare

loot *n, v*
▶ *n* spoils, booty, plunder, stolen money, stolen goods, pickings, riches, haul, prize
colloq. swag
▶ *v* steal, plunder, pillage, rob, steal (from), burgle, sack, rifle, raid, maraud, ransack, ravage
formal despoil

lop *v*
chop, cut (off), dock, prune, sever, trim, clip, crop, hack, shorten, curtail, detach, remove, take off, reduce, truncate

lope *v*
run, lollop, bound, spring, stride, canter, gallop

lop-sided *adj*
asymmetrical, unbalanced, askew, off balance, uneven, unequal, crooked, squint, tilting, one-sided
F3 balanced, symmetrical

loquacious *adj*
talkative, chatty, chattering, babbling, blathering, gossipy, wordy, garrulous
formal voluble, multiloquent, multiloquous
colloq. gabby, gassy
F3 succinct, taciturn, terse, reserved

loquacity *n*
talkativeness, chattiness, garrulity, effusiveness
formal volubility, multiloquence, multiloquy
colloq. gassiness
F3 succinctness, taciturnity, terseness

lord *n*
1 PEER, noble, nobleman, earl, duke, count, viscount, baron, aristocrat
2 MASTER, ruler, superior, overlord, leader, chief, captain, commander, governor, king, prince, sovereign, monarch, emperor
3 *God, the Lord*
God, Creator, Maker, King, Almighty, Holy One, Jehovah, Yahweh, Father, Eternal, Christ, Jesus Christ, the Word, Redeemer, Saviour, Son of God, Son of Man
▷ **lord it over** domineer, tyrannize, be overbearing, order around, queen it over, oppress, repress, pull rank, swagger; *formal* put on airs; *colloq.* act big, boss around

lordly *adj*
1 NOBLE, dignified, aristocratic, magnificent, splendid, majestic, grand, grandiose, stately, imperial, impressive, lofty
2 PROUD, arrogant, disdainful, haughty, imperious, condescending, patronizing, supercilious, dictatorial, high-handed, domineering, overbearing, over-confident
formal peremptory, hubristic
colloq. big-headed, stuck-up, high and mighty, uppity, toffee-nosed, hoity-toity, too big for your boots
F3 1 lowly 2 humble

lore *n*
knowledge, wisdom, learning, scholarship, traditions, folklore, teaching, beliefs, legends, stories, sayings, superstitions
formal erudition

lorry *n*
truck, trailer, articulated lorry, pantechnicon, removal van, vehicle, wagon, juggernaut, pick-up, float

lose *v*
1 MISLAY, misplace, forget, miss, not find, forfeit, drop
2 FAIL, fall short, suffer defeat, be defeated, be beaten, be conquered, go down, be unsuccessful
colloq. come to grief, throw in the towel
3 ELUDE, evade, throw off, shake off, leave behind, outrun
4 BE DEPRIVED OF, no longer have, stop having, be taken away, be bereaved of, be dispossessed of
formal be divested of

5 *lose an opportunity*
not take advantage of, fail to grasp, neglect, miss, disregard, ignore, waste, squander, fritter
6 *lose your way*
wander from, stray from, depart from, go astray, get lost, lose your bearings
7 WASTE, squander, spend, consume, use up, exhaust, expend, spend, drain
formal dissipate, deplete
F3 **1** find, keep, gain **2** win **3** win **5** grasp, take advantage of **6** find **7** make
▷ **lose yourself in something** be absorbed in, be preoccupied in, be occupied in, be taken up with, be engrossed in, be fascinated by, be enthralled by, be captivated by, be riveted by
▷ **lose out** suffer, miss out, be unsuccessful, be at a disadvantage, be disadvantaged

loser *n*
failure, runner-up, the defeated
colloq. also-ran, flop, no-hoper, washout, non-starter, write-off, has-been, dead loss
F3 winner

loss *n*
1 MISLAYING, misplacement, missing, forfeiture, forgetting, dropping
2 DEPRIVATION, disappearance, bereavement, dispossession, disadvantage, harm, hurt, impairment, undoing, waste
formal privation
3 *losses in war*
casualties, fatalities, death toll, dead, missing, wounded
4 *the business made a loss*
deficit, debt, deficiency
F3 **1** finding **2** gain **4** profit
▷ **at a loss** puzzled, perplexed, bewildered, mystified, not knowing what to do/say

lost *adj*
1 MISLAID, missing, vanished, disappeared, misplaced, astray, strayed, disoriented, disorientated, off course
2 CONFUSED, disoriented, bewildered, puzzled, baffled, perplexed, nonplussed, at a loss
3 WASTED, squandered, ruined, destroyed, wrecked, demolished, neglected, missed, frittered away, unrecoverable
4 *a lost civilization*
past, dead, defunct, extinct, bygone, long-forgotten, vanished, untraceable
5 *lost souls*
damned, fallen, condemned, doomed, cursed, irredeemable
6 *lost in thought*
absorbed, preoccupied, occupied, taken up with, engrossed, fascinated, enthralled, captivated, riveted, spellbound, absent-minded, dreamy
F3 **1** found

lot *n*
1 *lots of food; a lot of people*
large amount, great number, many, a quantity, a good/great deal
colloq. oodles, tons, loads, masses, heaps, piles, stacks, dozens, hundreds, thousands, millions, miles
2 COLLECTION, batch, bundle, assortment, quantity, group, set, consignment, crowd, gathering
colloq. bunch
3 SHARE, portion, allowance, ration, quota, percentage, part, piece, parcel

colloq. cut
4 *content with your lot in life*
destiny, fate, fortune, circumstances, situation
5 PLOT, allotment, parcel, piece of land, piece of ground
▷ **a lot** much, to a great extent/degree, often, frequently, for a long time
▷ **throw in your lot with** join forces, align yourself with, team up with, combine with, pitch in, take part in; *colloq.* muck in

lotion *n*
ointment, balm, balsam, cream, salve, emollient, embrocation, liniment

lottery *n*
1 DRAW, raffle, sweepstake, bingo, tombola, gambling game
2 SPECULATION, venture, risk, gamble, chance, hazard, luck

loud *adj*
1 NOISY, deafening, rowdy, booming, resounding, resonant, reverberating, roaring, ear-piercing, ear-splitting, piercing, penetrating, thundering, blaring, clamorous, insistent, emphatic, vehement, vociferous, strident, shrill, raucous, rowdy, aggressive, brazen, loud-mouthed, full-mouthed
formal stentorian
2 GARISH, gaudy, glaring, flashy, flamboyant, brash, showy, bold, obtrusive, ostentatious, tasteless, vulgar
colloq. flash
F3 **1** quiet, soft **2** subdued

loudly *adv*
noisily, strongly, deafeningly, resoundingly, clamorously, vehemently, shrilly, vigorously, uproariously, vociferously, lustily, stridently
technical fortissimo
formal streperously, strepitantly
F3 quietly, softly

loudmouth *n*
boaster, braggart, brag, blusterer, braggadocio, swaggerer
colloq. windbag, gasbag, big mouth

loud-mouthed *adj*
noisy, aggressive, bold, brazen, boasting, blustering, bragging, coarse, vulgar

lounge *v, n*
▶ *v* relax, loll (about), idle, laze, waste time, kill time, lie about/around, sprawl, recline, lie back, slump
formal repose
colloq. take it easy
▶ *n* sitting-room, living-room, drawing-room, day-room, parlour

lour, lower *v*
1 DARKEN, blacken, cloud over, threaten, menace, loom, impend, be brewing
2 SCOWL, frown, glare, glower
colloq. give a dirty look, look daggers

louring, lowering *adj*
menacing, threatening, forbidding, ominous, grim, impending, foreboding, gloomy, cloudy, overcast, dark, darkening, grey, black, heavy

lousy *adj*
1 BAD, rotten, poor, second-rate, no good, inferior, contemptible, miserable, low
colloq. awful, terrible, mingy; *slang* crap
2 ILL, unwell, sick, poorly, off-colour, seedy, queasy

colloq. awful, out of sorts, under the weather
E3 **1** excellent, superb **2** well

lout *n*
oaf, boor, dolt, barbarian, yahoo, gawk, lubber
colloq. clod, clodhopper, hick, hobbledehoy, slob, yob, yobbo, bumpkin

loutish *adj*
uncouth, oafish, boorish, doltish, ill-mannered, ill-bred, gawky, rude, coarse, rough, crude, vulgar, churlish, unmannerly, unrefined, uncivilized, gruff, impolite, rustic, uneducated, ignorant, bungling
colloq. clodhopping
E3 polite, refined, cultured, genteel

lovable *adj*
adorable, endearing, winsome, appealing, captivating, enchanting, bewitching, dear, charming, engaging, attractive, fetching, sweet, lovely, pleasing, delightful, likeable, cute
E3 detestable, hateful

love *v, n*
▶ *v* **1** *he loves his wife*
be fond of, like very much, adore, cherish, dote on, treasure, hold dear, be attracted to, feel affection for, be devoted to, care for, prize, desire, long for, be infatuated with, idolize, worship, think the world of, mean the world to someone
colloq. be mad on, be sweet on, be daft/nuts on, be sold on, have a crush on; *slang* have the hots for
2 *I love macaroons*
take pleasure in, enjoy, delight in, like very much, appreciate, desire, fancy, have a liking for, be partial to, savour, relish
E3 detest, hate
▶ *n* **1** FONDNESS, affection, adoration, attachment, care, regard, concern, liking, amorousness, ardour, intimacy, desire, devotion, adulation, passion, rapture, tenderness, warmth, inclination, infatuation, lust, delight, enjoyment, weakness, taste, friendship, brotherhood, sympathy, kindness
colloq. soft spot
2 *a love of power*
pleasure, enjoyment, delight, liking, appreciation, weakness, partiality, relish
colloq. soft spot
3 *come here, my love*
darling, beloved, dear, dear one, dearest, favourite, sweetheart, honey, angel, pet, treasure
E3 **1** hate, hatred, dislike **2** detestation, loathing
▷ **fall in love with** fall for, become infatuated with, burn with passion, take to, lose your heart to;
colloq. fall head over heels in love, have a thing for, fancy, be crazy about, have a crush on, take a shine to, have it bad
▷ **in love with** attracted to, smitten, sweet/soft on, besotted, charmed, doting, enamoured, infatuated;
colloq. mad/crazy/wild about, have a crush on, hooked, nuts about, stuck on
▷ **love affair** affair, romance, liaison, relationship, love, intrigue, passion; *old use* amour
▷ **make love** have sex with; *colloq.* sleep with, sleep together, go to bed with; *slang* have it off with, get your leg over; *taboo slang* fuck, screw, bang, bonk, shag
Related adjective: amatory

loveless *adj*
cold, cold-hearted, hard, icy, insensitive, unresponsive, unloved, unloving, passionless, unfeeling, unfriendly, unappreciated, friendless, disliked, frigid, forsaken, unvalued, heartless, uncherished
E3 passionate

lovelorn *adj*
infatuated, desiring, longing, pining, yearning, languishing, lovesick, unrequited in love

lovely *adj*
1 ATTRACTIVE, beautiful, charming, delightful, attractive, enchanting, pleasing, pleasant, good-looking, pretty, handsome, fair, adorable, sweet, winning, exquisite
2 MARVELLOUS, wonderful, enjoyable, pleasing, delightful, agreeable
E3 **1** ugly, hideous

love-making *n*
sexual intercourse, intercourse, sex, sexual relations, sexual union, copulation, intimacy, foreplay, mating
formal carnal knowledge, coition, coitus, congress
colloq. sleeping with someone, going to bed with someone

lover *n*
1 BELOVED, loved one, admirer, boyfriend, man friend, girlfriend, woman friend, sweetheart, partner, live-in partner, suitor, mistress, lady love, fiancé(e), other man, other woman, significant other
colloq. flame, bit on the side, vamp, wolf, bird, date, fella, toy boy, heart-throb
2 ENTHUSIAST, devotee, admirer, fan, supporter, follower, fanatic
colloq. buff, freak, fiend

lovesick *adj*
infatuated, desiring, longing, pining, yearning, languishing, lovelorn, unrequited in love

loving *adj*
amorous, affectionate, devoted, doting, fond, adoring, ardent, passionate, warm, warm-hearted, kind, tender, caring, friendly, sympathetic

low¹ *adj, n*
▶ *adj* **1** SHORT, small, squat, stunted, little, shallow
2 INADEQUATE, insufficient, deficient, poor, sparse, meagre, paltry, trifling, scant, scanty, little, insignificant, reduced
3 *low land*
close to the ground, sea-level, ground-level, depressed, deep, sunken, flat
4 LOWLY, humble, low-born, obscure, poor, plebeian, plain, simple, common, modest, ordinary, inferior, junior, low-ranking, peasant, meek, mild, mean, submissive, subordinate, unimportant
5 *have a low opinion of someone*
poor, unfavourable, bad, negative, adverse, hostile, opposing, antagonistic
6 *low notes*
DEEP, low-pitched, bass, resonant, sonorous, rich
7 *low achiever*
unintelligent, foolish, slow, dull, mediocre, inadequate, deficient, below standard
8 UNHAPPY, depressed, downcast, gloomy, low-spirited, miserable, despondent, sad, downhearted, disheartened, glum
formal disconsolate
colloq. down, down in the dumps, blue, fed up, cheesed off
9 BASE, coarse, vulgar, bad, evil, wicked, mean, contemptible, nasty, despicable, dishonourable, depraved, immoral, obscene, indecent, smutty
old use dastardly
formal heinous

10 CHEAP, inexpensive, reasonable, moderate, modest, reduced, slashed, sale, rock-bottom
11 SUBDUED, muted, soft, quiet, quietened, gentle, hushed, muffled, whispered
F3 **1** high **2** high **3** high **4** high, important **5** high, good **6** high **8** cheerful **9** honourable **10** high, exorbitant **11** loud, noisy
▶ *n* all-time low, lowest point, bottom, low point, low-watermark
F3 high
formal nadir

low² *v*
cattle lowing
bellow, moo

low-born *adj*
humble, poor, mean-born, plebeian, unexalted, lowly, low-ranking, peasant, obscure
F3 high-born, noble

lowbrow *adj*
ignorant, uncultivated, uncultured, unrefined, uneducated, unlearned, unscholarly, unlettered, crude, rude
F3 highbrow, intellectual

low-down *n*
information, news, facts, data, inside story, intelligence
colloq. dope, gen, info

lower¹ *adj, v*
▶ *adj* **1** *the lower jaw*
UNDER, bottom, undermost, nether
2 INFERIOR, lesser, subordinate, secondary, minor, second-class, low-level, lowly, junior
F3 **1** upper **2** higher
▶ *v* **1** DROP, depress, sink, descend, let down, let fall, take down
2 REDUCE, decrease, cut, lessen, diminish, curtail, slash, bring down, cheapen
formal abate
3 *lower your eyes*
look down, move downwards, set down, bring low
4 *lower your voice*
speak (more) quietly, quieten, hush
5 *not lower yourself by doing something*
debase, belittle, degrade, demean, disgrace, dishonour, abase
formal disparage
F3 **1** raise **2** increase **3** raise

lower² *see* lour.

lowering *see* louring.

low-grade *adj*
bad, inferior, poor, poor-quality, substandard, below standard, second-class, second-rate, third-rate, cheap-jack
colloq. not up to scratch
F3 good, quality

low-key *adj*
muted, quiet, restrained, subdued, understated, easy-going, relaxed, subtle, slight, soft
F3 showy, impressive

lowly *adj*
humble, low-born, obscure, poor, plebeian, plain, simple, common, modest, ordinary, inferior, junior, low-ranking, peasant, meek, mild, mean, submissive, subordinate, unimportant
F3 lofty, noble, pretentious

low-pitched *adj*
deep, low, bass, resonant, sonorous, rich
F3 high, high-pitched

low-spirited *adj*
depressed, gloomy, heavy-hearted, low, downhearted, despondent, dejected, discouraged, sad, unhappy, miserable, moody, glum
colloq. down, fed up, cheesed off, down in the dumps
F3 high-spirited, cheerful

loyal *adj*
true, faithful, steadfast, staunch, devoted, constant, firm, unchanging, trustworthy, truehearted, trusty, reliable, dependable, dedicated, committed, sincere, patriotic
F3 disloyal, treacherous

loyalty *n*
allegiance, faithfulness, fidelity, devotion, dedication, commitment, staunchness, steadfastness, constancy, trustworthiness, reliability, dependability, sincerity, patriotism
old use fealty
F3 disloyalty, treachery

lozenge *n*
pastille, gumdrop, tablet, cough-drop, jujube
technical troche, trochiscus, trochisk

lubber *n*
oaf, boor, dolt, barbarian, yahoo, gawk, lout
colloq. clod, clodhopper, hick, hobbledehoy, slob, yob, yobbo, bumpkin

lubberly *adj*
clumsy, awkward, blundering, gawky, ungainly, heavy-handed, bungling, churlish, loutish, oafish, uncouth, doltish, lumbering, clownish, lumpish, coarse, dense, crude
colloq. clodhopping

lubricant *n*
oil, grease, lubrication, fat, lard

lubricate *v*
oil, grease, smear, wax, polish, make smooth, lard

lucid *adj*
1 *lucid writing*
CLEAR, comprehensible, plain, explicit, distinct, intelligible, obvious, evident
2 CLEAR-HEADED, sane, rational, reasonable, intelligible, sensible, sober, sound, of sound mind, *compos mentis*
3 SHINING, bright, brilliant, beaming, transparent, translucent, gleaming, radiant, glassy, luminous, resplendent, crystalline, pure
formal diaphanous, effulgent, limpid, pellucid
F3 **1** unclear **2** unintelligible **3** dark, murky

luck *n*
1 CHANCE, fortune, accident, fate, the stars, hazard, destiny
formal fortuity, predestination
colloq. fluke
2 GOOD FORTUNE, good luck, success, prosperity, godsend
colloq. break
F3 **1** design **2** misfortune
▷ **in luck** fortunate, happy, favoured, successful, advantaged, timely, opportune; *formal* auspicious; *colloq.* jammy
▷ **out of luck** unlucky, unfortunate, luckless,

hapless, unsuccessful, disadvantaged;
formal inauspicious; *colloq.* down on your luck

luckily *adv*
as luck would have it, by good luck, by chance,
by accident, fortunately, happily, providentially
formal fortuitously
E3 unfortunately

luckless *adj*
unlucky, unfortunate, hopeless, ill-fated, ill-starred,
jinxed, cursed, doomed, hapless, star-crossed,
miserable, unhappy, unsuccessful, disastrous,
calamitous, catastrophic
formal unpropitious
E3 lucky, fortunate

lucky *adj*
fortunate, in luck, promising, favoured, charmed,
successful, prosperous, timely, opportune, expedient,
providential
formal auspicious, fortuitous, propitious
colloq. jammy
E3 unlucky

lucrative *adj*
profitable, well-paid, remunerative, profit-making,
money-making, high-paying, gainful, productive,
financially rewarding, advantageous, worthwhile
E3 unprofitable

lucre *n*
money, cash, riches, wealth, profit(s), gain(s),
proceeds, winnings, pay, income, remuneration,
spoils, mammon
slang dough, dosh, bread

ludicrous *adj*
absurd, ridiculous, preposterous, nonsensical,
laughable, farcical, silly, comical, comic, humorous,
amusing, hilarious, funny, droll, outlandish, zany, odd,
eccentric
formal risible
colloq. crazy
E3 serious

lug *v*
pull, drag, haul, carry, bear, tow, tote, heave, tug, hump

luggage *n*
baggage, belongings, paraphernalia
formal impedimenta
colloq. gear, things, stuff

Types of luggage include: case, suitcase, vanity-case,
bag, holdall, portmanteau, valise, overnight-bag,
kit-bag, flight bag, hand-luggage, travel bag,
Gladstone bag, grip, rucksack, knapsack,
haversack, backpack, briefcase, attaché case,
portfolio, satchel, basket, hamper, trunk, chest, box.

lugubrious *adj*
melancholy, morose, gloomy, glum, sad, woeful,
woebegone, sorrowful, sombre, serious, dismal,
doleful, dreary, mournful, funereal, sepulchral
E3 cheerful, jovial, merry

lukewarm *adj*
1 *lukewarm water*
tepid, slightly warm, warmish, cool
2 HALF-HEARTED, cool, apathetic, tepid,
indifferent, unenthusiastic, uninterested,
unresponsive, unconcerned, impassive, Laodicean

lull *n, v*
▶ *n* calm, calmness, peace, quiet, tranquillity,
stillness, let-up, pause, hush, silence
E3 agitation
▶ *v* soothe, subdue, calm, silence, hush, pacify,
quieten down, quiet, quell, still, allay, ease, compose
formal assuage
E3 agitate

lullaby *n*
cradle song, *berceuse*

lumber¹ *n, v*
▶ *n* 1 *store away lumber*
clutter, jumble, rubbish, refuse, bits and pieces, odds
and ends, junk, trash
2 TIMBER, wood
▶ *v* burden, encumber, saddle, land, load, hamper,
impose, charge

lumber² *v*
lumber round the house
clump, shamble, plod, shuffle, stump, stamp, trundle,
trudge, stumble

lumbering *adj*
awkward, clumsy, heavy-footed, ungainly, unwieldy,
heavy, blundering, bumbling, lumpish, ponderous,
hulking, massive, elephantine, bovine
colloq. like a bull in a china shop
E3 agile, nimble

luminary *n*
expert, authority, leader, leading light, celebrity, VIP,
dignitary, worthy, notable, personage, star, superstar
colloq. big name, bigwig

luminescent *adj*
glowing, bright, luminous, fluorescent, radiant,
shining
formal effulgent, luciferous, phosphorescent

luminous *adj*
glowing, illuminated, lit, lighted, radiant, shining,
glowing, dazzling, fluorescent, brilliant, lustrous,
bright
formal luminescent, effulgent

lump¹ *n, v*
▶ *n* 1 MASS, cluster, clump, clod, ball, dab, wad,
cluster, bunch, piece, chunk, cake, hunk, nugget,
wedge
2 SWELLING, growth, bulge, bump, protuberance,
bruise, protrusion, tumour, carbuncle
formal tumescence
▶ *v* collect, mass, gather, put together, cluster,
combine, pool, blend, fuse, coalesce, group,
consolidate, unite, mix together, conglomerate

lump² *v*
like it or lump it
put up with, bear (with), endure, tolerate, stand, suffer,
swallow, take, brook
Scot. thole
colloq. stomach

lumpish *adj*
awkward, heavy, clumsy, ungainly, hulking, gawky,
bungling, lumbering, lethargic, elephantine, stupid,
dull-witted, oafish, boorish, doltish, obtuse, stolid

lumpy *adj*
clotted, curdled, bunched, bumpy, cloggy, knobbly,
grainy, granular
formal nodous, nodose
E3 even, smooth

lunacy *n*

madness, insanity, aberration, derangement, dementia, dementedness, mania, idiocy, imbecility, folly, foolishness, absurdity, nonsense, stupidity, preposterousness, outrageousness, irresponsibility, silliness, inanity, ridiculousness, illogicality, irrationality, senselessness
formal imprudence
colloq. craziness
🔁 sanity

lunatic *n, adj*

▶ *n* psychotic, psychopath, madman, madwoman, insane person, imbecile, maniac, manic-depressive, neurotic
colloq. loony, nutcase, nutter, fruitcake, psycho, headcase, oddball; *slang* dipstick
▶ *adj* mad, insane, deranged, psychotic, unbalanced, disturbed, demented, irrational, foolish, idiotic, absurd, stupid, illogical, nonsensical, senseless, silly, inane
colloq. crazy, bonkers, loony, loopy, nuts, nutty, daft, barmy, potty, hare-brained, crackpot, off your rocker, round the bend/twist
🔁 sane

lunch *n*

midday meal, luncheon, light lunch, ploughman's lunch, packed lunch, brunch, Sunday lunch, dinner

lunge *v, n*

▶ *v* thrust, jab, stab, pounce, plunge, pitch into, charge, dart, dash, dive, poke, strike (at), fall upon, grab (at), hit (at), leap, spring, bound
▶ *n* thrust, stab, pounce, charge, jab, poke, pass, cut, spring, plunge, leap, bound

lurch *v*

roll, rock, pitch, sway, swerve, veer, stagger, totter, stumble, reel, list

lure *v, n*

▶ *v* tempt, entice, draw, attract, allure, induce, decoy, seduce, ensnare, beguile, lead on
formal inveigle
▶ *n* temptation, enticement, attraction, draw, allurement, bait, decoy, inducement, seduction
colloq. carrot

lurid *adj*

1 SENSATIONAL, shocking, startling, explicit, graphic, exaggerated, melodramatic
2 MACABRE, gruesome, gory, ghastly, grisly, horrific, revolting
3 BRIGHTLY COLOURED, garish, glaring, loud, showy, vivid, brilliant, dazzling, intense
🔁 **1** restrained **3** pale

lurk *v*

skulk, prowl, slink, lie in wait, crouch, lie low, hide, conceal yourself, snoop, sneak

luscious *adj*

1 *luscious food*
delicious, juicy, succulent, appetizing, mouth-watering, sweet, tasty, savoury
formal delectable
colloq. scrumptious, yummy, morish
2 *a luscious blonde*
attractive, beautiful, voluptuous, desirable, gorgeous, sensuous, stunning, ravishing, sexy
colloq. smashing

lush *adj, n*

▶ *adj* **1** FLOURISHING, luxuriant, abundant, prolific, teeming, dense, overgrown, green, profuse
formal verdant
2 SUMPTUOUS, opulent, ornate, plush, rich, luxurious, grand, lavish, extravagant, palatial
▶ *n* drunk, drunkard, alcoholic, inebriated, drinker, hard drinker, heavy drinker, dipsomaniac
colloq. tippler; *slang* boozer, wino, alkie, dipso, soak, piss artist, toper, sot, tosspot

lust *n*

1 SENSUALITY, sexual desire, libido, sexual drive, lechery, licentiousness, lewdness, lasciviousness
formal concupiscence, prurience
colloq. randiness, raunchiness, horniness, the hots
2 CRAVING, desire, appetite, longing, passion, greed, greediness, covetousness, hunger, yearning, avidity
formal cupidity
▷ **lust after** desire, crave, yearn for, want, need, hunger for, thirst for, covet, long for

lustful *adj*

sensual, passionate, licentious, lewd, lascivious, lecherous, carnal, unchaste, wanton, craving, hankering, salacious
old use lickerish
formal concupiscent, libidinous, prurient, cupidinous
colloq. horny, randy, raunchy

lustily *adv*

loudly, hard, robustly, strongly, vigorously, forcefully, powerfully, stoutly, with all your might
formal with might and main
🔁 weakly, feebly

lustiness *n*

power, robustness, sturdiness, vigour, health, healthiness, strength, energy, haleness, hardiness, toughness, stoutness, virility

lustre *n*

1 SHINE, gloss, sheen, gleam, glow, brilliance, brightness, radiance, sparkle, shimmer, resplendence, burnish, glitter, glint
formal refulgence, lambency
2 GLORY, honour, prestige, renown, distinction, fame, illustriousness, merit, credit

lustrous *adj*

bright, shiny, shining, glossy, glowing, dazzling, gleaming, glistening, glittering, shimmering, sparkling, twinkling, burnished, luminous, radiant
formal lambent
🔁 dull, lacklustre, matt

lusty *adj*

robust, strong, sturdy, vigorous, tough, hale, hearty, hale and hearty, healthy, blooming, energetic, lively, strapping, rugged, forceful, powerful, virile
colloq. gutsy
🔁 weak, feeble

luxuriance *n*

abundance, copiousness, lushness, denseness, rankness, fertility, lavishness, profusion, sumptuousness, richness, excess, exuberance
formal fecundity

luxuriant *adj*

1 ABUNDANT, prolific, lush, superabundant, sumptuous, profuse, plentiful, plenteous, overflowing, ample, lavish, teeming, thriving, rich, riotous, rank, copious, dense, productive, fertile
formal fecund
2 ELABORATE, extravagant, fancy, ornate, flamboyant, flowery, opulent, excessive, rococo,

baroque
formal florid
⊟ barren, infertile

⚠ **luxuriant** or **luxurious** ?
Luxuriant means 'abundant, prolific, growing
vigorously': *the luxuriant growth of the jungle plants.*
Luxurious means 'relating to luxury and riches,
expensive': *a luxurious house.*

---

luxuriate *v*
delight, enjoy, revel, relish, savour, thrive, bask,
abound, wallow, relax in, indulge, prosper, flourish,
grow, bloom, burgeon
colloq. live in the lap of luxury, live off the fat of the
land, live the life of Riley, live in clover, live on easy
street, have a ball

luxurious *adj*
sumptuous, opulent, lavish, de luxe, magnificent,
splendid, rich, expensive, costly, affluent,
self-indulgent, pampered, comfortable, grand,
well-appointed
colloq. plush, posh, cushy, glitzy, swanky
⊟ austere, spartan

luxury *n*
1 SUMPTUOUSNESS, opulence, hedonism, splendour,
affluence, richness, expensiveness, costliness,
magnificence, grandness, grandeur, pleasure,
indulgence, self-indulgence, gratification, comfort
colloq. lap of luxury

2 *life's little luxuries*
EXTRAVAGANCE, satisfaction, extra, treat
⊟ **1** austerity **2** essential

lying *adj, n*
▶ *adj* deceitful, dishonest, false, untruthful,
double-dealing
formal mendacious, dissembling, dissimulating
colloq. two-faced, crooked
⊟ honest, truthful
▶ *n* dishonesty, untruthfulness, deceit, falsity, perjury,
falsification, fabrication, invention, double-dealing
formal duplicity
colloq. fibbing, white lies, crookedness
⊟ honesty, truthfulness

lynch *v*
hang, hang by the neck, execute, put to death, kill
colloq. string up

lyric *adj*
emotional, passionate, personal, subjective, direct,
strong, poetic, musical

lyrical *adj*
1 POETIC, musical, romantic
2 ENTHUSIASTIC, emotional, rapturous, rhapsodic,
ecstatic, effusive, passionate, carried away, expressive,
impassioned, inspired

lyrics *n*
text, words, book, libretto

M

macabre *adj*
gruesome, chilling, grisly, grim, horrible, gory, horrific, frightful, frightening, terrifying, shocking, dreadful, morbid, ghostly, eerie, hideous, ghastly

mace *n*
rod, stick staff, club, cudgel

macerate *v*
soak, steep, soften, liquefy, mash, blend, pulp

Machiavellian *adj*
devious, crafty, designing, scheming, shrewd, sly, cunning, wily, artful, astute, calculating, deceitful, double-dealing, guileful, underhand, opportunist, foxy, intriguing, unscrupulous
formal perfidious

machination *n*
scheme, intrigue, plot, design, manoeuvre, conspiracy, tactic, wile, ruse, ploy, stratagem, trick, device, dodge, cabal
formal artifice
colloq. shenanigans

machine *n*
1 INSTRUMENT, device, contrivance, tool, contraption, mechanism, engine, motor, apparatus, appliance, gadget, hardware
2 AGENCY, organization, structure, instrument, tool, organ, vehicle, influence, catalyst, system, workings
3 AUTOMATION, robot, mechanical person, tool, mechanism, zombie, android

machine-gun *n*
See panel at weapons.

machinery *n*
1 INSTRUMENTS, mechanism, tools, apparatus, equipment, tackle, gear, gadgetry

> *Types of heavy machinery include*: all-terrain fork lift, bulldozer, caterpillar tractor, combine harvester, concrete mixer, concrete pump, crane, crawler crane, crawler tractor, digger, dragline excavator, dredger, dumper, dump truck, dustcart, excavator, fertilizer spreader, fire appliance, fork-lift truck, gantry crane, grader, grapple, gritter, hydraulic bale loader, hydraulic shovel, JCB®, muck spreader, pick-up loader, pile-driver, platform hoist, riding mower, road roller, road-sweeping lorry, Rotovator®, silage harvester, snowplough, straw baler, threshing machine, tower crane, tracklayer, tractor, tractor, tractor-scraper, truck crane, wheel loader.

2 ORGANIZATION, channel(s), structure, system, procedure, workings, agency

machinist *n*
worker, operator, operative, factory hand, mechanic

machismo *n*
masculinity, maleness, manliness, virility, toughness, strength

macrocosm *n*
universe, solar system, cosmos, creation, world, planet, society, civilization, community, culture, humanity, totality, (single) entity, system
🔄 microcosm

mad *adj*
1 INSANE, lunatic, unbalanced, psychotic, deranged, maniacal, demented, out of your mind, out of your senses, of unsound mind, unhinged, crazed, unstable, *non compos mentis*, frenzied, manic
colloq. crazy, nuts, nutty, nutty as a fruitcake, barmy, bonkers, batty, crackers, dippy, daffy, bananas, loony, loopy, off your rocker, off your head, off the wall, off your trolley, out to lunch, needing your head examined, round the bend, round the twist, having a screw loose, having bats in the belfry, having lost your marbles
2 ANGRY, furious, enraged, raging, infuriated, incensed, irate, blazing, fuming, livid, hopping mad, seeing red, hot under the collar
3 IRRATIONAL, illogical, unreasonable, absurd, ludicrous, preposterous, foolish, foolhardy, idiotic, insane, stupid, silly, nonsensical, wild
colloq. crazy, daft, barmy, potty, hare-brained, crackbrained, crackpot
4 FANATICAL, enthusiastic, infatuated, ardent, zealous, devoted, fond, keen, avid, passionate, wild
colloq. crazy, daft, nuts
5 UNCONTROLLED, wild, frantic, furious, reckless, violent, energetic, intense, rapid, hasty, hurried, unrestrained, frenzied, abandoned, excited
🔄 1 sane 2 calm 3 sensible 4 apathetic 5 controlled
▷ **like mad** energetically, quickly, furiously, wildly, frantically, hurriedly, enthusiastically, fanatically, zealously avidly

madcap *adj, n*
▶ *adj* foolhardy, rash, reckless, impulsive, silly, thoughtless, wild, lively, flighty, heedless, ill-advised, hotheaded, crazy
formal imprudent
colloq. bird-brained, hare-brained
▶ *n* adventurer, tearaway, hothead, daredevil, firebrand, fury, desperado
colloq. crackpot

madden *v*
anger, enrage, infuriate, incense, annoy, upset, agitate, exasperate, provoke, annoy, irritate, inflame, irk, vex
colloq. aggravate, bug, hassle, rub up the wrong way, get someone's blood up, make your blood boil, get on your nerves, get up your nose, get under your skin, get someone's goat, get on your wick, drive crazy/nuts, drive up the wall, drive round the bend/twist, get your back up, get your dander up
🔄 calm, pacify

maddening *adj*
infuriating, exasperating, annoying, troublesome, irritating, vexatious, galling, upsetting, disturbing

made-up *adj*
1 INVENTED, make-believe, unreal, untrue, false, fictional, imaginary, specious, fabricated, fairy-tale, mythical
colloq. trumped-up
2 WEARING MAKE-UP, painted, powdered, done up
E3 1 real, factual, true

madhouse *n*
1 BEDLAM, chaos, disarray, disorder, uproar, turmoil, pandemonium, Babel
2 MENTAL HOSPITAL, lunatic asylum, asylum, mental institution, psychiatric hospital
colloq. funny farm, loony bin, nut-house

madly *adv*
1 *he rolled his eyes madly*
insanely, dementedly, hysterically, frenziedly, deliriously, wildly, distractedly
colloq. crazily
2 *madly cleaning up*
wildly, excitedly, frantically, furiously, recklessly, violently, energetically, intensely, rapidly, hastily, fast, hurriedly
3 *madly in love*
intensely, wildly, fervently, devotedly, devoutly
4 EXTREMELY, wildly, exceedingly, exceptionally, utterly, unreasonably

madman, madwoman *n*
lunatic, psychotic, psychopath, maniac, imbecile
colloq. loony, nutter, nut, crackpot, crank, headcase, nutcase, fruitcake, screwball, oddball, basket case; *US* hook; *slang* psycho

madness *n*
1 INSANITY, lunacy, dementia, psychosis, mental instability, mania, derangement, distraction, delusion
colloq. craziness
2 FURY, rage, raving, frenzy, hysteria, anger, agitation, exasperation, wrath, ire
3 FOLLY, craziness, irrationality, unreasonableness, insanity, stupidity, silliness, inanity, absurdity, nonsense, foolishness, foolhardiness, preposterousness, wildness
colloq. daftness
4 KEENNESS, enthusiuasm, ardour, craze, abandon, zeal, wildness, unrestraint, uproar, riot, passion, excitement, fanaticism, infatuation, intoxication
E3 1 sanity 2 calmness 3 reasonableness

maelstrom *n*
confusion, disorder, turmoil, mess, pandemonium, tumult, uproar, bedlam, chaos, vortex, whirlpool, Charybdis

maestro *n*
expert, master, genius, prodigy, virtuoso
colloq. wizard, ace

magazine *n*
1 JOURNAL, periodical, publication, paper, weekly, monthly, quarterly, supplement, colour supplement
2 ARSENAL, storehouse, ammunition dump, depot, ordnance

magic *n, adj*
▶ *n* 1 SORCERY, enchantment, supernatural, occult, occultism, black magic, black art, witchcraft, wizardry, wonder-working, voodoo, hoodoo, magical powers, spell, curse
formal necromancy, thaumaturgy
2 CONJURING, illusion, sleight of hand, deception, trickery, legerdemain

formal prestidigitation
3 CHARM, fascination, glamour, enticement, allure, allurement, enchantment, magnetism, pull
▶ *adj* 1 SUPERNATURAL, occult, mysterious, demonic
2 CHARMING, enchanting, bewitching, fascinating, spellbinding, entrancing, captivating, irresistible, magnetic
3 WONDERFUL, excellent, great, tremendous, marvellous
colloq. terrific, smashing, brill, ace; *slang* mega, cool, wicked

magician *n*
1 SORCERER, miracle-worker, enchanter, wizard, witch, warlock, spellbinder, spellworker, wonder-worker
formal necromancer, thaumaturge
2 CONJURER, illusionist, juggler
3 GENIUS, maestro, expert, master, virtuoso
colloq. wizard, ace

magisterial *adj*
authoritative, commanding, masterful, assertive, authoritarian, domineering, imperious, high-handed, dictatorial, lordly, overbearing, arrogant, despotic
formal peremptory
colloq. bossy

magistrate *n*
judge, justice, justice of the peace, JP, stipendiary, bailiff, tribune, aedile
colloq. beak
Related adjective: magisterial

magnanimity *n*
generosity, liberality, open-handedness, benevolence, selflessness, unselfishness, charity, charitableness, big-heartedness, bountifulness, kindness, high-mindedness, nobility, philanthropy, altruism, mercy, forgiveness, largesse
formal beneficence, munificence
E3 meanness, vindictiveness

magnanimous *adj*
generous, liberal, open-handed, benevolent, selfless, charitable, big-hearted, bountiful, kind, kindly, noble, philanthropic, altruistic, unselfish, ungrudging, merciful, forgiving
formal beneficent, munificent
E3 mean

magnate *n*
tycoon, captain of industry, industrialist, mogul, entrepreneur, financier, plutocrat, baron, executive, personage, notable, leader
colloq. fat cat, moneybags, bigwig, big shot, big noise, big timer

magnet *n*
draw, bait, lure, allurement, charm, enticement, appeal, attraction, centre of attraction, focus, focal point, lodestone, solenoid
E3 repellent

magnetic *adj*
attractive, alluring, fascinating, appealing, enthralling, charming, engaging, mesmerizing, hypnotic, seductive, tempting, tantalizing, irresistible, entrancing, bewitching, enchanting, captivating, gripping, absorbing, charismatic
E3 repellent, repulsive

magnetism *n*
attraction, allure, fascination, enchantment,

captivation, charm, temptation, seductiveness, lure, appeal, drawing power, draw, pull, hypnotism, mesmerism, charisma, grip, magic, power, spell

magnification *n*
1 ENLARGEMENT, amplification, increase, expansion, intensification, enhancement, inflation, heightening, deepening, dilation, build-up, boost, extolment, lionization
formal aggrandizement, augmentation
2 EXAGGERATION, dramatization, overemphasis, overstatement, overdoing, embellishment, embroidery
E3 1 diminution, reduction

magnificence *n*
splendour, grandeur, impressiveness, glory, gorgeousness, brilliance, excellence, majesty, sumptuousness, nobility, luxuriousness, luxury, lavishness, pomp, stateliness
formal resplendence, opulence, sublimity
E3 modesty, plainness, simplicity

magnificent *adj*
splendid, grand, imposing, grandiose, impressive, striking, elegant, glorious, gorgeous, brilliant, dazzling, excellent, marvellous, wonderful, majestic, superb, sumptuous, noble, exalted, elegant, fine, lavish, luxurious, rich, royal, stately
formal resplendent, opulent, august, sublime
E3 modest, humble, poor

magnify *v*
1 ENLARGE, enlarge, amplify, increase, expand, intensify, enhance, boost, enhance, extend, greaten, heighten, broaden, deepen, dilate, build up
2 EXAGGERATE, dramatize, overemphasize, overplay, overstate, overdo, embellish, embroider
colloq. blow up, blow up out of all proportion, make a mountain out of a molehill
E3 1 reduce, diminish 2 belittle, play down

magniloquence *n*
pomposity, pretentiousness, bombast, loftiness, rhetoric, euphuism, turgidity, fustian
formal grandiloquence, orotundity
E3 simplicity, straightforwardness

magniloquent *adj*
pompous, high-sounding, lofty, overblown, elevated, exalted, bombastic, fustian, high-flown, pretentious, rhetorical, declamatory, euphuistic, sonorous, turgid, stilted
formal grandiloquent, orotund
E3 simple, straightforward

magnitude *n*
1 SIZE, extent, measure, amount, expanse, dimensions, mass, proportions, quantity, weight, volume, capacity, bulk, largeness, greatness, space, strength, amplitude
2 IMPORTANCE, consequence, significance, weight, greatness, eminence, fame, distinction, moment, note, intensity

magnum opus *n*
masterpiece, masterwork, chef d'oeuvre, *pièce de résistance*

maid *n*
servant, domestic, waitress, kitchenmaid, chambermaid, housemaid, girl, au pair, maidservant, serving-maid, lady's maid, handmaiden, soubrette, abigail, maid-of-all-work
colloq. skivvy

maiden *n, adj*
▶ *n* girl, young girl, young lady, young woman, virgin, lass, lassie, miss, nymph
formal damsel
▶ *adj* 1 *a maiden voyage*
FIRST, inaugural, new, introductory, initial, initiatory
2 CHASTE, decent, demure, gentle, girlish, female, modest, proper, pure, reserved, undefiled, unsullied, unbroached, vestal, virgin, unmarried, unwed, virginal, virtuous
old use seemly
formal decorous
E3 2 defiled, deflowered, unchaste

maidenly *adj*
becoming, chaste, decent, demure, gentle, girlish, female, modest, proper, pure, reserved, undefiled, unsullied, unbroached, vestal, virgin, unmarried, unwed, virginal, virtuous
old use seemly
formal decorous
E3 immodest

mail¹ *n, v*
▶ *n* 1 *deliver the mail*
post, letters, correspondence, communications, packages, parcels, packets, delivery, registered mail, recorded mail, special delivery, direct mail, airmail, surface mail, international mail, electronic mail, e-mail
colloq. junk mail, snail mail
2 POSTAL SERVICE, postal system, post, Post Office
▶ *v* post, send, dispatch, forward
Related adjective: postal

mail² *n*
chain mail
armour, chain mail, iron-cladding, panoply, protective covering

maim *v*
mutilate, disfigure, wound, incapacitate, injure, disable, hurt, impair, mar, cripple, lame, put out of action

main *adj, n*
▶ *adj* principal, chief, leading, first, foremost, major, key, predominant, dominant, pre-eminent, primary, most important, prime, premier, supreme, paramount, central, head, cardinal, outstanding, essential, critical, crucial, necessary, vital, fundamental, pivotal
E3 minor, unimportant, insignificant
▶ *n* pipe, duct, conduit, channel, cable, line
▷ **in the main** chiefly, mostly, on the whole, for the most part, generally, in general, especially, as a rule, by and large, commonly, usually, largely

mainly *adv*
primarily, principally, chiefly, first and foremost, in the main, mostly, on the whole, for the most part, generally, in general, especially, as a rule, by and large, commonly, usually, above all, largely, overall

mainspring *n*
motive, motivation, cause, reason, driving force, impulse, incentive, inspiration, origin, prime mover, generator, source, fountainhead, wellspring

mainstay *n*
support, buttress, bulwark, linchpin, prop, pillar, anchor, backbone, foundation, basis, base

mainstream *adj*
normal, average, central, general, typical, regular, standard, conventional, established, orthodox,

received, accepted, mainline
F3 heterodox, peripheral, marginal

maintain   *v*

1 CARRY ON, continue, keep (up), keep going, sustain, preserve, perpetuate, conserve, retain
2 CARE FOR, conserve, look after, keep (up), take care of, preserve, keep in good condition/repair
3 PROVIDE FOR, keep, support, finance, supply, feed, sustain, nourish, nurture
4 ASSERT, claim, profess, contend, declare, announce, hold, state, insist, believe, stand by, fight for, support
formal affirm, avow, aver, asseverate
F3 **2** neglect **4** deny

maintenance   *n*

1 CONTINUATION, continuance, carrying-on, preservation, conservation, perpetuation
2 CARE, conservation, preservation, support, repairs, protection, upkeep, running
3 KEEP, subsistence, feeding, sustenance, nourishment, nurture, living, livelihood, financing, support, upkeep, allowance, alimony, aliment
F3 **2** neglect

majestic   *adj*

magnificent, grand, glorious, dignified, distinguished, noble, royal, queenly, kingly, princely, lordly, stately, splendid, imperial, marvellous, impressive, elevated, exalted, awesome, imposing, regal, superb, lofty, monumental, pompous
formal resplendent, sublime, august
F3 lowly, unimpressive, unimposing

majesty   *n*

grandeur, grandness, glory, dignity, magnificence, beauty, awesomeness, nobility, nobleness, royalty, regality, splendour, stateliness, pomp, exaltedness, impressiveness, loftiness
formal resplendence, sublimity

major   *adj*

greater, chief, main, larger, bigger, higher, leading, outstanding, notable, supreme, prime, paramount, uppermost, significant, crucial, important, serious, key, keynote, great, senior, older, superior, pre-eminent, vital, weighty
F3 minor, unimportant, trivial

majority   *n*

1 BULK, mass, preponderance, (the) many, most, greater/larger part, more than half, nearly all
colloq. lion's share
2 ADULTHOOD, maturity, manhood, womanhood, legal age, age of consent, years of discretion
F3 **1** minority

make   *v, n*

▶ *v* **1** CREATE, manufacture, mass-produce, fabricate, construct, assemble, build, erect, produce, turn out, put together, put up, originate, compose, form, shape, fashion, mould, model
2 CAUSE, bring about, produce, accomplish, occasion, create, give rise to, engender, generate, render, perform
formal effect
3 CARRY OUT, accomplish, achieve, do, perform, undertake, discharge
formal effect, execute
colloq. deliver (the goods), get down to, wrap up
4 COERCE, force, urge, oblige, constrain, compel, impel, prevail upon, pressure, pressurize, press, drive, require, dragoon

colloq. bulldoze, strongarm, put the screws on
5 APPOINT, vote in, elect, select, designate, nominate, name, ordain, install, create, vote
6 COMPOSE, create, write, arrange, prepare, produce, devise, think up, form, formulate, frame, construct, draw up
7 EARN, gain, net, gross, obtain, acquire, get, bring in, secure, win, take home, clear
formal realize
8 CONSTITUTE, compose, comprise, add up to, amount to, come to, total
9 SCORE, gain, chalk up
colloq. notch up
10 PREPARE, get ready, put together, cook
US colloq. fix
11 CALCULATE, work out, compute, reckon (up), estimate
12 SERVE AS, have the qualifications for, become, act as, play the role/part of, achieve
F3 **1** dismantle **7** spend, lose
▷ **make away with** **1** STEAL, run off with, walk off with, snatch, seize, carry off, kidnap; *colloq.* pinch, lift, nick, nab, swipe **2** KILL, do away with, murder, slaughter, assassinate; *colloq.* do in, knock off, bump off
▷ **make believe** pretend, play, play-act, imagine, dream, enact, fantasize, act; *formal* feign; *colloq.* make castles in the air
▷ **make do** cope, manage, survive, get along, get by, improvise, make out, muddle through; *colloq.* scrape by, make the best of a bad job, keep your head above water
▷ **make for** **1** HEAD FOR, aim for, go towards, move towards **2** PRODUCE, lead to, promote, contribute to, facilitate, favour, forward, further, be conducive to
▷ **make it** succeed, be successful, get on, come through, arrive, pull through, reach, survive, prosper
F3 fail
▷ **make off** run off, run away, depart, bolt, leave, fly; *colloq.* cut and run, beat a hasty retreat, clear off, make a getaway, take to your heels, skedaddle, scarper, beat it
▷ **make off with** run off with, carry off, steal, swipe, walk off with, pilfer, kidnap, abduct; *formal* appropriate, purloin; *colloq.* filch, knock off, nab, nick, pinch
▷ **make out** **1** DISCERN, manage to see/hear, perceive, decipher, distinguish, recognize, see, detect, discover; *old use* espy **2** UNDERSTAND, work out, grasp, comprehend, follow, fathom **3** DRAW UP, complete, fill in, write out **4** MAINTAIN, imply, claim, assert, declare, describe, demonstrate, prove, establish; *formal* affirm, aver **5** MANAGE, get on, get along, get by, cope, progress, succeed; *formal* fare
6 WRITE OUT, fill in/out, complete
▷ **make over** transfer, sign over, convey, assign, bequeath, leave
▷ **make up** **1** CREATE, invent, devise, fabricate, construct, originate, formulate, frame, dream up, compose, think up, concoct, hatch **2** COMPLETE, fill, supply, provide, meet, supplement, round off **3** COMPRISE, constitute, compose, form **4** BE RECONCILED, make peace, settle differences, become friends again, shake hands, repent; *colloq.* bury the hatchet, forgive and forget, call it quits **5** PUT MAKE-UP ON, powder, rouge, perfume, paint; *colloq.* put on your face, doll up, tart up
▷ **make up for** compensate for, make amends for, make recompense for, offset, redress; *formal* atone for
▷ **make up to** curry favour with, toady to, court,

fawn on, butter up, make overtures to; *colloq.* chat up
▷ **make up your mind** decide, choose, determine, resolve, settle
🖃 waver
▷ **make way** allow to pass, make room/space for, stand back for, not stand in the way of, allow to succeed
▶ *n* brand, sort, type, style, variety, manufacture, model, mark, kind, form, structure

make-believe *n, adj*
▶ *n* pretence, imagination, fantasy, unreality, fabrication, play-acting, role-play, dream, dreaming, daydreaming, masquerade, charade
🖃 reality
▶ *adj* imaginary, imagined, made-up, imitated, pretended, fantasy, fantasized, dream, simulated, unreal, mock, sham
formal feigned
colloq. pretend
🖃 real

maker *n*
creator, manufacturer, constructor, builder, producer, director, architect, author, fabricator

makeshift *adj*
temporary, improvised, rough and ready, thrown together, cobbled together, provisional, substitute, stopgap, stand-by, expedient, make-do
🖃 permanent

make-up *n*
1 COSMETICS, paint, powder, greasepaint, maquillage
colloq. war paint
See panel at **cosmetics**.
2 CONSTITUTION, nature, composition, character, construction, form, format, formation, arrangement, organization, style, structure, assembly
formal configuration
3 PERSONALITY, temperament, temper, nature, character, disposition, style

making *n*
1 PRODUCTION, producing, creation, creating, manufacture, assembly, building, composition, construction, fabrication, modelling, moulding, forging
2 POTENTIAL, qualities, potentiality, promise, capability, capacity, possibilities, beginnings, materials, ingredients
3 EARNINGS, income, profits, proceeds, revenue, returns, takings
🖃 **1** dismantling
▷ **in the making** budding, potential, promising, coming, developing, emergent, up and coming; *formal* nascent, burgeoning, incipient

maladjusted *adj*
disturbed, unstable, confused, alienated, disordered, neurotic
formal estranged
colloq. dotty, round the bend, screwed-up;
slang schizo, psycho, gaga
🖃 well-adjusted; *colloq.* together

maladministration *n*
inefficiency, incompetence, mismanagement, mishandling, misrule, blundering, bungling, misgovernment, misconduct, corruption, dishonesty, malpractice, stupidity
technical malfeasance, misfeasance
formal malversation

maladroit *adj*
clumsy, awkward, bungling, unskilful, unhandy, gauche, graceless, inelegant, inept, inexpert, tactless, insensitive, thoughtless, inconsiderate, undiplomatic, ill-timed
formal untoward
colloq. cack-handed, ham-fisted
🖃 **1** skilful **2** adroit, tactful

malady *n*
illness, disease, sickness, complaint, infirmity, ailment, disorder, breakdown
formal affliction, malaise, indisposition
🖃 health

malaise *n*
uneasiness, unease, discontent, depression, discomfort, disquiet, weariness, anxiety, anguish, doldrums, *angst,* illness, disease, sickness, weakness
formal lassitude, melancholy, indisposition, enervation
🖃 happiness, well-being

malapropism *n*
wrong word, misuse, misapplication

malapropos *adj, adv*
▶ *adj* inappropriate, unsuitable, untimely, ill-timed, inopportune, misapplied, inapt, uncalled-for, tactless
formal inapposite, unseemly
🖃 appropriate, tactful
▶ *adv* inappropriately, unsuitably, inaptly, unseasonably, tactlessly, inopportunely
formal inappositely
🖃 appropriately, tactfully

malcontent *n, adj*
▶ *n* grumbler, complainer, moaner, rebel, agitator, mischief-maker, troublemaker
colloq. belly-acher, grouch, grouser, nit-picker, whinger
▶ *adj* dissatisfied, unhappy, unsatisfied, discontented, disgruntled, ill-disposed, disaffected, morose, rebellious, fault-finding, resentful
formal restive, dissentious
colloq. belly-aching
🖃 contented

male *adj*
masculine, manly, virile, boyish, he-, manlike
🖃 female

Male terms include: boy, lad, youth, man, gentleman, *colloq.* gent, bachelor, *colloq.* fellow, *colloq.* chap, *colloq.* bloke, *colloq.* guy, son, brother, boyfriend, beau, *colloq.* toy boy, fiancé, bridegroom, husband, father, uncle, nephew, grandfather, patriarch, godfather, widower, *colloq.* sugar daddy, *colloq.* hunk, gigolo, homosexual, gay, rent boy, *colloq.* male chauvinist pig (MCP); bull, dog, buck, tup, cock, cockerel, stallion, billy-goat, boar, dog fox, stag, ram, tom cat, drake, gander.

malediction *n*
curse, cursing, denunciation, anathema, anathematization, damnation, damning
formal execration, imprecation, malison
🖃 blessing, praise

malefactor *n*
law-breaker, criminal, offender, felon, convict, outlaw, delinquent, wrongdoer, evildoer, culprit, villain
technical misfeasor

formal miscreant, transgressor
colloq. crook

malevolence *n*
malice, malignancy, malignity, maliciousness, spite,
spitefulness, vindictiveness, vengefulness, ill-will,
hostility, unfriendliness, hate, hatred, bitterness,
venom, viciousness, fierceness, cruelty
formal rancour
⊟ benevolence

malevolent *adj*
malicious, malign, spiteful, vindictive, vengeful, ill-
natured, hostile, unfriendly, bitter, resentful, vicious,
fierce, cruel, venomous, pernicious, evil-minded
formal rancorous, baleful, maleficent
⊟ benevolent, kind

malformation *n*
deformity, misshapenness, disfigurement, irregularity,
distortion, warp

malformed *adj*
deformed, misshapen, irregular, disfigured, distorted,
twisted, warped, crooked, bent
⊟ perfect

malfunction *v, n*
▶ *v* break down, go wrong, fail, stop working
colloq. go kaput, pack up; *slang* conk out
▶ *n* fault, defect, failure, breakdown, flaw

malice *n*
maliciousness, enmity, hostility, animosity, ill-will,
hatred, hate, bad blood, spite, vindictiveness, venom,
spleen, bitterness, resentment
formal malevolence, animus, rancour
colloq. bone to pick, bloody-mindedness, bitchiness
⊟ love

malicious *adj*
ill-natured, hostile, malign, spiteful, venomous,
vicious, vengeful, evil, evil-minded, pernicious, bitter,
resentful
formal malevolent, baleful, rancorous
⊟ friendly, kind

malign *v, adj*
▶ *v* defame, slander, libel, abuse, harm, injure, insult
formal disparage, calumniate, vilify, traduce
colloq. run down, smear, slur, badmouth, stab in the
back, kick in the teeth, drag through the mud
⊟ praise
▶ *adj* harmful, malignant, bad, evil, hurtful,
injurious, destructive, hostile
formal malevolent
⊟ benign, kind

malignant *adj*
1 EVIL, hostile, malicious, spiteful, vicious,
venomous, spiteful, destructive, harmful, hurtful,
pernicious
formal malevolent, rancorous
2 FATAL, deadly, lethal, incurable, dangerous, life-
threatening, cancerous, uncontrollable, virulent
⊟ 1 kind 2 benign

malignity *n*
malice, maliciousness, harmfulness, hate, hurtfulness,
ill-will, hatred, bad blood, bitterness, deadliness,
perniciousness, gall, destructiveness, hostility,
wickedness, vengefulness, vindictiveness, spite,
venom, viciousness, animosity
formal animus, balefulness, malevolence, rancour
⊟ harmlessness, kindness

malinger *v*
pretend, pretend to be ill, slack
colloq. dodge, loaf, shirk, skive, put it on, swing the
lead
⊟ work

malingerer *n*
slacker
colloq. dodger, loafer, shirker, skiver, lead-swinger
⊟ worker

mall *n*
shopping centre, shopping precinct, galleria, plaza

malleable *adj*
1 SUPPLE, plastic, pliable, pliant, flexible, soft,
workable
formal ductile
2 IMPRESSIONABLE, manageable, receptive,
flexible, susceptible, persuadable, pliant, pliable,
adaptable, biddable, governable
formal compliant, tractile, tractable
⊟ 1 rigid 2 *formal* intractable

malnutrition *n*
starvation, undernourishment, underfeeding, hunger,
unhealthy diet, anorexia (nervosa)
formal inanition
⊟ nourishment

malodorous *adj*
foul-smelling, evil-smelling, fetid, nauseating, niffy,
offensive, putrid, rank, reeking, smelly, stinking
formal noisomemephitic, miasmal, miasmatic,
miasmatous, miasmic, miasmous,
⊟ sweet-smelling

malpractice *n*
misconduct, unethical behaviour, unprofessional
conduct, mismanagement, negligence, carelessness,
impropriety, wrongdoing, offence, abuse, misdeed
formal dereliction of duty

maltreat *v*
mistreat, ill-treat, treat badly, misuse, abuse, injure,
harm, damage, hurt, bully, hound, victimize, torture
⊟ care for

maltreatment *n*
mistreatment, ill-treatment, ill-usage, ill-use, abuse,
misuse, injury, harm, damage, hurt, bullying,
victimization, torture
⊟ care

mammal *n*

Mammals include: aardvark, African black
rhinoceros, African elephant, anteater, antelope,
armadillo, baboon, Bactrian camel, badger, bat,
bear, beaver, bushbaby, cat, chimpanzee, chipmunk,
cow, deer, dog, dolphin, duck-billed platypus,
dugong, echidna, flying lemur, fox, gerbil, gibbon,
giraffe, goat, gorilla, guinea pig, hamster, hare,
hedgehog, hippopotamus, horse, human being,
hyena, Indian elephant, kangaroo, koala, lemming,
leopard, lion, manatee, marmoset, marmot,
marsupial mouse, mole, mouse, opossum, orang
utan, otter, pig, porcupine, porpoise, rabbit,
raccoon, rat, sea cow, sea lion, seal, sheep, shrew,
sloth, squirrel, tamarin, tapir, tiger, vole, wallaby,
walrus, weasel, whale, wolf, zebra. *See also* **cat;
cattle; dog; horse; marsupial; monkey; rodent**.

mammoth *adj*
enormous, huge, vast, colossal, gigantic, giant,
massive, immense, stupendous, monumental, mighty,

prodigious, gargantuan, herculean, leviathan, Brobdingnagian
colloq. whopping, jumbo, bumper, ginormous
E3 tiny, minute

man *n, v*
▶ *n* **1** MALE, gentleman
colloq. guy, chap, bloke, boy, lad, fellow
Related adjective: male
2 HUMAN BEING, person, individual, adult, human, mortal
3 HUMANITY, human race, human beings, humankind, mankind, people, *Homo sapiens*, mortals
Related adjective: human
4 MANSERVANT, servant, worker, workman, labourer, employee, helper, hand, soldier, valet, houseman, houseboy, page, attendant, factotum, man-of-all-work, jack-of-all-trades, odd-jobman
5 PARTNER, husband, lover, boyfriend, spouse
colloq. fellow, bloke, guy, toy boy
▷ **to a man** without exception, unanimously, as one, with one voice, one and all, bar none
▶ *v* staff, crew, take charge of, be in charge of, work, operate, occupy

manacle *v*
handcuff, shackle, restrain, fetter, chain, put in chains, bind, curb, check, hamper, inhibit
E3 free, unshackle

manacles *n*
handcuffs, chains, fetters, cuffs, shackles, wristlets, irons, bonds
old use gyves
colloq. bracelets, darbies

manage *v*
1 ADMINISTER, direct, run, organize, command, govern, be in charge of, be responsible for, head (up), be head of, lead, guide, preside over, rule, superintend, supervise, control, oversee, conduct
2 ACCOMPLISH, succeed, achieve, bring about, bring off, engineer
formal effect
3 CONTROL, influence, deal with, master, handle, operate, manipulate, work, guide, use, wield
4 COPE, deal with, survive, get by, get along, get on, make do
formal fare
colloq. make out
E3 **1** mismanage **2** fail

manageable *adj*
1 *a manageable amount of work*
reasonable, doable, feasible, attainable, practicable, acceptable, viable, tolerable
2 CONTROLLABLE, governable, amenable, accommodating, yielding, submissive, docile, pliant, pliable, flexible
formal tractable
E3 **1, 2** unmanageable

management *n*
1 ADMINISTRATION, direction, control, government, command, leadership, organization, running, ruling, overseeing, superintendence, supervision, charge, care, handling, conduct
2 MANAGERS, directors, directorate, executive, executives, governors, board, owners, employers, proprietors, supervisors
colloq. bosses
E3 **1** mismanagement **2** workers

manager *n*
director, executive, employer, president, chairman, chief executive, managing director, administrator, controller, superintendent, supervisor, commissioner, overseer, governor, organizer, head, chief, head of department, comptroller
colloq. boss, gaffer, guv; *US* honcho

mandate *n*
order, command, decree, edict, injunction, dictate, charge, directive, direction, ordinance, ruling, law, statute, bidding, warrant, authorization, authority, instruction, commission, sanction

mandatory *adj*
obligatory, compulsory, binding, required, necessary, essential, imperative
formal requisite
E3 optional

manful *adj*
brave, manly, gallant, courageous, heroic, intrepid, bold, lion-hearted, determined, resolute, stalwart, stout, stout-hearted, valiant, strong, powerful, indomitable, hardy, daring, unflinching, vigorous, noble, noble-minded
E3 half-hearted, timid

manfully *adv*
bravely, courageously, valiantly, heroically, intrepidly, boldly, gallantly, pluckily, determinedly, hard, vigorously, strongly, powerfully, unflinchingly, desperately, resolutely, stalwartly, stoutly, steadfastly, nobly
E3 half-heartedly, timidly

manger *n*
trough, feeding trough, feeder, crib

mangle *v*
1 MUTILATE, disfigure, mar, maim, butcher, destroy, deform, wreck, twist, maul, distort, crush, cut, hack, tear, lacerate, rend
2 SPOIL, butcher, ruin, bungle
colloq. botch, mess up, make a mess of; *slang* screw up

mangy *adj*
seedy, shabby, scruffy, scabby, shoddy, moth-eaten, worn, filthy, dirty, mean
colloq. tatty

manhandle *v*
1 *the porters manhandled the baggage*
haul, heave, pull, push, shove, tug
colloq. hump
2 *the police manhandled the demonstrators*
maul, mistreat, maltreat, misuse, abuse, handle roughly, push, shove
colloq. knock about, rough up

manhood *n*
1 ADULTHOOD, maturity
2 MASCULINITY, virility, manliness, manfulness, maleness
colloq. machismo

mania *n*
1 MADNESS, insanity, lunacy, dementia, psychosis, derangement, disorder, aberration, frenzy, wildness, raving, hysteria
colloq. craziness

Manias (by name of disorder) include: dipsomania (*alcohol*), bibliomania (*books*), ailuromania (*cats*), demomania (*crowds*), necromania (*dead bodies*), thanatomania (*death*), cynomania (*dogs*), narcomania (*drugs*), pyromania (*fire-raising*), anthomania (*flowers*), hippomania (*horses*), mythomania (*lying and exaggerating*), egomania (*yourself*), ablutomania (*personal cleanliness*), hedonomania (*pleasure*), megalomania (*power*), theomania (*religion*), nymphomania (*sex*), monomania (*single idea or thing*), kleptomania (*stealing*), tomomania (*surgery*), logomania (*talking*), ergomania (*work*). *See also* **phobia**.

2 PASSION, craze, rage, obsession, compulsion, fetish, preoccupation, enthusiasm, infatuation, fixation, craving, urge, desire, fascination
colloq. fad

maniac *n*
1 LUNATIC, madman, madwoman, psychotic, psychopath, deranged person
colloq. loony, nutter, nut, nutcase, fruitcake, crackpot, crank, headcase; *US* hook; *slang* screwball, oddball, psycho
2 ENTHUSIAST, fan, fanatic
colloq. fiend, freak

manifest *adj, v*
▶ *adj* obvious, evident, clear, apparent, plain, open, patent, distinct, noticeable, conspicuous, perceptible, glaring, blatant, unmistakable, visible, unconcealed, transparent
🖃 unclear
▶ *v* show, exhibit, display, demonstrate, reveal, set forth, present, express, declare, indicate, expose, make clear/plain, prove, illustrate, establish
formal evince
🖃 conceal, hide

manifestation *n*
display, exhibition, demonstration, show, presentation, declaration, revelation, exposure, disclosure, appearance, expression, illustration, exemplification, evidence, sign, indication, token, mark
formal exposition

manifesto *n*
statement, declaration, announcement, proclamation, publication, policies, platform

manifold *adj*
many, several, numerous, varied, various, diverse, multiple, kaleidoscopic, abundant, copious
formal multifarious, multitudinous

manipulate *v*
1 MANOEUVRE, influence, control, exploit, work, engineer, guide, direct, steer, use/turn to your advantage, negotiate, capitalize on
colloq. wangle, cash in on, pull strings, have in the palm of your hand, twist round your little finger, have over a barrel, wheel and deal, frame, fit up
2 FALSIFY, rig, juggle with, massage, tamper with
colloq. doctor, cook, fiddle
3 HANDLE, control, wield, operate, work, knead, use, utilize, employ, process, ply

manipulator *n*
1 EXPLOITER, controller, manoeuvrer, influencer, schemer, engineer, director, negotiator
colloq. wheeler-dealer, smoothy, smart guy
2 HANDLER, operator, user, worker, controller, wielder

mankind *n*
human race, humanity, human beings, humankind, man, *Homo sapiens*, people, mortals

manliness *n*
masculinity, maleness, virility, manfulness, bravery, boldness, courage, valour, fearlessness, heroism, intrepidity, resolution, stout-heartedness, stalwartness, hardihood, independence, manhood, strength, vigour, mettle, firmness
formal fortitude
colloq. machismo
🖃 timidity, unmanliness

manly *adj*
masculine, male, virile, manful, brave, courageous, bold, intrepid, fearless, heroic, determined, strong, powerful, firm, tough, rugged, vigorous, sturdy, robust
colloq. macho

man-made *adj*
synthetic, manufactured, simulated, imitation, artificial
colloq. ersatz
🖃 natural

manner *n*
1 WAY, method, means, fashion, style, variety, procedure, technique, approach, practice, process, routine, form
formal mode
2 BEHAVIOUR, conduct, appearance, look, character, attitude, posture, stance
formal bearing, demeanour, air, mien, aspect, deportment
3 *good manners*
behaviour, conduct, way of behaving, etiquette, politeness, courtesy, protocol, good form, formalities, social graces
formal decorum, propriety, demeanour, bearing
colloq. p's and q's, the done thing

mannered *adj*
artificial, posed, pretentious, stilted, precious
formal affected, euphuistic
colloq. pseudo, put-on
🖃 natural

mannerism *n*
idiosyncrasy, peculiarity, characteristic, quirk, trait, feature, foible, habit

mannerly *adj*
polite, courteous, refined, well-behaved, well-bred, well-mannered, gentlemanly, ladylike, respectful, civil, civilized, deferential, gracious, formal, genteel, polished
formal decorous
🖃 unmannerly

mannish *adj*
masculine, unfeminine, unladylike, unwomanly, tomboyish, viraginian, viraginous, viragoish, Amazonian
formal virilescent
colloq. butch, laddish
🖃 womanish

mannishness *n*
masculinity, unfemininity, unladylikeness, unwomanliness, virilism
formal virilescence
colloq. butchness
🖃 womanishness

manoeuvre *v, n*
▶ *v* **1** MOVE, manipulate, handle, guide, pilot, steer, navigate, negotiate, jockey, direct, drive, exercise
2 CONTRIVE, engineer, plot, scheme, intrigue,

manipulate, manage, plan, devise, negotiate
colloq. wangle, pull strings, jockey for position
▶ *n* **1** EXERCISE, move, movement, operation, deployment, action
2 MANIPULATION, skilful plan, ploy, plot, ruse, stratagem, device, gambit, tactic, trick, scheme, subterfuge
formal machination, artifice
colloq. dodge, wangle

manor *n*
house, country house, seat, hall, villa, barony, château, Schloss, Hof
Related adjective: manorial

manse *n*
vicarage, rectory, parsonage, deanery, glebe-house

manservant *n*
butler, gentleman's gentleman, valet, retainer

mansion *n*
home, hall, house, manor, manor-house, castle, château, Schloss, villa, seat
formal abode, dwelling, habitation, residence

manslaughter *n*
killing, slaughter, murder, massacre, butchery, genocide, homicide, assassination, execution, slaying, extermination, carnage, bloodshed, elimination, destruction, fatality
formal patricide, matricide, infanticide, fratricide, sororicide, uxoricide
colloq. liquidation

mantle *n, v*
▶ *n* **1** CLOAK, cape, hood, shawl, veil, wrap, shroud, screen
2 COVER, covering, veil, shroud, blanket, layer, cloak, mask, cloud, envelope
▶ *v* cover, cloak, veil, mask, wrap, blanket, shroud, cloud, envelop, hide, disguise, conceal

manual *n, adj*
▶ *n* handbook, guide, guidebook, instruction book, instructions, ABC, companion, bible, prospectus, vade-mecum, directions
colloq. book of words
▶ *adj* hand-operated, by hand, (done) with your hands, physical, human
▣ mental, automatic

manufacture *v, n*
▶ *v* **1** MAKE, produce, construct, build, fabricate, create, assemble, mass-produce, put together, turn out, fashion, process, forge, model, form
2 INVENT, make up, devise, construct, frame, concoct, fabricate, think up, dream up
▶ *n* production, making, construction, building, fabrication, mass-production, assembly, processing, creation, formation, fashioning, modelling, forming

manufacturer *n*
maker, producer, industrialist, constructor, factory-owner, builder, creator

manure *n*
fertilizer, compost, muck, dung, animal excrement, droppings, guana, ordure
formal animal faeces

manuscript *n*
document, text, paper, parchment, scroll, vellum

many *adj, n*
▶ *adj* a lot of, a large number of, several, numerous, innumerable, countless, various, multiple, copious, varied, sundry, diverse
formal manifold, multitudinous
colloq. lots of, umpteen, scores, hundreds, thousands, millions, billions, zillions, masses, piles, heaps, stacks, oodles, scads, wads, tons
▣ few
▶ *n* a lot, a large number of people/things, a mass, a multitude, plenty
colloq. lots of, umpteen, scores, hundreds, thousands, millions, billions, zillions, masses, piles, heaps, stacks, oodles, scads, wads, tons

map *n, v*
▶ *n* chart, plan, town plan, street plan, street guide, road-map, atlas, gazetteer, graph, plot
▶ *v* chart, plot, plan, mark, sketch
formal delineate
▷ **map out** sketch, draw (up), draft, outline, work out

mar *v*
spoil, impair, harm, hurt, damage, blemish, deface, deform, disfigure, mutilate, injure, maim, scar, detract from, mangle, ruin, wreck, taint, tarnish, contaminate, stain
▣ enhance

maraud *v*
plunder, raid, ravage, ransack, loot, pillage, harry, forage, foray, sack
formal despoil, spoliate, depredate

marauder *n*
bandit, brigand, robber, raider, plunderer, looter, pillager, pirate, buccaneer, freebooter, outlaw, highwayman, ravager, predator, rustler, rover

march *v, n*
▶ *v* walk, file, parade, pace, step, tread, stride, tramp, hike, stalk, strut, swagger, forward, advance, progress, make headway
▶ *n* **1** STEP, pace, stride, walk, gait
2 WALK, route-march, trek, hike, tramp
colloq. footslog
3 PROCESSION, parade, demonstration
colloq. demo
4 ADVANCE, development, progress, evolution, passage, headway, evolution

margin *n*
1 BORDER, edge, boundary, bound, periphery, perimeter, frontier, demarcation line, rim, brim, brink, limit(s), confine(s), verge, side, skirt
2 ALLOWANCE, play, leeway, latitude, scope, room, room for manoeuvre, difference, differential, space, surplus, extra

marginal *adj*
borderline, doubtful, peripheral, on the edge, negligible, minute, minimal, insignificant, minor, slight, tiny, low, small
▣ central, core, mainstream

marijuana *n*
cannabis, hemp, hashish, bhang
colloq. dope, ganja, grass, hash, pot, spliff, puff, tea, kef; *slang* blow, weed, skunk, punk, leaf, *US* locoweed

marina *n*
dock, harbour, mooring, port, yacht station

marinade *v*
steep, soak, immerse, marinate, souse, saturate, imbue, permeate, infuse

marine *adj*
sea, maritime, naval, nautical, seafaring, seagoing, ocean-going, oceanic, saltwater, seawater, aquatic
formal pelagic, thalassian, thalassic

mariner *n*
sailor, seaman, seafarer, deckhand, navigator
colloq. tar, Jack Tar, matlo, matlow, matelot, sea dog, salt, limey

marital *adj*
conjugal, matrimonial, married, marriage, wedding, wedded
formal nuptial, connubial

maritime *adj*
marine, nautical, naval, seafaring, sea, seaside, seagoing, oceanic, coastal
formal littoral, pelagic

mark *n, v*
▶ *n* **1** SPOT, stain, blemish, patch, pimple, freckle, birthmark, blot, blotch, smudge, smear, dent, impression, trace, fingerprint(s), track(s), imprint, speck, notch, chip, cut, scar, scratch, bruise, score, line, nick
formal stigma
colloq. zit
2 SIGN, indication, character, symbol, stamp, token, characteristic, feature, quality, attribute, symptom, clue, proof, hint, evidence, impression, print
3 SCORE, grade, percentage, tick, assessment, evaluation, letter, number, symbol, emblem, brand, stamp, seal, badge, device, logo, trademark, motto, monogram
4 *inflation reaching the 5% mark*
point, level, stage, norm, standard, criterion, gauge, scale, measure, yardstick
5 TARGET, goal, aim, objective, object, purpose, end, intention, bull's-eye
▷ **make one's mark** succeed, be successful, prosper, get on; *colloq.* make it, hit/make the big time
▷ **wide of the mark** incorrect, inaccurate, imprecise, irrelevant, beside the point, off target
▶ *v* **1** STAIN, blemish, blot, smudge, discolour, dent, scar, scratch, bruise, dent, chip, cut, score, nick
2 BRAND, label, stamp, tag, flag, characterize, identify, distinguish
3 EVALUATE, assess, correct, grade
formal appraise
4 WRITE DOWN, note (down), indicate, name, label, specify, designate, jot down
5 CHARACTERIZE, identify, stamp, brand, typify, distinguish
6 *mark an event/occasion*
observe, remember, celebrate, commemorate, keep, honour, recognize
7 *mark my words*
listen, mind, note, spot, mind, observe, regard, see, notice, take note of, discern, pay attention to, bear in mind, take to heart
formal heed, take heed of
▷ **mark down** reduce, lower, decrease, cut;
colloq. slash
◼ mark up
▷ **mark out 1** *mark out a football pitch* draw lines, demarcate, show the boundaries of, fix, delimit
2 DISTINGUISH, differentiate, tell apart, set apart, discriminate, single out, tell the difference between
▷ **mark up** increase, raise, put up; *colloq.* hike up, jack up

marked *adj*
1 SPOTTED, spotty, stained, blemished, blotched, blotchy, scarred, pimply, freckled, bruised, scarred, scratched
2 NOTICEABLE, obvious, conspicuous, prominent, signal, evident, clear, pronounced, distinct, noted, decided, emphatic, considerable, remarkable, apparent, glaring, striking, blatant, unmistakable
3 SUSPECTED, watched, doomed, condemned
◼ **1** unnoticeable, slight

markedly *adj*
noticeably, obviously, conspicuously, prominently, signally, evidently, clearly, distinctly, decidedly, emphatically, considerably, remarkably, glaringly, strikingly, blatantly, unmistakably

market *n, v*
▶ *n* **1** *buy goods at the market*
mart, market-place, shopping centre, mall, bazaar, fair, exchange, outlet
formal agora
2 *no market for these goods*
demand, call, requirement, need, occasion, want, desire
3 BUSINESS, trade, trading, buying, selling, industry, dealings
Related adjective: nundinal
▶ *v* sell, retail, hawk, peddle, offer for sale
◼ buy
▷ **on the market** for sale, on sale, up for sale, available

marketable *adj*
in demand, sought after, wanted, saleable, sellable, merchantable
formal vendible
◼ unsaleable

marksman, markswoman *n*
crack shot, dead shot, sharpshooter, sniper, bersagliere

maroon *v*
abandon, strand, cast away, forsake, desert, put ashore, strand, leave (behind), isolate, turn your back on
colloq. leave in the lurch, leave high and dry

marriage *n*
1 *the marriage ceremony*
union, married relationship, married state, wedding
old use wedlock
formal matrimony, nuptials, spousage
2 UNION, alliance, partnership, merger, coupling, fusion, amalgamation, unification, combination, link, connection, association, confederation, affiliation
◼ **1** divorce **2** separation
Related adjectives: marital, matrimonial, conjugal, connubial

married *adj*
marital, wedded, united, wed, joined, husbandly, wifely, wived, yoked
formal conjugal, connubial, matrimonial, nuptial, spousal
colloq. hitched, spliced
◼ divorced, single

marrow *n*
essence, heart, nub, kernel, core, nucleus, centre, pith, soul, spirit, substance, quick, stuff, gist
formal quintessence
colloq. nitty-gritty, nuts and bolts
Related adjective: myeloid

marry *v*
1 WED, get married, become husband and wife, intermarry, elope
formal join in matrimony, become espoused
colloq. tie the knot, get hitched, get spliced, take the plunge, lead to the altar, make an honest woman of
2 UNITE, ally, join (together), merge, combine, amalgamate, couple, affiliate, match, link, connect, associate, weld, fuse, knit
Ⅎ **1** divorce **2** separate

marsh *n*
marshland, bog, swamp, fen, morass, mire, quagmire, slough
US bayou
Related adjective: paludal

marshal *v*
1 ARRANGE, dispose, order, line up, align, array, rank, organize, put in order, assemble, gather (together), muster, group, collect, draw up, deploy
2 GUIDE, lead, take, escort, conduct, usher, shepherd

marshy *adj*
boggy, fenny, fennish, swampy, quaggy, waterlogged, wet, muddy, squelchy, miry, slumpy, spongy
formal paludal, paludinal, paludine, paludinous
Ⅎ solid, firm, dry

marsupial *n*

Marsupials include: bandicoot, cuscus, kangaroo, rat kangaroo, tree kangaroo, wallaroo, koala, marsupial anteater, marsupial mouse, marsupial mole, marsupial rat, opossum, pademelon, phalanger, Tasmanian Devil, Tasmanian wolf, wallaby, rock wallaby, wombat.

martial *adj*
warlike, military, army, soldierly, militant, heroic, brave, belligerent, combative, aggressive
formal pugnacious, bellicose

martinet *n*
disciplinarian, stickler, tyrant, taskmaster, taskmistress, formalist
colloq. slave-driver

martyr *v*
put to death, make a martyr of, crucify, stone, persecute, torture, torment, burn at the stake, throw to the lions, put on the rack
colloq. give the works, give the third degree

martyrdom *n*
death, suffering, torture, torment, persecution, excruciation, ordeal, agony, anguish, witness

marvel *v, n*
▶ *v* wonder, gape, gaze, stare, goggle, not expect, be amazed at, stand in amazement
colloq. gawp, be flabbergasted, not believe your eyes, not know what to say
▶ *n* wonder, miracle, surprise, something amazing/incredible, phenomenon, prodigy, spectacle, sensation, genius
colloq. eye-opener, quite something

marvellous *adj*
1 WONDERFUL, excellent, splendid, superb, great, magnificent, terrific, super, fantastic
colloq. ace, brill, magic; *slang* awesome, wicked, bad, cool, mega
2 EXTRAORDINARY, amazing, surprising, astonishing, astounding, sensational, spectacular,

miraculous, remarkable, awesome, unbelievable, incredible, stupendous, glorious
Ⅎ **1** terrible, awful **2** ordinary, run-of-the-mill

masculine *adj*
1 MALE, manlike, manly, mannish, virile
colloq. macho, butch
2 VIGOROUS, strong, strapping, robust, powerful, muscular, rugged, red-blooded, bold, brave, gallant, fearless, heroic, determined, confident, resolute, stout-hearted
Ⅎ **1** feminine

masculinity *n*
manliness, maleness, virility, manfulness, bravery, boldness, courage, valour, fearlessness, heroism, intrepidity, resolution, stout-heartedness, stalwartness, hardihood, independence, manhood, strength, vigour, strength, mettle, firmness
formal fortitude
colloq. machismo
Ⅎ femininity

mash *v, n*
▶ *v* crush, pulp, beat, pound, purée, pulverize, pummel, grind, smash, squash
▶ *n* mush, pulp, crush, purée, squash, pap, paste

mask *n, v*
▶ *n* disguise, camouflage, fâcade, front, concealment, cover-up, cover, guise, pretence, semblance, cloak, veil, blind, screen, show, veneer, visor, goggles
▶ *v* disguise, camouflage, cover (up), conceal, cloak, veil, hide, obscure, screen, shield
Ⅎ expose, uncover

masquerade *n, v*
▶ *n* **1** MASQUE, masked ball, costume ball, fancy-dress party
2 DISGUISE, counterfeit, cover-up, cover, deception, front, pose, pretence, guise, cloak
▶ *v* disguise, impersonate, pose, pass yourself off, mask, play, pretend, profess
formal dissimulate

mass[1] *n, adj, v*
▶ *n* **1** HEAP, pile, load, accumulation, collection, combination, entirety, whole, total, totality, sum, lot, group, batch, bunch
formal aggregate, conglomeration, assemblage
2 QUANTITY, abundance, multitude, throng, troop, crowd, band, horde, mob
colloq. loads, heaps, bags, piles, lots, tons, scores, oodles
3 MAJORITY, body, bulk, greater part, most, preponderance
4 SIZE, dimension, magnitude, immensity, bulk, capacity
5 LUMP, piece, chunk, block, hunk
colloq. wodge
6 *the masses*
crowd, herd, mob, lower classes, working class(es), common people, proletariat, rabble, hoi polloi, the rank and file
colloq. plebs, riff-raff
▶ *adj* widespread, large-scale, extensive, comprehensive, general, universal, indiscriminate, popular, across-the-board, sweeping, wholesale, blanket
formal pandemic
Ⅎ limited, small-scale
▶ *v* collect, gather, assemble, congregate, amass, accumulate, draw together, come/bring together,

crowd, rally, cluster, muster, swarm, throng
🖅 separate

mass² *n*
go to mass
Eucharist, Communion, Holy Communion, Lord's
Supper, Lord's Table

massacre *n, v*
▶ *n* slaughter, murder, homicide, extermination,
carnage, butchery, wholesale slaughter, indiscriminate
killing, holocaust, bloodbath, annihilation, killing,
genocide, ethnic cleansing, pogrom, liquidation,
decimation
▶ *v* slaughter, butcher, murder, mow down,
exterminate, annihilate, kill (off), slay, decimate,
liquidate
colloq. wipe out

massage *n, v*
▶ *n* manipulation, kneading, rub, rubbing, rub-
down, pummelling, reflexology, aromatherapy,
acupressure, shiatsu, Jacuzzi®, osteopathy,
physiotherapy, Reichian therapy
▶ *v* manipulate, knead, rub (down), pummel

massive *adj*
huge, immense, enormous, vast, colossal, mammoth,
gigantic, big, bulky, monumental, solid, hulking, hefty,
weighty, substantial, heavy, large, large-scale, great,
extensive, mighty
colloq. whopping, jumbo, ginormous
🖅 tiny, small

mast *n*
pole, shaft, rod, bar, spar, boom, yard, heel, post, staff,
stick, upright, support

master *n, adj, v*
▶ *n* **1** RULER, chief, governor, head, lord, captain,
employer, commander, controller, director, manager,
superintendent, overseer, principal, overlord, owner
colloq. boss, gaffer, skipper, guv; *US* honcho
2 EXPERT, genius, professional, pundit, virtuoso,
past master, grand master, maestro, adept
colloq. dab hand, ace, pro, buff, egghead, wise guy;
US mavin, maven
3 TEACHER, tutor, mentor, instructor, schoolteacher,
schoolmaster, schoolmistress, guide, guru
formal pedagogue, preceptor
🖅 **1** servant, underling **2** amateur **3** learner,
pupil
▶ *adj* **1** CHIEF, principal, main, leading, foremost,
most important, prime, predominant, controlling,
great, grand
2 EXPERT, masterly, skilled, skilful, experienced,
proficient, practised, adept, dexterous
🖅 **1** subordinate **2** inept
▶ *v* **1** CONQUER, defeat, subdue, triumph over,
overcome, overpower, quell, suppress, rule, control,
govern, tame, bridle, check, curb
formal subjugate, vanquish
2 LEARN, grasp, acquire, manage
colloq. get the hang of

masterful *adj*
arrogant, authoritative, domineering, overbearing,
controlling, high-handed, despotic, dictatorial,
autocratic, tyrannical, powerful, dominating,
imperious
formal peremptory
colloq. bossy
🖅 humble, downtrodden; *colloq.* hen-pecked

⚠ **masterful** or **masterly** ?
Masterful means 'showing power, authority or
determination': *The directors show a masterful
approach to their employees. Masterly* means 'showing
the skill of a master': *a masterly display of
swordsmanship.*

masterly *adj*
expert, professional, accomplished, polished, skilled,
skilful, dexterous, adept, adroit, first-rate, excellent,
superb, superior, supreme
formal consummate
colloq. ace, crack, top-notch
🖅 inept, clumsy

mastermind *v, n*
▶ *v* devise, think up, contrive, engineer, direct,
organize, manage, originate, plan, conceive, design,
dream up, frame, hatch, forge, inspire, be behind
▶ *n* organizer, initiator, manager, planner, creator,
director, originator, authority, genius, intellect,
engineer, architect, prime mover, virtuoso
colloq. brains

masterpiece *n*
masterwork, *pièce de résistance, chef d'oeuvre*,
magnum opus, work of art, creation, jewel

mastery *n*
1 PROFICIENCY, skill, ability, capability, command,
expertise, virtuosity, knowledge, understanding,
comprehension, know-how, dexterity, familiarity,
grasp
formal prowess
2 CONTROL, command, domination, supremacy,
superiority, victory, triumph, dominion, authority,
sovereignty, rule, direction
formal ascendancy
colloq. upper hand
🖅 **1** incompetence **2** subjugation

masticate *v*
champ, chew, munch, chomp, crunch, eat, ruminate,
knead
formal manducate

masturbate *v*
colloq. jerk off, jack off, toss (it) off, play with yourself,
enjoy yourself; *slang* wank, frig

masturbation *n*
self-gratification, self-stimulation, autoeroticism,
onanism, self-abuse, tribadism, tribady
colloq. playing with yourself, enjoying yourself, hand
release; *slang* wank, wanking, frig, frigging, frottage

mat *n*
1 CARPET, doormat, felt, rug, underfelt, underlay,
drugget, table mat, place mat, coaster
2 TANGLE, knot, twist, cluster, mass

match¹ *n, v*
▶ *n* **1** CONTEST, competition, bout, game, test, trial,
event, meet, tournament
2 EQUAL, equivalent, peer, counterpart, fellow, mate,
rival, competitor, one of a pair, copy, double,
companion, complement, replica, lookalike, twin,
duplicate
colloq. dead ringer
3 MARRIAGE, alliance, union, combination,
partnership, affiliation, pairing, merger, coupling
▶ *v* **1** EQUAL, compare, measure up to, rival,
parallel, compete, oppose, contend, vie, keep up with,

pit against

2 FIT, go with, agree, suit, correspond, harmonize, tally, co-ordinate, blend, complement, adapt, go together, relate, tone with, accompany, connect
formal accord

3 JOIN, marry, unite, mate, link, couple, combine, ally, pair (up), yoke, team
colloq. hitch up

F3 **2** clash, conflict **3** separate, divorce

match² *n*
light the fire with matches
light, safety match, spill, taper, fuse, vesta

matching *adj*
corresponding, comparable, complementing, equivalent, parallel, like, identical, co-ordinating, blending, harmonizing, complementary, similar, duplicate, same, twin, paired, double, coupled
formal analogous

F3 clashing, conflicting

matchless *adj*
unequalled, without equal, peerless, incomparable, beyond compare, unmatched, unparalleled, unsurpassed, unexcelled, unrivalled, inimitable, perfect, unique

F3 ordinary

mate *n, v*
▶ *n* **1** FRIEND, companion, comrade, colleague, partner, fellow worker, coworker, workmate, associate
formal compeer
colloq. chum, crony, buddy, pal

2 PARTNER, husband, wife, spouse, boyfriend, girlfriend, companion
colloq. better half, other half, hubbie, missis, missus

3 ASSISTANT, helper, subordinate, apprentice, accomplice, partner

4 MATCH, fellow, twin, equivalent, counterpart
▶ *v* **1** COUPLE, pair, breed, copulate

2 JOIN, match, marry, wed

material *n, adj*
▶ *n* **1** STUFF, substance, body, matter, medium

2 FABRIC, textile, cloth, stuff

3 INFORMATION, facts, facts and figures, numbers, data, details, particulars, ideas, evidence, constituents, work, notes
colloq. low-down, gen, info
▶ *adj* **1** PHYSICAL, bodily, concrete, tangible, palpable, substantial, earthly, worldly
formal corporeal

2 RELEVANT, significant, important, momentous, consequential, meaningful, essential, vital, key, indispensable, serious, weighty
formal pertinent, germane, apposite

F3 **1** spiritual, abstract **2** irrelevant

materialistic *adj*
mercenary, money-grabbing, mammonist, mammonistic

F3 spiritual

materialize *v*
appear, arise, become visible, show/reveal yourself, take shape, turn up, happen, occur, take place, come into being

F3 disappear

materially *adv*
significantly, essentially, fundamentally, substantially, basically, considerably, seriously, gravely, greatly, much

F3 insignificantly

maternal *adj*
motherly, motherlike, nurturing, nourishing, loving, caring, kind, protective, vigilant, doting

F3 paternal

mathematics *n*

Mathematical terms include: acute angle, addition, algebra, algorithm, analysis, angle, apex, approximate, arc, area, argument, arithmetic, arithmetic progression, asymmetrical, average, axis, axis of symmetry, bar chart, bar graph, base, bearing, binary, binomial, breadth, calculus, capacity, cardinal number, Cartesian coordinates, chance, chord, circumference, coefficient, combination, commutative operation, complement, complementary angle, complex number, concave, concentric circles, congruent, conjugate angles, constant, continuous distribution, converse, convex, coordinate, correlation, cosine, covariance, cross section, cube, cube root, curve, decimal, degree, denominator, depth, derivative, determinant, diagonal, diameter, differentiation, directed number, distribution, dividend, division, divisor, edge, equal, equation, equidistant, even number, exponent, exponential, face, factor, factorial, Fibonacci sequence, formula, fraction, function, geometric progression, geometry, gradient, graph, greater than, group, harmonic progression, height, helix, histogram, horizontal, hyperbola, hypotenuse, identity, infinity, integer, integration, irrational number, latitude, length, less than, linear, line, locus, logarithm, longitude, magic square, matrix, maximum, mean, measure, median, minimum, minus, mirror image, mirror symmetry, Möbius strip, mode, modulus, multiple, multiplication, natural logarithm, natural number, negative number, number, numerator, oblique, obtuse angle, odd number, operation, ordinal number, origin, parabola, parallel lines, parallel planes, parameter, percentage, percentile, perimeter, permutation, perpendicular, pi, pie chart, place value, plane figure, plus, point, positive number, prime number, probability, product, proportion, protractor, Pythagoras's theorem, quadrant, quadratic equation, quadrilateral, quartile, quotient, radian, radius, random sample, ratio, rational number, real numbers, reciprocal, recurring decimal, reflection, reflex angle, regression, remainder, right-angle, right-angled triangle, root, rotation, rotational symmetry, sample, scalar segment, secant, sector, set, side, simultaneous equation, sine, speed, spiral, square, square root, standard deviation, statistics, straight line, subset, subtractor, supplementary angles, symmetry, tangent, three-dimensional, total, transcendental number, triangulation, trigonometry, unit, universal set, variable, variance, vector, velocity, Venn diagram, vertex, vertical, volume, whole number, width, zero. *See also* **shape**.

mating *n*
breeding, copulating, sexual intercourse, copulation, coupling, fusing, uniting, pairing, jointing, matching, twinning
formal coition

matrimonial *adj*
marital, marriage, wedding, married, wedded, spousal
formal nuptial, conjugal

matrimony *n*
marriage, married relationship/state, union
old use wedlock
formal espousals, nuptials, spousage

matted *adj*
knotted, tangled, entangled, tangly, tousled,

dishevelled, uncombed
F3 tidy, untangled

matter *n, v*
▶ *n* **1** SUBJECT, issue, topic, question, affair,
business, case, point, concern, event, occurrence,
happening, situation, proceeding, circumstance,
episode, incident, thing
2 IMPORTANCE, significance, consequence,
momentousness, interest, value, note, weight
formal import
3 *What's the matter?*
TROUBLE, problem, difficulty, distress, upset, worry,
bother, nuisance, inconvenience, shortcoming,
weakness
4 SUBSTANCE, stuff, material, medium, physical
elements, body, content
5 DISCHARGE, pus, secretion
formal purulence, suppuration
▶ *v* count, be important, be of importance, be
relevant, have influence, carry weight, make a
difference, mean something
colloq. make a stir, make waves, cut a lot of ice
▷ **as a matter of fact** in fact, actually, as it happens,
really, truly, in actual fact
▷ **no matter** never mind, it does not matter, it is
unimportant

matter-of-fact *adj*
unemotional, prosaic, down-to-earth, emotionless,
unsentimental, straightforward, sober, pedestrian,
unimaginative, lifeless, dry, dull, flat
colloq. deadpan
F3 emotional

mature *adj, v*
▶ *adj* **1** ADULT, grown-up, grown, full-grown, of
age, sensible, responsible, balanced, experienced,
wise, fully fledged, complete, finished, finalized,
perfect, perfected, well-developed, well-thought-out
2 RIPE, ripened, seasoned, mellow, ready
F3 **1** childish **2** immature
▶ *v* grow up, become adult, become sensible, come of
age, develop, be fully developed, become ripe, become
mellow, mellow, ripen, perfect, age, bloom, evolve, fall
due

maturity *n*
1 ADULTHOOD, full growth, majority, coming of age,
womanhood, manhood, wisdom, experience,
responsibility, sensibleness
2 RIPENESS, readiness, mellowness, perfection
F3 **1** childishness **2** immaturity

maudlin *adj*
sentimental, mawkish, emotional, tearful, half-drunk,
drunk, fuddled, tipsy
formal lachrymose
colloq. gushy, schmaltzy, mushy, sickly, slushy, soppy,
weepy
F3 pleasant

maul *v*
attack, abuse, ill-treat, mutilate, mangle, manhandle,
maltreat, assault, molest, paw, beat (up), claw, lacerate,
thrash
colloq. batter, wallop, belt, do over, mug, knock about,
rough up, knock someone's block off

maunder *v*
mutter, ramble, babble, blather, chatter, gabble
colloq. prattle, witter, natter, jabber, waffle, rabbit (on)

mausoleum *n*
tomb, crypt, vault, burial chamber, catacomb,
sepulchre, undercroft

maverick *n*
outsider, rebel, agitator, nonconformist, individualist
colloq. fish out of water

maw *n*
mouth, jaws, throat, stomach, gullet, gulf, abyss,
chasm

mawkish *adj*
sentimental, maudlin, emotional, offensive, nauseous,
nauseating, feeble, flat, disgusting, foul, loathsome
colloq. soppy, gushy, schmaltzy, mushy, sickly, slushy
F3 matter-of-fact, pleasant

maxim *n*
saying, proverb, adage, axiom, aphorism, saw,
epigram, motto, byword, precept, rule
formal gnome

maximum *adj, n*
▶ *adj* greatest, highest, largest, biggest, most,
utmost, supreme, top, topmost
F3 minimum
▶ *n* most, top (point), utmost, uttermost, upper limit,
peak, pinnacle, summit, height, ceiling, extremity
formal zenith, apogee, acme
F3 minimum

maybe *adv*
perhaps, possibly, conceivably, for all you know
formal perchance, peradventure
F3 definitely

mayhem *n*
chaos, disorder, confusion, disorganization, tumult,
disruption, uproar, riot, bedlam, madhouse, mess,
anarchy, lawlessness

maze *n*
labyrinth, network, tangle, jungle, web, mesh,
complex, confusion, puzzle, intricacy

meadow *n*
field, grassland, grass, pasture, pastureland, paddock,
green
old use lea, mead

meagre *adj*
1 SCANTY, sparse, inadequate, insufficient, deficient,
skimpy, paltry, negligible, small, poor, slight, stingy,
niggardly
formal exiguous
colloq. measly
2 THIN, puny, insubstantial, bony, emaciated,
scraggy, gaunt, scrawny, slight
F3 **1** ample **2** fat

meagreness *n*
scantiness, sparseness, inadequacy, insufficiency,
deficiency, smallness, slightness, stinginess, puniness
colloq. measliness

meal *n*

Meals include: breakfast, wedding breakfast,
colloq. elevenses, brunch, midday meal, lunch,
luncheon, tea, tea-break, tea-party, tiffin, afternoon
tea, cream-tea, high-tea, evening meal, dinner, TV
dinner, dinner party, supper, harvest supper, fork
supper, banquet, feast, spread, *colloq.* blow-out,
colloq. slap-up meal, barbecue, buffet, spread,
picnic, snack, *colloq.* bite, take-away, *formal* repast,
slang nosh-up.

mealy-mouthed *adj*
hestitant, indirect, mincing, over-squeamish,
overdelicate, reticent, plausible, equivocal, flattering,
smooth-tongued, euphemistic, prim, glib

mean¹ *v*
1 SIGNIFY, represent, stand for, symbolize, show,
designate, convey, express, suggest, indicate, imply,
intimate
formal denote, betoken, purport, connote
2 INTEND, aim, propose, design, purpose, plan,
aspire, wish, wont, have in mind, think of
3 CAUSE, give rise to, lead to, bring about, produce,
involve, entail, result in
formal effect
4 *it was meant to happen*
destine, fate, design, intend, appoint
formal ordain

mean² *adj*
1 MISERLY, niggardly, selfish, grasping, tight-fisted,
close-fisted
formal parsimonious
colloq. tight, stingy, penny-pinching, mingy
2 UNKIND, unpleasant, nasty, bad-tempered, cruel,
disagreeable, unfriendly, cross, spiteful
colloq. crotchety, crabby, grouchy
3 LOWLY, base, poor, humble, ordinary, common,
obscure, wretched, shabby, dirty, miserable, dismal,
squalid
FE 1 generous 2 kind 3 noble, splendid

mean³ *adj, n*
▶ *adj the mean score*
average, intermediate, middle, medium, middling,
halfway, median, normal
FE extreme
▶ *n* average, middle, mid-point, norm, median,
mode, compromise, middle course, middle way,
medium, happy medium, golden mean
FE extreme

meander *v*
1 WIND, zigzag, turn, twist, snake, bend, curve
2 WANDER, stray, amble, ramble, stroll, roam, rove,
ease, shuffle, inch
colloq. laze, mosey, mooch

meandering *adj*
wandering, winding, twisting, turning, rambling,
tortuous, circuitous, snaking, serpentine, sinuous,
indirect, roundabout, meandrous
formal convoluted
FE straight, direct

meaning *n*
1 SIGNIFICANCE, sense, implication, message,
expression, gist, drift, substance, essence, thrust,
trend, definition, explanation, interpretation
formal import, signification, connotation,
explication, elucidation
2 AIM, intention, purpose, plan, goal, object,
objective, aspiration, wish, idea
3 VALUE, worth, point, significance, purpose
Related adjective: semantic

meaningful *adj*
1 IMPORTANT, significant, relevant, valid, useful,
worthwhile, material, purposeful, serious
2 EXPRESSIVE, speaking, suggestive, eloquent,
pregnant, warning, pointed
FE 1 unimportant, worthless

meaningless *adj*
1 SENSELESS, pointless, purposeless, useless,
insignificant, incomprehensible, unintelligible,
aimless, motiveless, irrational, futile, insubstantial,
trifling, trivial
2 EMPTY, hollow, vacuous, vain, worthless,
nonsensical, absurd
FE 1 important, meaningful 2 worthwhile

meanness *n*
mean-spiritedness, miserliness, narrow-mindedness,
niggardliness, tight-fistedness, close-fistedness, close-
handedness, illiberality
formal parsimony, penuriousness
colloq. stinginess
FE generosity, kindness

means *n*
1 METHOD, way, manner, medium, course, agency,
process, instrument, avenue, channel, vehicle
formal mode
2 RESOURCES, funds, money, income, wealth,
capital, riches, substance, wherewithal, fortune,
affluence, assets, property
▷ **by all means** of course, naturally, certainly, surely,
with pleasure
▷ **by means of** using, with, through, via, with the
help of, with the aid of, as a result of; *formal* by dint of
▷ **by no means** certainly not, not at all, never;
colloq. no way

meantime, meanwhile *adv*
at the same time, for the time being, for now, for the
moment, in the meantime, in the meanwhile, in the
interim, in the interval, concurrently, simultaneously

measly *adj*
mean, miserable, paltry, meagre, pitiful, scanty,
skimpy, petty, poor, puny, trivial, ungenerous, miserly,
niggardly, beggarly, contemptible
colloq. stingy, piddling, pathetic, mingy
FE generous

measurable *adj*
perceptible, significant, quantifiable, noticeable,
appreciable, determinable, assessable, computable,
gaugeable, fathomable, material, quantitative
formal mensurable
FE measureless

measure *n, v*
▶ *n* 1 SIZE, quantity, magnitude, amount, degree,
extent, range, scope, proportion(s), dimension(s), area,
expanse, capacity, height, depth, length, width, weight,
volume, mass, bulk
2 RULE, gauge, ruler, scale, level, standard, system,
unit(s), criterion, norm, touchstone, yardstick,
benchmark, test, meter
3 STEP, course, action, act, deed, expedient,
procedure, proceeding, means, method, act, bill,
statute, resolution
4 PORTION, ration, share, piece, part, allocation,
quota, division, lot, allotment
colloq. rake-off, cut
▷ **beyond measure** beyond belief, immensely,
infinitely, endlessly, incalculably, inestimably
▷ **for good measure** as well, besides, in addition,
furthermore, over and above, as a bonus
▶ *v* quantify, evaluate, assess, weigh, value, gauge,
judge, sound, fathom, read, record, meter, time,
determine, calculate, estimate, size (up), rate, plumb,
survey, compute, measure out, measure off
formal appraise

▷ **measure off** mark out, measure (out), determine, fix, lay down, limit, pace out, delimit, demarcate; *formal* circumscribe
▷ **measure out** share out, divide, distribute, proportion, dispense, deal out, dole out, allot, apportion, hand out, mete out, parcel out, pour out, issue, assign
▷ **measure up** do, come up to standard, make the grade, pass muster, fit/fill the bill; *formal* suffice; *colloq.* come up to scratch, shape up
▷ **measure up to** equal, meet, live up to, come up to, match, match up to, compare with, touch, rival, make the grade
Related adjective: mensural

measured *adj*
deliberate, planned, reasoned, slow, unhurried, steady, regular, studied, well-thought-out, calculated, careful, considered, premeditated, precise

measureless *adj*
endless, immeasurable, inestimable, incalculable, innumerable, limitless, unbounded, infinite, boundless, bottomless, immense, vast
F3 measurable

measurement *n*
1 DIMENSION, size, extent, amount, proportion(s), amplitude, unit, magnitude, area, range, expanse, capacity, height, depth, length, width, weight, volume, mass, bulk, quantity

SI (Système International d'Unités) base units include: ampere, candela, kelvin, kilogram, metre, mole, second; *SI derivatives and other measurements include*: acre, angstrom, atmosphere, bar, barrel, becquerel, bushel, cable, calorie, centimetre, century, chain, coulomb, cubic centimetre, cubic foot, cubic inch, cubic metre, cubic yard, day, decade, decibel, degree, dyne, erg, farad, fathom, fluid ounce, fresnel, foot, foot-pound, furlong, gallon, gill, gram, hand, hectare, hertz, horsepower, hour, hundredweight, inch, joule, kilometre, knot, league, litre, lumen, micrometre, mile, millennium, millibar, millilitre, minute, month, nautical mile, newton, ohm, ounce, pascal, peak, pint, pound, pound per square inch, radian, rod, siemens, span, square centimetre, square foot, square inch, square kilometre, square metre, square mile, square yard, steradian, stone, therm, ton, tonne, volt, watt, week, yard, year.

2 ASSESSMENT, evaluation, estimation, computation, calculation, calibration, quantification, sizing, weighing, reading, gauging, judgement, appraisal, appreciation, survey

measuring instruments

Gauges include: cutting gauge, drill gauge, feeler gauge, gauge glass, gauge rod, gauge wheel, marking gauge, mortise gauge, paper gauge, pressure gauge, radius gauge, rain gauge, ring gauge, snap gauge, steam gauge, strain gauge, taper gauge, tide gauge, vacuum gauge, water gauge

Measuring instruments include: altimeter, ammeter, anemometer, audiometer, balance, barometer, bathometer, Breathalyser®, burette, callipers, calorimeter chronometer, clinometer, colorimeter, cyclometer, densitometer, galvanometer, gauge, Geiger counter, gravimeter, hourglass, hydrometer, hygrometer, hypsometer, manometer, measuring cylinder, meter, micrometer, multimeter, octant, optometer, pedometer, photometer, pipette, planimeter, plumb line, protractor, psychrometer, pyranometer, pyrometer, quadrant, radiosonde, rheometer, rule, saccharometer, salinometer, seismograph, sextant, speedometer, spherometer, sphygmomanometer, steelyard, stopwatch, tachometer, tachymeter, tape measure, tensiometer, theodolite, thermometer, vinometer, voltmeter, weighbridge, Wheatstone bridge.

meat *n*
1 FLESH

Kinds of meat include: beef, pork, lamb, mutton, ham, bacon, gammon, chicken, turkey, goose, duck, rabbit, hare, venison, pheasant, grouse, partridge, pigeon, quail; offal, liver, heart, tongue, kidney, brains, brawn, pig's knuckle, trotters, oxtail, sweetbread, tripe; steak, minced beef, sausage, rissole, faggot, beefburger, hamburger, black pudding, paté.

Cuts of meat include: shoulder, collar, hand, loin, hock, leg, chop, shin, knuckle, rib, spare-rib, breast, brisket, chine, cutlet, fillet, rump, scrag, silverside, topside, sirloin, flank, escalope, neck, saddle.

2 FOOD, rations, provisions, nourishment, sustenance, subsistence, fare, comestibles
formal viands, victuals
colloq. eats, eatables, tuck; *slang* grub, nosh
3 ESSENCE, substance, fundamentals, heart, kernel, marrow, core, crux, nub, nucleus, pith, point, gist

meaty *adj*
1 FLESHY, hearty, solid, heavy, brawny, beefy, burly, muscular, strapping, sturdy
colloq. hunky
2 SUBSTANTIAL, interesting, significant, meaningful, profound, rich, pithy

mechanic *n*
engineer, repairman, operative, operator, technician, machinist, mechanician, artificer

mechanical *adj*
1 *a mechanical device*
automatic, automated, machine-powered, power-driven, electric
2 AUTOMATIC, involuntary, instinctive, routine, machine-like, habitual, impersonal, emotionless, unemotional, unconscious, cold, matter-of-fact, unfeeling, perfunctory, lifeless, dead, dull
F3 2 conscious

mechanism *n*
1 MACHINE, machinery, engine, appliance, instrument, tool, contraption, motor, works, workings, action, movement, system, gadget, device, apparatus, contrivance, gears, components
colloq. guts
2 MEANS, method, agency, process, procedure, system, technique, medium, channel, structure, workings, operation, functioning, performance

medal *n*
award, medallion, prize, trophy, decoration, honour, reward
slang gong

meddle *v*
interfere, intervene, pry, intrude, butt in, tamper
colloq. poke/stick your nose in, stick/put your oar in, snoop

meddlesome *adj*
interfering, meddling, prying, intrusive, intruding,

mischievous
colloq. nosy

mediate   *v*
arbitrate, conciliate, intervene, referee, umpire,
intercede, moderate, reconcile, act as mediator/
intermediary/peacemaker, negotiate, resolve, settle,
step in
formal interpose

mediation   *n*
arbitration, reconciliation, negotiation, conciliation,
intercession, peacemaking, good offices, intervention
formal interposition

mediator   *n*
arbitrator, referee, umpire, intermediary, negotiator,
go-between, interceder, judge, arbiter, reconciler,
middleman, intervener, moderator, intercessor,
conciliator, peacemaker, Ombudsman

medical equipment

Medical and surgical equipment include: aspirator,
audiometer, aural speculum, auriscope, autoclave,
body scanner, bronchoscope, cannula, catheter,
CAT scanner, clamp, CT (computed tomography)
scanner, curette, defibrillator, disposable enema
pack, ear syringe, ECG (electrocardiograph),
electroencephalograph, endoscope, first aid kit,
forceps, haemodialysis unit, hypodermic needle,
hypodermic syringe, incubator, inhaler, instrument
table, iron lung, isolator tent, kidney dish,
laparoscope, laryngoscope, microscope, MRI
(magnetic resonance imaging) scanner, nebulizer,
obstetrical forceps, oesophagoscope, operating
table, ophthalmoscope, oxygen cylinder, oxygen
mask, rectoscope, respirator, resuscitator, retractor,
rhinoscope, scales, scalpel, sliding-weight scales,
specimen glass, speculum, sphygmomanometer,
sterile donor-pack, sterilizer, stethoscope, stomach
pump, surgical mask, surgical suture materials,
swabs, syringe, thermometer, tracheostomy tube,
traction apparatus, tweezers, ultrasound,
urethroscope, vaginal speculum, X-ray unit.

medical specialists

Medical specialists include: anaesthetist,
bacteriologist, cardiologist, chiropodist,
chiropractor, dentist, dermatologist, dietician,
doctor, embryologist, endocrinologist, forensic
pathologist, gastroenterologist, geriatrician,
gerontologist, gynaecologist, haematologist,
homoeopath, immunologist, microbiologist,
neurologist, obstetrician, oncologist,
ophthalmologist, optician (or optometrist),
orthodontist, orthopaedist, orthoptist,
paediatrician, pathologist, pharmacist,
pharmacologist, physiotherapist, psychiatrist,
psychologist, rheumatologist, toxicologist. *See also*
doctor; nurse; surgeon.

medical terms

Medical terms include: abortion, allergy,
amputation, analgesic, antibiotics, antiseptic,
bandage, barium meal, biopsy, blood bank, blood
count, blood donor, blood group, blood pressure,
blood test, caesarean, cardiopulmonary
resuscitation (CPR), case history, casualty,
cauterization, cervical smear, check-up, childbirth,
circulation, circumcision, clinic, complication,
compress, consultant, consultation, contraception,
convulsion, cure, diagnosis, dialysis, dislocate,
dissection, doctor, donor, dressings, enema,
examination, gene, health screening, home visit,

hormone replacement therapy (HRT), hospice,
hospital, immunization, implantation, incubation,
infection, inflammation, injection, injury,
inoculation, intensive care, labour, miscarriage,
mouth-to-mouth, nurse, ointment, operation,
paraplegia, post-mortem, pregnancy, prescription,
prognosis, prosthesis, psychosomatic, quarantine,
radiotherapy, recovery, rehabilitation, relapse,
remission, respiration, resuscitation, scan, side
effect, sling, smear test, specimen, splint,
sterilization, steroid, surgery, suture, symptom,
syndrome, therapy, tourniquet, tranquillizer,
transfusion, transplant, trauma, treatment, tumour,
ultrasound scanning, vaccination, vaccine, virus, X-
ray. *See also* **therapy**.

medicinal   *adj*
therapeutic, healing, remedial, health-giving, curative,
restorative, medical

medicine   *n*
medication, drug, cure, remedy, medicament,
prescription, pharmaceutical, panacea
technical analeptic

Types of medicine include: tablet, capsule, pill,
painkiller, lozenge, pastille, gargle, linctus, tonic,
laxative, suppository, antacid, ointment, arnica, eye
drops, ear drops, nasal spray, inhaler, Ventolin®,
antibiotic, penicillin, emetic, gripe-water,
paregoric. *See also* **drug**.

Forms of alternative medicine include: acupuncture,
aromatherapy, chiropractic, herbal remedies,
homeopathy, naturopathy, osteopathy, reflexology.

medieval   *adj*
1 *medieval history*
of the Middle Ages, of the Dark Ages, historic, old,
archaic
2 OLD-FASHIONED, obsolete, primitive, antiquated,
archaic, antique, antediluvian, old-world, outmoded,
unenlightened

mediocre   *adj*
ordinary, average, middling, medium, indifferent,
unexceptional, undistinguished, commonplace,
pedestrian, insignificant, second-rate, passable,
adequate, inferior, uninspired, tolerable
colloq. so-so, run-of-the-mill, fair to middling, not up
to much, not all that it is cracked up to be, nothing
much to write home about, no great shakes, not much
cop
E3 exceptional, extraordinary, distinctive

mediocrity   *n*
1 ORDINARINESS, unimportance, averageness,
unexceptionableness, adequacy, passableness,
insignificance, poorness, inferiority, indifference
2 NONENTITY, nobody, nothing
colloq. non-starter, no-hoper, dead loss
E3 **1** distinction, exceptionableness

meditate   *v*
reflect, ponder, ruminate, contemplate, muse, brood,
think (over), consider, deliberate, mull over, study,
concentrate, speculate, scheme, plan, devise, design,
intend, have in mind
formal cogitate
colloq. put on your thinking cap

meditation   *n*
contemplation, reflection, pondering, musing,
thought, ruminating, rumination, deliberation,

brooding, mulling over, speculation, study, reverie, concentration, brown study
formal cerebration, cogitation, excogitation

meditative *adj*
contemplative, deliberative, reflective, thoughtful, studious, museful, pensive, ruminant, ruminative
formal cogitative

medium *adj, n*
▶ *adj* average, middle, median, mean, medial, intermediate, middling, midway, midpoint, standard, fair
▶ *n* **1** AVERAGE, middle, median, mean, mode, intermediate point, midpoint, middle ground, norm, compromise, centre, happy medium, golden mean
2 MEANS, means of expression, way of expressing, agency, channel, vehicle, instrument, way, form, substance, material, stuff, avenue, organ
formal instrumentality, mode
3 ENVIRONMENT, element, setting, surroundings, atmosphere, conditions, habitat, circumstances, influences, ambience, milieu
4 PSYCHIC, spiritualist, spiritist, clairvoyant, necromancer

medley *n*
assortment, mixture, mix, miscellany, variety, melange, potpourri, hotchpotch, hodge-podge, confusion, farrago, salmagundi, smorgasbord, collection, pastiche, patchwork, gallimaufry, jumble
formal conglomeration
colloq. mixed bag, mishmash, omnium-gatherum

meek *adj*
modest, long-suffering, forbearing, humble, docile, patient, unassuming, quiet, lowly, mild, unpretentious, resigned, gentle, peaceful, tame, timid, submissive, yielding, deferential, weak, spiritless
formal compliant
colloq. spineless
🔁 arrogant, assertive, rebellious

meekness *n*
modesty, long-suffering, forbearance, humility, docility, patience, unpretentiousness, lowliness, mildness, gentleness, humbleness, peacefulness, submission, submissiveness, deference, tameness, softness, self-abasement, self-disparagement, self-effacement, timidity, spiritlessness, resignation, weakness
formal acquiescence, compliance
colloq. spinelessness
🔁 arrogance, assertiveness

meet *v*
1 ENCOUNTER, come across, run across, run into, make contact with, join up with, chance on
formal happen upon
colloq. bump into
2 GATHER, get together, collect, come together, muster, assemble, congregate, rally, rendezvous
formal convene, convoke, forgather
3 FULFIL, satisfy, match, answer, come up to, measure up to, equal, comply with, discharge, perform, execute
4 EXPERIENCE, encounter, face, come across, go through, undergo, bear, endure, suffer
5 *meet a challenge*
deal with, manage, handle, tackle, look after, cope with, get to grips with
6 *meet the cost*
pay (for), settle, discharge, honour

7 JOIN, converge, come together, connect, link (up), cross, intersect, touch, unite
formal abut, adjoin
🔁 **4** scatter, disperse **7** diverge, separate

meeting *n*
1 ENCOUNTER, confrontation, rendezvous, appointment, date, engagement, contact, assignation, introduction
formal tryst
2 ASSEMBLY, gathering, session

Types of meeting include: assembly, assignation, audience, audition, board, briefing, cabinet, committee, *formal* conclave, conference, congregation, congress, consultation, convention, *formal* convocation, council, debate, forum, *colloq.* get-together, interview, meet, panel, party, rally, rendezvous, reunion, seminar, service, session, social, soirée, summit, symposium, teleconference, workshop. *See also* **committee**.

3 CONVERGENCE, confluence, junction, intersection, union, venue, (point of) contact, interface, watersmeet
formal concourse, abutment, conjunction

megalomania *n*
overestimation, self-importance, exaggerated sense of power, delusions of grandeur, *folie de grandeur*, conceitedness

melancholy *adj, n*
▶ *adj* depressed, dejected, downcast, downhearted, downcast, gloomy, glum, low, low-spirited, heavy-hearted, sad, unhappy, despondent, dispirited, miserable, mournful, dismal, sorrowful, moody
formal disconsolate, lugubrious, woeful, woebegone
colloq. down, blue, down in the dumps, in the doldrums
🔁 cheerful, elated, joyful
▶ *n* depression, dejection, gloom, despondency, low spirits, sadness, unhappiness, sorrow, misery, pessimism
colloq. blues, doldrums, dumps
🔁 cheerfulness, elation, joy

melange *n*
assortment, mixture, mix, miscellany, variety, melange, potpourri, hotchpotch, hodge-podge, confusion, farrago, salmagundi, smorgasbord, collection, pastiche, patchwork, gallimaufry, jumble
formal conglomeration
colloq. mixed bag, mishmash, omnium-gatherum

melee *n*
1 BRAWL, rumpus, scuffle, set-to, fight, tussle, ruckus, ruction, broil, affray, fracas, fray, free-for-all, scrum
Scot. stramash
2 MUDDLE, confusion, chaos, disorganization, disorder, mess, mix-up, jumble, clutter, tangle

mellifluous *adj*
smooth, sweet-sounding, sweet, soothing, soft, tuneful, harmonious, dulcet, mellow, honeyed, silvery
formal canorous, euphonious
🔁 discordant, grating, harsh

mellow *adj, v*
▶ *adj* **1** MATURE, ripe, juicy, soft, tender, full-flavoured, sweet, luscious, mild
2 GENIAL, cordial, affable, pleasant, relaxed, easy-going, good-natured, amiable, amicable, placid, gentle, serene, tranquil, cheerful, happy, jolly, jovial, kind, kind-hearted

3 SMOOTH, melodious, tuneful, harmonious, smooth, rich, rounded, full, soft, sweet, dulcet
formal euphonious
F3 1 unripe **2** cold **3** harsh
▶ *v* mature, ripen, improve, sweeten, soften, temper, make/become less extreme, season, perfect

melodious *adj*
tuneful, musical, melodic, harmonious, dulcet, sweet, sweet-sounding, silvery
formal euphonious
F3 discordant, grating, harsh

melodramatic *adj*
histrionic, theatrical, overdramatic, exaggerated, extravagant, overemotional, sensational, overdone, stagy
colloq. hammy

melody *n*
1 TUNE, music, song, refrain, harmony, rhythm, theme, air, strain
2 TUNEFULNESS, musicality, musicalness, harmony, harmoniousness, sweetness
formal euphony

melt *v*
1 LIQUEFY, dissolve, thaw, defrost, unfreeze, fuse
formal deliquesce
2 *melt someone's heart*
soften, move, affect, touch, make/become tender, moderate, calm
F3 1 freeze, solidify **2** harden
▷ **melt away** disappear, vanish, fade (away), evaporate, dissolve, disperse; *formal* evanesce; *colloq.* disappear into thin air

member *n*
1 *members of a club*
adherent, associate, subscriber, representative, comrade, fellow
2 PART, limb, arm, leg, appendage, extremity, organ, element

membership *n*
1 *membership of a club*
affiliation, adherence, allegiance, participation, enrolment, fellowship
2 MEMBERS, associates, body, adherents, subscribers, representatives, comrades, fellows, fellowship

membrane *n*
sheet, film, skin, tissue, layer, veil, partition, diaphragm
technical integument, septum, velum, hymen

memento *n*
souvenir, keepsake, remembrance, reminder, token, memorial, trophy, record, vestige, relic

memoir *n*
account, biography, essay, journal, life, monograph, narrative, chronicle, record, register, report

memoirs *n*
reminiscences, recollections, memories, autobiography, life story, diary, diaries, chronicles, annals, journals, records, confessions, experiences

memorable *adj*
unforgettable, remarkable, significant, impressive, striking, notable, noteworthy, historic, extraordinary, important, consequential, distinguished, distinctive, special, outstanding, momentous, unique
F3 forgettable, trivial, unimportant

memorandum *n*
message, note, reminder
colloq. memo, memory-jogger

memorial *n, adj*
▶ *n* remembrance, monument, statue, stone, plaque, shrine, cenotaph, mausoleum, record, souvenir, memento
▶ *adj* commemorative, celebratory, monumental

memorize *v*
learn, learn by heart, learn by rote, commit to memory, remember
F3 forget

memory *n*
1 RECALL, powers of recall, retention, recollection, remembrance, reminiscence
2 COMMEMORATION, remembrance, tribute, honour, observance, recognition
F3 1 forgetfulness

menace *n, v*
▶ *n* **1** THREAT, intimidation, terrorism, ominousness, threatening behaviour, terrorizing, tyrannization, bullying, browbeating, coercion, pressure, warning
colloq. screws, frighteners, big stick
2 DANGER, peril, hazard, jeopardy, risk, threat
3 NUISANCE, annoyance, pest, bother, troublemaker
colloq. pain, thorn in your side/flesh
▶ *v* threaten, frighten, alarm, daunt, dismay, appal, intimidate, scare, terrorize, terrify, browbeat, coerce, press, pressure, pressurize, bully, loom, lour

menacing *adj*
threatening, intimidating, intimidatory, warning, ominous, alarming, frightening, dangerous, looming, sinister, grim, louring, Damoclean
formal impending, portentous, minacious, minatory

mend *v*
1 REPAIR, fix, renovate, restore, renew, refit, patch (up), put back together, cobble, darn, stick, sew, cure, heal, make whole
2 RECOVER, get better, improve, recuperate
3 REMEDY, correct, rectify, reform, revise, amend, improve, put right, put in order
formal ameliorate, emend
F3 1 break **2** deteriorate **3** destroy
▷ **on the mend** convalescing, convalescent, recovering, improving, recuperating, reviving, healing

mendacious *adj*
untruthful, untrue, false, fictitious, insincere, deceitful, deceptive, dishonest, lying, perjured, fraudulent
formal fallacious, perfidious, duplicitous
F3 honest, truthful; *formal* veracious

mendacity *n*
untruthfulness, untruth, lie, lying, misrepresentation, distortion, falsehood, falsification, insincerity, deceit, deceitfulness, dishonesty, fraudulence, perjury
formal inveracity, duplicity, perfidy
F3 honesty, truthfulness; *formal* veracity

mendicant *adj, n*
▶ *adj* begging, scrounging
formal petitionary, supplicant
colloq. cadging
▶ *n* beggar, supplicant, pauper, down-and-out, tramp, vagabond, vagrant, beachcomber
US hobo
colloq. bum, cadger, scrounger; *US* moocher

menial *adj, n*
▶ *adj* low, lowly, humble, base, dull, humdrum, routine, boring, degrading, demeaning, ignominious, unskilled, subservient, servile, slavish
▶ *n* servant, domestic, labourer, minion, attendant, drudge, slave, underling
colloq. skivvy, dogsbody

menstruation *n*
period, menstrual cycle, monthly flow, courses, flow, menses, menorrhoea
technical catamenia
colloq. monthlies, the usual, the curse

mensuration *n*
measurement, measuring, calibration, computation, estimation, calculation, assessment, evaluation, survey, surveying, valuation
technical metage

mental *adj*
1 INTELLECTUAL, abstract, unconscious, conceptual, theoretical, rational
formal cognitive, cerebral
2 MAD, insane, lunatic, crazy, deranged, psychotic, disturbed
colloq. (mentally) unbalanced, loony, nuts, barmy, bonkers, off your head, off your trolley, having a screw loose
E3 1 physical 2 sane

mentality *n*
1 FRAME OF MIND, mind, way of thinking, (mental) attitude, make-up, character, disposition, personality, psychology, outlook, mindset
2 INTELLECT, intelligence, understanding, mind, comprehension, faculty, rationality
colloq. brains, little grey cells, grey matter

mentally *adv*
intellectually, in the mind, inwardly, psychologically, rationally, temperamentally, subjectively, emotionally

mention *v, n*
▶ *v* 1 SPEAK OF, refer to, say, name, acknowledge, report, make known, impart, introduce, declare, communicate, divulge, disclose, broach, cite, reveal, state, quote
2 TOUCH ON, allude to, cite, refer to, speak about briefly, bring up, hint at, intimate, point out
▷ **don't mention it** not at all, don't worry, forget it, it was nothing, it's a pleasure, think nothing of it
▷ **not to mention** not including, to say nothing of, besides, as well as, let alone, not forgetting
▶ *n* reference, allusion, citation, observation, recognition, remark, statement, acknowledgement, announcement, notification, tribute, indication

mentioned *adj*
quoted, reported, stated, cited
formal above-mentioned, forementioned, forenamed, fore-quoted, foresaid, aforesaid, fore-cited

mentor *n*
teacher, tutor, adviser, counsellor, guru, swami, guide, coach, instructor, pedagogue, therapist

menu *n*
bill of fare, tariff, list, card, *carte du jour*

mercantile *adj*
trade, trading, commercial, merchantable, marketable, saleable

mercenary *adj, n*
▶ *adj* 1 GREEDY, covetous, grasping, acquisitive,

money-orientated, materialistic, mammonistic, sordid
formal avaricious
colloq. money-grubbing, on the make
2 HIRED, paid, venal
▶ *n* soldier of fortune, hired soldier, freelance, free companion, hireling, condottiere, galloglass, landsknecht, lansquenet
colloq. merc

merchandise *n, v*
▶ *n* goods, commodities, stock, produce, products, wares, cargo, freight, shipment
formal vendibles
▶ *v* 1 TRADE, deal in, market, retail, sell, buy and sell, carry, distribute, supply, traffic in, peddle
formal vend
2 ADVERTISE, publicize, promote, market, sell
colloq. push, plug, hype

merchant *n*
trader, dealer, broker, trafficker, wholesaler, distributor, retailer, seller, salesperson, salesman, saleswoman, sales executive, shopkeeper, vendor
Related adjective: mercantile

merciful *adj*
compassionate, forgiving, forbearing, humane, lenient, sparing, tender-hearted, soft-hearted, pitying, gracious, humanitarian, kind, liberal, tolerant, sympathetic, generous, mild
E3 hard-hearted, merciless

merciless *adj*
pitiless, relentless, unmerciful, ruthless, barbarous, hard-hearted, hard, heartless, implacable, inexorable, intolerant, inhumane, unforgiving, remorseless, unpitying, unsympathetic, unfeeling, unsparing, severe, rigid, stern, cruel, callous, harsh, inhuman
E3 compassionate, merciful

mercurial *adj*
volatile, temperamental, unpredictable, unstable, variable, changeable, inconstant, erratic, fickle, impetuous, impulsive, irrepressible, flighty, light-hearted, lively, spirited, sprightly, active, mobile
formal capricious
E3 saturnine

mercy *n*
1 COMPASSION, grace, forgiveness, forbearance, leniency, pity, humaneness, humanitarianism, kindness, tender-heartedness, tenderness, mildness, sympathy, generosity
formal clemency
2 BLESSING, godsend, boon, favour, good luck, stroke of good luck, relief
E3 1 cruelty, harshness
▷ **at the mercy of** in the control of, in the power of, in someone's clutches, defenceless against, unarmed against, exposed to, vulnerable to, unprotected against, at the whim of

mere *adj*
sheer, plain, simple, pure and simple, no more than, bare, utter, pure, absolute, complete, stark, unadulterated, common, paltry, petty

merely *adv*
simply, just, only, purely, nothing but, barely, hardly, scarcely

merge *v*
join, unite, combine, come/bring together, join forces, team up, converge, amalgamate, blend, coalesce, mix,

intermix, mingle, melt into, run into, fuse, meet, meld, be swallowed up in, be assimilated in, become lost in, be engulfed, incorporate, consolidate

merger *n*
amalgamation, union, fusion, combination, coalition, alliance, consolidation, confederation, incorporation, convergence, blend, assimilation

merit *n, v*
▶ *n* worth, excellence, value, quality, high quality, good, goodness, virtue, worthiness, asset, credit, advantage, strong point, talent, justification, reward, recompense, due, deserts, claim
colloq. plus
◪ fault, drawback; *colloq.* minus
▶ *v* deserve, be worthy of, be worth, earn, justify, have a right to, be entitled to, warrant

merited *adj*
deserved, earned, justified, entitled, fitting, appropriate, warranted, worthy, due, just, rightful
formal condign
◪ inappropriate, unjustified

meritorious *adj*
commendable, deserving, right, righteous, virtuous, excellent, good, honourable, praiseworthy, worthy, estimable, admirable, creditable, exemplary
formal laudable
◪ unworthy

merriment *n*
fun, jollity, hilarity, laughter, conviviality, high spirits, joyfulness, cheerfulness, gaiety, festivity, amusement, revelry, frolic, liveliness, joviality, buoyancy, carefreeness
formal mirthfulness, mirth, jocundity, blitheness
◪ gloom, seriousness

merry *adj*
1 JOLLY, light-hearted, jovial, joyful, happy, high-spirited, in good spirits, convivial, festive, cheerful, cheery, amusing, carefree, glad
formal mirthful, blithe
2 TIPSY, slightly drunk, happy, tiddly
colloq. squiffy
◪ 1 gloomy, melancholy 2 sober
▷ **make merry** have fun, enjoy yourself, celebrate, have a party, sing, dance, drink, carouse

merry-go-round *n*
roundabout, carousel, joy-wheel, whirligig

merrymaking *n*
merriment, celebration, fun, gaiety, jollification, rejoicings, conviviality, festivity, party, carousal, carousing, revel, revelry

mesh *n, v*
▶ *n* net, network, netting, lattice, latticework, tracery, trellis, web, tangle, entanglement, snare, trap
▶ *v* engage, interlock, dovetail, fit together (closely), connect, harmonize, match, co-ordinate, combine, go/come together

mesmerize *v*
transfix, hypnotize, magnetize, spellbind, hold spellbound, captivate, enthral, fascinate, grip, entrance, stupefy, benumb

mess *n*
1 CHAOS, untidiness, disorder, disarray, confusion, muddle, jumble, clutter, litter, turmoil, disorganization, mix-up, dirt, dirtiness, filth, filthiness, squalor

colloq. shambles, hole, dump, tip, dog's breakfast, pig's breakfast, dog's dinner
2 DIFFICULTY, trouble, predicament, plight, dilemma, quandary
colloq. fix, (tight) spot, jam, pickle, hiccup, hole, stew, hot/deep water, pretty pass
3 BOTCH, bungle, muddle, failure
colloq. farce, shambles, hash; *slang* cock-up, balls-up
◪ 1 order, tidiness
▷ **mess about/around** mess around, fool around, play, play around, play about, potter about, fiddle around; *colloq.* muck about, faff about/around; *slang* frig about/around; *taboo slang* fuck about/ around, piss about/around
▷ **mess about/around with** interfere with, treat badly, upset, bother, trouble, inconvenience, meddle with, play (about/around) with, fool about/around with, tamper with
▷ **mess up** 1 DISARRANGE, jumble, untidy, clutter up, throw into disorder, disrupt, confuse, muddle, tangle, dishevel, dirty, foul 2 BOTCH, bungle, spoil, ruin, make a mess of; *colloq.* muck up, bodge, botch, fluff, muff, foul up, make a hash of; *slang* louse up, cock up, screw up
◪ 1 order, tidy

message *n*
1 COMMUNICATION, bulletin, dispatch, communiqué, report, news, piece of information, word, errand, task, letter, memorandum, note, notice, fax, cable
formal missive, tidings, epistle
colloq. memo
2 MEANING, idea, sense, significance, point, theme, implication, gist, drift, essence, thrust, moral
formal purport
▷ **get the message** understand, take in, follow, see, grasp; *formal* comprehend; *colloq.* get it, get the point, get the idea, get the hang, catch the drift, catch on, latch onto, cotton on, tumble to

messenger *n*
courier, envoy, go-between, herald, runner, errand-boy, errand-girl, carrier, bearer, harbinger, agent, ambassador, Hermes
formal cmissary

messy *adj*
untidy, unkempt, dishevelled, disordered, disorganized, in disarray, chaotic, sloppy, slovenly, confused, muddled, dirty, grubby, filthy, muddled, cluttered, littered
colloq. shambolic, slobbish
◪ neat, ordered, tidy

metallic *adj*
1 *metallic elements*
copper, iron, tin, lead, nickel, steel, gold, silver, shiny, polished, gleaming
2 *metallic sounds*
harsh, grating, jarring, unpleasant, rough, dissonant, jangling

metamorphose *v*
change, alter, transform, remake, remodel, reshape, convert, modify, translate
technical mutate, transubstantiate
formal transmute, transfigure
colloq. transmogrify

metamorphosis *n*
change, alteration, rebirth, regeneration, transfiguration, conversion, modification,

change-over
technical mutation
formal transformation, transmutation
colloq. transmogrification

metaphor *n*
figure of speech, allegory, analogy, symbol, emblem,
emblematic, visual, picture, image, representation
formal trope

metaphorical *adj*
figurative, allegorical, symbolic, analogical,
emblematic, visual, representational
E3 literal

metaphysical *adj*
philosophical, theoretical, abstract, unreal, essential,
fundamental, basic, subjective, spiritual, supernatural,
transcendental, unsubstantial, insubstantial, general,
immaterial, speculative, intellectual, ideal, high-
flown, intangible, deep, profound, universal, eternal
formal abstruse, esoteric, impalpable, incorporeal,
recondite

mete *v*
▷ **mete out** allot, apportion, deal out, dole out,
hand out, measure out, share out, ration out, portion,
distribute, dispense, divide out, assign, administer

meteor *n*
meteorite, meteoroid, bolide, comet, shooting star,
fireball, aerolite, aerolith

meteoric *adj*
rapid, speedy, swift, quick, fast, sudden, lightning,
overnight, instantaneous, momentary, brief, transient,
spectacular, brilliant, dazzling, flashing

meteorologist *n*
weather forecaster, climatologist, weatherman,
weathergirl, weatherlady, met man, weather prophet

method *n*
1 WAY, approach, means, course, manner, fashion,
form, process, procedure, system, practice, route,
technique, style, plan, arrangement, scheme, rule,
programme, *modus operandi*
formal mode
2 ORGANIZATION, order, structure, system, pattern,
arrangement, form, design, plan, planning, regularity,
orderliness, routine

methodical *adj*
systematic, structured, organized, ordered, orderly,
well-ordered, logical, tidy, regular, planned, efficient,
disciplined, businesslike, deliberate, neat, scrupulous,
precise, meticulous, painstaking
E3 chaotic, irregular, confused

meticulous *adj*
precise, scrupulous, careful, conscientious, rigorous,
exact, punctilious, fussy, particular, detailed, accurate,
thorough, fastidious, painstaking, strict
E3 careless, slapdash

métier *n*
calling, vocation, line, line of business, business,
occupation, profession, sphere, field, forte, trade,
pursuit, speciality, specialty, craft

metropolis *n*
capital, city, main city, large city, municipality,
megalopolis, industrial/cultural centre

mettle *n*
1 CHARACTER, temperament, disposition, nature,
calibre, personality, personal qualities, make-up

2 SPIRIT, courage, bravery, vigour, nerve, boldness,
daring, intrepidity, indomitability, fearlessness, pluck,
nerve, resolve, determination, endurance, valour,
gallantry, fortitude
colloq. guts, backbone, spunk

mew *v*
miaow, meow, mewl, caterwaul, whine

mewl *v*
whine, whimper, whinge, cry, blubber, grizzle, snivel

miasma *n*
odour, smell, stench, stink, pollution, reek
formal fetor, effluvium, mephitis

miasmal *adj*
foul, noxious, putrid, reeking, smelly, stinking,
polluted, unwholesome
formal fetid, malodorous, noisome, mephitic,
miasm(at)ic, miasm(at)ous

microbe *n*
micro-organism, bacterium, bacillus, germ, virus,
pathogen
colloq. bug

microscopic *adj*
minute, tiny, extremely small, minuscule, infinitesimal,
indiscernible, imperceptible, negligible
E3 huge, enormous

midday *n*
noon, twelve, twelve o'clock, twelve noon, lunchtime
formal noonday, noontide
Related adjective: meridian

middle *adj, n*
▶ *adj* central, mid, midway, halfway, mean, medium,
medial, median, equidistant, intermediate, inner,
inside, intervening
▶ *n* centre, halfway point, midpoint, mean, median,
heart, core, midst, inside
colloq. bull's eye
E3 extreme, end, edge, beginning, border
▷ **in the middle of** busy with, during, engaged in,
in the process of, occupied with, surrounded by, while,
in the midst of, among

middle-class *adj*
conventional, suburban, professional, white-colour,
gentrified, bourgeois

middleman *n*
intermediary, go-between, negotiator, entrepreneur,
distributor, retailer, broker, fixer

middling *adj*
mediocre, medium, ordinary, moderate, average, fair,
unexceptional, unremarkable, run-of-the-mill,
indifferent, modest, adequate, passable, tolerable
colloq. so-so, OK

midget *n, adj*
▶ *n* person of restricted growth, pygmy, dwarf,
Lilliputian, Tom Thumb, gnome, manikin,
homunculus
E3 giant
▶ *adj* tiny, small, minute, diminutive, dwarf,
miniature, little, baby, pocket, pocket-sized, toy,
pygmy, Lilliputian
colloq. teeny, itsy-bitsy, teeny-weeny
E3 giant

midst *n*
middle, centre, midpoint, heart, core, bosom, nucleus,
hub, depths, thick, interior

▷ **in the midst** during, in the middle of, among, surrounded by, in the thick of

midway *adv*
halfway, in the middle, at the midpoint, in the centre, equidistant between, betwixt and between

mien *n*
appearance, look, manner, aspect, expression, air, complexion, presence, semblance, aura
formal bearing, carriage, countenance, demeanour, deportment

miffed *adj*
annoyed, irritated, displeased, aggrieved, nettled, hurt, offended, put out, resentful, upset, vexed, irked, disgruntled, chagrined, piqued
colloq. in a huff, narked, peeved
Ｅ delighted, pleased; *colloq.* chuffed

might *n*
power, strength, force, forcefulness, energy, powerfulness, ability, capability, capacity, sway, vigour, stamina, heftiness, muscularity, potency, valour, prowess
formal efficacy, puissance
colloq. clout, muscle

mightily *adv*
exceedingly, very, very much, much, extremely, greatly, highly, hugely, decidedly, intensely, powerfully, strongly, vigorously, energetically, forcefully, lustily, manfully, strenuously

mighty *adj*
1 STRONG, powerful, potent, forceful, vigorous, hefty, robust, tough, stalwart, stout, strapping, muscular, dominant, influential, doughty, grand, hardy, indomitable, lusty, manful,
old use puissant
2 LARGE, enormous, colossal, huge, immense, vast, massive, gigantic, great, tremendous, towering, titanic, stupendous, monumental, bulky, prodigious
Ｅ **1** frail, weak **2** small

migrant *n, adj*
▶ *n* traveller, wanderer, itinerant, emigrant, immigrant, rover, nomad, transient, globetrotter, drifter, Gypsy, tinker, vagrant
▶ *adj* travelling, wandering, peripatetic, itinerant, immigrant, roving, nomadic, shifting, transient, globetrotting, drifting, Gypsy, migratory, vagrant

migrate *v*
move, resettle, relocate, wander, roam, rove, journey, emigrate, travel, voyage, hike, trek, drift

migration *n*
movement, travel, journey, voyage, wandering, roving, emigration, shift, trek
technical diaspora
formal transhumance

migratory *adj*
travelling, wandering, peripatetic, itinerant, immigrant, roving, nomadic, shifting, transient, globetrotting, drifting, Gypsy, migrant, vagrant

mild *adj*
1 *mild manners*
gentle, calm, peaceable, placid, tender, tender-hearted, sensitive, soft, soft-hearted, good-natured, kind, sympathetic, warm, warm-hearted, meek, easy-going, amiable, lenient, humane, compassionate, merciful, forbearing
2 *mild weather*

calm, temperate, warm, balmy, clement, fair, moderate, pleasant
3 *mild food*
bland, mellow, smooth, subtle, soothing, tasteless, insipid
Ｅ **1** harsh, aggressive, fierce **2** cold, stormy
3 strong, sharp, spicy

mildewy *adj*
rotten, fusty, musty
formal fetid, mucedinous, mucid

mildness *n*
1 GENTLENESS, calmness, placidity, tenderness, softness, docility, kindness, sympathy, warmth, meekness, indulgence, leniency, lenity, compassion, mercy, forbearance, tranquillity, passivity
2 TEMPERATENESS, calmness, warmth, clemency, moderation
3 BLANDNESS, mellowness, smoothness, tastelessness, insipidness
Ｅ **1** harshness, aggressiveness, violence
2 storminess **3** sharpness

milieu *n*
environment, location, scene, setting, surroundings, background, locale, medium, arena, element, sphere

militant *adj, n*
▶ *adj* aggressive, belligerent, vigorous, fighting, combative, embattled, warring, assertive, activist
formal pugnacious
Ｅ pacifist, peaceful
▶ *n* activist, combatant, fighter, struggler, soldier, warrior, aggressor, belligerent, partisan

military *adj, n*
▶ *adj* martial, armed, army, soldierly, warlike, service, disciplined
▶ *n* army, armed forces, soldiers, forces, services, militia, air force, navy

Military terms include: about turn, absent without leave (AWOL), action stations, action, adjutant, aide-de-camp (ADC), air cover, air-drop, Airborne Warning and Control System (AWACS), allies, ambush, arm, armed forces, armistice, army, arsenal, artillery, assault course, atomic warfare, attack, attention, barracks, base, battle fatigue, battle, beachhead, billet, bivouac, blockade, bomb, bombardment, brevet, bridgehead, briefing, brigade, bugle call, call up, camouflage, camp, campaign, canteen, cease-fire, charge, citation, colours, combat, command, commission, company, conquest, conscript, conscription, corps, counter-attack, court-martial, crossfire, debriefing, decamp, decoration, defeat, defence, demilitarize, *colloq.* demob, demotion, depot, desertion, detachment, detail, disarmament, discharge, dispatches, division, draft, drill, duty, encampment, enemy, enlist, ensign, epaulette, evacuation, excursion, expedition, fall out, fatigues, firing line, first post, flank, fleet, flight, flotilla, foe, foray, forced march, front line, fusillade, garrison, guard, incursion, infantry, insignia, inspection, installation, insubordination, intelligence, invasion, kitbag, landing, last post, latrine, leave, left wheel, liaison, lines, logistics, manoeuvres, march, marching orders, march past, married quarters, martinet, minefield, mission, mobilize, munitions, muster, mutiny, national service, navy, Navy, Army and Air Force Institutes (NAAFI), nuclear warfare, observation post, offensive, operational command, operational fleet, operations, orders, ordnance, outpost, padre, parade, parade ground, parley, parole, patrol, pincer movement, platoon, posting, prisoner of war (POW), quartermaster, quarters, quick march, radar, range, rank, ration, rearguard, *colloq.* recce, recruit, regiment, reinforcements, requisition, retreat, reveille, rifle range, roll-call, rout, route march, salute, sentry, shell, shell-shock, signal, skirmish, slow march, sniper, sortie, squad, squadron, *slang* square-bashing, standard, stores, strategy, supplies, surrender, tactics, tank, target, task-force, tattoo, the front, training, trench, trench warfare, troop, truce, unit, vanguard, victory, wing. *See also* **armed services; rank, sailor; soldier.**

militate   *v*
▷ **militate against**   oppose, discourage, counter, counteract, go/count against, act/tell against, weigh against, be detrimental to, be harmful to, be disadvantageous to, damage, hurt, prejudice, be a decisive factor against, contend, resist
▷ **militate for**   help, promote, speak for, back, further, advance, aid

militia   *n*
reserve, reservists, Territorial Army, yeomanry, National Guard, minutemen
old use fencibles, trainband

milk   *v*
1 DRAIN, bleed, tap, extract, draw (off), exploit, use, express, press, pump, siphon, squeeze, wring
2 EXPLOIT, use, squeeze, wring, pump, take advantage of, oppress, impose on, manipulate
colloq. bleed, rip off

milksop   *n*
coward, weakling, namby-pamby, pansy, sissy
colloq. wimp, mummy's boy

milky   *adj*
white, milk-white, chalky, opaque, clouded, cloudy

mill   *n, v*
▶ *n* **1** FACTORY, plant, processing plant, works, workshop, shop, foundry
2 GRINDER, crusher, quern, roller
▶ *v* grind, pulverize, powder, pound, crush, crunch, roll, press, grate
formal comminute
▷ **mill around**   move about, crowd around, throng, swarm, stream, press around

millstone   *n*
burden, load, encumbrance, weight, obligation, duty, onus, trouble, affliction, grindstone, quernstone
colloq. cross to bear

mime   *n, v*
▶ *n* dumb show, pantomime, gesture, mimicry, mummery, charade
▶ *v* gesture, signal, indicate, act out, represent, simulate, impersonate, mimic, imitate

mimic   *v, n*
▶ *v* imitate, parody, caricature, copy, ape, parrot, impersonate, echo, mirror, resemble, simulate, look like
formal emulate
colloq. take off, send up
▶ *n* imitator, impersonator, impressionist, mimicker, caricaturist, parrot, copy, copyist
colloq. copycat

mimicry   *n*
imitation, imitating, impersonation, copying, parody, impression, caricature, aping, burlesque
colloq. take-off

mince   *v*
1 CHOP, cut, cut into very small pieces, hash, dice, grind, crumble
2 *not mince your words*
suppress, diminish, play down, tone down, speak indirectly, hold back, moderate, weaken, soften, spare
3 WALK AFFECTEDLY, attitudinize, pose, strike a pose, posture, ponce, simper, walk in an effeminate/a dainty way

mincing   *adj*
dainty, effeminate, nice, precious, foppish, pretentious, minikin, niminy-piminy, coxcombic(al)
formal affected
colloq. la-di-da, poncy, sissy

mind   *n, v*
▶ *n* **1** INTELLIGENCE, intellect, reason, powers of reasoning, judgement, sense, understanding, comprehension, wits, mentality, thinking, thoughts, subconscious, head, genius, concentration, application, attention, spirit, psyche
technical psyche
formal ratiocination
colloq. brains, brainbox, grey matter, little grey cells
Related adjective: mental
2 MEMORY, remembrance, recollection, recall, retention
3 OPINION, view, viewpoint, point of view, way of thinking, belief, attitude, judgement, outlook, feeling, sentiment
4 INCLINATION, disposition, tendency, will, wish, intention, desire, fancy, urge, notion
5 THINKER, intellect, intellectual, genius, mastermind, scholar, expert
colloq. egghead, brain, brainbox
▷ **be in two minds**   be uncertain, hesitate, be hesitant, be unsure, be undecided, waver, vacillate, dither; *colloq.* shilly-shally, dilly-dally
▷ **bear/keep in mind**   consider, remember, note, take note of, make a mental note of, take into account/ consideration, give thought to
▷ **cross your mind**   think of, remember, occur to, come to, strike, hit
▷ **make up your mind**   decide, come to/arrive at a decision, reach/make a decision, choose, determine, settle, resolve
▷ **mind's eye**   imagination, mind, head, contemplation, memory, recollection, remembrance
▶ *v* **1** OBJECT (TO), take offence (at), be offended by, be bothered by, be annoyed by, care about, resent, disapprove, dislike
2 *mind the traffic*
WATCH, be careful, heed, pay attention, pay heed to, regard, note, obey, respect, listen to, concentrate on, comply with, follow, mark, observe, watch
3 MAKE SURE, ensure, make certain, take care, remember, not forget, note
4 LOOK AFTER, take care of, watch over, guard, have charge of, attend to
colloq. keep an eye on
▷ **mind out**   be careful, take care, look out, watch out, watch, pay attention, beware, be on your guard, keep your eyes open
▷ **never mind 1** TAKE NO NOTICE OF, not bother about, don't worry, forget it **2** LET ALONE, not to mention, not forgetting, apart from, also, as well as, too

mindful   *adj*
aware, conscious, alive (to), alert, attentive, paying attention to, careful, watchful, wary, chary, heedful

⊟ heedless, inattentive
formal cognizant, sensible

mindless   *adj*
1 THOUGHTLESS, senseless, illogical, irrational, stupid, foolish, witless, dull, unintelligent, gratuitous, negligent
colloq. dumb, dopey, thick, bird-brained
2 MECHANICAL, automatic, tedious, routine, involuntary, instinctive
⊟ 1 thoughtful, intelligent

mine   *n, v*
▶ *n* 1 PIT, colliery, coalfield, excavation, quarry, well, vein, lode, seam, shaft, trench, deposit
2 SUPPLY, source, stock, store, storehouse, reserve, reservoir, quarry, fund, repository, hoard, treasury, wealth
3 LAND MINE, explosive, depth charge, bomb
▶ *v* excavate, dig for, dig up, delve, quarry, extract, unearth, tunnel, remove, undermine

miner   *n*
coalminer, collier, pitman

minerals   *n*

Minerals include: alabaster, albite, anhydrite, asbestos, aventurine, azurite, bentonite, blacklead, bloodstone, blue john, borax, cairngorm, calamine, calcite, calcspar, cassiterite, chalcedony, chlorite, chrysoberyl, cinnabar, corundum, dolomite, emery, feldspar, fluorite, fluorspar, fool's gold, French chalk, galena, graphite, gypsum, haematite, halite, haüyne, hornblende, hyacinth, idocrase, jacinth, jargoon, jet, kandite, kaolinite, lapis lazuli, lazurite, magnetite, malachite, meerschaum, mica, microcline, montmorillonite, olivine, orthoclase, peridot, plumbago, pyrites, quartz, rock salt, rutile, saltpetre, sanidine, silica, smithsonite, sodalite, spar, sphalerite, spinel, talc, uralite, uranite, vesuvianite, wurtzite, zircon.

mingle   *v*
1 MIX, intermingle, intermix, combine, blend, merge, unite, alloy, fuse, amalgamate, coalesce, join, compound
2 ASSOCIATE, socialize, circulate
formal commingle
colloq. hobnob, rub shoulders

miniature   *adj*
tiny, small, small-scale, scaled-down, minute, reduced, diminutive, midget, toy, dwarf, baby, pocket-sized, little
Scot. wee
colloq. pint-size(d), mini
⊟ giant

minimal   *adj*
least, smallest, minimum, slightest, littlest, negligible, minute, token, nominal

minimize   *v*
1 REDUCE, decrease, diminish, cut, curtail, shrink
colloq. slash
2 BELITTLE, make light of, make little of, deprecate, discount, play down, underestimate, underrate, trivialize, laugh off
formal disparage, decry
colloq. soft-pedal
⊟ 1 maximize 2 emphasize, play up

minimum   *n, adj*
▶ *n* least, lowest, lowest point, lowest number, smallest quantity, slightest, bottom
formal nadir
⊟ maximum
▶ *adj* minimal, least, lowest, slightest, smallest, littlest, tiniest
⊟ maximum

minion   *n*
1 ATTENDANT, follower, underling, lackey, flunkey, hireling, servant, menial, drudge
2 DEPENDANT, hanger-on, favourite, darling, sycophant, fawner, parasite, leech
colloq. yes-man, bootlicker

minister   *n, v*
▶ *n* 1 OFFICIAL, office-holder, politician, dignitary, diplomat, ambassador, delegate, legate, envoy, emissary, representative, consul, cabinet minister, agent, aide, administrator, executive, department secretary
2 CLERGYMAN, churchman, cleric, parson, priest, dean, pastor, vicar, rector, verger, curate, deacon, elder, chaplain, preacher, divine, padre
formal ecclesiastic
▶ *v* attend, serve, tend, take care of, look after, administer, wait on, cater to, accommodate, nurse
Related adjective: ministerial

ministration   *n*
help, aid, assistance, care, service, relief, supervision, backing, support, favour, patronage
formal succour

ministry   *n*
1 GOVERNMENT, cabinet, department, office, bureau, administration
2 THE CHURCH, holy orders, the priesthood
Related adjective: ministerial

minor   *adj*
lesser, secondary, small, smaller, inferior, subordinate, subsidiary, junior, younger, unimportant, insignificant, inconsiderable, unknown, little known, negligible, petty, trivial, trifling, second-class, unclassified, slight, light
⊟ major, significant, important

minstrel   *n*
singer, musician, troubadour, bard, rhymer, joculator, jongleur

mint   *v, adj, n*
▶ *v* 1 COIN, stamp, strike, cast, forge, punch, make, manufacture, produce, construct, devise, fashion
2 INVENT, make up, coin, fabricate, forge, falsify, fake, trump up, concoct, hatch
▶ *adj* perfect, brand-new, new, as new, fresh, immaculate, undamaged, unblemished, unused, excellent, first-class
▶ *n* fortune, wealth, riches
colloq. pile, packet, bomb, bundle, heap, stack, million

minuscule   *adj*
tiny, fine, little, very small, minute, miniature, microscopic, infinitesimal, diminutive, Lilliputian
colloq. teeny, teeny-weeny, itsy-bitsy
⊟ gigantic, huge

minute¹   *n*
1 *ten minutes*
moment, second, instant, short (length of) time, flash
colloq. jiffy, tick
2 *the minute something happens*
the moment, immediately, the instant, the point, directly, no sooner, as soon as

▷ **in a minute** soon, very soon, shortly, in a moment, in a flash, before long, in the near future;
colloq. pronto, in a jiffy/tick, in two shakes of a lamb's tail, before you can say Jack Robinson
▷ **up to the minute** latest, most modern, newest, most recent, fashionable; *colloq.* with it, in, all the rage

minute² *adj*
1 TINY, very small, infinitesimal, minuscule, microscopic, diminutive, miniature, inconsiderable, insignificant, infinitesimal, negligible, slight, trifling, trivial, Lilliputian
2 DETAILED, precise, accurate, exact, meticulous, painstaking, close, strict, critical, exhaustive, punctilious
3 **1** gigantic, huge **2** cursory, superficial

minutely *adv*
closely, in detail, meticulously, painstakingly, scrupulously, systematically, precisely, exactly, exhaustively, critically
colloq. with a fine-tooth comb

minutes *n*
proceedings, record(s), notes, memorandum, transcript, transactions, details, tapes

minutiae *n*
details, fine details, finer points, intricacies, complexities, particulars, niceties, subtleties, trifles, trivialities
colloq. small print

miracle *n*
wonder, marvel, prodigy, phenomenon
Related adjective: miraculous

miraculous *adj*
1 WONDERFUL, marvellous, phenomenal, extraordinary, remarkable, incredible, amazing, astounding, astonishing, unbelievable
2 SUPERNATURAL, inexplicable, unaccountable, phenomenal, extraordinary, remarkable, unbelievable, superhuman
3 natural, normal

mirage *n*
illusion, optical illusion, hallucination, fantasy, phantasm, phantasmagoria

mire *n, v*
▶ *n* **1** QUAGMIRE, quag, marsh, marshland, morass, bog, fen, swamp, slough
Scot. glaur
2 MUCK, mud, dirt, slime, ooze
3 DIFFICULTIES, trouble, mess
colloq. spot, jam, pickle, fix, hole, stew
▶ *v* sink, bog down, overwhelm, deluge

mirror *n, v*
▶ *n* **1** GLASS, looking-glass, reflector
2 REFLECTION, likeness, exact likeness, image, double, twin, copy, clone
colloq. dead ringer, spitting image
▶ *v* reflect, echo, imitate, copy, follow, represent, show, depict, mimic, parrot, ape
formal emulate
Related adjective: specular

mirth *n*
merriment, hilarity, gaiety, fun, laughter, enjoyment, pleasure, jollity, jocularity, amusement, frolics, revelry, glee, cheerfulness, light-heartedness, high spirits, buoyancy
formal blitheness
3 gloom, melancholy

mirthful *adj*
merry, hilarious, laughing, laughable, uproarious, pleasurable, jolly, jovial, amusing, funny, amused, happy, gay, cheerful, cheery, glad, gladsome, light-hearted, light-spirited, vivacious, buoyant, playful, sportive, frolicsome, festive
formal blithe, jocund
3 gloomy, glum, melancholy, mirthless

miry *adj*
marshy, swampy, boggy, fenny, muddy, mucky, dirty, oozy, slimy
Scot. glaury

misadventure *n*
bad luck, hard luck, accident, ill fortune, ill luck, misfortune, mischance, calamity, catastrophe, tragedy, mishap, disaster, failure, debacle, cataclysm, reverse, setback

misanthropic *adj*
antisocial, unfriendly, surly, unsociable, unsympathetic, malevolent, egoistic, inhumane
3 philanthropic

misanthropy *n*
antisociality, unsociableness, malevolence, egoism, inhumanity
3 philanthropy

misapply *v*
misuse, use unwisely/unsuitably, pervert, misappropriate, misemploy, abuse, exploit

misapprehend *v*
misunderstand, misinterpret, miscomprehend, misconceive, misconstrue, mistake, misread, get the wrong idea, get a false impression
colloq. get hold of the wrong end of the stick
3 apprehend

misapprehension *n*
misunderstanding, misconception, misinterpretation, misreading, error, mistake, wrong idea, false impression, fallacy, delusion

misappropriate *v*
steal, embezzle, pocket, thieve, pilfer, rob, swindle, misspend, misuse, misapply, abuse, pervert
formal peculate, defalcate
colloq. filch, pinch, nab, nick, have your fingers/hand in the till

misappropriation *n*
embezzlement, stealing, theft, pilfering, robbing, pocketing, misapplication, misuse
formal defalcation, peculation

misbegotten *adj*
1 DISHONEST, disreputable, stolen, unlawful, illicit, ill-gotten, shady
formal purloined
2 ILL-CONCEIVED, ill-advised, poorly thought-out, abortive
colloq. hare-brained
3 ILLEGITIMATE, natural, bastard, born out of wedlock

misbehave *v*
behave unacceptably/badly, be naughty, be rude, mess about, fool about/around, be beyond the pale, get up to mischief, offend, disobey, lapse, trespass

formal transgress
colloq. muck about, play up, act up, carry on

misbehaviour *n*
unacceptable/bad behaviour, misconduct, bad manners, disobedience, naughtiness, mischief, insubordination
formal misdemeanour, impropriety
colloq. mucking about, carryings-on

misbelief *n*
wrong belief, delusion, illusion, error, mistake, misapprehension, misunderstanding, misconception, fallacy, heresy, unorthodoxy, heterodoxy

miscalculate *v*
misjudge, get wrong, go wrong, make a mistake, slip up, blunder, err, miscount, overestimate, underestimate
colloq. boob

miscarriage *n*
1 *have a miscarriage*
spontaneous abortion
2 FAILURE, breakdown, abortion, aborting, mishap, mismanagement, error, perversion, ruination, disappointment
E3 2 success, fulfilment

miscarry *v*
1 *she miscarried*
abort, lose the baby, have a spontaneous abortion
2 FAIL, abort, come to nothing, fall through, go wrong, go amiss, misfire, founder, come to grief
colloq. flop, fold, not come off, come a cropper, bite the dust
E3 2 succeed

miscellaneous *adj*
mixed, varied, various, assorted, diverse, diversified, sundry, motley, jumbled, indiscriminate
formal heterogeneous, multifarious, variegated

miscellany *n*
assortment, mixture, mix, variety, collection, anthology, medley, potpourri, hotch-potch, jumble, diversity, pastiche, patchwork, gallimaufry, farrago, salmangundi, smorgasbord
formal conglomeration
colloq. mixed bag, mishmash, omnium-gatherum

mischance *n*
accident, misfortune, bad break, ill-chance, ill-fortune, ill-luck, misadventure, disaster, tragedy, calamity, mishap, blow, contretemps
formal infelicity

mischief *n*
1 TROUBLE, harm, hurt, evil, damage, injury, disruption
2 MISBEHAVIOUR, bad behaviour, naughtiness, impishness, roguishness, devilment, pranks, tricks, escapade, wrongdoing
colloq. monkey business, shenanigans, carry-on, hanky-panky, jiggery-pokery, funny business
3 IMP, monkey, rascal, rogue, stirrer, scallywag, scamp, nuisance, pest, tyke, villain, devil

mischievous *adj*
1 MALICIOUS, evil, spiteful, vicious, wicked, malignant, pernicious, destructive, harmful, hurtful, injurious, detrimental
2 NAUGHTY, badly-behaved, bad, disobedient, misbehaving, impish, rascally, roguish, playful,

teasing, frolicsome, troublesome
E3 1 kind 2 well-behaved, good

misconceive *v*
misunderstand, misapprehend, misinterpret, misread, misjudge, misconstrue, mistake
colloq. get hold of the wrong end of the stick

misconception *n*
misapprehension, misunderstanding, misreading, misinterpretation, error, mistake, fallacy, delusion, wrong idea, false impression
colloq. the wrong end of the stick

misconduct *n*
misbehaviour, bad/unacceptable behaviour, malpractice, unethical/unprofessional behaviour, mismanagement, wrongdoing
formal impropriety, misdemeanour

misconstrue *v*
misinterpret, misjudge, misread, misunderstand, misconceive, misapprehend, mistranslate, misreckon, mistake, take the wrong way
colloq. get hold of the wrong end of the stick

miscreant *n*
wrongdoer, criminal, evildoer, sinner, rogue, rascal, scoundrel, scamp, scallywag, villain, vagabond, wretch, reprobate, profligate, mischief-maker, knave, dastard, troublemaker
formal malefactor
E3 worthy

misdeed *n*
wrong, wrongdoing, crime, felony, offence, peccadillo, delinquency, error, fault, misconduct, villainy, sin, trespass
formal misdemeanour, transgression

misdemeanour *n*
wrongdoing, wrong, misdeed, offence, infringement, lapse, fault, error, indiscretion, misbehaviour, misconduct, trespass, peccadillo
formal malfeasance, transgression

miser *n*
niggard, skinflint, cheeseparer, Scrooge
colloq. penny-pincher, cheapskate, meanie, tightwad, money-grubber; *slang* tight arse
E3 spendthrift

miserable *adj*
1 UNHAPPY, sad, sorrowful, dejected, despondent, depressed, downcast, downhearted, heartbroken, low-spirited, wretched, distressed, crushed, desolate, forlorn, gloomy, glum
formal disconsolate, melancholic
colloq. down, down in the dumps, blue
2 *miserable weather*
CHEERLESS, depressing, dreary, gloomy, dismal, disagreeable, unpleasant, forlorn, joyless
3 *miserable living conditions*
impoverished, shabby, squalid, poor, wretched
4 CONTEMPTIBLE, despicable, ignominious, detestable, vile, base, mean, disgraceful, deplorable, low, shameful
5 MEAGRE, paltry, niggardly, scanty, poor, worthless, pathetic, pitiful
colloq. measly
6 GRUMPY, bad-tempered, ill-tempered, irritable, surly, sullen
colloq. grouchy, crotchety
E3 1 cheerful, happy 2 pleasant 3 happy
5 generous

miserliness *n*
meanness, niggardliness, tightness, tight-fistedness, close-fistedness, frugality, parsimony, penny-pinching, cheeseparing, covetousness, avarice
formal penuriousness
colloq. minginess, stinginess
❧ generosity, lavishness; *formal* prodigality

miserly *adj*
mean, niggardly, tight, tight-fisted, close-fisted, sparing, parsimonious, cheeseparing, beggarly
formal penurious
colloq. stingy, penny-pinching, mingy, money-grubbing
❧ generous, spendthrift

misery *n*
1 UNHAPPINESS, sadness, suffering, sorrow, distress, depression, discomfort, despair, anguish, agony, gloom, grief, wretchedness, adversity, misfortune
formal woe, melancholy, affliction
2 DEPRIVATION, hardship, poverty, want, oppression, destitution
formal privation, penury, indigence
3 SPOILSPORT, pessimist, killjoy, moaner, complainer, prophet of doom, Jeremiah
colloq. wet blanket, grouch, whiner, whinger, sourpuss
❧ 1 contentment 2 comfort

misfire *v*
miscarry, go wrong, go amiss, go awry, abort, fail, fall through, founder, fizzle out, come to grief
colloq. flop, not come off, come a cropper, bite the dust
❧ succeed

misfit *n*
individualist, nonconformist, eccentric, maverick, dropout, loner, lone wolf
colloq. oddball, weirdo, freak, odd one out, fish out of water, square peg in a round hole
❧ conformist

misfortune *n*
bad luck, mischance, mishap, ill-luck, hard luck, misadventure, setback, reverse, failure, calamity, catastrophe, disaster, blow, accident, tragedy, trouble, adversity, evil, sorrow, hardship, trial
formal tribulation, affliction, woe
❧ luck, success

misgiving *n*
doubt, uncertainty, unease, hesitation, qualm, reservation, apprehension, scruple, suspicion, distrust, second thoughts, niggle, anxiety, worry, fear
❧ confidence

misguided *adj*
misled, misconceived, ill-considered, ill-advised, ill-judged, imprudent, rash, misdirected, misinformed, misplaced, deluded, foolish, erroneous, wrong, mistaken
formal fallacious, injudicious
❧ sensible, wise

mishandle *v*
mismanage, make a mess of, bungle, misjudge, mess up
colloq. botch, make a hash of, make a pig's ear of, muff; *slang* balls up, make a balls of, screw up
❧ cope, manage

mishap *n*
misfortune, ill-fortune, stroke of bad luck, misadventure, accident, reverse, setback, calamity, catastrophe, disaster, adversity, blow, incident, trouble, trial
formal tribulation

mishmash *n*
hotchpotch, hodge-podge, jumble, medley, potpourri, pastiche, mess, muddle, salad, hash, farrago, gallimaufry, salmagundi, olla-podrida, olio
formal conglomeration

misinform *v*
mislead, misdirect, misguide, deceive, bluff, hoodwink
colloq. lead up the garden path, take for a ride, give a bum steer

misinformation *n*
disinformation, misleading, misdirection, nonsense, bluff, lies, baloney
colloq. bum steer, dope, eyewash, guff, hype

misinterpret *v*
misconstrue, misread, misunderstand, mistake, misjudge, misconceive, misapprehend, distort, garble, take the wrong way
colloq. get hold of the wrong end of the stick

misjudge *v*
miscalculate, mistake, misinterpret, misconstrue, misunderstand, overestimate, underestimate, have a wrong opinion about

mislay *v*
lose, misplace, miss, forget where you have put, lose sight of, lose track of, be unable to find, misfile

mislead *v*
misinform, misdirect, misguide, misrepresent, deceive, fool into, delude, lead astray, fool, hoodwink
colloq. send on a wild-goose chase, lead up the garden path, take for a ride, pull a fast one on, pull the wool over someone's eyes

misleading *adj*
deceptive, deceiving, confusing, unreliable, equivocal, ambiguous, biased, loaded, evasive, delusive, illusory
formal fallacious
colloq. tricky
❧ unequivocal, authoritative, informative

mismanage *v*
mishandle, botch, bungle, make a mess of, mess up, misrule, misspend, misjudge, foul up, mar, waste
colloq. botch, make a hash of, make a pig's ear of, muff; *slang* balls up, make a balls of, screw up

mismatched *adj*
clashing, discordant, ill-assorted, incompatible, unmatching, misallied, mismated, unsuited, unreconcilable, irregular
formal incongruous, disparate, antipathetic
❧ compatible, matching

misogynist *n*
woman-hater, anti-feminist, male chauvinist, male supremacist, sexist, misogamist
colloq. male chauvinist pig (MCP)
❧ feminist

misplace *v*
lose, mislay, miss, misapply, misassign, misfile, forget where you have put, lose sight of, lose track of, be unable to find

misprint *n*
mistake, error, literal, printing error, typographical error
formal corrigendum, erratum
colloq. typo

misquote *v*
misrepresent, misreport, muddle, misstate, twist, distort, pervert, falsify, garble, misremember

misrepresent *v*
distort, falsify, slant, pervert, twist, garble, misquote, exaggerate, minimize, misconstrue, misinterpret, misreport, misstate, give a false/wrong account of

misrule *n*
disorder, disorganization, maladministration, misgovernment, mismanagement, chaos, confusion, indiscipline, lawlessness, anarchy, riot, tumult, turmoil, turbulence, unreason

miss[1] *v, n*
▶ *v* **1** *miss a target*
FAIL, lose, let slip, let go, omit, fail, fail to hit/get/catch, miscarry, overlook, pass over, slip, leave out, mistake, trip, misunderstand, err
colloq. blow, muff
2 *miss a meeting*
be absent from, be away from fail to attend, not take part in, not go to, not go to see, not see, not be part of, be too late for
3 *miss an opportunity*
let go, let slip, fail to seize, not take advantage of, neglect, disregard, overlook
4 NOT NOTICE, not spot, fail to notice, fail to notice the absence of, overlook, disregard
5 AVOID, escape, evade, dodge, forego, skip, bypass, sidestep
formal circumvent
6 PINE FOR, long for, yearn for, regret, feel the loss of, grieve for, mourn, sorrow for, ache for, want, wish, need, lament
1 hit, get, catch **2** take part in **3** seize **4** notice, spot
▷ **miss out** bypass, dispense with, disregard, ignore, jump, leave out, omit, pass over, skip
▶ *n* failure, error, blunder, mistake, omission, oversight, fault, slip, fiasco
colloq. flop

miss[2] *n*
Miss Bancroft
girl, schoolgirl, young lady, young woman, teenager, Ms, mademoiselle, damsel, lass, maid, maiden

missal *n*
breviary, formulary, mass-book, office-book, prayerbook, servicebook, euchologion, Triodion

misshapen *adj*
deformed, distorted, twisted, malformed, warped, contorted, crooked, crippled, bent, misproportioned, grotesque, ugly, monstrous
E3 regular, shapely

missile *n*
projectile, shot, guided missile, ballistic, missile, arrow, shaft, dart, rocket, bomb, shell, flying bomb, grenade, torpedo, weapon

missing *adj*
absent, lost, lacking, gone, mislaid, unaccounted-for, wanting, disappeared, astray, gone astray, strayed, misplaced, nowhere to be found
E3 found, present

mission *n*
1 TASK, undertaking, assignment, operation, campaign, crusade, business, errand, work, duty, chore
2 CALLING, duty, purpose, vocation, *raison d'être*, aim, goal, quest, pursuit, charge, office, job, work

3 COMMISSION, ministry, delegation, deputation, task-force, legation, embassy

missionary *n*
evangelist, campaigner, preacher, converter, proselytizer, apostle, minister, crusader, propagandist, champion, promoter, emissary, envoy, ambassador

missive *n*
communication, dispatch, letter, line, message, report, note, bulletin, communiqué, memorandum
formal epistle
colloq. memo

misspent *adj*
wasted, frittered away, squandered, thrown away, idle, idled away, misused, profitless, misapplied, dissipated, unprofitable
formal prodigal
E3 profitable

misstate *v*
misreport, misrepresent, misquote, misrelate, pervert, twist, distort, falsify, garble, misremember

mist *n, v*
▶ *n* haze, fog, vapour, smog, cloud, condensation, film, spray, drizzle, mizzle, dew, steam, veil, dimness
▶ *v* ▷ **mist over/up** cloud over, become cloudy, become hazy, fog (up), dim, blur, become blurred, steam up, obscure, veil, glaze
E3 clear

mistake *n, v*
▶ *n* error, inaccuracy, slip, oversight, aberration, lapse, slip of the tongue, blunder, gaffe, fault, *faux pas*, indiscretion, misjudgement, miscalculation, misunderstanding, misapprehension, misprint, misspelling, misreading, mispronunciation
formal solecism, erratum, corrigendum
colloq. bloomer, howler, clanger, slip-up, muff, fluff, goof, botch-up, boob, booboo, a bad move, blooper
▶ *v* **1** MISUNDERSTAND, misapprehend, misconstrue, misjudge, misread, miscalculate, get wrong, slip up, blunder, err
colloq. muff, boob, goof (it), put your foot in it, get your wires crossed
2 *mistake a person for another*
confuse, mix up, confound, muddle (up)

mistaken *adj*
wrong, incorrect, in error, erroneous, inaccurate, inexact, untrue, unfounded, inappropriate, ill-judged, inauthentic, false, deceived, deluded, misguided, misinformed, misled, faulty, at fault
formal fallacious
colloq. having got hold of the wrong end of the stick, get the wrong idea, wide of the mark
E3 correct, right

mistakenly *adv*
wrongly, by mistake, erroneously, incorrectly, falsely, inaccurately, inappropriately, misguidedly, unfairly, unjustly
formal fallaciously
E3 appropriately, correctly, fairly, justly

mistimed *adj*
inconvenient, unfortunate, untimely, ill-timed, inopportune, unseasonable, unsynchronized, tactless
formal infelicitous, malapropos
E3 opportune

mistreat *v*
abuse, misuse, ill-treat, ill-use, maltreat, treat badly,

mishandle, harm, hurt, bully, batter, injure, molest, maul
colloq. knock about, beat up, walk (all) over
🔁 cosset, pamper

mistreatment *n*
maltreatment, abuse, ill-treatment, ill-use, harm, hurt, battering, injury, molestation, bullying, cruelty, unkindness, manhandling, mauling, mishandling, misuse, ill-usage, brutalization
🔁 cosseting, pampering

mistress *n*
1 LOVER, live-in lover, partner, girlfriend, kept woman, concubine, courtesan, paramour, woman, lady-love, inamorata, hetaera
colloq. bit on the side
2 TEACHER, schoolteacher, governess, tutor

mistrust *n, v*
▶ *n* distrust, doubt, suspicion, wariness, misgiving, reservations, qualm, hesitancy, chariness, caution, uncertainty, scepticism, apprehension
🔁 trust
▶ *v* distrust, doubt, have doubts about, have no faith in, suspect, be suspicious of, be wary of, beware, have reservations, have misgivings, fear
🔁 trust

mistrustful *adj*
distrustful, doubtful, dubious, hesitant, sceptical, suspicious, uncertain, wary, cautious, apprehensive, fearful, shy, chary, cynical
colloq. leery
🔁 trustful

misty *adj*
hazy, foggy, cloudy, blurred, fuzzy, murky, smoky, unclear, dim, indistinct, obscure, opaque, vague, nebulous, veiled
🔁 clear, distinct

misunderstand *v*
misapprehend, misconstrue, misinterpret, misread, misjudge, mistake, get wrong, get the wrong idea, get a false impression, miss the point, mishear,
colloq. get hold of the wrong end of the stick, not make head or tail of, get your wires crossed
🔁 understand

misunderstanding *n*
1 MISTAKE, error, misapprehension, misconception, misjudgement, misinterpretation, wrong idea, false impression, misreading, mix-up
colloq. the wrong end of the stick, crossed wires
2 DISAGREEMENT, argument, dispute, conflict, clash, difference, difference of opinion, breach, quarrel, rift, row, squabble
formal discord
colloq. falling-out, tiff
🔁 1 understanding 2 agreement

misunderstood *adj*
misappreciated, misconstrued, misjudged, misread, misrepresented, mistaken, unappreciated, unrecognized, misheard, misinterpreted, ill-judged

misuse *n, v*
▶ *n* mistreatment, maltreatment, mishandling, injury, abuse, wrong use, harm, ill-treatment, misapplication, misemployment, misappropriation, waste, squandering, perversion, corruption, exploitation
▶ *v* abuse, misapply, misemploy, ill-use, ill-treat, treat badly, harm, mistreat, wrong, distort, injure, hurt,

corrupt, pervert, waste, squander, misappropriate, exploit, dissipate

⚠ **misuse** or **abuse** ? *See panel at* **abuse**.

mite *n*
bit, trace, spark, whit, touch, atom, morsel, scrap, grain, jot, iota, modicum, ounce
colloq. smidgen, tad

mitigate *v*
moderate, temper, alleviate, reduce, lessen, calm, pacify, soften, soothe, still, subdue, tone down, weaken, placate, quiet, decrease, diminish, dull, check, ease, mollify, lighten, modify, blunt
formal abate, allay, appease, assuage, extenuate, palliate, remit, lenify
🔁 increase, exacerbate, aggravate

mitigating *adj*
extenuating, justifying, vindicating, tempering, modifying, qualifying, vindicatory
formal palliative

mitigation *n*
moderation, lessening, tempering, reduction, relief, easement, alleviation, decrease, diminution, qualification, mollification
formal abatement, allaying, appeasement, assuagement, extenuation, palliation, remission
🔁 increase, exacerbation, aggravation

mix *v, n*
▶ *v* 1 COMBINE, blend, mingle, put together, intermingle, intermix, amalgamate, compound, homogenize, synthesize, merge, join, unite, coalesce, fuse, alloy, incorporate, stir, whisk, mash, emulsify, infiltrate, introduce, fold in
formal interpolate
2 ASSOCIATE, consort, fraternize, socialize, meet others, mingle, join
colloq. hobnob
3 BE COMPATIBLE, harmonize, get along/on, agree, complement, go well with, suit
colloq. be on the same wavelength
🔁 1 divide, separate
▷ **mix in** add in, blend, merge, introduce, incorporate, infiltrate; *formal* interpolate
🔁 extract, isolate
▷ **mix up** confuse, bewilder, muddle (up), mistake, perplex, puzzle, confound, mix, jumble, get jumbled up, complicate, garble, involve, implicate, disturb, upset, snarl up
▶ *n* mixture, blend, amalgam, amalgamation, assortment, combination, union, compound, merger, coalition, alloy, fusion, synthesis, medley, composite
formal conglomerate
colloq. mishmash

mixed *adj*
1 *mixed race*
combined, hybrid, mingled, crossbred, mongrel, interbred, blended, composite, compound, incorporated, united, alloyed, amalgamated, fused
2 *mixed biscuits*
assorted, varied, miscellaneous, diverse, diversified, motley
3 *mixed feelings*
ambivalent, equivocal, conflicting, contradicting, uncertain, unsure
▷ **mixed up** 1 *a mixed-up person* maladjusted, disturbed, disordered, disoriented, distracted,

distraught, confused, bewildered, muddled, perplexed, puzzled, upset, chaotic, complicated, désorienté; *slang* screwed up **2** *mixed up in a crime* INVOLVED, embroiled, incriminated, caught up, entangled, implicated; *formal* inculpated; *colloq.* in on

mixer *n*
1 *a food mixer*
blender, food processor, liquidizer, beater, whisk
2 EXTROVERT, joiner, socializer, everybody's friend
colloq. life and soul of the party
3 INTERFERER, busybody, disrupter, meddler, mischief-maker, subversive, troublemaker
old use makebate
colloq. stirrer
≢ 2 introvert, loner, recluse **3** peacemaker

mixing *n*
1 AMALGAMATION, combination, synthesis, intermingling, coalescence, blending, union, fusion, hybridization, interbreeding, interflow
formal minglement
2 ASSOCIATION, fraternization, socializing, mingling
≢ 1 separation

mixture *n*
mix, blend, combination, amalgamation, amalgam, compound, composite, coalescence, alloy, brew, synthesis, union, fusion, concoction, cross, hybrid, assortment, variety, miscellany, medley, melange, farrago, smorgasbord, pastiche, patchwork, potpourri, jumble, hotchpotch
formal conglomeration
colloq. mixed bag, mishmash

mix-up *n*
mess, mistake, misunderstanding, muddle, nonsense, chaos, confusion, jumble, disorder, complication, snarl-up, tangle
colloq. foul-up; *slang* balls-up; *US* snafu

moan *n, v*
▶ *n* **1** GROAN, lament, lamentation, sob, wail, howl, whimper, whine
2 COMPLAINT, grumble, grievance, groan, dissatisfaction, annoyance, fault-finding, criticism, carping, censure, accusation, charge, representation
colloq. beefing, beef, belly-aching, grouse, gripe, bleating, whingeing, whinge
▶ *v* **1** GROAN, wail, sob, weep, howl, whimper, mourn, lament, sigh, grieve
2 COMPLAIN, grumble, whine, carp
colloq. whinge, gripe, grouse, bleat, belly-ache, beef, kick up a fuss
≢ 1 rejoice

mob *n, v*
▶ *n* **1** CROWD, mass, throng, multitude, horde, rabble, host, swarm, gathering, group, collection, body, flock, herd, drove, brood, pack, press, set, tribe, troop, company, crew, gang
formal assemblage
2 POPULACE, rabble, masses, hoi polloi, great unwashed, *canaille*
colloq. plebs, riff-raff
▶ *v* crowd, crowd round, surround, swarm round, gather round, jostle, overrun, set upon, fall upon, besiege, descend on, throng, pack, fill, pester, attack, charge

mobile *adj*
1 MOVING, movable, able to move, portable,

transportable, travelling, roaming, roving, itinerant, wandering, migrant
formal peripatetic, motile, locomotive, ambulatory
2 FLEXIBLE, adjustable, adaptable, supple, agile, active, energetic, nimble
3 CHANGING, changeable, ever-changing, expressive, lively
≢ 1 immobile

mobility *n*
movability, movableness, portability, flexibility, motion, expressiveness, vivacity, agility, animation, suppleness
formal locomobility, locomotion, locomotivity, motility, motivity
≢ immobility, inflexibility, rigidity

mobilize *v*
assemble, marshal, rally, conscript, muster, call up, enlist, call into action, activate, cause to take action, galvanize, organize, prepare, get ready, make ready, ready, summon, animate

mob rule *n*
lynch law, ochlocracy, Reign of Terror
colloq. mobocracy

mock *v, adj*
▶ *v* **1** RIDICULE, jeer, make fun of, poke fun at, laugh at, scoff, sneer, taunt, gibe, scorn, insult, tease, chaff
formal disparage, deride
colloq. kid, rib, rag, knock, take the mickey out of;
slang take the piss out of
2 IMITATE, simulate, mimic, ape, caricature, parody, burlesque, lampoon, satirize
formal emulate
colloq. send up, take off
▶ *adj* imitation, counterfeit, artificial, sham, simulated, synthetic, substitute, ersatz, false, fake, forged, fraudulent, bogus, pseudo, spurious, feigned, faked, pretended, dummy
colloq. phoney, pretend

mocker *n*
jeerer, ridiculer, scoffer, scorner, sneerer, satirist, tease, tormentor, flouter, lampooner, lampoonist, critic, detractor, pasquinader
formal derider, reviler, vilifier, iconoclast
≢ flatterer, supporter

mockery *n*
1 RIDICULE, jeering, scoffing, scorn, sneer, sneering, taunting, teasing, contempt, disdain, disrespect, sarcasm
formal derision, disparagement, contumely
colloq. kidding, ribbing, ragging, mickey-taking;
slang piss-taking
2 PARODY, satire, sham, travesty, caricature, farce, burlesque, lampoon, apology
formal emulation
colloq. send-up, take-off, spoof

mocking *adj*
scornful, derisive, derisory, contemptuous, sarcastic, satirical, taunting, scoffing, sardonic, sneering, insulting, irreverent, impudent, disrespectful, disdainful, cynical
colloq. snide

mode *n*
1 WAY, style, manner, approach, condition, method, form, plan, practice, procedure, process, technique, system, convention

2 FASHION, style, custom, trend, vogue, fad, look
colloq. craze, latest thing, rage, *dernier cri*

model *n, adj, v*
▶ *n* **1** COPY, replica, representation, facsimile,
image, imitation, mock-up, dummy
2 EXAMPLE, pattern, design, standard, ideal,
epitome, paragon, perfect example, embodiment,
mould, original, type, prototype, sample, template,
version
formal exemplar, archetype, paradigm
3 DESIGN, style, form, sort, kind, variety, type,
version, mark
formal mode
4 MANNEQUIN, fashion model, artist's model,
photographer's model, dummy, sitter, subject, poser
▶ *adj* exemplary, perfect, typical, ideal
formal archetypal, prototypical
▶ *v* **1** MAKE, form, fashion, mould, sculpt, carve,
cast, shape, work, create, design, plan, base
2 DISPLAY, wear, sport, pose, show off

moderate *adj, v, n*
▶ *adj* **1** MEDIOCRE, medium, modest, ordinary, fair,
fairish, indifferent, average, middling, adequate,
tolerable, passable, middle-of-the-road
colloq. so-so, fair to middling, not up to much, no great
shakes, not much cop, nothing much to write home
about
2 REASONABLE, restrained, fair, just, modest,
sensible, calm, steady, sober, controlled, temperate,
cool, mild, well-regulated
F3 1 exceptional, extreme **2** immoderate, excessive
▶ *v* control, regulate, decrease, lessen, slacken,
soften, restrain, tone down, play down, diminish, ease,
curb, calm, check, keep in check, keep under control,
modulate, repress, subdue, soft-pedal, tame, subside,
pacify, dwindle
formal attenuate, mitigate, allay, alleviate, abate,
appease, assuage, palliate
▶ *n* nonextremist, centrist, liberal, neutral person,
don't know
F3 extremist, hardliner

moderately *adv*
reasonably, somewhat, quite, rather, fairly, slightly,
passably, within reason, to some extent, to a certain
degree
F3 extremely

moderation *n*
1 RESTRAINT, self-control, self-restraint, caution,
control, composure, sobriety, abstemiousness,
temperance, temperateness, reasonableness
2 DECREASE, reduction, lessening, regulation,
curbing, subsidence
formal attenuation, mitigation, alleviation, abatement
F3 1 indulgence, self-indulgence
▷ **in moderation** within limits, within bounds,
within reason, moderately, with self-control
F3 to excess

modern *adj*
current, contemporary, up-to-date, existing, new,
fresh, latest, late, novel, present, present-day, recent,
up-to-the-minute, advanced, avant-garde, progressive,
modernistic, innovative, inventive, state-of-the-art,
go-ahead, forward-looking, futuristic, fashionable, in
fashion, stylish, in vogue, in style, voguish, modish
colloq. newfangled, in, trendy, with it, spanking new,
faddish, all the rage, the latest, hot off the press, hip,
cool

F3 old-fashioned, old, out-of-date, antiquated,
traditional

modernity *n*
innovation, innovativeness, newness, novelty,
originality, contemporaneity, fashionableness,
freshness, recentness
F3 antiquatedness, antiquity

modernize *v*
renovate, refurbish, rejuvenate, regenerate, streamline,
revamp, renew, make modern, update, bring up-to-
date, improve, do up, redesign, reform, remake,
remodel, refresh, transform, modify, progress
colloq. do over, do up, fix up, move with the times,
get with it
F3 regress

modest *adj*
1 UNASSUMING, humble, self-effacing,
self-deprecating, quiet, reserved, retiring,
unpretentious, discreet, bashful, shy, self-conscious,
coy, timid
2 MODERATE, ordinary, unexceptional, fair,
satisfactory, reasonable, tolerable, passable, adequate,
limited, small
3 *a modest house*
unassuming, unpretentious, simple, plain, inexpensive
4 *modest behaviour*
proper, discreet, decent, chaste, virtuous, demure
old use seemly
formal decorous
F3 1 immodest, conceited, arrogant **2** exceptional,
excessive **3** pretentious, expensive, extravagant

modesty *n*
1 HUMILITY, humbleness, self-effacement,
self-deprecation, reticence, reserve, quietness,
shyness, bashfulness, coyness, self-consciousness,
timidity
2 *modesty of behaviour*
decency, propriety, demureness, chasteness
old use seemliness
formal decorum
3 UNPRETENTIOUSNESS, simplicity, plainness,
inexpensiveness
F3 1 immodesty, vanity, conceit **3** extravagance

modicum *n*
little, bit, small amount, little bit, particle, molecule,
fragment, grain, scrap, shred, speck, touch, degree,
trace, tinge, atom, crumb, dash, drop, pinch, ounce,
hint, suggestion, inch, iota, mite
colloq. tad

modification *n*
adaptation, adjustment, alteration, change, revision,
variation, improvement, transformation, mutation,
refinement, reformation, reorganization, remoulding,
reworking, recasting, limitation, moderation,
qualification, restriction, tempering
formal modulation

modify *v*
1 CHANGE, alter, redesign, revise, vary, adapt, adjust,
transform, reform, convert, improve, reorganize,
reshape, remould, rework, recast
2 MODERATE, reduce, lessen, decrease, diminish,
temper, tone down, limit, soften, dull, qualify
formal abate, mitigate

modish *adj*
fashionable, stylish, smart, vogue, voguish,
contemporary, current, modern, modernistic,

avant-garde, chic, now, *à la mode*
colloq. all the rage, hip, in, jazzy, latest, mod, trendy, up-to-the-minute, with it
F3 dowdy, old-fashioned

modulate *v*
modify, adjust, balance, alter, soften, temper, moderate, lower, regulate, change, vary, harmonize, inflect, tune

modulation *n*
modification, adjustment, balance, alteration, softening, lowering, moderation, regulation, change, variation, harmonization, tuning, tone, shift, inflection, inflexion, intonation, accent, shade

modus operandi *n*
method, way, operation, plan, practice, procedure, process, manner, technique, system, rule, rule of thumb
formal praxis

mogul *n*
magnate, tycoon, baron, potentate, notable, personage, supremo
colloq. big cheese, big gun, big noise, big pot, big shot, big wheel, bigwig, Mr Big, top dog, VIP
F3 nobody

moist *adj*
damp, clammy, dank, humid, wet, wettish, dewy, rainy, dewy, muggy, marshy, drizzly, drizzling, watery, soggy, dripping
F3 dry, arid

moisten *v*
moisturize, dampen, damp, wet, make wet, soak, water, humidify, humify, lick, irrigate
F3 dry

moisture *n*
water, liquid, wetness, wet, wateriness, damp, dampness, dankness, humidity, vapour, rain, drizzle, dew, mugginess, condensation, soaking, steam, spray, perspiration, sweat
F3 dryness

mole¹ *n*
a mole on the skin
spot, blemish, blotch, speckle, freckle

mole² *n*
a mole in the organization
agent, infiltrator, secret agent, spy, double agent

mole³ *n*
a mole stretching out to sea
barrier, breakwater, pier, causeway, dyke, groyne, jetty, embankment

molest *v*
1 ANNOY, disturb, bother, harass, irritate, agitate, vex, exasperate, persecute, pester, nag, chivvy, harry, plague, tease, torment, hound, upset, fluster, worry, trouble, provoke, badger
colloq. aggravate, needle, hassle, bug
2 ATTACK, accost, assail, hurt, ill-treat, maltreat, mistreat, abuse, interfere with, (sexually) assault, rape, harm, injure
formal ravish

mollify *v*
placate, appease, calm, pacify, compose, conciliate, cushion, ease, relax, relieve, lessen, moderate, temper, modify, quell, soften, soothe, lull, quiet, blunt, sweeten, mellow

formal abate, allay, mitigate, assuage, propitiate
F3 aggravate, anger

mollusc *n*

Molluscs include: abalone, conch, cowrie, cuttlefish, clam, cockle, limpet, mussel, nautilus, nudibranch, octopus, oyster, periwinkle, scallop, sea slug, slug, freshwater snail, land snail, marine snail, squid, tusk shell, whelk.

mollycoddle *v*
pamper, coddle, indulge, spoil, overprotect, pander to, cosset, spoon-feed, mother, pet, baby, ruin
F3 ill-treat, neglect

moment *n*
1 *stop for a moment*
second, instant, (very) short time, less than no time, point in time, minute, split second, sec, flash, twinkling of an eye, trice
colloq. mo, jiffy, tick, two ticks, two shakes of a lamb's tail
2 *the moment something happens*
the minute, immediately, the instant, the point, directly, no sooner..., as soon as
3 IMPORTANCE, significance, substance, note, interest, value, worth, concern, consequence, gravity, seriousness, weight, weightiness
formal import
F3 3 insignificance

momentarily *adv*
briefly, for a moment, for a short time, for a second, for an instant, fleetingly, temporarily

momentary *adj*
brief, short, short-lived, temporary, transient, transitory, fleeting, hasty, quick, passing, spasmodic
formal ephemeral, evanescent
F3 lasting, permanent

momentous *adj*
significant, important, of importance, of consequence, of significance, critical, crucial, decisive, weighty, grave, serious, vital, consequential, fateful, historic, pivotal, earth-shaking, earth-shattering, world-shattering, epoch-making, eventful, major
F3 insignificant, unimportant, trivial

momentum *n*
impetus, force, energy, impulse, drive, power, driving-power, thrust, propulsion, speed, velocity, impact, incentive, stimulus, urge, strength, push

monarch *n*
sovereign, crowned head, ruler, king, queen, emperor, empress, prince, princess, tsar, potentate

monarchy *n*
1 KINGDOM, empire, principality, realm, sovereign state, domain, dominion
2 ROYALISM, sovereignty, kingship, autocracy, absolutism, despotism, tyranny
formal monocracy

monastery *n*
friary, priory, nunnery, convent, abbey, cloister, charterhouse, religious community
formal coenobium

monastic *adj*
reclusive, withdrawn, secluded, cloistered, canonical, austere, ascetic, celibate, meditative, contemplative

formal sequestered, eremitic, anchoritic, coenobitic
🔄 secular, worldly

monasticism *n*
asceticism, austerity, recluseness, reclusion, seclusion, monkhood
formal monachism, eremitism, coenobitism

monetary *adj*
financial, money, fiscal, budgetary, economic, capital, cash
formal pecuniary

money *n*
currency, cash, legal tender, banknotes, coin, funds, finances, assets, means, savings, resources, capital, riches, wealth, prosperity, affluence
colloq. the necessary, readies; *slang* megabucks, dough, dosh, bread, lolly, spondulicks, brass, loot, gravy, *US* greens, rhino, shekels, moolah, gelt
Related adjectives: monetary, pecuniary
▷ **in the money** rich, wealthy, affluent, prosperous, well-off, well-to-do; *colloq.* rolling in it, well-heeled, flush; *slang* loaded
🔄 poor

money-box *n*
cash box, chest, safe, coffer, piggy-bank

moneyed *adj*
wealthy, rich, affluent, comfortable, well-off, prosperous, well-to-do
formal opulent
colloq. flush, well-heeled, rolling in it; *slang* loaded
🔄 poor, impoverished

money-grubbing *adj*
acquisitive, grasping, miserly, mercenary, mammonish, mammonistic
formal quaestuary

money-making *adj*
profitable, profit-making, lucrative, commercial, remunerative, paying, successful

mongrel *n, adj*
▶ *n* cross, crossbreed, hybrid, half-breed, mixed breed, cur
▶ *adj* crossbred, hybrid, half-bred, bastard, mixed, of mixed breed, ill-defined
🔄 pure-bred, pedigree

monitor *v, n*
▶ *v* check, watch, keep track of, keep under surveillance, keep an eye on, keep track of, follow, track, supervise, oversee, observe, note, survey, trace, scan, record, plot, detect
▶ *n* **1** SCREEN, display, VDU, recorder, scanner, detector, security camera, CCTV
2 SUPERVISOR, watchdog, observer, overseer, invigilator, adviser, prefect, head boy, head girl

monk *n*
brother, religious, friar, frater, prior, abbot, hermit, monastic, mendicant, contemplative, cloisterer, coenobite, beguin, conventual, religieux, religionary, religioner, anchorite, gyrovague
Related adjectives: monastic, monasterial

monkey *n, v*
▶ *n* **1** PRIMATE, simian
Related adjective: simian

Monkeys include: ape, baboon, capuchin, colobus monkey, drill and mandrill, guenon, guereza, howler monkey, langur, leaf monkey, macaque, mangabey, marmoset, night monkey (or douroucouli), proboscis monkey, rhesus monkey, saki, spider monkey, squirrel money, tamarin, titi, toque, uakari (or cacajou), woolly monkey.

2 SCAMP, imp, urchin, brat, rogue, rascal, mischief-maker
colloq. scallywag
▷ **monkey business** mischief, tomfoolery, trickery, chicanery, clowning, pranks, dishonesty, skulduggery, legerdemain, sleight-of-hand, foolery; *colloq.* carry-on, hanky-panky, jiggery-pokery, monkey tricks, shenanigans, funny business
🔄 honesty
▶ *v* play, fool, tinker, tamper, trifle, fiddle, fidget, interfere, meddle, mess, potter

monochrome *adj*
black-and-white, monotone, sepia, monochromatic, monotonous
formal monochroic, unicolor, unicolorate, unicolorous, unicolour, unicoloured
🔄 kaleidoscopic, multicoloured

monocle *n*
eyeglass, glass

monogamous *adj*
having only one marriage partner
formal monandrous, monogamic, monogynous
🔄 bigamous, polygamous

monogamy *n*
state of having only one marriage partner, practice/custom of having only one marriage partner
formal monandry, monogyny
🔄 bigamy, polygamy

monolingual *adj*
speaking one language only, using/involving one language only, expressed in one language only
formal monoglot, unilingual
🔄 polyglot

monolith *n*
megalith, standing stone, shaft, menhir, sarsen

monolithic *adj*
massive, vast, colossal, gigantic, huge, monumental, giant, immovable, immobile, rigid, solid, unmoving, unchanging, inflexible, faceless, undifferentiated, fossilized, hidebound, intractable, unvaried

monologue *n*
speech, soliloquy, lecture, sermon, address, oration, homily
colloq. spiel
🔄 conversation, dialogue, discussion

monomania *n*
obsession, fixation, ruling passion, fanaticism, *idée fixe*, mania, neurosis, fetish
colloq. bee in one's bonnet, hobby-horse, thing

monopolize *v*
dominate, take over, keep to yourself, have (all) to yourself, corner, control, not share with others, have exclusive/sole rights, engross, occupy, preoccupy, take up, tie up
formal appropriate
colloq. hog
🔄 share

monopoly *n*
domination, control, corner, exclusive right(s), sole right(s)

technical monopsony
formal ascendancy

monotonous *adj*
boring, dull, tedious, uninteresting, unexciting,
tiresome, wearisome, unchanging, uneventful,
unvarying, unvaried, all the same, uniform, toneless,
flat, colourless, repetitive, repetitious, routine,
mechanical, plodding, humdrum, soul-destroying
colloq. run-of-the-mill, samey, deadly, ho-hum
F3 lively, varied, colourful

monotony *n*
tedium, dullness, boredom, sameness, tiresomeness,
uneventfulness, flatness, wearisomeness, uniformity,
routine, routineness, repetitiveness, repetition
F3 liveliness, colour, variety, excitement, interest

monster *n, adj*
▶ *n* **1** *sea monsters*
frightening creature, imaginary creature, mythical
creature, Frankenstein, dragon, Medusa, Gorgon,
Minotaur, Sphinx, hippocampus, kraken, wivern,
windigo
2 BEAST, fiend, brute, barbarian, savage, villain,
Frankenstein, giant, ogre, ogress, devil, troll
3 FREAK, freak of nature, monstrosity, mutant,
malformation, miscreation
formal teratism
4 MAMMOTH, jumbo, giant, colossus, leviathan,
behemoth, cyclops, Brobdingnagian
▶ *adj* huge, gigantic, giant, colossal, enormous,
immense, massive, monstrous, jumbo, mammoth,
vast, tremendous
colloq. whopping, ginormous, mega
F3 tiny, minute

monstrosity *n*
1 EYESORE, blot on the landscape, atrocity,
abnormality, enormity, freak, monster, mutant,
miscreation, obscenity
technical teras
2 DREADFULNESS, frightfulness, hideousness,
loathsomeness, horror, hellishness, evil
formal heinousness

monstrous *adj*
1 WICKED, evil, vicious, savage, cruel, criminal,
outrageous, scandalous, shocking, disgraceful,
abominable, atrocious, abhorrent, dreadful, frightful,
horrible, horrifying, grisly, terrible, vile, foul, nasty,
inhuman
formal heinous
2 UNNATURAL, inhuman, freakish, abnormal,
grotesque, hideous, gruesome, deformed, malformed,
misshapen
technical teratoid
3 HUGE, enormous, colossal, gigantic, vast,
immense, tremendous, massive, mammoth

monument *n*
memorial, cenotaph, headstone, gravestone,
tombstone, shrine, mausoleum, cairn, barrow, cross,
marker, obelisk, pillar, column, statue, relic,
remembrance, commemoration, witness, testament,
reminder, record, memento, evidence, token

monumental *adj*
1 IMPRESSIVE, imposing, striking, awe-inspiring,
awesome, overwhelming, significant, important,
epoch-making, historic, magnificent, remarkable,
majestic, memorable, unforgettable, notable,
outstanding, abiding, permanent, enduring,
immortal, lasting, classic

2 HUGE, immense, enormous, colossal, vast,
tremendous, extraordinary, massive, great, exceptional
3 COMMEMORATIVE, celebratory, memorial
F3 **1** insignificant, unimportant

mood *n*
1 DISPOSITION, frame of mind, state of mind,
temper, humour, vein, spirit, tenor, whim
2 BAD TEMPER, bad mood, sulk, the sulks, pique,
melancholy, low spirits, depression, doldrums
colloq. blues, dumps
3 ATMOSPHERE, feeling, feel, spirit, tenor, tone,
climate, ambience
▷ **in the mood for** wanting to do/have, feeling like,
willing to, eager to, keen on/to, inclined to, in the right
frame of mind to; *formal* disposed to

moody *adj*
changeable, temperamental, unpredictable, volatile,
unstable, irritable, short-tempered, bad-tempered,
crotchety, testy, touchy, morose, angry, broody,
irritable, irascible, cantankerous, petulant, mopy,
sulky, sullen, gloomy, melancholy, miserable,
downcast, in a huff, in a (bad) mood, doleful, glum,
impulsive, fickle, flighty
formal capricious
colloq. crabby, crusty
F3 equable, cheerful

moon *n, v*
▶ *n* ▷ **once in a blue moon** very rarely, seldom,
not often, hardly ever
▷ **over the moon** ecstatic, elated, blissful, joyful,
jubilant, rapturous, enraptured, overjoyed, euphoric,
delirious, frenzied, fervent
formal rhapsodic
colloq. jumping for joy, on cloud nine, in seventh
heaven, tickled pink, high as a kite
▶ *v* idle, loaf, languish, pine, mope, brood, daydream,
dream, fantasize
colloq. mooch

moonlike *adj*
lunar, moon-shaped, crescent, crescentic, moony
technical lunate
formal lunular, meniscoid, selenic

moonshine *n*
1 NONSENSE, rubbish, fantasy, stuff
colloq. hot air, guff, hogwash, baloney, blather,
blether, bosh, bunk, bunkum, claptrap, eyewash,
tommyrot, tosh, tripe, twaddle, piffle, rot;
slang bullshit, crap
2 SPIRITS, liquor, bootleg, hoo(t)ch, pot(h)een
F3 **1** sense

moor¹ *v*
to moor a boat
fasten, secure, tie up, drop anchor, anchor, berth, dock,
make fast, fix, fix firmly, hitch, lash, bind
F3 loose

moor² *n*
the Yorkshire moors
moorland, heath, fell, upland

moot *v, adj*
▶ *v* put forward, propose, suggest, submit, advance,
bring up, broach, introduce, pose, discuss, argue,
debate
formal propound
▶ *adj* controversial, problematic, difficult,
questionable, vexed, unsettled, unresolved,
unresolvable, undecided, undetermined, disputed,

disputable, arguable, doubtful, insoluble, knotty, open, open to debate, debatable, crucial, contestable, academic

mop *n, v*
▶ *n* **1** *a floor mop*
sponge, wiper, swab, squeegee
2 *a mop of hair*
head of hair, shock, mane, tangle, thatch, mat, mass
▶ *v* swab, sponge, wipe, clean, wash, absorb, soak
▷ **mop up 1** WIPE UP, wash, absorb, soak up, sponge, swab, clean up, tidy up **2** FINISH OFF, deal with, wipe up, dispose of, account for, round up, neutralize, eliminate, secure, take care of

mope *v, n*
▶ *v* brood, fret, sulk, pine, languish, droop, despair, grieve
▷ **mope about** idle, wander, moon, languish; *colloq.* mooch, lounge, loll
▶ *n* melancholic, misery, depressive, pessimist, killjoy, melancholiac, moaner, introvert
colloq. grouch, grump, moper

moral *adj, n*
▶ *adj* **1** ETHICAL, virtuous, good, right, principled, honourable, decent, upright, upstanding, straight, righteous, high-minded, honest, incorruptible, proper, blameless, chaste, clean-living, pure, just, noble
2 *give moral support*
encouraging, emotional, psychological
◨ **1** immoral
▶ *n* lesson, message, significance, teaching, point, dictum, meaning, maxim, adage, precept, saying, proverb, aphorism, epigram

morale *n*
confidence, spirit(s), *esprit de corps,* self-esteem, self-confidence, state of mind, heart, mood, optimism, hopefulness

morality *n*
ethics, morals, moral values, ideals, principles, principles of behaviour, principles of right and wrong, standards, virtue, righteousness, decency, purity, chastity, goodness, honesty, integrity, justice, uprightness, conduct, manners
formal rectitude, propriety
◨ immorality

moralize *v*
preach, lecture, pontificate, edify, sermonize
formal discourse, ethicize

morals *n*
morality, moral values, moral code, ethics, principles, principles of behaviour, principles of right and wrong, standards, ideals, integrity, scruples, behaviour, conduct, habits, manners

morass *n*
1 QUAGMIRE, bog, moss, marsh, marshland, swamp, slough, mire, fen, quag, quicksand
2 CONFUSION, clutter, chaos, mess, jam, jumble, muddle, mix-up, tangle
colloq. can of worms

moratorium *n*
delay, postponement, halt, freeze, suspension, stay, standstill, stoppage, respite, ban, embargo
◨ *colloq.* go-ahead, green light

morbid *adj*
1 GHOULISH, obsessed with death, ghastly,

gruesome, grisly, macabre, hideous, horrible, horrid, dreadful, grim
2 GLOOMY, pessimistic, melancholy, dejected, morose, sombre
formal lugubrious
3 SICK, ailing, diseased, unhealthy, unwholesome
formal insalubrious

mordant *adj*
biting, acid, caustic, bitter, astringent, critical, scathing, sharp, harsh, incisive, waspish, stinging, wounding, vicious, venomous, cutting, sarcastic, pungent, edged
formal acerbic, acrimonious, trenchant
◨ gentle, mild, sparing

more *adj, adv, pron*
▶ *adj* further, extra, additional, added, new, fresh, increased, other, another, supplementary, repeated, alternative, spare
◨ less
▶ *adv* further, longer, again, besides, moreover, better
◨ less
▶ *pron* greater number/quantity, additional people/things, extra

moreover *adv*
furthermore, further, besides, in addition, as well, also, additionally, what is more

morgue *n*
mortuary, funeral parlour, deadhouse, charnel house

moribund *adj*
1 DYING, failing, fading, expiring, declining, wasting away, senile, in extremis
technical comatose
colloq. on your last legs, on the way out, with one foot in the grave, not long for this world
2 WEAK, feeble, lifeless, declining, wasting away, waning, ebbing, stagnating, stagnant, obsolescent, doomed, dwindling, collapsing, crumbling
◨ **1** alive, lively; *formal* nascent **2** flourishing

morning *n*
before noon, a.m., dawn, sunrise, daybreak, break of day, daylight
Related adjectives: matutinal, antemeridian

moron *n*
fool, blockhead, fat-head, dolt, dunce, dimwit, simpleton, halfwit, idiot, cretin, imbecile, ignoramus, dupe, stooge, butt, laughing-stock, clown, comic, buffoon, jester
colloq. nincompoop, ass, chump, ninny, clot, dope, twit, nitwit, nit, sucker, mug, twerp, birdbrain; *slang* wally, jerk, dumbo, pillock, prat, dork, geek, plonker, prick; *US* schmuck

moronic *adj*
foolish, stupid, senseless, silly, absurd, ridiculous, ludicrous, nonsensical, unwise, ill-advised, ill-considered, shortsighted, half-baked, crazy, mad, insane, idiotic, hare-brained, half-witted, simple-minded, simple, ignorant, unintelligent, inept, inane, pointless, unreasonable
colloq. daft, crack-brained, gormless, dumb, dotty, potty, batty, barmy, nutty, not in your right mind, out of your mind, with a screw missing, needing to have your head examined

morose *adj*
ill-tempered, bad-tempered, moody, sombre, sullen, sulky, surly, gloomy, grim, gruff, sour, taciturn, glum,

saturnine, depressed, mournful, melancholic, pessimistic
formal lugubrious
colloq. grouchy, crabby
E3 cheerful, communicative

morsel *n*
bit, scrap, piece, fragment, crumb, bite, mouthful, nibble, taste, soupçon, titbit, slice, segment, fraction, modicum, grain, atom, part, particle

mortal *adj, n*
▶ *adj* **1** WORLDLY, earthly, bodily, fleshly, human, perishable, transient, temporal
formal corporeal, ephemeral
2 FATAL, lethal, deadly, killing, murderous
3 EXTREME, great, severe, intense, grave, awful, dire, terrible, unbearable
4 *mortal enemies*
implacable, relentless, unrelenting, deadly, cruel, bitter, vengeful
E3 1 immortal
▶ *n* human being, human, individual, person, man, woman, being, body, creature, earthling
E3 immortal, god

mortality *n*
1 HUMANITY, death, impermanence, worldliness, earthliness, perishability, transience
formal ephemerality
2 FATALITY, death, death rate, killing, slaughter, carnage, casualty, loss of life
E3 1 immortality

mortgage *n*
loan, pledge, security, bond, debenture
Scot. wadset
formal lien

mortification *n*
1 EMBARRASSMENT, humiliation, confounding, shame, disgrace, dishonour, loss of face, abasement, annoyance, chastening, vexation
formal chagrin, discomfiture, ignominy
2 DISCIPLINE, punishment, asceticism, control, self-control, denial, self-denial, conquering
formal subjugation

mortified *adj*
humiliated, horrified, shamed, ashamed, disgraced, dishonoured, humbled, embarrassed, crushed, confounded, defeated

mortify *v*
1 HUMILIATE, horrify, shame, put to shame, embarrass, offend, disgrace, dishonour, chastise, chasten, abash, confound, humble, bring low, crush, deflate, affront, annoy, disappoint
formal discomfit, chagrin
colloq. take down a peg or two
2 DISCIPLINE, restrain, suppress, deny, die, control, conquer, subdue

mortifying *adj*
embarrassing, humbling, humiliating, salutary, shaming, ignominious, overwhelming, crushing, chastening, punishing, thwarting
formal discomfiting

mortuary *n*
morgue, funeral parlour, deadhouse, charnel house

most *n*
bulk, mass, majority, overwhelming majority, preponderance, greatest/largest part, almost all,

nearly all
colloq. lion's share

mostly *adv*
mainly, on the whole, principally, especially, chiefly, generally, in general, usually, largely, predominantly, overall, for the most part, in the main, as a rule, above all

moth *n*

Types of moth include: brown-tail, buff-tip, burnet, six-spot, carpet, cinnabar, clothes, emperor, garden tiger, gypsy, death's head hawkmoth, privet hawkmoth, Kentish glory, lackey, lappet, leopard, lobster, magpie, oak hook-tip, pale tussock, peach blossom, peppered, puss, red underwing, silkworm, silver-Y, swallowtail, turnip, wax, winter.

moth-eaten *adj*
old, worn, worn-out, old-fashioned, obsolete, outdated, outworn, ragged, tattered, threadbare, dated, ancient, antiquated, archaic, decrepit, dilapidated, decayed, musty, shabby, stale, mouldy, mangy, moribund, seedy
E3 fresh, new

mother *n, v*
▶ *n* **1** PARENT, dam, matriarch, ancestor, matron
formal procreator, progenitress, materfamilias, mater
colloq. mum, mummy, ma, mam, mumsy, mamma, old woman; *US* mom, mommy
Related adjective: maternal
2 ORIGIN, source, spring, fount, foundation, base, cause, derivation, roots, wellspring
▶ *v* **1** BEAR, produce, bring forth, nurture, raise, rear, tend, nurse, care for, take care of, look after, cherish
2 PAMPER, spoil, baby, indulge, overprotect, fuss over

motherly *adj*
maternal, caring, comforting, affectionate, kind, loving, protective, warm, tender, gentle, fond
E3 neglectful, uncaring

motif *n*
theme, idea, topic, concept, pattern, design, figure, form, logo, shape, device, emblem, ornament, decoration

motion *n, v*
▶ *n* **1** MOVEMENT, action, mobility, moving, activity, locomotion, travelling, travel, transit, going, changing place(s), passage, passing, progress, change, flow, inclination
formal motility
Related adjective: kinetic
2 GESTURE, gesticulation, movement, act, action, indication, signal, sign, wave, nod
3 PROPOSAL, suggestion, recommendation, proposition, plan, scheme, project, manifesto, presentation, bid, offer
▷ **in motion** under way, moving, on the move, going, on the go, travelling, in progress, functioning, running, operational
E3 stationary, at rest
▶ *v* signal, gesture, gesticulate, sign, wave, nod, beckon, direct, usher

motionless *adj*
unmoving, still, stationary, static, immobile, unmovable, at a standstill, stock-still, fixed, halted, at rest, resting, standing, paralysed, inanimate, inert,

lifeless, frozen, transfixed, rigid, stagnant
F3 active, moving

motivate v
prompt, incite, impel, spur, provoke, stimulate, drive, lead, stir, urge, goad, push, propel, persuade, move, inspire, encourage, cause, trigger, actuate, activate, induce, kindle, draw, excite, arouse, bring, initiate
F3 deter, discourage, prevent, inhibit

motivation n
reason, incitement, inducement, prompting, spur, stimulus, provocation, drive, push, hunger, desire, wish, urge, impulse, incentive, ambition, inspiration, instigation, momentum, motive, persuasion, interest
F3 discouragement, prevention

motive n
ground(s), cause, reason, basis, purpose, motivation, occasion, object, intention, influence, rationale, thinking, incentive, impulse, stimulus, inspiration, incitement, inducement, urge, goad, spur, encouragement, inspiration, design, desire, attraction, lure, consideration, persuasion
F3 deterrent, disincentive

motley adj
1 ASSORTED, varied, mixed, miscellaneous, diverse, diversified, multifarious
formal heterogeneous
2 MULTICOLOURED, variegated, particoloured, colourful, many-hued, pied, piebald, tabby, dappled, brindled, mottled, spotted, striped, streaked
F3 1 uniform, homogeneous 2 monochrome

motor vehicle See car.

Parts of a motor vehicle include: ABS (anti-lock braking system), accelerator, airbag, air brake, air-conditioner, air inlet, antidazzle mirror, antiglare switch, anti-roll bar, antitheft device, ashtray, axle, *US* backup light, battery, bench seat, bezel, bodywork, bonnet, boot, brake drum, brake light, brake pad, brake shoe, bumper, car radio, car phone, catalytic converter, central locking, centre console, chassis, child-safety seat, cigarette-lighter, clock, clutch, courtesy light, crankcase, cruise control, dashboard, differential gear, dimmer, disc brake, door, door-lock, drive shaft, drum brake, electric window, emergency light, engine, exhaust pipe, *US* fender, filler cap, flasher switch, fog lamp, folding seat, four-wheel drive, fuel gauge, *US* gas tank, gear, gearbox, gear-lever (or gear-stick), glove compartment, grill, handbrake, hazard warning light, headlight, headrest, heated rear window, heater, *US* hood, horn, hub-cap, hydraulic brake, hydraulic suspension, ignition, ignition key, indicator, instrument panel, jack, jump lead, kingpin, *US* license plate, *US* lift gate, monocoque, number plate, oil gauge, overrider, parcel shelf, parking-light, petrol tank, pneumatic tyre, power brake, prop shaft, quarterlight, rack and pinion, radial-ply tyre, rear light, rear-view mirror, reclining seat, reflector, *colloq.* rev counter, reversing light, roof rack, screen-washer bottle, seat belt, shaft, shock absorber, sidelight, side-impact bar, side mirror, silencer, sill, solenoid, spare tyre, speedometer, spoiler, steering-column, steering-wheel, *US* stick shift, stoplight, sunroof, sun visor, suspension, temperature gauge, towbar, track rod, transmission, *US* trunk, tyre, vent, wheel, wheel arch, windscreen, windscreen-washer, windscreen-wiper, *US* windshield, wing, wing mirror. *See also* **engine**.

mottled adj
speckled, dappled, blotchy, blotched, flecked, piebald, stippled, streaked, marbled, splotchy, tabby, spotted, freckled, brinded, brindled, brindle, variegated
technical poikilitic
F3 monochrome, uniform

motto n
saying, slogan, maxim, watchword, cry, catchword, byword, precept, proverb, aphorism, saw, axiom, adage, formula, rule, golden rule, dictum, truism
formal epigram, gnome

mould¹ n, v
▶ *n* 1 CAST, form, shape, die, template, pattern, matrix, frame, framework, blister pack
2 SHAPE, form, format, pattern, structure, style, type, build, construction, formation, cast, cut, figure, design, kind, model, sort, stamp, arrangement, brand, frame, character, nature, quality, calibre, line, outline, make
formal configuration
▶ *v* 1 FORGE, cast, shape, stamp, make, form, fashion, create, design, construct, sculpt, carve, model, work, frame
2 INFLUENCE, affect, form, shape, direct, control

mould² n
a smell of mould
mildew, must, fungus, mouldiness, mustiness, blight, rot

moulder v
decay, decompose, perish, rot, waste, corrupt, crumble, disintegrate, turn to dust, humify

mouldy adj
mildewed, blighted, musty, decaying, corrupt, rotten, fusty, putrid, bad, spoiled, stale
F3 fresh, wholesome

mound n
1 HILL, hillock, hummock, rise, knoll, bank, dune, elevation, ridge, embankment, earthwork, tump, tumulus, barrow
2 HEAP, pile, stack, accumulation, collection, supply, store, hoard, abundance, mountain, lot, stack, bundle, stockpile

mount v, n
▶ *v* 1 PRODUCE, put on, set up, prepare, stage, exhibit, display, launch, arrange, organize, install
2 INCREASE, grow, build (up), accumulate, pile up, multiply, rise, intensify, escalate, soar, swell, accrue
3 CLIMB (UP), ascend, get up, go up, get on, clamber up, scale, climb on (to), jump on(to), get astride
F3 2 decrease, descend 3 descend, dismount, go down
▶ *n* 1 HORSE, steed
2 SUPPORT, mounting, backing, base, fixture, stand, frame

mountain n
1 HEIGHT, elevation, mount, peak, pinnacle, hill, fell, mound, alp, tor, massif
2 HEAP, pile, mound, stack, mass, abundance, accumulation, lot, stack, backlog

The highest mountains of the world include: Asia: Everest (Himalaya-Nepal/Tibet), K2 (Pakistan/India), Kangchenjunga (Himalaya-Nepal/India), Makalu (Himalaya-Nepal/Tibet), Dhaulagiri (Himalaya-Nepal), Nanga Parbat (Himalaya-India), Annapurna (Himalaya-Nepal); South America: Aconcagua (Andes-Argentina); North

America: McKinley (Alaska Range); Africa: Kilimanjaro (Tanzania); Europe: Elbruz (Caucasus), Mount Blanc (Alps-France); Antarctica: Vinson Massif; Australasia: Jaja (New Guinea).

mountainous *adj*
1 CRAGGY, rocky, hilly, high, highland, upland, alpine, soaring, lofty, towering, steep
2 HUGE, towering, enormous, immense, vast, colossal, massive, gigantic
🖃 1 flat 2 tiny

mountebank *n*
charlatan, swindler, cheat, fake, fraud, impostor, pretender, rogue, trickster
colloq. con man, phoney, pseud, quack

mourn *v*
grieve, lament, sorrow, bemoan, bewail, miss, regret, deplore, weep, wail, keen
🖃 rejoice

mourner *n*
griever, bereaved, sorrower, mute, keener

mournful *adj*
sorrowful, sad, unhappy, desolate, doleful, grief-stricken, heavy-hearted, heartbroken, broken-hearted, cast-down, downcast, miserable, tragic, melancholy, funereal, sombre, depressed, dejected, gloomy, dismal
formal woeful, lugubrious, disconsolate, elegiac
🖃 happy, joyful, cheerful

mourning *n*
grief, grieving, bereavement, lamentation, sadness, sorrow, sorrowing, desolation, weeping, wailing, keening
🖃 rejoicing

moustache *n*
whiskers, mustachio, handlebar moustache, toothbrush moustache, walrus
colloq. face fungus

mousy *adj*
1 BROWNISH, greyish, colourless, drab, dull, plain, uninteresting, diffident
2 SHY, quiet, timid, withdrawn, unassertive, unforthcoming, self-effacing
formal timorous
🖃 2 assertive, bright, extrovert, irrepressible

mouth *n, v*
▶ *n* 1 LIPS, jaws, embouchure
colloq. chops, kisser; *slang* trap, gob, traphole, cakehole
Related adjectives: oral, stomatic

Parts of the mouth and types of teeth include: cleft palate, gum, hard palate, hare lip, inferior dental arch, isthmus of fauces, labial commissure, lower lip, palatoglossal arch, palato-pharyngeal arch, soft palate, superior dental arch, tongue, tonsil, upper lip, uvula. *See also* **tooth**.

2 OPENING, aperture, cavity, vent, entrance, door, doorway, gateway, hatch, portal, inlet, estuary, outlet, delta
technical stoma
formal orifice
3 BOASTING, bragging, bragging, blustering, babble, empty/idle talk
colloq. hot air, gas
4 CHEEK, impudence, impertinence, insolence, disrespect, rudeness, backchat

formal effrontery
colloq. nerve, sauce, gall, lip, brass neck
▶ *v* enunciate, articulate, utter, say, pronounce, whisper, form

mouthful *n*
sample, morsel, spoonful, swallow, taste, bite, nibble, bit, gulp, sip, titbit, drop, forkful, slug, sup, bonne-bouche

mouthpiece *n*
spokesperson, spokesman, spokeswoman, representative, agent, delegate, propagandist, journal, periodical, publication, organ

movable *adj*
mobile, portable, transportable, changeable, alterable, adjustable, flexible, transferable
formal portative
🖃 fixed, immovable

movables *n*
belongings, possessions, goods, furniture, property
formal chattels, effects, impedimenta, plenishings
colloq. gear, stuff, things

move *v, n*
▶ *v* 1 GO, advance, travel, walk, shift, stir, change, pass, act, take action, proceed, progress, make strides
colloq. budge
2 TRANSPORT, carry, bring, take, fetch, relocate, transfer, shift, switch, shunt, swing
formal transpose
3 DEPART, go away, leave, transfer, decamp, migrate, remove, move house, move away, relocate
4 PROMPT, stimulate, incline, urge, impel, drive, cause, lead, propel, actuate, motivate, incite, excite, rouse, arouse, push, persuade, induce, inspire, influence, provoke
5 AFFECT, touch, agitate, stir, impress, excite, disturb, upset, agitate
6 PROPOSE, put forward, request, suggest, advocate, recommend
▶ *n* 1 MOVEMENT, motion, manoeuvre, gesture, gesticulation, activity
2 REMOVAL, relocation, migration, transfer, repositioning, change of address
3 MEASURE, step out, act, manoeuvre, action, activity, action, device, stratagem, tack
▷ **get a move on** hurry up, speed up, make haste; *colloq.* get cracking, shake a leg, put your food down
▷ **on the move** moving, travelling, journeying, progressing, advancing, moving forward, active, on the go, astir, under way

movement *n*
1 REPOSITIONING, move, moving, gesture, gesticulation, relocation, activity, act, action, agitation, stirring, shifting, transfer, transportation, passage
2 CHANGE, development, variation, advance, improvement, breakthrough, evolution, passage, current, drift, flow, current, fall, rise, swing, shift, progress, progression, trend, tendency
3 CAMPAIGN, crusade, drive, group, organization, party, coalition, faction, wing
4 MECHANISM, works, workings, system, action
colloq. guts
5 *a movement in a symphony*
section, part, division, piece, bit, portion, passage

movie *n*
film, motion picture, picture, feature film, video, silent, talkie, flick

moving *adj*

1 MOBILE, active, dynamic, in motion, astir, manoeuvrable
technical kinetic
formal motile
2 TOUCHING, affecting, poignant, impressive, emotive, arousing, stirring, emotional, inspiring, inspirational, exciting, thrilling, persuasive, stimulating, disturbing, upsetting, worrying, pathetic
3 *the moving force/spirit*
driving, motivating, leading, influential, dynamic, stimulating, inspiring, urging
E3 1 immobile, fixed **2** unemotional

mow *v*
cut, trim, crop, clip, shear, scythe
▷ **mow down** butcher, slaughter, massacre, shoot down, decimate, cut down, cut to pieces

much *adv, adj, n*
▶ *adv* greatly, to a great extent, a great deal, considerably, a lot, frequently, often
▶ *adj* copious, plentiful, ample, considerable, a lot, abundant, great, substantial, a great number of, extensive, widespread
colloq. lots
▶ *n* plenty, a great deal, a lot
colloq. lots, loads, heaps, lashings
E3 little

muck *n*
1 DIRT, mire, filth, mud, slime, grime, scum, sludge
colloq. gunge, yuck; *slang* grunge, crud
2 EXCREMENT, dung, manure, ordure, sewage
technical guano
formal faeces
▷ **muck about/around 1** FOOL AROUND, play around, play about; *colloq.* mess about/around, lark about/around **2** INCONVENIENCE, upset, bother, trouble; *colloq.* lead a merry dance, lead up the garden path, send on a wild goose chase, make life hell for **3** INTERFERE, tamper, meddle, untidy, disorder, disarrange, dishevel, mess up
▷ **muck up** ruin, wreck, spoil, mess up, make a mess of, botch, bungle; *slang* cock up, screw up, louse up

mucky *adj*
begrimed, bespattered, dirty, filthy, grimy, messy, miry, mud-caked, muddy, oozy, slimy, soiled, sticky
E3 clean

mucous *adj*
gelatinous, glutinous, gummy, viscous, viscid, slimy, snotty
formal mucilaginous

mud *n*
clay, mire, ooze, dirt, soil, sludge, silt

muddle *n, v*
▶ *n* chaos, confusion, disorganization, disorder, disarray, mess, mix-up, jumble, clutter, tangle
▶ *v* **1** DISORGANIZE, disorder, throw into disorder, mix up, mess up, jumble (up), scramble, tangle
2 CONFUSE, bewilder, bemuse, perplex, daze, puzzle, confound, befuddle
▷ **muddle through** get by, get along, cope, make

muddled *adj*
confused, chaotic, disorganized, disordered, jumbled, mixed-up, tangled, scrambled, disarrayed, messy, loose, higgledy-piggledy, disorient(at)ed, bewildered, perplexed, unclear, vague, woolly, befuddled,

stupefied, dazed, incoherent
colloq. at sea

muddy *adj, v*
▶ *adj* **1** DIRTY, filthy, foul, miry, mucky, grimy, grubby, slimy, slushy, oozy, marshy, boggy, swampy, quaggy, grimy
2 CLOUDY, indistinct, obscure, opaque, murky, turbid, hazy, smoky, blurred, fuzzy, dull, dingy
E3 1 clean **2** clear
▶ *v* **1** DIRTY, soil, smear, smirch, cloud, begrime, bespatter, bedash, bedaub
2 CONFUSE, cloud, make unclear, mix up, jumble (up), disorganize, scramble, tangle
E3 1 clean **2** clarify

muff *v*
botch, bungle, mess up, mismanage, miss, spoil, mishit
colloq. fluff

muffle *v*
1 WRAP, wrap up, envelop, cloak, swathe, swaddle, cover (up)
2 DEADEN, dull, quieten, soften, mute, hush, silence, stifle, dampen, muzzle, suppress, smother, gag
E3 2 amplify

mug[1] *n*
drink coffee from a mug
cup, beaker, pot, tankard

mug[2] *v*
mugged on his way home
set upon, attack, assault, waylay, steal from, rob, beat up, bash, jump (on), knock about
colloq. do over, rough up, batter, knock someone's block off, knock into the middle of next week

mug[3] *n*
like a mug, I agreed
fool, simpleton, gull
colloq. sucker, chump, muggins, soft touch

mug[4] *n*
his ugly mug
face, features
formal countenance, visage
colloq. kisser, mush, clock, phiz
▷ **mug up** bone up, con, cram, get up, study, swot

muggy *adj*
humid, sticky, stuffy, sultry, close, clammy, oppressive, airless, sweltering, moist, damp
E3 dry

mulish *adj*
obstinate, stubborn, defiant, difficult, headstrong, inflexible, self-willed, stiff-necked, unreasonable, wilful, perverse, rigid, wrong-headed
formal intractable, intransigent, recalcitrant, refractory
colloq. pig-headed

mull *v*
▷ **mull over** reflect on, ponder, contemplate, think over, think about, consider, weigh up, muse on, chew over, meditate, study, examine, deliberate; *formal* ruminate

multicoloured *adj*
variegated, particoloured, colourful, motley, pied, piebald, dappled, brindled, spotted, striped

multifarious *adj*
diverse, diversified, different, miscellaneous, varied, sundry, variegated, numerous, many, multiple,

multitudinous, legion
formal manifold, multiform

multiple *adj*
many, numerous, various, several, sundry, collective
formal manifold

multiplicity *n*
abundance, array, number, numerousness, profusion,
variety, diversity, mass, host, lot, myriad
formal manifoldness
colloq. heaps, loads, lots, oodles, piles, scores, stacks,
tons

multiply *v*
increase, proliferate, expand, grow, spread, reproduce,
propagate, breed, accumulate, intensify, extend, build
up, boost
formal augment
F3 decrease, lessen

multitude *n*
1 CROWD, throng, horde, swarm, mob, mass, herd,
congregation, assembly, host, lot, legion
colloq. lots
2 PUBLIC, people, populace, crowd, mob, common
people, rabble, hoi polloi, herd, common herd
colloq. plebs, riff-raff
F3 1 few, scattering

multitudinous *adj*
numerous, many, profuse, swarming, copious,
considerable, abundant, abounding, teeming,
innumerable, countless, great, infinite, legion, myriad
formal manifold
colloq. umpteen

mum *adj*
quiet, mute, dumb, silent, reticent, secretive, tight-
lipped, close-lipped, close-mouthed,
uncommunicative, unforthcoming

mumble *v*
murmur, rumble, talk to yourself, talk under your
breath, stutter, splutter, speak unclearly, speak softly,
speak in a low voice, slur

mumbo-jumbo *n*
nonsense, claptrap, gibberish, incantation, jargon,
magic, superstition, spell, chant, cant, charm, ritual,
rite, mummery, rigmarole, abracadabra
formal conjuration
colloq. double talk, gobbledygook, hocus-pocus,
humbug

munch *v*
eat, chew, crunch, champ, chomp
formal masticate

mundane *adj*
1 ORDINARY, banal, hackneyed, boring, stale, trite,
everyday, common, commonplace, usual, normal,
typical, regular, customary, prosaic, humdrum,
workaday, routine
2 WORLDLY, secular, earthly, terrestrial, fleshly,
temporal
F3 1 extraordinary 2 spiritual

municipal *adj*
civic, city, civil, town, metropolitan, urban, borough,
community, public

municipality *n*
city, town, township, borough, department, district,
precinct, council, local government, burgh,
département

munificence *n*
generosity, generousness, liberality,
magnanimousness, open-handedness, bounty,
benevolence, philanthropy, charitableness, altruism,
hospitality
formal largesse, beneficence, bounteousness
F3 meanness

munificent *adj*
generous, open-handed, big-hearted, bountiful, free-
handed, magnanimous, lavish, liberal, hospitable,
benevolent, philanthropical, charitable, altruistic,
rich, unstinting, princely
formal beneficent, bounteous
F3 mean

murder *n, v*
▶ *n* 1 KILLING, homicide, manslaughter, slaying,
slaughter, assassination, execution, massacre,
butchery, bloodshed, foul play
formal patricide, matricide, infanticide, fratricide,
sororicide, uxoricide
colloq. liquidation
2 *driving in town is murder*
hell, torment, torture, agony, ordeal, nightmare,
misery, wretchedness, suffering, anguish
▶ *v* 1 KILL, slaughter, slay, put to death, assassinate,
butcher, massacre
colloq. do in, bump off, eliminate, liquidate, knock off,
rub out, wipe out, take out, waste, blow away
2 RUIN, spoil, destroy, botch, mess up, wreck,
make a mess of
3 DEFEAT EASILY, beat, overwhelm, rout,
annihilate, outplay, outwit, outsmart, trounce
colloq. slaughter, hammer, clobber, lick, thrash,
wipe the floor with

murderer *n*
killer, homicide, slayer, slaughterer, assassin, butcher,
cut-throat

murderous *adj*
1 HOMICIDAL, brutal, barbarous, bloodthirsty,
bloody, cut-throat, killing, lethal, fatal, mortal, cruel,
savage, ferocious, deadly
2 DIFFICULT, exhausting, strenuous, arduous,
punishing, difficult, unpleasant, dangerous
colloq. killing

murky *adj*
1 DARK, dismal, gloomy, dreary, cheerless, dull,
overcast, misty, foggy, dim, cloudy, obscure, veiled,
grey
2 *murky water*
dirty, dark, dingy, cloudy, turbid
3 MYSTERIOUS, shady, dark, secret, suspicious,
questionable
F3 1 bright, clear, fine 2 clear

murmur *n, v*
▶ *n* 1 MUMBLE, muttering, whisper, undertone,
humming, rumble, drone, grumble
2 GRUMBLE, complaint, moan, grievance, protest,
objection, dissatisfaction, annoyance, fault-finding,
criticism, carping, censure
colloq. grouse, gripe, beefing, belly-aching, whingeing
▶ *v* 1 MUTTER, mumble, whisper, intone, buzz,
drone, hum, rustle, rumble, purr, purl, burble, babble
2 COMPLAIN, criticize, find fault, object, protest,
grumble, carp, fuss, whine
colloq. beef, belly-ache, grouse, gripe, whinge

murmuring *adj, n*
▶ *adj* mumbling, murmurous, muttering, rumbling,

whispering, buzzing, droning, purring
▶ *n* drone, mumble, mumbling, muttering,
rumble, rumbling, whisper(ing), buzz(ing),
purr(ing)
formal murmuration, susurrus

muscle *n, v*
▶ *n* **1** *strong muscles*
sinew, tendon, ligament
Related adjective: muscular

Muscles include: abdominal, biceps, deltoid,
gastrocnemius, gluteus, pectoralis major, pectoralis
minor, peroneal muscles, psoas, quadriceps, rectus,
rhomboideus, sartorius, scalenus, soleus, splenius,
trapezius, triceps.

2 FORCE, brawn, beef, power, forcefulness, strength,
stamina, potency, sturdiness, weight
colloq. clout
formal might
▶ *v* ▷ **muscle in** butt in, push in, shove, strongarm,
impose yourself, force your way in, elbow your way in,
jostle

muscular *adj*
brawny, sinewy, fibrous, athletic, powerfully built,
strapping, hefty, burly, powerful, husky, robust,
stalwart, rugged, sturdy, vigorous, strong, potent
colloq. beefy
◨ puny, flabby, weak

muse *v*
ponder, think, think over, meditate, mull over, weigh,
contemplate, consider, brood, reflect, review, chew,
dream, deliberate, speculate
formal cogitate, ruminate

mush *n*
1 PASTE, pulp, pap, dough, corn, slush, swill, mash,
cream, purée
2 SENTIMENTALITY, mawkishness
colloq. schmaltz

mushroom *v*
proliferate, shoot up, grow, increase, expand, flourish,
boom, spread, spring up, sprout, luxuriate
formal burgeon

mushrooms and toadstools

Types of mushroom and toadstool include: *edible*:
beefsteak fungus, blewits, boletus, chestnut boletus,
button mushroom, cep, champignon, chanterelle,
clouded agaric, common morel, cultivated
mushroom, dingy agaric, fairy ring, the goat's lip,
gypsy mushroom, honey fungus, horn of plenty,
horse mushroom, lawyer's wig, man on horseback,
march mushroom, oyster mushroom, parasol
mushroom, penny bun, saffron milk cap, shaggy
parasol, slippery jack, sweetbread mushroom,
truffle, trumpet agaric, velvet shank, winter
mushroom, wood hedgehog; *inedible/poisonous*:
amanita, common ink cap, copper trumpet, death
cap, destroying angel, devil's boletus, earth ball,
false morel, fly agaric, mower's mushroom, panther
cap, purple boletus, satan's mushroom, shaggy milk
cap, stinking parasol, sulphur tuft, verdigris agaric,
woolly milk cap, yellow-staining mushroom.

mushy *adj*
1 PULPY, pappy, pulpous, squashy, squelchy, squidgy,
soft, doughy, wet
2 SENTIMENTAL, sloppy, slushy, maudlin, mawkish,
saccharine, sugary, syrupy, weepy
colloq. schmaltzy

music *n*

Types of music include: acid house, ballet, ballroom,
bluegrass, blues, boogie-woogie, chamber, choral,
classical, country-and-western, dance, disco,
Dixieland, doo-wop, electronic, folk, folk rock,
colloq. funk, garage, gospel, grunge, hard rock,
heavy metal, hip-hop, honky-tonk, house,
incidental, instrumental, jazz, jazz-funk, jazz-pop,
jazz-rock, jive, karaoke, operatic, orchestral, pop,
punk rock, ragtime, rap, reggae, rhythm and blues
(R & B), rock and roll, rock, sacred, ska, skiffle, soft
rock, soul, swing, *slang* thrash metal. *See also* **jazz**.

musical *adj*
tuneful, melodious, melodic, harmonious, mellow,
dulcet, sweet-sounding, lyrical
formal euphonious, mellifluous
◨ discordant, unmusical

musical composition

Musical compositions include: arabesque, aubade,
bagatelle, bourrée, canon, capriccio, cavatina,
chaconne, concerto, concerto grosso, divertimento,
étude, extravaganza, fanfare, fantasia, fugue,
gavotte, humoresque, impromptu, intermezzo,
march, minuet, nocturne, opus, overture, partita,
pastorale, polonaise, prelude, requiem, rhapsody,
rondo, round, scherzo, serenade, sinfonietta,
sonata, sonatina, suite, symphony, toccata,
voluntary. *See also* **song**.

musical instruments

Musical instruments include: balalaika, banjo, cello,
double-bass, guitar, harp, hurdy-gurdy, lute, lyre,
mandolin, sitar, spinet, ukulele, viola, violin,
colloq. fiddle, zither; accordion, concertina,
colloq. squeeze-box, clavichord, harmonium,
harpsichord, keyboard, melodeon, organ,
Wurlitzer®, piano, grand piano, Pianola®, player-
piano, synthesizer, virginals; bagpipes, bassoon,
bugle, clarinet, cor anglais, cornet, didgeridoo,
euphonium, fife, flugelhorn, flute, French horn,
harmonica, horn, kazoo, mouth-organ, oboe, Pan-
pipes, piccolo, recorder, saxophone, sousaphone,
trombone, trumpet, tuba; castanets, cymbal,
glockenspiel, maracas, marimba, tambourine,
triangle, tubular bells, xylophone; bass-drum,
bongo, kettle-drum, snare-drum, tenor-drum,
timpani, tom-tom.

musical terms

Musical terms include: accelerando, acciaccatura,
accidental, accompaniment, acoustic, adagio, ad
lib, a due, affettuoso, agitato, al fine, al segno, alla
breve, alla cappella, allargando, allegretto, allegro,
al segno, alto, amoroso, andante, animato,
appoggiatura, arco, arpeggio, arrangement, a
tempo, attacca, bar, bar line, double bar line,
baritone, bass, beat, bis, breve, buffo, cadence,
cantabile, cantilena, chord, chromatic, clef, alto clef,
bass clef, tenor clef, treble clef, coda, col canto, con
brio, concert, con fuoco, con moto, consonance,
contralto, counterpoint, crescendo, crotchet, cross-
fingering, cue, da capo, decrescendo,
demisemiquaver, descant, diatonic, diminuendo,
dissonance, dolce, doloroso, dominant, dotted note,
dotted rest, downbeat, drone, duplet, triplet,
quadruplet, quintuplet, sextuplet, encore, ensemble,
expression, finale, fine, fingerboard, flat, double
flat, forte, fortissimo, fret, glissando, grave,
harmonics, harmony, hemidemisemiquaver, hold,
imitation, improvisation, interval, augmented

interval, diminished interval, second interval, third interval, fourth interval, fifth interval, sixth interval, seventh interval, major interval, minor interval, perfect interval, intonation, key, key signature, langsam, larghetto, largo, leading note, ledger line, legato, lento, lyric, maestoso, major, manual, marcato, mediant, medley, melody, metre, mezza voce, mezzo forte, microtone, middle C, minim, minor, moderato, mode, modulation, molto, mordent, movement, mute, natural, non troppo, note, obbligato, octave, orchestra, orchestration, ostinato, part, pause, pedal point, pentatonic, perdendo, phrase, pianissimo, piano, piece, pitch, pizzicato, presto, quarter tone, quaver, rallentando, recital, refrain, resolution, rest, rhythm, rinforzando, ritenuto, root, scale, score, semibreve, semiquaver, semitone, semplice, sempre, senza, sequence, shake, sharp, double sharp, slur, smorzando, solo, soprano, sostenuto, sotto voce, spiritoso, staccato, staff, stave, subdominant, subito, submediant, sul ponticello, supertonic, swell, syncopation, tablature, tacet, tanto, tempo, tenor, tenuto, theme, tie, timbre, time signature, compound time, simple time, two-two time, three-four time, four-four time, six-eight time, tone, tonic sol-fa, transposition, treble, tremolo, triad, trill, double trill, tune, tuning, turn, tutti, upbeat, unison, vibrato, vigoroso, virtuoso, vivace.

musician *n*

Musicians include: instrumentalist, accompanist, performer, player, composer, bard, virtuoso; bugler, busker, cellist, clarinettist, drummer, flautist, fiddler, guitarist, harpist, oboist, organist, pianist, piper, soloist, trombonist, trumpeter, violinist; singer, vocalist, balladeer, diva, prima donna; conductor, maestro; band, orchestra, group, backing group, ensemble, chamber orchestra, choir, duo, duet, trio, quartet, quintet, sextet, octet, nonet.

musing *n*
thinking, meditation, introspection, dreaming, daydreaming, wool-gathering, abstraction, absent-mindedness, contemplation, reflection, reverie, brown study
formal cerebration, cogitation, ponderment, rumination

muss *v*
ruffle, make untidy, dishevel, tousle, disarrange, make a mess of

must *n*
necessity, prerequisite, obligation, requirement, stipulation, essential, fundamental, imperative, duty, basic, provision, sine qua non
formal requisite

muster *v, n*
▶ *v* assemble, convene, gather (together), call together, mobilize, round up, marshal, bring/come together, congregate, collect, group, meet, rally, mass, throng, call up, summon (up), enrol
formal convoke
▶ *n* gathering, assembly, collection, congregation, convention, mass, mobilization, rally, round-up, meeting, parade, review, march past, throng, concourse
formal assemblage, convocation
▷ **pass muster** be acceptable, be accepted, come up to standard, measure up, fit/fill the bill, make the grade; *colloq.* come up to scratch, shape up

musty *adj*
mouldy, mildewy, mildewed, stale, stuffy, fusty, damp, dank, airless, decayed, decaying, smelly

mutability *n*
changeableness, interchangeability, alterability, variability, permutability, variation

mutable *adj*
changing, interchangeable, changeable, adaptable, alterable, vacillating, variable, volatile, wavering, inconsistent, uncertain, undependable, unreliable, unsettled, inconstant, fickle, flexible, irresolute, unstable, unsteady, permutable
F3 constant, invariable, permanent

mutation *n*
change, alteration, variation, modification, adaptation, transformation, deviation, anomaly, evolution
formal metamorphosis
colloq. transmogrification

mute *adj, v*
▶ *adj* silent, dumb, voiceless, uncommunicative, taciturn, wordless, speechless, unspoken, noiseless, unexpressed, unpronounced
technical aphasic
colloq. mum
F3 vocal, talkative
▶ *v* tone down, subdue, muffle, lower, moderate, dampen, deaden, dull, smother, quieten, stifle, suppress, soften, silence
colloq. soft-pedal
F3 intensify

muted *adj*
quiet, soft, softened, low-key, subtle, discreet, subdued, restrained, faint, dull, muffled, suppressed, dampened, stifled

mutilate *v*
1 MAIM, injure, dismember, disable, disfigure, lame, cripple, mangle, lacerate, cut to pieces, cut up, butcher, hack (up)
2 SPOIL, mar, damage, impair, ruin, distort, mangle, cut, censor
formal bowdlerize
colloq. hack, butcher

mutilation *n*
amputation, maiming, disfigurement, dismembering, damage
formal detruncation

mutinous *adj*
rebellious, insurgent, insubordinate, disobedient, disorderly, uncontrollable, ungovernable, seditious, revolutionary, riotous, anarchistic, subversive, unruly
formal refractory, contumacious
colloq. bolshie
F3 obedient, compliant

mutiny *n, v*
▶ *n* rebellion, insurrection, revolt, revolution, rising, uprising, insurgence, insubordination, disobedience, defiance, resistance, riot, strike, protest
▶ *v* rebel, revolt, rise up, resist, protest, disobey, defy, strike

mutt *n*
1 MONGREL, dog, cur, hound, bitch
colloq. pooch
2 FOOL, idiot, imbecile, ignoramus, moron, dolt
colloq. dunderhead, thickhead

mutter *v*
1 MUMBLE, murmur, talk to yourself, talk under your breath, stutter, splutter, rumble
2 COMPLAIN, grumble, criticize, find fault, object, protest, carp, fuss, whine
colloq. grouse, beef, belly-ache, gripe, whinge

mutual *adj*
reciprocal, shared, common, joint, collective, interchangeable, interchanged, exchanged, complementary

muzzle *v*
restrain, inhibit, check, stifle, suppress, gag, fetter, mute, silence, censor, choke

muzzy *adj*
1 GROGGY, tipsy, confused, dazed, befuddled, addled, muddled, bewildered
2 FUZZY, blurred, unfocused, unclear, indistinct, faint, hazy
E3 2 clear

myopic *adj*
1 *myopic vision*
short-sighted, near-sighted, purblind, half-blind
2 *myopic attitudes*
short-sighted, unwise, ill-considered, thoughtless, narrow, narrow-minded, localized, parochial, short-term
formal imprudent, uncircumspect
E3 2 far-sighted

myriad *adj, n*
▶ *adj* countless, innumerable, limitless, immeasurable, incalculable, untold, boundless
formal multitudinous
▶ *n* multitude, throng, horde, army, flood, host, swarm, sea
colloq. scores, thousands, millions, zillions, mountain

mysterious *adj*
1 ENIGMATIC, cryptic, mystifying, inexplicable, incomprehensible, puzzling, perplexing, obscure, strange, unfathomable, unsearchable, inscrutable, mystical, baffling, curious, hidden, insoluble
formal abstruse, arcane, recondite
2 SECRET, as if by magic, weird, secretive, veiled, dark, furtive, obscure, strange, mystical, baffling, curious, hidden, surreptitious, reticent
E3 1 straightforward, comprehensible

mystery *n*
1 ENIGMA, puzzle, secret, riddle, problem, conundrum, question, question mark
2 OBSCURITY, mystique, secrecy, ambiguity, curiosity, strangeness, weirdness, incomprehensibility, inexplicability, inscrutability, unfathomability, furtiveness, surreptitiousness, reticence

mystical *adj*
occult, arcane, mystic, esoteric, spiritual, supernatural, paranormal, other-worldly, transcendental, metaphysical, hidden, mysterious, obscure, incomprehensible, inexplicable, unfathomable, strange, weird, baffling
formal preternatural, abstruse, arcane, recondite
E3 rational, logical

mystify *v*
puzzle, bewilder, baffle, perplex, confound, confuse
colloq. bamboozle

mystique *n*
mystery, secrecy, fascination, glamour, magic, spell, charm, appeal, charisma, awe

myth *n*
1 LEGEND, fable, fairy tale, fairy story, allegory, parable, saga, story, tale, folk tale, bestiary
2 FICTION, fancy, fallacy, delusion, fantasy, invention, fabrication, lie, untruth, pretence
colloq. fib, tall story

mythical *adj*
1 MYTHOLOGICAL, legendary, fabled, fairytale, fictitious
formal chimerical, fabulous, fantastic
2 FICTITIOUS, imaginary, made-up, invented, non-existent, unreal, untrue, fantasy, fabricated, pretended, fanciful
colloq. make-believe, pretend, put-on, phoney
E3 1 historical **2** actual, real, true

mythological *adj*
legendary, mythical, traditional, mythic, fabled, fairytale, fictitious
formal fabulous, folkloric

Mythological creatures and spirits include: abominable snowman (or yeti), afrit, basilisk, bunyip, Cecrops, centaur, Cerberus, Chimera, cockatrice, Cyclops, dragon, dryad, Echidna, elf, Erinyes (or Furies), Fafnir, fairy, faun, Frankenstein's monster, genie, Geryon, Gigantes, gnome, goblin, golem, Gorgon, griffin, Harpies, hippocampus, hippogriff, hobgoblin, imp, kelpie, kraken, lamia, leprechaun, Lilith, lindworm, Loch Ness monster, Medusa, mermaid, merman, Minotaur, naiad, nereid, nymph, ogre, ogress, orc, oread, Pegasus, phoenix, pixie, roc, salamander, sasquatch, satyr, sea serpent, Siren, Sphinx, sylph, troll, Typhoeus, unicorn, werewolf, windigo, wivern.

mythology *n*
legend, myths, lore, tradition(s), stories, folklore, folk tales, tales

N

nab *v*
catch, arrest, capture, grab, seize, snatch
formal apprehend
colloq. collar, nail, nick, nobble

nabob *n*
celebrity, magnate, personage, tycoon, VIP,
millionaire, multimillionaire, billionaire, financier
formal luminary
colloq. bigwig

nadir *n*
low point, lowest point, minimum, zero, bottom,
depths, all-time low, low-watermark
colloq. rock bottom
E3 zenith, peak; *formal* acme, apex

nag¹ *v*
1 SCOLD, pester, badger, plague, torment, harass,
harry, vex, upbraid, pick on, keep on at, moan,
complain
formal berate
colloq. henpeck, hassle, grouse
2 NIGGLE, tease, worry, bother, trouble, annoy,
irritate
colloq. bug, aggravate, get someone's back up

nag² *n*
ride a nag
horse, hack, jade, keffel, rip, Rosinante
colloq. plug

nagging *adj*
1 *a nagging pain*
continuous, critical, distressing, upsetting, worrying,
irritating, niggling, painful, aching, persistent
2 SCOLDING, shrewish, critical, tormenting,
moaning
colloq. nit-picking

nail *v, n*
▶ *v* 1 FASTEN, attach, secure, pin, tack, fix, join,
hammer
2 CATCH, arrest, capture, grab, seize, trap, snatch,
corner, pin down
formal apprehend
colloq. collar, nick, nab, nobble
3 EXPOSE, detect, identify, reveal, uncover, unearth,
unmask
▶ *n* 1 FASTENER, pin, tack, rivet, brad, sprig, clout,
sparable, spike, skewer, screw
2 FINGERNAIL, toenail, nipper, pincer, claw, talon

naïve *adj*
unsophisticated, ingenuous, innocent, unaffected,
artless, guileless, simple, unrealistic, natural, frank,
childlike, inexperienced, immature, open, candid,
trusting, born yesterday, unsuspecting, unsuspicious,
unaffected, unworldly, gullible, unpretentious,
credulous, wide-eyed
formal jejune

colloq. green, wet behind the ears
E3 experienced, sophisticated

naïvety *n*
ingenuousness, innocence, inexperience, immaturity,
naturalness, artlessness, guilelessness, childlikeness,
simplicity, openness, frankness, candidness, gullibility,
credulity
E3 experience, sophistication

naked *adj*
1 NUDE, bare, with nothing on, undressed, unclothed,
uncovered, exposed, stripped, stark-naked, disrobed,
denuded
colloq. in the altogether, starkers, in your birthday suit,
in the raw, in the buff, not a stitch on, naked as the day
you were born
2 OPEN, unadorned, undisguised, unqualified,
unvarnished, plain, stark, bald, simple, evident, overt,
patent, blatant, flagrant, glaring, exposed
3 DEFENCELESS, exposed, unprotected, unguarded,
uncovered, weak, vulnerable, helpless, powerless
4 *a naked landscape*
denuded, stripped, grassless, treeless, exposed,
barren, bare, stark
E3 1 clothed, covered 2 concealed, veiled

nakedness *n*
1 NUDITY, bareness, undress, starkness
colloq. the altogether, the buff
2 PLAINNESS, openness, simplicity, baldness,
barrenness, bareness, starkness

namby-pamby *adj*
sentimental, feeble, spineless, weak, weedy, wet, wishy-
washy, mawkish, vapid, maudlin, insipid, colourless,
anaemic, pretty-pretty, prim, prissy

name *n, v*
▶ *n* 1 TITLE, designation, label, tag, style, term,
epithet, nickname
formal appellation, denomination, cognomen
colloq. handle, monicker
Related adjective: nominal

Kinds of name include: full name, first name, given
name, Christian name, baptismal name, second
name, middle name; surname, family name, last
name; maiden name; nickname, sobriquet,
agnomen, pet name, term of endearment,
diminutive; false name, pseudonym, alias, stage-
name, *nom-de-plume,* assumed name, pen-name;
proper name; place name; brand name, trademark;
code name.

2 REPUTATION, character, repute, renown, eminence,
prominence, fame, honour, prestige, distinction, note,
standing, popularity, celebrity
formal esteem
3 STAR, expert, authority, leading light, celebrity,
dignitary, VIP, luminary, hero
colloq. big noise, big name, bigwig, a somebody

▶ *v* **1** CALL, christen, baptize, give name to, term, title, entitle, dub, label, tag, style, identify
formal denominate
2 DESIGNATE, nominate, mention, cite, choose, pick, select, specify, classify, commission, appoint

named *adj*
called, known as, by the name of, labelled, termed, titled, entitled, dubbed, styled, baptized, christened, identified, designated, mentioned, chosen, picked, selected, singled out, specified, classified, commissioned, cited, nominated, appointed, dit
formal denominated
F∃ nameless

nameless *adj*
1 UNNAMED, anonymous, unidentified, untitled, unlabelled, unspecified, undesignated, unknown, obscure
formal innominate
2 INEXPRESSIBLE, indescribable, unutterable, unspeakable, unmentionable, unheard-of
F∃ **1** named

namely *adv*
that is, ie, specifically, viz, that is to say, in other words
formal to wit

nap¹ *n, v*
▶ *n* *have a nap*
rest, lie-down, doze, sleep, light sleep, siesta, catnap
colloq. snooze, forty winks, kip
▶ *v* doze, sleep, sleep lightly, nod (off), drop off, catnap, lie down, rest
colloq. snooze, kip, have forty winks, get some shut-eye

nap² *n*
the nap of the carpet
down, pile, weave, shag, surface, texture, fibre, grain, fuzz, downiness

nappy *n*
diaper, napkin, towel, serviette

narcissism *n*
self-love, egotism, egomania, egocentricity, self-centredness, self-regard, self-conceit, conceit, vanity

narcissistic *adj*
self-loving, egotistic, egomaniacal, egocentric, self-centred, conceited, vain

narcotic *n, adj*
▶ *n* drug, opiate, sedative, tranquillizer, sleeping pill, painkiller, analgesic, anodyne, anaesthetic, palliative, soporific
slang upper, downer
▶ *adj* soporific, sleep-inducing, hypnotic, sedative, analgesic, anaesthetic, tranquillizing, opiate, painkilling, numbing, dulling, pain-dulling, calming, stupefying
formal somnolent, stupefacient

narked *adj*
annoyed, bothered, irritated, piqued, irked, exasperated, provoked, riled, vexed, galled
colloq. bugged, miffed, nettled, peeved

narrate *v*
tell, read, report, describe, portray, unfold, recite, state, explain, set out, detail, chronicle
formal relate, recount, rehearse, set forth

narration *n*
account, story, tale, description, explanation, telling, report, statement, history, chronicle, detail, sketch,
portrayal, reading, recital, story-telling, voice-over
formal rehearsal, recountal

narrative *n*
story, tale, chronicle, account, history, report, description, sketch, portrayal, reading, detail, statement

narrator *n*
storyteller, chronicler, reporter, raconteur, anecdotist, commentator, writer, author, describer, relater, annalist
formal recounter

narrow *adj, v*
▶ *adj* **1** TIGHT, confined, constricted, cramped, small, slim, slender, thin, fine, spare, tapering, close
formal attenuated
2 LIMITED, restricted, cramped, squeezed, tight, close, meagre, scant
formal circumscribed, incommodious, exiguous
3 NARROW-MINDED, biased, bigoted, prejudiced, dogmatic, intolerant, illiberal, reactionary, hidebound, strait-laced, dyed-in-the-wool, close-minded, set, rigid, conservative, small-minded, insular, petty
4 *in the narrow sense of the word*
strict, literal, exact, precise, true, original
F∃ **1** wide **2** broad **3** broad-minded, tolerant **4** broad
▶ *v* constrict, limit, tighten, confine, restrict, cramp, reduce, diminish, taper, simplify
formal attenuate, circumscribe
F∃ broaden, widen, increase

narrowing *n*
compression, constriction, curtailment, contraction, reduction, tapering, thinning, emaciation, constipation
technical stenosis
formal attenuation
F∃ broadening, widening

narrowly *adv*
1 BARELY, scarcely, just, only just
colloq. by a hair's breadth, by a whisker
2 CAREFULLY, closely, strictly, scrutinizingly, precisely, exactly, painstakingly

narrow-minded *adj*
illiberal, biased, bigoted, prejudiced, reactionary, hidebound, strait-laced, dyed in the wool, opinionated, diehard, small-minded, close-minded, set, rigid, inflexible, entrenched, conservative, ultra-conservative, blimpish, intolerant, insular, provincial, parochial, twisted, warped, jaundiced, petty, petty-minded, exclusive, unreasonable
F∃ broad-minded, liberal, tolerant

narrowness *n*
1 THINNESS, tightness, slenderness, limitation, restrictedness, nearness, constriction, closeness, meagreness
formal attenuation
2 NARROW-MINDEDNESS, insularity, parochialism, exclusiveness, bias, bigotry, prejudice, intolerance, pettiness, small-mindedness, rigidity, conservatism
F∃ **1** breadth, width **2** broad-mindedness, tolerance

narrows *n*
straits, sound, channel, passage, waterway

nascent *adj*
budding, developing, growing, rising, young,

embryonic, beginning, evolving, advancing
formal burgeoning, incipient, naissant
⊟ dying

nastiness *n*
1 UNPLEASANTNESS, repulsiveness, horribleness,
disagreeableness, offensiveness, filth, dirtiness,
defilement, filthiness, foulness, impurity, pollution,
squalor, uncleanliness, unsavouriness
2 OBSCENITY, indecency, filth, pornography
colloq. porn, smuttiness
3 MALICE, spitefulness, spite, viciousness, meanness
formal malevolence

nasty *adj*
1 UNPLEASANT, awful, repulsive, hateful, loathsome,
objectionable, disagreeable, offensive, distasteful,
disgusting, obnoxious, revolting, sickening, horrible,
dirty, filthy, squalid, foul, vile, odious, polluted, rank
formal repellent, repugnant, noisome, malodorous
colloq. grotty, yucky
2 OBSCENE, offensive, indecent, dirty, filthy,
pornographic, ribald
colloq. blue, smutty
3 MALICIOUS, mean, spiteful, vicious, cruel, unkind,
bad-tempered, disagreeable, unpleasant
formal malevolent
4 SERIOUS, grave, critical, dangerous, worrying,
alarming, disquieting, unpleasant, difficult, tricky
5 *nasty weather*
stormy, wet, rainy, foggy, foul, disagreeable,
unpleasant, vile, filthy, awful
⊟ 1 agreeable, nice, pleasant, decent,
palatable 3 benevolent, kind 5 fine

nation *n*
country, people, race, tribe, state, kingdom, land,
realm, republic, population, community, society

national *adj, n*
▶ *adj* countrywide, civil, civic, domestic, nationwide,
state, internal, domestic, native, general,
governmental, federal, public, widespread,
comprehensive, social
▶ *n* citizen, native, subject, inhabitant, resident

nationalism *n*
patriotism, allegiance, loyalty, chauvinism,
xenophobia, jingoism

nationalistic *adj*
patriotic, loyal, chauvinistic, jingoistic, xenophobic
formal ethnocentrist

nationality *n*
race, nation, ethnic group, birth, tribe, clan

nationwide *adj*
national, countrywide, general, overall, extensive,
widespread, comprehensive, state, coast-to-coast

native *adj, n*
▶ *adj* 1 INDIGENOUS, local, domestic, vernacular,
home, home-grown, aboriginal, mother, original
formal autochthonous
2 INHERENT, inborn, innate, inbred, ingrained,
hereditary, inherited, congenital, instinctive, intuitive,
natural, built-in, intrinsic
formal natal, connate
▶ *n* inhabitant, resident, national, citizen, dweller,
aborigine
formal autochthon
⊟ foreigner, outsider, stranger, alien

nativity *n*
birth, childbirth, delivery
formal parturition

natter *v, n*
▶ *v* chat, chatter, gossip, talk, confabulate
colloq. blather, blether, confab, gab, gabble, jabber,
jaw, prattle, rabbit (on), chinwag, witter
▶ *n* chat, conversation, talk, gossip, prattle, chit-chat
colloq. blather, blether, chinwag, confab, gab, gabble,
jaw

natty *adj*
smart, neat, dapper, chic, elegant, well-dressed,
fashionable, spruce, stylish, trim
colloq. ritzy, snazzy, swanky

natural *adj*
1 ORDINARY, normal, common, regular, standard,
everyday, routine, run-of-the-mill, usual, typical
2 INNATE, inborn, inbred, ingrained, built-in,
normal, instinctive, intuitive, inherent, inherited,
congenital, native, indigenous
formal connate
3 *natural fibres*
genuine, pure, authentic, additive-free, chemical-free,
organic, raw, virgin, unrefined, unprocessed,
unmixed, plain, real, whole
4 SINCERE, unaffected, genuine, artless, ingenuous,
guileless, simple, unpretentious, unsophisticated,
frank, open, candid, spontaneous
⊟ 1 unnatural 2 acquired 3 artificial, man-
made, synthetic 4 affected, disingenuous, contrived

naturalist *n*
life scientist, plant scientist, botanist, biologist,
zoologist, ecologist, evolutionist, Darwinist,
creationist

naturalistic *adj*
natural, realistic, true-to-life, representational, lifelike,
graphic, real-life, photographic, factual
⊟ idealistic, unrealistic

naturalize *v*
introduce, adopt, incorporate, familiarize,
acclimatize, accept, assimilate, accustom, adapt,
enfranchise, domesticate
formal acclimate, acculturate, endenizen, habituate

naturally *adj*
1 OF COURSE, obviously, as a matter of course, simply,
logically, typically, certainly, absolutely, as you would
expect
colloq. natch
2 NORMALLY, genuinely, sincerely, instinctively,
spontaneously, artlessly, ingenuously, candidly, frankly

naturalness *n*
sincerity, genuineness, artlessness, ingenuousness,
simpleness, simplicity, plainness, pureness, purity,
wholeness, candidness, frankness, openness, realism,
unpretentiousness, unaffectedness, spontaneousness,
spontaneity, informality

nature *n*
1 ESSENCE, quality, character, essential quality/
character, identity, features, disposition, attributes,
personality, stamp, make-up, characteristic(s),
complexion, constitution, temperament, mood,
outlook, humour, temper
colloq. chemistry
2 KIND, sort, type, description, category, variety,
style, species, class, category
3 UNIVERSE, world, creation, cosmos, earth,

mother earth/nature, environment
4 COUNTRYSIDE, country, landscape, scenery, natural history

naught *n*
nothing, nothingness, zero, nought, nil
colloq. zilch

naughty *adj*
1 BAD, badly behaved, misbehaving, mischievous, disobedient, wayward, defiant, undisciplined, unruly, exasperating, playful, roguish, perverse, incorrigible
formal refractory
2 INDECENT, obscene, bawdy, risqué, vulgar, off-colour, coarse, ribald, lewd, smutty
colloq. blue
E∃ 1 good, well-behaved **2** decent

nausea *n*
1 VOMITING, sickness, retching, gagging, queasiness, biliousness, morning sickness, travel sickness, motion sickness, seasickness, carsickness, airsickness
colloq. throwing up, puking
2 DISGUST, revulsion, loathing, aversion, distaste, hatred
formal repugnance, abhorrence, detestation

nauseate *v*
sicken, make sick, disgust, revolt, repel, offend, make your gorge rise
colloq. turn off, turn your stomach; *US* gross out

nauseating *adj*
sickening, disgusting, repulsive, offensive, distasteful, repellent, odious, loathsome, nauseous, revolting
formal abhorrent, detestable, repugnant

nauseous *adj*
queasy, nauseated, sick, ill, travel sick, seasick, carsick, airsick
colloq. under the weather, about to throw up

nautical *adj*
naval, maritime, seagoing, sailing, oceanic, boating, yachting

Nautical terms include: afloat, aft, air-sea rescue, amidships, ballast, beam, bear away, beat, bow-wave, breeches buoy, broach, capsize, cargo, cast off, chandler, circumnavigate, coastguard, compass bearing, convoy, course, cruise, current, Davy Jones's locker, dead reckoning, deadweight, disembark, dock, dockyard, dry dock, ebb tide, embark, ferry, fleet, float, flotilla, flotsam, foghorn, fore, foreshore, go about, gybe, harbour, harbour-bar, harbour dues, harbour-master, haven, head to wind, heave to, heavy swell, heel, helm, high tide, inflatable life-raft, jetsam, jetty, knot, launch, lay a course, lay up, lee, lee shore, leeward, life buoy, life-jacket, life-rocket, list, low tide, make fast, marina, marine, maroon, mayday, moor, mooring, mutiny, navigation, neap tide, on board, pitch and toss, plane, put in, put to sea, quay, reach, reef, refit, ride out, riptide, roll, row, run, run aground, run before the wind, salvage, seafaring, sea lane, sea legs, seamanship, seasick, seaworthy, set sail, sheet in, shipping, shipping lane, ship's company, ship water, shipwreck, shipyard, shore leave, sink, slip anchor, slipway, stevedore, stowaway, tack, tide, trim, voyage, wake, wash, watch, wave, weather, weigh anchor, wharf, wreck. *See also* **sail**.

naval *adj*
marine, maritime, nautical, sea, seagoing, seafaring

navel *n*
umbilicus, centre, middle, hub
formal omphalos
colloq. belly-button, tummy-button
Related adjective: umbilical

navigable *adj*
passable, crossable, negotiable, open, clear, unblocked, unobstructed, surmountable
formal traversable

navigate *v*
steer, drive, direct, pilot, guide, handle, manoeuvre, negotiate, cruise, sail, voyage, journey, cross, helm, plot, plan
colloq. skipper

navigation *n*
sailing, steering, piloting, pilotage, directing, direction, guiding, guidance, cruising, voyaging, seamanship, helmsmanship, manoeuvring
Related adjective: nautical

Navigational aids include: astro-navigation, bell buoy, channel-marker buoy, chart, chronometer, conical buoy, Decca® navigator system, depth gauge, dividers, echo-sounder, flux-gate compass, Global Positioning System (GPS), gyrocompass, lighthouse, lightship, log, loran (long-range radio navigation), magnetic compass, marker buoy, nautical table, parallel ruler, pilot, radar, sectored leading-light, sextant, VHF radio.

navigator *n*
pilot, seaman, helmsman, mariner

navvy *n*
labourer, common labourer, worker, manual worker, workman, digger, ganger

navy *n*
fleet, ships, flotilla, armada, warships

nay *adv*
indeed, really, actually, in fact, in truth, certainly, absolutely, to be sure

near¹ *adj*
1 NEARBY, close, close by, within reach, within range, at hand, accessible, convenient, bordering, adjacent, alongside, local, neighbouring, surrounding
formal adjoining, contiguous
colloq. a stone's throw from
2 IMMINENT, close, impending, forthcoming, coming, looming, immediate, approaching, in the offing
formal proximate
3 DEAR, familiar, close, related, closely related, intimate, akin
4 SIMILAR, close, like, alike, comparable, corresponding
E∃ 1 far, far off, far-away **2** distant **3** remote
▷ **near thing** near miss, narrow escape, nasty moment, close call; *colloq.* close shave

near² *adv, prep, v*
▶ *adv* nearby, close, close by, not far away, at close quarters, alongside, within reach, at hand, within close range
colloq. a stone's throw away
▶ *prep* nearby, close to, next to, bordering on,

adjacent to, alongside, in the neighbourhood of, within reach of
formal adjoining, contiguous to
▶ *v* approach, get closer to, come nearer/closer, advance towards, come/move towards, draw near to, close in on, cling to
E∃ withdraw, keep your distance

nearby   *adj, adv*
▶ *adj* near, close, neighbouring, adjoining, adjacent, accessible, convenient, handy, within reach
E∃ faraway
▶ *adv* near, within reach, at close quarters, close at hand, not far away, a short distance away, in the vicinity
colloq. on your doorstep, in your own backyard

nearly   *adv*
almost, practically, virtually, as good as, closely, close to, approximately, more or less, all but, just about, roughly, well-nigh
E∃ completely, totally

nearness   *n*
1 CLOSENESS, vicinity, handiness, accessibility, availability, immediacy, imminence
formal proximity, contiguity, propinquity
2 INTIMACY, dearness, familiarity, closeness, chumminess

near-sighted   *adj*
short-sighted, myopic, half-blind, purblind

neat   *adj*
1 TIDY, orderly, ordered, well-ordered, organized, well-organized, straight, smart, spruce, dapper, trim, clean, shipshape
colloq. natty, spick-and-span, in apple-pie order, shipshape and Bristol fashion
2 DEFT, clever, adroit, nimble, skilful, practised, dexterous, expert
colloq. nifty
3 COMPACT, handy, dainty, convenient, efficient, well-designed, well-made, user-friendly
4 *a neat solution*
clever, convenient, nice, simple, apt, sensible, ingenious, elegant
5 GREAT, excellent, wonderful, marvellous, superb, admirable, tremendous, fantastic, fabulous
colloq. super, terrific, smashing; *slang* cool, mega, wicked
6 UNDILUTED, unmixed, unadulterated, straight, pure
E∃ 1 untidy, scruffy, shabby, slovenly **2** clumsy
6 diluted

neaten   *v*
tidy (up), straighten, smarten (up), spruce up, clean (up), arrange, trim, edge, round off, groom, put to rights

neatly   *adv*
1 TIDILY, smartly, stylishly, sprucely, methodically, systematically, efficiently
2 CLEVERLY, conveniently, handily, aptly, nicely, daintily, elegantly
3 DEFTLY, skilfully, adeptly, adroitly, agilely, nimbly, dexterously, effortlessly, expertly, precisely, accurately, gracefully
E∃ 1 untidily **2** inelegantly **3** unskilfully, inexpertly

neatness   *n*
1 TIDINESS, smartness, trimness, spruceness, stylishness, style, orderliness, straightness,

methodicalness
2 CLEVERNESS, aptness, efficiency, handiness, elegance, daintiness, niceness, nicety
3 SKILFULNESS, skill, adeptness, deftness, adroitness, agility, dexterity, gracefulness, grace, nimbleness, expertness, preciseness, precision, accuracy
E∃ 1 untidiness, disorderliness **2** inelegance

nebulous   *adj*
vague, hazy, imprecise, indefinite, indistinct, cloudy, misty, shadowy, obscure, uncertain, unclear, dim, ambiguous, confused, fuzzy, abstract, shapeless, unformed
formal amorphous, indeterminate
E∃ clear

necessarily   *adv*
inevitably, incontrovertibly, certainly, compulsory, by definition, inescapably, of necessity, inexorably, of course, naturally, consequently, automatically, therefore, thus, accordingly, axiomatically, willy-nilly, *nolens volens*
formal ineluctably, perforce

necessary   *adj*
needed, required, essential, compulsory, indispensable, vital, crucial, de rigueur, obligatory, needful, unavoidable, sure, inevitable, inescapable, inexorable, certain
old use needful
formal mandatory, imperative, requisite, ineluctable
E∃ unnecessary, inessential, unimportant

necessitate   *v*
require, involve, entail, make necessary, need, take, call for, demand, oblige, exact, force, constrain, compel

necessity   *n*
1 REQUIREMENT, obligation, prerequisite, essential, fundamental, indispensable, need, want, compulsion, demand
formal exigency, requisite, desideratum, sine qua non
colloq. must
2 INDISPENSABILITY, inevitability, certainty, inescapability, inexorability, obligation, needfulness
3 POVERTY, destitution, hardship, want, need, deprivation
formal penury, privation, indigence
E∃ luxury

neck   *n, v*
▶ *n* nape, scruff, scrag, halse
technical cervix
Related adjective: cervical
▶ *v* kiss, caress
colloq. smooch, canoodle; *slang* snog

necklace   *n*
chain, string, band, pearls, beads, jewels, choker, locket, pendant, lavallière, negligee, torque, torc, gorget, carcanet, rivière

necromancer   *n*
magician, conjurer, diviner, sorcerer, sorceress, witch, wizard, warlock, spiritist, spiritualist
formal thaumaturge, thaumaturgist

necromancy   *n*
divination, enchantment, wonder-working, magic, magical powers, black magic, black art, sorcery, witchcraft, witchery, spiritism, spiritualism, wizardry, demonology, voodoo, hoodoo
formal conjuration, thaumaturgy

necropolis *n*
cemetery, graveyard, burial ground, burial place, burial site, churchyard
formal charnel house, God's acre

need *v, n*
▶ *v* miss, lack, want, require, demand, call for, have need of, be necessary to have, have occasion for, have to, must, be compelled/obliged to, desire, crave, pine for, yearn for, be desperate for, cry out for, be dependent on, depend on, be reliant on, rely on
formal necessitate
▶ *n* **1** *a need for caution*
call, demand, obligation, want, wish, justification, requirement
formal exigency
2 *the country's needs*
essential, necessity, prerequisite
formal requisite, desideratum
3 *a need for equipment*
want, lack, insufficiency, inadequacy, neediness, demand, shortage
▷ **in need** poor, impoverished, in need, penniless, disadvantaged, deprived, poverty-stricken, underprivileged; *formal* destitute, penurious, indigent, impecunious; *colloq.* on the breadline, hard up, unable to keep the wolf from the door

needed *adj*
called for, desired, required, wanted, lacking, compulsory, necessary, obligatory, essential
formal requisite
E3 unnecessary, unneeded

needful *adj*
required, needed, necessary, essential, indispensable, vital, stipulated, needy
formal requisite
E3 excess, needless, superfluous

needle *n, v*
▶ *n* **1** *needle and thread*
knitting needle, pin, nib, bodkin, hypodermic needle, stylus
2 POINTER, indicator, arrow, marker, hand
3 THORN, prickle, spike, splinter, barb, spine, quill, briar, bristle, bramble
formal spicule
▶ *v* annoy, irritate, harass, pester, goad, spur, provoke, ruffle, prick, rile, bait, prod, nag, irk, taunt, torment, sting
colloq. aggravate, nettle, niggle, wind up, cheese off; *slang* piss off

needless *adj*
unnecessary, gratuitous, uncalled-for, unwanted, undesired, redundant, dispensable, superfluous, expendable, useless, pointless, purposeless, luxury
E3 necessary, essential, indispensable

needlework *n*
embroidery, fancywork, stitching, sewing, crocheting, tapestry, tatting, needlepoint

needy *adj*
poor, impoverished, in need, penniless, disadvantaged, deprived, poverty-stricken, underprivileged
formal destitute, penurious, indigent, impecunious
colloq. on the breadline, hard up, unable to keep the wolf from the door
E3 affluent, wealthy, well-off

ne'er-do-well *n*
good-for-nothing, idler, layabout, wastrel, waster
colloq. black sheep, loafer, shirker, skiver

nefarious *adj*
wicked, detestable, dreadful, evil, foul, loathsome, vile, vicious, shameful, outrageous, horrendous, terrible, odious, monstrous, villainous, abominable, atrocious, base, sinful, unholy, criminal, depraved, infamous, horrible, satanic, infernal
formal execrable, heinous, iniquitous, opprobrious
E3 exemplary

negate *v*
1 CANCEL, annul, invalidate, undo, neutralize, quash, reverse, wipe out, void, repeal
formal nullify, countermand, abrogate, retract, revoke, rescind
2 DENY, contradict, oppose, disprove, repudiate, renounce, reject, discredit
formal refute, gainsay
colloq. explode, squash
E3 2 affirm

negation *n*
1 CANCELLATION, repeal, neutralization, veto
formal disavowal, nullification, abrogation, countermanding
2 DENIAL, contradiction, rejection, renunciation, disclaimer
3 OPPOSITE, reverse, contrary
formal inverse, antithesis, converse
E3 2 affirmation

negative *adj, n*
▶ *adj* **1** CONTRADICTORY, contrary, denying, refusing, opposing, opposed, invalidating, neutralizing, annulling
formal nullifying, dissenting, gainsaying
2 UNCO-OPERATIVE, cynical, pessimistic, defeatist, gloomy, unenthusiastic, uninterested, unwilling, unhelpful, critical, weak, spineless
E3 1 affirmative, positive **2** constructive, positive
▶ *n* contradiction, denial, opposite, refusal, rejection
formal dissension

neglect *v, n*
▶ *v* **1** DISREGARD, ignore, overlook, leave alone, leave out, abandon, pass by, rebuff, scorn, disdain, slight, spurn
formal forsake
2 FORGET, fail (in), omit, overlook, let slide, shirk, skimp, be lax about
E3 1 cherish, appreciate **2** remember, pay attention to, attend to
▶ *n* negligence, disregard, carelessness, failure, inattention, disrepair, indifference, slackness, laxity, forgetfulness, ignoring, rebuff, scorn, disdain, slight, spurning, oversight, slight, disrespect
formal remissness, default, dereliction of duty, heedlessness
E3 care, attention, concern

neglected *adj*
uncared-for, disregarded, abandoned, derelict, overgrown, uncultivated, unmaintained, untended, untilled, unweeded, unhusbanded, underestimated, undervalued, unappreciated
E3 cherished, treasured

neglectful *adj*
uncaring, careless, inattentive, disregardful, forgetful, thoughtless, unmindful, indifferent, lax, negligent, oblivious

negligence *n*

formal heedless, remiss
colloq. sloppy
≠ attentive, careful

negligence *n*
inattentiveness, inattention, carelessness, laxity,
neglect, slackness, thoughtlessness, forgetfulness,
indifference, omission, oversight, disregard,
shortcoming, failure
formal default, remissness, dereliction of duty,
heedlessness
colloq. sloppiness
≠ attentiveness, care, regard

negligent *adj*
neglectful, inattentive, thoughtless, casual, lax,
cursory, careless, indifferent, offhand, nonchalant,
slack, uncaring, unmindful, forgetful
formal remiss, heedless, dilatory
colloq. sloppy
≠ attentive, careful, scrupulous

negligible *adj*
unimportant, insignificant, small, imperceptible,
inappreciable, trifling, trivial, petty, paltry, minor,
minute, tiny, not worth bothering about
≠ significant

negotiable *adj*
1 DEBATABLE, arguable, questionable, contestable,
open to discussion/question, undecided, unsettled
2 NAVIGABLE, passable, crossable, open, clear,
unblocked, unobstructed, surmountable
formal traversable
≠ 1 non-negotiable, fixed, definite

negotiate *v*
1 *negotiate an agreement*
deal, mediate, arbitrate, intervene, intercede, debate,
haggle, bargain, arrange, agree, come to an agreement,
hammer out, thrash out, pull off, transact, work out,
manage, complete, settle, fulfil, consult, contract, talk,
discuss, reach a compromise
formal confer, resolve, execute, conclude
colloq. parley, wheel and deal
2 GET ROUND, cross, clear, surmount, pass (over/
through)
formal traverse

negotiation *n*
mediation, arbitration, debate, conference, discussion,
diplomacy, bargaining, haggling, parleying,
transaction, reaching an agreement, thrashing-out,
hammering-out, pulling-off, talks
colloq. parley, wheeling and dealing

negotiator *n*
arbitrator, go-between, mediator, intermediary,
bargainer, haggler, moderator, intercessor,
adjudicator, broker, ambassador, diplomat
colloq. parleyer, wheeler-dealer

neigh *v*
whinny, hinny, bray, nicker

neighbourhood *n*
district, locality, vicinity, community, locale, quarter,
part, precinct, environs, confines, surroundings, area,
region
formal proximity, purlieus
▷ **in the neighbourhood of** near, close to, about,
roughly, almost, approximately, nearby, next to

neighbouring *adj*
adjacent, bordering, near, nearby, nearest, near at

hand, close at hand, local, connecting, next,
surrounding
formal adjoining, abutting, contiguous
≠ distant, remote, far away

neighbourly *adj*
sociable, friendly, amiable, kind, generous, helpful,
genial, warm, cordial, easy to get on/along with,
affable, hospitable, obliging, considerate,
companionable

nemesis *n*
retribution, vengeance, punishment, just punishment,
destruction, ruin, downfall, destiny, fate

neologism *n*
new word, new expression, new phrase, innovation,
coinage, novelty, vogue word

neophyte *n*
beginner, learner, novice, newcomer, apprentice,
probationer, trainee, recruit, raw recruit, new member,
tiro, rookie
formal noviciate, novitiate
colloq. greenhorn

nepotism *n*
favouritism, bias, partiality, preferential treatment,
keeping it in the family, looking after your own
colloq. jobs for the boys, old-boy network, old-school
tie

nerve *n, v*
▶ *n* 1 COURAGE, bravery, mettle, pluck, spirit,
vigour, intrepidity, valour, daring, fearlessness, cool-
headedness, hardihood, firmness, resolution,
steadfastness, will, determination, endurance, force
formal fortitude
colloq. guts, spunk, grit, bottle
2 AUDACITY, impudence, effrontery, brazenness,
gall, boldness, impertinence, insolence, presumption,
temerity
colloq. cheek, chutzpah, face, neck, brass neck, sauce,
mouth, lip
≠ 1 weakness 2 timidity
▶ *v* steel, strengthen, invigorate, encourage, bolster,
brace, hearten, embolden
formal fortify
≠ unnerve

nerveless *adj*
feeble, weak, flabby, inert, slack, nervous, spineless,
timid, unnerved, afraid, cowardly
formal debilitated, enervated
≠ bold, brave, strong

nerve-racking *adj*
harrowing, distressing, trying, stressful, tense,
maddening, worrying, anxious, disquieting, difficult,
frightening
colloq. nail-biting

nerves *n*
nervousness, tension, nervous tension, stress, anxiety,
worry, strain, fretfulness, apprehensiveness
colloq. jitters, butterflies, butterflies in your stomach,
collywobbles, willies, heebie-jeebies
Related adjective: neural

nervous *adj*
highly-strung, excitable, anxious, agitated, on edge,
edgy, tense, strained, fidgety, apprehensive, neurotic,
shaky, uneasy, worried, flustered, disquieted, fretful,
quaking, on tenterhooks, fearful, timid, timorous
formal perturbed

colloq. nervy, twitchy, het up, keyed up, wound up, jumpy, jittery, uptight, with butterflies in your stomach, on pins and needles, shaking like a leaf/jelly, with your heart in your mouth, in a sweat, in a stew, in a tizzy; *slang* screwed-up
E3 calm, relaxed

nervous breakdown *n*
mental breakdown, nervous disorder, neurosis, crisis, depression, clinical depression, melancholia
colloq. cracking-up

nervousness *n*
anxiety, tension, strain, stress, edginess, worry, uneasiness, disquiet, apprehensiveness, agitation, restlessness, fluster, excitability, timidity, timorousness, tremulousness
formal perturbation
colloq. habdabs, heebie-jeebies, touchiness, willies
E3 calmness, coolness

nervy *adj*
highly-strung, excitable, anxious, agitated, on edge, edgy, tense, strained, fidgety, apprehensive, neurotic, shaky, uneasy, worried, flustered, fearful
colloq. twitchy, het up, keyed up, wound up, jumpy, jittery, uptight, with butterflies in your stomach, on pins and needles, shaking like a leaf/jelly, with your heart in your mouth
E3 calm, relaxed

nescient *adj*
ignorant, uneducated, illiterate, innumerate, backward, unread, untaught, untrained, inexperienced, unschooled, unlearned, stupid, uninitiated, unenlightened, uninformed, ill-informed, unwitting, unaware, unfamiliar, unacquainted
colloq. clueless, dense, thick, thick as two short planks
E3 educated, knowledgeable, learned, clever; *formal* conversant

nest *n*
1 *a bird's nest*
breeding-ground, den, roost, perch, eyrie, lair, cote, dovecote, vespiary, nesting-box
US bird-house
formal nidification
2 RETREAT, refuge, shelter, haunt, hideaway, hideout, hiding-place, den, mew
Related adjective: nidal

nest egg *n*
fund(s), reserve(s), savings, store, cache, deposit, bottom drawer
colloq. money saved for a rainy day

nestle *v*
snuggle (up), huddle (together), cuddle (up), nuzzle, curl up

nestling *n*
fledgling, chick, suckling, weanling, baby

net¹ *n, v*
▶ *n* *a fishing net*
mesh, meshwork, web, webbing, network, netting, open work, tracery, lattice, latticework, filigree, lace, fishnet, drag, dragnet, drift, drift-net, drop-net, seine, seine net, snare, trap
formal reticulum
Related adjectives: retiary, reticular
▶ *v* catch, trap, capture, take captive, bag, ensnare, snare, enmesh, entangle
colloq. nab, collar, nick

net² *adj, v*
▶ *adj* **1** *a net salary*
nett, clear, after tax, after deductions, take-home, final, lowest
2 OVERALL, general, broad, total, inclusive, final, ultimate
E3 **1** gross
▶ *v* bring in, clear, earn, take, take home, raise, get, make, receive, gain, pocket, obtain, accumulate
formal realize
colloq. pull in, rake in

nether *adj*
1 LOWER, under, lower-level, bottom, below, beneath, underground
formal basal, inferior
2 INFERNAL, hellish, underworld, Plutonian, Stygian

nettle *v*
annoy, chafe, discountenance, exasperate, fret, goad, harass, incense, irritate, needle, pique, provoke, ruffle, sting, tease, torment, vex
colloq. bug, hassle, aggravate, get on someone's nerves, rub up the wrong way, get someone's blood/back up, drive round the bend/twist

nettled *adj*
annoyed, offended, irritated, angry, aggrieved, incensed, exasperated, cross, harassed, provoked, piqued, riled, ruffled, stung, vexed, galled, goaded, huffy, irritable
colloq. miffed, needled, peeved, narked

network *n*
1 NET, maze, mesh, labyrinth, circuitry, grill, meshwork, web, webbing, network, netting, open work, tracery, lattice, latticework, filigree, lace
formal convolution
2 SYSTEM, organization, arrangement, structure, interconnections, complex, grid, matrix, channels, tracks
formal nexus
colloq. grapevine, bush telegraph, Old-Boy network, old-school tie

neurosis *n*
(mental) disorder, psychological disorder, affliction, abnormality, disturbance, instability, maladjustment, derangement, deviation, fixation, obsession, phobia

neurotic *adj*
paranoid, irrational, disturbed, maladjusted, deranged, anxious, nervous, overwrought, hysterical, unstable, unhealthy, deviant, abnormal, compulsive, obsessive, phobic

neuter *v*
castrate, emasculate, doctor, geld, spay, dress, caponize, sterilize
colloq. fix

neutral *adj*
1 IMPARTIAL, uncommitted, unbiased, unprejudiced, non-aligned, disinterested, undecided, non-partisan, non-committal, objective, detached, indifferent, dispassionate, uninvolved, even-handed, open-minded
2 DULL, bland, inoffensive, unexceptionable, unremarkable, unassertive, ordinary, uninteresting, nondescript, colourless, insipid, drab, expressionless, indistinct, anodyne
3 *a neutral colour*
pale, pastel, indefinite, indistinct, grey, fawn, beige

◱ 1 biased, prejudiced, partisan 2 remarkable, exciting 3 colourful

neutrality *n*
unbiasedness, impartiality, impartialness, detachment, disinterest, disinterestedness, non-alignment, non-intervention, non-involvement

neutralize *v*
counteract, counterbalance, offset, balance, compensate for, make up for, negate, cancel (out), invalidate, annul, undo, frustrate, incapacitate
formal nullify

never *adv*
at no time, not ever, not for a moment, under no circumstances, not at all, on no account
colloq. not on your life, not on your nellie, when pigs fly, no way, not in a month of Sundays, not in a million years
◱ always

never-ending *adj*
everlasting, eternal, non-stop, endless, unending, without end, perpetual, unceasing, uninterrupted, continuous, unbroken, unremitting, interminable, incessant, unbroken, permanent, persistent, constant, unchanging, relentless, infinite, boundless, limitless
◱ fleeting, transitory

nevertheless *adv*
nonetheless, still, anyway, even so, yet, however, by any means, in any case/event, by some means, anyhow, but, regardless, for all that, all/just the same, at the same time
formal notwithstanding

new *adj*
1 MODERN, contemporary, current, latest, recent, state-of-the-art, present-day, up-to-date, up-to-the-minute, topical, modish, ultra-modern, futuristic, advanced, avant-garde
colloq. trendy, newfangled, way out
2 NOVEL, original, fresh, different, creative, resourceful, imaginative, innovative, pioneering, revolutionary, ground-breaking, experimental, ingenious, unfamiliar, strange, unconventional, unusual, brand-new, mint, unknown, unused, newly discovered, virgin, newborn
3 CHANGED, altered, modernized, improved, renewed, refreshed, reinvigorated, restored, remodelled, redesigned
colloq. born-again
4 ADDED, additional, another, further, extra, more, supplementary
5 *new to the work*
unfamiliar, unacquainted, unknown, inexperienced, unversed, unaccustomed, ignorant, a stranger, alien
◱ 1 out-of-date, old-fashioned, outdated 2 usual, ordinary, just another 3 old 5 familiar

newcomer *n*
1 IMMIGRANT, alien, foreigner, incomer, colonist, settler, (new) arrival, new arrival, outsider, intruder, stranger
2 NOVICE, beginner, learner, pupil, trainee, recruit, probationer, apprentice
formal neophyte
colloq. greenhorn, rookie

newfangled *adj*
modern, new, recent, state-of-the-art, contemporary, ultra-modern, futuristic, fashionable, modernistic, novel, gimmicky

colloq. trendy
◱ old-fashioned

newly *adv*
recently, lately, latterly, just, freshly, of late, afresh, anew

newness *n*
freshness, innovation, novelty, originality, oddity, uniqueness, unusualness, strangeness, unfamiliarity
formal recency
◱ oldness, ordinariness

news *n*
report, account, information, data, facts, intelligence, dispatch, message, communication, announcement, press release, communiqué, bulletin, news item, newsflash, newscast, gossip, hearsay, rumour, statement, story, word, latest, developments, scandal, revelation, exposé, disclosure, advice
formal tidings
colloq. lowdown, gen, info, dope

newspaper *n*
daily, paper, publication, broadsheet, tabloid, sheet, journal, periodical, magazine, weekly, press, gazette, organ
colloq. rag

newsworthy *adj*
reportable, hitting/making the headlines, important, significant, interesting, remarkable, stimulating, notable, noteworthy, arresting, unusual

next *adj, adv*
▶ *adj* 1 ADJACENT, neighbouring, bordering, along, alongside, beside, nearest, closest
formal adjoining, contiguous, tangential
2 FOLLOWING, succeeding, successive, ensuing, later
formal subsequent
◱ 2 previous, preceding
▶ *adv* afterwards, later, then
formal subsequently, thereafter

nibble *n, v*
▶ *n* bite, peck, gnaw, munch, morsel, taste, titbit, bit, crumb, snack, piece
▶ *v* bite, eat, peck, pick at, munch, gnaw
colloq. snack; *slang* nosh

nice *adj*
1 *have a nice time*
pleasant, agreeable, enjoyable, lovely, good, delightful, satisfying, acceptable, pleasurable, fine, appealing, amusing, entertaining, welcome
formal delectable
2 *he seems a nice man*
pleasant, agreeable, delightful, charming, likeable, attractive, good, good-natured, good-humoured, kind, kindly, friendly, genial, sweet, amiable, sympathetic, understanding, endearing, well-mannered, polite, respectable, civil, courteous
3 SUBTLE, delicate, fine, minute, fastidious, refined, particular, discriminating, scrupulous, meticulous, precise, exact, accurate, careful, strict, close
◱ 1 unpleasant, horrible 2 nasty, disagreeable, unpleasant 3 careless

nicely *adv*
satisfactorily, well, agreeably, delightfully, pleasurably, pleasantly, pleasingly, respectably, properly
◱ unpleasantly, disagreeably, nastily

niceness *n*

pleasantness, kindness, agreeableness, friendliness, delightfulness, likeableness, attractiveness, charm, amiability, politeness, respectability
F3 unpleasantness, disagreeableness, nastiness

nicety *n*

1 SUBTLETY, refinement, delicacy, distinction, nuance, fine point
2 PRECISION, accuracy, meticulousness, exactness, scrupulousness, minuteness, finesse

niche *n*

1 POSITION, place, vocation, calling, métier, slot, specialized/specialist area
2 RECESS, alcove, hollow, nook, cranny, cubbyhole, corner, opening

nick *n, v*

▶ *n* 1 NOTCH, indentation, chip, cut, groove, dent, scar, scratch, mark
2 PRISON, jail, jailhouse, police station
colloq. inside; *slang* clink, cooler, slammer, jug
3 *in good nick*
condition, shape, form, state, health, fettle
▶ *v* 1 NOTCH, cut, dent, indent, chip, score, scratch, scar, mark, damage, snick
2 STEAL, pilfer, take, pocket
colloq. knock off, pinch, swipe, lag, snitch
3 ARREST, catch, capture, pick up
formal apprehend
colloq. nab, collar, run in; *slang* bust

nickname *n*

pet name, familiar name, sobriquet, epithet, diminutive

nifty *adj*

slick, neat, clever, pleasing, enjoyable, excellent, quick, skilful, deft, chic, smart, stylish, spruce, sharp, adroit, agile, nippy, apt

niggardliness *n*

1 MEANNESS, miserliness, closeness, grudgingness, ungenerousness
formal parsimony
colloq. stinginess, tight-fistedness, cheese-paring
2 MEAGRENESS, paltriness, smallness, scantiness, skimpiness, inadequacy, insufficiency
F3 1 generosity 2 bountifulness

niggardly *adj*

1 MEAN, miserly, close, ungenerous, ungiving, sparing, grudging, hard-fisted
formal parsimonious
colloq. stingy, tight-fisted, cheese-paring
2 MEAGRE, small, miserable, scanty, skimpy, paltry, inadequate, insufficient
colloq. measly
F3 1 generous 2 bountiful

niggle *v*

1 BOTHER, worry, trouble, annoy, irritate, upset
colloq. bug
2 NAG, criticize, keep on at, pick on, complain, moan, carp, quibble
colloq. nit-pick, hassle, henpeck

night *n*

night-time, darkness, hours of darkness, dark, dead of night
F3 day, daytime
Related adjective: nocturnal

nightclub *n*

club, disco, discotheque, cabaret, nightspot
colloq. niterie, nitery

nightfall *n*

sunset, dusk, twilight, dark, evening, sundown
formal gloaming, crepuscule
F3 dawn, sunrise

nightmare *n*

1 BAD DREAM, hallucination
old use ephialtes
formal incubus
2 ORDEAL, horror, torment, torture, trial, calamity, agony, anguish, awful experience

nightmarish *adj*

terrifying, alarming, dreadful, frightening, harrowing, horrible, horrific, agonizing, disturbing, scaring, unreal
colloq. creepy

nihilism *n*

rejection, repudiation, negation, denial, pessimism, scepticism, nothingness, oblivion, emptiness, non-existence, lawlessness, anarchy, terrorism, disorder, agnosticism, atheism, cynicism, disbelief, negativism
formal abnegation, nullity, renunciation

nihilist *n*

pessimist, revolutionary, extremist, agitator, anarchist, terrorist, negationist, negativist, agnostic, atheist, disbeliever, cynic, sceptic, antinomian

nil *n*

nothing, zero, none, nought, naught, love
colloq. duck, zilch

nimble *adj*

1 AGILE, active, lively, sprightly, spry, smart, graceful, lithe, quick, quick-moving, brisk, deft, light-footed, prompt, ready, swift
colloq. nippy
2 ALERT, quick-witted, quick, quick-thinking, clever, smart, sharp-witted, sharp-eyed
F3 1 clumsy, slow 2 slow

nimbleness *n*

agility, adroitness, dexterity, grace, lightness, deftness, finesse, sprightliness, spryness, smartness, skill, alertness
formal alacrity
colloq. niftiness, nippiness

nimbly *adv*

smartly, agilely, fast, sharply, snappily, speedily, swiftly, spryly, quickly, readily, promptly, actively, proficiently, dexterously, deftly, briskly, easily, alertly, quick-wittedly
F3 awkwardly, clumsily

nincompoop *n*

fool, idiot, dunce, dimwit, simpleton, ignoramus, dolt
colloq. blockhead, nitwit, numskull, chump, clot, twit, twerp; *slang* nerd, plonker, wally

nip¹ *v*

1 BITE, pinch, squeeze, snip, clip, dock, lop, tweak, catch, grip, nibble
2 DASH, go, hurry, rush, fly, tear, run
colloq. pop
▷ **nip in the bud** halt, arrest, stop, stem, check, block, frustrate, obstruct, impede

nip² *n*

a nip of brandy

dram, draught, shot, swallow, mouthful, drop, sip, taste, portion

nipple *n*
teat, udder, breast, pap, papilla, dug
technical mamilla
slang tit

nippy *adj*
1 CHILLY, cold, biting, sharp, raw, nipping, piercing, stinging
2 FAST, quick, speedy, nimble, brisk, active, agile, sprightly, spry
F3 1 warm 2 slow

nirvana *n*
enlightenment, paradise, tranquillity, bliss, joy, peace, ecstasy, exaltation, serenity

nit-picking *adj*
quibbling, carping, finicky, fussy, hair-splitting, hypercritical, pedantic, captious, pettifogging, cavilling

nitty-gritty *n*
basics, essentials, fundamentals, main points, key points
colloq. bottom line, nuts and bolts, brass tacks

nitwit *n*
fool, idiot, dimwit, simpleton
colloq. dummy, nincompoop, ninny, numskull, nit, twit

no *adv*
not at all, not really, of course not, absolutely not, most certainly not, no thanks, under no circumstances
colloq. no way, nope, not on your life, over my dead body

nob *n*
VIP, aristocrat, personage
colloq. big shot, bigwig, fat cat, toff

nobble *v*
1 BRIBE, buy (off), influence, warn off, threaten, intimidate
2 DOPE, drug, interfere with, disable, incapacitate, hamstring
colloq. get at
3 CATCH, arrest, grab, seize
colloq. nab, collar, nick
4 STEAL, grab, take, pilfer, pinch
colloq. nick, knock off, snitch, swipe
5 THWART, frustrate, foil, check, defeat, hinder

nobility *n*
1 NOBLENESS, dignity, grandeur, grandness, illustriousness, stateliness, majesty, magnificence, splendour, impressiveness, eminence, excellence, superiority, uprightness, integrity, honour, virtue, worthiness, generosity, magnanimity
2 ARISTOCRACY, peerage, peers, nobles, gentry, elite, lords, high society
colloq. nobs, toffs
Related adjective: nobiliary
F3 1 baseness 2 proletariat

Titles of the nobility include: aristocrat, baron, baroness, baronet, count, countess, dame, dowager, duchess, duke, earl, governor, grand duke, knight, lady, laird, liege, liege lord, life peer, lord, marchioness, marquess, marquis, noble, nobleman, noblewoman, peer, peeress, ruler, seigneur, squire, thane, viscount, viscountess.

noble *n, adj*
▶ *n* aristocrat, peer, lord, lady, nobleman, noblewoman
F3 commoner
▶ *adj* 1 ARISTOCRATIC, high-born, titled, landed, high-ranking, patrician
colloq. blue-blooded, born with a silver spoon in your mouth
2 MAGNIFICENT, magnanimous, splendid, stately, generous, dignified, distinguished, fine, eminent, grand, great, exalted, lofty, honoured, honourable, venerated, imposing, impressive, majestic
3 VIRTUOUS, unselfish, honourable, worthy, excellent, elevated, fine, gentle, generous, self-sacrificing, magnanimous
F3 1 low-born 3 ignoble, base, contemptible

nobody *pron & n*
no one, nothing, nonentity, menial, cipher, mediocrity
colloq. lightweight
F3 somebody

nod *v, n*
▶ *v* 1 GESTURE, indicate, sign, signal, salute, acknowledge, incline, dip, bow
2 AGREE, approve, support, accept, say yes to
formal assent
3 SLEEP, fall asleep, doze (off), drowse, nap
formal slumber
colloq. drop off
▶ *n* gesture, indication, sign, signal, salute, greeting, beck, acknowledgement

node *n*
swelling, protuberance, lump, knob, knot, growth, bud, bump, nodule, carbuncle

noise *n, v*
▶ *n* sound, din, racket, row, clamour, clash, clatter, commotion, outcry, hubbub, uproar, cry, blare, talk, pandemonium, tumult, babble
F3 quiet, silence
▶ *v* report, rumour, publicize, announce, circulate

noiseless *adj*
silent, inaudible, soundless, quiet, mute, still, hushed
F3 loud, noisy

noisome *adj*
disgusting, offensive, repulsive, disagreeable, obnoxious, nauseating, harmful, hurtful, injurious, pernicious, bad, unhealthy, unwholesome, smelly, stinking, foul, putrid, reeking, poisonous
formal deleterious, fetid, malodorous, mephitic, noxious, pestiferous, pestilential
F3 balmy, pleasant, wholesome

noisy *adj*
booming, roaring, thundering, loud, deafening, blasting, blaring, ear-splitting, clamorous, piercing, vocal, tumultuous, rowdy, rumbustious, boisterous, obstreperous, clamorous, turbulent
formal vociferous
colloq. so loud you can't hear yourself think
F3 quiet, silent, peaceful

nomad *n*
traveller, wanderer, itinerant, transient, rambler, roamer, rover, migrant, vagabond, vagrant

nomadic *adj*
travelling, itinerant, wandering, roaming, migrant, migratory, drifting, roving, roaming, Gypsy, unsettled, vagrant
formal peregrinating, peripatetic

nom-de-plume *n*
pseudonym, pen-name, assumed name, alias

nomenclature *n*
naming, classification, vocabulary, terminology, phraseology
technical taxonomy
formal codification, locution

nominal *adj*
1 TITULAR, in name only, supposed, professed, ostensible, so-called, theoretical, formal, self-styled, puppet, symbolic
formal purported
2 TOKEN, minimal, trifling, trivial, insignificant, small, symbolic
E3 1 actual, genuine, real

nominate *v*
1 PROPOSE, designate, submit, suggest, recommend, present
colloq. put up
2 APPOINT, choose, select, name, elect, assign, commission, elevate, term

nomination *n*
1 PROPOSAL, submission, suggestion, recommendation
2 APPOINTMENT, choice, selection, designation, election

nominee *n*
candidate, entrant, contestant, appointee, runner, assignee

non-aligned *adj*
neutral, independent, impartial, non-partisan, uncommitted, undecided, uninvolved

nonchalance *n*
calm, cool, composure, indifference, detachment, unconcern, self-possession
formal equanimity, imperturbability, insouciance, sang-froid, aplomb, pococurant(e)ism
E3 anxiousness, worriedness

nonchalant *adj*
unconcerned, detached, dispassionate, offhand, blasé, indifferent, casual, cool, calm, collected, apathetic, careless
formal insouciant, imperturbable
colloq. laid-back, cool and collected, cool as a cucumber
E3 concerned, careful

non-committal *adj*
guarded, unrevealing, cautious, wary, reserved, ambiguous, discreet, equivocal, evasive, careful, neutral, indefinite, tactful, diplomatic, tentative, vague
formal circumspect, prudent, politic
colloq. sitting on the fence, playing your cards close to your chest

non compos mentis *adj*
of unsound mind, insane, mentally ill, deranged, unbalanced, unhinged, crazy
E3 sane, stable

nonconformist *n, adj*
▶ *n* dissenter, rebel, individualist, dissident, radical, protester, heretic, iconoclast, eccentric, maverick, seceder, secessionist
formal dissentient
colloq. fish out of water, square peg in a round hole
E3 conformist
▶ *adj* rebel, dissident, unco-operative, radical,

heretical, eccentric, individualist
formal dissentient

nonconformity *n*
unconventionality, originality, eccentricity, dissent, deviation, heterodoxy, heresy, secession
E3 conformity, conventionality

nondescript *adj*
featureless, indeterminate, undistinctive, undistinguished, indistinguishable, unexceptional, ordinary, outrage, commonplace, plain, dull, vague, bland, anaemic, insipid, uninspiring, uninteresting, unattractive, unremarkable, unclassified
colloq. run of the mill, common or garden
E3 distinctive, remarkable

none *pron*
no one, not any, not one, not even one, not a single one, nothing, nobody, not a soul, nil, zero

nonentity *n*
nobody, nothing, menial, cipher, mediocrity
colloq. lightweight
E3 somebody

non-essential *adj*
unnecessary, unimportant, superfluous, redundant, unneeded, inessential, peripheral, dispensable, excessive, extraneous, expendable, supplementary
E3 essential, necessary

nonetheless *adv*
nevertheless, still, anyway, even so, yet, however, anyhow, but, regardless
formal notwithstanding

non-existence *n*
unreality, fancy, illusion, illusiveness, insubstantiality, unbeing
formal chimera
E3 existence, reality

non-existent *adj*
missing, unreal, null, legendary, mythical, fictitious, fictional, fancied, fanciful, hallucinatory, illusory, hypothetical, imaginary, imagined, fantasy, immaterial, insubstantial
formal chimerical, incorporeal, suppositional
E3 actual, existing, real

non-flammable *adj*
not flammable, fire-proof, fire-resistant, flame-resistant, incombustible, uninflammable
E3 flammable, inflammable

non-intervention *n*
non-involvement, non-participation, non-alignment, non-interference, laissez-faire, inaction, inertia, passivity, apathy
colloq. hands-off policy

nonpareil *adj*
unparalleled, incomparable, beyond compare, without equal, unequalled, matchless, unrivalled, unique, inimitable

non-partisan *adj*
unbiased, unprejudiced, impartial, independent, neutral, objective, even-handed, detached, dispassionate
E3 partisan, biased, prejudiced

nonplus *v*
puzzle, perplex, take aback, baffle, bewilder, confound, confuse, dumbfound, stun, stump, astonish, astound, dismay, embarrass, disconcert, mystify

formal discomfit, discountenance
colloq. flabbergast, flummox, faze

nonplussed *adj*
disconcerted, confounded, taken aback, at a loss,
stunned, bewildered, astonished, astounded,
dumbfounded, perplexed, puzzled, baffled, dismayed,
embarrassed
colloq. stumped, flabbergasted, flummoxed, fazed,
floored, out of your depth

nonsense *n*
rubbish, trash, drivel, balderdash, gibberish,
gobbledygook, senselessness, stupidity, silliness,
foolishness, folly, blather, twaddle, ridiculousness
colloq. stuff and nonsense, double Dutch, mumbo-
jumbo, bunk, bunkum, claptrap, cobblers, poppycock,
piffle, waffle, flannel, rot, tripe, tosh, bosh, tommy-rot,
codswallop, baloney, humbug, hooey, bilge, bull;
slang crap, shit, balls, bullshit
≠ sense, wisdom

nonsensical *adj*
ridiculous, meaningless, senseless, foolish, stupid,
inane, irrational, silly, incomprehensible,
unintelligible, ludicrous, preposterous, absurd, fatuous
colloq. crazy, crackpot, potty, nutty, dotty, barmy, hare-
brained, wacky
≠ reasonable, sensible, logical

non-stop *adj, adv*
▶ *adj* never-ending, uninterrupted, continuous,
unceasing, ceaseless, incessant, constant, endless,
interminable, persistent, relentless, unending,
unbroken, without interruption, unfaltering, round-
the-clock, ongoing
≠ intermittent, occasional
▶ *adv* uninterruptedly, continuously, constantly,
incessantly, unceasingly, ceaselessly, endlessly,
interminably, unendingly, unbrokenly, round-the-
clock, unfalteringly, steadily, relentlessly,
unrelentingly, unremittingly
≠ intermittently, occasionally

non-violent *adj*
peaceable, peaceful, pacifist, passive, irenic, dovish
≠ violent

nook *n*
1 RECESS, alcove, corner, cranny, niche, cubbyhole
2 SHELTER, retreat, hideout, hideaway, den, refuge,
cavity, opening

noon *n*
midday, twelve o'clock, twelve noon, lunchtime

norm *n*
average, mean, standard, rule, usual rule, pattern, type,
criterion, gauge, model, yardstick, benchmark,
touchstone, measure, scale, reference

normal *adj*
usual, standard, general, commonplace, common,
ordinary, conventional, popular, average, regular,
routine, everyday, accepted, typical, mainstream,
natural, habitual, accustomed, well-adjusted, straight,
rational, reasonable
colloq. run of the mill
≠ abnormal, irregular, peculiar, deviant

normality *n*
usualness, commonness, ordinariness, regularity,
routine, conventionality, balance, adjustment,
averageness, typicality, naturalness, reason,

reasonableness, rationality
≠ abnormality, irregularity, peculiarity

normally *adv*
ordinarily, usually, as usual, as a rule, generally,
typically, commonly, conventionally, characteristically,
naturally, regularly, routinely
≠ abnormally, exceptionally

northern *adj*
north, northerly, polar, Arctic
old use septentrional
formal boreal, hyperborean
≠ southern

nose *n, v*
▶ *n* 1 *the animal's nose*
bill, neb
formal proboscis
colloq. beak, boko, hooter, schnozzle, snitch, snout,
snoot; *slang* conk
2 *a nose for a good story*
sense, flair, feel, perception, instinct
Related adjectives: nasal, rhinal
▶ *v* nudge, inch, edge, ease, push
▷ **nose around** poke around, search, pry;
colloq. snoop, rubberneck, poke your nose in
▷ **nose out** discover, detect, find out, uncover,
reveal, inquire; *colloq.* sniff out

nosedive *v, n*
▶ *v* plummet, dive, drop, plunge, decline, get worse,
go down, submerge, swoop
▶ *n* plummet, dive, drop, plunge, swoop, header,
purler

nosegay *n*
bouquet, posy, spray, bunch

nosh *n*
food, foodstuffs, comestibles, provisions, meals, stores,
rations, refreshments, sustenance, nourishment,
nutrition, nutriment, subsistence, feed, fodder, diet,
fare, dish, speciality, delicacy, cooking, cuisine, menu,
board, table
formal viands, victuals
colloq. eatables, eats, tuck; *slang* grub

nostalgia *n*
yearning, longing, wistfulness, regretfulness, regret(s),
remembrance, recollection(s), reminiscence(s),
homesickness, pining

nostalgic *adj*
yearning, longing, pining, wistful, emotional,
regretful, sentimental, homesick, reminiscent

nostrum *n*
medicine, pill, drug, potion, cure, remedy, elixir,
panacea, cure-all, cure for all ills, universal cure/
remedy

nosy *adj*
inquisitive, meddlesome, prying, interfering,
snooping, curious, eavesdropping, probing
colloq. snooping

notability *n*
1 NOTEWORTHINESS, impressiveness, importance,
significance, distinction, fame, eminence, renown
formal esteem
2 CELEBRITY, dignitary, magnate, worthy, luminary
formal notable, personage
colloq. somebody, VIP, bigwig, big shot, big noise,
heavyweight, top brass, someone
≠ nonentity

notable *adj, n*

▶ *adj* noteworthy, remarkable, noticeable, particular, striking, extraordinary, impressive, outstanding, special, important, significant, marked, unusual, uncommon, celebrated, distinguished, famous, great, illustrious, eminent, pre-eminent, well-known, momentous, notorious, memorable, renowned, unforgettable, rare
F3 ordinary, commonplace, usual
▶ *n* celebrity, notability, VIP, personage, somebody, dignitary, luminary, star, worthy
F3 nobody, nonentity

notably *adv*

markedly, noticeably, particularly, significantly, remarkably, strikingly, signally, conspicuously, distinctly, especially, impressively, outstandingly, extraordinarily, eminently, uncommonly

notation *n*

symbols, characters, code, cipher, signs, alphabet, system, script, hieroglyphics, noting, record, shorthand

notch *n, v*

▶ *n* **1** CUT, nick, indentation, incision, dent, score, groove, gouge, cleft, gash, scratch, mark, snip
2 DEGREE, grade, step, level, stage
▶ *v* cut, nick, score, dent, gouge, groove, indent, mark, gash, scratch
▷ **notch up** achieve, gain, attain, make, score, record, register; *colloq.* chalk up

notched *adj*

jagged, jaggy, pinked, serrate(d), serrulate(d), eroded
formal crenellate(d), emarginate, erose

note *n, v*

▶ *n* **1** MESSAGE, letter, communication, memorandum, reminder, line, jotting, account, record, comment
formal epistle, missive
colloq. memo
2 ANNOTATION, comment, commentary, explanation, gloss, footnote, remark
formal explication, marginalia
3 INDICATION, signal, element, tone, inflection, token, mark, symbol
4 EMINENCE, distinction, consequence, fame, renown, greatness, illustriousness, reputation, pre-eminence, prestige
5 HEED, attention, attentiveness, care, mindfulness, regard, notice, observation, consideration
▶ *v* **1** NOTICE, observe, perceive, heed, detect, mark, remark, mention, allude to, refer to, touch on, see, witness
2 RECORD, register, log, write down, enter, put in writing, put down, jot down

noted *adj*

famous, well-known, renowned, notable, celebrated, eminent, pre-eminent, prominent, great, of note, acclaimed, illustrious, distinguished, respected, recognized
F3 obscure, unknown

notes *n*

jottings, record, impressions, report, commentary, sketch, impressions, outline, synopsis, transcript, minutes, draft

noteworthy *adj*

remarkable, significant, important, notable, memorable, striking, exceptional, impressive,

extraordinary, unusual, outstanding, marked
F3 commonplace, unexceptional, ordinary

nothing *n*

1 NOUGHT, zero, not a thing, naught, nothingness
colloq. zilch, sweet Fanny Adams; *slang* bugger all, sod all; *taboo slang* fuck all
2 NON-EXISTENCE, emptiness, void, oblivion
formal nullity
colloq. lightweight
3 NOBODY, nonentity, menial, cipher, mediocrity
F3 something
▷ **for nothing 1** FREE, gratis, without charge, free of charge, at no cost; *colloq.* on the house **2** IN VAIN, unsuccessfully, futilely, needlessly, with no result, to no avail

nothingness *n*

non-existence, oblivion, vacuum, void, emptiness
formal nihilism, nihility, nullity
F3 life, existence

notice *v, n*

▶ *v* note, remark, perceive, observe, mind, see, discern, distinguish, make out, mark, detect, spot, become aware of, take note of, pay attention to
formal heed, take heed of, behold, espy
F3 ignore, overlook, miss
▶ *n* **1** ANNOUNCEMENT, notification, information, declaration, communication, intimation, intelligence, news, warning, instruction, advice, order
formal apprisal
2 ADVERTISEMENT, poster, sign, bill, handbill, bulletin, leaflet, pamphlet, circular, information sheet
3 REVIEW, comment, criticism, critique, write-up
colloq. crit
4 ATTENTION, observation, awareness, note, regard, thought, interest, watchfulness, consideration
formal heed, cognizance

noticeable *adj*

perceptible, observable, appreciable, unmistakable, conspicuous, visible, discernible, evident, clear, distinct, significant, striking, plain, patent, obvious, detectable, distinguishable, measurable
formal manifest
F3 inconspicuous, unnoticeable

notification *n*

announcement, information, notice, declaration, advice, warning, telling, informing, intelligence, message, publication, statement, communication, divulgence, disclosure

notify *v*

inform, tell, make known, advise, announce, declare, communicate, broadcast, warn, acquaint, caution, alert, publish, disclose, reveal, divulge
formal apprise

notion *n*

1 IDEA, thought, concept, conception, belief, impression, view, opinion, conviction, theory, hypothesis, assumption, understanding, apprehension
formal conceptualization
2 INCLINATION, desire, wish, whim, fancy, caprice

notional *adj*

theoretical, abstract, imaginary, hypothetical, illusory, conceptual, speculative, fanciful, fancied, unfounded, unreal, visionary, thematic, classificatory
formal ideational
F3 real

notoriety *n*
infamy, disrepute, dishonour, disgrace, scandal
formal ignominy, obloquy, opprobrium

notorious *adj*
infamous, disreputable, scandalous, dishonourable,
ill-famed, of ill repute, disgraceful, flagrant, blatant,
glaring, well-known
formal ignominious, egregious, opprobrious

notoriously *adv*
infamously, disreputably, scandalously, dishonourably,
disgracefully, flagrantly, blatantly, glaringly, overtly,
notably, obviously, openly, particularly, patently,
arrantly, spectacularly
formal egregiously, opprobriously, ignominiously

notwithstanding *adv & prep*
nevertheless, nonetheless, although, though, even so,
however, yet, despite, in spite of, regardless of

nought *n*
zero, nil, naught, nothing, nothingness
colloq. zilch

nourish *v*
1 NURTURE, feed, foster, care for, provide for, take
care of, sustain, support, attend to, tend, nurse, bring
up, rear, maintain, have, cherish
2 STRENGTHEN, encourage, promote, cultivate,
stimulate, foster, further, forward, advance, boost,
help, aid, assist

nourishing *adj*
nutritious, wholesome, healthful, health-giving, good,
beneficial, substantial, strengthening, invigorating
technical alimentative
formal nutritive

nourishment *n*
nutrition, food, sustenance, diet, nutriment,
subsistence
colloq. eats, tuck; *slang* grub, nosh

novel *adj, n*
▶ *adj* new, original, fresh, innovative, unfamiliar,
unique, rare, unusual, uncommon, different, creative,
imaginative, resourceful, ingenious, inventive,
unconventional, unorthodox, modern,
unprecedented, pioneering, ground-breaking, strange
ⴲ hackneyed, familiar, ordinary
▶ *n* fiction, story, tale, narrative, romance, book

novelty *n*
1 NEWNESS, originality, freshness, innovation,
unfamiliarity, unusualness, uniqueness, rareness,
difference, creativity, imaginativeness,
unconventionality, strangeness
2 GIMMICK, gadget, trifle, memento, knick-knack,
curiosity, souvenir, trinket, bauble, gimcrack

novice *n*
beginner, tiro, learner, student, pupil, trainee,
probationer, recruit, raw recruit, apprentice, amateur,
newcomer
formal neophyte, noviciate
colloq. greenhorn, rookie
ⴲ expert

noviciate *n*
apprenticeship, trainee period, training, initiation,
trial period

now *adv*
1 AT PRESENT, right now, just now, at the moment,
for the time being, at the present time, at the moment,

at this moment in time, at this time, currently,
nowadays, today, these days
US presently
2 IMMEDIATELY, at once, directly, instantly, straight
away, right away, promptly, without delay, next
▷ **now and then** at times, sometimes, from time to
time, now and again, occasionally, on and off, on
occasion, once in a while, periodically, infrequently,
intermittently, spasmodically, sporadically;
formal desultorily

nowadays *adv*
at present, today, at the present time, at the moment, at
this moment in time, at this time, currently, these days,
in this day and age
US presently

noxious *adj*
harmful, poisonous, pernicious, toxic, injurious,
unhealthy, deadly, destructive, ruinous, damaging,
detrimental, malignant, foul, disgusting, threatening,
menacing
formal noisome, deleterious
ⴲ innocuous, wholesome

nuance *n*
subtlety, suggestion, shade, shading, hint, suspicion,
gradation, (fine) distinction, overtone, refinement,
touch, trace, tinge, degree, nicety

nub *n*
centre, heart, core, nucleus, kernel, crux, gist, pith,
marrow, meat, pivot, focus, point, essence

nubile *adj*
mature, adult, marriageable, attractive, desirable,
voluptuous
colloq. sexy

nucleus *n*
centre, heart, nub, core, kernel, basis, marrow, meat,
pivot, focus, crux

nude *adj*
naked, bare, with nothing on, undressed, unclothed,
stripped, stark-naked, uncovered, exposed
colloq. starkers, in your birthday suit, in the altogether,
in the raw, in the buff, not a stitch on, naked as the day
you were born
ⴲ clothed, dressed

nudge *v & n*
poke, prod, jab, shove, dig, jog, prompt, push, elbow,
bump

nudity *n*
nakedness, bareness, undress, state of undress,
nudism, dishabille, déshabillé
colloq. in the altogether

nugatory *adj*
worthless, futile, useless, vain, valueless, unavailing,
null and void, invalid, inoperative, insignificant,
inconsequential, trifling, trivial, inadequate
formal ineffectual
ⴲ important, significant

nugget *n*
lump, mass, piece, chunk, clump, hunk, wad, wodge

nuisance *n*
annoyance, inconvenience, bother, irritation, irritant,
vexation, pest, bore, difficulty, problem, trial, trouble,
weight, burden, plague, inconvenience, drawback
formal affliction, tribulation
colloq. pain, drag, thorn in your side/flesh

null *adj*
void, invalid, invalidated, annulled, revoked, cancelled, useless, vain, worthless, powerless, inoperative
formal ineffectual, nullified, abrogated
🔄 valid

nullify *v*
annul, revoke, cancel, invalidate, declare null and void, abolish, rescind, quash, repeal, void, set aside, bring to an end, reverse, offset, counteract
formal abrogate, negate, countermand, renounce, discontinue
🔄 validate

nullity *n*
non-existence, voidness, characterlessness, immateriality, invalidity, powerlessness, uselessness, worthlessness
formal incorporeality, ineffectualness
🔄 validity

numb *adj, v*
▶ *adj* benumbed, insensible, unfeeling, dead, deadened, insensitive, without feeling, drugged, anaesthetized, stunned, dazed, frozen, paralysed, immobilized, in shock
formal insensible, insensate
🔄 sensitive
▶ *v* deaden, benumb, anaesthetize, drug, freeze, immobilize, paralyse, dull, daze, stupefy, stun
🔄 sensitize

number *n, v*
▶ *n* **1** FIGURE, numeral, digit, integer, unit, character, cipher, fraction, decimal, statistics, data
2 TOTAL, sum, aggregate, tally, score, count, sum, collection, amount, quantity, several, many, company, crowd, group, multitude, throng, horde
3 COPY, issue, edition, impression, imprint, volume, printing
▶ *v* **1** COUNT, calculate, enumerate, reckon, total, add (up to), compute, estimate, include
2 *your days are numbered*
limit, restrict, restrain, delimit, specify

numberless *adj*
innumerable, countless, endless, uncounted, many, unnumbered, unsummed, infinite, untold, myriad, immeasurable
formal multitudinous

numbness *n*
deadness, paralysis, anaesthetization, unfeelingness, dullness, insensitivity, stupefaction, stupor, torpor
formal insensateness, insensibility
🔄 sensitivity

numeral *n*
number, figure, digit, integer, unit, character, cipher

numerous *adj*
many, innumerable, countless, endless, abundant, several, quite a few, legion, plentiful, copious, profuse, various, sundry
formal manifold, multitudinous
colloq. a good few
🔄 few, scarce, rare

numerousness *n*
plentifulness, abundance, copiousness, countlessness, plurality, profusion
formal manifoldness, multiplicity, multitudinousness, multeity
🔄 scantiness, scarcity

numskull *n*
fool, dimwit, dunce, simpleton
colloq. clot, dummy, fat head, thickhead, twit, nit, nitwit, twerp, birdbrain

nun *n*
sister, abbess, prioress, vowess, mother superior, anchoress, ancress, canoness, vestal

nuncio *n*
representative, envoy, ambassador, legate

nunnery *n*
convent, priory, cloister, abbey

nuptial *adj*
wedding, wedded, marital, bridal
formal matrimonial, conjugal, connubial, hymeneal, epithalamial, epithalamic

nuptials *n*
wedding celebrations, wedding, marriage, bridal
formal matrimony, spousals, espousal

nurse *v*
1 TEND, care for, look after, treat, attend to, take care of
2 BREAST-FEED, feed, suckle, wet-nurse, nurture, nourish
3 PRESERVE, sustain, support, nourish, cherish, harbour, entertain, encourage, keep, foster, boost, promote, advance, further, nurture, help, aid, assist

Nurses include: charge nurse, children's nurse, dental nurse, district nurse, healthcare assistant, health visitor, home nurse, Iain Rennie nurse, locality manager, Macmillan nurse, matron, midwife, nanny, night nurse, night sister, nursemaid, nursery nurse, nurse tutor, occupational health nurse, psychiatric nurse, Registered General Nurse (RGN), school nurse, sister, staff nurse, State Enrolled Nurse (SEN), State Registered Nurse (SRN), theatre sister, ward sister, wet nurse.

nurture *n, v*
▶ *n* **1** FOOD, nourishment, nutrition, sustenance, diet, subsistence
colloq. eats, tuck; *slang* grub, nosh
2 REARING, upbringing, training, care, cultivation, stimulation, encouragement, fostering, promotion, help, aid, assistance, furtherance, advance, boosting, development, education, tending, feeding, schooling, discipline
▶ *v* **1** FEED, nourish, nurse, tend, care for, foster, support, sustain
2 BRING UP, rear, cultivate, develop, stimulate, promote, foster, help, aid, assist, further, advance, boost, educate, instruct, train, school, coach, tutor, discipline

nut *n*
1 *a bag of mixed nuts*
kernel, pip, seed, stone

Varieties of nut include: almond, beech nut, brazil nut, cashew, chestnut, cobnut, coconut, filbert, hazelnut, macadamia, monkey nut, peanut, pecan, pistachio, walnut.

2 MANIAC, insane person, lunatic, psychopath, madman, madwoman
colloq. loony, nutcase, nutter, fruitcake, basket-case; *slang* psycho, headcase, oddball
3 ENTHUSIAST, fan, fanatic, follower, supporter,

devotee, zealot, admirer, aficionado
colloq. buff, freak, fiend

nutriment *n*
food, nourishment, nutrition, sustenance, diet, subsistence
colloq. eats, tuck; *slang* grub, nosh

nutrition *n*
food, nourishment, sustenance, diet, nutriment, subsistence
colloq. eats, tuck; *slang* grub, nosh
Related adjective: trophic

nutritious *adj*
nourishing, nutritive, wholesome, healthful, health-giving, good, beneficial, strengthening, substantial, invigorating
F3 bad, unwholesome

nuts *adj*
1 MAD, crazy, insane, lunatic, unbalanced, disturbed, deranged, demented, crazed, wild, berserk, unhinged, out of your mind

colloq. loony, loopy, bonkers, nutty, nutty as a fruitcake, off your rocker, out to lunch, doolally, round the bend, round the twist

2 *nuts about computers*
crazy, enthusiastic, fanatical, zealous, devoted, fond, keen, avid, ardent, passionate, infatuated, enamoured, smitten, mad, wild
colloq. daft
F3 **1** sane **2** indifferent

nuts and bolts *n*
basics, essentials, fundamentals, details, components, bits and pieces, practicalities
colloq. nitty-gritty

nuzzle *v*
snuggle, cuddle, pet, nestle, fondle, nudge, burrow

nymph *n*
sprite, sylph, dryad, hamadryad, naiad, oread, undine, girl, damsel, lass, maid, maiden

O

oaf *n*
lout, boor, dolt, yahoo, barbarian, gawk, lubber
colloq. clod, hick, hobbledehoy, slob, yobbo, bumpkin

oafish *adj*
boorish, churlish, doltish, lumpish, lubberly, stolid,
swinish, uncouth, unmannerly, bungling, rough,
coarse, gross, ill-bred, ill-mannered, gawky, lumpen
colloq. clodhopping

oasis *n*
1 SPRING, watering-hole
2 REFUGE, haven, island, sanctuary, retreat,
hideaway, hideout
formal sanctum

oath *n*
1 VOW, pledge, promise, bond, word, assurance, word
of honour
formal affirmation, avowal, attestation
2 CURSE, swear-word, four-letter word, obscenity, bad
language, blasphemy
formal imprecation, profanity, expletive, malediction

obdurate *adj*
obstinate, stubborn, inflexible, hard-hearted,
implacable, iron, stiff-necked, stony, unfeeling,
immovable, unyielding, unbending, unrelenting,
persistent, dogged, headstrong, strong-minded, self-
willed, steadfast, firm, determined, adamant, wilful
formal intractable, intransigent
colloq. pig-headed, bloody-minded
E3 submissive, tender

obedience *n*
submissiveness, submission, respect, reverence,
amenableness, amenability, malleability, allegiance,
conformability, accordance, agreement, deference,
duty, dutifulness, passivity, subservience, observance,
docility
formal compliance, acquiescence, tractability
E3 disobedience, rebellion

obedient *adj*
submissive, docile, yielding, conforming, pliable,
malleable, amenable, dutiful, biddable, law-abiding,
deferential, respectful, well-trained, disciplined,
subservient, observant
formal compliant, acquiescent, tractable, obsequious
E3 disobedient, rebellious, wilful

obeisance *n*
respect, reverence, submission, deference, homage,
bow, curtsy, kowtow, salaam, salute
formal genuflection, salutation, veneration

obelisk *n*
pillar, column, monument, memorial, needle

obese *adj*
fat, overweight, tubby, stout, big, large, portly, fleshy,
round, well-endowed, paunchy, ponderous, plump,
podgy, chubby, roly-poly, heavy, bulky, outsize,

Falstaffian
formal corpulent, rotund
colloq. gross, flabby
E3 skinny, slender, thin

obesity *n*
fatness, overweight, stoutness, plumpness, portliness,
chubbiness, podginess, tubbiness, bulk
formal corpulence, rotundness
colloq. grossness, flabbiness
E3 thinness, slenderness, skinniness

obey *v*
1 *obey an order*
follow, observe, abide by, adhere to, conform, heed,
keep (to), mind, respond, submit, surrender, yield, be
ruled by, bow to, take orders from, do as you are told,
defer (to), respect, give way
formal comply, consent to, acquiesce in
colloq. stick to the rules, go by the book, toe the line
2 CARRY OUT, discharge, execute, act upon, fulfil,
perform
E3 1 disobey

obfuscate *v*
obscure, cover, blur, confuse, muddle, complicate,
conceal, cloud, hide, disguise, mask, overshadow,
shadow, shade, cloak, veil, shroud

object¹ *n*
1 THING, article, item, entity, body, something,
device, gadget, phenomenon
2 AIM, objective, purpose, goal, target, intention,
point, idea, motive, end, reason, ambition, design
formal intent
3 TARGET, focus, recipient, butt, victim

object² *v*
object to something
protest, oppose, take exception, disapprove, refuse,
complain, rebut, repudiate, withstand, resist, argue,
challenge, beg to differ, take issue, take a stand against
formal demur, expostulate, remonstrate
E3 agree, approve; *formal* acquiesce, accede, assent

objection *n*
protest, dissent, disapproval, opposition, complaint,
dissatisfaction, argument, challenge, grievance,
scruple
formal demur, expostulation, remonstration
E3 agreement, approval, assent

objectionable *adj*
unacceptable, unpleasant, offensive, obnoxious,
disagreeable, hateful, detestable, deplorable,
despicable, contemptible, intolerable, loathsome,
revolting, repulsive, nauseating, sickening
formal repugnant, abhorrent, repellent, reprehensible
E3 acceptable, pleasant, delightful

objective *adj, n*
▶ *adj* 1 IMPARTIAL, unbiased, detached,
unprejudiced, open-minded, equitable, dispassionate,

even-handed, neutral, disinterested, uninvolved, just, fair
2 *objective information*
factual, real, true, actual, authentic, genuine
🖃 **1** subjective
▶ *n* object, aim, goal, end, purpose, ambition, mark, target, intention, point, idea, design
formal intent

objectively *adv*
impartially, equitably, dispassionately, disinterestedly, even-handedly, neutrally, justly, fairly, with an open mind

objectivity *n*
impartiality, detachment, disinterest, disinterestedness, equitableness, even-handedness, justness, justice, fairness, open-mindedness, open mind
🖃 subjectivity, bias, prejudice

obligate *v*
compel, constrain, coerce, require, make, necessitate, force, impel, pressurize, pressure, press, bind

obligation *n*
duty, responsibility, onus, charge, task, function, assignment, job, commitment, liability, accountability, requirement, agreement, bond, deed, covenant, contract, debt, indebtedness, burden, trust, compulsion, demand, command, pressure, duress

obligatory *adj*
compulsory, statutory, required, binding, essential, necessary, unavoidable, enforced
formal mandatory, imperative, requisite
🖃 optional

oblige *v*
1 COMPEL, constrain, coerce, require, make, necessitate, force, impel, pressurize, pressure, press, bind, obligate, leave/be given no option
2 HELP, assist, accommodate, do someone a favour, serve, do someone a service, put yourself out for, gratify, please

obliged *adj*
under an obligation, indebted, in debt (to), grateful, thankful, gratified, appreciative, bound, forced, compelled, constrained, duty-bound, honour-bound, required, obligated, under compulsion
formal beholden

obliging *adj*
accommodating, co-operative, helpful, considerate, willing, generous, pleasant, agreeable, friendly, kind, good-natured, polite, courteous, civil, indulgent
formal complaisant
🖃 unhelpful

oblique *adj, n*
▶ *adj* **1** SLANTING, sloping, inclined, angled, tilted
2 INDIRECT, roundabout, circuitous, divergent, devious, rambling, winding, meandering, zigzag, tortuous, discursive
formal periphrastic, circumlocutory
▶ *n* diagonal, slant, slash, stroke
formal virgule

obliquely *adv*
1 DIAGONALLY, at an angle, aslant, aslope, askance, askant, slantwise
2 INDIRECTLY, in a roundabout way, circuitously, evasively, not in so many words

obliterate *v*
eradicate, destroy, eliminate, annihilate, strike out, delete, blot out, wipe out, rub out, erase
formal efface, expunge, extirpate

obliteration *n*
eradication, destruction, elimination, annihilation, blotting out, deletion, erasure
formal effacement, expunction, extirpation

oblivion *n*
1 UNCONSCIOUSNESS, blankness, darkness, stupor, void, limbo
2 OBSCURITY, nothingness, non-existence, disuse
3 UNAWARENESS, unconsciousness, inattentiveness, unmindfulness, absent-mindedness, carelessness, blindness, deafness, ignorance
🖃 **3** awareness
Related adjective: lethean

oblivious *adj*
unaware, unconscious, inattentive, unmindful, preoccupied, absent-minded, careless, forgetful, heedless, unheeding, blind, deaf, ignorant, negligent, unconcerned
formal insensible
🖃 aware, conscious

obloquy *n*
disgrace, dishonour, discredit, disfavour, shame, reproach, humiliation, criticism, attack, abuse, blame, censure, defamation, slander, detraction, bad press
formal animadversion, aspersion, calumny, contumely, ignominy, invective, odium, opprobrium, stigma, vilification

obnoxious *adj*
unpleasant, disagreeable, disgusting, offensive, objectionable, unacceptable, loathsome, nasty, horrid, horrible, odious, vile, repulsive, revolting, sickening, nauseating, hateful, detestable, contemptible, deplorable, intolerable
formal repugnant, abhorrent, repellent
🖃 pleasant

obscene *adj*
1 INDECENT, rude, improper, immoral, immodest, shameless, unchaste, impure, coarse, vulgar, filthy, dirty, foul, gross, vile, bawdy, lewd, licentious, pornographic, scurrilous, suggestive, sexy, risqué, smutty, off-colour, disgusting, foul
formal carnal, lubricious, prurient
colloq. near the knuckle/bone, blue, raunchy, fruity, sleazy
2 SHOCKING, shameless, offensive, outrageous, disgraceful, immoral, scandalous
🖃 **1** decent, wholesome

obscenity *n*
1 INDECENCY, immodesty, immorality, impurity, impropriety, unchasteness, lewdness, licentiousness, bawdiness, suggestiveness, eroticism, pornography, dirtiness, filthiness, foulness, coarseness, grossness, indelicacy, vulgarity, shamelessness, salaciousness, lasciviousness
formal carnality, prurience, lubricity
colloq. raunchiness, sleaze
2 ATROCITY, evil, outrage, offence, wickedness, vileness
formal heinousness
3 SWEAR-WORD, four-letter word, curse, bad language
formal profanity, expletive, imprecation, malediction

obscure *adj, v*

▶ *adj* **1** UNKNOWN, unimportant, insignificant, little-known, unheard-of, remote, out-of-the-way, God-forsaken, undistinguished, nameless, unsung, unrecognized, inconspicuous, humble, minor
colloq. off the beaten track
2 INCOMPREHENSIBLE, unclear, complex, involved, enigmatic, cryptic, opaque, mysterious, unexplained, inexplicable, unfathomable, impenetrable, deep, hidden, concealed, confusing, puzzling, perplexing
formal recondite, esoteric, arcane, abstruse
3 INDISTINCT, unclear, indefinite, uncertain, doubtful, shadowy, blurred, cloudy, faint, hazy, fuzzy, dim, misty, shady, vague, murky, dark, gloomy, dusky
E3 **1** famous, renowned **2** intelligible, straightforward **3** clear, definite
▶ *v* conceal, cloud, hide, cover, blur, confuse, muddle, complicate, disguise, mask, overshadow, shadow, shade, cloak, veil, shroud, darken, dim, eclipse, screen, block out
formal obfuscate
E3 clarify, illuminate

obscurity *n*

1 UNIMPORTANCE, insignificance, lowliness, namelessness, inconspicuousness, lack of fame/ recognition, inconspicuousness
2 INCOMPREHENSIBILITY, impenetrability, unclearness, complexity, intricacy, ambiguity, mystery, confusion, mysticism
formal abstruseness, reconditeness
E3 **1** fame **2** intelligibility, clarity, lucidity

obsequious *adj*

servile, ingratiating, grovelling, fawning, menial, sycophantic, cringing, toadying, deferential, flattering, unctuous, oily, submissive, subservient, slavish, abject;
colloq. smarmy, bootlicking, creepy; *slang* arse-licking

observable *adj*

noticeable, perceptible, discernible, appreciable, detectable, recognizable, measurable, significant, visible, apparent, clear, obvious, evident, open, patent, perceivable

observance *n*

1 ADHERENCE, performance, execution, obedience, keeping, following, fulfilment, honouring, notice, attention
formal compliance, heeding, discharge
2 RITUAL, custom, ceremony, rite, practice, tradition, formality, service, celebration, festival

observant *adj*

1 ATTENTIVE, alert, vigilant, on guard, watchful, mindful, perceptive, sharp, sharp-eyed, hawk-eyed, eagle-eyed, wide-awake, on the lookout
formal heedful
colloq. with your eyes skinned/peeled, with eyes like a hawk
2 DUTIFUL, committed, devoted, obedient, practising, orthodox
E3 **1** unobservant

observation *n*

1 ATTENTION, notice, noticing, seeing, viewing, examination, inspection, scrutiny, monitoring, study, review, watching, consideration, discernment, perception
2 REMARK, comment, utterance, thought, statement, pronouncement, declaration, reflection, opinion, finding, result, description, note, information, data
formal annotation

observe *v*

1 WATCH, see, view, spot, study, notice, note, contemplate, inspect, examine, monitor, keep an eye on, discern, perceive, detect, catch sight of, keep watch on, keep under surveillance
formal behold, espy
colloq. keep tabs on, miss nothing, keep an eye on, keep your eyes skinned/peeled, watch like a hawk
2 REMARK, comment, say, mention, utter, state, declare
3 *observe the law*
ABIDE BY, honour, keep, follow, obey, adhere to, fulfil, celebrate, mark, commemorate, remember, recognize, perform, conform to, respect, execute
formal comply with, discharge
E3 **1** miss **3** break, violate

observer *n*

watcher, spectator, viewer, witness, reporter, looker-on, onlooker, sightseer, eyewitness, commentator, bystander
formal beholder

obsess *v*

preoccupy, dominate, rule, control, monopolize, haunt, hound, torment, bedevil, grip, have a grip/hold on, plague, prey on, possess, engross, consume, be uppermost in your mind

obsessed *adj*

preoccupied, dominated, gripped, in the grip of, immersed in, haunted, hounded, plagued, infatuated, bedevilled, beset
colloq. hung up on
E3 detached, indifferent, unconcerned

obsession *n*

preoccupation, fixation, *idée fixe*, ruling passion, compulsion, fetish, infatuation, mania, complex, phobia, enthusiasm, fascination
colloq. hang-up, thing, one-track mind

obsessive *adj*

consuming, compulsive, gripping, fixed, haunting, tormenting, maddening

obsolescent *adj*

out of date, old-fashioned, outdated, dated, dying out, disappearing, declining, fading, waning, ageing, redundant, on the way out, past its prime, on the decline, on the wane
formal moribund

obsolete *adj*

outmoded, disused, in disuse, discarded, out of date, old-fashioned, out of fashion, *passé*, dated, outworn, old, ancient, antiquated, antique, superannuated, dead, extinct, bygone, behind the times, on the way out, past its prime
formal discontinued
colloq. past its sell-by date, old hat, on the shelf, out of the ark, antediluvian
E3 modern, current, up-to-date, in use

obstacle *n*

barrier, bar, obstruction, blockade, barricade, impediment, hurdle, hindrance, check, snag, stumbling-block, blockage, drawback, handicap, difficulty, hitch, catch, stoppage, stop, curb, interference, interruption, deterrent
colloq. hiccup, no-no, fly in the ointment, spanner in

the works
☞ advantage, help

obstinacy *n*
stubbornness, inflexibility, hard-heartedness, persistence, perseverance, resoluteness, tenacity, wilfulness, wrong-headedness, perversity, firmness, doggedness, relentlessness, mulishness
formal frowardness, intransigence, obduracy, pertinacity
colloq. pig-headedness
☞ co-operativeness, flexibility, submissiveness

obstinate *adj*
stubborn, inflexible, hard-hearted, immovable, unyielding, unbending, unrelenting, persistent, dogged, headstrong, strong-minded, self-willed, steadfast, firm, persevering, determined, adamant, wilful
formal intractable, intransigent, refractory, recalcitrant
colloq. pig-headed, bloody-minded, obstinate as a mule
☞ flexible, tractable

obstreperous *adj*
disorderly, unruly, tumultuous, unmanageable, undisciplined, wild, uncontrolled, out of hand, noisy, loud, boisterous, clamorous, raucous, riotous, rip-roaring, tempestuous, rowdy, rough, turbulent, uproarious, vociferous
formal refractory, restive, intractable
colloq. stroppy, bolshie, bloody-minded
☞ calm, disciplined, quiet

obstruct *v*
block, impede, hinder, prevent, check, frustrate, hamper, clog, choke, bar, barricade, stop, halt, bridle, stall, restrict, limit, thwart, encumber, hamstring, inhibit, hold up, brake, curb, arrest, slow down, delay, interrupt, interfere with, shut off, cut off, obscure
formal retard, arrest
☞ assist, further

obstruction *n*
barrier, blockage, bar, barricade, hindrance, impediment, obstacle, stumbling-block, check, stop, stoppage, restriction, embargo, sanction, difficulty, deterrent
☞ help

obstructive *adj*
hindering, delaying, blocking, stalling, unhelpful, unco-operative, awkward, difficult, restrictive, inhibiting, interrupting
☞ co-operative, helpful

obtain *v*
1 ACQUIRE, get, gain, gain possession of, come by, attain, secure, seize, earn, achieve
formal procure
colloq. get your hands on
2 PREVAIL, exist, hold, be in force, be the case, be effective, be in use, hold sway, stand, reign, rule, be prevalent

obtainable *adj*
available, at hand, ready, to be had, accessible, achievable, attainable, realizable, on call
formal procurable
colloq. on tap
☞ unobtainable, unavailable

obtrusive *adj*
1 PROMINENT, protruding, projecting, noticeable,

obvious, conspicuous, blatant, flagrant, bold, forward
2 INTRUSIVE, interfering, forward, prying, meddling
colloq. nosy, pushy
☞ 1 unobtrusive

obtuse *adj*
slow, slow-witted, stupid, unintelligent, dull, dense, crass, stolid, dull-witted, thick-skinned
colloq. thick, dumb, dim, dim-witted
☞ bright, sharp

obviate *v*
avert, prevent, divert, forestall, remove, counter, counteract, anticipate
formal preclude

obvious *adj*
evident, self-evident, manifest, patent, clear, crystal clear, plain, visible, distinct, transparent, undeniable, unmistakable, conspicuous, glaring, apparent, open, unconcealed, visible, noticeable, detectable, perceptible, pronounced, transparent, recognizable, self-explanatory, straightforward, clear-cut, prominent
colloq. as plain as a pikestaff, as clear as daylight, staring you in the face, sticking out a mile, right under your nose, shouting from the rooftops
☞ unclear, indistinct, obscure

obviously *adv*
plainly, clearly, evidently, noticeably, patently, undeniably, unmistakably, without doubt, undoubtedly, certainly, distinctly, of course
formal manifestly

occasion *n, v*
▶ *n* 1 EVENT, occurrence, incident, episode, experience, situation, circumstance, happening, affair, time, instance, point, chance, case, opportunity, juncture
2 REASON, cause, excuse, justification, call, ground(s)
3 CELEBRATION, function, affair, party
colloq. do, get-together
▶ *v* cause, bring about, bring on, make, produce, create, give rise to, generate, induce, lead to, provoke, prompt, evoke, elicit, influence, inspire, persuade, originate, engender
formal effect

occasional *adj*
periodic, intermittent, irregular, sporadic, infrequent, uncommon, incidental, odd, rare, casual
☞ frequent, regular, constant

occasionally *adv*
sometimes, on occasion, from time to time, at times, at intervals, now and then, now and again, irregularly, periodically, every so often, once in a while, off and on, on and off, infrequently, intermittently, sporadically
☞ frequently, often, always

occult *adj, n*
▶ *adj* mystical, supernatural, magical, magic, mysterious, concealed, obscure, secret, hidden, veiled, concealed
formal esoteric, arcane, recondite, abstruse, transcendental, preternatural
▶ *n* the supernatural, black arts, mysticism, supernaturalism

Terms associated with the occult include: amulet, astral projection, astrology, astrologer, bewitch, black cat, black magic, black mass, cabbala, charm, chiromancer, chiromancy, clairvoyance, clairvoyant, conjure, coven, crystal ball, curse, déjà vu, divination, diviner, divining-rod, dream, ectoplasm, evil eye, evil spirit, exorcism, exorcist, extrasensory perception (ESP), familiar, fetish, fortune-teller, garlic, Hallowe'en, hallucination, hoodoo, horoscope, horseshoe, hydromancer, hydromancy, illusion, incantation, jinx, juju, magic, magician, mascot, medium, necromancer, necromancy, obi, omen, oneiromancer, oneiromancy, Ouija board®, palmist, palmistry, paranormal, pentagram, planchette, poltergeist, possession, prediction, premonition, psychic, rabbit's foot, relic, rune, satanic, Satanism, Satanist, séance, second sight, shaman, shamrock, sixth sense, sorcerer, sorcery, spell, spirit, spiritualism, spiritualist, supernatural, superstition, talisman, tarot card, tarot reading, telepathist, telepathy, totem, trance, vision, voodoo, Walpurgis Night, warlock, white magic, witch, witchcraft, witch doctor, witch's broomstick, witch's sabbath.

occupancy n
tenancy, residence, tenure, term, occupation, owner-occupancy, ownership, possession, holding, use
formal domiciliation, habitation, inhabitancy

occupant n
occupier, owner-occupier, holder, inhabitant, resident, householder, tenant, user, renter, leaseholder, lessee, squatter, inmate, incumbent

occupation n
1 JOB, profession, work, career, vocation, employment, employ, trade, post, calling, business, field, line, province, pursuit, craft, walk of life, activity, métier
2 INVASION, seizure, conquest, control, possession, capture, overthrow, foreign rule, foreign domination, takeover
formal subjugation
3 OCCUPANCY, possession, holding, tenancy, tenure, residence, use
formal habitation

occupational adj
job-related, professional, vocational, career, work, employment, trade, business

occupied adj
1 UNAVAILABLE, in use, taken, busy, full, tenanted
2 ABSORBED, engrossed, taken up, employed, engaged, preoccupied, immersed, busy, working, tied up
colloq. hard at it
🖪 unoccupied, vacant

occupy v
1 INHABIT, live in, possess, reside in, stay in, make your home in, settle, people, tenant, take possession of, own
formal dwell in
2 ABSORB, take up, engross, employ, engage, hold, involve, preoccupy, immerse, amuse, entertain, busy, interest, divert
3 INVADE, seize, capture, overrun, take over, take possession of
4 FILL, take up, use (up), hold, have

occur v
1 HAPPEN, come about, take place, chance, come to pass, turn out, materialize, develop, crop up, turn up,

result
formal transpire, befall, eventuate
2 EXIST, be present, be found, have its being, arise, appear
formal obtain, manifest itself
3 *the idea occurred to me*
come to you, dawn on, strike, hit, suggest itself, come to mind, cross your mind, enter your head, present itself, spring to mind, sink in

occurrence n
1 INCIDENT, event, happening, affair, proceedings, circumstance, episode, instance, case, development, action
2 INCIDENCE, existence, appearance, arising, springing-up, development
formal manifestation

ocean n
main, profound, sea, the deep
colloq. briny, the drink
Related adjective: pelagic

The world's oceans and largest seas include: Pacific Ocean, Atlantic Ocean, Indian Ocean, Arctic Ocean, Antarctic (Southern) Ocean, South China Sea, Caribbean Sea, Mediterranean, Bering Sea, Gulf of Mexico, Sea of Okhotsk.

odd adj
1 UNUSUAL, strange, uncommon, peculiar, funny, abnormal, exceptional, curious, atypical, abnormal, different, queer, bizarre, eccentric, deviant, singular, idiosyncratic, remarkable, unconventional, uncanny, weird, irregular, wild, extraordinary, outlandish, rare
colloq. out of the ordinary, freaky, kinky, wacky, oddball, rum, zany, barmy, crackers, off the wall;
slang far-out, way-out
2 OCCASIONAL, incidental, haphazard, irregular, periodic, seasonal, random, casual, part-time, temporary
formal fortuitous
3 UNMATCHED, unpaired, single, spare, surplus, superfluous, left-over, remaining, sundry, various, miscellaneous
🖪 1 normal, usual 2 regular
▷ **odd one out** nonconformist, eccentric, odd man out, odd woman out; *colloq.* freak, oddball, weirdo, odd bod, fish out of water, square peg in a round hole

oddity n
1 ABNORMALITY, strangeness, peculiarity, queerness, rarity, eccentricity, idiosyncrasy, phenomenon, twist, quirk
2 CURIOSITY, anomaly, rarity, phenomenon, character, misfit
colloq. freak

oddment n
bit, scrap, piece, leftover, fragment, offcut, end, remnant, shred, snippet, patch

odds n
1 LIKELIHOOD, probability, chances
2 ADVANTAGE, edge, lead, superiority, supremacy
formal ascendancy
▷ **at odds** disagreeing, in disagreement, in conflict, differing, clashing, quarrelling, arguing, at loggerheads
▷ **odds and ends** litter, bits and pieces, bits, oddments, junk, remnants, rubbish, scraps, cuttings,

snippets, tatt, debris, flotsam and jetsam, leavings
colloq. odds and sods, this and that

odious *adj*
offensive, loathsome, unpleasant, disagreeable, obnoxious, disgusting, hateful, objectionable, repulsive, revolting, foul, detestable, horrible, horrid, vile, contemptible, despicable
formal repugnant, execrable, abhorrent, abominable, heinous
☒ pleasant

odium *n*
dislike, hatred, disapproval, disrepute, dishonour, shame, disgrace, disfavour, discredit, censure, condemnation, contempt
formal abhorrence, detestation, disapprobation, animosity, antipathy, obloquy, opprobrium, infamy, reprobation, execration

odorous *adj*
scented, sweet-smelling, balmy, aromatic, fragrant, perfumed, pungent
formal odoriferous, redolent
☒ odourless

odour *n*
smell, scent, aroma, fragrance, bouquet, perfume, stench
formal redolence
colloq. stink, pong, niff, whiff

odyssey *n*
journey, voyage, trek, travels, wandering, adventure
formal peregrination

off *adj, adv*
▶ *adj* **1** ROTTEN, bad, sour, turned, high, spoilt, rancid, mouldy, decomposed
2 CANCELLED, postponed, called off, abandoned, dropped
colloq. shelved, scrapped
3 AWAY, absent, gone, unavailable, unobtainable
4 SUBSTANDARD, below par, disappointing, unsatisfactory, slack, wrong, incorrect
▶ *adv* **1** AWAY, elsewhere, out, at a distance, apart, aside
2 ILL, out of sorts, unwell, sick, off form, poorly
formal indisposed
colloq. under the weather

offbeat *adj*
unorthodox, weird, unconventional, untraditional, abnormal, strange, unusual, bizarre, out of the ordinary
colloq. oddball, freaky, kooky, wacky; *slang* far-out, way-out

off-colour *adj*
1 ILL, out of sorts, unwell, sick, off form, poorly
formal indisposed
colloq. under the weather, run down
2 RUDE, indecent, improper, immoral, coarse, vulgar, impure, filthy, dirty, pornographic, suggestive, sexy, risqué, smutty

off-duty *adj*
off, off work, not at work, on holiday, free, at leisure
☒ on duty

offence *n*
1 *a criminal offence*
infringement, crime, trespass, wrong, wrongdoing, illegal act, breach of the law, sin
formal misdemeanour, transgression, violation,

misdeed, infraction
2 AFFRONT, insult, injury, hurt, outrage, snub, slight, indignity, atrocity, ire
3 RESENTMENT, indignation, anger, annoyance, exasperation, disapproval, pique, umbrage, outrage, hurt, hard feelings
formal antipathy
▷ **take offence** resent, be indignant, be angry, be annoyed, be exasperated, be hurt, be offended, be insulted, be upset, be/feel put out, take exception, take personally, take umbrage; *colloq.* be miffed, get huffy, get one's nose out of joint

offend *v*
1 HURT, insult, injure, affront, wrong, wound, displease, snub, upset, annoy, anger, outrage, exasperate, incense, provoke
colloq. miff, needle, put someone's back up, rub someone up the wrong way, put someone's nose out of joint, raise someone's hackles
2 DISGUST, repel, sicken, revolt, nauseate, put off
3 BREAK THE LAW, do wrong, sin, err, go astray
formal transgress, violate
☒ **1** please

offended *adj*
upset, hurt, resentful, disgruntled, affronted, displeased, angered, annoyed, exasperated, incensed, outraged, wounded, smarting, stung, piqued, pained, disgusted
colloq. huffy, in a huff, miffed, put out, touchy
☒ pleased, happy

offender *n*
wrongdoer, culprit, criminal, miscreant, guilty party, law-breaker, delinquent
formal malefactor, transgressor

offensive *adj, n*
▶ *adj* **1** DISAGREEABLE, unpleasant, objectionable, displeasing, disgusting, odious, obnoxious, revolting, loathsome, vile, sickening, nauseating, nasty, foul, detestable, abominable
formal repellent, repugnant, abhorrent
2 INSOLENT, abusive, rude, insulting, affronting, upsetting, hurtful, wounding, annoying, exasperating, impolite, disrespectful, discourteous, impertinent
☒ **1** pleasant **2** polite
▶ *n* attack, assault, onslaught, invasion, raid, drive, thrust, push, sortie, charge
formal incursion

offer *v, n*
▶ *v* **1** PRESENT, make available, advance, extend, put forward, submit, suggest, propose, recommend, hold out
formal propound, proffer
2 PROVIDE, give, supply, sell, put on the market
formal afford
3 *offer £100*
propose, bid, put in a bid, tender
4 VOLUNTEER, come forward, make yourself available, be at someone's service
colloq. show willing
5 *offer prayers/a sacrifice*
offer up, sacrifice, dedicate, present, worship, give, consecrate, celebrate
6 *offer resistance*
show, express, give, present, try, attempt
▶ *n* proposal, bid, submission, tender, suggestion, proposition, overture, approach, attempt, presentation

offering *n*

1 GIFT, present, donation, handout, contribution, subscription
2 SACRIFICE, dedicated, consecration, tithe, celebration
formal oblation

offhand *adj, adv*

▶ *adj* casual, unconcerned, uninterested, indifferent, unceremonious, discourteous, rude, brusque, abrupt, curt, terse, perfunctory, cursory, informal, cavalier, careless, blasé
colloq. take-it-or-leave-it, happy-go-lucky, free-and-easy, laid-back, couldn't-care-less
▶ *adv* impromptu, immediately, ad lib, without thinking about it, without checking
formal extempore
colloq. off the cuff, off the top of one's head
E∃ calculated, planned

office *n*

1 RESPONSIBILITY, duty, obligation, charge, commission, occupation, tenure, situation, post, position, employment, function, work, appointment, business, role, place, service
2 WORKPLACE, workroom, place of business, base, bureau
3 *through the offices of someone*
support, advocacy, help, aid, favour, recommendation, word, back-up, backing, patronage, mediation, intervention, referral
formal auspices, aegis, intercession

office equipment and furniture

Office equipment includes: acoustic hood, adhesive binder, answering machine, calculator, cash box, collating machine, comb binder, comb binding, computer, copy holder, data cartridge, date-stamp, desk organizer, desk-top display calculator, Dictaphone®, dictation machine, disk storage-system, diskette mailer, duplicator, dust cover, electric typewriter, electronic organizer, electronic typewriter, facsimile machine (or fax), flip-chart easel, guillotine, hole puncher, information board, inkpad, intercom, keyboard, laminator, laptop computer, letter-folding machine, letter opener, letter scales, letter tray, message board, microcassette, microcassette recorder, microfiche reader, monitor, monitor arm, mouse, mouse mat, notice-board, overhead projector (OHP), paper-folding machine, paper punch, parcel scales, photocopier, plan file, planner, planning board, printer, printwheel, projection screen, reference book, rotary filing-system, scanner, screen, screen filter, share certificate book, shredder, slide projector, stapler, staple-remover, switchboard, tacker, telephone, telephone directory, telephone index, telex machine, terminal trolley, textphone, thermal binder, time clock, trimmer, typewriter, visitors' book, visual display unit (VDU), wages book, waste-paper bin, wire bindings, wire-binding machine, word-processor.

Office furniture includes: boardroom table, computer desk, conference table, desk, desk lamp, display cabinet, draughtsman's chair, drawing-board, executive chair, executive desk, filing cabinet, filing cupboard, filing trolley, fire cupboard, fire-extinguisher, fire safe, lectern, partition, plan chest, printer stand, reception chair, safe, secretarial desk, stationery cupboard, stepstool, storage unit, swivel chair, typist's chair, work station, work table. *See also* **computer; stationery**.

officer *n*

official, office-holder, office-bearer, public servant, functionary, dignitary, bureaucrat, committee member, administrator, representative, executive, board member, agent, appointee, envoy, messenger, deputy

official *adj, n*

▶ *adj* **1** AUTHORIZED, authoritative, legal, lawful, legitimate, formal, accepted, recognized, licensed, certified, validated, endorsed, sanctioned, approved, authenticated, authentic, bona fide, proper
formal accredited
colloq. kosher
2 *official activities*
formal, ceremonial, stately, dignified, solemn, ritual
E∃ **1** unofficial
▶ *n* office-bearer, office-holder, officer, functionary

Officials include: administrator, agent, ambassador, bailiff, bureaucrat, captain, chairman (or chairwoman or chairperson), chancellor, chief, clerk, commander, commissar, commissioner, congressman, congresswoman, consul, coroner, councillor, delegate, diplomat, director, elder, envoy, equerry, Eurocrat, Euro-MP, executive, executor, gauleiter, governor, hakim, inspector, justice of the peace (JP), magistrate, manager, mandarin, marshal, mayor, mayoress, member of parliament, minister, monitor, notary, ombudsman, overseer, prefect, president, principal, proctor, proprietor, public prosecutor, registrar, representative, *US* senator, sheriff, steward, superintendent, supervisor, usher.

⚠ **official** or **officious** ?
Official means 'done by someone in authority; relating to authority': *We think she has won, but we're still waiting for the official result of the race. Officious* means 'too eager to meddle, offering unwanted advice or assistance' or, more often, 'holding too rigidly to rules and regulations': *An officious little man told us that we would have to move our bicycles.*

officiate *v*

preside, superintend, conduct, chair, take the chair, manage, oversee, run, be in charge, take charge

officious *adj*

obtrusive, domineering, dictatorial, intrusive, interfering, prying, meddlesome, meddling, inquisitive, over-zealous, self-important, forward, opinionated, bustling
formal importunate
colloq. bossy, pushy

⚠ **officious** or **official** ? *See panel at* **official**.

offing *n*

▷ **in the offing** imminent, near, coming/happening soon, coming up, (close) at hand, just round the corner, in sight, on the way, on the horizon; *colloq.* on the cards
E∃ far off

offish *adj*
standoffish, aloof, cool, haughty, unsociable
colloq. stuck-up
🔁 friendly, sociable

off-key *adj*
out of tune, discordant, unsuitable, inappropriate, out of keeping, inharmonious, jarring
formal dissonant
🔁 in tune

offload *v*
unburden, unload, jettison, dump, drop, deposit, get rid of, shift, discharge
formal disburden
colloq. dump, chuck

off-putting *adj*
intimidating, daunting, frightening, disconcerting, discouraging, disheartening, dispiriting, formidable, unnerving, unsettling, demoralizing, disturbing, upsetting
formal discomfiting

offset *v*
counterbalance, compensate for, cancel out, counteract, make up for, balance (out), neutralize
formal counterpoise, countervail

offshoot *n*
1 BRANCH, outgrowth, limb, arm
2 SPIN-OFF, by-product, product, result, consequence, outcome, development, branch, appendage

offspring *n*
child, children, young, young one(s), family, brood, heirs, successors, descendants
formal issue, progeny, fruit of your loins
colloq. kid(s), nipper(s)
🔁 parent(s)

often *adv*
frequently, repeatedly, regularly, generally, again and again, over and over again, time after time, time and (time) again, day in day out, week in week out, month in month out, many times, many a time, much
🔁 rarely, seldom, never

ogle *v*
eye, eye up, leer, make eyes at, look, stare

ogre *n*
1 GIANT, monster, devil, demon, troll, fiend, bogey, bogeyman
2 *his father is a bit of an ogre*
monster, beast, brute, villain, savage, barbarian, fiend

oil *v, n*
▶ *v* lubricate, grease, make smooth, anoint
▶ *n* lubricant, grease, ointment, lotion, liniment, cream, balm, salve
formal unguent

oily *adj*
1 GREASY, fatty, buttery
formal oleaginous
2 UNCTUOUS, smooth, smooth-talking, obsequious, ingratiating, glib, suave, urbane, flattering, servile, subservient
colloq. smarmy

ointment *n*
salve, balm, cream, gel, lotion, liniment
technical emollient
formal embrocation

OK *adj, n, v, interj*
▶ *adj* acceptable, all right, fine, permitted, in order, fair, satisfactory, reasonable, tolerable, passable, good, adequate, convenient, correct, accurate
colloq. not bad, so-so, up to par, up to scratch
▶ *n* authorization, approval, endorsement, permission, agreement, sanction
formal consent, approbation
colloq. go-ahead, green light, thumbs-up
▶ *v* approve, authorize, pass, rubber-stamp, agree to, say yes to
formal consent to
colloq. give the go-ahead to, give the green light to, give the thumbs-up to
▶ *interj* all right, fine, very well, very good, agreed, right, yes

old *adj*
1 AGED, ageing, elderly, advanced in years, mature, sensible, wise, past your prime, grey, senile
formal senescent
colloq. getting on, past it, no spring chicken, not as young as you were, not getting any younger, over the hill, (a bit) long in the tooth, not long for this world, gaga
2 ANCIENT, age-old, bygone, antique, classic, vintage, veteran, original, primitive, early, earlier, earliest, antiquated, primeval, prehistoric, primordial, primal
formal pristine
3 LONG-STANDING, long-established, long-lived, enduring, lasting, time-honoured, traditional, age-old
colloq. old as the hills
4 OBSOLETE, old-fashioned, unfashionable, out of date, behind the times, oudated, *passé*, archaic
colloq. on the way out, past it, past its sell-by date, Dickensian, out of the ark, antediluvian
5 WORN OUT, cast-off, torn, shabby, decayed, decaying, decrepit, broken down, crumbling, ramshackle, tumbledown
colloq. have seen better days
6 FORMER, previous, earlier, one-time, sometime, ex-
formal erstwhile, quondam
🔁 1 young 2 new 4 modern, contemporary, state-of-the-art, up-to-date, fashionable, new 5 new 6 current
▷ **old age** age, agedness, oldness, elderliness, advancing years, declining years, second childhood, senility, dotage, twilight of your life; *formal* senescence
🔁 youth
Related adjective: geriatric
▷ **old man** father, grandfather, husband, elder, OAP, senior citizen, employer, greybeard, white-beard, patriarch, elder statesman; *colloq.* old codger, old stager, old-timer, oldster, boss, gaffer, geezer, fuddy-duddy
▷ **old woman** mother, grandmother, granny, wife, OAP, senior citizen, old dear, complainer, grumbler; *colloq.* bag, fusspot, grouch, hag

old-fashioned *adj*
outmoded, out of date, outdated, dated, old, unfashionable, out of fashion, obsolete, past, bygone, ancient, old-time, dead, moth-eaten, written off, behind the times, antiquated, archaic, *passé*, obsolescent
colloq. antediluvian, out of the ark, fuddy-duddy, old hat, past it, square, past its sell-by date, on the way out
🔁 modern, up-to-date

old-time *adj*
old fashioned, outmoded, out of date, outdated, dated,

old, unfashionable, out of fashion, obsolete, past, bygone, behind the times, antiquated, archaic, *passé*

old-world *adj*
old fashioned, quaint, traditional, picturesque, antiquated, past, archaic, bygone

omen *n*
sign, warning, token, premonition, foreboding, indication, forecast, prediction, harbinger
formal portent, augury, auspice, presentiment, prodrome, prodromus
Related adjective: ominous

ominous *adj*
menacing, foreboding, sinister, fateful, unpromising, unlucky, unfavourable, threatening, sinister
formal portentous, inauspicious, unpropitious, minatory
E3 favourable; *formal* auspicious

omission *n*
exclusion, gap, exception, leaving-out, erasure, oversight, failure, lack, neglect, negligence, disregard, default, avoidance
formal lacuna, expunction, dereliction
E3 inclusion

omit *v*
leave out, exclude, miss (out), pass over, except, overlook, drop, skip, eliminate, forget, neglect, leave undone, fail, fail to mention, disregard, edit out, erase, delete, cross out, rub out
formal expunge
E3 include, mention

omnibus *adj, n*
▶ *adj* comprehensive, inclusive, wide-ranging, all-embracing, compendious, encyclopedic
E3 selective
▶ *n* anthology, collection, compilation, compendium, encyclopedia

omnipotence *n*
absolute/total power, complete authority, all-powerfulness, almightiness, divine right, invincibility, mastery, sovereignty, supremacy
formal plenipotence
E3 impotence

omnipotent *adj*
all-powerful, almighty, invincible, supreme
formal plenipotent
E3 impotent

omnipresent *adj*
universal, all-present, present everywhere, pervasive, all-pervasive, limitless, infinite, ubiquitous
formal ubiquitary

omniscient *adj*
all-knowing, all-seeing, all-wise
formal pansophic

omnivorous *adj*
all-devouring, eating anything, gluttonous, indiscriminate, undiscriminating

on *adv*
▷ **on and off** now and then, occasionally, on occasion, off and on, periodically, sometimes, from time to time, now and again, every so often, irregularly, at intervals, intermittently, spasmodically, sporadically, fitfully; *formal* discontinuously

once¹ *adv*
formerly, previously, in the past, at one time, on one occasion, at one point, one time, long ago, in times past, in times gone by, once upon a time, in the old days
▷ **at once 1** IMMEDIATELY, instantly, directly, right away, straightaway, without delay, now, right now, promptly; *formal* forthwith; *colloq.* pronto, before you know it, before you can say Jack Robinson, in two shakes of a lamb's tail, like a shot, yesterday **2** SIMULTANEOUSLY, together, at the same time, at the same moment
▷ **once and for all** permanently, decisively, definitively, conclusively, positively, finally, for good, for the last time
▷ **once in a while** now and again, now and then, at times, sometimes, from time to time, occasionally, on and off, on occasion, periodically, infrequently, intermittently, sporadically

once² *conj*
after, immediately after, as soon as, when

oncoming *adj*
approaching, advancing, upcoming, looming, nearing, onrushing, gathering

one *adj*
1 SINGLE, solitary, lone, individual, only, sole, ace
2 UNITED, joined, fused, bound, married, wedded, harmonious, like-minded, whole, entire, complete, equal, identical, alike

oneness *n*
singleness, unity, completeness, wholeness, identity, individuality, identicalness, sameness, consistency

onerous *adj*
oppressive, burdensome, demanding, tiring, wearying, laborious, arduous, strenuous, back-breaking, crushing, hard, taxing, difficult, troublesome, exacting, fatiguing, exhausting, heavy, weighty
formal exigent

oneself *pron*
▷ **by oneself 1** ALONE, by yourself, on your own, lonely, lonesome, deserted, isolated, abandoned, forsaken, forlorn, desolate, unaccompanied, unescorted, unattended, solo **2** ON YOUR OWN, independently, unaided, unassisted, without help, without assistance, singly, single-handed, unaccompanied

one-sided *adj*
1 UNBALANCED, unequal, uneven, lopsided
2 UNFAIR, unjust, prejudiced, biased, bigoted, partial, partisan, narrow-minded, discriminatory, inequitable
3 UNILATERAL, independent, one-way, separate, separated, disconnected
E3 **1** balanced **2** impartial **3** bilateral, multilateral

one-time *adj*
former, previous, ex-, late, sometime
formal erstwhile, quondam

ongoing *adj*
1 CONTINUING, continuous, unending, unbroken, uninterrupted, non-stop, constant, incessant
2 DEVELOPING, evolving, progressing, advancing, growing, in progress, current, unfinished, unfolding

onlooker *n*
bystander, observer, spectator, looker-on, eyewitness, witness, sightseer, watcher, viewer
colloq. rubberneck, gawper

only *adv, adj*
▶ *adv* just, at most, merely, simply, purely, barely, not more than, no more than, nothing but, exclusively, solely
▶ *adj* sole, single, one and only, solitary, lone, unique, exclusive, individual

onrush *n*
surge, rush, push, stream, flood, flow, charge, cascade, career, onset, onslaught, stampede

onset *n*
1 BEGINNING, start, outset, outbreak
formal commencement, inception
colloq. kick-off
2 ASSAULT, attack, onslaught, onrush, charge
E3 1 end, finish

onslaught *n*
attack, assault, offensive, charge, onrush, storming, raid, drive, push, thrust, foray, bombardment, blitz

onus *n*
burden, responsibility, weight, load, obligation, duty, charge, encumbrance, liability, task
colloq. millstone, albatross

onwards *adv*
forward(s), on, ahead, in front, beyond
formal forth
E3 backward(s)

oodles *n*
lots, masses, abundance
colloq. bags, heaps, lashings, loads, tons
E3 scarcity

oomph *n*
vitality, sparkle, vigour, energy, vivacity, enthusiasm, exuberance, animation
colloq. bounce, get-up-and-go, pep, pizzazz, zing, sexiness

ooze *v, n*
▶ *v* seep, exude, leak, percolate, escape, dribble, drip, trickle, drop, discharge, bleed, secrete, emit, flow, overflow with, pour forth, filter, drain
formal filtrate, excrete
▶ *n* sludge, silt, slime, muck, mire, mud, sediment, deposit
formal alluvium

oozy *adj*
sludgy, muddy, slimy, mucky, miry, dripping, dewy, moist, weeping, sweaty, sloppy
formal uliginous

opacity *n*
1 CLOUDINESS, opaqueness, dullness, unclearness, impermeability, milkiness, murkiness, filminess, density
2 OBSCURITY, impenetrability, incomprehensibility, unintelligibility
formal obfuscation
E3 1 transparency **2** clarity

opalescent *adj*
shimmering, sparkling, multicoloured, rainbow, rainbow-coloured, rainbow-like, prismatic, dazzling, glittering, shot, pearly, polychromatic
formal iridescent, variegated

opaque *adj*
1 CLOUDY, clouded, murky, unclear, dull, dim, hazy, misty, muddied, muddy, dingy, blurred, dense, thick, turbid

2 OBSCURE, unclear, impenetrable, unfathomable, incomprehensible, unintelligible, enigmatic, cryptic, difficult, confusing, baffling, puzzling
formal abstruse, recondite, esoteric
colloq. as clear as mud
E3 1 transparent **2** clear, obvious

open *adj, v*
▶ *adj* **1** UNCLOSED, ajar, gaping, wide open, uncovered, unfastened, unbolted, unlocked, unsealed, unbarred, unlatched, yawning, lidless, topless, coverless
2 UNRESTRICTED, free, unobstructed, unblocked, passable, navigable, unenclosed, unfenced, clear, accessible, exposed, unprotected, unsheltered, vacant, wide, obtainable, available, unoccupied
3 OVERT, obvious, plain, clear, visible, patent, evident, noticeable, apparent, flagrant, blatant, conspicuous, unhidden, unconcealed, undisguised
formal manifest
4 UNDECIDED, unresolved, unsettled, debatable, arguable, problematic, moot
5 FRANK, candid, honest, guileless, natural, simple, ingenuous, unreserved, forthright, blunt, direct
6 LOOSELY WOVEN, airy, holey, openwork, porous, honeycombed, cellular, spongelike
7 *an open secret*
widely known, well known, public, general, accessible, unrestricted
8 *open to misinterpretation*
liable, vulnerable, susceptible, receptive, exposed, disposed, accessible
E3 1 shut, closed **2** restricted **3** hidden, concealed **4** decided, resolved **5** reserved
6 close **7** private, closed
▶ *v* **1** UNFASTEN, undo, unlock, unlatch, uncover, unseal, untie, unbolt, unblock, uncork, crack, broach, break open, burst open, slide open, push open, force open, prise open, clear, expose
2 EXPLAIN, divulge, expose, disclose, bare, lay bare, pour out
3 EXTEND, spread (out), unroll, unfold, unfurl, flower, come apart, separate, split
4 BEGIN, start, commence, inaugurate, initiate, set in motion, launch
colloq. set the ball rolling, kick off, get cracking, take the plunge
E3 1 close, shut **2** hide **4** end, finish
▷ **open onto** give onto, overlook, lead to, command a view of, face

open-air *adj*
outdoor, out-of-doors, outside, afield, alfresco
E3 indoor

open-and-shut *adj*
straightforward, obvious, simple, clear, easily decided, easily solved

open-handed *adj*
generous, free, liberal, large-hearted, lavish, bountiful, unstinting
formal bounteous, eleemosynary, munificent
E3 tight-fisted

opening *n, adj*
▶ *n* **1** APERTURE, breach, gap, space, break, chink, crack, fissure, cleft, crevice, chasm, hole, cave, slot, split, inlet, outlet, vent, rupture
formal orifice, interstice
2 START, onset, beginning, outset, inauguration, birth, dawn, launch
formal inception

colloq. the word go, square one, kick-off, first base
3 OPPORTUNITY, chance, occasion, place, vacancy, job, position
colloq. break
F3 **2** close, end
▶ *adj* first, beginning, starting, introductory, initial, early, primary
formal commencing, inaugural
F3 closing

openly   *adv*
overtly, frankly, candidly, directly, forthrightly, bluntly, honestly, blatantly, flagrantly, plainly, unashamedly, brazenly, unreservedly, glaringly, in public, in full view, immodestly, shamelessly
colloq. with no holds barred
F3 secretly, slyly

open-minded   *adj*
unprejudiced, unbiased, broad-minded, broad, impartial, tolerant, liberal, receptive, reasonable, objective, free, catholic, dispassionate, enlightened
formal latidutinarian
F3 bigoted, intolerant, prejudiced, narrow-minded

open-mouthed   *adj*
amazed, astounded, spellbound, dumbfounded, shocked, clamorous, thunderstruck, expectant
colloq. flabbergasted

operate   *v*
1 *it operates on batteries*
function, act, perform, run, work, go
2 *she can operate that machine*
control, handle, manage, work, run, be in charge of, use, utilize, employ, manoeuvre

operation   *n*
1 FUNCTIONING, action, running, motion, movement, performance, working
2 INFLUENCE, manipulation, handling, control, working, running, management, use, using, utilization
3 UNDERTAKING, enterprise, affair, procedure, proceeding, process, exercise, activity, business, deal, job, task, transaction, effort
4 CAMPAIGN, action, task, manoeuvre, exercise, attack, assault, charge, raid
▷ **in operation** operational, in force, functioning, active, effective, efficient, in action, working, workable, viable, serviceable, functional, valid

operational   *adj*
working, in working order, in use, usable, functioning, functional, in action, going, viable, workable, ready, prepared, in service
F3 out of order

operative   *adj, n*
▶ *adj* **1** OPERATIONAL, in operation, in force, functioning, active, effective, efficient, in action, working, workable, viable, serviceable, functional, valid
2 KEY, crucial, important, relevant, significant, vital
F3 **1** inoperative, out of service
▶ *n* **1** WORKER, workman, employee, labourer, hand, mechanic, machinist, operator, artisan
2 DETECTIVE, private detective, (private) investigator
US operative
colloq. private eye, sleuth, gumshoe, shamus, dick
3 SECRET AGENT, agent, spy, double agent
US operative
colloq. mole

operator   *n*
1 OPERATIVE, worker, mechanic, machinist, technician, mover, driver, practitioner
2 TRADER, contractor, dealer, manager, director, administrator, handler
3 MANIPULATOR, machinator, punter, manoeuvrer, shyster, speculator
colloq. wheeler-dealer

opiate   *n*
drug, narcotic, sedative, pacifier, anodyne, tranquillizer, soporific, stupefacient, depressant, bromide
formal nepenthe
colloq. downer

opine   *v*
think, believe, suppose, suggest, guess, say, volunteer, presume, declare, judge, conceive, conclude, suspect, venture
formal conjecture, surmise

opinion   *n*
belief, judgement, view, point of view, viewpoint, thought, idea, perception, stance, standpoint, theory, impression, feeling(s), sentiment, assumption, assessment, conception, mind, notion, way of thinking, thought(s), school of thought, conviction, persuasion, attitude
formal estimation

opinionated   *adj*
dogmatic, doctrinaire, dictatorial, arrogant, inflexible, obstinate, stubborn, pigheaded, uncompromising, with preconceived ideas, single-minded, adamant, prejudiced, biased, bigoted, self-important, pompous, cocksure, pontifical
F3 open-minded

opponent   *n*
adversary, enemy, antagonist, foe, competitor, contestant, challenger, opposer, opposition, rival, contender, objector, dissident
formal dissentient
F3 ally, friend, supporter

opportune   *adj*
suitable, proper, convenient, appropriate, advantageous, apt, fit, seasonable, timely, well-timed, favourable, providential, fitting, fortunate, good, lucky, happy
formal auspicious, felicitous, pertinent, propitious
F3 unsuitable; *formal* inopportune

opportunism   *n*
exploitation, expediency, pragmatism, realism, taking advantage, unscrupulousness, Machiavellianism
colloq. making hay while the sun shines

opportunity   *n*
chance, opening, occasion, possibility, hour, moment
colloq. break, look-in

oppose   *v*
1 RESIST, withstand, counter, attack, combat, contest, challenge, contradict, disapprove of, argue against, disagree with, stand up to, take a stand against, be against, take issue with, confront, defy, face, fight, hinder, obstruct, bar, check, prevent, thwart
colloq. fly in the face of
2 COMPARE, contrast, match, offset, balance, counterbalance, set against, play off
formal juxtapose
F3 **1** defend, support

opposed *adj*
in opposition, against, hostile, conflicting, disagreeing, opposing, opposite, antagonistic, clashing, contrary, incompatible
formal averse, inimical
colloq. anti
E3 in favour

opposing *adj*
opposite, contrary, differing, at odds, at variance, rival, clashing, conflicting, irreconcilable, incompatible, opposed, contentious, enemy, hostile, antagonistic, fighting, contending, warring, combatant
formal antipathetic, disputatious, oppugnant

opposite *adj, n*
▶ *adj* **1** FACING, face to face, fronting, corresponding
2 OPPOSED, antagonistic, conflicting, contrary, hostile, contradictory, clashing, irreconcilable, unlike, reverse, inconsistent, different, contrasted, differing, at odds, at variance
formal adverse, antithetical, dissident
colloq. poles apart
E3 2 same
▶ *n* reverse, converse, contrary, contradiction, inverse
formal antithesis
colloq. flip side, the other side of the coin, the other side of the fence
E3 same

opposition *n*
1 ANTAGONISM, hostility, resistance, confrontation, obstructiveness, unfriendliness, dislike, disapproval
2 OPPONENT, adversary, enemy, antagonist, rival, foe, opposing side, other side, competition
E3 1 co-operation, support **2** ally, supporter

oppress *v*
1 OVERWHELM, subjugate, suppress, subdue, overpower, crush, trample, tyrannize, repress, enslave, quell, quash, persecute, maltreat, abuse
colloq. bring someone to their knees, treat like dirt, use as a doormat, walk all over; *slang* treat like shit
2 BURDEN, afflict, lie heavy on, weigh down, crush, harass, depress, sadden, discourage, dishearten, deject, dispirit, torment, vex
formal desolate

oppressed *adj*
tyrannized, burdened, downtrodden, enslaved, subject, crushed, repressed, harassed, abused, maltreated, misused, persecuted, troubled, disadvantaged, underprivileged
formal subjugated
E3 free

oppression *n*
tyranny, overwhelming, overpowering, subjection, repression, despotism, suppression, injustice, cruelty, brutality, ruthlessness, abuse, persecution, maltreatment, harshness, hardship
formal subjugation

oppressive *adj*
1 TYRANNICAL, despotic, overbearing, overwhelming, repressive, iron-fisted, domineering, crushing, harsh, unjust, inhuman, cruel, brutal, ruthless, pitiless, merciless, burdensome, onerous, intolerable, Draconian
2 AIRLESS, stuffy, close, stifling, suffocating, sultry, muggy, heavy
E3 1 just, gentle **2** airy

oppressor *n*
tyrant, bully, (hard) taskmaster, slave-driver, despot, dictator, persecutor, tormentor, torturer, intimidator, autocrat
formal subjugator

opprobrious *adj*
contemptuous, insulting, offensive, scandalous, abusive, damaging, defamatory, derogatory, insolent, scurrilous, vitriolic, venomous
formal calumniatory, calumnious, contumelious, invective, vituperative

opprobrium *n*
censure, disgrace, dishonour, reproach, disrepute, disfavour, discredit, degradation, debasement, shame, infamy, scurrility, stigma
formal calumny, contumely, ignominy, obloquy, odium
colloq. slur

opt *v*
choose, pick, decide (on), elect, prefer, select, settle on, single out
colloq. go for, plump for

optical instrument

Optical instruments and devices include: astronomical telescope, binoculars, camera, compound microscope, endoscope, field-glasses, film projector, laser, magnifying glass, opera-glass, periscope, photomicroscope, reflecting telescope, refracting telescope, sextant, simple microscope, slide projector, spyglass, stereocamera, telescope, telescopic sight, theodolite. *See also* **spectacles**.

optimistic *adj*
confident, assured, sanguine, hopeful, positive, cheerful, buoyant, bright, idealistic, expectant, bullish, pollyann(a)ish, Panglossian, Panglossic
colloq. upbeat, happy-go-lucky, looking on the bright side, through rose-coloured spectacles
E3 pessimistic

optimum *adj*
best, ideal, model, perfect, optimal, flawless, supreme, highest, superlative, top, choice, most favourable, utopian
E3 worst

option *n*
choice, alternative, preference, possibility, selection

optional *adj*
voluntary, discretionary, elective, free, unforced
E3 compulsory, required; *formal* mandatory

opulence *n*
1 RICHES, fortune, wealth, prosperity, affluence
colloq. easy street
2 SUMPTUOUSNESS, lavishness, richness, luxury, plenty
3 ABUNDANCE, fullness, copiousness, profusion, superabundance, luxuriance, cornucopia
E3 1 poverty; *formal* penury

opulent *adj*
1 RICH, wealthy, prosperous, affluent, well-to-do, well-off, moneyed
colloq. well-heeled, rolling in it
2 SUMPTUOUS, lavish, luxurious
colloq. plush, posh
3 ABUNDANT, copious, prolific, plentiful, profuse,

superabundant, luxuriant
⊟ 1 poor; *formal* penurious

opus *n*
work, piece, production, composition, creation, oeuvre, brainchild

oracle *n*
1 SEER, prophet, sage, soothsayer, wizard, sibyl, high priest, augur
2 AUTHORITY, adviser, mentor, expert, specialist
colloq. guru, mastermind, pundit
3 PROPHECY, vision, divination, prediction, revelation, answer, augury
formal prognostication

oracular *adj*
prophetic, wise, significant, positive, authoritative, dogmatic, dictatorial, grave, predictive, obscure, mysterious, cryptic, Delphic, venerable, ominous, portentous, ambiguous, equivocal, two-edged
formal arcane, abstruse, auspicious, haruspical, prescient, sage

oral *adj*
verbal, spoken, said, uttered, unwritten, vocal
⊟ written

orate *v*
speak, talk, hold forth, sermonize, pontificate, discourse, harangue, speechify
formal declaim

oration *n*
address, speech, lecture, sermon, discourse, harangue, homily
formal declamation
colloq. spiel

orator *n*
public speaker, speaker, lecturer, rhetorician, demagogue, declaimer, spellbinder, phrasemonger
colloq. spieler

oratorical *adj*
rhetorical, eloquent, sonorous, high-flown, elocutionary, silver-tongued, smooth-tongued, Ciceronian, Demosthenic
formal bombastic, declamatory, grandiloquent, magniloquent

oratory *n*
rhetoric, eloquence, public speaking, speech, speechifying, speech-making, diction, elocution, declamation
formal grandiloquence

orb *n*
ball, sphere, globe, circle, ring, mound, round, globule, spherule

orbit *n, v*
▶ *n* **1** CIRCUIT, cycle, circle, course, path, trajectory, track, revolution, rotation
formal circumgyration
2 RANGE, scope, reach, domain, influence, sphere of influence, sweep, ambit, compass
▶ *v* revolve, circle, encircle, circumnavigate

orchestrate *v*
arrange, co-ordinate, organize, stage-manage, put together, prepare, present, mastermind, fix, integrate, score, compose

ordain *v*
1 CONSECRATE, invest, appoint, call, elect, anoint, frock

2 DECREE, order, require, instruct, rule, set, lay down, fix, dictate, pronounce, will, fate, destine
formal foreordain, predestine, predetermine, prescribe

ordeal *n*
trial, test, trouble(s), suffering, anguish, distress, agony, pain, torment, persecution, torture, nightmare
formal tribulation(s), affliction

order *n, v*
▶ *n* **1** COMMAND, directive, decree, injunction, summons, writ, warrant, instruction, direction, edict, dictate, ordinance, stipulation, mandate, regulation, rule, precept, law
2 REQUISITION, request, requirement, booking, commission, reservation, application, demand, call, notification
3 ARRANGEMENT, organization, grouping, sequence, cycle, categorization, classification, codification, method, form, pattern, plan, system, rota, regularity, uniformity, symmetry, array, layout, line-up, set-up, structure
formal disposition
4 ORDERLINESS, neatness, tidiness, method, system
5 PEACE, quiet, calm, tranquillity, harmony, law and order, lawfulness, discipline
6 ASSOCIATION, society, club, community, fellowship, fraternity, brotherhood, sisterhood, sorority, lodge, guild, league, company, organization, denomination, sect, union, secret society
7 CLASS, kind, sort, type, group, variety, species, genus, rank, position, level, grade, degree, station, hierarchy, family, caste
colloq. pecking order
⊟ 3 disorder **4** confusion, chaos **5** anarchy
▷ **in order 1** WORKING, functioning, operative, mended **2** ORDERED, orderly, organized, tidy, neat, shipshape, arranged, well-organized, systematic, regular, methodical, categorized, classified, in sequence, in alphabetical order **3** ACCEPTABLE, proper, correct, right, lawful, allowed, permitted, suitable, appropriate, fitting, all right, done;
colloq. OK
▷ **in order to** with the purpose, with the intention of, intending to, to, with a view to, so that, with the result
▷ **out of order 1** BROKEN, broken down, not working, not functioning, inoperative, out of commission; *colloq.* gone phut, haywire, on the blink; *slang* conked out **2** DISORDERED, disorganized, untidy, messy, confused, muddled, out of sequence **3** UNSEEMLY, improper, un-called-for, incorrect, wrong, irregular, unacceptable, inappropriate, unsuitable, unlawful
Related adjective: ordinal
▶ *v* **1** COMMAND, instruct, direct, bid, decree, rule, legislate, require, authorize
formal prescribe, enjoin
2 REQUEST, reserve, book, apply for, call for, send away for, write off for
formal requisition
3 ARRANGE, organize, systematize, dispose, classify, group, marshal, tidy up, sort out, lay out, manage, control, regulate, catalogue, codify
▷ **order around** order about, domineer, dominate, tyrannize, bully, bulldoze, browbeat, boss around; *colloq.* push around, throw your weight about, lay down the law

orderly *adj*
1 ORDERED, systematic, neat, tidy, regular, methodical, efficient, businesslike, in order,

well-organized, well-regulated, trim
colloq. in apple-pie order
2 WELL-BEHAVED, controlled, disciplined, restrained, law-abiding, ruly
◨ 1 chaotic 2 disorderly

ordinance *n*
1 REGULATION, law, rule, ruling, command, decree, dictum, directive, injunction, canon, statute, edict, enactment, fiat
2 SACRAMENT, ceremony, order, practice, observance, rite, ritual, institution

ordinarily *adv*
as a rule, usually, commonly, normally, in general, generally, familiarly, customarily, habitually, conventionally

ordinary *adj*
normal, usual, customary, common, commonplace, regular, routine, standard, mainstream, average, everyday, workaday, quotidian, unexceptional, unremarkable, fair, typical, plain, familiar, habitual, simple, conventional, modest, mediocre, indifferent, uninteresting, dull, mundane, banal, bland, nondescript, pedestrian, prosaic, undistinguished, unpretentious, unmemorable
colloq. run-of-the-mill, common-or-garden
◨ extraordinary, unusual
▷ **out of the ordinary** usual, exceptional, remarkable, memorable, noteworthy, extraordinary, different, unique, rare, outstanding, surprising, unexpected

ordnance *n*
munitions, weapons, military supplies, arms, artillery, cannon, guns
colloq. big guns

ordure *n*
dirt, dung, excrement, excretion, waste matter, droppings, filth
technical egesta, frass, scats, guano
formal faeces, stool
slang crap, shit, poop

organ *n*
1 DEVICE, instrument, implement, tool, element, constituent, part, component, process, structure, unit, member
2 MEDIUM, agency, forum, vehicle, voice, mouthpiece, publication, newspaper, paper, magazine, periodical, journal

organic *adj*
1 *organic matter*
biological, living, animate, natural
technical biotic
2 *organic vegetables*
natural, not artificial, non-chemical, pesticide-free, additive-free
3 *an organic whole*
structured, organized, ordered, harmonious

organism *n*
1 LIVING THING, being, creature, entity, body, structure, cell, animal, plant, bacterium
2 SYSTEM, structure, entity, whole, unity, set-up

organization *n*
1 ASSOCIATION, institution, institute, society, company, firm, corporation, concern, operation, federation, group, body, union, league, club, confederation, consortium, conglomeration, syndicate, authority, council, outfit

2 ARRANGEMENT, management, running, co-ordination, administration, development, establishment
3 SYSTEM, classification, methodology, order, formation, grouping, method, plan, structure, unity, whole, set-up, pattern, composition, design
formal configuration

organize *v*
1 ARRANGE, co-ordinate, structure, manage, run, see to, administer, be in charge of, be responsible for, order, standardize, group, marshal, dispose, put in order, sort out, classify, systematize, tabulate, catalogue
2 ESTABLISH, found, set up, create, originate, start, begin, institute, prepare, develop, form, mould, frame, construct, assemble, put together, shape
◨ 1 disorganize

organized *adj*
arranged, neat, tidy, orderly, planned, ordered, well-ordered, structured, systematic, efficient, regular, methodical, businesslike, in order, well-organized, well-regulated
◨ disorganized

orgy *n*
1 PARTY, wild party, debauch, carousal, revelry, revel(s), bout, bacchanalia
colloq. binge, splurge
2 INDULGENCE, excess, spree, frenzy
colloq. binge, splurge

orient *v*
accustom, accommodate, familiarize, acclimatize, adapt, adjust, orientate, align, get your bearings
formal habituate

orientation *n*
1 SITUATION, bearings, location, direction, position, alignment, placement, attitude, inclination
2 INDUCTION, initiation, training, guiding, leading, acclimatization, familiarization, adaptation, adjustment, getting your bearings, settling-in

orifice *n*
opening, hole, gap, space, breach, break, inlet, pore, rent, slit, slot, vent, mouth, cleft, crack, rift, crevice, fissure, perforation
formal aperture

origin *n*
1 SOURCE, spring, fount, foundation, basis, base, cause, derivation, root(s), fountain, fountainhead, well-spring, etymology
formal provenance
2 BEGINNING, start, inauguration, foundation, launch, birth, dawn, dawning, creation, conception, emergence
formal commencement, inception, genesis
3 ANCESTRY, descent, extraction, heritage, family, lineage, parentage, pedigree, birth, paternity, stock
◨ 2 end, termination
Related adjective: genetic

original *adj, n*
▶ *adj* 1 FIRST, early, earliest, initial, primary, archetypal, rudimentary, embryonic, starting, opening, commencing, first-hand, primitive, primeval, primal, primordial
formal autochthonous
2 CREATIVE, innovative, new, novel, fresh, imaginative, ingenious, inventive, resourceful, unconventional, unorthodox, unusual, unique,

pioneering, ground-breaking
3 GENUINE, real, authentic, true
F3 **1** latest **2** hackneyed, unoriginal **3** copied
▶ *n* prototype, master, paradigm, model, pattern, archetype, standard, type
F3 copy

originality *n*
inventiveness, creativeness, creativity, imaginativeness, imagination, freshness, boldness, cleverness, creative spirit, daring, innovativeness, innovation, ingenuity, individuality, resourcefulness, newness, novelty, unconventionality, unorthodoxy, singularity, eccentricity

originally *adv*
initially, at first, at the start, at the outset, in the beginning, first, to begin with, in origin, by derivation, by birth

originate *v*
1 RISE, arise, spring, stem, issue, flow, emanate, proceed, derive, result, come, evolve, emerge, be born
2 CREATE, invent, inaugurate, introduce, give birth to, develop, discover, establish, begin, start, set up, set in motion, launch, pioneer, conceive, form, produce, generate, be the father/mother of
formal commence
F3 **1** end, terminate

originator *n*
architect, author, creator, designer, father, mother, founder, generator, developer, establisher, innovator, discoverer, inventor, initiator, pioneer, prime mover
colloq. the brains

ornament *n, v*
▶ *n* **1** ADORNMENT, decoration, embellishment, garnish, trimming, accessory, frill, pattern
2 TRINKET, decoration, bauble, jewel, accessory, gewgaw, furbelow, fallal
▶ *v* decorate, adorn, embellish, garnish, trim, beautify, brighten, dress up, deck, gild

ornamental *adj*
decorative, embellishing, adorning, embroidering, attractive, showy, fancy

ornamentation *n*
decoration, adornment, embellishment, embroidery, ornateness, elaboration, garniture, frills, fallalery

ornate *adj*
elaborate, ornamented, fancy, decorated, embellished, showy, ostentatious, baroque, rococo, florid, flowery, flamboyant, fussy, busy, grandiose, sumptuous
colloq. flash
F3 plain

orotund *adj*
1 *orotund voices*
full, loud, ground, powerful, strong, deep, rich, sonorous, booming, resonating
2 *orotund speaking*
dignified, imposing, ornate, pompous, strained, pretentious
formal magniloquent

orthodox *adj*
1 CONFORMIST, conventional, accepted, correct, official, traditional, usual, regular, well-established, established, received, customary, conservative, recognized, authoritative
2 *orthodox religious views*
sound, conservative, correct, true, faithful, devout,

traditional, strict
F3 **1** nonconformist, unorthodox

orthodoxy *n*
1 CONVENTIONALITY, conformity, conformism, correctness, properness, authoritativeness, received wisdom
2 TRADITIONALISM, soundness, conservatism, devoutness, devotion, trueness, faithfulness, inflexibility, strictness

oscillate *v*
fluctuate, vary, waver, sway, swing, vacillate, move backwards and forwards, move to and fro, vibrate, wigwag, go from one extreme to the other
colloq. seesaw, yo-yo

oscillation *n*
fluctuation, wavering, variation, vacillation, swinging, swing, instability
colloq. shilly-shallying, seesawing

ossify *v*
fossilize, harden, solidify, make/become fixed, make/become hard
formal indurate, petrify, rigidify

ostensible *adj*
alleged, apparent, presumed, seeming, supposed, so-called, professed, claimed, outward, pretended, superficial, specious
formal feigned, purported
F3 real, genuine

ostensibly *adv*
allegedly, apparently, professedly, supposedly, seemingly, reputedly, outwardly, superficially
formal purportedly

ostentation *n*
showiness, showing off, flamboyance, pretension, pretentiousness, show, flaunting, vaunting, pomp, exhibitionism, boasting, display, flourish, pageantry, parade, trappings, window-dressing
formal affectation
colloq. flashiness, swank, tinsel
F3 unpretentiousness

ostentatious *adj*
showy, pretentious, vulgar, loud, obtrusive, flaunting, demonstrative, garish, gaudy, flamboyant, conspicuous, extravagant
formal affected
colloq. flashy, flash, kitsch, glitzy, over the top, OTT
F3 restrained, modest

ostracism *n*
exclusion, isolation, rejection, barring, avoidance, banishment, boycott, exile, expulsion, excommunication
formal disfellowship, proscription
colloq. cold-shoulder
F3 acceptance, reinstatement, welcome

ostracize *v*
exclude, banish, exile, expel, excommunicate, reject, segregate, isolate, send to Coventry, shun, snub, boycott, bar, outlaw, avoid
colloq. cold-shoulder, cut
F3 accept, welcome

other *adj*
1 DIFFERENT, dissimilar, unlike, variant, separate, distinct, contrasting
formal disparate

2 MORE, further, extra, additional, supplementary, spare, alternative

otherwise   *adv*
1 UNLESS, if not, or, or else, failing that
2 DIFFERENTLY, in a different way, along different lines, in other respects

otherworldly   *adj*
dreamy, absent-minded, ethereal, preoccupied, rapt, bemused, fey
F3 worldly, mundane, solid, substantial

ounce   *n*
particle, scrap, speck, spot, trace, iota, jot, shred, whit, atom, crumb, drop, grain, modicum, morsel
Related adjective: uncial

oust   *v*
expel, eject, depose, displace, turn out, throw out, overthrow, evict, drive out, thrust out, force out, put out, get rid of, dismiss, unseat, dislodge, dispossess, disinherit, replace, topple
colloq. sack, fire, boot out, show the door to, give someone the boot/elbow
F3 install, settle

out   *adj*
1 AWAY, absent, elsewhere, not at home, gone, outside, abroad
2 UNCONSCIOUS, knocked out, out cold
technical comatose
formal insensible
colloq. KO'd
3 *the book is out*
published, available, obtainable, ready, in print
4 REVEALED, exposed, known, disclosed, divulged, public, evident, in the open
formal manifest
5 FORBIDDEN, unacceptable, impossible, excluded, inadmissible, unwelcome, undesirable, inappropriate, unsuitable
formal disallowed
6 OUT-OF-DATE, unfashionable, old-fashioned, dated, *passé*, antiquated, *démodé*
colloq. old hat
7 EXTINGUISHED, finished, expired, dead, not burning, doused, not shining, used up
8 *the flowers are out*
in bloom, in full bloom, blooming, blossoming, in flower
9 *out to make money*
determined, bent, insistent, intent, set
F3 **1** in, here, at home **2** conscious **3** out of print **4** hidden, concealed **5** allowed **6** up-to-date; *colloq.* in

out-and-out   *adj*
absolute, thorough, total, complete, utter, outright, perfect, downright, inveterate, thoroughgoing, unmitigated, unqualified, uncompromising
formal arrant, consummate
colloq. dyed-in-the-wool

outbreak   *n*
eruption, outburst, explosion, flare-up, upsurge, sudden start, flash, rash, burst, epidemic
formal recrudescence

outburst   *n*
outbreak, eruption, explosion, flare-up, outpouring, burst, fit, gush, surge, storm, spasm, seizure, gale, attack, fit of temper, paroxysm

outcast   *n*
castaway, exile, pariah, outsider, untouchable, leper, refugee, evacuee, reject, *persona non grata*

outclass   *v*
surpass, outshine, beat, excel over, be much better than, outrival, transcend, top, eclipse, outdo, outdistance, outrank, outstrip, overshadow, leave standing, put in the shade

outcome   *n*
result, consequence, upshot, conclusion, effect, after-effect, product, issue, sequel, end result

outcry   *n*
protest, complaint, protestation, objection, dissent, indignation, uproar, cry, exclamation, clamour, row, fuss, commotion, noise, tumult, hue and cry, outburst
colloq. hullaballoo, racket

outdated   *adj*
out of date, old-fashioned, out of fashion, dated, unfashionable, outmoded, behind the times, obsolete, obsolescent, superseded, antediluvian, antiquated, antique, archaic, *passé, démodé*
colloq. old hat, square, old-fogeyish
F3 fashionable, modern

outdistance   *v*
outstrip, outpace, outrun, pass, overtake, pull ahead of, shake off, overhaul, surpass, leave behind, leave standing

outdo   *v*
surpass, exceed, beat, excel, outstrip, outshine, get the better of, have the advantage over, come first, overcome, defeat, outclass, outdistance, eclipse, transcend
colloq. cap, gain the upper/whip hand over, stand/be head and shoulders above, run rings/circles round

outdoors   *adv*
out, outside, in the open air, out-of-doors, alfresco, en plein air, outdoors
F3 indoors

outer   *adj*
1 EXTERNAL, exterior, outside, outermost, outward, surface, superficial, peripheral
2 OUTLYING, distant, remote, further, fringe, peripheral, faraway
F3 **1** internal **2** inner

outface   *v*
brave, confront, defy, outstare, stare down, brazen out, beard
F3 capitulate; *formal* succumb

outfit   *n, v*
▶ *n* **1** CLOTHES, dress, suit, costume, ensemble
colloq. get-up, togs, garb, gear
2 EQUIPMENT, kit, tools, apparatus, rig, trappings, paraphernalia
colloq. gear
3 ORGANIZATION, firm, business, company, corporation, group, team, unit, set, set-up, clique, coterie, crew, gang, squad
▶ *v* fit out, furnish, provide, supply, equip, stock, turn out, fit up, kit out, appoint, provision
formal accoutre, apparel, attire

outfitter   *n*
tailor, clothier, costumer, costumier, dressmaker, sartor, modiste, haberdasher, couturier, couturière

outflow n
discharge, rush, spout, gush, jet, emergence, effusion, emanation, outrush, outpouring, drainage, ebb, outfall
formal debouchment, disemboguement, effluence, effluent, effluvium, efflux, effluxion
☞ inflow

outflowing adj
discharging, gushing, leaking, rushing, spurting, effluent, emanant
formal debouching

outgoing adj
1 SOCIABLE, friendly, unreserved, affable, amiable, warm, affectionate, approachable, expansive, open, talkative, extrovert, gregarious, cordial, genial, easy-going, communicative, demonstrative, sympathetic
2 DEPARTING, retiring, leaving, former, last, past, ex-
☞ 1 reserved 2 incoming

outgoings n
costs, expenditure, outlay, overheads, spending, expenses
formal disbursal, disbursement
☞ income

outgrowth n
1 CONSEQUENCE, effect, product, offshoot, by-product, spin-off, emanation
2 SWELLING, shoot, sprout
formal protuberance, excrescence

outing n
excursion, expedition, jaunt, pleasure trip, tour, mystery tour, spin, picnic
colloq. trip

outlandish adj
unconventional, unfamiliar, unheard-of, unknown, bizarre, strange, odd, unusual, peculiar, weird, eccentric, alien, exotic, curious, quaint, barbarous, grotesque, foreign, extraordinary, preposterous, unreasonable
colloq. freaky, oddball, wacky; *slang* way-out, far-out
☞ familiar, ordinary

outlandishness n
bizarreness, oddness, unusualness, strangeness, weirdness, queerness, eccentricity, exoticness, quaintness, grotesqueness
☞ commonplaceness, familiarity

outlast v
survive, come through, outlive, outstay, ride, weather

outlaw n, v
▶ n fugitive, bandit, brigand, robber, desperado, highwayman, criminal, marauder, pirate, outcast, exile
▶ v ban, disallow, forbid, prohibit, exclude, embargo, bar, debar, banish, excommunicate, condemn
formal proscribe, interdict
☞ allow, legalize

outlay n
expenditure, expenses, outgoings, payment, charge, cost, price, spending
formal disbursement
☞ income

outlet n
1 RETAILER, retail outlet, shop, store, market, supplier
2 EXIT, way out, vent, duct, escape, outfall, opening, release, valve, safety valve, channel, culvert, conduit
formal egress
3 *an outlet for your feelings*
channel, means of release, means of expression, safety valve
☞ 2 entry, inlet

outline n, v
▶ n 1 SUMMARY, sketch, synopsis, précis, résumé, main points, rough idea, bare facts, bare bones, thumbnail sketch, abstract
2 PROFILE, sketch, tracing, form, shape, design, layout, plan, contour, silhouette
formal configuration, delineation, lineament
▶ v sketch (out), summarize, draft, trace, rough out, give a rough idea of
formal delineate

outlive v
survive, outlast, come through, live through, weather
☞ predecease

outlook n
1 VIEW, viewpoint, point of view, attitude, perspective, frame of mind, interpretation, angle, slant, standpoint, opinion
2 EXPECTATIONS, future, forecast, prospect, prognosis
3 *a house with a pleasant outlook*
view, prospect, aspect, panorama

outlying adj
distant, remote, isolated, far-off, far-away, far-flung, outer, out-of-the-way, inaccessible, provincial
colloq. off the beaten track
☞ inner

outmanoeuvre v
outdo, outthink, outwit, outsmart, outfox, beat, outflank, outgeneral, get the better of
formal circumvent

outmoded adj
out of date, old-fashioned, out of fashion, dated, unfashionable, behind the times, obsolete, obsolescent, superseded, antediluvian, antiquated, archaic, *passé*, *démodé*
colloq. old hat, square, old-fogeyish
☞ modern, new, fashionable, fresh

out of date adj
old-fashioned, outdated, outmoded, out of fashion, dated, unfashionable, behind the times, obsolete, obsolescent, superseded, antediluvian, antiquated, archaic, *passé*, *démodé*
colloq. old hat, square, old-fogeyish
☞ modern, new, fashionable, fresh

out-of-the-way adj
remote, isolated, far-flung, far-off, far-away, distant, outlying, outer, inaccessible, lonely, little-known, obscure, unfrequented, peripheral
colloq. off the beaten track

out of work adj
unemployed, redundant, out of a job, jobless, idle, laid off, workless
colloq. on the dole
☞ employed, occupied, busy

outpace v
outstrip, outrun, outdistance, outdo, beat, pass, overtake, surpass, overhaul

outpouring n
flood, deluge, torrent, stream, spate, spurt, flow, outflow, flux, cascade, effusion, emanation

formal debouchment, disemboguement, effluence, efflux

output *n*
production, productivity, product, manufacture, achievement, performance, accomplishment, gain, yield, fruits, harvest, return

outrage *n, v*
▶ *n* **1** ANGER, fury, rage, indignation, shock, affront, horror, wrath
2 ATROCITY, offence, injury, enormity, barbarism, brutality, crime, violation, evil, scandal, horror, affront
▶ *v* **1** APPAL, anger, infuriate, affront, incense, enrage, madden, disgust, injure, offend, shock, horrify, scandalize
2 ASSAULT, violate, abuse, desecrate, defile, ravish, ravage

outrageous *adj*
1 ATROCIOUS, abominable, shocking, scandalous, offensive, disgraceful, dreadful, terrible, monstrous, unspeakable, horrible, ghastly, gruesome, vile, foul, unacceptable, intolerable, unbearable, insufferable
formal heinous
2 EXCESSIVE, exorbitant, immoderate, unreasonable, extortionate, scandalous, obscene, inordinate, preposterous
E3 **2** acceptable, reasonable

outré *adj*
unconventional, unusual, strange, odd, extraordinary, eccentric, weird, bizarre, shocking, outrageous
colloq. oddball, freaky; *slang* way-out, far-out

outrider *n*
advance guard, escort, attendant, guard, bodyguard, vanguard, herald, precursor

outright *adj, adv*
▶ *adj* **1** TOTAL, utter, absolute, complete, downright, out-and-out, unqualified, unconditional, unmitigated, perfect, pure, thorough, direct
2 CLEAR, definite, categorical, unequivocal, unmistakable, undeniable, straightforward
E3 ambiguous, indefinite
▶ *adv* **1** TOTALLY, absolutely, completely, wholly, entirely, categorically, utterly, thoroughly, openly, without restraint, straightforwardly, positively, directly, explicitly
2 *killed outright*
instantaneously, at once, there and then, instantly, immediately, straight away

outrun *v*
outstrip, outpace, outdistance, overtake, outdo, shake off, pass, overhaul, surpass, exceed, excel, beat, lose, leave behind

outset *n*
start, beginning, opening, inauguration
formal inception, commencement
colloq. kick-off
E3 end, conclusion

outshine *v*
outclass, outstrip, outdo, overshadow, transcend, eclipse, surpass, beat, best, upstage, excel, dwarf, outrank, top, put in the shade, put to shame

outside *adj, n*
▶ *adj* **1** EXTERNAL, exterior, outer, surface, superficial, outward, extraneous, outdoor, outermost, extreme
2 *an outside chance*
remote, marginal, distant, small, faint, slight, slim, slender, vague, negligible, improbable, unlikely
E3 **1** inside **2** likely, real, substantial
▶ *n* exterior, façade, front, surface, outer surface, face, appearance, cover
E3 inside

outsider *n*
stranger, intruder, alien, non-member, non-resident, foreigner, newcomer, visitor, emigrant, émigré, immigrant, outlander, intruder, interloper, misfit, gatecrasher
colloq. odd one out

outskirts *n*
suburbs, suburbia, vicinity, neighbourhood, environs, periphery, fringes, borders, boundary, limit, frontier, edge, margin, perimeter
E3 centre

outsmart *v*
outwit, outperform, outmanoeuvre, best, out-think, beat, get the better of, deceive, trick, dupe, outfox
colloq. kid, con, have on, take for a ride, pull a fast one on

outspoken *adj*
candid, frank, forthright, free, unreserved, unequivocal, unceremonious, plain-spoken, plain, direct, straightforward, explicit, blunt, brusque, rude
E3 diplomatic, reserved

outspread *adj*
spread out, outstretched, open, opened, wide, wide-open, unfolded, unfurled, stretched, extended, fanned out, flared, expanded

outstanding *adj*
1 EXCELLENT, distinguished, eminent, pre-eminent, famous, famed, well-known, renowned, celebrated, exceptional, superior, remarkable, prominent, superb, great, notable, impressive, striking, superlative, important, noteworthy, memorable, special, extraordinary, arresting
2 OWING, unpaid, due, unsettled, unresolved, uncollected, pending, payable, remaining, unfinished, ongoing, left-over
E3 **1** ordinary, unexceptional **2** paid, settled

outstandingly *adv*
exceptionally, remarkably, greatly, notably, extremely, especially, extraordinarily, impressively, strikingly, amazingly

outstrip *v*
surpass, exceed, better, outdo, beat, top, transcend, outshine, pass, gain on, leave behind, leave standing, outrun, outdistance, overtake, eclipse

outward *adj*
external, exterior, outer, outside, outermost, surface, superficial, visible, apparent, perceptible, noticeable, discernible, observable, evident, supposed, professed, public, obvious, ostensible
E3 inner, private

outwardly *adv*
apparently, externally, to all appearances, visibly, superficially, supposedly, seemingly, on the surface, on the outside, at first sight, as far as you can see, on the face of it

outweigh *v*
exceed, surpass, be greater than, be more than, be superior to, override, prevail over, overcome, take precedence over, cancel out, make up for,

compensate for, predominate
formal preponderate

outwit *v*
outsmart, outthink, outmanoeuvre, get the better of, be cleverer than, trick, better, beat, dupe, cheat, deceive, defraud, swindle
colloq. kid, con, have on, take for a ride, pull a fast one on

outworn *adj*
outdated, out of date, outmoded, ancient, antiquated, archaic, stale, discredited, defunct, old-fashioned, behind the times, hackneyed, rejected, obsolete, obsolescent, disused, rejected, exhausted, abandoned
colloq. old hat, moth-eaten, past its sell-by date
Ed fresh, new

oval *adj*
egg-shaped, elliptical, ovoid, ovate, ellipsoidal
technical obovate, oviform
formal vulviform

ovation *n*
applause, acclaim, acclamation, praise(s), tribute, clapping, handclapping, cheering, cheers, accolade, bravos
formal plaudits, laudation
colloq. bouquet
Ed abuse, catcalls

oven *n*
cooker, stove, microwave (oven), kiln

over *adj, adv, prep*
▶ *adj* finished, ended, at an end, done with, past, gone, no more, completed, closed, in the past, settled, up, forgotten, accomplished
formal concluded, terminated
colloq. over and done with, ancient history
▶ *adv* **1** ABOVE, beyond, overhead, on high
formal aloft
2 EXTRA, remaining, surplus, superfluous, left, left over, unclaimed, unused, unwanted, in excess, in addition
▷ **over and over (again)** again and again, repeatedly, frequently, often, continually, endlessly, time and (time) again, ad infinitum, ad nauseam
▶ *prep* **1** ABOVE, on, on top of, upon, in charge of, in command of, higher than, superior to
2 EXCEEDING, more than, in excess of
▷ **over and above** in addition to, on top of, together with, plus, along with, as well as, besides, added to, let alone, not to mention

overabundance *n*
surplus, surfeit, excess, glut, oversupply, *embarras de choix, embarras de richesse*
formal superfluity, superabundance, profusion, plethora
colloq. too much of a good thing
Ed lack, dearth

overact *v*
overplay, exaggerate, overdo
colloq. ham, lay/pile it on, lay/pile it on thick, lay/pile it on with a trowel
Ed underact, underplay

overall *adj, adv*
▶ *adj* total, all-inclusive, all-embracing, comprehensive, inclusive, complete, sweeping, general, universal, global, broad, all-over
colloq. blanket, umbrella
Ed narrow, specific

▶ *adv* in general, on the whole, by and large, broadly, generally speaking

overalls *n*
dungarees, coverall, boiler suit, workwear

overawe *v*
intimidate, daunt, dismay, disconcert, abash, frighten, scare, terrify, petrify, alarm, awe, unnerve, browbeat, cow
Ed reassure, comfort

overbalance *v*
lose your balance, fall over, tip over, topple over, trip, slip, tumble, upset, somersault, lose your footing, capsize, keel over, overturn, turn turtle

overbearing *adj*
imperious, domineering, arrogant, officious, dictatorial, despotic, lordly, tyrannical, high-handed, haughty, proud, cavalier, autocratic, dogmatic, oppressive, presumptuous, contemptuous, disdainful
colloq. bossy, la-di-da, snobby, snooty, snotty, stuck-up, toffee-nosed, too big for your boots, smart-ass
Ed meek, unassertive

overblown *adj*
overstated, overdone, overestimated, overcharge, excessive, extravagant, pretentious, embellished, amplified, bombastic, inflated, caricatured, burlesqued, exalted, self-important
colloq. over the top, OTT

overcast *adj*
cloudy, clouded (over), grey, dull, dark, darkened, sombre, gloomy, dreary, dismal, sunless, hazy, misty, foggy, leaden, louring
Ed bright, clear

overcharge *v*
surcharge, short-change, cheat, extort, swindle
colloq. rip off, sting, do, diddle, fleece, rook
Ed undercharge

overcoat *n*
See panel at **coat**.

overcome *v, adj*
▶ *v* conquer, defeat, beat, surmount, prevail, triumph over, get the better of, be victorious over, rise above, master, overpower, overwhelm, overthrow, subdue, trounce, best, worst, rout, outplay, outwit, outsmart, be more than a match for, have the edge on
formal vanquish, subjugate
colloq. hammer, slaughter, clobber, lick, thrash, wipe the floor with
▶ *adj* overwhelmed, overpowered, moved, broken, speechless
colloq. lost for words, bowled over, swept off your feet
formal affected

over-confident *adj*
arrogant, brash, cocksure, self-assured, blustering, swaggering, presumptuous, overweening, foolhardy, rash, incautious, over-optimistic, sanguine
formal hubristic, temerarious
colloq. cocky, uppity, uppish
Ed cautious, diffident

overcritical *adj*
overparticular, fault-finding, hypercritical, hard to please, pedantic, purist, captious, carping, cavilling, over-nice, Zoilean
formal ultra-crepidarian
colloq. nit-picking, pernickety, hair-splitting
Ed easy-going, tolerant, uncritical

overcrowded *adj*
congested, packed (out), crammed full, chock-full,
overpopulated, overloaded, swarming, teeming,
overrun, full to overflowing
colloq. jam-packed, packed like sardines
F3 deserted, empty

overdo *v*
exaggerate, go too far, carry to excess, overindulge,
overstate, overact, overplay
colloq. ham it, go overboard, camp it up, lay/pile it on,
lay/pile it on thick, lay/pile it on with a trowel, stretch a
point
▷ **overdo it** overwork, work too hard, do too much,
overstretch yourself, strain yourself, overreach
yourself, overexert yourself; *colloq.* sweat blood, burn
yourself out, bite off more than you can chew, run
yourself into the ground, burn the candle at both ends,
work your fingers to the bone, crack up

overdone *adj*
1 OVERCOOKED, burnt, spoiled, dried up,
overbaked, charred
colloq. burnt to a cinder, burnt to a frazzle
2 EXAGGERATED, overstated, overelaborate, undue,
unnecessary, overplayed, excessive, immoderate,
fulsome, effusive, gushing, inordinate, histrionic
colloq. over the top
F3 1 underdone, raw 2 underplayed, understated

overdraft *n*
overdrawn account, debt, arrears, liabilities,
borrowings, unpaid amounts, deficit, insufficient
funds

overdue *adj*
late, behindhand, behind schedule, delayed, owing,
unpaid, due, unsettled, pending, payable, unpunctual,
slow
formal tardy, belated
F3 early

overeat *v*
gorge, overindulge, guzzle, eat too much, go on a binge,
stuff yourself, gormandize
colloq. binge, make a pig of yourself, pig out, have eyes
bigger than your stomach
F3 abstain, starve

overeating *n*
guzzling, overindulgence, gluttony, bulimia,
hyperphagia, gourmandize, gourmandism,
gormandize, gormandism
colloq. bingeing
F3 abstemiousness, abstention

overemphasize *v*
exaggerate, overstress, lay/put too much emphasis on,
attach too much importance to, make too much of,
labour, belabour, overdramatize
colloq. make a mountain out of a molehill, blow up out
of all proportion
F3 minimize, play down, underplay, understate,
belittle

overexert *v*
▷ **overexert yourself** overdo it, overstrain yourself,
overtax yourself, overtire yourself, overwork, strain
yourself, wear yourself out, drive yourself too hard,
work too hard, run yourself into the ground, fatigue,
work yourself to death, push yourself too hard
colloq. burn the candle at both ends, knock yourself
out
F3 idle, laze

overflow *v, n*
▶ *v* spill (over), overrun, run over, pour over, well
over, flow over, brim over, bubble over, surge,
discharge, flood, cover, inundate, deluge, shower,
submerge, soak, swamp, teem
▶ *n* overspill, spill, inundation, flood, spillage,
overabundance, surplus

overflowing *adj*
crowded, filled, full, swarming, teeming, thronged,
bountiful, abounding, superabundant, brimful,
plentiful, copious, profuse, rife
formal inundant, plenteous
F3 lacking, scarce

overgrowth *n*
escalation, overabundance, overdevelopment,
superabundance
technical hypertrophy
F3 decline, failure, shrinkage, wasting

overhang *v*
jut (out), project, bulge (out), protrude, stick out, stand
out, extend, beetle

overhanging *adj*
projecting, protruding, jutting (out), bulging (out),
sticking out, standing out, beetling
formal pensile

overhaul *v, n*
▶ *v* 1 RENOVATE, repair, service, recondition,
revamp, mend, examine, inspect, investigate, check,
check over/up, survey, go over, re-examine, fix
2 OVERTAKE, pull ahead of, outpace, outstrip,
outdistance, gain on, pass, get ahead of
▶ *n* reconditioning, repair, renovation, check, check-
up, service, examination, inspection
colloq. going-over

overhead *adv, adj*
▶ *adv* above, up above, on high, upward
F3 below, underfoot
▶ *adj* elevated, aerial, overhanging, raised

overheads *n*
running costs, outgoings, operating costs, regular
costs, expenses, expenditure, burden, oncost
formal disbursement
F3 income, profit

overheated *adj*
angry, agitated, inflamed, fiery, flaming, overwrought,
passionate, roused, impassioned, excited, overexcited
F3 calm, cool, impassive, dispassionate

overindulge *v*
1 GORGE, gormandize, gluttonize, guzzle, debauch,
eat/drink too much, satiate, sate
colloq. binge, pig out, make a pig of yourself;
slang booze
2 PAMPER, mollycoddle, spoil, cosset, pander, pet
colloq. spoon-feed
F3 1 abstain

overindulgence *n*
excess, immoderation, overeating, intemperance,
surfeit, debauch
colloq. binge
F3 abstemiousness, abstention

overjoyed *adj*
delighted, elated, euphoric, ecstatic, in raptures,
joyful, enraptured, rapturous, thrilled, jubilant, in
transports of delight
colloq. over the moon, tickled pink, on cloud nine,

in seventh heaven, on top of the world, like a child with a new toy, pleased as Punch, high as a kite
F3 sad, disappointed

overlap *v*
coincide, cover, overlay, overlie, flap over
technical imbricate, shingle

overlay *v*
cover, wrap, envelop, blanket, inlay, decorate, ornament, adorn, veneer, varnish, laminate

overload *v*
burden, overburden, oppress, strain, tax, overtax, weigh down, overcharge, encumber, saddle, lumber

overlook *v*
1 FRONT ONTO, face, look onto, open onto, look over, command/have a view of
2 MISS, disregard, ignore, omit, neglect, pass over, leave, forget, take no notice of, let pass, let ride, slight
3 EXCUSE, forgive, pardon, condone, wink at, turn a blind eye to
F3 2 notice, observe 3 penalize, condemn

overlooked *adj*
unhonoured, unvalued, unregarded, unnoted, unremarked, unprized, unconsidered, unheeded
F3 appreciated, prized, sought-after, valued

overly *adv*
too, over, unduly, excessively, exceedingly, immoderately, unreasonably, inordinately
F3 inadequately, insufficiently

overnice *adj*
overfastidious, over-meticulous, overparticular, overprecise, oversensitive, overscrupulous, oversubtle, finical
colloq. nit-picking, pernickety
F3 casual, uncritical

overplay *v*
exaggerate, overstate, overdo, magnify, overemphasize, emphasize, stress, make too much of, dramatize, overdramatize, embellish, embroider, colour, stretch the truth, enlarge, amplify, enhance, oversell
formal aggrandize
colloq. lay/pile it on, lay/pile it on thick, lay/pile it on with a trowel, make a mountain out of a molehill, blow something up out of all proportion, shoot a line
F3 understate, play down

overpopulated *adj*
overcrowded, congested, packed (out), crammed full, chock-full, overloaded, swarming, teeming, overrun, full to overflowing
colloq. jam-packed, packed like sardines
F3 deserted, empty

overpower *v*
1 OVERWHELM, overcome, conquer, defeat, beat, trounce, rout, subdue, overthrow, quash, quell, crush, immobilize, master, gain mastery over, gain the upper hand over
formal vanquish, subjugate
2 *overpowered by a feeling*
move, affect deeply/strongly, touch, confuse, perplex, daze, stagger, dumbfound, leave speechless, take aback
colloq. bowl over, floor, flabbergast, knock for six

overpowering *adj*
overwhelming, powerful, strong, forceful, irresistible, undeniable, irrefutable, uncontrollable, compelling, extreme, oppressive, suffocating, stifling, unbearable, nauseating, sickening

overrate *v*
overestimate, overvalue, overpraise, magnify, overprize, make too much of, attach too much importance to
colloq. blow up
F3 underrate

overreach *v*
▷ **overreach yourself** overstretch yourself, try to do too much, overdo it, go too far, strain yourself
colloq. bite off more than you can chew, spread yourself too thinly, burn yourself out

override *v*
1 OUTWEIGH, be more important than, exceed, surpass, be greater than, be superior to, prevail over, overcome
2 OVERRULE, cancel, annul, set aside, supersede, quash, reverse, disregard, ignore, trample over
formal abrogate, countermand, nullify, rescind, vanquish
colloq. ride roughshod over

overriding *adj*
most important, most significant, principal, first, major, predominant, primary, prime, supreme, compelling, dominant, essential, final, ultimate, overruling, prior, prevailing, ruling, paramount, pivotal, cardinal, determining, number one
F3 insignificant, unimportant

overrule *v*
overturn, override, countermand, revoke, set aside, disallow, reject, reverse, invalidate, cancel, annul, vote down
formal abrogate, rescind, nullify

overrun *v*
1 INVADE, occupy, besiege, attack, storm, infest, overwhelm, inundate, permeate, penetrate, spread over, swamp, swarm over, surge over, ravage, overgrow
colloq. run riot, spread like wildfire
2 EXCEED, go over, overshoot, overstep, overreach

overseas *adj, adv*
▶ *adj* foreign, international, external, exotic, faraway, distant, remote
F3 domestic, home
▶ *adv* abroad, in/to a foreign country, out of the country, in/to foreign parts, in/to foreign climes, far and wide, widely

overseer *n*
supervisor, chief, foreman, forewoman, manager, manageress, superintendent
colloq. boss, gaffer

overshadow *v*
1 OBSCURE, cloud, darken, dim, mar, spoil, blight, veil, take the edge off, put a damper on
2 OUTSHINE, eclipse, excel, surpass, be superior to, dominate, dwarf, put in the shade, rise above, tower above

oversight *n*
1 LAPSE, omission, fault, error, slip-up, mistake, blunder, carelessness, neglect
formal dereliction
colloq. slip-up, howler, boob
2 SUPERVISION, responsibility, care, charge, control, custody, superintendence, handling, keeping, administration, management, surveillance, direction

overstate *v*
exaggerate, overdo, magnify, overemphasize,

emphasize, stress, make too much of, dramatize, overdramatize, embellish, embroider, colour, stretch the truth, enlarge, amplify, enhance, oversell
formal aggrandize
colloq. lay/pile it on, lay/pile it on thick, lay/pile it on with a trowel, make a mountain out of a molehill, blow something up out of all proportion, shoot a line
ﬀ understate, play down

overstatement *n*
exaggeration, overemphasis, emphasis, magnification, overestimation, excess, extravagance, embellishment, enlargement, pretentiousness, amplification, burlesque, caricature, parody
formal hyperbole
ﬀ meiosis, understatement

overt *adj*
open, plain, evident, patent, observable, obvious, noticeable, visible, conspicuous, apparent, public, professed, unconcealed, undisguised
formal manifest
ﬀ covert, secret

overtake *v*
1 PASS, go past, drive/run past, catch up with, outdistance, leave behind, outstrip, draw level with, pull ahead of, overhaul
2 COME UPON, happen to, happen suddenly/unexpectedly to, take by surprise, catch unawares, strike, overwhelm, engulf
formal befall

overthrow *v, n*
▶ *v* **1** DEPOSE, oust, bring down, topple, unseat, displace, dethrone, conquer, beat, defeat, crush, overcome, overpower, overwhelm, quash, quell, trounce, best, worst, subdue, master, abolish, upset
formal vanquish
2 OVERTURN, upset, upturn, tip over, topple, overbalance, keel over, knock over, spill, turn over, invert
ﬀ **1** install, protect, reinstate, restore
▶ *n* ousting, unseating, defeat, deposition, dethronement, fall, rout, undoing, suppression, downfall, end, humiliation, destruction, ruin
formal vanquishing

overtone *n*
suggestion, intimation, nuance, hint, undercurrent, insinuation, innuendo, connotation, hidden meaning, indirect reference, association, feeling, implication, sense, flavour

overture *n*
1 APPROACH, advance(s), offer, invitation, proposal, proposition, suggestion, signal, move(s), motion
2 PRELUDE, opening, introduction, opening move, (opening) gambit

overturn *v*
1 CAPSIZE, upset, upturn, tip over, topple, overbalance, keel over, knock over, spill, turn over, invert, skittle
2 OVERRULE, repeal, override, reverse, cancel, annul, abolish, destroy, quash, set aside, veto
formal abrogate, nullify, rescind, revoke
3 OVERTHROW, depose, oust, bring down, topple, unseat, displace, dethrone, conquer, beat, defeat, crush, overcome, overpower, overwhelm
formal vanquish

overused *adj*
overworked, hackneyed, trite, stereotyped, worn,

tired, unoriginal, stale, played out, commonplace, bromidic, clichéd, threadbare
formal platitudinous
ﬀ fresh, original, new

overweening *adj*
arrogant, conceited, haughty, proud, self-confident, supercilious, vain, presumptuous, overblown, high-handed, cocksure, excessive, immoderate, inflated, extravagant, swollen, opinionated, lordly, egotistical, cavalier, pompous, insolent
colloq. cocky
formal hubristic, vainglorious
ﬀ unassuming, modest, diffident

overweight *adj*
fat, plump, stout, massive, huge, chunky, obese, ample, hefty, bulky, outsize, podgy, portly, pot-bellied, fleshy, heavy, tubby, chubby, buxom
formal corpulent
colloq. flabby, gross, well-padded, well-upholstered
ﬀ underweight, thin, skinny, emaciated

overwhelm *v*
1 OVERCOME, overpower, overthrow, destroy, defeat, beat, trounce, worst, best, subdue, quash, quell, prevail, get the better of, be victorious over, outplay, outwit, outsmart, be more than a match for, have the edge on, crush, rout, devastate
formal vanquish, subjugate
colloq. hammer, slaughter, clobber, lick, thrash, wipe the floor with
2 OVERRUN, deluge, inundate, bury, submerge, overburden, swamp, engulf
colloq. snow under
3 CONFUSE, stagger, move, affect deeply/strongly, daze, touch
colloq. bowl over, floor, knock for six

overwhelming *adj*
1 OVERPOWERING, powerful, strong, forceful, irresistible, undeniable, irrefutable, uncontrollable, compelling, extreme, oppressive, suffocating, stifling, unbearable, nauseating, sickening
2 *an overwhelming majority*
great, large, vast, immense, huge
ﬀ **1** resistible **2** insignificant, negligible

overwork *v*
overstrain, overload, exploit, exhaust, overuse, overtax, strain, wear out, oppress, burden, weary, work too hard, overdo it, do too much, overstretch yourself, strain yourself, overreach yourself, overexert yourself
colloq. sweat blood, burn yourself out, bite off more than you can chew, run yourself into the ground, burn the candle at both ends, work your fingers to the bone, crack up

overworked *adj*
1 *overworked employees*
overstrained, exhausted, worn out, overtaxed
colloq. stressed out
2 *an overworked expression*
hackneyed, trite, stereotyped, worn, tired, unoriginal, stale, played out, commonplace, bromidic, clichéd, threadbare
formal platitudinous
ﬀ fresh, original, new

overwrought *adj*
tense, distraught, agitated, keyed up, on edge, edgy, worked up, wound up, nervous, highly, strung, frantic, overcharged, overexcited, excited, beside yourself

colloq. uptight, nervy
🖪 calm

owe *v*
be in debt to, be overdrawn, get into debt, run up debts, be indebted to, be in arrears to, be under an obligation to
colloq. be in the red, be up to your ears in debt

owing *adj*
unpaid, due, owed, in arrears, outstanding, payable, unsettled, overdue
▷ **owing to** because of, as a result of, on account of, thanks to

own *adj, v*
▶ *adj* personal, individual, private, particular, idiosyncratic
▷ **on your own** alone, isolated, by yourself, singly, unaccompanied, unaided, unassisted, independently; *colloq.* off your own bat, on your tod

▶ *v* possess, have, have got, have as your belongings/ property, have in your possession, have (all) to yourself, monopolize, hold, retain, keep, enjoy, use, occupy
▷ **own up** admit, confess, tell the truth, acknowledge; *colloq.* come clean, make a clean breast of it

owner *n*
possessor, holder, keeper, householder, home-owner, landlord, landlady, proprietor, proprietress, master, mistress, freeholder

ownership *n*
possession, proprietary rights, right of possession, proprietorship, rights, freehold, dominion
technical title

ox *n*
bull, bullock, steer, buffalo, bison, yak
Related adjective: bovine

P

pace *n, v*
▶ *n* **1** STEP, stride, walk, gait, tread
2 SPEED, movement, motion, progress, rate, rate of progress, velocity, quickness, rapidity, swiftness, tempo, measure
formal celerity
▶ *v* step, stride, walk, walk up and down, march, tramp, pound, patrol, mark out, measure

pacific *adj*
peaceable, peaceful, peace-loving, mild, peacemaking, pacifist, irenic, appeasing, friendly, gentle, equable, placid, still, unruffled, quiet, serene, tranquil, smooth, calm, conciliatory, nonbelligerent, nonviolent, diplomatic, dovelike, dovish
formal complaisant, pacificatory, placatory, propitiatory, halcyon
EJ belligerent, aggressive, contentious;
formal pugnacious

pacifism *n*
non-violence, pacificism, passive resistance, satyagraha

pacifist *n*
peacemaker, pacificist, peace-lover, conscientious objector, peace-monger, dove
colloq. conchy
EJ warmonger, hawk

pacify *v*
appease, conciliate, placate, mollify, calm, calm down, compose, soothe, assuage, allay, defuse, moderate, soften, lull, still, quiet, quieten, silence, quell, crush, put down, tame, subdue
formal propitiate
EJ anger

pack *n, v*
▶ *n* **1** PACKET, box, carton, container, parcel, package, bundle, truss, bale, burden, load
2 BAG, backpack, rucksack, haversack, knapsack, kitbag
3 GROUP, company, set, troop, crew, herd, flock, drove, band, bunch, crowd, gang, mob
▶ *v* **1** WRAP, wrap up, tie up, parcel, package, bundle, put in, cover, crate, stow, store
2 FILL, load, charge, cram, stuff, crowd, throng, mob, jam, press, squeeze, ram, wedge, compact, compress
▷ **pack in 1** CRAM IN, fill, load, charge, stuff, crowd, throng, mob, jam, press, squeeze, ram, wedge **2** STOP, end, give up, leave, resign;
colloq. throw in, jack in, chuck
▷ **pack off** send, dismiss, dispatch, bundle off
▷ **pack up 1** TIDY UP, tidy away, clear up, put things away **2** STOP, finish, end, give up;
colloq. throw in, jack in, wrap up, call it a day **3** BREAK DOWN, stop working, fail;
formal malfunction; *colloq.* seize up; *slang* conk out

package *n, v*
▶ *n* **1** PARCEL, pack, packet, box, container, carton, bale, consignment
2 WHOLE, unit, group, set, entity, package deal
▶ *v* parcel (up), wrap (up), pack (up), gift-wrap, box, batch

packaging *n*
container, box, packet, packing, wrapping(s), wrapper(s), presentation

packed *adj*
filled, full, crammed, jammed, crowded, congested, brimful, overflowing, overloaded
colloq. jam-packed, chock-a-block, packed like sardines
EJ empty, deserted

packet *n*
1 PACK, carton, box, bag, package, parcel, case, container, wrapper, wrapping, packing, padded bag, padded envelope, Jiffy bag®
2 *cost a packet*
a lot, lots, fortune, small fortune, king's ransom
colloq. mint, pile, pots, pretty penny, a bob or two, bomb, bundle, tidy sum

pact *n*
treaty, convention, covenant, bond, alliance, cartel, contract, deal, bargain, settlement, agreement, arrangement, entente, understanding
formal compact, concordat
EJ disagreement, quarrel

pad¹ *n, v*
▶ *n* **1** CUSHION, pillow, bolster, wad, wadding, buffer, padding, stuffing, protection
2 WRITING PAD, notepad, jotter, notebook, block
colloq. memo pad
3 *an animal's pad*
FOOT, paw, sole, print, footprint
4 HOME, place, room, rooms, quarters, penthouse, flat, apartment
colloq. hang-out
▶ *v* fill, stuff, wad, pack, wrap, line, cushion, protect
▷ **pad out** expand, inflate, fill out, amplify, elaborate, increase, flesh out, lengthen, stretch, spin out; *formal* augment, protract

pad² *v*
to pad softly
walk, move, step, run, tread, trudge, tramp, tiptoe, lope

padding *n*
1 FILLING, stuffing, wadding, packing, cushioning, lining, protection
2 VERBOSITY, verboseness, wordiness, bombast, hot air
formal verbiage, prolixity
colloq. waffle

paddle¹ *n, v*
▶ *n* *the paddles of a canoe*
oar, scull, sweep
▶ *v* row, oar, scull, propel, pull, punt, steer

paddle[2] *v*
children paddling in the water
wade, splash, slop, dabble, plunge

paddock *n*
enclosure, field, pen, fold, yard, pound, compound, stockade, corral

paddy *n*
rage, tiff, temper, tantrum, fit of temper, fury, passion, taking, bate
colloq. pet

padlock *n*
lock, mortise lock, spring lock, fastening, bolt, clasp, catch

padre *n*
chaplain, minister, priest, pastor, vicar, cleric, curate, reverend, father, parson, rector, deacon, deaconess, clergyman, churchman

paean *n*
eulogy, song of praise, ode to joy, hymn, doxology, anthem, psalm, ovation
formal dithyramb, encomium, panegyric
E3 denunciation, satire

pagan *n, adj*
▶ *n* heathen, atheist, unbeliever, nonbeliever, infidel, idolater
formal nullifidian
E3 believer
▶ *adj* heathen, irreligious, atheistic, godless, infidel, idolatrous, pantheistic
formal nullifidian

page[1] *n*
1 *write on a new page*
leaf, sheet, folio, side, recto, verso
2 *start a new page of your life*
episode, incident, event, period, stage, chapter, phase, era, epoch

page[2] *n, v*
▶ *n a page at a wedding*
pageboy, attendant, servant, messenger, bell-boy, footman
US bell-hop
▶ *v* call, ask for, send for, summon, bid, announce

pageant *n*
procession, parade, show, display, tableau, scene, play, representation, cavalcade, spectacle, extravaganza

pageantry *n*
pomp, ceremony, grandeur, magnificence, splendour, glamour, glitter, flourish, spectacle, parade, display, show, showiness, extravagance, theatricality, drama, melodrama

pail *n*
bucket, can, tub, bail, scuttle, pitcher, vessel, churn, piggin

pain *n, v*
▶ *n* 1 HURT, ache, throb, cramp, stitch, spasm, twinge, pang, stab, sting, smart, smarting, soreness, irritation, aching, throbbing, tenderness, discomfort, distress, suffering, trouble, anguish, agony, torment, torture
formal affliction
2 ANGUISH, grief, sorrow, agony, anxiety, desolation, distress, suffering, torment, torture, heartache, heartbreak, brokenheartedness, misery, pain, pang, rack, woe, wretchedness

formal tribulation
3 NUISANCE, bother, pest, annoyance, vexation, burden
colloq. bore, drag, headache, pain in the neck/backside; *slang* pain in the arse
▶ *v* 1 HURT, ache, be sore, sting, smart, irritate, be tender
2 AFFLICT, torment, torture, agonize, distress, worry, trouble, upset, make miserable, make anxious, sadden, grieve
E3 2 please, delight, gratify

pained *adj*
hurt, injured, wounded, stung, offended, aggrieved, reproachful, distressed, upset, worried, unhappy, sad, saddened, grieved, piqued, vexed
E3 pleased, gratified

painful *adj*
1 SORE, tender, hurting, irritating, inflamed, aching, throbbing, smarting, stabbing, agonizing, excruciating
2 *a painful experience*
unpleasant, disagreeable, distressing, upsetting, saddening, wretched, miserable, agonizing, disturbing, harrowing, traumatic
formal disquieting
3 EMBARRASSING, awkward, uncomfortable, disconcerting, distressing, upsetting, sensitive, mortifying, humiliating, shameful, shaming
formal discomfiting
colloq. touchy
4 HARD, difficult, tough, trying, exacting, laborious, tedious, arduous, rigorous, strenuous
E3 1 painless, soothing 2 pleasant, agreeable 4 easy, simple

painfully *adv*
distressingly, dreadfully, terribly, excessively, clearly, markedly, alarmingly, pitiably, pitifully, sadly, unfortunately, wretchedly, agonizingly, excruciatingly, woefully, deplorably

painkiller *n*
analgesic, anodyne, anaesthetic, palliative, sedative, drug, remedy, lenitive

painless *adj*
pain-free, trouble-free, effortless, easy, simple, undemanding
colloq. cushy, a piece of cake, child's play, like falling off a log, plain sailing
E3 painful, difficult

pains *n*
trouble, bother, effort, labour, care, diligence, assiduousness
▷ **be at pains** be anxious, be concerned, make every effort, try hard, take care, bother, go to great lengths

painstaking *adj*
careful, meticulous, scrupulous, thorough, conscientious, attentive, diligent, assiduous, industrious, hardworking, dedicated, devoted, persevering, searching
formal punctilious, sedulous
E3 careless, negligent

paint *n, v*
▶ *n* colour, colouring, pigment, colorant, vinyl wash, dye, tint, stain

Paints include: acrylic paint, colourwash, distemper, eggshell, emulsion, enamel, glaze, gloss paint, gouache, lacquer, masonry paint, matt paint, oil paint, oils, pastel, poster paint, primer, undercoat, varnish, watercolour, whitewash.

▶ *v* **1** COLOUR, dye, tint, stain, lacquer, varnish, glaze, apply, daub, wash, whitewash, coat, plaster, smear, cover, spray, respray, decorate, redecorate **2** PORTRAY, depict, tell, describe, narrate, draw, sketch, picture, evoke, represent
formal recount, delineate
▷ **paint the town red** celebrate, have/throw a party, rejoice, enjoy yourself, have fun, go out; *colloq.* rave, binge, have a ball, live it up, whoop it up, go out on the town, go on the razzle, kill the fatted calf, put the flags out

painter *n*
artist, colourist, oil painter, watercolourist, miniaturist, dauber, limner, depicter
formal delineator

painting *n*
oil painting, oil, watercolour, picture, portrait, landscape, portrayal, representation, likeness, still life, miniature, illustration, fresco, mural
formal delineation
Related adjective: pictorial

Painting terms include: abstract, alla prima, aquarelle, aquatint, art gallery, bleeding, bloom; brush, filbert brush, flat brush, round brush, sable brush; brush strokes, canvas, canvas board, capriccio, cartoon, charcoal, chiaroscuro, collage, composition, craquelure, diptych, drawing, easel, encaustic, facture, fête champêtre, fête galante, figurative, foreshortening, fresco, frieze, frottage, gallery, genre painting, gesso, gouache, grisaille, grotesque, hard edge, illustration, icon, impasto, landscape, mahlstick, miniature, monochrome, montage, mural, oil painting, paint, palette, palette knife, pastels, pastoral, paysage, pencil sketch, pentimento, perspective, picture, pieta, pigment, pochade box, pointillism, portrait, primer, scumble, seascape, secco, sfumato, sgraffito, silhouette, sketch, skyscape, still life, stipple, tempera, thinners, tint, tondo, tone, triptych, trompe l'oeil, turpentine, underpainting, vignette, wash, watercolour. *See also* **art, paint, picture**.

pair *n, v*
▶ *n* couple, brace, two, twosome, duo, twins, two of a kind, set
▶ *v* match (up), twin, team (up), mate, marry, wed, unite, splice, join (up), couple, link (up), bracket, put together, arrange in pairs
⊟ separate, part

paired *adj*
coupled, joined, linked, matched, double, twinned, in twos, yoked, mated, associated, bracketed
⊟ single

pal *n*
friend, comrade, companion, partner, confidant(e), intimate, soul mate
colloq. buddy, chum, crony, mate, sidekick
⊟ enemy, opponent

palace *n*
castle, château, mansion, stately home, basilica, dome

palatable *adj*
1 TASTY, appetizing, eatable, edible, flavoursome, flavorous, succulent, mouth-watering, savoury
formal delectable
colloq. yummy, morish, scrumptious, scrummy, done to a turn

2 ACCEPTABLE, satisfactory, pleasant, pleasing, nice, agreeable, enjoyable, attractive
⊟ **1** unpalatable **2** unacceptable, unpleasant, disagreeable

palate *n*
taste, sense of taste, appreciation, liking, relish, gout, enjoyment, enthusiasm, appetite, stomach, heart

palatial *adj*
grand, magnificent, splendid, majestic, regal, stately, grandiose, imposing, luxurious, de luxe, sumptuous, opulent, spacious
colloq. plush, posh, ritzy

palaver *n*
fuss, bother, fuss about nothing, rigmarole, procedure, carry-on, activity, business, bustle, commotion, fluster
colloq. song and dance, to-do, flap

pale¹ *adj, v*
▶ *adj* **1** PALLID, livid, ashen, ashy, white, whitish, colourless, chalky, pasty, pasty-faced, waxen, waxy, wan, peaky, sallow, anaemic, drained
colloq. washed out
2 *pale blue*
light, pastel, faded, bleached, colourless, insipid, vapid, weak, muted, feeble, thin, faint, dim, restrained, low-key
formal etiolated
colloq. washed-out
⊟ **1** ruddy **2** dark, strong, intense
▶ *v* **1** WHITEN, blanch, bleach, fade, dim, grow white, grow pale
2 *pale into insignificance*
fade, dim, lessen, diminish, melt, dwindle
⊟ **1** colour, blush

pale² *n*
▷ **beyond the pale** *such behaviour is beyond the pale* unacceptable, intolerable, unreasonable, improper, unsuitable, inappropriate, inadmissible;
formal unseemly

palisade *n*
fence, paling, defence, enclosure, barricade, bulwark, fortification, stockade

pall¹ *n*
a pall over a coffin; a pall of smoke
shroud, veil, mantle, cloak, cloud, shadow, gloom, damper
▷ **cast a pall over** spoil, mar, upset, impair, harm, ruin, destroy, wreck

pall² *v*
interest began to pall
wear off, tire, weary, become tired, become bored, lose its attraction, jade, sate, satiate, cloy, sicken

palliate *v*
ease, diminish, moderate, mollify, relieve, soften, soothe, temper, lessen, lighten, allay, alleviate, excuse, minimize, mitigate, cover, conceal, cloak
formal abate, assuage, extenuate, lenify

palliative *adj, n*
▶ *adj* sedative, soothing, mollifying, alleviative, calming, lenitive, calmative, anodyne
technical demulcent, paregoric
formal mitigative, mitigatory, assuasive
⊟ irritant
▶ *n* analgesic, anodyne, painkiller, sedative, tranquillizer, calmative, lenitive
technical demulcent, paregoric

pallid *adj*
1 PALE, pasty, whitish, sallow, colourless, pasty-faced, ashen, ashy, bloodless, anaemic, wan, waxen, waxy, whey-faced
Scot. peelie-wally
formal etiolated
2 UNEXCITING, weak, dull, boring, uninteresting, bland, uninspired, tame, sterile, tired, lifeless, insipid, spiritless, vapid
F3 **1** vigorous, ruddy, high-complexioned **2** lively, exciting

pallor *n*
paleness, whiteness, pallidness, wanness, sallowness, bloodlessness, chalkiness
formal etiolation
F3 ruddiness

pally *adj*
friendly, close, affectionate, familiar, intimate
colloq. chummy, thick
F3 unfriendly

palm *n, v*
▶ *n* hand
colloq. paw; *slang* mitt
Related adjectives: palmar, thenar, volar
▶ *v* take, grab, snatch, appropriate
▷ **palm off** foist, impose, fob off, thrust, offload, unload, pass off, get rid of

palmist *n*
fortune-teller, clairvoyant, palm reader

palmistry *n*
fortune-telling, clairvoyancy, palm reading, chirognomy, chiromancy

palmy *adj*
carefree, thriving, prosperous, flourishing, successful, fortunate, happy, glorious, triumphant, joyous, luxurious, golden
formal halcyon

palpable *adj*
1 SOLID, substantial, material, concrete, real, touchable, tangible
2 OBVIOUS, visible, apparent, clear, plain, evident, patent, conspicuous, glaring, blatant, unmistakable
formal manifest
F3 **1** intangible **2** impalpable, imperceptible, elusive

palpitate *v*
flutter, quiver, tremble, shiver, vibrate, quake, shake, beat, pulse, pulsate, pound, thump, thud, throb

paltry *adj*
meagre, derisory, contemptible, mean, low, miserable, wretched, poor, sorry, small, slight, trifling, inconsiderable, negligible, trivial, minor, contemptible, petty, unimportant, insignificant, puny, worthless
colloq. measly, piddling
F3 substantial, significant, valuable

pamper *v*
spoil, cosset, coddle, mollycoddle, humour, gratify, indulge, overindulge, pander, pet, fondle
colloq. spoon-feed, wait on someone hand and foot
F3 neglect, ill-treat

pampered *adj*
spoilt, cosseted, coddled, mollycoddled, indulged, overfed, high-fed, petted
F3 abused, neglected

pamphlet *n*
leaflet, brochure, booklet, folder, circular, handout, notice

pan[1] *n, v*
▶ *n pots and pans*
saucepan, frying-pan, fryer, pot, skillet, casserole, wok, container, vessel, pancheon
▶ *v* criticize, censure, flay, find fault with, hammer
colloq. knock, pull to pieces, roast, rubbish, slam, slate
F3 praise
▷ **pan out** work out, turn out, result, happen, yield, culminate, come to an end, be exhausted; *formal* eventuate

pan[2] *v*
pan the camera
sweep, scan, move, turn, follow, track, swing, circle
formal traverse

panacea *n*
cure-all, universal remedy, elixir, nostrum
formal catholicon, diacatholicon, panpharmacon

panache *n*
flourish, flamboyance, ostentation, style, flair, élan, dash, spirit, enthusiasm, zest, brio, energy, vigour, verve

pancake *n*
crêpe, waffle, wafer, blini, griddle-cake, tortilla
Scot. bannock
US battercake, flapjack

pandemic *adj*
widespread, extensive, general, common, prevalent, far-reaching, rife, pervasive, universal, global

pandemonium *n*
chaos, disorder, confusion, commotion, rumpus, turmoil, turbulence, tumult, uproar, din, bedlam, hubbub, hullaballoo, hue and cry
colloq. to-do
F3 order, calm, peace

pander *v*
▷ **pander to** humour, indulge, pamper, please, gratify, satisfy, fulfil, provide, cater to

panegyric *n, adj*
▶ *n* eulogy, praise, tribute, commendation, homage, accolade, citation
formal paean, encomium, eulogium
F3 censure, criticism
▶ *adj* eulogistic, favourable, flattering, glowing, praiseful, praising, complimentary, commendatory
formal encomiastic, laudatory, panegyrical
F3 censorious, critical, damning

panel *n*
1 *a wooden panel*
board, sheet, slab, plank, beam, timber, cartouche
2 *a panel of judges*
board, committee, council, jury, team, commission, directorate, trustees, advisory group
3 *a control panel*
board, console, dashboard, instrument panel, instruments, controls, switches, knobs, dials, buttons, levers

panelling *n*
panel-work, wainscot, wainscot(t)ing, dado

pang *n*
pain, ache, twinge, stab, sting, prick, stitch, gripe,

spasm, throe, misgiving, scruple, qualm, agony, anguish, uneasiness, discomfort, distress

panic *n, v*
▶ *n* agitation, alarm, dismay, fright, fear, horror, terror, frenzy, hysteria
formal consternation, disquiet, trepidation, perturbation
colloq. flap
E3 calmness, confidence
▶ *v* lose your nerve, lose your head, overreact, unnerve
colloq. flap, go to pieces, lose your cool, have kittens, get the jitters, get the shakes, get the willies, feel your hair stand on end, run round like a headless chicken
E3 relax

panic-stricken *adj*
alarmed, frightened, horrified, terrified, terror-stricken, petrified, scared, scared stiff, aghast, in a cold sweat, panicky, frantic, frenzied, hysterical
formal perturbed
colloq. in a tizzy
E3 relaxed, confident

panoply *n*
array, range, equipment, show, regalia, insignia, armour, dress, raiment, trappings
formal attire
colloq. garb, gear, get-up, turn-out

panorama *n*
view, wide-broad view, bird's eye view, vista, prospect, scenery, landscape, scene, spectacle, perspective, overview, survey

panoramic *adj*
scenic, wide, broad, sweeping, extensive, far-reaching, wide-ranging, widespread, overall, comprehensive, general, universal
E3 narrow, restricted, limited

pant *v, n*
▶ *v* **1** PUFF, blow, gasp, wheeze, breathe, sigh, heave, throb, palpitate
colloq. huff and puff
2 LONG, pine, desire, want, yearn, covet, crave, hanker, sigh, ache, thirst
colloq. yen
▶ *n* gasp, puff, huff, throb, wheeze

panting *adj*
1 PUFFED OUT, breathless, out of breath, gasping, short-winded, winded, puffing, puffed
2 ANXIOUS, eager, impatient, longing, craving, hankering

pantomime *n*
show, charade, farce, commedia dell'arte, harlequinade, masque
colloq. panto

pants *n*
1 UNDERPANTS, drawers, panties, briefs, knickers, camiknickers, teddy, panty girdle, Y-fronts, boxer shorts, trunks, shorts
colloq. undies, smalls, frillies
2 TROUSERS, slacks, jeans

pap *n*
1 MUSH, pulp, purée, soft food, semi-liquid food
colloq. goo
2 RUBBISH, drivel, trash, nonsense, gibberish
colloq. rot, claptrap; *slang* crap

paper *n, v*
▶ *n* **1** NEWSPAPER, daily, broadsheet, tabloid, magazine, periodical, weekly, journal, organ
colloq. rag
2 DOCUMENT, credential, authorization, identification, identity card, ID, certificate, record, deed, paperwork
colloq. red tape
3 *a paper on alternative medicine*
essay, composition, dissertation, thesis, treatise, article, study, report, work, examination, analysis
formal monograph
▷ **on paper 1** IN WRITING, written down, officially, on the record, recorded, in black and white **2** IN THEORY, hypothetically, ideally, theoretically, supposedly, seemingly, in your mind's eye

Types of paper include: art paper, bank, blotting paper, bond, carbon paper, cartridge paper, crêpe paper, graph paper, greaseproof paper, manila, notepaper, parchment, rice paper, silver paper, sugar paper, tissue paper, toilet paper, tracing paper, vellum, wallpaper, wrapping paper, writing-paper; card, cardboard, pasteboard; A4, foolscap, quarto, atlas, crown.

▶ *v* ▷ **paper over** hide, conceal, cover up, obscure, put out of sight, disguise, camouflage
Related adjective: papyraceous

papery *adj*
thin, paper-thin, light, lightweight, delicate, insubstantial, flimsy, fragile, frail, translucent

par *n*
level, standard, norm, usual, correspondence, similarity, equivalence, equal footing, equality, balance, equilibrium, accordance, average, mean
technical median
formal parity
▷ **below par 1** UNSATISFACTORY, inadequate, inferior, below average, not up to par; *colloq.* not up to scratch **2** UNWELL, under par, tired, out of sorts; *colloq.* under the weather
▷ **on a par with** equal to, equivalent to, as good as, the same standard as
▷ **par for the course** typical, normal, standard, usual, predictable, only to be expected

parable *n*
fable, allegory, lesson, moral tale, story, story with a moral

parade *n, v*
▶ *n* **1** PROCESSION, cavalcade, motorcade, march, column, file, train, progression, review, ceremony
2 SPECTACLE, pageant, show, display, demonstration, exhibition
formal array
▶ *v* **1** MARCH, process, file past
2 SHOW, display, exhibit, show off, vaunt, flaunt, brandish

paradigm *n*
pattern, model, example, original, ideal, framework, prototype
formal archetype, exemplar

paradise *n*
1 HEAVEN, home of God, bliss, next world, hereafter, life to come, afterlife, utopia, Elysium, elysium fields, happy hunting ground, Shangri-La, Eden, Garden of Eden
2 ECSTASY, rapture, bliss, happiness, complete

happiness, joy, delight, transports of delight
formal felicity
colloq. seventh heaven
E3 1 hell, Hades

paradox *n*
contradiction, inconsistency, absurdity, oddity, mystery, enigma, riddle, puzzle
formal incongruity, anomaly

paradoxical *adj*
self-contradictory, contradictory, conflicting, inconsistent, absurd, illogical, improbable, impossible, mysterious, enigmatic, puzzling, baffling
formal incongruous, anomalous

paragon *n*
ideal, epitome, model, pattern, crème de la crème, masterpiece, prototype, standard, criterion
formal exemplar, quintessence, archetype, nonpareil
colloq. the bee's knees

paragraph *n*
passage, section, part, portion, segment, subsection, subdivision, article, piece, clause, item

parallel *adj, n, v*
▶ *adj* 1 ALIGNED, equidistant, alongside, coextensive, collateral
2 SIMILAR, like, matching, resembling, equivalent, comparable, uniform, corresponding
formal analogous, homologous
E3 2 divergent, different
▶ *n* 1 MATCH, equal, twin, duplicate, equivalent, counterpart
formal analogue
2 SIMILARITY, resemblance, likeness, correspondence, equivalence, analogy, comparison
formal correlation
▶ *v* match, echo, be similar to, resemble, be like, be equivalent, equal, conform, agree, correspond, compare, liken
formal be analogous, correlate
E3 diverge, differ

paralyse *v*
1 *paralysed his leg*
cripple, lame, disable, incapacitate, immobilize, anaesthetize, numb, dull, deaden, freeze, shock, terrify, transfix
formal debilitate
2 *paralyse the transport system*
bring to a standstill, immobilize, cripple, halt, stop, disable

paralysed *adj*
paralytic, paraplegic, quadriplegic, crippled, lame, disabled, incapacitated, immobilized, numb
E3 able-bodied

paralysis *n*
1 *paralysis in the legs*
paraplegia, quadriplegia, palsy, numbness, deadness, immobility, powerlessness
technical paresis
formal debilitation
2 *paralysis of the transport system*
standstill, halt, stoppage, shutdown, breakdown, immobility

paralytic *adj*
1 CRIPPLED, disabled, paralysed, incapacitated, lame, immobilized, immobile, numb, palsied, quadriplegic, monoplegic, hemiplegic
2 DRUNK, inebriated, intoxicated

colloq. legless, plastered, pie-eyed; *slang* stoned, pissed, sloshed, smashed, stewed
E3 2 (stone-cold) sober

parameter *n*
variable, guideline, indication, criterion, specification, factor, limiting factor, limitation, restriction, framework, limit, boundary

paramount *adj*
supreme, highest, topmost, predominant, pre-eminent, prime, principal, main, chief, outstanding, cardinal, primary, first, foremost, first and foremost, most important, of greatest importance
E3 lowest, last

paramour *n*
lover, beloved, beau, courtesan, mistress, woman, kept woman, inamorato, inamorata, concubine, hetaera
colloq. fancy man, fancy woman, bit on the side

paranoia *n*
obsession, delusions, psychosis, megalomania, monomania, persecution complex

paranoid *adj*
suspicious, distrustful, bewildered, confused, afraid, fearful, fazed

parapet *n*
1 WALL, railing, fence, rail, paling, barrier
2 EMBANKMENT, defence, guard, battlement, bulwark, fortification, rampart, barbican, bastion

paraphernalia *n*
equipment, gear, tackle, apparatus, tools, implements, materials, accessories, trappings, belongings, possessions, stuff, things, baggage
formal effects, accoutrements
colloq. bits and pieces, odds and ends

paraphrase *v, n*
▶ *v* reword, rephrase, restate, put in other words, express differently, interpret, render, translate, gloss
colloq. rehash
▶ *n* rewording, rephrasing, restatement, different expression, other form of words, version, interpretation, rendering, translation, gloss

parasite *n*
1 LEECH, bloodsucker
technical endophyte, entozoon, endozoon, epiphyte, epizoon, epizoan
2 *parasites in society*
hanger-on, passenger, leech, drone, bloodsucker
colloq. sponger, scrounger, cadger, freeloader, bum, moocher

parasitic *adj*
1 *parasitic animals*
parasitical, biogenous, leechlike
technical epizoan, epizoic
2 *a parasitic person*
bloodsucking, freeloading
colloq. cadging, scrounging, sponging

parcel *n, v*
▶ *n* 1 PACKAGE, packet, pack, box, carton, bundle
2 *a parcel of land*
plot, patch, area, piece, portion, lot, allotment, tract
3 GROUP, company, troop, herd, flock, band, crowd, gang, mob
4 LOT, deal, transaction, package, pack, collection
▶ *v* package, pack (up), wrap (up), gift-wrap, bundle (up), tie up
▷ **parcel out** divide (out), carve up, apportion,

allocate, allot, share out, distribute, hand out, dispense, dole out, deal out, mete out

parch *v*
dry (up), dehydrate, bake, burn, scorch, sear, blister, wither, shrivel
formal desiccate

parched *adj*
1 ARID, waterless, dry, dried up, dehydrated, baked, burned, seared, blistered, scorched, withered, shrivelled
formal desiccated, sear, sere
colloq. dry as a bone
2 THIRSTY, dry, dehydrated
colloq. gasping

parchment *n*
scroll, vellum, document, certificate, charter, diploma, palimpsest
Related adjective: pergameneous

pardon *v, n*
▶ *v* forgive, condone, overlook, excuse, absolve, let off, reprieve, free, liberate, release
formal vindicate, acquit, remit, exonerate, exculpate
colloq. let off the hook
E3 punish, discipline
▶ *n* forgiveness, mercy, clemency, indulgence, forbearance, lenience, amnesty, excuse, absolution, reprieve, release, discharge
formal acquittal, condonation, exoneration, exculpation
E3 punishment, condemnation

pardonable *adj*
forgivable, excusable, justifiable, warrantable, understandable, allowable, permissible, slight, minor, venial, condonable
E3 inexcusable

pare *v*
peel, skin, shear, clip, trim, crop, cut, dock, lop, prune, cut back, whittle, reduce, decrease

parent *n, v*
▶ *n* **1** *a single parent*
father, mother, biological/birth parent, single parent, guardian, foster parent, custodial parent, dam, sire
old use begetter
formal progenitor, procreator
2 SOURCE, origin, root, cause, creator, originator, author, architect, prototype, forerunner
old use begetter
▶ *v* be the father/mother of, bring into the world, create, look after, take care of, nurture, bring up, raise, foster, educate, teach, train
old use beget
formal rear, procreate
Related adjective: parental

parentage *n*
family, birth, origin, source, stock, extraction, filiation, affiliation, ancestry, lineage, derivation, descent, line, race, pedigree, paternity
formal stirps

parenthetical *adj*
in parenthesis, incidental, qualifying, explanatory, bracketed, inserted, extraneous
formal elucidative, interposed, intervening
E3 basic, original

pariah *n*
outcast, outlaw, exile, castaway, leper, undesirable,

unperson, untouchable, Ishmael
colloq. black sheep

paring *n*
peel, peeling, skin, shaving, shred, clipping, trimming, fragment, cutting, flake, rind, slice, sliver, snippet, flaught

parish *n*
1 DISTRICT, community, village, town
2 PARISHIONERS, church, churchgoers, congregation, flock, fold
Related adjective: parochial

parity *n*
equality, equivalence, parallelism, consistency, conformity, analogy, agreement, correspondence, similarity, resemblance, likeness, sameness, uniformity, unity, semblance, affinity, par
formal congruence, congruity, consonance, similitude

park *n, v*
▶ *n* grounds, woodland, grassland

Types of park include: amusement park, arboretum, botanical garden, car park, estate, game reserve, industrial park, municipal park, national park, park-and-ride, parking lot, parkland, play area, playground, pleasance, pleasure garden, pleasure ground, recreation ground, reserve, sanctuary, theme park, wildlife park.

▶ *v* put, position, place, deposit, set, leave, stop
colloq. plonk

parlance *n*
phraseology, language, talk, speech, tongue, idiom, jargon, diction, argot, cant
colloq. lingo

parley *n, v*
▶ *n* talk(s), negotiation, meeting, conference, council, deliberation, discussion, get-together, dialogue, tête-à-tête
formal colloquy
colloq. confab, powwow
▶ *v* talk, speak, discuss, get together, negotiate, consult, deliberate
formal confer
colloq. powwow

parliament *n*
legislature, senate, congress, house, lower house, upper house, assembly, convocation, council, diet

parliamentary *adj*
governmental, senatorial, congressional, legislative, law-making, law-giving, elected, democratic, popular, representative, official, republican
formal legislatorial

parliaments and political assemblies

Names of parliaments and political assemblies include: House of Representatives, Senate (*Australia*); Nationalrat, Bundesrat (*Austria*); Narodno Sobraniye (*Bulgaria*); House of Commons, Senate (*Canada*); National People's Congress (*China*); Folketing (*Denmark*); People's Assembly (*Egypt*); Eduskunta (*Finland*); National Assembly, Senate (*France*); Bundesrat, Bundestag, Landtag (*Germany*); Althing (*Iceland*); Lok Sabha, Rajya Sabha (*India*); Majlis (*Iran*); Dáil, Seanad (*Ireland*); Knesset (*Israel*); Camera del Deputati, Senato (*Italy*); Diet (*Japan*); Staten-Generaal (*Netherlands*); House of Representatives (*New Zealand*); Storting (*Norway*); Sejm (*Poland*);

Cortes (*Portugal*); Congress of People's Deputies, Supreme Soviet (*Russia*); House of Assembly (*South Africa*); Cortes (*Spain*); Riksdag (*Sweden*); Nationalrat, Standerat, Bundesrat (*Switzerland*); Porte (*Turkey*); House of Commons, House of Lords (*UK*); House of Representatives, Senate (*US*); National Assembly (*Vietnam*).

parlour *n*
sitting-room, lounge, living-room, front room, drawing-room

parochial *adj*
insular, provincial, parish-pump, small-town, petty, small-minded, narrow-minded, narrow, inward-looking, blinkered, limited, restricted, confined
colloq. hick
F3 national, international

parochialism *n*
insularity, provincialism, small-mindedness, pettiness, narrow-mindedness, narrowness

parody *n, v*
▶ *n* caricature, lampoon, burlesque, satire, pasquinade, skit, mimicry, imitation, travesty, distortion, corruption, misrepresentation, perversion
colloq. send-up, spoof, take-off
▶ *v* caricature, lampoon, burlesque, satirize, mimic, imitate, ape
colloq. send up, spoof, take off

paroxysm *n*
fit, seizure, spasm, convulsion, attack, eruption, flare-up, outbreak, outburst, explosion

parrot *v, n*
▶ *v* repeat, copy, imitate, mimic, echo, rehearse, reiterate, ape
▶ *n* mimic, repeater, imitator, copy-cat, phraser, ape
Related adjective: psittacine

parrot-fashion *adv*
by rote, mechanically, mindlessly, unthinkingly, automatically

parry *v*
ward off, fend off, repel, repulse, rebuff, field, deflect, stave off, block, avert, turn aside, avoid, evade, keep/hold at bay, sidestep, steer clear of, shun
formal circumvent
colloq. duck, dodge

parsimonious *adj*
mean, niggardly, miserly, tight-fisted, stinting, sparing, scrimpy, saving, close, cheese-paring, close-fisted, close-handed, frugal, grasping
formal penurious
colloq. mingy, penny-pinching, stingy, tight
F3 generous, liberal, open-handed

parsimony *n*
meanness, miserliness, frugality, niggardliness, tight-fistedness
colloq. minginess, penny-pinching, stinginess, tightness
F3 generosity, liberality

parson *n*
vicar, rector, priest, minister, pastor, preacher, clergyman, reverend, cleric, churchman

part *n, v, adj*
▶ *n* 1 COMPONENT, constituent, module, element, factor, ingredient, side, dimension, aspect, facet, piece, bit, particle, fragment, slice, scrap, segment, fraction,

proportion, percentage, portion, extract, excerpt, share, section, division, department, branch, sector, wing
2 ROLE, character, duty, job, work, charge, task, responsibility, chore, office, function, capacity, involvement, participation
3 SECTION, chapter, volume, book, passage, scene, episode, instalment
4 AREA, district, sector, region, neighbourhood, territory, quarter
5 *a person of many parts*
skill, gift, talent, ability, capability, attribute, accomplishment, faculty, endowment, expertise, genius, intellect, intelligence, calibre
F3 1 whole, totality
▷ **for the most part** by and large, on the whole, generally, usually, mostly, mainly, in the main, chiefly, largely, commonly
▷ **in part** to some degree, partly, somewhat, to some extent, to a certain extent, to a certain degree, up to a point, slightly
▷ **take part in** join in, be involved in, participate in, share in, engage in, help with, assist in, play a part in, play a role in, contribute to; *formal* partake
▶ *v* 1 SEPARATE, detach, disconnect, sever, split, tear, break, break up, take apart, dismantle, come apart, split up, divide
formal disjoin, cleave
2 PART COMPANY WITH, split up from, separate from, divorce from, get divorced from, leave, withdraw from, go away from, go your separate ways, depart from, take your leave, say goodbye, get going
colloq. push along/off, split, scarper, clear off, take off, hit the road/trail, make tracks
3 DISPERSE, separate, diverge, disband, scatter, split up, break up
F3 1, 2 join
▷ **part with** relinquish, let go of, give up, yield, surrender, renounce, forego, abandon, discard, jettison
F3 hold onto
▶ *adj* partial, half, not complete, limited, restricted, imperfect, fragmentary, unfinished

partake *v*
take part, share, participate, be involved, engage, enter
▷ **partake of** 1 *partake of food* consume, eat, drink 2 *partake of the divine nature* receive, share, have, show, demonstrate, take, suggest, evoke; *formal* evince, manifest

partial *adj*
1 *a partial victory*
incomplete, in part, part, limited, restricted, imperfect, fragmentary, unfinished
2 BIASED, prejudiced, partisan, one-sided, discriminatory, preferential, unfair, unjust, inequitable, coloured, affected
formal predisposed
F3 1 complete, total 2 impartial, disinterested, unbiased, fair
▷ **partial to** fond of, liking, loving, keen on, taken with, with a weakness for; *formal* with a penchant for; *colloq.* crazy about, mad about, with a soft spot for

partiality *n*
1 BIAS, prejudice, discrimination, unfairness, injustice, inequity, inequitableness, partisanship
2 LIKING, fondness, love, inclination, preference
formal predilection, predisposition, proclivity

partially adv
incompletely, not fully, fractionally, somewhat, in part, partly

participant n
entrant, competitor, contestant, contributor, participator, member, party, co-operator, helper, associate, partner, worker, sharer, shareholder

participate v
take part, join in, contribute, engage, be involved, be associated, enter, share, play a part, play a role, co-operate, help, assist
formal partake

participation n
involvement, sharing, partnership, co-operation, contribution, assistance, association
formal partaking

particle n
bit, piece, fragment, scrap, trace, touch, shred, sliver, speck, morsel, mite, crumb, iota, whit, jot, tittle, atom, molecule, grain, drop
colloq. smidgen, tad

parti-coloured adj
motley, variegated, piebald
formal polychromatic, polychromic, versicoloured
F3 monochromatic, plain

particular adj, n
▶ *adj* **1** *on that particular day*
specific, precise, exact, distinct, certain, individual, special, peculiar
2 EXCEPTIONAL, remarkable, notable, marked, outstanding, thorough, unusual, uncommon, peculiar, notable, noteworthy
formal especial
3 FUSSY, discriminating, finicky, fastidious, selective, meticulous, painstaking, exacting
colloq. choosy, pernickety, picky
4 EXACT, detailed, thorough, precise, faithful, accurate
F3 1 general
▶ *n* detail, specific, point, feature, item, fact, circumstance
▷ **in particular** particularly, especially, specifically, exactly, precisely, to be specific, in detail

particularity n
feature, trait, detail, instance, fact, item, circumstance, characteristic, idiosyncrasy, individuality, point, property, distinctiveness, uniqueness, peculiarity, quirk, singularity

particularize v
detail, specify, itemize, stipulate, individualize, enumerate
formal individuate

particularly adv
especially, exceptionally, remarkably, notably, markedly, extraordinarily, unusually, uncommonly, surprisingly, in particular, specifically, explicitly, distinctly, expressly

parting n, adj
▶ *n* **1** DEPARTURE, going, leaving, leave-taking, farewell, goodbye, adieu
formal valediction
2 DIVERGENCE, separation, divorce, division, partition, rift, split, rupture, breaking, breaking-up
F3 1 meeting **2** convergence
▶ *adj* departing, leaving, farewell, goodbye, last,

dying, final, closing, concluding
formal valedictory
F3 first, arriving, opening

partisan n, adj
▶ *n* **1** SUPPORTER, devotee, adherent, follower, party man, disciple, backer, upholder, champion, fan, votary, stalwart
2 GUERRILLA, irregular, freedom fighter, resistance fighter
▶ *adj* biased, prejudiced, unfair, unjust, inequitable, partial, predisposed, discriminatory, one-sided, factional, sectarian
F3 impartial

partisanship n
bias, prejudice, partiality, partyism, sectarianism, factionalism
F3 impartiality

partition n, v
▶ *n* **1** DIVIDER, barrier, wall, dividing wall, panel, screen, room-divider, dividing screen, separator
technical membrane, diaphragm
2 DIVISION, break-up, splitting, separation, segregation, parting, severance, subdivision
Related adjectives: septiform, septiferous
▶ *v* **1** SEPARATE, separate off, divide, subdivide, bar, wall off, fence off, screen (off)
2 SHARE, divide (up), split up, break up, segregate, sever, parcel out

partly adv
somewhat, to some extent, to some degree, a little, to a certain extent, to a certain degree, up to a point, slightly, fractionally, in some measure, moderately, relatively, in part, partially, incompletely, half
F3 completely, totally, fully, wholly

partner n
1 ASSOCIATE, ally, confederate, colleague, co-worker, team-mate, collaborator, co-operator, accomplice, helper, mate, companion, comrade, consort, spouse, husband, wife
colloq. sidekick, oppo
2 *bring your partner to the party*
spouse, husband, wife, boyfriend, girlfriend, friend, companion, consort
colloq. other half

partnership n
1 *the partnership between teachers and parents*
association, alliance, co-operation, collaboration, participation, sharing, confederation, affiliation, combination, union, fellowship, fraternity, brotherhood
2 *a business partnership*
company, firm, corporation, syndicate, co-operative, association, society, conglomerate

party n
1 CELEBRATION, festivity, social, get-together, gathering, reunion, function, reception, at-home

Kinds of party include: acid-house party, barbecue, *slang* bash, *colloq.* beanfeast, *colloq.* beano, birthday party, *colloq.* bunfight, ceilidh, cocktail party, dinner party, disco, discotheque, *colloq.* do, flatwarming, garden party, *colloq.* gathering of the clan, Hallowe'en party, hen party, hooley, *US colloq.* hootnanny, housewarming, *colloq.* knees-up, orgy, picnic, pyjama party, rave, *colloq.* rave-up, *colloq.* shindig, shivoo, *US colloq.* shower, social, soirée, stag night, stag party, supper party, tea party, *colloq.* thrash, welcoming party.

2 *a search party*
team, squad, crew, gang, band, group, body, company, unit, contingent, detachment
3 *a political party*
faction, side, league, cabal, alliance, association, affiliation, grouping, camp, combination
4 PERSON, individual, litigant, plaintiff, defendant

parvenu *n*
upstart, pretender, climber, arriviste, *nouveau riche*, new rich, vulgarian

pass¹ *v, n*
▶ *v* **1** GO, move, proceed, travel, progress, flow, run, drive, make your way
2 OVERTAKE, go past, drive/run past, outdistance, outstrip, beat, lose, lap, leave behind, draw level with, pull ahead of, overhaul
3 GO THROUGH, go across, go over, get across, get over, run, move, traverse
4 *pass the salt*
hand, give, reach, let someone have, transfer, transmit
5 *time passes quickly*
go by, go past, elapse, proceed, advance, slip by, slip away, drag
6 *pass time wisely*
spend, fill, occupy, employ, use up, take up, devote, while away
7 EXCEED, surpass, go beyond, go over, outdo, outstrip
8 *pass an exam*
succeed, be successful in, get through, qualify, graduate, pass with flying colours, sail/breeze through, scrape through
9 *the examiner passed him*
declare successful, approve, accept, declare satisfactory
10 *pass a new law*
enact, ratify, validate, adopt, authorize, sanction, approve, vote for, agree to, accept
11 *pass from one state to another*
CHANGE, go, move, turn, become, develop, transfer, evolve
12 HAPPEN, take place, occur, come about
formal transpire, befall
13 *the estate passed to her daughter*
be left, be willed, be bequeathed, be inherited, be made over, be given, be handed down, be endowed, be granted, be consigned, transfer
14 *pass the ball*
throw, kick, move, swing, lunge
15 *pass urine*
discharge, expel, emit, let out, release
formal excrete
⊟ 2 fall behind **7** fail to reach **8** fail **9** fail
▷ **pass as/for** appear to be, be taken for, be mistaken for, be regarded as
▷ **pass away** die, pass on; *formal* expire, decease; *colloq.* give up the ghost, peg out, pop off, kick the bucket
▷ **pass off 1** HAPPEN, occur, take place, go off **2** *the effects passed off quickly* wear off, fade away, die down, disappear, vanish **3** FEIGN, counterfeit, fake, palm off
▷ **pass out 1** FAINT, lose consciousness, black out, collapse, drop; *old use* swoon; *colloq.* flake out, keel over **2** GIVE OUT, hand out, distribute, deal out, allocate, allot, share out, dole out
▷ **pass over** disregard, ignore, overlook, miss, omit, leave, neglect, forget, take no notice of, not take into consideration, turn a blind eye to, turn a deaf ear to

▷ **pass up** not take advantage of, ignore, miss, refuse, neglect, reject, let slip
▶ *n* **1** THROW, kick, move, lunge, swing
2 PERMIT, passport, visa, identification, ticket, licence, authorization, warrant, permission
3 *make a pass at someone*
advances, approach, overture, suggestion, proposition, play

pass² *n*
a pass through the mountains
col, defile, gorge, ravine, canyon, gap, passage

passable *adj*
1 SATISFACTORY, acceptable, allowable, tolerable, average, ordinary, unexceptional, moderate, fair, adequate, all right, mediocre
colloq. OK, run of the mill, so-so, nothing to write home about, not much cop, no great shakes
2 CLEAR, unobstructed, unblocked, open, navigable, traversable
⊟ 1 unacceptable, excellent **2** obstructed, blocked, impassable

passably *adv*
fairly, rather, somewhat, tolerably, relatively, reasonably, moderately, after a fashion

passage *n*
1 PASSAGEWAY, aisle, corridor, hall, hallway, lobby, vestibule, doorway, opening, entrance, exit
2 THOROUGHFARE, way, route, road, avenue, path, track, lane, alley
3 CHANNEL, duct, conduit, main, groove, furrow, trough, gutter, gully, canal, flume, watercourse, waterway, strait, neck, sound
4 MOVEMENT, flow, running, course
5 TRANSITION, progress, advance, change, transfer, turning, development
technical mutation, metamorphosis
6 *the passage of a bill*
acceptance, approval, adoption, authorization, validation, sanction, enactment, ratification
7 *grant passage through a country*
access, admission, permission to travel through, safe conduct
8 EXTRACT, excerpt, quotation, text, paragraph, section, piece, clause, verse
formal citation
9 JOURNEY, voyage, trip, crossing, tour, trek

passageway *n*
passage, corridor, hall, hallway, lobby, entrance, exit, aisle, lane, path, way, track, alley

passé *adj*
outdated, old-fashioned, out-of-date, dated, obsolete, outmoded, unfashionable, outworn, *démodé*, antiquated, past its best
colloq. old hat, out
⊟ fashionable, in

passenger *n*
1 TRAVELLER, voyager, commuter, rider, fare, fare-payer, hitchhiker
2 *get rid of passengers who don't work*
hanger-on, drone
colloq. freeloader, sponger, bum

passer-by *n*
bystander, witness, looker-on, onlooker, observer, spectator, witness, eyewitness
colloq. rubberneck, gawper

passing *adj, n*
▶ *adj* **1** SHORT-LIVED, temporary, momentary, transitional, fleeting, brief, short
formal ephemeral, transient
2 CASUAL, incidental, cursory, hasty, quick, slight, superficial, shallow
F3 1 lasting, permanent
▶ *n* death, departure, passing away, perishing, end, finish, loss
formal decease, demise, expiration, quietus, termination
▷ **in passing** incidentally, by the way, parenthetically, *en passant*; *colloq.* by the by(e)

passion *n*
1 FEELING, emotion, ardour, zeal, fervour, warmth, heat, spirit, intensity, fire, vehemence
2 OUTBURST, explosion, anger, indignation, wrath, rage, fit, temper, fury, tantrum
3 LOVE, desire, sexual desire, ardour, lust, adoration, infatuation, fondness, affection, craving
4 ENTHUSIASM, obsession, mania, craze, fascination, eagerness, keenness, avidity, zest, fanaticism, zeal
F3 1 coolness, indifference

passionate *adj*
1 ARDENT, fervent, eager, keen, avid, enthusiastic, fanatical, zealous, warm, hot, fiery, inflamed, aroused, excited, impassioned, intense, strong, fierce, vehement, violent, stormy, tempestuous, wild, frenzied
2 EMOTIONAL, excitable, hot-headed, intense, impetuous, impulsive, frenzied, quick-tempered, irritable
3 LOVING, affectionate, ardent, aroused, lustful, erotic, sexy, sensual, sultry
colloq. turned on, randy
F3 1 phlegmatic; *colloq.* laid back **3** frigid

passionless *adj*
emotionless, unfeeling, unemotional, unloving, impassive, calm, cold, cold-hearted, frigid, callous, frosty, icy, cold-blooded, apathetic, restrained, unresponsive, uncaring, indifferent, insensible, uninvolved, detached, dispassionate, impartial, neutral, withdrawn
F3 passionate, caring, sensitive, sympathetic

passive *adj*
1 DOCILE, receptive, unassertive, yielding, submissive, unresisting, non-violent, patient, resigned, compliant, long-suffering
2 UNEMOTIONAL, apathetic, lifeless, emotionless, unmoved, indifferent, detached, distant, uninvolved, unenterprising, non-participating, remote, aloof, dispassionate, inert, inactive
F3 1 involved, lively, active **2** responsive

passport *n*
1 *show your passport at the border*
travel documents, papers, identity card, ID, visa, permit, pass, authorization, laissez-passer
2 *the passport to success*
key, entry, door, doorway, avenue, path, way, route, admission, means of access

password *n*
watchword, signal, key, word, open sesame, parole, shibboleth, countersign

past *adj, n*
▶ *adj* **1** OVER, ended, finished, completed, done, over and done with
2 FORMER, previous, preceding, foregoing, foregone, late, sometime, last, latter, recent
formal erstwhile
3 ANCIENT, bygone, olden, early, gone, gone by, elapsed, long ago, no more, extinct, defunct, forgotten
F3 2 future, next
▶ *n* **1** *in the past*
history, former times, olden days, olden times, days gone by, bygone times/days, good old days, antiquity
formal days of yore
2 LIFE, background, experience, record, track record
F3 1 future

pasta *n*

Forms and shapes of pasta include: agnolotti, anelli, angel's hair, bombolotti, bucatini, cannelloni, capelletti, casarecci, conchiglie, crescioni, ditali, elbow macaroni, farfalline, fedelini, fettuccine, fiochetti, fusilli, gnocchi, lasagne, lasagne verde, linguini, lumache, macaroni, mafalde, manicotti, maruzze, mezzani, noodle, noodle farfel, penne, pennine, ravioli, rigatoni, ruoti, spaghetti, spaghetti bolognese, stelline, tagliatelle, tortellini, trofie, vermicelli, ziti.

paste *n, v*
▶ *n* **1** ADHESIVE, glue, gum, mastic, putty, cement
2 *fish paste*
pap, pulp, mush, blend, purée, spread, mixture
▶ *v* stick, glue, gum, cement, fix, fasten

pastel *adj, n*
▶ *adj* soft, soft-hued, light, light-coloured, pale, delicate, subtle, discreet, muted, low-key, subdued, faint
▶ *n* **1** CHALK, crayon, pastille
2 DRAWING, sketch, vignette

pastiche *n*
assortment, mixture, mix, miscellany, variety, melange, potpourri, hotchpotch, hodge-podge, confusion, farrago, salmagundi, smorgasbord, mish, collection, medley, patchwork, gallimaufry, jumble
formal conglomeration
colloq. mixed bag, mishmash, omnium-gatherum

pastille *n*
lozenge, pastel, sweet, tablet, cough sweet, cough drop, confection, jujube, troche

pastime *n*
hobby, activity, leisure activity, game, sport, recreation, play, fun, amusement, entertainment, diversion, distraction, relaxation
F3 work, employment

past master *n*
expert, proficient, virtuoso, adept, artist
colloq. ace, old hand, dab hand, wizard
F3 incompetent

pastor *n*
minister, clergyman, priest, rector, vicar, parson, cleric, churchman, canon, prebendary, divine, ecclesiastic
Related adjective: pastoral

pastoral *adj*
1 RURAL, country, rustic, agricultural, agrarian, simple, idyllic
formal bucolic
2 ECCLESIASTICAL, clerical, priestly, ministerial
F3 1 urban

pastry *n*

Types of pastry include: American crust, biscuit-crumb, cheese pastry, choux, Danish, filo, flaky, flan pastry, hot-water crust, one-stage pastry, pâte à savarin, pâte brisée, pâte frolle, pâte sablée, pâte sucrée, plain pastry, pork-pie pastry, puff, rich shortcrust, rough-puff, short, shortcrust, suetcrust, sweet pastry.

pasture *n*
grass, grassland, meadow, field, paddock, pasturage, grazing, grazing land
Related adjective: pastoral

pasty *adj*
sallow, pale, pallid, wan, anaemic, pasty-faced, sickly, unhealthy
E3 ruddy, healthy

pat *v, n, adj, adv*
▶ *v* tap, dab, slap, clap, touch, stroke, caress, fondle, pet
▷ **pat someone on the back** congratulate, praise, compliment, say well done to; *colloq.* take your hat off to
▶ *n* tap, dab, slap, touch, stroke, caress
▶ *adj* glib, fluent, smooth, slick, ready, easy, facile, simplistic
▶ *adv* precisely, exactly, perfectly, flawlessly, faultlessly, fluently
E3 imprecisely, inaccurately, wrongly

patch *n, v*
▶ *n* **1** *a patch of land*
bed, plot, lot, parcel, tract, area, piece, spot
2 COVER, material, cloth, covering, shield, protection
3 *go through a bad patch*
phase, period, stretch, time, term, spell
▶ *v* mend, repair, sew, stitch, fix, cover, reinforce

patchwork *n*
medley, jumble, mixture, farrago, gallimaufry, hash, hotchpotch, pastiche
colloq. mishmash

patchy *adj*
uneven, irregular, inconsistent, varying, variable, random, fitful, erratic, sketchy, bitty, spotty, blotchy
E3 even, uniform, regular, consistent

patent *adj, n*
▶ *adj* obvious, evident, conspicuous, clear, plain, transparent, apparent, visible, unmistakable, palpable, unequivocal, open, overt, blatant, flagrant, glaring
formal manifest
E3 hidden, opaque
▶ *n* privilege, right, certificate, licence, invention, copyright, registered trademark

paternal *adj*
fatherly, fatherlike, protective, benevolent, concerned, vigilant

path *n*
1 FOOTPATH, pathway, bridleway, trail, towpath, track, walk
2 ROUTE, course, direction, approach, way, circuit, passage, road, avenue, lane

pathetic *adj*
1 PITIABLE, poor, sorry, lamentable, miserable, wretched, sad, dismal, distressing, moving, affecting, touching, pitiful, poignant, plaintive, heart-rending, heartbreaking, woeful
2 CONTEMPTIBLE, derisory, deplorable, miserable, useless, worthless, inadequate, unsatisfactory, meagre, poor, sorry, feeble, woeful
E3 **1** cheerful **2** admirable, excellent, valuable

pathological *adj*
compulsive, habitual, inveterate, obsessive, confirmed, chronic, hardened, addicted, dependent, persistent

pathos *n*
poignancy, misery, sadness, pitiableness, pitifulness, plaintiveness, inadequacy

patience *n*
calmness, composure, self-control, equanimity, even-temperedness, restraint, tolerance, forbearance, endurance, fortitude, long-suffering, submission, resignation, stoicism, tranquillity, serenity, inexcitability, persistence, perseverance, diligence, doggedness, tenacity
formal imperturbability
colloq. unflappability, cool, stickability
E3 impatience, intolerance, exasperation

patient *adj, n*
▶ *adj* calm, composed, serene, self-possessed, self-controlled, restrained, even-tempered, mild, lenient, indulgent, understanding, forgiving, tolerant, accommodating, forbearing, long-suffering, uncomplaining, submissive, resigned, philosophical, stoical, persistent, persevering
formal imperturbable
colloq. patient as Job, unflappable, cool, hanging in there
E3 impatient, restless, intolerant, exasperated
▶ *n* invalid, sufferer, case, client

patois *n*
dialect, vernacular, local parlance, local speech, argot, cant, lingo, lingua franca, patter, slang, jargon,

patriarch *n*
elder, father, grandfather, paterfamilias, greybeard, founder, sire
colloq. grand old man

patrician *n, adj*
▶ *n* aristocrat, noble, nobleman, gentleman, grandee, peer
E3 commoner, plebeian
▶ *adj* aristocratic, noble, lordly, high-class, high-born, blue-blooded, gentle, thoroughbred, well-born
E3 common, humble

patrimony *n*
inheritance, legacy, bequest, heritage, estate, property, possessions, birthright, revenue, share, portion

patriot *n*
nationalist, loyalist, chauvinist, flag-waver, jingoist, jingo

patriotic *adj*
nationalistic, nationalist, chauvinistic, jingoistic, loyal, loyalist, flag-waving

patriotism *n*
chauvinism, flag-waving, jingoism, loyalty, nationalism

patrol *v, n*
▶ *v* police, guard, keep guard on, protect, defend, keep watch on/over, monitor, go the rounds, make/do the/your rounds, be on the beat, tour, inspect
▶ *n* **1** GUARD, patrolman, patrolwoman, sentry,

sentinel, police officer, security guard,
night-watchman, watchman
2 *on patrol*
watch, guard, vigil, surveillance, policing, patrolling,
protection, defence, round, beat

patron *n*
1 BENEFACTOR, philanthropist, sponsor, backer,
supporter, friend, promoter, sympathizer, advocate,
upholder, champion, defender, protector, guardian,
guardian angel, helper
colloq. angel, fairy godmother
2 CUSTOMER, client, frequenter, shopper, buyer,
purchaser, subscriber
colloq. regular

Occupations with a patron saint include: Accountants
(Matthew), Actors (Genesius; Vitus), Advertisers
(Bernardino of Siena), Architects (Thomas,
Apostle), Artists (Luke; Angelico), Astronauts
(Joseph of Cupertino), Astronomers (Dominic),
Athletes (Sebastian), Authors (Francis de Sales),
Aviators (Our Lady of Loreto), Bakers (Honoratus),
Bankers (Bernardino (Feltre)), Barbers (Cosmas and
Damian), Blacksmiths (Eligius), Bookkeepers
(Matthew), Book trade (John of God), Brewers
(Amand; Wenceslaus), Builders (Barbara; Thomas,
Apostle), Butchers (Luke), Carpenters (Joseph),
Chemists (Cosmas and Damian), Comedians
(Vitus), Cooks (Lawrence; Martha), Dancers (Vitus),
Dentists (Apollonia), Doctors (Cosmas and
Damian; Luke), Editors (Francis de Sales), Farmers
(Isidore), Firemen (Florian), Fishermen (Andrew;
Peter), Florists (Dorothy; Thérèse of Lisieux),
Gardeners (Adam; Fiacre), Glassworkers (Luke;
Lucy), Gravediggers (Joseph of Arimathea), Grocers
(Michael), Hotelkeepers (Amand; Julian the
Hospitaler), Housewives (Martha), Jewellers
(Eligius), Journalists (Francis de Sales), Labourers
(James; John Bosco), Lawyers (Ivo; Thomas More),
Librarians (Jerome; Catherine of Alexandria),
Merchants (Francis of Assisi), Messengers (Gabriel),
Metalworkers (Eligius), Midwives (Raymond
Nonnatus), Miners (Anne; Barbara), Motorists
(Christopher), Musicians (Cecilia; Gregory the
Great), Nurses (Camillus de Lellis; John of God),
Philosophers (Thomas Aquinas; Catherine of
Alexandria), Poets (Cecilia; David), Police
(Michael), Postal workers (Gabriel), Priests (Jean-
Baptiste Vianney), Printers (John of God), Prisoners
(Leonard), Radio workers (Gabriel), Sailors
(Christopher; Erasmus; Francis of Paola), Scholars
(Thomas Aquinas), Scientists (Albert the Great),
Sculptors (Luke; Louis), Secretaries (Genesius),
Servants (Martha; Zita), Shoemakers (Crispin;
Crispinian), Singers (Cecilia; Gregory), Soldiers
(George; Joan of Arc; Martin of Tours; Sebastian),
Students (Thomas Aquinas), Surgeons (Luke;
Cosmas and Damian), Tailors (Homobonus), Tax
collectors (Matthew), Taxi drivers (Fiacre), Teachers
(Gregory the Great; John Baptist de la Salle),
Theologians (Augustine; Alphonsus Liguori;
Thomas Aquinas), Television workers (Gabriel),
Undertakers (Dismas; Joseph of Arimathea), Waiters
(Martha), Writers (Lucy)

patronage *n*
1 SPONSORSHIP, funding, backing, support,
promotion, financial help/aid/assistance,
encouragement
2 CUSTOM, business, trade, commerce, buying,
purchasing, shopping, subscription

patronize *v*
1 LOOK DOWN ON, talk down to, despise, scorn, act/
speak condescendingly towards

formal disparage
colloq. look down your nose at, turn your nose up at
2 SPONSOR, fund, finance, back, support, maintain,
protect, help, assist, aid, promote, champion, foster,
encourage
3 FREQUENT, shop at, buy from, deal with
colloq. be a regular at

patronizing *adj*
condescending, stooping, overbearing, high-handed,
haughty, lofty, superior, snobbish, supercilious,
scornful, contemptuous, disdainful
colloq. snooty, toffee-nosed, stuck up, high-and-
mighty, on your high horse
E3 humble, lowly

patter[1] *v, n*
▶ *v rain pattering on the window*
tap, pat, pitter-patter, drum, pound, beat, pelt, trip,
scuttle, scurry
▶ *n* pattering, tapping, pitter-patter, beating

patter[2] *n*
a salesman's patter
chatter, gabble, jabber, line, pitch, jargon, monologue
colloq. spiel, lingo, yak

pattern *n, v*
▶ *n* **1** SYSTEM, method, order, plan, arrangement
2 DECORATION, ornamentation, ornament, figure,
motif, device, design, style, markings
3 MODEL, template, stencil, guide, plan, design,
instruction, original, prototype, blueprint, standard,
norm, ideal, example
4 *a book of fabric patterns*
sample, swatch
▶ *v* model, style, order, form, follow, imitate, match,
stencil, emulate, copy, decorate, design, shape, mould,
trim

patterned *adj*
decorated, ornamented, figured, printed, watered,
moiré
E3 plain

paucity *n*
lack, shortage, insufficiency, scarcity, scantiness,
poverty, rarity, fewness, sparseness, sparsity, want,
dearth, deficiency, smallness, slightness, slenderness,
meagreness, paltriness
formal exiguousness
E3 abundance

paunch *n*
fat stomach, abdomen, belly, pot-belly, beer-belly
colloq. corporation

paunchy *adj*
pot-bellied, fat, podgy, pudgy, portly, tubby
technical adipose
formal corpulent, rotund

pauper *n*
insolvent, down-and-out, have-not, bankrupt, beggar,
mendicant, church-mouse
formal indigent

pause *v, n*
▶ *v* halt, stop, break off, interrupt, adjourn, take a
break, rest, wait, delay, hold back, hesitate
formal cease, discontinue, desist
colloq. let up, take a breather, take a rest, take five
▶ *n* halt, stoppage, interruption, break, rest, lull, stay,
respite, gap, interval, interlude, intermission, wait,
delay, hesitation

formal cessation
colloq. breather, breathing space, let-up, time out

pave *v*
flag, tile, floor, surface, cover, asphalt, tar,
macadamize, tarmac, concrete
▷ **pave the way for**   get/make ready for, prepare for,
lead up to, introduce, take steps/measures, clear the
ground, lay the groundwork for, do the spadework for

pavement *n*
footpath, footway, path, way, floor, bed, causeway
US sidewalk

paw *n, v*
▶ *n*   foot, pad, forefoot, hand
▶ *v*   maul, touch, stroke, manhandle, mishandle,
molest
colloq. touch up

pawn[1] *n*
mere pawns in the power struggle
dupe, puppet, tool, instrument, toy, plaything
colloq. cat's paw, stooge

pawn[2] *v*
pawn your watch
deposit, pledge, stake, mortgage
formal impignorate
colloq. hock, pop, lay in lavender

pawnbroker *n*
pawnshop, lender, money-lender, usurer, gombeen-
man, *mont-de-piété, monte di pietà*
colloq. pop-shop; *slang* uncle

pay *v, n*
▶ *v*   **1** *pay money to someone*
spend, pay out, meet the cost of, lay out, outlay, hand
over, recompense, invest, reimburse, repay, refund,
settle, settle up, discharge, reward
formal remunerate, remit, expend, disburse,
indemnify
colloq. dip (your hand) into your pocket, foot the bill,
pick up the tab, fork out, shell out, cough up, stump up
2 BENEFIT, profit, pay off, bring in, produce, yield,
return, be beneficial to, be advantageous to, be
worthwhile to
colloq. rake in
3 ATONE, make amends, compensate, avenge
yourself on, pay back, answer, suffer
▷ **pay back 1** REPAY, refund, return, reimburse,
recompense, settle, pay off, give back, square
2 RETALIATE, get your own back, take revenge,
avenge yourself on, get even with, punish, repay,
reciprocate, counter-attack
▷ **pay for**   answer for, atone, be punished for,
compensate, make amends, suffer, pay a penalty for,
pay the price for, count the cost (of), cost dearly;
colloq. face the music, get your deserts
▷ **pay off 1** DISCHARGE, settle, square, clear,
meet, honour, repay, pay in full **2** DISMISS,
discharge, make redundant, lay off; *colloq.* fire,
sack **3** *the preparations paid off* succeed, be
successful, work, get results **4** BRIBE, buy off, take
care of; *colloq.* fix, grease, grease someone's palm
▷ **pay out**   spend, hand over, part with, lay out;
formal disburse, remit; *colloq.* fork out, shell out
▶ *n*   wages, salary, earnings, income, commission, fee,
stipend, honorarium, payment, reward, recompense,
compensation, reimbursement
formal remuneration, emoluments

payable *adj*
owed, owing, unpaid, to be paid, outstanding, in
arrears, due, mature

payment *n*
settlement, discharge, clearance, premium, outlay,
advance, deposit, instalment, amount, contribution,
donation, allowance, reward, pay, fee, hire, fare, toll
formal remittance, remuneration

pay-off *n*
1 RESULT, outcome, benefit, advantage, reward,
settlement, consequence, upshot
colloq. crunch, moment of truth, punchline
2 BRIBE, inducement, allurement, enticement
colloq. back-hander, sweetener, hush money, slush
fund, protection money

peace *n*
1 CALM, quiet, quietness, peacefulness, hush, silence,
still, stillness, rest, restfulness, relaxation, tranquillity,
calmness, serenity, composure, contentment, placidity
formal repose
2 ARMISTICE, truce, cease-fire, peace treaty, non-
violence, non-aggression, conciliation, harmony,
friendship, amicableness, goodwill, agreement, treaty
formal concord, amity, accord
⊟ 1 noise, disturbance **2** war, disagreement,
discord
Related adjective: irenic

peaceable *adj*
pacific, peace-loving, unwarlike, non-violent, non-
aggressive, conciliatory, friendly, cordial, even-
tempered, good-natured, irenic, amicable,
harmonious, inoffensive, gentle, placid, mild
colloq. easy-going
⊟ aggressive, quarrelsome, belligerent

peaceful *adj*
quiet, still, restful, relaxing, tranquil, serene, calm,
placid, sleepy, unruffled, undisturbed, untroubled,
friendly, harmonious, amicable, peaceable, pacific,
gentle
formal reposeful, in repose
⊟ noisy, disturbed, troubled, violent

peacemaker *n*
appeaser, conciliator, mediator, arbitrator, intercessor,
peace-monger, pacifier, pacifist

peacemaking *adj*
appeasing, conciliatory, pacific, irenic(al), mediating,
mediative, mediatorial, mediatory

peak *n, v*
▶ *n*   top, summit, pinnacle, crest, crown, zenith,
height, high point, elevation, mountain, mount, hill,
summit, pinnacle, maximum, climax, culmination,
apex, tip, point
formal apogee, zenith
⊟ trough; *formal* nadir
▶ *v*   climax, culminate, come to a head

peaky *adj*
pale, pallid, wan, ill, sick, unwell, off-colour, sickly,
poorly
colloq. under the weather, washed-out
⊟ healthy; *colloq.* in the pink

peal *n, v*
▶ *n*   chime, carillon, toll, knell, ring, clang, ringing,
reverberation, resounding, rumble, boom, roar, crash,
clap
formal tintinnabulation

▶ *v* chime, toll, ring (out), clang, resonate, reverberate, resound, rumble, boom, roll, roar, crash

peasant *n*
rustic, provincial, country person, yokel, bumpkin, oaf, boor, lout, churl
colloq. country bumpkin

pebble *n*
stone, agate, chip, gallet

peccadillo *n*
error, fault, indiscretion, lapse, slip, minor offence, misdeed, misdemeanour, delinquency
formal infraction
colloq. boob, slip-up

peck *v*
nip, jab, tap, rap, hit, strike, bite, prick, kiss

peculiar *adj*
1 *a peculiar sound*
strange, odd, curious, funny, queer, weird, bizarre, quaint, extraordinary, unusual, abnormal, exceptional, unconventional, offbeat, droll, eccentric, outlandish, freakish, grotesque, exotic
slang way-out
2 CHARACTERISTIC, distinctive, distinguishing, specific, particular, special, distinct, remarkable, individual, individualistic, personal, idiosyncratic, unique, singular
3 *feel peculiar*
unwell, ill, sick, poorly, out of sorts, dizzy
colloq. under the weather
F3 1 ordinary, normal **2** general
▷ **peculiar to** unique to, characteristic of, typical of, representative of

peculiarity *n*
oddity, bizarreness, weirdness, abnormality, exception, eccentricity, quirk, foible, mannerism, feature, trait, mark, hallmark, quality, attribute, property, characteristic, distinctiveness, particularity, idiosyncrasy

pecuniary *adj*
monetary, financial, fiscal, commercial
formal nummary, nummulary

pedagogic *adj*
educational, teaching, instructional, tuitional, academic, scholastic, didactic

pedagogue *n*
teacher, instructor, educator, master, mistress, educationalist, educationist, schoolmaster, schoolmistress, don, pedant, dogmatist, preceptor, dominie

pedagogy *n*
teaching, instruction, training, tuition, tutelage, didactics, pedagogics

pedant *n*
purist, formalist, literalist, perfectionist, precisionist, precisian, dogmatist, quibbler, casuist, doctrinaire, academic, intellectual, pettifogger, Dryasdust, scholastic
colloq. hair-splitter, nit-picker, egghead, highbrow

pedantic *adj*
stilted, fussy, purist, perfectionist, literalist, formalist, particular, precise, exact, meticulous, punctilious, scrupulous, quibbling, finical, pompous, pretentious, academic, intellectual, bookish, stuffy, erudite

colloq. hair-splitting, nit-picking
F3 imprecise, informal, casual

pedantry *n*
punctiliousness, exactness, meticulousness, cavilling, finicality, quibbling, pomposity, pretentiousness, academicness, intellectualism, bookishness, stuffiness, pedagogism, pedagoguishness, pedantism
colloq. hair-splitting, nit-picking

peddle *v*
sell, vend, hawk, tout, push, trade, traffic, market, offer/present for sale
colloq. flog

pedestal *n*
plinth, pillar, column, stand, support, mounting, foot, base, foundation, platform, podium
▷ **put on a pedestal** idolize, hero-worship, exalt, revere, admire, adulate

pedestrian *n, adj*
▶ *n* walker, foot-traveller, hicker
▶ *adj* dull, boring, flat, uninspired, unexciting, unimaginative, banal, mundane, commonplace, humdrum, ordinary, mediocre, indifferent, prosaic, stodgy, plodding, turgid
colloq. run-of-the-mill, not up to much, no great shakes, nothing much to write home about
F3 exciting, imaginative

pedigree *n, adj*
▶ *n* genealogy, family tree, lineage, ancestry, descent, line, line of descent, family, parentage, derivation, extraction, race, breed, stock, strain, blood
formal stirps
▶ *adj* pure-bred, pedigree, full-blooded, thoroughbred, aristocratic

pedlar *n*
seller, hawker, huckster, vendor, walker, street-trader, colporteur, chapman, gutter-man, gutter-merchant, boxwallah, cheap-jack
Scot. yagger

peek *v, n*
▶ *v* peep, glance, peer, spy, look
colloq. have a gander, have a look-see
▶ *n* peep, glance, glimpse, look, blink
colloq. dekko, look-see, shufti; *slang* gander

peel *v, n*
▶ *v* pare, skin, strip, scale, flake (off), take off, remove
formal decorticate, desquamate
▶ *n* skin, rind, zest, peeling
technical epicarp, exocarp, integument
▷ **keep your eyes peeled** watch closely, observe, monitor, keep a lookout for, be alert, keep your eyes skinned

peep¹ *v, n*
▶ *v* *peep through the keyhole*
look, peek, glimpse, spy, squint, peer, emerge, issue, appear
▶ *n* look, peek, glimpse, glance, squint
colloq. dekko, look-see, shufti; *slang* gander

peep² *v, n*
▶ *v* *birds peeping*
chirp, cheep, chirrup, pipe, tweet, chatter, twitter, warble, squeak
▶ *n* chirp, cheep, chirrup, pipe, tweet, chatter, twitter, warble, squeak, cry, utterance, sound, noise, word

peephole *n*
spyhole, keyhole, pinhole, hole, opening, aperture, slit,

chink, slink, crack, fissure, cleft, crevice, Judas-hole, Judas-window
formal interstice

peer[1] *v*
peer through the window
look, gaze, scan, scrutinize, examine, inspect, spy, snoop, peep, squint

peer[2] *n*
1 ARISTOCRAT, noble, nobleman, lord, duke, marquess, marquis, earl, count, viscount, baron, patrician
2 EQUAL, counterpart, equivalent, like, match, fellow, confrère, compeer

peerage *n*
aristocracy, nobility, lords and ladies
colloq. upper crust, top drawer

peeress *n*
aristocrat, noble, noblewoman, lady, dame, duchess, marchioness, countess, viscountess, baroness

peerless *adj*
matchless, without equal, unequalled, unexcelled, unmatched, incomparable, beyond compare, unparalleled, unrivalled, unsurpassed, unbeatable, unique, supreme, excellent, paramount, outstanding, superlative
formal nonpareil
colloq. second to none

peeve *v*
annoy, exasperate, irritate, vex, irk, exasperate, gall
colloq. rub someone up the wrong way, get someone's blood up, get on someone's nerves, get under your skin, drive up the wall

peeved *adj*
annoyed, irritated, exasperated, put out, upset, vexed, irked, galled, riled, sore, piqued, nettled
colloq. miffed, narked, got the hump, in a huff

peevish *adj*
petulant, querulous, fractious, fretful, touchy, complaining, irritable, cross, grumpy, crotchety, ill-tempered, in a bad mood, crabbed, cantankerous, crusty, snappy, short-tempered, moody, touchy, testy, tetchy, churlish, surly, sullen, sulky
colloq. ratty
F3 good-tempered

peevishness *n*
ill-temper, irritability, perversity, petulance, querulousness, testiness, pique, pet, captiousness, acrimony
formal protervity

peg *n, v*
▶ *n* pin, nail, screw, spike, brad, dowel, hook, knob, marker, post, stake
▷ **take/bring down a peg or two** humiliate, bring/cut down to size, put someone in their place, take the wind out of someone's sails
▶ *v* **1** FASTEN, secure, fix, attach, join, mark
2 *peg prices*
control, stabilize, limit, freeze, fix, set
▷ **peg away** apply yourself, work away, persevere, persist, plug away, beaver away, plod along;
colloq. hang in, keep at it, stick at it

pejorative *adj*
derogatory, disparaging, belittling, slighting, unflattering, uncomplimentary, unpleasant, bad, negative

formal deprecatory
F3 complimentary

pellet *n*
ball, shot, bullet, pill, drop, capsule, lozenge
colloq. slug

pell-mell *adv*
hurriedly, hastily, feverishly, precipitously, posthaste, recklessly, rashly, heedlessly, impetuously, at full tilt
colloq. helter-skelter, hurry-scurry

pellucid *adj*
clear, limpid, transparent, translucent, pure, glassy, bright

pelt[1] *v*
1 THROW, hurl, bombard, shower, attack, assail, batter, beat, hit, strike
2 POUR, teem
colloq. bucket (down), rain cats and dogs
3 RUSH, hurry, charge, tear, race, dash, run, speed, sprint, career
colloq. belt, zip

pelt[2] *n*
a beaver pelt
skin, coat, fur, fleece, hide, fell

pen[1] *n, v*
▶ *n* *write with a pen*
fountain pen, ballpoint, ballpoint pen, Biro®, felt-tip pen, felt-tip
▶ *v* write (down), compose, draft, scribble, jot down

pen[2] *n, v*
▶ *n* *a sheep pen*
enclosure, fold, pound, compound, stall, sty, coop, cage, hutch, mew, corral
▶ *v* enclose, fence, hedge, hem in, confine, cage, coop, shut (up)

penal *adj*
punitive, disciplinary, corrective, retaliatory, retributive, vindictive

penalize *v*
punish, discipline, correct, fine, disadvantage, handicap
formal castigate, chastise
F3 reward

penal servitude *n*
hard labour, stretch, time
colloq. bird, lag, porridge

penalty *n*
1 PUNISHMENT, retribution, sentence, fine, forfeit, chastisement
formal mulct, castigation
2 DISADVANTAGE, handicap, drawback, snag, weak point
colloq. downside, minus
F3 **1** reward **2** advantage, benefit

penance *n*
atonement, reparation, punishment, penalty, self-punishment, self-abasement, mortification
Related adjective: penitentiary

penchant *n*
fondness, liking, tendency, taste, preference, affinity, bent, inclination, leaning, bias, partiality, weakness, soft spot, proneness
formal disposition, predilection, predisposition, proclivity, propensity
F3 dislike

pendant *n*
medallion, locket, necklace

pendent *adj*
hanging, suspended, dangling, drooping, swinging
formal pendulous, pensile, nutant

pending *adj, prep*
▶ *adj* imminent, impending, in the offing,
forthcoming, coming, approaching, nearing, near,
undecided, unsettled, awaiting settlement, uncertain
colloq. in the balance, up in the air
Ea finished, settled
▶ *prep* until, till, to, before, so long as, while, whilst,
throughout

pendulous *adj*
sagging, hanging, suspended, dangling, drooping,
droopy, swaying, swinging
formal pendent

penetrable *adj*
clear, open, passable, permeable, pervious, porous,
fathomable, understandable, intelligible, accessible,
comprehensible, explicable
Ea impenetrable

penetrate *v*
1 PIERCE, stab, prick, perforate, puncture, spike,
probe, sink, bore
2 GET INTO, enter, infiltrate, make your way,
permeate, fill, seep, saturate, pervade, suffuse, imbue
3 GRASP, understand, fathom, comprehend, make
out, work out, see, register, sink in
colloq. crack, cotton on, twig, get to the bottom of

penetrating *adj*
1 PIERCING, stinging, biting, incisive, sharp
2 *a penetrating sound*
loud, clear, strident, shrill, piercing, carrying
3 *a penetrating mind*
keen, acute, shrewd, discerning, discriminating, wise,
perceptive, observant, profound, deep, searching,
probing
Ea 1 blunt

penetration *n*
1 PIERCING, puncturing, perforation, stabbing,
pricking, incision
2 ENTRANCE, entry, inroad, infiltration,
permeation, pervasion, invasion
formal interpenetration
3 DISCERNMENT, perception, insight, acumen,
astuteness, sharpness, keenness, acuteness,
shrewdness, wit
formal perspicacity

peninsula *n*
cape, point, mull, tongue, chersonese, doab

penis *n*
male organ of copulation
formal phallus, membrum virile
colloq. willy; *slang* pecker; *taboo slang* dick, cock,
prick, knob, tool, winkle, rod
Related adjective: penile

penitence *n*
repentance, contrition, sorrow, shame, remorse,
regret, self-reproach
formal compunction, ruefulness

penitent *adj*
repentant, contrite, sorry, sorrowful, apologetic,
remorseful, ashamed, regretful, conscience-stricken,
shamefaced, humble

formal rueful
Ea unrepentant, hard-hearted, callous

pen-name *n*
assumed name, pseudonym, stage-name, *nom de
plume*, false name
formal allonym

pennant *n*
flag, banner, ensign, standard, streamer, colours,
banderol, gonfalon, jack

penniless *adj*
poor, poverty-stricken, impoverished, destitute,
bankrupt, ruined, bust
formal indigent
colloq. broke, stony-broke, down and out, on the
breadline, cleaned out, strapped for cash, on your
beam-ends; *slang* skint
Ea rich, wealthy, affluent

penny-pincher *n*
miser, niggard, skinflint, cheeseparer, Scrooge
colloq. meanie, cheapskate, money-grubber

penny-pinching *adj*
miserly, mean, close, tight-fisted, niggardly, scrimping,
cheeseparing, ungenerous, frugal
formal parsimonious
colloq. mingy, stingy
Ea generous, open-handed

pension *n*
old-age pension, retirement pension, state pension,
personal pension, company pension, index-linked
pension, annuity, superannuation, support, welfare,
social assistance, income, allowance, benefit

pensioner *n*
retired person, old-age pensioner, senior citizen

pensive *adj*
thoughtful, reflective, contemplative, meditative,
thinking, pondering, musing, ruminative, absorbed,
preoccupied, absent-minded, dreamy, wistful, solemn,
serious, sober
formal cogitative
Ea carefree

pent-up *adj*
repressed, inhibited, restrained, bridled, curbed,
suppressed, stifled, held in
colloq. bottled-up

penurious *adj*
1 POOR, impoverished, destitute, poverty-stricken,
beggarly, penniless, hard up, in straitened
circumstances, inadequate
formal impecunious, indigent, parsimonious
colloq. tight, cheeseparing, bust, flat broke, stingy
2 MISERLY, mean, niggardly, close, close-fisted,
grudging, ungenerous
colloq. tight-fisted
Ea 1 wealthy, generous

penury *n*
poverty, destitution, pauperism, impoverishment,
insolvency, straitened circumstances, straits,
deficiency, need, want, dearth, beggary
formal indigence, mendicity
Ea prosperity

people *n, v*
▶ *n* 1 PERSONS, individuals, humans, human
beings, the human race, mankind, humankind,
humanity, mortals, folk(s)

2 CITIZENS, ordinary citizens, public, general public, populace, rank and file, population, men women and children, inhabitants, community, society, electorate, masses, mob, rabble
colloq. the plebs, riff-raff
3 NATION, race, tribe, clan
4 *his people are from Wales*
parents, relations, relatives, folks, family, kith and kin
▶ *v* populate, inhabit, occupy, settle, colonize

pep *n*
energy, vigour, verve, spirit, sparkle, vitality, life, liveliness, exuberance, effervescence, high spirits
formal ebullience
colloq. get-up-and-go, pizzazz
▷ **pep up** invigorate, vitalize, liven up, quicken, stimulate, animate, excite, exhilarate, inspire, energize
Ⅎ tone down

pepper *v*
1 BOMBARD, attack, assail, pelt, blitz
2 SPRINKLE, shower, scatter, spatter, bespatter, strew, dot

peppery *adj*
1 SPICY, hot, pungent, seasoned, piquant
2 QUICK-TEMPERED, hot-tempered, irritable, irascible, choleric, testy, fiery, grumpy, snappish
colloq. touchy
3 INCISIVE, sharp, sarcastic, biting, stinging, astringent, caustic, waspish
formal trenchant

perceive *v*
1 SEE, discern, make out, detect, discover, spot, catch sight of, glimpse, notice, observe, view, remark, note, distinguish, recognize
formal espy, behold
2 SENSE, feel, apprehend, learn, realize, appreciate, be aware of, discern, recognize, see, know, grasp, understand, gather, deduce, conclude, comprehend
formal be cognizant of
colloq. get wind of

perceptible *adj*
perceivable, discernible, detectable, appreciable, distinguishable, observable, noticeable, obvious, evident, conspicuous, clear, plain, distinct, patent, apparent, tangible, visible
formal manifest
Ⅎ imperceptible, inconspicuous

perception *n*
1 VIEW, interpretation, understanding, sense, feeling, impression, idea, conception, knowledge, apprehension
2 DISCERNMENT, awareness, consciousness, observation, recognition, insight, understanding, grasp, discrimination, sensitivity, responsiveness
formal cognizance

perceptive *adj*
discerning, observant, sensitive, responsive, aware, alert, quick, quick-witted, keen, sharp, sharp-eyed, astute, penetrating, discriminating, shrewd, understanding
formal perspicacious
Ⅎ unobservant

perch *v*
land, alight, settle, sit, roost, balance, rest

perchance *adv*
perhaps, maybe, possibly, conceivably, feasibly

percipience *n*
perception, discernment, astuteness, awareness, insight, intuition, understanding, sensitivity, penetration, judgement, alertness, acuteness
formal perspicacity, sagacity

percipient *adj*
perceptive, observant, discerning, discriminating, sharp, aware, alive, astute, alert, penetrating, quick-witted, knowing, intelligent, wide-awake
formal judicious, perspicacious
Ⅎ unaware, obtuse

percolate *v*
filter, strain, seep, ooze, leach, leak, drip, drain, sift, sieve, penetrate, pass through, spread (slowly) through, trickle through, permeate, pervade

perdition *n*
damnation, hell, everlasting punishment, condemnation, hellfire, destruction, doom, downfall, ruin, ruination, annihilation

peregrination *n*
travel, travelling, voyage, wandering, roaming, roving, journey, tour, expedition, exploration, trek, trekking, trip, excursion, globe-trotting, wayfaring, odyssey

peremptory *adj*
imperious, commanding, dictatorial, autocratic, tyrannical, lordly, authoritative, assertive, high-handed, overbearing, domineering, dogmatic, absolute, irrefutable, abrupt, curt, summary, arbitrary
colloq. bossy

perennial *adj*
lasting, enduring, abiding, everlasting, eternal, immortal, undying, imperishable, unceasing, endless, unending, incessant, never-ending, constant, continual, unchanging, uninterrupted, unfailing, perpetual, persistent, unfailing, permanent
formal ceaseless

perfect *adj, v*
▶ *adj* **1** FAULTLESS, impeccable, flawless, immaculate, sinless, unmarred, unblemished, spotless, blameless, pure, superb, wonderful, excellent, matchless, peerless, incomparable, superlative
2 IDEAL, model, textbook, exemplary, ultimate, expert, accomplished, finished, completed, experienced, skilful
formal consummate
colloq. just the job
3 EXACT, precise, accurate, right, correct, true, faithful
4 *perfect strangers*
utter, absolute, sheer, complete, entire, total, thorough, downright, out and out
Ⅎ **1** imperfect, flawed, blemished **2** inexperienced, unskilled **3** inaccurate, wrong
▶ *v* fulfil, complete, finish, better, improve, polish, refine, elaborate
formal consummate
Ⅎ spoil, mar

perfection *n*
1 EXCELLENCE, faultlessness, flawlessness, superiority, immaculateness, impeccability
2 IMPROVEMENT, betterment, polishing, refinement, completion, realization
formal consummation
3 IDEAL, model, paragon, crown, pinnacle, peak of perfection, ultimate, *ne plus ultra*, acme

colloq. one in a million
E3 3 imperfection, flaw

perfectionist *n*
idealist, purist, pedant, formalist, stickler, precisionist

perfectly *adv*
1 UTTERLY, absolutely, quite, thoroughly, completely,
entirely, wholly, totally, fully, altogether
2 FAULTLESSLY, flawlessly, immaculately, without
blemish, impeccably, ideally, wonderfully, superbly,
exactly, correctly, to perfection
E3 1 partially **2** imperfectly, badly

perfidious *adj*
treacherous, untrustworthy, deceitful, dishonest,
disloyal, double-dealing, double-faced, false,
traitorous, two-faced, unfaithful, faithless, corrupt,
Machiavellian, treasonous, Punic
formal duplicitous
E3 faithful, honest, loyal

perfidy *n*
treachery, betrayal, deceit, falsity, faithlessness,
infidelity, disloyalty, double-dealing, traitorousness,
treason
formal duplicity, perfidiousness
E3 faithfulness, honesty, loyalty

perforate *v*
hole, make holes in, punch, drill, bore, pierce, prick,
puncture, spike, stab, gore, burst, rupture, tear, split,
penetrate

perforated *adj*
pierced, holed, bored, drilled, punctured, punched,
porous
technical ethmoid, fenestrate(d), fenestrial,
foraminous

perforation *n*
hole, bore, prick, puncture, dotted line
technical fenestration, foramen

perforce *adv*
unavoidably, inevitably, necessarily, of necessity, willy-
nilly

perform *v*
1 DO, carry out, discharge, fulfil, satisfy, complete,
achieve, accomplish, conduct, bring off, pull off, bring
about
formal execute, effect
2 *perform a play*
stage, put on, present, enact, represent, act, do, play,
appear as
3 FUNCTION, work, operate, go, run, behave,
produce

performance *n*
1 SHOW, appearance, presentation, production,
interpretation, representation, portrayal, acting

Types of performance include: act, audition, benefit,
box-office hit, *US colloq.* bomb, charity concert,
command performance, concert, début, dress
rehearsal, dry run, encore, entertainment, exhibition,
farewell performance, first house, first night,
colloq. flop, full house, gala night, *colloq.* gig, last
night, last night at the Proms, matinée, one-night
stand, opening night, play, pop concert, première,
preview, production, readthrough, recital, rehearsal,
rendition, runthrough, second house, sell-out, short
run, show, sketch, *colloq.* smash hit, sneak preview,
theatre, turn. *See also* **theatrical**.

2 ACTION, deed, doing, carrying out,
implementation, discharge, fulfilment, conducting,
completion, achievement, accomplishment
formal execution, effecting
3 FUNCTIONING, operation, running, going,
behaviour, conduct

performer *n*
1 *circus performer*
actor, actress, player, musician, singer, dancer, comic,
comedian, clown, artiste, entertainer, trouper,
Thespian
See panels at **entertainer; musician; singers**.
2 ACHIEVER, doer, operator, author
formal executor

perfume *n*
scent, fragrance, smell, odour, aroma, bouquet,
sweetness, balm, essence, cologne, eau-de-cologne,
eau-de-toilette, toilet water, incense
formal redolence

perfunctory *adj*
quickly, careless, superficial, cursory, negligent,
offhand, slipshod, slovenly, inattentive, hurried,
heedless, automatic, mechanical, routine, stereotyped,
indifferent, brief, wooden
E3 carefully, enthusiastically

perhaps *adv*
maybe, possibly, conceivably, feasibly
formal perchance

peril *n*
danger, hazard, risk, jeopardy, uncertainty, insecurity,
threat, menace
E3 safety, security

perilous *adj*
dangerous, unsafe, hazardous, risky, chancy,
precarious, insecure, unsure, vulnerable, fraught with
danger, exposed, menacing, threatening, dire
E3 safe, secure

perimeter *n*
circumference, edge, border, boundary, frontier,
limit(s), outer limits, bounds, confines, fringe, margin,
periphery
E3 middle, centre, heart

period *n*
1 TIME, season, stretch, duration, space, span, spell,
stint, shift, term, while, turn, session, interval, cycle
2 STAGE, phase, era, epoch, age, eon, generation,
date, years
3 CLASS, lesson, lecture, seminar, tutorial,
instruction
4 *a woman's monthly period*
menstruation, menstrual flow, monthlies
formal menses
colloq. the curse
5 *a period at the end of the sentence*
full stop, full point, point
6 *you may not go, period*
full stop, stop, end, finish, conclusion

periodic *adj*
occasional, infrequent, sporadic, intermittent, once in
a while, recurrent, recurring, repeated, regular,
periodical, seasonal, cyclical, cyclic

periodical *n*
magazine, journal, publication, weekly, monthly,
quarterly, review, organ

peripatetic *adj*
travelling, itinerant, journeying, mobile, roaming, roving, migrant, migratory, nomadic, wandering, vagabond, vagrant
formal ambulant, ambulatory
F∃ fixed

peripheral *adj*
1 MINOR, secondary, lesser, incidental, unimportant, irrelevant, subsidiary, ancillary, unnecessary, marginal, borderline, surface, superficial
colloq. beside the point, neither here nor there
2 OUTLYING, outer, outermost, surrounding
F∃ 1 major, crucial **2** central

periphery *n*
edge, boundary, border, circumference, fringe, perimeter, brim, brink, rim, skirt, outskirts, outer regions, margin, verge, hem, circuit, ambit
F∃ centre, nub, middle

periphrastic *adj*
roundabout, indirect, circuitous, wandering, oblique, discursive, tortuous, rambling, long-drawn-out
formal circumlocutory

perish *v*
1 DIE, pass away, lose your life, depart, breathe your last
formal expire
colloq. peg out, bite the dust, pop off, have had it, kick the bucket
2 COLLAPSE, disintegrate, crumble, fail, fall, come to an end, disappear, vanish, die away, rot, decay, decompose, go off

perishable *adj*
destructible, biodegradable, decomposable, short-lived
F∃ imperishable, durable

perjure *v*
▷ **perjure yourself** lie, commit perjury, bear false witness/testimony, make false statements, give false evidence; *formal* forswear yourself

perjury *n*
false evidence, false testimony, false witness, false swearing, false oath, false statement, falsification
formal forswearing, mendacity

perk *n*
fringe benefit, benefit, bonus, advantage, dividend, gratuity, tip, extra, baksheesh
formal perquisite
colloq. plus, freebie, golden handshake
▷ **perk up** brighten (up), cheer up, take heart, revive, rally, liven up, make/become lively, rally, recover, improve, look up; *colloq.* buck up, pep up

perky *adj*
lively, jaunty, spirited, vivacious, sprightly, cheerful, cheery, gay, bright, animated, bouncy, buoyant, bubbly, effervescent, peppy, sunny
formal ebullient
F∃ cheerless, dull, gloomy

permanence *n*
fixedness, stability, imperishability, indestructibility, perpetuity, constancy, endurance, steadfastness, persistence, durability
F∃ impermanence, transience

permanent *adj*
1 LASTING, enduring, durable, imperishable, indestructible, unfading, eternal, everlasting, lifelong, perpetual, constant, steadfast, immutable, invariable, unchangeable, indelible, perennial, long-lasting
2 FIXED, stable, unchanging, constant, established
F∃ 1 temporary, fleeting; *formal* ephemeral

permanently *adv*
always, continually, constantly, ceaselessly, endlessly, eternally, perpetually, in perpetuity, incessantly, unceasingly, unremittingly, unendingly, once and for all, indelibly, everlastingly, ever more, for ever, for ever and ever, for all time
colloq. for keeps, till doomsday, till kingdom come, till the cows come home, till hell freezes over
F∃ temporarily

permeable *adj*
porous, absorbent, absorptive, penetrable, passable, spongy
F∃ impermeable, watertight

permeate *v*
pass through, soak through, filter through, seep through, spread through, penetrate, infiltrate, percolate, pervade, imbue, saturate, impregnate, fill, diffuse

permissible *adj*
permitted, allowable, allowed, admissible, all right, tolerable, acceptable, proper, authorized, sanctioned, lawful, legal, legitimate
colloq. OK, kosher
F∃ prohibited, banned, forbidden

permission *n*
consent, assent, agreement, approval, allowance, clearance, go-ahead, authorization, sanction, leave, warrant, permit, licence, dispensation, freedom, liberty
formal approbation
colloq. green light, thumbs up
F∃ prohibition

permissive *adj*
liberal, broad-minded, tolerant, forbearing, lenient, indulgent, overindulgent, lax, free
formal latitudinarian
colloq. easy-going
F∃ strict, rigid, narrow-minded

permit *v, n*
▶ *v* allow, let, consent, agree, admit, grant, authorize, enable, empower, sanction, warrant, license
colloq. give the go-ahead to, give the green light to, give the thumbs up to, give the nod to
F∃ prohibit, forbid
▶ *n* pass, passport, visa, licence, warrant, authorization, sanction, permission
F∃ prohibition

permutation *n*
alteration, change, shift, transformation, variation
formal transposition, configuration, transmutation, commutation

pernicious *adj*
harmful, damaging, dangerous, destructive, ruinous, detrimental, bad, hurtful, injurious, offensive, malicious, poisonous, venomous, pestilent, toxic, wicked, evil, malignant, fatal, deadly, unhealthy, unwholesome
formal deleterious, maleficent, malevolent, noisome, noxious
F∃ innocuous

pernickety *adj*
fussy, particular, over-particular, over-precise,
carping, nice, punctilious, fastidious, fiddly, finical,
finicky, exacting, detailed, careful, painstaking, fine,
tricky
colloq. choosy, picky, hair-splitting, nit-picking

peroration *n*
1 SUMMING-UP, summary, conclusion, closing
remarks, reiteration, recapitulation
colloq. recapping
2 SPEECH, lecture, talk, address
formal oration, diatribe, declamation

perpendicular *adj*
vertical, upright, erect, straight, at right angles, sheer,
steep, abrupt, precipitous, plumb
F3 horizontal

perpetrate *v*
commit, carry out, execute, do, be responsible for, be to
blame for, perform, inflict, wreak
formal effect, effectuate

perpetual *adj*
eternal, everlasting, infinite, endless, unending, never-
ending, interminable, ceaseless, unceasing, incessant,
continuous, unbroken, uninterrupted, unremitting,
constant, persistent, continual, repeated, recurrent,
perennial, permanent, lasting, enduring, abiding,
persisting, unchanging, unfailing, undying,
unvarying, intermittent
F3 temporary; *formal* ephemeral, transient

perpetually *adv*
eternally, endlessly, interminably, ceaselessly,
unceasingly, incessantly, unremittingly, constantly,
persistently, continually, permanently

perpetuate *v*
continue, keep up, maintain, sustain, preserve, keep
alive, keep going, immortalize, commemorate,
eternalize, memorialize

perpetuity *n*
▷ **in perpetuity** for ever, for ever and ever, for all
time, always, endlessly, eternally, perpetually, ever
more

perplex *v*
puzzle, baffle, mystify, stump, confuse, confound,
muddle, confound, bewilder, dumbfound
colloq. bamboozle, nonplus

perplexed *adj*
puzzled, baffled, bewildered, mystified, stumped,
confused, muddled, confounded, disconcerted,
fuddled, worried, at a loss
colloq. bamboozled, nonplussed

perplexing *adj*
puzzling, baffling, bewildering, confusing, mystifying,
amazing, complex, complicated, intricate,
inexplicable, hard, strange, weird, paradoxical,
difficult, taxing, involved, knotty, thorny, enigmatic,
mysterious
formal labyrinthine
F3 easy, simple

perplexity *n*
1 PUZZLEMENT, bafflement, bewilderment,
confusion, incomprehension, mystification, nonplus
2 COMPLEXITY, complication, difficulty, intricacy,
involvement, dilemma, enigma, mystery, puzzle,
paradox, obscurity, labyrinth
formal obfuscation

perquisite *n*
perk, fringe benefit, benefit, bonus, advantage,
dividend, gratuity, tip, extra, baksheesh, plus
colloq. freebie

persecute *v*
1 ILL-TREAT, abuse, mistreat, maltreat, oppress,
tyrannize, victimize, martyr, distress, afflict, torment,
torture, crucify
2 HARASS, hound, pursue, hunt, bother, worry,
annoy, pester, badger, molest
colloq. hassle
F3 1 pamper, spoil

persecution *n*
ill-treatment, mistreatment, abuse, maltreatment,
discrimination, oppression, harassment, molestation,
suppression, tyranny, victimization, punishment,
torture, martyrdom, crucifixion
formal subjugation

perseverance *n*
persistence, determination, resolution, resolve,
doggedness, tenacity, diligence, application, assiduity,
dedication, commitment, purpose, purposefulness,
constancy, steadfastness, stamina, endurance,
indefatigability
formal pertinacity, intransigence
colloq. stickability; *US* stick-to-it-iveness

persevere *v*
continue, carry on, go on, keep going, struggle on,
soldier on, persist, remain, be persistent, be
determined, be resolute, stand firm, stand fast, hold
on, hang on
colloq. stick at it, plug away, hang in there, go the whole
distance, stick to your guns, leave no stone unturned,
mean business
F3 give up, stop; *formal* discontinue

persist *v*
1 CONTINUE, carry on, go on, keep on, keep going,
soldier on, keep at it, persevere, stand firm, stand fast,
hold on, hang on, be persistent, be determined, be
resolute, insist
colloq. stick at it, plug away
2 REMAIN, keep on, hold, linger, last, endure,
continue
formal abide
F3 1 stop, give up; *formal* desist

persistence *n*
perseverance, determination, endurance, doggedness,
diligence, assiduousness, assiduity, constancy,
resolution, tenacity, steadfastness, tirelessness,
stamina, indefatigableness
formal pertinacity, sedulity
colloq. grit, stickability; *US* stick-to-it-iveness

persistent *adj*
1 INCESSANT, endless, never-ending, interminable,
continuous, unceasing, ceaseless, lasting, unrelenting,
relentless, unremitting, constant, steady, continual,
repeated, perpetual, lasting, enduring
2 *persistent effort*
persevering, determined, resolute, purposeful,
diligent, assiduous, dogged, tenacious, stubborn,
obstinate, steadfast, zealous, tireless, unflagging,
indefatigable
formal intractable, obdurate, pertinacious
colloq. US stick-to-it-ive

person *n*
individual, human being, human, being, man, woman,

mortal, body, soul, character, type, someone, somebody
▷ **in person** personally, face to face, bodily; *colloq.* in the flesh, as large as life

persona *n*
image, face, public face, role, part, character, personality, front, façade, mask

personable *adj*
pleasant, pleasing, likeable, presentable, nice, agreeable, amiable, affable, attractive, good-looking, handsome, charming, warm, winning, outgoing
E3 unpleasant, disagreeable, unattractive

personage *n*
celebrity, name, notable, worthy, public figure, personality, luminary, dignitary, headliner
colloq. VIP, big shot, somebody, big noise, bigwig

personal *adj*
1 *give you my personal attention*
individual, special, particular, exclusive, in person
2 *your personal style*
individual, idiosyncratic, peculiar, characteristic, distinctive, unique, own, subjective
3 PRIVATE, confidential, intimate, secret
4 *personal remarks*
offensive, insulting, critical, rude, abusive, hurtful, wounding, disrespectful, upsetting
E3 2 general, universal 3 public, official

personality *n*
1 CHARACTER, nature, disposition, temperament, temper, individuality, psyche, traits, make-up, charm, charisma, magnetism
2 CELEBRITY, notable, personage, public figure, dignitary, worthy, star
colloq. VIP

personally *adv*
1 INDIVIDUALLY, in person, specially, particularly, exclusively, solely, alone, independently, subjectively, idiosyncratically, distinctively, characteristically, uniquely, privately, confidentially
2 *take something personally*
directed against you, as personal criticism, as hurtful comments, insultingly, offensively

personification *n*
essence, embodiment, incarnation, likeness, image, representation, recreation, portrayal, semblance
formal delineation, manifestation, quintessence

personify *v*
embody, epitomize, typify, exemplify, symbolize, represent, mirror, be the incarnation of

personnel *n*
staff, workforce, workers, employees, crew, human resources, labour force, manpower, people, members
colloq. liveware

perspective *n*
1 VIEW, point of view, viewpoint, aspect, angle, slant, attitude, frame of mind, vantage point, standpoint, vista, scene, prospect, outlook
2 *get things into perspective*
proportion, relation, equilibrium

perspicacious *adj*
discerning, observant, sensitive, responsive, aware, alert, quick, quick-witted, keen, sharp, sharp-eyed, astute, penetrating, discriminating, shrewd, understanding

formal sagacious, percipient, judicious
E3 unobservant, obtuse

perspicacity *n*
discernment, astuteness, perceptiveness, discrimination, insight, acuteness, cleverness, sharpness, keenness, acumen, shrewdness, penetration, wit
formal percipience, perspicaciousness, perspicuity, sagaciousness, sagacity
colloq. brains

perspicuity *n*
clarity, clearness, plainness, precision, lucidity, straightforwardness, distinctness, explicitness, intelligibility, comprehensibility, comprehensibleness, penetrability, transparency
formal limpidity, limpidness

perspicuous *adj*
clear, crystal-clear, unambiguous, plain, obvious, self-evident, transparent, understandable, lucid, straightforward, apparent, explicit, distinct, intelligible, comprehensible
formal limpid, manifest

perspiration *n*
sweat, secretion, moisture, wetness
technical sudor, diaphoresis, hidrosis
formal exudation

perspire *v*
sweat, secrete, swelter, drip
technical sudate
formal exude

persuadable *adj*
amenable, agreeable, flexible, persuasible, malleable, pliable, receptive, susceptive, impressionable
formal acquiescent, compliant
E3 firm, inflexible, stubborn

persuade *v*
coax, prevail upon, cajole, wheedle, talk into, induce, bring round, win over, convince, satisfy, convert, lobby, sway, influence, tempt, lure, lead on, incite, prompt, urge, coerce
formal inveigle
colloq. lean on, sweet-talk, soft-soap, swing it, pull strings, twist someone's arm, put the screws on
E3 dissuade, deter, discourage, talk out of, put off

persuasion *n*
1 COAXING, prevailing, cajolery, wheedling, talking into, winning over, inducement, enticement, pull, power, influence, sway, conviction, conversion, incitement, prompting, urging, coercion
colloq. clout, sweet-talking, arm-twisting
2 OPINION, school (of thought), party, faction, side, camp, affiliation, philosophy, conviction, faith, belief, view, point of view, viewpoint, denomination, sect

persuasive *adj*
convincing, plausible, sound, valid, influential, forceful, weighty, effective, slick, telling, potent, compelling, moving, touching
formal cogent, effectual
colloq. pushy, smooth-talking
E3 unconvincing

pert *adj*
impudent, cheeky, presumptuous, impertinent, insolent, bold, brash, gay, forward, fresh, flippant, lively, spirited, brisk, daring, sprightly, jaunty, tossy

colloq. perky, saucy, cocky
E3 coy, shy

pertain *v*
relate, apply, be appropriate, be part of, be relevant, bear on, have a bearing on, befit, belong, come under, concern, refer, regard
formal appertain

pertinacious *adj*
persistent, persevering, determined, dogged, purposeful, tenacious, relentless, resolute, uncompromising, unyielding, wilful, headstrong, inflexible, obstinate, stubborn, self-willed, strong-willed, perverse, mulish
formal intractable, obdurate

pertinent *adj*
relevant, suitable, appropriate, fitting, apt, apposite, to the point, material, applicable
formal germane, apropos, *ad rem*
E3 inappropriate, unsuitable, irrelevant

pertness *n*
impudence, cheek, cheekiness, impertinence, insolence, presumption, rudeness, effrontery, forwardness, freshness, boldness, brashness, audacity, brazenness
colloq. sauciness, brass, cockiness, face, chutzpah

perturb *v*
worry, alarm, disturb, bother, trouble, upset, make anxious, disconcert, unsettle, discompose, disquiet, ruffle, fluster, confuse, agitate, vex
E3 reassure, compose

perturbed *adj*
worried, anxious, alarmed, upset, fearful, shaken, troubled, nervous, restless, disturbed, unsettled, discomposed, disconcerted, flustered, agitated, uncomfortable, uneasy, harassed, flurried
E3 calm, composed

perusal *n*
read, look, scrutiny, study, examination, inspection, check, browse, glance, skim, run-through

peruse *v*
study, pore over, read, scan, scrutinize, examine, inspect, check, browse, look through, run through, leaf through, glance through, skim

pervade *v*
affect, penetrate, permeate, percolate, charge, fill, pass through, spread through, be disseminated through, imbue, infuse, suffuse, diffuse, infiltrate, saturate, impregnate

pervasive *adj*
prevalent, common, extensive, widespread, general, universal, inescapable, rife, diffuse, ubiquitous
formal omnipresent, immanent

perverse *adj*
contrary, wayward, wrong-headed, wilful, headstrong, stubborn, obstinate, unyielding, disobedient, awkward, unruly, difficult, rebellious, troublesome, uncontrollable, unmanageable, pig-headed, ill-tempered, cantankerous, unreasonable, senseless, incorrect, improper, deviant
old use cussed
formal intransigent, obdurate, refractory, intractable
colloq. stroppy, bolshie, bloody-minded, nit-picking
E3 obliging, co-operative, reasonable

perversion *n*
1 CORRUPTION, depravity, debauchery, immorality, vice, wickedness, deviance, abnormality, irregularity
colloq. kinkiness
2 TWISTING, distortion, misrepresentation, travesty, misinterpretation, deviation, misuse, misapplication, falsification
formal aberration

perversity *n*
contrariness, waywardness, wrong-headedness, wilfulness, stubbornness, obstinacy, disobedience, awkwardness, unruliness, rebelliousness, troublesomeness, uncontrollability, unreasonableness, senselessness, contradictoriness, frowardness, gee
old use cussedness
formal contumacy, intransigence, obduracy, refractoriness

pervert *v, n*
▶ *v* **1** *pervert the truth*
twist, warp, distort, misrepresent, falsify, garble, misinterpret, misdirect, turn aside, deflect, avert
2 CORRUPT, lead astray, deprave, debauch, debase, degrade, warp, abuse, misuse, misapply
formal vitiate
▶ *n* deviate, deviant, debauchee, degenerate
colloq. weirdo, perv, oddball

perverted *adj*
corrupt, depraved, debauched, debased, immoral, evil, wicked, corrupted, deviant, unnatural, abnormal, unhealthy, twisted, warped, distorted
formal vitiated
colloq. kinky
E3 natural, normal

pessimism *n*
defeatism, fatalism, hopelessness, cynicism, depression, dejection, despair, gloom, gloominess, glumness, despondency, doomwatch, melancholy, negative thinking, distrust, Weltschmerz
colloq. looking on the black side
E3 optimism, hopefulness

pessimist *n*
defeatist, fatalist, alarmist, doubter, cynic, melancholic, worrier, prophet of doom, gloom-monger, doomster, doomwatcher, doubting Thomas
colloq. dismal Jimmy, gloom and doom merchant, killjoy, wet blanket, no-hoper
E3 optimist, hopeful

pessimistic *adj*
negative, cynical, fatalistic, defeatist, resigned, distrustful, suspicious, doubting, hopeless, alarmist, discouraging, depressing, off-putting, despairing, despondent, dejected, downhearted, glum, morose, melancholy, depressed, dismal, gloomy, bleak
colloq. looking on the black side
E3 optimistic

pest *n*
nuisance, bother, annoyance, irritation, irritant, vexation, trial, curse, scourge, bane, blight, bug
colloq. pain, pain in the neck, thorn in the flesh

pester *v*
nag, badger, hound, harass, plague, torment, provoke, worry, irk, fret, bother, disturb, annoy, irritate, pick on
colloq. hassle, get at, get on someone's nerves, drive round the bend, drive up the wall

pestilence *n*
plague, epidemic, disease, sickness, infection,

contagion, infestation, cholera
old use lues
formal pandemic
Related adjective: luetic

pestilent *adj*
1 HARMFUL, destructive, ruinous, diseased, disease-ridden, plague-ridden, poisonous, contaminated, contagious, infectious, infected, communicable, catching, corrupting, detrimental, pernicious
formal deleterious
2 INFURIATING, troublesome, annoying, bothersome, irritating, tiresome, vexing, irksome

pestilential *adj*
infuriating, troublesome, annoying, bothersome, irritating, tiresome, vexing, irksome, pernicious

pet¹ *n, adj, v*
▶ *n teacher's pet*
favourite, darling, idol, treasure, jewel
colloq. teacher's pet, apple of your eye, blue-eyed boy/girl
▶ *adj* favourite, favoured, preferred, dear, dearest, cherished, prized, preferred, chosen, special, particular, personal
▶ *v* stroke, caress, fondle, cuddle, embrace, kiss
colloq. neck, canoodle, smooch; *slang* snog

pet² *n*
in a pet
bad mood, bad temper, temper, sulk(s), tantrum
colloq. paddy, hump, huff, stew, grumps, the pits

peter *v*
▷ **peter out** dwindle, taper off, fade, wane, evaporate, ebb, diminish, fail, cease, stop, die away, come to an end, come to nothing; *colloq.* fizzle out

petite *adj*
dainty, small, slight, little, delicate, bijou, dinky
F3 big, large

petition *n, v*
▶ *n* appeal, round robin, protest, application, request, solicitation, plea, entreaty, prayer, supplication
formal invocation
▶ *v* appeal, call upon, ask, crave, solicit, bid, urge, press, implore, beg, plead, entreat, beseech, pray, request
formal supplicate, adjure, sue

pet name *n*
diminutive, endearment, term of endearment, nickname
formal hypocorisma

petrified *adj*
terrified, terror-stricken, aghast, horrified, horror-stricken, appalled, scared stiff, stunned, dumbfounded, shocked, speechless, stupefied, transfixed, numb, benumbed, dazed, frozen

petrify *v*
1 TERRIFY, horrify, frighten, alarm, panic, appal, paralyse, numb, stupefy, stun, dumbfound
2 TURN TO STONE, ossify, fossilize

petticoat *n*
slip, underskirt, jupon, kirtle

pettifogging *adj*
mean, petty, quibbling, paltry, captious, niggling, over-refined, subtle, sophistical, cavilling, casuistic,

equivocating
colloq. hair-splitting, nit-picking

pettish *adj*
peevish, sulky, irritable, petulant, thin-skinned, tetchy, grumpy, bad-tempered, ill-humoured, fractious, cross, fretful, querulous, snappish, waspish
formal splenetic
colloq. huffy, touchy

petty *adj*
1 MINOR, unimportant, insignificant, inconsequential, inessential, trivial, secondary, lesser, small, little, slight, trifling, paltry, inconsiderable, negligible
colloq. measly, grotty, piffling, piddling, no great shakes
2 SMALL-MINDED, narrow-minded, mean, ungenerous, grudging, spiteful
F3 1 important, significant **2** generous

petulance *n*
bad temper, irritability, ill-temper, ill-humour, sulkiness, sullenness, waspishness, peevishness, pique
formal procacity, querulousness, spleen
colloq. crabbedness, crabbiness

petulant *adj*
fretful, peevish, cross, irritable, snappish, bad-tempered, ill-humoured, complaining, impatient, moody, sullen, sulky, sour, ungracious
formal querulous
colloq. crotchety, crabby, crabbed, touchy, ratty, browned off, in a paddy, in a stew

phantom *n*
ghost, spectre, spirit, apparition, wraith, vision, hallucination, illusion, figment
formal revenant
colloq. spook

pharisaical *adj*
sanctimonious, self-righteous, holier-than-thou, formal, hypocritical, insincere, pietistic, preachy, moralizing
colloq. goody-goody

Pharisee *n*
hypocrite, fraud, pietist, whited sepulchre
formal dissembler, dissimulator
colloq. phoney, humbug

phase *n, v*
▶ *n* stage, step, time, juncture, period, spell, season, chapter, position, part, point, aspect, form, shape, state, condition
▶ *v* ▷ **phase in** introduce, ease in, bring in, start, start using, initiate
▷ **phase out** wind down, run down, ease off, taper off, wind up, eliminate, dispose of, get rid of, remove, withdraw, close, stop, stop using
formal terminate

phenomenal *adj*
marvellous, sensational, stupendous, amazing, astounding, astonishing, breath-taking, remarkable, extraordinary, exceptional, unprecedented, unparalleled, unique, singular, unheard of, unusual, unbelievable, incredible, wonderful, fantastic
colloq. mind-blowing, mind-boggling, too good to be true

phenomenon *n*
1 OCCURRENCE, happening, event, incident, episode, circumstance, fact, experience, appearance,

sight
2 WONDER, marvel, miracle, prodigy, rarity, curiosity, spectacle, sensation

philander *v*
womanize, flirt, dally, play/fool around, have an affair
colloq. sleep around

philanderer *n*
womanizer, ladies' man, flirt, dallier, libertine, playboy, Casanova, Don Juan
colloq. lady-killer, stud, wolf

philanthropic *adj*
humanitarian, public-spirited, altruistic, unselfish, selfless, benevolent, kind, kind-hearted, humane, charitable, alms-giving, generous, liberal, open-handed
formal munificent, bounteous, bountiful
F∃ misanthropic

philanthropist *n*
humanitarian, benefactor, patron, sponsor, giver, donor, helper, backer, contributor, alms-giver, altruist
F∃ misanthrope

philanthropy *n*
humanitarianism, public-spiritedness, altruism, unselfishness, selflessness, social concern/awareness, social conscience, benevolence, kind-heartedness, charity, alms-giving, giving, patronage, sponsorship, help, backing, generosity, liberality, open-handedness
formal beneficence, munificence, bounteousness, bountifulness
F∃ misanthropy

philippic *n*
diatribe, tirade, abuse, harangue, attack, onslaught, denunciation, criticism, insult, reviling, upbraiding, reproof, reprimand, rebuke
formal invective, vituperation

philistine *n, adj*
▶ *n* lowbrow, ignoramus, barbarian, bourgeois, vulgarian, yahoo
colloq. boor, lout
▶ *adj* uncultivated, uncultured, uneducated, unrefined, unread, unlettered, ignorant, lowbrow, tasteless, boorish, bourgeois, crass

philosopher *n*
philosophizer, thinker, theorist, theorizer, analyser, scholar, expert, guru, metaphysicist, sage, logician
technical epistemologist, dialectician
formal deipnosophist

philosophical *adj*
1 *a philosophical discussion*
metaphysical, abstract, theoretical, analytical, rational, logical, erudite, learned, wise, thoughtful, pensive, reflective, contemplative, meditative
2 RESIGNED, patient, stoic, stoical, self-possessed, dispassionate, unruffled, calm, composed, collected, cool, rational, logical, realistic
formal phlegmatic, imperturbable

philosophy *n*
1 *study philosophy*
reason, thought, thinking, wisdom, knowledge
2 IDEOLOGY, world-view, doctrine, beliefs, convictions, tenets, values, principles, attitude, viewpoint, point of view, view

Philosophical terms include: absolutism, aesthetics, agnosticism, altruism, antinomianism, a posteriori,

a priori, ascetism, atheism, atomism, behaviourism, deduction, deism, deontology, determinism, dialectical materialism, dogmatism, dualism, egoism, empiricism, entailment, Epicureanism, epistemology, ethics, existentialism, fatalism, hedonism, historicism, humanism, idealism, identity, induction, instrumentalism, interactionism, intuition, jurisprudence, libertarianism, logic, logical positivism, materialism, metaphysics, monism, naturalism, nihilism, nominalism, objectivism, ontology, pantheism, phenomenalism, phenomenology, positivism, pragmatism, prescriptivism, rationalism, realism, reductionism, relativism, scepticism, scholasticism, sensationalism, sense data, solipsism, stoicism, structuralism, subjectivism, substance, syllogism, teleology, theism, transcendentalism, utilitarianism.

phlegmatic *adj*
placid, stolid, impassive, calm, tranquil, cool, unemotional, unconcerned, indifferent, matter-of-fact, stoical, dispassionate
formal imperturbable
colloq. cool and collected
F∃ emotional, passionate, nervous

phobia *n*
fear, irrational fear, terror, dread, anxiety, neurosis, obsession, aversion, dislike, hatred, horror, loathing, revulsion, repulsion
formal antipathy, detestation
colloq. hang-up, thing
F∃ love, liking

Phobias (by name of fear) include: zoophobia (*animals*), apiphobia (*bees*), ailurophobia (*cats*), necrophobia (*corpses*), scotophobia (*darkness*), cynophobia (*dogs*), claustrophobia (*enclosed places*), panphobia (*everything*), pyrophobia (*fire*), xenophobia (*foreigners*), phasmophobia (*ghosts*), acrophobia (*high places*), hippophobia (*horses*), entomophobia (*insects*), astraphobia (*lightning*), autophobia (*loneliness*), agoraphobia (*open spaces*), toxiphobia (*poison*), herpetophobia (*reptiles*), ophiophobia (*snakes*), tachophobia (*speed*), arachnophobia (*spiders*), triskaidekaphobia (*thirteen*), brontophobia (*thunder*), hydrophobia (*water*).

phone *n, v*
▶ *n* **1** TELEPHONE, receiver, handset, mobile phone, car phone
colloq. blower
2 *give me a quick phone*
ring, call, phone call
colloq. buzz, tinkle, bell
▶ *v* telephone, ring (up), call (up), dial, contact, get in touch, give someone a call, make a call
colloq. give a buzz, give a tinkle, give a bell

phonetic alphabet

Communications code words for the letters of the alphabet are: Alpha, Bravo, Charlie, Delta, Echo, Foxtrot, Golf, Hotel, India, Juliet, Kilo, Lima, Mike, November, Oscar, Papa, Quebec, Romeo, Sierra, Tango, Uniform, Victor, Whisky, X-ray, Yankee, Zulu.

phoney *adj, n*
▶ *adj* fake, counterfeit, forged, fraudulent, bogus, trick, false, mock, spurious, assumed, feigned, simulated, affected, put-on, contrived, sham, imitation, ersatz
colloq. pseudo

⊟ real, genuine
▶ *n* impostor, pretender, fraud, sham, fake, faker, forgery, counterfeit, mountebank
colloq. humbug, pseud, quack

phosphorescent *adj*
glowing, bright, luminescent, luminous, radiant
technical noctilucent, noctilucous
formal refulgent

photocopy *v, n*
▶ *v* copy, duplicate, photostat, xerox, print, run off
▶ *n* copy, duplicate, facsimile, Photostat®, Xerox®

photograph *n, v*
▶ *n* photo, snap, snapshot, print, shot, still, slide, transparency, videotape, picture, image, likeness
colloq. mug shot
▶ *v* snap, take, take a picture of, take a photograph of, take a snapshot of, film, shoot, video, record, capture on film/videotape

photographic *adj*
1 *photographic equipment*
filmic, graphic, cinematic, pictorial
2 *photographic memory*
accurate, exact, detailed, faithful, precise, realistic, retentive, vivid, minute, visual, lifelike, natural, naturalistic, representational

Photographic equipment includes: camera, boom arm, flash umbrella, stand, tripod; developer bath, developing tank, dry mounting press, easel, enlarger, enlarger timer, film-drying cabinet, fixing bath, focus magnifier, light-box, negative carrier, print washer, contact printer, print-drying rack, paper drier, safelight, stop bath, Vertoscope®, viewer; slide viewer, slide projector, film projector, screen.

Photographic accessories include: air-shutter release, battery, cable release, camera bag, eye-cup, eyepiece magnifier, film, cartridge film, cassette film, disc film, film pack, filter, colour filter, heat filter, polarizing filter, skylight filter, flashbulb, flashcube, flashgun, flash unit, hot shoe, lens, afocal lens, auxiliary lens, close-up lens, fish-eye lens, macro lens, supplementary lens, telephoto lens, teleconverter, wide-angle lens, zoom lens, lens cap, lens hood, lens shield, light meter, exposure meter, spot meter, diffuser, barn doors, honeycomb diffuser, parabolic reflector, snoot, slide mount, viewfinder, right-angle finder; camcorder battery discharger/charger/tester, cassette adaptor, remote control, tele-cine converter, video editor, video light, video mixer. *See also* **camera**.

phrase *n, v*
▶ *n* construction, clause, idiom, expression, group of words, saying, utterance, remark, comment, language, phraseology, usage, way/style of speaking
▶ *v* word, formulate, frame, couch, present, put, express, say, utter, pronounce

phraseology *n*
terminology, phrase, phrasing, wording, expression, idiom, language, parlance, speech, writing, style, syntax, diction, argot, cant, patois

physical *adj*
1 BODILY, corporeal, fleshy, fleshly, carnal, incarnate, mortal, earthly, unspiritual
formal somatic
2 MATERIAL, concrete, solid, substantial, tangible, palpable, visible, real, actual
⊟ **1** mental, spiritual **2** abstract, theoretical

physician *n*
doctor, medical practitioner, general practitioner, GP, houseman, intern, registrar, consultant, specialist, healer
colloq. medic, doc, quack, medico

physics *n*

Terms used in physics include: absolute zero, acceleration, acoustics, alpha particles, analogue signal, applied physics, Archimedes principle, area, atom, beta particles, Big Bang theory, boiling point, bubble-chamber, capillary action, centre of gravity, centre of mass, centrifugal force, chain reaction, charge, charged particle, circuit, circuit-breaker, couple, critical mass, cryogenics, density, diffraction, digital, dynamics, efficiency, elasticity, electric current, electric discharge, electricity, electrodynamics, electromagnetic spectrum, electromagnetic waves, electron, energy, engine, entropy, equation, equilibrium, evaporation, field, flash point, force, formula, freezing point, frequency, friction, fundamental constant, gamma ray, gas, gate, grand united theory (GUT), gravity, half-life, heat, heavy water, hydraulics, hydrodynamics, hydrostatics, incandescence, indeterminacy principle, inertia, infrared, interference, ion, Kelvin effect, kinetic energy, kinetic theory, laser (light amplification by stimulated emission of radiation), latent heat, law, laws of motion, laws of reflection, laws of refraction, laws of thermodynamics, lens, lever, light, light emission, light intensity, light source, liquid, longitudinal wave, luminescence, Mach number, magnetic field, magnetism, mass, mechanics, microwaves, mirror, Mohs scale, molecule, moment, momentum, motion, neutron, nuclear, nuclear fission, nuclear fusion, nuclear physics, nucleus, optical centre, optics, oscillation, parallel motion, particle, periodic law, perpetual motion, phonon, photon, photosensitivity, polarity, potential energy, power, pressure, principle, process, proton, quantum chromodynamics (QCD), quantum electrodynamics (QED), quantum mechanics, quantum theory, quark, radiation, radioactive element, radioactivity, radioisotope, radio wave, ratio, reflection, refractor, relativity, resistance, resonance, rule, semiconductor, sensitivity, separation, SI unit, sound, sound wave, specific gravity, specific heat capacity, spectroscopy, spectrum, speed, states of matter, statics, substance, superstring theory, supersymmetry, surface tension, temperature, tension, theory, theory of relativity, thermodynamics, Thomson effect, transverse wave, ultrasound, ultraviolet, uncertainty principle, velocity, visible spectrum, viscosity, volume, wave, wave property, weight, white heat, work, X-ray. *See also* **atom**, **electricity**.

physiognomy *n*
face, features, look
old use visnomy
formal countenance, visage
colloq. clock, dial, mug, phiz, phizog, kisser

physique *n*
body, figure, shape, form, build, frame, structure, constitution, make-up

pick *v, n*
▶ *v* **1** SELECT, choose, go for, opt for, decide on, settle on, fix on, single out, prefer, favour, make up your mind
colloq. plump for
2 GATHER, collect, pluck, pull, harvest, cull, take in
3 *pick a lock/safe*
open, crack, break open, prise open, force open
4 *pick a quarrel*

cause, start, begin, provoke, produce, lead to, prompt, give rise to
▷ **pick at** nibble, peck, play with, toy with, eat small amounts of
▷ **pick off 1** SHOOT, hit, kill, remove, strike, fire at, take out **2** REMOVE, detach, take away, pull off
▷ **pick on** bully, torment, persecute, criticize, blame, find fault with, nag, bait; *colloq.* get at, needle
▷ **pick out** discern, make out, spot, notice, perceive, recognize, distinguish, tell apart, discriminate, separate, single out, hand-pick, choose, select
▷ **pick up 1** LIFT, raise, hoist, take up **2** *I'll pick you up at eight* call for, fetch, collect, give a lift/ride **3** LEARN, master, grasp, acquire, get to know, gather **4** IMPROVE, get better, rally, recover, make progress, make headway; *colloq.* perk up **5** ARREST, take into custody, apprehend; *colloq.* nick, nab, collar, run in, take in **6** RESUME, begin again, start again, continue, go on, carry on **7** OBTAIN, acquire, gain, learn, hear, find, discover, come across, buy, purchase; *formal* chance upon **8** *pick up an infection* catch, contract, get, become ill with, become infected with, go down with **9** *pick up a radio signal* receive, detect, get, hear
▶ *n* **1** CHOICE, selection, option, decision, preference, favour
2 BEST, cream, choicest, prize, flower, elite, elect, crème de la crème

picket *n, v*
▶ *n* **1** PICKETER, protester, objector, rebel, dissident, demonstrator, striker
2 GUARD, sentry, watch, patrol, lookout, outpost
3 STAKE, post, spike, upright, pike, stanchion, pale, paling
▶ *v* protest, demonstrate, boycott, blockade, go on a picket line, enclose, surround

pickings *n*
proceeds, profits, returns, rewards, earnings, yield, take, spoils, booty, loot, plunder
slang gravy

pickle *n, v*
▶ *n* **1** *cheese and pickle*
chutney, relish, vinegar, sauce, flavouring, seasoning, condiment
2 MESS, difficulty, dilemma, predicament, crisis, quandary, straits
formal exigency
colloq. bind, fix, hot water, jam, pinch, scrape, spot, tight spot
▶ *v* preserve, conserve, souse, marinade, steep, cure, salt

pick-me-up *n*
tonic, boost, refreshment, restorative, fillip, stimulant, stimulus, cordial
technical roborant
colloq. shot in the arm

pick-pocket *n*
thief, snatcher, pick-purse
old use file
colloq. dip, diver, wire

picnic *n*
1 *a picnic lunch*
outing, excursion, outdoor meal, *fête champêtre*, wayzgoose
2 *minding young children is no picnic*
colloq. child's play, cinch, doddle, piece of cake, pushover, walkover

pictorial *adj*
graphic, diagrammatic, schematic, representational, vivid, striking, expressive, illustrated, picturesque, scenic, in pictures, in photographs

picture *n, v*
▶ *n* **1** DESCRIPTION, portrayal, depiction, account, report, story, narrative, tale, semblance, impression
formal delineation, similitude
Related adjective: pictorial

Kinds of picture include: abstract, cameo, canvas, caricature, cartoon, collage, design, doodle, drawing, effigy, engraving, etching, fresco, graffiti, graphics, icon, identikit, illustration, image, kakemono, landscape, likeness, miniature, montage, mosaic, *colloq.* mugshot, mural, negative, oil-painting, old master, painting, passport photo, Photofit®, photograph, photogravure, pin-up, plate, portrait, print, representation, reproduction, self-portrait, silhouette, sketch, slide, *colloq.* snap, snapshot, still, still life, study, tableau, tapestry, tracing, transfer, transparency, triptych, trompe l'oeil, vignette, watercolour.

2 *the picture of health*
embodiment, personification, epitome, essence
formal archetype, exemplar, quintessence
3 FILM, motion picture
old use colloq. flick
4 *go to the pictures*
cinema, movies, picture-house, film theatre, entertainment centre, multiplex, picture-palace
old use colloq. flicks
▷ **get the picture** understand, grasp, take in, follow, see; *formal* comprehend; *colloq.* get the message, get it, get the idea, get the point, cotton on, tumble to
▷ **put someone in the picture** inform, tell, notify, communicate, explain, update; *colloq.* fill in, clue up, keep posted
▶ *v* **1** IMAGINE, envisage, envision, conceive, visualize, call to mind, see, see in your mind's eye
2 DEPICT, describe, represent, reproduce, show, portray, draw, sketch, paint, photograph, illustrate, appear
formal delineate

picturesque *adj*
1 ATTRACTIVE, beautiful, pretty, lovely, delightful, charming, pleasant, pleasing, quaint, idyllic, scenic
2 DESCRIPTIVE, graphic, vivid, colourful, striking, impressive
E3 1 unattractive **2** dull, boring

piddling *adj*
paltry, meagre, derisory, contemptible, mean, low, miserable, wretched, poor, sorry, small, slight, trifling, inconsiderate, negligible, trivial, minor, contemptible, petty, unimportant, insignificant, puny, worthless
colloq. measly, piffling
E3 substantial, significant, valuable

pie *n*
pastry, pie, tart
▷ **pie in the sky** daydream, dream, delusion, fantasy, reverie, romance, mirage, notion; *colloq.* jam tomorrow, hot air, castle in Spain, castle in the air

piebald *adj*
black and white, dappled, flecked, mottled, pied, spotted, speckled, variegated, brindled, skewbald

piece *n, v*
▶ *n* **1** FRAGMENT, bit, scrap, crumb, morsel, flake, speck, fleck, titbit, mouthful, bite, lump, chunk, wedge,

hunk, dollop, block, slab, bar, slice, sliver, snippet, chip, splinter, shred, offcut, length, sample, component, constituent, element, part, segment, section, unit, division, fraction, share, allocation, allotment, percentage, quota, portion, quantity
US tidbit
colloq. smithereen, cut, slice
2 ARTICLE, item, study, work, opus, story, review, composition, report, illustration, creation, specimen, example, instance
▷ **all in one piece** intact, unbroken, whole, complete, integral, entire, undamaged, unharmed, unhurt, uninjured
▣ broken, incomplete, damaged
▷ **go to pieces** lose control, break down, be overcome, collapse; *colloq.* crack up
▷ **in pieces** in bits, broken, damaged, disintegrated, ruined, shattered, smashed; *colloq.* kaput, in smithereens
▶ *v* ▷ **piece together** assemble, join, put together, unite, attach, compose, fit, mend, fix, repair, patch, restore

pièce de résistance *n*
masterpiece, masterwork, prize, showpiece, magnum opus, *chef-d'oeuvre*, jewel

piecemeal *adv, adj*
▶ *adv* little by little, intermittently, parcel-wise, partially, at intervals, slowly, bit by bit, by degrees, fitfully
colloq. in dribs and drabs
▣ completely, entirely, wholly
▶ *adj* fragmentary, intermittent, interrupted, partial, unsystematic, scattered, patchy, sporadic
formal discrete
▣ complete, entire, whole, wholesale

pied *adj*
flecked, irregular, motley, mottled, multicoloured, parti-coloured, piebald, dappled, brindle(d), spotted, streaked, skewbald, varicoloured, variegated

pier *n*
1 JETTY, breakwater, landing-stage, dock, quay, wharf
2 SUPPORT, upright, pile, pillar, post, column

pierce *v*
1 PENETRATE, enter, pass through, stick into, puncture, drill, bore, probe, perforate, punch, prick, stab, lance, bayonet, run through, spear, skewer, spike, impale, transfix
2 *pierce someone's spirit*
stab, sting, pain, hurt, move, prick, cut to the quick
3 *pierce the darkness*
burst through, penetrate, fill, enter, light up

pierced *adj*
perforated, impaled, punctured, stung
formal pertusate, pertuse(d)

piercing *adj*
1 *a piercing cry*
shrill, high-pitched, loud, ear-splitting, ear-piercing, penetrating, sharp, keen
2 PENETRATING, probing, searching, discerning, perceptive, shrewd, alert, astute, sharp, sharp-witted
3 COLD, bitter, raw, biting, numbing, keen, fierce, severe, wintry, frosty, freezing, Arctic
4 PAINFUL, agonizing, excruciating, extreme, severe, intense, stabbing, lacerating, shooting

piety *n*
piousness, devoutness, godliness, saintliness, holiness, sanctity, spirituality, religiousness, religion, faith, devotion, reverence, respect, deference
▣ impiety, irreligion

piffle *n*
nonsense, rubbish, trash, tripe, drivel, balderdash, rot, tarradiddle
colloq. bunk, bunkum, codswallop, guff, hooey, poppycock, tommy-rot, tosh, twaddle; *slang* balls, bullshit

pig *n, v*
▶ *n* **1** SWINE, hog, sow, boar, grunter, piglet
colloq. piggy
2 ANIMAL, beast, brute, boor
3 GLUTTON, gormandizer, gourmand
colloq. greedy guts, guzzler
▶ *v* gorge, guzzle, stuff
colloq. wolf
Related adjective: porcine

pigeonhole *n, v*
▶ *n* **1** COMPARTMENT, niche, slot, cubby-hole, cubicle, locker, box, place, section
2 CATEGORY, class, classification, compartment
▶ *v* **1** LABEL, compartmentalize, categorize, classify, sort, file, tag, slot, catalogue, alphabetize
2 SHELVE, defer, postpone, put off
colloq. put on the back burner

pig-headed *adj*
stubborn, obstinate, perverse, self-willed, stiff-necked, inflexible, contrary, mulish, stupid, unyielding, wilful, wrong-headed, headstrong, bull-headed
old use froward
formal intractable, intransigent
▣ flexible, tractable

pigment *n*
colour, hue, tint, dye, stain, paint, colouring, tincture

pile¹ *n, v*
▶ *n* **1** STACK, heap, bundle, mound, mountain, mass, accumulation, collection, assortment, hoard, stockpile, store
formal assemblage
2 LARGE QUANTITY, a great deal, a lot, quantities
colloq. loads, lots, lashings, stacks, heaps, oodles, millions, thousands, hundreds, tons
3 *make a pile*
fortune, wealth, riches
colloq. mint, packet, bundle, bomb; *slang* megabucks, big bucks
4 *a pile in the country*
large building, imposing/impressive building, edifice
▶ *v* **1** STACK, heap, mass, amass, accumulate, build up, gather, assemble, collect, hoard, stockpile, store, load
2 PACK, jam, crush, squeeze, crowd, flock, flood, stream, rush, charge
▷ **pile it on** exaggerate, overstate, overdo, magnify, overemphasize, emphasize, stress, make too much of, overplay, dramatize, overdramatize; *colloq.* lay it on, lay/pile it on thick, lay/pile it on with a trowel, make a mountain out of a molehill, blow something up out of all proportion
▣ understate, play down
▷ **pile up** mount up, increase, grow, accumulate, multiply, escalate, soar

pile² *n*
houses built on piles

post, piling, column, upright, support, bar, beam, foundation

pile³ *n*
the pile of a carpet
nap, shag, plush, fur, hair, fluff, fuzz, down, wool, (soft) surface, texture
Related adjectives: villose, villous

pile-up *n*
crash, accident, collision, bump, wreck
colloq. smash, smash-up, prang

pilfer *v*
steal, filch, shoplift, rob, thieve
formal purloin, peculate
colloq. pinch, nick, knock off, lift, nick, snaffle, swipe, nobble, have sticky fingers, snitch

pilgrim *n*
crusader, traveller, wanderer, wayfarer, worshipper, devotee, palmer, hadji

pilgrimage *n*
crusade, mission, expedition, journey, trip, tour, hadj

pill *n*
tablet, capsule, lozenge, pellet, ball, bolus

pillage *v, n*
▶ *v* plunder, raid, sack, vandalize, maraud, loot, spoil, ransack, ravage, raze, freeboot, rifle, rob, strip
formal depredate, despoil, spoliate
▶ *n* plunder, sack, devastation, marauding, harrying, seizure, spoils, robbery, loot, booty
formal depredation, rapine, spoliation

pillar *n*
1 COLUMN, shaft, pole, post, mast, pier, upright, pile, support, prop, stanchion
technical cippus
2 *a pillar of society*
mainstay, bastion, support, rock, tower of strength

pillory *v*
ridicule, mock, pour scorn on, laugh at, denounce, lash, hold up to shame, show up, brand, cast a slur on, stigmatize

pillow *n*
cushion, bolster, rest, headrest, bed

pilot *n, v, adj*
▶ *n* **1** FLYER, aviator, airman, airwoman, captain, commander, first officer, flight engineer, crew, aircrew
2 NAVIGATOR, steersman, helmsman, coxswain, captain, leader, director, guide
▶ *v* fly, drive, steer, direct, control, handle, manoeuvre, manage, operate, run, conduct, lead, guide, navigate
▶ *adj* experimental, trial, test, model

pimp *n*
pander, panderer, procurer, go-between, fancy man, fleshmonger, whoremonger, solicitor
old use bawd
slang hustler, mack

pimple *n*
spot, blackhead, boil, swelling, papula, papule, pustule
colloq. zit
Related adjectives: papulose, papulous

pin *v, n*
▶ *v* **1** TACK, nail, fix, stick, affix, attach, join, staple, clip, fasten, secure

2 HOLD DOWN, hold fast, restrain, constrain, press, immobilize
3 *pin the blame on someone*
attach, put, place, lay, attribute, ascribe
formal impute
▷ **pin down 1** PINPOINT, identify, define, determine, specify; *colloq.* nail down, put your finger on **2** FORCE, make, compel, press, pressurize, hold down, hold fast, restrain, constrain; *colloq.* nail down
▶ *n* tack, nail, screw, spike, rivet, bolt, peg, dowel, fastener, clip, staple, brooch

pincers *n*
forceps, tweezers, forfex

pinch *v, n*
▶ *v* **1** SQUEEZE, compress, crush, press, tweak, nip, hurt, confine, cramp, grip, grasp
2 STEAL, pilfer, filch, snatch
formal appropriate, purloin, peculate
colloq. nick, walk off with, knock off, lift
3 ECONOMIZE, save, cut back, budget, keep costs down, live on the cheap, scrimp and save
colloq. tighten your belt, cut your coat according to your cloth, scrape a living
4 ARREST, capture, catch, seize, detain
colloq. bust, nick, collar, nab, book, run in, pick up, nail
▶ *n* **1** SQUEEZE, tweak, nip
2 DASH, soupçon, trace, taste, bit, touch, speck, jot, mite
colloq. smidgen, tad
3 EMERGENCY, crisis, predicament, difficulty, hardship, pressure, stress
▷ **at a pinch** if necessary, if absolutely necessary, in an emergency, with great difficulty

pinched *adj*
pale, thin, drawn, haggard, gaunt, peaky, careworn, worn, narrowed, straightened, starved

pine *v*
1 YEARN, long, ache, sigh, wish, desire, crave, hanker, hunger, thirst
2 *pine away from grief*
grieve, mourn, fret, weaken, fade, languish, waste away

pinion *v*
pin down, tie, fasten, confine, bind, chain, fetter, manacle, shackle, hobble, immobilize, truss

pink¹ *adj, n*
▶ *adj* *pink flowers*
reddish, flushed, rose, rosy, salmon, roseate
▶ *n* perfection, height, peak, extreme, best, flower, summit, top, tiptop
formal acme
▷ **in the pink** fit, healthy, well, very well, in good shape/trim, in fine fettle, in perfect health, in the best of health; *colloq.* right as rain

pink² *v*
to pink cloth
cut, notch, serrate, perforate, score, incise, prick, punch, scallop
formal crenellate

pinnacle *n*
1 PEAK, summit, top, cap, crown, crest, apex, vertex, height, eminence, culmination
formal acme, zenith, apogee
2 SPIRE, steeple, turret, pyramid, cone, obelisk, needle

pinpoint v

identify, spot, distinguish, locate, place, home in on, pin down, discover, determine, specify, define
colloq. zero in on, nail down, put your finger on

pint-size *adj*

pint-sized, little, small, pocket, pocket-sized, tiny, diminutive, miniature, dwarf, midget
Scot. wee
🔃 giant, huge, enormous

pioneer *n, v*

▶ *n* **1** SETTLER, colonist, frontiersman, frontierswoman, explorer
2 *a pioneer in science*
developer, pathfinder, trail-blazer, ground-breaker, leader, innovator, inventor, discoverer, founder, founding father
▶ *v* invent, discover, originate, create, initiate, instigate, begin, start, launch, institute, introduce, found, establish, set up, develop, open up, prepare the way for, lead the way, spearhead, break new ground, blaze a trail, make the first move
colloq. set/start the ball rolling, pave the way

pious *adj*

1 DEVOUT, godly, saintly, holy, spiritual, religious, reverent, sanctified, faithful, dedicated, devoted, good, virtuous, righteous, moral
2 SANCTIMONIOUS, self-righteous, unctuous, hypocritical, insincere
colloq. holier-than-thou, goody-goody, pi
🔃 **1** impious, irreligious, irreverent

pipe *n, v*

▶ *n* **1** TUBE, hose, piping, tubing, pipeline, line, main, flue, duct, conduit, drainpipe, channel, passage, cylinder, conveyor, overflow
2 *pipe and tobacco*
clay, claypipe, hookah, hubble-bubble, kalian, water pipe, brier, dudeen, meerschaum, narghile, calumet, peace-pipe
▶ *v* **1** CHANNEL, funnel, siphon, carry, bring, take, convey, conduct, duct, transmit, supply, deliver
2 WHISTLE, chirp, tweet, cheep, chirrup, peep, twitter, sing, warble, trill, shrill, play, sound
▷ **pipe down** be quiet, stop talking; *colloq.* shut up

pipe-dream *n*

daydream, dream, delusion, fantasy, reverie, romance, mirage, notion
formal chimera, vagary
colloq. castle in Spain, castle in the air, pie in the sky

pipeline *n*

passage, pipe, tube, line, conduit, channel, duct, conveyor
▷ **in the pipeline** in preparation, planned, already started, under way

pipsqueak *n*

nobody, nonentity, nothing
colloq. upstart, squirt, twerp, whippersnapper, creep, hobbledehoy
🔃 somebody

piquancy *n*

1 SPICINESS, pungency, tang, pepperiness, spice, relish, flavour, sharpness, ginger, bite
2 LIVELINESS, excitement, interest, vigour, vitality, spirit, zest, colour, raciness, punch
colloq. edge, kick, pep, pizzazz, zip

piquant *adj*

1 *piquant sauce*
spicy, tangy, savoury, salty, peppery, seasoned, highly seasoned, pungent, zesty, sharp, biting, tart, stinging
2 LIVELY, spirited, stimulating, provocative, interesting, sparkling, intriguing, fascinating, sharp, racy, colourful
colloq. juicy
🔃 **1** bland, insipid **2** dull, banal

pique *n, v*

▶ *n* annoyance, anger, irritation, gall, vexation, displeasure, offence, resentment, grudge, umbrage
colloq. huff
▶ *v* **1** AROUSE, stimulate, excite, goad, rouse, provoke, stir, spur, whet, kindle, galvanize
2 ANNOY, anger, irritate, affront, displease, gall, irk, get, put out, rile, incense, offend, mortify, vex, wound, sting
formal miff, nettle, peeve

piqued *adj*

annoyed, irritated, vexed, riled, angry, displeased, offended, put out, resentful
colloq. miffed, peeved

piracy *n*

buccaneering, freebooting, bootlegging, robbery, stealing, theft, hijacking, infringement, plagiarism
formal rapine

pirate *n, v*

▶ *n* **1** BUCCANEER, brigand, freebooter, filibuster, corsair, marauder, raider, rover, picaroon, sea robber, sea rover, sea wolf, sea rat, water rat, marque
old use sallee-man
2 INFRINGER, plagiarist, plagiarizer
▶ *v* copy, reproduce illegally, steal, pinch, plagiarize, poach
formal appropriate
colloq. borrow, crib, lift, nick

pirouette *n, v*

▶ *n* gyration, spin, turn, twirl, whirl, pivot
▶ *v* gyrate, spin, turn, twirl, whirl, pivot

pistol *n*

gun, handgun, revolver, sidearm, six-shooter, Luger®, dag
US derringer
colloq. gat, iron, piece, rod

pit *n, v*

▶ *n* **1** *dig a pit*
hole, cavity, crater, pothole, gulf, chasm, abyss, mine, coalmine, quarry, diggings, trench, ditch, excavations, workings
2 HOLLOW, depression, dent, indentation, pockmark
▶ *v* pockmark, blemish, scar, mark, dent, notch, depress, indent, dimple, pothole
▷ **pit against** compete, match, oppose, set against

pitch¹ *v, n*

▶ *v* **1** THROW, fling, toss, cast, lob, bowl, hurl, heave, sling, fire, launch, aim, direct
colloq. chuck
2 PLUNGE, dive, plummet, drop, fall, fall headlong, topple, tumble
3 *pitch camp*
erect, put up, set up, place, station, settle, plant, fix
4 MOVE UP AND DOWN, lurch, sway, roll, reel, keel, list, flounder, wallow
▷ **pitch in** join in, co-operate, be involved, participate, help, lend a hand; *colloq.* muck in, do your bit
▶ *n* **1** *cricket pitch*

ground, field, sports field, playing-field, park, arena, stadium
2 SOUND, tone, timbre, tonality, modulation, frequency, level
3 GRADIENT, incline, slope, slant, tilt, angle, degree, inclination, steepness, cant
4 *reach a high pitch*
level, degree, extend, height, point, position, intensity, grade, mark
5 THROW, fling, toss, lob, hurl
colloq. chuck
6 TALK, patter, line, gabble, chatter, jargon
colloq. spiel, yak

pitch² *n*
to coat a surface with pitch
tar, bitumen, asphalt
Related adjective: piceous

pitch-black *adj*
pitch-dark, black, dark, jet-black, inky, coal-black, unilluminated, unlit

pitcher *n*
jug, ewer, jar, vessel, crock, bottle, can, container, urn

piteous *adj*
poignant, moving, touching, distressing, heart-breaking, heart-rending, plaintive, mournful, sad, sorrowful, woeful, wretched, pitiful, pitiable, pathetic

⚠ **piteous**, **pitiable** or **pitiful** ?
Pitiful means 'very sad, arousing or deserving pity': *She was a pitiful sight*; and also 'arousing or deserving contempt, very bad, very poor': *a pitiful attempt at catching the ball*. *Pitiable* means the same as *pitiful* but is less common: *He was in a pitiable condition; That was a pitiable attempt you made*. *Piteous* is a rather formal word meaning 'arousing or deserving pity': *She gave a piteous cry*.

pitfall *n*
danger, peril, hazard, trap, snare, stumbling-block, catch, snag, drawback, difficulty

pith *n*
gist, essence, essential part, salient point, point, crux, nub, heart, core, meat, kernel, marrow, importance, significance, moment, weight, value, consequence, substance, forcefulness, vigour, matter
formal import, quintessence

pithy *adj*
succinct, concise, compact, terse, short, brief, condensed, summary, pointed, expressive, meaningful, forceful, incisive, telling
formal trenchant, cogent
🖃 wordy, verbose

pitiable *adj*
contemptible, distressed, distressful, distressing, doleful, grievous, lamentable, miserable, mournful, piteous, poor, sad, sorry, woeful, woesome, wretched
colloq. pathetic

⚠ **pitiable**, **piteous** or **pitiful** ? *See panel at* **piteous**.

pitiful *adj*
1 PITEOUS, doleful, mournful, distressing, heart-breaking, heart-rending, affecting, moving, pathetic, pitiable, sad, miserable, wretched, poor, sorry
2 CONTEMPTIBLE, meagre, despicable, low, base, mean, poor, vile, shabby, miserable, deplorable,

lamentable, woeful, inadequate, hopeless, insignificant, paltry, worthless
colloq. pathetic

⚠ **pitiful**, **piteous** or **pitiable** ? *See panel at* **piteous**.

pitiless *adj*
merciless, cold-hearted, unsympathetic, unfeeling, uncaring, heartless, hard-hearted, callous, cruel, inhuman, inhumane, brutal, cold-blooded, ruthless, relentless, unremitting, inexorable, harsh, severe
🖃 merciful, compassionate, kind, gentle

pittance *n*
modicum, crumb, drop (in the ocean), trifle
colloq. chickenfeed; *slang* peanuts

pitted *adj*
dented, holey, potholed, pockmarked, blemished, scarred, marked, notched, depressed, indented, rough

pity *n, v*
▶ *n* **1** SYMPATHY, commiseration, regret, sorrow, sadness, distress, understanding, fellow-feeling, feeling, emotion, condolence, compassion, kindness, tenderness, mercy, forgiveness, grace
formal forbearance
2 *What a pity!*
shame, disappointment, misfortune, unfortunate thing, bad luck
colloq. crying shame
🖃 **1** cruelty, anger, scorn
▶ *v* feel sorry for, feel for, sympathize with, be sympathetic towards, empathize with, show understanding towards, feel/have compassion for, commiserate with, grieve for, weep for
▷ **take pity on** feel sorry for, feel for, sympathize with, be sympathetic towards, empathize with, show understanding towards, feel/have compassion for, commiserate with, show mercy, have mercy on, pardon, spare

pivot *n, v*
▶ *n* *the wheel turns on a pivot; the pivot of her life*
axis, hinge, axle, spindle, fulcrum, kingpin, linchpin, swivel, hub, central point, focal point, focus, centre, heart
▶ *v* **1** SWIVEL, turn, spin, revolve, rotate, swing
2 DEPEND, rely, revolve, hinge, hang, lie
formal turn, be contingent

pivotal *adj*
vital, important, focal, central, critical, crucial, decisive, determining, climactic, axial

pixie *n*
elf, brownie, goblin, leprechaun, fairy, sprite

placard *n*
poster, bill, notice, sticker, sign, advertisement
colloq. ad, advert

placate *v*
appease, pacify, conciliate, win over, mollify, calm (down), assuage, soothe, lull, quiet
formal propitiate
🖃 anger, enrage, incense, infuriate

placatory *adj*
appeasing, calming, soothing, mollifying, conciliatory, peace-making
formal pacificatory, propitiatory, propitiative

place *n, v*
▶ *n* **1** SITE, locale, venue, location, scene, setting,

situation, spot, point, position, part, whereabouts, seat, space, room
2 *a place name*
city, town, village, hamlet, locality, neighbourhood, whereabouts, district, area, region, state, country
3 BUILDING, establishment, hotel, restaurant, institution, property, accommodation, house, flat, apartment, home
formal dwelling, residence, abode, domicile
colloq. pad, digs
4 JOB, position, appointment, situation, role, part, niche, status, standing, grade, rank, footing
5 *not your place to comment*
role, function, task, duty, responsibility, right, concern, business
▷ **in place** arranged, in order, in the correct position, set up, working
▷ **in place of** instead of, in lieu of, as a replacement for, as an alternative to, in exchange for, as a substitute for, taking the place of
▷ **out of place** inappropriate, unsuitable, unfitting, improper, tactless, unbecoming; *formal* unseemly, inapposite
▷ **put someone in their place** humble, humiliate, shame, crush, deflate, bring low, bring/take someone down a peg or two, take the wind out of someone's sail
▷ **take place** happen, occur, come about, be held, come off, fall; *formal* transpire, come to pass, befall, betide
▷ **take the place of** replace, substitute for, supersede, stand in for, act for
▶ *v* **1** PUT, put down, set, set down, plant, fix, position, locate, situate, station, rest, settle, install, establish, lay, lay down, stand, deposit, lodge, leave
2 ARRANGE, put, class, sort, classify, categorize, group, rank, grade
3 *I can't quite place her*
recognize, know, remember, identify, establish, pinpoint, categorize
4 *place graduates in companies*
find a job for, find employment for, find accommodation for, allocate, assign

placement *n*
locating, location, installation, ordering, arrangement, deployment, appointment, positioning, ranking, stationing, distribution, classification, job, assignment, disposition, engagement, employment
formal emplacement

placid *adj*
1 *a placid person*
calm, composed, unmoved, undisturbed, unruffled, untroubled, unexcitable, cool, self-possessed, level-headed, imperturbable, mild, gentle, equable, serene, unemotional, even-tempered, peaceable, tranquil
colloq. easy-going, unflappable
2 *live in placid surroundings*
tranquil, still, quiet, calm, peaceful, restful
formal pacific
El 1 excitable, agitated, disturbed

plagiarism *n*
infringement, copying, reproduction, counterfeiting, piracy, theft
formal appropriation
colloq. borrowing, cribbing, lifting

plagiarist *n*
copier, robber, thief, pirate, imitator

plagiarize *v*
crib, copy, reproduce, imitate, counterfeit, pirate,

infringe copyright, poach, steal, lift, borrow
formal appropriate
colloq. crib, lift, nick

plague *n, v*
▶ *n* **1** PESTILENCE, epidemic, disease, sickness, infection, contagion, infestation, cholera, bubonic plague, pneumonic plague, Black Death
formal pandemic
2 *a plague of rats*
infestation, influx, swarm, invasion, huge number, epidemic
3 NUISANCE, annoyance, curse, scourge, trial, affliction, torment, calamity
colloq. thorn in the flesh, pain in the neck
▶ *v* annoy, vex, bother, disturb, trouble, distress, upset, irritate, worry, cause problems for, pester, harass, hound, dog, hamper, hinder, haunt, bedevil, afflict, torment, torture, persecute
colloq. bug, hassle, aggravate, cause headaches to

plain *adj, adv, n*
▶ *adj* **1** *plain cookery*
ordinary, basic, simple, unpretentious, unsophisticated, modest, unadorned, unelaborate, restrained, stark, austere, Spartan
2 *plain fabric*
undecorated, unadorned, unembellished, unpatterned, unvariegated, uncoloured, self-coloured, restrained, muted
3 OBVIOUS, evident, patent, clear, understandable, apparent, noticeable, perceptible, discernible, visible, overt, unmistakable transparent
formal manifest
colloq. plain as a pikestaff
4 UNATTRACTIVE, ordinary, unattractive, ugly, unprepossessing, unlovely
US homely
5 *plain language*
clear, intelligible, understandable, lucid, unambiguous, uncomplicated, simple, direct, straightforward, accessible
6 FRANK, candid, blunt, outspoken, direct, forthright, straightforward, unambiguous, plain-spoken, open, honest, sincere, truthful, simple, unassuming
El 1 fancy, elaborate **2** patterned **3** unclear, obscure **4** attractive, beautiful, good-looking **5** complicated, obscure **6** devious, deceitful
▶ *adv* completely, utterly, totally, thoroughly, undeniably, simply, quite
▶ *n* grassland, prairie, steppe, lowland, pampas, flat, flatland, plateau, tableland, savannah, tundra

plain-spoken *adj*
candid, frank, open, honest, blunt, outspoken, straightforward, direct, truthful, unequivocal, outright, explicit, forthright, downright

plaintive *adj*
doleful, mournful, melancholy, wretched, woeful, wistful, sad, unhappy, sorrowful, grief-stricken, heart-broken, piteous, pitiful, heart-rending, high-pitched
formal disconsolate

plan *n, v*
▶ *n* **1** IDEA, suggestion, intention, aim, arrangement, proposal, proposition, project, scheme, plot, system, method, means, way, policy, procedure, strategy, formula, programme, schedule, scenario
2 BLUEPRINT, layout, diagram, chart, map, drawing, scale drawing, sketch, representation,

illustration, design
formal delineation
▶ *v* **1** PLOT, scheme, design, invent, think of, devise, contrive, develop, formulate, frame, shape, draft, outline, sketch, map out, work out, prepare, organize, arrange, schedule, programme, mastermind
2 AIM, intend, want, wish, propose, purpose, mean, seek, contemplate, envisage, foresee
formal resolve

plane¹ *n, adj*
▶ *n* **1** FLAT SURFACE, level surface, flat, level
2 LEVEL, stage, position, class, condition, degree, rank, footing, rung, stratum, echelon
▶ *adj* level, smooth, uniform, regular, plain, flat, flush, even, horizontal
technical homaloidal
formal planar

plane² *n, v*
▶ *n* *travel by plane*
aeroplane, aircraft, jet, jumbo jet, jumbo, airliner, glider, bomber, fighter, seaplane, swing-wing, VTOL
US airplane
See also panel at **aircraft**.
▶ *v* skim, skate, fly, glide, sail, volplane, wing

planet *n*
Related adjective: planetary

Planets within the Earth's solar system (nearest the sun shown first) are: Mercury, Venus, Earth, Mars, Jupiter, Saturn, Uranus, Neptune, Pluto.

plant *n, v*
▶ *n* **1** *garden plants*
flower, shrub, herb, bush, vegetable
Related adjective: botanical

Plants include: annual, biennial, perennial, herbaceous plant, evergreen, succulent, cultivar, hybrid, house plant, pot plant; flower, herb, shrub, bush, tree, vegetable, grass, vine, weed, cereal, wild flower, air-plant, water-plant, cactus, fern, moss, algae, lichen, fungus; bulb, corm, seedling, sapling, bush, climber. *See also* **algae** and **lichen**; **bulb**; **flower**; **grass**; **leaf**; **poisonous**; **shrub**; **weed**; **wild flower**.

2 FACTORY, works, foundry, mill, shop, yard, workshop, machinery, apparatus, equipment, gear
▶ *v* **1** SOW, seed, scatter, implant, put into the ground, bury, transplant
2 INSERT, put, place, set, position, situate, fix, lodge, imbed, root, settle, found, establish
3 HIDE, put secretly, conceal, bury, disguise, put out of sight
formal secrete

plaque *n*
plate, slab, tablet, panel, sign, plaquette, brass, shield, medal, medallion, badge, brooch
technical cartouche

plaster *n, v*
▶ *n* **1** *apply plaster to walls*
stucco, mortar, plasterwork, gypsum, plaster of Paris, plasterboard
2 *put a plaster on a wound*
sticking-plaster, patch, dressing, adhesive dressing, bandage, Band-aid®, Elastoplast®
▶ *v* daub, bedaub, smear, coat, cover, cover thickly, overlay, spread

plastic *adj*
1 *plastic toys*
soft, pliable, flexible, supple, malleable, mouldable, ductile, shapeable
2 EASILY INFLUENCED, receptive, malleable, pliable, pliant, impressionable, manageable, mouldable
formal compliant, tractable
3 ARTIFICIAL, unnatural, false, synthetic, man-made
colloq. phoney
🢐🢐 **1** rigid, inflexible **2** inflexible;
formal intractable **3** natural

Types of plastic include: Bakelite®, Biopol®, celluloid®, epoxy resin, Perspex®, phenolic resin, plexiglass, polyester, polyethylene, polymethyl methacrylate, polynorbornene, polypropylene, polystyrene, polythene, polyurethane, PTFE (polytetrafluoroethylene), PVC (polyvinyl chloride), uPVC, silicone, Teflon®, transpolyisoprene, urea formaldehyde, vinyl.

plasticity *n*
flexibility, softness, suppleness, pliancy, pliableness, pliability, malleability
formal tractability
🢐🢐 inflexibility, rigidity

plate *n, v*
▶ *n* **1** DISH, platter, salver, helping, serving, portion, ashet
2 SHEET, slab, pane, panel, sign, plaque, tablet
formal lamina
3 ILLUSTRATION, photograph, picture, print, lithograph
▶ *v* coat, cover, overlay, veneer, laminate, electroplate, anodize, galvanize, platinize, gild, silver, tin

plateau *n*
1 *a grassy plateau*
plane, highland, tableland, table, upland, mesa
2 STABILITY, level, grade, stage

platform *n*
1 STAGE, podium, dais, rostrum, stand
colloq. soapbox
2 POLICY, party line, principles, tenets, manifesto, programme, objectives, aims, ideas, intentions, strategy

platitude *n*
banality, commonplace, truism, cliché, bromide, inanity, stereotype, hackneyed statement, trite expression, overworked phrase
colloq. chestnut

platitudinous *adj*
banal, commonplace, truistic, trite, clichéd, hackneyed, overworked, stale, stereotyped, set, stock, inane, tired, dull, flat, well-worn, vapid
colloq. corny

platonic *adj*
non-physical, spiritual, non-romantic, non-sexual, intellectual, ideal, idealistic, transcendent
formal incorporeal
🢐🢐 sexual

platoon *n*
company, group, patrol, battery, team, squad, squadron, outfit

platter *n*
plate, dish, salver, tray, charger, trencher

plaudits *n*
commendation, approval, praise, acclaim,
acclamation, applause, congratulations, hurrahs,
accolade, ovation, standing ovation, clapping
formal approbation
colloq. hand, bouquet, pat on the back, rave review,
good press
EJ criticism

plausible *adj*
credible, believable, reasonable, logical, likely,
possible, probable, imaginable, conceivable,
convincing, persuasive, smooth-talking, glib
formal cogent
EJ implausible, unlikely, improbable

play *v, n*
▶ *v* **1** AMUSE YOURSELF, have fun, enjoy yourself,
play games, occupy yourself, divert yourself, revel,
sport, romp, frolic, caper, gambol, frisk, cavort
2 PARTICIPATE, take part, join in, be involved in, do,
compete
3 *France played Italy*
oppose, compete against, vie with, rival, challenge,
take on
4 ACT, perform, play the part of, portray, represent,
impersonate
5 *light playing on the water*
dance, move lightly, flicker, twinkle, flash
EJ 1 work
▷ **play around with 1** FIDDLE WITH, toy with,
fidget with, meddle with, tamper with, interfere
with **2** DALLY WITH, mess around with, flirt with,
fool with, trifle with, womanize with, philander with
▷ **play at** pretend (to be), put on an act, make out;
formal affect; *colloq.* go through the motions
▷ **play down** minimize, make light of, gloss over,
underplay, downplay, understate, undervalue,
underestimate
EJ exaggerate, emphasize, play up
▷ **play on** exploit, take advantage of, turn to
account, profit by, trade on, capitalize on
▷ **play out** continue, go on, carry on, unfold, be
revealed, act, enact
▷ **play up 1** EXAGGERATE, highlight, spotlight,
accentuate, emphasize, stress, underline, point up, call
attention to **2** MISBEHAVE, be mischievous, be
naughty, give trouble, be difficult to control, trouble,
bother, annoy, hurt **3** MALFUNCTION, not work, go
wrong; *colloq.* go/be on the blink
EJ play down, underplay **3** work properly
▷ **play up to** flatter, ingratiate yourself, suck up to,
curry favour with, blandish, fawn, toady; *colloq.*
bootlick, butter up, soft-soap
▶ *n* **1** FUN, amusement, enjoyment, entertainment,
diversion, leisure, recreation, sport, game, hobby,
pastime, merrymaking
2 DRAMA, tragedy, comedy, farce, show, melodrama,
plot, performance
3 MOVEMENT, action, flexibility, give, freedom of
movement, slack, looseness, leeway, latitude, freedom,
liberty, free rein, margin, scope, range, licence, room,
space
colloq. give
4 ACTION, operation, exercise, interaction, interplay,
transaction
5 JEST, fun, joking, teasing, laugh
colloq. kicks
EJ 1 work

playboy *n*
philanderer, womanizer, ladies' man, lady-killer, rake,
libertine, roué, debauchee
colloq. man about town, socialite

player *n*
1 CONTESTANT, competitor, participant,
sportsman, sportswoman
2 PERFORMER, entertainer, artiste, actor, actress,
artist, comedian, trouper, player, musician,
instrumentalist, accompanist

playful *adj*
1 *as playful as a kitten*
frisky, sportive, frolicsome, lively, fun-loving, spirited,
mischievous, roguish, impish, puckish, kittenish
2 *a playful remark*
humorous, tongue-in-cheek, jesting, joking, facetious,
waggish, teasing
EJ serious

playground *n*
park, playing-field, play area, adventure playground,
amusement park, pleasure ground, recreation ground

playmate *n*
friend, companion, comrade, neighbour, playfellow
colloq. buddy, chum, pal

plaything *n*
toy, trifle, amusement, game, puppet, trinket, pastime,
bauble, gewgaw, gimcrack

playwright *n*
dramatist, writer, scriptwriter, screen writer,
dramaturge, dramaturgist, tragedian

plea *n*
1 APPEAL, petition, request, entreaty, supplication,
prayer
formal invocation, imploration
2 DEFENCE, justification, excuse, explanation,
claim, pretext
formal vindication

plead *v*
1 BEG, implore, entreat, appeal, petition, ask, request
formal beseech, solicit, make supplication
2 *plead ignorance*
assert, state, argue, maintain, claim, allege, put
forward
formal adduce

pleasant *adj*
1 *a pleasant chat*
ENJOYABLE, agreeable, nice, fine, lovely, delightful,
charming, amusing, pleasing, gratifying, satisfying,
acceptable, welcome, entertaining, refreshing
2 *a pleasant person*
FRIENDLY, amiable, affable, likeable, cheerful,
congenial, good-humoured, charming, nice, lovely,
winsome
EJ 1, 2 unpleasant, nasty **2** unfriendly

pleasantry *n*
1 *exchange pleasantries about the weather*
friendly remark, polite comment, casual remark
2 JOKE, jest, banter, badinage, quip, sally, witticism,
bon mot

please *v*
1 DELIGHT, make happy, give pleasure to, charm,
attract, appeal to, captivate, entertain, amuse, divert,
cheer (up), gladden, humour, indulge, gratify, satisfy,
fulfil, content, suit
2 WANT, will, wish, desire, like, prefer, choose, think

fit, see fit
🔳 **1** displease, annoy, anger, sadden

pleased *adj*
contented, satisfied, gratified, glad, happy, cheerful, delighted, thrilled, euphoric, elated
colloq. chuffed, over the moon, tickled pink
🔳 displeased, annoyed

pleasing *adj*
gratifying, satisfying, acceptable, good, pleasant, pleasurable, agreeable, nice, fine, delightful, enjoyable, amusing, entertaining, charming, attractive, engaging, winning
🔳 unpleasant, disagreeable

pleasurable *adj*
enjoyable, delightful, fun, good, lovely, nice, pleasant, gratifying, welcome, entertaining, amusing, diverting, agreeable, congenial
colloq. groovy
🔳 bad, disagreeable

pleasure *n*
1 HAPPINESS, contentment, joy, delight, gladness, enjoyment, satisfaction, gratification
formal solace
2 *the pleasure of playing a sport*
joy, delight, enjoyment, thrill, glory, treasure, prize, gem
3 *combine business with pleasure*
recreation, amusement, entertainment, leisure, fun
4 PREFERENCE, wish, will, desire, choice, inclination
🔳 **1** sorrow, pain, trouble, displeasure
2 disappointment, sadness

pleat *v*
tuck, fold, crease, flute, crimp, gather, pucker

plebeian *adj, n*
▶ *adj* **1** LOWER-CLASS, working-class, proletarian, low-born, peasant, mean
2 COMMON, uncultured, unrefined, uncultivated, coarse, base, ignoble, low
colloq. non-U
🔳 **1** aristocratic, noble, patrician **2** refined, sophisticated
▶ *n* common person, commoner, person in the street, proletarian, worker, peasant
colloq. pleb, prole
🔳 aristocrat, noble, patrician

plebiscite *n*
vote, referendum, ballot, poll, straw poll

pledge *n, v*
▶ *n* **1** PROMISE, vow, word of honour, word, oath, bond, covenant, guarantee, warrant, commitment, assurance, undertaking
2 DEPOSIT, security, surety, bail, guarantee, pawn
old use gage
formal collateral
▶ *v* **1** PROMISE, vow, give your word, swear, take an oath, commit, contract, engage, undertake, give an undertaking, vouch, guarantee, secure
2 GUARANTEE, mortgage
formal put up as collateral

plenary *adj*
full, complete, entire, open, absolute, unrestricted, whole, general, integral, unconditional, unlimited, unqualified, thorough, sweeping

plenipotentiary *n*
ambassador, envoy, minister, dignitary, emissary, legate, nuncio

plenitude *n*
abundance, plenty, plentifulness, profusion, fullness, completeness, copiousness, bounty, excess, wealth, cornucopia, entireness
formal amplitude, plenteousness, plethora, repletion
🔳 scarcity

plenteous *adj*
abundant, plentiful, bountiful, copious, fruitful, lavish, abounding, ample, generous, liberal, productive, fertile, profuse, prolific, overflowing, inexhaustible, infinite
formal bounteous, luxuriant
colloq. bumper
🔳 scarce, paltry

plentiful *adj*
ample, abundant, profuse, copious, production, overflowing, lavish, generous, liberal, bountiful, fruitful, productive, inexhaustible, infinite
formal bounteous
colloq. bumper
🔳 scarce, scanty, rare

plenty *n*
1 ABUNDANCE, profusion, copiousness, enough, fullness, sufficiency, quantity, mass, volume, fund, mine, store
formal plethora, plenteousness
2 AFFLUENCE, wealth, wealthiness, riches, fortune, substance, prosperity
🔳 **1** scarcity, lack, want **2** need
▷ **plenty of** many, large amount, large number, enough, more than enough, more than is needed;
colloq. lots, loads, masses, heaps, piles, stacks

plethora *n*
surfeit, surplus, excess, glut, overabundance, profusion, overfullness, superabundance
formal superfluity

pliability *n*
1 BENDABILITY, elasticity, flexibility, plasticity, ductility
2 ADAPTABILITY, amenability, susceptibility, malleability, suggestibility, impressionableness, docility
formal compliance, tractableness
🔳 **1,2** inflexibilty, rigidity

pliable *adj*
1 *pliable pieces of wood*
pliant, flexible, bendable, supple, lithe, malleable, elastic, plastic
colloq. bendy
2 *a pliable person*
yielding, adaptable, flexible, accommodating, manageable, docile, biddable, persuadable, responsive, receptive, impressionable, susceptible
formal tractable, compliant
🔳 **1** rigid, inflexible **2** headstrong

pliant *adj*
1 *pliant pieces of wood*
pliable, flexible, bendable, supple, lithe, malleable, elastic, plastic
colloq. bendy
2 *a pliant person*
yielding, adaptable, flexible, accommodating, manageable, docile, biddable, persuadable, responsive,

receptive, impressionable, susceptible
formal tractable, compliant
F∃ **1** rigid, inflexible **2** headstrong

plight¹ *n*
the plight of starving children
predicament, quandary, dilemma, extremity, trouble,
difficulty, difficult/distressing situation, straits, dire
straits, state, condition, situation, circumstances, case
colloq. jam, hole, tight spot, scrape, pickle

plight² *n*
plight your troth
promise, pledge, vow, swear, contract, covenant,
engage, guarantee, propose, vouch
old use affiance

plod *v*
1 TRUDGE, tramp, stump, clump, stomp, lumber,
walk heavily, plough through
2 DRUDGE, labour, toil, grind, slog, persevere, peg
away, plug away, soldier on

plodder *n*
drudge, dullard, toiler, slogger, mug, sap
F∃ high-flier

plot *n, v*
▶ *n* **1** CONSPIRACY, intrigue, scheme, plan, ruse,
stratagem, cabal
formal machination
2 STORY, narrative, action, subject, theme, storyline,
thread, outline, scenario
3 *plot of land*
patch, tract, area, allotment, lot, parcel
▶ *v* **1** CONSPIRE, intrigue, collude, connive, scheme,
hatch, lay, devise, contrive, plan, project, design, draft,
concoct, frame
formal machinate
colloq. cook up
2 CHART, map (out), mark, locate, draw, sketch,
calculate

plotter *n*
conspirator, intriguer, schemer, planner
formal machinator

plough *v*
cultivate, dig, till, work, ridge, spade, break, turn up,
furrow
▷ **plough into** crash into, drive into, smash into,
run/go into, hit, collide, bump into
▷ **plough through** plod through, move through
laboriously, trudge through, wade through

ploy *n*
manoeuvre, stratagem, tactic, move, device,
contrivance, scheme, game, trick, artifice, dodge, wile,
ruse, subterfuge

pluck *v, n*
▶ *v* **1** PULL, draw, tug, snatch, pull (off), remove,
extract, pick, collect, gather, take in, harvest
colloq. yank
2 *pluck a guitar*
pick, twang, strum, finger
▶ *n* courage, bravery, daring, boldness, spirit,
intrepidity, audacity, fearlessness, mettle, backbone,
resolution, determination
formal fortitude, valour
colloq. nerve, guts, grit
F∃ cowardice

plucky *adj*
brave, courageous, bold, daring, audacious, fearless,

intrepid, heroic, valiant, spirited, determined
colloq. gutsy, spunky, gritty
F∃ cowardly, weak, feeble

plug *n, v*
▶ *n* **1** STOPPER, bung, cork, seal, spigot
2 ADVERTISEMENT, publicity, commercial,
promotion, blurb, mention, puff, good word
colloq. hype, ad, push
3 *a plug of tobacco*
chew, wad, twist, cake
▶ *v* **1** STOP (UP), bung, cork, block, choke, close,
seal, fill, pack, stuff
colloq. hype, push
2 ADVERTISE, publicize, promote, market, tout,
mention
colloq. push
▷ **plug away** keep trying, preserve, plod on, slog
away, peg away, soldier on

plum *adj*
first-class, best, choice, prize, especially valued,
excellent
colloq. cushy

plumb *adv, v*
▶ *adv* **1** VERTICALLY, perpendicularly, sheer,
straight up, straight down, up and down
2 PRECISELY, right, exactly, dead
colloq. slap, bang, spot on
▶ *v* sound (out), fathom, measure, gauge, penetrate,
delve into, probe, search (out), examine, investigate,
explore
▷ **plumb the depths of** experience the worst
extremes of, hit the lowest point/level, reach rock
bottom

plumbing *n*

Plumbing materials and equipment include: auger,
back boiler, ballcock, ball valve, basin, basin
spanner, bath, bend, bidet, blowtorch, boiler, bowl,
ceiling joint, cistern, compression fitting, copper
pipe, copper tube, coupler, cylinder, draincock,
elbow joint, electric water heater, expansion (or
header) tank, *US* faucet, flare joint, float, flux, gas
water heater, gasket, gate valve, geyser, hose,
immersion heater, joint, jointing compound,
lavatory, lavatory chain, lever tap, lockshield valve,
mains pipe, mixer tap, monkey wrench, motorized
zone valve, nipple, nipple key, overflow bend, pan,
pedestal, pipe, pipe clip, pipe coupling, pipe wrench,
plug, plunger, programmer, P-trap, pump, radiator,
septic tank, shower, shower attachment, shower
head, sink, siphon washer, soil vent, solder, Stillson®
wrench, stopcock, sump pump, tank, tap, tee,
thermostat, thermostatic valve, toilet, trap, tube
cutter, tube flaring tool, U-bend, union, urinal,
washer, waste disposal unit, waste pipe, water closet,
WC, Y-branch.

plume *n*
feather, crest, pinion, quill, tuft, aigrette
technical pappus
▷ **plume yourself on** congratulate yourself, boast
about, pride yourself, preen yourself, exult in;
colloq. pat oneself on the back

plummet *v*
plunge, dive, nose-dive, descend, drop, fall, drop/fall
rapidly, decrease quickly, tumble, hurtle
F∃ soar

plump¹ *adj*
a plump person

fat, obese, dumpy, tubby, stout, round, well-rounded, portly, chubby, podgy, fleshy, full, ample, buxom
formal rotund, corpulent
colloq. well-upholstered, beefy, flabby, gross
F3 thin, skinny

plump² *v*
plump the sacks on the floor
put down, set down, deposit, drop, flop, sink, slump, collapse, descend, fall
colloq. dump
▷ **plump for** choose, select, prefer, opt for, back, side with, support, favour

plumpness *n*
fatness, fleshiness, chubbiness, stoutness, portliness, tubbiness, podginess, pudginess
formal corpulence, obesity, rotundity
F3 thinness, skinniness

plunder *v, n*
▶ *v* loot, pillage, ravage, lay waste, devastate, sack, raid, ransack, maraud, rifle, steal, rob, strip, fleece
formal despoil, depredate
▶ *n* loot, pillage, booty, spoils, pickings, ill-gotten gains, prize
slang swag
Related adjective: predatory

plunge *v, n*
▶ *v* **1** DIVE, jump, nose-dive, swoop, dive-bomb, plummet, descend, go down, sink, drop, fall, drop/fall rapidly, decrease quickly, throw, pitch, tumble, hurtle, career, charge, dash, rush, tear
2 THRUST, push, drive, stick, stab, shove, ram, jab
3 IMMERSE, submerge, dip, sink
▶ *n* dive, nose-dive, jump, swoop, descent, drop, fall, tumble, charge, rush, hurtle, immersion, submersion

plurality *n*
diversity, variety, number, numerousness, profusion, mass, bulk, majority, most
formal multiplicity, multitudinousness, preponderance
colloq. galaxy

plus *n, prep*
▶ *n* advantage, benefit, bonus, good point, asset, credit, gain, extra, surplus
colloq. perk
F3 disadvantage, drawback; *colloq.* minus
▶ *prep* and, with, together with, as well as, in addition to, over and above
colloq. not to mention
F3 minus

plush *adj*
luxurious, luxury, lavish, de luxe, palatial, stylish, affluent, sumptuous, costly, rich
formal opulent
colloq. ritzy, glitzy, posh, swanky

plutocrat *n*
rich man, capitalist, millionaire, tycoon, magnate, billionaire, multimillionaire, Dives, Croesus
colloq. fat cat, moneybags

ply¹ *v*
1 KEEP SUPPLYING, provide, supply, furnish, feed, lavish, assail, beset, bombard, harass, importune
2 TRAVEL, go, ferry, make regular journeys between/along
3 *ply a trade*
practise, carry on, follow, pursue, exercise, work at

4 *ply a tool*
use, employ, utilize, wield, handle, manipulate

ply² *n*
three-ply wool
thickness, strand, leaf, layer, sheet, fold

poach *v*
1 STEAL, pilfer, copy, take
formal appropriate
colloq. lift, borrow, nick
2 TRESPASS, encroach, infringe, intrude, catch/hunt illegally

pocket *n, adj, v*
▶ *n* **1** *a pocket on the back of the seat*
pouch, bag, envelope, receptacle, compartment, hollow, cavity
2 *the fees are a drain on my pocket*
resources, funds, means, money, finances, budget, assets, capital, wherewithal
3 *pocket of resistance/unemployment*
patch, small area, isolated area, small group
▶ *adj* small, little, concise, abridged, potted, compact, portable, miniature
colloq. mini, pint-size
▶ *v* take, gain, win unfairly, help yourself to, pilfer, filch, steal
formal appropriate, purloin
colloq. lift, nick, pinch

pockmark *n*
blemish, pock, pit, scar, pockpit

pod *n*
shell, husk, case, hull
technical legume

podgy *adj*
fat, chubby, paunchy, plump, fleshy, roly-poly, squat, chunky, dumpy, stout, tubby, stubby, stumpy
formal corpulent, rotund
F3 thin, skinny

podium *n*
dais, platform, stage, stand, rostrum

poem *n*

Types of poem include: ballad, bucolic, clerihew, couplet, ditty, eclogue, elegy, epic, epigram, epithalmium, epode, epopee, georgic, haiku, idyll, lay, limerick, lipogram, lyric, madrigal, monody, nursery rhyme, ode, palinode, pastoral, prothalamion, rhyme, rondeau, roundelay, song, sonnet, tanka, triolet, verse, verselet, versicle. *See also* song.

poet *n*
versifier, verse-maker, rhymer, rhymester, rhymist, lyricist, idyllist, sonneteer, balladeer, elegist, bard, minstrel, poetaster, poeticule

poetic *adj*
poetical, lyrical, moving, artistic, graceful, flowing, expressive, sensitive, beautiful, creative, imaginative, metrical, rhythmical, rhyming, prosaic, figurative, symbolic

poetry *n*
verse, lyrics, rhyme, rhyming, versing, poems, poesy, free verse, versification, vers libre, pennill, iambics, muse, Parnassus

pogrom *n*
slaughter, murder, homicide, extermination, carnage,

butchery, wholesale slaughter, indiscriminate killing, holocaust, bloodbath, annihilation, killing, genocide, ethnic cleansing, liquidation, decimation

poignancy *n*
pathos, feeling, sentiment, emotion, evocativeness, intensity, keenness, painfulness, piquancy, tenderness, piteousness, sharpness, pungency, sadness, pain, distress, tragedy, misery, wretchedness, bitterness

poignant *adj*
moving, touching, affecting, emotional, tender, distressing, tragic, upsetting, heartbreaking, heart-rending, heartfelt, piteous, pathetic, sorrowful, sad, tearful, painful, agonizing, miserable, wretched

point *n, v*
▶ *n* **1** *the main points of the argument*
issue, matter, subject, topic, question, item
2 FEATURE, attribute, quality, aspect, characteristic, trait, property, facet, detail, particular, item, subject, topic
3 *What's the point?*
use, sense, purpose, motive, reason, object, objective, intention, aim, end, goal, objective
4 ESSENCE, main point, crux, core, central point, heart, heart of the matter, pith, gist, nub, meat, marrow, thrust, meaning, significance, importance, theme, vein, tenor, drift, burden, keynote
5 PLACE, position, situation, location, locality, area, site, spot
6 MOMENT, instant, juncture, stage, time, period, position
7 DOT, spot, mark, speck, full stop, stop, full point, period, decimal point
8 *the point of a needle*
sharp end, end, extremity, tip, top, taper, spike, tine, nib
9 HEADLAND, head, foreland, promontory, cape, ness
10 MARK, score, goals, runs, hits, total
▷ **beside the point** irrelevant, immaterial, unrelated, unconnected, out of place; *colloq.* neither here nor there
▷ **in point of fact** actually, in fact, as a matter of fact, in reality, really
▷ **on the point of** on the verge of, about to, going to, ready to, preparing to
▷ **point of view 1** OPINION, view, belief, judgement, attitude, feeling, sentiment, position, standpoint, viewpoint **2** PERSPECTIVE, outlook, approach, angle, slant, aspect
▷ **to the point** relevant, related, connected, germane, applicable, appropriate; *formal* apposite, pertinent
▷ **up to a point** partly, somewhat, to some extent/degree, slightly
▶ *v* **1** *point a gun*
aim, direct, train, level
2 INDICATE, signal, gesture at/towards, show, signify, designate, suggest
formal denote, evidence
▷ **point out** show, indicate, draw/call attention to, point to, reveal, identify, specify, mention, bring up, allude to, remind
▷ **point up** emphasize, stress, underline, highlight, call attention to

point-blank *adv, adj*
▶ *adv* outright, directly, forthrightly, straightforwardly, straight, plainly, explicitly, openly, bluntly, frankly, candidly, rudely, abruptly,

unequivocally
▶ *adj* **1** OUTRIGHT, direct, forthright, straightforward, plain, explicit, open, unreserved, blunt, frank, candid
2 AT CLOSE RANGE, closely, close to, near, touching

pointed *adj*
1 SHARP, keen, edged, tapering, barbed
technical acicular, cuspidate(d)
formal aculeate(d), fastigiate, lanceolate(d), mucronate(d)
2 *a pointed comment*
cutting, incisive, biting, forceful, penetrating, telling, striking, clear, obvious
formal trenchant

pointer *n*
1 ARROW, indicator, needle, hand
2 TIP, recommendation, suggestion, sign, hint, guide, guideline, clue, indication, indicator, advice, piece of advice, warning, caution
3 STICK, rod, cane, pole

pointless *adj*
useless, futile, vain, fruitless, unproductive, unprofitable, worthless, senseless, valueless, absurd, ridiculous, nonsensical, foolish, inane, meaningless, insignificant, a waste of time/effort, aimless, to no avail, unavailing
colloq. a mug's game
F3 useful, profitable, meaningful

poise *n, v*
▶ *n* calmness, composure, self-control, self-possession, presence of mind, assurance, self-assurance, dignity, elegance, grace, serenity, balance, equilibrium
formal equanimity, aplomb
colloq. cool, coolness
▶ *v* balance, position, steady, hover, hang, suspend, support

poised *adj*
1 DIGNIFIED, graceful, calm, composed, collected, self-possessed, self-controlled, self-confident, assured, serene, suave, urbane
colloq. cool, cool calm and collected, unruffled, unflappable
2 *poised for action*
prepared, ready, set, all set, waiting, expectant

poison *n, v*
▶ *n* **1** *poison such as arsenic*
toxin, venom
2 *a poison spreading through society*
bane, blight, cancer, malignancy, contagion, pollution, contamination, corruption, canker
▶ *v* kill by poison, infect, contaminate, pollute, taint, adulterate, corrupt, deprave, defile, pervert, warp, spoil, blight

poisonous *adj*
1 TOXIC, venomous, lethal, deadly, fatal, mortal
2 HARMFUL, noxious, pernicious, malicious, vicious, spiteful, virulent, malignant, contaminating, corrupting, cancerous, cankerous

Poisonous plants include: aconite, amanita, anemone, banewort, belladonna, black nightshade, castor oil plant, common nightshade, cowbane, cuckoo pint, deadly nightshade, digitalis, dwale, foxglove, giant hogweed, helmet flower, hemlock, hemlock water dropwort, Jimsonweed, laburnum, lantana, lords-and-ladies, meadow saffron, monkshood, naked boys, naked lady, oleander, poison ivy, stinkweed, stramonium, thorn apple, wake-robin, wild arum, windflower, wolfsbane. *See also* **mushrooms and toadstools.**

poke *v, n*
▶ *v* prod, stab, jab, stick, thrust, push, shove, nudge, elbow, dig, butt, hit, punch
▷ **poke around** grope around, search for, look (all over) for, rummage around, rake through
▷ **poke fun at** ridicule, mock, jeer, make fun of, tease, parody
colloq. rag, rib, send up, spoof, take the mickey
▷ **poke out** stick out, jut out, protrude, project, overhang, extend, beetle, extrude
▷ **poke your nose into** meddle in, interfere in, tamper with, pry in; *colloq.* put/stick your oar in, butt in
▶ *n* prod, jab, thrust, shove, nudge, dig, butt, punch

poky *adj*
confined, cramped, small, tight, tiny, narrow, crowded
formal incommodious
F∃ spacious, roomy

polar *adj*
1 COLD, freezing, frozen, icy, glacial, arctic, Siberian
2 OPPOSITE, completely/utterly different, diametrically opposed, conflicting, ambivalent, contradictory
formal antithetical, dichotomous

polarity *n*
opposition, oppositeness, contradiction, ambivalence, contrariety, duality, paradox
formal antithesis, dichotomy

pole[1] *n*
a telegraph pole
bar, rod, stick, shaft, spar, upright, pillar, support, post, stake, mast, staff

pole[2] *n*
views that represent opposite poles
extremity, extreme, limit
▷ **poles apart** completely different, incompatible, irreconcilable, worlds apart; *colloq.* like chalk and cheese

polemic *n, adj*
▶ *n* argument, controversy, debate, dispute
▶ *adj* argumentative, contentious, controversial, polemical
formal disputatious, eristic(al)

polemicist *n*
debater, controversialist, arguer, contender, disputer, disputant, polemist
formal logomachist

polemics *n*
debate, dispute, argument, controversy, contention, argumentation
formal disputation, logomachy

police *n, v*
▶ *n* police force, constabulary
colloq. the Law, the Force, cops; *slang* the Bill, the fuzz, rozzers, pigs
▶ *v* 1 PATROL, guard, protect, defend, keep watch, keep the peace
2 CHECK, control, keep under control, regulate, monitor, watch, observe, supervise, oversee

police officer *n*
officer, policeman, policewoman, constable, PC
colloq. the Law, cop, copper, bobby, rozzer, boys in blue, the (old) Bill; *slang* pig, nark, the fuzz, flatfoot, bluebottle, bull

policy *n*
1 CODE OF PRACTICE, rules, guidelines, procedure, method, system, practice, custom, protocol
2 COURSE OF ACTION, line, course, plan, programme, scheme, schedule, stance, position, approach

polish *v, n*
▶ *v* 1 SHINE, brighten, smooth, rub (up), buff, burnish, furbish, clean, wax
2 IMPROVE, enhance, brush up, touch up, finish, perfect, refine, cultivate
F∃ 1 tarnish, dull
▷ **polish off** 1 EAT UP, consume, devour, put away, bolt, gobble, finish, complete, dispose of, down, stuff; *colloq.* wolf 2 MURDER, kill, eliminate; *colloq.* bump off, liquidate, rub out
▶ *n* 1 *a tin of polish*
wax, varnish
2 SHINE, gloss, sheen, lustre, brightness, brilliance, sparkle, smoothness, finish, glaze, veneer, burnish
3 REFINEMENT, cultivation, class, breeding, sophistication, finesse, style, elegance, grace, poise
F∃ 2 dullness 3 clumsiness

polished *adj*
1 SHINING, shiny, waxed, burnished, glossy, lustrous, gleaming, smooth, glassy, slippery
2 FAULTLESS, flawless, impeccable, perfect, outstanding, superlative, remarkable, excellent, masterly, expert, professional, skilful, accomplished, proficient, adept, perfected
formal consummate
3 REFINED, cultivated, genteel, well-bred, well-mannered, polite, sophisticated, civilized, urbane, suave, elegant, graceful
F∃ 1 tarnished 2 inexpert 3 gauche

polite *adj*
1 COURTEOUS, well-mannered, respectful, civil, well-bred, well-behaved, deferential, refined, cultured, gentlemanly, ladylike, gallant, chivalrous, gracious, obliging, thoughtful, considerate, tactful, diplomatic
2 *in polite society*
refined, cultured, genteel, well-bred, well-mannered, polite, sophisticated, civilized, urbane, suave, elegant
F∃ 1 impolite, rude, discourteous

politeness *n*
courtesy, manners, good manners, deference, cordiality, gentility, mannerliness, polish, refinement, elegance, courtliness, culture, thoughtfulness, cultivation, civility, considerateness, graciousness, grace, gentlemanliness, respect, respectfulness, diplomacy, tact, discretion, attention
formal complaisance
F∃ impoliteness, rudeness, discourtesy

politic *adj*
wise, prudent, shrewd, sensible, tactful, diplomatic, advisable, advantageous, opportune, expedient
formal judicious, sagacious, sage
F∃ impolitic

⚠ **politic** or **political** ?
Politic is a rather formal word meaning 'wise, sensible': *He considered it politic to leave before there*

was any further trouble. Political means 'relating to politics': *the political system of the USA; party political broadcasts.*

political *adj*

governmental, parliamentary, constitutional, ministerial, administrative, executive, bureaucratic, civil, public, judicial, party political

⚠ **political** or **politic** ? *See panel at* **politic**.

political ideology

Political ideologies include: absolutism, anarchism, authoritarianism, Bolshevism, Christian democracy, collectivism, communism, conservatism, democracy, egalitarianism, fascism, federalism, holism, imperialism, individualism, liberalism, Maoism, Marxism, nationalism, Nazism, neocolonialism, neo-fascism, neo-nazism, pluralism, republicanism, social democracy, socialism, syndicalism, Thatcherism, theocracy, totalitarianism, Trotskyism, unilateralism, Whiggism.

politics *n*

1 *go into politics*
public affairs, civics, affairs of state, statecraft, government, national government, regional government, local government, diplomacy, statesmanship, political science, party politics, political views/beliefs
2 *office politics*
power struggle, power game, power politics, manipulation, manoeuvring
formal machination(s)
colloq. wheeler-dealing

Terms used in politics include: alliance, apartheid, ballot, bill, blockade, cabinet, campaign, civil service, coalition, constitution, council, *coup d'état*, détente, election, electoral register, ethnic cleansing, general election, glasnost, go to the country, government, green paper, Hansard, judiciary, left wing, lobby, local government, majority, mandate, manifesto, nationalization, parliament, party, party line, perestroika, prime minister's question time, privatization, propaganda, proportional representation, rainbow coalition, referendum, right wing, sanction, shadow cabinet, sovereignty, state, summit, summit conference, term of office, trade union, veto, vote, welfare state, whip, three-line whip, white paper.

People in politics include: activist, ambassador, Black Rod, capitalist, Communist, *colloq.* commie, comrade, Conservative, Democrat, Deputy Speaker, dictator, dissident, *colloq.* dry, extremist, Green, high commissioner, independent, law-maker, *colloq.* lefty, legislator, Liberal, Liberal Democrat, loyalist, Marxist, Marxist-Leninist, member of parliament, minister, moderate, MP, party chairman, party member, party worker, *colloq.* pinko, politician, premier, president, prime minister, radical, *colloq.* red, Republican, revolutionary, secretary of state, Social Democrat, Socialist, speaker, statesman, stateswoman, Tory, Trotskyite, true-blue, *colloq.* wet, Whig.

Political parties include: Alliance, Communist, Conservative and Unionist, Co-operative, Democratic, Democratic Left, Democratic Unionist, Fianna Fáil, Fine Gael, Green, Labour, Liberal, Liberal Democratic, Militant Labour, National

Front, Parliamentary, Parliamentary Labour, Plaid Cymru, Progressive Democrats, Republican, Scottish Conservative and Unionist, Scottish Liberal Democratic, Scottish National, Sinn Féin, Social and Liberal Democratic, Social Democratic and Labour, Ulster Democratic Unionist, Ulster Popular Unionist, Ulster Unionist, Welsh Liberal Democratic. *See also* **government systems, parliaments and assemblies, political ideology**.

poll *n, v*

▶ *n* ballot, ballot-box, vote, voting, plebiscite, referendum, straw poll, straw vote, head count, show of hands, sampling, canvass, opinion poll, market research, Gallup poll, survey, returns, census, count, tally
▶ *v* **1** WIN, net, get, receive, return, gain, obtain
2 BALLOT, survey, canvass, sample, question, interview, solicit, electioneer, campaign
3 CLIP, cut, trim, shear, pollard, dod, dishorn

pollute *v*

contaminate, infect, poison, taint, adulterate, debase, corrupt, dirty, make dirty, foul, befoul, soil, defile, deprave, warp, sully, stain, tarnish, blacken, mar, spoil
formal vitiate

pollution *n*

impurity, contamination, infection, taint, adulteration, corruption, dirtiness, filthiness, foulness, fouling, defilement, debasement, depravity, sullying, staining, tarnishing, blackening
colloq. muckiness
F3 purification, purity, cleanness

polychromatic *adj*

multicoloured, many-coloured, kaleidoscopic, many-hued, mottled, motley, rainbow, variegated, varicoloured, polychrome, parti-coloured
technical poikilitic
F3 monochromatic, monochrome, black and white

polyglot *adj, n*

▶ *adj* multilingual, cosmopolitan, international, multiracial
formal polyglottal, polyglottic
F3 monoglot
▶ *n* linguist, multilinguist

polymath *n*

all-rounder, oracle, mine of information
formal pansophist, polyhistor
colloq. know-all, walking encyclopaedia
F3 ignoramus

pomp *n*

ceremony, ceremonial, ritual, solemnity, formality, ceremoniousness, state, grandeur, splendour, magnificence, pageantry, show, display, parade, spectacle, ostentation, flourish, brilliance, glory, majesty
colloq. glitter
F3 austerity, simplicity

pomposity *n*

1 VANITY, arrogance, self-importance, pride, haughtiness, presumption, pretension, pretentiousness, imperiousness, superciliousness, condescension, airs
formal affectation
2 BOMBAST, turgidity, rhetoric, stuffiness, preachiness
formal euphuism, fustian, grandiloquence,

magniloquence
F3 1 modesty **2** simplicity, economy

pompous *adj*
1 SELF-IMPORTANT, arrogant, proud, haughty, conceited, vain, presumptuous, grandiose, supercilious, patronizing, condescending, overbearing, imperious, magisterial, pretentious, ostentatious
formal affected
colloq. snooty
2 *pompous language*
elaborate, grant, bombastic, high-flown, overblown, windy, stilted, flowery, ostentatious, turgid, stuffy
formal euphuistic, magniloquent
colloq. preachy, la-di-da
F3 1 unassuming, modest, unaffected **2** simple

pond *n*
pool, puddle, pond, lake, mere, tarn, watering-hole, waterhole

ponder *v*
deliberate, give thought to, reflect, reason, think, contemplate, meditate, consider, brood, examine, analyse, study, ruminate over, weigh, muse, puzzle over, mull over
formal cerebrate, cogitate, excogitate, ratiocinate

ponderous *adj*
1 *ponderous writing*
dull, serious, dreary, tedious, stilted, long-winded, plodding, verbose, laborious, pedantic, pedestrian, stodgy, stolid, humourless, laboured, lifeless
formal prolix
2 CLUMSY, unwieldy, awkward, cumbersome, graceless, heavy, bulky, weighty, heavy-handed, heavy-footed, huge, massive, hefty, slow-moving, lumbering, elephantine
F3 1 light, simple **2** delicate

ponderousness *n*
seriousness, tedium, heaviness, laboriousness, stodginess, stolidity, weightiness, humourlessness, gravitas
F3 delicacy, lightness, subtlety

pontifical *adj*
1 PAPAL, apostolic, ecclesiastical, prelatic
2 SELF-IMPORTANT, pompous, overbearing, condescending, imperious, pretentious, magisterial, dogmatic, didactic, portentous, sermonizing
colloq. preachy
F3 2 reticent, unassuming

pontificate *v*
preach, hold forth, lecture, expound, pronounce, sermonize, sound off, harangue, dogmatize, moralize
formal declaim, perorate
colloq. lay down the law

pony *n*
See panel at **horse.**

pooh-pooh *v*
dismiss, scorn, make little of, belittle, brush aside, ridicule, disdain, disregard, slight, sneer, sniff at, scoff, spurn, reject, play down, minimize
formal deride, disparage
colloq. turn up your nose at
F3 exaggerate, magnify

pool¹ *n*
a pool of water
puddle, pond, lake, mere, tarn, watering-hole,

waterhole, paddling-pool, swimming-pool, swimming-bath(s)

pool² *n, v*
▶ *n* **1** FUND, reserve, supply, accumulation, bank, kitty, purse, pot, jackpot, ante
2 SYNDICATE, cartel, ring, combine, consortium, collective, group, team
▶ *v* share, merge, combine, amalgamate, contribute
colloq. chip in, muck in

poor *adj*
1 IMPOVERISHED, poverty-stricken, badly off, in need, hard-up, bankrupt, penniless, without means, without the wherewithal, destitute, deprived, underprivileged, disadvantaged, reduced, humble, lowly, mean, miserable, wretched, distressed, straitened, needy
formal penurious, impecunious, exiguous, indigent
colloq. broke, stony-broke, skint, on your uppers, on your beam ends, not having two pennies to rub together, not having a penny to your name, on the breadline, poor as a church mouse
2 BAD, substandard, unsatisfactory, inferior, mediocre, below standard, below par, low, low-quality, low-grade, second-rate, third-rate, shoddy, imperfect, defective, faulty, jerry, weak, feeble, sorry, worthless, fruitless, unproductive, barren
colloq. pathetic, rubbish, ropy, rotten, measly, crummy; *slang* naff
3 LACKING, deficient, inadequate, insufficient, scanty, skimpy, meagre, sparse, paltry, depleted, exhausted
4 UNFORTUNATE, unlucky, luckless, ill-fated, ill-starred, unhappy, miserable, wretched, sorry, sad, spiritless, pathetic, pitiable, pitiful
formal hapless
F3 1 rich, wealthy, affluent **2** good, superior, impressive **3** sufficient, ample **4** fortunate, lucky

poorly *adj, adv*
▶ *adj* ill, sick, unwell, indisposed, ailing, sickly, off colour, below par, seedy, groggy
colloq. out of sorts, under the weather, rotten
F3 well, healthy
▶ *adv* badly, inadequately, unsatisfactorily, unsuccessfully, faultily, incompetently, inexpertly, insufficiently, inferiorly, rottenly, shabbily, shoddily, meanly, feebly
F3 well

pop *v, n*
▶ *v* **1** BURST, explode, go off, bang, crack, snap
2 RUSH, dash, hurry, go quickly, leave quickly, go for a short time
colloq. nip
3 PUT, push, insert, slide, slip, thrust, drop, shove
▷ **pop off** die, pass away, pass on; *colloq.* peg out, have had it; *slang* snuff it, kick the bucket
▷ **pop up** appear, occur, materialize, crop up, turn up, show up, come along
▶ *n* **1** BANG, crack, snap, burst, explosion, boom
formal report
2 FIZZY DRINK, fizzy lemonade, cola, soda

pope *n*
pontiff, sovereign pontiff, Bishop of Rome, Holy Father, Vicar of Christ, His Holiness
Related adjectives: papal, pontifical

popinjay *n*
dandy, fop, beau, coxcomb, peacock, pansy, swell, dude

colloq. toff
☷ he-man, macho

poppycock *n*
nonsense, rubbish, trash, drivel, balderdash,
gibberish, gobbledygook, stupidity, silliness,
foolishness, folly, blather, twaddle
colloq. stuff and nonsense, bunk, rot, claptrap,
cobblers, piffle, waffle, flannel, rot, tripe, tosh, bosh,
tommy-rot, codswallop, baloney, humbug, hooey,
bilge, bull; *slang* crap, shit, balls, bullshit
☷ sense

populace *n*
inhabitants, natives, residents, citizens, occupants,
community, society, people, folk, general public,
crowd, masses, proletariat, public, mob, multitude(s),
common herd, canaille, hoi polloi
colloq. plebs, punters, rabble, rank and file
☷ aristocracy, élite, nobility

popular *adj*
1 WELL-LIKED, favourite, liked, favoured, in favour,
admired, wanted, desired, approved, in demand,
sought-after, fashionable, modish
colloq. trendy, in, hip, cool, big, all the rage
2 FAMOUS, well-known, celebrated, renowned,
acclaimed, noted, idolized
3 PREVAILING, current, accepted, usual, customary,
conventional, standard, stock, common, prevalent,
widespread, universal, general, generally recognized,
household
4 *a popular history of science*
general, non-specialist, non-technical,
understandable, accessible, simple, simplified,
ordinary, mass-market
☷ **1** unpopular, disliked, out of favour **2** unheard
of, obscure, unknown **3** rare, unusual **4** specialist,
technical, expert, professional

popularity *n*
approval, acceptance, recognition, reputation, favour,
vogue, kudos, mass appeal, regard, fame, renown,
currency, repute, acclaim, adoration, adulation, glory,
worship, idolization, lionization
formal approbation, esteem
☷ unpopularity

popularize *v*
spread, propagate, familiarize, universalize,
democratize, generalize, give currency to, simplify,
make understandable, make accessible

popularly *adv*
commonly, widely, universally, generally, usually,
customarily, ordinarily, regularly, conventionally,
traditionally

populate *v*
people, occupy, settle, colonize, inhabit, live in,
overrun
formal dwell

population *n*
inhabitants, natives, residents, citizens, occupants,
community, society, people, folk
formal populace

populous *adj*
crowded, packed, swarming, teeming,
crawling, densely populated, overpopulated,
overpeopled
☷ deserted, empty

porcelain *n*

Types of porcelain include: biscuit, bisque, blue and
white, bone china, Canton, Capodimonte,
chinoiserie, Compagnie des Indes, copper red,
eggshell, faience, famille-rose, famille-verte, First
Period Worcester, hard paste, Imari, Kakiemon,
Kraak, nankeen, Parian, saltglazed, soapstone paste,
soft paste, Yingqing.

Famous makes of porcelain include: Arita, Belleek,
Bow, Bristol, Caughley, Chantilly, Chelsea, Coalport,
Copeland, Derby, Dresden, Limoges, Meissen,
Ming, Minton, Nanking, Rockingham, Royal
Doulton, Royal Worcester, Satsuma, Sèvres, Vienna,
Wedgwood, Worcester.

porch *n*
vestibule, hall, hallway, entrance-hall, lobby, foyer

pore¹ *v*
▷ **pore over** *pore over a book* study, study intensely,
examine, examine closely, scrutinize, go over, read,
scan, contemplate, ponder, dwell on, brood
formal peruse

pore² *n*
sweating from every pore
hole, opening, perforation, aperture, outlet, vent
technical foramen
formal orifice

pornographic *adj*
obscene, indecent, dirty, filthy, blue, risqué, off-colour,
bawdy, coarse, gross, lewd, salacious, erotic, titillating
formal prurient
colloq. porn

pornography *n*
indecency, obscenity, filth, dirt, smut, erotica,
grossness, bawdiness, facetiae
colloq. porn, porno, sexploitation, girlie magazines

porous *adj*
permeable, pervious, penetrable, absorbent, spongy,
spongelike, honeycombed, cellular, holey, open, airy
technical foraminous, foveate
☷ impermeable, impervious

port *n*
seaport, harbour, jetty, dock, anchorage, harbourage,
haven, roads, roadstead, hithe

portable *adj*
movable, transportable, compact, lightweight,
manageable, conveyable, handy, convenient
☷ fixed, immovable

portend *v*
indicate, point to, be a sign of, be an indication of, warn
of, announce, forecast, predict, foretell, promise,
signify, threaten, herald
formal augur, bode, forebode, foreshadow, forewarn,
harbinger, bespeak, betoken, foretoken, prognosticate,
adumbrate, presage

portent *n*
sign, indication, warning, threat, omen, precursor,
forecast, foreboding, forerunner, prefiguration,
premonition
formal augury, signification, prognostication,
foreshadowing, forewarning, prognostic, presage,
presentiment, prodrome, harbinger

portentous *adj*
1 FOREBODING, ominous, sinister, menacing, threatening, momentous, fateful
2 REMARKABLE, significant, important, amazing, astounding, extraordinary, awe-inspiring, earth-shaking, epoch-making, miraculous, crucial
3 POMPOUS, ponderous, solemn, weighty, self-important, pontifical
E3 2 insignificant, unimportant, unimpressive

porter¹ *n*
a porter at a hotel
bearer, carrier, baggage-attendant, baggage-handler, baggage-carrier

porter² *n*
a porter at a college
doorman, commissionaire, door-keeper, gatekeeper, door attendant, janitor, caretaker, concierge

portion *n, v*
▶ *n* **1** SHARE, allocation, tranche, allotment, parcel, quantity, allowance, ration, quota, measure, part, section, division, fraction, percentage, bit, fragment, morsel, piece, segment, slice, wedge, serving, helping
colloq. cut, whack, rake-off
2 DESTINY, fate, lot, kismet, fortune, luck, chance
▶ *v* distribute, divide, deal, share out, allocate, allot, apportion, assign, slice up, parcel, partition
colloq. carve up, dole out

portliness *n*
ampleness, stoutness, roundness, plumpness, fatness, paunchiness, obesity, heaviness, fullness, dumpiness, tubbiness, chubbiness, fleshiness
formal corpulence, rotundity
colloq. beefiness

portly *adj*
stout, round, fat, plump, obese, overweight, stocky, ample, heavy, large
formal corpulent, rotund
E3 slim, thin, slight

portrait *n*
picture, painting, drawing, sketch, caricature, miniature, icon, photograph, likeness, image, representation, vignette, profile, study, thumbnail sketch, characterization, description, depiction, portrayal, story, account

portray *v*
1 DRAW, sketch, paint, illustrate, picture, represent
2 DESCRIBE, depict, picture, represent, characterize, illustrate, evoke
3 PLAY, act, play/act the part of, perform, impersonate, characterize, personify

portrayal *n*
representation, characterization, depiction, description, picture, painting, drawing, sketch, study, evocation, presentation, acting, performance, interpretation, rendering
formal delineation

pose *v, n*
▶ *v* **1** MODEL, sit, position, arrange
2 PRETEND, feign, act, put on an act, put on airs, masquerade, pass yourself off, impersonate, attitudinize
formal affect
3 *pose a question*
put forward, ask, submit, suggest, propose, put, set, advance
formal posit, postulate, propound

4 *pose a problem/threat*
create, present, cause, produce, give rise to, lead to, result in
▶ *n* **1** POSITION, stance, air, posture, attitude
formal bearing, carriage, deportment
2 PRETENCE, sham, façade, front, masquerade, airs, role, act, pretence
formal affectation

poser¹ *n*
he's a poser
poseur, poseuse, posturer, attitudinizer, exhibitionist, show-off, play-actor, charlatan, sham, impostor
colloq. pseud, phoney

poser² *n*
this is a poser
puzzle, riddle, conundrum, brainteaser, mystery, enigma, problem, dilemma, vexed question

poseur *n*
poser, poseuse, posturer, attitudinizer, exhibitionist, show-off, play-actor, charlatan, sham, impostor
colloq. pseud, phoney

posh *adj*
smart, stylish, fancy, fashionable, elegant, high-class, upper-class, grand, luxurious, lavish, sumptuous, luxury, de-luxe, rich, up-market, exclusive, select
formal opulent
colloq. la-di-da, swanky, classy, swish, plush
E3 inferior, cheap

posit *v*
put forward, pose, advance, state, submit, assert, assume, presume
formal postulate, predicate, propound

position *n, v*
▶ *n* **1** PLACE, situation, location, site, spot, scene, setting, area, locality, whereabouts, point
2 POSTURE, stance, pose, attitude, arrangement, disposition
formal bearing
3 JOB, post, occupation, employment, situation, appointment, office, duty, function, role, capacity
4 RANK, grade, level, place, status, standing, ranking, influence, prestige
5 SITUATION, state, condition, state of affairs, circumstances, case, factor(s), background, plight, predicament
6 OPINION, point of view, belief, view, outlook, viewpoint, attitude, stance, standpoint, stand
▶ *v* put, place, set, settle, fix, stand, arrange, dispose, lay out, deploy, station, locate, situate, site, install, establish
formal array

positive *adj*
1 SURE, certain, convinced, confident, assured
2 OPTIMISTIC, hopeful, confident, encouraged, cheerful, promising, encouraging
colloq. upbeat
3 *positive criticism*
helpful, constructive, practical, useful, productive
4 DEFINITE, decisive, conclusive, real, actual, concrete, clear, clear-cut, unmistakable, explicit, precise, unequivocal, express, direct, firm, emphatic, categorical, undeniable, indisputable, incontestable, incontrovertible
formal irrefutable
5 ABSOLUTE, utter, sheer, complete, rank, perfect, unmitigated, outright, out-and-out, thorough, veritable

formal consummate
F3 1 uncertain **2, 3** negative **4** indefinite, vague

positively *adv*
absolutely, definitely, categorically, firmly, finally,
decisively, emphatically, expressly, conclusively,
certainly, assuredly, surely, unmistakably,
unquestionably, incontestably, incontrovertibly,
indisputably, unequivocally, undeniably,
uncompromisingly

possess *v*
1 OWN, have, hold, be in possession of, acquire, gain,
get, enjoy, be endowed with, be gifted with
2 SEIZE, take, obtain, acquire, take over, take
possession of, get, occupy
3 INFLUENCE, control, dominate, bewitch, haunt,
enchant, infatuate, obsess

possessed *adj*
dominated, controlled, mesmerized, enchanted,
berserk, bedevilled, bewitched, haunted, cursed, hag-
ridden, frenzied, demented, crazed, maddened,
raving, consumed, infatuated, obsessed, besotted

possession *n*
OWNERSHIP, title, tenure, occupation, holding,
tenancy, custody, proprietorship, control, hold, grip

possessions *n*
lose your possessions
belongings, property, baggage, luggage,
paraphernalia, effects, goods, chattels, goods and
chattels, movables, assets, estate, wealth, riches
formal accoutrements
colloq. things, stuff, gear, (all your) worldly wealth

possessive *adj*
selfish, clinging, overprotective, domineering,
dominating, controlling, jealous, covetous, acquisitive,
grasping, greedy
F3 unselfish, sharing

possibility *n*
1 LIKELIHOOD, probability, odds, chance, risk,
danger, hazard, hope, prospect, potentiality,
conceivability, practicability, feasibility, attainability
2 *a place with possibilities*
promise, potential, prospects, advantages, capabilities,
expectations, talent
formal potentiality
3 OPTION, alternative, choice, preference, recourse
F3 1 impossibility, impracticability
2 disadvantages, liabilities

possible *adj*
likely, probable, promising, potential, imaginable,
conceivable, practicable, feasible, that can be done,
viable, tenable, credible, workable, achievable,
attainable, doable, accomplishable, realizable
colloq. on the cards, odds-on
F3 impossible, unthinkable, impracticable,
unattainable

possibly *adv*
perhaps, maybe, conceivably, by any means, at all, by
any chance
formal peradventure
colloq. hopefully

post¹ *n, v*
▶ *n a fence post*
pole, stake, picket, pale, pillar, column, shaft,
standard, support, prop, baluster, banister, palisade,
upright, newel, stanchion, strut, leg

▶ *v* **1** DISPLAY, stick up, pin (up), put up, attach, affix
2 ANNOUNCE, advertise, publicize, make known,
circulate, report, publish, broadcast

post² *n, v*
▶ *n a teaching post*
office, job, employment, position, situation, place,
vacancy, appointment, assignment, station, beat
▶ *v* station, locate, situate, position, place, put,
appoint, assign, second, transfer, move, send

post³ *n, v*
▶ *n deliver the post*
1 MAIL, letters, correspondence, communications,
packages, parcels, packets, delivery, registered mail,
recorded mail, special delivery, direct mail, airmail,
surface mail, international mail, electronic mail, e-
mail
colloq. junk mail, snail mail
2 POSTAL SERVICE, postal system, mail, Post Office
▶ *v* mail, send, dispatch, transmit, forward
▷ **keep someone posted** inform, keep up to date,
give the latest information; *colloq.* fill in, keep in the
picture

poster *n*
notice, bill, sign, placard, sticker, advertisement,
bulletin, announcement
colloq. ad, advert

posterior *adj, n*
▶ *adj* rear, rearward, behind, back, hind, hinder,
after, ensuing, following, subsequent, succeeding,
later, latter
technical dorsal, posticous
F3 anterior, front, previous
▶ *n* bottom, rear, behind, buttocks, rump, seat,
haunches, hinder end, hindquarters
colloq. backside, bum; *US* butt, tail, ass; *slang* arse
Related adjective: pygal

posterity *n*
descendants, successors, future generations, heirs,
offspring, seed, children
formal progeny, issue

posthaste *adv*
quickly, speedily, straightaway, immediately, at once,
directly, promptly, hastily, swiftly, with all speed
colloq. double-quick, full tilt, pronto
F3 eventually, gradually, slowly

postman, postwoman *n*
delivery officer, letter-carrier, mail-carrier, mail
handler, postal worker
US mailman
colloq. postie

post-mortem *n*
autopsy, dissection, necropsy, analysis, examination,
review

postpone *v*
put off, defer, put back, do later, hold over, delay,
adjourn, suspend, reschedule, shelve, pigeonhole,
freeze
formal prorogue, procrastinate
colloq. put on ice, put on the back burner, take a
raincheck on
F3 advance, forward, bring forward

postponed *adj*
put off, adjourned, deferred, shelved, suspended,
pigeonholed, frozen
formal in abeyance

colloq. on ice, on the back burner
E3 advanced

postponement *n*
adjournment, put-off, deferment, delay, deferral,
moratorium, freeze, suspension, stay, respite
formal prorogation

postscript *n*
addition, supplement, afterthought, addendum,
appendix, afterword, epilogue
technical codicil
colloq. PS
E3 introduction, prologue

postulate *v*
theorize, suppose, assume, presume, presuppose,
propose, advance, lay down, stipulate
formal hypothesize, posit

posture *n, v*
▶ *n* **1** POSITION, stance, pose, attitude, disposition
formal bearing, carriage, deportment
2 ATTITUDE, opinion, point of view, belief, view,
outlook, viewpoint, stance, standpoint, stand
▶ *v* pose, put on airs, show off, strike attitudes,
attitudinize, strut
formal affect

posy *n*
bouquet, spray, buttonhole, nosegay, corsage

pot *n*
1 RECEPTACLE, vessel, teapot, coffee pot, urn, jar,
vase, bowl, basin, pan, cauldron, crucible
2 KITTY, purse, fund, reserve

pot-bellied *adj*
bloated, corpulent, distended, fat, gor-bellied, obese,
overweight, paunchy, portly, tubby

pot-belly *n*
belly, beer belly, paunch, gut, pot
colloq. corporation, spare tyre

potency *n*
power, strength, force, influence, potential, vigour,
control, authority, effectiveness, persuasiveness,
energy, sway, capacity
formal cogency, efficaciousness, efficacy, might,
puissance
colloq. headiness, kick, muscle, punch
E3 weakness, impotence

potent *adj*
effective, powerful, mighty, strong, intoxicating,
pungent, impressive, convincing, persuasive, eloquent,
compelling, forceful, dynamic, energetic, vigorous,
authoritative, commanding, dominant, influential,
overpowering
formal cogent, efficacious, puissant
E3 impotent, weak

potentate *n*
ruler, monarch, sovereign, autocrat, head of state,
king, queen, despot, dictator, tyrant, emperor,
empress, prince, chief, chieftain, mogul, leader,
dynast, overlord

potential *adj, n*
▶ *adj* possible, likely, probable, prospective, future,
aspiring, would-be, promising, budding, developing,
embryonic, inherent, undeveloped, dormant, latent,
hidden, concealed, unrealized
▶ *n* possibility, ability, capability, capacity, aptitude,
gift, flair, talent, promise, powers, resources

potentiality *n*
likelihood, possibilities, potential, promise, prospect,
virtuality, ability, capability, aptitude, capacity

potion *n*
mixture, concoction, brew, beverage, drink, draught,
dose, medicine, tonic, elixir, philtre, potation

potpourri *n*
medley, mixture, assortment, jumble, hotchpotch,
miscellany, collection, melange, confusion,
smorgasbord, pastiche, patchwork, gallimaufry
colloq. mishmash

potter *v*
dawdle, amble, loiter
colloq. mess about, toddle, dilly-dally
▷ **potter about** tinker about/around, fiddle about/
around, fool about/around, play about/around;
colloq. mess about/around, muck about/around

pottery *n*
ceramics, crockery, china

Terms used in pottery include: armorial, art pottery,
basalt, blanc-de-chine, bronzing, celadon, ceramic,
china clay, cloisonné, crackleware, crazing,
creamware, delft, earthenware, enamel, faience,
fairing, figure, firing, flambé, flatback, glaze,
grotesque, ground, ironstone, jasper, kiln, lustre,
maiolica, majolica, maker's mark, mandarin palette,
model, monogram, overglaze, porcelain, sagger,
scratch blue, sgraffito, slip, slip-cast, spongeware,
Staffordshire, stoneware, terracotta, tin-glazed
earthenware, transfer printing, underglaze, Willow
pattern. *See also* **porcelain**.

potty *adj*
crazy, foolish, eccentric, demented, silly, touched, soft
colloq. daft, nuts, nutty, bananas, barmy, bonkers,
crackers, dippy, dotty

pouch *n*
bag, purse, pocket, container, receptacle, sack, wallet,
sporran, poke
technical marsupium, sac
formal reticule
Related adjectives: marsupial, saccate

pounce *v, n*
▶ *v* fall on, dive on, swoop, drop, descend, attack,
strike, ambush, spring, jump, leap, bound, lunge,
snatch, grab, take by surprise, catch/take unawares,
catch off guard
▶ *n* attack, assault, bound, dive, grab, jump, leap,
swoop, lunge, spring

pound[1] *n*
it cost 100 pounds
pound coin, £, pound sterling
colloq. quid; *slang* nicker, smacker, smackeroo, oncer,
sov

pound[2] *n*
keep animals in a pound
enclosure, compound, corral, yard, pen, fold

pound[3] *v*
1 STRIKE, thump, beat, drum, pelt, hammer, batter,
bang, bash, smash, pummel
2 PULVERIZE, powder, grind, mash, bray, pestle,
crush, beat, smash, granulate
formal levigate, comminute, triturate
3 *his heart was pounding*
throb, pulsate, palpitate, thump, thud

4 *pound the streets*
tread, tramp, walk, pace, trudge, plod, stomp

pour *v*
1 *pour a drink*
make flow, serve, pour out, decant, tip, spill, sprinkle
2 SPILL, issue, come out, discharge, flow, emit, leak,
ooze, stream, run, rush, spout, spew, jet, spurt, gush,
course, cascade, flood, crowd, throng, swarm
formal disgorge, disembogue
3 RAIN, team down, pelt down
colloq. rain cats and dogs, bucket down, come down in
buckets/stair rods/torrents; *slang* piss down

pout *v, n*
▶ *v* scowl, glower, lour, grimace, pull a face, sulk,
mope
E3 grin, smile
▶ *n* scowl, glower, grimace, long face, moue
E3 grin, smile

poverty *n*
poorness, impoverishment, insolvency, bankruptcy,
pennilessness, destitution, deprivation, distress,
hardship, need, necessity, want, lack, deficiency,
shortage, inadequacy, insufficiency, depletion, scarcity,
meagreness, paucity, dearth
formal penury, impecuniosity, indigence, privation
E3 wealth, richness, affluence, plenty

poverty-stricken *adj*
poor, penniless, impoverished, needy, destitute,
distressed, bankrupt, beggared
formal impecunious, obolary, indigent, penurious
colloq. broke, skint, stony, stony-broke, strapped, on
your beam-ends, on your uppers
E3 rich, affluent

powder *n, v*
▶ *n* dust, grains, pounce, bran, talc
formal triturate, pulvil, pulville, pulvil(l)io

Kinds of powder include: baking powder, chilli
powder, curry powder, soap powder, talcum powder,
washing powder.

▶ *v* **1** PULVERIZE, powder, grind, mash, bray, pestle,
crush, beat, smash, granulate
formal levigate, comminute, triturate
2 SPRINKLE, scatter, cover, dust, strew

powdery *adj*
dusty, sandy, grainy, granular, granulated, powdered,
pulverized, ground, fine, loose, dry, floury, crumbly,
chalky
formal friable, pulverulent, levigate

power *n*
1 COMMAND, authority, sovereignty, rule, dominion,
domination, control, say, influence, mastery,
supremacy, sway
formal ascendancy
colloq. clout, pull, muscle, teeth, clutches
2 RIGHT, authority, privilege, prerogative,
authorization, licence, warrant
3 POWERFULNESS, strength, intensity, energy, force,
forcefulness, effectiveness, vigour, potency
formal might
colloq. juice
4 ABILITY, capability, capacity, potential, faculty,
competence
formal potentiality
E3 **1** subjection **3** weakness,
impotence **4** inability

powerful *adj*
1 INFLUENTIAL, dominant, prevailing, leading,
high-powered, authoritative, commanding, potent,
effective, energetic, forceful, telling, impressive,
convincing, persuasive, compelling, winning,
overwhelming, all-powerful
2 STRONG, mighty, robust, tough, muscular, brawny,
strapping, burly, hardy
old use puissant
E3 **1** powerless, ineffective, impotent **2** weak

powerfully *adv*
strongly, vigorously, hard, forcefully, forcibly, potently,
convincingly, persuasively, impressively, tellingly
formal cogently, mightily, with might and main

powerless *adj*
helpless, unfit, unable, impotent, incapable,
ineffective, weak, having a say, feeble, frail, infirm,
incapacitated, disabled, paralysed, vulnerable,
defenceless, unarmed
formal debilitated, ineffectual
E3 powerful, influential, able, potent

practicability *n*
possibility, feasibility, practicality, viability,
workability, workableness, handiness, operability, use,
usefulness, value, utility
E3 impracticability

practicable *adj*
possible, feasible, performable, achievable, doable,
attainable, viable, workable, practical, realistic
E3 impracticable

⚠ **practicable** or **practical** ?
Practicable means 'able to be done, used, carried out,
etc': *a practicable plan. Practical,* when applied to
things, suggestions, etc also means 'able to be done,
used, or carried out' but has the further connotation
of 'efficient, sensible, useful': *Both these suggested
courses of action are practicable, but John's is certainly
the more practical of the two; High heels aren't very
practical for hill-walking.* Applied to people, *practical*
means 'able to do, make, or deal with things well or
efficiently': *He's not a very practical person: he has lots
of ideas for redesigning the bathroom but he doesn't
have a clue how to put up a shelf.*

practical *adj*
1 *put knowledge to practical use*
applied, hands on, real, actual
2 *a practical person*
down-to-earth, matter-of-fact, sensible, realistic,
pragmatic, hard-headed, businesslike, efficient,
experienced, trained, qualified, skilled,
accomplished, proficient
colloq. hard-nosed, having both feet on the ground
3 *practical ideas*
realistic, workable, feasible, sensible, commonsense,
applied, workaday, practicable
4 *wear practical shoes*
sensible, strong, suitable, utilitarian, functional,
working, everyday, ordinary, serviceable, useful, handy
5 *a practical walkover*
virtual, effective, essential
E3 **1** theoretical **2** impractical, unskilled
3, 4 impractical

⚠ **practical** or **practicable** ? *See panel at*
practicable.

practicality *n*
sense, common sense, realism, basics, experience,
practicability, pragmatism, practicalness,
serviceability, soundness, usefulness, utility,
workability, feasibility, practice
colloq. nitty-gritty, nuts and bolts

practically *adv*
1 ALMOST, nearly, well-nigh, virtually, all but, just
about, in principle, in effect, essentially,
fundamentally, to all intents and purposes
colloq. pretty much, pretty well
2 REALISTICALLY, sensibly, reasonably, rationally,
pragmatically, matter-of-factly

practice *n*
1 CUSTOM, tradition, convention, usage, habit,
routine, way, method, system, procedure, policy
formal wont
2 REHEARSAL, run-through, dry run, dummy run,
try-out, training, drill, exercise, work-out, study,
preparation, warm-up, experience
3 *in practice*
effect, reality, actuality, action, operation,
performance, use, exercise, application
4 *the practice of medicine*
business, work, profession, career, occupation,
employment, job, following, pursuit
F3 **3** theory, principle

practise *v*
1 DO, perform, implement, carry out, apply, put into
practice, observe, follow, pursue, engage in, undertake
formal execute
2 REHEARSE, run through, go through, go over,
repeat, drill, exercise, train, study, work on, work at,
prepare, perfect, refine, polish

practised *adj*
experienced, seasoned, veteran, trained, qualified,
accomplished, skilled, skilful, versed, knowing,
knowledgeable, able, adept, proficient, expert,
masterly, finished
formal consummate
F3 unpractised, inexperienced, inexpert

pragmatic *adj*
practical, realistic, sensible, matter-of-fact,
businesslike, efficient, utilitarian, hard-headed,
unsentimental
colloq. hard-nosed
F3 unrealistic, idealistic, romantic

pragmatism *n*
practicality, realism, utilitarianism, hard-headedness,
humanism, practicalism, opportunism, unidealism
F3 idealism, romanticism

pragmatist *n*
realist, utilitarian, opportunist, practicalist
F3 idealist, romantic

praise *v, n*
▶ *v* commend, congratulate, express approval of,
speak highly of, speak well of, admire, compliment,
flatter, sing the praises of, wax lyrical, extol, promote,
applaud, cheer, acclaim, hail, recognize, acknowledge,
pay tribute to, honour, glorify, magnify, exalt, worship,
adore, bless
formal eulogize, laud
colloq. rave over
F3 criticize, revile
▶ *n* approval, admiration, commendation,
congratulation, compliment, flattery, adulation,

applause, plaudits, ovation, cheering, acclaim,
recognition, testimonial, tribute, accolade, homage,
honour, glory, worship, adoration, devotion, thanks,
thanksgiving, hallelujah
formal approbation, eulogy, encomium, laudation,
panegyric
colloq. bouquets, puff
F3 criticism, revilement

praiseworthy *adj*
commendable, fine, excellent, admirable, exemplary,
worthy, deserving, honourable, reputable, estimable,
sterling
formal laudable
F3 blameworthy, dishonourable, ignoble

praising *adj*
approving, complimentary, congratulatory,
favourable, flattering, commendatory, adulatory,
recommendatory, promotional, worshipful
formal approbatory, eulogistic, encomiastic, laudative,
laudatory, panegyric, plauditory
F3 condemnatory, critical

prance *v*
1 LEAP, jump, spring, skip, dance, frisk, frolic,
gambol, cavort, caper, bound, romp, vault
2 SHOW OFF, strut, swagger, stalk, parade, curvet
colloq. swank

prank *n*
trick, practical joke, joke, stunt, caper, frolic, lark,
antic, escapade

prattle *v, n*
▶ *v* chat, chatter, witter, gabble, rattle, twitter,
twaddle, twattle, patter, drivel, gossip, blather, blether
colloq. babble, jabber
▶ *n* chat, chatter, gossip, talk, jaw, gab, tattle, blather,
blether, nonsense, prating, gibberish, foolishness,
drivel
colloq. hot air, bubble

prattler *n*
chatterer, talker, gossip, blether, gabbler, tatler, tattler,
magpie
colloq. babbler, blabbermouth, chatterbox,
loudmouth, windbag
F3 clam

pray *v*
1 *pray to God*
invoke, call on, commune with, talk to, speak to, say a
prayer, be at prayer, say your prayers, praise, worship,
adore, confess, thank
2 ENTREAT, implore, plead, beg, petition, ask,
request, crave, solicit
formal supplicate, beseech

prayer *n*
1 *prayer to God*
collect, litany, devotion, doxology, communion,
invocation, fellowship, intercession, praise, worship,
adore, confess, thank, the Lord's Prayer, Our Father,
Paternoster, Kyrie eleison, Hail Mary, Ave Maria,
Agnus Dei, Magnificat, Benedictus, Nunc Dimittis,
Sursum Corda, Gloria, Om, mantra
2 ENTREATY, plea, appeal, petition, request
formal supplication

prayer-book *n*
ordinal, service-book, missal, breviary, mahzor,
euchologion, euchology, formulary, Triodion

preach *v*
address, lecture, teach, proclaim, harangue,
pontificate, sermonize, evangelize, give a sermon,
spread the gospel, moralize, exhort, advise, admonish,
urge, advocate

preacher *n*
minister, clergyman, parson, evangelist, televangelist,
missionary, revivalist, sermonizer, moralizer,
pulpite(e)r, ranter, homilist, pontificater

preaching *n*
teaching, instruction, doctrine, precepts, message,
homiletics, homilies, dogma, gospel, sermons,
sermonizing, evangelism, pontificating
technical evangel, kerygma
formal exhortation
Related adjective: homiletic

preachy *adj*
moralizing, pontificating, sermonizing, religiose,
pietistic, pharisaic, pontifical, sanctimonious, self-
righteous, dogmatic, didactic, edifying, homiletic
formal exhortatory, hortatory
colloq. holier-than-thou

preamble *n*
introduction, lead-in, preliminaries, preparation,
prelude, foreword, preface, prologue, overture
formal exordium, proem, prolegomenon
▪ postscript, epilogue

precarious *adj*
unsafe, dangerous, treacherous, risky, hazardous,
chancy, uncertain, unsure, unsettled, dubious,
doubtful, unpredictable, unreliable, undependable,
unsteady, unstable, shaky, wobbly, insecure, vulnerable
colloq. chancy, dicey, dodgy, hairy, iffy, dicky
▪ safe, certain, stable, secure

precaution *n*
safeguard, security, preventive/preventative measure,
protection, insurance, providence, forethought, care,
caution, attentiveness, foresight, farsightedness,
anticipation, preparation, provision
formal prudence, circumspection

precautionary *adj*
safety, protective, preventive, preventative, provident,
cautious, far-sighted, preparatory, preliminary
formal prudent, judicious

precede *v*
come before, lead, come first, go before, go ahead of,
take precedence, introduce, herald, usher in, head,
preface
formal antecede, antedate, prevene
▪ follow, succeed

precedence *n*
priority, preference, pride of place, superiority,
supremacy, eminence, pre-eminence, lead, first place,
seniority, rank
formal ascendancy
▷ **take precedence over** take priority over, come
before, be more important than

precedent *n*
example, instance, case, parallel, pattern, model,
standard, criterion, yardstick
formal paradigm, exemplar

preceding *adj*
above, earlier, former, past, previous, prior, precedent,
foregoing, antecedent
formal aforementioned, aforesaid, supra, precursive,

anterior
▪ following, later

precept *n*
principle, axiom, command, commandment, charge,
direction, directive, ordinance, regulation, guideline,
order, injunction, institute, law, instruction, decree,
dictum, mandate, rule, statute, convention, canon,
maxim, motto, saying, sentence, rubric

precinct *n*
1 ZONE, area, district, quarter, sector, division,
section, shopping centre, mall, galleria
2 BOUNDARY, limit, bound, confine, enclosure,
close, court, neighbourhood, surrounds, locality,
vicinity, environs, milieu, purlieus

preciosity *n*
artificiality, pretentiousness, floweriness, over-
refinement, affectation, tweeness, chichi

precious *adj*
1 VALUED, treasured, prized, cherished, beloved,
dear, dearest, darling, favourite, loved, revered,
adored, idolized
2 VALUABLE, expensive, costly, high-priced, dear,
priceless, inestimable, rare, choice, fine
3 AFFECTED, overrefined, simulated, contrived,
artificial, mannered, pretentious, flowery, twee, chichi

precipice *n*
cliff, cliff face, bluff, brink, steep, escarpment, crag,
drop, height, escarp, scarp, krantz

precipitate *v, adj*
▶ *v* **1** HASTEN, hurry, speed (up), accelerate,
quicken, expedite, advance, further, bring about, bring
on, induce, trigger, cause, occasion
2 THROW, plunge, hurl, heave, thrust, fling
▶ *adj* sudden, unexpected, abrupt, quick, swift,
speedy, rapid, brief, hasty, hurried, headlong,
breakneck, frantic, violent, impatient, hot-headed,
impetuous, impulsive, rash, reckless, heedless,
indiscreet
▪ cautious, careful

⚠ **precipitate** or **precipitous** ?
Precipitate means 'hasty or too hasty': *precipitate
decision. Precipitous* means 'very steep, like a
precipice': *The path through the mountains is narrow
and precipitous.*

---

precipitation *n*

Types of precipitation include: dew, downpour, drizzle,
fog, hail, mist, rain, rainfall, rainstorm, shower, sleet,
snow, snowfall, snowflake.

precipitous *adj*
steep, sheer, perpendicular, vertical, abrupt, sharp,
high, sudden
▪ gradual

⚠ **precipitous** or **precipitate** ? *See panel at*
precipitate.

---

précis *n, v*
▶ *n* summary, abridgement, contraction,
abbreviation, condensation, synopsis, abstract, digest,
epitome, outline, résumé, sketch, compendium, run-
down, table
formal conspectus, encapsulation
▶ *v* summarize, shorten, sum up, outline, abstract,

abridge, condense, synopsize, digest, abbreviate, encapsulate, epitomize, contract, compress
F3 amplify, expand

precise *adj*
exact, accurate, right, punctilious, correct, factual, faithful, authentic, literal, word-for-word, actual, express, definite, explicit, unequivocal, unambiguous, clear-cut, distinct, detailed, blow-by-blow, minute, nice, particular, specific, fixed, rigid, strict, careful, scrupulous, punctilious, meticulous, conscientious, rigorous, fastidious
F3 imprecise, inexact, ambiguous, careless

precisely *adv*
exactly, absolutely, just so, accurately, on the dot, dead on, correctly, literally, verbatim, word for word, strictly, minutely, clearly, distinctly
US on the button
colloq. dead on, bang on, spot on, plumb, slap, smack, to a T

precision *n*
exactness, exactitude, accuracy, correctness, faithfulness, explicitness, distinctness, detail, particularity, rigour, care, reliability, meticulousness, scrupulousness, punctiliousness, conscientiousness, neatness, fastidiousness
F3 imprecision, inaccuracy

preclude *v*
prevent, exclude, eliminate, rule out, hinder, inhibit, prohibit, restrain, stop, avoid, check, debar, forestall
formal obviate
F3 incur, involve

precocious *adj*
forward, ahead, far ahead, advanced, early, premature, mature, developed, gifted, talented, clever, bright, brilliant, smart, quick, fast
F3 backward, slow, stupid

preconceive *v*
presuppose, presume, assume, anticipate, project, imagine, conceive, envisage, expect, visualize, picture

preconception *n*
presupposition, presumption, assumption, notion, anticipation, expectation, prejudgement, bias, prejudice
formal conjecture, predisposition

precondition *n*
condition, stipulation, requirement, prerequisite, essential, necessity
formal sine qua non
colloq. must

precursor *n*
forerunner, antecedent, sign, indication, prelude, herald, harbinger, messenger, usher, pioneer, trailblazer, curtain-raiser, ancestor, forebear
formal progenitor
F3 follower, successor

precursory *adj*
preceding, warning, introductory, antecedent, preliminary, preparatory, previous, prior, prefatory, anterior
formal preambulatory, precursive, preludial, prelusive, prevenient, prodromal
F3 following, resulting, subsequent

predatory *adj*
hunting, preying, voracious, carnivorous, greedy, acquisitive, avaricious, covetous, despoiling, thieving, ravaging, plundering, marauding, pillaging, wolfish, lupine, vulturine, vulturous
formal predacious, predative, rapacious, raptatorial, raptorial

predecessor *n*
ancestor, forefather, forebear, antecedent, forerunner, precursor
formal progenitor
F3 successor, descendant

predestination *n*
destiny, fate, lot, doom, foreordination
formal predetermination

predestine *v*
intend, mean, destine, fate, foreordain, preordain, pre-elect, doom, foredoom
formal predestinate, predetermine

predetermined *adj*
1 PREDESTINED, destined, fated, doomed, ordained, foreordained
2 PREARRANGED, arranged, agreed, fixed, set, settled

predicament *n*
situation, plight, trouble, mess, fix, quandary, dilemma, impasse, crisis, emergency
colloq. spot, tight spot, scrape, pickle, jam, hiccup, hole, stew, hot/deep water, can of worms, kettle of fish

predicate *v*
1 ASSERT, affirm, state, declare, proclaim, contend
formal aver, avouch, avow, posit, postulate, premise
2 BE DEPENDENT, rest, base, build, found, establish, maintain, ground

predict *v*
forecast, foretell, prophesy, foresee, project
formal prognosticate, vaticinate, augur, portend, presage, divine, auspicate
colloq. second-guess

predictable *adj*
foreseeable, expected, anticipated, likely, probable, imaginable, foreseen, foregone, certain, sure, reliable, dependable
colloq. on the cards, odds-on
F3 unpredictable, unforeseeable, uncertain

prediction *n*
prophecy, forecast, prognosis, fortune-telling, soothsaying
formal augury, divination, prognostication, auspication

predictive *adj*
prophetic, foretelling, diagnostic
formal augural, divinatory, prognostic

predilection *n*
fondness, preference, inclination, leaning, liking, affection, love, partiality, tendency, bent, bias, enthusiasm, fancy, taste, affinity, soft spot, weakness
formal penchant, predisposition, proclivity, propensity
F3 dislike, disinclination; *formal* antipathy

predispose *v*
dispose, incline, prompt, induce, make, make liable, sway, move, influence, persuade, affect, bias, prejudice

predisposed *adj*
inclined, liable, prepared, ready, susceptible, willing, disposed, well-disposed, minded, not unwilling, subject, agreeable, amenable, favourable, prone,

biased, prejudiced
F3 unwilling, reluctant, loath

predisposition *n*
likelihood, inclination, leaning, tendency, preference, disposition, bent, proneness, willingness, liability, susceptibility, vulnerability, bias, prejudice
formal penchant, potentiality, predilection, proclivity, propensity

predominance *n*
dominance, dominion, power, control, leadership, mastery, prevalence, superiority, supremacy, influence, sway, weight, hold, numbers
formal hegemony, ascendancy, paramountcy, preponderance, prepotence, prepotency, prepollence, prepollency
colloq. edge, upper hand
F3 ineffectiveness, weakness

predominant *adj*
dominant, prevailing, chief, main, principal, primary, capital, paramount, supreme, sovereign, ruling, controlling, in control, leading, powerful, potent, prime, important, most important, influential, forceful, strong, most noticeable, most obvious
formal preponderant, ascendant, in the ascendancy
F3 minor, lesser, weak

predominate *v*
prevail, dominate, outnumber, outweigh, override, overrule, overshadow, transcend, tell, reign, rule
formal obtain, preponderate

pre-eminence *n*
supremacy, distinction, excellence, fame, prestige, renown, repute, predominance, prominence, superiority, incomparability, peerlessness, matchlessness, paramountcy, transcendence

pre-eminent *adj*
supreme, unsurpassed, unrivalled, unequalled, unmatched, matchless, incomparable, inimitable, chief, first, most important, foremost, leading, eminent, distinguished, renowned, famous, prominent, outstanding, exceptional, excellent, superlative, transcendent, superior
F3 inferior, unknown

pre-eminently *adv*
especially, notably, particularly, exceptionally, eminently, signally, superlatively, singularly, strikingly, surpassingly, par excellence, exclusively, supremely, emphatically, conspicuously, incomparably, inimitably, matchlessly, peerlessly

pre-empt *v*
prevent, forestall, anticipate, assume, acquire, secure, seize, usurp
formal appropriate, arrogate

preen *v*
1 CLEAN, smooth, groom, plume, trim, spruce up, dress up, trick out, doll up, slick, prettify, adorn, beautify, deck, primp, prink
formal array
colloq. do up, tart up
2 CONGRATULATE, pride, exult, bask, plume, gloat, pique
colloq. pat yourself on the back

preface *n, v*
▶ *n* foreword, introduction, preamble, prologue, prelude, frontmatter, preliminaries
formal proem, prolegomenon, exordium

colloq. prelims
F3 epilogue, postscript
Related adjective: prefatory
▶ *v* precede, prefix, lead up to, introduce, launch, open, begin, start
F3 end, finish, complete

prefatory *adj*
introductory, opening, preparatory, preliminary, explanatory, antecedent
formal exordial, preambulatory, precursory, prefatorial, preludial, prelusive, prelusory, proemial, prolegomenal
F3 closing, final

prefect *n*
monitor, administrator, supervisor, praeposter, prepositor, praefect

prefer *v*
1 *I prefer tea to coffee*
favour, like better, would rather, would sooner, be partial to, want, wish, desire, choose, select, pick (out), opt (for), go for, single out, advocate, recommend, back, support, elect, adopt
colloq. plump for, fancy
2 PROMOTE, favour, advance, move up, raise, elevate, exalt, honour
formal aggrandize
3 *prefer charges*
bring, file, lodge, press, present, place
F3 1 reject 2 demote

preferable *adj*
better, superior, nicer, preferred, favoured, more desired, chosen, desirable, advantageous, advisable, recommended
F3 inferior, undesirable

preferably *adv*
rather, much rather, sooner, much sooner, from choice, for choice, by/for preference, first

preference *n*
1 FAVOURITE, first choice, choice, pick, selection, option, wish, desire
colloq. cup of tea
2 LIKING, fancy, inclination, bent, leaning, bias, discrimination, predilection, partiality, favouritism, priority, precedence, preferential treatment

preferential *adj*
better, superior, favoured, privileged, special, favourable, advantageous, partial, partisan, biased
F3 equal

preferment *n*
promotion, advancement, furtherance, improvement, rise, step up, betterment, dignity, elevation, exaltation, upgrading
formal aggrandizement
F3 demotion

preferred *adj*
favoured, selected, approved, choice, chosen, desired, recommended, authorized, sanctioned
formal predilect
F3 rejected, undesirable

pregnancy *n*
child-bearing, conception, fertilization, impregnation, gestation
technical parturition
formal gravidity
colloq. family way

pregnant *adj*
1 *a pregnant woman*
expectant, expecting
technical parturient
formal with child, enceinte
colloq. in the family way, in the club; *slang* preggers, with a bun in the oven, up the spout
2 *a pregnant pause*
meaningful, significant, eloquent, rich, expressive, suggestive, telling, pointed, charged, loaded, heavy, full, filled, fraught
formal replete
⊟ 2 jejune

prehistoric *adj*
primitive, primeval, primordial, earliest, early, ancient, archaic, antiquated, old, obsolete, out-of-date, outmoded
colloq. antediluvian, out of the ark, before the flood
⊟ modern

prejudge *v*
judge prematurely, anticipate, presume, assume, presuppose, forejudge
formal predetermine, prejudicate

prejudice *n, v*
▶ *n* **1** BIAS, partiality, partisanship, discrimination, preference, one-sidedness, unfairness, injustice, intolerance, narrow-mindedness, bigotry, chauvinism, racism, sexism, misogyny, ageism, xenophobia, misanthropy, anti-Semitism
2 HARM, damage, impairment, hurt, injury, detriment, disadvantage, loss, ruin
⊟ 1 fairness, tolerance **2** benefit, advantage
▶ *v* **1** BIAS, incline, sway, influence, condition, colour, jaundice, slant, distort, load, weight
formal predispose
2 HARM, damage, impair, be detrimental to, be disadvantageous to, hinder, undermine, hurt, injure, mar, spoil, ruin, wreck
⊟ 2 benefit, help, advance

prejudiced *adj*
biased, partial, subjective, partisan, one-sided, discriminatory, unfair, unjust, loaded, weighted, intolerant, narrow-minded, bigoted, blinkered, chauvinist, chauvinistic, xenophobic, anti-Semitic, racist, sexist, ageist, jaundiced, distorted, warped, influenced, conditioned, insular, parochial
formal predisposed
⊟ impartial, fair, tolerant

prejudicial *adj*
harmful, damaging, hurtful, injurious, detrimental, disadvantageous, counter-productive, unfavourable, inimical
formal deleterious, noxious
⊟ beneficial, advantageous

preliminary *adj, n*
▶ *adj* preparatory, prior, advance, exploratory, experimental, trial, test, pilot, early, earliest, first, initial, beginning, primary, qualifying, inaugural, introductory, opening, prefatory
formal precursory, exordial
⊟ final, closing
▶ *n* preparation, groundwork, foundations, basics, rudiments, formalities, introduction, preface, foreword, prelude, preamble, opening, beginning, start
formal proem, exordium, prolegomenon, prodrome

prelude *n*
overture, introduction, preface, foreword, preamble, prologue, opening, opener, preliminary, preparation, beginning, start, forerunner, herald, harbinger, precursor, curtain-raiser
formal proem, exordium, prolegomenon, prodrome, commencement
⊟ finale, epilogue
Related adjectives: preludial, preludious, proemial

premature *adj*
early, soon, too early, too soon, immature, green, unripe, embryonic, half-formed, incomplete, undeveloped, abortive, hasty, ill-considered, rash, impetuous, impulsive, precipitate, untimely, inopportune, ill-timed
colloq. jumping the gun
⊟ late; *formal* tardy

premeditated *adj*
planned, intended, intentional, deliberate, wilful, conscious, cold-blooded, calculated, considered, contrived, preplanned, prearranged, predetermined
⊟ unpremeditated, spontaneous

premeditation *n*
planning, prearrangement, purpose, intention, deliberation, deliberateness, determination, forethought, design, scheming, plotting
technical malice aforethought
formal predetermination
⊟ impulse, spontaneity

premier *n, adj*
▶ *n* head of government, prime minister, chief minister, first minister, chancellor, secretary of state
▶ *adj* principal, leading, highest, top, head, foremost, chief, primary, prime, main, supreme, paramount, pre-eminent, first, cardinal, earliest, original, initial

première *n*
first performance, first showing, opening, opening night, first night, début

premise *n, v*
▶ *n* proposition, statement, assertion, postulate, thesis, argument, basis, supposition, hypothesis, assumption
formal presupposition, postulate
▶ *v* lay down, state, assert, assume, stipulate, take as true, presuppose
formal hypothesize, posit, postulate, predicate

premises *n*
building, property, establishment, office, grounds, estate, site, place

premium *n*
1 *pay an insurance premium*
regular payment, instalment
2 *pay a premium rate*
extra sum/charge, surcharge, overcharging
colloq. an arm and a leg, daylight robbery
▷ **at a premium** scarce, rare, hard to come by, in short supply, in great demand, few and far between; *colloq.* like gold dust
▷ **put a premium on** value greatly, treasure, appreciate, favour, hold dear, attach great/special importance to, regard highly, set great store by

premonition *n*
feeling, intuition, sixth sense, hunch, idea, suspicion, sneaking suspicion, foreboding, misgiving, fear, apprehension, anxiety, worry, warning, omen, sign

formal presentiment, presage, portent
colloq. feeling in your bones, funny feeling, gut feeling

preoccupation *n*
1 OBSESSION, fixation, concern, interest, enthusiasm, hobby-horse
colloq. hang-up, thing, bee in your bonnet, one-track mind
2 DISTRACTION, absent-mindedness, daydreaming, reverie, abstraction, heedlessness, obliviousness, oblivion, inattentiveness, absorption, engrossment

preoccupied *adj*
1 OBSESSED, intent, immersed, engrossed, absorbed, engaged, taken up, wrapped up, involved, pensive, deep in thought
2 DISTRACTED, abstracted, absent-minded, daydreaming, absorbed, faraway, heedless, oblivious
formal distrait

preoccupy *v*
occupy, absorb, engage, take up, involve, obsess, occupy the attention of

preordain *v*
destine, prearrange, foreordain, doom, fate
formal predestine, predetermine

preparation *n*
1 *preparations for the wedding; in preparation for the event*
planning, plan, arrangement, organization, development, basics, rudiments, preliminaries, readiness, provision, supply, equipping, assembly, composition, construction, production, homework, foundation, groundwork, spadework
2 TRAINING, coaching, study, revision, practice
3 MIXTURE, compound, composition, concoction, potion, medicine, lotion, application, cosmetic

preparatory *adj*
preliminary, introductory, opening, initial, primary, basic, fundamental, rudimentary, elementary
formal precursory, prefatory
▷ **preparatory to** before, in advance of, in anticipation of, in expectation of, previous to, prior to, as a preparation for

prepare *v*
1 GET READY, make ready, make preparations for, set up, plan, organize, arrange, adjust, provide, supply, equip, fit out, rig out, prime, put together, construct, assemble, concoct, contrive, devise, draft, fashion, draw up, compose, pave the way, do your homework for, lay the foundations for, lay the groundwork for, do the spadework for, take the necessary steps for, set the scene for
colloq. gear up, psych up, tee up
2 TRAIN, exercise, coach, study, practise, prime, warm up, get into shape, make ready
3 *prepare a meal*
make, produce, concoct, put together, throw together, get ready
US fix
▷ **prepare yourself** brace yourself, steel yourself, gird yourself; *formal* fortify yourself, gird up your loins

prepared *adj*
ready, willing, disposed, waiting, set, fit, inclined, arranged, planned, organized, in order, fixed
formal predisposed
E3 unprepared, unready

preparedness *n*
readiness, preparation, order, fitness, alertness,

anticipation, expectancy
E3 unreadiness

preponderance *n*
dominance, supremacy, greater number, superiority, majority, bulk, mass, extensiveness, prevalence, predominance, domination, dominion, power, force, sway, weight
formal ascendancy
colloq. lion's share

preponderant *adj*
greater, larger, superior, predominant, prevailing, overriding, overruling, controlling, foremost, important, significant

preponderate *v*
dominate, predominate, prevail, outnumber, override, overrule, rule, tell, weigh with, turn the balance, turn the scales

prepossessing *adj*
attractive, charming, good-looking, winning, winsome, appealing, beautiful, likeable, lovable, amiable, delightful, fair, handsome, pleasing, striking, captivating, bewitching, enchanting, engaging, inviting, alluring, magnetic, fascinating, fetching, taking
E3 unattractive, unprepossessing

preposterous *adj*
incredible, unbelievable, absurd, ridiculous, ludicrous, foolish, farcical, crazy, nonsensical, irrational, unreasonable, senseless, monstrous, shocking, outrageous, asinine, intolerable, unthinkable, incredible, impossible
E3 sensible, reasonable, acceptable

prerequisite *n, adj*
▶ *n* condition, proviso, qualification, requirement, imperative, necessity, essential
formal precondition, requisite, sine qua non
colloq. must
E3 extra
▶ *adj* indispensable, necessary, obligatory, required, needed, needful, essential, basic, fundamental, vital, imperative
formal mandatory, requisite
E3 unnecessary, superfluous

prerogative *n*
privilege, right, authority, advantage, choice, sanction, exemption, immunity, liberty, due, claim, licence, carte blanche, birthright
technical droit

presage *v, n*
▶ *v* indicate, point to, be a sign of, be an indication of, warn of, announce, forecast, predict, foretell, promise, signify, threaten, herald, foretoken
formal augur, portend, bode, forebode, foreshadow, forewarn, harbinger, bespeak, betoken, adumbrate, prognosticate
▶ *n* sign, indication, warning, threat, omen, precursor, forecast, foreboding, forerunner, prefiguration, premonition
formal augury, portent, signification, prognostication, foreshadowing, forewarning, prognostic, presentiment, harbinger

prescience *n*
foreknowledge, foresight, far-sightedness, second sight, prophecy, clairvoyance, propheticness
formal precognition, prevision

prescient *adj*
foreknowing, far-sighted, far-seeing, prophetic,
foresighted, perceptive, discerning, clairvoyant,
divinatory, divining, psychic
formal previsional
F3 imperceptive

prescribe *v*
1 *prescribe medicine*
advise, act, specify, stipulate
2 *prescribe a duty*
ordain, decree, dictate, rule, command, order, require,
direct, specify, stipulate, lay down, set, appoint,
impose, fix, define, limit

⚠ **prescribe** or **proscribe** ?
To *prescribe* is to advise or order: *The doctor
prescribed a course of antibiotics; The law prescribes
severe penalties for such offences.* To *proscribe* is to
ban, outlaw or forbid: *This book was formerly
proscribed by the church; Such actions are proscribed
by law.*

---

prescribed *adj*
laid down, specified, stipulated, set, ordained,
assigned, decreed
formal formulary

prescription *n*
1 INSTRUCTION, direction, formula, recipe, advice,
recommendation, guideline(s)
2 MEDICINE, drug, preparation, mixture, remedy,
treatment

prescriptive *adj*
dictatorial, legislating, prescribing, didactic,
dogmatic, rigid, authoritarian, customary
formal preceptive

presence *n*
1 ATTENDANCE, company, companionship,
occupancy, residence, existence, being
2 AURA, air, appearance, dignity, poise, self-
confidence, self-assurance, attraction, personality,
charisma, appeal, magnetism
formal demeanour, bearing, carriage
3 NEARNESS, closeness, proximity, neighbourhood,
vicinity
formal propinquity
4 SPIRIT, ghost, phantom, spectre, apparition,
visitant, shadow
F3 **1** absence **3** remoteness, distance
▷ **presence of mind** calmness, self-possession,
composure, coolness, self-assurance, self-command,
level-headedness, alertness, poise; *formal* aplomb,
imperturbability, sang-froid; *colloq.* cool,
unflappability
F3 agitation, confusion

present[1] *adj, n*
► *adj* **1** ATTENDING, here, there, near, nearby, at
hand, close at hand, to hand, available, ready, existing
2 *at the present time*
current, contemporary, present-day, immediate,
instant, existent, existing
F3 **1** absent **2** past, out-of-date
▷ **the present day** today, now, nowadays, at this
time, currently
► *n* ▷ **at present** at the moment, now, at this time,
today, currently
▷ **for the present** for the time being, for the
moment, for now, in the meantime, pro tem

present[2] *v*
1 AWARD, grant, give, donate, hand over, entrust,
extend, hold out
formal confer, bestow
2 OFFER, tender, submit
formal proffer
3 SHOW, display, put on display, exhibit, demonstrate,
organize, mount, stage, perform, put on, introduce,
host, make known
5 *present a television show*
introduce, compère, host, announce
6 *the story presents her sympathetically*
DESCRIBE, depict, represent, portray, characterize,
picture
formal delineate
▷ **present oneself 1** *present yourself somewhere*
appear, arrive, attend, show up, turn up; *colloq.* pop
up **2** *an idea presents itself* occur, arise, crop up,
emerge, materialize, come to light, happen

present[3] *n*
Christmas presents
gift, offering, donation, contribution, handout, award,
grant, endowment, bounty, largesse, gratuity, tip,
favour
formal benefaction
colloq. prezzie, freebie, perk, sweetener

presentable *adj*
neat, tidy, clean, smart, smartly dressed, spruce,
respectable, decent, proper, suitable, acceptable,
satisfactory, tolerable
F3 unpresentable, untidy, shabby

presentation *n*
1 APPEARANCE, arrangement, organization,
structure, system, layout, form, format
2 AWARD, presenting, granting, donating, investiture
formal conferral, bestowal
3 TALK, address, lecture, speech, seminar
formal disquisition
4 SHOW, performance, production, staging, showing,
mounting, representation, rendition, display,
exhibition, demonstration, introduction, making
known, launch

present-day *adj*
current, present, existing, living, contemporary,
modern, up-to-date, fashionable
F3 past, future

presenter *n*
host, announcer, compère, anchorman,
anchorwoman, frontman, master of ceremonies, MC
colloq. emcee

presentiment *n*
premonition, intuition, apprehension, fear, feeling,
misgiving, hunch, anticipation, foreboding,
expectation, forecast, forethought
formal forebodement, presage
colloq. bad vibes

presently *adv*
1 SOON, shortly, in a short time, in a short while, in a
minute, before long, by and by
2 CURRENTLY, at present, now, at the moment, at the
present time, these days, at this moment in time

preservation *n*
protection, defence, maintenance, keeping, guarding,
safeguarding, safekeeping, safety, security,
conservation, storage, upkeep, support, retention,

upholding, continuation, perpetuation
E3 destruction, ruin

preserve *v, n*
▶ *v* **1** PROTECT, safeguard, guard, defend, shield, shelter, care for, look after, take care of, maintain, uphold, secure, sustain, continue, perpetuate, keep, retain, conserve, save, store
2 *preserve food*
bottle, tin, can, pickle, salt, cure, dry, smoke
E3 1 destroy, ruin
▶ *n* **1** *home made preserves*
conserve, jam, marmalade, jelly, pickle
2 DOMAIN, realm, sphere, area, field, speciality
3 RESERVATION, sanctuary, reserve, game reserve, safari park

preside *v*
chair, be in the chair, be the chairman/chairwoman/chairperson of, officiate, conduct, direct, manage, administer, control, run, head, lead, govern, rule, be responsible for, be in charge of
colloq. head up, call the shots

president *n*
head of state, ruler, leader, controller, governor, head, director, manager, principal, chief
colloq. boss
Related adjective: presidial

press *v, n*
▶ *v* **1** CRUSH, squash, squeeze, mash, pinch, knead, compress, stuff, jam, cram, crowd, push (down), depress, surge, swarm, throng, trample
2 *press clothes*
iron, smooth (out), flatten, roll
3 HUG, embrace, clasp, enfold, grasp, squeeze, caress, cuddle, crush
4 URGE, plead, petition, campaign, demand, call for, insist on, exhort, entreat, implore, push for, push forward, compel, constrain, force, coerce, pressure, pressurize, put pressure on, harass, besiege, afflict, vex, worry, trouble
formal supplicate
▷ **press on**   press ahead, continue, carry on, go on, go ahead, proceed
▶ *n* **1** CROWD, throng, multitude, mob, horde, troop, swarm, pack, crush, flock, push
2 JOURNALISTS, reporters, correspondents, photographers, paparazzi, newspapermen, newspaperwomen, pressmen, presswomen, the media, news media, newspapers, papers, Fleet Street, journalism, fourth estate
colloq. hacks
3 PRINTING PRESS, printing-machine, rotary press
4 *get a good/bad press*
coverage, treatment, articles, reviews, praise, criticism

pressed *adj*
1 FORCED, pressured, pressurized, coerced, bullied, browbeaten, constrained, hurried, pushed, rushed, harassed
2 *be pressed for time*
SHORT OF, having little, not having enough, lacking, deficient in
E3 1 unhurried **2** well-off

pressing *adj*
urgent, needing to be dealt with immediately, high-priority, burning, crucial, demanding, vital, essential, imperative, serious, important, critical, key
formal exigent
E3 unimportant, trivial

pressure *n*
1 FORCE, power, load, burden, weight, heaviness, compression, crushing, squeezing, stress, strain
2 COMPULSION, force, constraints, coercion, duress, bullying, harassment
3 STRESS, tension, difficulty, problem, demand, adversity, burden, trouble, constraint, obligation
colloq. hassle, aggro

pressurize *v*
force, compel, constrain, oblige, drive, bulldoze, dragoon, coerce, press, pressure, put pressure on, browbeat, bully
colloq. lean on, put the screws on

prestige *n*
status, reputation, standing, stature, eminence, distinction, regard, importance, authority, influence, fame, renown, kudos, credit, honour
formal esteem
E3 humbleness, unimportance

prestigious *adj*
respected, reputable, important, influential, distinguished, high-ranking, great, eminent, prominent, illustrious, renowned, celebrated, famous, well-known, exalted, imposing, impressive, up-market
formal esteemed
colloq. blue-chip
E3 humble, modest

presumably *adv*
most likely, very likely, in all likelihood, in all probability, as like as not, doubtless, doubtlessly, no doubt, probably, apparently, seemingly

presume *v*
1 ASSUME, take it, think, believe, imagine, suppose, surmise, infer, presuppose, deduce, take for granted
formal hypothesize
2 *presume to criticize*
dare, make so bold, have the audacity, take the liberty, go so far, venture, undertake
▷ **presume on**   count on, rely on, depend on, bank on, trust, take (unfair) advantage of, exploit

presumption *n*
1 ASSUMPTION, belief, opinion, surmise, deduction, inference, guess, likelihood, probability
formal hypothesis, presupposition, supposition, conjecture
2 PRESUMPTUOUSNESS, boldness, arrogance, effrontery, temerity, audacity, impertinence, impudence, insolence, forwardness, assurance
colloq. cheek, nerve
E3 2 humility

presumptive *adj*
expected, assumed, believed, designate, prospective, likely, possible, probable, reasonable, supposed, understood, believable, conceivable, credible, inferred, plausible
formal hypothetical
E3 known, unlikely

presumptuous *adj*
bold, audacious, impertinent, impudent, insolent, over-familiar, forward, arrogant, over-confident, conceited, cocksure
colloq. pushy, cheeky, cocky, big-headed, too big for your boots
E3 humble, modest

presuppose *v*
assume, presume, suppose, accept, consider, imply,

take for granted
formal posit, postulate, premise

presupposition *n*
assumption, presumption, belief, supposition, theory, preconception
formal hypothesis, premise, premiss

pretence *n*
show, display, appearance, cover, front, charade, façade, veneer, cloak, veil, mask, masquerade, guise, sham, feigning, faking, false show, semblance, hypocrisy, simulation, deception, trickery, wile, ruse, excuse, pretext, bluff, falsehood, deceit, lie, fabrication, invention, acting, play-acting, make-believe, posturing, posing, showiness, ostentation, pretentiousness
formal affectation, dissimulation, dissembling
E∃ honesty, openness

pretend *v*
1 *pretend to be asleep*
put on, assume, feign, sham, counterfeit, fake, fabricate, simulate, bluff, impersonate, pass yourself off, act, play-act, put on an act, mime, go through the motions
formal affect, dissemble
colloq. keep up appearances
2 CLAIM, allege, profess
formal purport
3 IMAGINE, make believe, suppose

pretended *adj*
artificial, put on, alleged, ostensible, professed, supposed, spurious, bogus, fake, false, feigned, sham, fictitious, counterfeit, so-called, imaginary, specious
formal affected, avowed, purported, supposititious
colloq. phoney, pretend, pseudo
E∃ real

pretender *n*
claimant, aspirant, claimer, candidate

pretension *n*
1 PRETENTIOUSNESS, pomposity, self-importance, airs, conceit, vanity, snobbishness, hypocrisy, pretence, show, showiness, floweriness, ostentation
formal affectation, magniloquence
2 CLAIM, profession, demand, aspiration, ambition
formal purporting
E∃ **1** modesty, humility, simplicity

pretentious *adj*
pompous, self-important, conceited, immodest, snobbish, twee, mannered, flaunting, showy, ostentatious, extravagant, flamboyant, elaborate, bombastic, exaggerated, high-sounding, artificial, inflated, grandiose, ambitious, overambitious
colloq. over-the-top, OTT
formal affected, magniloquent, vainglorious
E∃ modest, humble, simple, straightforward

pretentiousness *n*
ostentation, posing, pretension, show, theatricality, floweriness, floridness, flamboyance, attitudinizing
formal posturing
colloq. pseudery
E∃ humbleness, modesty, simplicity, straightforwardness

preternatural *adj*
extraordinary, unusual, exceptional, abnormal

pretext *n*
excuse, alleged/ostensible reason, ploy, ruse, cover,

cloak, mask, veil, guise, sham, semblance, appearance, pretence, show
colloq. red herring

prettify *v*
decorate, smarten up, ornament, adorn, beautify, bedeck, deck, deck out, embellish, gild, garnish, trick out, trim
colloq. do up, doll up, tart up
E∃ mar, uglify

pretty *adj, adv*
▶ *adj* attractive, good-looking, beautiful, fair, lovely, delightful, nice, cute, pleasant, pleasing, engaging, personable, prepossessing, winsome, appealing, charming, handsome, dainty, graceful, elegant, fine, delicate, nice
Scot. bonny
old use comely
E∃ plain, unattractive, ugly
▶ *adv* fairly, somewhat, rather, quite, reasonably, moderately, tolerably

prevail *v*
1 WIN, triumph, be victorious, succeed, overcome, overrule, conquer, reign, rule, gain mastery
formal gain ascendancy
colloq. carry the day
2 PREDOMINATE, abound, hold sway, occur, be common, be customary, be present, be normal, be accepted, be current
formal preponderate; obtain
E∃ **1** lose
▷ **prevail upon** persuade, talk into, prompt, induce, incline, sway, influence, convince, urge, win over, bring round, pressure, pressurize; *colloq.* sweet-talk, lean on, soft-soap, pull strings, twist someone's arm

prevailing *adj*
predominant, preponderant, main, principal, chief, supreme, dominant, controlling, powerful, compelling, influential, reigning, ruling, current, fashionable, in fashion, in vogue, popular, mainstream, accepted, established, set, usual, most usual, customary, general, common, most common, prevalent, widespread
formal prepotent, ascendant
E∃ minor, subordinate

prevalence *n*
commonness, currency, frequency, pervasiveness, acceptance, popularity, predominance, universality, regularity, rule, hold, mastery, sway, profusion
formal ascendancy, omnipresence, preponderance, primacy, ubiquity
E∃ uncommonness

prevalent *adj*
widespread, extensive, rampant, rife, pervasive, frequent, general, customary, usual, universal, established, accepted, set, ubiquitous, common, everyday, popular, current, prevailing, dominant
E∃ uncommon, rare

prevaricate *v*
equivocate, quibble, evade, shift, shuffle, lie, deceive
formal cavil, tergiversate
colloq. hedge, dodge, shilly-shally, waffle, pussy-foot, beat about the bush, sit on the fence

⚠ **prevaricate** or **procrastinate** ?
To *prevaricate* is 'to talk evasively in order to avoid telling the truth, coming to the point, or answering a question': *When faced with difficult questions,*

> *politicians usually prevaricate.* To *procrastinate* is to put off until later things that should be done immediately.

prevarication *n*
evasion, equivocation, pretence, quibbling, lie, falsehood, untruth, falsification, fibbing, fib(s), half-truth, misrepresentation, deception, deceit
formal cavilling, tergiversation

prevaricator *n*
evader, equivocator, quibbler, liar, hypocrite, deceiver
old use pettifogger
formal casuist, caviller, dissembler, sophist
colloq. dodger, fibber

prevent *v*
stop, avert, avoid, keep from, halt, arrest, hold back, inhibit, head off, ward off, fend off, stave off, intercept, forestall, anticipate, frustrate, thwart, restrain, hinder, hamper, impede, obstruct, block, check, hold in check, foil, balk, deter, bar
formal preclude, obviate
E∃ cause, help, foster, encourage, allow

prevention *n*
avoidance, halting, arresting, heading off, warding off, fending off, staving off, frustration, check, hindrance, impediment, obstruction, obstacle, bar, elimination, precaution, safeguard, deterrence, hampering, foiling, balking
technical prophylaxis
formal preclusion, obviation
E∃ cause, help

preventive *adj, n*
▶ *adj* preventative, anticipatory, pre-emptive, inhibitory, obstructive, precautionary, protective, counteractive, deterrent
technical prophylactic
E∃ causative, fostering
▶ *n* prevention, protection, precautionary measure, protective, impediment, hindrance, deterrent, block, obstruction, obstacle, safeguard, remedy, shield, neutralizer
technical prophylactic
E∃ cause, encouragement, incitement

previous *adj*
preceding, foregoing, earlier, prior, past, former, ex-, one-time, sometime, antecedent
formal erstwhile, quondam
E∃ following, subsequent, later

previously *adv*
formerly, once, earlier, until now, before, beforehand, at one time, in the past
formal heretofore, hitherto, erst, erstwhile
E∃ later

prey *n, v*
▶ *n* quarry, game, kill, victim, target
colloq. mug, fall guy
▶ *v* ▷ **prey on** **1** HUNT, kill, seize, catch, devour, eat, feed on, live off, exploit, take advantage of; *colloq.* con, fleece, bleed **2** *prey on one's mind* haunt, trouble, distress, worry, burden, weigh down, hang over, oppress, plague, torment

price *n, v*
▶ *n* **1** *the price of the car*
value, worth, cost, expense(s), outlay, expenditure, fee, charge, levy, toll, rate, bill, assessment, valuation, estimate, quotation, figure, amount, sum, payment, reward
2 *publicity is the price of fame*
penalty, forfeit, sacrifice, consequences, result
▷ **at a price** expensive, at a high price, at a high cost
▷ **at any price** at any cost, whatever it takes, whatever the cost, no matter what it costs
▶ *v* value, rate, cost, evaluate, assess, estimate, set/fix the price at
formal appraise, valorize

priceless *adj*
1 INVALUABLE, inestimable, incalculable, expensive, costly, dear, precious, valuable, prized, treasured, cherished, irreplaceable, incomparable, rare
colloq. worth its weight in gold
2 FUNNY, amusing, comic, hilarious, riotous, side-splitting
colloq. killing, rich, a scream
E∃ **1** cheap, run-of-the-mill

pricey *adj*
costly, dear, excessive, exorbitant, expensive, extortionate, high-priced
colloq. steep, over the odds, costing an arm and a leg
E∃ cheap

prick *v, n*
▶ *v* **1** PIERCE, puncture, perforate, punch, jab, jag, nick, slit, gash, wound, spike, bore, stab, sting, bite, prickle, itch, tingle, smart
2 *prick your conscience*
trouble, distress, worry, torment, plague, harass, harry, gnaw at, prey on
▶ *n* puncture, perforation, pinhole, hole, stab, jab, jag, nick, wound, pang, twinge, sting, pain, smarting, tingle, bite

prickle *n, v*
▶ *n* **1** THORN, spine, barb, spur, point, spike, needle, prong, tine
formal acantha
2 *feel a prickle of fear*
sensation, sting, stinging, itching, smarting, twinge, pang, tingle
technical paraesthesia
formal formication
colloq. pins and needles
▶ *v* tingle, itch, smart, sting, prick, nip

prickly *adj*
1 THORNY, brambly, spiny, barbed, spiky, spiked, pronged, bristly, rough, scratchy
2 IRRITABLE, edgy, touchy, grumpy, short-tempered, bad-tempered
colloq. stroppy, ratty, crabby, crotchety, grouchy
3 *a prickly subject*
complicated, difficult, hard, thorny, problematical, tough, troublesome, tricky
E∃ **1** smooth **2** relaxed; *colloq.* easy-going

pride *n, v*
▶ *n* **1** SATISFACTION, gratification, sense of achievement, pleasure, delight, joy
2 DIGNITY, self-respect, self-esteem, self-image, self-worth, ego, honour
3 CONCEIT, vanity, egotism, big-headedness, boastfulness, smugness, disdain, arrogance, self-importance, self-conceit, presumption, haughtiness, superciliousness, snobbery, pretentiousness
E∃ **1** shame **3** humility, modesty
▶ *v* ▷ **pride yourself on** take satisfaction in, congratulate yourself, flatter yourself, take pride in, revel in, glory in, exult in, vaunt, crow about, boast

about, brag about; *colloq.* pat yourself on the back for
F3 belittle, humble

priest *n*
minister, vicar, parson, pastor, padre, father, man/
woman of God, man/woman of the cloth, clergyman,
clergywoman, churchman, churchwoman, deacon,
deaconess
Related adjective: sacerdotal

priestess *n*
clergywoman, canoness, deaconess, nun, prioress,
sister, abbess, religious, vestal, beguine, mambo

priestly *adj*
clerical, ecclesiastical, canonical, pastoral, priestlike,
sacerdotal, Aaronic(al)
formal hieratic

prig *n*
prude, puritan, killjoy, precisian, old maid, Mrs
Grundy
colloq. goody-goody, holy Joe, holy Willie

priggish *adj*
smug, self-righteous, sanctimonious, puritanical,
prim, prudish, narrow-minded, starchy, stuffy, strait-
laced
colloq. goody-goody, holier-than-thou
F3 broad-minded

prim *adj*
prudish, strait-laced, formal, demure, proper,
priggish, prissy, fussy, particular, stuffy, starchy,
puritanical, precise, fastidious, school-marmish, old-
maidish
colloq. fuddy-duddy
F3 relaxed; *colloq.* easy-going

primacy *n*
supremacy, dominance, paramouncy, pre-eminence,
sovereignty, superiority, command, seniority,
dominion, leadership
formal ascendancy
F3 inferiority

primal *adj*
original, basic, earliest, fundamental, primitive, first,
primary, initial, major, greatest, highest, main,
central, chief, paramount, principal, prime
formal primeval, primordial
F3 later, minor

primarily *adv*
chiefly, principally, mainly, mostly, basically, first,
firstly, fundamentally, especially, particularly,
predominantly, essentially, in essence, in the main, in
the first place

primary *adj*
1 CHIEF, principal, main, dominant, leading,
foremost, supreme, prime, predominant, cardinal,
capital, paramount, greatest, highest, ultimate
2 FIRST, basic, fundamental, essential, radical,
rudimentary, elementary, simple, earliest, original,
initial, introductory, beginning, opening
formal elemental, primeval, primordial
F3 1 secondary, subsidiary, minor

prime¹ *adj, n*
▶ *adj* **1** BEST, choice, select, quality, first-class, first-
rate, excellent, top, top-grade, supreme, highest, pre-
eminent
2 CHIEF, principal, main, leading, foremost,
supreme, predominant
3 CLASSIC, typical, standard, characteristic

formal paradigmatic, quintessential
F3 second-rate, secondary
▶ *n* height, peak, pinnacle, zenith, heyday, flower,
blossom, bloom, culmination, best part, maturity,
perfection
formal acme

prime² *v*
1 PREPARE, equip, get ready, coach, train
2 BRIEF, inform, notify, fill, fill in
colloq. clue up, gen up

primer *n*
introduction, manual, textbook
formal prodrome, prodromus

primeval *adj*
earliest, first, original, early, old, ancient, prehistoric,
primitive, instinctive
formal primordial, autochthonal
F3 modern

primitive *adj*
1 CRUDE, rough, unsophisticated, uncivilized,
simple, natural, uncultured, undeveloped, barbarian,
wild, savage
2 EARLY, elementary, rudimentary, primary, first,
original, earliest, ancient
formal primeval, primordial
F3 1 advanced, sophisticated, civilized

primordial *adj*
earliest, first, original, early, old, ancient, prehistoric,
primitive, instinctive
formal primeval, autochthonal
F3 modern

primp *v*
groom, smarten, tidy, dress up, spruce up, beautify,
preen
colloq. titivate, doll up, tart up, put on your best bib and
tucker, put on your glad rags

prince *n*
lord, ruler, monarch, potentate, sovereign

princely *adj*
1 SOVEREIGN, imperial, royal, regal, majestic,
stately, grand, imposing, magnificent, splendid, noble
2 *princely sum*
handsome, generous, liberal, lavish, sumptuous,
magnificent, magnanimous
formal bounteous

principal *adj, n*
▶ *adj* main, chief, key, major, essential, cardinal,
primary, first, foremost, leading, controlling,
dominant, in charge, prime, paramount, pre-eminent,
most important, supreme, highest, arch
F3 minor, subsidiary, lesser, least
▶ *n* **1** HEAD, head teacher, headmaster,
headmistress, rector, chief, leader, director, manager,
superintendent, controller, ruler
colloq. boss
2 MONEY, capital, capital sum, capital funds, assets

⚠ **principal** or **principle** ?
As an adjective, *principal* means 'most important':
*Shipbuilding and coal-mining were two of Britain's
principal industries.* As a noun, *principal* means 'the
head of a school, college or university'. *Principle* can
only be used as a noun. It means 'a general rule' or
'the theory underlying a method or way of working':
the principles of economic theory.

principally _adv_
mainly, mostly, chiefly, primarily, predominantly, above all, particularly, especially, in the main, for the most part, first and foremost

principle _n_
1 RULE, formula, law, canon, axiom, dictum, precept, maxim, truth, tenet, doctrine, creed, dogma, code, theory, idea, standard, criterion, proposition, basis, fundamental, essential
formal postulate
2 _a man of principle_
honour, integrity, uprightness, virtue, decency, morality, morals, ethics, standards, scruples, conscience
formal rectitude
▷ **in principle** theoretically, in theory, ideally, in essence, _en principe_

⚠ **principle** or **principal** ? _See panel at_ **principal**.

principled _adj_
upright, virtuous, moral, ethical, high-minded, honourable, conscientious, decent, righteous, just, right-minded, scrupulous
🖵 unprincipled

print _v, n_
▶ _v_ mark, stamp, imprint, impress, engrave, etch, copy, reproduce, run off, publish, issue
colloq. put to bed
▶ _n_ **1** LETTERS, characters, lettering, type, typescript, typeface, fount
2 MARK, impression, fingerprint, footprint
3 COPY, reproduction, replica, design, picture, engraving, lithograph, photograph, photo, snapshot
colloq. snap
▷ **in print** published, available, obtainable, in circulation
🖵 out of print

Printing methods include: bubble-jet printing, collotype, colour-process printing, copper engraving, die-stamping, duplicating, electrostatic printing, engraving, etching, flexography, gravure, ink-jet printing, intaglio, laser printing, letterpress, lino blocking, litho, lithography, offset lithography, offset printing, photoengraving, rotary press, screen printing, silk-screen printing, stencilling, thermography, twin-etching, xerography.

Printing terms include: anodized plate, author's proof, back margin, backing-up, bad break, base alignment, batter, bi-directional printing, black printer, blanket-to-blanket press, bold face, bromide, camera-ready copy, carding, caret, cast-off, catchword, centre, character set, chase, cliché, cold composition, collograph, colour control bar, colour separation, column inch/centimetre, compose, composing room, composition size, compositor, condensed, copy, cylinder press, dampers, dot-etching, dot gain, drum printer, electrotype, em, en, end even, expanded type, feathering, finishing, first proof, flat-bed press, flong, font, forme, galley, gutter, hard hyphen, hot-metal typesetting, image printing, imposition, impression, indent, initial caps, inking roller, Intertype®, italic, justification, keep standing, kern, kiss impression, large print, leaders, leading, letterset, line printer, Linotype®, literal, logotype, lower-case, machine composition, machine proof, mackle, makeready, manuscript, margin, matrix, misprint, moiré, Monophoto®, Monotype®, mottling, newsprint, non-image area, non-impact printing, offprint, orphan, overprint, Ozalid®,

perfecting, phototypesetting, planographic, printing press, progressive proofs, proof, quoin, ragged right/left, registration, relief printing, reprint, roman, run-around, running head, running text, sans serif, see-through, signature, small capitals, soft hyphen, specimen page, spoilage, stereotype, stet, strike-on, strip in, take in, take over, text, thermal printer, tint, trim marks, type, typeface, type scale, typescript, typesetting, type spec, typo, _US_ typographer, upper-case, web-fed, web offset, widow, woodcut, wood engraving, zinco.

prior _adj_
earlier, preceding, foregoing, previous, former
🖵 later
▷ **prior to** before, preceding, earlier than, until
🖵 after, following

priority _n_
1 _a top priority_
most important thing, most urgent matter, matter of highest/greatest importance, main thing, supreme matter, first concern, primary issue, essential, requirement, pole position
colloq. top of the tree
2 PRECEDENCE, right of way, seniority, rank, superiority, pre-eminence, supremacy, paramouncy, the lead, first/highest place
🖵 **2** inferiority

priory _n_
monastery, abbey, cloister, friary, convent, nunnery, religious house, béguinage

prise _v_
lever, force, jemmy, pry, raise, lift, hoist, dislodge, shift, move, winkle

prison _n_
jail, penitentiary, cell, lock-up, cage, dungeon, imprisonment, confinement, detention, custody
colloq. nick, inside; _slang_ clink, cooler, slammer, jug, can, choky, quod

prisoner _n_
captive, hostage, convict, prisoner of war, POW, inmate, internee, detainee, recidivist
colloq. jailbird, con, lifer, (old) lag, yardbird

prissy _adj_
prim, squeamish, prudish, strait-laced, formal, demure, proper, priggish, fussy, particular, stuffy, starchy, puritanical, precise, fastidious, school-marmish, old-maidish
colloq. finicky, po-faced

pristine _adj_
1 IMMACULATE, undefiled, uncorrupted, untouched, virgin, unspoiled, unsullied
2 ORIGINAL, earliest, first, initial, former, primary, primitive, primal
formal primeval, primordial, primigenial
🖵 **1** spoiled **2** developed, later

privacy _n_
secrecy, confidentiality, independence, solitude, quietness, isolation, seclusion, privateness, concealment, retirement, retreat
formal sequestration
🖵 publicness, interruption, interference

private _adj, n_
▶ _adj_ **1** _private discussions_
CONFIDENTIAL, classified, secret, privileged, unofficial, off the record

colloq. hush-hush
2 *your private life/feelings*
personal, confidential, intimate, innermost, secret, individual
3 *a private bathroom*
exclusive, particular, own, special, individual, personal
4 *a private person*
quiet, reserved, withdrawn, independent, solitary, retiring, separate, self-contained
5 *a private place*
secluded, isolated, hidden, concealed, secret, remote, undisturbed, quiet, out-of-the-way
formal sequestered
6 *private industries*
independent, commercial, free-enterprise, privatized, non-governmental, denationalized, self-governing, self-determining
E3 1 official, public **5** public **6** public, state-controlled, state-run, nationalized
▶ *n* enlisted man, private soldier, Tommy, squaddy, swad, swaddy
colloq. Tommy Atkins
▷ **in private** privately, in confidence, confidentially, secretly, in secret, behind closed doors, in camera, *sub rosa*
E3 publicly, openly
▷ **private detective** private eye, private investigator, pinkerton, shamus
▷ **private parts** genitals, sexual organs, reproductive organs, vagina, womb, penis; *technical* pudenda; *formal* genitalia; *colloq.* privates; *slang* fanny, pussy, cunt, cock, prick, dick

privateer *n*
buccaneer, pirate, brigand, filibuster, freebooter, corsair, marque, sea robber, sea wolf

privation *n*
hardship, destitution, deprivation, affliction, neediness, poverty, suffering, lack, need, austerity, loss, misery, distress
formal indigence, penury, want
E3 affluence, wealth

privilege *n*
advantage, benefit, concession, birthright, title, due, right, prerogative, entitlement, honour, freedom, liberty, franchise, licence, sanction, dispensation, authority, immunity, exemption
E3 disadvantage

privileged *adj*
1 FAVOURED, advantaged, special, indulgent, sanctioned, authorized, immune, excepted, exempt, elite, honoured, ruling, powerful
2 CONFIDENTIAL, private, classified, secret, unofficial, off the record
E3 1 disadvantaged, under-privileged **2** public

privy *n*
toilet, lavatory, water closet, WC, public convenience, washroom, cloakroom, latrine
colloq. bog, loo
▷ **privy to** aware of, cognizant of, informed about, wise to; *formal* apprised of; *colloq.* in on, in the know about
E3 unaware of

prize *n, adj, v*
▶ *n* **1** REWARD, trophy, medal, award, winnings, jackpot, purse, premium, stake(s), honour, accolade, laurels, pennant

2 AIM, goal, gain, hope, desire, honour
3 BOOTY, loot, spoils, plunder, pickings, capture, pillage, trophy
▶ *adj* best, top, first-rate, excellent, outstanding, champion, winning, prize-winning, award-winning
colloq. top-notch, terrific, smashing, out of this world
E3 second-rate
▶ *v* treasure, value, appreciate, revere, cherish, love, hold dear, think highly of, hold in high regard, set great store by
formal esteem
E3 despise, undervalue

prize-winner *n*
winner, champion, cup-winner, medallist, prizeman, prizewoman, dux
colloq. champ

probability *n*
likelihood, likeliness, odds, chance(s), expectation, prospect, possibility
E3 improbability

probable *adj*
likely, expected, to be expected, anticipated, credible, believable, plausible, feasible, forseeable, predictable, possible, apparent, seeming
colloq. odds-on, on the cards, a fair bet
E3 improbable, unlikely

probably *adv*
in all likelihood, in all probability, likely, it looks like, the chances are, most likely, as likely as not, doubtless, presumably, possibly, perhaps, maybe
colloq. (as) like as not, a fair bet
E3 improbably

probation *n*
trial period, experimental period, trial, test, test period, apprenticeship, supervision

probe *v, n*
▶ *v* **1** INVESTIGATE, scrutinize, examine, study, inquire, analyse, research, go into, look into, search, sift, test
2 PROD, poke, pierce, penetrate, sound, plumb, check, explore, examine
▶ *n* **1** INQUIRY, inquest, investigation, exploration, examination, test, scrutiny, scrutinization, study, analysis, research
2 BORE, drill

probity *n*
uprightness, righteousness, integrity, honour, honourableness, virtue, morality, worth, honesty, goodness, equity, fairness, justice, truthfulness, trustworthiness, sincerity
formal fidelity, rectitude
E3 *formal* improbity

problem *n, adj*
▶ *n* **1** TROUBLE, worry, predicament, quandary, plight, dilemma, difficulty, complication, snag
colloq. hassle, hole, pickle, fix, mess, tight spot, dire straits, no-win situation, catch-22
2 QUESTION, issue, matter, poser, puzzle, brain-teaser, conundrum, riddle, enigma
▶ *adj* difficult, unmanageable, uncontrollable, unruly, troublesome, disobedient, delinquent
formal recalcitrant, intransigent
E3 well-behaved, manageable

problematic *adj*
1 DIFFICULT, fraught with difficulties, troublesome, awkward, hard, puzzling, perplexing, intricate,

involved, tricky, thorny, problematical, enigmatic, moot
colloq. a can of worms, a minefield
2 UNCERTAIN, questionable, debatable, doubtful, dubious
F3 1 easy, straightforward **2** certain

procedure *n*
routine, process, method, methodology, system, technique, custom, practice, means, measure, policy, formula, way, course, course of action, scheme, strategy, plan of action, move, step, action, conduct, operation, *modus operandi*, performance

proceed *v*
1 *the permission to proceed*
advance, go ahead, move on, go on, go forward, progress, continue, carry on, press on, make your way
2 START, begin, make a start, take steps, get under way, set in motion
3 ORIGINATE, derive, flow, start, stem, spring, arise, issue, emanate, result, ensue, follow, come
F3 1 stop, retreat

proceedings *n*
1 MATTERS, affairs, business, dealings, transactions, report, account, minutes, records, archives, annals
2 EVENTS, activities, happenings, deeds, doings, moves, steps, measures, action, course of action, operations, procedures, manoeuvres
3 *legal proceedings*
lawsuit, case, trial, action, process, litigation

proceeds *n*
revenue, income, returns, receipts, takings, earnings, gain, profit(s), yield, produce
F3 expenditure, outlay

process *n, v*
▶ *n* **1** PROCEDURE, operation, practice, action, method, system, technique, means, manner, way, stage, step
formal mode
2 COURSE, progression, advance, progress, development, change(s), evolution, formation, growth, movement, action, proceeding
▷ **in the process of** in the course of, in the middle of, being, in the making, in preparation
▶ *v* deal with, handle, treat, prepare, refine, transform, convert, change, alter

procession *n*
march, parade, cavalcade, motorcade, cortège, file, column, train, succession, stream, series, sequence, course, run

proclaim *v*
announce, declare, pronounce, give out, publish, advertise, circulate, broadcast, make known, notify, profess, testify, blazon, trumpet, show, indicate
formal affirm, promulgate

proclamation *n*
announcement, declaration, pronouncement, publication, circulation, advertisement, notice, notification, broadcast, manifesto, order, rule, command, decree, edict
formal affirmation, promulgation

proclivity *n*
tendency, leaning, inclination, weakness, disposition, bent, bias, liability, proneness, liableness
formal penchant, predilection, predisposition, propensity
F3 disinclination

procrastinate *v*
defer, put off, postpone, delay, stall, play for time, dally, drag your feet, prolong, protract
formal retard, temporize
colloq. dilly-dally
F3 advance, proceed

⚠ **procrastinate** or **prevaricate** ? *See panel at* **prevaricate**.

procrastination *n*
delaying, deferral, stalling, delaying tactics
formal temporizing
colloq. dilly-dallying

procreate *v*
reproduce, produce, father, mother, breed, conceive, generate, propagate, multiply, engender, sire, spawn
old use beget

procure *v*
1 ACQUIRE, buy, purchase, get, obtain, find, come by, pick up, lay hands on, earn, gain, win, secure, get hold of
formal appropriate, requisition
2 *procure a prostitute*
pimp, pander, solicit, importune
colloq. hook, hustle
F3 1 lose

procurer *n*
procuress, pimp, pander, panderer, bawd, madam, whoremonger

prod *v, n*
▶ *v* **1** POKE, jab, dig, elbow, nudge, push, butt, thrust
colloq. shove
2 URGE, goad, spur, prompt, stimulate, motivate, stir, move, encourage, incite
colloq. egg on
▶ *n* **1** POKE, jab, dig, elbow, nudge, push
colloq. shove
2 PROMPT, prompting, reminder, stimulus, spur, goad, motivation, encouragement

prodigal *adj, n*
▶ *adj* wasteful, extravagant, squandering, excessive, improvident, intemperate, unsparing, unthrifty, wanton, reckless, spendthrift, immoderate, lavish, profuse, sumptuous, exuberant, bountiful, copious
formal bounteous, luxuriant, profligate
F3 modest, thrifty, parsimonious
▶ *n* squanderer, waster, spendthrift, spendall, wastrel
formal profligate
colloq. big spender

prodigality *n*
wastefulness, extravagance, recklessness, squandering, waste, wantonness, unthriftiness, immoderation, intemperance, dissipation, excess, abandon, exuberance, richness, profusion, lavishness, sumptuousness, plenty, abundance
formal luxuriance, plenteousness, profligacy, bounteousness, amplitude, copiousness
F3 modesty, thrift, parsimony

prodigious *adj*
1 ENORMOUS, gigantic, huge, massive, vast, immense, colossal, giant, mammoth, immeasurable
2 EXTRAORDINARY, marvellous, startling, amazing, astounding, staggering, fabulous, fantastic, flabbergasting, striking, impressive, miraculous, wonderful, monumental, inordinate, spectacular,

remarkable, stupendous, tremendous, phenomenal, unusual, exceptional, abnormal

F∃ **1** small **2** commonplace, unremarkable

prodigy *n*
genius, virtuoso, child genius, wonder child, gifted child, mastermind, wonder, marvel, miracle, phenomenon, sensation, freak, curiosity, rarity
colloq. whizz kid

produce *v, n*
▶ *v* **1** CAUSE, occasion, give rise to, provoke, bring about, result in, create, evoke, originate, invent, develop, prepare, make, manufacture, fashion, fabricate, build, construct, put together, assemble, compose, generate, occasion, yield, bear, breed, grow, deliver
formal effect
2 ADVANCE, put forward, present, offer, give, supply, provide, furnish, bring out, bring forward, bring forth, show, exhibit, demonstrate, come up with
formal proffer
3 *produce a play*
direct, stage, present, perform, manage, organize, arrange, mount, put on
▶ *n* crop, harvest, yield, output, product(s), food, foodstuffs, fruit, vegetables, dairy products, eggs

producer *n*
director, presenter, impresario, manager, régisseur, manufacturer, maker, farmer, grower

product *n*
1 COMMODITY, merchandise, goods, wares, end-product, artefact, work, article, item, creation, invention, production, output, yield, produce, fruit, return
2 RESULT, consequence, effect, outcome, issue, upshot, fruit, offshoot, spin-off, by-product, legacy
F∃ **2** cause

production *n*
1 MAKING, manufacture, manufacturing, producing, building, fabrication, construction, assembly, creation, origination, preparation, formation, composition, development
2 OUTPUT, yield, harvest, fruit(s), return(s), productivity, manufacture, achievement, performance
3 *an amateur production*
staging, mounting, performance, presentation, direction, management, organization
4 SHOW, play, drama, concert, musical, opera, film, revue, presentation, performance
F∃ **1** consumption

productive *adj*
fruitful, profitable, rewarding, valuable, beneficial, worthwhile, useful, constructive, gainful, creative, inventive, fertile, prolific, rich, high-yielding, teeming, busy, energetic, vigorous, efficient, effective
formal fecund, fructiferous
F∃ unproductive, fruitless, useless

productivity *n*
productiveness, yield, output, production, capacity, work rate, efficiency

profane *adj, v*
▶ *adj* **1** SACRILEGIOUS, irreligious, blasphemous, idolatrous, godless, ungodly, irreverent, disrespectful, abusive, crude, vulgar, coarse, foul, filthy, unclean
2 SECULAR, temporal, lay, worldly, unconsecrated, unhallowed, unsanctified, unholy, impious
F∃ **1** sacred **2** religious, respectful

▶ *v* desecrate, pollute, contaminate, defile, debase, pervert, abuse, misuse, misemploy
F∃ revere, honour

profanity *n*
1 SACRILEGE, irreverence, profaneness, impiety, blasphemy, abuse
formal execration, imprecation, malediction
2 OBSCENITY, swear-word, swearing, expletive, curse, cursing
colloq. four-letter word
F∃ politeness, reverence

profess *v*
1 CLAIM, maintain, allege, lay claim to, make out, pretend
formal dissemble
2 DECLARE, admit, confess, acknowledge, own, confirm, certify, announce, proclaim, state, assert, affirm
formal aver, avow

professed *adj*
1 SELF-ACKNOWLEDGED, self-confessed, self-styled, so-called, *soi-disant*, confirmed, declared, certified, acknowledged, proclaimed
formal avowed
2 PRETENDED, supposed, ostensible, alleged, would-be
formal purported

profession *n*
1 CAREER, job, occupation, employment, business, line (of work), walk of life, craft, trade, vocation, calling, métier, craft, office, appointment, post, position, situation
2 ADMISSION, confession, acknowledgement, declaration, announcement, statement, testimony, assertion, affirmation, claim
formal averment, avowal

professional *adj, n*
▶ *adj* qualified, licensed, trained, experienced, practised, skilful, skilled, educated, expert, masterly, adept, proficient, competent, businesslike, efficient
F∃ amateur, unprofessional
▶ *n* expert, authority, specialist, master, past master, virtuoso
colloq. pro, dab hand, wizard, ace
F∃ amateur

proffer *v*
offer, tender, advance, extend, hold out, hand, suggest, present, propose, submit, volunteer
formal propound

proficiency *n*
skill, skilfulness, expertise, experience, mastery, talent, knack, dexterity, finesse, aptitude, accomplishment, capability, ability, competence, aptness, adeptness
F∃ incompetence

proficient *adj*
able, capable, skilled, qualified, trained, experienced, accomplished, expert, masterly, gifted, talented, clever, skilful, competent, efficient, effective, apt, adept
F∃ unskilled, incompetent

profile *n*
1 SIDE VIEW, outline, contour, silhouette, shape, form, line(s), figure, sketch, drawing, diagram, chart, graph
2 BIOGRAPHY, curriculum vitae, CV, thumbnail

sketch, vignette, portrait, sketch, study, analysis, examination, survey, review

profit *n, v*

▶ *n* **1** *the company's profits*
revenue, return, yield, proceeds, receipts, takings, earnings, winnings, dividend, interest, bonus, gain, surplus, excess, bottom line
colloq. fast buck, gravy, killing, rake-off
2 ADVANTAGE, benefit, gain, use, avail, value, worth
E3 1, 2 loss
▶ *v* gain, make money, pay, serve, avail, benefit
colloq. line your pockets
E3 lose
▷ **profit by/from** exploit, take advantage of, use, utilize, turn to advantage, put to good use, gain a benefit from, gain an advantage from, capitalize on, reap the benefit of; *colloq.* cash in on, milk

profitable *adj*

cost-effective, economic, commercial, money-making, lucrative, remunerative, paying, rewarding, successful, fruitful, productive, advantageous, beneficial, useful, valuable, worthwhile
formal gainful
colloq. in the black
E3 unprofitable, loss-making, non-profit-making

profiteer *n, v*

▶ *n* racketeer, exploiter, extortioner, extortionist
▶ *v* exploit, extort, racketeer, overcharge
colloq. fleece, make a fast buck, make a quick killing

profiteering *n*

exploitation, extortion, racketeering, Rachmanism

profitless *adj*

useless, worthless, fruitless, futile, vain, pointless, thankless, ineffective, idle, unavailing, unproductive, unprofitable, unremunerative, gainless
formal ineffectual
E3 profitable

profligacy *n*

1 WASTE, wastefulness, extravagance, excess, unrestraint, lavishness, unthriftiness, recklessness, squandering, improvidence, prodigality
2 IMMORALITY, promiscuity, corruption, debauchery, degeneracy, depravity, libertinism, licentiousness, wantonness, dissipation, dissoluteness
E3 morality, parsimony, thrift, uprightness

profligate *adj, n*

▶ *adj* **1** WASTEFUL, extravagant, squandering, immoderate, excessive, improvident, reckless, spendthrift, prodigal
2 IMMORAL, corrupt, dissolute, unprincipled, wicked, loose, dissipated, depraved, degenerate, debauched, iniquitous, promiscuous, licentious, wanton, libertine
E3 1 thrifty; *formal* parsimonious **2** upright, moral
▶ *n* **1** WASTER, wastrel, squanderer, spendthrift, prodigal
2 REPROBATE, debauchee, libertine, degenerate, rake, roué

profound *adj*

1 DEEP, great, intense, extreme, heartfelt, sincere, marked, thorough, thoroughgoing, far-reaching, radical, extensive, exhaustive
2 *a profound remark*
serious, weighty, deep, penetrating, discerning, thoughtful, philosophical, wise, learned, impenetrable

formal sagacious, erudite, esoteric, abstruse
E3 1 shallow, slight, mild **2** shallow

profoundly *adv*

deeply, intensely, extremely, seriously, acutely, greatly, heartily, thoroughly, keenly, sincerely
E3 slightly

profundity *n*

depth, profoundness, extremity, intensity, severity, strength, seriousness, penetration, learning, insight, intelligence, wisdom, perceptiveness, acumen
formal abstruseness, erudition, perspecuity, perspicacity, sagacity
E3 shallowness

profuse *adj*

ample, abundant, plentiful, copious, generous, liberal, lavish, rich, excessive, immoderate, extravagant, fulsome, unstinting, overabundant, superabundant, overflowing
formal luxuriant, inordinate
colloq. over the top
E3 inadequate, sparse

profusion *n*

abundance, copiousness, plenty, wealth, multitude, glut, riot, excess, surplus, superfluity, superabundance, extravagance
formal plethora, plenitude
colloq. loads, lots, heaps, tons
E3 inadequacy, scarcity

progenitor *n*

1 ANCESTOR, forebear, forefather, father, mother, parent
old use begetter
formal procreator, primogenitor
2 ORIGINATOR, forerunner, founder, instigator, precursor, predecessor, antecedent, source

progeny *n*

offspring, children, young, descendants, family, issue, lineage, race, breed, seed, stock, quiverful
formal posterity, scions

prognosis *n*

diagnosis, expectation, forecast, prediction, outlook, projection, assessment, evaluation, prospect, speculation, surmise
formal prognostication

prognosticate *v*

forecast, foreshadow, foretell, predict, prophesy, herald, indicate, soothsay, divine
formal augur, betoken, harbinger, portend, presage

prognostication *n*

prediction, projection, forecast, expectation, speculation, surmise, horoscope, prophecy
formal prognosis

programme *n, v*

▶ *n* **1** SCHEDULE, timetable, agenda, calendar, order of events, listing, list, line-up, plan, plan of action, scheme, project, syllabus, prospectus, curriculum
2 *radio programme*
broadcast, transmission, show, performance, production, presentation, episode, simulcast
▶ *v* arrange, plan, schedule, work out, formulate, itemize, lay on, line up, design, list, map out, book, prearrange

progress *n, v*

▶ *n* movement, progression, passage, going, journey,

way, advance, headway, step(s) forward, breakthrough, development, evolution, growth, increase, improvement, upgrading, betterment, promotion
formal advancement
F3 recession, deterioration, decline
▶ *v* proceed, advance, go forward, move forward, forge ahead, make progress, make headway, make your way, make strides, continue, go on, come on, develop, grow, mature, blossom, flourish, improve, better, recover, prosper, increase
colloq. be getting there, shape up
F3 deteriorate, decline
▷ **in progress** under way, proceeding, going on, happening, occurring, continuing, in preparation, not finished, not completed; *colloq.* in the pipeline, on the stocks

progression *n*
cycle, chain, string, succession, series, sequence, stream, train, order, course, advance, headway, passage, progress, development, forward movement
formal advancement

progressive *adj*
1 MODERN, avant-garde, advanced, forward-looking, forward-thinking, enlightened, liberal, radical, revolutionary, reformist, innovative, dynamic, enterprising, go-ahead, up-and-coming
2 ADVANCING, continuing, developing, growing, increasing, escalating, intensifying, accelerating
F3 1 conservative 2 regressive

prohibit *v*
forbid, ban, bar, veto, outlaw, rule out, prevent, exclude, stop, hinder, hamper, impede, obstruct, restrict
formal proscribe, preclude, interdict
F3 permit, allow, authorize

prohibited *adj*
forbidden, banned, barred, taboo, vetoed, embargoed, verboten
formal disallowed, interdicted, proscribed
F3 permitted, allowed

prohibition *n*
forbidding, forbiddance, ban, bar, constraint, veto, restriction, obstruction, exclusion, prevention, negation, embargo, injunction
formal disallowance, forbiddal, interdict, interdiction, proscription
F3 permission

prohibitionist *n*
teetotaller, abolitionist, dry, pussyfoot

prohibitive *adj*
forbidding, preposterous, excessive, exorbitant, extortionate, impossible, restrictive, restraining, suppressive, repressive, prohibiting, prohibitory
formal proscriptive
colloq. sky-high, steep
F3 encouraging, reasonable

project *n, v*
▶ *n* scheme, campaign, plan, venture, programme, design, proposal, assignment, contract, task, job, work, occupation, activity, enterprise, undertaking, idea, conception
▶ *v* 1 PREDICT, forecast, plan, propose, extrapolate, estimate, reckon, calculate, gauge, expect, design, map out
formal predetermine
2 THROW, fling, hurl, cast, launch, propel, discharge

3 PROTRUDE, stick out, stand out, extend, bulge, jut out, overhang
formal obtrude

projectile *n*
missile, rocket, shell, shot, grenade, bullet, ball, mortar-bomb

projecting *adj*
overhanging, protruding, protrusive, beetling
formal exsertile, extrusive, extrusory, protrudent

projection *n*
1 PREDICTION, forecast, expectation, extrapolation, estimate, estimation, reckoning, calculation, computation, plan, design
2 PROTUBERANCE, bulge, jutting, overhang, ledge, sill, shelf, ridge

proletariat *n*
working class, common people, masses, mob, lower classes, rabble, herd, hoi polloi, canaille, commoners, commonalty
colloq. great unwashed, plebs, proles, riff-raff

proliferate *v*
multiply, reproduce, grow quickly, breed, increase, build up, intensify, extend, escalate, mushroom, snowball, rocket, spread, expand, flourish, thrive
formal burgeon
F3 dwindle

proliferation *n*
multiplication, increase, intensification, escalation, expansion, spread, extension, build-up, concentration, duplication, mushrooming, snowballing, rocketing
F3 decrease

prolific *adj*
productive, fruitful, fertile, profuse, copious, abundant, rank
formal fecund, luxuriant
F3 unproductive

prolix *adj*
long-winded, verbose, lengthy, prolonged, prosy, discursive, digressive, long, diffuse, rambling, tedious, tiresome, wordy
technical pleonastic
formal protracted
F3 succinct

prolixity *n*
long-windedness, verboseness, verbiage, wordiness, prosiness, rambling, discursiveness, diffuseness, wandering, verbosity, boringness, tediousness
technical pleonasm
F3 succinctness

prologue *n*
introduction, foreword, preface, preamble, preliminary, prelude
formal exordium, proem, prolegomena, prooemion, prooemium

prolong *v*
lengthen, extend, elongate, stretch (out), protract, draw out, spin out, drag out, delay, continue, perpetuate
formal protract
F3 shorten

promenade *n, v*
▶ *n* 1 SEAFRONT, walkway, front, parade, esplanade, prom, boulevard, terrace
2 WALK, stroll, breather, airing, saunter, turn, walkabout

formal constitutional
▶ *v* walk, stroll, saunter, strut, swagger, sally forth, parade
formal perambulate
colloq. mosey

prominence *n*
1 FAME, celebrity, renown, eminence, pre-eminence, illustriousness, distinction, greatness, note, importance, conspicuousness, reputation, name, standing, stature, rank, prestige, weight, top billing
2 BULGE, protuberance, swelling, jutting, protruding, bump, hump, lump, mound, rise, elevation, projection, process, headland, promontory, pinnacle, crest, height, cliff, crag
🖅 1 unimportance, insignificance

prominent *adj*
1 NOTICEABLE, conspicuous, obvious, unmistakable, striking, eye-catching
2 BULGING, protuberant, projecting, jutting (out), standing out, sticking out, protruding, obtrusive, protrusive
3 *a prominent writer*
famous, well-known, celebrated, renowned, noted, notable, eminent, pre-eminent, distinguished, respected, illustrious, leading, foremost, chief, main, important, popular, outstanding, top, acclaimed
🖅 1 inconspicuous 3 unknown, unimportant, insignificant

promiscuity *n*
looseness, laxity, permissiveness, wantonness, immorality, dissoluteness, dissipation, licentiousness, debauchery, depravity
formal profligacy, protervity
🖅 chastity, morality

promiscuous *adj*
loose, immoral, licentious, dissolute, debauched, dissipated, abandoned, wanton, fast, of easy virtue, casual, random, haphazard, indiscriminate
formal profligate
🖅 chaste, moral

promise *v, n*
▶ *v* 1 VOW, pledge, swear, take an oath, contract, give an undertaking, undertake, give your word, vouch, warrant, guarantee, assure, give an assurance
2 *clouds that promise rain*
indicate, suggest, hint at, signify, denote, be a sign of
formal augur, presage, betoken
▶ *n* 1 VOW, pledge, oath, word, word of honour, bond, guarantee, assurance, contract, undertaking, engagement, commitment
formal compact, covenant
2 POTENTIAL, ability, capability, aptitude, talent, flair
3 *a promise of autumn sunshine*
sign, hint, suggestion, indication, evidence
▷ **promised land** paradise, Zion, land of milk and honey, Shangri-la

promising *adj*
favourable, rosy, bright, encouraging, optimistic, hopeful, talented, able, gifted, budding
formal auspicious, propitious
colloq. up-and-coming
🖅 unpromising, inauspicious, discouraging

promontory *n*
cliff, headland, head, foreland, bluff, precipice, point, projection, prominence, ridge, spur, cape, naze, ness, peninsula

promote *v*
1 UPGRADE, advance, move up, raise, elevate, exalt, honour
formal aggrandize, prefer
2 ENCOURAGE, recommend, advocate, champion, endorse, sponsor, support, back, help, aid, assist, advance, foster, nurture, further, forward, boost, stimulate, urge, contribute to
formal espouse
3 ADVERTISE, publicize, popularize, market, sell, push
colloq. plug, hype, puff up
🖅 1 demote, relegate 2 discourage, hinder; *formal* disparage

promotion *n*
1 ADVANCEMENT, upgrading, rise, elevation, exaltation, move-up
formal preferment, aggrandizement
2 ENCOURAGEMENT, support, recommendation, advocacy, urging, fostering, contribution, backing, furtherance, development, boosting
formal espousal
3 ADVERTISING, publicity, campaign, propaganda, marketing
colloq. plugging, hype, pushing
🖅 1 demotion 2 discouragement, obstruction; *formal* disparagement

prompt *adj, adv, v, n*
▶ *adj* punctual, on time, immediate, instantaneous, instant, direct, quick, swift, rapid, speedy, unhesitating, willing, ready, alert, eager, willing, responsive, timely, early
formal expeditious
🖅 slow, hesitant, late
▶ *adv* promptly, punctually, exactly, on time, on the dot, to the minute, sharp
colloq. dead on, bang on, spot on
▶ *v* cause, give rise to, result in, lead, occasion, produce, make, instigate, call forth, elicit, provoke, induce, incite, urge, encourage, inspire, move, stimulate, motivate, spur, impel, prod, remind
formal expedite
🖅 deter, dissuade
▶ *n* reminder, cue, refresher, encouragement, hint, help, jolt, prod, spur, stimulus

prompting *n*
encouragement, reminder, reminding, advice, assistance, hint, influence, jogging, prodding, pushing, suggestion, urging, persuasion, incitement, pressing, pressure
formal admonition, protreptic
🖅 dissuasion

promptly *adv*
1 IMMEDIATELY, instantly, directly, unhesitatingly, quickly, speedily, swiftly
formal forthwith
colloq. pronto
2 PUNCTUALLY, on time, on target, exactly, on the dot, to the minute, sharp, as soon as possible, posthaste
colloq. bang on, spot on, dead on, pronto, asap, pdq, pretty damn quick

promptness *n*
punctuality, quickness, readiness, speed, swiftness, willingness, briskness, dispatch, eagerness, alertness, haste
formal alacrity, expedition, promptitude
🖅 *formal* tardiness

promulgate *v*
announce, proclaim, declare, decree, promote, circulate, notify, communicate, publish, spread, publicize, broadcast, advertise, issue
formal disseminate

promulgation *n*
announcement, communication, declaration, proclamation, publication, publicizing, issuance, promulgating
formal dissemination

prone *adj*
1 LIKELY, given, inclined, disposed, bent, apt, liable, subject, susceptible, vulnerable
formal predisposed
2 *she lay prone*
face down, prostrate, flat, horizontal, full-length, stretched
formal recumbent, procumbent
EƎ 1 unlikely, immune 2 upright, supine

proneness *n*
inclination, leaning, tendency, susceptibility, aptness, bent, bias, disposition, liability, weakness
formal penchant, proclivity, propensity
EƎ dislike

prong *n*
point, spike, projection, spur, tine, tip, fork, grain

pronounce *v*
1 SAY, utter, speak, express, voice, vocalize, sound, enunciate, articulate, stress
2 DECLARE, announce, proclaim, decree, judge, affirm, assert

pronounceable *adj*
speakable, utterable, sayable, vocable, articulable, enunciable, expressible
EƎ unpronounceable

pronounced *adj*
clear, distinct, definite, positive, decided, marked, noticeable, conspicuous, evident, obvious, striking, unmistakable, strong, broad, thick
EƎ faint, vague

pronouncement *n*
declaration, statement, announcement, judgement, notification, proclamation, assertion, decree, edict, manifesto, dictum
formal pronunciamento, *ipse dixit*, promulgation

pronunciation *n*
speech, diction, elocution, enunciation, articulation, saying, uttering, voicing, vocalization, delivery, accent, stress, inflection, intonation, modulation

proof *n, adj*
▶ *n* evidence, documentation, demonstration, verification, confirmation, corroboration, certification, validation, substantiation, authentication
formal attestation
▶ *adj* impenetrable, impervious, proofed, repellent, resistant, strong, tight, treated, fireproof, weatherproof, waterproof, rainproof, leakproof, windproof, bombproof, bulletproof, childproof, foolproof, tamperproof, soundproof
EƎ permeable, untreated

prop *v, n*
▶ *v* 1 SUPPORT, sustain, uphold, hold up, maintain, shore (up), stay, brace, buttress, bolster (up), underpin, set, underwrite

2 *propped against the wall*
lean, rest, stand, balance, steady
▶ *n* 1 *a clothes prop*
support, stick, post, column, shaft, stay, mainstay, strut, buttress, upright, bolster, brace, truss, stanchion
2 *drink is the prop in his life*
mainstay, support, pillar, column, supporter, anchor

propaganda *n*
advertising, publicity, promotion, information, indoctrination, brainwashing, disinformation
colloq. hype

propagandist *n*
promoter, advocate, canvasser, publicist, pamphleteer, evangelist, proselytizer, indoctrinator
formal proponent
colloq. plugger

propagate *v*
1 SPREAD, transmit, broadcast, communicate, distribute, proclaim, diffuse, circulate, publish, publicize, promote
formal disseminate, promulgate
2 INCREASE, multiply, proliferate, grow, generate, produce, breed, spawn, reproduce
old use beget
formal procreate

propagation *n*
1 COMMUNICATION, spread, spreading, transmission, promotion, distribution, circulation, diffusion
formal dissemination, promulgation
2 INCREASE, generation, breeding, multiplication, proliferation, spawning, reproduction
old use procreation

propel *v*
move, drive, impel, force, thrust, push (forward), launch, shoot, send
colloq. shove
EƎ stop

propensity *n*
tendency, liability, susceptibility, inclination, leaning, disposition, aptness, proneness, bent, bias, readiness, foible, weakness
formal penchant, predisposition, proclivity
EƎ disinclination

proper *adj*
1 RIGHT, correct, accurate, exact, precise, true, genuine, real, actual
2 ACCEPTED, correct, suitable, appropriate, fitting, acceptable, conventional, orthodox, established, decent, respectable, polite, refined, genteel, strict, gentlemanly, ladylike, prim, prudish, formal
EƎ 1 wrong, incorrect 2 improper, indecent

property *n*
1 ESTATE, land, real estate, acres, premises, buildings, house(s), wealth, riches, resources, means, capital, assets, holding(s), belongings, possessions, goods, chattels, paraphernalia
formal effects
colloq. gear
2 FEATURE, trait, quality, attribute, characteristic, idiosyncrasy, quirk, peculiarity, mark

prophecy *n*
prediction, forecast, prognosis, second sight, fortune-telling, divination, soothsaying
formal augury, prognostication
Related adjective: vatic

prophesy *v*
predict, foresee, augur, foretell, forewarn, forecast
formal prognosticate, augur

prophet *n*
seer, soothsayer, foreteller, forecaster, oracle,
clairvoyant, fortune-teller
formal prognosticator
▷ **prophet of doom** pessimist, doomwatcher,
Jeremiah, Cassandra; *colloq.* doom merchant,
doomster

prophetic *adj*
forecasting, predictive, prognostic, foreshadowing,
oracular, fey
formal sibylline, presaging, prescient, augural,
divinatory, fatidical, mantic, vatic, vaticidal
E3 unprophetic

prophylactic *adj*
preventive, preventative, anticipatory, pre-emptive,
inhibitory, obstructive, precautionary, protective,
counteractive, deterrent
E3 causative, fostering

propinquity *n*
nearness, closeness, connection, tie, vicinity,
neighbourhood, proximity, adjacency, relation,
relationship, blood, kinship, affiliation, affinity
formal consanguinity, contiguity, kindredness,
kindredship
E3 remoteness

propitiate *v*
reconcile, pacify, placate, satisfy, appease, conciliate,
mollify, soothe
E3 anger, provoke

propitiation *n*
reconciliation, peacemaking, appeasement,
conciliation, mollification, pacification, placation,
pacifying
E3 angering, provocation

propitiatory *adj*
reconciliatory, peacemaking, soothing, pacifying,
pacificatory, appeasing, conciliatory, mollifying,
assuaging
formal placative, placatory, propitiative
E3 provocative

propitious *adj*
favourable, fortunate, advantageous, happy, friendly,
gracious, opportune, timely, promising, prosperous,
encouraging, reassuring, well-disposed, bright, lucky,
kindly, rosy, benign, beneficial, benevolent
formal auspicious
E3 inauspicious

proponent *n*
advocate, supporter, backer, proposer, subscriber,
apologist, partisan, defender, enthusiast, exponent,
upholder, vindicator, champion, friend, patron
formal propounder
E3 opponent, enemy

proportion *n*
1 PERCENTAGE, fraction, part, segment, portion,
measure, division, share, quota, amount
colloq. cut, split, whack, slice of the cake, piece of the
action
2 RATIO, relationship, correspondence, symmetry,
balance, distribution, quotient
3 *a task/building of huge proportions*
dimensions, measurements, size, magnitude, extent,

volume, capacity, bulk, mass, height, length, depth,
breadth, width, scale
E3 2 disproportion, imbalance

proportional *adj*
proportionate, relative, equivalent, commensurate,
consistent, corresponding, analogous, comparable,
equitable, even
E3 disproportionate

proportionally *adv*
proportionately, relatively, correspondingly,
comparably, commensurately, evenly, pro rata
E3 disproportionately

proposal *n*
plan, scheme, project, design, programme, manifesto,
presentation, proposition, suggestion,
recommendation, motion, bid, offer, tender, terms

propose *v*
1 SUGGEST, recommend, move, advance, put
forward, introduce, bring up, advocate, table, submit,
present, offer, tender
formal proffer, propound
2 INTEND, mean, aim, purpose, plan, design, have in
mind
3 NOMINATE, put up, name, recommend, suggest
4 *propose marriage*
ask to marry, ask for someone's hand in marriage
old use plight your troth
colloq. pop the question, go down on bended knee
E3 1 withdraw

proposition *n, v*
▶ *n* **1** PROPOSITION, proposal, suggestion, theory,
plan, project, programme, recommendation, scheme,
manifesto, motion, tender
formal theorem
2 TASK, activity, undertaking, venture
3 *a sexual proposition*
advance, overture, approach, indirect proposal/
suggestion, pass
▶ *v* accost, solicit, make sexual advances/overtures
to, make an indecent proposal to, make a pass at

propound *v*
put forward, suggest, propose, advance, set forth,
advocate, contend, lay down, present, submit
formal move, postulate
E3 oppose

proprietor, proprietress *n*
landlord, landlady, title-holder, freeholder,
leaseholder, landowner, owner, possessor, deed holder

propriety *n*
1 MODESTY, decorum, decency, civility, etiquette,
protocol, delicacy, respectability, refinement,
rightness, correctness, manners, good manners,
politeness, courtesy, breeding, appropriateness,
aptness, becomingness, suitableness, fitness,
gentlemanliness, ladylikeness
old use seemliness
formal punctilio, rectitude
2 *observe proprieties*
civility, standard, etiquette, convention, decency,
nicety
colloq. the done thing, p's and q's
E3 1, 2 impropriety

propulsion *n*
drive, driving force, power, pressure, push, thrust,
motive force, momentum, impetus, impulse, impulsion

prosaic *adj*
mundane, ordinary, routine, dull, stale, boring,
commonplace, humdrum, matter-of-fact,
unimaginative, uninspired, uninspiring,
monotonous, bland, tame, trite, banal, vacuous,
vapid, pedestrian, workaday, flat, dry, hackneyed,
everyday
🔁 imaginative, interesting

proscribe *v*
forbid, prohibit, ban, outlaw, bar, banish, condemn,
embargo, reject, exclude, boycott, censure, damn,
doom, black, blackball, denounce, deport, expel, exile,
excommunicate, expatriate, ostracize
formal interdict, disallow
🔁 allow, permit

⚠ **proscribe** or **prescribe** ? *See panel at* **prescribe**.

proscription *n*
prohibition, ban, bar, barring, embargo, outlawry,
censure, condemnation, damning, denunciation,
ostracism, rejection, banishment, boycott,
deportation, expulsion, ejection, eviction, exclusion,
exile, excommunication, expatriation
formal interdict
🔁 admission, allowing

prosecute *v*
accuse, sue, charge, bring charges, bring an action
against, prefer charges, take to court, litigate, summon,
put on trial, try
formal arraign, indict
🔁 defend

proselytize *v*
convert, evangelize, make converts, persuade, win
over, propagandize, spread the gospel, bring into the
fold, bring to God

prosody *n*

Forms of prosody include: abstract verse, Alcaic verse,
alexandrine, alliteration, amphibrach, amphimacer,
Anacreontic verse, anacrusis, analysed rhyme,
anapaest, antibacchius, antispast, Archilochian
verse, asclepiad, assonance, asynartete, ballade,
blank verse, bouts rimés, broken rhyme, caesura,
canto, catalexis, choliamb, choree, choriamb,
cinquain, couplet, dactyl, decastich, dipody,
dispondee, distich, ditrochee, dizain, dochmius,
elision, enjambment, envoy, epitrite, epode, eye
rhyme, false quantity, feminine caesura, feminine
ending, feminine rhyme, foot, free verse, galliambic,
glyconic, heptameter, heptapody, heroic couplet,
hexameter, hexastich, hypermetrical, iamb, ictus,
Ionic, kyrielle, laisse, Leonine rhyme, linked verse,
long-measure, macaronic, masculine ending,
masculine rhyme, metre, miurus, monometer,
monorhyme, paeon, pantoum, pentameter,
pentastich, Petrarchan sonnet, Pherecratean,
Pindaric, poulters' measure, pyrrhic, Pythian verse,
quatorzain, quatrain, reported verses, rhopalic,
rhyme royal, rime riche, rime suffisante, rondeau,
rondel, rove-over, Sapphic, senarius, septenarius,
sonnet, Spencerian stanza, spondee, sprung rhythm,
strophe, substitution, synaphea, tetrameter,
tetrapody, tetrastich, tribrach, trimeter, triolet,
tripody, triseme, trochee, villanelle, virelay.

prospect *n, v*
▶ *n* **1** *the prospect of rain*
chance(s), odds, probability, likelihood, likeness,
possibility, hope, expectation, anticipation, outlook,
future, promise

2 *a prospect of the bay*
outlook, vista, view, scene, panorama, aspect,
spectacle, perspective, landscape, opening
🔁 unlikelihood
▶ *v* explore, search, look for, seek, survey, examine,
inspect, quest, fossick
colloq. nose

prospective *adj*
future, -to-be, would-be, intended, designate, destined,
forthcoming, approaching, coming, imminent,
awaited, expected, anticipated, hoped-for, awaited,
likely, possible, probable, potential, aspiring

prospectus *n*
syllabus, manifesto, outline, synopsis, pamphlet,
leaflet, brochure, catalogue, list, literature, plan,
scheme, programme
formal conspectus

prosper *v*
boom, thrive, flourish, flower, bloom, succeed, be
successful, get on, get on well, do well, turn out well,
advance, progress, make progress, grow rich
formal burgeon
colloq. get ahead, get on in the world, go up in the
world, make your pile, hit, the big time, hit the jackpot,
live on easy street
🔁 fail

prosperity *n*
boom, plenty, affluence, wealth, riches, fortune, well-
being, luxury, success, good fortune
colloq. the good life, the life of Riley, easy street, bed of
roses, land of milk and honey, clover, lap of luxury
🔁 adversity, poverty

prosperous *adj*
booming, thriving, flourishing, blooming, successful,
fortunate, lucky, rich, wealthy, affluent, well-off, well-
to-do
formal burgeoning, opulent
colloq. well-heeled, rolling in it
🔁 unfortunate, poor

prostitute *n, v*
▶ *n* harlot, call-girl, woman of the streets, rent-boy,
woman of the town, woman of ill repute, loose woman,
fallen woman, floosie, wench, whore, trollop, street-
walker, strumpet, cocotte, courtesan, brass, bawd, *fille
de joie, fille des rues,* drab, grande cocotte, lorette
colloq. hooker, hustler, moll, pro, tart
▶ *v* cheapen, degrade, debase, demean, devalue,
pervert, misapply, misuse, profane

prostitution *n*
harlotry, whoredom, whoring, street-walking, vice,
meretriciousness
colloq. the game, the oldest profession

prostrate *adj, v*
▶ *adj* **1** FLAT, horizontal, prone, lying down, lying
flat, fallen
2 OVERCOME, overwhelmed, devastated, crushed,
paralysed, powerless, helpless, defenceless, laid low,
brought to your knees
🔁 **1** erect **2** triumphant
▶ *v* lay low, flatten, level, knock down, overcome,
overwhelm, crush, overthrow, bring to your knees, tire,
wear out, fatigue, exhaust, sap, drain, ruin
🔁 strengthen
▷ **prostrate yourself** bow down, kneel, kowtow,
submit, grovel, cringe, abase yourself

prostration *n*
collapse, abasement, kneeling, kowtow, submission, depression, desolation, despair, despondency, dejection, grief, helplessness, weakness, weariness, exhaustion, paralysis, bow
formal slough of despond, obeisance, genuflection
E3 elation, exaltation, happiness, triumph

protagonist *n*
hero, heroine, lead, principal, leader, main/chief/leading character, title role, prime mover, champion, advocate, supporter, banker, adherent, mainstay, standard-bearer, exponent, moving spirit
formal proponent
E3 critic, opponent

protean *adj*
ever-changing, changeable, versatile, inconstant, many-sided, variable, volatile, mercurial, multiform, mutable
technical polymorphic, polymorphous, amoebic
E3 stable, unchanging

protect *v*
safeguard, defend, guard, escort, cover, screen, shield, secure, watch over, look after, care for, take care of, support, shelter, harbour, keep, keep safe, conserve, preserve, save
E3 attack, neglect

protection *n*
1 *protection of the environment*
care, custody, charge, guardianship, safekeeping, conservation, preservation, safety, security, safeguard, defence
2 BARRIER, buffer, bulwark, defence, guard, shield, armour, screen, cover, shelter, safeguard, refuge, security, insurance
E3 1 neglect, attack

protective *adj*
1 *protective clothing*
waterproof, fireproof, insulating, covering, shielding, defensive
2 POSSESSIVE, defensive, motherly, maternal, fatherly, paternal, watchful, vigilant, careful, wary, over-protective
E3 2 aggressive, threatening

protector *n*
1 DEFENDER, benefactor, advocate, guardian, patron, champion, counsel, bodyguard, minder, father-figure
formal protectress, protectrix
2 GUARD, safeguard, shield, cushion, bolster, pad, buffer
E3 1 attacker, threat

protégé(e) *n*
pupil, student, ward, charge, dependant, discovery
colloq. blue-eyed boy
E3 guardian

protest *v, n*
▶ *v* **1** OBJECT, make/raise an objection to, speak out, take exception, complain, appeal, demonstrate, oppose, disapprove, disagree, argue, reject, take issue
formal remonstrate, demur
colloq. gripe, whinge, kick up a fuss
2 *protest your innocence*
assert, maintain, contend, insist, profess, proclaim, announce, declare
formal affirm, attest, avow
E3 1 accept

▶ *n* **1** OBJECTION, disapproval, disagreement, opposition, dissent, complaint, exception, protestation, outcry, fuss, appeal, demonstration, march, boycott, riot, civil disobedience
formal demurral, remonstration
colloq. demo
2 ASSERTION, contention, declaration, proclamation, announcement
formal affirmation, attestation, avowal
E3 1 acceptance

protestation *n*
statement, declaration, profession, pledge, vow, assurance, oath, objection, complaint, outcry, disagreement, protest, dissent
formal affirmation, asseveration, avowal, expostulation, remonstrance, remonstration

protester *n*
demonstrator, opposer, opponent, objector, complainer, agitator, striker, rebel, dissident, dissenter

protocol *n*
procedure, formalities, convention, custom, etiquette, manners, code of behaviour, civilities, good form
formal propriety, decorum
colloq. p's and q's

prototype *n*
original, model, mock-up, example, standard, type, pattern, precedent
formal archetype, exemplar, paradigm

protract *v*
continue, draw out, extend, keep going, lengthen, prolong, make longer, spin out, stretch out, sustain
colloq. drag out
E3 shorten

protracted *adj*
long, lengthy, prolonged, extended, drawn-out, long-drawn-out, stretched out, spun out, overlong, endless, interminable
E3 brief, shortened

protrude *v*
stick out, poke out, come through, bulge, jut out, project, extend, stand out, beetle
formal obtrude

protruding *adj*
jutting, prominent, protuberant, proud
formal exsertive, extrusive, extrusory, protrudent, protrusive
E3 flat, flush

protrusion *n*
lump, bulge, knob, bump, outgrowth, projection, protuberance, swelling, jut
formal obtrusion, process

protuberance *n*
lump, bump, bulge, bulb, knob, outgrowth, swelling, prominence, protrusion, projection, tumour, wart, welt, tuber, tubercle
technical apophysis
formal excrescence, process

protuberant *adj*
swelling, swollen, jutting, prominent, popping, bulging, bulbous, protruding, proud, beetling, bunched, gibbous
old use astrut
formal protrusive, exsertive, extrusive, extrusory, protrudent
E3 flat

proud *adj*
1 CONCEITED, vain, egotistical, big headed, boastful, smug, complacent, arrogant, self-important, cocky, presumptuous, haughty, full of yourself, scornful, high-handed, imperious, pompous, overweening, puffed up, overbearing, supercilious, snobbish
formal hubristic
colloq. high and mighty, snooty, toffee-nosed, stuck-up, jumped-up, too big for your boots
2 SATISFIED, contented, gratified, pleased, delighted, happy, glad, content, thrilled, honoured
3 DIGNIFIED, noble, honourable, worthy, self-respecting
4 *a proud moment*
satisfying, gratifying, pleasing, memorable, notable, splendid, marvellous, wonderful
colloq. red-letter
5 *a proud sight*
splendid, grand, imposing, glorious, magnificent, outstanding, notable, honourable, worthy
F≡ 1 humble, modest, unassuming **2** ashamed **3** deferential, ignoble

provable *adj*
demonstrable, establishable, confirmable, verifiable, testable
formal attestable, corroborable, evincible
F≡ unprovable

prove *v*
1 SHOW, demonstrate, verify, confirm, bear out, bear witness to, document, certify, authenticate, validate, justify, establish, determine, ascertain, try (out), test, check, examine, analyse
formal attest, corroborate, substantiate
2 TURN OUT, come about, be the case
formal transpire, eventuate
colloq. pan out
F≡ 1 disprove, discredit, falsify

proven *adj*
proved, confirmed, certified, checked, established, accepted, dependable, reliable, tested, tried, definite, authentic, trustworthy, valid, verified, undoubted
formal attested, corroborated
F≡ unproven

provenance *n*
source, origin, derivation, birthplace
formal provenience

provender *n*
food, provisions, foodstuffs, eats, supplies, rations, sustenance, groceries, edibles, comestibles, fare, feed, fodder, forage
formal victuals
colloq. eatables; *slang* grub, nosh

proverb *n*
saying, adage, aphorism, maxim, byword, dictum, precept, saw, gnome
formal apophthegm, paroemia

proverbial *adj*
axiomatic, accepted, conventional, traditional, customary, time-honoured, famous, famed, well-known, renowned, acknowledged, legendary, notorious, infamous, typical, archetypal

provide *v*
1 SUPPLY, furnish, stock, equip, outfit, kit out, prepare for, cater, serve, present, give, offer, contribute, yield, lend, add, bring

formal afford, impart
2 PLAN FOR, make plans for, allow, make provision, accommodate, arrange for, anticipate, take precautions, take measures/steps
3 STATE, specify, stipulate, lay down, require
F≡ 1 take, remove
▷ **provide for** support, maintain, sustain, look after, take care of, keep, endow, fend
F≡ ignore, neglect

provided *conj*
given, as/so long as, on condition, on the understanding, with the proviso

providence *n*
1 FATE, destiny, divine intervention, God's will, fortune, luck
2 PRUDENCE, far-sightedness, foresight, forethought, judgement, wisdom, caution, care, thrift, economy
formal sagacity, circumspection, judiciousness
F≡ 2 improvidence

provident *adj*
prudent, far-sighted, cautious, careful, thrifty, economical, frugal
formal sagacious, circumspect, judicious
F≡ improvident

providential *adj*
fortunate, lucky, fortuitous, opportune, timely, happy, convenient, welcome, heaven-sent
F≡ untimely

provider *n*
supplier, supporter, benefactor, wage-earner, breadwinner, earner, giver, donor, funder, source, mainstay
colloq. angel

providing *conj*
provided, given, as long as, on condition, on the understanding, with the proviso

province *n*
1 REGION, area, district, zone, county, shire, department, territory, state, colony, dependency
2 RESPONSIBILITY, concern, duty, office, business, role, function, charge, field, sphere, area, domain, department, line
colloq. pigeon

provincial *adj, n*
▶ *adj* **1** *a provincial theatre*
regional, local, rural, rustic, country
2 *provincial attitudes*
PAROCHIAL, insular, inward-looking, limited, intolerant, narrow, narrow-minded, small-minded, unsophisticated, home-grown, small-town, outlying, parish-pump
colloq. hick
F≡ 1 national, metropolitan, capital, cosmopolitan, urban **2** sophisticated
▶ *n* country bumpkin, yokel, rustic, peasant
colloq. hillbilly, hick

provincialism *n*
parochialism, provinciality, regionalism, sectionalism, insularity, localism, narrow-mindedness
F≡ sophistication

provision *n*
1 SUPPLY, giving, equipping, furnishing, preparation, service, contribution, outfitting
2 FACILITIES, amenities, services, recourses

3 PLAN, arrangement, preparation, measure, step, allowance, concession, precaution
4 STIPULATION, specification, proviso, condition, term, requirement, clause, qualification, rider
5 FOOD, foodstuff, groceries, sustenance, rations, supplies, stocks, stores
colloq. eatables

provisional *adj*
temporary, interim, transitional, stopgap, makeshift, conditional, tentative
colloq. pro tem
E3 permanent, fixed, definite

provisionally *adv*
for the time being, interim, meanwhile
colloq. pro tem

proviso *n*
condition, term, requirement, stipulation, qualification, reservation, restriction, limitation, provision, clause, rider
colloq. strings

provocation *n*
1 ANNOYANCE, enraging, angering, irritation, exasperation, vexation, grievance, offence, insult, affront, injury, taunt, challenge, dare
colloq. aggravation
2 CAUSE, grounds, justification, reason, motive, stimulus, stimulation, motivation, incitement, inducement, inspiration, eliciting, production, generation, instigation

provocative *adj*
1 ANNOYING, irritating, infuriating, exasperating, galling, outrageous, offensive, insulting, abusive
colloq. aggravating
2 STIMULATING, exciting, challenging
3 EROTIC, titillating, arousing, sexy, sexually arousing, seductive, alluring, tempting, inviting, tantalizing, teasing, suggestive
E3 1 conciliatory

provoke *v*
1 ANNOY, irritate, rile, offend, insult, anger, enrage, infuriate, incense, madden, exasperate, tease, taunt, pique, vex, nettle, harass
colloq. aggravate, needle, hassle, wind up, make someone's blood boil, get someone's back up
2 GOAD, stir, spur, prod, prompt, stimulate, motivate, incite, rouse, inflame, instigate
colloq. egg on
3 CAUSE, occasion, give rise to, produce, generate, induce, elicit, evoke, call forth, engender, promote, excite, inspire, move
E3 1 please, pacify **3** result

provoking *adj*
annoying, exasperating, infuriating, irritating, offensive, maddening, obstructive, tiresome, vexatious, vexing, irking, irksome, galling
colloq. aggravating
E3 pleasing

prow *n*
bow(s), fore, stem, front, head, nose, forepart, cut-water
E3 stern

prowess *n*
1 ACCOMPLISHMENT, attainment, ability, capability, aptitude, skill, skilfulness, expertise, facility, mastery, command, proficiency, talent, genius, dexterity, adeptness, adroitness

2 BRAVERY, courage, dauntlessness, fearlessness, daring, heroism, gallantry, pluck, valour, audacity, intrepidity
colloq. grit, nerve, guts, bottle, spunk

prowl *v*
creep, hunt, rove, roam, move stealthily, slink, sneak, stalk, lurk, skulk, steal, range, search, scavenge, cruise, patrol, nose, snook

proximity *n*
closeness, nearness, vicinity, neighbourhood, adjacency, juxtaposition
formal contiguity, propinquity
E3 remoteness

proxy *n*
agent, deputy, stand-in, substitute, surrogate, representative, delegate, attorney, factor

prude *n*
prig, old maid, puritan, school-marm, Mrs Grundy

prudence *n*
wisdom, judgement, good sense, common sense, care, foresight, forethought, far-sightedness, economy, heedfulness, preparedness, discretion, caution, vigilance, wariness, planning, providence, precaution, policy, canniness, frugality, saving, thrift, husbandry
formal circumspection, judiciousness, sagacity
E3 imprudence, rashness

prudent *adj*
wise, sensible, politic, shrewd, politic, discerning, careful, cautious, wary, vigilant, discreet, provident, far-sighted, frugal, economical, thrifty
formal judicious, circumspect, sagacious
E3 imprudent, unwise, careless, rash

prudery *n*
overmodesty, primness, squeamishness, starchiness, strictness, stuffiness, priggishness, prissiness, old-maidishness, puritanism, Grundyism
E3 laxness

prudish *adj*
overmodest, overnice, proper, prim, narrow-minded, squeamish, demure, starchy, strait-laced, stuffy, puritanical, school-marmish, old-maidish, prissy, priggish, po-faced, ultra-virtuous, Victorian
E3 lax; *colloq.* easy-going

prune *v*
clip, trim, snip, cut, dock, lop, pare, shape, reduce, shorten

prurient *adj*
salacious, lewd, dirty, obscene, indecent, lustful, desirous, itching, erotic, pornographic, lascivious, lecherous, voyeuristic
formal concupiscent, cupidinous, libidinous
colloq. smutty, blue
E3 decent

pry *v*
meddle, interfere, intrude, peep, peer, nose, ferret, dig, delve
colloq. snoop, poke/stick your nose in, put your oar in
E3 mind your own business

prying *adj*
meddlesome, meddling, interfering, intrusive, nosy, curious, inquisitive, spying, peering, peery
colloq. snooping, snoopy
E3 uninquisitive

psalm *n*
hymn, song, poem, prayer, chant, canticle, paean, paraphrase

pseud *n*
poser, poseur, trendy, fraud, humbug
colloq. phoney

pseudo *adj*
false, sham, mock, pretended, imitation, fake, counterfeit, bogus, artificial, spurious, ersatz, quasi-, ungenuine
colloq. phoney, pseud
F3 genuine, real, authentic

pseudonym *n*
false name, assumed name, alias, incognito, pen-name, *nom de plume*, stage name
formal allonym

psyche *n*
spirit, soul, mind, self, deepest feelings, heart of hearts, consciousness, personality, awareness, individuality, subconscious, intellect, intelligence, understanding
technical anima, pneuma

psychiatrist *n*
analyst, psychoanalyst, therapist, psychotherapist, psychologist, psychoanalyser
colloq. headshrinker, shrink, trick cyclist, head doctor, person in a white coat

psychic *adj*
1 *psychic power*
spiritual, supernatural, occult, mystic(al), clairvoyant, extrasensory, telepathic, telekinetic
2 MENTAL, psychological, intellectual, cognitive, spiritual

psychological *adj*
mental, intellectual, cognitive, emotional, subjective, subconscious, unconscious, psychosomatic, irrational, unreal, imaginary
formal cerebral
F3 physical, real

psychology *n*
1 *study psychology*
science of the mind, study of the mind, study of mental processes, science of human/animal behaviour
2 *the psychology of crowds*
mind, mental characteristics, behavioural characteristics, mental chemistry, make-up, attitudes, habits, motives, mindset
colloq. what makes someone tick

psychopath *n*
lunatic, mad person, maniac, sociopath, psychotic
colloq. psycho

psychopathic *adj*
lunatic, mad, insane, maniacal, psychotic, deranged, unbalanced, mentally disturbed, demented

pub *n*
public house, inn, tavern, bar, saloon, taproom, lounge, lounge bar, grill, brasserie, counter, table
colloq. local, hostelry, watering-hole; *slang* boozer

puberty *n*
pubescence, adolescence, teens, teenage years, youth, young adulthood, growing up, maturity
F3 childhood, immaturity, old age

public *adj, n*
▶ *adj* 1 *public buildings*
state, government, national, nationalized, official,
civil, community, social, civic, collective, communal, common, general, popular, universal, open, accessible, unrestricted
2 KNOWN, well-known, famous, important, influential, respected, eminent, illustrious, celebrated, popular, widespread, recognized, acknowledged, plain, overt, obvious, open, exposed, published
F3 1 private, privatized, personal 2 secret, exclusive
▷ **in public** publicly, openly, in the open, in full view, for all to see
F3 in secret
▶ *n* people, nation, country, population, populace, masses, citizens, society, everyone, community, voters, electorate, multitude, followers, supporters, fans, audience, spectators, patrons, clientèle, customers, buyers, consumers
▷ **public house** bar, saloon, inn, tavern, taproom, lounge, lounge bar, grill, brasserie, counter, table
colloq. pub, local, hostelry, watering-hole;
slang boozer

publican *n*
landlord, landlady, barman, barmaid, hotelier, hotel-keeper, innkeeper, taverner, mine host

publication *n*
1 *the publication of a book*
publishing, production, printing, distribution, circulation, release, issue
2 BOOK, newspaper, magazine, journal, periodical, weekly, monthly, daily, quarterly, booklet, leaflet, pamphlet, brochure, handbill
3 ANNOUNCEMENT, declaration, notification, reporting, proclamation, disclosure

publicity *n*
advertising, promotion, marketing, puff, propaganda, build-up, boost, attention, limelight, splash
colloq. plug, hype

publicize *v*
advertise, promote, market, spotlight, broadcast, make known, announce, make public, bring to the public's attention, blaze
formal disseminate, promulgate
colloq. plug, hype, push

public-spirited *adj*
community-minded, humanitarian, philanthropic, altruistic, charitable, unselfish, generous, conscientious
F3 selfish

publish *v*
1 *publish a book*
produce, print, issue, bring out, release, distribute, circulate, spread, diffuse
formal disseminate, promulgate
2 ANNOUNCE, declare, communicate, report, notify, make known, make public, proclaim, import, divulge, disclose, reveal, release, publicize, advertise

pucker *v, n*
▶ *v* gather, ruffle, wrinkle, pleat, ruckle, ruck, shrivel, crinkle, crumple, crease, furrow, purse, screw up, contract, compress
▶ *n* crinkle, crumple, fold, crease, ruck, wrinkle, ruckle, shirr

puckered *adj*
creased, gathered, rucked, ruckled, wrinkled, pursy
F3 smooth

puckish *adj*
impish, mischievous, naughty, playful, roguish, sly, waggish, whimsical, teasing, frolicsome, sportive
🖃 serious, solemn

pudding *n*
dessert, sweet, tart, pie, pastry
colloq. afters, pud

puddle *n*
pool, sop, plash, slop

puerile *adj*
childish, babyish, infantile, juvenile, immature, adolescent, irresponsible, silly, foolish, inane, trivial
🖃 mature

puff *n, v*
▶ *n* **1** BREATH, waft, whiff, draught, flurry, gust, blast
2 *a puff on a cigarette*
pull, drag
3 ADVERTISEMENT, publicity, promotion, marketing, push, commendation
colloq. plug
▶ *v* **1** BREATHE, pant, gasp, gulp, wheeze, blow, waft, inflate, expand, swell
2 *puff a cigarette*
smoke, pull, drag, draw, suck
3 ADVERTISE, praise, publicize, promote, market, push, commend
colloq. plug

puffed *adj*
out of breath, breathless, panting, winded, exhausted, gasping
colloq. done in
▷ **puffed up** arrogant, proud, swollen-headed, full of yourself, prideful; *colloq.* big-headed, high and mighty, too big for your boots
🖃 modest

puffy *adj*
puffed up, inflated, swollen, bloated, enlarged
technical oedematous
formal distended, dilated

pugilism *n*
boxing, fighting, prize-fighting, the noble art, the noble science, the ring, the prize-ring
colloq. the fancy, fistiana

pugilist *n*
boxer, fighter, prize-fighter
colloq. bruiser

pugnacious *adj*
hostile, aggressive, belligerent, contentious, antagonistic, argumentative, quarrelsome, bad-tempered, hot-tempered
formal disputatious, bellicose
🖃 peaceable

puke *v*
vomit, spew, retch, regurgitate, disgorge, heave
colloq. throw up

pull *v, n*
▶ *v* **1** TOW, drag, haul, trail, heave, draw, tug, jerk
colloq. yank
2 REMOVE, take out, draw out, extract, root out, pull out, pluck, uproot, pull up, rip, tear, wrench
3 ATTRACT, draw, bring in, pull in, lure, allure, entice, tempt, magnetize
4 DISLOCATE, sprain, wrench, strain, damage, tear
🖃 **1** push, press **3** repel, deter, discourage

▷ **pull apart 1** SEPARATE, part, dismember, dismantle, take to pieces, tear apart **2** CRITICIZE, take apart, attack; *colloq.* slate, slam, run down, pick holes in, pull to pieces, do a hatchet job on
🖃 **1** join
▷ **pull back** draw back, withdraw, retreat, fall back, retire, disengage, back out
▷ **pull down** destroy, demolish, knock down, dismantle, bulldoze, raze to the ground
🖃 build, erect, put up
▷ **pull in 1** STOP, arrive, draw in, pull up, park **2** ATTRACT, draw, bring in, lure, allure, entice **3** ARREST, capture, seize, apprehend, detain, take into custody; *colloq.* bust, nick, collar, nab, book, run in **4** EARN, receive, be paid, make, clear, take home; *colloq.* rake in
🖃 **1** pull away **2** repel **3** lose
▷ **pull off 1** ACCOMPLISH, achieve, bring off, succeed, manage, carry off, carry out **2** DETACH, remove, separate, take off, tear off, rip off
🖃 **1** fail **2** attach
▷ **pull out** retreat, withdraw, leave, depart, quit, move out, back out, evacuate, desert, abandon
🖃 join, arrive
▷ **pull through** recover, come through, rally, recuperate, survive, weather
▷ **pull together** co-operate, work together, collaborate, team up
🖃 fight
▷ **pull yourself together** control yourself, regain your self-control, get a grip on yourself
▷ **pull up 1** STOP, halt, come to a halt, park, draw up, pull in, pull over, brake **2** REPRIMAND, take to task, rebuke, scold, criticize; *colloq.* tell off, tick off, carpet
▶ *n* **1** TOW, drag, tug, haul, jerk, power, forcefulness, exertion
colloq. yank
2 ATTRACTION, lure, allurement, draw, drawing power, magnetism, influence, weight
colloq. clout, muscle

pulp *n, v*
▶ *n* flesh, marrow, paste, purée, mash, mush, pap
formal triturate
▶ *v* crush, squash, pulverize, mash, purée, liquidize, shred

pulpit *n*
platform, rostrum, lectern, dais
colloq. soapbox

pulpy *adj*
soft, sloppy, pappy, mushy, crushed, squashy, fleshy, succulent
🖃 hard

pulsate *v*
pulse, beat, throb, pound, hammer, drum, thud, thump, vibrate, oscillate, quiver

pulsating *adj*
vibrating, oscillating, pulsing, palpitating
formal pulsatile, pulsative, pulsatory, vibrative, vibratile

pulsation *n*
vibration, oscillation, palpitation, vibratiuncle
technical ictus

pulse *n, v*
▶ *n* beat, stroke, rhythm, throb, pulsation, beating, throbbing, thud, thudding, thump, thumping, pounding, drumming, vibration, oscillation

▶ *v* beat, drum, pulsate, vibrate, pound, thud, throb, tick

pulverize *v*
1 CRUSH, pound, grind, mill, powder, crumble, pulp, squash
formal triturate
2 DEFEAT, destroy, demolish, annihilate, smash
formal vanquish
colloq. thrash, hammer, wipe the floor with

pummel *v*
hit, knock, hammer, beat, batter, pound, punch, strike, thump, bang

pump *v*
1 PUSH, drive, force, send, inject, siphon, draw, drain
2 CROSS-EXAMINE, cross-question, interrogate, quiz
colloq. grill, give someone the third degree
▷ **pump out** bail out, drain, draw off, empty, force out, siphon
▷ **pump up** blow up, inflate, puff up, fill

pun *n*
play on words, *double entendre*, witticism, quip
technical paronomasia

punch¹ *v, n*
▶ *v* hit, strike, pummel, jab, bash, knock, clout, cuff, box, slug, thump, thwack
colloq. sock, wallop, bop, biff
▶ *n* 1 BLOW, jab, bash, knock, hit, clout, thump, thwack
colloq. sock, wallop, bop, biff
2 FORCE, strength, power, impact, effectiveness, drive, vigour, forcefulness, verve, panache
colloq. bite, pizzazz

punch² *v*
punch a hole
perforate, pierce, puncture, make a hole in, prick, bore, drill, hole, stamp, cut

punch-drunk *adj*
dazed, confused, befuddled, stupefied, unsteady, reeling, staggering, dizzy, groggy, woozy

punch-up *n*
stand-up fight, brawl, fight, row, free-for-all, argument, ruckus
colloq. scrap, set-to, ding-dong, dust-up, shindy

punchy *adj*
incisive, effective, forceful, aggressive, dynamic, lively, powerful, spirited, vigorous
colloq. zappy
🖃 feeble, weak

punctilio *n*
1 SCRUPULOUSNESS, strictness, exactness, ceremony, finickiness, formality, convention, punctiliousness, precision, meticulousness, refinement, preciseness
2 FINE POINT, detail, nicety, particular, exactitude, delicacy, distinction, particularity
🖃 1 informality

punctilious *adj*
scrupulous, conscientious, meticulous, careful, exact, precise, strict, formal, proper, particular, finicky, fussy
colloq. pernickety, choosy, picky, nit-picking
🖃 lax, informal

punctual *adj*
prompt, on time, exact, precise, well-timed, early, in

good time
colloq. on the dot, dead on time, bang on time, on cue
🖃 unpunctual, late

punctuality *n*
promptness, promptitude, regularity, readiness, strictness
🖃 unpunctuality

punctually *adv*
on time, prompt, promptly, precisely, exactly, sharp, to the minute, on the dot
colloq. dead on, bang on, spot on
🖃 unpunctually

punctuate *v*
interrupt, sprinkle, break, intersperse, pepper, emphasize, point, accentuate
formal interject

punctuation *n*

Punctuation marks include: apostrophe, asterisk, backslash, brackets, colon, comma, dash, exclamation mark, full stop, hyphen, inverted commas, oblique stroke, parentheses, period, question mark, quotation marks, *colloq.* quotes, semicolon, solidus, speech marks, square brackets, star.

puncture *n, v*
▶ *n* 1 FLAT TYRE, blow-out
colloq. flat
2 LEAK, hole, holing, piercing, perforation, cut, rupture, prick, nick, slit
▶ *v* 1 PRICK, pierce, penetrate, perforate, hole, bore, spike, cut, nick, burst, rupture
2 DEFLATE, flatten, let down, humiliate
colloq. put down

pundit *n*
authority, expert, master, teacher, maestro, guru, sage, savant
colloq. buff

pungent *adj*
1 *a pungent taste/smell*
strong, powerful, hot, peppery, fiery, spicy, aromatic, tangy, tart, piquant, sharp, keen, acute, sour, bitter, acid, acrid, caustic, stinging, burning, biting
2 *pungent comments*
cutting, incisive, pointed, piercing, penetrating, sarcastic, scathing, caustic, stinging, burning, biting
🖃 1 mild, bland, tasteless 2 mild, bland

punish *v*
1 PENALIZE, discipline, correct, scold, beat, make someone pay, smack, slap, flog, whip, scourge, lash, cane, spank, knee-cap, crucify, hang, fine, imprison
formal chastise, castigate
colloq. teach someone a lesson, make an example of, bring to book, throw the book at, give someone hell
2 BEAT, defeat, trounce, batter
colloq. hammer, thrash, rough up
3 MISUSE, maltreat, harm, damage, abuse
🖃 1 reward

punishable *adj*
criminal, convictable, chargeable, unlawful, blameworthy
formal culpable, indictable

punishing *adj*
arduous, strenuous, crippling, crushing, burdensome, taxing, grinding, demanding, hard, harsh, severe,

cruel, gruelling, fatiguing, tiring, wearying, exhausting, backbreaking
F3 easy

punishment *n*
discipline, correction, chastisement, penalty, sentence, deserts, retribution, revenge
colloq. short sharp shock
F3 reward
Related adjective: penal

Forms of punishment include: *slang* banging up, banishment, beating, belting, the birch, borstal, the cane, capital punishment, cashiering, chain gang, confinement, confiscation, corporal punishment, defrocking, demotion, deportation, detention, dressing-down, excommunication, execution, exile, expulsion, fine, flaying, flogging, gaol, gating, grounding, *colloq.* hiding, hitting, horsewhipping, house arrest, imprisonment, incarceration, internment, jail, jankers, keelhauling, *colloq.* larruping, lashing, leathering, lines, penal colony, prison, probation, *colloq.* being put away, the rack, rap across the knuckles, scourging, *colloq.* being sent down, being sent to Coventry, sequestration, slapping, the slipper, smacking, spanking, the stocks, suspension, *colloq.* tanning someone's hide, tarring and feathering, thrashing, torturing, transportation, unfrocking, walking the plank, walloping, whipping. *See also* **execution**.

punitive *adj*
1 PENAL, disciplinary, retributive, retaliatory, vindictive
formal chastising, castigatory
2 CRIPPLING, crushing, burdensome, demanding, hard, harsh, severe, cruel, gruelling, punishing, corrective

punter *n*
1 GAMBLER, better, backer, wagerer
2 CUSTOMER, client, consumer, person, individual, fellow, chap
colloq. guy, bloke

puny *adj*
weak, feeble, frail, sickly, undeveloped, underdeveloped, stunted, small, undersized, diminutive, little, tiny, insignificant, minor, inconsequential, trifling, petty, trivial
colloq. measly, piddling
F3 strong, sturdy, large, important

pupil *n*
student, scholar, schoolboy, schoolgirl, learner, apprentice, beginner, novice, disciple, protégé(e)
F3 teacher

puppet *n*
1 MARIONETTE, finger puppet, glove puppet, doll
2 *a mere puppet of a government*
tool, instrument, dupe, cat's-paw, pawn, quisling, stooge, gull, figurehead, mouthpiece, creature

purchase *v, n*
▶ *v* buy, pay for, invest in, acquire, obtain, get, pick up, shop for, go shopping, secure, gain, earn, win
formal procure
colloq. snap up, splash out on
F3 sell
▶ *n* **1** ACQUISITION, gain, buy, bargain, deal, investment, asset(s), possession(s), property, goods, holdings
formal emption

2 GRASP, foothold, grip, hold, advantage, leverage
F3 **1** sale

purchaser *n*
buyer, consumer, shopper, customer, client, hirer
formal vendee, emptor
F3 seller, vendor

pure *adj*
1 *pure gold*
unadulterated, unalloyed, unmixed, undiluted, 100%, flawless, perfect, neat, straight, solid, simple, natural, real, authentic, genuine, true
2 STERILE, uncontaminated, unpolluted, uninfected, germ-free, aseptic, antiseptic, disinfected, sterilized, hygienic, sanitary, clean, immaculate, spotless, clear, fresh, natural
3 SHEER, utter, complete, total, thorough, absolute, perfect, unqualified, unmitigated, downright
4 CHASTE, virgin, virginal, virtuous, undefiled, unsullied, moral, unblemished, upright, virtuous, honourable, honest, good, righteous, decent, noble, worthy, blameless, innocent
5 *pure mathematics*
theoretical, abstract, conjectural, speculative, academic
F3 **1** impure, adulterated **2** contaminated, polluted **4** immoral, corrupt, defiled **5** applied

pure-bred *adj*
pedigree, pedigreed, pure-blood, pure-blooded, thoroughbred, full-blooded, blooded
F3 cross-bred, hybrid, mixed, mongrel

purely *adv*
1 UTTERLY, completely, totally, entirely, wholly, thoroughly, absolutely
2 ONLY, simply, merely, just, solely, exclusively

purgative *n, adj*
▶ *n* laxative, enema, evacuant, purge
technical emetic, aperient, cathartic, eccoprotic
formal depurative
▶ *adj* cleansing, laxative, purging, evacuant
technical aperient, cathartic, cathartical, eccoprotic
formal abstersive, depurative

purge *v, n*
▶ *v* **1** PURIFY, cleanse, clean out, scour, clear, absolve
2 OUST, remove, get rid of, rid, eject, expel, depose, root out, clear (out), dismiss, eradicate, exterminate, wipe out, kill
▶ *n* removal, ejection, expulsion, witch hunt, eradication, rooting-out, extermination, cleansing, disposal, ousting

purification *n*
1 DECONTAMINATION, refinement, cleaning, cleansing, disinfection, filtration, sanitization, fumigation, deodorization, desalination
formal depuration, epuration
2 SANCTIFICATION, redemption, absolution, purge, cleansing
formal lustration, purgation
F3 **1** contamination, defilement, pollution

purify *v*
1 DECONTAMINATE, refine, filter, distil, clarify, clean, cleanse, sanitize, freshen, disinfect, sterilize, fumigate, deodorize, filtrate
formal depurate, lustrate
2 SANCTIFY, redeem, absolve, purge, cleanse, shrive

formal lustrate
E **1** contaminate, pollute, defile

purifying *adj*
cleansing, purificatory, refining, purging, purgative
technical cathartic
formal depurative, lustral, mundificative
E contaminating, defiling, polluting

purism *n*
fastidiousness, formalism, fussiness, over-precision,
pedantry, restraint, strictness, orthodoxy, austerity,
classicism, Atticism
E liberality, open-mindedness, tolerance

purist *n, adj*
▶ *n* pedant, literalist, formalist, precisionist,
dogmatist, stickler, quibbler
colloq. nit-picker
▶ *adj* fastidious, over-exact, over-fastidious, over-
meticulous, over-particular, over-precise, pedantic,
quibbling, uncompromising, strict, captious, finicky,
fussy, hypercritical, puristic
colloq. nit-picking
E liberal, open-minded, tolerant

puritan *n*
pietist, rigorist, disciplinarian, zealot, fanatic,
moralist, killjoy, spoilsport, prude
E hedonist, libertarian

puritanical *adj*
puritan, moralistic, disciplinarian, ascetic,
abstemious, austere, severe, stern, strict, strait-laced,
prim, proper, prudish, disapproving, stuffy, stiff, rigid,
narrow-minded, bigoted, fanatical, zealous
E hedonistic, liberal, indulgent, broad-minded

puritanism *n*
rigorousness, self-discipline, self-denial, strictness,
uncompromisingness, austerity, propriety, sternness,
severity, stiffness, rigidity, zealotry, fanaticism, bigotry,
narrow-mindedness, narrowness, priggishness,
primness, prudishness, abstemiousness, abstinence,
asceticism
E broad-mindedness, hedonism, indulgence,
liberality

purity *n*
1 CLEARNESS, clarity, cleanness, cleanliness,
freshness, untaintedness, flawlessness, wholesomeness
2 SIMPLICITY, authenticity, genuineness, truth,
perfection
3 CHASTITY, virginity, decency, morality, integrity,
rectitude, uprightness, goodness, virtue, virtuousness,
honour, honesty, decency, nobility, worthiness,
innocence, blamelessness
E **1** impurity, pollution, contamination
3 immorality

purlieus *n*
neighbourhood, surroundings, vicinity, suburbs,
environs, precincts, periphery, borders, bounds,
confines, limits, fringes, perimeter, outskirts

purloin *v*
steal, rob, remove, take, pilfer
formal appropriate
colloq. swipe, nick, pinch, filch, finger, lift, nobble,
pocket, snaffle, snitch, thieve

purport *v, n*
▶ *v* claim, allege, profess, seem, pose as, pretend,
imply, proclaim, show, mean, intend, indicate, denote,
signify, suggest, express, convey, declare, assert,

maintain
formal import, portend, betoken
▶ *n* meaning, significance, point, gist, drift, idea,
spirit, substance, theme, tendency, tenor, thrust,
bearing, direction, implication
formal import

purpose *n, v*
▶ *n* **1** INTENTION, aim, objective, end, goal, target,
plan, design, vision, idea, ambition, hope, wish, desire,
aspiration, point, object, reason, motive, motivation,
rationale, justification, principle, result, outcome,
basis
2 DETERMINATION, resolve, resolution, drive,
single-mindedness, firmness, dedication, devotion,
constancy, steadfastness, perseverance, persistence,
doggedness, tenacity, zeal
3 USE, function, application, good, advantage,
benefit, gain, effect, value, usefulness
▷ **on purpose** purposely, deliberately, intentionally,
consciously, knowingly, wittingly, wilfully, by design,
premeditatedly
E accidentally, impulsively, spontaneously
▶ *v* intend, mean, plan, propose, resolve, decide,
determine, settle, design, aspire, aim, desire,
contemplate, meditate

purposeful *adj*
determined, decided, resolved, resolute, single-
minded, constant, steadfast, persistent, persevering,
unwavering, unfaltering, tenacious, dogged, strong-
willed, positive, firm, deliberate
E purposeless, aimless

purposefully *adv*
resolutely, steadfastly, single-mindedly, persistently,
perseveringly, unwaveringly, unfalteringly, tenaciously

⚠ **purposefully** or **purposely** ?
Purposefully means 'obviously, or apparently, having
some purpose': *She stole purposefully towards him,
clearly intent on settling things once and for all.*
Purposely means 'intentionally, on purpose': *She
didn't want to go to college so she purposely failed her
exams.*

purposeless *adj*
pointless, senseless, aimless, objectless, empty,
goalless, thoughtless, gratuitous, unasked-for,
uncalled-for, unnecessary, useless, needless,
motiveless, nonsensical, vain, wanton, vacuous
E purposeful

purposely *adv*
on purpose, intentionally, deliberately, consciously,
calculatedly, by design, specifically, wilfully,
knowingly, premeditatedly, designedly, expressly, with
malice aforethought
E unintentionally, by accident, impulsively,
spontaneously

⚠ **purposely** or **purposefully** ? *See panel at*
purposefully.

purse *n, v*
▶ *n* **1** MONEY-BAG, wallet, pouch
2 MONEY, means, resources, finances, funds, coffers,
treasury, exchequer
3 REWARD, award, prize, present, gift
▶ *v* pucker, wrinkle, draw together, close, tighten,
contract, compress

pursuance *n*
discharge, pursuit, pursuing, performance, fulfilment, following, accomplishment, achievement, completion
formal effecting, effectuation, execution, prosecution

pursue *v*
1 CHASE, go after, run after, follow, track, stalk, trail, shadow, tail, dog, harass, harry, hound, hunt, seek, search for, investigate, inquire into
2 *pursue an activity*
perform, engage in, practise, conduct, follow, carry on, continue, keep on, keep up, maintain, persevere in, persist in, apply yourself to, hold to
3 STRIVE FOR, aspire to, aim for, seek, search for, try for, work towards, have your goal

pursuit *n*
1 CHASE, hue and cry, tracking, pursuing, stalking, trail, tailing, shadowing, hunt
2 SEARCH, quest, aim, aspiration, goal, investigation, following, continuance, persistence, perseverance
3 ACTIVITY, interest, hobby, pastime, occupation, trade, craft, line, speciality, vocation

purvey *v*
1 SUPPLY, cater, deal in, provide, furnish, stock, sell, retail, trade in
formal provision, victual
2 TRANSMIT, spread, communicate, publicize, publish, put about, pass on
formal propagate, disseminate

purveyor *n*
1 SUPPLIER, stockist, trader, dealer, provider, provisor, retailer
formal victualler
2 TRANSMITTER, communicator
formal disseminator, propagator

push *v, n*
▶ *v* 1 PROPEL, thrust, ram, shove, jostle, hustle, manhandle, butt, jolt, elbow, prod, nudge, poke, press, depress, squeeze, plunge, squash, cram, drive, force, constrain
2 PRESS (FOR), encourage, urge, incite, impel, spur, prod, goad, force, influence, persuade, press, pressurize, coerce, bully
colloq. egg on, twist someone's arm, put the screws on
3 PROMOTE, advertise, market, publicize, boost
colloq. hype, plug
◨ 1 pull 2 discourage, dissuade
▷ **push around** bully, torment, terrorize, intimidate, victimize, pick on
▷ **push off** go away, depart, leave, move;
colloq. push along, shove off, beat it, buzz off, clear off/out, make a move, make tracks
▶ *n* 1 KNOCK, shove, nudge, jolt, prod, poke, thrust, ram, jostle, butt
2 OFFENSIVE, assault, advance, charge, invasion, incursion, raid, foray
3 ENERGY, vigour, vitality, drive, effort, force, forcefulness, dynamism, enterprise, initiative, ambition, determination
colloq. go, get-up-and-go

pushed *adj*
short of, stretched, under pressure, harassed, rushed, hard-pressed, hard-up, hurried, in difficulties, strapped, pinched, pressed, harried

pushover *n*
1 *he's a pushover*
sucker, dupe, mug, stooge, gull

colloq. fall guy, sitting duck, sitting target, soft touch
2 *the job's a pushover*
colloq. child's play, cinch, doddle, picnic, piece of cake, walk-over
◨ 2 challenge, labour

pushy *adj*
assertive, self-assertive, ambitious, forceful, aggressive, over-confident, forward, bold, brash, arrogant, presumptuous, impertinent, assuming
colloq. bossy
◨ unassertive, unassuming

pusillanimity *n*
cowardliness, faint-heartedness, fearfulness, feebleness, timidity, timorousness, weakness, spinelessness, cravenness
formal poltroonery
colloq. gutlessness

pusillanimous *adj*
cowardly, faint-hearted, craven, fearful, timorous, scared, weak, weak-kneed, chicken-hearted, spineless, lily-livered, feeble, timid
colloq. chicken, gutless, yellow, wimpish
◨ brave, courageous, strong

pussyfoot *v*
1 PREVARICATE, equivocate, hedge
formal tergiversate
colloq. mess about, beat about the bush
2 CREEP, slink, tiptoe, prowl, pad, steal

pustule *n*
boil, pimple, abscess, carbuncle, eruption, fester, ulcer, pock, whitlow, blister, papule

put *v*
1 PLACE, lay (down), deposit, set (down), fix, settle, rest, establish, stand, position, dispose, situate, locate, station, post
colloq. plonk, dump
2 ARRANGE, place, class, sort, classify, categorize, group, rank, grade
3 APPLY, impose, inflict, levy, assign, subject, exact, demand, require
4 *put the blame on someone*
place, attribute, attach, fix, ascribe, assign, lay, pin, charge, impute
5 EXPRESS, word, phrase, formulate, frame, couch, say, speak, voice, pronounce, utter, state
6 *put a suggestion*
submit, present, offer, suggest, propose, tender, set/lay before, set forth, bring forward
formal proffer
7 *put money/energy into a project*
invest, spend, sink, devote, dedicate, give, contribute
8 TRANSLATE, transcribe, turn, render, convert
9 *put money on a horse*
bet, gamble, place, lay, risk, chance
▷ **put about** tell, spread, make known, circulate, announce; *formal* disseminate
▷ **put across** put over, get across/over, communicate, convey, express, explain, clarify, make clear, make understood, spell out, bring home to, get through to
▷ **put aside** put by, set aside, lay aside/by, keep, retain, save, reserve, keep in reserve, store, stow, stockpile, hoard, salt away, put to one side;
colloq. stash
▷ **put away** 1 CONSUME, devour, eat (up), drink, swallow, down; *colloq.* wolf, tuck in, guzzle, scoff, polish off 2 IMPRISON, jail, lock up, confine,

commit, certify; *colloq.* bang up, send down **3** SAVE, put aside/by, set aside, lay aside/by, keep, retain, save, reserve, keep in reserve, store, stow, stockpile

▷ **put back 1** DELAY, defer, postpone, reschedule, adjourn, suspend, shelve, freeze; *formal* procrastinate; *colloq.* put on ice **2** REPLACE, return, restore, reinstate, return to its place, clear away/up, tidy away/up

1 bring forward

▷ **put down 1** WRITE DOWN, note down, jot down, transcribe, enter, log, register, list, record **2** CRUSH, quash, suppress, defeat, quell, stop, stamp out, silence **3** *put down a sick dog* kill, destroy, put to sleep, put out of its misery **4** ASCRIBE, attribute, blame, charge, set down, fix, attach, lay **5** HUMILIATE, snub, slight, squash, deflate, humble, crush, shame, mortify; *formal* disparage, deprecate; *colloq.* take down a peg

▷ **put forward** advance, suggest, recommend, nominate, propose, move, table, introduce, present, submit, offer, tender; *formal* proffer

▷ **put in** insert, enter, input, submit, install, fit

▷ **put off 1** DELAY, defer, postpone, reschedule, adjourn, suspend, shelve; *formal* procrastinate; *colloq.* put on ice, put on the back burner **2** DETER, dissuade, talk out of, discourage, dishearten, demoralize, daunt, dismay, intimidate, disconcert, confuse, distract, sicken, nauseate **3** DISTRACT, divert, sidetrack, deflect, turn away/aside

2 encourage

▷ **put on 1** *put on new clothes* get dressed in, dress in, change into, get into, slip into, wear, don, try on; *colloq.* throw on, get dolled up in **2** ATTACH, affix, apply, place, add, impose **3** PRETEND, feign, sham, fake, simulate, affect, assume **4** STAGE, mount, produce, present, do, perform

1 take off

▷ **put out 1** PUBLISH, announce, broadcast, circulate, issue, disclose, make known, bring out **2** EXTINGUISH, quench, douse, smother, stamp out **3** INCONVENIENCE, cause inconvenience to, impose on, bother, disturb, trouble, disconcert, upset, hurt, offend, annoy, irritate, irk, anger, exasperate, provoke, infuriate, unsettle; *formal* perturb, discommode; *colloq.* faze

2 light

▷ **put through** accomplish, achieve, complete, conclude, finalize, execute, manage, bring off

▷ **put together** assemble, join, build, construct, fit/piece together

take apart

▷ **put up 1** ERECT, build, construct, assemble, raise **2** ACCOMMODATE, house, lodge, shelter, give a room to, provide with board and lodging **3** *put up prices* raise, increase, escalate; *colloq.* jack up, hike up, bump up **4** PAY, invest, give, advance, float, provide, supply, pledge, offer **5** *put up a candidate* nominate, put forward, propose, suggest, recommend, choose

1 take down, pull down **3** bring down

▷ **put up to** prompt, incite, encourage, urge, persuade, goad; *colloq.* egg on

discourage, dissuade

▷ **put up with** stand, bear, abide, stomach, endure, suffer, tolerate, allow, accept, stand for, take, brook; *colloq.* swallow, take lying down

object to, reject

▷ **put upon** impose on, exploit, take advantage of, take for granted, take liberties, inconvenience

putative *adj*
supposed, assumed, presumed, alleged, reported, reputed, hypothetical, theoretical, suppositional, reputative
formal conjectural, supposititious

put-down *n*
affront, humiliation, insult, slight, sneer, snub, rebuff, sarcasm, gibe
formal disparagement
colloq. slap in the face, dig

put-off *n*
deterrent, discouragement, disincentive, hindrance, constraint, curb, damper, obstacle, restraint

encouragement, incentive

putrefy *v*
rot, perish, go bad, decay, corrupt, mould, spoil, stink, taint, gangrene, decompose, deteriorate, fester, addle

putrescent *adj*
rotting, perishing, decaying, decomposing, putrefying, stinking, festering
formal mephitic

putrid *adj*
rotten, decayed, decomposed, mouldy, off, bad, rancid, addled, corrupt, contaminated, tainted, polluted, foul, rank, fetid, stinking

fresh, wholesome

put-upon *adj*
imposed on, taken advantage of, exploited, used, inconvenienced, abused, maltreated, persecuted

puzzle *v, n*
▶ *v* **1** BAFFLE, mystify, perplex, confound, confuse, stagger, bewilder
colloq. stump, floor, flummox, beat, nonplus
2 THINK, ponder, meditate, consider, brood, mull over, muse over, deliberate, figure, rack your brains

▷ **puzzle out** solve, work out, figure out, think out, decipher, decode, unravel, untangle, find the answer to, piece together, sort out, resolve, clear up; *colloq.* crack, get, suss (out)

▶ *n* question, poser, brainteaser, mind-bender, crossword, rebus, anagram, acrostic, riddle, conundrum, mystery, enigma, dilemma, paradox

puzzled *adj*
baffled, mystified, perplexed, confounded, at a loss, beaten, confused, bewildered, lost, in a haze
colloq. stumped, nonplussed, at sea, flummoxed, floored

clear

puzzlement *n*
bafflement, perplexity, bewilderment, confusion, disorientation, astonishment, mystification, surprise, wonder, uncertainty, doubt, doubtfulness
formal incertitude
colloq. bamboozlement

certainty, clarity, lucidity

puzzling *adj*
baffling, bewildering, confusing, perplexing, unclear, queer, peculiar, strange, bizarre, mystifying, mysterious, mystical, misleading, unaccountable, unfathomable, impenetrable, inexplicable, intricate, involved, ambiguous, equivocal, mind-bending, mind-boggling, curious, enigmatic, cryptic, tortuous, knotty, Sphinx-like
formal abstruse, labyrinthine

pygmy *n, adj*

▶ *n* person of restricted growth, dwarf, midget, Tom Thumb, Lilliputian, manikin, thumbling, fingerling
formal homunculus

E3 giant

▶ *adj* miniature, small, tiny, baby, diminutive, half-pint, undersized, minuscule, minute, pint-sized, pocket, elfin, stunted, dwarf, midget, dwarfish, toy, Lilliputian

Scot. wee

E3 gigantic

pyromaniac *n*
arsonist, incendiary, fire-raiser
colloq. firebug

Q

quack *n, adj*
► *n* charlatan, impostor, fraud, mountebank, pretender, masquerader, humbug, sham, fake, cowboy, swindler, trickster
old use quacksalver
colloq. phoney, pseud
► *adj* false, bogus, counterfeit, fake, pretended, fraudulent, spurious, supposed, sham, so-called, unqualified
colloq. phoney
E3 genuine, real

quackery *n*
charlatanism, mountebankery, mountebankism, fraud, fraudulence, sham, imposture
colloq. humbug, phoniness

quaff *v*
down, drink, gulp, knock back, swallow, swig, toss off, swill, carouse, drain
formal imbibe
colloq. booze, guzzle, tipple

quagmire *n*
1 BOG, marsh, quag, fen, swamp, morass, mire, slough, quicksand
2 MESS, problem, dilemma, quandary, perplexity
colloq. fix, hole, pickle, tight spot, hot/deep water

quail *v*
recoil, back away, shy away, shrink, flinch, pull back, draw back, cringe, cower, tremble, quake, shake, shiver, blench, shudder, falter

quaint *adj*
picturesque, charming, attractive, sweet, old-fashioned, antiquated, old-world, unusual, strange, odd, curious, droll, bizarre, fanciful, whimsical
colloq. twee, olde-worlde
E3 modern

quake *v*
shake, tremble, shudder, quiver, shiver, quail, vibrate, throb, pulsate, wobble, rock, sway, move, convulse, heave

qualification *n*
1 CERTIFICATE, diploma, degree, training, certification, skill, competence, proficiency, ability, capability, capacity, aptitude, suitability, fitness, suitability, accomplishment, eligibility
2 RESTRICTION, limitation, reservation, exception, allowance, exemption, condition, caveat, rider, provision, proviso, stipulation, modification, adjustment, adaptation

qualified *adj*
1 CERTIFIED, chartered, licensed, professional, trained, experienced, practised, skilled, accomplished, expert, knowledgeable, skilful, talented, proficient, competent, efficient, able, capable, adept, fit, fitted, equipped, prepared, eligible

2 *qualified praise*
reserved, guarded, cautious, restricted, limited, bounded, modified, conditional, provisional, equivocal
formal contingent, circumscribed
E3 **1** unqualified **2** unconditional, whole-hearted

qualify *v*
1 TRAIN, prepare, make ready, teach, instruct, equip, fit, coach, ground, pass, graduate, certify, empower, entitle, authorize, license, sanction, permit, allow, warrant
2 MODERATE, reduce, lessen, diminish, temper, soften, weaken, ease, adjust, modify, restrain, restrict, limit, delimit, make conditional, define, classify
formal mitigate, alleviate
E3 **1** disqualify

quality *n*
1 *of poor quality*
standard, grade, class, kind, sort, type, make, variety, calibre, status, rank, level, value, worth, merit, condition
2 EXCELLENCE, superiority, eminence, pre-eminence, distinction, merit, value, worth, refinement
3 CHARACTERISTIC, property, peculiarity, attribute, aspect, feature, trait, peculiarity, mark, nature, character, make-up

qualm *n*
misgiving, apprehension, fear, anxiety, worry, apprehension, concern, disquiet, uneasiness, scruple, hesitation, hesitancy, disinclination, reluctance, uncertainty, doubt
formal compunction

quandary *n*
dilemma, predicament, impasse, perplexity, confusion, bewilderment, muddle, mess, problem, difficulty
colloq. fix, hole, pickle, jam, tight spot

quantity *n*
1 AMOUNT, number, sum, total, aggregate, mass, lot, share, portion, quota, allotment, measure, dose, proportion, part, content, capacity, volume, weight, bulk, size, magnitude, expanse, extent, area, length, breadth
2 *quantities of food*
much, many, lots, masses
colloq. loads, heaps, stacks

quarantine *n*
detention, isolation, segregation, lazaret, lazaretto

quarrel *n, v*
► *n* row, argument, wrangle, squabble, tiff, misunderstanding, disagreement, dispute, dissension, controversy, difference, difference of opinion, conflict, clash, contention, strife, fight, brawl, fracas, feud, vendetta, schism
formal altercation, disputation
colloq. slanging match, scrap, set-to, dust-up,

punch-up
⊟ agreement, harmony
▶ *v* **1** ROW, argue, bicker, squabble, wrangle, be at loggerheads, fall out, disagree, dispute, dissent, differ, be at variance, clash, contend, fight, scrap, feud
2 FIND FAULT WITH, fault, criticize, dispute, censure
colloq. pick holes in, knock, slate, slam, pull to pieces
⊟ agree

quarrelling *n, adj*
▶ *n* bickering, contention, dissension, feuding, rowing, variance, strife, wrangling, disharmony, argumentation
formal altercation, discord, disputation, vitilitigation
colloq. argy-bargying
⊟ concord, harmony
▶ *adj* bickering, contending, fighting, squabbling, wrangling, warring, feuding, rowing, at odds, at variance, at loggerheads
formal discordant, dissentient
colloq. scrapping
⊟ amicable, friendly

quarrelsome *adj*
argumentative, disputatious, contentious, irascible, belligerent, ill-tempered, hot-tempered, irritable, ready for a fight
formal bellicose, pugnacious
⊟ peaceable, placid

quarry *n*
prey, victim, object, goal, target, game, kill, prize

quarter *n, v*
▶ *n* **1** DISTRICT, sector, zone, neighbourhood, accommodation, lodgings, billet, rooms, barracks, residence, station, locality, vicinity, area, region, province, territory, division, section, part, place, spot, point, direction, side
colloq. digs
2 MERCY, leniency, favour, pardon, pity, compassion, grace, indulgence, forgiveness, clemency
3 *living quarters*
accommodation, lodgings, billet, residence, rooms, barracks, station, post
formal dwelling, habitation, domicile
colloq. digs, pad
▶ *v* station, post, billet, accommodate, put up, lodge, board, house, shelter

quash *v*
1 ANNUL, revoke, rescind, cancel, void, invalidate, reverse, set aside, rescind, overturn, overrule, override
formal nullify, abrogate, countermand
2 CRUSH, squash, quell, suppress, subdue, defeat, overthrow
⊟ **1** confirm, vindicate, reinstate

quaver *v, n*
▶ *v* shake, tremble, quake, waver, shudder, quiver, vibrate, pulsate, oscillate, flutter, flicker, trill, warble
▶ *n* tremble, trembling, tremor, trill, break, quiver, shake, throb, sob, quaveriness, vibration, vibrato, warble, tremolo

quay *n*
wharf, pier, jetty, dock, harbour

queasy *adj*
sick, ill, unwell, queer, groggy, green, nauseated, sickened, bilious, squeamish, faint, dizzy, giddy
colloq. rough, under the weather, out of sorts

queen *n*
1 MONARCH, sovereign, ruler, majesty, princess, empress, consort
Related adjective: regal
2 BEAUTY, belle, idol, charm, Venus

queenly *adj*
sovereign, majestic, regal, royal, imperial, imperious, noble, stately, splendid, dignified, gracious, grand
formal august, monarchical, sublime
⊟ undignified

queer *adj, v*
▶ *adj* **1** ODD, mysterious, strange, unusual, uncommon, weird, unnatural, extraordinary, bizarre, eccentric, outlandish, peculiar, funny, puzzling, curious, unconventional, unorthodox, abnormal, deviant, remarkable
formal singular
2 *I feel queer*
unwell, ill, sick, queasy, light-headed, faint, giddy, dizzy
colloq. rough, under the weather, out of sorts
3 SUSPECT, suspicious, shifty, dubious, doubtful, irregular, peculiar, strange
colloq. shady, fishy, iffy
4 HOMOSEXUAL, gay, lesbian, bisexual
⊟ **1** ordinary, usual, common **2** well
4 heterosexual; *colloq.* straight
▶ *v* spoil, harm, ruin, upset, wreck, mar, botch, thwart, impair, foil, frustrate, endanger, jeopardize, stymie

queerness *n*
oddity, peculiarity, strangeness, unusualness, uncommonness, unconventionality, unnaturalness, bizarreness, anomalousness, curiousness, abnormality, irregularity, eccentricity, unorthodoxy
formal singularity

quell *v*
subdue, quash, crush, squash, suppress, rout, put down, overcome, conquer, defeat, overpower, moderate, allay, soothe, calm, pacify, appease, hush, quiet, silence, stifle, extinguish
formal mitigate, alleviate, vanquish

quench *v*
1 *quench one's thirst*
slake, satisfy, sate, cool
formal satiate
2 EXTINGUISH, stifle, smother, douse, put out, snuff out, stamp out

querulous *adj*
peevish, fretful, fractious, cross, irritable, complaining, grumbling, sour, testy, discontented, dissatisfied, critical, carping, captious, fault-finding, fussy, irascible
formal cantankerous, petulant
colloq. grouchy, shirty, ratty
⊟ placid, uncomplaining, contented

query *v, n*
▶ *v* ask, inquire, question, challenge, dispute, quarrel with, doubt, throw doubts on, suspect, be sceptical of, have suspicions about, distrust, mistrust, disbelieve
⊟ accept
▶ *n* question, inquiry, problem, uncertainty, doubt, suspicion, scepticism, reservation, hesitation, uneasiness, qualm(s), quibble

quest *n*
search, seeking, hunt, pursuit, investigation, inquiry,

purpose, aim, goal, mission, crusade, enterprise, undertaking, venture, journey, voyage, expedition, exploration, pilgrimage, adventure

question *v, n*
▶ *v* **1** INTERROGATE, quiz, grill, pump, interview, examine, cross-examine, cross-question, debrief, ask, inquire, investigate, probe, catechize
colloq. give the third degree to
2 QUERY, challenge, dispute, have doubts about, have reservations/qualms about, doubt, disbelieve
▶ *n* **1** QUERY, inquiry, poser, problem, difficulty
2 ISSUE, matter, problem, subject, theme, topic, point, point at issue, proposal, proposition, motion, debate, dispute, controversy
3 DOUBT, query, debate, dispute, argument, controversy, uncertainty
▷ **out of the question** impossible, unthinkable, unbelievable, absurd, ridiculous, unacceptable, not worth considering; *colloq.* not by any stretch of the imagination
▷ **without question** without arguing, immediately, unhesitatingly, unquestionably, without a shadow of doubt

questionable *adj*
debatable, disputable, unsettled, undetermined, unproven, uncertain, arguable, controversial, vexed, doubtful, dubious, suspicious, suspect
colloq. shady, fishy, iffy
E3 unquestionable, indisputable, certain

questioner *n*
interviewer, examiner, inquirer, inquisitor, interrogator, investigator, catechizer, catechist, disbeliever, doubter, sceptic, agnostic
formal interlocutor

questionnaire *n*
quiz, test, form, survey, opinion poll, market research

queue *n*
line, tailback, file, row, column, crocodile, procession, train, string, chain, succession, series, sequence, order
formal concatenation

quibble *v, n*
▶ *v* carp, cavil, split hairs, equivocate, avoid the issue, prevaricate
old use pettifog
colloq. nit-pick, split hairs
▶ *n* complaint, objection, criticism, query, protest, cavil, niggle, equivocation, prevarication
old use pettifogging
colloq. nit-picking

quibbler *n*
caviller, niggler, sophist, equivocator, casuist
old use pettifogger
colloq. hair-splitter, nit-picker

quibbling *adj*
niggling, critical, overnice, carping, captious, ambiguous, cavilling, evasive, casuistic, equivocating, logic-chopping
old use pettifogging
colloq. hair-splitting, nit-picking

quick *adj*
1 FAST, swift, rapid, speedy, nippy, express, hurried, hasty, cursory, fleeting, brief, perfunctory, prompt, ready, immediate, without delay, instant, instantaneous, sudden, brisk, nimble, sprightly, agile
formal expeditious
2 CLEVER, intelligent, quick-witted, smart, sharp,

sharp-witted, keen, shrewd, astute, discerning, perceptive, responsive, alive, receptive
E3 **1** slow, sluggish, lethargic **2** unintelligent, dull

quicken *v*
1 ACCELERATE, speed (up), hurry (up), hasten, dispatch, advance
formal precipitate, expedite
2 ANIMATE, enliven, invigorate, energize, galvanize, activate, incite, instigate, rouse, arouse, stimulate, stir (up), excite, kindle, inspire, whet, revive, refresh, reinvigorate, strengthen, revitalize, reactivate
formal revivify
E3 **1** slow, retard **2** dull

quickly *adv*
rapidly, quick, fast, speedily, swiftly, express, briskly, apace, hurriedly, hastily, immediately, instantaneously, readily, soon, abruptly, instantly, promptly, unhesitatingly, cursorily, posthaste
technical presto, prestissimo
formal expeditiously, perfunctorily
colloq. pronto, lickety-split, at a rate of knots, at the double, before you can say Jack Robinson, by leaps and bounds, hell for leather, like a bat out of hell, like the clappers, like greased lightning
E3 slowly; *formal* tardily

quickness *n*
1 SPEED, speediness, rapidity, swiftness, hastiness, immediacy, briskness, promptness, readiness, suddenness, instantaneousness, agility
formal expedition, precipitation, promptitude
2 INTELLIGENCE, shrewdness, sharpness, penetration, acuteness, astuteness, keenness, quick-wittedness, alertness
E3 **1** slowness; *formal* tardiness **2** dullness

quick-tempered *adj*
fiery, impatient, impulsive, hot-tempered, irascible, testy, touchy, irritable, explosive, volcanic, waspish, choleric, excitable, quarrelsome, shrewish, snappy, temperamental
formal splenetic, petulant
E3 cool, dispassionate

quick-witted *adj*
intelligent, clever, resourceful, keen, bright, sharp, shrewd, penetrating, acute, perceptive, smart, wide-awake, alert, astute, crafty, ingenious, witty, ready-witted, nimble-witted
E3 dull, slow, stupid

quiescent *adj*
quiet, at rest, resting, calm, peaceful, serene, placid, tranquil, undisturbed, untroubled, still, passive, silent, motionless, inactive, inert, sleeping, asleep, latent, dormant
formal in abeyance, reposeful
E3 active

quiet *adj, n*
▶ *adj* **1** SILENT, soundless, without a sound, noiseless, inaudible, hushed, soft, faint, indistinct, muffled, low
colloq. you could hear a pin drop
2 PEACEFUL, still, tranquil, serene, calm, mild, gentle, restrained, composed, undisturbed, untroubled, placid
3 SHY, reserved, reticent, uncommunicative, taciturn, placid, unforthcoming, undemonstrative, retiring, withdrawn, introvert, unexcitable, stoic, thoughtful, discreet, subdued, meek
formal imperturbable, phlegmatic

colloq. unflappable
4 *a quiet spot*
isolated, unfrequented, lonely, secluded, undisturbed, private, sleepy, peaceful
formal sequestered
colloq. off the beaten track
5 *quiet colours*
muted, subdued, soft, subtle, faint, restrained, low-key
F3 1 noisy, loud **2** excitable **3** extrovert
4 noisy **5** loud
▶ *n* quietness, silence, hush, peace, lull, stillness, soundlessness, noiselessness, tranquillity, serenity, calm, rest
formal repose
F3 noise, loudness, disturbance, bustle

quieten *v*
1 SILENCE, hush, shush, mute, soften, lower, diminish, reduce, stifle, muffle, deaden, dull
colloq. shut up
2 SUBDUE, pacify, quell, quiet, still, smooth, calm (down), tranquillize, soothe, compose, sober
F3 2 disturb, agitate

quietly *adv*
calmly, noiselessly, inaudibly, mutely, silently, softly, soundlessly, surreptitiously, placidly, tranquilly, peacefully, gently, mildly, meekly, unobtrusively, unostentatiously, undemonstratively, modestly, secretly, privately
F3 noisily, obtrusively

quietness *n*
calm, quiet, silence, serenity, tranquillity, calmness, hush, peace, placidity, lull, still, stillness, composure, inactivity, inertia, uneventfulness, dullness
formal quiescence, quietude, repose
F3 activity, bustle, commotion, disturbance, noise, racket

quietus *n*
release, end, silencing, discharge, dispatch, acquittance, death, death-blow, death-stroke, finishing stroke, *coup de grâce*, extinction
formal decease, demise

quilt *n*
bedcover, coverlet, bedspread, counterpane, eiderdown, duvet, continental quilt

quintessence *n*
embodiment, essence, core, distillation, marrow, pith, soul, spirit, extract, gist, heart, kernel, pattern, sum and substance
formal exemplar, quiddity

quintessential *adj*
essential, ideal, perfect, ultimate, complete, definitive, entire
formal archetypical, consummate, prototypical

quip *n, v*
▶ *n* joke, jest, crack, wisecrack, witticism, riposte, retort, gibe, epigram, pleasantry
colloq. gag, one-liner
▶ *v* jest, joke, retort, riposte, gibe, quirk, gag, wisecrack

quirk *n*
freak, eccentricity, curiosity, oddity, peculiarity, idiosyncrasy, mannerism, habit, trait, characteristic, feature, foible, whim, vagary, caprice, obsession, turn, twist, kink
colloq. thing, hang-up

quisling *n*
betrayer, traitor, turncoat, collaborator, renegade, fifth columnist, puppet, Judas
formal collaborationist

quit *v*
1 *quit smoking*
stop, end, abandon, drop, give up, leave off
formal cease, discontinue, desist, abstain
colloq. pack in
2 LEAVE, depart, go (away), exit, decamp, desert, abandon, renounce, relinquish, surrender, give up, resign, retire, withdraw
formal forsake

quite *adv*
1 MODERATELY, rather, somewhat, reasonably, fairly, relatively, comparatively, to some extent/degree
2 UTTERLY, absolutely, totally, completely, entirely, wholly, fully, perfectly, exactly, precisely

quits *adj*
equal, even, level, square
▷ **call it quits** stop, break off, make peace, stop fighting; *formal* cease, discontinue; *colloq.* call it a day, bury the hatchet, lay down your arms

quitter *n*
defector, delinquent, recreant, renegade, shirker, deserter, apostate
colloq. rat, skiver

quiver *v, n*
▶ *v* shake, tremble, shudder, shiver, quake, quaver, vibrate, pulsate, tingle, palpitate, flutter, flicker, oscillate, wobble
▶ *n* shake, tremble, shudder, shiver, tremor, throb, vibration, palpitation, quaver, pulsation, flutter, flicker, oscillation, wobble

quixotic *adj*
unrealistic, unworldly, idealistic, impracticable, visionary, extravagant, fanciful, Utopian, fantastical, romantic, starry-eyed, impetuous, impulsive, chivalrous
F3 hard-headed, practical, realistic

quiz *n, v*
▶ *n* questionnaire, test, examination, competition, questioning, cross-examination, cross-questioning
▶ *v* question, interrogate, examine, cross-examine, cross-question
colloq. grill, pump, give the third degree to

quizzical *adj*
questioning, inquiring, curious, amused, humorous, teasing, mocking, satirical, sardonic, sceptical, mystified, perplexed, puzzled, baffled

quota *n*
ration, allowance, allocation, assignment, share, portion, part, slice, percentage, proportion
colloq. cut, whack, slice of cake

quotation *n*
1 CITATION, extract, excerpt, line, passage, selection, piece, cutting, reference, allusion
colloq. quote
2 ESTIMATE, tender, figure, price, cost, charge, rate
colloq. quote

quote *v*
cite, refer to, mention, name, reproduce, echo, repeat, recite, recall, recollect, allude to

quoted *adj*
cited, referred to, reported, reproduced, stated,
above-mentioned
formal forementioned, instanced

quotidian *adj*
everyday, normal, ordinary, routine, workaday, regular,
daily, day-to-day, repeated, common, commonplace,
customary, recurrent, habitual
formal diurnal

R

rabbit *n, v*
▶ *n* bunny, cony, bunny rabbit, cottontail, daman, hyrax, dassie
Related adjective: oryctolagine
▶ *v* ▷ **rabbit on** chatter, go on (and on), blather, blether, maunder (on); *colloq.* natter, witter (on), waffle, gab, babble

rabble *n*
1 CROWD, throng, horde, herd, mob
2 MASSES, populace, crowd, herd, mob, common people, proletariat, hoi polloi
colloq. riff-raff, plebs

rabble-rouser *n*
agitator, troublemaker, incendiary, firebrand, demagogue, ringleader

Rabelaisian *adj*
satirical, exuberant, extravagant, coarse, bawdy, earthy, gross, vulgar, uninhibited, unrestrained, indecent, lewd, racy, ribald, risqué

rabid *adj*
1 FANATICAL, ferocious, extreme, burning, ardent, raging, fervent, frantic, unreasoning, intolerant, irrational, furious, obsessive, zealous, overzealous, bigoted, narrow-minded
2 MAD, hydrophobic, maniacal, wild, berserk, frenzied, crazed, violent, hysterical

rabies *n*
hydrophobia, rabidity, rabidness

race¹ *n, v*
▶ *n a horse race*
competition, contest, contention, rivalry, chase, pursuit, quest

> *Types of race and famous races include*: cycle race, cyclo-cross, road race, time trial, Milk Race, Tour de France; greyhound race, Greyhound Derby; horse race, Cheltenham Gold Cup, the Classics (Derby, Oaks, One Thousand Guineas, St. Leger, Two Thousand Guineas), Grand National, Kentucky Derby, Melbourne Cup, Prix de l'Arc de Triomphe, steeplechase, trotting race, *US* harness race; motorcycle race, motocross, scramble, speedway, Isle of Man Tourist Trophy (TT); motor-race, Grand Prix, Indianapolis 500, Le Mans, Monte Carlo rally, RAC Rally, scramble, stock car race; rowing, regatta, Boat Race; running, cross-country, *US* dash, hurdles, marathon, London Marathon, relay, sprint, steeplechase, track event; ski race, downhill, slalom; swimming race; walking race, walkathon; yacht race, Admiral's Cup, America's Cup; egg-and-spoon race, pancake race, sack race, wheelbarrow race.

▶ *v* run, sprint, dash, tear, fly, gallop, speed, career, dart, bolt, zoom, rush, hurry, hasten, accelerate, take part in a race
colloq. get a move on, go all out, get cracking, run like hell

race² *n*
a race of people
nation, people, ethnic group, racial group, colour, tribe, clan, house, dynasty, family, kindred, ancestry, line, lineage, blood, ancestry, extraction, stock, parentage, strain, stirps, genus, species, breed
Related adjective: ethnic

racecourse *n*
racetrack, course, track, circuit, lap, turf, speedway

racial *adj*
national, tribal, ethnic, folk, ethnological, genealogical, ancestral, inherited, genetic

raciness *n*
1 RIBALDRY, indecency, indelicacy, bawdiness, naughtiness, lewdness, smuttiness, suggestiveness, vulgarity, crudeness, coarseness
2 LIVELINESS, animation, zest, zestfulness, energy, exhilaration, freshness, dynamism
formal ebullience
colloq. pep

racism *n*
racialism, xenophobia, chauvinism, jingoism, discrimination, racial discrimination, prejudice, racial prejudice, apartheid, bias

racist *n, adj*
▶ *n* racialist, discriminator, bigot, chauvinist
▶ *adj* racialist, discriminatory, bigoted, intolerant

rack *n, v*
▶ *n* 1 HOLDER, shelf, stand, support, structure, frame, framework, trestle
2 SUFFERING, pain, misery, affliction, agony, anguish, distress, pangs, torment, torture, persecution
▶ *v* afflict, oppress, distress, agonize, pain, harass, convulse, shake, strain, stress, tear, stretch, wrench, wrest, wring, excruciate, harrow, lacerate, torment, torture, crucify

racket *n*
1 NOISE, din, uproar, row, fuss, outcry, clamour, shouting, yelling, tumult, commotion, disturbance, hullabaloo, pandemonium, hurly-burly, hubbub
2 SWINDLE, fraud, fiddle, deception, trick, dodge, scheme, business
colloq. con, game

raconteur *n*
narrator, storyteller, chronicler, reporter, anecdotist, commentator, describer, relater

racy *adj*
1 RIBALD, bawdy, risqué, vulgar, crude, rude, coarse, dirty, naughty, indecent, indelicate, suggestive, off-colour, smutty
colloq. blue
2 LIVELY, animated, spirited, vigorous, vivacious, fast-moving, energetic, dynamic, buoyant, enthusiastic, boisterous, sparkling

formal ebullience
colloq. peppy, zippy

raddled *adj*
haggard, drawn, gaunt, wasted, worn out,
unkempt, dishevelled, in a mess, the worse for
wear

radiance *n*
1 LIGHT, luminosity, radiation, brightness,
brilliance, shine, lustre, gleam, glow, glitter,
resplendence, splendour
technical incandescence
formal effulgence, refulgence
2 JOY, happiness, pleasure, delight, elation, ecstasy,
bliss, rapture

radiant *adj*
1 BRIGHT, luminous, shining, illuminated,
gleaming, glowing, beaming, glittering, sparkling,
brilliant, splendid, glorious
technical incandescent
formal resplendent, effulgent, refulgent
2 JOYFUL, happy, delighted, elated, pleased, blissful,
ecstatic, in raptures
colloq. in seventh heaven, on top of the world, over the
moon
E3 1 dull 2 miserable

radiate *v*
1 *radiate light/an emotion*
shine, gleam, glow, beam, shed, pour, send out/forth,
give off, emit, emanate, diffuse, issue
2 SPREAD (OUT), scatter, disperse, diverge, branch
formal disseminate, divaricate

radiation *n*
emanation, emission, rays, waves, transmission
technical insolation

radical *adj, n*
▶ *adj* 1 BASIC, fundamental, rudimentary, primary,
elementary, elemental, essential, natural, native,
innate, intrinsic, deep-seated, profound
2 *radical changes*
drastic, comprehensive, thorough, sweeping,
far-reaching, exhaustive, thoroughgoing, profound,
complete, absolute, total, entire, utter
3 FANATICAL, militant, extreme, extremist,
rebellious, revolutionary
E3 1 superficial 3 moderate
▶ *n* fanatic, militant, extremist, revolutionary, rebel,
reformer, reformist, fundamentalist

raffish *adj*
disreputable, dissipated, dissolute, cheap, tawdry,
vulgar, uncouth, trashy, bohemian, rakish, showy,
sporty, jaunty, casual, careless, devil-may-care,
improper, gross, flamboyant, flashy, garish, gaudy,
tasteless, loud, coarse
old use dashing
formal meretricious
E3 proper, sedate, staid; *formal* decorous

raffle *n*
draw, lottery, sweepstake, sweep, tombola

rag¹ *n*
1 *an old clothes rag*
cloth, flannel, floorcloth, duster, towel
2 *dressed in rags*
remnants, shreds, raggedness, tatters, tats,
clouts
colloq. duddery, duds

rag² *v*
rag the new boy
tease, badger, jeer, mock, ridicule, taunt, torment, bait
colloq. rib, kid, take the mickey out of

ragamuffin *n*
urchin, guttersnipe, waif, street arab, gamin

ragbag *n*
confusion, miscellany, assortment, mixture, mix,
jumble, medley, pastiche, hotchpotch, salad, potpourri
formal assemblage
colloq. omnium-gatherum

rage *n, v*
▶ *n* anger, wrath, fury, frenzy, raving, madness,
tumult, tantrum, temper, paroxysm
▷ **all the rage** fashionable, popular, the craze, in
vogue, stylish; *colloq.* the in thing, trendy
▶ *v* fume, seethe, rant, rave, storm, thunder, explode,
rampage
colloq. blow a fuse, blow your cool, blow your top, boil
over, burst a blood vessel, do your nut, explode, flip
your lid, fly off the handle, go mad, foam at the mouth,
go off the deep end, go up the wall, hit the roof, lose
your cool, lose your rag, raise hell, see red

ragged *adj*
1 *ragged clothes*
frayed, torn, ripped, tattered, in tatters, worn-out, in
holes, holey, threadbare, falling to pieces, tatty, shabby
old use rent
2 *ragged children*
scruffy, untidy, unkempt, poor, destitute, down and
out, down-at-heel
formal indigent
3 JAGGED, serrated, indented, notched, rugged,
rough, uneven, irregular
4 *a ragged group of people*
fragmented, erratic, disorganized, straggling

raging *adj*
1 VIOLENT, wild, stormy, turbulent, tumultuous
2 ANGRY, furious, enraged, infuriated, irate, fuming,
incensed, raving, seething, wrathful, frenzied, mad
formal fulminating, furibund, ireful

raid *n, v*
▶ *n* attack, onset, assault, charge, onslaught, inroad,
invasion, incursion, foray, sortie, sally, strike, blitz,
swoop, robbery, break-in, hold-up, smash-and-grab
raid
slang bust
▶ *v* loot, pillage, plunder, sack, ransack, forage, rifle,
maraud, break into, attack, assail, rush, set upon,
descend on, invade, storm
slang bust

raider *n*
attacker, invader, looter, plunderer, pillager,
ransacker, marauder, robber, thief, criminal, brigand,
villain, pirate
colloq. crook, shark

rail *v*
censure, criticize, attack, abuse, protest, decry,
upbraid, vociferate, mock, jeer, revile, ridicule, scoff
formal arraign, castigate, denounce, fulminate,
inveigh, vituperate

railing *n*
fence, fencing, paling, barrier, parapet, rail(s),
balustrade

raillery *n*
mockery, teasing, jeering, jesting, banter, chaff,
badinage, repartee, irony, joke, joking, ridicule, satire,
sport, pleasantry, persiflage
old use dicacity
formal diatribe, invective
colloq. kidding, ragging, ribbing, chiacking

railway *n*
track, line, rail(s)
US railroad

Types of railway include: branch line, broad gauge,
cable railway, cutting, electric railway, elevated
railway, express, feeder line, freight, funicular railway,
garden railway, goods line, high-speed line,
InterCity®, light railway, main line, marshalling
yard, metro, model railway, monorail, mountain
railway, narrow gauge, passenger line, rack-and-
pinion railway, rack railway, *US* railroad, rapid transit
system, siding, standard gauge, *US* subway, tramway,
trunk line, *colloq.* tube, underground.

rain *n, v*
▶ *n* **1** RAINFALL, precipitation, raindrops, drizzle,
mizzle, shower, cloudburst, downpour, deluge, torrent,
storm, rainstorm, thunderstorm, squall
2 *a rain of stones*
torrent, volley, shower, deluge
▶ *v* spit, drizzle, mizzle, sprinkle, shower, pour
(down), tipple down, teem, pelt, deluge
colloq. bucket (down), rain cats and dogs, come down
in buckets/sheets/stair rods/torrents, the floodgates/
clouds open; *slang* piss down
Related adjectives: pluvial, hyetal

rainbow *n, adj*
▶ *n* arc, arch, bow, spectrum, prism, iris
▶ *adj* rainbow-like, kaleidoscopic, prismatic,
variegated, spectral, opalescent
formal iridescent, irisated, irised
E3 monochrome

The colours of the rainbow are: red, orange, yellow,
green, blue, indigo, violet.

rainy *adj*
wet, damp, showery, drizzly
formal pluvial
E3 dry

raise *v*
1 LIFT, lift up, elevate, hoist, uplift, heave up, jack up,
put up, set up, erect, build, construct, weigh
2 INCREASE, escalate, put up, magnify, heighten,
strengthen, step up, intensify, amplify, boost, enhance,
upgrade
formal augment
colloq. jack up, bump up
3 *raise funds*
get, obtain, collect, gather, get together, amass,
accumulate, assemble, rally, muster, recruit
4 BRING UP, rear, breed, propagate, grow, cultivate,
educate, produce, develop, nurture
5 *raise a subject*
bring up, broach, introduce, present, put forward,
moot, suggest
6 PROVOKE, cause, create, arouse, rouse, activate,
evoke, excite, stir
E3 1 lower **2** decrease, reduce **5** suppress

raised *adj*
embossed, relief, applied, appliqué, cameo, relievo
E3 engraved, incised, intaglio

rake¹ *v*
1 *rake the grass*
scratch, hoe, scrape, graze, comb, level, smooth
2 SEARCH, scour, hunt, ransack, rifle, rummage,
comb
3 GATHER, collect, amass, accumulate

rake² *n, v*
▶ *n* degenerate, debauchee, playboy, roué, dissolute,
libertine, hedonist, lecher, sensualist, pleasure-seeker,
spendthrift, swinger
formal profligate, prodigal
E3 ascetic, puritan
▶ *v* ▷ **rake in** earn, receive, get paid, make;
colloq. bring in, pull in
▷ **rake up** remind, bring up, raise, mention, revive,
introduce, drag up

rake-off *n*
cut, share, slice, part, portion

rakish *adj*
stylish, sporty, smart, dapper, sharp, flamboyant,
flashy, jaunty, debonair, nonchalant, adventurous,
casual, breezy, devil-may-care, depraved, degenerate,
immoral, licentious, libertine, loose, dissipated,
abandoned, debauched, dissolute, lecherous, raffish,
sinful
old use dashing
formal prodigal, profligate
colloq. natty, snazzy

rally *n, v*
▶ *n* **1** GATHERING, assembly, convention,
convocation, conference, meeting, mass meeting,
jamboree, reunion, march, demonstration
formal assemblage
2 RECOVERY, recuperation, revival, comeback,
improvement, resurgence, renewal
▶ *v* **1** GATHER, collect, come/bring together, get
together, assemble, congregate, group, band together,
muster, summon, round up, unite, marshal, organize,
mobilize, reassemble, regroup, reorganize, reform
formal convene
2 RECOVER, recuperate, revive, improve, pick up, get
well, get better, gain strength, pull through
colloq. perk up, bounce back, get back on your feet, be
on the mend

ram *v*
1 HIT, strike, beat, butt, hammer, pound, drive,
drum, bump, crash, smash, dash, slam
2 FORCE, drive, thrust, cram, stuff, pack, crowd, jam,
squeeze, compress, wedge

ramble *v, n*
▶ *v* **1** WALK, hike, trek, tramp, traipse, stroll, amble,
saunter, stray, straggle, wander, roam, range, jaunt,
rove, diverge, meander, wind, zigzag
2 CHATTER, babble, blather, blether, digress,
wander, drift
formal expatiate
colloq. rabbit (on), witter (on), waffle, go off at a
tangent
▶ *n* walk, hike, trek, tramp, stroll, saunter, wander,
roam, amble, jaunt, tour, trip, excursion

rambler *n*
hiker, walker, traveller, stroller, rover, roamer,
saunterer, wanderer, drifter, wayfarer

rambling *adj*
1 SPREADING, sprawling, straggling, trailing
2 ROUNDABOUT, digressive, wandering, wordy,
long-winded, long-drawn-out, disjointed,
disconnected, incoherent
formal verbose, circuitous, periphrastic, errant
EӠ 2 direct

ramification *n*
1 RESULT, consequence, effect, upshot, outcome,
sequel
2 BRANCH, offshoot, limb, outgrowth, development,
implication, complication
formal divarication

ramp *n*
slope, incline, gradient, rise, grade
formal acclivity

rampage *v, n*
▶ *v* run wild, run amok, run riot, go berserk, rush,
rush violently/wildly, charge, tear, storm, rage, rant,
rave
▶ *n* rage, fury, frenzy, turmoil, mayhem, storm,
uproar, violence, destruction, furore
▷ **on the rampage** wild, amok, berserk, frenzied,
in a frenzy, violent(ly), wild(ly), out of control

rampant *adj*
unrestrained, uncontrolled, out of control, out of
hand, unbridled, unchecked, wanton, excessive, fierce,
violent, raging, wild, riotous, rank, profuse, rife,
widespread, prevalent, epidemic, pandemic
colloq. spreading like wildfire

rampart *n*
earthwork, embankment, bank, fence, barricade,
bastion, bulwark, defence, stronghold, guard, wall,
security, parapet, fort, fortification, breastwork,
vallum

ramshackle *adj*
dilapidated, tumbledown, broken-down, run-down,
crumbling, ruined, neglected, derelict, jerry-built,
unsafe, rickety, shaky, flimsy, unsteady, tottering,
decrepit, gone to rack and ruin
EӠ solid, stable

ranch *n*
farm, estate, plantation, station, hacienda, estancia

rancid *adj*
sour, off, bad, turned, high, overripe, unpleasant,
musty, stale, rank, foul, fetid, putrid, rotten
formal noxious, noisome, malodorous
EӠ sweet

rancorous *adj*
resentful, bitter, acerbic, hostile, spiteful, malignant,
vindictive, venomous, vengeful, implacable, virulent
formal acrimonious, malevolent, splenetic

rancour *n*
resentfulness, resentment, spite, hate, hatred,
animosity, malice, malignity, ill-feeling, ill-will,
hostility, bitterness, enmity, grudge, venom,
vindictiveness, spleen
formal acrimony, animus, antipathy, malevolence

random *adj*
arbitrary, chance, fortuitous, casual, incidental,
haphazard, irregular, sporadic, unsystematic,
unarranged, unplanned, unmethodical, accidental,
aimless, purposeless, indiscriminate, stray
formal serendipitous
colloq. hit-or-miss

EӠ systematic, deliberate
▷ **at random** haphazardly, incidentally, fortuitously,
arbitrarily, sporadically, irregularly, unsystematically,
unmethodically, aimlessly, purposelessly,
indiscriminately

randy *adj*
horny, sexy, raunchy, amorous, aroused, hot, lustful,
goatish, lascivious, lecherous, satyric
formal concupiscent
colloq. turned-on

range *n, v*
▶ *n* **1** *a range of fittings*
variety, diversity, assortment, selection, array, sort,
kind, type, class, order, species, genus, series, string,
chain, line, row, file
2 SCOPE, compass, scale, gamut, spectrum, radius,
sweep, spread, extent, distance, reach, span, confines,
limits, bounds, parameters, area, field, domain,
province, sphere, orbit
3 *a cooking range*
stove, cooker, oven
▶ *v* **1** EXTEND, stretch, reach, go, run, cover, spread,
vary, fluctuate
2 ALIGN, arrange, draw up, line up, order, rank, class,
classify, catalogue, group, categorize, grade,
pigeonhole, compartmentalize
formal dispose
3 ROAM, wander, stroll, stray, drift, amble, ramble

rangy *adj*
long-legged, leggy, lanky, gangling, skinny, weedy,
rawboned
EӠ compact, dumpy

rank¹ *n, v*
▶ *n* **1** GRADE, degree, class, caste, status, standing,
position, station, condition, estate, mark, echelon,
level, stratum, tier, classification, sort, type, group,
division
colloq. place in the pecking order
2 ROW, line, range, column, file, string, series, order,
formation

Ranks in the armed services include: air force:
aircraftsman, aircraftswoman, corporal, sergeant,
warrant officer, pilot officer, flying officer, flight
lieutenant, squadron-leader, wing commander,
group-captain, air-commodore, air-vice-marshal,
air-marshal, air-chief-marshal, marshal of the Royal
Air Force; army: private, lance-corporal, corporal,
sergeant, warrant officer, lieutenant, captain, major,
lieutenant-colonel, colonel, brigadier, major general,
lieutenant-general, general, field marshal; navy: able
seaman, rating, petty officer, chief petty officer,
sublieutenant, lieutenant, lieutenant-commander,
commander, captain, commodore, rear admiral,
vice-admiral, admiral, admiral of the fleet. *See also*
soldier.

▶ *v* **1** GRADE, class, rate, place, position, range, sort,
classify, categorize, order, arrange, organize, marshal
2 ALIGN, arrange, order, draw up, line up
formal dispose
▷ **rank and file 1** ORDINARY SOLDIERS, ordinary
men, soldiers, private soldiers **2** RABBLE, masses,
populace, crowd, herd, mob, common people,
proletariat, hoi polloi; *colloq.* riff-raff, plebs

rank² *adj*
1 UTTER, total, complete, absolute, unmitigated,
unqualified, thorough, sheer, downright, out-and-out,
arrant, gross, flagrant, glaring, blatant, outrageous
2 FOUL, repulsive, disgusting, unpleasant, offensive,

disagreeable, revolting, stinking, evil-smelling, acrid, pungent, putrid, fetid, rancid, stale
formal malodorous, mephitic, graveolent
3 *rank disobedience*
gross, coarse, shocking, outrageous, vile
4 OVERGROWN, lush, abundant, dense, profuse, vigorous
formal luxuriant

rankle *v*
annoy, irritate, rile, nettle, gall, irk, vex, peeve, fester, cause bitterness/resentment, embitter, anger
colloq. bug, get someone's blood, get someone's back up

ransack *v*
1 PLUNDER, rifle, raid, sack, strip, ravage, devastate, maraud, harry, loot, pillage
formal depredate
2 SEARCH, scour, comb, rummage through, go through, turn inside out, turn upside down
formal despoil

ransom *n, v*
▶ *n* **1** PAYMENT, price, money, pay-off
2 REDEMPTION, deliverance, rescue, freedom, setting free, liberation, restoration, release
▶ *v* buy off, buy/purchase the freedom of, redeem, deliver, rescue, liberate, free, set free, release

rant *v, n*
▶ *v* shout, cry, yell, roar, bellow, bluster, rave, harangue, rant and rave
formal declaim, vociferate
colloq. tub-thump
▶ *n* storm, shouting, crying, yelling, roaring, bluster, tirade, oration, harangue, rhetoric, bombast
formal declamation, diatribe, philippic, vociferation

rap *v, n*
▶ *v* **1** KNOCK, hit, strike, tap, whack, clout, clip, cuff, hammer, thump, bang, batter
2 REPROVE, reprimand, criticize, censure, punish, blame, scold
formal castigate
colloq. rail, slate, slam, knock
▶ *n* **1** KNOCK, hit, blow, tap, whack, clout, clip, cuff, hammer, thump, bang, batter
2 REBUKE, reprimand, censure, blame, punishment
formal castigation
colloq. flak, slating, slamming, knocking, stick

rapacious *adj*
uncaring, greedy, grasping, extortionate, preying, ravening, ravenous, voracious, plundering, predatory, marauding, insatiable, wolfish, wolvish, vulturish, vulturous, usurious
formal avaricious, esurient

rapacity *n*
greed, greediness, graspingness, avarice, insatiableness, predatoriness, rapaciousness, ravenousness, voraciousness, voracity, wolfishness, usury
formal avidity, esurience, esuriency
colloq. shark's manners

rape *v, n*
▶ *v* **1** *rape a woman*
violate, ravish, assault, assault sexually, abuse, maltreat, defile
2 *rape the land*
ravage, sack, ransack, strip, raid, loot, rob, pillage, plunder, devastate, violate, defile

formal despoil, depredate, spoliate
▶ *n* **1** *the rape of a young girl*
violation, assault, sexual assault, ravishment, abuse, maltreatment, date rape, gang rape
2 *rape of the countryside*
ravaging, sacking, ransacking, stripping, raid, looting, plundering, devastation, violation, defilement
formal rapine, despoliation, depredation, spoliation

rapid *adj*
swift, speedy, quick, fast, express, prompt, lively, brisk, hurried, hasty, headlong
formal precipitate, expeditious
colloq. like lightning
E3 slow, leisurely, sluggish; *formal* tardy

rapidity *n*
quickness, hurry, speed, speediness, rush, haste, briskness, swiftness, velocity, fleetness, promptness, dispatch
formal alacrity, celerity, expedition, expeditiousness, precipitateness, promptitude
E3 slowness

rapidly *adv*
fast, quickly, speedily, swiftly, hastily, hurriedly, briskly, promptly
formal expeditiously, precipitately
colloq. lickety-split
E3 slowly

rapine *n*
ravaging, sacking, ransacking, rage, stripping, raid, looting, plundering, devastation, violation, defilement
formal despoliation, depredation, spoliation

rapport *n*
bond, link, affinity, relationship, empathy, sympathy, understanding, good understanding, harmony

rapprochement *n*
reconcilement, increased friendliness, agreement, reconciliation, reunion, détente, softening, harmonization

rapt *adj*
engrossed, absorbed, preoccupied, intent, gripped, spellbound, enthralled, bewitched, captivated, preoccupied, concentrated, fascinated, entranced, charmed, enchanted, ecstatic, delighted, thrilled, ravished, enraptured, transported

rapture *n*
delight, happiness, joy, bliss, ecstasy, elation, exhilaration, enchantment, euphoria, exaltation, transport
formal delectation, felicity
colloq. seventh heaven, cloud nine, top of the world

rapturous *adj*
joyful, joyous, overjoyed, happy, delighted, enthusiastic, blissful, ecstatic, entranced, euphoric, exalted, ravished, transported, rhapsodic
colloq. over the moon, on cloud nine, in seventh heaven, tickled pink, on top of the world

rare *adj*
1 UNCOMMON, unusual, exceptional, scarce, sparse, sporadic, infrequent
colloq. thin on the ground, few and far between, like gold dust
2 EXQUISITE, superb, excellent, superlative, superior, outstanding, unparalleled, incomparable, matchless, exceptional, remarkable, precious, choice
E3 **1** common, abundant, frequent, ordinary, typical

rarefied *adj*
exclusive, select, private, esoteric, refined, high, noble, sublime, special

rarely *adv*
seldom, hardly ever, scarcely ever, infrequently, occasionally, little, scarcely, hardly, intermittently, sporadically, spasmodically
colloq. once in a blue moon
F∃ often, frequently

raring *adj*
eager, keen, enthusiastic, ready, willing, impatient, longing, itching, desperate

rarity *n*
1 CURIOSITY, curio, gem, pearl, treasure, find, marvel, wonder, nonpareil
2 UNCOMMONNESS, unusualness, strangeness, scarcity, shortage, sparseness, infrequency
F∃ 2 commonness, frequency

rascal *n*
rogue, scoundrel, scamp, scallywag, imp, devil, villain, good-for-nothing, ne'er-do-well, mischief-maker, wastrel

rascally *adj*
dishonest, wicked, mischievous, scoundrelly, unscrupulous, villainous, good-for-nothing, evil, vicious, disreputable, base, crooked, bad, knavish, low, mean, reprobate
colloq. furciferous

rash¹ *adj*
a rash action
impulsive, impetuous, hasty, reckless, ill-considered, foolhardy, ill-advised, madcap, hare-brained, hot-headed, headstrong, headlong, unguarded, unwary, indiscreet, adventurous, audacious, imprudent, careless, premature, heedless, unthinking
formal precipitate, temerarious
F∃ cautious, wary, careful

rash² *n*
1 *a rash on the skin*
eruption, outbreak, hives, nettlerash, heat rash, epidemic, plague
technical pompholyx, urticaria
2 *a rash of burglaries*
spate, flood, deluge, torrent, run, rush, wave

rashness *n*
impulsiveness, incaution, hastiness, foolhardiness, carelessness, incautiousness, recklessness, thoughtlessness, adventurousness, audacity, heedlessness, brashness, indiscretion
formal precipitance, precipitation, precipitancy, temerity
F∃ carefulness, cautiousness, wariness

rasp *n, v*
▶ *n* grating, scrape, grinding, scratch, harshness, hoarseness, croak
▶ *v* **1** GRATE, scrape, grind, file, sand, scour, scratch, abrade, rub
formal excoriate
2 IRRITATE, grate, jar
colloq. peeve, bug, get on your nerves
3 CROAK, screech, squawk, cackle

rasping *adj*
harsh, hoarse, creaking, croaking, grating, jarring, raspy, gravelly, gruff, husky, croaky, scratchy, rough,

raucous
formal stridulant

rate *n, v*
▶ *n* **1** SPEED, velocity, tempo, time, ratio, proportion, percentage, relation, degree, grade, rank, rating, standard, basis, measure, scale
2 CHARGE, fee, hire, toll, tariff, price, cost, value, worth, pay, payment, tax, duty, amount, figure, percentage
▷ **at any rate** in any case, anyway, in any event, nevertheless, regardless, at all
▶ *v* **1** JUDGE, regard, consider, deem, count, reckon, figure, estimate, evaluate, value, assess, weigh (up), measure, grade, rank, categorize, class, classify
formal appraise, esteem, adjudge
2 ADMIRE, respect, value, prize, have a high opinion of
formal esteem
3 DESERVE, merit, be worthy of, have a right to, warrant, justify, be entitled to

rather *adv*
1 MODERATELY, relatively, slightly, a bit, a little, somewhat, fairly, quite, to some degree/extent, pretty, noticeably, significantly, very
2 PREFERABLY, sooner, much rather, much sooner, instead, by/for preference, for/from choice

ratify *v*
approve, uphold, endorse, corroborate, sign, countersign, legalize, sanction, authorize, warrant, establish, affirm, agree to, confirm, certify, validate, authenticate
F∃ repudiate, reject

rating *n*
assessment, classification, category, score, mark, evaluation, class, rank, degree, status, standing, position, placing, order, grade, grading
formal appraisal, adjudging

ratio *n*
proportion, percentage, fraction, relation, relationship, correspondence, correlation, symmetry, balance

ration *n, v*
▶ *n* **1** QUOTA, allowance, allocation, allotment, share, proportion, percentage, portion, helping, part, measure, lot, amount
2 *rations in times of shortage*
food, foodstuffs, provisions, supplies, stores
formal viands, victuals
▶ *v* allot, allocate, budget, share, deal out, distribute, hand out, divide out, measure out, dole out, dispense, supply, issue, control, restrict, limit, conserve, save
formal apportion

rational *adj*
logical, reasonable, sound, well-founded, realistic, sensible, clear-headed, wise, sane, normal, balanced, lucid, reasoning, thinking, intelligent, enlightened
formal judicious, sagacious, circumspect, prudent, cognitive, cerebral, ratiocinative
F∃ irrational, illogical, insane, crazy

rationale *n*
logic, reasoning, philosophy, thesis, principle, basis, grounds, explanation, reason(s), purpose, *raison d'être*, motive, motivation, hypothesis, theory

rationalize *v*
1 JUSTIFY, excuse, vindicate, explain, account for, make allowances for, explain away

2 REORGANIZE, streamline, trim, modernize, update, make more efficient, cut back on, cut out waste

rattle *v*
1 CLATTER, jingle, jangle, clang, clank, clink, shake, vibrate, jolt, jar, bounce, bang, rap, bump, knock
2 UNNERVE, disconcert, unsettle, disturb, confuse, upset, put off/out, shake, alarm, throw off balance
colloq. faze, put someone's nose out of joint
▷ **rattle off** reel off, list, list quickly, run through, recite, repeat
▷ **rattle on** chatter, gabble, jabber, prate, prattle, blether, cackle; *colloq.* gab, rabbit on, witter, yack

ratty *adj*
irritable, annoyed, angry, cross, impatient, crabbed, testy, touchy, short, snappy, short-tempered
colloq. peeved
E3 calm, patient

raucous *adj*
harsh, rough, hoarse, husky, scratching, rasping, grating, jarring, screeching, piercing, ear-piercing, discordant, strident, shrill, sharp, noisy, loud

ravage *v, n*
▶ *v* destroy, devastate, lay waste, demolish, level, raze, wreck, ruin, leave in ruins, spoil, damage, loot, harry, maraud, pillage, plunder, sack, depredate
formal despoil
▶ *n* destruction, devastation, havoc, damage, ruin, ruination, looting, ransacking, desolation, wreckage, pillage, plunder
formal despoliation, depredation, spoliation

ravaged *adj*
devastated, destroyed, desolate, wrecked, ransacked, spoilt, shattered, war-worn, war-torn, battle-torn, war-wasted
E3 unspoilt

rave *v, adj, n*
▶ *v* **1** TALK WILDLY, rant and rave, shout, cry, yell, roar, bellow, babble, jabber, ramble
2 RAGE, storm, thunder, roar, rant, fume, seethe, explode, lose your temper
colloq. lose your cool, boil over, flip your lid, hit the roof
3 ENTHUSE, sing the praises of, wax lyrical, extol, acclaim, hail
colloq. be mad about
▶ *adj* enthusiastic, praising, rapturous, favourable, excellent, ecstatic, wonderful
formal laudatory
▶ *n* party, disco, celebration, carousal, orgy, acid-house party
colloq. do, knees-up, rave-up, bash, blow-out

ravenous *adj*
hungry, starving, starved, famished, greedy, voracious, insatiable, wolfish

rave-up *n*
party, celebration, carousal, debauch, orgy
colloq. bash, blow-out, do, shindig, thrash

ravine *n*
canyon, gorge, deep narrow valley, gully, canyon, abyss, gap, pass

raving *adj*
mad, insane, hysterical, delirious, deranged, demented, unbalanced, wild, frenzied, furious, berserk, irrational, out of your mind
colloq. crazy, barmy, batty, loony, loopy, round the

bend/twist
E3 rational, sane, balanced

ravish *v*
1 DELIGHT, enrapture, overjoy, enchant, charm, captivate, enthral, entrance, fascinate, spellbind, bewitch
2 RAPE, violate, assault, assault sexually, abuse, maltreat, defile

ravishing *adj*
delightful, enchanting, bewitching, enthralling, charming, lovely, beautiful, gorgeous, stunning, radiant, dazzling, alluring, seductive

raw *adj*
1 *raw vegetables*
uncooked, fresh
2 UNPROCESSED, unrefined, untreated, unprepared, unfinished, rough, crude, natural
3 PLAIN, bare, naked, basic, harsh, brutal, realistic, candid, blunt, outspoken, frank, forthright
4 SCRATCHED, grazed, scraped, abraded, chafed, open, bloody, sore, exposed, tender, sensitive
formal excoriated
5 COLD, chilly, chill, bitter, biting, nippy, piercing, freezing, bleak, wet, damp
6 *a raw recruit*
inexperienced, new, green, immature, callow, ignorant, naïve, untrained, untutored, unpractised, unskilled
colloq. wet behind the ears
E3 1 cooked, done **2** processed, refined, treated **5** warm **6** experienced, skilled

ray *n*
beam, shaft, flash, streak, stream, gleam, flicker, glimmer, twinkle, glint, spark, trace, hint, suggestion, indication

raze *v*
demolish, pull down, tear down, knock down, bulldoze, flatten, level, wreck, ruin, destroy, fell

razor *n*

Types of razor include: battery shaver, cut-throat, disposable razor, double-edged razor, electric razor, Ladyshave®, razor blade, rechargeable razor, safety razor, shaver, wet-and-dry shaver, wet razor.

re *prep*
about, concerning, regarding, with regard to, with reference to, on the subject of

reach *v, n*
▶ *v* **1** ARRIVE AT, get to, attain, achieve, make, make it to, amount to, come to, touch
colloq. hit
2 *reach for a pen*
stretch (out), extend, spread, touch, contact, grasp, hold, hit, strike
3 EXTEND, stretch, spread, project, continue, come to, go as far as, go down/up to, come down/up to
4 CONTACT, get in touch with, get hold of, communicate with, get through to, write to, speak to, get onto, telephone, phone, ring, call, fax
▶ *n* range, scope, compass, distance, span, spread, extent, extension, stretch, ambit, latitude, grasp, command, power, influence, authority, control, jurisdiction

react *v*
1 RESPOND, retaliate, reciprocate, reply, answer,

acknowledge, act, behave
2 *react against something*
rebel, rise up, oppose, defy, resist
formal dissent

reaction *n*
response, reply, answer, acknowledgement,
repercussion, counteraction, reflex, recoil,
reciprocation, counterbalance, reversal, reversion,
retaliation
colloq. feedback, backlash, kickback

reactionary *adj, n*
▶ *adj* conservative, ultraconservative, right-wing,
rightist, diehard, counter-revolutionary, traditional
◼ progressive, revolutionary
▶ *n* conservative, ultraconservative, right-winger,
rightist, diehard, counter-revolutionary, traditionalist
◼ progressive, revolutionary

read *v, n*
▶ *v* **1** STUDY, look at, pore over, scan, examine,
scrutinize, skim
formal peruse
colloq. dip into, browse through, leaf through, thumb
through, flick through
2 INTERPRET, understand, comprehend, decipher,
decode
formal construe
3 RECITE, declaim, deliver, speak, utter
4 *the gauge read zero*
indicate, show, display, register, record, measure
▷ **read into** interpret, deduce, infer, reason,
misinterpret, take out of context; *formal* construe;
colloq. read between the lines, get hold of the wrong
end of the stick
▶ *n* study, look, perusal, scan, scanning, skimming,
scrutiny, browsing

readable *adj*
1 LEGIBLE, decipherable, intelligible, clear, easy to
read, understandable, comprehensible
2 INTERESTING, enjoyable, worth reading,
entertaining, stimulating, captivating, enthralling,
gripping
colloq. unputdownable
◼ **1** illegible **2** unreadable

readily *adv*
willingly, unhesitatingly, happily, gladly, eagerly,
enthusiastically, promptly, quickly, swiftly, rapidly,
speedily, freely, smoothly, with ease, easily, effortlessly
◼ unwillingly, reluctantly, with difficulty

readiness *n*
willingness, preparedness, skill, preparation, aptitude,
fitness, eagerness, keenness, inclination, quickness,
rapidity, ease, promptness, facility, availability,
handiness
colloq. gameness
▷ **in readiness** in preparation, available, prepared,
on standby, standing by, on call, on full alert

reading *n*
1 STUDY, perusal, scrutiny, scan, browsing,
examination, inspection
2 INTERPRETATION, understanding, decoding,
deciphering, rendering, version, edition, rendition,
recital
3 *the reading on a meter*
indication, display, register, record, measurement,
figure
4 *a reading from the Bible*
passage, lesson

ready *adj, v*
▶ *adj* **1** *ready to go*
prepared, waiting, set, all set, fit, fitted out, equipped,
rigged out, arranged, organized, completed, finished
colloq. geared up
2 WILLING, inclined, disposed, happy, eager,
enthusiastic, keen
formal predisposed
colloq. game, psyched up
3 AVAILABLE, to hand, on hand, present, near,
accessible, convenient, handy, within reach
colloq. at your fingertips
4 ABOUT TO, on the point of, likely to, liable to, on the
verge of
5 PROMPT, immediate, quick, swift, rapid, speedy,
easy, sharp, astute, perceptive, discerning, alert,
resourceful
◼ **1** unprepared **2** unwilling, reluctant,
disinclined **3** unavailable, inaccessible **5** slow
▶ *v* prepare, organize, arrange, equip, order, prime,
set, alert

real *adj*
1 *in the real world*
actual, existing, physical, material, substantial,
tangible, concrete
2 *real leather*
genuine, authentic, bona fide, official, rightful,
legitimate, valid, true, factual, occurring, certain, sure,
positive, veritable
3 SINCERE, honest, truthful, genuine, true, from the
heart, fervent, heartfelt, unfeigned, unaffected
4 *this is a real mess*
right, complete, absolute, utter, thorough
◼ **1** unreal, imaginary **2** false,
imitation **3** insincere

realism *n*
1 ACTUALITY, practicality, pragmatism, sanity,
saneness, sensibleness, rationality
2 LIFELIKENESS, faithfulness, truthfulness,
authenticity, naturalness, genuineness

realistic *adj*
1 PRACTICAL, down-to-earth, commonsense,
sensible, matter-of-fact, level-headed, clear-sighted,
businesslike, hard-headed, pragmatic, matter-of-fact,
rational, logical, objective, detached, unsentimental,
unromantic
colloq. hard-boiled, hard-nosed
2 LIFELIKE, faithful, truthful, true, true-to-life,
vivid, genuine, authentic, natural, close, real, real-life,
graphic, representational
◼ **1** unrealistic, impractical, irrational,
idealistic **2** fake, imitation, unrealistic

reality *n*
truth, fact, certainty, realism, actuality, real world, real
life, existence, materiality, tangibility, substantiality,
genuineness, authenticity, validity
formal corporeality
◼ fiction, fantasy

realization *n*
1 UNDERSTANDING, comprehension, grasp,
recognition, discernment, perception, acceptance,
appreciation, awareness, consciousness
formal cognizance, apprehension
2 ACHIEVEMENT, accomplishment, fulfilment,
completion, implementation, performance
formal consummation
3 EARNING, selling, fetching, making, gain, clearing

realize *v*
1 UNDERSTAND, grasp, discover, learn, ascertain, catch on, take in, become aware/conscious of, recognize, perceive, discern, accept, appreciate, glean *formal* comprehend, apprehend
colloq. cotton on, twig, tumble to
2 ACHIEVE, accomplish, fulfil, complete, implement, perform, bring about
formal effect, effectuate, consummate
3 SELL FOR, fetch, make, earn, gain, produce, net, clear, bring in, encash

really *adv*
1 ACTUALLY, in fact, truly, honestly, sincerely, genuinely, positively, surely, certainly, undoubtedly, absolutely, categorically
2 VERY, extremely, exceptionally, intensely, remarkably, highly, severely, indeed

realm *n*
1 *defence of the realm*
kingdom, monarchy, principality, empire, country, state, land, territory, area, region, province, domain
2 *the realm of politics*
sphere, area, region, province, domain, world, orbit, field, department

reap *v*
1 HARVEST, cut, crop, gather, mow
formal garner
2 GAIN, obtain, secure, acquire, get, derive, collect, realize, win

rear *n, adj, v*
▶ *n* back, stern, end, hind, tail, rump, buttocks, posterior, behind, bottom
colloq. backside
E3 front
▶ *adj* back, hind, hindmost, rearmost, last, tail-end
E3 front
▶ *v* 1 *rear a child*
bring up, care for, look after, raise, breed, grow, cultivate, foster, nurse, nurture, instruct, train, educate, parent
2 RISE, rise up, loom, tower, soar, raise, elevate, lift (up), hoist

rearrange *v*
change, adjust, alter, shift, vary, reorder, reschedule, reposition, rejig

reason *n, v*
▶ *n* 1 CAUSE, motive, motivation, incentive, impetus, inducement, explanation, excuse, justification, defence, warrant, ground(s), basis, case, argument, aim, intention, purpose, object, end, goal
formal rationale, *raison d'être*
2 SENSE, logic, reasoning, rationality, sanity, mind, thought, wit, brain, intellect, intellectuality, intelligence, understanding, comprehension, wisdom, judgement, common sense, gumption
formal ratiocination
colloq. nous
▷ **within reason** within limits, in moderation, moderately, within bounds, with self-control
E3 to excess
▶ *v* work out, solve, reckon, resolve, conclude, deduce, infer, think, use your brain
formal celebrate, ratiocinate, cogitate, syllogize
▷ **reason with** urge, persuade, coax, move, argue with, debate with, discuss with, plead with;
formal remonstrate with

reasonable *adj*
1 SENSIBLE, wise, well-advised, sane, intelligent, rational, logical, practical, sound, fair, reasoned, understandable, well-thought-out, plausible, credible, possible, viable
formal sagacious, judicious
2 *a reasonable price*
acceptable, satisfactory, moderate, average, fair, just, modest, inexpensive, low
3 *a reasonable standard of work*
tolerable, acceptable, satisfactory, moderate, average, fair
colloq. OK, not a lot to write home about, no great shakes, not to be sneezed at
E3 1 unreasonable, irrational 2 exorbitant, expensive 3 poor, bad

reasoned *adj*
clear, logical, methodical, organized, rational, sensible, sound, systematic, well-thought-out
formal judicious
E3 illogical, unsystematic

reasoning *n*
logic, thinking, thought, analysis, interpretation, deduction, supposition, hypothesis, rationalization, argument, case, proof
formal rationale, ratiocination, cerebration
Related adjective: logistical

reassure *v*
comfort, cheer (up), encourage, hearten, inspirit, brace, bolster, buoy up, nerve, rally
formal inspirit
E3 alarm, unnerve

rebate *n*
refund, repayment, reduction, decrease, discount, deduction, allowance

rebel *n, v, adj*
▶ *n* 1 REVOLUTIONARY, agitator, insurgent, insurrectionary, guerrilla, freedom fighter, mutineer, revolter
2 DISSENTER, nonconformist, schismatic, apostate, heretic
old use recusant
▶ *v* revolt, mutiny, rise up, riot, run riot, dissent, disobey, oppose, defy, resist, recoil, shy away, pull back, shrink, flinch
E3 conform, obey
▶ *adj* revolutionary, insurgent, insurrectionary, mutinous, rebellious, defiant, disobedient, malcontent(ed)
formal insubordinate

rebellion *n*
revolt, revolution, rising, uprising, insurrection, insurgence, mutiny, riot, military takeover, coup, *coup d'état*, resistance, opposition, defiance, disobedience, civil disobedience, dissent, heresy
formal insubordination

rebellious *adj*
rebelling, resistant, defiant, disobedient, unruly, disorderly, ungovernable, unmanageable, obstinate, revolutionary, insurrectionary, insurgent, seditious, mutinous, rioting
formal contumacious, insubordinate, intractable, recalcitrant
E3 obedient, submissive

rebirth *n*
restoration, revival, renewal, regeneration,

renaissance, revitalization, rejuvenation, resurrection, reincarnation

rebound *v, n*
▶ *v* recoil, backfire, return, bounce (back), spring (back), ricochet, boomerang, fail, defeat itself, be self-defeating
colloq. come home to roost, score an own goal
▶ *n* recoil, backfiring, return, bounce, spring, ricochet, repercussion, reverberation, reflection

---

⚠ **rebound** or **redound** ?
To *rebound* is 'to bounce back', in either a neutral, a good, or a bad sense: *She was throwing the ball against the wall and catching it as it rebounded; His overweening ambition rebounded on him, as, having displaced his father from the throne, he was in turn ousted by those who would not accept him as the legitimate ruler.* To *redound* (now a rather old-fashioned or formal word) is 'to have advantageous or disadvantageous consequences': *His actions redounded to the credit of the regiment; A child's bad behaviour in public inevitably redounds on the parents.*

---

rebuff *v, n*
▶ *v* spurn, reject, refuse, decline, repudiate, turn down, repulse, discourage, snub, slight, cut
colloq. cold-shoulder, put down
▶ *n* rejection, refusal, repulse, check, discouragement, spurning, repudiation, snub, slight
colloq. brush-off, put-down, cold shoulder, slap in the face, kick in the teeth

rebuild *v*
restore, remake, remodel, renovate, reassemble, reconstruct, refashion, re-edify
E∃ demolish, destroy

rebuke *v, n*
▶ *v* reprove, chide, scold, reprimand, upbraid, rate, censure, blame, reproach
formal castigate, admonish, remonstrate
colloq. tell off, tick off, dress down, carpet, read the riot act to, throw the book at, give an earful, tear off a strip, come down on like a ton of bricks
E∃ praise, compliment
▶ *n* reproach, reproof, reprimand, scolding, lecture, censure, blame
formal admonition, castigation, remonstration
colloq. dressing-down, telling-off, ticking-off, carpeting
E∃ praise, commendation

rebut *v*
refute, quash, defeat, discredit, disprove, invalidate, negate, overturn, give the lie to
formal confute
colloq. explode

rebuttal *n*
refutation, negation, defeat, disproof, invalidation, overthrow
formal confutation

recalcitrant *adj*
disobedient, defiant, uncontrollable, ungovernable, unmanageable, unruly, wayward, wilful, contrary, obstinate, stubborn, unsubmissive, unwilling, unco-operative
formal contumacious, insubordinate, intractable, refractory, renitent
E∃ amenable, tractable

recall *v, n*
▶ *v* **1** REMEMBER, think of, call to mind, recollect, reminisce, think back to, cast your mind back, evoke, call up, summon up, bring back
2 ORDER BACK, summon (back), call back, order to return
3 CANCEL, revoke, withdraw, repeal, annul
formal rescind, retract, countermand, abrogate, nullify
▶ *n* **1** REMEMBRANCE, memory, recollection
2 CANCELLATION, annulment, repeal, withdrawal
formal abrogation, nullification, countermanding, retraction, revocation, recision

recant *v*
deny, disown, renounce, repudiate, rescind, apostatize, retract, revoke, withdraw, recall, unsay
formal abjure, abrogate, disavow, disclaim, forswear

recantation *n*
denial, renunciation, repudiation, apostasy, withdrawal, revocation, revoke, disownment
formal abjuration, disavowal, disclaimer, retractation

recapitulate *v*
recap, summarize, sum up, review, repeat, reiterate, restate, recount, run over, go over

recede *v*
1 GO BACK, return, retire, withdraw, move away, retreat
2 DIMINISH, decline, fade, dwindle, decrease, lessen, fall off, drop, shrink, slacken, subside, ebb, wane, sink
formal abate
E∃ **1** advance, approach **2** grow, increase

receipt *n*
1 VOUCHER, ticket, slip, proof of purchase, counterfoil, stub, acknowledgement
2 RECEIVING, reception, acceptance, getting, obtaining, deriving, gaining, delivery
3 MONEY RECEIVED, takings, income, earnings, proceeds, profits, gains, return(s), turnover

receive *v*
1 TAKE, take up, accept, get, obtain, derive, gain, acquire, come by, pick up, collect, gather, inherit
2 *receive guests*
admit, let in, greet, welcome, entertain, take, contain, hold, accommodate
3 EXPERIENCE, undergo, go through, suffer, bear, sustain, meet with, encounter
4 REACT TO, respond to, hear, find out about, be informed of, learn about, perceive
formal apprehend
E∃ **1** give, donate

receiver *n*
1 RECIPIENT, beneficiary, donee, assignee, grantee, legatee
2 RADIO, tuner, wireless, handset
E∃ **1** donor

recent *adj*
late, latest, current, present-day, contemporary, modern, up-to-date, up-to-the-minute, new, novel, fresh, young
E∃ old, out-of-date

recently *adv*
lately, of late, newly, freshly, in the last few days/weeks/months/years, in the past few days/weeks/months/years, not long ago, a short time ago, a little while back
E∃ long ago

receptacle *n*
container, vessel, holder
formal repository, reservatory

reception *n*
1 ACCEPTANCE, admission, greeting, recognition, welcome, entertaining, treatment, response, reaction, acknowledgement, receipt
2 PARTY, function, social, get-together, gathering, reunion, at-home, entertainment
colloq. do, bash, beano, shindig, rave-up

receptive *adj*
open-minded, open to reason, amenable, accommodating, suggestible, susceptible, flexible, willing, quick, sensitive, responsive, open, accessible, approachable, friendly, hospitable, welcoming, sympathetic, favourable, interested
E3 narrow-minded, resistant, unresponsive

recess *n*
1 BREAK, interval, intermission, rest, respite, time off, holiday, vacation
colloq. time out
2 ALCOVE, niche, nook, corner, bay, cavity, hollow, oriel, depression, indentation
3 *in the recesses of your mind*
innards, heart, depths, interior, reaches, bowels
formal penetralia

recession *n*
slump, depression, downturn, decline, slide, trough, collapse, crash, failure
E3 boom, upturn

recherché *adj*
refined, select, choice, rare, far-fetched, exotic
formal esoteric, abstruse, arcane
E3 commonplace

recipe *n*
formula, prescription, ingredients, instructions, directions, method, system, way, means, procedure, guide, process, technique

recipient *n*
receiver, beneficiary, assignee, donee, grantee, legatee
E3 donor, giver

reciprocal *adj*
mutual, joint, exchanged, shared, give-and-take, returned, requited, complementary, alternating, corresponding, equivalent, interchangeable, interdependent
formal correlative

reciprocate *v*
respond, reply, return, give in return, exchange, swap, repay, trade, match, equal, correspond, interchange, alternate
formal requite
colloq. do the same, give as good as you get

recital *n*
1 *a music recital*
performance, show, concert
2 RECITATION, reading, narration, report, telling, account, description, rendition, rendering, interpretation, repetition
formal declamation

recitation *n*
passage, reading, piece, party piece, poem, verse, monologue, narration, story, tale, recital, rendering, telling

recite *v*
repeat, tell, narrate, relate, recount, speak, say aloud, deliver, articulate, perform, reel off, rattle off, itemize, enumerate
formal declaim

reckless *adj*
heedless, thoughtless, mindless, careless, negligent, inattentive, irresponsible, imprudent, incautious, ill-advised, indiscreet, rash, hasty, foolhardy, desperate, daredevil, devil-may-care, wild, madcap, tearaway
formal precipitate
E3 cautious, wary, careful, prudent

recklessness *n*
carelessness, heedlessness, inattention, irresponsibility, irresponsibleness, negligence, rashness, thoughtlessness, incaution, imprudence, foolhardiness, mindlessness, madness, motorway madness
E3 carefulness, caution, prudence

reckon *v*
1 THINK, believe, imagine, fancy, suppose, assume, guess
formal surmise, conjecture
2 CONSIDER, regard, esteem, think of, look upon, value, rate, judge, evaluate, assess, estimate, gauge
formal deem, appraise
3 CALCULATE, compute, figure out, work out, add up, total, tally, count, number, enumerate
▷ **reckon on** rely on, depend on, bank on, count on, take for granted, trust in, hope for, expect, anticipate, foresee, plan for, bargain for, figure on, take into account, face
▷ **reckon with** anticipate, bargain for, consider, take into account, plan for, expect, foresee, handle, cope, deal, face, treat

reckoning *n*
1 *by my reckoning*
calculation, computation, addition, working-out, total, tally, score, number, enumeration, estimate
2 BILL, account, charge, due, score, paying, payment, settlement
3 JUDGEMENT, opinion, estimation, evaluation, assessment
formal appraisal
4 *the day of reckoning*
judgement, punishment, retribution, doom, damnation

reclaim *v*
recover, regain, get back, claim back, take back, recapture, retrieve, salvage, rescue, redeem, restore, reinstate, regenerate

recline *v*
rest, lean back, lie (down), lounge, loll, sprawl, stretch out
formal repose

recluse *n*
ascetic, hermit, solitary, loner, monk, eremite, stylite, solitarian, solitaire, anchorite, anchoret, anchoress

reclusive *adj*
isolated, solitary, withdrawn, secluded, retiring, recluse, cloistered, monastic, ascetic, eremitic, hermitical, anchoritic
formal sequestered

recognition *n*
1 IDENTIFICATION, detection, discovery, recollection, recall, remembrance, awareness,

knowing, knowledge, consciousness, perception, realization, admission, confession, understanding, placing, spotting
formal cognizance
2 ACCEPTANCE, allowing, admittance, endorsement, grating, approval, acknowledgement, validation, sanction
3 *receive recognition for your work*
appreciation, honour, reward, respect, salute, gratitude, thankfulness

recognize *v*
1 IDENTIFY, know, remember, recollect, recall, call to mind, pick out, tell, place, see, notice, spot, perceive, not miss, not mistake
2 *recognize your faults*
accept, acknowledge, admit, grant, concede, allow, endorse, appreciate, discern, perceive, understand, realize, confess, own, be aware of, be conscious of
formal apprehend
3 *recognize a qualification*
accept, allow, admit, endorse, grant, approve, acknowledge, adopt, validate, sanction
4 APPRECIATE, be thankful for, honour, respect, salute, show your gratitude/thankfulness

recoil *v, n*
▶ *v* move back, jump back, spring back, shy away, flinch, shrink, quail, rebound, react, falter, kick, backfire, boomerang, misfire
▶ *n* rebound, reaction, kick, backlash, repercussion

recollect *v*
recall, remember, call to mind, cast your mind back, reminisce

recollection *n*
memory, recall, remembrance, souvenir, reminiscence, (mental) impression

recommend *v*
commend, approve, endorse, praise, vouch for, advocate, urge, advise, counsel, guide, suggest, propose, put forward, advance, put in a good word for
formal exhort
colloq. plug
☒ disapprove

recommendation *n*
commendation, endorsement, approval, advice, counsel, guidance, suggestion, urging, proposal, advocacy, sanction, blessing, praise, tip, good word, special mention, reference, testimonial
formal exhortations
colloq. plug
☒ disapproval

recompense *n, v*
▶ *n* compensation, indemnification, damages, reparation, restitution, amends, requital, satisfaction, repayment, reward, payment, remuneration, pay, wages
formal guerdon
▶ *v* compensate, indemnify, remunerate, pay, reward, repay, redress, reimburse, requite, satisfy
formal guerdon

reconcile *v*
1 *be reconciled with someone*
reunite, conciliate, pacify, appease, placate, mollify, bring together, make (your) peace, put on friendly terms
formal propitiate
colloq. make up, bury the hatchet, become friends

again, shake hands, forgive and forget
2 *reconcile different aims*
harmonize, accommodate, adjust, resolve, settle, mend, remedy, put right, rectify, square
formal accord
colloq. patch up
3 *reconcile yourself to an unpleasant situation*
resign yourself to, face up to, accept, come to accept, submit
☒ **1** estrange, alienate

reconciliation *n*
reunion, conciliation, pacification, peace, mollification, appeasement, rapprochement, détente, settlement, agreement, harmony, harmonizing, accommodation, resolution, squaring, adjustment, compromise
formal propitiation, accord
☒ estrangement, separation

recondite *adj*
obscure, difficult, involved, complicated, intricate, mysterious, mystical, deep, profound, dark, concealed, hidden, secret
formal abstruse, arcane, esoteric
☒ simple, straightforward

recondition *v*
renovate, repair, restore, renew, refurbish, overhaul, fix, remodel, revamp

reconnaissance *n*
exploration, reconnoitring, scouting, survey, expedition, examination, inspection, probe, observation, scrutiny, scan, investigation, search, patrol
colloq. recce

reconnoitre *v*
explore, survey, scan, spy out, inspect, examine, scrutinize, investigate, patrol, observe, probe
colloq. recce, check out, see how the land lies, see the lie of the land

reconsider *v*
think over, rethink, review, revise, re-examine, think twice, modify, reassess, think better of, have second thoughts

reconstruct *v*
remake, rebuild, reassemble, re-establish, refashion, remodel, recondition, revamp, reform, reorganize, redo, recreate, restore, renovate, regenerate

record *n, v*
▶ *n* **1** REGISTER, log, chart, report, account, minutes, memorandum, note(s), entry, document(s), file, dossier, diary, logbook, journal, chronicle, memoir, memorial, history, annals, archives, documentation, data, evidence, photography, testimony, trace
2 RECORDING, disc, single, CD, compact disc, album, release, LP, cassette, tape
colloq. vinyl
3 *break the record*
fastest time, best performance, furthest distance, personal best, world record
4 BACKGROUND, history, previous performance, track record, curriculum vitae, career
▶ *v* **1** NOTE, enter, inscribe, write down, transcribe, register, log, chart, put down, take down, put on record, enrol, report, list, catalogue, minute, chronicle, document, keep, preserve
2 TAPE-RECORD, make a recording of, tape,

videotape, video, cut, edit
3 *the gauge records electrical activity*
show, register, indicate, display, read, express
▷ **off the record** unofficial, unofficially,
confidential, confidentially, private, privately;
formal sub rosa
◲ officially
▷ **on record 1** *the wettest April on record* noted,
documented, written down **2** *to go on record as
saying* officially recorded, publicly known,
documented

recorder *n*
1 REGISTRAR, archivist, annalist, chronicler, diarist,
historian, chronologer, secretary, clerk, stenographer,
scribe, scorer, score-keeper
2 TAPE RECORDER, cassette recorder, cassette-
player, video recorder, videocassette recorder
colloq. video

recording *n*

Types of recording include: album, audiotape,
cassette, CD, compact disc, digital recording, disc,
EP (extended play), 45, gramophone record,
long-playing record, LP, magnetic tape, mono
recording, record, 78, single, stereo recording, tape,
tape-recording, tele-recording, video, videocassette,
video disc, videotape, *colloq.* vinyl.

recount *v*
tell, relate, impart, communicate, report, narrate,
describe, depict, portray, unfold, detail, repeat,
rehearse, recite

recoup *v*
recover, retrieve, regain, get back, win back, make
good, repossess, repay, refund, indemnify, reimburse,
recompense, compensate

recourse *n*
appeal, resort, access, turning to, choice, option,
alternative, possibility, remedy, refuge, way out

recover *v*
1 *recover from illness*
get better, feel better, get well, improve, pick up, rally,
mend, heal, respond to treatment, get over, recuperate,
feel yourself again, revive, convalesce, gain strength,
get stronger, come round
formal ameliorate
colloq. pull through, bounce back, turn the corner, get
back on your feet, be on the mend
2 REGAIN, get back, win back, recoup, retrieve,
retake, recapture, repossess, reclaim, recycle, restore
◲ **1** worsen **2** lose, forfeit

recovery *n*
1 RECUPERATION, convalescence, rehabilitation,
mending, healing, improvement, upturn, rally,
rallying, revival, restoration
formal amelioration
2 RETRIEVAL, salvage, reclamation, recouping,
regaining, repossession, recapture, recycling
◲ **1** worsening **2** loss, forfeit

recreation *n*
fun, enjoyment, pleasure, amusement, diversion,
distraction, entertainment, hobby, pastime, game,
sport, play, leisure pursuit, leisure activity, leisure,
relaxation, refreshment

recrimination *n*
accusation, countercharge, counter-attack, reprisal,
retaliation, retort, bickering, quarrel

recruit *v, n*
▶ *v* enlist, draft, conscript, enrol, sign up, levy,
engage, take on, mobilize, raise, muster, gather,
assemble, put together, obtain, acquire
formal procure
▶ *n* beginner, newcomer, novice, new entrant,
initiate, learner, trainee, apprentice, tiro, conscript,
draftee, convert
colloq. greenhorn, rookie

rectify *v*
correct, put right, right, set right, make good, remedy,
cure, repair, fix, mend, reform, improve, better,
amend, adjust, reform
formal emend, ameliorate, redress

rectitude *n*
integrity, uprightness, virtue, honesty, honour,
goodness, justice, morality, incorruptibility,
irreproachability, exactness, decency, correctness,
righteousness, scrupulousness
formal probity

recumbent *adj*
lying down, lying, flat, horizontal, resting, reclining,
leaning, lounging, prostrate, prone, sprawling
formal supine
◲ erect, upright

recuperate *v*
recover, get better, get well, get stronger, regain your
strength, improve, pick up, pull through, rally, revive,
mend, convalesce
colloq. pull through, bounce back, turn the corner, get
back on your feet, be on the mend
◲ worsen

recur *v*
repeat itself, happen again, persist, return, reappear

recurrent *adj*
recurring, chronic, persistent, repeated, repetitive,
continual, habitual, regular, periodic, cyclical,
frequent, intermittent

recycle *v*
reuse, reprocess, reclaim, recover, salvage, save

red *adj*
1 SCARLET, vermilion, cherry, ruby, crimson, rose,
maroon, russet, pink, reddish, bloodshot, inflamed
2 RUDDY, florid, glowing, rosy, flushed, blushing,
embarrassed, shamefaced
technical rufescent
formal rubicund
3 *red hair*
ginger, carroty, auburn, chestnut, Titian
4 COMMUNIST, socialist, leftist, Bolshevik,
revolutionary
▷ **in the red** overdrawn, insolvent, bankrupt, in
debt, in arrears, owing money, penniless,
impoverished; *colloq.* on the rocks, broke, bust, gone
to the wall, on your beam ends
◲ in the black
▷ **see red** become angry, lose your temper, explode,
blow your cool, blow your top, boil over, burst a blood
vessel, fly into a rage, fly off the handle, go mad, lose
your cool, lose your rag

red-blooded *adj*
virile, strong, vigorous, manly, robust, hearty, lively,
lusty

redden *v*
blush, flush, colour, go red, crimson, suffuse

reddish *adj*
red, bloodshot, rosy, ruddy, russet, ginger, sandy, pink
technical rufescent
formal rubicund, rufous

redeem *v*
1 BUY BACK, repurchase, cash (in), convert, trade in, exchange, give in exchange, change, trade, ransom, reclaim, regain, get back, repossess, recoup, recover, recuperate, retrieve, salvage
2 COMPENSATE FOR, make up for, offset, outweigh
3 *Christ redeems sinners*
atone for, absolve, acquit, remove guilt from, discharge, release, liberate, emancipate, free, set free, deliver, rescue, save, ransom
formal expiate

redemption *n*
1 REPURCHASE, repossession, reclamation, recovery, reparation, retrieval, exchange, reinstatement, trade-in, fulfilment, compensation
2 ATONEMENT, deliverance, expiation, emancipation, freedom, rescue, salvation, ransom, liberation, release

redolent *adj*
1 EVOCATIVE, reminiscent, suggestive, remindful
2 AROMATIC, fragrant, perfumed, scented, sweet-smelling
formal odorous

redoubtable *adj*
formidable, fearsome, strong, terrible, powerful, resolute, mighty, awful, dreadful, fearful

redound *v*
contribute, ensue, reflect, result, tend
formal conduce, effect

⚠ **redound** or **rebound** ? *See panel at* **rebound**.

redress *v, n*
▶ *v* 1 RIGHT, put right, rectify, remedy, avenge, requite, recompense, make compensation for
2 ADJUST, amend, correct, balance, regulate
▶ *n* compensation, recompense, indemnification, remedy, relief, assistance, help, aid, correction, requital, restitution, satisfaction, reparation, payment, justice, atonement

reduce *v*
1 LESSEN, make less, make smaller, decrease, contract, shrink, slim, shorten, abbreviate, curtail, trim, minimize, downsize, lower, moderate, weaken, dilute, diminish, impair, deplete, take the edge off
formal mitigate
2 DRIVE, force, degrade, bring down, lower, downgrade, demote, humble, humiliate, impoverish, subdue, overcome, overpower, conquer, master
formal vanquish
3 *reduce prices*
lower, decrease, cut, slash, knock down, discount, rebate, halve
4 SLIM, diet, go on a diet, lose weight
colloq. weight-watch
🔄 1 increase, raise, boost

reduction *n*
decrease, drop, fall, decline, lessening, moderation, weakening, contraction, abbreviation, compression, shrinkage, downsizing, narrowing, shortening, curtailment, restriction, limitation, cutback, cut, discount, discounting, rebate, concession, allowance,

devaluation, depreciation, deduction, subtraction, loss
formal diminution
🔄 increase, rise, enlargement

redundancy *n*
1 DISMISSAL, notice, laying-off, discharge, removal, expulsion, marching-orders
colloq. papers, sacking, firing, sack, push, boot, elbow
2 SUPERFLUITY, surplus, uselessness, wordiness, excess, repetition, tautology
technical pleonasm
formal prolixity, verbosity
🔄 appointment, hiring

redundant *adj*
1 UNEMPLOYED, out of work, jobless, laid off, dismissed
colloq. sacked, fired
2 SUPERFLUOUS, surplus, excess, extra, unneeded, unnecessary, unwanted, inessential
formal supernumerary
3 WORDY, verbose, padded, repetitious, tautological
technical pleonastic
formal periphrastic
🔄 2 necessary, essential, required 3 concise

reef *n*
sandbank, sandbar, ridge, cay, key

reek *v, n*
▶ *v* smell, stink, fume
formal exhale
colloq. hum, pong
▶ *n* smell, odour, stink, stench, vapour, fume(s)
formal exhalation, effluvium, malodour, mephitis, fetor
colloq. pong

reel *v*
stagger, totter, wobble, rock, sway, waver, falter, stumble, fling, lurch, pitch, swim, roll, revolve, gyrate, spin, wheel, twirl, whirl, swirl

refer *v*
1 MENTION, allude, touch on, speak of, bring up, recommend, cite, quote, hint at
2 *refer to a catalogue*
consult, look up, turn to, look at, resort to
3 SEND, direct, point, guide, pass on, hand on, transfer, commit, deliver
formal remit
4 APPLY, concern, be relevant, relate, belong
formal pertain

referee *n, v*
▶ *n* umpire, judge, adjudicator, arbitrator, mediator
colloq. ref
▶ *v* umpire, judge, adjudicate, mediate, intercede, arbitrate

reference *n*
1 MENTION, remark, allusion, hint, citation, quotation, illustration, source, authority, instance, note, footnote
2 TESTIMONIAL, recommendation, endorsement, credentials, character
3 RELATION, applicability, regard, respect, connection, bearing
formal pertinence

referendum *n*
poll, vote, voting, plebiscite, survey

refine *v*
1 PURIFY, process, treat, clarify, filter, sift, strain,

distil, clear, cleanse
2 IMPROVE, polish, hone, perfect, elaborate, civilize, elevate, exalt

refined *adj*
1 CIVILIZED, cultured, cultivated, polished, sophisticated, stylish, urbane, genteel, gentlemanly, ladylike, well-bred, well-mannered, polite, civil, elegant, gracious, courtly, fine, delicate, subtle, precise, exact, sensitive, discriminating
2 PURIFIED, processed, treated, distilled, filtered, clear
E3 1 coarse, vulgar, rude

refinement *n*
1 MODIFICATION, alteration, amendment, addition, improvement
formal amelioration
2 CULTIVATION, sophistication, culture, urbanity, gentility, breeding, style, elegance, grace, civility, good manners, polish, taste, discrimination, subtlety, finesse
E3 1 deterioration **2** coarseness, vulgarity

reflect *v*
1 MIRROR, echo, imitate, reproduce, image, send back, throw back, bounce off
2 SHOW, portray, depict, reveal, display, exhibit, demonstrate, indicate, express, communicate
formal manifest, bespeak
3 THINK, ponder, consider, mull (over), dwell, brood, deliberate, contemplate, meditate, muse
formal ruminate, cogitate, cerebrate
4 *his behaviour reflects badly on the school*
discredit, disgrace, tarnish, put in a bad light, give a bad name to

reflection *n*
1 IMAGE, likeness, echo, mirror image
2 INDICATION, impression, expression, display, demonstration, portrayal, observation, view
formal manifestation
3 THINKING, thought, study, consideration, deliberation, contemplation, meditation, musing, view, opinion, impression, belief, viewpoint, idea, feeling(s)
formal rumination, cogitation, cerebration
4 DISCREDIT, slur, disgrace, shame, criticism, disrepute, blame, reproach
formal aspersion

reflective *adj*
thoughtful, contemplative, pondering, deliberative, meditative, pensive, reasoning, absorbed, dreamy
formal cogitating, ruminative

reflex *adj*
automatic, spontaneous, without thinking, unwilled, uncontrollable, involuntary, natural
colloq. knee-jerk

reform *v, n*
▶ *v* change, amend, improve, better, rectify, correct, mend, repair, revise, refashion, rehabilitate, rebuild, reconstruct, remodel, revamp, renovate, restore, regenerate, reconstitute, reorganize, revolutionize, purge
formal ameliorate
colloq. shake up
▶ *n* change, amendment, improvement, betterment, rectification, correction, rehabilitation, renovation, reorganization, revision, rebuilding, reconstruction, remodelling, restoration, purge
colloq. shake-up

reformer *n*
do-gooder, revolutionary
colloq. whistle-blower

refractory *adj*
stubborn, obstinate, headstrong, unmanageable, uncontrollable, naughty, unruly, wilful, unco-operative, perverse, mulish, difficult, disobedient, resistant, defiant, cantankerous, contentious
formal intractable, contumacious, recalcitrant, disputatious, restive
E3 co-operative, malleable, obedient

refrain¹ *v*
refrain from smoking
stop, give up, do without, leave off, renounce, avoid
formal cease, desist, abstain, forbear, eschew
colloq. quit

refrain² *n*
sing the refrain twice
chorus, response, burden, strain, melody, song, tune

refresh *v*
1 COOL, freshen, energize, stimulate, enliven, invigorate, revive, brace, restore, renew, rejuvenate, reanimate, revitalize, reinvigorate
formal fortify, revivify
colloq. breathe new life into
2 *refresh your memory*
jog, stimulate, stir, prompt, prod, arouse, activate, remind
E3 1 tire, exhaust

refreshing *adj*
1 *a refreshing bath*
invigorating, energizing, stimulating, inspiring, exhilarating, reviving, cool, thirst-quenching, bracing
2 *a refreshing change from routine*
different, fresh, freshening, new, novel, original, unexpected
colloq. not another

refreshment *n*
sustenance, food, drink(s), snack, freshening, stimulation, revival, restoration, renewal, reanimation, invigoration, reinvigoration, revitalization

refreshments *n*
aliment, drinks, food, provisions, snacks, elevenses, sustenance, titbits
colloq. eats; *slang* nosh, grub

refrigerate *v*
chill, cool, keep cold, freeze
E3 heat, warm

refuge *n*
sanctuary, asylum, shelter, protection, security, retreat, place of safety, hideout, hide-away, resort, harbour, haven, bolthole, island

refugee *n*
exile, émigré, displaced person, stateless person, fugitive, runaway, escapee

refulgent *adj*
brilliant, shining, beaming, bright, radiant, gleaming, glistening, glittering
formal irradiant, lambent, lustrous, resplendent

refund *v, n*
▶ *v* repay, pay back, reimburse, rebate, return, give back, restore
▶ *n* repayment, reimbursement, rebate, return

refurbish *v*
renovate, redecorate, re-equip, refit, remodel, revamp, repair, mend, overhaul, restore, recondition
colloq. do up

refusal *n*
rejection, turning-down, no, rebuff, spurning, repudiation, denial, negation, withholding
F⋥ acceptance, agreement

refuse¹ *v*
refuse to go; refuse permission
reject, turn down, say no, spurn, repudiate, rebuff, repel, deny, withhold
formal decline
colloq. pass up, knock back, shake your head, draw the line at, dig your heels in
F⋥ accept, agree, allow, permit, grant

refuse² *n*
piles of refuse
rubbish, waste, trash, garbage, junk, litter, debris, dregs, dross, scum, offscum
technical scoria, draff

refutation *n*
disproof, negation, rebuttal, overthrow
technical elenchus
formal confutation

refute *v*
disprove, rebut, give the lie to, discredit, counter, negate, overthrow, silence, deny (strongly)
formal confute

regain *v*
recover, get back, win back, recoup, reclaim, repossess, retake, take back, recapture, retrieve, return to

regal *adj*
majestic, kingly, queenly, princely, imperial, royal, sovereign, stately, magnificent, noble, lordly

regale *v*
amuse, entertain, delight, divert, captivate, fascinate, feast, ply, gratify, serve, refresh

regard *v, n*
▶ *v* **1** CONSIDER, judge, rate, value, gauge, estimate, think, believe, suppose, imagine, contemplate, weigh up
formal deem, appraise
2 LOOK AT, look upon, see, view, observe, watch, gaze at, scrutinize, eye
formal behold
colloq. give the once-over
2 HEED, listen to, observe, follow, note, bear in mind, take notice of, pay attention to, take into account/consideration
▶ *n* **1** CARE, concern, consideration, attention, notice, heed, respect, deference, honour, admiration, affection, love, sympathy, approval
formal esteem, approbation
2 *in this regard*
matter, subject, aspect, point, detail, particular
3 *send her my regards*
best wishes, good wishes, greetings, respects, compliments, salutations
F⋥ **1** disregard, contempt
▷ **with/in regard to** as regards, concerning, with reference to, with respect to, in relation to, in connection with, re, about, as to, on the subject of, apropos

regardful *adj*
attentive, mindful, thoughtful, noticing, observant, aware, careful, considerate, watchful, respectful, dutiful, heedful
formal circumspect
F⋥ heedless, inattentive, regardless, unobservant

regarding *prep*
with regard to, in regard to, as regards, concerning, with reference to, with respect to, in relation to, in connection with, re, about, as to, on the subject of, apropos

regardless *adj, adv*
▶ *adj* disregarding, heedless, unmindful, neglectful, negligent, inattentive, unconcerned, indifferent
F⋥ heedful, mindful, attentive
▶ *adv* anyway, nevertheless, nonetheless, no matter what, despite everything, come what may, anyhow
colloq. at any price/cost

regenerate *v*
revive, reinvigorate, reawaken, rekindle, renew, restore, reconstitute, reconstruct, re-establish, renovate, refresh, uplift, change, invigorate, rejuvenate, reproduce
formal inspirit, revivify

regeneration *n*
renewal, renovation, restoration, re-establishment, reinvigoration, reconstruction, reconstitution, rejuvenation, reproduction
formal homomorphosis

regime *n*
government, rule, administration, management, leadership, command, control, direction, reign, establishment, system

regiment *n*
army, brigade, cohort, battery, band, company, platoon, squadron, group, crew, gang, body

regimented *adj*
strict, disciplined, controlled, regulated, standardized, ordered, methodical, systematic, organized, systematized
F⋥ free, lax, disorganized

region *n*
land, terrain, sector, neighbourhood, range, scope, expanse, sphere, world, field, ambit, orbit, division, section, part, place

Types of geographical region and community include: Antarctic, Arctic, area, bailiwick, banana republic, basin, belt, Black Country, borough, built-up area, burgh, capital city, catchment area, city, coast, colony, commune, continent, country, countryside, county, county town, desert, development area, diocese, district, dockland, domain, dominion, duchy, East End, emirate, empire, estate, The Fens, forest, free state, ghetto, ghost town, grassland, green belt, hamlet, health resort, heartland, heath, hemisphere, home-town, hundred, industrial park, inner city, interior, jungle, kibbutz, kingdom, lowlands, manor, market town, marshland, metropolis, The Midlands, mission, municipality, nation, new town, no-man's land, old country, orient, outback, outpost, outskirts, pampas, parish, plain, port, postal district, prairie, principality, protectorate, province, quarter, realm, red-light district, region, republic, reservation, resort, riding, riviera, rural district, satellite town, savannah, scrubland, seaside, settlement, shanty town, shire, spa, state, steppe, subcontinent, suburb, territory, Third World, time zone, town, township, tract, tropics, tundra, urban district, veld, village, wasteland, West Country, West End, wilderness, woodland, zone. *See also* **park**.

▷ **in the region of** approximately, roughly, around, about, some, something like, odd, circa, more or less, loosely, round about, or thereabouts, approaching, close to, nearly, just about, not far off, in the neighbourhood/ vicinity of, in round numbers, rounded up/down; *colloq.* give or take
F∃ exactly

regional *adj*
district, local, localized, provincial, sectional, zonal, parochial
F∃ national, international, worldwide

register *n, v*
▶ *n* roll, roster, list, listing, index, catalogue, directory, log, diary, journal, record, chronicle, annals, archives, file(s), ledger, schedule, diary, almanac
▶ *v* **1** RECORD, note, log, enter, put in writing, put down, set down, take down, inscribe, mark, list, catalogue, chronicle, enrol, enlist, sign on, check in
2 SHOW, reveal, betray, display, exhibit, indicate, demonstrate, express, say
formal manifest
3 *the gauge registers a measurement*
read, indicate, record, show, display

registrar *n*
official, recorder, secretary, clerk, administrator, cataloguer, annalist, archivist, chronicler, protocolist

regress *v*
deteriorate, recede, relapse, retreat, return, revert, wane, backslide, degenerate, lapse, ebb
formal retrocede, retrogress
F∃ progress

regret *v, n*
▶ *v* feel sorry, wish that you had not done, be disappointed, be distressed, rue, repent, lament, bemoan, weep, mourn, grieve, deplore
▶ *n* remorse, contrition, repentance, penitence, self-reproach, shame, sorrow, grief, disappointment, bitterness
formal compunction

regretful *adj*
remorseful, rueful, repentant, contrite, penitent, conscience-stricken, ashamed, sorry, apologetic, sad, sorrowful, disappointed
F∃ impenitent, unashamed

⚠ **regretful** or **regrettable** ?
Regretful means 'full of regret, sad, sorry'; *regrettable* means 'causing regret, to be regretted': *It is regrettable that you have behaved so foolishly, and I feel regretful that I must now ask you to leave.*

regrettable *adj*
unfortunate, unlucky, unhappy, sad, disappointing, upsetting, distressing, lamentable, deplorable, disgraceful, shameful, sorry, wrong, ill-advised
formal reprehensible
F∃ fortunate, happy

⚠ **regrettable** or **regretful** ? *See panel at* **regretful**.

regular *adj*
1 ROUTINE, habitual, typical, usual, customary, time-honoured, classic, conventional, established, orthodox, correct, official, approved, proper, standard, normal, average, ordinary, common,

commonplace, daily, everyday
2 PERIODIC, rhythmic, frequent, recurring, hourly, daily, weekly, monthly, yearly, steady, constant, fixed, set, unchanging, unvarying, uniform, consistent, even, level, flat, evenly spread, smooth, balanced, symmetrical, orderly, systematic, methodical, well-organized
colloq. regular as clockwork
F∃ 1 unusual, unconventional **2** irregular, intermittent

regulate *v*
1 CONTROL, direct, guide, govern, rule, administer, oversee, superintend, supervise, manage, handle, conduct, run, organize, order, arrange, settle, square, monitor
2 ADJUST, set, synchronize, control, tune, moderate, balance

regulation *n, adj*
▶ *n* **1** RULE, statute, law, act, ordinance, by-law, edict, decree, order, ruling, directive, command, supervision, commandment, precept, dictate, dictum, pronouncement, ordinance, requirement, procedure
2 CONTROL, direction, guidance, rule, administration, superintendence, supervision, management
▶ *adj* standard, official, statutory, obligatory, required, fixed, set, orthodox, accepted, customary, usual, normal
formal prescribed, mandatory

regurgitate *v*
1 VOMIT, bring up, spew
formal disgorge
colloq. puke, throw up
2 REPEAT, say/tell again, restate, recapitulate
formal reiterate

rehabilitate *v*
restore, renew, reinvigorate, normalize, reform, reinstate, reconstitute, re-establish, renovate, reintegrate, recondition, rebuild, convert, adjust, clear, mend, reconstruct, save, redeem

rehash *n, v*
▶ *n* reworking, rearrangement, rejig, rejigging, restatement, reshuffle, rewrite
▶ *v* rework, change, alter, rearrange, rejig, rejigger, restate, reshuffle, refashion, rewrite

rehearsal *n*
practice, drill, exercise, trial run, run-through, preparation, reading, recital
colloq. dry run, dummy run

rehearse *v*
1 PRACTISE, drill, train, go over, run through, prepare, try out
2 REPEAT, recite, recount, relate, narrate, go over, enumerate

reign *v, n*
▶ *v* **1** RULE, be king/queen, sit on the throne, be in power, be in charge, be in control, govern, be in government, command, be in command
2 *silence reigns*
prevail, predominate, occur, hold sway, be present, exist, influence
formal obtain
▶ *n* rule, sway, monarchy, empire, sovereignty, supremacy, government, power, command, dominion, control, influence
formal ascendancy

reimburse *v*
refund, repay, pay back, give back, return, restore, recompense, compensate, indemnify, remunerate

rein *n, v*
▶ *n* check, control, curb, restraint, hold, overcheck, restriction, brake, bridle, harness
▶ *v* check, control, curb, restrain, restrict, limit, hold back, stop, hold, halt, arrest, bridle

reinforce *v*
1 STRENGTHEN, toughen, harden, stiffen, steel, brace, support, buttress, shore, prop, stay, supplement, increase
formal fortify, augment
2 EMPHASIZE, stress, underline, consolidate
F3 1 weaken, undermine

reinforcement *n*
1 STRENGTHENING, supplement, support, addition, increase, enlargement, prop, shore, stay, brace, buttress, emphasis, hardening, amplification
formal fortification, augmentation
2 *send reinforcements*
auxiliaries, reserves, additional soldiers/police officers, supplementaries, back-up, support, help

reinstate *v*
restore, return, give back, replace, recall, reappoint, reinstall, re-establish

reinstatement *n*
restoration, return, giving-back, replacement, recall, re-establishment

reiterate *v*
repeat, recapitulate, resay, restate, retell, emphasize, stress
formal iterate, rehearse
colloq. recap

reject *v, n*
▶ *v* 1 *reject a proposal*
refuse, deny, decline, turn down, say no to, veto, disallow, condemn, despise, spurn, rebuff, jilt, exclude, repudiate, repel
formal renounce
colloq. have nothing to do with, not have anything to do with, take a raincheck on, wash your hands of, turn your back on, turn your nose up at, not touch with a barge pole
2 DISCARD, scrap, jettison, eliminate, cast off, throw away, set aside
formal forsake
colloq. brush off, give the cold shoulder to
F3 1 accept, agree 2 choose, select
▶ *n* failure, second, discard, outcast, cast-off

rejection *n*
refusal, turning-down, denial, declining, veto, dismissal, rebuff, exclusion, discarding, jettisoning, repudiation, elimination
formal renunciation
colloq. brush-off, cold shoulder, Dear John letter
F3 acceptance, choice, selection

rejoice *v*
celebrate, revel, delight, be delighted/pleased, be joyful/happy, take pleasure, glory, exult, triumph
old use make merry
colloq. jump for joy, whoop it up

rejoicing *n*
celebration, revelry, festivity, happiness, gladness, joy, delight, pleasure, euphoria, elation, jubilation, glory,

exultation, triumph
old use merrymaking

rejoin *v*
retort, answer, reply, respond, quip, repartee, riposte

rejoinder *n*
retort, answer, reply, response, quip, repartee, riposte

rejuvenate *v*
revitalize, reinvigorate, reanimate, revive, renew, freshen up, refresh, restore, rekindle, recharge, regenerate
formal revivify

relapse *v, n*
▶ *v* worsen, deteriorate, degenerate, weaken, sink, fail, lapse, revert, regress, fall away, backslide
formal retrogress
▶ *n* worsening, deterioration, setback, recurrence, weakening, lapse, reversion, regression, backsliding
formal retrogression

relate *v*
1 LINK, connect, join, couple, ally, associate
formal correlate
2 REFER, apply, concern, have a bearing on, be relevant
formal pertain, appertain
3 *relate an anecdote*
tell, recount, narrate, report, describe, recite, present, communicate, detail
formal delineate
4 IDENTIFY, sympathize, empathize, understand, feel for, get on (well) with
colloq. hit it off, speak the same language, be on the same wavelength

related *adj*
kindred, akin, affiliated, allied, associated, connected, linked, interrelated, interconnected, accompanying, joint, mutual, relevant
formal concomitant, correlated, cognate, consanguineous, agnate
F3 unrelated, unconnected

relation *n*
1 LINK, linking, connection, bond, relationship, comparison, similarity, affiliation, alliance, interrelation, interconnection, interdependence
formal correlation
2 REGARD, reference, relevance, bearing, application
formal pertinence
3 RELATIVE, family, kin, kinsman, kinswoman, kinsfolk, kindred

relations *n*
1 RELATIVES, family, kin, kinsman, kinswoman, kinsfolk, kindred
colloq. folks
2 RELATIONSHIP, terms, rapport, liaison, interaction, affairs, dealings, connections, communications, contact(s), associations
formal intercourse
3 *sexual relations*
intercourse, sex, intimacy, intimate relations, love-making, copulation, carnal knowledge
formal coition, coitus
colloq. sleeping with someone, going to bed with someone

relationship *n*
1 CONNECTION, bond, link, tie(s), tie-up, association, alliance, liaison, rapport, friendship,

affinity, closeness, similarity, parallel, ratio, proportion
formal correlation
colloq. chemistry
2 AFFAIR, love affair, romance, intimacy, liaison,
friendship
colloq. fling

relative *adj, n*
▶ *adj* **1** COMPARATIVE, proportional,
proportionate, comparable, corresponding, respective,
parallel, reciprocal
formal commensurate, correlative
2 APPROPRIATE, relevant, applicable, related,
connected, interrelated, dependent
formal apposite, germane, pertinent
▶ *n* relation, family, kin, kinsman, kinswoman,
kinsfolk, kindred

relatively *adv*
comparatively, in/by comparison, fairly, quite, rather,
somewhat

relax *v*
1 *relax on holiday*
calm (down), rest, unwind, wind down, loosen up,
tranquillize, sedate
colloq. take it/things easy, let yourself go, make
yourself at home, let your hair down, put your feet up,
hang loose, cool it, chill out
2 *relax the rules*
moderate, soften, ease (off), lessen, reduce, diminish,
weaken, lower, slacken, loosen
formal abate, remit
E∃ 2 tighten

relaxation *n*
1 REST, unwinding, loosening up, refreshment,
leisure, recreation, fun, amusement, entertainment,
enjoyment, pleasure
formal repose
2 SLACKENING, loosening, weakening, lessening,
reduction, softening, easing, moderation, détente,
easing
formal abatement
colloq. let-up
E∃ 2 tension, intensification

relaxed *adj*
1 *feel relaxed*
at ease, comfortable, uninhibited, carefree, happy-go-
lucky, cool, calm, composed, restful, collected,
unhurried, leisurely
2 *a relaxed situation*
INFORMAL, casual, restful
colloq. laid-back, easy-going
E∃ 1 tense, nervous, worried **2** formal, tense

relay *n, v*
▶ *n* **1** BROADCAST, transmission, programme,
communication, message, dispatch
2 *work in relays*
shift, turn, stint, time, spell, period
▶ *v* broadcast, transmit, communicate, pass on, hand
on, send, circulate, spread, carry, supply

release *v, n*
▶ *v* **1** SET FREE, free, liberate, deliver, emancipate
2 LOOSEN, loose, unloose, let go, untie, undo, unlock,
unfasten, unchain, unbind, unshackle, unleash
3 EXCUSE, exempt, discharge, let go, let off, acquit,
absolve
formal exonerate
4 ISSUE, publish, make available, make known, make
public, announce, disclose, reveal, circulate, distribute,

present, launch, divulge, unveil
E∃ 1 imprison **3** detain
▶ *n* **1** FREEDOM, liberty, liberation, deliverance,
emancipation
formal manumission
2 ACQUITTAL, absolution, exoneration, exemption,
discharge
colloq. let-off
3 ISSUE, publication, publishing, disclosure,
revelation, declaration, bulletin, announcement,
proclamation
E∃ 1 imprisonment, detention

relegate *v*
demote, downgrade, degrade, reduce, consign, entrust,
assign, refer, dispatch, delegate, transfer, banish,
expatriate, deport, eject, exile, expel
E∃ promote

relent *v*
1 GIVE IN, give way, come round, yield, allow, change
your mind, capitulate
2 *the storm relented*
ease, let up, die down, slacken, soften, weaken, unbend,
relax
formal abate

relentless *adj*
unrelenting, unremitting, incessant, persistent,
unflagging, unceasing, ruthless, remorseless,
implacable, merciless, pitiless, cold-hearted,
hard-hearted, unforgiving, cruel, harsh, fierce, grim,
hard, punishing, uncompromising, inflexible,
unyielding, inexorable
E∃ merciful, yielding

relevant *adj*
material, significant, related, to the point, applicable,
apposite, apt, appropriate, suitable, fitting, proper,
admissible
formal pertinent, germane, congruous, apropos
E∃ irrelevant, inapplicable, inappropriate, unsuitable

reliable *adj*
unfailing, certain, sure, dependable, responsible,
trusty, trustworthy, dutiful, honest, true, devoted,
conscientious, faithful, constant, staunch, solid, safe,
sound, well-grounded, well-founded, stable, tested,
predictable, regular
E∃ unreliable, doubtful, untrustworthy

reliance *n*
dependence, trust, faith, belief, conviction, credit,
confidence, assurance

relic *n*
memento, souvenir, keepsake, token, reminder,
remembrance, survival, remains, artefact, heirloom,
antique, remnant, scrap, fragment, vestige, trace

relief *n*
1 *relief from pain*
respite, alleviation, easing, lessening, reduction,
soothing, release, cure, remedy, deliverance, remission
formal abatement, mitigation, allaying, assuaging,
palliation
2 COMFORT, reassurance, happiness, relaxation,
calmness, consolation
3 REST, refreshment, diversion, relaxation, respite,
break, interruption
formal repose
colloq. breather, let-up
4 *famine relief*
aid, help, assistance, rescue, saving, support,

back-up, sustenance
formal succour
5 SUBSTITUTE, replacement, reserve, stand-by,
stand-in, supply, locum, understudy, proxy, surrogate

relieve *v*
1 *relieve the pain*
alleviate, soothe, lessen, soften, slacken, reduce, cure,
heal, comfort, console, reassure
formal mitigate, abate, allay, assuage, palliate
2 DELIVER, set free, liberate, release, unburden,
discharge
3 SUBSTITUTE, replace, stand in for, take the place
of, take over from
4 HELP, aid, assist, rescue, save, support, sustain
formal succour
5 DISCHARGE, exempt, excuse, dismiss, expel,
remove, free, release
6 *relieve the tedium*
break (up), interrupt, pause, stop, bring to an end,
punctuate
formal discontinue
E3 1 aggravate, intensify

religion *n*

Religions include: Christianity, Church of England
(C of E), Baptists, Catholicism, Methodism,
Protestantism, Presbyterianism, Anglicanism,
Congregationalism, Calvinism, Salvation Army,
evangelicalism, Jehovah's Witnesses, Mormonism,
Quakerism, Amish; Bahaism, Buddhism,
Confucianism, Hinduism, Islam, Jainism, Judaism,
Sikhism, Taoism, Shintoism, Zen, Zoroastrianism,
voodoo, druidism. *See also* **scripture; worship.**

religious *adj*
1 SACRED, holy, divine, spiritual, devotional,
scriptural, theological, doctrinal
2 *a religious person*
believing, having a living faith, devout, godly, pious,
God-fearing, church-going, practising, committed,
reverent, righteous
3 CONSCIENTIOUS, scrupulous, rigorous,
meticulous, strict
E3 1 secular **2** irreligious, ungodly

religious officer

Religious officers include: abbess, abbot, archbishop,
archdeacon, bishop, canon, cardinal, chancellor,
chaplain, clergy, clergyman, clergywoman, curate,
deacon, deaconess, dean, elder, father, friar, minister,
monk, Monsignor, mother superior, nun, padre,
parson, pastor, pope, prelate, priest, prior, proctor,
rector, vicar; ayatollah, Dalai Lama, guru, imam,
muezzin, mullah, rabbi.

relinquish *n*
let go, release, hand over, surrender, yield, cede, give
up, resign, renounce, repudiate, waive, forego,
abandon, desert, drop, discard
formal forsake, cease, discontinue, desist, abstain,
abdicate
colloq. quit
E3 keep, retain

relish *v, n*
▶ *v* like, enjoy, savour, appreciate, adore, love, revel in,
delight in
▶ *n* **1** SEASONING, flavouring, condiment, sauce,
pickle, chutney, garnish, spice, flavour, piquancy, tang
2 ENJOYMENT, pleasure, delight, appreciation,

satisfaction, gusto, zest, liveliness, vivacity, vigour,
charm

reluctance *n*
unwillingness, hesitancy, hesitation, dislike, distaste,
loathing, aversion, backwardness
formal disinclination, indisposition, recalcitrance,
repugnance
E3 eagerness, enthusiasm, willingness

reluctant *adj*
unwilling, indisposed, hesitant, slow, backward, loath,
averse, unenthusiastic, grudging
formal disinclined
E3 willing, ready, eager, enthusiastic

rely *v*
depend, lean, be sure, count, bank, reckon, trust, swear
by

remain *v*
stay, rest, stand, last, endure, survive, stay behind, be
left over, prevail, persist, continue, linger, wait
old use bide
formal dwell, abide, tarry
E3 go, leave, depart

remainder *n*
rest, balance, surplus, excess, residue, leftovers,
remnant, remains, vestiges
formal superfluity, residuum

remaining *adj*
left, left over, spare, unused, unspent, unfinished,
residual, last, outstanding, surviving, persisting,
lingering, lasting, abiding

remains *n*
1 REST, remainder, residue, dregs, leavings, leftovers,
scraps, crumbs, fragments, remnants, oddments,
traces, vestiges, relics
formal detritus, reliquiae
colloq. odds and ends
2 CORPSE, body, dead body, cadaver, carcase, ashes,
debris

remark *v, n*
▶ *v* comment, observe, note, notice, mention, say,
state, assert, pronounce, declare
▶ *n* comment, observation, opinion, reflection,
mention, reference, utterance, statement, assertion,
pronouncement, acknowledgement, declaration,
notice

remarkable *adj*
striking, impressive, noteworthy, surprising, amazing,
strange, odd, unusual, uncommon, rare,
extraordinary, phenomenal, exceptional, memorable,
momentous, outstanding, notable, considerable,
conspicuous, prominent, important, significant, pre-
eminent, signal, surpassing, distinguished
formal singular
E3 average, ordinary, commonplace, usual

remedy *n, v*
▶ *n* cure, antidote, countermeasure, corrective,
restorative, medicine, medication, treatment, therapy,
relief, solution, answer, panacea
formal medicament, physic, nostrum
▶ *v* correct, put right, redress, control, counteract,
cure, heal, restore, treat, help, relieve, soothe, ease,
mend, repair, sort (out), fix, solve
formal rectify, mitigate

remember *v*
1 RECALL, recollect, summon up, think back,

think of, look back, hark back, cast your mind back, call to mind, reminisce, recognize, place
2 MEMORIZE, learn, learn by heart, commit to memory, make a mental note of, retain
3 COMMEMORATE, honour, mark, keep, recognize, celebrate, pay tribute to
4 *remember me to your parents*
send good/best wishes, send greetings, send your regards/respects
⊟ 1 forget

remembrance *n*
1 MEMORY, recollection, mind, reminder, recall, reminiscence, thought, testimonial, retrospect, nostalgia
2 COMMEMORATION, memorial, monument, souvenir, memento, token, keepsake, relic, recognition

remind *v*
prompt, nudge, hint, jog your memory, refresh your memory, bring to mind, call to mind, make you think of, call up, evoke

reminder *n*
prompt, nudge, hint, suggestion, note, memorandum, aide-mémoire, souvenir, memento
colloq. memo

reminisce *v*
remember, recall, recollect, think back, look back, hark back, review, retrospect

reminiscence *n*
memory, remembrance, memoir, anecdote, recollection, recall, retrospection, review, reflection

reminiscent *adj*
suggestive, evocative, nostalgic
formal redolent

remiss *adj*
careless, negligent, neglectful, forgetful, unmindful, heedless, lackadaisical, inattentive, indifferent, lax, slack, slipshod, sloppy, slow, thoughtless, casual, wayward
formal culpable, tardy, dilatory
⊟ careful, scrupulous

remission *n*
1 LESSENING, moderation, slackening, relaxation, release, weakening, decrease, reduction, respite, reprieve, ebb, lull
formal abatement, alleviation, diminution
colloq. let-up
2 CANCELLATION, repeal, annul, suspension
formal rescinding, abrogation, revocation
3 PARDON, forgiveness, acquittal, excuse, absolution, exemption, discharge, indulgence, amnesty
formal exoneration

⚠ **remission** or **remittance** ?
Remission means 'a lessening in force or effect': as in *Remissions in that form of cancer are not unknown*, 'the shortening of a prison sentence', 'the cancelling of a debt or punishment', and, in Christian theology, 'the forgiveness (of sins)'. *Remittance* is a formal word for the sending of money in payment for something, or for the money itself: *We are grateful for your remittance of the correct sum of money.*

remit *v, n*
▶ *v* **1** SEND, transmit, dispatch, post, mail, forward, pay, settle
2 REFER, transfer, direct, pass on

3 CANCEL, set aside, hold over, suspend, repeal
formal rescind, abrogate, revoke
▶ *n* brief, orders, instructions, guidelines, terms of reference, scope, authorization, responsibility

remittance *n*
sending, dispatch, payment, fee, allowance, consideration

⚠ **remittance** or **remission** ? *See panel at* **remission**.

remnant *n*
scrap, piece, bit, fragment, end, offcut, leftover, remainder, oddment, balance, residue, remains, shred, trace, vestige

remonstrance *n*
grievance, complaint, objection, opposition, protest, protestation, reprimand, reproof, exception, petition
formal expostulation

remonstrate *v*
protest, argue, challenge, oppose, take exception to, take issue with, complain, object, dispute
formal dissent, expostulate
colloq. gripe

remorse *n*
regret, ruefulness, repentance, penitence, contrition, self-reproach, shame, guilt, bad conscience, sorrow, grief
formal compunction

remorseful *adj*
guilty, regretful, repentant, ashamed, penitent, conscience-stricken, guilt-ridden, sorrowful, sorry, sad, apologetic, rueful, contrite
formal chastened, compunctious
⊟ impenitent, remorseless

remorseless *adj*
relentless, unrelenting, unremitting, unstoppable, undeviating, inexorable, implacable, pitiless, unforgiving, merciless, hard, hard-hearted, harsh, ruthless, savage, unmerciful, callous, cruel, stern, inhumane
⊟ sorry, remorseful

remote *adj*
1 DISTANT, far, faraway, far-off, outlying, out-of-the-way, inaccessible, God-forsaken, isolated, secluded, lonely
colloq. off the beaten track
2 DETACHED, aloof, distant, standoffish, unapproachable, uncommunicative, unconcerned, uninvolved, reserved, withdrawn
3 *a remote possibility*
slight, small, slim, poor, meagre, slender, faint, inconsiderable, negligible, doubtful, dubious, unlikely, improbable, insignificant, outside
⊟ 1 close, nearby, accessible **2** friendly, approachable **3** strong

removal *n*
1 MOVE, transferral, departure, relocation, uprooting, shift, shifting, transporting, conveyance
2 WITHDRAWAL, taking away, detachment, extraction, deletion, obliteration, abolition, purging
3 DISMISSAL, discharge, departure, riddance, ejection, ousting, eviction, expulsion, relegation, disposal
formal dislodgement
colloq. firing, sacking, sack, push, boot, elbow

remove   v
1 MOVE, transfer, relocate, take away, shift, dislodge, transport, carry, convey
2 TAKE AWAY, withdraw, take off, detach, tear off, pull off, amputate, destroy, cut off, lop off, take out, cut out, extract, excise, pull out, get out, strip, shed, doff
3 ELIMINATE, get rid of, erase, rub out, delete, strike out, cross out, obliterate, abolish, purge, blue-pencil
formal expurge, efface
4 DISMISS, discharge, eject, throw out, get rid of, oust, evict, expel, dislodge, unseat, depose, cast out, cashier, relegate
colloq. fire, sack, boot out

remunerate   v
pay, reimburse, recompense, compensate, reward, indemnify, redress, repay

remuneration   n
pay, wages, salary, emolument, stipend, fee, honorarium, retainer, earnings, income, profit, reward, recompense, payment, remittance, repayment, reimbursement, compensation, indemnity

remunerative   adj
profitable, lucrative, moneymaking, paying, rewarding, rich, (financially) worthwhile, gainful, fruitful

renaissance   n
revival, renewal, rebirth, reawakening, awakening, resurrection, rejuvenation, regeneration, re-emergence, restoration, new birth, new dawn, reappearance, resurgence
formal recrudescence, renascence

renascent   adj
revived, resurgent, renewed, re-emergent, reborn, resurrected, reawakened, reanimated
formal redivivus
colloq. born again

rend   v
tear, split, break, burst, divide, separate, rupture, sever, rip, fracture, pierce, shatter, smash, splinter, stab, lacerate
formal cleave

render   v
1 *they rendered it harmless*
make, cause to be, leave, change, turn
2 GIVE, provide, supply, tender, present, contribute, furnish, submit, hand over, deliver
formal proffer
3 TRANSLATE, transcribe, interpret, explain, clarify, represent, perform, play, sing
4 SHOW, describe, represent, display, exhibit, depict
formal manifest

rendezvous   n, v
▶ *n* 1 MEETING, appointment, engagement, assignation, date
old use tryst
2 MEETING-PLACE, venue, haunt, resort
old use trysting-place
▶ *v* meet, come together, gather, collect, assemble, rally, muster, converge
formal convene

rendition   n
performance, presentation, version, rendering, portrayal, reading, transcription, translation, interpretation, arrangement, construction, delivery, explanation, depiction
formal execution

renegade   n, adj
▶ *n* deserter, defector, traitor, turncoat, dissident, mutineer, outlaw, rebel, betrayer, apostate, backslider, runaway
formal tergiversator
▰ adherent, disciple, follower
▶ *adj* disloyal, rebel, rebellious, recreant, traitorous, unfaithful, apostate, backsliding, dissident, mutinous, outlaw, runaway
formal perfidious
▰ loyal, faithful

renege   v
default, repudiate, go back on your promise, backslide, apostatize, welsh, cross the floor

renew   v
1 RENOVATE, modernize, refurbish, refit, recondition, mend, repair, overhaul, remodel, reform, transform, recreate, reconstitute, re-establish, regenerate, revive, resuscitate, refresh, rejuvenate, reinvigorate, revitalize, restore, replace, replenish, restock
2 RESUME, repeat, restate, reaffirm, extend, prolong, continue, recommence, restart
formal reiterate

renewal   n
1 RENOVATION, reconditioning, re-creation, repair, refurbishment, reconstitution, reconstruction, reinvigoration, rejuvenation, revitalization, replenishment, resurrection, resuscitation
formal revivification
colloq. kiss of life
2 RESUMPTION, repetition, restatement, reaffirmation, continuance, recommencement
formal reiteration

renounce   v
abandon, give up, resign, relinquish, surrender, waive, sign away, discard, reject, spurn, shun, disown, forego, disinherit, repudiate, deny
formal forsake, disclaim, desist, abstain, eschew, abnegate, recant, abjure, abdicate
colloq. wash your hands of

renovate   v
restore, renew, recondition, repair, overhaul, modernize, refurbish, refit, redecorate, remodel, reform, rehabilitate, revamp, improve
colloq. do up, give a facelift

renovation   n
refurbishment, improvement, modernization, repair, restoration, renewal, reconditioning, refit
colloq. facelift

renown   n
fame, celebrity, stardom, acclaim, glory, eminence, pre-eminence, illustriousness, distinction, prestige, prominence, note, mark, reputation, repute, honour
formal esteem
▰ obscurity, anonymity

renowned   adj
famous, well-known, celebrated, acclaimed, famed, noted, eminent, pre-eminent, distinguished, prestigious, prominent, illustrious, notable, of repute
▰ unknown, obscure

rent¹   n, v
▶ *n*   *pay the rent*
rental, lease, hire, payment, fee
▶ *v* rent out, let (out), sublet, lease, hire (out), charter

rent[2] *n*
a world rent by conflict
tear, split, break, rip, slit, gash, chink, breach, perforation, rift, rupture, schism, slash, flaw, opening, hole, division, crack, cleavage, dissension, disunion

renunciation *n*
abandonment, giving up, relinquishment, surrender, waiving, discarding, rejection, spurning, shunning, disowning, disinheriting, repudiation, denial
formal forsaking, disclaiming, desistance, abstinence, abnegation, abdication

repair[1] *v, n*
▶ *v repair a faulty machine*
mend, fix, patch up, sew, darn, overhaul, refit, service, maintain, put right, rectify, adjust, redress, restore, make good, heal, renovate, renew
▶ *n* 1 MEND, patch, darn, overhaul, service, refit, maintenance, overhaul, restoration, adjustment, improvement
2 *in good/bad repair*
condition, shape, state, form, (working) order, fettle, kilter
colloq. nick

repair[2] *v*
repair to a place
go, move, turn, withdraw, retire, resort, remove, wend your way

reparable *adj*
recoverable, rectifiable, remediable, restorable, retrievable, salvageable, savable, corrigible, curable
☒ irreparable

reparation *n*
amends, redress, requital, restitution, satisfaction, renewal, compensation, recompense, damages, indemnity, atonement
technical solatium
formal propitiation

repartee *n*
banter, badinage, jesting, wit, riposte, retort

repast *n*
meal, snack, food, nourishment, spread, feed
formal refection, collation, victuals

repay *v*
1 REFUND, reimburse, pay back, compensate, recompense, reward, remunerate, pay, settle, settle up with, square
2 GET EVEN WITH, get back at, retaliate, reciprocate, revenge, avenge
colloq. get your own back on, settle the score, give as good as you get, not take it lying down

repayment *n*
1 REFUND, reimbursement, compensation, recompense, reward, remuneration, payment, reparation, redress, restitution, amends, requital, rebate
2 VENGEANCE, revenge, retribution, reciprocation, retaliation
colloq. tit for tat

repeal *v, n*
▶ *v* quash, annul, void, invalidate, cancel, set aside, recall, withdraw, reverse, abolish
formal revoke, rescind, abrogate, nullify, abjure, retract, countermand
☒ enact
▶ *n* cancellation, invalidation, quashing, reversal,

withdrawal, abolition, annulment
formal abrogation, nullification, rescinding, rescindment, rescission, revocation
☒ enactment, establishment

repeat *v, n*
▶ *v* restate, say again, go over, recapitulate, echo, parrot, quote, recite, relate, retell, reproduce, duplicate, renew, rebroadcast, reshow, replay, rerun, redo
formal reiterate, iterate, rehearse
colloq. recap
▶ *n* repetition, restatement, recapitulation, echo, reproduction, copy, duplicate, duplication, rebroadcast, reshowing, replay, rerun, ditto

repeated *adj*
frequent, constant, continual, regular, recurrent, periodic, rhythmical, persistent, recurring

repeatedly *adv*
time after time, time and (time) again, again and again, over and over, frequently, often

repel *v*
1 DRIVE BACK, repulse, check, hold off, ward off, parry, resist, keep at bay, oppose, fight, force back, beat back, push back, refuse, decline, reject, spurn, rebuff
2 DISGUST, revolt, nauseate, sicken, make you sick, offend
formal be repugnant to
colloq. turn off, turn your stomach
☒ 1 attract 2 delight

repellent *adj*
repulsive, revolting, disgusting, nauseating, sickening, offensive, shocking, distasteful, objectionable, off-putting, obnoxious, foul, vile, nasty, loathsome, abominable, abhorrent, contemptible, despicable, hateful, horrid, unpleasant, disagreeable
formal repugnant
☒ attractive, pleasant, delightful

repent *v*
regret, rue, feel remorse, sorrow, be sorry, be ashamed, be contrite, confess, lament, deplore, turn, be converted
formal recant
colloq. go down on your knees, beat your breasts, see the error of your ways, see the light, do a U-turn, wipe the slate clean

repentance *n*
penitence, confession, penance, contrition, remorse, regret, sorrow, grief, guilt, shame, conversion
formal compunction, recantation
colloq. U-turn

repentant *adj*
penitent, contrite, sorry, sorrowful, apologetic, remorseful, regretful, guilty, rueful, chastened, ashamed, conscience-stricken
☒ unrepentant

repercussion *n*
result, consequence, effect, reverberation, echo, rebound, recoil
colloq. backlash, ripple, shock wave

repertoire *n*
collection, list, range, repertory, reserve, reservoir, stock, store, supply
formal repository

repetition *n*
restatement, recapitulation, quoting, copying, echo,

echoing, return, reappearance, recurrence, duplication, redundancy, superfluity, tautology
technical echolalia
formal reiteration, iterance, iteration, rehearsal, reprise

repetitious *adj*
tedious, monotonous, boring, dull, unchanging, unvaried, redundant, tautological, long-winded, verbose, wordy, windy
technical pleonastic(al)
formal prolix

repetitive *adj*
recurrent, monotonous, tedious, boring, dull, mechanical, automatic, unchanging, unvaried
colloq. samey, soul-destroying

rephrase *v*
paraphrase, reword, put in other/different words, ask/say differently, rewrite, recast

repine *v*
grumble, complain, murmur, fret, lament, grieve, languish, moan, brood, sulk, mope
colloq. beef, grouse

replace *v*
1 *replace the lid*
put back, return, restore, make good, reinstate, re-establish
2 SUPERSEDE, take the place of, succeed, come after, follow, supplant, relieve, oust, deputize, substitute, stand in for, act for, fill in for

replacement *n*
substitute, stand-in, reserve, understudy, fill-in, supply, proxy, surrogate, successor

replenish *v*
refill, restock, reload, recharge, replace, restore, renew, supply, provide, furnish, stock, fill, fill up, top up, make up

replete *adj*
full, full up, filled, charged, abounding, brimful, brimming, sated, teeming, well-provided, well-stocked, glutted, gorged, jammed, stuffed, crammed
formal satiated
colloq. chock-a-block, chock-full, jam-packed

repletion *n*
fullness, overfullness, glut, completeness, superabundance, superfluity
formal plethora, satiation, satiety

replica *n*
model, imitation, reproduction, facsimile, copy, duplicate, clone

replicate *v*
repeat, duplicate, copy, mimic, follow, reduplicate, reproduce, recreate, clone, ape

reply *v, n*
▶ *v* answer, respond, retort, rejoin, react, acknowledge, return, come back, write back, echo, reciprocate, counter, retaliate, riposte
▶ *n* answer, response, retort, rejoinder, riposte, repartee, reaction, comeback, acknowledgement, return, echo, retaliation
colloq. comeback

report *n, v*
▶ *n* 1 ACCOUNT, article, piece, item, write-up, record, relation, narrative, description, story, tale, statement, communiqué, bulletin, register, chronicle,

minutes, write-up, declaration, announcement, communication, information, news, word, message, note, brief, file, dossier
formal delineation
2 GOSSIP, hearsay, rumour, talk
3 REPUTATION, honour, character, standing, stature, opinion, credit, repute, fame, renown, celebrity, distinction, name
formal esteem
4 EXPLOSION, shot, bang, crack, boom, crash, reverberation, noise
▶ *v* 1 STATE, announce, declare, proclaim, air, broadcast, relay, publish, circulate, pass on, communicate, notify, tell, recount, relate, narrate, describe, detail, set forth, disclose, divulge, cover, document, chronicle, record, note
formal delineate
2 COMPLAIN, inform on
colloq. tell on, shop, squeal, rat, split, blow the whistle on; *slang* grass

reporter *n*
journalist, correspondent, columnist, newspaperman, newspaperwoman, newscaster, commentator, announcer
colloq. hack

repose[1] *n, v*
▶ *n moments of repose*
rest, calm, peace, restfulness, ease, relaxation, respite, stillness, tranquillity, serenity, calmness, composure, inactivity, quietness, quiet, poise, equanimity, dignity, self-possession, sleep
formal aplomb, quietude, slumber
E3 activity, strain, stress
▶ *v* lie, lay, lean, rest, recline, relax, sleep
formal slumber
colloq. laze

repose[2] *v*
repose confidence in someone
place, put, set, store, lodge, deposit, confide, entrust, invest

repository *n*
store, storehouse, depository, depot, warehouse, safe, bank, treasury, vault, archive, container, receptacle, magazine

reprehensible *adj*
disgraceful, discreditable, objectionable, shameful, unworthy, blamable, blameworthy, bad, remiss, censurable, condemnable, delinquent, erring, errant, ignoble
formal culpable, opprobrious
E3 creditable, good, praiseworthy

represent *v*
1 STAND FOR, symbolize, designate, denote, mean, be, amount to, constitute, correspond to, be equivalent to
2 ACT FOR, stand for, speak for, act/speak on behalf of, act as representative of, act as spokesperson for, act/speak in the name of
3 EXEMPLIFY, typify, stand for, epitomize, embody, personify, show
4 DEPICT, portray, describe, picture, display, exhibit, draw, sketch, illustrate, evoke, characterize
5 ACT AS, enact, perform, appear as

representation *n*
1 LIKENESS, image, icon, picture, portrait, illustration, sketch, model, statue, bust, depiction, portrayal, description, account, explanation

formal delineation
2 REPRESENTATIVE, delegate, delegation, deputy, deputation, proxy, stand-in, spokesperson, spokesman, spokeswoman, envoy, ambassador, mouthpiece, MP, member of parliament, councillor
3 PERFORMANCE, production, presentation, play, show, spectacle
4 *make representations*
REQUEST, report, account, statement, allegation, protest, complaint

representative *n, adj*
▶ *n* delegate, delegation, deputy, deputation, proxy, stand-in, spokesperson, spokesman, spokeswoman, envoy, ambassador, mouthpiece, MP, member of parliament, councillor, commissioner, agent, salesman, saleswoman, traveller
colloq. rep
▶ *adj* **1** TYPICAL, illustrative, exemplary, characteristic, usual, normal, symbolic, indicative
formal archetypal
2 DELEGATED, chosen, elected, elective, nominated, appoint, commissioned, authorized, decentralized, devolved
▤ unrepresentative, atypical

repress *v*
1 INHIBIT, check, control, curb, restrain, suppress, bottle up, hold back, stifle, smother, muffle, silence
2 *repress a revolt*
quell, put down, crush, quash, subdue, overpower, overcome, master, dominate, domineer, oppress
formal subjugate, vanquish

repressed *adj*
frustrated, inhibited, withdrawn, introverted, self-restrained
colloq. uptight
▤ uninhibited, relaxed

repression *n*
1 OPPRESSION, suppression, quashing, quelling, crushing, suffocation, gagging, censorship, authoritarianism, dictatorship, despotism, tyranny, domination, control, constraint, coercion
formal subjugation
2 *repression of your feelings*
suppression, inhibition, restraint, control, holding-back, stifling, smothering, muffling

repressive *adj*
oppressive, authoritarian, despotic, tyrannical, dictatorial, dominating, autocratic, totalitarian, absolute, harsh, cruel, severe, strict, tough, coercive

reprieve *v, n*
▶ *v* pardon, forgive, acquit, show mercy/pity, spare, rescue, redeem, relieve, respite
colloq. let off, let off the hook, forgive and forget
▶ *n* pardon, amnesty, suspension, postponement, deferment, remission, respite, relief
formal abeyance, abatement
colloq. let-up

reprimand *v, n*
▶ *v* rebuke, reprove, reproach, scold, chide, lecture, criticize, censure, blame
formal admonish, berate, castigate
colloq. tell off, tick off, slate, give someone a ticking-off, give someone a dressing-down, haul over the coals, read the riot act, rap over the knuckles, give someone a rap over the knuckles, give someone a flea in their ear
▶ *n* rebuke, reproof, reproach, lecture, censure, blame

formal upbraiding, admonition, castigation
colloq. telling-off, ticking-off, talking-to, dressing-down, a flea in someone's ear, rocket, wigging, carpeting

reprisal *n*
retaliation, counter-attack, retribution, requital, revenge, vengeance, recrimination, redress
old use ultion
colloq. tit for tat, a taste of someone's own medicine

reproach *v, n*
▶ *v* rebuke, reprove, reprimand, upbraid, scold, chide, reprehend, blame, censure, condemn, criticize, find fault with, defame
formal disparage, admonish
colloq. give someone a dressing-down, give someone a ticking-off, haul over the coals, rap over the knuckles
▶ *n* **1** REBUKE, reproof, reprimand, scolding, blame, censure, condemnation, criticism, disapproval, scorn, contempt
formal admonition
2 DISGRACE, shame, disrepute, disrespect, discredit, stigma, dishonour, degradation, blemish, blot, smear, stain, slur
formal ignominy, opprobrium, obloquy

reproachful *adj*
reproving, upbraiding, scolding, censorious, critical, fault-finding, disapproving, disappointed, scornful
formal castigating, disparaging, opprobrious
▤ complimentary

reprobate *adj, n*
▶ *adj* immoral, corrupt, depraved, sinful, unprincipled, vile, wicked, bad, shameless, incorrigible, dissolute, degenerate, base, abandoned, hardened, damned
formal profligate, reprobative, reprobatory
▤ upright, virtuous
▶ *n* degenerate, miscreant, rake, *roué*, wrongdoer, criminal, evildoer, sinner, rogue, rascal, scoundrel, scamp, scallywag, villain, vagabond, wretch, mischief-maker, ne'er-do-well, knave, dastard, troublemaker
formal profligate

reproduce *v*
1 COPY, transcribe, print, duplicate, photocopy, Xerox®, Photostat®, mirror, echo, repeat, imitate, emulate, match, follow, cline, ape, mimic, simulate, recreate, remake, redo, reconstruct
formal replicate
2 BREED, spawn, bear young, give birth, generate, propagate, multiply, proliferate
formal procreate

reproduction *n*
1 COPY, print, picture, duplicate, photocopy, Xerox®, Photostat®, facsimile, replica, clone, imitation
2 BREEDING, generation, propagation, multiplication
formal procreation
▤ **1** original
Related adjective: genital

reproductive *adj*
generative, sexual, sex, genital, propagative
formal procreative, progenitive

reproof *n*
rebuke, reproach, reprimand, scolding, censure, condemnation, criticism
formal upbraiding, admonition, castigation,

disapprobation, berating
colloq. dressing-down, telling-off, ticking-off, rocket, wigging, carpeting
☲ praise

reprove *v*
rebuke, reproach, reprimand, scold, chide, reprehend, censure, condemn, criticize
formal upbraid, admonish, berate, castigate
colloq. tell off, tick off, slate, give someone a dressing-down, give someone a ticking-off, haul over the coals, rap over the knuckles
☲ praise

reptile *n*

> *Reptiles include*: adder, puff adder, grass snake, tree snake, asp, viper, rattlesnake, sidewinder, anaconda, boa constrictor, cobra, king cobra, mamba, python; lizard, frilled lizard, chameleon, gecko, iguana, skink, slow-worm; turtle, green turtle, hawksbill turtle, terrapin, tortoise, giant tortoise; alligator, crocodile. *See also* **dinosaurs**.

repudiate *v*
reject, denounce, deny, renounce, disown, discard, retract, reverse, revoke, cast off, desert, abandon, divorce
formal abjure, disaffirm, disavow, disclaim, disprofess, forsake, rescind
colloq. not touch with a barge pole, not have anything to do with, have nothing to do with, turn your back on
☲ admit, own

repudiation *n*
renunciation, renouncement, rejection, denial, disclaimer, disowning
formal abjuration, disaffirmance, disaffirmation, disavowal, recantation, retraction
☲ acceptance

repugnance *n*
reluctance, distaste, dislike, aversion, hatred, loathing, horror, repulsion, revulsion, nausea, disgust
formal abhorrence, odium, antipathy
☲ liking, pleasure, delight

repugnant *adj*
repellent, objectionable, obnoxious, offensive, unacceptable, antagonistic, antipathetic, hostile, averse, opposed, distasteful, inconsistent, incompatible, contradictory, adverse, disgusting, foul, vile, hateful, horrid, abominable, revolting, sickening, nauseating, loathsome, odious
formal abhorrent, inimical
☲ acceptable, consistent, pleasant

repulse *v, n*
▶ *v* repel, drive back, defeat, beat off, check, rebuff, reject, refuse, disregard, disdain, snub, spurn
▶ *n* check, defeat, disappointment, failure, rebuff, refusal, rejection, repudiation, reverse, snub, spurning
☲ acceptance, success

repulsion *n*
revulsion, disgust, distaste, hatred, aversion, loathing
formal repugnance, abhorrence, detestation, disrelish, repellence, repellency
☲ liking

repulsive *adj*
repellent, revolting, disgusting, nauseating, sickening, offensive, shocking, distasteful, objectionable, off-putting, obnoxious, foul, vile, nasty, loathsome, abominable, abhorrent, contemptible, despicable,

hateful, horrid, unpleasant, disagreeable, ugly, hideous, unattractive, forbidding
formal repugnant, reprehensible, heinous
☲ attractive, pleasant, delightful

reputable *adj*
respectable, respected, reliable, dependable, trustworthy, upright, honourable, honest, creditable, admirable, of high/good repute, well-thought-of, worthy, good, virtuous, excellent, irreproachable
formal esteemed, estimable
☲ disreputable, infamous

reputation *n*
1 NAME, opinion, credit, repute, character, standing, stature, status, rank, position, infamy, notoriety
formal estimation
2 FAME, renown, celebrity, distinction, prestige, image, character, good name, good standing, honour, respect, respectability
formal esteem

repute *n*
reputation, name, standing, stature, renown, fame, good name, celebrity, distinction
formal esteem, estimation
☲ infamy

reputed *adj*
alleged, supposed, said, rumoured, believed, thought, considered, regarded, reckoned, estimated, held, judged, seeming, assumed, presumed, apparent
formal ostensible
☲ actual, true

reputedly *adv*
allegedly, apparently, seemingly, supposedly, reputatively
formal ostensibly
☲ actually

request *v, n*
▶ *v* ask for, demand, require, seek, desire, beg, petition, apply for, call for, appeal
formal solicit, entreat, requisition, supplicate, beseech
colloq. put in for
▶ *n* appeal, call, demand, desire, application, suit, petition, petitioning, plea, pleading, prayer
formal requisition, solicitation, entreaty, supplication, imploration, behest

require *v*
1 NEED, want, wish, desire, crave, lack, miss, be short of, be deficient in
2 *you are required to attend*
oblige, force, compel, make, ask, request, call on, instruct, direct, command, order, demand, entail, insist on, take, involve
formal constrain, necessitate, enjoin

required *adj*
compulsory, essential, obligatory, recommended, demanded, necessary, stipulated, set, needed, unavoidable, vital
formal mandatory, prescribed, requisite
☲ optional, inessential

requirement *n*
need, necessity, essential, sine qua non, demand, lack, want, stipulation, condition, term, specification, proviso, qualification, provision
formal requisite, prerequisite, precondition
colloq. must

requisite *adj, n*
▶ *adj* required, needed, necessary, essential, obligatory, compulsory, set, vital
formal prescribed, prerequisite, mandatory
▶ *n* requirement, essential, due, necessity, need, condition, stipulation, specification, qualification, sine qua non
formal desideratum, prerequisite, precondition, desiderative
colloq. must
F3 inessential

requisition *v, n*
▶ *v* commandeer, take, take over, take possession of, use, confiscate, seize, occupy, request, put in for, demand, summons
formal appropriate
▶ *n* commandeering, confiscation, seizure, takeover, occupation, order, use, application, summons, request, call, demand
formal appropriation

requital *n*
amends, redress, restitution, satisfaction, recompense, compensation, indemnification, indemnity, repayment, payment, pay-off, reparation
formal quittance

requite *v*
repay, reciprocate, respond, retaliate, return, pay, recompense, reimburse, remunerate, reward, satisfy, redress, compensate, avenge

rescind *v*
cancel, set aside, overturn, quash, reverse, recall, repeal, annul, invalidate, void, negate
formal abrogate, countermand, nullify, retract, revoke
F3 enforce

rescission *n*
cancellation, negation, reversal, invalidation, annulment, recall, repeal
formal abrogation, nullification, rescindment, retraction, revocation, voidance
F3 enforcement

rescue *v, n*
▶ *v* save, recover, salvage, deliver, free, set free, liberate, emancipate, extricate, release, relieve, redeem, ransom
F3 capture, imprison
▶ *n* saving, recovery, salvage, deliverance, liberation, freeing, release, emancipation, relief, redemption, salvation
F3 capture

research *n, v*
▶ *n* investigation, inquiry, fact-finding, groundwork, examination, analysis, assessment, scrutiny, inspection, testing, test(s), study, review, search, probe, exploration, experiment, experimentation
▶ *v* investigate, examine, look into, analyse, scrutinize, study, inspect, search, probe, test, assess, review, explore, experiment

researcher *n*
investigator, student, analyst, inspector, inquirer, field worker, boffin

resemblance *n*
likeness, similarity, sameness, conformity, nearness, closeness, affinity, uniformity, parallel, parallelism, comparison, comparability, agreement, analogy, correspondence, image, facsimile

formal parity, similitude, congruity
F3 dissimilarity

resemble *v*
be like, look like, be similar to, bear resemblance to, take after, favour, mirror, echo, duplicate, parallel, approach
F3 differ from

resent *v*
grudge, begrudge, envy, feel bitter about, feel aggrieved at, be angry at, take offence at, take umbrage at, take amiss, object to, grumble at, take exception to, dislike
F3 accept, like

resentful *adj*
grudging, envious, jealous, bitter, embittered, hurt, wounded, offended, aggrieved, put out, piqued, incensed, in high dudgeon, indignant, angry, irritated, irked, vindictive, malicious, spiteful
colloq. miffed, peeved
F3 satisfied, contented

resentment *n*
grudge, envy, jealousy, bitterness, spite, malice, ill-will, ill-feeling, bad feelings, hard feelings, (high) dudgeon, animosity, hostility, hurt, umbrage, pique, offence, displeasure, irritation, indignation, annoyance, ire, vexation, anger, vindictiveness
F3 contentment, happiness

reservation *n*
1 DOUBT, scepticism, misgiving, qualm, scruple, hesitancy, hesitation, second thoughts
formal demur
2 BOOKING, engagement, appointment, arrangement, order, prearrangement
3 RESERVE, preserve, park, sanctuary, homeland, enclave, tract
4 PROVISO, stipulation, qualification, condition, limitation

reserve *v, n, adj*
▶ *v* 1 SET ASIDE, earmark, keep, retain, hold back, keep back, save, store, lay aside, set apart, stockpile, hoard, accumulate
2 *reserve a seat*
book, engage, order, arrange for, secure, prearrange
3 DELAY, postpone, defer, put off, suspend, shelve, hold over, adjourn
F3 1 use up
▶ *n* 1 STORE, stock, supply, fund, stockpile, pool, reservoir, bank, cache, hoard, accumulation, savings
2 SUBSTITUTE, replacement, stand-in, understudy, fill-in, supply, proxy, surrogate, successor
3 RESERVATION, preserve, park, area, sanctuary, tract, enclave
4 SHYNESS, reticence, unresponsiveness, secretiveness, coldness, coolness, aloofness, detachment, modesty, restraint, self-restraint, distance, remoteness, unapproachability
F3 4 friendliness, openness, approachability
▷ **in reserve** for use when needed, available, to hand, in hand, unused, stored, spare, set aside
▶ *adj* spare, substitute, additional, auxiliary, alternative, extra, secondary

reserved *adj*
1 BOOKED, engaged, ordered, arranged, prearranged, taken, spoken for, set aside, earmarked, meant, intended, designated, destined, saved, held, kept, retained
2 SHY, retiring, reticent, unresponsive, unforthcoming, uncommunicative, secretive, silent,

taciturn, unsociable, cool, cold, aloof, standoffish, unapproachable, modest, diffident, restrained, cautious, distant, remote
Ea 1 unreserved, free, available **2** friendly, open

reservoir *n*
1 LAKE, pond, pool
Scot. loch
2 TANK, cistern, vat, basin, container, receptacle
3 STORE, stockpile, stock, supply, source, reserves, accumulation, fund, holder, bank
formal repository, reservatory

reshuffle *n, v*
▶ *n* reorganization, shake-up, upheaval, redistribution, regrouping, rearrangement, realignment, restructuring, revision, change, interchange
▶ *v* reorganize, restructure, shake up, change, interchange, shift, shuffle, revise, rearrange, regroup, realign, redistribute

reside *v*
1 LIVE, inhabit, lodge, stay, board, occupy, settle, remain
formal dwell, sojourn
2 BE PRESENT, exist, lie, rest, be inherent, be contained
formal dwell, abide

residence *n*
home, house, flat, apartment, seat, place, lodgings, quarters, hall, manor, mansion, palace, villa, country house, country seat, stay, lodging
formal dwelling, habitation, domicile, abode, sojourn
colloq. pad, digs

resident *n, adj*
▶ *n* inhabitant, citizen, local, householder, occupant, occupier, tenant, lodger, guest, patient, inmate, client
formal resider, dweller, sojourner
Ea non-resident
▶ *adj* live-in, living-in, dwelling, local, permanent, inhabiting, neighbourhood, settled, en poste
old use gremial
Ea non-resident

residential *adj*
commuter, suburban, dormitory
formal exurban

residual *adj*
remaining, left-over, unused, unconsumed, net, excess, surplus

residue *n*
remainder, remains, remnant, rest, surplus, excess, extra, overflow, balance, difference, lees, dregs, leftovers
formal residuum
Ea core

resign *v*
stand down, retire, step down, leave, abdicate, vacate, give up, hand in your notice, give in your notice, forego, waive, surrender, yield, abandon
formal renounce, relinquish, forsake
colloq. quit
Ea join
▷ **resign yourself** reconcile yourself, accept, bow, submit, yield, come to terms; *formal* comply, acquiesce
Ea resist

resignation *n*
1 STANDING-DOWN, stepping-down, abdication, retirement, departure, notice, letter of resignation, surrender, giving-up, waiving
formal renunciation, relinquishment
2 ACCEPTANCE, reconciliation, submission, non-resistance, passivity, patience, stoicism, yielding, defeatism
formal acquiescence, compliance
Ea 2 resistance

resigned *adj*
reconciled, philosophical, stoical, patient, long-suffering, unprotesting, unresisting, passive, submissive, yielding, defeatist
formal acquiescent
Ea resistant, protesting

resilience *n*
1 FLEXIBILITY, elasticity, springiness, spring, pliability, plasticity, suppleness, give, bounce, recoil
2 STRENGTH, toughness, hardiness, adaptability, buoyancy, irrepressibility, unshockability
Ea inflexibility, rigidity

resilient *adj*
1 *resilient material*
flexible, pliable, supple, plastic, elastic, springy, bouncy, rubbery
2 STRONG, tough, hardy, adaptable, buoyant, irrepressible, unshockable
Ea 1 rigid, brittle **2** weak

resist *v*
oppose, defy, confront, fight, struggle, contend, battle, combat, weather, withstand, stand up to, hold out against, obstruct, repel, counter, counteract, check, stop, halt, avoid, refuse, prevent, hinder, obstruct, thwart, impede, restrain, curb, stem
Ea submit, accept

resistance *n*
opposition, defiance, confrontation, fight, fighting, struggle, combat, contention, counteraction, battle, withstanding, repulsion, avoidance, refusal, prevention, thwart, hindrance, obstruction, impedance, impediment, restraint
formal intransigence
Ea acceptance, submission

resistant *adj*
1 OPPOSED, antagonistic, defiant, unyielding, unwilling
formal intransigent
2 PROOF, impervious, immune, unaffected, invulnerable, unsusceptible, tough, strong
Ea 1 compliant, yielding

resolute *adj*
determined, resolved, intent, decided, dedicated, constant, serious, earnest, adamant, stalwart, set, fixed, unwavering, unyielding, unswerving, inflexible, staunch, firm, steadfast, relentless, single-minded, persevering, dogged, tenacious, stubborn, obstinate, strong-willed, undaunted, unflinching, bold
formal obdurate
Ea irresolute, weak-willed, half-hearted

resolution *n*
1 DECISION, judgement, finding, declaration, proposition, motion, decree, verdict, declaration
2 DETERMINATION, resolve, willpower, commitment, dedication, devotion, dedication, constancy, firmness, intentness, seriousness,

earnestness, steadfastness, persistence, perseverance, doggedness, inflexibility, tenacity, zeal, courage, boldness
3 SOLVING, answer, solution, unravelling, disentangling, working out, sorting out
E3 2 half-heartedness, uncertainty, indecision

resolve *v, n*
▶ *v* **1** DECIDE, make up your mind, determine, fix, settle (on), conclude
2 SOLVE, answer, unravel, disentangle, sort out, work out
3 BREAK UP, break down, analyse, reduce, divide, separate, dissolve, disintegrate, detail, convert, anatomize, itemize
▶ *n* determination, willpower, commitment, dedication, devotion, constancy, firmness, intentness, seriousness, earnestness, steadfastness, persistence, perseverance, doggedness, inflexibility, tenacity, zeal, courage, boldness, sense of purpose
E3 indecision

resonant *adj*
deep, strong, sonorous, ringing, booming, rich, vibrant, full, plummy, resounding, reverberant, reverberating, echoing
formal canorous
E3 weak, faint

resort *v, n*
▶ *v* go, visit, frequent, patronize, haunt
formal repair
▷ **resort to** turn to, use, utilize, make use of, avail yourself of, fall back on, have recourse to, employ, exercise
▶ *n* **1** HOLIDAY CENTRE, centre, spot, health resort, spa
2 RECOURSE, refuge, course (of action), measure, step, alternative, option, chance, possibility
formal expedient

resound *v*
resonate, reverberate, echo, re-echo, ring, sound, boom, thunder

resounding *adj*
1 RESONANT, reverberating, echoing, ringing, loud, sonorous, booming, resonating, thunderous, full, rich, vibrant
2 *a resounding victory*
decisive, conclusive, impressive, striking, outstanding, great, memorable, remarkable, notable, emphatic, thorough
E3 1 faint

resource *n*
1 *a shortage of resources*
materials, supplies, reserves, holdings, funds, money, wealth, riches, capital, assets, property, means, power, wherewithal
2 SUPPLY, reserve, supply, pool, accumulation, stockpile, store, fund, source, contrivance, device, course, resort
formal expedient
3 RESOURCEFULNESS, initiative, enterprise, ingenuity, inventiveness, wit, imagination, talent, ability, capability

resourceful *adj*
ingenious, imaginative, creative, inventive, enterprising, innovative, original, versatile, clever, bright, sharp, quick-witted, witty, able, capable, talented, adroit

resourceless *adj*
inadequate, useless, hopeless, helpless, feeble, feckless, shiftless
E3 unimaginative

respect *v, n*
▶ *v* **1** ADMIRE, regard, have a good opinion of, think highly of, hold in high regard, set great store by, appreciate, value, praise, honour, approve of, revere
formal esteem, venerate
2 OBEY, observe, heed, follow, adhere to, honour, fulfil
formal comply with
3 CONSIDER, show consideration for, pay attention to, take into account, show regard for
formal take cognizance of
E3 1 despise, scorn **2** ignore, disobey
▶ *n* **1** ADMIRATION, appreciation, recognition, honour, deference, reverence, high opinion, regard, high regard, homage
formal esteem, veneration, approbation, obeisance
2 CONSIDERATION, attention, attentiveness, notice, regard, heed, thoughtfulness, politeness, courtesy
formal cognizance
3 GREETINGS, compliments, regards, salutations, best wishes, good wishes
formal devoirs
4 *in every respect*
point, aspect, facet, feature, characteristic, particular, detail, sense, matter, way, regard, reference, bearing, relation, connection
E3 1 disrespect

respectable *adj*
1 REPUTABLE, honourable, worthy, respected, dignified, upright, honest, above-board, trustworthy, worthy, decent, good, presentable, neat, tidy, clean, clean-living
formal decorous
2 ACCEPTABLE, tolerable, passable, adequate, fair, reasonable, all right, appreciable, considerable
colloq. not bad, OK
E3 1 dishonourable, disreputable **2** inadequate, paltry

respected *adj*
admired, valued, highly regarded, highly valued, held in high regard, thought highly of
formal esteemed, highly esteemed

respectful *adj*
deferential, reverent, reverential, humble, polite, well-mannered, courtly, dutiful, courteous, civil, subservient
E3 disrespectful

respecting *prep*
about, concerning, considering, in respect of, with regard to, regarding, with respect to

respective *adj*
corresponding, relevant, various, several, separate, individual, personal, own, specific, particular, special

respite *n*
1 PAUSE, rest, relief, break, adjournment, intermission, recess, relaxation, interval, interruption, halt, gap, lull
formal cessation, hiatus
colloq. breather, let-up
2 DELAY, reprieve, postponement, deferment, remission, stay, suspension, moratorium
formal abatement

resplendent *adj*
dazzling, shining, radiant, brilliant, bright, irradiant,
luminous, beaming, gleaming, glittering, glorious,
splendid
formal effulgent, fulgent, lustrous, refulgent
colloq. splendiferous
🖃 dull

respond *v*
answer, reply, acknowledge, retort, rejoin, answer
back, react, return, counter, reciprocate

response *n*
answer, reply, acknowledgement, retort, rejoinder,
riposte, return, reaction, feedback
colloq. comeback
🖃 query

responsibility *n*
1 DUTY, obligation, burden, onus, charge, care, role,
task, authority, power trust, business, affair, concern
colloq. baby, pidgin
2 FAULT, blame, guilt, answerability, accountability
formal culpability
3 DEPENDABILITY, reliability, conscientiousness,
honesty, soundness, maturity, adulthood, stability

responsible *adj*
1 IN CHARGE OF, in control of, controlling,
managing, leading, accountable, answerable
2 *a responsible citizen*
guilty, at fault, to blame, blameworthy, liable,
answerable, accountable
formal culpable
3 DEPENDABLE, reliable, conscientious,
trustworthy, honest, sound, steady, sober, mature,
adult, stable, reasonable, sensible, rational, sane, level-
headed
4 IMPORTANT, authoritative, powerful, executive,
decision-making
colloq. high-level
🖃 2 irresponsible, unreliable, untrustworthy

responsive *adj*
alert, aware, sensitive, awake, open, sharp, reactive,
amenable, receptive, susceptible, sympathetic,
perceptive, forthcoming, impressionable, alive,
respondent
formal responsorial
colloq. on the ball, with it
🖃 unresponsive

rest¹ *n, v*
▶ *n* 1 LEISURE, relaxation, lie-down, sleep, snooze,
nap, siesta, idleness, inactivity, ease, motionlessness,
standstill, stillness, tranquillity, calm
formal repose, quietude, slumber
2 BREAK, pause, breathing-space, intermission,
interlude, interval, recess, holiday, vacation, time off,
halt, lull, respite
formal cessation
colloq. breather
3 SUPPORT, prop, stand, base, holder
🖃 1 action, activity 2 work
▶ *v* 1 PAUSE, halt, stop
formal cease
2 RELAX, sit (down), recline, lounge, laze, lie down,
sleep, snooze, doze
formal repose
colloq. put your feet up, take it easy, recharge your
batteries
3 DEPEND, rely, hinge, hang, lie, be based

4 LEAN, prop, support, stand, steady
🖃 1 continue 2 work

rest² *n, v*
▶ *n the rest of us stayed behind*
remainder, others, balance, surplus, excess, residue,
remains, leftovers, remnant(s)
formal residuum
▶ *v* continue, remain, stay, last, endure, persist

restaurant *n*

Types of restaurant include: bistro, brasserie, buffet,
burger bar, café, cafeteria, canteen, carvery,
colloq. chippy, coffee bar, *US* diner, dining-car,
dining-room, eating-house, fish-and-chip shop,
slang greasy spoon, grill, grill room, health food
restaurant, ice-cream parlour, *US* luncheonette,
McDonald's®, mess room, milk bar, motorway café,
NAAFI (Navy, Army and Air Force Institutes),
pizzeria, pull-in, refectory, sandwich bar, self-service
restaurant, snack-bar, steakhouse, teahouse, tea
room, tea shop, transport café, trattoria.

restful *adj*
relaxing, soothing, calming, calm, tranquil, serene,
peaceful, quiet, still, placid, undisturbed, relaxed,
comfortable, leisurely, unhurried
formal languid
🖃 tiring, restless

restitution *n*
amends, reparation, requital, restoration, restoring,
return, satisfaction, redress, repayment, damages,
compensation, recompense, remuneration, refund,
reimbursement, indemnification, indemnity

restive *adj*
1 UNRULY, impatient, wayward, wilful, turbulent,
uncontrollable, undisciplined, unmanageable
formal recalcitrant, refractory
2 RESTLESS, agitated, fidgety, fidgeting, unsettled,
nervous, uneasy, anxious, fretful, tense, edgy
colloq. jumpy, uptight
🖃 2 calm, relaxed

restless *adj*
1 FIDGETY, fidgeting, unruly, turbulent, impatient,
changeable
formal restive
2 AGITATED, nervous, anxious, worried, uneasy,
fretful, edgy, troubled, unsettled
colloq. jittery, jumpy, uptight
3 SLEEPLESS, uncomfortable, broken, disturbed,
tossing and turning
🖃 1 still 2 calm, relaxed 3 restful, comfortable

restlessness *n*
agitation, disturbance, unsettledness, uneasiness,
unrest, turbulence, turmoil, worriedness, anxiety,
nervousness, fitfulness, insomnia, fretfulness, bustle,
disquiet, hurry, activity, instability, movement,
inconstancy, transience
formal inquietude, restiveness
colloq. edginess, jitters, jumpiness, heebie-jeebies
🖃 calmness, relaxation

restoration *n*
1 RENOVATION, repair, refurbishing, rebuilding,
reconstruction, renewal, rehabilitation
2 REVIVAL, refreshment, rejuvenation,
revitalization, recovery
colloq. kiss of life
3 RETURN, replacement, reinstallation, restitution,

reinstatement, re-establishment
≡ 1 damage 2 weakening 3 removal

restore v

1 *restore a building*
renovate, renew, rebuild, reconstruct, redecorate,
refurbish, retouch, recondition, rehabilitate, revamp,
repair, mend, fix
colloq. do up
2 REVIVE, refresh, recover, rejuvenate, revitalize,
strengthen, build up
formal revivify
3 REPLACE, return, give back, hand back, reinstate,
re-establish, reintroduce, re-impose, re-enforce
≡ 1 damage 2 weaken 3 remove

restrain v

restrain your feelings; restrain a prisoner
hold back, keep back, suppress, subdue, repress,
inhibit, check, hold in check, curb, bridle, stop, arrest,
prevent, hinder, obstruct, impede, bind, tie, chain,
fetter, manacle, imprison, detain, jail, confine, restrict,
regulate, control, keep under control, govern
colloq. bottle up
≡ encourage, liberate

restrained adj

1 CALM, controlled, steady, self-controlled,
self-restrained, unemotional, formal, cold, aloof,
uncommunicative
2 *restrained decorations*
tasteful, moderate, temperate, mild, subdued, subtle,
muted, quiet, soft, low-key, unobtrusive, discreet
≡ 1 emotional, demonstrative 2 *colloq.* loud

restraint n

behave with restraint; no restraints in modern life
moderation, inhibition, self-control, self-discipline,
hold, grip, check, curb, rein, bridle, suppression,
bondage, captivity, confinement, imprisonment,
bonds, chains, fetters, straitjacket, restriction, control,
constraint, limit(s), restriction(s), duress, block,
barrier, stint, limitation, tie, hindrance, prevention
formal judiciousness, prudence
≡ liberty

restrict v

limit, bound, demarcate, control, keep under control,
keep within limits, regulate, confine, contain, cramp,
constrain, impede, hinder, hamper, handicap, tie,
restrain, curtail
colloq. hem in
≡ broaden, free

restricted adj

1 SMALL, narrow, cramp, confined, tight
2 SECRET, private, limited, exclusive, controlled,
regulated

restriction n

limit, bound, confine, limitation, constraint,
handicap, check, curb, restraint, ban, stint, embargo,
control, regulation, rule, stipulation, qualification,
condition, proviso
≡ freedom

result n, v

▶ *n* effect, consequence, sequel, repercussion,
reaction, implication, outcome, upshot, end, issue,
end-product, by-product, side effect, fruit(s), score,
grade, mark, answer, verdict, judgement, decision,
conclusion
colloq. pay-off, spin-off
≡ cause

▶ *v* follow, ensue, happen, occur, issue, emerge, arise,
spring, derive, stem, flow, evolve, emanate, proceed,
come out of, develop, end, finish, terminate, culminate
formal eventuate
≡ cause

resume v

restart, start again, begin again, recommence, reopen,
reconvene, re-occupy, continue, carry on, go on,
proceed, take up (again)
≡ cease

résumé n

summary, précis, synopsis, outline, sketch,
breakdown, abstract, digest, recapitulation, review,
overview, run-down, epitome

resumption n

restart, recommencement, reopening,
re-establishment, renewal, resurgence, continuation,
proceeding
≡ cessation

resurgence n

re-appearance, re-emergence, resumption, return,
rebirth, resurrection, revival, renaissance
formal renascence, recrudescence, revivification,
risorgimento
≡ decrease

resurrect v

1 *Jesus Christ was resurrected*
bring back to life, raise from the dead, restore, restore
to life, revive
2 *resurrect an old idea*
restore, revive, resuscitate, reactivate, bring back,
reintroduce, re-establish, re-install, renew, revitalize
≡ 1 kill, bury

resurrection n

1 *the resurrection of Jesus Christ*
bringing back to life, raising/rising from the dead,
restoration to life, return from the dead
2 *resurrection of former procedures*
restoration, revival, resuscitation, renaissance, rebirth,
renewal, revitalization, re-establishment, resurgence,
reappearance, return, comeback

resuscitate v

revive, bring round, resurrect, save, rescue, reanimate,
quicken, reinvigorate, breathe new life into, revitalize,
restore, renew
formal revivify
colloq. give the kiss of life to

resuscitated adj

restored, revived, resurrected
formal redivivus, redintegrate(d)

retain v

1 KEEP, hold, keep hold of, grasp, grip, reserve,
hold back, hold fast to, save, continue, maintain,
preserve
colloq. hang on to
2 *retain information*
remember, recall, recollect, memorize, bear in mind,
keep in mind, call to mind
3 EMPLOY, engage, hire, pay, commission
≡ 1 release 2 forget 3 dismiss

retainer n

1 FEE, retaining fee, deposit, advance
2 SERVANT, lackey, footman, domestic, attendant,
supporter, valet, dependant, vassal, menial

retaliate *v*
reciprocate, counter-attack, get back at, pay someone back, hit back, strike back, fight back, avenge, take revenge
colloq. get your own back, get even with, give as good as you get, return like for like, give someone a taste of their own medicine

retaliation *n*
reprisal, counter-attack, revenge, vengeance, retribution, reciprocation
formal ultion
colloq. tit for tat, like for like, an eye for an eye and a tooth for a tooth, a taste of your own medicine

retard *v*
slow down, delay, hold up, decelerate, brake, put a/the brake on, handicap, incapacitate, obstruct, hinder, impede, check, curb, restrict
🗲 speed up, accelerate

retardation *n*
slowness, slowing, incapability, mental handicap, deficiency, incapacity, impeding, hindering, hindrance, delay, lag, obstruction, dullness
formal retardment
🗲 advancement

retch *v*
vomit, heave, reach, disgorge, regurgitate, gag
colloq. puke, spew, throw up

retching *n*
vomiting, nausea, reaching, gagging
formal vomiturition
colloq. puking

reticence *n*
reserve, restraint, quietness, uncommunicativeness, unforthcomingness, secretiveness, silence, taciturnity, muteness, diffidence
🗲 communicativeness, forwardness, frankness

reticent *adj*
reserved, shy, restrained, uncommunicative, unforthcoming, tight-lipped, secretive, taciturn, silent, quiet, diffident
🗲 communicative, forward, frank

retinue *n*
entourage, following, followers, personnel, staff, suite, train, attendants, escort, cortège, aides, servants

retire *v*
stop work, stop working, leave work, give up work, resign, leave, depart, go away, withdraw, retreat, recede, move, go, decamp
colloq. bow out, be put out to pasture
🗲 join, enter, advance

retired *adj*
former, ex-, emeritus, past

retirement *n*
withdrawal, retreat, exit, departure, resignation, solitude, loneliness, seclusion, privacy, obscurity

retiring *adj*
shy, bashful, timid, shrinking, quiet, reticent, reserved, self-effacing, unassertive, diffident, coy, modest, unassuming, humble
🗲 bold, forward, assertive

retort *v, n*
▶ *v* answer, reply, respond, rejoin, return, counter, retaliate

▶ *n* answer, reply, response, rejoinder, riposte, repartee, quip

retract *v*
take back, withdraw, recant, reverse, cancel, repeal, repudiate, disown, disclaim, deny, renounce, renege
formal revoke, rescind, disavow, abjure, abrogate
🗲 assert, maintain

retreat *v, n*
▶ *v* draw back, pull back, fall back, recoil, shrink, withdraw, decamp, give ground, give way, retire, leave, depart, flee
colloq. turn tail, quit
🗲 advance
▶ *n* **1** WITHDRAWAL, drawing back, pulling back, falling back, departure, evacuation, flight
2 SECLUSION, privacy, solitude, retirement, hideaway, hideout, den, refuge, asylum, sanctuary, shelter, harbour, haven
🗲 **1** advance, charge

retrench *v*
cut back, economize, cut, slim down, live more economically, save, reduce, lessen, limit, decrease, diminish, curtail, trim, pare, prune, husband
colloq. tighten your belt
🗲 increase

retrenchment *n*
cutback, cutting back, cut, economy, reduction, pruning, curtailment, cost-cutting, run-down, contraction, shrinkage
colloq. tightening your belt
🗲 increase

retribution *n*
punishment, reckoning, justice, satisfaction, retaliation, requital, reward, reprisal, redress, repayment, payment, compensation, recompense, revenge, vengeance, Nemesis
old use talion
colloq. just deserts

retrieve *v*
recover, get back, fetch, bring back, regain, recapture, repossess, recoup, reclaim, put to rights, make good, salvage, save, rescue, redeem, restore, remedy, return, mend, repair
🗲 lose

retrograde *adj*
backward, reverse, retrogressive, negative, downward, worsening, declining, deteriorating
🗲 progressive

retrogress *v*
regress, retrograde, return, revert, relapse, withdraw, recede, drop, ebb, fall, sink, wane, retire, retreat, backslide, decline, deteriorate, worsen, degenerate
🗲 progress, advance

retrogression *n*
regression, regress, return, relapse, decline, worsening, deterioration, drop, ebb, fall
formal recidivism, retrogradation
🗲 increase, progress

retrospect *n*
hindsight, afterthought, thinking back, reflection, re-examination, review, survey, recollection, remembrance
🗲 prospect
▷ **in retrospect** retrospectively, with hindsight,

looking back, thinking back, on reflection, with the wisdom of hindsight

retrospective *adj*
backward-looking, retro-active, retro-operative

return *v, n*
▶ *v* **1** COME BACK, reappear, recur, go back, get back, come home, come again, backtrack, regress, revert
2 GIVE BACK, hand back, send back, take back, deliver, put back, replace, reinstate, restore
formal remit
3 *return a favour*
reciprocate, repay, refund, reimburse, recompense, exchange, match, equal, correspond
formal requite
colloq. do the same
4 ANSWER, reply, respond, rejoin, retort, riposte, counter
5 *return a verdict*
announce, pronounce, declare, deliver, bring in
1 leave, depart **2** take
▶ *n* **1** REAPPEARANCE, recurrence, home-coming
colloq. comeback
2 REPAYMENT, recompense, replacement, restoration, reinstatement, reciprocation
3 REVENUE, income, proceeds, takings, yield, gain, profit, interest, reward, advantage, benefit
4 *the return of the books*
giving back, handing back, taking back, reinstatement, restoration, delivery, replacement
1 departure, disappearance **2** removal **3** payment, expense, loss

re-use *v*
recycle, reconstitute

revamp *v*
renovate, recondition, rebuild, reconstruct, repair, restore, revise, refit, refurbish, rehabilitate, overhaul, recast
colloq. do up

reveal *v*
expose, bring to light, make aware, uncover, unveil, unmask, unearth, expose to view, show, display, exhibit, lay bare, manifest, disclose, divulge, give away, betray, leak, tell, let out, let slip, impart, communicate, publicize, broadcast, publish, make public, make known, announce, proclaim
hide, conceal, mask

revealing *adj*
1 *a revealing interview*
indicative, significant, revelatory, give-away
2 *a revealing dress*
low-cut, daring, see-through, diaphanous, sheer

revel *v, n*
▶ *v* **1** *revel in an experience*
enjoy, delight, take delight, take pleasure, relish, glory, joy, indulge, thrive, wallow, savour, bask, rejoice, lap up, gloat, crow, luxuriate
2 *revelling through the night*
celebrate, carouse, have a party, make merry, roist, roister
colloq. live it up, whoop it up, paint the town red, push the boat out, raise the roof
1 dislike
▶ *n* celebration, party, carousal, carouse, festivity, spree, gala, merrymaking, jollification, bacchanal, debauch, saturnalia
colloq. rave, rave-up

revelation *n*
1 UNCOVERING, unveiling, unearthing, bring to light, exposure, unmasking, show, display, exhibition, disclosure, divulgence, confession, admission, betrayal, broadcasting
formal manifestation
2 NEWS, fact, detail, information, secreted/confidential information, communication, giveaway, publication, announcement, proclamation, leak

reveller *n*
celebrator, party-goer, pleasure-seeker, merrymaker, carouser, roisterer, wassailer, bacchanal

revelry *n*
celebration, festivity, party, merrymaking, fun, carousal, jollity, jollification, debauchery
sobriety

revenge *n, v*
▶ *n* vengeance, satisfaction, reprisal, retaliation, requital, retribution, redress, vendetta
old use avengement
colloq. tit for tat, eye for an eye and a tooth for a tooth, a taste of someone's own medicine
▶ *v* avenge, repay, retaliate, settle a score/an old score, pay someone back, put someone back in their own court, get back at, hit back, fight back
colloq. get your own back, get even with, give as good as you get

revengeful *adj*
bitter, resentful, implacable, vengeful, vindictive, malignant, spiteful, malicious, merciless, unmerciful, pitiless, unforgiving
formal malevolent
forgiving, merciful

revenue *n*
income, return, yield, interest, profit(s), gain, proceeds, receipts, rewards, takings
expenditure

reverberate *v*
echo, re-echo, resound, resonate, ring, boom, vibrate

reverberation *n*
1 ECHO, re-echoing, resounding, resonance, ringing, vibration, wave, rebound, recoil, reflection
2 *reverberations following the resignation*
repercussion, effect, consequence, result
colloq. shock wave, ripple

revere *v*
respect, admire, honour, look up to, think highly of, pay homage to, worship, reverence, adore, exalt
formal esteem, venerate
despise, scorn

reverence *n, v*
▶ *n* respect, deference, honour, homage, admiration, awe, worship, exaltation, adoration, devotion
formal veneration, (high) esteem
contempt, scorn
▶ *v* admire, respect, honour, acknowledge, revere, adore, worship
formal venerate
despise, scorn

reverent *adj*
reverential, respectful, admiring, deferential, humble, dutiful, devoted, awed, solemn, pious, devout, adoring, worshipping, loving
irreverent, disrespectful

reverie *n*
daydream, daydreaming, musing, trance, abstraction, absent-mindedness, inattention, preoccupation, brown study, woolgathering

reversal *n*
1 NEGATION, cancellation, annulment, nullification, countermanding, repeal, reverse, turnabout, turnaround, volte-face, upset
formal revocation, rescinding
colloq. U-turn
2 MISFORTUNE, mishap, misadventure, adversity, affliction, hardship, trial, blow, disappointment, upset, setback, check, delay, problem, difficulty, failure, defeat
E3 1 advancement, progress

reverse *v, n, adj*
▶ *v* **1** *reverse a car*
back, move backwards, drive backwards, retreat, backtrack, withdraw
formal regress
2 *reverse a decision*
undo, negate, set aside, cancel, annul, invalidate, overrule, repeal, quash, overthrow
formal countermand, revoke, rescind, retract
3 TRANSPOSE, turn round, invert, up-end, overturn, turn upside-down, put back to front, upset, change, change round, swap, alter
E3 1 go forwards **2** advance, enforce
▶ *n* **1** UNDERSIDE, other side, back, rear, inverse, counter, converse, contrary, opposite
formal antithesis
2 MISFORTUNE, mishap, misadventure, adversity, affliction, hardship, trial, blow, disappointment, upset, setback, check, delay, problem, difficulty, failure, defeat, reversal
formal vicissitude
▶ *adj* opposite, contrary, converse, inverse, inverted, backward, back, rear, verso

revert *v*
return, go back, resume, lapse, relapse, regress

review *n, v*
▶ *n* **1** CRITICISM, critique, assessment, evaluation, appraisal, judgement, report, commentary, examination, scrutiny, analysis, study, survey, rating, recapitulation, reassessment, re-evaluation, re-examination, revision
formal recension
colloq. rethink
2 MAGAZINE, periodical, journal
▶ *v* **1** CRITICIZE, assess, evaluate, judge, weigh (up), discuss, examine, view, inspect, scrutinize, analyse, study, survey, recapitulate
formal appraise
2 *review the situation*
reassess, re-evaluate, re-examine, reconsider, rethink, revise, take stock of
colloq. size up

reviewer *n*
commentator, critic, judge, observer, connoisseur, arbiter, essayist

revile *v*
despise, hate, scorn, slander, libel, defame, abuse, smear, reproach, malign, blackguard
formal calumniate, denigrate, traduce, vituperate, vilify
E3 praise

revise *v*
1 *revise your opinion*
change, alter, modify, amend, correct, update, edit, rewrite, reword, redraft, recast, revamp, reconsider, re-examine, review
formal emend
2 STUDY, learn, memorize
colloq. swot up, cram, bone up on, mug up

revision *n*
1 CHANGE, amendment, editing, modification, alteration, correction, recast, recasting, re-examination, reconstruction, review, rewriting, rereading
formal emendation
2 STUDYING, memorizing, homework, learning, updating
colloq. swotting

revitalize *v*
revive, renew, restore, refresh, reactivate, reanimate, rejuvenate, resurrect
formal revivify
E3 dampen, suppress

revival *n*
resuscitation, revitalization, restoration, re-establishment, reintroduction, renewal, renaissance, rebirth, resurrection, reawakening, resurgence, upsurge, upturn
colloq. the kiss of life, comeback

revive *v*
resuscitate, bring round, reanimate, revitalize, restore, renew, refresh, animate, invigorate, quicken, rouse, awaken, recover, rally, comfort, cheer up, reawaken, breathe new life into, rekindle, reactivate, re-establish, reintroduce
colloq. give the kiss of life to
E3 weary

revivify *v*
revive, revitalize, invigorate, restore, resuscitate, refresh, renew, reactivate, reanimate
formal inspirit
E3 dampen, depress

reviving *adj*
refreshening, invigorating, reinvigorating, exhilarating, bracing, stimulating, tonic, reanimating, enheartening, regenerating
formal revivescent, revivifying, reviviscent
E3 disheartening, exhausting

revocation *n*
revoking, repeal, repealing, quashing, reversal, withdrawal, annulment, nullification, invalidation, negation, cancellation, abolition, repudiation
formal countermanding, rescinding, rescission, retractation, retraction
E3 enforcement

revoke *v*
repeal, quash, annul, nullify, invalidate, negate, cancel, abolish, reverse, withdraw
formal rescind, abrogate, countermand, retract
E3 enforce

revolt *n, v*
▶ *n* revolution, rebellion, mutiny, rising, uprising, insurrection, putsch, coup (d'état), secession, defection
▶ *v* **1** REBEL, mutiny, rise, rise up, riot, resist, defect, take up arms, take to the streets
formal dissent
2 DISGUST, sicken, nauseate, repel, turn your stomach,

offend, shock, outrage, scandalize
☐ **1** submit **2** please, delight

revolting *adj*
disgusting, sickening, nauseating, repulsive, repellent,
obnoxious, nasty, horrible, vile, hateful, foul,
loathsome, abhorrent, abominable, distasteful, off-
putting, offensive, shocking, appalling
formal repugnant, reprehensible, heinous
☐ pleasant, delightful, attractive, palatable

revolution *n*
1 REVOLT, rebellion, mutiny, rising, uprising,
insurrection, insurgence, putsch, coup (d'état)
2 CHANGE, reformation, transformation,
innovation, upheaval, cataclysm
technical metamorphosis
colloq. sex change
3 ROTATION, turn, spin, wheel, whirl, cycle, circuit,
round, circle, orbit, gyration

revolutionary *n, adj*
▶ *n* rebel, mutineer, insurgent, insurrectionist,
anarchist, revolutionist
▶ *adj* **1** REBEL, rebellious, mutinous, insurgent,
insurrectionary, subversive, seditious, extremist,
anarchistic
formal extremist
2 *revolutionary ideas*
new, innovative, progressive, experimental, avant-
garde, different, drastic, radical, thoroughgoing,
complete
☐ **1** conservative

revolutionize *v*
transform, reform, restructure, cause radical changes
in, reorganize, transfigure, turn upside-down

revolve *v*
1 ROTATE, turn, go, move, pivot, swivel, spin, wheel,
whirl, gyrate, circle, orbit
2 *his life revolves around sport*
centre on, focus on, concentrate on, be preoccupied
with, turn on, hinge on, hang on

revolver *n*
gun, handgun, firearm, pistol, rifle, shotgun, airgun,
six-shooter
colloq. shooter

revolving *adj*
rotating, turning, spinning, whirling, gyrating,
gyratory
☐ stationary

revulsion *n*
disgust, distaste, dislike, repulsion, aversion, hatred,
hate, loathing, nausea, abhorrence, recoil,
abomination
formal repugnance, detestation
☐ delight, pleasure, approval

reward *n, v*
▶ *n* **1** *a reward for long service*
present, prize, honour, medal, decoration, bounty,
pay-off, bonus, premium, payment, remuneration,
recompense, repayment, compensation, gain, profit,
return, benefit, merit, desert
2 REQUITAL, punishment, retribution
colloq. just deserts
▶ *v* pay, remunerate, recompense, repay, requite,
compensate, honour, decorate
☐ punish

rewarding *adj*
profitable, remunerative, lucrative, productive, fruitful,
worthwhile, valuable, advantageous, beneficial,
satisfying, gratifying, pleasing, fulfilling, enriching,
edifying
☐ unrewarding

rewording *n*
rephrasing, paraphrase, revision
technical metaphrase, metaphrasis

rewrite *v*
revise, rework, reword, redraft, recast, correct, edit
formal emend

rhetoric *n*
eloquence, oratory, bombast, pomposity, hyperbole,
verbosity, wordiness, long-windedness, fustian
formal grandiloquence, magniloquence, prolixity

rhetorical *adj*
oratorical, bombastic, pompous, high-sounding, long-
winded, verbose, wordy, grand, high-flown, flowery,
florid, flamboyant, showy, pretentious, artificial,
insincere
formal grandiloquent, magniloquent, declamatory,
prolix
☐ simple

Rhetorical devices include: abscission, alliteration,
amplification, anacoluthon, anadiplosis, anaphora,
anastrophe, anticlimax, antimetabole,
antimetathesis, antiphrasis, antithesis, antonomasia,
aporia, apostrophe, asyndeton, auxesis, bathos,
catachresis, chiasmus, climax, diallage, diegesis,
dissimile, double entendre, dramatic irony,
dysphemism, ellipsis, enantiosis, enumeration,
epanadiplosis, epanalepsis, epanaphora, epanodos,
epanorthosis, epigram, epiphonema, epistrophe,
epizeuxis, erotema, erotetic, euphemism, figure of
speech, hendiadys, hypallage, hyperbole,
hypostrophe, hypotyposis, hysteron-proteron,
increment, innuendo, irony, litotes, meiosis,
metalepsis, metaphor, metonymy, mixed metaphor,
onomatopoeia, oxymoron, parabole, paradox,
paraleipsis, parenthesis, pathetic fallacy,
personification, prolepsis, pun, rhetorical question,
simile, syllepsis, symploce, synchoresis, synchrysis,
synecdoche, synoeciosis, tautology, transferred
epithet, trope, vicious circle, zeugma.

rhyme *n*
poetry, verse, poem, ode, limerick, jingle, song, ditty

rhythm *n*
beat, pulse, time, throb, tempo, metre, measure,
movement, harmony, flow, lilt, swing, accent, cadence,
pattern

rhythmic *adj*
rhythmical, metric, metrical, pulsating, throbbing,
flowing, lilting, periodic, regular, repeated, steady

rib *n*
bone, band, bar, support, vein, moulding, ribbing,
ridge, shaft, welt, wale
formal costa

ribald *adj*
rude, obscene, risqué, racy, off-colour, bawdy, earthy,
coarse, smutty, vulgar, filthy, foul-mouthed, gross,
base, scurrilous, low, mean, lewd, disrespectful,
licentious, indecent, irreverent, satirical, jeering,
mocking, derisive, Rabelaisian
colloq. blue, naughty
☐ polite

ribaldry *n*
rudeness, obscenity, bawdiness, raciness, vulgarity, smut, smuttiness, earthiness, coarseness, filth, grossness, lowness, baseness, licentiousness, indecency, scurrility, jeering, derision, mockery
colloq. naughtiness

ribbon *n*
band, cord, cloth, line, sash, strip, braid, shred, tatter, jag, hair-band, headband, fillet, taenia
Related adjectives: taeniate, taenioid

rich *adj*
1 WEALTHY, affluent, moneyed, prosperous, well-to-do, well-off
colloq. flush, well-heeled, made of money, in the money, rolling in it, with money to burn; *slang* loaded, filthy rich, stinking rich
2 EXPENSIVE, precious, valuable, priceless, costly, lavish, magnificent, sumptuous, luxurious, lush, splendid, grand, gorgeous, palatial, fine, elaborate, ornate
formal opulent
3 PLENTIFUL, abundant, abounding, copious, profuse, prolific, ample, full, high, packed, steeped, overflowing, well-provided, well-supplied
formal replete, plenteous
4 FERTILE, fruitful, productive, lush
formal fecund
5 *rich food*
creamy, fatty, oily, full-bodied, heavy, full-flavoured, strong, spicy, savoury, tasty, delicious, luscious, juicy, sweet
6 *rich colours*
deep, intense, vivid, strong, bright, brilliant, vibrant, warm
7 IRONIC, laughable, ridiculous, outrageous, preposterous
8 *a rich voice*
deep, mellow, full, sonorous, resonant
formal mellifluous
E3 **1** poor, impoverished **2** plain **4** barren, infertile **5** plain, bland **6** dull, soft

riches *n*
wealth, affluence, prosperity, money, gold, treasure, fortune, assets, property, substance, resources, means
old use (filthy) lucre
formal opulence
E3 poverty

richly *adv*
1 LAVISHLY, splendidly, gorgeously, sumptuously, elegantly, elaborately, expensively, exquisitely, luxuriously, palatially
formal opulently
2 FULLY, thoroughly, completely, well, strongly, suitably, appropriately, properly
E3 **1** poorly, scantily

rickety *adj*
unsteady, wobbly, shaky, unstable, insecure, flimsy, jerry-built, decrepit, ramshackle, broken-down, dilapidated, derelict
E3 stable, strong

rid *v*
free, deliver, relieve, unburden, clear, purge, cleanse, purify
▷ **get rid of** throw away, throw out, dispose of, discard, dump, scrap, jettison, abolish, put an end to, eliminate, do away with; *colloq.* chuck (out), ditch, junk

riddance *n*
deliverance, release, relief, removal, freedom, elimination, clearance, disposal, ejection, expulsion, extermination, purgation
E3 burdening

riddle¹ *n*
tell me a riddle
enigma, mystery, conundrum, brainteaser, puzzle, poser, problem
technical koan

riddle² *v*
1 PERFORATE, pierce, puncture, pepper, fill, permeate, pervade, infest
2 SIFT, sieve, strain, filter, mar, winnow

ride *v, n*
▶ *v* sit, move, go, progress, travel, journey, gallop, trot, pedal, drive, steer, control, dominate, handle, manage
formal bestride
▶ *n* journey, trip, outing, jaunt, spin, drive, lift

ridge *n*
band, escarpment, hill, hummock, lump, arête, drum, drumlin, esker, yardang, sastruga, hog's back, reef, ripple, saddle, knurl, wale, welt, crinkle
formal costa

ridicule *n, v*
▶ *n* mockery, jeering, laughter, scorn, derision, taunting, teasing, chaff, banter, badinage, satire, irony, sarcasm
E3 praise
▶ *v* laugh at, mock, make fun of, jeer, scorn, gibe, scoff, deride, sneer, tease, humiliate, taunt, satirize, send up, caricature, lampoon, burlesque, parody
colloq. rib, kid, rag, pull someone's leg, pooh-pooh, take the mickey out of
E3 praise

ridiculous *adj*
ludicrous, absurd, nonsensical, silly, foolish, stupid, contemptible, derisory, laughable, facetious, farcical, comical, funny, humorous, droll, hilarious, outrageous, shocking, preposterous, incredible, unbelievable
formal risible
E3 sensible

rife *adj*
abundant, abounding, rampant, teeming, swarming, overflowing, raging, epidemic, prevalent, widespread, predominant, extensive, general, common, frequent, ubiquitous
E3 scarce

riff-raff *n*
mob, rabble, hoi polloi, scum, dregs, undesirables, canaille
colloq. rent-a-mob

rifle¹ *n*
shoot with a rifle
gun, airgun, firearm, shotgun, musket, carbine, firelock, flintlock, fusil, bundook

rifle² *v*
rifle through some files
search, rummage, sack, pillage, plunder, ransack, rob, maraud, loot, strip, burgle, gut
formal despoil

rift *n*
1 SPLIT, breach, break, fracture, crack, fault, chink,

cleft, fissure, slit, cavity, cranny, crevice, gap, space, opening, hole
2 DISAGREEMENT, difference, fight, split, row, feud, conflict, breach, separation, division, schism, alienation
formal estrangement, altercation
⊟ 2 unity

rig *n, v*
▶ *n* equipment, kit, outfit, gear, tackle, apparatus, machinery, fittings, fixtures
formal accoutrements
▶ *v* falsify, tamper with, doctor, fiddle, distort, twist, pervert, manipulate, massage, misrepresent, forge, fake
colloq. cook
▷ **rig out 1** EQUIP, kit out, outfit, fit (out), supply, provide, furnish, make ready **2** CLOTHE, dress (up), wear, put on, get into, garb, robe, trim, turn out; *formal* array, accoutre, attire; *colloq.* get up
▷ **rig up** arrange, build, assemble, construct, erect, fit up, fix up, put together, improvise; *colloq.* knock up, throw together, cobble together
⊟ dismantle

right *adj, adv, n, v*
▶ *adj* **1** *the right answer*
correct, accurate, exact, precise, true, factual, actual, real, genuine, authentic, valid
colloq. spot on, bang on
2 PROPER, fitting, correct, accepted, approved, becoming, appropriate, suitable, fit, fitting, admissible, acceptable, satisfactory, reasonable, desirable, favourable, preferable, advantageous, convenient, opportune
old use seemly
formal propitious, auspicious
colloq. the done thing
3 FAIR, just, equitable, lawful, legal, honest, upright, good, virtuous, righteous, moral, ethical, proper, principled, honourable, impartial
4 RIGHT-WING, conservative, Tory, reactionary, true-blue
5 *he's a right fool*
complete, absolute, utter, real, thorough
⊟ 1 wrong, incorrect, erroneous **2** improper, unsuitable **3** unfair, wrong **4** left-wing
▶ *adv* **1** CORRECTLY, accurately, exactly, precisely, factually, properly, satisfactorily, well, favourably, fairly
colloq. by the book
2 *right to the bottom*
straight, in a straight line, directly, as the crow flies, completely, utterly, entirely, absolutely, wholly, totally, all the way
colloq. slap bang
3 *I'll be right back*
straight, immediately, without delay
⊟ 1 wrongly, incorrectly, unfairly
▷ **right away** straight away, immediately, at once, now, instantly, directly, forthwith, without delay, promptly; *colloq.* from the word go
⊟ later, eventually
▶ *n* **1** JUSTICE, legality, lawfulness, good, goodness, virtue, righteousness, morality, ethics, honour, honesty, integrity, uprightness, truthfulness, impartiality, fairness
formal rectitude, propriety
2 PRIVILEGE, prerogative, due, claim, entitlement, birthright, business, authority, power, permission, warrant, freedom, opportunity, licence, charter, sanction, title deed

technical droit
formal lien
⊟ 1 wrong
▷ **by rights** rightfully, correctly, properly, rightly, justifiably, justly, lawfully, legally, legitimately; *technical* de jure
▷ **in the right** justified, right, warranted, vindicated
⊟ in the wrong, at fault
▷ **put/set to rights** rectify, correct, put in order, fix, settle, straighten (out)
▷ **within your rights** justified, entitled, permitted, allowed, reasonable, right
▶ *v* rectify, correct, put right, put in order, fix, repair, redress, vindicate, avenge, settle, straighten (out), stand up

righteous *adj*
1 *a righteous person/action*
just, good, virtuous, moral, worthy, honourable, upright, fair, ethical, equitable, honest, law-abiding, blameless, irreproachable, incorrupt, guiltless, God-fearing, saintly, pure, sinless
2 *righteous anger*
justifiable, defensible, excusable, warranted, reasonable, supportable, justified, lawful, legal, legitimate, acceptable, explainable, valid, well-founded, proper
⊟ 1 unrighteous **2** unjustifiable

righteousness *n*
goodness, honesty, honour, virtue, uprightness, morality, integrity, justice, blamelessness, faithfulness, equity, ethicalness, purity, holiness, sanctification
technical dharma
formal probity, rectitude
⊟ unrighteousness

rightful *adj*
legitimate, lawful, legal, just, bona fide, true, real, genuine, valid, authorized, correct, proper, suitable, due
⊟ wrongful, unlawful

rightfully *adv*
correctly, properly, rightly, by rights, justifiably, justly, lawfully, legally, legitimately
technical de jure
⊟ incorrectly, unjustifiably

rigid *adj*
1 STIFF, inflexible, inelastic, unbending, cast-iron, hard, firm, set, fixed, unyielding, unalterable, invariable
2 *a rigid political system*
austere, harsh, severe, inflexible, unrelenting, strict, rigorous, stringent, stern, uncompromising, unyielding, Spartan
formal intransigent
⊟ 1 flexible, elastic, bending, malleable **2** variable, weak

rigmarole *n*
process, bother, performance, fuss, palaver, nonsense, jargon, gibberish, twaddle
colloq. carry-on, hassle, red tape, to-do

rigorous *adj*
1 EXACT, precise, accurate, meticulous, painstaking, scrupulous, conscientious, punctilious, laborious, thorough
2 STRICT, stringent, rigid, firm, tough, harsh, hard, severe, stern, austere, exacting, uncompromising, Spartan

formal intransigent
F3 1 lax, superficial

rigour *n*

1 *the rigours of war*
TRIAL, hardship, severity, suffering, ordeal
formal privation
2 THOROUGHNESS, exactness, meticulousness,
accuracy, preciseness, precision, conscientiousness,
punctiliousness, inflexibility
3 STRICTNESS, stringency, rigidity, firmness,
toughness, harshness, hardship, hardness, severity,
sternness, austerity
formal intransigence
F3 3 leniency, mildness

rig-out *n*

clothing, clothes, garments, outfit, uniform, dress,
costume, habit, livery
formal apparel, raiment
colloq. clobber, garb, gear, get-up, togs

rile *v*

annoy, irritate, nettle, pique, put out, upset, irk, vex,
anger, exasperate
colloq. peeve, aggravate, bug
F3 calm, soothe

rim *n*

lip, edge, brim, brink, verge, margin, border,
circumference
F3 centre, middle

rind *n*

peel, skin, husk, crust
formal epicarp, integument

ring¹ *n, v*

▶ *n* **1** CIRCLE, round, loop, hoop, disc, halo, band,
circlet, belt, girdle, collar, circuit, area, arena,
enclosure, atoll
2 GROUP, cartel, syndicate, association,
organization, league, alliance, combine, society, club,
fraternity, sorority, gathering, circle, gang, crew, mob,
band, cell, clique, coterie
▶ *v* surround, encircle, gird, loop, encompass,
enclose, cage in, hem in
formal circumscribe

ring² *v, n*

▶ *v* **1** CHIME, peal, toll, knell, ding, ding-dong,
tinkle, clink, jingle, clang, sound, resound, resonate,
echo, reverberate, buzz
2 TELEPHONE, phone, call, ring up
colloq. give a buzz, give a tinkle, give a bell
▶ *n* **1** CHIME, peal, toll, knell, tinkle, clink, jingle,
clang, ding-dong
2 PHONE CALL, call
colloq. buzz, tinkle, bell

ringleader *n*

leader, spokesman, spokeswoman, spokesperson,
mouthpiece, chief, fugleman, bell-wether
colloq. brains

rinse *v*

swill, bathe, wash, wash clean, clean, cleanse, flush
(away), wet, dip

riot *n, v*

▶ *n* **1** *a riot in the streets*
insurrection, rising, uprising, revolt, rebellion,
insurgence, anarchy, lawlessness, fight, brawl, fray,
fracas, melee, affray, disturbance, turbulence, disorder,
confusion, commotion, tumult, turmoil, uproar, row,

quarrel, strife
2 REVELRY, feasting, partying, indulgence,
debauchery, orgy
old use merrymaking
colloq. rave, rave-up
3 *a riot of colour*
display, show, flourish, exhibition, extravaganza
4 LAUGH
colloq. scream, hoot
F3 1 order, calm
▷ **run riot** rampage, run wild, run amok, go berserk,
rush wildly, charge, tear, storm, rage, rant, rave
▶ *v* revolt, rebel, mutiny, rise up, run riot, run wild,
run amok, go berserk, rush wildly, charge, tear, storm,
rage, rant, rave, rampage, go on the rampage

riotous *adj*

1 WILD, violent, uncontrollable, unrestrained,
unruly, rebellious, lawless, insurrectionary,
insubordinate, disorderly, mutinous, ungovernable,
wanton
2 NOISY, loud, rowdy, tumultuous, boisterous,
uproarious
F3 1 orderly, restrained

rip *v, n*

▶ *v* tear, rend, split, separate, rupture, burst, cut,
shred, slit, slash, gash, lacerate, hack
▷ **rip off** overcharge, swindle, defraud, cheat, diddle,
trick, dupe, exploit; *colloq.* do, fleece, con; *slang* sting
▶ *n* tear, rent, split, cleavage, rupture, cut, ladder, slit,
slash, gash, hole

ripe *adj*

1 RIPENED, mature, mellow, seasoned, grown, fully-
grown, developed, fully-developed, complete,
finished, perfect
2 READY, suitable, fit, right, advantageous,
favourable, timely, opportune
formal auspicious, propitious
F3 2 untimely, inopportune; *formal* inauspicious

ripen *v*

develop, mature, bring/come to maturity, mellow,
season, age

rip-off *n*

robbery, exploitation, cheat, swindle, theft, fraud,
diddle
colloq. con, con trick, daylight robbery; *slang* sting

riposte *n, v*

▶ *n* retort, rejoinder, repartee, quip, answer, reply,
response, return, sally, comeback
▶ *v* retort, rejoin, quip, reciprocate, answer, reply,
respond, return

ripple *n, v*

▶ *n* **1** WAVE, disturbance, eddy, gurgle, lapping,
ripplet, undulation, burble, babble, purl, wimple
2 REPERCUSSION, effect, result, consequence,
reverberation
colloq. shock wave
▶ *v* ruffle, wrinkle, flow, undulate, purl, wimple,
crease, pucker, crumple

rise *v, n*

▶ *v* **1** GO UP, move upwards, ascend, climb (up),
mount, slope (up), soar, tower, loom, grow, get higher,
increase, escalate, swell, intensify, rocket
2 STAND UP, get up, arise, jump up, leap up, spring
up, get to your feet, get out of bed
3 ADVANCE, progress, make progress, approach,
improve, prosper, be promoted

4 ORIGINATE, spring, flow, issue, emanate, emerge, appear, start, begin
formal commence
5 REBEL, revolt, mutiny, riot, resist, defect, take up arms, take to the streets
formal dissent
6 *rise to the challenge*
attempt, try, do your best, respond, react to, exert yourself
Ea 1 fall, descend **2** sit down **3** declare
▶ *n* **1** ASCENT, climb, slope, soaring, towering, incline, hill, elevation
formal acclivity
2 INCREASE, growth, escalation, leap, increment, upsurge, upturn, advance, progress, improvement, advancement, promotion
US raise
formal amelioration, aggrandizement
Ea 1 descent, valley **2** fall

risible *adj*
ridiculous, ludicrous, funny, hilarious, humorous, laughable, absurd, amusing, comic, comical, droll, farcical
colloq. rib-tickling, side-splitting
Ea serious, unfunny

rising *n, adj*
▶ *n* riot, revolution, revolt, uprising, insurrection
▶ *adj* ascending, growing, increasing, intensifying, mounting, soaring, swelling, advancing, emerging, approaching
Ea decreasing

risk *n, v*
▶ *n* danger, peril, jeopardy, hazard, threat, chance, possibility, uncertainty, gamble, speculation, venture, adventure
Ea safety, certainty
▶ *v* endanger, imperil, jeopardize, put in jeopardy, hazard, chance, take a chance, gamble, venture, dare
colloq. chance it, put on the line, go for broke, stick your neck out, play with fire

risky *adj*
dangerous, unsafe, perilous, hazardous, chancy, uncertain, touch-and-go, high-risk, tricky, precarious
colloq. dicey, dodgy, iffy
Ea safe

risqué *adj*
indecent, improper, rude, immodest, indelicate, suggestive, coarse, crude, earthy, dirty, bawdy, racy, smutty, naughty, ribald, off-colour
colloq. adult, blue, near the knuckle
Ea decent, proper

rite *n*
ceremony, custom, act, usage, office, form, formality, ceremonial, ordinance, practice, procedure, ritual, service, worship, liturgy, sacrament, observance

ritual *n, adj*
▶ *n* custom, tradition, convention, usage, practice, habit, wont, routine, procedure, ordinance, prescription, form, formality, ceremony, ceremonial, solemnity, rite, sacrament, service, liturgy, celebration, observance, act
▶ *adj* customary, traditional, conventional, habitual, routine, procedural, prescribed, set, formal, ceremonial
Ea informal

rival *n, adj, v*
▶ *n* competitor, contestant, contender, challenger, opponent, opposition, adversary, antagonist, vier, fellow, match, equal, peer
Ea colleague, associate
▶ *adj* competitive, competing, in competition, in conflict, conflicting, opposed, opposing, in opposition
Ea associate
▶ *v* compete with, contend with, vie with, oppose, compare with, measure up to, emulate, match, equal, parallel
Ea co-operate

rivalry *n*
competitiveness, competition, contest, contention, conflict, struggle, strife, vying, opposition, antagonism
Ea co-operation

river *n*
waterway, watercourse
Related adjectives: fluvial, potamic

Forms of river or watercourse include: beck, billabong, bourn, broads, brook, burn, canal, channel, confluence, creek, cut, delta, estuary, firth, frith, inlet, mountain stream, mouth, rill, rillet, rivulet, runnel, source, stream, tributary, wadi, waterway.

The world's longest rivers include: Nile (Africa), Amazon (South America), Yangtze (Asia), Mississippi-Missouri (North America), Yenisey-Angara-Selenga (Asia), Amur-Argun-Kerulen (Asia), Ob-Irtysh (Asia), Plata-Parena-Grande (South America), Yellow (Asia), Zaire (Africa).

riveting *adj*
fascinating, absorbing, interesting, exciting, gripping, arresting, captivating, engrossing, enthralling, spellbinding, magnetic, hypnotic
Ea boring

road *n*

Types of road include: A-road, alley, arterial road, autobahn, avenue, B-road, boulevard, bridle path, bridle way, broadway, bypass, byroad, byway, carriageway, cart-track, cartway, causeway, circle, circus, clearway, close, course, crescent, cul-de-sac, dead end, dirt-road, dirt-track, drive, driveway, dual carriageway, *US* expressway, flyover, *US* freeway, grove, high street, *US* highway, lane, main road, motorway, one-way street, *US* overpass, parade, passage, path, pathway, primary route, ring road, roadway, route, service road, side road, side street, single-track road, slip road, square, street, terrace, thoroughfare, toll road, towpath, track, trail, trunk road, *US* turnpike, unadopted road, underpass, walk, way.

roam *v*
wander, rove, range, travel, traverse, walk, tramp, trek, ramble, meander, stroll, amble, prowl, drift, stray
formal ambulate, perambulate, peregrinate
Ea stay

roar *v, n*
▶ *v* **1** BELLOW, yell, shout, cry, scream, shriek, bawl, howl, hoot, guffaw, thunder, crash, blare, rumble
2 LAUGH, burst out laughing, shriek with laughter, guffaw, hoot
colloq. split your sides, fall about, break up, crease up, laugh like a drain
Ea 1 whisper

▶ *n* bellow, yell, shout, cry, scream, shriek, bawl, howl, hoot, guffaw, thunder, crash, blare, rumble

rob *v*
steal from, hold up, raid, burgle, loot, pillage, plunder, sack, rifle, ransack, swindle, cheat, defraud, deprive
colloq. rip off, do, mug; *slang* sting, heist

robber *n*
thief, burglar, stealer, hijacker, bandit, swindler, embezzler, fraud, cheat, plunderer, raider, pirate, highwayman, looter, brigand
colloq. con man, mugger

robbery *n*
theft, stealing, larceny, break-in, housebreaking, hold-up, pilferage, raid, burglary, pillage, plunder, fraud, embezzlement, swindle
colloq. rip-off, mugging; *slang* stick-up, heist

robe *n, v*
▶ *n* costume, gown, vestment, habit, bathrobe, dressing-gown, housecoat, peignoir, wrap, wrapper
▶ *v* clothe, dress, drape, garb, vest
formal apparel, attire

robot *n*
automaton, machine, android, zombie

robust *adj*
1 STRONG, sturdy, tough, hardy, energetic, vigorous, powerful, muscular, well-built, strapping, stalwart, athletic, fit, healthy, well
2 *robust opinions*
strong, forceful, vigorous, straightforward, direct
colloq. no-nonsense
3 COARSE, earthy, rude, crude, ribald, risqué, raw
F3 2 weak, feeble, unhealthy

rock¹ *n*
rocks rolling down the hill
boulder, stone, pebble, crag, outcrop

Rocks include: basalt, breccia, chalk, coal, conglomerate, flint, gabbro, gneiss, granite, gravel, lava, limestone, marble, marl, obsidian, ore, porphyry, pumice stone, sandstone, schist, serpentine, shale, slate.

rock² *v*
1 SWAY, swing, tilt, tip, shake, wobble, roll, undulate, pitch, toss, lurch, reel, stagger, totter, oscillate, move to and fro
2 *news that rocked the nation*
shock, stun, stagger, bewilder, daze, dumbfound, astound, astonish, surprise, startle, take back

rocket *v*
soar, tower, increase quickly/suddenly, escalate, shoot up

rocky¹ *adj*
rocky moorland
stony, pebbly, craggy, rugged, rough, hard, flinty
F3 smooth, soft

rocky² *adj*
a rocky marriage
unsteady, shaky, wobbly, wobbling, staggering, tottering, unstable, unreliable, uncertain, weak
F3 steady, stable, dependable, strong

rod *n*
bar, shaft, strut, pole, stick, baton, wand, cane, switch, staff, mace, sceptre
Related adjective: rhabdoid

rodent *n*

Kinds of rodent include: agouti, bandicoot, beaver, black rat, brown rat, cane rat, capybara, cavy, chinchilla, chipmunk, cony, coypu, dormouse, ferret, fieldmouse, gerbil, gopher, grey squirrel, groundhog, guinea pig, hamster, hare, harvest mouse, hedgehog, jerboa, kangaroo rat, lemming, marmot, meerkat, mouse, muskrat, musquash, pika, porcupine, prairie dog, rabbit, rat, red squirrel, sewer-rat, squirrel, vole, water rat, water vole, woodchuck.

rogue *n*
scoundrel, rascal, scamp, villain, miscreant, deceiver, swindler, fraud, fraudster, cheat, reprobate, good-for-nothing, wastrel, ne'er-do-well
colloq. crook, con man, nasty piece of work

roguish *adj*
mischievous, playful, cheeky, impish, knavish, rascally, waggish, frolicsome, coquettish, swindling, villainous, deceiving, deceitful, dishonest, criminal, crooked, fraudulent, shady, unprincipled, unscrupulous
F3 honest, serious

roister *v*
revel, rollick, celebrate, carouse, frolic, romp, strut, swagger, brag, bluster, boast
old use make merry
colloq. paint the town red, whoop it up

roisterer *n*
reveller, carouser, ranter, roister, swaggerer, boaster, braggart, blusterer

roisterous *adj*
loud, noisy, wild, rowdy, uproarious, disorderly, exuberant, boisterous, clamorous, obstreperous
F3 orderly, restrained

role *n*
part, character, representation, portrayal, impersonation, function, capacity, task, duty, job, post, position, situation, place

roll *v, n*
▶ *v* **1** ROTATE, revolve, turn (round), go round, spin, wheel, twirl, whirl, gyrate, move, go, run, pass
2 WIND, coil, furl, twist, curl, wrap, envelop, fold, enfold, bind
3 *the ship rolled*
rock, sway, swing, pitch, toss, lurch, reel, billow, tumble, stagger, wallow, undulate
4 PRESS, press down, flatten, crush, smooth, level
5 RUMBLE, roar, thunder, boom, resound, reverberate
▷ **roll up** arrive, assemble, gather, congregate, convene
F3 leave
▶ *n* **1** ROLLER, cylinder, drum, reel, spool, bobbin, scroll
2 REGISTER, roster, census, list, inventory, index, catalogue, directory, schedule, record, file, chronicle, annals
3 ROTATION, revolution, cycle, turn, spin, wheel, twirl, whirl, gyration, undulation
4 RUMBLE, roar, thunder, boom, resonance, reverberation
5 SWELL, pitching, tossing, rocking, reeling, billowing, undulation

rollicking *adj*
lively, noisy, light-hearted, hearty, romping, sprightly, exuberant, frolicsome, jovial, carefree, boisterous, joyous, merry, spirited, sportive, jaunty, cavorting, devil-may-care, roisterous, roisting, frisky, playful, rip-roaring, swashbuckling
E restrained, serious

rolling *adj*
heaving, surging, waving, rippling, undulating, undulant
E flat

roly-poly *adj*
fat, plump, chubby, overweight, rounded, tubby, buxom, podgy, pudgy
formal rotund
E slim

romance *n, v*
▶ *n* **1** LOVE AFFAIR, affair, relationship, liaison, attachment, intrigue, amour, passion
2 LOVE STORY, romantic fiction, novel, story, tale, fairytale, legend, idyll, fiction, fantasy, whimsy
3 ADVENTURE, excitement, melodrama, mystery, charm, fascination, glamour, sentiment
▶ *v* **1** LIE, fantasize, exaggerate, overstate
2 GO OUT WITH, court, see
colloq. date, go steady with

romantic *adj, n*
▶ *adj* **1** IMAGINARY, fictitious, fanciful, fantastic, legendary, fairy-tale, idyllic, utopian, optimistic, idealistic, quixotic, visionary, starry-eyed, dreamy, unrealistic, impractical, improbable, unlikely, wild, extravagant, exciting, fascinating, mysterious
2 SENTIMENTAL, loving, amorous, passionate, tender, fond, soppy, mushy, sloppy
colloq. lovey-dovey
E **1** real, practical **2** unromantic, unsentimental
▶ *n* sentimentalist, dreamer, visionary, idealist, utopian
E realist

Romeo *n*
lover, ladies' man, Don Juan, Casanova, lady-killer, gigolo

romp *v, n*
▶ *v* gambol, frolic, skip, sport, frisk, caper, cavort, revel, rollick, roister
▶ *n* caper, frolic, lark, rig, spree

roof *n*
Related adjective: tectiform

Types of roof include: bell roof, conical broach roof, cupola, dome, flat roof, French roof, gable roof, gable-and-valley roof, gambrel roof, geodesic dome, helm roof, hip roof, imbricated roof, imperial roof, lean-to roof, mansard roof, monitor roof, ogee roof, onion dome, pavilion roof, pendentive dome, pitched roof, saddle roof, saucer dome, sawtooth roof, sloped turret, span roof, thatched roof.

rook *v*
cheat, swindle, defraud, overcharge
colloq. rip off, do, fleece, diddle, con, bilk, sting

room *n*
space, volume, capacity, area, headroom, legroom, elbow-room, scope, range, extent, expanse, volume, leeway, latitude, margin, allowance, chance, opportunity

Types of room include: attic, loft, box-room, bedroom, boudoir, spare room, dressing-room, guest room, nursery, playroom, sitting-room, lounge, front room, living-room, drawing-room, parlour, salon, reception room, chamber, lounge-diner, dining-room, study, *colloq.* den, library, kitchen, kitchen-diner, kitchenette, breakfast room, larder, pantry, scullery, bathroom, en suite bathroom, toilet, lavatory, WC, *colloq.* loo, cloakroom, laundry, utility room, porch, hall, landing, conservatory, sun lounge, cellar, basement; cabin, cubicle, cell, chambers; classroom, music-room, laboratory, office, sick-room, dormitory, workroom, studio, workshop, storeroom, waiting-room, anteroom, foyer, mezzanine, family room, games room.

roomy *adj*
spacious, large, sizeable, broad, wide, extensive, ample, generous
formal capacious, voluminous, commodious
E cramped, small, tiny

root¹ *n, v*
▶ *n* **1** TUBER, rhizome, stem, radical, radicle, radix
2 ORIGIN, source, derivation, reason, cause, starting point, fount, fountainhead, seed, germ, kernel, nucleus, heart, core, nub, essence, seat, base, bottom, basis, foundation, fundamental
3 *tracing your family roots*
beginning(s), origins, family, heritage, background, birthplace, home
▷ **root and branch** completely, entirely, wholly, totally, utterly, thoroughly, radically, finally
E not at all, slightly
▶ *v* anchor, moor, fasten, fix, set, stick, implant, embed, entrench, establish, ground, base
▷ **root out** unearth, dig out, uncover, discover, uproot, eradicate, eliminate, put an end to, exterminate, destroy, abolish, clear away, remove, get rid of; *formal* extirpate
Related adjective: radical

root² *v*
root around in the cupboard
▷ **root around** rummage, ferret, poke, pry, nose, dig, delve, burrow, forage, hunt

root³ *v*
root for your team
support, shout, cheer (on), encourage, applaud, hail
US pull

rooted *adj*
entrenched, established, felt, firm, fixed, deep, deeply, deep-seated, ingrained, confirmed, rigid, radical
E superficial, temporary

rope *n, v*
▶ *n*

Kinds of rope include: bobstay, bowline, brace, bridle, buntline, cable, clew-line, cord, cordage, cringle, dragline, dragrope, gantline, guy, guy-rope, hackamore, halter, halyard, hawser, head rope, hobble, lanyard, lariat, lashing, lasso, line, marline, noose, painter, ratline, stay, strand, string, tack, tackle, tether, towrope, vang, warp, widdy.

▶ *v* tie, bind, lash, fasten, hitch, moor, tether
▷ **rope in** enlist, engage, involve, persuade, talk into; *formal* inveigle
Related adjective: funicular

ropy *adj*
poor, substandard, deficient, inadequate, inferior,

unsatisfactory, rough, unwell, off colour
colloq. below par
⊟ good, well

roster *n*
rota, schedule, register, roll, list, listing, index,
directory

rostrum *n*
platform, stage, dais, podium

rosy *adj*
1 PINK, reddish, red, rose, rose-coloured, rose-hued,
roselike, rose-pink, rose-red, rose-scented, roseate,
glowing, fresh, sunny, healthy-looking, blooming,
blushing, ruddy, flushed, florid, inflamed, bloodshot
formal rubicund
2 PROMISING, cheerful, bright, encouraging,
optimistic, hopeful, reassuring, favourable
formal auspicious
⊟ 2 depressing, sad, unhappy

rot *v, n*
▶ *v* decay, decompose, fester, perish, corrode, spoil,
go bad, go off, degenerate, go sour, deteriorate,
crumble, disintegrate, taint, corrupt
formal putrefy
▶ *n* 1 DECAY, decomposition, deterioration,
disintegration, corrosion, rust, mould
formal putrefaction
2 NONSENSE, rubbish, drivel, claptrap
colloq. poppycock, bunk, bunkum, baloney, humbug,
piffle, tosh, bosh, codswallop

rotary *adj*
rotating, revolving, turning, spinning, whirling,
gyrating, gyratory
⊟ fixed

rotate *v*
1 REVOLVE, turn (round), spin (round), go round,
move round, reel, whirl, gyrate, pivot, swivel, roll
2 ALTERNATE, take (it) in turns, interchange,
reciprocate

rotation *n*
revolution, turn, turning, spin, spinning, swivel,
swivelling, whirl, whirling, gyration, orbit, cycle,
alternation, sequence, succession

rotten *adj*
1 DECAYED, decomposed, putrid, addled, bad, off,
sour, spoilt, tainted, mouldy, fetid, stinking, rank, foul,
rotting, decaying, disintegrating, mouldering
formal putrescent
2 INFERIOR, bad, poor, inadequate, low-grade,
lousy, mean
colloq. crummy, ropy
3 NASTY, evil, wicked, horrible, beastly, dirty,
despicable, contemptible, dishonourable, dishonest,
immoral, corrupt, unprincipled
4 ILL, sick, unwell, poorly, awful, off colour
colloq. grotty, rough, ropy
⊟ 1 fresh 2, 3 good 4 well

rotter *n*
scoundrel, cad, blackguard, dastard, cur
colloq. bounder, blighter, stinker, swine, rat, fink,
louse

rotund *adj*
1 FAT, round, stout, tubby, full, fleshy, plump, podgy,
portly, chubby, roly-poly, heavy, obese, spherical,
globular, spheric, spheral, spherular, bulbous
formal corpulent, rotundate, orbicular

2 RESONANT, rich, sonorous, full, rounded
formal grandiloquent, magniloquent, orotund
⊟ 1 flat, slim, gaunt

roué *n*
rake, lecher, libertine, profligate, wanton, debauchee,
sensualist, rakehell

rough *adj, n, v*
▶ *adj* 1 UNEVEN, bumpy, lumpy, stony, rugged,
craggy, jagged, irregular, gnarled, coarse, bristly,
hairy, shaggy, scaly, prickly, scratchy
2 BOISTEROUS, forceful, energetic, lively, disorderly,
violent, wild, noisy, rowdy, raucous
3 HARSH, severe, stern, tough, hard, difficult,
insensitive, unfeeling, merciless, cruel, brutal, drastic,
extreme, vulgar, impolite, coarse, brutish, brusque,
curt, sharp
4 *in a rough voice*
husky, throaty, gruff, harsh, hoarse, rasping, croaking,
guttural, raucous, discordant, strident
5 APPROXIMATE, estimated, imprecise, inexact,
hazy, vague, general, quick, cursory, hasty, sketchy,
incomplete, unfinished, unpolished, unrefined, crude,
basic, rudimentary
6 *rough sea*
choppy, agitated, turbulent, stormy, tempestuous,
violent, wild
7 ILL, sick, unhealthy, unwell, poorly, off colour
colloq. below par, rotten, grotty
⊟ 1 smooth 2 gentle 3 mild 5 accurate,
exact 6 calm, smooth 7 well
▶ *n* 1 SKETCH, mock-up, outline, draft, model
2 THUG, hooligan, bully, rowdy, ruffian, bruiser,
roughneck, tough
slang yob, yobbo
▶ *v* ▷ **rough out** sketch, draft, draw in rough,
outline, mock up, give a summary of
▷ **rough up** beat up, maltreat, manhandle, mistreat;
colloq. do in, knock about, bash, mug

rough-and-ready *adj*
approximate, crude, sketchy, simple, makeshift, make-
do, provisional, stop-gap, hurried, unpolished,
unrefined
⊟ exact, refined

rough-and-tumble *n*
scuffle, struggle, fight, fracas, rumpus, affray, brawl,
melee
colloq. dust-up, punch-up, scrap

roughen *v*
abrade, asperate, coarsen, granulate, graze, harshen,
rough, chafe, chap, rasp, ruffle, scuff
⊟ smooth

roughneck *n*
tough, thug, rough, rowdy, ruffian, hooligan, lout,
bully boy, bruiser, keelie

round *adj, n, v*
▶ *adj* 1 SPHERICAL, globular, ball-shaped, circular,
ring-shaped, disc-shaped, disklike, globelike,
hooplike, cylindrical, rounded, curved
formal spheroid, discoid, discoidal, orbicular, globate
2 ROTUND, plump, stout, portly, ample
formal corpulent
3 APPROXIMATE, rough, imprecise, estimated
▶ *n* 1 CIRCLE, ring, band, hoop, circlet, disc, sphere,
cylinder, globe, ball, orb
2 CYCLE, series, sequence, succession, period, bout,
session, heat, game, level, stage
3 BEAT, circuit, route, path, lap, course, routine

▶ *v* go round, move past, circle, skirt, travel round, flank, bypass

▷ **round off** finish (off), complete, end, close, conclude, cap, crown, top off

E3 begin

▷ **round on** turn on, set upon, attack, lay into, abuse

▷ **round up** bring together, herd, marshal, assemble, gather, rally, muster, collect, group

E3 disperse, scatter

roundabout *adj*
circuitous, tortuous, twisting, winding, meandering, indirect, oblique, devious, evasive
formal periphrastic, circumlocutory
E3 straight, direct

roundly *adv*
completely, thoroughly, forcefully, violently, vehemently, fiercely, intensely, rigorously, severely, sharply, bluntly, openly, frankly, outspokenly
E3 mildly

round-up *n*
summary, survey, overview, précis, collation, collection, assembly, gathering, herding, marshalling, muster, rally
E3 dispersal

rouse *v*
1 WAKE (UP), awaken, arouse, call, stir, get up
2 EXCITE, move, start, disturb, agitate, anger, provoke, stimulate, instigate, incite, inflame, impel, induce, kindle, evoke, call up, galvanize, whip up
E3 2 calm

rousing *adj*
stimulating, exciting, inspiring, lively, moving, spirited, stirring, vigorous, exhilarating, brisk, electrifying
E3 dull, boring, calming

rout *n, v*
▶ *n* defeat, conquest, overthrow, beating, trouncing, drubbing, flight, retreat, stampede
formal subjugation
colloq. thrashing
E3 win
▶ *v* defeat, conquer, overthrow, crush, beat, trounce, put to flight, chase, dispel, scatter
formal vanquish, subjugate
colloq. hammer, thrash, lick, slaughter, wipe the floor with

route *n, v*
▶ *n* course, run, path, road, avenue, way, flight path, direction, itinerary, journey, passage, circuit, round, beat
▶ *v* direct, send, forward, convey, dispatch

routine *n, adj*
▶ *n* **1** PROCEDURE, way, method, system, order, pattern, schedule, programme, formula, practice, usage, custom, wont, habit, rut
2 *comedy routine*
act, piece, programme, performance, lines
colloq. patter, spiel, yak
▶ *adj* customary, habitual, usual, typical, ordinary, run-of-the-mill, normal, standard, common, wonted, workaday, conventional, unoriginal, predictable, familiar, everyday, banal, humdrum, dull, boring, monotonous, tedious, tiresome, hackneyed
E3 unusual, different, exciting, inspiring

rove *v*
roam, wander, ramble, range, meander, drift, cruise,
stroll, stray, gallivant, traipse
Scot. stravaig
E3 stay

rover *n*
rambler, wanderer, transient, vagrant, traveller, drifter, itinerant, ranger, nomad, Gypsy, gadabout
Scot. stravaiger
E3 stay-at-home

row[1] *n*
a row of seats
line, tier, bank, rank, range, column, file, queue, string, chain, series, sequence, arrangement

row[2] *n, v*
▶ *n* **1** ARGUMENT, quarrel, disagreement, dispute, controversy, squabble, tiff, fight, conflict, fracas, brawl
formal altercation
colloq. slanging match, falling-out, set-to, scrap, dust-up
2 NOISE, racket, din, uproar, commotion, clamour, disturbance, rumpus, hubbub, tumult
E3 2 calm
▶ *v* argue, quarrel, wrangle, bicker, squabble, fight
colloq. scrap

rowdy *adj, n*
▶ *adj* noisy, loud, rough, boisterous, disorderly, unruly, unrestrained, riotous, wild, obstreperous
E3 quiet, peaceful, restrained
▶ *n* rough, ruffian, tough, tearaway, hooligan, lout, brawler, apache, keelie
colloq. hoodlum; *slang* yahoo, yob, yobbo

royal *adj*
regal, majestic, kingly, kinglike, queenly, queenlike, princely, imperial, monarchical, sovereign, august, grand, impressive, imposing, stately, magnificent, splendid, superb

rub *v, n*
▶ *v* **1** STROKE, caress, fondle, pat, massage, scratch, knead
formal embrocate
2 CLEAN, smooth, polish, buff (up), burnish, shine
3 SCOUR, scratch, scrape, scrub, wipe, clean, abrade
4 PUT ON, apply, work in, spread, smear
5 CHAFE, grate, scrape, pinch
▷ **rub in** emphasize, stress, underline, highlight, make much of, insist on, harp on
▷ **rub off on** influence, affect, have an effect on, change, alter, transform
▷ **rub out 1** ERASE, obliterate, delete, cancel;
formal efface **2** KILL, assassinate, murder, put to death, finish off, do away with; *colloq.* do in, bump off, eliminate, liquidate
▷ **rub up the wrong way** annoy, anger, irk, irritate, get, vex, niggle, get to; *colloq.* bug, get one's goat, get under one's skin, needle, peeve
E3 calm
▶ *n* **1** MASSAGE, stroke, caress, kneading
2 POLISH, shine, wipe, clean
3 DIFFICULTY, drawback, hindrance, trouble, impediment, problem, obstacle, hitch, catch
colloq. snag

rubbish *n*
1 REFUSE, junk, litter, scrap, waste, dross, debris, rubble, flotsam and jetsam
US garbage, trash
formal detritus
2 NONSENSE, drivel, twaddle, gibberish, gobblydegook, balderdash

colloq. stuff and nonsense, claptrap, poppycock, rot, cobblers, bunk, bunkum, piffle, rot, tripe, tosh, bosh; *slang* crap, shit, bull, bullshit

📧 2 sense

rubbishy *adj*
worthless, valueless, trashy, cheap, tawdry, third-rate, grotty, paltry, petty, shoddy, throw-away, gimcrack, tatty, twopenny-halfpenny

📧 high-quality, classy

ruction *n*
protest, quarrel, trouble, fracas, fuss, row, rout, rumpus, disturbance, dispute, commotion, racket, uproar, storm, brawl, rookery, ruffle
formal altercation
colloq. scrap, to-do

📧 calm

ruddy *adj*
red, reddish, scarlet, crimson, blushing, flushed, rosy, glowing, healthy, blooming, florid, fresh, sunburnt
formal rubicund

📧 pale, unhealthy

rude *adj*
1 IMPOLITE, discourteous, disrespectful, bad-tempered, impertinent, impudent, insolent, offensive, insulting, abusive, ill-mannered, ill-bred, unpleasant, uncouth, uncivilized, unrefined, unpolished, uneducated, untutored, uncivil, curt, brusque, abrupt, sharp, short
colloq. cheeky
2 *a rude joke*
obscene, vulgar, coarse, improper, indecent, indelicate, dirty, filthy, risqué, ribald, lewd, bawdy, naughty, gross
colloq. near the bone
3 *get a rude shock*
unpleasant, harsh, disagreeable, nasty, unexpected, sudden
4 SIMPLE, rough, crude, primitive, rudimentary, rough-and-ready
5 IGNORANT, illiterate, uncivilized, unrefined, uneducated, untutored, unpolished, uncouth, rough

📧 1 polite, courteous, civil 2 clean, decent 3 pleasant 4 advanced, well-developed 5 educated

rudimentary *adj*
1 BASIC, primary, initial, introductory, elementary, fundamental
2 PRIMITIVE, undeveloped, embryonic, crude, simple, rough

📧 1 advanced 2 developed

rudiments *n*
basics, fundamentals, essentials, principles, elements, ABC, beginnings, foundations

rue *v*
regret, be regretful, be sorry, mourn, grieve, lament, deplore, feel remorse for, bemoan, bewail, repent

📧 rejoice

rueful *adj*
regretful, remorseful, penitent, sad, melancholy, repentant, sorrowful, sorry, mournful, dismal, apologetic, grievous, conscience-stricken, doleful, pitiable, pitiful, plaintive, self-reproachful
formal contrite, lugubrious, woebegone, woeful

📧 glad, joyful

ruffian *n*
villain, scoundrel, bully, bully-boy, brute, thug, lout, rowdy, rogue, cut-throat, rascal, roughneck, hooligan, bruiser
formal miscreant
colloq. hoodlum, rough, tough, yobbo; *slang* yob

ruffle *v*
1 RUMPLE, dishevel, tangle, tousle, wrinkle, crease, pucker, crumple, ripple
formal disarrange
2 ANNOY, upset, irritate, anger, put out, vex, irk, exasperate, fluster, rile, nettle, confuse, trouble
formal discompose, perturb
colloq. aggravate, bug, hassle, rattle

📧 1 smooth 2 pacify

rugged *adj*
1 ROUGH, bumpy, uneven, irregular, jagged, rocky, stony, craggy, stark
2 STRONG, robust, hardy, tough, sturdy, stalwart, vigorous, burly, well-built, muscular, sinewy, weather-beaten, furrowed
3 DETERMINED, strong, robust, tough, resolute, firm, tenacious, unflinching, unwavering

📧 1 smooth

ruin *n, v*
▶ *n* 1 DESTRUCTION, devastation, wreckage, havoc, damage, disrepair, decay, disintegration, breakdown, collapse, fall, downfall, failure, defeat, overthrow, ruination, undoing
2 *financial ruin*
insolvency, bankruptcy, loss, failure, crash, disaster
formal indigence, penury
3 *the ruins of the castle*
remains, debris, rubble, fragments, traces, vestiges, relics, remnants, chaos, devastation, havoc, shambles
formal detritus

📧 1 development, reconstruction

▶ *v* 1 DAMAGE, harm, spoil, mar, botch, break, smash, shatter, injure, wreck, wreak havoc, destroy, demolish, raze, devastate, lay waste, overwhelm, overthrow, defeat, cripple, crush
colloq. mess up
2 IMPOVERISH, bankrupt, make bankrupt, make insolvent, cripple

📧 1 develop, restore

ruinous *adj*
1 *ruinous costs*
exorbitant, extortionate, excessive, unreasonable, immoderate, crippling
2 RUINED, in ruins, damaged, dilapidated, broken-down, ramshackle, decrepit, destroyed, devastated, wrecked, shattered, catastrophic, calamitous, devastating, cataclysmic

📧 1 low 2 beneficial

rule *n, v*
▶ *n* 1 REGULATION, law, statute, ordinance, decree, ruling, order, command, commandment, direction, guide, corrective, restriction, precept, tenet, canon, maxim, axiom, truth, truism, principle, formula, guideline, direction, instruction, standard, criterion
2 REIGN, sovereignty, supremacy, kingship, queenship, dominion, mastery, influence, sway, power, authority, command, direction, control, influence, regime, administration, government, leadership, jurisdiction
3 CUSTOM, convention, practice, standard, routine, procedure, protocol, form, habit, wont
▷ **as a rule** usually, normally, mainly, in the main, ordinarily, generally, in general, on the whole, by and large, for the most part

▶ *v* **1** *rule a country*
reign, govern, command, lead, preside over, officiate, administer, manage, direct, guide, control, be in control, administer, regulate, prevail, dominate
colloq. call the shots, sit in the driving seat
2 JUDGE, adjudicate, decide, find, settle, determine, resolve, establish, decree, direct, order, lay down, pronounce
▷ **rule out** exclude, eliminate, reject, dismiss, prevent, ban, prohibit, forbid, disallow;
formal preclude

ruler *n*

Titles of rulers include: Aga, begum, caesar, caliph, commander, consul, controller, duce, emir, emperor, empress, Führer, governor, governor-general, head, head of state, kaiser, khan, king, leader, lord, maharajah, maharani, mikado, monarch, nawab, nizam, overlord, pharaoh, potentate, president, prince, princess, queen, rajah, rani, regent, shah, sheikh, shogun, sovereign, sultan, sultana, suzerain, tsar, viceroy.

ruling *n, adj*
▶ *n* judgement, adjudication, verdict, decision, finding, resolution, decree, pronouncement
▶ *adj* **1** REIGNING, sovereign, on the throne, supreme, governing, controlling, in control, in charge, commanding, leading
2 MAIN, chief, leading, principal, dominant, predominant, most influential

rum *adj*
strange, unusual, odd, peculiar, abnormal, bizarre, curious, weird, funny, freakish, queer, suspect, suspicious
formal singular
colloq. funny-peculiar

rumbustious *adj*
boisterous, loud, noisy, rowdy, disorderly, clamorous, exuberant, unmanageable, unruly, uproarious, wild, rough, wayward, wilful, robust, roisterous, roisting
formal obstreperous, refractory
E₃ quiet, restrained, sensible

ruminate *v*
ponder, think, reflect, meditate, mull over, muse, brood, consider, contemplate, deliberate, chew over
formal cogitate

rummage *v, n*
▶ *v* root (around), search, turn over, poke around, hunt, explore, examine, delve, ransack, forage, rifle
▶ *n* jumble, junk, tat, bric-à-brac, odds and ends

rumour *n, v*
▶ *n* hearsay, gossip, talk, speculation, whisper, scandal, word, information, news, report, story
formal tidings
colloq. grapevine, bush telegraph, buzz
▶ *v* say, tell, hint, put about, noise abroad, report, publish, gossip, circulate, whisper, bruit

rump *n*
1 BUTTOCKS, backside, bottom, rear, seat, dock, hindquarters, haunch, nache, croup
colloq. bum, posterior; *US colloq.* butt
2 LEFTOVERS, remains, remainder, residue, trace, vestige

rumple *v*
wrinkle, crease, pucker, crumple, ruffle, dishevel,

disorder, tousle, crinkle, crush, derange, scrunch
E₃ smooth

rumpus *n*
disturbance, noise, uproar, confusion, commotion, disruption, furore, rout, row, tumult, fuss, fracas, brawl, brouhaha, ruction
colloq. kerfuffle
E₃ calm

run *v, n*
▶ *v* **1** SPRINT, jog, race, charge, career, tear, dash, hurry, rush, speed, bolt, dart, gallop, trot, scoot, scuttle, scamper, scurry
colloq. step on it
2 GO, pass, move, travel, proceed, issue, flow
3 FUNCTION, work, go, operate, be in operation, perform, progress
4 *run a company*
head, lead, administer, direct, operate, own, carry on, carry out, conduct, manage, superintend, supervise, organize, co-ordinate, oversee, control, be in control of, regulate, be in charge of
5 COMPETE, contend, stand, enter, take part in, put yourself forward, challenge
6 LAST, continue, go, go on, extend, reach, stretch, proceed, spread, range
7 FLOW, stream, glide, roll, course, pour, gush, issue, jet, spurt, cascade, drip, trickle
8 *run your hand over something*
move, pass, spread, slide, cross
9 *run you to the station*
DRIVE, take, convey, transport, give a lift
10 *run a car*
own, possess, have, drive, use, keep, maintain
11 *the play ran for four years*
be performed, be presented, be produced, be staged, be mounted, be played, last, go on
12 *the newspaper ran a story*
publish, print, carry, feature, include, communicate, broadcast
▷ **run across** meet, encounter, come across, run into; *formal* chance upon; *colloq.* bump into
▷ **run after** chase, pursue, follow, tail
E₃ flee
▷ **run away 1** ESCAPE, flee, abscond, decamp, bolt, run off, make off; *colloq.* scarper, beat it, clear off, make a run for it **2** *run away from problems* avoid, ignore, disregard, evade, neglect, overlook, take no notice of, brush aside; *colloq.* shut your eyes to, turn your back on **3** *run away with your neighbour's wife* run off, elope, make off with, leave **4** *run away with the money* make off with, walk off with, steal, pocket; *formal* appropriate, purloin; *colloq.* pinch, nick, lift
E₃ 1 stay **2** deal with
▷ **run down 1** CRITICIZE, denounce, attack, belittle, disparage, defame; *formal* denigrate
colloq. knock, slate, slag off, rubbish **2** RUN OVER, knock down, knock over, knock to the ground, hit, strike **3** TIRE, weary, exhaust, weaken **4** *run down production* reduce, decrease, drop, cut, cut back on, trim, curtail
E₃ 1 praise **4** increase
▷ **run for it** escape, flee, fly, make off, retreat, bolt; *colloq.* scarper, scram, do a bunk, skedaddle
E₃ stay
▷ **run in** arrest, jail; *formal* apprehend; *colloq.* nick, pick up, nab, lift, pinch, bust, collar
▷ **run into 1** MEET, encounter, run across; *formal* chance upon; *colloq.* bump into **2** HIT,

strike, collide with, bump into, crash, ram

E∃ 2 miss

▷ **run off 1** RUN AWAY, escape, make off, abscond, bolt, decamp, elope; *colloq.* scarper, skedaddle **2** DUPLICATE, print, produce, xerox, photostat

E∃ 1 stay

▷ **run off with** run away with, make off with, elope with

▷ **run on** continue, go on, carry on, last, extend, reach

▷ **run out** expire, terminate, end, close, finish, be finished, exhaust, be exhausted, dry up, give out, fail; *formal* cease

▷ **run out on** abandon, leave, strand, maroon; *formal* forsake; *colloq.* walk out on, jilt, ditch, chuck, dump, leave in the lurch

▷ **run over 1** HIT, knock down, run down, strike **2** REPEAT, go over, run through, practise, rehearse, review, overflow, survey; *formal* reiterate

▷ **run through 1** REHEARSE, go through, run over, practise, read, review, survey, examine **2** SPEND, waste, squander, exhaust, fritter away; *formal* dissipate

▷ **run to** amount to, add up to, total, come to, equal, afford, have enough of

▷ **run together** join, mix, unite, blend, combine, fuse, merge, mingle, amalgamate, coalesce; *formal* commingle

E∃ separate

▶ *n* **1** JOG, gallop, race, sprint, spurt, dash, rush, hurry **2** DRIVE, ride, jaunt, excursion, outing, trip, journey *colloq.* spin **3** SERIES, sequence, string, cycle, chain, course, round, succession, spell, stretch, period **4** COURSE, route, way, line, track, road, flight path **5** ENCLOSURE, coop, pen, pound, fold, sty, paddock, yard **6** *a run on a currency* demand, need, call, rush, clamour, pressure **7** POINT, goal, hit, mark, score **8** *different from the average run of things* sort, kind, type, class, set, variety, category **9** *a run in a stocking* ladder, rip, tear, cut, hole, split, slit, slash, snag, gash

▷ **in the long run** eventually, ultimately, at last, in the end; *colloq.* when all is said and done, at the end of the day

runaway *n, adj*

▶ *n* escaper, escapee, fugitive, absconder, truant, deserter, refugee

▶ *adj* escaped, fugitive, loose, out of control, uncontrolled, wild

run-down *n, adj*

▶ *n* **1** REDUCTION, decrease, curtailment, decline, drop, cut, cutback **2** SUMMARY, résumé, synopsis, analysis, outline, sketch, briefing, review, recap, run-through

▶ *adj* **1** WEAK, tired, weary, drained, exhausted, fatigued, worn-out, unhealthy, grotty, seedy, peaky *formal* debilitated, enervated **2** NEGLECTED, uncared-for, dilapidated, tumble-down, ramshackle, broken-down, decrepit, dingy, shabby

E∃ 1 healthy **2** well-kept

run-in *n*

fight, quarrel, argument, dispute, set-to, wrangle, skirmish, tussle, confrontation, difference of opinion, brush, contretemps

formal altercation

colloq. dust-up

runner *n*

1 JOGGER, sprinter, athlete, competitor, participant, **2** COURIER, messenger, racer, dispatch rider, bearer **3** STEM, shoot, offshoot, sprout, tendril, sprig, sarmentum, stolon

technical flagellum

running *n, adj*

▶ *n* **1** SPRINTING, jogging, racing, rushing **2** ADMINISTRATION, direction, management, organization, co-ordination, superintendency, supervision, leadership, charge, control, controlling, regulation **3** FUNCTIONING, working, operation, performance, conduct **4** *out of the running* contention, contest, competition

▶ *adj* **1** UNBROKEN, uninterrupted, continuous, constant, perpetual, ceaseless, incessant, moving, flowing

formal unceasing

2 IN SUCCESSION, successive, consecutive, in a row

colloq. on the trot

E∃ 1 broken, occasional

runny *adj*

flowing, fluid, liquid, liquefied, melted, molten, watery, diluted

E∃ solid

run-of-the-mill *adj*

ordinary, common, normal, everyday, average, unexceptional, mediocre, middling, tolerable, fair, unremarkable, undistinguished, unimpressive

colloq. so-so, not up to much, no great shakes

E∃ exceptional, remarkable

rupture *n, v*

▶ *n* **1** SPLIT, tear, burst, puncture, break, breaking, breach, fracture, crack **2** DIVISION, separation, split, schism, rift, disagreement, quarrel, falling-out

old use rent

formal estrangement

colloq. bust-up

▶ *v* split, tear, burst, puncture, break, fracture, crack, sever, separate, divide, cut off

old use rend

rural *adj*

country, rustic, pastoral, agricultural, agrarian, bucolic, sylvan

E∃ urban

ruse *n*

plan, trick, deception, hoax, imposture, stratagem, tactic, manoeuvre, ploy, plot, scheme, wile, subterfuge, artifice, device, blind, sham

colloq. dodge

rush *v, n*

▶ *v* **1** HURRY, dash, hasten, quicken, accelerate, speed (up), press, push, dispatch, bolt, dart, shoot, fly, tear, career, race, run, sprint, scramble, gallop, stampede, charge

old use make haste

colloq. get a move on

2 ATTACK, charge, assault, storm, raid, strike

▶ *n* **1** HURRY, haste, urgency, speed, rapidity, swiftness, dash, race, scramble, stampede, charge, flow,

flood, surge, stream, gush
2 BUSTLE, activity, hustle and bustle, stir,
commotion, excitement, flurry, hurry, hurly-burly
colloq. hive of activity, comings and goings
3 ATTACK, charge, onslaught, assault, storm, raid,
strike
4 DEMAND, call, need, run, clamour, pressure

rushed *adj*
busy, hurried, emergency, careless, cursory,
superficial, quick, fast, rapid, swift, brisk, hasty,
prompt, urgent
formal expeditious

rust *n, v*
▶ *n* corrosion, oxidation, verdigris, stain, decay
▶ *v* corrode, oxidize, tarnish, deteriorate, decline,
decay, rot

rust-coloured *adj*
rusty, reddish-brown, brown, red, reddish, coppery,
copper, auburn, chestnut, russet, ginger, gingery,
sandy, tawny, titian

rustic *adj, n*
▶ *adj* **1** PASTORAL, sylvan, bucolic, countrified,
country, countryside, rural
2 PLAIN, simple, rough, crude, coarse, rude, clumsy,
awkward, artless, homespun, ingenuous,
unsophisticated, unrefined, uncultured, provincial,
uncouth, graceless, indelicate, boorish, clodhopping,
oafish
formal maladroit
⊟ 1 urban **2** urbane, sophisticated, cultivated,
polished
▶ *n* bumpkin, countryman, countrywoman, oaf,
peasant, provincial, yokel, boor, churl, clodhopper,

clod, country cousin
colloq. hayseed, hick, hillbilly
⊟ sophisticate, dandy

rustle *v, n*
▶ *v* crackle, whoosh, swish, whisper, sigh
formal susurrate
▶ *n* crackle, crinkling, rustling, swish, whoosh,
whisper, whispering
formal crepitation, crepitus, susurration, susurrus

rusty *adj*
1 CORRODED, rusted, rust-covered, oxidized,
tarnished, discoloured, dull
2 RUST-COLOURED, reddish-brown, brown, red,
reddish, coppery, copper, auburn, chestnut, russet,
ginger, gingery, sandy, tawny, titian
3 UNPRACTISED, out of practice, weak, poor,
impaired, deficient, dated, old-fashioned, outmoded,
antiquated, stale, stiff, creaking

rut *n*
1 DITCH, channel, furrow, groove, gutter,
indentation, trough, track, gouge, pothole, wheelmark
2 ROUTINE, habit, pattern, system, humdrum, grind,
daily grind, treadmill, same old round/place, no
change of scenery

ruthless *adj*
merciless, pitiless, hard-hearted, hard, heartless,
unforgiving, unmerciful, unfeeling, unsparing,
callous, cruel, inhuman, grim, stern, vicious, brutal,
savage, barbarous, fierce, ferocious, relentless,
remorseless, unrelenting, inexorable, implacable,
harsh, severe, draconian
colloq. cut-throat, dog-eat-dog
⊟ merciful, compassionate

S

sable *adj*
dark, black, coal-black, pitch-black, pitch-dark, pitchy, ebony, inky, jet, dusky, sombre, midnight

sabotage *v, n*
► *v* damage, spoil, mar, disrupt, vandalize, wreck, destroy, thwart, ruin, scupper, cripple, incapacitate, disable, undermine, impair, weaken
► *n* vandalism, damage, impairment, disruption, wrecking, destruction, ruin, spoiling, crippling, disabling, weakening

sac *n*
bag, pocket, pouch, pod, bladder, capsule, follicle, cyst, saccule, vesicle
technical bursa, theca, vesica, vesicula
Related adjective: thecal

saccharine *adj*
sickly, sweet, sentimental, honeyed, cloying, maudlin, mawkish, nauseating, oversweet, sugary, syrupy, sickly-sweet
colloq. soppy, sloppy, mushy, gushy, schmaltzy
🔁 bitter, tart

sack¹ *v, n*
► *v sack 100 workers*
dismiss, fire, discharge, lay off, make redundant
colloq. axe, send packing, boot out, fire, give someone their cards, give someone the sack/push/boot/elbow, show someone the door
► *n* dismissal, discharge, your cards, notice, marching orders
colloq. the boot, the push, the elbow, the axe, the chop, papers, sacking, firing

sack² *v, n*
► *v the army sacked the town*
destroy, raid, plunder, ravage, raze, lay waste, waste, level, devastate, desecrate, demolish, maraud, pillage, rifle, rob, loot, ruin, rape, spoil, strip
formal depredate, despoil
► *n* destruction, devastation, ravage, razing, ruin, waste, levelling, looting, plunder, plundering, marauding, desecration, rape, pillage
formal depredation, despoliation, rapine

sacred *adj*
1 HOLY, divine, heavenly, blessed, hallowed, sanctified, consecrated, dedicated
2 RELIGIOUS, spiritual, devotional, ecclesiastical, priestly, saintly, godly
3 REVERED, venerable, respected, sacrosanct, inviolable, defended, protected, hallowed, untouchable, impregnable, secure
🔁 1 profane, secular 2 temporal

sacredness *n*
holiness, divinity, godliness, sanctity, solemnity, saintliness, sacrosanctity, invulnerability, inviolability
🔁 profaneness, worldliness

sacrifice *v, n*
► *v* 1 *sacrifice an animal in a religious ceremony*
offer, offer up, slaughter, immolate
2 GIVE UP, surrender, forfeit, relinquish, let go, abandon, renounce, forego
► *n* 1 OFFERING, immolation, slaughter, victim
formal oblation
2 GIVING-UP, destruction, surrender, abandonment, renunciation, loss

sacrificial *adj*
atoning, votive
formal oblatory, propitiatory, expiatory, reparative, piacular

sacrilege *n*
blasphemy, profanity, heresy, desecration, profanation, violation, outrage, irreligion, impiety, irreverence, disrespect, mockery
🔁 piety, reverence, respect

sacrilegious *adj*
blasphemous, profane, heretical, desecrating, disrespectful, irreverent, impious, irreligious, godless, ungodly, unholy
formal profanatory
🔁 pious, reverent, respectful

sacrosanct *adj*
sacred, hallowed, untouchable, inviolable, impregnable, protected, secure

sad *adj*
1 UNHAPPY, sorrowful, tearful, grief-stricken, heavy-hearted, upset, distressed, miserable, low-spirited, in low spirits, downcast, glum, long-faced, crestfallen, dejected, down-hearted, despondent, melancholy, depressed, mournful, doleful, wistful, joyless, gloomy, dismal, wretched
formal woebegone, disconsolate
colloq. fed up, blue, low, down, down in the dumps, (at) rock bottom
2 *sad news*
upsetting, distressing, painful, depressing, touching, poignant, heart-rending, heart-breaking, tragic, grievous, lamentable, regrettable, miserable, sorry, sorrowful, unfortunate, unhappy, serious, grave, calamitous, disastrous
3 *in a sad state*
grievous, lamentable, regrettable, deplorable, disgraceful, shameful, sorry, unfortunate, wretched, pitiful, pitiable
colloq. pathetic
🔁 1 happy, cheerful 2 fortunate, lucky 3 good

sadden *v*
upset, distress, grieve, depress, deject, dismay, discourage, dishearten, cast down, dispirit, break your heart, drive to despair
colloq. get someone down
🔁 cheer, please, gratify, delight

saddle *v*

burden, encumber, lumber, land, impose, tax, charge, load

sadism *n*

cruelty, inhumanity, brutality, savagery, viciousness, heartlessness, ruthlessness, unnaturalness, sado-masochism, spite, callousness, barbarity, bestiality
formal malevolence

sadistic *adj*

cruel, inhuman, brutal, savage, vicious, merciless, pitiless, barbarous, bestial, unnatural, perverted

sadness *n*

unhappiness, sorrow, sorrowfulness, grief, misery, misfortune, despondency, desolation, depression, dejection, cheerlessness, bleakness, joylessness, dolefulness, dismalness, poignancy, sombreness, mournfulness, distress, low spirits, glumness, gloominess, tearfulness, wretchedness, tragedy, pain, regret, pathos
formal disconsolateness, lugubriousness, melancholy, woe
colloq. heartache
🔁 happiness, cheerfulness, delight

safe *adj, n*

▶ *adj* **1** HARMLESS, innocuous, non-toxic, non-poisonous, uncontaminated
2 UNHARMED, undamaged, unscathed, uninjured, out of danger, unhurt, intact, secure, sound, protected, sheltered, defended, guarded, impregnable, invulnerable, unassailable, immune
colloq. out of harm's way, safe and sound, safe as houses, in good hands
3 DEPENDABLE, reliable, trustworthy, responsible, honest, honourable, sure, proven, tried, tested, sound, upright
4 UNADVENTUROUS, unenterprising, cautious, conservative
formal prudent, circumspect
🔁 **1** dangerous, harmful **2** vulnerable, at risk, exposed **3** risky **4** adventurous
▶ *n* cash box, deposit box, safety-deposit box, strongbox, chest, coffer, vault, depository, repository

safe-conduct *n*

authorization, pass, passport, permit, safeguard, warrant, licence, convoy, laissez-passer

safeguard *v, n*

▶ *v* protect, preserve, defend, look after, take care of, guard, shield, screen, shelter, secure
🔁 endanger, jeopardize
▶ *n* protection, defence, shield, security, surety, guarantee, assurance, insurance, cover, precaution, preventive, preventative

safekeeping *n*

protection, care, custody, keeping, charge, trust, guardianship, surveillance, supervision, ward, wardship

safety *n, adj*

▶ *n* **1** PROTECTION, security, safeguard, immunity, welfare, sanctuary, impregnability, safeness, harmlessness, soundness, reliability, dependability, trustworthiness
2 SANCTUARY, refuge, shelter, cover
🔁 **1** danger, jeopardy, risk
▶ *adj* precautionary, preventive, preventative, protective, fail-safe

sag *v, n*

▶ *v* **1** HANG LOOSELY, bend, give, bag, droop, hang
2 *prices/her spirits started to sag*
fall, drop, sink, dip, decline, slump, subside, flop, fail, flag, falter, weaken, wilt
🔁 **1** bulge **2** rise
▶ *n* drop, fall, low, low point, reduction, slump, slip, slide, dip, decline, depression, downturn, dwindling
🔁 peak, rise

saga *n*

chronicle, epic, history, narrative, adventure, story, tale, yarn, romance, soap opera, roman fleuve
formal epopee, epopeia, epos

sagacious *adj*

wise, discerning, insightful, penetrating, perceptive, far-sighted, able, intelligent, knowing, acute, sharp, astute, canny, quick, shrewd, smart, wary, wide-awake, wily, fly
formal prudent, judicious, percipient, perspicacious, sage, sapient
🔁 foolish, obtuse

sagacity *n*

wisdom, discernment, understanding, judgement, insight, foresight, penetration, sense, sharpness, shrewdness, acumen, knowingness, astuteness, acuteness, canniness, wariness, wiliness
formal prudence, judiciousness, percipience, perspicacity, sapience
🔁 folly, foolishness, obtuseness

sage *n, adj*

▶ *n* wise person, wise man, wise woman, teacher, master, expert, authority, pundit, savant, guru, maharishi, oracle, elder, philosopher, wiseacre, Solomon, mahatma, hakam
🔁 ignoramus
▶ *adj* wise, intelligent, discerning, knowing, learned, knowledgeable, astute, canny, politic, sensible
formal judicious, perspicacious, prudent, sagacious, sapient
🔁 foolish

sail *v*

1 *sail for France*
embark, set sail, leave port, weigh anchor, put to sea, put off, cruise, yacht, boat, ship, voyage
2 CAPTAIN, skipper, pilot, navigate, steer
3 GLIDE, plane, sweep, float, drift, coast, skim, scud, fly, wing, soar
▷ **sail into** attack, lay into, let fly, set about, tear into, turn on, assault
▷ **sail through** deal with successfully, succeed in/pass easily, romp through
🔁 scrape through

Types of sail include: Bermuda rig, canvas, course, foreroyal, foresail, forestaysail, foretop, fore-topgallant, fore-topsail, gaff sail, gaff-topsail, genoa, headsail, jib, jigger, kite, lateen sail, lugsail, main course, mainsail, maintopsail, mizzen, moonraker, rig, fore-and-aft rig, jury rig, royal, skysail, spanker, spinnaker, spritsail, square sail, staysail, studdingsail, topgallant, topsail, trysail.

sailor *n*

seafarer, mariner, seaman

Types of sailor include: AB, able seaman, bargee, bluejacket, boatman, boatswain, bosun, buccaneer, cabin boy, captain, cox, coxswain, crewman, deck hand, fisherman, galiongee, *US slang* gob, hearty, helmsman, Jack tar, lascar, leatherneck, *US colloq.* limey, marine, master, mate, *slang* matelot, navigator, oarsman, pilot, pirate, purser, rating, rower, salt, sculler, sea dog, skipper, *colloq.* tar, *Scot.* tarry-breeks, water rat, Wren, yachtsman, yachtswoman.

saintliness *n*
godliness, piety, devoutness, holiness, spirituality, blessedness, purity, spotlessness, faith, innocence, blamelessness, sinlessness, virtue, selflessness, morality, goodness, righteousness, sanctity, chastity, self-denial, self-sacrifice, asceticism, uprightness, unselfishness
E3 godlessness, unholiness, wickedness

saintly *adj*
saintlike, godly, pious, devout, God-fearing, holy, religious, spiritual, believing, blessed, angelic, pure, spotless, innocent, blameless, sinless, virtuous, moral, ethical, good, upright, worthy, righteous
E3 godless, unholy, wicked

sake *n*
benefit, advantage, good, welfare, wellbeing, gain, profit, behalf, interest, account, regard, respect, purpose, aim, goal, object, objective, cause, reason, consideration

salacious *adj*
prurient, bawdy, indecent, improper, obscene, scurrilous, pornographic, lecherous, lewd, carnal, coarse, erotic, horny, ribald, wanton, randy, lustful, raunchy, ruttish
formal concupiscent, lascivious, libidinous, lubricious
colloq. blue, smutty, steamy
E3 clean, decent, proper

salaried *adj*
paid, remunerated, waged, stipendiary
formal emolumental, emolumentary
E3 unpaid, voluntary, honorary

salary *n*
pay, remuneration, emolument, stipend, honorarium, wages, earnings, income, fee

sale *n*
selling, marketing, vending, bargaining, disposal, trade, market, traffic, transaction, deal
▷ **for sale** on sale, up for sale, available, obtainable, on the market, in the shops; *colloq.* up for grabs

Types of sale include: auction, autumn sale, bargain offer, bazaar, bazumble, boot-sale, bring-and-buy, car-boot sale, charity sale, church bazaar, clearance sale, closing-down sale, cold-call, end-of-line sale, end-of-season sale, exhibition, exposition, fair, fleamarket, forced sale, garage sale, grand opening sale, introductory offer, January sale, jumble sale, mail order, market, mid-season sale, on-promotion, open market, pre-season sale, private sale, public sale, pyramid selling, remainder sale, rummage sale, sale of bankrupt stock, sale of the century, sale of work, second-hand sale, special offer, spring sale, stocktaking sale, summer sale, tabletop sale, telesales, trade show, trash and treasure sale, winter sale.

saleable *adj*
marketable, merchantable, sought-after, desirable
formal vendible
E3 unmarketable, unsaleable

salesperson *n*
salesman, saleswoman, saleslady, sales assistant, clerk, salesclerk, shop assistant, shop-boy, shop-girl, salesgirl, shopkeeper, representative
colloq. rep

salient *adj*
important, significant, chief, main, principal, striking, arresting, conspicuous, noticeable, obvious, prominent, pronounced, outstanding, signal, remarkable

sallow *adj*
yellowish, pale, pallid, wan, waxen, pasty, sickly, jaundiced, unhealthy, anaemic, colourless
E3 rosy, healthy

sally[1] *v, n*
▶ *v* **1** RUSH, surge, attack, sortie, charge, breeze, venture, erupt, foray, issue
2 SAUNTER, stroll, wander, promenade
colloq. mosey
E3 **1** retreat
▶ *n* **1** RUSH, raid, assault, attack, foray, incursion, offensive, surge, sortie, thrust, venture, dash
2 EXCURSION, jaunt, wander, trip, drive, frolic, escapade
E3 **1** retire, retreat

sally[2] *n*
JOKE, retort, riposte, witticism, wisecrack, jest, crack, quip, *bon mot*, jeu d'esprit

salt *n, adj, v*
▶ *n* **1** *add a pinch of salt*
seasoning, taste, flavour, savour, relish, piquancy, pungency, smack, punch, rock-salt, sea-salt
2 LIVELINESS, zest, interest, wit, vigour, zip
formal trenchancy
3 SAILOR, seafarer, mariner, seaman, marine, rating
▶ *adj* salted, saltish, salty, saline, brackish, briny
E3 fresh
▶ *v* ▷ **salt away** store up, hoard, save, stash, stockpile, collect, cache, bank, accumulate, amass, hide
E3 spend, squander

salty *adj*
1 SALT, salted, saline, briny, brackish, savoury, spicy, piquant, tangy
2 LIVELY, vigorous, witty, exciting, stimulating, animated
formal trenchant
E3 fresh, sweet

salubrious *adj*
sanitary, hygienic, health-giving, healthy, healthful, wholesome, pleasant, beneficial, salutary, refreshing, invigorating

salutary *adj*
1 GOOD, beneficial, advantageous, profitable, valuable, helpful, useful, practical, timely
2 HEALTHY, sanitary, hygienic, health-giving, refreshing, invigorating

salutation *n*
greeting, address, welcome, salute, reverence, respects, homage
formal obeisance

salute *v, n*
▶ *v* **1** GREET, acknowledge, recognize, wave, hail, address, nod, bow, honour, present arms
2 HONOUR, acknowledge, recognize, mark,

celebrate, pay tribute to
▶ *n* **1** GREETING, acknowledgement, recognition, welcome, wave, gesture, hail, address, handshake, nod, bow, reverence
2 HONOUR, celebration, recognition, acknowledgement, tribute, homage

salvage *v*
save, preserve, conserve, rescue, recover, recuperate, retrieve, get back, reclaim, redeem, repair, restore, retain
F3 waste, abandon

salvation *n*
deliverance, liberation, rescue, saving, preservation, lifeline, redemption, reclamation
technical soteriology
Related adjective: soterial
F3 loss, damnation

salve *n, v*
▶ *n* ointment, lotion, cream, balm, liniment, medication, preparation, application
formal embrocation
▶ *v* ease, lighten, relieve, calm, comfort, soothe

same *adj, n*
▶ *adj* **1** IDENTICAL, twin, indistinguishable, equal, selfsame, the very same, one and the same, very, alike, like, similar, duplicate, carbon copy, comparable, equivalent, matching, corresponding, mutual, reciprocal, interchangeable, unchanging, substitutable, synonymous
formal aforementioned
2 UNCHANGING, consistent, uniform, unvarying, unvariable, changeless, unchanged
F3 **1** different **2** inconsistent, variable, changeable
▷ **all the same** nevertheless, nonetheless, still, anyway, even so, yet, however, by any means, in any case/event, by some means, anyhow, but, regardless, for all that; *formal* notwithstanding
▶ *n* the above-mentioned, the above-named, ditto
formal the aforementioned, the aforesaid

sameness *n*
changelessness, invariability, consistency, monotony, predictability, repetition, tedium, uniformity, standardization, resemblance, similarity, indistinguishability, likeness, identicalness, identity, oneness, duplication, déjà vu
F3 variety, difference

sample *n, v, adj*
▶ *n* specimen, example, cross-section, representative, model, pattern, type, test, sampling, swatch, piece, demonstration, illustration, instance, sign, indication, foretaste
▶ *v* try, test, taste, sip, inspect, examine, experience
▶ *adj* representative, specimen, demonstrative, illustrative, typical, dummy, trial, test, pilot

sanctify *v*
1 HALLOW, consecrate, make holy, make sacred, bless, anoint, dedicate, set apart, cleanse, purify, wash, absolve, exalt, canonize
2 SANCTION, authorize, allow, permit, approve, ratify, confirm, support, back, endorse, underwrite, accredit, license, warrant, legitimize
F3 **1** desecrate, defile **2** veto, forbid, disapprove

sanctimonious *adj*
self-righteous, holier-than-thou, pious, pietistic, moralizing, smug, superior, hypocritical, priggish, pharisaical
formal unctuous
colloq. goody-goody
F3 humble

sanctimoniousness *n*
self-righteousness, moralizing, righteousness, hypocrisy, self-satisfaction, priggishness, pietism, preachiness, complacency, cant, smugness, humbug, pharisaism
formal unctuousness
F3 humility

sanction *n, v*
▶ *n* **1** AUTHORIZATION, permission, agreement, approval, ratification, confirmation, support, backing, endorsement, licence, authority
formal approbation, accreditation
colloq. OK, go-ahead, green light, thumbs-up
2 *impose sanctions on a country*
restriction, boycott, embargo, ban, prohibition, penalty, deterrent, punishment, sentence
▶ *v* authorize, allow, permit, approve, ratify, confirm, support, back, endorse, underwrite, accredit, license, warrant, legitimize
formal accredit
colloq. OK, give the go-ahead to, give the green light to, give the thumbs-up to
F3 veto, forbid, disapprove

sanctity *n*
holiness, sacredness, inviolability, piety, godliness, saintliness, blessedness, religiousness, devotion, grace, spirituality, purity, goodness, virtue, righteousness
F3 unholiness, secularity, worldliness, godlessness, impurity

sanctuary *n*
1 CHURCH, temple, tabernacle, shrine, altar, place of worship, holy place, holy of holies
formal sanctum, sanctum sanctorum
2 ASYLUM, refuge, protection, shelter, haven, retreat, hideout, hideaway
3 SAFETY, protection, security, safeguard, immunity
4 RESERVE, reservation, park, area, enclave, tract, preserve

sanctum *n*
1 HOLY PLACE, holy of holies, shrine, sanctuary
formal sanctum sanctorum
2 REFUGE, retreat, den, hideaway, hideout, study, cubbyhole

sand *n*
beach, shore, strand, sands, seashore, desert, wilderness, grit, rock
Related adjectives: arenaceous, sabulous

sandbank *n*
dune, reef, sand bar, sandhill, bar, hurst, key, yardang

sandy *adj*
gritty, ginger, rusty, tawny, reddish, reddish-yellow, yellow, yellowish, yellowy, gingerous, gingery, auburn, coppery, red, titian
technical arenaceous, psammitic

sane *adj*
normal, rational, right-minded, balanced, lucid, in your right mind, of sound mind, stable, sound, sober, level-headed, sensible, responsible, wise, reasonable, moderate
formal judicious
colloq. all there
F3 insane, mad, crazy, foolish

sang-froid *n*
composure, self-control, poise, self-possession, indifference, equanimity, assurance, calmness, dispassion, cool-headedness, nonchalance, coolness, imperturbability
formal aplomb, phlegm
colloq. nerve, cool, unflappability
E3 discomposure, excitability, hysteria, panic

sanguinary *adj*
bloody, bloodied, gory, grim, bloodthirsty, brutal, cruel, merciless, murderous, savage, pitiless, ruthless

sanguine *adj*
1 CHEERFUL, confident, hopeful, lively, expectant, optimistic, over-confident, over-optimistic, assured, animated, ardent, buoyant, spirited, unabashed, unbowed
2 RUDDY, rosy, florid, red, pink, fresh-complexioned, fresh, flushed
formal rubicund
E3 1 cynical, depressive, gloomy, melancholy, pessimistic 2 pale, sallow

sanitary *adj*
clean, pure, uncontaminated, unpolluted, aseptic, antiseptic, germ-free, disinfected, sterile, hygienic, healthy, wholesome
formal salubrious
E3 insanitary, unwholesome

sanity *n*
normality, rationality, reason, sense, common sense, good sense, balance of mind, soundness of mind, lucidity, right-mindedness, stability, soundness, level-headedness, wisdom, responsibility
formal judiciousness, prudence
E3 insanity, madness

sap *v, n*
▶ *v* bleed, drain, exhaust, weaken, wear down/away, erode, enfeeble, undermine, deplete, reduce, diminish, impair
formal enervate, debilitate
E3 strengthen, build up, increase
▶ *n* 1 *sap in a plant*
lifeblood, vital fluid, juice, essence, vigour, energy
2 FOOL, idiot, imbecile, moron
colloq. clot, twit, nit, nitwit; *slang* jerk, prat, git, fink

sarcasm *n*
irony, satire, mockery, sneering, ridicule, scoffing, derision, scorn, contempt, gibing, cynicism, resentment, acidity, spitefulness, bitterness
formal acrimony, trenchancy

sarcastic *adj*
ironical, satirical, mocking, snide, taunting, sneering, derisive, derisory, scornful, sardonic, jeering, scoffing, scathing, cynical, incisive, cutting, biting, caustic
formal disparaging, acrimonious, acerbic, mordant
colloq. sarky

sardonic *adj*
mocking, jeering, sneering, derisive, scornful, contemptuous, sarcastic, dry, biting, cruel, heartless, malicious, cynical, bitter
formal acrimonious, acerbic, mordant

sash *n*
belt, girdle, waistband, cummerbund, cincture

Satan *n*
the Devil, the Enemy, the Adversary, the Evil One, the Tempter, Beelzebub, Lucifer, Old Nick, Prince of Darkness, Mephistopheles, Belial, Apollyon, Abaddon

satanic *adj*
satanical, diabolical, devilish, demonic, fiendish, hellish, infernal, damned, accursed, inhuman, wicked, evil, sinful, abominable, black, dark
formal malevolent, iniquitous
E3 holy, divine, godly, saintly, benevolent

sate *v*
satisfy, overfill, saturate, surfeit, fill, glut, gorge, gratify, cloy, sicken, slake
formal satiate
E3 deprive, dissatisfy, starve

satellite *n*
1 ORBITING BODY, natural/artificial satellite, spacecraft, moon, planet, spaceship, sputnik
2 DEPENDANT, hanger-on, parasite, sycophant, subordinate, follower, attendant, aide, adherent, disciple, minion, lackey, sidekick, retainer, vassal
colloq. puppet

satiate *v*
sate, overfill, overfeed, satisfy, gorge, slake, glut, cloy, engorge, stuff, surfeit, jade, nauseate
E3 deprive, dissatisfy, underfeed

satiety *n*
satiation, saturation, satisfaction, gratification, fullness, over-fullness, overindulgence, surfeit
formal repleteness, repletion

satire *n*
ridicule, irony, sarcasm, wit, burlesque, lampoon, skit, parody, caricature, travesty
colloq. send-up, spoof, take-off, mickey-taking;
slang piss-taking

satirical *adj*
ironical, sarcastic, mocking, ridiculing, irreverent, taunting, derisive, sardonic, incisive, cutting, biting, caustic, cynical, bitter
formal trenchant, acerbic, mordant, acrimonious

satirist *n*
cartoonist, mocker, parodist, ridiculer, caricaturist, lampooner, lampoonist
formal pasquilant, pasquiler, pasquinader

satirize *v*
ridicule, mock, make fun of, poke fun at, burlesque, lampoon, parody, caricature, criticize
formal deride
colloq. send up, take off, take the mickey out of;
slang take the piss out of
E3 acclaim, honour

satisfaction *n*
1 GRATIFICATION, contentment, happiness, pleasure, enjoyment, delight, comfort, ease, well-being, fulfilment, self-satisfaction, pride, sense of achievement
2 SETTLEMENT, compensation, reimbursement, indemnification, indemnity, damages, reparation, amends, redress, recompense, requital, vindication, restitution
E3 1 dissatisfaction, displeasure

satisfactory *adj*
acceptable, passable, up to the mark, all right, fair, average, competent, adequate, fine, sufficient, suitable, proper
colloq. OK, up to scratch
E3 unsatisfactory, unacceptable, inadequate

satisfied *adj*
1 HAPPY, contented, pleased, self-satisfied, content, smug
2 CONVINCED, reassured, persuaded, sure, certain, positive, pacified
3 FULL, sated, satiated
formal replete
1 dissatisfied; *colloq.* disgruntled
2 unconvinced **3** hungry

satisfy *v*
1 GRATIFY, indulge, content, please, delight, appease, quench, slake, sate, satiate, surfeit
formal assuage
2 *satisfy requirements*
meet, fulfil, discharge, settle, answer, fill, be sufficient for, be adequate for, serve, qualify
formal comply with, suffice
3 ASSURE, reassure, convince, persuade
4 COMPENSATE FOR, indemnify, make reparation for
formal appease, placate, requite
1 dissatisfy **2** fail

satisfying *adj*
pleasing, fulfilling, gratifying, cheering, pleasurable, satisfactory, convincing, persuasive, filling, cool, refreshing
dissatisfying, frustrating, unsatisfactory

saturate *v*
1 SOAK, make wet through, wet, steep, flood, souse, drench, waterlog
2 IMPREGNATE, permeate, imbue, pervade, suffuse, fill, overfill, sate, glut, surfeit

saturated *adj*
1 SOAKED, soaking, sopping, dripping, soused, steeped, drenched, flooded, wringing, waterlogged, sodden
2 IMBUED, impregnated, permeated, suffused

saturnine *adj*
morose, gloomy, unfriendly, sombre, severe, austere, dismal, dour, dull, grave, melancholy, moody, glum, stern, heavy, withdrawn, taciturn, uncommunicative, phlegmatic
cheerful, jovial

sauce *n*
1 DRESSING, relish, condiment, flavouring, dip, mayonnaise
2 CHEEKINESS, cheek, impudence, impertinence, presumption, presumptuousness, audacity, freshness, flippancy, pertness, backchat, brazenness, insolence, disrespectfulness, disrespect, irreverence, rudeness, sass
formal malapertness
colloq. brass, lip, nerve, sauciness, mouth
2 politeness, respectfulness

saucy *adj*
impertinent, impudent, insolent, brazen, presumptuous, disrespectful, irreverent, rude, pert, forward, presumptuous, flippant
colloq. cheeky, fresh, lippy; *US* sassy
polite, respectful

saunter *v, n*
▶ *v* stroll, amble, wander, ramble, meander
old use promenade
colloq. mosey, mooch
▶ *n* stroll, amble, walk, constitutional, ramble

old use promenade
colloq. mosey, mooch

savage *adj, n, v*
▶ *adj* wild, untamed, undomesticated, uncivilized, primitive, barbaric, barbarous, fierce, ferocious, vicious, beastly, cruel, terrible, inhuman, grim, brutal, sadistic, bloodthirsty, bloody, murderous, pitiless, merciless, ruthless, harsh
old use fell
formal feral
colloq. cut-throat, dog-eat-dog
tame, civilized, humane, mild
▶ *n* brute, boor, churl, beast, monster, barbarian, wild person, wild man, wild woman
▶ *v* **1** *savaged by a dog*
attack, bite, claw, tear, tear to pieces, lacerate, maul, mangle
2 *savaged by the critics*
attack, denounce
colloq. slate, slam, run down, tear to pieces, tear to shreds

savagery *n*
cruelty, fierceness, ferocity, viciousness, wildness, roughness, barbarity, bestiality, brutality, inhumanity, ruthlessness, mercilessness, pitilessness, murderousness, bloodthirstiness, brutishness, sadism, primitiveness
formal ferity
civilization, civility, humanity

savant *n*
authority, scholar, intellectual, pundit, guru, mastermind, man/woman of letters, master, philosopher
formal sage
amateur, ignoramus

save *v*
1 RESCUE, come to the rescue of, deliver, liberate, free, set free, release, get someone out of, redeem, salvage, recover, reclaim
colloq. bail out
2 *save food*
conserve, preserve, keep, retain, hold, reserve, store, lay up, set aside, put by, put aside, hoard, stockpile, collect, gather
colloq. stash
3 ECONOMIZE, cut back, cut costs, use less, budget, buy cheaply, live on the cheap, be thrifty, scrimp and save
colloq. tighten your belt, cut your coat according to your cloth
4 PROTECT, guard, screen, keep, shield, safeguard, keep safe, preserve, spare, prevent, hinder
formal obviate
2 waste, discard **3** spend, squander

saving *adj, n*
▶ *adj* **1** ECONOMICAL, careful, sparing, thrifty, frugal
2 *a saving grace*
qualifying, compensatory, extenuating, mitigating
▶ *n* **1** ECONOMY, thrift, discount, reduction, bargain, cut, conservation, preservation
2 *put your savings in the bank*
capital, investments, nest egg, fund, store, reserves, resources
1 expense, loss, waste **2** expenditure

saviour *n*
1 RESCUER, deliverer, redeemer, liberator,

emancipator, guardian, protector, defender, champion
2 *Jesus Christ, the Saviour*
Redeemer, Deliverer, Lamb of God, Mediator, Emmanuel
F3 1 destroyer

savoir-faire *n*

capability, ability, accomplishment, confidence, assurance, discretion, expertise, finesse, poise, diplomacy, tact, urbanity
colloq. know-how
F3 awkwardness, clumsiness, incompetence, inexperience

savour *n, v*

▶ *n* **1** TASTE, flavour, smack, tang, piquancy, salt, spice, relish, zest
2 SMELL, aroma, bouquet, fragrance, perfume, scent
3 TRACE, hint, suggestion, touch, smattering
▶ *v* **1** RELISH, taste to the full, enjoy, enjoy to the full, delight in, take pleasure in, revel in, like, appreciate
2 SMACK, suggest, speak, spell, seem like, have all the signs of, have the hallmarks of
F3 1 shrink from

savoury *adj, n*

▶ *adj* **1** TASTY, flavoursome, appetizing, delicious, mouthwatering, luscious, palatable
colloq. yummy, scrumptious
2 *savoury pancakes*
salty, spicy, aromatic, piquant, tangy
F3 1 unappetizing, tasteless, insipid **2** sweet
▶ *n* appetizer, snack, hors d'oeuvre, bonne-bouche, canapé

saw[1] *n*
use a saw to cut wood

> *Kinds of saw include*: band-saw, bench saw, chainsaw, circular saw, compass saw, coping-saw, crosscut saw, fretsaw, hacksaw, handsaw, jigsaw, panel saw, power-driven saw, pruning-saw, rabbet saw, radial-arm saw, ripsaw, scroll-saw, tenon saw.

saw[2] *n*
SAYING, byword, proverb, maxim, aphorism, adage, axiom, dictum, epigram, commonplace, gnome, mot
formal apophthegm

say *v, n*

▶ *v* **1** EXPRESS, phrase, put, put into words, speak, mention, render, utter, voice, articulate, enunciate, pronounce, deliver, speak, rehearse, recite, repeat, perform, read, indicate
formal orate
2 ANSWER, reply, respond, rejoin, retort, exclaim, comment, remark, observe, mention, add, drawl, mutter, grunt
formal ejaculate
3 TELL, instruct, order, communicate, convey, intimate, report, announce, declare, state, assert, affirm, maintain, claim, allege, rumour, suggest, imply, signify, reveal, disclose, divulge
4 GUESS, estimate, reckon, judge, imagine, suppose, assume, presume, surmise
▷ **that is to say** ie, that is, in other words

> *Other words for say include*: accuse, acknowledge, add, admit, admonish, advise, affirm, agree, allege, announce, answer, argue, ask, assert, assume, *formal* aver, *formal* avow, babble, banter, bark, bawl, beg, begin, bellow, blare, blaspheme, blurt, boast, brag, call, chant, chatter, claim, coax, *colloq.* come out with, command, comment, communicate,

> complain, conclude, confide, *formal* conjecture, continue, contradict, convey, correct, counter, croak, cry, curse, declare, demand, deny, describe, detail, disclose, dispute, divulge, echo, elaborate, elucidate, emphasize, enjoin, estimate, exclaim, expostulate, express, falter, finish, flounder, gasp, greet, groan, growl, grumble, grunt, guess, hint, howl, imagine, implore, imply, indicate, infer, inform, inquire, insinuate, insist, instruct, interrogate, interrupt, intervene, intimate, jeer, jest, joke, laugh, lecture, lie, maintain, make known, make public, mention, mimic, moan, mock, mouth, mumble, murmur, mutter, nag, observe, offer, orate, order, persist, persuade, phrase, pipe, plead, point out, predict, press, presume, proclaim, profess, proffer, prompt, pronounce, propose, protest, *colloq.* put about, query, question, quote, rage, rail, rant, read, reassure, rebuke, recite, reckon, recommend, rehearse, reiterate, rejoice, relate, remark, remonstrate, renounce, repeat, reply, report, respond, request, resolve, respond, retaliate, retort, retract, reveal, roar, rumour, scoff, scold, scream, screech, shout, shriek, snap, snarl, speak, specify, speculate, squeak, stammer, state, storm, stutter, submit, suggest, suppose, surmise, swear, sympathize, taunt, tease, tell, testify, thunder, urge, utter, venture, voice, volunteer, vow, whine, whisper, wonder, yell.

▶ *n* **1** *have a say in something*
voice, word, opinion, vote, right to express yourself, opportunity to speak, turn/chance to speak
2 *have no say in the matter*
influence, power, authority, sway, weight
colloq. clout

saying *n*
adage, proverb, dictum, precept, axiom, aphorism, maxim, motto, slogan, phrase, catch phrase, cliché, platitude, expression, quotation, epigram, statement, remark, word/pearl of wisdom
formal apophthegm

say-so *n*
authorization, permission, agreement, approval, affirmation, authority, backing, assertion, assurance, word, guarantee, ratification, sanction
formal asseveration, consent, dictum
colloq. OK

scaffold *n*
1 PLATFORM, framework, scaffolding, gantry, tower
2 GALLOWS, gibbet, the rope

scald *v*
burn, sear, brand, scorch, blister
formal cauterize

scale[1] *n, v*
▶ *n* **1** *the Richter scale*
graduation, calibration, system of measurement, measuring system, register
2 EXTENT, level, degree, measure, spread, reach, range, scope, compass, spectrum, gamut
3 *What is the scale of the map?*
ratio, proportion, relative size
4 SEQUENCE, series, gamut, progression, hierarchy, ranking, order, ladder
colloq. pecking order
▶ *v* climb, go up, ascend, mount, clamber, scramble, shin up, conquer, surmount
▷ **scale down** decrease, make less, lessen, reduce, cut back/down, drop, contract, shrink

scale[2] *n*
scale in a kettle; scales on a fish
encrustation, deposit, crust, layer, coat, coating, limescale, tartar, plaque, film, lamina, plate, flake,

scurf, furfur
formal squama
Related adjective: squamose

scaliness *n*
dandruff, flakiness, furfur, scurfiness, scabrousness
formal squamosity

scaly *adj*
flaky, scurfy, scabby, scabrous, rough, branny
formal lepidote, furfuraceous, furfurous, squamose,
squamous, squamulose, desquamative, desquamatory

scamp *n*
rogue, rascal, scallywag, monkey, mischief-maker,
troublemaker, imp, devil, wretch
colloq. whippersnapper

scamper *v*
scuttle, scurry, scoot, dart, dash, run, sprint, rush,
hurry, race, scramble, fly, romp, frolic, gambol
formal hasten

scan *v, n*
▶ *v* 1 EXAMINE, scrutinize, inspect, study, search,
survey, sweep, investigate, check
2 SKIM, have a quick look at, browse through,
run through, run over, go over, glance at, flick through,
flip through, thumb through, leaf through, run your
eye over
▶ *n* screening, examination, scrutiny, inspection,
search, probe, check, study, investigation, test, survey,
review

scandal *n*
1 OUTRAGE, offence, outcry, uproar, furore, discredit,
dishonour, disgrace, shame, embarrassment,
ignominy
formal obloquy, opprobrium
2 GOSSIP, rumours, libel, slander, smear, dirt
formal defamation, calumny
colloq. dirty linen/washing/laundry, skeleton in the
cupboard
3 DISGRACE, shame, pity, reproach, blot, slur, smear,
stain, black mark
colloq. crying shame

scandalize *v*
shock, horrify, appal, dismay, disgust, repel, revolt,
offend, insult, affront, outrage

scandalmonger *n*
gossip, gossip-monger, tattler, tattle, talebearer,
busybody, quidnunc
formal calumniator, defamer, traducer
colloq. muck-raker, nosy parker

scandalous *adj*
shocking, appalling, atrocious, abominable,
monstrous, unspeakable, outrageous, blatant, flagrant,
disgraceful, shameful, disreputable, dishonourable,
infamous, improper, malicious, scurrilous,
slanderous, libellous, untrue
formal unseemly, defamatory, opprobrious
colloq. juicy

scant *adj*
little, sparse, limited, little or no, bare, deficient,
minimal, hardly any, inadequate, insufficient
formal exiguous
colloq. measly
🖙 adequate, ample, sufficient

scanty *adj*
deficient, short, inadequate, insufficient, scant, little,
limited, restricted, narrow, poor, meagre,

insubstantial, thin, skimpy, sparse, bare
🖙 adequate, sufficient, ample, plentiful, substantial

scapegoat *n*
victim, whipping-boy, sucker
colloq. fall guy; *US slang* patsy

scar *n, v*
▶ *n* mark, lesion, wound, injury, shock, trauma,
defacement, disfigurement, discolouration, blemish,
blotch, stigma
▶ *v* mark, deface, disfigure, discolour, spoil, damage,
injure, shock, traumatize, brand, stigmatize

scarce *adj*
few, rare, infrequent, uncommon, unusual, sparse,
scanty, scant, meagre, in short supply, too little, not
enough, insufficient, inadequate, deficient, lacking
colloq. few and far between, like gold dust
🖙 plentiful, common

scarcely *adv*
1 *I can scarcely hear you*
hardly, barely, only just
2 *that is scarcely a reason to hit him*
hardly, not, not at all, certainly not, definitely not

scarcity *n*
lack, shortage, dearth, deficiency, insufficiency,
rareness, rarity, infrequency, uncommonness,
sparseness, scantness, scantiness
formal paucity, want, exiguity
🖙 glut, plenty, abundance, sufficiency, enough

scare *v, n*
▶ *v* frighten, startle, alarm, make afraid, make
frightened, dismay, daunt, intimidate, unnerve,
threaten, menace, terrorize, shock, appal, panic,
terrify, petrify
formal perturb
colloq. rattle, scare out of your wits, make your blood
run cold, scare the living daylights out of, make your
hair stand on end, make your flesh creep, make
someone jump out of their skin, put the frighteners on,
put the wind up; *slang* scare the shit out of
🖙 reassure, calm
▶ *n* fright, start, shock, alarm, panic, hysteria,
horror, terror, fearfulness
🖙 reassurance, comfort

scared *adj*
afraid, frightened, fearful, nervous, anxious, worried,
startled, alarmed, cowed, shaken, panic-stricken,
panicky, quivery, terrified, petrified, terrorized,
terror-stricken, unnerved, jittery, nervous
colloq. scared out of your wits, scared to death,
with your heart in your mouth, shaking like a leaf,
having kittens, in a blue funk
🖙 confident, reassured

scaremonger *n*
alarmist, pessimist, prophet of doom, doom and
gloom merchant, doomwatcher, jitterbug, Cassandra

scarf *n*
headscarf, headsquare, kerchief, neckerchief, muffler,
necktie, shawl, stole, cravat, babushka

scarper *v*
leave, depart, go, run away, vanish, disappear, abscond,
bolt, escape, flee, decamp, flit
colloq. clear off, beat it, bunk off, run for it, scram,
skedaddle, vamoose, hightail it, do a bunk

scary *adj*
frightening, alarming, daunting, formidable,

fearsome, forbidding, intimidating, disturbing, shocking, horrifying, terrifying, petrifying, hair-raising, bloodcurdling, spine-chilling, chilling, creepy, eerie
colloq. spooky, hairy

scathing *adj*
sarcastic, scornful, critical, cutting, biting, stinging, caustic, acid, vitriolic, ferocious, fierce, severe, bitter, harsh, brutal, savage, unsparing
formal trenchant, mordant
F∃ complimentary

scatter *v*
disperse, dispel, dissipate, disband, disunite, separate, divide, break up, disintegrate, diffuse, broadcast, spread, sprinkle, sow, strew, fling, shower
formal disseminate
F∃ gather, collect

scatterbrained *adj*
forgetful, absent-minded, empty-headed, feather-brained, hare-brained, careless, inattentive, thoughtless, unreliable, impulsive, irresponsible, wool-gathering, frivolous, slaphappy, carefree
colloq. scatty, having your head in the clouds
F∃ sensible, sober, efficient, careful

scattering *n*
sprinkling, few, handful, smattering, break-up
F∃ mass, abundance

scavenge *v*
forage, rummage, rake, search, look for, hunt, scrounge

scavenger *n*
rummager, scavager, forager, scrounger, raker

scenario *n*
1 SITUATION, scene, circumstances, state, state of affairs, sequence of events, plan, programme
2 OUTLINE, synopsis, summary, résumé, storyline, script, screenplay, plot, scheme, plan, programme, projection, sequence

scene *n*
1 PLACE, area, spot, location, locale, site, situation, position, whereabouts, locality, environment, milieu, setting, context, background, backdrop, arena, set, stage
2 LANDSCAPE, scenery, panorama, view, vista, outlook, prospect, sight, spectacle, picture, tableau, pageant
3 EPISODE, incident, proceeding, part, division, act, clip
4 *don't make a scene*
fuss, commotion, outburst, furore, performance, drama, exhibition, display, show
colloq. to-do, kerfuffle
5 *not my scene*
area of interest, area of activity, field, area, speciality

scenery *n*
landscape, terrain, panorama, view, vista, outlook, prospect, scene, background, setting, surroundings, backdrop, set, *mise-en-scène*

scenic *adj*
panoramic, picturesque, attractive, pretty, beautiful, grand, striking, impressive, spectacular, breathtaking, awe-inspiring
F∃ dull, dreary

scent *n, v*
▶ *n* 1 FRAGRANCE, aroma, perfume, bouquet, smell, odour
formal redolence
2 PERFUME, essence, cologne, eau-de-cologne, eau-de-toilette, toilet water
3 *follow the scent*
track, trail, trace, spoor
F∃ 1 stink
▶ *v* 1 SMELL, sniff (out), nose (out), track, trail, trace
2 SENSE, become aware of, become conscious of, perceive, detect, discern, recognize

scented *adj*
perfumed, fragrant, sweet-smelling, aromatic
F∃ malodorous, stinking

sceptic *n*
doubter, unbeliever, disbeliever, agnostic, atheist, rationalist, questioner, scoffer, cynic, doubting Thomas
F∃ believer

sceptical *adj*
doubting, doubtful, unconvinced, unbelieving, disbelieving, incredulous, questioning, distrustful, mistrustful, hesitating, hesitant, dubious, suspicious, scoffing, cynical, pessimistic
F∃ convinced, confident, trusting

scepticism *n*
doubt, unbelief, disbelief, hesitancy, agnosticism, atheism, rationalism, distrust, doubtfulness, dubiety, suspicion, incredulity, cynicism, pessimism
F∃ belief, faith

schedule *n, v*
▶ *n* timetable, programme, agenda, diary, calendar, itinerary, plan, scheme, list, syllabus, inventory, catalogue, table, form
▶ *v* timetable, time, table, programme, plan, organize, arrange, appoint, assign, book, list

schematic *adj*
diagrammatic, representational, symbolic, illustrative, graphic

scheme *n, v*
▶ *n* 1 PROGRAMME, schedule, plan, project, strategy, tactics, system, method, procedure, course of action, idea, proposal, proposition, suggestion, draft, outline, blueprint, schema, diagram, chart, map, layout, sketch, pattern, design, shape, arrangement
formal configuration, disposition, delineation
2 INTRIGUE, plot, conspiracy, device, stratagem, ruse, ploy, shift, manoeuvre, tactic(s), strategy
formal machinations
▶ *v* plot, conspire, connive, collude, intrigue, manoeuvre, manipulate, pull strings, mastermind, plan, project, contrive, devise, frame, work out
formal machinate

schemer *n*
plotter, intriguer, politician, conniver, deceiver, mastermind, intrig(u)ant(e), Machiavelli, Machiavellian, éminence grise, fox
formal machinator
colloq. wangler, wheeler-dealer, wire-puller

scheming *adj*
crafty, cunning, deceitful, sly, underhand, unscrupulous, wily, devious, artful, calculating, conniving, designing, insidious, tricky, slippery, foxy, Machiavellian
formal duplicitous
F∃ artless, honest, open, transparent

schism *n*
1 DIVISION, split, rift, rupture, break, breach, disunion, separation, severance, discord
formal estrangement
2 SPLINTER, group, faction, sect, detachment

scholar *n*
1 STUDENT, pupil, learner, schoolchild, schoolboy, schoolgirl
2 ACADEMIC, intellectual, authority, expert, philosopher, mastermind, pundit
colloq. egghead, bookworm

scholarly *adj*
learned, erudite, lettered, academic, scholastic, school, intellectual, highbrow, bookish, studious, knowledgeable, well-read, conscientious, analytical, scientific
E3 uneducated, illiterate

scholarship *n*
1 LEARNING, learnedness, knowledge, wisdom, education, schooling, academic achievements/attainments
formal erudition
2 *a scholarship to a public school*
grant, award, bursary, endowment, fellowship, exhibition

scholastic *adj*
academic, scholarly, educational, pedagogic, learned, lettered, literary, bookish, analytical, pedantic, precise

school *n, v*
▶ *n* **1** *go to school*
college, academy, institute, institution, university, seminary, faculty, department, division, discipline, class, group, pupils, students, yeshiva(h),
See also **educational establishments**.
2 *a school of artists*
group, set, circle, clique, coterie, faction, association, club, society, guild, league, company
▶ *v* educate, teach, instruct, tutor, coach, train, discipline, drill, verse, prime, prepare, indoctrinate

schooling *n*
education, learning, book-learning, teaching, instruction, tuition, coaching, training, drill, preparation, grounding, guidance, indoctrination

schoolteacher *n*
teacher, instructor, educator, schoolmaster, master, schoolmistress, mistress, schoolmarm, pedagogue

science *n*
technology, discipline, specialization, knowledge, skill, proficiency, expertise, technique, dexterity, art

Sciences include: acoustics, aerodynamics, aeronautics, agricultural science, anatomy, anthropology, archaeology, astronomy, astrophysics, behavioural science, biochemistry, biology, biophysics, botany, chemistry, chemurgy, climatology, computer science, cybernetics, diagnostics, dietetics, domestic science, dynamics, earth science, ecology, economics, electrodynamics, electronics, engineering, entomology, environmental science, food science, genetics, geochemistry, geographical science, geology, geophysics, graphology, hydraulics, information technology, inorganic chemistry, life science, linguistics, macrobiotics, materials science, mathematics, mechanical engineering, mechanics, medical science, metallurgy, meteorology, microbiology, mineralogy, morphology, natural science, nuclear physics, organic chemistry, ornithology, pathology, pharmacology, physics, physiology, political science, psychology, radiochemistry, robotics, sociology, space technology, telecommunications, thermodynamics, toxicology, ultrasonics, veterinary science, zoology.

scientific *adj*
methodical, systematic, controlled, regulated, orderly, analytical, mathematical, exact, precise, accurate, scholarly, thorough

scientific instruments

Types of scientific instrument include: absorptiometer, barostat, cathode ray oscilloscope, centrifuge, chronograph, coherer, collimator, cryostat, decoherer, dephlegmator, dipleidoscope, electromyograph, electrosonde, eudiometer, fluoroscope, Fresnel lens, Geissler tube, heliograph, heliostat, hodoscope, humidistat, hydrophone, hydroscope, hydrostat, hygrograph, hygrostat, iconoscope, image converter, image tube, interferometer, microtome, nephograph, optical character reader, oscillograph, oscilloscope, pantograph, parametric amplifier, phonendoscope, radarscope, radiosonde, rheocord, rheostat, slide-rule, spectroscope, stactometer, stauroscope, strobe, stroboscope, tachistoscope, tachograph, teinoscope, telemeter, telethermoscope, tesla coil, thermostat, thyratron, torsion-balance, transformer, transponder, tunnel diode, vernier, zymoscope. *See also* **laboratory apparatus; measuring instruments; medical equipment**.

scintillate *v*
sparkle, spark, shine, flash, gleam, glint, glisten, glitter, twinkle, blaze, wink
formal coruscate

scintillating *adj*
sparkling, glittering, flashing, bright, shining, brilliant, dazzling, exciting, stimulating, lively, animated, vivacious, witty, exhilarating, invigorating
formal ebullient
E3 dull

scion *n*
1 CHILD, descendant, offspring, heir, successor
2 OFFSHOOT, shoot, branch, sprout, graft, twig

scoff[1] *v*
scoff at something
mock, ridicule, laugh at, poke fun, taunt, tease, jeer, sneer, gibe, scorn, despise, revile, belittle
formal deride, disparage
colloq. rib, pooh-pooh, knock
E3 praise, compliment, flatter

scoff[2] *v, n*
▶ *v* *scoff food*
eat, consume, devour, finish off, gobble, guzzle, bolt, gulp
colloq. put away, wolf
▶ *n* food, foodstuffs, comestibles, provisions, meal, refreshments, sustenance, nourishment, nutrition, nutriment, subsistence
colloq. eatables, eats, tuck; *slang* grub, nosh, nosh-up; *US* chow

scoffing *adj*
mocking, taunting, sneering, derisive, scathing, cynical, sarcastic, fiendish, Mephistophelian
formal disparaging

scold *v*
reprimand, reprove, rebuke, chide, take to task,

reproach, blame, censure, lecture, nag
formal admonish, upbraid, castigate, berate, lambaste
colloq. tell off, tick off, give someone a piece of your mind, give a dressing-down, read the riot act to, haul over the coals, rap over the knuckles
F3 praise, commend

scolding *n*
telling-off, reprimand, reproof, rebuke, lecture, talking-to
formal castigation, upbraiding
colloq. a piece of your mind, ticking-off, dressing-down, carpeting, wigging, earful
F3 praise, commendation

scoop *n, v*
▶ *n* **1** LADLE, spoon, dipper, bailer, bucket, shovel
2 EXCLUSIVE, coup, inside story, revelation, exposé, sensation
colloq. latest
▶ *v* gouge, scrape, hollow, empty, excavate, dig, shovel, remove, ladle, spoon, dip, bail

scoot *v*
rush, hurry, dash, dart, career, bolt, shoot, run, sprint, zip, scurry, scud, scuttle, tootle
colloq. vamoose, skedaddle, beat it, scarper

scope *n*
1 RANGE, compass, field, area, sphere, ambit, terms of reference, realm, confines, limits, reach, orbit, extent, span, sweep, breadth, coverage
2 *scope for improvement*
room, space, capacity, elbow-room, latitude, leeway, freedom, liberty, opportunity

scorch *v*
burn, singe, char, blacken, discolour, scald, roast, sear, parch, shrivel, wither, dry up

scorching *adj*
burning, roasting, sizzling, blistering, sweltering, torrid, tropical, searing, red-hot
colloq. boiling, baking

score *n, v*
▶ *n* **1** RESULT, goals, runs, hits, total, sum, tally, points, marks, record, outcome
2 SCRATCH, line, groove, mark, cut, gouge, incision, nick, notch, gash, slit, scrape
3 *scores of people*
crowds, lots, masses, multitudes, hundreds, thousands, millions, myriads, swarms, shoals, droves, hosts, legions
4 REASON, grounds, basis, motives, explanation, case, argument
5 *no worries on that score*
matter, subject, question, issue, concern, aspect
6 *settle old scores*
grievance, grudge, complaint, dispute, quarrel, argument, bone of contention
▶ *v* **1** RECORD, register, get, count, total, keep a tally, make, earn, gain, achieve, attain, win, have the advantage, have the edge, be one up
colloq. chalk up, notch up, hit the jackpot
2 SCRATCH, scrape, graze, mark, groove, gouge, cut, incise, engrave, indent, nick, slit, gash, slash, notch
3 *score a piece of music*
set, arrange, adapt, write, orchestrate, instrument
▷ **score off** gain an advantage over, make a clever reply to, humiliate, have the edge; *colloq.* get one over on
▷ **score out** cross out, cancel, remove, strike out, erase, delete; *formal* efface, expunge, obliterate

F3 reinstate, restore

scorn *n, v*
▶ *n* contempt, scornfulness, disdain, sneering, derision, mockery, haughtiness, ridicule, sarcasm, disgust
formal disparagement, contumely
F3 admiration, respect
▶ *v* despise, look down on, disdain, sneer at, sniff at, scoff at, mock, laugh at, slight, rebuff, spurn, refuse, shun, reject, dismiss
formal deride, disparage
F3 admire, respect

⚠ **scorn** or **spurn** ?
In *scorn*, the main focus is on contempt for someone or something: *Courbet had little formal art training and scorned the rigid classical outlook of the time*. In *spurn*, the emphasis is on the rejection rather than the contempt: *Spurned by her family, she moved to London; He spurned their offer of help.*

scornful *adj*
contemptuous, disdainful, supercilious, haughty, arrogant, sneering, scoffing, derisive, mocking, jeering, sarcastic, scathing, insulting, slighting, dismissive
formal disparaging
F3 admiring, respectful

scornfully *adv*
contemptuously, disdainfully, superciliously, haughtily, arrogantly, scathingly, slightingly, sneeringly, derisively, dismissively, witheringly
formal disparagingly
F3 admiringly, respectfully

scot-free *adj*
clear, unpunished, unrebuked, unreprimanded, unreproached, unharmed, unhurt, unscathed, undamaged, safe, ininjured, without a scratch

scoundrel *n*
rogue, rascal, villain, vagabond, ruffian, ne'er-do-well, good-for-nothing, miscreant, scamp, scallywag, cheat, reprobate
old use blighter, bounder, dastard, rotter, stinker
colloq. rat, swine; *slang* louse, scab

scour[1] *v*
scour pots and pans
scrub, scrape, clean, wash, cleanse, purge, flush, rub, polish, wipe, burnish
formal abrade

scour[2] *v*
scour the hillside
search, hunt, comb, drag, ransack, rummage, turn upside-down, forage, rake

scourge *n, v*
▶ *n* **1** AFFLICTION, misfortune, torment, terror, torture, bane, evil, curse, menace, plague, trial, penalty, nuisance, punishment, thorn in your side
2 WHIP, lash, strap, flail, birch, cat-o'-nine-tails, switch, flagellum
F3 **1** blessing, godsend, boon
▶ *v* **1** AFFLICT, torment, torture, burden, curse, plague, devastate, punish, chastise, discipline
2 WHIP, flog, beat, lash, strap, birch, cane, flail, thrash

scout *v, n*
▶ *v* spy out, reconnoitre, explore, investigate,

check out, survey, inspect, spy, snoop, search, seek, hunt, probe, look (for), watch, observe
colloq. recce; *slang* case
▶ *n* spy, reconnoitre, vanguard, advance guard, outrider, escort, lookout, recruiter, spotter, talent spotter

scowl *v, n*
▶ *v* frown, glower, glare, grimace, pout, lour, look daggers at
🖃 smile, grin, beam
▶ *n* frown, glower, glare, grimace, pout
colloq. dirty/black look
🖃 smile, grin, beam

scrabble *v*
clamber, scramble, scrape, scratch, claw, grope, grub, paw, dig, root

scraggy *adj*
scrawny, skinny, thin, lean, lanky, bony, raw-boned, angular, gaunt, undernourished, emaciated, wasted
🖃 plump, sleek

scram *v*
go away, leave, depart, disappear, flee
colloq. take to your heels, clear out, clear off, quit, beat it, shove off, skedaddle, vamoose, do a bunk, scarper, scoot, bolt

scramble *v, n*
▶ *v* **1** CLIMB, scale, clamber, crawl, shuffle, scrabble, grope
2 RUSH, hurry, run, push, jostle, jockey, struggle, tussle, strive, vie, contend, compete, battle
formal hasten
3 MIX, jumble, mix up, infuse, disturb, disorganize
▶ *n* **1** CLAMBER, climb, scrabble, shuffle, scaling
2 RUSH, hurry, race, dash, hustle, bustle, scurry, commotion, confusion, muddle, struggle, tussle, vying, competition, free-for-all, mêlée

scrap[1] *n, v*
▶ *n* **1** *a scrap of paper*
bit, piece, fragment, part, fraction, crumb, morsel, bite, mouthful, sliver, shred, snippet, tatter, atom, iota, grain, particle, mite, trace, vestige, remnant, leftover, waste, junk
2 *scraps of meat*
leftovers, bits, scrapings, leavings, remains, residue
colloq. bits and pieces, odds and ends; *slang* odds and sods
▷ **on the scrap heap** discarded, forgotten, jettisoned, redundant, rejected, written off;
colloq. ditched, dumped
▶ *v* discard, throw away, get rid of, jettison, shed, abandon, drop, dump, cancel, axe, demolish, break up, write off
colloq. chuck out, ditch, junk
🖃 recover, restore

scrap[2] *n, v*
▶ *n* *a scrap in the school playground*
fight, scuffle, brawl, quarrel, row, argument, squabble, wrangle, dispute, disagreement, tiff, fracas
colloq. dust-up, set-to, punch-up
🖃 peace, agreement
▶ *v* fight, brawl, quarrel, argue, fall out, squabble, bicker, row, wrangle, disagree
🖃 agree

scrape *v, n*
▶ *v* **1** GRATE, grind, rasp, file, scour, rub, clean, remove, erase, scrabble, claw

formal abrade
2 SCRATCH, graze, skin, cut, bark, scuff
▷ **scrape by** just manage to live, get by, scrimp, skimp, scarcely have enough to live on
▷ **scrape through** just pass, only just/barely win, just succeed in; *colloq.* get through by a whisker
▷ **scrape together** get together, round up, pool together, get with difficulty, collect with difficulty, obtain with difficulty, just manage to get
▶ *n* **1** GRAZE, scratch, rub, abrasion, scuff, shave
2 DIFFICULTY, dilemma, predicament, trouble, plight, distress
colloq. fix, mess, pickle, tight spot, pretty kettle of fish

scrappy *adj*
bitty, disjointed, piecemeal, fragmentary, incomplete, untidy, disorganized, sketchy, superficial, slapdash, slipshod
🖃 complete, finished

scratch *v, n, adj*
▶ *v* claw, gouge, score, mark, cut, nick, incise, etch, engrave, scrape, rub, scuff, graze, gash, skin, tear, lacerate
formal abrade
▶ *n* mark, line, scrape, scuff, abrasion, graze, gash, wound, laceration
▷ **up to scratch** good enough, satisfactory, adequate, acceptable, reasonable, tolerable, competent; *colloq.* OK
🖃 unsatisfactory
▶ *adj* improvised, impromptu, unrehearsed, rough-and-ready, rough, haphazard
🖃 polished

scrawl *v, n*
▶ *v* scribble, write quickly, pen, jot (down), dash off, doodle
▶ *n* scribble, squiggle, writing, handwriting, bad/illegible handwriting, scratch, scrabble
formal cacography

scrawny *adj*
scraggy, skinny, thin, lean, lanky, angular, bony, raw-boned, underfed, undernourished, emaciated
🖃 fat, plump

scream *v, n*
▶ *v* shriek, screech, cry, shout, yell, bawl, roar, howl, wail, squeal, yelp, squawk
colloq. holler; *US* yawp
🖃 whisper
▶ *n* **1** SHRIEK, screech, cry, shout, yell, bawl, roar, howl, wail, squeal, yelp, squawk
colloq. holler; *US* yawp
2 *he's a scream*
joker, comic, comedian, wit
colloq. character, hoot, laugh, riot
🖃 **1** whisper **2** bore

screech *v, n*
▶ *v* squeal, cry, scream, shriek, howl, yell, squawk, yelp
🖃 whisper
▶ *n* squeal, cry, scream, shriek, howl, yell, squawk, yelp
🖃 whisper

screen *n, v*
▶ *n* **1** PARTITION, divider
2 SHIELD, guard, protection, cover, mask, veil, cloak, shroud, concealment, front, façade, disguise, camouflage, shelter, shade, curtain, blind, awning, canopy, net, netting, mesh

▶ *v* **1** *screen a film*
show, present, broadcast
2 SHIELD, protect, safeguard, defend, guard, cover, mask, veil, cloak, shroud, hide, conceal, disguise, camouflage, shelter, shade
3 SORT, grade, sift, sieve, riddle, filter, process, evaluate, test, check, investigate, gauge, examine, scan, vet
F3 2 uncover, expose
▷ **screen off** partition (off), separate (off), divide (off), fence off, hide, conceal

screw *n, v*
▶ *n* fastener, pin, tack, nail, rivet, brad, bolt
▷ **put the screws on** pressurize, force, compel, constrain, dragoon, coerce; *colloq.* lean on
▶ *v* **1** FASTEN, adjust, tighten, clamp, fix, contract, compress, squeeze, turn, wind, twist, wring, distort, wrinkle
F3 1 unscrew
2 *screw money out of him*
extract, extort, force, constrain, pressurize
colloq. bleed, milk
▷ **screw up 1** *screw up your face* wrinkle, distort, tighten, knot, crumple, contract, pucker, contort
2 MESS UP, spoil, botch, bungle, mishandle, mismanage; *colloq.* make a hash of; *slang* louse up, cock up
F3 2 manage

screwy *adj*
crazy, eccentric, mad, odd, weird, queer
colloq. daft, dotty, nutty, batty, crackers, round the twist, round the bend
F3 sane

scribble *v, n*
▶ *v* write, pen, jot (down), dash off, scrawl, doodle
▶ *n* squiggle, writing, handwriting, bad/illegible handwriting, scratch, scrabble
formal cacography

scribbler *n*
writer
colloq. hack, pen-pusher, pot-boiler

scribe *n*
writer, author, reporter, copyist, transcriber, amanuensis, secretary, clerk, recorder
colloq. hack, pen-pusher

scrimmage *n*
brawl, fight, riot, row, struggle, scuffle, skirmish, squabble, disturbance, fray, free-for-all, affray, shindy, melee
colloq. bovver, dust-up, scrap, set-to

scrimp *v*
skimp, save, economize, cut back on, limit, reduce, restrict, scrape, curtail, shorten, stint, pinch
colloq. tighten your belt, cut your coat according to your cloth
F3 spend

script *n*
1 *a film script*
text, lines, words, manuscript, dialogue, screenplay, libretto, book
2 WRITING, handwriting, hand, longhand, calligraphy, letters, manuscript, copy

scripture *n*

The sacred writings of religions include: the word of God, the word, Holy Bible, the Gospel, Old Testament, New Testament, Epistle, Torah, Pentateuch, Talmud, Koran, Bhagavad-Gita, Veda, Granth, Zend-Avesta.

scroll *n*
paper, parchment, roll, volume, list, inventory

Scrooge *n*
miser, skinflint, niggard
colloq. cheapskate, meanie, money-grubber, penny-pincher, tightwad
F3 spendthrift

scrounge *v*
cadge, beg, borrow
colloq. sponge, bum, bludge

scrounger *n*
cadger, parasite, beggar, borrower
colloq. sponger, bum, freeloader, bludger, moocher

scrub[1] *v*
1 *scrub the floor*
rub, brush, clean, wash, cleanse, wipe, scour
2 ABOLISH, cancel, delete, abandon, give up, drop, forget
formal discontinue
colloq. axe

scrub[2] *n*
an area of scrub
scrubland, bush, backwoods, brush

scruffy *adj*
untidy, messy, unkempt, dishevelled, bedraggled, ungroomed, run-down, tattered, shabby, down-at-heel, disreputable, slatternly, worn-out, ragged, seedy, squalid, slovenly
colloq. sloppy; *slang* sluttish
F3 tidy, well-dressed

scrumptious *adj*
delicious, appetising, tasty, mouth-watering, succulent, luscious, delightful, exquisite, magnificent
formal delectable
colloq. morish, yummy, scrummy
F3 unappetizing; *colloq.* yucky

scrunch *v*
crunch, crumple, twist, crush, grate, grind, screw (up), mash, squash, chew, champ

scruple *n, v*
▶ *n* **1** RELUCTANCE, hesitation, doubt, qualm, reservation, misgiving, second thoughts, uneasiness, difficulty, perplexity
formal vacillation, compunction
2 *has no scruples*
standards, principles, morals, ethics
▶ *v* hesitate, be reluctant, think twice, hold back, shrink, balk
formal vacillate

scrupulous *adj*
1 PAINSTAKING, meticulous, conscientious, careful, rigorous, thorough, strict, exact, precise, minute, fastidious, nice
formal punctilious
2 PRINCIPLED, high-principled, moral, ethical, honourable, honest, upright
F3 1 superficial, careless, reckless **2** unscrupulous, unprincipled

scrutinize *v*
examine, inspect, study, scan, go over, go through, look over, look through, run over, run through, analyse, sift,

investigate, probe, search, explore
formal peruse

scrutiny *n*
examination, inspection, study, analysis, investigation,
inquiry, search, exploration, probe
formal perusal

scud *v*
sail, skim, race, blow, fly, speed, shoot, dart

scuff *v*
scrape, scratch, graze, rub, brush, drag
formal abrade

scuffle *v, n*
▶ *v* fight, quarrel, tussle, brawl, come to blows,
grapple, struggle, contend, clash
colloq. scrap
▶ *n* fight, tussle, brawl, fray, rumpus, commotion,
disturbance, affray, row, quarrel
colloq. scrap, set-to, dust-up

sculpt *v*
sculpture, carve, chisel, hew, cut, model, mould, cast,
form, shape, fashion, represent

sculpture *n*

> *Types of sculpture include*: bas-relief, bronze, bust,
> carving, caryatid, cast, effigy, figure, figurine,
> group, head, herm, high-relief, maquette, marble,
> moulding, plaster cast, relief, statue, statuette,
> telamon, waxwork.

scum *n*
1 *scum floating on a liquid*
froth, foam, film, layer, covering, impurities, dross,
dregs
2 *they're the scum of the earth*
rabble, dregs of society, undesirables, lowest of the low,
rubbish, trash
colloq. riff-raff, plebs, the great unwashed

scupper *v*
1 *scupper a plan*
foil, wreck, ruin, scuttle, disable, demolish, defeat,
destroy, overthrow, overwhelm
colloq. put a spanner in the works
2 *scupper a ship*
sink, destroy, submerge, torpedo
EЭ 1 advance, promote

scurf *n*
scale, scaliness, dandruff, flakiness, furfur,
scabrousness
Related adjective: furfuraceous

scurfy *adj*
scaly, flaky, scabby, scabrous
old use scaberulous, scabrid
formal furfuraceous, furfurous, lepidote

scurrility *n*
scurrilousness, rudeness, offensiveness, vulgarity,
nastiness, obscenity, coarseness, foulness, indecency,
grossness, abuse, abusiveness
formal invective, obloquy, vituperation
EЭ politeness

scurrilous *adj*
rude, vulgar, coarse, foul, obscene, indecent, salacious,
offensive, abusive, insulting, slanderous, libellous,
scandalous
formal disparaging, defamatory, vituperative
EЭ polite, courteous, complimentary

scurry *v, n*
▶ *v* dash, rush, hurry, bustle, scramble, scuttle,
scamper, scoot, dart, run, sprint, trot, race, fly, skim,
scud
formal hasten
▶ *n* rush, bustling, hurry, flurry, scampering, whirl
colloq. hustle and bustle
EЭ calm

scurvy *adj*
contemptible, vile, dirty, shabby, worthless,
dishonourable, sorry, ignoble, despicable, rotten,
pitiful, mean, low, bad, base
formal abject
colloq. low-down
EЭ good, honourable

scuttle *v*
scurry, hurry, rush, scutter, bustle, scamper, scramble,
scud, run
formal hasten

sea *n, adj*
▶ *n* **1** OCEAN, main, deep
colloq. briny
See also **ocean**.
Related adjectives: marine, maritime, thalassic, pelagic
2 *a sea of faces*
large number, multitude, abundance, profusion, host,
mass, expanse
▶ *adj* marine, maritime, ocean, oceanic, salt,
saltwater, aquatic, seafaring, afloat
EЭ land, air
▷ **at sea** adrift, lost, confused, bewildered, baffled,
puzzled, perplexed, mystified

seafaring *adj*
sea-going, ocean-going, oceanic, sailing, nautical,
naval, marine, maritime

seal *v, n*
▶ *v* **1** *seal a jar*
close (up), shut, stop (up), plug, cork, stopper,
waterproof, fasten, secure, tighten, make airtight/
watertight
2 SETTLE, conclude, finalize, confirm, ratify, stamp
colloq. clinch
EЭ 1 unseal
▷ **seal off** block up, cordon off, close off, shut off,
fence off, cut off, segregate, isolate, quarantine
EЭ open up
▶ *n* stamp, signet, insignia, imprimatur,
authentication, assurance, confirmation, ratification
formal attestation

sealed *adj*
closed, shut, corked, plugged, hermetic
EЭ unsealed

seam *n*
1 JOIN, joint, junction, weld, closure, line
2 *coal seam*
layer, stratum, vein, lode

seaman *n*
sailor, rating, seafarer, steersman, AB, tar, deck hand,
Jack tar, sea dog
slang matelot

seamy *adj*
disreputable, sordid, squalid, unsavoury, rough, dark,
low, nasty, unpleasant
colloq. sleazy
EЭ respectable, wholesome, pleasant

sear *v*
burn, scorch, char, singe, brown, fry, sizzle, seal,
brand, parch, shrivel, wither, wilt, dry-up
formal cauterize

search *v, n*
▶ *v* **1** SEEK, look, look through, go through, hunt,
rummage, rifle, ransack, forage, scour, comb, sift
colloq. go through with a fine-tooth comb, turn upside-
down/inside-out
2 EXAMINE, probe, explore, examine, scrutinize,
inspect, check, investigate, inquire, pry
colloq. frisk
▶ *n* **1** HUNT, hunt, quest, pursuit, rummage, rifling,
forage, ransacking
2 EXAMINATION, exploration, probe, scrutiny,
inspection, investigation, inquiry, research, survey

searching *adj*
penetrating, piercing, alert, discerning, observant,
keen, sharp, close, intent, probing, thorough, minute
E3 vague, superficial

seaside *n*
coast, shore, seashore, beach, sands
Related adjective: littoral

season *n, v*
▶ *n* period, spell, phase, term, time, span, interval
▷ **in season** available, obtainable, growing
plentifully, growing, on the market
▶ *v* **1** *season food*
flavour, spice, salt, add flavouring, add pepper to, add
herbs to, add relish/sauce to
colloq. pep up
2 AGE, mature, ripen, mellow, harden, toughen, train,
prime, prepare, condition, treat
3 TEMPER, moderate, tone down

seasonable *adj*
timely, well-timed, welcome, opportune, providential,
convenient, suitable, appropriate, fitting
E3 unseasonable, inopportune

seasoned *adj*
mature, experienced, practised, established, well-
versed, veteran, long-serving, battle-scarred, old,
hardened, toughened, conditioned, acclimatized,
weathered
formal habituated
E3 inexperienced, novice

seasoning *n*
flavouring, spice, condiment, salt, pepper, herbs,
relish, sauce, dressing

seat *n, v*
▶ *n* **1** CHAIR, bench, pew, stool, throne, stall, form,
settle
2 *country seat*
residence, house, mansion, stately home
formal abode
3 PLACE, site, situation, location, headquarters,
centre, heart, hub, axis, source, cause, origin, reason,
bottom, base, foundation, footing, ground
▶ *v* **1** SIT, place, put, position, deposit, set, locate,
install, fit, fix, settle
2 *the theatre seats 1000*
accommodate, hold, contain, take, have room for

seating *n*
seats, chairs, places, room, accommodation

seaweed *n*
alga, seaware, varec(h), vraic

Related adjective: fucoid

Seaweed species include: carrageen, coral weed,
gulfweed, Irish moss, laver, oarweed, peacock's tail,
sargasso, sea moss, tangle, thongweed; wrack,
bladder wrack, channelled wrack.

secede *v*
separate, split off, withdraw, break away, break, resign,
retire, leave, disaffiliate, turn your back on
formal apostatize
colloq. quit
E3 join, unite with

secession *n*
seceding, split, withdrawal, defection, break,
breakaway, disaffiliation, schism
formal apostasy
E3 amalgamation, unification

secluded *adj*
private, cloistered, shut away, cut off, isolated, lonely,
unfrequented, solitary, remote, out-of-the-way,
sheltered, hidden, concealed
formal sequestered
E3 public, accessible

seclusion *n*
privacy, retirement, withdrawal, retreat, isolation,
solitude, remoteness, shelter, secrecy, hiding,
concealment
formal sequestration

second¹ *adj, n, v*
▶ *adj* **1** NEXT, following, subsequent, succeeding
2 ADDITIONAL, further, extra, supplementary,
alternative, other, alternate, back-up
3 DUPLICATE, twin, double, repeated
4 SECONDARY, subordinate, lower, inferior, lesser,
supporting
▶ *n* helper, assistant, backer, supporter, attendant,
second-in-command, right-hand man/woman
▶ *v* approve, agree with, endorse, back, back up,
support, help, assist, aid, further, advance, forward,
promote, encourage

second² *n*
in ten seconds
minute, moment, instant, flash, split second,
twinkling, twinkling of an eye, trice
colloq. tick, jiffy, two shakes of a lamb's tail

second³ *v*
seconded to Australia for a year
transfer, relocate, change, move, shift, assign, send

secondary *adj*
subsidiary, subordinate, lower, inferior, lesser, minor,
unimportant, non-essential, ancillary, auxiliary,
supporting, relief, back-up, reserve, spare, extra,
second, alternative, indirect, derived, derivative,
resulting
E3 primary, main, major, essential

second-class *adj*
second-best, second-rate, mediocre, inferior,
unimportant, indifferent, uninspiring,
undistinguished, uninspired
E3 valuable

second-hand *adj*
used, old, nearly-new, worn, hand-me-down,
borrowed, derivative, secondary, indirect, vicarious
E3 brand-new

second-in-command *n*
helper, assistant, backer, supporter, attendant, right-hand man/woman

second-rate *adj*
inferior, substandard, lesser, unimportant, second-class, second-best, poor, low-grade, shoddy, cheap, tawdry, mediocre, undistinguished, uninspired, uninspiring
colloq. tacky, lousy, tinpot, ropy
F3 first-rate

secrecy *n*
privacy, seclusion, confidentiality, confidence, disguise, covertness, concealment, camouflage, furtiveness, surreptitiousness, stealthiness, stealth, mystery
F3 openness

secret *adj, n*
▶ *adj* **1** PRIVATE, discreet, covert, hidden, concealed, unseen, shrouded, covered, disguised, camouflaged, undercover, furtive, surreptitious, stealthy, sly, underhand, under-the-counter, underground, backstairs, back-door
formal clandestine
colloq. cloak-and-dagger, hole-and-corner, closet
2 CLASSIFIED, restricted, confidential, sensitive, unpublished, undisclosed, unrevealed, unknown
colloq. hush-hush, top secret, between you and me, between you, me and the gatepost
3 CRYPTIC, mysterious, occult, deep
formal arcane, recondite, abstruse
4 CONCEALED, private, cloistered, shut away, cut off, isolated, lonely, unfrequented, solitary, remote, close, sheltered, hidden, retired, secluded, out-of-the-way
formal sequestered
F3 1 public, open **2** well-known **4** public, accessible
▶ *n* **1** CONFIDENTIAL MATTER, confidence, private matter, mystery, enigma
colloq. inside story
2 *the secret of eternal youth*
code, key, answer, solution, formula, recipe
▷ **in secret** confidentially, in confidence, in private, in secret, under cover, privately, quietly, surreptitiously, stealthily, unobserved, covertly, furtively, on the quiet; *formal* clandestinely, in camera, privily; *colloq.* on the q.t., on the sly, behind closed doors, hugger-mugger
F3 openly

secretary *n*
personal assistant, PA, office administrator, executive assistant, typist, stenographer, clerk, person Friday, amanuensis

secrete[1] *v*
secrete a weapon
hide, conceal, bury, cover, cover up, cache, screen, shroud, veil, disguise, take, appropriate
formal sequester
colloq. stash away
F3 uncover, reveal, disclose

secrete[2] *v*
secrete a liquid
exude, discharge, release, excrete, give off, emit, send out, emanate, produce, leach, leak, ooze

secretion *n*
exudation, discharge, release, emission, emanation, leakage, oozing
technical osmosis

secretive *adj*
tight-lipped, close, uncommunicative, unforthcoming, reticent, taciturn, reserved, withdrawn, intent, quiet, deep, cryptic, enigmatic
colloq. cagey, playing your cards close to your chest
F3 open, communicative, forthcoming

secretly *adv*
confidentially, in confidence, in private, in secret, under cover, privately, quietly, surreptitiously, stealthily, unobserved, covertly, furtively, on the quiet
formal clandestinely, in camera, privily
colloq. on the q.t., on the sly, behind closed doors
F3 openly

sect *n*
denomination, cult, division, subdivision, group, splinter group, order, faction, camp, wing, party, school

sectarian *adj, n*
▶ *adj* factional, partisan, cliquish, exclusive, narrow, hidebound, limited, parochial, insular, narrow-minded, bigoted, prejudiced, fanatical, extreme, doctrinaire, dogmatic, rigid
F3 non-sectarian, broad-minded
▶ *n* bigot, fanatic, partisan, zealot, dogmatist, extremist, fractionalist

section *n*
division, subdivision, chapter, paragraph, passage, instalment, part, component, fraction, fragment, bit, piece, slice, portion, segment, sector, zone, district, area, region, department, branch, wing
F3 whole

sectional *adj*
separate, divided, exclusive, factional, separatist, regional, local, localized, partial, class, racial, sectarian
F3 general, universal

sector *n*
zone, district, quarter, area, region, branch, field, category, section, division, subdivision, part
F3 whole

secular *adj*
lay, temporal, worldly, earthly, civil, state, non-religious, non-spiritual, profane
F3 religious, spiritual

secure *adj, v*
▶ *adj* **1** SAFE, unharmed, undamaged, protected, sheltered, shielded, immune, impregnable, fast, tight, closed, sealed, fastened, locked
formal fortified
colloq. out of harm's way
2 CONFIDENT, assured, reassured, safe, comfortable, relaxed, happy, contented
3 FIXED, immovable, stable, steady, sturdy, solid, firm
4 CERTAIN, sure, well-founded, reliable, dependable, steadfast, conclusive, definite, established, settled
F3 1 insecure, vulnerable **2** uneasy, ill at ease, embarrassed, uncomfortable
▶ *v* **1** OBTAIN, acquire, gain, get, get hold of
formal procure
colloq. come by, land
2 FASTEN, attach, fix, make fast, tie (up), moor, lash, chain, lock (up), shut, close, padlock, bolt, batten down, nail, rivet
3 PROTECT, make safe, strengthen, guard, safeguard, defend, cover, shield, screen

4 GUARANTEE, assure, ensure, establish, confirm, sponsor, underwrite, endorse
⊟ 1 lose **2** unfasten

security *n*
1 SAFETY, immunity, asylum, sanctuary, refuge, cover, protection, defence, protection, invulnerability, surveillance, safe-keeping, preservation, care, custody
2 *security for a loan*
collateral, surety, pledge, guarantee, warranty, assurance, insurance, precaution(s), safeguard(s), protection, defence
old use gage
3 CONFIDENCE, assurance, ease, peace of mind, conviction, certainty, positiveness
⊟ 1 insecurity, danger **3** anxiety, worry, embarrassment

sedate *adj, v*
▶ *adj* staid, dignified, solemn, grave, stiff, serious, earnest, sober, proper, demure, composed, unruffled, serene, tranquil, calm, quiet, unexciting, dull, cool, collected, deliberate, slow-moving
old use seemly
formal decorous, imperturbable
colloq. unflappable
⊟ undignified, lively, agitated
▶ *v* tranquillize, calm, calm down, quieten down, soothe, relax, pacify

sedative *adj, n*
▶ *adj* calming, soothing, anodyne, lenitive, tranquillizing, relaxing, soporific, depressant
⊟ rousing
▶ *n* tranquillizer, sleeping-pill, narcotic, barbiturate, opiate, calmative, depressant
colloq. downer

sedentary *adj*
sitting, seated, desk-bound, inactive, still, stationary, immobile, unmoving
⊟ active

sediment *n*
deposit, residue, grounds, lees, dregs, silt
formal precipitate, residuum

sedition *n*
agitation, rabble-rousing, subversion, disloyalty, treachery, treason, mutiny, rebellion, revolt
formal insubordination, fomentation, incitement to riot
⊟ calm, loyalty

seditious *adj*
agitating, inciting, rabble-rousing, subversive, disloyal, traitorous, mutinous, rebellious, revolutionary
formal insubordinate, dissident, insurrectionist, fomenting, refractory
⊟ calm, loyal

seduce *v*
entice, lure, allure, attract, tempt, charm, beguile, ensnare, lead astray, mislead, deceive, corrupt, dishonour, deprave, ruin
formal inveigle
colloq. get into bed
⊟ repel

seducer *n*
charmer, philanderer, womanizer, flirt, deceiver, libertine, Don Juan, Casanova, Lothario
colloq. wolf, goat

seduction *n*
enticement, lure, allure, allurement, attraction, appeal, temptation, charm, beguilement, corruption, deception, misleading, ruin
colloq. come-on

seductive *adj*
enticing, alluring, luring, attractive, appealing, tempting, tantalizing, inviting, flirtatious, sexy, provocative, beguiling, charming, captivating, bewitching, deceiving, misleading, irresistible, sultry
colloq. come-hither
⊟ unattractive, repulsive

seductress *n*
femme fatale, temptress, siren, Lorelei, Circe
colloq. vamp

sedulous *adj*
diligent, industrious, conscientious, painstaking, persevering, persistent, laborious, busy, constant, assiduous, tireless, untiring, unflagging, unremitting, resolved, determined
⊟ half-hearted

see *v*
1 PERCEIVE, catch sight of, set eyes on, glimpse, discern, spot, make out, recognize, distinguish, identify, sight, notice, observe, watch, view, look at, get a look at, witness, mark, note
old use espy, behold
2 *I see your point*
understand, comprehend, grasp, fathom, follow, know, take in, make out, realize, recognize, appreciate, regard, consider, reflect, deem
colloq. get, latch onto, cotton onto
3 IMAGINE, picture, visualize, envisage, forecast, foresee, predict, anticipate
4 DISCOVER, find out, ask, learn, ascertain, investigate, inquire, determine, decide
5 ACCOMPANY, usher, lead, show, take, escort
6 VISIT, consult, speak to, interview, meet, encounter
formal chance upon
colloq. bump into, run into, come across
7 GO OUT WITH, court, date, take out, keep company with
▷ **see about** arrange, attend to, deal with, take care of, look after, organize, manage, be responsible for, do, fix, repair, sort out
▷ **see through 1** *see through a trick* realize, understand, fathom, penetrate, not be deceived by, not be taken in by; *colloq.* get wise to **2** *see a task through* stick out, continue, persist, persevere, not give up; *colloq.* hang in
▷ **see to** attend to, deal with, take care of, look after, arrange, organize, manage, be responsible for, do, fix, repair, sort out, mind, ensure, make sure, make certain

seed *n*
1 *the seeds of a plant*
pip, stone, kernel, nucleus, grain, germ, sperm, ovum, egg, ovule, spawn, embryo, semen, spermatozoon
Related adjective: seminal
2 *the seeds of rebellion*
source, start, beginning, root, origin, cause, reason(s)
3 OFFSPRING, child, children, young, young one(s), family, heirs, successors, descendants
▷ **go/run to seed** deteriorate, decay, decline, degenerate, get worse; *colloq.* go downhill, got to pot, go to the dogs, go down the tubes

seedy *adj*
1 SHABBY, dirty, untidy, scruffy, tatty, mangy, squalid,

run-down, dilapidated, decaying
colloq. grotty, crummy, sleazy
2 UNWELL, ill, sick, poorly, ailing, off-colour
colloq. groggy, rough, under the weather, out of sorts
E3 2 well

seek *v*
look for, search for, try to find, hunt for, pursue, follow,
inquire, ask, invite, request, beg, petition, want, desire,
aim, try, attempt, endeavour, strive
formal solicit, entreat, aspire

seeker *n*
inquirer, searcher, student, disciple, novice
formal chela, zetetic

seem *v*
appear, look, have/give the appearance of being, look
like, come across as, have the look of, show signs of,
give the impression of being, strike you as, feel, sound,
pretend to be

seeming *adj*
apparent, outward, external, superficial, surface,
supposed, pretended, quasi-, pseudo, specious
formal ostensible, assumed
E3 real

seemingly *adv*
apparently, superficially, on the surface, on the face of
it, as far as you can see, outwardly, allegedly
formal ostensibly
E3 really

seemly *adj*
appropriate, proper, suitable, suited, befitting, fit,
fitting, decent, nice, attractive, handsome, maidenly,
becoming, *comme il faut*
old use comely, meet
formal decorous
E3 unseemly

seep *v*
ooze, leak, exude, well, trickle, drip, dribble, percolate,
drain, permeate, soak

seepage *n*
leak, leakage, dripping, oozing, exudation, percolation
technical osmosis

seer *n*
augur, prophet, soothsayer, sibyl, spaeman, spaewife

seesaw *v*
alternate, swing, go from one extreme to the other,
fluctuate, oscillate, teeter, pitch
colloq. yo-yo

seethe *v*
1 BOIL, simmer, bubble, effervesce, fizz, foam, froth,
ferment, rise, swell, surge, teem, swarm
2 RAGE, fume, smoulder, storm, be furious, be
outraged, be livid, be incensed
colloq. explode, boil over, see red, foam at the mouth

see-through *adj*
transparent, translucent, sheer, filmy, gauzy,
gossamer(y), flimsy
E3 opaque

segment *n, v*
▶ *n* section, division, compartment, part, bit, piece,
slice, portion, wedge
E3 whole
▶ *v* cut up, separate, divide, split, slice, halve,
anatomize

segregate *v*
separate, keep apart, set apart, cut off, isolate,
dissociate, ostracize, quarantine, set apart, exclude
formal sequester
E3 unite, join

segregation *n*
separation, setting apart, isolation, quarantine,
dissociation, apartheid, discrimination
formal sequestration
E3 unification

seize *v*
1 GRAB, snatch, grasp, clutch, grip, hold, get/take
hold of, grab hold of
2 *seize property/a plane*
take, confiscate, impound, usurp, appropriate,
commandeer, hijack, annex, kidnap, abduct
formal sequestrate
3 *seize a criminal*
catch, capture, arrest, apprehend
colloq. nab, collar, nail, nobble
E3 1, 2 let go, release, hand back

seizure *n*
1 FIT, attack, convulsion, paroxysm, spasm
2 TAKING, confiscation, commandeering, hijack,
annexation, abduction, snatching, capture, arrest,
apprehension
formal appropriation, sequestration
E3 2 release, liberation

seldom *adv*
rarely, infrequently, occasionally, hardly ever, scarcely
ever
colloq. once in a blue moon
E3 often, usually

select *v, adj*
▶ *v* choose, pick, single out, decide on, settle on,
appoint, elect, favour, prefer, opt for, invite
▶ *adj* selected, choice, top, prime, first-class, first-
rate, best, finest, supreme, high-quality, hand-picked,
élite, exclusive, limited, privileged, special, excellent,
superior
colloq. posh
E3 second-rate, ordinary, general

selection *n*
1 CHOICE, pick, option, preference
2 ASSORTMENT, variety, choice, range, line-up,
miscellany, medley, potpourri, collection, anthology

selective *adj*
particular, careful, fussy, finicky, fastidious,
discerning, discriminating
colloq. choosy, picky, pernickety
E3 indiscriminate

self *n*
ego, personality, identity, I, person, inner being, soul
colloq. the real me, heart of hearts

self-assertive *adj*
forceful, pushing, aggressive, authoritarian,
commanding, dictatorial, overbearing, heavy-
handed, high-handed, overweening, domineering
formal peremptory
colloq. bossy, pushy, not backward in coming forward
E3 compliant

self-assurance *n*
confidence, overconfidence, belief in yourself, self-
confidence, assurance, self-possession, positiveness,
aplomb, cocksureness

colloq. cockiness
⊟ humility, unsureness

self-assured *adj*
self-confident, confident, assured, sure of oneself, self-collected, self-possessed, overconfident, cocksure
colloq. cocky
⊟ humble, unsure

self-centred *adj*
selfish, self-seeking, self-serving, self-interested, egotistic(al), narcissistic, self-absorbed, egocentric, thinking only of yourself, wrapped up in yourself
⊟ altruistic

self-confident *adj*
confident, self-reliant, self-assured, assured, self-possessed, composed, cool, bold, fearless, positive, unabashed
⊟ unsure, self-conscious

self-conscious *adj*
uncomfortable, ill at ease, awkward, embarrassed, blushing, shamefaced, sheepish, shy, diffident, bashful, coy, retiring, timid, shrinking, self-effacing, nervous, insecure
formal timorous
⊟ natural, unaffected, confident

self-control *n*
calmness, composure, patience, self-restraint, restraint, self-denial, temperance, self-discipline, self-mastery, willpower
colloq. cool

self-denial *n*
moderation, temperance, abstemiousness, asceticism, self-sacrifice, unselfishness, selflessness
formal self-abnegation, self-renunciation
⊟ self-indulgence

self-esteem *n*
ego, self-respect, self-regard, self-assurance, self-confidence, pride, self-pride, dignity, *amour-propre*
⊟ inferiority complex

self-evident *adj*
obvious, clear, undeniable, axiomatic, unquestionable, incontrovertible, inescapable
formal manifest

self-glorification *n*
self-exaltation, self-aggrandizement, self-admiration, self-advertisement, egotism, egotheism
⊟ humility

self-government *n*
autonomy, independence, home rule, democracy, self-sovereignty
formal autarchy
⊟ subjection

self-importance *n*
arrogance, pompousness, conceit, conceitedness, vanity, pomposity, big-headedness, self-opinion, donnism, self-consequence
colloq. cockiness, pushiness, bumptiousness
⊟ humility

self-important *adj*
arrogant, pompous, big-headed, conceited, egoistic, vain, proud, overbearing, swaggering, strutting, self-consequent, swollen-headed
colloq. cocky, pushy, bumptious
⊟ humble

self-indulgence *n*
extravagance, excess, self-gratification, sensualism, dissoluteness, intemperance, high living, hedonism
formal dissipation, profligacy
⊟ self-denial

self-indulgent *adj*
hedonistic, dissolute, extravagant, intemperate, immoderate
formal dissipated, profligate
⊟ abstemious

self-interest *n*
selfishness, self-love, self-regard, self-serving, self
⊟ selflessness

selfish *adj*
self-interested, self-seeking, self-serving, mean, miserly, mercenary, greedy, covetous, self-centred, inconsiderate, egocentric, egotistic(al)
colloq. thinking of nobody except yourself
⊟ unselfish, selfless, generous, considerate

selfishness *n*
self-centredness, self-seeking, self-serving, self-love, self-interest, self-regard, greed, meanness, egotism
⊟ selflessness

selfless *adj*
unselfish, altruistic, self-denying, self-sacrificing, generous, philanthropic
formal magnanimous
⊟ selfish, self-centred

self-possessed *adj*
self-assured, self-collected, calm, collected, composed, confident, unruffled, poised
colloq. cool, unflappable, together
⊟ worried

self-possession *n*
calmness, confidence, composure, self-confidence, coolness, self-command, poise
formal aplomb, sang-froid
colloq. cool, unflappability

self-reliance *n*
independence, self-support, self-sufficiency, self-sustenance, self-sustainment
technical autarky
formal self-sustentation
⊟ dependence

self-reliant *adj*
independent, self-supporting, self-sufficient, self-sustaining
technical autarkic(al)
⊟ dependent

self-respect *n*
pride, dignity, self-esteem, self-assurance, self-confidence, self-regard, *amour-propre*
⊟ inferiority complex

self-restraint *n*
self-discipline, self-denial, self-control, patience, forbearance, moderation, abstemiousness, self-government, temperance, self-command, willpower
formal encraty
⊟ licence

self-righteous *adj*
smug, complacent, superior, priggish, pious, sanctimonious, holier-than-thou, pietistic, hypocritical, pharisaical

colloq. goody-goody, pi
▆ humble

self-righteousness *n*
priggishness, piousness, goodiness,
sanctimoniousness, pharisaicalness, pharisaism
colloq. goody-goodiness
▆ humility

self-sacrifice *n*
self-denial, selflessness, altruism, unselfishness,
generosity
formal self-abnegation, self-renunciation
▆ selfishness

self-satisfaction *n*
smugness, complacency, contentment, pride,
self-appreciation, self-approval
formal self-approbation
▆ humility

self-satisfied *adj*
smug, complacent, self-congratulatory, self-righteous,
proud
colloq. puffed up
▆ humble

self-seeking *adj*
mercenary, self-interested, selfish, self-loving,
self-serving, self-endeared, opportunistic, acquisitive,
calculating, careerist, fortune-hunting, gold-digging
colloq. on the make
▆ altruistic

self-styled *adj*
self-appointed, self-titled, professed, so-called,
soi-disant, would-be, pretended

self-supporting *adj*
self-sufficient, self-financing, independent,
self-reliant, self-sustaining
▆ dependent

self-willed *adj*
stubborn, obstinate, stiff-necked, opinionated,
self-opinionative, self-opinionated, headstrong,
pig-headed, ungovernable, wilful, bloody-minded
formal intractable, refractory
colloq. cussed
▆ complaisant

sell *v*
1 *sell cars*
exchange, trade, barter, auction, dispose of, vend,
retail, hawk, peddle, tout
colloq. flog
2 STOCK, handle, deal in, carry, market, trade in,
traffic in, merchandise, import, export
3 PROMOTE, advertise, market, get support/approval
for, persuade, win over
colloq. push, hype
▆ **1** buy
▷ **sell out 1** *sell out of fruit* run out of, have none
left, be out of stock **2** BETRAY, fail, double-cross;
colloq. rat on, sell down the river, stab in the back;
slang fink on

seller *n*
vendor, merchant, trader, supplier, stockist
▆ buyer, purchaser

Types of seller include: agent, auctioneer, bagman,
barrow-boy, broker, cold caller, colporteur,
commercial traveller, costermonger, dealer,
demonstrator, door-to-door salesman/saleswoman,
estate agent, factor, hawker, huckster, jobber, knight
of the road, market trader, merchandiser, milkman,
milklady, pedlar, *US* peddler, *colloq.* rep,
representative, retailer, sales assistant, sales clerk,
sales executive, saleslady, salesman, salesperson,
saleswoman, sales staff, shop assistant, shopkeeper,
store clerk, storekeeper, street trader, tallyman,
telephone sales-person, ticket agent, tout,
tradesman, tradeswoman, traveller, wholesaler. *See
also* **shops**.

selling *n*
dealing, marketing, trading, transactions, traffic,
trafficking, merchandising, salesmanship, promotion
formal vendition
▆ buying

semblance *n*
appearance, air, show, pretence, guise, mask, front,
façade, veneer, look, aspect, image, resemblance,
likeness, similarity
formal apparition

seminal *adj*
influential, major, important, original, innovative,
productive, creative, formative, imaginative,
seminary
▆ derivative

seminary *n*
college, institute, institution, training-college,
academy, school

send *v*
1 POST, mail, get off, address, put in the post/mail,
dispatch, consign, forward, redirect, convey, deliver
formal remit
2 TRANSMIT, broadcast, beam, relay, communicate,
convey, radio, televise
3 PROPEL, drive, move, throw, cast, fling, hurl,
launch, fire, shoot, discharge, project, emit, direct
4 THRILL, stimulate, excite, arouse, give pleasure to
colloq. turn on, give a buzz/kick
▷ **send for** summon, call for, request, order,
command
▆ dismiss
▷ **send up** satirize, mock, ridicule, parody, mimic,
imitate; *colloq.* take off, take the mickey out of;
slang take the piss out of

send-off *n*
goodbye, farewell, leave-taking, departure, start
▆ arrival

send-up *n*
mockery, parody, skit, satire, imitation
colloq. mickey-take, spoof, take-off

senile *adj*
old, aged, doddering, decrepit, failing, confused
formal senescent
colloq. gaga

senility *n*
old age, infirmity, dotage, second childhood, senile
dementia, decrepitude, anility
formal paracme, caducity, senescence

senior *adj*
older, elder, higher, superior, high-ranking, first,
major, chief
formal doyen(ne), âiné(e)
▆ junior

seniority *n*
priority, precedence, rank, standing, status, age,
superiority, importance

sensation *n*
1 FEELING, sense, impression, perception, awareness, consciousness, emotion
colloq. vibes
2 *the report caused a sensation*
commotion, stir, agitation, excitement, thrill, furore, outrage, scandal
3 SUCCESS, hit, triumph
colloq. winner, wow

sensational *adj*
1 EXCITING, thrilling, electrifying, breathtaking, startling, stirring, amazing, astounding, staggering, dramatic, spectacular, impressive, exceptional, excellent, wonderful, superb, marvellous
colloq. smashing, fantastic, terrific, fabulous
2 SCANDALOUS, shocking, horrifying, revealing, melodramatic, lurid
E3 1 ordinary, run-of-the-mill

sense *n, v*
▶ *n* 1 FEELING, sensation, impression, perception, awareness, consciousness, appreciation, faculty
formal sensibility
2 REASON, logic, mind, brain(s), wit(s), wisdom, common sense, intelligence, cleverness, understanding, comprehension, apprehension, discernment, judgement, appreciation, intuition
formal prudence, judiciousness
colloq. gumption, nous, savvy
3 MEANING, significance, definition, interpretation, implication, drift, tenor, nuance, point, purpose, substance
formal denotation, import, purport
E3 2 foolishness 3 nonsense
▷ **make sense of** understand, grasp, make out, comprehend, make much of; *colloq.* figure out, fathom, make head or tail of
▶ *v* feel, suspect, be aware of, be conscious of, discern, perceive, detect, experience, notice, observe, recognize, realize, appreciate, understand, comprehend, grasp
formal intuit, divine
colloq. pick up

senseless *adj*
1 FOOLISH, stupid, unwise, silly, idiotic, mad, crazy, moronic, ridiculous, ludicrous, absurd, meaningless, nonsensical, fatuous, irrational, illogical, unreasonable, mindless, pointless, purposeless, futile
colloq. daft, dotty, batty
2 UNCONSCIOUS, stunned, anaesthetized, deadened, numb, unfeeling
formal insensible, insensate
colloq. out, out cold
E3 1 sensible, meaningful, intelligent 2 conscious

sensibility *n*
1 *show sensibility*
sensitiveness, sensitivity, susceptibility, discernment, perceptiveness, appreciation, awareness, responsiveness, insight, intuition, delicacy, taste
2 *offend someone's sensibilities*
feelings, emotions, sentiments, susceptibilities, sensitivities
E3 1 insensibility

sensible *adj*
1 WISE, well-advised, shrewd, sharp, far-sighted, intelligent, clever, mature, level-headed, down-to-earth, commonsense, commonsensical, sober, sane, rational, logical, reasonable, realistic, practical,

functional, sound
formal prudent, judicious, sagacious
colloq. with both feet on the ground, with your head screwed on (the right way)
2 SENSITIVE, responsive, aware, perceptive, discerning, susceptible, vulnerable
3 *wear sensible shoes*
practical, ordinary, everyday, working, serviceable, hard-wearing, strong, tough
E3 1 senseless, foolish, unwise 2 insensitive
3 impractical, fashionable, decorative
▷ **sensible of** sensitive to, understanding, conscious of, aware of, acquainted with, mindful of, observant of, alive to, convinced of; *formal* cognizant of
E3 unaware of

sensitive *adj*
1 SUSCEPTIBLE, vulnerable, impressionable, tender, emotional, thin-skinned, temperamental, touchy, irritable, sensitized, responsive, reactive, aware, perceptive, discerning, appreciative
formal sentient
2 DELICATE, fine, fragile, soft, exact, precise
3 *a sensitive issue*
delicate, tricky, controversial, difficult, problematic, awkward, touchy
4 *needs sensitive handling*
tactful, delicate, diplomatic, careful, considerate, sympathetic, discerning, discreet, well-thought-out
E3 1 insensitive, thick-skinned 2 imprecise, approximate

sensitivity *n*
1 SUSCEPTIBILITY, vulnerability, responsiveness, awareness, perceptiveness, receptiveness, reactiveness, discernment, appreciation, sympathy
2 DELICACY, fineness, fragility, softness
E3 1 insensitivity

sensual *adj*
self-indulgent, voluptuous, sultry, worldly, physical, animal, carnal, fleshly, bodily, sexual, erotic, sexy, lustful, lecherous, lewd, licentious
colloq. randy
E3 ascetic

⚠ **sensual** or **sensuous** ?
Sensual means 'of or concerning the physical senses and the body rather than the mind', and is used especially with a connotation of sexuality or sexual arousal: *a full, sensual mouth; a strong desire for sensual pleasure. Sensuous* means 'perceived by or affecting the senses, especially in a pleasant way', as in *I find his music very sensuous; Her sculptures have a certain sensuous quality to them.*

---

sensuality *n*
voluptuousness, lewdness, lustfulness, salaciousness, sexiness, licentiousness, libertinism, eroticism, carnality, animalism, lasciviousness, debauchery, lecherousness, gourmandize
formal profligacy, prurience
E3 asceticism, Puritanism

sensuous *adj*
pleasurable, gratifying, pleasing, pleasant, voluptuous, rich, lush, luxurious, sumptuous, aesthetic
E3 ascetic, plain, simple

⚠ **sensuous** or **sensual** ? *See panel at* **sensual**.

---

sentence *n, v*
▶ *n* judgement, decision, verdict, condemnation, pronouncement, ruling, decree, order, punishment
▶ *v* judge, pass judgement on, impose a sentence on, condemn, doom, punish, penalize

sententious *adj*
1 MORALIZING, moralistic, judgemental, sanctimonious, canting, pompous
2 BRIEF, concise, compact, pithy, short, terse, succinct, pointed, epigrammatic, aphoristic, laconic, axiomatic, gnomic
colloq. preachy
🖃 1 humble 2 verbose

sentient *adj*
conscious, aware, sensitive, responsive, live, living, reactive
🖃 *formal* insentient

sentiment *n*
1 THOUGHT, idea, feeling, opinion, view, point of view, judgement, belief, persuasion, attitude
2 EMOTION, sensibility, tenderness, soft-heartedness, softness, romance, romanticism, sentimentality, mawkishness

sentimental *adj*
tender, soft-hearted, emotional, loving, gushing, sugary, touching, pathetic, tear-jerking, maudlin, mawkish, nostalgic, romantic, affectionate, sloppy, soppy
colloq. weepy, lovey-dovey, slushy, mushy, schmaltzy, corny, sickly, gushy
🖃 unsentimental, realistic, cynical

sentimentality *n*
tenderness, sentimentalism, emotionalism, romanticism, mawkishness, nostalgia
formal bathos
colloq. corniness, gush, mush, pulp, schmaltz, sloppiness, slush

sentry *n*
sentinel, guard, picket, watchman, watch, lookout

separable *adj*
divisible, detachable, removable, distinguishable, distinct, independent, different, particular
🖃 inseparable

separate *v, adj*
▶ *v* divide, sever, take/come apart, keep apart, break off, break up, part, split (up), divorce, part company, diverge, dismantle, disconnect, uncouple, disunite, disaffiliate, disentangle, single out, segregate, isolate, cut off, partition, abstract, remove, detach, withdraw, secede
old use sunder
formal disjoin, become estranged
🖃 join, unite, combine
▶ *adj* different, distinct, unattached, unconnected, unrelated, single, individual, particular, independent, alone, solitary, segregated, isolated, apart, divorced, divided, disunited, disconnected, disjointed, detached, sundry
formal disparate, discrete, several, autonomous
🖃 together, attached

separated *adj*
separate, split up, divided, disconnected, parted, isolated, disunited, disassociated, apart, segregated
old use sundered
🖃 attached, together

separately *adv*
independently, individually, singly, apart, discriminately, discretely, alone, personally
formal severally
🖃 together

separating *adj*
divisive, isolating, dividing, intervening, partitioning, segregating
🖃 unifying

separation *n*
division, parting, parting of the ways, leave-taking, farewell, split-up, break-up, divorce, split, rift, schism, gap, divergence, disconnection, uncoupling, disengagement, dissociation, segregation, isolation, apartheid, detachment
formal severance, estrangement, disseverment
🖃 unification

septic *adj*
infected, poisoned, festering, putrefying, putrid
formal putrefactive, suppurating

sepulchral *adj*
gloomy, grave, melancholy, sombre, cheerless, mournful, sad, solemn, dismal, funereal, morbid, deep, hollow
formal lugubrious, sepulchrous, woeful
🖃 happy, cheerful

sepulchre *n*
tomb, grave, burial place, vault, mausoleum

sequel *n*
follow-up, continuation, development, result, consequence, outcome, issue, upshot, pay-off, end, conclusion

sequence *n*
succession, series, run, progression, chain, string, train, line, procession, order, arrangement, consequence, course, track, cycle, set

sequester *v*
1 ISOLATE, set apart, seclude, insulate, detach, remove, alienate, shut away, shut off
2 SEQUESTRATE, seize, confiscate, impound, take, commandeer
formal appropriate

sequestered *adj*
isolated, secluded, lonely, outback, out-of-the-way, private, remote, quiet, retired, unfrequented, cloistered
🖃 public, busy, frequented

sequestrate *v*
seize, confiscate, impound, take, commandeer, sequester
formal appropriate

seraphic *adj*
seraphical, angelic, heavenly, celestial, holy, divine, pure, saintly, innocent, blissful
formal beatific, sublime
🖃 demonic

serendipity *n*
chance, coincidence, happy coincidence, accident, luck, fortune, good fortune
formal fortuity

serene *adj*
calm, tranquil, cool, composed, placid, untroubled, undisturbed, unclouded, unruffled, still, quiet, peaceful
formal halcyon, imperturbable

colloq. unflappable
⊟ troubled, disturbed

serenity *n*
calm, calmness, stillness, tranquillity, cool,
composure, placidity, peace, peacefulness, quietness
formal quietude
colloq. unflappability
⊟ anxiety, disruption

serf *n*
slave, servant, thrall, villein, bondservant, bond-slave,
bond(s)man, bond(s)woman, bondmaid, helot
⊟ master

series *n*
set, cycle, succession, sequence, run, progression, row,
chain, string, line, train, stream, order, arrangement,
course
formal concatenation

serious *adj*
1 IMPORTANT, significant, weighty, momentous,
crucial, critical, urgent, pressing, acute, grave,
worrying, difficult, life-and-death, grim, severe, deep,
far-reaching
formal of consequence, consequential
colloq. no joke, no laughing matter
2 UNSMILING, long-faced, humourless, unlaughing,
grim, dour, solemn, sober, sombre, grave, grim, stern,
thoughtful, quiet, pensive, preoccupied, earnest,
genuine, honest, sincere
colloq. heavy
3 *serious injuries*
severe, acute, critical, grave, bad, dangerous,
precarious, life-and-death, grievous
formal perilous
⊟ **1** trivial **2** smiling, laughing, joking, light-
hearted, facetious, frivolous **3** slight, trivial

seriously *adv*
1 SOLEMNLY, thoughtfully, earnestly, sincerely,
joking apart
2 ACUTELY, gravely, badly, severely, critically,
dangerously, sorely, distressingly, grievously
⊟ **1** casually **2** slightly

seriousness *n*
1 IMPORTANCE, significance, urgency, weight,
gravity
formal moment
2 SOLEMNITY, earnestness, humourlessness,
sternness, staidness, sedateness
formal sobriety, gravitas
⊟ **1** triviality, slightness **2** casualness

sermon *n*
address, discourse, lecture, talk, message, harangue,
homily
formal oration, exhortation, declamation
colloq. talking-to

serpentine *adj*
winding, twisting, tortuous, meandering, coiling,
crooked, sinuous, snakelike, snaking, snaky
formal serpentiform
⊟ straight

serrated *adj*
toothed, notched, indented, jagged, sawlike,
saw-toothed, saw-edged
formal serratulate, serrulated
⊟ smooth

serried *adj*
dense, close, close-set, crowded, compact, massed
⊟ scattered

servant *n*
attendant, retainer, hireling, help, helper, assistant,
ancillary
Related adjectives: menial, servile
⊟ master, mistress

Kinds of servant include: au pair, barmaid, barman,
batman, *US* bell-hop, boots, butler, care assistant,
carer, chambermaid, *colloq.* char, charlady,
chauffeur, chauffeuse, chef, cleaner, coachman,
commissionaire, cook, *colloq.* daily,
colloq. dogsbody, domestic, domestic help, drudge,
equerry, errand boy, factotum, fag, flunkey,
footman, governess, groom, henchman,
henchperson, henchwoman, home help, house boy,
housekeeper, housemaid, kitchen-maid, lackey,
lady-in-waiting, lady's maid, maid, manservant,
menial, nanny, ostler, page, page-boy, parlour-maid,
scullery maid, scullion, seneschal, *colloq.* skivvy,
slave, steward, stewardess, *colloq.* tweeny, valet,
waiter, waitress, wet nurse.

serve *v*
1 WAIT ON, attend, minister to, be employed by, work
for, help, aid, assist, be of assistance to, benefit, be of
benefit to, further, support, be of use to
formal succour
colloq. do a good turn to
2 *serve a purpose*
fulfil, complete, answer, satisfy, perform, carry out, go
through, act, function, do the work of
formal discharge, suffice
3 DISTRIBUTE, give out, dish up, wait, dole out,
present, deliver, take care of, provide, supply

service *n, v*
▶ *n* **1** EMPLOYMENT, work, labour, business, duty,
duties, job, function, performance, activity, assistance
2 USE, usefulness, utility, advantage, benefit, help,
assistance
colloq. turn
3 SERVICING, maintenance, repair(s), overhaul,
check
4 *church service*
worship, observance, ceremony, rite, ritual, sacrament,
ordinance
5 *armed services*
forces, air force, navy, army
See also panel at **armed services**.
6 *railway/postal services*
facilities, amenities, resources, utilities
▶ *v* maintain, overhaul, check, repair, go over,
recondition, tune

serviceable *adj*
usable, useful, helpful, profitable, advantageous,
beneficial, utilitarian, simple, plain, unadorned,
strong, tough, durable, hard-wearing, dependable,
efficient, functional, practical, sensible, convenient
⊟ unserviceable, unusable

servile *adj*
obsequious, toadying, cringing, fawning, grovelling,
bootlicking, slavish, subservient, subject, submissive,
humble, abject, low, lowly, mean, base, menial
formal sycophantic
⊟ assertive, aggressive

servility *n*
obsequiousness, toadyism, grovelling, fawning,

bootlicking, self-abasement, slavishness, submissiveness, subservience, meanness, unctuousness, abjection, abjectness, baseness
formal sycophancy
⊟ aggressiveness, boldness

serving *n*
helping, portion, share, amount, plateful, bowlful, spoonful, ration

servitude *n*
slavery, enslavement, bondage, obedience, bonds, chains, serfdom, thrall, thraldom, vassalage, villeinage
formal subjugation
⊟ freedom, liberty

session *n*
1 MEETING, sitting, hearing, assembly, conference, discussion
2 PERIOD, stretch, spell, time, term, semester, year

set *v, n, adj*
▶ *v* **1** PUT, place, lay (down), locate, situate, position, station, arrange, prepare, make ready, install, lodge, insert, fix, stick, park, deposit, rest
colloq. plonk, dump
2 SCHEDULE, appoint, arrange, organize, designate, specify, name, prescribe, ordain, assign, allocate, impose, fix, establish, determine, stipulate, decide, conclude, confirm, settle, agree on, resolve
3 ADJUST, regulate, synchronize, co-ordinate, harmonize, put right
4 *set the table*
lay, prepare, get ready, arrange, set out
5 *set something in motion*
cause, start, begin, occasion, bring about, produce, prompt, set off, give rise to, lead to, result in, trigger (off)
6 *set someone a task*
assign, allocate, give, grant, delegate, choose, select, consign
7 *set a record/precedent*
establish, provide, inaugurate, start, begin, create, bring into being
8 *set a trap*
prepare, arrange, organize, lay, set up, plan, devise
9 *set words to music*
arrange, score, adapt, write, orchestrate, harmonize
10 *the sun sets*
go down, go below the horizon, sink, dip, decline, subside, disappear, vanish
11 CONGEAL, thicken, gel, stiffen, become firm/ hard, solidify, harden, cake, coagulate, crystallize
⊟ **10** rise
▷ **set about** begin, start, get down to, embark on, undertake, tackle, attack; *formal* commence; *colloq.* set the ball rolling
▷ **set against 1** BALANCE, compare, contrast, weigh; *formal* juxtapose **2** OPPOSE, divide, disunite, alienate; *formal* estrange
▷ **set apart** distinguish, make different, differentiate, mark off, put aside, separate
▷ **set aside 1** PUT ASIDE, lay aside, lay by, keep (back), put away, save, keep in reserve, reserve, set apart, separate, select, earmark, mothball; *colloq.* stash away **2** ANNUL, cancel, reverse, overturn, overrule, reject, ignore, discount, discard; *formal* abrogate, revoke
▷ **set back** delay, hold up, slow, thwart, check, hinder, impede; *formal* retard
▷ **set down 1** LAY DOWN, record, stipulate, assert,

affirm, state, establish, formulate, prescribe
2 WRITE DOWN, note (down), record, put in writing
▷ **set forth 1** EXPLAIN, expound, describe, present, set out, clarify; *formal* delineate, elucidate, explicate **2** *set forth on a journey* depart, set out, set off, leave, start out
▷ **set in** begin, start, come, arrive;
formal commence
▷ **set off 1** LEAVE, depart, set out, start (out), set forth, begin **2** DETONATE, blow up, light, ignite, touch off, trigger off, explode **3** ACTIVATE, trigger (off), touch off, prompt, encourage, initiate, set in motion **4** DISPLAY, show off, enhance, contrast, throw into relief, heighten, intensify
▷ **set on** set upon, attack, assault, turn on, go for, fall upon, lay into, mug; *colloq.* beat up
▷ **set out 1** LEAVE, depart, set off, start (out), begin **2** ARRANGE, lay out, display, exhibit, present, describe, explain
▷ **set up 1** BUILD, raise, elevate, erect, construct, assemble, compose; *formal* dispose, array **2** START, form, create, establish, institute, found, inaugurate, initiate, begin, introduce, bring into being, organize, arrange, prepare **3** FRAME, trap, incriminate, accuse falsely; *colloq.* fit up
▶ *n* **1** COLLECTION, batch, series, sequence, kit, outfit, compendium, assortment, class, category
formal array, assemblage
2 *a set of people*
group, band, gang, crowd, circle, clique, faction
3 *the set of a film*
setting, background, scene, scenery, backdrop, wings, *mise-en-scène*
4 *the set of someone's face/body*
expression, turn, look, position, posture
formal bearing
▶ *adj* **1** FIXED, established, scheduled, appointed, arranged, prearranged, specified, decided, agreed, settled, firm, strict, rigid, inflexible, ingrained, entrenched
formal predetermined, prescribed, ordained
2 REGULAR, routine, usual, customary, everyday, traditional, habitual, standard, stock, stereotyped, conventional
3 READY, prepared, equipped, arranged, organized, completed, finished, all set
⊟ **1** undecided, movable **2** spontaneous
3 unprepared

setback *n*
delay, problem, hitch, hiccup, reverse, reversal, stumbling-block, impediment, hindrance, obstruction, misfortune, upset, disappointment, defeat
colloq. hold-up, snag, blow
⊟ boost, advance, help, advantage

setting *n*
mounting, frame, surroundings, milieu, environment, background, context, perspective, period, position, location, locale, site, scene, scenery, *mise-en-scène*

setting-up *n*
start, establishment, institution, initiation, inauguration, foundation, founding, introduction, creation
formal inception
⊟ abolition, termination

settle *v*
1 AGREE (ON), decide, resolve, reconcile, solve, compromise, fix, establish, determine, decide (on),

settle on, choose, confirm, appoint, arrange
colloq. patch up, clinch
2 ARRANGE, order, put in order, organize, adjust, complete, conclude
3 SINK, subside, drop, fall, come down, descend, land, alight, light upon
formal repose
4 COLONIZE, occupy, populate, people, inhabit, live, make your home, put down roots
formal reside
5 *settle a bill*
pay, clear, discharge, settle up, square (up)
colloq. fork out, cough up, foot
▷ **settle down** calm down, make comfortable, quieten, still, soothe, compose

settlement *n*
1 RESOLUTION, agreement, arrangement, contract, decision, conclusion, reconciliation, satisfaction
formal termination
colloq. patching up
2 ARRANGEMENT, ordering, organization, completion, conclusion
3 PAYMENT, clearance, clearing, liquidation, discharge
formal defrayal
4 COLONY, outpost, community, kibbutz, camp, encampment, hamlet, village, plantation, establishment, colonization, occupation, population

settler *n*
colonist, colonizer, pioneer, frontiersman, frontierswoman, planter, immigrant, incomer, newcomer, squatter
F3 native

set-to *n*
argument, quarrel, conflict, fight, row, squabble, wrangle, disagreement, exchange, fracas, brush, contest, slanging-match
formal altercation
colloq. argy-bargy, barney, dust-up, scrap, spat

set-up *n*
system, structure, organization, composition, arrangement, format, framework, business, conditions, circumstances
formal disposition

sever *v*
1 CUT, split, part, separate, divide, break off, tear off, lop off, chop (off), hack, cut off, amputate, detach, disconnect, disjoin, disunite
old use rend
formal cleave
2 *sever a relationship*
dissociate, alienate, break off, dissolve, end
formal cease, terminate, estrange
F3 **1** join, combine, attach, unite

several *adj*
some, many, a number of, (quite) a few, various, assorted, sundry, diverse, different, distinct, separate, particular, individual
formal disparate

severally *adv*
separately, individually, singly, discretely, particularly, respectively, specifically, seriatim, apiece
F3 simultaneously, together

severe *adj*
1 EXTREME, acute, intense, fierce, violent, strong, forceful, powerful, cruel, pitiless, merciless, relentless, inexorable, harsh, tough, hard, difficult, grim, forbidding, rigorous, stringent, drastic, draconian, tyrannical
2 STRICT, rigid, unbending, stern, grim, dour, cold, unsympathetic, disapproving, sober, serious, unsmiling, strait-laced
3 AUSTERE, ascetic, plain, simple, modest, start, Spartan, undecorated, unembellished, unadorned, functional
4 *a severe illness*
serious, grave, critical, acute, dangerous, perilous
5 HARD, difficult, demanding, rigorous, arduous, burdensome, taxing, exacting, punishing
F3 **1** mild, kind, compassionate, sympathetic
2 lenient **3** decorated, ornate **4** minor **5** easy, simple

severely *adv*
1 EXTREMELY, acutely, intensely, badly, critically, dangerously, gravely
2 STRICTLY, rigorously, disapprovingly, sternly, hard, harshly, sharply, sorely, grimly, bitterly, coldly, unsympathetically, dourly

severity *n*
1 EXTREMITY, acuteness, severeness, intensity, strength, forcefulness, fierceness
2 HARSHNESS, hardness, toughness, sharpness, ungentleness, ruthlessness, pitilessness, mercilessness, grimness, stringency, coldness, sternness, strictness, seriousness, gravity
3 AUSTERITY, plainness, rigour, asceticism, simplicity, bareness, plainness, Spartanism
F3 **1** mildness **2** compassion, kindness, leniency

sew *v*
stitch, tack, baste, hem, darn, mend, seam, embroider
Related adjectives: sutorial, sutorian

sex *n*
1 GENDER, sexuality, sex appeal, sexual desire, libido, sex attraction, sensuality, desirability, allure, seductiveness, glamour, sexiness, magnetism, voluptuousness
formal nubility
colloq. it
2 SEXUAL INTERCOURSE, intercourse, sexual relations, copulation, lovemaking, fornication, reproduction, union, intimacy, intimate relations
formal consummation, coitus, coition
colloq. sleeping with someone, going to bed with someone; *taboo slang* fuck, fucking, screw, screwing, shag, shagging
Related adjective: sexual

sexless *adj*
asexual, unsexual, unsexed, unfeminine, unmasculine, undersexed, neuter
technical parthenogenetic

sexton *n*
caretaker, verger, grave-digger, grave-maker, fossor, sacristan

sexual *adj*
sex, reproductive, procreative, genital, coital, venereal, carnal, sensual, erotic

sexuality *n*
sexual instincts, sexual urge, sexual orientation, sexual desire, sexiness, sensuality, desire, carnality, eroticism, virility, lust, voluptuousness

Sexual orientations include: bisexual, *slang* AC/DC; hermaphrodite, unisexual; heterosexual; homosexual, gay, *slang* queer, *colloq.* cissy, *slang* pretty boy, *slang* nancy, *slang* nancy boy, *slang* pansy, *US slang* faggot, rent boy, lesbian, *slang* lez, *slang* dyke, *colloq.* butch; transsexual, transvestite, cross-dresser.

sexy *adj*
alluring, desirable, attractive, sensual, voluptuous, nubile, seductive, inviting, flirtatious, arousing, stimulating, slinky, provoking, provocative, titillating, pornographic, erotic, salacious, suggestive
colloq. raunchy, beddable
F3 sexless

shabby *adj*
1 RAGGED, tattered, frayed, threadbare, worn, worn-out, mangy, moth-eaten, faded, scruffy, tatty, dowdy, disreputable
2 DILAPIDATED, run-down, broken-down, tumbledown, ramshackle, seedy, dirty, squalid, dingy, poky, in disrepair
colloq. tacky
3 *a shabby trick*
unfair, contemptible, despicable, rotten, mean, low, cheap, shoddy, unworthy, shameful, dishonourable
F3 1, 2 smart **3** honourable, fair

shack *n*
hut, cabin, shanty, hovel, shed, hutch, lean-to
colloq. dump, hole

shackle *v, n*
▶ *v* **1** HAMPER, inhibit, impede, encumber, limit, restrict, restrain, secure, thwart, bind, tie, constrain, obstruct, handicap, hamstring
2 CHAIN, handcuff, bind, restrain, manacle, fetter, trammel, tether
old use gyve
▶ *n* bond, tether, chain, fetter, iron, handcuff, rope, manacle, trammel
old use gyve
colloq. bracelets, darbies

shade *n, v*
▶ *n* **1** SHADINESS, shadow(s), darkness, obscurity, semi-darkness, dimness, gloom, gloominess, murkiness, twilight, dusk, gloaming
2 AWNING, canopy, cover, covering, shelter, protection, screen, blind, curtain, veil, shield, visor, umbrella, parasol
3 COLOUR, hue, tint, tone, tinge
4 TRACE, dash, hint, suggestion, suspicion, touch, memory, reminder, nuance, gradation, degree, difference, amount, variety
colloq. tad
5 GHOST, spectre, phantom, spirit, apparition, semblance
▶ **a shade** a little, a bit, rather, slightly, a touch, a trifle
▶ **put in the shade** outshine, outclass, surpass, beat, excel, eclipse, outrank, top, dwarf
▶ *v* shield, screen, protect, cover, shroud, veil, hide, conceal, obscure, block light from, cloud, dim, darken, shadow, overshadow

shadow *n, v*
▶ *n* **1** SHADE, darkness, obscurity, inconspicuousness, semi-darkness, dimness, gloom, twilight, dusk, gloaming, cloud, cover, protection
formal tenebrosity
2 SILHOUETTE, shape, outline, image,

representation
3 *cast a shadow over the proceedings*
cloud, gloom, sadness, blight, foreboding
4 FOLLOWER, companion, inseparable companion, pal, detective, sleuth
colloq. sidekick
5 TRACE, hint, suggestion, suspicion, vestige, remnant
▶ **a shadow of your former self** vestige, remnant, weaker version, poor imitation
▶ *v* **1** OVERSHADOW, overhang, shade, shield, screen, obscure, darken
2 FOLLOW, tail, dog, stalk, trail, watch

shadowy *adj*
1 DARK, gloomy, murky, obscure, dim
formal crepuscular, tenebrous, tenebrose, tenebrious
2 VAGUE, faint, indistinct, ill-defined, indistinguishable, indeterminate, unclear, hazy, nebulous, intangible, unsubstantial, ethereal, ghostly, spectral, phantom, illusory, dreamlike, imaginary, unreal, mysterious

shady *adj*
1 SHADED, shadowy, shielded, screened, protected, covered, shrouded, veiled, dim, dark, obscure, clouded, cool, leafy, bowery
old use caliginous
formal umbrageous, umbratile, umbratilous, umbriferous, umbrose, umbrous, tenebrous, tenebrose, tenebrious
2 DUBIOUS, questionable, suspect, suspicious, dishonest, crooked, unreliable, untrustworthy, disreputable, unscrupulous, unethical, underhand
colloq. fishy, slippery, iffy
F3 1 sunny, sunlit, bright **2** honest, trustworthy, honourable

shaft *n*
1 PASSAGE, duct, tunnel, well, flue
2 HANDLE, shank, stem, upright, pillar, pole, rod, bar, stick, arrow
3 *a shaft of light*
ray, dart, pencil, beam, duct, passage
technical winze

shaggy *adj*
hairy, long-haired, hirsute, bushy, woolly, unshorn, dishevelled, unkempt
formal crinose
F3 bald, shorn, close-cropped

shake *v, n*
▶ *v* **1** *the windows are shaking in the wind*
rattle, jolt, jerk, bump, roll, bounce, judder, wag, agitate, twitch, convulse, heave, throb, vibrate, oscillate
2 TREMBLE, quiver, quake, wobble, totter, sway, rock, shiver, shudder, judder, convulse
3 WAVE, swing, flourish, brandish, wield
4 *the news shook her*
upset, distress, alarm, shock, shake up, frighten, unnerve, intimidate, disturb, unsettle, agitate, stir, rouse
formal discompose, perturb
colloq. rattle, faze
5 *shake someone's confidence*
weaken, undermine, reduce, diminish, lower, lessen
▶ **shake a leg** hurry, get a move on; *colloq.* get cracking, step on it, look lively
▶ **shake off** get rid of, dislodge, lose, elude, escape, give the slip, leave behind, outdistance, outstrip
▶ **shake up 1** *the accident shook me up* upset, distress, alarm, shock, unnerve, unsettle;

colloq. rattle **2** *shake up an organization*
reorganize, rearrange; *colloq.* reshuffle
▶ *n* **1** JOLT, rattle, roll, bounce, rocking, jerk, judder,
twitch, throbbing, vibration, oscillation
2 TREMBLING, convulsion, quiver, quake, quaking,
shiver, shivering, shudder, shuddering
3 SHOCK, upset, alarm, disturbance, jolt, unsettling

shake-up *n*
reorganization, rearrangement, disturbance, upheaval
colloq. reshuffle

shaky *adj*
1 TREMBLING, quivering, quavery, faltering,
unsteady, wobbly, tottering, tottery, staggering,
doddering, tentative, uncertain
formal tremulous
2 UNSTABLE, unsteady, insecure, precarious, wobbly,
rocky, tottery, rickety, weak
3 DUBIOUS, questionable, suspect, weak, flimsy,
unreliable, unsound, unfounded, ungrounded,
unsupported, untrustworthy
E3 2 firm, strong

shallow *adj*
1 *shallow water/containers*
superficial, surface, skin-deep
2 *a shallow person*
superficial, slight, flimsy, trivial, frivolous, foolish,
idle, empty, petty, trifling, meaningless, unscholarly,
ignorant, simple, insincere
E3 1 deep, profound **2** deep, profound, serious,
careful

sham *n, adj, v*
▶ *n* **1** PRETENCE, fraud, counterfeit, imposture,
forgery, fake, copy, imitation, simulation, feigning,
hoax
colloq. humbug
2 IMPOSTOR, fraud, fake, charlatan, impersonator,
pretender, deceiver, cheat, swindler
colloq. phoney, con man
▶ *adj* false, fake, counterfeit, spurious, bogus,
pretended, feigned, make-believe, put-on, simulated,
artificial, mock, imitation, synthetic
colloq. phoney
E3 genuine, authentic, real
▶ *v* pretend, feign, put on, make believe, simulate,
imitate, fake, counterfeit
formal affect, dissemble

shaman *n*
magician, sorcerer, witch doctor, medicine man,
medicine woman, powwow, pawaw, angekok

shamble *v*
shuffle, scrape, drag, falter, limp, toddle, doddle,
hobble

shambles *n*
mess, chaos, muddle, confusion, disorganization,
disorder, havoc, anarchy, bedlam, wreck
formal disarray
colloq. madhouse, pigsty

shambling *adj*
awkward, clumsy, unsteady, ungainly, lumbering,
lurching, shuffling, unco-ordinated, disjointed, loose
E3 agile, neat, nimble, spry

shame *n, v*
▶ *n* **1** HUMILIATION, degradation,
shamefacedness, remorse, guilt, embarrassment,
mortification
formal compunction

2 DISGRACE, dishonour, discredit, stain, stigma,
disrepute, infamy, scandal
formal ignominy, opprobrium
3 *it's a shame*
pity, disappointment, misfortune, unfortunate thing,
bad luck
E3 1 pride **2** honour, credit, distinction
▷ **put to shame** show up, humiliate, humble,
embarrass, mortify, disgrace, upstage, outshine,
outclass, outstrip, surpass, eclipse
▶ *v* embarrass, mortify, abash, confound, humiliate,
ridicule, humble, put to shame, show up, disgrace,
dishonour, discredit, debase, degrade, sully, taint, stain

shamefaced *adj*
ashamed, conscience-stricken, guilty, regretful,
penitent, remorseful, contrite, apologetic, sorry, red-
faced, blushing, embarrassed, mortified, abashed,
humiliated, uncomfortable
colloq. sheepish
E3 unashamed, proud

shameful *adj*
1 *a shameful waste of money*
disgraceful, outrageous, shocking, scandalous,
indecent, abominable, atrocious, wicked, mean, base,
low, vile, reprehensible, dishonourable, discreditable,
inglorious, contemptible, unworthy, ignoble
formal heinous
2 EMBARRASSING, mortifying, shaming,
humiliating
formal ignominious
E3 1 honourable, creditable, worthy

shameless *adj*
1 UNASHAMED, unabashed, unrepentant,
unregretful, impenitent, barefaced, flagrant, blatant,
brazen, brash, audacious, insolent, imprudent,
defiant, hardened, incorrigible
2 IMMODEST, indecent, improper, unprincipled,
wanton, dissolute, corrupt, depraved
formal unbecoming, indecorous, unseemly
E3 1 ashamed, shamefaced, contrite **2** modest

shanty *n*
hut, cabin, shed, shack, lean-to, hovel, bothy, hutch

shape *n, v*
▶ *n* **1** FORM, outline, outward appearance,
silhouette, profile, model, mould, pattern, cut, lines,
contours, figure, physique, build, structure, frame,
design, format
formal configuration
2 APPEARANCE, guise, likeness, form, look, aspect,
image, air, guise, semblance
3 *in good shape*
condition, state, form, health, trim, fettle, kilter
4 PATTERN, mould, model, format, structure,
character
formal configuration

Geometrical shapes include: circle, semicircle,
quadrant, oval, ellipse, crescent, triangle, equilateral
triangle, isosceles triangle, scalene triangle,
quadrilateral, square, rectangle, oblong, rhombus,
diamond, kite, trapezium, parallelogram, polygon,
pentagon, hexagon, heptagon, octagon, nonagon,
decagon, polyhedron, cube, cuboid, prism, pyramid,
tetrahedron, pentahedron, octahedron, cylinder,
cone, sphere, hemisphere.

▶ *v* form, fashion, model, mould, cast, forge, sculpt,
sculpture, carve, whittle, make, guide, influence,
develop, produce, construct, create, design, define,

devise, frame, block, plan, prepare, organize, develop, adapt, adjust, regulate, accommodate, alter, modify, remodel
▷ **shape up** develop, come on, take shape, progress, make progress, move forward, make headway, flourish

shapeless *adj*
formless, amorphous, unformed, unfashioned, undeveloped, unframed, nebulous, unstructured, irregular, misshapen, badly proportioned, ill-proportioned, deformed, dumpy

shapely *adj*
elegant, pretty, attractive, well-formed, well-proportioned, well-turned, trim, neat, graceful, gainly, curvaceous, voluptuous
old use comely

shard *n*
fragment, piece, bit, part, chip, particle, splinter, shiver

share *v, n*
▶ *v* divide, split, go halves, partake, participate, have a share in, share out, distribute, dole out, give out, hand out, deal out, allot, allocate, assign
formal apportion
colloq. go fifty-fifty, go Dutch, carve up
▶ *n* portion, ration, quota, allowance, allocation, allotment, lot, part, division, proportion, percentage, dividend, due, contribution
colloq. cut, whack, rake-off, slice of the cake, piece/slice of the action
▷ **share out** give out, distribute, hand out, mete out, divide up, parcel out, allot, apportion, assign
◨ monopolize

shark *n*
1 *a man-eating shark*

Types of shark include: basking, blue, dogfish, fox, ghost, goblin, great white, Greenland, grey reef, hammerhead, leopard, mackerel, mako, man-eating, nurse, porbeagle, requiem, saw, thresher, tiger, whale.

2 CROOK, extortioner, swindler, parasite, slicker
colloq. fleecer, sponger, wheeler-dealer

sharp *adj, adv*
▶ *adj* **1** *a sharp needle*
pointed, keen, edged, knife-edged, razor-edged, razor-sharp, needle-like, cutting, serrated, jagged, barbed, spiky
2 QUICK-WITTED, quick, clever, bright, intelligent, alert, shrewd, astute, perceptive, observant, discerning, penetrating
3 HARSH, brusque, incisive, cutting, biting, cruel, hurtful, malicious, caustic, sarcastic, sardonic, scathing, vitriolic, venomous
formal trenchant, acrimonious
4 CLEAR, clear-cut, well-defined, distinct, crisp
5 SUDDEN, abrupt, unexpected, violent, fierce, rapid, tight, intense, extreme, severe, keen, acute, piercing, stinging, shooting, stabbing
6 PUNGENT, strong, piquant, sour, tart, vinegary, bitter, biting, acerbic, acid, acidic, burning, acrid
7 CRAFTY, clever, deceptive, dishonest, cunning, artful, wily, sly
8 *a sharp dresser*
neat, tidy, smart, elegant, stylish, fashionable
colloq. snappy, natty
◨ **1** blunt **2** slow, stupid **3** mild **4** blurred **5** gentle **6** bland **8** shabby
▶ *adv* punctually, promptly, on the dot, exactly,

precisely, abruptly, suddenly, unexpectedly
◨ approximately, roughly

sharpen *v*
edge, whet, hone, grind, file, keen, strop
formal acuminate
◨ blunt, blur

sharp-eyed *adj*
observant, perceptive, noticing, eagle-eyed, hawk-eyed, keen-sighted
◨ short-sighted, unobservant

sharpness *n*
1 DISCERNMENT, penetration, acuteness, keenness, astuteness, shrewdness, observation, perceptiveness, incisiveness, eagerness
2 INTENSITY, fierceness, severity
3 HARSHNESS, brusqueness, cruelty, incisiveness, sarcasm, vitriol, venom
4 CLARITY, definition, precision, crispness

shatter *v*
1 BREAK, break, smash, splinter, shiver, crack, split, burst, explode, blast, crush, demolish, smash/blow to smithereens
formal pulverize
2 *shatter your hopes*
destroy, devastate, dash, crush, wreck, ruin, disappoint, overturn
3 *shattered by her death*
upset, devastate, crush, overwhelm, break your heart

shattered *adj*
1 OVERWHELMED, devastated, crushed, broken
2 WORN OUT, exhausted, weary, tired out
colloq. all in, dead beat, dog-tired, done in, knackered, zonked

shattering *adj*
devastating, damaging, crushing, overwhelming, paralysing, severe

shave *v*
cut, trim, barber, shear, crop, fleece, graze, brush, touch, pare, cut, plane, scrape

sheaf *n*
bundle, bunch, armful, truss

sheath *n*
1 SCABBARD, case, sleeve, envelope, shell, wrapping, casing, covering
2 CONDOM, protective contraceptive,
US prophylactic
slang rubber, French letter, johnnie
Related adjective: thecal

shed¹ *v*
1 DROP, cast (off), moult, discard, slough, spill
2 GET RID OF, pour, spill, scatter, diffuse, emit, shower, throw, radiate, shine

shed² *n*
a garden shed
hut, outhouse, lean-to, building, shack

sheen *n*
lustre, gloss, shine, gleam, sparkle, shimmer, brightness, brilliance, shininess, polish, burnish
formal patina
◨ dullness, tarnish

sheep *n*
ram, ewe, lamb, wether, tup, bell-wether
Austral. colloq. jumbuck
Related adjective: ovine

sheepish *adj*
ashamed, shamefaced, embarrassed, mortified,
chastened, abashed, uncomfortable, self-conscious,
silly, foolish
E3 unabashed, brazen, bold

sheer[1] *adj*
1 UTTER, complete, total, absolute, thorough, mere,
pure, unadulterated, downright, out-and-out, rank,
veritable, thoroughgoing, unconditional, unqualified
formal unmitigated
2 *a sheer drop*
vertical, perpendicular, precipitous, abrupt, steep,
sharp
3 THIN, fine, light, delicate, flimsy, gauzy, gossamer,
translucent, transparent, see-through
formal diaphanous
E3 2 gentle, gradual **3** thick, heavy

sheer[2] *v*
sheer away to the right
swerve, turn, bend, veer, swing, shift, drift, deviate,
diverge, deflect

sheet *n*
1 *cotton sheets*
cover, blanket, bed-linen
2 COVERING, coating, coat, film, layer, stratum,
skin, membrane, veneer, overlay, plate, piece, panel,
slab, plate, pane
formal lamina
3 *a sheet of paper*
leaf, page, folio
4 *a sheet of ice*
expanse, stretch, reach, sweep, surface

shelf *n*
1 *put books on the shelf*
ledge, mantelpiece, mantelshelf, sill, step, bench,
bracket, counter, bar
2 *the shelf on the seabed*
bank, sandbank, reef, ledge, terrace, continental shelf,
sand bar, bar, step, shoal

shell *n, v*
▶ *n* **1** COVERING, covering, hull, husk, pod, rind,
crust, case, carapace, casing, body, chassis, frame,
framework, structure, skeleton
technical integument
US shuck
Related adjective: conchoidal
2 EXPLOSIVE, bullet, shot, pellet, missile, grenade
▶ *v* **1** *shell nuts*
hull, husk, pod
US shuck
2 BOMB, bombard, fire on, barrage, blitz, attack
▷ **shell out** pay out, spend, lay out, give, contribute,
donate, expend; *formal* disburse; *colloq.* ante, cough
up, fork out

shelter *n, v*
▶ *n* cover, roof, shade, shadow, protection, shield,
screen, defence, guard, security, safety, sanctuary,
asylum, haven, refuge, harbour, retreat,
accommodation, lodging
E3 exposure
▶ *v* cover, shroud, screen, shade, shadow, protect,
defend, guard, safeguard, shield, harbour, hide,
conceal, accommodate, put up
E3 expose

sheltered *adj*
covered, shaded, shady, shielded, protected, screened,
cosy, snug, warm, quiet, secluded, isolated, retired,

withdrawn, reclusive, cloistered, unworldly
E3 exposed

shelve *v*
postpone, defer, put off, suspend, halt, put aside, lay
aside, pigeonhole, mothball
colloq. put on ice, put on the back burner
E3 expedite, implement

shepherd *n, v*
▶ *n* shepherdess, herdess, shepherdling, herdsman,
protector, shepherd boy, herdboy, guardian
Related adjective: pastoral
▶ *v* guide, lead, conduct, convoy, escort, usher, steer,
marshal, herd

shield *n, v*
▶ *n* buckler, defence, bulwark, rampart, support,
screen, guard, cover, shelter, protection, protector,
safeguard, targe
technical escutcheon
▶ *v* defend, guard, protect, safeguard, screen, shade,
shadow, cover, shelter
E3 expose

shift *v, n*
▶ *v* **1** CHANGE, vary, fluctuate, alter, adjust, modify,
move, budge, relocate, reposition, rearrange, transfer,
carry, switch, swerve, veer
formal transpose
2 REMOVE, dislodge, displace, get rid of
▶ *n* **1** CHANGE, variation, fluctuation, alteration,
modification, move, movement, removal, switch,
displacement, relocation, rearrangement, transfer
formal transposition
colloq. U-turn
2 *work shifts*
period, spell, time, stretch, span, stint

shiftless *adj*
lazy, idle, unambitious, unenterprising, resourceless,
aimless, directionless, goalless, incompetent,
inefficient, irresponsible, inept, feckless
formal indolent, ineffectual, slothful
colloq. good-for-nothing, lackadaisical
E3 enterprising, ambitious, aspiring, eager

shifty *adj*
untrustworthy, dishonest, deceitful, scheming,
contriving, tricky, wily, crafty, cunning, devious,
evasive, furtive, underhand, dubious
formal duplicitous
colloq. shady, slippery, iffy
E3 dependable, honest, open

shilly-shally *v*
dither, hesitate, vacillate, waver, fluctuate, falter, teeter,
seesaw
formal prevaricate
colloq. dilly-dally, hem and haw, mess about

shimmer *v, n*
▶ *v* glisten, gleam, sparkle, glimmer, glint, glitter,
scintillate, glow, flicker, twinkle
▶ *n* lustre, gleam, sparkle, glint, glimmer, glitter,
glistening, glow, flicker, twinkle
formal iridescence

shimmering *adj*
glittering, glowing, glistening, gleaming, shining,
shiny, lustrous, luminous
technical aventurine
formal incandescent, iridescent
E3 dull, matt

shin *v*
climb, mount, soar, scramble, ascend, clamber, scale, shoot, swarm

shine *v, n*
▶ *v* **1** BEAM, radiate, glow, flash, glare, dazzle, gleam, glint, glitter, flicker, sparkle, twinkle, shimmer, glisten, glimmer, give off, emit
formal incandesce
2 POLISH, burnish, gloss, buff, brush, rub (up), wax
3 *shine at athletics*
excel, stand out, be brilliant, be excellent, be outstanding, be pre-eminent
▶ *n* **1** LIGHT, radiance, glow, brightness, glare, dazzle, flash, gleam, sparkle, shimmer, glitter, glint, flicker, twinkle
formal effulgence, luminescence, incandescence, lambency
2 GLOSS, polish, burnish, gleam, sheen, lustre, glaze
formal patina

shininess *n*
brightness, gleam, glitter, shine, sheen, polish, lustre, glossiness, burnish
formal effulgence
F3 dullness

shining *adj*
1 BRIGHT, radiant, glowing, beaming, flashing, gleaming, glittering, glinting, glistening, shimmering, twinkling, sparkling, flickering, luminous, brilliant, splendid, glorious
formal phosphorescent, resplendent, effulgent, incandescent
2 *a shining example*
conspicuous, outstanding, splendid, magnificent, glorious, brilliant, leading, eminent, pre-eminent, celebrated, distinguished, illustrious
F3 **1** dark

shiny *adj*
polished, burnished, shining, sheeny, lustrous, glossy, silky, sleek, bright, gleaming, glistening, shimmering
F3 dull, matt

ship *n*
vessel, craft, liner, steamer, tanker, trawler, ferry, boat, yacht

Parts of a ship include: anchor, berth, bilge, boiler room, bollard, bridge, brig, bulkhead, bulwarks, bunk, cabin, capstan, chain locker, chart room, cleat, companion ladder, companion way, crow's nest, davit; deck, after deck, boat deck, flight deck, gun deck, lower deck, main deck, poop deck, promenade deck, quarter deck, top deck; engine room, figurehead, forecastle (fo'c'sle), funnel, galley, gangplank, gangway, gunwale (gunnel), hammock, hatch, hatchway, hawser, head, hold, keel, landing, mast, oar, paddle wheel, pilot house, Plimsoll line, port, porthole, prow, quarter, radio room, rigger, rowlock, rudder, sail, stabilizer, stanchion, starboard, stateroom, stern, superstructure, tiller, transom, wardroom, waterline, wheel, winch. *See also* **boat; sail**.

shipshape *adj*
tidy, neat, orderly, spruce, trim, well-organized, well-planned, businesslike, well-regulated, spick and span, trig
F3 disorderly, untidy

shirk *v*
dodge, get out of, evade, avoid, shun, shrink from, play truant, slack
colloq. duck, skive

shirker *n*
dodger, slacker, idler, layabout, loafer, absentee, truant, malingerer, shirk
colloq. quitter, skiver

shiver¹ *v, n*
▶ *v* *shivering with cold*
shudder, tremble, quiver, quake, shake, vibrate, palpitate, flutter
▶ *n* shudder, quiver, shake, tremor, twitch, start, vibration, flutter

shiver² *n, v*
▶ *n* *shivers of light*
splinter, piece, bit, fragment, shred, sliver, shaving, chip, shard
colloq. smithereen(s)
▶ *v* shatter, break, smash, splinter, crack, split

shivery *adj*
cold, chilly, trembly, shuddery, shaking, quivery, quaking, chilled, nervous, fluttery

shoal *n*
group, mass, multitude, mob, throng, swarm, horde, flock
formal assemblage

shock *v, n*
▶ *v* disgust, revolt, repel, sicken, offend, nauseate, appal, outrage, scandalize, outrage, horrify, startle, astound, stagger, amaze, stun, daze, stupefy, numb, paralyse, traumatize, jolt, jar, shake, agitate, unsettle, upset, distress, disquiet, unnerve, bewilder, take aback, confound, dumbfound, dismay
formal perturb
colloq. bowl over
F3 delight, please, gratify, reassure
▶ *n* **1** FRIGHT, fright, start, jolt, surprise, blow, trauma, upset, distress, dismay, disgust, outrage, horror
formal consternation, perturbation
colloq. bombshell, thunderbolt, bolt from the blue, rude awakening
2 IMPACT, crash, collision, blow, shake, jolt, jarring, jerk
F3 **1** delight, pleasure, reassurance

shocking *adj*
appalling, outrageous, scandalous, offensive, horrifying, disgraceful, deplorable, intolerable, unbearable, atrocious, abominable, monstrous, vile, foul, unspeakable, detestable, abhorrent, dreadful, loathsome, awful, terrible, frightful, ghastly, hideous, horrible, horrific, disgusting, revolting, repulsive, sickening, nauseating, unsettling, disquieting, distressing
formal perturbing, repugnant
F3 acceptable, satisfactory, pleasant, delightful

shoddy *adj*
inferior, second-rate, cheap, tawdry, tatty, trashy, rubbishy, poor, poor-quality, careless, slipshod, slapdash, cheapjack
colloq. ropy, tacky, rubbish
F3 superior, well-made

shoe *n*
See **footwear**.

shoemaker *n*
cobbler, bootmaker, snob, snab

shoemaking   *n*
bootmaking, cobblery, cobbling

shoot   *v, n*
▶ *v* **1** FIRE, discharge, launch, propel, kick, hit,
throw, hurl, fling, lob, project, let off, aim, direct
2 HIT, kill, injure, wound, open fire, blast, bombard,
gun down, shell, snipe at, pick off
colloq. zap
3 DART, bolt, dash, tear, rush, race, sprint, speed,
hurry, charge, fly, hurtle, streak, whisk, whiz
4 *shoot a film*
film, photograph, take photographs of, video
colloq. snap
5 GROW, germinate, shoot up, sprout, burgeon, bolt,
bud, stretch
▶ *n* sprout, bud, offshoot, branch, twig, sprig,
cutting, slip, scion, graft, tendron

shop   *n, v*
▶ *n* store, retail outlet
formal emporium

Types of shop include: bazaar, market, indoor market,
stall, mini-market, general store, corner shop,
shopping precinct, shopping mall, arcade, complex,
mall, plaza, galleria, chain store, department store,
supermarket, superstore, hypermarket, cash-and-
carry; butcher, baker, grocer, greengrocer,
fishmonger, dairy, delicatessen, health-food shop,
farm shop, fish and chip shop, take-away, off-licence,
tobacconist, sweet shop, confectioner, tuck shop;
bookshop, newsagent, stationer, chemist, pharmacy,
tailor, outfitter, dress shop, boutique, milliner, shoe
shop, haberdasher, draper, florist, jeweller, toy shop,
hardware shop, ironmonger, saddler, radio and TV
shop, video shop; launderette, hairdresser, barber,
betting shop, bookmaker, *colloq.* bookie,
pawnbroker, post office.

▶ *v* **1** *shop for clothes*
go shopping, buy, buy things, do the shopping, stock up
on, get, purchase
2 INFORM ON, betray
colloq. tell on, split, squeal, rat, blow the whistle on;
slang grass

shore¹   *n*
walk along the shore
seashore, beach, sand(s), shingle, strand, waterfront,
front, promenade, coast, seaside, seaboard, foreshore,
lakeside, bank
Related adjective: littoral

shore²   *v*
shore up a building
support, hold (up), prop (up), stay, underpin, buttress,
brace, strengthen, reinforce

shorn   *adj*
cut, cropped, shaved, shaven, stripped, bald,
beardless, crew-cut, deprived

short   *adj, adv*
▶ *adj* **1** BRIEF, cursory, fleeting, momentary, short-
lived, transitory, temporary, concise, succinct, terse,
crisp, pithy, to the point, compact, compressed,
shortened, condensed, truncated, curtailed,
abbreviated, abridged, summarized, summary
formal ephemeral, evanescent
2 SMALL, little, low, petite, slight, minuscule,
diminutive, squat, dumpy, stubby
Scot. wee
colloq. teeny, pint-size(d)
3 INADEQUATE, insufficient, deficient, lacking,

wanting, low, poor, meagre, scarce, scanty, scant,
sparse
colloq. tight
4 BRUSQUE, curt, gruff, snappy, sharp, abrupt, terse,
blunt, direct, rude, impolite, discourteous, uncivil
E◀ **1** long, lasting **2** tall **3** adequate, ample
4 polite
▶ *adv* unexpectedly, suddenly, abruptly
▷ **fall short** be less than required, be lacking,
be insufficient, be inadequate
▷ **in short** in brief, in a word, in a few words, in
conclusion, summarizing, concisely; *colloq.* in a
nutshell, to cut a long story short
▷ **short of** deficient in, lacking, missing, short on,
less than, low on, other than; *formal* wanting;
colloq. pushed for

shortage   *n*
inadequacy, insufficiency, deficiency, shortfall, deficit,
lack, want, need, scarcity, poverty, absence, dearth
formal paucity
E◀ sufficiency, abundance, surplus

shortcoming   *n*
defect, imperfection, fault, flaw, drawback, failing,
weak point, weakness, frailty, foible

shorten   *v*
cut (down), trim, prune, crop, dock, pare (down),
curtail, truncate, abbreviate, abridge, condense,
compress, contract, sum up, reduce, lessen, decrease,
diminish, take up
E◀ lengthen, enlarge, amplify

shortened   *adj*
abridged, condensed, summarized, abbreviated,
abstracted
formal abbreviatory
E◀ amplified

short-lived   *adj*
brief, momentary, passing, short, temporary, transient,
transitory, fleeting, impermanent
technical caducous
formal ephemeral, evanescent, fugacious
E◀ abiding, enduring, lasting, long-lived

shortly   *adv*
1 SOON, in a little while, in a while, before long,
presently, by and by
2 BRUSQUELY, curtly, gruffly, sharply, abruptly,
tersely, bluntly, directly, rudely, impolitely,
discourteously, uncivilly

short-sighted   *adj*
1 MYOPIC, near-sighted
2 IMPROVIDENT, unwise, unthinking, impolitic,
ill-advised, thoughtless, careless, rash, heedless, hasty,
ill-considered
formal imprudent, injudicious, uncircumspect
E◀ **1** long-sighted, far-sighted

short-staffed   *adj*
shorthanded, understaffed, with insufficient staff,
below strength

short-tempered   *adj*
bad-tempered, impatient, irritable, hot-tempered,
quick-tempered, fiery, irascible, choleric, crusty
colloq. ratty, testy, touchy
E◀ calm, patient, placid

short-winded   *adj*
breathless, gasping, panting, puffing

shot¹ n

1 GUNFIRE, discharge, blast, bang, crack, explosion
2 BULLET, ammunition, missile, projectile, ball, pellet
colloq. slug
3 *have a shot at goal*
kick, hit, throw, fling, lob
4 PHOTOGRAPH, photo, snap, snapshot, print, picture, image
5 ATTEMPT, try, effort, endeavour, guess, turn
colloq. go, bash, whack, crack, stab
6 INJECTION, inoculation, immunization, vaccination, dose
colloq. jab; *slang* fix
▷ **call the shots** be in charge, lead, give a lead, head (up), manage, direct, supervise, command
▷ **like a shot** without delay, without hesitation, immediately, instantly, at once, eagerly, enthusiastically, willingly
▷ **shot in the arm** encouragement, stimulus, boost, fillip, lift, uplift, impetus, fresh talent
▷ **shot in the dark** guess, guesswork, wild guess, blind guess, conjecture, speculation

shot² adj
shot fabric
variegated, mottled, watered, moiré, iridescent

shoulder v

1 ACCEPT, assume, take on, take upon yourself, bear, carry, sustain, support
2 PUSH, shove, jostle, thrust, press, force, elbow
▷ **rub shoulders with** meet with, associate with, socialize with, mix with, fraternize with; *colloq.* hobnob with
▷ **shoulder to shoulder** side by side, hand in hand, together, co-operatively, working together, closely, in alliance

shout v, n

▶ v call (out), cry (out), scream, shriek, yell, raise your voice, rant and rave, squawk, roar, bellow, bawl, howl, bay, cheer
colloq. holler; *US* yawp
▶ n call, cry, scream, shriek, yell, squawk, roar, bellow, bawl, howl, bay, cheer
colloq. holler; *US* yawp

shove v, n

▶ v push, thrust, drive, propel, force, barge, jolt, jostle, elbow, shoulder, press, crowd
▷ **shove off** leave, depart; *colloq.* beat it, clear off, push off, get lost, scram, scarper, clear out, skedaddle, vamoose, do a bunk
▶ n push, thrust, jolt, jostle, elbow, shoulder

shovel n, v

▶ n spade, scoop, bucket
▶ v dig, excavate, scoop, dredge, clear, move, shift, spade, heap

show v, n

▶ v 1 REVEAL, expose, uncover, disclose, divulge, make visible, make clear, make plain, make known
formal manifest
2 EXPRESS, mean, indicate, signify, register, record, portray, depict, make it clear, be evidence, bear witness to, suggest
formal manifest
3 TEACH, instruct, clarify, make clear, elucidate, point out, explain, demonstrate, prove, illustrate, exemplify
formal expound

4 DISPLAY, exhibit, demonstrate, set out, present, produce, offer
5 *show him out*
lead, guide, direct, conduct, steer, take, usher, escort, accompany, attend
6 *he didn't show*
appear, arrive, come, turn up
🔁 1 hide, cover (up)
▷ **show off** parade, strut, swagger, brag, boast, flaunt, brandish, display, exhibit, demonstrate, show to advantage, advertise, set off, enhance; *colloq.* swank
▷ **show up** 1 REVEAL, show, make visible, expose, unmask, lay bare, highlight, pinpoint
2 HUMILIATE, embarrass, mortify, shame, put to shame, disgrace, let down 3 ARRIVE, come, turn up, appear; *colloq.* materialize
▶ n 1 ENTERTAINMENT, performance, programme, production, staging, showing, spectacle, extravaganza
2 EXHIBITION, fair, parade, presentation, demonstration, display, spectacle
formal exposition
colloq. expo
3 DISPLAY, representation, demonstration, presentation, sign, indication, arrangement
formal manifestation, array
4 PRETENCE, semblance, façade, front, illusion, ostentation, parade, flamboyance, panache, showiness, exhibitionism, pose
formal affectation
colloq. window dressing, play-acting, pizzazz
5 APPEARANCE, air, impression, guise, display, profession
6 *Who's running the show?*
affair, proceedings, organization, undertaking, operation

showdown n
confrontation, clash, crisis, climax, moment of truth, culmination, dénouement, face-off

shower n, v
▶ n rain, drizzling, stream, torrent, sprinkling, deluge, hail, volley, barrage
▶ v spray, sprinkle, rain, pour, fall, deluge, inundate, overwhelm, load, heap, lavish

showiness n
flamboyance, pretentiousness, glitter, glitz, ostentation, razzle-dazzle
colloq. flashiness, pizzazz, razzmatazz, swank
🔁 restraint

showing n, adj
▶ n display, evidence, impression, representation, record, presentation, performance, exhibition, show, staging, account, statement, appearance, past performance
colloq. track record
▶ adj explanatory, demonstrative, descriptive, illustrative, indicative, representative, significant, symbolic
formal explicatory, elucidative, revelatory

showing-off n
boasting, self-advertisement, bragging, exhibitionism, braggadocio, swagger, egotism, peacockery
formal vainglory
colloq. swank
🔁 modesty

showman n
performer, entertainer, impresario, publicist,

ring-master, self-advertiser
colloq. show-off

show-off *n*
swaggerer, braggart, boaster, exhibitionist, peacock,
poser, poseur, egotist
colloq. swanker, know-all

showy *adj*
flashy, flamboyant, ostentatious, gaudy, garish,
glittering, loud, tawdry, fancy, ornate, pretentious,
pompous
colloq. swanky, flash
E∃ quiet, restrained

shred *n*
1 SCRAP, ribbon, tatter, rag, snippet, sliver, bit, piece,
fragment, remnant, particle, modicum, speck
2 JOT, iota, atom, grain, mite, whit, trace, whisp

shred *v*
cut (up), tear (up), rip (up), chop, slice

shrew *n*
dragon, nag, scold, termagant, virago, vixen,
Xanthippe, harridan, henpecker, spitfire, Fury
slang bitch

shrewd *adj*
astute, well-advised, calculated, far-sighted, smart,
clever, intelligent, sharp, keen, acute, alert, perceptive,
observant, discerning, discriminating, knowing,
calculating, cunning, crafty, wily, canny, artful, sly
formal callid, judicious, sagacious, perspicacious
E∃ unwise, obtuse, naïve, unsophisticated

shrewdly *adv*
astutely, cleverly, far-sightedly, wisely, knowingly,
perceptively, craftily, cannily, artfully, slyly
formal judiciously, sagaciously, perspicaciously

shrewdness *n*
discernment, intelligence, perceptiveness, sharpness,
acuteness, astuteness, grasp, judgement, penetration,
wisdom, acumen, canniness
formal perspicacity, astucity, callidity, sagacity
colloq. smartness
E∃ foolishness, naïvety, obtuseness

shrewish *adj*
scolding, bad-tempered, ill-tempered, ill-humoured,
ill-natured, nagging, peevish, quarrelsome,
complaining, discontented, fault-finding, henpecking,
petulant, captious, sharp-tongued, vixenish
formal querulous
E∃ affectionate, peaceable, placid, supportive

shriek *v, n*
▶ *v* scream, screech, squawk, squeal, cry (out), shout,
yell, wail, howl
▶ *n* scream, screech, squawk, squeal, cry, shout, yell,
wail, howl

shrill *adj*
high, high-pitched, treble, sharp, acute, piercing,
penetrating, screaming, screeching, strident,
ear-splitting
E∃ deep, low, soft, gentle

shrine *n*
holy place, sacred place, chapel, sanctuary, church,
tabernacle, temple, martyry, fane, dome, delubrum,
dagoba, stupa, tope, darga, vimana

shrink *v*
1 CONTRACT, shorten, grow/become smaller,
narrow, decrease, lessen, reduce, diminish, drop off,

fall off, dwindle, shrivel, wrinkle, wither, atrophy
2 RECOIL, draw back, back away, shy away, withdraw,
retire, balk, quail, cower, cringe, wince, flinch, start
back, shun
E∃ 1 expand, stretch 2 accept, embrace

shrivel *v*
wrinkle, pucker (up), wither, wilt, shrink, dwindle,
parch, dry (up), dehydrate, desiccate, scorch, sear,
burn, frizzle
Scot. gizzen

shrivelled *adj*
wrinkled, puckered, shrunken, withered, emaciated,
wizened, dried up, dry, desiccated
old use writhled
Scot. gizzen
formal sere

shroud *v, n*
▶ *v* wrap, envelop, swathe, cloak, veil, screen, cloud,
hide, conceal, enshroud, blanket, cover
E∃ uncover, expose
▶ *n* winding-sheet, cloth, graveclothes, cerecloth,
cerement, pall, mantle, cloak, veil, screen, cloud,
blanket, covering

shrouded *adj*
wrapped, enveloped, swathed, cloaked, enshrouded,
hidden, concealed, covered, clouded, blanketed,
veiled
E∃ exposed, uncovered

shrub *n*

Shrubs include: azalea, berberis, broom, buddleia,
camellia, clematis, cotoneaster, daphne, dogwood,
euonymus, firethorn, flowering currant, forsythia,
fuchsia, heather, hebe, holly, honeysuckle,
hydrangea, ivy, japonica, jasmine, laburnum, laurel,
lavender, lilac, magnolia, mallow, mimosa, mock
orange, peony, privet, musk rose, rhododendron,
rose, spiraea, viburnum, weigela, wistaria, witch
hazel. *See also* **flower; plant**.

shrug *v*
▷ **shrug off** brush off, ignore, disregard, dismiss,
neglect, take no notice of

shrunken *adj*
reduced, shrunk, shrivelled, contracted, emaciated,
gaunt
formal cadaverous
E∃ full, generous, rounded, sleek

shudder *v, n*
▶ *v* shiver, shake, tremble, quiver, quake, heave,
convulse
▶ *n* shiver, quiver, tremble, quake, heave, tremor,
spasm, convulsion

shuffle *v*
1 MIX (UP), intermix, jumble (up), confuse, disorder,
rearrange, reorganize, move around, shift around,
switch
2 *shuffle across the room*
shamble, scuffle, scrape, drag, falter, limp, toddle,
doddle, hobble

shun *v*
avoid, evade, elude, steer clear of, shy away from, keep
away from, spurn, ignore, ostracize
formal eschew
colloq. give a wide berth to, cold-shoulder
E∃ accept, embrace

shut *v*

close, slam, seal, fasten, secure, seal, put the lid on, lock, latch, bolt, bar

🔁 open

▷ **shut down** close (down), stop, halt, suspend, switch off, inactivate; *formal* cease, terminate, discontinue

▷ **shut in** enclose, box in, hem in, fence in, confine, imprison, cage (in), keep in, restrain; *formal* immure

▷ **shut off** seclude, isolate, cut off, separate, segregate

▷ **shut out 1** EXCLUDE, bar, debar, lock out, ostracize, banish, outlaw, exile **2** HIDE, conceal, cover (up), block out, mask, screen, veil

▷ **shut up 1** SILENCE, gag, quiet, quieten, hush (up), hold your tongue; *colloq.* pipe down, clam up, keep mum

Colloquial ways of telling someone to shut up include: belt up!, button it!, cut the cackle!, drop dead!, dry up!, enough said!, get knotted!, give it a rest!, give over!, hold your peace!, not another word!, one more word out of....!, pack it in!; pipe down!, put a sock in it!, say no more!, shut up!, shut your face!, shut your gob!, shut your mouth!, wrap up!

2 CONFINE, lock up, cage in, coop up, imprison, jail, intern; *formal* incarcerate, immure

shutter *n*

screen, shade, blind, louvre, jalousie

shuttle *v*

go to and fro, travel, ply, alternate, commute, shunt, shuttlecock, seesaw

shy *adj, v*

▶ *adj* timid, bashful, reticent, reserved, demure, diffident, introverted, retiring, diffident, coy, self-conscious, embarrassed, inhibited, modest, self-effacing, shrinking, withdrawn, hesitant, cautious, chary, suspicious, nervous
formal timorous
colloq. mousy, backward in coming forward
🔁 bold, assertive, confident

▷ **fight shy of** avoid, steer clear of, shun, spurn; *formal* eschew; *colloq.* give a wide berth to, keep at arm's length

▶ *v* ▷ **shy away** avoid, balk, shrink, recoil, wince, back away, flinch, swerve, start quail, rear, buck

shyness *n*

timidity, timidness, hesitancy, diffidence, bashfulness, reticence, self-consciousness, inhibition, embarrassment, modesty, constraint, nervousness, coyness
formal timorousness
colloq. mousiness
🔁 boldness, assertiveness, confidence

sibling *n*

brother, sister, german, twin

sibyl *n*

wise woman, oracle, prophetess, seer, seeress, sorceress, Pythia, pythoness

sick *adj*

1 ILL, unwell, laid up, poorly, ailing, sickly, weak, feeble
formal indisposed
colloq. under the weather, rough, groggy, off colour, out of sorts

2 VOMITING, retching, nauseous, queasy, bilious, travel-sick, carsick, seasick, airsick

colloq. throwing up, spewing up, puking

3 *sick of waiting*
bored, tired, weary, disgusted, nauseated
colloq. fed up

4 DISGUSTED, annoyed, angry, enraged, disgruntled
colloq. fed up, sick and tired, cheesed off, browned off, hacked off; *slang* pissed off

5 *a sick joke*
cruel, black, tasteless, vulgar, gross, in bad taste
🔁 **1** well, healthy

sicken *v*

1 NAUSEATE, revolt, disgust, repel, appal, put off
colloq. turn off, turn your stomach

2 BECOME ILL, catch, develop, pick up, get, go down with, come down with, become infected with, become ill with
formal contract, succumb to
🔁 **1** delight, attract

sickening *adj*

nauseating, revolting, disgusting, offensive, appalling, shocking, distasteful, off-putting, foul, vile, loathsome, nauseous, repulsive, repellent, stomach-turning
🔁 delightful, pleasing, attractive

sickly *adj*

1 UNHEALTHY, infirm, delicate, weak, feeble, frail, wan, pale, pallid, ailing, indisposed, sick, bilious, faint, languid
colloq. washed out

2 NAUSEATING, revolting, sweet, syrupy, cloying, mawkish
colloq. soppy, schmaltzy, gushy, mushy, slushy
🔁 **1** healthy, robust, sturdy, strong

sickness *n*

1 ILLNESS, disease, ailment, complaint, ill-health, indisposition, disorder, infirmity
formal malady, affliction
colloq. bug, virus

2 VOMITING, retching, nausea, queasiness, biliousness, travel sickness, motion sickness, morning sickness, carsickness, seasickness, airsickness
colloq. throwing up, spewing up, puking
🔁 **1** health

side *n, adj, v*

▶ *n* **1** *the side of an object*
face, facet, surface, end, profile

2 EDGE, margin, fringe, periphery, border, boundary, limit, end, verge, rim, brink, bank, shore, flank, hand
technical jamb
Related adjective: lateral

3 *the other side of the city*
district, quarter, area, region, sector, neighbourhood, section, zone

4 ASPECT, angle, slant, facet, standpoint, view, viewpoint, point of view, profile

5 STANDPOINT, viewpoint, view, aspect, angle, slant

6 TEAM, party, faction, wing, camp, sect, splinter group, cause, interest

▷ **side by side** next to each other, close to each other, alongside each other, shoulder to shoulder

▶ *adj* **1** LATERAL, flanking, wing

2 MINOR, marginal, secondary, subsidiary, subordinate, lesser, incidental

3 OBLIQUE, oblique, wideward, wideways, sidelong

▶ *v* ▷ **side with** agree with, team up with, take someone's side, be on the side of, support, give your support, back, give your backing, join with, vote for, favour, prefer

sidelong *adj*
indirect, oblique, sideward, sideways, covert
F3 direct, overt

sidestep *v*
avoid, find a way around, dodge, evade, elude, skirt, bypass
formal circumvent
colloq. duck, shirk, give a miss
F3 tackle, deal with

sidetrack *v*
deflect, head off, lead away from, divert, distract

sideways *adv, adj*
▶ *adv* from side to side, sidewards, edgeways, edgewise, crabwise, laterally, obliquely, askance, athwart
▶ *adj* sideward, side, lateral, slanted, oblique, indirect, sidelong

sidle *v*
slink, edge, inch, creep, sneak

siege *n*
blockade, encirclement, besiegement, beleaguerment
Related adjective: obsidional

siesta *n*
rest, sleep, relaxation, nap, doze
formal repose
colloq. catnap, forty winks, snooze

sieve *v, n*
▶ *v* sift, strain, filter, screen, riddle, separate, remove, sort, winnow
▶ *n* colander, strainer, filter, sifter, riddle, screen
Related adjectives: cribrate, cribrose, ethmoid

sift *v*
1 SIEVE, strain, filter, riddle, screen, winnow, separate, sort
2 EXAMINE, scrutinize, investigate, analyse, study, pore over, probe, review

sigh *v*
1 BREATHE, moan, complain, lament, grieve
old use suspire
formal exhale
2 *the wind sighing through the valley*
rustle, whisper, crackle, swish
formal susurrate
▷ **sigh for** grieve, lament, languish, long, mourn, pine, weep, yearn, cry

sight *n, v*
▶ *n* 1 VISION, eyesight, seeing, ability to see, faculty/sense of sight, observation, perception
2 VIEW, look, glance, glimpse, range, field of vision, range of vision, visibility
3 APPEARANCE, spectacle, show, display, exhibition, scene, monstrosity
colloq. eyesore, fright
4 *see the sights of London*
places of interest, amenities, beauties, features, curiosities, wonders, splendours, marvels
▷ **catch sight of** see, perceive, notice, note, watch, view, look at, mark, glimpse, discern, make out, recognize, spot, identify
▷ **lose sight of** forget, omit, fail to remember, neglect, overlook, disregard, ignore, put aside, slip your mind
▷ **set your sights on** aim at, plan for, seek to, intend to, strive for, aspire towards, work towards
▶ *v* see, observe, spot, glimpse, perceive, discern,

distinguish, make out
old use espy, behold
Related adjective: visual

sightseer *n*
tourist, visitor, holidaymaker, tripper, excursionist
US rubberneck

sign *n, v*
▶ *n* 1 SYMBOL, token, character, figure, code, cipher, representation, emblem, badge, insignia, logo
2 INDICATION, mark, signal, gesture, evidence, proof, clue, pointer, token, hint, suggestion, trace, symptom
formal manifestation
3 GESTURE, signal, movement, motion, wave, indication, act, action, gesticulation
4 NOTICE, poster, board, placard, signpost, marker, indicator
5 PORTENT, omen, forewarning, foreboding
formal augury, prognostication, harbinger, presage
▶ *v* 1 *sign your name*
autograph, countersign, initial, endorse, write
formal inscribe
2 SIGNAL, wave, gesticulate, gesture, beckon, wink, motion, nod, indicate, express, show, mark, communicate
▷ **sign over** make over, transfer, turn over, surrender, entrust, deliver, convey, consign
▷ **sign up** enlist, enrol, join (up), join the services, volunteer, register, sign on, put your name down for, recruit, take on, hire, engage, employ

signal *n, v, adj*
▶ *n* sign, indication, mark, gesture, evidence, clue, message, symptom, pointer, token, hint, light, alert, warning, tip-off
colloq. shot across the bows

Kinds of signal and warning include: alarm, burglar alarm, car alarm, fire alarm, personal alarm, security alarm; alarm-bell, alarm clock, amber light, beacon, Belisha beacon, lighthouse beacon; bell, bicycle bell, curfew bell; bleeper, buoy, buzzer, cue, distress signal, drumbeat, final warning, fire, flag, flare, flashing light, foghorn, gale warning, go-ahead, gong, green light, hand signal, heliograph, honk, hooter, horn, car horn; hurricane warning, indicator, klaxon, knell, larum, larum-bell, Lutine bell, mayday, Morse code, pager, password, red alert, red flag, red light, reveille, rocket, semaphore signal, a shot across the bows, shout, signal box, signal letters, siren, smoke signal, SOS, starter's gun, storm cone, storm signal, storm warning, tattoo, time signal (pips), tocsin, toot, trafficator, traffic lights, Very light, vigia, warning light, whistle, police whistle; winker, written warning, yellow card, yellow flag.

▶ *v* wave, gesticulate, gesture, beckon, wink, motion, nod, sign, indicate, express, show, mark, communicate
formal signify
▶ *adj* significant, important, exceptional, notable, noteworthy, outstanding, extraordinary, impressive, memorable, momentous, remarkable, striking, eminent, distinguished, conspicuous, glorious, famous

signature *n*
autograph, name, initials, mark, endorsement, inscription
US colloq. John Hancock

significance *n*
importance, relevance, consequence, seriousness, solemnity, magnitude, matter, interest, consideration, weight, force, meaning, implication(s), sense, essence,

gist, point, message
formal significance, import, purport
E3 insignificance, unimportance, pettiness

significant *adj*

1 IMPORTANT, relevant, consequential, momentous, memorable, weighty, serious, noteworthy, material, critical, vital, crucial, key, fateful, marked, considerable, appreciable
2 MEANINGFUL, symbolic, expressive, suggestive, indicative, symptomatic, eloquent, pregnant, ominous
E3 1 insignificant, unimportant, trivial
2 meaningless

significantly *adj*

1 VITALLY, crucially, considerably, appreciably, noticeably, perceptibly, critically, materially
2 MEANINGFULLY, eloquently, meaningly, knowingly, suggestively

signify *v*

1 MEAN, symbolize, be a sign of, represent, stand for, indicate, show, exhibit, signal, express, convey, transmit, communicate, declare, proclaim, intimate, imply, suggest
formal denote, betoken, portend
2 MATTER, count, be of importance, be important, be relevant, have influence, carry weight
colloq. make waves

signpost *n*

sign, pointer, marker, indicator, placard, guidepost, finger-post, handpost, waypost, clue

silence *n, v*

▶ *n* quiet, quietness, hush, peace, peacefulness, stillness, still, calm, calmness, tranquillity, lull, noiselessness, soundlessness, muteness, dumbness, speechlessness, wordlessness, voicelessness, taciturnity, uncommunicativeness, reticence, reserve, secretiveness
E3 noise, sound, din, uproar
▶ *v* quiet, quieten, hush, mute, strike dumb, deaden, muffle, stifle, gag, muzzle, suppress, subdue, quell, still, dumbfound
formal abate
colloq. be able to hear a pin drop

silent *adj*

inaudible, noiseless, soundless, quiet, peaceful, still, calm, hushed, muted, mute, dumb, speechless, tongue-tied, tight-lipped, taciturn, reticent, reserved, secretive, tacit, unspoken, implicit, implied, unexpressed, understood, unvoiced, voiceless, wordless
colloq. mum
E3 noisy, loud, talkative

silently *adv*

noiselessly, quietly, calmly, inaudibly, soundlessly, speechlessly, wordlessly, unheard, dumbly, mutely, tacitly

silhouette *n, v*

▶ *n* outline, contour, shape, form, profile, shadow
formal delineation, configuration
▶ *v* outline, shadow, shape, profile, stand out
formal delineate, configurate, configure

silky *adj*

silken, fine, sleek, lustrous, glossy, satiny, smooth, soft, velvety
formal diaphanous

silly *adj, n*

▶ *adj* foolish, stupid, unintelligent, unwise, senseless, pointless, thoughtless, idiotic, ridiculous, ludicrous, preposterous, absurd, meaningless, unreasonable, irrational, illogical, frivolous, childish, puerile, inane, fatuous, immature, irresponsible, foolhardy, rash, reckless, scatterbrained
formal imprudent, injudicious
colloq. daft, soft, dotty, loopy, barmy, potty, loony, nutty
E3 wise, sensible, sane, mature, clever, intelligent
▶ *n* fool, idiot, ignoramus, simpleton, ninny, half-wit
colloq. dumbo, silly-billy, clot, dope, duffer, twit, wally, goose

silt *n, v*

▶ *n* sediment, deposit, residue, sludge, mud, ooze
formal alluvium
▶ *v* ▷ **silt up** block, clog, dam, choke, congest

silvan *adj*

leafy, tree-covered, wooded, woodland
formal arboreous, forestal, forested, forestine
E3 treeless

similar *adj*

like, alike, close, much the same, related, akin, corresponding, equivalent, comparable, uniform
technical homologous
formal analogous, homogeneous
E3 dissimilar, different

similarity *n*

likeness, resemblance, sameness, closeness, relation, kinship, correspondence, parallelism, equivalence, comparability, compatibility, agreement, affinity, uniformity
formal similitude, congruence, analogy, homogeneity, concordance
E3 dissimilarity, difference, clash

similarly *adv*

in the same way, likewise, correspondingly, uniformly, by the same token, by analogy
E3 differently

similitude *n*

similarity, likeness, resemblance, sameness, closeness, relation, correspondence, parallelism, equivalence, comparability, compatibility, agreement, affinity, uniformity
formal congruence, analogy

simmer *v*

1 BOIL GENTLY, bubble, cook gently, seethe, stew
2 *simmer with anger*
fume, rage, seethe, burn, smoulder
▷ **simmer down** calm down, cool down, subside, lessen, control yourself, collect yourself

simpering *adj*

self-conscious, silly, coy, giggling, missish, schoolgirlish
formal affected

simple *adj*

1 *a simple question; in simple language*
easy, elementary, straightforward, uncomplicated, uninvolved, effortless, clear, lucid, plain, understandable, comprehensible
colloq. cushy, easy-peasy, rough and ready, a cinch, a doddle, a piece of cake, a pushover, as easy as falling off a log
2 BASIC, plain, crude, primitive, natural, undecorated, unadorned, unembellished, unsophisticated, ordinary, unpretentious, unfussy,

classic, rudimentary, stark, austere, Spartan
colloq. low-tech, no-frills
3 *the simple fact is …*
plain, basic, straightforward, bald, stark, direct,
unambiguous, open, honest, sincere, candid, blunt
4 UNSOPHISTICATED, natural, innocent, artless,
guileless, ingenuous, naïve, green
5 FOOLISH, stupid, silly, idiotic, half-witted, simple-
minded, feeble-minded, slow, backward, retarded
🖃 1 difficult, hard, complicated, intricate
2 elaborate, fancy, luxurious **4** sophisticated,
worldly, artful **5** clever

simple-minded *adj*
unsophisticated, simple, natural, artless, stupid,
foolish, idiot, idiotic, imbecile, moronic, cretinous,
brainless, backward, retarded, dim-witted, feeble-
minded, addle-brained
colloq. dopey, goofy
🖃 bright, clever

simpleton *n*
idiot, fool, moron, ninny, imbecile, dolt, dullard,
dunce, dupe, jackass, flathead
colloq. dope, nincompoop, numskull, nitwit, stupid,
twerp, clot, twit, greenhorn, soft-head, goose,
blockhead, booby
🖃 brain

simplicity *n*
simpleness, ease, easiness, facility,
straightforwardness, uncomplicatedness,
elementariness, clarity, purity, plainness, lucidity,
intelligibility, restraint, starkness, naturalness, clean
lines, innocence, guilelessness, naïvety, artlessness,
directness, frankness, candour, openness, sincerity,
honesty, directness
🖃 difficulty, complexity, intricacy, sophistication,
elaborateness

simplify *v*
disentangle, untangle, unravel, decipher, make easy/
easier, make easier to understand, make (more)
comprehensible, remove complexities in, explain,
clarify, paraphrase, abridge, reduce, sort out,
streamline
🖃 complicate, elaborate

simplistic *adj*
oversimplified, superficial, shallow, sweeping, facile,
simple, naïve, pat
🖃 analytical, detailed

simply *adv*
1 MERELY, just, only, solely, purely, utterly, completely,
totally, wholly, altogether, absolutely, positively, quite,
really, undeniably, unquestionably, unreservedly,
unconditionally, clearly, plainly, obviously
2 EASILY, straightforwardly, directly, intelligibly,
plainly, clearly, lucidly, naturally

simulate *v*
pretend, assume, put on, act, feign, sham, fake,
counterfeit, reproduce, duplicate, copy, imitate, mimic,
parrot, echo, reflect, parallel
formal affect
colloq. make believe

simulated *adj*
pretended, feigned, artificial, assumed, imitation, put-
on, sham, fake, mock, make-believe, bogus, spurious,
substitute, synthetic, man-made, inauthentic,
insincere

colloq. phoney, pseudo
🖃 real, genuine

simultaneous *adj*
happening at the same time, existing at the same time,
done at the same time, synchronous, synchronic,
coexistent, coinciding, parallel
formal concurrent, contemporaneous, concomitant
🖃 asynchronous

sin *n, v*
▶ *n* wrong, offence, misdeed, lapse, fault, error,
crime, wrongdoing, sinfulness, wickedness, badness,
evil, impiety, immorality, ungodliness,
unrighteousness, irreligiousness, guilt
formal transgression, trespass, misdemeanour,
iniquity
▶ *v* offend, commit a sin, lapse, err, misbehave, go
wrong, do wrong, stray, go astray, fall, fall from grace
formal transgress, trespass

sincere *adj*
genuine, true, real, honest, truthful, unfeigned,
bona fide, trustworthy, candid, frank, open, direct,
straightforward, plain-spoken, serious, fervent,
earnest, heartfelt, wholehearted, pure, unadulterated,
unmixed, natural, artless, ingenuous, guileless, simple
formal unaffected
colloq. no-nonsense, above board, up front
🖃 insincere, hypocritical, affected

sincerely *adv*
genuinely, honestly, earnestly, in earnest, seriously,
really, simply, truly, truthfully, wholeheartedly,
unfeignedly
formal unaffectedly

sincerity *n*
genuineness, honour, integrity, probity, uprightness,
honesty, truth, truthfulness, candour, frankness,
openness, directness, straightforwardness,
seriousness, earnestness, wholeheartedness,
trustworthiness, artlessness, ingenuousness,
guilelessness
🖃 insincerity

sinecure *n*
soft option
colloq. plum job, picnic, doddle, cinch, cushy job,
money for jam, money for old rope, gravy train

sinewy *adj*
muscular, burly, brawny, strapping, stalwart, strong,
sturdy, robust, vigorous, athletic, wiry, stringy

sinful *adj*
wrong, wrongful, criminal, evil, bad, wicked, erring,
fallen, immoral, corrupt, depraved, impious, ungodly,
unholy, unrighteous, irreligious, guilty
formal iniquitous
🖃 sinless, righteous, godly

sinfulness *n*
immorality, wickedness, sin, ungodliness,
unrighteousness, impiety, corruption, guilt
formal iniquity, depravity, peccability, peccancy,
transgression
🖃 righteousness

sing *v*
chant, intone, vocalize, burst into song, croon,
serenade, yodel, trill, warble, chirp, quaver, pipe,
whistle, hum
▷ **sing out** shout, yell, cry (out), call, bawl, bellow,
cooee; *colloq.* holler

singe *v*
scorch, char, blacken, burn, sear

singer *n*

Singers include: vocalist, songster, songstress, warbler, balladeer, minstrel, troubadour, opera singer, diva, prima donna, soloist, precentor, choirboy, choirgirl, chorister, chorus, folk-singer, pop star, pop singer, chanteuse, crooner, carol-singer; soprano, coloratura soprano, castrato, tenor, treble, contralto, alto, baritone, bass.

single *adj, v*
▶ *adj* **1** ONE, unique, singular, individual, particular, exclusive, sole, only, one and only, by yourself/itself, lone, solitary, isolated, separate, distinct, unshared, undivided, unbroken, simple, one-to-one, person-to-person, man-to-man, woman-to-woman
2 UNMARRIED, unwed, free, unattached, celibate, on your own, by yourself, available
🗲 **1** multiple **2** married
▶ *v* ▷ **single out** choose, select, pick, hand-pick, distinguish, identify, separate (out), set apart, decide on, isolate, highlight, pinpoint

single-handed *adj, adv*
by yourself, on your own, alone, solo, independent(ly), without help, unaided, unassisted, unaccompanied

single-minded *adj*
determined, resolute, dogged, persevering, tireless, unwavering, fixed, set, unswerving, undeviating, steadfast, dedicated, committed, devoted, obsessive, monomaniacal

singly *adv*
one by one, on their own, one at a time, individually, separately, distinctly, solely, independently

singular *adj*
1 REMARKABLE, exceptional, unusual, extraordinary, noteworthy, unique, unparalleled, pre-eminent, outstanding, eminent, conspicuous
2 PECULIAR, odd, queer, unusual, strange, uncommon, curious, eccentric, atypical
🗲 **1** usual **2** normal

singularity *n*
peculiarity, strangeness, queerness, quirk, particularity, oddness, oddity, abnormality, curiousness, eccentricity, idiosyncrasy, irregularity, extraordinariness, uniqueness, oneness, twist
🗲 normality

singularly *adv*
remarkably, exceptionally, extraordinarily, notably, outstandingly, particularly, uncommonly, unusually, especially, surprisingly, signally, conspicuously, prodigiously, bizarrely

sinister *adj*
ominous, menacing, threatening, disturbing, disquieting, terrifying, frightening, unlucky, evil, harmful, cruel, wicked, vicious
formal inauspicious, malevolent, portentous
🗲 harmless, innocent; *formal* auspicious

sink *v*
1 DESCEND, slip, fall, drop, go down, slump, lower, go lower, slump, plummet, plunge, stoop, succumb, lapse, droop, sag, dip, set, disappear, vanish
2 DECREASE, lessen, subside, abate, dwindle, diminish, ebb, fade, flag, weaken, fail, decline, worsen, degenerate, degrade, decay, collapse, fall (in)

formal abate
colloq. go downhill, go to pot
3 FOUNDER, dive, plunge, plummet, capsize, submerge, immerse, engulf, drown
4 *sink a well*
bore, drill, penetrate, dig, excavate, drive, put down, embed, lay, conceal
5 *sink money into a project*
invest, put in, lay out, fund, risk, plough
6 RUIN, destroy, wreck, devastate, demolish, foil, scupper, scuttle
colloq. put a spanner in the works
🗲 **1** rise **2** increase, improve **3** float

sinless *adj*
innocent, virtuous, faultless, guiltless, immaculate, pure, unblemished, uncorrupted, undefiled, unsullied, unspotted, impeccable
🗲 sinful

sinner *n*
wrongdoer, offender, criminal, backslider, reprobate, evil-doer
formal malefactor, miscreant, transgressor, trespasser

sinuous *adj*
lithe, slinky, curved, curving, wavy, undulating, tortuous, twisting, winding, bending, turning, meandering, serpentine, coiling, curling, ogee
🗲 straight

sip *v, n*
▶ *v* taste, sample, drink, drink slowly, sup
▶ *n* taste, drop, drink, spoonful, mouthful

siren *n*
1 ALARM, tocsin, burglar alarm, car alarm, fire alarm, personal alarm, security alarm
2 SEDUCTRESS, *femme fatale*, temptress, vamp, charmer, Lorelei, Circe

sissy *n, adj*
▶ *n* baby, coward, weakling, pansy, softy, mummy's boy, milksop
colloq. wimp, namby-pamby, wet
▶ *adj* unmanly, weak, soft, cowardly, effeminate, feeble, pansy
colloq. wimpish, namby-pamby, wet

sister *n*
1 *brothers and sisters*
sibling, blood-sister, relation, relative
2 *sisters in the struggle against injustice*
comrade, friend, partner, colleague, associate, fellow, companion
3 *sisters in a convent*
nun, abbess, prioress, vowess
Related adjective: sororal

sit *v*
1 SETTLE, sit down, take your seat, be seated, lie, hang, rest, squat (down), place, deposit, position, situate, locate, stand, perch, roost, brood, pose
2 SEAT, accommodate, hold, contain, have room/space for
3 MEET, assemble, gather, convene, consult, deliberate, be in session

site *n, v*
▶ *n* **1** LOCATION, place, spot, position, situation, locality, station, setting, scene
2 PLOT, lot, ground, area
▶ *v* locate, place, position, situate, station, put, set, install

sitting *n*
session, period, spell, meeting, assembly, hearing, consultation

situate *v*
locate, place, position, station, put, set, install

situation *n*
1 SITE, location, position, place, spot, seat, locality, locale, setting, environment, milieu, scenario
2 STATE OF AFFAIRS, case, circumstances, predicament, affairs, environment, climate, set-up, state, state of play, condition(s), status, rank, station
colloq. scenario, lie of the land, picture, what's going on, score
3 JOB, post, office, position, place, employment

size *n, v*
▶ *n* magnitude, measurement(s), dimensions, proportions, volume, bulk, mass, expanse, height, length, area, extent, range, scale, amount, greatness, largeness, bigness, vastness, immensity
▶ *v* ▷ **size up** gauge, assess, evaluate, judge, weigh up, estimate, rate, measure; *formal* appraise; *colloq.* suss out

sizeable *adj*
substantial, fairly large, considerable, respectable, goodly, largish, biggish, decent, generous
E∃ small, tiny

sizzle *v*
hiss, crackle, spit, sputter, fry, frizzle

skeletal *adj*
skin-and-bone, wasted, drawn, emaciated, gaunt, haggard, hollow-cheeked, shrunken, fleshless
formal cadaverous

skeleton *n, adj*
▶ *n* bones, frame, structure, framework, support, bare bones, outline, blueprint, plan, draft, sketch
▶ *adj* smallest, lowest, minimum, reduced, basic

sketch *v, n*
▶ *v* draw, depict, portray, represent, pencil, paint, outline, delineate, draft, rough out, block out
▶ *n* drawing, vignette, design, plan, diagram, outline, skeleton, plan, abstract, draft, representation, description
formal delineation, *croquis*, *ébauche*, *esquisse*

sketchily *adv*
roughly, vaguely, incompletely, inadequately, imperfectly, patchily, cursorily, perfunctorily, hastily
E∃ fully

sketchy *adj*
rough, vague, incomplete, unpolished, unfinished, scrappy, crude, provisional, patchy, bitty, imperfect, inadequate, insufficient, defective, deficient, slight, superficial, cursory, meagre, perfunctory, hasty
E∃ full, complete

skilful *adj*
able, capable, adept, competent, proficient, efficient, good, dexterous, deft, adroit, handy, expert, (well-) versed, masterly, clever, smart, accomplished, skilled, gifted, talented, practised, experienced, trained, professional, tactical, cunning
E∃ inept, clumsy, awkward

skill *n*
skilfulness, ability, aptitude, facility, handiness, adeptness, deftness, adroitness, talent, knack, art, technique, training, experience, expertise, expertness,

professionalism, finesse, mastery, proficiency, competence, efficiency, accomplishment, cleverness, smartness, intelligence

skilled *adj*
trained, schooled, qualified, professional, experienced, practised, accomplished, gifted, talented, expert, masterly, proficient, competent, efficient, able, capable, good, adept, skilful
E∃ unskilled, inexperienced

skim *v*
1 BRUSH, touch, skate, plane, float, sail, glide, graze, fly, skip, bounce
2 SCAN, look through, glance at, skip, read (through) quickly, run through/over, have a quick look at, browse through, flick through, flip through, thumb through, leaf through
3 CREAM, separate
formal despumate

skimp *v*
economize, be economical, cut back on, scrimp, pinch, stint, withhold
colloq. cut corners, tighten your belt, cut your coat according to your cloth
E∃ squander, waste

skimpy *adj*
small, scanty, short, sparse, thin, tight, sketchy, meagre, miserly, niggardly, inadequate, insufficient, insubstantial, beggarly
formal exiguous
colloq. measly
E∃ generous

skin *n, v*
▶ *n* hide, fleece, fell, pelt, membrane, film, coating, layer, surface, covering, cover, outside, peel, rind, husk, hull, pod, casing, crust
technical corium, derma, dermis, cutis, integument, tegument, epidermis
formal cuticle
Related adjectives: dermatoid, cutaneous
▶ *v* flay, fleece, strip, peel, scrape, graze
▷ **by the skin of your teeth** narrowly, barely, only just; *colloq.* a near/close thing

skin-deep *adj*
shallow, superficial, surface, external, outward, artificial, empty, meaningless

skinflint *n*
miser, niggard, cheeseparer, Scrooge
old use tightwad
colloq. meanie, penny-pincher
E∃ spendthrift

skinny *adj*
thin, lean, scrawny, scraggy, skeletal, emaciated, underfed, undernourished
colloq. (all) skin-and-bone
E∃ fat, plump

skip *v*
1 HOP, jump, leap, dance, spring, bounce, bob, bound, cavort, gambol, frisk, caper, prance
2 *skip a page*
miss (out), omit, leave out
colloq. dodge, cut
3 *skip from one thing to another*
move quickly, jump, rush, pass, dart, tear, race

skirmish *n, v*
▶ *n* fight, combat, battle, engagement, encounter,

confrontation, conflict, clash, brush, affray, fracas, mêlée, tussle, argument, dispute, difference of opinion
formal altercation
colloq. scrap, set-to, dust-up, punch-up
▶ *v* clash, fight, tussle, brawl, scuffle, combat, battle, contend, argue, quarrel, wrangle
colloq. scrap, fall out, be at each other's throats

skirt *v*
1 CIRCLE, move/go round, border, edge, flank
formal circumnavigate
2 AVOID, evade, bypass, find a way round
formal circumvent

skit *n*
satire, parody, caricature, burlesque, sketch
colloq. spoof, take-off, send-up, mickey-taking;
slang piss-taking

skittish *adj*
nervous, excitable, fidgety, lively, playful, playful, jumpy, highly-strung, frivolous, fickle
formal restive

skittles *n*
ninepins, pins, tenpin, skittle-pins, kettle-pins

skive *v*
dodge, laze, idle, shirk, malinger, skulk, slack
colloq. swing the lead

skiver *n*
dodger, idler, do-nothing, shirker, slacker, loafer, malingerer

skulduggery *n*
trickery, swindling, fraudulence, double-dealing, underhandedness, unscrupulousness, chicanery
formal duplicity, machinations
colloq. jiggery-pokery, shenanigans, hanky-panky

skulk *v*
lurk, hide, prowl, sneak, creep, slink, lie in wait, steal, slide, pad, pussyfoot, loiter

sky *n*
space, atmosphere, air, heavens, the blue, firmament
formal vault of heaven, empyrean, welkin
Related adjectives: celestial, supernal, empyreal

slab *n*
piece, block, lump, chunk, hunk, brick, briquette, wedge, slice, portion
colloq. wodge

slack *adj, n, v*
▶ *adj* **1** LOOSE, relaxed, flexible, limp, hanging, sagging, flapping, flabby, baggy
formal flaccid
2 *a slack period*
sluggish, slow, quiet, idle, lazy, inactive
3 NEGLECTFUL, negligent, careless, inattentive, permissive, lax, relaxed
formal remiss, tardy
colloq. easy-going, sloppy
F≡ 1 tight, taut, stiff, rigid **2** busy **3** diligent
▶ *n* looseness, give, play, room, leeway, excess, spare capacity
▶ *v* idle, shirk, dodge, malinger, neglect
colloq. skive

slacken *v*
▷ **slacken off** loosen, release, relax, ease, moderate, reduce, lessen, get less, decrease, diminish, slow (down), become slower, become less

intense/active; *formal* abate; *colloq.* take it easy
F≡ tighten, increase, intensify, quicken

slacker *n*
idler, shirker, dawdler, loafer, malingerer, clock-watcher, good-for-nothing, layabout
colloq. skiver

slag *v*
▷ **slag off** criticize, abuse, mock, malign, insult;
formal berate, deride, lambaste; *colloq.* slam, slate

slake *v*
satisfy, satiate, quench, moisten, sate, gratify, allay, reduce, extinguish, moderate
formal abate, assuage, mitigate

slam *v*
1 BANG, crash, dash, smash, thump, slap, throw, hurl, fling
2 CRITICIZE, attack, denounce, find fault with
colloq. slate, pan, rubbish, run down, pull/tear to pieces, tear to shreds, do a hatchet job on

slander *n, v*
▶ *n* defamation, misrepresentation, libel, scandal, smear, smear campaign, slur, denigration, backbiting
formal aspersion, disparagement, calumny, vilification, traducement, obloquy
colloq. muck-raking, mudslinging
▶ *v* defame, malign, disparage, libel, smear, blacken the name of, slur, backbite
formal vilify, cast aspersions on, denigrate, vilipend, calumniate, traduce
colloq. sling/throw mud at, drag someone's name through the mud; *US* badmouth
F≡ praise, compliment

⚠ **slander** or **libel** ? *See panel at* **libel**.

slanderous *adj*
defamatory, false, untrue, libellous, damaging, malicious, abusive, insulting, backbiting
formal aspersory, aspersive, calumniatory, calumnious

slang *n*
cant, jargon, argot, patois, patter, cockney, cockney rhyming slang, vulgarism, doublespeak, gobbledygook, colloquialism, informal expressions
colloq. lingo, mumbo-jumbo

slanging match
argument, row, quarrel, dispute, shouting match
formal altercation
colloq. argy-bargy, barney, set-to, spat

slant *v, n*
▶ *v* **1** TILT, slope, incline, lean, list, dip, skew, be askew, angle, shelve
2 DISTORT, twist, warp, bend, weight, bias, skew, colour
▶ *n* **1** SLOPE, incline, inclination, leaning, gradient, ramp, camber, pitch, tilt, dip, angle, diagonal
2 BIAS, prejudice, distortion, twist, one-sidedness, emphasis, attitude, angle, opinion, view, viewpoint, point of view

slanting *adj*
sloping, tilting, tilted, inclining, leaning, listing, dipping, on an incline, at a slant, askew, oblique, diagonal

slap *n, v, adv*
▶ *n* smack, spank, cuff, blow, hit, bang, clap, thump,

whack, punch
colloq. wallop, clout, biff, sock, clobber
▷ **slap in the face** insult, humiliation, blow, affront, rejection, repulse, snub, rebuke, rebuff, indignity;
colloq. put-down
▶ *v* **1** SMACK, spank, hit, strike, thump, whack, punch, cuff, bang, clap
colloq. clout, wallop, biff, sock, clobber
2 PUT DOWN, set (down), plump, plonk, slam, stick
3 DAUB, plaster, spread, apply
▶ *adv* right, directly, straight, exactly, precisely, dead, plumb
colloq. bang, slap-bang, smack

slapdash *adj*
careless, thoughtless, haphazard, slovenly, disorderly, clumsy, offhand, negligent, messy, slipshod, thrown-together, untidy, hurried, last-minute, hasty, rash, perfunctory
formal sloppy
E3 careful, orderly

slap-happy *adj*
casual, irresponsible, boisterous, haphazard, reeling, happy-go-lucky, nonchalant, reckless, slapdash, hit-or-miss, dazed, giddy, punch-drunk, woozy

slapstick *n*
comedy, farce, buffoonery, tomfoolery, knockabout, horseplay

slap-up *adj*
excellent, splendid, lavish, elaborate, first-class, first-rate, magnificent, superb, sumptuous, luxurious, princely, superlative

slash *v, n*
▶ *v* **1** *slash your wrists*
cut, slit, gash, lacerate, knife, rip, tear, hack, score, rend
2 *slash costs*
cut, reduce, decrease, curb, curtail, prune
colloq. axe
▶ *n* cut, incision, slit, gash, laceration, score, rip, tear, rent

slate *v*
scold, rebuke, reprimand, berate, censure, blame, criticize
colloq. slam, pan, rubbish, run down, pull/tear to pieces, tear to shreds, do a hatchet job on
E3 praise

slatternly *adj*
slovenly, sloppy, dirty, slipshod, untidy, unkempt, unclean, dowdy, bedraggled, frowzy, frumpish, frumpy, sluttish

slaughter *v, n*
▶ *v* kill, put to death, slay, butcher, murder, massacre, exterminate, liquidate, annihilate
▶ *n* killing, putting to death, murder, massacre, extermination, liquidation, annihilation, butchery, carnage, blood-bath, bloodshed

slave *n, v*
▶ *n* servant, drudge, menial, lackey, vassal, serf, villein, captive, thrall, bondservant, bond-slave, bond(s)man, bond(s)woman
colloq. skivvy
Related adjective: servile
▶ *v* toil, labour, drudge, sweat, grind, slog, work your fingers to the bone, work your guts out

slaver *v*
dribble, drivel, slobber, drool
formal salivate

slavery *n*
servitude, bondage, yoke, captivity, enslavement, serfdom, vassalage, thrall, thraldom
formal subjugation
E3 freedom, liberty

slavish *adj*
1 UNORIGINAL, imitative, unimaginative, uninspired, literal, strict
2 SERVILE, abject, submissive, sycophantic, obsequious, deferential, grovelling, cringing, fawning, menial, low, mean
E3 1 original, imaginative **2** independent, assertive

slay *v*
kill, butcher, massacre, murder, dispatch, destroy, eliminate, execute, slaughter, annihilate, assassinate, exterminate
colloq. rub out

slaying *n*
murder, killing, butchery, slaughter, assassination, massacre, destruction, dispatch, elimination, annihilation, extermination
formal mactation

sleazy *adj*
disreputable, low, seedy, sordid, squalid, crummy, run-down
colloq. tacky

sleek *adj*
shiny, glossy, lustrous, smooth, silky, silken, soft, well-groomed, stylish, thriving, prosperous
E3 rough, unkempt

sleep *v, n*
▶ *v* be asleep, get some sleep, fall asleep, doze, hibernate, drop off, go off, drift off, nod off, nap, rest
formal slumber, repose
colloq. snooze, have a snooze, have forty winks, be in the land of Nod, sleep like a log, flake out, crash out, go out like a light; *slang* kip, doss (down)
▶ *n* doze, nap, catnap, hibernation, rest, siesta
formal slumber, repose
colloq. snooze, forty winks, shut-eye; *slang* kip
Related adjectives: hypnic, hypnoid, hypnoidal

sleepiness *n*
drowsiness, doziness, heaviness, lethargy, torpor
formal languor, oscitancy, oscitation, somnolence
E3 alertness, wakefulness

sleeping *adj*
asleep, daydreaming, idle, inactive, unaware, becalmed, passive, off guard, inattentive, dormant, hibernating
formal slumbering
E3 alert, awake

sleepless *adj*
unsleeping, awake, wide-awake, alert, vigilant, watchful, wakeful, restless, disturbed, insomniac

sleeplessness *n*
insomnia, wakefulness
formal insomnolence

sleepwalker *n*
somnambulist, noctambulist

sleepwalking *n*
somnambulism, somnambulation, noctambulism, noctambulation

sleepy *adj*
1 DROWSY, tired, weary, heavy, slow, sluggish, torpid, lethargic, inactive, quiet, dull, soporific, hypnotic
technical comatose
formal somnolent, languid, languorous
2 *a sleepy little village*
quiet, dull, peaceful, still, isolated, lonely, unfrequented, undisturbed
formal sequestered
colloq. off the beaten track
E3 1 awake, alert, wakeful, restless

sleight of hand
trickery, skill, artifice, dexterity, legerdemain, deception, magic, adroitness, manipulation
formal prestidigitation

slender *adj*
1 SLIM, thin, lean, slight, svelte, graceful, trim, sylphlike, willowy, willowish
2 *a slender chance*
faint, remote, small, little, slim, slight, inconsiderable, tenuous, flimsy, feeble, deficient, inadequate, insufficient, meagre, scant, scanty
E3 1 fat **2** appreciable, considerable, ample

sleuth *n*
detective, private investigator, shadow, tail, tracker
colloq. private eye, bloodhound, dick, gumshoe

slice *n, v*
▶ *n* piece, sliver, wafer, rasher, tranche, slab, wedge, segment, section, hunk, chunk, part, share, portion, allocation, allotment, helping
colloq. cut, whack, slice of the cake
▶ *v* carve, cut (up), chop, sever, divide, separate, segment

slick *adj*
1 GLIB, plausible, easy, simplistic, deft, adroit, sharp, dexterous, skilful, smooth, professional, efficient, masterly
2 SMOOTH, sleek, glossy, shiny, polished, quick, streamlined, well-oiled, well-organized
3 INSINCERE, glib, smarmy, smooth-speaking, smooth-talking, persuasive, polished, sophisticated, suave, unctuous

slide *v*
1 MOVE SMOOTHLY, go smoothly, slip, slither, skid, skate, ski, toboggan, glide, plane, coast, skim
2 DETERIORATE, lessen, decrease, decline, fall, drop, plummet, plunge, lapse, worsen, get worse, depreciate

slight *adj, v, n*
▶ *adj* **1** MINOR, unimportant, insignificant, inconsequential, negligible, inappreciable, imperceptible, trivial, petty, scant, paltry, subtle, modest, small, little, minute, inconsiderable, insubstantial
2 SLENDER, slim, small, dainty, diminutive, petite, frail, fragile, delicate, elfin
E3 1 major, significant, noticeable, considerable
2 large, muscular
▶ *v* scorn, despise, disdain, insult, affront, offend, snub, spurn, slur, cut, ignore, disregard, neglect
formal disparage
colloq. giving the cold shoulder to, cold-shoulder
E3 respect, praise, compliment, flatter

▶ *n* insult, affront, scorn, slur, snub, rebuff, rudeness, discourtesy, disrespect, contempt, disdain, indifference, disregard, neglect
colloq. cold shoulder, slap in the face, kick in the teeth

slighting *adj*
disdainful, disrespectful, belittling, insulting, scornful, offensive, defamatory, derogatory, slanderous, abusive, supercilious, uncomplimentary
formal disparaging
E3 complimentary

slightly *adj*
rather, quite, a little, a bit, to some degree, to some extent

slim *adj, v*
▶ *adj* **1** SLENDER, thin, slight, lean, svelte, trim, graceful, sylphlike, willowy, willowish
2 SLIGHT, remote, faint, poor, small, little, scant, scanty, meagre, inconsiderable, tenuous, flimsy, insufficient, inadequate
E3 1 fat, chubby **2** strong, considerable
▶ *v* lose weight, diet, go on a diet, reduce

slime *n*
mud, ooze, muck, mess,
colloq. goo, gunk, yuck

slimy *adj*
1 MUDDY, miry, sludgy, oozy, sticky, mucous, viscous, oily, greasy, slippery
2 SERVILE, obsequious, sycophantic, toadying, ingratiating, grovelling, creeping, oily, unctuous
colloq. smarmy

sling *v, n*
▶ *v* **1** THROW, hurl, fling, catapult, heave, pitch, lob, toss, shy
colloq. chuck
2 HANG, suspend, dangle, swing
▶ *n* bandage, loop, strap, support, band, catapult

slink *v*
sneak, steal, creep, sidle, slip, lurk, prowl, skulk

slinky *adj*
close-fitting, figure-hugging, clinging, skin-tight, sleek, sinuous

slip[1] *v, n*
▶ *v* **1** SLIDE, glide, skate, skid, stumble, lose your balance, trip, lose your footing, fall, slither, slink, sneak, steal, creep
2 *slip into/out of clothes*
put on, get dressed in, change into, get into, take off, change out of, pull on, wear, don
3 *standards are slipping*
fall, drop, sink, decrease, decline, plummet, plunge, slump, deteriorate, worsen, lapse, get worse
colloq. go to the dogs, go to pot, go down the tube
▷ **let slip** let out, reveal, divulge, give away, betray, leak, tell
▷ **slip up** make a mistake, go wrong, get wrong, miscalculate, bungle, blunder, err, stumble;
colloq. boob, botch, goof, fluff; *slang* cock up, screw up
▶ *n* **1** MISTAKE, error, blunder, fault, indiscretion, omission, oversight, failure
colloq. slip-up, bloomer, boob, booboo, howler, clanger; *slang* cock-up
2 PETTICOAT, underskirt, jupon, kirtle
▷ **give someone the slip** escape from, run away from, get away from, flee from, break loose from,

shake off; *colloq.* slip through someone's fingers, dodge, duck

slip² *n*
a slip of paper
piece, strip, paper, note, voucher, chit, coupon, certificate
▷ **a slip of a** small, thin, slender, slim, slight, delicate, fragile, young

slipper *n*
houseshoe, moccasin, mule, flip-flop, sandal, pump, loafer, pabouche, pantof(f)le, pantoufle, pantable
Scot. panton

slippery *adj*
1 SLIPPY, icy, wet, greasy, oily, slimy, glassy, smooth, dangerous, treacherous, perilous
colloq. skiddy
2 *a slippery character*
dishonest, untrustworthy, unreliable, false, two-faced, crafty, cunning, devious, clever, shifty, deceitful, foxy, evasive, smooth, smarmy
formal duplicitous, perfidious
E3 1 rough **2** trustworthy, reliable

slipshod *adj*
careless, slapdash, sloppy, slovenly, untidy, disorganized, negligent, lax, casual
E3 careful, fastidious, neat, tidy, methodical, organized

slip-up *n*
slip, mistake, error, blunder, fault, indiscretion, omission, oversight, failure
colloq. bloomer, boob, booboo, howler, clanger; *slang* cock-up

slit *v, n*
▶ *v* cut, gash, slash, slice, split, pierce, lance, knife, rip, tear
formal rend
▶ *n* opening, aperture, fissure, vent, cut, incision, gash, slash, split, rip, tear
formal rent

slither *v*
slide, skid, slip, glide, slink, creep, snake, worm

sliver *n*
flake, shaving, paring, slice, wafer, shred, fragment, piece, bit, scrap, chip, splinter, shiver, shard

slob *n*
lout, oaf, sloven, churl, boor, philistine
colloq. yob

slobber *v*
drool, dribble, drivel, slaver, foam at the mouth
formal salivate

slog *v, n*
▶ *v* **1** HIT, strike, thump, belt
formal smite
colloq. bash, slosh, slug, sock, wallop
2 PERSEVERE, labour, slave, work, plough through, toil, plod, trudge, trek, tramp
▶ *n* struggle, effort, exertion, grind, labour, hike, trek, trudge, tramp

slogan *n*
jingle, motto, catch phrase, catchword, watchword, battle-cry, rallying cry, war cry, logo

slop *v*
spill, overflow, slosh, splash, splatter, spatter

slope *n, v*

Words used for slopes include: *up:* acclivity, ascent, climb, incline, rise, uphill, upward; *down:* decline, declivity, descent, dip, downgrade, downhill, downward, drop, fall; *up and down:* bajada, brae, cant, escalator, escarp, glacis, gradient, inclination, pitch, ramp, scarp, slant, staircase, stairs, stairway, steps, tilt, versant.

▶ *v* slant, lean, tilt, tip, dip, pitch, incline, rise, fall (away), drop
▷ **slope off** slip away, sneak off, steal away, leave quietly

sloping *adj*
inclined, inclining, slanting, leaning, oblique, tilting, askew, angled, canting, bevelled
formal acclivitous, acclivous, declivitous, declivous
E3 level

sloppy *adj*
1 WATERY, wet, liquid, runny, soggy, splashy, mushy, slushy
2 *sloppy work*
careless, hit-or-miss, slapdash, slipshod, hurried, hasty, slovenly, untidy, disorganized, messy, clumsy, amateurish
3 SENTIMENTAL, gushy, gushing, mawkish, maudlin
colloq. mushy, soppy, schmaltzy, slushy, sickly, corny
E3 1 solid **2** careful, exact, precise, organized, methodical

slosh *v*
1 SPLASH, wade, slop, slog, pour, shower, flounder, spray, swash
2 HIT, strike, thump, thwack, slap, swipe, punch
colloq. bash, biff, slug, sock, wallop

slot *n, v*
▶ *n* **1** HOLE, opening, aperture, crack, slit, vent, notch, groove, channel
2 *a slot in your schedule*
gap, space, time, vacancy, place, opening, spot, position, niche
colloq. window
▶ *v* insert, fit, put, install, place, position, assign, pigeonhole

sloth *n*
laziness, idleness, inactivity, slackness, listlessness, slothfulness, sluggishness, torpor, inertia
formal indolence, acedia, accidie, fainéance
E3 diligence, industriousness; *formal* sedulity

slothful *adj*
lazy, idle, inactive, inert, slack, listless, sluggish, workshy, torpid, do-nothing
formal indolent, fainéant
colloq. skiving
E3 diligent, industrious; *formal* sedulous

slouch *v*
stoop, hunch, bend, droop, slump, lounge, loll, shuffle, shamble

slovenly *adj*
sloppy, careless, slipshod, untidy, messy, disorganized, scruffy, unclean, dirty, unkempt, slatternly, sluttish
E3 careful, tidy, neat, smart

slow *adj, v*
▶ *adj* **1** LEISURELY, unhurried, lingering, loitering, lagging, dawdling, lazy, sluggish, slow-moving, slow-

motion, ponderous, creeping, gradual, deliberate, measured, plodding, at a snail's pace, delayed, late
formal tardy, dilatory
2 STUPID, unintelligent, slow-witted, dim, dull, dull-witted, dense, retarded, daft
colloq. thick, dumb, dopey
3 PROLONGED, time-consuming, protracted, long-drawn-out, tedious, boring, dull, tiresome, wearisome, uninteresting, uneventful
4 QUIET, sleepy, dull, slack, sluggish, stagnant, dead
5 *slow to anger*
unwilling, reluctant, hesitant, averse, disinclined, loath, indisposed
E3 **1** fast, quick, swift, rapid, speedy **2** bright, clever, intelligent **3** brief, exciting **4** brisk, lively, exciting
▶ *v* brake, decelerate, ease up, reduce speed, put the brakes on, delay, hold up, handicap, check, curb, detain, keep/hold back, restrict
formal retard
E3 speed, accelerate

slowly *adv*
leisurely, at a leisurely pace, slowly but surely, unhurriedly, gradually, little by little, by degrees, steadily, lazily, ploddingly, ponderously, sluggishly, at a snail's pace
technical lento, adagio, largo, larghetto
E3 fast, quickly

sludge *n*
mud, ooze, mire, muck, residue, sediment, silt, slime, slush, swill, slop, slag, dregs
colloq. gunge, gunk

sluggish *adj*
lethargic, listless, torpid, heavy, dull, slow, slow-moving, slothful, languid, lazy, idle, inactive, apathetic, lifeless, unresponsive, phlegmatic
formal languorous, indolent, somnolent
E3 brisk, vigorous, lively, dynamic

sluggishness *n*
lethargy, listlessness, torpor, phlegm, heaviness, inertia, dullness, slowness, slothfulness, apathy, drowsiness, stagnation, lassitude
formal indolence, languor, somnolence, fainéance
E3 dynamism, eagerness, quickness

sluice *v*
wash, cleanse, drain, flush, swill, drench, irrigate, slosh

slumber *n, v*
▶ *n* sleep, rest, doze, nap
formal repose
colloq. snooze, forty winks, shut-eye; *slang* kip
▶ *v* doze, drowse, nap, rest, sleep
formal repose
colloq. snooze

slummy *adj*
run-down, squalid, dirty, decayed, seedy, sleazy, sordid, ramshackle, overcrowded, wretched

slump *v, n*
▶ *v* **1** COLLAPSE, fall, go down, decrease, drop, plunge, plummet, sink, subside, nosedive, decline, deteriorate, worsen, crash, fail
colloq. go down hill
2 DROOP, sag, bend, stoop, slouch, loll, lounge, flop
▶ *n* recession, depression, stagnation, devaluation, downturn, slide, low, lowering, trough, downswing, decline, deterioration, worsening, fall, drop, decrease,

plunge, collapse, crash, failure
E3 boom, upturn

slur *n, v*
▶ *n* smear, slight, insult, disgrace, discredit, reproach, slander, libel, affront, stain, blot, innuendo, insinuation, stigma
formal aspersion, calumny
▶ *v* mumble, speak unclearly, splutter, stumble

slush *n*
1 SNOW, melting snow, wet snow
2 SENTIMENTALITY, emotionalism, romanticism, mawkishness
colloq. mush, gush, pulp, schmaltz, soppiness, sloppiness

slut *n*
loose woman, slattern, sloven, trollop, hussy, drab, prostitute
colloq. hooker, floosie; *slang* tart, scrubber, slag

sly *adj*
wily, foxy, crafty, cunning, artful, guileful, clever, canny, shrewd, smart, astute, knowing, subtle, devious, shifty, tricky, furtive, stealthy, surreptitious, insidious, underhand, covert, secret, secretive, scheming, conniving, mischievous, impish, roguish
formal clandestine
colloq. sneaky
E3 honest, frank, candid, open
▷ **on the sly** in secret, secretly, in private, under cover, privately, stealthily, surreptitiously, underhandedly, furtively, covertly;
formal clandestinely; *colloq.* on the q.t.
E3 openly

smack¹ *v, n, adv*
▶ *v* *Do you ever smack your children?*
hit, strike, slap, spank, clap, box, thump, punch, bang, crash, thud, cuff, pat, tap
colloq. whack, thwack, belt, clout, wallop, biff, sock, clobber, put over your knee, give a hiding to
▶ *n* blow, slap, spank, box, thump, punch, bang, crash, thud, cuff, pat, tap
colloq. whack, thwack, belt, clout, wallop, biff, sock, clobber
▶ *adv* bang, slap-bang, right, plumb, straight, directly, exactly, precisely
▷ **smack your lips** enjoy, relish, savour, drool over, delight in, anticipate

smack² *v, n*
▶ *v* *his attitude smacks of hypocrisy*
suggest, savour of, hint at, give the impression of, intimate, evoke, bring to mind, remind you of
▶ *n* **1** TASTE, flavour, savour, tang, relish, piquancy, zest
2 SUGGESTION, hint, trace, impression, intimation, tinge, touch, dash, speck, whiff, nuance

small *adj*
1 LITTLE, tiny, minute, minuscule, short, slight, puny, petite, diminutive, compact, pocket, cramped, poky, miniature, microscopic, infinitesimal, teeny, mini, pocket, pocket-sized, young
Scot. wee
colloq. pint-size(d), knee-high to a grasshopper
2 PETTY, trifling, trivial, unimportant, insignificant, minor, inconsiderable, inappreciable, negligible
3 INADEQUATE, insufficient, scanty, meagre, paltry, mean, limited
4 *make you feel small*
humiliated, ashamed, embarrassed, crushed, broken,

deflated, degraded, disgraced, stupid, unimportant, insignificant
F3 **1** big, large, tall, huge **2** great, major, considerable **3** ample

small-minded *adj*
petty, mean, ungenerous, illiberal, intolerant, bigoted, narrow-minded, prejudiced, biased, parochial, insular, rigid, hidebound
F3 liberal, generous, tolerant, broad-minded, open-minded

small-time *adj*
unimportant, minor, insignificant, petty, piddling, inconsequential, no-account
F3 important, major, big-time

smarminess *n*
obsequiousness, unctuousness, oiliness, servility, sycophancy, toadying, suavity
formal unctuosity

smarmy *adj*
smooth, oily, unctuous, servile, obsequious, sycophantic, bootlicking, suave, toadying, ingratiating, crawling, fawning

smart *adj, v*
▶ *adj* **1** *smart clothes*
elegant, stylish, chic, fashionable, modish, neat, tidy, spruce, trim, presentable, dapper, well-dressed, well-groomed, well-turned-out
colloq. natty, cool, snazzy
2 CLEVER, intelligent, bright, sharp, acute, shrewd, astute
3 *a smart hotel*
fashionable, elegant, expensive, stylish, chic, modish
colloq. posh, glitzy, ritzy
F3 **1** dowdy, unfashionable, untidy, scruffy **2** stupid, slow **3** cheap
▷ **smart alec** know-all, wise guy, wiseacre;
colloq. clever clogs, clever dick, smartypants, smartyboots; *slang* smart-arse
▶ *v* sting, hurt, prick, burn, nip, ache, tingle, twinge, throb

smarten *v*
neaten, make neat, tidy (up), make tidy, spruce up, groom, clean, polish, beautify

smash *v, n*
▶ *v* **1** *smash a window*
break, shatter, crack, splinter, disintegrate, shiver, ruin, wreck, demolish, destroy, dash, defeat, crush
formal pulverize
2 CRASH, collide, wreck, strike, bang, bump, drive, go, run, knock, hit, plough, bash, thump
▶ *n* accident, crash, collision, pile-up, bump, wreck
colloq. smash-up, prang

smashing *adj*
excellent, wonderful, marvellous, superb, terrific, tremendous, great, fantastic, magnificent, sensational, superlative, stupendous, super, exhilarating, first-class, first-rate, fabulous

smattering *n*
bit, modicum, dash, sprinkling, basics, rudiments, elements

smear *v, n*
▶ *v* **1** DAUB, plaster, spread, cover, slap, coat, rub, smudge, streak
2 SULLY, blacken, stain, tarnish, slur, taint
formal defame, malign, vilify, calumniate

colloq. drag someone's name through the mud;
US badmouth
▶ *n* **1** STREAK, smudge, blot, spot, patch, blotch, splodge, splotch, daub
2 *a smear campaign against a politician*
taint, slur, stain, slander, libel
formal defamation, aspersion, vilification, obloquy
colloq. mudslinging, muck-raking

smell *n*

Words used for types of smell include: *pleasant:* aroma, ouquet, fragrance, incense, nose, odour, pot pourri, perfume, redolence, scent; *unpleasant:* b.o. (body odour), fetor, *US* funk, hum, malodour, mephitis, miasma, *slang* niff, *colloq.* pong, pungency, reek, sniff, stench, stink, whiff.

Related adjective: olfactory

smelly *adj*
stinking, reeking, foul, bad, off, putrid, high, strong-smelling
formal malodorous, fetid, mephitic, noisome
colloq. pongy, humming

smile *n*
grin, beam, simper, smirk, leer, sneer, laugh, chuckle, giggle, snigger, titter
colloq. someone's face lights up, be all smiles

smirk *n*
grin, sneer, snigger, leer, simper

smitten *adj*
obsessed, bewitched, beguiled, charmed, attracted, enthusiastic, captivated, infatuated, enamoured, afflicted, plagued, struck, troubled, burdened, beset
colloq. bowled over

smog *n*
fog, pea-souper, smoke, pollution, exhaust, fumes, haze, mist, vapour

smoke *n, v*
▶ *n* fumes, exhaust, gas, vapour, mist, fog, smog
▶ *v* fume, draw (on), puff (on), light up, smoulder, preserve, cure, dry

smoky *adj*
sooty, black, grey, dark, grimy, murky, cloudy, hazy, foggy, smoggy

smooth *adj, v*
▶ *adj* **1** LEVEL, plane, even, flat, horizontal, flush
2 STEADY, even, unbroken, uninterrupted, continuous, flowing, regular, uniform, rhythmic, easy, simple, effortless, problem-free, trouble-free
colloq. plain sailing
3 SHINY, polished, burnished, glossy, silky, silken, velvety, sleek, like a mirror, glassy
4 CALM, still, undisturbed, serene, tranquil, peaceful
5 SUAVE, agreeable, smooth-talking, urbane, sophisticated, over-confident, glib, plausible, persuasive, slick, unctuous, ingratiating, crawling, fawning
colloq. smarmy
F3 **1** rough, coarse, lumpy **2** troublesome, irregular, erratic, unsteady **4** bumpy, rough, choppy
▶ *v* **1** IRON, press (down), roll, flatten, plaster (down), slick, rub down, level, plane, even (out), file, sand, grind, polish
2 EASE, alleviate, pacify, soothe, allay, calm (down), palliate, mollify
formal assuage, mitigate, appease

3 *smooth the way*
make easier, facilitate, ease, help, assist, aid, encourage, clear the way for
◨ **1** roughen, wrinkle, crease

smoothly *adv*
evenly, calmly, steadily, soothingly, peacefully, tranquilly, serenely, pleasantly, mildly, easily, effortlessly, equably, fluently

smoothness *n*
1 LEVELNESS, evenness, flatness
2 STEADINESS, evenness, flow, regularity, rhythm, unbrokenness, ease, efficiency, effortlessness, facility, fluency, finish
3 SHINE, polish, silkiness, velvetiness, sleekness, glassiness, serenity, calmness, stillness, softness
◨ **1** roughness, coarseness

smooth-talking *adj*
persuasive, plausible, slick, suave, silver-tongued, facile, glib, bland
colloq. smooth

smother *v*
suffocate, asphyxiate, strangle, throttle, choke, stifle, put out, extinguish, snuff, damp (down), dampen, muffle, inundate, overwhelm, suppress, repress, keep back, hide, conceal, cover, shroud, cocoon, envelop, surround, wrap

smoulder *v*
burn, smoke, fume, rage, foam, boil, seethe, fester, simmer

smudge *n, v*
▶ *n* (dirty) mark, blot, blotch, stain, spot, blemish, blur, smear, streak, smutch
▶ *v* blur, smear, streak, daub, mark, spot, stain, dirty, make dirty, soil, blacken, besmirch

smug *adj*
complacent, self-satisfied, superior, holier-than-thou, self-righteous, pleased with yourself, priggish, conceited
◨ humble, modest

smuggler *n*
runner, contrabandist, moonshiner, courier
colloq. bootlegger, mule

smutty *adj*
dirty, crude, coarse, filthy, indecent, improper, indelicate, obscene, pornographic, risqué, racy, bawdy, suggestive, vulgar, gross, lewd, salacious, ribald
formal prurient
colloq. blue, off colour, raunchy, sleazy
◨ clean, decent

snack *n*
refreshment(s), light meal, sandwich, bite, nibble(s), titbit, buffet
colloq. elevenses, bite to eat, pick-me-up

snag *n, v*
▶ *n* disadvantage, inconvenience, drawback, catch, problem, difficulty, complication, setback, hitch, obstacle, stumbling-block
▶ *v* catch, rip, tear, hole, ladder

snap *v, n, adj*
▶ *v* **1** *the twig snapped*
break, crack, split, splinter, fracture, separate, crackle
2 BITE, nip, bark, growl, snarl, retort, crackle
3 SNATCH, seize, catch, grasp, grip
4 *speak angrily to*

growl at, snarl at, lash out at, bark at, speak sharply/brusquely to
5 PHOTOGRAPH, take, film, shoot, record
▷ **snap up** grab, grasp, seize, snatch, pounce on, pick up, pluck; *colloq.* nab
▶ *n* **1** BREAK, crack, bite, nip, flick, fillip, crackle
2 *a cold snap*
spell, period, time, stretch, span, stint
3 PHOTOGRAPH, photo, snapshot, print, shot, still, picture
▶ *adj* sudden, immediate, instant, on-the-spot, abrupt

snappy *adj*
1 SMART, stylish, chic, elegant, fashionable, up-to-date, up-to-the-minute, modish
colloq. trendy, snazzy, natty
2 QUICK, hasty, brisk, lively, energetic
3 CROSS, irritable, edgy, touchy, brusque, bad-tempered, quick-tempered, ill-tempered, ill-natured, irascible, crabbed, testy, crotchety
◨ **1** dowdy **2** slow

snare *v, n*
▶ *v* trap, ensnare, entrap, catch, capture, seize, net
▶ *n* trap, wire, net, noose, gin, springe, catch, pitfall

snarl¹ *v*
the dog snarled
growl, show your teeth, snap, bark, howl, yelp, lash out at, grumble, complain

snarl² *v*
TANGLE, knot, ravel, twist, entangle, enmesh, entwine, embroil, confuse, muddle, jumble, complicate

snarl-up *n*
muddle, tangle, mess, mix-up, jumble, confusion, entanglement, traffic jam, gridlock

snatch *v, n*
▶ *v* grab, seize, steal, kidnap, abduct, take as hostage, make off with, take, take/get hold of, pluck, pull, wrench, wrest, gain, win, clutch, pounce on, grasp, grip, secure
colloq. nab, swipe, bag, collar, nail
▶ *n* part, piece, bit, section, segment, fraction, fragment, smattering, snippet, spell

snazzy *adj*
stylish, showy, fashionable, smart, attractive, flamboyant, raffish, sporty, dashing, sophisticated
colloq. flashy, jazzy, ritzy, snappy, swinging, with it
◨ drab, unfashionable

sneak *v, n, adj*
▶ *v* **1** CREEP, steal, slip, slink, sidle, slide, skulk, pad, lurk, prowl, smuggle, spirit
2 TELL TALES, inform on
colloq. split, squeal, snitch, blow the whistle on, shop, rat; *slang* grass on
▶ *n* tell-tale, informer
colloq. squealer, mole, rat, whistle-blower; *slang* grass
▶ *adj* secret, surprise, quick, covert, furtive, stealthy, surreptitious
formal clandestine

sneaking *adj*
private, secret, furtive, surreptitious, hidden, lurking, suppressed, unvoiced, unexpressed, grudging, nagging, niggling, persistent, worrying, uncomfortable, intuitive

sneaky *adj*
shady, shifty, furtive, dishonest, devious, guileful,

deceitful, unethical, unreliable, unscrupulous, untrustworthy, sly, snide, double-dealing, base, contemptible, cowardly, nasty, mean, low, low-down, malicious
formal disingenuous
colloq. slippery
F∃ honest, open; *colloq.* up front

sneer   *v, n*
▶ *v* scorn, disdain, look down on, scoff, jeer, mock, ridicule, insult, taunt, slight, gibe, laugh, snigger, snicker, smirk
formal deride
▶ *n* scorn, disdain, derision, jeer, mockery, ridicule, insult, taunt, slight, gibe, snigger, snicker, smirk

snicker   *v & n*
snigger, laugh, giggle, titter, chuckle, chortle, sneer

snide   *adj*
derogatory, sarcastic, cynical, scornful, sneering, hurtful, mocking, taunting, jeering, scoffing, derisive, scathing, biting, caustic, unkind, nasty, mean, spiteful, malicious, ill-natured
formal disparaging
F∃ complimentary

sniff   *v, n*
▶ *v* **1** BREATHE, inhale, snuff, snuffle
2 SMELL, nose, scent, whiff, get a whiff of
▷ **sniff at** look down on, disdain, sneer at, scoff at, mock, laugh at, slight, spurn, refuse, shun, reject, dismiss, disregard, overlook; *formal* deride, disparage
F∃ admire, respect
▶ *n* **1** SMELL, scent, whiff, aroma
2 HINT, whiff, suggestion, trace, impression, intimation

sniffy   *adj*
snobbish, snobby, contemptuous, scoffing, sneering, scornful, condescending, superior, supercilious, disdainful, haughty

snigger   *v, n*
snicker, laugh, giggle, titter, chuckle, chortle, sneer, smirk

snip   *v, n*
▶ *v* cut, clip, trim, crop, dock, prune, slit, nick, snick, notch, incise
▶ *n* **1** CUT, clip, trim, crop, prune, slit, clipping
2 BIT, fragment, piece, scrap, shred, snippet
3 BARGAIN, giveaway, special offer, good buy, discount, reduction, value for money
colloq. steal

snippet   *n*
piece, scrap, bit, cutting, clipping, fragment, particle, shred, snatch, part, portion, segment, section

snivel   *v*
cry, weep, bawl, sniff, sniffle, snuffle, sob, blub, blubber, whimper, grizzle, moan, whinge, whine

snivelling   *adj*
crying, weeping, sniffling, snuffling, blubbering, whimpering, grizzling, moaning, whingeing, whining

snobbery   *n*
snobbishness, superciliousness, airs, loftiness, arrogance, haughtiness, pride, pretension, condescension, superiority, disdain, airs and graces
colloq. snootiness, uppishness, side

snobbish   *adj*
supercilious, disdainful, proud, haughty, snobby,

superior, lofty, high and mighty, arrogant, pretentious, affected, condescending, patronizing
colloq. snooty, stuck-up, toffee-nosed, uppity, jumped-up, hoity-toity, too big for your boots

snoop   *v, n*
▶ *v* spy, sneak, pry, nose, interfere, meddle
colloq. poke/stick your nose in, stick/put your oar in
▶ *n* **1** *have a snoop around*
sneak, pry, nose, interference, meddling
2 SNOOPER, spy, busybody, pry, meddler
colloq. nosy parker, Paul Pry

snooper   *n*
snoop, spy, busybody, pry, meddler
colloq. nosy parker, Paul Pry

snooze   *v, n*
▶ *v* nap, drop off, nod off, catnap, doze, sleep
formal slumber
colloq. have forty winks; *slang* kip
▶ *n* nap, catnap, doze, siesta, sleep
formal slumber, repose
colloq. forty winks, shut-eye; *slang* kip

snout   *n*
nose, muzzle, neb, trunk
formal proboscis
colloq. schnozzle, snitch

snow   *n*
snowfall, snowstorm, snowflakes, snowdrift, blizzard, snow flurries, sleet, slush, ice
Related adjective: niveous

snub   *v, n*
▶ *v* rebuff, shun, spurn, insult, disregard, ignore, brush off, cut, slight, rebuke, put down, squash, humble, shame, humiliate, mortify
formal affront
colloq. cold-shoulder, give the cold-shoulder to, slap in the face, kick in the teeth
▶ *n* rebuff, brush-off, slight, affront, insult, rebuke, put-down, humiliation
colloq. slap in the face, kick in the teeth

snug   *adj*
cosy, warm, comfortable, homely, friendly, intimate, sheltered, secure, tight, skintight, close-fitting, figure-hugging
colloq. comfy, snug as a bug in a rug

snuggle   *v*
nestle, nuzzle, curl up, cuddle, embrace, hug

soak   *v*
wet, drench, saturate, penetrate, permeate, infuse, bathe, marinate, souse, steep, submerge, immerse, imbue, ret

soaking   *adj*
soaked, soaked to the skin, wet through, drenched, sodden, waterlogged, saturated, sopping, sopping wet, wringing, dripping, streaming
F∃ dry

soar   *v*
fly, wing, glide, plane, tower, rise, take off, ascend, climb, mount, escalate, spiral, rocket, skyrocket
F∃ fall, plummet

sob   *v*
cry, weep, shed tears, bawl, howl, blubber, snivel
colloq. boohoo

sober   *adj*
1 TEETOTAL, temperate, moderate, abstinent,

abstemious, clear-headed
colloq. sober as a judge, dry, drying out, stone-cold sober, on the wagon, off the bottle, having signed the pledge
2 SOLEMN, dignified, serious, earnest, grave, thoughtful, staid, steady, sedate, quiet, serene, calm, composed, unruffled, unexcited, cool, dispassionate, level-headed, practical, realistic, reasonable, rational, clear-headed, self-controlled
3 *sober dress*
sombre, staid, drab, dull, dark, plain, severe, austere, subdued, restrained
F3 1 drunk, intemperate **2** frivolous, excited, unrealistic, irrational **3** flashy, garish

sobriety *n*
1 ABSTEMIOUSNESS, soberness, abstinence, moderation, temperance, teetotalism
2 SOLEMNITY, seriousness, staidness, steadiness, calmness, composure, level-headedness, coolness, sedateness, restraint, self-restraint, gravity
F3 1 drunkenness **2** excitement, frivolity

so-called *adj*
alleged, supposed, ostensible, nominal, self-styled, professed, would-be, pretended, *soi-disant*
formal purported

sociability *n*
friendliness, companionability, congeniality, conviviality, cordiality, affability, neighbourliness, gregariousness
colloq. chumminess

sociable *adj*
friendly, outgoing, gregarious, affable, companionable, genial, convivial, cordial, warm, hospitable, neighbourly, approachable, accessible, familiar
colloq. chummy
F3 unsociable, withdrawn, unfriendly, hostile

> ⚠ **sociable** or **social** ?
> *Sociable* is usually applied to people and means 'friendly, fond of the company of others': *Our new neighbours aren't very sociable; He's a cheerful, sociable sort of bloke. Social* means 'of or concerning society': *Problems such as this are social rather than medical in origin; social class. Social* also means 'concerning the gathering together or meeting of people for recreation and amusement': *a social club; His reasons for calling round were purely social.*

social *adj, n*
▶ *adj* **1** *social policies*
communal, public, community, civic, common, general, collective, group, organized
2 *social activities*
leisure, entertainment, amusement
▶ *n* party, get-together, gathering, dance
colloq. do

> ⚠ **social** or **sociable** ? *See panel at* **sociable**.

socialism *n*
leftism, communism, welfarism, Leninism, Marxism, Stalinism, Trotskyism

socialist *adj, n*
▶ *adj* left-wing, leftist, communist, Trotskyist, Trotskyite
colloq. commie, leftie, red, Trot
▶ *n* left-winger, leftist, communist, welfarist,

Trotskyist, Trotskyite
colloq. commie, leftie, red, Trot

socialize *v*
mix, mingle, be sociable, meet people, meet socially, fraternize, get together, go out, entertain
colloq. hobnob

society *n*
1 COMMUNITY, population, culture, civilization, nation, public, people, mankind, humanity, human race, humankind
2 CLUB, circle, group, band, body, association, organization, company, corporation, federation, alliance, league, union, guild, fellowship, fraternity, brotherhood, sisterhood, sorority
3 FRIENDSHIP, companionship, camaraderie, fellowship, company
4 UPPER CLASSES, high society, aristocracy, gentry, nobility, elite
colloq. nobs, toffs, swells, top drawer, the smart set, the upper crust, Sloane Rangers

sodden *adj*
wet, soaking, soaked, wet, drenched, saturated, sopping, waterlogged, soggy, marshy, boggy, miry
Scot. drookit
F3 dry

soft *adj*
1 YIELDING, pliable, flexible, pliant, elastic, springy, plastic, supple, malleable, tender, spongy, squashy, mushy, squelchy, pulpy
formal ductile
colloq. squishy
2 *soft colours; speak in a soft voice*
pale, light, pastel, delicate, subdued, shaded, muted, restrained, quiet, low, low-key, whispered, hushed, dim, faint, diffuse, mild, bland, gentle, flowing, soothing, sweet, mellow, melodious, dulcet, pleasant
formal mellifluous
3 FURRY, downy, fleecy, velvety, silky, silken, smooth
4 LENIENT, lax, liberal, permissive, indulgent, tolerant, forgiving, forbearing, weak
colloq. easy-going, spineless,
5 TENDER, kind, generous, sympathetic, affectionate, gentle, merciful, soft-hearted, sensitive
6 *a soft life*
easy, comfortable, luxurious, successful, prosperous
colloq. cushy, easy-going, a bed of roses, all beer and skittles
F3 1 hard, firm **2** harsh, hard, sharp, bright, loud **3** rough **4** hard, strict, severe
5 unsympathetic, cruel **6** hard
▷ **soft spot** fondness, liking, partiality, weakness; *formal* penchant

soften *v*
1 MODERATE, temper, lessen, diminish, alleviate, ease, cushion, soothe, palliate, quell, subdue, mollify, appease, calm (down), still, relax
formal mitigate, abate, assuage
2 MELT, liquefy, dissolve, reduce
3 CUSHION, pad, muffle, quicken, lower, lighten
▷ **soften up** persuade, conciliate, disarm, win over, weaken, melt; *colloq.* butter up, soft-soap

soft-hearted *adj*
sympathetic, compassionate, gentle, kind, benevolent, charitable, generous, warm-hearted, tender, affectionate, sentimental
F3 hard-hearted, callous

soft-pedal *v*
moderate, go easy, play down, subdue, tone down
F3 highlight, emphasize

soggy *adj*
wet, damp, moist, soaked, soaking, drenched, sodden,
waterlogged, saturated, sopping, sopping wet,
dripping, heavy, boggy, spongy, pulpy

soil¹ *n*
1 EARTH, clay, loam, humus, dirt, dust, ground
Related adjective: edaphic
2 LAND, region, country, territory
formal terra firma

soil² *v*
1 DIRTY, begrime, stain, spot, smudge, smear, foul,
muddy, pollute, defile
2 *soil your reputation*
besmirch, stain, smear, sully, tarnish, defile

soiled *adj*
dirty, grimy, stained, spotted, sullied, polluted,
tarnished
formal maculate
colloq. manky
F3 clean, immaculate

sojourn *n, v*
▶ *n* stay, rest, visit, stop, stopover
formal peregrination
▶ *v* lodge, rest, stay, stop
formal dwell, reside, abide, tarry, tabernacle

solace *n, v*
▶ *n* comfort, consolation, relief, alleviation, support,
condolence, cheer
formal succour
▶ *v* comfort, console, support, allay, alleviate, soften,
soothe
formal mitigate, succour

soldier *n, v*

Types of soldier include: cadet, private, sapper, NCO,
orderly, officer, gunner, infantryman, trooper,
fusilier, rifleman, paratrooper, sentry, guardsman,
marine, commando, tommy, dragoon, cavalryman,
lancer, hussar, conscript, recruit, regular, private,
Territorial, *US* GI, warrior, mercenary, legionnaire,
guerrilla, partisan, centurion; fighter, serviceman,
troops. *See also* **rank¹**.

Related adjective: military
v ▷ **soldier on** continue, persevere, keep on, keep
going, remain, hold on, hang on; *colloq.* keep at it, stick
at it, plug away

sole *adj*
only, unique, exclusive, individual, single, singular,
one, lone, solitary, alone
F3 shared, multiple

solecism *n*
error, mistake, blunder, lapse, gaucherie, impropriety,
absurdity, cacology, *faux pas*
technical anacoluthon
formal incongruity, indecorum
colloq. boob, boo-boo, howler, gaffe

solely *adv*
exclusively, only, singly, uniquely, merely, completely,
entirely, alone, single-handedly

solemn *adj*
1 *a solemn expression*
serious, grave, sober, sedate, sombre, glum, thoughtful,

earnest, formal, awed, reverential
2 GRAND, stately, majestic, ceremonial, ritual,
formal, ceremonious, pompous, dignified, august,
venerable, awe-inspiring, impressive, imposing,
momentous
3 *a solemn promise*
sincere, formal, earnest, genuine, wholehearted,
committed, grave
F3 **1** light-hearted **2** frivolous

solemnity *n*
1 SERIOUSNESS, earnestness, gravity, sacredness,
sanctity, momentousness, dignity, impressiveness,
grandeur, stateliness
formal portentousness
2 CEREMONY, celebration, observance, rite, ritual,
ceremonial, proceedings, formalities
F3 **1** frivolity

solemnize *v*
keep, honour, observe, commemorate, celebrate,
dignify

solicit *v*
ask (for), request, crave, beg, implore, plead, pray,
apply (for), petition, canvass
formal seek, beseech, entreat, supplicate, sue,
importune
colloq. tout, hustle

solicitor *n*
lawyer, advocate, attorney, barrister, QC

solicitous *adj*
caring, attentive, considerate, concerned, anxious,
worried, apprehensive, uneasy, troubled, eager,
earnest, zealous

solicitude *n*
care, concern, attentiveness, considerateness,
consideration, regard, worry, anxiety, uneasiness,
disquiet, trouble

solid *adj*
1 HARD, firm, dense, thick, compact, compressed,
strong, concrete, sturdy, substantial, stable, sound,
well-built, durable, long-lasting, unshakable
2 RELIABLE, dependable, trusty, trustworthy,
worthy, decent, upstanding, upright, sensible,
level-headed, steadfast, stable, serious, sober,
respectable
3 *solid evidence*
reliable, sound, valid, strong, firm, authoritative,
weighty, well-grounded, well-founded
formal cogent
4 REAL, genuine, pure, concrete, tangible,
unadulterated, unmixed, unalloyed
5 *a solid white line*
unbroken, continuous, undivided, uninterrupted
F3 **1** liquid, gaseous, hollow **2** unreliable,
unstable **3** unsound, unreliable **4** unreal
5 broken, dotted

solidarity *n*
unity, agreement, accord, unanimity, consensus,
harmony, concord, cohesion, like-mindedness, single-
mindedness, camaraderie, team spirit, *esprit de corps*,
soundness, stability
F3 discord, division, schism

solidify *v*
harden, go/become hard, set, gel, jell, congeal,
coagulate, clot, cake, crystallize
F3 soften, liquefy, dissolve

solitary *adj, n*
▶ *adj* **1** LONELY, sole, single, lone, alone, lonesome, by yourself, friendless, companionless, unsociable, introverted, reclusive, hermitical, withdrawn, retired **2** REMOTE, lonely, separate, isolated, desolate, out-of-the-way, inaccessible, cloistered, secluded, unfrequented, unvisited, untrodden
formal sequestered
EB 1 accompanied, gregarious, busy **2** accessible
▶ *n* loner, individualist, hermit, recluse, ascetic, monk, anchorite, anchoress, ancress, eremite, stylite
colloq. lone wolf

solitude *n*
aloneness, loneliness, singleness, friendlessness, lonesomeness, introversion, unsociability, reclusiveness, retirement, privacy, seclusion, isolation, remoteness, desolation
EB companionship

solution *n*
1 ANSWER, result, explanation, resolution, key, remedy, way out, panacea, cure-all, clarification, decipherment, disentanglement, unfolding, unravelling
formal elucidation
colloq. (quick) fix
2 MIXTURE, blend, mix, compound, suspension, emulsion, liquid, solvent

solve *v*
work out, figure out, puzzle out, decipher, crack, disentangle, unravel, unfold, answer, resolve, put right, remedy, settle, clear up, clarify, explain, interpret, get to the bottom of
formal rectify, expound
colloq. fathom, crack

solvent *adj*
sound, financially sound, able to pay, creditworthy, out of debt, unindebted
colloq. in the black
EB insolvent

sombre *adj*
dark, funereal, drab, dull, dim, obscure, shady, shadowy, gloomy, dismal, dingy, melancholy, mournful, sad, depressed, doleful, morose, joyless, sober, serious, grave, solemn
formal funereal, lugubrious
EB bright, cheerful, happy

somebody *n*
someone, celebrity, dignitary, name, personage, star, superstar, VIP, notable, luminary, magnate, mogul, heavyweight, nabob, panjandrum
colloq. household name, bigwig, big noise, big shot, big wheel
EB nobody

someday *adv*
sometime, at some time in the future, one day, one of these (fine) days, sooner or later, later, later on, in due course, by and by, eventually, ultimately
EB never

somehow *adv*
by some means, one way or another, come what may
colloq. by fair means or foul, by hook or by crook, come hell or high water

sometime *adv, adj*
▶ *adv* someday, one day, at some time in the future, at some time in the past, another time, in the past, then, previously, earlier

▶ *adj* former, previous, one-time, late, retired, emeritus
formal erstwhile, quondam
colloq. ex

sometimes *adv*
occasionally, on occasion(s), now and again, now and then, on and off, off and on, every so often, once in a while, at times, from time to time
EB always, never

somnolent *adj*
sleepy, drowsy, dozy, half-awake, heavy-eyed, soporific, torpid
technical comatose
formal oscitant

son *n*
boy, child, lad(die), offspring, descendant, inhabitant, native, disciple
Related adjective: filial

song *n*

Types of song include: air, anthem, aria, ballad, barcarole, bird call, bird song, blues, calypso, cantata, canticle, cantilena, canzone, canzonet, carol, chanson, chansonette, chant, chorus, descant, dirge, dithyramb, ditty, elegy, epinikion, epithalamium, folk-song, gospel song, hymn, jingle, lay, love-song, lied, lilt, lullaby, lyric(s), madrigal, melody, number, nursery rhyme, ode, plainchant, plainsong, pop song, psalm, recitative, refrain, requiem, rock and roll, roundelay, serenade, shanty, spiritual, Negro spiritual, threnody, tune, war song, wassail, yodel. *See also* poem.

▷ **song and dance** commotion, stir, fuss, bother, ado, to-do, tumult, furore, performance; *colloq.* flap, hoo-ha, kerfuffle, pother, tizzy

songster *n*
singer, vocalist, chorister, balladeer, chanteuse, minstrel, troubadour, crooner, warbler

sonorous *adj*
resonant, resounding, ringing, rich, rounded, orotund, ororotund, full, full-mouthed, full-voiced, full-throated, loud, sounding, high-flown, high-sounding
formal grandiloquent, plangent

soon *adv*
shortly, presently, in a little while, in no time (at all), in a short time, in a minute, in a moment (or two), any minute (now), before long, in the near future
colloq. pronto, in a jiffy, in a tick, in two shakes of a lamb's tail, before you can say Jack Robinson

soothe *v*
alleviate, relieve, ease, salve, comfort, allay, calm (down), compose, tranquillize, settle (down), still, quiet, quieten (down), hush, lull, pacify, mollify, soften, palliate, temper
formal appease, assuage, mitigate
EB aggravate, irritate, annoy, vex

soothing *adj*
relaxing, restful, calming, easeful, emollient, lenitive, balmy, palliative, balsamic
technical anetic
formal assuasive, demulcent
EB annoying, irritating, vexing

soothsayer *n*
prophet, diviner, foreteller, seer, sibyl, augur, Chaldee
formal haruspex

sophisticated *adj*
1 URBANE, cosmopolitan, worldly, worldly-wise, experienced, seasoned, cultured, cultivated, stylish, elegant, refined, polished, suave
2 *sophisticated technology*
advanced, highly-developed, complicated, complex, intricate, elaborate, delicate, subtle
⊟ 1 unsophisticated, naïve 2 primitive, simple

sophistication *n*
urbanity, worldliness, culture, experience, elegance, finesse, poise, *savoir-faire*, *savoir-vivre*
⊟ naïvety, simplicity

sophistry *n*
casuistry, sophism, quibble, fallacy
technical paralogism, elenchus

soporific *adj, n*
▶ *adj* sleep-inducing, hypnotic, sedative, opiate, narcotic, tranquillizing, sleepy
formal somnolent
⊟ stimulating, invigorating
▶ *n* tranquillizer, sleeping pill, sleeping tablet, sedative, opiate, narcotic, hypnotic, anaesthetic, hypnic
⊟ stimulant

soppy *adj*
sentimental, overemotional, mawkish, maudlin, cloying, soft, crazy, wild, silly
colloq. slushy, mushy, sloppy, lovey-dovey, weepy, schmaltzy, corny, wet, wimpish, daft

sorcerer *n*
sorceress, wizard, warlock, witch, magician, enchanter, magus, mage, magian, reim-kennar, necromancer, voodoo, angek(k)ok
formal thaumaturgist
Related adjective: magian

sorcery *n*
magic, black magic, witchcraft, wizardry, necromancy, voodoo, spell, incantation, charm, enchantment, pishogue
formal thaumaturgy

sordid *adj*
1 DIRTY, filthy, unclean, foul, vile, squalid, grimy, stained, soiled, sleazy, mucky, seamy, seedy, disreputable, shabby, tawdry
2 CORRUPT, degraded, degenerate, immoral, debased, dishonest, dishonourable, disreputable, debauched, low, base, vile, foul, despicable, shameful, wretched, mean, miserly, niggardly, grasping, mercenary, self-seeking
formal abhorrent, ignominious
⊟ 1 clean, pure 2 honourable, upright

sore *adj, n*
▶ *adj* 1 PAINFUL, hurting, aching, smarting, stinging, burning, chafed, tender, sensitive, inflamed, red, reddened, bruised, injured, raw, wounded
2 ANNOYED, irritated, vexed, angry, upset, hurt, wounded, afflicted, aggrieved, offended, bitter, resentful, distressed
⊟ 2 pleased, happy
▶ *n* wound, cut, graze, laceration, lesion, scrape, abrasion, chafe, swelling, inflammation, boil, abscess, ulcer

sorrow *n, v*
▶ *n* 1 SADNESS, unhappiness, grief, mourning, misery, woe, distress, suffering, pain, dejection, anguish, heartache, heartbreak, misfortune, wretchedness
formal affliction, disconsolateness, dolour
2 TROUBLE, misfortune, hardship, worry, trial, regret, remorse
formal tribulation, affliction
⊟ 1 happiness, joy 2 joy
▶ *v* grieve, lament, bewail, bemoan, be/feel sad, be/feel miserable, weep, agonize, moan, mourn, pine
⊟ rejoice

sorrowful *adj*
miserable, mournful, sad, unhappy, tearful, sorry, distressing, depressed, dejected, wretched, painful, lamentable, woeful, melancholy, grievous, doleful, heartbroken, heart-rending, heavy-hearted, piteous, rueful
Scot. wae
formal afflicted, disconsolate, lugubrious, woebegone
⊟ happy, joyful

sorry *adj*
1 APOLOGETIC, regretful, ashamed, remorseful, contrite, penitent, repentant, conscience-stricken, guilt-ridden, shamefaced
2 *sorry to hear the news*
sad, unhappy, upset, distressed
colloq. down
3 SYMPATHETIC, compassionate, understanding, pitying, concerned, moved
4 *in a sorry state*
pathetic, pitiful, poor, wretched, miserable, sad, unhappy, dismal, grievous, heart-rending, shameful
⊟ 1 impenitent, unashamed 2 happy, pleased
3 uncaring 4 happy, cheerful

sort *n, v*
▶ *n* kind, type, genre, ilk, family, race, breed, species, variety, order, class, set, breed, category, group, denomination, style, make, brand, stamp, quality, nature, character, description
technical genus
formal genre
▷ **out of sorts** 1 UNWELL, ill, sick, poorly, laid up, ailing, off-colour, seedy, queasy, diseased, unhealthy, infirm, frail, weak, feeble, bedridden; *colloq.* in a bad way, dicky, below par, down in the dumps, down in the mouth, under the weather, run down, rough, groggy
2 BAD-TEMPERED, irritable, cross, snappy, quick-tempered, grumpy, fractious, in a (bad) mood, narky, impatient, choleric; *colloq.* crotchety, crabbed, crabby, grouchy, stroppy, shirty, ratty, in a huff, in a sulk
▶ *v* class, group, categorize, distribute, divide, separate, segregate, sift, screen, grade, rank, order, classify, catalogue, arrange, put in order, organize, systematize
▷ **sort out** 1 ARRANGE, order, put in order, organize, work out 2 CLASSIFY, class, group, categorize, rank, order, grade, separate, divide, segregate, choose, select 3 RESOLVE, clear up, work out, put right, solve

sortie *n*
foray, raid, offensive, attack, charge, assault, sally, swoop, invasion, rush

so-so *adj*
average, middling, moderate, indifferent, fair, adequate, ordinary, respectable, neutral, tolerable, unexceptional, undistinguished, passable
colloq. fair to middling, not bad, OK, run-of-the-mill

soul *n*
1 SPIRIT, psyche, mind, reason, intellect, character,

inner being, inner self, essence, life, life-giving
principle, vital force
colloq. heart of hearts
2 INDIVIDUAL, person, human being, man, woman,
creature
colloq. character
3 *a singer with no soul*
sensitivity, sympathy, compassion, feeling, humanity,
understanding, appreciation, tenderness, inspiration
4 *he's the soul of discretion*
epitome, personification, embodiment, essence,
model, example
F∃ 1 body

soulful *adj*
sensitive, emotional, expressive, heartfelt, moving,
profound, mournful, meaningful, eloquent
F∃ soulless

soulless *adj*
unfeeling, spiritless, unsympathetic, inhuman, lifeless,
cold, callous, cruel, unkind, dead, uninteresting,
ignoble, mean, mean-spirited, soul-destroying,
mechanical
F∃ soulful

sound¹ *n, v*
▶ *n* *hear a tapping sound*
noise, din, report, resonance, reverberation, tone,
timbre, tenor, description
Related adjective: sonic
▶ *v* **1** RING, toll, chime, peal, resound, resonate,
reverberate, echo, go off
2 ARTICULATE, enunciate, pronounce, voice,
express, utter, say, declare, announce

Sounds include: bang, beep, blare, blast, bleep,
boom, bubble, buzz, chime, chink, chug, clack,
clang, clank, clap, clash, clatter, click, clink, crack,
crackle, crash, creak, crunch, cry, drone, echo,
explode, fizz, grate, grizzle, groan, gurgle, hiccup,
hiss, honk, hoot, hum, jangle, jingle, knock, moan,
murmur, patter, peal, ping, pip, plop, pop, rattle,
report, reverberate, ring, roar, rumble, rustle,
scrape, scream, screech, sigh, sizzle, skirl, slam,
slurp, smack, snap, sniff, snore, snort, sob, splash,
splutter, squeak, squeal, squelch, swish, tap, throb,
thud, thump, thunder, tick, ting, tinkle, toot, twang,
wail, whimper, whine, whirr, whistle, whoop, yell.

Animals sounds include: bark, bay, bellow, bleat,
bray, cackle, caw, chirp, chirrup, cluck, coo, croak,
crow, gobble, growl, grunt, hiss, hoot, howl, low,
mew, miaow, moo, neigh, purr, quack, roar, screech,
snarl, squawk, squeak, tweet, twitter, warble,
whinny, woof, yap, yelp, yowl.

sound² *adj*
1 FIT, well, healthy, in good health, in good
condition/shape, vigorous, robust, sturdy, firm, solid,
whole, sane, complete, intact, perfect, disease-free,
unbroken, undamaged, unimpaired, unhurt,
uninjured
colloq. in fine fettle, sound as a bell
2 VALID, well-founded, well-grounded, reasonable,
rational, logical, orthodox, authoritative, weighty,
right, true, proven, reliable, dependable, trustworthy,
secure, substantial, solid, sturdy, thorough, good,
complete
formal judicious, cogent
F∃ 1 unfit, ill, shaky **2** unsound, unreliable, poor

sound³ *v*
to sound the depths
measure, plumb, fathom, probe, examine, test, inspect,
investigate
▷ **sound out** ask, canvass, examine, investigate,
research, survey, probe, pump, question; *colloq.* suss
out

sound⁴ *n*
the Sound of Jura
channel, estuary, inlet, passage, strait, firth, fjord, voe

soup *n*
broth, potage, consommé, stock, chowder, bisque,
cockieleekie, borsch, gazpacho, mulligatawny,
julienne

sour *adj, v*
▶ *adj* **1** TART, sharp, acid, tangy, acidy, aciduous,
acetic, pungent, vinegary, bitter, rancid, curdled,
turned
colloq. off, bad
2 EMBITTERED, bad-tempered, surly, churlish, ill-
tempered, peevish, crusty, resentful, unpleasant, nasty,
disagreeable
formal acrimonious
colloq. crabbed, grouchy, shirty, ratty
F∃ 1 sweet, sugary **2** good-natured, generous
▶ *v* disenchant, embitter, make better, exacerbate,
exasperate, alienate, spoil, envenom

source *n*
origin, derivation, beginning, start, cause, root, rise,
spring, wellspring, fountainhead, wellhead, supply,
mine, originator, author, authority, informant
technical ylem
formal commencement, provenance, primordium,
fons et origo

sourpuss *n*
misery, grumbler, killjoy, shrew, whiner, kvetch
colloq. crosspatch, grouse, grump, whinger

souse *v*
douse, drench, dunk, sink, immerse, marinate,
marinade, pickle, plunge, soak, saturate, steep, dip,
submerge

souvenir *n*
memento, reminder, remembrance, keepsake, relic,
token, trophy

sovereign *n, adj*
▶ *n* ruler, monarch, king, queen, emperor, empress,
tsar, chief
formal potentate
▶ *adj* **1** RULING, royal, kingly, queenly, princely,
imperial, majestic, absolute, unlimited, supreme,
paramount, predominant, principal, chief, dominant,
independent, autonomous, self-governing, self-ruling
2 UNRIVALLED, outstanding, utmost, extreme,
unequalled

sovereignty *n*
autonomy, independence, supremacy, domination,
sway, dominion, kingship, queenship, regality,
primacy, raj
formal ascendancy, imperium, suzerainty

sow *v*
plant, seed, scatter, strew, bestrew, spread, distribute,
disperse, broadcast, lodge, implant
formal disseminate

space *n, v*
▶ *n* **1** ROOM, place, seat, accommodation, capacity,

area, volume, extent, expanse, sweep, stretch, expansion, latitude, scope, range, play, clearance, elbow-room, leeway, margin
formal amplitude
Related adjective: spatial
2 BLANK, omission, gap, break, empty space, opening, interval, intermission, chasm
formal lacuna, interstice
Related adjective: lacunary
3 *in a short space of time*
period, stretch, span, spell, time, shift, stint
4 OUTER SPACE, the Milky Way, galaxy, universe, cosmos, solar system, deep space
Related adjective: cosmic
▶ *v* arrange, order, put in order, range, be apart, set apart, space out, stretch out, string out, place at intervals
formal array, dispose

spacious *adj*
roomy, ample, big, large, sizable, broad, wide, huge, vast, immense, extensive, expansive, open, uncrowded
formal capacious, commodious
E3 small, narrow, cramped, confined; *colloq.* poky

spadework *n*
foundation, groundwork, homework, preparation, labour, drudgery
colloq. donkey-work

span *n, v*
▶ *n* spread, stretch, reach, range, scope, compass, extent, length, distance, duration, time, interval, term, period, spell
▶ *v* arch, vault, bridge, link, cross, traverse, range, extend, stretch, last, cover, include
formal bestride

spank *v*
smack, slap, thrash, slipper, cane
colloq. wallop, whack, thwack, tan, put over your knee

spanking *adj, adv*
▶ *adj* brisk, fast, quick, lively, smart, speedy, swift, vigorous, energetic, snappy, invigorating, fine, gleaming
E3 slow
▶ *adv* absolutely, completely, utterly, totally, exactly, strikingly, positively, brand

spar *v*
argue, dispute, contest, fall out, contend, wrangle, squabble, bicker, wrestle, box, skirmish
colloq. scrap, spat, tiff

spare *adj, v*
▶ *adj* **1** RESERVE, emergency, extra, additional, supplementary, leftover, remaining, unused, over, surplus, surplus to requirements, superfluous, supernumerary, auxiliary, unwanted
2 *spare time*
free, unoccupied, leisure
3 LEAN, thin, skinny, bony, gaunt, lank, slim, slender, scraggy, scrawny
colloq. all skin and bones
4 FRUGAL, scanty, scant, meagre, modest, sparing
E3 **1** necessary, vital, used **3** fat
▷ **to spare** left over, remaining, extra, in reserve, unused, surplus
▶ *v* **1** PARDON, let off, reprieve, show mercy to, forgive, release, free
2 GRANT, allow, provide, give, afford, part with, do without, manage without
formal dispense with

3 NOT HARM, protect, save, guard, safeguard, secure, take care of, defend

sparing *adj*
economical, thrifty, careful, frugal, meagre, miserly, tight-fisted, close-fisted
formal prudent, penurious
colloq. stingy, mingy
E3 unsparing, liberal, lavish

spark *n, v*
▶ *n* **1** FLASH, flare, gleam, glint, glimmer, flicker
2 *not a spark of intelligence*
flicker, hint, trace, vestige, scrap, bit, touch, suggestion, iota, atom, jot
▶ *v* ▷ **spark off** kindle, set off, trigger (off), start (off), cause, touch off, occasion, prompt, provoke, stimulate, stir, incite, excite, inspire; *formal* precipitate

sparkle *v, n*
▶ *v* **1** TWINKLE, glitter, scintillate, flash, flicker, gleam, glint, glisten, glow, glimmer, shimmer, shine, beam
formal coruscate
2 EFFERVESCE, fizz, bubble
3 BE LIVELY, be animated, be spirited, be enthusiastic, be witty, be vivacious, be effervescent
formal be ebullient
colloq. be bubbly
▶ *n* **1** TWINKLE, glitter, flash, shimmer, gleam, glow, shine, glint, flicker, spark, radiance, brilliance, dazzle
formal coruscation
2 SPIRIT, vitality, life, animation, vivacity, liveliness, energy, dash, enthusiasm
formal ebullience
colloq. get-up-and-go, vim, pizzazz

sparkling *adj*
1 EFFERVESCENT, fizzy, carbonated, bubbly
2 TWINKLING, flashing, glittering, glistening, gleaming
formal coruscating
3 LIVELY, animated, scintillating, witty
E3 **1** flat **3** dull

sparse *adj*
scarce, scanty, meagre, slight, scattered, infrequent, sporadic
E3 plentiful, thick, dense

spartan *adj*
austere, harsh, severe, rigorous, strict, disciplined, self-denying, ascetic, abstemious, stringent, temperate, frugal, plain, simple, bleak, joyless
E3 luxurious, self-indulgent

spasm *n*
burst, eruption, outburst, frenzy, fit, bout, convulsion, seizure, attack, paroxysm, contraction, cramp, jerk, twitch, tic
formal access

spasmodic *adj*
sporadic, occasional, intermittent, erratic, periodic, irregular, fitful, jerky
E3 continuous, uninterrupted

spate *n*
flood, deluge, torrent, rush, outpouring, flow

spatter *v*
splatter, splash, splodge, spray, sprinkle, shower, speckle, scatter, daub, bedaub, bestrew, besprinkle, bespatter, dirty, soil

spay *n*
neuter, sterilize, castrate, emasculate, doctor, geld

speak *v*
talk, say, state, declare, express, utter, voice, articulate, enunciate, pronounce, tell, chat, communicate, address, lecture, harangue, hold forth, argue, discuss
formal converse, declaim
colloq. have a word with, chatter, gab, witter, yak
▷ **speak for** speak on behalf of, represent, act for, stand for, act as spokesperson for
▷ **speak of** refer to, make reference to, mention, make mention of, discuss
▷ **speak out/up** say publicly, speak openly, defend, support, protest; *colloq.* stand up and be counted
▷ **speak to** rebuke, reprimand, scold, warn, lecture, accost, address; *formal* admonish, upbraid; *colloq.* bring to book, dress down, tell off, tick off
▷ **speak up** talk (more) loudly, raise your voice, make yourself heard

speaker *n*
talker, lecturer, orator, spokesperson, spokesman, spokeswoman, mouthpiece
formal prolocutor

spearhead *v, n*
▶ *v* lead, head, initiate, launch, front, pioneer
▶ *n* vanguard, front line, leading position, pioneer, trailblazer, leader, guide, overseer
colloq. van, cutting edge

special *adj*
1 *a special occasion*
important, significant, momentous, major, noteworthy, notable, distinguished, distinctive, memorable, remarkable, extraordinary, outstanding, exceptional, unusual
colloq. out of the ordinary, red-letter
2 DIFFERENT, distinctive, characteristic, peculiar, individual, unique, exclusive, select, choice, particular, exact, specific, precise, detailed
formal singular
E3 1 normal, ordinary, usual; *colloq.* run of the mill
2 general, common

specialist *n*
consultant, authority, expert, master, professional, connoisseur
colloq. brains

speciality *n*
strength, feature, forte, talent, gift, field/area of study, field, *pièce de résistance*
US specialty

specially *adv*
for a special purpose, for a particular purpose, particularly, exclusively, uniquely, in particular, specifically, explicitly, distinctly, expressly

species *n*
class, kind, breed, sort, type, category, variety, genus, group, collection, description

specific *adj*
precise, exact, fixed, set, limited, determined, particular, special, definite, well-defined, unequivocal, clear-cut, detailed, explicit, express, unambiguous
E3 vague, approximate, unspecific

specification *n*
requirement, condition, qualification, stipulation, instruction, description, listing, naming, statement,

designation, item, particular, detail
formal delineation

specify *v*
stipulate, spell out, set out, define, particularize, detail, itemize, particularize, enumerate, list, mention, state, cite, name, designate, indicate, describe
formal delineate

specimen *n*
sample, example, instance, illustration, model, pattern, type, representative, copy, exhibit
formal paradigm, exemplar

specious *adj*
false, misleading, unsound, untrue, deceptive, plausible
formal fallacious, casuistic, sophistic, sophistical
E3 valid, true

speck *n*
mark, fleck, dot, speckle, shred, grain, particle, bit, blot, defect, blemish, fault, flaw, stain, spot, atom, mite, iota, jot, trace, whit, tittle

speckled *adj*
spotted, spotty, flecked, dotted, dappled, mottled, sprinkled, stippled, brinded, brindle(d), fleckered, freckled
technical lentiginous

spectacle *n*
show, performance, display, exhibition, parade, pageant, extravaganza, scene, sight, picture, curiosity, wonder, marvel, phenomenon

spectacles *n*

Types of spectacles include: bifocals, diving mask, eyeglass, goggles, half-glasses, lorgnette, monocle, pince-nez, Polaroid® glasses, quizzing glass, reading glasses, safety glasses, shooting glasses, sports spex, sunglasses, trifocals, varifocals.

spectacular *adj, n*
▶ *adj* grand, splendid, magnificent, sensational, impressive, glorious, striking, stunning, staggering, amazing, astonishing, extraordinary, outstanding, remarkable, dramatic, daring, breathtaking, dazzling, eye-catching, colourful, ostentatious, flamboyant
formal resplendent, opulent
E3 unimpressive, ordinary
▶ *n* extravaganza, show, display, exhibition, pageant, spectacle

spectator *n*
watcher, viewer, onlooker, looker-on, bystander, passer-by, witness, eye-witness, observer
formal beholder
US slang rubberneck
E3 player, participant

spectral *adj*
ghostly, incorporeal, insubstantial, disembodied, supernatural, unearthly, weird, uncanny, phantom, shadowy, eerie
colloq. spooky

spectre *n*
1 GHOST, phantom, spirit, wraith, apparition, vision, presence, shade, shadow, revenant, visitant
old use larva
colloq. spook
2 THREAT, menace, fear, dread

spectrum *n*
See **rainbow**.

speculate *v*
1 GUESS, wonder, contemplate, meditate, muse, reflect, consider, deliberate, theorize, suppose
formal conjecture, surmise, hypothesize, cogitate
2 GAMBLE, risk, hazard, venture

speculation *n*
1 GUESS, guesswork, consideration, supposition, theory, hypothesis, contemplation, deliberation, flight of fancy
formal conjecture, surmise
2 GAMBLE, gambling, hazard, risk

speculative *adj*
conjectural, hypothetical, theoretical, notional, indefinite, vague, abstract, academic, tentative, risky, hazardous, uncertain, unpredictable, unproven
formal suppositional
colloq. iffy, chancy, dicey

speech *n*
1 COMMUNICATION, spoken communication, language, dialogue, conversation, talk, articulation, pronunciation, diction, enunciation, elocution, accent, delivery, utterance, voice, tongue, parlance, dialect, jargon
colloq. lingo
2 *make a speech*
oration, address, discourse, talk, lecture, harangue, patter, conversation, dialogue, monologue, soliloquy, tirade
formal diatribe, philippic
colloq. spiel

speechless *adj*
dumbfounded, dumbstruck, thunderstruck, amazed, astounded, shocked, aghast, tongue-tied, inarticulate, mute, dumb, silent, mum
formal obmutescent
F3 talkative

speed *n, v*
▶ *n* velocity, rate, pace, tempo, momentum, quickness, swiftness, promptness, rapidity, alacrity, haste, hurry, dispatch, rush, acceleration
formal celerity, expeditiousness
F3 slowness, delay
▶ *v* race, tear, zoom, career, bowl along, sprint, gallop, hurry, rush, dash, accelerate, quicken
formal hasten
colloq. belt, hurtle, pelt, put your foot down, step on it/ the gas/the juice
F3 slow, delay
▷ **speed up** 1 ACCELERATE, quicken, speed, drive faster, go faster, pick up/gather speed, gain momentum; *colloq.* open up, put your food down, step on it/the gas/the juice, put on a spurt 2 *speed up a process* hurry, step up, stimulate, facilitate, advance, further, promote, spur on, forward; *formal* hasten, expedite, precipitate

speedily *adv*
fast, quickly, rapidly, swiftly, hastily, hurriedly, promptly, posthaste
F3 slowly

speedy *adj*
fast, quick, swift, rapid, nimble, express, prompt, immediate, hurried, hasty, cursory, summary
formal precipitate, expeditious

colloq. nippy, zippy
F3 slow, leisurely

spell[1] *v*
his expression spelt trouble
signal, suggest, mean, indicate, imply, promise, signify, herald
formal augur, portend, presage
▷ **spell out** explain, clarify, make clear, elucidate, emphasize, detail, stipulate, specify

spell[2] *n*
a spell of sunny weather
period, time, bout, session, term, season, interval, extent, course, stretch, span, patch, turn, shift, stint

spell[3] *n*
1 CHARM, incantation, abracadabra, magic, sorcery, witchery, bewitchment, enchantment, trance
2 FASCINATION, charm, glamour, pull, attraction, drawing power, allure, magnetism

spellbinding *adj*
gripping, fascinating, riveting, enthralling, captivating, enchanting, bewitching, entrancing, mesmerizing

spellbound *adj*
transfixed, hypnotized, mesmerized, fascinated, enthralled, gripped, entranced, riveted, captivated, bewitched, transported, enraptured, enchanted, charmed, rapt

spend *v*
1 *spend money*
pay out, invest, lay out, waste, squander, fritter, expend, consume, use up, exhaust, finish
formal disburse
colloq. fork out, shell out, splash out, blow, spend like water, dip/dig into your pocket
2 *spend time*
pass, fill, occupy, use (up), take up, while away, put in, employ, apply, devote
colloq. do, kill
F3 1 save, hoard

spendthrift *n, adj*
▶ *n* squanderer, prodigal, wastrel
formal profligate
F3 miser, hoarder, saver
▶ *adj* improvident, extravagant, prodigal, wasteful, squandering
formal profligate

spent *adj*
1 USED (UP), finished, expended, exhausted, consumed, gone
2 TIRED OUT, exhausted, weary, wearied, drained, weakened
formal debilitated, effete
colloq. worn out, fagged (out), burnt out, all in, bushed, dead beat, dog-tired, done in, jiggered, knackered, shattered, whacked, zonked

spew *v*
vomit, spit out, spurt, gush, issue, retch, regurgitate, disgorge, belch
colloq. puke, throw up

sphere *n*
1 BALL, globe, orb, round, globule
2 DOMAIN, realm, province, department, territory, discipline, speciality, field, area, range, scope, compass, extent, rank, function, capacity

3 *a sphere of people*
circle, class, group, set, band, crowd, clique

spherical *adj*
round, ball-shaped, globe-shaped, globular
formal rotund, globoid, globate, globose, orbicular

spice *n, v*
▶ *n* **1** FLAVOURING, seasoning, piquancy, relish, savour, tang
See also **herbs.**
2 EXCITEMENT, life, colour, zest, gusto
colloq. kick, pep, zap, zip
▶ *v* liven (up), enliven, vitalize, put life into, rouse, invigorate, animate, energize, brighten, stir (up)
colloq. buck up, pep up, perk up, hot up

spick and span
tidy, clean, polished, scrubbed, trim, well-kept, neat, immaculate, spotless, spruce, shipshape
F3 dirty, untidy

spicy *adj*
1 PIQUANT, hot, peppery, pungent, sharp, tangy, tart, seasoned, well-seasoned, flavoured, strongly flavoured, flavoursome, aromatic, fragrant
2 RACY, risqué, ribald, suggestive, indelicate, indecent, improper, scandalous, sensational
formal indecorous, unseemly
colloq. raunchy, juicy, blue, adult, near the bone/ knuckle
F3 1 bland, insipid **2** decent

spiel *n*
patter, pitch, sales patter, speech, recital
formal oration

spike *n, v*
▶ *n* point, prong, projection, tine, spine, barb, nail, stake, rowel
▶ *v* **1** IMPALE, stick, prick, spear, skewer, spit
2 *spike a drink*
lace, drug, add, mix in, contaminate

spill *v, n*
▶ *v* overturn, upset, slop, flow, overflow, disgorge, run (out/over), pour, tip, discharge, well, shed, scatter
▷ **spill the beans** inform, tell (on); *colloq.* blab, rat, split, squeal, grass, blow the gaff, give the game away, let the cat out of the bag
▶ *n* fall, accident, tumble, overturn, upset
colloq. cropper

spin *v, n*
▶ *v* **1** TURN (ROUND), go round, revolve, rotate, circle, twist, gyrate, twirl, swivel, pirouette, wheel, whirl, whirr, swirl, reel
2 *spin a story/yarn*
tell, narrate, relate, make up, invent, fabricate, dream up
▷ **spin out** prolong, extend, lengthen, amplify, pad out; *formal* protract
▶ *n* **1** TURN, revolution, rotation, circle, twist, gyration, twirl, swivel, pirouette, wheel, whirl, swirl, reel
2 COMMOTION, agitation, panic
colloq. flap, state, dither, fluster, tizzy, tizz
3 DRIVE, ride, run, trip, journey, outing, jaunt

spindle *n*
axis, pivot, pin, rod, axle
technical arbor, fusee

spindly *adj*
long, thin, lanky, gangly, gangling, skinny, spidery,

skeletal, spindle-shanked
formal attenuate(d)
colloq. weedy
F3 stocky, thickset

spine *n*
1 BACKBONE, spinal column, vertebral column, vertebrae, dorsum, rachis
Related adjective: vertebral
2 THORN, barb, prickle, bristle, spike, needle, quill, rachis
3 STRENGTH OF CHARACTER, courage, bravery, determination, spirit, resolution, mettle, pluck
formal fortitude
colloq. guts, bottle, grit, spunk

spine-chilling *adj*
frightening, hair-raising, horrifying, scary, terrifying, bloodcurdling, eerie
colloq. spooky

spineless *adj*
weak, feeble, irresolute, indecisive, ineffective, cowardly, faint-hearted, spiritless, lily-livered, soft, submissive, weak-kneed, timid
formal timorous
colloq. chicken, yellow, wet, wimpish
F3 strong, brave, courageous

spiny *adj*
thorny, thistly, prickly, briery
formal spinose, spinous, acanthaceous, acanthous, spinigerous, spiniferous, spicular, spiculate

spiral *adj, n, v*
▶ *adj* winding, twisting, coiled, corkscrew, helical, whorled, scrolled, circular
technical cochlear
formal cochleate(d)
▶ *n* coil, helix, corkscrew, screw, twist, whorl, convolution, wreath, curlicue
technical cochlea
formal gyre, volute, volution, volute(d)
Related adjective: helical
▶ *v* **1** WIND, twist, coil, circle, screw, whorl, wreathe, gyrate, gyre
2 *costs spiralling*
rise, increase, go up, soar, climb, escalate, rocket, skyrocket

spire *n*
steeple, belfry, tower, turret, pinnacle, peak, summit, crest, top, tip, point, spike

spirit *n, v*
▶ *n* **1** SOUL, psyche, inner being, inner self, mind, breath, life, life-giving principle, vital force, *élan vital*
2 GHOST, spectre, phantom, apparition, supernatural being, presence, wraith, shade, shadow, renevant, visitant, angel, demon, fiend, devil, fairy, sprite
colloq. spook
3 MOOD, atmosphere, air, humour, temper, disposition, temperament, character, complexion, feeling(s), morale, make-up, quality, state/frame of mind, attitude, outlook
4 DETERMINATION, strength of character, resolution, willpower, courage, bravery, backbone, mettle, pluck, dauntlessness, stoutheartedness
colloq. guts, bottle, grit, spunk
5 TENDENCY, characteristic, principle, essence, essential quality, force
6 LIVELINESS, vivacity, animation, sparkle, vigour, energy, zest, fire, ardour, motivation, enthusiasm, zeal,

enterprise
colloq. pizzazz, zip, kick
7 *the spirit of the law*
meaning, sense, substance, essence, drift, gist, tenor, implication, character, quality
formal purport
▶ *v* ▷ **spirit away** remove, capture, carry, convey, abstract, seize, kidnap, steal, whisk; *formal* purloin; *colloq.* abduct, snaffle

spirited *adj*
lively, vivacious, animated, sparkling, high-spirited, vigorous, energetic, fiery, passionate, active, ardent, zealous, bold, determined, resolute, courageous, valiant, mettlesome, plucky, confident
formal valorous
colloq. feisty
⊟ spiritless, lethargic, cowardly

spiritless *adj*
apathetic, weak, lifeless, listless, dull, unenthusiastic, unmoved, lacklustre, anaemic, despondent, depressed, dejected, dispirited, low, melancholy, torpid, droopy
formal languid
colloq. wishy-washy
⊟ spirited

spirits *n*
1 LIQUOR, alcohol, strong drink, strong liquor, moonshine
colloq. fire-water, hooch, the hard stuff
2 FEELINGS, emotions, mood, temperament, temper, attitude, humour

spiritual *adj*
1 UNWORLDLY, incorporeal, immaterial, ethereal, otherworldly, intangible
2 RELIGIOUS, devotional, heavenly, divine, holy, sacred, ecclesiastical
⊟ **1** physical, material, temporal **2** secular

spit *v, n*
▶ *v* eject, discharge, issue, rasp, hawk, splutter, hiss
formal expectorate
▷ **spitting image** likeness, exact likeness, double, lookalike, picture, replica, spit, twin, clone;
colloq. dead spit, dead ringer, ringer
▶ *n* spittle, saliva, slaver, drool, dribble, sputum, phlegm
formal expectoration

spite *n, v*
▶ *n* spitefulness, malice, maliciousness, venom, gall, bitterness, resentment, rancour, animosity, ill-feeling, ill-will, grudge, vengeance, vindictiveness, ill nature, hostility, evil, hate, hatred
formal malevolence, malignity
colloq. hard feelings
⊟ goodwill, compassion, affection
▷ **in spite of** despite, regardless of, undeterred by, against, defying, in the face of;
formal notwithstanding
▶ *v* annoy, irritate, irk, vex, provoke, gall, hurt, upset, injure, wound, offend, put out

spiteful *adj*
malicious, venomous, snide, barbed, resentful, bitter, cruel, hostile, rancorous, vindictive, vengeful, ill-natured, ill-disposed, nasty
formal malevolent, malignant
colloq. catty, bitchy
⊟ charitable, affectionate

splash *v, n*
▶ *v* **1** BATHE, wallow, paddle, wade, dabble, plunge, wet, wash, shower, spray, squirt, sprinkle, spatter, splatter, splodge, splotch, scatter, spread, daub, plaster, slop, slosh, plop, surge, break, dash, beat, strike, batter, buffet, smack
2 PUBLICIZE, show, display, exhibit, flaunt, blazon, trumpet, plaster
▷ **splash out** invest in, lash out, spend, splurge, be extravagant; *colloq.* push the boat out
▶ *n* **1** SPOT, patch, splatter, splodge, splotch, splurge, stain, burst, touch, streak, dash, beating
2 PUBLICITY, display, ostentation, effect, impression, impact, stir, excitement, sensation
colloq. splurge

spleen *n*
anger, bad temper, bitterness, resentment, hatred, hostility, ill-will, ill-humour, spite, spitefulness, vindictiveness, peevishness, venom, malignity, wrath, pique, rancour, bile, biliousness, gall, animosity
formal acrimony, animus, malevolence, malice, petulance

splendid *adj*
brilliant, dazzling, glittering, lustrous, bright, radiant, glowing, glorious, magnificent, gorgeous, sumptuous, luxurious, lavish, rich, fine, grand, stately, imposing, impressive, great, distinguished, illustrious, renowned, celebrated, outstanding, remarkable, exceptional, sublime, supreme, superb, excellent, first-class, wonderful, marvellous, admirable
formal resplendent, opulent, refulgent
colloq. fabulous, terrific, super
⊟ drab, ordinary, run-of-the-mill

splendour *n*
brightness, radiance, brilliance, dazzle, glow, gleam, lustre, glory, luxury, sumptuousness, magnificence, richness, grandeur, majesty, illustriousness, solemnity, pomp, ceremony, display, show, spectacle
formal resplendence, opulence
⊟ drabness, squalor

splenetic *adj*
angry, cross, bad-tempered, irritable, irascible, sullen, spiteful, choleric, morose, peevish, churlish, fretful, bilious, envenomed, acid, crabby, sour, testy, touchy
old use atrabilious
formal petulant, rancorous
colloq. bitchy, crabbed, ratty

splice *v*
join, fasten, connect, marry, bind, tie, plait, braid, interweave, interlace, intertwine, entwine, mesh, knit, graft
▷ **get spliced** get married, wed, become husband and wife; *colloq.* get hitched, tie the knot, take the plunge

splinter *n, v*
▶ *n* sliver, shiver, chip, shard, fragment, bit, piece, shred, flake, shaving, paring
colloq. smithereens
▶ *v* split, break, break into pieces, fracture, smash, shatter, shiver, crumble, fragment, disintegrate
formal cleave

split *v, n, adj*
▶ *v* **1** *split the logs; the cloth split*
break, cut, splinter, shiver, crack, burst, rupture, tear, rip, chop, slit, slash, open
old use rend
formal cleave

2 *split in two*
divide, separate, partition, halve, bisect, share
3 *split the profits*
share, separate, divide, halve, allocate, allot,
apportion, distribute, hand out, dole out, parcel out
colloq. carve up
4 PART COMPANY, part, disunite, disband, break up,
set apart, dissociate from, divide, separate, divorce,
become estranged, become alienated
5 INFORM ON, betray, incriminate
colloq. tell on, shop, squeal, rat, blow the whistle on;
slang grass
▷ **split hairs** find fault, quibble, pettifog, over-
refine, cavil; *colloq.* nit-pick
▷ **split up** part, part company, disband, break up,
separate, divorce, get divorced
▶ *n* **1** DIVISION, separation, partition, break, cut,
breach, gap, cleft, crevice, crack, fissure, rupture, tear,
rip, rift, slit, slash
old use rent
2 SCHISM, disunion, dissension, discord, difference,
division, separation, rupture, estrangement,
alienation, divergence, break-up
▶ *adj* divided, cleft, bisected, dual, twofold, broken,
fractured, cracked, ruptured
formal cloven

split-up *n*
break-up, separation, divorce, estrangement,
alienation, parting, parting of the ways

spoil *v*
1 MAR, upset, wreck, ruin, destroy, damage, bodge,
impair, harm, hurt, injure, deface, disfigure, blemish,
taint, contaminate, pollute, foul, tarnish, deform,
obliterate, poison
colloq. mess up, throw a spanner in the works, pour
cold water on, put a damper on, cast a shadow over;
slang louse up, screw up
2 *spoil a child*
indulge, overindulge, pamper, cosset, coddle,
mollycoddle, baby, spoon-feed
colloq. wait on hand and foot
3 DETERIORATE, go bad, go off, go sour, sour, turn,
curdle, decay, decompose, rot, go/become rotten
▷ **spoil for** be eager for, be keen on, be intent on,
long for, yearn for

spoils *n*
plunder, loot, booty, haul, gain, benefit, profit,
acquisitions, prizes, winnings
formal spoliation
colloq. pickings; *slang* swag

spoil-sport *n*
misery, killjoy, party-pooper, meddler, damper
colloq. dog in the manger, wet blanket, wowser

spoken *adj*
verbal, oral, voiced, said, stated, told, uttered,
phonetic, expressed, declared, unwritten, viva voce
🖅 unspoken, unexpressed, written

spokesman, spokeswoman *n*
spokesperson, representative, delegate, agent, voice,
negotiator, arbitrator, intermediary, mediator,
go-between, broker, mouthpiece, propagandist

sponge *v*
1 WIPE, mop, clean, wash, swab
2 *sponge off/on other people*
cadge, beg, borrow, scrounge
colloq. bum, bludge, freeload

sponger *n*
cadger, scrounger, parasite, hanger-on, beggar,
borrower
colloq. freeloader, bum, moocher, bludger

spongy *adj*
soft, cushioned, cushiony, yielding, elastic, resilient,
springy, squashy, porous, absorbent, light

sponsor *n, v*
▶ *n* patron, supporter, backer, friend, promoter,
subsidizer, underwriter, guarantor, surety
colloq. angel
▶ *v* finance, fund, bankroll, subsidize, patronize,
be a patron of, back, support, promote, underwrite,
guarantee, put up the money for

spontaneous *adj*
1 UNPLANNED, voluntary, unprompted,
uncompelled, impromptu, extempore, unrehearsed,
unpremeditated, free, willing, unhesitating
colloq. spur of the moment, knee-jerk
2 NATURAL, unforced, untaught, instinctive,
impulsive
🖅 **1** planned, deliberate **2** forced, studied

spontaneously *adv*
voluntarily, willingly, freely, impromptu, extempore,
impulsively, on impulse, unplanned, unprompted,
instinctively, of your own accord, on the spur of the
moment
colloq. off the cuff, off the top of your head

spoof *n*
joke, hoax, game, travesty, trick, prank, fake,
deception, caricature, bluff, burlesque, parody,
mockery, satire, lampoon
colloq. send-up, take-off, con, leg-pull

spooky *adj*
creepy, chilling, frightening, hair-raising, ghostly,
scary, mysterious, spine-chilling, supernatural, weird,
unearthly, uncanny, eerie

spoon-feed *v*
indulge, overindulge, cosset, pamper, spoil,
mollycoddle, baby, featherbed
colloq. wait on hand and foot

sporadic *adj*
occasional, intermittent, infrequent, isolated,
spasmodic, erratic, irregular, uneven, random,
scattered
🖅 frequent, regular

sport *n, v*
▶ *n* **1** GAME, exercise, activity, physical activity,
pastime, amusement, entertainment, diversion,
recreation, pleasure, fun, play
2 FUN, mirth, humour, joking, jesting, banter,
teasing, mockery, ridicule, sneering
colloq. kidding

Sports include: badminton, fives, lacrosse, squash,
table-tennis, *colloq.* ping-pong, tennis; American
football, baseball, basketball, billiards, boules,
bowls, cricket, croquet, football, golf, handball,
hockey, netball, pétanque, pitch and putt, polo, pool,
putting, rounders, Rugby, snooker, soccer, tenpin
bowling, volleyball; athletics, cross-country,
decathlon, discus, high-jump, hurdling, javelin, long-
jump, marathon, pentathlon, pole vault, running,
shot put, triple-jump; angling, canoeing, diving,
fishing, rowing, sailing, skin-diving, surfing,
swimming, synchronized swimming, water polo,
water-skiing, windsurfing, yachting; bobsleigh,

curling, ice-hockey, ice-skating, skiing, speed skating, tobogganing (luging); aerobics, fencing, gymnastics, jogging, keep-fit, roller-skating, trampolining; archery, darts, quoits; boxing, judo, jujitsu, karate, kung fu, tae kwon do, weightlifting, wrestling; climbing, mountaineering, rock-climbing, walking, orienteering, pot-holing; cycle racing, drag-racing, go-karting, motor racing, speedway racing, stock-car racing, greyhound-racing, horse-racing, show-jumping, trotting, hunting, shooting, clay-pigeon shooting; gliding, sky-diving.

▶ *v* wear, display, exhibit, show off

sporting *adj*
sportsmanlike, decent, modest, considerate, fair, reasonable, respectable, just, honourable, gentlemanly, ladylike
E3 unsporting, ungentlemanly, unfair

sportive *adj*
playful, lively, frisky, frolicsome, gamesome, gay, jaunty, merry, skittish, sprightly, prankish, rollicking, coltish, kittenish

sports equipment

Kinds of sports equipment: ball, basketball, boule, bowl, jack, wood, football, netball, rugby ball, tenpin bowling ball, volleyball; fishing-rod, fly rod, spinning rod, fishing-line, paternoster, reel, fly reel, hook, gaff, gang-hook, jig, trace, lure, bait, fly, float, net, keep-net, priest, disgorger; bow, arrow, crossbow, bolt; badminton racket, shuttlecock, net; baseball bat, baseball, mitt, catcher's glove; boxing glove, gum shield, punch-bag, punch-ball; cricket bat, cricket ball, wicket, stump, bail, nets; épée, foil, sabre, face-guard, mask; discus, hammer, javelin, shot; golf club, golfball, tee, golfing glove; asymmetrical bars, horizontal bar, isometric bar, parallel-bars, beam, balance-beam, mat, pommel horse, vaulting horse, rings, rope, springboard, trampoline; hockey stick, hockey ball, ice-hockey stick, puck, hockey skate; curling stone; ice-skate, roller-skate, rollerblade, roller boot, speed skate, skateboard; ski, ski stick, snow board, toboggan; snooker ball, billiard ball, cue ball, table, cue, rest, bridge, rack, chalk; squash racket, squash ball; table-tennis bat, table-tennis ball, net; tennis racket, tennis ball, net, racket press; oar, aqualung, snorkel, water-ski, sailboard, surfboard. *See also* **golf club**.

sporty *adj*
1 ATHLETIC, fit, energetic, outdoor
2 STYLISH, jaunty, showy, loud, flashy, casual, informal
colloq. trendy, natty, snazzy

spot *n, v*
▶ *n* 1 DOT, speckle, fleck, mark, speck, blotch, blot, splodge, splotch, smudge, daub, splash, stain, discoloration, blemish, flaw
2 PIMPLE, blackhead, boil, pock, papula, papule, pustule
3 PLACE, point, position, situation, location, site, scene, setting, locality, local, area
4 *have a spot of lunch*
bit, little, some, small amount, bite, morsel
5 *have a spot on television*
slot, niche, opening, position, place, time, airtime, show, programme
6 PLIGHT, predicament, quandary, difficulty, trouble, mess
colloq. fix, hole, jam, scrape, pickle
▶ *v* 1 NOTICE, see, observe, detect, discern, identify, recognize, make out, catch sight of

formal descry, espy
2 MARK, dot, speckle, fleck, soil, blemish, taint, stain

spotless *adj*
immaculate, clean, white, gleaming, shining, spick and span, unmarked, unstained, unblemished, unsullied, untainted, pure, chaste, virgin, virginal, untouched, innocent, blameless, faultless, irreproachable
E3 dirty, impure

spotlight *v, n*
▶ *v* emphasize, stress, accentuate, focus on, highlight, underline, illuminate, feature, point up, draw attention to, give prominence to, throw into relief
E3 tone down, play down
▶ *n* attention, public attention, public eye, fame, emphasis, notoriety, interest
colloq. limelight

spotted *adj*
dotted, speckled, flecked, mottled, dappled, brindled, pied, piebald, polka-dot, spotty
formal macular, guttate(d)

spotty *adj*
1 PIMPLY, pimpled, blotchy, spotted, dotted, speckled, flecked, mottled, dappled, pied, piebald
2 PATCHY, uneven, inconsistent, varying, erratic, bitty

spouse *n*
husband, wife, partner, companion, consort, mate
colloq. better half, other half, hubby, missus

spout *v, n*
▶ *v* 1 SPURT, jet, squirt, spray, shoot, gush, flow, stream, pour, surge, erupt, emit, discharge, disgorge, spew
2 *spouting poetry*
pontificate, go on, rant, hold forth, spout off/forth
formal expatiate, sermonize, orate
colloq. spiel, rabbit on, waffle, witter (on)
▶ *n* stream, jet, fountain, geyser, gargoyle, outlet, nozzle, rose, spray

sprawl *v*
1 *sprawl on the couch*
flop, slump, stretch, slouch, recline
formal repose
colloq. loll, lounge
2 STRAGGLE, spread, stretch, trail, ramble

spray[1] *n, v*
▶ *n* 1 MOISTURE, drizzle, mist, foam, froth, spume, shower, jet, spindrift
2 AEROSOL, atomizer, sprinkler, vaporizer
▶ *v* shower, spatter, spout, sprinkle, scatter, diffuse, disperse, gush, jet, wet, drench
formal disseminate

spray[2] *n*
a spray of flowers/leaves
sprig, branch, corsage, posy, nosegay, bouquet, garland, wreath

spread *v, n*
▶ *v* 1 STRETCH, extend, sprawl, broaden, widen, dilate, enlarge, develop, grow, increase, advance, expand, grow/become bigger, swell, mushroom, proliferate, escalate, spill over, open (out), unroll, unfurl, unfold, fan out, cover, lay (out), order, set, arrange
2 SCATTER, strew, diffuse, radiate, fan out, broadcast, transmit, communicate, propagate, make public, make known, publicize, advertise, publish, circulate,

go/get round, distribute
formal disseminate, promulgate
3 COAT, cover, put on, apply, smear, layer
⊞ **1** close, fold **2** suppress
▶ *n* **1** STRETCH, reach, span, extent, expanse, sweep, compass
2 *the spread of disease*
advance, development, expansion, increase, proliferation, escalation, swelling, mushrooming, diffusion, dispersion, distribution, transmission, broadcasting, communication, propagation
formal dissemination
3 LARGE MEAL, banquet, feast, party, dinner, dinner party, treat
formal repast
colloq. blow-out

spree *n*
bout, fling, orgy, revel, carouse, debauch
colloq. binge, splurge, razzle, razzle-dazzle, bender

sprig *n*
twig, stem, spray, shoot, branch, bough

sprightly *adj*
agile, nimble, spry, active, energetic, lively, animated, spirited, vivacious, hearty, brisk, jaunty, playful, frolicsome, cheerful, light-hearted, blithe, airy
colloq. perky
⊞ doddering, inactive, lifeless

spring *v, n*
▶ *v* **1** JUMP, leap, vault, bound, hop, bounce, rebound, recoil
2 ORIGINATE, derive, come, stem, arise, start, proceed, issue, descend, emerge, emanate, appear, sprout, grow, develop
3 *spring the news on someone*
tell unexpectedly, reveal suddenly, present without warning
▷ **spring up** appear suddenly, come into existence, come into being, develop, grow, shoot up, sprout up, proliferate, mushroom
▶ *n* **1** JUMP, leap, vault, bound, hop, bounce, rebound, recoil
2 SPRINGINESS, resilience, give, flexibility, elasticity, bounciness, buoyancy
3 LIVELINESS, energy, spirit, briskness, cheerfulness, light-heartedness, animation
4 SOURCE, origin, beginning, basis, cause, root, fountainhead, wellhead, wellspring, well, geyser, spa

springy *adj*
bouncy, resilient, flexible, elastic, stretchy, rubbery, spongy, buoyant, tensible, tensile
⊞ hard, stiff, rigid

sprinkle *v*
shower, spray, spatter, splash, trickle, scatter, strew, dot, pepper, dust, powder

sprinkling *n*
few, handful, dash, scattering, scatter, smattering, sprinkle, trickle, touch, trace, dusting
formal admixture

sprint *v*
run, race, dash, tear, fly, dart, career, shoot
colloq. belt, scoot, zip

sprite *n*
spirit, elf, fairy, goblin, imp, kelpie, nymph, naiad, puck, pouke, pixie, sylph, brownie, leprechaun, dryad, apparition

sprout *v*
shoot, bud, germinate, grow, develop, come up, put forth, spring up

spruce *adj, v*
▶ *adj* smart, elegant, neat, trim, dapper, well-dressed, chic, well-turned-out, well-groomed, sleek
colloq. natty, cool, snazzy
⊞ scruffy, untidy
▶ *v* ▷ **spruce up** neaten, tidy (up), smarten up, groom, preen, primp, titivate

spry *adj*
sprightly, quick, alert, agile, energetic, brisk, ready, nimble, active, supple
colloq. nippy, peppy
⊞ doddering, inactive, lethargic

spume *n*
foam, froth, lather, suds, head, bubbles, fizz, effervescence

spunk *n*
courage, nerve, spirit, pluck, resolution, toughness, gameness, heart, mettle, chutzpah
colloq. guts, grit, bottle, backbone
⊞ *colloq.* funk

spur *v, n*
▶ *v* stimulate, prompt, incite, drive, propel, impel, urge, induce, encourage, motivate, goad, prod, poke, prick
⊞ curb, discourage
▶ *n* incentive, encouragement, inducement, motive, motivation, stimulus, stimulant, urge, incitement, impetus, prompt, fillip
⊞ curb, disincentive, discouragement
▷ **on the spur of the moment** on impulse, impulsively, impetuously, spontaneously, impromptu, unexpectedly, suddenly, thoughtlessly, unpremeditatedly, without planning; *colloq.* on the spot

spurious *adj*
false, fake, counterfeit, forged, fraudulent, deceitful, contrived, bogus, mock, sham, feigned, pretended, simulated, imitation, artificial
colloq. make-believe, pseudo, phoney, trumped-up
⊞ genuine, authentic, real

spurn *v*
reject, turn down, turn away, say no to, scorn, condemn, despise, disdain, rebuff, repulse, repudiate, slight, snub, ignore, disregard
colloq. cold-shoulder, look down on
⊞ accept, embrace

⚠ **spurn** or **scorn** ? *See panel at* **scorn.**

spurt *v, n*
▶ *v* gush, spray, squirt, jet, shoot, pour, stream, well, burst, erupt, issue, surge
▶ *n* **1** JET, gush, stream, spray, squirt, outpouring, welling, eruption
2 *a spurt of activity*
burst, rush, surge, rush, increase, spate, fit, access

spy *n, v*
▶ *n* secret agent, undercover agent, foreign agent, enemy agent, double agent, fifth columnist, scout, snooper
colloq. mole
▶ *v* spot, glimpse, notice, see, observe, discern, discover, make out, catch sight of

formal espy, descry
▷ **spy on** watch, observe (closely), keep an eye on, keep tabs on, keep under surveillance

squabble *v, n*
▶ *v* bicker, wrangle, fight, quarrel, row, argue, dispute, have words, clash, brawl
colloq. scrap, set to
▶ *n* row, clash, dispute, fight, argument, disagreement, spat
colloq. barney, scrap, set-to, tiff

squad *n*
crew, team, gang, band, group, company, unit, brigade, platoon, troop, force, outfit

squalid *adj*
1 DIRTY, filthy, unclean, grimy, grubby, mucky, foul, disgusting, repulsive, sordid, seedy, dingy, untidy, slovenly, unkempt, broken-down, run-down, ramshackle, dilapidated, neglected, uncared-for
colloq. sleazy, grotty
2 REPULSIVE, low, mean, nasty, sordid, unpleasant, wretched, vile, shameful, obscene, offensive, disgraceful
🖅 1 clean, attractive 2 pleasant

squall *n, v*
▶ *n* wind, storm, gale, gust, hurricane, blow, tempest, windstorm
▶ *v* wail, yell, cry, howl, yowl, moan, groan

squally *adj*
windy, stormy, rough, wild, gusty, blowy, blustery, tempestuous, turbulent

squalor *n*
squalidness, dirtiness, dirt, filthiness, filth, uncleanness, grime, griminess, grubbiness, muckiness, foulness, dinginess, decay, neglect, meanness, wretchedness
colloq. sleaziness

squander *v*
waste, misspend, misuse, lavish, fritter away, throw away, dissipate, scatter, spend, expend, consume
colloq. splash out on, splurge, throw/pour down the drain, spend money like water, spend money as if it grows on trees, spend money as if it's going out of style/ fashion, spend money like there's no tomorrow
slang blow

square *n, v, adj*
▶ *n* 1 QUADRANGLE, market square, town square, plaza
colloq. quad
2 TRADITIONALIST, conservative, conventionalist, conformer, conformist, diehard
colloq. fuddy-duddy, (old) fogey, stick-in-the-mud
▶ *v* settle (up), reconcile, tally, agree, harmonize, conform, correspond, match, be compatible with, balance, straighten, level, align, even, make equal, adjust, regulate, set/put right, adapt, tailor, fit, suit
formal accord, be congruous with
▶ *adj* 1 QUADRILATERAL, rectangular, right-angled, perpendicular, straight, true, even, level
2 FAIR, equitable, just, ethical, upright, straight, honourable, honest, genuine, above-board
colloq. on the level
3 TRADITIONALIST, conservative, conventionalist, conformist, diehard, old-fashioned, strait-laced
colloq. fuddy-duddy

squash *v*
1 CRUSH, flatten, press, squeeze, compress, crowd,

pack, jam, trample, stamp, pound, grind, pulp, mash, smash, distort
formal macerate, pulverize
2 SUPPRESS, silence, quell, quash, crush, annihilate, put down, squelch, snub, humiliate
🖅 1 stretch, expand

squashy *adj*
soft, spongy, squelchy, mushy, pappy, pulpy, squishy, yielding
🖅 firm

squat *v, adj*
▶ *v* crouch, stoop, bend, kneel, hunch, sit on your haunches, sit
▶ *adj* short, stocky, thickset, dumpy, chunky, stubby
🖅 slim, lanky, slender

squawk *v, n*
screech, shriek, cry, scream, yelp, croak, cackle, crow, hoot

squeak *v, n*
squeal, whine, creak, peep, cheep, pipe

squeal *v, n*
▶ *v* 1 CRY, shout, yell, howl, yelp, wail, scream, screech, shriek, squawk
2 INFORM, tell tales, sneak, betray
colloq. tell, shop, snitch, split, rat; *slang* grass
▶ *n* cry, shout, yell, howl, yelp, wail, scream, screech, shriek, squawk

squeamish *adj*
queasy, nauseated, nauseous, sick, delicate, fastidious, finicky, particular, punctilious, prudish, strait-laced, scrupulous

squeeze *v, n*
▶ *v* 1 PRESS, squash, crush, pulp, mash, pinch, nip, tighten, compress, twist, wring, extract, grip, clasp, clutch, pinch, hold tight, hug, embrace, enfold, cuddle
2 *squeeze into a corner*
cram, stuff, pack, crowd, crush, squash, wedge, jam, force, ram, push, thrust, shove, jostle
3 WRING, wrest, extort, milk, force, pressurize, pressure
colloq. bleed, lean on, put the screws on
▶ *n* 1 PRESS, squash, crush, crowd, congestion, jam
2 HUG, embrace, cuddle, hold, grasp, grip, clutch, clasp

squint *adj*
crooked, indirect, oblique, off-centre, aslant, askew, awry, cockeyed
technical strabismic
colloq. skew-whiff
🖅 straight
Related adjective: strabismal

squirm *v*
wriggle, twist, writhe, squiggle, move, shift, wiggle, fidget, agonize, flounder

squirt *v, n*
▶ *v* spray, spurt, jet, shoot, spout, gush, stream, spew (out), ejaculate, discharge, issue, pour, well, surge, emit, eject, expel
▶ *n* spray, spurt, jet, stream, gush, surge

stab *v, n*
▶ *v* pierce, puncture, cut, wound, injure, gore, knife, spear, skewer, slash, bayonet, transfix, stick, push, jab, thrust
▷ **stab in the back** betray, deceive, let down, slander, double-cross, inform on, sell out;

colloq. sell down the river
▶ *n* **1** ACHE, pang, pain, spasm, throb, twinge, prick
2 CUT, puncture, incision, slash, gash, injury, wound, jab
3 TRY, attempt, go, endeavour, venture
formal essay
colloq. bash, crack, shot, whirl

stabbing *adj*
shooting, stinging, piercing, throbbing, painful, acute

stability *n*
steadiness, firmness, secureness, soundness, sturdiness, solidity, reliability, durability, uniformity, constancy, regularity, unchangeability
E3 instability, unsteadiness, insecurity, weakness

stable *adj*
1 *a stable structure*
balanced, fixed, static, steady, firm, secure, fast, sound, strong, sturdy, solid, sure, reliable
2 *a stable government/relationship*
established, well-founded, deep-rooted, lasting, long-lasting, durable, enduring, abiding, permanent, dependable, reliable, unchangeable, invariable, unwavering, unswerving
3 *the patient's condition is stable*
regular, uniform, steady, constant, unchanging
E3 **1** wobbly, shaky, weak, unstable **2** unstable
3 irregular, erratic, unstable

stack *n, v*
▶ *n* **1** HEAP, pile, mound, mass, load, collection, accumulation, store, hoard, stock, stockpile
2 *stacks of money*
a large amount, lot, great numbers, many, a good/great deal
colloq. oodles, tons, loads, masses, heaps, piles
▶ *v* heap, pile, load, amass, accumulate, assemble, gather, save, hoard, stockpile

stadium *n*
sports ground, sports field, field, arena, bowl, ring, track, pitch

staff *n, v*
▶ *n* **1** *member of staff*
personnel, workforce, employees, workers, crew, team, teachers, officers
2 STICK, pole, cane, crook, rod, baton, crutch, wand, truncheon, prop, crosier
▶ *v* man, work, operate, occupy, provide, supply, equip

stage *n, v*
▶ *n* **1** PHASE, point, juncture, step, time, period, division, lap, leg, length, level, floor
2 PLATFORM, podium, dais, rostrum, stand, apron
colloq. soapbox
3 ARENA, setting, scene, sphere, field, realm, background, backdrop
▷ **the stage** theatre, drama, the play, dramatics, theatrics, show business; *formal* Thespian art; *colloq.* the boards, the footlights, rep
▶ *v* mount, put on, lay on, put together, present, produce, give, do, perform, direct, arrange, organize, stage-manage, orchestrate, engineer

stagger *v*
1 LURCH, totter, teeter, wobble, sway, rock, roll, pitch, reel, falter, hesitate, waver
2 SURPRISE, amaze, astound, astonish, stun, stupefy, dumbfound, shake, shock, confound, overwhelm
colloq. flabbergast, nonplus, bowl over

staggering *adj*
amazing, astounding, astonishing, surprising, dramatic, shocking, stunning, stupefying, unexpected, unforeseen
colloq. mind-boggling

stagnant *adj*
1 *stagnant water*
still, motionless, unflowing, standing, brackish, stale, foul, dirty, filthy, smelly, unhealthy
2 *a stagnant economy*
inactive, slow, quiet, dull, sluggish, torpid, lethargic
E3 **1** fresh, moving **2** busy

stagnate *v*
vegetate, become stagnant, idle, languish, do nothing, decline, deteriorate, degenerate, decay, rot, putrefy, fester, rust

staid *adj*
sedate, calm, composed, sober, demure, solemn, serious-minded, serious, proper, formal, grave, sombre, quiet, steady, stiff, starchy, prim
formal decorous
E3 jaunty, debonair, frivolous, adventurous

stain *v, n*
▶ *v* **1** MARK, spot, blemish, blot, blotch, smear, smudge, discolour, dirty, soil, taint, contaminate, corrupt, sully, tarnish, blacken, disgrace, damage, injure
formal besmirch
2 DYE, tint, tinge, colour, paint, varnish
▶ *n* mark, spot, blemish, blot, blotch, smear, splodge, smudge, discoloration, smear, slur, taint, disgrace, shame, dishonour, damage, injury

stake[1] *n, v*
▶ *n* *a stake supporting a young tree*
post, pole, standard, picket, pale, paling, spike, stick, rod
▶ *v* **1** SUPPORT, fasten, brace, tie, tie up, prop (up), secure, hold (up), tether, pierce
2 *stake a claim*
establish, lay claim to, state, declare, demand, put in
formal requisition
▷ **stake out** demarcate, define, delimit, stake off, mark out, outline, reserve, survey, watch, keep an eye on

stake[2] *n, v*
▶ *n* **1** INVESTMENT, share, claim, involvement, concern, (financial) interest, bet, wager, pledge
colloq. ante
2 *the leadership stakes*
contest, competition, race, prize, winnings
▶ *v* risk, gamble, bet, wager, pledge, chance, hazard, venture
colloq. ante

stale *adj*
1 *stale bread*
dry, hard, hardened, old, musty, mouldy, fusty, flat, insipid, tasteless, sour
colloq. (gone) off
2 OVERUSED, hackneyed, corny, clichéd, cliché-ridden, stock, stereotyped, tired, jaded, worn-out, unoriginal, uninspired, flat, trite, insipid, banal, commonplace
formal platitudinous
colloq. run of the mill
E3 **1** crisp, fresh **2** new, original, imaginative

stalemate *n*
draw, tie, deadlock, impasse, standstill, halt, blockade, stand-off, *zugzwang*
F3 progress

stalk¹ *n*
the stalk of a flower
stem, shoot, twig, branch, trunk
technical peduncle, petiole
Related adjective: peduncular

stalk² *v*
stalk a person/an animal
1 TRAIL, track, hunt, chase, give chase, follow, pursue, shadow, track down, tail, haunt
2 STRIDE, walk, step, pace, march

stall¹ *v*
stall them to give you more time
temporize, play for time, delay, hold up, put off, defer, postpone, hedge, equivocate, obstruct, stonewall
colloq. beat about the bush, drag your feet, put on ice, put on the back burner

stall² *n*
1 STAND, table, booth, kiosk, counter, surface, place, platform
2 CUBICLE, compartment, enclosure, coop, pen

stalwart *adj*
1 STAUNCH, loyal, faithful, devoted, committed, steady, trusty, steadfast, reliable, dependable, vigorous, valiant, daring, intrepid, indomitable, determined, resolute
2 STRONG, sturdy, robust, rugged, stout, hardy, strapping, muscular, athletic, brawny, burly
F3 **1** disloyal, unfaithful **2** weak, feeble, timid

stamina *n*
energy, vigour, strength, power, force, grit, resilience, resistance, endurance, indefatigability, staying power
formal fortitude
colloq. grit
F3 weakness

stammer *v, n*
▶ *v* stutter, stumble, falter, hesitate, splutter, lisp, mumble, gibber, babble
▶ *n* stutter, speech impediment, speech defect

stamp *v, n*
▶ *v* **1** TRAMPLE, tread, crush, beat, pound, pulp, mash, squash
2 IMPRINT, impress, print, inscribe, engrave, emboss, mark, brand, fix, label, categorize, designate, identify, characterize
▷ **stamp out** eradicate, suppress, crush, quell, quash, put down, scotch, destroy, eliminate, end, extinguish, quench, kill; *formal* extirpate
▶ *n* print, imprint, impression, seal, signature, authorization, mark, hallmark, tag, label, brand, cast, mould, cut, form, fashion, sort, kind, type, quality, variety, breed, character, description
formal attestation

stampede *n, v*
▶ *n* charge, rush, onrush, dash, sprint, flight, rout, scattering
▶ *v* charge, rush, dash, tear, run, race, sprint, gallop, shoot, fly, flee, scatter

stance *n*
position, posture, deportment, carriage, bearing, stand, standpoint, viewpoint, policy, angle, slant, line, point of view, opinion, attitude

stanch *v*
stem, stop, check, block, arrest, stay, halt, plug, dam
F3 increase, promote

⚠ **stanch** or **staunch**?
In the sense of 'to stop the flow of', either form is correct, but *staunch* is the commoner: *staunched the flow of blood from the wound; staunch the decline of royal authority; This helped to staunch the Danish invasion.* As an adjective, the form to use is *staunch,* meaning 'loyal, trusty, steadfast': *a staunch ally/ Catholic/opponent.*

stand *v, n*
▶ *v* **1** RISE, rise to your feet, get on/to your feet, get up, stand up, be on your feet, straighten up, be erect, be upright
2 PUT, place, set, erect, up-end, place, position, station, locate
3 *I can't stand it*
bear, tolerate, put up with, cope with, endure, allow, brook, suffer, experience, live with, undergo, withstand, weather
formal abide
colloq. stomach
4 *the offer still stands*
exist, be, remain, hold, be valid, be in effect, be in force
formal prevail, obtain
▷ **stand by** support, back, champion, defend, stand up for, stick up for, uphold, side with, adhere to, hold to, stick by
F3 let down
▷ **stand down** step down, resign, abdicate, quit, give up, retire, withdraw
F3 join
▷ **stand for 1** REPRESENT, symbolize, mean, signify, denote, indicate; *formal* betoken **2** *not stand for such nonsense* put up with, tolerate, bear, endure, allow, brook; *colloq.* stomach
▷ **stand in for** deputize for, cover for, understudy, replace, take the place of, substitute for; *colloq.* hold the fort for
▷ **stand out** show, be noticeable, be obvious, be conspicuous, stick out, jut out, extend, project, poke out; *colloq.* catch the eye, stick out a mile
▷ **stand up 1** RISE, rise to your feet, get up, get to your feet, straighten up, stand **2** COHERE, hold up, hold water, stand; *colloq.* wash
▷ **stand up for** defend, stick up for, side with, fight for, stand by, support, protect, champion, uphold, adhere
F3 attack
▷ **stand up to** defy, oppose, resist, withstand, challenge, endure, face, face up to, confront, brave
F3 give in to
▶ *n* **1** BASE, pedestal, support, shelf, case, frame, rack
2 STALL, booth, counter, table, stage, dais, platform, place
3 STANCE, position, standpoint, viewpoint, policy, angle, slant, line, point of view, opinion, attitude

standard *n, adj*
▶ *n* **1** NORM, average, type, model, pattern, example, sample, guide, guideline, benchmark, touchstone, yardstick, principle, rule, measure, gauge, criterion, requirement, specification, grade, level, quality
formal archetype, paradigm, exemplar
2 PRINCIPLE, scruple, ethic, moral, code, ideal
3 FLAG, ensign, pennant, pennon, streamer, colours,

banner, gonfalon
technical vexillum
▶ *adj* normal, average, typical, stock, classic, basic, staple, usual, ordinary, customary, habitual, popular, prevailing, regular, approved, accepted, recognized, official, authoritative, orthodox, conventional, set, fixed, established, definitive
E3 abnormal, unusual, irregular

standard-bearer *n*
ensign, standard, gonfalonier, cornet, vexillary

standardize *v*
normalize, equalize, systematize, regiment, regularize, homogenize, stereotype, mass-produce
E3 differentiate

stand-in *n*
deputy, representative, delegate, proxy, substitute, surrogate, second, second-in-command, understudy, locum

standing *n, adj*
▶ *n* **1** REPUTATION, status, rank, position, seniority, eminence, station, repute, experience, footing
2 DURATION, existence, continuance
▶ *adj* **1** UPRIGHT, erect, perpendicular, vertical, up-ended, on your feet
2 PERMANENT, perpetual, lasting, fixed, regular, repeated
E3 1 horizontal, lying **2** temporary

stand-off *n*
deadlock, impasse, standstill, halt, blockade

standoffish *adj*
aloof, remote, distant, unapproachable, unsociable, unfriendly, uncommunicative, withdrawn, detached, reserved, cold, cool
E3 friendly, approachable

standpoint *n*
viewpoint, angle, slant, point of view, perspective, position, station, vantage point, stance

standstill *n*
stop, halt, pause, lull, rest, stoppage, jam, log-jam, hold-up, dead stop, impasse, deadlock, stalemate
formal cessation
E3 advance, progress

staple *adj*
basic, fundamental, primary, key, main, chief, major, important, foremost, principal, essential, indispensable, vital, necessary, standard
E3 minor, dispensable

star *n, adj*
▶ *n* **1** *the stars in the sky*
asteroid, planet, sun, moon, heavenly/celestial body, sphere, orb, satellite
Related adjectives: stellar, astral, sidereal

Types of star include: nova, supernova, pulsar, quasar, falling-star, shooting-star, meteor, comet, Halley's comet, red giant, supergiant, white dwarf, red dwarf, brown dwarf, neutron star, Pole Star, Polaris, North Star. *See also* **constellation**.

2 CELEBRITY, personage, luminary, idol, lead, leading man, leading lady, superstar, principal
colloq. household name, big name, bigwig, big shot, leading light
▶ *adj* brilliant, well-known, famous, leading, illustrious, celebrated, prominent, talented, principal,

major, pre-eminent, paramount
E3 minor

starchy *adj*
formal, stiff, prim, punctilious, ceremonious, conventional, stuffy, strait-laced
E3 informal

stare *v, n*
▶ *v* gaze, look, watch, gape, gawp, gawk, goggle, glare
▶ *n* gaze, look, glare, gawp
▷ **be staring you in the face** be very obvious, be glaringly obvious, be blatant, be conspicuous;
colloq. stick out a mile

stark *adj, adv*
▶ *adj* **1** *faced with the stark reality*
bald, bare, plain, simple, blunt, harsh, grim, severe, undecorated, unembellished, unadorned
2 *a stark landscape*
bare, barren, desolate, bleak, austere, forsaken, empty, harsh, severe, grim, dreary, gloomy, depressing
3 UTTER, complete, unmitigated, unqualified, total, absolute, sheer, pure, downright, thorough, out-and-out, flagrant, arrant
formal consummate
▶ *adv* completely, entirely, wholly, totally, absolutely, altogether, quite, utterly, clean
E3 mildly, slightly

stark-naked *adj*
naked, nude, in the nude, stripped, undressed
formal unclad
colloq. in the altogether, in the buff, in your birthday suit, in the raw, starkers
E3 clothed, dressed

start *v, n*
▶ *v* **1** BEGIN, originate, initiate, introduce, pioneer, create, embark on/upon, bring/come into being, bring/come into existence, get under way, found, establish, set up, institute, inaugurate, launch, pioneer, open, instigate, activate, turn on, trigger (off), set off, get going, set out, leave, depart, appear, arise, issue
formal commence
colloq. kick off, set the ball rolling, get things moving, get cracking, fire away
2 JUMP, jerk, leap, twitch, flinch, shrink, wince, recoil
E3 1 stop, finish, end
▶ *n* **1** BEGINNING, outset, dawn, birth, break, outburst, onset, origin, origination, initiation, introduction, foundation, institution, inauguration, launch, opening, emergence
formal commencement, inception
colloq. kick-off
2 JUMP, jerk, leap, twitch, flinch, wince, spasm, convulsion, fit
E3 1 stop, finish, end

startle *v*
surprise, amaze, astonish, astound, shock, make you jump, scare, frighten, alarm, agitate, upset, unsettle, disturb
formal perturb
E3 calm

startling *adj*
surprising, astonishing, astounding, extraordinary, shocking, staggering, unexpected, sudden, dramatic, alarming, unforeseen, electrifying
E3 boring, calming, ordinary

starvation *n*
hunger, extreme hunger, undernourishment,

malnutrition, famine, fasting, death
🗷 plenty, excess

starve *v*
hunger, fast, diet, deprive, deny, die, perish, faint
🗷 feed, gorge

starving *adj*
(very) hungry, underfed, undernourished, ravenous,
famished, faint, dying

stash *v, n*
▶ *v* store, hide, conceal, hoard, closet, lay up, save up,
stockpile, stow, cache
formal secrete
colloq. salt away
🗷 bring out, uncover
▶ *n* hoard, store, collection, accumulation, mass,
heap, pile, fund, reservoir, reserve, stockpile, cache

state *n, v, adj*
▶ *n* 1 CONDITION, shape, situation, position,
circumstances, case, predicament
2 NATION, country, land, territory, kingdom,
republic, realm, government, federation
3 PANIC, bother, plight, predicament
colloq. fluster, flap, tizzy
4 GOVERNMENT, administration, authorities,
parliament, council, Establishment
5 POMP, ceremony, dignity, majesty, grandeur, glory,
splendour, display
▷ **in a state** agitated, anxious, worried, distressed,
troubled, upset, worked up, panic-stricken, ruffled;
colloq. flustered, hassled, het up, in a stew, in a tizzy
🗷 calm
▷ **state of affairs** case, situation, position,
circumstances, condition, plight, predicament, crisis,
juncture; *colloq.* kettle of fish, lie of the land
▶ *v* say, declare, tell, announce, report, communicate,
assert, affirm, specify, present, express, put, set out,
make known, proclaim, formulate, articulate, voice,
utter, reveal, divulge, disclose
formal aver, promulgate
▶ *adj* national, governmental, parliamentary, public,
official, formal, ceremonial, pompous, stately
🗷 private, commercial

stately *adj*
grand, imposing, impressive, splendid, glorious,
magnificent, elegant, majestic, regal, royal, imperial,
noble, lofty, pompous, dignified, measured, deliberate,
solemn, ceremonial, ceremonious, graceful
formal august
🗷 informal, unimpressive

statement *n*
account, report, bulletin, communiqué,
announcement, declaration, assertion, proclamation,
communication, presentation, utterance, revelation,
divulgence, disclosure, testimony
formal affirmation, averment, promulgation

statesman, stateswoman *n*
politician, leader, elder statesman, diplomat, GOM
colloq. grand old man

static *adj*
stationary, motionless, immobile, unmoving, still, at a
standstill, inert, resting, fixed, constant, steady,
changeless, unchanging, undeviating, unvarying,
stable
🗷 dynamic, mobile, varying

station *n, v*
▶ *n* 1 *a bus/railway station*

stop, stopping-place, halt, fare-stage, terminus,
exchange, park-and-ride
2 OFFICE, base, depot, headquarters
3 *your station in life*
status, standing, position, rank, level, grade, class
4 PLACE OF DUTY, post, place, site, location,
position
▶ *v* locate, set, establish, install, garrison, post, send,
appoint, assign

stationary *adj*
motionless, immobile, unmoving, still, at a standstill,
static, constant, inert, standing, resting, parked,
moored, fixed
🗷 mobile, moving, active

stationery *n*

Items of stationery include: account book, address
book, adhesive tape, blotter, bulldog clip, calendar,
carbon paper, card index, cartridge ribbon, cash
book, clipboard, computer disk, copying paper,
correcting paper, correction fluid, correction
ribbon, desk-diary, diary, divider, document folder,
document wallet, drawing pin, dry-transfer
lettering, elastic band, envelope, brown manila
envelope, reply-paid envelope, self-seal envelope,
window envelope, eraser, expanding file, file, file
tab, filing tray, Filofax®, flip chart, floppy disk,
folder, graph paper, headed notepaper, index card,
ink, Jiffy bag®, label, lever arch file, marker, memo
pad, notepaper, paper clip, paper fastener, paper
knife, pen, pencil, pencil-sharpener, personal
organizer, pin, pocket calculator, pocket folder,
Post-it note®, printer label, printer paper, printer
ribbon, reinforcement ring, ring binder, rubber,
rubber band, rubber stamp, ruler, scissors,
Sellotape®, shorthand notebook, spiral notebook,
stamp pad, staple, suspension file, tape dispenser,
Tipp-Ex®, toner, treasury tag, typewriter ribbon,
wall chart, writing paper. *See also* **paper**.

statue *n*
figure, head, bust, effigy, image, idol, statuette,
figurine, carving, sculpture, bronze, representation

statuesque *adj*
dignified, imposing, impressive, majestic, stately,
regal, handsome
🗷 small

stature *n*
1 HEIGHT, tallness, elevation, attitude, loftiness, size
2 IMPORTANCE, reputation, standing, prominence,
prestige, fame, renown, eminence, rank, consequence,
weight
🗷 2 unimportance

status *n*
1 POSITION, rank, grade, degree, level, class, station,
standing, state, condition
2 IMPORTANCE, prestige, eminence, distinction,
reputation, consequence, weight
🗷 2 unimportance, insignificance

statute *n*
law, rule, regulation, act, decree, ordinance, edict,
enactment, ukase
formal interlocution

staunch¹ *adj*
a staunch supporter
loyal, faithful, devoted, hearty, strong, stout, firm,
resolute, sound, sure, constant, true, trusty,
trustworthy, committed, reliable, dependable,

steadfast

⊟ unfaithful, weak, unreliable

⚠ **staunch** or **stanch** ? *See panel at* **stanch**.

staunch² *v*
staunch the flow of blood
stem, stop, check, block, arrest, stay, halt, plug
⊟ increase, promote

⚠ **staunch** or **stanch** ? *See panel at* **stanch**.

stave *v*
▷ **stave off** fend off, ward off, avoid, avert, deflect, repel, repulse, turn aside, parry, foil, keep back, keep at bay
⊟ cause, encourage

stay¹ *v, n*
▶ *v* **1** REMAIN, last, continue, endure, linger, persist, keep, stay put
formal abide, tarry
2 *stay in a hotel*
live, settle, stop, board, lodge, put up, rest, halt, pause, wait, visit, be accommodated at, take a room at
formal reside, dwell, sojourn
3 *stay judgement*
suspend, halt, postpone, put off, delay, defer, adjourn, reprieve
formal prorogue
4 *stay your anger*
control, restrain, arrest, check, curb, stop, halt, prevent, hinder, block, obstruct
▶ *n* **1** VISIT, holiday, vacation, stopover
formal sojourn
2 *a stay of execution*
suspension, postponement, deferment, delay, reprieve
formal remission

stay² *n*
a stay supporting a mast
prop, brace, buttress, reinforcement, stanchion, support, shoring

staying power
stamina, energy, vigour, strength, power, force, grit, resilience, resistance, endurance, indefatigability, fibre
formal fortitude
colloq. grit

steadfast *adj*
firm, fixed, resolute, stable, steady, intent, single-minded, loyal, faithful, stout-hearted, sturdy, dedicated, constant, dependable, staunch, reliable, established, persevering, unswerving, unwavering, unfaltering, implacable, unflinching
⊟ unreliable, wavering, weak

steady *adj, v*
▶ *adj* **1** *hold the camera steady*
stable, balanced, well-balanced, poised, fixed, secure, immovable, unmoving, motionless, firm
2 *make steady progress*
regular, even, uniform, consistent, unvarying, unvariable, unchanging, ceaseless, perpetual, constant, persistent, uninterrupted, unbroken, unfaltering, unwavering
formal incessant, unremitting
3 CALM, stable, settled, controlled, self-controlled, well-balanced, still, imperturbable, unexcitable, unexcited
colloq. unflappable

4 RELIABLE, dependable, balanced, well-balanced, serious, sober, sensible, steadfast
5 *a steady boyfriend*
regular, constant, usual, customary, established, habitual
⊟ **1** unsteady, shaky, wobbly **2** uneven, irregular, variable, wavering **3** excitable, worried
4 unreliable
▶ *v* **1** STABILIZE, balance, fix, secure, brace, support
2 COMPOSE, control, soothe, relax, tranquillize, still, subdue, check, restrain

steal *v, n*
▶ *v* **1** *steal a car*
thieve, pilfer, filch, take, misappropriate, snatch, break in, swipe, pocket, shoplift, poach, embezzle, kidnap, abduct, plagiarize
formal appropriate, purloin, peculate
colloq. pinch, nick, lift, snaffle, knock up, nobble, rip off, knock off, help yourself to, make off/away with, run off with, go/walk off with, have your fingers in the till;
slang heist
2 CREEP, tiptoe, slip, slink, slide, slither, sneak
⊟ **1** return, give back
▶ *n* bargain, giveaway, special offer, good buy, value for money, discount, reduction
colloq. snip

stealing *n*
theft, robbery, thieving, shoplifting, pilfering, pilferage, burglary, break-in, embezzlement, larceny, misappropriation, plagiarism, poaching, piracy, thievery
formal peculation, appropriation, purloining
colloq. rip-off, filching, pinching, nicking, stick-up job

stealth *n*
stealthiness, furtiveness, surreptitiousness, covertness, secrecy, slyness, sneakiness, unobtrusiveness

stealthy *adj*
surreptitious, covert, secret, unobtrusive, secretive, quiet, furtive, sly, cunning, sneaky, underhand
formal clandestine

steam *n, v*
▶ *n* **1** VAPOUR, mist, haze, exhalation, condensation, moisture, dampness
2 *run out of steam*
energy, activity, enthusiasm, eagerness, liveliness, vigour, stamina
▷ **under your own steam** by your own efforts, independently, by yourself, alone, without (other's) help
▶ *v* ▷ **get steamed up** get annoyed, get angry, get flustered, get excited; *colloq.* get het up, boil over, fly into a rage
▷ **steam up** mist up, fog up, become covered with steam, become covered with mist

steamboat *n*
steamer, steamship, steam-packet, steam vessel, packet-boat, packet-ship, packet, paddle-boat, paddle-steamer, vaporetto

steamy *adj*
1 HUMID, hot, steaming, sweltering, hazy, muggy, sticky, misty, sweaty, close, damp, sultry, stewy, vaporous, vapourish, vapoury, gaseous
formal vaporiform
2 EROTIC, passionate, sensual, lustful, amorous, seductive
colloq. sexy, raunchy, blue

steed *n*
horse, charger, hack, mount, nag, jade, Rosinante

steel *v*
brace, harden, toughen, nerve, prepare
formal fortify
E∃ weaken

steely *adj*
1 GREY, steel-coloured, steel-blue, blue-grey
2 DETERMINED, firm, resolute, strong, hard, harsh, inflexible, pitiless, merciless, unyielding

steep¹ *adj*
1 *a steep slope*
sheer, precipitous, headlong, abrupt, sudden, sharp, vertical, perpendicular
formal acclivitous, declivitous
2 EXCESSIVE, extreme, stiff, unreasonable, uncalled-for, high, exorbitant, extortionate, inordinate, expensive, costly, dear, overpriced
colloq. over the top
E∃ 1 gentle, gradual 2 moderate, low

steep² *v*
steep something in liquid
saturate, seethe, soak, moisten, damp, souse, submerge, suffuse, drench, fill, imbrue, imbue, immerse, infuse, permeate, pervade, marinate, pickle, brine, macerate

steeple *n*
spire, beltry, tower, turret

steer *v*
pilot, guide, direct, control, drive, govern, conduct, navigate, cox, lead, usher
▷ **steer clear of** avoid, shun, evade, bypass, escape, skirt; *formal* circumvent, eschew; *colloq.* dodge, give a wide berth to
E∃ seek

stem¹ *n, v*
▶ *n the stem of a plant*
stalk, shoot, stock, branch, trunk
technical peduncle
Related adjective: cauline
▶ *v* come, develop, flow, originate, derive, emanate, spring, issue, arise
E∃ give rise to, cause

stem² *v stem the flow of blood*
stop, halt, arrest, stanch, staunch, block, dam, check, curb, restrain, contain, resist, oppose
E∃ encourage

stench *n*
stink, reek, smell, odour, whiff
formal mephitis, miasma
colloq. pong; *slang* niff

stentorian *adj*
loud, strong, booming, thunderous, thundering, resonant, sonorous, ringing, full, vibrant, reverberating, strident

step *n, v*
▶ *n* 1 PACE, stride, footstep, walk, gait, tread, tramp, footprint, print, impression, trace, track
2 MOVE, act, action, course of action, deed, measure, procedure, process, proceeding, progression, advance, development, movement, maneouvre, expedient, effort, stage, rank, grade, level, phase, degree
3 RUNG, stair, level, rank, point
▷ **in step** together, in agreement, in harmony, in unison

▷ **out of step** in disagreement, not in step, having different opinions, at odds, at loggerheads
▷ **step by step** gradually, slowly, progressively, bit by bit, gradatim
▷ **watch your step** be careful, look out, watch out, take care, be attentive; *colloq.* mind how you go
▶ *v* pace, stride, tread, stamp, walk, move, advance, progress
▷ **step down** stand down, resign, abdicate, quit, leave, retire, withdraw, give up your post
▷ **step in** intervene, mediate, arbitrate, intercede, interfere, interrupt, intrude, involve yourself in
▷ **step up** increase, raise, boost, build up, intensify, escalate, accelerate, speed up; *formal* augment
E∃ decrease

stereotype *n, v*
▶ *n* formula, convention, mould, pattern, model, cliché, hackneyed expression, conventional/ standardized image, fixed set of ideas
▶ *v* typecast, pigeonhole, standardize, formalize, tag, label, conventionalize, mass-produce, categorize
E∃ differentiate

stereotyped *adj*
conventional, stereotypical, standardized, standard, unoriginal, stock, overused, mass-produced, hackneyed, clichéed, cliché-ridden, banal, stale, trite, tired, threadbare, corny
formal platitudinous
E∃ different, unconventional

sterile *adj*
1 GERM-FREE, germless, clean, pure, aseptic, sterilized, disinfected, antiseptic, uncontaminated, uninfected
2 INFERTILE, barren, arid, bare, unproductive, unprofitable, fruitless, unfruitful, pointless, futile, vain, useless, unyielding, abortive
formal infecund, ineffectual
E∃ 1 septic 2 fertile, fruitful

sterility *n*
1 CLEANNESS, purity, disinfection
technical asepsis
2 INFERTILITY, barrenness, unfruitfulness, unproductiveness, impotence, fruitlessness, futility, pointlessness, uselessness, ineffectiveness
technical atocia
formal inefficacy, unfecundity
E∃ 1 infection, contamination 2 fertility, fruitfulness

sterilize *v*
1 DISINFECT, fumigate, purify, clean, cleanse
2 MAKE INFERTILE, castrate, neuter, doctor, geld, spay
E∃ 1 contaminate, infect

sterling *adj*
excellent, great, superlative, first-class, genuine, real, sound, standard, authentic, true, pure, worthy
E∃ false, poor

stern¹ *adj*
a stern look/person
strict, severe, authoritarian, rigid, inflexible, unyielding, hard, tough, rigorous, demanding, exacting, stringent, harsh, cruel, tyrannical, draconian, unsparing, relentless, unrelenting, grim, sombre, forbidding, stark, austere
E∃ kind, gentle, mild, lenient

stern² *n*
the stern of the ship
rear, back, tail, tail end, poop
E3 bow

stew *v, n*
▶ *v* **1** *stew the meat*
boil, simmer, braise, cook, casserole
2 *let him stew in his own juice*
worry, sweat, fret, fuss, agonize
▶ *n* **1** *beef stew*
casserole, goulash, pot-au-feu, daube, ragout, hash, chowder, lobscouse, bouillabaisse
2 FLUSTER, worry, fuss, bother, agitation, pother, fret
colloq. tizzy

steward *n*
attendant, flight attendant, air hostess, waiter, waitress, official, butler, supervisor, overseer, custodian, caretaker, marshal, factor, chamberlain, manciple, *major-domo, homme d'affaires, maître d'hôtel*

stick¹ *v*
1 THRUST, poke, stab, jab, push, pierce, prick, penetrate, insert, puncture, spear, impale, transfix
2 GLUE, gum, paste, cement, bond, fuse, weld, solder, tape, adhere, grip, cling, hold, attach, affix, fasten, secure, fix, pin, tack, join, bind
3 PUT, place, lay, position, site, locate, set (down), install, deposit, drop
4 *the car got stuck in the mud*
fix, jam, clog (up), get bogged down, trap, stop, come to a halt, come to a standstill
5 REMAIN, stay, linger, persist, continue, carry on, rest, last, endure
formal dwell, abide
6 TOLERATE, bear, stand, endure, put up with
formal abide
colloq. stomach
▷ **stick at 1** PERSEVERE, persist, continue, keep at; *colloq.* plug away **2** HESITATE, recoil, shrink from, stop at, doubt, pause, balk, scruple; *formal* demur; *colloq.* draw the line at
E3 1 give up
▷ **stick by** stand by, support, back, champion, defend, stand up for, stick up for, uphold, side with, adhere to, hold to
E3 let down
▷ **stick it out** persevere, persist, continue; *colloq.* plug away, see things through to the end, keep at it, hang in there
▷ **stick out** protrude, jut out, poke out, bulge, project, extend, be noticeable, be obvious, be conspicuous
▷ **stick up for** stand up for, speak up for, fight for, stand by, defend, protect, champion, support, uphold, take the side/part of
E3 attack

stick² *n*
gather dry sticks
1 BRANCH, branch, twig, switch

Types of stick include: alpenstock, baton, birch, bludgeon, cane, club, cosh, crook, crutch, cudgel, hockey stick, lathi, lug, pike, pole, post, rod, sceptre, shillelagh, staff, stake, tripod stick, truncheon, waddy, walking stick, wand, whip.

2 CRITICISM, hostility, punishment, reproof, blame, abuse
colloq. flak

E3 praise
▷ **the sticks** remote areas, backwoods, bush, outback; *colloq.* middle of nowhere, end of the earth, hickdom, yokeldom; *US* boondocks, boonies

stickiness *n*
adhesiveness, gumminess, glueyness, tackiness, syrupiness
formal glutinousness, viscidity
colloq. goo, gooeyness

stick-in-the-mud *adj, n*
▶ *adj* fuddy-duddy, unadventurous, conservative, fossilized, fogeyish, outmoded, antiquated, antediluvian, Victorian
colloq. square
E3 adventurous, modern
▶ *n* fuddy-duddy, conservative
colloq. (old) fogey, back number, fossil

stickler *n*
fanatic, maniac, perfectionist, pedant, purist, precisianist, fusspot
colloq. nut

sticky *adj*
1 ADHESIVE, gummed, tacky, gluey, gummy, viscous
formal glutinous, viscoid
colloq. gooey
2 *a sticky situation*
difficult, tricky, thorny, unpleasant, awkward, embarrassing, delicate, sensitive, ticklish
3 HUMID, clammy, muggy, close, oppressive, sweltering, sultry
E3 1 dry **2** easy **3** fresh, cool

stiff *adj*
1 RIGID, unbending, unyielding, inflexible, hard, solid, hardened, solidified, firm, tight, taut, inelastic, tense
2 *stiff muscles/joints*
aching, arthritic, rheumatic, tight, tense, rheumaticky
3 DIFFICULT, hard, tough, tiring, harsh, arduous, laborious, awkward, demanding, exacting, challenging, rigorous
4 FORMAL, ceremonial, ceremonious, reserved, pompous, stand-offish, cold, chilly, awkward, prim, priggish
formal decorous
5 SEVERE, extreme, rigorous, hard, harsh, tough, demanding, austere, strict, drastic, strigent, draconian
6 *a stiff breeze*
strong, fresh, brisk, windy, forceful, vigorous
7 *a stiff drink*
large, alcoholic, strong, intoxicating
E3 1 flexible, supple **3** easy **4** informal, relaxed, friendly **6** light

stiffen *v*
1 HARDEN, solidify, tighten, tense (up), starch, thicken, congeal, coagulate, jell, set
2 STRENGTHEN, steel, brace, harden, reinforce
formal fortify

stiff-necked *adj*
proud, stubborn, obstinate, arrogant, haughty, uncompromising, opinionated
formal contumacious,
E3 humble, flexible

stifle *v*
1 *stifle opposition*
repress, silence, hush, suppress, quell, quash, check, curb, restrain, keep in, hold back, smother, crush,

subdue, extinguish, muffle, dampen, deaden
2 SMOTHER, suffocate, asphyxiate, strangle, choke
▣ **1** encourage

stigma *n*
brand, mark, stain, blot, spot, blemish, slur, taint,
disgrace, shame, dishonour
▣ credit, honour

stigmatize *v*
stain, mark, blemish, disgrace, shame, condemn,
denounce, discredit, brand, label, mark
formal vilify, vilipend
▣ praise

still *adj, v, adv, n*
▶ *adj* **1** STATIONARY, motionless, immobile,
unmoving, unstirring, static, stock-still, lifeless,
stagnant, inert, inactive, sedentary
2 QUIET, undisturbed, unruffled, calm, smooth,
tranquil, serene, mild, restful, peaceful, hushed, silent,
noiseless
▣ **1** moving, active **2** disturbed, agitated, noisy
▶ *v* calm, soothe, allay, tranquillize, subdue, restrain,
hush, quieten, silence, pacify, settle, moderate, smooth
formal assuage, appease, abate
▣ agitate, stir up
▶ *adv* **1** UNTIL NOW, up to the present time, up to
this time, yet
2 YET, but, even so, though, although, nevertheless,
nonetheless, however, in spite of this/that, for all that
formal notwithstanding
▶ *n* stillness, quiet, quietness, hush, peace,
peacefulness, silence, noiselessness, serenity,
tranquillity
▣ agitation, disturbance, noise

stilted *adj*
artificial, unnatural, laboured, stiff, wooden, forced,
constrained
▣ natural, relaxed, fluent, flowing

stimulant *n*
tonic, restorative, reviver
technical analeptic
colloq. pick-me-up, pep pill

⚠ **stimulant** or **stimulus** ?
Stimulant is normally used only of a drug or medicine
which makes a person more alert or part of their body
more active: *Tea and coffee contain stimulants; a
powerful heart stimulant*. *Stimulus* is used to mean
'something which causes or encourages a person to
make greater efforts': *Many people think that children
need the stimulus of competition to make them work well
at school.*

stimulate *v*
rouse, arouse, animate, quicken, kindle, fan, fire,
inflame, excite, inspire, motivate, encourage, induce,
fillip, urge, impel, spur, prompt, goad, provoke, incite,
instigate, trigger (off)
colloq. whip up
▣ discourage, hinder, prevent

stimulating *adj*
inspiring, rousing, stirring, interesting, exciting,
exhilarating, intriguing, provoking, provocative,
thought-provoking, galvanic
▣ uninspiring, boring, depressing

stimulus *n*
incentive, encouragement, impetus, inducement, spur,

goad, prod, provocation, incitement, fillip, drive,
push, jolt, jog
colloq. shot in the arm
▣ discouragement

⚠ **stimulus** or **stimulant** ? *See panel at* **stimulus**.

sting *v, n*
▶ *v* **1** *bees sting*
bite, prick, hurt, injure, wound
2 SMART, tingle, burn, pain, irritate
3 HURT, distress, wound, upset, offend, annoy,
grieve, torment, provoke, exasperate, incense, needle,
nettle
4 CHEAT, swindle, defraud, deceive, trick, fiddle
colloq. do, fleece, rip off, con, take for a ride, take to the
cleaners
▶ *n* **1** PRICK, bite, nip, wound, injury, hurt, pain,
smart, tingle, irritate
2 *the memory lost its sting*
sharpness, viciousness, spite, malice, pungency,
incisiveness, sarcasm, causticness, causticity, edge, bite

stinging *adj*
burning, smarting, tingling, irritating, hurtful,
injurious, wounding, offensive, distressing
formal urent, urticant, aculeate(d)
▣ mild, soothing, comforting

stingy *adj*
mean, miserly, niggardly, cheeseparing
formal parsimonious, penurious
colloq. tight-fisted, penny-pinching, mingy
▣ generous, liberal

stink *v, n*
▶ *v* **1** SMELL, reek
colloq. pong, hum
2 *the whole set-up stinks*
be bad, be awful, be nasty, be unpleasant, be despicable
▶ *n* **1** SMELL, bad/foul smell, odour, stench
formal malodour
colloq. pong; *slang* niff
2 FUSS, trouble, bother, furore, row, commotion, stir,
fluster
colloq. hassle, hoo-ha, flap, song and dance

stinker *n*
1 PROBLEM, difficulty, predicament, plight,
impediment, horror, shocker
2 SCOUNDREL, creep, cur, rotter
old use bounder, cad, dastard
slang rat, swine

stinking *adj*
bad, unpleasant, vile, awful, nasty, contemptible,
disgusting, foul, rotten
▣ good, pleasant

stint *n, v*
▶ *n* spell, stretch, period, time, shift, turn, bit, share,
quota
▶ *v* economize, save, withhold, pinch, begrudge,
scrimp
colloq. skimp on

stipulate *v*
specify, lay down, set down, require, demand, insist on

stipulation *n*
specification, requirement, point, demand, condition,
proviso
formal precondition, prerequisite

stir *v, n*

▶ *v* **1** MOVE, budge, shift, rouse, disturb, agitate, shake, tremble, twitch, quiver, flutter, rustle
2 MIX, blend, whip, beat
3 AFFECT, touch, inspire, excite, thrill
▷ **stir up** encourage, rouse, arouse, awaken, waken, inspire, animate, quicken, kindle, fire, inflame, excite, stimulate, spur, motivate, drive, impel, prompt, provoke, incite, instigate, agitate, electrify, galvanize
E3 calm, discourage
▶ *n* activity, movement, bustle, flurry, commotion, ado, fuss, uproar, tumult, disturbance, disorder, agitation, excitement, ferment
colloq. to-do, hoo-ha, flap, kerfuffle, tizzy, song and dance
E3 calm

stirring *adj*
rousing, exciting, spirited, inspiring, stimulating, moving, animating, thrilling, exhilarating, heady, emotive, dramatic, lively, impassioned, intoxicating
E3 calming, uninspiring

stitch *v*
sew, stitch, tack, darn, mend, repair, seam, embroider, hem
See panel at **embroidery**.

stock *n, adj, v*
▶ *n* **1** GOODS, merchandise, wares, commodities, inventory, repertoire, quantity, collection, range, selection, variety, assortment, source, supply, quantity, fund, reservoir, store, reserve, cache, stockpile, hoard, heap, pile, amassment, accumulation
2 *stocks and shares*
investment, holding, shares, bonds, securities, equities, portfolio, money, capital, funds, assets
3 PARENTAGE, ancestry, genealogy, background, descent, extraction, family, relatives, line, lineage, pedigree, race, breed, strain, species, blood
4 LIVESTOCK, animals, farm animals, cattle, cows, pigs, horses, sheep, herds, flocks
▷ **in stock** available, for sale, on sale, on the market, on the shelves
▷ **take stock** assess, reassess, estimate, review, survey, evaluate, re-evaluate, re-examine, size up, weigh up; *formal* appraise
▶ *adj* standard, basic, regular, routine, ordinary, average, run-of-the-mill, usual, common, customary, essential, basic, traditional, conventional, set, stereotyped, tired, worn-out, hackneyed, clichéed, overused, banal, trite
E3 original, unusual
▶ *v* keep, carry, sell, market, trade in, traffic in, merchandise, deal in, handle, carry, supply, provide, furnish, equip
formal accoutre
colloq. kit out
▷ **stock up** gather, accumulate, amass, lay in, fill (up), load, store (up), buy (up), put aside, put away, save, hoard, stockpile, stack up, pile up, heap (up);
formal provision, replenish; *colloq.* salt away, stash away

stockpile *v, n*
▶ *v* hoard, store (up), save, gather, accumulate, amass, pile up, heap (up), keep, put aside, put away
▶ *n* store, hoard, fund, reservoir, reserve, cache, pile, heap, amassment, accumulation

stock-still *adj*
motionless, unmoving, unstirring, static, still, immobile, inactive, inert, stationary

stocky *adj*
sturdy, solid, thickset, chunky, broad, short, squat, dumpy, stubby, stumpy
formal mesomorphic
E3 tall, skinny

stodgy *adj*
1 *stodgy food*
solid, heavy, indigestible, filling, starchy, substantial
2 STUFFY, unimaginative, uninspired, unexciting, unenterprising, solemn, heavy, boring, dull, tedious, staid, formal, leaden, laboured, turgid, spiritless
colloq. fuddy-duddy
E3 exciting, informal, light

stoical *adj*
patient, long-suffering, uncomplaining, accepting, resigned, philosophical, indifferent, impassive, unexcitable, unemotional, dispassionate, self-disciplined, self-controlled, forbearing, cool, calm, imperturbable
formal phlegmatic
E3 excitable, anxious

stoicism *n*
patience, long-suffering, resignation, indifference, dispassion, unexcitability, impassivity, calmness, acceptance, forbearance, imperturbability, stolidity, fatalism
formal fortitude, ataraxia, ataraxy
E3 anxiety, depression, fury

stolid *adj*
slow, heavy, dull, bovine, wooden, blockish, lumpish, impassive, unemotional, uninspiring, unimaginative, solemn, indifferent, apathetic
formal phlegmatic
E3 lively, interested

stomach *n, v*
▶ *n* **1** GUT, inside(s), belly, abdomen, paunch, pot-belly
colloq. tummy, corporation; *slang* bread basket
Related adjective: gastric
2 *have the stomach for food*
desire, relish, hunger, appetite, taste, zest
3 *not have the stomach for a fight*
courage, determination, desire, inclination, liking, passion, appetite
colloq. guts
▶ *v* tolerate, bear, stand, endure, suffer, approve of, submit to, take, brook, put up with
formal abide

stone *n*
1 ROCK, boulder, cobble, pebble
formal concretion
Related adjectives: lapidarian, lithic
2 *precious stones*
jewel, gemstone, gem, lapis
3 GRAVESTONE, tombstone, headstone, slab, flagstone, set(t)
4 PIP, kernel, pit, seed
technical endocarp

stony *adj*
1 *stony beach*
pebbly, shingly, rocky, gravelly, gritty
2 BLANK, expressionless, deadpan, poker-faced, hard, cold, frigid, icy, frosty, chilly, indifferent, unfeeling, heartless, adamant, steely, unresponsive, callous, merciless, pitiless, severe, stern, unforgiving, inexorable, hostile
E3 **2** warm, soft-hearted, friendly

stooge *n*
puppet, pawn, lackey, henchman, dupe, foil, butt
colloq. cat's paw, fall guy

stoop *v, n*
▶ *v* **1** HUNCH, bow, bend, lower, incline, lean, duck, squat, crouch, kneel
2 *stoop to blackmail*
descend, sink, lower yourself, resort, go so far as, condescend, go so low as, deign
formal vouchsafe
▶ *n* droop, hunching, round-shoulderedness, sag, slouch, slump, bending, inclination, lowering, ducking

stop *v, n*
▶ *v* **1** HALT, end, finish, conclude, discontinue, abandon, bring/come to an end, suspend, interrupt, pause, quit
formal cease, terminate, arrest, refrain, desist
colloq. quit, wind up, pack in, kick, knock off, leave off, give over
2 PREVENT, bar, frustrate, thwart, intercept, hinder, impede, obstruct, block, check, restrain, stall
3 SEAL, close, plug, block, bung, stop up, cover, obstruct, arrest, stem, stanch, staunch
4 STAY, live, settle, lodge, board, visit, put up, rest, pause, break your journey
formal reside, dwell, sojourn
▣ **1** begin, start, continue
▶ *n* **1** HALT, standstill, stoppage, end, finish, close, conclusion
formal cessation, termination, discontinuance, discontinuation
2 STATION, halt, bus stop, fare stage, stopping-place, terminus, destination
3 REST, break, stay, pause, stage, stopover, visit
formal sojourn
▣ **1** start, beginning, continuation

stopgap *n, adj*
▶ *n* improvisation, makeshift, substitute, temporary substitute, expedient, resort, shift
▶ *adj* improvised, makeshift, provisional, temporary, emergency, impromptu
formal expediential
colloq. rough-and-ready
▣ finished, permanent

stopover *n*
stop-off, stop, visit, rest, break, overnight stay
formal sojourn

stoppage *n*
1 STOP, halt, standstill, arrest, blockage, obstacle, obstruction, check, hindrance, interruption
formal cessation, termination, discontinuance, discontinuation, occlusion
2 STRIKE, shutdown, closure, walk-out, sit-in, industrial action
3 DEDUCTION, subtraction, reduction, decrease, taking away/off, withdrawal, removal, discount, allowance
▣ **1** start, continuation

stopper *n*
cork, bung, plug, seal, spigot
old use stopple

store *v, n*
▶ *v* save, keep, put aside, lay by, reserve, stock, stock up with, lay in, deposit, put down, lay down, lay up, bank, gather, collect, accumulate, hoard, stockpile
colloq. salt away, stash, save for a rainy day
▣ use

▶ *n* **1** STOCK, supply, provision, fund, reserve, mine, reservoir, hoard, cache, stockpile, heap, load, accumulation, amassment, deposit, quantity, abundance, plenty, lot
2 SHOP, retail outlet, supermarket, hypermarket, chain store, department store, corner shop
See panel at **shop**.
3 STOREROOM, storehouse, warehouse, repository, depository, larder, buttery
▣ **1** scarcity
▷ **set/lay store by** value, think highly of, consider highly, admire, hold in high regard;
formal esteem

storehouse *n*
repository, warehouse, treasury, wealth, vault, depository, depot, garner, granary, hold, cellar, armoury, arsenal, fund, entrepot, repertory, barn, buttery, larder, pantry, silo

storey *n*
floor, level, stage, tier, flight, deck
formal stratum

storm *n, v*
▶ *n* outburst, uproar, furore, outcry, row, rumpus, commotion, disturbance, clamour, tumult, brouhaha, turmoil, stir, agitation, rage, roar, outbreak, offensive, attack, assault, onslaught
colloq. to-do, kerfuffle
▣ calm

Kinds of storm include: blizzard, buran, cloudburst, cyclone, downpour, dust-devil, dust-storm, electrical storm, gale, haboob, hailstorm, hurricane, monsoon, rainstorm, sand storm, snow storm, squall, tempest, thunderstorm, tornado, typhoon, whirlwind. *See also* **wind**.

▶ *v* **1** *storm a citadel*
CHARGE, rush, attack, assault, assail
2 RAGE, roar, rant, rave, shout, fume, thunder, explode, seethe
colloq. hit the roof, lose your cool, foam at the mouth
3 *storm out of the room*
charge, rush, stamp, tear, flounce

stormy *adj*
tempestuous, squally, rough, choppy, turbulent, rainy, wild, raging, windy, gusty, blustery, foul
▣ calm, peaceful

story *n*
1 TALE, fiction, anecdote, episode, plot, storyline, narrative, history, chronicle, record, account, relation, recital, report, item, article, feature

Types of story include: adventure story, anecdote, bedtime story, *colloq.* blockbuster, children's story, comedy, black comedy, crime story, detective story, fable, fairy story, fairy tale, fantasy, folk tale, ghost story, historical novel, horror story, legend, love story, Mills & Boon®, mystery, myth, novel, novella, parable, romance, saga, science fiction, *colloq.* sci-fi, short story, spiel, spine-chiller, spy story, supernatural tale, tall story, thriller, western, *colloq.* whodunit, *colloq.* yarn.

2 LIE, falsehood, untruth
colloq. rib, untruth

storyteller *n*
narrator, writer, author, novelist, raconteur, raconteuse, anecdotist, chronicler, bard, romancer, tell-tale

stout *adj*

1 FAT, stocky, plump, fleshy, portly, obese, overweight, heavy, tubby, bulky, big, brawny, beefy, hulking, thickset, burly, muscular, athletic
formal corpulent
2 *stout packaging*
strong, tough, durable, thick, solid, heavy, sturdy, substantial, robust, hardy, vigorous
3 BRAVE, courageous, valiant, plucky, tough, fearless, bold, gallant, heroic, intrepid, dauntless, resolute, stalwart, determined, strong, forceful, fierce
formal valorous
colloq. gutsy, spunky, gritty
⬛ 1 thin, lean, slim **2** weak **3** cowardly, timid, afraid

stove *n*

cooker, oven, range, furnace, kiln, grill, heater

stow *v*

put away, store, place, deposit, load, pack, cram, bundle, stuff
colloq. stash
⬛ unload

straggle *v*

stray, wander, drift, lag, amble, loiter, ramble, roam, rove, trail, range, scatter, spread, string out
colloq. dilly-dally

straggly *adj*

untidy, rambling, drifting, straying, straggling, aimless, disorganized, irregular, random, spreading, loose, strung out
⬛ tidy, organized, grouped

straight *adj, adv*

▶ *adj* **1** *a straight line*
DIRECT, undeviating, unswerving, unbending, unbent, uncurving
2 LEVEL, even, flat, horizontal, upright, vertical, aligned, true, right
3 FRANK, honest, candid, blunt, forthright, direct, outspoken, straightforward
4 CONSECUTIVE, successive, continuous, unbroken, uninterrupted, one after the other
5 TIDY, neat, in order, orderly, shipshape, arranged, organized
6 HONOURABLE, honest, law-abiding, respectable, upright, trustworthy, reliable, upstanding, decent, straightforward, fair, just, faithful, sincere, conventional
7 *straight whisky*
undiluted, neat, pure, unadulterated, unmixed
⬛ 1 bent, crooked, curved, wavy, curly
2 sloping **3** evasive **5** untidy **6** dishonest
7 diluted
▶ *adv* **1** DIRECTLY, with no changes of direction, without deviating, as the crow flies
2 IMMEDIATELY, directly, instantly, promptly, right away, without delay, at once, as soon as possible
colloq. pronto
3 *tell someone straight*
frankly, honestly, candidly, bluntly, directly, plainly, clearly, forthrightly, straightforwardly, point-blank
colloq. not pulling any punches, straight from the shoulder
4 CONSECUTIVELY, successively, continuously, uninterruptedly, one after the other
colloq. on the trot
▷ **straight away** at once, immediately, instantly, right away, directly, without delay, now, there and then;

colloq. pronto
⬛ later, eventually

straighten *v*

unbend, align, tidy (up), neaten, order, arrange, adjust, put in order, put right
⬛ bend, twist
▷ **straighten out** clear up, sort out, settle, resolve, correct, realign, disentangle, regularize, tidy up, put in order, put right; *formal* rectify
⬛ confuse, muddle
▷ **straighten up** stand up, stand, stand erect, stand upright, straighten your back/body

straightforward *adj*

1 EASY, simple, uncomplicated, clear, elementary, unexacting, undemanding
colloq. child's play, a piece of cake, like falling off a log
2 HONEST, truthful, sincere, genuine, open, frank, candid, direct, forthright, outspoken, plain-speaking
⬛ 1 difficult, complicated, tricky **2** evasive, devious

strain¹ *v, n*

▶ *v* **1** PULL, heave, tug, wrench, twist, sprain, hurt, injure, wrick, tear, stretch, extend, elongate, tighten, tauten
formal distend
2 SIEVE, sift, screen, separate, filter, percolate, riddle, purify, drain, wring, squeeze, compress, express
3 WEAKEN, tire, fatigue, tax, overtax, overwork, pressure, labour, try, endeavour, struggle, strive, exert, force, drive, push to/beyond the limit, make every effort, do your utmost
colloq. go all out, put your heart and soul into, pull out all the stops
▶ *n* **1** SPRAIN, pull, wrench, twist, injury, wrick
2 PRESSURE, tension, stress, anxiety, worry, duress, effort, struggle, exertion, pressure, force, burden, demand. tiredness, weariness, fatigue, exhaustion, overwork
⬛ 2 relaxation

strain² *n*

1 STOCK, ancestry, descent, extraction, breed, family, lineage, pedigree, blood, variety, type, sort, kind
2 TRAIT, streak, quality, characteristic, vein, tendency, way, trace, element, suggestion, suspicion
formal disposition, proclivity
3 *the strains of music*
theme, tune, melody, song, air

strained *adj*

forced, constrained, laboured, false, artificial, unnatural, stiff, wooden, tense, unrelaxed, uneasy, uncomfortable, awkward, embarrassed, self-conscious
⬛ natural, relaxed

strainer *n*

sieve, colander, sifter, filter, screen, riddle

strait *n*

1 *the Straits of Gibraltar*
sound, narrows, inlet, channel, kyle
2 *in desperate straits*
crisis, difficulty, emergency, hardship, predicament, plight, perplexity, distress, dilemma, embarrassment, extremity, poverty
colloq. hole, mess, fix, pickle

straitened *adj*

poor, reduced, difficult, distressed, limited, restricted, impoverished, embarrassed
⬛ easy, well-off

strait-laced *adj*
prudish, stuffy, starchy, prim, priggish, proper, strict, narrow, narrow-minded, puritanical, moralistic
▣ broad-minded

strand¹ *n*
1 FIBRE, filament, wire, thread, string, piece, length
2 *the strands of a theory*
element, feature, component, factor, ingredient

strand² *n*
walk along the strand
shore, beach, seashore, foreshore, sand(s), waterfront, front

stranded *adj*
marooned, high and dry, abandoned, helpless, penniless, aground, grounded, beached, shipwrecked, wrecked
formal forsaken
colloq. (left) in the lurch

strange *adj*
1 ODD, peculiar, curious, queer, weird, bizarre, eccentric, abnormal, irregular, uncommon, unusual, unexpected, exceptional, remarkable, fantastic, extraordinary, unreal, surreal, mystifying, perplexing, unexplained, inexplicable, uncanny
formal singular
colloq. funny, freaky, wacky, oddball, offbeat, kinky
2 NEW, novel, untried, unknown, unheard-of, unfamiliar, unaccustomed, unacquainted, foreign, alien, exotic
▣ 1 ordinary, common 2 well-known, familiar

strangeness *n*
oddity, oddness, peculiarity, bizarreness, extraordinariness, irregularity, abnormality, queerness, eccentricity, uncanniness, eeriness, exoticness
formal singularity
▣ ordinariness

stranger *n*
newcomer, new arrival, visitor, guest, non-member, outsider, incomer, foreigner, alien
▣ local, native
▷ **a stranger to** unfamiliar with, inexperienced in, unversed in, unacquainted with, unaccustomed to

strangle *v*
1 THROTTLE, choke, asphyxiate, suffocate, stifle, smother
2 SUPPRESS, gag, repress, inhibit, restrain, check, keep in, hold back, stifle, smother

strap *n, v*
▶ *n* thong, tie, band, belt, cord, leash
▶ *v* 1 BEAT, lash, whip, flog, belt, scourge
2 FASTEN, secure, tie, bind, truss, lash, bandage

strapping *adj*
brawny, strong, sturdy, well-built, beefy, big, burly, hefty, robust, hulking, husky
colloq. hunky
▣ puny

stratagem *n*
plan, scheme, plot, intrigue, ruse, ploy, trick, deception, dodge, manoeuvre, device, tactic, artifice, wile, subterfuge
formal machination

⚠ **stratagem** or **strategy** ?
A *stratagem* is a plan or trick, intended to deceive someone or gain an advantage over them: *He was a master of the cunning stratagem and the bare-faced lie.* *Strategy* is used to describe tactics, especially in a long-term plan of campaign: *adopt a strategy of civil disobedience; guerrilla tactics were replaced by a strategy of conventional warfare.*

strategic *adj*
important, key, critical, decisive, crucial, vital, essential, tactical, planned, calculated, deliberate, politic, diplomatic
▣ unimportant

strategy *n*
tactics, planning, policy, approach, procedure, plan, plan of action, programme, schedule, design, scheme
colloq. blueprint, game, plan

⚠ **strategy** or **stratagem** ? *See panel at* **stratagem**.

stratum *n*
1 LEVEL, grade, class, rank, table, tier, category, bracket, caste, station, group, region
2 LAYER, seam, vein, lode, bed, stratification

stray *v, adj*
▶ *v* wander (off), get lost, err, go astray, ramble, saunter, amble, roam, range, meander, straggle, drift, diverge, deviate, digress, go off the subject
colloq. go off at a tangent
▶ *adj* 1 LOST, abandoned, homeless, wandering, roaming, drifting
2 RANDOM, chance, occasional, accidental, freak, odd, erratic, scattered, isolated

streak *n, v*
▶ *n* 1 LINE, stroke, smear, band, stripe, strip, layer, vein
2 TRACE, dash, touch, element, strain
3 *on a lucky streak*
spell, time, period, stint, stretch
▶ *v* 1 BAND, stripe, mark, fleck, smear, smudge, daub
formal striate
2 SPEED, tear, rush, hurtle, sprint, race, gallop, fly, dart, dash, flash, whistle, zoom, whizz, sweep, scurry

streaked *adj*
flecked, fleckered, streaky, lined, banded, barred, brinded, brindle(d)
formal striate

stream *n, v*
▶ *n* 1 RIVER, creek, brook, beck, burn, rill, rillet, rivulet, tributary
2 *a stream of traffic*
course, drift, flow, surge, current, outpouring, jet, run, gush, rush, tide, flood, deluge, cascade, torrent, volley, burst
formal efflux
▶ *v* 1 ISSUE, well, surge, run, flow, course, pour, spout, gush, flood, cascade, crowd, spill, shed
2 *streaming in the wind*
float, trail, flap, fly, flutter

streamer *n*
ribbon, banner, pennant, pennon, flag, ensign, standard, gonfalon
formal vexillum

streamlined *adj*
1 AERODYNAMIC, smooth, sleek, graceful
2 EFFICIENT, well-run, smooth-running,

rationalized, time-saving, organized, modernized, slick
colloq. up-to-the-minute
E3 2 clumsy, inefficient

street *n*
See panel at **road**.
▷ **man in the street** woman in the street, ordinary person, ordinary citizen, average person, Mr/Mrs Average, average punter; *colloq.* Joe Bloggs, person/man/woman on the Clapham omnibus

strength *n*
1 POWER, force, energy, vigour, brawn, muscle, sinew, stoutness, toughness, stamina, fitness, health, vigour
colloq. clout
2 TOUGHNESS, resilience, robustness, sturdiness, impregnability, durability, solidity, solidness, resistance, firmness, soundness, hardiness
3 DETERMINATION, resolution, forcefulness, firmness, assertiveness, persistence, spirit, bravery, courage
formal fortitude
colloq. guts
4 INTENSITY, depth, vividness, graphicness, sharpness, keenness, pungency, passion, fervency, ardour, vehemence
5 FORCEFULNESS, effectiveness, power, force, potency, persuasiveness, weight, validity, soundness, urgency
formal cogency
6 STRONG POINT, talent, gift, aptitude, advantage, asset, bent, forte, specialty, speciality, métier
colloq. thing
E3 1 weakness, frailty **2** weakness **3** weakness, feebleness **4** mildness, blandness, faintness
5 weakness, ineffectiveness **6** weakness
▷ **on the strength of** because of, because of the influence of, on account of, based on, on the basis of;
formal by virtue of

strengthen *v*
reinforce, brace, steel, buttress, build up, prop up, shore up, bolster, support, back up, toughen, harden, stiffen, consolidate, substantiate, corroborate, confirm, encourage, hearten, refresh, restore, rally, invigorate, nourish, increase, heighten, intensify
formal fortify
colloq. beef up
E3 weaken, undermine

strenuous *adj*
1 *strenuous work*
hard, tough, demanding, gruelling, taxing, difficult, laborious, heavy, uphill, arduous, tiring, exhausting, weighty
2 ACTIVE, energetic, vigorous, eager, keen, earnest, tenacious, determined, forceful, resolute, spirited, bold, tireless, indefatigable
E3 1 easy, effortless

stress *n, v*
▶ *n* **1** PRESSURE, strain, tension, worry, uneasiness, apprehension, anxiety, distress, difficulty, trouble, weight, burden, trauma
colloq. hassle
2 EMPHASIS, accent, accentuation, beat, force, weight, value, priority, importance, significance
technical ictus
E3 1 relaxation
▶ *v* emphasize, accentuate, highlight, underline, underscore, point up, spotlight, repeat, exaggerate

E3 understate, play down, moderate, downplay, tone down

stretch *v, n*
▶ *v* **1** LENGTHEN, extend, make/become longer, broaden, widen, make/become wider, expand, spread, elongate, prolong, draw out
formal protract
2 *stretch from one point to another*
reach, extend, spread, unfold, unroll, continue, project, go as far as, go/come down/up to, last, range
3 TIGHTEN, pull, tauten, strain
4 REACH OUT, straighten, extend, hold out, present, offer
formal proffer
5 *the job will stretch you*
challenge, extend, push, test, tax, try
E3 1 shorten, condense, compress
▷ **stretch your legs** exercise, go for a walk, move about, stroll, take a walk, take the air;
formal promenade; *colloq.* take a breather
▷ **stretch out** extend, relax, hold out, put out, lie down, sprawl, reach; *formal* recline
E3 draw back
▶ *n* **1** EXPANSE, spread, sweep, reach, extent, distance, space, area, tract
2 PERIOD, time, term, spell, stint, run

strew *v*
scatter, spread, disperse, bestrew, litter, sprinkle, toss
old use bespread, besprinkle
E3 gather

stricken *adj*
affected, afflicted, hit, struck, injured, wounded, smitten
E3 unaffected

strict *adj*
1 *a strict teacher*
stern, authoritarian, no-nonsense, hard, firm, rigid, inflexible, uncompromising, stringent, rigorous, disciplinarian, harsh, tough, severe, austere, narrow
2 EXACT, precise, accurate, clear, clear-cut, literal, faithful, close, true, absolute, utter, total, complete, thoroughgoing, meticulous, scrupulous, conscientious, particular, orthodox, religious
E3 1 liberal, soft, flexible; *colloq.* easy-going
2 loose

strictness *n*
1 STERNNESS, authoritarianism, firmness, harshness, rigidity, rigidness, severity, stringency, stringentness, austerity
2 EXACTNESS, precision, accuracy, meticulousness, rigorousness, rigour, scrupulousness
E3 1 flexibility, mildness

stricture *n*
1 CRITICISM, rebuke, reproof, blame, censure
formal animadversion
colloq. flak
2 RESTRICTION, limit, bound, confine, constraint, restraint, control, tightness
E3 1 praise

stride *v, n*
▶ *v* walk, step, pace, tread, advance, progress
▶ *n* step, pace, walk, tread, movement, advance, progression

strident *adj*
loud, thundering, roaring, booming, clamorous, vociferous, harsh, rough, raucous, grating, rasping,

shrill, screeching, unmusical, discordant, clashing, jarring, jangling
formal stentorian, stridulant
F3 quiet, soft

strife *n*
conflict, disagreement, discord, dissension, controversy, animosity, hostility, friction, rivalry, contention, ill-feeling, ill-will, quarrel, quarrelling, row, argument, dispute, bickering, wrangling, struggle, fighting, combat, battle, warfare
F3 peace

strike *n, v*
▶ *n* **1** INDUSTRIAL ACTION, work-to-rule, go-slow, stoppage, sit-in, walk-out, mutiny, revolt
2 HIT, blow, stroke, slap, smack, thump, thwack
colloq. wallop, clobber, whack, belt, biff
3 ATTACK, charge, aid, storming, assault, rush, ambush, trap
▶ *v* **1** STOP WORK, down tools, take industrial action, work to rule, walk out, protest, mutiny, revolt
2 HIT, knock, collide with, slap, smack, cuff, thump, thwack, thrash, rap, beat, bang, pound, punch, box, hammer, buffet, batter
colloq. clout, wallop, sock, clobber, swipe, whack, belt, biff
3 ATTACK, charge, storm, assail, assault, raid, rush, set about, pounce on, ambush, trap
4 FIND, discover, come upon, unearth, uncover, encounter, reach
formal chance upon, happen upon
5 *the idea suddenly struck me*
occur to, hit, come to, come to mind, dawn on, register
6 *it strikes me as odd*
seem, appear, look, look like, feel, sound, give the impression, impress, affect, touch, have the look of
7 *strike a particular pose*
adopt, take on, assume, embrace, affect
8 *strike a bargain*
reach, come to, agree on, come to an agreement on, settle on, arrive at, achieve
colloq. clinch
▷ **strike back** retaliate, hit back, fight back, reciprocate, get back at, pay someone back; *colloq.* get your own back, get even with
▷ **strike down** afflict, ruin, destroy, kill, murder, assassinate; *formal* slay, smite
▷ **strike out** cross out, delete, rub out, erase, strike through, cancel, strike off, remove, obliterate
F3 add
▷ **strike up** begin, start, initiate, instigate, introduce, establish; *formal* commence; *colloq.* kick off

striking *adj*
1 NOTICEABLE, conspicuous, obvious, evident, salient, outstanding, remarkable, extraordinary, memorable, distinct, visible, impressive, dazzling, arresting, astonishing, stunning
2 ATTRACTIVE, stunning, beautiful, good-looking, gorgeous, pretty, glamorous
F3 **1** unimpressive **2** ugly

string *n, v*
▶ *n* **1** *a piece of string*
twine, cord, rope, yarn, cable, line, strand, fibre
2 SERIES, succession, sequence, chain, line, row, column, file, queue, procession, stream, train
3 *with no strings attached*
qualifications, conditions, limitations, restrictions, stipulations, provisos, obligations, requirements,

catches
formal prerequisites
▶ *v* thread, link, connect, fasten, tie up, sling, hang, suspend, festoon, loop
▷ **string along** deceive, fool, bluff, dupe, play (someone) false, hoax, humbug; *colloq.* play fast and loose with, put one over on, take for a ride
▷ **string out** space out, spread out, stretch out, straggle, fan out, disperse, extend, lengthen, wander; *formal* protract
F3 gather, shorten
▷ **string up** hang, kill, lynch, send to the gallows/ scaffold/gibbet; *colloq.* top

stringent *adj*
binding, strict, severe, rigorous, tough, firm, rigid, inflexible, uncompromising, exacting, demanding, tight, hard, harsh
F3 lax, flexible

stringy *adj*
tough, gristly, chewy, fibrous, sinewy, leathery, wiry, ropy
F3 tender

strip *v, n*
▶ *v* **1** UNDRESS, take your clothes off, unclothe, remove your clothes, uncover, expose, lay bare
formal disrobe, denude
2 CLEAN OUT, clear, empty, divest, deprive, dispossess, gut, ransack, pillage, plunder, loot
3 PEEL, skin, flay, flake off
formal excoriate
4 DISMANTLE, take apart, disassemble, separate, pull apart, take to pieces
F3 **1** clothe, dress, get dressed **2** cover, fill **4** assemble, put together
▶ *n* ribbon, thong, strap, belt, sash, band, bar, stripe, swathe, lath, slat, piece, bit, slip, shred

stripe *n*
band, line, bar, chevron, flash, streak, fleck, strip, belt

striped *adj*
banded, barred, streaky, stripy, variegated, striated, vittate

stripling *n*
boy, fledgling, lad, teenager, adolescent, youth, youngster
colloq. young'un

strive *v*
1 TRY, attempt, endeavour, struggle, strain, work, toil, labour, try hard, campaign, exert yourself, give your all, do your best, do your utmost
2 FIGHT, battle, contend, engage, contest, combat, do battle, vie, compete

stroke *n, v*
▶ *n* **1** CARESS, pat, rub
2 BLOW, hit, knock, swipe, slap, thwack, thump, smack
colloq. wallop, clobber, whack, belt, biff
3 SWEEP, flourish, movement, action, move, motion, line
4 ACCOMPLISHMENT, achievement, coup
5 COLLAPSE, shock, spasm, attack, seizure, thrombosis, cerebral haemorrhage
▶ *v* caress, fondle, pet, touch, pat, rub, massage

stroll *v, n*
▶ *v* saunter, amble, dawdle, ramble, wander, meander, go for a walk

colloq. stretch your legs
▶ *n* walk, saunter, amble, constitutional, turn, ramble

stroller *n*
saunterer, rambler, walker, wanderer, dawdler

strong *adj*
1 POWERFUL, mighty, potent, lusty, strapping, sturdy, stout, burly, well-built, beefy, brawny, muscular, sinewy, athletic, fit, well, healthy
2 TOUGH, resilient, durable, hard-wearing, heavy-duty, solid, long-lasting, well-built, well-protected, reinforced, robust, hardy, sturdy, vigorous, stalwart, rugged
3 DETERMINED, forceful, firm, confident, resolute, assertive, aggressive, formidable, strong-willed, strong-minded, single-minded, persistent, brave, courageous
colloq. gutsy
4 *a strong colour/point*
INTENSE, deep, vivid, graphic, fierce, violent, powerful, sharp, heady, keen, pungent, piquant, biting, highy-flavoured, highly-seasoned, hot, spicy
5 *a strong impression*
marked, clear, clear-cut, obvious, evident, remarkable, pronounced
6 *take strong action*
decisive, firm, positive, active, severe, resolute, forceful
7 *a strong interest in railways*
keen, enthusiastic, eager, devoted, committed, passionate
8 *a strong case/argument*
convincing, persuasive, powerful, potent, plausible, valid, sound, effective, telling, forceful, weighty, compelling, urgent
formal efficacious
9 *strong feelings*
intense, passionate, fervent, great, powerful, deep, profound, ardent, vehement
10 UNDILUTED, concentrated, potent
E3 1 weak, frail, sickly, unhealthy 2 weak, insubstantial 3 feeble, weak 4 weak, faint, mild, bland 6 weak, indecisive 8 weak, unconvincing 9 weak, feeble 10 diluted
▷ **strong point** strength, talent, gift, aptitude, advantage, asset, bent, forte, speciality, specialty, métier; *colloq.* thing

strongarm *adj*
forceful, physical, violent, oppressive, terror, aggressive, bullying, coercive, threatening, intimidatory, thuggish
E3 gentle

stronghold *n*
citadel, bastion, fort, fortress, castle, tower, keep, refuge

strong-minded *adj*
resolute, steadfast, strong-willed, tenacious, firm, determined, independent, iron-willed, uncompromising, unbending, unwavering
E3 weak-willed

strong-willed *adj*
stubborn, obstinate, intractable, wayward, inflexible, wilful, self-willed
formal obdurate, refractory, recalcitrant, intransigent

stroppy *adj*
bad-tempered, difficult, unhelpful, unco-operative, perverse, awkward, bloody-minded, quarrelsome, rowdy, cantankerous, obstreperous

formal refractory
E3 co-operative, sweet-tempered

structural *adj*
design, constructional, organizational
technical tectonic
formal configurational, formational

structure *n, v*
▶ *n* 1 *the structure of society*
framework, frame, construction, fabric, form, shape, design, make-up, formation, arrangement, organization, composition, constitution, system, set-up
formal configuration, conformation
2 BUILDING, construction, edifice, erection
▶ *v* construct, assemble, build, form, shape, design, arrange, organize

struggle *v, n*
▶ *v* 1 STRIVE, work, toil, labour, strain, try hard, exert yourself, give your all, do your best, do your utmost, agonize
2 FIGHT, battle, wrestle, grapple, engage, contest, combat, contend, compete, vie
E3 2 yield, give in
▶ *n* difficulty, problem, effort, exertion, trouble, pains, agony, work, labour, toil, clash, conflict, strife, fight, battle, skirmish, encounter, combat, scuffle, brawl, hostilities, contest, competition
E3 ease, submission, co-operation

strut *v*
parade, prance, stalk, swagger, peacock
colloq. swank

stub *n*
end, stump, remnant, butt, counterfoil
colloq. fag end, dog-end

stubborn *adj*
obstinate, stiff-necked, mulish, pig-headed, rigid, uncompromising, inflexible, unbending, unyielding, dogged, persistent, tenacious, headstrong, self-willed, strong-willed, adamant, hidebound, wilful, difficult, unmanageable, stubborn as a mule, not listening/open to reason
formal obdurate, intransigent, refractory, intractable, recalcitrant
E3 compliant, flexible, yielding

stubby *adj*
stumpy, dumpy, chunky, short, squat, thickset
E3 long, tall, thin

stuck *adj*
1 FAST, jammed, firm, fixed, embedded, rooted, fastened, unmovable, immobile, joined, glued, cemented
colloq. bogged down
2 BEATEN, baffled
colloq. stumped, perplexed, at a loss, at your wits' end, nonplussed
E3 1 loose
▷ **get stuck into** set about, tackle, get down to, start, begin, embark on
▷ **stuck on** fond of, enthusiastic about, keen on, obsessed with, infatuated with, wild about, crazy about; *colloq.* dotty about, mad on, nuts on
E3 indifferent to

stuck-up *adj*
snobbish, supercilious, haughty, patronizing, condescending, proud, arrogant, conceited
colloq. snooty, bigheaded, toffee-nosed, high and

mighty, hoity-toity, uppish
F3 humble, modest

studded *adj*
dotted, flecked, set, spotted, speckled, sprinkled, ornamented, spangled, scattered
old use bejewelled, bespangled

student *n*
undergraduate, postgraduate, scholar, schoolboy, schoolgirl, pupil, disciple, learner, probationer, trainee, apprentice

studied *adj*
deliberate, conscious, wilful, intentional, premeditated, planned, purposeful, calculated, contrived, forced, affected, unnatural, artificial, over-elaborate
F3 unplanned, impulsive, natural

studio *n*
workshop, workroom, school, atelier

studious *adj*
scholarly, academic, intellectual, bookish, serious, thoughtful, reflective, diligent, hard-working, industrious, meticulous, thorough, assiduous, careful, attentive, earnest, eager
formal sedulous
F3 lazy, idle, negligent

study *v, n*
▶ *v* read, learn, train, revise, cram, read up, research, major in, investigate, analyse, survey, scan, examine, scrutinize, peruse, pore over, contemplate, meditate, ponder, consider, deliberate
colloq. swot, mug up, bone up
▶ *n* 1 READING, homework, preparation, learning, scholarship, revision, cramming, research, investigation, inquiry, analysis, examination, scrutiny, inspection, contemplation, thought, consideration, attention
colloq. swotting

Subjects of study include: accountancy, agriculture, anatomy, anthropology, archaeology, architecture, art, astrology, astronomy, biology, botany, building studies, business studies, calligraphy, chemistry, CDT (craft, design and technology), civil engineering, the Classics, commerce, computer studies, cosmology, craft, dance, design, domestic science, drama, dressmaking, driving, ecology, economics, education, electronics, engineering, environmenal studies, ethnology, eugenics, fashion, fitness, food technology, forensics, genetics, geography, geology, heraldry, history, home economics, horticulture, information technology (IT), journalism, languages, law, leisure studies, lexicography, linguistics, literature, logistics, management studies, marketing, mathematics, mechanics, media studies, medicine, metallurgy, metaphysics, meteorology, music, mythology, natural history, oceanography, ornithology, pathology, penology, personal and social education (PSE); personal, health and social education (PHSE), pharmacology, philosophy, photography, physics, physiology, politics, pottery, psychology, religious studies, science, shorthand, social sciences, sociology, sport, statistics, surveying, technology, theology, typewriting, visual arts, word processing, writing, zoology.

2 REPORT, essay, thesis, paper, monograph, work, survey, review, critique
3 OFFICE, studio, library, workroom
colloq. den

stuff *v, n*
▶ *v* 1 PACK, stow, load, fill, pad, press, cram, crowd, force, push, ram, thrust, wedge, jam, squeeze, stow, compress, block, obstruct, bung up
colloq. shove
2 GORGE, gormandise, overindulge, guzzle, gobble, sate, satiate
colloq. pig out, gross out, make a pig of yourself
F3 1 unload, empty 2 nibble
▶ *n* 1 MATERIAL, fabric, matter, substance, essence
2 BELONGINGS, possessions, things, objects, articles, items, goods, luggage, paraphernalia, kit, tackle, equipment, materials
colloq. gear, clobber

stuffing *n*
padding, wadding, quilting, packing, kapok, filling, forcemeat, farce

stuffy *adj*
1 *a stuffy room*
musty, stale, airless, unventilated, suffocating, stifling, oppressive, heavy, close, muggy, sultry, fuggy
2 STAID, strait-laced, prim, conventional, old-fashioned, pompous, dull, dreary, uninteresting, stodgy, stiff, starchy
colloq. fuddy-duddy
F3 1 airy, well-ventilated 2 informal, modern, lively

stultify *v*
blunt, dull, stupefy, numb, smother, stifle, suppress, thwart, invalidate, negate, nullify
formal hebetate
F3 prove, sharpen, electrify

stumble *v*
1 TRIP, slip, fall, lurch, reel, stagger, flounder, blunder, lose your balance
2 STAMMER, stutter, hesitate, falter
▷ **stumble on** come across, find, discover, encounter; *formal* chance upon, happen upon

stumbling-block *n*
obstacle, hurdle, barrier, bar, obstruction, hindrance, impediment, difficulty, snag

stump *n, v*
▶ *n* end, remnant, trunk, stub, butt, remains
colloq. fag end, dog-end
▶ *v* defeat, outwit, confound, perplex, puzzle, baffle, mystify, confuse, bewilder, dumbfound, foil
colloq. flummox, bamboozle, nonplus
F3 assist
▷ **stump up** pay, pay out/up, hand over, donate, contribute; *colloq.* fork out, shell out, chip in, cough up
F3 receive

stumped *adj*
perplexed, stuck, baffled
colloq. floored, bamboozled, flummoxed, nonplussed, stymied

stumpy *adj*
chunky, heavy, short, squat, stocky, stubby, thickset, thick, dumpy
F3 long, tall, thin

stun *v*
amaze, astonish, astound, stagger, shock, daze, stupefy, dumbfound, overcome, overpower, confound, confuse, bewilder
colloq. flabbergast, knock out, knock for six, bowl over, take your breath away

stunned *adj*
amazed, astounded, devastated, dumbfounded, dazed, numb, shocked, staggered, stupefied
colloq. flabbergasted, floored, gobsmacked
🔁 indifferent

stunner *n*
beauty, charmer, good-looker, sensation, dazzler, heart-throb, looker, *femme fatale*, lovely, siren
colloq. smasher, knock-out, peach, wow, eye-catcher

stunning *adj*
beautiful, lovely, gorgeous, ravishing, dazzling, brilliant, striking, impressive, spectacular, remarkable, extraordinary, amazing, wonderful, marvellous, great, sensational, incredible, staggering
colloq. smashing, fabulous
🔁 ugly, awful

stunt¹ *n*
a publicity stunt
feat, exploit, act, deed, action, enterprise, trick, turn, performance
colloq. wheeze

stunt² *v*
stunt someone's growth
stop, arrest, check, restrict, curb, slow, hinder, hamper, impede, dwarf
formal retard
🔁 promote, encourage

stunted *adj*
small, little, tiny, undersized, diminutive, dwarfed, dwarfish
🔁 large, sturdy

stupefaction *n*
daze, numbness, state of shock, blackout, senselessness, bewilderment, wonder, bafflement, amazement, astonishment

stupefy *v*
daze, stun, numb, dumbfound, shock, devastate, stagger, dull, amaze, astound
colloq. knock out, knock for six, bowl over

stupendous *adj*
huge, enormous, immense, gigantic, colossal, vast, phenomenal, tremendous, breathtaking, wonderful, extraordinary, overwhelming, staggering, stunning, amazing, astounding, fabulous, superb, marvellous
formal prodigious
colloq. fantastic
🔁 ordinary, unimpressive

stupid *adj*
1 SILLY, foolish, irresponsible, ill-advised, indiscreet, foolhardy, rash, senseless, mad, lunatic, brainless, mindless, half-witted, idiotic, imbecilic, moronic, feeble-minded, simple-minded, slow, dim, dull, dull-witted, dense, crass, inane, fatuous, puerile, futile, pointless, meaningless, nonsensical, absurd, ludicrous, laughable
formal injudicious
colloq. gormless, thick, dumb, dopey, not all there, slow on the uptake, thick as a plank/two short planks
2 DAZED, groggy, stupefied, stunned, sluggish, semiconscious, unconscious
🔁 1 sensible, wise, clever, intelligent 2 alert

stupidity *n*
silliness, folly, foolishness, foolhardiness, irresponsibility, indiscretion, rashness, senselessness, madness, lunacy, denseness, crassness, absurdity,

dimness, asininity, feeble-mindedness, dullness, puerility, fatuousness, fatuity, futility, impracticality, brainlessness, idiocy, imbecility, inanity, ineptitude, naïvety, obtuseness, pointlessness, ludicrousness, slowness
colloq. dopiness, doziness, dumbness, thickness
🔁 intelligence, alertness, cleverness

stupor *n*
daze, state of shock, stupefaction, lethargy, inertia, trance, blackout, coma, numbness, oblivion, insensibility, unconsciousness
formal torpor
🔁 alertness, consciousness

sturdy *adj*
strong, robust, durable, well-made, stout, substantial, solid, well-built, powerful, muscular, athletic, hardy, vigorous, flourishing, hearty, staunch, stalwart, steadfast, firm, resolute, determined, tenacious
formal mighty
🔁 weak, flimsy, puny

stutter *v*
stammer, hesitate, splutter, falter, stumble, mumble

style *n, v*
▶ *n* 1 APPEARANCE, cut, design, pattern, shape, form, sort, type, kind, variety, category
formal genre
2 ELEGANCE, smartness, chic, flair, panache, stylishness, dash, taste, polish, refinement, sophistication, urbanity, suaveness, fashion, vogue, trend, mode, dressiness, flamboyance, wealth, affluence, comfort, luxury, grandeur
3 *style of working*
technique, approach, method, methodology, manner, fashion, way, custom
formal mode
4 WORDING, phrasing, expression, language, tone, tenor
🔁 2 inelegance, tastelessness
▶ *v* 1 DESIGN, cut, tailor, fashion, make, shape, produce, adapt
2 DESIGNATE, term, name, call, address, title, dub, tag, label
formal denominate

stylish *adj*
chic, fashionable, *à la mode*, modish, in vogue, voguish, snappy, dressy, smart, elegant, polished, refined, sophisticated, urbane
colloq. trendy, natty, snazzy, classy, ritzy
🔁 old-fashioned, shabby

stylus *n*
needle, pointer, pen, index, hand, style, probe
formal graphium

stymie *v*
foil, frustrate, hinder, stump, thwart, defeat, confound, baffle, balk, mystify, puzzle
colloq. bamboozle, flummox, nonplus, snooker
🔁 help, assist

suave *adj*
debonair, refined, polite, courteous, charming, civil, civilized, agreeable, affable, soft-spoken, smooth, polished, bland, unctuous, glib, sophisticated, urbane, worldly
🔁 rude, unsophisticated

suavity *n*
refinement, politeness, courtesy, sophistication, urbanity, charm, civility, agreeability, blandness,

smoothness, unctuousness, worldliness
❳ coarseness

subaquatic adj
underwater, undersea, submersed, submarine
formal subaqua, subaqueous, demersal

subconscious adj, n
▶ *adj* subliminal, unconscious, intuitive, instinctive, inner, innermost, deep, hidden, latent, underlying, repressed, suppressed
❳ conscious
▶ *n* psyche, unconscious, unconscious self, ego, super-ego, id

subdue v
overcome, quell, suppress, repress, overpower, crush, quash, defeat, conquer, overrun, subject, gain mastery over, get the better of, humble, break, tame, master, discipline, control, check, stifle, restrain, moderate, reduce, soften, quieten, damp, mellow
formal vanquish, subjugate
❳ arouse, awaken

subdued adj
1 SAD, downcast, dejected, crestfallen, depressed, quiet, unexcited, lifeless, serious, grave, solemn
colloq. down in the dumps
2 QUIET, muted, hushed, silent, noiseless, still, soft, softened, pastel, dim, shaded, sombre, sober, restrained, delicate, unobtrusive, low-key, subtle, toned down
❳ 1 lively, excited 2 bright, loud, striking, obtrusive

subject n, adj, v
▶ *n* 1 TOPIC, theme, matter, issue, question, aspect, point, substance, case, affair, business, discipline, area of study, field, field of study, motif
2 NATIONAL, citizen, participant, client, patient, victim
3 SUBORDINATE, vassal, liegeman, inferior, dependant, captive
colloq. underling
❳ 3 monarch, ruler, master
▶ *adj* 1 LIABLE, disposed, prone, susceptible, vulnerable, likely, apt, open, exposed
2 *subject to a law*
captive, bound, constrained, obedient, answerable, accountable, subordinate, inferior, subservient, submissive
formal subjugated
3 DEPENDENT, conditional
formal contingent
❳ 1 invulnerable 2 free, superior
3 unconditional
▶ *v* expose, lay open, submit, subdue, submit
formal subjugate

subjection n
captivity, bondage, slavery, oppression, domination, mastery, defeat, enslavement, chains, shackles
formal subjugation

subjective adj
biased, prejudiced, bigoted, personal, individual, idiosyncratic, emotional, intuitive, instinctive
❳ objective, unbiased, impartial

subjugate v
conquer, overpower, overcome, master, overthrow, gain mastery over, get the better of, crush, defeat, subdue, suppress, oppress, quell, reduce, enslave, tame, thrall

formal vanquish
❳ free, liberate

sublimate v
channel, divert, transfer, redirect, turn, exalt, heighten, elevate, purify, refine
formal transmute
❳ let out

sublime adj
1 GLORIOUS, exalted, elevated, high, lofty, noble, majestic, great, grand, imposing, magnificent, transcendent, spiritual
2 SUPREME, great, intense, extreme, complete, utter
❳ 1 lowly, base

submerge v
submerse, immerse, plunge, plummet, duck, dip, dunk, sink, go down, go/put under water, drown, engulf, overwhelm, swamp, overflow, flood, inundate, deluge, bury
❳ surface

submerged adj
submersed, immersed, underwater, sunk, sunken, drowned, swamped, inundated, hidden, concealed, cloaked, veiled, unseen

submission n
1 SURRENDER, giving in, capitulation, resignation, agreement, acquiescence, compliance, obedience, deference, submissiveness, meekness, passivity
formal assent
2 PRESENTATION, offering, contribution, entry, introduction, tendering, tabling, tender, suggestion, proposal, statement, assertion
formal averment
❳ 1 resistance, opposition, intransigence, intractability 2 withdrawal

submissive adj
yielding, unresisting, resigned, patient, uncomplaining, accommodating, malleable, biddable, compliant, acquiescent, obedient, deferential, ingratiating, subservient, resisting, servile, humble, meek, self-effacing, docile, weak, weak-willed, downtrodden, subdued, passive
formal supine
❳ intractable, assertive; *formal* intransigent

submit v
1 YIELD, give in, give way, surrender, lay down your arms, capitulate, knuckle under, bow, bend, stoop, succumb, agree, comply, defer, acquiesce
formal accede
2 PRESENT, tender, offer, put forward, suggest, propose, introduce, table, move, state, claim, assert, argue
formal proffer, propound, aver
❳ 1 resist, oppose 2 withdraw

subnormal adj
below normal, below average, low, backward, inferior, slow, retarded, feeble-minded
❳ gifted

subordinate adj, n
▶ *adj* secondary, auxiliary, ancillary, subsidiary, dependent, inferior, lower, lower in rank, lower-ranking, junior, minor, lesser, subservient, lowly
❳ superior, senior
▶ *n* inferior, junior, assistant, attendant, second, deputy, aide, dependant, menial, vassal
colloq. underling, sidekick, skivvy, dogsbody,

second fiddle
▣ superior, boss

subordination *n*
inferiority, subjection, submission, dependence,
servitude, subservience
▣ superiority

subscribe *v*
1 *subscribe to a magazine*
pay for regularly, buy regularly, receive/take regularly
2 DONATE, give, contribute, pledge
colloq. shell out, fork
3 *subscribe to a theory*
support, endorse, back, approve, agree, underwrite
formal advocate, consent, accede

subscription *n*
membership fee, dues, payment, donation,
contribution, offering, gift

subsequent *adj*
following, later, future, next, succeeding, consequent,
resulting, ensuing
▣ previous, earlier, prior

subsequently *adv*
later, after, afterwards, consequently
▣ previously

subservient *adj*
1 SERVILE, deferential, submissive, fawning,
ingratiating, unctuous, obsequious, toadying
formal sycophantic
colloq. bootlicking
2 SUBORDINATE, less important, secondary,
ancillary, auxiliary, subsidiary, dependent, inferior,
lower, junior, minor, lesser, conducive, useful,
instrumental
▣ 1 domineering, rebellious 2 superior, senior,
more important, unhelpful

subside *v*
1 DECREASE, lower, get lower, lessen, diminish,
dwindle, decline, wane, ebb, recede, moderate, die
down, quieten, let up, fall, slacken, ease
formal abate
colloq. peter out
2 SINK, collapse, cave in, settle, descend, lower, fall,
drop
▣ 1 rise, increase

subsidence *n*
decline, decrease, descent, settlement, sinking,
slackening, lessening, ebb, de-escalation, settling
formal abatement, detumescence, diminution
▣ increase

subsidiary *adj, n*
▶ *adj* auxiliary, supplementary, additional,
supplementary, ancillary, assistant, supporting,
contributory, secondary, subordinate, subservient,
lesser, minor
▣ primary, chief, major
▶ *n* branch, offshoot, division, section, part, wing

subsidize *v*
support, back, endorse, underwrite, sponsor, finance,
fund, invest in, give a subsidy to, pay part of the cost of,
contribute to, aid, promote

subsidy *n*
grant, allowance, assistance, help, aid, contribution,
sponsorship, finance, funding, investment, support,
backing, endorsement, underwriting
formal subvention

subsist *v*
exist, continue, endure, hold out, live, survive, remain,
last, eke out an existence

subsistence *n*
living, survival, existence, continuance, livelihood,
maintenance, support, keep, sustenance,
nourishment, food, provisions, rations, aliment

substance *n*
1 MATTER, material, stuff, fabric, essence, mass,
medium, entity, body, solidity, materiality, tangibility,
concreteness, reality, actuality, ground, foundation
formal corporeality
2 SUBJECT, subject matter, matter, topic, theme, text,
burden, pith, gist, meaning, meaningfulness,
significance, validity, truth, foundation, ground, basis,
force, power, weight
formal import
3 *a person of substance*
wealth, money, prosperity, riches, assets, means,
resources, affluence, power, influence

substandard *adj*
second-rate, inferior, imperfect, damaged, shoddy,
poor, inadequate, unacceptable
colloq. below par, not up to scratch
▣ first-rate, superior, perfect

substantial *adj*
1 LARGE, big, sizable, ample, generous, great,
considerable, significant, important, meaningful,
notable, remarkable, weighty, worthwhile, valuable
colloq. tidy
2 WELL-BUILT, solid, stout, sturdy, strong, tough,
durable, sound
3 TANGIBLE, material, existing, concrete, real,
actual, true
formal corporeal
4 BASIC, essential, central, primary, main, principal,
fundamental, inherent, intrinsic
5 WEALTHY, prosperous, rich, successful, affluent,
powerful, influential
▣ 1 small, insignificant 2 flimsy 3 insubstantial,
imaginary 5 poor

substantially *adv*
1 SIGNIFICANTLY, largely, considerably, to a great
extent
2 ESSENTIALLY, fundamentally, mainly, in the main,
materially, to all intents and purposes
▣ 1 slightly

substantiate *v*
prove, verify, confirm, uphold, support, back up, bear
out, authenticate, validate
formal corroborate
▣ disprove, refute

substitute *v, n, adj*
▶ *v* 1 CHANGE, exchange, swap, switch, interchange,
replace, use instead
2 STAND IN, cover, deputize, understudy, relieve,
take over, take the place of, double, act instead of
colloq. fill in, sub
▶ *n* reserve, stand-by, supply, locum, understudy,
stand-in, replacement, relief, surrogate, proxy, agent,
deputy, makeshift, stopgap
formal locum tenens
colloq. temp, fill in
▶ *adj* reserve, temporary, relief, acting, deputy,
surrogate, proxy, replacement, alternative, stand-by,
stand-in

substitution *n*
change, exchange, replacement, interchange, swap,
swapping, switch, switching

subterfuge *n*
trick, stratagem, scheme, ploy, ruse, wile, intrigue,
expedient, manoeuvre, deviousness, evasion,
deception, artifice, pretence, excuse, pretext
formal machination, duplicity
colloq. dodge,
E✸ openness, honesty

subtle *adj*
1 DELICATE, understated, implied, indirect, low-key,
slight, minute, tenuous, elusive, faint, indistinct,
indefinite, mild, toned down, fine, nice, refined,
sophisticated, deep, profound
2 ARTFUL, cunning, crafty, sly, devious, wily, indirect,
shrewd, astute, discreet, discriminating, tactful, clever,
strategic, intricate, complex
E✸ **1** blatant, obvious **2** artless, open, indiscreet,
tactless

subtlety *n*
1 DELICACY, nicety, nuance, refinement, finesse,
faintness, indistinctness, indefiniteness, mutedness,
sophistication
2 ARTFULNESS, cunning, wiliness, guile,
deviousness, craftiness, cleverness, discernment,
astuteness, skill, discrimination, intricacy, slyness,
acuteness, acumen
formal sagacity

subtract *v*
deduct, take away, remove, dock, withdraw, debit,
detract, diminish
E✸ add

suburb *n*
suburbia, outskirts, commuter belt, residential area,
dormitory town
formal purlieus
E✸ centre, heart

suburban *adj*
1 *a suburban railway*
commuter, residential
2 *suburban attitudes*
conventional, dull, unimaginative, narrow, narrow-
minded, parochial, provincial, insular, bourgeois,
middle-class

subversive *adj, n*
▶ *adj* seditious, treasonous, treacherous, traitorous,
revolutionary, inflammatory, incendiary, disruptive,
troublemaking, riotous, weakening, undermining,
discrediting, destructive
E✸ loyal
▶ *n* seditionist, terrorist, dissident, traitor, quisling
colloq. freedom fighter, fifth columnist

subvert *v*
undermine, destroy, ruin, pervert, corrupt, confound,
deprave, demoralize, contaminate, poison, overturn,
upset, disrupt, invalidate, wreck, demolish, debase,
raze, sabotage
formal vitiate
E✸ boost, uphold

subway *n*
1 UNDERGROUND RAILWAY, underground, metro
colloq. tube
2 UNDERPASS, tunnel, pedestrian tunnel,
underground passage

succeed *v*
1 TRIUMPH, do well, be successful, thrive, flourish,
prosper, make good, manage, carry out, complete,
achieve, accomplish, reach, realize, attain, fulfil,
prevail, work, work out, get results
colloq. make it, get on, bring off, pull off, turn up
trumps, take over, steal the show, go places, win the
day, land/fall on your feet, bring home the bacon,
strike gold, hit the jackpot
2 *winter succeeds autumn*
follow, come after, replace, take the place of, result,
ensue
E✸ **1** fail; *colloq.* flop **2** precede
▷ **succeed to** come into, enter upon, inherit,
replace, take over, supersede; *formal* accede, assume
E✸ abdicate, precede

succeeding *adj*
following, next, subsequent, ensuing, coming, to come,
later, successive
E✸ previous, earlier, prior

success *n*
1 TRIUMPH, victory, positive result, luck, fortune,
prosperity, happiness, fame, eminence, completion,
achievement, accomplishment, realization,
attainment, fulfilment
2 CELEBRITY, star, winner, bestseller, hit, sensation
colloq. somebody, VIP, big name, bigwig, big shot,
wow, sell-out, box-office hit
E✸ **1** failure, disaster **2** failure, loser;
colloq. write-off, flop, dead loss

successful *adj*
1 VICTORIOUS, triumphant, winning, lucky,
fortunate, prosperous, wealthy, affluent, thriving,
flourishing, booming, moneymaking, lucrative,
profitable, rewarding, satisfying, fruitful, productive
2 *a successful writer*
famous, well-known, popular, leading, bestselling,
top, unbeaten
E✸ **1** unsuccessful, unprofitable, fruitless
2 unknown

successfully *adv*
great, fine, well, victoriously, beautifully, famously
colloq. swimmingly
E✸ unsuccessfully

succession *n*
1 SERIES, sequence, order, progression, run, chain,
string, cycle, continuation, flow, course, line, train,
procession
2 *the succession to the throne*
accession, attaining, elevation, inheritance
formal assumption
▷ **in succession** successively, consecutively,
sequentially, uninterruptedly, running, one after the
other; *colloq.* on the trot

successive *adj*
consecutive, sequential, following, succeeding,
running, serial

successively *adv*
consecutively, in succession, sequentially,
uninterruptedly, running, one after the other
colloq. on the trot

successor *n*
replacement, substitute, relief, descendant,
beneficiary, heir, co-heir, inheritor, next in line

succinct *adj*
concise, short, brief, terse, crisp, pithy, compact,

condensed, summary, to the point, in a word
☰ long, lengthy, wordy, verbose

succour *n, v*
▶ *n* help, aid, assistance, support, comfort, relief
formal ministrations
colloq. helping hand
▶ *v* help, help out, aid, assist, comfort, encourage,
support, relieve, foster, minister to, nurse, befriend
☰ undermine

succulent *adj*
fleshy, juicy, moist, luscious, mouthwatering, lush,
rich, mellow
☰ dry

succumb *v*
1 GIVE IN, give way, yield, submit, knuckle under,
surrender, capitulate, collapse, fall
2 *succumb to an illness*
catch, go down with, pick up, die of
formal contract
☰ 1 overcome, overwhelm, master

suck *v*
draw (in), imbibe, absorb, blot up, soak up, extract,
drain
▷ **suck up to** fawn, flatter, ingratiate, toady, curry
favour, truckle; *colloq.* lick someone's boots

sucker *n*
fool, victim, dupe, stooge, sap, leech
colloq. pushover, mug, butt, cat's-paw

suckle *v*
breastfeed, feed, nurse

sudden *adj*
unexpected, unforeseen, unanticipated, surprising,
startling, dramatic, abrupt, sharp, quick, fast, swift,
rapid, speedy, meteoric, immediate, instantaneous,
prompt, hurried, hasty, rash, impetuous, impulsive
colloq. snap, spur-of-the-moment
☰ expected, predictable, gradual, slow

suddenly *adv*
unexpectedly, all of a sudden, quickly, abruptly,
sharply, immediately, instantaneously, without
warning
colloq. out of the blue, from out of nowhere

suddenness *n*
unexpectedness, abruptness, hurriedness, haste,
hastiness, impulsiveness
☰ slowness

suds *n*
bubbles, soapiness, lather, froth, foam

sue *v*
1 PROSECUTE, charge, bring charges against,
take (legal) action against, indict, take to court,
bring to trial
2 SUMMON, solicit, appeal, beg, petition, plead
formal beseech

suffer *v*
1 HURT, ache, be in pain, be afflicted, agonize, grieve,
sorrow
colloq. go through the mill
2 UNDERGO, experience, go through, feel, meet with,
endure, sustain
3 BEAR, support, stand, put up with, tolerate, endure
formal abide

suffering *n*
pain, discomfort, hurt, hurting, agony, anguish,

affliction, distress, misery, hardship, wretchedness,
plight, adversity, ordeal, torment, torture
☰ ease, comfort

suffice *v*
do, satisfy, be sufficient, be adequate, answer, measure
up, serve, content
colloq. fit/fill the bill

sufficiency *n*
adequateness, adequacy, enough, plenty, satiety,
competence
formal sufficience
☰ insufficiency, inadequacy

sufficient *adj*
enough, adequate, ample, plenty, satisfactory, effective
colloq. decent
☰ insufficient, inadequate

suffocate *v*
asphyxiate, smother, stifle, choke, strangle, throttle,
be/make breathless

suffrage *n*
franchise, right to vote, right of representation
formal enfranchisement

suffuse *v*
spread, imbue, infuse, permeate, pervade, steep,
transfuse, cover, flood, mantle, bathe, colour, redden

sugar *n*

Kinds of sugar include: beet sugar, brown sugar, cane
sugar, caster sugar, crystallized sugar, demerara,
dextrose, fructose, glucose, golden syrup,
granulated sugar, icing sugar, invert sugar, jaggery,
lactose, maltose, maple syrup, molasses, powdered
sugar, refined sugar, sucrose, sugar loaf, sugar lump,
sweets, *US* candy, *US* sugar candy, syrup, treacle,
unrefined sugar.

Artificial sweeteners include: acesulfame K,
aspartame, Canderel®, cyclamate, Hermesetas®,
NutraSweet®, saccharin, sorbitol, Sweetex®. *See
also* **sweets**.

sugary *adj*
sentimental, emotional, gushing, touching, maudlin,
mawkish, sloppy, soppy
colloq. lovey-dovey, slushy, mushy, schmaltzy, corny,
sickly, gushy

suggest *v*
1 PROPOSE, put forward, advocate, recommend,
submit, advise, counsel, move, table, nominate
colloq. float
2 IMPLY, insinuate, hint, intimate, evoke, bring to
mind, indicate, give the impression

suggestion *n*
1 PROPOSAL, proposition, motion, recommendation,
submission, idea, plan, hint, piece of advice, pointer
2 IMPLICATION, insinuation, intimation, innuendo
3 HINT, intimation, suspicion, trace, touch,
indication

suggestive *adj*
1 EVOCATIVE, reminiscent, expressive, meaning,
indicative
formal redolent
2 *a suggestive remark*
indecent, immodest, improper, indelicate, titillating,
off-colour, sexual, risqué, bawdy, dirty, smutty, ribald,

lewd, provocative
colloq. blue
F∃ **1** inexpressive **2** decent, clean

suicide *n*
killing yourself, self-destruction, self-murder, taking of your (own) life, self-slaughter, hara-kiri, suttee
formal felo de se, self-immolation
colloq. topping yourself, ending it all

suit *n, v*
▶ *n* **1** *wear a suit*
outfit, costume, dress, clothing, set of clothes, ensemble
2 LAWSUIT, action, case, cause, dispute, argument, contest, prosecution, litigation, proceedings, process, trial
▶ *v* **1** GO WELL WITH, complement, match, tally with, agree with, harmonize with, fit, befit, become, look good/attractive on, flatter
2 PLEASE, satisfy, answer, gratify
3 BE CONVENIENT FOR, be suitable for, be appropriate, be applicable, be acceptable, be satisfactory, qualify
formal suffice
colloq. fit/fill the bill
F∃ **1** clash **2** displease **3** be unsuitable for, be inconvenient for

suitability *n*
appropriateness, aptness, fitness, fittingness, opportuneness, timeliness, convenience, rightness
formal appositeness
F∃ unsuitability, inappropriateness

suitable *adj*
appropriate, fitting, convenient, opportune, suited, in keeping, right, compatible, well-suited, well-matched, due, apt, relevant, applicable, fit, adequate, satisfactory, acceptable, befitting, becoming, seemly, proper, right
old use seemly
formal apposite, pertinent
colloq. (right/just) up someone's street
F∃ unsuitable, inappropriate

suitably *adv*
appropriately, fittingly, properly, fitly, acceptably, accordingly, quite
F∃ unsuitably

suitcase *n*
case, vanity-case, bag, holdall, portmanteau, valise, overnight-bag, flight bag, hand-luggage, travel bag, attaché case, portfolio, trunk

suite *n*
1 APARTMENT, rooms, set of rooms, household
2 SET, series, collection, sequence, train, furniture
3 ATTENDANTS, retinue, entourage, escort, followers, retainers, servants

suitor *n*
admirer, boyfriend, lover, young man, wooer, beau, follower, pretendant
old use swain

sulk *v, n*
▶ *v* mope, brood, pout, grouse, grump
colloq. be miffed, be in a huff
▶ *n* mood, temper, bad mood, bad temper, pique
colloq. huff, miff

sulky *adj*
brooding, moody, morose, resentful, grudging,

disgruntled, put out, cross, moping, grumpy, out of sorts, bad-tempered, sullen, aloof, unsociable
colloq. miffed, ratty, huffy
F∃ cheerful, good-tempered, sociable

sullen *adj*
1 SULKY, moody, morose, glum, gloomy, silent, uncommunicative, surly, sour, cross, churlish, perverse, obstinate, stubborn, resentful
2 DARK, gloomy, sombre, dismal, cheerless, dull, leaden, heavy
F∃ **1** cheerful, happy **2** fine, clear

sullenness *n*
moroseness, sulkiness, surliness, moodiness, brooding, glowering, sourness, glumness, heaviness
F∃ cheerfulness

sully *v*
dirty, soil, defile, pollute, contaminate, taint, spoil, mar, spot, blemish, besmirch, stain, tarnish, damage, disgrace, dishonour
old use befoul
F∃ cleanse, honour

sultry *adj*
1 *sultry weather*
hot, sweltering, stifling, stuffy, oppressive, suffocating, close, airless, humid, muggy, sticky
2 SENSUAL, voluptuous, passionate, attractive, sexy, provocative, seductive, tempting, alluring
F∃ **1** cool, cold

sum *n, v*
▶ *n* total, sum total, aggregate, whole, entirety, number, quantity, amount, tally, reckoning, score, result, answer, summary, culmination
▶ *v* ▷ **sum up 1** SUMMARIZE, review, recapitulate, conclude, close; *colloq.* put in a nutshell **2** EPITOMIZE, embody, encapsulate, exemplify

summarily *adv*
immediately, promptly, speedily, swiftly, without delay, hastily, abruptly, arbitrarily
formal expeditiously, peremptorily, forthwith

summarize *v*
outline, précis, condense, abridge, abbreviate, shorten, sum up, epitomize, encapsulate, review, sketch, outline
colloq. recap
F∃ expand (on)

summary *n, adj*
▶ *n* synopsis, résumé, outline, main points, abstract, précis, condensation, digest, compendium, abridgement, summing-up, review, recapitulation, overview, plan
colloq. rundown
▶ *adj* short, succinct, brief, cursory, swift, speedy, hasty, prompt, without delay, immediate, instant, instantaneous, direct, unceremonious, without formality, arbitrary
formal peremptory
F∃ lengthy, careful

summerhouse *n*
belvedere, gazebo, pavilion

summit *n*
top, peak, pinnacle, point, crest, crown, head, vertex, acme, climax, culmination, height
formal apex, zenith, apogee
F∃ bottom, foot, nadir

summon *v*
call, send for, order, demand, invite, bid, beckon, gather, assemble, convene, rally, muster, mobilize, rouse, arouse
formal convoke
🖅 dismiss
▷ **summon up** gather, assemble, convene, rally, muster, mobilize, rouse, arouse, evoke, revive, call to mind

summons *n*
writ, subpoena, citation, order, call, injunction

sumptuous *adj*
luxurious, plush, lavish, extravagant, rich, costly, expensive, dear, splendid, magnificent, gorgeous, superb, grand, de luxe
formal opulent
🖅 plain, poor

sun *n, v*
▶ *n* star, daystar, sunlight, light, daylight, sunshine
Related adjective: solar
▶ *v* sunbathe, tan, brown, bake, bask
formal insolate

sunbathe *v*
sun, bask, tan, brown, bake, sunbake
formal insolate

sunburnt *adj*
brown, tanned, sun-tanned, bronzed, weather-beaten, burnt, red, blistered, blistering, peeling, inflamed
🖅 pale

sunder *v*
split, separate, divide, part, cut, chop, sever
formal cleave, dissever, dissunder
🖅 join

sundry *adj*
various, diverse, miscellaneous, assorted, varied, different, several, some, a few

sunk *adj*
failed, lost, ruined, finished, doomed
colloq. done for, up the creek, up the spout, in a fix/jam

sunken *adj*
1 SUBMERGED, buried, recessed, lower, lowered, below ground level
2 *sunken eyes*
depressed, concave, hollow, haggard, drawn

sunless *adj*
bleak, overcast, dark, cloudy, grey, hazy, gloomy, depressing, dismal, dreary, sombre, cheerless
🖅 sunny, bright

sunny *adj*
1 FINE, cloudless, unclouded, clear, summery, sunshiny, sunlit, bright, brilliant
2 CHEERFUL, happy, joyful, smiling, cheery, glad, bright, merry, beaming, radiant, light-hearted, bubbly, bouncy, buoyant, optimistic, hopeful, pleasant
formal blithe
🖅 1 sunless, cloudy, dull 2 gloomy

sunrise *n*
dawn, crack of dawn, break of day, daybreak, daylight, first light, sun-up, cock-crow, aurora

sunset *n*
sundown, dusk, twilight, gloaming, evening, close of day, nightfall

super *adj*
great, excellent, superb, wonderful, outstanding, marvellous, magnificent, glorious, incomparable, peerless, matchless, sensational
colloq. smashing, terrific, top-notch, neat, ace, brill; *slang* mega, cool, wicked
🖅 poor; *colloq.* lousy

superannuated *adj*
antiquated, old, elderly, pensioned off, obsolete, senile, retired, aged, decrepit
formal moribund
colloq. past it, put out to grass
🖅 young

superb *adj*
excellent, first-rate, first-class, superior, superlative, choice, fine, exquisite, brilliant, gorgeous, magnificent, splendid, lavish, grand, wonderful, great, outstanding, remarkable, unrivalled, unsurpassed, marvellous, admirable, impressive, breathtaking, dazzling
colloq. fabulous, smashing, terrific, neat, ace, brill
🖅 bad, poor, inferior

supercilious *adj*
arrogant, condescending, patronizing, overbearing, scornful, lofty, lordly, imperious, insolent, proud, disdainful, haughty, contemptuous
formal vainglorious
colloq. snooty, snotty, stuck-up, toffee-nosed, uppish, uppity, hoity-toity, jumped up, too big for your boots
🖅 humble, self-effacing

superficial *adj*
surface, external, exterior, peripheral, outward, outer, apparent, alleged, seeming, cosmetic, skin-deep, shallow, slight, trivial, facile, lightweight, insignificant, frivolous, casual, cursory, sketchy, careless, slapdash, perfunctory, hasty, hurried, passing
formal ostensible
🖅 internal, deep, thorough

superficially *adv*
externally, on the surface, apparently, seemingly, casually, carelessly, hurriedly
formal ostensibly
🖅 in depth

superfluity *n*
redundancy, excess, surfeit, surplus, extra, exuberance, glut, superabundance, excessiveness
technical pleonasm
formal plethora
🖅 lack

superfluous *adj*
extra, spare, excess, surplus, remaining, redundant, to spare, unnecessary, unneeded, needless, gratuitous, unwanted, unwarranted, uncalled-for, excessive
formal supernumerary
🖅 necessary, needed, required, wanted, essential

superhuman *adj*
great, immense, supernatural, herculean, heroic, stupendous, divine, paranormal, phenomenal
formal preternatural, prodigious
🖅 average, ordinary

superintend *v*
supervise, oversee, overlook, inspect, run, manage, administer, direct, be in charge of, be responsible for, control, be in control of, handle, steer

superintendence *n*
supervision, oversight, inspection, direction, control, government, charge, care, management, administration, running, guidance, surveillance

superintendent *n*
supervisor, overseer, director, governor, controller, conductor, administrator, manager, inspector, chief, curator
colloq. gaffer, boss

superior *adj, n*
▶ *adj* **1** EXCELLENT, first-class, first-rate, high-class, high-quality, exclusive, prime, quality, prize, choice, select, fine, de luxe, admirable, distinguished, exceptional, unrivalled, par excellence
colloq. top-notch, top-flight
2 BETTER, preferred, greater, higher, higher in rank, senior
3 HAUGHTY, lordly, lofty, pretentious, snobbish, supercilious, disdainful, condescending, patronizing
colloq. snooty, stuck-up, toffee-nosed, uppish, uppity, jumped up, too big for your boots
E3 1 inferior, average **2** inferior, worse, lower **3** humble, self-effacing
▶ *n* senior, elder, better, boss, chief, principal, director, manager, foreman, supervisor, chief
E3 subordinate, inferior, junior, assistant

superiority *n*
advantage, lead, edge, supremacy, pre-eminence, eminence, dominance, predominance
formal ascendancy
E3 inferiority

superlative *adj*
best, greatest, highest, first-class, first-rate, supreme, unbeatable, unrivalled, unparalleled, matchless, peerless, unsurpassed, unbeaten, excellent, brilliant, magnificent, outstanding
formal transcendent, consummate
colloq. ace, brill
E3 poor, average, mediocre

supernatural *adj*
paranormal, unnatural, abnormal, otherworldly, metaphysical, spiritual, psychic, mystic, mystical, occult, hidden, mysterious, miraculous, magical, magic, phantom, ghostly, eerie, weird
formal preternatural
E3 natural, normal

supernumerary *adj*
superfluous, surplus, redundant, spare, excess, excessive, extra, extraordinary
E3 necessary

supersede *v*
succeed, replace, supplant, usurp, oust, displace, take the place of, take over from, remove

superstition *n*
myth, old wives' tale, fallacy, delusion, illusion, magic

superstitious *adj*
mythical, false, fallacious, irrational, groundless, delusive, illusory
E3 rational, logical, factual

supervise *v*
oversee, watch (over), look after, keep an eye on, inspect, superintend, run, manage, administer, direct, guide, conduct, preside over, be in charge of, be responsible for, be in control of, control, handle

supervision *n*
surveillance, care, charge, superintendence, oversight, running, management, administration, direction, control, guidance, inspection, instruction

supervisor *n*
overseer, inspector, superintendent, boss, chief, director, administrator, manager, steward, foreman, forewoman

supervisory *adj*
administrative, managerial, executive, overseeing, superintendent
formal directorial

supine *adj*
1 PROSTRATE, flat, horizontal
formal recumbent
2 LAZY, idle, inactive, lethargic, careless, heedless, resigned, bored, uninterested, apathetic, indifferent, sluggish, slothful, inert, languid, negligent, passive, listless, spiritless, unresisting
formal indolent, torpid
colloq. spineless
E3 1 upright **2** alert

supper *n*
dinner, evening meal, tea, snack

supplant *v*
replace, supersede, usurp, oust, displace, take the place of, take over from, remove, overthrow, topple, unseat

supple *adj*
flexible, bending, stretching, elastic, pliant, pliable, plastic, lithe, supple, limber, graceful, loose-limbed, double-jointed
E3 stiff, rigid, inflexible

supplement *n, v*
▶ *n* addition, additive, extra, insert, pull-out, add-on, addendum, appendix, rider, postscript, sequel
technical codicil
▶ *v* add to, boost, reinforce, increase, fill up, top up, complement, extend, eke out
formal augment
E3 deplete, use up

⚠ **supplement, complement** or **compliment** ? *See panel at* **complement**.

supplementary *adj*
additional, extra, added, auxiliary, secondary, attached, complementary, accompanying

⚠ **supplementary, complementary** or **complimentary** ? *See panel at* **complementary**.

suppliant *adj*
begging, entreating, imploring, supplicating, craving
formal beseeching, importunate

supplicant *n*
petitioner, pleader, suitor, applicant, suppliant
formal postulant

supplicate *v*
request, entreat, appeal, petition, plead, pray, solicit
formal invoke, beseech

supplication *n*
request, appeal, entreaty, petition, plea, pleading, prayer, orison, suit
formal invocation, imploration, solicitation, rogation

supplicatory *adj*
begging, petitioning, supplicating, imploring
formal beseeching, imprecatory, precative, precatory

supplier *n*
dealer, seller, vendor, wholesaler, retailer, outfitter, provider, contributor, donor

supply *v, n*
▶ *v* provide, furnish, equip, outfit, fit out, stock, fill, replenish, give, donate, grant, endow, contribute, yield, produce, sell
formal endue, proffer
F3 take, receive
▶ *n* **1** STOCK, source, amount, quantity, fund, reservoir, store, reserve, heap, mass, pile, stockpile, hoard, cache
2 PROVISIONS, stores, food, rations, equipment, materials, necessities
F3 **1** lack

support *v, n*
▶ *v* **1** BACK, second, defend, champion, advocate, further, be in favour of, be in sympathy with, be behind/with, promote, foster, help, aid, assist, rally round
formal espouse
colloq. run with, throw your weight behind
2 HELP, encourage, comfort, motivate, befriend, care for, sympathize with, be kind to, give strength to, give moral support to, be supportive to
3 HOLD UP, bear, carry, take the weight of, sustain, brace, reinforce, strengthen, prop (up), shore up, buttress, underpin, bolster (up)
4 MAINTAIN, keep, look after, take care of, provide for, sustain, feed, nourish
5 *support a statement*
endorse, confirm, back up, bear out, verify, authenticate, substantiate, validate, ratify, document
formal corroborate
6 FINANCE, fund, subsidize, underwrite, back, sponsor, contribute to, give a donation to
F3 **1** oppose **4** live off **5** contradict
▶ *n* **1** BACKING, allegiance, loyalty, defence, protection, patronage, approval, encouragement, comfort, relief, help, aid, assistance
formal espousal
2 PROP, stay, post, pillar, brace, buttress, bolster, trestle, crutch, foundation(s), underpinning, substructure, skeleton, base
3 HELP, encouragement, comfort, care, sympathy, motivation, strength, friendship, moral support
colloq. tower of strength
4 MAINTENANCE, keep, provision, sustenance, food, subsistence
5 FINANCE, funding, sponsorship, grant, donation, subsidy, contribution, patronage
6 EVIDENCE, confirmation, backing, verification, authentication, substantiation, validation, ratification
F3 **1** opposition, hostility

supporter *n*
fan, follower, adherent, advocate, champion, defender, promoter, sympathizer, seconder, patron, sponsor, donor, contributor, partner, co-worker, helper, ally, friend, voter, well-wisher, apologist
F3 opponent

supportive *adj*
helpful, caring, attentive, sympathetic, understanding, comforting, reassuring, encouraging
F3 discouraging

suppose *v*
1 THINK, guess, believe, consider, imagine, reckon, fancy, judge, expect, infer, conclude, take for granted
formal conjecture, surmise
2 ASSUME, presume, imply, require
formal postulate, hypothesize, posit, presuppose

supposed *adj*
alleged, reported, rumoured, assumed, presumed, reputed, so-called, believed, imagined, hypothetical
formal putative
▷ **supposed to** meant to, intended to, expected to, required to, obliged to

supposition *n*
assumption, presumption, guess, speculation, theory, idea, notion
formal conjecture, surmise, postulation, hypothesis, presupposition
F3 knowledge

suppress *v*
crush, stamp out, put an end to, quash, squash, quell, subdue, stop, silence, censor, stifle, smother, strangle, conceal, withhold, hold back, control, keep under control, contain, restrain, check, keep in check, repress, inhibit
formal vanquish
colloq. crack/clamp down on
F3 encourage, incite

suppression *n*
crushing, quashing, quelling, elimination, prohibition, censorship, check, inhibition, dissolution, smothering, cover-up, termination, extinction
colloq. clampdown, crackdown
F3 encouragement, incitement

suppurate *v*
gather, discharge, fester, ooze, weep
technical maturate

suppuration *n*
festering, pus, mattering
technical diapyesis

supremacy *n*
dominance, domination, dominion, mastery, lordship, rule, power, control, predominance, primacy, sovereignty, sway, pre-eminence
formal ascendancy, hegemony, paramountcy

supreme *adj*
1 GREATEST, best, highest, excellent, top, crowning, culminating, first, first-rate, first-class, leading, foremost, chief, principal, head, sovereign, pre-eminent, predominant, prevailing, world-beating, unsurpassed, second-to-none, incomparable, peerless, matchless, consummate, transcendent, superlative, prime
2 *the supreme sacrifice*
utmost, extreme, ultimate, final, last, greatest, highest
F3 **1** lowly, poor

sure *adj*
1 CERTAIN, convinced, assured, confident, decided, positive, definite, unmistakable, unfaltering, unwavering, clear, accurate, precise, unquestionable, indisputable, undoubted, undeniable, irrevocable, inevitable, guaranteed, bound
colloq. as sure as eggs is eggs
2 SAFE, secure, fast, solid, firm, steady, stable, guaranteed, reliable, dependable, tested, loyal, faithful, trustworthy, steadfast, unwavering, unerring, unfailing, never-failing, infallible, effective, foolproof

formal efficacious
colloq. home and dry, sure-fire, sure-footed, safe as houses
F3 1 unsure, uncertain, hesitating, doubtful
2 unsafe, insecure

surely *adv*
certainly, without doubt, doubtlessly, undoubtedly, unquestionably, indubitably, definitely, assuredly, firmly, confidently, inevitably, inexorably

surety *n*
guarantee, indemnity, pledge, security, safety, warrant, warranty, certainty, bail, insurance, mortgagor, sponsor, bond, deposit, guarantor, hostage, bondsman

surface *n, v, adj*
▶ *n* outside, outward appearance, exterior, façade, veneer, covering, skin, top, side, face, plane
F3 inside, interior
▷ **on the surface** superficially, externally, apparently, seemingly; *formal* ostensibly
▶ *v* rise, arise, come up, come to the surface, emerge, appear, reappear, materialize, come to light
F3 sink, disappear, vanish
▶ *adj* superficial, outer, outside, outward, exterior, external, apparent
F3 interior

surfeit *n, v*
▶ *n* surplus, superfluity, excess, glut, satiety, superabundance, overindulgence
formal plethora
colloq. bellyful
F3 lack
▶ *v* fill, overfill, overfeed, stuff, cram, glut, gorge, satiate

surge *n, v*
▶ *n* **1** RUSH, gush, stream, sweep, pouring, flow, wave(s), billow, breaker, roller, swell, eddy
formal efflux
2 INCREASE, upswing, upsurge, rise, escalation, intensification
▶ *v* **1** RUSH, gush, stream, sweep, pour, flow, break, swell, swirl, eddy, heave, roll, seethe
2 INCREASE, rise, escalate

surgeon *n*

Types of surgeon include: brain surgeon, cosmetic surgeon, dental surgeon, eye surgeon, general surgeon, heart surgeon, house surgeon, neurosurgeon, oral surgeon, plastic surgeon, tree surgeon, veterinary surgeon.

surly *adj*
gruff, brusque, churlish, ungracious, uncivil, ill-natured, bad-tempered, cross, grouchy, crusty, grumpy, testy, cantankerous, irascible, sullen, sulky, morose
colloq. crabbed, crotchety
F3 friendly, polite

surmise *v, n*
▶ *v* infer, suppose, presume, assume, conclude, deduce, imagine, fancy, guess, consider, speculate, suspect
formal conjecture, opine
F3 know
▶ *n* inference, conclusion, deduction, assumption, presumption, speculation, guess, idea, suspicion, thought, opinion, notion, possibility

formal conjecture, hypothesis, supposition
F3 certainty

surmount *v*
overcome, get over, conquer, master, triumph over, prevail over, surpass, exceed
formal vanquish

surpass *v*
beat, outdo, exceed, outstrip, outclass, better, excel, transcend, tower above, outshine, overshadow, eclipse

surpassing *adj*
exceptional, incomparable, outstanding, matchless, unrivalled, unsurpassed, rare, inimitable, extraordinary, supreme, phenomenal, transcendent
F3 poor

surplus *n, adj*
▶ *n* excess, residue, remainder, balance, superfluity, glut, surfeit, leftovers
F3 lack, shortage
▶ *adj* excess, superfluous, redundant, extra, spare, remaining, unused, left over

surprise *v, n*
▶ *v* **1** AMAZE, startle, astonish, astound, stagger, take aback, stun, bewilder, confuse, disconcert, dismay
colloq. flabbergast, nonplus, bowl over, wow, knock for six, knock someone down with a feather, take someone's breath away
2 CATCH RED-HANDED, catch in the act, catch unawares, expose, unmask, startle, burst in on, find (out)
colloq. catch someone with their pants/trousers down
▶ *n* amazement, astonishment, incredulity, wonder, bewilderment, dismay, shock, start, revelation
colloq. bombshell, thunderbolt, bolt from the blue
F3 composure

Expressions of surprise include: bless my soul!, blow me down!, by Jove!, come off it!, did you ever!, fancy that!, for goodness sake!, for heaven's sake!, good heavens!, Gordon Bennett!, great Scott!, heavens above!, holy smoke!, how about that, then!, I ask you!, I don't know!, I'll be blessed!, I'll be damned!, imagine that!, in heaven's name!, just a moment!, my eye!, my foot!, my goodness!, my word!, no kidding!, of all the …!, oh mother!, oh my!, stone me!, that'll be the day!, that's news to me!, the (very) idea!, to think!, well, did you ever!, well, I'll be blowed!, well I never!, wonders will never cease!, would you believe!, you don't say!, you're joking!, you're kidding!

surprised *adj*
startled, amazed, astonished, astounded, staggered, thunderstruck, dumbfounded, speechless, lost for words, open-mouthed, shocked, stunned
colloq. flabbergasted, nonplussed, gobsmacked
F3 unsurprised, composed

surprising *adj*
amazing, astonishing, astounding, staggering, stunning, incredible, extraordinary, remarkable, wonderful, startling, unexpected, unforeseen, unlooked-for
F3 unsurprising, expected

surrender *v, n*
▶ *v* capitulate, submit, resign, concede, yield, give in, cede, give up, leave behind, let go of, relinquish, abandon, renounce, abdicate, forego, waive
formal succumb

colloq. quit, throw in the towel/sponge
▶ *n* capitulation, resignation, submission, yielding, relinquishment, renunciation, abandonment, abdication, waiving
formal cession

surreptitious *adj*
furtive, stealthy, sly, covert, veiled, hidden, secret, underhand, unauthorized
formal clandestine
colloq. sneaky
⊟ open, obvious

surrogate *n*
substitute, replacement, representative, stand-in, deputy, proxy

surround *v*
encircle, ring, go round, gird, girdle, encompass, confine, envelop, encase, enclose, fence in, hem in, besiege, beset
formal environ

surrounding *adj*
encircling, bordering, adjacent, adjoining, neighbouring, nearby

surroundings *n*
neighbourhood, vicinity, locality, scene, setting, environment, habitat, environs, background, milieu, element, ambience

surveillance *n*
watch, observation, inspection, superintendence, supervision, vigilance, stewardship, guardianship, monitoring, scrutiny, check, care, charge, control, direction, regulation

survey *v, n*
▶ *v* 1 VIEW, contemplate, observe, look at, look over, supervise, scan, scrutinize, examine, inspect, study, research, poll, review, consider
2 ASSESS, estimate, evaluate, measure, plot, plan, map, chart, reconnoitre
formal appraise
colloq. size up, recce
▶ *n* 1 REVIEW, overview, scrutiny, examination, inspection, consideration, study, poll, appraisal, assessment, measurement, valuation
2 QUESTIONNAIRE, quiz, test, form, study, probe, opinion poll, market research

surveyor *n*
inspector, examiner, assessor
technical geodesist

survive *v*
outlive, outlast, endure, last, continue, persist, stay, remain, live (on), exist, withstand, hold out, cope, manage, weather, recover, rally
formal be extant
colloq. pull through, make it, keep your head above water
⊟ succumb, die

susceptibility *n*
liability, openness, vulnerability, defencelessness, weakness, proneness, responsiveness, sensitivity, suggestibility, gullibility, tendency
formal predisposition, proclivity, propensity
⊟ impregnability, resistance

susceptible *adj*
liable, prone, inclined, disposed, given, subject, receptive, responsive, impressionable, easily led, credulous, gullible, suggestible, weak, vulnerable,

defenceless, open, sensitive, tender
⊟ resistant, immune

suspect *v, adj*
▶ *v* 1 DOUBT, have doubts about, distrust, mistrust, be wary of, have misgivings/qualms about, be uneasy about, call into question
old use misdoubt
colloq. smell a rat
2 *I suspect you're right*
believe, fancy, feel, guess, suppose, speculate, consider, conclude, infer
formal conjecture, surmise
colloq. have a hunch, get it into your head
▶ *adj* suspicious, doubtful, dubious, questionable, debatable, unreliable
colloq. iffy, dodgy, fishy
⊟ acceptable, reliable

suspend *v*
1 HANG, dangle, swing
2 ADJOURN, interrupt, delay, defer, postpone, put off, arrest, shelve, pigeonhole
formal discontinue, cease, put in abeyance, prorogue
colloq. put on ice, put on the back burner, take a raincheck on
3 EXPEL, dismiss, exclude, remove, debar, keep out, shut out, unfrock
⊟ 2 continue, carry on 3 restore, reinstate

suspended *adj*
1 HANGING, dangling
formal pendent, pensile
2 POSTPONED, delayed, deferred, put off, shelved, pending
colloq. put on ice

suspense *n*
uncertainty, insecurity, doubt, doubtfulness, anxiety, tension, nervousness, apprehension, anticipation, expectation, expectancy, excitement
⊟ certainty, knowledge

suspension *n*
1 ADJOURNMENT, interruption, break, intermission, respite, remission, stay, moratorium, delay, deferral, deferment, postponement
formal cessation, abeyance
2 EXPULSION, dismissal, exclusion, removal, debarment, unfrocking
⊟ 1 continuation

suspicion *n*
1 DOUBT, scepticism, distrust, mistrust, chariness, wariness, qualm(s), caution, misgiving(s), apprehension
2 TRACE, hint, suggestion, soupçon, touch, tinge, shade, glimmer, shadow, scintilla
3 IDEA, notion, feeling, belief, opinion
colloq. hunch, sixth sense, funny feeling
⊟ 1 trust

suspicious *adj*
1 DOUBTFUL, sceptical, unbelieving, disbelieving, suspecting, unsure, distrustful, mistrustful, wary, chary, apprehensive, uneasy
2 DUBIOUS, questionable, suspect, irregular, strange, odd, funny, peculiar, dishonest, guilty, shifty
colloq. shady, dodgy, fishy, iffy
⊟ 1 trustful, confident 2 trustworthy, innocent

sustain *v*
1 NOURISH, feed, provide for, nurture, foster, help, aid, assist, comfort, encourage, relieve, support,

uphold, give strength to, endorse, bear, carry
2 MAINTAIN, keep going, keep up, carry on, continue, prolong, hold
formal protract
3 SUFFER, go through, experience, undergo, endure, receive, happen to

sustained *adj*
prolonged, long-drawn-out, steady, continuous, continuing, constant, perpetual
formal protracted, unremitting
E∃ broken, interrupted, intermittent, spasmodic

sustenance *n*
nourishment, food, provisions, fare, maintenance, subsistence, support, livelihood
formal refection, aliment, comestibles, provender, viands, victuals
colloq. grub, nosh, scoff

svelte *adj*
slender, slim, lithe, elegant, graceful, lissom, willowy, sylphlike, shapely, sophisticated, urbane, polished
E∃ bulky, ungainly

swagger *v, n*
▶ *v* bluster, boast, crow, brag, prance, parade, strut
colloq. swank, show off, play to the gallery, make an exhibition of yourself, go over the top
▶ *n* bluster, show, ostentation, arrogance, prancing, parading

swallow *v*
1 CONSUME, devour, eat, gobble up, drink, quaff, gulp
formal ingest
colloq. guzzle, knock back, down, scoff, swig, polish off
2 ACCEPT, believe, trust, be certain of
colloq. buy, fall for, swallow hook line and sinker
3 STIFLE, smother, repress, hold back, contain, suppress
4 TOLERATE, put up with, accept, endure, stand, take, abide, bear
colloq. stomach
▷ **swallow up** overwhelm, overrun, engulf, enfold, envelop, absorb, assimilate

swamp *n, v*
▶ *n* bog, marsh, fen, slough, quagmire, quag, quicksand, mire, morass, mud
▶ *v* flood, inundate, deluge, engulf, submerge, sink, drench, saturate, waterlog, wash out, weigh down, overload, overwhelm, besiege, beset

swampy *adj*
boggy, marshy, wet, miry, fenny, soggy, quaggy, squelchy, waterlogged
formal paludal, uliginous
E∃ arid, dehydrated, dry

swank *v, n*
▶ *v* brag, boast, show off, strut, swagger, parade, posture, preen yourself, attitudinize
▶ *n* bragging, boastfulness, pretentiousness, showing-off, show, display, ostentation, conceit, conceitedness, swagger, self-advertisement
formal vainglory
E∃ modesty, restraint

swanky *adj*
glamorous, ostentatious, fashionable, expensive, luxurious, rich, lavish, smart, grand, stylish, showy, exclusive, de luxe, sumptuous, fancy, pretentious
colloq. flash, flashy, plush, plushy, posh, ritzy, swish
E∃ discreet, unobtrusive

swap, swop *v*
exchange, transpose, switch, interchange, substitute, barter, trade, bandy, traffic

swarm *n, v*
▶ *n* crowd, throng, mob, mass, stream, body, multitude, myriad, host, army, horde, pack, herd, flock, drove, shoal
▶ *v* flock, flood, surge, stream, mass, congregate, crowd, throng
▷ **be swarming with** be crowded with, be teeming with, be overrun with, be crawling with, be bristling with, be thronged with, abound in

swarthy *adj*
dark, dark-complexioned, dark-skinned, tanned, dusky, brown, black
E∃ fair, pale

swashbuckling *adj*
daring, courageous, adventurous, bold, spirited, swaggering, exciting, gallant, flamboyant, dare-devil, dashing, robust
E∃ tame, unadventurous, unexciting

swathe *v*
wrap, bandage, bind, wind, cloak, envelop, drape, enshroud, enwrap, fold, shroud, swaddle, lap, sheathe, furl
E∃ unwind, unwrap

sway *v, n*
▶ *v* **1** ROCK, roll, reel, lurch, stagger, swing, wave, shake, wobble, oscillate, fluctuate, bend, incline, lean, divert, veer, swerve
2 INFLUENCE, affect, persuade, win over, bring round, induce, convince, convert, overrule, rule, direct, dominate, govern
formal prevail upon
▶ *n* control, command, authority, power, influence, leadership, government, rule, sovereignty, dominion, predominance, jurisdiction
technical hegemony
formal ascendancy, preponderance
colloq. clout

swear *v*
1 VOW, promise, promise solemnly, pledge, pledge yourself, take an oath, be on/under oath, take the oath, testify, affirm, assert, declare, insist
formal avow, attest, asseverate, aver, abjure
2 CURSE, blaspheme, utter profanities, use bad language, blind, take the Lord's name in vain, turn the air blue
formal imprecate, maledict
colloq. cuss, eff, eff and blind
▷ **swear by** believe in, trust in, depend on, rely on, have confidence in, have faith in

swearing *n*
bad language, foul language, cursing, profanity, expletives, blasphemy
technical coprolalia
formal imprecations, maledictions
colloq. cussing, effing and blinding

swear-word *n*
expletive, four-letter word, curse, oath, obscenity, profanity, blasphemy, swearing, bad language, foul language
formal imprecation

sweat *n, v*
▶ *n* **1** PERSPIRATION, moisture, stickiness
technical sudor, diaphoresis, hidrosis

Related adjective: sudatory
2 ANXIETY, worry, agitation, panic, fuss, dither
colloq. fluster, flap, tizzy
3 TOIL, labour, drudgery, chore, effort
▶ *v* perspire, secrete, swelter, drip, break out in a sweat
technical sudate
formal exude
colloq. sweat like a pig, sweat buckets

sweaty *adj*
damp, moist, clammy, sticky, sweating, perspiring
F3 dry, cool

sweep *v, n*
▶ *v* **1** *sweep the floor*
brush, dust, clean (up), clear (up), remove, vacuum
2 PUSH, thrust, drive, move quickly, spread quickly, force, shove, drag, jostle, elbow, poke
3 PASS, sail, fly, glide, scud, skim, glance, whisk, race, whip, tear, hurtle
▶ *n* **1** ARC, curve, bend, swing, stroke, move, movement, action, gesture, stroke
formal curvature
2 SCOPE, compass, range, extent, span, stretch, vastness, immensity, expanse, vista

sweeping *adj*
general, global, all-inclusive, all-embracing, broad, wide, wide-ranging, extensive, far-reaching, comprehensive, thorough, thoroughgoing, radical, wholesale, indiscriminate, oversimplified, simplistic
colloq. blanket, across-the-board
F3 specific, narrow

sweepstake *n*
draw, lottery, gambling, sweep, sweepstakes

sweet *adj, n*
▶ *adj* **1** SUGARY, syrupy, sickly, sickly sweet, sweetened, honeyed, candied, glacé, saccharine, luscious, delicious, ripe
2 AROMATIC, fragrant, perfumed, balmy, sweet-scented
formal ambrosial, odoriferous, odorous, redolent
3 *sweet music*
melodious, tuneful, harmonious, sweet-sounding, euphonious, musical, dulcet, soft, mellow
formal mellifluous
4 PLEASANT, delightful, pleasing, lovely, attractive, beautiful, pretty, winsome, winning, cute, engaging, appealing, likeable, lovable, adorable, charming, agreeable, amiable, affectionate, tender, kind, kindly, treasured, precious, cherished, dear, darling
5 FRESH, clean, wholesome, pure, clear
F3 **1** savoury, salty, sour, bitter **2** foul
3 discordant **4** unpleasant, nasty, ugly **5** foul
▷ **sweet on** fond of, liking, keen on, having a soft spot for, infatuated with, ravished with; *colloq.* crazy about, mad about, far gone on
▶ *n* **1** DESSERT, pudding
colloq. afters
2 BONBON, candy, sweetmeat, confectionery
formal confection
colloq. sweetie

Sweets include: barley sugar, bull's eye, butterscotch, caramel, chewing-gum, chocolate, fondant, fruit pastille, fudge, gobstopper, gumdrop, humbug, jelly, jelly bean, Kit-Kat®, liquorice, liquorice allsort, lollipop, Mars®, marshmallow, marzipan, nougat, peppermint, praline, rock, Edinburgh rock, toffee, toffee apple, truffle, Turkish delight.

sweeten *v*
1 SUGAR, add sugar to, honey
2 MELLOW, soften, soothe, mollify, appease
3 TEMPER, cushion, alleviate, ease, relieve
formal mitigate
F3 **2** sour, embitter

sweetheart *n*
darling, dear, boyfriend, girlfriend, love, lover, truelove, suitor, valentine, admirer, beloved, betrothed, follower, inamorata, inamorato, Romeo
old use swain
colloq. flame, steady, sweetie

sweetness *n*
1 SUGARINESS, syrup, succulence, lusciousness, mellowness, freshness
2 FRAGRANCE, balminess, aroma
3 KINDNESS, amiability, winsomeness, tenderness, sweet temper, love, loveliness, charm
4 HARMONY, euphony
formal dulcitude
F3 **1** saltness, sourness, bitterness, acidity
2 foulness **3** nastiness **4** cacophony

sweet-smelling *adj*
aromatic, fragrant, perfumed, balmy, sweet-scented
formal ambrosial, odoriferous, odorous, redolent
F3 fetid, malodorous

swell *v, n, adj*
▶ *v* **1** EXPAND, inflate, blow up, puff up, bloat, fatten, bulge, balloon, billow
formal dilate, distend
2 RISE, surge, mount, increase, enlarge, grow larger, escalate, extend, grow, step up, accelerate, mushroom, proliferate, snowball, skyrocket, heighten, intensify
formal augment
F3 **1** shrink, contract **2** decrease, dwindle
▶ *n* **1** BILLOW, wave, undulation, surge, rise, increase, enlargement
2 DANDY, fop, beau, dude, cockscomb
colloq. bigwig
F3 **2** down-and-out, scarecrow, tramp
▶ *adj* great, grand, smart, stylish, exclusive, fashionable, de luxe
colloq. flashy, posh, ritzy, swanky
F3 seedy, shabby

swelling *n*
lump, tumour, bump, bruise, blister, boil, inflammation, bulge, protuberance, puffiness, enlargement
formal distension, tumescence

sweltering *adj*
hot, tropical, baking, boiling, roasting, scorching, torrid, stifling, suffocating, airless, oppressive, sultry, clammy, muggy, steamy, sticky, humid
colloq. baking, roasting, sizzling
F3 cold, cool, fresh, breezy, airy

swerve *v*
change direction suddenly, turn, bend, incline, veer, swing, twist, shift, deviate, stray, wander, diverge, deflect, skew, sheer

swift *adj*
fast, quick, rapid, brisk, speedy, express, flying, hurried, hasty, short, brief, sudden, abrupt, immediate, prompt, ready, agile, lively, nimble
old use fleet
formal expeditious

colloq. nippy
▰ slow, sluggish, unhurried

swiftly *adj*
quickly, posthaste, fast, rapidly, speedily, express,
hurriedly, instantly, promptly, at full tilt
formal expeditiously
colloq. double-quick, hotfoot
▰ slowly; *formal* tardily

swiftness *n*
quickness, rapidity, speed, speediness, suddenness,
velocity, immediacy, immediateness, instantaneity,
readiness, promptness, dispatch
old use fleetness
formal alacrity, celerity, expedition
▰ delay, slowness; *formal* tardiness

swill *v, n*
▶ *v* drink, swallow, swig, quaff, gulp, guzzle, drain,
consume
formal imbibe
colloq. knock back, toss off
▷ **swill out** wash out, wash down, rinse, clean,
cleanse, drench, flush, sluice
▶ *n* **1** DRINK, gulp, swallow, swig
2 WASTE, slops, hogwash, pigswill, scourings, refuse

swim *v*
bathe, take a dip, tread water, float, bob, snorkel
Related adjective: natatorial

The main swimming strokes include: backstroke,
breaststroke, butterfly, crawl, doggy-paddle,
sidestroke

swimming-pool *n*
swimming-bath, leisure pool, lido, swimming-pond

swimsuit *n*
swimming costume, bathing costume, bathing suit,
bikini, trunks

swindle *v, n*
▶ *v* cheat, defraud, diddle, overcharge, exploit, fleece,
trick, deceive, dupe
colloq. do, rip off, con, bamboozle, sting, rook, do one
over on, take for a ride, take to the cleaners, pull the
wool over someone's eyes
▶ *n* fraud, fiddle, diddle, racket, sharp practice,
double-dealing, trickery, deception
colloq. con, rip-off, scam

swindler *n*
cheat, fraud, fiddler, impostor, trickster, rogue, rascal,
charlatan, mountebank
colloq. con man, shark, rook, hustler, hood, hoodlum

swine *n*
1 PIG, beast, boar, hog
2 SCOUNDREL, rogue, rascal, good-for-nothing,
brute, boor

swing *v, n*
▶ *v* **1** HANG, dangle, wave, spin, rotate, pivot, sway,
rock
2 SWERVE, veer, turn, twist, wind, curve, bend,
incline, lean, oscillate, fluctuate, change, vary
formal pendulate
3 ARRANGE, achieve, get, set up, make, organize
colloq. fix (up)
▶ *n* sway, rock, oscillation, waving, vibration,
fluctuation, variation, change, shift, move, movement,
motion, stroke, rhythm

swingeing *adj*
harsh, severe, stringent, drastic, serious, punishing,
devastating, excessive, extortionate, exorbitant,
oppressive, heavy, draconian
colloq. thumping
▰ mild

swinging *adj*
lively, exciting, dynamic, fashionable, contemporary,
modern, up-to-date, up-to-the-minute, stylish
colloq. jet-setting, trendy, with it; *slang* hip
▰ old-fashioned, fuddy-duddy

swipe *v, n*
▶ *v* **1** HIT, strike, lunge, lash out, slap
colloq. whack, wallop, sock, biff, clout
2 STEAL, pilfer, lift
colloq. pinch, whip, nick, filch
▶ *n* stroke, blow, slap, smack
colloq. clout, whack, wallop, biff

swirl *v*
churn, agitate, spin, revolve, circulate, twirl, whirl,
wheel, eddy, twist, curl

swish¹ *v*
the horses swished their tails
flourish, whisk, swing, swirl, thrash, flog, lash, birch,
whip, rustle, twirl, whizz, swoosh, wave, brandish,
whirl, whistle, whoosh

swish² *adj*
a swish hotel
smart, grand, fashionable, exclusive, plush, stylish,
elegant, sumptuous, de luxe
colloq. flash, posh, ritzy, swanky, swell
▰ seedy, shabby

switch *v, n*
▶ *v* change, exchange, swap, trade, barter,
interchange, substitute, replace, shift, rearrange, turn,
put, veer, deviate, divert, deflect
formal transpose
colloq. chop and change
▶ *n* **1** CHANGE, alteration, shift, exchange, swap,
interchange, substitution, replacement, reversal,
about-turn
2 TWIG, shoot, branch, cane, rod, birch, lash, twitch,
whisk, whip, thong

swivel *v*
pivot, spin, rotate, revolve, turn, twirl, pirouette,
gyrate, wheel

swollen *adj*
bloated, inflated, tumid, puffed up, puffy, inflamed,
enlarged, expanded, bulbous, bulging
formal distended, dilated, tumescent
▰ shrunken, shrivelled

swoop *v, n*
▶ *v* dive, plunge, drop, fall, descend, stoop, pounce,
lunge, rush
▶ *n* dive, plunge, drop, descent, pounce, lunge, rush,
attack, onslaught

swop *see* **swap**.

sword *n*
blade, foil, rapier, sabre, scimitar, steel, épée, katana
▷ **cross swords** disagree, argue, quarrel, fight,
contend, dispute, contest, wrangle, bicker, be at odds,
be at loggerheads

sworn *adj*
devoted, confirmed, eternal, implacable, inveterate,

relentless
formal attested

swot *v*
study, work, learn, memorize, revise, cram
colloq. mug up, bone up, burn the midnight oil

sybarite *n*
parasite, pleasurer, pleasure-seeker, sensualist, bon
vivant, epicure, epicurean, hedonist, playboy,
voluptuary, one of the idle rich
E∃ ascetic, toiler

sybaritic *adj*
easy, pleasure-loving, pleasure-seeking, self-
indulgent, sensual, voluptuous, hedonistic, epicurean,
luxurious, parasitic
E∃ ascetic

sycophancy *n*
cringing, fawning, flattery, toadyism, grovelling,
servility, slavishness, kowtowing, backscratching,
adulation, truckling
formal obsequiousness
colloq. bootlicking; *slang* arse-licking

sycophant *n*
cringer, fawner, flatterer, groveller, backscratcher,
slave, parasite, hanger-on, toady, toad-eater, truckler
colloq. bootlicker, sponger, yes-man; *slang* arse-licker

sycophantic *adj*
cringing, fawning, flattering, grovelling, servile,
slavish, ingratiating, parasitical, backscratching, slimy,
toad-eating, toadying, time-serving, unctuous,
truckling
formal obsequious
colloq. bootlicking, smarmy; *slang* arse-licking

syllabus *n*
curriculum, course, programme, schedule, plan,
outline

syllogism *n*
deduction, argument, proposition
technical epicheirema

sylph-like *adj*
slim, slight, slender, elegant, graceful, lithe, willowy,
streamlined, svelte
E∃ bulky, plump

symbiotic *adj*
co-operative, interactive, interdependent
technical endophytic, epizoan, epizoic, epizootic
formal commensal, synergetic

symbol *n*
sign, token, representation, mark, emblem, badge,
logo, character, ideograph, figure, image
formal type

Symbols include: badge, brand, cipher, coat of arms,
crest, emblem, hieroglyph, icon, ideogram, insignia,
logo, logogram, monogram, motif, pictograph,
swastika, token, totem, trademark; ampersand,
asterisk, caret, dagger, double-dagger, obelus.

symbolic *adj*
symbolical, representative, typical, illustrative,
emblematic, token, figurative, metaphorical,
allegorical, meaningful, significant

symbolize *v*
represent, stand for, denote, mean, signify, typify,

exemplify, epitomize, personify
formal betoken

symmetrical *adj*
balanced, even, regular, well-proportioned, parallel,
uniform, consistent, harmonious, corresponding,
proportional
E∃ asymmetrical, irregular

symmetry *n*
balance, evenness, regularity, parallelism,
correspondence, proportion(s), harmony, uniformity,
consistency, agreement
formal congruity
E∃ asymmetry, irregularity

sympathetic *adj*
understanding, appreciative, supportive, comforting,
encouraging, consoling, commiserating, pitying,
interested, concerned, caring, compassionate,
tolerant, tender, kind, kindly, warm, warm-hearted,
kind-hearted, well-disposed, affectionate, agreeable,
favourable, considerate, solicitous, friendly, pleasant,
likeable, companionable, congenial, sociable,
neighbourly, like-minded, compatible
formal solicitous
E∃ unsympathetic, indifferent, callous, antipathetic

sympathetically *adv*
appreciatively, supportively, understandingly,
compassionately, comfortingly, consolingly,
responsively, sensitively, warmly, warm-heartedly,
feelingly, kindly, pityingly

sympathize *v*
understand, comfort, console, encourage, be
supportive, appreciate, show concern/interest, care
for, offer condolences, commiserate, pity, feel sorry for,
feel for, your heart goes out, empathize, identify with,
respond to
E∃ ignore, disregard

sympathizer *n*
supporter, friend in need, condoler, admirer, backer,
adherent, well-wisher, fan, fellow-traveller, partisan
E∃ enemy, opponent, adversary

sympathy *n*
1 UNDERSTANDING, comfort, encouragement,
support, appreciation, consolation, condolences,
commiseration, pity, compassion, tenderness,
kindness, warmth, warm-heartedness, thoughtfulness,
empathy, fellow-feeling, closeness, consideration,
affinity, rapport
formal solace
2 AGREEMENT, approval, correspondence,
harmony
formal accord, approbation
E∃ 1 indifference, insensitivity, callousness
2 disagreement

symptom *n*
sign, indication, signal, evidence, expression, display,
demonstration, note, feature, characteristic, mark,
token, warning
technical prodrome, prodromus
formal manifestation

symptomatic *adj*
indicative, typical, characteristic, associated,
suggesting, suggestive

syndicate *n*
association, alliance, combination, group, bloc, cartel,
ring, combine

synonymous *adj*
interchangeable, substitutable, the same, identical, similar, comparable, tantamount, equivalent, corresponding
E3 antonymous, opposite

synopsis *n*
outline, abstract, summary, sketch, résumé, précis, condensation, digest, abridgement, review, recapitulation, compendium
formal summation, conspectus
colloq. run-down

synthesis *n*
amalgamation, combination, compound, fusion, integration, union, welding, blend, alloy, amalgam, coalescence, composite, pastiche
formal unification

synthesize *v*
unite, combine, amalgamate, integrate, merge, blend, compound, alloy, fuse, weld, coalesce, unify
E3 separate, analyse, resolve

synthetic *adj*
manufactured, man-made, simulated, artificial, ersatz, imitation, fake, bogus, mock, sham, pseudo
E3 genuine, real, natural

syrupy *adj*
1 SWEET, sugary, sickly sweet, sweetened, honeyed, saccharine
2 SENTIMENTAL, emotional, loving, gushing, sugary, pathetic, tear-jerking, maudlin, mawkish, romantic, affectionate, sloppy, soppy
colloq. weepy, lovey-dovey, slushy, mushy, schmaltzy, corny, sickly, gushy

system *n*
1 METHOD, technique, procedure, process, routine, practice, approach, way, means, usage, rule, *modus operandi*
formal mode
2 ORGANIZATION, structure, set-up, systematization, co-ordination, orderliness, methodology, logic, classification, arrangement, network, framework, order, plan, scheme, apparatus, mechanism

systematic *adj*
methodical, logical, ordered, well-ordered, planned, well-planned, organized, well-organized, structured, systematized, standardized, scientific, orderly, businesslike, efficient
E3 unsystematic, arbitrary, disorderly, inefficient

systematize *v*
arrange, order, structure, plan, organize, rationalize, methodize, standardize, schematize, regulate, regiment, classify, tabulate, make uniform
formal dispose

T

tab *n*
flap, tag, marker, label, sticker, ticket
▷ **keep tabs on** watch closely, keep an eye on, observe, keep a close watch on, keep a close check on

tabby *adj*
stripy, striped, streaked, wavy, mottled, variegated, banded, brindled

table *n, v*
▶ *n* **1** BOARD, slab, counter, bar, worktop, desk, bench, stand
2 DIAGRAM, chart, figure, graph, timetable, schedule, programme, plan, list, inventory, catalogue, tabulation, index, register, record
3 FOOD, board, diet, fare, dish, speciality, menu
colloq. tuck; *slang* grub, nosh; *US* chow
▶ *v* propose, suggest, submit, put forward, move

tableau *n*
representation, picture, portrayal, scene, spectacle, vignette, diorama, *tableau vivant*

tablet *n*
pill, capsule, lozenge, pellet, ball, bolus

taboo *adj, n*
▶ *adj* forbidden, prohibited, banned, ruled out, vetoed, sacrosanct, unacceptable, unmentionable, unthinkable
formal proscribed
🔁 permitted, acceptable
▶ *n* ban, prohibition, veto, restriction, anathema, curse
formal interdiction, proscription
🔁 permission, acceptance

tabulate *v*
order, arrange, arrange in columns, chart, classify, list, sort, systematize, table, catalogue, categorize, range, index, codify, tabularize

tacit *adj*
unspoken, unexpressed, unstated, unvoiced, silent, wordless, understood, implicit, implied, inferred
🔁 express, explicit

taciturn *adj*
silent, quiet, uncommunicative, unforthcoming, close-mouthed, tight-lipped, reticent, reserved, withdrawn, aloof, detached, distant, cold, dumb, mute
🔁 talkative, communicative, forthcoming

tack *n, v*
▶ *n* **1** NAIL, pin, drawing-pin, staple
US thumbtack
2 COURSE, path, bearing, heading, direction, line, line of action, course of action, approach, method, way, technique, procedure, process, policy, strategy, plan, tactic, attack
▶ *v* **1** ADD, append, attach, annex
2 FIX, fasten, affix, nail, pin, staple, stitch, sew, baste

tackle *n, v*
▶ *n* **1** *a rugby tackle*
attack, challenge, interception, intervention, block
2 EQUIPMENT, tools, implements, apparatus, rig, outfit, gear, things, trappings, paraphernalia, harness
formal accoutrements
colloq. stuff
▶ *v* **1** BEGIN, embark on, set about, go about, try, attempt, undertake, take on, challenge, confront, encounter, face up to, grapple with, get to grips with, apply yourself to, address, deal with, attend to, handle, grab, seize, grasp, take hold of
2 INTERCEPT, block, take, halt, stop, deflect, catch, grapple with, obstruct
🔁 **1** avoid, sidestep

tacky¹ *adj*
tacky paint
sticky, adhesive, gluey, gummy
colloq. gooey

tacky² *adj*
1 SHABBY, scruffy, tatty, threadbare, shoddy, dingy, tattered, ragged, untidy, messy, sloppy
colloq. grotty
2 TASTELESS, vulgar, tawdry, flashy, gaudy, kitschy
colloq. naff

tact *n*
tactfulness, diplomacy, discretion, prudence, delicacy, subtlety, sensitivity, perception, discernment, judgement, understanding, thoughtfulness, consideration, skill, dexterity, adroitness, finesse, *savoir-faire*
formal judiciousness
🔁 tactlessness, indiscretion

tactful *adj*
diplomatic, discreet, politic, prudent, careful, delicate, subtle, sensitive, perceptive, discerning, thoughtful, understanding, considerate, polite, skilful, adroit
formal judicious
🔁 tactless, indiscreet, thoughtless, rude

tactic *n*
1 APPROACH, course, course of action, way, means, method, procedure, plan, stratagem, scheme, ruse, ploy, subterfuge, trick, device, shift, expedient, move, manoeuvre
2 *military tactics*
strategy, campaign, plan, policy, approach, line of attack, moves, manoeuvres

tactical *adj*
strategic, planned, calculated, artful, cunning, shrewd, adroit, skilful, clever, smart, prudent, politic
formal judicious

tactician *n*
strategist, orchestrator, planner, politician, diplomat, director, campaigner, co-ordinator, mastermind
colloq. brain

tactless *adj*
undiplomatic, indiscreet, indelicate, unsubtle,
inappropriate, impolitic, imprudent, careless, clumsy,
awkward, blundering, gauche, insensitive, unfeeling,
hurtful, unkind, thoughtless, inconsiderate, rude,
rough, impolite, discourteous
formal injudicious, maladroit
Ea tactful, diplomatic, discreet

tactlessness *n*
insensitivity, impoliteness, indelicacy, indiscretion,
thoughtlessness, discourtesy, rudeness, ineptitude,
bad timing, clumsiness, gaucherie, boorishness
formal maladroitness
Ea tact, tactfulness, diplomacy

tag *n, v*
▶ *n* **1** LABEL, sticker, tab, ticket, mark,
identification, note, slip, docket
2 IDENTIFICATION, label, description, name, title,
nickname, epithet, badge
3 QUOTATION, saying, expression, phrase, maxim,
moral, motto, proverb, dictum, epithet, allusion,
stock phrase
colloq. quote
▶ *v* **1** LABEL, mark, identify, designate, term, title,
entitle, call, name, christen, nickname, style, dub
2 ADD, attach, append, annex, adjoin, affix, fasten,
tack
▷ **tag along** follow, shadow, tail, trail, accompany

tail *n, v*
▶ *n* **1** END, extremity, rear, rear end, bottom, back,
rump, appendage, conclusion
formal termination
colloq. behind, posterior, backside
Related adjective: caudal, cercal
2 DETECTIVE, (private) investigator
colloq. private eye, sleuth, gumshoe, shamus
▷ **turn tail** run away, escape, flee, abscond, decamp,
bolt; *colloq.* skedaddle, scarper, beat it
▶ *v* follow, pursue, shadow, dog, stalk, track, trail,
dog
▷ **tail off** decrease, decline, drop (off), fall away,
fade, wane, dwindle, taper off, peter out, die (out)
Ea increase, grow

tailor *n, v*
▶ *n* outfitter, dressmaker, costumer, costumier,
couturier, seamster, seamstress, modiste, clothier
Related adjective: sartorial
▶ *v* fit, suit, cut, trim, style, fashion, shape, mould,
alter, modify, convert, adapt, adjust, accommodate

tailor-made *adj*
made-to-measure, custom-built, bespoke, ideal,
perfect, right, suited, fitted
Ea off the peg, ready-made

taint *v, n*
▶ *v* contaminate, infect, pollute, adulterate, corrupt,
deprave, stain, blemish, blot, smear, tarnish, blacken,
dirty, soil, muddy, defile, sully, harm, damage, injure,
blight, spoil, ruin, shame, disgrace, dishonour
formal befoul
▶ *n* contamination, infection, contagion,
adulteration, pollution, corruption, stain, blemish,
fault, flaw, defect, spot, blot, smear, stain, stigma,
shame, disgrace, dishonour

take *v, n*
▶ *v* **1** SEIZE, grab, snatch, clutch, grasp, hold, get
hold of, grip, catch, capture, get, obtain, acquire,
secure, gain, receive, win, derive, adopt, assume, pick,
choose, select, decide on, settle on, accept, receive
formal procure
2 REMOVE, eliminate, take away, subtract, deduct,
steal, seize, kidnap, abduct, carry off, confiscate
formal purloin, appropriate
colloq. filch, nick, pinch, lift, have your fingers in the
till
3 *take me home*
convey, carry, bring, fetch, deliver, drive, transport,
ferry, accompany, escort, show, lead, guide, conduct,
usher, shepherd
formal bear
colloq. whisk
4 BEAR, tolerate, put up with, stand, stomach, abide,
endure, suffer, undergo, experience, withstand
5 *the journey takes 6 hours*
NEED, necessitate, require, demand, call for, use (up),
last
6 CAPTURE, win, seize, conquer, occupy
formal vanquish
7 *take pleasure in something*
derive, obtain, draw, gain, receive, attain, secure,
achieve, be given, come by, get
formal procure
8 *take the blame/responsibility*
accept, bear, be responsible for, admit, acknowledge,
undertake
9 CONSIDER, believe, assume, presume, suppose,
note, remember, examine, bear in mind
10 UNDERSTAND, comprehend, grasp, gather,
apprehend, follow, fathom (out)
colloq. cotton on, twig
11 *take the news badly*
react to, accept, respond to, cope with, deal with,
handle
12 *take him for a fool*
believe, think, consider, regard, look upon, view,
reckon, suppose, hold
formal deem
13 *the hall takes 400 people*
hold, contain, accommodate, seat, have a capacity of,
have room for, have space for
14 *take a measurement*
find out, discover, measure, establish, determine,
ascertain
15 BUY, purchase, rent, hire, lease, pay for, book,
receive
16 *take a subject at university*
study, learn, pursue, be taught, research, read, major in
17 *take the new road*
use, travel along, drive along, go along, follow
18 *take food/drink*
consume, swallow, eat, drink, devour
formal imbibe
colloq. tuck in, guzzle, scoff
19 *Will the drug take?*
succeed, work, produce results, be effective
formal be efficacious
Ea 1 leave, refuse **2** replace, put back **6** lose
15 sell **19** fail
▷ **take aback** surprise, astonish, astound, stagger,
stun, shock, startle, disconcert, bewilder, dismay,
upset
▷ **take after** resemble, look like, be like, be similar
to, favour, mirror, echo
▷ **take against** dislike, object to, disapprove of,
despise, regard with distaste
Ea take to
▷ **take apart** take to pieces, separate, dismantle,
analyse; *formal* disassemble

▷ **take back** 1 WITHDRAW, retract, recant, repudiate, renounce, disclaim, deny; *colloq.* eat one's words 2 REPOSSESS, reclaim, regain, get back 3 RETURN, replace, restore, give back, hand back, send back

▷ **take down** 1 DISMANTLE, disassemble, demolish, raze, level, lower 2 NOTE, make a note of, record, write down, put down, set down, get down, transcribe, put on paper
🖃 put up

▷ **take in** 1 ABSORB, assimilate, digest, realize, appreciate, understand, comprehend, grasp 2 ACCOMMODATE, admit, receive, shelter, welcome 3 INCLUDE, contain, comprise, incorporate, embrace, encompass, cover 4 DECEIVE, fool, dupe, mislead, trick, hoodwink, cheat, swindle; *colloq.* con, bamboozle, lead up the garden path

▷ **take off** 1 *watch the plane take off* depart, fly, lift off, ascend, climb, rise, soar, mount, become airborne 2 REMOVE, undress, get undressed, strip, divest, shed, discard, detach, pull off, throw off, tear off, drop, doff 3 SUBTRACT, take away, remove, deduct, discount 4 LEAVE, depart, go, run away, decamp, disappear, flee, abscond; *colloq.* skedaddle, scarper, bunk off, do a runner 5 IMITATE, mimic, parody, caricature, satirize, mock; *colloq.* send up 6 *the project has really taken off* succeed, work, do well, become fashionable, become popular, catch on, prosper, flourish; *colloq.* make it, become all the rage, go places, hit the jackpot, strike gold

▷ **take on** 1 ACCEPT, assume, acquire, undertake, tackle, face 2 COMPETE WITH, contend with, fight, oppose, vie with, tackle 3 *take on staff* employ, hire, enlist, recruit, engage, enrol, retain

▷ **take out** 1 REMOVE, extract, get out, detach, excise, cut out, pull out 2 *take someone out to a restaurant* go with, go out with, accompany, escort, see 3 *take out a loan* arrange, organize, set up, settle on, work out; *colloq.* fix 4 *take out a book from the library* borrow, use temporarily, have a loan, be lent

▷ **take over** gain control of, take charge of, become responsible for, assume responsibility for, buy out

▷ **take to** 1 LIKE, find pleasant, find attractive, become friendly with, become keen on, appreciate 2 BEGIN, start, launch into, undertake, set about; *formal* commence

▷ **take up** 1 OCCUPY, fill, engage, engross, absorb, become interested in, monopolize, use (up), consume 2 RAISE, lift, pick up 3 *take up a hobby* start, begin, embark on, pursue; *formal* commence 4 RESUME, carry on, continue, pick up; *colloq.* pick up the threads 5 ACCEPT, adopt, assume, agree to
🖃 5 refuse

▶ *n* 1 CATCH, gate, haul, bag, yield 2 INCOME, revenue, takings, proceeds, profit(s), receipts, return(s), yield, gate, gate-money

take-off *n*
1 DEPARTURE, flight, flying, lift-off, ascent, climbing 2 IMITATION, mimicry, impersonation, parody, caricature, travesty
colloq. spoof, send-up

takeover *n*
gaining of control, merger, amalgamation, combination, incorporation, buyout, coalition, coup

taking *adj, n*
▶ *adj* catching, attractive, charming, pleasing, delightful, winning, winsome, appealing, fascinating, fetching, engaging, enchanting, compelling, alluring, beguiling, captivating, intriguing, prepossessing
🖃 repellent, repulsive, unattractive
▶ *n* receipts, proceeds, profits, gain, returns, income, revenue, yield, income, earnings, winnings, pickings, gate, gate money

tale *n*
1 STORY, yarn, anecdote, narrative, account, report, rumour, tall story, old wives' tale, superstition, fable, myth, legend, epic, saga, parable, allegory
colloq. spiel
2 LIE, falsehood, untruth, fabrication
colloq. fib, whopper, porky, tall story, cock-and-bull story

talent *n*
gift, endowment, genius, flair, feel, knack, bent, aptitude, faculty, facility, skill, ability, capacity, aptness, power, strength, strong point, forte
🖃 inability, weakness

talented *adj*
gifted, brilliant, well-endowed, versatile, accomplished, able, capable, proficient, adept, adroit, deft, artistic, clever, skilful
🖃 inept

talisman *n*
amulet, charm, fetish, mascot, totem, symbol, idol, ju-ju, phylactery, periapt, abraxas

talk *v, n*
▶ *v* 1 SPEAK, say, utter, articulate, voice, communicate, express, have a conversation/discussion
formal converse, confer, orate
colloq. natter, jabber, babble, prattle, chinwag, jaw
2 NEGOTIATE, discuss, bargain, haggle, work out an agreement
3 GOSSIP, spread rumours, chat, chatter, natter
4 *talk to the police*
tell, confess, give (secret) information to, inform on
colloq. tell tales, squeal, blab, spill the beans, let the cat out of the bag, give the game away; *slang* grass

▷ **talk back** answer back, answer rudely, be cheeky to, retort, riposte, retaliate

▷ **talk big** bluster, boast, brag, show off, crow, exaggerate, swank, vaunt

▷ **talk down to** patronize, speak condescendingly towards, look down on, despise

▷ **talk into** encourage, coax, sway, persuade, convince, bring round, win over
🖃 dissuade, talk out of

▷ **talk out of** discourage, deter, put off, prevent, stop, dissuade
🖃 persuade, convince, talk into

▶ *n* 1 CONVERSATION, dialogue, discussion, chat, chatter, tête-à-tête
colloq. natter, confab, jaw, chinwag
2 *give a talk*
lecture, seminar, symposium, speech, address, discourse, sermon
formal disquisition, oration
colloq. spiel
3 GOSSIP, hearsay, rumour, tittle-tattle
4 *the two sides are holding talks*
NEGOTIATION, discussion, interview, meeting, consultation, debate, conference, summit conference, dialogue, seminar, symposium, bargaining, haggling
formal conclave
5 LANGUAGE, dialect, slang, cant, jargon, speech, utterance, words

technical idiolect
colloq. lingo

talkative *adj*
garrulous, vocal, communicative, forthcoming, unreserved, expansive, chatty, gossipy, verbose, wordy, longwinded
formal voluble, loquacious
colloq. gabby, gassy, mouthy, can talk the hind legs of a donkey
ᴇᴈ taciturn, quiet, reserved

talker *n*
speaker, conversationalist, communicator, lecturer, speech-maker
formal orator
colloq. chatterbox

talking-to *n*
lecture, scolding, reprimand, rebuke, reproof, reproach, criticism
colloq. dressing-down, telling-off, carpeting, ticking-off
ᴇᴈ praise, commendation

tall *adj*
1 HIGH, lofty, elevated, soaring, towering, sky-high, lanky, big, great, giant, gigantic
2 *a tall story*
unlikely, unbelievable, incredible, improbable, remarkable, implausible, absurd, far-fetched, exaggerated, dubious, preposterous, overblown
3 *a tall order*
difficult, demanding, exacting, taxing, hard, challenging, trying
ᴇᴈ 1 short, low, small 2 reasonable 3 easy

tallness *n*
altitude, height, loftiness, stature

tally *n, v*
▶ *n* 1 RECORD, count, total, sum, score, enumeration, reckoning, account, register, list, roll
2 COUNTERFOIL, counterpart, duplicate, ticket, tag, tab, stub
▶ *v* 1 AGREE, concur, tie in, square, accord, harmonize, coincide, correspond, match, conform, suit, fit
formal concur
2 ADD (UP), total, count, reckon, figure
ᴇᴈ 1 disagree, differ

tame *adj, v*
▶ *adj* 1 *a tame rabbit*
domesticated, broken in, trained, disciplined, manageable, tractable, amenable, gentle, docile, meek, subdued, submissive, unresisting, obedient, biddable
2 DULL, boring, tedious, uninteresting, unexciting, humdrum, flat, bland, insipid, weak, feeble, uninspired, unadventurous, unenterprising, wearisome, lifeless, spiritless, vapid
ᴇᴈ 1 wild, unmanageable, rebellious 2 exciting, adventurous
▶ *v* domesticate, house-train, break in, train, discipline, master, overcome, conquer, bring to heel, bridle, curb, repress, suppress, quell, subdue, temper, soften, mellow, calm, pacify, humble
formal subjugate

tamper *v*
interfere, meddle, tinker, fiddle, manipulate, juggle, alter, damage
colloq. mess about, muck about, monkey, fix, rig, poke/stick your nose in, stick/put your oar in

tan *adj, v*
▶ *adj* brown, light brown, yellowish brown
▶ *v* 1 BROWN, go/turn brown, make/become darker, bronze, sunburn
2 BEAT, flog, lash, thrash, whip, flay, cane, birch, strap, spank
colloq. wallop, whack, belt, clout

tang *n*
1 SHARPNESS, piquancy, spice, pungency, taste, flavour, savour, smack, smell, aroma, scent, whiff
colloq. bite, edge, kick, pep, punch
2 TINGE, touch, trace, hint, suggestion, overtone

tangible *adj*
touchable, palpable, solid, concrete, material, substantial, physical, real, actual, hard, perceptible, discernible, visible, evident, definite, well-defined, unmistakable, positive
formal tactile, manifest
ᴇᴈ intangible, abstract, unreal

tangle *n, v*
▶ *n* 1 KNOT, snarl-up, twist, coil, mesh, mat, web, maze, labyrinth
formal convolution
2 MESS, muddle, jumble, mix-up, confusion, entanglement, embroilment, complication, imbroglio
▶ *v* 1 ENTANGLE, knot, snarl, ravel, twist, coil, interweave, interlace, intertwine, intertwist, catch, ensnare, entrap, enmesh
formal convolve
2 INVOLVE, embroil, ensnare, entrap, enmesh, implicate, muddle, confuse
ᴇᴈ 1, 2 disentangle

tangled *adj*
1 *tangled hair*
knotty, knotted, twisted, snarled, matted, tousled, dishevelled, messy, entangled
2 CONFUSED, muddled, jumbled, twisted, tortuous, involved, mixed up, complicated, complex, intricate
formal convoluted

tangy *adj*
sharp, biting, acid, tart, spicy, piquant, pungent, strong, fresh
ᴇᴈ tasteless, insipid

tank *n*
1 *a hot-water tank*
container, reservoir, receptacle, cistern, aquarium, vat, basin
2 *anti-tank missiles*
armoured car, armoured vehicle, panzer

tantalize *v*
tease, taunt, torment, torture, provoke, lead on, titillate, tempt, allure, entice, beguile, bait, balk, frustrate, thwart, disappoint
ᴇᴈ gratify, satisfy, fulfil

tantamount *adj*
as good as, equivalent, equal, synonymous, the same as
formal commensurate

tantrum *n*
temper, rage, fury, storm, outburst, fit, fit of temper, flare-up, pet, scene, paroxysm
colloq. paddy

tap[1] *v, n*
▶ *v* *tap someone on the shoulder*

hit, strike, knock, rap, beat, drum, pat, touch
► *n* knock, rap, beat, pat, touch, light blow

tap² *n, v*
► *n* **1** STOPCOCK, valve, faucet, spigot, spout
2 STOPPER, plug, bung
3 BUG, listening device, hidden microphone, receiver
▷ **on tap** available, ready, on/at hand, handy,
accessible
► *v* use, utilize, exploit, mine, quarry, siphon, bleed,
milk, drain

tape *n, v*
► *n* **1** BAND, strip, string, binding, ribbon
2 VIDEO, videotape, cassette, videocassette,
recording, tape-recording, video recording,
audiotape, magnetic tape
3 *with tape over their mouths*
adhesive tape, Sellotape®, masking tape, sticky tape
► *v* **1** BIND, secure, tie, fasten, stick, seal
2 RECORD, tape-record, video, video-record

taper *v, n*
► *v* narrow, make/become narrow, thin, thin out,
make/become thin, slim, decrease, reduce, lessen,
diminish, dwindle, fade, wane, peter out, tail off,
die away/off
formal attenuate
◳ widen, flare, swell, increase
► *n* spill, candle, wick

tardily *adv*
late, slowly, unpunctually, sluggishly, late in the day,
at the last minute
formal belatedly
colloq. at the eleventh hour
◳ promptly, punctually

tardiness *n*
lateness, delay, slowness, unpunctuality, sluggishness,
dawdling
formal procrastination, dilatoriness, belatedness
◳ promptness, punctuality

tardy *adj*
slow, slack, sluggish, late, unpunctual, overdue,
delayed, dawdling, loitering, behindhand, backward,
last-minute, eleventh-hour
formal belated, dilatory, procrastinating, retarded
◳ prompt, punctual

target *n*
1 MARK, aim, goal, bull's eye, victim, butt, game,
prey, quarry
2 AIM, object, objective, end, purpose, intention,
ambition, goal, destination

tariff *n*
1 TOLL, tax, levy, customs, excise, duty
2 PRICE LIST, schedule, (list of) charges, menu,
bill of fare, rate

tarnish *v, n*
► *v* discolour, corrode, rust, dull, dim, darken,
blacken, sully, taint, stain, blemish, spot, blot, mar,
spoil
formal befoul, besmirch
◳ polish, brighten
► *n* blemish, spot, stain, taint, blot, discoloration,
blackening, film, rust, patina
◳ brightness, polish

tarry *v*
linger, remain, stay, stop, rest, wait, pause, delay, lag,
dally, dawdle, loiter
formal abide, bide, sojourn

tart¹ *n, v*
► *n* **1** *cherry tart*
pie, flan, pastry, tartlet, patty, quiche, strudel
2 PROSTITUTE, call girl, loose woman, fallen woman,
slut, strumpet, street-walker, broad, whore, harlot,
scarlet woman, trollop, drab, *fille de joie*
colloq. floosie, hooker; *slang* scrubber, tramp
► *v* ▷ **tart up** smarten (up), renovate, decorate,
redecorate, embellish; *colloq.* doll up

tart² *adj*
1 *the food tastes tart*
sharp, acid, sour, bitter, vinegary, tangy, piquant,
pungent
formal acidulous
2 *tart remarks*
biting, sharp, cutting, sarcastic, incisive, caustic, acid,
acerbic, scathing, sardonic
formal trenchant, astringent
◳ **1** bland, sweet **2** kind

task *n*
job, chore, duty, charge, imposition, assignment,
commission, exercise, mission, engagement, errand,
undertaking, enterprise, business, occupation,
activity, employment, work, piece of work, labour, toil,
burden
▷ **take to task** reprimand, rebuke, criticize, blame,
scold, reproach, reprove, censure, lecture;
formal upbraid; *colloq.* tell off, tick off
◳ commend, praise

taste *n, v*
► *n* **1** FLAVOUR, savour, relish, smack, tang
Related adjective: gustative, gustatory

Ways of describing taste include: acid, acrid,
appetizing, bitter, bittersweet, citrus, creamy,
delicious, flavoursome, fruity, hot, meaty, moreish,
colloq. mouth-watering, peppery, piquant, pungent,
salty, sapid, savoury, *colloq.* scrumptious, sharp,
sour, spicy, sugary, sweet, tangy, tart, tasty, vinegary,
colloq. yummy.

2 SAMPLE, bit, piece, morsel, titbit, bite, nibble,
mouthful, sip, drop, dash, soupçon
3 *a taste for adventure*
liking, fondness, partiality, preference, inclination,
bent, leaning, hankering, desire, hunger, thirst, appetite
formal penchant, predilection
4 DISCRIMINATION, discernment, judgement,
perception, appreciation, sensitivity, refinement, polish,
culture, cultivation, breeding, decorum, stylishness,
etiquette, finesse, style, grace, elegance, tastefulness,
propriety
◳ **1** blandness **3** distaste **4** tastelessness
► *v* **1** SAMPLE, nibble, sip, try, test
2 SAVOUR, smack, relish
3 EXPERIENCE, undergo, feel, encounter, meet, know
4 DIFFERENTIATE, distinguish, discern, make out,
perceive

tasteful *adj*
refined, polished, cultured, cultivated, elegant,
pleasing, charming, smart, stylish, aesthetic, artistic,
harmonious, beautiful, pretty, exquisite, delicate,
graceful, restrained, well-judged, correct, fastidious,
discriminating
formal judicious
◳ tasteless, garish, tawdry

tasteless *adj*
1 FLAVOURLESS, insipid, bland, mild, weak, thin, watery, watered-down, flat, plain, stale, dull, boring, uninteresting, vapid
2 INELEGANT, graceless, unseemly, improper, unfitting, indiscreet, crass, rude, tactless, crude, vulgar, kitsch, cheap, tawdry, flashy, showy, gaudy, garish, loud, uncouth
colloq. tacky; *slang* naff
F3 1 tasty 2 tasteful, elegant

tasting *n*
testing, sampling, trial, assay, assessment
formal gustation

tasty *adj*
luscious, palatable, appetizing, mouth-watering, delicious, flavoursome, succulent, tangy, spicy, piquant, savoury, sweet, delectable
formal flavorous
colloq. scrumptious; *slang* yummy
F3 tasteless, insipid

tatter *n*
▷ **in tatters** 1 IN RAGS, in shreds, in ribbons, in pieces, in bits 2 DESTROYED, ruined, wrecked, broken, shattered, devastated

tattered *adj*
ragged, frayed, threadbare, ripped, torn, tatty, shabby, scruffy
F3 smart, neat

tattler *n*
gossip, busybody, tell-tale, scandalmonger, tale-teller, newsmonger, rumour-monger, talebearer

taunt *v, n*
▶ *v* tease, torment, provoke, bait, goad, jeer, mock, ridicule, make fun of, poke fun at, gibe, deride, sneer, insult, revile, reproach
colloq. rib
▶ *n* jeer, catcall, gibe, dig, barb, sneer, insult, reproach, taunting, teasing, provocation, mockery, ridicule, sarcasm, derision, censure
colloq. brickbat

taut *adj*
tight, stretched, tightened, contracted, strained, tense, tensed, unrelaxed, stiff, rigid
F3 slack, loose, relaxed

tautological *adj*
repetitive, superfluous, redundant, wordy
technical pleonastic
formal verbose
F3 succinct, economical

tautology *n*
repetition, repetitiveness, duplication, superfluity, redundancy
technical pleonasm, perissology
formal iteration, verbosity

tavern *n*
public house, local, inn, bar, alehouse, tap-house, roadhouse
colloq. dive, hostelry, joint, pub; *slang* boozer

tawdry *adj*
cheap, vulgar, tasteless, fancy, showy, flashy, gaudy, garish, tinselly, glittering
colloq. tacky
F3 fine, tasteful

tawny *adj*
golden, golden brown, khaki, sandy, yellow, tan, fawn
formal fulvous, fulvid, xanthous

tax *n, v*
▶ *n* 1 LEVY, charge, rate, duty, tariff, customs, contribution
formal imposte
Related adjective: fiscal

Taxes include: airport tax, capital gains tax, capital transfer tax, capitation, community charge, corporation tax, council tax, customs, death duty, estate duty, excise, income tax, inheritance tax, insurance tax, PAYE, poll tax, property tax, rates, surtax, tithe, toll, value added tax (VAT).

2 BURDEN, load, strain, stress, pressure, imposition, weight
▶ *v* 1 LEVY, charge, demand, exact, assess, impose
2 BURDEN, weigh (down), load, overload, strain, stretch, encumber, impose, exact, try, test, tire, wear out, weary, exhaust, drain, sap, weaken, make demands on
formal enervate

taxi *n*
cab, minicab, taxicab, hansom-cab, hackney coach, fiacre

taxing *adj*
burdensome, exacting, demanding, exhausting, punishing, stressful, heavy, tough, hard, tiring, trying, onerous, draining, wearing, wearying, wearisome
formal enervating
F3 easy, gentle, mild

teach *v*
instruct, train, coach, tutor, lecture, drill, give lessons, ground, verse, discipline, school, educate, enlighten, edify, inform, impart, indoctrinate, condition, brainwash, advise, counsel, guide, direct, show, demonstrate
formal inculcate
F3 learn

teacher *n*
schoolteacher, educator, guide
F3 pupil

Kinds of teacher include: adviser, coach, college lecturer, counsellor, crammer, dean, demonstrator, deputy head, doctor, don, duenna, fellow, form teacher, governess, guru, head of department, head of year, headmaster, headmistress, headteacher, housemaster, housemistress, instructor, lecturer, maharishi, master, mentor, middle school teacher, mistress, nursery school teacher, pastoral head, pedagogue, pedant, preceptor, preceptress, primary school teacher, principal, private tutor, professor, pundit, reception teacher, school-ma'am, schoolmaster, schoolmistress, schoolteacher, secondary school teacher, senior lecturer, student teacher, subject co-ordinator, supply teacher, trainer, tutor, university lecturer, upper school teacher.

teaching *n*
1 INSTRUCTION, tuition, education, pedagogy

Methods of teaching include: apprenticeship, briefing, coaching, computer-aided learning, correspondence course, counselling, demonstration, distance learning, drilling, familiarization, grounding, guidance, hands-on training, home-learning, indoctrination, induction training, in-service training, instruction, job training, lecturing, lesson, master-class, on-the-job training, practical, preaching, private tuition, role play, rote learning, schooling, seminar, shadowing, special tuition, theory, training, tuition, tutelage, tutorial, vocational training, work experience.

2 DOGMA, doctrine, tenet, precept, principle
Related adjective: doctrinal

team *n, v*
▶ *n* side, line-up, squad, shift, crew, gang, band, group, set, troupe, bunch, company, stable
▶ *v* ▷ **team up** join, unite, couple, combine, band together, co-operate, collaborate, work together, match, yoke

teamwork *n*
collaboration, co-operation, co-ordination, joint effort, team spirit, fellowship, *esprit de corps*
F3 disharmony, disunity

tear¹ *v, n*
▶ *v* 1 RIP, rend, divide, pull apart, break apart, split, ladder, rupture, sever, shred, scratch, claw, gash, wound, injure, lacerate, slash, mutilate, mangle
old use sunder
2 PULL, snatch, grab, seize, pluck, wrest
colloq. yank
3 *tear down the street*
dash, rush, hurry, speed, race, run, sprint, fly, shoot, dart, bolt, career, gallop, charge
colloq. belt, nip, rip, whizz, vroom, zap, zing, zip, zoom, step on it
▶ *n* rip, rent, slit, hole, split, run, rupture, scratch, gash, wound, injury, laceration, slash, mutilation

tear² *n*
▷ **in tears** crying, weeping, sobbing, wailing, whimpering, blubbering, sad, sorrowful, upset, distressed, emotional
colloq. weepy
Related adjective: lachrymal

tearaway *n*
rough, tough, rowdy, ruffian, rascal, daredevil, delinquent, hooligan, hoodlum, hothead, madcap, roughneck
colloq. good-for-nothing

tearful *adj*
crying, weeping, sobbing, whimpering, blubbering, sad, sorrowful, upset, distressed, emotional, upsetting, distressing, mournful, doleful
formal lachrymose
colloq. weepy
F3 happy, smiling, laughing

tease *v*
taunt, provoke, bait, goad, annoy, vex, irritate, badger, worry, pester, plague, torment, tantalize, mock, ridicule, gibe, banter
colloq. aggravate, needle, rag, kid, rib

technical *adj*
mechanical, scientific, technological, electronic, computerized, specialist, specialized, practical, applied, expert, professional

technique *n*
1 METHOD, system, procedure, manner, fashion, style, way, means, approach, course, performance, execution, *modus operandi*
formal mode
2 SKILL, skilfulness, ability, capability, delivery, artistry, mastery, craftsmanship, dexterity, skill,

facility, proficiency, expertise, art, craft, knack, touch
colloq. know-how

tedious *adj*
boring, monotonous, uninteresting, unexciting, dull, dreary, uninspired, unvaried, lifeless, flat, drab, banal, routine, humdrum, tiresome, wearisome, wearying, tiring, laborious, long-winded, long-drawn-out
formal prosaic
colloq. run-of-the-mill, samey
F3 lively, interesting, exciting

tedium *n*
boredom, tediousness, monotony, dullness, dreariness, lifelessness, drabness, banality, sameness, routine, prosiness, ennui, vapidity
F3 excitement, interest

teem *v*
swarm, bristle, crawl, burst, proliferate, abound, increase, multiply, overflow, produce, bear, brim
formal pullulate
F3 lack, want

teeming *adj*
swarming, crawling, alive, bristling, seething, full, packed, brimming, overflowing, bursting, numerous, abundant, fruitful, thick
formal replete, pullulating
colloq. chock-a-block, chock-full
F3 lacking, sparse, rare

teenage *adj*
teenaged, adolescent, young, youthful, juvenile, immature

teenager *n*
young person, young adult, adolescent, youth, boy, girl, minor, juvenile

teeny *adj*
tiny, minute, minuscule, miniature, diminutive, microscopic
Scot. wee
colloq. titchy, teeny-weeny, teensy-weensy

teeter *v*
sway, rock, roll, reel, stagger, totter, shake, tremble, waver, wobble, balance, lurch, pitch, pivot, seesaw

teetotal *adj*
temperate, abstinent, abstemious, sober
colloq. on the wagon

teetotaller *n*
non-drinker, abstainer, nephalist, Rechabite, water-drinker

telegram *n*
Telemessage®, cable, telex, fax, telegraph
colloq. wire

telegraph *n, v*
▶ *n* cable, teleprinter, telex, telegram, radiotelegraph
colloq. wire
▶ *v* send, transmit, signal, cable, telex
colloq. wire

telepathy *n*
mind-reading, thought transference, sixth sense, ESP, extrasensory perception, clairvoyance

telephone *n, v*
▶ *n* phone, handset, receiver
colloq. blower, hot line

Types of telephone include: Ansaphone®, answering machine, caller display phone, cardphone, carphone, cashphone, cellphone, cellular phone, corded phone, cordless phone, fax, fax-phone, hazardous area phone, Minicom®, mobile phone, pager, payphone, push-button telephone, system phone, textphone, tone-dialling phone, Touchtone®, Uniphone®, videophone, weather-resistant phone.

▶ *v* phone, ring (up), call (up), dial, contact, get in touch
colloq. buzz, give a buzz, give a tinkle, give a bell

telescope *v*
contract, shrink, compress, condense, abridge, squash, squeeze, crush, shorten, compact, curtail, truncate, abbreviate, reduce, cut, trim, concertina

televise *v*
broadcast, screen, show, put on, transmit, air, beam, relay, cable

television *n*
TV, receiver, set, small screen
colloq. telly, the box, goggle-box, idiot box, the tube; *US* boob tube

tell *v*
1 INFORM, notify, let know, brief, mention, acquaint, impart, communicate, make known, report, speak, utter, say, state, confess, divulge, show, disclose, reveal, announce, broadcast, declare, proclaim
formal apprise
colloq. give the low-down
2 *tell a story*
narrate, recount, relate, recite, report, announce, describe, sketch, portray, mention
formal delineate
3 ORDER, command, direct, instruct, require, charge, bid, dictate, advise, authorize, decree
4 DIFFERENTIATE, distinguish, discriminate, tell apart, discern, recognize, identify, discover, see, perceive, make out, understand, comprehend
5 AFFECT, have an effect on, take its toll of, exhaust, drain, change, transform, alter
6 INFORM ON, talk, betray, denounce
colloq. rat, squeal, tell tales, blab, blow the whistle on, spill the beans, let the cat out of the bag, give the game away; *slang* grass, shop
▷ **tell off** scold, chide, reprimand, rebuke, reprove, lecture, reproach, censure; *formal* upbraid, berate; *colloq.* tick off, dress down, give a talking-to

teller *n*
cashier, clerk, bank clerk, banker, treasurer

telling *adj*
revealing, significant, impressive, marked, effective, powerful, convincing, persuasive, impressive
formal cogent

telling-off *n*
scolding, chiding, rebuke, reprimand, reproach, reproof, lecture, row
formal castigation, upbraiding
colloq. dressing-down, ticking-off, bawling-out

tell-tale *adj, n*
▶ *adj* revealing, meaningful, revelatory, noticeable, perceptible, unmistakable
colloq. give-away
▶ *n* informer, secret agent, sneak, spy
Scot. clype
colloq. squealer, snake in the grass, snitch, snitcher; *slang* grass

temerity *n*
presumption, impudence, impertinence, effrontery, gall, audacity, boldness, daring, rashness, recklessness, impulsiveness
colloq. cheek, nerve
🖪 caution, prudence

temper *n, v*
▶ *n* 1 MOOD, humour, nature, temperament, character, attitude, disposition, constitution, frame/state of mind
2 ANGER, bad mood, rage, fury, passion, tantrum, fit of temper, scene, storm, annoyance, resentment, irritability, petulance, ill-humour
colloq. paddy, wax, flare-up
3 CALM, calmness, composure, self-control, tranquillity
slang cool
🖪 2 calmness, self-control 3 anger, rage
▷ **lose your temper** get angry, boil over, get all steamed up, foam at the mouth, fly off the handle, go mad, see red, get up in arms, get aggravated, blow a fuse, blow a gasket, blow your cool, blow your top, burst a blood vessel, do your nut, explode, flip your lid, fly into a rage, go off the deep end, go up the wall, hit the ceiling, hit the roof, lose your cool, lose your rag, lose your patience, raise hell, throw a tantrum, throw a wobbly
▶ *v* 1 MODERATE, lessen, weaken, reduce, calm, soothe, allay, alleviate, palliate, modify, soften
formal mitigate, assuage
colloq. tone down
2 HARDEN, roughen, toughen, strengthen
technical anneal
formal fortify

temperament *n*
1 CHARACTER, nature, personality, disposition, tendency, bent, constitution, make-up, complexion, soul, spirit, mood, humour, temper, frame/state of mind, attitude, outlook
2 MOODINESS, excitability, sensitivity, touchiness, irritability, impatience, fieriness, explosiveness, hot-headedness, volatility

temperamental *adj*
1 MOODY, emotional, over-emotional, neurotic, highly-strung, sensitive, hypersensitive, touchy, irritable, impatient, passionate, fiery, excitable, explosive, hot-blooded, hot-headed, petulant, volatile, mercurial, capricious, unpredictable, unreliable
2 NATURAL, inborn, innate, inherent, constitutional, ingrained, congenital
🖪 1 calm, level-headed, steady

temperance *n*
teetotalism, prohibition, abstinence, abstemiousness, sobriety, continence, moderation, restraint, self-restraint, self-control, self-discipline, self-denial, austerity
🖪 intemperance, excess

temperate *adj*
1 *temperate climate*
mild, clement, balmy, fair, equable, balanced, stable, moderate, gentle, pleasant, agreeable
2 TEETOTAL, abstinent, abstemious, self-denying, sober, continent, moderate, restrained, self-restrained, controlled, self-controlled, even-tempered, calm, composed, reasonable, sensible
🖪 2 intemperate, extreme, excessive

tempest *n*
1 STORM, gale, squall, tornado, typhoon, hurricane, cyclone
2 FURORE, upheaval, uproar, ferment, disturbance, commotion, tumult

tempestuous *adj*
stormy, windy, gusty, blustery, squally, turbulent, tumultuous, rough, wild, uncontrolled, violent, furious, raging, heated, boisterous, impassioned, fierce, feverish, passionate, intense
F꜉ calm, peaceful, quiet

temple *n*
place of worship, shrine, sanctuary, church, tabernacle, mosque, pagoda
See also **worship**.

tempo *n*
time, rhythm, metre, measure, beat, cadence, pulse, throb, speed, velocity, rate, pace

temporal *adj*
secular, profane, worldly, earthly, terrestrial, material, carnal, fleshly, mortal
F꜉ spiritual

temporarily *adv*
for the time being, momentarily, in the interim, pro tem, transiently, transitorily, briefly, fleetingly
F꜉ permanently

temporary *adj*
impermanent, provisional, interim, short-term, fill-in, makeshift, stopgap, pro tem, temporal, transient, transitory, passing, fleeting, brief, short-lived, momentary
formal ephemeral, evanescent, fugacious
F꜉ permanent, everlasting

temporize *v*
delay, hang back, pause, stall, equivocate, play for time
formal procrastinate, tergiversate
colloq. hum and haw

tempt *v*
1 ENTICE, coax, cajole, persuade, woo, bait, lure, educe, provoke, incite, egg on
formal inveigle
2 ALLURE, attract, draw, invite, tantalize
colloq. make someone's mouth water
F꜉ 1 discourage, dissuade 2 repel

temptation *n*
enticement, inducement, incitement, coaxing, cajolery, persuasion, urging, bait, lure, allure, appeal, attraction, influence, draw, pull, seduction, invitation

tempting *adj*
attractive, inviting, alluring, tantalizing, enticing, appetizing, mouthwatering, seductive
F꜉ unattractive, uninviting

temptress *n*
enchantress, seductress, siren, vamp, flirt, sorceress, *femme fatale*, coquette, Delilah

tenable *adj*
credible, defensible, justifiable, reasonable, rational, sound, arguable, believable, defendable, plausible, maintainable, supportable, viable, feasible
F꜉ untenable, indefensible, unjustifiable

tenacious *adj*
1 DETERMINED, persistent, dogged, firm, single-minded, adamant, resolute, purposeful, steadfast, relentless, unyielding, unshakeable, unswerving, obstinate, stubborn
formal intransigent, obdurate
2 ADHESIVE, cohesive, sticky, clinging, secure, firm, tight, fast
F꜉ 1 loose, slack, weak

tenacity *n*
determination, persistence, single-mindedness, firmness, fastness, perseverance, doggedness, resoluteness, resolution, resolve, steadfastness, staunchness, toughness, diligence, power, solidity, solidness, strength, force, forcefulness, inflexibility, indomitability, application, stubbornness, obstinacy
formal intransigence, obduracy, pertinacity
F꜉ looseness, slackness, weakness

tenancy *n*
occupancy, possession, renting, residence, tenure, holding, lease, leasehold, occupation, incumbency

tenant *n*
renter, lessee, leaseholder, occupier, occupant, resident, inhabitant, landholder, incumbent

tend¹ *v*
tends to arrive late
incline, lean, show a tendency, bend, bear, head, aim, point, lead, go, move, gravitate

tend² *v*
tend someone who is ill
look after, take care of, care for, cultivate, keep, maintain, see to, manage, handle, guard, protect, watch (over), keep an eye on, mind, nurture, nurse, minister to, serve, attend (to), wait on
F꜉ neglect, ignore

tendency *n*
trend, drift, movement, course, direction, trend, bearing, heading, bias, partiality, readiness, liability, susceptibility, proneness, inclination, leaning, bent, aptness, disposition
formal predisposition, propensity, proclivity, conatus

tender¹ *adj*
1 KIND, gentle, caring, humane, generous, benevolent, considerate, compassionate, sympathetic, warm, kindly, fond, affectionate, loving, amorous, romantic, sentimental, emotional, evocative, sensitive, vulnerable, tender-hearted, soft-hearted
2 YOUNG, youthful, immature, green, raw, new, early, callow, inexperienced, impressionable, vulnerable
3 SOFT, succulent, fleshy, juicy, dainty, delicate, fragile, frail, sensitive, weak, feeble
4 SORE, painful, aching, smarting, bruised, throbbing, inflamed, red, raw, sensitive
F꜉ 1 hard-hearted, callous 2 mature 3 tough, hard

tender² *v, n*
▶ *v tender an apology*
offer, extend, give, present, submit, propose, suggest, advance, volunteer, bid, proffer
▶ *n* 1 *legal tender*
currency, money
2 OFFER, bid, estimate, quotation, price, proposal, proposition, suggestion, submission

tender-hearted *adj*
caring, gentle, kind, kind-hearted, kindly, mild, warm, warm-hearted, sympathetic, soft-hearted, feeling, considerate, compassionate, benevolent, loving, fond, affectionate, responsive, sensitive, humane, merciful, pitying, sentimental, benign
F꜉ callous, cruel, hard-hearted, unfeeling

tenderness *n*
1 KINDNESS, gentleness, warmth, warm-
heartedness, tender-heartedness, sympathy, sweetness,
sensitivity, loving-kindness, humaneness,
benevolence, attachment, devotion, affection,
fondness, amorousness, love, liking, mercy, pity, care,
compassion, consideration, humanity, sentimentality,
soft-heartedness, vulnerability
2 YOUTH, youthfulness, immaturity, callowness,
greenness, inexperience
3 SOFTNESS, weakness, delicateness, frailness,
fragility, feebleness
4 SORENESS, rawness, bruising, sensitiveness, ache,
aching, inflammation, irritation, pain, painfulness
F3 1 cruelty, hardness, harshness   2 maturity
3 toughness, hardness

tenet *n*
principle, belief, precept, presumption, conviction,
opinion, teaching, rule, thesis, view, doctrine, dogma,
maxim, creed, credo, canon, article of faith

tenor *n*
meaning, tendency, theme, trend, essence, substance,
gist, aim, point, direction, drift, purpose, sense, spirit,
intent, course, path, way, burden
formal purport

tense *adj, v*
▶ *adj* 1 TIGHT, taut, stretched, strained, stiff, rigid
2 NERVOUS, anxious, worried, strained, distraught,
under pressure, jittery, uneasy, apprehensive, edgy,
fidgety, restless, jumpy, overwrought, keyed up
colloq. edgy, uptight, stressed out; *slang* screwed up
3 STRESSFUL, exciting, worrying, uneasy, strained,
charged, fraught, nerve-racking, nail-biting
F3 1 loose, slack   2 calm, relaxed
▶ *v* tighten, contract, brace, stretch, strain, stiffen,
work
F3 loosen, relax

tension *n*
1 TIGHTNESS, tautness, stiffness, rigidity, strain,
straining, stretching, stress, pressure
2 NERVOUSNESS, anxiety, worry, strain, stress,
pressure, uneasiness, apprehension, edginess,
restlessness, agitation, disquiet, distress, suspense
colloq. nerves
3 CONFLICT, disagreement, friction, quarrel,
dissension, dispute, opposition, antagonism, hostility,
strife, unrest, confrontation, feud, discord, contention,
ill-will, difference of opinion, variance, clash
formal antipathy
F3 1 looseness   2 calm(ness), relaxation
3 harmony

tent *n*

Types of tent include: barrel-vaulted tent, bell tent,
big top, bivvy, black tent, box tent, canopy, canvas,
conical tent, crossover pole tent, dome tent, double-
A pole mountain tent, frame tent, hooped bivvy,
kata, lodge, marquee, mat tent, ridge tent, single
hoop tent, sloping ridge tent, sloping wedge tent,
tabernacle, tepee, touring tent, trailer tent, tunnel
tent, tupik, wigwam, yaranga.

tentative *adj*
1 PROVISIONAL, experimental, exploratory,
speculative, test, trial, pilot, indefinite, unconfirmed,
unproven
formal conjectural
2 HESITANT, wavering, faltering, cautious, unsure,

uncertain, timid, doubtful, undecided
F3 1 definite, conclusive, final, firm   2 decisive,
confident

tenterhooks *n*
▷ **on tenterhooks** anxious, in suspense, impatient,
nervous, excited, waiting, watchful, eager, with bated
breath

tenuous *adj*
thin, slim, slender, fine, slight, insubstantial, flimsy,
fragile, delicate, weak, vague, hazy, shaky, indefinite,
doubtful, dubious, questionable
F3 strong, substantial

tenure *n*
possession, proprietorship, residence, tenancy, term,
time, holding, occupancy, occupation, incumbency
formal habitation

tepid *adj*
lukewarm, cool, warmish, half-hearted, indifferent,
unenthusiastic, apathetic
F3 cold, hot, passionate

term *n, v*
▶ *n* 1 WORD, name, title, epithet, phrase, expression
formal designation, denomination, appellation,
locution
2 TIME, period, course, duration, spell, span, stretch,
interval, space, semester, session, season
3 *on good terms*
relations, relationship, footing, standing, position
4 *the terms of the contract*
conditions, points, details, specifications, stipulations,
clauses, provisos, provisions, qualifications,
particulars
5 CHARGES, rates, fees, prices, costs, tariff
6 END, interval, conclusion, limit, finish, duration,
period, culmination, close, bound, boundary, fruition,
terminus
▷ **come to terms** become reconciled, reconcile
yourself, resign yourself, accept, come to accept,
submit
▷ **in terms of** in relation to, as regards, with/in
regard to, with respect to
▶ *v* call, name, dub, style, designate, label, tag, title,
entitle
formal denominate

terminal *adj, n*
▶ *adj* 1 LAST, final, concluding, ultimate, extreme,
utmost, ending, confining, limiting
2 *terminal illness*
fatal, deadly, lethal, mortal, incurable, dying, killing
F3 1 initial, first
▶ *n* 1 END, extremity, limit, termination, boundary,
depot, terminus
2 *a computer terminal*
VDU, computer workstation, input-output device,
keyboard, console, monitor

terminate *v*
finish, bring/come to an end, complete, conclude, end,
stop, close, cut off, result, put an end to, abort, lapse,
run out, expire
formal cease, discontinue
colloq. wind up
F3 begin, start, initiate

termination *n*
end, ending, finish, conclusion, close, abortion,
completion, issue, result, consequence, effect,
dénouement, expiry, finale, finis

formal demise, cessation, discontinuation
F3 beginning, initiation, start

terminology *n*
language, jargon, phraseology, vocabulary, words, expressions, terms, nomenclature

terminus *n*
end, close, termination, extremity, limit, boundary, destination, goal, target, depot, station, garage, terminal

terrain *n*
land, ground, territory, country, countryside, landscape, topography

terrestrial *adj*
earthly, worldly, global, mundane
F3 cosmic, heavenly

terrible *adj*
1 BAD, awful, frightful, dreadful, shocking, appalling, outrageous, disgusting, revolting, repulsive, nasty, offensive, abhorrent, hateful, horrid, horrible, unpleasant, obnoxious, foul, vile, hideous, gruesome, horrific, harrowing, grim, distressing, unspeakable, harsh, grave, desperate, incompetent, poor, incorrigible
2 EXTREME, serious, severe, great, intense, exceptional, big, large
colloq. frightful, awful
F3 1 excellent, wonderful, superb

terribly *adv*
very, much, greatly, extremely, exceedingly, thoroughly, desperately, decidedly, seriously
colloq. frightfully, awfully

terrific *adj*
1 EXCELLENT, wonderful, great, marvellous, super, remarkable, outstanding, brilliant, magnificent, superb, sensational, amazing, stupendous, breathtaking
colloq. smashing, fabulous, fantastic, smashing, neat, ace, brill, crack, out of this world; *slang* mega, cool, wicked, awesome, crucial
2 HUGE, enormous, gigantic, tremendous, great, intense, extreme, excessive, extraordinary
F3 1 awful, terrible, appalling

terrified *adj*
frightened, petrified, scared, scared stiff, panic-stricken, intimidated, horrified, horror-struck, dismayed, appalled, alarmed, awed
colloq. scared out of your wits, scared to death, having kittens, in a blue funk

terrify *v*
petrify, horrify, appal, shock, terrorize, intimidate, frighten, scare, scare stiff, panic, alarm, dismay, paralyse, numb
colloq. rattle, scare out of your wits, make your blood run cold, scare the living daylights out of, make your hair stand on end, make someone jump out of their skin, put the frighteners on, put the wind up; *slang* scare the shit out of

territorial *adj*
geographical, area, district, zonal, regional, sectional, topographic, localized
formal domainal

territory *n*
country, land, state, dependency, province, domain, preserve, jurisdiction, sector, region, area, district, county, zone, tract, terrain, field

terror *n*
1 FEAR, panic, dread, trepidation, horror, shock, fright, alarm, dismay, terrorism, intimidation
formal consternation
colloq. blue funk
2 *that child's a terror*
rascal, rogue, horror, tearaway
3 FIEND, monster, devil, demon

terrorize *v*
threaten, menace, intimidate, oppress, coerce, bully, browbeat, frighten, scare, alarm, terrify, petrify, horrify, shock
colloq. strongarm, put the frighteners on, put the wind up

terse *adj*
short, brief, succinct, concise, to the point, compact, crisp, elliptical, condensed, pithy, incisive, snappy, curt, blunt, brusque, abrupt, laconic
formal epigrammatic, elliptical, gnomic
F3 long-winded, verbose

test *v, n*
▶ *v* 1 *test them on spelling*
try (out), experiment, examine, assess, evaluate, check, scrutinize, inspect, investigate, study, analyse, screen, sample, prove, verify
formal appraise, assay
colloq. probe
2 *test someone's patience*
strain, burden, load, overload, stretch, encumber, impose, exact, try, test, tire, wear out, weary, exhaust, drain, sap, weaken, make demands on
formal enervate
▶ *n* trial, try-out, experiment, examination, audition, pilot study, assessment, evaluation, questions, questionnaire, quiz, check, check-up, scrutinization, investigation, inspection, analysis, exploration, proof, probation, ordeal

testament *n*
testimony, witness, demonstration, proof, evidence, exemplification, tribute, will, earnest
formal attestation

testicles *n*
taboo slang balls, bollocks, goolies, nuts, rocks
Related adjective: testicular

testify *v*
give evidence, state, declare, assert, swear, vouch, certify, confirm, verify, establish, demonstrate, substantiate, show, bear witness, back up, support, endorse
formal depose, avow, attest, corroborate, affirm

testimonial *n*
reference, character, credential, certificate, (letter of) recommendation, endorsement, commendation, tribute

---

⚠ **testimonial** or **testimony** ?
A *testimonial* is a letter describing a person's character and abilities. A *testimony* is a statement of evidence, for example that of a witness at a trial: *He was convicted mainly by the testimony of his former partner; Her book is a remarkable testimony to her vision for the future of her country.*

---

testimony *n*
evidence, statement, submission, declaration, profession, assertion, support, proof, verification,

confirmation, witness, demonstration, indication
technical affidavit, deposition
formal attestation, affirmation, corroboration,
manifestation

> ⚠ **testimony** or **testimonial** ? *See panel at*
> **testimonial**.

testy *adj*
bad-tempered, cross, quarrelsome, crusty, quick-
tempered, short-tempered, irritable, impatient,
grumpy, irascible, snappish, snappy, waspish, sullen,
fretful, peevish, splenetic, petulant, captious
formal cantankerous
colloq. crabbed, tetchy, touchy, crotchety, stroppy,
shirty, ratty
▣ even-tempered, good-humoured

tetchy *adj*
irritable, irascible, peevish, bad-tempered, crusty,
grumpy, short-tempered, snappish
colloq. touchy, crotchety, shirty, ratty

tête-à-tête *n*
conversation, chat, talk, heart-to-heart, dialogue
colloq. confab, natter

tether *n, v*
▶ *n* chain, rope, cord, line, lead, leash, bond, fetter,
shackle, restraint, fastening
▶ *v* tie, fasten, secure, restrain, chain, rope, leash,
bind, lash, fetter, shackle, manacle

text *n*
1 WORDS, wording, content, matter, main matter,
body
2 SUBJECT, subject matter, topic, theme, issue, point
3 READING, passage, verse, chapter, paragraph,
sentence
4 BOOK, set book, textbook, source

texture *n*
consistency, feel, touch, surface, finish, grain,
appearance, weave, tissue, fabric, structure,
composition, constitution, character, quality

thank *v*
say thank you, be grateful, show/express your
gratitude, express your thanks, appreciate, show your
appreciation, acknowledge, recognize, credit

thankful *adj*
grateful, appreciative, obliged, indebted, pleased,
contented, relieved
formal beholden
▣ ungrateful, unappreciative

thankless *adj*
unrecognized, unappreciated, unacknowledged,
unrequited, unrewarded, unrewarding, unprofitable,
useless, fruitless
▣ rewarding, worthwhile

thanks *n, interj*
▶ *n* gratitude, gratefulness, appreciation,
acknowledgement, recognition, credit, thanksgiving,
thank-offering
▷ **thanks to** because of, owing to, due to,
on account of, as a result of, through
▶ *interj* many thanks, bless you, much obliged,
that's very kind of you, that's very good of you,
you shouldn't have
colloq. cheers, ta

thaw *v*
1 MELT, defrost, defreeze, de-ice, soften, liquefy,
dissolve, warm, heat up
2 BECOME FRIENDLIER, become more relaxed,
relax, loosen up
▣ **1** freeze

theatre *n*
1 *go to the theatre*
auditorium, hall, playhouse, amphitheatre, lyceum,
odeon, opera house
2 DRAMA, the stage, dramatics, theatrics, show
business
formal Thespian art
colloq. the boards, the footlights, rep

> *Parts of a theatre include*: apron, auditorium,
> backstage, balcony, border, box, bridge, catwalk,
> circle, coulisse, cut drop, cyclorama, decor,
> downstage, flat, flies, forestage, fourth wall, gallery,
> *colloq.* the gods, green room, grid, leg drop, lights,
> floats, floods, footlights, spots, loge, loggia, logum,
> mezzanine, open stage, opposite prompt, orchestra
> pit, picture-frame stage, pit, prompt side,
> proscenium, proscenium arch, revolving stage,
> rostrum, safety curtain, scruto, set, stage, stalls,
> tormentor, trapdoor, upper circle, upstage, wings.

theatrical *adj*
1 DRAMATIC, thespian

> *Theatrical forms include*: ballet, burlesque, cabaret,
> circus, comedy, black comedy, comedy of humours,
> comedy of manners, comedy of menace, commedia
> dell'arte, duologue, farce, fringe theatre, Grand
> Guignol, kabuki, Kitchen-Sink, legitimate drama,
> masque, melodrama, mime, miracle play,
> monologue, morality play, mummery, music hall,
> musical, musical comedy, mystery play, Noh, opera,
> operetta, pageant, pantomime, play, Punch and Judy,
> puppet theatre, revue, street theatre, tableau, theatre-
> in-the-round, Theatre of the Absurd, Theatre of
> Cruelty, tragedy. *See also* **performance**.

2 MELODRAMATIC, histrionic, dramatic, mannered,
affected, unreal, artificial, forced, pompous,
ostentatious, showy, extravagant, emotional,
exaggerated, overdone

theft *n*
robbery, thieving, burglary, stealing, pilfering, larceny,
shoplifting, kleptomania, fraud, swindling,
embezzlement
formal purloining
colloq. pinching, nicking, swiping, lifting, nobbling

thematic *adj*
conceptual, notional, classificatory
formal taxonomic

theme *n*
1 SUBJECT, topic, subject matter, thread, motif,
keynote, idea, gist, essence, burden, argument
formal leitmotif
2 THESIS, paper, dissertation, composition, essay,
text, matter
3 MELODY, tune, motif

then *adv*
1 AT THAT TIME, at that point, at that moment,
in those days, by that time
formal whereupon
2 AFTERWARDS, after, next, soon, subsequently, at a
later date
3 IN ADDITION, additionally, also, as well,

moreover, besides, too, further, furthermore
4 THEREFORE, so and so, accordingly, consequently, as a result
formal thus

theological *adj*
religious, divine, doctrinal, ecclesiastical, scriptural
technical hierological

theorem *n*
formula, principle, rule, statement, deduction, proposition, hypothesis
formal dictum, postulate

theoretical *adj*
hypothetical, speculative, abstract, conceptual, notional, academic, doctrinaire, pure, ideal
formal conjectural, suppositional
colloq. on paper
E3 practical, applied, concrete

theorize *v*
suppose, guess, speculate, formulate
formal hypothesize, conjecture, postulate, propound

theory *n*
hypothesis, supposition, assumption, presumption, surmise, guess, speculation, idea, view, opinion, notion, abstraction, philosophy, thesis, plan, proposal, scheme, system
formal conjecture, postulation
E3 certainty, practice

therapeutic *adj*
remedial, curative, healing, curing, restorative, tonic, medicinal, corrective, good, advantageous, beneficial, salutary, health-giving
formal ameliorative, sanative
E3 harmful, detrimental

therapy *n*
treatment, remedy, cure, healing, tonic

Types of therapy include: acupressure, acupuncture, Alexander technique, aromatherapy, art therapy, aversion therapy, beauty therapy, behaviour therapy, biofeedback, chemotherapy, chiropractic, cognitive therapy, confrontation therapy, drama therapy, electro-convulsive therapy, electrotherapy, faith healing, family therapy, Gestalt therapy, group therapy, heat treatment, herbalism, homeopathy, hormone-replacement therapy, horticulture therapy, hydrotherapy, hypnotherapy, irradiation, moxibustion, music therapy, naturopathy, occupational therapy, csteopathy, phototherapy, physiotherapy, play therapy, primal therapy, psychotherapy, radiotherapy, reflexology, regression therapy, reminiscence therapy, Rolfing, sex therapy, shiatsu, speech therapy, ultrasound, zone therapy.

thereabouts *adv*
about, approximately, roughly, near that number, near that date

thereafter *adv*
subsequently, afterwards, after that, after that time, next

therefore *adv*
so and so, then, accordingly, consequently, as a result
formal thus, ergo

thesaurus *n*
dictionary, lexicon, wordbook, vocabulary, synonymy, encyclopedia, storehouse, repository, treasury

thesis *n*
1 *doctoral thesis*
dissertation, essay, composition, treatise, paper, monograph
formal disquisition
2 SUBJECT, topic, theme, idea, opinion, view, theory, hypothesis, proposal, proposition, premise, statement, argument, contention

thick *adj, n*
▶ *adj* **1** WIDE, broad, fat, stout, chunky, heavy, bulky, deep, big, substantial, stiff, solid, dense, impenetrable, close, compact, concentrated, condensed, viscous, coagulated, creamy, lumpy, clotted
2 FULL, packed, crowded, filled, overflowing, swarming, teeming, bristling, brimming, crawling, bursting, numerous, abounding, abundant
colloq. chock-a-block
3 *thick fog*
impenetrable, dense, heavy, murky, smoggy, soupy, opaque, concentrated
4 *a thick voice*
husky, rough, unclear, indistinct, throaty, guttural, croaky, croaking, gruff, gravelly, rasping
5 *a thick accent*
strong, pronounced, broad, marked, definite, obvious, noticeable, striking
6 STUPID, foolish, slow, dense, dull, dim-witted, brainless, simple
colloq. dumb, gormless, dopey, thick as a plank/two short planks
E3 **1** thin, slim, slender, slight **2** sparse
4 clear **5** faint, vague **6** clever, intelligent;
colloq. brainy
▶ *n* middle, centre, focus, midst, hub, heart

thicken *v*
1 *thicken a soup*
make/become more solid, solidify, stiffen, condense, congeal, coagulate, clot, cake, gel, jell, set
2 *the plot thickens*
become more mysterious, become more complicated, become more involved, become more intricate
E3 **1** thin

thicket *n*
wood, copse, coppice, grove, spinney, maquis

thickhead *n*
fool, idiot, dunce
colloq. nitwit, twit, numskull, fathead, blockhead, dimwit, dope, clot, dummy, pinhead, chump, imbecile, moron

thick-headed *adj*
stupid, foolish, dense, slow, brainless, obtuse, dim-witted, dull-witted, idiotic, imbecilic, moronic, asinine, doltish, slow-witted
colloq. blockheaded, dopey, thick, gormless
E3 clever, intelligent, sharp; *colloq.* brainy

thickness *n*
1 WIDTH, breadth, diameter, extent, density, viscosity, consistency, bulk, bulkiness, body, solidness, closeness
2 LAYER, stratum, seam, vein, band, deposit, bed, ply, sheet, coat, film, lamina
E3 **1** thinness

thickset *adj*
stocky, heavy, heavily built, well-built, sturdy, powerful, strong, muscular, burly, solid, bulky, squabby, squat, dense

colloq. beefy, brawny,
E3 lanky

thick-skinned *adj*
insensitive, unfeeling, callous, tough, invulnerable,
hardened, case-hardened, inured
colloq. hard-boiled, hard-nosed, tough as old boots
E3 thin-skinned, sensitive, vulnerable

thief *n*
robber, bandit, pickpocket, shoplifter, burglar, housebreaker, plunderer, poacher, stealer, pilferer,
kleptomaniac, fraud, fraudster, swindler, embezzler,
brigand
colloq. mugger, filcher, nicker, nobbler

thieve *v*
steal, rob, pinch, cheat, swindle, misappropriate,
embezzle, pilfer, plunder, poach, abstract
formal peculate, purloin
colloq. make/run off with, nobble, snaffle, filch, knock
off, lift, nick, rip off, swipe; *slang* heist

thieving *n*
stealing, theft, robbery, burglary, pilferage, pilfering,
shoplifting, plundering, embezzlement, larceny,
thievery, banditry, crookedness, piracy
formal peculation
colloq. mugging, knocking off, ripping off, lifting,
nicking, filching

thievish *adj*
dishonest, fraudulent, crooked, light-fingered,
thieving, larcenous, predatory
formal furacious, rapacious
colloq. sticky-fingered

thin *adj, v*
▶ *adj* **1** LEAN, slim, slender, fine, light, svelte,
narrow, paper-thin, wafer-thin, attenuated, slight,
skinny, bony, skeletal, scraggy, scrawny, spindly, lanky,
gaunt, spare, anorexic, wasted, shrunken,
underweight, undernourished, emaciated
colloq. thin as a rake
2 *thin fabric*
fine, delicate, light, flimsy, filmy, gauzy, gossamer,
sheer, see-through, transparent, translucent
formal diaphonous
3 SPARSE, scarce, scattered, scant, paltry, meagre,
poor, inadequate, deficient, scanty, skimpy, straggly,
wispy
4 WEAK, feeble, runny, watery, diluted, dilute
colloq. wishy-washy
5 *the evidence is thin*
weak, flimsy, unconvincing, implausible, feeble, lame,
inadequate, inconclusive, untenable, defective,
deficient
6 *a thin voice/sound*
high-pitched, soft, quiet, weak, faint
E3 **1** fat, broad **2** substantial, thick, dense, solid
3 thick, plentiful, abundant **4** strong, thick
5 strong, substantial
▷ **on thin ice** precarious, unsafe, at risk, vulnerable,
insecure, in jeopardy, open to attack
▶ *v* **1** DIMINISH, reduce, dwindle, decrease, lessen,
make/become less in number, trim, narrow, weed out
formal attenuate
2 WEAKEN, dilute, make more watery, water down,
rarefy, refine

thing *n*
1 ARTICLE, item, object, entity, creature, body,
substance
2 DEVICE, contrivance, gadget, tool, implement,

instrument, apparatus, machine, mechanism
colloq. gismo, doodah, thingy, thingummy, thingamy,
thingummyjig, thingummybob, what-d'you-call-it,
whatsit, what's-its-name
3 *take your things with you*
clothes, clothing, garments, belongings, possessions,
paraphernalia, goods, luggage, baggage, equipment,
tools, apparatus, tackle, oddments, odds and ends,
bits and pieces
formal apparel, attire, effects
colloq. stuff, gear, togs, bits and bobs, clobber
4 ASPECT, detail, particular, characteristic, trait,
feature, quality, property, factor, element, attribute,
point, fact, concept, notion, thought, idea
5 ACT, deed, feat, exploit, action, undertaking, job,
chore, task, responsibility, problem
6 CIRCUMSTANCE, situation, eventuality,
happening, occurrence, event, episode, matter,
incident, phenomenon, affair, proceeding,
arrangement, condition
7 OBSESSION, preoccupation, fixation, *idée fixe*,
fetish, phobia, dislike, fear, horror, aversion
colloq. hang-up, one-track mind
8 LIKING, fondness, love, affection, preference,
partiality, affinity, taste, attraction, appreciation,
proneness, inclination, tendency, bias, leaning, bent,
desire, weakness, fancy
formal predilection, penchant, propensity, proclivity
colloq. soft spot
▷ **the thing** fashionable, popular, in vogue, current,
latest, modish; *colloq.* the latest, all the rage, hip, cool

think *v, n*
▶ *v* **1** BELIEVE, hold, consider, regard, judge,
estimate, reckon, calculate, determine, conclude,
reason
formal esteem, deem, opine
colloq. figure, reckon
2 CONCEIVE, imagine, suppose, guess, presume,
expect, foresee, envisage, visualize, anticipate
formal surmise, conjecture
3 *think it over*
ponder, mull over, chew over, brood, ruminate,
meditate, contemplate, muse, reflect, concentrate,
deliberate, weigh up, recall, review, take stock,
recollect, remember
formal cogitate, cerebrate
colloq. sleep on it
▷ **think better of** change your mind about, think
again, think twice, reconsider, rethink, revise, have
second thoughts about, decide not to do; *colloq.* get
cold feet
▷ **think much of** think highly of, admire, prize,
respect, value, set store by, rate; *formal* esteem
E3 abominate
▷ **think nothing of** consider normal, consider
usual
▷ **think over** reflect upon, consider, weigh up,
contemplate, meditate, ponder, chew over, ruminate,
mull over
▷ **think up** devise, contrive, dream up, imagine,
conceive, visualize, invent, design, create, concoct
▶ *n* consideration, contemplation, deliberation,
reflection, meditation, assessment, evaluation
formal cogitation

thinkable *adj*
likely, imaginable, possible, feasible, reasonable,
supposable, conceivable
formal cogitable
E3 unthinkable

thinker *n*
philosopher, scholar, theorist, ideologist, intellect, sage, mastermind
colloq. brain

thinking *n, adj*
▶ *n* reasoning, philosophy, thought(s), conclusion(s), theory, idea, opinion, view, outlook, position, judgement, assessment, evaluation, appraisal
▶ *adj* reasoning, rational, sensible, intellectual, intelligent, cultured, sophisticated, philosophical, analytical, logical, reflective, contemplative, meditative, thoughtful

thin-skinned *adj*
sensitive, easily upset, snappish, soft, susceptible, tender, vulnerable, hypersensitive, irritable
colloq. touchy
ε≡ thick-skinned, unfeeling, callous

third-rate *adj*
low-grade, low-quality, poor, bad, awful, inferior, unsatisfactory, mediocre, indifferent, slipshod, shoddy, cheap and nasty
colloq. ropy; *slang* naff
ε≡ first-rate

thirst *n, v*
▶ *n* **1** THIRSTINESS, dryness, drought, parchedness, aridity, drouth, drouthiness
2 DESIRE, longing, yearning, hankering, craving, hunger, appetite, lust, passion, eagerness, keenness
colloq. yen
▶ *v* hunger, desire, long, yearn, hanker, crave, lust

thirsty *adj*
1 DRY, dehydrated, arid
colloq. parched, gasping
2 *thirsty for knowledge*
desirous, longing, yearning, hankering, craving, hungry, thirsting, burning, itching, dying, eager, keen, avid, greedy

thong *n*
band, strip, belt, cord, lash, strap

thorn *n*
spike, point, barb, prickle, spine, bristle, needle
Related adjective: spiniform

thorny *adj*
1 SPIKY, pointed, sharp, barbed, prickly, spiny, bristly
formal acanthous, spinous, spinose
2 *a thorny problem*
difficult, troublesome, irksome, vexed, worrying, trying, upsetting, problematic, knotty, complex, intricate, tough, awkward, delicate, tricky, ticklish
formal convoluted

thorough *adj*
1 *a thorough person*
painstaking, scrupulous, meticulous, careful, conscientious, efficient, methodical
2 *thorough research*
sweeping, all-embracing, comprehensive, all-inclusive, exhaustive, scrupulous, meticulous, extensive, deep, thoroughgoing, intensive, widespread, in-depth
3 *a thorough waste of time*
full, complete, total, entire, utter, absolute, perfect, pure, sheer, unqualified, unmitigated, out-and-out, downright
ε≡ **1, 2** partial, superficial, careless

thoroughbred *adj*
pedigree, pedigreed, pure-blood, pure-blooded, full-blooded, blooded
ε≡ cross-bred, hybrid, mixed, mongrel

thoroughfare *n*
road, street, roadway, way, highway, avenue, motorway, passage, passageway, access, turnpike, boulevard, concourse

thoroughly *adv*
1 CAREFULLY, painstakingly, meticulously, scrupulously, intensively, conscientiously, assiduously, efficiently, comprehensively, sweepingly, exhaustively, root and branch, inside out
2 FULLY, perfectly, completely, absolutely, downright, entirely, quite, totally, utterly
colloq. every inch, with a fine-tooth comb
ε≡ **1** carelessly, haphazardly **2** partially

though *conj, adv*
▶ *conj* although, even if, while, allowing, granted
formal notwithstanding
▶ *adv* however, but, nevertheless, nonetheless, yet, still, even so, for all that
colloq. all the same

thought *n*
1 THINKING, attention, care, heed, regard, consideration, reasoning, study, scrutiny, introspection, meditation, pondering, contemplation, musing, rumination, reflection, deliberation
formal cogitation, cerebration
2 IDEA, notion, concept, conception, belief, conviction, opinion, view, point of view, feeling, judgement, theory, assessment, estimation, appraisal, conclusion, plan, design, intention, purpose, reason, aim, hope, dream, prospect, expectation, anticipation, aspiration
3 THOUGHTFULNESS, consideration, kindness, care, concern, regard, compassion, sympathy, tenderness, gesture, touch
formal solicitude

thoughtful *adj*
1 PENSIVE, wistful, dreamy, abstracted, reflective, contemplative, introspective, thinking, absorbed, studious, serious, solemn, quiet, lost in thought, deep, profound
formal cogitative
colloq. in a brown study
2 CONSIDERATE, kind, unselfish, helpful, caring, compassionate, sympathetic, tender, attentive, mindful, careful, prudent, cautious, wary
formal heedful, solicitous
ε≡ **2** thoughtless, insensitive, selfish

thoughtless *adj*
1 INCONSIDERATE, unthinking, insensitive, unfeeling, tactless, undiplomatic, indiscreet, unkind, rude, impolite, selfish, uncaring
2 ABSENT-MINDED, inattentive, heedless, mindless, foolish, stupid, silly, rash, hasty, reckless, ill-considered, ill-advised, unwise, imprudent, careless, negligent, remiss
formal precipitate
ε≡ **1** thoughtful, considerate **2** careful

thrall *n*
thraldom, power, bondage, enslavement, servitude, slavery, subjection, serfdom, vassalage
formal subjugation
ε≡ freedom

thrash v
1 PUNISH, beat, whip, lash, flog, scourge, cane, spank, clobber, lay into
colloq. wallop, tan, whack, belt
2 DEFEAT, beat, trounce, drub, be more than a match for, have the edge on, crush, overwhelm, rout
formal vanquish
colloq. hammer, slaughter, clobber, lick, wipe the floor with
3 THRESH, flail, hit, flog, toss, jerk, swish, writhe
▷ **thrash out** discuss, debate, negotiate, hammer out, settle, resolve, clear the air

thrashing n
1 PUNISHMENT, flogging, lashing, caning, hiding, beating, tanning, whipping, leathering, pasting
formal chastisement
colloq. belting
2 DEFEAT, drubbing, beating, rout, crushing, trouncing, lamming
colloq. hammering, clobbering, licking

thread n, v
▶ n 1 YARN, strand, fibre, filament, string, line, strip, streak
Related adjective: fibrillary, fibrillous

Types of thread include: button thread, cotton, coton à broder, mercerized cotton, pearl cotton, machine twist, quick-match, stranded cotton, embroidery thread, machine embroidery thread, embroidery silk, embroidery wool, floss, metallic thread, polyester, purl, silk, wool, knitting wool, 2-ply, 3-ply, 4-ply, baby wool, chunky wool, double-knitting, tapestry wool, crewel wool, Persian wool.

2 COURSE, direction, drift, tenor, theme, subject, motif, plot, storyline, train of thought
▶ v pass, ease, move, push, inch, meander, wind, string, weave

threadbare adj
1 *threadbare clothes*
worn, frayed, ragged, moth-eaten, scruffy, tatty, tattered, shabby
2 HACKNEYED, overused, old, stale, tired, trite, worn-out, well-worn, cliché-ridden, commonplace, stock, stereotyped
colloq. corny
🖪 1 new 2 fresh

threat n
menace, warning, ultimatum, omen, foreboding, danger, risk, hazard, peril
formal portent, presage, commination

threaten v
1 MENACE, intimidate, browbeat, cow, pressurize, bully, extort, blackmail, terrorize, warn, warn (off), endanger, jeopardize, imperil
colloq. push around, lean on, put the frighteners on, put the screws on
2 BE IMMINENT, be in the offing, approach, loom (up), forebode, foreshadow
formal portend, presage, augur, comminate

threatening adj
menacing, intimidatory, warning, cautionary, ominous, foreboding, sinister, grim, looming
formal inauspicious, impending, minacious, minatory

threesome n
trio, trilogy, triple, triplet, triumvirate, triad, triune, troika, trinity, triptych

threshold n
doorstep, sill, doorway, door, entrance, entry, brink, verge, starting-point, dawn, beginning, start, commencement, outset, opening
formal inception

thrift n
economy, husbandry, saving, conservation, frugality, carefulness
formal prudence, parsimony
colloq. scrimping and saving
🖪 extravagance, waste

thriftless adj
extravagant, lavish, spendthrift, unthrifty, wasteful, prodigal
formal imprudent, improvident, dissipative, profligate
🖪 thrifty

thrifty adj
economical, saving, frugal, sparing, careful, conserving
formal prudent, parsimonious
🖪 extravagant, profligate, prodigal, wasteful

thrill n, v
▶ n excitement, adventure, pleasure, delight, joy, stimulation, charge, sensation, feeling, glow, tingle, throb, frisson, shudder, flutter, vibration, quiver, tremor
colloq. kick, buzz
▶ v excite, exhilarate, rouse, arouse, move, stir, stimulate, electrify, galvanize, flush, glow, tingle, throb, shudder, flutter, vibrate, tremble, shiver, quiver, shake
colloq. give a buzz/kick to
🖪 bore

thrilling adj
exciting, stimulating, stirring, rousing, riveting, sensational, exhilarating, gripping, electrifying, rip-roaring, heart-stirring, soul-stirring, shaking, shuddering, shivering, trembling, vibrating, quaking
colloq. hair-raising

thrive v
flourish, prosper, boom, grow, increase, advance, develop, bloom, blossom, gain, profit, succeed, do well, make progress, make headway
formal burgeon
🖪 languish, stagnate, fail, die

thriving adj
prosperous, successful, blossoming, booming, developing, flourishing, growing, healthy, wealthy, affluent, well, comfortable, blooming
formal burgeoning
🖪 ailing, failing, languishing, stagnating, dying

throat n
throttle, windpipe, gullet, gorge, oesophagus, craw, thropple, fauces, halse
old use weasand
Scot. thrapple
colloq. the Red Lane
Related adjective: guttural, jugular

throaty adj
guttural, hoarse, rasping, raucous, low, husky, deep, gruff, thick

throb v, n
▶ v pulse, pulsate, beat, palpitate, vibrate, pound, thump, drum

▶ *n* pulse, pulsation, beat, palpitation, vibration, pounding, thumping, drumming

throe *n*
convulsion, fit, pain, pang, paroxysm, seizure, spasm, stab, suffering, distress, agony, anguish, torture
formal travail

throng *n, v*
▶ *n* crowd, mass, mob, multitude, pack, press, crush, jam, swarm, flock, congregation, herd, bevy, horde, host
formal assemblage
▶ *v* flock, fill, crowd, cram, converge, herd, press, swarm, pack, bunch, congregate, jam
colloq. mill around

throttle *v*
1 STRANGLE, strangulate, choke, asphyxiate, suffocate, smother, stifle
2 SUPPRESS, gag, silence, inhibit, restrain, check, keep in, hold back, strangle, stifle, smother

through *prep, adj*
▶ *prep* 1 ACROSS, all the way across, from one side of to the other, from one end of to the other
2 BETWEEN, by, with the help of, via, by way of, by means of, using, through the agency of
formal through the good offices of, by virtue of
3 *all through the night*
throughout, during, in, to/until the end of, from the beginning to the end of, without a break/interruption in
4 BECAUSE OF, as a result of, owing to, due to, thanks to, on account of, by virtue of
▷ **through and through** completely, totally, thoroughly, utterly, wholly, entirely, fully, unreservedly, altogether, to the core, from top to bottom
▶ *adj* 1 FINISHED, ended, completed, done, no longer having anything to do with, no longer involved with
formal terminated
2 *through train*
direct, express, non-stop

throughout *adv, prep*
▶ *adv* everywhere, in every part, extensively, widely, completely, from beginning to end
formal ubiquitously
▶ *prep* 1 DURING, during/in the whole of, all through, in the course of, for the duration of
2 IN ALL PARTS, in every part of, all over, all round, everywhere

throw *v, n*
▶ *v* 1 HURL, heave, lob, pitch, sling, cast, fling, toss, shy, launch, project, propel, catapult, send
colloq. chuck
2 MOVE QUICKLY, fling, turn, force, put, cast
3 *throw light*
shed, cast, project, send, direct, cause to fall, emit, radiate, give off
4 BRING DOWN, floor, fell, prostrate, upset, overturn, dislodge, unseat, unsaddle, unhorse
5 *throw a switch*
put on, switch on, operate, work
6 PERPLEX, baffle, confound, disturb, put out, confuse, disconcert, surprise, astonish, dumbfound
formal discomfit
colloq. floor
7 *throw a party*
arrange, organize, give, put on, lay on
▷ **throw away** 1 DISCARD, jettison, get rid of,

reject, scrap, dispose of, throw out; *formal* dispense with; *colloq.* dump, ditch, chuck away/out 2 WASTE, lose, squander, fritter away; *slang* blow
🔁 1 keep, preserve, salvage, rescue 2 exploit, make use of, capitalize on
▷ **throw off** shed, cast off, drop, abandon, shake off, free yourself from, get rid of, discard, jettison, elude, escape from
▷ **throw out** 1 EVICT, turn out, expel, eject; *colloq.* turf out 2 REJECT, discard, dismiss, turn down, jettison, throw away, scrap; *formal* dispense with; *colloq.* dump, ditch 3 EMIT, emit, radiate, give off, emanate, exude, send out, diffuse, produce
4 MENTION, speak about, refer to, bring up, point out, introduce
▷ **throw over** abandon, desert, discard, drop, finish with, jilt, leave, reject; *formal* forsake; *colloq.* chuck, quit
▷ **throw up** 1 VOMIT, spew, regurgitate, disgorge, retch, heave, gag; *colloq.* puke 2 ABANDON, renounce, resign, quit, leave; *formal* relinquish; *colloq.* chuck in, pack in, jack in
▶ *n* heave, lob, pitch, sling, fling, toss, cast
colloq. chuck

throwaway *adj*
1 *throwaway comments*
careless, casual, offhand, passing, unemphatic, undramatic
2 *a throwaway product*
disposable, cheap, expendable, non-returnable, biodegradable

thrust *v, n*
▶ *v* 1 PUSH, shove, butt, ram, jam, wedge, stick, poke, prod, jab, lunge, pierce, stab, plunge, drive, press, force, impel, drive, propel
2 IMPOSE, press, urge, force, inflict, burden, saddle, encumber, foist
▶ *n* 1 PUSH, shove, poke, prod, lunge, jab, ram, prod, stab
2 DRIVE, motive, power, force, pressure, impetus, momentum
3 *the thrust of an argument*
gist, essence, drift, tenor, theme, message, point, substance

thud *n, v*
thump, clump, knock, clunk, clonk, smack, bash, crash, bang, thunder
colloq. wallop, wham

thug *n*
ruffian, tough, rough, roughneck, robber, bandit, killer, murderer, cut-throat, assassin, hoodlum, gangster, hooligan, villain
colloq. mugger

thumb *v*
▷ **thumb through** glance at, scan, skim, peruse, browse through, flick through, flip through, leaf through

thumbnail *adj*
short, brief, concise, pithy, quick, small, compact, succinct, miniature

thumbs-down
refusal, rejection, disapproval, negation, rebuff, no, turn-down
🔁 thumbs-up

thumbs-up
approval, encouragement, acceptance, yes, sanction

formal affirmation
colloq. go-ahead, green light, OK
▣ thumbs-down

thump   *v, n*
▶ *v* **1** HIT, strike, knock, punch, box, cuff, smack,
thrash, slap, rap, thwack, crash, bang, thud, batter
colloq. clout, whack, wallop
2 THROB, pound, hammer, beat, pulsate, palpitate
▶ *n* knock, blow, punch, box, cuff, smack, rap,
thwack, crash, bang, thud, beat, throb
colloq. clout, whack, wallop

thumping   *adj, adv*
▶ *adj* big, enormous, great, intense, extreme, severe,
immense, massive, huge, colossal, monumental,
terrific, thundering, tremendous, impressive,
mammoth, excessive, exorbitant, gigantic, towering,
gargantuan, titanic
colloq. whopping
▣ insignificant, petty, trivial; *colloq.* piddling
▶ *adv* extremely, very, intensely, really, greatly,
severely, unusually

thunder   *n, v*
▶ *n* boom, reverberation, crash, crashing, bang,
crack, clap, peal, rumble, roll, roar, outburst, blast,
explosion
▶ *v* boom, resound, reverberate, crash, bang, crack,
clap, peal, rumble, roll, roar, bellow, blast

thundering   *adj, adv*
▶ *adj* great, enormous, excessive, remarkable,
monumental, tremendous, unmitigated
▶ *adv* extremely, very, intensely, really, greatly,
severely, unusually

thunderous   *adj*
booming, resounding, reverberating, roaring,
rumbling, loud, noisy, deafening, tumultuous,
ear-splitting

thunderstruck   *adj*
stunned, shocked, staggered, amazed, astonished,
astounded, dazed, dumbfounded, open-mouthed,
paralysed, aghast, agape, petrified
colloq. flabbergasted, floored, flummoxed,
nonplussed, bowled over, knocked for six

thus   *adv*
1 THEREFORE, so, consequently, then, accordingly
formal hence, ergo
2 LIKE THIS, in this way, so, as follows

thwack   *v, n*
▶ *v* beat, bash, hit, flog, smack, thump, slap, buffet,
cuff
colloq. clout, wallop, whack
▶ *n* blow, bash, slap, thump, smack, cuff, buffet
colloq. wallop, whack

thwart   *v*
frustrate, foil, defeat, hinder, hamper, impede,
obstruct, block, balk, check, baffle, stop, prevent,
oppose, cross, nobble
colloq. stymie
▣ help, assist, aid

tic   *n*
jerk, spasm, twitch, tic douloureux

tick   *n, v*
▶ *n* **1** CLICK, tap, stroke, beat, tick-tock
2 *wait a tick*
moment, instant, flash, second, minute, twinkling
colloq. jiffy, sec, trice

3 MARK, line, stroke
US check
▶ *v* **1** MARK, indicate, choose, select
US check
2 CLICK, tap, beat
▷ **tick off** **1** *tick off items on a list* put a tick against,
mark, indicate; *US* check (off) **2** SCOLD, chide,
reprimand, rebuke, reproach, reprove;
formal upbraid; *colloq.* tell off, give someone a
dressing-down, haul over the coals, tear off a strip
▣ **2** praise, compliment

ticket   *n*
pass, card, certificate, token, voucher, coupon, docket,
stub, counterfoil, slip, label, tag, sticker

tickle   *v*
touch, stroke, excite, thrill, delight, please, gratify,
amuse, entertain, divert, interest, stimulate

ticklish   *adj*
sensitive, touchy, delicate, thorny, awkward,
problematic, difficult, tricky, knotty, critical, risky,
hazardous, precarious
colloq. dodgy
▣ easy, simple, straightforward

tide   *n, v*
▶ *n* **1** CURRENT, ebb, flow, stream, flux, movement
2 COURSE, movement, run, direction, drift, trend,
tendency, tenor
▶ *v* ▷ **tide over** help (through), assist, aid, see
through, keep going, help out

tidings   *n*
news, communication, report, bulletin, message,
advice, word, information, intelligence, greetings
colloq. dope, gen

tidy   *adj, v*
▶ *adj* **1** NEAT, orderly, methodical, efficient,
businesslike, systematic, organized, in order, well-
ordered, ordered, uncluttered, clean, spick-and-span,
immaculate, shipshape, smart, spruce, trim, well-
groomed, well-kept
2 *a tidy sum*
large, substantial, sizeable, considerable, fair,
respectable, good, generous, ample
▣ **1** untidy, messy, disorganized **2** small,
insignificant
▶ *v* neaten, straighten (out), straighten up, order,
arrange, clean (up), clear up, smarten, spruce up,
groom

tie   *v, n*
▶ *v* **1** FASTEN, knot, fix, secure, moor, tether, attach,
join, connect, link, couple, unite, rope, lash, strap,
chain, bind
2 RESTRAIN, restrict, confine, limit, curb, constrain,
hamper, impede, hinder, cramp, shackle
3 DRAW, be equal, be even
colloq. be all square
▷ **tie down** restrain, constrain, restrict, confine,
limit, hamper, hinder
▷ **tie up** **1** MOOR, tether, attach, fasten, secure,
rope, lash, chain, bind, connect, truss, wrap up,
restrain; *colloq.* do up **2** CONCLUDE, settle, finalize;
formal terminate; *colloq.* wind up, wrap up
3 OCCUPY, engage, engross, keep busy
▶ *n* **1** KNOT, fastening, link, band, bond, ribbon,
tape, clip
2 CONNECTION, link, liaison, relationship, bond,
friendship, affiliation, allegiance, kinship
3 OBLIGATION, commitment, duty, restraint,

constraint, restriction, limit, limitation, hindrance
4 DRAW, dead heat, stalemate, deadlock

tie-in *n*
connection, relationship, link, relation, co-ordination,
association, liaison, tie-up, affiliation
colloq. hook-up

tier *n*
floor, storey, level, stage, layer, stratum, belt, zone,
band, echelon, rank, row, line, bank

tiff *n*
disagreement, squabble, row, difference, difference of
opinion, quarrel, words, dispute, temper, ill-humour,
sulk, tantrum
colloq. falling-out, huff, scrap, set-to, pet, barney, spat

tight *adj*
1 TAUT, stretched, tense, strained, strained, rigid,
stiff, firm, fixed, fast, secure, close, cramped, clenched,
constricted, compressed, limited, restricted, compact,
snug, close-fitting, skin-tight, figure-hugging
2 SEALED, hermetic, sound-proof, impervious,
impenetrable, airtight, watertight
3 *tight security*
strict, tough, firm, severe, stringent, rigorous, hard,
harsh, rigid, inflexible
4 *money is tight*
scarce, limited, insufficient, inadequate, too little,
not enough, in short supply
5 *a tight contest*
close, evenly matched, well-matched, hard-fought
colloq. neck and neck
6 *in a tight corner/spot*
difficult, awkward, problematic, tricky, delicate
colloq. dodgy
7 MEAN, stingy, miserly, niggardly, penny-pinching
formal parsimonious
colloq. tight-fisted
8 DRUNK, intoxicated, tipsy
colloq. under the influence, sloshed, sozzled,
plastered, tiddly, merry, well-oiled, legless;
slang pissed, stoned, tanked up, smashed
⊟ 1 loose, slack   **2** open   **3** lax   **4** plentiful
6 easy   **7** generous   **8** sober

tighten *v*
tauten, stretch, pull tight, tense, stiffen, fix, fasten,
make fast, secure, narrow, close, cramp, constrict,
crush, squeeze
formal rigidify, constringe
⊟ loosen, relax

tight-fisted *adj*
mean, stingy, miserly, niggardly, penny-pinching,
sparing, grasping
formal parsimonious
colloq. mingy, tight
⊟ generous, charitable

tight-lipped *adj*
silent, uncommunicative, unforthcoming, close-
lipped, close-mouthed, quiet, reticent, taciturn,
reserved, secretive, mum, mute
⊟ talkative, forthcoming, garrulous

till [1] *prep*
till the end of June
until, up to, to, up to the time of, all through
US through

till [2] *v*
till the land
cultivate, work, plough, dig, farm

tilt *v, n*
▶ *v* **1** SLOPE, incline, slant, pitch, list, tip, lean, cant
2 ATTACK, charge, rush, fight, contend, encounter,
clash, duel, spar, joust
▶ *n* **1** SLOPE, incline, angle, inclination, slant, pitch,
list
2 ATTACK, charge, fight, contest, encounter, combat,
clash, duel, spar, joust, tournament
▷ **at full tilt** very quickly, very fast, at full speed, at
top speed, at full blast, at full pelt, with full force;
colloq. all out, flat out

timber *n*
1 WOOD, trees, forest
US lumber
2 BEAM, lath, plank, pole, spar, board, log

timbre *n*
quality, voice quality, tone, tonality, resonance, ring,
colour
technical klang

time *n, v*
▶ *n* **1** SPELL, stretch, period, term, season, session,
span, duration, interval, space, while
2 TEMPO, beat, rhythm, metre, measure
3 MOMENT, point, juncture, stage, instance, instant,
occasion, date
4 AGE, era, epoch, life, lifetime, lifespan, generation,
heyday, peak
Related adjective: temporal

Periods of time include: eternity, eon, era, age,
generation, period, epoch, millennium, chiliad,
century, lifetime, decade, decennium,
quinquennium, year, light-year, yesteryear, quarter,
month, fortnight, week, midweek, weekend, long
weekend, day, today, tonight, yesterday, tomorrow,
morrow, weekday, hour, minute, second, moment,
instant, millisecond, microsecond, nanosecond;
dawn, sunrise, sun-up, the early hours, *colloq.* wee
small hours, morning, morn, a.m., daytime, midday,
noon, high noon, p.m., afternoon, tea-time, evening,
twilight, dusk, sunset, nightfall, bedtime, night,
night-time; season, spring, summer, midsummer,
autumn, *US* fall, winter.

▷ **all the time** continually, constantly, perpetually,
incessantly, interminably, always, forever
⊟ never
▷ **at one time** once, formerly, previously, at one
point, long ago, in times past
▷ **at the same time 1** SIMULTANEOUSLY, all
together, in parallel; *formal* concurrently
2 NEVERTHELESS, nonetheless, still, but, however,
anyway, even so, for all that
▷ **at times** sometimes, on occasions, from time to
time, now and again, now and then, off and on, every so
often
▷ **behind time** late, overdue, unpunctual, delayed,
behind, behind schedule; *formal* tardy
⊟ early
▷ **behind the times** old-fashioned, out of date,
dated, old, unfashionable, out of fashion, obsolete, past;
colloq. fuddy-duddy, old hat, past its sell-by date
⊟ up to date
▷ **for the time being** at present, for now, right now,
just now, at the moment, for the moment, for the
present, at the present time, temporarily, (in the)
meantime, meanwhile, pro tem
▷ **from time to time** now and again, now and then,
at times, sometimes, occasionally, on occasion, once in
a while, periodically, intermittently, spasmodically,

sporadically, every now and then, every so often

▣ constantly, always

▷ **in good time** early, with time to spare, ahead of time, ahead of schedule, punctually, on time

▣ late

▷ **in time** not too late, early enough, punctually, on time

▷ **on time** punctually, promptly, exactly, precisely, sharp, on the dot; *colloq.* dead on, bang on, spot on

▣ late

▷ **play for time** delay, hesitate, stall, temporize, stonewall, hang fire, filibuster; *formal* procrastinate; *colloq.* drag your feet

▷ **time after time** repeatedly, frequently, often, recurrently, many times, on many occasions, time and (time) again, again and again, over and over again

▶ *v* **1** ARRANGE, set, schedule, programme, timetable, fix

2 MEASURE, clock, calculate, count, meter, regulate, control, adjust

time-honoured *adj*
age-old, traditional, long-established, usual, accustomed, conventional, customary, established, fixed, old, ancient, historic, venerable

timeless *adj*
ageless, immortal, deathless, everlasting, eternal, endless, permanent, lasting, enduring, changeless, unchanging, unending, indestructible, imperishable
formal immutable, abiding

timely *adj*
well-timed, at the right time, seasonable, suitable, appropriate, convenient, opportune, prompt, punctual
formal propitious, felicitous
▣ ill-timed, unsuitable, inappropriate

timetable *n, v*
▶ *n* schedule, programme, agenda, calendar, diary, rota, roster, list, listing, curriculum
▶ *v* schedule, programme, diarize, set, fix, arrange, list

time-worn *adj*
worn, old, aged, dog-eared, out of date, *passé*, outworn, ruined, well-worn, tired, trite, stock, stale, threadbare, bromidic, clichéed, hackneyed, weathered, dated, decrepit, ancient, broken-down, run-down, shabby, ragged, hoary, wrinkled, lined
▣ fresh, new

timid *adj*
shy, bashful, modest, shrinking, retiring, nervous, apprehensive, afraid, scared, frightened, fearful, cowardly, faint-hearted, spineless, irresolute
formal timorous, pusillanimous
colloq. chicken, yellow, gutless, wimpish, lily-livered
▣ brave, bold, confident

timorous *adj*
shy, timid, bashful, afraid, fearful, scared, frightened, apprehensive, shrinking, retiring, faint-hearted, nervous, diffident, coy, tentative, irresolute, modest, unadventurous, cowardly, trembling
formal pusillanimous
colloq. mousy
▣ assertive, assured, bold

tincture *n, v*
▶ *n* trace, flavour, touch, tinge, tint, colour, hint, hue, dash, suggestion, shade, stain, seasoning, smack, aroma

▶ *v* flavour, scent, season, stain, tinge, tint, colour, dye, infuse, permeate, imbue, suffuse

tinge *n, v*
▶ *n* **1** TRACE, touch, suggestion, hint, smack, flavour, pinch, drop, dash, bit, sprinkling, smattering
2 TINT, dye, colour, shade, wash, tincture
▶ *v* tint, dye, stain, colour, flavour, shade, suffuse, imbue

tingle *v, n*
▶ *v* sting, prickle, tickle, itch, prick, thrill, throb, tremble, quiver, vibrate
▶ *n* stinging, prickling, tickle, tickling, itch, itching, thrill, tremor, throb, quiver, shiver, gooseflesh, goose-pimples
colloq. pins and needles

tinker *v, n*
▶ *v* fiddle, play, toy, trifle, potter, dabble, meddle, fool about/around, tamper
colloq. mess about/around
▶ *n* itinerant, Gypsy, fixer, mender, botcher, bungler

tinkle *v, n*
▶ *v* ring, ding, jingle, jangle, clink, chink, peal, chime
▶ *n* **1** *the tinkle of the bell*
ring, ding, jingle, jangle, clink, chink, peal, chime
2 *give you a tinkle*
ring, phone call, call
colloq. buzz, bell

tinsel *adj, n*
▶ *adj* showy, ostentatious, cheap, gaudy, tawdry, trashy, superficial, specious, gimcrack, sham
formal meretricious
colloq. flashy
▶ *n* glitter, spangle, frippery, show, triviality, display, ostentation, flamboyance, garishness, gaudiness, sham, worthlessness, artificiality, meaninglessness, insignificance, pretension

tint *n, v*
▶ *n* dye, stain, rinse, wash, colour, hue, shade, tincture, tinge, tone, cast, streak, trace, touch
▶ *v* dye, colour, tinge, streak, stain, taint, affect

tiny *adj*
minute, microscopic, infinitesimal, minuscule, small, little, slight, trifling, negligible, insignificant, diminutive, petite, dwarfish, midget, pocket, miniature, Lilliputian
Scot. wee
colloq. pint-sized, mini, teeny, teeny-weeny, itsy-bitsy
▣ huge, enormous, immense

tip¹ *n, v*
▶ *n* *the tip of a finger*
end, extremity, point, nib, apex, peak, pinnacle, summit, acme, top, cap, crown, head
▶ *v* cap, crown, top, surmount

tip² *v, n*
▶ *v* *tip your head*
lean, incline, slant, list, tilt, cant, topple (over), capsize, upset, overturn, spill, pour (out), empty, unload, dump
▶ *n* dump, rubbish-heap, refuse-heap, slag heap, midden

tip³ *n, v*
▶ *n* **1** HINT, pointer, clue, suggestion, advice, recommendation, warning, tip-off, information, inside information, forecast
2 GRATUITY, gift, bonus, reward, gift, present, baksheesh, *pourboire*

formal perquisite
colloq. perk
▶ *v* **1** ADVISE, suggest, warn, caution, forewarn, tip off, inform, tell
2 *tip the driver*
reward, remunerate

tip-off *n*
hint, pointer, clue, suggestion, warning, information, inside information

tipple *v, n*
▶ *v* drink, imbibe, indulge, quaff, bib
colloq. swig, booze
▶ *n* drink, regular drink, favourite drink, alcohol, liquor
colloq. booze, poison, usual

tippler *n*
drinker, hard drinker, drunk, drunkard, dipso(maniac), bibber, inebriate, wine-bag
colloq. boozer, sponge; *slang* lush, soak, sot, toper, wino

tipsy *adj*
drunk, under the influence
colloq. merry, happy, mellow, squiff(y), tiddly, tight
🖅 sober

tirade *n*
harangue, diatribe, denunciation, abuse, lecture, outburst, rant
formal fulmination, invective, philippic

tire *v*
weary, fatigue, wear out, tire out, exhaust, tax, strain, drain, drop, flag, bore
formal enervate
🖅 enliven, invigorate, refresh

tired *adj*
1 WEARY, drowsy, sleepy, flagging, fatigued, wearied, worn out, exhausted, dog-tired, drained, jaded
formal enervated
colloq. fagged out, bushed, whacked, shattered, beat, dead-beat, all in, knackered, ready to drop, washed-out, hardly able to keep your eyes open
2 *tired of waiting*
bored, sick
colloq. fed up, sick and tired
3 HACKNEYED, old, stale, worn-out, trite, clichéd
colloq. corny, past its sell-by date
🖅 **1** lively, energetic, rested, refreshed **3** new

tireless *adj*
untiring, unwearied, unflagging, indefatigable, energetic, vigorous, diligent, industrious, resolute, determined
🖅 tired, lazy, unenthusiastic

tiresome *adj*
troublesome, trying, annoying, irritating, exasperating, irksome, vexatious, wearisome, dull, boring, routine, humdrum, tedious, monotonous, uninteresting, unexciting, tiring, fatiguing, laborious
🖅 interesting, stimulating, easy

tiring *adj*
wearying, wearisome, fatiguing, exhausting, draining, demanding, hard, tough, difficult, exacting, taxing, arduous, strenuous, laborious
formal enervating

tiro, tyro *n*
beginner, novice, apprentice, freshman, learner, pupil, starter, student, trainee, tenderfoot, greenhorn,

initiate, neophyte, novitiate, catechumen
🖅 veteran; *colloq.* old hand

tissue *n*
1 MATTER, substance, material
2 *a box of tissues*
paper handkerchief, disposable handkerchief, Kleenex®, facial tissue, toilet paper, toilet tissue
3 *tissue paper*
fabric, stuff, gauze, gossamer
4 *a tissue of lies*
web, mesh, network, structure, texture

tit for tat
blow for blow, retaliation, revenge, requital, measure for measure, counterblow, counterbuff, countercharge
formal quid pro quo, lex talionis
colloq. like for like, an eye for an eye and a tooth for a tooth, a taste of your own medicine

titan *n*
colossus, giant, superman, Hercules, Atlas, leviathan

titanic *adj*
colossal, huge, enormous, massive, vast, immense, giant, gigantic, jumbo, mammoth, monumental, prodigious, stupendous, towering, mountainous, monstrous, herculean, cyclopean
formal mighty
🖅 insignificant, small

titbit *n*
morsel, scrap, appetizer, snack, delicacy, dainty, treat, bonne-bouche

tithe *n, v*
▶ *n* tenth, tax, levy, duty, tariff, toll, tribute, rent, assessment, impost
▶ *v* give, hand over, pay, take in, tax, assess, charge, levy, rate

titillate *v*
stimulate, arouse, excite, thrill, tickle, provoke, tease, tantalize, intrigue, interest
colloq. turn on

titillating *adj*
stimulating, arousing, exciting, sexy, erotic, seductive, lewd, lurid, thrilling, provocative, sensational, suggestive, intriguing, interesting, teasing, captivating

titivate *v*
smarten up, touch up, refurbish, preen, make up, primp, prink
colloq. doll up, tart up

title *n, v*
▶ *n* **1** NAME, term, designation, form of address, label, epithet, nickname, sobriquet, pseudonym, *nom-de-plume*, rank, status, office, position
formal appellation, denomination
colloq. handle, moniker
Related adjective: titular
2 HEADING, headline, caption, legend, inscription, credit(s)
3 RIGHT, prerogative, privilege, claim, entitlement, ownership, proprietorship, deeds
4 CHAMPIONSHIP, match, contest, competition, game, prize, trophy, stakes, laurels, crown
▶ *v* entitle, name, call, dub, style, term, designate, tag, label

titter *v, n*
▶ *v* giggle, snigger, snicker, chuckle, cackle, laugh, chortle, mock

▶ *n* giggle, snigger, snicker, chuckle, cackle, laugh, chortle

tittle-tattle *n, v*
▶ *n* gossip, rumour, hearsay, chatter, cackle, prattle
colloq. chitchat, babble, blather, blether, jaw, natter, twaddle, ya(c)k, yackety-yak
▶ *v* gossip, chat, chatter, cackle, prattle
colloq. chitchat, tell tales, witter, babble, blather, blether, jaw, natter, ya(c)k, yackety-yak

titular *adj*
nominal, token, so-called, self-styled, honorary, formal, official
formal putative
colloq. puppet

toadstool *n*
See panel at **mushrooms and toadstools**.

toady *n, v*
▶ *n* fawner, flatterer, sycophant, groveller, lackey, minion, parasite, flunkey, jackal
colloq. yes-man, sucker, bootlicker, crawler, creep, hanger-on, truckler; *slang* arse-licker
▶ *v* curry favour, crawl, flatter, grovel, fawn, creep, cringe, kowtow
colloq. bootlick, bow and scrape, butter up, kiss the feet, suck up, truckle

toast *v, n*
▶ *v* **1** *toast bread*
grill, brown, roast, crisp, bake, heat (up), warm (up), barbecue
2 *toast the bride and groom*
drink to, drink the health of, honour, salute, pledge
▶ *n* drink, pledge, tribute, salute, salutation, compliment(s), best wishes, health

Toasts include: all the best!, *auf Ihre Gesundheit*, *à votre santé*, bottoms up!, cheers!, down the hatch!, good health!, good luck!, happy landings!, here's how!, here's looking at you!, here's mud in your eye!, here's to …!, here's to you!, *prosit!*, skoal!, *slàinte!*, to absent friends!, your health!

tobacco *n*

Forms of tobacco include: *colloq.* baccy, cheroot, chewing tobacco; cigar, Havana cigar; cigarette, cork-tipped cigarette, filter-tip cigarette, king-size cigarette, menthol cigarette, Russian cigarette; *colloq.* ciggie, *slang* coffin nail, *colloq.* fag; cigarette end, cigarette butt, *slang* dog-end, *slang* fag end; cigarillo, corona, high-tar, low-tar, panatella, plug, snuff, flake tobacco, pipe tobacco, shag tobacco, Turkish tobacco, Virginia tobacco, *colloq.* the weed.

Tobacco accessories include: ashtray, cigar box, cigar case, cigar cutter, cigar-holder, cigarette box, cigarette case, cigarette- holder, cigarette lighter, gas lighter, petrol lighter, cigarette machine, cigarette paper, cigarette roller, humidor, match, matchbook, box of matches, match striker, pipe, chibouk, church-warden, clay pipe, hookah, meerschaum, narghile, peace pipe (pipe of peace), tobacco pipe, pipe-cleaner, pipe-rack, pipe-rest, smoker's companion, snuffbox, tobacco-pouch, vesta.

today *n, adv*
1 THIS DAY, the present day, this very day, the present time, this morning, this afternoon, this evening
2 AT THIS MOMENT, at this moment in time, now,

right now, just now, at the present time, these days, nowadays

toddle *v*
walk/move unsteadily, totter, wobble, stagger, waddle, reel, lurch, stumble, falter, waver, teeter, sway, rock, shake

to-do *n*
commotion, fuss, furore, bother, disturbance, flurry, stir, tumult, turmoil, uproar, unrest, excitement, bustle, agitation, rumpus, ruction, quarrel
colloq. performance, brouhaha, flap, hoo-ha, stew

together *adv, adj*
▶ *adv* **1** UNITED, collectively, jointly, mutually, in concert, in unison, working together, in collaboration, in conjunction, as one, as a partnership, as a team
2 *travel together*
side by side, shoulder to shoulder, hand in hand, in a row
3 SIMULTANEOUSLY, at the same time, at one time, all at once
formal concurrently
4 CONTINUOUSLY, consecutively, successively, in succession, without a break, without interruption, on end
colloq. on the trot, back to back
E3 1 separately, individually **2** alone
▶ *adj* well-balanced, well-adjusted, stable, well-organized, organized, level-headed, sensible, down-to-earth, composed, calm, commonsensical
colloq. cool

toil *n, v*
▶ *n* labour, hard work, slog, drudgery, sweat, slaving, industry, application, effort, exertion
colloq. donkey-work, graft, elbow grease
▶ *v* labour, work, slave, drudge, sweat, grind, push yourself, slog, persevere, strive, struggle
colloq. graft, plug away, work like a Trojan, work your fingers to the bone

toiler *n*
worker, workaholic, drudge, grafter, slogger, struggler, slave, workhorse, labourer, menial, navvy
E3 idler, loafer, shirker

toilet *n*
lavatory, WC, bathroom, cloakroom, washroom, public convenience, urinal, latrine, convenience, powder room
US rest room
colloq. loo, bog, the ladies, the gents; *slang* kazi; *US* john

toilsome *adj*
difficult, hard, laborious, arduous, burdensome, backbreaking, fatiguing, painful, tough, wearisome, severe, strenuous, taxing, tedious, tiresome, uphill, herculean

token *n, adj*
▶ *n* **1** SYMBOL, emblem, representation, mark, sign, indication, demonstration, expression, evidence, proof, recognition, clue, warning, signal, index, reminder, remembrance, memorial, memento, souvenir, keepsake
formal manifestation
2 *gift token*
voucher, coupon, counter, disc
▶ *adj* symbolic, emblematic, nominal, slight, minimal, perfunctory, superficial, cosmetic, hollow, insincere

tolerable *adj*
1 BEARABLE, endurable, sufferable
2 ACCEPTABLE, satisfactory, passable, adequate, reasonable, fair, fairly good, average, all right, mediocre, indifferent, unexceptional, ordinary, middling
colloq. OK, so-so, run-of-the-mill, not bad, nothing (much) to write home about, no great shakes, not much cop
E3 intolerable, unbearable, insufferable

tolerance *n*
1 TOLERATION, patience, forbearance, open-mindedness, broad-mindedness, liberalism, sympathy, understanding, leniency, lenity, laxness, indulgence, permissiveness
formal magnanimity
2 VARIATION, fluctuation, allowance, clearance
colloq. play, give, swing
3 RESISTANCE, resilience, toughness, endurance, stamina
formal fortitude
E3 1 intolerance, prejudice, bias, bigotry, narrow-mindedness

tolerant *adj*
patient, forbearing, long-suffering, open-minded, fair, unprejudiced, broad-minded, catholic, liberal, charitable, kind-hearted, sympathetic, understanding, forgiving, lenient, compliant, indulgent, permissive, lax, soft
formal magnanimous
colloq. easy-going
E3 intolerant, biased, prejudiced, bigoted, unsympathetic

tolerate *v*
endure, suffer, put up with, bear, stand, swallow, take, receive, accept, admit, allow, permit, warrant, sanction, condone, indulge
formal abide, countenance
colloq. stomach

toleration *n*
1 PATIENCE, forbearance, open-mindedness, broad-mindedness, liberalism, sympathy, understanding, leniency, lenity, laxness, indulgence, permissiveness
formal magnanimity
2 RESISTANCE, resilience, toughness, endurance, stamina
formal fortitude
3 ACCEPTANCE, allowance, endurance, sufferance, sanction, indulgence

toll¹ *v*
the bell tolls
ring, peal, chime, knell, sound, strike, clang, announce, call, signal, warn, herald

toll² *n*
1 *motorway tolls*
charge, fee, payment, levy, tax, duty, tariff, rate, cost, penalty, demand
2 *the casualty toll*
cost, loss, damage, injury, death

tomb *n*
grave, burial-place, vault, crypt, sepulchre, catacomb, mausoleum, cenotaph
Related adjective: sepulchral

tombstone *n*
gravestone, headstone, stone, memorial, monument

tome *n*
book, volume, work, opus

tomfoolery *n*
mischief, horseplay, silliness, stupidity, messing about, messing on, foolishness, childishness, idiocy, inanity, skylarking, clowning, buffoonery, hooey
colloq. larking about, larks, shenanigans

tone *n, v*
▶ *n* 1 *tone of voice*
note, timbre, pitch, sound, quality, volume, expression, intonation, modulation, inflection, accent, accentuation, stress, emphasis, force, strength
2 TINT, tinge, colour, hue, shade, cast, tonality, tincture
3 AIR, manner, attitude, mood, spirit, humour, temper, character, quality, feel, style, effect, vein, tenor, drift
Related adjective: tonal
▶ *v* match, co-ordinate, suit, blend, harmonize, go (well) with
▷ **tone down** moderate, temper, subdue, restrain, soften, lighten, dim, dampen, play down, reduce, alleviate; *formal* assuage, mitigate; *colloq.* soft-pedal
▷ **tone up** shape up, touch up, trim, tune up, sharpen up, limber up, freshen, invigorate, brighten

tongue *n*
language, speech, discourse, talk, utterance, articulation, vernacular, idiom, dialect, patois, jargon, slang, argot, cant
formal parlance
colloq. lingo
Related adjective: lingual, glottic

tongue-tied *adj*
speechless, dumbstruck, inarticulate, silent, mute, dumb, wordless, voiceless, lost for words
E3 talkative, garrulous, voluble

tonic *n*
cordial, pick-me-up, restorative, refresher, bracer, stimulant, analeptic, boost, fillip
colloq. shot in the arm

too *adv*
1 ALSO, as well, in addition, furthermore, besides, moreover, likewise
2 EXCESSIVELY, inordinately, unduly, over, overly, unreasonably, ridiculously, extremely, very

tool *n, v*
▶ *n* 1 IMPLEMENT, instrument, utensil, gadget, device, contrivance, contraption, apparatus, artefact, appliance, machine, means, vehicle, medium, agency, agent, intermediary
colloq. gismo
2 PUPPET, pawn, dupe, stooge, flunkey, minion, hireling, cat's paw

Types of tool include: axe, bolster, caulking-iron, crowbar, hod, jackhammer, jointer, mattock, pick, pick-axe, plumb-line, sledgehammer; chaser, clamp, dividers, dolly, drill, hacksaw, jack, pincers, pliers, protractor, punch, rule, sander, scriber, snips, socket-wrench, soldering-iron, spraygun, tommy bar, vice, wrench; auger, awl, bevel, brace and bit, bradawl, chisel, file, fretsaw, hammer, handsaw, jack-plane, jig-saw, level, mallet, plane, rasp, saw, screwdriver, set-square, spirit level, tenon-saw, T-square; billhook, chainsaw, chopper, dibber, fork, grass-rake, hay fork, hoe, pitchfork, plough, pruning-knife, pruning-shears, rake, scythe, secateurs, shears, shovel, sickle, spade, thresher, trowel; needle, scissors, pinking-shears, bodkin, crochet hook, forceps, scalpel, tweezers, tongs, cleaver, steel, gimlet, mace, mortar, pestle, paper-cutter, paper-knife, stapler, pocket-knife, penknife

▶ *v* work, machine, cut, shape, decorate, fashion, ornament, chase

tooth *n*
cog, denticle, denticulation, dentil, fang, incisor, jag, masticator, molar, prong, tush, tusk

Types of tooth include: baby tooth, back tooth, bicuspid, bucktooth, canine, carnassial, dog-tooth, eye tooth, fang, first tooth, gold tooth, grinder, incisor, central incisor, lateral incisor, milk tooth, molar, first molar, second molar, third molar, premolar, first premolar, second premolar, snaggletooth, tush, tusk, wisdom tooth; false tooth, false teeth, bridge, cap, crown, denture, dentures, plate.

toothsome *adj*
appetizing, delicious, tasty, tempting, mouth-watering, palatable, nice, agreeable, flavoursome, sweet, luscious, savoury, dainty, delectable
colloq. scrumptious, yummy
🗲 disagreeable, unpleasant

top *n, adj, v*
▶ *n* **1** HEAD, tip, highest point, apex, crest, crown, peak, pinnacle, summit, climax, culmination, height
technical vertex, acme, zenith, apogee
2 LID, cap, cover, cork, stopper
3 *a sleeveless top*
blouse, shirt, sweatshirt, T-shirt, tee shirt, jumper, jersey, sweater, pullover, tank top, smock
🗲 **1** bottom, base, nadir **3** bottoms
▷ **on top of the world** thrilled, happy, overjoyed, ecstatic, elated, exhilarated, exultant; *colloq.* on cloud nine, over the moon
▷ **over the top** excessive, immoderate, inordinate, extreme, too much, undue, uncalled-for, disproportionate, unreasonable, lavish, exorbitant, extravagant; *colloq.* a bit much
▶ *adj* highest, topmost, uppermost, upper, superior, head, chief, leading, main, first, foremost, principal, sovereign, ruling, pre-eminent, dominant, prime, paramount, utmost, greatest, maximum, best, finest, supreme, crowning, culminating
🗲 bottom, lowest, inferior
▶ *v* **1** TIP, cap, crown, cover, finish (off), decorate, garnish
2 BEAT, exceed, outstrip, better, excel, best, surpass, eclipse, outshine, outdo, surmount, transcend
3 HEAD, lead, be first in, rule, command
▷ **top up** refill, recharge, reload, add to, supplement, increase, boost; *formal* replenish, augment

topic *n*
subject, subject matter, theme, issue, question, argument, matter, point, talking point, thesis, text

topical *adj*
current, contemporary, up-to-date, up-to-the-minute, recent, newsworthy, relevant, popular, familiar

topmost *adj*
uppermost, highest, loftiest, top, upper, supreme, first, leading, foremost, principal, maximum, paramount, dominant
technical apical
🗲 bottom, bottommost, lowest

top-notch *adj*
first rate, first-class, second-to-none, matchless, peerless, top, top-flight, leading, supreme, superior, prime, excellent, outstanding, superlative, premier, exceptional, splendid, superb, fine, admirable
colloq. super, A1, ace, crack, out of this world;
slang wicked, way-out, cool, radical, mega

topple *v*
1 OVERBALANCE, totter, tumble, fall (over), collapse, upset, tip over, knock over/down, keel over, overturn, capsize
2 OVERTHROW, oust, bring down, unseat, displace, dethrone

topsy-turvy *adj*
confused, in confusion, jumbled, chaotic, inside out, upside down, disorganized, disarranged, disorderly, in disorder, untidy, mixed-up, messy
🗲 ordered, tidy

torch *n*
light, firebrand, brand, flambeau
US flashlight
old use cresset

torment *n, v*
▶ *n* **1** ANGUISH, distress, misery, affliction, suffering, pain, agony, ordeal, worry, torture, persecution
2 ANNOYANCE, provocation, irritation, vexation, bane, scourge, curse, pest, trouble, bother, nuisance, harassment, worry
colloq. thorn in the flesh, pain in the neck
▶ *v* **1** AFFLICT, plague, distress, trouble, distress, harrow, pain, torture, persecute
2 ANNOY, tease, provoke, irritate, vex, trouble, worry, harass, hound, pester, bother, plague, badger, bedevil

torn *adj*
1 CUT, ragged, ripped, slit, split, rent, lacerated
2 DIVIDED, uncertain, undecided, unsure, irresolute, vacillating, wavering, dithering

tornado *n*
storm, cyclone, gale, hurricane, whirlwind, typhoon, monsoon, tempest, squall
colloq. twister

torpid *adj*
sluggish, lethargic, slow, dull, lifeless, inert, inactive, apathetic, lazy, passive, listless, drowsy, sleepy, dead, deadened, numb, nerveless, insensible
formal languorous, somnolent, supine, indolent
🗲 active, lively, vigorous

torpor *n*
torpidity, sluggishness, lethargy, listlessness, slowness, dullness, lifelessness, inactivity, inertia, inertness, drowsiness, sleepiness, numbness, apathy, laziness, passivity, sloth
formal indolence, languor, somnolence, hebetude
🗲 activity, vigour, enthusiasm

torrent *n*
1 *torrent of water*
stream, gush, rush, flood, storm, outburst, volley, barrage, inundation, spate, deluge, cascade, downpour
2 *a torrent of abuse*
outburst, volley, barrage, stream, gush, rush, flood, storm, inundation, spate, deluge
🗲 **1, 2** trickle

torrid *adj*
1 HOT, blazing, sweltering, blistering, boiling,

sizzling, scorching, tropical, stifling, arid, parched, scorched, waterless, desert
2 PASSIONATE, erotic, red-hot, sexy, amorous
colloq. steamy

tortuous *adj*
1 *a tortuous road*
twisting, winding, meandering, curving, serpentine, zigzag, circuitous, roundabout, indirect
formal sinuous
2 COMPLICATED, involved, serpentine, zigzag, circuitous, roundabout, indirect
formal convoluted
⊟ 1 straight **2** straightforward

torture *v, n*
▶ *v* pain, agonize, excruciate, crucify, rack, martyr, persecute, abuse, ill-treat, mistreat, torment, harrow, plague, punish, afflict, worry, distress, trouble
▶ *n* pain, agony, suffering, affliction, distress, punishment, misery, anguish, torment, abuse, ill-treatment, mistreatment, martyrdom, persecution

toss *v, n*
▶ *v* **1** FLIP, cast, fling, throw, pitch, heave, sling, hurl, lob, shy
colloq. chuck
2 ROLL, heave, sway, pitch, lurch, jolt, shake, jerk, agitate, rock, thrash, squirm, writhe, wriggle
▶ *n* flip, cast, fling, throw, pitch
colloq. chuck

tot¹ *n*
1 TODDLER, child, infant, mite, baby
Scot. bairn
2 *a tot of whisky*
DRAM, measure, nip, shot, slug, finger

tot² *v*
▷ **tot up** add (up), calculate, compute, count (up), reckon, mount (up), sum, tally, total

total *n, adj, v*
▶ *n* sum, whole, entirety, grand total, subtotal, totality, all, lot, mass, amount
formal aggregate
▶ *adj* full, complete, entire, whole, comprehensive, integral, all-out, utter, absolute, unconditional, unqualified, outright, undisputed, perfect, thoroughgoing, rank, sheer, downright, thorough
formal consummate, unmitigated
⊟ partial, limited, restricted
▶ *v* add (up), sum (up), tot up (up), count (up), reckon, amount to, come to, reach, make

totalitarian *adj*
authoritarian, one-party, despotic, dictatorial, oppressive, tyrannous, monolithic, undemocratic
formal omnipotent, monocratic
⊟ democratic

totality *n*
total, sum, whole, wholeness, entirety, entireness, everything, fullness, completeness, all, cosmos, universe
formal aggregate, pleroma

totally *adv*
completely, fully, wholly, entirely, perfectly, utterly, quite, thoroughly, wholeheartedly, absolutely, unconditionally, comprehensively, undividedly, undisputedly
formal consummately, unmitigatedly
⊟ partially

totter *v*
1 STAGGER, waddle, move unsteadily, reel, lurch, stumble, falter, waver, teeter, sway, roll, rock, shake, wobble, quiver, tremble
2 *the economy is tottering*
be unstable, be unsteady, be insecure, be shaky, be precarious, be about to collapse
colloq. wobble

touch *v, n*
▶ *v* **1** FEEL, handle, hold, finger, run your finger over, brush, skim, graze, stroke, caress, fondle, pet, tickle, pat, tap, hit, strike, contact
2 ADJOIN, bring/come into contact, meet, abut, border, impinge
formal be contiguous to
3 MOVE, stir, upset, sadden, disturb, impress, inspire, influence, affect, have an effect on, have an influence/impact on, involve, concern, regard
4 EQUAL, match, rival, better, come near, approach
colloq. hold a candle to
5 REACH, attain, make, come to
colloq. hit
6 *not touch alcohol*
consume, use, eat, drink, take, devour
7 MENTION, broach, speak of, remark on, refer to, allude to, cover, deal with
▷ **touch off** spark off, trigger (off), begin, cause, set off, initiate, provoke, foment, fire, ignite, inflame, light, arouse; *formal* actuate
▷ **touch up** renovate, improve, brush up, retouch, revamp, enhance, finish off, round off, patch up, perfect, polish up
▶ *n* **1** FEEL, brush, stroke, caress, pat, tap, blow, hit, contact, tactility
Related adjective: tactile, haptic
2 TEXTURE, feel, surface, finish, grain, weave
3 SKILL, art, knack, flair, craftsmanship, dexterity, style, method, manner, technique, approach, direction
4 *finishing touches*
DETAIL, feature, point, addition, aspect, nicety, minutiae
5 *keep/lose touch*
contact, communication, correspondence, connection, association
6 *a touch of garlic*
trace, spot, dash, pinch, taste, soupçon, suspicion, hint, suggestion, bit, speck, jot, tinge, smack
colloq. whiff

touch-and-go *adj*
close, critical, dangerous, uncertain, hazardous, near, nerve-racking, offhand, perilous, dire, precarious, risky, sticky, tricky
formal parlous
colloq. dodgy, hairy

touched *adj*
1 MOVED, stirred, inspired, influenced, affected, impressed, disturbed, upset
2 MAD, crazy, insane, deranged, disturbed, eccentric, unbalanced
colloq. dotty, daft, barmy, nutty, bonkers, batty, loopy

touchiness *n*
bad temper, irritability, grouchiness, grumpiness, irascibility, peevishness, pettishness, surliness, testiness, tetchiness, petulance, crabbedness, captiousness

touching *adj*
moving, stirring, impressive, affecting, upsetting, disturbing, poignant, pitiable, pitiful, heart-breaking,

heart-rending, pathetic, sad, emotional, tender
formal piteous

touchstone *n*
criterion, standard, test, norm, proof, measure, gauge, guide, model, pattern, template, benchmark, yardstick

touchy *adj*
irritable, bad-tempered, quick-tempered, grumpy, cross, over-sensitive, thin-skinned, peevish, grouchy, crabbed, captious, irascible
colloq. edgy, prickly
🖃 calm, imperturbable

tough *adj, n*
▶ *adj* **1** STRONG, durable, resilient, resistant, firm, hardy, sturdy, solid, rigid, stiff, inflexible, hard, leathery
2 *tough criminal*
rough, violent, disorderly, rowdy, vicious, callous, hardened, obstinate
3 HARSH, severe, strict, stern, firm, resolute, adamant, determined, tenacious, unyielding, uncompromising
4 ARDUOUS, strenuous, laborious, exacting, hard, taxing, grim, difficult, puzzling, perplexing, baffling, knotty, thorny, troublesome
colloq. uphill
5 FIT, muscular, hardy, burly, well-built, robust, sturdy, rugged, vigorous, stalwart
6 *the meat is tough*
rubbery, chewy, fibrous, gristly
colloq. tough as leather
7 *tough luck*
hard, unpleasant, unfortunate, unlucky, uncomfortable, distressing
🖃 **1** fragile, delicate, weak, tender **2** gentle, soft **3** gentle **4** easy, simple **5** weak **6** tender **7** good
▶ *n* brute, thug, bully, ruffian, hooligan, lout, bully, rowdy, roughneck
slang yob

toughen *v*
strengthen, harden, reinforce, brace, stiffen, considerate, substantiate, make stricter
formal fortify

toughness *n*
strength, resilience, resistance, firmness, hardiness, sturdiness, tenacity, determination, inflexibility, ruggedness, obduracy
colloq. grit
🖃 weakness, vulnerability, softness, liberality

tour *n, v*
▶ *n* circuit, round, visit, expedition, journey, trip, outing, excursion, inspection, drive, ride, jaunt, course
formal peregrination
colloq. walkabout
▶ *v* visit, go round, sightsee, explore, travel round, journey through, drive through, ride

tourist *n*
holidaymaker, visitor, sightseer, tripper, day-tripper, excursionist, traveller, voyager, globetrotter
formal sojourner
US slang rubberneck

tournament *n*
championship, series, competition, contest, match, event, meeting, meet, joust

tousled *adj*
dishevelled, ruffled, messed up, disordered, disarranged, tangled, rumpled, tumbled

tout *v*
1 SELL, hawk, peddle, trade
2 ADVERTISE, promote, market, solicit, petition, ask, appeal, seek
colloq. plug, hype, push

tow *v, n*
▶ *v* pull, tug, draw, trail, drag, lug, haul, transport
▶ *n* pull, tug, haul, trail, lug
▷ **in tow** following closely, accompanying, by your side, in convoy

towards *prep*
1 TO, in the direction of, on the way to, approaching, nearing, close to, nearly, almost, -wards
2 *his feelings towards her*
regarding, with regard to, with respect to, concerning, about, for

tower *n, v*

Types of tower include: barbican, bastille, bastion, belfry, bell tower, belvedere, campanile, castle, church tower, citadel, column, demi-bastion, donjon, Eiffel Tower, fort, fortification, fortress, gate-tower, high-rise building, hill-fort, keep, lookout tower, martello tower, minar, minaret, mirador, pagoda, peel-tower, scaffold tower, skyscraper, smock mill, spire, steeple, stronghold, tower block, tower mill, Tower of London, Tower of Pisa, turret, watchtower, water tower.

▶ *v* rise, rear, ascend, mount, soar, loom, overlook, dominate, surpass, transcend, overshadow, eclipse, exceed, excel, top, cap

towering *adj*
1 HIGH, soaring, tall, lofty, elevated, monumental, colossal, gigantic, great
2 MAGNIFICENT, imposing, impressive, outstanding, sublime, supreme, incomparable, unrivalled, surpassing, overpowering, extraordinary, extreme, inordinate
🖃 **1** low, small, tiny **2** minor, trivial

town *n*
borough, village, municipality, burgh, market town, county town, new town, city, suburbs, outskirts, conurbation, metropolis, urban district, settlement, township, pueblo
Related adjective: urban
🖃 country

town-dweller *n*
citizen, townsman, townswoman, burgher, urbanite
formal oppidan
colloq. towny
🖃 country-dweller, rustic

toxic *adj*
poisonous, harmful, noxious, unhealthy, dangerous, deadly, lethal, baneful
🖃 harmless, safe

toy *n, v*
▶ *n* plaything, knick-knack, trinket, trifle, bauble

Kinds of toy include: Action Man®, activity centre, aeroplane, baby-bouncer, baby-walker, ball, balloon; bicycle, *colloq.* bike, mountain bike; blackboard and easel, boxing-gloves, building-block, building-brick, catapult, climbing-frame, computer game, crayon; doll, Barbie doll®, kewpie doll, rag-doll,

Sindy doll®, Tiny-Tears doll®, doll's buggy, doll's cot, doll's house, doll's pram; drum set, electronic game, executive toy, farm, fivestones, football, fort, Frisbee®, game, garage, glove puppet, go-kart, golliwog, guitar, gun, cap-gun, pop-gun, gyroscope, hobby-horse, hula-hoop, jack-in-the-box, jigsaw puzzle, kaleidoscope, kite, box-kite, Lego®, marble, Matchbox®, Meccano®, model car, model kit, model railway, modelling clay, musical box, ocarina, paddling-pool, paints, pantograph, pedal-car, peashooter, Plasticene®, Play-Doh®, playhouse, pogo stick, Power Rangers®, puzzle, rattle, rocker, rocking-horse, Rubik's Cube®, sandpit, Scalextric®, scooter, seesaw, sewing machine, shape-sorter, skateboard, skipping-rope, slide, soft-toy, spacehopper, Space Invaders®, spinning top, Subbuteo®, swing, swingball, teaset, teddy-bear, toy soldier, train set, trampoline, tricycle, *colloq.* trike, Turtles®, typewriter; video game, Game Boy®, Nintendo®, Sega®, Super Mario®; *colloq.* walkie-talkie, water pistol, Wendy house, yo-yo. *See also* **game**.

▶ *v* play, tinker, fiddle, sport, trifle, dally, flirt
colloq. mess about/around

trace *n, v*
▶ *n* **1** *leave traces of blood*
hint, suggestion, suspicion, soupçon, dash, pinch, drop, spot, bit, jot, touch, tinge, shadow, smack
2 MARK, token, sign, indication, evidence, record, relic, remains, remnant, vestige, trail, track, spoor, footprint, footmark, scent
▶ *v* **1** FIND, discover, detect, unearth, track (down), uncover, dig up, trail, track, stalk, hunt, seek, follow, pursue, dog, shadow
colloq. run down
2 COPY, draw, draft, sketch, outline, show, depict, mark (out), record, map, chart
formal delineate

track *n, v*
▶ *n* **1** WAY, rail, path, way, route, orbit, line, trail, trajectory, slot, groove, course, drift, sequence, argument
2 FOOTPRINT, footstep, footmark, scent, spoor, trail, wake, mark, trace
▷ **keep track of** monitor, check, watch, follow, observe, record, keep an eye on
⊟ lose track of
▷ **make tracks** leave, go, depart, make off, dash (off), disappear; *colloq.* scram, beat it, hit the road
▶ *v* stalk, trail, hunt, trace, follow, pursue, chase, dog, tail, shadow
▷ **track down** find, discover, trace, hunt down, run to earth, nose out, sniff out, ferret out, turn up, dig up, uncover, unearth, expose, catch, capture; *colloq.* run down

tract *n*
1 *a tract of land*
stretch, extent, expanse, plot, lot, territory, area, region, zone, district, quarter
2 *a religious tract*
booklet, leaflet, brochure, pamphlet, treatise, sermon, essay, dissertation, homily, discourse, monograph
formal disquisition

tractable *adj*
pliant, pliable, manageable, obedient, persuadable, willing, submissive, docile, controllable, amenable, biddable, governable, malleable, compliant, yielding, workable, tame, tractile
formal complaisant
⊟ headstrong, intractable, obstinate, refractory, stubborn, unruly, wilful

traction *n*
drawing, pull, pulling, haulage, propulsion, drag, draught, grip, friction, adhesion

trade *n, v*
▶ *n* **1** COMMERCE, traffic, trafficking, business, dealing, buying, selling, marketing, shopkeeping, barter, exchange, switch, swap, transactions, custom
Related adjective: mercantile
2 OCCUPATION, employment, job, work, business, line (of work), profession, career, calling, vocation, métier, craft, skill
▶ *v* do business, deal, transact, buy, sell, run, traffic, peddle, market, merchandise, barter, exchange, swap, switch, bargain

trademark *n*
1 *a registered trademark*
brand, brand name, tradename, proprietary name, proprietary brand, label, name, sign, symbol, logo, insignia, crest, emblem, badge
2 HALLMARK, stamp, mark, speciality, typical quality, (distinctive) feature, attribute, characteristic, idiosyncrasy, peculiarity, quirk

trader *n*
merchant, tradesman, tradeswoman, broker, dealer, buyer, seller, marketeer, marketer, vendor, supplier, wholesaler, retailer, shopkeeper, trafficker, peddler

tradesman, tradeswoman *n*
1 SHOPKEEPER, retailer, buyer, seller, merchant, dealer, vendor
2 ARTISAN, craftsman, craftswoman, worker, mechanic, journeyman

tradition *n*
convention, custom, belief, ceremony, usage, way, habit, routine, practice, observance, ritual, rite, institution, folklore
formal praxis

traditional *adj*
conventional, customary, habitual, usual, routine, accustomed, ceremonial, established, fixed, set, long-established, time-honoured, old, age-old, historic, folk, oral, unwritten
⊟ unconventional, innovative, new, modern, contemporary

traduce *v*
misrepresent, slander, revile, deprecate, decry, defame, blacken, abuse, insult, malign, smear
formal disparage, detract, asperse, denigrate, depreciate, calumniate, vilify
colloq. knock, run down, slag

traducer *n*
defamer, slanderer, disparager, abuser, smearer
formal asperser, calumniator, denigrator, deprecator, detractor, vilifier
colloq. knocker, mud-slinger

traffic *n, v*
▶ *n* **1** VEHICLES, cars, shipping, transport, transportation, freight, passengers
2 TRADE, commerce, business, dealing, trading, trafficking, buying and selling, peddling, barter, exchange
3 COMMUNICATION, dealings, relations, contact
formal intercourse
▶ *v* peddle, buy, sell, trade, do business, deal, peddle, bargain, barter, exchange

trafficker *n*
dealer, merchant, trader, broker, peddler, monger

tragedy *n*
adversity, misfortune, unhappiness, affliction, blow, calamity, disaster, catastrophe
🖅 success, triumph

tragic *adj*
calamitous, disastrous, catastrophic, deadly, fatal, sad, sorrowful, miserable, terrible, unhappy, wretched, unfortunate, unlucky, ill-fated, pitiable, pathetic, heartbreaking, shocking, appalling, dreadful, awful, deplorable, dire
🖅 happy, comic, successful

trail *n, v*
▶ *n* track, path, footpath, road, route, way, wake, footprints, footmarks, scent, spoor, sign, trace
▶ *v* 1 DRAG, pull, tow, haul, draw, droop, dangle, hang, extend, reach, stream, sweep, straggle, dawdle, lag, loiter, linger
2 TRACK, stalk, hunt, follow, pursue, chase, dog, shadow, tail
▷ **trail away** decrease, die away, diminish, disappear, dwindle, fade (away), fall away, melt away, lessen, peter out, shrink, sink, subside, tail off, taper off, trail off, weaken

train *n, v*
▶ *n* 1 *a train of events*
sequence, succession, series, progression, order, set, suite, string, chain, trail, line, path, track, stream, file, procession, column, convoy, cortège, caravan
formal concatenation
2 RETINUE, entourage, attendants, court, household, staff, followers, following, cortège
▶ *v* 1 TEACH, instruct, coach, tutor, educate, improve, school, indoctrinate, discipline, prepare, drill, ground, exercise, work out, practise, rehearse, groom
formal inculcate
2 LEARN, study, be trained, be taught, be prepared
3 POINT, direct, aim, focus, level

trainer *n*
teacher, instructor, coach, tutor, handler, educator

training *n*
teaching, instruction, coaching, tuition, tutoring, education, schooling, learning, lessons, discipline, preparation, grounding, drill, exercise, workout, working-out, practice, learning, apprenticeship

traipse *v, n*
▶ *v* trudge, tramp, plod, slouch, trail
▶ *n* trudge, trek, slog, plod, tramp

trait *n*
feature, attribute, quality, property, characteristic, idiosyncrasy, peculiarity, quirk

traitor *n*
betrayer, informer, deceiver, double-crosser, double-dealer, turncoat, renegade, deserter, defector, quisling, collaborator, fifth columnist, Judas
colloq. back-stabber, two-timer
🖅 loyalist, supporter, defender

traitorous *adj*
disloyal, unfaithful, faithless, false, untrue, treasonable, dishonourable, double-crossing, double-dealing, renegade, treacherous, apostate
formal perfidious, seditious
🖅 faithful, loyal, patriotic

trajectory *n*
line, orbit, path, route, flight, flight path, course, track, trail

trammel *n, v*
▶ *n* bar, block, bond, fetter, rein, shackle, check, clog, chain, hamper, curb, handicap, hindrance, impediment, obstacle, stumbling-block
▶ *v* bar, block, clog, restrict, restrain, fetter, catch, check, tie, enmesh, ensnare, entrap, shackle, inhibit, impede, hinder, handicap, hamper, curb, capture, net

tramp *n, v*
▶ *n* 1 VAGRANT, vagabond, hobo, down-and-out, derelict
slang dosser, bum
2 TRUDGE, march, tread, walk, trek, hike, ramble
3 LOOSE WOMAN, prostitute, wench, trollop, whore
slang slut, tart, scrubber
▶ *v* walk, march, tread, stamp, stomp, stump, plod, trudge, traipse, trail, trek, hike, ramble, roam, rove

trample *v*
tread, stamp, crush, squash, flatten

trance *n*
dream, reverie, daze, stupor, unconsciousness, catalepsy, spell, ecstasy, rapture

tranquil *adj*
calm, peaceful, quiet, serene, composed, cool, imperturbable, unexcited, even-tempered, placid, sedate, relaxed, restful, still, undisturbed, untroubled, hushed, silent
formal reposeful
colloq. laid-back, unflappable
🖅 agitated, disturbed, troubled, noisy

tranquillity *n*
calm, peace, peacefulness, serenity, calmness, composure, quiet, quietness, rest, restfulness, stillness, hush, silence, imperturbability, coolness, equanimity, sedateness, placidity
technical ataraxia, ataraxy
formal quietude, repose
🖅 disturbance, agitation, noise

tranquillize *v*
calm, quiet, pacify, relax, sedate, soothe, quell, lull, compose
technical narcotize, opiate
🖅 disturb, agitate, upset

tranquillizer *n*
sedative, calmative, sleeping pill, opiate, narcotic, barbiturate
colloq. downer

transact *v*
carry out, conduct, do, perform, settle, handle, manage, carry on, accomplish, negotiate, conclude, dispatch, discharge, enact, execute
formal prosecute

transaction *n*
1 *bank transactions*
deal, bargain, agreement, arrangement, negotiation, business, affair, matter, proceeding, enterprise, undertaking, deed, action, handling, settlement, enactment, execution, discharge
2 *the transactions of a learned society*
reports, proceedings, record, minutes, concerns, annals, affairs, doings
colloq. goings-on

transcend *v*
surpass, excel, outshine, eclipse, outdo, outstrip, leave behind, beat, surmount, exceed, go beyond, rise above, overstep

transcendence *n*
transcendency, superiority, supremacy, pre-eminence, predominance, incomparability, matchlessness, paramoun(t)cy, excellence, greatness
formal ascendancy, sublimity

transcendent *adj*
1 SURPASSING, supreme, sublime, superlative, excelling, excellent, magnificent, incomparable, matchless, peerless, unparalleled, unsurpassable
2 SUPERHUMAN, supernatural, spiritual
formal ineffable, numinous

transcendental *adj*
supernatural, spiritual, otherworldly, metaphysical, mystical, mysterious
formal preternatural

transcribe *v*
write out, write up, copy out, copy up, reproduce, rewrite, transliterate, translate, render, take down, note, record

transcript *n*
transcription, copy, reproduction, duplicate, transliteration, translation, version, note, record, manuscript

transfer *v, n*
▶ *v* 1 CHANGE, transpose, move, shift, remove, relocate, transplant, transport, carry, take, convey
2 *transfer land*
assign, convey, transmit, consign, grant, hand over
▶ *n* change, changeover, transposition, move, shift, removal, relocation, displacement, transmission, handover, assignment, transference
technical conveyance

transfigure *v*
transform, change, alter, convert, exalt, glorify, idealize
formal transmute, translate, metamorphose, apotheosize

transfix *v*
1 FASCINATE, spellbind, mesmerize, hypnotize, paralyse, stun, hold, engross, rivet, petrify
2 IMPALE, pierce, run through, spear, skewer, spike, stick

transform *v*
change, alter, adapt, convert, remodel, rebuilt, reconstruct, renew, transfigure, revolutionize
formal transmute, metamorphose
colloq. transmogrify
🖪 preserve, maintain

transformation *n*
change, alteration, conversion, transfiguration, revolution
technical metastasis
formal mutation, transmutation, metamorphosis
colloq. sea change, transmogrification
🖪 preservation, conservation

transfuse *v*
transfer, imbue, pervade, instil, permeate, suffuse

transgress *v*
break, offend, sin, contravene, disobey, misbehave, overstep, exceed, violate, breach, defy, infringe,

encroach, lapse, err
formal trespass
🖪 keep, obey

transgression *n*
wrong, wrongdoing, offence, infringement, lapse, crime, sin, violation, fault, error, iniquity, misdeed, peccadillo, misbehaviour, misdemeanour, breach, contravention, encroachment, debt
formal infraction, trespass

transgressor *n*
lawbreaker, offender, wrongdoer, evil-doer, criminal, culprit, delinquent, debtor, miscreant, felon, sinner, villain
formal trespasser, malefactor

transience *n*
transitoriness, shortness, briefness, brevity, impermanence, deciduousness
technical caducity
formal ephemerality, evanescence, fugacity, fugitiveness
colloq. fleetingness
🖪 permanence

transient *adj*
transitory, passing, flying, fleeting, brief, short, momentary, short-lived, temporary, short-term, impermanent
formal ephemeral, evanescent, fugacious
🖪 lasting, permanent

transit *n*
passage, journey, journeying, travel, crossing, route, movement, transfer, transportation, conveyance, carriage, haulage, shipment
▷ **in transit** en route, on the way, travelling, by road, by rail, by air, by sea

transition *n*
passage, passing, progress, progression, development, evolution, move, movement, flux, change, change-over, alteration, conversion, transformation, shift, switch
formal metamorphosis, transmutation

transitional *adj*
provisional, temporary, passing, intermediate, developmental, evolutionary, changing, fluid, unsettled
🖪 initial, final

transitory *adj*
transient, passing, flying, fleeting, brief, short, momentary, short-lived, temporary, short-term, impermanent
formal ephemeral, evanescent, fugacious
🖪 lasting, permanent

translate *v*
1 *translate into German*
put, render, paraphrase, reword, explain, interpret, simplify, decode, decipher, transliterate, transcribe
formal construe
2 CHANGE, alter, convert, transform, improve, move, transfer, relocate, shift
formal transmute
colloq. transmogrify

translation *n*
1 *a translation from Spanish*
rendering, version, rendition, explanation, interpretation, gloss, crib, rewording, rephrasing, paraphrase, simplification, transliteration,

transcription
formal metaphrasis
2 CHANGE, alteration, conversion, transformation, move, transfer, shift
formal transmutation, metamorphosis
colloq. transmogrification

translator *n*
linguist, polyglot, paraphraser, interpreter, glosser, dragoman
formal exegete, exegetist, glossarist, glossator, metaphrast, paraphrast

translucent *adj*
transparent, clear, see-through, pellucid, translucid, limpid
formal diaphanous
E3 opaque

transmigration *n*
transformation, rebirth, reincarnation
formal metempsychosis, Pythagoreanism

transmission *n*
1 BROADCASTING, diffusion, spread, communication, conveyance, carriage, transport, shipment, sending, dispatch, relaying, transfer, transference, imparting
formal dissemination
2 *a live transmission*
broadcast, programme, show, performance, production, presentation, episode, simulcast, signal
E3 1 reception

transmit *v*
communicate, impart, convey, carry, bear, impart, transport, send, pass on, dispatch, forward, relay, transfer, broadcast, radio, network, diffuse, spread
formal disseminate, remit
E3 receive

transmute *v*
transform, alter, change, convert, remake, transfigure, transverse
formal metamorphose, translate
colloq. transmogrify
E3 retain

transparency *n*
1 CLEARNESS, clarity, translucence, translucency, sheerness, gauziness, filminess, pellucidity, pellucidness, perspicuousness, limpidity, limpidness, translucidity, water
formal diaphanousness
2 PLAINNESS, clearness, clarity, obviousness, apparentness, distinctness, unambiguousness, straightforwardness, directness, openness, patentness, frankness, forthrightness, explicitness, candidness
3 *holiday transparencies*
slide, photograph, photo, picture
E3 1 opacity **2** ambiguity, unclearness

transparent *adj*
1 *transparent plastic*
clear, see-through, translucent, sheer, pellucid, diaphanous, gauzy, filmy
2 PLAIN, distinct, clear, lucid, explicit, unambiguous, unequivocal, unmistakable, apparent, visible, obvious, noticeable, discernible, perceptible, evident, patent, undisguised, open, direct, forthright, candid, straightforward
formal manifest
E3 1 opaque **2** unclear, ambiguous

transpire *v*
1 BECOME KNOWN, turn out, come to light, come out, be disclosed, become apparent, appear, prove
2 HAPPEN, occur, take place, ensue, arise, come about, come to pass
formal befall

transplant *v*
move, shift, displace, remove, uproot, graft, transfer, relocate, resettle, repot, replant
E3 leave

transport *v, n*
▶ *v* **1** CONVEY, carry, bear, take, fetch, bring, move, run, shift, transfer, ship, haul, remove, deport, exile
2 DELIGHT, enrapture, entrance, captivate, electrify, spellbind
colloq. carry away
▶ *n* **1** CONVEYANCE, transit, vehicle, carriage, transfer, transportation, shipment, shipping, haulage, freight, removal
2 *transports of delight*
rapture, ecstasy, bliss, euphoria, elation, exhilaration, frenzy, fit
colloq. seventh heaven

transportation *n*
conveyance, transit, carriage, transfer, shipment, shipping, haulage, freight

transpose *v*
swap, exchange, switch, interchange, transfer, shift, invert, rearrange, reorder, change, convert, alter, move, substitute

transverse *adj*
cross, crossways, crosswise, transversal, diagonal, oblique

trap *n*
▶ *n* snare, net, mesh, noose, springe, gin, booby-trap, pitfall, danger, hazard, ambush, trick, wile, ruse, stratagem, device, trickery, ploy, artifice, subterfuge, deception
▶ *v* snare, net, entrap, ensnare, enmesh, confine, catch, take, ambush, lure, beguile, corner, trick, deceive, dupe
formal inveigle

trapped *adj*
caught, beguiled, cornered, ensnared, ambushed, snared, stuck, netted, surrounded, tricked, deceived, duped
formal inveigled
E3 free

trapper *n*
hunter, huntsman, backwoodsman, frontiersman, voyageur

trappings *n*
ornaments, accompaniments, clothes, adornments, dress, decorations, fripperies, equipment, paraphernalia, fixtures, fittings, furnishings, housings, finery, livery, gear, trimmings
formal accoutrements, panoply, raiment
colloq. things

trash *n*
1 RUBBISH, garbage, refuse, junk, waste, litter, sweepings, offscourings, scum, dregs
2 NONSENSE, rubbish, garbage, junk, drivel, balderdash, gibberish, gobbledygook
colloq. bunk, rot, tripe, bull

3 UNDESIRABLES, riff-raff, rabble, scum, dregs, *canaille*

trashy *adj*
rubbishy, worthless, shabby, tawdry, tinsel, flimsy, third-rate, cheap, cheap-jack, kitschy, shoddy, inferior
formal meretricious
colloq. grotty, naff
E3 first-rate

trauma *n*
injury, wound, hurt, lesion, damage, pain, suffering, anguish, agony, torture, distress, ordeal, shock, disorder, jolt, upset, disturbance, upheaval, strain, stress
E3 healing

traumatic *adj*
painful, harmful, hurtful, injurious, wounding, shocking, agonizing, upsetting, distressing, disturbing, unpleasant, frightening, stressful
E3 healing, relaxing

travail *n*
1 TOIL, hardship, exertion, effort, drudgery, slog, strain, stress, suffering, distress, grind, tears, sweat
formal tribulation
2 LABOUR PAINS, childbirth, birth-pangs, labour, throes
E3 rest

travel *v, n*
▶ *v* journey, voyage, tour, make a trip, explore, go, go abroad/overseas, wend, make your way, move, advance, proceed, progress, wander, ramble, roam, rove, tour, cover, cross, traverse
colloq. see the world
E3 stay, remain

Methods of travel include: fly, aviate, pilot, shuttle, sail, cruise, punt, paddle, row, steam, ride, cycle, *colloq.* bike, freewheel, drive, motor, bus, tour, walk, hike, march, ramble, trek, orienteer, hitch-hike, commute.

Forms of travel include: flight, cruise, sail, voyage, ride, drive, march, walk, hike, ramble, excursion, holiday, jaunt, outing, tour, trip, visit, expedition, safari, trek, circumnavigation, exploration, journey, migration, mission, pilgrimage.

▶ *n* **1** TRAVELLING, touring, journeying, tourism
colloq. globetrotting
2 *travels abroad*
voyage, expedition, passage, journey, trip, excursion, sightseeing, tour, wanderings
colloq. globetrotting

traveller *n*
1 TOURIST, explorer, voyager, globetrotter, sightseer, holidaymaker, tourer, excursionist, passenger, commuter, wanderer, rambler, hiker
colloq. tripper
2 WANDERER, wayfarer, migrant, nomad, Gypsy, itinerant, tinker, vagrant, tramp, drifter
3 SALES REPRESENTATIVE, salesman, saleswoman, representative, commercial traveller, agent
colloq. rep

travelling *adj*
touring, wandering, roaming, roving, wayfaring, migrating, migrant, migratory, nomadic, itinerant, mobile, moving, vagrant, homeless, unsettled

formal peripatetic
E3 fixed, settled

travel-worn *adj*
weary, tired, jet-lagged, saddle-sore, travel-weary, footsore, waygone, wayworn
E3 fresh

traverse *v*
cross, pass over/through, go across/through, travel across/through, negotiate, bridge, span, ford, ply, range, roam, wander
formal peregrinate

travesty *n*
mockery, parody, burlesque, farce, caricature, perversion, corruption, distortion, misrepresentation, sham, apology
colloq. take-off, send-up, wind-up, spoof, tall story

treacherous *adj*
1 TRAITOROUS, disloyal, unfaithful, faithless, unreliable, untrustworthy, false, untrue, deceitful
formal duplicitous, perfidious
colloq. double-crossing, back-stabbing, two-timing
2 *treacherous roads*
dangerous, hazardous, risky, perilous, precarious, unsafe, icy, slippery
E3 **1** loyal, faithful, dependable **2** safe, stable

treacherously *adv*
deceitfully, falsely, disloyally, faithlessly
formal perfidiously
E3 loyally

treachery *n*
treason, betrayal, sabotage, unfaithfulness, faithlessness, disloyalty, infidelity, falseness, deceitfulness
formal duplicity, perfidity
colloq. double-dealing, double-crossing, back-stabbing, two-timing
E3 loyalty, dependability

tread *v, n*
▶ *v* walk, step, pace, stride, march, go, hike, trek, tramp, trudge, plod, stamp, trample, walk on, press (down), crush, squash, flatten
▷ **tread on someone's toes** offend, hurt, upset, vex, irk, annoy, infringe, injure, affront, bruise, inconvenience; *formal* discommode;
colloq. disgruntle
E3 soothe
▶ *n* walk, footstep, step, pace, stride, tramp, gait, footprint, footmark, footfall

treason *n*
treachery, disloyalty, subversion, mutiny, rebellion, disaffection, lese-majesty
formal perfidy, duplicity, sedition
E3 loyalty

treasonable *adj*
traitorous, disloyal, false, unfaithful, faithless, subversive, seditious, mutinous, rebellious
formal perfidious
E3 loyal

treasure *n, v*
▶ *n* **1** FORTUNE, wealth, valuables, riches, money, cash, gold, jewels, gems, hoard, cache
2 *she's a real treasure*
gem, prize, masterpiece, pride and joy, darling, *pièce de résistance*, crème de la crème
▶ *v* prize, value, hold dear, revere, worship, love,

adore, idolize, dote on, cherish, think highly of, preserve, guard
formal esteem
🗲 disparage, belittle

treasurer *n*
bursar, cashier, purser

treasury *n*
bank, exchequer, repository, resources, revenues, finances, capital, money, funds, assets, coffers, cache, hoard, vault, store, storehouse, thesaurus, corpus

treat *n, v*
▶ *n* indulgence, gratification, pleasure, delight, enjoyment, fun, entertainment, amusement, excursion, outing, party, celebration, feast, banquet, gift, present, surprise, thrill
▶ *v* **1** DEAL WITH, manage, handle, use, attend to, behave towards, view, regard, consider, study, discuss, cover, review
2 TEND, nurse, minister to, attend to, care for, look after, heal, cure, medicate
3 PAY FOR, buy, stand, give, pay/foot the bill, provide, take out, entertain, amuse, delight, regale, feast
4 *wood treated with creosote*
put on, apply, spread on, lay on, cover with, paint, smear, rub

treatise *n*
essay, dissertation, thesis, monograph, paper, pamphlet, tract, study, discourse
formal exposition, disquisition, prodrome

treatment *n*
1 HEALING, cure, remedy, medication, medicament, therapy, surgery, care, nursing, manipulation, therapeutics
2 MANAGEMENT, handling, dealing(s), use, usage, conduct, behaviour, action, discussion, coverage

treaty *n*
pact, convention, agreement, covenant, compact, negotiation, bargain, contract, deal, pledge, bond, alliance
formal concordat

treble *adj*
1 HIGH, high-pitched, shrill, sharp, piping
2 TRIPLE, threefold
🗲 **1** deep

tree *n*
bush, shrub, evergreen, conifer
Related adjective: arboreal

Trees include: acacia, acer, alder, almond, apple, ash, aspen, balsa, bay, beech, birch, blackthorn, blue gum, box, cedar, cherry, chestnut, coconut palm, cottonwood, cypress, date palm, dogwood, Dutch elm, ebony, elder, elm, eucalyptus, fig, fir, gum, hawthorn, hazel, hickory, hornbeam, horse chestnut, jacaranda, Japanese maple, larch, laurel, lime, linden, mahogany, maple, monkey puzzle, mountain ash, oak, palm, pear, pine, plane, plum, poplar, prunus, pussy willow, redwood, rowan, rubber tree, sandalwood, sapele, sequoia, silver birch, silver maple, spruce, sycamore, tamarisk, teak, walnut, weeping willow, whitebeam, willow, witch hazel, yew, yucca; bonsai, conifer, deciduous, evergreen, fruit, hardwood, ornamental, palm, softwood.

trek *v, n*
▶ *v* hike, journey, walk, march, tramp, traipse, trudge, plod, slog, journey, ramble, rove, roam

▶ *n* hike, walk, march, tramp, ramble, journey, trip, expedition, safari, odyssey

trellis *n*
framework, mesh, grid, net, network, lattice, grate, grating, grille
formal reticulation

tremble *v, n*
▶ *v* shake, vibrate, quake, shiver, shudder, judder, wobble, rock
▶ *n* shake, vibration, quake, shiver, shudder, judder, quiver, tremor, wobble
🗲 steadiness

trembling *n*
shaking, vibration, quaking, quavering, quivering, shuddering, juddering, shivering, heart-quake, oscillation, rocking
colloq. shakes
🗲 steadiness

tremendous *adj*
1 WONDERFUL, marvellous, stupendous, remarkable, sensational, spectacular, exceptional, extraordinary, great, amazing, incredible, impressive
colloq. terrific, smashing, out of this world;
slang wicked
2 HUGE, immense, vast, great, enormous, massive, colossal, gigantic, towering, formidable
🗲 **1** ordinary, unimpressive

tremor *n*
shake, quiver, tremble, trembling, shiver, quake, quaver, wobble, vibration, agitation, thrill, shock, earthquake
🗲 steadiness

tremulous *adj*
unsteady, shaking, wavering, vibrating, trembling, shivering, jumpy, jittery, quavering, quivering, quivery, agitated, trembly, afraid, scared, frightened, fearful, nervous, anxious, excited, timid
🗲 steady, firm, calm

trench *n*
ditch, channel, excavation, trough, waterway, earthwork, furrow, gutter, pit, cut, drain, rill, sap, entrenchment, fosse

trenchant *adj*
1 INCISIVE, pungent, caustic, biting, scathing, acerbic, penetrating, acute, astute, sharp, clear, perceptive, effective, clear-cut
formal mordant, perspicacious
2 FORTHRIGHT, vigorous, forceful, emphatic, blunt, terse, unequivocal
colloq. no-nonsense
🗲 woolly

trend *n*
1 TENDENCY, course, flow, current, drift, direction, bearing, inclination, leaning
2 FASHION, craze, vogue, mode, style, look
colloq. rage, fad, latest

trendy *adj*
fashionable, latest, modish, stylish, up to the minute, voguish
colloq. all the rage, natty, hip, cool, funky, in, groovy, with it
🗲 unfashionable

trepidation *n*
fear, apprehension, alarm, dread, anxiety, worry, unease, qualms, disquiet, misgivings, dismay,

uneasiness, excitement, emotion, trembling, nervousness, shaking, agitation, quivering, tremor, palpitation, fright
formal consternation, perturbation
colloq. butterflies, cold sweat, jitters, nerves
❊ calm

trespass   *v, n*
▶ *v* invade, intrude, encroach, impinge, poach, infringe, violate, offend, sin, wrong
formal obdurate, transgress
❊ obey, keep to
▶ *n* invasion, intrusion, encroachment, poaching, infringement, violation, wrongdoing, contravention, offence, sin, misdemeanour
formal transgression

trespasser   *n*
intruder, encroacher, poacher, offender, criminal, delinquent, evil-doer, sinner
formal transgressor

tress   *n*
hair, curl, lock, braid, bunch, plait, pigtail, ringlet, tail

trial   *n, adj*
▶ *n* 1 LITIGATION, case, lawsuit, hearing, inquiry, examination, tribunal, appeal, retrial
2 EXPERIMENT, test, examination, check, dummy run, try-out, practice, rehearsal, audition, contest, competition, selection, probation
formal assay
colloq. dry run
3 SUFFERING, grief, misery, distress, adversity, hardship, ordeal, trouble, nuisance, annoyance, burden, vexation, bother, bane, cross, cross to bear
formal affliction, tribulation
colloq. hassle, pest, pain in the neck, thorn in the flesh
❊ 3 relief, happiness
▶ *adj* experimental, test, testing, pilot, exploratory, provisional, probationary, dummy
colloq. dry

triangle   *n*

Types of triangle include: acute-angled, congruent, equilateral, isosceles, obtuse-angled, right-angled, scalene, similar.

triangular   *adj*
triangle-shaped, three-sided, three-cornered, trilateral
technical trigonous
formal trigonal, trigonic

tribal   *adj*
ethnic, family, native, indigenous, class, group, sectional

tribe   *n*
race, nation, people, clan, sept, family, house, dynasty, blood, stock, group, ethnic group, caste, class, division, branch

tribulation   *n*
suffering, grief, pain, sorrow, vexation, ordeal, misery, unhappiness, misfortune, wretchedness, worry, care, woe, burden, blow, distress, heartache, trial, reverse, adversity, hardship, trouble, curse
formal affliction, travail
❊ happiness, rest

tribunal   *n*
court, committee, hearing, examination, inquisition, trial, bar, bench

tribute   *n*
1 PRAISE, commendation, compliment, high/good opinion, good word, accolade, present, gift, homage, respect, honour, applause, testimonial, credit, acknowledgement, evidence, proof, recognition, gratitude
formal eulogy, paean, panegyric, enconium
2 PAYMENT, levy, charge, tax, tariff, duty, gift, offering, contribution

trice   *n*
moment, minute, second, instant, flash, twinkling
colloq. jiffy, sec, shake, tick

trick   *n, adj, v*
▶ *n* 1 FRAUD, swindle, deception, deceit, artifice, ploy, ruse, dodge, subterfuge, trap, device, manoeuvre
colloq. con, rip-off, scam, diddle
2 HOAX, practical joke, joke, prank, antic, caper, frolic, gag, jape, feat, stunt
colloq. leg-pull, frame-up, fast one, scam
3 ILLUSION, apparition, mirage, fantasy, trick of light, legerdemain
4 KNACK, gift, talent, technique, skill, art, flair, ability, capability, faculty, facility, capacity, secret, genius
colloq. know-how, hang
▶ *adj* false, mock, artificial, imitation, ersatz, fake, forged, counterfeit, feigned, sham, bogus
❊ real, genuine
▶ *v* deceive, delude, dupe, fool, hoodwink, beguile, mislead, take in, bluff, hoax, cheat, swindle, diddle, defraud, trap, outwit
colloq. con, pull someone's leg, kid, have on, do, take for a ride, pull a fast one on, pull one over, lead up the garden path, pull the wool over someone's eyes
▷ **trick out** decorate, spruce up, ornament, adorn, dress up; *formal* array, attire, bedeck; *colloq.* do up, doll up, tart up

trickery   *n*
deception, deceit, cunning, illusion, sleight of hand, pretence, artifice, guile, wiliness, subterfuge, deceit, dishonesty, cheating, swindling, fraud, imposture, double-dealing, monkey business, chicanery, skulduggery
formal duplicity
colloq. funny business, hanky-panky, jiggery-pokery, hocus-pocus, shenanigans
❊ straightforwardness, honesty

trickle   *v, n*
▶ *v* dribble, run, leak, seep, ooze, flow slowly, exude, drip, drop, filter, percolate
❊ stream, gush
▶ *n* dribble, drip, drop, leak, seepage
❊ stream, gush

trickster   *n*
cheat, swindler, deceiver, fraud, hoaxer, impostor, joker, pretender, tricker, cozener
old use tregetour
formal dissembler
colloq. con man, diddler

tricky   *adj*
1 *a tricky problem*
difficult, awkward, problematic, complicated, knotty, thorny, sensitive, delicate, ticklish
colloq. dodgy
2 CRAFTY, artful, cunning, sly, wily, foxy, subtle, devious, slippery, scheming, deceitful

colloq. dodgy
▣ **1** easy, simple **2** honest

tried *adj*
tested, proved, reliable, dependable, trusted, trustworthy, established

trifle *n, v*
▶ *n* **1** LITTLE, bit, small amount, spot, drop, dash, touch, trace
2 TOY, plaything, trinket, bauble, knick-knack, triviality, nothing, trivia, inessential, minor consideration
▶ *v* toy, play, sport, flirt, treat frivolously, dally, dabble, fiddle, meddle, fool, potter
colloq. mess about/around

trifling *adj*
small, paltry, slight, negligible, inconsiderable, unimportant, insignificant, minor, trivial, superficial, petty, silly, foolish, frivolous, idle, empty, shallow, worthless
formal inconsequential
▣ important, significant, serious

trigger *v, n*
▶ *v* cause, start, initiate, activate, bring about, set off, spark off, provoke, prompt, elicit, generate, produce, set in motion
colloq. set/start the ball rolling
▶ *n* lever, catch, switch, spur, stimulus

trim *adj, v, n*
▶ *adj* **1** NEAT, tidy, orderly, shipshape, in good order, spick-and-span, spruce, smart, well-turned-out, well-groomed, well-dressed, presentable, dapper
colloq. natty, cool, snazzy
2 SLIM, slender, svelte, streamlined, fit, compact
▣ **1** untidy, scruffy
▶ *v* **1** CUT, clip, crop, dock, snip, prune, pare, shave, shear, chop
2 DECREASE, reduce, cut (down), cut back on, diminish, curtail, contract, scale down
3 DECORATE, ornament, embellish, garnish, adorn, festoon, dress, fringe, edge, adjust, arrange, order, neaten, tidy (up)
formal array
▶ *n* **1** CONDITION, state, order, form, shape, fitness, health, fettle
2 TRIMMING, braid, border, edging, fringe, frill

trimming *n*
1 ADORNMENT, decoration, braid, border, edging, fringe, frill, embellishment, garnish, ornamentation, trim, extra, accessory, piping, falbala, frou-frou, passement, passementerie
technical fimbriation
old use furbelow
2 CUTTING, clipping, paring, end

trinket *n*
bauble, jewel, ornament, knick-knack, trifle, gimcrack, gewgaw, bagatelle, whim-wham

trio *n*
threesome, triad, trinity, triune, triunity, triplet, triplicity, trilogy
formal triumvirate, troika

trip *n, v*
▶ *n* **1** OUTING, excursion, tour, jaunt, ride, drive, spin, run, journey, voyage, expedition, foray
2 FALL, slip, stumble, tumble, false step
3 ERROR, blunder, mistake, inaccuracy, slip, gaffe, *faux pas*

colloq. howler, bloomer, clanger, booboo
4 HALLUCINATION, illusion, vision, apparition, fantasy, dream, experience
slang freak-out, buzz
▶ *v* **1** STUMBLE, slip, slide, fall, tumble, stagger, totter, lose your footing
2 DANCE, skip, gambol, hop, spring, caper, tiptoe
▷ **trip up** catch (out), trap, snare, ensnare, ambush, waylay, outsmart, outwit, surprise, trick

tripe *n*
rubbish, nonsense, bunkum, drivel, garbage, inanity, claptrap, trash, guff
colloq. balderdash, hogwash, twaddle, tosh, rot, poppycock, blah, bosh; *slang* balls, bullshit
▣ sense

triple *adj, v, n*
▶ *adj* treble, three times, triplicate, threefold, three-ply, three-way, tripartite
▶ *v* treble, triplicate
▶ *n* trio, threesome, triad, trinity, triune, triunity, triplet, triplicity, trilogy
formal triumvirate, troika

tripper *n*
tourist, sightseer, traveller, voyager, holidaymaker, excursionist
colloq. grockle

trite *adj*
banal, commonplace, common, ordinary, run-of-the-mill, stale, tired, worn, worn-out, threadbare, unoriginal, uninspired, dull, routine, hackneyed, overdone, overused, stock, stereotyped, clichéed
formal platitudinous
colloq. corny
▣ original, new, fresh, imaginative, inspired

triumph *n, v*
▶ *n* **1** WIN, victory, conquest, walk-over, success, mastery, achievement, accomplishment, attainment, feat, coup, masterstroke, hit, sensation
colloq. walkover
2 EXULTATION, jubilation, rejoicing, celebration, elation, joy, happiness
▣ **1** failure
▶ *v* **1** WIN, succeed, prosper, conquer, defeat, beat, overcome, overwhelm, gain mastery, dominate
formal vanquish, prevail
colloq. win the day
2 CELEBRATE, rejoice, glory, gloat, exult, revel, swagger, crow
formal jubilate
▣ **1** lose, fail

triumphant *adj*
winning, victorious, conquering, successful, prize-winning, exultant, jubilant, rejoicing, celebratory, glorious, elated, joyful, proud, boastful, gloating, swaggering
colloq. cock-a-hoop
▣ defeated, humble

trivia *n*
details, trifles, trivialities, irrelevancies, minutiae
colloq. pap
▣ essentials

trivial *adj*
unimportant, insignificant, incidental, minor, petty, paltry, trifling, flimsy, small, little, inconsiderable, negligible, worthless, meaningless, frivolous, banal, trite, commonplace, everyday

formal inconsequential
colloq. measly, piddling, no great shakes, cutting no ice
E3 important, significant, profound, substantial

triviality *n*
unimportance, insignificance, pettiness, smallness,
worthlessness, meaninglessness, foolishness, frivolity,
trifle, detail, technicality
E3 importance, essential

trivialize *v*
minimize, play down, underestimate, underplay,
undervalue, devalue, belittle, depreciate, scoff at
E3 exalt

troop *n, v*
▶ *n* **1** *send in troops*
army, military, soldiers, armed forces, servicemen,
servicewomen
2 *a troop of soldiers/children*
contingent, squadron, unit, division, company, squad,
team, crew, gang, band, bunch, group, body, pack,
squad, herd, flock, horde, crowd, throng, mob,
gathering, multitude
formal assemblage
▶ *v* go, march, parade, stream, flock, swarm, throng,
traipse, trudge

trophy *n*
cup, prize, laurels, award, spoils, souvenir, memento

tropical *adj*
hot, torrid, sultry, boiling, sweltering, stifling, steamy,
humid
E3 arctic, cold, cool, temperate

trot *v, n*
▶ *v* jog, canter, run, pace, scamper, scuttle, bustle,
scurry
▷ **trot out** bring out, bring up, drag up, relate,
repeat, bring forward, exhibit, reiterate;
formal adduce, recite, rehearse
▶ *n* jog, canter, run

troubadour *n*
singer, minstrel, balladeer, cantabank, jongleur, poet,
trouvère, trouveur, Minnesinger

trouble *n, v*
▶ *n* **1** PROBLEM, difficulty, struggle, annoyance,
irritation, vexation, bother, nuisance, inconvenience,
hardship, misfortune, adversity, trial, torment, burden,
pain, suffering, distress, grief, woe, heartache,
concern, unease, uneasiness, worry, anxiety, agitation
formal tribulation, affliction, disquiet
colloq. hassle, headache, hot water, mess, corner, fix,
scrape, jam, pickle, tight spot
2 UNREST, strife, fighting, tumult, commotion,
disturbance, disorder, upheaval
3 *back trouble*
disorder, complaint, ailment, illness, disease,
disability, defect
4 *engine trouble*
problem(s), failure, breakdown, cutting-out,
shutdown, stopping, stalling
formal malfunction
colloq. packing-up; *slang* conking-out
5 EFFORT, exertion, pains, care, attention, thought,
thoughtfulness, bother, fuss, ado, inconvenience
colloq. hassle
E3 **1** relief, calm **2** order **3** health
▶ *v* annoy, vex, harass, torment, bother, make the
effort, inconvenience, disturb, upset, distress, sadden,
pain, afflict, weigh (down), burden, worry, agitate,

irritate, disconcert, perplex
formal discommode, perturb
colloq. put out, hassle
E3 reassure, help

troublemaker *n*
agitator, rabble-rouser, incendiary, instigator, inciter,
ringleader, stirrer, *agent provocateur*, mischief-maker
E3 peacemaker

troublesome *adj*
1 ANNOYING, irritating, vexatious, irksome,
bothersome, worrisome, disturbing, inconvenient,
difficult, hard, awkward, tricky, thorny, taxing,
demanding, exacting, laborious, tiresome, wearisome
formal perturbing
2 UNRULY, mischievous, rowdy, turbulent, trying,
unco-operative, insubordinate, rebellious
E3 **1** easy, simple **2** helpful

trough *n*
1 MANGER, feeding trough, feeder, crib
2 GUTTER, conduit, drain, trench, ditch, gully,
channel, duct, groove, furrow, flame, hollow,
depression

trounce *v*
defeat, rout, beat, thrash, overwhelm, paste, punish,
best, crush
colloq. wallop, wipe the floor with, slaughter, hammer,
clobber, lick, drub

troupe *n*
company, group, set, band, cast, troop

trouper *n*
actor, performer, player, theatrical, artiste,
entertainer, veteran
formal thespian
colloq. old hand

trousers *n*
slacks, jeans, denims, Levis®, flannels, dungarees,
breeches, shorts
US pants

truancy *n*
absence, absenteeism, shirking, malingering, French
leave
colloq. skiving
E3 attendance

truant *n, adj, v*
▶ *n* absentee, deserter, runaway, idler, shirker,
dodger, malingerer
colloq. skiver
▶ *adj* absent, missing, runaway
▶ *v* play truant, desert, dodge, shirk, malinger
colloq. skive, skive off, play hooky

truce *n*
cease-fire, peace, armistice, cessation, moratorium,
suspension, stay, respite, lull, rest, break, interval,
intermission
colloq. let-up
E3 war, hostilities

truck¹ *n*
heavy trucks on the road
lorry, heavy goods vehicle (HGV), van, wagon, float

truck² *n*
have no truck with someone
contact, communication, connection, relations,
dealings, business, trade, commerce, traffic, exchange
formal intercourse

truculent *adj*
aggressive, belligerent, defiant, disobedient, quarrelsome, antagonistic, contentious, hostile, violent, savage, combative, fierce, argumentative, rude, bad-tempered, ill-tempered, sullen, cross, obstreperous, discourteous, disrespectful
formal bellicose, pugnacious
E3 co-operative, good-natured

trudge *v, n*
▶ *v* tramp, plod, clump, stump, lumber, traipse, slog, toil, labour, trek, hike, walk, march, shuffle
▶ *n* tramp, traipse, slog, haul, trek, hike, walk, march

true *adj, adv*
▶ *adj* **1** REAL, genuine, authentic, actual, veritable, exact, precise, accurate, close, correct, right, factual, truthful, veracious, sincere, honest, legitimate, faithful, unerring, valid, rightful, proper
formal veracious
2 FAITHFUL, loyal, constant, steadfast, fast, staunch, firm, dependable, reliable, trustworthy, trusty, honourable, sincere, dedicated, devoted
E3 1 false, wrong, untrue, incorrect, inaccurate
2 unfaithful, faithless
▶ *adv* accurately, exactly, correctly, faithfully, honestly, precisely, rightly, truly, truthfully, unerringly, properly, perfectly, veritably
formal veraciously
E3 falsely, inaccurately

true-blue *adj*
card-carrying, committed, confirmed, constant, dedicated, devoted, dyed-in-the-wool, faithful, loyal, orthodox, staunch, true, trusty, uncompromising, unwavering
E3 superficial, wavering

truism *n*
platitude, self-evident truth, truth, commonplace, cliché, bromide, axiom

truly *adv*
very, greatly, extremely, exceptionally, really, genuinely, sincerely, honestly, constantly, steadfastly, truthfully, surely, definitely, certainly, undoubtedly, undeniably, indeed, in fact, in reality, actually, exactly, precisely, correctly, rightly, properly
formal indubitably
E3 slightly, falsely, incorrectly

trump *v*
▷ **trump up** invent, fake, fabricate, create, devise, make up, concoct, contrive
colloq. cook up

trumped-up *adj*
false, fabricated, fake, faked, falsified, invented, made-up, untrue, cooked-up, concocted, contrived, spurious
colloq. phoney
E3 genuine, real, true

trumpery *adj*
worthless, useless, valueless, shabby, trifling, showy, cheap, flashy, nasty, rubbishy, shoddy, tawdry, trashy
formal meretricious
colloq. grotty
E3 first-rate

trumpet *n, v*
▶ *n* bugle, horn, clarion, blare, blast, roar, bellow, cry, call
▶ *v* blare, blast, roar, bellow, bay, shout, proclaim, announce, herald, broadcast, advertise

truncate *v*
shorten, abbreviate, curtail, reduce, diminish, cut, lop, dock, prune, pare, clip, trim, crop
E3 lengthen, extend

truncheon *n*
baton, club, cudgel, cosh, stick, staff, shillelagh, knobkerrie

trunk *n*
1 STEM, shaft, stock, stalk
2 CASE, suitcase, chest, coffer, box, crate, portmanteau
3 SNOUT, nose
technical proboscis
4 TORSO, body, frame

truss *v, n*
▶ *v* tie, strap, bind, pinion, fasten, tether, secure, bundle, wrap, pack
E3 untie, loosen
▶ *n* binding, bandage, pad, support, brace, prop, stay, shore, buttress, strut, joist

trust *n, v*
▶ *n* **1** FAITH, belief, credence, credit, hope, expectation, reliance, confidence, assurance, conviction, certainty
2 CARE, charge, custody, safekeeping, guardianship, trusteeship, protection, obligation, responsibility, duty, commitment
E3 1 distrust, mistrust, scepticism, doubt
Related adjective: fiduciary
▶ *v* **1** RELY ON, depend on, put your confidence in, have confidence in, be sure of, count on, bank on, swear by
2 BELIEVE, imagine, assume, presume, suppose, hope, expect
formal surmise
3 ENTRUST, commit, consign, confide, give, assign, turn over, delegate
E3 2 distrust, mistrust, doubt, disbelieve

trustee *n*
keeper, administrator, agent, custodian, guardian, executor, executrix, fiduciary, depositary

trusting *adj*
trustful, credulous, gullible, naïve, innocent, ingenuous, unquestioning, unsuspecting, unguarded, unwary
E3 distrustful, suspicious, cautious

trustworthy *adj*
honest, upright, honourable, principled, ethical, dependable, reliable, steadfast, stable, staunch, true, committed, devoted, faithful, loyal, responsible, sensible, level headed
colloq. (as) good as your word
E3 untrustworthy, dishonest, unreliable, irresponsible

trusty *adj*
faithful, dependable, reliable, responsible, strong, supportive, firm, honest, loyal, staunch, trustworthy, true, solid, straightforward, steady, upright
E3 unreliable

truth *n*
1 TRUTHFULNESS, candour, frankness, honesty, sincerity, genuineness, authenticity, realism, exactness, precision, correctness, accuracy, validity, legitimacy, rightness, honour, honourableness, integrity, uprightness, faithfulness, loyalty, constancy
formal veracity, fidelity

2 *tell the truth*
facts, reality, actuality, fact, the gospel truth, axiom, maxim, principle, truism
colloq. home truth
E **1** deceit, dishonesty, falseness **2** lie, falsehood

truthful *adj*
frank, candid, straight, honest, open, forthright, true, sincere, veritable, exact, precise, right, factual, accurate, correct, valid, realistic, faithful, trustworthy, reliable
formal veracious
E untruthful, deceitful, false, untrue

truthfulness *n*
frankness, candour, honesty, openness, sincerity, straightness, uprightness, righteousness
formal veracity
E untruthfulness

try *v, n*
▶ *v* **1** ATTEMPT, endeavour, venture, undertake, seek, strive, aim
formal assay
colloq. have a go, have a bash/crack/shot/stab, give something your best shot, give something a whirl
2 HEAR, judge
3 EXPERIMENT, test, try out, sample, taste, inspect, examine, investigate, evaluate
formal appraise
4 *try someone's patience*
tax, make demands on, strain, stress, tire, wear out, weary, exhaust, drain, sap, weaken, stretch
▷ **try out** test, evaluate, try on, check out, inspect, sample, taste; *formal* appraise
▶ *n* **1** ATTEMPT, endeavour, effort
colloq. go, bash, crack, shot, stab, whirl
2 EXPERIMENT, test, trial, evaluation, ample, taste
formal appraisal

trying *adj*
annoying, irritating, vexatious, exasperating, troublesome, tiresome, wearisome, bothersome, difficult, hard, tough, arduous, taxing, demanding, testing
colloq. aggravating
E easy

tub *n*
bath, bathtub, basin, vat, tun, butt, cask, barrel, keg, hogshead

tubby *adj*
chubby, plump, portly, podgy, paunchy, stout, pudgy, roly-poly, fat, overweight, obese, buxom, well-upholstered
formal corpulent, rotund
E slim

tube *n*
hose, pipe, cylinder, duct, conduit, spout, channel, shaft, inlet, outlet

tubular *adj*
tubelike, pipelike, pipy
formal tubulous, tubulate, tubiform, tubate, vasiform

tuck *v, n*
▶ *v* **1** INSERT, push, ease, thrust, stuff, cram
2 FOLD, pleat, gather, crease, ruffle
▷ **tuck away** stash away, save (up), store, hide, conceal, hoard
▷ **tuck in/into** eat, eat up, gorge, devour, dine, feast; *colloq.* gobble, scoff, wolf down
▷ **tuck in/up** put to bed, make comfortable, make snug, cover up, wrap up, fold in/under

▶ *n* **1** FOLD, pleat, gather, pucker, crease
2 FOOD, comestibles, meals, snack(s)
colloq. eats; *slang* grub, nosh, scoff

tuft *n*
crest, beard, tassel, truss, knot, clump, cluster, bunch, wisp
formal flocculus

tug *v, n*
▶ *v* pull, draw, tow, haul, drag, lug, heave, wrench, jerk, pluck
colloq. yank
▶ *n* pull, tow, haul, heave, wrench, jerk, pluck
colloq. yank

tuition *n*
teaching, instruction, coaching, training, guidance, lessons, schooling, education

tumble *v, n*
▶ *v* **1** FALL, trip (up), topple, stumble, drop, flop, knock down, unseat, overthrow
2 PITCH, roll, toss, lurch, sway, reel, heave
3 *prices are tumbling*
decrease, fall, decline, collapse, slide, plummet, dive, nosedive, plunge, fall headlong
▷ **tumble to** understand, realize, grasp, perceive, become aware of; *colloq.* cotton on to, twig
▶ *n* **1** FALL, stumble, trip, drop, roll, toss
2 DECREASE, fall, decline, collapse, slide, dive, nosedive

tumbledown *adj*
broken-down, ramshackle, rickety, dilapidated, unstable, unsteady, shaky, unsafe, ruinous, ruined, crumbling, crumbly, disintegrating, decrepit, tottering
E well-kept

tumbler *n*
1 ACROBAT, gymnast, contortionist
2 DRINKING-GLASS, glass, beaker, cup, drinking-glass, goblet, mug

tumid *adj*
1 SWOLLEN, enlarged, bulging, protuberant, bloated, puffed up, bulbous
formal distended, tumescent
2 BOMBASTIC, pompous, affected, overblown, grandiose, high-flown, inflated, pretentious, fulsome, flowery, stilted, turgid
formal euphuistic, grandiloquent, magniloquent
E **1** flat **2** simple

tumour *n*
cancer, growth, lump, swelling
technical carcinoma, melanoma, lymphoma, myeloma, sarcoma, neoplasm

tumult *n*
commotion, turmoil, disturbance, upheaval, stir, agitation, unrest, disorder, confusion, chaos, pandemonium, bedlam, babel, noise, clamour, shouting, din, racket, hubbub, hullabaloo, row, rumpus, uproar, riot, fracas, brawl, affray, strife
formal disarray
E peace, calm, composure

tumultuous *adj*
turbulent, stormy, raging, frenzied, fierce, violent, wild, vehement, fervent, hectic, boisterous, rowdy, noisy, loud, deafening, clamorous, disorderly, unruly, riotous, uncontrolled, restless, agitated, troubled, disturbed, excited
E calm, peaceful, quiet

tune   *n, v*
▶ *n* melody, theme, motif, song, air, strain
▷ **change your tune** change your mind, change your attitude/opinions, change your approach
▷ **in tune with** in agreement with, in sympathy with, agreeing with, in harmony with; *formal* in accord with
▶ *v* pitch, harmonize, set, regulate, adjust, adapt, temper, synchronize
formal attune

tuneful   *adj*
melodious, melodic, catchy, musical, euphonious, harmonious, pleasant, agreeable, mellow, sonorous
formal mellifluous
◧ tuneless, discordant

tuneless   *adj*
unmelodic, unmelodious, unmusical, unpleasant, disagreeable, harsh, clashing, discordant, cacophonous, dissonant
formal atonal, horrisonant
◧ tuneful

tunnel   *n, v*
▶ *n* passage, underground passage, passageway, gallery, subway, underpass, burrow, hole, mine, shaft, chimney
▶ *v* burrow, dig, excavate, mine, bore, penetrate, undermine, sap

turbid   *adj*
cloudy, clouded, hazy, dense, dim, foggy, fuzzy, muddy, murky, unclear, thick, muddled, opaque, confused, disordered, turbulent, unsettled, impure, incoherent, foul
formal feculent
◧ clear

turbulence   *n*
roughness, storm, unrest, boiling, upheaval, agitation, turmoil, tumult, confusion, commotion, chaos, disorder, disruption, instability, pandemonium
◧ calm

turbulent   *adj*
rough, choppy, foaming, stormy, blustery, tempestuous, raging, furious, violent, wild, tumultuous, unbridled, boisterous, rowdy, disorderly, unruly, undisciplined, obstreperous, rebellious, mutinous, riotous, agitated, in turmoil, unsettled, unstable, confused, disordered
◧ calm, composed

turf   *n, v*
▶ *n* grass, clod, sod, divot, sward, green, lawn, glebe
▶ *v* ▷ **turf out** discharge, dismiss, eject, turn out, throw out, evict, banish, fling out, expel, oust; *formal* dispossess; *colloq.* kick out, chuck out, elbow, fire, sack, give the elbow to

turgid   *adj*
pompous, bombastic, flowery, fulsome, grandiose, high-flown, inflated, ostentatious, extravagant, overblown, pretentious, stilted, affected
formal grandiloquent, magniloquent
◧ simple

turmoil   *n*
confusion, disorder, tumult, commotion, disturbance, trouble, disquiet, agitation, turbulence, stir, ferment, flurry, bustle, chaos, pandemonium, bedlam, noise, din, hubbub, row, uproar, upheaval
formal disarray
◧ calm, peace, quiet

turn   *v, n*
▶ *v* **1** REVOLVE, circle, spin, go round, go round and round, go round in circles, twirl, whirl, spiral, wind, reel, twist, gyrate, pivot, hinge, swivel, rotate, roll, move, shift, invert, reverse, bend, veer, swing, swerve, pass, point, direct, aim, divert **2** MAKE, transform, change, alter, modify, convert, adapt, adjust, fit, mould, shape, cast, form, fashion, remodel
formal mutate, transmute, metamorphose
3 *turn cold*
go, become, grow, come to be
4 RESORT, have recourse, apply, appeal
5 SOUR, curdle, spoil, go off, go bad, make, become rancid
▷ **turn against** dislike, disapprove of, distrust, make/become hostile to
◧ like, trust, support
▷ **turn aside** deviate, depart, diverge, deflect, ward off, fend off, parry, avert
▷ **turn away** reject, avert, deflect, deviate, depart, move away; *colloq.* cold shoulder
◧ accept, help, receive
▷ **turn down 1** *turn down an offer* reject, decline, refuse, spurn, rebuff, repudiate, veto **2** LOWER, decrease, reduce, lessen, make quieter, quieten, soften, mute, muffle
◧ **1** accept **2** turn up
▷ **turn in 1** GO TO BED, retire; *colloq.* hit the hay, hit the sack **2** HAND IN, give in, tender, submit, return, give back, hand over, give up, surrender, deliver
◧ **1** get up **2** keep
▷ **turn off 1** BRANCH OFF, leave, depart from, deviate, divert, go along a different road; *colloq.* quit **2** SWITCH OFF, turn out, stop, shut down, unplug, disconnect, pull off **3** REPEL, sicken, nauseate, disgust, offend, displease, disenchant, alienate, bore, discourage, put off, turn against
◧ **1** join **2** turn on **3** *colloq.* turn on
▷ **turn on 1** SWITCH ON, start (up), activate, plug (in), connect **2** AROUSE, stimulate, excite, thrill, please, attract **3** HINGE ON, depend on, rest on, hang on; *formal* be contingent on **4** ATTACK, round on, fall on, set upon, lay into
◧ **1** turn off **2** *colloq.* turn off
▷ **turn out 1** HAPPEN, come about, ensue, result, end up, become, develop, emerge; *formal* transpire; *colloq.* pan out **2** SWITCH OFF, turn off, unplug, disconnect **3** APPEAR, present, dress, clothe **4** ATTEND, turn up, come, go, arrive, appear, be present; *colloq.* show up **5** PRODUCE, make, manufacture, fabricate, assemble; *colloq.* churn out **6** EVICT, throw out, expel, deport, banish, dismiss, discharge, drum out; *colloq.* chuck out, kick out, turf out, sack, fire **7** *turn out the attic* empty, clear (out), clean out
◧ **2** turn on **6** admit, receive **7** fill
▷ **turn over 1** THINK OVER, think about, mull over, ponder, deliberate, reflect on, contemplate, consider, examine; *formal* ruminate **2** HAND OVER, surrender, deliver, transfer, assign, consign **3** OVERTURN, upset, upend, turn turtle, invert, reverse, capsize, keel over
▷ **turn over a new leaf** change, change your ways, improve, mend your ways, amend, reform, begin again; *colloq.* pull one's socks up
◧ persist
▷ **turn up 1** ATTEND, turn out, come, arrive, appear, be present; *colloq.* show up **2** AMPLIFY, make louder, intensify, raise, increase **3** DISCOVER,

find, uncover, unearth, dig up, expose, disclose, reveal, show, bring to light
E3 1 stay away **2** turn down
▶ *n* **1** REVOLUTION, cycle, round, circle, rotation, spin, twirl, whirl, twist, swivel, gyration, bend, curve, corner, loop, reversal
2 CHANGE, alteration, shift, variation, difference, deviation, divergence
3 *it's your turn*
go, chance, opportunity, occasion, time, stint, period, spell
colloq. crack, stab, bash
4 ACT, appearance, routine, performance, performer
5 TREND, tendency, inclination, direction, bias, leaning, drift
formal propensity
6 *gave her quite a turn*
illness, nervousness, faintness, shock, fright, scare
▷ **to a turn** perfectly, exactly, correctly, precisely, to perfection
▷ **turn of events** incident, happening, occurrence, result, affair, outcome, phenomenon
▷ **turn of phrase** expression, idiom, saying, style, diction, metaphor, phraseology; *formal* locution

turncoat *n*
traitor, defector, deserter, renegade, renegate, seceder, backslider, blackleg
formal apostate, tergiversator
colloq. fink, rat, scab

turning *n*
turn-off, junction, crossroads, fork, bend, curve, turn

turning-point *n*
crossroads, watershed, crux, crisis, critical/decisive moment, moment of truth

turnout *n*
1 ATTENDANCE, audience, gate, crowd, gathering, assembly, congregation, number
formal assemblage
2 APPEARANCE, outfit, dress, clothes
formal attire, array
colloq. gear, clobber, togs, get-up

turnover *n*
income, profits, productivity, business, production, output, yield, volume, outturn, change, movement, flow, replacement

turpitude *n*
baseness, corruption, badness, corruptness, evil, criminality, immorality, vileness, wickedness, viciousness, depravity, degeneracy, foulness, sinfulness, villainy
formal flagitiousness, nefariousness, iniquity
E3 honour

tussle *v, n*
▶ *v* struggle, battle, wrestle, compete, vie, fight, contend, grapple, scrap, brawl, scuffle, scramble
▶ *n* struggle, battle, conflict, contest, scramble, fight, brawl, bout, fracas, fray, melee, punch-up, scrap, scuffle, scrum, set-to, competition, contention, scrimmage
colloq. dust-up

tutelage *n*
guidance, charge, custody, care, protection, guardianship, wardship, patronage, vigilance, eye, teaching, instruction, education, schooling, tuition, preparation
formal aegis

tutor *n, v*
▶ *n* teacher, instructor, coach, educator, lecturer, supervisor, guide, mentor, guru, guardian
▶ *v* teach, instruct, train, drill, coach, educate, school, lecture, supervise, direct, guide

tutorial *n, adj*
▶ *n* class, lesson, seminar, teach-in
▶ *adj* coaching, didactic, educative, educatory, guiding, instructional, teaching

TV *n*
television, receiver, set, small screen
colloq. telly, the box, goggle-box, idiot box, the tube; *US* boob tube

twaddle *n*
drivel, rubbish, nonsense, trash, garbage, gabble, waffle, blather, blether, guff, gossip, tattle, balderdash, bunk, bunkum, claptrap, inanity, gobbledygook, poppycock, stuff
colloq. balls, hogwash, hot air, piffle, rot, tosh
E3 sense

tweak *v, n*
twist, pinch, squeeze, nip, pull, tug, jerk, twitch

twee *adj*
sweet, cute, pretty, dainty, quaint, sentimental, affected, precious

twiddle *v*
turn, twirl, swivel, twist, wiggle, adjust, fiddle, finger

twig¹ *n*
dried twigs
branch, spring, spray, shoot, offshoot, stick, wattle, whip, withe, withy
formal ramulus

twig² *v*
then I twigged
understand, see, get, comprehend, grasp, fathom, rumble
colloq. catch on, cotton on, tumble to

twilight *n, adj*
▶ *n* dusk, half-light, gloaming, gloom, dimness, sunset, evening, decline, ebb
formal crepuscule
▶ *adj* darkening, dim, declining, evening, shadowy, final, last, ebbing, dying
formal crepuscular

twin *n, adj, v*
▶ *n* double, look-alike, likeness, duplicate, clone, match, counterpart, equivalent, complement, fellow, mate
formal corollary
colloq. (dead) ringer
▶ *adj* identical, matching, corresponding, symmetrical, parallel, matched, paired, double, dual, duplicate, twofold
▶ *v* match, pair, couple, link, join, yoke

twine *n, v*
▶ *n* string, cord, thread, yarn
▶ *v* wind, coil, spiral, loop, curl, bend, twist, tangle, wreathe, wrap, surround, encircle, entwine, plait, braid, knit, weave

twinge *n*
pain, pang, throb, spasm, ache, throe, stab, stitch, cramp, pinch, prick

twinkle *v, n*
▶ *v* sparkle, glitter, shimmer, glisten, glimmer, flicker, wink, flash, glint, gleam, shine, scintillate
formal coruscate
▶ *n* sparkle, scintillation, glitter, shimmer, glisten, glimmer, flicker, wink, flash, glint, shining, gleam, light
formal coruscation

twinkling *adj, n*
▶ *adj* bright, sparkling, glittering, shimmering, glistening, glimmering, flickering, gleaming, flashing, blinking, scintillating, shining, winking, polished
formal coruscating, nitid
▶ *n* moment, flash, instant, second
colloq. sec, tick, jiff, jiffy, mo, trice, shake, no time, two shakes of a lamb's tail

twirl *v, n*
▶ *v* spin, whirl, pirouette, wheel, rotate, revolve, swivel, pivot, turn, curl, twist, gyrate, wind, coil
▶ *n* spin, whirl, pirouette, rotation, revolution, turn, curl, twist, gyration, convolution, spiral, coil

twirling *adj*
spinning, whirling, pirouetting, rotating, revolving, pivoting, pivotal, gyratory, swivelling
formal gyral, rotatory

twist *v, n*
▶ *v* **1** TURN, screw, wring, spin, rotate, revolve, swivel, wind, zigzag, bend, coil, spiral, curl, wreathe, twirl, twine, entwine, intertwine, weave, braid, plait, entangle, wriggle, squirm, writhe, skew
2 *twist your ankle*
wrench, rick, sprain, strain
3 CHANGE, alter, garble, falsify, misquote, misrepresent, misreport, distort, contort, warp, bend, misshape, deform, pervert
▷ **twist someone's arm** persuade, force, intimidate, pressurize, bulldoze, bully, coerce, dragoon; *colloq.* lean on, put the screws on
▶ *n* **1** TURN, screw, spin, roll, bend, curve, arc, kink, curl, loop, zigzag, coil, spiral, convolution, squiggle, tangle
2 WRENCH, rick, sprain, strain
3 CHANGE, variation, break, turn, surprise, turnabout
4 PERVERSION, distortion, contortion, imperfection, defect, flaw
formal aberration
5 QUIRK, oddity, peculiarity, idiosyncrasy, foible, freak, whim

twisted *adj*
winding, wavy, squiggly, warped, perverted, deviant, unnatural, strange, peculiar, odd
formal sinuous
▣ straight

twister *n*
swindler, cheat, crook, fraud, rogue, deceiver, trickster, scoundrel, blackguard
colloq. con man, phoney

twit *n*
idiot, fool, simpleton, blockhead, clown,
colloq. ass, ninny, halfwit, dope, twerp, nitwit, clot, nincompoop, chump

twitch *v, n*
▶ *v* jerk, jump, start, blink, tremble, quiver, flutter, shake, pull, tug, tweak, snatch, pluck
▶ *n* spasm, convulsion, tic, tremor, shiver, quiver, flutter, jerk, jump, start

twitter *v, n*
▶ *v* **1** CHIRP, chirrup, tweet, cheep, sing, warble, whistle, chatter
2 PRATTLE, witter, gabble, gossip, twaddle, blather, blether
▶ *n* chirping, chirruping, tweeting, song, cry, warble, chatter

two-faced *adj*
hypocritical, insincere, false, lying, deceitful, treacherous, double-dealing, devious, untrustworthy, Janus-faced
formal perfidious, dissembling, duplicitous
▣ honest, candid, frank

tycoon *n*
industrialist, entrepreneur, captain of industry, magnate, mogul, baron, supremo, capitalist, financier
colloq. fat cat, big noise, big cheese, moneybags, moneyspinner

type *n*
1 SORT, kind, form, set, style, variety, strain, species, breed, group, class, category, subdivision, classification, description, designation, stamp, mark, order, brand, model, make, standard
technical genus
formal genre
2 EMBODIMENT, prototype, original, model, pattern, specimen, example
formal archetype, exemplar, quintessence
3 PRINT, printing, character(s), letter(s), number(s), symbol(s), lettering, face, fount, font

typhoon *n*
whirlwind, cyclone, tornado, hurricane, tempest, storm, squall
colloq. twister

typical *adj*
standard, normal, usual, average, ordinary, conventional, orthodox, classic, true, stereotype, stock, model, representative, illustrative, indicative, characteristic, distinctive
formal archetypal, quintessential
colloq. run-of-the-mill
▣ atypical, unusual

typically *adv*
usually, normally, ordinarily, characteristically, customarily, routinely, habitually, as a rule
formal quintessentially

typify *v*
embody, epitomize, encapsulate, personify, characterize, exemplify, symbolize, indicate, represent, illustrate

tyrannical *adj*
dictatorial, despotic, autocratic, absolute, totalitarian, arbitrary, authoritarian, domineering, overbearing, high-handed, imperious, magisterial, ruthless, harsh, severe, strict, cruel, oppressive, repressive, overpowering, unjust, unreasonable, Neronian
formal peremptory
▣ liberal, tolerant

tyrannize *v*
oppress, crush, intimidate, terrorize, coerce, repress, suppress, dictate, domineer, enslave, browbeat, bully, lord it over
formal subjugate

tyranny *n*
dictatorship, despotism, autocracy, absolutism,
authoritarianism, imperiousness, high-handedness,
ruthlessness, harshness, severity, strictness, cruelty,
oppression, injustice
🔁 democracy, freedom

tyrant *n*
dictator, despot, autocrat, absolutist, authoritarian,
bully, oppressor, slave-driver, taskmaster, martinet

tyro *see* tiro.

U

ubiquitous *adj*
ever-present, everywhere, universal, global, pervasive, common, frequent
formal omnipresent
E3 rare, scarce

ubiquity *n*
commonness, pervasiveness, universality, frequency, popularity, prevalence
formal omnipresence
E3 rarity

ugliness *n*
1 UNATTRACTIVENESS, unloveliness, plainness, unsightliness, hideousness, monstrosity, deformity
US homeliness
2 UNPLEASANTNESS, repulsiveness, offensiveness, frightfulness, enormity, horridness, horror, vileness
formal heinousness
3 DANGER, evil, nastiness, menace
E3 1 beauty, charm, goodness 2 pleasantness

ugly *adj*
1 UNATTRACTIVE, unsightly, plain, unlovely, unprepossessing, ill-favoured, hideous, revolting, repulsive, grotesque, monstrous, misshapen, deformed
US homely
colloq. ugly as sin
2 UNPLEASANT, disagreeable, nasty, horrid, hideous, objectionable, offensive, shocking, disgusting, loathsome, revolting, foul, repulsive, vile, frightful, obnoxious, terrible
3 DANGEROUS, threatening, alarming, sinister, grave, nasty, hostile, evil
E3 1 attractive, good-looking, beautiful, handsome, pretty 2 pleasant

ulcer *n*
sore, open sore, fester, abscess, boil, canker, ulceration, noma
old use impostume
Related adjective: helcoid

ulterior *adj*
secondary, hidden, concealed, undisclosed, unexpressed, unrevealed, covert, secret, private, personal, selfish
E3 overt, declared

ultimate *adj, n*
▶ *adj* 1 FINAL, last, closing, concluding, eventual, terminal, furthest, end, remotest, extreme
2 RADICAL, basic, fundamental, primary
formal elemental
3 BEST, utmost, greatest, topmost, highest, supreme, superlative, maximum, perfect
▶ *n* best, greatest, peak, perfection, summit, culmination, greatest achievement, masterpiece, *chef d'oeuvre*, height, extreme
formal consummation, epitome
colloq. daddy of them all, last word

ultimately *adv*
1 FINALLY, eventually, at last, in the end, after all, sooner or later
2 BASICALLY, fundamentally, primarily

ultra- *prefix*
extremely, excessively, especially, exceptionally, unusually, extraordinarily, remarkably, extra

ululate *v*
howl, wail, screech, moan, lament, keen, mourn, cry, scream, weep, sob, holler, hoot

umbrage *n*
▷ **take umbrage** take offence, resent, be angry, be annoyed, be exasperated, be hurt, be offended, be insulted, be upset, be/feel put out, take exception, take personally
colloq. be miffed, get huffy, get your nose out of joint

umbrella *n*
1 *put up your umbrella*
parasol, sunshade
colloq. brolly, gamp
2 PROTECTION, cover, patronage, agency
formal aegis

umpire *n, v*
▶ *n* referee, linesman, judge, adjudicator, arbiter, arbitrator, mediator, moderator
colloq. ref
▶ *v* referee, judge, adjudicate, arbitrate, mediate, moderate, control

umpteen *adj*
numerous, very many, plenty, thousands, millions, countless, innumerable
colloq. a good many
E3 few

unabashed *adj*
unashamed, unembarrassed, brazen, blatant, bold, confident, undaunted, unconcerned, undismayed
E3 abashed, sheepish

unable *adj*
incapable, powerless, impotent, unequipped, unqualified, unfit, incompetent, inadequate
formal ineffectual
E3 able, capable; *colloq.* up to

unabridged *adj*
complete, entire, full-length, full, whole, uncondensed, unshortened, uncut, unexpurgated
E3 abridged, shortened

unacceptable *adj*
intolerable, inadmissible, unsatisfactory, unsuitable, disappointing, undesirable, unwelcome, objectionable, disagreeable, offensive, unpleasant, obnoxious
E3 acceptable, satisfactory

unaccommodating *adj*
inflexible, uncompromising, unco-operative,

unyielding, unbending, obstinate, stubborn, perverse, rigid, disobliging
formal intransigent, uncomplaisant
E3 flexible, obliging

unaccompanied *adj*
alone, unescorted, unattended, by yourself, on your own, lone, solo, single, single-handed
E3 accompanied

unaccountable *adj*
1 INEXPLICABLE, unexplainable, unfathomable, impenetrable, insoluble, incomprehensible, baffling, puzzling, mysterious, astonishing, extraordinary, strange, odd, peculiar, singular, curious, bizarre, queer, unusual, uncommon, unheard-of
2 *unaccountable to the public*
not responsible, not answerable, free, immune
E3 1 explicable, explainable 2 accountable, bound

unaccustomed *adj*
1 *unaccustomed to such luxury*
unused, unacquainted, unfamiliar, unpractised, inexperienced
formal unwonted
2 STRANGE, unusual, uncommon, different, new, unexpected, surprising, extraordinary, remarkable, unfamiliar, uncharacteristic, unprecedented
E3 1 accustomed, familiar 2 customary

unacquainted *adj*
unfamiliar, unaccustomed, unused, inexperienced, strange, ignorant

unadorned *adj*
plain, simple, straightforward, undecorated, unornamented, unembellished, unvarnished, severe, stark, restrained
E3 decorated, embellished, ornate

unaffected *adj*
1 UNMOVED, unconcerned, indifferent, impervious, untouched, unchanged, unaltered
2 UNSOPHISTICATED, artless, naïve, ingenuous, guileless, unspoilt, plain, simple, straightforward, natural, unpretentious, unassuming, candid, true, sincere, honest, genuine
E3 1 moved, impressed, influenced 2 affected, pretentious, insincere

unafraid *adj*
fearless, confident, daring, dauntless, brave, courageous, imperturbable, intrepid, unshakable
E3 afraid, fearful, nervous

unalterable *adj*
unchangeable, invariable, unchanging, immutable, final, inflexible, unyielding, rigid, fixed, permanent
E3 alterable, flexible

unanimity *n*
consensus, unity, agreement, concurrence, like-mindedness, consistency, harmony, unison, concert
formal accord, concord, congruence
E3 disagreement, disunity

unanimous *adj*
united, concerted, joint, common, as one, in agreement, like-minded, consistent, harmonious
formal in accord, concordant
E3 disunited, divided

unanimously *adv*
unopposed, without opposition, without exception, as one, of one mind, with one voice, by common consent,

in concert, *nem con*
formal conjointly

unanswerable *adj*
incontestable, incontrovertible, indisputable, unarguable, undeniable, absolute, final, conclusive
formal irrefragable, irrefutable
E3 answerable, refutable

unappetizing *adj*
unpleasant, tasteless, unpalatable, off-putting, distasteful, disagreeable, uninviting, unsavoury, insipid, unappealing, unattractive, unexciting, uninteresting
E3 appetising

unapproachable *adj*
inaccessible, remote, distant, aloof, remote, standoffish, withdrawn, reserved, unsociable, unfriendly, unresponsive, uncommunicative, forbidding, cold, cool
E3 approachable, friendly

unapt *adj*
unsuitable, unfit, unfitted, unsuited, inappropriate, inapplicable, untimely, unseasonable, inapt
formal inapposite, malapropos
E3 apt

unarmed *adj*
defenceless, unprotected, exposed, open, vulnerable, weak, helpless
E3 armed, protected

unashamed *adj*
shameless, unabashed, impenitent, unrepentant, unconcealed, undisguised, open, honest, blatant
E3 ashamed, abashed

unasked *adj*
uninvited, unbidden, unrequested, unsought, unsolicited, unwanted, voluntary, spontaneous, unannounced
E3 invited, wanted

unassailable *adj*
invulnerable, incontestable, impregnable, incontrovertible, indisputable, secure, sound, positive, proven, absolute, conclusive, invincible, inviolable, undeniable, well-armed
formal irrefutable, well-fortified
E3 assailable

unassertive *adj*
self-effacing, unassuming, backward, bashful, quiet, retiring, shy, timid, meek, mousy, diffident, timorous
E3 assertive

unassuming *adj*
unassertive, self-effacing, retiring, modest, shy, demure, humble, meek, quiet, reticent, unobtrusive, unpretentious, simple, natural, restrained
E3 presumptuous, assertive, pretentious

unattached *adj*
unmarried, unengaged, uncommitted, single, on your own, by yourself, free, available, footloose, fancy-free, independent, unaffiliated
E3 engaged, committed

unattended *adj*
ignored, disregarded, abandoned, neglected, forgotten, unguarded, unwatched, unsupervised, unaccompanied, unescorted, alone
formal forsaken
E3 attended, escorted, looked after

unattractive *adj*
unappealing, disagreeable, unlovely, plain,
unpleasant, unprepossessing, uninviting, unexciting,
unsightly, ugly, objectionable, offensive, disgusting,
distasteful, off-putting, undesirable, ill-favoured,
uncomely, unwelcome, unpalatable, unsavoury,
repellent, unappetizing
US homely
E3 attractive

unauthorized *adj*
unofficial, unlicensed, unlawful, forbidden,
prohibited, illegal, illicit, illegitimate, irregular,
unapproved, unsanctioned, unwarranted
E3 authorized, legal; *formal* accredited

unavailing *adj*
unsuccessful, failed, abortive, vain, futile, useless,
ineffective, fruitless, unproductive, unprofitable,
sterile, luckless, unlucky, unfortunate, losing, beaten,
defeated, frustrated, thwarted
E3 successful, effective

unavoidable *adj*
inevitable, inescapable, inexorable, certain, sure, fated,
destined, predestined, obligatory, required,
compulsory, necessary
formal mandatory, ineluctable
E3 avoidable

unaware *adj*
oblivious, unconscious, ignorant, uninformed,
unenlightened, in the dark, unknowing, unsuspecting,
unmindful, heedless, blind, deaf
formal insentient
E3 aware, conscious

unawares *adv*
off guard, by surprise, accidentally, inadvertently,
mistakenly, suddenly, unexpectedly, aback, abruptly,
unintentionally, unconsciously, unknowingly,
unprepared, unthinkingly, unwittingly, insidiously
colloq. on the hop

unbalanced *adj*
1 INSANE, mad, lunatic, deranged, disturbed,
demented, irrational, unsound, unstable, mentally ill
colloq. crazy, barmy, crackers, round the bend/twist,
needing your head examining
2 *an unbalanced report*
biased, prejudiced, one-sided, partisan, unfair, unjust,
unequal, uneven, asymmetrical, lopsided, unsteady,
unstable
formal inequitable
E3 **1** sane, sound **2** unbiased

unbearable *adj*
intolerable, unacceptable, insupportable, insufferable,
unendurable, excruciating
colloq. too much, too bad, the limit, the last straw, the
straw that broke the camel's back
E3 bearable, acceptable

unbeatable *adj*
invincible, unconquerable, unstoppable,
unsurpassable, matchless, supreme, best, excellent
formal indomitable

unbeaten *adj*
undefeated, unconquered, victorious, winning,
supreme, triumphant, unsubdued, unsurpassed,
unbowed
formal unvanquished
E3 defeated; *formal* vanquished

unbecoming *adj*
unseemly, improper, unsuitable, inappropriate,
unbefitting, indelicate, ungentlemanly, unladylike,
unattractive, unsightly
formal indecorous, unseemly
E3 suitable, attractive

unbelief *n*
atheism, agnosticism, scepticism, doubt, incredulity,
disbelief
E3 belief, faith

unbelievable *adj*
incredible, inconceivable, unthinkable, unimaginable,
amazing, astonishing, staggering, extraordinary,
impossible, improbable, unlikely, implausible,
unconvincing, far-fetched, preposterous, outlandish
E3 believable, credible

unbeliever *n*
disbeliever, agnostic, atheist, doubter, doubting
Thomas, sceptic, infidel
formal nullifidian
E3 believer, supporter

unbelieving *adj*
sceptical, suspicious, disbelieving, distrustful,
doubtful, doubting, dubious, unconvinced,
unpersuaded, incredulous
formal nullifidian
E3 credulous, trustful

unbend *v*
loosen up, relax, become less formal/strict, thaw,
unfreeze, unbutton, uncoil, uncurl, straighten
E3 stiffen, withdraw

unbending *adj*
rigid, inflexible, strict, tough, uncompromising,
unyielding, resolute, firm, formal, formidable,
stubborn, severe, stiff, stern, hard-line, forbidding,
aloof, distant, reserved
formal intransigent
E3 approachable, friendly, relaxed

unbiased *adj*
impartial, unprejudiced, objective, just, fair,
fair-minded, open-minded, independent, equitable,
even-handed, disinterested, dispassionate, neutral,
uninfluenced, uncoloured
E3 biased

unbidden *adj*
spontaneous, unforced, free, voluntary, unsolicited,
unprompted, uninvited, willing, unasked, unwanted,
unwelcome
E3 invited, solicited

unbind *v*
untie, unfasten, unloose, unloosen, unchain, undo,
unshackle, free, liberate, loose, loosen, release, unyoke,
unfetter
E3 bind, restrain

unblemished *adj*
untarnished, unspotted, unstained, unsullied,
unimpeachable, unflawed, pure, clear, perfect,
spotless, immaculate, irreproachable, flawless
E3 blemished, flawed, imperfect

unblinking *adj*
steady, unfaltering, unflinching, unshrinking,
unwavering, imperturbable, emotionless,
unemotional, fearless, unafraid, assured, calm,
impassive, cool, composed
E3 fearful, cowed

unblushing *adj*
shameless, brazen, blatant, bold, immodest,
unabashed, unashamed, unembarrassed, amoral,
conscience-proof
🖃 abashed, ashamed

unborn *adj*
embryonic, *in utero*, expected, awaited, coming, to-
come, future, subsequent, succeeding

unbosom *v*
unburden, confess, admit, reveal, tell, lay bare, divulge,
disclose, confide, uncover, let out, pour out, bare
colloq. tell all
🖃 hide, conceal, suppress

unbounded *adj*
boundless, limitless, unlimited, unrestricted,
unrestrained, uncontrolled, unchecked, unbridled,
infinite, endless, immeasurable, vast
🖃 limited, restrained

unbreakable *adj*
indestructible, shatterproof, toughened, resistant,
shatterproof, durable, strong, tough, rugged, solid
formal infrangible
🖃 breakable, fragile

unbridled *adj*
immoderate, excessive, rampant, riotous, wild,
uncontrolled, unrestrained, unconstrained,
ungoverned, uncurbed, unchecked, intemperate,
licentious, profligate

unbroken *adj*
1 INTACT, whole, entire, complete, solid, undivided
2 UNINTERRUPTED, continuous, endless, non-stop,
ceaseless, incessant, unceasing, constant, perpetual,
progressive, successive
formal unremitting
3 *unbroken record*
unbeaten, unsurpassed, unrivalled, unequalled,
unmatched
🖃 1 broken, damaged 2 intermittent, fitful

unburden *v*
confess, admit, reveal, tell, lay bare, divulge, offload,
disclose, confide, uncover, let out, pour out, bare
colloq. tell all
🖃 hide, conceal, suppress

uncalled-for *adj*
unwarranted, gratuitous, unprovoked, unjustified,
unasked, unsought, unsolicited, unprompted,
undeserved, unwelcome, unnecessary, needless
🖃 timely

uncanny *adj*
weird, strange, queer, odd, bizarre, mysterious,
unaccountable, incredible, remarkable, exceptional,
extraordinary, fantastic, unnatural, unearthly,
supernatural, eerie, creepy
Scot. eldritch
formal preternatural
colloq. spooky

uncaring *adj*
unconcerned, unmoved, unsympathetic,
inconsiderate, unfeeling, cold, callous, indifferent,
uninterested
🖃 caring, concerned

unceasing *adj*
ceaseless, incessant, unending, endless, never-ending,
non-stop, continuous, unbroken, constant, perpetual,
continual, persistent, relentless, unrelenting,

unremitting
🖃 intermittent, spasmodic

unceremonious *adj*
1 INFORMAL, casual, relaxed, unofficial
colloq. easy-going, laid-back
2 DIRECT, abrupt, sudden, impolite, rude,
undignified, disrespectful, discourteous

uncertain *adj*
1 UNSURE, unconvinced, doubtful, dubious,
undecided, unresolved, open, equivocating,
ambivalent, hesitant, wavering, vacillating
colloq. in two minds
2 INCONSTANT, changeable, variable, erratic,
irregular, shaky, fitful, unsteady, unreliable
3 UNPREDICTABLE, unforeseeable, undetermined,
unsettled, unresolved, unconfirmed, unknown,
unclear, speculative, indefinite, vague, insecure, risky
colloq. iffy, up in the air, touch and go, (hanging) in the
balance, in the lap of the gods
🖃 1 certain, sure 2 steady 3 predictable

uncertainty *n*
doubt, scepticism, irresolution, dilemma, ambiguity,
ambivalence, hesitation, misgiving, qualm(s),
uneasiness, confusion, vagueness, bewilderment,
perplexity, puzzlement, unreliability, unpredictability,
riskiness, insecurity
🖃 certainty

unchallengeable *adj*
absolute, conclusive, incontestable, indisputable,
incontrovertible, final, impregnable
formal irrefutable, irrefragable, inappellable
🖃 inconclusive

unchangeable *adj*
changeless, unchanging, invariable, irreversible,
permanent, final, eternal
formal immutable, intransmutable
🖃 changeable

unchanging *adj*
unvarying, changeless, same, invariable, steady,
steadfast, constant, perpetual, lasting, enduring,
abiding, eternal, permanent
🖃 changing, changeable

uncharitable *adj*
unkind, cruel, hard-hearted, callous, hard, harsh,
stern, severe, unfeeling, insensitive, unsympathetic,
uncompassionate, unfriendly, mean, ungenerous,
unforgiving
🖃 kind, sensitive, charitable, generous

uncharted *adj*
unexplored, unsurveyed, undiscovered, unplumbed,
foreign, alien, strange, unknown, unfamiliar, new,
virgin
🖃 familiar

unchaste *adj*
immoral, depraved, defiled, dissolute, dishonest,
impure, immodest, promiscuous, fallen, loose,
licentious, wanton, lewd
🖃 chaste

uncivil *adj*
rude, impolite, discourteous, disrespectful, bad-
mannered, ill-mannered, ill-bred, uncouth,
unmannerly, ungracious, churlish, brusque, abrupt,
gruff, curt, boorish, bearish, surly
🖃 civil, polite

uncivilized *adj*
primitive, barbaric, barbarian, savage, wild, rough, boorish, brutish, untamed, uncultured, unrefined, unsophisticated, unenlightened, uneducated, illiterate, uncouth, antisocial
F3 civilized, cultured

unclassifiable *adj*
doubtful, indistinct, uncertain, undefinable, indescribable, unidentifiable, vague, elusive, ill-defined, indefinable, indefinite, indeterminate
F3 conformable, definable, identifiable

unclean *adj*
dirty, soiled, filthy, grimy, grubby, foul, polluted, contaminated, tainted, impure, unhygienic, unwholesome, corrupt, adulterated, defiled, sullied, bad, evil, wicked
F3 clean, hygienic

unclear *adj*
indistinct, hazy, foggy, dim, obscure, vague, indefinite, ambiguous, equivocal, uncertain, undetermined, unsettled, unsure, doubtful, dubious
colloq. iffy
F3 clear, evident

unclothed *adj*
naked, nude, stripped, undressed, bare
formal disrobed, unclad
colloq. stark naked, in your birthday suit, in the altogether, in the buff, starkers,
F3 clothed, dressed

uncomfortable *adj*
1 CRAMPED, hard, cold, ill-fitting, irritating, painful, disagreeable
2 AWKWARD, embarrassed, self-conscious, nervous, uneasy, tense, troubled, worried, anxious, disturbed, distressed, disquieted, conscience-stricken
formal discomfited
colloq. on edge
F3 1 comfortable 2 relaxed

uncommitted *adj*
unattached, uninvolved, undecided, available, free, fancy-free, floating, non-aligned, non-partisan, neutral
F3 committed

uncommon *adj*
rare, scarce, infrequent, unusual, abnormal, atypical, unfamiliar, strange, odd, peculiar, queer, singular, curious, bizarre, extraordinary, remarkable, notable, outstanding, striking, exceptional, distinctive, special
colloq. thin on the ground, few and far between, like gold dust
F3 common, usual, normal

uncommonly *adv*
exceptionally, abnormally, peculiarly, remarkably, strangely, unusually, occasionally, singularly, rarely, seldom, infrequently, extremely, outstandingly, particularly, very
F3 commonly, frequently

uncommunicative *adj*
silent, taciturn, tight-lipped, close, secretive, unforthcoming, unresponsive, curt, brief, reticent, quiet, reserved, shy, retiring, diffident, withdrawn, aloof, unsociable
F3 communicative, forthcoming, talkative, conversational

uncomplicated *adj*
simple, easy, straightforward, direct, uninvolved, clear, undemanding
F3 complicated, complex, involved

uncompromising *adj*
unyielding, unbending, inflexible, unaccommodating, rigid, firm, stiff, strict, tough, hard-line, immovable, inexorable, stubborn, obstinate, die-hard
formal obdurate, intransigent
F3 flexible, yielding

unconcealable *adj*
insuppressible, irrepressible, uncontrollable, indistinguishable, obvious, plain, clear, insistent
formal manifest

unconcealed *adj*
open, obvious, patent, evident, conspicuous, overt, undistinguished, admitted, visible, blatant, frank, apparent, noticeable, unashamed, ill-concealed, self-confessed
formal manifest
F3 hidden, secret

unconcern *n*
aloofness, detachment, remoteness, apathy, nonchalance, indifference, uninterestedness, negligence, callousness
formal insouciance, pococurantism
F3 concern

unconcerned *adj*
indifferent, apathetic, uninterested, nonchalant, carefree, relaxed, casual, complacent, cool, composed, untroubled, unworried, unruffled, unmoved, uncaring, unsympathetic, callous, aloof, remote, distant, detached, dispassionate, uninvolved, oblivious
formal unperturbed, insouciant, pococurante
F3 concerned, worried, interested

unconditional *adj*
unqualified, unreserved, unrestricted, unlimited, absolute, utter, full, plenary, total, complete, entire, whole-hearted, thoroughgoing, downright, outright, out-and-out, positive, define, conclusive, categorical, unequivocal
F3 conditional, qualified, limited

unconfirmed *adj*
unproven, unproved, unratified, unverified, unauthenticated, unsubstantiated
formal uncorroborated
F3 confirmed

unconformity *n*
discontinuity, irregularity, unconformability
formal disconformity
F3 conformability

uncongenial *adj*
unfriendly, uninviting, unappealing, unattractive, unpleasant, displeasing, disagreeable, antagonistic, unsympathetic, incompatible, unsuited, unsavoury, discordant, distasteful
formal antipathetic
F3 congenial

unconnected *adj*
1 IRRELEVANT, unrelated, beside/off the point, inappropriate, unattached, detached, separate, independent .
colloq. neither here nor there
2 DISCONNECTED, incoherent, irrational, illogical,

confused, unco-ordinated, disjointed
F3 1 connected, relevant

unconquerable *adj*
irrepressible, enduring, ingrained, inveterate,
undefeatable, unbeatable, invincible, unyielding,
insuperable, insurmountable, irresistible,
overpowering
formal indomitable
F3 weak, yielding

unconscionable *adj*
unprincipled, amoral, outrageous, unethical,
unjustifiable, unscrupulous, unreasonable,
unwarrantable, unpardonable, preposterous, criminal,
exorbitant, extreme, extravagant, excessive,
immoderate, inordinate

unconscious *adj*
1 STUNNED, knocked out, dazed, out, fainted,
collapsed, drugged, in a coma, concussed, blacked
out, senseless, asleep
technical comatose
formal insensible
colloq. out cold, out for the count, zonked,
dead to the world
2 UNAWARE, oblivious, blind, deaf, heedless,
unmindful, ignorant
formal insensible, incognizant
3 *an unconscious reaction*
involuntary, automatic, reflex, instinctive, impulsive,
innate, subconscious, subliminal, repressed,
suppressed, latent, unthinking, unwitting, inadvertent,
accidental, unintentional
F3 1 conscious 2 aware 3 intentional

unconstraint *n*
unreserve, unrestraint, openness, freedom, liberality,
relaxation, abandon, laissez-faire

uncontrollable *adj*
ungovernable, unmanageable, unruly, out of control,
disorderly, wild, mad, furious, violent, strong,
irrepressible
formal intractable
F3 controllable, manageable

uncontrolled *adj*
unrestrained, unbridled, unchecked, rampant, violent,
wild, boisterous, riotous, unruly, uncurbed,
undisciplined, unhindered
F3 controlled, restrained

unconventional *adj*
unorthodox, alternative, different, offbeat, eccentric,
bohemian, idiosyncratic, individual, original, odd,
unusual, uncommon, rare, uncustomary, irregular,
abnormal, bizarre
colloq. fringe, out of the ordinary, freaky, wacky,
oddball, zany; *slang* way-out, far-out
F3 conventional, orthodox

unconvincing *adj*
implausible, unlikely, improbable, questionable,
doubtful, dubious, suspect, weak, feeble, flimsy, lame
colloq. fishy
F3 convincing, plausible

unco-ordinated *adj*
clumsy, awkward, ungainly, ungraceful, bungling,
bumbling, clodhopping, inept, disjointed
formal maladroit
F3 graceful

uncouth *adj*
coarse, crude, vulgar, rude, bad-mannered, ill-
mannered, impolite, improper, clumsy, awkward,
boorish, loutish, gauche, graceless, unrefined,
uncultivated, unsophisticated, uncultured,
uncivilized, rough
formal unseemly
F3 polite, refined, urbane

uncover *v*
unveil, unmask, unwrap, strip, bare, lay bare, open,
peel, expose, reveal, bring to light, show, disclose,
divulge, make known, leak, unearth, dig up, exhume,
discover, detect
F3 cover, conceal, suppress

uncritical *adj*
undiscerning, undiscriminating, unselective,
unquestioning, credulous, accepting, trusting,
gullible, naïve, non-judgemental, unfussy, superficial
F3 discerning, discriminating, sceptical

unctuous *adj*
1 INSINCERE, fawning, ingratiating, smooth, suave,
sycophantic, gushing, slick, plausible, glib,
sanctimonious, obsequious, servile, pietistic
colloq. smarmy
2 GREASY, oily, creamy

uncultivated *adj*
fallow, wild, rough, natural
F3 cultivated

uncultured *adj*
unsophisticated, unrefined, uncultivated, uncivilized,
unintellectual, rough, uncouth, boorish, rustic, hick,
coarse, crude, ill-bred
F3 cultured, sophisticated

undaunted *adj*
undeterred, undiscouraged, undismayed, unbowed,
unflagging, resolute, steadfast, brave, courageous,
fearless, bold, brave, unalarmed, intrepid, dauntless,
indomitable
F3 discouraged, timorous

undecided *adj*
uncertain, unsure, unknown, ambivalent, doubtful,
hesitant, dithering, equivocating, wavering, irresolute,
uncommitted, unestablished, indefinite, vague,
dubious, debatable, moot, unresolved, unsettled, open
colloq. in two minds, the jury is still out on, up in the air
F3 decided, certain, definite

undecorated *adj*
plain, simple, severe, stark, austere, unadorned,
unornamented, unembellished, functional, classical
formal inornate
F3 decorated, ornate

undefeated *adj*
unbeaten, unconquered, victorious, winning,
supreme, triumphant, unsubdued, unsurpassed,
unbowed
formal unvanquished
F3 defeated; *formal* vanquished

undefended *adj*
defenceless, exposed, vulnerable, unprotected,
unguarded, open, unarmed, naked, pregnable
formal unfortified
F3 armed, defended; *formal* fortified

undefiled *adj*
pure, spotless, unblemished, unsoiled, unspotted,
immaculate, flawless, sinless, chaste, clean, clear,

unstained, unsullied, intact, virginal
formal inviolate

undefined *adj*
vague, hazy, ill-defined, indefinite, unclear, unexplained, unspecified, indistinct, inexact, imprecise, woolly, nebulous, formless, shadowy, tenuous
formal indeterminate
F3 definite, precise

undemonstrative *adj*
aloof, distant, remote, withdrawn, reserved, reticent, uncommunicative, unresponsive, stiff, formal, cool, cold, unemotional, restrained, impassive, phlegmatic
F3 demonstrative, communicative

undeniable *adj*
indisputable, incontrovertible, unquestionable, sure, certain, undoubted, indubitable, beyond doubt, beyond question, definite, positive, proven, clear, obvious, patent, evident, unmistakable
formal irrefutable, manifest
F3 questionable

undependable *adj*
unreliable, inconsistent, changeable, erratic, uncertain, fickle, capricious, irresponsible, inconstant, unpredictable, unstable, untrustworthy, variable, mercurial, treacherous, fair-weather
F3 dependable, reliable

under *prep, adv*
▶ *prep* **1** BELOW, underneath, beneath, lower than, less than
2 INFERIOR TO, secondary to, junior to, subordinate to, subservient to
F3 **1** over, above
▶ *adv* below, underneath, beneath, down, downward, less, lower

underclothes *n*
underwear, underclothing, undergarments, underlinen, frillies, lingerie
colloq. smalls, undies, unmentionables

undercover *adj*
secret, private, confidential, sly, intelligence, underground, surreptitious, stealthy, furtive, covert, hidden, concealed
formal clandestine
colloq. hush-hush
F3 open, unconcealed

undercurrent *n*
1 *an undercurrent in the sea*
undertow, underflow
2 FEELING, undertone, overtone, hint, suggestion, tinge, flavour, aura, atmosphere, sense, movement, tendency, trend, drift, undertow

undercut *v*
1 UNDERPRICE, undersell, undercharge, underbid, undermine
2 EXCAVATE, hollow out, mine, gouge out, scoop out

underestimate *v*
underrate, undervalue, misjudge, miscalculate, fail to appreciate, minimize, belittle, dismiss, look down on, sell short, trivialize
formal disparage
colloq. play down
F3 overestimate, exaggerate

undergo *v*
experience, suffer, sustain, submit to, go through,

put up with, tolerate, bear, stand, endure, weather, withstand

underground *adj, n, adv*
▶ *adj* **1** *an underground passage*
subterranean, buried, sunken, covered, hidden, concealed
2 SECRET, covert, furtive, surreptitious, undercover, revolutionary, subversive, radical, experimental, avant-garde, alternative, unorthodox, unofficial, illegal
formal clandestine
▶ *n* subway, metro
colloq. tube
▶ *adv* below the surface, below ground level, below ground

undergrowth *n*
brush, brushwood, scrub, vegetation, ground cover, bracken, thicket, bushes, brambles, briars

underhand *adj*
unscrupulous, unethical, immoral, improper, sly, crafty, sneaky, stealthy, secret, surreptitious, furtive, devious, dishonest, deceitful, deceptive, fraudulent, scheming
formal clandestine
colloq. crooked, shady
F3 honest, open; *colloq.* above board

underline *v*
mark, underscore, stress, emphasize, draw attention to, accentuate, italicize, highlight, point up
F3 play down, soft-pedal

underling *n*
minion, subordinate, inferior, lackey, menial, nonentity, flunkey, hireling, servant, slave, nobody
F3 boss, leader, master

underlying *adj*
basic, fundamental, essential, primary, elementary, root, intrinsic, latent, hidden, concealed, lurking, veiled
formal basal

undermine *v*
1 WEAKEN, make less secure, destroy, erode, wear away, sap, damage, sabotage, subvert, injure, mar, impair
formal vitiate
2 MINE, tunnel, dig, excavate
F3 **1** strengthen, fortify

underprivileged *adj*
disadvantaged, deprived, poor, needy, in need, in distress, in want, impoverished, destitute, oppressed
formal impecunious
F3 privileged, fortunate, affluent

underrate *v*
underestimate, undervalue, fail to appreciate, belittle, depreciate, dismiss, look down on, sell short
formal disparage
F3 overrate, exaggerate

undersell *v*
undercharge, undercut, cut, mark down, reduce, slash, sell short, depreciate, play down, understate
formal disparage

undersized *adj*
little, small, tiny, minute, miniature, pygmy, dwarf, stunted, underdeveloped, underweight, puny, runtish, atrophied
technical achondroplastic

colloq. pint-(sized)
F3 oversized, big, overweight

understand *v*
1 *I don't understand*
grasp, take in, follow, fathom, penetrate, make out, figure out, discern, perceive, see, realize, recognize, appreciate, accept
formal comprehend, apprehend
colloq. get, cotton on, click, twig, tumble to, latch onto, get the hang of, rumble, suss out, get the message, get the picture, get wise, get your head/mind round;
slang savvy
2 SYMPATHIZE, empathize, commiserate, comfort, feel sorry for, feel for, identify with, support
3 BELIEVE, think, know, hear, learn, gather, assume, presume, suppose, conclude
F3 1 misunderstand

understanding *n, adj*
▶ *n* **1** GRASP, knowledge, wisdom, intelligence, intellect, sense, judgement, discernment, insight, appreciation, awareness, impression, feeling, perception, view, belief, idea, notion, opinion, interpretation
formal comprehension, apprehension
2 AGREEMENT, arrangement, pact, bargain, harmony
formal accord, compact, entente
3 SYMPATHY, empathy, compassion, comfort, support, consolation, commiseration, trust
▶ *adj* sympathetic, compassionate, kind, considerate, supportive, sensitive, thoughtful, tender, loving, patient, lenient, tolerant, forbearing, forgiving
F3 unsympathetic, insensitive, impatient, intolerant

understate *v*
underplay, play down, minimize, make light of, belittle, dismiss
colloq. soft-pedal
F3 exaggerate, emphasize

understatement *n*
minimization, restraint, underplaying, dismissal
technical litotes, meiosis
F3 overstatement, exaggeration

understood *adj*
accepted, assumed, presumed, implied, implicit, inferred, tacit, unstated, unspoken, unwritten

understudy *n*
stand-in, double, substitute, replacement, reserve, deputy, relief, locum
colloq. fill in

undertake *v*
1 PLEDGE, promise, guarantee, agree, contract, covenant
2 BEGIN, embark on, tackle, set about, try, attempt, endeavour, take on, accept, assume
formal commence

undertaker *n*
funeral director, funeral furnisher
US mortician

undertaking *n*
1 ENTERPRISE, venture, business, affair, task, project, operation, attempt, endeavour, effort, job, plan, campaign, scheme
2 PLEDGE, commitment, promise, vow, word, assurance, guarantee, warrant

undertone *n*
hint, suggestion, whisper, murmur, intimation, trace, tinge, touch, flavour, feeling, aura, atmosphere, undercurrent

undervalue *v*
underrate, underestimate, misjudge, minimize, depreciate, dismiss, look down on, sell short
formal disparage
F3 overrate, exaggerate

underwater *adj*
subaquatic, undersea, submarine, immersed, submerged, sunken
formal subaqueous

underwear *n*
underclothes, undergarments, lingerie, frillies
colloq. undies, smalls, unmentionables

underweight *adj*
thin, undersized, underfed, undernourished, half-starved
F3 overweight

underworld *n*
1 CRIMINAL WORLD, organized crime, gangland
slang the mob
2 NETHER WORLD, infernal regions, Hades, hell, the Inferno
Related adjectives: chthonian, chthonic

underwrite *v*
endorse, authorize, sanction, approve, confirm, back, guarantee, insure, sponsor, support, fund, finance, subsidize, subscribe, sign, initial, countersign

undesirable *adj*
unwanted, unwelcome, unacceptable, unwished-for, disliked, unsuitable, unpleasant, disagreeable, distasteful, offensive, objectionable, foul, nasty, obnoxious
formal repugnant
F3 desirable, pleasant

undeveloped *adj*
1 *undeveloped countries*
developing, underdeveloped, less advanced, Third World
2 UNFORMED, embryonic, potential, latent, immature, stunted, dwarfed
formal inchoate, primordial
F3 1 advanced, industrialized **2** developed, mature

undignified *adj*
inelegant, ungainly, clumsy, foolish, improper, unsuitable, inappropriate, unbecoming
formal unseemly, indecorous
F3 dignified, elegant

undisciplined *adj*
wild, unrestrained, unruly, uncontrolled, wayward, disobedient, obstreperous, wilful, unpredictable, unreliable, unschooled, unsteady, untrained, disorganized, unsystematic
F3 disciplined, self-controlled

undisguised *adj*
unconcealed, open, overt, explicit, frank, genuine, apparent, patent, obvious, evident, transparent, blatant, naked, unadorned, stark, utter, outright, thoroughgoing
formal manifest
F3 secret, concealed, hidden

undisguisedly *adj*
overtly, outright, openly, obviously, transparently, patently, unreservedly, frankly, blatantly
🖅 secretly

undisputed *adj*
uncontested, unchallenged, unquestioned, undoubted, indisputable, incontrovertible, undeniable, accepted, acknowledged, recognized, sure, certain, conclusive
formal irrefutable
🖅 debatable, uncertain

undistinguished *adj*
unexceptional, unremarkable, unimpressive, ordinary, everyday, common, pedestrian, banal, indifferent, mediocre, inferior
colloq. run-of-the-mill, so-so, not up to much, not all that it is cracked up to be, nothing much to write about, no great shakes, not much cop
🖅 distinguished, exceptional, remarkable

undisturbed *adj*
untouched, calm, composed, equable, collected, even, quiet, placid, serene, tranquil, untroubled, motionless, unconcerned, unaffected, uninterrupted, unruffled
formal unperturbed
🖅 disturbed, interrupted

undivided *adj*
solid, unbroken, intact, whole, total, entire, full, complete, combined, united, unanimous, unqualified, unreserved, concentrated, exclusive, wholehearted, serious, dedicated, sincere

undo *v*
1 UNFASTEN, untie, unbuckle, unbutton, unhook, unzip, unlock, unwrap, unwind, open, free, release, loose, loosen, separate, disentangle
2 ANNUL, invalidate, cancel, offset, neutralize, reverse, overturn, repeal, revoke, set aside, upset, quash, defeat, undermine, subvert, mar, spoil, ruin, wreck, crush, shatter, destroy, obliterate
formal nullify
🖅 1 fasten, do up

undoing *n*
downfall, ruin, ruination, collapse, destruction, defeat, overthrow, reversal, weakness, shame, disgrace

undomesticated *adj*
wild, untamed, uncivilized, natural, savage
formal feral
🖅 domesticated, tame

undone *adj*
1 UNACCOMPLISHED, unfulfilled, unfinished, uncompleted, incomplete, outstanding, left, omitted, neglected, ignored, forgotten, passed over
2 UNFASTENED, untied, unlaced, unbuttoned, unlocked, open, loose
3 RUINED, lost, destroyed, betrayed
🖅 1 done, accomplished, complete 2 fastened

undoubted *adj*
unchallenged, undisputed, acknowledged, uncontested, unquestionable, indisputable, incontrovertible, undesirable, sure, certain, definite, obvious, patent
formal indubitable, irrefutable

undoubtedly *adv*
certainly, definitely, doubtless, without doubt, no doubt, beyond doubt, surely, of course, undeniably,

unquestionably, unmistakably, assuredly
formal indubitably

undreamed-of *adj*
undreamt, inconceivable, unheard-of, unhoped-for, unimagined, unexpected, incredible, unforeseen, unsuspected, amazing, astonishing, miraculous

undress *v, n*
▶ *v* strip, disrobe, take off, remove, shed, unclothe
formal divest
colloq. peel off
▶ *n* nakedness, nudity, dishabille, déshabillé
formal disarray

undressed *adj*
unclothed, disrobed, stripped, naked, stark naked, nude
🖅 clothed

undue *adj*
unnecessary, needless, uncalled-for, unwarranted, undeserved, unjustified, unreasonable, disproportionate, excessive, immoderate, inordinate, extreme, superfluous, extravagant, improper, inappropriate
🖅 reasonable, moderate, proper

undulate *v*
rise and fall, swell, roll, surge, wave, ripple, billow, heave

undulating *adj*
rolling, wavy, rippling, billowing, sinuous
formal flexuose, flexuous, undate, undulant
🖅 flat

unduly *adv*
too, over, excessively, immoderately, inordinately, disproportionately, out of all proportions, unreasonably, unjustifiably, unnecessarily
🖅 moderately, reasonably

undutiful *adj*
negligent, neglectful, careless, disloyal, remiss, slack, defaulting, delinquent
formal unfilial
🖅 dutiful

undying *adj*
eternal, deathless, lasting, perpetual, everlasting, immortal, infinite, continuing, constant, perennial, permanent, unending, unfading, indestructible, inextinguishable, imperishable, undiminished
formal abiding, sempiternal
🖅 impermanent, inconstant

unearth *v*
dig up, exhume, disinter, excavate, uncover, expose, reveal, bring to light, find, discover, detect
🖅 bury

unearthly *adj*
1 SUPERNATURAL, ghostly, phantom, eerie, uncanny, weird, strange, spine-chilling, other-worldly
Scot. eldritch
formal preternatural
colloq. creepy
2 *at this unearthly hour*
unreasonable, preposterous, appalling, outrageous, ungodly
colloq. horrendous
🖅 2 reasonable

uneasiness *n*
anxiety, alarm, apprehension, apprehensiveness,

worry, doubt, qualms, unease, misgiving, nervousness, suspicion, disquiet, dis-ease, agitation
formal inquietude, perturbation
E3 calm, composure

uneasy *adj*
1 UNCOMFORTABLE, anxious, worried, alarmed, apprehensive, tense, strained, nervous, agitated, shaky, edgy, upset, troubled, disturbed, unsettled, restless, impatient, unsure, insecure
formal perturbed
colloq. on edge, nervy, twitchy, keyed up, wound up, jittery
2 WORRYING, troubling, disturbing, unsettling, unnerving, disconcerting
formal perturbing
E3 1 calm, composed

uneconomic *adj*
unprofitable, uncommercial, loss-making, non-profit-making
E3 economic, profitable, profit-making, remuneration

uneducated *adj*
unschooled, untaught, unread, ignorant, illiterate, uncultivated, uncultured, philistine, benighted
E3 educated

unemotional *adj*
cool, cold, unfeeling, impassive, reserved, indifferent, apathetic, passionless, unresponsive, undemonstrative, unexcitable, phlegmatic, detached, objective, dispassionate
E3 emotional, excitable

unemphatic *adj*
understated, unobtrusive, underplayed, played-down, unostentatious
colloq. down-beat, soft-pedalled

unemployed *adj*
jobless, out of work, laid off, redundant, unwaged, idle, unoccupied
colloq. on the dole
E3 employed, occupied

unending *adj*
endless, never-ending, unceasing, ceaseless, incessant, interminable, continuous, uninterrupted, constant, continual, perpetual, everlasting, eternal, undying
formal unremitting
E3 transient, intermittent

unendurable *adj*
intolerable, unbearable, overwhelming, shattering, insufferable, insupportable
E3 bearable, endurable

unenthusiastic *adj*
uninterested, unimpressed, cool, half-hearted, apathetic, bored, neutral, nonchalant, indifferent, unmoved, unresponsive, blasé, lukewarm, Laodicean
E3 enthusiastic

unenviable *adj*
undesirable, unpleasant, disagreeable, uncongenial, uncomfortable, thankless, difficult, dangerous
E3 enviable, desirable

unequal *adj*
1 DIFFERENT, varying, dissimilar, unlike, unfair, unjust, biased, inequitable, discriminatory
2 UNMATCHED, uneven, unbalanced, lopsided, disproportionate, asymmetrical, irregular
3 *unequal to a task*

incapable, unqualified, inadequate, unsuited, unfitted, incompetent
colloq. not up to, not cut out for
E3 1, 2, 3 equal

unequalled *adj*
unmatched, unsurpassed, unrivalled, peerless, unique, paramount, matchless, incomparable, unparalleled, pre-eminent, surpassing, transcendent, supreme, exceptional, inimitable
formal nonpareil

unequivocal *adj*
unambiguous, explicit, clear, plain, evident, distinct, unmistakable, express, direct, straight, straightforward, definite, positive, categorical, incontrovertible, absolute, outright, unqualified, unreserved
E3 ambiguous, vague, qualified

unerring *adj*
unfailing, perfect, impeccable, infallible, faultless, exact, certain, sure, accurate, uncanny
colloq. dead
E3 fallible

unerringly *adv*
unfailingly, infallibly, accurately
colloq. bang, dead

unethical *adj*
unprofessional, immoral, improper, wrong, wicked, evil, unscrupulous, unprincipled, dishonourable, disreputable, illegal, illicit, dishonest, underhand
colloq. shady
E3 ethical

uneven *adj*
1 *uneven ground*
rough, bumpy, lumpy, stony, rugged, craggy, jagged, irregular, coarse
2 ODD, unequal, inequitable, unfair, unbalanced, one-sided, ill-matched, asymmetrical, lopsided, crooked
3 IRREGULAR, intermittent, spasmodic, fitful, jerky, unsteady, variable, changeable, fluctuating, erratic, inconsistent, patchy
E3 1 even, flat, level 2 even, equal 3 regular, consistent

uneventful *adj*
uninteresting, unexciting, quiet, unvaried, boring, monotonous, tedious, dull, routine, humdrum, ordinary, everyday, commonplace, unremarkable, unexceptional, unmemorable
colloq. run-of-the-mill
E3 eventful, memorable, remarkable

unexampled *adj*
unprecedented, never before seen, incomparable, unequalled, unparalleled, unheard-of, unmatched, unique, novel

unexceptional *adj*
unremarkable, unmemorable, typical, average, normal, usual, ordinary, common, everyday, indifferent, mediocre, unimpressive, undistinguished
colloq. run-of-the-mill, so-so, not up to much, not all that it is cracked up to be, nothing much to write about, no great shakes, not much cop
E3 exceptional, impressive

unexcitable *adj*
self-possessed, cool, composed, relaxed, serene, calm, contained, dispassionate, impassive, passionless,

unimpassioned, phlegmatic
formal imperturbable
colloq. easy-going, laid-back
⊟ excitable

unexpected *adj*
unforeseen, unanticipated, unpredictable, unlooked-
for, chance, accidental, fortuitous, sudden, abrupt,
surprising, startling, amazing, astonishing, unusual
⊟ expected, predictable

unexpectedly *adv*
suddenly, surprisingly, unpredictably, without
warning, abruptly, by chance, fortuitously
colloq. out of the blue

unexpressive *adj*
expressionless, emotionless, impassive, inexpressive,
inscrutable, vacant, blank, dead-pan, immobile
⊟ expressive, mobile

unfading *adj*
lasting, imperishable, durable, enduring, undying,
unfailing, fadeless, fast, evergreen
formal abiding, immarcescible
⊟ changeable, transient

unfailing *adj*
constant, certain, dependable, reliable, sure, steady,
true, steadfast, faithful, loyal, staunch, undying,
unfading, inexhaustible, infallible
⊟ fickle, impermanent, transient

unfair *adj*
1 UNJUST, partial, biased, prejudiced, bigoted,
discriminatory, unbalanced, weighted, one-sided,
slanted, partisan, arbitrary, undeserved, unmerited,
unwarranted, unreasonable, uncalled-for
formal inequitable
2 UNETHICAL, unscrupulous, unprincipled,
wrongful, deceitful, dishonest
colloq. crooked, shady, bent, below the belt
⊟ 1 fair, just, unbiased, deserved 2 honest, ethical

unfairness *n*
injustice, inequity, one-sidedness, partiality,
partisanship, prejudice, bigotry, bias, discrimination
⊟ fairness, equity

unfaithful *adj*
disloyal, treacherous, false, untrue, insincere, deceitful,
dishonest, untrustworthy, unreliable, fickle,
inconstant, adulterous, cheating, double-dealing,
faithless, unbelieving, godless
formal duplicitous, perfidious
colloq. two-timing
⊟ faithful, loyal, reliable

unfaltering *adj*
unfailing, unwavering, unyielding, unswerving,
untiring, tireless, unflagging, unflinching, constant,
firm, indefatigable, steady, steadfast, resolute, fixed
formal pertinacious
⊟ faltering, uncertain, wavering

unfamiliar *adj*
1 STRANGE, unusual, uncommon, curious, alien,
foreign, uncharted, unexplored, unknown, different,
new, novel
2 UNACCUSTOMED, unacquainted, uninformed,
inexperienced, unpractised, unskilled, unversed,
unconversant
⊟ 1 familiar, customary 2 conversant

unfashionable *adj*
outmoded, dated, out of date, out, *passé*, old-

fashioned, *démodé*, antiquated, obsolete, unpopular
colloq. old hat, square
⊟ fashionable

unfasten *v*
undo, untie, loosen, unwrap, unclasp, unlock, open,
uncouple, disconnect, separate, detach
⊟ fasten, do up, bolt, lock

unfathomable *adj*
inexplicable, incomprehensible, impenetrable,
baffling, fathomless, immeasurable, unknowable,
mysterious, deep, profound, hidden, bottomless,
unplumbed, unsounded, inscrutable, indecipherable
formal abstruse, esoteric
⊟ comprehensible, explicable, penetrable

unfavourable *adj*
1 UNPROMISING, ominous, threatening,
discouraging, inopportune, untimely, unseasonable,
ill-suited, unfortunate, unlucky, disadvantageous, bad,
poor, adverse, contrary, negative
formal inauspicious
2 HOSTILE, critical, adverse, negative, bad, poor,
unfriendly, uncomplimentary
formal inimical
⊟ 1 favourable, promising; *formal* auspicious
2 friendly, complimentary, good

unfeeling *adj*
insensitive, cold, hard, stony, callous, heartless, hard-
hearted, harsh, cruel, inhuman, pitiless, uncaring,
unsympathetic, apathetic
⊟ sensitive, sympathetic

unfeigned *adj*
genuine, natural, pure, real, sincere, unaffected, frank,
spontaneous, wholehearted, unforced, heartfelt
⊟ insincere, pretended, feigned

unfettered *adj*
unconstrained, free, unhampered, unrestrained,
unhindered, unconfined, unchecked, unbridled,
uninhibited, unshackled, untrammelled
⊟ constrained, fettered

unfinished *adj*
incomplete, uncompleted, half-done, sketchy, rough,
crude, imperfect, lacking, wanting, deficient, undone,
unaccomplished, unfulfilled
⊟ finished, perfect

unfit *adj*
1 UNSUITABLE, inappropriate, unsuited, inapt,
ill-equipped, unqualified, ineligible, untrained,
unprepared, unequal, incapable, unable, incompetent,
inadequate, ineffective, useless
2 UNHEALTHY, out of condition, flabby, feeble,
weak, decrepit
formal debilitated
⊟ 1 fit, suitable, competent 2 healthy, fit

unflagging *adj*
unfaltering, unfailing, untiring, tireless, unswerving,
unceasing, undeviating, persevering, persistent, never-
failing, indefatigable, constant, steady, fixed, single-
minded, staunch
formal unremitting
⊟ faltering, inconstant

unflappable *adj*
calm, collected, composed, level-headed, unworried,
unexcitable, unruffled, equable, cool, impassive, self-
possessed, phlegmatic
formal imperturbable

excitable, nervous, temperamental;
colloq. panicky

unflattering *adj*
unbecoming, uncomplimentary, unfavourable,
unprepossessing, critical, honest, blunt, candid,
outspoken
E3 complimentary, flattering

unflinching *adj*
steady, unfaltering, unwavering, unshaken,
unshrinking, unswerving, firm, fixed, determined,
constant, staunch, steadfast, sure, bold, resolute,
stalwart, unblinking
E3 unsteady, scared

unfold *v*
1 DEVELOP, evolve, grow, work out, come about,
result, emerge
2 REVEAL, disclose, show, present, tell, relate, make
known, describe, explain, clarify, elaborate, narrate
3 *unfold a map*
open (out), spread (out), flatten, straighten (out),
stretch out, undo, unfurl, unroll, uncoil, unravel,
unwrap, uncover
E3 2 withhold, suppress **3** fold, wrap

unforeseen *adj*
unpredicted, unpredictable, unexpected,
unanticipated, unlooked-for, surprising, amazing,
astonishing, startling, sudden, unavoidable, unusual
E3 expected, predictable

unforgettable *adj*
memorable, momentous, historic, noteworthy,
notable, impressive, remarkable, significant,
exceptional, extraordinary, striking, important,
special, distinctive
E3 unmemorable, unexceptional

unforgivable *adj*
unpardonable, inexcusable, unjustifiable, indefensible,
intolerable, shameful, outrageous, disgraceful,
deplorable, contemptible
formal reprehensible
E3 forgivable, venial

unforgiven *adj*
unredeemed, unabsolved, unregenerate, unrepentant
E3 absolved, forgiven

unfortunate *adj*
1 UNLUCKY, luckless, unsuccessful, poor, wretched,
unhappy, doomed, ill-fated, hopeless, calamitous,
disastrous, ruinous, adverse, unpleasant,
disadvantageous, untoward
formal hapless
2 REGRETTABLE, lamentable, deplorable, adverse,
unfavourable, unsuitable, inappropriate, inopportune,
untimely, ill-timed, ill-advised
formal injudicious
E3 1 fortunate, happy **2** favourable, appropriate

unfortunately *adv*
regrettably, unhappily, unluckily, sadly, alas, sad to say,
sad to relate
colloq. worse luck
E3 fortunately

unfounded *adj*
baseless, groundless, unsupported, unsubstantiated,
unproven, unjustified, idle, false, spurious, trumped-
up, fabricated, without foundation
formal uncorroborated, conjectural
E3 substantiated, justified

unfrequented *adj*
lonely, remote, secluded, uninhabited, unvisited,
isolated, deserted, desolate, solitary, lone, God-
forsaken
formal sequestered
E3 busy, crowded, populous

unfriendly *adj*
unsociable, standoffish, aloof, distant,
unapproachable, inhospitable, uncongenial,
unneighbourly, unwelcoming, unkind, cold, chilly,
cool, frosty, hostile, strained, aggressive, quarrelsome,
antagonistic, ill-disposed, unpleasant, disagreeable,
surly, sour
formal inimical, inauspicious
E3 friendly, amiable, agreeable

unfrock *v*
dismiss, depose, degrade, demote, suspend
E3 restore, reinstate

unfruitful *adj*
unproductive, fruitless, barren, exhausted,
impoverished, infertile, sterile, arid, unprofitable,
unprolific, unrewarding
formal infecund, infructuous
E3 fruitful, productive

ungainly *adj*
clumsy, awkward, gauche, inelegant, ungraceful,
gawky, unco-ordinated, lumbering, gangling,
unwieldy, uncouth, loutish
formal maladroit
E3 graceful, elegant

ungodly *adj*
1 UNREASONABLE, outrageous, preposterous,
intolerable, unearthly, unsocial
colloq. horrendous
2 IMPIOUS, irreligious, godless, blasphemous,
profane, immoral, corrupt, depraved, sinful, wicked
formal iniquitous

ungovernable *adj*
uncontrollable, wild, disorderly, unmanageable,
unrestrainable, unruly, ungoverned, rebellious,
masterless
formal refractory

ungracious *adj*
discourteous, uncivil, impolite, rude, disrespectful,
graceless, bad-mannered, ill-bred, unmannerly,
offhand, boorish, churlish
E3 gracious, polite

ungrateful *adj*
unthankful, unappreciative, rude, impolite, uncivil,
ill-mannered, ungracious, selfish, thankless, heedless
E3 grateful, thankful

unguarded *adj*
1 *in an unguarded moment*
unwary, careless, inattentive, off guard, incautious,
indiscreet, undiplomatic, thoughtless, unthinking,
heedless, foolish, foolhardy, rash, ill-considered
formal imprudent, impolitic, uncircumspect
2 UNDEFENDED, unprotected, exposed, vulnerable,
defenceless, unpatrolled
E3 1 guarded, cautious **2** defended, protected

unhappily *adv*
unfortunately, regrettably, unluckily, sadly, alas, sad to
say, sad to relate
colloq. worse luck
E3 fortunately

unhappy *adj*
1 SAD, sorrowful, miserable, melancholy, depressed, dispirited, glum, despondent, dejected, downcast, crestfallen, long-faced, gloomy, mournful
formal woebegone, disconsolate
colloq. down, blue, fed up, low, down in the dumps
2 UNFORTUNATE, unlucky, ill-fated, ill-starred, unsuitable, inappropriate, inapt, ill-chosen, ill-advised, tactless, awkward, clumsy
formal hapless, injudicious
E3 1 happy **2** fortunate, suitable

unharmed *adj*
undamaged, unhurt, uninjured, unscathed, untouched, whole, intact, safe, sound
E3 harmed, injured, hurt

unhealthy *adj*
1 UNWELL, sick, ill, poorly, ailing, sickly, infirm, invalid, weak, feeble, frail, unsound
formal indisposed, debilitated
2 UNWHOLESOME, insanitary, unhygienic, harmful, injurious, insalutary, detrimental, noxious, morbid, unnatural
formal insalubrious
E3 1 healthy, fit **2** wholesome, hygienic, natural

unheard-of *adj*
1 UNTHINKABLE, inconceivable, unbelievable, unimaginable, undreamed-of, unprecedented, extraordinary, exceptional, unacceptable, offensive, shocking, outrageous, preposterous
2 UNKNOWN, unfamiliar, new, unusual, obscure, unsung, unheralded, undiscovered
E3 1 normal, acceptable **2** famous

unheeded *adj*
ignored, disregarded, disobeyed, unnoticed, unnoted, unobserved, unremarked, overlooked, neglected, forgotten
E3 noted, observed

unheralded *adj*
unsung, unrecognized, unproclaimed, unpublicized, unnoticed, surprise, unadvertised, unannounced, unexpected, unforeseen
E3 advertised, publicized, trumpeted, acclaimed

unhesitating *adj*
immediate, instant, instantaneous, prompt, ready, automatic, spontaneous, unquestioning, unwavering, unfaltering, wholehearted, confident, implicit
E3 hesitant, tentative

unhinge *v*
unbalance, unnerve, unsettle, upset, confuse, distract, disorder, drive mad, madden, craze, derange

unholy *adj*
1 IMPIOUS, irreligious, godless, ungodly, blasphemous, sinful, immoral, corrupt, depraved, wicked, evil
formal iniquitous
2 *an unholy mess*
unreasonable, shocking, outrageous, ungodly, unearthly
colloq. horrendous
E3 1 holy, pious, godly **2** reasonable

unhoped-for *adj*
unexpected, unforeseen, unanticipated, unimaginable, unlooked-for, unbelievable, undreamed-of, incredible, surprising

unhurried *adj*
slow, leisurely, deliberate, easy, relaxed, calm, sedate
colloq. easy-going, laid-back
E3 hurried, hasty, rushed

unhurt *adj*
unharmed, uninjured, unscathed, untouched, whole, intact, safe, sound
E3 hurt, injured

unhygienic *adj*
insanitary, unclean, impure, unhealthy, unsanitized, dirty, dirtied, contaminated, polluted, infected, disease-ridden, filthy, foul, infested
formal unhealthful, noisome, noxious, insalubrious, feculent
E3 hygienic, sanitary, clean

unidentified *adj*
unknown, unrecognized, unmarked, unnamed, nameless, anonymous, incognito, unfamiliar, strange, mysterious, obscure, unclassified
E3 identified, known, named

unification *n*
union, uniting, merger, alliance, amalgamation, combination, federation, fusion, incorporation, coalescence, coalition, confederation
formal enosis
E3 separation, split, division

uniform *n, adj*
▶ *n* outfit, costume, livery, insignia, regalia, robes, dress, suit, regimentals
colloq. garb, rig
▶ *adj* same, identical, like, alike, similar, homogeneous, consistent, regular, equal, smooth, even, flat, monotonous, unvarying, unchanging, constant, unbroken, stable, invariable, undeviating
E3 different, varied, changing

uniformity *n*
sameness, constancy, invariability, regularity, similarity, evenness, flatness, monotony, drabness, dullness, tedium
formal homogeneity, homomorphism, similitude
E3 difference, dissimilarity, variation

unify *v*
unite, bring/come together, join, bind, combine, integrate, mix, blend, merge, amalgamate, consolidate, coalesce, fuse, weld
E3 separate, divide, split

unifying *adj*
uniting, reconciling, combinatory, consolidative
technical esemplastic
formal unific, henotic
E3 divisive

unimaginable *adj*
inconceivable, unbelievable, incredible, amazing, astonishing, staggering, extraordinary, preposterous, impossible, fantastic, undreamed-of, unthinkable, unheard-of, implausible, unlikely, unconvincing, far-fetched, outlandish
colloq. mind-boggling

unimaginative *adj*
uninspired, unoriginal, predictable, hackneyed, banal, mundane, pedestrian, ordinary, dull, boring, routine, usual, dry, barren, lifeless, stale, unexciting, tame
colloq. matter-of-fact, samey
E3 imaginative, creative, original

unimpeachable *adj*
blameless, perfect, unblemished, spotless, faultless, immaculate, impeccable, irreproachable, unchallengeable, unquestionable, unassailable, reliable, dependable
🎙 blameworthy, faulty

unimpeded *adj*
unrestrained, unconstrained, free, open, clear, unhindered, unblocked, unchecked, unhampered, uninhibited, untrammelled
colloq. all-round
🎙 hampered, impeded

unimportant *adj*
insignificant, inconsequential, irrelevant, immaterial, insubstantial, minor, secondary, incidental, marginal, peripheral, trivial, trifling, petty, slight, negligible, worthless
formal nugatory
colloq. no great shakes, no big deal, not worth mentioning
🎙 important, significant, relevant, vital

unimpressive *adj*
unspectacular, undistinguished, unexciting, unexceptional, unremarkable, uninteresting, dull, ordinary, common, average, commonplace, indifferent, mediocre
🎙 impressive, memorable, notable, special

uninhabited *adj*
unoccupied, vacant, empty, deserted, abandoned, desolate, unpeopled, unpopulated, unsettled

uninhibited *adj*
unconstrained, unreserved, unselfconscious, liberated, free, unrestricted, uncontrolled, unrestrained, abandoned, natural, spontaneous, frank, outspoken, candid, open, relaxed, informal
🎙 inhibited, repressed, constrained, restrained

uninspired *adj*
ordinary, boring, commonplace, dull, indifferent, stale, trite, stock, unexciting, unimaginative, uninspiring, uninteresting, undistinguished, unoriginal, pedestrian, prosaic, humdrum
🎙 original, inspired, exciting

unintelligent *adj*
stupid, foolish, silly, slow, half-witted, empty-headed, fatuous, unreasoning, unthinking, dense, dull, obtuse, brainless
colloq. thick, dumb, gormless
🎙 intelligent

unintelligible *adj*
incomprehensible, incoherent, inarticulate, garbled, scrambled, jumbled, muddled, indecipherable, unreadable, illegible, impenetrable, unfathomable, puzzling, mysterious, obscure, complicated, complex, involved
colloq. double Dutch
🎙 intelligible, comprehensible, clear

unintentional *adj*
unintended, accidental, inadvertent, unplanned, unpremeditated, uncalculated, involuntary, unconscious, unwitting, careless
formal fortuitous
🎙 intentional, deliberate

uninterested *adj*
indifferent, unconcerned, uninvolved, bored, listless, apathetic, unenthusiastic, blasé, impassive, distant,

unresponsive
🎙 interested, concerned, enthusiastic, responsive, curious

⚠ **uninterested** or **disinterested** ? *See panel at* **disinterested**.

uninteresting *adj*
boring, tedious, monotonous, humdrum, dull, drab, dreary, dry, flat, tame, stale, prosaic, pedestrian, uneventful, unexciting, uninspiring, unimpressive, tiresome, wearisome
🎙 interesting, exciting, entertaining

uninterrupted *adj*
unbroken, continuous, non-stop, unending, unceasing, ceaseless, endless, constant, continual, steady, sustained, undisturbed, peaceful
formal unremitting
🎙 broken, intermittent

uninvited *adj*
unasked, unsought, unsolicited, unwanted, unwelcome
🎙 invited

uninviting *adj*
unappealing, unattractive, undesirable, unpleasant, unwelcoming, repellent, repulsive, offensive, off-putting, unsavoury, disagreeable, distasteful, unappetizing
🎙 inviting, welcome

uninvolved *adj*
unattached, uncommitted, unengaged, free, independent, footloose, fancy-free, unhampered, unhindered, untrammelled
🎙 attached, committed

union *n*
1 FUSION, unification, unity, alliance, coalition, league, association, confederation, amalgamation, merger, combination, joining, juncture, consolidation, mixture, synthesis, blend
2 ASSOCIATION, trade union, alliance, coalition, league, club, federation, confederacy, consortium, confederacy
3 AGREEMENT, harmony, unity, unanimity
formal accord, concurrence
4 MARRIAGE, wedding
old use wedlock
formal matrimony, nuptials
🎙 1 separation, alienation; *formal* estrangement
4 divorce

unique *adj*
single, one-off, sole, only, one and only, one of a kind, lone, solitary, unmatched, matchless, peerless, unequalled, unparalleled, unrivalled, incomparable, unprecedented, inimitable
formal nonpareil, *sui generis*
🎙 common

unison *n*
concert, co-operation, unanimity, unity
formal accord, concord

unit *n*
item, part, element, constituent, piece, component, module, section, segment, portion, entity, whole, one, system, assembly

unite *v*
join, connect, link, couple, marry, ally, co-operate,

band, associate, federate, confederate, combine, join forces, pool, amalgamate, merge, blend, unify, consolidate, coalesce, weld, fuse
colloq. pull together
E∃ separate, sever

united *adj*
allied, affiliated, corporate, unified, combined, amalgamated, pooled, collective, concerted, one, unanimous, agreed, in agreement, like-minded, co-operative
formal in accord
E∃ disunited

unity *n*
1 AGREEMENT, harmony, peace, consensus, unanimity, solidarity
formal accord, concord, concert
colloq. togetherness
2 UNION, integrity, oneness, wholeness, amalgamation, unification
E∃ 1 disunity, disagreement, discord, strife

universal *adj*
worldwide, global, cosmic, all-embracing, all-inclusive, general, comprehensive, common, across-the-board, total, whole, entire, all-round, unlimited
formal ubiquitous, omnipresent

universality *n*
commonness, comprehensiveness, all-inclusiveness, entirety, totality, completeness, generalization, generality, predominance, prevalence
formal ubiquity

universally *adv*
always, everywhere, uniformly, invariably
formal ubiquitously

universe *n*
cosmos, world, nature, creation, firmament, heavens
formal macrocosm

university *n*
college, institute, varsity, academy
formal academia

unjust *adj*
unfair, wrong, partial, biased, prejudiced, one-sided, partisan, unreasonable, unjustified, undeserved
formal inequitable
E∃ just, fair, reasonable

unjustifiable *adj*
indefensible, inexcusable, unforgivable, unpardonable, unreasonable, uncalled-for, unwarranted, immoderate, excessive, unacceptable, outrageous
E∃ justifiable, acceptable

unkempt *adj*
dishevelled, tousled, rumpled, uncombed, ungroomed, untidy, disordered, messy, scruffy, shabby, slovenly
colloq. sloppy, shambolic, slobbish
E∃ well-groomed, tidy

unkind *adj*
cruel, harsh, inhuman, inhumane, callous, hard-hearted, cold-hearted, heartless, unfeeling, insensitive, thoughtless, inconsiderate, uncharitable, pitiless, ruthless, nasty, malicious, vicious, snide, spiteful, mean, unfriendly, uncaring, unsympathetic
formal malevolent
colloq. shabby, bitchy
E∃ kind, kindly, considerate, generous, sympathetic

unkindness *n*
cruelty, harshness, uncharitableness, unfriendliness, inhumanity, callousness, hard-heartedness, insensitivity, maliciousness, meanness, spite
E∃ kindness, friendship

unknowable *adj*
unimaginable, unpredictable, untold, unascertainable, unfathomable, unforeseeable, incalculable, infinite
colloq. in the lap of the gods

unknown *adj*
unfamiliar, unheard-of, strange, alien, foreign, mysterious, dark, obscure, hidden, concealed, undisclosed, secret, undivulged, untold, new, uncharted, unexplored, undiscovered, unrevealed, unidentified, unnamed, nameless, anonymous, unheard-of, incognito
E∃ known, familiar

unlawful *adj*
illegal, criminal, illicit, illegitimate, against the law, unconstitutional, outlawed, banned, prohibited, forbidden, unauthorized, unlicensed, unsanctioned
E∃ lawful, legal, allowed, permitted

unleash *v*
loose, let loose, free, release, unloose, untie, untether
E∃ restrain

unlettered *adj*
illiterate, ignorant, uneducated, unlearned, unschooled, untaught, untutored, unlessoned
E∃ educated

unlike *adj, prep*
▶ *adj* dissimilar, different, distinct, opposite, opposed, incompatible, contrasted, ill-matched, unrelated, unequal, divergent, diverse
old use difform
formal disparate
E∃ similar, related
▶ *prep* dissimilar to, different from, in contrast to, as opposed to, as against
E∃ like

unlikely *adj*
1 IMPROBABLE, implausible, far-fetched, unconvincing, unbelievable, incredible, inconceivable, unimaginable, unexpected, doubtful, dubious, questionable, suspect, suspicious
2 SLIGHT, faint, remote, distant, slim, small, inconsiderable
E∃ 1 likely, plausible

unlimited *adj*
limitless, unrestricted, unbounded, boundless, illimitable, infinite, endless, countless, incalculable, immeasurable, untold, vast, immense, extensive, great, indefinite, absolute, total, unconditional, unqualified, all-encompassing, total, complete, full, unconstrained, unhampered, unimpeded, uncontrolled, unchecked
E∃ limited

unload *v*
unpack, empty, discharge, dump, offload, unburden, relieve
E∃ load

unlock *v*
unbolt, unlatch, unfasten, undo, unbar, open, free, release
E∃ lock, fasten

unlooked-for *adj*
unexpected, unforeseen, unanticipated, unpredicted, unhoped-for, unthought-of, undreamed-of, surprising, surprise, fortunate, chance, lucky
formal fortuitous
⊟ expected, predictable

unloved *adj*
unpopular, disliked, hated, detested, unwanted, rejected, spurned, loveless, uncared-for, neglected
formal forsaken
colloq. dumped
⊟ loved

unlucky *adj*
1 UNFORTUNATE, luckless, unsuccessful, poor, wretched, unhappy, miserable, ill-fated, ill-starred, star-crossed, jinxed, doomed, cursed
formal hapless
colloq. down on your luck
2 UNFAVOURABLE, adverse, unfortunate, unpleasant, unpromising, doomed, ill-fated, ominous, disadvantageous, untoward, calamitous, disastrous, catastrophic
formal inauspicious, unpropitious
⊟ **1** fortunate, lucky **2** favourable, lucky

unmanageable *adj*
1 UNWIELDY, bulky, cumbersome, awkward, inconvenient, unhandy
formal incommodious
2 UNCONTROLLABLE, wild, unruly, disorderly, ungovernable, obstreperous, difficult
formal recalcitrant, refractory
⊟ **1** manageable **2** controllable

unmanly *adj*
effeminate, dishonourable, feeble, weak, weak-kneed, soft, weedy, cowardly, chicken-hearted, craven, namby-pamby
colloq. sissy, wet, yellow, wimpish
⊟ manly

unmannerly *adj*
impolite, rude, uncivil, uncouth, discourteous, ill-mannered, badly-behaved, bad-mannered, disrespectful, graceless, ungracious, ill-bred, boorish, low-bred
⊟ polite

unmarried *adj*
single, unwed, divorced, celibate, unattached, available, lone, on your own
⊟ married

unmask *v*
unveil, uncloak, uncover, bare, expose, reveal, show, disclose, discover, detect
⊟ mask, conceal

unmatched *adj*
unrivalled, unique, unparalleled, unequalled, unsurpassed, incomparable, beyond compare, matchless, supreme, peerless, paramount, unexampled
formal consummate, nonpareil

unmentionable *adj*
unspeakable, unutterable, taboo, immodest, indecent, embarrassing, unpleasant, shocking, scandalous, shameful, disgraceful, abominable

unmerciful *adj*
merciless, pitiless, ruthless, cruel, brutal, hard, callous, sadistic, heartless, implacable, relentless, remorseless, unrelenting, unsparing, uncaring, unfeeling
⊟ merciful

unmethodical *adj*
unorganized, confused, muddled, disorderly, haphazard, illogical, irregular, unsystematic, unco-ordinated, random
formal desultory
⊟ methodical

unmindful *adj*
heedless, careless, negligent, remiss, unheeding, neglectful, lax, slack, indifferent, inattentive, unaware, unconscious, oblivious, forgetful, blind, deaf, regardless
⊟ mindful, aware, heedful

unmistakable *adj*
clear, plain, distinct, pronounced, obvious, evident, patent, glaring, blatant, striking, explicit, conspicuous, clear-cut, well-defined, unambiguous, unequivocal, positive, definite, sure, certain, unquestionable, beyond question, indisputable, undeniable
formal manifest, indubitable
⊟ unclear, ambiguous

unmitigated *adj*
utter, absolute, complete, pure, rank, perfect, outright, downright, out-and-out, thorough, thoroughgoing, sheer, relentless, persistent, intense, unqualified, unalleviated, unrelieved, unbroken, unrelenting, unredeemed, unmodified, undiminished, harsh, grim
formal arrant, consummate, unabated, unremitting

unmoved *adj*
unaffected, untouched, unshaken, unstirred, dry-eyed, unfeeling, cold, dispassionate, indifferent, impassive, unresponsive, unconcerned, unimpressed, firm, adamant, inflexible, unbending, undeviating, unwavering, steady, unchanged, resolute, resolved, determined
⊟ moved, affected, shaken

unnatural *adj*
1 ABNORMAL, anomalous, freakish, irregular, unusual, strange, odd, peculiar, queer, bizarre, extraordinary, uncommon, uncanny, supernatural, inhuman, perverted
2 AFFECTED, feigned, artificial, false, insincere, unspontaneous, contrived, laboured, stilted, forced, strained, staged, self-conscious, stiff
⊟ **1** natural, normal **2** sincere, fluent

unnecessary *adj*
unneeded, needless, uncalled-for, unrequired, wasted, unwanted, gratuitous, non-essential, inessential, dispensable, expendable, superfluous, redundant, tautological
⊟ necessary, essential, indispensable

unnerve *v*
daunt, intimidate, frighten, scare, alarm, discourage, deject, demoralize, dishearten, dismay, disconcert, put out, disquiet, unsettle, upset, worry, shake, confound, fluster, unman
formal perturb
colloq. rattle
⊟ nerve, brace, steel

unnoticed *adj*
unobserved, unremarked, unseen, unrecognized, undiscovered, overlooked, ignored, disregarded,

neglected, unheeded
🔄 noticed, noted

unobtrusive *adj*
inconspicuous, unnoticeable, unassertive, self-effacing, humble, modest, unassuming, unaggressive, unostentatious, unpretentious, restrained, low-key, subdued, quiet, retiring
🔄 prominent, obtrusive, ostentatious

unobtrusively *adv*
inconspicuously, quietly, modestly, on the quiet, unostentatiously, surreptitiously, humbly, unpretentiously
🔄 obtrusively, ostentatiously, showily, aggressively

unoccupied *adj*
1 UNINHABITED, vacant, empty, deserted
formal forsaken
2 JOBLESS, free, idle, inactive, workless, unemployed
🔄 1 occupied 2 busy

unofficial *adj*
unauthorized, illegal, informal, off-the-record, personal, private, confidential, undeclared, unconfirmed, unratified
🔄 official, ratified; *formal* accredited, substantiated, corroborated

unoriginal *adj*
unimaginative, uninspired, hackneyed, stale, trite, copied, cliché-ridden, derivative, cribbed, second-hand, derived
🔄 original, imaginative, creative, innovative, fresh

unorthodox *adj*
unconventional, nonconformist, heterodox, alternative, fringe, irregular, abnormal, unusual, eccentric, creative, innovative, new, novel, fresh
🔄 orthodox, conventional

unpaid *adj*
1 *unpaid bills*
outstanding, overdue, unsettled, owing, due, payable, pending, uncollected, remaining
2 *unpaid work*
voluntary, honorary, unsalaried, unwaged, unremunerative, free
🔄 1 paid

unpalatable *adj*
1 UNAPPETIZING, distasteful, insipid, bitter, uneatable, inedible, unsavoury, disgusting
2 UNPLEASANT, disagreeable, unattractive, distasteful, unsavoury, offensive, nasty, repellent
formal repugnant
🔄 1 palatable 2 pleasant

unparalleled *adj*
unequalled, without equal, unmatched, matchless, peerless, beyond compare, incomparable, unrivalled, unsurpassed, supreme, superlative, rare, unique, exceptional, unprecedented

unpardonable *adj*
unforgivable, inexcusable, unjustifiable, indefensible, outrageous, deplorable, disgraceful, shocking, shameful, scandalous
formal irremissible, reprehensible, unconscionable
🔄 forgivable, understandable

unperturbed *adj*
calm, unexcited, unflustered, untroubled, unworried, undisturbed, unruffled, unflinching, self-possessed, composed, collected, tranquil, serene, placid, poised,

cool, impassive
🔄 anxious, perturbed

unpleasant *adj*
1 *an unpleasant smell*
disagreeable, nasty, objectionable, offensive, distasteful, unpalatable, unappetizing, unattractive, repulsive, bad, foul, troublesome, disgusting, undesirable
formal repugnant, noisome
2 *an unpleasant person*
unfriendly, unkind, disagreeable, rude, impolite, discourteous, bad-tempered, ill-natured, nasty, objectionable, hostile, aggressive, quarrelsome, surly, sour, mean
🔄 1, 2 pleasant, agreeable, nice

unpleasantness *n*
annoyance, nastiness, trouble, upset, bother, embarrassment, fuss, furore, ill-feeling, scandal

unpolished *adj*
unfinished, unworked, rough and ready, sketchy, unrefined, unfashioned, unsophisticated, uncultivated, uncultured, uncivilized, coarse, crude, rough, home-bred, rude, uncouth, vulgar
🔄 finished, polished, refined

unpopular *adj*
disliked, hated, detested, unloved, friendless, undesirable, unattractive, unsought-after, unfashionable, undesirable, unwelcome, unwanted, rejected, shunned, avoided, ignored, neglected
🔄 popular, fashionable

unprecedented *adj*
new, original, revolutionary, unknown, unheard-of, exceptional, remarkable, extraordinary, abnormal, unusual, uncommon, freakish, unparalleled, unrivalled, unequalled
🔄 usual

unpredictable *adj*
unforeseeable, unexpected, changeable, variable, inconstant, unreliable, fickle, unstable, volatile, erratic, random, chance
formal mercurial, capricious
🔄 predictable, foreseeable, constant, reliable

unprejudiced *adj*
unbiased, fair, fair-minded, impartial, just, objective, non-partisan, open-minded, even-handed, balanced, detached, uncoloured, dispassionate, enlightened
🔄 prejudiced, narrow-minded

unpremeditated *adj*
spontaneous, unintentional, unplanned, unprepared, unrehearsed, offhand, impulsive, impromptu, extempore
formal fortuitous
colloq. off-the-cuff, spur-of-the-moment
🔄 premeditated

unprepared *adj*
unready, surprised, unsuspecting, ill-equipped, unwilling, unfinished, incomplete, half-baked, unplanned, unrehearsed, spontaneous, improvised, ad-lib
colloq. off-the-cuff
🔄 prepared, ready

unpretentious *adj*
unaffected, natural, plain, simple, ordinary, unobtrusive, honest, straightforward, humble, modest,

unassuming, unostentatious
E3 pretentious, show, ostentatious

unprincipled *adj*
unscrupulous, unprofessional, unethical, dishonest,
dishonourable, immoral, underhand, deceitful,
devious, corrupt, discreditable
colloq. crooked
E3 ethical, principled

unproductive *adj*
infertile, sterile, barren, dry, arid, unfruitful, fruitless,
futile, vain, idle, worthless, useless, ineffective,
unprofitable, unremunerative, unrewarding
formal inefficacious, otiose
E3 productive, fertile

unprofessional *adj*
amateurish, inexpert, unskilled, incompetent,
inexperienced, untrained, inefficient, casual,
negligent, lax, unethical, unprincipled, unscrupulous,
improper, unacceptable, inadmissible
formal unseemly, indecorous
colloq. sloppy
E3 professional, skilful

unpromising *adj*
unfavourable, adverse, discouraging, gloomy,
depressing, doubtful, dispiriting, inauspicious,
ominous
formal unpropitious
E3 promising, favourable, auspicious

unprotected *adj*
defenceless, unguarded, unattended, undefended,
unfortified, unarmed, unshielded, unsheltered,
uncovered, exposed, open, naked, vulnerable, liable,
helpless
E3 protected, safe, immune

unprovable *adj*
unverifiable, indemonstrable, undemonstrable,
indeterminable, unascertainable
E3 verifiable

unqualified *adj*
1 UNTRAINED, inexperienced, amateur, ineligible,
unlicensed, unfit, incompetent, incapable,
unprepared, ill-equipped
2 ABSOLUTE, categorical, utter, total, complete,
perfect, positive, thorough, downright, unmitigated,
unreserved, wholehearted, outright, out and out,
unconditional, unequivocal, unrestricted
formal consummate
E3 1 qualified, professional 2 conditional, tentative

unquestionable *adj*
unequivocal, beyond question, incontestable, faultless,
flawless, indisputable, obvious, patent, clear,
conclusive, definite, absolute, sure, certain, self-
evident, unchallenged, undeniable, unmistakable
formal incontrovertible, indubitable, irrefutable,
manifest
E3 dubious, questionable

unquestioning *adj*
implicit, unhesitating, questionless, unconditional,
unqualified, wholehearted
E3 doubtful

unravel *v*
unwind, undo, untangle, disentangle, free, extricate,
separate, unknot, straighten out, resolve, sort out, clear
up, solve, work out, figure out, puzzle out, penetrate,

interpret, explain
E3 tangle, complicate

unreadable *adj*
unintelligible, too difficult to read, incomprehensible,
incoherent, inarticulate, garbled, scrambled, jumbled,
muddled, indecipherable, unreadable, illegible,
impenetrable, unfathomable, puzzling, mysterious,
obscure, complicated, complex, involved
colloq. double Dutch
E3 intelligible, comprehensible, clear

unreal *adj*
false, artificial, synthetic, mock, fake, sham,
imaginary, visionary, fanciful, make-believe, fictitious,
made-up, fairy-tale, legendary, mythical, fantastic,
bizarre, illusory, immaterial, insubstantial, nebulous,
hypothetical, non-existent
formal chimerical, phantasmagorical
colloq. pretend
E3 real, genuine, authentic

unrealistic *adj*
impractical, idealistic, theoretical, romantic, quixotic,
impracticable, unworkable, unreasonable, impossible,
over-optimistic
E3 realistic, pragmatic

unreasonable *adj*
1 UNFAIR, unjust, biased, unjustifiable, unjustified,
unwarranted, unacceptable, undue, uncalled-for
2 IRRATIONAL, illogical, inconsistent, arbitrary,
absurd, nonsensical, ludicrous, far-fetched,
outrageous, preposterous, mad, senseless, silly, foolish,
stupid, headstrong, opinionated, perverse
3 *unreasonable prices*
excessive, immoderate, extravagant, outrageous,
expensive, exorbitant, extortionate, undue
colloq. steep
E3 1 reasonable, fair 2 rational, sensible
3 moderate

unrecognizable *adj*
unidentifiable, disguised, incognito, changed, altered,
unknowable
formal incognizable

unrecognized *adj*
unnoticed, unobserved, unremarked, unseen,
undiscovered, overlooked, ignored, disregarded,
neglected, unheeded
E3 recognized, noticed, noted

unrefined *adj*
raw, untreated, unprocessed, unpurified, unfinished,
unpolished, crude, coarse, vulgar, unsophisticated,
uncultivated, uncultured
E3 refined, finished

unregenerate *adj*
unconverted, hardened, impenitent, stubborn,
obstinate, unreformed, unrepentant, persistent,
abandoned, shameless, wicked, sinful
formal intractable, obdurate, incorrigible,
recalcitrant, refractory
E3 reformed, repentant

unrelated *adj*
unconnected, unassociated, irrelevant, beside/off the
point, extraneous, different, dissimilar, unlike,
distinct, foreign, separate, independent
formal disparate
colloq. neither here nor there
E3 related, similar

unrelenting *adj*
relentless, uncompromising, inexorable, unceasing, ceaseless, endless, unbroken, continuous, constant, continual, perpetual, steady, remorseless, ruthless, cruel, unmerciful, merciless, pitiless, unforgiving, unsparing
formal unremitting, incessant, unabated, intransigent
⊟ spasmodic, intermittent

unreliable *adj*
unsound, fallible, deceptive, false, mistaken, erroneous, inaccurate, doubtful, unconvincing, implausible, uncertain, undependable, untrustworthy, unstable, fickle, irresponsible
colloq. iffy, slippery
⊟ reliable, dependable, trustworthy, sound

unremitting *adj*
unrelenting, unceasing, ceaseless, relentless, remorseless, tireless, constant, continual, continuous, perpetual, unbroken
formal incessant, unabated
⊟ spasmodic, intermittent

unrepentant *adj*
impenitent, unapologetic, unabashed, unashamed, shameless, confirmed, hardened, callous
formal incorrigible, obdurate
⊟ repentant, penitent, ashamed

unreserved *adj*
unqualified, unrestrained, unconditional, unhesitating, uninhibited, unlimited, complete, full, absolute, free, total, open, wholehearted, entire, frank, forthright, direct, candid, demonstrative, extrovert, outgoing, outspoken
⊟ inhibited, tentative, hesitant

unreservedly *adv*
completely, entirely, utterly, wholeheartedly, outright, unhesitatingly

unresisting *adj*
submissive, docile, obedient, passive, meek
colloq. like a lamb to the slaughter
⊟ resisting, protesting

unresolved *adj*
undecided, unanswered, undetermined, unsettled, unsolved, vexed, undetermined, vague, indefinite, doubtful, problematical, pending, moot
colloq. up in the air
⊟ definite, determined

unresponsive *adj*
unaffected, unmoved, unsympathetic, uninterested, indifferent, aloof, apathetic, cool
⊟ responsive, sympathetic

unrest *n*
protest, rebellion, turmoil, agitation, disorder, restlessness, dissatisfaction, dissension, worry, turmoil, disquiet, discontent, unease, uneasiness
formal disaffection, discord, perturbation
⊟ peace, calm

unrestrained *adj*
unbridled, uncontrolled, unhindered, uninhibited, unrepressed, unreserved, unchecked, unconstrained, unbounded, irrepressible, inordinate, immoderate, intemperate, free, natural, rampant, abandoned, boisterous
⊟ restrained, inhibited

unrestricted *adj*
unlimited, unbounded, unopposed, unhindered,

unimpeded, unobstructed, clear, free, open, public, unconditional, absolute
colloq. free-for-all
⊟ restricted, limited

unripe *adj*
unripened, green, immature, undeveloped, unready
⊟ ripe, mature

unrivalled *adj*
unequalled, unparalleled, unmatched, matchless, peerless, incomparable, unsurpassed, without equal, beyond compare, supreme, superlative
formal inimitable, nonpareil

unruffled *adj*
undisturbed, untroubled, imperturbable, collected, composed, cool, calm, tranquil, serene, peaceful, smooth, level, even
formal unperturbed
⊟ troubled, anxious

unruly *adj*
uncontrollable, unmanageable, ungovernable, disorderly, wild, rowdy, riotous, rebellious, mutinous, lawless, insubordinate, disobedient, wayward, wilful, headstrong, obstreperous
formal recalcitrant, refractory, intractable
⊟ manageable, orderly

unsafe *adj*
dangerous, perilous, risky, high-risk, hazardous, treacherous, chancy, unreliable, uncertain, unsound, unstable, precarious, insecure, vulnerable, exposed, defenceless
colloq. dicey, hairy
⊟ safe, secure

unsaid *adj*
unspoken, unstated, unexpressed, unvoiced, unmentioned, undeclared, unuttered, unpronounced
⊟ spoken

unsatisfactory *adj*
unacceptable, imperfect, defective, faulty, inferior, poor, mediocre, weak, inadequate, insufficient, deficient, unsuitable, displeasing, dissatisfying, unsatisfying, frustrating, disappointing
colloq. leaving a lot to be desired
⊟ satisfactory, adequate, pleasing

unsavoury *adj*
distasteful, disagreeable, unpleasant, disgusting, nauseating, revolting, sickening, nasty, undesirable, repulsive, objectionable, obnoxious, offensive, repellent, unattractive, sordid, squalid, unpalatable, unappetizing
formal repugnant
⊟ palatable, pleasant

unscathed *adj*
unhurt, uninjured, unharmed, undamaged, untouched, whole, intact, safe, sound
⊟ hurt, injured, harmed

unscrupulous *adj*
unprincipled, ruthless, shameless, dishonourable, dishonest, corrupt, immoral, unethical, improper
colloq. crooked
⊟ scrupulous, ethical, proper

unseasonable *adj*
seasonable, inappropriate, ill-timed, unsuitable, untimely, mistimed
formal inopportune, intempestive, malapropos
⊟ timely

unseasoned *adj*
unprepared, unprimed, unmatured, untreated, untempered
colloq. green

unseat *v*
remove, depose, dethrone, dismount, displace, dismiss, discharge, oust, throw, overthrow, topple, unhorse, unsaddle, dishorse

unseemly *adj*
improper, indelicate, unbecoming, undignified, unrefined, disreputable, discreditable, undue, inappropriate, unsuitable, unbefitting
formal indecorous
E3 seemly, decorous

unseen *adj*
unnoticed, unobserved, undetected, unobtrusive, invisible, hidden, concealed, veiled, obscure, lurking
E3 visible

unselfish *adj*
selfless, altruistic, self-denying, self-sacrificing, self-forgetting, disinterested, noble, kind, generous, open-handed, liberal, charitable, philanthropic, public-spirited, humanitarian
formal magnanimous
E3 selfish

unsentimental *adj*
realistic, practical, pragmatic, hard-headed, tough, unemotional, unfeeling, unromantic, level-headed
E3 sentimental, idealistic

unsettle *v*
disturb, upset, trouble, bother, discompose, ruffle, fluster, unbalance, destabilize, shake, agitate, disconcert, confuse
formal perturb, discomfit
colloq. rattle, throw

unsettled *adj*
1 DISTURBED, upset, troubled, agitated, anxious, uneasy, tense, edgy, fidgety, flustered, shaken, unnerved, disoriented, confused
colloq. on edge
2 UNRESOLVED, undetermined, undecided, to be decided, open, uncertain, doubtful
colloq. up in the air, in the balance
3 *unsettled weather*
changeable, variable, unpredictable, inconstant, unstable, uncertain, insecure, unsteady, shaky
4 UNPAID, outstanding, owing, in arrears, payable, overdue
5 UNINHABITED, unoccupied, deserted, abandoned, desolate, unpeopled, unpopulated
E3 **1** composed **2** decided, certain
3 settled **4** paid **5** settled, peopled

unshakable *adj*
firm, well-founded, fixed, stable, immovable, unassailable, unswerving, unwavering, constant, steadfast, staunch, sure, resolute, determined
E3 insecure

unsightly *adj*
ugly, unattractive, unprepossessing, hideous, revolting, repulsive, repugnant, off-putting, unpleasant, disagreeable
E3 attractive

unskilful *adj*
unskilled, amateurish, inexperienced, unprofessional, unqualified, untaught, untrained, uneducated,

untalented, unpractised, incompetent, awkward, clumsy, fumbling, bungling, inept, inexpert, gauche
formal maladroit
E3 skilful, skilled

unskilled *adj*
untrained, unqualified, inexperienced, unpractised, inexpert, unprofessional, amateurish, incompetent
E3 skilled, professional

unsociable *adj*
unfriendly, aloof, distant, standoffish, withdrawn, introverted, reclusive, solitary, retiring, reserved, taciturn, unforthcoming, uncommunicative, cold, chilly, cool, uncongenial, unneighbourly, inhospitable, hostile
E3 sociable, friendly, congenial

unsolicited *adj*
unrequested, unsought, uninvited, unasked, unwanted, unwelcome, uncalled-for, unasked-for, gratuitous, voluntary, spontaneous
E3 requested, invited

unsophisticated *adj*
1 *an unsophisticated person*
artless, guileless, innocent, ingenuous, naïve, inexperienced, simple, unworldly, childlike, natural, unaffected, unpretentious
2 CRUDE, unrefined, plain, simple, basic, straightforward, rudimentary, undeveloped, uncomplicated, uninvolved
E3 **1** sophisticated, worldly **2** complex

unsound *adj*
1 *unsound reasoning*
faulty, flawed, defective, ill-founded, unfounded, false, weak, erroneous, invalid, illogical, shaky
formal fallacious
2 UNHEALTHY, unwell, ill, diseased, weak, ailing, delicate, frail, unbalanced, deranged, unhinged
3 UNSTABLE, unsteady, rickety, wobbly, shaky, insecure, broken, dangerous, unsafe, unreliable
E3 **1** sound **2** well **3** stable

unsparing *adj*
1 GENEROUS, lavish, liberal, open-handed, ungrudging, unstinting, plenteous, abundant, bountiful, profuse
formal munificent
2 HARSH, hard, merciless, unmerciful, ruthless, severe, stern, relentless, implacable, uncompromising, unforgiving
E3 forgiving, mean, sparing

unspeakable *adj*
unutterable, inexpressible, indescribable, awful, dreadful, frightful, terrible, horrible, shocking, appalling, monstrous, inconceivable, unimaginable, unthinkable, unbelievable
formal execrable

unspectacular *adj*
unremarkable, unimpressive, unexciting, uninteresting, dull, boring, ordinary, common, average, plodding
E3 spectacular, impressive, memorable

unspoilt *adj*
preserved, unchanged, untouched, natural, unaffected, unsophisticated, unharmed, undamaged, unimpaired, unblemished, perfect
E3 spoilt, affected

unspoken *adj*
unstated, undeclared, unuttered, unexpressed, unsaid, voiceless, wordless, silent, tacit, implicit, implied, inferred, understood, assumed
stated, explicit

unstable *adj*
1 CHANGEABLE, variable, fluctuating, vacillating, wavering, fitful, erratic, moody, inconsistent, volatile, inconstant, unpredictable, unreliable, untrustworthy
formal capricious, mercurial
2 UNSTEADY, wobbly, shaky, rickety, insecure, unsafe, risky, precarious, tottering, unbalanced
3 *emotionally/mentally unstable*
deranged, insane, mad, disturbed, unsound, unhinged
colloq. crazy, barmy, crackers
1 stable 2 steady 3 stable, sane

unsteady *adj*
unstable, wobbly, shaky, rickety, doddery, insecure, unsafe, treacherous, precarious, tottering, unreliable, inconstant, irregular, flickering
steady, firm, stable

unstinting *adj*
abounding, abundant, ample, bountiful, full, generous, large, lavish, liberal, plentiful, profuse, ungrudging, unsparing
formal munificent, prodigal
grudging, mean

unsubstantiated *adj*
unconfirmed, debatable, dubious, questionable, disputable, unestablished, unproved, unproven, unsupported, unverified
formal unattested, uncorroborated
proved, proven

unsuccessful *adj*
failed, abortive, vain, futile, useless, ineffective, unavailing, fruitless, unproductive, unprofitable, sterile, luckless, unlucky, unfortunate, losing, beaten, defeated, frustrated, thwarted
formal ineffectual
successful, effective, fortunate, winning

unsuitable *adj*
inappropriate, inapt, unsuited, unfit, unacceptable, out of place, improper, incompatible
formal unseemly, unbecoming, incongruous, inapposite, infelicitous, malapropos
suitable, appropriate

unsullied *adj*
untainted, unspotted, spotless, unstained, stainless, untarnished, unblemished, uncorrupted, undefiled, unspoiled, unsoiled, untouched, perfect, clean, pure, immaculate, intact, unblackened
formal pristine
dirty, stained

unsung *adj*
unhonoured, unpraised, unacknowledged, uncelebrated, unhailed, unacclaimed, unknown, unrecognized, overlooked, disregarded, neglected, forgotten, unknown, anonymous, obscure
honoured, famous, renowned

unsure *adj*
1 *unsure of yourself*
uncertain, hesitant, insecure, lacking self-confidence, tentative, doubtful, dubious, suspicious, sceptical, unconvinced, unpersuaded, undecided
2 *unsure about what to do*
undecided, uncertain, unknown, ambivalent,

doubtful, hesitant, dithering, equivocating, wavering, irresolute, uncommitted, indefinite, vague
colloq. in two minds
1 confident, sure, certain 2 sure, certain, decided

unsurpassed *adj*
surpassing, supreme, transcendent, unbeaten, unexcelled, unequalled, unparalleled, unrivalled, incomparable, matchless, superlative, exceptional
surpassed

unsurprising *adj*
expected, anticipated, promised, hoped-for, predicted, forecast, foreseen, forseeable, looked-for, wished-for
colloq. just as you thought
surprising, unexpected

unsuspecting *adj*
unwary, unaware, off guard, unconscious, trusting, trustful, unsuspicious, credulous, gullible, ingenuous, naïve, innocent
suspicious, knowing

unswerving *adj*
unflagging, unwavering, unfaltering, untiring, undeviating, staunch, steadfast, dedicated, devoted, steady, sure, true, firm, constant, fixed, immovable, resolute, single-minded, direct
irresolute, tentative

unsympathetic *adj*
unpitying, unconcerned, uncaring, unmoved, unresponsive, indifferent, insensitive, unfeeling, cold, heartless, pitiless, soulless, hard-hearted, harsh, callous, cruel, inhuman, unkind, hard, stony, hostile, antagonistic
sympathetic, compassionate

unsystematic *adj*
unmethodical, unco-ordinated, irregular, disorganized, unorganized, unplanned, disorderly, untidy, haphazard, illogical, confused, muddled, jumbled, chaotic, indiscriminate, random, slapdash, shambolic
colloq. sloppy
logical, systematic

untamed *adj*
wild, fierce, savage, undomesticated, unmellowed, untameable, barbarous
formal feral
domesticated, tame

untangle *v*
disentangle, extricate, unravel, undo, resolve, solve, work out, straighten out
tangle, complicate

untarnished *adj*
unblemished, unstained, stainless, unspotted, spotless, unsullied, unsoiled, unspoilt, clean, immaculate, impeccable, intact, bright, pure, burnished, shining, glowing, polished, unimpeachable
formal pristine
tarnished, blemished

untenable *adj*
indefensible, unreasonable, unmaintainable, unsound, unjustifiable, inexcusable, insupportable, unsustainable, flawed, illogical, fallacious, rocky, shaky
tenable, sound

unthinkable *adj*
inconceivable, unimaginable, unheard-of,
unbelievable, incredible, impossible, improbable,
unlikely, implausible, unreasonable, illogical, absurd,
preposterous, outrageous, shocking, staggering

unthinking *adj*
thoughtless, inconsiderate, insensitive, tactless,
indiscreet, undiplomatic, unkind, rude, impolite,
heedless, careless, negligent, rash, impulsive,
instinctive, involuntary, unconscious, automatic,
mechanical
E≡ considerate, conscious

untidy *adj*
messy, cluttered, disorderly, muddled, jumbled,
unsystematic, chaotic, haywire, disorganized,
shambolic, topsy-turvy, scruffy, bedraggled, rumpled,
dishevelled, unkempt, slovenly, slipshod
colloq. sloppy, higgledy-piggledy
E≡ tidy, neat

untie *v*
undo, unfasten, unhitch, unknot, unbind, unwrap,
free, release, loose, loosen
E≡ tie, fasten

untimely *adj*
early, premature, unseasonable, ill-timed,
inopportune, inconvenient, awkward, unsuitable,
inappropriate, unfortunate
formal inauspicious, infelicitous, malapropos
E≡ timely, opportune

untiring *adj*
unflagging, unfaltering, tireless, indefatigable,
dogged, persevering, persistent, tenacious,
determined, resolute, devoted, dedicated, constant,
incessant, unceasing, steady, staunch, unfailing
formal unremitting
E≡ inconstant, wavering

untold *adj*
1 *cause untold damage*
indescribable, unimaginable, inconceivable,
inexpressible, unutterable
2 COUNTLESS, uncounted, unnumbered,
unreckoned, incalculable, innumerable, uncountable,
infinite, measureless, immeasurable, boundless,
inexhaustible, undreamed-of, unimaginable

untouched *adj*
unharmed, undamaged, unimpaired, unhurt,
uninjured, unscathed, safe, intact, unchanged,
unaltered, unaffected, unimpressed, unstirred
E≡ damaged, affected

untoward *adj*
unfortunate, troublesome, inconvenient, annoying,
adverse, unfavourable, unexpected, unsuitable,
unfitting, untimely, vexatious, irritating, worrying,
awkward, disastrous, improper, contrary, unlucky,
inappropriate, inauspicious, ominous, ill-timed
formal indecorous, inopportune, unbecoming,
unpropitious, unseemly
E≡ suitable, auspicious

untrained *adj*
unskilled, untaught, unschooled, uneducated,
inexperienced, unpractised, unqualified, amateur,
unprofessional, inexpert, incompetent
E≡ trained, expert

untried *adj*
untested, unproved, unestablished, experimental,

exploratory, new, novel, innovative, innovatory
E≡ tried, tested, proven

untroubled *adj*
unworried, unconcerned, undisturbed, unexcited,
unstirred, unflustered, unruffled, steady, calm,
composed, peaceful, impassive, cool, placid, serene,
tranquil
formal unperturbed
colloq. unflappable
E≡ anxious, troubled

untrue *adj*
1 FALSE, fallacious, deceptive, misleading, wrong,
incorrect, inaccurate, inexact, mistaken, erroneous,
fabricated
colloq. made-up, trumped-up
2 UNFAITHFUL, disloyal, untrustworthy, dishonest,
deceitful, fraudulent, untruthful
formal perfidious
colloq. two-faced
E≡ 1 true, correct 2 faithful, honest

untrustworthy *adj*
dishonest, deceitful, untruthful, disloyal, unfaithful,
faithless, treacherous, false, untrue, dishonourable,
capricious, fickle, fly-by-night, unreliable, untrusty
formal duplicitous
colloq. two-faced
E≡ trustworthy, reliable

untruth *n*
lie, story, tale, fiction, invention, fabrication,
falsehood, lying, untruthfulness, deceit, perjury
colloq. fib, whopper, porky, tall story, made-up story,
cock-and-bull story
E≡ truth

untruthful *adj*
lying, deceitful, dishonest, hypocritical, insincere,
false, untrue, fictional, fabricated, invented,
erroneous, fallacious
formal mendacious, unveracious
colloq. crooked, two-faced
E≡ truthful, honest

untwine *v*
unravel, uncoil, untwist, unwind, disentwine
E≡ twine, wind

untwist *v*
uncoil, unravel, untwine, unwind
E≡ twist

untutored *adj*
untrained, unschooled, unpractised, uneducated,
unlearned, unversed, inexperienced, inexpert,
illiterate, ignorant, unrefined, unsophisticated,
simple, artless, unlessoned
E≡ educated, trained

unused *adj*
1 LEFTOVER, remaining, surplus, extra, spare,
available, new, fresh, blank, clean, untouched,
unexploited, untapped, unemployed, idle
2 UNACCUSTOMED, unacquainted, unfamiliar,
unpractised, inexperienced
formal unwonted
E≡ 1, 2 used

unusual *adj*
uncommon, rare, unfamiliar, strange, odd, curious,
queer, bizarre, weird, unconventional, unorthodox,
irregular, abnormal, atypical, phenomenal,
extraordinary, out of the ordinary, remarkable, special,

exceptional, different, anomalous, surprising, unexpected, unprecedented
formal singular
colloq. offbeat
E≩ usual, normal, ordinary

unutterable *adj*
unspeakable, indescribable, unimaginable, extreme, overwhelming, ineffable
formal egregious, nefandous

unvarnished *adj*
unembellished, unadorned, straightforward, undisguised, simple, sincere, plain, candid, frank, bare, naked, honest, pure, sheer, stark
E≩ disguised, embellished, exaggerated

unveil *v*
uncover, expose, lay open, bare, lay bare, unmask, betray, reveal, disclose, divulge, bring to light, bring out into the open, make known, discover
colloq. take the lid off
E≩ cover, hide

unwanted *adj*
undesired, uninvited, unwelcome, outcast, rejected, unrequired, unneeded, unnecessary, surplus, extra, superfluous, redundant, useless
technical otiose
formal unsolicited
E≩ wanted, needed, necessary

unwarranted *adj*
unjustified, undeserved, unprovoked, uncalled-for, gratuitous, unnecessary, groundless, unreasonable, unjust, wrong, inexcusable, unjustifiable, indefensible
E≩ warranted, justifiable, deserved

unwary *adj*
unguarded, off guard, incautious, careless, indiscreet, thoughtless, unthinking, heedless, reckless, rash, hasty
formal imprudent
E≩ wary, cautious

unwavering *adj*
unswerving, unshakable, unfaltering, undeviating, unshaken, untiring, unflagging, unquestioning, staunch, steadfast, steady, sturdy, dedicated, consistent, determined, resolute, single-minded, tenacious
E≩ wavering, fickle

unwelcome *adj*
1 UNWANTED, undesirable, unpopular, uninvited, excluded, rejected
2 *unwelcome news*
unpleasant, disagreeable, upsetting, worrying, distasteful, unpalatable, unacceptable
E≩ 1 welcome, desirable 2 pleasant

unwell *adj*
ill, sick, poorly, off-colour, ailing, sickly, unhealthy, unfit
formal indisposed, debilitated
colloq. in a bad way, dicky, out of sorts, under the weather, run down, rough, groggy, like death warmed up
E≩ well, healthy

unwholesome *adj*
unhealthy, bad, harmful, demoralizing, evil, wicked, immoral, degrading, depraving, corrupting, perverting, sickly, tainted, unhygienic, poisonous, insanitary, innutritious, pasty, noxious, wan, pale, pallid, anaemic

formal insalubrious, insalutary
colloq. junk
E≩ salubrious, wholesome

unwieldy *adj*
unmanageable, inconvenient, awkward, clumsy, ungainly, bulky, massive, hefty, hulking, weighty, ponderous, cumbersome
formal incommodious
E≩ handy, dainty

unwilling *adj*
reluctant, disinclined, hesitant, resistant, opposed, averse, loath, slow, unenthusiastic, grudging
formal indisposed, loathful
E≩ willing, enthusiastic

unwillingness *n*
reluctance, disinclination, hesitancy, slowness, lack of enthusiasm, backwardness
formal indisposition, loathfulness, nolition
E≩ enthusiasm, willingness

unwind *v*
1 UNROLL, unreel, unwrap, undo, uncoil, untwist, unravel, disentangle
2 RELAX, wind down, calm down
colloq. take it/things easy, let yourself go, make yourself at home, let your hair down, put your feet up, hang loose, cool it, chill out
E≩ 1 wind, roll

unwise *adj*
ill-advised, inadvisable, inexpedient, short-sighted, improvident, ill-considered, ill-judged, foolish, stupid, silly, senseless, thoughtless, indiscreet, foolhardy, irresponsible, rash, reckless
formal impolitic, imprudent, injudicious
E≩ wise, sensible; *formal* prudent

unwitting *adj*
1 UNAWARE, unknowing, unsuspecting, unthinking, unconscious, involuntary
2 INADVERTENT, accidental, chance, unintentional, unintended, unplanned
E≩ 1 knowing 2 conscious, deliberate

unwonted *adj*
unusual, uncommon, unfamiliar, unexpected, unheard-of, strange, rare, peculiar, infrequent, exceptional, extraordinary, unaccustomed, uncustomary, atypical
formal singular
E≩ wonted, usual

unworldly *adj*
1 NAÏVE, visionary, idealistic, impractical, unsophisticated, inexperienced, innocent, gullible, ingenuous
colloq. green
2 SPIRITUAL, transcendental, metaphysical, otherworldly, extra-terrestrial
E≩ 1 sophisticated, worldly 2 worldly, materialistic

unworried *adj*
untroubled, undismayed, unruffled, unabashed, composed, collected
formal unperturbed
E≩ worried, anxious

unworthy *adj*
undeserving, inferior, ineligible, unsuitable, inappropriate, unfitting, improper, unprofessional, shameful, disgraceful, dishonourable, disreputable, discreditable, ignoble, base, contemptible, despicable

formal unbecoming, unseemly, unbefitting, incongruous
E3 worthy, commendable

unwritten *adj*
verbal, oral, word-of-mouth, unrecorded, tacit, implicit, understood, accepted, recognized, traditional, customary, conventional
E3 written, recorded

unyielding *adj*
unrelenting, uncompromising, relentless, unwavering, unbending, immovable, inflexible, hard-line, adamant, steadfast, stubborn, obstinate, tough, firm, determined, resolute, staunch, rigid, solid
formal implacable, inexorable, intractable, intransigent, obdurate
E3 yielding, flexible

up-and-coming *adj*
promising, ambitious, eager, assertive, enterprising
colloq. go-getting, pushing

upbeat *adj*
positive, buoyant, hopeful, optimistic, encouraging, favourable, promising, forward-looking, bright, cheerful, heartening, cheery, rosy
colloq. bullish
E3 downbeat, gloomy

upbraid *v*
reprimand, admonish, rebuke, reprove, reproach, scold, chide, criticize, censure
formal castigate, berate
E3 praise, commend

upbringing *n*
bringing-up, raising, rearing, breeding, parenting, care, nurture, cultivation, tending, education, training, instruction, teaching

update *v*
modernize, revise, amend, correct, renew, renovate, revamp, upgrade

upgrade *v*
improve, make better, better, modernize, enhance, promote, advance, elevate, raise
formal ameliorate
E3 downgrade, demote

upheaval *n*
disruption, disturbance, upset, chaos, confusion, disorder, turmoil, revolution, overthrow
colloq. shake-up

uphill *adj*
hard, difficult, arduous, tough, taxing, strenuous, laborious, tiring, wearisome, exhausting, gruelling, punishing, burdensome, onerous
E3 easy, downhill

uphold *v*
support, maintain, confirm, keep, hold to, stand by, defend, champion, advocate, promote, back, endorse, sustain, strengthen, justify, vindicate
formal fortify
E3 abandon, reject

upkeep *n*
1 MAINTENANCE, preservation, conservation, care, running, repair, support, sustenance, subsistence, keep
2 RUNNING COSTS, expenditure, outlay, overheads, operating costs, oncosts, expenses
E3 1 neglect

uplift *v, n*
▶ *v* improve, better, boost, upgrade, advance, enlighten, exalt, inspire, elate, lift, elevate, raise, hoist, heave, refine, cultivate, edify, civilize
formal ameliorate
▶ *n* improvement, lift, enlightenment, enrichment, advancement, enhancement, refinement, edification, boost, cultivation
formal betterment

upper *adj*
higher, loftier, superior, greater, senior, top, topmost, uppermost, high, elevated, exalted, eminent, important
E3 lower, inferior, junior
▷ **upper hand** advantage, dominance, control, sway, supremacy, superiority, mastery, domination, dominion; *formal* ascendancy; *colloq.* edge

upper-class *adj*
aristocratic, noble, well-bred, well-born, high-born, high-class, patrician, blue-blooded, exclusive, elite
colloq. swanky, top-drawer
E3 humble, working-class

uppermost *adj*
highest, loftiest, top, topmost, greatest, supreme, first, primary, foremost, leading, principal, main, major, chief, dominant, predominant, paramount, pre-eminent
E3 lowest

uppity *adj*
arrogant, self-important, conceited, presumptuous, snobbish, supercilious, impertinent, affected, assuming, big-headed, overweening, bumptious, cocky
colloq. hoity-toity, stuck-up, swanky, toffee-nosed
E3 unassertive, diffident

upright *adj*
1 VERTICAL, perpendicular, erect, straight, at right angles, sheer, steep
2 RIGHTEOUS, good, virtuous, upstanding, noble, worthy, decent, respectable, reputable, honourable, moral, ethical, principled, high-minded, incorruptible, honest, trustworthy
E3 1 horizontal, flat 2 dishonest

uprising *n*
rebellion, revolt, mutiny, rising, overthrow, insurgence, insurrection, revolution, *coup d'état*, putsch

uproar *n*
noise, din, racket, hubbub, hullabaloo, brouhaha, pandemonium, tumult, turmoil, turbulence, commotion, confusion, disorder, mayhem, bedlam, clamour, outcry, furore, riot, rumpus, fracas, ruction

uproarious *adj*
hilarious, riotous, rip-roaring, side-splitting, hysterical, boisterous, noisy, loud, rollicking, rowdy, confused, clamorous, deafening, wild, unrestrained
colloq. killing, rib-tickling
E3 quiet

uproot *v*
pull up, rip up, root out, weed out, remove, displace, eradicate, destroy, wipe out

upset *v, n, adj*
▶ *v* 1 DISTRESS, grieve, dismay, trouble, worry, agitate, disturb, hurt, bother, fluster, ruffle, sadden, discompose, shake (up), unnerve, disconcert, put out, confuse, disorganize

formal perturb
2 TIP, spill, overturn, capsize, topple, knock over, overthrow, destabilize, unsteady
▶ *n* **1** TROUBLE, worry, agitation, distress, disturbance, bother, disruption, upheaval, reverse, surprise, shock
formal perturbation
colloq. shake-up
2 *stomach upset*
disorder, complaint, illness, sickness, ailment
formal malady
colloq. bug
▶ *adj* distressed, grieved, hurt, annoyed, dismayed, troubled, worried, agitated, disturbed, unsettled, discomposed, put out, flustered, bothered, shaken, disconcerted, confused
formal perturbed
colloq. in a state, het up, uptight, worked up

upshot *n*
result, consequence, outcome, issue, end, conclusion, finish, culmination, dénouement
colloq. pay-off

upside down
inverted, upturned, up-ended, wrong way up, wrong side up, upset, overturned, disordered, muddled, jumbled, confused, topsy-turvy, chaotic
colloq. messed up

upstanding *adj*
upright, honest, honourable, strong, true, trustworthy, ethical, moral, principled, incorruptible, erect, good, virtuous, firm, four-square
F3 untrustworthy

upstart *n*
social climber, arriviste, parvenu, parvenue, *nouveau riche*, nobody

uptight *adj*
edgy, tense, uneasy, anxious, hung-up, irritated, nervy
colloq. prickly, on edge
F3 calm, cool, relaxed

up-to-date *adj*
current, contemporary, modern, present-day, fashionable, in fashion, prevalent, latest, recent, new
colloq. trendy, in, all the rage, cool, state-of-the-art
F3 out-of-date, old-fashioned

upturn *n*
revival, recovery, upsurge, upswing, rise, increase, boost, improvement, betterment
formal amelioration
F3 downturn, drop

urban *adj*
town, city, inner-city, metropolitan, municipal, civic, built-up
formal oppidan
F3 country, rural

⚠ **urban** or **urbane** ?
Urban means 'of a town': *urban development; urban life; urban violence. Urbane* means 'cultured, elegant, refined': *urbane wit.*

urbane *adj*
cultivated, suave, sophisticated, refined, polished, mannerly, civilized, courteous, cultured, debonair, well-bred, well-mannered, civil, elegant, smooth
F3 gauche, uncouth

⚠ **urbane** or **urban** ? *See panel at* **urban**.

urbanity *n*
refinement, cultivation, sophistication, suavity, mannerliness, polish, ease, smoothness, grace, elegance, culture, civility, courtesy, charm, worldliness
old use eutrapelia
F3 awkwardness, gaucheness

urchin *n*
brat, guttersnipe, ragamuffin, waif, gamin, street Arab, kid

urge *v, n*
▶ *v* **1** PERSUADE, encourage, press, push, incite, drive, impel, prod, goad, spur, constrain, compel, force, hasten, induce, instigate, stimulate
colloq. egg on
2 BEG, entreat, appeal, implore, plead
formal beseech
3 ADVISE, counsel, recommend, advocate, encourage
formal exhort
F3 **1** discourage, dissuade, deter, hinder
▶ *n* desire, wish, inclination, fancy, longing, yearning, impulse, compulsion, need, impetus, drive, eagerness
colloq. itch, yen
F3 disinclination

urgency *n*
hurry, haste, pressure, stress, priority, importance, seriousness, extremity, gravity, imperativeness, need, necessity
formal exigency, importunity

urgent *adj*
1 PRESSING, immediate, instant, top-priority, important, critical, necessary, vital, essential, crucial, imperative
formal exigent
2 COMPELLING, persuasive, earnest, serious, grave, eager, insistent, persistent
F3 **1** unimportant

urinate *v*
pass water, relieve yourself
formal micturate
colloq. leak, pee, piddle, spend a penny, tinkle, wee; *slang* piss

usable *adj*
working, operational, serviceable, functional, fit to use, practical, exploitable, available, current, valid
F3 unusable, useless

usage *n*
1 TREATMENT, handling, management, control, running, operation, employment, application, use
2 TRADITION, custom, practice, habit, convention, etiquette, rule, regulation, form, routine, procedure, way, method
formal mode

use *v, n*
▶ *v* **1** UTILIZE, employ, make use of, exercise, service, practise, operate, work, apply, ply, wield, handle, deal with, treat, manoeuvre, enjoy, resort to, draw on, take advantage of, bring into play, make use of, put to use
2 EXPLOIT, manipulate, take advantage of, impose on, misuse, abuse, take liberties with
colloq. cash in on, bleed, milk, wrap/twist someone

round your little finger

3 CONSUME, exhaust, get through, go through, expend, spend, waste

▷ **use up** finish, exhaust, drain, sap, deplete, consume, devour, absorb, waste, squander, fritter

▷ **used to** accustomed to, adjusted to, in the habit of, familiar with, acclimatized to, given to, prone to; *formal* habituated to, inured to, wont to; *colloq.* at home with, no stranger to

▶ *n* **1** USAGE, application, employment, operation, exercise, utilization, manipulation, exploitation

2 USEFULNESS, value, worth, profit, service, advantage, benefit, good, avail, help, point, object, end, purpose

3 *have the use of the car* right, permission, privilege, ability

4 EXPLOITATION, manipulation, imposition, misuse, abuse

5 NEED, cause, occasion, necessity, demand, call

used *adj*
second-hand, cast-off, hand-me-down, nearly new, worn, dog-eared, soiled
F∃ unused, new, fresh

useful *adj*
1 CONVENIENT, handy, all-purpose, practical, effective, productive, fruitful, profitable, valuable, worthwhile, rewarding, advantageous, beneficial, helpful, functional, general-purpose
colloq. nifty
2 SKILLED, proficient, practised, experienced, expert, able, skilful, handy
F∃ 1 useless, ineffective, worthless

usefulness *n*
utility, use, value, worth, profit, advantage, benefit, good, help, avail, service, convenience, practicality, efficiency, fitness, serviceableness
formal efficacy

useless *adj*
1 FUTILE, fruitless, unproductive, vain, idle, unavailing, to no avail, hopeless, unhelpful, pointless, worthless, unusable, unprofitable, broken-down, unworkable, impractical
formal ineffectual, inefficacious
colloq. clapped-out
2 INCOMPETENT, ineffective, incapable, inefficient, bad, weak
colloq. hopeless
F∃ 1 useful, helpful, effective **2** good

uselessness *n*
futility, hopelessness, impracticality, incompetence, ineffectiveness, ineptitude, idleness
formal ineffectuality, inutility
F∃ effectiveness, usefulness

usher *n, v*
▶ *n* usherette, doorkeeper, attendant, escort, guide
▶ *v* escort, accompany, conduct, lead, direct, guide, show, pilot, steer
▷ **usher in** herald, inaugurate, initiate, introduce, launch, precede, announce, ring in, pave the way for

usual *adj*
normal, typical, stock, standard, regular, routine, habitual, customary, conventional, traditional, orthodox, accepted, recognized, accustomed, established, familiar, common, everyday, general, ordinary, average, unexceptional, expected, predictable

formal wonted
F∃ unusual, strange, rare

usually *adv*
normally, generally, as a rule, ordinarily, typically, traditionally, regularly, routinely, commonly, by and large, on the whole, mainly, chiefly, mostly, for the most part, on average, in the main
colloq. nine times out of ten
F∃ exceptionally

usurer *n*
extortionist, money-lender, Shylock
colloq. loan-shark

usurp *v*
take over, assume, arrogate, seize, take, take possession of, annex, appropriate, commandeer, steal

usury *n*
money-lending, extortion, interest

utensil *n*
tool, implement, instrument, device, contrivance, gadget, apparatus, appliance

utilitarian *adj*
functional, practical, convenient, serviceable, sensible, useful, unpretentious, effective, efficient, pragmatic, down-to-earth, lowly
F∃ decorative, impractical

utility *n*
usefulness, use, value, worth, profit, advantage, benefit, good, help, avail, service, convenience, practicality, efficiency, fitness, serviceableness
formal efficacy

utilize *v*
use, employ, make use of, put to use, resort to, take advantage of, turn to account, exploit, adapt

utmost *adj, n*
▶ *adj* **1** *with the utmost care* extreme, maximum, most, greatest, highest, supreme, paramount
2 FARTHEST, furthest, furthermost, remotest, outermost, ultimate, final, last
▶ *n* best, hardest, most, maximum, top, peak

Utopia *n*
paradise, Eden, Garden of Eden, bliss, Elysium, heaven, heaven on earth, Shangri-la
colloq. seventh heaven

Utopian *adj*
ideal, idealistic, illusory, imaginary, perfect, visionary, wishful, fanciful, fantastic, airy, dream, romantic, unworkable, impractical, Elysian
formal chimerical

utter¹ *v*
not utter a word
speak, say, voice, vocalize, verbalize, put into words, express, articulate, enunciate, sound, pronounce, deliver, state, declare, announce, proclaim, tell, reveal, divulge

utter² *adj*
to my utter amazement
absolute, complete, total, entire, thoroughgoing, thorough, out-and-out, downright, sheer, stark, arrant, unmitigated, unqualified, positive, categorical, perfect, consummate

utterance *n*
statement, remark, comment, opinion, expression, word, articulation, delivery, speech, declaration, announcement, proclamation, pronouncement, enunciation

utterly *adv*
absolutely, completely, totally, fully, entirely, wholly, thoroughly, downright, perfectly, categorically

U-turn *n*
about-turn, volte-face, reversal, backtrack

V

vacancy *n*
opportunity, opening, position, post, job, place, room, situation

vacant *adj*
1 EMPTY, unoccupied, unfilled, free, available, void, not in use, unused, deserted, abandoned, uninhabited
2 BLANK, expressionless, vacuous, inane, poker-faced, straight-faced, deadpan, impassive, inattentive, absent, absent-minded, unthinking, dreamy
F∃ 1 occupied, engaged, in use, busy

vacate *v*
leave, depart, evacuate, abandon, withdraw
colloq. quit

vacation *n*
holiday, trip, leave, leave of absence, time off, break, rest, recess, furlough

vacillate *v*
waver, hesitate, fluctuate, shilly-shally, sway, oscillate, keep changing your mind, haver, temporize
formal tergiversate

vacillating *adj*
wavering, hesitant, irresolute, uncertain, unresolved, shilly-shallying, shuffling, oscillating
F∃ resolute, unhesitating

vacillation *n*
wavering, inconstancy, hesitancy, hesitation, fluctuation, irresolution, shilly-shallying, indecision, indecisiveness, unsteadiness, temporization
formal tergiversation

vacuity *n*
emptiness, space, nothingness, blankness, vacuousness, vacuum, void, apathy, inanity, incomprehension, incuriosity
formal incognizance

vacuous *adj*
empty, blank, vacant, void, unfilled, inane, unintelligent, stupid, uncomprehending, incurious, apathetic, idle

vacuum *n*
emptiness, void, nothingness, hollowness, vacuity, space, chasm, gap
formal lacuna

vagabond *n*
vagrant, tramp, wanderer, wayfarer, down-and-out, hobo, rascal, beggar, rover, runabout, itinerant, migrant, outcast, nomad
slang bum

vagary *n*
fancy, notion, prank, quirk, whim, whimsy, humour, crotchet
Scot. megrim
formal caprice

vagrancy *n*
wandering, travelling, shiftlessness, rootlessness, unsettledness, nomadism, itinerancy, homelessness

vagrant *n, adj*
▶ *n* tramp, wanderer, drifter, itinerant, stroller, hobo, beggar
Scot. gangrel
colloq. rolling stone; *slang* bum
▶ *adj* wandering, vagabond, travelling, shiftless, rootless, unsettled, roaming, roving, nomadic, itinerant, homeless

vague *adj*
1 ILL-DEFINED, blurred, unfocused, out of focus, indistinct, hazy, dim, faint, shadowy, foggy, misty, fuzzy, nebulous, obscure
formal amorphous
2 INDEFINITE, imprecise, unclear, unsure, uncertain, undefined, undetermined, unspecific, unspecified, rough, approximate, generalized, inexact, ambiguous, evasive, loose, lax, woolly
formal indeterminate
F∃ 1 clear 2 definite, precise, specific

vaguely *adv*
slightly, imprecisely, faintly, dimly, inexactly, obscurely, vacantly, absent-mindedly

vagueness *n*
unclearness, fuzziness, haziness, uncertainty, dimness, faintness, obscurity, imprecision, looseness, ambiguity, inexactitude, woolliness
formal amorphousness
F∃ clarity, precision

vain *adj*
1 *a vain attempt*
useless, worthless, futile, fruitless, pointless, unproductive, unprofitable, unavailing, hollow, groundless, empty, idle, trivial, insubstantial, unimportant, insignificant
formal abortive, nugatory
2 CONCEITED, proud, haughty, self-satisfied, arrogant, self-important, self-conceited, self-glorious, egotistical, affected, pretentious, ostentatious, swaggering, narcissistic, peacockish
colloq. big-headed, swollen-headed, stuck-up, snooty, high and mighty
F∃ 1 fruitful, successful 2 modest, self-effacing
▷ **in vain** to no avail, unsuccessfully, uselessly, fruitlessly, vainly; *formal* ineffectually
F∃ successfully

valediction *n*
goodbye, farewell, leave-taking, adieu
colloq. send-off
⊟ welcome, greeting

valedictory *adj*
farewell, parting, departing, final, last

valet *n*
manservant, man, gentleman's gentleman, body
servant, *valet de chambre*

valetudinarian *adj*
sickly, invalid, infirm, weakly, feeble, frail, delicate,
hypochondriac, neurotic

valiant *adj*
brave, courageous, gallant, fearless, intrepid, bold,
dauntless, audacious, heroic, plucky, staunch, stout-
hearted, lion-hearted
formal indomitable, valorous
⊟ cowardly, fearful, dismayed

valid *adj*
1 LOGICAL, well-founded, well-grounded,
reasonable, justifiable, sound, good, convincing,
telling, conclusive, credible, reliable, substantial,
forceful, weighty, powerful, just
formal cogent
2 OFFICIAL, legal, lawful, legitimate, authentic,
effective, bona fide, genuine, binding, contractual,
proper
⊟ 1 false, weak 2 unofficial, invalid

validate *v*
confirm, authenticate, endorse, legalize, authorize,
substantiate, underwrite, ratify, certify
formal attest, corroborate

validity *n*
soundness, legality, lawfulness, legitimacy, foundation,
grounds, justifiability, strength, power, force, weight,
substance, logic, point, authority
formal cogency
⊟ invalidity

valley *n*
dale, vale, dell, glen, hollow, cwm, depression, slade,
gulch
Scot. strath

valorous *adj*
brave, bold, heroic, courageous, fearless, plucky, lion-
hearted, stout-hearted, valiant, intrepid, gallant,
hardy, mettlesome, dauntless, doughty, stalwart
⊟ cowardly, weak

valour *n*
boldness, courage, bravery, heroism, intrepidity, lion-
heartedness, fearlessness, mettle, spirit, gallantry,
hardiness, doughtiness
formal fortitude
⊟ cowardice, weakness

valuable *adj*
1 *valuable necklace*
precious, prized, valued, costly, expensive, dear, high-
priced, treasured, cherished, priceless, estimable
colloq. worth a pretty penny, worth its weight in gold
2 *valuable suggestions*
helpful, worthwhile, useful, beneficial, invaluable,
constructive, fruitful, profitable, advantageous,
important, serviceable, worthy, handy
⊟ 1 worthless 2 useless

valuation *n*
evaluation, assessment, estimate, computation, survey
formal appraisement

value *n, v*
▶ *n* 1 COST, price, rate, worth
2 WORTH, use, usefulness, utility, merit, importance,
desirability, benefit, advantage, significance, good,
profit, gain, avail
3 *moral values*
morals, principles, moral, principles, standards, ethics
▶ *v* 1 PRIZE, appreciate, treasure, hold dear, admire,
respect, cherish, set great store by
formal esteem
2 EVALUATE, assess, estimate, price, put a price on,
survey, rate
formal appraise
⊟ 1 disregard, neglect 2 undervalue

valued *adj*
highly regarded, cherished, treasured, prized,
respected, dear, loved, beloved
formal esteemed

van *n*
lorry, truck, wagon, trailer, carriage

vanguard *n*
forefront, most advanced part, front, front line, firing
line, spearhead, lead, fore, leading/foremost position

vanish *v*
disappear, fade, fade away/out, dissolve, evaporate,
disperse, melt (away), die out, leave, depart, exit, fizzle
out, peter out
formal evanesce
⊟ appear, materialize

vanity *n*
1 CONCEIT, conceitedness, pride, arrogance,
haughtiness, self-conceit, self-love, self-satisfaction,
self-glorification, narcissism, egotism, pretension,
ostentation, affectation, airs
colloq. big-headedness, swollen-headedness,
snootiness
2 WORTHLESSNESS, uselessness, emptiness, futility,
pointlessness, unreality, unproductiveness,
unprofitableness, hollowness, fruitlessness, triviality,
idleness, unimportance, insignificance
⊟ 1 modesty, worth

vanquish *v*
defeat, conquer, beat, triumph over, overcome,
overpower, overwhelm, subdue, humble, master,
repress, quell, confound, crush, rout
formal subjugate
colloq. hammer, slaughter, clobber, wipe the floor with

vapid *adj*
vacuous, uninteresting, lifeless, dead, banal, bland,
boring, dull, tedious, flat, insipid, limp, stale, tame,
flavourless, tasteless, watery, wishy-washy, colourless,
tiresome, trite, weak, uninspiring
old use jejune
⊟ interesting, vigorous

vaporous *adj*
1 STEAMY, misty, gaseous, fumy, fumous, foggy
2 FANCIFUL, flimsy, insubstantial, vain
formal chimerical
⊟ 2 substantial

vapour *n*
steam, mist, fog, smoke, breath, fumes, haze, damp,
dampness, exhalation

variable *adj, n*
▶ *adj* changeable, inconstant, varying, shifting, mutable, unpredictable, fluctuating, fitful, unstable, unsteady, uneven, wavering, vacillating, temperamental, fickle, flexible
formal chameleonic, protean
E3 fixed, invariable, stable
▶ *n* factor, parameter

variance *n*
1 VARIATION, difference, discrepancy, divergence, inconsistency, disagreement
2 DISAGREEMENT, disharmony, conflict, discord, division, dissent, dissension, quarrelling, opposition, strife, odds
E3 1 agreement 2 agreement, harmony

variant *n, adj*
▶ *n* alternative, variation, modification, development, deviant, rogue
▶ *adj* alternative, different, divergent, modified, derived, deviant, exceptional
E3 normal, standard, usual

variation *n*
diversity, variety, deviation, discrepancy, diversification, alteration, change, difference, vacillation, fluctuation, departure, modification, modulation, inflection, novelty, innovation
E3 monotony, uniformity

varied *adj*
assorted, diverse, miscellaneous, mixed, various, sundry, motley, different, wide-ranging
formal heterogeneous, multifarious
E3 standardized, uniform

variegated *adj*
multicoloured, many-coloured, parti-coloured, varicoloured, speckled, mottled, dappled, pied, streaked, marbled, jaspe, motley
technical poikilitic
E3 monochrome, plain

variety *n*
1 ASSORTMENT, miscellany, mixture, collection, medley, pot-pourri, range
2 DIVERSITY, difference, dissimilarity, discrepancy, variation
formal multiplicity, multifariousness
3 SORT, kind, class, category, species, type, breed, brand, make, strain, classification
E3 2 uniformity; *formal* similitude

various *adj*
different, differing, dissimilar, unlike, diverse, varied, varying, assorted, miscellaneous, distinct, diversified, mixed, many, several, motley
formal heterogeneous, disparate, variegated

varnish *n, v*
▶ *n* lacquer, lac, glaze, enamel, shellac, resin, polish, gloss, coating, veneer, japan
▶ *v* lacquer, glaze, enamel, shellac, polish, gloss, coat, veneer, japan

vary *v*
1 CHANGE, alter, modify, modulate, diversify, reorder, transform, alternate, inflect, permutate
formal metamorphose
2 DIFFER, diverge, disagree, depart, fluctuate, be dissimilar, clash, be in conflict, be at odds

vase *n*
container, jar, jug, pitcher, urn, vessel, ewer, amphora, hydria

vassal *n*
serf, slave, subject, thrall, bondman, bondsman, bondservant, retainer, villein, liege, liegeman

vassalage *n*
dependence, bondage, servitude, slavery, subjection, serfdom, thraldom, villeinage
formal subjugation

vast *adj*
huge, immense, massive, gigantic, enormous, great, colossal, bulky, extensive, tremendous, sweeping, extensive, unlimited, fathomless, limitless, boundless, immeasurable, never-ending, monumental, monstrous, far-flung
formal prodigious

vat *n*
barrel, tank, tub, container, kier, keeve

vault¹ *v*
vault over the wall
leap, spring, bound, clear, jump, hurdle, leap-frog

vault² *n*
1 CELLAR, crypt, strongroom, repository, cavern, depository, wine-cellar, underground chamber, basement, tomb, mausoleum
2 ARCH, roof, span, concave

vaunt *v*
boast, brag, exult in, flaunt, parade, trumpet, crow
colloq. show off, swank, blow your own trumpet;
US blow your own horn
E3 belittle, minimize

veer *v*
swerve, swing, change, shift, diverge, deviate, wheel, turn, sheer, tack

vegetable *n*

Vegetables include: artichoke, asparagus, aubergine, bean, beetroot, broad bean, broccoli, Brussels sprout, butter bean, cabbage, calabrese, capsicum, carrot, cauliflower, celeriac, celery, chicory, courgette, cress, cucumber, *US* eggplant, endive, fennel, French bean, garlic, kale, leek, lentil, lettuce, mange tout, marrow, mushroom, okra, onion, parsnip, pea, pepper, petit pois, potato, *colloq.* spud, pumpkin, radish, runner bean, shallot, soya bean, spinach, spring onion, swede, sweetcorn, sweet-potato, turnip, watercress, yam, *US* zucchini.

Vegetable dishes include: aubergine roll, baba ganoush, bhaji, onion bhaji, bubble and squeak, cauliflower cheese, champ, chillada, colcannon, coleslaw, couscous, crudités, dal, dolma, duchesse potatoes, fasolia, felafel, fondue, gado-gado, gnocchi, guacamole, gumbo, hummus, imam bayildi, latke, macaroni cheese, macedoine, mushy peas, nut cutlet, paella, pakora, pease pudding, peperonata, pilau, pissaladière, polenta, ratatouille, raita, risotto, rosti; salad, caesar salad, green salad, hot salad, mixed salad, salad nicoise, Waldorf salad, winter salad; sauerkraut, stovies, stuffed marrow, stuffed mushroom, succotash, tabbouleh, tahina, tsatsiki, vegetable chilli, vegetable curry, vegetable soup, vegetarian goulash, vichyssoise.

vegetate *v*
stagnate, degenerate, deteriorate, rusticate, go to seed, idle, rust, languish, moulder, do nothing

vegetation *n*
plants, trees, flowers, flora, green plants, greenery
formal herbage, verdure

vehemence *n*
passion, energy, enthusiasm, keenness, fervency, eagerness, earnestness, emphasis, strength, power, animation, intensity, zeal, verve, vigour, ardour, fervour, force, forcefulness, urgency, impetuosity, violence, warmth, heat, fire
F3 indifference

vehement *adj*
impassioned, passionate, ardent, fervent, intense, forceful, emphatic, heated, strong, powerful, spirited, vigorous, urgent, enthusiastic, animated, eager, keen, earnest, forcible, fierce, violent, zealous
formal fervid
F3 apathetic, indifferent

vehicle *n*
1 CONVEYANCE, transport

Vehicles include: plane, boat, ship, car, taxi, hackney-carriage; bicycle, *colloq.* bike, cycle, tandem, tricycle, *colloq.* boneshaker, penny-farthing, motor-cycle, motor-bike, scooter; bus, omnibus, minibus, *colloq.* double-decker, coach, charabanc, caravan, caravanette, camper; train, Pullman, sleeper, wagon-lit, tube, tram, monorail, maglev, trolleybus; van, Transit®, lorry, truck, juggernaut, pantechnicon, trailer, tractor, fork-lift truck, steam-roller, tank, wagon; bobsleigh, sled, sledge, sleigh, toboggan, troika; barouche, brougham, dog-cart, dray, four-in-hand, gig, hansom, landau, phaeton, post-chaise, stagecoach, sulky, surrey, trap; rickshaw, sedan-chair, litter. *See also* **aircraft; boats and ships; car**.

2 MEANS, agency, channel, medium, mechanism, instrument, organ

veil *v, n*
▶ *v* screen, cloak, cover (up), mask, mantle, blanket, shadow, shield, obscure, conceal, hide, shroud, disguise, shade, camouflage
F3 expose, uncover
▶ *n* cover, covering, cloak, curtain, mask, mantle, blanket, screen, disguise, film, blind, shade, canopy, shroud, purdah

vein *n*
1 STREAK, stripe, stratum, seam, lode, blood vessel

Veins and arteries include: aorta, axillary, brachial, carotid, femoral, frontal, gastric, hepatic, iliac, jugular, portal, pulmonary, radial, renal, saphena, subclavian, superior, temporal, tibial.
Related adjective: venous

2 MOOD, tendency, bent, strain, streak, temper, tenor, tone, frame of mind, humour, mode, style, disposition, temperament, attitude, inclination

veined *adj*
streaked, variegated, marbled, mottled, jaspe

velocity *n*
speed, rate, quickness, rapidity, pace, impetus, swiftness
old use fleetness
formal celerity

venal *adj*
corrupt, corruptible, bribable, mercenary, grafting, simoniacal
colloq. bent, buyable
F3 incorruptible

vendetta *n*
feud, blood-feud, enmity, rivalry, quarrel, bad blood, bitterness

vendor *n*
seller, trader, salesperson, merchant, supplier, stockist
See panel at **seller**.

veneer *n*
1 FAÇADE, front, appearance, display, show, mask, gloss, camouflage, pretence, guise
2 LAYER, coating, surface, finish, gloss, covering

venerable *adj*
respected, revered, honoured, venerated, dignified, grave, wise, august, aged, worshipped
formal esteemed, hallowed

venerate *v*
revere, respect, honour, worship, adore
formal esteem, hallow
F3 despise, anathematize

veneration *n*
respect, reverence, deference, adoration, awe, worship, devotion
formal esteem

vengeance *n*
retribution, revenge, retaliation, reprisal, requital
colloq. tit for tat, an eye for an eye and a tooth for a tooth
F3 forgiveness
▷ **with a vengeance 1** FORCEFULLY, violently, vigorously, powerfully, energetically, furiously; *colloq.* flat out, like crazy **2** TO A GREAT DEGREE, greatly, to a great extent, fully, to the full, to the utmost; *colloq.* with no holds barred

vengeful *adj*
spiteful, unforgiving, vindictive, avenging, revengeful, retaliatory, relentless, retributive, punitive, implacable
formal rancorous
F3 forgiving

venial *adj*
forgivable, excusable, pardonable, slight, minor, insignificant, trivial, trifling, negligible
F3 mortal, unforgivable, unpardonable

venom *n*
1 POISON, toxin
2 RANCOUR, ill-will, malice, vindictiveness, spite, bitterness, resentment, hate, enmity, hostility, animosity, virulence
formal malevolence, acrimony

venomous *adj*
1 POISONOUS, toxic, lethal, deadly, fatal, virulent, harmful
formal noxious
2 MALICIOUS, spiteful, vicious, vindictive, bitter, resentful, baleful, hostile, malignant, baneful
formal rancorous, malevolent
F3 1 harmless

vent *n, v*
▶ *n* opening, hole, aperture, outlet, gap, passage, orifice, duct

▶ *v* air, express, voice, utter, release, discharge, emit, let out, pour out

ventilate *v*
1 *ventilate a room*
air, aerate, freshen, cool
2 *ventilate your feelings*
express, air, broadcast, debate, discuss, bring out into the open

venture *v, n*
▶ *v* 1 DARE, advance, go, make bold, put forward, presume, suggest, volunteer
2 RISK, hazard, chance, endanger, imperil, jeopardize, put in jeopardy, speculate, gamble, wager, stake
▶ *n* risk, chance, hazard, speculation, gamble, undertaking, project, adventure, exploit, endeavour, enterprise, operation, fling

venturesome *adj*
adventurous, enterprising, courageous, bold, brave, daring, fearless, intrepid, spirited, plucky, audacious, dauntless, doughty
colloq. daredevil
E3 unenterprising, cowardly

veracious *adj*
truthful, true, trustworthy, genuine, frank, honest, reliable, credible, dependable, straightforward, exact, factual, faithful, accurate
E3 untruthful

veracity *n*
truthfulness, truth, trustworthiness, integrity, honesty, frankness, precision, accuracy, candour, credibility, exactitude
formal probity, rectitude
E3 untruthfulness

verbal *adj*
spoken, oral, said, uttered, vocal, linguistic, verbatim, unwritten, word-of-mouth
E3 written

verbatim *adv*
word for word, exactly, literally, to the letter, precisely, closely

verbiage *n*
repetition, verbosity, waffle
formal circumlocution, pleonasm, periphrasis, prolixity
E3 succinctness, briefness

verbose *adj*
long-winded, wordy, windy, garrulous, diffuse
formal prolix, loquacious, circumlocutory, periphrastic, pleonastic
E3 succinct, brief

verbosity *n*
verboseness, windiness, wordiness, long-windedness, garrulity, logorrhoea, verbiage
formal loquaciousness, loquacity, multiloquy, prolixity
E3 economy, succinctness

verdant *adj*
lush, green, grassy, fresh, leafy
formal viridescent, virid, graminaceous, gramineous

verdict *n*
decision, judgement, conclusion, finding, adjudication, assessment, opinion, ruling, sentence

verdure *n*
grass, greenery, greenness, herbage, foliage, leafage,

pasture, meadows
formal verdancy, viridity, viridescence

verge *n, v*
▶ *n* border, edge, margin, limit, rim, brim, brink, boundary, threshold, brink, extreme, extremity, edging
▶ *v* ▷ **verge on** approach, border on, come close to, near, tend towards

verification *n*
confirmation, checking, proof, substantiation, validation, authentication
formal attestation, corroboration

verify *v*
confirm, substantiate, authenticate, bear out, prove, support, endorse, validate, testify
formal corroborate, attest, accredit
E3 invalidate, discredit

verisimilitude *n*
authenticity, credibility, resemblance, realism, likeliness, plausibility, semblance, colour
colloq. ring of truth
E3 implausibility

verity *n*
truth, truthfulness, validity, factuality, actuality, authenticity, soundness
formal veracity
E3 untruth

vernacular *adj, n*
▶ *adj* indigenous, local, native, popular, vulgar, informal, colloquial, common
▶ *n* language, speech, tongue, parlance, dialect, idiom, cant, jargon
colloq. lingo

versatile *adj*
adaptable, flexible, all-round, all-purpose, multipurpose, multifaceted, adjustable, many-sided, general-purpose, functional, resourceful, handy, variable
E3 inflexible

verse *n*
poetry, rhyme, stanza, strophe, metre, doggerel, jingle
See panel at **pocm**.

versed *adj*
skilled, proficient, practised, experienced, familiar, acquainted, learned, read, knowledgeable, conversant, seasoned, qualified, competent, accomplished

versifier *n*
poet, poetess, poetaster, rhymer, rhymester, rhymist, verser, verse-maker, verse-monger, verse-smith, versificator, poeticule

version *n*
1 RENDERING, reading, interpretation, understanding, account, report, translation, paraphrase, adaptation, portrayal
2 TYPE, kind, variant, form, model, style, design, reproduction

vertex *n*
peak, top, apex, summit, height, highest point, pinnacle, culmination, crown, extremity
technical acme, apogee, zenith
E3 nadir

vertical *adj*
upright, perpendicular, straight up, upstanding, sheer, erect, on end
E3 horizontal

vertigo *n*
dizziness, giddiness, light-headedness, sickness
Related adjective: dinic

verve *n*
vitality, vivacity, animation, energy, dash, élan,
liveliness, sparkle, vigour, passion, fervour,
enthusiasm, gusto, life, relish, spirit, force, brio
colloq. pizzazz, zip
Ƒ apathy, lethargy

very *adv, adj*
▶ *adv* extremely, greatly, highly, deeply, truly,
remarkably, excessively, exceeding(ly), exceptionally,
acutely, particularly, really, quite, absolutely,
noticeably, unbelievably, incredibly, exceptionally,
unusually, uncommonly
colloq. pretty, terribly, dreadfully, awfully
Ƒ slightly, scarcely
▶ *adj* actual, real, same, selfsame, identical, true,
genuine, simple, utter, sheer, pure, perfect, ideal, plain,
mere, bare, exact, suitable, appropriate, fitting

vessel *n*
1 SHIP, boat, craft, barque
2 CONTAINER, bowl, receptacle, holder, jar, pot,
pitcher, jug

vest *v*
give, endow, supply, grant, empower, authorize,
sanction
formal bestow, confer

vestibule *n*
foyer, hall, entrance, entrance hall, entranceway, lobby,
porch, anteroom, portico

vestige *n*
trace, suspicion, touch, indication, sign, mark, track,
impression, print, hint, evidence, inkling, glimmer,
token, scrap, remains, remainder, remnant, residue,
relics
colloq. whiff

vestigial *adj*
remaining, surviving, rudimentary, undeveloped,
imperfect, incomplete, reduced, functionless

vet *v*
investigate, examine, check (out), scrutinize, scan,
inspect, survey, review, audit
formal appraise

veteran *n, adj*
▶ *v* master, pastmaster, old hand, old stager, old-
timer, warhorse
colloq. pro
Ƒ novice, recruit
▶ *adj* experienced, practised, seasoned, long-
serving, expert, adept, proficient, old, battle-scarred
Ƒ inexperienced

veto *v, n*
▶ *v* reject, turn down, forbid, ban, prohibit, rule out,
block
formal disallow, proscribe, interdict
colloq. give the thumbs-down to
Ƒ approve, sanction
▶ *n* rejection, ban, embargo, prohibition
formal proscription
colloq. thumbs-down
Ƒ approval, assent

vex *v*
irritate, annoy, provoke, pester, trouble, upset, worry,
bother, harass, disturb, distress, agitate, enrage,

exasperate, torment, fret
formal perturb
colloq. put out, hassle, aggravate, needle, bug, get
someone's blood up, get someone's back up
Ƒ calm, soothe

vexation *n*
annoyance, exasperation, displeasure, chagrin, anger,
fury, pique, dissatisfaction, frustration, nuisance,
misfortune, irritant, problem, trouble, upset, worry,
bother, difficulty, bore
colloq. headache, pain, bind, thorn in the flesh,
aggravation; *slang* pain in the backside/arse; *US* pain
in the ass/butt

vexatious *adj*
annoying, irritating, troublesome, upsetting,
worrying, irksome, nagging, exasperating, infuriating,
distressing, disappointing, bothersome, burdensome,
disagreeable, unpleasant, trying, worrisome,
provoking, teasing, tormenting, afflicting
formal pestiferous
colloq. aggravating, pesky
Ƒ pleasant, soothing

vexed *adj*
1 IRRITATED, annoyed, provoked, upset, troubled,
worried, irate, incensed, infuriated, put out,
exasperated, bothered, confused, perplexed, harassed,
ruffled, riled, disturbed, flustered, distressed,
displeased, agitated
colloq. nettled, aggravated, hassled, peeved, miffed,
narked
2 *a vexed question*
difficult, controversial, contested, disputed, in dispute,
debated
formal moot

viable *adj*
feasible, practicable, possible, workable, usable,
operable, achievable, sustainable, sound
Ƒ impossible, unworkable

vibes *n*
atmosphere, aura, ambience, feel, feelings, emotions,
vibrations, reaction, response, emanation

vibrant *adj*
1 ANIMATED, vivacious, lively, energetic, vigorous,
responsive, sparkling, spirited, sensitive, thrilling,
dynamic, electrifying, electric
2 *vibrant colours*
vivid, bright, brilliant, colourful, striking

vibrate *v*
quiver, pulsate, shudder, shiver, resonate, reverberate,
resound, throb, oscillate, tremble, undulate, sway,
swing, shake

vibration *n*
quiver, pulsation, pulse, shudder, judder, juddering,
resonance, reverberation, resounding, throb,
throbbing, oscillation, trembling, tremor, shaking,
frisson

vicar *n*
minister, priest, chaplain, clergyman, clergywoman,
parson, pastor, rector

vicarious *adj*
indirect, second-hand, substituted, surrogate,
delegated, deputed, acting, commissioned
formal empathetic

vice *n*
1 EVIL, evil-doing, wrongdoing, immorality,

depravity, immorality, wickedness, sin, corruption, degeneracy
formal iniquity, profligacy, transgression
2 FAULT, failing, defect, shortcoming, weakness, imperfection, foible, flaw, blemish, bad habit, besetting sin
🔁 **1** virtue, morality

vice versa
reciprocally, oppositely, contrariwise, the other way round, inversely

vicinity *n*
neighbourhood, surroundings, area, locality, district, precincts, environs, proximity
formal propinquity

vicious *adj*
1 SAVAGE, wild, violent, fierce, barbarous, brutal, cruel, ferocious, dangerous
2 MALICIOUS, spiteful, vindictive, virulent, cruel, mean, nasty, slanderous, venomous, caustic, defamatory
formal malevolent
colloq. bitchy, catty
3 WICKED, bad, wrong, immoral, depraved, unprincipled, degenerate, diabolical, corrupt, debased, perverted, vile, heinous
formal profligate
🔁 **1** gentle **2** kind **3** virtuous

viciousness *n*
savagery, brutality, cruelty, ferocity, virulence, spite, spitefulness, venom, malice, wickedness, badness, immorality, corruption, sinfulness, depravity
formal profligacy, rancour
colloq. bitchiness
🔁 goodness, gentleness, virtue

vicissitude *n*
change, variation, alteration, alternation, shift, turn, revolution, deviation, divergence, fluctuation, twist
formal mutation

victim *n*
sufferer, casualty, prey, quarry, scapegoat, martyr, sacrifice, fatality
colloq. dupe, sucker, fall guy, sitting target, sucker
🔁 offender, attacker

victimize *v*
1 OPPRESS, persecute, discriminate against, pick on, prey on, bully, exploit, take (unfair) advantage of
2 CHEAT, deceive, trick, defraud, dupe, hoodwink, fool
colloq. swindle

victor *n*
winner, conqueror, champion, first, prize-winner
formal subjugator, vanquisher, victor ludorum
colloq. champ, top dog
🔁 loser; *formal* vanquished

victorious *adj*
conquering, champion, triumphant, winning, unbeaten, successful, prize-winning, top, first
formal vanquishing
🔁 defeated, unsuccessful

victory *n*
conquest, win, triumph, success, superiority, mastery, vanquishment, subjugation, overcoming
🔁 defeat, loss, failure

victuals *n*
food, provisions, supplies, stores, edibles, bread,

rations, sustenance, comestibles
formal aliment, viands
colloq. eatables, eats, tuck; *slang* grub, nosh

vie *v*
strive, compete, contend, struggle, contest, fight, rival

view *n, v*
▶ *n* **1** OPINION, attitude, belief, judgement, point of view, viewpoint, angle, thought, conviction, estimation, feeling, sentiment, impression, idea, notion
2 SIGHT, scene, vision, range of vision, vista, spectacle, outlook, prospect, perspective, panorama, landscape, composition
3 SURVEY, inspection, examination, observation, study, contemplation, scrutiny, scan, assessment, review
4 DESCRIPTION, account, impression, picture, portrait, portrayal, sketch
5 GLIMPSE, look, sight, perception
▷ **in view of** considering, bearing in mind, taking into account, taking into consideration
▶ *v* **1** OBSERVE, watch, see, look at, examine, inspect, look at, gaze at, scrutinize, scan, survey, witness, perceive
2 CONSIDER, regard, contemplate, judge, reflect on, think about, speculate

viewer *n*
spectator, watcher, observer, onlooker

viewpoint *n*
attitude, position, perspective, slant, standpoint, stance, opinion, angle, feeling

vigil *n*
watch, wakefulness, wake, lookout, sleeplessness, stake-out
formal pernoctation

vigilance *n*
watchfulness, alertness, attentiveness, observation, carefulness, caution, guardedness, wakefulness
formal circumspection

vigilant *adj*
watchful, alert, attentive, observant, on your guard, on the lookout, cautious, aware, careful, wide-awake, sleepless, unsleeping
formal circumspect
🔁 careless

vigorous *adj*
1 HEALTHY, energetic, active, lively, strong, strenuous, tough, athletic, robust, lusty, sound, vital
2 DYNAMIC, forceful, forcible, powerful, stout, spirited, full-blooded, effective, efficient, brisk, enterprising, flourishing, lively, animated, sparkling, intense
🔁 **1, 2** weak, feeble

vigorously *adv*
briskly, hard, forcefully, energetically, eagerly, heartily, powerfully, strongly, strenuously, lustily
🔁 feebly, weakly

vigour *n*
energy, vitality, liveliness, health, robustness, stamina, strength, resilience, sturdiness, toughness, soundness, spirit, verve, gusto, activity, animation, power, potency, force, forcefulness, might, dash, dynamism
formal vivacity
colloq. zip, oomph, pep, brio
🔁 weakness

vile *adj*
1 *vile weather; a vile meal*
disgusting, foul, nasty, unpleasant, disagreeable, horrible, horrid, nauseating, sickening, repulsive, repugnant, revolting, obnoxious, offensive, distasteful, loathsome
formal noxious
2 EVIL, base, contemptible, debased, low, depraved, degenerate, bad, wicked, wretched, worthless, sinful, miserable, mean, impure, corrupt, despicable, disgraceful, degrading, vicious, appalling
formal iniquitous
E3 **1** pleasant, lovely **2** pure, worthy

vileness *n*
foulness, nastiness, unpleasantness, dreadfulness, meanness, offensiveness, outrage, ugliness, wickedness, corruption, depravity, baseness, evil, profanity
formal degeneracy, noxiousness

vilification *n*
criticism, defamation, abuse, denigration, scurrility
formal aspersion, calumniation, calumny, contumely, disparagement, invective, revilement, vituperation
colloq. mud-slinging

vilify *v*
criticize, revile, denigrate, denounce, slander, defame, stigmatize, abuse, smear, debase
formal malign, disparage, asperse, berate, calumniate, decry, traduce, vilipend, vituperate
colloq. badmouth, slate, slam
E3 praise, compliment, adore, eulogize, glorify

village *n*
hamlet, community, settlement, town
colloq. one-horse town

villain *n*
evildoer, wrongdoer, scoundrel, rogue, criminal, reprobate, knave, rascal, wretch, devil
formal miscreant, malefactor
colloq. baddy
E3 hero, heroine; *colloq.* goody

villainous *adj*
wicked, bad, criminal, evil, sinful, vicious, notorious, cruel, inhuman, vile, depraved, debased, degenerate, disgraceful, terrible, fiendish
formal heinous, nefarious, iniquitous, opprobrious
E3 good

villainy *n*
wickedness, viciousness, badness, crime, criminality, delinquency, atrocity, depravity, baseness, vice, sin, rascality, roguery, knavery
formal iniquity, turpitude

vindicate *v*
1 CLEAR, acquit, excuse, absolve, rehabilitate
formal exonerate, exculpate
2 JUSTIFY, uphold, support, back, maintain, sustain, champion, defend, establish, advocate, assert, verify, confirm, warrant
formal corroborate

vindication *n*
justification, defence, plea, excuse, assertion, apology, support, maintenance, substantiation, verification, rehabilitation, extenuation
formal exculpation, exoneration
E3 accusation, conviction

vindictive *adj*
spiteful, unforgiving, implacable, vengeful, relentless, unrelenting, revengeful, resentful, punitive, venomous, malicious
formal malevolent, rancorous
E3 forgiving

vintage *n, adj*
▶ *n* year, period, era, epoch, generation, time, origin, harvest, gathering, crop
▶ *adj* choice, best, fine, prime, quality, high-quality, select, superior, supreme, rare, mature, old, ripe, enduring, classic, venerable, veteran

violate *v*
1 CONTRAVENE, disobey, disregard, break, flout, infringe, breach
formal transgress, infract
2 OUTRAGE, debauch, defile, rape, ravish, molest, dishonour, desecrate, profane, invade, disturb, interfere with, disrupt, invade, wreck
E3 **1** observe

violation *n*
breach, contravention, offence, outrage, infringement, trespass, abuse, disruption, encroachment, profanation, sacrilege, defilement, desecration
formal infraction, spoliation, transgression
E3 obedience, observance

violence *n*
1 FORCE, strength, power, forcefulness, vehemence, intensity, passion, ferocity, fierceness, severity, tumult, turbulence, wildness
formal might
2 BRUTALITY, aggression, roughness, destructiveness, cruelty, bloodshed, murderousness, savagery, passion, wildness, fighting, frenzy, fury, hostilities

violent *adj*
1 INTENSE, strong, severe, sharp, acute, extreme, great, dramatic, harmful, destructive, devastating, injurious, powerful, painful, agonizing, excruciating, forceful, forcible, harsh, ruinous, rough, vehement, passionate, tumultuous, turbulent
2 CRUEL, brutal, aggressive, fierce, ferocious, bloodthirsty, impetuous, hot-headed, headstrong, murderous, savage, wild, vicious, unrestrained, uncontrollable, ungovernable, passionate, furious, intemperate, maddened, outrageous, riotous, fiery, destructive
E3 **1** calm, moderate **2** peaceful, gentle

VIP *n*
celebrity, luminary, magnate, somebody, notable, personage, dignitary, star, headliner, lion
colloq. bigwig, big name, big noise, big shot, big cheese, heavyweight
E3 nobody, nonentity

virago *n*
shrew, termagant, vixen, tartar, scold, harridan, dragon, fury, gorgon, Xanthippe
colloq. battle-axe

virgin *n, adj*
▶ *n* girl, maiden, celibate, vestal
▶ *adj* virginal, chaste, intact, immaculate, maidenly, pure, modest, new, fresh, spotless, stainless, undefiled, unblemished, untainted, untouched, unspoilt, unsullied

virginal *adj*
pure, spotless, virgin, untouched, undefiled,

uncorrupted, undisturbed, stainless, white, snowy, vestal, immaculate, chaste, fresh, celibate, maidenly
formal pristine

virginity *n*
purity, chastity, chasteness, maidenhood, virtue

virile *adj*
man-like, masculine, male, manly, robust, muscular, strapping, vigorous, potent, lusty, red-blooded, forceful, strong, rugged
colloq. macho
E3 effeminate, impotent

virility *n*
manhood, manliness, masculinity, ruggedness, vigour, huskiness, potency, machismo
E3 effeminacy, impotence, weakness

virtual *adj*
effective, in effect, essential, practical, for all practical purposes, in all but name, implied, implicit, potential, prospective

virtually *adv*
practically, effectively, in effect, almost, nearly, as good as, more or less, for all practical purposes, in all but name, in essence, conceivably

virtue *n*
1 GOODNESS, morality, uprightness, worthiness, righteousness, integrity, honesty, honour, incorruptibility, justice, high-mindedness, excellence
formal rectitude, probity
2 QUALITY, worth, merit, advantage, benefit, asset, credit, strength
colloq. plus
E3 1 vice
▷ **by virtue of** because of, on account of, by means of, owing to, with the help of, thanks to, by way of;
formal by dint of

virtuosity *n*
skill, mastery, expertise, artistry, brilliance, polish, finesse, flair, panache, éclat, finish, wizardry, bravura

virtuoso *n, adj*
▶ *n* expert, master, maestro, prodigy, genius
▶ *adj* skilful, masterly, expert, brilliant, excellent, dazzling,

virtuous *adj*
good, moral, righteous, upright, upstanding, worthy, honourable, honest, irreproachable, incorruptible, exemplary, unimpeachable, ethical, high-principled, blameless, respectable, decent, clean-living, excellent, innocent, angelic
E3 immoral, vicious

virulence *n*
1 POISON, venom, toxicity, deadliness
2 HOSTILITY, bitterness, resentment, hurtfulness, harmfulness, spite, vindictiveness, viciousness, acrimony, antagonism, malevolence, malice, malignancy, spleen, vitriol, hatred
formal rancour

virulent *adj*
1 POISONOUS, toxic, venomous, deadly, fatal, lethal, malignant, injurious, pernicious, severe, intense, extreme
2 HOSTILE, resentful, spiteful, acrimonious, bitter, vicious, vindictive, malicious, vitriolic
formal malevolent, rancorous
E3 1 harmless

viscera *n*
innards, insides, intestines, vitals, bowels, entrails, gralloch

viscous *adj*
sticky, adhesive, gluey, thick, clammy, mucous, tacky, syrupy, treacly, gummy, tenacious, viscid
formal gelatinous, glutinous, mucilaginous
colloq. gooey
E3 runny, thin, watery

visible *adj*
perceptible, discernible, detectable, apparent, noticeable, observable, perceivable, recognizable, distinguishable, discoverable, evident, unconcealed, undisguised, unmistakable, conspicuous, showing, clear, exposed, obvious, open, overt, palpable, plain, patent
formal manifest
E3 invisible, indiscernible, hidden

vision *n*
1 SIGHT, seeing, eyesight, perception, discernment, far-sightedness, foresight, penetration
2 IDEA, ideal, conception, insight, perception, intuition, view, picture, image, mental image, mental picture, imagination, fantasy, dream, daydream
3 APPARITION, hallucination, dream, illusion, optical illusion, delusion, mirage, phantom, ghost, chimera, spectre, wraith

visionary *adj, n*
▶ *adj* idealistic, impractical, romantic, dreamy, unrealistic, utopian, quixotic, unreal, fanciful, prophetic, perceptive, discerning, far-sighted, speculative, unworkable, illusory, imaginary
colloq. moonshiny, ivory-tower
▶ *n* idealist, romantic, dreamer, daydreamer, fantasist, prophet, mystic, seer, utopian, Don Quixote, rainbow-chaser, theorist
E3 pragmatist

visit *v, n*
▶ *v* 1 *visit her brother*
call on, call in, go and see, go round/over to, stay with, stay at, look in, look up, see, spend time with
colloq. drop in on, drop by, stop by, pop in, blow in
2 INFLICT, punish, trouble, afflict, curse, plague
old use smite
▶ *n* call, stay, stop, excursion
formal sojourn

visitation *n*
1 VISIT, inspection, examination
2 INFLICTION, punishment, retribution, catastrophe, disaster, calamity, bane, blight, scourge, ordeal, trial, cataclysm
3 APPEARANCE, manifestation

visitor *n*
caller, guest, company, tourist, traveller, holidaymaker

vista *n*
view, prospect, panorama, perspective, outlook, scene, vision

visual *adj*
visible, observable, discernible, perceptible, optical
formal ocular, optic, specular

visualize *v*
picture, envisage, imagine, conceive, see, conceive of, contemplate

vital *adj*
1 CRITICAL, crucial, important, imperative, key,

significant, basic, fundamental, essential, necessary, indispensable, urgent, life-and-death, decisive, forceful
formal requisite
2 LIVELY, alive, living, life-giving, invigorating, spirited, vivacious, vibrant, vigorous, forceful, dynamic, animated, energetic
formal quickening
E3 1 inessential, peripheral **2** dead

vitality *n*
life, liveliness, animation, vigour, energy, vivacity, spirit, sparkle, exuberance, zest, strength, stamina
colloq. go, get-up-and-go, oomph, pizzazz

vitamin *n*

Vitamins include: retinol, aneurin (thiamine), riboflavin, pantothenic acid, nicotinic acid (niacin), pyridoxine (adermin), cyanocobalamin, folic acid, pteroic acid, ascorbic acid, calciferol, cholecalciferol, ergocalciferol, tocopherol, linoleic acid, linolenic acid, biotin, phylloquinone, menadione, bioflavonoid/citrin.

vitiate *v*
spoil, mar, weaken, undermine, deteriorate, harm, injure, blemish, ruin, sully, taint, corrupt, pervert, pollute, debase, contaminate, blight, defile, invalidate, nullify, devalue, deprave, impair

vitriolic *adj*
bitter, abusive, virulent, vicious, venomous, malicious, caustic, biting, sardonic, scathing, destructive
formal acrimonious, acerbic, mordant, trenchant, vituperative

vituperate *v*
blame, revile, reproach, censure, denounce, abuse
formal berate, castigate, upbraid, vilify
colloq. slam, slate, slag off
E3 praise, applaud, extol

vituperation *n*
censure, rebuke, reprimand, reproach, blame, abuse, fault-finding, scurrility
formal castigation, invective, obloquy, revilement, contumely, diatribe, philippic, vilification, objurgation
colloq. flak, stick
E3 acclaim, praise

vituperative *adj*
censorious, harsh, insulting, abusive, scornful, derogatory, defamatory, scurrilous, withering, belittling, sardonic
formal calumniatory, denunciatory, fulminatory, opprobrious
E3 laudatory

vivacious *adj*
lively, animated, spirited, high-spirited, effervescent, cheerful, jolly, merry, sparkling, light-hearted
formal ebullient
colloq. bubbly

vivacity *n*
liveliness, spirit, animation, energy, quickness, vitality, dynamism, activity, élan, effervescence, light-heartedness, merriness
formal ebullience
colloq. brio

vivid *adj*
1 BRIGHT, colourful, intense, strong, rich, vibrant,

brilliant, glowing, dazzling, glaring, lurid, vigorous, expressive, dramatic, flamboyant, animated, dynamic, lively, lifelike, spirited
2 MEMORABLE, powerful, graphic, clear, distinct, striking, dramatic, lively, sharp, realistic
E3 1 colourless, dull **2** vague

vividness *n*
intensity, strength, glow, brilliancy, brightness, lucidity, radiance, realism, clarity, sharpness, immediacy, life, liveliness, distinctness
formal refulgence, resplendence
E3 dullness, lifelessness

vocabulary *n*
language, words, glossary, lexicon, dictionary, word-book, thesaurus, idiom
technical lexis

vocal *adj*
1 SPOKEN, said, oral, uttered, expressed, voiced
2 ARTICULATE, eloquent, expressive, noisy, clamorous, shrill, strident, outspoken, frank, blunt, forthright, plain-spoken, vociferous
E3 1 unspoken **2** inarticulate

vocation *n*
calling, pursuit, career, métier, mission, profession, occupation, trade, employment, work, craft, role, line, post, job, business, office

vociferous *adj*
noisy, vocal, clamorous, loud, obstreperous, strident, vehement, thundering, shouting, outspoken, frank, blunt, forthright
E3 quiet

vogue *n*
fashion, style, taste, craze, popularity, trend, prevalence, acceptance, custom
formal mode
colloq. fad, the latest, the rage, the thing
▷ **in vogue** fashionable, modish, popular, stylish, trendy, up-to-the-minute, voguish, current, prevalent; *colloq.* in, with it

voice *n, v*
▶ *n* **1** SPEECH, utterance, articulation, language, words, sound, tone, intonation, inflection, expression, mouthpiece, agency, vehicle, medium, instrument, organ
Related adjective: vocal
2 SAY, vote, opinion, view, decision, option, will, desire, wish, airing
▶ *v* express, say, utter, air, articulate, speak of, talk of, mention, verbalize, assert, convey, disclose, divulge, declare, enunciate

void *adj, n, v*
▶ *adj* **1** EMPTY, emptied, free, unfilled, unoccupied, vacant, clear, bare, blank, drained, lacking, devoid
2 ANNULLED, inoperative, invalid, cancelled, nullified, ineffective, futile, useless, vain, worthless, nugatory
E3 1 full **2** valid, binding
▶ *n* emptiness, vacuity, vacuum, abyss, chasm, blank, blankness, space, lack, want, cavity, gap, hollow, opening
formal lacuna
▶ *v* **1** NULLIFY, cancel, annul, invalidate, rescind
formal abnegate
2 DISCHARGE, eject, defecate, emit, empty, drain, evacuate
E3 1 validate **2** fill

volatile *adj*
changeable, inconstant, unstable, variable, erratic, irregular, temperamental, unsteady, unsettled, fickle, whimsical, unpredictable, fitful, restless, giddy, flighty, lively, volcanic, explosive
formal mercurial, capricious
colloq. up and down
E∃ constant, steady

volcano *n*

> The world's active volcanoes include: Mayon (Philippines); Hudson (Chile); Kilauea (Hawaii); Pinatubo, Mt (Philippines); Vulcano (Italy), St Helens, Mt (USA); Etna (Italy); Ruapehu (New Zealand); Stromboli (Italy); Klyuchevskoy (Russia); Mauna Loa (Hawaii); Nyamuragira (Zaire); Hekla (Iceland); Krakatoa (Sumatra); Taal (Philippines); Vesuvius (Italy).

Related adjective: volcanic

volition *n*
will, free will, choice, choosing, determination, option, election, preference, discretion, purpose, resolution

volley *n*
barrage, salvo, bombardment, cannonade, fusillade, hail, shower, burst, blast, discharge, explosion

volte-face *n*
about-turn, about-face, (complete) reversal, turnabout
formal enantiodromia
colloq. U-turn

voluble *adj*
fluent, glib, articulate, talkative, forthcoming, garrulous
formal loquacious
colloq. chatty

volume *n*
1 BULK, size, capacity, space, dimensions, amount, mass, quantity, aggregate, amplitude, sound, loudness, body
2 BOOK, tome, publication; *formal* omnibus

voluminous *adj*
roomy, big, ample, spacious, billowing, vast, full, bulky, huge, large
formal capacious

voluntarily *adv*
willingly, freely, intentionally, consciously, deliberately, purposely, spontaneously, of your own free will, by choice, on your own initiative, of your own accord
E∃ involuntarily, unwillingly

voluntary *adj*
1 FREE, gratuitous, optional, spontaneous, unforced, willing, volunteer, unpaid, honorary
2 CONSCIOUS, deliberate, purposeful, intended, intentional, wilful, optional, of your own free will
formal of your own volition
E∃ 1 compulsory, obligatory 2 involuntary

volunteer *v*
offer, propose, put forward, present, suggest, step forward, advance, tender
formal proffer

voluptuary *n*
hedonist, sensualist, epicurean, pleasure-seeker, libertine, sybarite, debauchee, *bon vivant*
formal profligate

colloq. playboy
E∃ ascetic

voluptuous *adj*
1 SENSUAL, licentious, luxurious, self-indulgent, hedonistic, sensuous, opulent
2 EROTIC, shapely, buxom, full-figured, seductive, provocative, enticing
colloq. sexy

vomit *v*
be sick, bring up, heave, retch, regurgitate
colloq. throw up, puke, spew, heave, fetch; *US slang* barf

vomiting *n*
sickness, retching, regurgitation, emission, ejection, chundering
technical emesis
colloq. puking, spewing; *US slang* barfing

voracious *adj*
insatiable, greedy, hungry, gluttonous, acquisitive, avid, devouring, ravenous, ravening, uncontrolled, unquenchable
formal edacious, omnivorous, prodigious, rapacious

voracity *n*
greed, hunger, ravenousness, eagerness, acquisitiveness, avidity
formal edacity, rapacity

vortex *n*
whirlpool, maelstrom, eddy, whirlwind, whirl

votary *n*
believer, follower, disciple, devotee, addict, adherent

vote *n, v*
▶ *n* 1 *to cast your vote*
ballot, poll, election, franchise, referendum, plebiscite
2 *give everyone the vote*
franchise, suffrage, enfranchisement
E∃ disenfranchisement
▶ *v* elect, ballot, go to the polls, re-elect, choose, opt, plump for, suggest, put in, declare, return

vouch *v*
▷ **vouch for** guarantee, assure, warrant, support, back, endorse, confirm, answer for, certify, affirm, verify, assert, speak for, swear to, uphold
formal attest to, asseverate

voucher *n*
coupon, token, ticket, document, paper

vouchsafe *v*
give, grant, impart, deign, yield, cede
formal bestow, confer, accord

vow *v, n*
▶ *v* promise, pledge, swear, give your word, undertake, dedicate, devote, profess, consecrate, affirm
▶ *n* promise, oath, pledge

voyage *n, v*
▶ *n* journey, travel(s), trip, passage, expedition, crossing, cruise, sail, tour, safari
formal odyssey
▶ *v* journey, travel, go, cruise, sail, tour

vulgar *adj*
1 INDECENT, obscene, coarse, improper, dirty, filthy, crude, suggestive, risqué, rude, indelicate, distasteful, offensive, off-colour, ribald, lewd, bawdy
colloq. near the bone

2 UNREFINED, uncouth, coarse, rude, rough, common, crude, ill-bred, impolite, boorish
formal indecorous
3 TASTELESS, flashy, showy, ostentatious, kitsch, garish, loud, gaudy, tawdry
colloq. cheap and nasty, tacky, glitzy
4 ORDINARY, general, popular, vernacular, common, low, unsophisticated, uncultured
Ⅎ 1 decent **2** correct **3** tasteful, refined **4** sophisticated

vulgarity *n*
1 CRUDENESS, indecency, crudity, dirtiness,

rudeness, suggestiveness, ribaldry, coarseness
2 TASTELESSNESS, tawdriness, gaudiness, showiness, ostentation, garishness
Ⅎ 1 decency, politeness **2** tastefulness

vulnerable *adj*
unprotected, exposed, unguarded, insecure, defenceless, susceptible, weak, powerless, helpless, sensitive, open, open to attack, wide open
Ⅎ protected, strong, safe

W

wacky *adj*
crazy, silly, wild, eccentric, irrational, odd, unpredictable, zany, erratic, daft
colloq. goofy, loony, loopy, nutty, screwy, off beat
Ⅎ sensible

wad *n*
chunk, plug, roll, bundle, ball, lump, hunk, mass, block
colloq. wodge

wadding *n*
packing, padding, stuffing, filling, filler, lining, cottonwool

waddle *v*
toddle, totter, wobble, sway, rock, shuffle

wade *v*
cross, ford, loll, lie, wallow, roll, welter, lurch, flounder, splash
formal traverse
▷ **wade in** pitch in, launch in, tear in, set to, get stuck in, wade through, trawl through, plough through

waffle *v, n*
▶ *v* jabber, prattle, blather, babble
colloq. rabbit on, witter on
▶ *n* blather, prattle, wordiness, padding, nonsense
formal verbosity
colloq. gobbledygook, hot air, guff

waft *v, n*
▶ *v* drift, float, glide, blow, transport, carry, transmit
▶ *n* breath, puff, draught, current, breeze, scent, whiff

wag *v, n*
▶ *v* shake, waggle, wave, sway, swing, bob, nod, wiggle, oscillate, wobble, flutter, vibrate, quiver, rock
▶ *n* wit, joker, humorist, jester, comic, comedian, clown, fool, droll, banterer

wage *n, v*
▶ *n* pay, fee, earnings, salary, wage-packet, payment, stipend, remuneration, allowance, reward, hire, compensation, returns, recompense
formal emolument
▶ *v* carry on, conduct, engage in, undertake, execute, practise, pursue

wager *v, n*
▶ *v* bet, gamble, chance, risk, speculate, venture, stake, pledge, lay odds, hazard, punt

▶ *n* bet, gamble, speculation, stake, venture, hazard, pledge, punt, flutter

waggish *adj*
amusing, mischievous, playful, sportive, funny, humorous, comical, droll, facetious, witty, impish, roguish, jesting, frolicsome, puckish, merry, jocular, jocose, bantering
formal risible
Ⅎ grave, serious, staid

waggle *v*
wiggle, wobble, shake, jiggle, wave, oscillate, wag, bobble, flutter

wagon *n*
cart, dray, carriage, truck, van, train, float, buggy

waif *n*
orphan, stray, foundling

wail *v, n*
▶ *v* moan, cry, howl, lament, weep, sob, complain, groan, keen
formal ululate
colloq. yowl
▶ *n* moan, cry, howl, lament, complaint, groan, weeping, sob
formal ululation

wait *v, n*
▶ *v* delay, linger, hold back, hesitate, pause, remain, rest, stand by, sit out, stay, await
formal abide, tarry, bide your time
colloq. hang around, hang on, hang fire
Ⅎ proceed, go ahead

Colloquial ways of telling someone to wait include: all in good time, bear with me, half a mo, half a moment, half a tick, hang on, hold on, hold your horses, I'll be right with you, just a jiffy, just a minute, just a moment, just a second, just a tick, wait a minute, wait a moment.

▷ **wait on** serve, attend to, minister to, look after, take care of, tend, work for
▶ *n* hold-up, hesitation, delay, interval, pause, halt

waiter, waitress *n*
server, attendant, steward, stewardess, host, hostess, butler

waive *v*
give up, do without, abandon, set aside, resign,

surrender, yield, cede, postpone, defer
formal renounce, relinquish, forego
F∃ enforce, claim, maintain

waiver *n*
disclaimer, postponement, resignation, surrender, abandonment
formal abdication, deferral, relinquishment, remission, renunciation

wake¹ *v, n*
▶ *v* **1** RISE, get up, arise, waken, awake, awaken, rouse, stir, came to, bring round
2 STIMULATE, stir, activate, arouse, animate, excite, fire, galvanize, prod, goad, whet
colloq. egg on
3 ALERT, notify, warn, signal, make/become aware of, make/become conscious of
F∃ **1** sleep
▶ *n* funeral, death-watch, vigil, watch, funeral

wake² *n*
in the wake of the ship
trail, track, path, aftermath, backwash, wash, rear, train, waves

wakeful *adj*
sleepless, restless, insomniac, unsleeping, watchful, vigilant, observant, heedful, attentive, alert, wary
F∃ inattentive, sleepy, unwary

waken *v*
wake, rise, get up, awake, awaken, arouse, rouse, stimulate, stir, whet, quicken, animate, activate, enliven, kindle, fire, ignite, galvanize

walk *v, n*
▶ *v* **1** *walk along the street*

Ways of walking include: amble, clump, crawl, creep, dodder, *colloq.* go by shanks's pony, hike, hobble, *colloq.* hoof it, limp, lope, lurch, march, mince, *colloq.* mooch, pace, pad, paddle, parade, patter, *formal* perambulate, plod, potter, promenade, prowl, ramble, roam, saunter, scuttle, shamble, shuffle, slink, sneak, stagger, stalk, steal, step, stomp, *colloq.* stretch your legs, stride, stroll, strut, stumble, swagger, tiptoe, *colloq.* toddle, totter, traipse, tramp, trample, tread, trek, trip, troop, trot, trudge, trundle, waddle, wade, wander, *colloq.* yomp.

2 ACCOMPANY, escort, guide, lead, conduct, usher, shepherd
▷ **walk off/away with** go off with, walk away with, make off with, run off with, steal, pocket; *colloq.* pinch, nick, lift
▷ **walk out** go on strike, strike, stop work, down tools, protest, mutiny, revolt, take industrial action
▷ **walk out on** abandon, desert; *formal* forsake; *colloq.* run out on, jilt, dump, leave in the lurch, leave high and dry
▶ *n* **1** *he has an odd walk*
carriage, gait, step, pace, stride
2 *go for a walk*
stroll, amble, ramble, saunter, march, hike, tramp, promenade, trek, traipse, trudge, trail
3 *a tree-lined walk*
footpath, path, walkway, avenue, pathway, promenade, alley, esplanade, lane, drive, track, pavement, sidewalk
4 BEAT, round, rounds, circuit, way, path, route, trail
▷ **walk of life** occupation, profession, trade, field, area, sphere, line, activity, arena, course, pursuit, career, vocation, calling, métier, background

walker *n*
pedestrian, rambler, hiker

walk-out *n*
strike, stoppage, industrial action, protest, rebellion, revolt

walk-over *n*
colloq. pushover, doddle, child's play, piece of cake, cinch

walkway *n*
path, pathway, passage, footpath, lane, pavement, promenade, esplanade
US sidewalk

wall *n*

Types of wall and famous walls include: abutment, bailey, barricade, barrier, block, breeze-block wall, brick wall, bulkhead, bulwark, buttress, cavity wall, curtain wall, dam, dike, divider, embankment, enclosure wall, fence, flying buttress, fortification, garden wall, Great Wall of China, Hadrian's Wall, hedge, inner wall, load-bearing wall, mural, obstacle, outer bailey, paling, palisade, parapet, partition, party wall, rampart, retaining wall, screen, sea-wall, shield wall, stockade, stud partition, wall of death.

Related adjective: mural

wallet *n*
pouch, purse, folder, holder, case, notecase, pochette
US bill-fold

wallop *v, n*
▶ *v* beat, hit, smack, punch, pummel, buffet, swat, swipe, bash, strike, thrash, thump, pound, clobber, batter, thwack, defeat, crush, trounce, rout, drub, hammer
formal vanquish
colloq. clout, belt, lick, paste, whack
▶ *n* blow, hit, kick, thump, thwack, whack, swat, swipe, smack, punch, bash

wallow *v*
1 *wallow in mud*
loll, lie, roll, wade, welter, lurch, flounder, splash
2 *wallow in nostalgia*
indulge, relish, revel, bask, enjoy, glory, delight
formal luxuriate

wan *adj*
pale, washed out, ashen, white, weak, discoloured, faint, colourless, anaemic, ghastly, feeble, whey-faced, waxen, pallid, pasty, sickly, bleak, mournful, weary

wand *n*
rod, baton, staff, stick, sprig, mace, sceptre, twig

wander *v, n*
▶ *v* **1** ROAM, rove, ramble, meander, saunter, stroll, prowl, drift, range, traipse, stray, straggle
formal peregrinate
2 DIGRESS, diverge, deviate, depart, go astray, stray, swerve, veer, err, lose your way
3 RAMBLE, rave, babble, gibber, talk nonsense
▶ *n* excursion, ramble, amble, stroll, saunter, meander, prowl, cruise

wanderer *n*
itinerant, traveller, voyager, drifter, rover, rambler, stroller, stray, straggler, ranger, wayfarer, nomad, Gypsy, vagrant, vagabond
colloq. rolling stone

wandering *adj, n*
▶ *adj* itinerant, travelling, rambling, wayfaring,

roving, strolling, voyaging, rootless, homeless, unsettled, drifting, migratory, nomadic, vagabond, vagrant
formal peripatetic
▶ *n* travels, drift(ing), journey(ing), meander(ing), walkabout
formal odyssey, peregrination

wane *v, n*
▶ *v* diminish, decrease, decline, weaken, subside, fade (away), dwindle, ebb, lessen, abate, sink, drop, taper off, peter out, dim, droop, contract, shrink, fail, wither, vanish
formal abate
F∃ increase, wax
▶ *n* fading, dwindling, decline, decrease, lessening, sinking, ebb, contraction, subsidence, weakening, decay, degeneration, failure, fall, drop, tapering off, atrophy
formal abatement, diminution
F∃ increase
▷ **on the wane** deteriorating, declining, degenerating, weakening, withering, fading, subsiding, dwindling, lessening, ebbing, tapering off, dropping, on the decline, obsolescent;
formal moribund; *colloq.* on its last legs, on the way out

wangle *v*
manipulate, arrange, contrive, engineer, fix, scheme, manoeuvre, work, pull off, manage
colloq. fiddle, wheel and deal

want *v, n*
▶ *v* **1** DESIRE, wish, like, feel like, crave, covet, fancy, hope for, long for, pine for, yearn for, hunger for, thirst for
2 NEED, require, demand, lack, miss, be without, be deficient in, call for
▶ *n* **1** DESIRE, demand, longing, pining, yearning, craving, coveting, hunger, thirst, requirement, wish, need, lust, appetite
2 LACK, dearth, insufficiency, absence, deficiency, shortage, inadequacy, scarcity, scantiness
formal paucity
3 POVERTY, destitution
formal privation, indigence, penury

wanting *adj*
1 ABSENT, missing, lacking, short, insufficient
2 INADEQUATE, imperfect, faulty, defective, substandard, poor, deficient, unsatisfactory, unacceptable, disappointing
colloq. not up to scratch
F∃ 1 sufficient **2** adequate

wanton *adj, n*
▶ *adj* **1** *a wanton action*
malicious, arbitrary, unprovoked, unjustifiable, groundless, gratuitous, pointless, unrestrained, rash, reckless, wild, extravagant
formal malevolent
2 *a wanton woman*
immoral, promiscuous, shameless, immodest, impure, abandoned, dissipated, dissolute, lewd, lecherous
▶ *n* slut, harlot, strumpet, trollop, prostitute, whore, voluptuary, debauchee, lecher, libertine, rake, roué, Don Juan, Casanova
slang tart

war *n, v*
▶ *n* warfare, hostilities, fighting, fight, battle, combat, conflict, clash, skirmish, strife, struggle, bloodshed,

contest, confrontation, campaign, contention, enmity, antagonism, ill-will
Related adjective: martial
F∃ peace, cease-fire

Types of war include: ambush, armed conflict, assault, attack, battle, biological warfare, blitz, blitzkrieg, bombardment, chemical warfare, civil war, cold war, counter-attack, engagement, germ warfare, guerrilla warfare, holy war, hot war, invasion, jihad, jungle warfare, limited war, manoeuvres, nuclear war, private war, resistance, skirmish, state of siege, struggle, total war, trade war, war of attrition, war of nerves, world war.

Famous wars include: American Civil War (Second American Revolution), American Revolution (War of Independence), Boer War, Cod wars, Crimean War, Crusades, English Civil War, Falklands War, Franco-Prussian War, Gulf War, Hundred Years War, Indian Wars, Iran-Iraq War, Korean War, Mexican War, Napoleonic War, Opium Wars, Peasants' War, Russo-Finnish War (Winter War), Russo-Japanese War, Russo-Turkish Wars, Seven Years War, Six-Day War, Spanish-American War, Spanish-American Wars of Independence, Spanish Civil War, Suez Crisis, Thirty Years War, Vietnam War, War of 1812, War of the Pacific, Wars of the Roses, World War I (the Great War), World War II.

▷ **war cry** rallying-cry, battle cry, war-song, slogan, watchword
▶ *v* wage war, fight, take up arms, cross swords, make war, battle, clash, combat, strive, skirmish, struggle, contest, contend

warble *v, n*
▶ *v* sing, chirrup, chirp, twitter, quaver, yodel, trill
▶ *n* song, cry, call, chirp, chirrup, quaver, trill, twitter

ward *n, v*
▶ *n* **1** ROOM, apartment, compartment, cubicle, unit
2 DIVISION, area, district, quarter, precinct, zone
3 CHARGE, dependant, protégé(e), pupil, minor
▶ *v* ▷ **ward off** avert, fend off, deflect, parry, repel, drive back, stave off, thwart, beat off, forestall, evade, turn aside, turn away, block, avoid; *colloq.* dodge

warden *n*
keeper, custodian, guardian, protector, warder, caretaker, curator, ranger, steward, watchman, superintendent, supervisor, overseer, administrator, janitor

warder *n*
jailer, keeper, prison officer, guard, wardress, custodian, warden
slang screw

wardrobe *n*
1 CUPBOARD, closet
2 CLOTHES, outfit
formal attire, apparel

warehouse *n*
store, storehouse, depot, depository, repository, stockroom, entrepot

wares *n*
goods, merchandise, commodities, stock, products, produce, stuff

warfare *n*
war, fighting, hostilities, battle, arms, combat, strife, struggle, passage of arms, contest, confrontation,

campaign, conflict, contention, discord, blows
E3 peace

warily *adv*
cautiously, carefully, guardedly, watchfully, vigilantly,
hesitantly, apprehensively, gingerly, cagily, charily,
suspiciously, uneasily, distrustfully
formal circumspectly
E3 heedlessly, recklessly, thoughtlessly, unwarily

wariness *n*
caution, carefulness, attention, mindfulness, alertness,
care, heedfulness, watchfulness, vigilance, foresight,
discretion, caginess, apprehension, hesitancy,
suspicion, distrust, unease
formal circumspection, prudence
E3 heedlessness, recklessness, thoughtlessness

warlike *adj*
martial, belligerent, aggressive, combative,
bloodthirsty, war-mongering, militaristic, militant,
hostile, antagonistic, hawkish, unfriendly
formal bellicose, pugnacious
E3 friendly, peaceable

warlock *n*
witch, wizard, sorcerer, enchanter, conjurer, magician,
demon
formal necromancer

warm *adj, v*
▶ *adj* **1** HEATED, tepid, lukewarm
2 ARDENT, passionate, fervent, vehement, intense,
earnest, eager, enthusiastic, heart-felt, sincere, zealous
3 *warm colours*
rich, intense, mellow, cheerful, relaxing
4 FRIENDLY, amiable, cordial, affable, kind, kindly,
genial, hearty, hospitable, caring, sympathetic, loving,
affectionate, tender
5 FINE, sunny, balmy, temperate, close
E3 **1** cool **2** indifferent **3** cold, cool
4 unfriendly **5** cool
▶ *v* **1** HEAT (UP), make warm, reheat, melt, thaw
2 ANIMATE, interest, please, delight, stimulate, liven
up, enliven, put some life into, stir, rouse, excite, cheer
up
E3 **1** cool
▷ **warm up** limber up, loosen up, exercise, prepare

warm-blooded *adj*
passionate, enthusiastic, excitable, fervent, hot-
blooded, emotional, ardent, earnest, lively, spirited,
vivacious, impetuous, rash

warm-hearted *adj*
kind, kind-hearted, kindly, affectionate, loving,
sympathetic, tender, tender-hearted, compassionate,
generous, cordial, ardent, genial
E3 cold, unsympathetic

warmth *n*
1 WARMNESS, heat, hotness, fire
2 FRIENDLINESS, affection, cordiality, tenderness,
kindness, kindliness, care, love, compassion,
sympathy, hospitality
3 ARDOUR, enthusiasm, passion, fervour, zeal,
vehemence, intensity, eagerness, sincerity
E3 **1** coldness **2** unfriendliness **3** indifference

warn *v*
1 INFORM, notify, tell, let know, advise, alert, give
(advance) notice, put on your guard, sound the alarm
formal forewarn
colloq. tip off
2 ADVISE, counsel, urge, caution, exhort

3 REBUKE, caution, reprimand, reprove
formal admonish

warning *n, adj*
▶ *n* **1** CAUTION, alert, advice, notification,
information, notice, advance notice, counsel, hint,
lesson, alarm, threat
formal admonition
colloq. tip-off, shot across the bows
2 OMEN, threat, sign, signal
formal augury, premonition, presage, portent
▶ *adj* ominous, threatening, cautionary
formal admonitory, premonitory, monitory

warp *v, n*
▶ *v* twist, bend, contort, deform, distort, kink,
misshape, pervert, corrupt, deviate
E3 straighten
▶ *n* twist, bend, contortion, deformation, distortion,
bias, kink, irregularity, turn, bent, defect, deviation,
quirk, perversion

warrant *n, v*
▶ *n* authorization, authority, sanction, validation,
permit, permission, licence, guarantee, warranty,
security, pledge, commission, voucher
formal consent
▶ *v* **1** GUARANTEE, pledge, swear, certify, assure,
declare, affirm, vouch for, answer for, underwrite,
uphold, support, back, endorse
formal avouch
2 AUTHORIZE, entitle, empower, sanction, permit,
allow, license, justify, excuse, approve, support, call for,
commission, require
formal necessitate, consent to

warrantable *adj*
permissible, allowable, defensible, excusable,
justifiable, right, reasonable, proper, legal, lawful,
accountable, necessary
E3 indefensible, unjustifiable, unwarrantable

warranty *n*
guarantee, contract, certificate, bond, authorization,
assurance, pledge, justification
formal covenant

warring *adj*
fighting, hostile, opposing, opposed, conflicting,
contending, combatant, embattled, belligerent, at war,
at daggers drawn

warrior *n*
fighter, soldier, fighting man, combatant, champion,
warhorse, wardog

wart *n*
growth, lump, protuberance, verruca
formal excrescence

wary *adj*
cautious, guarded, careful, chary, on your guard, on the
lookout, distrustful, suspicious, heedful, attentive,
alert, on the alert, watchful, vigilant, wide-awake,
cagey
formal prudent, circumspect
E3 unwary, careless, heedless

wash *v, n*
▶ *v* **1** CLEAN, cleanse, launder, shampoo, scrub,
mop, swab down, sponge, wipe, rinse, soak, swill
2 BATHE, bath, freshen up, get cleaned up, have a
wash, have a bath, shower, have a shower, douche,
shampoo
3 FLOW, sweep, wave, swell, stream, beat, splash,

dash

4 *that excuse won't wash*
be unbelievable, be implausible, not be accepted, hold, stand up, bear examination, bear scrutiny, carry weight, pass muster
colloq. stick
▷ **wash your hands** abandon, give up on, have nothing to do with, leave to your own devices, abdicate responsibility
▶ *n* **1** CLEANING, cleansing, bath, bathe, laundry, laundering, scrub, shower, shampoo, washing, rinse
2 FLOW, roll, sweep, wave, swell, surge
3 LAYER, coat, coating, rinse, stain

washed-out *adj*
pale, pallid, blanched, bleached, faded, wan, colourless, drained, drawn, exhausted, tired-out, fatigued, worn-out, weary, spent, flat, lacklustre, haggard
colloq. all in, dead on your feet, dog-tired, knackered

washout *n*
failure, disaster, disappointment, fiasco, debacle, messy
colloq. flop, lead balloon
F3 success, triumph

waspish *adj*
critical, irritable, bad-tempered, cross, ill-tempered, captious, irascible, peevish, snappish, testy, grumpy
formal cantankerous, petulant
colloq. bitchy, crabbed, crabby, crotchety, grouchy, prickly, touchy

waste *v, n, adj*
▶ *v* **1** SQUANDER, misspend, misuse, fritter away, lavish, spend, throw away, get through, go through
formal dissipate
colloq. blow, splurge
2 CONSUME, erode, exhaust, drain, destroy, spoil, devastate
3 WITHER, shrivel, shrink, become emaciated
formal atrophy, debilitate
4 LAY WASTE, desolate, ravage, destroy, devastate, raze, ruin, sack, spoil, pillage, rape
formal depredate, despoil
F3 **1** economize **2** preserve
▶ *n* **1** SQUANDERING, wastefulness, extravagance, loss
formal dissipation, prodigality
2 MISAPPLICATION, misuse, abuse, neglect
3 RUBBISH, refuse, leftovers, debris, dregs, effluent, litter, scrap, slops, offscouring(s), dross
US trash, garbage
F3 **1** thriftiness
▶ *adj* **1** USELESS, worthless, unwanted, unused, left-over, superfluous, extra
formal supernumerary
2 BARREN, desolate, empty, uninhabited, bare, devastated, uncultivated, unprofitable, unproductive, wild, dismal, bleak, dreary

wasted *adj*
1 UNNECESSARY, needless, useless, unrequired
2 EMACIATED, withered, weak, weakened, shrivelled, shrunken, gaunt, washed-out, spent
formal atrophied
F3 **1** necessary **2** robust

wasteful *adj*
extravagant, spendthrift, prodigal, uneconomical, thriftless, unthrifty, ruinous, lavish, improvident

formal profligate
F3 economical, thrifty

wasteland *n*
wilderness, desert, barrenness, waste, wild(s), void, emptiness, barrenness

wasting *adj*
destroying, emaciating, enfeebling, devastating
technical marasmic
F3 strengthening

wastrel *n*
good-for-nothing, idler, layabout, loafer, ne'er-do-well, malingerer, spendthrift
formal profligate
colloq. lounger, shirker, skiver

watch *v, n*
▶ *v* **1** OBSERVE, see, look at, look on, regard, note, notice, mark, stare at, peer at, gape at, contemplate, scan, survey, gaze at, view
2 GUARD, look after, keep an eye on, mind, protect, superintend, inspect, take care of, keep
colloq. keep tabs on, not take your eyes off
3 PAY ATTENTION, be careful, take care, take heed, look out
▷ **watch out** notice, be vigilant, look out, keep a lookout, keep your eyes open; *colloq.* keep your eyes peeled, keep your eyes skinned
▷ **watch over** guard, protect, stand guard over, keep an eye on, look after, take care of, mind, shield, defend, shelter, preserve
▶ *n* **1** TIMEPIECE, wristwatch, clock
formal chronometer
2 VIGILANCE, watchfulness, vigil, guard, observation, surveillance, notice, lookout, attention, heed, alertness, inspection, supervision

watchdog *n*
1 GUARD DOG, house-dog
2 MONITOR, inspector, scrutineer, vigilante, ombudsman, guardian, custodian, protector

watcher *n*
spectator, observer, onlooker, looker-on, viewer, (member of the) audience, lookout, spy, witness

watchful *adj*
vigilant, attentive, heedful, observant, alert, guarded, on your guard, wide awake, keep your eyes open/peeled/skinned, on the lookout, suspicious, wary, chary, cautious
formal circumspect, on the qui vive
F3 unobservant, inattentive

watchfulness *n*
vigilance, alertness, attention, attentiveness, heedfulness, caution, cautiousness, circumspection, suspicion, suspiciousness, wariness
F3 inattention

watchman *n*
guard, security guard, caretaker, custodian, caretaker

watchword *n*
catch phrase, slogan, catchword, maxim, password, motto, rallying-cry, battle-cry, signal, byword, buzz word, magic word, shibboleth

water *n, v*
▶ *n* rain, sea, ocean, lake, river, current, stream, moisture, flooding, torrent
Related adjective: aqueous
▶ *v* wet, moisten, dampen, soak, spray, sprinkle, irrigate, saturate, drench, flood, hose, douse

⊟ dry out, parch
▷ **water down** dilute, thin, water, weaken, adulterate, mix, tone down, play down, soften, qualify; *formal* mitigate; *colloq.* soft-pedal

watercourse *n*
river, stream, channel, ditch, canal, wadi, water-channel

waterfall *n*
fall, falls, cascade, chute, cataract, torrent

waterproof *adj*
impervious, water-resistant, damp-proof, rubberized, impermeable, water-repellent, coated, proofed
⊟ leaky

watertight *adj*
1 WATERPROOF, sound, hermetic
2 IMPREGNABLE, unassailable, airtight, flawless, foolproof, firm, sound, incontrovertible, indisputable
⊟ 1 leaky

watery *adj*
1 LIQUID, fluid, moist, wet, damp
technical hydrous
formal aqueous
2 WEAK, watered-down, diluted, adulterated, insipid, tasteless, thin, runny, soggy, squelchy, flavourless, washy
colloq. wishy-washy
⊟ 1 dry

wave *v, n*
▶ *v* 1 BECKON, gesture, gesticulate, indicate, sign, signal, direct
2 BRANDISH, flourish, flap, flutter, stir, shake, sway, swing, waft, quiver, ripple, surge, move from side to side
formal undulate
▷ **wave aside** dismiss, brush aside, disregard, reject, set aside, shelve, spurn; *colloq.* pour cold water on
▶ *n* 1 BREAKER, roller, billow, ripple, comber, foam, froth, swell, surf, tidal wave, wavelet, undulation
colloq. white horse
2 SURGE, sweep, swell, flow, upsurge, ground swell, current, drift, movement, rush, tendency, trend, stream, flood, outbreak, rash

waver *v*
1 VACILLATE, falter, hesitate, dither, fluctuate, vary, seesaw, equivocate
colloq. shilly-shally, hum and haw
2 TREMBLE, oscillate, shake, sway, wobble, stagger, teeter, totter, rock
⊟ 1 decide

waverer *n*
ditherer, doubter, haverer, wobbler
colloq. shilly-shallier

wavering *adj*
hesitant, doubting, doubtful, dithering, dithery, havering, in two minds
colloq. shilly-shallying
⊟ determined

wavy *adj*
undulating, rippled, curly, curling, curvy, curving, ridged, sinuous, winding, zigzag

wax *v*
grow, increase, get bigger, rise, swell, develop, enlarge, expand, extend, spread, magnify, broaden, widen,

mount, fill out, become
⊟ decrease, wane

waxen *adj*
pale, colourless, ashen, wan, white, whitish, pallid, ghastly, anaemic, bloodless, livid
⊟ ruddy

waxy *adj*
soft, pallid, pasty, waxen, impressible, impressionable
formal ceraceous, cereous

way *n*
1 METHOD, approach, manner, technique, process, plan, course of action, strategy, procedure, means, instrument, tool, system, style, fashion, lines
formal mode, instrumentality
2 CUSTOM, practice, behaviour, manner, habit, usage, characteristic, idiosyncrasy, peculiarity, mannerism, personality, temper, temperament, disposition, trait, style, conduct, nature
formal wont
3 DIRECTION, course, route, path, pathway, road, channel, access, avenue, track, passage, highway, roadway, street, thoroughfare, lane
▷ **by the way** incidentally, in passing, secondarily, parenthetically, *en passant*
▷ **give way** 1 COLLAPSE, break, fall in, sink, disintegrate, subside, cave in 2 GIVE IN, yield, surrender, capitulate, submit, concede
▷ **under way** in progress, moving, in motion, going, begun, started, in operation, afoot
▷ **way of life** lifestyle, life, living conditions, position, situation, world
▷ **ways and means** methods, procedure, way, resources, wherewithal, capability, capacity, tools, cash, funds, reserves, capital

wayfarer *n*
traveller, walker, wanderer, journeyer, globetrotter, rover, trekker, voyager, itinerant, nomad, Gypsy
⊟ resident, stay-at-home

wayfaring *adj*
journeying, walking, travelling, wandering, rambling, roving, drifting, itinerant, voyaging, nomadic
formal peripatetic
⊟ resident, stay-at-home

waylay *v*
lie in wait for, ambush, attack, accost, set upon, surprise, catch, hold up, intercept, seize, buttonhole

way-out *adj*
weird, crazy, bizarre, outlandish, unusual, unorthodox, unconventional, fantastic, eccentric, wild, experimental, avant-garde, progressive
colloq. far-out, freaky, off-beat
⊟ ordinary

wayward *adj*
wilful, perverse, contrary, changeable, fickle, unpredictable, stubborn, self-willed, unmanageable, ungovernable, headstrong, obstinate, disobedient, rebellious, insubordinate, unruly, incorrigible
formal intractable, obdurate, contumacious, refractory, capricious
⊟ tractable, good-natured

weak *adj*
1 FEEBLE, frail, infirm, shaky, unhealthy, sickly, puny, delicate, exhausted, worn out, fatigued, fragile, flimsy
formal debilitated, indisposed, enervated
colloq. weedy
2 VULNERABLE, unprotected, unguarded,

defenceless, exposed
3 POWERLESS, impotent, spineless, cowardly,
indecisive, irresolute, poor, flimsy, feeble, lacking,
lame, inadequate, faulty, imperfect, useless, defective,
deficient, inconclusive, unconvincing, unsound,
untenable
formal ineffectual
4 FAINT, slight, dim, low, soft, muffled, stifled, dull,
imperceptible
5 INSIPID, tasteless, watery, thin, diluted, runny,
adulterated
F3 1 strong **2** secure **3** powerful, determined
4 strong **5** strong

weaken v
1 ENFEEBLE, tire, exhaust, sap, undermine,
incapacitate, disable, paralyse, cripple, incapacitate,
dilute, diminish, lower, lessen, reduce, moderate,
mitigate, temper, soften (up), thin, water down
formal debilitate, enervate
2 TIRE, flag, fail, give way, droop, fade, ease up,
dwindle
formal abate
F3 1 strengthen

weakening n
fading, failing, flagging, reduction, diminishment,
dwindling, easing, lessening, lowering, moderation,
dilution, waning
formal abatement
F3 strengthening

weakling n
coward, underling, underdog, mouse
colloq. wimp, wet, wally, weed, drip, doormat, sissy
F3 hero, stalwart

weak-minded adj
pliable, faint-hearted, irresolute, persuasible,
submissive, compliant, weak-kneed, persuadable
formal complaisant, pusillanimous
colloq. spineless
F3 strong-willed

weakness n
1 FEEBLENESS, infirmity, impotence, incapacity,
delicateness, frailty, powerlessness, vulnerability
formal debility, enervation
2 FAULT, failing, flaw, imperfection, shortcoming,
blemish, defect, deficiency, foible, weak point,
Achilles' heel
3 LIKING, inclination, fondness, passion
formal penchant, predilection, proclivity,
predisposition
colloq. soft spot
F3 1 strength **2** strength **3** dislike

weal n
welt, stripe, streak, scar, ridge, mark, wound,
contusion, cicatrice, cicatrix

wealth n
1 MONEY, cash, riches, assets, affluence, prosperity,
funds, mammon, fortune, treasure, capital, finance,
means, substance, resources, goods, possessions,
property, estate
formal opulence
2 ABUNDANCE, plenty, mass, bounty, fullness, store,
copiousness
formal cornucopia, profusion, plenitude
F3 1 poverty

wealthy adj
rich, prosperous, affluent, well-off, moneyed,

comfortable, well-heeled, well-to-do
formal opulent
F3 poor, impoverished
colloq. flush, rolling in it, made of money;
slang loaded, filthy rich, stinking rich

weapon n

Weapons include: gun, airgun, pistol, revolver,
automatic, Colt®, Luger®, magnum, Mauser, six-
gun, six-shooter, rifle, air rifle, Winchester® rifle,
carbine, shotgun, blunderbuss, musket, elephant
gun, machine-gun, kalashnikov, submachine-gun,
tommy-gun, sten gun, Bren gun, cannon, field gun,
gatling-gun, howitzer, mortar, turret-gun; knife,
bowie knife, flick-knife, stiletto, dagger, dirk,
poniard, sword, épée, foil, rapier, sabre, scimitar,
bayonet, broadsword, claymore, lance, spear, pike,
machete; bomb, atom bomb, H-bomb, cluster-
bomb, depth-charge, incendiary bomb, Mills bomb,
mine, land-mine, napalm bomb, time-bomb; bow
and arrow, longbow, crossbow, blowpipe, catapult,
boomerang, sling, harpoon, bolas, rocket, bazooka,
ballistic missile, Cruise missile, Exocet®,
colloq. Scud, torpedo, hand grenade, flame-
thrower; battleaxe, pole-axe, halberd, tomahawk,
cosh, cudgel, knuckleduster, shillelagh, truncheon;
gas, Agent Orange, CS gas, *US* Mace®, mustard
gas, tear-gas.

wear v, n
▶ *v* **1** DRESS IN, be dressed in, have on, put on, be
clothed in, don, sport, carry, bear, have, display, show,
exhibit, assume
2 DETERIORATE, erode, corrode, consume, fray,
become thinner, become weaker, become threadbare,
rub, abrade, waste, grind
▷ **wear down** reduce, rub away, corrode, abrade,
erode, grind down, chip away at, consume, undermine,
diminish, lessen, overcome; *formal* macerate
▷ **wear off** decrease, dwindle, diminish, subside,
wane, weaken, fade, lessen, ebb, peter out, disappear;
formal abate
F3 increase
▷ **wear on** go on, go by, pass, elapse
▷ **wear out 1** EXHAUST, fatigue, tire (out), strain,
stress, drain, sap; *formal* enervate
2 DETERIORATE, wear through, erode, impair,
consume, fray
▶ *n* **1** CLOTHES, clothing, dress, garments, outfit,
costume
formal attire
2 DETERIORATION, erosion, corrosion, damage,
wear and tear, friction, abrasion
3 USE, service, employment, usefulness, utility,
durability

weariness n
fatigue, tiredness, exhaustion, lassitude, lethargy,
ennui, drowsiness, sleepiness, listlessness, prostration
formal enervation, languor
F3 freshness

wearing adj
exhausting, fatiguing, tiring, tiresome, wearisome,
trying, taxing, oppressive, irksome, exasperating,
erosive
F3 refreshing

wearisome adj
tiresome, troublesome, wearing, fatiguing, exhausting,
dreary, burdensome, bothersome, boring,
monotonous, humdrum, tedious, annoying, trying,

exasperating, irksome, vexatious, dull
☒ refreshing

weary *adj, v*
▶ *adj* **1** TIRED, exhausted, fatigued, sleepy, worn
out, drained, drowsy, jaded
colloq. all in, done in, fagged out, knackered, bushed,
pooped, dead beat, whacked, dog-tired
2 *weary of trying to please him*
bored, unenthusiastic, tired, uninterested, unexcited
colloq. sick and tired, bored to tears, browned off,
brassed of, cheesed of
☒ **1** refreshed **2** excited, interested
▶ *v* tire, tire out, wear out, fatigue, bore, fail, jade, sap,
sicken, drain, burden, fade, annoy, irritate, exasperate,
irk, tax
formal debilitate, enervate
colloq. bug, fag

wearying *adj*
tiring, fatiguing, exhausting, wearisome, wearing,
taxing, draining, trying
☒ refreshing

weather *n, v*
▶ *n* climate, conditions, temperature, humidity,
dryness, windiness, sunniness, cloudiness,
meteorological reports, atmospheric conditions,
forecast, outlook

Types of weather include: breeze, wind, squall, gale,
hurricane, tornado, typhoon, monsoon, cyclone,
whirlwind, chinook, mistral; cloud, mist, dew, fog,
smog; rain, drizzle, shower, deluge, downpour,
rainbow; sunshine, heatwave, haze, drought; storm,
tempest, thunder, lightning; frost, hoar frost; hail,
sleet, snow, snowstorm; ice, black ice, thaw, slush. *See
also* **precipitation, wind**.

▷ **under the weather** ill, sick, poorly, queer, ailing,
off-colour, the worse for wear, seedy, groggy, below par,
squeamish, nauseous, hung over, out of sorts;
formal indisposed
▶ *v* **1** ENDURE, survive, live through, come through,
get through, ride out, rise above, stick out, withstand,
surmount, stand, brave, overcome, resist, pull through,
suffer
2 EXPOSE, toughen, season, harden, dry
☒ **1** succumb

weave *v*
1 INTERLACE, lace, plait, braid, intertwine, spin,
knit, entwine, intercross, interwork, fuse, merge,
unite
2 CREATE, compose, construct, contrive, make up,
put together, fabricate
3 WIND, twist, zigzag, criss-cross

web *n*
network, net, netting, lattice, lacework, mesh,
complex, webbing, interlacing, weft, snare, knot,
tangle, trap

wed *v*
1 MARRY, get married, yoke
formal espouse
colloq. get hitched, splice, tie the knot,
2 JOIN, unite, unify, coalesce, blend, ally, combine,
link, interweave, fuse, merge
formal commingle
☒ **1** divorce

wedded *adj*
married, marital, joined, husbandly, wifely

formal conjugal, connubial, matrimonial, nuptial,
spousal

wedding *n, adj*
▶ *n* marriage, union, marriage service, marriage
ceremony, celebration of marriage
old use wedlock
formal matrimony, nuptials
☒ divorce
▶ *adj* marriage
formal bridal, matrimonial, nuptial, hymeneal,
hymenean, epithalamic

wedge *n, v*
▶ *n* lump, block, piece, chunk, wodge, chock, triangle
▶ *v* jam, cram, pack, ram, squeeze, stuff, push, lodge,
fit, block, thrust, crowd, force

wedlock *n*
marriage, union
formal holy matrimony, matrimony

wee *adj*
small, little, tiny, miniature, minute, negligible,
insignificant, diminutive, minuscule, microscopic,
midget, Lilliputian
colloq. itsy-bitsy, teeny, teeny-weeny, weeny
☒ big, large

weed *n, v*

Weeds include: annual nettle, bindweed, birdsfoot
trefoil, bracken, broad-leaved dock, burnet saxifrage,
Canadian pondweed, chickweed, cinquefoil,
coltsfoot, common burdock, common chickweed,
common persicaria, common plantain, common
reed, couch grass, creeping buttercup, creeping
thistle, creeping yellow cress, curled dock, daisy,
dandelion, deadnettle, dock, duckweed, fat hen, field
wood rush, greater or rat-tailed plantain, ground
elder, ground ivy, groundsel, hairy bittercress,
horsetail, Japanese knotgrass, knapweed, knotgrass,
large bindweed, lesser celandine, lesser yellow trefoil,
liverwort, meadow grass, mind your own business,
moss, mouse-ear chickweed, oxalis, pearlwort,
perennial nettle, perennial oat-grass, petty spurge,
pineapple weed, ragweed, ribwort, rough hawkbit,
salad burnet, self-heal, shepherd's purse, sheep's
sorrel, small bindweed, snakeweed, sow thistle,
speedwell, spurge, stemless thistle, sun spurge, thale
cress, vetch, white clover, yarrow. *See also* **wild flower**.

▶ *v* ▷ **weed out** get rid of, remove, root out,
eradicate, eliminate, purge; *formal* extirpate
☒ add, fix, infiltrate

weedy *adj*
thin, skinny, puny, scrawny, undersized, gangling,
weak, feeble, frail, weak-kneed, insipid
colloq. wet, wimpish
☒ strong

weekly *adv, adj*
▶ *adv* every week, by the week, once a week
formal hebdomadally
▶ *adj formal* hebdomadal, hebdomadary

weep *v, n*
▶ *v* cry, sob, be in tears, shed tears, moan, lament,
wail, mourn, grieve, bawl, blubber, snivel, whine,
whimper
colloq. blub
☒ rejoice
▶ *n* cry, sob, moan, snivel, blub, lament

weepy *adj, n*
▶ *adj* crying, tearful, sobbing, blubbering, weeping,

teary
formal labile, lachrymose
▶ *n* melodrama, sob-stuff, tear-jerker

weigh   *v*
1 *weigh the apples*
measure the weight of, see/measure how heavy
something is
2 BEAR DOWN, oppress, burden, depress, afflict,
trouble, worry
colloq. get down
3 CONSIDER, contemplate, evaluate, meditate on,
mull over, ponder, think over, examine, reflect on,
deliberate
▷ **weigh down** oppress, overload, load, burden,
bear down, weigh upon, press down, depress, afflict,
trouble, worry
colloq. get down
E∃ lighten, hearten
▷ **weigh up** assess, examine, size up, evaluate,
balance, compare, consider, contemplate, deliberate,
mull over, ponder, think over, discuss
colloq. chew over

weight   *n, v*
▶ *n* **1** HEAVINESS, gravity, burden, load, pressure,
mass, quantity, force, ballast, tonnage, poundage
formal avoirdupois
2 IMPORTANCE, significance, substance,
consequence, impact, moment, influence, force, value,
authority, power, consideration
formal preponderance
colloq. clout
3 BURDEN, load, onus, responsibility, duty, worry,
trouble, strain, encumbrance
E∃ **1** lightness
▶ *v* **1** LOAD, weigh down, burden, oppress, handicap
2 BIAS, unbalance, slant, prejudice, angle, load, twist,
sway

weightless   *adj*
light, insubstantial, airy
formal imponderous
E∃ heavy

weighty   *adj*
1 HEAVY, substantial, massive, bulky, hefty
2 IMPORTANT, significant, consequential, crucial,
critical, momentous, vital, serious, influential,
authoritative, grave, solemn
3 DEMANDING, burdensome, onerous, difficult,
exacting, taxing
E∃ **1** light **2** unimportant, significant

weird   *adj*
strange, uncanny, bizarre, eerie, creepy, supernatural,
unnatural, ghostly, freakish, mysterious, queer,
grotesque
formal preternatural
colloq. spooky, far-out, way-out
E∃ normal, usual

weirdo   *n*
eccentric, freak, crank, cure
colloq. crackpot, oddball, nutcase, loony, fruitcake,
nut, nutter, queer fish

welcome   *adj, n, v*
▶ *adj* acceptable, desirable, popular, pleasing,
pleasant, agreeable, gratifying, appreciated, delightful,
refreshing
E∃ unwelcome
▶ *n* reception, greeting, acceptance, hospitality
colloq. salutation, red carpet

▶ *v* greet, hail, receive, salute, meet, accept, approve
of, be pleased with, be satisfied with, embrace
colloq. roll out the red carpet for
E∃ reject, snub

weld   *v, n*
▶ *v* fuse, unite, bond, join, solder, bind, connect, seal,
link, cement
E∃ separate
▶ *n* joint, bond, seal, seam

welfare   *n*
1 WELL-BEING, health, prosperity, happiness,
comfort, soundness, security, benefit, good, fortune,
advantage, interest, profit, success
2 *live off welfare*
benefit, income, allowance, pension, sick pay, payment

well¹   *adv, adj*
▶ *adv* **1** *speak Czech well*
competently, skilfully, properly, ably, expertly,
proficiently, effectively, adeptly, excellently, rightly,
correctly, successfully
2 *everything turned out well*
satisfactorily, adequately, suitably, fittingly, sufficiently
3 *treat someone well*
kindly, genially, generously, hospitably, agreeably,
pleasantly, happily
4 *Did you know her well?*
thoroughly, properly, carefully, industriously, fully,
deeply, profoundly, closely, completely, greatly,
considerably
5 *live well*
successfully, prosperously, comfortably, splendidly,
luckily, fortunately
6 *think/speak well of someone*
highly, approvingly, favourably, glowingly, warmly
7 *well over a thousand people*
substantially, considerably, very much, to a great
extent, far
8 *you may well be right*
conceivably, quite possibly, very likely, probably,
certainly
E∃ **1** badly, inadequately, incompetently, wrongly
2, 3 badly **5** poorly **6** unfavourably
▷ **as well** too, also, in addition, furthermore,
besides, moreover; *colloq.* into the bargain
▷ **as well as** in addition to, together with, along
with, including, over and above, not to mention, to say
nothing of
▷ **well done** bravo, congratulations, hurrah, encore
▶ *adj* **1** HEALTHY, in good health, fit, able-bodied,
sound, robust, strong, thriving, flourishing, hale and
hearty
2 SATISFACTORY, right, all right, good, pleasing,
proper, agreeable, fine, lucky, fortunate
colloq. OK
E∃ **1** ill **2** bad

well²   *n, v*
▶ *n* *dig a well*
spring, well-spring, fountain, fount, source, reservoir,
pool, well-head

> *Types of well include*: artesian well, borehole, draw-
> well, gas well, geyser, gusher, hot spring, inkwell, lift-
> shaft, mineral spring, oil-well, pump-well, stairwell,
> thermal spring, waterhole, wishing-well.

▶ *v* flow, spring, surge, gush, stream, brim over, jet,
spout, spurt, swell, issue, rush, pour, flood, ooze, run,
trickle, rise, seep

well-advised *adj*
wise, reasonable, sensible, sound, far-sighted, long-sighted, shrewd, politic
formal prudent, judicious, sagacious, circumspect

well-balanced *adj*
1 RATIONAL, reasonable, level-headed, well-adjusted, stable, sensible, sane, sound, sober
colloq. together
2 SYMMETRICAL, even, harmonious, balanced, well-proportioned, well-ordered
E3 1 unbalanced, maladjusted 2 asymmetrical, disordered

well-behaved *adj*
well-mannered, good, polite, respectful, under control, obedient, considerate, co-operative
formal compliant
colloq. good as gold
E3 disobedient, naughty

well-being *n*
welfare, happiness, comfort, health, good health, good

well-bred *adj*
well-mannered, polite, well-brought-up, mannerly, courteous, civil, refined, cultivated, cultured, genteel, gentlemanly, ladylike, aristocratic, blue-blooded, upper-crust, gallant, urbane
E3 ill-bred

well-built *adj*
strong, muscular, brawny, strapping, burly, beefy, stout

well-deserved *adj*
deserved, due, just, justified, merited, rightful, appropriate
old use meet
formal condign
E3 undeserved

well-disposed *adj*
favourable, friendly, well-placed, sympathetic, agreeable, amicable, well-arranged, well-minded, well-aimed
E3 ill-disposed

well-dressed *adj*
smart, well-groomed, elegant, fashionable, chic, stylish, neat, trim, dapper, spruce, tidy
colloq. natty
E3 badly dressed, scruffy

well-founded *adj*
justifiable, reasonable, acceptance, reasonable, warranted, sustainable, right, sensible, sound, proper, fit, valid, plausible

well-groomed *adj*
neat, tidy, smart, trim, spruce, dapper, well-turned-out, well-dressed

well-known *adj*
famous, renowned, celebrated, famed, eminent, notable, noted, illustrious, familiar, widely-known, usual, common
E3 unknown

well-nigh *adv*
almost, nearly, practically, virtually, all but, just about, to all intents and purposes

well-off *adj*
1 RICH, wealthy, affluent, prosperous, well-to-do, moneyed, thriving, successful, comfortable
colloq. well-heeled, flush, rolling in it; *slang* loaded, filthy rich, stinking rich

2 FORTUNATE, lucky, prosperous, thriving, successful, comfortable
E3 1 poor, badly-off 2 unfortunate, unlucky

well-read *adj*
educated, literate, well-informed, knowledgeable, cultured, lettered

well-spoken *adj*
articulate, fluent, eloquent, clear, coherent, well-expressed

well-thought-of *adj*
respected, highly regarded, admired, looked up to, honoured, revered
formal esteemed, venerated
E3 despised, looked down on

well-to-do *adj*
rich, wealthy, affluent, moneyed, prosperous, well-off, comfortable
colloq. flush, well-heeled, rolling in it; *slang* loaded
E3 poor

well-versed *adj*
knowledgeable, familiar, acquainted, experienced, conversant, *au fait*, trained

well-wisher *n*
supporter, sympathizer, fan, well-willer

well-worn *adj*
1 *a well-worn phrase*
timeworn, stale, tired, trite, overused, unoriginal, hackneyed, commonplace, stereotyped, threadbare
colloq. corny
2 *well-worn clothing*
threadbare, worn, worn out, frayed, ragged, scruffy, shabby
E3 1 original 2 new

welsh *v*
cheat, defraud, swindle
colloq. diddle, do

welt *n*
weal, scar, mark, ridge, contusion, wound, streak, stripe, cicatrice, cicatrix

welter *v, n*
▶ *v* roll, flounder, pitch, toss, wallow, splash, wade, lurch, heave
▶ *n* mess, confusion, jumble, muddle, tangle, web, hotchpotch
colloq. mish-mash

wend *v*
▷ **wend your way** go, move, make your way, proceed, progress, travel, walk, hike, wander, trudge, plod, meander
E3 stay

wet *adj, n, v*
▶ *adj* 1 DAMP, moist, soaked, soaking, sodden, saturated, soggy, sopping, sopping wet, watery, waterlogged, drenched, dripping, spongy, dank, clammy
2 RAINING, rainy, showery, teeming, pouring, drizzling, dank, damp, humid
3 WEAK, feeble, weedy, spineless, soft, namby-pamby, irresolute
formal ineffectual, timorous, effete
colloq. pathetic, wimpish
E3 1 dry 2 dry 3 strong
▷ **wet behind the ears** new, untrained, inexperienced, immature, raw, innocent, naïve,

callow; *colloq.* green
◼ experienced
▶ *n* **1** WETNESS, moisture, moistness, damp, dampness, liquid, water, clamminess, condensation, humidity, rain, drizzle
2 *don't be such a wet*
fool, idiot, softy, weakling, milksop
colloq. wimp, wally, drip; *slang* jerk, nerd
◼ **1** dryness
▶ *v* moisten, damp, dampen, soak, saturate, drench, steep, flood, swamp, water, irrigate, spray, splash, sprinkle, imbue, douse, dip
◼ dry

wetness *n*
damp, dampness, moisture, wet, water, liquid, soddenness, sogginess, condensation, dankness, clamminess, humidity
◼ dryness

whack *v, n*
▶ *v* hit, strike, smack, thrash, slap, beat, bang, cuff, thump, box, buffet, rap
colloq. bash, wallop, belt, clobber, clout, sock
▶ *n* **1** SMACK, slap, blow, hit, rap, stroke, thump, cuff, box, bang
colloq. clout, bash, wallop
2 SHARE, portion, quota, allowance, allocation, lot, part, division, stint, proportion, percentage
colloq. cut, rake-off, slice of the cake

wharf *n*
dock, quay, quayside, jetty, landing-stage, dockyard, marina, pier

what's-its-name *n*
thingummy, thingummyjig, thingummybob, what-d'you-call-it
colloq. whatsit, doodah, whatnot

wheedle *v*
cajole, coax, persuade, talk into, win over, charm, flatter, beguile, entice, induce, court, draw
formal inveigle
◼ force

wheel *n, v*
▶ *n* turn, revolution, circle, rotation, gyration, pivot, roll, spin, twirl, whirl

Types of wheel include: balance-wheel, big wheel, buff-wheel, cartwheel, castor, Catherine wheel, charka, cogwheel, crown-wheel, drive-wheel, escape wheel, Ferris wheel, flywheel, gearwheel, idle wheel, mill wheel, paddle wheel, potter's wheel, prayer wheel, ratchet-wheel, roulette wheel, spinning-jenny, spinning-wheel, sprocket, spur gear, steering-wheel, wagon wheel, water-wheel, wheel of fortune, worm wheel.

▷ **at the wheel 1** DRIVING, steering, behind the wheel, in the driver's seat, turning **2** IN CHARGE, at the helm, in control, in command, responsible, directing; *colloq.* heading up
▶ *v* turn, rotate, circle, gyrate, orbit, spin, go round, pivot, twirl, whirl, swing, roll, revolve, swivel

wheeze *v, n*
▶ *v* pant, gasp, cough, hiss, rasp, whistle
▶ *n* **1** RASP, gasp, cough, hiss, whistle
2 TRICK, joke, gag, crack, prank, ruse, practical joke, ploy, scheme, plan, stunt, idea, story, anecdote, catch phrase
colloq. chestnut, one-liner, wrinkle

whereabouts *n*
location, position, place, situation, site, vicinity

wherewithal *n*
means, resources, supplies, money, cash, funds, capital, necessary
colloq. readies

whet *v*
1 SHARPEN, hone, file, grind, edge
2 STIMULATE, stir, rouse, arouse, excite, provoke, kindle, quicken, incite, awaken, titillate, increase
◼ **1** blunt **2** dampen

whiff *n*
1 *a whiff of fresh air*
breath, puff, hint, trace, blast, gust, draught, odour, smell, aroma, sniff, scent, reek, stink, stench
2 *a whiff of scandal/danger*
trace, hint, suspicion, suggestion, touch

while *n, v*
▶ *n* time, period, spell, stretch, season, span, interval
▶ *v* ▷ **while away** spend, pass, occupy, use (up), devote

whim *n*
fancy, caprice, notion, idea, quirk, freak, humour, conceit, fad, craze, passion, vagary, urge, impulse

whimper *v, n*
▶ *v* cry, sob, weep, snivel, sniffle, whine, grizzle, mewl, moan, groan
colloq. whinge
▶ *n* sob, cry, snivel, whine, moan, groan

whimsical *adj*
fanciful, quirky, playful, mischievous, impulsive, unpredictable, eccentric, funny, droll, curious, queer, unusual, weird, odd, peculiar, quaint
formal capricious
colloq. dotty

whine *v, n*
▶ *v* **1** CRY, sob, whimper, grizzle, moan, wail
2 COMPLAIN, carp, grumble, moan, groan, grouse
colloq. gripe, whinge, grouch, beef, belly-ache
▶ *n* **1** CRY, sob, whimper, moan, wail
2 COMPLAINT, moan, grumble, groan, grouse
colloq. gripe, grouch, beef, belly-ache

whinge *v, n*
▶ *v* complain, grumble, moan, carp
colloq. gripe, grouse, beef, belly-ache
▶ *n* complaint, grumble, moan, groan, grouse
colloq. gripe, beef, belly-ache

whip *v, n*
▶ *v* **1** BEAT, flog, lash, scourge, birch, cane, strap, thrash, punish, discipline
formal flagellate, chastise, castigate
colloq. tan, belt, whack, clout, wallop, give someone a good hiding
2 PULL, jerk, snatch, whisk, flash
colloq. yank
3 DASH, dart, rush, tear, flit, fly
4 *whip the cream*
stir, mix, whisk, beat
5 GOAD, drive, spur, prod, push, urge, stir, rouse, agitate, incite, invoke, prompt, instigate
▷ **whip up** stir up, work up, agitate, excite, arouse, incite, inflame, kindle, instigate, provoke, foment;
colloq. psych up
◼ dampen, deter

▶ *n* lash, scourge, switch, birch, cane, horsewhip, crop, riding-crop, cat-o'-nine-tails

whippersnapper *n*
scamp, scallywag, imp, rascal, nipper, hobbledehoy

whipping *n*
beating, punishment, spanking, flogging, lashing, thrashing, birching, caning
formal castigation, flagellation
colloq. belting, hiding, tanning, walloping

whirl *v, n*
▶ *v* spin, swirl, turn, twist, twirl, pivot, pirouette, swivel, wheel, rotate, revolve, turn round, reel, roll, gyrate, circle
▶ *n* **1** SPIN, twirl, twist, gyration, revolution, pirouette, swirl, turn, wheel, rotation, circle, reel, pivot, roll
2 BUSTLE, flurry, round, series, succession, merry-go-round, commotion, agitation, hubbub, hurly-burly, confusion, daze, muddle, jumble, giddiness, tumult, uproar
▷ **give something a whirl** try, attempt, strive, endeavour, venture; *colloq.* have a go, have a bash/crack/shot/stab

whirlpool *n*
maelstrom, vortex
Scot. weel

whirlwind *n, adj*
▶ *n* tornado, cyclone, vortex
▶ *adj* hasty, impulsive, quick, rapid, speedy, swift, lightning, headlong, impetuous, rash
🔄 deliberate, slow

whisk *v, n*
▶ *v* **1** WHIP, beat, stir, mix
2 DART, dash, rush, hurry, speed, fly, tears, bolt, hasten, race, shoot, dive, whip
3 BRUSH, sweep, flick, wipe, twitch
▶ *n* beater, brush, swizzle-stick

whisky *n*
whiskey, Scotch, bourbon, rye, usquebaugh, moonshine, malt

whisper *v, n*
▶ *v* **1** MURMUR, mutter, mumble, say/speak quietly, breathe, hiss, rustle, sigh, sough
formal susurrate
2 HINT, intimate, insinuate, gossip, divulge
🔄 **1** shout
▶ *n* **1** MURMUR, soft/quiet/low voice, undertone, sigh, hiss, rustle, sough
2 HINT, suggestion, suspicion, breath, whiff, rumour, report, innuendo, insinuation, trace, tinge, soupçon, buzz

whistle *v, n*
▶ *v* pipe, sing, call, cheep, chirp, warble
▶ *n* song, call, cheep, warble, chirp, siren, hooter

whit *n*
atom, little, drop, bit, scrap, shred, piece, fragment, particle, crumb, pinch, speck, trace, iota, jot, grain, mite, modicum, dash, hoot
🔄 lot

white *adj*
1 PALE, light-skinned, pallid, wan, ashen, colourless, anaemic, pasty, waxen
2 LIGHT, snowy, milky, creamy, ivory, hoary, silver, grey

3 PURE, immaculate, spotless, stainless, undefiled
🔄 **1** black, dark, ruddy **2** dark **3** defiled

white-collar *adj*
executive, office, professional, salaried, clerical, non-manual
🔄 blue-collar, manual

whiten *v*
bleach, blanch, whitewash, pale, fade, whitewash
formal etiolate
🔄 blacken, darken

whitewash *n, v*
▶ *n* cover-up, concealment, deception, camouflage
🔄 exposure
▶ *v* **1** COVER UP, conceal, hide, make light of, suppress, gloss over, camouflage
2 THRASH, beat, crush, drub, best
colloq. clobber, hammer, lick, paste, trounce
🔄 **1** expose

whittle *v*
1 CARVE, cut, scrape, shave, trim, pare, hew, shape
2 ERODE, eat away, wear away, diminish, consume, use (up), reduce, undermine

whole *adj, n*
▶ *adj* **1** COMPLETE, entire, integral, full, total, unabridged, uncut, undivided, unedited
2 INTACT, unharmed, undamaged, unbroken, perfect, sound, in one piece, mint, uninjured, unhurt
formal inviolate
3 WELL, healthy, fit, sound, strong
🔄 **1** partial **2** damaged **3** ill
▶ *n* total, aggregate, sum total, entirety, all, fullness, totality, ensemble, entity, unit, lot, piece, everything
🔄 part
▷ **on the whole** generally, mostly, in general, generally speaking, in the main, as a rule, for the most part, all in all, all things considered, by and large, predominantly

wholehearted *adj*
enthusiastic, earnest, committed, dedicated, devoted, hearty, passionate, heartfelt, emphatic, warm, sincere, unfeigned, genuine, unreserved, unstinting, unqualified, complete, true, real, zealous
🔄 half-hearted

wholesale *adj, adv*
▶ *adj* comprehensive, far-reaching, extensive, sweeping, wide-ranging, mass, broad, all-inclusive, outright, total, massive, indiscriminate
🔄 partial
▶ *adv* indiscriminately, totally, extensively, comprehensively, massively, en bloc
🔄 partially

wholesome *adj*
1 *wholesome food; a wholesome climate*
good, healthy, healthful, hygienic, sanitary, nutritious, nourishing, beneficial, salutary, refreshing, invigorating, bracing
formal salubrious
2 *wholesome entertainment*
moral, decent, clean, proper, improving, edifying, uplifting, pure, virtuous, righteous, beneficial, helpful, ethical, honourable, respectable
🔄 **1** unhealthy **2** unwholesome, immoral

wholly *adv*
completely, entirely, fully, purely, absolutely, totally, utterly, comprehensively, altogether, perfectly, thoroughly, all, exclusively, only, in every respect

colloq. one hundred per cent
F3 partly

whoop *v, n*
shout, cry, yell, cheer, scream, shriek, roar, hoop, hoot, hurrah
colloq. holler

whopper *n*
lie, falsehood, fabrication, untruth, fable
colloq. cracker, fairy story, tall story

whopping *adj*
large, big, huge, massive, extraordinary, immense, vast, great, mammoth, tremendous, staggering, monumental, enormous, giant, gigantic, whacking
formal prodigious
F3 tiny

whore *n*
prostitute, harlot, call girl, scarlet woman, trollop, wench, strumpet, fallen woman, street-walker, woman of the town, *fille de joie*, courtesan
colloq. hooker, hustler; *slang* tart

whorehouse *n*
brothel, bordello, bawdy-house, house of ill repute, bagnio
slang knocking-shop; *US* cat-house

whorl *n*
spiral, twist, turn, coil, helix, vortex, corkscrew
formal convolution

wicked *adj*
1 EVIL, sinful, immoral, bad, depraved, corrupt, vicious, unprincipled, debased, abominable, ungodly, devilish, unrighteous, shameful, black-hearted, villainous
old use facinorous
formal iniquitous, heinous, dissolute, egregious, nefarious
2 BAD, unpleasant, harmful, offensive, scandalous, vile, worthless, difficult, terrible, dreadful, distressing, awful, atrocious, severe, intense, nasty, injurious, troublesome, terrible, foul, fierce
3 NAUGHTY, mischievous, roguish, impish, rascally
4 EXCELLENT, admirable
colloq. cool
F3 1 good, upright 2 harmless

wickedness *n*
evil, depravity, vileness, atrocity, abomination, corruption, corruptness, foulness, fiendishness, immorality, shamefulness, sin, sinfulness, impiety, unrighteousness, devilishness, enormity, amorality
formal dissoluteness, heinousness, iniquity, reprobacy
F3 uprightness

wickerwork *n*
wicker, basket-work, wattle, wattle-work

wide *adj, adv*
▶ *adj* 1 BROAD, roomy, spacious, extensive, vast, immense, ample
2 DILATED, expanded, full
3 EXTENSIVE, wide-ranging, comprehensive, great, broad, vast, immense, far-reaching, general
4 LOOSE, baggy, full, roomy
formal capacious
5 OFF-TARGET, off-course, off the mark, distant, remote
F3 1 narrow 3 restricted 5 near
▶ *adv* 1 ASTRAY, off course, off target, off the mark

2 FULLY, completely, to the full extent, all the way
F3 1 on target

⚠ **wide** or **broad** ? *See panel at* **broad**.

wide-awake *adj*
conscious, aware, fully awake, wakened, observant, watchful, vigilant, wary, sharp, alert, astute, roused, heedful, keen, quick-witted, on your toes, on the alert, on the qui vive
colloq. on the ball
F3 asleep

widely *adv*
broadly, extensively, generally, comprehensively

widen *v*
broaden, expand, extend, spread, increase, stretch, enlarge
formal distend, dilate
F3 narrow

wide-open *adj*
open, gaping, wide, outspread, outstretched, spread, unprotected, vulnerable, defenceless, exposed, susceptible
formal unfortified
F3 closed, narrow

wide-ranging *adj*
far-reaching, broad, extensive, widespread, comprehensive, thorough, important, significant, momentous, sweeping

widespread *adj*
extensive, prevalent, rife, general, sweeping, universal, wholesale, far-reaching, unlimited, broad, common, pervasive, far-flung
F3 limited

width *n*
breadth, broadness, diameter, wideness, compass, thickness, largeness, span, scope, range, measure, girth, beam, amplitude, extent, extensiveness, reach

wield *v*
1 *wield a weapon*
brandish, flourish, swing, wave, handle, ply, shake, manage, manipulate
2 *wield power*
have, hold, possess, employ, exert, exercise, use, utilize, control, maintain, command

wife *n*
partner, spouse, companion, mate, bride
colloq. better half, other half, missus
Related adjective: uxorial

wiggle *v & n*
jiggle, shake, jerk, wriggle, wag, waggle, twist, squirm, twitch, writhe

wild *adj*
1 UNTAMED, undomesticated, savage, barbarous, primitive, uncivilized, natural, unbroken, ferocious, fierce, brutish
formal feral
2 UNCULTIVATED, natural, desolate, waste, barren, forsaken, unpopulated, uninhabited, unsettled, rugged, inhospitable
3 UNRESTRAINED, unruly, undisciplined, unmanageable, violent, turbulent, rowdy, lawless, out of control, uncontrollable, ungovernable, rampant, disorderly, riotous, boisterous
4 STORMY, tempestuous, raging, rough, furious,

violent, blustery, choppy, turbulent
5 UNTIDY, unkempt, messy, dishevelled, tousled, uncombed
6 RECKLESS, rash, impulsive, foolish, foolhardy, impracticable, irrational, outrageous, preposterous, wayward, extravagant, fantastic, unwise
formal imprudent
7 MAD, frenzied, distraught, demented, berserk, frantic, beside yourself
colloq. crazy, nuts, nutty, bonkers, bananas
8 ANGRY, furious, raging, enraged, infuriated, incensed, blazing, fuming
colloq. crazy, mad, hopping mad, foaming at the mouth
9 ENTHUSIASTIC, keen, fervent, vehement, passionate, excited, fanatical
colloq. crazy, mad, nuts, daft, potty
EƎ 1 tame, civilized **2** cultivated **3** restrained **4** calm **5** tidy **6** sensible **7** sane

wilderness *n*
desert, wasteland, waste, wilds, jungle

wild flower

Wild flowers include: Aaron's rod, ale hoof, bird's foot trefoil, birth-wort, bistort, black-eyed susan, bladder campion, bluebell, broomrape, butter-and-eggs, buttercup, campion, celandine, clary, clustered bellflower, clover, columbine, comfrey, common evening-primrose, common mallow, common toadflax, cowslip, crane's bill, crowfoot, cuckoo flower, daisy, edelweiss, field cow-wheat, foxglove, goatsbeard, goldcup, goldenrod, great mullein, harebell, heartsease, heather, horsetail, lady's slipper, lady's smock, lungwort, marguerite, masterwort, moneywort, multiflora rose, New England aster, oxeye daisy, oxslip, pennyroyal, poppy, primrose, ragged robin, rock rose, rough-fruited cinquefoil, self-heal, shepherd's club, solomon's seal, stiff-haired sunflower, stonecrop, teasel, toadflax, violet, water lily, white campion, wild chicory, wild endive, wild gladiolus, wild iris, wild orchid, wild pansy, wood anemone, yarrow, yellow rocket. *See also* weed.

wildlife *n*
animals, fauna

wilds *n*
outback, remote areas, wasteland, wilderness, desert
colloq. the back of beyond, the sticks, the middle of nowhere, the boondocks

wiles *n*
trick, stratagem, ruse, ploy, device, contrivance, guile, manoeuvre, subterfuge, cunning, deceit, deception, cheating, trickery, fraud, craftiness, artfulness, chicanery
colloq. dodge
EƎ guilelessness

wilful *adj*
1 DELIBERATE, conscious, intentional, voluntary, calculated, planned, premeditated
2 SELF-WILLED, headstrong, obstinate, stubborn, pig-headed, mulish, inflexible, unyielding, uncompromising, perverse, wayward, contrary, determined, dogged
formal obdurate, refractory, intransigent, intractable
EƎ 1 unintentional, spontaneous **2** good-natured

will *n, v*
▶ *n* **1** VOLITION, choice, option, preference, decision, discretion

2 WISH, desire, inclination, feeling, fancy, disposition, mind
3 PURPOSE, resolve, resolution, determination, purposefulness, willpower, single-mindedness, aim, intention, command
▶ *v* **1** WANT, desire, wish, intend, choose, compel, direct, command, decree, order, ordain
2 BEQUEATH, leave, hand down, pass on, pass down, dispose of
formal transfer, confer

willing *adj*
disposed, inclined, agreeable, ready, prepared, consenting, content, amenable, biddable, co-operative, pleased, well-disposed, so-minded, favourable, happy, glad, eager, enthusiastic, keen
formal compliant
colloq. game
EƎ unwilling, disinclined, reluctant

willingly *adv*
readily, unhesitatingly, eagerly, freely, happily, cheerfully, by choice, voluntarily, gladly, nothing loth
EƎ unwillingly

willingness *n*
readiness, inclination, will, wish, consent, desire, favour, enthusiasm, agreeableness, agreement, disposition, volition
formal complaisance, compliance
EƎ unwillingness

willowy *adj*
slender, slim, graceful, svelte, sylph-like, limber, lissom, lithe, lithesome, supple
EƎ buxom

willpower *n*
determination, resolution, resolve, single-mindedness, commitment, will, self-control, self-discipline, self-mastery, self-command, persistence, doggedness, drive
colloq. grit

willy-nilly *adv*
necessarily, compulsorily, of necessity
formal perforce

wilt *v*
droop, sag, wither, shrivel, flop, flag, dwindle, weaken, faint, diminish, lessen, grow less, fail, fade, languish, ebb, sink, wane
EƎ perk up

wily *adj*
shrewd, cunning, scheming, artful, sharp, crafty, foxy, intriguing, tricky, underhand, shifty, deceitful, cheating, deceptive, astute, sly, guileful, designing, crooked
colloq. fly
EƎ guileless

wimp *n*
fool, softy, clown, milksop
colloq. clot, drip, wally, wet; *slang* jerk, nerd

win *v, n*
▶ *v* **1** BE VICTORIOUS, triumph, succeed, achieve, success, prevail, overcome, conquer, come (in) first, carry off, finish first
colloq. win the day, win hands down, come out on top, turn up trumps, strike gold, hit the jackpot
2 GAIN, acquire, achieve, attain, accomplish, receive, secure, obtain, get, earn, collect, catch, net
formal procure
EƎ 1 fail, lose

▷ **win over** persuade, convince, influence, convert, sway, talk round, bring round, charm, allure, attract; *formal* prevail upon
▶ *n* victory, triumph, conquest, success, mastery
F₃ defeat

wince *v, n*
▶ *v* start, jump, draw back, recoil, flinch, jerk, shrink, cringe, blench, cower, quail
▶ *n* start, cringe, flinch, jerk

wind¹ *n*
blowing in the wind
air, breeze, draught, gust, puff, breath, air-current, blast, current, bluster, gale, hurricane, tornado

Types of wind include: anticyclone, austral wind, berg wind, bise, bora, Cape doctor, chinook, cyclone, doctor, east wind, El Nino, etesian, Favonian wind, fohn, gregale, harmattan, helm wind, khamsin, levant, libeccio, meltemi, mistral, monsoon, north wind, nor'wester, pampero, prevailing wind, samiel, simoom, sirocco, snow eater, southerly, southerly buster, trade wind, tramontana, westerly, wet chinook, williwaw, willy-willy, zephyr, zonda.

Related adjective: aeolian
▷ **in the wind** likely, probable, expected, about to happen; *colloq.* on the cards
▷ **put the wind up** scare, frighten, discourage, alarm, unnerve, startle, panic, agitate, daunt, sound the alarm; *formal* perturb

wind² *v, n*
▶ **1** CURVE, bend, loop, spiral, zigzag, twine, snake, deviate, meander, ramble
2 COIL, wrap, twist, turn, curl, twine, encircle, furl, wreathe, roll, reel
▷ **wind down 1** SLOW (DOWN), slacken off, lessen, reduce, subside, diminish, dwindle, decline, stop, bring/come to an end **2** RELAX, unwind, quieten down, ease up, calm down
F₃ 1 increase
▷ **wind up 1** CLOSE (DOWN), end, finalize, finish, stop, bring to a close, bring to an end, liquidate; *formal* conclude, terminate **2** END UP, finish up, find yourself, settle **3** ANNOY, irritate, disconcert, fool, trick, make fun of; *colloq.* kid, pull someone's leg, rub someone up the wrong way
F₃ 1 begin
▶ *n* bend, curve, turn, twist, zigzag, meander

windbag *n*
boaster, gossip, bore, braggart, blether
colloq. gasbag, big-mouth

winded *adj*
puffed out, breathless, out of breath, panting, puffed, out of puff
F₃ fresh

windfall *n*
stroke of luck, bonanza, godsend, jackpot, treasure-trove, stroke of luck, find, manna, pennies from heaven

winding *adj*
curving, turning, twisting, bending, crooked, tortuous, indirect, roundabout, spiral, circuitous, meandering, serpentine
formal sinuous, sinuate(d), flexuose, flexuous, anfractuous, convoluted
F₃ straight

window *n*
pane, light, opening

Types of window include: bay, bow, bull's eye, casement, Catherine wheel, compass, decorated, dormer, double-glazed, double-glazing, early English, fanlight, French, lancet, louvre window, lucarne, mullioned window, Norman, oeil-de-boeuf, oriel, patio door, perpendicular, porthole, quarterlight, rose window, sash, secondary-glazed, shop window, skylight, sliding window, stained glass window, ticket window, windscreen, windowpane.

windpipe *n*
throat, pharynx
old use weasand
technical trachea
Related adjective: tracheal

windy *adj*
1 *windy weather*
breezy, blowy, blustery, squally, windswept, stormy, wild, tempestuous, gusty
2 *windy speech*
long-winded, wordy, verbose, garrulous, rambling, turgid, pompous, bombastic
formal prolix
3 NERVOUS, uneasy, afraid, frightened, scared, timid
colloq. chicken, nervy, on edge
F₃ 1 calm, windless **3** fearless

wine *n*

Types of wine include: alcohol-free, dry, brut, sec, demi-sec, sweet, sparkling, table wine, house wine, red wine, *colloq.* house red, white wine, *colloq.* house white, rosé, blush wine, fortified wine, mulled wine, tonic wine, vintage wine, *colloq.* plonk; sherry, dry sherry, fino, medium sherry, amontillado, sweet sherry, oloroso; port, ruby, tawny, white port, vintage port.

Varieties of wine include: Alsace, Asti, Auslese, Beaujolais, Beaujolais Nouveau, Beaune, Bordeaux, Burgundy, cabernet sauvignon, Chablis, Chambertin, champagne, Chardonnay, Chianti, claret, Côtes du Rhône, Dao, Douro, Frascati, Graves, hock, Lambrusco, Liebfraumilch, Mâcon, Madeira, Malaga, Marsala, Mateus Rosé, Médoc, Merlot, moselle, Muscadet, muscatel, Niersteiner, retsina, Riesling, Rioja, Sauterne, Sekt, Soave, Spatlese, Tarragona, Valpolicella, vinho verde.

Related adjective: vinous

wine-bottle sizes

Sizes of wine-bottles include: magnum, flagon, jeroboam, methuselah, rehoboam, salmanazar, balthazar, nebuchadnezzar.

wine glass *n*
glass, goblet, flute, schooner

wing *n, v*
▶ *n* **1** SECTION, branch, arm, faction, group, grouping, flank, circle, coterie, set, segment, side
2 ANNEXE, adjunct, extension, attachment, side
▶ *v* fly, glide, flit, hurry, move, travel, pass, speed, race, soar, zoom
formal hasten

wink *v, n*
▶ *v* blink, flutter, glimmer, glint, glitter, twinkle,

gleam, sparkle, flicker, flash
formal nictate, nictitate
▷ **wink at** ignore, disregard, overlook, neglect, pass over, condone, take no notice of; *colloq.* turn a blind eye to
▶ *n* **1** BLINK, flutter, sparkle, twinkle, glimmering, gleam, glitter, glint, flash
formal nictation, nictitation
2 INSTANT, moment, second, split second, flash

winkle *v*
extract, extricate, draw out, worm, force, prise, flush

winner *n*
champion, victor, prizewinner, medallist, title-holder, world-beater, conqueror
formal vanquisher
colloq. champ
⊟ loser

winning *adj*
1 CONQUERING, triumphant, unbeaten, undefeated, victorious, successful
formal vanquishing
2 WINSOME, charming, attractive, captivating, engaging, beguiling, bewitching, fetching, enchanting, endearing, delightful, amiable, alluring, lovely, pleasing, sweet
⊟ **1** losing **2** unappealing

winnings *n*
jackpot, gains, proceeds, profits, takings, prize(s), booty, spoils
⊟ losses

winnow *v*
sift, separate, screen, divide, cull, select, sort, part, comb, fan

winsome *adj*
charming, attractive, captivating, engaging, beguiling, bewitching, fetching, enchanting, endearing, delightful, amiable, alluring, lovely, pleasing, pretty, prepossessing, sweet
old use comely
formal delectable
⊟ unattractive

wintry *adj*
1 *wintry weather*
cold, chilly, bleak, cheerless, biting, piercing, raw, desolate, dismal, harsh, snowy, arctic, frosty, freezing, frozen, icy, glacial
formal hibernal, hiemal
2 UNFRIENDLY, hostile, bleak, cheerless, desolate, dismal, cold, frosty, icy, cool, harsh

wipe *v, n*
▶ *v* **1** RUB, clean, dry, dust, brush, mop, swab, sponge, clear
2 REMOVE, erase, take away, take off, get rid of
▷ **wipe out** eradicate, obliterate, destroy, massacre, exterminate, annihilate, erase, expunge, raze, abolish, blot out, demolish; *formal* efface, extirpate
▶ *n* rub, clean, dry, dust, brush, mop, sponge, swab

wire-pulling *n*
scheming, plotting, influence, intrigue, conspiring, manipulation, pull, Machiavellianism
colloq. clout

wiry *adj*
1 SINEWY, muscular, lean, tough, strong
2 *wiry hair*

coarse, wavy, rough
⊟ **1** puny, flabby **2** soft

wisdom *n*
discernment, penetration, reason, sense, astuteness, comprehension, enlightenment, judgement, insight, common sense, understanding, knowledge, learning, intelligence, foresight
formal sagacity, judiciousness, erudition, prudence, circumspection, sapience
⊟ folly, stupidity

wise *adj*
1 DISCERNING, perceptive, rational, informed, well-informed, understanding, enlightened, knowing, educated, knowledgeable, intelligent, clever, aware, experienced
formal sagacious, erudite, sapient
2 WELL-ADVISED, reasonable, sensible, sound, far-sighted, long-sighted, shrewd, politic
formal prudent, judicious, sagacious, circumspect
⊟ **1** foolish, stupid **2** ill-advised
▷ **put wise** inform, notify, tip off, warn, tell, alert, fill in, intimate to, put in the picture, clue in; *formal* apprise; *colloq.* wise up

wiseacre *n*
wise guy, wiseling
colloq. smart alec, smartypants, clever dick

wisecrack *n*
quip, joke, jest, funny, witticism, gag, barb, gibe, pun, in-joke
colloq. one-liner

wish *v, n*
▶ *v* **1** DESIRE, want, yearn, long, hanker, pine, covet, crave, aspire, hope, fancy, hunger, thirst, prefer, need, lust
colloq. yen
2 ASK, bid, require, order, instruct, direct, command
▶ *n* **1** DESIRE, want, hankering, aspiration, inclination, longing, craving, hunger, thirst, liking, fondness, preference, yearning, urge, whim, hope, fancy
colloq. yen
2 REQUEST, desire, bidding, order, instruction, command, will

wishy-washy *adj*
feeble, weak, insipid, thin, watered-down, watery, flat, bland, ineffective, vapid, tasteless
formal ineffectual
colloq. namby-pamby
⊟ strong, firm

wisp *n*
shred, strand, thread, twist, piece, lock

wispy *adj*
thin, straggly, frail, fine, insubstantial, light, flimsy, fragile, delicate, ethereal, gossamer, faint
formal attenuated
⊟ substantial

wistful *adj*
1 THOUGHTFUL, pensive, musing, reflective, wishful, contemplative, dreamy, dreaming, meditative
2 MELANCHOLY, sad, forlorn, longing, yearning, mournful
formal disconsolate

wit *n*
1 HUMOUR, funniness, repartee, facetiousness, drollery, banter, badinage, jocularity, levity,

waggishness
2 INTELLIGENCE, cleverness, sense, reason, common sense, wisdom, understanding, judgement, insight, shrewdness, astuteness, faculties, intellect
formal sagacity
colloq. brains, gumption, nous, marbles
3 HUMORIST, comedian, comic, satirist, joker, wag
F3 **1** seriousness **2** stupidity

witch   *n*
sorceress, enchantress, occultist, magician, hex, hag
formal necromancer

witchcraft   *n*
sorcery, magic, wizardry, occultism, the occult, the black art, black magic, enchantment, voodoo, spell, incantation, divination
formal necromancy, conjuration

witch doctor
magician, medicine man, medicine woman, shaman, angekok

witch hunt
hounding, hue and cry, McCarthyism

with it
fashionable, vogue, modern, contemporary, progressive, up-to-date, up-to-the-minute, modish
colloq. cool, hip, in, trendy, groovy
F3 out-of-date

withdraw   *v*
1 REMOVE, take away, pull back, draw back, draw out, pull out, extract
2 DEPART, go (away), absent yourself, retire, remove, leave, back out, draw back, fall back, recede, drop out, retreat, secede, scratch
3 RECANT, disclaim, take back, revoke, retract, cancel, recall, take away
formal rescind, abjure, nullify, annul
4 RECOIL, shrink back, draw back, pull back

withdrawal   *n*
1 REMOVAL, taking away, pulling back, drawing back/out, extraction
2 DEPARTURE, exit, exodus, falling back, retirement, retreat, evacuation, disengagement
3 REPUDIATION, recantation, disclaimer, revocation, recall, secession
formal disavowal, abjuration

withdrawn   *adj*
1 RESERVED, unsociable, shy, introvert, introverted, quiet, retiring, aloof, detached, shrinking, private, uncommunicative, unforthcoming, taciturn, silent
2 REMOTE, isolated, distant, secluded, out-of-the-way, private, hidden, solitary
F3 **1** extrovert, outgoing, forthcoming

wither   *v*
shrink, shrivel, dry (up), wilt, droop, weaken, decay, disintegrate, dwindle, wane, perish, die (off), disappear, fade (away), languish, decline, waste
F3 flourish, thrive

withering   *adj*
scornful, contemptuous, scathing, snubbing, humiliating, mortifying, wounding, destructive, deadly, death-dealing, devastating
F3 encouraging, supportive

withhold   *v*
keep back, retain, hold back, suppress, restrain, repress, control, curb, check, keep in check, reserve, deduct, refuse, hide, conceal

formal decline
F3 give, accord

withstand   *v*
resist, oppose, stand fast, stand your ground, stand, stand up to, stand firm/fast, fight, confront, brave, face, cope with, take on, thwart, defy, hold your ground, hold out, last out, hold off, endure, bear, tolerate, put up with, survive, weather
F3 give in, yield

witless   *adj*
stupid, mindless, foolish, silly, senseless, inane, crazy, imbecilic, idiotic, moronic, daft, gormless, dull, empty-headed, half-witted, cretinous
F3 intelligent

witness   *n, v*
▶ *n* **1** *witness in a court*
testifier
formal attestant, deponent
2 ONLOOKER, eye-witness, looker-on, observer, spectator, viewer, watcher, bystander
▶ *v* **1** SEE, observe, notice, note, view, watch, look on, mark, perceive
2 TESTIFY, bear witness, give evidence, confirm, prove, verify, support, endorse, be evidence of, bear out
formal attest, depose, corroborate, affirm
3 ENDORSE, sign, countersign

witticism   *n*
quip, riposte, pun, repartee, pleasantry, *bon mot*, wisecrack, epigram
colloq. one-liner

witty   *adj*
humorous, amusing, comic, sharp-witted, droll, whimsical, original, brilliant, clever, ingenious, lively, sparkling, funny, facetious, waggish, fanciful, jocular
F3 dull, unamusing

wizard   *n, adj*
▶ *n* **1** SORCERER, magician, warlock, enchanter, occultist, witch, conjurer
formal necromancer, thaumaturge
2 EXPERT, adept, virtuoso, ace, master, maestro, prodigy, genius
colloq. star, whiz, hotshot
▶ *adj* fantastic, wonderful, great, good, marvellous, brilliant, enjoyable, tremendous, super, superb, smashing, sensational
colloq. fab, terrific, smashing

wizened   *adj*
shrivelled, shrunken, dried up, withered, wrinkled, gnarled, thin, worn, lined

wobble   *v, n*
▶ *v* shake, oscillate, tremble, quake, sway, stagger, teeter, totter, rock, seesaw, vibrate, waver, quiver, dodder, fluctuate, hesitate, dither, vacillate
colloq. shilly-shally
▶ *n* shake, unsteadiness, tremor, quaking, rock, tremble, vibration, oscillation

wobbly   *adj*
unstable, shaky, rickety, unsteady, quavering, trembling, teetering, tottering, doddering, doddery, uneven, unbalanced, unsafe
colloq. wonky
F3 stable, steady

woe   *n*
misery, adversity, distress, sadness, sorrow, unhappiness, wretchedness, grief, melancholy,

misfortune, suffering, hardship, trouble, pain, agony, anguish, gloom, curse, trial, depression, dejection, burden, disaster, calamity, heartache, heartbreak, tears
formal affliction, tribulation
E≡ joy

woebegone *adj*
miserable, wretched, sad, sorrowful, troubled, downcast, downhearted, gloomy, forlorn, grief-stricken, long-faced, dejected, crestfallen, mournful, doleful, dispirited, tearful, tear-stained
formal disconsolate, lugubrious
colloq. blue, down in the mouth
E≡ joyful

woeful *adj*
1 SAD, miserable, wretched, mournful, sorry, unhappy, gloomy, grieving, grievous, heartbreaking, heart-rending
formal disconsolate, doleful
2 DISTRESSING, disappointing, lamentable, pitiable, disgraceful, deplorable, shocking, sorrowful, tragic, cruel, hopeless, inadequate, mean, paltry, feeble, dreadful, appalling, awful, bad, terrible, poor, rotten, calamitous, catastrophic, disastrous
colloq. lousy, pathetic
E≡ joyful

wolf *n, v*
▶ *n* womanizer, seducer, ladies' man, lady-killer, lecher, philanderer, Casanova, Don Juan, Romeo
▶ *v* ▷ **wolf down** put away, pack away, gobble, gulp, devour, cram, bolt, stuff, gorge, scoff
E≡ nibble

woman *n*
female, lady, girl, maiden, maid
Related adjective: female

womanhood *n*
1 ADULTHOOD, maturity
formal muliebrity
2 WOMANKIND, woman, womenkind, womenfolk(s)

womanizer *n*
philanderer, seducer, wolf, lady-killer, ladies' man, lecher, Casanova, Don Juan, Romeo

womanly *adj*
feminine, female, ladylike, womanish, motherly, kind, warm, tender, effeminate

wonder *n, v*
▶ *n* 1 AWE, amazement, astonishment, admiration, wonderment, fascination, surprise, pleasure, bewilderment
2 MARVEL, phenomenon, miracle, prodigy, sight, spectacle, rarity, curiosity
formal nonpareil

The seven wonders of the world are: Pyramids of Egypt, Hanging Gardens of Babylon, Statue of Zeus at Olympia, Temple of Artemis at Ephesus, Mausoleum of Halicarnassus, Colossus of Rhodes, Pharos of Alexandria.

▶ *v* 1 ASK YOURSELF, meditate, speculate, ponder, question, puzzle, inquire, query, doubt, think, reflect
formal conjecture
2 MARVEL, gape, be amazed, be surprised, be astonished, be astounded, stand in awe, be dumbfounded, be lost for words

wonderful *adj*
1 MARVELLOUS, magnificent, outstanding,

excellent, superb, admirable, delightful, phenomenal, sensational, stupendous, tremendous
colloq. super, terrific, brilliant, great, fabulous, fantastic, smashing, ace, out of this world; *slang* cool, wicked
2 AMAZING, astonishing, astounding, startling, surprising, extraordinary, incredible, remarkable, staggering, awesome, strange
E≡ 1 appalling, awful, dreadful 2 ordinary

wonky *adj*
shaky, wobbly, weak, wrong, unsound, unsteady, askew, skew-whiff, amiss
E≡ stable, straight, balanced

wont *adj, n*
▶ *adj* inclined, used, accustomed, given
formal habituated
▶ *n* habit, custom, routine, practice, rule, use, way

wonted *adj*
usual, customary, familiar, normal, regular, common, daily, frequent, routine, accustomed, conventional
formal habitual
E≡ unwonted

woo *v*
1 *woo a lover*
court, pay court to, chase, pursue, seek the hand of
2 *woo custom*
encourage, cultivate, attract, look for, seek, pursue

wood *n*
1 TIMBER, lumber, planks

Types of wood include: timber, *US* lumber, hardwood, softwood, heartwood, sapwood, seasoned wood, green wood, bitterwood, brushwood, cordwood, firewood, kindling, matchwood, plywood, pulpwood, whitewood, chipboard, hardboard, wood veneer; afrormosia, ash, balsa, beech, cedar, cherry, chestnut, cottonwood, deal, ebony, elm, mahogany, African mahogany, maple, oak, pine, redwood, rosewood, sandalwood, sapele, satinwood, teak, walnut, willow. *See also* **tree**.

Related adjective: ligneous
2 FOREST, woods, woodland, trees, plantation, thicket, grove, coppice, copse, spinney
Related adjective: sylvan
▷ **out of the wood(s)** out of danger, safe, safe and sound, secure, in the clear, out of difficulty, home and dry

wooded *adj*
forested, timbered, woody, tree-covered
formal sylvan
E≡ open

wooden *adj*
1 TIMBER, woody
2 EMOTIONLESS, expressionless, awkward, clumsy, stilted, stodgy, lifeless, spiritless, graceless, impassive, unemotional, unresponsive, stiff, rigid, leaden, deadpan, blank, empty, vacant, vacuous, slow
E≡ 2 lively

woodland *n*
wood(s), forest, trees, plantation, thicket, grove, coppice, copse, spinney
formal boscage

woody *adj*
wooded, wooden, forested, tree-covered
formal bosky, ligneous, sylvan, xyloid
E≡ open

wool *n*
fleece, down, hair, floccus, yarn
Related adjective: lanate
▷ **pull the wool over someone's eyes** deceive,
fool, trick, hoodwink, take in, bamboozle, delude,
dupe; *colloq.* con, lead up the garden path, pull a fast
one on, put one over on

wool-gathering *n*
absent-mindedness, day-dreaming, forgetfulness,
distraction, inattention, preoccupation

woolly *adj, n*
▶ *adj* **1** WOOLLEN, fleecy, woolly-haired, hairy,
downy, fluffy, shaggy, fuzzy, frizzy
formal flocculent
2 UNCLEAR, indistinct, ill-defined, hazy, fuzzy,
blurred, foggy, cloudy, confused, muddled, vague,
indefinite, nebulous
F3 2 clear, distinct
▶ *n* jumper, sweater, jersey, pullover, cardigan

woozy *adj*
dazed, dizzy, nauseated, fuddled, confused, blurred,
wobbly, unsteady, rocky, befuddled, bemused, tipsy
F3 alert

word *n, v*
▶ *n* **1** NAME, term, expression, designation,
utterance
formal vocable
Related adjectives: verbal, lexical
2 CONVERSATION, chat, talk, discussion,
consultation, tête-à-tête
3 INFORMATION, news, report, communication,
notice, message, bulletin, communiqué, intelligence,
statement, utterance, dispatch, declaration, comment,
assertion, account, remark, advice, warning
formal tidings
colloq. gen, info, low-down, dope
4 PROMISE, pledge, oath, assurance, honour, vow,
guarantee, undertaking
5 COMMAND, signal, order, decree, will,
commandment, mandate
colloq. go-ahead, green light, thumbs-up
6 RUMOUR, hearsay, gossip, talk, speculation,
scandal, whisper
7 *the words of a song*
lyrics, libretto, script, text, book
▷ **have words** argue, dispute, quarrel, disagree,
row, squabble, bicker
▷ **in a word** briefly, in short, in brief, to be brief, to
put it briefly, concisely, succinctly, summarizing, to
sum up; *colloq.* in a nutshell, to cut a long story short
▷ **word for word** verbatim, literally, exactly,
precisely, accurately, closely
▶ *v* phrase, express, couch, put, say, state, explain,
write

wordiness *n*
verbiage, wordage, logorrhoea, verbal diarrhoea
formal perissology

wording *n*
words, choice of words, language, phrasing,
expression, phraseology, terminology, style, diction,
wordage, verbiage

word-perfect *adj*
accurate, faithful, exact, spot-on, letter-perfect
F3 inaccurate

wordplay *n*
puns, punning, wit, witticisms, repartee
technical paronomasia

wordy *adj*
verbose, long-winded, garrulous, rambling, diffuse,
discursive
formal loquacious, prolix
F3 concise

work *n, v*
▶ *n* **1** OCCUPATION, job, employment, profession,
trade, business, career, calling, vocation, pursuit, field,
line, line of business, métier, livelihood, craft, skill, art,
workmanship
2 TASK, assignment, undertaking, job, chore,
responsibility, duty, charge, mission, commission
3 TOIL, labour, drudgery, trouble, effort, exertion,
industry
formal travail
colloq. slog, graft, elbow grease
4 CREATION, production, achievement,
accomplishment, composition, piece, poem, painting,
book, play, writing, œuvre, opus
5 *steel works*
factory, plant, workshop, mill, foundry, shop
6 *good works*
actions, acts, doings, deed
7 *the works of a clock*
machinery, mechanism, workings, action, movement,
parts, working parts, installations
colloq. innards, guts
F3 1 play, rest, hobby
▶ *v* **1** BE EMPLOYED, have a job, earn your living
2 LABOUR, toil, exert yourself, drudge, slave
colloq. slog, peg away, plug away, work your fingers to
the bone, slog your guts out
3 FUNCTION, go, operate, perform, run, handle
4 OPERATE, run, handle, manage, use, drive, control
5 BRING ABOUT, accomplish, perform, execute,
achieve, create, do, cause
formal effect
colloq. pull off
6 BE SUCCESSFUL, succeed, be effective, be
satisfactory, have the desired effect, go well, prosper
7 MANIPULATE, manoeuvre, engineer, arrange,
contrive
colloq. fix, fiddle, wangle
8 *work your way forward*
shift, guide, edge, move, make, penetrate, manoeuvre
9 CULTIVATE, farm, dig, till
10 MOULD, manipulate, knead, shape, form, fashion,
model, make, process
F3 1 be unemployed **2** play, rest **3** fail
▷ **work out 1** SOLVE, resolve, calculate, figure out,
puzzle out, sort out, understand, clear up
2 DEVELOP, evolve, go well, succeed, be effective,
prosper, turn out; *colloq.* pan out **3** PLAN, devise,
organize, arrange, contrive, invent, construct,
formulate, develop, put together **4** ADD UP TO,
amount to, total, come out, come to **5** EXERCISE,
train, drill, practise, keep fit, warm up
▷ **work up 1** *work up a crowd* excite, agitate, incite,
arouse, stir up, move **2** *work something up* incite, stir
up, rouse, arouse, animate, move, stimulate, build up,
inflame, spur, instigate, kindle, agitate, generate, whet

workable *adj*
practicable, feasible, possible, practical, realistic,
viable, doable
F3 unworkable

workaday *adj*
everyday, ordinary, routine, work-day, working,
practical, mundane, humdrum, dull, common,
commonplace, familiar, labouring, toiling
colloq. run-of-the-mill
🔁 exciting

worker *n*
employee, labourer, working man, working woman,
member of staff, artisan, workman, workwoman,
craftsman, craftswoman, tradesman, hand, operative,
wage-earner, breadwinner, proletarian
colloq. workhorse, workaholic

workforce *n*
workers, employees, personnel, labour force, staff,
labour, manpower, work-people, shop floor

working *n, adj*
▶ *n* **1** FUNCTIONING, operation, running, routine,
manner, process, system, method, action
2 *mine workings*
mine, quarry, pit, shaft, diggings, excavations
3 *the workings of a clock*
works, machinery, mechanism, action, movement,
parts, working parts, installations
colloq. innards, guts
▶ *adj* **1** FUNCTIONING, operational, running,
operating, operative, going, in working order
colloq. up and running
2 EMPLOYED, active
🔁 **1** inoperative **2** idle

workman, workwoman *n*
worker, employee, labourer, hand, artisan, craftsman,
craftswoman, operative, tradesperson, mechanic,
journeyman, navvy, artificer

workmanlike *adj*
efficient, proficient, satisfactory, careful, adept, skilful,
skilled, thorough, painstaking, expert, professional,
masterly
🔁 amateurish

workmanship *n*
skill, craft, craftsmanship, expertise, art, artistry,
handicraft, handiwork, technique, execution,
manufacture, work, finish

workmate *n*
colleague, associate, co-worker, fellow-worker, work-
fellow, yoke-fellow

workout *n*
exercise, training, drill, practice, warm-up, aerobic,
gymnastics, isometrics, eurhythmics, callisthenics

workshop *n*
1 WORKS, workroom, atelier, studio, garage, factory,
plant, mill, shop
2 STUDY GROUP, seminar, symposium, discussion
group, class

world *n*
1 EARTH, globe, sphere, planet, star, heavenly body,
universe, cosmos, creation, nature
2 EVERYBODY, everyone, people, human race,
humankind, humanity, mankind, man
3 SPHERE, realm, field, area, domain, department,
division, section, group, system, society, province,
kingdom
4 TIMES, epoch, era, period, age, days, life
5 WAY OF LIFE, life, reality, existence, experience,
situation
Related adjectives: terrestrial, global, mondial

▷ **out of this world**   wonderful, excellent,
incredible, marvellous, remarkable, great, fantastic,
superb, unbelievable, phenomenal, indescribable;
colloq. fabulous

worldly *adj*
1 TEMPORAL, earthly, material, mundane,
terrestrial, physical, secular, unspiritual, profane,
carnal
formal corporeal
2 WORLDLY-WISE, sophisticated, urbane,
cosmopolitan, experienced, knowing
colloq. streetwise
3 MATERIALISTIC, selfish, ambitious, grasping,
greedy, covetous, avaricious
🔁 **1** spiritual, eternal **2** unsophisticated

worldwide *adj*
international, global, general, universal, catholic
formal mondial, ubiquitous
🔁 local

worn *adj*
1 SHABBY, threadbare, worn-out, tatty, tattered, in
tatters, frayed, ragged
2 EXHAUSTED, tired, weary, spent, fatigued,
careworn, drawn, strained, haggard, jaded
colloq. done in, all in, dog-tired, bushed, knackered
🔁 **1** new, unused **2** fresh
▷ **worn out 1** SHABBY, threadbare, useless, used,
tatty, tattered, on its last legs, ragged, moth-eaten,
frayed, decrepit
2 TIRED OUT, exhausted, weary
colloq. done in, all in, dog-tired, bushed, knackered
🔁 **1** new, unused **2** fresh

worried *adj*
anxious, troubled, uneasy, ill at ease, apprehensive,
concerned, bothered, upset, fearful, afraid,
frightened, overwrought, tense, strained, nervous,
disturbed, distraught, distracted, disquieted,
dismayed, fretful, distressed, agonized
formal perturbed
colloq. on edge, uptight, (all) hot and bothered;
slang wired
🔁 calm, unworried, unconcerned

worrisome *adj*
worrying, upsetting, anxious, troublesome,
frightening, bothersome, agonizing, distressing,
uneasy, disturbing, insecure, fretful, apprehensive,
vexing, irksome, disquieting, jittery
formal perturbing
colloq. nail-biting
🔁 calm, reassuring

worry *v, n*
▶ *v* **1** BE ANXIOUS, be troubled, be distressed,
agonize, fret
2 IRRITATE, plague, pester, torment, upset, unsettle,
agitate, annoy, bother, disturb, trouble, concern, vex,
tease, nag, harass, harry
formal perturb
colloq. aggravate, bug, hassle
3 ATTACK, go for, tear at, bite, savage
🔁 **1** be unconcerned **2** comfort
▶ *n* **1** PROBLEM, trouble, responsibility, burden,
concern, care, trial, annoyance, nuisance, pest,
plague, irritation, vexation
2 ANXIETY, apprehension, trouble, distress, disquiet,
concern, unease, misgiving, fear, fearfulness, tension,
stress, strain, disturbance, agitation, torment, anguish,
misery, perplexity

formal perturbation
colloq. hang-up, tizzy, tiz, stew
⊟ 2 comfort, reassurance

worrying *adj*
anxious, troublesome, trying, unsettling, upsetting,
niggling, disturbing, distressing, harassing,
disquieting, worrisome, uneasy
formal perturbing
colloq. nail-biting
⊟ calm, reassuring

worsen *v*
1 AGGRAVATE, exacerbate, intensify, increase,
heighten
2 GET WORSE, weaken, deteriorate, degenerate,
decline, slip, sink
colloq. go from bad to worse, go down the tube(s),
go to pot, go downhill
⊟ improve

worsening *n*
deterioration, decline, degeneration, decay,
retrogression
formal exacerbation, pejoration
⊟ improvement

worship *v, n*
▶ *v* revere, reverence, adore, exalt, glorify, honour,
praise, idolize, adulate, admire, love, extol, respect,
pray to, deify
formal venerate, laud
⊟ despise, hate
▶ *n* reverence, adoration, devotion(s), homage,
honour, glory, glorification, exaltation, praise,
prayer(s), respect, regard, love, adulation, deification,
idolatry
formal veneration, laudation

Places of worship include: abbey, bethel, cathedral,
chantry, church, fane, kirk, masjid, meeting-house,
minster, mosque, pagoda, shrine, shul, synagogue,
tabernacle, temple, wat. *See also* **religions**.

worst *v*
beat, defeat, get the better of, overcome, overpower,
overthrow, conquer, crush, master, subdue, drub,
whitewash, best
formal subjugate, vanquish

worth *n*
worthiness, merit, value, benefit, profit, gain,
advantage, importance, significance, eminence, use,
usefulness, utility, service, quality, good, virtue,
excellence, credit, desert(s), cost, rate, price, help,
assistance, avail
⊟ worthlessness

worthless *adj*
1 VALUELESS, useless, pointless, meaningless, futile,
unavailing, unimportant, insignificant, trivial,
unusable, cheap, poor, rubbishy, trashy, trifling, paltry
formal ineffectual, nugatory
slang naff
2 CONTEMPTIBLE, despicable, good-for-nothing,
corrupt, vile, low, useless
⊟ 1 valuable **2** worthy

worthwhile *adj*
profitable, useful, valuable, worthy, good, helpful,
advantageous, beneficial, constructive, gainful,
justifiable, productive
⊟ worthless

worthy *adj, n*
▶ *adj* praiseworthy, creditable, commendable,
valuable, worthwhile, admirable, reliable, fit,
deserving, appropriate, respectable, trustworthy,
reputable, good, moral, honest, honourable, excellent,
decent, upright, righteous, virtuous
formal laudable, meritorious
⊟ unworthy, disreputable
▶ *n* dignitary, personage, name, luminary, notable
colloq. bigwig, big cheese, big noise, big shot

would-be *adj*
aspiring, budding, striving, endeavouring, ambitious,
enterprising, keen, eager, hopeful, optimistic, wishful,
longing

wound *n, v*
▶ *n* **1** INJURY, trauma, hurt, cut, gash, graze,
scratch, lesion, laceration, scar
2 HURT, distress, trauma, torment, heartbreak, blow,
harm, damage, pain, ache, anguish, grief, shock
▶ *v* **1** DAMAGE, harm, hurt, injure, hit, cut, gash,
tear, graze, scratch, lacerate, slash, stab, puncture,
pierce
2 DISTRESS, hurt, offend, shock, insult, pain,
traumatize, mortify, upset, slight, grieve

wraith *n*
ghost, spirit, phantom, apparition, spectre, revenant,
shade
colloq. spook

wrangle *n, v*
▶ *n* argument, quarrel, dispute, controversy,
squabble, tussle, tiff, bickering, disagreement, clash,
contest
formal altercation
colloq. row, slanging match, set-to, barney, argy-bargy
⊟ agreement
▶ *v* argue, quarrel, disagree, dispute, bicker, contend,
have words, clash, row, squabble, scrap, fight, spar
formal altercate
colloq. fall out
⊟ agree

wrap *v, n*
▶ *v* envelop, fold, enfold, enclose, cover, pack,
shroud, wind, surround, package, parcel (up), muffle,
cocoon, encase, cloak, roll up, bind, bundle up, swathe,
immerse
⊟ unwrap
▷ **wrap up 1** WRAP, pack up, package, parcel (up)
2 CONCLUDE, finish off, end, bring to a close,
terminate, wind up, complete, round off **3** SHUT UP,
colloq. dry up, belt up, pipe down, give it a rest, hold
your tongue, put a sock in it, shut your mouth
▶ *n* shawl, stole, cape, robe, cloak, mantle

wrapper *n*
wrapping, packaging, envelope, Jiffy bag®, cover,
covering, jacket, dust jacket, sheath, casing, case,
sleeve, paper

wrapping *n*
packaging, wrapper, envelope, Jiffy bag®, paper, case,
carton, blister card, blister pack, bubble pack,
Cellophane®, foil, tinfoil, silver paper

wrath *n*
anger, bitterness, rage, fury, exasperation, indignation,
irritation, annoyance, temper, resentment, passion,
displeasure, spleen, choler
formal ire
⊟ calm, pleasure

wrathful *adj*
angry, furious, incensed, enraged, infuriated, raging, indignant, bitter, displeased, irate, ireful
formal furibund
colloq. in a paddy, on the warpath
◼ calm, pleased

wreak *v*
inflict, exercise, create, cause, bring about, perpetrate, vent, unleash, express, execute, carry out
formal bestow

wreath *n*
garland, coronet, chaplet, festoon, crown, band, loop, ring, circle, circlet

wreathe *v*
encircle, surround, enfold, entwine, twine, twist, wind, coil, wrap, envelop, crown, adorn, shroud, enwrap, festoon, intertwine, interweave

wreck *v, n*
▶ *v* destroy, ruin, demolish, devastate, shatter, smash, break, sink, spoil, mar, play havoc with, torpedo, ravage, write off
◼ conserve, repair
▶ *n* ruin, destruction, devastation, shattering, smashing, breaking, mess, demolition, ruination, write-off, disaster, loss, undoing, disruption, shipwreck, derelict, debris, remains, rubble, ruin, fragments, flotsam, pieces

wreckage *n*
debris, remains, rubble, ruin, fragments, flotsam, pieces
formal detritus

wrench *v, n*
▶ *v* yank, wrest, jerk, pull, tug, force, sprain, strain, rick, tear, twist, wring, rip, distort
▶ *n* **1** PULL, jerk, tear, twist, tug, sprain, pain, ache, pang
2 UPROOTING, upheaval, shock, sorrow, sadness, blow

wrest *v*
seize, force, extract, pull, take, win, wring, wrench, twist, strain

wrestle *v*
struggle, strive, fight, scuffle, grapple, tussle, combat, contend, contest, vie, battle

wretch *n*
scoundrel, rogue, villain, good-for-nothing, ruffian, rascal, vagabond, miscreant, outcast, devil
colloq. rat, swine, worm

wretched *adj*
1 MISERABLE, sad, unhappy, sorry, melancholy, depressed, dejected, disconsolate, downcast, forlorn, gloomy, doleful, distressed, broken-hearted, crestfallen
2 PATHETIC, pitiable, pitiful, sad, unhappy, miserable, piteous, unfortunate, unlucky, sorry, hopeless, poor
formal hapless
3 CONTEMPTIBLE, despicable, vile, worthless, shameful, inferior, bad, low, base, mean, vile, paltry
4 ATROCIOUS, awful, deplorable, appalling, shocking, outrageous, dreadful, terrible, horrible
◼ **1** happy **2** enviable **3** worthy **4** excellent

wriggle *v, n*
▶ *v* squirm, writhe, wiggle, worm, twist, snake, slink, crawl, edge, sidle, manoeuvre, squiggle, dodge, extricate, zigzag, waggle, turn

▶ *n* wiggle, twist, squirm, writhe, jiggle, jerk, turn, twitch

wring *v*
1 SQUEEZE, twist, wrench, wrest, extract, mangle, screw
2 EXACT, extort, coerce, force
3 DISTRESS, pain, hurt, rack, tear, rend, pierce, torture, wound, lacerate, stab, tear

wrinkle *n, v*
▶ *n* furrow, crease, corrugation, line, ridge, fold, gather, pucker, crumple, rumple, wimple, frounce
▶ *v* crease, corrugate, furrow, line, fold, crinkle, crumple, rumple, shrivel, gather, pucker

wrinkled *adj*
crumpled, wrinkly, crinkled, creased, furrowed, ridged, puckered, rivelled, rumpled, crinkly
formal rugose, rugate, rugous
◼ smooth

writ *n*
court order, summons, decree, subpoena

write *v*
pen, inscribe, record, register, jot down, note (down), set down, put down, take down, make a note of, transcribe, print, scribble, scrawl, correspond, communicate, draft, draw up, copy, compose, create
colloq. dash off, put down in black and white
▷ **write off 1** DELETE, cancel, cross out, wipe out, disregard; *formal* annul, nullify **2** WRECK, destroy, crash, demolish, smash (up)

writer *n*

Writers include: annalist, author, autobiographer, bard, biographer, calligraphist, chronicler, clerk, columnist, composer, contributor, copyist, copywriter, correspondent, court reporter, diarist, dramatist, editor, essayist, fabler, fiction writer, ghost writer, hack, historian, journalist, leader-writer, lexicographer, librettist, lyricist, novelist, pen-friend, penman, pen-pal, *colloq.* penpusher, penwoman, playwright, poet, poet laureate, reporter, rhymer, satirist, scribbler, scribe, scriptwriter, short-story writer, sonneteer, stenographer, *colloq.* storyteller.

writhe *v*
squirm, wriggle, thresh, thrash, twist, wiggle, jerk, toss, coil, contort, struggle
colloq. twist and turn

writing *n*
1 HANDWRITING, calligraphy, script, penmanship, scrawl, scribble, hand, text, words, print
2 DOCUMENT, composition, work, opus, volume, publication

Types of writing include: account, advertising copy, annals, article, autobiography, biography, book, chronicle, commentary, confessions, copywriting, correspondence, criticism, critique, curriculum vitae, diary, discourse, dissertation, documentary, drama, editorial, epistle, essay, feature, history, journal, legal document, letter, life story, literature, lyric, memoir, monograph, narrative, news, newspaper column, paper, parable, poem, profile, propaganda, record, report, review, satire, scientific writing, script, sketch, sonnet, statement, story, study, tale, thesis, travelogue, treatise, yearbook. *See also* **book; literature; poem; story; sacred writings**.

Related adjective: literary

writing instrument

Types of writing instruments include: pen, ballpoint, Biro®, calligraphy pen, cartridge pen, dip pen, eraser pen, felt-tip pen, fountain pen; marker pen, rollerball pen; writing brush, pencil, chinagraph pencil, coloured pencil, crayon, ink pencil, lead-pencil, propelling pencil, board marker, laundry marker, permanent marker, highlighter; cane pen, quill, reed, Roman metal pen, steel pen, stylus; brailler, typewriter, word-processor.

written *adj*

set down, recorded, drawn up, transcribed, documented, documentary
formal documental
🔁 unwritten, verbal

wrong *adj, adv, n, v*

▶ *adj* **1** INACCURATE, incorrect, mistaken, erroneous, false, in error, imprecise
formal fallacious
colloq. wide of the mark, off beam, off target
2 INAPPROPRIATE, unsuitable, improper, unconventional, unfitting, inapt
formal unseemly, indecorous, incongruous, infelicitous, inapposite, malapropos
colloq. hardly the place/time
3 UNJUST, unethical, unfair, unlawful, immoral, illegal, illicit, dishonourable, unjustified, dishonest, criminal, blameworthy, guilty, to blame, bad, wicked, sinful, evil
formal reprehensible, iniquitous, felonious
colloq. crooked
4 DEFECTIVE, faulty, out of order, amiss, awry
colloq. up the spout
5 REVERSE, opposite, inside, inverse, inverted, back, contrary
🔁 **1** correct, right **2** suitable, right **3** good, moral **4** in order **5** right, front
▶ *adv* amiss, astray, awry, inaccurately, incorrectly, inexactly, imprecisely, wrongly, mistakenly, faultily, badly, erroneously, improperly
🔁 right
▷ **go wrong 1** BREAK DOWN, stop working, fail; *formal* malfunction; *colloq.* pack up, conk out, seize up **2** FAIL, be unsuccessful, collapse, come to grief, come to nothing, stray, go astray; *colloq.* not make it,

come a cropper, become unstuck
▶ *n* sin, misdeed, offence, crime, immorality, sinfulness, wickedness, unlawfulness, wrongdoing, grievance, abuse, injustice, iniquity, inequity, infringement, unfairness, error
formal transgression, trespass, injury
🔁 right
▷ **in the wrong** at fault, guilty, in error, mistaken, to blame, blameworthy
🔁 in the right
▶ *v* abuse, ill-treat, mistreat, maltreat, injure, ill-use, hurt, harm, discredit, dishonour, misrepresent, malign, oppress, cheat

wrongdoer *n*

offender, law-breaker, criminal, delinquent, felon, miscreant, evil-doer, sinner, trespasser, culprit
formal transgressor, malefactor

wrongdoing *n*

crime, offence, error, evil, misdeed, fault, felony, immorality, delinquency, sin, sinfulness, wickedness, mischief
formal iniquity, maleficence, transgression

wrongful *adj*

immoral, improper, unfair, unethical, unjust, unlawful, illegal, illegitimate, illicit, dishonest, criminal, blameworthy, dishonourable, wrong, unjustified, unwarranted, reprehensible, wicked, evil
🔁 rightful

wrongly *adv*

incorrectly, mistakenly, badly, by mistake, in error, inaccurately, erroneously
🔁 rightly

wrought *adj*

shaped, fashioned, hammered, beaten, made, manufactured, ornamental, ornate, decorative, ornamented

wry *adj*

1 *wry humour*
ironic, sardonic, dry, witty, sarcastic, mocking, droll
2 TWISTED, distorted, deformed, contorted, warped, uneven, askew, crooked
🔁 **2** straight

xenophobia *n*

racism, ethnocentrism, racialism, xenophoby
🔁 xenomania

xenophobic *adj*

racist, racialist, parochial, ethnocentrist

xerox *v*

photocopy, copy, duplicate, Photostat®, reproduce, print, run off

Xerox® *n*

photocopy, duplicate, facsimile, Photostat®

yack *v, n*

▶ *v* chatter, gossip, prattle, tattle, twattle, jabber, witter on, blather

colloq. jaw, gab, yap
▶ *n* chat, gossip, prattle, rant, harp on, twattle, jaw, blather

colloq. blah, chinwag, confab, hot air, yackety-yack

yank   *v & n*
jerk, tug, pull, wrench, snatch, haul, heave

yap   *v*
1 BARK, yelp
2 CHATTER, jabber, babble, prattle, yatter
colloq. jaw, gab

yard   *n*
courtyard, court, garden, quadrangle
colloq. quad

yardstick   *n*
measure, gauge, criterion, standard, scale, guideline,
benchmark, touchstone, comparison

yarn   *n*
1 THREAD, fibre, strand
2 STORY, tale, anecdote, fable, fabrication
colloq. tall story, cock-and-bull story

yawning   *adj*
gaping, wide, wide-open, huge, vast, cavernous

yearly   *adj, adv*
▶ *adj* annual, per year, per annum, perennial
▶ *adv* annually, every year, once a year, perennially

yearn   *v*
long, pine, desire, want, wish, crave, covet, hunger,
thirst, hanker, ache, fancy, languish, itch
colloq. yen

yearning   *n*
longing, pining, desire, wish, craving, hunger, thirst,
hankering, fancy
colloq. yen

yell   *v, n*
▶ *v* shout, scream, cry (out), bellow, roar, bawl,
shriek, squeal, howl, screech, squall, yelp, yowl, whoop
colloq. holler
E3 whisper
▶ *n* shout, scream, cry, roar, bellow, shriek, howl,
screech, squall, whoop
colloq. holler
E3 whisper

yellow   *adj*
lemon, gold, golden, buff, tawny, canary, primrose,
saffron, flaxen
technical xanthous, xanthic, xanthochroic,
xanthomelanous, vitellary, vitelline
formal flavescent, fulvous, fulvid

yelp   *v, n*
▶ *v* yap, bark, squeal, cry, yell, yowl, bay
▶ *n* yap, bark, yip, squeal, cry, yell, yowl

yen   *n*
longing, yearning, hunger, desire, craving, hankering,
itch, passion, lust
colloq. thing
E3 dislike

yes   *adv*
right, quite, absolutely, certainly, agreed, of course,
affirmative
colloq. yeah, yep
E3 no

yes-man   *n*
sycophant, crawler, toady, lackey, minion, bootlicker
old use toad-eater
slang arse-licker

yet   *adv, conj*
▶ *adv* 1 UP TILL NOW, until now, up to this time, up
till then, by now, by then, now, already, as yet
formal thus far, hitherto, heretofore
2 IN ADDITION, still, even, too, also, furthermore,
besides, moreover
colloq. into the bargain
▶ *conj* but, however, nevertheless, nonetheless,
anyway, even so, all/just the same, for all that
formal notwithstanding

yield   *v, n*
▶ *v* 1 SURRENDER, give up, abandon, abdicate,
cede, part with
formal relinquish, forego, renounce
2 GIVE WAY, capitulate, surrender, concede, submit,
succumb, give in, admit defeat, bow, cave in, knuckle
under, resign yourself, go along with, permit, allow,
accede, agree, comply, consent
formal acquiesce
colloq. throw in the towel/sponge
3 PRODUCE, bear, supply, provide, give, generate,
bring in, bring forth, furnish, return, earn, fetch, pay,
net, gross
formal fructify, fructuate
E3 1 hold 2 resist, withstand
▶ *n* return, product, earnings, harvest, crop, produce,
output, profit, revenue, takings, proceeds, income,
haul

yielding   *adj*
1 FLEXIBLE, pliable, pliant, resilient, elastic, springy,
soft, supple, spongy, quaggy
2 SUBMISSIVE, obedient, amenable, biddable,
obliging, unresisting, accommodating, easy
formal acquiescent, complaisant, compliant, tractable
E3 1 solid 2 obstinate

yoke   *n, v*
▶ *n* 1 HARNESS, bond, link, tie, coupling
2 BURDEN, bondage, enslavement, slavery, tyranny,
oppression, servility
formal servitude, subjugation
▶ *v* couple, link, join, tie, bond, harness, hitch,
bracket, connect, unite

yokel   *n*
country bumpkin, clodhopper, country cousin, hick,
peasant, rustic, boor, bucolic
colloq. hillbilly
E3 sophisticate, towny

young   *adj, n*
▶ *adj* 1 YOUTHFUL, juvenile, childlike, baby, infant,
junior, small, little, teenage, adolescent
colloq. kid
2 IMMATURE, childish, early, new, recent, green,
growing, fledgling, unfledged, inexperienced,
undeveloped
E3 1 adult, old 2 mature, old
▶ *n* offspring, babies, little ones, issue, litter, brood,
children, family
formal progeny

youngster   *n*
child, boy, lad, girl, lass, toddler, young person,
young adult, young man, youth, young woman,
teenager, adolescent
colloq. kid, shaver

youth   *n*
1 ADOLESCENT, teenager, youngster, juvenile, boy,
lad, young man
colloq. kid

2 YOUNG PEOPLE, the young, younger generation
3 ADOLESCENCE, teenage years, teens, childhood, immaturity, inexperience, boyhood, girlhood
F3 3 adulthood, maturity

youthful *adj*
young, boyish, girlish, childish, immature, juvenile, inexperienced, fresh, active, vigorous, lively, sprightly, spry, well-preserved
F3 aged

youthfulness *n*
liveliness, vigour, spryness, sprightliness, vivaciousness, freshness, juvenileness, juvenility

formal vivacity
F3 agedness, languor

yowl *v, n*
▶ *v* wail, yell, yelp, cry, howl, screech, squall, bay, caterwaul
formal ululate
▶ *n* wail, cry, howl, screech, yell, yelp

yucky *adj*
disgusting, revolting, horrible, unpleasant, messy, mucky, filthy, dirty, foul, sickly, sentimental, saccharine
colloq. grotty
F3 nice

Z

zany *adj* comical, funny, amusing, eccentric, odd, absurd, ridiculous, droll, clownish
colloq. crazy, daft, loony, wacky; *US* kooky
F3 serious

zap *v*
kill, destroy, hit, shoot, finish off
colloq. do in, bump off, rub out, wipe out

zeal *n*
enthusiasm, ardour, fervour, passion, warmth, fire, devotion, spirit, energy, vigour, keenness, zest, eagerness, earnestness, dedication, commitment, vehemence, intensity, fanaticism, gusto, verve
F3 apathy, indifference

zealot *n*
fanatic, radical, extremist, bigot, militant, partisan

zealous *adj*
ardent, fervent, impassioned, passionate, devoted, burning, fiery, enthusiastic, intense, warm, fanatical, militant, keen, committed, dedicated, eager, earnest, spirited
formal fervid
F3 apathetic, indifferent

zenith *n*
summit, peak, height, pinnacle, apex, high point, highest point, top, optimum, climax, culmination, meridian
technical acme, vertex, apogee
F3 nadir

zero *n, v*
▶ *n* nothing, nought, naught, nil, nadir, bottom, cipher, duck, love
colloq. zilch
▶ *v* ▷ **zero in on** aim for, concentrate on, converge on, home in on, direct at, level at, pinpoint, fix on, focus on, train on, head for

zest *n*
1 GUSTO, appetite, enthusiasm, enjoyment, relish, keenness, zeal, eagerness, liveliness, vigour, exuberance, interest, *joie de vivre*
colloq. zing
2 FLAVOUR, taste, relish, savour, spice, tang,

piquancy
F3 1 apathy

zigzag *v, adj*
▶ *v* meander, snake, wind, twist, curve
▶ *adj* meandering, crooked, serpentine, sinuous, twisting, winding
F3 straight

zing *n*
liveliness, life, energy, vitality, vigour, spirit, animation, zest, sparkle, élan, joie de vivre
colloq. go, oomph, pizzazz, zip, dash, brio
F3 listlessness

zip *n, v*
▶ *n* energy, verve, vitality, life, liveliness, enthusiasm, drive, sparkle, spirit, vigour, zest, gusto, élan
colloq. go, get-up-and-go, oomph, pizzazz, pep, punch, zing
F3 listlessness
▶ *v* fly, dash, tear, rush, race, hurry, speed, shoot, flash, scoot, zoom
colloq. whiz, whoosh

zodiac *n*

> *The signs of the zodiac (with their symbols) are*: Aries (Ram), Taurus (Bull), Gemini (Twins), Cancer (Crab), Leo (Lion), Virgo (Virgin), Libra (Balance), Scorpio (Scorpion), Sagittarius (Archer), Capricorn (Goat), Aquarius (Water-bearer), Pisces (Fishes).

zone *n*
region, area, district, territory, province, section, sector, belt, sphere, tract, stratum

zoo *n*
zoological gardens, safari park, animal park, aquarium, aviary, menagerie

zoom *v*
race, rush, tear, dash, speed, fly, hurtle, streak, flash, shoot, whirl, dive, buzz, zip
colloq. go all out, vroom, whiz, zap